Encyclopedia of North Carolina

Editor : William S. Powell

Associate Editor : Jay Mazzocchi

Consulting Editor : William S. Price Jr.

Illustrations Editor : Jerry Cotten

Cartographer : Mark Anderson Moore

Editorial Interns :

Charles Battle	Philip McFee
Greg Behr	Sarah Mobley
Allyson C. Criner	Cecelia Moore
Lisa Coston Hall	Laura Morgan
Laura Hegyi	Dena Ratner
Ruth E. Homrighaus	Erin Sommerville
Kelly Kress	Robert Blair Vocci
Nathan McCamic	

Encyclopedia of **North Carolina**

WILLIAM S. POWELL, *Editor*

Jay Mazzocchi, *Associate Editor*

Published in Association with the

University of North Carolina at Chapel Hill Library

THE UNIVERSITY OF NORTH CAROLINA PRESS

Chapel Hill

© 2006 The University of North Carolina Press
All rights reserved

Designed by Richard Hendel
Set in Arnhem and The Serif types
by Tseng Information Systems, Inc.
Manufactured in the United States of America

The paper in this book meets the guidelines for
permanence and durability of the Committee on
Production Guidelines for Book Longevity of the
Council on Library Resources.

Library of Congress Cataloging-in-Publication Data
Encyclopedia of North Carolina / William S. Powell,
editor ; Jay Mazzocchi, associate editor.
    p. cm.
"Published in Association with the University of
North Carolina at Chapel Hill Library."
Includes bibliographical references and index.
ISBN-13: 978-0-8078-3071-0 (cloth : alk. paper)
ISBN-10: 0-8078-3071-2 (cloth : alk. paper)
1. North Carolina—Encyclopedias. 2. North Carolina—
Civilization—Encyclopedias. 3. North Carolina—
History—Encyclopedias. I. Powell, William Stevens,
1919– . II. Mazzocchi, Jay. III. University of North
Carolina at Chapel Hill. Library.
F254.E54 2006
975.6'003—dc22   2006011352

10 09 08 07 06   5 4 3 2 1

To Ida and William Friday,

whose tireless devotion to the

University of North Carolina

has been of enormous benefit

to North Carolina and all its

citizens

Contents

Maps

Preface

After devoting nearly half a century to the study of North Carolina history, I have, with the publication of the *Encyclopedia of North Carolina*, been afforded the opportunity to review what I have learned. Without doubt, North Carolina has changed dramatically during my lifetime in the areas of urbanization, population growth, technology, economy and industry, race relations, and ethnic and cultural diversity. In 2006 the state is as likely to be noted by those living in other regions of the country for its prominence in banking and finance as for the quality of its pork barbecue, for its many successful residential developments in cities and suburbs as for its beautiful countryside, and for its role in the information technology industry as for its tobacco farms and agricultural products. Historians have a growing number of subjects to occupy them, as today's evolving issues cast new light on events of the past.

Yet, despite all of these changes, many things in North Carolina have remained the same. The state that I have known my whole life continues to be a place where a small-town attitude prevails. People work hard at their jobs. Parents remain devoted to nurturing and educating their children. Neighbors and co-workers still take an interest in each others' lives. In times of need, no people on earth are more generous than North Carolinians—whether they have lived here for generations or have recently relocated here from other places. Even with all the exciting opportunities and pursuits and entertainments of modern-day life, the North Carolina of previous generations has never really been lost.

The *Encyclopedia of North Carolina* is a means by which all of us can view our state in its entirety and perhaps plan a future based on a better understanding of our common history. I think the need for such a book first came to me when I was newly out of the army at the end of World War II and happily employed as the researcher on the staff of the North Carolina Department of Archives and History in Raleigh. It was my responsibility to reply to requests for information on historical, geographical, and biographical subjects. I spoke to many people who sought information about North Carolina and wanted definitive answers to a variety of questions—some of which were quite simple and easily answered, but others of which could be resolved only through research, experience, or long pondering.

The need for a ready source of information arranged in an easy-to-use form began to intrigue me. Years later, through the work of many hundreds of people, that idea has taken shape as the *Encyclopedia of North Carolina*—a comprehensive reference work designed to capture the distinctive historical and cultural personality of the Tar Heel State. I have envisioned this encyclopedia as the final installment of a series of three works,

the first two being the *North Carolina Gazetteer* (1968) and the *Dictionary of North Carolina Biography* (six volumes, 1979–96). The *Gazetteer* provides information on some 20,000 of the state's places, including counties and towns, lakes, mountains, and other named places or natural features. The *Dictionary of North Carolina Biography* contains more than 3,500 articles on the lives of significant North Carolinians and others born outside the state who played important roles in its history. I wanted the *Encyclopedia of North Carolina* to be both a completely new document and an extension of these previous works.

With the support of many friends and colleagues as well as the University of North Carolina Press, I began to work in earnest on the encyclopedia in the early 1990s. During the initial stages of the project, I prepared a list of more than 3,500 topics that I believed would be important and interesting to a wide range of people. I sent the list to fellow historians, specialists in various fields, librarians, teachers, politicians, members of local historical societies, and many others, asking them to comment on the topics. Many of these people added subjects to the list that had not occurred to me, while others suggested removing certain subjects. As work progressed, the evolving list was sent to writers, requesting their collaboration. Looking back now on the more than 560 authors—academics, professional writers, and amateur historians motivated solely by lifelong interest—who volunteered to contribute without compensation, I am still amazed by the cooperative spirit of people who seized on the opportunity to tell the state's stories. In keeping with that spirit, I am pleased to think of this as *our* encyclopedia rather than *my* encyclopedia.

As the number of completed articles increased, many editorial decisions were made with the goal of creating a factual, balanced, and useful book that would suit the needs of its intended audience—indeed, the needs of anyone interested in North Carolina's past and present. Over time, the realization grew that not all of the several thousand subjects could be included in individual articles. Faced with limited space and a practically endless list of noteworthy historic homes, cemeteries, schools, towns, academies, businesses, artistic groups, and other institutions—all arguably important and dear to many North Carolinians—we were constantly confronted with the daunting task of reviewing which of these subjects would merit individual articles in the encyclopedia, which would be mentioned within related articles, and which would be left out altogether. In some cases it became editorially necessary to condense or revise multiple articles into a single piece.

Regrettably, we also faced the difficult decision of omitting some articles after they had been commissioned and completed. Finally, recent events and new historical findings made it necessary to update and expand articles on a number of topics that were originally completed earlier in the project's development. My colleagues and I have done all that is humanly possible to bring fairness and good judgment to this challenging editorial process. We benefited immensely during this process from the wisdom of expert scholars, anonymous peer reviewers, and other advisers who carefully considered not only articles themselves but also the underlying questions of how best to represent a seemingly infinite body of knowledge in a finite space.

I believe that we—contributors and editors—have succeeded in making the *Encyclopedia of North Carolina* a comprehensive work representing all that is essential in understanding the formation and modern characteristics of the Tar Heel State. The scope of the subjects covered is perhaps the encyclopedia's most exciting feature. Never before have the entire history and culture of North Carolina been so thoroughly and skillfully explained in a single volume. The encyclopedia features information on practically every aspect of the state, including its discovery, exploration, and settlement; the national and ethnic origins of its people; politics and government; military history; the judiciary; education; religion; recreation and sports; business and industry; fine and folk art; customs and manners; agriculture; language and literature; transportation; geology; the natural environment; and legends and folklore.

Readers will find answers to thousands of North Carolina–related questions, both serious and amusing, in the encyclopedia. What happened to the once-thriving Carolina parakeet? Why are there so many Scottish place-names in the southeastern section of the state? Who were the Exodusters? What role did women play in the Regulator Movement? Why is the North Carolina coastline nicknamed the "Graveyard of the Atlantic"? What famous inventions were made by North Carolinians? Which North Carolina governor boxed naked with members of his council and a visiting South Carolina dignitary? Which local festival celebrates the attributes of mules? What Durham native is known as the "First Lady of Gospel"? When was electricity first made widely available to rural families? Which now-prosperous North Carolina city did George Washington call a "trifling place" while traveling through the state? What are North Carolina's largest American Indian tribes? How many

state flags has North Carolina officially flown? Why have North Carolinians at various times in history battled over inoculations, ticks, moonshine, oysters, and pork barbecue?

There are articles on some topics that have never appeared in a work of this kind and stand as curious footnotes to North Carolina history. These include peculiar events, groups, and cultural oddities, as well as esoteric subjects such as field names, pseudonyms, and reported sightings of angels. Some supposedly factual statements, formerly accepted as reliable, have been explained and rejected, including the belief that rock walls in Rowan County were built by prehistoric men; that Napoleon's Marshal Ney escaped a firing squad and came to North Carolina; and that residents of Mecklenburg County declared independence from England in 1775.

Of course, in a work of this size—and despite the strict attention and multiple layers of editorial review every article in the encyclopedia has received—factual errors may on occasion be found. The editors accept responsibility for any errors and welcome correspondence concerning possible corrections that may need to be made. It should also be said that I myself regret that certain subjects were not able to be included in the book, and I expect some readers will be similarly disappointed that a particular topic has been left out. To those, I pledge our intention to enhance and improve the information offered here, insofar as may be possible, through future work.

In summary, I hope and believe that the *Encyclopedia of North Carolina* as it has evolved is a resource in which anyone connected with the state might take pride, a reference anyone might find fascinating and informative. The encyclopedia stands ready to serve the North Carolina historian, teacher, student, government worker, journalist, librarian, farmer, businessperson, and any other who desires to explore, in whole or in part, the history of the state. Those outside its borders will perhaps come to understand through the encyclopedia's articles why natives and residents appreciate their state so much, readily finding the significance, beauty, and vitality of North Carolina within these pages. Undoubtedly, the encyclopedia will be a good starting place for research about the state for many years to come.

William S. Powell

Acknowledgments

I am reminded of a line from the poem "Ulysses" by Alfred Lord Tennyson, which I learned as a boy and have remembered ever since: "I am a part of all that I have met." No words could better describe my feelings toward the people and institutions that I have encountered during my lifetime. Some of those who have aided my search for information about North Carolina may be surprised to know that I am still appreciative of their influence. In 1929, for example, when I was ten years old, I began talking with "old-timers" and keeping notes about subjects they remembered from their own youth. This initial spark of historical curiosity has remained within me, and I have been pleased to witness a similar exuberance in the several hundred writers and editorial interns who have made the *Encyclopedia of North Carolina* such a monumental work. I am deeply grateful for their essential contributions to the project.

This has been a cooperative effort from first to last, and while a complete list of all the colleagues who have offered their time and talent on behalf of the encyclopedia over the past 15 years is too long to include here, I would like to express my gratitude to Robert G. Anthony Jr., John L. Bell, Lindley S. Butler, Jerry C. Cashion, Jeffrey J. Crow, H. G. Jones, Jaquelin Drane Nash, Thomas C. Parramore, George Stevenson, Bland Simpson, David Stick, Beverly Tetterton, and Wiley J. Williams for their extensive and unfailing support. In addition to these professionals, several scholars in various fields have read parts of the manuscript and helped revamp it where necessary, and I am grateful for their important suggestions and critiques. I would particularly like to thank William S. Price Jr. for his invaluable insight and intense scrutiny during a key time in the project's development and Jerry Cotten for his extraordinary work in securing the many unique and enlightening illustrations included in the encyclopedia.

A few groups and individuals joined our editorial efforts on practically a daily basis, offering administrative support and answering the countless questions that came up in the course of writing and editing the hundreds of articles in the encyclopedia. These include University of North Carolina at Chapel Hill Library administrators Sarah C. Michalak, Joe Hewitt, and Larry Alford and the staffs of the North Carolina Collection, the Davis Library Reference and Circulation Departments, and the Southern Historical Collection. On a statewide level, the staffs of the North Carolina State Archives and the North Carolina Museum of History have been important allies. Many members of the Historical Society of North Carolina also have been of enormous assistance in this long and exciting process. Numerous other librarians, journalists, public relations specialists, educators, curators of local museums, and history enthusiasts have added greatly to the quality of the manuscript.

I would like to recognize the perceptive and enthusiastic support of David Perry, Mark Simpson-Vos, and others at the University of North Carolina Press during the progression of the *Encyclopedia of North Carolina* from its earliest stages to its publication.

The mind and body that has kept the encyclopedia workshop active and flourishing during the last several years has been Jay Mazzocchi, a Virginian by birth but as complete a Tar Heel as exists. With degrees from the University of North Carolina at Chapel Hill and Duke Divinity School, Jay recalls the facts of North Carolina history like a native, while also keeping me updated on modern music, theater, literature, sports, and other matters. For his excellent work in bringing the project to its final form, I am very grateful.

Unlike many faculty wives who profess to feel that their college degrees were probably not a good investment, my wife Virginia is frequently reminded that hers certainly were. A native of North Carolina with majors in English, history, and library science as well as experience and skill at typewriters and computers, she has been an indispensable consultant, guide, and "assistant memory" during the entire production of the *Encyclopedia of North Carolina*.

William S. Powell

Organization and Use of the Encyclopedia

North Carolina is, and always has been, a diverse state with a complex character. Even the land itself reflects that complexity and has reinforced it: the people of the Coastal Plain, Piedmont, and Mountain regions have all developed their own unique identities, mirroring the particular natural resources and terrain found in each. From the time Native Americans, European settlers, and enslaved Africans first encountered one another more than four centuries ago, North Carolina's people have created distinctive yet interwoven histories that mark the present and continue to evolve, even as new people come to the state, seemingly from every corner and continent on the globe.

How, then, to represent all of these people, their institutions, their stories, and the events that have shaped their experiences, in a single volume like this one? It is a challenge faced by every individual or group that has conceived of an encyclopedia. In this case, the editors have answered the challenge by attempting to echo something of the state's geographical and regional complexity. Despite centuries of change, North Carolina remains in many ways what it always has been: a place defined by hundreds of smaller communities linked by culture, institutions, economies, and modes of transportation to larger towns and cities of moderate size. While modern highways and high-speed telecommunications hasten our travel and enhance our connections to the larger world, it is not unreasonable to suggest that most North Carolinians still retain a strong awareness of their region, their county, their hometown, and the people with whom they interact daily.

The metaphor of small places linking to larger ones seems apt for this encyclopedia, since all of the seemingly disconnected stories that make up the state's history are, in reality, part of one comprehensive narrative—that of North Carolina itself, a place whose history stretches back more than 400 years and continues to evolve during each new day of the twenty-first century. In this volume, more than 560 contributors—living from the mountains to the sea—offer articles written from their own perspectives and addressing approximately 2,000 individual topics of interest. But the stories are bound together, literally and figuratively, and within the larger alphabetical organization of the work are also topical connections. Short articles on subjects of specific or more local interest link topically to longer articles on broader issues, and these in turn connect to the longest essay-length articles on major topics.

The process of assembling and editing the encyclopedia to suggest these connections has undoubtedly been more art than science. Just as North Carolina has cities that retain a "cozy" feel and tiny hamlets that nevertheless have played major roles in the state's history, this encyclopedia has articles that, for their own reasons, do not adhere neatly to length expectations. But in the end, taken together, they represent the editors' best efforts to tell the whole story of North Carolina in a straightforward and valuable way.

While the *Encyclopedia of North Carolina* features numerous articles on the natural environment, scientific pursuits, technological advancements, and similar subjects, it takes a primarily humanities-based approach, addressing subjects from the perspective of their importance and impact in human history and culture. The editors have endeavored to address the broad sweep of North Carolina history, indeed even its prehistory, from the time before European contact until the present day; but, inevitably the focus is on recorded history from exploration and colonial settlement forward. Where the question of whether or not to include an article has arisen—and of course it has arisen often—the editors have consistently erred on the side of addressing subjects with a firm geographical or cultural connection to North Carolina and an enduring impact on the state's history. In the area of business and industry, for example, articles on large, multinational firms with relatively brief or limited ties to the state may have been omitted in favor of articles on smaller businesses based in North Carolina for their entire history.

The editors devoted considerable time and energy to the matter of geography and the best way to address it in this encyclopedia. They were guided first by the availability of geographical information in the *North Carolina Gazetteer*, which provides information on some 20,000 places, including counties, cities, towns, small crossroads communities, lakes, rivers, mountains, sounds, and inlets. Second, the editors were guided by the fact that North Carolina has developed, not within the shadow of a single huge metropolis or other central urban area, but through the history and progress of its counties and its many small communities, towns, and mid-sized cities. Reflecting this, the encyclopedia includes short articles on all 100 North Carolina counties and select cities and towns. The latter have been chosen by the editors on the basis of their significance in the early history of the state or for their key contributions to its modern composition and character. North Carolina's largest cities also have individual articles by virtue of the criteria just mentioned as well as their importance in the state's modern-day economy and culture.

Because of the large number of subjects included and the desire of the editors to make the encyclopedia as user-friendly as possible, articles are in many instances connected through a system of cross-references, enabling readers to explore related topics quickly and efficiently. Cross-referencing has been undertaken with readers' good sense in mind and should not be considered a complete list of every related subject referred to in a particular article.

Authorship and Point of View

Most of the articles in the *Encyclopedia of North Carolina* have been written by a single contributor, but in some cases two or more authors are credited. In such cases, authors are listed in order of their contribution, the first author having written the majority of the article and any that follow a lesser but still substantial portion. Other authors whose work was relied upon to complete an article in some way are credited as having contributed additional research.

The editors of the *Encyclopedia of North Carolina* have attempted to preserve the narrative voice of individual authors and allowed some stories to be told in a style suited to the subject matter. Consequently, the articles on moonshine or the Devil's Tramping Ground may touch the ear in a completely different way from the articles on exports or the Federalist Party. Although most articles are relatively brief, sometimes historical or editorial arguments—often presented by the contributors—compelled the editors to devote a larger amount of space to a given topic.

References

Rather than simply offering a list of works cited, the bibliographic references following the majority of articles in the encyclopedia represent works that the authors and/or editors believe would well serve readers in search of more information on the subject and would likely be readily available to the general population. Personal papers and other limited-availability sources have been omitted in most cases. In addition to scholarly works directly treating the subject, popular histories sometimes have been included to assist readers who may desire to approach the subject within the wider scope of North Carolina history. The editors acknowledge that these references are suggestive rather than comprehensive. Readers are always encouraged to consult general histories of the state and the collections of North Carolina's excellent libraries for additional information.

Statistics and Names

Statistical information in the encyclopedia—such as population and economic figures—is current at least through the 2000 U.S. Census and in most cases through 2005 estimates. Names of towns, schools, and businesses generally appear as they were during the era covered in an article, with parenthetical reference to their modern names as seems helpful. All named cities and towns are in North Carolina unless otherwise noted, with the exception of well-known U.S. cities that require no further identification.

Abbreviations

The following abbreviations are used in the references and illustration credits:

NCC
North Carolina Collection, University of North Carolina at Chapel Hill Library

NCHR
North Carolina Historical Review

NCOA&H
North Carolina Office of Archives and History, Raleigh

UNC
University of North Carolina

A

Aberdeen & Rockfish Railroad Company (A&R), chartered on 22 June 1892, became one of North Carolina's most colorful and successful "short-line" railroads. It was founded by Aberdeen businessman and Civil War veteran John Blue, who owned and controlled substantial tracts of longleaf pine forestland east of Aberdeen and needed a way to transport his lumber and turpentine stores to the rail head at Aberdeen. From there they could be shipped to market on the Raleigh & Augusta Air Line Railroad (which later became part of the Seaboard Air Line Railway).

Construction on the standard-gauge line began immediately, and by June 1893 the railroad had reached "Buffalo," nine miles from Aberdeen. Over the next few years the main line pushed to Endon in an area later included in Fort Bragg at the headwaters of Rockfish Creek. On 30 June 1897 a branch line arrived in Raeford, where on the same day John Blue and railroad surveyor Hector Smith laid out Main Street.

Over the years, the Aberdeen & Rockfish was one of the more innovative railroads. It was among the first to use gasoline-powered rail cars to carry passengers (1921), to provide door-to-door delivery for package freight (1931), to convert to diesel power for freight trains (1947), to use radio for train operations (1966), and to computerize accounting (1967). In 1987 the A&R acquired a branch line from CSX between Dunn and Erwin and formed the Dunn & Erwin Railway, which served a large denim mill in Erwin. A short time later, a second line opened at Bennettsville, S.C.; called the Pee Dee River Railway, it served a paper mill and board plant. The A&R also provided service to a chemical resin plant, a cosmetics company, a newspaper, a scrap dealer, and a variety of other shippers. These three lines made up the A&R of the 1990s until the Dunn-Erwin line shut down in 1998.

At the beginning of the twenty-first century, the family of founder John Blue still maintained control of the A&R, one of the most profitable short lines operating in the United States. Continuing to serve the south-central region of North Carolina and businesses in Moore, Hoke, and Cumberland Counties, it carried such commodities as industrial chemicals, coal, oil, scrap metal, newsprint, fertilizer, lumber and building materials, plastics, and steel beams. According to the Railway Association of North Carolina, the A&R operates 46 miles of track, employs about 30 people, and moves 4,000 carloads (385,000 tons) of freight a year. It has connections with CSX, the Norfolk Southern Railroad, and three short-line carriers, as well as an intermodal truck-to-rail and rail-to-truck system. The company's motto is "The Road of Personal Service."

Reference: Jim Wrinn and Edward Lewis, *The Road of Personal Service: A Centennial History* (1992).

Edward A. Lewis

Aberdeen, Carolina, and Western Railroad. In 1889 the Aberdeen & West End Railroad was chartered to build a line from Aberdeen to Star, while the Asheboro & Montgomery built a line from Asheboro to Star from the other direction in 1896. These lines, along with the Jackson Springs Railroad, were formally merged as the Aberdeen & Asheboro (A&A) in 1907. Five years later, the Raleigh, Charlotte, and Southern was established by the Norfolk Southern Railroad (NS) to take control of the A&A. Afterward, construction continued west from Mount Gilead to Charlotte, a distance of 52 miles, until completion on 1 Dec. 1913.

The NS operated the Charlotte-Raleigh line as part of the Western Division until 1974, when the Southern Railway Company incorporated the NS into its system. Southern continued operations until 1982, when abandonment proceedings were begun for the line from Star to Aberdeen.

An agreement was reached with the Southern in 1983 to operate this section of the old NS as the Aberdeen & Briar Patch (A&BP) under the control of Willard Formyduvall. The A&BP was in service for five years before it was sold in 1987 to Robert M. Menzie, who changed the name to the Aberdeen, Carolina, and Western Railroad (AC&W). Menzie soon realized that the relatively short section of track was greatly dependent on both the Southern Railway and the Aberdeen & Rockfish for survival. He therefore leased the section of the old NS from Charlotte through Star to Gulf, a distance of 105 miles. The resulting AC&W became a vibrant short line headquartered in Star, finding a niche hauling traffic once thought too light for the big systems.

By 2004, serving businesses in Montgomery, Moore, Mecklenburg, Cabarrus, Chatham, and Stanly Counties, the road carried lumber and forest products, grain and agricultural products, plastics, building materials, propane gas, and solite rock products. Since its inception, the AC&W has upgraded more than 30 miles of its track with 132-pound, continuous-welded rail to handle modern larger-capacity freight cars. In the early 2000s it had connections with four railroads (CSX, Norfolk Southern, Aberdeen & Rockfish, and Winston-Salem Southbound), operated 160 miles of track, had 20 employees, and carried 12,000 carloads (about 1.2 million tons) a year with its 12 locomotives.

Reference: R. E. Prince, *Norfolk Southern Railroad—Old Dominion Line and Connections* (1972).

Larry K. Neal Jr.

Abolitionism. SEE Colonization Societies; Manumission Societies; Underground Railroad.

A. C. Monk and Company was founded in Farmville in 1907 by Albert Coy Monk. Initially, Monk and one assistant bought tobacco and shipped it in hogsheads from the Farmville railroad station. After weathering the panic of 1907, the company flourished by concentrating on foreign markets and steadily grew to become one of the world's largest independent dealers and exporters of flue-cured tobacco. A. C. Monk and Company built a larger warehouse in 1913, replacing an earlier structure purchased in 1907. The company initially packed its product green in hogsheads on the warehouse floor, but subsequently it built a small redrying room and finally a full-scale processing plant on Horne Avenue. In 1933 the company expanded this plant to double its capacity.

By the 1980s the company occupied a 55-acre landscaped tract with a processing plant covering 10 acres, and it employed approximately 70 buyers, more than 30 salesmen, and an in-season labor force of approximately 1,000. Its buying organization covered every American tobacco belt, as well as markets in Guatemala, Italy, Brazil, Korea, and Canada, and it sold tobacco throughout the world. To remain competitive, Monk and Company continued to expand, doubling its size in 1990 by acquiring Austin Company, a Greeneville, Tenn.-based tobacco merchant.

In November 1992 the Monk-Austin company went public, trading on the New York Stock Exchange, but Monk family members retained more than 70 percent of the shares. In April 1993 the company expanded again by acquiring its joint-venture partner, Centerleaf (Malawi) Limited, and the tobacco division of T. S. Ragsdale Leaf Company of Lake City, S.C. In 1994 the company diversified when Albert C. Monk III forged a merger with Dibrell Brothers of Danville, Va., leading to the creation on 1 Apr. 1995 of DIMON, Inc. The new enterprise, headquartered in Danville, became the world's second-largest leaf tobacco dealer as well as the world's largest importer and exporter of fresh cut flowers. In 1997 DIMON acquired Intabex Holdings Worldwide, S.A., the world's fourth-largest leaf merchant, and in September 1998 it sold its flower business. By 2004 DIMON had more than $1 billion in assets.

Charles H. McArver

Act of Pardon and Oblivion was passed at Hillsborough by the North Carolina General Assembly of 1783, the state's first legislature to convene after the Revolutionary War. The act embodied the most important of several 1783 measures regarding the treatment of North Carolina Tories, or Loyalists. It originated as a moderate bill, drawn up by Archibald Maclaine and introduced in the House of Commons (Lower House) by William Cumming. Both men were members of the House Committee on Public Bills. Maclaine's desire for clemency for Loyalists was grounded in the Wilmington lawyer's conservative philosophy and shaped by his friendship with several Loyalists.

The bill passed the first reading in both Houses of the legislature on 7 May 1783. No further action was taken on it until after Maclaine left Hillsborough just three days prior to the end of the session. At that point the bill underwent significant changes that reflected a harsher stance toward Loyalist concerns. Prior to the Declaration of Independence, a series of laws passed in the state had confiscated first movable goods and later all property of persons who joined or aided the British. After the war, the emerging peace treaty with Britain called such laws into question. Already the November 1782 Preliminary Articles had stipulated that the Continental Congress would urge states to allow Loyalists to return home and regain their confiscated property. In North Carolina, the final form of the Act of Pardon and Oblivion, while pardoning all but a specifically designated class of Loyalists, also confirmed the state's earlier anti-Loyalist legislation in the face of the peace treaty, protecting past, present, and future purchasers of confiscated land from any attempt of the Continental Congress to fulfill its treaty obligation.

The final clause of the act listed categories of exclusion from the projected pardon, including those who had become officers in the British army or had left the state with the British and stayed away for more than a year. Loyalists Samuel Andrews, Peter Mallet, and David Fanning were specifically excluded. The act concluded by also withholding pardon for those who had committed "willful and deliberate murder, robbery and house-burning."

Almost as soon as it was passed, the Act of Pardon and Oblivion was used successfully by nine defendants accused of treason in the May 1783 term of the Wilmington District Superior Court. Each of the nine, after pleading the act, was discharged after paying court fees. Significantly, Mallet's treason case in the same court was handled differently. Mallet did not appeal to the Act of Pardon and Oblivion since its exclusions named him. Instead, he underwent a trial in which the jury agreed that he had met the conditions of the governor's proclamation of pardon. Apparently this referred to a December 1781 proclamation in which Governor Alexander Martin had offered pardon to Loyalists who would enlist in Continental service by 10 Mar. 1782.

The Act of Pardon and Oblivion was only one way in which the 1783 General Assembly addressed the issue of Loyalist property and legal status. Another 1783 act gave county courts more supervision over commissioners of confiscated property. In addition, a new law suspended the statute of limitations for the period between 4 July 1776 and 1 June 1784. Suspension enabled creditors to sue for debts that had been unrecoverable during the war. Its final clause, however, denied any benefit of the act to persons either "included within the description of

... the confiscation laws" or who "have withdrawn themselves from the common defense of the country during the war" or to their agents or heirs. Thus creditors could sue Loyalist and British debtors for old debts, but Loyalist and British creditors (most conspicuously British merchants) could not reciprocate. Another act made it clear that persons who had been active Loyalists could not become citizens simply by taking the oath that the state required for militia service.

Reference: Walter Clark, ed., *The State Records of North Carolina* (16 vols., 1895–1906).

Carole Watterson Troxler

Adjutant General. The Militia Acts passed in 1792 and 1795 by the U.S. Congress required the North Carolina legislature in 1806 to establish the Department of the Adjutant General to better organize and train the state militia. The modern adjutant general, appointed by the governor, is director of the North Carolina National Guard. As head of the state's military force, the appointee must have had at least five years' commissioned service in an active status in one of the nation's armed forces. The North Carolina National Guard is subject to the call of the governor for state matters and of the U.S. president in times of national emergency.

Jeffrey Allen Howard

SEE ALSO National Guard.

Admiralty Courts in the colonial era dealt with maritime issues requiring adjudication, including both criminal and noncriminal matters. Although the royal Charters of 1663 and 1665 granted power to the Lords Proprietors to create courts of admiralty, they never did so. The Navigation Act of 1696, however, provided that the High Court of Admiralty in England could create vice-admiralty courts in the various colonies to enforce the act. One such court established in Virginia in 1697 claimed jurisdiction over North Carolina, but the assertion was successfully resisted by the latter's Governor Henderson Walker. The colony's governor and council thereafter appointed the court's judge, who tried cases without a jury and named the register and other officials. The judge also could designate surrogates for ports where he did not hold court in person. Although few records of the vice-admiralty courts survive for the colonial period or after, it is known that they tried several prize cases during wartime and libeled vessels for violation of the Navigation Acts. The courts also tried cases relating to mercantile activity, such as suits for wages.

In June 1776 the Council of Safety assumed the power of appointing vice-admiralty judges and other court officials for the various ports in North Carolina, a duty to which the General Assembly fell heir after independence. North Carolina's ratification of the U.S. Constitution in 1789 brought state control of admiralty courts to an end, since that document extended the judicial power of the United States to "all cases of admiralty and maritime jurisdiction."

Reference: Carl W. Ubbelohde Jr., "The Vice-Admiralty Court of Royal North Carolina, 1729–1759," *NCHR* 31 (October 1954).

Robert J. Cain

Adoption, according to a 1996 North Carolina law, is "the creation by law of the relationship of parent and child between two individuals." Adoption and guardianship are legal ways for a responsible adult to provide the necessary care and nurture to children or incompetent adults when the parent is unable to fulfill this responsibility. This is crucial to ensure that some level of care, supervision, and guidance is available to the children and other citizens.

In North Carolina, the adoption of children can occur when parental rights are terminated through relinquishment (the voluntary surrender of a child to an agency for adoption) or through consent (the voluntary surrender of a child for adoption by a parent or guardian in a direct or independent placement). Any minor or child may be adopted, as well as adults or children who have been emancipated. However, the legal requirements are quite different for these procedures. The major difference between guardianship and adoption is that in adoption the child is viewed legally the same as a birth child.

Any adult (defined as a person over age 18) may adopt or be appointed guardian in North Carolina. Public agencies may also be appointed as guardian, usually when incompetent adults have no family, relative, or friend capable and willing to serve as guardian. Children are placed for adoption by child welfare agencies, a guardian, or the birth parent(s). The adoption of Indian children in the state is governed by the federal Indian Child Welfare Act. Special policies and procedures apply to this group.

Many children available for adoption are in the custody of the Division of Social Services within the North Carolina Department of Health and Human Services. These children typically were found by a local court to have been abused or neglected. They were removed from their parent(s) and placed in substitute care to ensure their protection from further serious abuse or neglect. In severe cases, and in situations where the parent fails to make the necessary changes for the child to be returned home, authorities may file a termination-of-parental-rights petition asking the court to grant the agency the authority to seek an adoptive placement for the child. If the court determines that there is adequate evidence to terminate parental rights, the child is freed for adoption. This severing of parental ties occurs only in the most serious cases.

References: I. B. Nelson, ed., *Children and the Law: A Casebook for Practice* (1992); North Carolina Division of Social Services, *Family Services Manual* (1996).

Lisa C. Shaffer

Ad Valorem Taxation of Slaves was a major political issue in antebellum North Carolina and continued during the Civil War as a manifestation of the divisions between the planter class and the nonslaveholding majority. Until the issue was resolved, slaves were taxed as persons rather than as property. Based on the Constitutional Convention of 1835, no levy was imposed on slaves under age 12 and over age 50; all others were assessed at an amount not to exceed the poll tax for white men. As long as property and poll taxes remained low, this provision raised no particular concern. By the late 1850s, however, when assessments were increased to support railroad construction and other internal improvements, small farmers and laborers felt that they were bearing an unfair share of the tax burden.

In 1858 the remnants of the disintegrating Whig Party took the fight for ad valorem taxation of slaves to the state legislature. Senator Moses A. Bledsoe of Wake County led the effort to have slaves taxed as property rather than as persons. Although his attempt failed, it aroused strong feelings on both sides of the issue. In 1860, when Whig candidate John Pool ran against incumbent Democratic governor John W. Ellis, ad valorem taxation was the major plank of Pool's platform. Ellis narrowly won reelection by a vote of 59,396 to 53,303. The fact that 17,000 more votes were cast for governor than for president suggests the intensity of the debate.

The Secession Convention of May 1861 finally amended the state constitution to provide for ad valorem taxation of slaves. Forced to act, the legislature passed a bill that provided for a $500 exemption and ad valorem taxation based on estimates of value established by the slave owners. When it met again in 1862, the convention eliminated the $500 exemption. In early 1863 the legislature stipulated that the value of slaves was to be determined by the same agency that assessed real estate.

Although the proponents of the new tax won the debate, the long delay in ad valorem taxation illustrates the power of the tiny planter minority in North Carolina. On the other hand, the triumph of ad valorem advocates demonstrates the growing democratization of state politics.

References: William K. Boyd, "Ad Valorem Slave Taxation, 1858–1860," *Historical Papers, Historical Society of Trinity College* (repr., 1970); Donald C. Butts, "A Challenge to Planter Rule: The Controversy over the Ad Valorem Taxation of Slaves in North Carolina, 1858–1862" (Ph.D. diss., Duke University, 1978); Butts, "'Irrepressible Conflict': Slave Taxation and North Carolina's Gubernatorial Election of 1860," *NCHR* 58 (January 1981).

Ronnie W. Faulkner

Advance was the first and most famous of four blockade-running vessels that the state of North Carolina operated in partnership with the Alexander Collie Company of London and Manchester during the Civil War. Originally a passenger steamer named the *Lord Clyde* that plied the waters between Dublin, Ireland, and Glasgow, Scotland, the ship was converted to a blockade-runner in 1863. After its first run into Wilmington, it was renamed the *Advance*, a name that would often be confused with the ship's sponsor, Governor Zebulon B. Vance. The vessel became one of the war's most successful blockade-runners, although its career in that dangerous business did not exceed 15 months. In early September 1864 the *Advance*, after running Cape Fear's New Inlet, was overtaken by the *Santiago de Cuba*, one of the Union's swiftest blockaders, and forced to surrender. Given to the Union navy and renamed the *Frolic*, the steamer was converted to a blockader and returned to the waters off Wilmington, where ironically it was used to intercept Confederate runners.

References: Dawson Carr, *Gray Phantoms of the Cape Fear: Running the Civil War Blockade* (1998); Kenneth Wayne Robinson, "North Carolina's Blockade-Running Partnership: An Effort toward Self-Sufficiency during the Civil War" (M.A. thesis, North Carolina State University, 1973); Stephen R. Wise, *Lifeline of the Confederacy: Blockade-Running during the Civil War* (1988).

William C. Harris

Advancement School. The North Carolina Advancement School in Winston-Salem was one of the education initiatives of Governor Terry Sanford (1961–65), who conceived it as a counterpart to the Gifted and Talented Programs begun in 1962. With North Carolina's school dropout rate among the nation's highest at 40 percent, Sanford wanted to address the needs of academic underachievers—those with average or above average abilities who were nevertheless performing poorly in school and likely to drop out. Sanford charged Ralph McCallister, formerly of Syracuse University and the Chautauqua Institute, with assembling educational experts to design a strategy to keep such underachievers in school. With a planning grant from the U.S. Office of Education, McCallister, working principally with Sanford adviser John Ehle and Harold Howe II, former superintendent of public schools in Scarsdale, N.Y., developed and proposed the Advancement School.

The Advancement School, like the North Carolina School of the Arts and the Governor's School for the Gifted, was to be a residential facility and a teaching laboratory and research center with three fundamental tasks: to assemble existing materials and techniques used to teach students achieving from one to three grades below national norms, to develop new materials and techniques to further students' achievement levels and educational aspirations, and to work with classroom teachers so that materials could be transferred from the residence-school setting to local schools.

In a unique arrangement, the Learning Institute of North Carolina (LINC), headed by Howe and located at the Quail

Roost Conference Center in Rougemont, contracted with the State Board of Education to operate the Advancement School until 30 June 1967. With a combination of state funds and grants from the U.S. Office of Education and the Carnegie Corporation, Advancement School director Gordon L. McAndrew leased the vacated City Memorial Hospital from Winston-Salem. The Advancement School opened its doors to 82 boys for a six-week pilot session on 8 Nov. 1964.

In addition to instructional techniques, the Advancement School pioneered in race relations. Ten years after the landmark Supreme Court case *Brown v. Board of Education*, only about 6 percent of the state's black children attended integrated schools. In the Advancement School's pilot session, there were 51 white children, 22 blacks, and 9 Native Americans. During the regular sessions, African American enrollment averaged 25 percent to 30 percent of the student body. The Advancement School established firm ties with schools in Hoke and Robeson Counties, and Native American enrollment in at least one session constituted about 40 percent of the student body. Donald G. Hayes, the assistant director, made room assignments without consideration to racial identity, a practice continued throughout the life of the school.

From November 1964 through June 1967, the Advancement School enrolled 2,331 students from 133 of the state's 169 school systems. Although the legislature approved continuation of the Advancement School beyond 1967, it drastically reduced the budget and placed the school under the supervision of the State Board of Education. The school enrolled only 144 students in January 1968, and after the spring 1969 session, enrollment dropped below 100. A nonresidency component was added, and after 1971 the school only enrolled day students. In its final three years, the Advancement School continued as a year-round day school for Winston-Salem students. In 1975 a budget crisis forced the legislature to make massive cuts. The state provided the Advancement School only enough funds to prepare a final report. A skeleton staff moved to Graylyn Estate on the campus of Wake Forest University, where it conducted a few more workshops, completed its report, and closed the school in 1976.

References: John N. Bridgman Jr. and Ernestine M. Godfrey, *The Investigation and Treatment of Underachievement in North Carolina: Final Report, 1964–1976: The North Carolina Advancement School, Winston-Salem* (1976); Chester Davis, "North Carolina Advancement School: A New Approach to the Student Who Can Do . . . but Doesn't," *Southern Education Report* (July–August 1965); Terry Sanford, *But What about the People?* (1966).

Paul E. Kuhl

Advertising. Mass advertising in North Carolina began with the founding of the printing trade in the eighteenth century. James Davis, the state's first printer, established the *North-*

Advertisements appearing in the 4 Nov. 1820 issue of the *Cape-Fear Recorder* in Wilmington. Newspapers were a primary outlet for advertisers from the state's early days well into the twentieth century. NCC.

Carolina Gazette in New Bern in August 1751. To make the paper successful, Davis focused on subscriptions but found them to be an unreliable source of revenue. Far more lucrative were the advertisements that soon appeared, not only in Davis's *Gazette* but in other colonial newspapers, such as Andrew Steuart's *North-Carolina Gazette* (1764–67) and Adam Boyd's *Cape-Fear Mercury* (1769–76). Newspapers between 1751 and 1778 featured ads relating to property and trade (the buying and selling of slaves and servants; the buying, selling, and

Advertisements painted on the sides of buildings, Kinston, ca. 1922. NCC.

leasing of real estate; the importation and exportation of commodities) as well as cultural and social affairs.

Broadsides were a popular advertising medium throughout the colonial and antebellum periods. Unlike newspapers, broadsides were printed on only one side of a sheet of paper. They were handed out individually and were used to advertise everything from theatrical performances, railroad schedules, store openings, and rewards for runaway slaves to the messages of poets and other writers, political parties and candidates, religious societies, reform organizations, and businesses.

Magazines (periodicals or journals) began appearing in North Carolina around the middle of the nineteenth century. The decision to include advertising varied with the publication, with many accepting ads relevant to their trade or profession. For example, the *North Carolina Journal of Education*, established in 1857 under the editorship of Calvin H. Wiley, ran ads for schoolbooks, booksellers, academies, and book and job printing. The *Medical Journal of North Carolina*, begun just prior to the Civil War, included ads for medical books, druggists, and the Medical College of Virginia and its hospital. Other magazines such as the *North Carolina Historical Review*, *Popular Government*, or *Appalachian Journal* did not include advertising.

North Carolina entered the world of radio advertising in April 1922 with the establishment of the state's first commercial radio station, WBT in Charlotte. Advertisers increasingly employed the power of radio, and by the 1950s, television, to carry their message to thousands, even millions, of North Carolinians in an instant.

The first advertising agency in North Carolina is believed to have been Bennett Advertising, established in 1922 in High Point by Harold C. Bennett. The firm continued under that name until the 1970s, when, following Bennett's retirement, it became Behrends and Company, with Richard D. Behrends as president. Most of Bennett's accounts were with out-of-state clients. By 1965 there were more than 50 reported advertising agencies in North Carolina. By 2000 the number of agencies

capable of assuming responsibility for complete advertising campaigns in the state had reached 626.

Modern advertising in North Carolina, as in every U.S. state, is sustained by the growth of high-tech media, which still includes radio and television but since the mid-1990s has become increasingly dominated by the Internet. Even the somewhat homely, old-fashioned highway billboard has been updated: many now feature computerized screens capable of changing images to advertise a variety of products from one location. Controversy has developed over the legality and suitability of these billboards and other low-tech versions in certain sections of the state's highway system. Various public policy groups have fought against billboard usage with the backing of the federal Highway Beautification Act, an environmental law passed by Congress in 1965.

References: Ray O. Hummel, *Southeastern Broadsides before 1877: A Bibliography* (1971); Wesley H. Wallace, "Cultural and Social Advertising in Early North Carolina Newspapers," *NCHR* 33 (July 1956).

Wiley J. Williams

Advisory Budget Commission (ABC) was created when the General Assembly of 1925 enacted the Executive Budget Act to vest the governor with more direct supervision of state agencies and institutions. The act also enabled the chief executive to initiate a balanced budget for presentation before each session of the legislature. The ABC was part of the Budget Bureau, established by the legislature within the governor's office. The governor was designated as the Budget Bureau's director and ex officio head and was authorized to appoint a budget officer as an assistant.

The ABC superseded the Budget Commission (created by the General Assembly in 1919) and assisted, but was subordinate to, the governor. It included the chairs of the appropriations and finance committees of the General Assembly and two gubernatorial appointees. In addition to advisory duties concerning state expenditures and finance, the ABC assisted the director in the preparation of the budget. The legislature has from time to time altered the duties, responsibilities, and membership of the ABC, but its role in the state's fiscal decisions has remained essentially the same.

Reference: Clyde L. Ball, *The Advisory Budget Commission* (rev. ed., 1983).

Wiley J. Williams

African American Dance Ensemble, founded in Durham in 1984 by Raleigh native Chuck Davis, seeks to preserve and promote traditional African and American dance and music while entertaining and educating its audiences. A pioneer in the African heritage movement and internationally acclaimed as a dancer and choreographer, Davis was the artistic director of the New York City–based Chuck Davis Dance Company when he received an invitation from Charles Reinhardt, director of the American Dance Festival (ADF), to return to North Carolina in 1980 to be on the ADF faculty and to lead its Community Outreach Program. Davis brought along his New York dancers and decided to stay. Within four years the African American Dance Ensemble (AADE), by then made up largely of dancers trained in North Carolina, had emerged to become a mainstay of the state's dance community.

In addition to its mission of preserving African dance heritage, the AADE promotes cross-cultural understanding and respect for all peoples, carrying this message to audiences across North Carolina and the United States and abroad. The AADE has an impressive record for concert work and activities in schools and communities far beyond the borders of the state. Its repertoire includes traditional and contemporary African and American dance. Donald McKayle's *Games* was presented as part of the ADF's Black Tradition in American Modern Dance Project, which began in 1987. Davis and other choreographers create original, non-African pieces for the ensemble. In 1997 Ronald K. Brown choreographed *Free*, which the AADE premiered on a program with other works. The Lila Wallace Reader's Digest Program for Leading Dance Centers supported this endeavor as part of the ADF Dance and Community Project.

Patricia L. Pertalion

African Americans in North Carolina, as in other southern states, have experienced a difficult, often tragic, but uniquely inspiring journey from their introduction into the region as slaves in the seventeenth century to the modern day. Critical eras in black history have thrown light on both the evils and the graces of North Carolina society, particularly blacks' liberation from the inhumanity of the nineteenth-century slave system and entry into a postemancipation culture generally unwilling to accept them as legal or social equals. The struggle of African Americans for equality and prosperity defined much of the state's history throughout the twentieth century, leading to the seismic changes created by the civil rights movement of the 1950s and 1960s. Their fight persisted in the twenty-first century through various lawsuits involving the constitutionality of congressional voting districts and school busing plans, as well as numerous educational and political programs. As a result of the progress made, and despite continuing poverty, racism, and social injustice, by the early 2000s the professional, economic, social, and personal lives of a growing number of African Americans in North Carolina differed little from the lives of other citizens.

Life under Slavery and the Achievements of Free Blacks

The eight Lords Proprietors who received the Carolina charter from England's King Charles II in 1663 planned from the beginning to employ slave labor in their colony. The Fundamental Constitutions drafted in 1669 explicitly mention the slave status of Africans. Barbadians, who were among the first colonists to invest in Carolina, persuaded the Proprietors to institute a headright system under which settlers received a certain amount of acreage for each "Negro-Man or Slave" and "Woman-Negro or Slave" brought to the province.

Yet slavery grew slowly in North Carolina. The colony's treacherous coastline and poor harbors forced planters to purchase slaves in Virginia or South Carolina and to transport them overland or along inland water routes. Relatively few slaves were imported directly by sea, and those who were usually came from other mainland colonies or the West Indies. A small number arrived straight from Africa. In 1712 the entire black population of North Carolina was estimated to be only 800. But as the eighteenth century progressed, the number of enslaved Africans in the colony exploded—from an estimated 6,000 in 1730 to about 41,000 in 1767. After the American Revolution and by the time of the first decennial census in 1790, the 100,572 slaves in North Carolina comprised one-fourth of its total population. From 1820 to 1860 the black population stabilized at between 32 and 33 percent of the aggregate population, reaching 331,059 in 1860.

Most slaves lacked adequate clothing, shelter, and nutrition and worked long hours. Slaveholders issued clothes twice a year, in the spring and autumn. Rations consisted of meat, meal, molasses, and potatoes. To supplement their diet, slaves planted their own gardens, hunted, and fished. In the rice-growing districts, a task system had become fairly standard by the 1840s, and most work could be completed by midafternoon. During the harvest season, however, men, women, and children labored from dawn to dusk seven days a week. Working in gangs, often under black drivers, slaves cleared new ground, rolled logs into heaps, planted crops, hoed, harvested, threshed, and transported crops to market.

The North Carolina legislature enacted the basic slave codes defining the social, economic, and physical place of bondservants in 1715 and 1741. In the ensuing years modifications followed. Slave patrols were instituted in 1753. Jurisdiction over slaves changed from special slave courts before 1791, to county courts, and finally to superior courts in 1816. It was not murder to kill a slave until 1817. By the 1850s the slave code prohibited slaves from engaging in a wide range of behaviors and activities, such as being disrespectful to whites, trespassing against whites, intermarrying or cohabiting with free blacks, running away, producing forged papers, hiring themselves out, hunting with a gun, and preaching at a prayer meeting where slaves of different masters were gathered. Slave codes also forbade whites to teach slaves or free blacks to read and write (teaching rudimentary math skills was allowed).

Periodically, rumors of slave revolts swept North Carolina. The most serious incidents occurred in 1775–76 at the outset

A rocking chair, bureau, and washstand made by free black cabinetmaker Thomas Day for David S. Reid, governor of North Carolina from 1851 to 1854. North Carolina Museum of History.

of the American Revolution and in 1780–81 as British troops under Lord Charles Cornwallis advanced across the state; in 1802, during the religious ferment of the Second Great Awakening, when slaves in both Virginia and North Carolina tried to organize a conspiracy; and in 1830–31, when the dual impact of David Walker's *Appeal* (1829) and the Nat Turner Rebellion in Virginia (1831) was felt. In each instance, white hysteria sometimes magnified the actual danger, and many innocent slaves were persecuted, transported, or murdered.

Yet blacks' desire for freedom was powerful, and their efforts to achieve it were often relentless. Runaways were frequent, and maroons in the Great Dismal Swamp lived for years unmolested by whites. For most blacks, release from bondage was a distant dream. Strict manumission laws across the South permitted emancipation only for "meritorious services" as determined by the courts. Quakers circumvented the law by giving slaves the "full benefit of their labour" or assigning liberated blacks to agents who would arrange for their transport to Haiti, Liberia, or the free-soil North. A few slaves managed to buy their own freedom and that of their families. John Carruthers Stanly of New Bern was emancipated in 1795, bought the freedom of his wife and family, and eventually became the largest black slaveholder in the South, owning at one time 163 slaves. From 1790 to 1860, manumission of African Americans steadily increased but never kept pace with the rise in slave numbers.

By the 1830s hundreds of free blacks—some whose freedom had been bought, others whose legal status was determined by the fact that their birth mother had been free —owned businesses and property in North Carolina; some prospered and became an integral part of the economic community. The cabinetmaking business of free black Thomas Day, headquartered in Caswell County, became one of the most successful enterprises in antebellum North Carolina. The population of free blacks was largest in the east and the Piedmont, and many freedpeople resided in towns. Around the end of the eighteenth century a significant number of free blacks in Virginia migrated to counties such as Halifax, Bertie, and Northampton in northeastern North Carolina; they were later joined by freedpeople from elsewhere in the state. From this demographic group would emerge the black leaders of the Reconstruction era. When North Carolina opted to leave the Union at the start of the Civil War, the state was home to more than 30,000 free blacks. That number, one of the largest in the nation, North or South, represented about 10 percent of the state's total African American population.

Religion was another aspect of colonial society that had attracted free blacks who aspired to leadership and influence, and by the late 1700s many whites had accepted their participation in church affairs as nonthreatening to the social order. Such tolerance was encouraged by the First Great Awakening that swept the colonies in the mid-eighteenth century. The crusading zeal of Baptists, Methodists, and Presbyterians for the lowly and disinherited made thousands of converts in the decades leading to the Revolutionary War.

John Chavis was North Carolina's most prominent antebellum black minister. Born free in Oxford, Chavis received training at Princeton University and Washington Academy (now Washington and Lee University) before he was recognized in 1801 by the General Assembly of the Presbyterian Church. After serving as a missionary outside the state for several years, he was appointed minister to Presbyterian churches in Granville, Wake, and Orange Counties. As he traveled his circuit for more than 20 years, Chavis drew general praise for his "prudence and piety." Perhaps his more lasting contribution was the organization of a school in Raleigh, where Chavis taught white children by day, including future political leaders, and free blacks in the evening. His school was considered one of the best in the state.

The activities of North Carolina's free blacks were nevertheless limited by many laws and customs. At various times during the antebellum era, freedpeople were not allowed to carry guns, to testify against whites in court, or to compete in business on an equal basis with whites. Their movements and right to assemble were also restricted. Until 1835, freedmen could vote in North Carolina, but the new state constitution of that year disfranchised them while extending more direct representation to white males. This marked the beginning of additional restrictions for free blacks as well as slaves, culminating in the 1861 law prohibiting African Americans from owning or controlling slaves—and by extension making it impossible for freedpeople to redeem others from slavery. In the years prior to the Civil War, free blacks in North Carolina faced further hardships as their rights were systematically diminished.

Emancipation and the Freedmen's Fight for Civil Rights

The conditions of African Americans changed dramatically after the outbreak of the Civil War. The Confederates used black slave labor to operate railroads, to construct earthworks and fortifications, and—in the closing days of the conflict—to fight in their army. Many slaves defected to Union forces in eastern North Carolina. A sizable number joined the African Brigade, first organized in New Bern, to bear arms for the Federal army. Perhaps as many as 5,000 black North Carolinians fought for the Union.

With the Emancipation Proclamation of 1863, nearly 4 million slaves were free people by the end of the war, more than 360,000 of them in North Carolina. Despite their lack of schooling, these African Americans demonstrated a clear vision of what they wanted and a strong determination to get it. Like their fellow citizens, they demanded independence and the opportunity to own their own farms, businesses, and homes, and they were willing to work as hard as necessary to achieve these goals. They also desired education for themselves and their children, making great sacrifices toward this end; a full and rewarding social life, surrounded by family and friends; and protection from physical abuse, intimidation, and discriminatory laws.

The majority of North Carolina's white population sought to keep African Americans in a subservient position, politically and economically. The state's 1865 black code restricted their movements, economic opportunities, and civil rights. Blacks were limited in their right to testify in court, received discriminatory penalties for crimes, and could not vote. Planters sought a stable labor force through restrictive contracts, low wages, apprenticeship, physical intimidation, and, in some cases, abuse of the court system. Most blacks worked peacefully but with determination to change attitudes and policies.

Socially, thousands of the state's African Americans reunited their families and married the person with whom they had previously cohabited. They deserted white churches and formed new ones, either affiliating with white northern or African Methodist Episcopal churches. Black churches quickly became the center not only for religious worship but also for educational instruction and community pride. Blacks also organized a rich cultural life, forming bands and lodges, sponsoring parades and exhibits, holding balls and dances, and establishing a few newspapers to serve their communities. Moreover, North Carolina's freedpeople exhibited a "mania"

An engraving from the 31 Jan. 1863 edition of *Harper's Weekly* shows former slaves who took refuge at a Union camp on Roanoke Island. The Federally occupied island quickly became a formal colony for newly freed slaves after issuance of the Emancipation Proclamation on 1 Jan. 1863.

for education. Almost immediately after the war, blacks in many areas began to raise money to build schools, buy books, and pay teachers. Within two years, more than 150 schools taught approximately 13,000 black children.

Freedmen held two statewide conventions (1865 and 1866), in addition to numerous mass meetings throughout the state. At these gatherings, they praised the work of congressional Republicans and the Freedmen's Bureau and called for full civil and political rights. They also pressed for more economic equality, complaining of physical abuse and intimidation, nonpayment of wages, mistreatment by their former masters, low pay, and the unavailability of land for them to purchase. Blacks established the Freedmen's Educational Association of North Carolina to promote black education and an Equal Rights League to advance their civil rights. Many of the state's traditionally black colleges were established in this era. Freedmen also organized one of the South's most successful Union Leagues, which became the basis for political education once black suffrage was instituted. They protested abuse of the apprenticeship system, whereby children were removed from their parents and apprenticed to their former owners. Taking their grievances to the Freedmen's Bureau and to state courts, they finally won a victory in 1867, when the North Carolina Supreme Court voided the apprenticeship contracts of Harriet and Eliza Ambrose to Daniel L. Russell and delivered a strong censure of those who violated due process of law.

When black men gained the vote in 1867, their political activity increased in North Carolina. Between 1876 and 1894, 52 African Americans were sent to the Lower House of the General Assembly. The Second Congressional District, known as the "Black Second," served as a political stronghold between 1872 and 1900, electing such representatives as John A. Hyman, the first African American in North Carolina to sit in the U.S. Congress; James E. O'Hara, the state's second black congressman; and George H. White, the last former slave to serve in Congress.

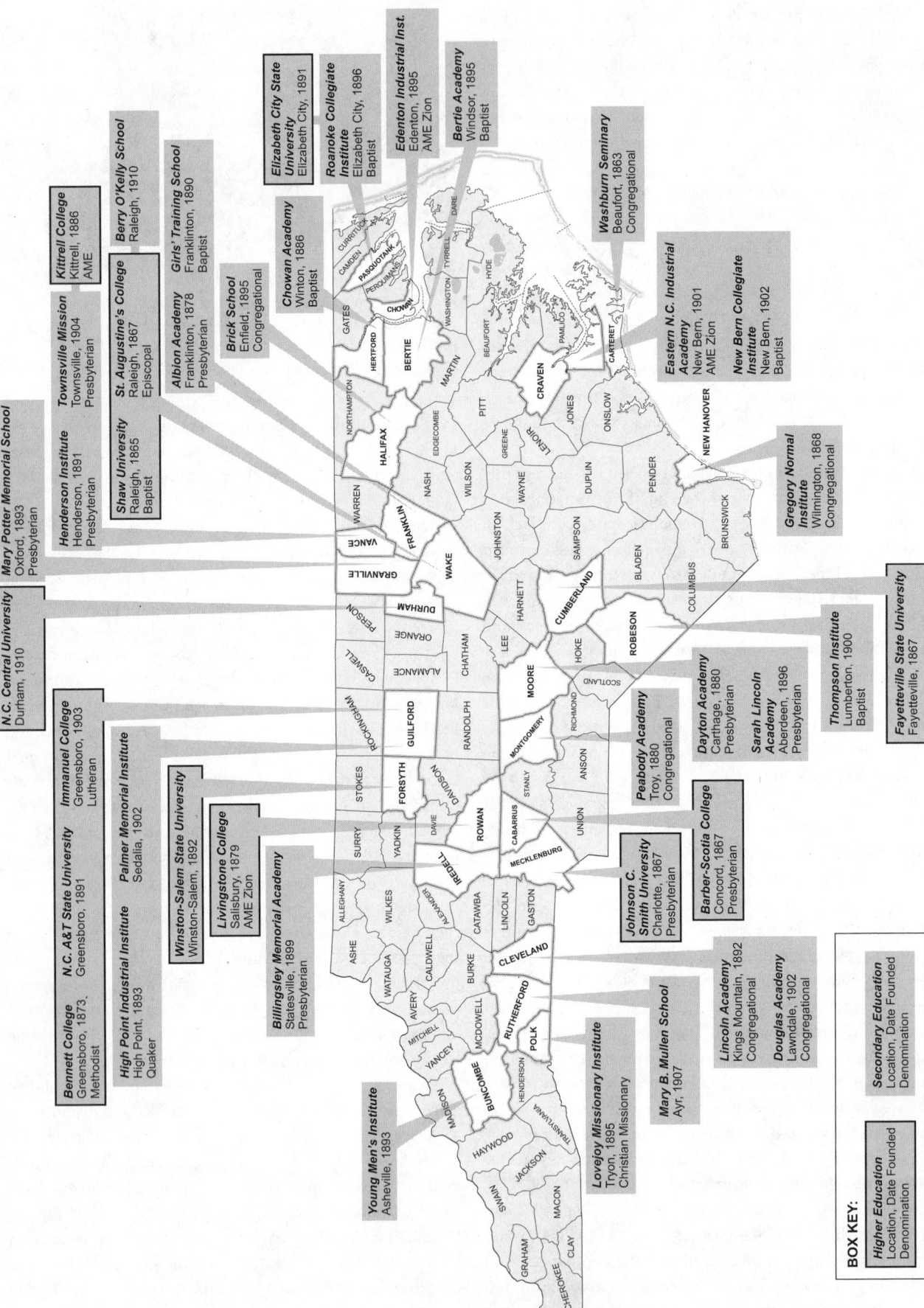

BOX KEY:

Higher Education
Location, Date Founded
Denomination

Secondary Education
Location, Date Founded
Denomination

African American educational institutions founded between Emancipation and 1910. Map by Mark Anderson Moore, courtesy NCOA&H.

N.C. Central University
Durham, 1910

Bennett College
Greensboro, 1873,
Methodist

N.C. A&T State University
Greensboro, 1891

Immanuel College
Greensboro, 1903,
Lutheran

High Point Industrial Institute
High Point, 1893
Quaker

Palmer Memorial Institute
Sedalia, 1902

Winston-Salem State University
Winston-Salem, 1892

Livingstone College
Salisbury, 1879
AME Zion

Billingsley Memorial Academy
Statesville, 1899
Presbyterian

Young Men's Institute
Asheville, 1893

Lovejoy Missionary Institute
Tryon, 1895
Christian Missionary

Mary B. Mullen School
Ayr, 1907

Lincoln Academy
Kings Mountain, 1892
Congregational

Douglas Academy
Lawndale, 1902
Congregational

Johnson C. Smith University
Charlotte, 1867
Presbyterian

Barber-Scotia College
Concord, 1867
Presbyterian

Peabody Academy
Troy, 1880
Congregational

Dayton Academy
Carthage, 1880
Presbyterian

Sarah Lincoln Academy
Aberdeen, 1896
Presbyterian

Thompson Institute
Lumberton, 1900
Baptist

Fayetteville State University
Fayetteville, 1867

Mary Potter Memorial School
Oxford, 1893
Presbyterian

Henderson Institute
Henderson, 1891
Presbyterian

Townsville Mission
Townsville, 1904
Presbyterian

Kittrell College
Kittrell, 1886
AME

Berry O'Kelly School
Raleigh, 1910

St. Augustine's College
Raleigh, 1867
Episcopal

Shaw University
Raleigh, 1865
Baptist

Girls' Training School
Franklinton, 1890
Baptist

Albion Academy
Franklinton, 1878
Presbyterian

Brick School
Enfield, 1895
Congregational

Chowan Academy
Winton, 1886
Baptist

Elizabeth City State University
Elizabeth City, 1891

Roanoke Collegiate Institute
Elizabeth City, 1896
Baptist

Edenton Industrial Inst.
Edenton, 1895
AME Zion

Bertie Academy
Windsor, 1895
Baptist

Washburn Seminary
Beaufort, 1863
Congregational

Eastern N.C. Industrial Academy
New Bern, 1901
AME Zion

New Bern Collegiate Institute
New Bern, 1902
Baptist

Gregory Normal Institute
Wilmington, 1868
Congregational

St. Stephen AME Church in Wilmington was formed by a community of former slaves after the Civil War. The church's edifice was begun in 1880 and completed in 1886; most of the construction, including the Gothic Revival interior woodwork, was done by church members. Photograph by Tim Buchman. Courtesy of Preservation North Carolina.

Life for black North Carolinians following Reconstruction appeared to be liberal by late nineteenth-century standards. After the passage of the national Civil Rights Act of 1875, many African Americans exercised their new freedom in railroad cars, steamboats, hotels, theaters, and other public venues. Their political gains came at great cost, however, and were muted by the return of Democrats to power in 1876. The new-found freedoms enjoyed by blacks fueled a brutal backlash by angry whites. North Carolina saw the eruption of widespread violence by groups such as the Ku Klux Klan, whose purpose was to terrorize blacks and diminish their newly won political rights. When the Republican and Populist Parties collaborated in the mid-1890s to again oust the Democrats, their "Fusion" government yielded blacks more funds for education and direct election of local officials, as well as a wealth-based tax system.

In response, brutal white supremacy campaigns in 1898 and 1900 enabled the Democratic Party—through fraud, intimidation, violence, and racist rhetoric—to return to power in North Carolina. The Democrats then set out to prevent any future challenges to white supremacy, a move grounded in African American disfranchisement. Building on the "separate-but-equal" doctrine established in the 1896 U.S. Supreme Court decision in *Plessy v. Ferguson*, North Carolina Democrats in 1899 passed Jim Crow laws instituting a system of legal segregation. The next year, white citizens approved a state constitutional amendment requiring all voters to pay a poll tax and pass a literacy test unless an ancestor had voted in an election prior to 1 Jan. 1867. Intended to disfranchise the African American population, the amendment succeeded in eliminating black North Carolinians from traditional politics.

Segregation and the Struggle for Equality

During the Jim Crow era, racial segregation combined with disfranchisement maintained the second-class citizenship of black North Carolinians. Segregation defined the physical place of blacks in society, as well as their position in the accepted social order. Blocked from political participation, many African American leaders of the middle class—comprised of teachers, clergymen, and businessmen—endorsed patience and accommodation. While they attempted to cultivate a spirit of cooperation with whites, other blacks simply worked to overcome continuing gross inequities, building successful businesses and educational institutions despite the lack of white support. Durham became a center for the black professional class in the early twentieth century. The North Carolina Mutual Life Insurance Company, headquartered there under the direction of John H. Merrick and Aaron M. Moore, was a prime example of African American achievement during the era. Mutual Life was the first black-owned insurance company in the state and the largest and most successful in the nation.

Building on the traditional role of women as the moral protectors of society, female African Americans proved to be particularly adept in this adverse political environment. With more than 30 years of involvement in temperance societies, Republican aid groups, and churches, black women in North Carolina became critical spokespersons for their communities and managed to turn the Progressive crusade for public cleanliness into a means to improve the living conditions of many African Americans. Regardless of these efforts, however, most white North Carolinians sought only to refine the Jim Crow system and retain systematic segregation.

Early in the twentieth century, organized resistance to segregation began to take form and gradually intensify. In 1932 black ministers in Raleigh refused to participate in the dedication of the new War Memorial Auditorium because African Americans would be confined to a small section of the balcony. In 1938 Greensboro students boycotted local theaters that supported the censure of "the appearance of colored people in scenes with whites on an equal basis."

Opposition to segregation began to grow more rapidly during and after World War II. In 1942 Montford Point Camp was established at Camp Lejune near Jacksonville to train the first African American members of the U.S. Marine Corps. Although Montford Point itself was separated from the rest of the camp, the training of black marines and their integration into the corps was a defining moment in ending federally sanctioned segregation. As they returned from service abroad in the armed forces, black men and women increasingly challenged their lack of complete freedom in the postwar society. Organizations such as the North Carolina chapter of the National Association for the Advancement of Colored People, which held its first state convention in 1943, became

A meeting of the Phyllis Wheatley YWCA in Charlotte, ca. 1940s. Founded in 1916, the Phyllis Wheatley Branch was the first African American YWCA branch in the United States. Photograph courtesy of Floretta Douglas Gunn. Carolina Room, Public Library of Charlotte and Mecklenburg County.

effective instruments for leading opposition to segregation of the races. In 1946 hundreds of students marched in downtown Lumberton to protest inadequate educational opportunities. In 1949 students from the North Carolina College for Negroes (modern-day North Carolina Central University) picketed the State Capitol to demand better law school facilities at the Durham institution. Limited desegregation of higher education occurred as the University of North Carolina School of Medicine at Chapel Hill accepted Edward O. Diggs as a student; four other black men entered the law school in 1951. By 1957 seven black activists led by Douglas E. Moore, a Methodist minister, sought service in the white section of a local ice cream parlor in Durham. Although these activists were arrested and convicted of trespassing, similar events elsewhere presaged more positive results as pressure for change increased and resistance gradually diminished.

Other, more reluctant North Carolina communities followed these examples, but it took more than three decades of court-ordered desegregation to deinstitutionalize the racial policies of the Jim Crow era. In the case of *Blue v. Durham Board of Education* (1951), a North Carolina court found that in the matter of unequal public school facilities, black children had been discriminated against because of their race. As a result of that finding, school officials conceded the existence of disparities between facilities for white and black children and the need for more equitable resources.

The 1954 ruling by the U.S. Supreme Court in *Brown v. Board of Education of Topeka, Kansas* that segregation in public schools solely on the basis of race was unconstitutional caused even greater consternation within North Carolina's white political community. In response, Governor William B. Umstead established a Special Advisory Committee on Education to "keep the law, keep the peace, and keep the schools." In December 1954 the committee recommended "that North Carolina try to find means of meeting the requirements of the Supreme Court's decision within our present school system before consideration is given to abandoning or materially altering it." It also proposed that the authority to make pupil assignments to individual schools be transferred from the State Board of Education to the appropriate local boards of education. The General Assembly adopted the committee's proposals in March 1955.

The following month the legislators created a seven-member North Carolina Advisory Committee on Education. New governor Luther H. Hodges appointed its members and named Thomas J. Pearsall as chair. The Pearsall Committee, as it became known, put forward a plan in which it recommended that educational expense grants be allocated from state or local public funds for the private schooling of any child who was assigned to an integrated school against the wishes of his or her parent or guardian. Moreover, local communities would be permitted—by majority vote—to suspend the operation of public schools if conditions became intolerable because of forced integration. The General Assembly adopted the plan in July 1956, and white voters overwhelmingly ratified the amendment in September. Although it purported to give local officials the authority to make decisions regarding their own school systems, the Pearsall Plan actually served to discourage or at least delay integration.

In the late summer of 1957, a dozen black students were enrolled in the previously all-white public schools of Charlotte, Greensboro, and Winston-Salem. From this small beginning, integration continued at a modest pace; in 1961, just over 200 black children attended classes with their white counterparts in 11 school districts. With the passage of the U.S. Civil Rights Act of 1964—providing that federal funds be withheld from school districts where racial discrimination continued to be practiced—North Carolina began more rigorous efforts to integrate its public school system.

Many people believed that the landmark decision in *Brown* applied to segregation in all accommodations, not just the public schools. In later cases, the U.S. Supreme Court upheld this view, but actual change was agonizingly slow in North Carolina, forced at almost every juncture by black activists. In one celebrated episode, four African American students from the North Carolina Agricultural and Technical College staged a sit-in at the lunch counter at Woolworth's in Greensboro in February 1960. They were soon joined by other blacks, and by the end of the week more than 300 students were participating in the protest, which had extended to other stores that served food. The movement spread to cities across the state, and after prolonged negotiations, all the stores involved agreed to make their food service available without regard to race. On 25 July 1960, the first African American was served at Woolworth's lunch counter in Greensboro.

Similar activities by young African Americans and their supporters integrated the state's theaters, hotels, motels, and restaurants in 1963. In the same year the General Assembly voted to desegregate the National Guard. With the federal Civil Rights Act of 1964 prohibiting discrimination in most public facilities, soon even municipal cemeteries were integrated, as were the athletic teams of many previously all-white colleges and universities. In 1966 the U.S. Supreme Court declared North Carolina's Pearsall Plan unconstitutional. Although none of the powers granted under the plan were ever invoked, supporters argued that it had served its purpose as a "safety valve." No schools were closed in North Carolina to avoid integration. Such cases as *Swann v. Charlotte-Mecklenburg Board of Education* (1971) gave federal judges and liberal educators a new tool—busing—not only to desegregate but to fully integrate the public schools.

Dancer at the Community Village on South State Street during a Kwanzaa celebration in Raleigh, 17 Dec. 1999. Photograph by Bernard Thomas. *Durham Herald-Sun.*

Emerging Roles and New Challenges for African Americans

The 1960s saw the end of legal segregation in North Carolina and every other state, but most blacks still experienced deep racial prejudice in many aspects of their lives. Given this frustration, militant activities often replaced nonviolent political strategies. A notable example was the firebombing of a grocery store in Wilmington in 1972 and the subsequent trial of the so-called Wilmington Ten. From the 1970s on, however, black political power grew both locally and nationally. Between 1970 and 1997, 506 black North Carolinians served as county commissioners, school board members, mayors, state legislators, and judges; two African Americans—Eva Clayton in the First Congressional District and Mel Watt in the Twelfth—won seats in the U.S. House of Representatives. Henry E. Frye was appointed to the Supreme Court of North Carolina in 1983 and became chief justice in 1999. Ralph Campbell Jr. was elected state auditor in 1992, 1996, and 2000, and former Charlotte mayor Harvey Gantt ran as the Democratic candidate for U.S. senator against incumbent Republican Jesse Helms in 1990 and 1996 (Gantt lost the races by 52 to 48 percent and 53 to 47 percent margins, respectively).

Between 1876, when the *Star of Zion*, the organ of the African Methodist Episcopal Zion Church, first appeared in Salisbury, and 1995, more than 250 African American newspapers were published in North Carolina. In the early 2000s there were 16 black papers in the state, including the *Asheville Advocate* (since 1987), *Charlotte Post* (1918), *Carolina Times* (Durham, 1919), *Fayetteville Press* (1987), *Iredell County News* (1980), and *Winston-Salem Chronicle* (1947).

In 2006 African Americans comprised about 22 percent of the North Carolina population. Economically, they made impressive if erratic progress in the late twentieth and early twenty-first centuries—although their per capita income remained well behind that of whites and their poverty level was significantly higher. Increasingly, black youths have attended four-year colleges. The number of blacks in all professions, in-

cluding medicine, dentistry, and law, has continued to rise, and successful African American businesses have grown in number. According to the June 2000 issue of *Black Enterprise*, 10 of the nation's largest black firms were headquartered in North Carolina: 2 companies in the industrial/service category, 4 automobile dealers, 2 banks, an insurance company (North Carolina Mutual Life Insurance Company), and an affiliated asset management firm (NCM Capital Management Group, Inc.). Hundreds of other smaller black enterprises existed among the approximately 2,000 minority businesses statewide.

References: Roberta Sue Alexander, *North Carolina Faces the Freedmen: Race Relations during Presidential Reconstruction, 1865–1867* (1985); Eric Anderson, *Race and Politics in North Carolina, 1872–1901: The Black Second* (1981); Lerone Bennett Jr., *Before the Mayflower: A History of Black America* (1993); William H. Chafe, Raymond Gavins, and Robert Korstad, eds., *Remembering Jim Crow: African Americans Tell about Life in the Segregated South* (2001); Jeffrey J. Crow, Paul D. Escott, and Flora J. Hatley, *A History of African Americans in North Carolina* (2002); W. McKee Evans, *Ballots and Fence Rails: Reconstruction on the Lower Cape Fear* (1966); John Hope Franklin, *The Free Negro in North Carolina, 1790–1860* (1943); Franklin and Alfred A. Moss Jr., *From Slavery to Freedom: A History of Negro Americans* (6th ed., 1988); Glenda Elizabeth Gilmore, *Gender and Jim Crow: Women and the Politics of White Supremacy in North Carolina, 1896–1920* (1996); Herbert G. Gutman, *The Black Family in Slavery and Freedom, 1750–1925* (1976); Timothy J. Minchin, *Hiring the Black Worker: The Racial Integration of the Southern Textile Industry, 1960–1980* (1999); R. Drew Smith, *Long March Ahead: African American Churches and Public Policy in Post–Civil Rights America* (2004); Timothy B. Tyson, *Blood Done Sign My Name: A True Story* (2004); Walter B. Weare, *Black Business in the New South: A Social History of the North Carolina Mutual Life Insurance Company* (rev. ed., 1993).

Roberta Sue Alexander
Rodney D. Barfield
Steven E. Nash
Additional research provided by
Joseph W. Wescott II and Wiley J. Williams.

SEE ALSO Black Codes; Black Freemasonry; Civil Rights
Movement; Colonization Societies; Disfranchisement;
Emancipation; Equal Rights League; Exodusters;
Fourteenth Amendment; Freedmen's Bureau; Freedmen's
Conventions; Greensboro Sit-Ins; Manumission Societies;
Maroons; North Carolina Mutual Life Insurance
Company; Slave Narratives; Slavery; *State v. John Mann*;
State v. Negro Will; *Swann v. Charlotte-Mecklenburg Board
of Education*; Underground Railroad; Walker's *Appeal*;
Wilmington Race Riot; Wilmington Ten.

African Brigade. SEE Union Volunteer Regiments.

African Methodist Episcopal (AME) Church is a Christian denomination dating back to 1787, when a number of black worshippers withdrew from the interracial St. George's Methodist Episcopal Church in Philadelphia after the removal of a black member, Absalom Jones, while he was praying. Led by Richard Allen, a local black preacher in the Methodist Episcopal Church, the group formed the Free African Society and, in 1793, established the Bethel AME Church in Philadelphia. In 1816 representatives from the Bethel AME Church and African American churches in four other cities officially organized the AME Church in Philadelphia, elected Allen their bishop, and adopted the doctrine and form of government of the Methodist Episcopal Church with minimal changes.

As a result of its active role in the antislavery movement, the AME Church was restricted almost entirely to northern states during its first 50 years. After South Carolina whites came to suspect the AME Church of masterminding the thwarted Denmark Vesey plot of 1822—in which Vesey, a wealthy ex-slave, had attempted to organize a massive slave revolt to kill whites in Charleston and burn the city—slaveholders did not allow the church to operate among slaves in the South. Not until the Civil War and emancipation did the AME Church advance into North Carolina and other southern states. Through its work with recently liberated blacks after the war, the denomination grew considerably. The North Carolina Annual Conference of the AME Church, organized in Wilmington in 1868, enlarged to such an extent that the Western North Carolina Conference branch was added in 1900. In 1886 the AME Church established Kittrell College in Vance County; the institution provided blacks a higher education until 1975.

The *Christian Recorder*, the official organ of the AME Church, is the oldest newspaper in the United States continuously circulated by people of African descent. North Carolina, located in the church's Second Episcopal District, hosts two annual conferences: the North Carolina Conference and the Western North Carolina Conference. In the early 2000s there were more than 150 active AME churches in the state.

References: Reginald F. Hildebrand, *The Times Were Strange and Stirring: Methodist Preachers and the Crisis of Emancipation* (1995); Daniel A. Payne, *History of the African Methodist Episcopal Church* (1968); Richard R. Wright Jr., *Centennial Encyclopaedia of the African Methodist Episcopal Church* (1916).

Allyson C. Criner

African Methodist Episcopal Zion Church (AME Zion Church) traces its roots to 1796, when Peter Williams, Christopher Rush, James Varick, and other African Americans left the white John Street Methodist Church in New York City to form a black church. Five years later, the group was chartered as the African Methodist Episcopal Church ("Zion" was added in 1848). Unable to penetrate the white-dominated South during slavery, the AME Zion Church was primarily a northern institution for decades. It became known as the "freedom church" because of its efforts to help slaves escape from their masters, and because its membership included celebrated black leaders Harriet Tubman, Sojourner Truth, and Frederick Douglass.

After the Civil War, congregations developed in many North Carolina towns, and by the late nineteenth century the AME Zion Church had achieved an important religious status in the state. In 1876 the *Star of Zion*, its official newspaper, was established to provide news and information on events in local churches, district and annual conferences, evangelistic efforts, educational meetings, and ecumenical participation. Since 1894 the organ has been published in Charlotte, which also is the home of the AME Zion Publishing House. Throughout its more than 125-year history, the *Star of Zion* has advocated greater citizenship rights and educational and economic

Members of the Board of Directors of the AME Zion Publishing House, Charlotte, 1916. Carolina Room, Public Library of Charlotte and Mecklenburg County.

opportunities for African Americans, who, the church teaches, carry much of the responsibility for their own progress. Prior to the election of President Franklin D. Roosevelt in 1932, the paper's political orientation had a Republican cast; since then, it has reflected the Democratic view of government as an ally in the fight for justice and equal rights for racial and other minorities.

In the early 2000s, more than 300,000 members of the AME Zion Church worshipped in approximately 600 congregations across North Carolina. The offices of the AME Zion general secretary and the publishing house are located in a Charlotte facility constructed in 1966 to replace a 1911 structure. The church also maintains six institutions of higher learning, including two in North Carolina—Livingstone College and Hood Theological Seminary, both in Salisbury.

References: David Henry Bradley, *A History of the A.M.E. Zion Church* (2 vols., 1956–70); David B. Van Leeuwen, "Saving the White Man's Christianity: William Jacob Walls and Twentieth-Century African American Christianity" (Ph.D. diss., UNC-Chapel Hill, 1995); William Jacob Walls, *The African Methodist Episcopal Zion Church* (1974).

Wiley J. Williams

SEE ALSO Livingstone College.

Agricultural Experiment Stations. The legislative act of 27 Feb. 1877 that established the North Carolina Department of Agriculture (NCDA) and a Board of Agriculture also created the North Carolina Agricultural Experiment Station, the first such station in the South and the second in the nation (Connecticut's station began in 1875). The station began work on 19 Apr. 1877 in a one-room chemistry laboratory at the University of North Carolina in Chapel Hill. In the summer of 1881 it was transferred to the old State Agricultural Building in Raleigh.

The original legislation directed the experiment station to conduct research on plant nutrition and growth, to ascertain which fertilizers were best suited to specific crops, and to conduct other needed investigations. The initial movement to establish field testing stations began in 1885, when the General Assembly directed the Board of Agriculture to secure prices on lands and machinery. The board obtained 35 acres on Hillsborough Street in Raleigh, and the job of clearing land, laying out test plots, and constructing buildings began. On 8 Sept. 1889 management of the station was formally transferred to the North Carolina College of Agriculture and Mechanic Arts (precursor to modern-day North Carolina State University). The federal Hatch Act (1887), which had provided $15,000 to each state for agricultural research, had specified that the money be directed to land grant colleges. In establishing the College of Agriculture and Mechanic Arts, the legislature had provided that it would receive all land grant benefits.

Apple Research Laboratory, Wilkes County, 1941. North Carolina State University Archives Photograph Collection.

While the NCDA maintained its relationship with the agricultural experiment station, it shifted its effort to establishing other stations, or "test farms," in various locations statewide. The purpose was to experiment with different crop-fertilizer-soil combinations to find the most suitable for certain areas. The first two research stations were in Edgecombe and Robeson Counties. In all, 15 stations were opened—in locations including Whiteville, Clayton, Castle Hayne, Clinton, Kinston, Oxford, Salisbury, Plymouth, Laurel Springs, and Reidsville—and the NCDA began to conduct research on farming practices, livestock, poultry, and crops at these sites.

The NCDA and N.C. State University continue to operate these experiment stations cooperatively. The NCDA owns nine stations and provides administrative support. N.C. State owns the other six and provides scientists for various research projects. The Center for Environmental Farming Systems at Cherry Farm in Goldsboro, dedicated in February 1994, studies organic, no-till optimized yields and sustainable agriculture.

Reference: *A Century of Service: The North Carolina Agricultural Experiment Station at Raleigh* (1979).

Wiley J. Williams

Agricultural Organizations. SEE Agricultural Society; Farm Bureau Federation; Farmers' Alliance; Farmers Union; Grange; North Carolina Crop Improvement Association; *North Carolina Farmer*; North Carolina Farmers' Association; *Progressive Farmer*.

Agricultural Society. The Agricultural Society of North Carolina was organized in December 1818 in Raleigh with Governor John Branch as ex officio president and Joseph Gales Sr., publisher of the *Raleigh Register*, as secretary. This initial organization survived only a few years. A second organization, the North Carolina Agricultural Society, was established in Raleigh on 8 Oct. 1852 and survived until the late 1920s. This second society created and sponsored the first North Carolina State Fair in October 1853. The state fair was the Agricultural Society's principal agency for the promotion of both scientific agriculture and industry. The success of the organization resulted in large part because some of the state's more enlightened planters and farmers were members. These included Thomas Ruffin Sr., a lawyer, judge, former chief justice of the North Carolina Supreme Court, and prominent Alamance County planter; John S. Dancy of Panola Plantation in Edgecombe County; and Kenneth Raynor, a Hertford County planter and prominent Whig politician.

In addition, the North Carolina Agricultural Society issued publications—including its official but short-lived *Farmer's Journal* (1852–54), edited by John F. Tompkins—to encourage farmers to adopt improved cultivation practices such as fertilizing, crop rotation, deep plowing, and contour plowing. The society also deserves considerable credit for the University of North Carolina's establishment in 1854 of a chair of applied chemistry to deal with agricultural matters and, soon afterward, the creation of an experimental farm south of what is now South Building.

With the appointment of the first State Fair Board by Governor Angus McLean in 1925, the North Carolina Agricultural Society gave up sponsorship of and financial responsibility for the fair, and before the end of the decade the society had disbanded.

References: Melton A. McLaurin, "The Nineteenth Century North Carolina State Fair as a Social Institution," *NCHR* 59 (July 1982); Elizabeth Reid Murray, *Wake: Capital County of North Carolina* (1983); North Carolina Agricultural Society, *Charter and By-Laws of the North Carolina Agricultural Society, Organized 1852* (rev. ed., 1925).

Wiley J. Williams

SEE ALSO State Fair.

Agriculture has been a principal component of North Carolina's economy and culture throughout its history. For centuries before European settlement, the region's Native

Picking cotton, ca. 1930. Photograph by Bayard Wootten. NCC.

Americans had cultivated a variety of crops, such as corn, sunflowers, squash, pumpkins, and beans. Over time Indians situated their communities near rivers and streams to take advantage of the fertile soil, and many native cultural traditions grew out of the seasonal rhythms associated with agriculture.

The land that Roanoke governor Ralph Lane in 1585 described as the "goodliest soil under the cope of heaven" beckoned to European settlers. After gaining title to a tract in the backcountry, typically through a land grant, these early American farmers cleared the forests by the process of "slash and burn," or girdling, so the soil in which they grew could be planted with crops. Colonists brought from Europe fruits, grains, and vegetables and, under the guidance of the Indian population, added corn, potatoes, and varieties of peas and beans.

Precolonial and colonial North Carolina was characterized by an agrarian economy that involved approximately 90 percent of its inhabitants—primarily small farmers, often referred to as "yeomen," who engaged in subsistence farming. This trend continued through the antebellum period and beyond, as North Carolina remained a state of small farms. In some instances the agricultural labor force, largely comprised of indentured servants and slaves, enabled a land-owning, or gentry, class to attain wealth and profit in a growing export economy.

In the twentieth century, the state's agriculture underwent

Farmers line up to sell strawberries at the market in Chadbourn, a traditional center for production of the crop in North Carolina, ca. 1920. NCC.

a seismic transformation. Advances in farming techniques and technology, as well as shifting social and economic realities, left only a fraction of the small farms that once occupied practically every North Carolina county. Trends in the industry were reflected by the new name given to the state agency charged with overseeing farms: in 2001, with the election of the first female commissioner of agriculture, Meg Scott Phipps, the agency was recast as the Department of Agriculture and Consumer Services. Despite these changes, agriculture in various forms has remained a large segment of the economic bottom line in North Carolina. Including crops, floriculture, livestock, and forest products, it contributed approximately $60 billion annually to the state's economy in the early 2000s, when about 20 percent of the workforce was employed in agriculture-related industries, including 56,000 farmers growing more than 80 different commercial products.

Improvements in Farming Technology and the Burgeoning of "Mega Farms"

For the vast majority of North Carolinians involved in agriculture, the farming life was hard, bitterly so in many instances, with problems ranging from insect infestations to plant diseases and exhausted soil. By the 1820s, in fact, many North Carolinians—most of them descendants of original settlers—had moved west to greener pastures in Alabama and

Mississippi. Efforts to lift farmers and their families from the lower rungs of society and improve farming practices took many forms in the state. In nineteenth-century North Carolina, as elsewhere in the South, considerable activity went toward agricultural reform, including the creation of the State Agricultural Society in 1818, a centralized state agricultural department in 1877, and the North Carolina College of Agriculture and Mechanic Arts (present-day North Carolina State University), the state's major land grant institution, in 1887.

The twentieth century brought further efforts to assist farm families. Agricultural extension agents in every county taught farmers the principles of crop rotation, deeper plowing, improved seed selection, crop diversity, and the correct use of fertilizer. Rural youths were served by a host of organizations. Governor O. Max Gardner, elected in 1928, stated in his inaugural address that "one of the major aims of my administration shall be to improve agricultural and rural life in North Carolina." This led to a proliferation of experiment stations designed to give farmers up-to-date information about a variety of subjects. The modern-day Department of Agriculture and Consumer Services offers an array of educational and professional services to farmers in North Carolina.

North Carolinians in some cases were slow to adapt to new discoveries and inventions that promised more efficient and productive farms, choosing instead to continue traditional methods. Many early farmers relied on hoes and other hand tools—rather than plows—to till the land. Early plows were expensive, inefficient, and frustrating to maintain. Some farmers believed that the iron points and moldboards poisoned the soil. Many large-scale planters rejected plows, claiming that their slaves and other laborers often ruined them by improper use.

Improvements in iron and steel technology in the mid-nineteenth century finally produced affordable and properly shaped plows that reduced drag and were self-cleaning. Around the outbreak of the Civil War, a revolution in plowing began to take place, and new designs—including "gang" plows, with several working plow bottoms, and steam-powered riding or "sulky" plows—enabled farmers to plow larger fields more quickly and efficiently.

Mechanization and improved fertilization and crop-growing techniques shaped the agricultural revolution of the twentieth century. In 1924 the invention of the Farmall row-crop tractor led to further advancements in farming methods and production. Now tractors could be used not only to plow fields but also to draw cultivators through standing crops. The use of tractors led to greater use of larger tillage implements, such as disk harrows for field preparation and rotary hoes for cultivation. The widespread use of tractors also significantly reduced the need for beasts of burden, although many growers continued to depend on walking plows and other simple, old-fashioned implements to work their farms.

By the mid-twentieth century, commercial agriculture on huge "mega farms" with high-tech equipment began to supplant individual, family-owned farming in North Carolina. Yields for crops such as corn, tobacco, wheat, cotton, soybeans, and peanuts rose dramatically with improved fertilization and hybrid development, requiring much less land and fewer workers. This trend continued through the end of the twentieth century, with the number of farms in the state dropping from 301,000 in 1950 to fewer than 60,000 in 2000. North Carolina farms continue to be lost at the rate of 2,000 per year.

Decades, and in some cases centuries, of plowing fields had devastating effects in North Carolina. Years of spring and fall plowing combined with excessive cultivating practices created severe soil erosion and infertility. Although efforts to combat soil erosion began in earnest in the 1930s, it was not until the 1980s, with the introduction of new tillage equipment and methods, that centuries-old plows were wholly replaced by less invasive implements. "No-till" or "minimum-till" agriculture was developed to reduce soil erosion, chemical runoff, and the use of costly fuel. No longer is the soil literally turned over, spring and fall, exposing it to erosion-causing wind and rain. Some modern farmers only chisel their fields once a year in preparation for planting, and no-till planters do not require any soil preparation. But tobacco farmers still rely to a greater extent on moldboard plows to prepare their character-istic ridged fields than do farmers who grow corn, soybeans, and cotton.

Modern farming and the associated practices of drainage, fertilization, mechanization, and mass production for special markets have produced a revolutionary efficiency in North Carolina agriculture. Although the state has above-average rainfall, there are critical periods when several weeks of drought may determine success or failure for the season's crops. Irrigation on its current scale is relatively new to the state, largely a phenomenon of the last decades of the twentieth century. In the United States as a whole, more water is withdrawn from rivers, lakes, and wells for agriculture than for any other use. About 47 percent of these freshwater withdrawals are for irrigation, using methods such as coordinated sprinkler systems, trickle-and-drip systems, and underground pipes.

Changes in the Agricultural Labor Force

For much of North Carolina's history, the primary source of agricultural labor for the vast majority of small farms was the farmer's own family, including small children, whose abilities and productivity grew with age. Indentured servants frequently worked on larger farms and plantations, outnumbering African slaves throughout the colony's first half century. As the lowest class of whites, these "Christian" servants had voluntarily bound themselves to a master by a written contract for a predetermined number of years to "redeem" their passage to the colony. Also included in this group were people who had been taken against their will: political prisoners, criminals, and other convicts sold into bondage in lieu of incarceration in England. Their length of service depended on the nature of the contract but generally lasted between three and five years. At the end of this period, a servant usually received 50 acres of land from the colony, along with food, clothing, tools, and other farming supplies from the master. Some contracts stipulated that the servant be taught a trade as well as to read and write. The colony enacted laws that prohibited harsh treatment of indentured servants.

As the agricultural economy grew during the colonial period, its progress was restricted by insufficient labor. Indentured servitude was simply not a viable resource because of the limited number of white servants available in the colony. In an effort to mature and expand the fledgling economy, North Carolina began to draw on black slave labor.

The majority of planters who wished to increase their labor supply preferred slaves over free blacks or white laborers. North Carolina's slave population grew slowly; smaller than that of any other southern colony, it comprised only 25 percent of the state's inhabitants, compared to 60 percent of South Carolina's. Slavery was more prevalent in the eastern half of North Carolina because of its fertile soil and amenable terrain; in some counties, slaves outnumbered whites.

It was often difficult for North Carolina planters to determine the number of acres that could profitably be cultivated by slaves, since every planter was an autonomous entity and had little knowledge of his neighbors' experiences until the last two decades of slavery. Some planters permitted their slave population to increase beyond the point of efficiency, which, consequently, left the slaves with little to do and caused plantations to operate at a loss. Some growers attempted to plant over twice the amount of land that their slaves could reasonably cultivate. According to the *Farmers' Journal*, North Carolina's nineteenth-century farmers were far more likely to understaff their plantations than to amass surplus labor. The *Journal* believed that North Carolina's "low state of agriculture" during the last half of the antebellum period resulted from a tendency to cultivate too much land as well as poor management practices.

Free blacks were another source of agricultural labor in the antebellum period, working as day laborers, farm tenants, and farm operators. As farmhands, some free blacks found steady employment and lived on a plantation much like slaves, or they worked only during the harvest season. A few owned slaves and used them in the same way as white slave owners did. The census of 1830 indicates that 192 free blacks in North Carolina owned from 1 to 41 slaves. Many of these black owners had married slaves, hoping later to obtain their emancipation. In 1828 the legislature required planters to pay a poll tax on the free blacks who lived on their plantations, just as they paid on their slaves.

After the Civil War, sharecropping and other forms of tenant farming emerged from the ashes of slavery. In the harsh postbellum economy, sharecropping was a natural choice for landowners without capital to pay wages and for poor black and white families who lacked both land and capital but who could furnish a suitable labor supply. This system allowed planters to maintain their farming operations, to pay for labor with a share of the crop, and to entice workers to remain on the farm until harvest. The tenants' share varied according to locality and crop, but it generally depended on their contribution to the enterprise. If the landowner furnished farm tools, animals, fertilizer, seeds, a house, and food and the tenant provided only labor, the owner would probably take three-fourths of the crop. If the sharecropper brought his own provisions, he received one-half of the harvest.

Sharecropping in North Carolina extended well into the twentieth century, often leading to debt and impoverishment for a huge number of tenants and their families. White tenants always outnumbered black tenants, but the percentage of whites was less than that of blacks. In 1920, 33 percent of white farmers and 71 percent of black farmers were tenants. A survey of 351 rural families in Chatham County in 1923 found that half of them were tenants, few of whom had running water. In 1929 a University of North Carolina sociologist described

"much that is ugly" about rural life: "Many of our North Carolina farmers are desperately poor, live in wretched houses, and are scantily provided with even the necessities of life. There is poverty, illiteracy, uncouthness, narrowness, and excessive individualism. Tenancy and cash crop farming have failed to provide prosperity, culture, or social unity."

Tenancy tended to decrease farm size and efficiency, deplete soil fertility, discourage the use of machinery, perpetuate the one-crop system and crop liens, and inhibit the growth of rural organization and cooperative ventures. However, it continued to thrive well into the 1940s, especially in the Coastal Plain, where good tobacco prices and high land values minimized labor arrangements. As better applications of fertilizer on the most suitable tobacco land created higher yields per acre, landlords increased their tenant units to accommodate increased production. As late as 1954, the tenancy rate in Wilson County remained about 75 percent of all farmers.

With ever-expanding mechanization in the 1960s, the need for agricultural hand labor during the growing season decreased. In time the increased use of labor-saving devices led to an exodus from the farm. A 1929 study of sons and daughters of white farmers in Wake County found that 80 percent chose to stay within a 50-mile radius of where they grew up. As machinery did the work formerly performed by family members, tenants, and hired workers, the rural workforce moved to urban areas. Exhausted or eroded soil caused others to leave the farm.

With tenancy and the farm population decreasing, North Carolina growers used different types of workers and labor-saving equipment. When higher-paying work became available in manufacturing plants, the able-bodied took advantage of a steady income. For a time, farmers recruited youthful urban workers from the area. Throughout the 1970s, both urban and rural youths, black and white, were able to find work on many North Carolina tobacco farms.

By the 1980s and 1990s the agricultural labor system again evolved to accommodate changing economic trends. As young workers found jobs in area businesses and the school year began earlier, the farm workforce declined. Growers often found acceptable day laborers lacking. At this time migrant labor began proliferating in the state; many workers came from Mexico and Central America in search of higher wages and stability. By the end of the twentieth century and the early twenty-first, migrants comprised the vast majority of agricultural laborers in North Carolina.

Field Crops, Livestock, and Other Agricultural Products

Although for centuries tobacco was North Carolina's premier crop, other products—including field crops, vegetables, livestock, and Christmas trees—have come to comprise much of the state's agricultural industry. However, tobacco is still important. In the early 2000s North Carolina continued to lead the nation in both flue-cured (flavorful and aromatic) and burley (dark-leaf filler) tobacco production, with about 125,000 harvested acres yielding 275 million pounds of product worth more than $600 million annually. Tobacco growing has remained a way of life for thousands of North Carolina farmers.

The importance of several other crops and products has increased over the years. Cotton was by far the state's major commercial crop before the Civil War; it was grown for household use almost from the earliest days of settlement. North Carolina's nineteenth-century "cotton kingdom" consisted of about a dozen eastern counties bounded by the towns of Halifax, Goldsboro, and Washington and the southern counties bordering South Carolina from Robeson to Mecklenburg. Of these counties, 12 produced more than 4,000 bales of cotton in 1860. Cotton production underwent several fluctuations and finally diminished during the Great Depression. Nevertheless, the quality of North Carolina cotton lint has generally remained above average, and the yield per acre is usually the highest in the South. By the early 2000s, cotton accounted for approximately $300 million of the state's gross farm production.

Soybeans have long been grown in North Carolina for livestock forage and as a soil-building crop. Many other modern uses—including the soy products in baby foods and cereals, candies, vegetarian meat substitutes, baked goods, pet foods, soy milk, soy sauce, and a variety of food flavorings—have led to a massive increase in soybean production approaching 50 million bushels worth $290 million annually in the early 2000s. The state's other important field crops include corn ($182 million annually), sweet potatoes ($90 million), peanuts ($77 million), wheat ($73 million), and hay ($20 million). Fruits and vegetables include blueberries ($32 million), cucumbers ($31 million), tomatoes ($18 million), apples ($18 million), strawberries ($16 million), and Irish potatoes ($15 million).

North Carolina's livestock, plant, and forest products experienced the greatest increases in the last few decades of the twentieth century and the early years of the twenty-first. Livestock such as hogs ($2 billion), broiler chickens ($2 billion), turkeys ($449 million), cattle ($258 million), as well as by-products such as eggs ($240 million) and milk ($171 million), have come to dwarf other commodities in total production and value. Greenhouse and nursery products, including garden and bedding plants, potted foliage and flowering plants, and perennials, account for about $830 million of the state's agricultural yield. North Carolina has also become one of the nation's leading producers of Christmas trees, with approximately 1,600 growers accounting for about $100 million worth of trees annually.

References: Cornelius O. Cathey, *Agricultural Developments in North Carolina, 1783–1860* (1956); "Country Life in North Carolina," University of North Carolina Extension Bulletin 9 (September 1929); Pete Daniel, *Breaking the Land: The Transformation of Cotton, Tobacco, and Rice Cultures since 1880* (1985); C. Horace Hamilton, "What's Happening to North Carolina Farms and Farmers?" Agricultural Experiment Station Bulletin 403 (August 1958); Robert Hinton, *Cotton Culture on the Tar River: The Politics of Agricultural Labor in the Coastal Plain of North Carolina, 1862–1902* (1993); Lu Ann Jones, "'The Task That Is Ours': White North Carolina Farm Women and Agrarian Reform, 1886–1914" (M.A. thesis, UNC-Chapel Hill, 1983); Jack Temple Kirby, *Rural Worlds Lost: The American South, 1920–1960* (1987); Jane Simpson McKimmon, *When We're Green We Grow* (1945).

Michael Hill
Additional research provided by
Peter A. Coclanis, Stephanie Hall,
Will M. Heiser, Charles LeCount, and W. W. Yeargin.

SEE ALSO Agricultural Experiment Stations; Agriculture and Consumer Services, Department of; Extension Service; Farm Bureau Federation; Farmers' Alliance; Hog Farming; Live-at-Home Program; Migrant Workers; North Carolina Farmers' Association; Poultry; *Progressive Farmer*; Sharecropping; Slavery; Threshing; Tobacco; Tobacco Auctions.

Agriculture and Consumer Services, Department of.

As early as 1860, North Carolina governor John W. Ellis urged the General Assembly to set up a board of agriculture. Legislators ignored the request because of their concern over the impending Civil War. The foundation for establishing an agriculture department was laid in the state constitution of 1868, which called for the creation of a Bureau of Statistics, Agriculture, and Immigration within the office of the secretary of state. But this agency did not provide for the real needs of agriculture and failed to satisfy farmers, who wanted an independent department.

At a state constitutional convention in 1875, the General Assembly was charged with organizing a Department of Agriculture, Immigration, and Statistics "under such regulations as may best promote the agricultural interests of the State and shall enact laws for the adequate protection and encouragement of sheep husbandry." The legislature did so in March 1877, when it also created a Board of Agriculture to supervise the new department's activities. Col. Leonidas LaFayette Polk, who had been instrumental in the department's formation, was named the first commissioner of agriculture on 2 Apr. 1877. Polk is well remembered as founder in 1886 of the *Progressive Farmer*, which sought to teach farmers better agricultural methods and urged them to form clubs to increase their political influence. Through these farmers' clubs, Polk secured the establishment in 1887 of a state college of agriculture, the modern North Carolina State University in Raleigh.

The position of commissioner of agriculture became an elected office in 1899. Through the decades, the state's Agriculture Department—the modern Department of Agriculture and Consumer Services—expanded its services to meet a wide variety of agricultural needs. By the early 2000s it consisted of 15 divisions, including Agricultural Statistics, Agronomic Services, Aquaculture and Natural Resources, Food Distribution, Food and Drug Protection, Human Resources, Livestock Marketing, Structural Pest Control, and Veterinary Services. The Agriculture Department also oversees the annual North Carolina State Fair in Raleigh. Employing about 1,400 people, it holds broad responsibilities for regulating public health, safety, and welfare as well as for protecting, maintaining, and enhancing agriculture in the state.

Wiley J. Williams

Air-Conditioning

Air-Conditioning greatly changed the nature of life in North Carolina and the rest of the South. Willis H. Carrier, who had created an experimental cooling system in New York in 1902, installed the first air-conditioning system in the South in 1906 at Chronicle Cotton Mills in Belmont. Prior to the 1920s, the use of air-conditioning was restricted almost entirely to industrial settings, where it was hailed as a boon to worker productivity; by the 1930s, however, air-conditioned movie theaters and railway cars became common. After World War II commercial use increased, and, with the invention of the window unit in 1951, residential application boomed. While it is difficult to quantify the effects of the widespread availability of air-conditioning, historians have recognized it as an important contributor to the reversal of migration from the South in the latter half of the twentieth century. It also helped spark a variety of other social and cultural changes as increasing numbers of North Carolinians moved off their porches during the hot summer months, choosing instead the comforts of controlled indoor temperatures.

Stuart W. Cramer, born in Thomasville, played an important role in the development of air-conditioning. A leading figure in the textile industry at the turn of the twentieth century and the holder of more than 60 patents, Cramer pioneered humidity control and ventilating equipment for cotton mills and installed scores of such systems across the South. In a paper read before an American Cotton Manufacturers Association convention in 1906, Cramer—for whom the Gaston County town of Cramerton is named—is believed to have coined the term "air-conditioning." The industry's trade organization within the state, the North Carolina Association of Plumbing-Heating-Cooling Contractors, was formed in 1910; L. L. Hackney of Charlotte was the group's first president.

References: Raymond Arsenault, "The End of the Long Hot Summer: The Air Conditioner and Southern Culture," *Journal of Southern History* 50 (November 1984); Charles Reagan Wilson and William Ferris, eds., *Encyclopedia of Southern Culture* (1989).

Michael Hill

Airmail Service

Airmail Service developed after the Wright brothers' first flight at Kill Devil Hill in 1903, as aviators began to anticipate airplanes' practical uses, such as carrying mail. The first official airmail was flown from North Carolina on 2 Jan. 1911. Later that year, a group of Wilmington businessmen headed by Frank Herbst made plans to bring an airplane to the city on New Year's Day, 1912. Morris Caldwell, president of the Wilmington Driving Association, assisted the group. The Wright Exhibition Company also agreed to send an aircraft and a pilot, and the U.S. postmaster general granted permission for the plane to carry mail. Nearly 1,700 people gathered to watch the plane take off. The 1,600 pieces of mail carried a special "Aeroplane Mail Service" postmark. The pilot flew three miles to Winter Park Gardens, where he dropped the mail pouch from about 500 feet to Wilmington post office employee E. L. Lee. The mail then moved through normal delivery channels.

Full-time airmail service did not begin in North Carolina until May 1928, when contract airmail route 19 was given to Pitcairn Aviation, Inc. The service carried mail from Boston and New York City to Atlanta, Miami, and New Orleans, with stops in New Bern, Wilmington, Raleigh-Durham, Charlotte, Greensboro–High Point, and Winston-Salem. The inauguration of jet airliners in the 1960s provided even faster delivery. By the end of the century, almost all nonlocal mail went by plane, well overshadowing the railroad and highway postal system.

Airmail required special stamps to pay the additional postage. Of the more than 130 different U.S. airmail stamps, 2 saw their first day of issue in North Carolina. On 17 Dec. 1948 a

Commemorative envelope postmarked 1 Nov. 1940, the day airmail service began in Rocky Mount (via a flight that originated in Norfolk, Va., and had stops in Rocky Mount, Raleigh, Greensboro, and Asheville before terminating in Knoxville, Tenn.). Photograph courtesy of Tony Crumbley.

The first powered airplane flight at Kitty Hawk, 17 Dec. 1903. Courtesy of NCOA&H.

six-cent stamp was issued to honor the 46th anniversary of the Wright brothers' flight. Its first-day ceremonies were held at Kitty Hawk, where 378,585 first-day covers were processed. Again on 15 May 1971, a nine-cent airmail stamp bearing the image of a Delta Wing airplane had its first-day ceremonies at Kitty Hawk; 379,442 first-day covers were processed.

Reference: Thomas J. O'Sullivan, *The Pioneer Airplane Mails of the United States* (1985).

Tony L. Crumbley

Airplane, First Flight of. At 10:35 A.M. on 17 Dec. 1903, the first powered flight of an airplane was made from the base of Kill Devil Hill, a sand dune four miles south of the village of Kitty Hawk on the Outer Banks. The feat was achieved by Wilbur and Orville Wright, brothers in their early thirties from Dayton, Ohio, with Orville at the controls. The Wrights first became interested in flying when reading about the work of Otto Lilienthal, a pioneering German aviator who made about 2,000 successful glider flights before being killed in an air crash in August 1896. Enthusiastic bicycle builders and competitive racers, they took up gliding as a hobby in 1899 but soon considered the possibility of powered, heavier-than-air flight.

In mid-1899 Wilbur Wright undertook a systematic study of contemporary knowledge on the subject. Three elements emerged as the fundamentals of flight: wings to lift a machine from the ground, a motor for power, and a way to control a plane in flight. Lilienthal appeared to have solved the first requirement with his cambered wings, and several experimenters had achieved brief liftoff with steam or other types of motors. The unresolved problem was control in the air.

Observing the flight of pigeons near Dayton in July 1899, Wilbur theorized that their wingtips enabled them to direct their movements in the air. Tilting a wing upward increased the wind on its underside; simultaneously, tilting the other downward increased the wind on its upperside. The result allowed the bird to turn, rise, and descend at will. The question, then, was whether these movements could be duplicated mechanically.

A few days later, Wilbur was fiddling with a cardboard inner tube box in his bicycle shop. Idly pressing the corners of the box's long sides at one end and those of the short sides at the other, he noticed that this distortion of the box mimicked the action of pigeons' wings. He promptly built a model biplane glider to test whether altering its wings in flight would control it. Flying the glider as a kite, he found that strings tied to the wings (cambered like Lilienthal's) could manipulate the plane. This, he realized, was the key to heavier-than-air flight.

The Wright brothers then set about building a man-carrying machine. As it neared completion, and seeking sites for experiments, they contacted the National Weather Service in Washington, D.C. The ideal place would have steady winds, hills, soft ground, and few trees or bushes to avoid. From a list of proposed sites, they wrote to weather stations at Kitty Hawk, N.C., and Myrtle Beach, S.C.; only the former replied. Bill Tate, assistant weatherman at Kitty Hawk, had just read a magazine article on flight and was eager to host the Wrights. His letter stressed that there were sites well suited to their purposes nearby and that he could provide temporary accommodations at his home.

Wilbur Wright arrived unannounced at Tate's door on 12 Sept. 1899. He had brought with him the crated glider, as Orville remained briefly in Dayton to close their shop. After Orville arrived, the brothers set up camp at Kill Devil Hill, the tallest dune on the Outer Banks. Over the next 39 months, the Wrights returned to Kill Devil Hill for several months each year to test a series of gliders, each of which had been altered based on previous lessons learned.

During this time, the brothers broke virtually all existing glider records. A flight by Wilbur in October 1902 covered 622 feet in 21 seconds, both the distance and time setting American records. In achieving these results, the Wrights were assisted by a host of Outer Bankers, who helped prepare takeoff sites, launch gliders, build hangars and living quarters, bring in materials for experiments, and send and receive messages, among other things. Bill Tate's brother Dan was the Wrights' only paid employee.

In early December 1903 the Wright brothers attached to their latest glider a 12-horsepower motor, built under their direction at Dayton. They targeted 14 December for their first attempt at powered flight. They hoped to fly to Kitty Hawk that day, but Wilbur made only a 60-foot, gravity-aided downhill hop, splitting an elevator support. Nevertheless, the publicity-shy Wrights wired home: "Success assured keep quiet."

The second attempt occurred on 17 December. At 10:00 A.M. a red flag was hoisted as usual to summon available men from the nearby Lifesaving Station, most of whom were far up the beach watching efforts to refloat a beached submarine. Three men—John T. Daniels, Adam D. Ethridge, and William S. Dough—responded. With them came W. C. Brinkley, of Manteo, who was trying to salvage lumber, and John T. Moore, a 17-year-old out looking for crabs.

The Wrights had assembled a monorail of two-by-fours on level sand at the base of the dune, the plane being equipped with a grooved wheel at each end. They set up a tripod camera and asked Daniels to photograph the plane as it left the track, although he had never taken a picture before and never did again. Orville won the coin toss to fly the machine, and men were assigned to balance it by holding its left wing and tail while Wilbur held the right wing. The Wrights each turned a propeller to start the motor, and Orville lay on his stomach between the wings. At 10:35 A.M. the plane moved along its track, lifting as it reached the end into a 27-mile-per-hour wind. Bucking and lurching with an excited Orville struggling to keep control, the plane in the next 12 seconds darted forward for about 120 feet—a ludicrously short flight, but an astonishing historical event.

The witnesses, several of whom had assisted glider take-offs, saw a flight that differed little from the others except that it was shorter and not as well-controlled as most. John Daniels later candidly told reporters, "I didn't think it amounted to much." But three more flights that morning, the final one lasting for 59 seconds and covering 852 feet, demonstrated that the world was at the threshold of a technological revolution. The Wrights left the next day for Dayton and renown of mythical proportions. In 2003 a variety of celebrations marking the 100th anniversary of their achievement took place throughout North Carolina.

References: Fred E. C. Culik and Spencer Dunmore, *On Great White Wings: The Wright Brothers and the Race for Flight* (2001); Thomas C. Parramore, *First to Fly: North Carolina and the Beginnings of Aviation* (2002).

Thomas C. Parramore

SEE ALSO Wright Brothers National Memorial.

Airports. SEE Aviation.

Alamance, Battle of. The Regulator Movement, also known as the War of the Regulation, involved the violent actions of discontented North Carolinians from several western counties who were fighting what they viewed as corrupt and unfair practices of the colonial government. The uprising culminated in a battle three miles south of the town of Alamance in present-day Alamance County. In January 1771, responding to Regulator violence, the Assembly passed Johnston's Riot Act, which, among other stipulations, empowered royal governor William Tryon to call out the militia to maintain order and enforce the law. In March 1771 judges of the superior court at Hillsborough informed Tryon that they would be unable to hold court without protection from the provincial militia. In response, Tryon called out the militia to undertake an expedition against the Regulators.

Encouraged by a bounty of 40 shillings, the militiamen assembled at New Bern and on 22 April began marching toward Hillsborough. Other militia companies joined Tryon's force, and by 3 May, when the troops reached Smith's Ferry on the Neuse River in Johnston County, the army had grown to 1,068 men. Gen. Hugh Waddell commanded a second detachment that proceeded from Cape Fear to Salisbury, where he planned to enlist western militia, suppress Regulators in the Yadkin River Valley, and then join Tryon at Hillsborough. Unable to recruit men in the west, Waddell left Salisbury on 9 May and advanced toward Hillsborough. At the Yadkin River his army of approximately 300 men was met by a larger number of Regulators, who forced his troops to return to Salisbury.

On 11 May Tryon and his force left Hillsborough for Salisbury on a route through the heart of Regulator country. Three days later, they encamped on Alamance Creek. Meanwhile, three miles west of their position approximately 2,000 Regulators gathered on the plantation of Michael Holt. On 16 May 1771, after several failed attempts at communication to avoid bloodshed, Tryon directed the militiamen to move toward the Regulator encampment.

As his force approached the Regulators, Tryon sent a proclamation ordering the insurgents to disperse within the hour. Tryon's men, numbering approximately 1,000, advanced to an open clearing where their front lines were almost touching the front lines of the Regulators. Slowly these Regulators withdrew into a wooded area to join their main force, thereby leaving the provincial army in the clearing and within 25 yards of a Regulator line that had formed at the edge of the woods. After a final warning by Tryon and continued Regulator defiance, the battle began. Some contemporary accounts state that when Tryon gave the order to fire, the militia hesitated. The governor repeated his command, shouting "Fire, fire on them or on me!" and the troops turned their weapons on the insurgents.

Though greater in number, the Regulators, who did not have a true commander or sufficient ammunition for a lengthy engagement, were no match for Tryon's militia and artillery, which included two field pieces and four swivel guns. The Regulators' initial fire forced the provincial army to fall back. Some Regulators rushed forward and seized one of the cannons, but without ammunition or skill in firing it they were soon driven from their position by Tryon's force. Grapeshot from the two cannons was instrumental in dispersing the Regulators. In his report to Lord Hillsborough, secretary of state for the American colonies, Tryon wrote that after about half an hour the Regulators "took to tree fighting" and that he then advanced his first line to force the Regulators from their cover and pursued them "a mile beyond their camp."

Tryon reported 9 militiamen killed and 61 wounded. Regulator casualties were more numerous: estimates range from 9 killed and an undetermined number wounded to as high as 300 killed and wounded.

Tryon took 15 prisoners, one of whom was hanged on the battlefield that evening. In trials at Hillsborough, 12 Regulators were found guilty of treason; 6 of these were executed and the others pardoned. On the day following the battle, Tryon offered to pardon all Regulators who would swear allegiance to the Crown. Within six weeks, more than 6,000 backcountry settlers had taken the oath and received pardons from the new royal governor, Josiah Martin.

References: William S. Powell, *The War of the Regulation and the Battle of Alamance, May 16, 1771* (1965); Powell, James K. Huhta, and Thomas J. Farnham, eds., *The Regulators in North Carolina: A Documentary History, 1759–1776* (1971).

George W. Troxler

SEE ALSO Johnston's Riot Act.

Alamance Battleground.

On 16 May 1771 the North Carolina militia, under the command of royal governor William Tryon, defeated backcountry farmers known as the Regulators in a two-hour engagement at a site six miles south of present-day Burlington. The Regulators represented the more violent, radical faction of the growing number of colonists—mainly in the western part of the colony—who were unhappy with the provincial government. Their grievances included high tax rates, dishonest sheriffs, illegal fees, and a scarcity of paper money. Although not the first battle of the American fight for independence, the battle at Alamance contributed to the revolutionary fervor building in the colonies. It also generated a greater westward migration of people into the areas now comprised by the states of Tennessee and Kentucky.

As early as the 1850s, Benson J. Lossing sketched the site of the battle, known as the Alamance Battleground, for his famous pictorial history of the American Revolution. In 1880 citizens of Alamance County erected a granite monument to mark the site. A little more than 50 years later, Alamance Battleground was among the first sites awarded a state highway historical marker. The battleground, now a North Carolina State Historic Site, is located on a 40-acre rural tract on N.C. 62. A visitors center displays maps and museum objects and provides an overview of the battle and its background. A 1780 log house provides a further glimpse at the Regulator movement and life in the backcountry during this period. Flags marking battle positions and the Regulator campsite, monuments, a cannon, and informational plaques are on the battlefield. Demonstrations and special programs are presented at various times at the site.

References: Richard F. Knapp, ed., *North Carolina's State Historic Sites: A Brief History and Status Report* (1995); William S. Powell, James K. Huhta, and Thomas J. Farnham, eds., *The Regulators in North Carolina: A Documentary History, 1759–1776* (1971).

Bryan Dalton

Alamance County, located in the Piedmont region of north central North Carolina, was formed in 1849 out of Orange County. The county was named for either the Great Alamance Creek or the Battle of Alamance (16 May 1771), the decisive battle in the War of the Regulation. Early inhabitants of the area included the Saxapahaw and Sissipahaw Indians, followed by English, Scotch-Irish, German, Welsh, and Pennsylvania Quaker settlers. Graham, the county seat, was incorporated in 1851 and named for William A. Graham, a former North Carolina governor. Other important communities in Alamance County include Burlington, Green Level, Haw River, and Mebane. Elon College (now Elon University) was established in the county in 1889.

Beginning in 1837, when Edwin M. Holt opened the first large-scale textile mill in the county and began producing the widely popular Alamance Plaids, the textile industry has been a principal part of the Alamance County economy. Burlington Industries, founded in 1923 by J. Spencer Love, dominated the textile industry for much of the twentieth century. Other important manufactured goods have included furniture, biomedical products, chemicals, foundry products, and building supplies. Burlington, with its numerous outlet stores, draws shoppers from a wide surrounding area. Alamance County also produces a variety of agricultural goods, such as tobacco, poultry, eggs, vegetables, soybeans, beef cattle, and hogs. Notable physical features of the county include the Haw River, Stony Creek Mountain, the Stony Creek Reservoir, and Great Alamance Creek.

Alamance County is home to many landmarks and historic sites, such as Glencoe Mill Village Historic District, a nineteenth-century cotton mill village; the Southern Railway Passenger Depot; and the Burlington Historic District, which features examples of early North Carolina architecture. The outdoor drama *The Sword of Peace*, based on the activities of local Quakers during the Revolution, is produced in Snow Camp during the summer. Cultural institutions include the Alamance Battleground Museum, the Gallery Players, the Burlington Artists League, the McDade Wildlife Museum, and Cedarock Historic Farm. July Fourth in Snow Camp is one of the county's largest festivals. In 2004 Alamance County had an estimated population of slightly more than 137,000.

Reference: Elinor Samons Euliss, ed., *Alamance County: The Legacy of Its People and Places* (1984).

Jay Mazzocchi

SEE ALSO Alamance, Battle of; Burlington Industries; Company Shops; Glencoe; Regulator Movement.

Alamance Mills. The original Alamance Cotton Mill was founded by Edwin M. Holt and William A. Carrigan on Big Alamance Creek near Burlington in 1837, at the site of several small, water-powered operations, including a gristmill and a sawmill. The fourth cotton mill in North Carolina, it became famous as the first southern mill to manufacture dyed, woven cotton cloth. Thomas M. Holt, Edwin Holt's second son, learned the basic techniques of cotton dyeing from an itinerant French dyer in the 1850s and later learned more advanced techniques from a Philadelphia dyer. Under Thomas Holt's direction, workers at the mill began to dye cotton yarn before weaving it into cloth. In 1853 Holt's mill began producing a woven, dyed cotton cloth called Alamance Plaids, which became the state's best-known textile product in the antebellum period.

The Holt family was prominent in the development of North Carolina's textile industry in the nineteenth century. The descendants of Edwin Holt—sons, sons-in-law, nephews, and cousins—transformed Alamance County from a rural community based on agriculture to a series of small villages along the Haw River and its tributaries. After the 1837 establishment of Alamance Mills, family members developed sites at Haw River, Glencoe, Ossipee, Saxapahaw, and Graham over the next 45 years. In addition to rural mill sites, the Holt family also developed five mills between 1883 and 1893 in the Company Shops area, which became the city of Burlington in 1887. The original Alamance Mill burned in 1871 but was rebuilt and remained part of the Holt family enterprises until 1927, when it was sold to John Shoffner to become the Standard Hosiery Mill.

Thomas M. Holt, the most notable of Holt's sons, became the proprietor of Granite Mills in Haw River and the governor of North Carolina from 1891 to 1893.

References: Bess Beatty, *Alamance: The Holt Family and Industrialization in a North Carolina County, 1837–1900* (1999); Brent D. Glass, *The Textile Industry in North Carolina: A History* (1992).

Brent D. Glass
Additional research provided by Eileen McGrath.

Albemarle, CSS. The CSS *Albemarle*, an ironclad ram, was one of the Confederacy's most successful ironclads. This vessel and its sister ship, the CSS *Neuse*, were designed to wrest control of North Carolina's sounds from the Federal forces that had dominated the region since early 1862. The *Albemarle* was a twin propeller ship mounting two 6.4-inch Brooke rifles in an armored casemate. Construction of the new ironclad began in a cornfield at Edward's Ferry on the Roanoke River in January 1863. To ensure rapid completion of the *Albemarle*, the Confederate navy sent its chief builder (and designer of the ship) John L. Porter to oversee construction. Abandoned railroad rails were scrounged from across the state to be rolled into armor plates, and sawmills and a blacksmith shop were established on site. The work was aided by a newly developed drill that reduced the time for drilling holes in the armor plate from 20 minutes to 4 minutes.

In late 1863 Cdr. James Cooke was sent to take over Porter's supervision duties. Cooke, who would later command the *Albemarle* in action, became known as the "ironmonger captain" for his relentless efforts to gather iron of all sorts that could be rolled into plating. But despite all attempts to accelerate the vessel's construction, there were delays. The keel of the new ship was damaged during launching, requiring extensive repairs, and railroad delivery of iron from the foundries was exceedingly slow.

By April 1864 the gunboat was nearing completion. Brig. Gen. Robert F. Hoke was planning an infantry attack on the town of Plymouth near the mouth of the Roanoke and required the cooperation of the ironclad. Early on 17 April, as Hoke's infantry assaulted the outermost Union positions, the *Albemarle* started out. Workmen swarmed over its deck and casemate to fasten down the last layer of armor even as it steamed downriver. While under way the engines broke down, necessitating several hours of repairs. Finally, the ship reached Plymouth early on the morning of 19 Apr. 1864.

Waiting for it were the USS *Miami* and *Southfield*, the most powerful of several wooden gunboats at Plymouth. Chains had been strung between the two ships in an attempt to ensnare the *Albemarle* and batter it with their combined fire. But Cooke recognized the trap and avoided it. He then made for the *Southfield*, plunging the ironclad's armored bow deep into the wooden vessel and sinking it so quickly that the ram almost followed the victim. The *Miami*, along with the other Union gunboats, soon withdrew after shot and shell from its 6.4-inch rifles and 9-inch smoothbore guns glanced harmlessly off the *Albemarle*'s four inches of iron plating. With the opposing fleet dispersed, the *Albemarle* bombarded the last remaining strongholds in Plymouth, helping force a Federal surrender.

Hoke next focused his attention on New Bern. The ironclad *Neuse* had run aground en route to New Bern, and so the *Albemarle* was called upon to provide naval support for the operation. On 5 May it steamed out of Plymouth, but as the rebel ironclad reached Albemarle Sound, 7 Federal gunboats mounting a total of 55 guns attacked. The massed artillery of the fleet failed to penetrate the armor, but the *Albemarle*'s smokestack was nearly destroyed and the muzzle of one gun was shot away. In the melee the *Albemarle* itself was rammed by one of the wooden gunboats. Its steering gear was damaged, and, because of the mangled smokestack, it was necessary to feed bacon, lard, and butter into the boilers to keep up steam pressure. Despite having damaged each of the Federal ships, Cooke had no choice but to limp back to Plymouth.

The *Albemarle* was repaired and remained at its mooring until 27 Oct. 1864, when it was sunk by a torpedo in a daring raid led by Lt. William Cushing. With their ironclad gone, the Confederate forces evacuated Plymouth on 31 October. In March 1865 the Union navy raised the ship and towed it to Norfolk, Va., the following month. The *Albemarle* remained an officially commissioned U.S. Navy ship until 15 Oct. 1867, when it was sold at auction to J. N. Leonard and Company for $3,200.

Reference: William N. Still Jr., *Iron Afloat: The Story of the Confederate Armorclads* (1985).

Dan Blair

Albemarle and Chesapeake Canal, a man-made waterway connecting Albemarle Sound with the Chesapeake Bay, was proposed initially by William Byrd II in 1728. Surveys were made, but engineering complications held up the project until the 1850s. Upon its opening on 9 Jan. 1859, the canal provided an economic link between North Carolina and Virginia. The full canal was 75 miles long, but only 14 miles cut through land. Of those, 5 miles were in North Carolina, essentially bisecting Currituck County at Coinjock. The rest of the canal followed natural channels and dredged rivers.

Construction was authorized by bills introduced in the North Carolina and Virginia legislatures in 1854. Bonds to pay for the project, totaling just over $1 million, were sold in the two states. Whereas 50 years before, the nearby Dismal Swamp Canal had been dug by hand, newly invented steam dredges (known as "Iron Titans") were used to cut through massive stumps, roots, and buried logs. During the Civil War the canal was the site of partisan action, with ships sunk at its mouths to block entry.

After the war, commercial use of the canal increased, especially by steamship lines. By 1892, 7,717 vessels (including 4,061 steamers) used the waterway. On 30 Apr. 1913 the canal's operation—a private venture until that point—was taken over by the federal government. In 1988 a new high-level bridge replaced the old swing span at Coinjock. By the early 2000s the canal was used largely by pleasure craft as part of the Intracoastal Waterway.

References: Alexander Crosby Brown, *Juniper Waterway: A History of the Albemarle and Chesapeake Canal* (1981); Clifford Reginald Hinshaw Jr., "North Carolina Canals before 1860," *NCHR* 25 (January 1948); David Stick, *The Outer Banks of North Carolina, 1584–1958* (1958).

Michael Hill

Albemarle County. The name "Albemarle" was applied to the section or region of northeastern North Carolina that was the earliest permanently settled part of the colony. Settlers began moving there about the middle of the seventeenth century, settling along the northern shore of the sound that was first called the Sea of Roanoke (1609) or Roanoke Sound (1657) and, for a very short time, Carolina River (1663). It is known today as Albemarle Sound. In 1664 a county of 1,660 square miles with imprecise boundaries was created and named Albemarle for George Monck, duke of Albemarle, one of the Lords Proprietors of Carolina. The county was divided into Chowan, Currituck, Pasquotank, and Perquimans Precincts in 1668. Albemarle County ceased to exist as a unit of government in 1689, and the precincts came to be recognized as counties. In time additional counties were created in the region, but the northeastern corner of North Carolina is still referred to as the Albemarle region.

Although the Albemarle region of North Carolina was by the 1660s the site of the only structured government in the colony, there were several factors that slowed its development. Communication with other colonies, except Virginia, was virtually impossible for the area. The Outer Banks prevented direct navigation. The waters surrounding the Albemarle region would not support large ships, which further inhibited growth. Also, many of the Lords Proprietors focused their energies and finances on the easier-to-settle southern part of the colony, blaming the Albemarle residents for a lack of interest in development.

Government leaders of the Albemarle region attempted to overcome these serious obstacles in a number of ways. Several laws were enacted in an effort to entice new settlers to the region. A proclamation by the governor brought land ownership laws into accord with Virginia's, making movement from one colony to another easier and encouraging migration. To distribute land ownership more equally (and probably to prevent speculating), ownership by one party of more than 660 acres was prohibited, except by direct grant from the Lords Proprietors. Trading privileges with the Native Americans in the area were reserved for official residents of the colony, which stimulated the economy and encouraged traders to make Albemarle a permanent home.

The legislature approved acts that excused new settlers from taxes for one year and also pardoned new settlers from paying any debt accrued inside or outside the colony for five years. These measures allowed new settlers to establish themselves and their families before burdening themselves with large debt payments. Some Virginia authorities, however, viewed the law as encouraging only debtors to settle in the Albemarle region.

There were few religious leaders in Albemarle, yet the government wanted to encourage family development and settlement. As a result, the legislature also approved licenses for civil officials to perform marriage ceremonies. This unconventional measure, along with the region's reputation as a haven for ne'er-do-wells of all sorts, provoked insulting epithets from Albemarle's Virginia neighbors, the most popular being "Rogue's Harbor."

Reference: William S. Powell, ed., *Ye Countie of Albemarle in Carolina* (1958).

Laura Young Baxley
William S. Powell

Albemarle Steam Navigation Company was incorporated in 1860 as the Albemarle Steam Packet Company. Its 24 initial investors included Edward Wood, Henry A. Bond, Joseph Norcom, and others of the town of Edenton and counties bordering the Chowan River. The group planned to operate one or more boats between Edenton and the Seaboard & Roanoke Railroad station at Franklin, Va., on the Blackwater River. In 1860 it ordered a 155-foot passenger and freight boat, the *Virginia Dare*, to be built by Harlan and Hollingsworth of Wilmington, Del. Not quite finished when the Civil War began, the vessel was purchased by the U.S. Navy, converted into a gunboat, and renamed the *Delaware*. Ironically, the *Delaware* became the flagship of Vice Adm. L. M. Goldsborough's squadron, which participated in the capture of Roanoke Island in early 1862 and cleared Albemarle Sound and its tributaries of Confederate traffic.

Edward Wood headed the investors who incorporated the Albemarle Steam Navigation Company (ASN) in 1866 for the same Blackwater-Chowan route. The company began operations with a former Civil War blockade-runner, the 170-foot side-wheeler *Ells*. Over the next six decades, the ASN provided service for the Edenton-Franklin and other routes in the Albemarle Sound area, connecting with various steamboat companies plying the waters between Norfolk and the Cape Fear River.

The firm was recognized for relatively reliable, fast, and safe service, but it experienced perhaps the worst disaster in North Carolina's steam transportation history. On the night of 16 Feb. 1903, its 130-foot *Olive* was capsized by a line squall about a mile from Holley's Wharf on the Chowan River. The loss of 17 lives is said to have been the only fatal accident in the ASN's history. Apparently a later victim of railroad competition, the company ceased operations in 1929.

Reference: Thomas C. Parramore, "Yankees Converted Steamboat into a Gunboat," *Raleigh News and Observer*, 14 Apr. 1968.

Thomas C. Parramore

Alcoholic Beverage Control Commission was created by the General Assembly in 1937 to regulate the sale of alcoholic beverages in North Carolina after the repeal of the Eighteenth Amendment (Prohibition). The modern commission consists of a chair and two associate members appointed by the governor. Its duties include supervising local ABC stores for the sale of spirituous liquors, determining what brands of alcoholic beverages may be sold, maintaining the state ABC warehouse for the distribution of spirituous liquors, regulating the sale of wine and beer, and issuing permits for wineries, breweries, wholesalers, and retailers. The ABC Commission also sets standards and adopts rules for malt beverages, unfortified wine, fortified wine, and spirituous liquors to protect the public against beverages containing harmful or impure substances.

Armistead Jones Maupin

Alexander County, located in the western Piedmont region, was formed from sections of Caldwell, Iredell, and Wilkes Counties in 1847. The county took its name from William Julius Alexander, Speaker of the North Carolina House of Commons. Taylorsville, the county seat, was named for either John Louis Taylor, the first chief justice of the North Carolina Supreme Court, or U.S. president Zachary Taylor. Other communities of note in the county include Hiddenite, Stony Point, Bethlehem, Little River, and Millersville.

Approximately two-thirds of Alexander County is farmland. Although agriculture employs only a small segment of the county's population (most jobs are provided by the manufacturing and service sectors), agricultural production remains strong. The county ranks third in the state for its poultry output, fifth in apples (apples produced in the county won first prize at the 1900 Paris World's Fair), sixth in dairy products, and tenth in beef cattle.

Alexander County is home to a wide variety of minerals. The Hiddenite Gems Emerald Hollow Mine is rich with emeralds, sapphires, garnets, aquamarine, smoky and clear quartz, tourmaline, sillimanite, monazite, and rutile. In 1969 the largest emerald in North America (subsequently given the name "Carolina") was unearthed in Hiddenite. The town also hosts the Hiddenite Celebration of the Arts, which features an eclectic program of musical performances. Other Alexander County events include the Apple Festival, the Taylorsville Lions Club Agricultural Fair, Stony Point Day, Mayfest, and the Vashti Fourth of July Parade. Alexander County had an estimated population of 35,000 in 2004.

Reference: Sara C. Allen, ed., *The Heritage of Alexander County, North Carolina* (1985).

Robert Blair Vocci

Alexander Railroad Company was organized by Alexander County business interests on 30 Nov. 1945 to operate an 18-mile Southern Railway branch line from Statesville to Taylorsville that was being abandoned. Constructed in 1887 as the Statesville & Western Railroad, the road had been acquired by the Richmond & Danville in 1894 as part of the new Southern Railway System. After the discovery of the precious gem hiddenite near Taylorsville, a local attorney named Limney exclaimed that there was such wealth "even a June bug could fly away with it." As a result, trains on the line came to be known as "June Bugs." The affectionate term remained in use, although hopes for great wealth were never quite realized.

Operations were resumed by the Alexander Railroad on 7 Feb. 1946 under the direction of L. P. Zachary and, later, his son Sam Zachary. Beginning with a locomotive rented from the Southern, the Alexander soon acquired a 45-ton General Electric diesel, no. 6, as its motive power. The Alexander became known to the general public by its conspicuous name on a bridge over Interstate 40 near Statesville.

By the early 2000s the Junebug Line was an 18-mile road headquartered in Taylorsville with connections to the Norfolk Southern Railroad in Statesville, serving businesses in Iredell and Alexander Counties. The railroad's four locomotives moved commodities such as grain, pulpboard, plastics, lumber, waste paper, fertilizer, and liquefied petroleum gas.

Reference: Lou Harshaw, *Trains, Trestles, and Tunnels* (1977).

George A. Kennedy

Alleghany County, located in the Blue Ridge Mountains of northwestern North Carolina and bordering Virginia, was formed in 1859 from Ashe County through an act of the North Carolina legislature. Its earliest peoples were Cherokee and Shawnee Indians; English, German, and Scotch-Irish settlers subsequently arrived in the area. The county name comes from either the Allegewi Indian tribe or the Delaware Indian word "oolikhanna" (beautiful stream). The county seat, Sparta, was established in 1825, with the original name of Bower's Store. Its name was changed to Gap Civil (1846) before becoming Sparta in 1879, named for the Greek city. Other important communities located in Alleghany County are Piney Creek, Glade Valley, Laurel Springs, Roaring Gap, Twin Oaks, and Stratford. In addition to the mountains of the Blue Ridge, the county's other significant physical features include the New River (one of the world's oldest rivers), the Little River, and a part of the Eastern Continental Divide.

The construction of the Blue Ridge Parkway in the 1930s —made possible by the political efforts of longtime U.S. Congressman and Alleghany County native Robert Lee Doughton —brought increased tourism and growth to Alleghany County. However, the county remains North Carolina's fifth-smallest in land area (233 square miles) and its sixth-smallest in population (about 11,000 residents in 2004). Christmas trees make up a large portion of the agricultural goods produced by Alleghany County, generating an annual income in excess of $17 million. The production of dairy and beef cattle and other livestock is also a multimillion-dollar industry in Alleghany County.

Alleghany County hosts several annual cultural festivals and events rooted in the region's mountain heritage, including the Blue Ridge Mountain Fair, the Mountain Heritage Festival, the Blue Ridge Mountains Crafts Fair, and Choose and Cut Day (for Christmas tree buyers).

Reference: Alleghany Historical-Genealogical Society, *Alleghany County Heritage* (1983).

Bernadette Rider

Alligators. In North Carolina the American alligator inhabits fresh and estuarine bodies of water as far west as Robeson and Cumberland Counties, building dens with submerged entrances at the water's edge. Alligators are concentrated in the lower Cape Fear and Neuse River Valleys but roam over much of the Coastal Plain south of the 36th parallel, which splits Albemarle Sound lengthwise. A few atypical creatures, such as the one evicted from a golf course near Kings Mountain, penetrate far into the Piedmont. Escaped pets, including spectacled caimans imported from the tropics, account for some sightings.

Alligator populations are greatest in places with restricted human activity, such as military bases and state and federal parks, but the stress of living around the northern limits of their range has limited the animals' survival, growth, and reproduction in North Carolina even in these areas. Consequently, the species has not responded as well to official protection in North Carolina as in other southern states. Nevertheless, alligators are useful predators and are believed to help maintain healthy environments for fish and other wildlife in the lakes and ponds they inhabit (in particular, by retarding the eutrophication of these bodies of water).

Exactly how far north alligators once ventured is difficult to assess. William Byrd, who traversed the Great Dismal Swamp in 1728, mentioned tales of the species there but did not record direct sightings. Alligators have left their mark on North Carolina geography, however. Named for them are two bays in Onslow and Brunswick Counties; two river branches in Columbus and Brunswick Counties; five creeks in Brunswick, Camden, Carteret, Pamlico, and Tyrrell Counties; a lake in Hyde County; a river and a swamp in Brunswick County; a township in Tyrrell County; the Great Alligator Dismal Swamp, which covers much of the Albemarle-Pamlico Peninsula; and other land forms in the state.

Reference: Bernard S. Martof and others, *Amphibians and Reptiles of the Carolinas and Virginia* (1980).

Wynne Dough

Almanacs. In early North Carolina an almanac and a Bible were often the only publications owned by a family. North Carolina residents relied on almanacs for information on such things as planting seasons, phases of the moon, religious and civil anniversaries, and other subjects. Almanacs also provided an important source of entertainment, as they included essays, humor, and reprinted "news" from other parts of the country and world. The margins or blank pages in the alma-

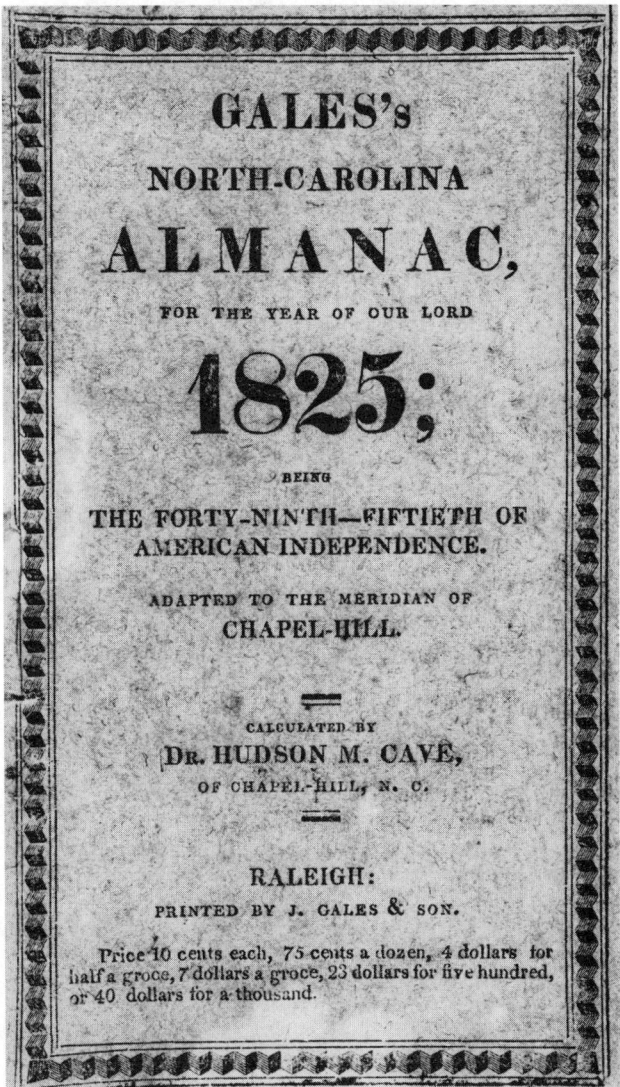

Front cover of *Gale's North Carolina Almanac* for the year 1825. NCC.

nac might be used to record important information such as the date of a destructive storm or flood, the breeding of livestock, or even family births and deaths. Extant copies of family almanacs in libraries, museums, and archives offer a valuable source of information on North Carolina, particularly before the twentieth century.

In the Albemarle region of North Carolina, the Taylor family had almanacs from England beginning in 1663. In August 1768 the *Virginia Gazette* in Williamsburg advertised copies of the *North-Carolina Almanack for the Year of Our Lord 1769* for sale by William Scarborough in Edenton. In 1800 John M. Slump of Lincolnton published an almanac in German, while in 1802 Joseph Gales published an English-language one in Raleigh. Other early almanacs that have survived were published by William Boylan in Raleigh (1805), Francis Coupee in Salisbury (1808), and Thomas Henderson in Raleigh (1812). Most North Carolina almanacs obtained their information from

GALES's ALMANAC FOR 1825.

An infallible remedy for Whitloes.

Make a strong lie of vine ashes, and in this, warmed, let the finger soak a good while. To keep up an equal degree of warmth, every minute pour into the vessel a little more hot lie. Repeat this operation two or three times, and you will soon find the good effect of it.

Cure for the Fever and Ague.

Take thirty grains of salts of wormwood, twenty grains of Virginia Snake root, half an ounce of Red Bark, mix them together in one gill of molasses; take one third of this mixture when the fit is first coming on, one-third four hours later, and one-third four hours after that. It would be advisable, first, to take an emetic.

For Indigestion, Weak Stomach, Head Ache, &c.

One tea-spoonful, salt tart. one table spoonful cream tart, ground together—a tea-spoonful of this mixture, in a wine glass of water for a dose—repeat the same until you are relieved.

Burns, Gout and Rheumatism.

The efficacy of cotton in cases of burns has been well attested. In attacks of gout and rheumatism, cotton carded and laid upon the part affected, has likewise been found to afford a relief which could be obtained from no other application.

Cure for Cancer.—Sheep sorrel, (leaf like that of a clover)—express the juice on a pewter plate; expose it to the sun, until it assumes the consistency of salve; apply this as a plaster to a cancer, and change it occasionally as necessity may require. It will fully and entirely extract the cancer. If the disease be really the cancer, the application will cause pain; if not, no pain will ensue.

For Frost or Chilblains.—Take an equal quantity of hartshorn and sweet oil, shake them together in a phial, which will make a liniment, then rub the part affected with it hard three or four times a day. Always use it cold and in a few days it will make a perfect cure.

Home remedies as detailed in *Gale's North Carolina Almanac* for the year 1825. NCC.

the almanacs of other states, but Philip Brooks, who identified himself as an astronomer of Richmond County, compiled one himself for 1815. Boylan and Colin McIver of Fayetteville (1823) also prepared their own information. In Raleigh in 1828 the American Tract Society published a *Christian Almanac for North Carolina*. Several almanacs were published regularly for many years; for example, the *Blum's Farmers' and Planters' Almanac* was published in Salem from 1829 to 1947, when it was absorbed by *Turner's North Carolina Almanac*.

Reference: Douglas C. McMurtrie, *Eighteenth-Century North Carolina Imprints, 1749–1800* (1938).

William S. Powell

Aluminum Company of America (Alcoa) established

an aluminum smelting plant in east Tennessee in 1914. Alcoa

purchased sites on the Little Tennessee River in North Carolina between 1910 and 1925 in order to build hydroelectric generating stations for its smelting operation. A complex of dams constructed in the North Carolina–Tennessee borderlands supplied electricity to the reduction plant at Alcoa, Tenn. The company subsequently perceived a growing demand for electric power by individuals and communities in far western North Carolina. In response, the Nantahala Power and Light Company was formed as a state public utility in 1929, bringing the first electricity to a number of the state's western farms and towns.

Alcoa's Badin Reduction Works in Stanly County and the Alcoa, Tenn., plant have employed North Carolinians and contributed to the local economies since early in the twentieth century. The French-owned Southern Aluminum Company first chose the Badin site on the Yadkin River. Unable to complete construction because of the war in Europe, the French company sold the partially built dam and powerhouse to Alcoa in 1915. Alcoa finished the Yadkin Narrows hydroelectric plant and constructed the Badin Works, which has operated regularly since its opening in July 1917. Over the years, the company expanded hydroelectric capacity with generating facilities at Yadkin Falls and High Rock. The Badin Works now produces primary aluminum, cast sheet, and high purity aluminum.

In 1986 Alcoa moved a wholly owned subsidiary, Permatech, from Pittsburgh, Pa., to the town of Graham. Permatech manufactures ceramic products used in handling molten aluminum, and about two-thirds of its output goes to other Alcoa plants. In the early 2000s, Alcoa also operated Alcoa Distribution and Industrial Products in Catawba, Six R Communications, L.L.C., in Monroe, and T.I.C.S. Corporation in Charlotte. The relationship between Nantahala Power and Light Company and Alcoa was severed in 1971, when demand from North Carolina customers exceeded Nantahala's production. Alcoa agreed to cease purchasing electricity from Nantahala, and in 1988 the electric company was sold to Duke Power Company of Charlotte.

References: Charles C. Carr, *Alcoa: An American Enterprise* (1952); George David Smith, *From Monopoly to Competition: The Transformation of Alcoa, 1888–1986* (1988).

Susan Bales
Additional research provided by James L. Hunt.

Amadas and Barlowe Expedition was the first of the

English voyages to Roanoke Island in the 1580s and was one of Sir Walter Raleigh's attempts to establish a colony in the New World. The expedition, led by Capt. Philip Amadas and Master Arthur Barlowe, left England with two ships piloted by veteran Portuguese navigator Simon Fernándes on 27 Apr. 1584. Amadas, who commanded the flagship (which may have been

Construction of the Narrows Dam and powerhouse on the Yadkin River near Badin, a project of the Aluminum Company of America, 1917. NCC.

Raleigh's 200-ton vessel *Bark Raleigh*), was a member of Raleigh's official household, where he may have studied instrumental navigation and related mathematics under Thomas Harriot. Barlowe, commander of the other vessel (possibly a smaller sailboat named the *Dorothy*), had become one of Raleigh's "owne servants" in Ireland as early as 1580–81.

After sailing through the Canary Islands and the Caribbean, the two ships reached the mainland American coast on 4 July 1584. They sailed northward until they reached an "entrance, or River issuing into the Sea." According to a later account by one Richard Butler, they landed first near present-day Ocracoke Island, though Barlowe's journal suggests an initial landing farther north, nearer present-day Oregon Inlet. The exact location is difficult to determine because of centuries of change in the barrier islands. After anchoring, the explorers went ashore in boats to view and take possession of the "lande next adjoyning" for Queen Elizabeth I and their patron, Raleigh. Barlowe's journal provides an almost lyrical description of the land and its exploration.

In addition to extolling the natural bounty and beauty of the coastal region (perhaps too favorably), Barlowe sympathetically portrayed the Algonquian Indians whom the Englishmen soon encountered and with whom they almost immediately began to trade. Barlowe also tried to give a rough idea of the geography of the region as best he and his companions could understand it from the Indians, who called the area "Wingandacoa." He recounted a visit to the town of Roanoke, whose name the island would carry for over four centuries. After perhaps as long as six weeks exploring and trading, the expedition returned to England, taking with it two local Indians: the Croatoan Manteo and the Roanoke Wanchese.

The wide-ranging information acquired by Amadas and Barlowe, as well as what they learned from their association with Manteo and Wanchese, gave Raleigh and his associates sufficient encouragement to continue their plans to establish the first English colony in America in 1585.

References: David B. Quinn, *The Roanoke Voyages, 1584–1590* (2 vols., 1955); Quinn, *Set Fair for Roanoke: Voyages and Colonies, 1584–1606* (1985); David Stick, *Roanoke Island: The Beginnings of English America* (1983).

Phillip W. Evans

American Association of University Women. The North Carolina Chapter of the American Association of University Women (NCAAUW) was founded in 1927, 46 years after the national organization. It has maintained a strong presence at the state's colleges and universities. The organization's three main charges are to promote equity for females of all ages, to provide an outlet for lifelong education and self-development, and to provide a means for positive societal change. Anyone possessing at least a bachelor's degree from an accredited college or university is eligible for membership. Undergraduates enrolled in an accredited institute of higher learning may obtain student membership.

The first of North Carolina's 31 NCAAUW branches was formed in Chapel Hill in 1923 after the merger of the Southern Association of College Women and the Association of Collegiate Alumnae. Seventeen women met in the home of Mrs. Harry Woodburn Chase, the wife of the University of North Carolina president; Louise Venable, the daughter of former university president Francis Venable and future wife of botany professor William C. Coker, was elected to serve as the first chapter president.

At the University of North Carolina, the organization's efforts began with an initiative to locate a physical education instructor as well as provide a place for female students to exercise. As community involvement increased, the group later played a vital role in establishing the Chapel Hill Public Library, which opened its doors in 1958. Membership grew to include women from Durham, Orange, and Chatham Counties. The Carrie Heath Schwenning Scholarship Fund was formed to provide financial assistance for female graduate students at the university who display outstanding academic performance.

Nationally, the AAUW includes programs geared to offer services and support for females of all ages. The Educational Foundation provides funding for research, community projects, and grants. The Legal Advocacy Fund offers legal support to women faced with sexual discrimination cases in higher education. In 1953 the NCAAUW established the AAUW Award for Juvenile Literature. A plaque—on which the names of winners are engraved—was given to the North Carolina Literary and Historical Association, and a cup is presented to the annual winner who has published in book form "an original work of juvenile literature of outstanding excellence . . . most worthy of recognition." The competition, open to residents of North Carolina, is handled through the secretary of the North Carolina Literary and Historical Association.

In addition to its Chapel Hill chapter, the NCAAUW has chapters in university and college settings in Raleigh, Asheville, Brevard, Greensboro, Charlotte, Winston-Salem, Statesville, Wilmington, and other North Carolina cities.

H. G. Jones
Additional research provided by Susan L. Blalock.

American Dance Festival (ADF) is a six-week summer gathering of dance students, choreographers, and dance professionals of emerging and legendary status who work together in an exchange of dance craft, creativity, and experimentation, giving North Carolinians the opportunity to see important dance companies and innovators in a number that exceeds what is available in most larger metropolitan areas. The mission of the ADF is to promote all forms of modern

Dancers rehearse in the Reynolds Industries Theater at Duke University during the 2001 American Dance Festival. Photograph by Kevin Seifert. *Durham Herald-Sun.*

dance, both classic and new. What became the ADF began in 1934 in Bennington, Vt., when Martha Hill invited modern dance choreographers Martha Graham, Doris Humphrey, Charles Weidman, and Hanya Holm to teach and choreograph new works at the School of Dance of Bennington College. Since that time the ADF's prestigious list of faculty and premiered masterworks has continued to grow and is unrivaled in the history of dance. The festival moved to Duke University in Durham in 1978.

The ADF sponsors technique classes in dance forms and choreography; presents emerging and established dance companies in public performances; and sponsors workshops for dance teachers, critics, videographers, and movement therapists. In the 1980s the ADF began to move beyond the boundaries of America by presenting modern dance companies and artists from other countries, sponsoring the International Choreographers Residential Program, and holding "miniature" ADF programs in Japan, Korea, and Russia. In addition, the ADF started collaborative programs with existing dance institutions in China, South America, Africa, Poland, the Philippines, and other regions of the world.

The ADF's Black Tradition in American Modern Dance Project began in 1987 to preserve works created by African American choreographers. More than 20 such works have been reconstructed by leading American companies and presented in concert throughout the United States. The ADF Archival Project documents and preserves the performances and special events of the festival and provides access to these archives, which date back to the 1930s. The ADF video collection is housed in Lilly Library at Duke University, and the ADF continues to add to this collection by videotaping performances and interviews with choreographers. The ADF also has issued a series of publications.

Reference: Jack Anderson, *American Dance Festival* (1987).

Patricia L. Pertalion

American Indians have populated the region that includes modern-day North Carolina continuously since the Paleo-Indian period (13,000–8000 B.C.). The historical and archaeological record, as interpreted by scholars and by American Indians themselves, has shown that North Carolina was home to many flourishing communities of indigenous peoples before the arrival of European explorers and colonists in the sixteenth and seventeenth centuries. After the first arrival of Europeans, however, these native cultures changed decisively as natives interacted—sometimes productively but often violently—with European settlers. Since European contact, the history of American Indians in North Carolina, as elsewhere in the United States, often has been marked by conflict and struggle, not only between Indians and whites but also among and within Indian groups. During the early nineteenth century, North Carolina's government joined the federal government in its official policy of removal of American Indian people to reservations in Oklahoma and elsewhere, and this struck a terrible blow to the state's indigenous population. Nevertheless, communities of American Indians remained in the state, even during the era of removal, and native peoples' cultures and identities have persisted and evolved in the face of complex and often conflicting relationships with their nonnative neighbors. Today, the state is home to two of the largest Indian tribes east of the Mississippi River, the Eastern Band of Cherokee Indians and the Lumbee Indians, along with a number of smaller recognized tribes and unaffiliated Indian groups. Many American Indians have established themselves as vital participants in the state's social, cultural, economic, and political spheres.

American Indians before European Contact

The history of American Indians before European contact is broadly divided into three major periods: the Paleo-Indian period, the Archaic period (8000–1000 B.C.), and the Woodland period (1000 B.C.–1600 A.D.). The limited evidence available about the Paleo-Indian period suggests that the first Indians in the Southeast, as elsewhere, were nomadic, hunting and defending themselves with stone tools (knives and scrapers), clubs, and spears, which were at times tipped with well-crafted, fluted stone points. During the Archaic period, basketry, bone tools, and finer stone tools appeared. Archaic peoples also began to develop more specialized knowledge of their local environments and the animals and plants that lived there. Though they did not generally travel far beyond these familiar environments, American Indians during this period did begin to establish trade and migration routes that brought the native peoples of the Carolinas in contact with other bands and tribes.

Scholars suggest that small-scale agriculture began to develop among American Indians in the Southeast around 1000 B.C., marking a slow transition to what is known as the Woodland period. During the early Woodland period, native peoples began to concentrate settlements near streams and rivers, where the rich soil allowed successful farming. This Woodland tradition took root among Indians in the Carolina region. Many Woodland people planted crops such as sunflowers, corn, pumpkins, squash, and beans and built permanent wooden homes. Nevertheless, Indians in the Woodland period still relied primarily on hunting, fishing, and gathering. Among the enormous variety of animal resources available, deer was a primary staple, providing food, clothing, blankets, and tools made of antler and bone. Fishing methods included the use of hooks, spears (sometimes poisoned), nets, traps, weirs, and dugout canoes. In most tribes, work was shared by men and women. Indian housing typically consisted of lodges made of bark or thatch, at times raised off the ground. Some

Indians, including the Cherokee, also built earthen winter homes without windows. Homes were furnished with straw or cane mats, pottery, basketry, and wooden utensils. As family groups and larger bands formed around productive agricultural or hunting grounds, villages developed. Some villages were surrounded by protective palisades, and most included a council house for public gatherings.

Use of the bow and arrow probably evolved during the middle and late Woodland period; the oldest examples of arrow points in North Carolina have been located near the Yadkin River in the Piedmont. Tobacco pipes of stone and clay, beads, and other ornaments made of shell and clay also came into common use. Pottery began to appear, as did a clear concern for the dead, evidenced in some regions by burial or effigy mounds and earthen enclosures. In some cases, the dead were placed in round or oval pits and buried with grave goods.

The Woodland Indians of North Carolina, though scattered and in many ways diverse, shared a number of cultural traits. Tribal societies were generally organized by leaders rather than rulers, governed by consensus rather than decree, and directed by a sense of community more than by individualism. Community rituals for marking the passage of time and seasons and for personal cleanliness and purification developed along with religious beliefs about the ability of individuals to tap into the supernatural world, which was seen as full of spirits.

Sometime around the middle of the Woodland period (ca. 700 A.D.), an important American Indian cultural tradition known as the Mississippian tradition took shape along the Mississippi River and its tributaries. Over time, Mississippian tribal groups began to migrate into the Southeast, including North Carolina. While Mississippian peoples had many similarities to Woodland peoples, there were also important differences. Mississippian cultures were rooted more deeply in farming than were Woodland cultures, and Mississippians developed large town sites that served as hubs for religious ceremonies and trade. These towns often included large pyramid-shaped mounds topped by temples and meetinghouses, and the mounds were surrounded by public grounds for games and public rituals. Individual houses, often made of wood, surrounded these public grounds, and beyond the homes were often extensive cultivated fields. Town Creek Indian Mound, located in modern-day Montgomery County, is one North Carolina example of a mound that was at the heart of a town site built by Mississippian people.

Mississippian peoples also developed more formal systems of governance, called chiefdoms, and extensive religious rituals and ceremonies related to agricultural cycles of planting and harvest. One particularly important ritual was the Green Corn Ritual. This rite celebrated the ripened corn crop in the late summer and served as a period for village members to cleanse their environment and start anew on a personal and spiritual level. Typically, the Green Corn Ritual involved the cleaning of the council house and family homes, fasting, bathing, forgiving past wrongs, and the symbolic extinguishing of old fires and the creation of new ones. The Indians' respect for their environment, and their vision of their community as grateful recipients of nature's bounty, was shown through the destruction of accumulated foodstuffs from the previous year.

The chiefdoms of the Mississippian tradition came to dominate American Indian culture in the Southeast as the time of European contact approached, and differences between Mississippian and Woodland Indians almost certainly sparked conflict as cultures met in North Carolina and elsewhere. But scholars believe that many Woodland people simply adapted Mississippian practices over time. Other Woodland tribes likely moved to more isolated lands and maintained their cultural practices, sometimes reclaiming their traditional territories when Mississippian tribes themselves relocated to new planting grounds. Certainly European explorers, when they began to encounter the native people of North Carolina, found groups practicing both Woodland and Mississippian ways of life.

Indian Tribes from European Contact to the Era of Removal

Whether speaking in a historical context or of the present day, there are many ways to define an American Indian tribe. In its most widely understood form, however, an American Indian tribe is a group of bands, often (though not always) related by family ties, sharing common territories and having a feeling of unity deriving from similarities in culture, frequent friendly contacts, and other shared interests. More or less elaborate types of formal tribal organization may be defined within these basic outlines, but tribal groups can exist and function without them. One important way scholars have defined tribes for the purpose of study is by linguistic group. Many North Carolina tribes disappeared or merged with other groups before their languages were recorded, but word lists, town and tribal names, and other indicators suggest that by the sixteenth century, when European explorers first arrived in the region, native tribes populating North Carolina, both Mississippian and Woodland, comprised three linguistic groups: Iroquoian, Siouan, and Algonquian. The two most prominent Iroquoian tribes were the Cherokee, occupying the Blue Ridge Mountains and regions west and south, and the Tuscarora, occupying the Coastal Plain between Ocracoke Island and Topsail Island inland to the central Piedmont. The Neusioc and Coree, also Iroquoian, occupied the Cape Lookout environs of modern Carteret and Craven Counties.

Tribes of the Siouan linguistic group flourished throughout the central Piedmont, the Pee Dee River Valley, and the Lower Cape Fear region. These tribes included the Cape Fear, Catawba, Keyauwee, Occaneechi, Pee Dee (or Pedee), Saponi,

Sissipahaw, Saura (Cheraw), Tutelo, Waxhaw, and Waccamaw peoples. Algonquian tribes settled and hunted the northeastern region of the state, including the Outer Banks north of Ocracoke and the Albemarle and Pamlico Sounds inland to the approximate western limit of the Coastal Plain. Representative tribes of the Algonquian group include the Chowanoac, Hatteras, Moratuc, Croatan, Secotan, Pamlico, Roanoke, and Weapemeoc (Yeopim).

Early European explorers and settlers to the land that would become North Carolina documented some of their encounters with the native peoples, providing firsthand descriptions of their appearance and demeanor. In July 1524 Giovanni da Verrazano, a Florentine navigator, became the first European to report on the characteristics of the Coastal Plain peoples. He described the natives he encountered on Bogue Banks and at the mouth of the Cape Fear River as "of a russet color," tall, strong, and sporting long black hair worn "like a little tail." The Indians were at first uneasy but soon became friendly toward the visitors.

The 1584 expedition sent by Sir Walter Raleigh and led by Philip Amadas and Arthur Barlowe was the first group of Englishmen to encounter natives on the Carolina coast. Arriving on Hatteras Island, the explorers were met by a friendly and curious people, with whom they exchanged gifts. The following year, a colony led by Ralph Lane was temporarily established in the region. Through the work of two of its members —scientist Thomas Harriot and artist John White—much information and documentation was gathered about the indigenous people. Reflecting the attitude of virtually all Englishmen of the era, Harriot described a people who were "very ingenious" and yet clearly inferior and in need of being brought "to civilities." More than a century later, John Lawson, in *A New Voyage to Carolina* (1709), wrote at great length about the characteristics and customs of the Indians. Lawson's attitude toward them remained similar to Harriot's, stressing the need to treat the Indians well in order to encourage them to adopt the "worthier" customs of the English people.

The European discovery and settlement of the Carolina region signaled an era of radical change for local Indians, one marked by the toppling of the previous Indian way of life and a tragic and unrelenting decline in their population. The various strains of European diseases such as smallpox, bubonic plague, typhus, and measles inflicted severe misery upon many Indian tribes, which had no immunity against them. A massive smallpox epidemic in 1695 among the Pamlico Indians, and a similarly devastating outbreak that wiped out nearly half of the Cherokee in 1738, are but two examples of the deadly effects these diseases had on the Indian population.

At the same time that European settlement brought violent conflict between whites and Indians, it also increased the occurrence of warfare between Indian tribes. There were sev-

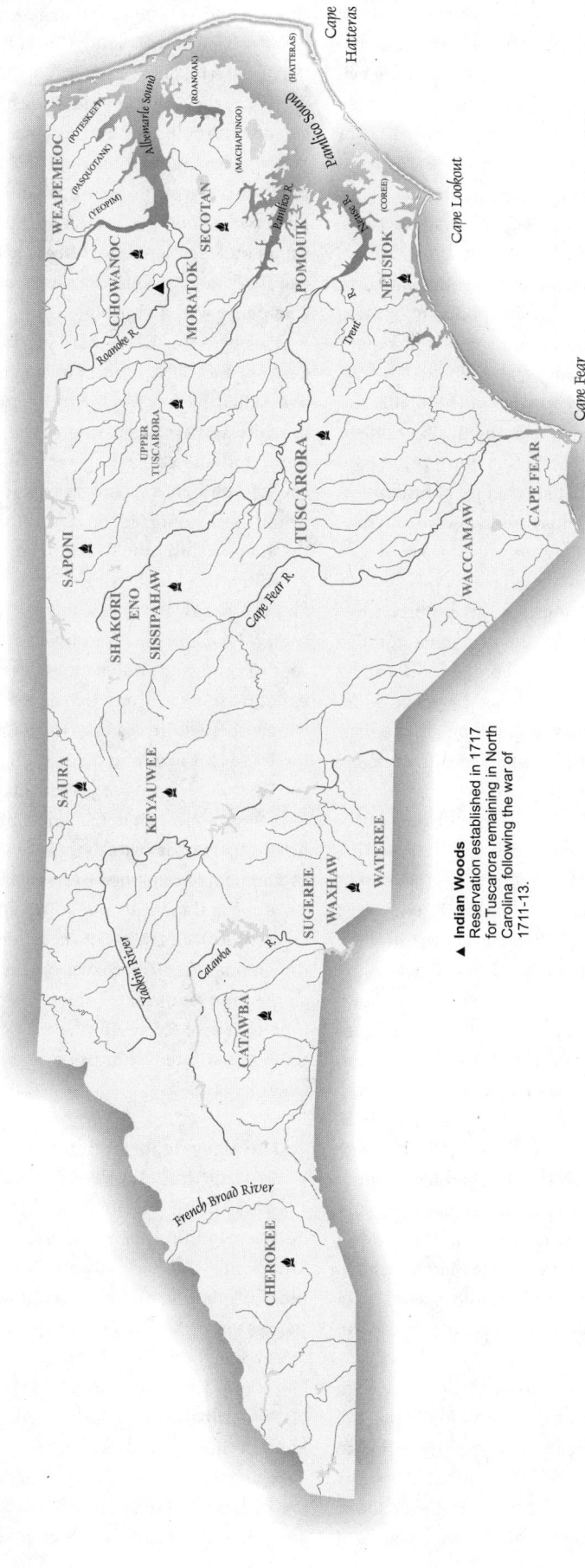

Principal American Indian tribes at the time of the Tuscarora War. (Tribes largely displaced by European settlement shown in parentheses.) Map by Mark Anderson Moore, courtesy NCOA&H.

▲ **Indian Woods**
Reservation established in 1717 for Tuscarora remaining in North Carolina following the war of 1711-13.

CHEROKEE

French Broad River

CATAWBA

Catawba R.

Yadkin River

SAURA

KEYAUWEE

SUGEREE

WAXHAW

WATEREE

SAPONI

SHAKORI
ENO
SISSIPAHAW

UPPER
TUSCARORA

TUSCARORA

Cape Fear R.

WACCAMAW

CAPE FEAR

Cape Fear

WEAPEMEOC
(POTESKEET)
(PASQUOTANK)
(YEOPIM)

CHOWANOC

Roanoke R.

MORATOK

SECOTAN
(MACHAPUNGO)

(ROANOAC)
(HATTERAS)

Albemarle Sound

Pamlico R.

POMOUIK

Pamlico Sound

NEUSIOK
(COREE)

Neuse R.

Trent R.

Cape Hatteras

Cape Lookout

eral factors influencing these hostilities. Many historians have concluded that a central cause of the problem was trade between the natives and the newcomers. Initially, there is evidence to suggest that North Carolina's native peoples worked and lived cooperatively with the Europeans, teaching them agricultural techniques for corn, tobacco, and other cultivation as well as fishing and other necessary survival skills. In return, the white settlers offered the Indians manufactured goods from their homeland. But this trade led to a massive upheaval in both the ways Indians related to each other and how they came to view the white settlers. The introduction of these items resulted in the Indians' becoming increasingly reliant on products such as metal knives, hoes, and hatchets as well as guns and ammunition. The acceptance of these effective new tools and other trade products made them vulnerable to manipulation by white traders and colonial authorities, who often turned one native tribe against another for political, economic, or other purposes. Many unscrupulous white traders also charged unfairly high prices for their wares, giving rise to ill feelings among natives that often led to conflict.

Furthermore, providing the Europeans with commodities that they needed—not only products like deerskins but also Indian slave labor—caused tremendous competition among Indian tribes and often resulted in violence between them. The pressure exerted on the Indian population by the constant expansion of European settlements also caused many hostile acts on both parts. The Tuscarora War of 1711–13 represented an early pinnacle of Indian resistance against European encroachment. At the outbreak of this conflict, the Tuscarora were the most powerful tribe in the eastern portion of North Carolina, with alliances that stretched both northward and southward into what are now Virginia and South Carolina. After German and Swiss colonists founded New Bern on the Neuse River in Tuscarora lands, the Tuscarora, led by Chief Hancock, attacked the town and nearby settlements in September 1711. The Tuscarora warriors killed 120 colonists and captured others, destroyed houses and barns, and confiscated crops and livestock. For the next year and a half, many individual battles occurred, sparked by both sides, until the Tuscarora were finally defeated at the village of Neoheroka in March 1713. The long conflict took a severe toll on the Tuscarora, and surviving tribal members who chose to remain in North Carolina were forced onto a reservation near Lake Mattamuskeet, in what is today Hyde County. Over time, many of these southern Tuscarora traveled to New York and Canada to join the Iroquois Confederacy.

The defeat and subsequent relocation of the Tuscarora resulted in even greater westward expansion of white settlements during the eighteenth century. This expansion led to increased conflict with the inland tribes, particularly the Cherokee, with more than 40 towns and six times as many people as the Tuscarora, occupying the mountainous lands of southwestern North Carolina as well as parts of what are now eastern Tennessee, South Carolina, northern Georgia, and northeastern Alabama. During the French and Indian War (1754–63) the Cherokee sided with the French, and they later sided with the British in the American Revolution as a result of a royal proclamation that prohibited colonial settlement in the lands west of the Appalachian Mountains. Many colonists consequently considered the Cherokee hostile, and assaults on Cherokee towns became exceedingly brutal. Cherokee fields and storehouses were often destroyed, and many Cherokees were left to starve.

Through the latter part of the eighteenth century, the Cherokee and the other native people of the Carolinas were compelled by force or by treaty to cede much of their land to white settlers. Adjusting to these extreme circumstances, many Indians adopted aspects of Western culture, creating schools, churches, businesses, and forms of governance that would be recognized by non-Indians. Most famous among these efforts was the development of a written language, or syllabary, by the Cherokee Sequoyah. Despite these changes and the positive impression they might have had on whites, Indian land remained a target of white desire, and the concept of removing Indians to western lands continued to gain support. In 1830 Congress passed the Indian Removal Act, which opened the way for North Carolina and other states to force the Cherokee and their neighbors to relocate. Removal of the Cherokee people to present-day Oklahoma began in May 1838, and approximately 4,000 Cherokee people died on the infamous Trail of Tears to their new home. Nevertheless, some Indian people remained in North Carolina, maintaining a distinct cultural identity and autonomy in the face of enormous challenges. The largest of these remaining groups, known as the Oconaluftee Cherokee, claimed North Carolina citizenship rather than membership in the Cherokee Nation, and therefore avoided removal. The Oconaluftee Cherokee eventually constituted what became the modern Eastern Band of Cherokee Indians.

The Struggle for Indian Sovereignty and Cultural Identity

While North Carolina's native tribes retained a hard-won degree of cultural and even political independence during the nineteenth and early twentieth centuries, the lives of most Indians grew ever more impoverished and practically inconsequential in the eyes of the growing white community. The story of the Lumbee tribe, living in Robeson, Hoke, and Scotland Counties, is an example of this trend. Although the facts of their tribal history have been the subject of debate, the Lumbee likely are descendants of Saura and other Siouan-speaking natives who survived the European onslaught by living in swampy lands unattractive to white settlers. They had adopted much of white settler culture—most notably, speaking English and adopting Christian beliefs—by the time white North Carolinians began to take note of the Lumbee as culturally different in the first decades of the nineteenth century. For a time, the Lumbee people maintained their rights of citizenship. When North Carolina enacted a new state constitution in 1835, however, which restricted the rights of "persons of color," nearly all Lumbee civil rights were taken away. Through much of the remainder of the nineteenth and twentieth centuries, the Lumbee people were victimized by prejudice and segregation, and they were left without the meager protections secured by other tribes through treaties with the federal government.

American Indians in North Carolina played a complex role in the secession crisis and Civil War. The Oconaluftee Cherokee, encouraged by secessionist and Indian agent William Holland Thomas, offered soldiers to the Confederate cause, and other North Carolinians of Indian descent undoubtedly fought for the Confederacy. But among the Lumbee people, a band led by Henry Berry Lowry did what it could to further the Union cause. Lowry organized attacks on Confederate leaders as well as wealthy whites. His exploits, which lasted until the early 1870s, made him a popular hero among the Lumbee as well as with some blacks and poor whites.

While Reconstruction and the push for new civil rights for people of color initially offered some hope of improved circumstances for American Indians in North Carolina, this promise quickly disappeared. The federal and state governments did, however, offer some limited educational and other benefits to the state's native peoples. In 1885 the state officially recognized the Indian people living around Robeson County with the name "Croatan" (the name "Lumbee" did not officially designate the tribe until 1953), and separate schools were provided for their use, beginning with the Croatan Normal Indian School in Robeson County in 1887. This school, which granted its first college degree in 1940, became part of the University of North Carolina system in 1969 as Pembroke State University and later the University of North Carolina at Pembroke, offering crucial opportunities to Indian people.

Among the Cherokee, Chief Nimrod Jarrett Smith negotiated with the North Carolina government on behalf of the Oconaluftee, and in 1889 they were recognized by the state as the Eastern Band of Cherokee Indians with a status that allowed the tribe to function as a separate political body. Later, in the 1930s, the federal government extended a number of economic, educational, and other programs to Cherokee people. These programs improved the circumstances of many Cherokees while allowing the tribe to retain elements of its political and cultural autonomy. With the development of large-scale tourism in western North Carolina coinciding with the opening of the Great Smoky Mountains National Park in 1934, some Cherokee people capitalized on the opportunity to promote their cultural heritage as a part of the region's appeal.

While the Cherokee were drawn out of their regional isolation and afforded modest economic gains, some changes did not benefit the tribe. Tourists' expectations of encountering "cigar store Indians" reinforced stereotypes among non-Indian visitors, and increased contact with the larger world presented Cherokee people with new struggles in their efforts to maintain traditional ways of life.

Despite some achievements in the first half of the twentieth century, the majority of American Indians in North Carolina continued to suffer from a lack of economic opportunities, poor access to education and health benefits, a sharply limited political voice, and persistent racism. Many American Indian people who had in the nineteenth century moved to marginal lands that were not valued by whites to avoid removal or other confrontation remained mired in relative obscurity. This was particularly true of the state's smaller Indian tribes.

Nevertheless, many Indian people created businesses, churches, schools, newspapers, and other institutions in North Carolina, finding ways to promote their own sense of culture and identity while insisting upon a greater voice in state affairs. Indian leaders often concentrated their efforts on the development of separate schools. Members of the Waccamaw tribe, whose territory is centered in modern-day Bladen and Columbus Counties, first established a tribal school with their own funds in 1891 and maintained it through much of the next century. The East Carolina Indian School, founded in 1942 in Sampson County, was another important institution for the state's Indian people. Occasional advances were also made politically. The predominantly Lumbee town of Pembroke elected its first Indian mayor in 1947. Sometimes Indian people found it necessary to confront opposition forcefully. In one notable instance of Indian resistance to white racism, a large group of armed Lumbee Indians confronted a Ku Klux Klan rally held on 18 Jan. 1958 near the town of Maxton. The Lumbees drove off Klan members and effectively put an end to Klan activity against Indian people in the area, drawing attention from state and national media who viewed the events in the context of the emerging civil rights movement.

North Carolina Indians Today

Sparked in part by the national civil rights movement and its gains, and also by the continued building of cultural identity and institutions among Indians themselves, a new surge of interest in the status of North Carolina's American Indian people marked the last third of the twentieth century. In 1971 the North Carolina Commission of Indian Affairs was established in response to requests from concerned native people in the state. The commission serves as the primary advocate for American Indian rights in North Carolina and assists Indian communities in establishing programs and associations for the improvement of their health, education, housing, and economic situation.

Through legislative and other action, the state of North Carolina officially recognizes eight American Indian tribes and several chartered Indian groups. These include the Coharie tribe, the Cumberland County Association for Indian People, the Eastern Band of Cherokee Indians, the Guilford Native American Association, the Haliwa-Saponi tribe, the Sappony, the Meherrin Indian tribe, the Metrolina Native American Association, the Occaneechi Band of Saponi Nation, the Triangle Native American Society, the Lumbee tribe, and the Waccamaw-Siouan tribe. North Carolina also is home to people who identify with or are enrolled members of many other American Indian tribal groups, some of which continue to seek fuller recognition from the state. These include the Tuscarora Nation of North Carolina, the Southern Band Tuscarora Indian tribe, Cherokee Indians of Hoke County, and the Hattadare Indian Nation.

In 2002 Governor Michael Easley proclaimed November as Indian Heritage Month in North Carolina. Special events were planned during that month to draw attention to the contributions native people have made to the state and to their particular cultural heritage. Other annual and seasonal events celebrate American Indian culture and history in the state. Two outdoor dramas portray aspects of the history of Indian people in the state: *Unto These Hills*, performed in Cherokee, tells the story of the Eastern Band of Cherokee Indians at the time of removal, and *Strike at the Wind!*, performed at the North Carolina Indian Cultural Center near Lumberton, focuses on the history and legend surrounding Henry Berry Lowry. Cultural events such as powwows are held throughout the year; these celebrations have become increasingly popular as an opportunity for native and nonnative people alike to participate in and observe traditional storytelling, dance, singing, crafts, and drumming. A number of fairs and festivals are held in and around the Cherokee community. These include the Spring Ramp Festival, held each April to celebrate the arrival of ramps, a member of the onion and garlic family with deep ties to the foodways and traditional medicinal practices of the Cherokee people, and the Cherokee Fall Fair, held the first week of October and featuring crafts, food, storytelling, and traditional stickball games.

By the early 2000s the Indian population in North Carolina was just under 100,000 people, or approximately 1.24 percent of the total population. This was the largest Indian population of any state east of the Mississippi River and the eighth largest in the United States. American Indians live in all 100 North Carolina counties. The only tribe in North Carolina recognized fully by the U.S. government remains the Eastern Band of Cherokee Indians, whose territory is officially known as Qualla Boundary. In March 1997, to boost their local economy, the tribe followed the lead of other Indian groups across the nation and opened a casino. The successful Harrah's Cherokee Great Smoky Mountains Casino significantly increased the business of motels, cabins, campgrounds, retail shops, and restaurants in and around the region. Tribal attractions such as the Oconaluftee Indian Village and the Museum of the Cherokee Indian offer tourists a more complete picture of Cherokee life and history than was previously available. Of the other state-recognized tribes and organizations, only the Lumbee (with more than 42,000 enrolled members, the largest tribe by far in the state) have achieved a degree of federal recognition, but by 2005 the tribe had not yet achieved full recognition from the Bureau of Indian Affairs. Efforts to secure full recognition and tribal benefits from the federal government were ongoing.

References: Adolph L. Dial and David K. Eliades, *The Only Land I Know: A History of the Lumbee Indians* (1996); Barbara R. Duncan and Brett H. Riggs, *Cherokee Heritage Trails Guidebook* (2003); Tom Hartley, *The Dividing Paths: Cherokees and South Carolinians through the Era of Revolution* (1993); Theda Perdue, *Native Carolinians: The Indians of North Carolina* (1985); Douglas L. Rights, *The American Indian in North Carolina* (1947); Timothy Silver, *A New Face on the Countryside: Indians, Colonists, and Slaves in South Atlantic Forests, 1500–1800* (1990); Stanley A. South, *Indians in North Carolina* (1980); H. Trawick Ward and R. P. Stephen Davis Jr., *Indian Communities on the North Carolina Piedmont, A.D. 1000 to 1700* (1993); Ruth Y. Wetmore, *First on the Land: The North Carolina Indians* (1975).

William G. DiNome
Additional research provided by Joffre L. Coe, Michael D. Green, Louis P. Towles, and Rich Weidman.

SEE ALSO Catawba Indians; Cherokee Indians; Commission of Indian Affairs; Great Trading Path; Indian Museum of the Carolinas; Indian Trading Paths; Lumbee Indians; Museum of the Cherokee Indian; Town Creek Indian Mound; Tuscarora Indians.

American Legion maintains an important presence in North Carolina, a state that is home to several large military bases and thousands of active and retired soldiers. The U.S. Congress officially granted a national charter for the American Legion on 16 Sept. 1919, although the organization had already begun operations before that time. The first national convention was held in Minneapolis, Minn., later that year. Since then, the American Legion has pushed for increased and improved care for disabled and sick veterans and was a major force in the establishment of government-funded hospitals to care for veterans. The legion also played a role in the creation of the Veterans Administration in 1930, of the Department of Veterans Affairs in 1989, and in the passing of the original GI Bill of Rights for veterans of World War II and subsequent wars.

North Carolina's first American Legion Post was established in Raleigh on 20 July 1919 and was designated Raleigh

Post, No. 1. Thereafter, there was a proliferation of posts in North Carolina. The first North Carolina American Legion state convention was held in Raleigh on 20 Oct. 1919. The first women's auxiliary post was chartered in Winston-Salem in 1920, and others quickly followed. In keeping with period social codes, posts for African American legionnaires were originally formed separately from ones for white legionnaires. The first post for blacks in North Carolina was Post No. 4 in Wilmington, and Post No. 124 in Pembroke in Robeson County was composed of Native Americans.

By 1929 North Carolina had 101 active white posts and 16 black posts. Total membership in 1929 was 12,001, with 682 of these being African American members. Henry L. Stevens Jr., from Post 109 in Warsaw, served as the American Legion national commander in 1931–32. A fiftieth-anniversary convention for the North Carolina American Legion was held in Winston-Salem in June 1969, with Governor Robert W. Scott as one of the principal speakers. That year approximately 25,000 of the 40,000 members in North Carolina attended the convention. An evening banquet and dance was held at the Robert E. Lee Hotel in Winston-Salem.

The American Legion in North Carolina is currently divided into five divisions, with each of these subdivided into five districts. By the early 2000s there were approximately 40,000 legionnaires in 200 posts across North Carolina. Ray G. Smith from Post 109 in Benson was elected national commander for the years 2000–01. Many prominent North Carolinians, such as Governor R. Gregg Cherry, Governor Luther H. Hodges, Senator Samuel J. Ervin Jr., State Treasurer Edwin M. Gill, U.S. Representative Lawrence H. Fountain, and others, have been proud members of the American Legion.

References: A. L. Fletcher, *History of the American Legion and American Legion Auxiliary: Department of North Carolina, 1919–1929* (1930); Wendy Hower, "Doug Tyson's Duty," *Raleigh News and Observer* (28 May 2000); Thomas A. Rumer, *The American Legion: An Official History, 1919–1989* (1990).

Tom Belton

American Missionary Association (AMA) was a Christian educational organization founded on 3 Sept. 1846 in Albany, N.Y., through the antislavery coalition of the Union Missionary Society, the Committee for West Indian Missions, and the Western Evangelical Missionary Society. The organization was born amid the protests of Christian abolitionists critical of the refusal of American churches and benevolent societies to adopt and act on abolitionist principles. The AMA's founders maintained that slaveholding was a personal sin no matter what the reasons or motives underlying it and that all blacks were members of the "equal brotherhood in the family of Christ." This belief distinguished them from many other abolitionists, including William Lloyd Garrison, who was outspokenly antichurch and who believed in using violence if necessary to achieve freedom for enslaved blacks.

The AMA began its activities in North Carolina in 1863, when schools were established in black churches on Roanoke Island and in Federally occupied cities such as New Bern, Beaufort, Morehead City, Washington, and Plymouth. After the Civil War, AMA schools were started in several other towns, including Raleigh, Fayetteville, Wilson, Wilmington, McLeansville, Charlotte, Murfreesboro, Franklinton, Ahoskie, and Winston (now Winston-Salem). Initially, the AMA's focus was on elementary education; in North Carolina and elsewhere in the South, it had been illegal to teach a slave to read, so the level of illiteracy among blacks was high. The AMA's concept of educational equality eventually included full access for all blacks in the areas of elementary education, industrial and technical training, higher education for teachers, professional training, and liberal arts education at the collegiate level for those capable and interested. The AMA firmly supported the public school system, and its long range objective was to help the public understand its responsibility in educating all of its citizens, both black and white.

The year 1865 marked the beginning of the end of the AMA's nondenominational status and the start of its cooperation with the Freedmen's Bureau. That year the AMA received $250,000 from the National Council of Congregational Churches, which previously had adopted the AMA as its agent in matters related to freedmen's welfare and the channel for much of its antislavery effort. In 1865 the AMA also became the first organization to employ black teachers in North Carolina. Most were North Carolina natives, and some had been slaves. White teachers employed by the AMA to educate blacks were often treated with disdain by local communities.

Many citizens at first turned their backs on white teachers from the North who were looking for room and board or seeking to buy land. In some North Carolina counties, the Ku Klux Klan actively disrupted the efforts of AMA teachers. A short-lived whites-only school was established by the AMA in Beaufort in 1867; it was subsequently closed because of the backlash in the black community.

With many of its North Carolina schools being incorporated into the state public school system during the late nineteenth century, the AMA turned its attention to a special institution at Bricks, a community in Edgecombe County near the boundaries of Halifax and Nash Counties. On land deeded to the AMA by Julia Elma Brewster Brick, the Joseph Keasley Brick Agricultural, Industrial, and Normal School was established for blacks in 1895. From a simple rural elementary institution, the school grew into a high school, and, in 1926, a junior college. Until it closed in 1933, the school specialized in training in agriculture, farm industries, and homemaking, maintaining a great influence among local farmers and providing a valuable educational service by training teachers.

In 1937 the AMA became part of the Board of Home Missions of the Congregational Christian Church, which had been created in 1931. By 1957 the AMA was working under the direction of the United Church of Christ, which had absorbed the Congregational Christian Church.

References: Joyce Hollyday, *On the Heels of Freedom* (2005); Maxine Deloris Jones, "'A Glorious Work': The American Missionary Association and Black North Carolinians, 1863–1880" (Ph.D. diss., Florida State University, 1982); A. Knighton Stanley, *The Children Is Crying: Congregationalism among Black People* (1979).

Wiley J. Williams

American Party, also known as the Know-Nothing Party, was organized in North Carolina by Kenneth Rayner during the winter of 1854–55. Its opponents referred to it as the "Know-Nothing Party" because initially it began in the Northeast as a fraternal organization whose members were bound to secrecy. Consisting mainly of Whigs whose national organization had been shattered by the slavery issue, the American Party sought to continue Whig principles without alignment with the northern antislavery wing of the old party. North Carolina Whigs, along with other southern and northern conservative Whigs, were searching for another political party to oppose the dominant Democrats in the South and to reduce sectional strife in the nation. In addition, nativism—an expression mainly of anti-Catholicism—was part of the American Party appeal, attracting many non-Whigs who were disturbed by the large influx of Irish Catholics into the United States (though relatively few came to North Carolina).

Vilified by the Democrats for their intolerance and secrecy, the North Carolina Know-Nothings abandoned their nativism in time to win three congressional seats in 1855. The next year, however, with the rising threat of the antislavery Republican Party in the presidential election, North Carolina voters rejected American Party candidate Millard Fillmore and rallied behind Democrat James Buchanan as the better defender of southern rights and slavery. Although it won approximately 40 percent of the state vote in the presidential election and in an earlier 1856 gubernatorial contest, the American Party soon collapsed, having failed to achieve a moderate alternative to the sectional Republican and Democratic Parties.

References: William A. Griffin, *Ante-Bellum Elizabeth City* (1970); William C. Harris, *North Carolina and the Coming of the Civil War* (1988); W. Darrell Overdyke, *The Know-Nothing Party in the South* (1950).

William C. Harris

American Revolution was fought on several critical battlefronts across North Carolina and near its borders, altering the lives of all North Carolinians and creating social and political upheaval within practically every community. The progression to full-scale war in North Carolina, as in other American colonies, was a slow process marked by years of emerging unrest among its citizens. Crises such as the violent resistance to the 1765 Stamp Act—as well as the adoption of anti-British documents, or "resolves," by some local political leaders who believed England's economic policies toward the colonies to be unfair and overly punitive—created a spirit of revolution well before any significant battles took place within the province. By the time war erupted after the bloodshed in Lexington and Concord, Mass., on 19 Apr. 1775, which left the British with 273 dead, wounded, or missing compared to 100 American casualties, many North Carolinians had already been anticipating the fight to gain their independence.

First North Carolina Conflicts and the Establishment of a Provincial Government

A month before the "shot heard 'round the world," North Carolina's royal governor Josiah Martin had asked for weapons from Gen. Thomas Gage in Massachusetts, but his letter was intercepted by the Whigs, or Patriots, as the radicals were now called. On 31 May 1775 the Mecklenburg County Committee of Safety issued the Mecklenburg Resolves, which asserted that all laws and commissions issued by the British Crown were null and void and that the people should establish their own government and military forces. That same day, Martin sent his children and pregnant wife to New York for protection. During the night of 31 May 1775, Martin left New Bern for the safety of Fort Johnston. The fort was not safe enough, however, and the Patriots began making moves to capture Martin, who barely escaped to a British warship. Three days later, on 18 July 1775, John Ashe and Cornelius Harnett led 500 militia in burning down Fort Johnston. The destruction of the British fort was the first act of war in the North Carolina colony.

On 20 Aug. 1775 the Provincial Congress (the third held since the previous August) met in Hillsborough to further organize North Carolina's war efforts. Headed by Samuel Johnston and including representatives from every county and town, the body agreed to establish a new government and an army, with the Provincial Congress itself being the highest ruling body. When the congress was not in session, a 13-member Provincial Council served as the chief executive authority. Local affairs were managed by the various Committees of Safety.

Two Continental Army regiments were authorized with Cols. James Moore and Robert Howe as commanders. North Carolina was divided into six military districts with a regiment of 100 minutemen each, and the local militia was reorganized with officers commissioned in each county. The colony's new armed forces were quickly put to work. North Carolina troops were dispatched to join with other Patriot troops in Virginia to help prevent that colony's royal governor, Lord Dunmore, from carrying out his plan to arm the slaves against their

Patriot masters. The Americans were successful, and Dunmore was defeated at the Battle of Great Bridge on 9 Dec. 1775. On 22 December 700 North Carolina troops moved into South Carolina, joining with soldiers from that colony in defeating a group of Loyalists known as the "Scovellites" in what became known as the Snow campaign.

After these two campaigns outside of North Carolina, the colony's troops were soon fighting closer to home. Governor Martin had drawn up elaborate plans for winning back North Carolina from the Patriot forces, beginning with the important port of Brunswick. His plan called for building an army composed of local Tories (Loyalists), former Regulators, and Scottish Highlanders, all supported by British regulars. Gen. Donald McDonald led his 1,600 Highlanders in a drive toward Brunswick but was met by 1,100 Patriots at Moore's Creek Bridge in present-day Pender County on 27 Feb. 1776. When the battle ended, one Patriot was wounded and another lay dead. The Highlanders, on the other hand, lost about 70 dead and wounded. The Tory force broke and ran all the way back to its base camp, pursued by the Patriots. The remaining Tories surrendered without firing a shot. That day the Crown lost hundreds of guns, swords, knives, wagons, and supplies, as well as 850 soldiers captured, including General McDonald. The Battle of Moore's Creek Bridge was hailed as the "Lexington and Concord of the South."

North Carolina's Role in the Continental Congresses

Although the war for independence from Great Britain had essentially begun, the 13 colonies had not categorically affirmed their mutual intention to establish a new country on the American continent. Beginning in September 1774, the colonies sent delegates to Philadelphia to serve in the First Continental Congress, whose purpose was to discuss Britain's oppression of the colonies, formulate a careful statement of colonial rights, apply economic pressure to the English Parliament, and forge a strong colonial union. Representatives from 30 of North Carolina's 36 counties, meeting in North Carolina's First Provincial Congress in New Bern in August 1774, had elected three delegates to represent them in Philadelphia. They were William Hooper, Joseph Hewes, and Richard Caswell. Their instructions were to examine the present state of the British colonies, describe colonists' rights, repair any infractions to those rights, and protect the colonists from future violations. The delegates were vested with authority to act on behalf of the colony.

The First Continental Congress accomplished its mission with the adoption of the Declaration of Rights and Grievances to protest British trade legislation and the Continental Association plan, a nonimportation, nonconsumption, nonexportation agreement. The Congress began to unify the colonies on a permanent basis as the United Colonies. Representatives to the Second Continental Congress, convened in May 1775, did not agree on the question of independence. Whereas some delegates vehemently argued in support of total separation, others opposed cutting all ties with Britain. Hooper and Hewes continued to serve throughout the second congress along with John Penn, a Granville County lawyer who replaced Caswell when he resigned to become treasurer for the Southern District of North Carolina. Penn's election to the delegation may have been an attempt to placate those backcountry settlers who were likely to support the Crown in an armed struggle, as well as to ease east-west sectional tensions within the North Carolina Provincial Congress.

Hooper and Hewes initially supported reconciliation with Britain. Fearful that separation would wreak financial and commercial turmoil, Penn also briefly endorsed a rapprochement. But as colonial relations with Britain deteriorated and King George III declared the colonies to be in rebellion, the North Carolina delegates advocated withholding their colony's naval stores from British use, strengthening the Revolution, and forming a Carolina militia. As the Continental Congress moved from reconciliation toward insurrection, North Carolina strengthened its position on independence.

North Carolina's Fourth Provincial Congress, meeting in Halifax during April-May 1776, empowered its delegates to the Second Continental Congress to concur with delegates from the other colonies in declaring independence and establishing foreign alliances. This was the first official colonial action to secure independence. Although North Carolina made the first formal provincial endorsement for separation with the Halifax Resolves of April 1776, Hewes waited to present the resolves until 27 May, the same day the Virginia delegates presented their resolves. On 2 July the congress adopted the motion by Virginian Richard Henry Lee to make the colonies free and independent states. On 4 July 1776 the Second Continental Congress approved the final draft of the Declaration of Independence. Hooper, Hewes, and Penn all signed the historic document. By the time it adjourned in December 1776, the congress had voted for independence and had begun the transformation of the 13 American colonies into a national government.

Conflict with the Cherokees and British Invasion of the South

North Carolina witnessed little fighting within its boundaries from 1776 to 1780, with one exception. The Cherokee Indians in the western part of the colony were compelled to join forces with the British, who had promised to remove American encroachers from Cherokee land and, ultimately, to ensure greater tribal independence. In response to Cherokee attacks on Americans living in the western frontiers of North Carolina and Virginia, Gen. Charles Lee, commander of the Continental forces in the South, organized a coordinated attack on the Cherokee towns that populated the region. In the

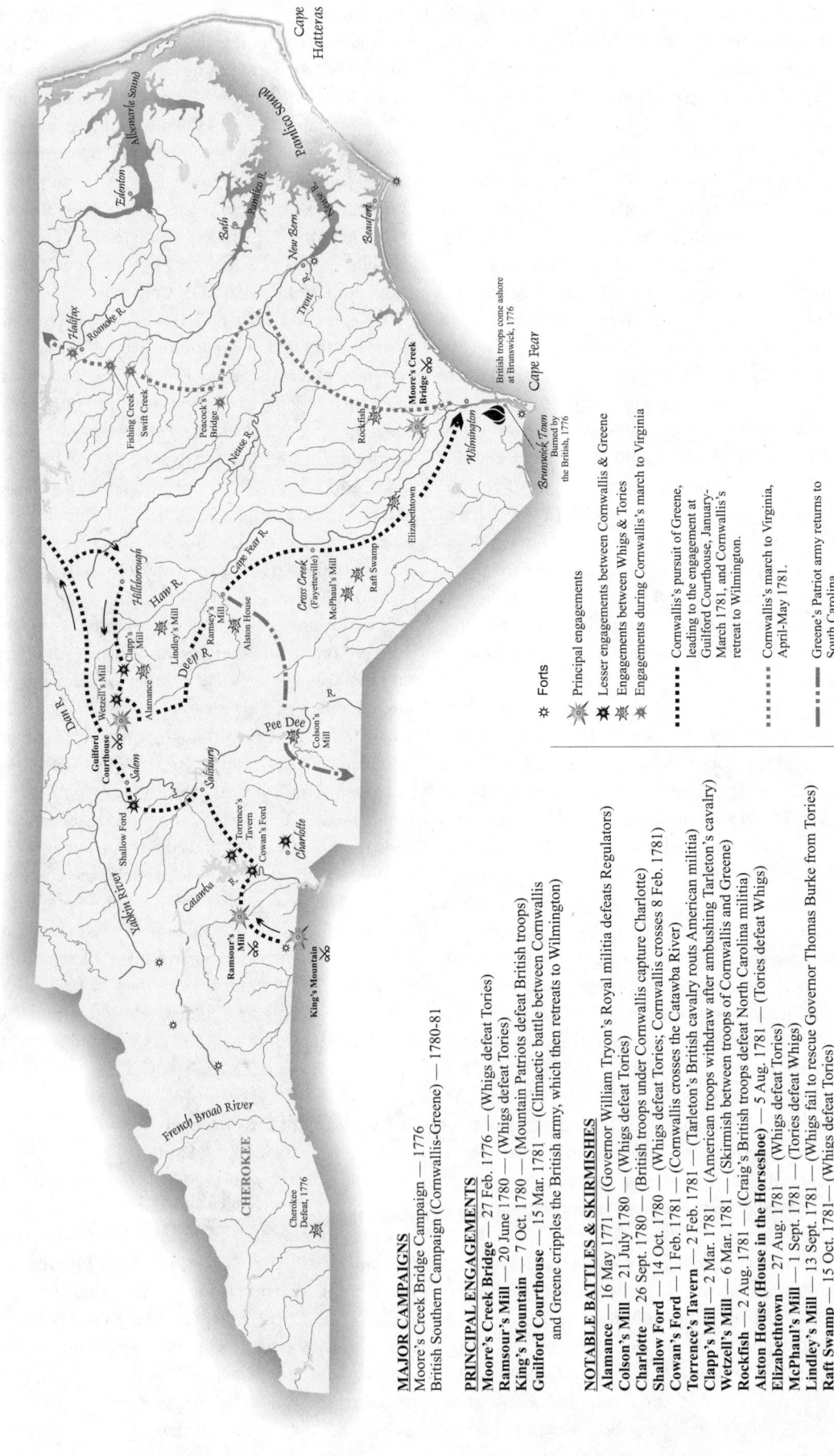

MAJOR CAMPAIGNS

Moore's Creek Bridge Campaign — 1776
British Southern Campaign (Cornwallis–Greene) — 1780–81

PRINCIPAL ENGAGEMENTS

Moore's Creek Bridge — 27 Feb. 1776 — (Whigs defeat Tories)
Ramsour's Mill — 20 June 1780 — (Whigs defeat Tories)
King's Mountain — 7 Oct. 1780 — (Mountain Patriots defeat British troops)
Guilford Courthouse — 15 Mar. 1781 — (Climactic battle between Cornwallis and Greene cripples the British army, which then retreats to Wilmington)

NOTABLE BATTLES & SKIRMISHES

Alamance — 16 May 1771 — (Governor William Tryon's Royal militia defeats Regulators)
Colson's Mill — 21 July 1780 — (Whigs defeat Tories)
Charlotte — 26 Sept. 1780 — (British troops under Cornwallis capture Charlotte)
Shallow Ford — 14 Oct. 1780 — (Whigs defeat Tories; Cornwallis crosses 8 Feb. 1781)
Cowan's Ford — 1 Feb. 1781 — (Cornwallis crosses the Catawba River)
Torrence's Tavern — 2 Feb. 1781 — (Tarleton's British cavalry routs American militia)
Clapp's Mill — 2 Mar. 1781 — (American troops withdraw after ambushing Tarleton's cavalry)
Wetzell's Mill — 6 Mar. 1781 — (Skirmish between troops of Cornwallis and Greene)
Rockfish — 2 Aug. 1781 — (Craig's British troops defeat North Carolina militia)
Alston House (House in the Horseshoe) — 5 Aug. 1781 — (Tories defeat Whigs)
Elizabethtown — 27 Aug. 1781 — (Whigs defeat Tories)
McPhaul's Mill — 1 Sept. 1781 — (Tories defeat Whigs)
Lindley's Mill — 13 Sept. 1781 — (Whigs fail to rescue Governor Thomas Burke from Tories)
Raft Swamp — 15 Oct. 1781 — (Whigs defeat Tories)

✵ Forts
⊛ Principal engagements

⊛ Lesser engagements between Cornwallis & Greene
⊛ Engagements between Whigs & Tories
⊛ Engagements during Cornwallis's march to Virginia

········ Cornwallis's pursuit of Greene, leading to the engagement at Guilford Courthouse, January–March 1781, and Cornwallis's retreat to Wilmington.

········ Cornwallis's march to Virginia, April–May 1781.

—·—·— Greene's Patriot army returns to South Carolina.

Revolutionary War campaigns and battles. Map by Mark Anderson Moore, courtesy NCOA&H.

summer of 1776 Gen. Griffith Rutherford and 2,400 troops, backed by soldiers from Virginia and South Carolina, savagely fought and defeated the Cherokees in western North Carolina, leaving town after town devastated and many survivors without basic necessities. The Cherokees finally surrendered and on 20 July 1777 signed the Treaty of Long Island, in which they agreed to cede lands to the Americans and promised not to resume fighting.

Frustrated by their unsuccessful attempts to defeat America's Gen. George Washington in the North, the British in 1778 undertook a new strategy of crushing the independence movement in the South. Gen. Robert Howe, the highest-ranking North Carolinian in the Continental Army, was commander of the entire Southern Department. When the British unleashed a powerful assault on Georgia in December 1778, however, Howe's defensive measures were inadequate. Savannah was the first major southern town to fall into British hands, with the rest of Georgia quickly following. Howe was later court-martialed and forced to resign over his failure to protect the state.

The British next moved into South Carolina, which fell in turn. The loss of Charles Towne (now Charleston, S.C.) led to the surrender of Gen. Benjamin Lincoln and his entire Patriot army, which included 815 Continentals and 600 militiamen from North Carolina. Now nothing stood in the way of a British invasion of North Carolina. Governor Richard Caswell (1776–80) and his successor, Abner Nash (1780–81), worked feverishly to prepare to meet the enemy forces, which were now commanded by Lord Charles Cornwallis. Caswell was placed in charge of the state's entire military force by the North Carolina General Assembly.

Although British victories in Georgia and South Carolina bolstered the spirits of North Carolina Loyalists, the defeat of the Tories at Ramsour's Mill (near present-day Lincolnton) and at Hanging Rock, S.C., impeded Cornwallis's efforts to subdue South Carolina and necessitated an invasion of North Carolina. The Continental Congress had tapped Gen. Horatio Gates, hero of the Battle of Saratoga, as the man to stop Cornwallis. On 25 July 1780 Gates arrived at Hillsborough and assumed command of the Southern Department of the Continental Army. Gates led his 3,000 Continentals and 1,200 raw militia troops, under Caswell and Rutherford, on a poorly planned march to Camden, S.C. The troops had inadequate food, and many became ill on the long and difficult journey. On 6 August Gates and Cornwallis fought the Battle of Camden, with disastrous results for the Americans. Many of the raw North Carolina militiamen panicked and fled the battlefield. The Continentals suffered 800 dead and 1,000 captured. Gates was forced to retreat to Charlotte and then back to Hillsborough as Cornwallis prepared to launch his long-awaited invasion of North Carolina.

On 28 Sept. 1780 Cornwallis and his army entered Char-

lotte. North Carolina militia forces, led by Col. William R. Davie, harassed the British but could not stop them. Cornwallis was accompanied by the exiled Josiah Martin, who was so anxious to be reinstalled as royal governor of North Carolina that he almost immediately proclaimed the restoration of British rule. But Martin's announcement was premature. The people of Charlotte and the surrounding area did not welcome the return of royal rule, as the British had hoped they would. In addition, a 1,100-man Tory force led by a British regular, Maj. Patrick Ferguson, was defeated by a force of nearly 1,800 backcountry men along the North Carolina–South Carolina border. The American victory, known as the Battle of King's Mountain, forced Cornwallis to change his plan to remain in North Carolina for fear that in his absence the same backcountry men who had defeated Ferguson would slip in behind him and retake South Carolina. Therefore, Cornwallis reluctantly returned to South Carolina. King's Mountain saved North Carolina for the time being and bolstered Patriot morale throughout the 13 colonies.

Gen. Nathanael Greene and the Battle of Guilford Courthouse

The Patriots got another boost on 3 Dec. 1780, when Gen. Nathanael Greene replaced Horatio Gates as commander of the Southern Department of the Continental Army. Greene arrived in Charlotte and quickly went to work rebuilding the army that Gates had lost at Camden, S.C. Greene, who would prove to be one of the most skillful American generals in the Revolutionary War, was aided by outstanding subordinates such as Daniel Morgan, William Washington, William R. Davie, and Henry "Light Horse Harry" Lee.

Cornwallis sent Lt. Col. Banastre Tarleton and his British Legion in pursuit of one of Greene's smaller units under Morgan. The overconfident Tarleton, who had a reputation for brutality first earned at the Battle of the Waxhaws in South Carolina in May 1780, was soundly defeated by Morgan at the Battle of Cowpens in South Carolina on 17 Jan. 1781. Tarleton's rout forced Cornwallis and his 3,000-man army to pursue Morgan into North Carolina. General Greene saw this as an opportunity to destroy Cornwallis and ordered his scattered units to rejoin him. Rather than taking on the British commander at this point, however, Greene conducted a brilliant strategic retreat, marching as far north as Virginia, which worked to wear down Cornwallis and elongate his supply lines. A weary and frustrated Cornwallis at last gave up chasing Greene and marched into Hillsborough, where he again proclaimed the restoration of royal rule. Hillsborough residents were no more receptive to this decree than the citizens of Charlotte had been, and Patriot forces began attacking isolated British troops.

The situation was no better for North Carolina's Tories in the region. On 25 Feb. 1781 about 90 Tory militiamen, led by

Col. John Pyle, were killed in an ambush by Light Horse Harry Lee and his American Legion while on their way to join Cornwallis in Hillsborough. Lee's men were dressed in short green jackets similar to those worn by Tarleton's British Legion. Lee permitted the unsuspecting Pyle to approach, thinking Lee was Tarleton before springing the trap in what became known as "Pyle's Massacre."

Greene at last felt ready to face Cornwallis directly and moved his army to Guilford Courthouse on 15 Mar. 1781. Greene's optimism was well founded. While his army had grown to 4,400 men, of whom 2,200 were battle-hardened Continentals, Cornwallis's weary force had been reduced from 3,000 to 2,252 troops.

The contest was fierce; at one point a desperate Cornwallis knowingly ordered cannons to be fired too close to his own lines, killing some of his men in order to prevent defeat. By the battle's end, American casualties were heavy. Because Greene retreated, leaving the enemy in possession of the field, Cornwallis won the tactical contest. In fact, however, the Battle of Guilford Courthouse proved to be a Pyrrhic victory for the British, who lost 93 soldiers killed, 439 wounded, and 26 missing. When word of the battle reached England, Charles James Fox declared in Parliament that "another such victory would destroy the British Army."

A tired and battered Cornwallis now retreated to Wilmington to be resupplied, but the Americans were determined not to let him travel there in peace and harassed him at numerous points. Light Horse Harry Lee skirmished with the British at Ramsour's Mill, and Col. Alexander Lillington and the Bladen County militia were responsible for about 35 British casualties between Cross Creek and Wilmington. Once in Wilmington, Cornwallis again announced the restoration of British rule and the reappointment of Martin as royal governor, although Martin soon gave up and sailed for England, claiming sickness.

Cornwallis determined that the best way to secure North Carolina was to invade Virginia. He and his Tory allies made a strong march north through eastern North Carolina, fighting various skirmishes and destroying Patriot property along the way. In May 1781 Cornwallis and his army left North Carolina and headed for Yorktown, Va., where he was finally defeated by Gen. George Washington and the French at the climactic Battle of Yorktown on 19 Oct. 1781. When the news reached North Carolina, the British began withdrawing, with the last royal troops departing from Wilmington on 18 Nov. 1781. The last North Carolina soldier was released from duty in April 1783.

At the close of the war, the British held as prisoners a number of North Carolina soldiers who had been captured at Charles Towne. These men suffered untold privations aboard sweltering British prison ships moored near the city or in the British West Indies. To escape the inhumane conditions, many of these North Carolinians enlisted on the side of the British in its ongoing war with Spain.

In response to concerns voiced by friends and families of the prisoners, the General Assembly passed a resolution in 1782 authorizing Governor Alexander Martin to negotiate the release of the captive North Carolinians with Gen. Alexander Leslie, the British commander at Charles Towne. By the time the legislature met in 1783, Martin was able to report that his negotiations were successful in securing the release of North Carolina Patriots in exchange for certain North Carolinians who had remained loyal to the Crown during the war. The governor described such Loyalists as "disaffected inhabitants guilty of Military offenses only."

A Troubled Aftermath

Although the formal war with the British had ended, the new state of North Carolina faced many problems. Social and political chaos reigned where a new, well-organized government had yet to form. Bands of marauders, both Whigs and Tories, wreaked havoc, burning houses, murdering, and robbing indiscriminately. For more than a year, various groups of Loyalists continued the so-called Tory War, fighting violently in numerous neighborhood encounters. Under the inspiration of Loyalist leader David Fanning, who shortly before the end of the war had reorganized the Loyal militia, these men ranged across central North Carolina engaging in a program of violence and destruction. Several truces were arranged, but neither side fully supported them. It was only after Fanning married a local woman in April 1782 and left the state that peace prevailed.

Through the rest of the 1780s, North Carolina remained a troubled aggregation of factions that had yet to achieve the unity and communal identity that would eventually characterize the state. The road to recovery was long and arduous. Economic conditions were extremely unstable, and commerce was practically nonexistent. Many of the state's businesses and important institutions, such as schools and newspapers, were in ruins. The Church of England and several other Protestant denominations struggled to assert the same moral influence as before. Political bitterness and distrust between social classes were rampant. All of these issues needed to be resolved before North Carolina would fully and successfully participate in the emerging national government.

References: John Buchanan, *The Road to Guilford Courthouse: The American Revolution in the Carolinas* (1997); Robert O. DeMond, *The Loyalists in North Carolina during the Revolution* (1964); Robert L. Ganyard, "Threat from the West: North Carolina and the Cherokees, 1776–1778," NCHR 45 (January 1968); John Hairr, *Colonel David Fanning: The Adventures of a Carolina Loyalist* (2000); David T. Morgan and William J. Schmidt, *North Carolinians in the Continental Congress* (1976); Dan L. Morrill, *Southern Campaigns of the American Revolution* (1992); John S. Pancake, *This Destructive*

War: The British Campaign in the Carolinas, 1780–1782 (1985); Anthony J. Scotti Jr., *Brutal Virtue: The Myth and Reality of Banastre Tarleton* (2002).

Alan K. Lamm
Additional research provided by David K. Davis and Carolyn Sparks Whittenburg.

SEE ALSO Guilford Courthouse, Battle of; Loyalists; Moore's Creek Bridge, Battle of; Resolves, Prerevolutionary; Rutherford's Campaign; Wilmington Campaign of 1781.

American Revolution Bicentennial Observance in

North Carolina in 1976 involved many different events and was preceded by several years of planning. A state agency, the North Carolina Bicentennial Commission, was created in the Division of Archives and History of the Department of Cultural Resources, and it worked throughout the state to help plan the nation's 200th anniversary celebration. Individuals and organizations planned and carried out programs of social, historic, and artistic interest. Five major events of statewide historic significance took place during the bicentennial year. These included events commemorating the Battle of Moore's Creek Bridge (27 Feb. 1776), the Halifax Resolves (12 Apr. 1776), the Battle of Guilford Courthouse (15 Mar. 1781), the Fourth of July, and the Battle of Kings Mountain (7 Oct. 1780), jointly observed with South Carolina.

Other activities and celebrations were staged across the state. A Bicentennial Mall in Raleigh (between the State Capitol and the state legislative buildings) was completed and became the site of a time capsule containing items made in the state. (The capsule, containing a Bic pen, Salem cigarettes, cellophane tape, razor blades, L'eggs pantyhose, Goody's headache powder, and other objects, is to be opened at the nation's tricentennial.) Newspapers, magazines, and radio and television stations generously covered events in local areas and across the state. In Durham, the Greater Durham Chamber of Commerce sponsored a Bicentennial Folk Life Festival. The North Carolina Symphony and other musical groups performed several times throughout the year, and a symphony and an opera were composed and performed for the bicentennial celebration.

The bicentennial also sparked publication of a number of works on North Carolina, many of which remain in print and are influential for their contribution to the history of the state. Examples of these include the first comprehensive history of North Carolina's colonial period, *Colonial North Carolina*, by Hugh T. Lefler and William S. Powell, published in 1973 as a volume in Scribner's *History of the American Colonies* series; and the state's official bicentennial book, a history of North Carolina before the Revolution titled *Spirit up the People: North Carolina, the First Two Hundred Years*, written by Taylor Lewis and Joanne Young and published in 1975.

Reference: North Carolina Bicentennial Commission, *North Carolina Bicentennial Newsletter*, vols. 1–3 (1973–76).

Wiley J. Williams

American Tobacco Company, one of the first giant hold-

ing companies in American industry, was incorporated in North Carolina on 31 Jan. 1890 by James B. Duke. Duke's father, Washington, had become a successful small manufacturer of tobacco after the Civil War. His son Brodie, seeing little opportunity in a small rural tobacco factory, moved to Durham in 1869. There he began to produce smoking tobacco; five years later, Washington and his two other sons, James B. and Benjamin N., moved to Durham and combined forces with Brodie to build a factory for their joint use. The Dukes formed the firm of W. Duke, Sons and Company in 1878 to raise needed capital for the growth of their business. Soon substantial profits were pouring in, and the Dukes reinvested the money in the business for continued expansion. During this period, the youngest son, James, emerged as the true leader of the enterprise.

The leading manufacturer of smoking tobacco in Durham at the time was the William T. Blackwell Company, with its famous Bull Durham label. The sales of W. Duke, Sons and Company's brand Duke of Durham lagged behind that of Bull Durham. James B. Duke, always the visionary, realized the cigarette had great potential for the future if a machine for mass production could be perfected. In the early 1880s, James Bonsack of Virginia invented such a machine. Before the end of the decade, James B. Duke had gained exclusive control of the Bonsack machine and soon had a monopoly on the American cigarette industry. He took over the nation's five major cigarette manufacturers, which were centered in Richmond, Va., and New York City. Duke's newly formed American Tobacco Company (or Trust) encompassed practically all of the small smoking tobacco firms and most of the chewing tobacco producers in the nation. Major firms absorbed in North Carolina included R. J. Reynolds of Winston-Salem, W. T. Blackwell of Durham, and F. R. Penn of Reidsville. In 1904 Duke reorganized his many tobacco firms into a single corporation. By 1906 American Tobacco controlled four-fifths of the entire domestic tobacco industry other than cigars.

In 1907 a federal court ruled that American Tobacco had a monopoly on licorice, a flavoring, and that the company was guilty of violating the Sherman Antitrust Act. After a long trial, the court prohibited the company from enjoying interstate trade until conditions were corrected. The ruling was appealed to the U.S. Supreme Court, which decided on 29 May 1911 that the company had to be dissolved. On 16 Nov. 1911 the Supreme Court issued a decree that the company had to be divided into three major parts: American Tobacco, Liggett and Myers, and P. Lorillard. The control of R. J. Reynolds Tobacco Company of Winston-Salem was also relinquished. James B. Duke, a multi-millionaire by then, retired from active management of the American companies and turned his attention to other interests, including the generation of hydroelectric power and the creation of Duke University in Durham.

After the breakup of American Tobacco in 1911, the restructured company concentrated its tobacco manufacturing in Durham and Reidsville, N.C.; Louisville, Ky.; and Richmond, Va. The Durham facility had been built by the Duke family and included the former William T. Blackwell plant. The Reidsville plant was the former F. R. Penn Tobacco Company, which the American Tobacco Company had purchased shortly before the dissolution of the American Tobacco Trust in 1911.

American Tobacco purchased the Penn plant in 1911, and Penn's sons, Charles and T. Jeff, continued to work for the corporation. Charles A. Penn became a director of American Tobacco in 1911 and the vice president of manufacturing in 1916. He perfected the blend for a new cigarette known as Lucky Strike, which was later to become one of the leading brands in the history of the industry. Mainly through Charles Penn's efforts, the former Penn plant was enlarged for the production of Lucky Strike, and Reidsville soon became one of American Tobacco's four major production centers.

American Tobacco Company began to diversify in the 1960s and moved into other fields, including distilled spirits, life insurance, office supplies, cosmetics, and hardware. In 1968 the various components of the company were reorganized into a new corporation, American Brands, Inc. As its older tobacco manufacturing plants became outmoded, the company began to concentrate its cigarette production in Reidsville. It closed its Louisville plants in 1971, its Richmond plants in 1981, and its Durham plants in 1987. The manufacturing complex in Reidsville was expanded to accommodate the increased production. In 1986 the American Tobacco Company became a subsidiary of American Brands, making it one of the largest cigarette producers in the United States. As Gallaher, Ltd., it also became the leading cigarette producer in the United Kingdom.

Through the work of the Historic Preservation Society of Durham and various developers in the 1980s, the tobacco district of downtown Durham began to be restored and transformed into a thriving urban center featuring apartment complexes, restaurants, and unique retail stores. The 14 acres of the American Tobacco Historic District was at the heart of Durham's renewal. By 2004 its massive red-brick buildings had undergone a $200 million renovation financed by Capital Broadcasting Company and was serving as attractive office space for a variety of tenants.

References: American Tobacco Company, *The American Tobacco Story* (1962); Robert F. Durden, *The Dukes of Durham, 1865–1929*

(1975); Durden, *Bold Entrepreneur: A Life of James B. Duke* (2003); Michael Orey, *Assuming the Risk: The Mavericks, the Lawyers, and the Whistleblowers Who Beat Big Tobacco* (1999).

Robert W. Carter Jr.

SEE ALSO W. Duke, Sons and Company.

America's Four Hundredth Anniversary Observance.

Between 1984 and 1987, North Carolina commemorated the quadricentennial of the attempts by Sir Walter Raleigh to colonize what are now the Outer Banks of North Carolina in the years between 1584 and 1587. Created by the North Carolina General Assembly in 1978 as part of the North Carolina Department of Cultural Resources, America's Four Hundredth Anniversary Committee was charged with planning and carrying out the celebrations and events. County committees created for the anniversary also focused on local history as part of the celebration.

In April 1984 the celebration began in Plymouth, England, when a North Carolina delegation led by Governor James B. Hunt Jr. unveiled a plaque in memory of the colonists and explorers. In July of that year, Her Royal Highness the Princess Anne came to North Carolina, where she began the American phase of the celebration. Events over the next two years included celebrations of the arrival of the first colony in 1585 and Sir Francis Drake carrying the colony back to England in 1586. In April 1987 Governor James G. Martin led a delegation to Portsmouth, England, to commemorate the departure of the "lost colonists" from that port city. The celebration ended in August 1987 with the commemoration of the 400th anniversary of the baptism of Croatoan Indian leader Manteo and

Ceremonies commemorating the four hundreth anniversary of the Roanoke voyages began at Plymouth, England, in April 1984 with the unveiling of a plaque on the waterfront commemorating the 27 Apr. 1584 departure of the colonists and explorers. Shown here are the lord mayor of Plymouth, Peter Whitfield, and his wife (left) and North Carolina governor James B. Hunt and Mrs. Hunt. NCC.

the birth of Virginia Dare, the first child of English parentage born in the New World. For Dare's birthday, an enormous cake was displayed and enjoyed in the visitor center at Fort Raleigh on Roanoke Island. Each of these events was broadcast live on television through the efforts of WRAL-TV of Raleigh, the North Carolina Association of Broadcasters, and the UNC Center for Public Television.

With the goal of making people aware of the significance of the Roanoke voyages, the anniversary committee left many legacies, the most tangible of which are the sixteenth-century-style ship *Elizabeth II*, its visitor center, and the Outer Banks History Center in Manteo. An impressive array of publications —5 books, 10 pamphlets, and 30 folders—also won the praise of scholars and lay people alike. The committee sponsored symposia and teacher workshops and worked with school-teachers and librarians for the timely return of the teaching of North Carolina history to the school curriculum.

Together with the North Carolina Museum of History in Raleigh, the Four Hundredth Anniversary Committee sponsored the exhibition Raleigh and Roanoke, which was held at the British Library in London, the North Carolina Museum of History, and the New York Public Library in New York City. Included in the exhibition were John White watercolors, painted on the coast of North Carolina in 1585. More than 100,000 people saw the exhibition in Raleigh alone.

Archaeology played an important role in the celebration. Major archaeological work took place at sites in Hertford and Hyde Counties, and information obtained at both locations added greatly to the knowledge about Native Americans who lived in northeastern North Carolina in the sixteenth century. In 1986 the committee celebrated the "Year of the Native American" in an effort to make the people of North Carolina aware of the heritage of the state's Indian population.

Although state funds were used to finance many of the events surrounding America's Four Hundredth Anniversary Observance, corporations, foundations, and individuals also contributed more than $2 million in private funds for the activities.

John D. Neville

Amusement Parks began to appear in North Carolina in the late 1800s and grew in popularity during the first half of the twentieth century. Some parks started out as swimming holes and picnic groves, with rides and other attractions later added to entice larger crowds. So-called trolley parks, usually located at the end of a streetcar line, were popular and provided additional revenues during the weekends and holidays when the streetcar business was otherwise slow. Utility companies, which often owned both the trolley lines and trolley parks, benefited by selling power to these "electric parks," which came alive at night with hundreds of lights decorating rides, buildings, and trees. Brookside Park, a trolley park lo-

The carousel at Pullen Park in Raleigh, 1983. Courtesy of NCOA&H.

cated in Raleigh just north of Oakwood Cemetery and near the end of a streetcar line, opened for business in 1892 and became one of the state's earliest amusement parks. Attractions included a dance pavilion and a lake with rental boats. Bloomsbury Park, established in 1912 and located near Lassiter Mill in northwest Raleigh, was the capital city's most ambitious effort to provide outdoor amusements, boasting a carousel, a roller coaster, a penny arcade, refreshment stands, a lake for boating, and a shaded picnic area.

Asheville, Burlington, Raleigh, Rocky Mount, and other North Carolina towns had city parks with swimming pools, dance pavilions, and other attractions. Like Raleigh's Pullen Park, some operated a few rides. A Gustave A. Dentzel carousel, moved to Pullen Park from Bloomsbury Park in 1921, continues to be Pullen's most popular attraction and one of only 14 such carousels in the United States. (North Carolina's other Dentzel carousel is in a city park in Burlington.) Although small in comparison to Coney Island and Atlantic City, North Carolina's seaside resorts with amusement attractions also became popular during the early to mid-1900s. Principal seaside amusement parks of this era included those at Carolina Beach, Wrightsville Beach, and Atlantic Beach.

As North Carolina's economy and population grew during the second half of the twentieth century and family motor travel became commonplace, the entertainment and tourism industry burgeoned, resulting in the establishment of many new amusement parks and other attractions throughout the state. Located near natural attractions in the mountains such as Chimney Rock, Grandfather Mountain, and Mount Mitchell, and along the North Carolina coast, privately developed carnival parks with rides, water parks, miniature golf courses, and expansive electronic arcades grew in number and popularity. Increasingly high-budget theme parks also were developed, some with investors outside the state. In western North Carolina, Ghost Town in the Sky (Maggie Valley), Gold City Amusement Park (Franklin), Santa's Land (Cherokee), and

Tweetsie Railroad (Blowing Rock) have attracted generations of North Carolinians and tourists from beyond the state.

North Carolina's largest amusement park is Paramount's Carowinds, a 105-acre theme and water park that straddles the North Carolina–South Carolina line near Charlotte. Initially consisting of seven themed areas that included references and reflections of Carolina history, culture, and heritage, it was inspired by Charlotte businessman E. Pat Hall's 1956 trip to Disneyland and his desire to see his home state have such a park. Carowinds opened in 1973, attracting 1.23 million visitors in its first season. In addition to amusement park features, Carowinds from the beginning included campgrounds and picnic and recreational areas.

In January 1975 Carowinds was bought for $16 million by Family Leisure Centers, a new company formed by Ohio-based Taft Broadcasting Company, which already owned Kings Island in Cincinnati and was building Kings Dominion near Richmond, Va. More than $108 million was invested in Carowinds from 1973 to 2003, including $60 million since Paramount purchased the facility in 1992. The largest investment for a new product in the history of the park occurred in 1999, when the park spent more than $10 million to introduce Top Gun: The Jet Coaster, themed after the 1986 hit Paramount movie. It remains the most popular attraction among Carowinds's numerous roller coasters.

References: Norman D. Anderson, *Ferris Wheels: An Illustrated History* (1992); William F. Mangels, *The Outdoor Amusement Industry: From the Earliest Times to the Present* (1952).

Norman D. Anderson

SEE ALSO Tweetsie Railroad.

Andrew Jackson Birthplace.

Although the actual birthplace of Andrew Jackson, the seventh president of the United States, is still disputed, some North Carolina historians believe its location to be a cabin that was owned by the Jackson family near the head of Ligget's Branch, a tributary of Twelve Mile Creek in the Catawba River region of North Carolina. Jackson's Irish immigrant parents settled in the Waxhaw region of Union (then Mecklenburg) County. His father died in 1767 or 1768 and was buried in South Carolina, about 12 miles from their home. Following a visit to family in South Carolina, Elizabeth Jackson gave birth to their son, Andrew, on 15 Mar. 1767. It is unknown whether she made it home or stopped at the home of South Carolina relatives along the way to give birth. Jackson himself believed he was born in South Carolina, and North Carolina did not claim to be his birthplace until 15 years after his death.

Reference: Burke Davis, *Old Hickory: A Life of Andrew Jackson* (1977).

Jeffrey Allen Howard

Andrew Johnson Birthplace.

The birthplace of Andrew Johnson, seventeenth president of the United States, is believed to be a small, one-story house with a loft structure now standing in Mordecai Historic Park near downtown Raleigh. The building originally stood on the back side of lot 162, where Casso's Inn was located. Its exact date of construction cannot be documented, but architectural experts believe that it could date from the late eighteenth century. The kitchen-turned-dwelling generally conforms to several structures described as outbuildings by Peter Casso in 1809 (the year of Johnson's birth), but if it is one of those structures, it managed to escape the devastating fires that ravaged the east side of Fayetteville Street in 1816 and 1821. Extensive research has neither proved nor disproved the validity of the Andrew Johnson Birthplace, and it has not solved one of the most intriguing mysteries related to the house. In 1867, when the president returned to Raleigh to dedicate a monument at his father's grave, his itinerary was meticulously detailed in the local newspapers; yet, no mention whatsoever was made of a visit to, inquiry about, or interest in the house in which he was born.

Whether the authentic building or one constructed at a later date, the house known as the Andrew Johnson Birthplace stood on its original site until the early 1880s. Sometime between 1880 and 1884 Catherine Pool purchased the structure, moved it to lot 33 on Cabarrus Street, and rented it to a black family. Around 1887 the house was first identified as the birthplace of Johnson—a designation promoted, if not created, by Col. Frederick A. Olds, who later founded the Hall of History (precursor to the North Carolina Museum of History). The association of the house with Johnson inspired the Wake County Chapter of the North Carolina Society of the Colonial Dames of America to buy it, for $100, in 1904 and arrange with the city of Raleigh to have it moved to Pullen Park, where it could be preserved as part of the state's heritage.

Located at first near the railroad, the birthplace was later moved to a second site in the park for better protection. A restoration project was undertaken, and the house opened to the public in 1940. Closed during World War II, it reopened in 1948 while restoration continued. In 1975 the Andrew Johnson Birthplace traveled to its fourth and perhaps final location in Mordecai Historic Park, where it stands as an exhibit on the early history of Raleigh.

References: James A. Hagerty Jr., "Historical Research Report: Andrew Johnson Birthplace, Raleigh, North Carolina," revised by Jerry L. Cross (1976); Robert W. Winston, *Andrew Johnson: Plebeian and Patriot* (1928).

Jerry L. Cross

Andrews Geyser,

a massive artificial fountain located near the town of Old Fort in McDowell County, was created as a dramatic tourist attraction during the early years of the Western

Andrew Johnson's birthplace, ca. 1906. The photograph was likely taken before the house was moved from its original site. NCC.

North Carolina Railroad (WNCR). In 1855 the North Carolina legislature issued a charter to the WNCR to run from Salisbury to "some point on the French Broad River, beyond the Blue Ridge," and eventually farther west. Hoping to achieve commercial success as well as bring the state's mountain-dwelling citizens closer to the rest of North Carolina, the company reached Old Fort, at the foot of the mountains, in 1869. But the steep grades of the Eastern Continental Divide thwarted the builders and, unable to provide through service, the railroad soon foundered. In 1875 the state bought it at auction, hired builders, and legislated the leasing of convict labor to take the track over the hills.

By 1879 rail had been laid through Swannanoa Gap and into Asheville, though the process had cost numerous lives due to accidents and disease. The grade required seven tunnels between Old Fort and Black Mountain, passages cut with the first use of nitroglycerine in the southeastern United States. Around 1885 in Round Knob, a secluded cove looped by the railroad, private investors built a five-story resort hotel that

quickly became a popular stop on the new rail line. A pond was dammed above the hotel and buried pipe dropped down the mountain, feeding a seemingly natural geyser that shot nearly 80 feet into the air in front of the lodge. When Round Knob Lodge burned in 1903, both the cove and its geyser fell into disuse.

In 1910 George Fisher Baker, a wealthy New York City banker, missed seeing the geyser on his train rides through the area. He asked the Southern Railway, then owner of the line, to let him restore it in honor of his friend, Alexander Boyd Andrews, who had served as president of the WNCR. By 1911 Baker had bought the land at Round Knob and restored the geyser, now named Andrews Geyser, constructing a five-lobed pool around its base. He donated the set-up to the Southern Railway, which promised to maintain it.

Economic conditions led the railroad to cease upkeep of Andrews Geyser in the early 1970s, soon after which the pipeline broke in pieces, the basin filled with mud, and the cove became overgrown. In 1975 the town of Old Fort asked the rail-

Andrews Geyser and Round Knob Lodge, ca. 1890s. NCC.

road for the property so it could be reclaimed, and the Southern complied. In May 1976 a restored Andrews Geyser and its surrounding area were opened to the public. The lake that supplies the modern-day geyser's water belongs to the Inn on Mill Creek.

References: Burke Davis, *The Southern Railway: Road of the Innovators* (1985); Luke Dixon, "The Mountain and the Fountain," *Sky-Land* 1 (October 1913).

Whitmel M. Joyner

Andy Griffith Show was broadcast on CBS Television from October 1960 to September 1968 (a total of 249 episodes), making it one of the most enduring and influential shows in American television history. The series starred North Carolinian and University of North Carolina graduate Andy Griffith as Sheriff Andy Taylor of Mayberry, a fictional North Carolina town. Mayberry represented the ideal small southern community, where gossip often ran rampant but where the citizens were genuinely concerned about one another. The exact location of

Mayberry was never clear, although the real town of Siler City was often referred to as a neighboring community. Another frequently mentioned neighbor was "Mt. Pilot," presumably based on the town of Pilot Mountain, which was in the proximity of Griffith's hometown, Mount Airy (Surry County).

The *Andy Griffith Show* was instantly popular nationally, achieving in its first season Nielsen ratings of first among situation comedies and fourth among all shows. By the final season, the series was number one in the overall ratings. Although much of its success can be attributed to the quality of its writing and the talent of its cast, the *Andy Griffith Show* also offered viewers a gentle, warmhearted vision of the South that directly countered the real-life turmoil characterizing the region throughout the 1960s. Although its scripts did not deal with issues of race and civil rights overtly, they consistently advocated decency, fairness, justice, humanity, and equality — alternatives to the "dark side" of the South that was so unsettlingly apparent in the unrest, demonstrations, and violence of the era.

Most episodes centered on the difficulties and misunder-

Two in a series of *Andy Griffith Show* trading cards produced in 1990 by Pacific Trading Cards, Inc. Pictured on the cards are (left to right) Opie (Ron Howard), Aunt Bea (Frances Bavier), Andy (Andy Griffith) and Deputy Barney Fife (Don Knotts). Pacific Trading Cards Inc.; Viacom International Inc. NCC.

standings that arose among friends and neighbors in the community. Andy Taylor was a widower raising his young son Opie (Ron Howard), and Bee Taylor (Frances Bavier), his aunt, lived with them. Supporting characters included Deputy Barney Fife (Don Knotts, who earned five Emmy Awards in the role), town drunk Otis Campbell (Hal Smith), barber Floyd Lawson (Howard McNear), gas station attendants Gomer and Goober Pyle (Jim Nabors and George Lindsey), and two of Andy's "sweethearts," drugstore clerk Ellie Walker (Elinor Donahue) and teacher Helen Crump (Anita Corsaut), whom he eventually married. By the end of most episodes, Andy had used his charm and homespun wisdom to settle disturbances in Mayberry and restore its peacefulness and order. Some episodes revolved around Andy's domestic life; he always worked to build Opie's character and to reassure Aunt Bee of her value to both the community and his household. Other episodes involved Andy's tact in dealing with Barney's incompetence and eccentricities.

When Griffith left the series in 1968, it continued for 78 episodes (23 Sept. 1968–6 Sept. 1971) in its Monday time slot as *Mayberry R.F.D.*, with Ken Berry in the principal role as a small-town councilman. Spin-offs included CBS's other rural comedy series, *The Beverly Hillbillies*, *Petticoat Junction*, *Green Acres*, and *Gomer Pyle, U.S.M.C.* In 1971 CBS—seeking younger, more urban audiences—dropped all southern-oriented series. The *Andy Griffith Show* was subsequently syndicated as *Andy of Mayberry*. In April 1986 NBC aired *Return to Mayberry*, a nostalgic TV movie that reunited most of the original cast of the *Andy Griffith Show* (with the exception of Frances Bavier, who was ill, and Howard McNear, who had died in 1969). Individual stations throughout the country continued to offer reruns of the *Andy Griffith Show*, which has remained extremely popular decades after the original series began.

References: Ken Beck and Jim Clark, *The Andy Griffith Show Book: From Miracle Salve to Kerosene Cucumbers: The Complete Guide to One of Television's Best-Loved Shows* (1995); Richard Michael Kelly, *The Andy Griffith Show* (rev. ed., 1984); Stephen J. Spignesi, *Mayberry, My Hometown: The Ultimate Guidebook to America's Favorite TV Small Town* (1991).

Jo Ann Williford
Additional research provided by Wiley J. Williams.

Angels. The existence of angels, spiritual beings believed to be similar to human beings but without corporeal bodies, has been proposed by practically all peoples from the earliest days of human awareness. Presumed likenesses or emblems of angels have been found in crude native art as well as in the most refined forms of Western sculpture, painting, and music. Angels are not bound by creed or philosophy but have a place in the beliefs of Christians, Jews, Muslims, and other faiths.

Following the Moravians' settlement of the Wachovia and Salem communities in North Carolina beginning in 1753, angels and the acts they performed in the lives of people were frequently mentioned. Many of these instances are recorded in the published *Records of the Moravians* (edited by Adelaide L. Fries and others). On the morning of 21 Jan. 1773, for example, Jacobus van der Merk said that he would "go home [that is, die] this evening about six o'clock . . . that many angels would be present, that he had already seen in his room, dressed in a beautiful white robe, the little Jacob Blum, who went home some years ago and he would like to be able himself to take part in the last blessing." At Bethania in 1775 angels purportedly guarded the people from various dangers; the *Salem Memorabilia* in 1778 reported that correspondence with Moravians in Bethlehem and Lititz, Pa., came safely to hand through the protection of angels. In 1861 some children from Bethania went into the woods to look for Christmas greenery and one of them became lost. Some men later found the girl concealed under a tree; she told them an angel had protected her from panthers known to have been in the vicinity.

Angels have also appeared in the artistic efforts of North Carolinians, including the poem "Angel in the Cloud" (1871) by Edwin W. Fuller and the novel *Look Homeward, Angel* (1929) by Thomas Wolfe. A magnificent bronze memorial near the center of downtown Salisbury depicts a natural-size angel raising a Confederate soldier. In 1958 angels were referred to by Billy Graham, a North Carolina Christian evangelist, as "God's secret agents."

References: Geddes MacGregor, *Angels: Ministers of Grace* (1988); H. C. Moolenburgh, *Meetings with Angels* (1991).

William S. Powell

Anglican Church. SEE Church of England.

Animals. SEE Wildlife.

Anson County, located on the eastern edge of North Carolina's Piedmont region, along the South Carolina border, was formed in 1750 with the division of Bladen County. The county takes its name from George Lord Anson (1697–1762), then First Lord of the British Admiralty. For a time, Anson County was one of the largest territories in the colony, with borders that theoretically extended westward as far as the Mississippi

River. Later, portions of Anson County became Mecklenburg, Montgomery, Richmond, and Union Counties. Its county seat, Wadesboro, was established in 1783 and was known as New Town until 1787, when it was renamed for Revolutionary War soldier and North Carolina legislator Col. Thomas Wade. Other communities in the county include Ansonville, Cedar Hill, Lilesville, McFarlan, Morven, Peachland, Polkton, Pee Dee, and White Store.

Anson County was home to a considerable population of Catawba and Cheraw Indians, whose settlements along the Pee Dee River offered important trading outposts for British and Scotch-Irish immigrants who came to the region. Today, the Pee Dee River region in the county's northeast is home to the 8,443-acre Pee Dee National Wildlife Refuge, one of ten such refuges in the state.

Anson County remained largely rural throughout the eighteenth and nineteenth centuries. Leonidas L. Polk, North Carolina's first commissioner of agriculture and president of the National Farmers' Alliance, was born in the county and founded the town of Polkton in 1875. As in other Piedmont counties, textile production became an increasingly important part of the local economy in the nineteenth century. Anson County was the site of the nation's first soil conservation district, Brown Creek, established in 1937.

In the middle and late twentieth century, growth in nearby Charlotte and surrounding areas led to some increased growth in Anson County. By the early twenty-first century it remained largely rural and small in overall population, but a growing number of residents were moving to the county for its quiet lifestyle within a relatively short distance of the Charlotte-Mecklenburg metropolitan area. Anson County's population was estimated to be 25,700 in 2004.

Reference: Mary L. Medley, *History of Anson County, North Carolina, 1750–1976* (1976).

Peter Bangma

Anti-Federalists. During the debates over the ratification of the U.S. Constitution in the late 1780s, supporters and opponents of the Constitution evolved into two opposing political parties. Those who endorsed the Constitution were soon called Federalists; those who opposed it or favored waiting until the document was revised to address their concerns about preserving individual rights were termed Anti-Federalists. The Anti-Federalists only became a party when the Constitution was being voted on by the states and it ended soon after opposition to ratification ceased, but the roots of the party went back for many years.

Many Anti-Federalists preferred a weak central government because they equated a strong government with British tyranny. Others wanted to encourage democracy and feared a strong government that would be dominated by the wealthy.

They felt that the states were giving up too much power to the new federal government. Another major objection was the lack of guarantees of individual rights in the Constitution as it then stood. Until the adoption of the Bill of Rights in December 1791, there was no right of trial by jury or freedom of assembly, speech, religion, or the press.

North Carolina was strongly Anti-Federalist. Most citizens were small farmers who, while self-reliant and independent, were also by and large provincial and uneducated. They were concerned with their families, crops, and local matters; they gave little thought to the other states or foreign countries; and they were content with the weak government of the Confederation. The state's Anti-Federalist leaders included Willie Jones, David Caldwell, Lemuel Burkitt, Thomas Person, Samuel Spencer, and Timothy Bloodworth.

While most of the state was Anti-Federalist, Federalist sympathies dominated the Albemarle and Pamlico Sound regions and the port towns of Edenton, New Bern, Halifax, and Wilmington, where navigable rivers encouraged trade and access to the outside world and helped connect these areas with the rest of the states. Somewhat unexpectedly, the Cape Fear River region, home of many wealthy planters and an area also dependent on trade, was strongly Anti-Federalist. Only in Wilmington was there much Federalist support.

The split between Federalists and Anti-Federalists continued even after North Carolina joined the Union. Many citizens distrusted the Federalists, who strengthened the central government and began to persecute political dissenters. At the suggestion of Thomas Jefferson, the Anti-Federalists began calling themselves Republicans. Under this name, they grew in strength until they won the presidential election of 1800. In North Carolina, Republicans dominated state politics, and Federalists declined and practically disappeared after the War of 1812.

References: John C. Cavanagh, *Decision at Fayetteville: The North Carolina Ratification Convention and the General Assembly of 1789* (1989); Cecilia M. Kenyon, ed., *The Antifederalists* (1966); Jackson Turner Main, *The Antifederalists: Critics of the Constitution, 1781–1788* (1961); Louise Irby Trenholme, *The Ratification of the Federal Constitution in North Carolina* (1932).

David A. Norris

Anti-Saloon League. The North Carolina Anti-Saloon League was organized in 1902, with J. W. Bailey as chairman of its executive committee. Bailey, a native of Warrenton, was also a U.S. senator. Those involved in the temperance forces in the state had successfully eliminated the legal sale of liquor in many towns by using local option elections, a campaign led by Bailey.

Many rural communities also eliminated the sale of liquor ·by obtaining acts of incorporation by the General Assembly.

The Democratic-controlled legislature, at the urging of the Anti-Saloon League, passed the Watts Act in 1903. This law prohibited the manufacture and sale of liquor except in incorporated towns. In 1907 the Anti-Saloon League launched a successful campaign for statewide prohibition: in May 1908 voters approved a measure that made North Carolina the first state in the nation to enact a total ban on the manufacture and sale of alcohol. In January 1919 the Eighteenth Amendment of the Constitution was ratified by Congress, making Prohibition a national policy.

References: Hugh T. Lefler, *North Carolina History Told by Contemporaries* (1948); William S. Powell, *North Carolina through Four Centuries* (1989).

Ginny Orvedahl

Appalachian Industrial School was a coed grammar school founded in Penland in 1912 by Episcopal minister Rufus Morgan. Sponsored by the Diocese of Western North Carolina of the Episcopal Church, the school was situated on more than 200 acres of land originally occupied by Seven Springs Baptist Industrial School. The school's curriculum included English (as required in the North Carolina Course of Study), Bible study, nature study, music, folk dancing, sewing, and manual training. Boys and girls interested in farm life could help with essential activities such as milking, haying, and vegetable gardening. Games were played on the playground, and, when they reached an appropriate age, students were instructed in gardening, cooking, housekeeping, care of farm animals and pets, and taking care of their own clothing. In a shop, some children worked with wood, leather, clay, and paints.

The school year ran from September to June, and during the summer the property was used for a summer camp. Morgan's sister, Lucy, was principal of the school from 1920 to 1923. She is, however, remembered more as the founder of the Penland School of Crafts. The Appalachian Industrial School was closed in July 1964, and the property was purchased from the Episcopal diocese by the Penland School of Crafts.

References: Appalachian School, *The Appalachian School* (1933); Lucy C. Morgan and LeGette Blythe, *Gift from the Hills: Miss Lucy Morgan's Story of Her Unique Penland School* (1958).

Wiley J. Williams

SEE ALSO Penland School of Crafts.

Appalachian Regional Commission. The Appalachian Regional Development Act—the first of President Lyndon B. Johnson's Great Society measures to be passed by Congress —was signed into law on 9 Mar. 1965. The act created the Appalachian Regional Commission (ARC), a federal-state-local partnership designed to help the Appalachian region emerge permanently from backwardness and poverty. The region was initially defined as all of West Virginia and parts of Alabama, Georgia, Kentucky, Maryland, North Carolina, Ohio, Pennsylvania, South Carolina, Tennessee, and Virginia; by 1967 selected counties in New York and Mississippi had been added, bringing the total to 399 counties.

The primary purpose of the ARC was to assist in the preparation of coordinated economic development plans for the region, which included 29 counties in western North Carolina. The commission received special federal financial aid (in addition to other congressionally authorized and state and local funds) to help the area obtain the primary public facilities needed for economic expansion, such as roads and health facilities. The ARC also aided in restoring natural resources ravaged by neglect and misuse, such as timber and water resources and land ruined by strip mining or poor agricultural practices.

The ARC greatly influenced the economy and culture of western North Carolina. In mid-1968 Senator Sam Ervin Jr. reported that in the commission's first three years, the 29 western counties had attracted more than $68 million in facilities and services. According to Ervin, the ARC was "one of the few federal programs which recognizes that the ultimate solution of Appalachian problems lies with the economy's private sector." In North Carolina, he noted, it funded interstate highways and local access roads, high school vocational education facilities, hospital inpatient and outpatient facilities, public libraries, community colleges, industrial education centers, sewage treatment plants, and airport facilities. Later, as the funds for nonhighway or social service programs exceeded those for roads, ARC-approved grants were applied to job development programs, medical and dental care, day-care facilities, family planning information, housing improvements, and the Smart Start program of Governor James B. Hunt. By the mid-1990s, on the eve of the ARC's thirtieth year, North Carolina's Appalachian counties had received more than $351 million.

Reference: Michael John Bradshaw, *Appalachian Regional Commission: Twenty-Five Years of Government Policy* (1992).

Wiley J. Williams

Appalachian State University had its origins as Watauga Academy, which, under the leadership of Dauphin Disco Dougherty and Blanford Barnard Dougherty, opened in Boone in September 1899. Blanford Dougherty, a Watauga County native with an undergraduate degree from Carson Newman College in Tennessee and a degree in philosophy from the University of North Carolina in Chapel Hill, served as principal of the academy and assumed the title of president when the institution changed its name to Appalachian Training School for Teachers.

In spite of initial opposition from the North Carolina educational establishment and General Assembly, Appalachian Training School came under public control in 1903, with the town of Boone beating out Blowing Rock, Globe, Montezuma, and Valle Crucis for the campus. Among the school's early benefactors was Greensboro textile magnate Moses Cone. In 1921 the Training School implemented a two-year curriculum; four years later, in 1925, Appalachian Training School became Appalachian State Normal School. In 1929 the name again changed, this time to Appalachian State Teachers College, and the school began to offer Bachelor of Science degrees in elementary education plus physical education, mathematics, and science on the secondary level.

By 1946 Appalachian State was offering majors in business education, English, French, history, home economics, library science, and music. In 1948 the American Association for Colleges of Teacher Education granted Appalachian the distinction of being the first southern state teachers college to award graduate degrees. On 1 July 1967, Appalachian State Teachers College became Appalachian State University, and in 1972 the school became part of the consolidated University of North Carolina System.

As a public university located in the mountains of northwestern North Carolina, Appalachian State has historically possessed a commitment to its region. The university is one of several founding members of the Appalachian Consortium, which seeks to promote the culture of the Southern Highlands. The school also sponsors the Appalachian Summer Festival during July of each year; the North Carolina Symphony is one of a number of ensembles that perform at this event. Other programs include the Appalachian-Foothills Regional Service Center of the North Carolina Small Business and Technology Development Center; the Appalachian Mathematics and Science Education Center, which offers resources to mathematics and science teachers throughout North Carolina; the Appalachian Regional Bureau of Government, which serves as a resource and offers courses on local government and law enforcement issues; the Center for Appalachian Studies, which offers collegiate programs in the field and publishes the *Appalachian Journal*; and the National Center for Developmental Education, which deals with the needs of academically challenged students.

By the early 2000s Appalachian State's campus comprised approximately 80 buildings on 250 acres, with about 12,000 students (86 percent of whom are from North Carolina) enrolled. The university has approximately 580 full-time and 173 part-time faculty members (88 percent of whom hold doctorates or terminal degrees—the highest percentage in the University of North Carolina System). Students pursue 190 majors in 17 different degree programs, including a doctorate in education. Appalachian State University is a member of the Southern Conference; the school's mascot is the Mountaineer, and 19 varsity sports are offered.

References: William R. Dunlap and others, *Remembrances: Watauga Academy, Appalachian Training School, Appalachian State Normal School, Appalachian State Teachers College, and Appalachian State University* (1975); Richard D. Howe, ed., *Leaders of the Appalachian Alumni Family* (1986); Ruby J. Lanier, *Blanford Barnard Dougherty: Mountain Educator* (1974).

James I. Martin Sr.

Appalachian Trail, a marked, rustic footpath built by volunteers between 1922 and 1937, runs more than 2,100 miles through 14 states from Georgia to Maine. One of the most popular hiking trails in the nation, the Appalachian Trail is a prime tourist destination in North Carolina, where it passes through the Pisgah and Nantahala National Forests and along the highest ridges of the Great Smoky Mountains National Park (see map, p. 56). Steep and narrow in many places, the trail generally follows the North Carolina–Tennessee border for a total distance of around 200 miles, traversing Clingman's Dome, the highest peak on the trail. Each year more than 4 million people hike part of the Appalachian Trail for short stretches during a day or a weekend, and about 2,500 hearty "through-hikers" attempt to traverse it in its entirety. Late spring through early fall is the trail's busiest season.

The Appalachian Trail has been part of the national park system since 1968. Federal or state ownership protects 99 percent of the trail, though its maintenance is carried out by groups and volunteers coordinated by the Appalachian Trail Conference, whose regional office (covering Tennessee, North Carolina, and Georgia) is in Asheville.

Wiley J. Williams

SEE ALSO Great Smoky Mountains National Park.

Apparel Industry. SEE Textiles.

Appian Way of North Carolina was a plank road built by the Fayetteville and Western Plank Road Company that extended 129 miles from Fayetteville to Bethania. Completed to Salem in 1853, it reached Bethania on 28 Oct. 1854 and at the time was the longest plank road in the world. The road's descriptive name suggests its importance—the ancient road of the same name built in Italy in A.D. 312 extended 132 miles from Rome to modern Santa Maria Capua Vetere. Eventually continued into southern Italy, the Appian Way was considered to be the "queen of long-distance roads."

References: Kenneth G. Hamilton, ed., *Records of the Moravians in North Carolina*, vol. 11 (1969); Robert B. Starling, "The Plank Road Movement in North Carolina," *NCHR* 16 (January–April 1939).

William S. Powell

Apprenticeship, the system of binding a child to a master to learn a craft, trade, or occupation, has taken two forms in North Carolina. Compulsory apprenticeship was used from the last quarter of the seventeenth century into the beginning of the twentieth century. Voluntary apprenticeship has been in use from the earliest days to the present.

Compulsory apprenticeship had as its immediate objective the relief of indigent orphans, abandoned or illegitimate children, and the children of impoverished parents—the support and maintenance of whom would otherwise have fallen to the community. Its long-term objective was to train children in an occupation so that they could support themselves as adults. Such children, white or free black, male or female, were bound under court order to a master. The master stood in loco parentis and was entitled to the child's obedience and service, while being expected to offer moral instruction and paternal control. The courts sometimes removed apprentices from cruel masters. Boys were apprenticed to learn skilled crafts such as carpentry or farming, while girls were usually apprenticed to learn housekeeping or "feminine arts" such as weaving. In England only master craftsmen, certified by local guilds, had been able to take an apprentice, but in America —where trained artisans were fewer and social institutions were weaker—a more informal system evolved in which anyone could train apprentices. In North Carolina and the rest of the South, widespread use of indentured servants and slaves weakened the practice of apprenticeship, especially in rural areas.

With the end of slavery in 1865, the Freedmen's Bureau preempted the courts' power to apprentice indigent black children and orphans. From September 1865 to September 1867, the bureau apprenticed hundreds of these children ranging in age from infancy to late teens. Some were bound to learn skilled trades, many to learn farming and housekeeping, and a great number merely to serve as "apprentices or servants."

Although the system of compulsory apprenticeship lasted into the early 1900s, it was used less and less as the number of orphanages with their own agricultural, mechanical, industrial, and commercial training programs increased. The system was dropped altogether upon passage of the Child Welfare Act in 1919.

Voluntary apprenticeship in North Carolina was based on common law rather than statute law until the twentieth century. A father, white or free black, being entitled to the service and obedience of his child until age 21, was able to forge a binding agreement that his child should serve another for one or more years. The Apprenticeship Act of 1889 forbade voluntary apprenticing of children younger than 14 and set the term of their apprenticeship at three to five years. Since 1939 apprentices have been required to be 16 or older.

When slaves were apprenticed, the right of the slave owner to the services of his slave was absolute, and assent of the slave

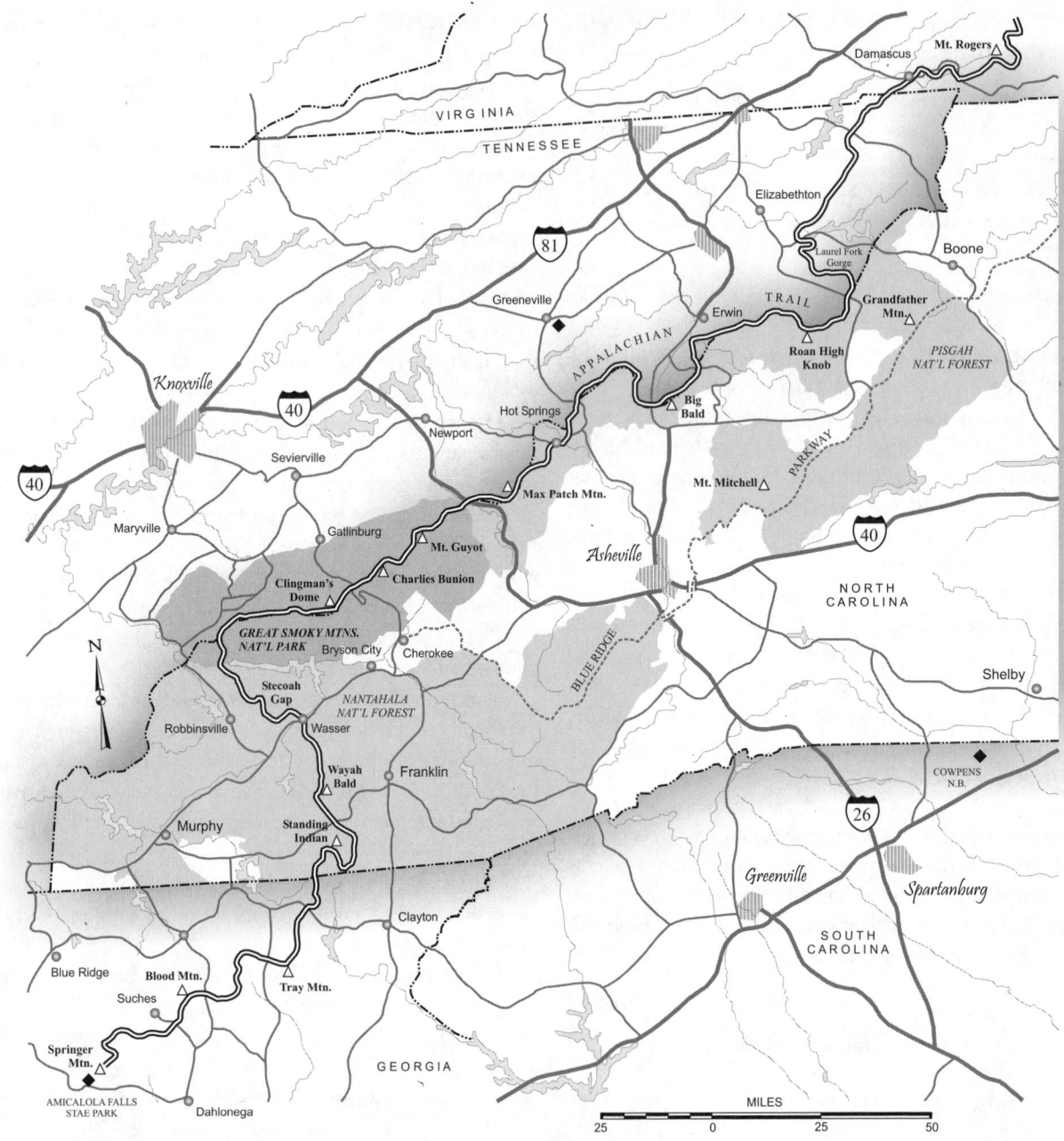

The Appalachian Trail in North Carolina. Map by Mark Anderson Moore, courtesy NCOA&H.

was unnecessary. Apprenticed slaves were generally made to learn skilled crafts that could not be learned on the plantation, such as shipbuilding, house carpentry, and coach making. Although slave craftsmen could not be masters of apprentices, they were sometimes the teachers from whom other African American apprentices learned.

Labor union policies, reluctance of employers to train apprentices who then sought employment elsewhere, and unfair wages and terms of apprenticeship led to the National Apprenticeship Act (or Fitzgerald Act) of 1937. In North Carolina provisions of the federal act were implemented in the 1939 Voluntary Apprenticeship Act, which provided for the creation of apprenticeship committees to work with school authorities, employers, and employees in setting up local programs. Agreements were to be signed by the apprentice (and, if a minor, by his or her father) and the employer, and to become effective only after review by the director of apprenticeship.

By the twentieth century's end, only those occupations that remained essentially on a handicraft basis (such as machining and the building trades) or those industries where production varies from unit to unit (such as printing, tool and die making, and molding work) needed apprentices. North Carolina's modern apprenticeship program, coordinated under the Department of Labor, is supported by cooperating industries and businesses, labor unions, technical institutes, and high schools.

References: Guion G. Johnson, *Ante-Bellum North Carolina: A Social History* (1937); W. J. Rorabaugh, *The Craft Apprentice from Franklin to the Machine Age in America* (1985).

George Stevenson
Jeremy T. Canipe

Aquaculture. SEE Fishing, Commercial.

Aquariums owned and operated by the state of North Carolina are found in three locations along the Atlantic Coast. First opened in 1976, primarily as research facilities whose focuses shifted due to public interest, these facilities explore the natural history and marine resources of their respective regions. The North Carolina Aquarium at Fort Fisher is the southernmost aquarium, and its exhibits explain the diverse aquatic life in the vicinity of Cape Fear and Frying Pan Shoals. The North Carolina Aquarium at Pine Knoll Shores is located in Carteret County and houses exhibits depicting aquatic life in the waters of the central coast in the vicinity of Bogue Banks and Cape Lookout. The North Carolina Aquarium at Roanoke Island stands on the shores of Croatan Sound and features exhibits depicting the aquatic life of the coast, sounds, and estuaries of the Outer Banks and the northeastern portion of the state.

Major expansion of the North Carolina aquariums was undertaken beginning in the late 1990s, through a $53 million program—financed primarily by state funds, but with $6 million coming from the North Carolina Aquarium Society—that more than doubled their size and expanded displays, exhibits, and educational programs. In 2000, the Roanoke Island facility reopened after two years of construction as a 68,000-square-foot facility on 14 acres, complete with a nature trail, shoreline boardwalk with observation decks, and outdoor exhibits. Beginning at the Alligator River, exhibits focus on the fresh- and saltwater marshes of northeastern North Carolina and the offshore waters of the Gulf Stream, including a look at the Great Dismal Swamp. The centerpiece of the new facility is a 285,000-gallon ocean tank that includes a re-creation of the wreckage of the Civil War ironclad the USS *Monitor*, along with large sharks, sea turtles, spadefish, cobia, drum, and groupers.

The North Carolina Aquarium at Fort Fisher reopened as an 84,000-square-foot facility in 2002 after more than two years and $17.5 million worth of construction. Featured is a 235,000-gallon, two-story, Cape Fear Shoals Open Ocean Tank with multilevel viewing, complete with large sharks, barracudas, loggerhead turtles, colorful tropical fish, and other sea creatures swimming around re-created Cape Fear rock ledges. (Before renovation, the largest aquarium at Fort Fisher was 17,000 gallons.) In all, the facility's varied exhibit areas opened with 250 species and 2,500 specimens of animal and plant life. Its 24 acres also features a marsh area and nature trail.

Pine Knoll Shores originally housed the largest of the state's aquariums, 35,000 square feet located in 298 acres of maritime forest in the Theodore Roosevelt Natural Area, including a marsh area and two nature trails. The aquarium was closed in 2004 for renovations and was scheduled for reopening in 2006. The new facility will be three times larger and feature a 306,000-gallon ocean tank and many new exhibits.

John Hairr

Arator, or the *Plowman*, was an agricultural periodical published monthly by its editor Thomas J. Lemay from 1855 to 1857. Lemay had been prevailed on by the North Carolina State Agricultural Society to start the magazine as its official publication, although the *Arator* was never accorded that designation. Lemay had previously owned and edited the *North Carolina Farmer* and the *North Carolina Star*.

Like other agricultural journals of the day, the *Arator* aimed to educate farmers as well as provide them with up-to-date information on all phases of farming. It also included information to appeal to housewives and young farmers-to-be. The readership was never large, and the decline of Lemay's health along with his financial assets ended the *Arator*'s short life.

Reference: Richard Bardolph, "A North Carolina Farm Journal of the Middle Fifties," NCHR 25 (January 1948).

Jean B. Anderson

Archaeology. After World War II, professional archaeologists began to show increased interest in North Carolina's rich cultural remains, beginning with the region along the Atlantic Coast. Between 1947 and 1953 the National Park Service sponsored excavations on Roanoke Island to expose and reconstruct the remains of Fort Raleigh, the first English settlement in North Carolina and the site of the "Lost Colony." In the decades that followed, more than 27,000 recorded archaeological sites across the state were discovered and researched. These sites can be categorized both by geographic region (coastal plain, piedmont, and mountains) and by cultural eras, which include the Paleo-Indian period (before 8000 B.C.); the Archaic period (8000–1000 B.C.); the Woodland period (1000 B.C.–1600 A.D.); the Mississippian period (1000–1400 A.D., piedmont and mountains only); and the Historic, or Contact, period (after 1540 A.D.).

The North Carolina Archaeological Society, a nonprofit organization dedicated to the study and protection of the state's archaeological heritage, was established in 1933 as the Archaeological Society of North Carolina. Douglas L. Rights of Winston-Salem was elected as its first president. In 1991 the Archaeological Society of North Carolina and the Friends of North Carolina Archaeology, another nonprofit organization with similar goals, merged to form the North Carolina Archaeological Society (NCAS). The principal office of the NCAS is at the North Carolina Office of State Archaeology in Raleigh. For a time in the 1930s, the society published the *Bulletin of the Archaeological Society of North Carolina*, and it continues to put out a newsletter (begun in 1938) and a journal, *Southern Indian Studies* (begun in 1949).

Archaeological Research in the Coastal Plain

In 1883 geologist J. A. Holmes was the first to report on the archaeological remains of the North Carolina coastal plain. In 1955 a program to develop the Cape Hatteras National Seashore Park was undertaken and an archaeological survey of the northeastern coastal region was done under the direction of William Haag. Since then numerous excavations have been made, piecing together a cultural history of the southern and northern coastal areas.

During the Paleo-Indian period, most of the North Carolina coast was situated several miles east of its present location. As a consequence, many Paleo-Indian sites lie submerged, and those that are found represent what was then the inland coastal plain region. There are few recorded sites, and settlement patterns of the Paleo-Indian period are still unknown. It is hypothesized that some of the sites were located on major streams or probably served as base camps, but this does not represent a settlement model. Fifteen fluted Paleo-Indian spear points have been found in the coastal plain, one-third of them in Camden and Pasquotank Counties. The others were scattered, isolated finds that reveal little in terms of a distributional pattern.

Numerous Archaic period Indian sites have been discovered on the North Carolina coast and coastal plain. Many spear point styles have been identified from this period, including the Palmer corner-notched and Kirk corner-notched points, Stanly stemmed points, and Guilford Lanceolate points. These points represent different times within the Archaic period. There were also different types of campsites occupied by bands of hunters and gatherers reacting to specific food-source and environmental changes. The Late Archaic period seems to reflect a shift in settlement location to the mouths of major rivers. Camps were more sedentary, and the rudiments of pottery making and horticulture began. Large groups began to settle and live in the same spot through most of the year.

The northern coastal plain was occupied by Algonquian- and Iroquoian-speaking groups when the first English colonists arrived. The southern portion, extending from just south of the Neuse River basin to the modern South Carolina state line, was inhabited by Siouan-speaking tribes. The central part, today comprised primarily of Onslow and Carteret Counties, reflected an area of cultural overlap and transition between the northern and southern coastal plain. Most archaeologists usually define the onset of the Woodland period by the appearance of pottery making and use the various styles of pottery to chronologically order artifact assemblages and to study relationships among Woodland cultures. The use of cultivated plants and advancing agricultural practices also define the time periods within this era. With growing populations came more conflicts, and evidence of stockades to repel attackers has been found.

The first permanent European settlers on the coast were English. Settlements grew out of port towns such as Edenton, Bath, New Bern, Beaufort, Brunswick, and Wilmington. Most of these white inhabitants came from Virginia. The Albemarle Sound region was settled around 1650, and later the Cape Fear region.

There is abundant evidence of North Carolina's maritime heritage buried in mud and sediment throughout the waterways and ocean. Indian wooden dugout canoes, ships, paddlewheel steamboats, fishing boats, and more indicate the activities of these past people up to the present.

Current archaeological sites on the coast include those on Hatteras Island, the Amity site, the Contentnea Creek drainage, Neoheroka Fort, the Eden House site, and Brunswick Town (a State Historic Site). These and other maritime archaeological sites are monitored by the Office of State Archaeology (OSA), Division of Historical Resources.

Discoveries of the North Carolina Piedmont

Paleo-Indian sites remain elusive in the piedmont, but their presence is occasionally indicated by sporadic surface discoveries of fluted projectile points. The most notable exception is the Hardaway site, discovered and excavated since 1948 by the Research Laboratories of Anthropology of the University of North Carolina at Chapel Hill. Unfortunately, almost every serious relic collector has also "excavated" the site, and by 2003 a great deal of its potential had been destroyed.

In contrast to the Paleo-Indian inhabitants, the bearers of Archaic culture covered the piedmont landscape, leaving a network of tracks that has been easily followed. In almost every plowed field some trace of the Archaic period can be found. Archaic cultures did not live in permanent villages and did not make pottery. They were organized in small groups of 20 to 30 individuals who usually moved within well-defined territories to take advantage of seasonal food resources.

There are several known Archaic sites, including the Doerschuk site on the east bank of the Yadkin River, the Gaston site in Halifax County on the Roanoke River, and the Lowder's Ferry site in Stanly County. These sites each had distinctive styles of spear points, from which archaeologists could define specific time periods.

The Late Archaic period saw a dramatic increase in the population of the piedmont and a gradual trend toward a more sedentary life due to improved climatic conditions. Cultivation of squash, gourds, sunflowers, maygrass, and chenopodium was evident, and permanent camps were found. The Late Archaic is distinguished from earlier periods by the presence of ground and polished stone tools, steatite bowls, and decorated bone and shell ornaments. The most characteristic artifact of that period is a large, broad-bladed spear point with a square stem called the Savannah River stemmed point. These points were probably multipurpose tools used for a variety of cutting tasks as well as for spear tips.

The Early Woodland and Middle Woodland periods (1000 B.C.–800 A.D.) came into being with the introduction of pottery making and the cultivation of gardens. One of the earliest archaeological phases in the Piedmont Village Tradition is called Badin, named for the small Stanly County town of Badin in the southern piedmont. Its pottery, defined as the Badin ceramic series, was well made and tempered with sediments of clay that were welded together using a cord- or fabric-wrapped paddle. Vessels were simple, straight-sided jars with conical bases.

In the Early and Middle Woodland periods, the piedmont seems to have been an area of merging influences from different regions. The Roanoke Rapids Reservoir sites suggest that freshwater mollusks and other aquatic resources were important food resources during the first half of the Woodland period. Birds and mammals were also eaten. The bow and arrow completely replaced the atlatl as the weapon of choice. The earliest evidence of these new arrow points for the use of the new weapon appeared along the Yadkin River. Another distinguishing feature of the Early and Middle Woodland periods was the Woodland people's concern for the dead. The Thelma site reflects the presence of group burials.

In the Late Woodland period (800–1600 A.D.), major cultural changes took place. This was a time of population consolidation and the beginning of intertribal conflicts. Larger villages were often surrounded by stockades to protect inhabitants from raids from hostile neighbors. Linguistic and tribal groups described by European explorers could begin to be identified by archaeologists. Late Woodland locations include the Dan River, Eno River, Haw River drainage, Uwharrie River, Hillsborough, and Town Creek sites.

The southern piedmont saw the arrival of new ideas and innovations from the south during the later Woodland period. This infusion of knowledge is known as Pee Dee culture. The Pee Dees built mounds on which they placed temples but chiefly residences. Pee Dee people participated in a cultural tradition known as South Appalachian Mississippian (1000–1400 A.D.), which was felt from Minnesota to Florida and from Texas to Georgia. The cultural pattern revealed highly stratified political systems headed by a hereditary elite.

In the late seventeenth century, the trade of pelts, thousands of ornaments, and controlled firearms spread between Europeans and Piedmont Indian tribes, which were generally hostile to the European presence. In 2003 Piedmont archaeological sites included the Town Creek Indian Mound, Neuse Levee, Occaneechi Town, Historic Bethabara Park, Central Catawba River Valley, Latta Plantation in Mecklenburg County, Confederate Prison in Salisbury, and Brattonville in Rock Hill (scientists at the last three sites have used thermal imaging or infrared camera technology as a noninvasive form of archaeology).

Mountain Archaeological Sites and Discoveries

Evidence of the Paleo-Indians in the North Carolina mountain region is rare. No buried or stratified sites have been found. The only indication has been the find of eight fluted points from the Appalachian Summit, reported by Phil Perkinson in 1973. These specimens were made of local material, suggesting that Paleo-Indians did occupy the region and were not just passing through.

Little Archaic period research has been conducted in the Appalachians. Most archaeologists have drawn their conclusions on this period from two Early Archaic sites: the Warren Wilson site in Buncombe County and the Tuckasegee site in Jackson County. Both contained Archaic artifacts including scrapers, tools, and a possible mano (grinding stone).

As in the piedmont, the Late Archaic period in the mountains was a time of rapid population growth and larger and more numerous sites. In the Upper Watauga Valley a wide range of habitats were discovered; at higher elevations, only a few small hunting camps were uncovered. In the Warren Wilson site, extensive Late Archaic occupation was evident. Based on its location and the large number of spear points and butchering and hide-working tools at the site, it is thought that fish, turtles, and game were important to the Late Archaic people. They also harvested acorns and hickory nuts. There is evidence that sunflowers, maygrass and chenopodium, and squash and gourds were cultivated at the end of this period.

The Woodland period in the mountains was a time of increasing cultural diversity stimulated by ideas from outside the region. It is apparent that ceramics were introduced during the Early Woodland period, or Swannanoa phase. These vessels were cord-marked or fabric-impressed. Weapon points were also used by archaeologists to chronologically place this period. In the Middle Woodland period, or Pigeon phase, ceramics had crushed quartz as temper, compact paste, and a well-burnished interior produced by rubbing with a steatite pebble. Settlement patterns reveal that food was harvested and processed in floodplain areas, as well as in upland valleys, coves, and ridge tops.

People who lived during the second half of the Middle Woodland period—the Connestee phase—produced another pottery series as well as engaged in mound construction. A site reflecting this era is the Garden Creek Mounds in Haywood County. The Late Woodland is poorly understood, and differences between that and the Mississippian period are vague. From excavation of the Cane Creek site in Mitchell County, it is clear that the pottery was significantly different from the Connestee phase pottery. Much of the information is speculative about burial practices, as Cane Creek's site was badly disturbed and there was a great deal of relic collecting before archaeologists examined it.

The cultural evolution in the Mississippian period, or Pisgah phase, appears even more abrupt, as evidenced by its ceramics, stockade villages, substructure mounds, and agricultural economy. Sites that reflect this period are the Garden Creek site (Mound 1) and the Brunk Site in northern Buncombe County.

The Late Mississippian period, or Qualla phase, is characterized by smaller points and other chipped stone tools, as well as weaponry influenced by Europeans in the later Qualla phase, such as chipped gunflints. This phase reflects the archaeology of the very late prehistoric and early historic Cherokee culture. The artifact styles, house and mound forms, and civic and ceremonial life of the Pisgah and Qualla cultures displayed continuity, but the diagnostic artifacts, as well as community structure and regional settlement patterns, of the two phases were significantly different.

A reconstruction of Hernando de Soto's exploration route offered a broad interpretation of archaeological data for much of the mountains and piedmont in North Carolina. This reconstruction was a result of President Franklin D. Roosevelt's appointment of a commission to document De Soto's route in 1935. Some of these "route sites" reflect fourteenth-, fifteenth-, and sixteenth-century occupation by Europeans.

A sampling of mountainous archaeological sites by 2003

were Kituhwa in Bryson City (the thermal imaging technique for noninvasive archaeology was used at this site before actual digs occurred), Blue Rock Soapstone Quarry in Yancey County, the Deaver site in Transylvania County, the Donnaha site in Yadkin County, the Time Tunnel in Watauga County, and the Appletree site in Macon County.

Underwater Archaeology

Underwater archaeology was first conducted in North Carolina in the early 1960s, when U.S. Navy divers, working in cooperation with the North Carolina Department of Cultural Resources, recovered several thousand artifacts from sunken Civil War blockade-runners in the Wilmington vicinity. In 1963 the state established a preservation laboratory at the Fort Fisher State Historic Site to treat those artifacts, and in 1967 the General Assembly passed a law to protect submerged cultural resources in the state. That statute claimed North Carolina's ownership of all cultural material unclaimed in state waters for more than ten years. Further, the law authorized the Department of Cultural Resources to establish a professional staff and regulations for managing those submerged resources, and to develop a system for permitting qualified individuals, groups, and institutions to conduct investigations and recovery projects of underwater archaeological sites.

The North Carolina Underwater Archaeology Unit maintains extensive files on over 4,000 historically documented shipwrecks, as well as a wide variety of water-related subjects such as bridge and ferry crossings, historic ports, plantation landings, riverine and coastal trade, harbor development, and improvements to navigation. Historical research can be used to define a search area where a specific shipwreck should be located or to identify a site that has been located by other means. Over the past three decades, researchers have documented more than 700 underwater archaeological sites in North Carolina that include prehistoric dugout canoes, colonial sailing vessels, beached shipwreck remains, dozens of

Archaeologists on a recovery ship secure a 763-pound cannon brought to the surface by divers from a wreck believed to be Blackbeard's flagship, the *Queen Anne's Revenge*, which sank in Beaufort Harbor in 1718. The site, discovered in 1996, yielded a wide variety of artifacts as well as parts of the ship itself. Courtesy of NCOA&H.

Civil War shipwrecks, and nineteenth- and twentieth-century steamboats.

Underwater archaeologists use a variety of means to locate and document shipwrecks and other submerged sites. Occasionally, sites can be visually observed in shallow water and are reported by fishermen, boaters, or recreational scuba divers. To locate shipwrecks in deeper water, archaeologists rely on remote sensing equipment such as magnetometers and side-scan sonar. The remote sensing equipment is operated from a research vessel that systematically searches the survey area. Ideally, an electronic positioning system is used to maintain and record the vessel's position during the survey.

The position of all artifacts must be carefully recorded, and, once recovered, the artifacts should be stored in water until they reach the preservation laboratory. A variety of methods are employed to stabilize artifacts recovered from an underwater environment, depending on the composition of the material and whether it came from fresh or salt water. Water-logged organic materials, such as wood, are normally preserved by replacing the water with a bulking agent such as polyethylene glycol (PEG) or sugar. Ferrous metals are ordinarily stabilized through electrolytic reduction. For large objects, like cannons, this process can take several years to complete.

References: George F. Bass, *Ships and Shipwrecks of the Americas: A History Based on Underwater Archaeology* (1988); Linda Crawford Culberson, *Arrowheads and Spear Points in the Prehistoric Southeast: A Guide to Understanding Cultural Artifacts* (1993); Mark A. Mathis and Jeffrey J. Crow, eds., *The Prehistory of North Carolina: An Archaeological Symposium* (1983); Theda Perdue, *Native Carolinians: The Indians of North Carolina* (1985); Burton L. Purrington, *Ancient Mountaineers: An Overview of the Prehistoric Archaeology of North Carolina's Western Mountain Region* (1983); Trawick H. Ward and R. P. Stephen Davis Jr., *Time before History: The Archaeology of North Carolina* (1999).

Joan E. Freeman
R. P. Stephen Davis Jr.
Additional research provided by Richard W. Lawrence.

SEE ALSO American Indians; Cherokee Indians; Shell Mounds; Shipwrecks; Tuscarora Indians.

Architecture in North Carolina has been transformed over four centuries by ever-evolving design trends, techniques, and purposes. In the late seventeenth and early eighteenth centuries, the first generations of British and African settlers in North Carolina built small frame buildings and log structures. Such short-lived and expedient buildings met the immediate needs of the frontier settlement in the subtropical forest. Later in the eighteenth century, colonists began to construct larger buildings and employ more permanent materials and methods that required the skilled labor of trained artisans.

The small, brick Newbold-White House in Perquimans County typifies the modest scale of the earliest durable houses, including its two-room plan with an entrance directly into the principal room. Representing the most elaborate work of the mid-eighteenth century is the Cupola House in Edenton, a massive frame house with the eccentric combination of a cupola and an overhanging jetty.

Architectural Influences and Achievements in Early North Carolina

During the late colonial period, the most ambitious North Carolina buildings showed the growing influence of the Georgian style derived from then-current English models. The most spectacular architectural statement in the colony appeared in New Bern, when Governor William Tryon employed English architect John Hawks to design and superintend construction of the governor's residence, known as Tryon Palace, which burned in 1798 and was reconstructed in the 1950s.

Meanwhile, in the developing Piedmont, colonists of German and Scotch-Irish as well as English and African origins established settlements. The most prevalent construction material was log, both in the frontier years and for decades to come. A few more substantial buildings were erected before the American Revolution, notably stone houses such as the German Michael Braun House in Rowan County and the Scotch-Irish Hezekiah Alexander House in Mecklenburg County. Best known are the traditional Germanic buildings built by the Moravians, who established the Wachovia settlement around present-day Winston-Salem. Although building in log at first, they eventually raised traditional European "fachwerk," or half-timbered buildings roofed in tile, as seen in the Single Brothers House in Salem.

From the 1780s to the 1820s, the state experienced a widespread rebuilding. Traditional forms endured, while in towns and a few plantation sections English and American builders' guides spread the influence of classical styles. Carpenters and bricklayers erected sturdy frame and brick buildings in unprecedented numbers. Two-story houses became more numerous. Especially along the coast, the use of one- and two-story porches was distinctive and prevalent, while builders working in brick traditions developed great virtuosity in the Piedmont.

Farmsteads developed characteristic layouts, from formal plantation complexes to informal small farms. Farmers typically built many small outbuildings and barns around the farmhouse rather than build big barns or extend farm buildings as in some northern and European settings. Built of log or frame, domestic outbuildings stood near the house and usually included a separate kitchen, smokehouse, corncrib, and perhaps a washhouse and dairy, often surrounded by a fence delineating the domestic yard.

Among the most stylish buildings, the robust classical

forms of the Palladian-influenced Georgian style persisted through the eighteenth century and into the early nineteenth century. But by the early nineteenth century the lighter, more delicate forms of the Federal style took precedence. Various artisans created a series of elegant Federal-style buildings in the early nineteenth century in New Bern, then the largest town in the state.

Greek Revival, Gothic Revival, and Other Nineteenth-Century Trends

During North Carolina's antebellum period, the construction of railroads made building materials more accessible, boosted the economy, and supported the development of factories to mass-produce lumber and other construction components. In leading towns and progressive rural areas, North Carolinians adopted the nationally popular Greek Revival, Gothic Revival, and Italianate styles. Reflecting the development of the architectural profession, key buildings were designed by architects. Prime landmarks of the era are the State Capitol (1833–40) and Christ Episcopal Church (1848–52) in Raleigh. Elaborate Greek Revival and Italianate plantation houses and town houses, such as Coolmore near Tarboro, were built for corn, cotton, and tobacco planters along the rivers and railroads. Farther west, completion of the Buncombe Turnpike from South Carolina to Henderson and Buncombe Counties encouraged construction of houses and churches in Gothic Revival, Italianate, and Greek Revival modes.

The Civil War and its aftermath brought a hiatus in construction. As the state's economy and transportation system recovered, the Industrial Revolution transformed the building industry. Mass production of all construction elements, made possible by the development of rail networks and large-scale steam-powered factories, meant that bricks, framing timbers, finishing and decorative elements, nails, glass, and every other component were produced at speeds and low costs unimaginable earlier in the nineteenth century.

A troubled agricultural economy and the shift from a slave to a tenant system of labor kept most rural building simple and unpretentious, but thousands of modest frame farmhouses, barns, sheds, and other structures were built with factory-produced lumber, nails, bricks, and hardware. Like the small houses built for workers moving into growing towns to find jobs, most of these buildings continued along earlier forms and plans, even as they incorporated new construction methods. With the development of flue-cured bright leaf tobacco culture, a distinctive building form appeared on the landscape: the flue-cure tobacco barn. These small, tightly built structures allowed farmers to cure tobacco with carefully regulated heating stages. Such barns appeared first in the Old Belt in the northern Piedmont, then grew numerous eastward as tobacco culture began to replace cotton in the Coastal Plain in the late nineteenth and early twentieth centuries.

Monuments of the Industrial Revolution appeared in textile mills and other factories. Mill architecture combined practical concerns of function and fire resistance with popular stylistic devices adapted from the Italianate style—low-pitched roofs, arched windows, campanile-like towers, and ornate brickwork. Textile industrialists also built residential villages of regularly placed one- or two-story dwellings near the mill to house employees.

The picturesque Italianate and Gothic Revival styles continued their popularity, joined by the nationally popular Second Empire style with its distinguishing mansard roof and, later, the eclectic Queen Anne style. For key public building projects, the state engaged Philadelphia architect Samuel Sloan. Sloan designed the Western North Carolina Hospital for the Insane (later Broughton Hospital) at Morganton in the elaborate, dramatic Queen Anne style, as well as the ornate, brick Executive Mansion in Raleigh. The design of the era appears at its most magnificent at Biltmore near Asheville. Built in the 1890s for industrial heir George Washington Vanderbilt, the immense house was designed in a French château style by leading American architect Richard Morris Hunt, while the estate was planned by Frederick Law Olmsted, the great American landscape architect.

Twentieth-Century Innovations and the Rise of the Architectural Profession

With the turn of the twentieth century, improved rail networks and highways, industrial growth, and urbanization combined to rebuild and expand the leading towns. Influenced by the classical emphasis of the Ecole des Beaux Arts and a reaction against the late nineteenth century's expressiveness, architectural leaders revived classical ideals and advocated greater simplicity. A growing interest in city planning encouraged the City Beautiful Movement's formal layouts and separation of functions and uses. In southern cities, this ideal complemented growing emphasis on segregation of races and of industrial and residential areas.

The architectural profession grew rapidly, and regional and local architectural firms emerged as architects established offices in Asheville, Charlotte, Greensboro, Winston-Salem, Raleigh, Durham, Wilson, Wilmington, and other cities. Towns continued rebuilding commercial districts, using Neoclassical as well as Italianate styles for banks, city halls, and especially courthouses. Urban aspirations took vivid form in small skyscrapers such as Charlotte's Independence Building (1908).

The Gothic Revival maintained its popularity in church architecture, along with the round-arched Romanesque style and a renewed use of classical elements such as domes and porticoes. Beaux Arts classicism shaped major public building projects, from the expansion of the University of North Carolina in Chapel Hill to Duke University in Durham. Facilitated by trolleys and automobiles, and following the trend toward city planning and segregation, residential suburbs developed at the edges of the principal cities.

In the early 1900s, architects such as Herbert Woodley Simpson of New Bern and C. C. Hook of Charlotte initially combined Queen Anne–style massing with classical columns and other "colonial" motifs, but they soon turned to more restrained and symmetrical forms as the Colonial Revival grew into the favored residential style. Also popular in the 1920s, especially in western North Carolina, was the Tudor Revival style, with its half-timbered effects and picturesque outline, as well as other various naturalistic and rustic modes regarded as suitable to the rugged landscape.

Especially numerous among smaller houses was the shotgun plan, a narrow, one-story house type built most often in neighborhoods developed for black families who had moved to growing towns to find work. Some scholars attribute the form to Caribbean meldings of French and African concepts. The nationally popular bungalow gained wide use. This informal house form and style, developed from progressive and Craftsman ideals and associated with California, was promoted through magazines and catalogs. The bungalow typically had a low-slung silhouette, simple detailing including tapered porch posts and rafter ends, natural materials, and a porch. Another widely built Progressive Era style of residence was the foursquare house, typically two stories with a low hip roof, a simple porch, and unpretentious detailing. While most of these houses were built on site by local contractors, both types were also available in precut kits, in which standardized manufactured elements were shipped to the customer for speedy erection on the site.

The Great Depression brought building nearly to a standstill in North Carolina. Gradually federal employment projects put builders back to work. Prominent among the federal works projects of the era were schools and small post offices, typically in red brick or native stone with simple classical detailing. The Civilian Conservation Corps erected a number of rustic stone and timber recreational buildings in state and national parks and forests. Most spectacular was the creation and construction of the Blue Ridge Parkway, a beautiful feat of engineering and landscape design threaded along the eastern edge of the Appalachian Mountains.

North Carolina Architecture after World War II

The tribulations of World War II saw the construction of the great Tennessee Valley Authority (TVA) dams to generate hydroelectric power for the war effort and for the region, of which the largest and most famous is Fontana Dam, designed in a monumental modernist form by TVA architect Roland Wank. World War II brought another hiatus in nonmilitary construction. Rapid, vast undertakings such as the expansion of Fort Bragg and the construction of the huge naval air station docks near Elizabeth City required practically endless supplies of labor and materials. After the war, the urgency to rebuild again brought a building boom. The era saw the creation of shopping centers—Cameron Village in Raleigh was the first in the Southeast—as well as the construction of veterans' housing and new suburbs and the design of practical modern dwellings for farmers (such as the work of North Carolinian Woodley Warrick, who designed the "Number 90" ranch house for the Farmers Home Administration).

Although North Carolinians continued their conservative architectural preferences, the postwar years also ushered in an important chapter in the history of progressive, advanced architectural ideals. In 1948 the School of Design (later renamed the College of Design) was established at North Carolina State University in Raleigh. Under founding dean Henry Kamphoefner, the school's Department of Architecture established a strong modernist presence. Other modernist landmarks also appeared across the state as the postwar building boom gained momentum in the 1950s and early 1960s; these included A. G. Odell's coliseum in Charlotte and Mitchell/Giurgola's visitors center, a Mission 66 building, at the Wright Brothers National Memorial.

The public reaction to the spread of architectural modernism was mixed. Before his death in 1950, N.C. State Architecture Department head Matthew Nowicki designed the famed Dorton Arena, an innovative building that eventually won over the hearts of Raleigh's citizens, even being named a National Historic Monument in 1972. When architect I. M. Pei planted his Akzona (now Biltmore) Building on Asheville's Pack Square in 1980, it was criticized for being bland or inconsistent with the town's architectural stylings. Bold glass structures loosely influenced by the "skin and bone" style of modernist Ludwig Mies van der Rohe, including the Blue Cross and Blue Shield headquarters in Chapel Hill and Durham's newest skyscrapers, the People's Security Building and University Tower, have received mixed reviews. Arenas, once designed solely for capacity but sometimes lambasted for their outward appearance, have become more ornamental, as evidenced by comparison between Raleigh's RBC Center and the University of North Carolina at Chapel Hill's Dean E. Smith Center, built more than a decade earlier.

Public opinion has yet to stem the tide of bold new designs as North Carolina's population and need for business and cultural centers expands. The year 1999 saw plans scrapped for a 100-story skyscraper in Charlotte that would have housed the headquarters of First Union Bank. Charlotte's downtown district, however, continues to grow as it develops into the South's leading banking center. In 2005 Duke University opened its Nasher Museum of Art, a modern structure with a minimalist approach designed by reputed architect Rafael Viñoly. North Carolina will, no doubt, continue to play host to shifting architectural ideas, whether they are brought to reality in its cities or taught at its design schools.

References: John V. Allcott, *Colonial Homes in North Carolina* (repr., 1975); Catherine W. Bishir, *North Carolina Architecture* (1990); Bishir and others, *Architects and Builders in North Carolina: A History of the Practice of Building* (1990); Bishir and Michael T. Southern, *A Guide to the Historic Architecture of Eastern North Carolina* (1996); Frances Benjamin Johnston and Thomas T. Waterman, *The Early Architecture of North Carolina* (1941); Mills Lane, *Architecture of the Old South: North Carolina* (1985).

Catherine W. Bishir

SEE ALSO Barns; Biltmore House; Christ Episcopal Church; College of Design; Cupola House; Independence Building; State Capitol.

Archives and History, Office of.

The North Carolina Office of Archives and History is the third-oldest state historical agency in the nation, and one of the largest such agencies. It is a direct descendant of the North Carolina Historical Commission, established in 1903 on the heels of similar actions by Alabama in 1901 and Mississippi in 1902. That these agencies were established in the old Confederacy during the rise of the New South was no accident. Many southerners believed that in order to direct their future they had to preserve their past. In 1943 the North Carolina agency was designated the Department of Archives and History. With the reorganization of state government between 1971 and 1973, the agency became the North Carolina Division of Archives and History within the Department of Cultural Resources. In 2001 it was renamed the Office of Archives and History.

From its beginnings—when a young Raleigh attorney named William J. Peele began pressing for the creation of a state historical agency in 1900 and met with success three years later—the organization has enjoyed notable leadership. Among its directors have been R. D. W. Connor (who went on to become the first archivist of the United States), Albert Ray Newsome (first president of the Society of American Archivists), C. Christopher Crittenden (first president of the American Association for State and Local History), and H. G. Jones (twice recipient of the national Waldo Gifford Leland Award for excellence in archival history, theory, or practice). Through the years, the Office of Archives and History has established award-winning programs in archives and records management, museums, highway markers, historic sites, historic preservation, archaeology (including underwater archaeology), and publications. The degree of professionalism has remained high, largely because of the supervision of the North Carolina Historical Commission, an 11-member body made up of five historians and six laypersons appointed by the governor for six-year staggered terms. In 2003 a number of events were held in observance of the organization's centennial year.

The North Carolina State Archives is the state's depository for historically valuable documents and information. The agency collects, preserves, and makes available for public use historical and evidential materials relating to North Carolina. The archives' holdings consist of official records of state and local governmental units and copies of federal and foreign government materials. County records comprise a large part of the collection, including county court records, wills, estate records, marriage bonds, and tax records. The archives also houses some military records such as pay vouchers, pensions, and accounts from the Revolution to World War II.

Patrons can also access microfilm copies of the Federal Census from 1790 to 1920 (excluding the burned 1890 census) as well as bound volumes of county lists from the censuses. In addition to these official records, the archives possesses private collections, maps, pamphlets, sound recordings, photographs, motion picture film, and a small reference library. In all, the North Carolina State Archives houses more than 50,000 linear feet of permanently valuable materials, containing millions of individual items. New records are acquired as they become available. Counties and government agencies deposit records periodically, while the archives obtains other collections through donations and purchases financed by the Friends of the Archives.

The North Carolina State Archives received the first Distinguished Service Award of the Society of American Archivists in 1964, and *The Way We Lived in North Carolina*, a five-volume series of richly illustrated books examining the social history of the state with a special emphasis on its historic sites, won the James Harvey Robinson Prize of the American Historical Association for its outstanding contribution to the teaching and learning of history in 1984.

References: *Biennial Reports of the North Carolina Historical Commission* (1903 to present); Ansley Herring Wegner, *History for All the People: One Hundred Years of Public History in North Carolina* (2003).

William S. Price Jr.
Additional research by Jeffrey Allen Howard.

Area Health Education Centers.

SEE Public Health.

Argyll Colony

was the first colony of Highland Scots to settle in the Upper Cape Fear. Settled in 1739, the colony was named for the shire in western Scotland from which its members came. They were the vanguard of what began as a trickle and grew into a flood of Highland immigrants to Bladen County (later divided into Cumberland, Moore, Robeson, Harnett, and Hoke Counties). By the 1770s Highland Scots comprised one-third of the population of that region, earning for it the sobriquet "Valley of the Scots."

The Argyll Colony sailed from Scotland in June 1739, arriving in North Carolina during September. They probably spent most of their first winter in or near Newton (soon to be renamed Wilmington) because they had not yet decided on a specific location for settlement. On 10 Nov. 1739 James Murray, a local merchant, wrote Henry McCulloh that four of the party had traveled upriver to inspect vacant land near his (McCulloh's) land, presumably a 100,000-acre tract in present-day Guilford and Alamance Counties. The Murray letter also implies that the Argyll colonists had previously negotiated with McCulloh, a London merchant and large-scale land speculator in North Carolina, about purchasing some of his land.

By February 1740 the colony's five leaders—Duncan Campbell, Daniel McNeill, Dugald McNeill, Neill McNeill, and Coll McAlister—had petitioned the colonial Assembly for an exemption from all taxes for ten years and a grant of £1,000 to be distributed among them. This indicates that by that date they probably had decided on which land to settle and had made entries for the property that was granted them the following June. In return for the favors requested, they had pledged to encourage their friends and neighbors to immigrate to the province. Exemption from taxes was granted but the award of £1,000 was not.

There is a persistent tradition that Governor Gabriel Johnston, himself a Lowland Scot, played a leading role in bringing the Argyll Colony to Cape Fear, but there is no evidence of this. Another popularly held but untenable tradition claims that other Highland Scots had preceded the Argyll Colony and that the colony on its arrival was greeted by kinsmen and former neighbors. Without doubt, the first Argyll colonists could not have envisioned the number of Scots who would follow them, although they certainly encouraged their peers to emigrate. The place they chose to settle became a Mecca for succeeding generations of Scottish immigrants; indeed, the Valley of the Scots became home to the largest aggregation of that nationality in the continental United States.

References: Duane Meyer, *The Highland Scots of North Carolina, 1752–1776* (1957); Jennie M. Patten, *The Argyle Patent and Accompanying Documents* (1979).

William C. Fields

Armorial Bearings were coats of arms, crests, and other insignias formerly borne on shields by knights and later granted by the Crown or other designated officials to individuals, public and local authorities, and corporate bodies such as guilds. Before the American Revolution, persons in North Carolina entitled to bear arms would use a seal to impress their family arms in wax when sealing a document such as a deed or will. Among the surviving examples of documents authenticated with seals are those pertaining to Thomas Harvey (1699) of Albemarle County; William Boyce (1703) of Perquimans County; Frederick Jones (1722) of Chowan County; Emanuel Low (1727) of Pasquotank County;

Roger Mason (1752) of Hyde County; and Thomas Symons (1757) of Pasquotank County. Many people used seals depicting only a single object, perhaps from the crest of their arms. For example, Jacob Ternell's seal in 1713 had a swan, Grace Pilson's in 1743 had a watchdog, and James Sumner's in 1750 had a castle.

After the Revolution, coats of arms, except as used by descendants of original grantees, ceased to have any authentic purpose. In the twentieth century prints and drawings of coats of arms, plaques, and signet rings with an intaglio seal began to be offered for sale commercially without regard to descent of the purchaser or entitlement.

References: J. Bryan Grimes, *North Carolina Wills and Inventories* (1912); Mary Hilliard Hinton, "Heraldry and Its Usage in the Colony of North Carolina," *North Carolina Booklet* 14 (July 1914).

William S. Powell

Armories. References to armories, where matériel for common defense is stored and used in training troops, appear at various times in the records of Asheville, Edenton, Fayetteville, Salisbury, Wilmington, and other North Carolina locations. In 1755, for example, during the French and Indian War, the Assembly asked the governor "to appoint some person to provide a sufficient Store House for . . . safe keeping the Arms sent by his Majesty for the Use of this province and keep the same clean and in good Order."

On 15 June 1776 the Council of Safety authorized the treasurer to pay James Dupree £150 to purchase tools for an armory that would serve Continental troops in North Carolina. Governor Richard Caswell's correspondence at this time suggests that munitions were manufactured there. After the Revolutionary War North Carolina congressman Hugh Williamson pointed out that the Continental Congress had built arsenals in the North but none in the South, and there was concern about the disposition of North Carolina's share of remaining military supplies; the state worried about potential attacks by Indians or the Spanish.

In an effort to strengthen the new republic's defenses after the War of 1812, more than 20 arsenals were approved for the Atlantic coastline, including one at Fayetteville. In 1836 the U.S. Congress made the initial appropriations for this site, officially named the North Carolina Arsenal, and the cornerstone for the first building was laid on 19 Apr. 1838. The arsenal was completed in 1859 after various periods of construction, although poor transportation left it largely unused except for the storage of vintage arms.

In April 1861 Governor John Ellis rejected President Abraham Lincoln's request for troops and ordered the seizure of all Federal property in North Carolina. The capture of 37,000 stands of arms stored at the arsenal provided weapons for thousands of volunteers. Acting on Ellis's offer to transfer the North Carolina Arsenal to the Confederacy, President Jefferson Davis requested that Virginia loan the Harpers Ferry rifle machinery to North Carolina for use at Fayetteville. In July 1861 a Confederate officer was ordered there to take command of the newly named Fayetteville Arsenal and Armory for the government in Richmond.

The arsenal was expanded far beyond its original boundaries to utilize large amounts of captured machinery. Surpassed only by facilities in the Confederate capital, Fayetteville became the second most important source of rifles in the South; as many as 10,000 rifles were made there during the war. The arsenal was razed during William T. Sherman's occupation in March 1865. By the early 2000s the buildings and grounds of the Museum of the Cape Fear covered part of the site.

The Wilmington Armory began as a Greek Revival–style house built about 1847 for James Allan Taylor, a shipping and railroad industrialist, city alderman, president of the Wilmington Bank, and a director of Oakdale Cemetery. The structure, designed by Benjamin Gardner, was valued at $40,000 in 1850. In 1876 it became the property of Charles Stedman, a former Confederate army major who later was lieutenant governor of North Carolina and ultimately a U.S. congressman.

On 16 May 1893 the house was acquired by the Wilmington Light Infantry (WLI), the state's second oldest military organization, dating from 1853. The militia group, which eventually became part of the Army Reserve Corps and National Guard, served in every war from the Civil War through World War II. The WLI used the building as its armory until 1951, when the city of Wilmington bought it for use as a public library, reserving a room in the basement for meetings and social gatherings. The WLI added to the landmark by placing small cannons on the roof.

In 1981 city planning and development offices replaced the New Hanover County Public Library. New federal laws requiring handicapped access in public buildings forced the city to sell the building in 1996 to neighboring First Baptist Church. The sale stipulated that the WLI could continue to meet in the building until its last member died.

As a part of the federal program for economic recovery in the 1930s, National Guard armories were among the buildings planned for construction to provide employment for out-of-work men. The armories proved to be useful when state troops were called into national service. Afterward, they provided a site for functions such as concerts, lectures, athletic events, and rallies.

References: Thomas W. Belton, "A History of the Fayetteville Arsenal and Armory" (M.A. thesis, North Carolina State University, 1979); Walter Clark, *Histories of the Several Regiments and Battalions from North Carolina in the Great War, 1861–65*, vol. 4

(1901); Tony P. Wrenn, *Wilmington, North Carolina: An Architectural and Historical Portrait* (1984).

William S. Powell
Additional research provided by
Tom Belton and Beverly Tetterton.

SEE ALSO Asheville Armory.

Army Worm was the term applied to extortionists who followed the invading Federal army in the South during the Civil War.

William S. Powell

Arrears, when applied to quitrents and taxes in colonial North Carolina, meant that certain fees were unpaid and overdue. Arrears represented the amount owed and any additional fees. During Governor William Tryon's time in North Carolina (1765–71), John Rutherfurd, receiver general of quitrents, expressed his frustration to Tryon that because of more than 50 years of inadequate quitrent and tax rolls, the king was due large amounts of money in outstanding debts from quitrents, taxes, and the arrears fees.

In 1767 Tryon, in a dispatch to the earl of Shelburne, stated the need for Rutherfurd to have assistance in preparing adequate books so that proper quitrent fees, taxes, and the amounting arrears could be collected. In January 1769 Rutherfurd cautioned Tryon that arrears were in such default that more money was owed than the land was worth; because no cash was readily available, attempting to resell the land or collect the arrears would result in chaos and anarchy. All of these factors contributed to much unrest in North Carolina.

Joanne G. Carpenter

Artesian Wells, more abundant in southern North Carolina than in the state's northern counties, consist of ground water sufficiently concentrated and under enough natural pressure to flow to the surface through fabricated pipes without need of artificial pumping. Through these pipes, inserted at precise locations, steady streams of water flow at rates of 8 to 400 gallons per hour. The depth of artesian wells ranges from 50 to 350 feet; the temperature of the water is constant year round, but the quality of the water varies. In North Carolina, examples of successful artesian wells may be found in Brunswick, Columbus, Craven, Cumberland, Duplin, New Hanover, Pamlico, Pender, Richmond, Sampson, and Wayne Counties.

William S. Powell

Artificial Reefs have been used for decades in North Carolina waters to concentrate game fish by providing shelter for their prey, as shipwrecks and some natural formations do.

Cities, counties, chambers of commerce, and sport-fishing clubs, most of them in Carteret County and the Cape Fear area, were responsible for such structures until 1973, when the North Carolina General Assembly allowed the Division of Marine Fisheries to use 0.125 percent of boaters' unrebated fuel taxes for building and inspecting reefs and conducting creel censuses.

State and federal support has been inconsistent through the years, but local governments and private agencies continue to obtain permits for new reefs and to donate dock space, labor, equipment, and materials. Consequently, North Carolina has developed one of the nation's most effective artificial reef programs without oil and gas rigs. By the early 2000s the Division of Marine Fisheries was overseeing several dozen oceanic and estuarine reefs, which provided good homes for fish and also resting places for decommissioned ships, worn-out railroad cars, rubble from demolished bridges, and hundreds of thousands of automobile tires that otherwise would take up valuable landfill space.

Reference: Elizabeth B. Noble, *The North Carolina Artificial Reef Master Plan* (1988).

Wynne Dough

Arts Festivals. SEE Folk Festivals.

Ashe County is located in the northwestern corner of North Carolina, bordered by Tennessee and Virginia. Nestled in the Appalachian Mountains, the county was formed in 1799 from portions of Wilkes County and named for Samuel Ashe, governor of North Carolina from 1795 to 1798. Its county seat, Jefferson, was founded in 1803 and named for President Thomas Jefferson. Other communities in the county include West Jefferson, Lansing, Todd, and Glendale Springs.

From 1784 to 1790, the region including Ashe County was part of the State of Franklin, an autonomous area formed by mountain settlers in present-day western North Carolina and eastern Tennessee under the leadership of John Sevier. Violent disputes with neighboring Cherokee and other Indian groups led the region's whites to seek protection from North Carolina and its state militia, which led to the county's formation. It remained lightly populated through the nineteenth century, with small farming communities located along the New River and in neighboring valleys. Copper and iron were found in the area in the late nineteenth century, and for a brief time the copper mine at Ore Knob was the largest producer of that metal in the United States. Dairy production increased in the early twentieth century as woodlands were converted to pasture, and today Ashe County is known for its cheese production. Corn, tobacco, cattle, and poultry remain important agricultural products, and the county is also home to some 600 Christmas tree farms. Manufactures include lumber, furni-

ture, textiles and clothing, and rubber products. Small businesses in the county also produce a significant number of ambulances and small delivery trucks by building on existing truck chassis.

At the end of the twentieth century, tourism was an increasingly important force in the county. Land development along the Blue Ridge Parkway, which skirts the county's southeastern edge, and around the towns of Jefferson and West Jefferson brought economic growth and change as an increasing number of people built second homes in the county or moved there permanently for the mountain lifestyle. Ashe County had an estimated population of 25,000 in 2004.

The county is home to New River State Park, a well-known destination for paddling, and Mount Jefferson State Natural Area, which offers excellent opportunities for hiking and other outdoor activities. Many artists and traditional craftspeople live and work in Ashe County, and frescoes by well-known North Carolina artist Ben Long adorn Episcopal churches near West Jefferson and Glendale Springs. Each August, mountain music traditions are celebrated at the Ashe County Old Time Fiddler's Convention. The region's fiddle and banjo music can also be enjoyed at the weekly Mountain Music Jamboree in Glendale Springs and at impromptu jams and gatherings elsewhere in the county.

Peter Bangma

SEE ALSO Franklin, State of; Ore Knob Copper Mine.

Asheville, located in Buncombe County in western North Carolina, is situated on a plateau with an average altitude of 2,216 feet and guarded from severe temperature extremes by staggered mountain chains. The city was settled soon after the American Revolution at a crossroads of trails and on hunting grounds along the French Broad River seized from the Cherokee Indians. While still a frontier outpost, it was incorporated in 1797 and named for North Carolina governor Samuel Ashe (1795–98). In 1792 Buncombe County had been created as an entity so vast that it was called the "State of Buncombe." Asheville was selected as the site for a courthouse and has remained the county seat ever since. Asheville began to be opened up to the outside world when the Buncombe Turnpike came to town in 1827; three years later its population totaled 350. The Western Turnpike converged with the Buncombe Turnpike at Asheville in 1850, by which time the population had grown only to 520 people.

No strong secession sentiment stirred Asheville before the Civil War. Nonetheless, the Confederate government established a commissary, post office, and hospital there. In 1870, with a population of slightly more than 1,500, Asheville became an important mountain tobacco center and remained one until the late 1890s. It was, however, the coming of the Western North Carolina Railroad in 1880 that really gave Asheville a boost. The start of regular rail service ushered in a cycle of economic booms and busts.

Tourism, boosted by the region's renown as a haven for those seeking better health, became a major industry in Asheville beginning in the late nineteenth century. With the growth in tourism came an expansion of civic activities, public utilities, and educational and cultural facilities. An electric streetcar system that began operating in Asheville in 1887 was the second such system in the nation.

In the same year George Washington Vanderbilt commissioned architect Richard Morris Hunt and landscape architect Frederick Law Olmsted to create Biltmore House. The original estate covered 125,000 acres, and the mansion included 250 rooms. Completed in 1895, it was, at the time, one of the world's most technologically advanced houses as well as the largest private residence in the United States. After the completion of Biltmore House, many artisans stayed on in Asheville to work on other structures, and downtown Asheville boasts many noteworthy public and commercial buildings. Clayton native Douglas D. Ellington perhaps left the grandest mark, designing most of Asheville's Art Deco edifices, including the City Hall, the main building of the Lee Edwards High School, the s&w Cafeteria, and the First Baptist Church. Today, among U.S. cities, Asheville ranks second only to Miami Beach, Fla., in the number of surviving Art Deco buildings. Along with outstanding architecture there are several first-class hotels—including the famous Grove Park Inn—and historic sites—such as the Thomas Wolfe House—to remind visitors and townspeople alike of Asheville's rich history.

Tourism continues to account for about 25 percent of the Asheville metropolitan area's economy. Manufacturing, finance, government, health care, and education also provide significant numbers of jobs. Asheville is the home of several institutions of higher learning, most notably the University of North Carolina at Asheville. The Education, Arts, and Science Center is a downtown complex containing galleries, museums, performance spaces, and shops. In 2005 Asheville was North Carolina's tenth-largest city, with a population of more than 70,000.

References: Martha Norburn Allen, *Asheville and the Land of the Sky* (1960); Mitzi Tessier Schaden, *Asheville: A Pictorial History* (1982).

Charles H. Bowman Jr.

SEE ALSO Biltmore House; Buncombe Turnpike; Grove Park Inn; Thomas Wolfe Memorial; University of North Carolina at Asheville.

Asheville, Battle of.

Asheville, Battle of. One of the last Civil War actions, the Battle of Asheville was a five-hour standoff between Union and Confederate forces that occurred on the northern outskirts of the city during the afternoon and evening of 6 Apr. 1865.

The site of Confederate recruitment camps and a rifle factory, Asheville had once aspired to be the "capital of the Confederacy" because of its geographic centrality. Yet it was spared in Federal raids from East Tennessee until the war's final month. Col. Isaac B. Kirby led 900 Union troops of the 101st Ohio Infantry from Greeneville, Tenn., into North Carolina, moving down the French Broad Valley with orders to "scout in the direction of Asheville, N.C." Along the way, Kirby's men burned bridges, stole horses, confiscated rations, and added Confederate deserters to their ranks. Only as they reached the Sondley and Woodfin farms within four or five miles of Asheville were local residents alerted to their approach.

Confederate colonel John B. Palmer, stationed in the city as an administrator of the state's Western District, was able to muster only 100 to 150 men, some regular troops home on leave and the rest Home Guardsmen. They moved out of the city with two or three cannons in time to encounter Kirby's forces on a field previously fortified with trenches and earthworks beside the French Broad River. Details of the battle remain sketchy, but the trenches and cannon fire seem to have led the Ohioans to assume that they faced a more formidable force than was actually the case. Kirby also received false reports listing 2,000 men and 20 cannons in Asheville, with reinforcements moving in from surrounding areas. Darkness and stormy weather led him to abandon further efforts to take Asheville; instead, he ordered his men to retreat.

The local victory proved short-lived. Two weeks later Maj. Gen. George H. Stoneman's cavalry raid, which moved through western North Carolina and Virginia in March and April, approached Asheville, moving west from Burke and McDowell Counties. Although no official word of Robert E. Lee's surrender at Appomattox had reached either Stoneman or local Confederates, both sides agreed on 24 April that Union forces would march unchallenged through Asheville en route back to Tennessee. But the same Federal troops returned to Asheville a day later, this time pillaging the town, burning the armory, and harassing both male and female residents.

References: John G. Barrett, *The Civil War in North Carolina* (1963); F. A. Sondley, *A History of Buncombe County, North Carolina*, vol. 2 (1930).

John C. Inscoe

Asheville, uss. The city of Asheville had four naval warships named in its honor during the twentieth century. The uss *Asheville* (PG-21) was the first warship built at the Charleston Naval Shipyard in Charleston, S.C. Launched on 4 July 1918 and commissioned on 6 July 1920, the vessel's assignments included duty in the Caribbean and the Pacific, with a considerable amount of time spent patrolling Chinese waters, particularly during 1932–40. In the late 1930s author Richard McKenna, later a resident of Chapel Hill, served on the PG-21,

The USS Asheville, ca. 1937. Courtesy of Walter F. Ashe, Asheville.

where he was introduced to various accounts of the Chinese Revolution (1925–27) that he incorporated in his nationally acclaimed book *The Sand Pebbles* (1962), which was made into a motion picture in the mid-1960s. In December 1940 the PG-21 was sent to the Philippines for inshore patrol at Manila, but by May 1941 it was back in Chinese waters. After experiencing engine trouble in early July, it was towed to the Philippines for repairs.

Following the Japanese attack on Pearl Harbor on 7 Dec. 1941, the USS *Asheville* and its sister ship, the USS *Tulsa*, were ordered to proceed to Java. On 27 Feb. 1942 the Japanese won the Battle of the Java Sea, and on 1 March the *Asheville* and the *Tulsa* were ordered to Australia to seek refuge from an overwhelming enemy force. A number of ships, including the *Asheville* and the *Tulsa*, were to rendezvous 500 miles south of Tjilatjap, Java. The two ships were spotted by the Japanese on 2 March, prompting them to part company. The PG-21, once again experiencing engine trouble, continued to the rendezvous point, hoping to join other ships of the Asiatic Fleet for protection. But the Japanese had detected the order to rendezvous, and two destroyers and one cruiser were lying in wait on 3 March. Within 30 minutes they sank the PG-21 in 2,700 fathoms of water. Only one survivor, Fred Brown of Fort Wayne, Ind., was picked up by the Japanese, presumably to identify the sunken ship. Brown was held in a Japanese prison camp until his death from pellagra, heart trouble, and dysentery in March 1945. The only details of the sinking of the PG-21 were recounted by another prisoner of war who heard them from Brown before he died. At a ceremony held on 7 Sept. 1942 in the Asheville City Auditorium, 160 men enlisted in the navy—enough to replace the crew lost at sea.

The second USS *Asheville* (PF-1) was constructed by Canadian Vickers, Ltd., of Montreal. It was part of the Lend-Lease program and was originally named HMS *Adur*. Taken over by the United States during construction, the ship was launched as the USS *Asheville* on 22 Aug. 1942 and commissioned on 1 Dec. 1942. The PF-1 was initially assigned to the Eastern Sea Frontier, escorting convoys between New York and Guantanamo Bay, Cuba; during the winter of 1943–44, it patrolled the waters off Cape Hatteras. After a refitting in Boston, the PF-1 took part in antisubmarine warfare experiments at Quonset Point, R.I., and Port Everglades, Fla. It served as an experimental radar ship during its final phase of duty and was decommissioned at the Norfolk Navy Yard on 14 Jan. 1946.

The third USS *Asheville* (PG-84) was a patrol gunboat constructed by the Tacoma Boatbuilding Company of Tacoma, Wash. Launched on 1 May 1965 and commissioned on 6 Aug. 1966, the PG-84 was assigned to South Vietnamese waters in May 1967. As part of the coastal surveillance force, it provided gunfire support for the U.S. and South Vietnamese armies and blockaded the coast in an attempt to cut the flow of arms and supplies to the North Vietnamese. Although the ship's involvement in Vietnam ended in December 1972, it remained in the central and western Pacific until June 1974. The PG-84 spent the rest of its active career on the Great Lakes as a training platform for Naval Reserve personnel. It was decommissioned on 31 Jan. 1977.

The fourth USS *Asheville* (SSN-758) is a nuclear attack submarine constructed by Newport News Shipbuilding, with parts manufactured by its subsidiary, Asheville Industries, located in Arden, a suburb of Asheville. Launched on 5 Feb. 1990 and commissioned on 28 Sept. 1991, the SSN-759 is equipped with vertical launch cruise missiles, 21-inch torpedo tubes, an advanced combat control system, a satellite direction-finding system, retractable bow planes, and a hardened sail. These features enable the ship to function in every ocean in the world, including the icy Arctic and Antarctic waters. It continues to serve as a memorial to the sailors who died on the first USS *Asheville* at the beginning of World War II.

Ron Holland
Walter Ashe

Asheville Armory. Three Asheville businessmen—Robert Pulliam, Ephraim Clayton, and George Whitson—established the Asheville Armory in 1862. By November of that year, they were employing 107 workers and had produced 200 rifles. But the rifles were of poor quality, and Josiah Gorgas, chief of ordnance for the Confederate army, seized control of the works. He dispatched Capt. Benjamin Sloan from the Tredegar Works outside of Richmond, Va., to take over the armory's operations.

Sloan was unable to significantly improve production despite a workforce that grew to approximately 125 by January 1863. The increased number of workers, however, was offset by a high level of turnover among the personnel. Consequently, many workers failed to gain the expertise and experience essential for learning the complex production process. Sloan soon resorted to using enslaved African American workers, who were prohibited from leaving the premises and were accustomed to skilled work. Even with more reliable labor, however, arms production did not improve, in part because of raids by native Unionists and the Federal army located in Knoxville, Tenn.

An angry Gorgas replaced Sloan with Capt. C. C. McPhail, a stern disciplinarian. Before McPhail's arrival had any significant impact, Federal raids intensified and the decision was made to transfer the armory equipment to Columbia, S.C. Only 900 rifles were ever manufactured at the Asheville works, and extant examples are rare.

References: William B. Floyd, "The Asheville Armory and Rifle," *Bulletin of the American Society of Arms Collectors* 44 (1981); Gordon B. McKinney, "Premature Industrialization in Appalachia: The Asheville Armory, 1862–1863," in Kenneth W. Noe and Shannon H. Wilson, eds., *The Civil War in Appalachia: Collected Essays* (1997).

Gordon B. McKinney

Asheville Citizen-Times was founded as the *Asheville Citizen* in 1870 by Randolph Abbott Shotwell, who conceived the newspaper as a voice for Conservative-Democratic politics. After the Western North Carolina Railroad reached Asheville in 1880, the circulation and influence of the *Citizen* grew with the town. It became a daily in 1885. Over the next several decades the newspaper, as the only morning daily west of Charlotte and Winston-Salem, was a consistent advocate of economic progress in the Mountain region.

Over the years, the *Citizen* experienced a number of changes, becoming one of the first newspapers to have a linotype machine in the state. It changed ownership many times until 1930, when then-owner Charles A. Webb formed the Asheville Citizen-Times Company with Don S. Elias, publisher of the afternoon *Asheville Times*. One Sunday edition of both papers was consolidated under the name *Citizen-Times*, although the editorial staffs remained separate and followed independent policies. The *Citizen* continued to support regional development, especially concerning the Great Smoky Mountains National Park and the Blue Ridge Parkway. In 1954 the Peace family of South Carolina acquired the company and in 1969 consolidated it with the Greenville News–Piedmont Company and Southeast Broadcasting Corporation to form Multimedia, Inc. In 1991 the *Citizen* and the *Times* merged into one newspaper, the *Asheville Citizen-Times*, and four years later Multimedia, Inc., was purchased by the giant communications corporation, the Gannett Company.

Reference: Foster A. Sendley, *History of Buncombe County, North Carolina* (2 vols., 1930).

John L. Bell

Asheville Female College was one of the first educational institutions established in western North Carolina. During several decades in the nineteenth century it was considered an advanced school, endeavoring "to instruct young ladies in the languages and the arts so that they may be able to perform more fully their duties in circles of refinement and culture." At its peak, the college had an enrollment of more than 300 students and attracted young women from 23 different states.

The school's early history is not well documented, but it is believed to have been the outgrowth of a seminary for young ladies founded in 1835 by Samuel Dickson, a Presbyterian minister. Later school catalogs date the establishment of Asheville Female College to 1842, which is the year the school came under the direction of the Holston Conference of the Methodist Church. The school was incorporated as the Holston Conference Female College in February 1855 and operated under the direction of the Reverend Anson W. Cummings.

The college was forced to close during the Civil War, but it was reopened in 1866 by James S. Kennedy. Financial problems ensued, and the community grew concerned that "the property [might] pass into private hands and be appropriated to other purposes than that of Female Education." In March 1869 a joint stock company was incorporated as Asheville Female College to buy out the financially strapped Holston Conference Female College. James Atkins was appointed president of the college in 1879 and supervised the construction of a new building, completed in 1888. Atkins left the school in 1889 but returned in 1893 for three more years.

In 1896 the school was purchased by Archibald M. Jones and operated as the Asheville College for Girls and Young Women until it closed permanently in 1901. The college building, on Oak Street between Woodfin and College Streets, was sold to the city of Asheville in 1907 for use as a high school.

Reference: Charles Lee Raper, *The Church and Private Schools of North Carolina* (1898).

Ann S. Wright

Asheville Normal and Collegiate Institute was an outgrowth of the Home Industrial School, an elementary school started in 1887 by Louis M. Pease and his wife. The Peases directed the school, and Florence Stephenson was its first principal, holding the post for 30 years. From the beginning, the school emphasized home training and religious instruction for girls and young women in addition to regular academic work. Within a few weeks of opening, it was filled to capacity, with 75 boarding students and 45 day pupils. High school grades were added later. With the improvement of the public school system, the elementary grades were gradually phased out, and the high school department was discontinued in 1930.

In 1892 the campus was expanded and renamed the Asheville Normal and Collegiate Institute, with the goals of providing higher education for young women from the southern Appalachians and of training teachers, particularly for rural schools. Thomas Lawrence was the first principal of the normal school and served in that role until 1907. Pease House opened on the campus in 1908 to serve as a home for girls under the age of 12 "who cannot be trained in homes of their own"; the girls were taught by seniors from the normal school. Pease House operated until 1925.

Edward R. Childs directed the school from 1907 to 1916, when John E. Calfee took over and presided over a period of rapid institutional growth. In 1921 the Asheville Normal and Associated Schools consolidated the Presbyterian missionary schools in the area; it included Asheville Normal, Home School, and Pease House on the central campus in Asheville and the Farm School for boys in Swannanoa. By 1926 the school had evolved from a two-year normal school into a four-year teachers college. In 1931 the name was changed to Asheville Normal and Teachers College.

In 1940 the Presbyterian Board of Missions withdrew its support of the college. The Asheville community attempted unsuccessfully to take on the financial burden of operating the school. Asheville College, as it had been renamed, closed at the end of the term in 1944. The campus was taken over for use by Memorial Mission Hospital, and school records were transferred to the Farm School (now Warren Wilson College).

References: Cordelia Camp, *A Thought at Midnight* (1959); Mary Kestler Clyde, *Flashbacks to Dawn: Eye Openers in Preparatory School, Circa 1914–1922* (1983).

Ann S. Wright

Asheville School. The Asheville School for Boys, renamed the Asheville School when it became coeducational in 1972, was one of the first boarding college preparatory schools in North Carolina. An outgrowth of the University School of Cleveland, Ohio, the nation's first country day school, the Asheville School was founded by Newton Mitchell Anderson and Charles Andrew Mitchell, who had also founded the University School.

Opening with 50 students in the fall of 1900, the Asheville School was, like its forerunner, distinctive in the way it combined classical studies with manual training—thus preparing boys to attend any college or technical school in the country. The school prospered until the mid-1920s, when financial difficulties led to its sale to a Pittsburgh resident who sought to change the school's orientation (and did change its name to the Asheville School for Training in Christian Leadership). However, in 1933 a group of alumni led by trustee chairman Philip R. Clarke raised $350,000, bought the school, and returned it to its original college preparatory curriculum. As the years passed the school expanded its mission, first admitting

day students and then girls in 1972. The Asheville School—named to the National Register of Historic Places in 1996 and passing its centennial in 2000—enrolled about 218 students in the early 2000s, including 111 females and 107 males, most of whom boarded on the 300-acre campus of the school. Annual fees for tuition, room, and board were more than $26,000.

Reference: Milton Ready, *Asheville: Land of the Sky* (1986).

William H. Pruden III

Assemblies of God, headquartered in Springfield, Mo., and maintaining substantial membership in North Carolina, is one of the largest of the Pentecostal sects, with more than 12 million members worldwide. Like several other Pentecostal groups, the Assemblies of God have their roots in the Azusa Street Revival (1906–11), which was named for the Azusa Street Mission in Los Angeles, Calif., where it took place. Members of the Assemblies of God consider the revival one of the most significant events in the history of the Pentecostal Church. There, many Pentecostals believe, the Holy Spirit descended on those who sought a "baptism of the spirit," which was evidenced by their speaking in tongues (glossolalia). This and other beliefs distinguish the Pentecostals from many other Protestant denominations.

The North Carolina District of the Assemblies of God was formed, staffed, and commissioned in Dunn in 1944. The district council consisted of 29 charter members. The decades following the 1940s saw considerable growth in the Assemblies of God in North Carolina. Aided by the "charismatic movement" of the 1960s and the creation of Christian television programming, Pentecostal churches began to attract members from mainline denominations. Diversity marked Assemblies of God churches in North Carolina, as local congregations ranged from traditional to charismatic in structure and methodology, though all remained united in Pentecostal doctrine.

In 1987 the Assemblies of God experienced and survived a "crisis of integrity" as a series of scandals enveloped television evangelist Jim Bakker and his Charlotte-based PTL (Praise the Lord) Club ministry. Some Pentecostal churches experienced a reduction in membership as a result of the scandals, although the setback proved temporary. By 2004 the North Carolina District Council of the Assemblies of God, with headquarters in Selma, included 249 individual churches, with approximately 49,000 members throughout the state.

Reference: Charles H. Cookman and others, *Never Let Go: The Dramatic Story of the North Carolina District of the Assemblies of God* (1994).

Helen Losse

Atlantic & Western Railway Company was chartered on 7 Mar. 1899 under sponsorship of the Edwards family of

Sanford. It took over the operation of a line extending 12 miles west from Hope Mills that had been built by the Enterprise Land & Improvement Company. Between 1903 and 1913 it built its own line east from Sanford to Lillington (26 miles); plans to continue to Goldsboro were never realized. In 1926 the company was sold under foreclosure and reorganized as the Atlantic & Western Railway (A&W), which continued to operate a line between Sanford and Lillington until 15 Dec. 1961, when all but three miles from Sanford to Jonesboro were abandoned.

The A&W was reorganized on 1 Jan. 1970 as the Atlantic & Western Corporation. Since 1988, it has been the property of Rail Management and Consulting, based in Florida. In 1990 the A&W acquired the former Cape Fear & Yadkin Valley Railroad line between Sanford and Greensboro, long operated by the Southern Railway. What began as a link between Sanford and the east has thus become a route to the west. By the early 2000s the railroad operated ten miles of track and had connections with CSX and the Norfolk Southern Railroad.

Reference: S. David Carriker, *Railroading in the Carolina Sandhills*, vol. 2 (1987).

George A. Kennedy

Atlantic Coast Line Railroad

Atlantic Coast Line Railroad (ACL), one of three major railroads that served North Carolina during the twentieth century, traced its roots to a holding company called the American Improvement and Construction Company, incorporated in Connecticut on 19 Apr. 1889. The organizers of the ACL—like their competitors, the founders of the Seaboard Air Line Railway—were largely businessmen from Baltimore who began developing a transportation system in eastern North Carolina, South Carolina, and Virginia after the Civil War. On 5 May 1893 the Connecticut legislature approved a name change from the American Improvement and Construction Company to the Atlantic Coast Line Company as a step toward outright purchase of the various individual roads in the alliance.

North Carolina's Wilmington & Weldon Railroad, Norfolk & Carolina Railroad, and Southeastern Railroad, as well as the ACL of Virginia and the ACL of South Carolina, merged on 23 Apr. 1900 into the Atlantic Coast Line Railroad, a system of more than 1,500 miles. In April 1902 another 1,700 miles were added with acquisition of the Savannah, Florida, and Western Railway, whose main line ran from Charleston, S.C., to Tampa, Fla. North Carolina railroads that were eventually incorporated into the ACL included the Wilmington, Onslow, and East Carolina Railway, the Wilmington & Manchester Railroad, and the Red Springs & Northern Railway.

The ACL was profitable throughout most of its history, reporting deficits only in the Depression years of 1933–35 and in 1938. Its creation by merger brought a number of advantages to North Carolina. General offices of the railroad were established in Wilmington and remained there until 1960, when

they moved to Jacksonville, Fla. The excellent transportation service attracted industry to the state, and traffic agencies of the railroad throughout the country developed new business for its lines. The north-south main line across the state—through Rocky Mount, Wilson, and Fayetteville—was doubletracked and maintained to the highest standards. It offered dependable passenger service with modern equipment, including dining and sleeping cars on many trains.

As Florida's popularity as a retirement and vacation destination grew, new deluxe trains traveled between the Northeast and Florida cities, primarily in the winter season. The ACL fiercely competed with the parallel Seaboard Air Line Railway for the Florida traffic, and although the Seaboard had the advantage of reaching both coasts of Florida, its route was longer and hillier. The straight and level route of the ACL across the Carolinas and Georgia made possible some of the fastest travel in the country. In the late 1930s and 1940s new streamlined, diesel-powered trains called the "Champions" were introduced between Florida and New York. Even in the 1960s, when many roads sought to discourage passengers, the ACL remained passenger-oriented, though local and branch line service had been curtailed.

Beginning in the 1960s, the Interstate Commerce Commission and other regulatory agencies approved mergers by parallel railroads seeking greater efficiency through coordination or reduction of overlapping services. By the 1950s the revenues of the ACL had been eclipsed by those of the Seaboard, which had long been the weaker system. In 1959 a study commissioned by the two railroads recommended merger, and stockholders approved the move on 18 Aug. 1960. A lengthy court battle followed in which other interests, including the city of Tampa, tried to prevent the merger. The U.S. Supreme Court ultimately decided in favor of it, and on 1 July 1967 the ACL and the Seaboard Air Line Railway became the Seaboard Coast Line Railroad (SCL).

In November 1972 the name "Family Lines Rail System" was adopted as a marketing device by the SCL and other lines. The Family Lines provided an integrated freight service, running trains from points on one of the railroads to points on another, and maintained joint agencies for soliciting business. The name also replaced those of the individual railroads on some diesel locomotives and other equipment. In January 1983 the Family Lines Rail System was merged with the Seaboard System. In July 1986 the Seaboard System, in turn, was merged with the northern-based Chessie System into the CSX Corporation, which took over what remained of the ACL.

Reference: R. E. Prince, *Atlantic Coast Line Railroad: Steam Locomotives, Ships, and History* (1966).

George A. Kennedy

SEE ALSO Seaboard Air Line Railway; Wilmington & Weldon Railroad.

Atlantic Collegiate Institute. In 1878 Samuel Lloyd Sheep, a Pennsylvanian who had recently arrived in Elizabeth City, opened the Elizabeth City Academy. The history of the academy in its earliest years is unknown, but records show that the building was used during the Civil War to house Federal troops and was later torn down and destroyed. Under Sheep, the school operated successfully for 16 years. In 1894 the school's name was changed to Atlantic Collegiate Institute, and its curriculum was expanded to include primary, preparatory, and collegiate departments (the latter to prepare students to enter colleges with advanced standing). Among its students were two who would distinguish themselves in North Carolina politics: John C. B. Ehringhaus, governor from 1933 to 1937, and Robert Bruce Etheridge, state legislator for 11 terms between 1903 and 1959 and director of the North Carolina Department of Conservation and Development from 1933 to 1949.

In 1907 Elizabeth City took over the institute and converted it into a public school. Sheep remained superintendent for 20 years, except for a four-year interval (1914–18) during which he was superintendent of schools in Helena, Ark. In 1940 the Elizabeth City Board of Education named the school after Sheep, who had devoted nearly 50 years of his life to the education of the youth of Elizabeth City and the Albemarle section of North Carolina.

Reference: Robert Temple Ryland, "Education in Pasquotank" (M.A. thesis, UNC-Chapel Hill, 1928).

Wiley J. Williams

Attachment Clause in North Carolina colonial law allowed for the garnishment of the property of nonresidents in certain cases of debt. The controversy surrounding British attempts to delete this clause from the court laws—often referred to as the "Court Quarrel"—provoked severe anti-British sentiment in the colony immediately preceding the outbreak of the American Revolution.

As early as 1746, the colonial Assembly had included in the court laws a clause that allowed creditors to attach property owned in North Carolina by nonresidents of the province in order to satisfy their debts. The British Board of Trade ignored the clause until 1770, when a newly appointed legal adviser raised objections to certain aspects of the attachment provision. The board thereupon took the position that attachment as specified in the North Carolina legislation violated acceptable legal practice. The British ministry in 1770 urged the governor to "induce" the Assembly to amend the foreign Attachment Clause or to omit it entirely from the court law. Governor Josiah Martin, newly arrived in North Carolina, was convinced that the provincial government favored colonists at the expense of the British and that the Attachment Clause was proof of the impropriety of their views.

North Carolina lawmakers were determined that the Attachment Clause would be retained regardless of the governor's opposition, and the issue became a crucial factor around which anti-British sentiment developed in the colony. Without the clause, North Carolina creditors would be forced to sue in English courts to gain satisfaction for debts owed by non–North Carolinians; the impracticality of such a procedure was more than they were willing to accept. The Attachment controversy, in the minds of North Carolinians, had become a symbol of the British government's conscious effort to destroy the colony's constitution.

The North Carolina House both appealed to King George III and asked former governor William Tryon (now governor of New York) to intercede with the king on the colony's behalf. Governor Martin, the Board of Trade, and the North Carolina Assembly tried repeatedly to craft compromise legislation, without success. By the spring of 1775, the British Board of Trade was responsive to memorials presented by North Carolina agents in London. The fact that all other colonies utilized foreign attachments without being challenged was a major consideration, as were promises that North Carolina lawmakers would modify the language in their Attachment legislation. By this juncture, however, royal government in North Carolina had collapsed, the governor was no longer in control of the province, and the issue was lost in the rush toward revolution.

References: Charles A. Bennett and Donald R. Lennon, *A Quest for Glory: Major General Robert Howe and the American Revolution* (1991); H. Braughn Taylor, "The Foreign Attachment Law and the Coming of the Revolution in North Carolina," *NCHR* 52 (January 1975).

Donald R. Lennon

Atticus was the pseudonym employed by the author of a scathing, 4,500-word letter printed on the front page of the 7 Nov. 1771 issue of the *Virginia Gazette* (Williamsburg). Atticus accused North Carolina royal governor William Tryon of mishandling the Regulator uprising and called for an end to prosecution of the movement's leaders. Tryon's response to backcountry grievances, according to Atticus, exhibited a rashness, an arrogance, and a vindictiveness that infuriated the Regulators, deepened their antipathy toward the establishment, and contributed to continuing disorder.

Beginning with Francis X. Martin in his 1829 *History of North Carolina from the Earliest Period*, many historians have identified Atticus as Maurice Moore Jr., a colonial jurist, Whig pamphleteer, and member of an illustrious Lower Cape Fear planter family. Neither Martin nor subsequent historians, however, have offered documentation to support their claim. As colonel of a troop of Gentlemen Volunteer Light Dragoons, Moore accompanied Tryon in his first military expedition against the Regulators in the hinterlands. If indeed Atticus was Moore, Atticus's call for leniency reversed his earlier opposition to the Regulators as evidenced by his participation in Tryon's expedition against them.

References: William S. Powell, ed., *The Correspondence of William Tryon* (2 vols., 1981); William S. Price Jr., "Maurice Moore Jr.," *Dictonary of North Carolina Biography*, vol. 4 (1991).

Richard Rankin

Attorney General is North Carolina's chief legal officer. The first attorney general in the Carolina colony was appointed in 1677 by the English Crown. In 1776 the office was made appointive by the General Assembly, and the North Carolina Constitution of 1868 made it elective by the people. In 1971 the attorney general was placed in the executive branch of the state government as head of the newly created Department of Justice for a four-year term.

The attorney general's ultimate responsibilities are in legal services and law enforcement. The legal services of the Department of Justice are the concern of several divisions, including criminal; civil; trade and commerce; administrative, with separate sections relating to particular clients or areas of the law, such as mental health/medical facilities, health and public assistance, elections, and the Real Estate Commission; special litigation (for example, the Education Section represents the State Board of Education, the Department of Public Instruction, and the State Board of Community Colleges); victims' rights, child and elder abuse, domestic violence and family matters; and environmental issues. The attorney general has also played a crucial role in enforcing laws relating to public health and safety as well as the state's natural resources by advising and representing in legal proceedings a variety of state departments and agencies, including the Department of Labor, the Department of Insurance, the Marine Fisheries Commission, the Wildlife Commission, and the Pesticide Board.

Law enforcement in the Department of Justice is addressed by two departments: the State Bureau of Investigation and the Division of Training and Standards. Training and Standards includes four major units: the North Carolina Justice Academy at Salemburg, the Criminal Justice Standards Division, the Sheriffs' Standards Division, and the Law Enforcement Liaison Section.

Wiley J. Williams

SEE ALSO State Bureau of Investigation.

Auditor, State. The North Carolina state auditor, an elected official, is responsible for monitoring state agencies' financial records for accuracy and for determining their compliance with state law and administrative policy. The auditor also conducts performance reviews of agency programs as well as special investigations for alleged embezzlement or misuse of state property. In 1862 the General Assembly created the Office of Public Accounts, supervised by an auditor elected every two years by the legislature. Under the North Carolina Constitution of 1868, the auditor became popularly elected every four years and, moved from the legislative to the executive branch, a member of the Council of State. The office's original duties included providing an annual report on the state's receipts and expenditures and making projections for the next fiscal year, keeping the general accounts of state government, recommending ways to improve the management of public money, settling claims against the state and accounts of persons indebted to the state, providing certification of the state treasurer's balances, and issuing warrants for all disbursements from the state treasury.

In the 1920s and 1930s, as the state began to exert better control over agency expenditures and track local government indebtedness more closely, the state auditor assumed new responsibilities. In 1955 the General Assembly transferred to the Budget Bureau (established in 1925) all preaudit functions, particularly the issuance of warrants for disbursements—a primary duty since 1868. The revised constitution and subsequent Executive Organization Act in 1971 left the office virtually unchanged, except for the creation of a new Department of State Auditor.

In 1985 the General Assembly transferred to a new office of state controller all functions of the state auditor relating to development, installation, and maintenance of state agency accounting systems. The modern Department of State Auditor is organized into two divisions: general administration and auditing.

K. Todd Johnson

Audubon Society of North Carolina. For a relatively brief period, the Audubon Society of North Carolina (ASNC) was perhaps the most important of the state Audubon societies formed as a part of the bird protection movement generated by the American Ornithologists' Union (AOU). The movement began in the 1880s, when the AOU noted that the killing of game birds (birds generally regarded as suitable for eating) was regulated by numerous states but that few had laws protecting nongame birds; furthermore, what little nongame bird protection legislation existed seemed to be totally ignored. Consequently, many bird species in America were rapidly declining in number. Birds were killed for sport, collected for study and amusement, and destroyed as nuisances. A few extremely poor people ate birds of any species. Millions of birds were killed each year for the millinery industry. By the 1880s almost every woman's hat was decorated with wild bird feathers. To meet the demand, several species of the gull and heron families, including the populations in North Carolina, had been hunted almost to extinction.

The ASNC was founded in 1902 by AOU member T. Gilbert Pearson, a biology professor at what is now the University of North Carolina at Greensboro. Pearson had begun writing and making speeches about the need to protect birds while a Guilford College preparatory student. Only 28 years old when he founded the ASNC, he had already developed into the most persuasive speaker and lobbyist among the nation's ornithologists.

Public support for the ASNC in its first year emboldened Pearson to draft a bird protection bill incorporating most of the AOU model law's provisions and authorizing the society to enforce the proposed protection for birds and all North Carolina game laws. Largely because Pearson lobbied persuasively, his bill, known as the Audubon Act, passed easily in both houses, became law on 6 Mar. 1903, and took effect immediately. Thereupon, the ASNC, a private organization endowed with public authority, became the first state wildlife commission in the South.

The ASNC flourished for six years as a combination educational organization and law enforcement agency. Armed with natural history books, its wardens taught people about birds and game and regulations relating to them. Anyone apprehended in violating the regulations, after warnings, was arrested. Pearson provided small natural history libraries to interested schools and enticed teachers to establish Junior Audubon Societies in their classrooms. He gave frequent lectures illustrated with color stereopticon slides. The state commissioner of agriculture joined the ASNC board of directors, and his summer institutes for farmers took on a teacher employed by the ASNC to talk to joint meetings of farm men and women about the value of birds to agriculture.

Although North Carolinians in general complied with the Audubon Act, there were problems—particularly along the coast, where ASNC wardens struggled to nurture the nearly depleted gull and heron colonies and stop illegal hunting of ducks and geese for shipment to northern markets. Pearson bought for the ASNC four small coastal islands where gulls and terns could be given special protection. Their populations increased with gratifying speed. Within a few years, the largest least tern colonies in the eastern United States were breeding on the Audubon islands.

Enforcement of the game laws in the coastal counties gradually aroused strong resentment. In 1909 a senator from Beaufort County introduced in the legislature a bill to remove Beaufort and Currituck Counties from the ASNC's jurisdiction. The idea immediately appealed to other eastern legislators. Pearson's supporters on the game committees of the House and Senate tried to trap the bill but were outvoted. It was brought to the floor of both houses and amended many times. When finally enacted into law, it removed 52 counties from the ASNC's jurisdiction.

Thereafter, the ASNC declined steadily. After two years, Pearson resigned from office and moved to New York to take charge of the National Association of Audubon Societies (now the National Audubon Society). In 1911, and for the next 16 years, Pearson collaborated with the ASNC in urging the North Carolina legislature to abolish the society and create a fully public agency. This effort finally succeeded in 1927, when the legislature passed an act creating a State Game Commission, abolishing the ASNC, and transferring its property to the new commission.

Subsequent changes resulted in the establishment of the modern North Carolina Wildlife Resources Commission. Apart from the ASNC's being the antecedent of the Wildlife Resources Commission, the Audubon movement is now represented in North Carolina by a state office and several chapters of the National Audubon Society, which guards 20 bird sanctuaries on the North Carolina coast.

References: Frank Graham, *The Audubon Ark* (1990); Oliver H. Orr Jr., *Saving American Birds: T. Gilbert Pearson and the Founding of the Audubon Movement* (1992); T. Gilbert Pearson, *Adventures in Bird Protection* (1937).

Oliver H. Orr Jr.

Augusta Conference. In response to orders from King George III, the leaders of Virginia, North Carolina, South Carolina, and Georgia met with representatives of the southern Indians (Creek, Cherokee, Choctaw, Chickasaw, and Catawba) at Augusta, Ga., on 5 Nov. 1763. Present were 25 Indian chiefs and 700 warriors, 3 colonial governors, the lieutenant governor of Virginia, and John Stuart, the superintendent of Indian affairs in the Southern District. After six days of oratory, eating, drinking, and distributing presents from the king, the group signed a "Treaty of Perfect and Perpetual Peace and Friendship." The document provided for the mutual forgiveness of all past offenses and injuries; the establishment of satisfactory trade relations; the punishment, by each party, of offenders of its own race for crimes against members of the other race; and the fixing of boundaries of a reservation of about 15 square miles for the Catawba Indians.

Reference: William S. Powell, *North Carolina through Four Centuries* (1989).

Wiley J. Williams

Automobiles revolutionized the American way of life, giving people previously unimagined mobility and greater freedom to live, work, and travel where they wanted. Exactly when the first automobile appeared in North Carolina is uncertain, although there is evidence to suggest that a steam-powered vehicle was used in the state as early as 1881 and perhaps even 1874. In all likelihood, the first automobiles to come to North

Carolina used steam or electric motors to travel the few passable roads that existed at that time. The earliest vehicles were called "horseless carriages" because, except for the steering tiller mounted in the front and the engine tucked beneath the seat, they looked very much like a buggy without a horse. It is estimated that there may have been as many as 50 such "high-wheelers" in the state by 1900.

As automobiles changed design and became less expensive, their numbers quickly increased. Aside from a few scattered attempts by state car builders to create their own versions of the famous Ford Model-T or other automobiles between 1900 and 1920, there were no serious manufacturing competitors in North Carolina. Only the Corbitt Motor Company of Henderson was able to market a production model, which never sold more than 100 units.

By 1909, the first year in which the state required licensing of autos, 1,600 vehicles existed in North Carolina. In 1912 the number of registrations had reached 6,000, and by 1919 it had leaped to 109,000. With the rapid expansion of the state highway system after 1921 came a steady growth of automobile use, reaching 473,623 registrations by 1928.

As the twentieth century marched on, North Carolinians' love affair with the car led to the growth of suburbs, motels, shopping centers, highways, theme parks, drive-in restaurants, service stations, and other now-common features of the state's economy and culture. Beginning with World War I, motor vehicles including trucks also changed the face of the military. The automobile spurred many support industries ranging from oil and parts production to insurance, vehicle inspection, auto racing, and state regulation of drivers. At the state level, vehicle safety inspection is ultimately the responsibility of the North Carolina Department of Transportation and its Division of Motor Vehicles.

References: Frank Coffey, *America on Wheels: The First 100 Years, 1896–1996* (1996); Robert E. Ireland, *Entering the Auto Age: The Early Automobile in North Carolina, 1900–1930* (1990); Capus Waynick, *North Carolina Roads and Their Builders*, vol. 1 (1952).

Robert E. Ireland

SEE ALSO Highways; Roads; Trucks and Trucking.

Auto Racing in North Carolina has grown from occasional competitions among speed-hungry moonshiners during the 1930s to a billion-dollar industry operating under the sponsorship of major corporations and attracting legions of devoted followers. As the availability of cars increased in the first decades of the twentieth century, organized races and auto rallies began to be held in northern and midwestern cities. In the rural South, where fewer people could afford cars, racing was slower to develop. An early advocate of the sport in North Carolina was automobile dealer Osmond Long Barringer Sr.,

Driver Herb Thomas of Sanford and his pit crew during a race in 1954. Courtesy of NCOA&H.

who in 1924 built a one-mile pinewood track near Pineville (today part of the Charlotte metropolitan area).

Many of North Carolina's original racing competitions matched law officers against local moonshiners who, with the fastest cars and the most innovative equipment, became formidable high-speed drivers capable of astounding—and often dangerous—maneuvers during their nightly liquor deliveries. Beginning in the mid-1930s, weekly races among moonshiners and others driving muscular cars were held at various rough-hewn tracks throughout the state. As these races grew in number and attendance increased, some ex-moonshiners became racing legends. Robert Glen "Junior" Johnson, born in Wilkes County in 1931, was the embodiment of the cunning, gritty southern renegade who drew the admiration of fans as auto racing began to develop into an organized spectator sport during the 1940s. Johnson learned the moonshine trade from his bootlegger father. He began competing in local races at age 15, and by his mid-twenties he had become a major talent on the growing racing circuit. Among Johnson's 50 career professional victories was the 1960 Daytona 500; he is also credited as the first driver to successfully use "drafting"—gaining additional speed by driving close behind another driver—to overcome faster cars during races.

The "down-home" appeal of auto racing was a key element in its growing popularity in North Carolina and other southern states during the latter half of the twentieth century. Although North Carolinians have participated in all types of motor sports, including drag racing and competing with "sprint" cars, "midget" cars, and karts, stock car racing—today featuring high-tech versions of commercial, assembly-line autos with V-8 engines and 700-plus horsepower—emerged as the most popular form of auto racing in the state. While heroes abounded in all sports, stock car drivers' personalities, re-

Richard Petty with one of his race cars and some of his many trophies in the Petty Museum at Level Cross. Photograph courtesy of the North Carolina Division of Tourism, Film, and Sports Development.

gional allegiances, and other personal qualities became as important to many racing fans as the types of cars they drove or their success on the track. With its speed, noise, and danger, stock car racing came to be an affirmation of the most thrilling aspects of small-town southern life. These characteristics also contributed to its early reputation as a sport appealing predominately to rural white males.

Over the years, many North Carolina communities have had auto racing tracks—sometimes dirt, sometimes paved—where drivers and mechanics alike showcased their skills and built their reputations. The concentration of these local tracks, many of which have now closed or fallen into disrepair, was particularly high in the western Piedmont and Mountain region. But the local, rough-and-tumble nature of auto racing in the state began to shift decisively in 1947, when businessmen William France Sr. and Ed Otto formed the National Association for Stock Car Auto Racing (NASCAR). NASCAR quickly established itself as the sanctioning body for races and race tracks; it also established tight control over the kinds of modifications that would be allowed in racing vehicles. The first official NASCAR event was held on 19 June 1949 at the three-quarter-mile dirt speedway in Charlotte. In NASCAR's first decade, much of the sport's attention was focused on glamorous races outside the state at "superspeedways" in Darling-

ton, S.C., Talladega, Ala., and Daytona Beach, Fla. But in 1959, Charlotte businessman O. Bruton Smith and early driving star Curtis Turner joined to build Concord's 1.5-mile Charlotte Motor Speedway, and as the host of a 600-mile race that was longer than any other NASCAR event, the track helped return North Carolina to a central place in the sport.

For much of its history, NASCAR sanctioned three tracks in North Carolina: the Charlotte Motor Speedway, the one-mile oval North Carolina Speedway in Rockingham, and the half-mile "short track" North Wilkesboro Speedway. In 1972 NASCAR began a 33-year relationship with Winston-Salem's R. J. Reynolds Tobacco Company and its Winston cigarette brand, naming its top circuit the "Winston Cup." The Petty family of Level Cross came to be considered by many as the "first family" of stock car racing during this era, thanks to the exploits of Lee Petty, who won three NASCAR championships (1954, 1958, 1959), and his son Richard, who won 200 races during his career and earned the Winston Cup championship seven times (1964, 1967, 1971–72, 1974–75, and 1979). Kannapolis native Dale Earnhardt was one of the few drivers to rival Richard Petty's dominance, winning seven Winston Cup titles (1980, 1986–87, 1990–91, 1993–94) before his death in an accident during the final lap of the 2001 Daytona 500, the sport's premier race. Many of NASCAR's other champions and leading drivers have been born in North Carolina or call the state home today.

The 1990s were a decade of change and expansion for auto racing in North Carolina and across the nation. Although the stereotypical image of the racing fan as a blue-collar, white male remained intact, the sport's fan base grew in diversity, encompassing men from all economic and social backgrounds as well as an increasing number of women. Professionals at the highest levels of auto racing, however, have remained exclusively white males: by the early 2000s, no African Americans had successfully competed in NASCAR, and only two women were competing in NASCAR's Craftsman Truck Series.

Charlotte Motor Speedway nearly tripled its seating capacity to 167,000 in the early 1990s, and a lighting system for night racing was installed in 1992. The speedway became the first of its kind to offer lavish VIP suites and on-track condominiums. In 1995 Howard "Humpy" Wheeler, president and general manager of Charlotte Motor Speedway, and speedway owner Bruton Smith put the first publicly owned motor sports company, Speedway MotorSports, on the New York Stock Exchange. That company operates facilities in Charlotte and several other cities across the United States. In 1999 North Wilkesboro–based Lowe's Companies, Inc., secured the naming rights to the track, which is known today as Lowe's Motor Speedway. The 600-mile races run at Lowe's Motor Speedway remain the longest in the sport.

But the 1990s and the early 2000s also saw NASCAR shift

away from its North Carolina roots. In 1996 the legendary short track at North Wilkesboro hosted its last Winston Cup race, as NASCAR moved that track's events to a speedway in New Hampshire, built as a part of an ongoing effort to diversify the sport's geographic base. And on 19 June 2003, the anniversary of North Carolina's first NASCAR event, the sport announced it would end its relationship with R. J. Reynolds in favor of a new partnership with wireless telecommunications provider Nextel Communications. Beginning in 2004 the sport's top circuit became known as the Nextel Cup. NASCAR officials cited the decision as a result of new limitations on the marketing of cigarettes, though many assume the decision was also tied to the larger effort to capture a more affluent national audience.

By the early 2000s, even as stock car racing expanded beyond its traditional southern base to tracks in many other regions of the country, it remained an annual billion-dollar industry in North Carolina, including brand product, television, restaurant, and hotel revenues, as well as money generated by the races themselves. Stock car racing has begun to receive media attention on a par with professional football, basketball, and baseball and is considered the nation's fastest-growing sport.

References: Jerry Bledsoe, *The World's Number One, Flat-Out, All-Time Great Stock Car Racing Book* (1995); Pete Daniel, *Lost Revolutions: The South in the 1950s* (2000); Peter Golenbock, *American Zoom: Stock Car Racing* (1993); Randal L. Hall, "Before NASCAR: The Corporate and Civic Promotion of Automobile Racing in the American South, 1903–1927," *Journal of Southern History* 68 (August 2002); Joe Menzer, *The Wildest Ride: A History of NASCAR* (2002); Daniel S. Pierce, "The Most Southern Sport on Earth: NASCAR and the Unions," *Southern Cultures* 7, no. 2 (2001); Sylvia Wilkinson, *Dirt Tracks to Glory: The Early Days of Stock Car Racing as Told by the Participants* (1983).

Jay Mazzocchi
Additional research provided by Wiley J. Williams.

Averasboro, Battle of. The Battle of Averasboro was a costly delaying action that began in Harnett County on 15 Mar. 1865, near the end of the Civil War. Maj. Gen. William T. Sherman's Union army of 60,000 men was moving northward from Fayetteville in two columns. On 15 March Gen. Joseph E. Johnston ordered Lt. Gen. William J. Hardee's 6,000 Confederate troops to engage the enemy while Maj. Gens. Robert F. Hoke and Daniel H. Hill marched from Kinston. Johnston needed time to consolidate his forces for a major battle. About five miles south of Averasboro, Hardee deployed his troops in three defensive lines to impede Sherman's left wing.

At 6:00 A.M. the next day, in the driving rain, the Federal attack began with an artillery barrage and cavalry charge. Skirmishers were driven back, but the Confederates rallied and

charged. They had the upper hand until Maj. Gen. Henry W. Slocum, commander of Sherman's left wing, ordered up additional infantry led by Col. William Hawley. By 11:00 A.M. the Confederate right on the first line had been turned, forcing the Rebels back to their second line of defense. At 1:00 P.M., after another Union attack, the Confederates withdrew to their third line. Union shelling continued, followed by several costly charges. At 8:00 P.M. Hardee ordered a withdrawal along the road to Smithfield, leaving Maj. Gen. Joseph Wheeler's dismounted cavalry to cover the retreat. At daybreak Wheeler withdrew.

The fight delayed the Union advance, but Hardee's small force was no match for Sherman's left wing. Union casualties were reported at 682 killed, wounded, and missing. Confederate casualties were, Hardee asserted, "between 400 and 500." The fight near Averasboro was only a small battle; nonetheless, it effectively stalled Slocum's advance for one day, enabling Johnston to concentrate his forces and launch a full-scale attack against the Union left wing at Bentonville three days later.

References: John G. Barrett, *The Civil War in North Carolina* (1963); Barrett, *Sherman's March through the Carolinas* (1956); Mark L. Bradley, *Last Stand in the Carolinas: The Battle of Bentonville* (1996); J. S. Smith, "On the Battlefield at Averasboro," *Confederate Veteran* (February 1926).

Ronnie W. Faulkner

Avery County, located in North Carolina's Mountain region and bordered in part by Tennessee, was formed in 1911 from parts of Mitchell, Caldwell, and Watauga Counties. Avery was the one-hundredth and final county to be created in North Carolina. The county was named after Col. Waightstill Avery, a Revolutionary War officer and the first attorney general of North Carolina. The earliest inhabitants of Avery County were the Cherokee Indians, followed by German, Scotch-Irish, and English settlers. Newland, the county seat, was incorporated in 1913 and named for William Calhoun Newland, the lieutenant governor of North Carolina from 1909 to 1913. Newland is situated at an elevation of 3,589 feet, making it the highest county seat in the eastern United States. Other communities in Avery County include Banner Elk, Crossnore, Elk Park, and Linville. Lees-McRae College was established in Banner Elk in 1900.

The terrain of Avery County is perhaps its most significant feature and is the basis for its primary industry, tourism. Located in a region known as the "High Country," it is a very popular destination for vacationers, including hikers, hang gliders, and other outdoor enthusiasts, who flock to the county throughout the year, particularly in the fall and summer, to enjoy the rugged beauty of the region. Several important landmarks draw thousands of other visitors, including the much-visited Grandfather Mountain, Linville Caverns, and

Beech Mountain. The Blue Ridge Parkway's Linn Cove Viaduct, a 1,234-foot curved bridge near Grandfather Mountain, represents one of the most complex engineering feats in the United States. Major events such as the Grandfather Mountain Highland Games, Beech Mountain Storytelling and Crafts Festival, and Banner Elk Art Festival are some of Avery County's most popular annual attractions.

Avery County produces lumber, tobacco, potatoes, and beef cattle. It has been called a "Christmas tree capital" for its supplying of large numbers of the popular Fraser fir variety of tree used for this purpose (and now the official state Christmas tree). The county also produces such minerals as kaolin, mica, iron, and feldspar. In 2004 Avery County's population was estimated to be 18,000.

Jay Mazzocchi

SEE ALSO Beech Mountain/Land of Oz; Grandfather Mountain; Highland Games; Lees-McRae College; Linn Cove Viaduct.

Aviation. The history of aviation and the airline industry in North Carolina encompasses more than Orville and Wilbur Wright's momentous flight at Kitty Hawk in December 1903. Before that, North Carolina inventors built and tried to fly several kinds of aircraft. Henry Gatling's 1873 hand-cranked monoplane in Hertford County and Daniel Asbury's 1881 steam-driven monoplane in Mecklenburg County were perhaps the best known. Jacob A. Hill built a dirigible at Winston-Salem in 1902, and Louis H. Kromm of Reidsville designed a huge dirigible the same year but was unable to finance it. In the wake of the first Wright brothers flight, North Carolina remained a leader in the field of aviation for nearly 20 years.

While the Wrights struggled at Kitty Hawk, Luther Paul of the Davis community in Carteret County designed and built a twin-rotor helicopter. In 1907 this machine, unmanned and tethered to the ground, lifted itself between four and five feet, making North Carolina the site of the world's first vertical as well as horizontal heavier-than-air flights. A model helicopter, built at Wilmington in 1910, was intended to lead to a full-sized machine, but the project failed.

Spurred by Louis Bleriot's 1909 flight across the English Channel and the onset of exhibition flying, North Carolinians between 1910 and 1912 built and flew six planes and projected over a dozen more. Wilmington and Charlotte craftsmen were responsible for at least five of those that were built, but only M. F. H. Gouverneur and Harold M. Chase's four-winged multiplane actually flew (on 10 Nov. 1910 at Shell Island near Wilmington). A Santos-Dumont "Demoiselle" monoplane, built by three Kinstonians in 1911, failed to fly because of its underpowered automobile motor. Greensboro's W. F. Johnson in 1910 became the first African American to design an aircraft (an electric biplane), but only a model was built.

While these and other projects—including David Palmgren's unique "aero-car" at Wilmington—proceeded within the state, two North Carolinians who went north seeking greater industrialization and ready capital achieved more impressive results. William W. W. Christmas, a Warrenton native, claimed to be the first American after the Wrights to build and fly a plane (in northern Virginia in March 1908). The claim was never validated, but he built biplanes at College Park, Md., in 1910 and 1912; both achieved successful flights. In 1914 Christmas took out the first patent on an inset aileron, a device used by virtually every plane since that time. Meanwhile, Lenoir's James S. Spainhour built and flew a "self-balancing" biplane near Pittsburgh in 1911. By the 1920s, aircraft building had become too complex and expensive to be a large-scale industry in North Carolina. Small companies built planes at High Point, Asheville, and perhaps elsewhere, but the major expansion of the industry took place outside the state.

Exhibition flyers roared into North Carolina in 1910, beginning with flights by Eugene Ely and J. A. D. McCurdy in Curtiss planes at Raleigh on 10 November. Lincoln Beachey gave an exhibition at Wilmington on 9 Mar. 1911 and briefly opened a flight school at Pinehurst for the golfing set that spring. He flew at Durham, Asheville, Greensboro, Winston-Salem, and other towns, generating huge popularity for aviation. Charles C. Witmer, Charles F. Walsh, Harry LeVan, and J. B. McCauley were among numerous others who exhibited in North Carolina prior to 1914. In 1913 Tiny Broadwick of Oxford became the first woman to parachute from an airplane. At Greensboro in 1911, entrepreneur Lindsey Hopkins of Reidsville started the Lindsey Hopkins Aviation Company, paid for the flight lessons of auto mechanic Thornwell H. Andrews of Charlotte, bought a Curtiss airplane, and sponsored exhibitions across the country.

Because many of its youth were familiar with cars and planes, the state contributed more than 300 pilots to World War I. Reidsville's Opie Lindsey shot down six German planes to qualify as an ace, and James McConnell of Carthage and Kiffin Rockwell of Asheville founded the Lafayette Escadrille, volunteers who fought for France before America entered the war in 1917. Both died in air battles.

In 1918 the U.S. Navy established a seaplane base at Morehead City and the Signal Corps Air Service began work on Pope Field near Fayetteville. The Carolina Airplane Company, founded in 1918 by veteran pilot Harry Atwood, built Curtiss seaplanes at Raleigh, Smithfield, and Goldsboro, but they proved to be underpowered and the navy rejected them. Planes were assembled and flown at Camp Greene, outside Charlotte. Also in 1918 Christmas designed and built what he expected to be America's first pursuit plane, the "Christmas Bullet," but two prototypes crashed, killing their pilots.

Belvin Maynard of Harrell's Store was regarded by many as the world's best pilot at the war's close. A test pilot during the

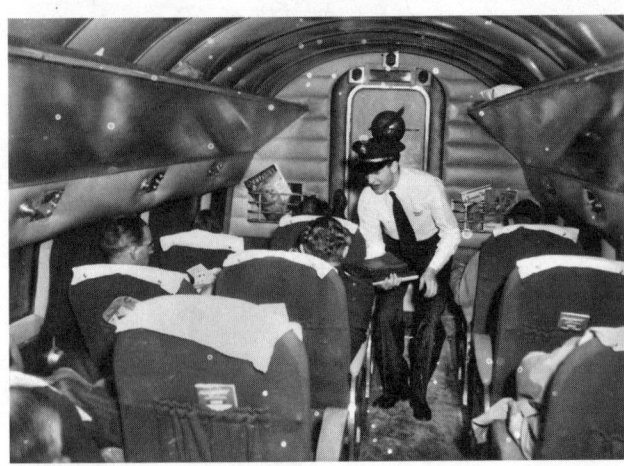
Interior of a Piedmont Airlines plane, 1950. Courtesy of NCOA&H.

conflict, Maynard set an as-yet unchallenged record in early 1919 by performing 318 consecutive inside loops in 67 minutes with a Sopwith Camel at a French airfield. He was home in time to fly in the army's round-trip endurance races between Long Island and Toronto and across North America that fall, the longest air races held to that time. Maynard won both events, the second despite a forced landing in rural Nebraska and the overnight replacement of his burned-out engine. He died in a Vermont air crash in 1922.

As air travel developed from experimental to military to commercial use in the twentieth century, many airlines have served North Carolina travelers. Piedmont Airlines, founded by Tom Davis in Winston-Salem on 1 Jan. 1948, became one of the nation's leading carriers. The airline grew out of Piedmont Aviation, Inc., established by Davis in July 1940 as a sales and service outlet for the Southeast's burgeoning aircraft business. Authorized to begin operations by the Civil Aeronautics Board on 4 Apr. 1947, Piedmont made its first flight on 20 Feb. 1948 from Wilmington to Cincinnati, Ohio. There was one paying passenger on board, a man named Bill Turner, and his fare was $34.35.

Limited by government regulations to regional routes during the daytime, Piedmont nonetheless thrived. By 1958 it was carrying nearly 200,000 passengers annually, and within another four years it was granted access to Atlanta from its bases in Columbia, S.C.; Washington, D.C.; and Baltimore. The number of passengers carried annually rose to 664,000. In November 1966 Piedmont inaugurated flights to New York's La Guardia Airport; within three years it was carrying more than 2 million passengers a year. Within a decade it added routes to Miami, Tampa, and Boston.

Truly phenomenal growth occurred in the wake of the federal government's decision in August 1978 to deregulate the nation's air carriers. Liberalized route and fare policies meant that strongly positioned regional carriers like Piedmont could branch out quickly and competitively. Los Angeles, Denver,

Dallas, San Francisco, and Phoenix were added to Piedmont's system; in less than a decade the airline inaugurated international service with flights to London. The immediate consequence of deregulation was a dramatic increase in Piedmont's size as an airline and in its number of passengers. In 1969 it served 78 cities and carried 2.2 million passengers. In 1984 it carried 13 million passengers and passed the $1 billion mark in revenues. By 1987 it was carrying 23 million passengers a year to 235 destinations.

By the time of deregulation, however, Piedmont's future was becoming more uncertain. Despite Davis's long-held belief that growth was best achieved internally, Piedmont was an increasingly attractive target in a number of take-over bids. The first, launched by Air Florida in 1978, failed. Next came the Norfolk & Western Railroad, which offered $1.5 billion and $65/share for the airline in 1986. That bid was upset by US Airways's subsequent bid of $1.6 billion, based on stock buy-outs ranging from $68/share to $71/share. On 9 Mar. 1987 the merger between US Air and Piedmont was announced, a decision that created the nation's seventh-largest air carrier.

Aviation has allowed for much faster travel for North Carolinians and other Americans, but it has sometimes resulted in the tragic loss of lives. The first crash of a commercial aircraft in North Carolina occurred near Bolivia on 6 Jan. 1960, involving a National Airlines flight from New York to Miami. The plane had just passed Wilmington and was over the ocean when a bomb exploded on board. Despite the damage, the plane headed back toward Wilmington. Before it could reach the airport, however, the plane disintegrated and crashed, killing all 34 people on board. The bomb had been carried onto the plane by passenger Julian Frank of New York, who was in a web of complicated business deals and under investigation by the district attorney for embezzlement. A few months earlier, he had taken out nearly $1 million in life insurance. His death was ruled a suicide and his wife did not collect.

On 19 July 1967 a Piedmont Boeing 727 and a private Cessna 310 collided near Hendersonville. All 79 people in the jetliner and all 3 in the Cessna were killed. The Piedmont flight had just taken off from Asheville when the Cessna, preparing to land, crashed into it. On board the jet was secretary of the navy designate John T. McNaughton, who was to be sworn in a week later. The collision was a result of pilot confusion and unclear air traffic control instructions.

The state's largest air accident to date occurred on 11 Sept. 1974, when an Eastern Airlines DC-9 crashed while attempting to land at Charlotte. Of the 82 people on board, 71 died, including CBS news editor John Merriman. There was patchy fog as the plane tried to land, but the primary cause of the wreck was error by both pilots (one of whom survived). Other tragic airplane accidents in the state include the July 1994 crash of a US Airways DC-9 near Charlotte, killing 37 people, and the December 1994 crash of an American Eagle Jetstream Super

31 four miles southwest of Raleigh-Durham International Airport, in which 15 of 20 passengers died.

North Carolina airports have gained and then lost several airline hubs through the years, in particular those of American Airlines and Midway Airlines (both located at Raleigh-Durham International Airport). Today, North Carolina's major carriers include United, Delta, Southwest, and US Airways (which has a hub in Charlotte). The state has about 75 publicly owned airports and nearly 300 more that are privately owned. There are also approximately 50 flight schools in North Carolina, educating the state's more than 15,000 privately licensed pilots. Nine airports have regularly scheduled airline service, and four are international (Charlotte/Douglas International Airport, Raleigh-Durham International Airport, Wilmington International Airport, and Greensboro-Piedmont Triad International Airport). By the early 2000s, more than 35 million passengers flew to and from North Carolina each year, and more than 800 million pounds of air freight originated annually in the state.

References: Richard Hallion, *Taking Flight: Inventing the Aerial Age from Antiquity through the First World War* (2003); Thomas C. Parramore, *First to Fly: North Carolina and the Beginnings of Aviation* (2002); William Stockton, *Final Approach: The Crash of Eastern 212* (1977).

Thomas C. Parramore
Additional research provided by
Clyde Ellis and Stephen Moyer.

SEE ALSO Airmail Service; Airplane, First Flight of.

Azalea Festival. The North Carolina Azalea Festival is held every April in Wilmington as a celebration of the beauty of the abundant azalea flowers in the vicinity. In the 1930s Houston Moore, interested in the beautification of Wilmington's Greenfield Lake and Park, suggested to civic organizations that a "festival with pageantry and color" be established. Municipal officials secured support from the New Deal's Works Project Administration for the beautification of the lakeside park, and when it was completed, upkeep was turned over to civic leaders. By 1937 the city government of Wilmington had accepted responsibility for the park. Ten years later, the idea for an extensive festival arose, and the organizers incorporated. The first Azalea Festival was launched in 1948 with a parade, dance, community sing, and flower show. A motion picture star, Jacqueline White, served as the festival's "queen," and about 60,000 people attended.

The Azalea Festival soon expanded to include such attractions as concerts, tours of local houses and gardens, and a street fair on the Cape Fear River waterfront. Movie actors, musicians, and other celebrities have attended the festival as honored guests, including Ronald Reagan, who was master of ceremonies in 1958. Other famous entertainers featured at the festival have been Andy Griffith, Michael Landon, Frankie Avalon, Pat Boone, Bob Hope, Barbara Mandrell, and Wayne Newton.

By 2006 the North Carolina Azalea Festival was attracting more than 300,000 people annually and generating more than $5 million for Wilmington and surrounding areas.

Craig M. Stinson

B

Babies Hospital was a seaside pediatric institution that operated in New Hanover County from 1920 until 1978. Medical professionals had long proclaimed the benefits of ocean breezes for childhood ailments and had often instructed parents to take their sick children or infants on a trip aboard the daily steamer from Wilmington to Southport to take advantage of the air's curative powers. Acting on such beliefs, Wilmington physician J. Buren Sidbury in 1920 opened the Babies Hospital on the sound just across from Wrightsville Beach overlooking the modern Intracoastal Waterway. In his appeals for contributions, Sidbury, believed to be only the second doctor in the state to specialize in pediatrics, cited the success of similar resort hospitals in Virginia Beach, Va., and Atlantic Beach, N.J. Until Duke Hospital opened in Durham in 1930, Sidbury's hospital was the only pediatric care facility in North Carolina.

In its 58-year history, the Babies Hospital never received public funds. The original cottage housing the facility burned in 1927 (with no loss of life or injuries) and was replaced the next year by a fireproof structure directly across the road. The new building featured 22 rooms, a spacious ward, and a roof garden with high walls for sunning. Through 1939 the hospital was open only during the summer months. From 1942 to 1967 the Babies Hospital conducted a nurses' training program where senior student nurses statewide received three months of pediatric training. Pediatric supervisors throughout North Carolina and South Carolina were also trained there. Although the hospital served primarily the eastern parts of North Carolina and South Carolina, it was not unusual for patients to be referred from other East Coast states.

In 1954 a third floor was added to the building, in 1955 a nurses' dormitory was built, and in 1962 a pediatric research center was completed (since used by UNC-Wilmington for marine biomedical research). Patient use of the Babies Hospital peaked in 1967. In 1978 the board of directors closed the facility, as progress in the treatment of children's diseases had made its traditional sea-breeze therapy obsolete. The 1928 structure was subsequently leased for commercial office space.

References: Diane Cashman, *The Lonely Road: A History of the Physicks and Physicians of the Lower Cape Fear, 1735–1976* (1978); Lockert B. Mason, "Babies Hospital, 1920–1978," *North Carolina Medical Journal* 45 (January 1984).

Michael Hill

Backcountry was the term used during the early settlement and colonial periods for the vast interior of North Carolina, located away from the coastline and including both the modern-day Piedmont and Mountain regions. The backcountry was first explored by John Lederer in 1670 and was penetrated gradually by Virginia Indian traders. Not until the mid-eighteenth century did large numbers of Scotch-Irish and Germans begin to spread across the region, following the "Great Wagon Road" from Pennsylvania down through the Shenandoah Valley of Virginia. The interior population rapidly swelled to become 40 percent of the colony's total, and backcountry settlers' inadequate political representation in the colonial assembly was a factor in the increasing east-west sectional friction that led to the Regulator Movement (1765–71) and other conflicts. The backcountry was the last area of the state to be settled and, consequently, the most volatile region of North Carolina society for many years.

References: Carl Bridenbough, *Myths and Realities: Societies of the Colonial South* (1952); C. Christopher Crittenden, *The Commerce of North Carolina* (1936); Richard J. Hooker, ed., *The Carolina Backcountry on the Eve of the Revolution* (1953).

Lindley S. Butler

Balanced Budget Amendment, sponsored by Rep. John Gamble of Lincoln County, was adopted as part of the North Carolina Constitution in 1977. The amendment requires that the state conduct its fiscal affairs on a cash basis, at least on the revenue side of the ledger, and that state government as a whole may not spend in any given fiscal period more money than is added to the state treasury during that period. The amendment gave constitutional sanction to what had been statute law since enactment of the Executive Budget Act in 1925.

Both the state constitution and Section 143-25 of the General Statutes of North Carolina, a portion of the Executive Budget Act, require the governor (designated by the state constitution as director of the budget) to "continually survey the collection of the revenue" and "effect the necessary economies in state expenditures" to prevent expenditures from exceeding available revenue. The governor recommends and the General Assembly enacts a balanced budget by estimating revenue and appropriating expenditures for specific purposes. Once the budget is enacted, only the expenditure side of the equation can be controlled with any degree of certainty. The constitution and statutes, therefore, direct the governor to observe the balanced budget requirement by curtailing expenditures if revenues fail to materialize in the anticipated amounts.

Joseph Ferrell

Bald Head is the southernmost part of a complex of sandy islands and marshland at the mouth of the Cape Fear River known as Smith Island. Fixing the precise location of Bald Head is difficult. Some North Carolinians apply the name to an entire island, while others use it to refer to only a small part of that island. Those who have studied the area and its history generally use the name Bald Head Island to refer to the part of the Smith Island complex that extends from Cape Fear on the east to the Cape Fear River on the west, with the Atlantic Ocean stretching away to the south. They reserve the name Bald Head for the area near the river on which Bald Head Lighthouse is located.

Initially, the island complex was shown on maps as Cape Island, or Cape Fear Island, and even earlier it was said to have been known as Cedar Island. In time, all of the land in the area located east of the Cape Fear River was claimed by Landgrave Thomas Smith, a South Carolina merchant who perfected his title in 1713 with a grant from the North Carolina authorities. Within a few years cartographers were showing the name on their maps as Landgrave Thomas Smith's Island, leading in time to the current name of Smith Island. Bald Head itself was a large sand hill on the southwest part of the island from which Cape Fear River pilots could get an early view of ocean-going vessels heading toward the mouth of the river. It appeared as "Barren Head" on the 1733 Mosely map, but by the time the Collet map was published in 1770 it was shown as Bald Head.

By then, maritime traffic had become so heavy that there was a clamor to build North Carolina's first lighthouse at Bald Head. In 1784 the General Assembly levied a special six-pence-per-ton duty on all vessels entering the Cape Fear River, with the proceeds to go toward building a lighthouse. Five years later, before the lighthouse was completed, the U.S. government took over responsibility for the "establishment and support of light-houses, beacons, buoys and public piers," with the expenses to come from the federal treasury. The lighthouse at Bald Head, begun by the state and finished by the federal government, was first lighted in 1795, but the structure was built so close to the Cape Fear River that it was threatened by erosion and had to be abandoned 15 years later. A second Bald Head Lighthouse was built in 1818, this time well back from the water; it remains the oldest standing lighthouse in North Carolina. The first Cape Fear Lifesaving Station was built on the East Beach near the lighthouse in 1882, and for the next half-century crewmen from the isolated shore station participated in many rescues of shipwrecked mariners.

Efforts to develop Bald Head Island as a tourist destination began as early as 1916, when Thomas Frank Boyd paid $45,000 for the entire Smith Island complex, consisting of Bald Head Island, Middle Island, Bluff Island, and assorted patches of migratory marshland. Calling his development Palmetto Island, Boyd built a long pier (to accommodate river

The lighthouse on Bald Head Island, late 1980s. Photograph by Tim Buchman. Courtesy of Preservation North Carolina.

steamers) and a combination pavilion and hotel. He subsequently lost this entire property for nonpayment of taxes during the Depression. In 1938 title to the complex was acquired by Frank O. Sherrill, who retained ownership for three decades and periodically talked of development plans. His 1960 plan to build a resort city for 60,000 people—in the process dredging up virtually all of the Smith Island marshland—never got past the talking stage, although there was considerable public uproar over the prospect of the destruction of Bald Head's unique natural resources.

When a newly formed company called Carolina Cape Fear Corporation announced in 1970 that it had acquired the Sherrill property for development purposes, spokesman William R. Henderson was careful to emphasize that it planned to proceed in a "very responsible manner," with special emphasis on protecting the ecology and environment of the island. The project failed, but two subsequent owners—first Walter R. Davis and then the family of George P. Mitchell—proceeded with the carefully planned development of Smith Island. The owners have worked closely with the state of North Carolina, federal agencies, and environmental groups to protect and preserve most of Smith Island's approximately 17,000 acres— habitat for an amazing number of plant and animal species, many of them threatened or endangered.

Reference: David Stick, *Bald Head: A History of Smith Island and Cape Fear* (1985).

David Stick

"Ballad of Tom Dooley." Thomas C. Dula was born in Wilkes County on 20 June 1844, the son of Mary Dula. In 1862 he enlisted in the 42nd Regiment, North Carolina Infantry, as a private. Dula was captured at Kinston and was a prisoner of war at Cape Lookout, Md., where he was released in 1865. He returned to Wilkes County, where he resumed a liaison with Ann Melton, begun when he was 15 years old. In 1866 he cohabited with Laura Foster, from whom he eventually contracted syphilis.

On the morning of 25 May 1866, locals saw Foster on Stony Fork Road riding her father's mare with a bundle of clothing on her lap. The next morning, the mare returned alone to the Foster home, and a search began for Laura. On 18 June, searchers found Laura in a shallow grave, dead from a stab wound. Dula fled to Watauga County and then to Tennessee, where he was captured about three weeks later and returned to Wilkes County.

Dula and Melton went to trial for murder in Wilkes County, but the case was moved to Iredell County, where Dula was convicted. A second trial was held after the North Carolina Supreme Court reversed the decision, and Dula was again found guilty. He was hanged in Statesville on 1 May 1868.

Even before Dula's execution, locals in Wilkes and Watauga Counties sang a ballad about the incident, featuring the following lyrics:

Hang down your head, Tom Dula,
Hang down your head and cry;
You killed poor Laura Foster,
And now you're bound to die.

The Kingston Trio revived and popularized the folk song in the 1950s as "The Ballad of Tom Dooley."

References: Henry M. Belden and Arthur Palmer Hudson, eds., *The Frank C. Brown Collection of North Carolina Folklore*, vol. 2 (1952); John Foster West, *The Ballad of Tom Dula* (1971).

Thornton W. Mitchell

Ballads. SEE Folk Music.

Ballast Stones, whose weight stabilized empty ships, have been found at various colonial landing sites along the North Carolina coast. Although there are no known records, residents and local historians believe that these stones, found in coastal counties along the shore and under water, were used as ballast in early sailing vessels. In the colonies, the market for manufactured goods from abroad was limited, but local produce such as lumber, naval stores, grain, and tobacco was exported from North Carolina. On the westbound voyage, ships needed weight to lower them in the water to keep them from capsizing; large stones filled the ships' hold, but after they arrived this ballast was thrown overboard to be replaced by products from the colony.

Jettisoned stones began to clog the harbors so badly that in 1769 North Carolina political leader Richard Caswell presented a bill in the colonial Assembly to appoint a ballast master who would regulate this activity in the vicinity of Ocracoke Inlet. The problem persisted, however, and in 1784 the General Assembly passed an act that prohibited ballast stones from being thrown into the channel of the Cape Fear River. Thereafter, before docking, ships were required to dispose of their ballast prior to reaching the low watermark. Stones left in shallower water undoubtedly provided the cobblestones still seen in some of the streets along the river in Wilmington.

References: Walter Clark, ed., *State Records of North Carolina*, vol. 24 (1905); C. Christopher Crittenden, *The Commerce of North Carolina, 1763–1789* (1936).

William S. Powell

Bandy was a popular sport on North Carolina's college and school campuses prior to the Civil War. The sport, which closely resembled modern field hockey, featured two teams of varying numbers using a curved stick to knock a ball into a goal. The likelihood of a player having his shins hit with the stick led to an alternate name for the sport: "shinny." It was unorganized, without the printed rules, designated teams, or other features of modern sports that developed after the end of the war in such campus sports as baseball and football. The popularity of the latter sports resulted in the decline of bandy.

One particularly good description of an antebellum bandy contest came from J. R. Cole, a student at Trinity College (later Duke University). Describing games involving as many as 40 students, Cole wrote: "as the big hard ball is thrown up or down, see them rush up to it with uplifted clubs, and strike right and left crying 'shin on your side' and see them jump into the air to avoid a savage blow, and the ball is knocked whirlin, and all rush for it, and sticks fly, and hands are hurt, and limbs are bruised, and heads are struck." Not surprisingly, bandy did not meet with much favor with school officials across the state. Occasional attempts were made to ban the activity.

Jim L. Sumner

Bank Holiday of 1933. Between the stock market crash of October 1929 and mid-March 1933, 215 North Carolina banks, with a combined $110,854,000 in assets, failed. Bank runs had increased in early 1933, prompting the General Assembly to give authority to N.C. Banking Commissioner Gurney P. Hood to limit withdrawals. However, only a few banks made use of this power, and runs continued to occur.

Customers crowd in front of the Raleigh Banking and Trust Company during the crisis that prompted President Roosevelt to declare a bank holiday, temporarily closing all banks. Courtesy of NCOA&H.

To stem panic and help prevent bank runs, individual governors around the country began to declare bank holidays. After a New York State bank holiday was proclaimed on 4 Mar. 1933, Hood met with state bankers to plan a similar action for North Carolina. Between 6 and 8 March of that year, Governor John C. B. Ehringhaus proclaimed a bank holiday, making North Carolina the last state to suspend bank activity. The day after his inauguration President Franklin D. Roosevelt called a national bank holiday to extend from 5 to 9 March (it was later extended for an indefinite time). Congress moved quickly to pass the Emergency Banking Act, which authorized the bank holiday and established a mechanism for the orderly reopening of all banks. The act also created the Federal Deposit Insurance Corporation (FDIC) and put more authority and responsibility in the Federal Reserve Board, thus providing for more rigid control over capital requirements in state banks. The move proved to be successful. By 18 March, it was announced that 222 banks were back in operation in North Carolina.

Reference: T. Harry Gatton, *Banking in North Carolina: A Narrative History* (1987).

Robert E. Ireland

Banking, although important to North Carolina's economic health and stability for two centuries, became a major industry in the state only during the latter half of the twentieth century. The emergence of interstate banking, spurred by the 1985 U.S. Supreme Court decision upholding it, helped drive this growth. Led by mammoth corporations such as Bank of America, First Union, and Wachovia, North Carolina's banking industry has been characterized by mergers and acquisitions as well as increased competition through the establishment of new state-chartered banks.

North Carolina chartered its first banks in 1804, making it the last of the original 13 states to do so. That year the General Assembly chartered the Bank of Cape Fear as the state's first bank, followed later in the year by the Bank of New Bern. Limited wealth provided little opportunity for the accumulation of substantial capital. To provide services for small businesses, provisions were made for branch banks in other towns. This early practice made North Carolina a "bank branching" state, a concept that has persisted.

There were opposing views within the General Assembly on the proposed structure of a banking industry. One faction, consisting largely of Federalists, favored the establishment of private local banks such as the Bank of New Bern over a state bank, which it saw as a product of "the monied aristocracy." An opposing argument, made largely by Republicans, was for the establishment of a central state bank with branches throughout the state, owned and controlled jointly by the state and by individuals.

In 1810 the legislature chartered the State Bank of North Carolina. The bank's capital was set at $1.6 million, and the state treasurer was authorized to subscribe $250,000 in bank stock. The act required the state treasurer to use the full amount of the dividends from the state's stock to redeem paper currency issued earlier by the state. The headquarters of the State Bank of North Carolina was in Raleigh, with branches in several cities.

The State Bank of North Carolina quickly moved to cripple the operations of the Bank of New Bern and the Bank of Cape Fear by securing and presenting their notes for redemption. Instead of joining the State Bank, however, the Bank of New Bern was permitted in 1814 to establish branches in Raleigh, Halifax, and Milton, and the legislature granted the bank's request for recharter to 1835.

Public concern prompted the General Assembly to investigate the practices of state-chartered banks during the 1820s. A major examination of banking practices in 1828–29 was highly critical of state banks, and in the case of the Bank of New Bern, it exposed some irregularities and possible violations of its charter. By 1832, after some anxious years and with the help of generous creditors, the bank had paid off its obligations, but it was liquidated upon the expiration of its charter in 1835.

In 1791 U.S. Treasury Secretary Alexander Hamilton had persuaded Congress to charter the first Bank of the United States, essentially a private bank operating under a federal charter. Headquartered in Philadelphia, the bank had eight branches in major cities but none in North Carolina. The bank closed when it failed to have its charter renewed in 1811. Financial problems associated with the War of 1812, however, led to renewed plans for a central bank, and the federal government authorized the Second Bank of the United States on 10 Apr. 1816. Its capital was set at $35 million; stock subscriptions were sold in Raleigh, and a branch opened in Fayetteville in January 1817.

This was a major turning point in North Carolina's financial history, as the structural problems of the federal bank would significantly affect the state's banking industry. When President Andrew Jackson vetoed the bank charter renewal bill in 1832, the Fayetteville branch of the Second Bank of the United States closed. Following its demise, the regulation of bank credit and the nation's currency was left to state banks until the Civil War. In 1835 the Bank of the State of North Carolina was chartered as a successor to the State Bank of North Carolina. A new charter was granted in 1859 and the name was changed to the Bank of North Carolina, which finally closed its doors in 1866.

When North Carolina seceded from the Union on 20 May 1861, the state needed to raise funds immediately to support the military. Finance was a critical matter, and banks were induced to increase loans to the state. One step was to authorize the treasurer to borrow $1 million from the banks at 6 percent interest; the loan amount increased almost immediately to $3 million. That figure was increased to $8.4 million, one-third of the state's bank capital in 1862, as the war progressed. Financing the war was a major challenge to both the Confederate and state governments. In 1865 there was over $4 million in unpaid interest on state bonds. Surrender in 1865 did not stop the cost of the war. The banks had survived, but their doom was sealed when the U.S. Congress levied a 10 percent tax on all notes issued by state banks. Every bank in the state ceased operation, including the state's first bank, the Bank of Cape Fear.

National banking came to North Carolina when the First National Bank of Charlotte was chartered on 1 Aug. 1865, followed on 12 September by the Raleigh National Bank of North Carolina. In 1866 three additional national charters were granted for banks in New Bern, Wilmington, and Salem. There were no banks chartered by the state until the Bank of Greensboro on 7 Apr. 1869. The state continued to struggle with the economic effects of the Civil War. In the 30 banks in operation in the state in 1875, total deposits were only $250,000.

Banks remained private businesses unsupervised by the state until 1887, when a law was passed to make banks report to the state treasurer twice annually. The North Carolina Corporation Commission was created in 1899, and authority over banks was given to the new body with provisions for regulation and examination. In 1921 the commission established a banking department.

During banking's "glory days" of the 1920s, almost every town in the state desired a bank. After the Great Depression began in 1929 with the crash of the stock market, smaller banks began to fail. Governor O. Max Gardner, backed by the North Carolina Bankers Association, won the battle for regulation, and Gurney P. Hood became the state's first commissioner of banks in May 1931. North Carolina was the last state to close its banks for the national bank holiday announced by President Franklin D. Roosevelt on 5 Mar. 1933. Within a few days most of the banks in North Carolina were reopened; the remainder were liquidated under the provisions of the order. From 1921 to 1933, 316 banks failed in the state.

Building on Charlotte's history as a financial center, several North Carolina banking institutions emerged as national and international leaders during the second half of the twentieth century. By the early 2000s, Charlotte had become the nation's second-largest financial hub, ranked behind only New York City. In an era that saw job losses and diminished economic health in industries such as manufacturing and farming, North Carolina banking has continued to play a vital role in the state's economy. By 2004 there were nearly 100 state-chartered banks and many other bank and trust companies in North Carolina licensed to offer financial services in the state.

References: T. Harry Gatton, *Banking in North Carolina: A Narrative History* (1987); William S. Powell, "Beginning of Banking in North Carolina," *ESC Quarterly* 7 (Winter 1949).

T. Harry Gatton
Additional research provided by Bryna R. Coonin.

SEE ALSO Bank of America; Bank of Cape Fear; Branch Banking and Trust Company; Central Carolina Bank & Trust Company; State Bank of North Carolina; Wachovia Corporation.

Bank of America, the fifth-largest corporation in the world in 2004, has its roots in the 1957 merger of two Charlotte institutions, the American Trust Company and the Commercial National Bank. The newly formed American Commercial Bank, under the leadership of Addison Reese, merged three years later with Security National Bank of Greensboro. The new entity, North Carolina National Bank (NCNB), had assets of about $500 million. After an aggressive acquisition of a bank with the same name that was headquartered in Jacksonville, N.C., NCNB, with 40 branch offices in 20 North Carolina communities, was the second-largest bank in the state behind Wachovia Bank of Winston-Salem.

In a three-way contest with Wachovia and First Union Bank Corporation, NCNB began an aggressive policy of constructing new branch offices, merging with other banks, and expanding its assets. Reese was first in the state to enroll his bank in the new national BankAmericard program. The bank credit card gave customers a more efficient way of managing their money and enabled the bank to earn a transaction fee and attract new customers. By 1973 NCNB had surpassed Wachovia as the largest bank in the state. NCNB often led the way in social and community causes, helping, for example, in the redevelopment of downtown Charlotte, putting branches in poor areas of the city and aggressively hiring African Americans and women.

After Tom Storrs became its CEO in 1974, NCNB expanded its international commitment by opening branches in England, South Africa, Australia, and Hong Kong. By 1976, with the Charlotte giant controlling 20 percent of the state's retail banking market, NCNB moved into interstate banking.

Through ownership of the Trust Company of Florida, NCNB purchased the First National Bank of Lake City and quickly established a presence throughout Florida. In 1983 Hugh L. McColl Jr. became CEO of NCNB, succeeding Storrs. The son and grandson of bankers, McColl immediately consolidated acquisitions in Florida while moving into Georgia, South Carolina, Maryland, and Virginia. By 1987 NCNB was the largest bank in the Southeast.

The 1989 acquisition of First Republic Bank, the largest bank in Texas, made NCNB the nation's ninth-largest bank. In 1992 NCNB merged with Atlanta-based C&S and Sovran, the country's twelfth-largest bank, to become NationsBank, with nearly 2,000 offices and more than 59,000 employees. Through the $1.38 billion purchase of MNC Financial Corp. in 1993, merger with Boatman's Bankshares of St. Louis in 1996, and the purchase of Florida-based Barnett Banks in 1997, NationsBank became the third-largest banking entity in America.

McColl completed the process of transforming a regional bank into the first nationwide bank in 1998, when NationsBank merged with BankAmerica Corporation, which was based in California, to form the new Bank of America, then the largest banking institution in the nation. When McColl's tenure began, NCNB operated in two states, employed 7,600 people, and had assets of $12 billion. By 2006 the Bank of America Corporation, which remained headquartered in Charlotte, employed more than 175,000 people, managed total assets in excess of $475 billion, had operations in 29 states and the District of Columbia, and provided financial services to clients in 150 countries worldwide.

References: Howard E. Covington Jr. and Marion A. Ellis, *The Story of NationsBank* (1993); John Monk, "The Billion Dollar Man," *Carolina Lifestyle* (September 1983); Howard Troxler, "The Tortoise and the Hare," *Tar Heel* (June 1982).

Julian M. Pleasants

Bank of Cape Fear was the first private state bank chartered in North Carolina and one of the state's largest banks until the Civil War. Created by an act of the General Assembly in 1804, the bank was authorized initial capital of $250,000 with notes and debts not to exceed $750,000. In addition to its headquarters in Wilmington, it was permitted to open a branch in Fayetteville. In 1807 the General Assembly authorized the state treasurer to borrow from the bank, and the state exercised its statutory option to buy 250 shares of its stock. Throughout much of the antebellum era, income from Bank of Cape Fear shares represented a major source of state revenue. On 8 Apr. 1807, the bank announced the opening of a Raleigh branch.

Supported by Federalists, the bank and its sister institution, the Bank of New Bern, angered Republicans by reissuing old state notes, which led to specie hoarding and currency depreciation. This prompted the General Assembly to levy a 1 percent tax on private bank stock in 1809 and helped push the chartering of the public State Bank of North Carolina in 1810.

Additional branches had opened in Charlotte, Halifax, Hillsborough, Milton, and Salem by 1835 and in Asheville, Fayetteville, Greensboro, Raleigh, Salem, Salisbury, Washington, and Wilmington by 1859. By 1861 Bank of Cape Fear capital had reached $2.5 million. The bank remained open throughout the Civil War, and the Wilmington branch purportedly prospered from the blockade-running trade. However, the postwar repudiation of state war debts and a new federal tax on state bank notes forced its liquidation late in 1865, with a 25 percent payoff to investors.

References: T. Harry Gatton, *Banking in North Carolina: A Narrative History* (1987); William S. Powell, "Beginning of Banking in North Carolina, 1804–1860," *ESC Quarterly* 7 (Winter 1949).

Bennett L. Steelman

Baptist Children's Homes of North Carolina, Inc., founded in 1885, is one of the largest residential child care facilities in the South. The idea to establish an orphanage was first brought before the North Carolina Baptist State Convention in 1884 but was rejected primarily because of the cost of such an enterprise, the existence of the Oxford Masonic Orphanage (which Baptists had helped organize), and the tendency among many North Carolina Baptists to reject any type of missionary efforts beyond the local church. Within a year, however, supporters of the idea had appointed John Haymes Mills as the first general superintendent and commissioned him with the task of raising money and finding a site. A site was selected in Thomasville, and the first resident of the Baptist Orphanage was admitted in 1885.

Baptist Children's Homes of North Carolina, Inc., became an important ministry of the Baptist denomination, receiving a great deal of support from the North Carolina Baptist State Convention. In the early 2000s, the organization had 12 facilities throughout the state, aiding more than 1,200 children and their families through residential group care, crisis emergency care, maternity services for unmarried women, and other support programs.

Glenn Jonas

Baptists, with a theology rooted in the Reformation, represent the largest Protestant denomination in North Carolina among both blacks and whites. Baptists are unique among Christian sects in their rejection of infant baptism (waiting instead until individuals are old enough to choose for themselves) and their requiring of full immersion as the method of baptism. They also refute any religious or moral authority other than that of the Bible as interpreted by individual believers. Baptists also believe a true church can be formed only by a congregation of believing, baptized members who together are the sole source of authority for that congregation.

As a result of this individualistic approach to their faith, Baptists historically have developed into a variety of sects, each espousing a theology that is unique in some way. They are often connected to each other through Baptist associations, which are meetings of delegates from various churches that have agreed to cooperate to achieve certain designated goals. Several Baptist groups have played significant roles in North Carolina's religious history, including the General Baptists, the Free Will Baptists, the Particular Baptists, and the Separate Baptists.

General Baptists are the oldest Baptist group that originated in England. They were so named because of their Arminian belief that the death of Christ was a "general atonement," available to all humans and not just God's "elect." They were tolerant not only of differing beliefs within a congregation but of members whose baptism might have come before an experience of grace. The General Baptist tradition in North Carolina began in the 1720s with the work of Paul Palmer, who established Baptist churches based on the theology of free will, as opposed to the doctrine of predestination advocated by more Calvinistic Baptists at the time.

Free Will Baptists are a remnant of General Baptists in North Carolina and the South. They assumed a separate identity and the name Original Free Will Baptists in about 1828, after having been designated "freewillers" by their detractors as early as 1803. In 1830 the annual meeting of Free Will Baptists divided North Carolina into two conferences—Bethel (Pitt, Wayne, Greene, Orange, and Duplin Counties) and Shiloh (Craven and Beaufort Counties). In 1842, after a number of Free Will Baptists had withdrawn from the Bethel Conference and joined the more ecumenical Campbellites (later the Disciples of Christ), the remnants of both conferences reunited as the General Conference. After the Civil War, a conference for African American Free Will Baptists was organized. As a result, a number of historically black associations of Free Will Baptists continue to exist in North Carolina, particularly in the state's eastern counties.

Particular Baptists emerged during the middle of the eighteenth century, insisting on the concept that salvation was given by God only to those who were chosen and that these individuals were predetermined, leaving no room for individual choice by the believer. For them a church was a closely organized and disciplined congregation of believers who had agreed to accept these concepts as defined in a church covenant. They also insisted that an experience of grace—difficult to define but implying that the believer had been touched by God and was sure of his or her salvation—precede baptism. A particularly antimissionary group of these Baptists became known as Primitive Baptists and dominated Baptist affairs in eastern North Carolina during much of the nineteenth century.

Separate Baptists and their closely related brethren, Missionary Baptists, are rooted in the First Great Awakening of the mid-eighteenth century. Their enthusiasm for the emotional revivalism and missionary activity of the era separated them from other Baptists, including the General and Particular Baptists. Their brand of faith tended to thrive in rural areas of North Carolina. Missionary Baptists responded to the Great Awakening by promoting an increase in missionary work, not only at home but also in many other countries. In doing so, they parted company with the Particular Baptists and went on to win an increasing number of members and become the dominant body of the so-called Regular Baptists, a term used to designate mainstream Baptists. Over time, most Particular, Missionary, and Separate Baptists also became part of the mainstream Baptists.

The Baptist State Convention of North Carolina, formed in 1830, is the largest organization of Baptists in the state. The denomination's activity in the state had grown since the organization of its first association, the Sandy Creek Baptist Association, by Shubal Stearns in 1758. The move toward formal organization as a state Baptist body was gradual. Early attempts were made to provide a permanent apparatus for the support of home and foreign missions by North Carolina Baptists. Each attempt failed, however, and it was determined that a better plan was needed to solicit support from all North Carolina Baptists.

In 1826 such a proposal was made by Martin Ross of the Chowan Association. He died before his proposal came to fruition, but his suggestion was not forgotten. On 26 Mar. 1830 the newly formed North Carolina Baptist Benevolent Society unanimously adopted a resolution that the society be transformed into a state convention. Thomas Meredith presented a draft of a constitution, and it was adopted as he read it, article by article. The objective of the Baptist State Convention was to aid in providing ministerial education and both domestic and foreign mission support.

By the early 2000s, approximately 3,500 churches were affiliated with the Baptist State Convention of North Carolina, which was headquartered in Cary. The convention also supported six educational institutions: Mars Hill College, Gardner-Webb University, Campbell University, Chowan College, Wingate College, and Fruitland Baptist Bible Institute. Early in 1997, Meredith College severed its relationship with the convention rather than continue to allow it even partial control over the college's direction.

The Baptist State Convention of North Carolina supports a weekly periodical, the *Biblical Recorder*, which is published in Raleigh and has provided news and information to North Carolina Baptists since 1835—the year it was founded by Baptist leader Thomas Meredith. Since its founding, the paper has been published continuously except for two brief interruptions, one in the 1840s and the other during the Civil War. The *Biblical Recorder* continues to inform Baptists in the state about issues of concern to the denomination as well as publicize the resource needs of, and opportunities in, missionary work. During the last years of the twentieth century and the first years of the twenty-first, the *Biblical Recorder* also voiced opposition to efforts by some members of the North Carolina General Assembly to liberalize the state's liquor and gambling laws.

The Baptist State Convention of North Carolina also supports several social service institutions, such as the Baptist Children's Homes of North Carolina, the Baptist Retirement Homes of North Carolina, and the North Carolina Baptist Hospital. A variety of mission projects and other agencies have been initiated by the convention, and it was instrumental in the formation of the North Carolina Baptist Historical Society in 1885. The society's constitution invests in its executive committee the responsibility for holding and managing the society's property and providing "a suitable place for preserving books, manuscripts and other materials that may be collected." Now a joint project of Wake Forest University and the state convention, the North Carolina Baptist Historical Collection (formally named the Ethel Taylor Crittenden Collection in Baptist History) is located in a wing of the university's Z. Smith Reynolds Library along with the University Archives.

Many North Carolina Baptists consider themselves part of the wider group known as Southern Baptists, separated from their northern counterparts since the mid-1800s. Much controversy has surrounded the relationship between the Baptist State Convention of North Carolina and the Southern Baptist Convention, which was founded in 1845 and has maintained a theologically conservative stance since the late 1970s. Southeastern Baptist Theological Seminary in Wake Forest became a battleground in the mid-1980s between conservatives (often fundamentalists) and moderates, frustrating many North Carolina Baptists. The state convention, however, has tried to maintain a balance between conservatives and moderates, continuing to focus on the common ground of missionary and philanthropic work.

References: Maloy A. Huggins, *History of North Carolina Baptists, 1727–1932* (1967); George Washington Paschal, *History of North Carolina Baptists* (2 vols., 1938); Robert G. Torbet, *A History of the Baptists* (1950).

Anne Moore
James I. Martin Sr.
Additional research provided by
Lloyd Johnson, Glenn Jonas, and Michael R. Pelt.

SEE ALSO Cragmont Assembly; Kehukee Baptist Association; New Lights; North Carolina Baptist Historical Collection; Sandy Creek Baptist Association.

Barbecue is one of North Carolina's most popular foods as well as a beloved cultural icon. The word is thought to have entered the English language through the Spanish, who encountered in the West Indies the Taino (Arawakan) word "barbacoa," for a method of drying meat over a fire on a frame of wooden sticks. By the late 1600s, at about the time settlers introduced swine to the northeastern Albemarle area of North Carolina, English speakers began using the word "barbecue" to denote the wooden grill used widely by Indians and depicted by Jacques Le Moyne and John White in drawings in the previous century. North Carolinians probably had discovered the usefulness of this apparatus for cooking pork by 1728, when William Byrd wrote, "The only business here is raising of Hogs, which is manag'd with the least Trouble, and affords the Diet they are most fond of." In North Carolina, the unmodified noun "barbecue" has come to mean not just the grill or the method of cooking but also the pork cooked.

Grudging agreement on usage, however, has not prevented North Carolinians from engaging in generations-long arguments about which style of barbecue can truly be considered worthy of the state. North Carolinians in the Coastal Plain generally understand barbecue to refer to its simplest and eldest form: a split hog roasted over a pit of coals, basted with a mixture of cider vinegar, red pepper, and salt, and then boned,

A traditional North Carolina barbecue meal, with pulled pork, coleslaw, hush puppies, fried squash, hot sauce, and iced tea. Photograph courtesy of North Carolina Division of Tourism, Film, and Sports Development.

A barbecue cook in Franklin County applies sauce to pigs being grilled over an open pit, ca. 1941. Photograph by Albert Barden. NCC.

chopped, or shredded and seasoned further with the basting sauce. The modern-day "pig pickin'" is representative of this barbecue style. Few commercial barbecue pits today are dug in the ground, and mass-produced pepper sauces are often applied after cooking, but a whole hog sopped with locally made vinegar-pepper formulas remains the recipe of choice for most pig pickin' devotees. In some areas, bits of skin are considered integral to the finished product. In the southeastern quadrant of the state, as in eastern South Carolina, Worcestershire sauce, sweeteners, and other ingredients are often added to the basic vinegar and pepper mixture. Baked corn sticks, fried hush puppies, Brunswick stew, and white or yellow coleslaw (often added to barbecue sandwiches) are common side dishes.

Lexington, home to a popular barbecue festival, is the inspirational center of the western-style barbecue of the Piedmont and Mountains, where chopped or sliced pork shoulders or butts with a thin, tomato-based sauce are favored. Economy, fastidiousness, and health regulations prevent many vendors from basting with this more-combustible sauce, but it is served at table; hence its popular name, "dip." Hush puppies and red coleslaw ("barbecue slaw"), colored with ketchup or dip, are common accompaniments. On the fringes of its range, Lexington-style barbecue merges with the red barbecues of adjacent states.

A third style of barbecue, pork with mustard-based sauce, has crossed the South Carolina line and found admirers farther north. Some North Carolinians also follow their southern neighbors in segregating skin, the dry "outside meat," and the juicier "inside meat." The fourth variety of barbecue common in North Carolina and confined to no area in particular is a composite of midwestern and other regional specialties: practically any meat chunked, chopped, or sliced, covered in one of a multitude of thick homemade or store-bought tomato-based barbecue sauces, and grilled over an open flame. Even the most open-minded partisans of this style seldom use the term barbecue alone for chicken or ribs, which are usually prepared with the same sauces.

By the early twenty-first century, native and immigrant varieties of barbecue had merged, evolved, and traveled widely within and without North Carolina. All contained generous amounts of salt, cholesterol, tars, and saturated fats, substances known or suspected to be harmful. Nevertheless, North Carolina barbecue has kept its several identities through change, neglect, and rediscovery, and its following has continued to grow despite occasional health fads and alarms.

References: Marion Brown, *Marion Brown's Southern Cookbook* (1968); Lolis Eric Elie, *Smokestack Lightning: Adventures in the Heart of Barbecue Country* (1996); Bob Garner, *Bob Garner's Guide to North Carolina Barbecue* (2002); Ernest Matthew Mickler, *White Trash Cooking* (1986); Manuel Roig-Franzia, "On N.C. Barbecue, East and West Don't Meet—Except to Argue," *Washington Post*, 23 May 2005.

Wynne Dough

Barbers. By the time North Carolina was colonized, the French custom of having barbers do surgery was never practiced in the colonies. Striped barber poles were abandoned, only to be revived by the appearance of barber shops as a business following the Civil War. Although haircutting was practiced by specialists in ancient civilizations such as Egypt, it was not regarded as a career in early North Carolina. Among the upper classes, people were hired to cut hair in order to improve a person's appearance. Members of the lower classes generally relied on the help of friends and family, with most men depending on the haircutting skills of their wives or daughters. Shaving was a personal task, the need for which was reduced by many men by growing a beard that could be cut only after it grew long. Straight razors were available, as were stones and leather straps on which they were sharpened. Safety razors, a later invention, did not become popular until the early twentieth century.

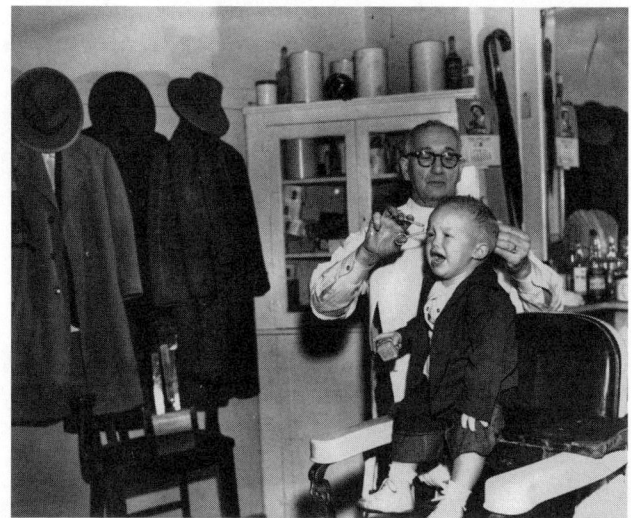

A North Carolina barber at work (date unknown). Courtesy of NCOA&H.

Slaveholders frequently used individual slaves as house laborers, drawing on their ability to perform many functions, including haircutting. As the wearing of wigs was never practiced in North Carolina as an aid to attractiveness, talents such as haircutting were in demand. Slaves' success as haircutters sometimes led to their freedom: at the end of the Civil War, there were 25 freed blacks who practiced the profession of barbering. Working at the house of the customer, they practiced the only profession that was open to blacks at that time.

At the start of the twentieth century, shops specializing in haircuts and shaves spread throughout the state. These were generally open to male customers only, while women went to separate establishments called beauty shops or parlors. Barbershops served at times as male sanctuaries, private clubs for male companionship often being unavailable to the majority of men. Social and political as well as tonsorial reasons often were motivations for visits to barbershops.

Specialized barber chairs, lifted by gears and later by hydraulic power, were often installed. Boards were placed across the arms of the chairs for young patrons. Early haircutting was confined to scissor cutting, although clippers appeared at about the same time as barbershops. Early hand-operated clippers caused many barbers to complain of arthritic hands. These early clippers were replaced by the electric versions that have remained almost unchanged from their original appearance. The shops also provided showers, and a bath with hot water was much more desirable than the cold water found in the majority of homes. Perfumed products such as hair tonics and soaps were used, and Bay Rum was the standard aftershave lotion.

After World War II, new types of establishments appeared that had great growth in the latter part of the century. So-called unisex hair dressing shops offered a variety of styles not available in the older barbershops. Haircuts in the latest styles were available at a cost of five to ten times the barbershop rate. The new shops also worked by appointment, which had great appeal for employed people and busy professionals.

Although barbershops of the old style still existed in North Carolina by the early 2000s, their number had declined precipitously. Modern unisex hairstyle businesses, often large chains, could be found in practically every North Carolina mall. As the ambiance of the old barbershops has been replaced by the largely impersonal service of the newer establishments, some social observers have concluded that the freewheeling conversation on which democracy thrives has been markedly diminished.

References: Robert Archibald, "The Barber, Baker, Candlemaker Help Create Community," *St. Louis Business Journal* 17 (9 Dec. 1996); Michael Kermap, "Short on the Top, Clippers on the Side and Taper the Back," *Smithsonian* (May 1991).

William S. Powell

Barber-Scotia College was founded in Concord in 1867 as Scotia Seminary, a Presbyterian preparatory school for young, newly freed African American women. For more than a generation the institute prepared these women to become teachers, social workers, and members of other professions. Over time the school grew, and significant changes in programs and policy were initiated. In 1916 the curriculum was expanded and the school's name changed to Scotia's Women's College. In 1930 the college merged with Barber Memorial College of Anniston, Ala., and the name Barber-Scotia College was adopted two years later. The first bachelor's degrees were awarded by Barber-Scotia in 1945.

Barber-Scotia College became coeducational in 1954. By the early 2000s the college was an accredited four-year liberal arts institution, continuing its historical relationship with the Presbyterian Church (U.S.A.). The student population continues to be primarily from North Carolina and South Carolina, although students have come from many states, the U.S. Virgin Islands, and several foreign countries.

References: "Barber-Scotia College," in W. Augustus Low and Virgil A. Clift, eds., *Encyclopedia of Black America* (1981); "Barber-Scotia Junior College," *Crisis* 49 (August 1942); Charles I. Brown, "The Male Student at Barber-Scotia College," *Quarterly Review of Higher Education among Negroes* 25 (July 1957).

Charles W. Wadelington

Bare Boxing Incident. The loose structure of government institutions in colonial North Carolina at times resulted in lapses of decorum that appear outrageous and humorous from a modern perspective. An early example of the sometimes coarse behavior of the colony's leaders was that of several members of the North Carolina Council during the Tuscarora Indian War (1711–13).

John Barnwell, an ally from South Carolina who was bringing troops to assist his northern neighbor, arrived in the colony in April 1712. Soon after his arrival he reported to the council, then in session in Perquimans Precinct (a section of the original County of Albemarle). To celebrate the occasion two or three members provided alcohol-laden punch. Present were Governor Edward Hyde, Councilman Thomas Boyd, and the Reverend John Urmston, an Anglican missionary. After drinking the potent punch for an extended time, the council voted on resolutions and addresses of thanks, then soon "strip'd naked & boxt it fairly two & two, all the same day." Paired off were Hyde and Boyd, Urmston and Hyde (who was also Speaker of the Council), and the provost marshal with another assemblyman. Neither the outcome of the matches nor the visiting Barnwell's reaction to them are known, although it can be surmised that little official business was attended to after the boxing had begun.

Reference: John Barnwell to "Your Honr," 20 Apr. 1712, "The Tuscarora Expedition: Letters of Colonel John Barnwell," *South Carolina Historical and Genealogical Magazine* (January 1908).

William S. Powell

Bark, generally from oak trees, was an unusual export to Great Britain from the forests of the Carolina-Virginia backcountry in the eighteenth century. As new regions were inhabited, bark from numerous felled oak trees became valuable as a source of tannic acid used in tanning the large number of deerskins and other pelts being shipped to England at that time. Edward Moseley's 1738 map of North Carolina included bark as one of the colony's significant products.

Stripping bark from logs, however, appears to have been a lengthy process. The *Virginia Gazette* of 18 Dec. 1766 referred to bark mills and bark pits in Edenton, as well as to bark houses where the bark was stored prior to local use or shipment. Thomas Hart of Hillsborough advertised in 1779 that he had for sale "a Tan yard with three or four hundred hides now in tan bark-houses &c." In June 1781 George Hartmann of Salem went to Salisbury to haul bark, presumably for use in the tannery operated by the Moravians.

William S. Powell

Barns have been used in North Carolina to protect farm animals and store crops and farm equipment since the early days of European settlement. The design of a barn was strongly related to the immigrant ethnic group who built it. In the 1600s the English constructed their primitive dwellings without using floor plans and using only unfamiliar local materials. The Germans (Lutheran, Moravian, and Reformed Protestants of diverse European origin) who settled into the sparsely populated western Piedmont region in the late seventeenth century built barns similar to European hillside barns, which

Looping tobacco in Granville County, ca. 1930. Photograph by Albert Barden. NCC.

allowed for easy access to upper levels. There was also the *Grundscheier*, a ground barn that was a single-level structure with two log cribs separated by the threshing. At about the same time, Scotch-Irish immigrants came to North Carolina, bringing their unique style of architecture to the land. In the late nineteenth century, as farming became more technologically advanced, barn designs became less individual and more practical.

The size of a barn usually indicates the size of the farm on which it stands. The hill country of Appalachia and the western region of North Carolina were earlier known for crib barns, the simplest barn structure of all—a pen or crib made of rough logs held together at the corners by notches. On larger farms in the same region, cantilevered double-crib barns with lofts overhanging the cribs (usually in the front and back) were common. The lofts were used for hay storage.

The barn most easily identified with North Carolina, having changed little over several decades, is the flue-cured tobacco barn. These square buildings typically measure from 16 to 20 feet per side, with a height of around 20 feet. Tobacco barns were at one time so numerous in the state that an astute ob-

server counted 200 of them on a 60-mile stretch of Highway 86 from Hillsborough to Danville, Va. These buildings were constructed in relation to roads, fields, and other farm buildings and were never placed near a house. The construction of one was a major social event, taking 12 to 15 men an entire day.

Early flue-cured tobacco barns resembled log cabins, especially in their small size (about 16 square feet). Like cabins, they were square log buildings (constructed using similar notching techniques) with no floor plan, and the spaces between their logs were filled with mud or mortar chinking. They had gabled roofs and a door in the center. The internal structural supports had to bear the inside load as well as withstand strong windstorms. Since bundled tobacco leaves are hung in tiers and fresh tobacco is 80 percent water, the internal structure of a tobacco barn 20 square feet in size must support nearly five tons of weight. The inside also had to be airtight, as ventilation control was critical to proper curing. Some tobacco barns had sheds alongside that served three purposes: they provided a shady place for the stringing operation during the very hot harvest months of July through September; they protected the furnace from rain; and they gave shelter to the attendant who slept overnight at the barn during the curing process.

While the earlier tobacco barns were constructed of pine logs, later builders were forced to try other materials because of the scarcity of good pine; their efforts generally proved unsatisfactory. Frame barns were poorly insulated and needed siding; sheet metal was used, but this wasted heat. Stucco did not allow moisture to escape, and many buildings made of this material simply collapsed. By 1925, Coastal Plain tobacco barns were being built of concrete, which provided a superior method of construction. In the Piedmont region, however, the newer frame barns could not compare to the high quality of the older log tobacco barns.

References: W. A. Foster and D. G. Carter, *Farm Buildings* (1922); Amos Long, *Farmsteads and Their Buildings* (1972).

Laura Harris

Barton College, originally called Atlantic Christian College, dates to 1886, when the Committee on Education for the Disciples of Christ expressed a desire to establish a collegiate institute in North Carolina. Predecessors to Atlantic Christian College included Carolina Christian Institute (Beaufort County) and Carolina Christian College (Pitt County). In 1901 the North Carolina Christian Missionary Convention (Disciples of Christ) acquired Kinsey Seminary in Wilson, which had opened in 1897 but closed four years later. In 1902 Atlantic Christian College was incorporated by the state of North Carolina and opened in September of that year with 107 students (20 men, 87 women) and seven faculty. The following year Carolina Christian College in Ayden closed, and the land and buildings were sold. Among the first instructors at Atlantic Christian was Abdullah Ben Kori, a Syrian linguist who supervised the Language Department. Atlantic Christian inaugurated a four-year curriculum in 1923 and was accredited by the Southern Association of Colleges and Schools in 1953.

In 1990, in recognition of Barton Warren Stone (1772–1844), one of the progenitors of the Disciples of Christ denomination—and also in an attempt to dispel any perceptions of fundamentalism—Atlantic Christian changed its name to Barton College. The school in the early 2000s enrolled approximately 1,300 students representing 26 states and 24 foreign countries. Barton awards the Bachelor of Arts, Bachelor of Science, Bachelor of Fine Arts, Bachelor of Liberal Studies, Bachelor of Science in Nursing, and Bachelor of Social Work degrees. The college also offers Lifelong Education and Weekend College Programs, along with study abroad opportunities in Japan, South Korea, and Switzerland. From one building on a five-acre campus, the college has come to include 23 buildings on a 32-acre main campus, with an athletic complex located on an additional 30-acre tract.

Barton College's presidents since its inception have in-

cluded James Caswell Coggins (1902–4), namesake of the Coggins Cup for academic achievement; John James Harper (1904–8), who gave Atlantic Christian College its name and was honored, along with other members of his family, with the dedication of Harper Hall in 1950; and Howard Stevens Hilley (1920–49), a Rhodes scholar and Oxford graduate who, during his lengthy tenure, witnessed the construction of the Hardy Alumni Hall (1935), the gymnasium (1935–39), and Howard Chapel (1939).

References: Griffith Hamlin, "Educational Activities of the Disciples of Christ in North Carolina, 1852–1902," *NCHR* 23 (July 1956); Charles Crossfield Ware, *A History of Atlantic Christian College: Culture in Coastal Carolina* (1956).

James I. Martin Sr.

SEE ALSO Carolina Christian College.

Baseball has been popular in North Carolina since the late nineteenth century. Baseball's antecedent, rounders, was widely played in antebellum North Carolina. Modern baseball was apparently introduced to North Carolina during the Civil War by Union troops, who played the game as prisoners at Salisbury Prison and in other places. Baseball spread rapidly across the state in the years after the war. By the end of the nineteenth century, virtually every town in North Carolina had one or more amateur or semiprofessional teams, and the game was a mainstay on college and high school campuses. North Carolina became a hotbed of textile league baseball during the first half of the twentieth century.

Professional minor leagues became a fixture in North Carolina, with more than 70 cities and towns hosting a team at one

A play from the Durham Bulls–Scranton Barons game at the Durham Bulls Athletic Park, 25 May 2003. Photograph by Sara Davis. *Durham Herald-Sun.*

time or another, a total surpassed only by Texas. The Piedmont League (1920–55) and the Carolina League, started in 1945, are among the more successful North Carolina–based minor leagues. Durham attorney William G. Bramham was president of the National Association of Professional Baseball Leagues, the governing body of the minor leagues, from 1932 to 1946. During this period the association was headquartered in Durham.

North Carolina is the birthplace of about 300 major league baseball players, including six members of the sport's Hall of Fame: Luke Appling (High Point), Rick Ferrell (Durham), Jim "Catfish" Hunter (Hertford), Buck Leonard (Rocky Mount), Enos Slaughter (Roxboro), and Hoyt Wilhelm (Huntersville). Leonard played in the Negro Leagues during the period when organized baseball was racially segregated. Although the Negro Leagues did not have an extensive minor league system, some North Carolina cities did have black minor league teams. North Carolina's minor leagues were integrated in the 1950s, as were most of the state's college and high school teams in the next decade.

Minor league baseball in the state experienced a boom during the 1980s, when the Durham Bulls received national attention by way of the hit movie *Bull Durham* (1988), starring Kevin Costner, Susan Sarandon, and Tim Robbins. In 1998, after 45 seasons in the Carolina League, the Bulls joined the International League as a Class-AAA affiliate of the Tampa Bay Devil Rays. By the early 2000s the state was home to 9 minor league teams, a far cry from the 49 teams that operated in 1949. In addition to the Bulls, North Carolina's minor league teams were the Asheville Tourists (Class-A, Colorado Rockies), the Winston-Salem Warthogs (Class-A, Chicago White Sox), the Greensboro Grasshoppers (Class-A, Florida Marlins), the Burlington Indians (rookie team, Cleveland Indians), the Kannapolis Intimidators (Class-A, Chicago White Sox), the Charlotte Knights (Class-AAA, Chicago White Sox), the Kinston Indians (Class-A, Cleveland Indians), and the Carolina Mudcats (Class-AA, Florida Marlins).

Youth baseball leagues continue to thrive in North Carolina, and college baseball remains a popular sport, although not at the level of college basketball and football. Adult recreational baseball has been largely superseded by the more accessible sport of slow-pitch softball.

References: J. Chris Holaday, *Professional Baseball in North Carolina: An Illustrated City-by-City History, 1901–1996* (1998); Jim Sumner, *A History of Sports in North Carolina* (1990).

Jim L. Sumner

Basketball. The game of basketball is much more than a popular spectator and participant sport in North Carolina. Like football in other southern states such as Texas and Alabama, basketball is a statewide obsession that cannot be understood purely by focusing on the histories of individual players, coaches, and teams, statistics for participation in youth and recreational leagues, or other traditional measures. From the sport's first appearance in the late 1890s, basketball has been a vibrant and influential strand in North Carolina's cultural fabric.

The date of the first organized basketball game in North Carolina is not known, but the sport initially appeared in local YMCAs during the 1890s, possibly through the efforts of Charlotte YMCA official John Mahan, who had played in the first games organized in Springfield, Mass., by basketball's inventor, James Naismith. Within a few years, the game was being played at virtually every level of competition. Amateur and recreational games were sponsored by the YMCA and Amateur Athletic Union, and schools were encouraged to adopt the game as a part of their physical education programs. The North Carolina High School Athletic Association was founded in 1912 and has sanctioned state basketball championships since 1915. By 1920 virtually every college and university in the state had a men's team.

Records conflict about the date and location of the first intercollegiate men's game played in the state, but it seems certain that Wake Forest College was one of the participants. Information from that school's archives points to a game played on 6 Feb. 1906 at Guilford College in which the home team defeated Wake Forest by a 26-19 score. But official athletic department records at Duke University (then Trinity College) state that the first game in the state was played between Trinity and Wake Forest on 2 Mar. 1906, with Wake Forest prevailing 24-10.

Basketball was a popular addition to student life at North Carolina's women's colleges from its earliest years of existence. By the 1920s girls' high school teams were also widespread. The first recorded intercollegiate game in Charlotte was played in April 1907 between two women's colleges, Elizabeth College and Presbyterian College; reporters from the *Charlotte Observer* described the game from second-hand accounts, however, because no one from the all-male reporting staff was allowed to observe. While female athletes were expected to dress modestly on the court during this period, usually in skirts and bloomers, basketball offered young women a rare opportunity for equal access until the 1950s, when they were increasingly steered into more "feminine" activities such as cheerleading. Nevertheless, the women's Hanes Hosiery team of Winston-Salem earned national acclaim by winning the National American Amateur Association championship in 1951, 1952, and 1953.

The Southern Conference, Everett Case, and the Rise of the "Big Four"

While the game spread quickly at all levels throughout North Carolina, it was the remarkable popularity of college basketball that came to define the history of the sport in the state. In the early years, games were generally played between local schools, but in the 1910s and 1920s North Carolina teams also competed against teams from Tennessee, Virginia, South Carolina, and Georgia. The first significant effort to organize competition between college teams came when the Southern Conference was founded in 1921 with 14 charter members, including the University of North Carolina and North Carolina State College. UNC was the winner of the first Southern Conference Tournament in 1922, led by Cartwright Carmichael, the university's first All-American athlete in any sport (1923). With the realignment of the Southern Conference in the 1930s, intrastate rivalries among basketball teams increased as Davidson College and Wake Forest College joined the league.

There was no formal national tournament or championship in these early years of the game, but the press often recognized national champions based on the results of games between top regional teams. The University of North Carolina's 1924 team, led by Carmichael and fellow All-American Jack Cobb, won all 26 of its games and was voted national champion by the Helms Athletic Foundation. In 1926 Cobb went on to become the first national player of the year to play for a North Carolina college or university.

Duke University moved to elevate the profile of its sports programs by joining the Southern Conference in 1928. In that year Eddie Cameron became the school's head basketball coach, and he went on to establish the program as an annual front-runner in the league, delivering its first conference championship in 1938. Cameron coached at Duke for 14 years before becoming athletic director at the school. Legend has it that Cameron drew up plans for the university's indoor basketball stadium on the cover of a matchbook in 1935; the stadium was rededicated in Cameron's name in 1972. As the home of the "Cameron Crazies," as Duke's enthusiastic student fans are popularly known, Cameron Indoor Stadium is now regarded as one of the most exciting venues to watch any sport, collegiate or professional, in the nation.

In 1946 two significant events marked the start of a transition for the sport in North Carolina. First, UNC finished second in the 1946 National Collegiate Athletic Association (NCAA) tournament. Horace "Bones" McKinney, a schoolboy star from Durham who began his college days at North Carolina State before transferring to Chapel Hill, was a key player on that team; he went on to become a successful coach at Wake Forest College in the 1950s and 1960s, as well as one of the most colorful basketball personalities in the state. Also in 1946, North Carolina State hired Everett Case, an Indiana high school coach, as its head coach. At the time, North Carolina State's program lagged behind Duke, UNC, and Wake Forest, but Case quickly changed the tone in Raleigh, and with it, the place of the sport in the state.

Everett Case, nicknamed the Old Gray Fox, and his North Carolina State basketball team after defeating Wake Forest 82–80 at Reynolds Coliseum in Raleigh to win the first ACC title on 6 Mar. 1954. *Raleigh News and Observer.*

Case was known for meticulous game preparation, fast-paced tempo on offense, and high-pressure defense, and his teams quickly established dominance over archrival UNC, including 15 consecutive wins in a six-year span during the late 1940s and early 1950s. More important, Case recognized that if he wanted to lure the best athletes to his program year after year, he would have to change the way the sport and the college were perceived. He spoke freely with the media and relentlessly sold himself and his team to the general public, making a show of such things as pregame player introductions and encouraging previously unknown traditions such as cutting down the basketball nets after big wins. Case also insisted that North Carolina State build a new arena that would showcase the program. When Reynolds Coliseum was completed in 1949, it seated more than 12,400 fans—by far the most of any venue in the state or region—and regularly boasted attendance figures greater than those at Madison Square Garden in New York City. With the opening of the new arena, one prominent local sports editor opined that Raleigh had become "the basketball capital of the world."

With the new venue for his program complete, Case spearheaded the creation of a new tournament, the Dixie Classic, to be held at Reynolds Coliseum each December. The single-elimination tournament featured the state's "Big Four" Southern Conference teams—Duke, UNC, Wake Forest, and North Carolina State—against four of the best teams in the country. The tournament, which was played for 12 years before being canceled in the wake of a point-shaving scandal, proved enormously popular not just with students and alumni around the state but with the general public, who followed games on statewide radio. Closely fought games not only cemented rivalries among the Big Four schools but also raised the national profile of the teams, elevating them to a level above other Southern Conference programs and putting them on par with contemporary national powerhouses such as Kansas, Kentucky, and Indiana.

The Atlantic Coast Conference Takes Center Stage

In 1953 North Carolina's Big Four left the unwieldy Southern Conference to become charter members of the new Atlantic Coast Conference (ACC) with three other teams; an eighth team was added later that same year. While the main impetus for the shift in conference alignment was to group the best football programs from the Southern Conference in a new league, in the following decades the ACC became known instead as the premier college basketball conference in the country. With the start of the new conference looming, UNC determined it could no longer abide the basketball dominance of Case's North Carolina State teams. Case had successfully established a pipeline that brought the best talent from around the nation (and particularly from his home state of Indiana) to Raleigh, including players such as Norm Sloan and Vic Bubas, who went on to become prominent coaches at North Carolina State and Duke, respectively. UNC responded in 1953 by hiring a coach who could establish a talent pipeline of his own: New York City's Frank McGuire, who left a successful program at St. John's University to lead the Tar Heels.

McGuire, with his "underground railroad" of New York area talent, took only a few years to build a program that rivaled Case's. Case's and McGuire's teams regularly played close contests on the court, and the two coaches extended the rivalry by taking sometimes pointed jabs at one another in comments to reporters. Local sportswriters thrived on the appearance of hostility between the two outspoken men, building them into personalities that rivaled other prominent sports figures of the day. The teams traded wins throughout the 1950s, with the underdog in each meeting routinely upsetting the higher-ranked team. But in 1957 McGuire achieved the ultimate success. Led by star forward and Bronx native Lennie Rosenbluth —a player Case recruited but decided not to sign— McGuire's Tar Heels finished an incredible 32-0 to win the first NCAA championship for a basketball program in the state, besting a Wilt Chamberlain–led Kansas team 54-53 in a final game that featured three overtime periods. Rosenbluth went on to earn first-team All-American honors and was named Helms Foundation National Player of the Year.

UNC's championship was a watershed for basketball in North Carolina for many reasons, but perhaps the most significant is that it helped cement ties between the sport and television broadcasting in the state. In 1955 public television station UNC-TV made a UNC-Wake Forest basketball game its first experimental broadcast, shown on delay from Woollen Gymnasium in Chapel Hill. McGuire supported the experiment, which was also encouraged by Philadelphia-based sports television pioneer C. D. Chesley. When UNC earned its berth in the 1957 Final Four, Chesley returned to his friend McGuire for support as he quickly assembled a small network of fledgling television stations in North Carolina to broadcast the games from Kansas City. The broadcasts were an enormous success in the state, turning the UNC coaches and players into media stars. Among those who watched the broadcasts were executives from Pilot Life Insurance in Greensboro, who quickly arranged to sponsor a series of 10 ACC games to be televised the following season over the same small network. The network grew quickly in subsequent years to cover much of the state and region, which further increased the league's local media exposure and helped expand its popularity.

Recruitment of out-of-state players increased during this period, further improving the quality of the game and the national reputation of North Carolina basketball. Bones McKinney, who became the head coach at Wake Forest in 1957, brought two-time All-American Len Chappell to his program and led the Demon Deacons to ACC titles in 1961 and 1962 as well as the 1962 Final Four. From 1969 to 1971 McKinney also coached the state's first professional franchise, the Carolina Cougars of the American Basketball Association (ABA). In 1959 Duke University hired former North Carolina State player and assistant coach Vic Bubas to become the program's head coach. Bubas recruited players such as Art Heyman, Jeff Mullins, and Bob Verga to Durham, and they rewarded their coach with three trips to the NCAA Final Four in four years from 1962 to 1966. But while Duke and Wake Forest surged, the programs at North Carolina State and UNC suffered a series of major scandals that resulted in NCAA sanctions. Case weathered the storms until 1964, when poor health forced him to resign only two games into the season. When Case left North Carolina State, McGuire had already been gone from the ACC for three years. In 1961, after he saw his program placed on NCAA probation for offering illegal benefits to recruits, McGuire left UNC for a position as head coach of the National Basketball Association's (NBA) Philadelphia Warriors. By all accounts, supporters of the UNC program were eager to see McGuire leave, but few would have predicted the astounding success of their next coach, Dean Smith.

Basketball and Civil Rights

Men's college basketball in the state underwent another dramatic transformation beginning in the late 1960s, when previously all-white college teams began recruiting black players. Prior to and after racial integration, North Carolina's African American colleges attracted numerous outstanding collegians. Cal Irvin at North Carolina A&T, John McClendon at North Carolina College (later North Carolina Central University), and Clarence "Big House" Gaines at Winston-Salem State University established extremely successful programs. Gaines coached Winston-Salem State to the NCAA Division II National Championship in 1967.

Given the popularity and prominence of ACC basketball, when North Carolina's Big Four began recruiting African American athletes, it marked a sea change. Wake Forest's Norwood Todman became the first black scholarship player to take the court when he joined that school's freshman team in 1966. Then, in 1967, UNC's Charlie Scott became the first African American to play varsity basketball in the ACC; he went on to lead the program to back-to-back Final Four appearances in 1968 and 1969. In 1971 Wake Forest's Charlie Davis became the first African American player to be named ACC Player of the Year.

After several decades of decline, women's basketball received a new spark in the state when the U.S. Congress passed the Education Amendment Act in 1972. The law, popularly known as Title IX, mandated increased spending on women's collegiate athletic programs and led to the development of scholarship basketball programs on most of the state's college campuses. The majority of North Carolina's high schools followed suit and began to support girls' teams again. Many credit Title IX with the success of women's college basketball in North Carolina and the United States today. North Carolina's ACC and other teams have been some of the strongest in the nation. The UNC women's basketball team, coached by Sylvia Hatchell, won the 1994 NCAA women's championship, and N.C. State head coach Kay Yow coached the U.S. Olympic women's team to the 1988 gold medal. Duke University's women's team under coach Gail Goestenkors reached the NCAA Final Four in 2002 and 2003. Many of the state's female college players have gone on to play professionally in the United States and overseas.

While the story is less well known, basketball has also proven to be a major source of community pride among the Lumbee Indians in the southeastern region of the state. The college gymnasium at Pembroke State College, for many years the only four-year college in the nation for American Indians, hosted a basketball league for local athletes. The most accomplished Lumbee basketball player was John "Ned" Sampson, who Duke All-American Dick Groat once called the best athlete he had ever competed against. Sampson went on to become head coach at Pembroke State College. His players there included his son, Kelvin, a four-time letter winner who went on to a successful career as a head coach at the University of Oklahoma.

North Carolina NCAA Champions and Charlotte's Professional Franchises

The men's 1974 NCAA Final Four was held in Greensboro, where N.C. State, coached by Norm Sloan, upended seven-time defending champion UCLA in a dramatic semifinal game and captured the championship against Marquette. Sloan's Wolfpack team was led by schoolboy legend and Boiling Springs native David Thompson, a three-time All-American who today is generally regarded as the greatest high school and collegiate player the state has produced. Two years later, UNC coach Dean Smith led the U.S. men's team to the Olympic Gold Medal in basketball, with a squad that included several UNC players—among them Rocky Mount's Phil Ford, UNC's own three-time All-American and 1978 National Player of the Year. Smith, whose legendary system stressed unselfish team play, intelligent decision making, and precision passing, also coached UNC to the NCAA championship in 1982 and 1993 before retiring in 1997 with the most wins (879) in NCAA Division I coaching history. Smith's 1982 championship was famously won with two plays involving North Carolinians—the game-winning shot by then-freshman and Wilmington native Michael Jordan, and an errant pass secured by Gastonia native James Worthy. Worthy would go on to a successful career with the Los Angeles Lakers of the NBA. Jordan used his three-year career at UNC as the launching pad for even greater heights, becoming arguably the most famous male athlete of all time, in any sport, after a long career in professional basketball with the NBA Chicago Bulls and Washington Wizards. The list of other North Carolina natives who have gone on to success in college and professional basketball grows longer by the year.

North Carolina State, coached by Jim Valvano, surprised the basketball world by capturing the NCAA title again in 1983, defeating the University of Houston 54-52 in what many consider the greatest upset in NCAA tournament history. Duke coach Mike Krzyzewski arrived in Durham in 1981 and subsequently coached the Blue Devils to numerous Final Four appearances, winning NCAA titles in 1991, 1992, and 2001 with teams that stressed defensive intensity and excellent perimeter shooting. In 2005 Asheville native Roy Williams coached UNC to the school's fourth national title.

North Carolina's first major professional basketball team, the Carolina Cougars, played in the ABA from 1969 through 1974. The Cougars divided their home games among Charlotte, Greensboro, and Raleigh, boasting a roster than included many players who had starred at local area colleges. The Cougars enjoyed good attendance and fair success on the court until owners moved the franchise to St. Louis in 1975. The Charlotte Hornets returned professional play to the state in 1988, greeted by an enthusiastic reception by fans. But a series of disputes between the team's owners and Charlotte leaders led the owners to relocate the franchise to New Orleans in 2002. A second NBA franchise, the Charlotte Bobcats, began play in 2004 under owner Robert Johnson, the first African American to own a major professional sports franchise. As a franchise in the Women's National Basketball Association, the Charlotte Sting played their first season in the summer of 1997, during which they achieved a 15-13 record and earned a trip to the playoffs.

References: Smith Barrier, *On Tobacco Road: Basketball in North Carolina* (1983); Tim Brayboy and Bruce Barton, *Playing before an*

Michael Jordan, as a UNC freshman, launches the winning shot against the Georgetown Hoyas in the 1982 NCAA championship game in New Orleans. Photograph by Allen Dean Steele. *Raleigh News and Observer*.

Overflow Crowd: The Story of Indian Basketball in Robeson, North Carolina, and Adjoining Counties (2002); Pamela Grundy, *Learning to Win: Sports, Education, and Social Change in Twentieth-Century North Carolina* (2001); Joe Menzer, *Four Corners: How UNC, N.C. State, Duke, and Wake Forest Made North Carolina the Center of the Basketball Universe* (2004); Ron Morris, *ACC Basketball: An Illustrated History* (1988); Jim L. Sumner, *A History of Sports in North Carolina* (1990).

Mark Simpson-Vos

Basket Making has likely been a part of North Carolina's history as long as human beings have inhabited the region. Although the fragility of basket materials means that few related artifacts still exist, the Native Americans of North Carolina's Paleo-Indian period (13,000 B.C. to 8000 B.C.) probably used baskets that they constructed from native materials for transporting items and gathering food. Archaeological evidence confirms that Indians used baskets widely in the early archaic period (8000 B.C. to 6000 B.C.). Basket making presumably spread as settlements stabilized and agricultural practices developed. Observations from the De Soto and Pardo expeditions in the sixteenth century note the existence of baskets among Southern Appalachian Indians. Early eighteenth-century ac-

counts by European explorers and traders describe a developed Indian basket-making tradition.

Basket-making traditions from the eighteenth century to the modern era in North Carolina possess Native American, European, and African origins. The history of the craft reflects social, economic, and environmental changes faced by its practitioners. The variety of cultures in the state influenced each other. Older forms of basket making were adapted to newer materials even as older basket makers passed on their knowledge and traditions to younger generations. Baskets were an essential part of most households into the early twentieth century, used for gathering, storing, transporting, and measuring. Basket makers typically made their baskets after the planting or harvesting seasons and used such indigenous materials to color them as bloodroot (orange), yellow root (yellow), black walnut (brown), and butternut (black).

Once crucial to the agricultural and fishing economies of North Carolina, basket making diminished in importance during the twentieth century as inexpensive and readily available galvanized buckets, plastic containers, and paper bags became popular for gathering, transporting, and storing household items. Although no longer crucial to the typical North Carolina household, the basket-making tradition continues.

Baskets are part of a vibrant material folk culture and arts and crafts movement and a core part of Cherokee economic development programs. Indian and artisan cooperatives continue to bring new attention to North Carolina's basket-making tradition.

Traditional North Carolina baskets include several types made from native materials. White oak split baskets were made from pliable and sturdy young white oak trees, which had straight bark that yielded easily. Basket makers cut trees into sections and divided the sections into narrow strips called splits. The basket maker weaved the splits around a rib frame constructed of larger oak strips. White oak split baskets dominated basket making in North Carolina due to the tree's abundance, strength, and durability. Baskets made by Thurman Strickland, winner of a North Carolina Folk Heritage Award in 1991, typify the state's split oak tradition.

Rivercane baskets, made from the once-plentiful plant that thrived along the banks of North Carolina's rivers and streams, were primarily made by the Cherokee Indians. They harvested rivercane after it reached eight feet in height, peeling off the outer layer and soaking the cane to make it pliable. The Cherokee wove in single- and double-weave patterns. Emma Taylor and Eva Wolfe, 1989 North Carolina Folk Heritage Award recipients, continue to work in the Cherokee rivercane basket-making tradition. Honeysuckle baskets did not become popular until the twentieth century. Not a strong material, honeysuckle is best suited for decorative baskets. Coiled baskets made from rye straw, broomcorn, and pine needles were popular among German immigrants and others. Many basket makers preferred North Carolina's plentiful longleaf pine needles as coiled basket material. The basket maker bundled the needles and coiled them in a tight spiral, binding the rows together with raffia or nylon string. Bark baskets were also common, often made of two pieces of hickory, poplar, or birch bark connected securely with hickory or birch lacing.

References: Jan Arnow, *By Southern Hands: A Celebration of Craft Traditions in the South* (1987); Betty J. Duggan and Brett H. Riggs, *Studies in Cherokee Basketmaking* (1991); John Rice Irwin, *Baskets and Basket Makers in Southern Appalachia* (1982).

Dennis W. Cross

Bassett Affair significantly enhanced the ideal of academic freedom in North Carolina and the nation. The controversy involved Tarboro native John Spencer Bassett, who taught history at Trinity College (precursor to Duke University) for ten years and was the founding editor of the *South Atlantic Quarterly*. This journal encouraged faculty dialogue and scholarship by promoting the literary, social, and historical development of the South.

By 1903 the white supremacy campaign had proven successful in North Carolina politics. Democrats used this campaign to disfranchise blacks, thus enabling party members to monopolize political power. In this climate of promoting the separation of the races, Bassett wrote an article in his journal titled "Stirring up the Fires of Race Antipathy," reacting to a racial incident that had occurred in Hamlet. This incident began when a group of African American travelers—including prominent black leader Booker T. Washington—stopped for a prearranged breakfast at a hotel there. At the hotel, the blacks were given the main dining room, and the whites used a small improvised dining room. This arrangement offended Augustus O. Bacon, a U.S. senator from Georgia who refused to eat breakfast under the circumstances. In his article, Bassett exalted Washington—who had been involved in a similar incident in Washington, D.C., when he attended a dinner with President Theodore Roosevelt—calling him "the greatest man, save General Lee, born in the South in a hundred years." The statement provoked a very heated response from Josephus Daniels, editor of the *Raleigh News and Observer*. In an editorial, Daniels called for the trustees at Trinity to fire Bassett and urged parents not to send their children to the college until it removed Bassett from the faculty. Daniels's campaign to oust Bassett spread to other newspapers, and it began to affect the friends and trustees of Trinity.

Bassett received support from Trinity's faculty, alumni, and students as well as its president, John Carlisle Kilgo, a militant and inspired Methodist minister who promoted high standards and scholarship. Kilgo supported Bassett on the grounds of academic freedom. During the controversy, Bassett submitted a letter of resignation to Trinity's trustees. The trustees met on 1 December, finally voting 17–7 to keep Bassett at Trinity and reject his offer to resign. Most of the trustees believed that it was better for Trinity College to suffer temporary political pressure than to enter upon a policy of coercion and intolerance. Thus, the Bassett affair represented a major precedent concerning academic freedom in the United States.

References: Joseph L. Morrison, "Josephus Daniels and the Bassett Academic Freedom Case," *Journalism Quarterly* 39 (Spring 1962); Earl W. Porter, "The Bassett Affair: Something to Remember," *South Atlantic Quarterly* 72 (Autumn 1973); William S. Powell, *North Carolina through Four Centuries* (1989).

Lloyd Johnson

Bastardy, as a legal term, designates the civil condition of a child born under illegitimate circumstances. Under English common law, children born out of lawful wedlock were classed as bastards. In the eyes of the law they had no parents, no kindred, and no ancestors. They were not, then, entitled to a surname except such as they won for themselves by reputation, and they were heirs-at-law of no one. Although the early history of North Carolina furnishes occasional examples of illegitimate children who achieved fame and fortune, throughout the seventeenth and eighteenth centuries the great majority of them were apprenticed at a tender age to a master and condemned to a lowly existence.

In North Carolina, whose legal foundation was in common law, bastards ordinarily assumed the surnames of their birth mothers, but they otherwise suffered all of the common-law disabilities. Bastard children were thus disadvantaged from their birth. Bastardy proceedings were held to determine the probable paternity of an illegitimate child likely to become a charge on the public and to oblige the putative father to support the child. From as early as 1700, the mother of an illegitimate child could voluntarily appear before two justices of the peace and name the father of her child in a sworn statement, or she could be summoned by them and interrogated as to the father. By force of the mother's sworn testimony, the man was usually adjudged the putative father and was compelled to enter into a bond with sureties, called a "bastardy bond," to support the child at a set amount. Or, if the man resisted the nomination, he could be bound over to a full session of the county court, but even there the matter was, for more than a century, summarily dealt with. Many a young man "went west" rather than submit to the proceedings.

In 1814 an amendment to the bastardy law made the mother's sworn testimony prima facie evidence rather than conclusive evidence, granted the putative father a trial by jury, and required the proceedings to be brought within three years of the child's birth. (An act of 1850 strengthened the sworn testimony of the mother by making her evidence presumptive rather than prima facie.) Gradually the minimum age to which the child had to be supported was raised to 10 (the age stipulated by the bastardy act of 1933), then to 14 in 1937, and to 18 in 1951.

In 1917 the General Assembly enacted a provision that automatically legitimated all children of parents who married each other either before or after the birth of the child. Legitimation by private act, by court order, and under the 1917 law entitled a child to the use of the father's surname and made him or her heir to, but not through, the father. By an act of 1955, legitimated children were made heirs-at-law to and through both mother and father, and were thus given complete families. Under the law, children born under illegitimate circumstances whose births are not legitimated by court order or by marriage of their birth parents remain without kindred and without ancestors.

George Stevenson

Bath became the first incorporated town in North Carolina in 1705. The town also boasted the state's first library (1701), church (1734), and free school (ca. 1753). Bath is thought to be on or near the site of the sixteenth-century Indian town of Secotan, an area that late in the seventeenth century was inhabited by the Pamlico Indians. Colonial settlers came to the site by the 1690s. Located at the tip of a peninsula formed by Bath (Old Town) and Back (Adam's) Creeks, Bath possessed a good harbor and easy access to the Pamlico River and Ocracoke Inlet. The first settlers were French Huguenots, who were followed by settlers of English extraction from the Albemarle Sound region, Virginia, New England, and England itself.

Early agricultural products from the Bath area included cattle, swine, and corn. Tar, turpentine, shingles, and staves were produced locally and exported to New England and the West Indies. A small sloop was built for commercial purposes at Bath as early as 1707. Bath had 12 houses when it was incorporated and grew slowly but steadily during the early part of the eighteenth century. Wharves and warehouses dotted the waterfront. By 1706 Bath was the seat of Bath County, established in 1696. Court was initially held in the home of the sheriff, Thomas Bonner. A courthouse was built in 1723 and then replaced by a newer one by 1769. Bath County was split in 1738, and Bath became the county seat of the new Beaufort County. The flow of court business, and the arrival and departure of ships, provided customers for several inns and taverns. Three early governors, Robert Daniel, Thomas Cary, and Charles Eden, lived in Bath.

The town was the center of the Anglican parish of St. Thomas, formed in 1701. In that year, the parish received a gift of 1,000 books from the Society for the Propagation of the Gospel in Foreign Parts, thus having a library even before it had a church building or regular minister. Construction of St. Thomas Episcopal Church in Bath, the first church building in North Carolina, did not begin until 1734.

Bath's early days were tumultuous, with the upheaval of the Cary Rebellion, followed by the Tuscarora uprising of 1711. Refugees from destroyed farms and settlements throughout the region filled the town, which shortly thereafter acquired its most famous and notorious citizen, the pirate Blackbeard (whose real name was Edward Drummond, Edward Teach, or Edward Thatch). Arriving in Bath sometime after Charles Eden was appointed governor of the colony in 1714, the "reformed" pirate befriended the governor, reportedly married a local woman, and settled at Plum Point, across Adam's Creek from the town. He soon returned to piracy, sailing the Caribbean and the Atlantic, using Bath as a base and a place to dispose of his spoils. It was widely believed that Governor Eden shared in Blackbeard's spoils in exchange for protection. Blackbeard was killed by Capt. Robert Maynard of the Royal Navy in a battle at Ocracoke Inlet in 1718. Tobias Knight, secretary of the colony, was implicated as a receiver of stolen goods but acquitted, probably through Eden's influence. For some years, an amphitheater on the waterfront in Bath was home to a modern outdoor drama, *Blackbeard*.

Bath had passed its peak of importance by the late colonial period, as other ports less hampered by sandbars and shallow water took over the state's ocean trade, and traffic on the rivers pushed farther inland, closer to populous new settlements. In 1743, 1744, and 1752, the General Assembly met at Bath, which was considered when a location for the permanent capital of the colony was chosen, but it lost out to New Bern. In 1785, Bath lost its courthouse when the seat of Beaufort County was moved to Washington.

In 1925 the Adams Floating Palace, one of the last operating showboats in the country, was docked in Bath. Author Edna Ferber visited Bath for several days to do research for her novel, *Showboat*, which inspired the famous stage and film musicals of the same name.

The modern Historic Bath State Historic Site occupies 13 acres in 5 tracts of the town. Following the observance of Bath's 250th anniversary in 1955, the Historic Bath Commission was created in 1959 to acquire, develop, and restore historic property. In addition to St. Thomas Church, a number of other buildings, notably the 1751 Palmer-Marsh House, the ca. 1808 Van Der Veer House, and the 1830 Bonner House, have been restored and opened to the public. There is also a visitor center with artifacts on display.

References: Richard F. Knapp, ed., *North Carolina's State Historic Sites: A Brief History and Status Report* (1995); Herbert R. Paschal Jr., *A History of Colonial Bath* (1955); Linda Reeves, *Bath Town Guidebook* (1977); L. A. Squires, "Little Washington and Show Biz," *The State* 47 (November 1979).

David A. Norris

SEE ALSO Palmer-Marsh House; St. Thomas Episcopal Church.

Bathing, for most North Carolinians until the twentieth century, was an irregular practice often regarded as unhealthy. William Byrd's "secret history" of the surveying of the dividing line between North Carolina and Virginia in 1727 noted that one of the commissioners, Col. Harvey Harrison, "refreshes himself every morning" in a cold bath. It was in a building "about 5 Feet Square, & as many deep, thro which a pure Stream continually passes, & is covered with a little House just big enough for the Bath & a Firing Room." The other eight members of the survey party took turns bathing but seemed more interested in the rum they had afterward and the carpet they walked on going to bed than in the novel experience of a cold bath.

At the Moravian Boys' School in 1823 it was noted that the youth bathed twice a week—on Wednesday and Saturday.

William S. Powell

Battle of the Atlantic. SEE Submarine Attacks.

Battle of the Bees. SEE McIntyre's Farm, Battle of.

The USS *New Jersey* after being hit by one of several bombs that sank the ship off the North Carolina coast, 5 Sept. 1923. NCC.

Battleships Bombed by Billy Mitchell. In 1923 two surplus navy battleships were bombed and sunk by aircraft under the command of Brig. Gen. William "Billy" Mitchell off Cape Hatteras to determine the effectiveness of air power against heavy surface ships. Mitchell, an outspoken advocate of air power, had demonstrated in 1921 what many naval strategists considered impossible—that battleships could be destroyed from the air—when he used airplanes to sink an old surplus battleship. Two years later, he set up the experiment off Cape Hatteras to determine if battleships could be sunk by high-level bombing and to measure the potential for aircraft being called into combat from long distances to intercept a hostile warship. The target vessels, which were to be scrapped under postwar naval limitation treaties, were the 14,949-ton *New Jersey* and *Virginia*, built between 1902 and 1906 at a cost of $6 million each and anchored 18 miles southeast of Cape Hatteras.

The attacks began on the morning of 5 Sept. 1923. While officers and dignitaries watched from another ship, the first planes flew directly into action from Langley Airfield, Va., a distance of 175 miles, demonstrating the feasibility of long-range attack. The remaining planes under Mitchell flew from a temporary airfield on Hatteras. The *New Jersey* was shelled with 600-pound bombs from 10,000 feet, which left the ship damaged and leaking. The attack then shifted to the *Virginia*, which was sunk with thirteen 1,100-pound bombs from 3,000 feet in only 30 minutes. That afternoon the planes returned to send the *New Jersey* to the bottom in only a few minutes.

The experiment proved both the benefit of high-altitude bombing and aircraft long-range strike capability. However, debate over the use of air power against ships continued until World War II conclusively demonstrated the value of air power.

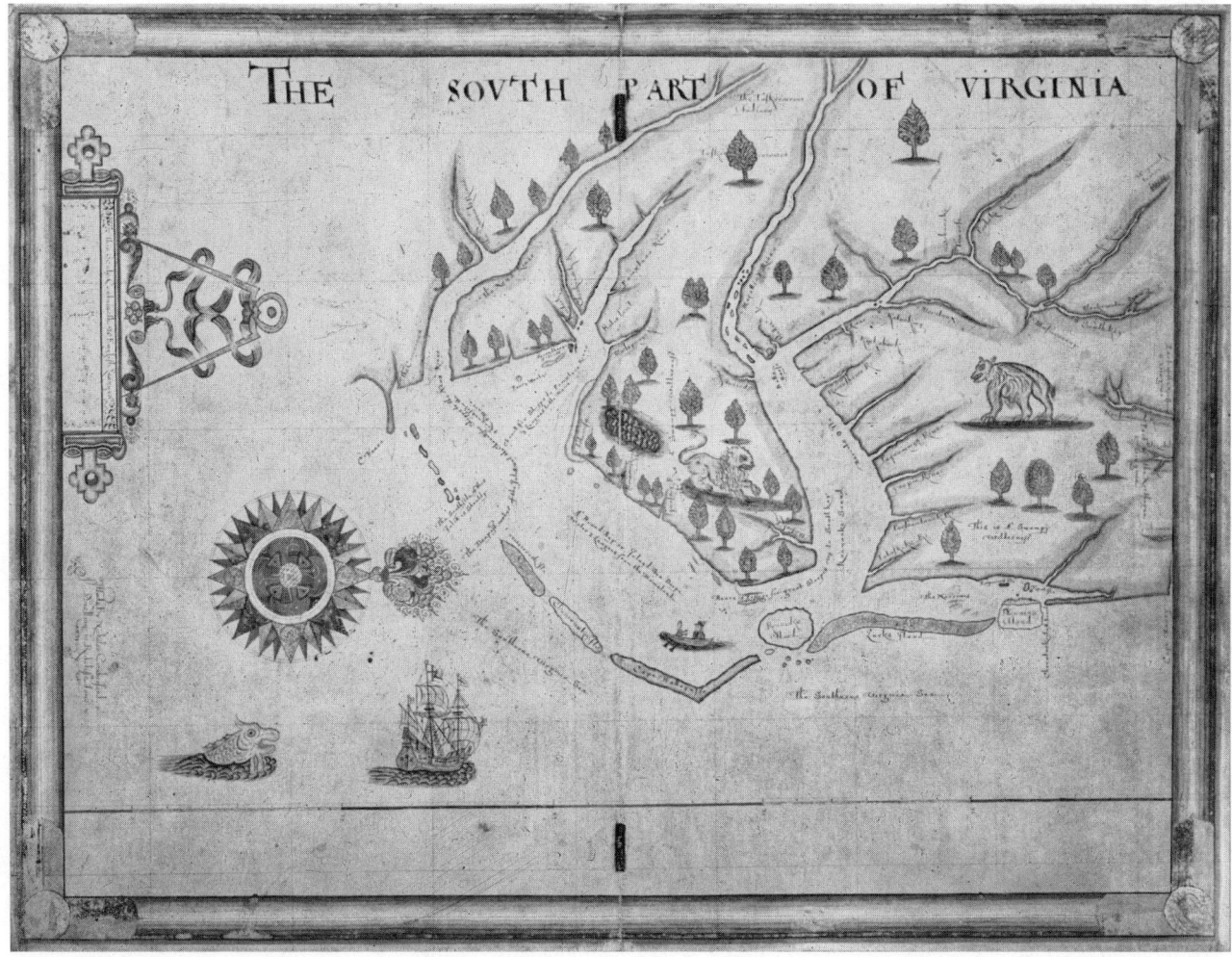

The Nicholas Comberford map of 1657 shows the house of Nathaniell Batts near the confluence of the Morattico (Roanoke) and Choan (Chowan) Rivers. Copyright National Maritime Museum, London.

References: Burke Davis, *The Billy Mitchell Story* (1969); Emile Gauvreau and Lester Cohen, *Billy Mitchell: Founder of Our Air Force and Prophet without Honor* (1942); William Schwarzer, *The Lion Killers: Billy Mitchell and the Birth of Strategic Bombing* (2003).

Paul Branch

Batts House. Fur trader Nathaniell Batts, reputedly North Carolina's first permanent white settler, apparently worked for George Yeardley of Lynnhaven River, Va. (modern-day Virginia Beach), who in 1653 sent Batts to explore the Albemarle Sound area of what is now North Carolina to identify fertile lands that Yeardley might acquire for development. Batts's efforts led to an arrangement between Yeardley and Chief Kiscatanewh of the Pasquotank Indians for Yeardley's purchase of an extensive tract, probably at the mouth of the Pasquotank River. As part of the arrangement, Yeardley would build an English-style house furnished with English goods for Kiscatanewh. In the spring of 1655, Yeardley employed carpenter Robert Bodnam to travel south with five workmen and build Kiscatanewh's

house and another for Nathaniell Batts "to live in and trade with the Indians." Bodnam made two trips, probably one for each house, and spent a total of five months in the Albemarle Sound area. Yeardley died while the work was in progress.

Batts's house, evidently erected on the south side of the mouth of Salmon Creek, measured 20 feet square, with two rooms and a chimney. Batts used the house primarily during fur-trading seasons and after 1655 made his home on Lynnhaven River with his wife and family. Batts later moved to Albemarle and apparently settled at the site of present-day Edenton, where he owned land. Batts told George Fox in 1672 that he was formerly a "governor" in Carolina, perhaps referring to some authority he may have held, under Proprietary governors, over a handful of settlers who occupied land on Salmon Creek until driven off by the Tuscarora Indians around 1667.

The Batts house on Salmon Creek, or its replacements, was probably the center of fur trade between whites and the Tuscarora and other area Indians for more than half a century. John Lawson, visiting the site around 1708, described there "a House made of Logs, (such as the Swedes in America very often make, and are very strong)," which Governor Seth Sothel, owner in the 1680s of a large tract of Salmon Creek land, had used as a fur-trading facility. The site of the house is indicated on Nicholas Comberford's 1657 map of the "South Part of Virginia."

References: Hugh T. Lefler, ed., *A New Voyage to Carolina by John Lawson* (1967); Elizabeth Gregory McPherson, "Nathaniell Batts: Landholder on Pasquotank River, 1660," NCHR 43 (January 1966).

Thomas C. Parramore

Bayard v. Singleton was possibly the first legal decision in the United States in which a court nullified a law because it was found to be unconstitutional. During the American Revolution the government confiscated the land of Loyalists to raise money for the war. People whose land was seized were those who refused to swear an oath of allegiance to North Carolina, maintaining their loyalty to Great Britain instead. Although born in America, Samuel Cornell, a Loyalist, lost his land when it was confiscated by North Carolina. It was later purchased in part by Spyres Singleton. In 1786 Cornell's daughter, Elizabeth Cornell Bayard, to whom Cornell had willed this property, sued Singleton for the portion of her father's property that had been left to her. In response, Singleton's attorneys cited a law passed by the North Carolina legislature in 1785 that said that those who held land purchased under the state's Confiscation Acts of 1777 and 1779 could not be sued for the return of their land.

After lengthy consideration, the state court—composed of Judges Samuel Ashe, Samuel Spencer, and John Williams—citing the state constitution, declared that the 1785 act was unconstitutional and those whose property had been seized were entitled to a trial by jury. Although Singleton was able to keep the land based on the state Confiscation Acts, the significance of the case resulted from the court's overruling of an established act of the legislature. This ruling by the court was an early example of the system of checks and balances vital to the new American democracy. *Bayard v. Singleton* set a precedent for judicial review, as applied by the U.S. Supreme Court in the 1803 case of *Marbury v. Madison*.

References: Lindley S. Butler and Alan D. Watson, eds., *The North Carolina Experience: An Interpretive and Documentary History* (1984); Don Higginbotham, "James Iredell's Efforts to Preserve the British Empire," NCHR 49 (1972); Quinton Holton, "History of the Case of *Bayard v. Singleton*" (M.A. thesis, UNC-Chapel Hill, 1948).

Andy Hollins

Beaches. SEE Resorts.

Beards of two North Carolinians attracted worldwide attention during their lifetimes. Sam G. Brinkley (1850–1929), a schoolteacher at Magnetic Hill (renamed Buladean) in Mitchell County, had facial hair that grew so fast he gave up shaving while a young man. As his beard grew to his waist, he began attracting attention, and when it reached his knees and toes, he claimed to have the longest beard in the world. He was such a curiosity, in fact, that he wore his rolled-up beard beneath his shirt and charged a dime to reveal it. He was about 40 years old when he was hired by the Barnum & Bailey Circus, and during the next two decades he was exhibited throughout the country as the world's authority in pogonotrophy, or the cultivation of beards. He made extra cash by selling picture postcards of himself. Embedded in his tombstone at the Presbyterian Church in Buladean is a photograph revealing his flowing beard, nearly six feet long.

Beards are usually associated with men, but a North Carolina female also became famous for facial hair. Jane Barnell, born in Wilmington in 1871 with heavy down on her face, was an embarrassment to her mother, who, while her husband was away on an extensive trip, sold the child to a small circus as it passed through the town. Jane, billed as a bearded princess throughout the southern states, was taken to Europe later and, during a serious illness, was committed to an orphanage. When George Barnell learned of his daughter's whereabouts, he retrieved the girl and gave her to his mother-in-law, a Catawba Indian living in Mecklenburg County. There Jane grew to womanhood, regularly shaving off her beard as if she were a young man. A neighbor, William Heckler, a seasonal strongman with the John Robinson Circus, persuaded Jane to accept her beard as a gift of nature and to join the traveling circus. Thus, at age 21 she was unveiled to the world as "Lady Olga, the Bearded Woman." With that title, she was employed later by other circuses, and in 1932 she played the role of the bearded lady in Tod Browning's infamous film *Freaks*. She gave her last circus performance with the Ringling Brothers Circus in New York in 1938 but continued until her death to appear in dime museums in and around the city.

References: H. G. Jones, "In Light of History," *Statesville Record and Landmark* (14 Oct. 1982); E. Wayne Massey, "North Carolina Medical Curiosities: Modern Bearded Lady," *North Carolina Medical Journal* 42 (June 1981); Joseph Mitchell, "Profiles: Lady Olga," *New Yorker* (3 Aug. 1940).

H. G. Jones

Bear River Indians, an Algonquian tribe also known as the Bay River Indians, lived between the Pamlico and Neuse Rivers in the late seventeenth and early eighteenth centuries. They were neighbors of the Pamlico, and there is some evidence they were related to the Machapunga Indians. Both the Bear River and Pamlico Indians may have been descendants of the Indians that the Raleigh colonists of 1585–86 found living in the area. In 1709 the Bear River Indians occupied a single town, Raudauquaquank, which contained 50 warriors.

The colonists complained of depredations and threats from this tribe, which apparently helped instigate the massacre that began the Tuscarora War (1711–13). During that uprising, colonial leaders enslaved a number of the tribe's women and children, and the Bear River chief was tortured to death by Indian allies of the colonists. At the end of the war, the Tuscarora turned on their former allies, promising in the peace treaty to destroy them, sparing no males more than 14 years old.

References: F. Roy Johnson, *The Tuscaroras* (2 vols., 1968); Ruth Y. Wetmore, *First on the Land: The North Carolina Indians* (1975).

Ruth Y. Wetmore

Beat the Bounds. To "beat the bounds," or "do procession," meant walking the boundaries of a property and, in ancient times, striking certain places with a rod in the presence of witnesses. In the American colonies, landowners would walk the bounds of their property showing their sons (or others) its limits. Notches or blaze marks on trees would be recut if needed. Parish bounds were also so determined. This practice is mentioned in England as early as 1570, and in North Carolina it was established by an act of the Assembly in 1703 by direction of the Lords Proprietors. The act read: "Inhabitants of this Government shall some time in the month of April next & from thenceforth in April Every Four Years Meet as Many of the Neighborhood as Conveniently come and go in procession and Remark the Lines of the Land belonging to Each person of the Neighborhood under penalty of Forty Shillings to be paid by the Delinquent to the Use of the Poor of the Neighborhood." The practice was continued into the twentieth century, especially for forested tracts.

References: J. R. B. Hathaway, ed., *North Carolina Historical and Genealogical Register*, vol. 3 (1903); David M. Walker, *Oxford Companion to Law* (1980).

William S. Powell

Beaufort, Battle of. Claimed by some to be the last engagement of the Revolutionary War, the Battle of Beaufort took place as a result of a British raid on the town in April 1782. The surrender of Lord Charles Cornwallis's British army at Yorktown in October 1781 had brought an end to major military operations in the war, and treaty negotiations were under way to conclude it. But the British continued to hold New York, Charles Towne (present-day Charleston), and Savannah, and their navy's ships continued to operate out of these ports. In late March 1782 four vessels led by Cdr. D. McLean left Charleston for the North Carolina coast to take prizes and capture a quantity of public stores believed to be in Beaufort. On 4 April the British fleet entered Beaufort Harbor without identifying itself and seized all of the pilots and townspeople who

went out to greet the ships. In the early morning hours of 5 April, a landing party commanded by Maj. Isaac Stuart rowed ashore and captured Beaufort itself, driving off the handful of local militia who had turned out under Col. John Easton. The British spent the next five days plundering the town and skirmishing with local militiamen, who had begun to gather in increasing force from neighboring communities.

In the Beaufort fighting the British had lost one man killed, a few wounded, and a number captured. On 10 April they returned to their ships but remained in the harbor. During that time their attempts to land on adjacent Bogue and Shackleford Banks for water were repulsed by the militia. After an exchange of prisoners, the British fleet finally departed on the afternoon of 17 April and the threat was ended. The raid spawned fears that the British might be encouraged to launch other expeditions against more promising areas such as New Bern and Edenton, but this was not the case. In November 1782 initial articles of peace were signed between the United States, its allies, and Great Britain, followed by the formal treaty of peace on 3 Sept. 1783 that recognized American independence.

Reference: Jean Bruyere Kell, ed., *North Carolina's Coastal Carteret County during the American Revolution, 1765–1785* (1976).

Paul Branch

Beaufort County, located on Pamlico Sound in North Carolina's Coastal Plain region, was originally formed as Pamptecough Precinct, a part of Bath County, in 1705. In 1712 it took its present name from Henry Somerset, duke of Beaufort, one of the Lords Proprietors. Its county seat, since 1785, has been the city of Washington, founded in 1770s as Forks of the Tar and called Washington as early as 1776. Washington is believed to be the first town in the United States named for President George Washington. The county, rich in history and coastal traditions, also includes the town of Bath, North Carolina's oldest incorporated town, as well as Aurora, Belhaven, Chocowinity, Pantego, and Pinetown. In 2004 Beaufort County's population was estimated at 45,000.

As early as the 1580s, English explorers visited the lands that became Beaufort County, encountering the Tuscarora and other Indians who lived in the Pamlico River basin. The first permanent settlements were established in the 1690s, and Bath was incorporated in 1705. The area, at a junction of coastal and inland rivers, continued as a key center of growth for the Carolina colony. Washington, established by colonist James Bonner on his farm bordering the Tar/Pamlico River, became an important port in the late eighteenth century and, during the Revolutionary War, served as a strategic supply point for the Continental Army. Washington remained the economic and cultural center of the county, with a thriving shipbuilding trade, through the first half of the nineteenth century.

John Gray Blount (1752–1833), merchant and land speculator, kept his home in Washington. In April 1864 the city was devastated when a fire set by Union troops to burn a cache of naval stores blazed out of control and consumed much of the central district. Residents rebuilt the city after the war, only to see much of it destroyed again in a fire that swept through the town in September 1900. The city was rebuilt once more, and today the few remaining structures from the 1700s and early 1800s and the late Victorian architecture of the restored downtown district are preserved and listed on the National Register of Historic Places.

The fortunes of Beaufort County began to wane with the decline of the shipping trade in the early twentieth century, but it remains an important center for the state's seafood industry, with a number of commercial fishing enterprises located in Belhaven. Coastal and cultural heritage tourism also plays an important role in the local economy. Fossil beds on the southern banks of the Pamlico River are considered to be among the richest on the Atlantic Coast; prehistoric sharks' teeth and other fossils recovered from the beds are on display at the Aurora Fossil Museum. The county also holds an important place in North Carolina folklore. Edward Teach, known as the pirate Blackbeard, lived briefly in Bath and is said to have buried treasure in the county before being killed in a battle with British sailors at Ocracoke Inlet in 1718.

Peter Bangma

SEE ALSO Bath.

Beauty Shops,

or beauty parlors, have had a notable impact on the lives of North Carolina women since the early twentieth century. Cosmetologists delivered more than better looks; they became confidantes and comforters, offering a listening ear and a healing touch while at the same time enhancing the personal image of their customers. Beauty shops emerged in North Carolina just after 1900, although professional beauty care was available in the state at least as early as the 1880s. For instance, Samuel Fowler, a barber and hairdresser in Hendersonville, placed an ad in an 1885 promotional brochure. Advertisements from an 1884 newspaper indicate that Mrs. L. Quonts of Concord and Wilson & Burwell of Charlotte were available to do hair work and hair dyeing. It is not clear whether they were itinerant operators, going from house to house, or whether they offered beauty services in their own home "parlors." What is known is that at this time and all over the nation, women's beauty regimens moved out of the privacy of their homes and into the beauty parlors of hairdressers.

During the 1920s, home beauty shops appeared in significant numbers in response to social changes that came in the wake of World War I. In 1919 Congress gave women the right to vote at about the same time that the automobile gave them greater mobility. Further, as the Victorian disdain for makeup and revealing clothing dissipated, women exercised their new freedoms by shortening their skirts, cutting their hair, and painting their faces. Short hair created a demand for professional coiffing.

By the late 1920s and early 1930s, beauty services began to move into commercial space in downtown areas, becoming known as beauty shops or "salons." This move was due primarily to advances in hairdressing technology, particularly after the hot-blast hair dryer was invented in 1892, the marcel curling iron in 1897, and the permanent wave machine in 1905. Because of the hazards of working with sharp instruments, electrical appliances, and chemicals, the industry and state governments recognized the need for regulation. In North Carolina, a State Board of Barber Examiners was established in 1929. Women's beauty shops became regulated in 1933 when a Board of Cosmetology, originally made up of three experienced cosmetologists, was created to grant licenses to beauty schools, individual cosmetologists, apprentices, manicurists, instructors, salons, and shops.

In towns of all sizes, even during the era of the Depression, beauty shops were fixed elements in the lives of women in North Carolina and all over America. By 1939 U.S. Department of Commerce figures showed 87,270 salons across the nation, with a payroll of $81 million. In High Point, for example, a population of about 37,000 in 1935 had at least eight beauty shops, advertising permanents for one dollar and up and shampoo and finger waves for 50 cents. One beauty school offered classes day and night.

After World War II, the beauty business embraced the fashion industry, and together they campaigned to encourage American women to be more style-conscious and to pursue professional beauty care. With an increasing number of women working outside the home and lacking the time to take care of their hair themselves, professional beauty services were more in demand than ever. One factory in North Carolina even added a beauty parlor in 1967 to serve its 500 female employees, hoping to reduce absenteeism.

Increased automobile ownership allowed beauty shops to drift away from downtown locations to outlying strip malls during the decades following World War II. During the 1960s, social change once again brought benefits to the beauty industry. Barbers lacked the know-how and inclination to deal with the longer hair being worn by men. Moreover, they found that the time it took to groom long hair was not cost-effective. The result was that men began going to women's beauty shops to get their hair cut. Ultimately, beauty shops embraced barbering and became unisex, soon catering to the specific needs of virtually all groups.

The 1960s and 1970s ushered in an era of new style consciousness for American women. A wide range of hairstyles was available, many of them bearing the names of the female celebrities who first wore them. Many beauty shops began to move to indoor malls. Customers chose from a range of services that might include not only cuts, roller-sets, and hair texturing (curling or relaxing) but also hair coloring, hair extensions, manicures, artificial nails, facials, and even tanning. The stressful lives of women trying to manage both careers and families also created a market for the full-service day spa, specializing in "client pampering."

By the end of the twentieth century and the early years of the twenty-first, the ownership and management of beauty shops had changed. With the exception of the chains, which still earned a percentage of each operator's business, almost all shops went to the booth rental system, with operators establishing their own fees and paying for their own supplies, turning cosmetologists into entrepreneurs. A large percentage of North Carolina's beauty shops were also one-chair operations, often in rural settings. Women with training in cosmetology who wanted to stay at home and continue working set up beauty shops by adapting their homes to accommodate a business, much as women did in the early decades of the century.

References: Julia Cherry Spruill, *Women's Life and Work in the Southern Colonies* (repr., 1972); Mary Trasko, *Daring Do's: A History of Extraordinary Hair* (1994).

Virginia Gunn Fick

Beavers—the largest North American rodents, recognized by their rich brown fur, webbed hind paws, and large, flat tails—were trapped almost to extinction in North Carolina as well as in much of eastern North America during the colonial period, their valuable pelts being an important item of trade in the colonies. The last reported native North Carolina beaver was seen in Stokes County in 1897.

In 1939 the agency that became the North Carolina Wildlife Resources Commission released 29 Pennsylvania beavers in the Coastal Plain in what is now the Sandhills Game Land. The beavers thrived, and by 1953 their population, estimated at 1,000 animals, stretched into seven counties. Because their pelts remained valuable, the stocking program was continued between 1951 and 1956, with 54 beavers released in nine other counties. By the early 2000s, beavers—natural engineers that take down trees to create dams and shallow ponds—had become so successful that regulated trapping was necessary in some regions to diminish timber damage and flooding in populated or agricultural areas. Although sometimes causing damage, beaver ponds also provide ideal habitats for creatures such as kingfishers, muskrats, and wood ducks. In fact, North Carolina's native wood duck population and harvests have increased concurrent with the rise in the beaver population.

Laura Hegyi

Enlargement of the obverse of a five-dollar gold coin believed to have been struck between 1834 and 1837 by Christopher Bechtler Sr. The actual diameter of the coin is 24.7 mm. NCC.

Bechtler Mint. Before gold was discovered in California in 1848, North Carolina was the leading gold-producing state. Although gold was found in some abundance in North Carolina, gold coins as a medium of exchange were not. Gold dust, nuggets, and jewelry often circulated as money since state and federal currency were scarce. The arrival in Rutherford County in 1830 of Christopher Bechtler, his son Augustus, and a nephew Christopher soon brought a change. They were experienced German metalworkers from the Grand Duchy of Baden who had gone to Pennsylvania in 1829. After a brief stay there they moved to North Carolina and settled near the center of a gold-producing area west of the Yadkin River that also included a small portion of northwestern South Carolina and northern Georgia.

Soon after opening a jewelry shop in Rutherfordton, the elder Bechtler realized that the regional economy was hindered by the lack of gold in circulation. Congress had rejected a petition for the establishment of a branch of the U.S. Mint in the area, so Bechtler, "at the suggestion of several gentlemen of highest standing" among the miners, decided to coin gold himself.

The Bechtlers manufactured their own dies and press and by July 1831 began striking coins in $2.50 and $5.00 pieces. For several weeks beginning on 2 July 1831, Christopher Bechtler advertised in the *North Carolina Spectator and Western Advertiser* in Rutherfordton that he had established a mint 3½ miles north of the town. In 1832 he began to produce $1.00 gold coins, the first gold dollar to be produced in the United States. The senior Bechtler died in 1842, and family members continued to produce gold coins until the late 1840s. In addition to coins, the Bechtlers were known for their collar buttons, cuff links, clocks, watches, watch chains, necklaces, brooches, rings, and firearms. They also operated a gold mine nearby but little is known about its production.

References: Rodney Barfield and Keith Strawn, *The Bechtlers and Their Coinage: North Carolina Mint Master of Pioneer Gold* (1980); Fletcher M. Green, "Gold Mining: A Forgotten Industry of Antebellum North Carolina," *NCHR* 14 (January 1937).

Ron Holland

Beech Mountain/Land of Oz.

Beech Mountain in Avery County is the eastern United States' highest town, at 5,606 feet above sea level. Local residents share the mountain with several resort communities and Ski Beech, a popular ski resort. During the 1970s Beech Mountain was also home to the Land of Oz, a theme park that has taken its place amid the rich folklore of the Appalachian Mountains.

Throughout the early part of the twentieth century, Beech Mountain was part of an important logging industry. While sparsely populated, it was dotted with small cabins where loggers lived during the week while they worked. Skiing came to the mountain starting in the 1930s, with students from nearby Lees-McRae College using skis produced in the college's wood shop.

The Robbins brothers—Grover, Harry, and Spencer—purchased a large tract of land on top of the mountain in 1962. The Robbinses, who also owned Tweetsie Railroad and the Hound Ears Resort, joined with other investors to create the Carolina Caribbean Corporation in 1965. Carolina Caribbean planned a 10,000-acre resort with homesites for 9,000 families, an eight-slope ski resort, a summer recreation area, a golf course, and a theme park. Grover Robbins enlisted Charlotte artist and designer Jack Pentes to develop an idea for a theme park that would draw people to the mountain during the off-season. Pentes dreamed of a place that would enchant people and allow them to escape the harsh realities of the late 1960s.

For inspiration Pentes drew upon L. Frank Baum's classic children's tale of enchantment and escape, *The Wizard of Oz*, having noted the similarity between gnarled beech trees on the property and the talking apple trees in the story. With the help of two fellow Charlotteans, composer Loonis McGlohon and choreographer Alice Lamar, Pentes created the 16-acre Land of Oz theme park. When its first season ended in the fall of 1970, attendance had hit the six-figure mark. From hot air balloons and the magical cyclone to flying monkeys and happy songs, the Land of Oz allowed visitors to live every moment of the famous adventure for themselves as they walked the 55,000 bricks of the park's yellow brick road. Visitors were joined by each of the beloved characters as they visited Kansas, Munchkinland, the Wicked Witch's Castle, and the Emerald City.

In 1975 the Carolina Caribbean Corporation went bankrupt. Shortly afterward, vandals set fire to the Emerald City and stole Judy Garland's original dress along with other artifacts from the park's Oz museum. The Land of Oz, already hit by a lack of repeat visitors, never recovered. As the property changed hands, the park fell victim to a lack of consistent management and poor funding, closing in 1980.

The property was purchased in 1990 by the Emerald Mountain development corporation, which created homesites on 450 acres around the old theme park. Each fall, Emerald Mountain holds an Autumn at Oz party, where fans of the Land of Oz may take a nostalgic stroll down the yellow brick road and see remnants of the theme park that have been carefully preserved. Other artifacts from the park are on display at the Appalachian Cultural Museum in Boone.

Beech Mountain was incorporated as a town in 1981. The mountain is home to a shopping village, the 14-slope Ski Beech ski resort, and two golf courses, including one designed by Jack Nicklaus.

Reference: Robert R. Gottfried, *The Impact of Recreational Communities on Land Prices in the Local Communities: The Case of Beech Mountain* (1981).

Elizabeth Scheld Glynn

Beer and Breweries.

The brewing of beer in the region that would become North Carolina began long before the first Europeans arrived. According to John Lawson's *A New Voyage to Carolina* (1709), Native Americans made beer from cedar berries and corn. In *The Natural History of North Carolina* (1737), John Brickell observed that the Indians "likewise make Beer of Mollosses, or common Treacle."

The first English colonists in North America brewed beer in their settlement on Roanoke Island in 1585. An account written by one of the settlers reported: "Wee make of the same in the country some mault, whereof was brued as good ale as was to be desired." Beer was a mainstay of the colonial diet. Most brewing occurred in private homes and was often carried out by housewives, but taverns served local or country beer along with a few imports from England and some "Northward beer" from New York and Philadelphia. Commercial brewing was rare until the 1800s, although one resident of Old Salem advised in 1773 that "the distillation of strong drink should not be extended too much because beer is not only much more wholesom for our brethren but also neighbors would buy quantities of it."

Brewing in North Carolina diminished significantly after the Revolutionary War for several reasons. Where transportation was poor, especially along the frontier, farmers found it easier to turn their excess grain into whiskey than beer. Whiskey kept better, took up less room, and could be carried in small bottles or flasks. In the 1840s the introduction and growing popularity of German lager beer—with its emphasis on lightness, dryness, and sparkle—along with technological advancement in the brewing process, revolutionized the industry. Large breweries in areas of significant German migration such as St. Louis, Milwaukee, and Cincinnati overwhelmed the small local producers of traditional English-style ales. In antebellum North Carolina growing racial tensions and white fears led the government to restrict African Americans' consumption and retailing of alcohol. During the Civil War the state outlawed all brewing to save grains for food.

The temperance and prohibition movements that swept across the state and country at various times severely limited beer production. County courts and later local governments restricted alcohol consumption and retail through licensing, fees, and prohibitions. In the 1870s the state legislature expanded the power of local option, and by 1881, 68 communities in North Carolina were described as "dry." In 1908 North Carolina became the first state to adopt Prohibition by a direct vote of the people, foreshadowing adoption of the Eighteenth Amendment to the U.S. Constitution in 1919. In 1933, 300,054 North Carolinians voted against repeal of the Eighteenth Amendment, compared to only 115,526 who cast ballots to support the successful national movement to end Prohibition. Responding to such strong temperance sentiments, the legislature returned to its policy of local option, experimenting with Alcoholic Beverage Control (ABC) programs as early as 1935.

After World War II, consumption of beer rose dramatically in North Carolina. A number of factors contributed to the skyrocketing demand for beer, including increased availability as more communities voted to allow beer sales, a high rate of migration into the state, a younger population, increased advertising, more tolerant attitudes toward alcohol, and higher incomes. By 1989 North Carolina had a higher per capita consumption of malt beverages than New York, and it collected more tax revenues from packaged beer as well.

Commercial brewing also returned to North Carolina in the second half of the twentieth century. In 1948 Atlantic Beer and Ale in Charlotte was the lone brewery in the state producing beer for sale and distribution, but by the 1970s the new Schlitz (later Stroh's) brewery in Winston-Salem became one of the top 20 most-productive breweries in the country. Miller opened a major new facility in Eden in 1976. In the 1980s and 1990s, North Carolinians participated in the microbrew trend in the brewing industry. Microbreweries— small breweries generally producing fewer than 15,000 barrels of beer and ale a year—and brewpubs, which produce and sell beer for consumption only on the premises, spread rapidly across the state. The success of these small, local establishments was accompanied by increased consumer demand for darker and heavier English-style beers like those popular 200 years before. By the early 2000s North Carolina's approxi-

mately 30 microbrewers had successfully reestablished many of the state's colonial brewing traditions.

References: Stanley Baron, *Brewed in America: A History of Beer and Ale in the United States* (1962); Daniel Jay Whitener, *Prohibition in North Carolina, 1715–1945* (1946).

Karl E. Campbell

Belk. Charlotte-based Belk, Inc., the nation's largest privately owned department store organization, began in Monroe in 1888 as one small store named the New York Racket. The 25-year-old founder, William Henry Belk, who had worked in the dry goods trade in Monroe since he was 12, invested his life savings of $750, borrowed $500, and used $3,000 of consigned merchandise to launch his store. It realized a profit in its first year of operation, largely because of Belk's innovative business techniques. He insisted that all merchandise bear clearly marked prices—no haggling—since sales were cash only. No credit or barter terms were allowed, although customers were guaranteed a full refund on any purchase if later dissatisfied. These principles were unusual in 1888, when North Carolinians were poor and struggling during the post-Reconstruction era. The store opened early and closed late to accommodate the lifestyle of the working-class customer. Economical or "bargain" items were always stocked. Advertising was another concept Belk introduced in the retail trade to his advantage.

Belk depended on the small profit on the overall volume of sales rather than on individually sold items. The New York Racket thrived, and in 1891 Belk convinced his brother, John Belk, a medical doctor practicing in nearby Anson County, to join him as a partner in the management and operation of the retail business. The store underwent a formal name change to the Belk Brothers Company as a result of this partnership.

In 1893 a second Belk Brothers Company store opened in Chester, S.C. The Monroe store remained the operational center of the expanding Belk Brothers Company until 1895, when the fourth and largest Belk's opened in Charlotte. Other Belk stores opened during the early twentieth century, often in partnership with former employees who had gained experience and established their own stores with the help of Henry Belk. Among these were the first Parks-Belk Company, opened in Concord in 1911; the first Hudson-Belk Company, opened in Raleigh in 1915; the first Belk-Stevens Company, opened in Winston-Salem in 1916; and the first Gallant-Belk Company, opened in Anderson, S.C., in 1919.

In the second half of the twentieth century, Belk modernized and expanded its retail trade. Beginning in the 1950s, Belk developed a private label program that launched successful brands such as Archdale shirts for men, Sweetbriar clothing for women, and Nursery Rhyme for toddlers and infants. The traditional Belk principle of no credit ended in 1967, when the first Belk-only credit card was issued, valid at all

Belk stores. Mail-order sales, sophisticated computerization of the merchandising system, and modern managerial techniques followed. In the 1970s Belk continued the dominant modern trend of the retail trade by locating stores in shopping malls.

In 1998 Belk consolidated all of its stores into one corporation, Belk, Inc. Behind-the-scenes cost cutting helped Belk avoid a national trend among retailers in the first quarter of 2002 by achieving record income. In early 2005 Belk, Inc., still owned and operated by William Henry and John Belk's descendants, had 275 stores in 16 southeastern, mid-Atlantic, and southwestern states, employing 17,900 people and posting annual sales of more than $2.5 billion.

References: Henderson Belk, *Early Belk Partners: Ordinary People Who Did the Extraordinary* (1994); Howard E. Covington Jr., *Belk: A Century of Retail Leadership* (1988).

J. Elizabeth Furr

Belmont Abbey College, located in Belmont (Gaston County), is a Benedictine Catholic college that was founded in 1876. In that year, Father Jeremiah O'Connell purchased the 500-acre Caldwell Place, and under the sponsorship of Abbot Boniface Wimmer and the Benedictine monks of St. Vincent Abbey in Latrobe, Penn., the order established a monastery and college. Four students constituted the college's first class. Nine years later, in 1885, Abbot-elect (later bishop) Leo Michael Haid came to head the fledgling school; he would serve as abbot and president of the college until his death in 1924. In April 1886 the state of North Carolina chartered the abbey/school as Saint Mary's College with degree-granting status; in 1913 Saint Mary's adopted the Belmont Abbey name.

Under the leadership of Vincent George Taylor, a Virginian who succeeded Bishop Haid as abbot and president of the college, Belmont Abbey, though temporarily reduced to junior college status, was accredited by the Southern Association of Colleges and Schools in 1936. In September 1952 the college resumed offering bachelor's degrees and was accredited as a baccalaureate institution five years later.

In 1970 Father Edmund McCaffery assumed the role of *abbot nullius* and college chancellor while Father John Bradley became the first non-Benedictine president of the college. It was during McCaffery's and Bradley's tenure, in 1972, that women residents were first admitted to Belmont Abbey. During the 1990s the college initiated a master's program in education and restored the Lourdes Grotto. The 650-acre complex is home to the college, the monastery, and the Abbey Basilica. By the early 2000s, 40 full-time faculty members served a student body of approximately 1,000 students in pursuit of a wide variety of undergraduate degrees, some through the Adult Degree Program.

References: Paschal Baumstein, *A Carolina Basilica: A History of the Monastic Church at Belmont Abbey, North Carolina, Belmont, North*

Carolina (1999); Baumstein and Debra Estes, *Blessing the Years to Come: Belmont Abbey—A Pictorial Perspective* (1997); John P. Bradley, *The First Hundred Years: Belmont Abbey College* (1976).

James I. Martin Sr.

Benefit of Clergy was a colonial legal term rooted in medieval English law that allowed a person convicted of a capital crime to receive a special pardon and escape execution. Initially, only clergymen—who were often the only members of their communities who could read and write and consequently faced prejudicial decisions by illiterate judges and juries in the common courts—were eligible for benefit of clergy. Over time, any illiterate person could claim the privilege, although not always successfully. Some felonies were so heinous that benefit of clergy was not allowed. By the mid-eighteenth century, for example, North Carolina followed the English law on horse stealing, making it a nonclergyable offense. During the last years of the colonial era, every recorded sentence for horse theft reflected the penalty required by law—death without benefit of clergy. Mixed larceny, stealing from a person or a house, robbery, and burglary were also not clergyable crimes.

In general, benefit of clergy was permitted in North Carolina "in all Cases where Clergy is not expressly taken away, or where the Offender has not once before had Clergy allow'd." Judges never deviated from the law on this point. Throughout the colonial era, no offender was extended the privilege if the law did not allow it. The earliest recorded case in which a North Carolina court granted benefit of clergy was the theft conviction of Elijah Stanton at the Edenton General Court in 1727. Stanton "pray'd the Benefit of the Act of Parliament . . . wherein the Clergy is allow'd." He was then sentenced to "be burnt on the hand with the letter T." A later beneficiary of this form of pardon was Charles Dent, indicted in 1743 for killing his infant daughter. A General Court found him guilty of manslaughter, a clergyable offense, for which he was burned on the hand. At times it was even possible for an offender to evade the required branding on the thumb. This was the experience of Roger Snell, a convicted thief who escaped the traditional branding because "of his very grievous sickness and weakness of Body." From a modern-day perspective, benefit of clergy was a means to mitigate the sometimes harsh penalties rendered under colonial law.

References: Bradley Chapin, *Criminal Justice in Colonial America, 1606–1660* (1983); Donna J. Spindel, *Crime and Society in North Carolina, 1663–1776* (1989).

Donna J. Spindel

Bennett College, in Greensboro, began in 1873 as a coeducational academy for African American youth. The school was founded through the motivation of newly freed slaves,

An 1865 engraving depicting the meeting between Gens. Joseph E. Johnston and William T. Sherman at Bennett Place. NCC.

but the Freedman's Aid and Southern Education Society of the Methodist Episcopal Church assumed responsibility for its support. Philanthropist Lyman Bennett gave the first $10,000 to purchase land and erect a building large enough to house classrooms and also serve as a dormitory. Shortly thereafter he died of pneumonia, and the school was named Bennett Seminary in his honor. The seminary achieved college status in 1889 and began graduating both men and women who assumed positions of leadership in all walks of life. Two of the first African American bishops in the Methodist Episcopal Church were graduates of Bennett College.

During the early part of the twentieth century, the Women's Home Missionary Society decided to build an academy for the education of young black females. To assist the venture, the church's Board of Education offered Bennett College for this purpose. Thereafter the school was operated jointly by the Missionary Society and the Board of Education. In 1926 the school was reorganized solely to educate women. That same year Bennett became a senior college with a physical plant that consisted of nine buildings and 38 acres, serving 151 high school and 10 college students. In 1930 the school graduated its first college class of four women. Several thousand women graduates followed through the years.

By the early 2000s Bennett College was a fully accredited four-year liberal arts college that continued to serve primarily young African American women. Special features of the col-

lege include an integrated program in women's studies and intensive personal counseling, academic advising, and career guidance services. The school also offers satellite telecommunications programming to enhance curricular offerings and uses cooperative arrangements with neighboring institutions for enrollment in Army/Air Force ROTC and for dual degree programs in electrical or mechanical engineering and nursing. Bennett provides interdisciplinary studies in communications media and public relations; learning laboratories to reinforce classroom experiences; computer-assisted instruction; and intercollegiate athletics.

References: Virginia Simmons, "Bennett History," *MS.* (June 1939); Lois Taylor, "Social Action at Bennett College," *Opportunity* 20 (January 1942); Frank Trigg, "Bennett College," *Southern Workman* 55 (February 1926).

Charles W. Wadelington

Bennett Place in western Durham was the locale of negotiations that led to the largest troop surrender of the Civil War. The farmhouse of James and Nancy Bennitt (as they spelled their name) was on the Hillsborough Road, seven miles from Durham Station and about midway between the Confederate army commanded by Gen. Joseph E. Johnston and the Union army commanded by Maj. Gen. William T. Sherman. Under a flag of truce the two commanders met at the farm

An engraving from *Frank Leslie's Illustrated Newspaper*, 22 Apr. 1865, showing Bentonville the morning after the battle. NCC.

three times to discuss a peaceful conclusion to a tragic war. After Sherman's initial agreement was disapproved by President Andrew Johnson, terms of a military surrender acceptable to both sides were reached on 26 Apr. 1865, 17 days after Gen. Robert E. Lee had surrendered his army to Gen. Ulysses S. Grant at Appomattox Courthouse in Virginia. Johnston's surrender affected 89,270 soldiers in the two Carolinas, Georgia, and Florida. It also spared North Carolina the destruction that had befallen neighboring states.

North Carolinians, who did not like to recall the surrender, neglected the site for years. It was not until 1919 that Samuel T. Morgan of Richmond, Va., acquired the farm and talked of a park there; but the house, except for its stone chimney, burned in 1921, and Morgan died before the plans materialized. R. O. Everett of Durham, a member of the General Assembly, secured an agreement by which the state would erect a monument and maintain the site in return for a grant of 3½ acres. A Bennett Place Memorial Commission was created for this purpose, and in 1923 the Unity Monument was raised. Rather than mark the site of a surrender, it proclaimed national unity as demonstrated in the agreement between Johnston and Sherman.

With the approach of the Civil War centennial, interest in the Bennett Place was revived in the 1950s and a reconstruction project was begun in 1960. A condemned house about the same age, size, and interior arrangement as the Bennett house was discovered in the vicinity. It was acquired and moved to the site for restoration. Declared a North Carolina State Historic Site, the restored house and separate kitchen were dedicated in 1962. An 1860 smokehouse was later moved to the site, and in 1982 a visitors center with an auditorium, library/research room, and museum were built.

References: Mark L. Bradley, *This Astounding Close: The Road to Bennett Place* (2000); Richard F. Knapp, ed., *North Carolina's State Historic Sites: A Brief History and Status Report* (1995); Arthur C. Menius III, "James Bennitt: Portrait of an Antebellum Yeoman,"

NCHR 58 (October 1981); William M. Vatavuk, *Dawn of Peace: The Bennett Place State Historic Site* (1989).

William S. Powell

Bentonville, Battle of. The largest Civil War land engagement in North Carolina, the Battle of Bentonville took place during 19–21 Mar. 1865 in rural Johnston County. The encounter was one of the Confederacy's last attempts to defeat the Union army before the South capitulated. With reports that Maj. Gen. William T. Sherman's 60,000-man army was marching toward Goldsboro in two columns, Gen. Joseph E. Johnston concentrated about 21,000 men near the community of Bentonville. His aim was to defeat the Union left wing before it could be reinforced by the right. Johnston thus hoped to prevent or delay Sherman's junction with Maj. Gen. John M. Schofield's Federal forces at Goldsboro.

Confederate cavalry skirmished with Federal troops on 18 March, impeding their advance while Johnston moved toward Bentonville from Smithfield and Averasboro. On 19 March Johnston deployed his troops in a sickle-shaped formation across and above the Goldsboro road. On the left was Gen. Braxton Bragg's command, Hoke's Division, which included the 17- and 18-year-olds of the North Carolina Junior Reserves; it was the largest brigade in Johnston's army. On the right were the troops led by Lt. Gen. William J. Hardee, most of them veterans of the Army of Tennessee.

On the morning of 19 March, Confederate cavalry was again attacked by advancing Union foragers but repulsed them. At 7:00 A.M. the Union left wing under Maj. Gen. Henry W. Slocum began to advance, but it soon encountered the same Confederate cavalry that had stalled the foraging details. Acting on a false report that the main Confederate force was near Raleigh, the Union left wing brushed aside the cavalry and then came under heavy fire. After the Confederates repulsed a Union probing attack, three gray-clad deserters came through the Union lines and informed Slocum that he was confronting Johnston's entire army. Undeceived, Slocum decided to dig in and summon reinforcements, a portion of which arrived by 2:00 P.M. In Johnston's words, his troop deployments "consumed a weary time," so the Confederate attack did not begin until 3:15 P.M. One Union officer stated that "the onward sweep of the rebel lines was like the waves of the ocean, resistless." The Federal left broke and fell back in confusion. Instead of taking advantage of the gaps in the remaining Federal lines, the Confederate units either attempted a frontal assault or became disorganized and failed to attack at all. During the attacks, however, fresh Union troops came up to meet them. Reinforcements likewise bolstered the collapsed Federal left, which had fallen back to a position anchored by four Union batteries. After several determined strikes failed to budge the Federal defenders, the Confederates withdrew to their original lines at sundown.

When word of the battle reached Sherman late on 19 March, he sent the Union right wing under Maj. Gen. Oliver O. Howard to Slocum's support. Johnston redeployed his lines into a *V* to prevent being outflanked and to guard his only route of retreat. By 4:00 P.M. on 20 March, most of the Union right wing had reached Bentonville. Johnston was forced to deploy cavalry on his flanks to give the appearance of a strong front. Uncertain of Johnston's strength, Sherman decided against a general attack and instead ordered his subordinates to probe the Confederate defensive line. The Federal commander expected Johnston to retreat under cover of darkness, but dawn the next day revealed that the Confederates still held their entrenchments.

There was more intense skirmishing on 21 March despite the onset of heavy rain. During the afternoon, a Union attack nearly cut off Johnston's line of retreat before being repulsed by a hastily mounted Confederate counterattack. The Rebels thus escaped from Bentonville mainly because Sherman did not launch a general assault. That night the Confederates withdrew, removing as many of the wounded as possible, and returned to Smithfield. Lt. Gen. Wade Hampton's cavalry was ordered to cover the retreat, engaging in lively skirmishing with the Union forces. Total casualties at Bentonville were 1,527 Federals and 2,606 Confederates. After the battle, Sherman resumed the Union march toward Goldsboro, arriving there on 23 March.

References: John G. Barrett, *The Civil War in North Carolina* (1963); Barrett, *Sherman's March through the Carolinas* (1956); Mark L. Bradley, *Last Stand in the Carolinas: The Battle of Bentonville* (1996).

Ronnie W. Faulkner

Bentonville Battlefield, a North Carolina State Historic Site located in southern Johnston County, consists of 150 of the 6,000 acres on which the Civil War Battle of Bentonville (19–21 Mar. 1865) was fought. This was the last major Confederate open-field offensive of the war and the largest land battle ever fought in North Carolina. A monument to mark the common grave of 360 Confederates was erected by the Goldsboro Rifles in 1893, and in 1927 the United Daughters of the Confederacy commemorated the battle by erecting the North Carolina Junior Reserves monument near the point where the main Confederate line crossed the Goldsboro road.

Frequent attempts were made to acquire, mark, and preserve the battleground, but only in anticipation of the centennial of the battle did the General Assembly appropriate funds and authorize the development of 51 acres as a North Carolina State Historic Site. Included in the purchase were the Harper House, which had been used as a hospital during the battle, the cemetery, and part of the Union earthworks. Interested citizens came forward and raised funds to erect a visitors center, and in 1961, the General Assembly provided additional funds. Further support from state and private sources became available. In 1996, with the assistance of the National Park Service, Bentonville Battleground State Historic Site was designated a National Historic Landmark. In the same year, a grant from the Recreation and Natural Heritage Trust Fund resulted in the purchase of an additional 21 acres.

Historical material is displayed in the visitors center, and on the grounds there are several monuments, reproduced field fortification exhibits, and historic entrenchments. Summer "living history" programs are held at the battlefield, as well as Confederate Memorial Day (10 May) ceremonies and artillery demonstrations. Every five years, the site sponsors a major reenactment of the battle on the weekend closest to its anniversary.

References: Mark L. Bradley, *Last Stand in the Carolinas: The Battle of Bentonville* (1996); Richard F. Knapp, ed., *North Carolina's State Historic Sites: A Brief History and Status Report* (1995).

William S. Powell

Bernice Bienenstock Furniture Library in High Point is considered to be one of the largest and most comprehensive furniture publications libraries in the world. Founded in 1970, the collection and its ancillary services had their origins in the personal collections of Nathan (Sandy) Bienenstock of Pennsylvania. Bienenstock's family-owned *Furniture World* magazine began publication in New Rochelle, N.Y., in the 1920s. His company subsequently bought the *Southern Furniture News* in High Point and renamed it *Furniture South*, a subsidiary publication of *Furniture World*.

Bienenstock retired in 1970, leaving the publication business to his son and moving to High Point. He brought his invaluable collection of furniture publications, which dated back to the eighteenth century and included the complete original volumes published by Thomas Chippendale, George Hepplewhite, and Thomas Sheraton. In High Point, Bienenstock purchased the handsome Colonial Revival home that houses the library from the estate of Charles S. Grayson, a physician and four-term mayor of the city. It was one of the few remaining homes from the city's early development along its main thoroughfare.

A special display case in the Bienenstock Library holds Chippendale's first, second, and third editions of *Gentlemen & Cabinet-Makers Director*, published from 1754 to 1762. Along with those editions are Hepplewhite's *Cabinet-Maker and Upholsterer's Guide* and Sheraton's *Cabinet-Makers and Upholsterer's Drawing Book*, all dated from the mid- to late 1700s. While the entire collection of nearly 6,000 books is officially valued at about $2.5 million, these volumes and a number of others are considered priceless.

Bienenstock's wife Bernice died in 1984, and the library was formally named for her by the Furniture Library Association. The building in which it is housed is on the National Register of Historic Places.

Joe Exum Brown

Bertie County, located in the northeastern Coastal Plain region of North Carolina, was formed in 1722 from Chowan County. Nathaniell Batts, the first permanent white settler in North Carolina, lived in the region of Salmon Creek beginning in 1655. The county was named for Lords Proprietors James and Henry Bertie. Early inhabitants of Bertie County included the Tuscarora Indians, followed by English settlers. Windsor, the county seat, was incorporated in 1766, although it had been settled 40 years earlier. The town was named for Windsor Castle, a residence of the British royal family. Other communities in Bertie County include Lewiston-Woodville, Aulander, Colerain, and Roxobel. The county's important physical features include the Cashie River, the Roanoke River, Albemarle Sound, Conine Island, and the Roanoke River wetlands.

Because of its location and the large amount of water within and surrounding it, Bertie County's soil is rich and ideal for agriculture. The county's major agricultural crops include tobacco, corn, peanuts, cotton, wheat, hay, and soybeans. Livestock produced include beef cattle, swine, and poultry. The county also produces sand, gravel, and clay. Seafood is an important product, and among the county's manufactures are clothing, lumber, farm equipment, and woodstoves.

Bertie County's historic sites include the Hope Plantation (the home of early nineteenth-century North Carolina governor and U.S. senator David Stone), the King-Bazemore House (1763), the Sans Souci Ferry, and a "new" (1858) Windsor Castle. Eden House, alongside the Chowan River, was a colonial estate and home to government; it is now a site of archaeological work. Popular events such as the Fun Day in the Park at Windsor, the Sea and Tee Festival, and Chicken on the Cashie attract many natives of the county as well as tourists.

The population of Bertie County was estimated to be 19,700 in 2004.

Reference: Alan D. Watson, *Bertie County: A Brief History* (1982).

Jay Mazzocchi

SEE ALSO Batts House.

Bethabara is the site of the first Moravian settlement in North Carolina. Located just north of present-day Winston-Salem, Bethabara, meaning "house of passage," was established on 17 Nov. 1753 by 15 Moravian men sent down the Great Wagon Road from Pennsylvania. At first Bethabara was nothing more than a small abandoned cabin located in the northwest part of Wachovia, a 99,000-acre tract of land purchased by the Moravians.

Each of the first colonists had a special skill needed to build a settlement in the backcountry wilderness. Within a few years they and additional church members sent from Pennsylvania had built a thriving community of log and stone structures, including a church, a tannery, and a mill. English, Scotch-Irish, and other German non-Moravian settlers from near and far came to Bethabara to trade. Given its location along the Great Wagon Road and the number of craftsmen making up the settlement, Bethabara became an important economic center on the North Carolina frontier.

When the French and Indian War broke out in 1754, refugees from the outer settlement areas began to arrive at Bethabara looking for shelter and protection. By July 1756 the war was going so badly for the colonists that the Moravians built a stockade around the Bethabara village. As the Indian attacks came closer to Bethabara, the number of refugees grew, soon outstripping the Moravian population. In April 1758 another stockade was built around the mill to protect it and the approximately 200 refugees gathered there. Not until 1761, when the war slowly wound down, did the refugees leave and life at Bethabara return to normal.

After the war Bethabara continued to grow. In 1765 the community received instructions from church leaders to begin construction of the new town of Salem, more in the center of the Wachovia tract. Perhaps the last notable event in the history of the thriving Bethabara village came in June 1771, when Governor William Tryon encamped his army nearby after his victory over the Regulators at the Battle of Alamance. Within months all of the key industries and craft operations were moved to Salem along with most of Bethabara's population.

During the Revolutionary War, Lord Cornwallis marched his English army through Bethabara in February 1781, causing great consternation by confiscating livestock and supplies. By then the few Moravians that remained at Bethabara worked primarily on the farm or at the mill or distillery. By 1820 most of the buildings in Bethabara were gone. The few people left farmed open land that once held a thriving community of industry and activity; for all intents and purposes, the first Moravian settlement site in North Carolina had ceased to exist.

References: C. Daniel Crews, *Through Fiery Trials: Moravians and the Revolution* (1996); Crews, *Villages of the Lord: The Moravians Come to Carolina* (1995); Kenneth G. Hamilton, *History of the Moravian Church* (1967).

R. Jackson Marshall III

SEE ALSO Salem.

Bethel Regiment

Bethel Regiment was the popular name of the first regiment of volunteers raised in North Carolina at the beginning of the Civil War. Commanded by Col. Daniel Harvey Hill, it played a significant role in winning the first land battle of the conflict at Bethel, Va., on 10 June 1861. The first Confederate soldier from the state to be killed in action, Henry Lawson Wyatt, died there.

References: Edward J. Hale, "The 'Bethel Regiment': The First North Carolina Volunteers," in Walter Clark, ed., *Histories of the Several Regiments and Battalions from North Carolina in the Great War, 1861–1865*, vol. 1 (1901).

William S. Powell

Better Baby Contests

Better Baby Contests were held throughout the nation, including in North Carolina, during the early decades of the twentieth century. The contests were a part of both the larger infant welfare movement, which sought to combat high rates of infant mortality and morbidity, and the efforts of various reformers to modernize rural lifestyles and home environments. Designed to measure child health and educate mothers in better child-rearing practices, the contests were held at a variety of venues, including county and state fairs and in mill villages. *Woman's Home Companion* magazine and the *Child Welfare Magazine* of the National Congress of Mothers provide the most complete coverage of better baby contests nationwide. The *Companion* reported that by 1914 all but three states in the country had held at least one baby health contest, and that by 1915 more than 200,000 babies had participated in the contests.

Child participants were initially limited in age from 6 to 36 months, but after 1914 children up to age five were allowed to compete. In spite of some variety in location and organization, North Carolina's better baby contests all followed similar procedures for determining which babies were "better" and which were not. *Woman's Home Companion* developed the Better Babies Standard Score Card in conjunction with physicians, distributed pamphlets with instructions on how to hold contests, and created a wall chart for judges that explained the scoring system and how to make the required measurements.

Scorecards included analyses of such physical characteristics as height; weight; symmetry; quality of skin, fat, and bones; length of head; and shape and size of ears, lips, forehead, and nose. Psychological measurements included disposition, energy, facial and ocular expression, and attention. Using the categories of the scorecard and the typical measurements for normal boys and girls, physicians across the country served as judges, examining babies in order to score and rank them, often differentiating between boys and girls, and urban and rural children. *Woman's Home Companion* also distributed the same prizes to winners across the country, including cash awards of $25 to $100; Better Babies medals in gold, silver, and bronze; and Better Babies certificates of award.

References: Marilyn Irvin Holt, *Linoleum, Better Babies and the Modern Farm Woman, 1890–1930* (1995); Richard A. Meckel, *Save the Babies: American Public Health Reform and the Prevention of Infant Mortality* (1990); Anna Steese Richardson, "A Year of Better Babies," *Woman's Home Companion* (March 1914).

Susan Pearson

Bettis's Bridge, Battle of

Bettis's Bridge, Battle of. Bettis's Bridge (also known as Betti's or Beattie's Bridge), located near the present crossing of the Lumber River (formerly Drowning Creek) by U.S. Highway 401 between Raeford and Wagram at the Hoke County–Scotland County line, was the site of one or more skirmishes between Whig and Loyalist forces during the last days of the American Revolution. The battle has also been called the Battle of Drowning Creek and the Battle of McPhaul's Mill. The bridge, with a narrow causeway through Raft Swamp on both sides of Drowning Creek, was one of the few places where the stream could be crossed with relative ease, and the causeway formed an ideal place for ambush.

Confusion created by conflicting reports by participants, misnaming of geographic locations, and differing interpretations by later writers make it impossible to say with certainty when and where these skirmishes took place, but it appears that there may have been at least two encounters at Bettis's Bridge. The action of 4 Aug. 1781 was brought on by Col. Thomas Wade and his Anson County militia, who were determined to disperse a rumored large Loyalist muster at McPhaul's Mill. Wade pursued the Loyalist force, commanded by Cols. Hector McNeil and Duncan Ray, to Bettis's Bridge, where in an evening engagement that ended at midnight the Loyalists were defeated. Wade had 4 men wounded, and the Loyalists suffered 12 killed and 15 wounded.

The more significant Battle of Bettis's Bridge of 1 Sept. 1781 again involved Wade, who had followed up his previous victory by ravaging the Loyalist region with a large militia. Hearing word of a post of Loyalists with Colonel McNeil near Bettis's Bridge, Wade rode to attack them. Col. David Fanning, the noted Loyalist commander, was passing through the area en route from Wilmington to his interior command in Randolph and Chatham Counties. On receiving word that the Loyalists were defeated at Elizabethtown and that Wade was threatening McNeil, Fanning responded immediately to reinforce McNeil, arriving at dawn on the day of the battle. Although sources differ on the numbers engaged on both sides, there is agreement that Fanning faced a force twice the size of his command, and he credited Wade with 450 men.

After crossing a causeway in the swamp, Fanning dispatched McNeil to the right flank of Wade's position on a nearby hill to block the Whig escape route over the bridge. Fanning then proceeded to the Whig left flank, but an accidental discharge of a musket prematurely began the action at 11:00 A.M. Vigorous assaults over 90 minutes finally unnerved the Whig line, and it broke into a headlong, confused flight. Fanning's men pursued the Whigs for seven miles, taking 50 prisoners and 250 horses. The battle was superbly conducted by Fanning and would have resulted in the total destruction of Wade's force had McNeil succeeded in blocking the retreat as he was ordered. Fanning had 4 wounded and 1 man killed. He counted 23 Whig dead. This victory suppressed the Whigs in southeastern North Carolina and emboldened the Loyalists under Fanning to attack the temporary state capital at Hillsborough 12 days later.

References: Lindley S. Butler, ed., *The Narrative of Colonel David Fanning* (1981); Blackwell P. Robinson, *Battles and Engagements of the American Revolution in North Carolina* (1961).

Lindley S. Butler
Henry A. McKinnon Jr.

Big Ore Bank is a bed of iron ore found in eastern Lincoln County. Worked extensively in the first half of the nineteenth century, this bed was described by Denison Olmsted in 1824 as "extending from the base of Little Mountain on the north, to the foot of King's Mountain on the south." Exploitation of the iron deposits began in 1789, when Peter Forney obtained grants to a large section of barren hills. Soon, others joined in the operations, including Alexander Brevard, Joseph Graham, and John Davidson. Forges, furnaces, and bloomeries were established along the Big Ore Bank, and by 1810 Lincoln County was home to six iron bloomeries.

By the 1820s the Big Ore Bank led the state in the production of iron. Most of it was utilized locally for such things as cooking implements, tools, hinges, and nails. Bar iron was turned out for use by local blacksmiths. But lack of adequate transportation limited the market for the Big Ore Bank iron. Despite this drawback, the iron works in Lincoln County prospered between 1820 and 1840, generating up to 900 tons of iron per year.

The coming of the railroads flooded the market in North Carolina with cheaper iron from Pennsylvania, and the operations along the Big Ore Bank declined. They were no longer economically viable and ceased to function following the Civil War.

References: W. H. Kerr, *Report of the Geological Survey of North Carolina* (1875); William Sherrill, *Annals of Lincoln County, North Carolina* (1932).

John Hairr

Biltmore Forest School, established near Asheville in 1898, was the first school for the scientific study of forestry in the United States. The history of the school began when George Washington Vanderbilt, who had been plagued with a lingering case of pneumonia, traveled to a popular health spa in Asheville. While basking in the fresh air and sunshine of the North Carolina mountains, young Vanderbilt, a multimillionaire via inheritance from his grandfather, Cornelius Vanderbilt, spied Mount Pisgah looming beautifully on Asheville's western horizon. That view so captivated him that he decided to purchase all the land in sight and build a European-style chateau, fully incorporating the scene.

Utilizing a New York attorney to execute the purchases secretly, Vanderbilt began to buy the desired lands in May 1888 and simultaneously launched plans for constructing his chateau. Desiring an estate similar to those he had frequently seen in Europe—ancestral seats owned by landed aristocrats—he secured the services of skilled consultants, including architect Richard Morris Hunt and America's most renowned landscape architect, Frederick Law Olmsted, creator of New York City's Central Park.

When Vanderbilt took Olmsted to the site of his chateau and explained what he desired, the landscape architect quickly informed him that the woodlands in view were so miserable that it would be extremely difficult to transform them into a European-style park. Olmsted instead recommended that European forestry methods be applied. When Vanderbilt agreed to the concept, Olmsted implemented two moves that were to have monumental significance. First, he personally began managed forestry on the estate by ordering the planting of white pine seedlings and a series of selective cuttings to improve the existing woodlands. More important, he suggested that Vanderbilt hire a professional forester, leading to the hiring of a brilliant young American of French descent, Gifford Pinchot, fresh from forestry school in Europe. Pinchot considered himself the first American to undertake a professional career in forestry and was determined, as he said, "to break new ground."

In 1892 the Biltmore lands became Pinchot's laboratory. Utilizing knowledge gained in European forestry schools and improvising with American ingenuity when faced with new challenges, he conceived and implemented the first working plans for the woodlands, thereby establishing the first scientifically managed private forestry program in America. In addi-

Carl Schenck (with a moustache, near the middle of the back row) and his forestry students, 14 June 1912. NCC.

tion, Pinchot skillfully publicized what he was doing by preparing and exhibiting the Biltmore forestry story at the Chicago World's Fair in 1893.

The resulting publicity brought so much fame to Pinchot that he asked Vanderbilt to secure another forester who could assist him. The Biltmore forests thus acquired a second young forester, Carl Alwin Schenck, who had a Ph.D. from a renowned German forestry school and ambition equal to that of Pinchot.

After Pinchot was called to Washington, D.C., to found what became the U.S. Forest Service, Schenck became Vanderbilt's chief forester. As publicity conscious as Pinchot, Schenck cultivated friendships with the nation's leading forestry and conservation officials. Building on Pinchot's pioneering efforts, he was determined to make the Biltmore forests models for the rest of the nation. One unexpected result was that numerous young men interested in careers as foresters applied for the opportunity to serve as interns to Schenck. Their pleading influenced Schenck to establish what he called the Biltmore Forest School in 1898, the first formal school of forestry in America.

Schenck preached "practical forestry," which emphasized profit. Without formal textbooks, he devised his own curriculum, sought prominent authorities as lecturers, and diligently exposed his students to a combination of theoretical and practical forestry. Designed as a one-year finishing school, his institution sought the enrollment of sons of influential men involved in the timber industry. His recruiting catalogs stipulated that an applicant be male, at least 20 years old, a high school graduate, and preferably experienced in practical lumbering.

Eager applicants, especially from the New England region, flocked to Schenck's school, spending part of their time in the classroom and part in actual forest activities. The remote "Pink Beds" section of Vanderbilt's holdings became their popular summer working classroom. Schenck labored diligently and successfully to instill a strong esprit de corps in his students, and they proudly responded, calling themselves "Schenck's Foresteers."

From 1898 to 1909 the Biltmore Forest School was conducted on the Biltmore estate. In 1909 Schenck and Vanderbilt had a disagreement over management practices, and Schenck was forced to leave the Biltmore estate. He found an alternate site for his school at Sunburst, one of Champion Paper Company's holdings. For some four years he led his students in pursuit of practical forestry, carrying them all across the nation to observe his forestry techniques at work. In the meantime numerous universities such as Yale (with financial assistance from Pinchot) and Cornell had established sound professional forestry schools and had made such inroads into Schenck's clientele that he decided in 1913 to close his school and return to Germany.

Graduates of Biltmore Forest School attained prominent forestry-related positions throughout the nation and the world. Their old working field at the Pink Beds became, in 1914, part of Pisgah National Forest (the first eastern national forest). In 1968 Congress recognized the significance of Schenck's, Pinchot's, and Vanderbilt's contributions and officially established 6,540 acres of the Pisgah National Forest, centering in the Pink Beds, as the "Cradle of Forestry in America." Schenck's Biltmore Forest School was reconstructed and in 1976 designated as a National Historic Site.

Reference: Carl Alwin Schenck, *The Birth of Forestry in America: Biltmore Forest School, 1898–1913* (1974).

Harley E. Jolley

Biltmore House. George Washington Vanderbilt, inheritor of part of the huge Vanderbilt fortune accrued by his grandfather, steamship and railroad magnate Cornelius Vanderbilt, first visited Asheville in 1889 for health reasons. Although remote, the area around Asheville functioned as the center for a growing health industry that capitalized on good water, a pleasant climate, and a relaxing atmosphere. George Vanderbilt seemed to have little interest in his family's business. He was, however, an accomplished scholar, with a special interest in languages, philosophy, literature, architecture, and landscaping. Inheriting his father's appreciation of art, George

Biltmore House, late 1980s. Photograph by Tim Buchman.
Courtesy of Preservation North Carolina.

often accompanied him on buying trips. He fell in love with the western North Carolina mountains and chose to build a southern country home in an area near the village of Best, just south of Asheville. Upon completion, Vanderbilt's "country home" included 255 rooms and over 125,000 acres of property, the largest residence ever built by a private citizen in the United States.

Vanderbilt purchased the town of Best in 1889 and renamed it Biltmore Village. The name Biltmore derived from "Bildt," the region in Holland from which the Vanderbilt family originated, and "more," an old English word for rolling upland country. When Vanderbilt purchased Best, it consisted of a railway station, two small inns, a gristmill, and a few homes. By 1896, construction of Biltmore Village was under way, and the new village included cottages, shops, carpentry and other traditional craft schools, an Episcopal church, a post office, a laundry, a hospital, and the Biltmore Office Building. Architect Richard Morris Hunt, designer of New York's Tribune Building and the base of the Statue of Liberty, modeled Biltmore Village after a Swiss village.

Vanderbilt originally had no style in mind for his house. When Hunt arrived, he and Vanderbilt agreed that the property, located where the Swannanoa and French Broad Rivers meet, resembled the French Loire Valley. The site's similarity to the French region prompted the house's Francis I style, reminiscent of sixteenth-century chateaux in the Loire Valley. Hunt equipped the chateau with all the modern conveniences possible, and he and Vanderbilt went on buying trips to supplement Vanderbilt's existing collection of art, books, and antiques. Well known for his problem-solving ability, Hunt fulfilled his client's extravagant requests. Vanderbilt wanted his house on a promontory with a back porch looking out onto a view of Mount Pisgah, even though he chose a site in a valley. Hunt suggested a plan to fill in the valley and build Vander-

bilt's promontory, and workers hauled sufficient rock and soil to create a hill on which to build the house.

The house's majesty necessitated matching grounds, and Vanderbilt issued the challenge of creating them to landscape designer Frederick Law Olmsted. Best known for designing New York City's Central Park, Olmsted achieved a greater triumph at Biltmore, a property nine times larger than Central Park. Olmsted drew plans for formally landscaping the 200 acres immediately surrounding the house, laying out the English Walled Garden, the Italian Garden, and a manmade lake called the Lagoon. He also planned to refurbish forests and create farms and a nursery on the rest of the land.

Gifford Pinchot managed the reforestation project. The first trained forester in the United States, Pinchot planned New York State's Adirondack Park and founded the U.S. Forest Service. Vanderbilt's forest, named Pisgah Forest, began about 10 miles from Biltmore and extended 60 miles to the west. Pinchot established the Biltmore Forest School and developed a comprehensive plan to continue the tree nursery, reforestation, and harvest projects. His principles of sustained yield, which struck a balance between cutting timber and growing new trees, first developed at Biltmore and remain standard practice in forestry today. The estate also had a dairy farm, a pig farm, and a poultry farm on site.

Construction of the house, completed by hundreds of laborers, took place between 1890 and 1895 and provided employment for much of the local population. Workers built a spur railway to bring in supplies from the depot in Biltmore Village to the construction site three miles away. Limestone, the fundamental building stone used in the house, was shipped from Indiana, and workers built a brick factory and a woodworking factory on site as well. The finished masterpiece included walk-in refrigeration, electricity, advanced plumbing, and central heating, all at a time when many of Vanderbilt's neighbors still used outhouses.

The house was officially opened on Christmas Eve 1895, with 350 family members and friends in attendance. Stacks of gifts for employees' children stood under a 30-foot Christmas tree in the enormous banquet hall. The party set a precedent for entertaining at Biltmore, and in following years, the house became a haven of amusement for the Vanderbilts—George Vanderbilt married Edith Stuyvesant Dresser in 1898, and their only child, Cornelia, was born in 1900—and their wealthy friends. Guests enjoyed formal dinners and balls, or slipped into the extensive library for reading and study. The gymnasium, bowling alley, swimming pool, and ping-pong table provided a variety of diversions. Outdoor activities included hunting, fishing, riding, hiking, croquet, archery, and strolling the grounds. The Vanderbilts' lifestyle at Biltmore depended tremendously on the service staff, with about 80 servants required to run the house and stables efficiently.

In later years, the Vanderbilt family spent more and more

time away from the estate. The 1902 depression hit the family fortune hard. With Biltmore's operating costs reaching roughly $6,000 a month, the family shut down the estate and sailed to Europe. Despite the financial crisis, Mrs. Vanderbilt later set up a school at Biltmore to teach domestic arts and crafts to local women.

George Vanderbilt died in March 1914. His daughter Cornelia inherited a trust fund left by her father, while Edith inherited Biltmore's house and lands. Edith sold the federal government a large part of Pisgah Forest, which now makes up the core of Pisgah National Forest, reducing the Biltmore property to a more manageable 8,000 acres. A flood destroyed Olmsted's nursery in 1916, but the dairy thrived and paid for the estate's maintenance.

Cornelia married British diplomat John Francis Amherst Cecil in 1924, and their sons George and William spent much of their childhood at Biltmore. Edith married Senator Peter G. Gerry in 1925 and moved out of Biltmore, leaving its operations to the Cecils. During the First World War and the Great Depression, Junius Adams, a local judge, was employed to manage the property. He incorporated Biltmore and opened the house to visitors for the first time in 1930.

Edith died in 1958, and in 1960 the Cecil sons split the Biltmore property. George took the dairy and a portion of the estate, while William took the house and the part of the estate known as Biltmore Forest. William became head of the Biltmore Company and a leading historic preservation advocate. Although the U.S. government has declared Biltmore a National Historic Landmark, it operates without federal grants or subsidies and pays property taxes. The property also contributes significantly to the economy of Asheville and western North Carolina. Roughly 750,000 visitors each year come to the estate and take the self-guided tour, which includes 85 rooms of the house as well as the grounds.

References: Mead Parce, *Twice-Told True Tales of the Blue Ridge and Great Smokies* (1995); Susan M. Ward and Michael K. Smith, eds., *Biltmore Estate: House, Gardens, Winery* (1990); Robert Wernick, "Here's the House that Lots and Lots of Jack Built," *Smithsonian* (September 1992).

Brooke Calton

Biltmore Industries. The origins of Biltmore Estate Industries can be traced to Eleanor Vance and Charlotte Yale, missionaries who moved from the North to Biltmore Village near Asheville in 1901. Both women desired to work with young people, and shortly after arriving in Biltmore they organized a Boys' Club that later became affiliated with All Souls Church. Vance taught the craft of wood carving. At about this time, George and Edith Vanderbilt of the nearby Biltmore Estate became interested in establishing an industrial school to "make it possible for native girls and boys to become productive and useful citizens of their own community." Biltmore Estate Industries was subsequently established, combining the talents of Vance and Yale with the resources of the Vanderbilts. Because George Vanderbilt was occupied with other pursuits, Edith Vanderbilt became the driving force behind the effort.

By 1905 there were 20 boys and girls in training at Biltmore Industries, and a year later the business made the transition from a cottage craft enterprise to a successful craft industry. Early products were baskets, needlework, and hand-carved articles, including small pieces of furniture and cabinets. Edith Vanderbilt was extremely interested in establishing a weaving project, and in 1907 the homespun operation began. The quality, however, was not what Vanderbilt had envisioned. Consequently, she sent Vance and Yale to study production methods in England and Ireland. In addition to returning with improved methods, they brought back a loom from Scotland as a model for the woodworking class to replicate. By 1909 Biltmore homespun had become the most popular sales item of Biltmore Industries. It subsequently became popular with several presidential families. Mrs. Calvin Coolidge selected for her wardrobe a red homespun, which became known as "Coolidge Red." Suits for President Herbert Hoover were made of "Hoover Grey," a wool blend of 85 percent black and 15 percent white material. Some of Franklin D. Roosevelt's white suits were made of Biltmore homespun. Eleanor Roosevelt was so interested in the homespun operations that she visited Biltmore Industries in 1934.

Although the Vanderbilts subsidized the business early on, Biltmore Industries had begun to make a profit by 1909. By 1921 the company claimed to be the "largest hand-weaving industry in the world." Biltmore Industries was purchased by Harry Blomberg in 1953, and the Asheville entrepreneur oversaw the operations of its looms for the next 30 years. After his death in 1991, Blomberg's heirs renovated some of the original buildings and grounds and opened a craft showplace named the Grovewood Gallery, several craft studios, and the Grovewood Cafe. By the early 2000s Biltmore Industries was still producing a small amount of high-quality wool fabrics using original equipment and techniques.

Reference: Frances Louisa Goodrich, *Mountain Homespun* (1931).

Ron Holland

Bingham School was actually a series of classical academies overseen by three generations of the Bingham family over a period of 135 years. The esteem in which these teachers were held was such that any school they managed came to be known as the Bingham School. The first schoolmaster in the line was Presbyterian minister William Bingham, born in Ireland and educated in Scotland. He emigrated to Wilmington and set up a school in 1793. After serving in a number of educational posts, he established a school of his own at Mount Re-

I RESIDENCE OF MAJ. R BINGHAM. SUPT.
II BATH HOUSE & WATER WORKS.
III GYMNASIUM & SOCIETY HALLS.
IV ACADEMY.
V BOILER HOUSE.
VI GAS HOUSE.

VII PLAY GROUND.
VIII BARRACKS.
(1ST TO 3TH GALLERIES.)
IX MESS HALL
X CONSERVATORY.
XI MRS WM BINGHAMS RESIDENCE.

BINGHAM SCHOOL,

BINGHAM SCHOOL P.O. ORANGE CO. N.C.

Bingham School P.O., Orange Co. N.C. Month 4 Day 23 1885

The buildings and grounds of Bingham School at Mebane as depicted in an engraving on the school's letterhead, 1885. NCC.

pose, northwest of Hillsborough, where he had settled as early as 1816. A log cabin served as the school building, and other cabins accommodated his 35 to 40 students. During the spring term in 1826 Bingham died, and his son William James Bingham finished the term in his place.

The younger Bingham, university educated and trained in law by legislator and jurist Archibald D. Murphey, found teaching to his liking and became principal of the Hillsborough Academy in 1827. Under his direction the school thrived and attained a national reputation for excellence. In 1840 his brother John Archibald Bingham joined the school's administration.

In 1844 William James Bingham moved to Oaks, southwest of Hillsborough, to establish what he called a select classical and mathematical school. Bingham reduced the enrollment from the 100-plus students at Hillsborough to some 30 in order to give them closer personal attention. He also managed a model farm to experiment with new strains of seed and new methods of cultivation. Bingham's illness in 1855 closed the school. In 1857, however, Bingham's sons William and Robert joined him in partnership, and the school reopened, with double the enrollment, as W. J. Bingham and Sons.

In 1863 the elder Bingham's illness and Robert Bingham's

absence in the army obliged William Bingham the younger to take over operations. In 1864 all three Binghams and their families moved with the school to a new location on the North Carolina Railroad east of the town of Mebane, where it became officially known as the Bingham School.

In 1866 William James Bingham died, and his sons took over the school. William Bingham, admired for his musical and literary accomplishments as well as his pedagogy, wrote textbooks that became standard works in American schools, including a Latin grammar (1863), an English grammar (1867), and an edition of Caesar's *Commentaries* (1864). He died in 1873. His brother Robert made several improvements to the school, both in its buildings and curriculum. His efforts, however, were undermined by serious family complications regarding financial interests in the school, and in 1891 he established his own Bingham School on 250 acres overlooking the French Broad River in Asheville. This incarnation of the Bingham School featured the first gymnasium and swimming pool built in the South specifically for school use. The Bingham School operated successfully until its closing in 1928, one year after Robert Bingham's death.

References: Sallie Bingham, *Passion and Prejudice: A Family Memoir* (1989); Robert I. Curtis, "The Bingham School and

Classical Education in North Carolina, 1793–1873," *NCHR* 53 (July 1996); Robert H. Stone, *A History of Orange Presbytery, 1770–1970* (1970).

Jean B. Anderson

Biotechnology. North Carolina is home to one of the most dynamic biotechnology industries in the United States. In the early 2000s, 10 percent of all biotechnology firms were based in the state, and North Carolina employed nearly 1 in 10 biotechnology workers. Leading pharmaceutical companies GlaxoSmithKline and Merck & Co. operated facilities in North Carolina, as did firms such as Bayer, Wyeth, Baxter, and Biogen Idec. Many of these companies' facilities in North Carolina are the largest of their type in the world. Additionally, as of the early 2000s, four of the world's largest contract research organizations and testing companies—LabCorp, Quintiles Transnational, PPD, and AAI—were based in North Carolina, representing one of the heaviest concentrations of such companies in the world.

The growth of the biotechnology industry in North Carolina has been encouraged by several factors, including the state's excellent research universities and medical schools and the continuing influence of the Research Triangle Park, a world-renowned research facility located between Raleigh and Durham. The industry has also benefited from generous public investment at the state and local levels. In 1984 the General Assembly created the North Carolina Biotechnology Center, a private nonprofit corporation to promote the industry's development. The center works in three main areas: science and technology development, business and technology development, and education and training. It also works with universities and companies to secure grants, loans, and technical assistance in the biotechnology field. In the early 2000s, in an effort to serve a larger portion of the state, the center established branch offices in Greenville, Wilmington, Winston-Salem, Asheville, and Charlotte.

North Carolina has seen its biotechnology sector increase at annual rates of between 10 and 15 percent through the early 2000s, generating approximately $3 billion in annual revenue. It is believed that the state's biotechnology industry will continue to expand to meet the needs of the nation's aging population and to combat the threats of global pandemics and bioterrorism.

Robert Blair Vocci

Birds. SEE Audubon Society of North Carolina; Waterfowl; Wildlife.

Bishop of Durham Clause. The Carolina charters of 1663 and 1665 contained an important provision conferring upon the eight Lords Proprietors of Carolina and their successors the power to "have, hold, use, exercise, and enjoy" all the "Rights, Jurisdictions, privileges, prerogatives, Royalties, liberties, Immunities, and Franchises" as those "heretofore had, held, used, or enjoyed" by "any Bishop of Durham, in our Kingdom of England." Such powers also had been included in the grant of "Carolana" to Sir Robert Heath in 1629.

In the eleventh century the Crown erected the Bishopric of Durham into a "county palatine" and invested it with extraordinary, almost regal, powers because of the bishopric's proximity to the untamed and often turbulent region bordering Scotland. Although in theory subject to the central authority, the palatinate had its own judicial system, mint, powers of legislation, and other trappings of sovereignty.

Lord Baltimore's charter of 1632 granting him the territory of Maryland contained a similar provision, including the major concession that powers were to be those of "any" bishop of Durham. That single word meant that an act of Parliament of 1536 greatly reducing the bishops' temporal authority, or "regalia," did not apply to Baltimore's grant or to those of the eight Lords Proprietors. Instead, the Proprietors of both Maryland and Carolina could claim the regalia of the fourteenth century, when the palatinate of Durham enjoyed its greatest independence.

The practical effect of the Bishop of Durham clause on the governing of Carolina was, however, not great. Virtually all of the powers exercised by the Lords Proprietors in the Fundamental Constitutions and other instruments of governance, such as commissions and instructions to governors and other officials, had been specifically granted by the Crown in various other clauses in the charters.

References: Charles M. Andrews, *The Colonial Period of American History* (4 vols., 1934–38); Mattie Erma Edwards Parker, ed., *North Carolina Charters and Constitutions, 1578–1698* (1963).

Robert J. Cain

Bishop of London. During the seventeenth and eighteenth centuries, the bishop of London had extradiocesan responsibility for Anglican congregations and clergy outside the British Isles. The precise legal and ecclesiastical terms of the bishop's duties concerning the American colonies were never officially or legally spelled out (except briefly during Edmund Gibson's tenure from 1723 to 1748), and colonial affairs necessarily took a back seat to the primary concerns of the bishop of London as an officer of state, a member of the House of Lords, and the spiritual and temporal administrator of a large, critically important, and demanding diocese.

Anglican clergy serving in North Carolina, as in all other British overseas possessions, had to secure a license from the bishop of London identifying their charge and qualifying them to receive the king's (or queen's) bounty, which helped to cover travel expenses. Prospective clergy, including increasing numbers of colonials, attracted to overseas ministry looked to the bishop of London for ordination. The responsibility for licensing and ordination added substantially to the bishop's workload, but the registers, correspondence, recommendations, and credentials collected at Fulham Palace, the bishop's official residence, now afford scholars the most important manuscript collection for the study of colonial Anglicanism.

References: George MacLaren Brydon, *Virginia's Mother Church and the Political Conditions under Which It Grew* (2 vols., 1947); Arthur Lyon Cross, *The Anglican Episcopate and the American Colonies* (1902).

John K. Nelson

Black and Tan Constitution was a derisive label used by many white Democrats to characterize the North Carolina Constitution of 1868. The term referred to the individuals who were believed to have a primary influence on the framing of the constitution—recently arrived northern whites ("carpetbaggers"), southern white Unionists ("scalawags"), and blacks who were thought to be mainly of mixed blood. Conservative Democrats throughout the South applied the epithet to other state constitutions drafted at Republican conventions during Reconstruction.

Although labeled "black and tan" by opponents, the Constitution of 1868 was a progressive document for its time, providing for a number of important changes. For example, it gave all male adults, including blacks, the right to vote and extended some nonpolitical rights to women. Voters were to elect state executive officers, judges, and county officials, and all property and taxation requirements for holding office and apportioning seats in the State Senate were eliminated. The governor's term of office was extended from two to four years, and separate public school systems for both blacks and whites were established.

Ratified by a vote of 93,086 to 74,016, the 1868 constitution was frequently amended and remained the state's fundamental law until 1971.

References: William C. Harris, *William Woods Holden: Firebrand of North Carolina Politics* (1987); Otto H. Olsen, *Carpetbagger's Crusade: The Life of Albion Winegar Tourgée* (1965).

William C. Harris

Black Codes. Soon after the Civil War, southern states governed by Presidential Reconstruction (1865–67) adopted racially discriminatory laws, called "black codes," to maintain close control over the newly freed slaves, thereby retaining as much of the elements of slavery as possible. North Carolina's black code was arguably not as stringent as those of states with larger black populations, but that would have made little practical difference to the state's newly emancipated black citizens, who were refused most privileges of citizenship. Approved in 1866 after a vigorous debate in the General Assembly, the North Carolina code—actually a series of laws—denied blacks the right to vote, serve on juries, and testify against whites in court; provided for the apprenticing of young blacks to their former owners; established capital punishment for blacks convicted of raping white women; attempted to restrict their movement into and out of the state; and prohibited them from owning or carrying firearms or other weapons unless they obtained a license one year before the purchase. The black code also prohibited interracial marriages, and it applied the same criminal and civil laws, including those relating to the ownership of property, to the former slaves as to whites. The code was enforced by loosely organized (and generally unrestrained) county militias.

Strong northern and black opposition to the southern black codes contributed to the termination of Presidential Reconstruction in 1867 and the imposition of Congressional, or Military, Reconstruction in the former Confederate states, including North Carolina. The new political order nullified the black codes and attempted to institute civil and political equality for African Americans, but it did little to address the underlying social and economic inequities. After Reconstruction ended in 1877, southern white politicians returned to practices that disfranchised blacks and perpetuated their status as second-class citizens. In fact, many Jim Crow laws of the early twentieth century found their origins in the black codes.

References: Roberta Sue Alexander, *North Carolina Faces the Freedmen: Race Relations during Presidential Reconstruction, 1865–1867* (1985); Jane Dailey and others, *Jumpin' Jim Crow: Southern Politics from Civil War to Civil Rights* (2000); Eric Foner, *Reconstruction: America's Unfinished Revolution, 1863–1877* (1988).

William C. Harris

Black-Eyed Pea is a small, cream-colored, kidney-shaped legume with a black "eye" (hilum) at its inner curve. It is also known as a cow pea or field pea. Under the "southern peas" classification, black-eyed peas are cultivated in North Carolina for both fresh and dried markets. Traditionally, dried black-eyed peas have been valued for their long shelf life and preferred for special occasions that can accommodate the overnight soak and half-day simmer they require. Consumption of fresh black-eyed peas has grown due to modern demands for foods that can be more quickly prepared. Postharvest handling and marketing of fresh southern peas must adhere to strict grading and shipping standards; consequently, the fresh market product is more expensive. Like other beans, black-eyed peas are typically also available frozen and in cans.

Black-eyed peas and other southern pea varieties are grown extensively across the southern half of the United States, but production is not limited to the southern regions. Both California and Michigan are large commercial producers of the dried varieties. North Carolina cultivates southern peas from the coast to the mountains, but they are not a major source of income for growers. Most of the crop is for local consumption.

Several magical properties and superstitions have been connected to black-eyed peas in North Carolina and elsewhere. Hoppin' John, a dish made with black-eyed peas and rice, is traditionally eaten on New Year's Day to obtain good luck throughout the coming year. Black-eyed peas are also considered helpful for medicinal purposes, as one technique suggested for the removal of warts demonstrates: "If you rub a black-eyed pea over your wart, then throw it over your left shoulder and go away without looking back, the wart will go away."

Carmena B. Zimmerman

Black Freemasonry, like its white counterpart, promotes fellowship within a membership that engages in a wide variety of social and benevolent activities. Although black freemasonry dates back to the American Revolution, it was not until 1866—during a period of tremendous antiblack sentiment following the Civil War—that the first African American lodge appeared in North Carolina. Within five years of the founding of King Solomon Lodge in New Bern, lodges were also created in Wilmington, Fayetteville, and Raleigh. In 1870 these four groups established a state organization, the Most Worshipful Grand Lodge of the State of North Carolina, with headquarters in Fayetteville.

As black freemasonry spread across the state, the composition of its membership changed. Whereas most of the original members were urban residents, the fraternal organization gradually reached the countryside. Because black masons were often businessmen and landowners, there was a close relationship between freemasonry and black economic enterprise. Such membership increased personal and business contacts and promulgated valuable skills about property management. Black lodges often rented their property to black businessmen.

During the late nineteenth century, black freemasonry in North Carolina continued to grow in size and extend the range of its social and benevolent activities. From 37 lodges and 1,000 members in 1880, the organization grew to 358 lodges and more than 10,000 members by 1910. The fraternal society offered short-term financial assistance to members experiencing financial problems, provided insurance for the widows of deceased members, and established a black orphanage in Oxford. It also made substantial contributions to the United Negro College Fund, the Legal Defense Fund of the National Association for the Advancement of Colored People, a scholarship program for black students, and a number of black North Carolina colleges. By 2005 the Most Worshipful Prince Hall Grand Lodge Free and Accepted Masons of North Carolina and

Jurisdictions, Inc., headquartered in Durham, was the state's central organization of black lodges, which numbered more than 320.

Robert C. Kenzer

Black Mountain College, an experimental school situated near Asheville, was founded in 1933 by John Andrew Rice, Theodore Dreier, and several others who had previously taught at Rollins College in Winter Park, Fla., but who had either been fired or resigned for various reasons. Inspired by the progressive educational ideals of John Dewey, the founders developed an innovative "whole-student" concept, featuring a community that not only learned together but lived and worked (typically farming) together as well. There were no required courses, no formal graduation, and no social distinctions between the faculty and the student body. The institution was run not by administrators but by its professors and students (the latter participated in all but financial and "purely educational" decisions).

During the college's twenty-three-year existence, it had fewer than 1,200 students, of which only 55 actually graduated with formal degrees. But Black Mountain College became renowned for its commitment to individualized programs of study, creative expression in the classroom, and development of students' artistic abilities to support learning in any subject. Josef Albers, a leading figure in the Bauhaus artistic movement and an emigrant from Nazi Germany, became the school's first art teacher. Beginning in 1944, the college began offering special summer sessions in the arts, which attracted prominent artists such as Willem de Kooning and Robert Motherwell (both former students of Albers) as visiting faculty. Other professors included experimental composer John Cage and visionary inventor Buckminster Fuller, who began work on his famous geodesic dome design while teaching at Black Mountain. Albert Einstein and poet William Carlos Williams were among the school's many distinguished guest lecturers.

Throughout its history, Black Mountain College struggled to support its thriving community of artists, who were often more concerned with their own creative freedom than the practical problems of maintaining a small arts college. An influx of World War II veterans, empowered by the GI Bill to pursue their higher education aspirations, rescued the school from its funding drought during the war, but the conservative climate of the 1950s proved inhospitable to its unconventional and progressive approach to education. Despite the energetic leadership of poet Charles Olson, Black Mountain College closed in 1956.

With the encouragement of former students, many of them accomplished artists and scholars in their own right, the Black Mountain College Museum and Arts Center was erected in 1993 to commemorate the school's revolutionary principles and preserve its legacy. The Asheville facility—supported by

Summer Institute at Black Mountain College, 1946. Left to right: Leo Amino, Jacob Lawrence, Leo Lionni, Theodore Dreier, Nora Lionni, Beaumont Newhall, Gwendolyn Lawrence, Ise Gropius, Jean Varda (in tree), Nancy Newhall (sitting), Walter Gropius, Mary Gregory, Josef Albers, and Anni Albers. Courtesy of NCOA&H.

the North Carolina Arts Council, the North Carolina Department of Cultural Resources, Western Carolina University, the Asheville Arts Council, and others affiliated with Black Mountain College—maintains exhibits, archives, and faculty and alumni collections and sponsors a variety of programs dedicated to their work.

References: Martin Duberman, *Black Mountain: An Exploration in Community* (1972); Mary Emma Harris, *The Arts at Black Mountain College* (1987); H. G. Jones, *North Carolina Illustrated, 1524–1984* (1983); John A. Rice, *I Came Out of the Eighteenth Century* (1942; rev. ed., 1957).

Wiley J. Williams
Robert Blair Vocci

Black Panther Party was founded in Oakland, Calif., in October 1966. The controversial organization espoused black

pride and black control of neighborhood institutions, preached self-defense against alleged police brutality in African American communities, and developed educational and food programs for the local black poor. The Black Panther Party quickly drew national media attention, and chapters formed in such cities as Chicago, New York City, Des Moines, and Denver.

In North Carolina, Greensboro had some Black Panther adherents, and Charlotte supporters formed the Afro-American Unity Organization, which failed to receive official recognition by the Oakland party headquarters. Benjamin Chavis, a future defendant in the Wilmington Ten case, served as an officer in the short-lived Charlotte organization. It was Winston-Salem, however, that became home to the state's most organized Panther chapter, which operated a Free Breakfast for Children program; provided free clothing, free ambulance service, and classes in black consciousness; and held small rallies to promote its causes. The Winston-Salem office also established a satellite Community Information Center in nearby High Point, where a local police officer was wounded during a gun battle in February 1971.

Wherever it settled, including in Charlotte and Winston-Salem, the Black Panther Party attracted the heavy scrutiny of the Federal Bureau of Investigation. The bureau did not close its counterintelligence program files on the Black Panthers in North Carolina until the mid-1970s. By then, the Winston-Salem chapter, like many other Black Panther affiliates nationwide, was badly hampered by lack of funds, internal dissension, and the incarceration of its members.

Reference: Philip S. Foner, ed., *The Black Panthers Speak* (2002).

J. Christopher Schutz

SEE ALSO Wilmington Ten.

Black Second. SEE Congressional Districts.

Black Tongue is the familiar name for the often fatal effects of a deficiency of the vitamin niacin (once designated Vitamin B^3, now B^5), found chiefly in liver, lean meat, poultry, fish, and beans. The term, seldom used since the mid-twentieth century, is generally synonymous with pellagra in humans; it was sometimes, although imprecisely, identified as anthrax in livestock. Recorded as early as 1820, Black Tongue became a serious problem in North Carolina and other southern states around the beginning of the twentieth century with the spread of rural poverty that accompanied tenant and share-crop farming and low-wage employment in cotton mills. Economic slumps increased the incidence.

Black Tongue, which occurred anywhere that diets consisted almost entirely of corn, was perhaps the most acute vitamin deficiency the United States has known. The affliction caused diarrhea, mental confusion, loss of weight and strength, irritation inside the mouth and stomach lining, and painful lesions of the skin, especially areas exposed to sunlight. The affected tissue would darken, thicken, and become scaly; cases were sometimes misdiagnosed as leprosy. Symptoms could progress to depression, stupor, and an irrational violence. Until foods containing niacin were determined a cure, as many as two of every three Black Tongue patients died of its effects.

By 1914, Black Tongue was epidemic in the South and Congress legislated an investigation. That year, 551 deaths from the disease were recorded in North Carolina; in 1915 the state's death toll rose to 831. Wide experimentation in 1915, typically on prison and asylum inmates and orphan children, revealed to federal public health professional Joseph Goldberger that certain foods cured pellagra, although the simple niacin compound was not identified as the agent until 1937. Annual deaths in the state peaked at 1,015 in 1930. The yearly total stayed well into the hundreds through the Depression and beyond; it did not fall to double digits until 1944. The first year that the state recorded no Black Tongue deaths was 1960. The discovery of vitamins and their nutritional roles began the disease's rapid decline; in modern times it has been almost unknown in the United States.

Reference: Alan M. Kraut, *Goldberger's War: The Life and Work of a Public Health Crusader* (2003).

Whitmel M. Joyner

Bladen County lies in the Coastal Plain region of southeastern North Carolina. It was formed in 1734 from New Hanover County and named for English commissioner of trade and plantations Martin Bladen. Its earliest inhabitants were the Waccamaw Indians. Colonial newcomers to the region included Highland Scots and English settlers. Bladen County has been named the "Mother of Counties" because all or part of 55 of North Carolina's modern counties were formed from its original land. It remains one of the state's largest counties. The county seat, Elizabethtown, was established in 1773 and incorporated in 1895. The town was named for either the "sweetheart" of Isaac Jones, owner of the land the town was built on, or for Queen Elizabeth I of England. "Tory Hole," near Elizabethtown, was the site of a key Revolutionary War battle in August 1781. Other communities located in Bladen County are Clarkton, White Lake, East Arcadia, Bladenboro, Dublin, and Tar Heel.

The county's physical features include the Cape Fear, South, and Black Rivers and the Bladen Lakes State Forest and Game Land. In former times, the county contained as many as 1,000 lakes; today, it has far fewer, but these include White and Jones Lakes, examples of the famous (and scientifically mysterious) Carolina Bays.

Bladen County farms produce swine, tobacco, blueberries, peanuts, and cotton. Industrial enterprises include peanut processing and the manufacture of textiles and clothing, plastics, and resin products. Bladen County hosts a number of annual festivals and events, such as the East Coast Delta Kite and Glider Competition. In 2004 the population of Bladen County was estimated to be 33,000.

Bernadette Rider

SEE ALSO Carolina Bays; Elizabethtown, Battle of.

Blakeley Silver Service. Word that Captain Johnston Blakeley and the men of the U.S. sloop of war *Wasp* had defeated the British sloops *Reindeer* and *Avon* in the summer of 1814 proved welcome news for Americans hungry for military and naval successes during the War of 1812. The good news was particularly welcome in North Carolina, since Blakeley

The Blakeley tea and coffee service. Photograph courtesy of the North Carolina Museum of Art, Raleigh. Gift of Mr. and Mrs. Charles Lee Smith Jr., in honor of Dr. Robert Lee Humber.

had grown up in Wilmington. Eager to add its voice to those praising the young hero, the General Assembly on 7 Dec. 1814 voted "to present to Captain Blakely [*sic*], on his return to the United States, a superb sword, appropriately adorned, in the name and on behalf of his fellow citizens." Unfortunately, Blakeley never made it back to the United States. He, his crew, and the *Wasp* were last seen on 9 Oct. 1814. Although rumors abounded, their loss remained a mystery.

The General Assembly waited to acknowledge Blakeley's death until 28 Dec. 1816, when it resolved that the sword intended for the captain should be delivered to his widow, Jane Hoope Blakeley. They located Mrs. Blakeley in Boston, but instead of sending a sword they wrote her and asked if some other gift might be appropriate since the captain's only child, Udney Maria Blakeley, was a daughter. "You have been so kind as to desire my opinion on the subject of a present more proper than a sword for a female," she replied; "allow me to propose a set of tea-plate." The General Assembly endorsed the change of plan and agreed to spend as much as $500 for the gift.

The French-style tea service was completed in 1819 and presented to Maria Blakeley on her sixteenth birthday. Consisting of a teapot, a coffee pot, a milk jug, a slop or waste basin, and a sugar bowl with cover and tongs, the service was the work of Anthony Rasch, a German-born and -trained silversmith who worked in Philadelphia from 1804 until 1820. Rasch's classically derived design may have been inspired by plate 34 in *Recueil de Décorations Intérieures*, an 1802 publication by Charles Percier and Pierre F. L. Fontaine, designers to Napoleon's court. The eagle finials that the larger vessels bore and the crossed anchors engraved on the back of each piece represented Blakeley's naval exploits and presumed death.

The silver service remained outside of North Carolina for a century and a half before returning permanently in 1968 as a gift to the North Carolina Museum of Art in Raleigh. Inherited by descendants of Maria Blakeley's widower and his second wife, the tea set was acquired through art dealers and donated to the museum by Mr. and Mrs. Charles Lee Smith Jr. of Raleigh in honor of Robert Lee Humber of Greenville. The Museum of Art has lent the Blakeley service for numerous exhibitions in other American museums. Its usual location is the building's board room.

References: Wendy A. Cooper, *Classical Taste in America, 1800–1840* (1993); H. G. Jones, "N.C. 'Adopted' Girl in 1817," *Goldsboro News-Argus*, 23 Mar. 1972; A. R. Newsome, "Udney Maria Blakeley,"

NCHR 4 (April 1927); David B. Warren, *Marks of Achievement: Four Centuries of American Presentation Silver* (1987).

Thomas J. Farnham
Additional research provided by Elizabeth Reid Murray.

Bland Expedition. Edward Bland, a Virginia merchant, explored the region between the Meherrin and Roanoke Rivers in North Carolina in the late summer of 1650. A Tuscarora Indian chief in the lower Roanoke River country had invited trade with Virginia, and Bland hoped to negotiate with the Tuscarora for that purpose. Leaving Fort Henry (now Petersburg, Va.) in August, Bland and a party of Virginians rode southeast on horseback along the north side of Blackwater River, turned south through Nottoway Indian country, and crossed the Nottoway and Meherrin Rivers before entering present-day North Carolina on 31 August. The party's immediate destination was what was known to Bland as the Hocomawananck (Roanoke) River and renamed by him Blandina River.

After a night camping three or four miles above the falls of the Roanoke, the party moved south to the falls and approximately opposite the present town of Roanoke Rapids. Here they were disappointed in not making contact with the Tuscarora chief who had invited the Virginians to his territory. Warned that the Indians might have dangerous suspicions as to the whites' intentions, Bland's expedition turned back northward on 1 September. They made inquiries among the Roanoke Tuscarora about an unidentified "Englishman amongst them, and . . . an English woman cast away long since." Although apparently nothing was learned of the woman, the man was said to be at a Tuscarora village some distance farther on. Before leaving, Bland's party wrote "to the Englishman in English, Latin, Spanish, French and Dutch," there being evidently some question as to his nationality. (Three years later, explorers from Lynnhaven River learned from Tuscarora near the mouth of the Roanoke that a Spaniard lived at a nearby Tuscarora village.)

The Bland Expedition is of interest because it establishes the location of the Tuscarora village known to the first Jamestown settlers as Ocamahawan. It was the understanding of John Smith and others that not only some Spaniards but also several refugees from John White's 1587 Lost Colony resided at one time or another at Ocamahawan during or before 1611. In any event, soon after 1650 Virginia traders were successful in establishing a fur trade with the Tuscarora, and for the next half century this tribe remained an important factor in Virginia's commerce.

References: Clarence Alvord and Lee Bidgood, eds., *The First Explorations of the Trans-Allegheny Region by the Virginians* (1912); Lewis R. Binford, "An Ethnohistory of the Nottoway, Meherrin and Weanock Indians of Southeastern Virginia," *Ethnohistory* 14 (Summer–Fall 1967).

Thomas C. Parramore

Blandwood was the Greensboro home of North Carolina governor John Motley Morehead (1841–45). The original structure consisted of a wooden dwelling that was constructed in approximately 1825. In 1844 Morehead contracted innovative architect Alexander Jackson Davis to expand the residence, and Davis devised a Tuscan-style addition of four rooms centered around a tower. A kitchen and an office were connected to the main house by vaulted arches.

Upon Morehead's death in 1866, the mansion remained in the family until 1896, when a drug and alcohol rehabilitation organization known as the Keeley Institute of North Carolina leased, and later purchased, Blandwood. The building served as a rehabilitation center until the 1960s, but by 1965 the property stood empty and in danger of demolition.

The trustees of Guilford College acquired Blandwood in 1965 and served as a holding agency until the newly created Greensboro Preservation Society could raise the funds to maintain the property. In 1968 the society purchased Blandwood from the college with the aid of a grant from the Department of Housing and Urban Development, and the next year the General Assembly appropriated money for renovation. The National Register of Historic Places listed Blandwood in 1970, and by 1975 it was substantially restored, furnished with original and period items, and available for public visits. The restored carriage house serves as a gathering place for meetings and social events. The oldest example of Italian villa architecture in the United States, Blandwood is operated as a house museum by the private, nonprofit organizations Preservation Greensboro, Inc., and the Blandwood Guild.

Reference: Mary Lewis Rucker Edmonds, *Governor Morehead's Blandwood and the Family Who Lived There* (1976).

Alexander R. Stoesen

Blank Patents were warrants to survey land for grants that had blank spaces to be filled in later with the description of the land. They were issued by colonial land office officials for their own convenience, since blank patents freed them from having to appear in person to sign each patent individually. The receiver of the blank patent subsequently wrote a description of the land he desired. This gave the individual a claim to a specific piece of property while allowing him to avoid paying taxes until the land was actually surveyed and recorded.

Predictably, untaxed land held under blank patents became a cause of concern to royal officials. In North Carolina, corrupt use of patents was an issue of considerable controversy in the 1720s and 1730s.

William S. Powell

Blind Tiger was a term of unknown origin applied to establishments that sold liquor during Prohibition. Newspapers and other publications in North Carolina in the 1920s used

Blandwood, late 1980s. Photograph by Tim Buchman. Courtesy of Preservation North Carolina.

it as a synonym for "speakeasy," and North Carolina author Thomas Wolfe also used it in his novel *The Web and the Rock* (1938). With the repeal of Prohibition in 1933, the term became obsolete.

William S. Powell

Blockade-Running. At the outset of the Civil War, the Union navy was faced with the monumental task of blockading the Confederate coast from Virginia to Texas, a coastline measuring almost 4,000 miles and containing 189 harbors. President Abraham Lincoln's proclamations of 19 and 27 Apr. 1861 made the blockade of the South complete, but only on paper. When the war started there were only 42 Union warships in commission, a far cry from the number required to close the Confederate ports. In May only two Federal vessels guarded the entire coast of North Carolina, and it was not until 20 July that the blockader *Daylight* took up station off the Cape Fear River. Twelve months later Adm. S. P. Lee had three cordons of Union ships guarding the mouth of the river. The first line was semicircular, reaching along the coast in either di-

rection and far out to sea. In this cordon he placed sluggish, barely seaworthy vessels, whose orders were not to give chase but to signal the position of the blockade-runners to the faster ships patrolling in the second group or to the few cruisers even farther out. Still, he found it difficult to prevent ships from slipping through the blockade.

Wilmington, situated 570 miles from Nassau and 674 miles from Bermuda, was ideally situated for blockade-running. Located 28 miles up the Cape Fear River, it was free from enemy bombardment as long as the forts at the mouth of the river remained in Confederate hands. Moreover, Smith Island and Frying Pan Shoals jutted out into the Atlantic Ocean for approximately 25 miles, which made guarding Cape Fear's two navigable entrances very difficult. A fleet patrolling the two channels was required to cover a 50-mile arc and at the same time stay out of range of Confederate shore batteries. Protecting New Inlet, the passage preferred by most vessels, was massive Fort Fisher.

Few southerners were engaged in the business of blockade-running. It was monopolized by English and Scottish mer-

Harper's Weekly illustration from 3 Dec. 1864 showing Union ships off New Inlet blocking the approach to Wilmington via the Cape Fear River. Fort Fisher is in the background. NCC.

chants who had ships and capital to invest in this hazardous but lucrative trade. British firms dispatched both luxury items and war matériel to the West Indies in regular merchant ships for transfer to blockade-runners, which would arrive in port loaded with cotton. With the South's leading staple crop selling for around 3 cents a pound in the Confederacy and 45 cents to one dollar a pound in Europe, enormous profits were to be made. On only eight trips through the blockade the British steamer *Banshee*, the first steel-hulled ship to cross the Atlantic, earned for its stockholders 700 percent profit.

After experiencing the tribulations of purchasing supplies from privately owned blockade-runners, North Carolina governor Zebulon B. Vance sent agents to England to purchase a steamer. They contracted for the *Advance*, which from 26 June 1863, the date of its maiden voyage to Wilmington, until its capture at sea a little over a year later, contributed much to North Carolina's war effort.

References: Dawson Carr, *Gray Phantoms of the Cape Fear: Running the Civil War Blockade* (1998); Thomas E. Taylor, *Running the Blockade: A Personal Narrative of Adventures, Risks, and Escapes during the American Civil War* (1896); Stephen R. Wise, *Lifeline of the Confederacy: Blockade Running during the Civil War* (1988).

John G. Barrett

SEE ALSO *Advance; Modern Greece.*

Bloc Voting generally refers to a clique or coalition of legislators who vote similarly on issues, such as the farm vote or the big-city vote. In North Carolina, and elsewhere in the South, it also refers to factions or groups of the general electorate that vote in mass with a high degree of cohesiveness. Historically, some white candidates in the state have used the term in a derogatory way to describe the cohesiveness of black voters in support of particular candidates.

In the late New Deal era, as urban blacks began to identify with the civil rights stance of the national Democratic Party and President Franklin D. Roosevelt, they switched their allegiance from the Republican Party to the Democratic Party. To elect their candidate into office, blacks began voting in "bloc" for the Democrats. One of the most famous instances of bloc voting in North Carolina politics occurred in the racially charged Democratic senatorial primary of 1950 between Frank Porter Graham and Willis Smith. Smith supporters used the term to describe and explain Graham's showing in Durham precincts with large numbers of black voters. Smith's forces successfully used race as an attack issue at the end of the first primary and extensively in the run-off primary, especially in the east, to present Graham as "one who favors mixing the races." Smith won in the runoff.

In 1964 bloc voting reemerged as an issue in the Democratic gubernatorial run-off primary. Dan Moore, a moderate conservative, said that his opponent Richardson Preyer, a progressive, "owed his first primary lead and the major part of his entire vote to the bloc of Negro votes . . . and this vote hangs like a millstone around his neck." On the Monday after the first primary, then–TV editorialist Jesse Helms used his nightly *Viewpoint* editorial, broadcast across the east on WRAL-TV, to claim that if it had not been for the black ballot, Preyer would have received fewer votes than Moore or segregationist candidate I. Beverly Lake Sr. The tactic worked again, as Moore easily defeated Preyer in the run-off primary. Decrying the black bloc vote was used by Helms himself in his 1984 U.S. Senate campaign against Governor James B. Hunt Jr., as well as his 1990 Senate campaign against Harvey Gantt, former black mayor of Charlotte.

References: Samuel Lubell, *The Future of American Politics* (1956); Julian M. Pleasants and Augustine M. Burns III, *Frank Porter Graham and the 1950 Senate Race in North Carolina* (1990); William P. Snider, *Helms and Hunt: The North Carolina Senate*

Race, 1984 (1985); James R. Spence, *The Moore-Pryer-Lake Primaries of 1964: The Making of a Governor* (1968).

W. Lee Johnston Jr.

SEE ALSO Helms-Hunt Senate Race; Smith-Graham Senate Race.

Blossom's Ferry was located on the Northeast Cape Fear River on the border between New Hanover and Pender Counties, one mile east-northeast of the community of Castle Hayne and approximately nine miles north of Wilmington. There is evidence of ferry activity as early as 1731 on the Northeast Cape Fear; a drawbridge and a ferry were sometimes operated in conjunction with each other in that vicinity. When Jackson Wood bought the property in 1866, the title included only "the ferry known as Big Bridge Ferry." Wood and his nephew John E. Wood operated a ferry there until 1882, when the property and ferry concession were purchased by Margaret Sophia Blossom. She and her husband Samuel continued the ferry service until his death in 1926. By that time the construction of a state-maintained bridge less than a mile west of the site eliminated the need for a ferry, ending 200 years of transportation activity. Archaeological research conducted at the ferry site from 1981 to 1983 by the East Carolina University Program in Maritime History and Underwater Research revealed the remains of two ferries, one dating from the mid-eighteenth century and the other from the late eighteenth or early nineteenth century.

Reference: Gordon P. Watts Jr. and Wesley K. Hall, *An Investigation of Blossom's Ferry on the Northeast Cape Fear River* (East Carolina University Department of History, ECU Research Report no. 1, January 1986).

Beverly Tetterton

Blue Cross and Blue Shield of North Carolina. In 1927 Wilburt C. Davison, dean of the newly created Duke Medical School, began to tackle the problem of inadequate medical care in North Carolina. With the assistance of Watson S. Rankin, director of the Hospital and Orphan Sections of the Duke Endowment, Davison investigated a Roanoke Rapids medical plan that required employees of the area's textile mills to prepay Roanoke Rapids Hospital 25¢ per week per family, entitling them to receive basic minimum care at the hospital. Davison then called on George Watts Hill Sr., a Durham banker-philanthropist and president of the board of directors of Watts Hospital, and other Durham businessmen and doctors to arouse their interest in setting up a plan on a community-wide basis with all community hospitals participating.

In August 1933 Davison and others established the Hospital Care Association in Raleigh, a voluntary plan of prepaying hospital bills. Unlike other prepayment plans, this one was open to citizens all across the state. By pooling funds, Hospital Care provided members access to hospital treatment and provided hospitals much-needed financial support. Having foundered in Raleigh by November 1933, the organization reorganized and moved to Durham, where Hill's interest in the prepayment idea continued and Duke and Watts hospitals provided credit extensions.

In November 1935 a competitive hospital prepayment plan, Hospital Saving Association, was established in Chapel Hill. Three years later, both Hospital Saving and Hospital Care were approved by the American Hospital Association to display the Blue Cross symbol. In 1941 the General Assembly enacted Chapter 57 of the General Statutes of North Carolina (recodified as part of Chapter 58 in 1987), which became the legal enabling act governing the operation of both plans. The spirit of competition resulted in both associations expanding their choices of hospital, medical, and surgical benefits; and each added group, life, and related benefits by organized subsidiaries to compete with commercial package plans for major medical benefits. Between 1946 and 1956, combined membership of the Hospital Saving and Hospital Care plans tripled.

On 2 Jan. 1968 the two organizations finally merged as North Carolina Blue Cross and Blue Shield, and the North Carolina Department of Insurance subsequently gave its approval. The present name, Blue Cross and Blue Shield of North Carolina, Inc. (BCBSNC), was adopted in 1973.

Beginning in the 1990s, pressure grew to convert BCBSNC to a for-profit company. To further these efforts and to produce greater profits and continue to increase its membership, the company acquired Partners National Health Plan, the state's largest for-profit health maintenance organization, in October 2001. The BCBSNC Foundation was established in November 2000, and its first gift of $1 million went to the ECU CARE program at the Brody School of Medicine of East Carolina University; this was an attempt to strengthen the company's claim that becoming a for-profit business would help the organization compete with larger companies as well as aid the people of North Carolina. As of 2006, BCBSNC remained a not-for-profit health care company with more than 3,000 employees and 3.2 million members. The company is headquartered in Chapel Hill, with field offices in Charlotte, Raleigh, Winston-Salem, Hickory, Greenville, and Wilmington.

References: Blue Cross and Blue Shield of North Carolina, *Fifty and Forward* (1983); V. H. Hart, "The History of Blue Cross and Blue Shield of North Carolina," in Dorothy Long, ed., *Medicine in North Carolina: Essays in the History of Medical Sciences and Medical Services, 1524–1960* (1972); Jeff Zimmer, "Blue Cross Still Awash in Green," *Durham Herald-Sun* (16 Nov. 2002).

Wiley J. Williams

A performance at MerleFest in Wilkesboro, 29 Apr. 2001. Left to right: Brad Davis (guitar), Earl Scruggs (banjo), Gary Scruggs (bass guitar), and Marty Stuart (mandolin). Photograph by David Schenk.

Bluegrass Music. Whether lightning-paced and exuberant or slow and mournful, the songs of bluegrass music are immediately recognizable by their tight vocal harmonies; precisely arranged string band instrumentation featuring banjo, fiddle, mandolin, and guitar; and legendary "high lonesome sound." An essential differentiation between bluegrass and the "old-time" country music that preceded it is that of the banjo-playing styles in the two genres. In old-time music, the banjo player employs the "clawhammer" style, also known as "frailing" or "drop-thumb," while bluegrass utilizes the three-finger roll or crawl style developed by Earl Scruggs of North Carolina's Cleveland County. This style of American folk music takes its name from its most famous early practitioners, Bill Monroe and the Blue Grass Boys, with Kentuckian Monroe long known as the "Father of Bluegrass Music."

After 1945 the bluegrass sound exemplified by Monroe and the Blue Grass Boys, with the revolutionary banjo playing of Scruggs, swept North Carolina with its exciting new music displaying strong roots in the brother duet and string band styles. Scruggs, who received a North Carolina Folk Heritage Award in 1996, helped make bluegrass internationally popular through his work as a member of Monroe's band and subsequently in his own duo with Lester Flatt (Flatt and Scruggs), an act that called Raleigh home for a time after World War II. Although virtually every important band from the early days of bluegrass music featured North Carolinians or performed on radio stations in the state, few North Carolina–based bands achieved fame at the time. Among the best known were Hack Johnson and His Tennesseans, the Church Brothers, and the Murphy Brothers. At the end of the 1960s, Raleigh's ephemeral New Deal String Band became the first progressive, "hippie" bluegrass ensemble to achieve widespread notoriety. Burlington's Bass Mountain Boys stood among the most popular nationally touring acts in bluegrass from the late 1980s until their 1996 breakup. New Vintage from Raleigh also earned extensive national airplay.

Another North Carolinian considered an American bluegrass ambassador to the world is Arthel "Doc" Watson, the great banjo player and flat-picking guitarist from Deep Gap, to whom the University of North Carolina at Chapel Hill awarded an Honorary Doctor of Letters degree in 1997. Other North Carolinians well known in the world of folk and acoustic music include Charlotte's Arthur C. Smith and such ensembles as the Bluegrass Experience, the Sons of Ralph (Lewis) Featuring Ralph, and the Shady Grove Band. Other important twentieth-century North Carolina banjo players performing in bluegrass and related genres include Charlie Poole, Tommy Jarrell (a National Folk Heritage Award winner), Fred Cockerham, Bascom Lamar Lunsford, George Pegram, Kyle Creed, Clarence Tom Ashley, Dink Roberts, John Snipes, Odell Thompson, Jan Davidson, Don Lewis, Lynn Smathers, Nancy Sluys, and Union Grove old-time banjo champion, Hollow Rock String Band member, and Red Clay Ramblers founder Tommy Thompson.

Bluegrass festivals large and small occur all over North Carolina and the South from early spring until late fall. One of the leading events is late April's Merle Watson Festival, popularly called MerleFest, in Wilkesboro, named and held in memory of Doc Watson's late son.

Bland Simpson
Art Menius

SEE ALSO MerleFest; Old-Time String Band Music.

Blue Laws

Blue Laws refer to statutes designed to enforce morality as some lawmakers understand it, such as restricting the hours that stores can open on Sundays or the sale of alcoholic beverages. The term "blue law" originated in the eighteenth-century New Haven colony in Connecticut, where the laws were so called because of the color of paper on which they were printed or bound. In the early 1960s North Carolina experimented briefly with a statewide Sunday blue law (effective October 1961) that had the support of the North Carolina Merchants Association and various religious groups. Four Charlotte discount stores—G.I. Surplus Store, Mecklenburg Surplus Company, Clark's Charlotte, Inc., and Atlantic Mills of North Carolina—brought an action to toss out the law, and in May 1962 the North Carolina Supreme Court ruled unanimously that it was "unconstitutionally vague, uncertain, and indefinite."

Local jurisdictions continued to maintain an array of blue laws, particularly those related to Sundays. In Lincolnton and elsewhere, an ordinance at one time permitted convenience stores, but not supermarkets, to open on Sunday mornings. For a while in Goldsboro and Wilmington, certain types of businesses—such as cigar and tobacco shops, fruit stands, service stations, auto parts stores, grocery stores, hotels, motels, restaurants, and pharmacies—could open on Sundays, whereas clothing, appliance, hardware, and musical instrument stores could not. Businesses with "brown-bagging" permits authorized by local ordinances could operate, but stores and restaurants could not sell alcoholic beverages. Because of the inequities in these Sunday blue laws, such regulations were abolished in most cities and towns by the end of the twentieth century, though a number of them remain in force.

Reference: David N. Laband and Deborah Hendry Heinbuch, *Blue Laws: The History, Economics, and Politics of Sunday Closing Laws* (1987).

Wiley J. Williams

Blue Lodges

Blue Lodges were secret groups organized to defend slavery and the "southern way of life" in response to the Kansas-Nebraska Act of 1854. The new law, sponsored by Senator Stephen A. Douglas of Illinois and supported by President Franklin Pierce, allowed settlers in the Kansas and Nebraska territories to decide for themselves whether to permit slavery, striking down the Missouri Compromise of 1820, which had designated Missouri as the legal boundary of the institution.

The 1854 legislation prompted groups on both sides of the issue to hurriedly recruit homesteaders for Kansas. The New England Emigrant Aid Society sent hordes of free-state settlers to the territory, whereas the pro-slavery forces had less success in finding southerners, other than Missourians, who were willing to move there. Consequently, pro-slavery leaders from Missouri organized Blue Lodges in North Carolina and other southern states where their supporters met secretly to raise money and recruit volunteers to rush to Kansas and vote illegally as settlers. Promising "free ferry, a dollar a day, and liquor," the Blue Lodges set up bogus communities, which were little more than places for the phony settlers to gather just before an election. Blue Lodge members wore a bit of hemp in their lapels and used the password phrase, "Sound on the goose."

In the 1855 election, illegal pro-slavery voters from Missouri and other states captured the first Kansas territorial legislature and legalized slavery. Free-state settlers, knowing they had been cheated, met in Topeka to draft an antislavery constitution and elect their own governor and representatives. Kansas now had two governments, neither legitimate. Rather than call for a new, legal election, Pierce chose to support the pro-slavery territorial legislature. The sporadic bloodshed between the opposing groups quickly escalated into gun battles, rampant pillaging, torture, and murder. "Bleeding Kansas" foreshadowed the terrible destruction to come when the nation fell into civil war in 1861.

Reference: Nicole Etcheson, *Bleeding Kansas: Contested Liberty in the Civil War Era* (2004).

Barry McGee

Blue Mold

Blue Mold, a fungal disease, decreases or destroys tobacco quality. Initially it was diagnosed in 1921 in tobacco plant beds in Georgia, and by 1931 it had found its way southward to Florida and northward to South Carolina, North Carolina, and Virginia. The mold enters the tobacco plant through the leaves or systemically through the soil. It is promoted by cool, damp, and rainy weather. By 1940 blue mold had become a serious and widespread plant bed problem in North Carolina, severely damaging the supply of regional tobacco plants and forcing farmers to transport plants from other states. This resulted in the spreading of blue mold, along with other diseases, throughout the flue-cured and burley tobacco areas of North Carolina.

The Blue Ridge Parkway near Doughton Park, ca. 1950s. Photograph by Gus Martin. NCC.

By the late 1970s blue mold had spread from plant beds into tobacco fields, costing farmers in North Carolina and other states over $252 million in lost market value. Scientific research during the last years of the twentieth century, however, proved reasonably successful in controlling the disease and the damage it causes.

Reference: Furney A. Todd, *Tobacco in the United States* (rev. ed., 1979).

W. W. Yeargin

Blue Ridge Parkway traverses 469 miles of the southern Appalachian Mountains beginning in Virginia in the Shenandoah National Park and proceeding south into North Carolina. It passes through parts of 12 of the state's counties and the Pisgah National Forest and ends in the Great Smoky Mountains National Park. The parkway was first planned as the "Crest of the Blue Ridge Highway," a visionary project conceived in 1909 by Col. Joseph Hyde Pratt, director of the North Carolina Geo-

logical and Economic Survey. From his position of leadership in the Good Roads movement, Pratt began the political and engineering work needed to build a scenic toll road extending about 350 miles from Marion, Va., to Cornelia, Ga. The route was chosen to provide views of the finest mountain scenery in the eastern United States, so that a trip along the highway would be an experience "never to be forgotten." From White Top Mountain in Virginia, the road was to run through the high country by Boone, Blowing Rock, Grandfather Mountain, Linville, and Little Switzerland, and from there through Buck Creek Gap, Stepp's Gap, Balsam Gap, and the Great Craggy Mountains into Asheville. To maximize scenic values, the route was to be located as near the summits of the mountains as possible. South of Asheville the highway would connect to Henderson, Brevard, Lake Toxaway, and Highlands, and into Georgia near Rabun Gap, finally ending beyond Tallulah Falls.

Pratt intended the road to be 24 feet wide, with a sand-clay or gravel surface and a gradient not exceeding 4.5 percent. The estimated cost was $5,000 per mile. Portions of the

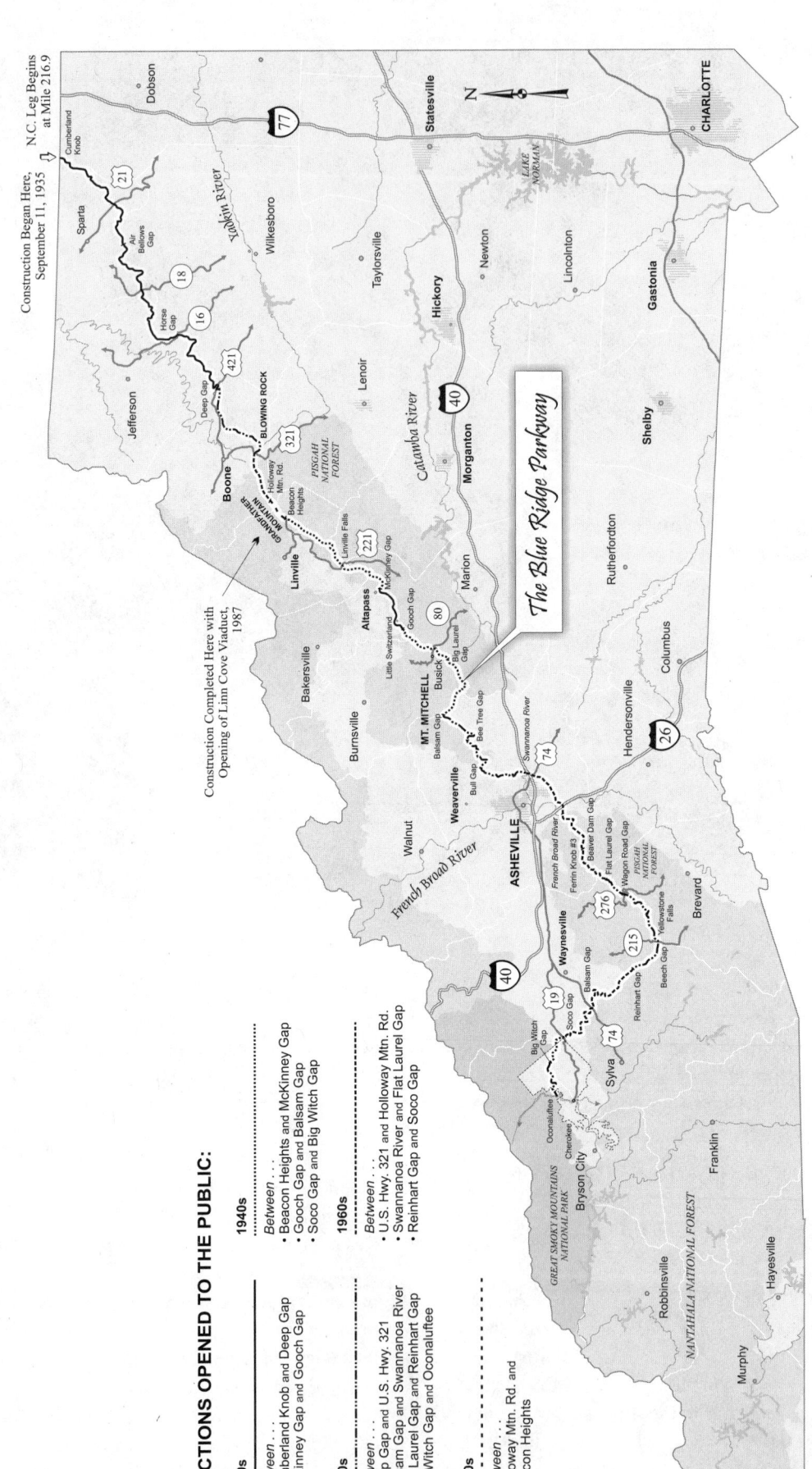

SECTIONS OPENED TO THE PUBLIC:

1930s

Between . . .
- Cumberland Knob and Deep Gap
- McKinney Gap and Gooch Gap

1940s

Between . . .
- Beacon Heights and McKinney Gap
- Gooch Gap and Balsam Gap
- Soco Gap and Big Witch Gap

1950s

Between . . .
- Deep Gap and U.S. Hwy. 321
- Balsam Gap and Swannanoa River
- Flat Laurel Gap and Reinhart Gap
- Big Witch Gap and Oconaluftee

1960s

Between . . .
- U.S. Hwy. 321 and Holloway Mtn. Rd.
- Swannanoa River and Flat Laurel Gap
- Reinhart Gap and Soco Gap

1980s

Between . . .
- Holloway Mtn. Rd. and Beacon Heights

Construction Began Here,
September 11, 1935

N.C. Leg Begins
at Mile 216.9

Construction Completed Here with
Opening of Linn Cove Viaduct,
1987

The Blue Ridge Parkway

The Blue Ridge Parkway in North Carolina. Map by Mark Anderson Moore, courtesy NCOA&H.

route had already been constructed, such as the Yonahlossee Road around Grandfather Mountain's south flank from Blowing Rock to Linville, but the more technically daunting segments through the Black Mountains and Great Craggies had not been laid out until the summer of 1910, when a surveying crew began work. Pratt apparently planned to use convict labor to help keep the costs as low as possible, although he recognized that the expense of laying the road through these rugged mountains might exceed $12,000 per mile.

Construction of new segments began by July 1912, under charter to Pratt's Appalachian Highway Company of Chapel Hill, but by World War I the Crest of the Blue Ridge project had been abandoned, presumably because of financial pressures and resource shortages. In the 1930s federal plans for the Blue Ridge Parkway, linking the Shenandoah and the Great Smoky Mountains National Parks, incorporated much of the concept and some of the actual route proposed by Pratt. In 1935 the roadway was resurrected as a project of the New Deal's Public Works Administration.

Construction of the parkway began on 11 Sept. 1935 and was completed 52 years later to the day, with the Linn Cove Viaduct dedication in 1987. Breathtaking scenery and numerous recreational opportunities make the Blue Ridge Parkway one of the most popular attractions of the national park system and an enormous boon to the local tourism industry and local land developers.

References: Harley E. Jolley, *Blue Ridge Parkway: The First Fifty Years* (1985); Ina Van Noppen and John Van Noppen, *Western North Carolina since the Civil War* (1973); Capus Waynick, *North Carolina Roads and Their Builders*, vol. 1 (1952).

Robert E. Ireland
Marcus B. Simpson Jr.

Blues. North Carolina boasts significant contributions to the musical tradition known as the blues. Throughout its formative decades, the blues was the music of solo artists rather than groups, with the guitar as the dominant instrument. Blues players generally picked the guitar with the thumb and one or two fingers, allowing them to play several strings at different times in complex patterns.

In the Carolinas, African American musicians around the first decade of the twentieth century developed a style of music known as the Piedmont blues. An important form of traditional music in North Carolina, the Piedmont blues is characterized by a guitar style that contains a distinct bass line played on the lower strings of the guitar as well as a melody picked on the higher strings. The bouncy, fingerpicked guitar style of Piedmont blues distinguishes it from Delta blues, which is often slow and mournful. Vocals, often paralleled by the melody played on the guitar, tell about the triumphs and trials of everyday life, such as work, love, heartbreak, loneliness, and the pitfalls of drinking and other overindulgences.

Elizabeth Cotten performs at the North Carolina Folklife Festival at Eno River State Park in Durham, 1978. Photograph by Jerry Cotten. NCC.

In the 1930s and 1940s, Durham was an important center of blues culture as a result of tobacco's unprecedented success. Rural African Americans flocked to the city, drawn by the comparatively high wages paid by the American Tobacco Company. Alden "Tarheel Slim" Bunn, Richard and William Trice, and Floyd Council are some of the well-known North Carolinians who earned their livings playing the blues at private parties and local clubs in Durham and the Piedmont during this time.

"Blind" Gary Davis, a South Carolinian later known as Reverend Gary Davis after his ordination, moved to Durham in the early 1930s and was a major influence on perhaps the best-known bluesman from North Carolina, Blind Boy Fuller. Born Fulton Allen in Wadesboro, Fuller moved to Durham in 1929 and soon became a regular among the street musicians on Pettigrew Street and near the booming tobacco warehouses. By the mid-1930s, Fuller moved into the clubs and recording studios. Having assembled an outstanding lineup of bluesmen that included the famous harmonica player Sonny Terry, himself blind, and his former mentor Davis, Fuller went on to record 135 songs on a number of labels, scoring minor hits with "Rag Mama Rag" and "I'm a Rattlesnakin' Daddy."

Within the Piedmont blues tradition, women developed a distinctive sound, and many of the best exponents of this tradition were North Carolinians, including Etta Baker of

Morganton, Alga Mae Hinton of Johnston County, and Elizabeth Cotten of Carrboro. Cotten's inimitable picking style and heartbreaking vocals on "Freight Train" and other songs evoked the hard life shared by many southern, rural African Americans.

On the coast, Richard "Big Boy" Henry, born in Beaufort, grew up listening to bluesmen playing on the streets of New Bern, where his family moved during the Depression. Henry learned to sing and play guitar from itinerant South Carolinian Fred Miller, and the two played together at house parties and fish fries. When Miller relocated to New York City, Henry visited frequently, where he met fellow North Carolinians Sonny Terry and Brownie McGhee. The three recorded together in 1951, but the recording was not released until decades later. Disenchanted, Henry put music aside during the 1950s and 1960s, but he picked up his guitar upon returning to Beaufort in 1971. Henry's song "Mr. President," written in response to cuts in social welfare programs in the 1980s, earned him a W. C. Handy Award from the Blues Foundation. Interested in folklorists' attempts to document the work songs sung by himself and other African Americans who fished on menhaden boats, in 1988 he helped organize a group of retired fishermen known as the Menhaden Chanteymen to re-create the singing and share it with the public.

A social analysis of blues culture, the first of its kind, was undertaken by University of North Carolina sociologists Howard Odum and Guy B. Johnson in the 1920s and 1930s. Their *Negro Workaday Songs* (1925) remains a classic examination of the social and cultural roots of the blues. Durham's rise as an important stop on the growing blues circuit proved beneficial to Odum, who began collecting lyrics and melodies of folk blues as early as 1905. Odum's research revealed important links between blues lyrics of the younger performers and the dislocation of many African Americans caused by the poverty of southern agriculture and the lure of northern industry. The recurring themes of traveling and prison reflected the rise of a segregated South that imposed strict vagrant laws and used chain gangs to keep cheap African American labor in the region.

The blues continue to thrive in North Carolina. The rise of the Chicago blues, which featured electrified instruments, led to the formation of full blues bands by the 1950s, and eventually these influences migrated to the state. By the 1990s the state boasted a number of strong amplified blues ensembles, including Skeeter Brandon and Highway 61 and Steady Rollin' Bob Margolin. The Durham Blues Festival, one of the first blues festivals held in the South, began in 1973 and features nationally recognized blues acts. Raleigh and Charlotte are regular stops for big names such as Buddy Guy, while Durham, Winston-Salem, and Greensboro all offer steady diets of local performers and blues societies for aficionados.

References: William Barlow, *"Looking up at Down": The Emergence of Blues Culture* (1989); Bruce Bastin, *Red River Blues: The Blues Tradition in the Southeast* (1986); Lawrence Cohn, *Nothing But the Blues: The Music and Musicians* (1993); David Evans, *Big Road Blues: Tradition and Creativity in the Folk Blues* (1982).

Charles J. Holden
Bruce E. Baker

SEE ALSO Menhaden Chanteymen.

Board of Trade was the agency of the British government principally concerned with matters relating to the colonies. Established in 1695, the board maintained correspondence with provincial and royal governors, compiled statistics and other data, and prepared reports and recommendations regarding administration of the colonies. Although technically subordinate to the Privy Council, of which it was a committee, and to the secretary of state, who also had oversight of colonial affairs, the Board of Trade wielded much influence in the formulation and implementation of colonial policy. The board's involvement in the governing of North Carolina increased markedly with the establishment of royal government in 1731, and it remained substantial until the creation in 1768 of the position of secretary of state concerned exclusively with the colonies.

Robert J. Cain

Board of War. The imminent invasion of North Carolina following the British Revolutionary War victory at Camden, S.C., on 16 Aug. 1780 precipitated a crisis in the state government. Governor Abner Nash asked the General Assembly to create a "council" to assist in the conduct of the war. On 13 September, just before adjourning, the legislature named five of its members to a Board of War, which would remain constantly in session with broad authority to direct military affairs, such as mobilizing troops and procuring and delivering provisions and military supplies to state and Continental forces.

Nash, who had returned to his home on the Trent River above New Bern following the adjournment of the Assembly, complained that the Board of War infringed upon his executive authority. When the Assembly reconvened at Halifax in late January 1781, he suggested that the board's creation had subverted the state constitution and deprived him of rightful powers. Nash threatened to resign unless the legislature restored his lawful authority. Lawmakers assured Nash that if it was necessary to retain the Board of War, its powers would be defined to avoid conflict with the governor. Before adjourning, they created a three-member Council Extraordinary and empowered the governor with the concurrence of the council to exercise the emergency powers formerly vested in the Board of War.

The four and a half months that the Board of War directed

the state's military affairs constituted a period of crisis. Board members corresponded with commanders of the Continental forces in North Carolina and South Carolina and with Governor Thomas Jefferson of Virginia, directing the movement of men and supplies. On at least 11 occasions they sent letters to Nash at his residence near New Bern, reporting their actions, forwarding correspondence from the military officers, and requesting the governor's attention to specific needs. The Battle of King's Mountain on 7 Oct. 1780, the Battle of Cowpens on 17 Jan. 1781, and the food, clothing, and military supply demands of Nathanael Greene's army operating in the Carolinas strained the state's meager resources.

George W. Troxler

Boll Weevils, or cotton boll weevils, were a significant problem to North Carolina cotton growers during much of the twentieth century. The boll weevil (*Anthonomus grandis*) came to the attention of the U.S. Department of Agriculture in October 1894, when a resident of Corpus Christi, Tex., mailed a specimen to the department. The insects, which feasted on the boll, or pod, of the cotton plant, were spreading north and east into Texas's prime cotton-growing areas. By the 1910s they had expanded their territory as far east as North Carolina.

The first year of severe boll weevil destruction in North Carolina was 1922, when the pest claimed 13 percent of the state's cotton crop. In 1929, 21 percent of the crop was lost; the damage was substantial but considerably less than in other states' worst years. The problem persisted throughout the middle decades of the twentieth century. North Carolina's northeastern counties participated in an experimental boll weevil eradication project covering 15,000 acres beginning in 1978. At the time, North Carolina's cotton acreage had sunk to 42,000 acres, its lowest level in years. The project's combination of chemical, biological, and cultural methods of eradicating the boll weevil proved successful, and subsequently a federal, state, and university program in North Carolina and South Carolina was launched to destroy the pests. These efforts were also successful, and North Carolina was declared free of boll weevils by 1985.

References: Douglas Helms, "Just Lookin' for a Home: The Cotton Boll Weevil and the South" (Ph.D. diss., Florida State University, 1977); Helms, "Revision and Reversion: Changing Cultural Control Practices for the Cotton Boll Weevil," *Agricultural History* 54 (1980).

Douglas Helms

Bonnie Blue Flag, a rectangular blue field with a single five-pointed star in the center, is the familiar name of a flag that dates from 16 Sept. 1810, when it was used by the short-lived Republic of West Florida. The flag was also the flag of the Republic of Texas for three years and of the Republic of Mississippi before it became a part of the Confederacy. Although never approved by the Confederate Congress, it was adopted by the southern people and flew as the national flag in North Carolina during the time of the Confederacy. The Bonnie Blue Flag is also referred to as the flag of secession, as it was used before the Civil War by citizens who believed in secession. In 1861 Harry Macarthy wrote "The Bonnie Blue Flag," a song that he performed before a packed house in New Orleans. The crowd loved the song, and its popularity quickly spread across the South. It became the Confederate soldiers' favorite marching song. After the war, anyone singing it in the occupied South was subject to arrest.

William S. Powell

Book Publishing. The growth of book publishing in North Carolina came late relative to other states, primarily because of the state's early agricultural economy. Most books owned in colonial North Carolina were imported. The first recorded printer of books in North Carolina was James Davis, a Virginian who established a shop in New Bern in 1749 at the behest of the colonial Assembly and published mostly legislative acts.

The marketing and distribution of books was limited in North Carolina until the early nineteenth century as a result of the state's high illiteracy rate. Considering the effort involved in transporting books on long sea voyages or overland journeys, it is clear that books owned by early American settlers were valued possessions. Settlers needed books to fulfill practical purposes, and their meager libraries contained volumes on subjects such as exploration, religion, and law. Books exclusively for entertainment were not popular until later in the eighteenth century.

Several booksellers existed in North Carolina during the late eighteenth and early nineteenth centuries, and many printed the books that they sold. In the eastern part of the state, booksellers were active in Edenton, New Bern, Swansboro, and Wilmington; farther west, Salisbury, Salem, and Morganton all had booksellers. Raleigh featured two successful printers and booksellers, Edwards & Broughton and Branson & Farrar. Selling books by subscription was common in the state from the early eighteenth century to the mid-nineteenth century. The interests of North Carolinians had by then expanded to include history, poetry, biography, literature, essays, geography, travel, science, foreign language, and shorthand as well as religion and law.

Records of nineteenth-century publishing endeavors are scarce and frequently do not distinguish among printers, royalty publishers, and self-publishing authors. E. J. Hale & Son, founded in 1825 in Fayetteville, published mostly books of local interest and soon became one of the most important book publishers in the South, as well as the publisher of a newspaper, the *Observer*. A study of the importation into North Carolina of books published by Ticknor & Fields in the United

Kingdom suggests a small but active book trade based in Raleigh and Wilmington around 1856. However, it would not be until nearly the start of the twentieth century that book publishing in North Carolina would thrive with permanence. In 1888 the trade journal *Publishers Weekly* listed only one North Carolina firm, Alfred Williams & Company of Raleigh, in its publishing directory. In 1900 three firms were listed, including one in Charlotte. By 1919 the journal listed publishing enterprises in Asheville, Charlotte, Concord, Chapel Hill, and Raleigh.

In the early twentieth century, university presses became important publishing entities throughout the United States. The University of North Carolina Press, founded in 1922, was the first university press in the South and a pioneer in the publication of books on regional topics. The UNC Press list has featured groundbreaking studies of the South, including books about African American life and works on regional folkways as well as popular works such as cookbooks and nature guides. The press at Trinity College in Durham began as an intermittent program, originally publishing papers of the historical society of the undergraduate division. After the founding of Duke University, Trinity College Press became Duke University Press, issuing its first book, E. Malcolm Carroll's *Origins of the Whig Party*, in 1925. Duke University Press continues to publish more scholarly than regional works, as well as a few medical titles and a large number of scholarly journals.

Book publishing in North Carolina was further enhanced by John F. Blair, Publisher, which was established in 1954. As an editor at the UNC Press, Blair had come to believe that many worthwhile and entertaining regional works went unpublished because of the strict scholarly requirements of university presses. Blair subsequently published hundreds of books of North Carolina poetry, literature, and folklore as well as popular regional cookbooks and travel guides. John F. Blair, Publisher, has also distributed titles from other publishers, including Down Home Press, Bank Channel Books, and Crane Hill Publishers.

At least 25 notable book publishers, including university presses, operated in North Carolina in the early 2000s. Most were located in the Triangle area (Raleigh, Durham, and Chapel Hill) or the Triad (Winston-Salem, High Point, and Greensboro). Many commercial houses produce hardcovers and trade paperbacks (originals and reprints) of mainly regional nonfiction and some fiction. McFarland & Company, Inc., Publishers, based in Jefferson, is the state's most prolific commercial publisher, averaging about 135 titles per year (nonfiction, primarily reference, technical, and educational resources). Algonquin Books of Chapel Hill was founded in 1982 by Louis D. Rubin Jr., a respected author, critic, editor, and authority on southern literature at the University of North Carolina at Chapel Hill. Algonquin specializes in fiction and literary nonfiction and has published the works of many important local authors, including Clyde Edgerton, Lee Smith, Jill McCorkle, and Kaye Gibbons. Other large publishers in the state include the Carolina Academic Press (legal casebooks and academic studies); Lark Books (nonfiction on crafts and leisure); and SAS Institute, Inc. (nonfiction, including technical titles, computer resources, and textbooks).

References: John Tebbel, *A History of Book Publishing in the United States* (4 vols., 1972); Michael Winship, *American Literary Publishing in the Mid-Nineteenth Century: The Business of Ticknor & Fields* (1995).

William G. DiNome
Additional research provided by John F. Ansley.

Boon's Mill, Battle of. Located in Northampton County, Boon's (or Boone's) Mill was the site of a Civil War Federal repulse by Confederate forces under Brig. Gen. Matt W. Ransom on 28 July 1863. Boon's Mill was situated on the main road from Jackson, the county seat, to Garysburg and Weldon, where the vitally important Wilmington & Weldon Railroad ran north to Petersburg, Va. It was by this road that the Federal force hoped to capture and burn the Weldon Bridge, thus disrupting the flow of supplies from Wilmington to Petersburg, Richmond, and the Army of Northern Virginia.

On 26 July Federal ships off Winton unloaded regiments from Massachusetts, New York, New Jersey, and Rhode Island commanded by Maj. Gen. John G. Foster to support Col. Samuel P. Spear and a brigade of cavalry expected hourly from Virginia. This combined Union force totaled approximately 5,000 men.

Spear's arrival on 27 July, as well as Foster's the day before, was quickly discovered by Confederate intelligence. Orders were then passed to recently promoted Brig. Gen. Matt W. Ransom to move his brigade southward from its camp near Petersburg, where it had been helping to defend Richmond from Federal forces that occupied Williamsburg.

Ransom's brigade, consisting of elements of the 24th, 35th, and 49th North Carolina Regiments and two guns of Georgia Artillery, reached Garysburg around daybreak of 28 July. Ransom ordered his force of about 200 men to Boon's Mill, choosing this site because it was located on the main road running through Gumberry Swamp. The pond and swamp made it an excellent defensive position. Ransom and his staff left the men and rode to Jackson in an attempt to gather information about Spear's Federal force. On their return, one-half mile from Jackson, Union cavalry exploded from the county seat to give chase. With the Federals not more than 250 yards behind, it was literally a horse race back to the mill for Ransom and his staff, who were fired upon the entire way. Dashing across the bridge at Boon's Mill, Ransom ordered his men to take up the planks and to form ranks.

Spear brought up his artillery and shelled the Confederate

position for over an hour. Then he ordered his dismounted cavalrymen to attack down the road toward the mill; however, concentrated Confederate fire broke this initial advance. Next Spear attempted flanking movements to the left and right, hoping that the dense undergrowth of the swamp would offer cover. But Ransom moved his guns forward and swept the woods with grape and canister. This maneuver, along with Confederate infantry fire, forced Spear to call off his assault after five hours of fighting. Convinced that he could not break through and aware that the entire area was aware of his presence, Spear retreated back to Jackson under the cover of darkness.

Federal casualties from the fight at Boon's Mill were listed at 11 dead, buried on the field. Confederate losses were reported as 1 soldier from the 49th Regiment killed and 3 from the 24th Regiment wounded.

References: John G. Barrett, *The Civil War in North Carolina* (1963); Walter Clark, ed., *Histories of the Several Regiments and Battalions from North Carolina in the Great War, 1861–1865*, vols. 2–4 (1901).

Fred W. Kiger

Borough Towns were towns that were entitled to send a member to the legislature of North Carolina. These towns sent representatives to the colonial Assembly, the five Provincial Congresses, the postrevolutionary General Assembly, and the Constitutional Conventions of 1788 and 1789. In 1715 the North Carolina Assembly passed a law that gave each town with more than 60 families the right to send a representative. The law's intent was to perpetuate the forms of British government—Parliament had, for centuries, had borough members, in special consideration of cities' dense population and commercial interests—and to encourage the growth of towns and commerce. At that time, North Carolina had only two towns, neither of which had 60 families. New Bern had been nearly wiped out during the Tuscarora War in 1711, and Bath had not grown much since incorporation in 1706.

Edenton officially became the first borough town when it sent two representatives to the Assembly of 1725. The Assembly of 1731 had members from three borough towns, Edenton, Bath, and New Bern. Wilmington joined that group in 1740.

The legality of borough representation in North Carolina was doubtful for much of the eighteenth century, as the towns were granted this right only by the Assembly. English borough towns were granted that right by a charter from the Crown, and British authorities at times regarded borough charters granted only by a colonial assembly as invalid. In practice, the British usually allowed North Carolina's borough charters but made it clear that towns held that right through the Crown. Instructions for Governor Arthur Dobbs dated 17 June 1754 allowed Bath, Edenton, New Bern, and Wilmington representation in the Assembly but forbade the addition of other borough towns. However, Brunswick began sending a representative later that year. Rather than spark a fight with the Assembly, Dobbs granted permission for Brunswick to be a borough.

In 1760 the town of Halifax on its own accord elected a member to the Assembly. The Board of Trade disallowed the election, whereupon the member applied to Dobbs for a charter, which the governor granted. The Board of Trade eventually came to accept the law of 1715, which it cited in other cases involving borough representation. Marking growth and settlement in the western part of the colony, Campbellton began sending representatives to the Assembly in 1768, Salisbury in 1769, and Hillsborough in 1771. Tarboro sent a representative in 1773, but the town election was disallowed by the Assembly on the grounds of insufficient population. Nixonton (in 1766) and Beaufort (in 1773) made unsuccessful attempts to elect their own representatives to the colonial Assembly.

After North Carolina and other colonies achieved independence, the concept of borough representation continued in the Provincial Congresses and the General Assembly, although Bath, Brunswick, and Campbellton lost their seats. Towns held seats in the new State House of Commons but not in the Senate. Campbellton, as part of Fayetteville, regained its seat in 1789. Towns had different economic interests from rural areas, being more dependent on trade than agriculture, as was sometimes reflected in the voting patterns of borough representatives. Boroughs tended to elect Federalists and supporters of internal improvements.

Borough town representatives formed only a small percentage of the membership of the state's legislature from 1722 to 1835. However, they provided urban and commercial interests a voice in a legislature dominated by rural and agricultural interests. Without borough town votes, the bill proposing the Constitutional Convention of 1835 would not have passed in the House. Ironically, then, the most lasting effect of borough representation on North Carolina history was in permitting the convention that drafted a constitution abolishing borough towns.

References: John L. Cheney Jr., comp., *North Carolina Government, 1585–1979: A Narrative and Statistical History* (1981); Harold J. Counihan, "The North Carolina Constitutional Convention of 1835: A Study in Jacksonian Democracy," NCHR 46 (October 1969); Mary Phlegar Smith, "Borough Representation in North Carolina," NCHR 7 (April 1930).

David A. Norris

Bostian Bridge Train Wreck occurred on 27 Aug. 1891, just west of Statesville. The accident took the lives of 23 people, making it one of the worst railroad disasters in North Carolina history. Richmond & Danville Railroad (R&D) engine number 9 left Statesville at approximately 2:30 A.M., pulling six cars: a

The locomotive and remains of wooden passenger cars at the base of the 60-foot-high Bostian Bridge over Third Creek near Statesville. Photograph by William Stimson, courtesy of Betty Boyd. NCC.

tender, a baggage car, a second-class car, a first-class coach, a Pullman sleeper, and the private car of the R&D's superintendent. According to station hands, engineer William West was 34 minutes late and left Statesville in a hurry, obviously intending to make up time.

Less than five minutes after leaving Statesville, the train plunged off Bostian Bridge, a 60-foot-high, five-span brick tower bridge crossing Third Creek. Because of its speed—later estimated at 35 to 40 miles per hour by the coroner's jury—the train, according to survivors, was literally airborne when it derailed. The sleeping car hit the ground 153 feet from where it left the bridge.

Several battered survivors walked back to Statesville to announce the disaster, and all normal activity ceased that day as the town immersed itself in the rescue effort. The injured were transported to Statesville, which had no hospital, and placed in private homes. The dead were taken to a tobacco warehouse to be viewed for identification.

Once the rescue effort ended, the wreck site became a magnet for the curious. Thousands of people arrived to stare off the bridge at the wreck or to prowl among the debris. Photographers William Stimson of Statesville and a Mr. VanNess of Charlotte took pictures and, according to the Statesville paper the *Landmark*, sold hundreds in the coming weeks. A story of the wreck with a VanNess photograph appeared in *Frank Leslie's Weekly*, an illustrated newspaper. The *Police Gazette* of Boston carried a story illustrated with what the *Landmark* called "one of its loud imaginary pictures."

Four days after the accident, a coroner's inquest concluded that it was caused by unknown persons removing spikes from the rails, though some blamed the track's neglected condition. Inasmuch as the R&D was experiencing financial troubles, officials, fearing huge damage suits, worked feverishly to find the alleged train wreckers. For months, railroad detectives swarmed over the area. Several people were detained and questioned but eventually released. In 1897 two men already in the state penitentiary were convicted of causing the tragedy on the strength of their supposed confessions to other inmates.

Bill Moose

Boundaries, State.

North Carolina borders the Atlantic Ocean to the east, Virginia to the north, Tennessee to the west, and Georgia and South Carolina to the south. The state claims jurisdiction of the waters of the Atlantic to a distance of "one marine league eastward of the extreme low-tide mark." The boundaries shared by North Carolina and neighboring states were the cause of controversy and violence during the eighteenth and nineteenth centuries, and minor disagreements were still being addressed during the twentieth century.

Northern Boundary. The Albemarle Sound settlements were separated from Virginia when Charles II granted the new province of Carolina to the Lords Proprietors. The provinces were divided at the 36th parallel by the Carolina charter of 1663; the Carolina charter of 1665 moved the line northward to 36°30', adding a 30-mile-wide strip to Carolina. By 1680 Virginia authorities were becoming irritated by residents along the boundary region who refused to pay their Virginia quitrents. The Virginians preferred to ignore the provisions of the 1665 Carolina charter and considered that the boundary should be at the 36th parallel, as outlined in 1663, which would place the most heavily populated districts of Carolina in Virginia.

Attempts at surveying a boundary were frustrated by various private interests and objections from Virginia, which feared that a boundary survey would extinguish their claims to the land around the Albemarle settlements. Virginia even ordered a secret survey in 1705 to see how much land would be lost by an accurate survey. When North Carolina became a royal colony as the Lords Proprietors sold their rights to the province, the Crown insisted on a boundary survey. In 1728 commissioners and surveyors from both provinces began work on settling the location of the boundary. The line was begun at Currituck Inlet on 5 Mar. 1728, and 73 miles were surveyed when work halted six weeks later. Work was resumed in the fall. After an additional 50 miles were surveyed, the North Carolina commissioners left for home, declaring that it was a waste of time to survey so far inland and so far from any settlers. The Virginia party continued surveying for another 72 miles, getting as far as present-day Stokes County.

The Virginian point of view of the 1728 survey was set forth by William Byrd II in his famous *History of the Dividing Line betwixt Virginia and North Carolina* (published in 1841). Byrd noted the plight of planters whose lands were divided by the line, "which made the Owners accountable to both Governments." He also wrote that many settlers in the area preferred to belong to North Carolina, where the grasp of the government was weak and taxes for the province and the church were lower. Further surveys in 1749 and 1779 traced the remainder of the boundary. The surveys simply continued the line surveyed in Byrd's time, with little controversy.

Southern Boundary. The series of boundary disputes with South Carolina was long and bitter. The Proprietary province of Carolina was considered two separate colonies by the late 1600s, but no official boundary was specified for many years. Nothing was done to settle the location of the boundary until North Carolina and South Carolina became royal colonies. An agreement reached in 1730 called for the boundary to start 30 miles south of the mouth of the Cape Fear River and run northwest parallel to the river. Governor George Burrington of North Carolina later refused to allow funding for the survey, claiming that it would be a wasteful expense and that the Pee Dee River was a better dividing line. Had Burrington allowed that survey, North Carolina would have lost nearly all of the country west of the Cape Fear River and much of the present area of the state.

In 1735, after Gabriel Johnston took office as governor of North Carolina, commissioners from both colonies agreed on a new plan for the boundary. The line was to run diagonally northwest from a cedar stake driven into the Atlantic shore to the 35th parallel, then straight west to the South Seas (Pacific Ocean), making only such detours as needed to place Catawba or Cherokee lands in South Carolina. Surveys in 1735 and 1737 brought the diagonal line beyond the settled regions to a remote meadow that was thought to lie on the 35th parallel, and work on the boundary was halted until 1764.

As the lands west of the end of the 1737 line were settled, conflict between the Carolinas grew. By the 1750s, both provinces had issued grants to some of the same properties. Government authority in the disputed areas broke down as officials of one colony were arrested or driven away by authorities or residents of the other as they tried to perform their duties. Governor Arthur Dobbs later bitterly denounced South Carolina sheriffs and tax collectors in the disputed area as an "invasive force."

In 1764 another survey began at the same meadow where the line had ended in 1737 and ran the boundary to the Salisbury-Charlotte road, about 62 miles to the west and at the edge of lands held by the Catawba Indians. The entire 1764 survey was made in error. The terminus of the 1737 survey, which later surveyors used as their starting point, was about 11 miles too far south of the 35th parallel. North Carolina ended up with a wide strip of extra land containing more than 600 square miles.

Work began on the boundary again in 1772. Surveyors, under instructions from the Board of Trade, continued the 1764 line by following the Salisbury road for about eight miles north, then cutting diagonally around the Catawba lands to the forks of the Catawba River (leaving that peculiar "notch" in the state's southern line), then running straight west as far as the Cherokee line of 1767. West of the Catawba lands, the line was run at 35°09', in effect giving South Carolina land north of the 35th parallel to make up for the territory lost by the earlier surveying error. After years of disagreements, both states finally accepted the 1764 and 1772 survey lines, reasoning that what each state lost in one survey was made up for by the other. A survey in 1815 completed the far western part of the boundary, ending at Ellicott's Rock on the Chattooga River, the meeting place of the boundaries of North Carolina, South Carolina, and Georgia.

A boundary dispute between North Carolina and Georgia reached such extremes that North Carolina militia companies clashed with Georgians before the differences were resolved. Georgia had ceded its western lands to the United States and in turn received a 12-mile-wide strip of land ceded by South Carolina south of the 35th parallel. A surveying error led Georgia to start granting land in a region, named Walton County, that was legally in North Carolina north of the 35th parallel. Virtual anarchy resulted as citizens and officials of both states clashed, with neither side gaining complete control; outlaws took advantage of the lack of law enforcement, and law-abiding citizens fled the region during the so-called Walton War. It took several years before the two states could agree on the location of the boundary. The present boundary between North Carolina and Georgia was surveyed in 1819 and 1821. The 1819 survey line is slightly north of the 35th parallel and the 1821 line is slightly south of it, but both states accepted these slight variations rather than continue the quarrel.

Western Boundary. North Carolina ceded its western lands that became the state of Tennessee to the federal government in 1789. The act of cession decreed that the boundary between the two states would begin at Stone Mountain, on the Virginia line, and follow the highest ridges of various mountain ranges until reaching the Georgia boundary. A survey in 1795 plotted the boundary for 151 miles but halted when the surveyors reached some Cherokee lands. The southern section of the boundary was not surveyed until 1819.

The location of much of the boundary was of little importance until settlers began moving to the area after the Cherokees were forced off of the land in that region in 1836. By that time, many of the old survey marks had been lost. There were places along the boundary where Smoky Mountain, the high ridge of which had been used to determine the location of the boundary, split into two or more ridges. Both North Carolina and Tennessee issued land grants for some of the same property in the valleys between these ridges, causing lawsuits. The Federal District Court in 1900 and 1902, and the U.S. Supreme Court in 1914, upheld North Carolina's claims in the disputed areas.

References: Darin E. Fields, *William Byrd's Histories of the Dividing Line betwixt Virginia and North Carolina Run in the Year of Our Lord 1728: A Genetic Text* (1992); Alexander S. Salley Jr., *Boundary Line between North Carolina and South Carolina* (1929); Marvin L. Skaggs, *North Carolina Boundary Disputes Involving Her Southern Line* (1933); Samuel Cole Williams, "The North Carolina–Tennessee Boundary Line Survey," *Tennessee Historical Magazine* 6 (July 1920).

David A. Norris

SEE ALSO Carolinas, Separation of; *History of the Dividing Line*; Tennessee, Formation of; Walton War.

Bounties, or grants, were implemented by Great Britain in the eighteenth century to encourage the production of vital or hard-to-obtain goods. Although rewards were given for the production of silk and indigo, the most important bounties in North Carolina were those paid for naval stores, including tar, pitch, turpentine, and rosin. The practice of paying bounties for naval stores, which were essential to maintain Britain's large fleet, began in the early 1700s with the realization that it was dangerous to depend entirely on northern countries (Norway, Sweden, and Denmark) for such goods. Knowing that England's colonies could not hope to compete commercially with these nations without governmental assistance, Parliament in 1705 offered a bounty of four pounds sterling per ton of tar and pitch produced and three pounds sterling for rosin and turpentine.

Louis P. Towles

Bourbons were conservative Democrats who came to power in North Carolina after Reconstruction, which officially ended in 1877. They were also sometimes known as "Redeemer" Democrats because they purportedly "redeemed" the state from Republican Reconstruction. Created by political opponents, the term "Bourbons" evoked Talleyrand's comment that the French royal family of that name, when restored to the throne in 1814, had apparently learned nothing from the French Revolution. North Carolina's Bourbons, like their counterparts in other southern states, supposedly had not changed their views despite the Civil War experience.

In reality, the southern defeat greatly influenced the economic policies of the North Carolina Bourbons. While continuing to honor the "Lost Cause" of the Confederacy, they sought a new economic order for the state modeled after the victorious North, including agricultural diversification and industrialization. To maintain northern goodwill and prevent the reenactment of Reconstruction, these conservatives promised to abide by the provisions of the Fourteenth and Fifteenth Amendments (ratified in 1868 and 1870, respectively) protecting black rights. They generally ignored this promise, although they were careful to avoid racial violence that could result in federal intervention.

In their efforts to promote industrialization and secure northern capital, conservative leaders ignored the plight of poor farmers. Their retrenchment policies for public services, especially education, came at a severe cost to the majority of

North Carolinians still recovering from the Civil War. Further-more, Bourbons, in attempting to retain power, resorted to ballot-box fraud. During the 1890s a coalition of farmers, organized as the Populist Party, and Republicans, consisting mainly of black voters, overturned the rule of the Bourbons.

References: Alan B. Blomberg, "The Redeemer Period in North Carolina, 1876–1894" (Ph.D. diss., University of Virginia, 1977); Robert F. Durden, "North Carolina in the New South," in Lindley S. Butler and Alan D. Watson, eds., *The North Carolina Experience: An Interpretive and Documentary History* (1984); C. Vann Woodward, *Origins of the New South, 1877–1913* (1951).

William C. Harris

Box Suppers were a popular feature of many social gatherings at schools and churches in rural North Carolina. Girls often decorated boxes with ribbons and whatever colorful trim was at hand and filled them with such popular favorites as fried chicken, ham biscuits, cakes, and cookies. The boxes were then auctioned to the boys, who had been saving pennies for the event. A girl sometimes tipped off a special boy as to which box was hers and then waited, wondering, as the bidding went higher, whether her chosen recipient would be able to afford her box. The competition between boys occasionally led to physical combat. According to one account, the boxes that brought the highest price often belonged not to the most popular young ladies but to the daughters of prominent local citizens.

The proceeds from the bidding were for the benefit of the church or school. At Yadkin College, for instance, the box supper was a regular part of commencement. Money collected from box suppers went to pay for medals awarded in the declamation contests.

Beyond functioning as fund-raisers, box suppers also served as entertainment for the group and as a courting ritual for the young.

Reference: Rhoda H. Wynn, ed., *Paul Green's Wordbook: An Alphabet of Reminiscence* (1990).

Virginia Gunn Fick

Boy Scouts of America. The scouting movement, incorporating personal integrity, preparedness, and philanthropic ideals, was founded in 1907 by retired British army officer Lord Robert Baden-Powell following his founding of an experimental camp on Brownsea Island off the southern coast of England. The first scout troops in the United States were organized before the establishment of a national office; they were informal programs modeled on Baden-Powell's handbook. The Boy Scouts of America (BSA) was incorporated on 8 Feb. 1910 by William D. Boyce, a Chicago publisher who had been in London the previous year and was impressed with the group.

Scouting in North Carolina began in 1910 in Greensboro, with the founding of what seems to be the state's first scout troop. The Greensboro Area Council of the BSA was formed in 1918. Scouting increased greatly in the state after Boyce established a separate organization, the Lone Scouts, which offered a scouting program to boys in rural areas. The Lone Scout program became a part of the BSA in 1924. The program thrived in rural North Carolina. A Lone Scout Museum at the John J. Bernhardt Scout Camp near New London in Stanly County preserves mementos of the program.

The first scout troop in Winston-Salem was formed at Fairview Moravian Church in 1911. By 1918 at least 16 troops had been organized in Winston-Salem and a Winston-Salem council had been organized. The following year the council employed a full-time scout executive and opened a council office. Land for a permanent camp was donated to the council in 1923. In 1928 the Winston-Salem Council assumed oversight of scout troops in six other counties, and to reflect the larger geographical jurisdiction the council name was changed to Old Hickory in 1941. The following year Stokes County transferred from the Cherokee Council, headquartered at the time in Reidsville. Like many of the first council camps, the 43-acre camp in Forsyth County could not meet the expanding program needs of the growing council, and in 1953–54 land was purchased in Surry County. The first summer camp was held at the council's new camp, Raven Knob, in the summer of 1954. Currently, the Old Hickory Council serves Forsyth, Stokes, Yadkin, Surry, Wilkes, Alleghany, Ashe, and Watauga Counties.

Each North Carolina council operates one or more year-round camping facilities that offer a resident summer camp program and are available for unit activities throughout the year. Councils are subdivided into districts. Each district is served by a professional staff member who works through a volunteer district committee to provide organizational training and program support for individual cub scout packs, scout troops, explorer posts, and varsity scout teams.

During scouting's early years, segregation was the law in the southern states. Most North Carolina councils had a single black district, which served all African American scout units in that council and operated separate camps for them. Because these districts covered a wide area, and because the camps lacked the resources available at the white camps, there never was a proportionate number of African American scouts in the segregated South. Nevertheless, committed volunteers and professionals made possible outstanding scouting programs in a few of North Carolina's black communities. One of the earliest African American troops in the South was organized in Elizabeth City in 1911.

Cub scouting became an official part of the BSA in 1930, although programs for younger boys modeled on Baden-Powell's *Wolf Cub's Handbook* had operated for a decade without official sanction of the national office. The first Sea Scouting program for older boys began in 1911. Since then, the BSA has developed a number of programs for older youth, including Rover Scouts, Explorer Scouts, Air Explorers, Exploring, and Varsity Scouts. In 1969 girls became participants in explorer activities, and two years later they were registered as Explorers.

In the early 2000s, the BSA had hundreds of troops and 31 camps in North Carolina, involving thousands of scouts at various levels. Camps in the state that are the property of the BSA include Bonner Scout Reservation in Washington, Camp Daniel Boone in Canton, Mecklenburg Scout Reservation in Nebo, and Occoneechee Scout Reservation in Carthage. BSA members also use facilities at North Carolina's various state parks and wilderness areas.

References: William Hillcourt, *Baden-Powell: The Two Lives of a Hero* (1964); Robert W. Peterson, *The Boy Scouts: An American Adventure* (1984).

George W. Troxler

Boys Road Patrol was chartered by the General Assembly in 1915 under the aegis of J. Hampton Rich "to look after the maintenance of the stretch of road indigenous to each member of the patrol, dragging and ditching same by the use of machinery placed in the care of the patrol by the State and county." For ten years the program fell under the Department of Agriculture, but in 1925 it was transferred to the State Board of Education. It apparently was most active in Forsyth and Davie Counties, where Rich personally directed the work. Before paved roads, the patrol, with the slogan "A Boy on Every Mile," helped keep country roads dragged and drained. A simple road drag formed the patrol's seal. With the advent of improved roads in the 1930s, the organization (in essence, Rich himself) preached traffic and pedestrian safety.

H. G. Jones

Bragg Committee. In 1868–69 North Carolina's Reconstruction government extended $27.83 million in the form of bonds and stocks to 18 railroad companies in the state. Although it was mainly zeal for internal improvements that accounted for the state's generosity, some of the more extravagant and ill-advised aid measures resulted from the activities of a railroad "ring" operating primarily through the Republican-controlled General Assembly. The ringleaders were lobbyist Milton S. Littlefield, a suave transplanted northerner, and George W. Swepson, an erstwhile North Carolina banker. Swepson had gained the confidence of Republican governor William W. Holden, who foolishly believed that tax revenues would be adequate to meet the interest on the bonds.

By 1870 the bond market had virtually collapsed, leaving North Carolina with a heavy debt and few new railroad miles to show for it. With the state's credit standing deteriorating,

both reform Republicans and Conservatives (Democrats) in the General Assembly demanded an investigation of the railroad scandal. The Senate appointed a three-member investigating committee headed by former governor Thomas Bragg, a respected Conservative. Influenced by Holden, who believed that the fraud charges were politically motivated, Republicans in the Senate limited the scope of the committee's work and thus prevented a thorough inquiry into the scandal. The Bragg Committee did reveal the need for an extended, unrestricted investigation of the charges. When the Conservatives assumed power later in 1870, they appointed a committee known as the Shipp Commission, which subsequently uncovered numerous incidents of fraud and bribery—some involving Conservatives—in the issuance of railroad bonds and stocks. Neither Swepson nor Littlefield, the chief perpetrators of the corruption, were brought to justice.

References: William C. Harris, *William Woods Holden: Firebrand of North Carolina Politics* (1987); Charles L. Price, "Railroads and Reconstruction in North Carolina, 1865–1871" (Ph.D. diss., UNC-Chapel Hill, 1959).

William C. Harris

Branch Banking and Trust Company was established in Wilson in 1872, when Alpheus Branch and Thomas Jefferson Hadley formed Branch and Hadley, a private banking firm. In 1887 Branch bought Hadley's interest in the company for $81,000, which is believed to have been the largest check written in Wilson County up to that time. The company's name was changed to Branch and Company Bankers, then to Wilson Banking and Trust Company (1889), the State Bank of Wilson (1891), and finally Branch Banking Company (1893). Branch Banking operated as a private institution until 1900, when it began operating under a charter. In 1907 it became the first bank in the state to engage in trust activities, and in 1913 its charter was amended to change the company's name to Branch Banking and Trust Company (BB&T).

BB&T was the only bank in Wilson to survive the Great Depression. The tenure of BB&T president Herbert Dalton Bateman (1924–52) saw, among other accomplishments, the establishment of 17 branch offices throughout the state. Dramatic growth, through mergers, acquisitions, and interstate banking, took place from the 1960s into the 1990s, and by 1994 BB&T was the state's fourth-largest bank.

BB&T's 1995 "merger of equals" with Southern National Bank, based in Winston-Salem and at the time the state's fifth-largest bank, marked the beginning of the modern BB&T Corporation. Southern National had its origins in the Bank of Lumberton, founded in 1897 by Angus Wilton McLean. The acquisition of neighboring banks and expansion of branches caused the bank to change its name several times, culminating in 1963 with the name of Southern National Bank of

North Carolina. By 1965 the bank had 22 offices in 13 eastern North Carolina communities, and it had moved into other business lines, such as credit cards, mortgages, and leases. Southern National's headquarters moved to Winston-Salem in 1993, although corporate headquarters and several other divisions remained in Lumberton.

After the Southern National merger, BB&T Corporation had 437 branches in 220 locations in the Carolinas and Virginia. Other acquisitions, including Maryland Federal Bancorp (1998), First Citizens Corporation (Georgia, 1999), Matewan Bancshares (West Virginia, 1999), BankFirst Corporation (Tennessee, 2000), FirstSpartan Financial Corporation (South Carolina, 2001), and MidAmerica Bancorp (Kentucky, 2002), signaled the company's continued growth outside of North Carolina. By 2006 BB&T Corporation employed more than 28,000 people, had $110 billion in assets, and operated more than 1,400 branches in 11 states and Washington, D.C.

References: Vidette Bass, *BB&T: A Tradition with a Future* (1992); Clint Johnson, *Service—None Better: The History of Southern National Bank* (1997); Hugh T. Lefler, ed., *North Carolina History Told by Contemporaries* (4th ed., 1965).

Ginny Orvedahl
Additional research provided by Barry McGee.

Branchhead Boys.

In his gubernatorial campaign of 1948, W. Kerr Scott strongly appealed to voters whose roots were in the soil. Scott called them "Branchhead Boys," referring to people who lived at the head of the branch of a creek—in other words, rural people isolated in the backwoods. They were the "farmers and townspeople who know the bust of day, coffee that's saucered and blowed, folks who made a good stagger at honest toil and plowed to the end of the row." Scott campaigned to "get the farmer out of the mud," he said, "so farmers could get to church and farm children to school."

These so-called Branchhead Boys became a political force, backing Scott in a surprising victory over Charles M. Johnson and supporting the new governor's populist and progressive legislation. Scott implemented a range of new programs under his "Go-Forward" plan, astonishing the state by proposing a $200 million bond issue (more than $1.5 billion in 2005) to pave rural roads in North Carolina. Additionally, his programs advanced rural electrification and improved state schools and health facilities.

References: John W. Coon, "Kerr Scott, the Go Forward Governor: His Origins, His Programs, and the North Carolina General Assembly" (M.A. thesis, UNC-Chapel Hill, 1968); Roy Wilder Jr., "Unrest among the Branchhead Boys," in Jack Claiborne and William Price, eds., *Discovering North Carolina: A Tar Heel Reader* (1991).

Wiley J. Williams

Breads

Breads of various types have been essential elements of the foodways of North Carolinians since long before European settlement. Corn was the base ingredient for North Carolina's earliest Indian breads. Many centuries ago, American Indians in the region made cornbread by frying it in bear fat or boiling it into a type of dumpling. In another method, a small loaf or a round "pone" was put in the bottom of a large pot. A smaller pot was then placed upside-down over it and covered with hot coals. Early Indian ways of making cornbread were later adapted by European settlers and became the basis of an important part of traditional southern cooking.

"Indian corn" quickly became the staple crop of the early European settlers in North Carolina. Corn was easier to grow than wheat in most of North Carolina and the southern region, and the crude early gristmills did a better job of grinding corn than wheat. Cornbread was also easier to make than wheat bread, as it did not require the use of yeast and long waits for the dough to rise. Its main disadvantage was that it did not keep well, which seems to be the beginning of the southern preference for hot bread at meals. Cooks could add milk, eggs, shortening, or even wheat flour to increase the variety of cornbreads. White cornmeal was the traditional favorite in North Carolina and throughout the South.

There were several traditional forms of cornbread, most of which are still popular in North Carolina. Ashcakes were baked in the hot coals of a fireplace. The burnt outside of the cake was scraped off before eating. Hoecakes were originally baked on the blade of a hoe, although later the name was applied to other kinds of cornbread. Johnnycake differed from other forms of cornbread in that it was cooked on a plank before an open fire to provide sustenance for travelers over extended paths and trails. It was also cooked indoors, especially at the hearths of Piedmont and Mountain cabins. The name reflects the frontier pronunciation of "journey-cake," the chief early American trail food.

Corn pone, based on the Indian way of making cornbread, was a simple loaf of cornbread usually made without eggs or milk. Cracklin' bread was made with the crisp "cracklins" left over from rendering pork lard added to the batter. Hush puppies were small deep-fried balls of cornmeal batter, often flavored with onions. The name allegedly came from the practice of cooks tossing the tasty bits of fried corn dough to dogs to keep them quiet. Finally, spoon bread was a soft bread made with cornmeal, eggs, milk, and shortening; it is served with a spoon.

Wheat was grown in North Carolina as early as the seventeenth century. John Lawson wrote of seeing fine crops of wheat in the colony. He was surprised on one occasion when, at the home of some Waxhaw Indians, he was served "white-bread as any *English* would have done." Antebellum North Carolina grew more wheat than most of the other southern states, although its production was dwarfed by the output of the midwestern states. Wheat flour was more expensive than cornmeal, and the state's slaves and poor farmers rarely had any bread but cornbread. Even the richest North Carolinians (and southerners in general), though, never seemed to grow tired of cornbread, and many families had various kinds of corn or wheat bread at the same meal.

Most early North Carolina families had to do their baking with their fireplace and a Dutch oven, but wealthier families might have a brick oven built into or next to the kitchen fireplace chimney. During the middle of the nineteenth century, families began to switch from cooking in the fireplace to using iron stoves. Biscuits became especially popular after the Civil War with the appearance of the woodstove, commercial baking powder, and the availability of cheap white flour from the Midwest. Biscuits were such common dinner table fare in North Carolina that one usually finds few recipes for them in old cookbooks. While there are numerous recipes for breads and muffins, biscuits remained relatively basic. Most housewives prepared them three times a day, not bothering to measure ingredients. When girls stood beside their mothers to study the culinary skills required in a kitchen, biscuit making was one of the first challenges.

While families ate home-baked bread during most of North Carolina's history, commercial bakeries existed as early as the eighteenth century. The Winkler Bakery (1800) was still operating in Old Salem by the early 2000s. Taverns and ordinaries in the colonial era and afterward baked bread to serve guests as well as prisoners in the county jails. In later times, home delivery helped make bakery products popular in towns. Bakeries were aided by new inventions, such as automatic wrapping machines in the 1910s and a practical bread slicer in 1928. After World War I, it became fashionable to have toast instead of biscuits for breakfast.

Commercial breads became more popular as the twentieth century unfolded, although "store-bought" bread was initially considered inferior to home-baked bread. Farm families tended to bake their own bread for years after town households switched to buying commercially baked bread. The increase in the number of women who worked outside the home, rising incomes, and the ease of transporting baked goods by truck on a growing state road system all contributed to the decline in home baking and the rapid growth of the baking industry. This trend was greatly accelerated during World War II, as many more women entered the wartime workplace and had little time for making their own bread. The trend away from home baking continued after the war, as North Carolina consumers enjoyed the convenience and ever-increasing variety of commercial bakery goods.

References: Sam Bowers Hilliard, *Hog Meat and Hoecake: Food Supply in the Old South, 1840–1860* (1972); William G. Panschar, *Baking in America: Economic Development* (2 vols., 1956); Barbara E. Taylor, ed., *A Taste of the Past: Early Foodways of the Albemarle Region, 1585–1830* (1991); Joe Gray Taylor, *Eating, Drinking, and Visiting in the South: An Informal History* (1982); Roger L. and Linda K. Welsch, *Cather's Kitchens: Foodways in Literature and Life* (1987).

David A. Norris
Additional research provided by
Jerry Leath Mills and Marilyn Wright.

Brevard College, a United Methodist institution located in the mountain town of Brevard, was named for Ephraim Brevard, a teacher and one of the local leaders that produced the Mecklenburg Resolves in 1775. Brevard College traces its origins to three institutions: Weaver College, a two- and four-year school founded in Buncombe County in 1853 by the "Brothers of Temperance"; Rutherford College, founded as the Owl Hollow School in 1853 in Burke County; and Brevard Institute, a high school inaugurated in 1895 by Asheville businessman Fitch Taylor and his wife Sarah. During the depression-ridden 1930s, all three institutions closed their doors, leading to the creation of Brevard College in 1934.

The college, which enrolled 394 students taught by 24 faculty when it opened, was designed to provide opportunities for Mountain residents who otherwise would not have been able to secure secondary and postsecondary training. This was reflected in the school motto, "Labor, Learn, Live." The first president of the new college was Eugene J. Coltrane. During Coltrane's 16-year tenure, Brevard College had its own farm, garden, and dairy; students were responsible for much of the day-to-day operation of these facilities. The curriculum, in keeping with the college's regional outlook, included classes in agriculture, home economics, and industrial arts; there were also traditional academic courses in the arts and sciences.

The administration of President Emmett K. McLarty (1957–68) marked several noteworthy events, including the adoption of a new college seal and motto, *Cognosce Ut Prosis* ("Learn in order that you might serve"), creation of the Concerned Student Activist Movement, and the admission of the college's first African American students.

Brevard College in the early 2000s enrolled approximately 650 students, and although it still offered associate degrees, it was primarily a four-year institution offering a variety of majors. (The vast majority of the students completing an associate degree go on to four-year colleges.) A number of unique programs, including the School of Wilderness Education's Certificate in Outdoor Leadership Areas, keep the college vibrant. The institution holds membership in the National Association of Music Schools and has an Intensive English Institute for international students.

References: Dan F. Brewster and G. Ross Freeman, eds., *Higher Education in the Southeastern Jurisdiction of the United Methodist*

Church, 1787–1984 (1984); George W. Bumgardner and James E. Carroll, *The Flowering of Methodism in Western North Carolina* (1984).

James I. Martin Sr.

Brevard Music Center, often called the "Summer Music Capital of the South," is the site of an annual festival featuring musicals, operas, symphonies, and choral programs that attracts thousands of people each summer to Brevard, near the Pisgah National Forest in the mountains of Transylvania County. Concurrent with the festival is a summer camp that enrolls 300–400 of the country's best high school and college musicians in a vigorous program of instruction and performance. The center was the brainchild of James Christian Pfohl, the son of a bishop of the Moravian Church, head of the music department at Davidson and Queens Colleges, and conductor of the Charlotte Symphony. Pfohl moved his music camp for boys from Queens College in Charlotte in 1945 to the site of an abandoned boys' camp he had found while vacationing in the North Carolina mountains. The natural beauty of the area, he believed, would form a perfect backdrop for a music camp. He convinced interested Brevard citizens to form the Brevard Music Foundation Festival Association, and in 1946 the association began sponsoring a festival symphony orchestra, with Pfohl conducting. In 1947 the camp, then known as the Transylvania Music Camp, and the association came together to form the Brevard Music Foundation, possibly the first nonprofit organization of its kind.

Under Pfohl's tutelage the festival continued to grow and, in 1955, the name Brevard Music Center was adopted to encompass both the camp and the festival. Over the years, the Brevard Music Festival has featured some of the world's leading performers, such as violinist Isaac Stern, guitarist Carlos Montoya, and soprano Eileen Farrell. By 2006 the 140-acre Brevard Music Center boasted a nationally recognized summer music camp, a 1,600-seat, open-sided concert hall, and a seven-week concert and opera season.

Angelyn H. Patteson

Brick Making techniques were introduced in North Carolina from northern colonies, especially from Jamestown, Va., when settlers began to locate along the Albemarle coastal area in the 1660s. The abundant supply of clay and oyster shells necessary to make lime mortar enabled wealthier settlers to build brick houses in North Carolina before 1700. James Long's will, dated 15 Nov. 1711 and probated in Chowan County, listed in it "the brick house plantation." John Lawson, the surveyor general for the colonial government, wrote a report in 1714 stating that in the region "good bricks and tiles are made and several sorts of useful Earths as Boles, Fuller's-Earth, Oakers and Tobacco-pipe Clay [are found] in great plenty."

Bricks were made during the 1700s in more than a dozen North Carolina counties. Examples of early brick structures include the Newbold-White House, Perquimans County (about 1730); St. Thomas Church, Bath (1734); and Tryon Palace, New Bern (1767–70). Early methods of making bricks by hand involved packing locally found clay into dampened cedar wood mold boxes, the insides of which were sanded to give the brick texture and releasing qualities. Radical changes in brick making occurred in the last half of the nineteenth century with the development of extrusion machines using "star" cutters to end-cut brick. These cutters could cut through small sticks and stones often found in alluvial clays. Auger extrusion machines replaced the hand-mold or pressed-brick methods that had been used almost universally for thousands of years.

In the 1860s tunnel kilns were patented, revolutionizing the brick industry for mass production. The first successful tunnel kiln in North Carolina was built by Isenhour Brick and Tile Company in Spencer in 1938. A North Carolinian, James Columbus Steele, played an important part during the late nineteenth century in developing American-based brick manufacturing equipment by supplying brick machinery parts for manufacturers. He also designed in 1887 and patented in 1889 a two-wheeled, hand-operated "brick truck," which enabled a person to carry freshly made "green" bricks to the dryer and then the kiln for firing. Steele's four sons further developed innovative machinery such as clay feeders and reel cutters to side-cut the brick so that the header ends would match the faces. J. C. Steele & Sons eventually became one of the most successful brick machinery corporations in the world.

As the twentieth century approached, brick manufacturing plants were built all over the state. For a time after World War II, North Carolina was the leading brick-producing state in the United States. By 1960 the industry had 30 plants in 20 counties, most near large cities accessible to rail lines and major highways. The state's manufacturers in 2004 produced approximately 10 percent of the nation's brick, or about 1 billion bricks annually.

References: Brick Institute of America, *Profile of the Brick Industry* (1990); J. C. Steele & Sons, *A History of J. C. Steele and Sons, Inc.* (1989).

Clegg M. Furr

British Cemetery on Ocracoke Island is a small cemetery containing the graves of four British navy personnel killed while helping defend the North Carolina coast against German U-boats (submarines) in World War II. In March 1942, the 900-ton HMS *Bedfordshire* was one of 24 armed trawlers sent by Great Britain to help the U.S. Navy defend the Atlantic coast of the United States against U-boat attacks. On 11 May 1942, the *Bedfordshire* was torpedoed and sunk by U-558 southeast of Cape Lookout with a loss of all 37 crew members. The bodies

The British Cemetery of Ocracoke. Photograph courtesy of North Carolina Division of Tourism, Film, and Sports Development.

British Debts.

British Debts. Debts owed by North Carolina merchants and planters to British merchants before the Revolutionary War were disputed by the United States and England until 1802. The colonial merchants and planters bought practically all of their manufactured articles from British merchants and depended on their trade and crops, respectively, to pay the balances due in England. From 1763 to 1775, as their indebtedness grew, North Carolina merchants and planters often did not pay their debts purposely as a way of undermining the authority of Parliament and the mother country over colonial matters.

The peace treaty between Great Britain and the United States, signed at Paris on 3 Sept. 1783, which consummated American independence, included a guarantee against legal obstacles to the collection of private prewar debts to British creditors. The states, including North Carolina, circumvented this guarantee, and so the debt controversy remained unresolved. With the adoption of the U.S. Constitution in 1789, the dispute entered a new phase, with the courts facilitating the collection of some of the debts. Also, the George Washington administration, by sending Thomas Jefferson to Paris between 1784 and 1785, hoped to negotiate more effectively with England regarding the infractions of the 1783 treaty. Negotiations between George Hammond, the English minister, and Jefferson, however, failed to settle the debt question.

Nothing more was done until the strained British-American relations of 1792–93 led to the mission of John Jay and Jay's Treaty. No policy or action of President Washington resulted in more criticism in North Carolina than did Jay's Treaty with England, which was negotiated in 1794 and ratified in 1795. Both of the state's U.S. senators voted against confirming Jay as peace commissioner, and both voted against ratification of the completed treaty. Every North Carolina congressman in the U.S. House of Representatives except W. B. Grove also voted against it. North Carolinians across the state complained of the treaty's "sins."

A five-member commission (three British, two American members) to adjudicate the claims of British merchants sat at Philadelphia from May 1797 to July 1799, when the Americans walked out during a particularly bitter debate. The commissioners were unable to agree on such matters as the commission's jurisdiction, the nature of legal impediments, the question of the solvency of debtors, and wartime interest on the debts. Finally, a settlement was negotiated by Rufus King (the U.S. diplomat who helped to prevent a break in severely strained British-American relations) and Henry Addington (British prime minister). King convinced the British government on 8 Jan. 1802 to accept a payment of £600,000 from the United States for the full satisfaction of all claims recoverable at the end of the Revolutionary War that could not be recouped through ordinary legal procedures. Furthermore, in the future U.S. courts would be open to British creditors. A British com-

of two crew members, Lt. Thomas Cunningham and Ordinary Telegraphist Stanley Craig, washed ashore on Ocracoke, and the Coast Guard buried them in a small cemetery plot donated by a local family. A week later, two additional *Bedfordshire* crew members, unidentified, washed up and were also buried in the plot.

Later fitted with permanent markers and enclosed by a white picket fence, the four graves have since become well known as the British Cemetery of Ocracoke. Currently, a bronze plaque engraved with words from Rupert Brooke rests on the fence, serving as a fitting tribute to the four men who died in war far from home:

> If I should die think only this of me,
> That there's some corner of a foreign field,
> That is forever England.

Reference: L. VanLoan Naisawald, *In Some Foreign Field: Four British Graves and Submarine Warfare on the North Carolina Outer Banks* (rev. ed., 1997).

Paul Branch

mission sat until 1811 adjusting the claims. It found that only about 20 to 25 percent of the claims were good, but even so it was able to pay, with the £600,000, only about 45 percent of the approved claims.

References: Samuel Flagg Bemis, *Jay's Treaty: A Study in Commerce and Diplomacy* (1924); Hugh T. Lefler and Albert R. Newsome, *North Carolina: The History of a Southern State* (3rd ed., 1973).

Wiley J. Williams

Broadsides, or broadsheets, single sheets of paper with printed text on one or both sides, were used in England as early as 1575 to communicate various kinds of information. The earliest known broadside printed in North Carolina, probably at the press of public printer James Davis in New Bern, appeared in 1757. It was a proclamation from royal governor Arthur Dobbs prohibiting the payment of taxes with notes or bills issued by James Murray and John Rutherfurd. Broadsides often dealt with strictly local matters such as politics, crime, religion, business, slavery, railroads, canals, education, real estate, military affairs, and upcoming entertainments.

References: Ray O. Hummel Jr., ed., *Southeastern Broadsides before 1877: A Bibliography* (1971); Douglas C. McMurtrie, *Eighteenth Century North Carolina Imprints, 1749–1800* (1938).

William S. Powell

Brookings Institution, a private, nonprofit organization devoted to public policy analysis based in Washington, D.C., played an instrumental role in helping North Carolina cope with the effects of the Great Depression. In the process, the organization helped the state dramatically reshape its system of government. At the time North Carolina, like the rest of the country, was struggling to cope with economic hard times. Shrinking revenues and a desperate need for tax relief put great pressure on Governor O. Max Gardner to devise a plan that would enable the state to efficiently provide necessary public services while at the same time relieving the tax burden of North Carolina's citizens. Searching for solutions, Governor Gardner turned to the Brookings Institution for help, requesting that the institution undertake a study of North Carolina state and county government and make recommendations for implementing such a plan.

After careful study and analysis, the Brookings research staff created their report and presented it to Governor Gardner in December 1930. In it they described a scheme of government within which all agencies would function as parts of a whole, complementing rather than contradicting or duplicating each other's efforts. The report also suggested ways of shifting financial responsibility for some public services from the counties to the state in order to help reduce local property taxes.

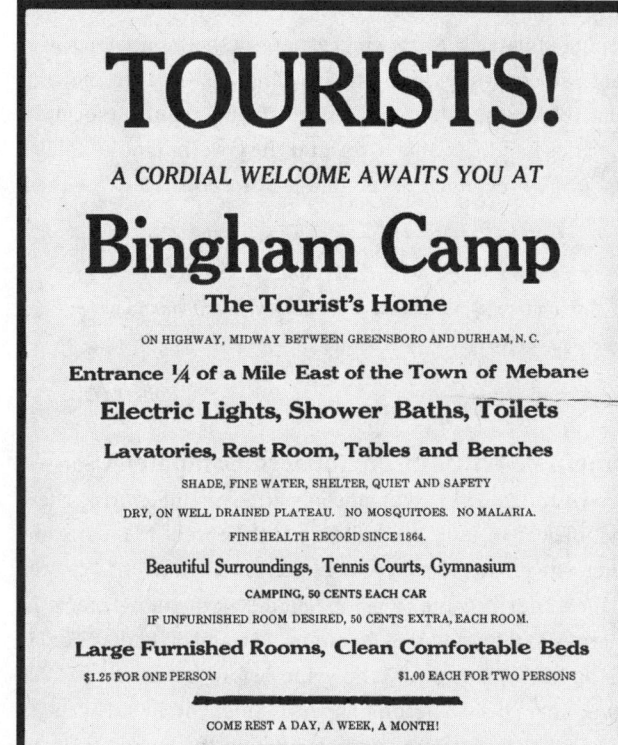

Broadside advertising the Bingham Camp for tourists at Mebane, ca. 1930. NCC.

At first many North Carolinians were shocked at what they felt was the radical nature of some of the institute's recommendations. Among the controversial proposals was one for a "short ballot," so called because it would have reduced the number of elective administrative offices in state government from 13 to 3. Also of concern were recommendations for the merging of several counties and the transfer of many responsibilities and prerogatives from the counties to the state.

Despite such concerns, the desperate needs of the times demanded change. When the governor presented his program to the 1931 legislature, it included a number of the Brookings report proposals. Nearly all of these were enacted into law. Among the most significant of the proposals adopted in that legislative session was a plan for consolidation of the University of North Carolina in Chapel Hill, North Carolina State College in Raleigh, and the North Carolina College for Women in Greensboro. Lawmakers consented to the creation of a State Division of Purchasing and Contract and the creation of a State Department of Personnel. The legislature also agreed that the state would assume much of the responsibility for roads and prisons and the financing of local schools.

The adoption of the Brookings Institution recommendations in 1931 marked the beginning of a dramatic shift of power in North Carolina. As subsequent legislatures enacted further changes based on the report, more responsibilities and authority would shift from the county seats to the state capital of Raleigh. Surprisingly, many of these initiatives were met with relatively little protest. This was because the state was able to provide many services better than the local authorities had been able to do, and the government in Raleigh also took over much of the financial responsibility for these services.

References: Paul V. Betters, ed., *State Centralization in North Carolina* (1932); William S. Powell, *North Carolina through Four Centuries* (1989).

Robert D. Weaver

Brown & Williamson Tobacco Company. George T. Brown and Robert L. Williamson started manufacturing chewing tobacco in 1894 in a building at the corner of Liberty and First Streets at the southern border of the town of Winston (which later became Winston-Salem). Both young men's fathers were tobacco manufacturers. Williamson had worked in his father's plant near Yanceyville before he moved to Winston, where he had become superintendent of the T. L. Vaughn Tobacco Company. Brown speculated in the buying and selling of leaf tobacco. When the financial panic of 1893 left him with 100,000 pounds of tobacco for which he could find no buyers, he and Williamson, his brother-in-law, who had practical experience in tobacco manufacturing, decided to go into business together as partners. They named their company Brown & Williamson, with Williamson's brother-in-law Walter R. Leak as treasurer.

During the new firm's first year, Brown & Williamson took over the T. F. Williamson & Son company and its brands of Red Juice and Red Crow twist chewing tobacco and Golden Grain granulated smoking tobacco. To these they added their own products, including Bloodhound, Bugler, Kite, and Shot chewing tobacco. All of these became immensely popular brands, and the young firm grew so fast that in 1906 it was incorporated as Brown & Williamson Tobacco Company, with Brown as president, Williamson as vice president, and Leak as treasurer.

In 1925 Brown & Williamson bought the J. G. Flynt Tobacco Company and its Sir Walter Raleigh pipe tobacco brand, which had been manufactured since 1884. The firm expanded further in April 1926 by buying R. P. Richardson Jr. & Company of Reidsville, which manufactured the Old North State brand of smoking tobacco, dating to 1873. Richardson also made cigarettes with the brand name of Old North State. With the purchase of this company, then, Brown & Williamson entered the field of cigarette manufacturing.

In 1929 all divisions of Brown & Williamson except chewing tobacco and snuff were moved to Louisville, Ky., and headquarters for the company remain there. The company merged with R. J. Reynolds Tobacco in 2004 to form Reynolds American, Inc.

Anna Withers Bair

Brown Bagging was the widespread practice of customers bringing liquor into restaurants in brown paper bags, purchasing soft drink set-ups and then mixing their own drinks at the table. Brown bagging was legalized in North Carolina in 1967. Until then, public drinking of liquor had been illegal since 1908. The first liquor-by-the-drink sale in the state occurred amidst much fanfare in Charlotte in November 1978.

Brown bagging originally was Air Force slang for a married man who carried his lunch in a brown paper bag. A "brown-bagger" eventually came to mean simply a married man in the military.

Reference: Luther Hodges, "Not 'If' But 'When': Liquor by the Drink," *Charlotte Magazine* (Spring 1976).

Alex Coffin

Brown Mountain Lights are unexplained phenomena that appear low in the air under favorable atmospheric conditions, grow in size, and then linger for a few minutes before fading away. Brown Mountain is located on the Burke-Caldwell county line, approximately half a mile west of Wilson Creek and northwest of Morganton. The lights have been documented since 1833, prompting investigation and inspiring song and story. As few as one and as many as a dozen lights might be seen at one time. They are mostly white but occasionally show a red, blue, or yellowish tinge. The lights appear most often on clear, warm, summer evenings, beginning shortly after dark.

Although various authorities have studied the Brown Mountain Lights, no entirely satisfactory scientific explanation has been offered. The U.S. Geological Survey has suggested that the lights may be the result of refraction of headlights on trains or automobiles in the valley. The National Geographic Society reports that discharges of static electricity might be the source of the lights. Folklorists credit an Indian brave searching by torchlight for his lost love.

The lights are best seen from the Lost Cove overlook on the Blue Ridge Parkway, near Milepost 310 on the southeast side of the road, northeast of its junction with N.C. 181.

References: John Harden, *Tar Heel Ghosts* (1954); Nancy Roberts, *North Carolina Ghosts and Legends* (1991).

Robert J. Dodge

Brown's Marsh, Battle of. The Battle of Brown's Marsh was the last in a long line of military encounters in North Carolina at the end of the Revolutionary War, following Loyalist colonel David Fanning's capture of Whig governor Thomas

Burke at Hillsborough on 12 Sept. 1781. The precise site of the battle, as well as its exact date, is currently unknown, but it likely took place sometime between 28 Sept. and 2 Oct. 1781 near present-day Clarkton in Bladen County. While attempting to convey their valuable prisoners to the British garrison at Wilmington, Fanning's command was ambushed by Gen. John Butler's Whig army at Lindley's Mill in what is now Alamance County on 13 Sept. 1781. The Loyalists managed to extricate themselves, but Fanning was severely wounded and his command devolved to Col. Archibald McDugald.

McDugald led his army and prisoners through the Sandhills en route to Wilmington, stopping at the Loyalist stronghold of McPhaul's Mill to regroup and turn over the captives to a swifter party commanded by Col. Duncan Ray (although some of the Loyalists escorting the prisoners from Hillsborough continued on the journey). Hearing news of the successful raid, Maj. James Craig, leader of the British force in Wilmington, went up River Road to meet the Loyalists. Governor Burke and his fellow prisoners were delivered to Craig at Livingston Creek by 23 Sept. 1781.

Meanwhile, Butler had gathered what militia he could and set off to overtake the Loyalists and liberate the governor. When word of Butler's plans reached the British at Wilmington, Craig dispatched a Major Manson and 180 British regulars from the Wilmington garrison to accompany the Loyalists as far as Brown's Marsh. Scouts soon brought news of Butler's exact location back to Manson, who planned to attack the Whigs before they found out that the Loyalists had been reinforced.

The British rode all night through swamps and forests that required expert guides to negotiate. When close to Butler's camp, Manson divided his force into three wings: the British regulars, the Highlanders, and a contingent of Fanning's command under Capt. Steven Holloway. Each wing was accompanied by an experienced guide who was believed to be able to bring the respective units into position for the attack but who ultimately proved unprepared for the task.

As the British were groping about in Brown's Marsh, the Whigs had been alerted to their presence and hastily prepared defensive positions. Heedless of this setback, Manson ordered an attack in the predawn darkness. From the outset, consternation reigned in the Whig camp. As he had at Lindley's Mill, Butler ordered a retreat soon after the fighting began, but once again Col. Robert Mebane stepped forward to stop the Whigs' flight—though on this occasion, even with the help of Col. Thomas Owen, his efforts were only temporary.

In less than an hour, the Battle of Brown's Marsh was over. The British had routed the Whigs and were now in possession of their camp, while the Whigs were fleeing north to safety with Butler at their head. The victory cost the British two killed and five wounded—both deaths coming from Fanning's men, including their leader, Captain Holloway. The Battle of Brown's Marsh capped a successful campaign in what was to be the high point of the Loyalists' efforts during the Revolutionary War.

References: Lindley S. Butler, ed., *The Narrative of Colonel David Fanning* (1981); John Hairr, *Colonel David Fanning: The Adventures of a Carolina Loyalist* (2000).

John Hairr

Broyhill Furniture. Modern-day Broyhill Furniture Industries, Inc., grew out of the Lenoir Chair Company, founded in 1926 by James Edgar Broyhill in Lenoir. Broyhill upholstered chairs on consignment, but he believed that he could operate on his own. His chair company was immediately successful, and Broyhill expanded his product line in the early 1940s by buying six small furniture plants in Lenoir and nearby towns, organizing them all under the name of Broyhill Furniture Factories. The emphasis in early years was on the production of inexpensive to medium-priced bedroom and upholstered furniture.

A slump in furniture sales in the 1940s and 1950s caused Broyhill to make changes. These included a paid sales staff, modernized factories, the production of more expensive and stylish products, quality control, national advertising, and the production of plastic and ready-to-assemble furniture. Sales more than tripled to $265 million in the years from 1966 to 1979. In 1980 Interco, Inc., of St. Louis, a shoe and clothing manufacturer, bought Broyhill, Ethan Allen, Inc., and later Lane Home Furnishings. In 1991 Interco, overextended and seeking bankruptcy protection from creditors, began to concentrate on furniture as its primary product. The company subsequently established Broyhill Showcase Galleries to show and sell Broyhill furnishings. By the early 2000s, there were 340 of these galleries, as well as 475 Broyhill Furniture Centers, around the nation. Broyhill Furniture Industries, Inc., as a subsidiary of Interco's latest incarnation, Furniture Brands International, remains one of the world's largest manufacturers of medium-priced furniture.

References: Elizabeth Rourke, "Broyhill Furniture Industries, Inc.," *International Directory of Business Histories*, vol. 10 (1995); William Stevens, *Anvil of Adversity: Biography of a Furniture Pioneer* (1968).

John L. Bell

Bruce's Cross Roads, Battle of. Bruce's Cross Roads, located in northern Guilford County in the present community of Summerfield, was the site of a Revolutionary War skirmish on 12 Feb. 1781 between American forces commanded by Lt. Col. Henry Lee and British troops under Lt. Col. Banastre Tarleton. Following the American council of war at Guilford Courthouse on 8–10 Feb. 1781, Lee's cavalry was assigned to a 750-man contingent that was detached from the main body of Gen. Nathanael Greene's army for the purpose of staying in front of the British army so that Greene could safely cross the Dan River. In carrying out their mission, Lee and his cavalrymen were frequently within rifle range of Tarleton's troopers.

About noon on 12 February, Lee, who was suffering from a lack of sleep and food, paused for a meal at the home of Charles Bruce, a local Patriot. The dwelling was located approximately one-half mile south of the crossroads named for Bruce. As the meal was being prepared for Lee, Isaac Wright, an area resident, appeared at the Bruce home in an agitated state with news that a detail of British dragoons was two to three miles away. Lee promptly dispatched a Captain Armstrong, one of his most trusted and skilled officers, to confirm the report. Wright, who was ordered by Lee to act as a guide, received permission to exchange his slow-gaited pony for the speedy horse of Lee's teenage bugler, James Gillies. To ensure that he would not lose his horse, the bugler accompanied Armstrong, Wright, and several other soldiers on the scouting expedition.

After traveling some distance, Armstrong grew skeptical of the report, but Wright prevailed upon young Gillies and two other soldiers to proceed a bit farther. They rode only another quarter mile when they encountered the British dragoons. The small group of Americans immediately began to retreat with the enemy in hot pursuit. Because he was mounted on Wright's pony, the unarmed teenage bugler was no match for the speedy British pursuers. He was overtaken, pulled from his pony, and slashed to pieces while begging for quarter.

Captain Armstrong and a squadron of Americans arrived on the scene about the time the youth was being butchered. During the ensuing melee, Armstrong's men killed seven British soldiers. Tarleton, alerted by the sounds of the fight, closed in with his cavalry at full speed. The Americans retreated to the crossroads, where Lee had concealed his command in a most favorable position. A portion of Tarleton's corps slammed into Lee's waiting forces. The British soldiers were routed, suffering 13 dead and several captured.

Much of the British army camped on the Bruce plantation on the night of 12 February. James Gillies, the lone American casualty in the skirmish, was buried at the Bruce family cemetery. Charles Bruce was later buried near the young bugler. In 1922 a monument was erected by the Daughters of the American Revolution at Bruce (Guilford Muster Ground) Park in Summerfield to honor the two Patriots.

References: John Buchanan, *The Road to Guilford Courthouse: The American Revolution in the Carolinas* (1997); Eli Washington Caruthers, *Revolutionary Incidents and Sketches of Character Chiefly in the Old North State* (1856).

Daniel W. Barefoot

Brunswick County, located in the Coastal Plain region of southeastern North Carolina, was formed in 1764 from New Hanover and Bladen Counties. The county was named after King George I, who was also the duke of Brunswick and Lunenburg. Early inhabitants of Brunswick County included the Cape Fear Indians, followed by English and French Huguenot settlers. The county seat is now (since 1975) Southport, but for most of the county's history, Bolivia (incorporated in 1911) served in that role. Situated along the Atlantic Coast, Brunswick County has some of North Carolina's most accessible and popular ocean communities, including Sunset Beach, Ocean Isle Beach, Holden Beach, and Bald Head Island. Cape Fear lies at the southern tip of Bald Head Island, and the Cape Fear River runs along the county's eastern border. The Intracoastal Waterway passes through the county as well.

Brunswick County is home to a number of historic sites, including Orton Plantation and Gardens, dating to ca. 1730; Bald Head Island Lighthouse, fondly known as "Old Baldy"; and the Brunswick Inn, built in 1859. Fort Johnston, completed in 1764, served as a refuge for royal governor Josiah Martin in 1775. Brunswick Town/Fort Anderson State Historic Site interprets the colonial and Civil War history of the region. Other cultural institutions include the Southport Maritime Museum, the Brunswick County Historical Society, and the Bald Head Island Conservatory. Well-attended annual events in Brunswick County include the North Carolina Fourth of July Festival, the Christmas-by-the-Sea Festival, the North Carolina Festival-by-the-Sea, and the North Carolina Oyster Festival.

Brunswick County agricultural products include tobacco, vegetables, berries, corn, oats, sweet potatoes, swine, beef cattle, and poultry; and manufactured products include polyester fibers, children's clothes, lumber, and citric acid. In addition to the beaches that draw millions of vacationers, the county's numerous golf courses are a popular attraction for visitors (as well as a growing number of retirees). Charter boat fishing on the Intracoastal Waterway is another important recreational activity in the region. Brunswick County's population was estimated to be 85,000 in 2004.

References: Lawrence Lee, *The History of Brunswick County, North Carolina* (1980); David Stick, *Bald Head: A History of Smith Island and Cape Fear* (1985).

William S. Powell

SEE ALSO Bald Head; Brunswick Town; Cape Fear; Cape Fear River Settlements; Resorts.

Brunswick Town was the first permanent European settlement on the Lower Cape Fear River. Founded in 1725 by Col. Maurice Moore (son of James Moore, the royal governor of South Carolina) on part of a 1,500-acre grant, Brunswick was made a township, the seat of New Hanover Precinct, and a port of entry in 1729. Although the General Assembly never

The ruins of St. Philip's Episcopal Church at Brunswick Town State Historic Site. Photograph by Tim Buchman. Courtesy of Preservation North Carolina.

met there, the Governor's Council sometimes did; since it was the seat of the colony's executive branch, Brunswick during its early years essentially served as the capital of North Carolina.

The town was situated on a low bluff on the western bank of the Cape Fear River near Town Creek, approximately 20 miles north of the river's mouth—a site that was less than ideal because of nearby swamps and exposure to attack but commercially viable since it was accessible by oceangoing vessels. The town was named in honor of George I of England, a member of the German House of Brunswick-Hanover, and its earliest residents were mostly planters from South Carolina and the Albemarle, merchants, and seamen. The town became a center of commerce—with tobacco, lumber, naval stores, furs, and other products being shipped out—as well as the home of a number of prominent persons. Russellborough, home of two royal governors, Arthur Dobbs and William Tryon, stood just outside the town's limits.

Brunswick Town originally covered about 360 acres consisting of a commons and 336 half-acre lots organized into 24 town squares. Lots were reserved for a church, a cemetery, a courthouse and a jail, but no formal courthouse or jail was ever built. About a dozen households were reported standing in 1730. St. Philip's Parish was established in 1741, but harsh living conditions and rivalry with St. James Parish in Wilmington left Brunswick frequently without a minister. The construction of St. Philip's Church began in 1754, but because of public apathy, monetary problems, and natural disaster, it was not completed until 1768. In fact, after 1739—with the founding of the upriver port of Newton (Wilmington)—Brunswick Town entered a period of decline. Slowly eclipsed economically by its rival port, it was also beset by other troubles, including the 1748 attacks of two Spanish privateers and a destructive 1761 hurricane. Nonetheless, the town became the seat of

Brunswick County when that county was created in 1764 out of New Hanover and Bladen Counties.

In February 1766, a peaceful assault on Governor Tryon's home was organized in opposition to the Stamp Act, forcing the resignation of the Comptroller of the Customs, William Pennington. During the early years of the Revolution, Brunswick Town was nearly abandoned, and it was partially burned by the British soon after. When the county seat was moved to a safer location in 1779, Brunswick ceased to exist as a political center, and by 1783 it lay mostly in ruins. Some merchants remained to serve heavy vessels that had to lighten cargo before proceeding to Wilmington due to river shallows, but the deepening of the river channel in later years ensured the town's complete demise.

Between 1768 and 1770, a Swiss surveyor and engineer, Claude Joseph Sauthier, mapped ten North Carolina towns. His map of Brunswick is one of those that survives in the British Library, and many of the buildings that he depicted have been marked on the ground. Streets are indicated and the plan and function of this early eighteenth-century town may be studied. During the Civil War, the Confederate army built Fort Anderson on the site. Much of the modern-day Brunswick Town/Fort Anderson State Historic Site was excavated by archaeologists during the 1950s and 1960s. The ruins of St. Philip's Church remain, with brick walls 3 feet thick and 25 feet high. Portions of other businesses and homes exist, as well as the remains of Fort Anderson. A visitors center reveals the history of Brunswick Town through a variety of exhibits and artifacts.

References: Elizabeth A. Fenn and Peter H. Wood, *Natives and Newcomers: The Way We Lived in North Carolina before 1770* (1983); Richard F. Knapp, ed., *North Carolina's State Historic Sites: A Brief History and Status Report* (1995); Lawrence Lee, "The History of Brunswick, North Carolina: The Political and Economic Development of a Colonial Town" (M.A. thesis, UNC-Chapel Hill, 1951); Lee, *The Lower Cape Fear in Colonial Days* (1965).

William G. DiNome
Additional research provided by Ron Gooding.

SEE ALSO St. Philip's Church.

Buck Dancing is a folk dance that originated among African Americans during the era of slavery. It was largely associated with the North Carolina Piedmont and, later, with the blues. The original buck dance, or "buck and wing," referred to a specific step performed by solo dancers, usually men; today the term encompasses a broad variety of improvisational dance steps.

In contemporary usage, "buck dancing" often refers to a variety of solo step dancing to fiddle-based music done by dancers primarily in the Southern Appalachians. Among North Carolinians, buck dancing is differentiated from clogging and flatfooting by the use of steps higher off the floor, a straight and relatively immobile torso, and emphasis on steps that put the dancer on his or her toes rather than heels.

Reference: Mike Seeger and Ruth Pershing, *Talking Feet: Buck, Flatfoot, and Tap: Solo Southern Dance of the Appalachian, Piedmont, and Blue Ridge Mountain Regions* (1992).

Bruce E. Baker

SEE ALSO Clogging; Step Dancing.

Buffaloes were local Unionists engaged in guerrilla warfare and terrorist tactics during the Civil War, especially in eastern North Carolina. Similar to "bushwhackers" in the western part of the state, in portions of Appalachia, and on the war's western frontier, buffaloes consisted of Confederate deserters, draft resisters, escaped prisoners, and lawless white men and boys. They formed bands (which were compared with "herds of buffaloes") that hid out in swamps and forests and, often in league with fugitive slaves, gathered arms and raided local communities and plantations, harassing civilians and stealing or destroying their property and foodstuffs.

Wingfield plantation, on the Chowan River north of Edenton, became a fortified encampment that served as the base of buffalo operations and provided a refuge for deserters, fugitive slaves, and Union sympathizers throughout the northeastern corner of the state. Local Confederates assaulted it in a series of attacks in the winter of 1862–63. By the third strike, although the fort itself was destroyed, most buffaloes had escaped by Federal gunboat.

Farther down the coast, burning and pillaging by black and white guerrillas was sufficiently aggravating that Confederate commander George E. Pickett (reassigned to the New Bern area after the Battle of Gettysburg) resorted to extreme measures. In February 1864 Pickett captured 22 deserters engaged in guerrilla activity, all of them dressed as Union soldiers. After a court-martial for desertion from the Confederate army, Pickett marched the prisoners west to Kinston, where most of them had lived. There he ordered them hanged in front of their wives, children, and other family members, an action that put Pickett in the midst of yet another major military controversy.

References: John G. Barrett, *The Civil War in North Carolina* (1963); W. Scott Boyce, *Economic and Social History of Chowan County, North Carolina* (1917); Wayne K. Durrill, *War of Another Kind: A Southern Community in the Great Rebellion* (1990).

John C. Inscoe

Building and Loan Associations are the direct descendants of English building societies, which began in Birmingham, England, in 1781. In America, organizations such as the Oxford Provident Building Association in Pennsylvania (1831) were created to allow subscribers, most of whom were tex-

tile workers, to build or purchase houses on a monthly payment plan. A homestead and building associations bill was ratified by the North Carolina General Assembly in 1870. A decade passed, however, before the first building and loan association was organized in the state. The work of A. G. Brenizer led to the formation of the Mutual Building and Loan Association in Charlotte in April 1881. Mechanics Perpetual Building and Loan Association of Charlotte followed in February 1883. With the exception of the Wilmington area, most of the state's early building and loan activity was in the Piedmont, as the associations gave the hope of home ownership to wage-earners lured from rural areas by manufacturing and service jobs in the state's growing cities. Associations were also formed in Monroe (1885); Salisbury (1886); Statesville (1887); and Concord, Rutherfordton, and Lenoir (1888). A strong Wilmington market produced three building and loan associations there, organized in 1885, 1887, and 1889, respectively.

Building and loan associations were welcomed by local communities because they significantly increased the number of home-owning citizens. The editor of the local newspaper in Concord opined on 1 June 1888 that "nothing that has been started in our town for years will accomplish half as much towards giving homes to the people and improving the town as this B. & L. Association. A poor man can buy his home and pay for it with very little advance on his present monthly payments for rent."

By 1911, only 30 years after the founding of the first building and loan association in North Carolina, there were 113 such organizations, with 25,174 members and assets of nearly $8.5 million. Building and loan associations survived both the Great Depression and the Second World War. During the late 1940s and 1950s they provided capital so that the young couples who produced the "baby boom" could purchase their own homes. The years that followed saw a dramatic change in the industry, however, as the associations moved from their traditional roles into offering diverse banking services. Many converted to stock-owned institutions. Deregulation produced a fiercely competitive climate and forced changes in the marketing of services. North Carolina's well-managed building and loan institutions survived the widespread national savings and loan failures in 1988, which were followed by adverse publicity and intensive regulation.

References: Henry Morton Bodfish, ed., *History of Building and Loan in the United States* (1931); Josephine Hedges Ewalt, *A Business Reborn: The Savings and Loan Story, 1930–1960* (1962).

Clarence E. Horton Jr.

Bull Durham Tobacco. Seeking a name for his manufactured smoking tobacco shortly after the Civil War, John R. Green of Durham drew inspiration from a popular brand of mustard made in Durham, England, that featured the head of

An 1879 advertisement for Durham's W. T. Blackwell & Co. features the company's trademark bull, used to popularize its tobacco products. NCC.

a Durham bull on its label. Green chose to use the image of a whole bull, and his trademark—soon the subject of extensive litigation to protect it—became one of the most recognizable product advertisements in the country. Green made William T. Blackwell his partner in 1867, and when Green died two years later, Blackwell bought the entire business from the Green estate. Subsequently, with James R. Day and Julian S. Carr as his partners, Blackwell led the William T. Blackwell Company to a dominant position in Durham's burgeoning tobacco industry. Bull Durham smoking tobacco was widely advertised and was one of the world's best-known American products of the late nineteenth and early twentieth centuries. The 1988 blockbuster film *Bull Durham*, starring Kevin Costner, Susan Sarandon, and Tim Robbins, brought national attention to both the famous tobacco moniker and the Durham Bulls, Durham's popular minor league baseball team.

References: William K. Boyd, *The Story of Durham: City of the New South* (1927); Nannie M. Tilley, *The Bright-Tobacco Industry, 1860–1929* (1948).

Robert F. Durden

Buncombe. The word "Buncombe" has, along with its variations of "bunk" and "bunkum," entered American slang as a term synonymous with meaningless speech. The popular term for pretentious and nonsensical talk originated with Felix Walker, a U.S. congressman (1817–23) who represented a region in western North Carolina that included Buncombe County. Walker gave a high-sounding speech on a militia pension bill to a nearly empty congressional chamber. Afterward, when questioned about his reasons for the verbiage, he reportedly stated that he was "speaking . . . to Buncombe." This elicited the response: "And buncombe your talk certainly was." Thereafter the term was used to refer to insincere political speech but was later expanded to include any trivial and overblown application of language.

References: John P. Arthur, *Western North Carolina: A History, 1730–1913* (1914); Richard Walser, *The North Carolina Miscellany* (1962).

Ronnie W. Faulkner

Buncombe County, nicknamed "Land of the Sky" for its rugged mountain beauty, is located in the Mountain region of western North Carolina. Buncombe's land includes parts of the Great Craggy Mountains and the Blue Ridge Mountains, and a section of the Eastern Continental Divide passes through it. Buncombe County was formed from Burke and Rutherford Counties in 1791. It was named for Edward Buncombe, a Revolutionary War colonel. Its earliest residents were the Cherokee Indians, who were later joined by Scottish, German, and English settlers, who came to populate the region.

Asheville, the county seat, was in 2005 North Carolina's tenth-largest city and the Mountain region's cultural, economic, and educational center. Asheville was incorporated in 1797 and named for Samuel Ashe, then governor of North Carolina. The city's many historic and cultural institutions include the Biltmore House, the Grove Park Inn, and the Thomas Wolfe Memorial. The University of North Carolina at Asheville adds to the cultural life of Buncombe County, as do Warren Wilson College and Montreat College, both near Asheville. Black Mountain College was one of the Southeast's most influential artistic centers from 1933 to 1956.

Tourism is one of Buncombe County's principal industries. The county's agricultural products include milk and dairy products, burley tobacco, swine, honey, and many berries, fruits, and nuts. Minerals mined in Buncombe County include garnet, corundum, kyanite, and moonstone, and manufactures produced there include hosiery, glass products, textiles and apparel, baby foods, and electronics. Buncombe County is home to the Southern Highland Craft Guild's Folk Art Center and the Mountain Dance and Folk Festival, as well as Culturefest, the Sourwood Festival, the Poetry Festival, and the Swannanoa Music Festival. In 2004 the population of Buncombe County stood at just over 215,000.

References: Foster A. Sondley, *A History of Buncombe County, North Carolina* (1930); Douglas Swaim, ed., *Cabins and Castles: The History and Architecture of Buncombe County, North Carolina* (1981).

Jay Mazzocchi

SEE ALSO Asheville; Biltmore House; Black Mountain College; Buncombe; Montreat; Mountain Dance and Folk Festival; Southern Highland Craft Guild; University of North Carolina at Asheville.

Buncombe Turnpike, a 75-mile route through North Carolina from the South Carolina border to the Tennessee border constructed between 1824 and 1828, opened the western part of the state to settlement and trade. David L. Swain, then a Buncombe County legislator, sponsored a bill in 1824 "for the purpose of laying out and making a turnpike road from the Saluda Gap . . . by the way of . . . Warm Springs to the Tennessee line." Three Asheville men—James Patton, Samuel Chunn, and George Swain—were authorized to sell $50,000 of stock in the company. The collection of tolls further financed the project.

South of Asheville, the Buncombe Turnpike followed approximately the same course as present-day U.S. 25 Business through the communities of Flat Rock and Hendersonville. North of Asheville, its route followed the east bank of the French Broad River across Beaver Dam, Reems, Flat, Ivy, and Laurel Creeks to Paint Rock and the Tennessee state line. Well constructed and maintained, the highway was called the finest of its day in North Carolina.

The turnpike's effects on western North Carolina commerce and development were striking. The Mountain region, long isolated, was opened to settlement. Stagecoaches and mail delivery established regular routes. The resort business began to flourish. Other roads were developed to feed into the turnpike. Fowl and livestock were driven to markets in Charleston, S.C., and Augusta, Ga., via the turnpike, and corn planting increased to feed the large droves. In 1849 William A. Lenoir spent the night in an inn south of Asheville with, he wrote, 5,000 hogs and 75 people. By 1850 the heavy animal traffic had necessitated repairs, and sections were converted into plank roads. In the post–Civil War period the railroad, following much the same route, supplanted the turnpike as the principal commercial transportation artery.

References: Ora Blackmun, *Western North Carolina: Its Mountains and Its People to 1880* (1977); John C. Inscoe, *Mountain Masters, Slavery, and the Sectional Crisis in Western North Carolina* (1989); F. A. Sondley, *A History of Buncombe County, North Carolina* (1930).

Michael Hill

Burial Customs. The nature of the specific burial customs that may have existed among the people inhabiting the North Carolina region prior to European settlement can only be guessed at based on the artifacts and burial sites that remain. Funerary mounds ascribed to the Mississippian, or Temple Mound Builder, culture (1000–1500 A.D.) remain in the central Piedmont, notably in the Catawba River Valley. Town Creek Indian Mound in Montgomery County is an example of a restored temple mound complex that includes a burial mound. While Mississippian natives are known to have buried their dead in cemeteries, mound burials were evidently reserved for the elite. Interments included elaborate grave goods, including pottery, weavings, beads, pipes, mica, and carved stone, and the deceased were placed in the fetal position or in a sitting position facing east.

Grave and grave shed in northeastern Union County. Photograph (taken ca. 1990) courtesy of Douglas Helms.

In the Coastal Plain, low mounds known as tumuli were common. These are roughly circular, ranging from 15 to 40 feet in diameter and standing about 3 feet high. Tumuli often contain only bones, but sometimes also pot shards, charcoal, shell beads found in bunches near skulls and breastbones, and "killed" shell cups, their bottoms broken out upon the death of their owner presumably to prevent use by nonsanctified persons or to free the spirit of the cup to accompany the deceased. Bones are often found distributed throughout the mound. Few skeletons are found singly; oftentimes they are crowded one upon another. Skeletons are often in the fetal position.

European settlers brought to North Carolina their own burial customs and, with some variations, these remained the customs practiced through modern times. Prior to the wide availability of embalming, burials usually took place the day following death. In most communities throughout the eighteenth and nineteenth centuries, the corpse was never left alone during the wake period preceding burial, with family and friends "sitting up" through the night with the dead at home. The preparation, or "laying out," of the corpse was traditionally performed by neighbors, permitting the immediate family time to grieve. The corpse was stretched flat upon a hard surface, usually a cloth-draped board, sometimes called a cooling board. Sometimes this necessitated tying the body down or even breaking bones. The mouth was tied closed and weights (sometimes coins) were used to close the eyelids.

In some areas, especially among African Americans, plates of salt and ashes (thought to be a preservative and to absorb disease, respectively) were placed beneath the cooling board; both were later buried with the body. Bathing of the body, frequently limited to the extremities, was typically performed by the women and was accomplished using any of various materials such as lye soap, soda water, camphor, vinegar, or alcohol. Hair was seldom washed, but men's faces were usually shaved. Prior to the mid-1800s the dead were usually dressed in shrouds of black or white cloth, open at the back. Later they were dressed in their own clothing, often the deceased's favorite or "Sunday best."

Although embalming had been popularized by the tour of President Abraham Lincoln's body from Washington, D.C., to Springfield, Ill., the procedure was not introduced into western North Carolina until the turn of the twentieth century and did not become widely popular for another 50 years afterward. Funeral directors first became licensed embalmers late in the nineteenth century. In modern times embalming is the standard practice.

While women were sometimes buried with a flower in hand, large displays of flowers during the wake or burial ceremony were rare until recently. A wreath or small flower arrangement was sometimes hung on or near the front door of the home or business, a custom often observed still. Common superstitions, such as covering mirrors in the home of the deceased, or preventing very young children from viewing the corpse, are matters of folkloric record. In some towns, bell-ringing (tolling) provided notification of a death to the community; often the tolling communicated the age of the deceased.

No coffins were used by early settlers; rather, a sheet (often linen or wool dipped in wax), a blanket, or a quilt was provided by women friends or family. Early coffins were fashioned out of hollow tree sections. Burials in the Appalachians went without coffins or caskets much later than elsewhere in the state. Woven burial baskets have also been known. Early wooden coffins were frequently beautified with paint or cloth on inside and outside surfaces, and coffin linings, typically quilts or inexpensive cloth, soon became commonplace. Coffins were built by the family of the deceased in early years, then by tradesmen, and finally by specialists. Metal coffins were introduced in the early 1800s, not without some protest, and by the 1900s (the 1930s or 1940s in the Mountains), durable metal caskets had become popular, as had coffins with elaborately designed handles, nails, and carvings. In the rural western part of the state, grave sheds, or grave houses, often complete with windows and rain gutters, were sometimes erected over the burial site. As church grounds became filled, perpetual-care cemeteries, both municipal and private, became the norm.

Despite its growing popularity in America since the first modern crematory furnace was perfected in 1873, cremation generally has never been the preferred burial method in North Carolina. This is likely due to scripturally based, Judeo-Christian attitudes about the sanctity of the human body. The first crematory in North Carolina is thought to have been founded by Thos. Shepherd & Son Funeral Directors in 1970 at Shepherd Memorial Park in Hendersonville. Although still rare in Mountain communities, cremation by 2004 was provided by nearly 40 crematories in the state, and cremation was chosen in approximately 25 to 38 percent of all North Carolina deaths. Higher percentages occurred in locales where retirees are numerous, particularly among retirees who have migrated from the North, where cremation has long been available.

Most burial customs now practiced in North Carolina are essentially the same as those practiced elsewhere in the United States. These customs also exhibit a similar trend toward diminishing family cohesion and solidarity and a lesser role of neighbors in funerary procedures.

References: James K. Crissman, *Death and Dying in Central Appalachia: Changing Attitudes and Practices* (1994); M. Ruth Little, *Sticks and Stones: Three Centuries of North Carolina Gravemarkers* (1998); Mildred J. Miller and Pat M. Crooks, *Time Is, Time Was: Gravestone Art, Burial Customs and History: Iredell County, North Carolina* (1990).

William G. DiNome

SEE ALSO Funerals; Town Creek Indian Mound.

Burke County is located in west central North Carolina, in the state's Mountain region. It was formed in 1777 and named for Thomas Burke, delegate to the Continental Congress and governor of the state (1781–82). The county originally comprised substantial territory in the western part of the state, and portions of it later formed counties including Alexander, Buncombe, Caldwell, Catawba, Madison, Mitchell, McDowell, and Yancey. Its present borders have been settled since 1834. Morganton, the county seat and largest city, was incorporated in 1784 and named for Gen. Daniel Morgan, the Revolutionary War hero who led Continental troops at the Battles of King's Mountain and Cowpens. Other Burke County communities include Connelly Springs, Drexel, Glen Alpine, Hildebran, Rhodhiss (on the Caldwell County line), and Valdese. A small western portion of the city of Hickory also lies within Burke County, although most of the city is located in neighboring Catawba County.

Catawba and Cherokee Indians were the primary inhabitants of the lands that became Burke County when English, Scotch-Irish, and German settlers first moved into the area. During the late eighteenth and early nineteenth centuries, many of these settlers came from Pennsylvania, having traveled south through the Shenandoah Valley along what came to be known as the Great Wagon Road. After the Civil War, the development of the Southern Railroad through Burke County led to increased contact with the rest of the state and region and brought industrial development to Morganton and the county's smaller communities.

The county's economy today is diversified. Industrial products include furniture, chemicals, machine parts, and textiles, although the textile industry in Burke County has diminished sharply in recent years, mirroring developments elsewhere in the state. The county is also home to a significant agricultural processing industry, and it is one of the state's largest producers of forest products, including Christmas trees, and ornamental plants. Burke County has the highest proportion of state government employees outside of Raleigh. Important state institutions in the county include the North Carolina School for the Deaf; Broughton Hospital and Western Carolina Hospital, which serve the state's mental health needs; and Western Correctional Center, a state prison. The Historic Burke Foundation operates Quaker Meadows, the Revolutionary-era home of the McDowell family, and Western Piedmont Community College houses the library and re-created office of Senator Sam J. Ervin Jr.

Burke County is known for its natural resources and parklands, which contribute to a thriving tourism industry. Lake James State Park and South Mountains State Park are both located in the county, as is a portion of the Pisgah National Forest. Because of the size of these park and forest lands, the U.S. government and the state of North Carolina are two of the three largest landholders in the county. (The third is Duke Energy, whose predecessor companies created 6,510-acre Lake James in the 1910s and which today operates several hydroelectric facilities in the county.) The Blue Ridge Parkway runs through the far northwestern corner of the county, past the Linville Gorge Wilderness Area and its popular Linville Falls as well as other destinations for hiking, camping, mountain biking, and nature study. The population of Burke County in 2004 was estimated to be 89,000.

Reference: Edward W. Phifer Jr., *Burke County: A Brief History* (1979).

Peter Bangma

Burlington Industries.

Burlington Industries. In 1923 J. Spencer Love founded a textile company located on the outskirts of Burlington. Love and his father contributed $50,000 worth of machinery from a previously owned mill and $200,000 from the sale of its real estate, while Burlington citizens subscribed to an additional $200,000 worth of stock in the new company. Early in 1924 construction began for the first mill, the Pioneer Plant, and for a village of 70 houses known as Piedmont Heights.

The success and rapid expansion of Burlington Industries is closely associated with rayon. Love's was one of the first American-owned mills to produce rayon, which saw spectacular growth in the post–World War I fashion revolution. Originally known as artificial silk, rayon was the only synthetic fiber then available. Rayon bedspreads, one of the earliest fruits of Love's experimentation with the new synthetic, became a huge seller. By 1928 four additional mills in the Piedmont Heights area and new wide Jacquard looms were producing rayon upholstery goods, draperies, bedspreads, and dress goods.

In 1929 Burlington Industries engaged its own selling agent in New York, thereby establishing more direct contact with

Inspectors examine newly woven fabric at the Burlington Industries mill in Mooresville, ca. 1960. NCC.

its customers. With a commitment to the modernization of plants and machinery, the company expanded during the 1930s by acquiring mills that had been closed during the Depression. The corporate headquarters was moved to Greensboro in 1935, and two years later, following reorganization to consolidate the various associated companies, stock in Burlington Mills was listed on the New York Stock Exchange.

A pioneer in the production of synthetic fabrics, Burlington Industries produced a variety of goods, such as nylon parachute cloth for the federal government during World War II. The company was a leader in the process of forward integration, converting its products into finished goods. When Love died in 1962, Burlington's manufacturing operations included more than 130 plants in 16 states and 7 foreign countries, employing approximately 65,000 workers.

Burlington Industries remained one of the largest and most diversified manufacturers of textile products in the world at the end of the twentieth century. Its close connection with the high-tech Nano-Tex, L.L.C., beginning in 1998 allowed the company to create and use new fabrics in its products as well as improve older ones. Its products included synthetic yarns, denim fabrics, cotton and cotton-blend knits, wool worsted fabrics, and fabrics for draperies, upholstery, mattress coverings, and carpets. However, the economic struggles affecting the textile industry in North Carolina, struggles rooted mainly in the adoption of various trade agreements that led to a massive increase in foreign imports, caused Burlington Industries to declare bankruptcy in 2001. In March 2004 the company was bought by New York financier Wilbur L. Ross, becoming, along with Cone Mills (also in bankruptcy), a part of the massive International Textile Group, headquartered in Greensboro.

References: Jacquelyn Dowd Hall and others, *Like a Family: The Making of a Southern Cotton Mill World* (1987); Peter Wood,

Southern Capitalism: The Political Economy of North Carolina, 1880–1980 (1986).

George W. Troxler

Reference: Fred A. Coe Jr., *Burroughs Wellcome Co., 1880–1980: Pioneer of Pharmaceutical Research* (1980).

Cecelia Moore

Burroughs Wellcome Fund (BWF) is an independent private foundation whose mission is to advance the medical sciences by supporting research and other scientific and educational activities. It was founded in 1955 in the United States as an extension of the England-based Wellcome Trust, from which it became completely independent in 1993. From its headquarters in Research Triangle Park, the fund grants about $25 million annually across the United States and Canada for biomedical sciences, the study of infectious diseases, and other scientific fields. In North Carolina, BWF grants have been particularly important in the area of science education. Among other successful efforts, BWF funds helped establish the North Carolina Science, Mathematics, and Technology Education Center, which has been instrumental in helping to strengthen science, math, and technology education in secondary schools across the state.

The Burroughs Wellcome Fund and its original English parent, the Wellcome Trust, grew from the pharmaceutical company Burroughs Wellcome, established in England in 1880. The company's founders, Silas Mainville Burroughs (1846–95) and Henry Wellcome (1853–1936), were American pharmacists who traveled to England to explore a new method of medicine delivery—compressed pills. The company soon began manufacturing its own medicines and quickly established an in-house research facility, a first among pharmaceutical companies. Burroughs Wellcome opened U.S. operations in New York City in 1908 and a manufacturing facility in Tuckahoe, N.Y., in 1919. Growth considerations led the company to relocate its U.S. operations to North Carolina in 1970, building research facilities in Research Triangle Park and a manufacturing facility in Greenville.

Henry Wellcome's will set up a complex ownership for the Burroughs Wellcome Company. It also created the Wellcome Trust as the sole shareholder of the Wellcome Foundation, Ltd., the parent company. The company's profits went to the trustees to support medical research around the world. The Wellcome Trust remains the largest British charity supporting medical research today.

From its creation in 1955 as an arm of the Wellcome Trust until 1993, the Burroughs Wellcome Fund operated as a corporate foundation, supporting scientific research. In 1993 the trustees made a $400 million gift to the Burroughs Wellcome Fund and gave it independence. The fund has no direct ties to the Wellcome Foundation, Ltd., or to GlaxoSmithKline, the modern incarnation of the company. In the early 2000s its assets were more than $575 million.

Burwell School in Hillsborough was established in 1837 by the Reverend Robert Amistead Burwell and his wife, Margaret Anna Burwell. The Burwells opened the Presbyterian school for young females shortly after arriving from Petersburg, Va. The school enrolled 40 girls aged 8 to 18 in its first year, at a tuition rate of $17.50 per term. By 1848, when the building that housed the school was enlarged a second time, the school's catalog boasted 107 pupils from as far away as New York. In 1857, however, the Burwells moved to Charlotte to become directors of the Charlotte Female Institute (later to become Queens College). In 1871, after the death of Margaret Burwell, Robert and his son John Bott Burwell presided over Peace Institute (later Peace College). The original Burwell School in Hillsborough was purchased by the Historic Hillsborough Commission in 1965 and became a public museum.

References: Hugh T. Lefler and Paul Wager, eds., *Orange County, 1752–1952* (1953); M. C. S. Noble, *A History of the Public Schools of North Carolina* (1930).

Robert E. Ireland

Business Directories have been published in North Carolina since the beginning of the nineteenth century. Many extant directories provide a valuable contemporary portrait of the business community of the entire state as well as other interesting county and municipal information. One of the earliest examples of a directory of North Carolina businesses is the *Commercial Directory*, published by J. C. Kayer & Company (Philadelphia) in 1823. This publication, based on the 1820 U.S. census, lists businesses in three of the state's largest towns: New Bern, Fayetteville, and Wilmington. Pre-1900 city directories also exist for Wilmington (1860–61 edition), Asheville (1883), Charlotte (1875), Durham (1887), Greensboro (1879), New Bern (1880), Raleigh (1880), and the Winston-Salem area (including Greensboro, 1879). Typically, these volumes have an alphabetical list of the names and addresses of residents and businesses, a street address directory, and a classified business directory. These directories usually include a numerical list of telephone subscribers.

Between 1867 and 1897, Levi Branson, one of North Carolina's leading publishers and booksellers, compiled and published nine editions of *Branson's North Carolina Business Directory*. Organized by county, *Branson's Directory* includes the names of business firms under such headings as blacksmiths, grocers, dry goods stores, and restaurants. The names of all municipal and county officeholders, as well as U.S. officials who held posts such as customs collectors, are also listed.

In addition, the volumes include the names of a wide variety of other professionals and institutions in each county, such as schools, attorneys, ministers, physicians, and postmasters. Importantly, the directories also note if businessmen and other community figures were African American.

Some leading annual directories of modern North Carolina businesses and manufacturers are the *North Carolina Business Directory* (1988–), *North Carolina Manufacturers Directory* (1993–), *North Carolina Manufacturers Register* (1994–), and *Regional Industrial Buying Guide: Greater Carolinas* (1990–). The 1998–99 edition of the *North Carolina Business Directory* covers some 300,000 businesses. The *North Carolina Manufacturers Directory*, covering about 11,000 companies and more than 26,000 personnel, is compiled in cooperation with the N.C. Department of Commerce.

Wiley J. Williams
Additional research provided by Robert C. Kenzer.

Busing. SEE *Swann v. Charlotte-Mecklenburg Board of Education.*

Buttermilk, the liquid left when milk or cream is churned into butter, has long added to the richness of North Carolina cuisine. It is the essential ingredient in the buttermilk biscuit —a southern staple that has become a popular part of breakfasts across the nation, particularly since being promoted by several major fast food chains. Buttermilk is also a main ingredient in such traditional foods as buttermilk pie, hush puppies, rolls, and cornbread.

Evidence of buttermilk's role in North Carolina culture is its use in several place names. These include Buttermilk Creek, which flows from Caswell County into Alamance County and the Haw River, and Buttermilk Mountain in Henderson County.

Athena Masci

C

Cabarrus Black Boys were nine young men from Rowan and Mecklenburg (later Cabarrus) Counties who took part in an infamous raid against a royal governmental military convoy during the Regulator Movement in North Carolina in the years before the American Revolution. On 9 May 1771 Gen. Hugh Waddell left Salisbury en route to Hillsborough to assist Governor William Tryon in quelling the Regulator uprising. After crossing the Yadkin River, Waddell's militia encountered a numerically superior body of Regulators and began to fall back to Salisbury. A small band of Regulators, disguised as Indians, attacked a convoy that was carrying gunpowder from South Carolina to Waddell. The group burned two powder wagons as well as destroyed some blankets, leggings, kettles, and other supplies.

The men involved in this episode were either blackened by their Indian disguises or by the powder as they emptied it from kegs, and the name "Black Boys of Cabarrus" was applied to them at a later time. By a proclamation of 11 June 1771, Tryon offered amnesty to certain categories of Regulators, but this did not apply to those who were involved in blowing up Waddell's gunpowder. James Ashmore, who lived near the site, swore under oath that the Cabarrus Black Boys, in addition to himself, were Robert Caruthers, Benjamin Cockran, Robert Davis, Joshua Hadley, James White Jr., John White Jr., William White, and another William White, identified as the "son of the Widow White."

Reference: William S. Powell, James K. Huhta, and Thomas J. Farnham, eds., *The Regulators in North Carolina: A Documentary History, 1759–1776* (1971).

William S. Powell

Cabarrus County, located in North Carolina's south central Piedmont, was formed in 1792 from Mecklenburg County and named for Stephen Cabarrus, then Speaker of the North Carolina House of Commons. Catawba Indians were the primary inhabitants of the area when Scotch-Irish and German immigrants began traveling the Great Wagon Road to the North Carolina backcountry in significant numbers in the middle of the eighteenth century. These immigrants settled in the region that became Cabarrus County, separated by language, religion, and other cultural barriers. Concord, the county seat, was founded in 1798; its name celebrates the settlement of long-term disputes between ethnic groups and agreement over the town as the site for the courthouse. Other communities in the county include Georgeville, Harrisburg, Kannapolis, Mount Pleasant, and Stanfield.

Growth in the county received a boost when gold was discovered for the first time in the United States in 1799 at Reed Gold Mine near modern-day Georgeville. North Carolina was the leading producer of gold in the nation until the California gold rush of 1848. Reed Gold Mine is now a North Carolina State Historic Site.

For much of the late nineteenth and twentieth centuries, the county was a leading producer of textiles. Kannapolis, which celebrated its centennial in 2006, was built around the then-thriving Cannon Mills textile company. Concord's Coleman Manufacturing Company, which operated from 1896 to 1904, was the nation's first textile company owned and operated by African Americans. The rapid growth of neighboring Charlotte and Mecklenburg County in the middle and late twentieth century brought spillover growth to Cabarrus County, which benefited from economic diversification and took on an increasingly suburban character.

When international competition caused the fortunes of North Carolina's textile industry to decline sharply at the end of the twentieth century, many Cabarrus County residents felt the effects. Kannapolis in particular suffered from declining wages and lost jobs. An especially severe setback came in 2003, when Pillowtex, the company that had purchased Cannon Mills in 1997, closed its doors and laid off nearly 5,000 people statewide, including 1,500 in Cabarrus County alone. In 2005 a regional partnership between several public and private entities was formed to support a major redevelopment of Kannapolis, focusing on turning the shuttered Cannon Mills facility into a research campus for biotechnology and health science.

In the early 2000s Cabarrus County, with an estimated population of 147,000 (2004), was one of the largest and fastest growing counties in North Carolina. It is strongly identified with the history of auto racing in the state. Legendary driver Dale Earnhardt was born in Kannapolis, and a number of the sport's leading teams have been based in the county. Concord's Lowe's Motor Speedway, built in 1959 as one of the first "superspeedway" tracks in America, today hosts tens of thousands of fans each year for races sponsored by NASCAR (the National Association for Stock Car Auto Racing).

Peter Bangma

SEE ALSO Auto Racing; Cannon Mills; Coleman Manufacturing Company; Gold Rush; Reed Gold Mine.

Cabinet of Minerals was a collection of native ores assembled in the antebellum period to illustrate their potential commercial value to the state. The original collection was completed in 1856 and displayed in the State Capitol. A second, larger cabinet, put together after the Civil War primarily for exhibition and education, played a major role in establishing a state-supported museum of natural history. The collection contained specimens large enough to show the potential for commercial mining as well as a few fossils. No inventory of the cabinet has been found, but it is believed to have included gold, coal, mica, copper, iron, tungsten, zinc, granite, marble, lead, nickel, kaolin, and limestone.

In 1865 the state donated the collection to the University of North Carolina in Chapel Hill, where other collections were added, exhibited, and culled until the original cabinet of minerals was no longer distinguishable. After the Civil War, state geologist W. C. Kerr decided to build a second cabinet from the renewed geological survey. The capitol building again became home for the exhibit, but the display area was hampered by boxes of materials stored by the military department. By 1877 the new cabinet of minerals had become larger in both scope and size than its predecessor.

Leonidas L. Polk, commissioner of the North Carolina Department of Agriculture, conceived the idea of a museum of natural history in 1879, and the legislature transferred jurisdiction of the mineral collection to his agency. It was removed from the capitol and became part of a larger collection that frequently was broken apart for various exhibits over the next two years. By 1881 the second cabinet had suffered the same fate as the first; no longer could its parts be separated and identified. It had been swallowed by what was to become the State Museum and later the Museum of Natural Sciences.

References: Margaret Martin, *A Long Look at Nature* (2001); Stuart Noblin, "Leonidas Lafayette Polk and the North Carolina Department of Agriculture," NCHR 20 (April–July 1943); State Board of Agriculture, *North Carolina and Its Resources* (1896).

Jerry L. Cross

Calabash is a fishing and resort town situated on the Calabash River in southwestern Brunswick County. Dubbed the "Seafood Capital of the World" by a food editor of the *New York Times*, the small town can boast of more seafood restaurants than any place of its size in the United States. Settled in the early 1700s, the site now occupied by Calabash evolved into a village known as Pea Landing, named for the peanut crops brought to the river for shipment by area planters. In 1873, the name was changed to Calabash for the drinking gourds that hung at wells in the area.

The first of the restaurants that have brought the town international fame opened in the early 1940s, featuring lightly battered and deep fried shrimp, oysters, flounder, and other seafood. Over the ensuing half century, some two dozen other restaurants have been built, serving seafood dinners to more than 1.25 million patrons each year. The special method of seafood preparation in the town has become popular in other parts of the United States, and the town has thus lent its name to "Calabash-style" seafood.

Local tradition holds that legendary entertainer Jimmy Durante made reference to the town each time he closed his radio and television shows with the famous line, "Goodnight, Mrs. Calabash, wherever you are." Durante dined often at a Calabash restaurant in the 1940s. Since its incorporation in 1973, Calabash has undergone significant commercial and resort development.

References: Daniel W. Barefoot, *Touring the Backroads of North Carolina's Lower Coast* (1995); Jerry Bledsoe, *Carolina Curiosities* (1984).

Daniel W. Barefoot

Calcium Carbide, a chemical compound used in the commercial manufacture of acetylene gas, was discovered accidentally during experiments in aluminum processing in Spray (now Eden) in Rockingham County. A local entrepreneur, James Turner Morehead, formed a partnership with Thomas L. Willson, a Canadian chemist, to develop an economical method for producing aluminum. Using existing water-power resources in Spray, the Willson Aluminum Company constructed the first electric arc furnace in the United States to procure the high temperatures necessary to reduce aluminum. Combining aluminum oxide and carbon in the furnace was not successful, but the company did commercially produce alloys of copper and aluminum.

In the course of the experimentation, a mixture of lime and coal tar was introduced with calcium for the purpose of producing metallic calcium as a reduction agent in the aluminum process. Following the routine procedure of quenching the results in water for rapid cooling, a large quantity of gas was observed on 2 May 1892. Morehead's son, John Motley Morehead III, a chemistry graduate of the University of North Carolina in Chapel Hill, identified the new substance as calcium carbide. Lacking gas analysis equipment, they sent a sample to Chapel Hill, where Professor F. P. Venable and an assistant, William Rand Kenan, identified the gas as acetylene. In spite of initially lacking a practical use for the new compound or gas, the elder Morehead continued to produce and experiment, believing that the gas had commercial possibilities for energy and especially lighting use. His heavily mortgaged businesses were lost in the panic of 1893, and he was left with little more than samples of calcium carbide.

In 1894 Morehead and Willson convinced New York investors to form the Electric Gas Company to produce calcium carbide and acetylene. Additional experimentation in Spray with alloys led to the development of ferrochromium and ferrosilicon, which were used in the hardening of steel. These steel alloys were important in the development of armor plate and armor-piercing projectiles, which were significant in the late nineteenth-century naval arms buildup. Later power development by Morehead on the James River in Virginia and the Kanawba River in West Virginia, as well as patents in chemical processes and metal alloys, led to the formation of Union Carbide Corporation in Chicago in 1898. Union Carbide was founded with the purpose of producing acetylene gas for use in household lighting and streetlamps, providing an alternative to coal gas and kerosene. The company expanded into producing oxyacetylene for welding in 1911. The 1917 merger of Union Carbide, Linde Air Products, Prest-O-Lite Company, and National Carbon Company created Union Carbide and Carbon Corporation, which quickly developed into a producer of petrochemicals, metal alloys, antifreeze, and synthetics. The company is also known for its role in the horrific 1984 pesticide plant disaster that killed 3,500 people in Bhopal, India.

References: William R. Kenan Jr., *Discovery and Identification of Calcium Carbide in the U.S.A.* (1939); Herbert T. Pratt, "The History of Willson Aluminum Company, Spray, North Carolina, 1891–1896," *Journal of Rockingham County History and Genealogy* 17 (June 1992).

Lindley S. Butler
Kimberley Hewitt

Caldwell County, located in the Mountain region of western North Carolina, was formed from Burke and Wilkes Counties in 1841. It was named for Joseph Caldwell, the first president of the University of North Carolina in Chapel Hill. Early inhabitants of Caldwell County included Cherokee and Siouan Indians, followed by German, Scotch-Irish, and English settlers. The county seat, Lenoir, was incorporated in 1851 and named for Revolutionary War general William Lenoir. Other communities in Caldwell County include Hudson, Granite Falls, Rhodhiss (on the Burke County line), Cajah Mountain, and Gamewell. Part of Blowing Rock is also in Caldwell County.

The mountainous terrain attracts thousands of tourists to Caldwell County each year, and a large portion of the county is covered by the Blue Ridge Mountains and Pisgah National Forest. The Catawba, Yadkin, and Little Rivers flow through the county.

Caldwell County is one of the leading producers of furniture in the world. Other manufactured products include labels and tape, twines, yarn, and thread and cordage. Agricultural products from Caldwell County include broilers, hatching eggs, hay, soybeans, oats, barley, and landscape nursery plants.

Historic sites in Caldwell County include the county courthouse, constructed in 1905; Fort Defiance (1790), the home of General Lenoir; the Eli Corpening House, built in 1856; and Little House, built in 1872. Cultural institutions include the Foothills Performing Arts Community Theatre, the Unifour Jazz Ensemble, and the Caldwell County Heritage Museum. The Overmountain Victory National Historic Trail traverses the county. In 2004 the population of Caldwell County was estimated to be 78,500.

Jay Mazzocchi

SEE ALSO Fort Defiance; Overmountain Victory National Historic Trail.

Caldwell Institute, originally located in Guilford County, grew out of the determined effort of the Presbyterian Church to establish a school providing a classical education imbued with Christian principles. In 1833 a committee appointed by the Orange Presbytery selected Greensboro as the site for the proposed institution, but not until 21 Jan. 1837 did the General Assembly ratify the charter of incorporation for the Caldwell Institute. The name honored Joseph Caldwell (1773–1835), the first president of the University of North Carolina, whose distinguished career in education spanned more than four decades.

The Caldwell Institute's school year consisted of two sessions of five months each, with one-month vacations in April and August that coincided with the planting and harvesting seasons. The trustees chose not to construct a dormitory on campus because they believed that living in homes under family restraints would offer fewer temptations to students. Everyone attending the institute was required to attend public worship on Sundays and to spend time Sunday afternoon reciting from the Bible and Westminster Catechism.

The Caldwell Institute flourished for eight years, and, according to local tradition, attracted students from surrounding states as well as North Carolina. An outbreak of typhoid fever in Greensboro in 1845 prompted the trustees to move the school to Hillsborough, where classes were held in the recently repaired and enlarged Hillsborough Academy building. The Caldwell Institute, under the continuing leadership of Alexander Wilson, thrived for three years, reaching a peak enrollment of 100 in 1848. The next year attendance dropped back to 68, and in 1850 the trustees voted to discontinue the school.

References: Ethel Stephens Arnett, *Greensboro, North Carolina: The County Seat of Guilford* (1955); Ruth Blackwelder, *The Age of Orange: Political and Intellectual Leadership in North Carolina, 1752–1861* (1961); Bettie D. Caldwell, *Founders and Builders of Greensboro* (1925); Charles L. Coon, *North Carolina Schools and Academies, 1790–1840: A Documentary History* (1915).

Jerry L. Cross

Caldwell School. The David Caldwell School, also known as "Log College," was established in what is now Greensboro in 1767 by David Caldwell, a Presbyterian minister, self-taught physician, and patriot. As a spiritual leader of the growing Scotch-Irish population in rural North Carolina, Caldwell saw a need for an institution that would raise the level of education of people in the "backwoods." For the first 20 years, he operated the school out of his home. At an unknown date after the American Revolution, a separate school building was erected. The idea of a permanent school with boarders was unusual in the state, as it ran against the tradition of itinerant teachers.

Caldwell's curriculum was adapted to each student's needs. Advanced students received instruction in math and mechanical sciences, English writing and grammar, Latin, Greek, and Hebrew. Instruction in metaphysics was derived by Caldwell from notes he had taken at Princeton. Seeking to involve students in practical matters, Caldwell had them build a mill and dam. Heavy emphasis was placed on a firm appreciation and understanding of the Protestant religious heritage. Caldwell's instruction was considered good enough to allow several students to enter the junior year at the University of North Carolina.

Most early accounts of the Log College place the number of students between 50 and 60, but more recent studies estimate that the number was between 12 and 20. Figures given by early local writers were inflated to give the impression that it was the equal of later academies in the Piedmont. Graduates entered the learned professions at a rate unknown by other schools. Many went into professions such as law and medicine. Others went into politics with success, with five becoming governors, including John Motley Morehead (1841–45).

In 1795 Caldwell's prominence as an educator led the trustees of the University of North Carolina to offer him the presidency of the university, which he declined. He died in 1824, still active in the operation of his Log College.

References: Ethel Stephens Arnett, *David Caldwell* (1976); Aubrey Lee Brooks, "David Caldwell and His Log College," *NCHR* 28 (October 1951); Eli W. Caruthers, *Sketch of the Life of the Rev. David Caldwell* (1842).

Alexander R. Stoesen

Camden, Battle of. In April 1780, at the height of the Revolutionary War, Gen. George Washington ordered Gen. Johann de Kalb to march the Maryland and Delaware Continentals from their encampment in Morristown, N.J., to Charleston (then Charles Towne), S.C. The British army had besieged the city and, unless American reinforcements arrived, it would soon fall. When de Kalb arrived in Hillsborough on 22 June, he learned that Charleston had fallen on 12 May. De Kalb's troops became the only force of Continentals in the South.

After remaining in North Carolina for a time, de Kalb was replaced by Gen. Horatio Gates in June 1780. The Continental Congress opted for Gates to command the force because de Kalb was a foreigner and was unlikely to win local support; moreover, Gates had won a stupendous victory at Saratoga, N.Y., in 1777. On assuming command, Gates examined a letter addressed to de Kalb from Thomas Sumter, South Carolina's upstate partisan leader. Sumter's message detailed the scattered postings of British forces in South Carolina, listing the strength of their garrison at Camden at 700. On this information, Gates decided to take Camden.

Moving south with his men through the intense summer heat, Gates received a major boost when Maj. Gen. Richard Caswell and the North Carolina militia of more than 2,000 men joined his troops at Rugeley's Mill on 6 August, boosting Gates's complement to more than 3,000. The British soon learned of Gates's advance, and Lord Rawdon, commander of the Camden garrison, notified Lord Charles Cornwallis in Charleston. Cornwallis decided to fight for the town for several reasons. Camden contained military storehouses and industry vital to the British war effort in the South. Additionally, Cornwallis would have had to abandon several hundred sick and wounded soldiers to Gates if he relinquished Camden. Finally, a British retreat from Camden could begin the deterioration of royal hegemony in South Carolina and Georgia that had taken over a year to reclaim, as well as delay a subsequent British advance into North Carolina. Cornwallis rushed reinforcements to Camden, boosting his strength to 2,300, and waited for Gates.

The Battle of Camden erupted on 16 Aug. 1780. Both commanders decided to lead with the attack in the morning. The opposing armies formed their battle lines astride the Charlotte road north of town. Gates posted his Maryland and Delaware Continentals on the right flank and his North Carolina and Virginia militia on the left flank. Cornwallis deployed his British infantry on the right flank and his Provincials on the left. Cornwallis had two North Carolina Loyalist units in his force—Col. Morgan Bryan's North Carolina Volunteers and Col. John Hamilton's Royal North Carolina Regiment.

At dawn, Gates ordered the Virginia militia to advance against the British infantry. When the militiamen faltered, Cornwallis ordered his regulars to attack. Both the Virginia and North Carolina militia fled. Gates expected too much from his militia, and shortly after the battle began his left wing had evaporated. The British infantry then wheeled left and attacked the Continentals. The Continentals, along with Col. Henry Dixon's North Carolina militia regiment, defended their position gallantly, but they were forced to retreat with heavy losses. General de Kalb was killed in the battle, and Gen. Griffith Rutherford was captured. The bulk of the militia, along with Gates, raced back to North Carolina, and 700 Continentals reformed at Hillsborough. British forces remained in control of South Carolina, ready to advance into North Carolina. Combined with victories at Savannah, Ga., and Charleston, S.C., the British had squelched most organized resistance in the Carolinas and marked the nadir for the American cause in the South.

References: Peter Lumpkin, *From Savannah to Yorktown: The American Revolution in the South* (1981); Dan L. Morrill, *Southern Campaigns of the American Revolution* (1993); Hugh F. Rankin, *The North Carolina Continentals* (1971).

Dennis Isenbarger

Camden County, located in the Coastal Plain region of northeastern North Carolina and bordered in part by the state of Virginia and Albemarle Sound, was formed in 1777 from Pasquotank County and named for Sir Charles Pratt, earl of Camden, in gratitude for the support he gave to the colonists. The Tuscarora and Weapemeoc Indians, who left North Carolina in 1774, were the first inhabitants of the area; by 1650 English settlers had arrived, many drifting south from Virginia. The county seat, Camden, dates to 1740, when it was known as Plank Bridge. Its name was changed to Jonesborough in 1792 and, by 1840, to Camden. Other Camden County communities include South Mills, Belcross, and Shiloh.

The Great Dismal Swamp National Wildlife Refuge covers parts of Camden County, and farmland makes up 33 percent of the total acreage of the county. Important agricultural products are corn, potatoes, wheat, swine, soybeans, oats, barley, chickens, cotton, and beef cattle. Because the Camden County terrain features a great amount of water, North Carolinians and others travel there for boating, fishing, swimming, and waterfowl observance. The large wild turkey population also attracts hunters.

Historic sites in Camden County include the county courthouse (1847); Sanderlin-Prichard House (1851); Milford (1744–46), North Carolina's oldest remaining two-story brick house; and Shiloh Baptist Church (1729), the state's oldest Baptist church. In 2004 Camden County's population was estimated to be 8,500.

Jay Mazzocchi

SEE ALSO Great Dismal Swamp.

Cameron Village, the first shopping center built in the Southeast, opened in Raleigh in 1949. It was part of a 158-acre development that also included single-family residential areas and apartments, mostly constructed between 1948 and 1953 and reflecting postwar economic and demographic changes. By 1954 the shopping center included 40 stores, 38 offices, a movie theater, and parking for 1,500 cars on its 36 acres. Its success symbolized and profited from the rapid westward expansion of Raleigh following World War II. Unlike later shopping centers that brought "downtown" indoors, Cameron Village provided an improved "horizontal" downtown, with unique stores side by side, attractive facades and sidewalks, and convenient parking.

Cameron Village, 1950. Photograph courtesy of York Properties, Inc., Raleigh.

During the 1960s, Cameron Village featured numerous large fashion and clothing retailers, department stores, a supermarket, and dozens of specialty shops and offices. By the early 1970s, the shopping center had to adapt to competition from nearby malls such as North Hills and Crabtree Valley, which featured newer, larger, and often national chain stores and indoor, multilevel parking decks. Cameron Village has remained successful with a mixture of national and local tenants, undergoing a $17 million overhaul in the early 1990s.

Reference: Nan Hutchins, *Cameron Village: A History, 1949–1999* (2001).

Arthur Menius

Campbell University, a Baptist institution of higher learning located in Buies Creek, started as Buies Creek Academy in 1887 with an enrollment of 21 students. The school was founded by James Archibald Campbell, a Baptist minister and graduate of Wake Forest College, to fulfill his desire to offer Christian education to the youth of the area without regard to financial status. By 1898 the academy had three buildings, including a large wooden tabernacle where commencements were held. On 20 Dec. 1900, a fire destroyed all the buildings except the tabernacle. Zachary Taylor Kivett came to visit after the fire and found Campbell "in bed and discouraged to the limit." Kivett said, "Why are you in bed? I thought Campbells had Humps on them." This comment is thought to be the source of the institution's unusual mascot, the Fighting Camel. Kivett pledged to build a new brick building; Kivett Hall, completed in 1903 and extensively renovated since, remains the oldest building at Campbell University.

In 1926 Buies Creek Academy was elevated to junior college status and its name changed to Campbell College in honor of its founder. In 1961 the college became a senior institution, and it achieved university status in 1979. The Campbell University School of Law was established in 1976, and the Lundy-Fetterman School of Business in 1983. The Schools of Pharmacy and Education were launched in 1985. By the early 2000s the school had an enrollment of more than 9,700 students, including those in both the main campus and extension campuses. Extension programs included not only students in Sanford, Fayetteville, Raleigh, Goldsboro, Rocky Mount, and Jacksonville, but 1,028 students at Tunku Abdul Rahman College in Kuala Lumpur, Malaysia.

Campbell University educates more teachers than any other private college in North Carolina. Famous alumni include Pulitzer Prize–winning author Paul Green and baseball legends James and Gaylord Perry.

References: Everett M. Kivette, *The McNeill's Ferry Chronicle and Campbell University* (1983); J. Winston Pearce, *Campbell College: Big Miracle in Little Buies Creek, 1887–1974*, vol. 2 (1985); James R. Spence, *Portrait of a Place and Time* (1991); William P. Tuck, ed., *A Mosaic of Memories of Campbell University, 1887–1987* (1986); Tuck, *A Mosaic of Memories of Leslie Hartwell Campbell, 1892–1970* (1992).

Ronnie W. Faulkner

Camp Lejeune, near Jacksonville, home of the Second Marine Expeditionary Force, was established just before the United States entered World War II. The installation was named in December 1942 in honor of Gen. John Archer Lejeune, who had died a month earlier. Lejeune was the first Marine Corps officer to lead a U.S. Army division (during World War I) and commander of the Marine Corps in the 1920s.

The site, chosen in the 1930s for an East Coast fleet Marine Corps headquarters and training facility in anticipation of a war with Germany and Japan, was on the New River in Onslow County close to the Marine Air Station at Cherry Point and accessible to two deepwater ports: Morehead City and Wilmington. The process of acquiring the rights to 174 square miles (111,155 acres), including 11 miles of beachfront, meant displacing 720 families—a total of more than 2,400 persons—and delayed the beginning of the camp's construction until April 1941. The following month Lt. Col. W. P. T. Hill assumed command of the base, originally named Marine Barracks, New River. A converted beach cottage served as his headquarters, and the most imposing structure on the base was a large tobacco barn that the marines used as a warehouse. When the First Marine Division, under Brig. Gen. Philip H. Torrey, arrived at New River in September 1941, tents were the only quarters available for the troops, although by then 8,000 civilian workers were toiling seven days a week to build permanent barracks and other facilities.

Camp Lejeune Railroad, also named in December 1942, began operations in 1941 to meet immediate requirements for a track connecting the new base with the Atlantic Coast Line Railroad in Jacksonville. Within 60 days, an eight-mile section between the camp and Jacksonville was hauling materials for the facility's construction and supplies for the marines, as well as providing access to both the Wilmington port and the Marine Corps Air Station at Cherry Point. From Havelock, where the Cherry Point station was located, the railroad cars from Camp Lejeune could continue to Morehead City on the tracks of the Atlantic & Eastern North Carolina Railroad. The Cherry Point branch, with its sidings, switches, and yards, was fully operational by 2 Dec. 1943. During World War II thousands of marines began their journey from North Carolina to the battlefront on the Camp Lejeune Railroad.

Camp Lejeune provided a broad range of instruction, excepting only general recruit and officer training. Thousands of new marines, fresh from boot camp, arrived to attend infantry school. In 1942 the Marine Corps Engineering School moved from Quantico, Va., to the base and established the Marine Corps Service Support Schools. A year later the Field Medical Service School and the Naval Hospital began to operate there. Lejeune was the only facility that offered recruit and officer training for women marines and the only recruit depot and training center for African American marines (at Montford Point Camp, established in the summer of 1942). Before the war ended, Peterfield Point (later Marine Corps Air Station New River) had been commissioned. Although some of these schools and Peterfield Point were decommissioned immediately after the war, all were eventually reestablished at Lejeune, most of them during the Korean War.

The Second Marine Division, formed in 1941, endured some of the deadliest combat of World War II, fighting at Guadalcanal, Tarawa, Tinian, and Okinawa. At the end of the war, after a short stay in Japan as part of the U.S. occupying force, the division made Camp Lejeune its permanent home. Along with the Second Marine Aircraft Wing, the Second Force Service Support Group, and the Second Surveillance, Reconnaissance, and Intelligence Group, it constituted the Second Marine Expeditionary Force.

By the early 2000s Camp Lejeune, expanded to 233 square miles (151,000 acres) with 450 miles of paved roads, 50 miles of sidewalks, and 6,946 buildings, accommodated the largest single contingent of marines and sailors in the world. More than 43,000 marines were assigned to the camp, and almost 5,000 civilians worked on the base. In addition to the Second Marine Expeditionary Force, Camp Lejeune was home to the Second Marine Expeditionary Brigade and the Fourth Marine Expeditionary Brigade (Anti-Terrorism), which was reactivated in September 2001. The 22nd, 24th, and 26th Marine Expeditionary Units were also based there. Camp Lejeune marines continued to serve in U.S. conflicts, including Operation Iraqi Freedom (begun in March 2003).

References: Gertrude S. Carraway, *Camp Lejeune Leathernecks: Camp Lejeune, N.C., Marine Corps' Largest All-Purpose Base* (1946); Tucker R. Littleton, "A Civilian History of the Camp Lejeune Area from Earliest Settlement to 1941," *Archaeological and Historical Survey of U.S.M.C. Base Camp Lejeune*, vol. 2 (1981).

Thomas J. Farnham

SEE ALSO Cherry Point Marine Corps Air Station.

Camp Meetings

Camp Meetings were religious gatherings of North Carolinians who congregated in rural camps for an extended length of time to live and worship together. The events were born out of the spiritual and social needs of a people who lived a basically isolated existence on the frontier and embraced any opportunity to gather in community. They were also a natural outgrowth of the spiritual revivalism that swept through America in the early and mid-eighteenth century. Besides being places of spiritual awakening, camp meetings were also a primary place for politicians to campaign, families to hold reunions, and young people to meet their future mates.

The first camp meetings in the United States were staged at the end of the eighteenth century by Presbyterians. Methodists, however, soon became the most influential force in the camp meeting movement, as the concept had great appeal for the itinerant "circuit riders" who welcomed the opportunity to be in community with each other. Preaching was the central activity of the meetings, and services were held throughout the day and into the night.

Notable North Carolina camp meetings that have early origins include those held at Rehobeth Church in Lincoln County, at Shepherds Crossroads in Iredell County, at Town Creek near Wilmington, and at Wesley Chapel Camp Ground in Catawba County. Although camp meetings were held both in the eastern and western parts of North Carolina, only the western camp meetings had any lasting influence, with the greatest concentration of meetings being in the Piedmont area of the state. Several of these camp meetings remain active. The Rock Springs Camp Meeting in Denver (which sprang from the Rehobeth Church meeting) has met every year since 1829 or 1830. With the exception of the year 1890, Balls Creek Camp Meeting near Maiden in Catawba County has met continuously since it was established in 1853. Both meet in the month of August.

References: Elmer T. Clark, *Methodism in Western North Carolina* (1966); John James Powell, *The Origins and History of the Methodist Camp Meeting Movement in North Carolina* (1943).

Lynne S. Lepley

Canals

Canals. Since the eighteenth century, canals and canal building have been an important part of Tidewater North Carolina history. Between the American Revolution and the Civil War, many political leaders—Hillsborough representative Archibald D. Murphey prime among them—viewed canals as the state's best hope for overcoming such natural barriers to coastal navigation and mercantile trade as shifting inlets, shallow harbors, and broad shoals. Alarmed by declining maritime trade and a high rate of outmigration in the early nineteenth century, Murphey and other progressives pinned their hopes on large canals that would allow sailing vessels to avoid the Outer Banks, as well as on smaller canals around the falls of rivers to extend shipping farther into the North Carolina interior. Some of their canal-building schemes were truly magnificent. One route that seized the General Assembly's imagination in varying guises for several decades would have linked the Chesapeake Bay with Old Topsail Inlet near Beaufort, a route that bypassed Cape Hatteras and Cape Lookout altogether. Variations called for as many as five canals spanning 90 miles. Unrealistic at the time for financial and technological reasons, the plan was a testament to how profoundly the state's boosters placed their hopes in canal building before the advent of railroads.

Smaller canals, whose purpose was drainage, were vital for coastal agriculture as well as commerce, for much of the coastal plain was too soggy for farming or settlement without draining pocosins and other swamplands. Heavy ditching and canalization of wetlands has continued into the modern era as a way to make them usable for large-scale agriculture and even larger-scale monocultural forestry. One of the earliest shipping canals ever proposed for the North American continent was the Dismal Swamp Canal (initially suggested by the 1728 North Carolina–Virginia boundary line commissioner William Byrd II of Westover), a waterway to connect Chesapeake Bay with North Carolina's Albemarle Sound. This massive, 20-mile-long project was eventually undertaken between 1794 and 1805; the canal was then widened and deepened a generation later.

Camp meeting at Pleasant Grove Campground near Mineral Springs, 1983. Courtesy of NCOA&H.

The steamer *Albemarle* in a lock of the Albemarle and Chesapeake Canal (date unknown). Courtesy of NCOA&H.

In the same era, the Lake Company used slave labor to dig canals and drain for agriculture thousands of acres on the north side of Lake Phelps, creating the plantation Somerset Place and, just to the west, the Pettigrew family's Bonarva. Other navigation projects from the historical canal-building era include the Harlowe and Clubfoot Creek Canal, dug as a ship canal between 1795 and 1828 but never more than a workboat route between Beaufort and New Bern; the Roanoke Canal, circumnavigating the Great Falls, a 90-foot drop in the Roanoke River between Rock Landing and Weldon; the Cape Fear River canals near Averasboro and Fayetteville; and the Albemarle and Chesapeake Canal, connecting Hampton Roads with the Albemarle by way of North Landing River and Currituck Sound and serving as a competitor to the Dismal Swamp Canal.

Built between 1855 and 1859, the Albemarle and Chesapeake, while employing slave labor, was the state's first canal built with hydraulic dredges rather than axes, mattocks, and shovels. Several Lake Mattamuskeet canals established communication between the vast natural lake and outer waters. An early twentieth-century canal serving the massive New Holland pumping station drained the 10,000-acre lake's waters for nearly a generation, allowing the lake bed to be farmed from the mid-1910s until the fall of 1932.

A twentieth-century fulfillment of the earlier interior navigation dream is the Intracoastal Waterway, a U.S. Army Corps of Engineers project that traversed all of eastern North Carolina by 1936. Major sections of the "Big Ditch" include the Dismal Swamp Canal and the Albemarle and Chesapeake Canal as alternate routes from Virginia to North Carolina waters; the Alligator River-to-Pungo River cut; the Adams Creek-to-Core Creek cut, connecting the Neuse River to the Newport and Bogue Sound; and Snow's Cut, joining Myrtle Grove Sound and the Cape Fear River, near Carolina Beach. In the second half of the twentieth century, canals were employed as never before in important agricultural clearing and draining projects, including the 350,000-acre First Colony Farms venture of the 1970s on the Albemarle-Pamlico peninsula, as well

as the smaller, but still enormous, Open Grounds Farms and North River Farms projects in eastern Carteret County. These projects drained most of the largest remaining pocosin wetlands in North America. A brief enforcement moratorium on wetlands protection in 2000–2001 resulted in a drainage spree in southeastern North Carolina affecting more than 10,000 acres.

Unintended negative environmental consequences of farmland drainage have involved both the lowering of groundwater levels and the rapid runoff of pesticides and herbicides into fish and shellfish estuarine nursery areas. Even prior to the Civil War, pioneering agronomist Edmund Ruffin argued that the Dismal Swamp Canal had lowered water levels in the surrounding swamplands and dried out the peaty soils, which, when combusted, nourished unusually hot wildfires. Ironically, much of the land cleared by First Colony Farms eventually became part of the system of national wildlife refuges, the Alligator River National Wildlife Refuge and the Pocosin Lakes National Wildlife Refuge, following the same progression that saw the creation of the Lake Mattamuskeet National Wildlife Refuge after the collapse of the lakebed farming experiment. Efforts to protect estuarine water quality by restoring wetlands have been under way in that area since the early 1990s, and, as of the early twenty-first century, at North River Farms in eastern Carteret County as well.

Well before the modern era of draglines and V-ditches, though, canal building was notorious for being the most miserable labor imaginable in the slave South. The old canals, still in use or merely ruins and remnants, stand as monuments to those who performed the hardest, most brutal task under the harshest conditions, working in water and struggling constantly with snakes, insects, roots, stumps, and buried trees.

References: Peggy Jo Cobb Braswell, *The Roanoke Canal: A History of the Old Navigation and Water Power Canal of Halifax County, North Carolina* (1987); David S. Cecelski, *The Waterman's Song: Slavery and Freedom in Maritime North Carolina* (2001); Bland Simpson, *The Great Dismal: A Carolinian's Swamp Memoir* (1998).

David S. Cecelski
Bland Simpson

SEE ALSO Albemarle and Chesapeake Canal; Dismal Swamp Canal; Roanoke Canal.

Canebrakes were large tracts of giant cane plants (*Arundinaria gigantea*), an evergreen relative of bamboo that once grew across great stretches of North Carolina and the Southeast, often along rivers and streams. A perennial plant that flowers and dies every few years, leaving seeds to grow in its place, the cane plant can reach a height of 20 feet. It often multiplies into thick patches with an extensive network of roots that can crowd out nearly all other forms of vegetation.

Cane was a valuable food for livestock, especially in the winter and early spring. Other uses for cane included chair bottoms, weavers' shuttles, tubing, cattle feed, and fishing poles. In *A New Voyage to Carolina* (1709), John Lawson records Indians using cane for "Mats, Baskets, and Dressing-boxes," canoe poles, and special mats used to wrap the dead for funerals. Canebrake ecosystems are highly vulnerable to fire, a method often used by settlers to clear them. Lawson witnessed Indians setting a canebrake on fire to drive game out into the open. The popping sounds coming from the burning cane were so loud that Lawson at first thought he was witnessing a battle between two parties of Indians armed with guns.

Canebrakes have largely disappeared from the South. They were easily cleared by settlers seeking farming and grazing land. The name appears in several land forms in North Carolina, however, including 14 separate Cane Creeks in the state.

References: F. P. Porcher, *Resources of Southern Fields and Forests* (1991); B. W. Wells, *The Natural Gardens of North Carolina* (rev. ed., 2002).

David A. Norris

Cane Creek Connection refers to the large number of Quaker (Society of Friends) settlers that arrived in the Piedmont region of North Carolina in the mid-eighteenth century, primarily from Pennsylvania, Maryland, and western Virginia after traveling along the Great Wagon Road. The Cane Creek region included an area that ranged across much of modern-day Guilford, Alamance, and Orange Counties and the northern parts of Randolph and Chatham Counties. As the area became more settled, other Quaker groups, known as monthly meetings, were established. As a result, many members who belonged to the original Cane Creek monthly meeting became members of more localized meetings without moving. But some of these pioneers were restless and lived in the Cane Creek area for only a short while. From the 1750s until about 1800, Quaker migration continued further south into piedmont South Carolina and coastal Georgia. One group initially living near Hillsborough moved almost en masse between 1768 and 1779 to Newberry County, S.C., and Wilkes County, Ga. Several other families from throughout the area followed this pattern. The Cane Creek Connection, then, eventually came to influence the settlement of a wide swath of the United States.

While it is not possible to name every family involved in the migration to and from Cane Creek, many names are preserved in the records of the Cane Creek monthly meeting. The Cane Creek meeting has had an uninterrupted ministry from the time of the earliest settlements to the present. The meetinghouse is still at its original location, with the burial ground adjoining, in Snow Camp. To prepare for its sesquicentennial in 2001, the Cane Creek meeting established a "heritage room" with many family histories and memorabilia. The meeting also has solicited additional family updates to add to this collection.

Reference: Bobbie T. Teague, *Cane Creek: Mother of Meetings* (1995).

John Allen

Cannon Award. The Ruth Coltrane Cannon Award, North Carolina's most prestigious award for historic preservation achievement, was established by Ruth Coltrane Cannon and her husband, Charles A. Cannon, in 1948. The North Carolina Society for the Preservation of Antiquities originally administered the award, and for many years playwright Paul Green made the formal presentation on behalf of the society. Recipients' names are engraved on a silver bowl prominently displayed in the North Carolina Museum of History in Raleigh, and engraved silver replicas of a Revolutionary War camp cup are given to winners.

In 1974 the North Carolina Society for the Preservation of Antiquities changed its name to the Historic Preservation Society of North Carolina, Inc. A restructuring in 1984 prompted another name change to the Historic Preservation Foundation of North Carolina, Inc. Popularly known as Preservation North Carolina, the organization continues to administer the Cannon Awards. From 1948 to 1982, a total of 161 awards were given to individuals and organizations, but since 1982 only a single Cannon Award is given each year.

The first Cannon Award winners in 1948 were Gertrude Carraway, C. Christopher Crittenden, Inglis Fletcher, Adelaide Fries, Paul Green, Archibald Henderson, Mrs. J. E. Latham, Douglas L. Rights, and Charles Lee Smith. The list of subsequent winners includes Kathryn Page Cloud, Marie W. Colton, Marion Stedman Covington, Chalmers G. Davidson, Cecil B. DeMille, Gordon Gray, James A. Gray, John Sprunt Hill, A. L. Honeycutt Jr., Mrs. Ernest Ives, H. G. Jones, Joye E. Jordan, Margaret M. Kluttz, Kay Kyser, Hugh T. Lefler, Jeanelle C. Moore, Clarence Poe, William S. Powell, William S. Price Jr., John L. Sanders, Virginia S. Stevens., Robert E. Stipe, and Banks C. Talley Jr.

Reference: David L. S. Brook, *A Lasting Gift of Heritage: A History of the North Carolina Society for the Preservation of Antiquities, 1939–1974* (1997).

T. Harry Gatton

Cannon Mills, producer of all-purpose cloth and kitchen, bathroom, and bedroom textile products, was founded by James William Cannon, a 35-year-old cotton broker and general merchandiser, in 1887 in Concord. Costing $75,000 and employing 4,000 spindles, the steam-powered Cannon Manufacturing Company produced its first yarn on 1 Apr. 1888. Instead of spinning yarn and sending it to be woven into fabric in northern factories (as was then the rule among southern cotton mills), Cannon began with raw cotton, spun the yarn, and wove it into a finished product called Cannon Cloth. An inexpensive item, this cloth was popular with housewives who sewed items such as shirts and pillowcases at home.

When it became clear that factory-sewn pieces would eventually replace simple fabrics, Cannon surveyed the textile industry and decided to fill the towel-making niche. Cannon Manufacturing Company produced its first towels in 1890. The company's early towels, made out of a flat (also known as huck) weave, were designed to be completed by the housewife, who cut and hemmed them to desired sizes. Around the turn of the century, Cannon began to weave a more absorbent towel known as terry or Turkish cloth, a new product for the company and the South that became popular during World War I. By the end of the war, Cannon had become the nation's largest towel producer.

The Cannon textile enterprise expanded rapidly. With various partners, James William Cannon organized Cabarrus Cotton Mills (1892), Patterson Manufacturing Company (1893), Kesler Manufacturing Company (1895), Gibson Manufacturing Company (1901), and Coleman Mills in Concord (1906), which had been founded by a former slave and had employed only blacks. In 1906 Cannon bought 600 acres of land located about seven miles north of his first plant in Concord, where he built a planned community that included rental houses and a school. The community became the quintessential "company town" of Kannapolis.

A 1928 consolidation of nine textile plants into the Cannon Mills Company helped the business survive the Depression. Cannon continued to add to its family of mills throughout most of the twentieth century, buying such companies as Maiden Knitting Mills (1969), Wiscassett Mills Company (1978), and Beacon Manufacturing (1978). Cannon Mills' low debt, fully funded retirement plan, large amount of attractive real estate, and lack of firm family control created an opportunity for a leveraged buyout and hostile takeover. In 1982 David Murdock, a California industrialist, financier, and real estate developer, offered $44 per share for the approximately 9.4 million Cannon shares then selling for $28.92 each. Within 34 days, Murdock controlled 98 percent of Cannon Mills stock at a cost of $413 million.

Murdock reorganized management, invested $200 million in capital improvements, redesigned the company's product lines, and made dramatic changes in Kannapolis by donating parkland, spurring the creation of a senior center and library, and renovating the business district. He also sold company housing and tore down the YMCA, one of the centers of town life.

Negotiations for the sale of Cannon Mills began in 1985, and Fieldcrest Mills, Inc., of Eden, bought Cannon's bath and bedding operations in January 1986 for $250 million. This purchase included 12 plants and 14 sales offices, which employed nearly all of the company's workers, and created a new corporation, Fieldcrest Cannon, Inc., under the leadership of Joseph B. Ely II. The resulting modernization and automation of production equipment led to a reduction in the number of employees. With the purchase, Fieldcrest doubled in size and became one of the largest producers of home furnishings and textile products in the world. Murdock retained that portion of nonindustrial property owned by Cannon Mills and managed it under the name of Atlantic American Properties.

In December 1997 Pillowtex, Inc., a Dallas-based manufacturer of Ralph Lauren, Martha Stewart, Disney, and other brand-name fabrics and home furnishings, purchased Fieldcrest Cannon for $700 million. Pillowtex's Kannapolis-based operations, which employed approximately 4,000 people, were closed in 2003.

References: *Cannon Mills Company, 1887–1987: A Century of Progress* (1987); Paul R. Kearns, *Weavers of Dreams* (1995); James Lewis Moore and Thomas Herron Wingate, *Cabarrus Reborn: A Historical Sketch of the Founding and Development of Cannon Mills Company and Kannapolis* (1940).

Kevin Cherry

Canoes have provided a primary form of transportation on the sounds, rivers, and bays of coastal North Carolina for centuries. In the 1580s the explorers and colonists sent to Roanoke Island by Sir Walter Raleigh found Indians traveling throughout the labyrinth of estuarine waters in long, narrow log canoes, some large enough to carry 20 men and their gear. Lacking iron tools, the Native Americans used fire and sharp shells to build their canoes in a time-consuming process that began by maintaining a small, controlled fire near the base of a selected tree until the tree fell down. They repeated the process, burning through the fallen trunk at the chosen spot. They elevated the log on a frame and, using gum and rosin to stoke the fire, burned deep enough to form coals that were scraped away with the shells. This process was repeated until the desired depth was reached.

One of the preferred woods used for canoes appears to have been juniper (white cedar), which grew in great profusion throughout swampy areas of coastal North Carolina. Juniper is still valued by local boatbuilders because it is soft, lightweight, and extremely resistant to rot. So impressed were the Europeans with the finished products that one of Raleigh's men said the natives "knowe how to make them as handsomelye . . . as ours."

When permanent settlers arrived, it was logical for them to use locally available juniper wood for their own small craft. With sharp axes and other tools, it was no doubt easier to make a canoe out of a single log than to have the log cut into boards in order to construct a more traditional small boat from scratch. Following the lead of earlier settlers in the

Chesapeake Bay area, North Carolina settlers began to adapt the dugout canoe technique used for small boats to larger ones that could carry more cargo. Early efforts resulted in a process in which a log was split down the middle and another piece was added between the two original canoe halves, more than doubling the capacity of the little craft. Concurrent with this innovation was the development and use of what was called a "tobacco canoe." This simple form of catamaran consisted of two log canoes lashed together side by side, across which as many as eight or nine hogsheads of tobacco could be placed. A more sophisticated form of the two-log dugout canoe evolved with the selection of matching logs (often cypress as juniper became more difficult to find) and the fitting of the two together in the construction process. The smaller of these were called kunners; the larger ones became known as periaugers.

In time, canoe builders began producing three-log canoes, not just because they were larger than the earlier dugouts but also because it was sometimes considered easier to work with several small logs than with a single large one. In time, even more logs—as many as five and possibly more—were utilized, until dugouts were being used in the North Carolina sounds and rivers and, in some cases, in trade with other East Coast ports and even with the Caribbean. The widespread use of dugout canoes continued through the nineteenth century, and dugouts used as workboats, as well as more sleek models designed for canoe racing, remained popular well into the twentieth century.

Flat-bottomed skiffs and stick-built canoes gradually replaced smaller dugout canoes, including those known as punts. In recent years, the popularity of one-man canoes has faded. The craft has been replaced on the sounds and rivers by a first cousin, the one-man kayak. In the modern era, there are probably more kayaks on North Carolina's coastal waters than there were Indian dugout canoes when the Europeans first discovered the area.

References: Michael B. Alford, *Traditional Work Boats of North Carolina* (1990); M. V. Brewington, *Chesapeake Bay Log Canoes and Bugeyes* (1963).

David Stick

Cape Fear in modern-day Brunswick County projects into the Atlantic Ocean at the southeastern tip of Smith Island, near the mouth of the Cape Fear River and adjacent to the area known as Bald Head. The Frying Pan Shoals extend another 20 miles outward from Cape Fear. Known during various eras as Cape Feare, Cape Fair, and Cape Fayre, the cape maintains a significant place in North Carolina history. Sailing under the French flag, Italian explorer Giovanni da Verrazano may have been the first to encounter Cape Fear in 1524. During the period of the English Roanoke explorations, Sir Richard

Grenville reported in June 1585 that the ship *Tiger*, en route to Roanoke Island, was nearly wrecked "on a breache called the Cape of Feare." In 1587 artist John White also nearly wrecked "upon the breach called Cape of Fear" on one of his voyages.

The southernmost point explored by the English during this period is designated as "Promontorium tremendum" on the 1590 de Bry map and has mistakenly been identified as Cape Fear in the past. Current cartographic researchers have established this cape as modern-day Cape Lookout and not Cape Fear. Other maps drawn during the seventeenth century—including those by Comberford (1657), Horne, (1666), Ogilby (1672), Gascoyne (1682), and Lea (1695)—show Cape Fear by name.

The name "Cape Fair" was used at times in the seventeenth century, when colonists were encouraged to settle the Carolina region. Under the leadership of William Hilton, explorers encountered Cape Fear in 1662 and sailed up the present Cape Fear River, then called the Charles, to the mouth of Town Creek, where they established a brief settlement. In his 1663 "Letter of the English Adventurers to the Lords Proprietors," Hilton referred to the "Point of Cape Fair River." Hilton's notes became the basis for the first accurate map of the region, prepared by Nicholas Shapley. In addition to Hilton's report, other sources that made mention of Cape Fair included the history and map of John Lawson, surveyor general in 1709, and Wimble's map of 1738. The name Cape Fair was not permanently accepted, and by the American Revolution Cape Fear had become the common designation both for the cape itself and for the region surrounding the lower basin of the Cape Fear River.

References: William P. Cumming, *The Southeast in Early Maps* (3rd ed., 1998); Lawrence Lee, *Lower Cape Fear in Colonial Days* (1965); James Sprunt, *Chronicles of the Cape Fear River, 1660–1916* (1992).

Claude V. Jackson

Cape Fear and Deep River Navigation Company
aimed to provide improved water access to the naval stores of the Upper Cape Fear Valley and to the coal deposits of Moore and Chatham Counties. Originally, the Cape Fear Navigation Company sought to enhance the navigability of the Cape Fear River above Fayetteville—including the Deep and Haw Rivers—but after receiving little benefit from its expenditures, it abandoned the Upper Cape Fear by 1830 to concentrate on the river between Fayetteville and Wilmington. In the 1840s residents of Moore and Chatham Counties attempted once again to open the Upper Cape Fear and Deep Rivers to navigation; Wilmington, which hoped to benefit from increased river trade, supported the effort. A meeting in Pittsboro in August 1848 authorized a survey of the watercourses and appointed a committee to petition the legislature for a charter of incorporation. The General Assembly complied in 1849, promising state financial assistance.

Work on improvements began in 1850 but progressed haltingly due to winter freshets that destroyed locks and dams, a labor shortage that resulted from the unsuccessful utilization of immigrants, and, despite state aid, insufficient funds. In 1855 company officials persuaded the legislature, still enthusiastic about the prospects of tapping coal deposits in Chatham County, to permit them to issue $300,000 in bonds with the state acting as security.

Following the 1855 legislation, the little-changed "New Company" continued to suffer not just from labor shortages and unsatisfactory engineers but from fundamental problems such as improperly designed and decaying locks and dams, internal dissension, and mismanaged funds—raising arguments from the editor of the *Fayetteville Observer* concerning the greater utility of railroads compared to river navigation. To protect the public interest in the face of the company's looming bankruptcy, the legislature authorized the 23 Apr. 1859 purchase of the company for $365,000. The Board of Managers of the newly renamed Cape Fear and Deep River Navigation Works hired the capable and conscientious Elwood Morris as chief engineer. He and his crew finished the improvements on the Cape Fear by April 1860 and those on Deep River six months later, finally completing the project after a decade of turmoil.

Before Morris could leave, though, a series of freshets in November seriously damaged the works. In February 1861 an exasperated legislature restricted expenditures on behalf of the company to $30,000 annually and sought to sell the works. Rather than pursue repairs, the governor directed Morris to suspend operations. In 1873 the state sold to the Deep River Navigation Company the navigation works from Foxes Island in the Cape Fear River to the junction of the Deep and Haw and up both of those rivers.

References: Wade H. Hadley Jr., *The Story of the Cape Fear and Deep River Navigation Company, 1849–1873* (1980); Elsie Faye Russ, "The Cape Fear and Deep River Navigation Company, 1849–1873" (M.A. thesis, Wake Forest University, 1970).

Alan D. Watson

Cape Fear Club is a business and professional men's club, founded on 3 Mar. 1866 in Wilmington and incorporated on 8 Feb. 1872. It is generally recognized as the oldest social club of its kind in continuous existence in North Carolina and one of the oldest in the Southeast. The club was largely organized by former Confederates; its 1868 membership roster listed 1 former brigadier general (William MacRae), 10 colonels, 5 majors, and 13 captains. Several of the founders had previously belonged to a gentleman's club called the Hollowleg Club, organized in Wilmington in 1852 and dissolved at the outbreak of the Civil War.

From the start, the Cape Fear Club had close ties to the railroad industry. Guilford Lafayette Dudley, its first president, was general freight agent for the Wilmington & Weldon Railroad. Champion McDowell Davis, the longtime president of the Atlantic Coast Line Railway, was president of the club from 1922 to 1926. Officially nonpartisan, the club has nevertheless exerted strong influence in Wilmington affairs. At its centennial in 1966, its members included the mayor, the city manager, two city councilmen, and executives of most of the area's largest companies. During the 1980s the club's lack of black and women members was sometimes raised as a political issue.

The club owns a number of seventeenth-century Italian paintings donated anonymously (probably by Henry Walters, a club member, chairman of the board of the Atlantic Coast Line and founder of the Walters Art Gallery in Baltimore). It also has an extensive collection of U.S. Navy, Coast Guard, and maritime memorabilia, acquired in part through its long association with the U.S. Navy League.

References: Leslie N. Boney Jr., ed., *The Cape Fear Club, 1967–1983* (1984); Tony P. Wrenn, *Wilmington, N.C.: An Architectural and Historical Portrait* (1984).

Bennett L. Steelman

Cape Fear Indians were likely associated with North Carolina's eastern Siouan tribes, possibly the Waccamaw, but it is not clear whether they were independent or part of some other tribe. The native name for the tribe is unknown, and no vocabulary has been preserved. Although five Cape Fear Indian villages were reported to have existed in 1715, the only village mentioned by name is Necoes, located approximately 20 miles from the mouth of the Cape Fear River, probably in modern-day Brunswick County. The tribe's population in 1600 was estimated at 1,000. Contact with the Cape Fear Indians was made by several early voyagers, including Giovanni da Verrazano in 1524 and William Hilton in 1661 and 1663. Hilton is reported to have met with Watcoosa, "king" of the Cape Fear Indians, at Crane Island (now Big Island, about 13 miles below Wilmington). Watcoosa is said to have sold Hilton the river and contiguous lands. In 1664, after settlers seized some Indian children and sent them away, evidently into slavery, the Indians drove the settlers away.

Threatened by increasing European settlement, the Cape Fear Indians in 1695 asked Governor John Archdale for protection, which was granted. A few Cape Fear Indian scouts accompanied John Barnwell during the Tuscarora War in 1711–12. Many Cape Fear Indians were driven out of the Cape Fear region by Col. Maurice Moore and a force of Tuscaroras during the Yamassee War in 1715. A Cape Fear Indian settlement at Big Sugar Loaf (now in Carolina Beach State Park, on the east bank of the Cape Fear River) was decimated by Roger Moore in 1725, after an alleged Indian raid on his Orton Plantation.

Little presence of the tribe is reported on the Lower Cape Fear River after 1730. Remnants of the tribe were said to have joined with the Peedee in South Carolina. No mention is made of the Cape Fear Indians after 1808.

References: John Reed Swanton, *The Indians of the Southeastern United States* (1946); Ruth Y. Wetmore, *First on the Land: The North Carolina Indians* (1975).

William G. DiNome

Cape Fear Museum

Cape Fear Museum in Wilmington began as the Confederate Museum, started by the Wilmington chapter of the United Daughters of the Confederacy in 1898. It was originally located in a room on the second floor of the Wilmington Light Infantry armory building. During World War I, space in the armory was in demand, so in 1918 the collection was moved for safekeeping and placed in the care of Frederick A. Olds in Raleigh, where it was displayed in the Hall of History (forerunner of the North Carolina Museum of History). After the war ended, the New Hanover Historical Commission worked through the 1920s to have the collection returned to Wilmington. In 1929 their efforts were rewarded. Stewardship changed hands from the United Daughters of the Confederacy to the North Carolina Sorosis, a local women's group, which secured the use of the second floor of the New Hanover County Courthouse Annex for the museum. The group broadened the collection to include artifacts related to regional and maritime history and established Wednesday afternoons as the regular time for public visitation of what became known as the New Hanover Museum.

By the early 1960s, the museum needed larger quarters. Its fourth home became the third floor of the city police station, and a grand opening was held in 1963. The first professional director was hired, and the museum's name was changed to the Wilmington–New Hanover Museum. The museum continued to grow in the late 1960s, and the collection was moved to the National Guard Armory building in 1970. In 1979 the museum's first clear-cut mission statement—"to make available to the public the history, natural history, and culture of the Lower Cape Fear area through interpretive exhibits and educational programs"—was adopted. Eight years later New Hanover County voters approved a $4.2 million bond referendum to increase the museum's space from 12,750 square feet to approximately 42,000 square feet. The long-term exhibition "Waves & Currents," designed by Ralph Applebaum & Associates of New York City, was part of the project.

The museum, renamed the Cape Fear Museum, opened on 17 Jan. 1992. Its continuing mission is to preserve and interpret southeastern North Carolina's human and natural history. The Michael Jordan Discovery Gallery, named for the lead donor and Wilmington-born basketball star, opened in 1995 to allow children and families to explore the ecology of the Lower Cape Fear region.

References: Cape Fear Museum, *The Official Museum Directory* (2002); Ida Brooks Kellam, "New Hanover County Museum," *Lower Cape Fear Historical Society Newsletter* (1961); Harry Warren, *Cape Fear Museum, Wilmington, NC* (1994).

Beverly Littlejohn

Cape Fear River

Cape Fear River is formed in central North Carolina at the Chatham-Lee County line by the convergence of the Deep and Haw Rivers, flowing southeast and touching parts of Harnett, Cumberland, Bladen, Columbus, Pender, Brunswick, and New Hanover Counties before emptying into the Atlantic Ocean at Cape Fear (part of Bald Head Island) south of Wilmington. The river also receives the Black and Northeast Cape Fear Rivers near Wilmington. Its 202-mile length makes the Cape Fear the longest river to run entirely within the state's boundaries.

The Cape Fear River has been one of North Carolina's most important natural resources since it was first dubbed "Rio Jordan" by Spanish explorers in 1526. Its subsequent names included the Charles River and the Clarendon River; it appears to have been commonly known as the Cape Fear River by at least 1733. The Cape Fear was the site of many initial European settlements and served as a key transportation route for colonial pioneers traveling into the North Carolina backcountry. The Cape Fear and Deep River Navigation Company, operating in the nineteenth century, was financed by state and private funds to improve the river's navigability. Control of the Cape Fear River during the Civil War became a coveted prize for both Confederate and Union forces.

The Cape Fear River system is the largest in North Carolina, encompassing a 9,000-square-mile basin that includes streams flowing within 29 of the state's 100 counties. With about 27 percent of the state's population and dozens of municipalities situated within its boundaries—including Greensboro, Burlington, Chapel Hill, Sanford, Fayetteville, Dunn, Clinton, Warsaw, Burgaw, and Wilmington—the Cape Fear River Basin is one of the most industrialized regions in North Carolina. These and other cities and towns rely on the river and its tributaries for freshwater, transportation, recreation, natural habitats for abundant wildlife species, and other uses. The Cape Fear Estuary—a 35-mile section of the river between Wilmington and the Atlantic Ocean—features saline waters that are important habitats and breeding grounds for many saltwater animals, including fish, crabs, and shrimp. The estuary is also part of the Atlantic Intracoastal Waterway.

Reference: Philip Gerard, "Cape Fear: Historic Gateway to the Atlantic," *Wildlife in North Carolina* 63 (November 1999).

Jay Mazzocchi

SEE ALSO Cape Fear and Deep River Navigation Company; Cape Fear River Settlements.

Cape Fear River Settlements. Attempts to explore and colonize North Carolina's Cape Fear region (now Brunswick, New Hanover, and other southeastern counties) spanned 200 years prior to the permanent occupation of the area by English settlers. Although first discovered by Giovanni da Verrazano on behalf of France in 1524, a Spanish expedition under Lucas Vasquez de Ayllon entered the river in 1526 and explored its banks before moving farther south to establish an ill-fated settlement. In 1662 William Hilton explored the river on behalf of Massachusetts Bay colonists. As a result of Hilton's report, New England Puritans went to the area in 1663, only to leave almost immediately after posting a notice at the point of Cape Fear disparaging the land along the river.

By the early summer of 1664, a group of "adventurers" from Barbados, led by John Vassall, settled in Lower Cape Fear, encouraged by a second voyage to the river by Hilton. Vassall and his party proceeded to the newly created Clarendon County without awaiting the outcome of negotiations with the Lord Proprietors for the terms of settlement. Vassall's colony founded Charles Towne about 20 miles upstream near the mouth of what later became Town Creek. The settlement rapidly grew to almost 800 persons, but untenable terms for settlement by the Lords Proprietors led to its decline. After negotiations with the Proprietors failed, the Proprietors appointed Vassall's rival, Sir John Yeamans, as governor of Clarendon County. Yeamans, who preferred a settlement farther south, discouraged colonization on Cape Fear. Because of the unfavorable decisions from the Lords Proprietors, along with growing hostility among the local Indian population, settlers fled the region. By early 1667 Clarendon County was inhabited only by its Native American population.

The earliest permanent settlement of the Cape Fear Valley took place in the spring of 1726, when Maurice Moore occupied lands on the south side of the river and laid off the town of Brunswick about 12 miles above its mouth. After the failure of the Vassall colony, the region had remained uninhabited except by native tribes until 1724–25, when Governor George Burrington spent the winter exploring the Cape Fear River and contemplating its potential development. In 1725 he issued grants for almost 9,000 acres in the area, primarily to a powerful group of settlers who were joined by blood and marriage. "The Family," as they came to be known, included Maurice, Roger, James, and Nathaniel Moore of South Carolina, along with the prominent North Carolina Allen, Porter, Moseley, and Swann families, all of whom were joined by marriage.

Although these important families acquired more than 100,000 acres along the river and dominated the initial landholdings in the region, rival settlers poured into Cape Fear during the 1730s, establishing the town of Wilmington and pressing upriver on both the northwest and northeast branches of the river. Wilmington, located on the east bank of the river near the fork in its branches, quickly replaced Brunswick Town as the center of commerce for Lower Cape Fear and as the seat for New Hanover County. By the outbreak of the American Revolution, the younger town was vying to become the leading municipality in the province, whereas Brunswick would soon be taken over by the forest that bordered the river.

The arrival of Gabriel Johnston in 1734 as governor of the colony of North Carolina ushered in a period of rapid growth in the Cape Fear region. Thousands of Scottish Highlanders settled as far as 100 miles above Wilmington. By 1760 a community known as Cross Creek was established at the head of navigation for the river, and two years later the town of Campbellton was founded nearby. The communities were combined as Fayetteville in 1783.

In addition to the English and Scottish Highlander colonists, a variety of other nationalities attempted to settle in the region. A group of Welsh homesteaders sought to occupy the area between Cape Fear (Northwest Branch) and the Northeast River. Although little is known about the venture or its degree of success, their location continued to be known as the Welsh Tract as late as the Revolutionary War period. Developers also looked for substantial tracts of land on which to establish settlements of Irish Protestants and Swiss. Although the Scotch-Irish occupied a tract on the Northeast River, the Swiss colonization effort failed.

A plantation economy developed from the beginning of settlement, and considerable numbers of African slaves were transported to the area from the West Indies, South Carolina, and other colonies. In 1790, when the first federal census was taken, more than 38 percent of the population of the Lower Cape Fear counties of New Hanover, Bladen, Brunswick, Duplin, and Onslow consisted of black slaves. Naval stores and lumber—the products of vast acreages of pine barrens—became the primary exports, although animal skins, rice, and grain contributed to the region's export economy.

The forest and farm environment of Cape Fear was not conducive to the development of an urban environment, and Wilmington and Campbellton remained the only substantial towns in the region. Attempts to establish the towns of New Exeter and South Washington on the Northeast River were largely unsuccessful, and efforts to develop a town as the seat of Bladen County finally resulted in the establishment of the village of Elizabeth Town in 1773 between Campbellton and Wilmington. Otherwise, the Cape Fear region had no significant community or commercial center until after the American Revolution.

References: Lawrence Lee, *The Lower Cape Fear in Colonial Days* (1965); Hugh T. Lefler and William S. Powell, *Colonial North Carolina: A History* (1973).

Donald R. Lennon

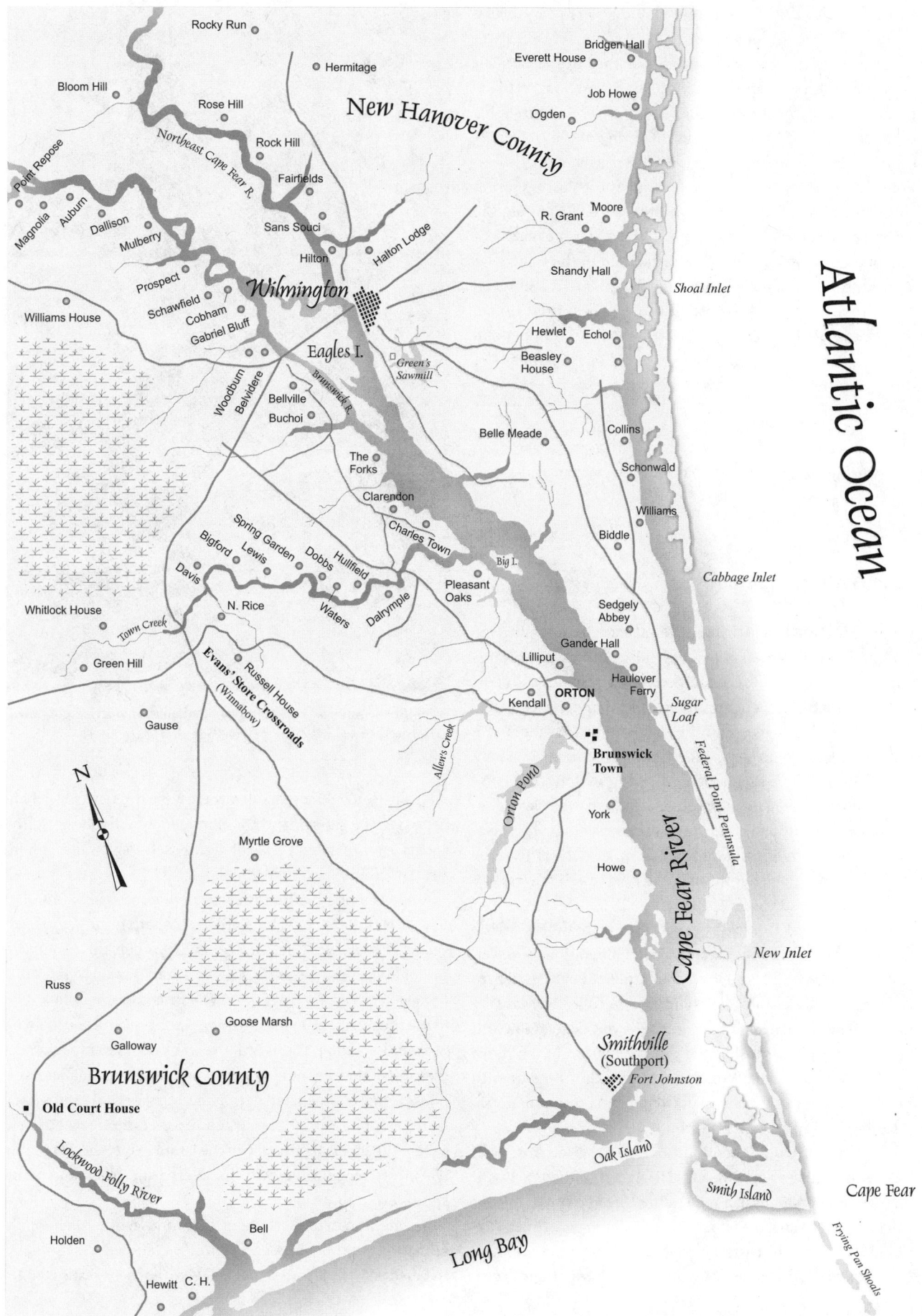

Plantations and communities of the Lower Cape Fear, ca. 1720–1760. Map by Mark Anderson Moore, courtesy NCOA&H.

Cape Fear Valley Scottish Festival, held in Fayetteville on 19–24 Nov. 1939, commemorated the 200th anniversary of the arrival of the Scottish Highlanders in the Cape Fear Valley as well as the 150th anniversary of North Carolina's ratification of the U.S. Constitution, the cession of the western lands that became Tennessee, and the chartering of the University of North Carolina in Chapel Hill. Dignitaries including Governor Clyde R. Hoey spoke at the festival, but its lasting legacy was that playwright Paul Green wrote *The Highland Call*, the second of his outdoor "symphonic dramas," for the occasion. The play dealt with the Scottish settlement in the Cape Fear Valley and was a blend of history, music, spectacle, and social commentary. A second Scottish festival was held from 14 Oct. to 2 Nov. 1940, but despite ongoing interest in Cumberland County's Scottish heritage, the festival did not remain an annual event, being overshadowed by similar festivals elsewhere in the state.

References: Emily Ann Colandson, *Scottish Highland Games in America* (1986); John A. Oates, *The Story of Fayetteville and the Upper Cape Fear* (3rd ed., 1981).

Wiley J. Williams

Cape Hatteras Lighthouse. SEE Lighthouses.

Cape Hatteras National Seashore, embracing the southern portion of Bodie Island and nearly all of Hatteras and Ocracoke Islands to the south, contains some 28,500 acres and more than 70 miles of unbroken ocean frontage on North Carolina's Outer Banks. Authorized as the first national seashore by Congress in 1937, Cape Hatteras National Seashore was established in 1953 and formally dedicated in 1958. Land acquisition for the park was originally through voluntary donation and later through condemnation proceedings. Preservation of the beaches, sand dunes, and other natural features was achieved very largely through the Depression-era work of the Civilian Conservation Corps.

Cape Hatteras has long been known to mariners as the "Graveyard of the Atlantic." Its fame and reputation, however, come not from the cape itself, but from the succession of ever-shifting underwater sandbars, known collectively as Diamond Shoals, that extend seaward to the very edge of the Gulf Stream. They are formed by the violent collision of the warm tropical waters flowing northward in the Gulf Stream with much colder currents coming down the coast from the north, resulting in almost constant turbulence.

There are three different shoals off Cape Hatteras, each with a distinctive name officially designated by the U.S. Board on Geographic Names in a 1949 ruling. The one spreading out from shore is Hatteras Shoal, the middle one is Inner Diamond Shoal, and the easternmost one, touched by the tropical Gulf Stream waters, is Outer Diamond Shoal. Experienced sea-

Fishing in the surf near Cape Hatteras Lighthouse. Photograph courtesy of North Carolina Division of Tourism, Film, and Sports Development.

men have known for years that there were two navigable channels, Hatteras Slough and Diamond Slough, that bisected the shoals, thus making it possible for vessels to pass through instead of around Diamond Shoals.

Cape Hatteras National Seashore is accessible by automobile via N.C. Route 12, which proceeds south from Nags Head, across the Oregon Inlet Bridge, and through the communities of Rodanthe, Waves, Salvo, Avon, and Buxton to the cape. Long before getting that far, however, visitors are usually able to see the top of the spiraling Cape Hatteras Lighthouse rising near the shoreline. The lighthouse was built in 1870 as the successor to a number of lightships and an earlier, smaller lighthouse, none of which had been effective in warning ships away from Diamond Shoals. The structure towers 208 feet above the sand—the tallest lighthouse in the United States and arguably the most recognizable, with its alternating black and white spirals extending around the tower.

In addition to Cape Hatteras Lighthouse, other man-made attractions within the Cape Hatteras National Seashore are the Bodie Island and Ocracoke Lighthouses, restored lifesaving stations, and the visible remains of numerous shipwrecks. Natural attractions include unspoiled beaches, sand dunes, salt marshes, maritime forests, and a rich diversity of wildlife. Pea Island National Wildlife Refuge, located within the park, has become a favorite destination of bird-watchers. Available activities at the Cape Hatteras National Seashore include surf fishing, boating, sunbathing, swimming, hiking, camping, and nature study. Long popular with sportsmen and -women and vacationers from throughout the nation and the world, the park attracts more than 2 million visitors annually.

References: Walter C. Biggs Jr. and James F. Parnell, *State Parks of North Carolina* (1989); David Stick, *Dare County: A History* (1970); Stick, *The Outer Banks of North Carolina, 1584–1958* (1958).

Wilson Angley
Additional research provided by David Stick.

SEE ALSO Lighthouses.

Cape Lookout National Seashore

Cape Lookout National Seashore encompasses 28,000 acres of land and water and extends for 55 miles along the North Carolina coast from Ocracoke Inlet to Beaufort Inlet. Included within its boundaries are Shackleford Banks, Cape Lookout, Core Banks, and the site of the deserted village of Portsmouth, which was the first town established on the Outer Banks (1753). Established in 1966, the park is one of the most remote of the nation's 10 national seashores and one of the least visited, lacking paved roads, restaurants, hotels, and private residences. It has been described as a vast nature preserve, established to protect one of the few remaining unaltered barrier island systems in the world while at the same time encouraging visitors who are willing to "rough it" in exchange for unique fishing, hiking, swimming, camping, and other outdoor experiences in a completely natural setting. Cape Lookout is entirely different from its sister park to the north, the older Cape Hatteras National Seashore (1953), which is traversed by a modern highway for almost its entire length and has accommodations for thousands of tourists at private facilities in the eight villages within its borders.

The headquarters of the Cape Lookout National Seashore is located at the end of the paved road on Harkers Island, east of Beaufort. The National Park Service provides no public access to the park, but passenger ferries from Harkers Island to Cape Lookout, Ocracoke to Portsmouth, and Davis or Atlantic to Core Banks are operated by concessionaires. Vehicular traffic is permitted in certain sections of the park, but only immediately adjacent to the ocean beach or on designated sand trails.

A ranger station is maintained at Portsmouth village, where visitors can see the restored church, several residences, and the historic Portsmouth Coast Guard Station. A self-guided walking tour provides information on the history of the village and the individual structures that remain. Portsmouth and Ocracoke Inlet gained prominence in the eighteenth century as the only deepwater port on the northern North Carolina coast. A fort, described as "a fascine battery on pilings," was built there in the 1750s, with a barracks building for housing 40 men, but it was abandoned after brief use. Portsmouth served for many years as an official commodity inspection point, and in 1806, just three years before the official census listed the population of Portsmouth as 387, there was an "academy" in the town. A post office was established at Portsmouth in 1840, the same year that a marine hospital was built there, but that marked the turning point in Portsmouth's fortune. With the opening of nearby Hatteras Inlet, the maritime traffic through Ocracoke Inlet began to decline, as did the population of Portsmouth, but it was more than a century later before the last permanent residents of Portsmouth left the island, leaving behind their homes and family cemeteries.

Unlike other sections of the park, Shackleford Banks, which extends from Lookout Light to Beaufort Inlet, is prohibited for vehicular traffic. Until late in the nineteenth century, Shackleford Banks was the location of a community known as Diamond City (because of the distinctive checkered pattern of the nearby lighthouse), and for many years it was the base for shore whaling along the North Carolina coast. Whenever a whale was harpooned and brought ashore, just about everybody in the community, from children to old persons, participated in the activity of cutting up and boiling the blubber in the process of "trying out" the whale oil. Diamond City and Shackleford Banks were abandoned in the 1890s following a succession of disastrous hurricanes, and most of the residents moved to Harkers Island, Salter Path, or a section of Morehead City they called the "Promised Land."

References: Walter C. Biggs Jr. and James F. Parnell, *State Parks of North Carolina* (1989); David Stick, *The Outer Banks of North Carolina, 1584–1958* (1958).

David Stick
Additional research provided by Dan Blair.

Capital Punishment

Capital Punishment. North Carolina's administration of the death penalty dates back to the colonial era, when capital punishment was regulated by English common law and legislation enacted by the colonial Assembly. Though arguably more humane than it was two centuries ago, when several slaves were executed by burning at the stake, the death penalty nevertheless remains controversial in North Carolina.

Hanging was the method of execution until 1910, when the state took over the task from the counties and began using the electric chair. In the eighteenth and nineteenth centuries, public hangings were social occasions that attracted spectators from far and near. In anticipation of the event, a wife might prepare a cake, fried chicken, and deviled eggs while her husband made sure he had plenty of liquor. They hitched the team to the wagon, and soon the whole family would be on their way to watch the gruesome event.

Electrocution, in contrast to hanging, was believed by many people to be painless. The method was certainly more efficient, and state and prison officials were satisfied with its performance until Republican legislator C. A. Peterson introduced a bill to replace it with the gas chamber. A popular lawmaker, Peterson persuaded the Democratic majority that the gas chamber, then used by three states, was both more efficient and more humane than the electric chair. Asphyxiation by lethal gas thus became the preferred means of administering the death penalty in 1936, although the electric chair remained in use as late as 1938.

Between 1910 and 1961 North Carolina executed 362 persons, two of them women. During this period capital punishment became more controversial, with death sentences increasingly challenged in the state and federal courts. In 1972 the U.S. Supreme Court declared the death penalty "cruel and unusual punishment" and a violation of the Eighth Amendment when juries were permitted to exercise complete discretion in imposing it, often resulting in arbitrary sentencing. The North Carolina Supreme Court responded by declaring that certain crimes would result in mandatory death sentences, taking responsibility out of the hands of the jury. In the 1976 decision in *Woodson v. North Carolina*, the U.S. Supreme Court struck down this practice on the grounds that it failed to give juries sufficient standards or discretion in determining whether convicted criminals should live or die. As a result of this and other related U.S. Supreme Court rulings, 120 inmates awaiting execution in North Carolina had their sentences vacated. Many received new trials, and most were resentenced to life in prison.

Although a revised capital punishment law, which became effective on 1 June 1977, restored the death penalty for first-degree murder, no executions were carried out in North Carolina from 1962 to 1984. But in the 1980s, national attitudes about capital punishment began to swing again toward harsh penalties for criminals, and beginning in 1984 the number of death sentences and executions in North Carolina began to rise. The General Assembly initially gave death row inmates the option to choose between death by lethal gas or lethal injection, but in 1998 legislation eliminated the former, leaving lethal injection as the state's sole method of execution. Between 1984 and 2004, 34 prisoners, including one woman, were executed. All death sentences have been carried out at Raleigh's Central Prison.

Opponents of capital punishment have continued to criticize the practice as cruel, and they have frequently suggested that socioeconomic and racial inequities distinguish those given the death penalty and others who receive nonlethal punishments for similar crimes. The late 1990s, in particular, saw a growing condemnation of capital punishment and new questions about its place in civilized society, with churches and organizations such as Carrboro-based People of Faith

against the Death Penalty forcefully joining the debate. In 2004 the highly publicized acquittal of death row inmate Alan Gell, who was granted a retrial after an appeals court uncovered prosecutorial misconduct and overturned his 1998 conviction, lent weight to charges that the state's system of administering the death penalty was flawed and in need of review. Legislators, however, failed to enact a moratorium on executions. On 2 Dec. 2005 North Carolina carried out the nation's one-thousandth execution since reinstatement of the death penalty.

Reference: Matthew Eisley, "Acquittal Fuels Moratorium Push," *Raleigh News and Observer*, 20 Feb. 2004; Mark Grossman, *Encyclopedia of Capital Punishment* (1998); Joseph Neff, "Death Row Inmate Granted New Trial," *Raleigh News and Observer*, 9 Dec. 2003; Isaac Unah, *Race and the Death Penalty in North Carolina: An Empirical Analysis, 1993–1997* (2001).

Noel Yancey
Additional research provided by Robert Blair Vocci.

Capitals, Colonial and State. Several locations served as the seat of government for the colony and state of North Carolina before Raleigh was designated as its permanent capital. For most of the colonial period, the capital was situated in whatever town the governor lived. The colony's records, stored at different locations, were carted from place to place, often suffering loss and damage in the process.

From April 1692 to March 1712, North Carolina and South Carolina were combined into the single province of Carolina, of which Charles Towne (Charleston, S.C.) served as the official seat of government. In subsequent years, sharp competition between different regions of North Carolina made it difficult to agree on the site for a permanent capital. The Assembly had no fixed location for most of the colonial period; only fragmentary records remain of the sessions of the seventeenth and much of the early eighteenth century. The legislature met in Edenton in 1708. Before and for a few years after that date, it evidently met in various private homes and public buildings in the colony. For example, the Executive Council called for the Assembly of 1715–16 to meet at the home of Capt. Richard Sanderson in Little River, "instead of the Church in Chowan which was the place of ye last meeting."

From 1725 to 1736 the Assembly again met at Edenton. Later sessions were held there, as well as at New Bern, Wilmington, and Bath. In 1746 the legislature passed an act to make New Bern the permanent capital. The measure was vetoed by the royal government, partly because of objections from the northern counties. The Assembly in 1758 located the capital at Tower Hill, a place on the Neuse River near modern Kinston, where a new town, to be called George City, was to be built. The plan stalled and was dropped. New Bern at last was made the permanent capital in 1766, when the Assembly voted to build what came to be known as Tryon Palace, colonial governor William Tryon's mansion.

After the American Revolution began, the seat of government was considered to be wherever the legislature met. Before an Assembly for the rebels was organized, the Provincial Council met at the "court house in Johnston County" in 1775–76. In 1776 the Council of Safety met at Wilmington, "William Whitfield's in Dobbs County," "Joel Lane's in Wake County," Salisbury, and Halifax (twice). During 1774–76 the Provincial Congress of North Carolina met twice in New Bern, once in Hillsborough, and twice in Halifax.

The General Assembly of 1777 met in New Bern; during 1778–81, it convened in New Bern, Hillsborough, Halifax, Smithfield, and Wake Court House. In 1781 officials chose Hillsborough as the permanent capital. When the town was raided later that year by Loyalist forces under David Fanning, the legislature determined that it was not a safe location for a capital. After the Revolution, the General Assembly continued to move, holding sessions at Hillsborough, New Bern, Fayetteville, and Tarboro.

In 1788 the lawmakers decided to resolve the issue of a permanent state capital once and for all. At a convention in Hillsborough to consider ratification of the U.S. Constitution that summer (the measure would fail), they created a committee, led by Willie Jones, to fix an "unalterable seat of government of this state" within ten miles of Isaac Hunter's plantation in Wake County. Willie Jones and the committee favored this location but left the choice of a particular site to the legislature. Advocates of Fayetteville as the capital kept the issue alive by delay tactics. When the proposal came to a vote on 29 Mar. 1790, the House and Senate split evenly, with the House Speaker voting for Wake County and the Senate Speaker in opposition. On 5 December the legislature finally approved the Wake County site and appointed a nine-member commission to purchase a tract of land. After visiting more than a dozen farms, the commissioners continued to put off a decision. Joel Lane, however, gave a lavish dinner for them, and his property soon was chosen. Most historians credit Governor Alexander Martin with suggesting that the site be named to honor Sir Walter Raleigh, the leader of England's early colonization efforts. The General Assembly met in Raleigh for the first time during 1794–95 and a capitol building was finished in 1796. As a state law required the governor to live in Raleigh, a house for the chief executive was provided by 1797.

References: Candy Lee Metz Beal, *Raleigh: The First 200 Years* (1992); William K. Boyd, *History of North Carolina, Vol. 2: The Federal Period* (1919); John L. Cheney Jr., ed., *North Carolina Government, 1585–1979: A Narrative and Statistical History* (1981); Elizabeth Reid Murray, *Wake: Capital County of North Carolina* (1983); William S. Powell, *North Carolina through Four Centuries*
(1989); James Vickers, *Raleigh, City of Oaks: An Illustrated History* (1992).

David A. Norris
Additional research provided by
Wiley J. Williams and Jo Ann Williford.

SEE ALSO Raleigh; State Capitol.

Cardinal. A year-round resident of North Carolina, the northern cardinal was designated as the official state bird by the General Assembly in 1943. The cardinal is sometimes called the winter redbird because it stands out greatly during the winter, when it is the only red bird active. It is one of the most common birds in the state, frequenting meadows, yards, gardens, and woodlands. The male cardinal is completely red, except for its throat and the black region around its bill, and its head is conspicuously crested. The female is olive in color, with the red confined mostly to the crest, wings, and tail. That both the male and the female of the species are fine singers makes the cardinal unusual among birds. Its nest, generally not more than four feet above the ground, is an untidy construction of weed stems, grass, and similar materials. The usual number of eggs laid in the spring is three in North Carolina and four farther north. The cardinal is by nature a seed eater, but it also eats small fruits and insects.

Alex Coffin

Carnegie Libraries. Between 1886 and 1923, industrialist Andrew Carnegie and the Carnegie Corporation donated funds for more than 1,600 public library buildings in the United States. Ten of those libraries were constructed in North Carolina. Charlotte was the first North Carolina city to apply for Carnegie funds; its application for $25,000 was approved in 1901. Greensboro applied next, in 1902, and Winston-Salem (1903), Rutherford College (1907), Hendersonville (1911), Andrews (1914), Murphy (1916), Durham (1917), and Hickory (1917) followed. In 1915 Charlotte received an additional grant of $15,000 to add a children's room and an auditorium. After several false starts, Greensboro was given a second grant in 1922 to construct a branch for African Americans.

Carnegie's generosity spurred the creation and institutionalization of public library service in many communities. However, most towns eventually outgrew their original Carnegie buildings. In North Carolina, the period after World War II saw an expansion of collections and services that forced many of the nine towns with Carnegie libraries to build new facilities. The Carnegie libraries in Andrews, Charlotte, and Rutherford College were torn down, as was the white Carnegie library in Greensboro. Greensboro's second Carnegie library is now part of the Bennett College campus. The Carnegie buildings in Durham, Hendersonville, Hickory, Murphy, and Winston-Salem still stand, but none is used as a library.

References: Mary E. Anders, "The Contributions of the Carnegie Corporation and the General Education Board to Library Development in the Southeast" (M.A. thesis, UNC-Chapel Hill, 1950); George S. Bobinski, *Carnegie Libraries: Their History and Impact on American Public Library Development* (1969); Wendell W. Smiley, *Library Development in North Carolina before 1930* (1971).

Eileen McGrath

Carolana, "land of Charles," referred to the area south of Virginia granted on 30 Oct. 1629 by King Charles I to his attorney general, Sir Robert Heath. The grant was part of the Crown policy to expand England's overseas empire at little royal expense or effort by distributing Proprietary charters to individuals who were then obligated to develop their holdings. Carolana included the territory between 31° and 36° north latitude, and Heath was given broad authority for self-government under the Bishop of Durham clause, although his legislative power was limited by requiring "the counsel, assent & approbation of the Freeholders." The Carolana grant apparently was motivated by the inquiries into colonization by French Huguenot refugee M. de Belavane, an agent of the Baron de Sancé. Also involved in the venture was a Puritan merchant of Huguenot ancestry, Samuel Vassall, who began the Vassall family's interest in colonization of the region that extended into the Carolina Proprietary of 1663.

The Sancé group received permission to settle in Carolana on 19 Mar. 1630. Although plans moved forward to establish a colony, no expedition succeeded in reaching the area. Vassall then took the initiative to keep the project alive by engaging Henry Taverner, master of the ship *Thomas*, to look for suitable colonizing sites along the Carolana coast. Following his exploration, Taverner transported colonists from England in the fall of 1633 but was unable to reach Carolana, leaving them stranded in Virginia. Heath, in 1632, had assigned the patent to Carolana to Henry Frederick Howard, Lord Maltravers, who in 1637–38 founded the county of Norfolk and appointed a deputy governor, Henry Hartwell, for the northern half of the province. Despite his plans, there is no evidence that Lord Maltravers was any more successful than Heath had been. The onset of civil war in England ended the interest in colonial ventures by courtiers. The Carolana grant is important because it signifies the first time the area south of Virginia was envisioned as a separate colonial territory, and it is the original source for the name "Carolina."

References: Paul E. Kopperman, "Profile of Failure: The Carolana Project, 1629–1640," *NCHR* 59 (January 1982); William S. Powell, "Carolana and the Incomparable Roanoke: Explorations and Attempted Settlements, 1620–1663," *NCHR* 51 (January 1974).

Lindley S. Butler

Carolina was a Proprietary colony established by England's King Charles II through the charter of 24 Mar. 1663 that granted eight Lords Proprietors all of the land on the North American continent between the latitudes of 31° and 36° north, extending west to the South Seas (Pacific Ocean). This was the same territory that had been conferred by Charles I in 1629 to Sir Robert Heath as the Carolana Proprietary, which was nullified by the new charter. Named in honor of Charles II, the Carolina Proprietary rewarded courtiers and loyalists who had helped make the 1660 restoration of the monarchy possible. To encompass the settlement north of Albemarle Sound, a second charter was issued on 30 June 1665 that expanded the colony to 36°30′ and 29° north latitude, which located the northern boundary on the present Virginia–North Carolina border and the southern boundary in mid-Florida.

References: Hugh T. Lefler and William S. Powell, *Colonial North Carolina: A History* (1973); Powell, *The Carolina Charter of 1663* (1954).

Lindley S. Butler

Carolina Ballet. SEE Dance.

Carolina Bays are oval depressions in the earth's surface concentrated on either side of the North Carolina–South Carolina boundary. They are most numerous in Bladen County, although some are found as far away as Georgia and Maryland. Once thought to number in the hundreds of thousands, there are now fewer than 900 notable Carolina Bays, with about 80 percent of these located in North Carolina. They are oriented in a northwest-southeast direction and frequently have a sand rim on the southeast portion. Varying in size from a few hundred feet to about six miles in length, some of the Carolina Bays, such as those forming Lake Waccamaw, Bay Tree Lake, White Lake, Little Singletary Lake, and Horseshoe Lake, still hold water. Others have become bogs or pocosins of peat or black loam soil or have completely dried up. Lake Waccamaw, the largest, is about 20 feet deep, while White Lake reaches a depth of 15 feet. The depth of the peat in some of the bays that are no longer filled with water measures between 11 and 50 feet.

These unusual formations were first given special attention by geologists in 1895 after L. C. Glenn noticed the shape and other similarities they shared. Popular scientific opinion once held that the bays are the result of a shower or successive showers of meteorites hitting the earth at an angle, although other theories of their origin included ice fragments from a Hudson River basin meteor impact and the tail-fanning of a huge fish. The current formation theory holds that the wave-motion of the receding ocean created pools of standing water that were then elliptically shaped by winds blowing in the same direction for a long period of time.

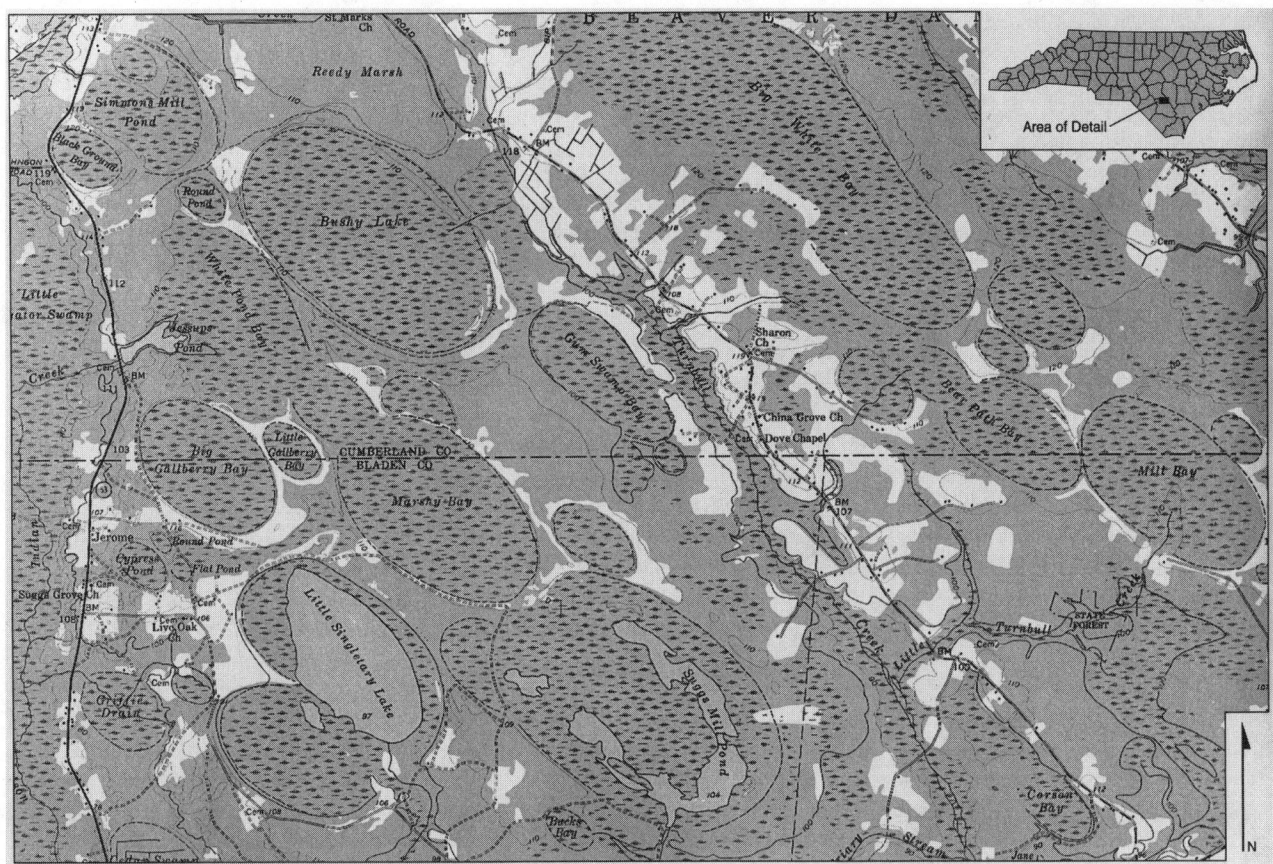

Carolina Bays as shown on a U.S. Geological Survey map of the border area between Bladen and Cumberland Counties. U.S. Geological Survey, Roseboro, N.C., 1:62,500 Quadrangle N3445–W830/15, 1959.

References: Kevin Krajick, "Riddle of the Carolina Bays," *Smithsonian* 28 (September 1997); Timothy Nifong, *An Ecosystematic Analysis of Carolina Bays in the Coastal Plain of the Carolinas* (1998); Thomas E. Ross, *Carolina Bays: An Annotated and Comprehensive Bibliography, 1844–2000* (2000).

William S. Powell

Carolina Central Railway began in 1855 as the Wilmington & Charlotte Railroad Company, soon changing its name to the Wilmington, Charlotte, and Rutherford Railroad (WC&R) to reflect its intended course. Construction of the road began on 1 Jan. 1857 at Navassa, on the west bank of the Cape Fear River near Wilmington. By April 1861 the company had completed 112 miles of track from Navassa west to Rockingham and another 31 miles from Charlotte west to Lincolnton. The Civil War interrupted construction, which was not resumed until 1870. By 1873 the WC&R had failed financially and was sold at foreclosure to new owners organized as the Carolina Central Railway Company. By the close of 1874 they were able to complete the line between Rockingham and Charlotte and also extend it west from Lincolnton to Shelby. But the new owners, like their predecessors, were unable to make the road profitable, and in 1876 the firm was once again sold at fore-

closure, emerging this time as the Carolina Central Railroad Company (CCRR).

The following year, the Seaboard & Roanoke Railroad—which was beginning the expansion that led to the formation of the Seaboard Air Line system—began acquiring control of the CCRR, and the line eventually became part of that larger system. In 1887 the last section of the railroad was completed from Shelby to Rutherfordton, establishing a 267-mile link from coastland to foothills across southern North Carolina. By 1890 the line had been relaid with steel rails, and by 1900 the CCRR had lost its separate identity.

Despite its stormy history, the line has fared well in modern times compared to other Wilmington lines. Most through traffic between the north and east on the former Atlantic Coast Line and former Seaboard lines to the west and southwest has been diverted to the former CCRR's line to and from Hamlet. The entire route has remained in service, with the main portion operated by CSX Corporation, successor to the Seaboard Air Line and other companies that had merged. West of Bostic in Rutherford County, the old CCRR is operated by the Thermal Belt Railway, an independent short line. A distinguishing feature of the CSX portion is a 79-mile straight track from a point near East Arcadia west of Wilmington to a point near Laurel

The first page of the Carolina charter of 1663. In the charter, Charles II (shown at upper left) conveyed vast lands extending to the Pacific Ocean and including what is now North Carolina to eight of his supporters, known subsequently as the Lords Proprietors. Courtesy of NCOA&H.

Hill in Scotland County. It is the longest stretch of main-line railroad without a curve in the United States.

References: S. D. Carriker, *Railroading in the Carolina Sandhills* (1985); Robert Wayne Johnson, *Through the Heart of the South: The Seaboard Air Line Railroad Story* (1995); Edward A. Lewis, *American Shortline Railway Guide* (1996).

Wingate Lassiter
George A. Kennedy

SEE ALSO Seaboard Air Line Railway.

Carolina Charters (1663, 1665).

Shortly after his restoration as English monarch in 1660, King Charles II granted the territory of Carolina to a number of supporters who had helped him regain the throne. The resultant charter (or "letters patent") of 1663 granted to the eight Lords Proprietors all of the territory between 31° and 36° north latitude from the Atlantic Coast to the Pacific Ocean, or in effect from about 70 miles south of the border of present-day Florida to about 40

miles south of the present northern boundary of North Carolina. King Charles I had granted the same territory to his attorney general, Sir Robert Heath, in 1629. Inactivity under that grant led to its presumed lapse, although a succession of unsuccessful claimants under the Heath grant pressed their suits well into the next century.

A further grant to the Proprietors in 1665 extended the northern boundary 30 minutes, to the present border of North Carolina and Virginia. The Proprietors held the land in "free and common soccage," which meant that instead of being required to furnish armed knights to serve the king when necessary, a substantial annual payment constituted the service. (Several decades later the Lords Proprietors were so far behind in their payments that the Crown threatened to revoke the grant.)

The charters of 1663 and 1665 granted not only the soil of Carolina but extensive rights of governance as well. Many powers bestowed upon the Lords Proprietors derived from the clause in the charter granting them those prerogatives traditionally enjoyed by the bishop of Durham, who in the Middle Ages was in effect a viceroy in the turbulent border region of northern England. The Proprietors were empowered to make laws, "with the advice, assent, and approbation" of the freemen or their representatives, and to make orders and ordinances without such approval. They could also establish courts; appoint judges and other officials; grant lands; erect towns, seaports, and forts; make war; and create and bestow titles of honor. Most of the charter's provisions were later incorporated into the Fundamental Constitutions of Carolina, including one permitting a generous measure of religious tolerance.

In 1949 the state of North Carolina acquired the Carolina charter of 1663 from a bookseller in England at a cost of slightly more than $6,000; it is in the possession of the North Carolina State Archives.

References: Mattie Erma Edwards Parker, ed., *North Carolina Charters and Constitutions, 1578–1698* (1963); William S. Powell, *The Carolina Charter of 1663* (1954).

Robert J. Cain

Carolina Charter Tercentenary Commission was established by the 1959 General Assembly in order to plan for observations of the 300th anniversary of the signing of the Carolina charter in 1663. The celebration centered on educational and public observances of the first century of the colony's official existence. Pamphlets, brochures, and leaflets were prepared for various age levels. A 30-minute motion picture was produced, as was a one-act historic opera (*The Sojourner and Mollie Sinclair*, by Carlisle Floyd), and a symphony (*North State*). A mobile Museum of History toured the state displaying historical artifacts. A literary competition, religious commemorations, a commemorative postage stamp, and local county observances were important components of the celebration.

One enduring contribution of the Tercentenary Commission was the construction of a building to house the State Archives, a museum of history, and other historical agencies. The groundbreaking ceremony for such an edifice took place in October 1963. The commission also sparked a new edition of *The Colonial Records of North Carolina*; in 1961 the North Carolina Colonial Records Project came into being, and the first of the project's nine volumes was published for the tercentenary in 1963.

Robert J. Cain

Carolina Christian College, a precursor of present-day Barton College in Wilson, was established by the Disciples of Christ in 1893 in the Pitt County town of Ayden, where it operated until 1903. By the late nineteenth century the Disciples had established a number of academies in eastern North Caro-

lina and directed their convention president to seek a site for an institution of higher learning. Bids were received from Wilson's Mills, Dunn, Grifton, and Ayden. The trustees accepted the Ayden offer of $500 and five acres. Incorporated in 1890, the town was on the railroad and, importantly for the Disciples of Christ, was centrally located in the eastern counties where the greatest strength of the denomination rested.

At a trustees meeting in the spring of 1893 the name Carolina Christian College was chosen, and construction soon commenced on two buildings. Classes were held in the fall of 1893, with 17 students on the rolls. The first principal was L. L. Rightsell (1862–1927), a minister and Indiana native. In 1901 the annual convention of the Disciples of Christ (also known as the Christian Church) voted to establish a larger college in Wilson on the campus of the former Kinsey Institute. Atlantic Christian College opened in 1902; the following year the school in Ayden closed and the land and buildings were sold. In 1990 Atlantic Christian was renamed Barton College for church founder Barton W. Stone.

Reference: C. C. Ware, *A History of Atlantic Christian College* (1956).

Michael Hill

Carolina College for Women, located at Maxton, was chartered by the North Carolina Methodist Conference in 1907. The Reverend S. E. Mercer and Euclid H. McWhorter, pastor of the Maxton Methodist Church, led the efforts to establish the school. With funds from the Methodist Conference and local contributions, a stately main building was constructed, and the school began operations in 1912. It was a liberal arts school, with emphasis on spiritual development and education in the arts. Mercer was the first president, and others who served in that position were R. B. John and S. E. Green.

The college operated until 1926, when it closed for financial reasons. Its properties were acquired by the North Carolina Synod of the Presbyterian Church for the establishment of Presbyterian Junior College.

References: Dorothy Collins, "Three Schools on a Maxton Campus," in *Maxton, North Carolina, 1874–1974: Maxton Area Centennial, March 29–April 6, 1974* (1974); Maud Thomas, *Away Down Home: A History of Robeson County, North Carolina* (1982).

Henry A. McKinnon Jr.

Carolina Comments began in 1952 as a newsletter of the North Carolina Department of Archives and History. The newsletter reported on historical activities in the department and around the state and served as an organ of the North Carolina Literary and Historical Association. Much of the information that had been appearing in the "Historical News" section of the *North Carolina Historical Review* was absorbed by *Caro-*

lina Comments. In the late 1970s the newsletter took on a more structured format, with regular reports from each section in the Division of Archives and History; news from state, county, and local historical organizations as well as colleges and universities; feature stories; and occasional articles. It continues to be published six times a year (January, March, May, July, September, and November).

Jeffrey J. Crow

Carolina Female College was established in Anson County by an act of the North Carolina legislature in 1850. At the time of its founding, it was one of 13 schools for young women in the state. Women ages 10 to 20, described mostly as "preacher's daughters," were enrolled. Course offerings emphasized the classics, including Latin and ancient history.

The school was first owned by a local village stock company that gave money and political support for its establishment and funded the erection of the original three-story school building. Its promoters included Joel Tyson, John McLendon, Joseph Medley, W. A. Smith, Christopher Watkins, and David Carpenter. The first president of the college was the Reverend Alexander Smith, and the first president of the Board of Trustees was Col. Wm. G. Smith. While the college began as a privately owned enterprise, it was offered in 1861 to the South Carolina Methodist Conference on obligation of a $10,000 debt.

An outbreak of typhoid fever and the ongoing Civil War combined to close the school in 1862. It enjoyed a brief comeback from 1864 to 1868, but the burden of Reconstruction and a lack of enrollment were too much for the small, struggling operation. The original 13-room school building stood for about 100 years and was finally demolished in the 1950s. The president's home remained nearby as a private residence.

References: Mary Medley, *History of Anson County, N.C., 1760–1976* (1976); W. A. Smith, "Old Carolina College," *North Carolina Booklet* 22 (1922).

Deena Deese Kilmon

Carolina Hotel. In June 1895 James W. Tufts, a successful Boston manufacturer, came to North Carolina seeking a healthy and mild climate. After purchasing 5,890 acres for approximately $1.00 per acre in the Sandhills area of Moore County, Tufts hired Frederick Law Olmsted, the distinguished landscape artist who designed Central Park in New York City and the grounds of Biltmore House, to draw up plans for a village named Pinehurst. Tufts put in cottages, a power plant, a post office, a department store, and the 250-room Carolina Hotel. The huge structure, the largest frame hotel in the state, contained 49 suites with bath and a music room for 400 guests, which featured daily concerts by the hotel orchestra. The hotel opened on 1 Jan. 1901 and boasted every modern comfort and convenience, including electric lights, elevators, and telephones in each room. Tufts also built a trolley line from the Seaboard Railway station in nearby Southern Pines to transport passengers to the Carolina Hotel.

In 1898 Tufts hired golf architect Donald J. Ross to build a nine-hole golf course. By 1919 Ross had designed four courses, including the famed Pinehurst Number 2 course, and golf became the essential pastime for Pinehurst's tourists. The hotel also provided tennis courts, horseback riding, polo, croquet, and trap shooting. Sharpshooter Annie Oakley ran the Pinehurst Gun Club for ten years. Guests of the Carolina Hotel included Warren G. Harding, J. Pierpont Morgan, Amelia Earhart, John D. Rockefeller Sr., Theodore Roosevelt, John Philip Sousa, and Will Rogers. From 1895 until 1920, James Tufts ran Pinehurst and the hotel as a sole proprietorship. In 1920 a charter for Pinehurst, Inc., was obtained from the state. By 1980 Pinehurst was a municipality, no longer a "company town."

In 1980 Malcolm McLean of Diamondhead Corporation purchased Pinehurst, Inc. McLean built a new front entrance and thoroughly refurbished and repaired the hotel, now known as the Pinehurst Hotel. Diamondhead defaulted on bank loans in 1982, and the Club Corporation of America bought the hotel, golf courses, and clubhouse two years later. Restored to its former splendor, the Pinehurst Resort and Country Club was in the early 2000s a AAA Four-Diamond Resort, with eight golf courses, a tennis complex, and other amenities.

References: Raymond North, *The Pinehurst Story: June 1895–June 1984* (1985); Lee Pace, "Getting Back on Course," *Business North Carolina* (August 1988); Manly Wade Wellman, *The County of Moore* (1962).

Julian M. Pleasants

Carolina Indian Voice, a weekly newspaper published in Pembroke, was established on 18 Jan. 1973. It serves the interests of the Lumbee Indians in Robeson County, who make up approximately one-third of the county's population. Bruce Barton, who served as editor, founded the paper with a $500 loan. Its masthead states that the paper is "Dedicated to the Best in All of Us," and the *Carolina Indian Voice* refers to itself as "the newspaper for all Indians and their friends everywhere."

Barton's editorials, under the title "As I See It," have argued for greater Indian representation in the county educational system, local government jobs, and all aspects of public life. The *Indian Voice*'s usual eight pages include a front-page feature, an editorial and opinion page, and such regular columns as "Educational Views," "According to Scripture," and "Pembroke News." A columnist with the pseudonym Ol' Reasonable Locklear contributes from time to time, "depending on his gout." A mix of local advertising supports the paper. Barton was succeeded as editor by his sister, Connie Braboy, in 1988. As of the early 2000s the newspaper's weekly circulation was approximately 6,000.

Edwin H. Mammen

Carolina Israelite, a newspaper published in Charlotte from 1944 to 1968, was the creation of journalist, social critic, and humorist Harry Golden (1902?–81). Golden, who changed his name from Harry Goldhurst after serving a prison sentence for postal law violations, grew up on New York's Lower East Side. He moved south for what he thought would be temporary work at the *Charlotte News* but settled permanently in Charlotte in 1941. The actual date of the first edition of the *Carolina Israelite* is unknown, but it is generally considered to be February 1944. The front page of the first issue featured a masthead with symbols of a menorah and a Torah; under the title was the statement: "To Break Down the Walls of Misunderstanding—And to Build Bridges of Good Will." The headline celebrated Brotherhood Week, recently proclaimed by President Franklin D. Roosevelt.

The *Carolina Israelite* consisted almost exclusively of essays and writings by Golden, as well as advertisements. Some exceptions were letters to the editor, a column on men in the armed forces, a few guest essays, and in later years occasional columns and book reviews by Golden's sons. The prototype of the *Carolina Israelite* was the *American Freeman*, a personal journal published by Golden's friend Emanuel Haldeman-Julius in Kansas, in which the publisher discoursed on atheism, socialism, literature, and his boyhood experiences. Golden himself largely adhered to this structure throughout the years of the *Israelite*, which reflected his personal commitment to liberal causes and civil rights, a lifetime of voracious reading, and the Jewish immigrant experience of his boyhood.

Golden often used humor to clarify his points. In the wake of the Supreme Court school desegregation decisions, he introduced his "Vertical Negro Plan" in the May–June 1956 issue of the *Israelite*. He pointed out that in the South, whites and blacks had no trouble *standing* next to each other at the same bank tellers' windows, walking side by side through the same five-and-dime stores, or wheeling carts through the aisles of the same supermarkets. He argued that "vertical integration" had thus been achieved; it was when these different races tried sitting next to each other that problems arose. So Golden suggested some minor changes, such as replacing seats in schools with stand-up desks and removing seats at lunch counters. With everyone vertical, he explained, peaceful integration would be assured. When *Time* magazine publicized the tongue-in-cheek Vertical Negro Plan in 1957, the *Israelite*'s subscription list included 20 U.S. senators, 40 members of Congress, and such luminaries as William Faulkner, Earl War-

ren, Ernest Hemingway, Bertrand Russell, Harry Truman, and Golden's longtime friend Carl Sandburg.

Golden lived and worked in a rented office on the north side of Elizabeth Avenue in Charlotte. He was lecturing in New Jersey early in 1958 when a predawn fire caused by a faulty flue destroyed his home, his books, and all material relating to the *Israelite*—including much of the subscription list that took him 15 years to build. Parts of the list were restored with the assistance of the laboratories of the Charlotte Police Department, and the remainder was rebuilt by the use of extensive publicity asking subscribers to notify Golden. He announced that due to the fire, the next issue would be a little late (although, as the *Charlotte Observer* pointed out, issues were always a little late).

Later in 1958, Golden signed a contract with World Publishing to publish a collection of essays from the *Israelite*, which became his best seller *Only in America*. This book made Golden famous and eased his financial burdens. It also led to regular appearances on the *Tonight Show* with Jack Paar, which Golden credited with increasing the circulation of the *Carolina Israelite* to more than 40,000 subscribers at its peak in the late 1950s and early 1960s.

After the fire, Golden moved to a white Victorian home on the south side of Elizabeth Avenue, where he remained until the paper folded in 1968. The final issue (vol. 25, no. 6, January–February 1968) contained an advertisement from the *Nation* lamenting the departure of the *Carolina Israelite* but promising that "Harry Golden will continue to be heard through our pages."

References: Harry Lewis Golden, *The Best of Harry Golden* (1967); "Golden Rule," *Time*, 1 Apr. 1957; Tom Hanchett, "Remembering Harry Golden: Food, Race, and Laughter," *Southern Cultures* 11 (Summer 2005); Dannye Romine, "Activist Writer Harry Golden Dies," *Charlotte Observer*, 3 Oct. 1981.

Bryna R. Coonin

Carolina Panther. Previously identified as *Felis concolor couguar* but more recently as *Puma concolor couguar*, the cautious and intelligent Carolina panther, once prevalent in North Carolina, is now considered extinct in the wild by most zoologists despite consistent rumors of sightings and species resurgence. The variety historically present in North Carolina was likely the eastern puma or cougar, though the range of the Florida panther extended through most of the Southeast and certainly into parts of South Carolina. When the New World was first explored, panthers were found from coast to coast and from southern Canada to Tierra del Fuego. Thomas Harriot in 1588 recorded that the Indians sometimes hunted and ate them. On 25 Apr. 1861 the *Raleigh Weekly Ad Valorem Banner* reported that a panther, measuring 7 feet 4 inches long and 2.5 feet tall, had been killed at the head of the Pungo River.

Carolina panthers, showing little fear of humans, lived in close proximity to people if their needs for food, water, shelter, and an escape route were met.

By the early twentieth century, extensive hunting combined with a decrease in the population of the panther's primary prey, white-tailed deer, and deforestation in its natural habitat, had made the panther very rare throughout the Southeast except in a small area of southern Florida. Reports of panthers in North Carolina continued, however, and increased when the North Carolina Wildlife Resources Commission implemented a program to reestablish a deer herd for hunting. Between 1937 and 1993, 121 adult panthers and 17 panther kittens were claimed to have been sighted, though reports have generally been unverifiable and attempts to lure the cats into camera range have proved fruitless.

References: David S. Lee, "Unscrambling Rumors: The Status of the Panther *Felis Concolor* in North Carolina," *Wildlife in North Carolina* 41 (July 1977); Leonard Lee Rue III, "American Wildcats," *American Hunter* (August 1991); Stanley P. Young, *The Puma: Mysterious American Cat* (1964).

Charles R. Humphreys

Carolina Parakeet (*Conuropsis carolinensis*), now extinct, was found in large numbers in the region of the Carolinas and Virginia when the first European colonists arrived. Sir Walter Raleigh mentioned the bird in his 1596 book on the discovery of Guiana in South America, noting its similarity to the "paraquitos" of Central America and Italy. Captain John Smith, a leader in the settlement of Virginia in 1607, likewise made reference to parrots. When William Byrd surveyed the boundary between Carolina and Virginia in 1728, he was amazed at the large number of parakeets he encountered. "Carolina" became a part of the bird's everyday name sometime after the 1663 chartering of the Carolina colony.

The Carolina parakeet was 12.5 inches long with a wingspan of about 22 inches. The bird was mostly green with an orange head, a yellow neck, and white legs, its tail feathers giving the impression of being long and pointed. Though skilled climbers, parakeets seemed reluctant to walk from place to place, instead going airborne even to turn around. Sometimes human traits such as laziness were ascribed to these birds. Their voice was said to be loud, harsh, and grating. Though generally not adept at speaking, occasionally the parakeet imitated sounds or words, and some trainers who began with very young birds were successful in teaching them to mimic a limited number of words from human speech.

Parakeets were thought to mate for life and show signs of close attachment to their own kind. Some, in fact, were acclaimed "love birds." When a parakeet died or was killed, a host of chattering birds promptly surrounded its body. Although no evidence seems to suggest that these birds mi-

Lithograph of Carolina parakeets from a drawing by John James Audubon. NCC.

grated, they often flew off together around their territory in such large flocks that they were said to have blotted out the sun.

Carolina parakeets ate thistle seeds and cockleburs, birch buds in April, and beechnuts and chinquapins in the autumn. They also preferred to drink salty seawater when it was available. Orchards of European settlements were very appealing to flocks of parakeets, whose bills were ideal for splitting the fruit to get at the seeds. Raided orchards were stripped bare and the ground underneath covered with broken fruit that soon spoiled.

The Carolina parakeet rapidly declined in the late nineteenth century. Landowners began hunting the birds, which had become pests and were also prized as food and for their colorful feathers, with which Victorian milliners decorated women's hats. Parakeets seemed to possess an uncommon degree of curiosity, and they appeared to be attracted rather than dispersed by gunshots. Their communal reaction to their dead also made them easy targets. In addition, the increasing human population in the rural regions of the southeastern United States began to deprive these birds of their natural habitat. The species probably fled North Carolina by the 1780s but may have lingered in South Carolina until the 1860s. A few later reports of sightings from Tennessee, South Carolina, and Florida appear credible, but Carolina parakeets were described as endangered soon after 1900 and became extinct in the wild early in the twentieth century, the final captive specimen dying in the Cincinnati Zoo on 21 Feb. 1918.

References: Alan Feduccia, *Catesby's Birds of Colonial America* (1985); Eloise F. Potter, James E. Parnell, and Robert P. Teulings, *Birds of the Carolinas* (1980).

William S. Powell
Additional research provided by Wynne Dough.

Carolina Peacemaker, an African American weekly newspaper published in Greensboro since 1967, was the creation of John Marshall Stevenson, its editor and publisher. The paper was intended to address the needs and interests of African Americans in Greensboro and the rest of North Carolina. In the summer of 1974, Stevenson legally changed his name to "Kilimanjaro," stating that to keep the name of his great grandfather's master would lend itself to the "glorification of one who exploited and denigrated a great but unfortunate people."

The first issue of the *Peacemaker* appeared on 30 Mar. 1967; in his editorial, titled "The Other Side of the Tracks," Kilimanjaro stated that he had founded the paper because the "Negro citizens of Greensboro had had their hopes of achieving political representation on both the local and state levels dashed unceremoniously to the ground" in the 1960s. There was a need to unify the black community, and he intended to provide the "journalistic vehicle through which the hopes, ambitions, fears, and aspirations of the entire citizenry regarding social, economic, and civic affairs might be expressed."

In the mid-1970s a column titled "UP and DOWN MARKET STREET" appeared, using a caricature of a "black" dialect. Written by "Ole Nosey," a typical leadoff sentence began: "Lawd, lawd! Mastah, when I turned on my teevee and heerd where them jokers over yonder at the Big Schoolhouse is done somehow managed to git theyself almost nelly bout half a million dollars in the hole for them tuitions and stuff." These lines, from the 1 Feb. 1975 issue, were aimed at A&T State University—often a target of the column. The commentary has long since been discontinued, although its writer possessed an artistry seldom found in the genre.

True to its calling, the *Peacemaker* has consistently focused on the black community, especially in the areas of civil rights and politics. Its reporters have specialized in the activities of local government and have addressed economic questions facing black businessmen and entrepreneurs. The paper has offered editorials by its own writers, along with the syndicated columns of nationally prominent figures like Vernon Jordan, Roy Wilkins, and Julian Bond. A page on religion has included many articles by notable church figures.

The *Peacemaker* has also provided information and practical advice on nonpolitical subjects such as cooking, black health matters, vacations, shopping, educational opportunities, entertainment, and sex and marriage. These articles have demonstrated an intense interest in anything that might be of concern to black people, with an emphasis on brotherhood and the need for unity. Every issue since its founding has carried the following quotation by Martin Luther King Jr.: "Americans must learn to live together as brothers, lest we all die together as fools."

In 2004 the *Carolina Peacemaker* had a circulation of about 25,000 and was a member of the National Newspaper Publishers Association, the North Carolina Black Publishers Association, and the North Carolina Press Association. Over the years the number of classified ads and the volume of legal notices in the *Peacemaker* has grown considerably, reflecting its importance in the economic life of Greensboro.

Alexander R. Stoesen

Carolina Political Union (CPU) was formed at the University of North Carolina at Chapel Hill in the spring of 1936 to carry out an idea formulated by Floyd Fletcher, a senior from Raleigh, and other students in Professor E. J. Woodhouse's political science class. This nonpartisan student organization, whose first faculty adviser was Woodhouse, sought to encourage the development of greater student reasoning and investigation into politics and government by placing emphasis on open forums following speeches and on small discussion groups either before or after speakers' visits. The CPU stressed cooperation with similar university organizations, such as the Young Democrats and Young Republicans, both clubs that it founded.

The CPU was not intimidated by controversy, as is evident by the speakers it brought to Chapel Hill. These speakers included Earl Browder, leader of the Communist Party; Hiram W. Evans, Grand Wizard of the Ku Klux Klan; President Franklin D. Roosevelt; Norman Thomas, leader of the Socialist Party; Edwin S. Smith of the National Labor Relations Board; and many other prominent political and social leaders. The CPU survived until the mid-1950s.

Reference: William S. Powell, *The First State University: A Pictorial History of the University of North Carolina* (3rd ed., 1992).

Wiley J. Williams

Carolina Power & Light Company (CP&L) was chartered by the state on 13 July 1908. The creation of CP&L represented the merger of three existing companies, the Raleigh

CP&L's Shearon Harris Nuclear Power Plant in Wake County.
Photograph courtesy of Progress Energy.

Electric Company, the Central Carolina Power Company, and the Consumer Light and Power Company. The fledgling CP&L had 983 Raleigh customers billed at a base rate of $1 per month and 15¢ per kilowatt-hour. Early expansion was in the Henderson and Oxford area with the 1911 acquisition of the Oxford Electric Company. The following year, CP&L gained controlling interest in the Asheville Power and Light Company and bought the Goldsboro system, thus forming the basic service area of the company for years to come.

The World War I period was one of increased commercial use of electricity, particularly in cotton mills and fertilizer factories. Expansion was somewhat hampered by scarcity of materials as a result of the war effort, and few transmission lines were expanded during that time. Following the war and through the 1920s, uses for electricity increased, particularly at the domestic level. Refrigerators, irons, washing machines, and ranges dramatically changed lifestyles at home, while electric trolley cars changed the urban environment. In 1926 CP&L received a new charter, consolidating its holdings into one new company.

At a May 1941 meeting on national defense, the CP&L board of directors authorized numerous expansion programs geared to providing increased service to mills and serving the growing number of military installations within the company's service area. The expansion also provided a base for meeting the domestic demand following the war's end.

In its first 50 years of operation, the company relied on power from coal, oil, and water for electric production. In 1955 the company began investigating nuclear energy possibilities by sending 30 employees to study at North Carolina State University, the first campus in the country to have a nuclear reactor. CP&L entered the nuclear age in 1966, when construction began at the Robinson Plant near Hartsville, S.C.

The 1970s and 1980s were marked by the increased emphasis on nuclear generation due to the threat imposed by the oil embargo. Nuclear power, however, was not popular with the public, especially after the 1979 accident at Three Mile Island Nuclear Power Plant near Harrisburg, Pa. Difficulties in operation of CP&L's Brunswick Plant—the state's first nuclear power plant, completed in 1975—and the increased cost of the Shearon Harris Nuclear Power Plant near New Hill created difficult times for CP&L. Increased regulation, public opposition, and the positive effects of conservation measures caused the company to reconsider its nuclear program. Planned to have four reactors, the Shearon Harris Plant was ultimately scaled back to only one.

In November 2000 CP&L acquired Florida Progress Corporation; the merger resulted in the formation of Progress Energy, a Fortune 250 company headquartered in Raleigh that includes subsidiaries CP&L, Florida Power, NCNG, Progress Telecom, SRS, and Energy Ventures. In January 2003 CP&L became Progress Energy Carolinas, operating 18 plant sites and serving more than 1.3 million customers living in over 34,000 square miles in eastern North Carolina and South Carolina. By 2006 its parent company, Progress Energy, had $10 billion in annual revenues, maintained more than 24,000 megawatts of generation capacity, and served approximately 3 million electricity and gas customers in North Carolina, South Carolina, and Florida.

References: Carolina Power & Light Company, *A Brief History of Carolina Power and Light Company* (n.d.); Jack Riley, *Carolina Power & Light Company, 1908–1958: A Corporate Biography* (1958).

William J. McCrea

Carolina Quarterly. SEE Literary Journals.

Carolinas, Separation of. The province of Carolina given by England's King Charles II to the Lords Proprietors in 1663 and 1665 constituted a single grant. In 1664 the northeastern portion of the province, at that time the only part settled by Europeans, became the county of Albemarle, and a few years later, in 1670, another colony was established at Charles Towne (now Charleston, S.C.) on the Ashley River. Separate governmental structures—governors, councils, assemblies, and courts—came into being for the two settlements, although technically the province of Carolina was a united entity with neither of its two colonies being considered superior to the other.

In 1691, in a halfhearted attempt to centralize authority in response to unrest in both settlements, the Lords Proprietors decreed that the governor of Carolina would reside in Charles Towne and appoint a deputy for the northern part of the colony. The practical effect of the measure was at best negligible. Although the innovation resulted in the chief executives of North Carolina being styled "deputy governor" as a result of the change, their subordination to the "governor" at Charles Towne seems to have been merely formal. In addition, the legislatures and courts of both parts of the province continued their separate and independent existences. In 1710, however, the Proprietors ceased naming a governor for all of Carolina, and in 1712 Edward Hyde took the oath as governor of "No. Carolina." Nevertheless, various formal documents issued by the Lords Proprietors well after 1712 continued to refer to the "Province of Carolina" as if it were an undivided unit, as well as to the "Province of North Carolina" and the "Province of South Carolina."

References: Hugh T. Lefler and William S. Powell, *Colonial North Carolina: A History* (1973); Powell, *The Carolina Charter of 1663* (1954).

Robert J. Cain

Carowinds. SEE Amusement Parks.

Carpetbaggers. SEE Reconstruction.

Carson House, located in the community of Pleasant Gardens alongside Buck Creek four miles west of Marion in McDowell County, exemplifies nineteenth-century Piedmont North Carolina life. From 1843 to 1845 the home served as the seat of county government. The oldest section of the house consists of a single-pen, two-story log building over a full cellar, built by planter John Carson in 1793. After inheriting the property in 1841, Carson's son Jonathan Logan Carson oversaw major renovations, including an imposing double-porch facade and interior and exterior features in the Greek Revival style.

John Carson immigrated to America from Ireland in 1773 at age 21. A member of the Fayetteville convention that approved the federal Constitution in 1789 and a state legislator in 1805 and 1806, Carson married twice and fathered 12 children. Three of his sons also served in the state legislature. His son Samuel Price Carson served three terms in Congress and later became the first secretary of state of the Republic of Texas. After Jonathan Logan Carson's widow sold the house in 1884, the John Seawell Brown family owned the property for 23 years. In the twentieth century, the house passed through several owners before a group of local citizens bought it. Led by sisters Mary and Ruth Greenlee, the group restored the home in 1963, and the building now operates as a historical house museum filled with household and plantation artifacts.

References: Moffitt Sinclair Henderson, *A Long, Long Day for November* (1972); Michael Hill, *Historical Research Report: The Carson House of Marion, North Carolina* (1982).

Michael Hill

Cartagena Expedition. SEE Jenkins' Ear, War of.

Carteret County, located in the Coastal Plain region of eastern North Carolina, was formed in 1722 from Craven County and was named for Lord Proprietor John Carteret. It is a largely coastal county that incorporates the southern end of the Outer Banks, including Cape Lookout. Early inhabitants of Carteret County included the Hatteras, Core, Neuse, and Tuscarora Indians, followed by French Huguenot, English, Scotch-Irish, and German settlers. The county seat is Beaufort, which was laid out by 1713 and incorporated in 1723, making it one of the state's oldest towns; it was originally called Fishtown but was renamed for the duke of Beaufort, Henry Somerset.

Carteret County is home to many of North Carolina's most popular and prosperous coastal communities and beaches, among them Morehead City (location of an official North Carolina state port), Emerald Isle, Indian Beach, Atlantic Beach, Cedar Point, Newport, and Harkers Island. The Beaufort area hosts marine research facilities associated with the University of North Carolina at Chapel Hill and Duke University. Tourism and recreational pursuits are principal elements of the county's economic life. The county also raises agricultural products such as corn, soybeans, tobacco, wheat, hay, potatoes, cotton, vegetables, poultry, and beef cattle. Manufactured goods produced in Carteret County are fish meal, concrete products, clothing, roofing products, and jewelry.

The Cape Lookout Lighthouse, erected in 1859 and now part of the Cape Lookout National Seashore, and Fort Macon State Park are two of Carteret County's important historic landmarks. A small wild horse population exists on Shackleford Banks, just south of Harkers Island. A state aquarium is located at Pine Knoll Shores along Salter Path. Other cultural institutions include the North Carolina Maritime Museum and the Carteret County Historical Society, which operates a historical park in Beaufort. Among popular annual events and festivals in Carteret County are the summertime outdoor drama *Worthy Is the Lamb* (Swansboro), the Beaufort Old Homes Tour, the Emerald Isle St. Patrick's Day Festival, and the North Carolina Seafood Festival. The population of Carteret County was estimated to be 62,000 in 2004.

Reference: Pat Dala Davis and Kathleen Hill Hamilton, eds., *The Heritage of Carteret County, North Carolina* (2 vols., 1982–84).

Jay Mazzocchi

SEE ALSO Cape Lookout National Seashore; Fort Macon; Harkers Island Boats; Hoi Toiders.

Cary Rebellion is named for Thomas Cary, chief executive of North Carolina from March 1705 until October 1707 and from October 1708 until January 1711, when he was displaced by Edward Hyde. During his first term as deputy governor, Cary had been allied with the Anglican faction dominating the legislature and endeavoring to exclude dissenters (chiefly Quakers) from public office. However, after dissenters successfully appealed to the Lords Proprietors for Cary's removal in 1707, he began seeking a political alliance with dissenters and with Bath County residents who resented the legislative dominance of Albemarle leaders.

Through skillful maneuvering, Cary became chief executive again late in 1708. Soon he liberalized land grant policy to favor Bath County, lowered its quitrent rate, and replaced some local officials with dissenters. The colonial Assembly repealed all laws requiring test oaths.

When Edward Hyde arrived as deputy governor early in 1711, Cary withdrew to his home in Bath County. That March, when Hyde asked the legislature to pass new laws against dissenters and urged Cary's arrest, Cary rallied his supporters—dissenters and Bath County residents—to take up arms. In May Hyde led a force of 150 men to seize Cary, but he repulsed them with artillery. In June Cary outfitted a brigantine to sail into Albemarle Sound and overthrow Hyde. After a series of indecisive engagements, Governor Alexander Spotswood of Virginia sent troops to assist Hyde, and by 17 July Cary had been forced to flee North Carolina.

Captured in late July in Tidewater, Va., Cary and his lieutenants (all Bath County men but not all dissenters) were sent to England to stand trial before the Lords Proprietors. Because no one appeared to press charges, Cary was released after a year and returned to North Carolina early in 1713. He spent the rest of his life in apparent tranquility in Bath County, dying in about 1720.

Sometimes portrayed as chiefly an Anglican-dissenter struggle, the Cary Rebellion was more complex than that. Of equal or greater importance were the opposition of newcomers in Bath County to the established political dominance of Albemarle men and the conflict of the mercantile interests of Indian traders with the agricultural predominance of planters.

References: William S. Price Jr., ed., *North Carolina Higher-Court Minutes, 1709–1723* (1977); Price, ed., *North Carolina Higher-Court Records, 1702–1708* (1974).

William S. Price Jr.

Cassidey's Shipyard was the smaller of two Confederate shipyards in Wilmington during the Civil War and the construction site of the ironclad CSS *Raleigh*. The yard was founded when James Cassidey (1792–1866), a ship's carpenter, bought a waterfront lot at the foot of Church Street on the east bank of the Cape Fear River. By the late 1830s he was operating a yard on the site, and by 1846 he was advertising a marine railway. By 1850 the yard was repairing and copper-bottoming sailing ships on the West Indies trade.

Work on the *Raleigh*, a four-gun steam sloop sometimes classified as a ram, began in mid-1862, about the same time it began on the CSS *North Carolina* at Beery's Shipyard across the river. However, the *Raleigh*'s construction was frequently stalled. Crews fled the yellow fever epidemics of 1862 and 1863, and workers went on strike when pay was delayed by the Confederate Navy Department. Finally, by 30 Apr. 1863 the *Raleigh* was in commission.

After the war, Cassidey's Shipyard merged with Benjamin W. Beery's adjoining works at the foot of Nun Street and was renamed Cassidey & Beery. In 1881 S. W. Skinner took over the facility, and by 1911 the Cape Fear Machine Works had moved onto the site.

References: William N. Still Jr., *Iron Afloat: The Story of the Confederate Armorclads* (1985); Tony P. Wrenn, *Wilmington, North Carolina: An Architectural and Historical Portrait* (1984).

Bennett L. Steelman

Castle McCulloch Gold Mill is a restored gold refinery in Jamestown listed on the National Register of Historic Places. Built by Charles McCulloch, a Cornish engineer who brought the new steam engine technology to North Carolina from England, the structure was completed in 1823 and restored in the early 1980s. It is a granite castle, complete with drawbridge, moat, and 70-foot tower. Using locally quarried granite, McCulloch and stonemason Elizier Kersey created a Cornish Rock Engine House for the refining of gold ore, with a "Walking Beam" steam engine that powered Chilean mill ore crushers.

After years of ownership within the McCulloch family, the site passed through several hands and fell into disrepair before being bought and rebuilt by Richard Harris during the mid-1980s. It is maintained by the McCulloch Foundation. The site is popular for such occasions as weddings, receptions, and corporate events. In 1997 the Crystal Garden was built nearby, with Victorian-style beveled glass walls, a crystal chandelier, and a veranda with a view across a lake to the castle. The gold mill—which operated on the grounds of the castle for its first three decades—offers gem and gold panning, historical tours, and rock quarry visits.

References: Elizabeth Hines, "McCulloch's Rock Engine House: An Antebellum Cornish-style Gold Ore Mill near Jamestown, North Carolina," *Material Culture* 27 (1995); Grimsley T. Hobbs, *Exploring the Old Mills of North Carolina* (1985); Alexander R. Stoesen, *Guilford County: A Brief History* (1993).

Lisa Coston Hall

Caswell County, located in the northern Piedmont region of North Carolina and partially bordering the state of Virginia, was formed from Orange County in 1777 and named for Richard Caswell, the first governor of North Carolina. Early inhabitants of the region included the Occaneechi and other Siouan Indians, followed by German and English settlers. The county seat, Yanceyville, was established in 1791 as Caswell Court House. The name was changed to Yanceyville in 1833 after Bartlett Yancey, a U.S. congressman and state senator. Other Caswell County communities include Milton, Anderson, Pelham, Casville, Leasburg, and Providence. The Dan River flows through a section of the county, and Hyco Lake is an important water source as well as a popular recreational site.

Caswell County agricultural products include tobacco, soybeans, corn, wheat, oats, barley, hay, alfalfa, beef cattle, sheep, swine, and chickens. Manufactured goods include clothing, textiles, and electronics. The county also produces several minerals, such as mica, microcline, beryl, graphite, corundum, and soapstone.

Caswell County's historic sites include the White House, built ca. 1800; Pascal House, built ca. 1840; and Brown's Store, dating from the eighteenth century. The county was, in 1837, the scene of the accidental discovery—by a slave named Stephen on the farm of Abisha and Elisha Slade—of the process of flue-curing for tobacco, and, between 1824 and 1861, the home of Thomas Day, a successful free black furniture maker who worked in Milton, where his shop in Union Tavern is preserved. Cultural institutions include the Caswell County Historical Association, the Caswell County Historical Museum, and the Caswell Council for Arts and History. Annual festivals and events include the Brightleaf Hoedown, the Thomas Day House Annual Heritage Tour of Homes, and the Milton Old-Fashioned Fourth of July Celebration. The Caswell County population was estimated at 23,600 in 2004.

Reference: William S. Powell, *When the Past Refused to Die: A History of Caswell County, North Carolina, 1777–1977* (1977).

William S. Powell

Cataloochee Ranch and Ski Area, the first ski slope south of Virginia, encompasses approximately 1,000 acres on a ridge above Maggie Valley in Haywood County. Forester Tom Alexander and his wife Judith Barksdale Alexander opened the original Cataloochee Ranch in 1933 as a rustic trout fishing, horseback riding, and pack tripping resort in the Cataloochee Valley. They leased a farm there from the National Park Service, which had acquired the land for inclusion in the fledgling Great Smoky Mountains National Park.

In 1938 Tom Alexander purchased the present property on Fie Top, just across the Cataloochee Divide from old Cataloochee and adjoining the national park. The Alexanders employed local residents and developed the tract as a working sheep and cattle farm and a guest facility. The new Cataloochee Ranch opened to visitors in 1939. It accommodates guests in the main ranch house, a lodge, and individual cabins and offers horseback riding, hiking, and fishing in a serene, scenic 5,000-foot-high setting near the remains of several former pioneer settlements.

In 1961 the Alexanders acquired four snow-making machines and opened skiing facilities. Winter skiing subsequently became extremely popular in the region. Cataloochee Ski Area expanded and moved to 5,400-foot-elevation Moody Top in 1968. Both the ranch and the ski area continue to operate under the management of the Alexanders' children and grandchildren.

References: Tom Alexander, *Mountain Fever* (1995); Faris Jane Corey, *Exploring the Mountains of North Carolina* (1972); Sara Pacher and Lynda McDaniel, *The Insiders' Guide to the North Carolina Mountains* (1996).

Kathleen B. Wyche
Additional research provided by Marilyn Wright.

Cataloochee Trail is part of the remains of a once-thriving community located in the present-day Great Smoky Mountains National Park. The entire valley had originally belonged to Col. Robert Love, a post–Revolutionary War speculator who, in order to hold the land, had "granted homesteads to those who would settle and improve" it. In 1814 the first recorded homestead went to the Caldwell family, followed by others to the Hannah, Bennett, Noland, Palmer, Franklin, Woody, and Barnes families. By the 1850s the community known as Cataloochee was well populated, and by 1900 almost 200 buildings dotted the cove.

In the mid-1930s, however, the families of Cataloochee were relocated as their community was incorporated into the Great Smoky Mountains National Park, the first park of its kind not established solely on public land. Although the Cataloochee residents received compensation for the loss of their property, many resented having to leave their homes. Some of the log houses were moved to the Pioneer Farmstead at Oconaluftee, though most structures were burned or dismantled in accordance with the park's original policy of allowing the land to revert to wilderness.

Only four houses remain along the Cataloochee Trail, one of which serves as the ranger station. The trail leads past these houses and passes the Will Messer barn, Beech Grove School, and Palmer Chapel. Dwindling down to little more than a footpath, the trail continues by Hannah's cabin and the Little Cataloochee Church and ends beyond the ruins of the apple house at the Cook place. This small array of structures is the only remnant of North Carolinians' brief but memorable tenure in the region.

References: Carlos C. Campbell, *Birth of a National Park in the Great Smoky Mountains* (rev. ed., 1993); Elizabeth Powers with Mark Hannah, *Cataloochee: Lost Settlement of the Smokies* (1982).

Rosemary Clifford Neill

Catalpa Tree in North Carolina belongs to the southern species *Catalpa bignonioides*, native to Georgia and Florida but thoroughly naturalized throughout the southeastern quarter of the United States. It is widely cultivated as an ornamental tree because of its rapid growth, its amenability to transplantation, its broad, heart-shaped leaves, and the abundant white and yellow spotted blossoms it produces in late May and early June. The catalpa's leaves, unlike those of most other trees, are reddish brown rather than light green when they first appear, turning to dark green within a month. The tree attains a maximum height of about 30 feet and produces wood useful for fence posts, though for little else.

The catalpa tree is especially valued by North Carolina fishermen for its role as host to the catalpa worm, a three-inch, green and black caterpillar that is the larval stage of a butterfly that lays its eggs on the undersides of catalpa leaves. The caterpillars reach maturity within two weeks of hatching and devour their natal leaves before burrowing into the earth around the roots for a pupal stage of about a year's duration; the tree grows new foliage at a fast rate and can produce several crops of worms in a summer. These worms are unrivaled as bait for bream, bass, and catfish, and they fetch handsome prices at country stores and bait and tackle shops during the season. In North Carolina, they are sometimes misnamed "catawba worms," as well as other imaginative spellings such as "katabo worms" and "cadawber worms."

Reference: Hal Porter, "The Fishing Tree," *Wildlife in North Carolina* 53 (July 1989).

Jerry Leath Mills

Catawba College was founded in Newton in 1851 by the German Reformed Church. During the Civil War the college became an academy, operating at Catawba High School from 1865 to 1885, when it resumed operation under its original charter as Catawba College. In 1890 it became a coeducational institution. A move from Newton to Salisbury came about in response to an offer of a partially constructed dormitory/administration building and several acres of land in Salisbury. College, trustee, and church officials closed the Newton campus in 1923 and reopened the school in Salisbury in 1925.

The modern-day Catawba College, affiliated with the United Church of Christ, offers bachelor's degrees (Arts, Business Administration, Fine Arts, and Science) and a Master of Education degree. It also offers cooperative programs in deaf education with Appalachian State University, in forestry and environmental science with Duke University, and in physician assistant and medical technician training with Wake Forest University. The college has grown from 1 building to 27 buildings on 210 acres, with another 150 acres devoted to an ecological preserve. The student body in the early 2000s was approximately 1,100, evenly divided by gender.

References: Francis B. Dedmond, *Catawba: The Story of a College* (1989); Jacob C. Leonard, *History of Catawba College* (1927).

Wiley J. Williams

Catawba County, located in the western Piedmont region of North Carolina in the foothills of the Blue Ridge Mountains, was formed in 1842 from Lincoln County. The county was named for the Catawba Indians, who once inhabited the land. After the Catawba, other early inhabitants included German, Swiss, and Scotch-Irish settlers. The county seat is Newton, incorporated in 1855 and named for Isaac Newton Wilson, a member of the North Carolina General Assembly who first proposed formation of the county in the legislature. Other communities in the county include Hickory, Maiden, Brookford, Claremont, and Longview. Physical features influencing the culture and character of Catawba County include the Catawba River, Lake Hickory, Lookout Shoals Lake, Mountain Creek, and Anderson Mountain. Lake Norman, a massive reservoir, is a popular destination for recreational boaters, swimmers, and fishers.

Catawba County—in particular Hickory—has been an important furniture manufacturing region for decades. Other manufactures include textiles, gloves, cables, and telecommunications equipment. County agricultural products include corn, soybeans, barley, livestock feed, swine, poultry, and both beef and dairy cattle. Catawba County was part of the short but lucrative North Carolina gold rush of the mid-1800s.

Catawba County has a host of historic landmarks, including the Hickory Motor Speedway; Bunker Hill Covered Bridge (1895); Maple Grove (ca. 1875), an Italianate-style home in Hickory; and Shuford Memorial Gardens. Catawba College was founded in Newton in 1851, and 40 years later Lenoir-Rhyne College was established in Hickory. Cultural institutions include the Maiden Public Library, the Catawba County Council for the Arts, the Western Piedmont Symphony, and the Green Room Community Theatre. The Hickory Museum of Art is North Carolina's second-oldest museum, boasting one of the finest collections of American art in the Southeast. Catawba County's popular annual events include Octoberfest, the Old Soldiers Reunion Celebration, Big Sunday at Balls Creek Camp Grounds, and the Strawberry Festival and Craft Show. Catawba County's population was estimated to be 148,000 in 2004.

References: Gary R. Freeze, *The Catawbans: Crafters of a North Carolina County* (1995); Sidney Halma, *Catawba County: An Architectural History* (1991).

Elizabeth Bayley

SEE ALSO Catawba College; Lenoir-Rhyne College.

Catawba Indians are often referred to as the Catawba Nation—a term that describes an eighteenth-century amalgamation of different peoples that included the Catawba Indians. Historically, the Indians who came to be called "Catawba" occupied the Catawba River Valley above and below the present-day North Carolina–South Carolina border. They are descended from a large group of independent peoples in the Catawba Valley who spoke a Siouan language.

From the time of the settlement of Charles Towne (modern-day Charleston, S.C.) in 1670, the Esaw, Catawba, and Sugaree tribes experienced the difficult and disruptive consequences of Euro-American frontier expansion. The politics of trade and settlement, and the concern for protection from other Indians (especially the Iroquois), were the major forces that dictated the Catawba's relations with the Carolina and Virginia colonies. Some historians believe that the location of the Catawba on the trading paths was advantageous in that it enabled them to deal with both Virginia and Charles Towne. Also helpful was the Catawba ability to remain generally neutral during the colonial trading wars between 1690 and 1710. This placed the Catawba in the position of having some control over trading access and also served as a motivation to maintain their position. Those who joined the Catawba often did so for protection, not only from the Iroquois but also from the Catawba themselves.

On the whole, the Tuscarora War (1711–13) and the Yamassee War (1715) proved to be devastating for Indians of the Carolinas, including the Catawba. The actions of abusive fur traders and the constant threat of Indian slave traders enraged many of the Indian tribes, especially those living in proximity to colonial settlements. In 1713 the Catawba actively joined with the Yamassee in a concerted attack against the lowcountry colonists in South Carolina. The onset of the so-called Yamassee War again reflected the abuses and politics of the Indian trade between the North Carolina and South Carolina colonies. The Yamassee and their allies were savagely repulsed, with many of the smaller Indian groups disappearing in the aftermath. The Catawbas retreated to their northern towns and again absorbed refugees from the defeated tribes.

The Catawba Nation at the end of the Yamassee War included remnants from as many as 30 other Indian tribes, among them the Esaw, Saura (Cheraw), Sugaree, Waxhaw, Congaree, Shakori, Keyauwee, and Sewee. Despite the continual influx of refugees, diseases and warfare had taken a terrible toll on the Catawba, and their population in 1728 was believed

Catawba Indian–made pan with hand-painted floral decoration, ca. 1880s. Courtesy of the Research Laboratories of Archaeology, UNC-Chapel Hill.

to have been only around 1,400. A smallpox epidemic in 1738 appears to have killed nearly one-half of the nation's population. During the 1750s, the Catawba were embattled by northern war parties that effectively ended the tribe's ability to compete for deerskins. They lost a series of crops to drought and excessively hot summers, and disease continued to take its toll. The Catawba regained some strength during the French and Indian War, during which they sided with the British. However, a second devastating smallpox epidemic struck in 1759, reducing their population to a mere 500 people.

Reeling from the effects of Anglo-American settlement and the epidemic, in 1759 the Catawba gathered together, abandoning their towns around Sugar Creek and establishing a unified town at Twelve Mile Creek. They also negotiated a land deal with South Carolina that established clear title to a reservation 15 miles square. Though they established their reservation, this period marked the beginning of the end of Catawba influence in colonial affairs. When the French and Indian War concluded in 1763, the English colonies had little need for the services of the small and struggling Catawba Nation.

By the time of the American Revolution, the Catawba had adjusted uneasily to their circumstances, surrounded by and living among the Euro-American settlers, who did not consider them a threat. In September 1775, the Catawba pledged their allegiance to the colonies. Catawba warriors fought against the Cherokee and against Lord Charles Cornwallis in North Carolina. When the English captured Charles Towne (1780) and moved north, the Catawbas fled into North Carolina. Upon their return in 1881, they found their village destroyed and plundered. By the end of the eighteenth century, it appeared to most observers that the Catawba people would soon be extinct. By 1826 only 30 families lived on the reservation. Despite constant complaints about unfair settlement within their reservation, the Catawba could get little satisfaction from the South Carolina government.

Both sides agreed to meet at Nation Ford in March 1840. The Catawba agreed to give up their lands in exchange for a government pledge to spend $5,000 to purchase land for them elsewhere. After an abortive attempt to relocate them near the Cherokee in North Carolina, a 630-acre tract was selected on the west bank of the Catawba River within the boundaries of the old reservation; by 1850, 100 Catawbas were living there.

The small enclave of Catawba Indians persevered through poverty and oppression. Some served with the Confederacy in the Civil War. They remained poor and relatively isolated from their neighbors but retained a strong Catawba cultural identity. During the late 1800s, many Catawba converted to Mormonism and moved to southern Colorado, founding Mormon towns such as Fox Creek, La Jara, and Sanford. During this diaspora period, others of the Catawba left South Carolina for Oklahoma and Texas.

The Catawba maintained their identity into the twentieth century, and in 1941 they became a federally recognized tribe. They chose to terminate their tribal status in 1959, however, and received individual landholdings in 1962. Tribal membership that year was slightly more than 600. The federal termination policy proved to have disastrous effects for all tribes that were terminated, and the Catawbas were no exception. They soon realized that termination had led to a weakened cultural identity and a decreased ability to maintain their community. As a result, the Catawba decided to fight their terminated status.

In 1973 the Catawba reorganized a tribal council, and the tribe was recognized by the state of South Carolina. In 1993, following a nearly 20-year court case, the Catawba regained their status as a federally recognized tribe and began the process of establishing a tribal roll. The Catawba Indian Nation tribal council administers a wide variety of programs, including social services and a very active cultural preservation program. In the early 2000s, approximately 2,200 Catawba Indians were living on reservation lands near Rock Hill, S.C.

References: Douglas Summers Brown, *The Catawba Indians: The People of the River* (1966); Charles Hudson, *The Catawba Nation* (1970); James H. Merrell, *The Indians' New World: Catawbas and Their Neighbors from European Contact through the Era of Removal* (1989).

David G. Moore

Catawba River rises in the Blue Ridge Mountains of McDowell County, approximately 20 miles east of Asheville, flowing east-northeast above Hickory until turning southward into the massive Lake Norman Reservoir. It then continues south, flowing west of Charlotte and following the North Carolina–South Carolina border for about 10 miles before entering South Carolina. The river flows east of Rock Hill, through the Fishing Creek Reservoir; once it reaches the Lake Wateree Reservoir (about 30 miles northeast of Columbia, S.C.), the Catawba River becomes the Wateree River. In all, the river is 224 miles long, and its watershed of 3,279 square miles contains nearly 40 municipalities, both large and small.

The flow of the modern Catawba River is blocked by 11 dams, 7 of which are in North Carolina. Its water is used for drinking, electrical power, and recreation. The river also is home to a variety of fish, including smallmouth and largemouth bass, catfish, and carp. Industrialization is the key threat to the health of the Catawba, as some areas are polluted with waste from nearby cities and towns, farms, and manufacturing plants. Private and governmental efforts to protect the Catawba River Basin from further environmental strain are ongoing.

Reference: Tim Mead, "River of Change," *Wildlife in North Carolina* 63 (November 1999).

Elizabeth Bayley

Cathey's Fort was built in McDowell County by William Cathey in 1776. Cathey had purchased land near Turkey Cove at the foot of the mountains and there, where Cove Creek joined the North Fork of the Catawba River, he made his home. The fort was raised to protect Cathey's family and his neighbors from the Cherokee Indians. Until Davidson's Fort was built soon afterward in what is now Old Fort, Cathey's Fort was the farthest western military outpost in North Carolina during the Revolutionary War. Both forts played a part in the western campaigns of the war, including events leading up to the Battle of King's Mountain on 7 Oct. 1780.

References: Pat Alderman, *The Overmountain Men* (1986); Lyman C. Draper, *King's Mountain and Its Heroes: History of the Battle of King's Mountain, October 7th 1780 and the Events Which Led to It* (repr., 1967).

Steve Suther

Cat-Throwing Incident in the colonial Assembly of North Carolina is an example of the disorderly behavior of legislators and of the arbitrary response to personal comments among them. The incident was mentioned in political discussions and personal correspondence at various times after its occurrence, creating more interest than it probably warranted. Charles Cogdell of Carteret County apparently was present merely as an observer at the session of the Assembly meeting in Wilmington in April 1761. James Hasell, president of the council, was speaking in the temporary absence of the governor in favor of raising troops in support of the French and Indian War. A disturbance arose in which Cogdell was described as being "guilty of a contempt and indignity of this House by throwing a Cat upon Mr. Charles Robinson," a member of the House.

Taken into custody by the sergeant at arms, Cogdell was escorted to the bar of the House, where he "Confest that a Cat leaping upon his shoulders from a Stare Case, he on a surprise, threw her from him, which might fall on Mr. Robinson, but with no design or contempt to any of the Members of the House." It was ordered that Cogdell withdraw and remain in custody until further instructed. Later Cogdell was called in and reprimanded by the Speaker of the House. He also asked the pardon of the House in general and of Robinson in particular. After paying the fees imposed, he was discharged.

At the next meeting of the House, member Blake Baker of Halifax County charged that one John Fergus, not a member, was also guilty of contempt and breach of the privileges of the House for saying that he, Baker, was a scoundrel for moving the House against Cogdell. Fergus also said that if he were Cogdell, he would give Robinson "a genteel flogging." Fergus was subsequently brought before the House, and it was revealed that he had, indeed, spoken in support of Cogdell. By way of punishment, Fergus was ordered on his knees to ask forgiveness of the House in general and of the Speaker in particular. Having done so, he was returned to the custody of the sergeant at arms until he paid the fees for his offense.

References: John L. Cheney Jr., *North Carolina Government, 1585–1974* (1975); William L. Saunders, ed., *Colonial Records of North Carolina*, vol. 6 (1888).

William S. Powell

Cattle Drives, made famous in western states such as Texas and Oklahoma during the nineteenth century, were actually undertaken in North Carolina before the end of the colonial period. Tens of thousands of cattle every year were driven along roads and paths from North Carolina to seaports such as Charleston or Norfolk, to Philadelphia, and to New York City by cattle drovers. The cattle were gathered from the forests and meadows into areas called "cow pens," branded, and walked to market.

Lee Plummer Templeton

SEE ALSO Drovers.

Caucasian was one of the state's most prominent reform publications in the late nineteenth and early twentieth centuries. Founded in Clinton in 1884 as the weekly organ of the local Democratic Party, the paper in 1888 acquired as editor Marion Butler, an aggressive young Sampson County schoolteacher and future U.S. senator. Butler, its chief editor for the next 25 years, transformed the *Caucasian* into a mouthpiece for the Farmers' Alliance and one of the dominant voices of the North Carolina People's Party.

In 1893, after the paper's original plant was burned in a suspicious fire, Butler changed its venue to Goldsboro in an effort to expand readership. Following the Populist-Republican Fusion triumph in the election of 1894, he moved the paper again, this time to Raleigh. For a brief period it functioned as a daily, the only Populist paper of its kind ever published in the state. The *Caucasian* was also the only North Carolina paper and one of a few in the United States to promote populism continuously from 1892 until the party collapsed in the election of 1900. Mirroring Butler's political career, the newspaper generally endorsed Republicans after 1904, although it supported Theodore Roosevelt's Progressive Party campaign in 1912 before finally folding as a result of financial problems in early 1913.

At its peak in the mid-1890s, the *Caucasian* had more than 10,000 subscribers from all sections of the state and across the nation, from Maine to California. Between 1888 and 1913 it championed the full panoply of Populist and Progressive causes, including agricultural cooperatives, government ownership of railroads, the subtreasury plan, federal control of the money supply, a federal income tax, more money for education, and the direct election of U.S. senators. Ironically, the *Caucasian* was comparatively liberal on racial issues, opposing the Democrats' disfranchisement legislation of 1898–1900.

Reference: James L. Hunt, "Marion Butler and the Populist Ideal, 1863–1938" (Ph.D. diss., University of Wisconsin, 1990).

James L. Hunt

Caves and Caverns. Nearly 900 caves and caverns are known to exist in North Carolina, although only a small number are accessible to the public. Linville Caverns, which lies deep within Humpback Mountain in McDowell County, is the most popular underground system in the state. The caverns, which stay at a consistent 52 degrees year round, have been developing intricate stalactite and stalagmite formations over the centuries with names like Frozen Waterfall, Natural Bridge, Franciscan Monk, Monster's Hands, and Shepherd. An underground stream running through the caverns is home to blind trout. Small bats cling to the cavern walls.

The first recorded exploration of Linville Caverns was made by H. E. Colton, a native of eastern North Carolina, and his local guide, Dave Franklin, in the mid-1800s. During the Civil

Rock formation in Linville Caverns known as Gilkey's Column. Photograph courtesy of Linville Caverns.

narrow, and explorers must crawl along most of the passage-way. Legendary frontiersman Daniel Boone is said to have hid-den from Indians in the cave, which was also known as "Devil's Den."

Other well-known North Carolina cave and cavern systems include Rock House Cave in Onslow County, Old Blockhouse Cave in Jones County, the Caves in Rumbling Bald Mountain in Rutherford County, Tories Den in Stokes County, and the Wolf's Den in Watauga County.

Reference: Fred Beyer, *North Carolina, the Years before Man: A Geologic History* (1991).

Rich Weidman

Cement, calcium oxide produced by heating carbonate rock or shell and used as a hardening and binding agent when mixed with water and sand, was manufactured from lime-stone, marl, and shell deposits for local use in antebellum North Carolina. On a commercial basis, the Blue Ridge Lime Company of Buncombe County was producing cement as early as 1903. The limestone deposits at Castle Hayne in New Han-over County supplied a series of cement plants in the late twentieth century and early twenty-first centuries. Work at these deposits also provided many interesting fossil speci-mens for collectors.

Reference: William F. Wilson, P. Albert Carpenter III, and Stephen G. Conrad, *North Carolina Geology and Mineral Resources: A Foundation for Progress*, North Carolina Geological Survey Educational Series No. 4 (1976).

Jean H. Seaman

Cemeteries, National and State. North Carolina's four national cemeteries are located in New Bern, Raleigh, Salis-bury, and Wilmington. From the end of the Civil War until the First World War, these cemeteries were often referred to as "Yankee cemeteries" and ignored by the majority of the local residents, who continued to memorialize their Confederate dead. The cemeteries were frequented by local Grand Army of the Republic members on Decoration Day (Memorial Day) and at other times of patriotic celebration.

Prior to the Civil War, the U.S. government buried its mili-tary dead in a designated corner of the garrison at which the death occurred. Soldiers who died far away from their home post were buried near the place of death, often on the side of a lonely road or trail. Sailors were buried at sea. They all, however, received proper military burials. The large number of casualties that occurred during the Civil War focused pub-lic attention on providing a decent burial for those who gave their lives in defense of the Union. Therefore, on 17 July 1862, the 37th Congress of the United States passed the Omnibus Act that established the National Cemetery System. Section 18

War, the caverns served as a refuge for deserters from both Union and Confederate armies. According to local legend, an old man lived in the caverns, making and mending shoes for the soldiers. Linville Caverns opened as a tourist attrac-tion on 1 July 1939. Less than a year later, a flood devastated the site and destroyed many nearby homes and businesses. Linville Caverns eventually reopened, becoming one of the most popular attractions in the northern mountains or "High Country."

Comprised of igneous and metamorphic rocks, Bat Cave in Henderson County is the largest tectonic cave in the state. Mapped passages extend nearly 1.4 miles, and the largest chamber on record is 330 feet long and about 85 feet high. Bat Cave was once the home of a large flock of bats, but most have been driven away or killed by intruders. Rattlesnakes are said to take refuge in the cave during the winter. Privately owned, the cave is protected by the North Carolina Nature Conser-vancy, which restricts visitors to occasional guided tours.

Another well-known site is Boone's Cave, which overlooks the Yadkin River in 110-acre Boone's Cave State Park in David-son County. The cave's entrance is 2 to 3 feet high; the cave it-self is about 80 feet long and varies in height from 4.5 feet near the entrance to less than 1 foot near its farthest point. It is very of the act provided "that the President of the United States shall have power, whenever in his opinion it is expedient, to purchase cemetery grounds and cause them to be securely enclosed, to be used as a national cemetery for the soldiers who shall die in the service of the country."

The first national cemeteries were established to bury the dead from general hospitals located near large troop training camps and to bury the battlefield dead, who had generally been buried where they fell. After the Civil War, a search was conducted of every possible battlefield, isolated churchyard, farm, or railroad siding at which the Union dead might lie. Cemeteries were established near large battlegrounds, hospitals, or prison camps and the Union dead were brought to the nearest cemetery. By 1873 Congress extended the right of burial in a national cemetery to all honorably discharged Union veterans of the Civil War. No Confederate dead were allowed burial there. By the Spanish-American War (1898), burial was available to those who died on foreign soil by disinterring the body and shipping it home to a national cemetery. Eventually burial was offered to veterans of all wars.

The New Bern National Cemetery (1711 National Avenue) was established on 1 Feb. 1867. It contains 7.7 acres of land and became closed to new interments in the early 1990s. New Bern and the surrounding coastal area fell to Union occupiers early in the Civil War. By 1862, Gen. A. E. Burnside was using the area as a base of operations for his blockade of the North Carolina coast. After the war, Union dead were moved to the cemetery from New Bern, Beaufort, Morehead City, Kinston, Hatteras, Roanoke Island, and other places along the coast. Four special monuments have been erected in the cemetery to commemorate servicemen from Connecticut (1898), New Jersey (1905), Massachusetts (1908), and Rhode Island (1909).

The Raleigh National Cemetery (501 Rock Quarry Road) was established in 1865 shortly after Gen. William T. Sherman's army occupied the city. It was situated on the site of Camp Green, a Union military post. Remains of Union veterans were brought there from Averasboro, Smithfield, Bentonville, Goldsboro, Greensboro, Franklin, Henderson, and other places within the state. By 2005 the seven-acre cemetery had more than 5,900 interments of U.S. military personnel, including Medal of Honor recipient William Maud Bryant, who was killed in Vietnam in 1969.

The Salisbury National Cemetery (202 Government Road) was designated a national cemetery in 1865, although Union prisoners of war had been buried there since 1863. Salisbury, the largest town in western North Carolina at the time, had been chosen to house a Confederate prison because of its proximity to a major rail center. Early in the war, an elaborate scheme to exchange prisoners of war was practiced, but by late 1864 the facility housed as many as 10,000 prisoners. That winter, over 5,000 fell victim to starvation and disease. More than 11,000 men who perished at the prison during 1864 and 1865

are buried in 18 trenches, each about 240 feet long. A monument 39 feet tall was erected to their memory in 1876. Following the end of the Civil War, 412 remains were moved to the national cemetery from Lexington, Charlotte, Morganton, and other nearby places. By the 2000s the cemetery covered 11.2 acres of land and had more than 15,800 interments.

The Wilmington National Cemetery (2011 Market Street) covers 5.1 acres of land, which were purchased in 1867 and 1877. Wilmington, the last port open to incoming Confederate supplies, did not fall until February 1865. The heavily armed Fort Fisher, located about 28 nautical miles from the city, protected the harbor and the blockade-runners who frequented the port. Two major battles at Fort Fisher, which occurred in December 1864 and January 1865, left a large number of Union dead. Other deaths occurred during the Federal march from the Fort to Wilmington, during the city's occupation, and among the large numbers of prisoners of war that were sent there during the closing days of the war. Original interments in the cemetery were remains removed from the city of Wilmington, the Lutheran churchyard in Wilmington, Fort Fisher, Fort Johnson, Fayetteville, and Smithville (Southport), and from 12 miles along the Wilmington & Weldon and the Wilmington & Manchester Railroads.

By 1985 two of the four national cemeteries in the state, those at Wilmington and Raleigh, were slated to be closed to burials; those at New Bern and Salisbury were also near capacity. The U.S. Department of Veterans Affairs had decided not to enlarge or establish any more cemeteries, instead establishing a grant program to provide matching funds to states interested in building and operating state veterans' cemeteries.

In 1989 the North Carolina General Assembly appropriated funds to construct two state military cemeteries. The Western Carolina State Veterans Cemetery was opened in Black Mountain in October 1993, and the Coastal Carolina State Veterans Cemetery was opened in Jacksonville in December 1993. In 1995 funds were appropriated to construct the Sandhills State Veterans Cemetery, which was completed and opened in Spring Lake in June 1997. All three cemeteries operate with funds appropriated by the General Assembly to the North Carolina Division of Veterans Affairs for that purpose.

References: Dean W. Holt, *American Military Cemeteries: A Comprehensive Illustrated Guide to the Hallowed Grounds of the United States, Including Cemeteries Overseas* (1992); National Cemetery System, *Interments in VA National Cemeteries* (1997).

William S. Powell
Beverly Tetterton

Central Carolina Bank & Trust Company

Central Carolina Bank & Trust Company traces its roots to a 1903 charter for the Durham Loan and Trust Company, which focused mainly on insurance and real estate. Its first president was John Sprunt Hill, and its directors included such prominent Durham businessmen as George W. Watts, Benjamin N. Duke, and James S. Manning. A banking department was added in 1915. In 1937 the company became the Durham Bank & Trust Company and moved into a new building on Corcoran Street, which it has continued to occupy. The company grew through mergers and acquisitions, changing its name in 1961 to the Central Carolina Bank & Trust Company (CCB).

CCB's growth continued primarily through new acquisitions. In 1993 alone, CCB acquired the ten offices of Greensboro's First Home Federal, Graham Savings Bank, and Mutual Savings Bank and Citizens Savings, both in Lenoir. In 2000 Memphis-based National Commerce Bancorporation (with about 400 offices in nine states) acquired CCB Financial Corporation (with more than 200 offices), combining the institutions into a $15 billion enterprise. Memphis became the headquarters for the combined companies under the banner of National Commerce Bancorporation, and Durham remained CCB operations headquarters.

Reference: Central Carolina Bank & Trust Co., *Our Sixtieth Year of Service to Central Carolina* (1963).

Wiley J. Williams

Central Prison in Raleigh has played a significant role in the North Carolina criminal justice system since the nineteenth century. It was established in 1884, after the North Carolina Constitution of 1868 mandated the creation of a state prison to address concerns about inconsistent and cruel punishment and mounting costs at county jails. The legislature subsequently ratified an act appointing commissioners to buy land and direct construction using convict labor as much as possible. In 1870 a 22-acre site near Raleigh was purchased, and prisoners housed in temporary structures on the property began building the prison. The entire gothic-style complex was completed in 1884. Stone carver W. O. Wolfe, father of novelist Thomas Wolfe, was among the professional artisans hired to help with construction.

In 1968 an inmate riot at Central Prison resulted in the death of 6 inmates and injuries to more than 70 others. The prisoners demanded the formation of a grievance committee that included inmate members and the return of inmates confined to higher-security areas to the general prison population. In the course of the riot, prisoners burned several buildings and assembled a huge cache of weapons.

The original complex has undergone extensive renovation. In the 1940s a prison industries facility was erected to house a state license plate fabrication operation and print shop, and in the 1960s an acute care hospital opened, supplemented by two mental health wings built in the 1970s. A nearly $38 million renovation project of the North Carolina Department of Corrections in the 1980s added additional inmate housing and administrative office space.

Central Prison's infirmary and mental health facility serve the inmate population from across the state, and it is the intake facility for all male felons over the age of 22 with sentences longer than 20 years. The prison also contains the state's execution chamber, deathwatch area, and men's death row. Inmates receive a variety of job assignments in prison industries, the kitchen, or laundry; they also work as barbers, janitors, and clerks. The prison offers substance abuse therapy, GED and college courses, and worship services.

Lisa D. Smith
Additional research provided by Jo White Linn.

Chain Gang. From the Reconstruction era to the late 1950s, the use of prisoners in chain gangs to perform hard labor, especially in building and maintaining public roads, was a common practice in North Carolina and throughout the South. Established by law as a means of punishment in the late nineteenth century, working on a chain gang became a standard sentence for vagrancy and petty larceny, although in North Carolina it was also inflicted on any able-bodied male prisoner serving a sentence of up to ten years.

Living conditions for chain gang convicts were frequently horrific, with sanitation practically nonexistent and diseases and illnesses common. This was especially true if prisoners were housed in temporary living quarters—often railroad boxcars or caged vehicles easily transported from site to site. Prisoners frequently suffered at the hands of brutal overseers. Over time, the image of men, many of them African Americans, shackled with leg irons to prevent their escape came to symbolize the cruelties of imprisonment as well as the injustices associated with racial and economic inequality in the segregated South.

The most extensive use of chain gangs in North Carolina coincided with the rapid growth of highway construction accompanying the Auto Age, from 1900 to 1950. A number of

Chain gang working on a railroad near Asheville, 1915.
Copied from a postcard. Courtesy of NCOA&H.

reforms in the 1920s were intended to end the worst practices of chain gangs. Eventually, the chain gang was operated as a daily road crew that lived in permanent prison facilities nearby. With the advent of more mechanized heavy equipment for road building, the need for labor gangs decreased. After this, contracted paid laborers constructed state roads, and prisoners began working primarily in beautification projects and litter control.

Reference: Jesse F. Steiner and Roy M. Brown, *The North Carolina Chain Gang: A Study of County Convict Road Work* (1927).

Robert E. Ireland

Chambers of Commerce are associations of business people attempting to promote the interests of their members and of local businesses in general. These organizations work to bring new industries to their communities and also provide information about the localities that may help those planning to move there. Chambers often work closely with the state tourism agency, convention and visitors bureaus, and economic development organizations. In 2004 there were approximately 180 chambers of commerce in North Carolina. Some communities have more than one such organization. Charlotte, for example, has the Carolinas Asian-American Chamber, a French American Chamber, and the Charlotte Chamber; Kannapolis has the Cabarrus Regional Chamber as well as a city chamber; and Raleigh has the Carolinas Association of Chambers, the Hispanic Chamber, and the Greater Raleigh Chamber. The North Carolina Citizens for Business and Industry is the state affiliate of the U.S. Chamber of Commerce and the National Association of Manufacturers.

Wiley J. Williams

Champion Paper and Fibre Company was formed in 1935 by the merger of Champion Coated Paper of Hamilton, Ohio, and the Champion Fibre Company of Canton, N.C. The paper company had been organized in 1893 by Peter Thomson, a retired printer. The fiber company had been established in 1906 by Reuben B. Robertson, Thomson's son-in-law, to provide wood pulp for the Ohio paper mill. Robertson's company pioneered several developments: it was the first mill to make white pulp from chestnut wood and one of the first mills to establish a paper chemistry research laboratory (1920s); it installed and operated the world's largest book-paper machine in 1933; and, by 1934, it had become the first mill to make high-quality white pulp from southern pine.

In 1931 Champion Fibre Company sold approximately 90,000 acres of forest land to the government to create the Great Smoky Mountains National Park. The company received $3 million for the land, which enabled it to buy new equipment and sustain profitable operations during the Great Depression. Other factors contributing to profitability were family control of the company, the production of high-quality writing and printing paper at low cost, and the extraction and sale of by-products from pulp and paper manufacture. After World War II, the company expanded its products to include kraft, cardboard, and drink-carton paper and also opened a pulp mill in Brazil.

Falling profits in the 1950s led the Thomson family to relinquish management to Karl Bendetson, who took drastic action to restore profitability. In 1967 Champion merged with U.S. Plywood to make more efficient use of both companies' timber resources. The new company was named U.S. Plywood-Champion Papers, but in 1972 the name was changed to Champion International Corporation. In 1984 Champion acquired St. Regis Corporation, a large producer of newsprint and magazine paper. This gave the company 6.4 million acres of forestland, making it one of the largest private landholders in the nation. The company sold some 2 million acres to raise capital. In the 1990s, Champion maintained extensive wood and paper operations in the United States, Canada, and Brazil. In 1999 Champion sold the Canton mill and other operations to its employees in a $200 million union-led buyout. The resulting company, Blue Ridge Paper Products, is an important producer of envelope papers, writing and printing papers, and packaging products.

References: Champion Paper and Fibre Company, *The Story of the Canton Division, The Champion Paper and Fibre Company, Canton, North Carolina* (1948); Angela Woodward, "Champion International Corporation," *International Directory of Company Histories*, vol. 4 (1995).

John L. Bell

Chancery Court, or the Court of Equity and Conscience, was the highest of several courts—Admiralty, Chancery, Claims, Palatine, and General Court—that originated in the Grand Council of early North Carolina as part of a general grant of juridical powers made by the English Crown to the Lords Proprietors in the Carolina charters of 1663 and 1665. The court was composed of the governor, at least five deputies (including a chancery clerk, originally the provincial clerk of court), and sheriffs of the adjacent counties, who were responsible for enforcing all decrees.

The Chancery Court, which did not possess an independent identity prior to the 1690s, held final jurisdiction over lands, wills, administrations, guardianships, and misconduct in high office. These matters were handled on a day-to-day basis by the clerks and justices of the county courts, but—especially in the case of suspected fraud, a complicated trust, or an accidental death—a caveat, or legal protest, might be issued by one party, and for the sum of 40 shillings and assorted fees the case could be appealed to the Chancery Court.

The Chancery Court functioned alongside superior and inferior courts until the onset of the American Revolution, when the departure of the royal governor and most of his deputies made the court inoperable. An attempt was made in 1778 to revive chancery, but it failed. Four years later superior courts were clearly empowered to "be and act as a Court of Equity for the same district . . . that the court of chancery" had been. In 1806 the Supreme Court of North Carolina was created to deal with equity as part of its duties.

Reference: William S. Price Jr., ed., *North Carolina Higher-Court Records, 1702–1708* (1974).

Louis P. Towles

Charles B. Aycock Birthplace. The Charles B. Aycock Birthplace in northern Wayne County stands as a memorial to a man who from 1901 to 1905 earned the moniker "North Carolina's education governor" because of his many contributions to the state's public school system. Aycock was born near the town of Fremont (then called Nahunta) on 1 Nov. 1859, the youngest of ten children of Benjamin and Serena Aycock. He graduated from the University of North Carolina in Chapel Hill, where he earned a reputation as a skilled orator, in 1880 and opened a law practice in Goldsboro. He soon became a rising star in the Democratic Party and was elected governor in 1900. His ability to rouse people to support education at the local level and his passionate advocacy of universal access to public, though racially segregated, education for all North Carolina children stimulated the construction of approximately 1,100 schools—one for every day he was in office.

Aycock's birthplace became a North Carolina State Historic Site in 1958. In addition to a mid-nineteenth-century farmstead, including a house, kitchen, and other outbuildings furnished with period pieces, the site includes stables and barns, a one-room schoolhouse (ca. 1893) moved to the site to represent the grassroots educational revival pushed by Aycock, and a visitors center. A number of living history demonstrations are offered throughout the year, as well as educational programs aimed particularly at students studying North Carolina history.

References: Edwin Anderson Alderman, "Charles Brantley Aycock: An Appreciation," *NCHR* 1 (July 1924); Richard F. Knapp, ed., *North Carolina's State Historic Sites: A Brief History and Status Report* (1995).

Lisa Coston Hall

Charles Towne on the Cape Fear River was the first overseas effort to colonize the Carolinas after the 1663 Carolina grant from Charles II to the eight Lords Proprietors. As early as 1662, William Hilton had explored the Cape Fear River (briefly called the Charles River) for the Adventurers about Cape Fayre, a group of Puritans from the Massachusetts Bay Colony. Following Hilton's favorable report, the Puritans sent a colonizing expedition early in 1663 that remained only a short time.

Meanwhile on Barbados, which was already plagued by overcrowding, the Corporation of Barbadian Adventurers petitioned the Lords Proprietors for permission to settle in Carolina. Hilton, having shifted his base to the Caribbean colony, set forth again in August 1663 for the Carolina coast. Although there was greater interest in the more southerly Port Royal Sound area, on 29 May 1664 John Vassall landed a colony of Barbadians and possibly a few New Englanders on the Cape Fear, founding Charles Towne. The settlement was included in the newly formed Clarendon County, with Sir John Yeamans of Barbados as governor and Vassall as deputy governor. The two earliest governmental documents for Carolina, the Declaration and Proposals of 1663 and the Concessions and Agreement of 1665, were developed essentially for the promotion and governance of Charles Towne.

A fortified compound was established on the east side of the river just upstream from the mouth of Old Town Creek. The colony grew rapidly, and by 1666 it was described as containing some 800 inhabitants scattered up and down the river on individual homesteads, producing agricultural products for export primarily to Barbados. With increased interest for settling further south, Charles Towne became a base for exploratory voyages of the southern coast.

In the fall of 1665, Sir John Yeamans arrived in the settlement en route to a second colony in the Port Royal region, but his plans foundered in an untimely shipwreck at Cape Fear in which most of the public supplies were lost. England's loss of interest and lack of support, resulting from problems at home and a war with the Dutch, coupled with internal dissension, prompted most of the settlers to drift away. By the fall of 1667 Vassall wrote that the colony had been abandoned. In spite of the failure, many Barbadians involved in the Cape Fear colony became the driving force behind the founding of the second Charles Towne in southern Carolina in 1670 (modern-day Charleston, S.C.). Charles Towne on the Cape Fear is significant as the first Proprietary colonizing experience, as the first overseas expansion of the Caribbean to the mainland, and as the predecessor of the second and longer-lived Charles Towne.

References: Lawrence Lee, *The Lower Cape Fear in Colonial Days* (1965); Alexander S. Salley Jr., ed., *Narratives of Early Carolina* (1911).

Lindley S. Butler

Charlotte was a small country crossroads whose dramatic growth into a major city reflects the emergence of Piedmont North Carolina as a leading area of commercial development in the United States. By the mid-eighteenth century, newly arrived European immigrants, mostly German and Scotch-Irish, had traveled the Great Wagon Road south from Philadelphia into the Carolina backcountry and established small communities along the busy thoroughfare that was bringing thousands of settlers to the interior of the southern colonies. Mecklenburg County was created in 1762 to accommodate these new settlements, and a county seat was to be established on a tract donated by George Augustus Selwyn in an attempt to stimulate immigration to his vast holdings. Enterprising individuals catering to traffic on the Great Wagon Road had already sparsely settled this area, and they named their village after the wife of King George III. Charlotte received its town charter in 1768 and subsequently became the county seat, mainly through the efforts of local citizens who hastily erected a pillared courthouse and other necessary public offices.

During the Revolutionary War, Charlotte acquired a reputation as a Patriot stronghold. The town revealed its strategic importance to the British when it was occupied by Lord Charles Cornwallis in 1780. The unfriendly reception accorded the general and his troops, highlighted by the so-called Battle of Charlotte, caused Cornwallis to withdraw and dismiss the place as a "hornet's nest."

After the war, North Carolina's hinterland began to flourish. The discovery of gold nearby led to increased settlement in the Charlotte area. Mining activity, including several pits dug almost in the center of town, fueled Charlotte's growth, and proximity to the mines led to the establishment of a branch of the national mint in Charlotte in 1837. Concurrently, several banks were opened in the town, which by the end of the antebellum era was becoming the economic heart of the Carolina backcountry.

In the 1850s Charlotte became the southern terminus of the North Carolina Railroad, anchoring one end of the "urban crescent" of commercial and manufacturing activity that would later arc across the middle of the state. During the Civil War, Charlotte's access to the railroad allowed it to host a concentration of important Confederate military installations. Confederate president Jefferson Davis held his last formal cabinet meeting in Charlotte and there received the news of Abraham Lincoln's assassination. Like most other North Carolina cities, Charlotte emerged from the war with its infrastructure largely intact, ready for renewed growth.

In the postwar years, Charlotte became one of the leading cities of the New South. North Carolina's booming textile industry, powered by the Piedmont's swift-flowing rivers and streams, intensified economic activity throughout the area, and Charlotte experienced rapid development. Prosperity and a growing population brought cultural advances to the city and led to the establishment of important educational and medical facilities or the growth of existing institutions, such as Queen's College, which had been founded in 1771. By the 1870s Charlotte, along with Greensboro, pioneered the development of public graded schools in North Carolina. The city's racial tolerance encouraged the establishment of several colleges and institutions for African Americans, notably the Biddle Institute, later renamed Johnson C. Smith University.

In the twentieth century, Charlotte continued to expand and modernize, mirroring the dramatic rise of central North Carolina as one of the nation's most prosperous economic districts. Numerous industries have relocated to Charlotte to take advantage of the city's position as a major transportation hub. It is also home to some of the nation's largest banking institutions, most notably the financial giant, Bank of America. In the early 2000s, Charlotte continued its heritage of educational and cultural advancement. The University of North Carolina at Charlotte, initially founded as Charlotte College, was one of the fastest-growing campuses in the state's university system. In 1936 the old federal mint facility was transformed into the Mint Museum of Art, and the Levine Museum of the New South was incorporated in 1991. Charlotte has also become a center for professional sports, with deep roots in auto racing (in 2006 the city was chosen as the site of the NASCAR Hall of Fame) and new facilities built to accommodate the city's minor league baseball team, NBA team, and NFL franchise. Charlotte is North Carolina's largest city, with a population topping 600,000 in 2005.

References: LeGette Blythe and Charles Raven Brockmann, *Hornet's Nest: The Story of Charlotte and Mecklenburg County* (1961); Mary Norton Katt, *Charlotte: Spirit of the New South* (1980).

David L. Cockrell

SEE ALSO Banking; Bank of America; Charlotte, Battle of; Levine Museum of the New South; Queens University of Charlotte; University of North Carolina at Charlotte.

Charlotte, Battle of. On 26 Sept. 1780 the Revolutionary War battle at Charlotte pitted the British troops of Lord Charles Cornwallis against a greatly outnumbered but surprisingly combative force of North Carolina Patriots. The militia in western North Carolina was commanded by Gen. William Lee Davidson. On encountering the British army, Davidson ordered most of his small force to retreat, sending a detachment under Col. William R. Davie to delay Cornwallis at Charlotte. Davie later wrote that his force of 150 "mounted Infantry and dragoons" was joined by 14 volunteers under Capt. Joseph Graham. (Graham later gave the number of his command as 50.)

Charlotte at that time, as later described by Davie, was a town of "about twenty houses, built on two streets, which cross each other at right angles, at the intersection of which stands the court-house." This is the present intersection of Trade and Tryon Streets, a spot shaded by Charlotte's tallest skyscrapers. The wooden courthouse stood on eight 10-foot-high brick pillars, which were connected by a 3½-foot-high stone wall. The partially enclosed ground floor of the courthouse served as a marketplace. Davie placed "one company" under the courthouse and two more companies 80 yards ahead, under the cover of houses and gardens.

The British cavalry formed a line of battle about 300 yards from Davie's men and charged. As the infamous Col. Banastre Tarleton was "indisposed" from the previous night's march, his men were led by Maj. George Hanger. The Americans held their fire until Hanger's cavalrymen were 60 yards away. The rebel musket fire stunned the British, and Hanger's men reeled back in confusion. Pressure from the British infantry forced Davidson to pull his outlying men into line with the courthouse, but they repelled two more cavalry charges. Despite the failure of the cavalry, the steadier British light infantry pressed the American flanks until Davie began withdrawing his men. Davie's troops moved back stubbornly, covering each other and drawing away in good order.

Graham's men served as the rear guard and skirmished with the British units that pursued them. Four miles from Charlotte, near Sugar Creek Church, the British charged and scattered the rear guard. Graham was critically wounded and Lt. George Locke was killed. After this clash, the British advance force turned back to join the main body of troops at Charlotte. Davie continued to withdraw until his force crossed the Rocky River, 16 miles from Charlotte and 4 miles in front of Davidson's army.

Patriot casualties at Charlotte were given by Davie as "Lt. Locke and 4 privates killed [and] Major Graham and five privates wounded." Davie reported the British losses as "twelve non-commissioned officers killed and wounded; Major Hanger and Captains Campbell and McDonald wounded, with about thirty privates." Two dead British soldiers were reported to have been found near Sugar Creek Church.

The Battle of Charlotte itself was not decisive, but the stubborn resistance of the outnumbered Americans symbolized the resolve of the people of Mecklenburg County and led to the region receiving a famous new nickname. Lord Cornwallis, after 16 humiliating days in the Charlotte area, was heard to say as he prepared to depart: "Let's get out of here; this place is a damned hornet's nest." So honored were Charlotteans with the epithet given to their city by Cornwallis that they adopted it for perpetuity. The official city seal features a hornet's nest, and many local organizations and clubs carry the name. Hornet's Nest Park is located on Beatties Ford Road not far from the battle site, which is marked by a monument and a self-guiding trail.

References: Daniel W. Barefoot, *Touring North Carolina's Revolutionary War Sites* (1998); Hugh F. Rankin, *North Carolina in the American Revolution* (1959); Phillips Russell, *North Carolina in the Revolutionary War* (1965).

David A. Norris
Daniel W. Barefoot

Charlotte Country Day School,

the oldest independent school in Mecklenburg County, was founded in 1941. The school began with 18 students in the preschool through sixth grades and met in the home of Stuart Cramer. Over the next several years, classes were added through the ninth grade, and enrollment grew steadily to 126 students in 1951. To accommodate growth, the school moved several times during its early years before settling on its Sardis Road campus from 1945 to 1960.

From 1955 to 1969 headmaster David L. Howe led Country Day through important changes. In 1960 the school moved to a new 30-acre campus, later expanded to 60 acres, on Carmel Road. The successive additions of the tenth, eleventh, and twelfth grades between 1960 and 1962 completed the upper school. In 1969 the school included eight administrative staff members, 52 faculty members, and 557 students.

Charlotte Country Day experienced tremendous growth pressures in the 1970s as it was flooded with "white flight" applications in the wake of the *Swann v. Charlotte-Mecklenburg Board of Education* decision (1971), which imposed busing to achieve integration in the public schools of Mecklenburg County. In 1980 Country Day merged with Carmel Academy, one of three independent schools established in the county after the *Swann* decision.

In the early 2000s enrollment figures showed approximately 1,600 students in grades K–12 attending classes on two campuses. With the vast majority of its graduates attending college, Charlotte Country Day possesses a reputation for academic rigor and excellence. Its alumni have been notably successful in public life and particularly influential in Charlotte and Mecklenburg County.

Reference: Julia Moody Britt, *Charlotte Country Day School: The First Fifty Years* (1991).

Richard Rankin

Charlotte Hawkins Brown Museum

is located in eastern Guilford County at the site of the former Palmer Memorial Institute, which Brown founded in 1901 as a private school for black children. Brown was born in Henderson in 1883 but grew up in Cambridge, Mass., and graduated from a public high school there. She returned to North Carolina in 1901 to teach in a church school at Sedalia under the American Missionary Association. The school closed after one year, but in 1902, after obtaining financial support from friends in New England, Brown opened the Palmer Memorial Institute, naming it after the president of Wellesley College, Alice Freeman Palmer, who had befriended her back home. It began in a log house, but by 1908 the school owned three substantial buildings and 200 acres of land. Later it became a preparatory school for middle- and upper-class blacks.

An excellent teacher and fund-raiser, Brown received sup-

Early faculty members at Palmer Memorial Institute. Charlotte Hawkins Brown is in the center on the back row. Courtesy of NCOA&H.

port from blacks and whites in both the South and the North. New England businessman and philanthropist Galen L. Stone and his family were by far the most generous supporters of her school. As the years passed, Brown suffered age-related problems but retained ultimate power as the school's financial officer for several years after giving up the presidency that she had held for 50 years. She died on 11 Jan. 1961, the recipient of six honorary degrees.

Described as "one of the most significant experiments in Negro education in the country," Palmer Institute fell victim to the desegregation of education in North Carolina. The school lost the generosity of previous contributors, who were uninterested in supporting what undoubtedly would remain a segregated school, and a new generation of African Americans saw little need for the school's continued operation. Thus, both the white and the black communities began to abandon Palmer for other interests and schools.

After the Alice Freeman Palmer Building burned to an empty shell in February 1971, questions about the school's future became acute. Although plans for the new year were complete, the trustees abruptly closed the institute in the summer of 1971. The property was ceded to Bennett College, which sold a portion of it to the Chicago-based American Muslim Mission in 1973. The Muslim Mission intended to use it as a training center for missionaries, but by 1980 internal difficulties within the mission ended long-term plans for the site. A few years later a group of alumni and friends of Palmer Memorial Institute made plans to preserve it as a memorial to Charlotte Hawkins Brown. They began to raise money and to seek state funding to purchase the buildings and grounds.

In 1983 the General Assembly appropriated funds for the purchase of the site and its 14 buildings. Four years later, the Charlotte Hawkins Brown Museum was designated a North Carolina State Historic Site; in 2006 it remained the only state historic site dedicated specifically to the achievements of an African American and a woman. Five of the site's buildings are official projects of Save America's Treasures, a public-private partnership dedicated to the preservation of the country's irreplaceable cultural and historic resources.

References: Richard F. Knapp, ed., *North Carolina's State Historic Sites: A Brief History and Status Report* (1995); Constance H. Marteena, *The Lengthening Shadow of a Woman: A Biography of Charlotte Hawkins Brown* (1977); Sandra N. Smith and Earle H. West, "Charlotte Hawkins Brown," *Journal of Negro Education* 51 (Summer 1982); Charles W. Wadelington and Richard F. Knapp, *Charlotte Hawkins Brown and Palmer Memorial Institute: What One Young African American Woman Could Do* (1997).

Alexander R. Stoesen

Charlotte Navy Yard. Charlotte became one of the Confederate navy's most important manufacturing centers during the Civil War. The incongruity of a landlocked city housing a navy yard is explained by its location in North Carolina, where it was relatively safe from potential Federal activity. The city was also an important rail center that facilitated movement of matériel throughout the South.

In May 1862 the Confederacy established a navy yard in Charlotte to replace the one lost at Norfolk, Va. Early that year, fearing that it might be forced to abandon the facility, Confederate secretary of the navy Stephen Mallory quietly instructed the commander at Norfolk to begin planning for the relocation of machine tools and equipment that were not required for current projects. Charlotte was selected for the new site because of its rail connections with coastal cities. The government in Richmond purchased property and immediately began planning to establish a navy yard in the city. In early May the first equipment, including lathes, planers, and a small steam hammer, was moved to the new facility.

The importance of the new yard can hardly be overestimated. It manufactured nearly all of the propellers, shafts, and anchors for the Confederate navy. Additionally, although power plants complete with boilers and engines were not made there, many of the parts for them were. The Charlotte Navy Yard was the only Confederate facility capable of such heavy forging. It also produced ordnance for vessels, including gun carriages. In June 1863 Charlotte became responsible for casting all of the shot and shell for the vessels in Charleston and Savannah. Further, the yard was capable of forging specialized wrought-iron shot for use against Union ironclads. The Charlotte Navy Yard remained in operation until the final flight of the Confederate government in April 1865.

References: Ralph W. Donnelly, "The Charlotte, North Carolina, Navy Yard, C.S.N.," *Civil War History*, vol. 5 (1959); William N. Still Jr., *Confederate Shipbuilding* (1987).

Dan Blair

Charlotte Observer, founded in 1869, has the largest circulation of any newspaper in North Carolina. A consistent advocate of economic progress in Charlotte and the surrounding region, the paper, in the mid-twentieth century, also became a strong voice for racial and gender equality in the South.

At the close of the Civil War, four Confederate veterans and now-unemployed printers moved to Charlotte from nearby towns and began doing business as Smith, Watson & Company. Their firm first issued the *Observer* on 25 Jan. 1869. Unlike many other newspapers, this publication was politically independent and tended to avoid the controversies of the day. Nevertheless, the paper clearly disapproved of Reconstruction, the policies of Reconstruction governor William W. Holden, and the Fourteenth and Fifteenth Amendments. From the beginning, the *Observer* linked its future to that of Charlotte and the Piedmont Carolinas.

In September 1872 James H. Smith, the last of the four founding printers to retain an interest in the *Observer*, sold the paper to Johnstone Jones, a lawyer and newspaper publisher. Jones's progressive editorials promoted industry and commerce, public schools, and public improvements. They envisioned a reviving South, a conception soon embraced in the New South creed pioneered by Henry W. Grady's *Atlanta Constitution* and Henry Watterson's *Louisville Courier-Journal*. Jones also introduced telegraphic news, replaced a hand press with a rotary press, and, by hiring Joseph P. Caldwell as city editor in 1872, greatly enhanced local and regional news coverage.

In the depths of the depression caused by the panic of 1873, the *Observer* was sold in the spring of 1874 to Col. Charles R. Jones and Fred H. Pendleton. Restless under the stand-pat policies of state Democrats, Jones editorially applauded the rise of independent journals across the country and the advantage they enjoyed over party newspapers. He continued to openly fight against Democratic leadership and early in 1886 announced his candidacy for Congress as an Independent. Acting on the advice of Democratic leaders, William S. Hemby founded the *Charlotte Chronicle* (March 1886) as an evening alternative to the morning *Observer*. Hemby's paper soon switched to a morning daily in order to compete directly against Jones and the *Observer*. The strategy worked, and the *Observer* ceased publication on 1 Aug. 1887.

When the *Chronicle*'s fortunes began to decline, the paper was sold (in January 1892) to Joseph Caldwell, the former city editor of the old *Observer*, and Daniel A. Tompkins, an engineer, financier, and promoter. On 13 Mar. 1892 the *Chronicle* appeared without warning as the *Charlotte Daily Observer*. With Caldwell as editor and Tompkins as publisher, the *Observer* underwent an expansion that propelled it from country reporting to modern journalism. The two men recruited a staff of fine writers and reporters; installed the latest news-gathering and printing equipment; broadened coverage to include books, music, drama, finance, architecture, and medicine; and made their paper a vigorous advocate of education and industrialism. They promoted manufacturing but opposed labor unions, urged a diverse agriculture but rejected the agrarian Populists (who supported William Jennings Bryan for president), and befriended individual blacks but endorsed white supremacy laws that denied blacks the right to vote and ultimately produced a harsh segregation. Caldwell, as editor, maintained extremely high editorial standards, and by 1904 the *Observer* was considered the state's best newspaper.

In June 1912, a few months after Caldwell's death, Wade Harris was appointed the paper's editor, a position he held until his own death in 1935. His editorials, however, were never as forceful as Caldwell's; often they were mere news summaries with scant opinion. After Tompkins died in October 1914, the paper was briefly owned by two bankers, George Stephens and Word H. Wood, founders of the American Trust Company. They sold the *Observer* in 1916 to Curtis B. Johnson, owner of the *Knoxville Sentinel* and widely admired as a conservative southern publisher. (That year, "Daily" was also dropped from the paper's name.) Under Johnson, the *Charlotte Observer* became the largest newspaper in the Carolinas, with circulation rising from nearly 13,000 daily (over 16,000 on Sundays) in 1916 to about 134,000 at the time of the publisher's death on 6 Oct. 1950. Johnson made these gains by modernizing the paper's plant, expanding its delivery system (and consequently enhancing Charlotte's reputation as a distribution center), and improving its news coverage and features. His efforts to make the *Observer* the newspaper of record in the Carolinas earned it the appellation "the *New York Times* of the South."

Johnson's widow then assumed active leadership of the *Observer*. At her urging, it became one of a handful of southern newspapers to react positively to the U.S. Supreme Court's landmark decision, *Brown v. Board of Education of Topeka*, on 17 May 1954. The paper's call for compliance was another step in its long, slow departure from the South's oppression of blacks, and it helped to strengthen the climate for moderation in Charlotte.

In 1955 the *Observer* was bought by Knight Newspapers, Inc. (which became Knight-Ridder Newspapers in 1974), for $7.5 million, becoming one of several North Carolina papers owned by large conglomerates. From 1955 to 1990 the *Observer* supplied editorial and managerial talent to many other newspapers across the country, including chief executive officers for Knight-Ridder and McClatchy chains; publishers in Philadelphia, Akron, Providence, Winston-Salem, and Anderson, S.C.; and editors in Wichita, Miami, Philadelphia, and other cities.

The *Charlotte Observer*, through its constant promotion, has helped make Charlotte a business capital and the largest city in the Carolinas. The paper has also received high praise from the journalism community, receiving four Pulitzer Prizes —two for meritorious public service (its 1981 series on brown lung disease, which afflicted textile workers in the Charlotte area, and its 1988 coverage of the scandal surrounding the "Praise the Lord" ministry of Jim and Tammy Bakker). In the early 2000s the *Observer* had a daily circulation of about 235,500 (291,000 on Sundays), 1,200 employees, 5 regional bureaus in North Carolina (Hickory, Gastonia, Concord, Monroe, and Statesville), a regional bureau in York, S.C., and offices in Raleigh, Columbia, S.C., and Washington, D.C.

Reference: Jack Claiborne, *The Charlotte Observer: Its Time and Place, 1869–1986* (1986).

Wiley J. Williams

Charlotte Three was the term applied by journalists in the 1970s to James Grant, T. J. Reddy, and Charles Parker, African American civil rights activists who were arrested and convicted in 1972 as political terrorists on charges of barn burning by federal agents of the Alcohol, Tobacco, and Firearms division of the U.S. Treasury Department. Their case was representative of racial unrest that marked Mecklenburg County at the time. The three men were placed in the custody of North Carolina because the barn was located near Charlotte. The case dragged on for several years, and the men were sentenced to 25, 20, and 10 years, respectively; additional men were charged with participating in the unrest associated with this and related incidents. Two years after the trial, two witnesses revealed that the federal government had paid them $4,000 each as a "relocation fee" following their testimony against the accused. After numerous appeals and hearings, the sentences of the Charlotte Three were adjusted, and in time the prisoners were placed on work release or paroled.

References: A. L. May, "Hunt Reduces Jail Sentences for Charlotte Three," *Raleigh News and Observer*, 21 July 1979; J. Christopher Schutz, "The Burning of America: Race, Radicalism, and the 'Charlotte Three' Trial in 1970s North Carolina," NCHR 76 (January 1999).

William S. Powell

Chatham County, located in the Piedmont region of North Carolina, was formed from Orange County in 1771 in response to troubles stemming from the War of the Regulation. The county was named for William Pitt, earl of Chatham, who defended American rights in the British Parliament. Early inhabitants of Chatham County included Iroquoian and Siouan Indians, who were followed by Scottish, English, and German settlers. The county seat is Pittsboro—also named for William Pitt—which was incorporated in 1778 as Chatham but renamed Pittsboro in 1787. Other communities in Chatham County include Goldston, Siler City, Bennett, Brickhaven, Silk

Hope, Moncure, Bynum, and Mount Vernon Springs. Physical features of the county include B. Everett Jordan Lake, a sprawling reservoir popular as a recreation area, and the Cape Fear, Deep, Haw, Rocky, and New Hope Rivers.

On the western edge of the booming Triangle area that includes Raleigh, Durham, Chapel Hill and environs, Chatham County is growing at a rapid rate. Nonetheless it still raises many agricultural products, including swine, tobacco, corn, soybeans, hay, poultry, and beef cattle. Manufactured products from the county include textiles, yarns, fabrics, furniture, and lumber. Sandstone, shale, coal, and iron are mined in the county.

Chatham County's historic landmarks include the Green Womack House (ca. 1819), the Pittsboro Masonic Lodge (ca. 1840), and the London Cottage (1861). The Devil's Tramping Ground, a mysterious and legendary 40-foot circular path in which no vegetation will grow, is located in Chatham County near Siler City. The Carnivore Preservation Trust is a sanctuary for unique endangered species located in Pittsboro and open to the public by appointment. The county's cultural institutions include the Chatham Theatre Guild and the Siler City Arts Council. Popular annual events and festivals include the Silk Hope Old Fashion Farm Days, Deep River Crescent Celebration, and Siler City Chicken Festival. In 2004 the population of Chatham County was estimated to be 55,000.

Jay Mazzocchi

SEE ALSO Devil's Tramping Ground.

Chatham Manufacturing Company, one of North Carolina's oldest textile firms, was established in the late 1860s, when Alexander Chatham and Thomas L. Gwyn, owners of a store and grain mill in Elkin, began to process local wool into yarn and cloth. By the time Chatham and Gwyn formed a partnership in 1877, their Elkin Mills produced woolen blankets, flannels, jeans, and knitting yarns. After a railroad line was completed to Elkin in 1890, the operation was enlarged and reorganized. Alexander Chatham retired from the business, Gwyn sold his interest to the Chatham family, and Hugh Gwyn Chatham, Alexander's son, became president. The new operation was incorporated as Chatham Manufacturing Company in 1894. Modern buildings with new machinery were built in the 1890s. The company's famous products included woollen "Chatham Blankets," which were sold in all parts of the United States.

In 1907 a second factory was built in Winston-Salem. Sales offices were established in large urban centers throughout the United States. Large amounts of blankets and uniform cloth were produced for American armies in World Wars I and II. In 1936 Chatham Manufacturing abandoned its primary reliance on blanket sales and began to produce upholstery material for automobiles. In 1960 the company extended its upholstery business to include furniture fabrics. After World War II, a bitter fight took place over the unionization of Chatham's employees. In 1965 Chatham workers in Elkin chose to be represented by the Textile Workers Union of America.

In the late 1980s, Chatham Manufacturing owned plants in Elkin, Eden, and Charlotte. About two-thirds of the company's more than $125 million in sales in 1987 derived from upholstery products, while most of the rest of the company's revenues were from the sale of bedding products, including blankets. A majority of the company's stock was still owned by descendants of Alexander Chatham. However, in 1988, Northern Feather, Ltd., a Danish textile maker, outbid family members and senior management for control of Chatham Manufacturing and purchased the blanket-maker for more than $92 million. This ended the company's more than 110 years of North Carolina ownership. Northern Feather went bankrupt within four years, however, and Chatham Manufacturing was sold to CMI Industries of Columbia, S.C., in 1992. In 2000 Atlanta-based Interface, Inc., acquired the firm from CMI Industries, and, as Chatham, Inc., it became part of the Interface Fabrics Group, with a focus on upholstery for commercial and residential uses.

Reference: "Mr. Chatham's Mill," *Rohn & Haas Reporter* 17 (November–December 1959).

James L. Hunt

Chautauqua was an adult educational program established in 1874 by leaders of the Methodist Episcopal church on the shores of Lake Chautauqua, N.Y. From this base, programs spread to many parts of the nation where, for a week or so in the summer, benches and large tents were erected for afternoon and evening programs. Initially formed to train Sunday school teachers, the Chautauqua program quickly expanded its objective and attracted a wide following to its correspondence and university extension courses and "great books" discussion programs. By the early years of the twentieth century

Tent of the Redpath Chautauqua at Goldsboro, ca. 1915. NCC.

and into the 1920s, these programs were being presented in many North Carolina communities. People gathered in a resort setting for classes, lectures, musical programs, and other forms of instruction and entertainment. Prominent lecturers, preachers with national reputations, and noted musicians, actors, and magicians appeared throughout the state. The Chautauqua program was often the entertainment and intellectual highlight of the year for many North Carolinians who had little disposable income to spend on such pursuits.

The term "Chautauqua" actually originated in North Carolina. It had been the name of the Tuscarora Indian village where the town of New Bern arose following the arrival of Swiss settlers in 1710. Tuscaroras who migrated to New York soon afterward took the name with them.

References: Lida Tunstall Rodman, "The Name Chautauqua of North Carolina Origin," *Daughters of the American Revolution Magazine* 47 (July 1915); John H. Vincent, *The Chautauqua Movement* (1886).

William S. Powell

Cheerwine. In 1913 L. D. Peeler and several other investors in Salisbury purchased stock in the Kentucky-based Mint-Cola Bottling Company, and Peeler started the local bottling franchise of the company. When the parent company went bankrupt in 1917, the Salisbury investors purchased their local branch and renamed it the Carolina Beverage Corporation. In the same year, in response to a sugar shortage during World War I, Peeler sought ways to make a cola drink with less sugar. After experimenting with different formulas, he added wild cherry flavoring to a cola to create Cheerwine. The name comes from the drink's cherry flavor and burgundy wine color.

The exact formula for Cheerwine has never been revealed, and the company that produces it is still owned and operated by Peeler descendants. The popularity of the new drink was so great that the bottling company changed its name in 1924 to the Piedmont Cheerwine Bottling Company. For many years the drink was available only in western North Carolina, where it is still enormously popular, but in 1981 the company began to expand beyond its traditional market into neighboring states. In January 2003 Cheerwine became available in Europe for the first time through a licensing agreement with a local bottling company in Norway.

Eileen McGrath

Cherohala Skyway. SEE Highways.

Cherokee Botanical Garden, first opened to the public in May 1953, adjoins Oconaluftee Indian Village on the Cherokee Indian Reservation (Qualla Boundary) in western North Carolina. The garden is a project of the nonprofit Cherokee Historical Association, incorporated in 1948 to research and publicize the history and traditions of the Cherokee. Its other endeavors include *Unto These Hills*, an outdoor drama tracing Cherokee history produced each summer since 1950 in the Mountainside Theater. The association also owns the Museum of the Cherokee Indian, believed to house the most complete collection of Cherokee artifacts in existence. These artifacts, rescued from burial grounds and ancient campsites, date back some 10,000 years.

Along the half-mile nature trail of the Cherokee Botanical Garden are many of the flora of the Smoky Mountains, including rhododendrons, mountain laurel, bloodroot, jewel weed, squirrel corn, Dutchman's breeches, hepatica, wild white hydrangeas, asters, pink flowering raspberry, sunflowers, goldenrods, shad-bush, sassafras, tulip trees, and azaleas. Huckleberry, mountain ash, various sumacs, vegetables (Indian corn, pole beans, turnips, and others), zinnias, marigolds, and other plant varieties are included in the 150 species represented. Each is identified by its botanical and common names and grows in a spot that is well suited to its particular needs; many of the plants are growing where they were before the garden's inception. Care has been taken to disturb the natural growth as little as possible and to put new species and replacements in their natural habitats. Paths lead up and around mossy rocks, through which water trickles slowly downward.

References: Aubry Jennings, "Cherokee Indian Garden," *The State* 30 (August 1962); Marguerite Schumann, *Tar Heel Sights* (1983); Ginny Turner, ed., *North Carolina Traveler* (4th ed., 1997).

Wiley J. Williams

Cherokee Clay. Georgia potter Andrew Duche first made porcelain in 1739 after discovering the essential ingredients in porcelain, kaolin and petunze, in the clay found in Cherokee Indian country near present-day Franklin. English potter Josiah Wedgwood learned of the so-called Cherokee clay and requested a sample in 1766. Unsuccessful in his request, Wedgwood commissioned Thomas Griffiths to obtain some of the clay. Griffiths brought five tons of Cherokee clay to London in April 1768. Wedgwood took out a patent for encaustic ornamentation using the clay in 1769. Wedgwood's supply lasted at least until 1783, when he wrote that Cherokee clay was the basis for the new biscuit porcelain (jasper) he was making. The discovery of suitable clay in Cornwall, England, ended the demand for more Cherokee clay. However, in the summer of 1985, the Wedgwood firm in England received additional Cherokee clay from western North Carolina to cast limited edition bowls and plates commemorating the 400th anniversary of English colonization efforts on Roanoke Island.

References: William L. Anderson, "Cherokee Clay, from Duche to Wedgwood: The Journal of Thomas Griffiths, 1767–1768," NCHR 63 (October 1986); Ann Finer and George Savage, eds., *The Selected Letters of Josiah Wedgwood* (1965).

William L. Anderson

Cherokee County, located in the Mountain region of North Carolina and partially bordering the states of Tennessee and Georgia, is the state's westernmost county. It was formed in 1839 from Macon County and named for the Cherokee Indians who inhabited its lands before European settlement by Scotch-Irish, English, and German immigrants. Murphy, the county seat, was incorporated in 1851 and named for Archibald D. Murphey, one of North Carolina's most progressive political leaders, an advocate for internal improvements and other reform initiatives. Cherokee County's land includes large portions of the Nantahala National Forest, punctuated by the centrally located and enormous reservoir, Lake Hiwassee. This body of water was created by a Tennessee Valley Authority project, which constructed Hiwassee Dam between 1936 and 1940.

Cherokee County farms produce grains, tobacco, corn, soybeans, hay, swine, beef and dairy cattle, and chickens. Manufactured products include apparel, truck brakes, furniture, fertilizers, and textiles.

Cherokee County attractions include the Fields of the Wood, the assembly grounds for the Church of God of Prophecy featuring the world's largest Ten Commandments, written in concrete letters on the side of a mountain. Cultural institutions include the Cherokee County Museum and Cherokee County Arts and Historical Council. The county hosts a number of festivals and annual events, such as the Nation's Oldest Wagon Train on the Fourth of July, the Folk School Fall Festival, and Great Smoky National Railway excursion trips. Cherokee County had an estimated population of 25,600 in 2004.

References: Alice D. White and Nell A. White, *Heritage of Cherokee County, North Carolina* (2 vols., 1987); Michael Ann Williams, *Marble and Log: The History and Architecture of Cherokee County* (1984).

Jay Mazzocchi

Cherokee Indians once occupied an area encompassing approximately 140,000 square miles that became parts of North Carolina, Tennessee, South Carolina, Georgia, and Alabama. The Cherokee thrived in North Carolina well into the late eighteenth century, but as Euro-American settlers steadily moved into and near Cherokee lands, sharp conflicts arose between Cherokees and whites and between Cherokees themselves, as leaders with competing claims to speak for the tribe secured treaties and formed other agreements with white settlers that were not acknowledged by all Cherokee people. In 1838–39, the U.S. government forcibly removed the Cherokee from their lands in North Carolina, leading them on the

Goingback Chiltoskey carving animal figures from wood, 1967. NCC.

infamous Trail of Tears to the Indian Territory (present-day Oklahoma). A small number of Cherokee people successfully resisted removal, however, by claiming North Carolina citizenship and by maintaining the right to remain on lands they owned. These people and their descendants were recognized in 1868 by the federal government as the Eastern Band of Cherokee Indians. In the early 2000s these Cherokee, living on the Qualla Boundary in the western part of the state, were the only Indian tribe in North Carolina fully recognized by the federal government. The tribe has more than 13,000 enrolled members.

Cherokee Origins and First European Contact

The Cherokee, members of the Iroquoian language group, are descended from the native peoples who occupied the southern Appalachian Mountains beginning in approximately 8000 B.C. By 1500 B.C., a distinct Cherokee language had developed, and by 1000 A.D. the Cherokee were living a Woodland lifestyle with unique cultural characteristics influenced by Mississippian religious traditions. The growing and harvesting of corn, or *selu*, beans, and squash—the Cherokee "three sisters"—were ascribed deep spiritual significance, as were other occupations, including hunting, the care and cleaning of homes, the gathering of other essential foods, games,

dances, and religious ceremonies. The central philosophy of *duyuktv*, meaning "the right way," prescribed that the Cherokee attempt to obtain harmony and balance in every aspect of their lives, particularly with respect to the natural world. Communal responsibility and sacrifice were essential to the Cherokee vision of life, as symbolized by the central plaza—used for public ceremonies—and the council house, or town house, which held the "sacred fire," embodying the spiritual essence of the town. Besides food, the environment provided all that the people needed, including medicine, clothing, weapons, shelter, musical instruments, and personal adornments. The governing of Cherokee towns was through democratic consensus as well as the leadership of priests, war chiefs, and peace chiefs. Familial ties and clan affiliations came through Cherokee women, who owned the houses and fields and passed them on to their daughters.

Although initial contact took place during Hernando De Soto's expedition in 1540, sustained relations between Europeans and the Cherokee were not established until the late seventeenth century by traders from Virginia and South Carolina. During the seventeenth century, Cherokees living in what became North Carolina were distributed among the "Middle Towns" along the Little Tennessee River, the "Valley Towns" along the Hiwassee and Valley Rivers, and the "Out Towns" on the Tuckasegee and Oconaluftee Rivers. As British and French colonial aspirations began to clash, the Cherokee became increasingly important as a buffer and continued to alternate alliances between the two nations. In 1730 Alexander Cuming took seven Cherokees to England, reinforcing Cherokee alliances with the English that had been established through a treaty signed at the Town of Neguassee. The increasing pressure of European expansion, and the subsequent loss of much of their territory, led the Cherokee to initiate hostilities as the French and Indian War (1754–63) progressed. Virginian hostility toward the Cherokee led to the Cherokee War of 1760–61, a war in which the tribe suffered extensive losses.

Disease, Destruction, and the Loss of Cherokee Land

Smallpox and other diseases brought by Europeans and enslaved Africans were more devastating to the Cherokee and other southeastern Indians than war. Since the Indians did not have the immune system the Europeans had built up after centuries of contact with these diseases, simple contact could set off an epidemic. Cherokee people were exposed to smallpox for a period spanning over three centuries. Probably their first exposure was in 1698, when a smallpox epidemic decreased their population measurably. In 1738–39 the tribe experienced its worst epidemic from smallpox, when the disease was brought by traders or was brought back from an expedition in which the Cherokee aided the British against the Spanish in Florida. Between 7,000 and 10,000 Cherokees died, representing about one-half of the tribe's population. Since medicine men were unable to provide a cure, the Cherokee tried a traditional method of purification—sweat houses followed by plunging into icy streams. This practice only added to the number who died. Others who survived the disease were horror stricken by their disfigurement and killed themselves rather than live in disgrace.

In addition to population losses, the 1738–39 epidemic had other consequences for the Cherokee. Towns were relocated, Cherokee distrust of the English increased, and the French gained a foothold among the tribe. The epidemic also brought a deterioration of Cherokee culture by challenging religious beliefs, almost destroying the medicine man's perceived power. Smallpox struck the Cherokee people again in 1759–60 during the French and Indian War.

Although the Cherokee first made land cessions to Europeans in 1721 and 1755, British victory in the French and Indian War in 1763 ended the need for the tribe as a buffer and brought increasing pressure of colonial expansion. Although the Proclamation Line of 1763 officially prohibited white settlers from entering Indian territory, white encroachment on Cherokee lands continued after the establishment of the line. The years 1768, 1770, 1773, and 1775 saw a series of "voluntary" land cessions made by the Cherokee. The 1775 cession, led by land speculator Judge Richard Henderson, involved most of the upper half of Cherokee hunting grounds and included most of what is modern-day Kentucky. In all during this period, the Cherokee people ceded almost 50,000 square miles of land.

The Revolutionary War, Cherokee Defeat, and Additional Land Cessions

When the Revolutionary War erupted in 1775, John Stuart, British superintendent of the South, planned to use Indian tribes in conjunction with English troops against the colonists. White encroachers at the Tennessee–North Carolina border along the Watauga, Nolichucky, and Holston Rivers, as well as a delegation of Shawnee and other northern Indians urging the Cherokee to fight against the Americans, inspired their decision to aid the British. The Upper Cherokee planned a three-pronged attack on the intruders along the North Carolina and Virginia frontiers. The Cherokee Middle Towns were to attack North Carolina, while the Lower Towns were to attack South Carolina and Georgia. The Lower and Middle settlements met with limited success. In reaction to these attacks, Gen. Charles Lee, commander of the southern Continental forces, urged a joint punitive expedition, known as the Cherokee Campaign of 1776. Under Col. Andrew Williamson, South Carolina troops moved against the Lower Towns and then traveled northwest to join the North Carolina forces under Gen. Griffith Rutherford in devastating the Middle and Valley Towns. Virginia troops under Col. William Christian crushed the Overhill Towns in present-day Tennessee. More than 50 Cherokee towns were destroyed in the summer of 1776, and the survivors were left without food or shelter.

These attacks devastated the Cherokee people, who sued for peace, giving up huge parcels of land in the process. The treaties signed after the Cherokee Campaign of 1776 marked the first forced land cessions by the Cherokee, and for the first time the land ceded was not unsettled hunting grounds but the sites of some of the tribe's oldest towns, in which the Cherokee people had lived for centuries. The Cherokee Campaign of 1776 also caused a schism between the old chiefs and young warriors. Many of the latter withdrew to Tennessee and northern Alabama, where they became known as the Chickamauga Cherokee and continued to fight white Americans until 1794.

While the American Revolution brought independence to white North Carolinians, the region's Indians, including the Cherokee, were a conquered people. Nevertheless, the Cherokee managed to maintain a semblance of political independence and cultural integrity despite military defeat. With the Treaty of Holston (1791), the United States initiated a "civilization" program aimed at assimilating the Cherokee people into the mainstream of American society. To a great extent this meant the adoption of sedentary agriculture. Consequently, with Indians living by means of farming, their huge hunting grounds would no longer be needed and whites could easily acquire more Cherokee land. The Tellico Treaty was signed in 1798 as a result of the movement of settlers into Cherokee territory in western North Carolina, west of the 1791 Holston Treaty line. The Tellico Treaty specified that a line, called the Meigs-Freeman Line, was to be drawn from the "Great Iron" or "Smokey" mountain in a southeasterly direction so as to exclude settlers from Cherokee territory. War Department agent Return Jonathan Meigs supervised the running and Thomas Freeman the surveying of the line from July through October 1802. They were assisted by Cherokee leaders and settlers. The line ran from the peak of Mount Collins (located between Clingman's Dome and Newfound Gap) to a point on the North Carolina–South Carolina border near the southwestern corner of Transylvania County.

Within their newly established boundaries, the Cherokee took the lead in adopting Euro-American ways in the early nineteenth century, establishing schools and a bicameral tribal legislature. In the 1820s, the Cherokee Sequoyah invented a syllabary that enabled his people to read and write in their own language, and a bilingual newspaper, the *Cherokee Phoenix*, soon began publication. Cherokee men and women took up farming of cotton, flax, and livestock, and engaged widely in trade with whites. Some Cherokees even built columned plantation houses and bought slaves. Historians have referred to this period of recovery as the "Cherokee renaissance."

Despite the successes of this period, which saw the Cherokee willingly embrace white culture, seeds were also planted for a new and even greater crisis for the Cherokee people. In an attempt to save land that had been lost after the Creek War of 1813, the Cherokee signed two more treaties in 1817 and 1819. The 1817 treaty was the first Cherokee treaty that included a provision for their removal from North Carolina lands. The treaty proposed exchanging Cherokee lands in the Southeast for territory west of the Mississippi River. The government promised assistance in resettling those Cherokees who chose to remove, and approximately 1,500–2,000 did. The Treaty of 1817 also contained a proposal for an experiment in Cherokee citizenship. Cherokees who wished to remain on ceded land in the East could apply for a 640-acre reserve and legal rights as American citizens.

In 1819 the remaining Cherokees who opposed removal negotiated still another treaty. During the period from 1783 to 1819, the Cherokee people had lost an additional 69 percent of their remaining land. Although the tribe ceded almost 4 million acres by the 1819 treaty, they hoped that this additional cession would end any further removal effort. In fact, the Cherokee National Council agreed that they would not enter into any more negotiations involving the giving up of "even one foot of land." The continuing westward movement of North Carolina settlers usually brought whites into conflict with Indians, however, especially those on whose land gold was discovered in 1828. These whites were reaching into lands that treaties supposedly had guaranteed to the Cherokee. Yet instead of enforcing the treaties, the U.S. government —with President Andrew Jackson leading the way—decided to relocate the Cherokee people.

The Trail of Tears and the Creation of the Eastern Band of Cherokees

In 1830 Congress passed the Indian Removal Act, setting the stage for the forced removal of the Cherokee and the infamous Trail of Tears. In 1835, a small, unauthorized group of about 100 Cherokee leaders (known as the Treaty Party) signed the Treaty of New Echota (Georgia), giving away all remaining Cherokee territory in the Southeast in exchange for land in northeastern Oklahoma. Principal Cherokee Chief John Ross collected more than 15,000 signatures, representing almost the entire Cherokee Nation, on a petition requesting the U.S. Senate to withhold ratification of this illicit treaty. The Senate, however, approved the treaty by a margin of one vote in 1836. The treaty gave the Cherokee people two years to vacate their mountain homeland and go west to Oklahoma.

By May 1838, few Cherokees were prepared to move, so President Martin Van Buren, who had succeeded Jackson in 1837, dispatched federal soldiers commanded by Gen. Winfield Scott to round up Cherokees in North Carolina, Tennessee, Georgia, and Alabama and place them in various internment camps and stockades. The horrible conditions facing his

people at these poorly planned facilities led Ross to appeal to the president for a delay in the removal until fall, when water and game would be more plentiful. Van Buren agreed, and between October 1838 and March 1839, the Cherokee moved west. The journey was mismanaged; there was a shortage of supplies; and the troops rushed the Indians onward, refusing to allow them to minister to their sick or bury their dead. Of the approximately 15,000 who began the trek, an estimated 4,000 perished.

Approximately 300 to 400 Cherokees remained in North Carolina, hiding in the mountains. One of their leaders, Tsali, was captured and executed for killing two federal soldiers pursuing him and his family, but some of his followers and other Cherokees (who had possibly aided in Tsali's capture) were allowed to remain. Between removal of the Cherokee Nation in 1838 and the end of the Civil War, many Cherokees gave their money to William Holland Thomas, their agent and later their only white chief, to purchase land for them. Thomas acquired many of the tracts that would make up the modern-day Qualla Boundary, the official name of the Cherokee Indian Reservation in North Carolina. These Cherokees—together with the hundreds who had hidden in the mountains, who already legally owned land through the Treaty of 1817, or who had escaped the Trail of Tears and returned—formed the nucleus of what would become the Eastern Band of Cherokee Indians.

Federal Recognition and the Fight for Cherokee Rights

During the Civil War, the most serious Cherokee losses resulted not from the conflict itself but from smallpox brought by a returning tribal member who had joined the Union forces. The vaccine provided by a doctor proved ineffective. Disillusioned by white medicine, the Cherokee attempted traditional cures again, which as before proved no match for the deadly disease. After the war, Thomas sought official permission for the Cherokee to remain in North Carolina. In 1866—in recognition of Cherokee ownership of land as well as their efforts to aid the Confederacy during the Civil War—North Carolina acknowledged the legal right of the Cherokee people to reside in the state. Two years later, the U.S. Congress recognized the Eastern Band of Cherokee Indians as a separate entity from their brethren in Oklahoma and directed the secretary of the interior to assume the same guardianship of the tribe. The Eastern Band adopted a constitutional government in the 1870s that provided for two chiefs and for council representatives from each Cherokee community. The Cherokee received the right to vote, although they were disfranchised along with African Americans by the 1900 North Carolina General Assembly. Soon the first English-language schools for the Cherokee were established; these, however, often attempted to destroy traditional beliefs and practices, forbidding the children to use the Cherokee language. This situation was not reversed

Cherokee Indian family, ca. 1900. NCC.

the timber boom ended in the mid-1920s, Cherokee people had little to fall back upon. Tourism became an important economic boost to the Cherokee beginning at this time. Substantial economic relief came only when the New Deal programs of the mid-1930s provided jobs and the opening of the Great Smoky Mountains National Park near Cherokee land brought large numbers of visitors to the area.

In 1953 a new federal policy was designed to extend civil and criminal protection to reservation Indians in specific states. This policy ultimately failed; it was followed by the 1968 Civil Rights Act, which provided specific protections for individual tribal members and limitations on tribal governments. In 1971 the North Carolina General Assembly created the Commission of Indian Affairs to deal with a broad range of Indian concerns. Subsequent decades have witnessed renewed interest in and respect for Indian culture. The commission was created to assist Cherokees and other Indians in gaining access to local, state, and federal funds; to help tribal communities establish social, educational, and economic development programs and enhance economic self-sufficiency; to protect Indian rights and interests when necessary; and to ensure that Indians are permitted to pursue their cultural and religious traditions.

Modern-Day Cherokee Life and Culture

Despite many acts of Congress and more than 40 court decisions specifically related to the Cherokee in North Carolina, questions have continued to arise concerning tribal, state, and federal jurisdictions. The modern charter and governing document of the Eastern Band was adopted in 1986 and has 24 sections covering tribal officers, qualifications for office, and council meetings. The Cherokee code, published in 1998, consists of 36 chapters on a wide range of subjects. Court cases may be handled in tribal, state, or federal court, depending on the persons and subject matter in question. A Tribal Council of 12 members and a principal and vice chief carry out the executive and legislative functions, while a Court of Indian Offenses handles judicial matters not under federal jurisdiction. The largest section of the Qualla Boundary, approximately 50,000 acres, surrounds the Swain County town of Cherokee. Sixty miles away, in Graham County, a parcel of 2,250 acres is occupied by about 400 members of the Cherokee's Snowbird Community. Another 5,575 acres of Cherokee land lies in various parts of Cherokee County. Individual Cherokees can sell or exchange their land only to other Eastern Band tribal members.

The Eastern Band's approximately 13,000 tribal members, those living on or off the Qualla Boundary, were by the early 2000s leading lives reflective of both their Cherokee heritage and the diversity of American culture and society. Working as business owners, teachers, police officers, medical professionals, and homemakers as well as Cherokee histori-

until late in the twentieth century, when the Cherokee school system reintroduced courses in Cherokee language and culture.

In the early twentieth century, a shift in federal emphasis encouraged the coexistence of tribal membership with state and federal citizenship. Eastern Cherokee citizenship status had not been fully resolved when World War I began, but approximately 70 members of the Eastern Band of Cherokee Indians were drafted or joined the armed forces. The largest single group served in the 321st Infantry Regiment, which also included some Lumbee Indians from eastern North Carolina. On 16 Nov. 1919, a congressional act granted citizenship to Indians who had served in the armed forces during World War I. In spite of this, the Cherokees fully regained voting rights only in 1946, with the return of Cherokee veterans from World War II.

In 1924 the Eastern Band of Cherokee Indians and the federal government agreed to put Cherokee tribal lands in trust. As a result, North Carolina state law did not apply to Cherokee lands within the Qualla Boundary. While most Indian reservations were carved out of existing federal property and set aside for individual tribes, the federal government never owned the lands comprising the Qualla Boundary in North Carolina.

The economy of western North Carolina in the early twentieth century was dominated by the timber industry, and when

Cherokee stickball game at the Fading Voices Festival, held annually in the Snowbird community near Robbinsville. Photograph by Murray Lee.

ans, storytellers, and craftsmen, modern Cherokee people are bound by their desire to remain faithful to Cherokee traditions. This desire often informs many of the decisions made by tribal leaders.

The town of Cherokee is both the spiritual and governmental center of the Eastern Band and a thriving tourist spot dedicated to enlightening visitors about Cherokee culture, tradition, and current affairs. The Oconaluftee Indian Village Living History Museum, the Museum of the Cherokee Indian, the Qualla Arts and Crafts Mutual, and many important historic and natural sites around the town offer opportunities for first-hand, authentic encounters with Cherokee history. *Cherokee One Feather*, a weekly broadsheet newspaper owned and published by the Eastern Band of Cherokee Indians in Cherokee, was launched in 1966 as a three-to-four-page weekly under the supervision of a tribal publications committee. Its content is tightly focused on matters of tribal interest, including local news, commentary, arts and entertainment, sports, and community announcements.

Cherokee festivals and events include the presentation,

during the summer months, of *Unto These Hills*, an outdoor drama portraying the history surrounding the Trail of Tears; the Cherokee Fall Fair; the annual Ramp Festival in April; and the Cherokee Voices Festival in June. Cherokee artisans have been widely recognized for their traditional basketry, weaving, and stamped pottery. The Qualla Arts and Crafts Mutual, a Cherokee-operated artists' cooperative, plays an important role in promoting the quality and authenticity of Cherokee crafts. Traditional storytelling in the Cherokee language, as well as in English, also remains an important part of the living heritage of the Cherokee. The legality of gaming on Indian land, established by the Indian Gaming Act of 1988, has had a huge economic impact on the Cherokee, as thousands of people from around the country visit the Harrah's Cherokee Great Smoky Mountains Casino and other establishments in Cherokee every year. The growth of business interests surrounding the casinos, such as hotels and restaurants, has allowed more tribal members access to higher salaries and benefits, as well as improved health care and educational opportunities.

References: William L. Anderson, *Cherokee Removal: Before and After* (1991); Barbara R. Duncan and Brett H. Riggs, *Cherokee Heritage Trails Guidebook* (2003); John Ehle, *Trail of Tears: The Rise and Fall of the Cherokee Nation* (1988); John R. Finger, *The Eastern Band of Cherokee, 1819–1900* (1984); Tom Hartley, *The Dividing Paths: Cherokees and South Carolinians through the Era of Revolution* (1993); William G. McLaughlin, *Cherokee Renascence in the New Republic* (1986); James H. O'Donnell III, *The Cherokees of North Carolina in the American Revolution* (1976); Theda Perdue, *The Cherokee* (1988); Timothy Silver, *A New Face on the Countryside: Indians, Colonists, and Slaves in South Atlantic Forests, 1500–1800* (1990); Russell Thornton, *The Cherokees: A Population History* (1990).

William L. Anderson
Ruth Y. Wetmore
Additional research provided by John L. Bell.

SEE ALSO Etchoe, Battle of; Museum of the Cherokee Indian; Oconaluftee Indian Village.

Cherry Point Marine Corps Air Station

Cherry Point Marine Corps Air Station was established on 6 Aug. 1941 on 8,000 acres south of New Bern. On 20 May 1942 the field was named Cunningham Field to honor Lt. Col. Alfred A. Cunningham, the first marine aviator. It was later renamed Marine Corps Air Station, Cherry Point, in reference to a local post office situated among cherry trees. During World War II Cherry Point trained units and individual marines for service in the Pacific theater. The air station also served as a base for antisubmarine operations, with an Army Air Corps and Navy unit each sinking a German U-boat just off the North Carolina coast in 1943. The Ninth Marine Aircraft

Wing was based at Cherry Point during the war but replaced with the Second Marine Aircraft Wing in 1946.

Throughout the Korean War (1950–53), the base provided a steady stream of trained aviators and air crewmen, as well as maintenance and support personnel as replacements to forward deployed aviation units. During the Vietnam War (1957–75), Cherry Point deployed three A-6 Intruder squadrons to the Far East and again provided a constant source of replacements for aircrews and enlisted aviation personnel. In Operation Desert Storm (1991), Cherry Point deployed three AV-8B Harrier squadrons, two A-6E Intruder squadrons, one KC-130 Hercules squadron, one EA-6B Prowler squadron, and headquarters detachments from Marine Air Group 14, Marine Air Group 32, and the Second Marine Aircraft Wing. Following the terrorist attacks of 11 Sept. 2001 in New York City, Cherry Point marines and sailors participated in strike missions and operations in Afghanistan and Iraq.

By the early 2000s, the largest command at Cherry Point was the Second Marine Aircraft Wing. Other units housed there were Marine Aircraft Group 14, Marine Wing Support Group 27, and Marine Air Control Group 28. Marine Aircraft Group 14's flying squadrons included three AV-8B Harrier squadrons, four EA-6B Prowler squadrons, and one KC-130 Hercules refueling squadron. The Marine Corps's only Harrier training squadron and only Hercules training squadron were also located at the air station. The air station proper consisted of 13,164 acres, with an additional 15,975 auxiliary acres, including Marine Corps Auxiliary Landing Field Bogue, situated along Bogue Sound in Carteret County. Approximately 7,486 marines and sailors were stationed at Cherry Point.

Reference: William R. Evinger, ed., *Directory of U.S. Military Bases Worldwide* (1995).

John L. Bell

Chicamacomico Lifesaving Station.

SEE *Mirlo* Rescue.

Child Labor. North Carolina children have worked, often alongside their parents, on family farms or elsewhere since colonial times. As the South industrialized, children began to leave home to find work in factories and mills. By 1900, 25 percent of all southern mill workers were between the ages of 10 and 16; even younger children worked in the state's textile mills. The so-called street trades employed large numbers of boys in North Carolina cities. A 1918 study found that many African American boys as young as 9 were working at shoeshine stands, acting as barkers to aggressively procure customers. Boys also delivered orders for drugstores and department stores, and many older boys (aged 14 to 16) worked as messengers for companies such as Western Union.

By far the most common street trade was selling newspapers. "Newsies" got up before dawn to pick up the papers they hawked on street corners, in hotel lobbies, and outside train stations. (Asheville author Thomas Wolfe delivered newspapers as a child for his older brother Fred, who supervised a group of young boys peddling the *Saturday Evening Post* in the early 1900s.) Both boys and girls worked as servers, busboys, and counter help in restaurants and ice cream parlors, often spending long hours on their feet and sometimes until very late at night.

Statistics from the 1900 census indicate that North Carolina mills employed more children between the ages of 10 and 15 than any other mills in the United States, and half of the state's mill-family children were illiterate. When the North Carolina Child Labor Committee was organized in 1906, only one child labor law had been passed in the state. The 1903 statute included only those provisions sanctioned by mill owners: no child under 12 could work in a mill, and no one under 18 could work more than 66 hours a week. There were no restrictions on night work, and no provision was made for enforcement of the law.

The state Child Labor Committee was a volunteer organization that campaigned for ten years (1906–16) to inform public opinion and to obtain regulatory legislation to protect the health and welfare of young textile factory workers. For most of that time, Clarence H. Poe served as chairman. Reflecting the humanitarianism of the progressive reform movement, the committee was composed of individuals who were interested in the child labor issue from a moral and educational perspective. The committee achieved limited progress in advocating for legislative restrictions on child labor: the maximum workweek was reduced from 66 to 60 hours, no child under 16 could work at night, and no child under 13 could be employed in the mills, although 12-year-olds could work in an "apprenticeship capacity." The organization was unsuccessful in raising the minimum age to 14 and in obtaining measures for effective enforcement of factory inspections, as North Carolina's child labor regulations continued to lag behind those of most states.

By 1916 the Child Labor Committee had been absorbed into a larger social reform organization, the North Carolina Conference for Social Service (formed in 1912–13). The broader campaign against illiteracy, led by Governor Charles B. Aycock and others, resulted in a 1913 law making school attendance compulsory at least four months of each year for all children between the ages of 8 and 12. Meanwhile, organizations such as the National Child Labor Committee, founded by reformers Alexander J. McKelway of North Carolina and Edgar Gardner Murphy of Alabama, lobbied Capitol Hill for a National Child Labor Reform Law. Although Congress first considered the issue in 1906, it did not pass legislation until 1916, when the Owen-Keating Bill established a minimum age requirement

Children are well represented in this photograph of the employees of a textile mill at West Monbo in Catawba County, ca. 1913. NCC.

of 14 years by closing interstate and foreign commerce to the products of child labor.

Some business leaders in North Carolina and other southern states accused reformers of using child labor laws to sabotage the South's economic recovery. They claimed that white sharecroppers and tenant farmers had a better life in the mills than they did trying to survive on worn-out land. Manufacturers argued before Congress that children had to be taught how to spin at a young age for the industry to maintain a skilled labor force. In western North Carolina, one of the most important textile districts in the United States, mill owners maintained that the 1916 law prevented them from meeting the demands of their customers.

On 3 June 1918 the U.S. Supreme Court, in a five-to-four decision, declared the Owen-Keating Bill unconstitutional because it did not represent a legitimate exercise of congressional power. Although the ruling was a major setback for child advocates, the case did elevate the issue to the national political arena. Twenty years later, in 1938, passage of the federal Fair Labor Standards Act (FLSA) marked the beginning of

effective child labor reform. The FLSA and subsequent amendments, which remain in effect today, established legal standards for wages, hours of employment, and occupations for working-age children (those 14 and older).

In 1979 the North Carolina legislature enacted the Wage and Hour Act (WHA) authorizing additional measures governing child labor. By the early 2000s, labor laws stipulated a variety of controls that applied to nonagricultural occupations for children under age 18. Generally, however, as children moved from ages 14 to 18, employment regulations, including working hours, became less restrictive. On the other hand, occupations that were hazardous or "detrimental to the health and well-being" of youths were banned. In this category were practically all manufacturing jobs involving power-driven tools or equipment, such as woodworking, saw mining, coal mining, and meat packing, as well as jobs that required operating motorized vehicles. Among acceptable occupations for 14- and 15-year-olds were office work, cashiering, bagging groceries, and stocking shelves. Restrictions on the total number of working hours—during the school year and the summer

Chimney Rock, with Lake Lure in the distance. Photograph by Charles E. Jones. North Carolina Department of Transportation.

months as well as for youth employment generally—were also covered by FLSA and WHA regulations.

References: Elizabeth Huey Davidson, *Child Labor Legislation in the Southern Textile States* (1939); W. H. Swift, *Child Welfare in North Carolina: An Inquiry by the National Child Labor Committee for the North Carolina Conference for Social Service* (1918); George-Anne Willard, "Charles Lee Coon: North Carolina Crusader for Social Justice" (M.A. thesis, East Carolina University, 1966).

Kirstin Reimer
George-Anne Willard

Children of the Confederacy is an organization for both male and female descendants of those who honorably served the Confederate States of America during the Civil War. Sponsored and supervised by the United Daughters of the Confederacy, children under the age of 21 who meet the same genealogical requirements as the Daughters of the Confederacy are eligible for membership. The purpose, goals, and activities of the Children of the Confederacy are much the same as those of the United Daughters of the Confederacy. Pride in one's heritage, a willingness to give to others, and a sense of responsibility are but a few of the lessons the organization seeks to instill in its members. There are 23 chapters of the Children of the Confederacy in North Carolina, including chapters in Butner, Charlotte, Concord, Fayetteville, Jacksonville, Lexington, Shelby, and Wilson.

Charles C. Davis

Chimney Rock is a monolith rising 225 feet from the surrounding mountainside and overlooking Hickory Nut Gorge and Lake Lure in western Rutherford County. The American Indians of the region used it as a landmark for many years, and it is believed that explorer Hernando De Soto passed through the gorge and became the first European to view the monolith in 1539. Locals claim that Chimney Rock also served as a marker on an Underground Railroad line through the area before the Civil War. Between January and mid-summer 1874, shocks from an apparent earthquake disturbed the area, causing many citizens to move from the valley in fear that the rock and mountains might collapse. It was determined later that the shocks were of the nature of volcanic disturbances.

The first development of Chimney Rock as a tourist attraction came in July 1916, when Lucius B. Morse built a stairway to the top and a series of trails leading to nearby points of interest, including Hickory Nut Falls, the state's tallest waterfall. Three years later he opened the Cliff Dwellers' Inn, which was replaced by the Sky Lounge in 1949. That year, an elevator was opened to make Chimney Rock more accessible. For a number of years, an annual "hill climb" to the top of the rock was held.

In 1922 Morse conceived of the idea of building a large summer resort in the valley below the rock. After putting his plan before a number of Rutherford County area businessmen, he incorporated the enterprise as Chimney Rock Mountains, Inc., capitalized at $4 million, the largest corporation granted charter in North Carolina up to that time. The corporation secured option on approximately 8,000 acres of land and began the construction of a dam and powerhouse. The dam was completed in 1926, and the resultant body of water, Lake Lure, with a 27-mile shoreline, complemented the recreational facilities of the Hickory Nut Gorge. At the same time, the state began to build a new highway, N.C. 20 (later U.S. 64-74) through the gorge, and the Lake Lure Inn was opened, making the Chimney Rock–Lake Lure region one of the state's major tourist areas.

References: John Preston Arthur, *Western North Carolina: A History, 1730–1914* (1914); Clarence W. Griffin, *The History of Rutherford County, 1936–1951* (1952).

Paul L. McCraw

China Connection,

China Connection, a term referring to North Carolina's relationship with China, was used in the state for a century following the 1847 arrival in Shanghai of Matthew T. Yates of Wake County as a Baptist missionary. Yates was followed by other Baptists as well as missionaries sponsored in increasing numbers by Episcopal, Presbyterian, and Methodist churches, and occasionally by others. North Carolina workers supported by the YMCA and YWCA also served there. Only men were missionaries in the beginning, but women who had accompanied their husbands and helped to establish family life served as teachers of Chinese women and children. Correspondence between these expatriates and people who remained at home often led other North Carolinians to move to China. When missionaries returned, they often proved to be the first important contact North Carolinians had with people from a foreign country.

Schools, colleges, and hospitals were established initially in Shanghai, and soon business leaders became aware of trade possibilities between the countries. Tobacco and textiles became important items of commerce.

References: "The Chinese, 100 Years in the South" and "The China Connection," *Southern Exposure* 12 (July–August 1984); North Carolina China Council, *North Carolina's "China Connection," 1840–1849: A Record* (1981).

William S. Powell

Chinquapin, or "chinkapin," is a diminutive cousin of the American chestnut. Although their name derives from eastern-dwelling Algonquian Indian language, chinquapin trees are known as far west as Texas, and several species exist. In North Carolina the principal chinquapin tree, *Castanea pumila*, occurs in the Piedmont and Mountain regions. Small and shrublike in nature and often with several trunks, a chinquapin seldom grows above 20 to 30 feet in height. The wood of chestnuts and chinquapins is extremely rot resistant and has been used in making railroad ties and posts and rails for fences. The occasional split-rail zigzag fences along the Blue Ridge Parkway are fashioned mostly from these trees.

Chinquapin husks contain a single kernel that, when ripe in the fall, is a tasty foodstuff for humans as well as animals. Kemp P. Battle, the president of the University of North Carolina from 1876 to 1891, remarked that there were two local delicacies that students dependably would raid: scuppernong grapes and chinquapins. In his day a convenient grove of chinquapins stood near the intersection of Columbia and Franklin Streets, main corners of modern-day Chapel Hill. In the early 1950s it was possible to buy a bag of chinquapins at roadside stands in hilly, rural North Carolina counties such as Stokes and Surry. The bag was approximately the same size as a bag of peanuts sold at a ball game and usually cost a nickel. At the end of the decade the price had increased to a quarter a bag, if one could find them for sale at all.

References: William C. Coker and Henry R. Totten, *Trees of the Southeastern States, including Virginia, North Carolina, South Carolina, Georgia, and Northern Florida* (1934); J. S. Holmes, *Common Forest Trees of North Carolina: A Pocket Manual* (rev. ed., 1995).

David Southern

Chowan College, a four-year institution affiliated with the Baptist State Convention of North Carolina, is located in Murfreesboro in the northeastern part of the state. The college traces its origins to the May 1848 Chowan Baptist Association Meeting, where Baptist deacon and physician Godwin Cotton Moore of Hertford County, along with A. J. Askew, William Watson Mitchell, A. J. Perry, and S. J. Wheeler, recommended that a regional school for girls be created. On 11 Oct. 1848, Chowan Female Institute opened with 11 students. First situated in the old Banks School Building in Murfreesboro, the school changed its name in 1850 to Chowan Female Collegiate Institute and occupied the $30,000 McDowell Columns (the present administration building). The curriculum included algebra, arithmetic, astronomy, botany, drawing, English composition and grammar, French, geography, guitar, history, Latin, logic, "natural and moral philosophy," needlework, painting, and piano; tuition was $113 for five months. During the Civil War, the institute remained open with 81 students.

The school was renamed Chowan College in 1910 and, by this time, was granting B.A. and B.S. degrees; in 1925 the school received state accreditation as a senior college, as well as a $13,750 endowment from the North Carolina Baptist Convention. In 1927 the college was able to raise $25,000 to match a gift offered the previous year by tobacco magnate Benjamin N. Duke. In 1931, after a failed attempt at merging with Meredith College in Raleigh, Chowan began admitting men. The travails of the Great Depression forced Chowan to retrench to two-year status in 1937, and from 1943 through 1949 the college was closed.

In 1949 Chowan College reopened as a coeducational two-year institution. The school provided liberal arts education on the junior college level for the next four decades. New curricular offerings included secretarial courses (1949), graphic arts (1952), and a short-lived agriculture and mechanics curriculum (1953).

Throughout the 1980s the faculty and trustees debated the merits of transforming Chowan into a four-year school. Initially, the board refused to sanction this change, but in 1992 the college again began offering baccalaureate programs and awarded bachelor's degrees in 1994. In the early 2000s Chowan had approximately 750 full-time students served by 82 faculty members.

References: Herman W. Gatewood and R. Hargus Taylor, eds., *Through the Years: A Pictorial History, Issued in Observance of the 125th Academic Year in the Life of Chowan College, Murfreesboro, North Carolina* (1972); Edgar V. McKnight and Oswald Creech, *A History of Chowan College* (1964); R. Hunt Parker, *Chowan College: Yesterday and Today* (n.d.).

James I. Martin Sr.

Chowan County, known as the "cradle of the colony," is located in the Coastal Plain region of northeastern North Carolina. The county was formed in 1668 by English settlers and was originally called Shaftesbury Precinct of Albemarle County. It was renamed Chowan Precinct around 1681 for the Chowan River, itself named for the Chowanoac Indians who inhabited the region. Chowan County is partially bordered by the Albemarle Sound and the Chowan River. The county seat, Edenton, was known as the Town on Queen Anne's Creek until it was incorporated as Edenton in 1722; the city is named for Charles Eden, a North Carolina royal governor. Edenton served as the capital of the colony of North Carolina from 1722 to 1743. It was also the location of the famous Edenton Tea Party (25 Oct. 1774) at which a group of Edenton women pledged unity against oppressive British rule as part of the foment leading up to the American Revolution. Other communities in Chowan County include Tyner, Ryland, Valhalla, and Hancock.

Chowan County, where pride of place is a distinguishing trait, has been called an "architectural treasure house." With Historic Edenton State Historic Site as its center, the county is home to a number of structures that were built more than 200 years ago. These historic places include St. Paul's Church (ca. 1736), the Chowan County Courthouse (1767), the James Iredell House (ca. 1773), the Cupola House (ca. 1758), the Barker House (1782), the Williams-Flurry House (ca. 1779), and Bennett's Inn (ca. 1765). Harriet Jacobs, a fugitive slave, lived her early life in Edenton and depicted that life in her memoir, *Incidents in the Life of a Slave Girl* (1861). Chowan County also hosts many annual events and festivals, such as the Tea Party Celebration, the Peanut Festival, and the Edenton Christmas Candlelight Tour.

Notable physical features of Chowan County's geography include Edenton Bay, Bear Swamp, Dillard Mill Pond, Bluff Point, and Cherry Point. Among the county's agricultural products are oats, tobacco, wheat, sweet potatoes and Irish potatoes, cotton, sorghum, chickens, and beef cattle. Its manufactured products include elastics, fishmeal, motor yachts, and carded cotton. The population of Chowan County was estimated to be 14,400 in 2004.

Reference: Thomas C. Parramore, *Cradle of the Colony: The History of Chowan County and Edenton* (1967).

William S. Powell

SEE ALSO Albemarle County; Edenton; Edenton Tea Party.

Chowan County Courthouse was built in 1767, after the North Carolina Assembly ordered the construction of a new courthouse in Edenton to replace the deteriorating 1719 wood frame structure. The first courthouse was located on lot 5, later known as Courthouse Square or the Green, and constructed in compliance with the Assembly's order to build "a Court House to hold the Assembly in, at the fork of Queen Anne's Creek, commonly called Matchacamak Creek in Chowan Precinct."

John Hawks, architect of Tryon Palace and other public structures in the 1760s, is believed to have been the designer of the 1767 classic Georgian-style courthouse. The original design provided a large central room with adjoining offices and a semicircular apse in the rear. The upper floor housed a large paneled meeting room used by Edenton's political leaders during the American Revolution. In 1970 the Chowan County Courthouse, the finest of its kind in the South and a key attraction in the modern Historic Edenton State Historic Site, was recognized as a National Historic Landmark.

References: Catherine W. Bishir, *North Carolina Architecture* (1990); Marc D. Brodky, *The Courthouse at Edenton* (1989); Thomas R. Butchko, *Edenton: An Architectural Portrait* (1992).

Deborah Joy

Chowanoac Indians were a tribe of Indians of the Algonquian language group living along both banks of the present-day Chowan River in northeastern North Carolina at the time of European settlement in the sixteenth and seventeenth centuries. The name is said to be Carolina Algonquian for "people at the south," possibly indicating some migration on their part just prior to contact with Europeans. Their tribal lands encompassed much of modern Gates, Hertford, Bertie, and Chowan Counties. Their villages, farms, and fisheries were bounded by their Iroquoian Mangoak (later Tuscarora) neighbors south and west of Salmon Creek in Bertie County, their Algonquian Weapemeoc neighbors east of Rockyhock Creek in Chowan County, and their Algonquian Nansemond and Iroquoian Nottoway, Meherrin, and Wyanoke neighbors north of the convergence of the Meherrin and Blackwater Rivers on the present North Carolina–Virginia border. The swampy lowlands of these watercourses were shared "hunting quarters" for these various groups of Woodland Indians. At the time of Sir Walter Raleigh's colonization efforts from 1584 to 1590, the Chowanoac were probably the most powerful of the Carolina Algonquians.

By 1666 the Chowanoac were beginning to respond to English encroachment into their lands. Violence broke out that year, with losses to the settlers on the west side of the Chowan River. Peace was once again established, leading to the Chowanoac's essentially abandoning their lands west of the river to rapid English settlement. The Chowanoac were apparently involved to some degree in the warfare that ignited Bacon's Rebellion in Virginia in 1676, but they were "wholly subdued" in late 1677. Numbering perhaps less than 200, the Chowanoac were placed on a reservation of 12 square miles in modern Gates County. They, like other coastal Indians, began to live among the English, but they continued to suffer from the encroachment of the colonials. They were amenable to the teachings of Christian missionaries, notably the Quaker George Fox.

By the time of the Tuscarora War of 1711–13, the once mighty Chowanoac could muster only 15 fighting men to go on expeditions to fight with the English against their historic Iroquoian neighbors to the west. During the period they suffered both at the hands of their enemy and their English allies. Chowanoac Chief John Hoyter petitioned the colonial government for protection, only to have the tribe lose some of its best land when the reservation was reduced to six square miles. By 1734 the Chowanoac were too few to farm even this land, and a petition signed by four tribal leaders asked the colonial government for permission to sell some 2,050 acres. They continued to sell land over the next two decades and ceased to exist as a functioning tribe around 1751.

References: David B. Quinn, *The Roanoke Voyages, 1584–1590* (2 vols., 1955); Quinn, *Set Fair for Roanoke: Voyages and Colonies, 1584–1606* (1985); Ruth Y. Wetmore, *First on the Land: The North Carolina Indians* (1975).

Phillip W. Evans

Christ Episcopal Church, a handsome yet unassuming Gothic Revival–style stone church standing at the eastern edge of Capitol Square in Raleigh, enjoys landmark status in both the architectural history of North Carolina and the history of Episcopal Church architecture. Erected between 1848 and 1852 and consecrated on 5 Jan. 1854, the church is the second building raised as a house of worship for Raleigh's first Episcopal congregation. Since its organization in 1821, Christ Church Parish has shared the fortunes of the city through both the character of its congregation and its location at the geographic center of state government. In 1826, when the congregation set about erecting its first church, it turned to the English-born architect William Nichols, who had completed a remodeling of the statehouse in 1824.

For the church that would be a companion landmark to the State Capitol, the congregation of Christ Church turned to the leading New York–based architect, Richard Upjohn (1802–78). In a letter of 12 Jan. 1846, Bishop Levi Silliman Ives of the Episcopal Diocese of North Carolina approached Upjohn for the design of a new building, "a neat Gothic Church edifice," to replace the small frame church standing in the shadow of the splendid new State Capitol. Upjohn completed the plans in the autumn of 1846, and Richard Mason, rector of Christ Church and chairman of its building committee, signed a contract on 7 June 1848 with James Puttick, Robert Findlater, and Justin Martindale for a church to be built of locally quarried granite. The tower, a part of the original plan, was undertaken separately in about 1859 and completed in 1861. Fifty years later, in 1911, the congregation of Christ Church approached Upjohn's grandson, Hobart Brown Upjohn, for the design of a parish house. Completed in 1914 and linked to the antebellum church by an arched cloister, the parish house shares with the church a remarkable and unique physical, stylistic, and familial relationship.

Along with Thomas U. Walter's St. James Church in Wilmington (1840), Christ Church firmly established the Gothic Revival as the favored style for Episcopal churches in North Carolina, serving as the prototype for a succession of important cross-plan churches until the mid-twentieth century. In addition to this distinction, and that of having introduced the cruciform plan in its design, Christ Church became the first of a trio of churches designed by Richard Upjohn to be built in North Carolina, the other two being the chapel at St. Mary's School in Raleigh and Grace Church in Plymouth. These three churches—the first erected in stone, the second in board-and-batten sheathed frame construction, and the third in brick—represent the possibilities of Gothic Revival church architecture in mid-nineteenth-century North Carolina and served as models for a succession of later buildings. Of the three, Christ Church continues to evoke a much-deserved admiration and no little envy for its spare elegance and unpretentious beauty.

References: Davyd Foard Hood, *To the Glory of God: Christ Church, 1821–1997* (1997); Lawrence Foushee London and Sarah McCulloh Lemmon, eds., *The Episcopal Church in North Carolina, 1701–1959* (1987); Everard M. Upjohn, *Richard Upjohn: Architect and Churchman* (1939).

Davyd Foard Hood

Christian and Missionary Alliance

Christian and Missionary Alliance (CMA), an international, evangelical Protestant denomination, traces its origins to the ministry of Albert B. Simpson (1843–1919), a Canadian Presbyterian clergyman who, after serving congregations in Hamilton, Ontario; Louisville, Ky.; and New York City, created an interdenominational missionary society in 1887. The alliance, which remained a society rather than a denomination until 1971, represents an amalgamation of Christians from a variety of ethnic and religious backgrounds. Since 1989 the denomination has been headquartered in Colorado Springs, Colo. As of the early 2000s, the Christian and Missionary Alliance included nearly 2,000 churches with 389,000 members and missionaries in 54 countries.

North Carolina, Georgia, and South Carolina comprise the South Atlantic District of the CMA. The district, founded in 1938, initially had its headquarters in High Point, the home of its first superintendent, R. L. Staley. Later, the district moved its central office to Durham and finally to Charlotte, where it remains today. There are approximately 40 CMA groups in North Carolina, including intercultural ministries. The oldest active congregations include First Alliance, Winston-Salem (1888); Durham Alliance (1889); Lumberton Newgate Community Church (1899); First Alliance, Asheville (1927); High Point Christian Community (1931); Reidsville Alliance (1940); First Alliance, Raleigh (1940); Lumberton Mt. Haven Alliance (1940); and Wilmington Alliance (1944). Golden Valley (Rutherford County) Academy, founded in 1907 by R. A. Forrest, was the initial predecessor of Toccoa Falls College, a fully accredited institution located in northern Georgia. The CMA also established youth camps at Deep River (Randolph County), Lo-Ma-Co (Asheville area), and Toccoa Falls.

The CMA has sponsored ministries for minorities in North Carolina for more than a century. As early as 1900, the society enlisted the services of African American evangelist E. M. Colette (1852–1923) in order to promote the Gospel among blacks residing in Virginia and North Carolina. In 1906 the alliance established the Lovejoy Missionary School in Mill Springs (Polk County); the institution relocated to Boydton, Va., five years later. The Mary B. Mullen School was founded at Uree (Rutherford County) at about the same time as Lovejoy and remained active through the 1950s.

The CMA has also sponsored significant Native American ministries. In 1958 Eugene and Carol Hall were appointed as pastors of the Indian Chapel in Lumberton. As a result of the generosity of benefactor Jane Hargreaves, the service projects of CMA teenagers, and the work of women's groups, the society was able to construct a new facility for this specialized ministry. The Halls served until 1961, after which they were succeeded in turn by Wayne Damron, Lowell Halbert, and, in 1966, J. C. Huggins, the first Native American to pastor what is now the Lumberton Mt. Haven Alliance Church.

In the 1980s and 1990s, the CMA began ministering to a growing number of "nontraditional" minorities. Dega (Vietnam) Alliance churches have existed in Charlotte, Greensboro, and Raleigh since 1987. There are Cambodian Alliance missions in Charlotte (1991) and Lexington (1991) and Hmong (Laos) churches in Hickory (1989) and Salisbury (1988). In 1994 the South Atlantic District also inaugurated a ministry in Raleigh for recent arrivals from Zaire.

References: Troy Damron, *A Tree God Planted* (1982); Robert Niklaus and others, *All for Jesus: God at Work in the Christian and Missionary Alliance* (1986); Charles H. Williams, *Nineteen Eighty Four Report of the Black Field of the Christian and Missionary Alliance*.

James I. Martin Sr.

Christian Church in the South

Christian Church in the South was a schismatic North Carolina–Virginia offshoot of the Methodist Church. In 1792 the Reverend James O'Kelly broke away from the Methodists in a dispute over issues of hierarchical authority, and in 1794 he and his followers organized a new polity. At first called O'Kellyites and later Republican Methodists, the group finally settled on the name Christian Church in the South to underscore its nondenominational, nonsectarian character and its identification with the primitive Christianity of the early church. Born in controversy, the new church struggled to define itself. Sweeping away intervening Christian tradition, O'Kelly meant to return to what he felt certain had been the Christocentric faith of the early church, in which all believers had direct personal access to Jesus, "the king and head of the people," and Christian fellowship reflected "the all sufficiency of a Bible government."

In 1810 the nascent denomination split into two conferences, one in eastern Virginia and the other in the rest of Virginia and North Carolina. The Eastern Virginia Conference maintained ties with similar churches in New England, although differences over baptism by immersion, which the New England churches practiced but O'Kelly opposed, thwarted union between the church bodies. In 1856 the Eastern Virginia and Virginia–North Carolina churches merged to form the Southern Christian Convention, and in 1858 the convention became loosely affiliated with Christian Conferences in Alabama, Mississippi, and Missouri.

From the 1850s until 1900, the Christian Church in the South continued to struggle with problems of identity and visibility. At the beginning of the twentieth century, North Carolina's Christian Church in the South poured its limited resources into two projects—Elon College, founded near Burlington in 1889, and the Christian Orphanage, opened in the same area in 1905. In 1931 the church merged with the Congregational Church, which in 1957 joined with the Evangelical and Reformed Church to form the United Church of Christ—a denomination that stresses salvation through faith alone, a theology that probably would have suited O'Kelly and his followers.

Reference: Durward T. Stokes and William T. Scott, *A History of the Christian Church in the South* (1973).

Robert M. Calhoon

Christian Science, or the Church of Christ, Scientist, was established in Boston in 1879 by Mary Baker Eddy, whose theology evolved from her study of the Bible and her belief that she herself was healed through faith in God. Her subsequent writings defined the church's doctrines, which are based on the principle that God alone encompasses everything that is real; what is not of God—evil, sin, sickness, and suffering—is therefore unreal and able to be eliminated through wholly spiritual means.

The Christian Science Church first came to North Carolina in August 1894, when Mary Hatch Harrison of New Bern was reportedly healed of a paralytic affliction through her study of the Bible and Eddy's writings. Harrison began holding meetings in her home but later secured a meeting room. In August 1902 a church was organized with 18 members, and its edifice, the first of the denomination to be built in the state, was dedicated in 1907.

Eddy, who lived in Wilmington for a brief time in 1844, seems to have been particularly interested in the establishment of her church in North Carolina and participated actively in the building of the New Bern church. At her behest, John Swinson, owner of a quarry in Concord, N.H., cut and donated the granite block for the cornerstone. Eddy sent copies of all of her writings to be placed in the stone, as well as a gift of $3,000 for the building fund.

Meanwhile, in 1897 seven Christian Scientists held their first service in Asheville, and in 1912 their church edifice was completed. Elizabeth Earl Jones was one of the seven charter members; she became a Christian Scientist practitioner, devoting much of her time to the public practice of healing through prayer.

The Christian Science Society in Chapel Hill was recognized in May 1956; the well-known bandleader James K. "Kay" Kyser was one of the 16 charter members and eventually became a Christian Science practitioner, teacher, and lecturer. At the beginning of the twenty-first century, there were 29 Christian Science churches in North Carolina.

References: Stephen Gottschalk, *The Emergence of Christian Science in American Religious Life* (1973); Anne Russell, Marjorie Megivern, and Kevin Coughlin, *North Carolina Portraits of Faith: A Pictorial History of Religions* (1986).

Tess Bradstreet

Christ School in Arden was founded in 1900 by the Reverend Thomas Cogdill Wetmore. Established on the site of an old plantation called Struan, Christ School was originally open to boys and girls in the Mountain region and was primarily an industrial school. Students could pay their tuition through work. An industrial curriculum that included carpentry, telegraphy, and bookkeeping complemented the academic courses for the students, many of whom walked as many as ten miles to get to the school.

The school was initially supported by the General Fund of the Episcopal Church Diocese as well as private donations. However, it soon moved beyond its local orientation. Indeed, having limited its enrollment to boys, and finding the area's improved public schools drawing away students who had once opted for Christ School, the institution expanded its accommodations and started to accept students from other states. By 1928, as the public school system in the area became fully established, Christ School switched its focus and became a college preparatory school for boys; staying true to its roots, it remained affiliated with the Episcopal Church. The school is located on a 500-acre campus in the town of Arden, approximately 11 miles south of Asheville. A nonprofit institution, Christ School is governed by a 27-member board of trustees. In a Christian environment reflective of its religious ties and heritage, the school provides a traditional college preparatory curriculum based in an overall program that seeks to develop and educate the whole person. In the early 2000s it enrolled approximately 175 boys in grades 8–12, and the campus featured five new buildings that were added after 1995.

Reference: Ina and John J. Van Noppen, *Western North Carolina since the Civil War* (1973).

William H. Pruden III

Church Camps. Many churches of a variety of denominations maintain facilities throughout North Carolina used for recreational camping, meetings, retreats, and other events. Mountain areas have been attractive to such groups because of their cool evenings and beautiful scenery, while seaside camps have provided church members with good swimming, sandy beaches, and some privacy for their programs. The United Methodist Church maintains one of the shining lights of church camping facilities in North Carolina—the Lake Junaluska Conference and Retreat Center in Haywood County. The site includes youth facilities, an open-air auditorium, hotels, and hundreds of private dwellings. Drawing patrons from Methodist churches throughout the Southeast, a town has grown up around the lake, which is the reservoir formed by a dam built in the early part of the twentieth century.

There is no accurate census of mountain church camps, but it is believed that more than 15 established denominational camps exist in the Blue Ridge Mountain area. Montreat, a sprawling facility near Black Mountain (Buncombe County), has been a significant part of the worship and ecclesiastical life of southern Presbyterians since its purchase by the church in 1906. The Black Mountain area is also home to church camps run by Free Will Baptists and Disciples of Christ. Nearby is Ridgecrest, a Southern Baptist Camp serving North Carolina churches. The Episcopal Church maintains Kanuga in the mountains (a retreat center for all ages in the Brown Summit area), Vade Mecum for youth, and Camp Leach in the east.

The most prominent seaside camp is at a former military installation called Fort Caswell, in Brunswick County, where the Southern Baptists have developed a thriving camp that is used by youth, families, and individual churches. The Neuse River has provided sailing as well as water sports for camps like Don Lee (a United Methodist camp) and Camp Caroline (a Disciples of Christ camp). Lakes have been the site of several camps, such as the Rockfish Camp near Fayetteville and Camp Chestnut Ridge near Eno. Several church camps have been established at Lake Norman and other lakes near Charlotte. The Roman Catholic Church is particularly interested in retreat centers and has expanded its program and facilities throughout North Carolina.

In addition to Christian groups, Buddhists have established Zen centers both in the mountains and in the Chapel Hill area, and Muslims have begun to enter the religious camp trend in the state.

Gene Purcell

SEE ALSO Cragmont Assembly; Montreat.

Churches of Christ are theologically conservative congregational churches bound together by association rather than a formal denominational structure. These churches resulted from the so-called restoration movement of the early nineteenth century. This movement was led by James O'Kelly in North Carolina and Virginia, Barton Stone in Kentucky, and Thomas and Alexander Campbell in West Virginia. Together these men sought primarily to promote scripture, particularly the New Testament, as the only source of truth among the faithful. Secondarily, they hoped to achieve individual church liberty and a union of similarly believing churches. The Churches of Christ pattern their organization and their

form of worship upon an interpretation of the early Christian church. Services are simple, with the choir singing without instrumental accompaniment. The Lord's Supper is held weekly, believer baptism is by immersion, and members are expected to have a strong prayer and preaching commitment.

As of the early 2000s, there were more than 1.25 million baptized members in approximately 13,000 Churches of Christ in the United States. In North Carolina there are some 15,000 baptized believers in about 190 Churches of Christ.

Louis P. Towles

Church Homecomings have been held in North Carolina since colonial times, offering people a sense of communal pride, renewal, shared history, and fellowship with other church members and with God. Quintessentially southern, they typically take place in small towns and rural regions, and they are a significant and continuing part of the religious heritage of North Carolina. Most homecomings in North Carolina are held during late August and early September, although they may be held as early as June or as late as November. They are frequently scheduled to coincide with the start of the church year.

Church homecomings almost always include two events: preaching and a communal meal. A common practice is to have a former pastor or special guest minister deliver the sermon, and occasionally, a new minister will make an inaugural presentation. Some homecomings are connected to revival services. This is the practice, for example, of Smokemont Baptist Church in an old logging community in the Great Smoky Mountains National Park. The church is used once a year in August for a weeklong revival, which culminates in a homecoming program attended by people from throughout western North Carolina. Many attendees wear period clothing and listen to "old fashioned" preaching prior to a hearty meal on Sunday.

A number of churches use homecomings as a time to remember the deceased of the past year with a memorial service. Another typical homecoming activity is to have a groundbreaking ceremony or the dedication of a new building. The First Baptist Church of Greensboro has intermittent homecomings to memorialize prominent church leaders of the past and follows the service with dinner on the grounds.

Several Quaker meetings in eastern North Carolina and the Piedmont hold homecomings that are similar to those of other denominations in the state. Some churches, such as Westover United Methodist Church in Raleigh, prefer a relaxed atmosphere for the time after dinner and make it a "time for music and memories." Mt. Pelier Presbyterian Church in Rowland has an annual daylong homecoming that includes a call for contributions to a special offering for cemetery upkeep. Such maintenance is an activity at numerous homecomings.

Alexander R. Stoesen

Churchman was a term applied to those who were members or supporters of the Church of England, or Anglican Church. It was in use in England by 1677 and in North Carolina by 1711, when missionary John Urmston observed that there were a few churchmen serving in the Assembly. Differences between churchmen and dissenters contributed to the Cary Rebellion, which erupted in 1711. With the end of the American Revolution and the disestablishment of the Anglican Church, the term, as it had been understood, ceased to be meaningful.

William S. Powell

Church of England, or the Anglican Church, arrived in North Carolina with the initial colonists venturing to Roanoke Island under Sir Walter Raleigh. In 1585 Manteo, a Native American, and Virginia Dare, the first English child born in America, were baptized, indicating the presence of an Anglican priest. The Carolina charter of 1663 permitted religious toleration of other Protestant groups but provided for the establishment of parishes of the Church of England in the colony. However, the Church of England neither supplied clergymen nor began to build churches until the eighteenth century. The sparse organized religion of seventeenth-century North Carolina was provided by the Quakers.

In 1701 the Assembly passed the first Vestry Act, which divided the colony into five parishes. Each parish had a vestry of 12 men, who elected 2 of their members as wardens. The vestries were supposed to start building churches, care for widows and orphans, and levy a tax on property owners to provide funding for the church.

In December 1701 the nucleus of St. Paul's vestry met at the home of Thomas Gilliam, near what later became Edenton, and soon began to build a church on an acre of land donated by Edward Smithwick. This church, the first one in North Carolina, was "very sorrily put together." Ten years after work began, cattle and swine continually wandered into the building, which had neither a floor nor a lock. The first substantial Anglican church in the colony was St. Thomas's in Bath, begun in 1734, followed by St. Paul's in Edenton, begun in 1736. Both buildings remain standing as popular historic sites.

Even with a succession of other Vestry Acts, church growth was slow. There was no Anglican bishop in America. Few clergymen were appointed for North Carolina, and of those selected, many were unfit for or dissatisfied with their posts. The first Anglican clergyman in the colony, Daniel Brett, was one of several reputed to indulge in immoral behavior. Another early missionary, John Blair, became disgusted with the colony—"the most barbarous place on the continent"—before he quit, and Governor Arthur Dobbs, an ardent church advocate, despaired of the "deluded depraved colony." Some Anglican priests in North Carolina were accused of wholly ungodly behavior, such as stealing, public drunkenness, and adultery.

By 1765 only 5 Anglican Church buildings existed in North Carolina. Of these, only the New Bern church was "in good repair"; those in Brunswick and Wilmington were unfinished, and those in Bath and Edenton were in need of repair. Most parishes either had no building at all or only a small chapel served by lay readers and occasionally visited by traveling missionaries or ministers from distant towns. The Reverend Alexander Stewart not only supervised the construction of St. Thomas's Church in Bath but also preached at 13 chapels in Beaufort, Pitt, and Hyde Counties. One minister complained that the "chapels" in his parish were merely "people's houses where we are obliged to attend." Another chapel was "a most miserable old house . . . [where] ev'ry shower of Rain or blast of wind blows quite through it."

The Church of England in North Carolina received only limited financial support from England and from the government of the colony. Many so-called dissenters—Quakers, Baptists, Moravians, Presbyterians, Lutherans, and others—objected to compulsory taxation to fund an "established church" to which they did not belong. Before 1751 vestrymen were appointed by the Assembly; afterward, they were elected by the freeholders of each parish. Vestrymen were not required to be members of the Church of England.

Despite many obstacles, the Church of England accomplished much good in the North Carolina colony. Vestries helped support widows and orphans and arranged apprenticeships for needy children. The church helped establish some of the few schools in the colony, including the one opened by Charles Griffin in Pasquotank County in 1705, the first recorded school in North Carolina. Stewart dedicated much of his time to the conversion and education of the Indians of eastern North Carolina. Some Anglican clergymen preached to the colony's slaves, although their early efforts were thwarted by the false belief of planters that baptism meant emancipation. Missionary efforts in the antebellum period were also hampered by the scarcity of clergy and the resistance of many masters to any education or religious training of their slaves.

Never overly vigorous in North Carolina, the Church of England lagged behind other, more popular denominations by the time of the American Revolution. The North Carolina Constitution of 1776 stated that no state church would be established and that church attendance and payments would be voluntary. The Church of England's ties with the royal government caused it to fall from favor after the Revolution. Following the departure of many Anglican clergymen and church members, the church nearly disappeared in North Carolina. It was not until 1817 that the former Church of England, now known in the United States as the Episcopal Church, established a diocese in North Carolina and began to develop the modern church, which includes several congregations that refer to themselves as "Anglican."

References: Lawrence F. Brewster, *A Short History of the Diocese of East Carolina, 1883–1972, with Its Background in the Heritage of the Anglican Church in the Colony and the Protestant Episcopal Church in North Carolina* (1975); Lawrence Foushee London and Sarah McCulloh Lemmon, *The Episcopal Church in North Carolina, 1701–1959* (1987); Alice E. Matthews, *Society in Revolutionary North Carolina* (1976); Alan D. Watson, *Society in Colonial North Carolina* (1975).

David A. Norris

SEE ALSO Episcopal Church; St. Thomas Episcopal Church; Society for the Propagation of the Gospel in Foreign Parts.

Church of God in Christ,

founded in 1897 and with its world headquarters in Memphis, Tenn., is the largest black Pentecostal denomination and the second-largest of all black Christian groups in the United States. It possesses a rich spiritual heritage with roots in both the African American experience and the spiritual revival that manifested itself among black and white Christians at the beginning of the twentieth century. The church, a "Pentecostal holiness" denomination, emphasizes a life of holiness in the Methodist tradition while adding the "necessity" of the Pentecostal baptism with the Holy Spirit to its dogma. The denomination also is Arminian in theology (against the Calvinist concept of predestination) and Wesleyan in doctrine.

The Church of God in Christ was founded by Charles Harrison Mason, who had been dismissed by his black Baptist church in Arkansas because of his beliefs concerning sanctification. The movement toward a deeper spiritual experience, which sprang from Baptist and Methodist theology, was both interdenominational and antisectarian. Mason's group, however, experienced an early break with major black Baptist conventions over issues of culture, personality, and class differentiation. Mason, who became the "General Overseer and Chief Apostle" (later, senior bishop) of the denomination, envisioned a "Pentecostal empowerment" that would, through the gifts of the Holy Spirit, equip the poor for both personal survival and social growth.

The Church of God in Christ celebrates its anniversary based on 1907 as the founding date. It was during that year that Mason began to seek more diligently the "fullness of God." Like many others, he was attracted to the Los Angeles, Calif., Azusa Street Mission (1906–11), where the Holy Spirit was believed to be descending daily upon those who sought a "baptism of the spirit." In 1907 Mason visited the mission and was filled with the spirit, reportedly speaking in tongues.

In the same year Levi Bazemore, who was living near Newport News, Va., came to North Carolina to visit relatives. After he had introduced them to the Pentecostal concept of "baptism of the Holy Spirit," his family established Cedarfolk, the state's first Church of God in Christ congregation, in Bertie County. Churches later were established in Edenton, Center Hill, Washington, Parmele, and other communities. Many local church members in North Carolina experienced great suffering, for Pentecostal groups were often considered dangerous outsiders by mainline Christian churches (both black and white). Ministers of the Church of God in Christ were sometimes beaten, threatened, and jailed.

Although the gift of tongues came to both black and white Christians at the Azusa Street Mission, racial conflict and secular social pressures soon caused white Christians to separate themselves from the Church of God in Christ (some of them formed the Assemblies of God in 1914). The period during which black and white Pentecostals worshipped together ended in 1924. Mason emphasized the value of prophetic black Christianity (one of the contributing factors in the separation of whites from the denomination). Women are considered spiritually equal to men and are allowed free expression of their spiritual gifts. Women and men also share social responsibility within the community. The church established its Women's Department in 1911. The work of women has been instrumental in the establishment of local churches throughout the country, especially in the South.

Following Mason's death in 1961, the Church of God in Christ struggled to find focus and identity. Under the guidance of new leaders, however, the church emerged from its insular roots to become one of the world's fastest-growing and influential Pentecostal denominations. In the early 2000s the Church of God in Christ had more than 8 million members worldwide, with a large presence in North Carolina.

References: Bishop Ithiel C. Clemmons, *Bishop C. H. Mason and the Roots of the Church of God in Christ* (1996); Lucille J. Cornelius, *The History of the Church of God in Christ* (1975); C. Eric Lincoln and Lawrence H. Mamiya, *The Black Church in the African American Experience* (1995).

Helen Losse

Circuit Riders

were itinerant preachers who traveled from place to place ministering to the spiritual needs of the people. The term came to be synonymous with Methodist preachers, followers of the teachings of John Wesley, who had begun the Methodist movement in eighteenth-century England as a way of bringing reform to the Church of England.

In the geographical area of North Carolina, there were many famous itinerant preachers who left their mark. The nationally and internationally known evangelist George Whitefield preached in the eastern towns of New Bern (1739) and Bath (1748). Other itinerants with denominational ties such as Charles Woodmason (Anglican) and Francis Makemie (Presbyterian) traveled from place to place in North Carolina and other states establishing congregations. It was the Meth-

Arrival of the Barnum & Bailey Circus train at Durham, 1940. NCC. Courtesy of J. Marvin Black.

odists, however, who brought new order to the idea of itinerancy, with preachers, or circuit riders, as they came to be known, assigned to a specific area of parishes, called "circuits." The minister "rode the circuit" by traveling from community to community and from church to church within his appointed area.

Under the leadership of the American bishop Francis Asbury, the circuits became the basic organizing unit of the Methodist movement in North Carolina and throughout America. Asbury himself was probably the greatest of the Methodist circuit riders. From 1771 to his death in 1816, he rode some 228,000 miles throughout the country. Asbury visited many of the established Methodist preaching places in North Carolina.

The Brunswick Circuit, formed in 1774 and served by the Reverend Robert Williams, was the first Methodist Circuit that included North Carolina in its boundaries. The Carolina Circuit (1775) was served by three circuit riders. It was probably the first circuit to be formed completely within the geographical bounds of the state, although the exact boundaries of the circuit are not known.

As the population moved westward, so did the circuit riders. Other circuits that were formed as part of this westward movement in North Carolina were the Yadkin Circuit (1780), the Salisbury Circuit (1783), and the Lincoln Circuit (1790). By

1802 the Methodist Church in North Carolina had 200 circuits and 358 itinerant preachers appointed to minister to its 86,734 members.

With the invention of more modern modes of transportation and increased population density, the old-time circuit rider, who covered a large territory on horseback, became a thing of the past. Increasingly, ministers were appointed to much smaller, more densely populated areas and thus were able to take up residence in the communities that they served.

References: Elmer T. Clark, *Methodism in Western North Carolina* (1966); Timothy D. Hall, *Contested Boundaries: Itinerancy and the Reshaping of the Colonial American Religious World* (1994).

Lynne S. Lepley

Circuses were considered by many to be both educational and entertaining when they began to appear in early nineteenth-century North Carolina. Along with dancing and the theater, the circus came to be regarded as a place of "worldly amusement." Precursors of the circus were collections of drawings or paintings of wild animals displayed in rural settings around the country. They were followed by small menageries, often consisting of a single animal such as a lion, elephant, or rhinoceros. There were some who regarded these menageries as sinful because they wasted both time and money. Nevertheless, it was at a circus or menagerie that many of the wonders of the world were revealed to people who had little or no knowledge of other countries. Acrobats and performing horses soon began to appear, followed by such other recognizable circus features as tightrope walkers, trained animals, and circus music. On 3 Apr. 1823, one source reported, one "Mr. Keller, a native of North Carolina, '42 years old, 36 inches tall, double-jointed, possessing extraordinary strength for a man of his size,'" would perform "feats of agility."

In 1830 the Moravians in North Carolina initially declined to allow the appearance of a menagerie in their midst, but when "the circus men, out of respect for our town," moved it to a nearby site, local residents attended in large numbers. In the future, the circus owners assured Moravian leaders, they would not "present improper theatrical scenes," and in 1834, with "a procession of wagons," they presented an acceptable performance. It may have been while he was on this circuit that a young circus man, P. T. Barnum, made an important move. His autobiography recounts that on 12 Nov. 1836 the troupe camped in a grove by the river at Rocky Mount. Here Barnum used his savings to purchase the financially strapped circus and set off on a successful career under his own management. Elsewhere in North Carolina, it was estimated that on 9 May 1856 there were 1,100 spectators to see a menagerie, circus, and other attractions at Bethabara. It was around the same time that Alonzo T. Mial of Wake County bought tickets and took all of his slaves to the circus.

While no national-level circuses have originated in North Carolina, the state has seen a continuous stream of both small and large groups visit many cities from the coast to the mountains. The Ringling Brothers and Barnum & Bailey Circus, a regular visitor to Raleigh, Charlotte, and other North Carolina cities, offers a special educational show catering to school groups. A growing movement in support of circuses that do not feature animal acts—based on the belief that such acts are dangerous and degrading to the animals involved—gained momentum in the 1990s and early 2000s.

References: P. T. Barnum, *Struggles and Triumphs; or, Forty Years' Recollections of P. T. Barnum* (repr., 1981); Guion G. Johnson, *Ante-Bellum North Carolina: A Social History* (1937); George Speaight, *A History of the Circus* (1980).

William S. Powell

Cisterns, large receptacles built for the storage of water, were used in North Carolina for potables or fire protection in all types of urban and rural buildings prior to the advent of modern plumbing. Unlike a well, a cistern must be deliberately filled with water because it does not connect to a natural underground water source. By the last quarter of the nineteenth century, fire insurance maps for many North Carolina small towns and cities documented the location of public and private cisterns.

Cistern construction probably reached its peak between 1880 and 1900, following advances in biological sciences and the emergence of a new breed of "sanitarians" fighting for social reforms and a healthier standard of living. One of the major health concerns in coastal North Carolina during the last quarter of the nineteenth century was the outbreak and control of malarial fever epidemics. In 1895 Dr. Richard Lewis, then secretary of North Carolina's Board of Health, published a booklet titled *Drinking Water in Its Relation to Malarial Diseases*, in which he endorsed the use of cisterns instead of shallow wells for drinking water. Testimonials published in the book indicated that cistern use was rising throughout the state, and health improvements were the result.

Two shapes of cisterns have been noted in different geophysical regions of North Carolina. A low-vaulted, rectangular-shaped cistern was constructed in the Coastal Plain (the Ziegler House cisterns in Edenton are of this type), while a dome-topped, conical-shaped cistern was used in the Piedmont and the Mountains (the Thomas Wolfe House cistern in Asheville is of this type). This difference was likely related to soil types and, more important, levels of the natural underground water table. Numerous other extant and archaeological cisterns have been recorded and examined in locations around the state, including the campus of the University of North Carolina at Chapel Hill (in front of New West building), Somerset Place (a plantation house in Washington County), houses in Raleigh's historic Oakwood neighborhood, the Beldon-Horne House in Fayetteville, and houses in Elizabeth City and New Bern. Archaeological excavations have revealed that these underground reservoirs, once fallen into disuse or replaced by modern plumbing, often were converted into garbage receptacles. Excavations of the Thomas Wolfe cistern fill produced more than 15,000 artifacts and interesting insights into the cultural behaviors of the house's former occupants. Cisterns can still be found in some rural homesteads where fire hydrants never existed and where potable water for livestock, gardens, or washing is needed.

Reference: Benjamin Earle Washburn, *A History of the North Carolina State Board of Health, 1877–1925* (1966).

Linda F. Carnes-McNaughton

City Beautiful Movement, a loosely connected grassroots organization devoted to urban renewal, was influential nationwide in the late nineteenth and early twentieth centuries. Reacting to the perceived ugliness of their urban environment resulting from industrialization, individuals and groups began to work for improvements. The immediate catalyst for the City Beautiful movement was the 1893 Chicago World's Fair, which exhibited an idealized urban setting of white classical architecture in a formal symmetrical arrangement with canals and lagoons designed under the direction of Daniel H. Burnham and Frederick Law Olmsted. The "White City" of the World's Fair starkly contrasted with the "Black City" of industrial Chicago and showed the benefits of planned urban settings. Many people who attended the fair returned to their hometowns with a new vision of urban beautification.

The primary goals of the City Beautiful movement were to enhance urban areas and make them more sanitary. Its leaders proposed that public buildings reflect classical architecture, that streets be lined with trees, and that towns provide landscaped public parks with fountains and statuary. They also called for paved and lighted streets, underground wiring, regular garbage collection, and adequate water and sewer systems. These objectives were further popularized in the magazines of civic groups distributed throughout the United States.

In North Carolina—a state without large, highly populated urban areas but with several medium-sized cities, as well as small towns and villages centered around textile mills—the City Beautiful movement was spearheaded by local civic groups, especially women's clubs. As chair of the North Carolina exhibit at the Chicago World's Fair of 1893, Sallie Southall Cotten, the wife of Robert Randolph Cotten, saw the possibilities of urban beautification in her own state. In 1902 she was instrumental in organizing the North Carolina Federation of Women's Clubs, which had designated village improvement as one of its original goals. By 1912, 95 women's clubs across the state were engaged in civic work, much of which involved city beautification. They awarded prizes for the loveliest flower gardens along the streets, raised money to fix up schoolyards, and urged local governments to clean streets and sidewalks and to develop more public parks and playgrounds.

A notable movement developed among textile mill owners to improve company towns in North Carolina. Earle S. Draper, a landscape architect in Charlotte, planned or upgraded numerous mill villages in the state from 1917 into the 1930s. His design of Spindale for Tanner Mills in 1919 incorporated the basic principles of the City Beautiful movement and made it a model textile community for that time. Draper also designed the Rowan Cotton Mills in Salisbury, Richmond Cotton Mills in Laurel Hill, Carolina Cotton and Woolen Mill in Spray (now Eden), and others.

Influenced by the City Beautiful movement, North Carolina municipalities hired consultants to prepare city plans. An example is the Asheville Plan developed by John Nolen, who proposed that Asheville City Hall and Buncombe County Courthouse, both constructed in 1927, be part of a civic complex. The plans drawn up in the 1920s had government financing and were implemented until the Great Depression drastically curtailed revenue.

References: Kay Haire Huggins, "City Planning in North Carolina, 1900–1929," *NCHR* 46 (October 1969); Huggins, "Planned Communities in the South: The Works of Earle S. Draper, 1913–1930," in *Proceedings: First National Conference on American Planning History* (1986); William H. Wilson, *The City Beautiful Movement* (1994).

Kay Haire Huggins

City Planning. When European powers established colonies in the New World, they often gave significant attention to town planning, especially the selection of sites for towns and their designs. In North Carolina most colonial towns—including Bath, New Bern, Beaufort, Edenton, Brunswick, and Wilmington—were laid out in a rectangular grid oriented toward the waterfront. Raleigh, the capital city laid out in 1792, was also a gridiron, but had a distinctive design with a central square for the capitol building and four additional squares.

To control the physical development of towns, the colonial Assembly passed numerous regulations. The concept of planning towns common in the eighteenth century gave way in the nineteenth century to laissez-faire and haphazard urban development. A concern for planning reemerged in the late nineteenth and early twentieth centuries, when a significant number of planned communities were developed by private enterprise. In North Carolina these included mill villages, resort towns, and suburbs.

Two outstanding planned communities were Pinehurst, a resort town, and Biltmore Village, a residential and business area for Biltmore Estate workers, both designed by Frederick Law Olmsted and his firm in the 1890s. After 1900 some suburbs were also developed with carefully planned layouts. One of the best examples was Myers Park in Charlotte, begun during the 1910s and designed by Bostonian John Nolen with the assistance of Earle S. Draper, a landscape architect from Charlotte. Both of these designers achieved national prominence—Nolen as the designer of many extraordinary neighborhoods and Draper as a similarly successful designer as well as the head of planning for the Tennessee Valley Authority and the director of the Federal Housing Authority. In North Carolina, Draper planned such early twentieth-century communities as Hayes-Barton in Raleigh, Emerywood in High Point, and Irving Park in Greensboro.

Draper also did extensive work in the planning and redesign of mill villages during the late 1910s and 1920s. Before then, mill villages, or "company towns," were often hastily constructed and poorly designed, but more attention was paid to design and landscaping after 1915 as a result of the City Beautiful movement. The first phase of the public city planning movement, the City Beautiful movement began in the 1890s and emphasized classical architecture for public buildings, the development of parks, and the planting of trees. The main leaders of the movement were women's clubs. The Woman's Club of Raleigh hired Charles Mulford Robinson to draw up the first modern city plan in the state in 1913, but women lacked the means for implementation since they did not have the vote. Draper employed many of the principles of the City Beautiful movement in his designs for new or existing mill villages, including Spindale, Rowan Cotton Mills, and Richmond Cotton Mills in Laurel Hill.

The second phase of the public planning movement, the City Useful movement, which emphasized well-planned street systems, efficient and economical city government, adequate water and sewage systems, and rational land development, was supported by many chambers of commerce. By 1917 the chambers of larger cities had city planning committees. Chambers encouraged municipalities to appoint city planning commissions, as was done first in High Point in 1917. In 1919 the General Assembly passed an enabling act that officially provided municipalities with the legal power to establish city planning commissions, and by 1930, 12 cities in the state had done so. City planning became a part of government because of the strong support of chambers of commerce and other civic groups and because it seemed a rational approach to the rapidly increasing urban population and the expanding presence of automobiles in the 1920s.

City planning commissions, composed of volunteer citizens who usually had little technical knowledge of city planning, often contracted with a planner or engineer for a plan. Before 1930 Asheville, Durham, and High Point had comprehensive plans prepared and other cities had specialized transportation or zoning studies done. The plans emphasized better street systems, attractive settings for public buildings, the development of parks, and zoning.

In 1923 the General Assembly passed a statewide enabling act for zoning. Zoning had been recommended by professional planners and was promoted by chambers of commerce and some municipal officials. By 1930 at least eight cities had zoning laws. City planning commissions often handled zoning appeals and reviewed plans for new subdivisions, which left little time for long range planning.

The New Deal and World War II put unprecedented emphasis on planning at all levels of government. The National Planning Board was created in 1933 to prepare a national public works program, and a state planning board was appointed in 1935. The North Carolina State Planning Board encouraged the development of local planning boards and extended numerous aids to them, especially between 1944 and 1947. The first city in the state to hire a full-time professional planner was Durham in 1944. Other organizations that actively promoted city planning in the 1940s were the North Carolina League of Municipalities, chambers of commerce, women's clubs, and the Department of City Planning at the University of North Carolina at Chapel Hill (established in 1946 as the first such department in the South). In 1946 the number of local planning boards in the state was over 100. By 1950 the state's five largest cities had professional planners, and gradually smaller cities hired planners as well.

By the 1960s, North Carolina had a complex hierarchy of planning boards, including city, county, joint city-county, regional, and state. The concept and practice of city planning continued to evolve, but planning had become an accepted part of local government in North Carolina—a continuous process with full-time professional planners and broad goals. By the 2000s, in North Carolina as in other states, addressing the environmental, economic, and social issues resulting from urban sprawl—the tremendous expansion of North Carolina's larger urban areas—had become one of the profession's greatest challenges.

References: Kay Haire Huggins, "City Planning in North Carolina, 1900–1929," *NCHR* 46 (October 1969); Huggins, "Town Planning in North Carolina, 1704–1920," *North Carolina Architect* (November/December 1973); John W. Reps, *The Making of Urban America: A History of City Planning in the United States* (1965).

Kay Haire Huggins

Civic Clubs play a significant role in the social, economic, and cultural life of North Carolina women and men and have done so for decades. In the early 1800s, people from different professions and occupations began coming together in weekly meetings for fellowship. The origin of these voluntary associations in the United States is usually credited to Reformation leaders such as Martin Luther and John Calvin. Calvin, for instance, taught that all believers should participate equally in church decisions, seeing the church as a free and voluntary association of members. In America, this democratic church model developed first in New England towns with the local Congregationalist church as the exemplar of volunteerism. When insightful French intellectual Alexis de Tocqueville penned *Democracy in America* (1835), based on his tour of America in the early 1830s, he especially noticed the degree to which Americans formed groups to serve personal interests and solve both large and small problems. He was particularly impressed by New England town meetings, in which the gathered citizens voted on projects such as caring for the poor.

Over time, voluntary associations of men and women came to represent the civic conscience of their communities, and they were designated civic or service clubs. These nonprofit organizations work for the public benefit independently and separately from governments and private businesses, perhaps earning profits but always using funds in excess of their operating expenses to further the public purposes expressed in their charters, whether that means serving a particular group or working to aid the whole community. Most boards of directors of these groups are volunteers who oversee the work without compensation. The twentieth century provided an enormous proliferation of voluntary associations with different missions and aims but with a shared commitment to community service.

The Benevolent and Protective Order of Elks was founded by 15 actors and entertainers in New York City in 1868 as a social and patriotic association. Goldsboro's lodge, the oldest in North Carolina, dates to 1902. Through the years the Elks have shed much of their secrecy, but still the lodge rituals remain unknown and membership strictly fraternal. The group's constitution states the Elks' objectives, which all involve charity, patriotism, and fraternity. The Improved Benevolent Protective Order of Elks of the World, founded in 1898, is an international fraternal organization of primarily African American members. With headquarters in Winton, N.C., it champions civil liberties and equal opportunity.

In 1914, when the Rotary Club opened its first North Carolina chapter in Raleigh, the then-nine-year-old organization already was well on its way to being part of the largest social service movement in the world. Started in Chicago, the Rotarians were businessmen dedicated to rekindling small-town fellowship. The club is so named because members met in rotation at their various places of business. Under the motto "Service Above Self," the international organization has grown to 1.1 million members in more than 25,800 clubs. In the early 2000s North Carolina had 13,800 Rotarians in 230 clubs, almost all of which are descended from the original Raleigh club. North Carolina alone now hosts six Rotary districts and has had three district governors serve as presidents of Rotary International. In their efforts to promote good will and peace via service, North Carolina Rotarians also have contributed to all-ages service and scholarship initiatives, including supporting the international PolioPlus campaign to eradicate polio by the year 2005—Rotary International's 100th anniversary. More than $230 million was raised in this campaign among Rotarians worldwide, a reflection of the group's commitment to furthering international humanitarian efforts.

The Kiwanis Clubs of North Carolina date back to 1919 and are an integral part of Kiwanis International, which was founded in 1915 in Detroit, Mich., by businessmen seeking to network. Behind clubs in Asheville and Charlotte, regional groups bonded together to form the Carolinas District, of which almost one-third of its members are South Carolinians. The club's motto, "We Build," has seen fruition in the lives of the children it seeks to aid. In one year, clubs sponsored 147,000 service projects, the culmination of $70 million in funds raised and 6.2 million hours of volunteer time. In North Carolina, Kiwanis initiatives include the Terrific Kids reward program, started in Black Mountain, and the Golden K Kiwanis Club for retirees. North Carolina clubs, representing membership of all ages, have raised millions in support of programs around the world, including the 96 nations that host chapters.

Civitan International, a service club whose members have included Thomas Edison and Presidents Harry S Truman and John F. Kennedy, was organized in 1917 in Birmingham, Ala.

Worldwide since 1920, Civitan is an association dedicated to the task of building better citizenship through fellowship, knowledge, and service: gaining strength by sharing responsibility and knowledge in a group setting. Among their initiatives, Civitans are strong supporters of the Special Olympics and many other avenues for helping individuals with developmental disabilities. North Carolina District West, which includes 67 clubs, lays claim to being the largest in the world. The numerous state Civitan clubs have long supported the Boys and Girls Homes of North Carolina, a sanctuary for at-risk children located at Lake Waccamaw.

Also started in Chicago, 12 years after the Rotary Club's 1905 founding, Lions Clubs first came to North Carolina in 1922, when ten clubs were organized in the state. By the late 1960s, there were 430 North Carolina Lions Clubs with a total membership of 14,400. By the beginning of the twenty-first century, there were 10,600 members in the state. These clubs perform a variety of community activities but are most noted for assisting visually impaired and blind citizens. Behind events such as the annual White Cane Drive, the Lions of North Carolina have raised millions of dollars, which, along with the hundreds of millions raised nationally, are put toward funds for eye exams, glasses, white canes, radios, hearing aids, and college scholarships for children of blind parents. North Carolina Lions built and have maintained Camp Dogwood, a $3 million facility located on the eastern shore of Lake Norman. This camp is used for week-long vacations for approximately 850 blind and deaf individuals each summer.

The Optimist Club is an international civic service club established in Louisville, Ky., in 1919, later making its way to Asheville in 1923. Now based in St. Louis, and active in France, England, and throughout the Caribbean, the club is dedicated to youth and community service, advocating "youth safety" and aiding in the development of sports skills. The organization is active in about 150 communities in North Carolina, focusing its broader efforts on eradicating childhood cancer in the world.

Sertoma Clubs appeared in North Carolina as early as 1925. Affiliated with Sertoma International and founded in 1912 in Kansas City, Mo., Sertoma is an acronym for "Service to Mankind." Club members have considerable latitude in the kinds of programs and projects they sponsor. In the greater Durham area, individuals have donated hearing aids, restored homes, given scholarships, sponsored "career days," and promoted various educational events. The club's Service to Mankind Award has been given to multiple North Carolinians, including eminent UNC-Chapel Hill academic Louis Round Wilson.

Ruritan, a rural community service organization, first appeared in North Carolina in 1935, seven years after its initial founding, when it was organized at Sunbury. By 1946, the same year Swindell Lowery of Pasquotank County was elected national president of Ruritan, 12 new clubs were organized in the state, giving North Carolina in January 1947 a total of 219 clubs and 7,872 members. Illustrative of Ruritan's goal of encouraging leadership from among rural people are the variety of fields in which its members have been active: extension directors, Farm Bureau roles, parent-teacher positions, school board leadership, Boy Scout guidance, and leadership in allied activities such as insurance and merchandising. Work and experience with Ruritan has helped advance many members in industrial management, local government, and the military, often through experience in public speaking.

Pilot Club International, a women's service club, was begun in Macon, Ga., in 1921; the first club in North Carolina was organized in Winston-Salem in 1934. Three presidents of this international organization have been North Carolinians. Among the projects sponsored or supported in the state by the club have been those pertaining to schools, hospitals, nursing homes, group homes, the Red Cross, Alzheimer's disease wards, Head Start, bicycle helmets, bulletproof vests for law enforcement officers, flags for classrooms and outside poles, the Special Olympics, Habitat for Humanity, and other causes. In the early 2000s, of the more than 600 Pilot Clubs worldwide, 38 were in North Carolina.

Exchange Clubs originated in Detroit in 1896, when a group of men began meeting for a friendly luncheon to exchange ideas on fellowship, friendship, and business, civic, and family interests. In time, they came to see themselves as service oriented. In 1911 they formed a civic club called the Exchange Club. The first Exchange Club in North Carolina was formed in Wilmington in 1924 with 23 members. The club was active in getting the River Road built to what is now the North Carolina State Port. The club raised funds to help the completion of the inland waterways in the Wilmington area. Other clubs were formed in Winston-Salem, Raleigh, and Greensboro in 1935. Durham and Reidsville clubs were formed in 1941, and Henderson, Roxboro, Hillsborough, Wilson, Murfreesboro, Kernersville, and Elon College Clubs soon followed.

Over the next decades, Exchange Clubs were formed over all of North Carolina. By the early 2000s, 46 clubs made up the North Carolina District Exchange Clubs, representing 1,200 members and working in areas that include crime prevention, fire prevention, youth of the month/year awards, "Give a Kid a Flag to Wave," Book of Golden Deeds Award, community service awards, and the Freedom Shrine project. North Carolina Exchange Clubs have conducted many fund-raising and service projects to provide community services. The National Exchange Club Foundation for the Prevention of Child Abuse was set up in 1979 and works through local clubs to form Child Abuse Centers. The Winston-Salem center, which opened in 1981, was the first in North Carolina and the second in the nation.

References: Albert Coates, *By Her Own Bootstraps: A Saga of Women in North Carolina* (1975); Coates, *Citizens in Action: Women's Clubs, Civic Clubs, Community Chests; Flying Buttresses to Governmental Units* (1976); Robert D. Putnam, *Bowling Alone: The Collapse and Revival of American Community* (2000); Alvin J. Schmidt, *Fraternal Organizations* (1980).

Wiley J. Williams
Additional research provided by Jerry S. Bates, Sue Cause, Ronnie W. Faulkner, Roy W. Kelley, J. B. Morris, Willis H. Overby, and Clarence E. Whitefield.

Civil Rights Movement. In North Carolina and throughout the United States, African Americans have endured a long, turbulent, and sometimes violent struggle for social, political, and economic equality and justice. Segregation, born of slavery and descended from the black codes of the pre–Civil War South, was legal in the state from its embodiment in the North Carolina Constitution of 1868 to its undoing by the federal Civil Rights Act of 1964; de facto separation of the races and the legacy of racism have endured well beyond 1964. At practically every turn, the attempts of blacks to overcome an unjust status quo were met by white resistance and an unwillingness to change without the prodding of judicial authority or local activism. By the early 2000s, nevertheless, tremendous progress had been achieved.

In North Carolina the civil rights movement extends from the heady days following emancipation when blacks first won political representation and the legal right to self-determination, through the struggles of the late nineteenth and early twentieth centuries when these initial gains were rolled back by white supremacy and the repressions of Jim Crow, to the small, grassroots movements of the 1940s and the landmark victories of the 1950s and 1960s. Even after the legal framework of segregation fell, however, its legacy was proved hard to dispel in practice, requiring regular interventions by the federal government, state legislators, and the courts. At every stage, African Americans led the way, not just at the federal and state level but also locally, one place and one issue at a time. Beginning in the 1960s and 1970s, Indians, women, gays and lesbians, and other groups struggled similarly for equal legal and social access in the state and the nation, with various levels of success. These movements continued through the final decades of the twentieth century, and in some regards they continue to the present day.

The Roots of Civil Rights Activism in North Carolina

Although emancipation formally ended slavery and the Fourteenth and Fifteenth Amendments guaranteed the rights of citizenship to African Americans, in everyday life segregation continued to have an impact on whites, blacks, and Native Americans in North Carolina after the Civil War. During the Reconstruction era blacks took advantage of their newfound freedoms to found schools and colleges, begin businesses, and create a variety of social and political organizations. Formal political representation came as blacks were elected to offices at the state and federal levels, particularly from the Black Belt region in the northeastern part of the state, where newly freed slaves joined significant numbers of freeborn blacks to establish a powerful political and social force.

Practically all of the political advances made by black North Carolinians began to erode, however, with the end of Reconstruction and were rolled back altogether in the state's white supremacy campaigns of 1898 and 1900. After Democrats in the General Assembly crafted new voting restrictions that disfranchised black voters in 1899, the state's last remaining black congressman, Bladen County native George Henry White, recognizing the inevitability of his defeat, decided not to run in the 1900 election. For decades after that, African Americans struggled to regain what they had lost, to end segregation, and to enjoy the full rights and freedoms of citizenship on an equal footing with whites.

Black North Carolinians began working to recover their civil rights almost immediately after they were taken away at the opening of the twentieth century. Individuals and groups worked most often on the community level to effect change. The state's first chapters of the National Association for the Advancement of Colored People (NAACP) were established in 1917, and their members advocated antilynching legislation, fair employment practices, equal educational funding and access, and voting rights. Black churches and schools were also important early incubators for civil rights activism. In 1932 a group of black ministers gained notoriety by protesting at the dedication of Raleigh's new War Memorial Auditorium because they were required to sit in the balcony. During the 1930s, student groups in Greensboro and elsewhere in the state initiated boycotts of theaters for similar restrictions on seating for blacks and for their failure to show racially balanced movies. These early boycotts laid the groundwork for similar tactics used later to protest segregation in department stores and other commercial establishments.

In the 1940s the statewide movement for civil rights gained new momentum, particularly as black veterans returned home from World War II in the second half of the decade, declaring that their service to the nation had earned them an equal voice in politics and other walks of life. The NAACP grew significantly in the state during this time, and local activists who had come of age in the 1920s and 1930s took on new leadership positions in the national civil rights movement. Among these leaders was Ella Baker, a native of Virginia who was raised in Littleton and attended Raleigh's Shaw University before becoming national branch director for the NAACP. In 1943 Baker persuaded the state's branch presidents to form the North Carolina Conference of Branches and helped revitalize several of the state's local civil rights organizations.

In addition to the NAACP, other civil rights groups emerged and developed tactics in the 1940s that contributed to later successes of the movement. During this period, union activists in Winston-Salem linked concerns for the civil rights of black tobacco industry workers with their push for workers' rights at R. J. Reynolds Tobacco Company. Elsewhere in the state, similar alliances were formed between labor and civil rights activists, with both communities pushing for improved working conditions and equal pay. Meanwhile, in 1947, eight white men and eight black men began a bus pilgrimage through the South to test the U.S. Supreme Court ruling that declared segregation in interstate travel unconstitutional. The Congress of Racial Equality (CORE), another key civil rights organization, organized the "Journey of Reconciliation," whose members were arrested several times, including in North Carolina. A precursor of the Freedom Rides of the 1960s, the Journey of Reconciliation was an early example of the "direct action" strategy CORE and other civil rights groups employed from the 1950s to the late 1960s.

Individuals such as E. V. Wilkins also effected change in their communities. In 1952, after a long struggle led by Wilkins and his sister, Wilie Mae Winfield, black citizens in the Washington County community of Roper successfully overturned the community's "literacy" test (which amounted to an arbitrary evaluation of penmanship) and regained the right to vote. Such local gains mirrored and in many cases anticipated national developments.

Brown v. Board of Education and White Resistance to School Desegregation

A watershed moment in the modern civil rights movement came on 17 May 1954, when the U.S. Supreme Court, in *Brown v. Board of Education of Topeka, Kansas*, unanimously ruled that racial segregation in public schools was unconstitutional. The decision expressly rejected the separate-but-equal doctrine contained in the Court's 1896 *Plessy v. Ferguson* decision. The 1954 decision declared that separate facilities were inherently unequal and state laws and constitutional provisions upholding segregation denied African American children the equal protection of the laws guaranteed in the Fourteenth Amendment.

In North Carolina the winds of change had first been felt in the area of educational segregation in 1951, when the University of North Carolina at Chapel Hill was ordered by federal courts to admit blacks to its law, medical, and graduate schools. Under this court order, Floyd B. McKissick, Harvey Beech, J. Kenneth Lee, and James Lassiter became the first African Americans admitted to the university's law school. Primary and secondary school systems remained segregated, however, and in the same year the Pamlico County NAACP filed a lawsuit for school equalization or integration. At the time, the national NAACP was readying the court challenge that would lead to the *Brown* decision.

Following the 1954 *Brown* decision, which ordered states' compliance "with all deliberate speed," North Carolina lawmakers moved with extraordinary caution in the face of virulent white opposition to the decision. Under the leadership of Lieutenant Governor Luther H. Hodges, the state developed a series of legal and administrative barriers that blocked school integration in the interest of "local choice" without appearing to openly violate the Supreme Court ruling. The most significant of these policies were the Pupil Assignment Act of 1955 and the Pearsall Plan of 1956.

The Pupil Assignment Act placed authority for public education in the hands of local school districts to deter a statewide lawsuit by the NAACP. It also hampered black students' efforts to transfer to white schools by establishing a series of vague criteria by which school boards could deny black students admission, without citing race as the reason. The act thus divided the state school system into numerous potential legal targets and gave local schools ways to avoid school desegregation that were legal under state statutes. Meanwhile, the Pearsall Plan —which comprised six laws, one resolution, and a constitutional amendment—further forestalled integration by making it voluntary by establishing private tuition grants from the state for white parents who did not wish their children to attend an integrated school. The plan was said by whites to have "softened the blow" of integration in North Carolina and to have given the state time to initiate progressive desegregation programs without incident. However, the plan was bitterly opposed by blacks, who recognized its shortcomings, and by most whites, who continued their hostile protests at the few previously all-white schools to which blacks were admitted.

In 1957 North Carolina admitted only 11 black students to previously all-white schools. In 1958 the school boards in Charlotte, Greensboro, and Winston-Salem (which had first admitted blacks to white schools the year before) admitted a few additional blacks without incident. But even these modest gains for African Americans in the public schools were achieved in only a few counties by the mid-1960s. A few towns near military bases, where black officers asserted their influence in local schools, were an exception to the general pattern, but overall in North Carolina, the combination of the Pearsall Plan and the Pupil Assignment Act allowed local school boards to delay segregation for more than a decade.

North Carolina saw a significant rise in racial violence and membership in the Ku Klux Klan (KKK) in reaction to school desegregation and social change in the 1950s. Some blacks and other minorities involved in the movement for civil rights met white backlash with equal force. Robert F. Williams, president of the Monroe chapter of the NAACP, began organizing squads of black citizens to arm themselves against the KKK in 1957. The national NAACP, which embraced Martin Luther King Jr.'s doctrine of nonviolent direct action, disapproved of Williams's philosophy of armed self-defense and suspended him from the organization. But Williams was undeterred and remained an important advocate for black armed resistance on the state and national level.

Integration Efforts in the Workplace, Sit-Ins, and Other Nonviolent Protests

Progress toward school desegregation was painfully slow, but schools were not the only battle front in the civil rights movement in North Carolina. Integration of the workplace was, for example, another significant focus of the movement. In 1957 delegates from the American Friends Service Committee (AFSC), a Quaker organization dedicated to social justice, successfully pressured and encouraged textile manufacturers to hire black employees in one of their North Carolina factories. Though the African Americans were placed in clerical positions, the move laid a foundation for future advances. In 1958 the AFSC reported that it had assisted in the appointment of a black supervisor at a large textile mill in Greensboro. In 1959 a textile manufacturer in High Point agreed to hire five black men as production workers. Some white workers left the mill when the blacks started, but the mill owner remained steadfast and the experiment succeeded. The exclusion of blacks remained widespread, however, until the pressure of the Civil Rights Act of 1964 forced companies to relent. Soon after the act went into effect, Southerland Mills in Mebane hired some of the state's first black female textile workers.

Civil rights activists fought racism in their communities by standing up for themselves and using all the tools and tactics of the national civil rights movement; civil disobedience, strikes, picket lines, and economic boycotts (methods also utilized by the labor movement) were hallmarks of the 1950s and 1960s. The use of nonviolent protests in such forms as marches and sit-ins led to important progress in the integration of North Carolina's theaters, hotels, and restaurants by 1963. That year the General Assembly voted to desegregate the National Guard. Municipal cemeteries were eventually integrated as well.

Although sit-ins had occasionally been staged during labor strikes and other civil actions earlier on, they were not a widespread form of protest until the 1960s. Sit-ins were attempted in North Carolina as early as 1943 without publicity. In 1957 seven African American students led by the Reverend Douglas E. Moore went into the Royal Ice Cream Company shop in Durham using a whites-only entrance. They took seats inside, only to be arrested and fined $25.00 apiece.

A sea change for the sit-in movement occurred in Greensboro on 1 Feb. 1960. Four black students from the North Carolina Agricultural and Technical State University walked into an F. W. Woolworth's in downtown Greensboro at about 4:30 in the afternoon. Ezell A. Blair (now Jibreel Khazan), Franklin E. McCain, Joseph A. McNeil, and David L. Richmond

Durham pastor and civil rights leader Douglas E. Moore gives communion to five of the local youths who sat-in at the Royal Ice Cream Company shop in 1957. Courtesy Virginia Williams and the Civil Rights Heritage Project, Durham County Library.

made various purchases from different departments of the store, thereby becoming paying customers. They then proceeded to Woolworth's luncheonette counter and requested to be served. In reply they were told that blacks were not served in that establishment, but they could order food at a stand nearby. As black workers behind the counter shook their heads, calling the boys foolish, and white workers asked the four to leave, the youths remained seated at the counter until the store was closed. The next day the number of protesters increased to 15, which became about 150 on the third day and then mushroomed to nearly 1,000 the day after that. The protests soon spread to other downtown lunch counters. The nonviolent protesters, including area white students as well, augmented their sit-ins with economic boycotts. Finally, on 25 July 1960, it was announced that Woolworth's, Kress, and Meyers lunch counters would henceforth serve blacks.

After the initial Greensboro sit-in, other such protests followed around the state and the South: in the short term, a week later they spread to Durham and Winston-Salem and then to communities in South Carolina, Florida, Virginia, and Tennessee, while, in the long-term, they remained an effective tactic for many years. Charlotte and Salisbury both saw successful sit-in movements, and in 1964 sit-ins came to Brady's Restaurant and the Colonial Drug Store, two popular eateries in Chapel Hill. These events heralded the collective entrance of young people into the civil rights movement as high school and college students participated en masse in sit-ins around the country. Organizations such as CORE held workshops for sit-in planners, and protesters always adhered to certain guidelines. For example, they faced straight ahead at the counter, dressed well, generally did not talk among themselves, and always remained calm and nonviolent.

In April 1960 a new organization emerged from the North

Carolina sit-ins. Ella Baker, who by then worked for the Southern Christian Leadership Conference (SCLC), invited a number of southern university students, some of whom had participated in sit-ins, to Shaw University in Raleigh. The Student Nonviolent Coordinating Committee (SNCC) grew out of these meetings, with the purpose of coordinating the use of nonviolent direct action against segregation and other forms of racism. Over the course of the 1960s, SNCC's importance in local efforts increased with its growing profile and significance in the national movement, in which it played a leading role in the Freedom Rides, the Mississippi Freedom Summer, and the Mississippi Freedom Democratic Party.

Community activism continued in North Carolina, often without attention from the national press, and a number of local black leaders formed movements within their own communities. Golden Frinks, a member of the NAACP and SCLC, was one of the most important civil rights organizers in eastern North Carolina in the 1960s. Frinks was a leader in the 1961–62 Edenton Movement, a campaign distinguished by its location and supporters. Unlike most of the prominent civil rights protests up to that point, the Edenton Movement took place in an isolated, mostly rural area rather than a city. Its leadership came not from a college-educated or middle-class population, but from poor, uneducated people. Frinks used the strategies of civil disobedience, picket lines, slowdowns, strikes, and boycotts developed in Edenton, the small eastern North Carolina town where the movement began, to drive the Williamston Freedom Movement that included 32 straight days of demonstrations and sit-ins in the nearby town of that name. Activists also staged an economic boycott of downtown businesses and attempted to enroll black students at the local white high school. Their efforts won important concessions. The degrading "colored/white" signs were removed from public places, and hospitals, libraries, and schools were integrated.

In 1962 and 1963 a coalition of SNCC, the SCLC, CORE, and the NAACP—called the Council of Federated Organizations—was formed to register black voters all over the South. Several local organizations also participated. In North Carolina, the Halifax County Voters Movement exemplified the organized efforts of blacks to shape politics in their communities. The organization's aims included increased black voter registration, more blacks running for office, and improved relations with white officials. Similar groups soon appeared in nearby Bertie and Northampton Counties. Meanwhile, demands for equal political participation resounded throughout the nation, pressuring President Lyndon B. Johnson to support two important pieces of legislation aimed at securing full civil and voting rights for African Americans. Both the national Civil Rights Act of 1964 (which included policies such as affirmative action) and the Voting Rights Act of 1965 addressed the need for black voter registration. The latter act—coming in the

Demonstrators block the entrance to Colonial Drug Store in Chapel Hill in 1964 to protest its policy of serving whites only. NCC.

wake of the dramatic, and in many ways climactic, Selma-to-Montgomery March of 21–25 Mar. 1965—is generally considered the culmination of one phase of the civil rights movement, as the coalition of civil rights organizations of the early 1960s soon began to unravel as a result of disagreements over strategies—including white involvement in the movement—and personalities.

Forced School Desegregation and the Rise of the Black Power Movement

In 1967 new antiterror laws made it a felony in North Carolina to burn crosses or wear masks for the purpose of intimidation or to burn occupied buildings. The law also allowed the governor to offer rewards of up to $10,000 for information leading to the arrest and conviction of felons. With prodding by President Johnson, the Civil Rights Act of 1964 was broadened in 1968 to include, in addition to African Americans, American Indians, Hispanics, Puerto Ricans, and Asian

Americans. North Carolina followed the federal lead, although reluctantly in a number of cases. The General Assembly created a Commission of Indian Affairs to deal "fairly and effectively" with a broad range of Indian concerns and in 1971 passed an equal opportunity law applying to all units of state and local government. It was the first such law in a southern state.

Little meaningful integration had occurred in the state's public school systems by the late 1960s. Gains in education for African Americans in North Carolina were very slow in coming and encountered a great deal of opposition at both the community and state level and from both official school district policies and private actions, such as organized intimidation campaigns led by the KKK and other groups. Only as result of pressure from the U.S. Department of Health, Education, and Welfare, bolstered by a 1966 federal court decision declaring the Pearsall Plan unconstitutional, did mandatory desegregation begin to arrive in North Carolina counties. Even then, in counties where schools were desegregated, the formerly black schools were commonly shut down and the black teachers fired. This one-way integration essentially erased the historic and cultural heritage of the black schools and their leaders, ensuring that black students would be taught by whites only. When blacks in Hyde County learned that the local school board had endorsed such a desegregation plan, they boycotted the public schools for the entire 1968–69 academic year. Only in 1969, under pressure from the federal government and the courts, did the state enter negotiations with the leaders of the boycott. Ultimately, black families won a victory by ensuring that the traditionally black schools in the district would remain open and black teachers would keep their jobs.

While major victories were won in the late 1960s, the assassination of Martin Luther King Jr. in 1968 was a tragedy that proved pivotal in the overall direction of the national civil rights movement, which had begun to experience divisive tensions even before King's death. Robert F. Williams, advocate of armed self-defense, became a prominent voice in the 1960s in the national debate over nonviolence and armed resistance as strategies for obtaining civil rights. Williams, in self-exile in Cuba, broadcast his ideas for armed self-defense and black liberation in a radio show called *Radio Free Dixie*, which could be received throughout the South. Williams's ideas influenced a new generation of civil rights activists and organizations such as the Black Panthers, a militant black nationalist group that rose to prominence in the late 1960s. King's assassination helped galvanize this shift in the national civil rights movement, which by the 1970s began to give way to the Black Power movement. Black Power organizations found fertile ground in North Carolina, with Black Panther Party affiliates forming in several of the state's cities and remaining active through the mid-1970s.

Continued Civil Rights Battles in the State

The shift in strategy after the 1960s did not alter the fundamental goals of civil rights workers. Legislation born of the movement eliminated the practice of legal segregation, but activists still fought racism and de facto segregation in North Carolina and the rest of the nation. Individuals, groups, and organizations continued that battle for social, educational, and political equality through both peaceful and nonpeaceful means. And white resistance and violence continued to greet the state's African Americans, with racially charged incidents continuing into the 1970s. One of the most notorious occurred in 1970 in Oxford, when Henry "Dickie" Marrow, a 23-year-old black veteran, was murdered by Robert Teel, a white man with KKK connections, and his sons. Teel's subsequent acquittal led to anger, violence, and unrest among the town's African American population. Similarly, a week of racial tension in Wilmington in early February 1971, rooted in dissatisfaction among black students who boycotted a public school,

Marchers from Hyde County and elsewhere around the state enter Raleigh on 14 Feb. 1969 to protest Hyde County's school desegregation plan. Courtesy of NCOA&H. The *Raleigh News and Observer* files.

left two men dead and others wounded and resulted in the use of the National Guard and the imposition of a citywide curfew. A white-owned grocery store was fire-bombed, and and a year later nine black men and a white woman (nicknamed the "Wilmington Ten") were convicted of the crime. In 1980 a federal court overturned the convictions on technical grounds. Unrest was pronounced in the state following the 1971 U.S. Supreme Court ruling in the case of *Swann v. Charlotte-Mecklenburg Board of Education* that forced cities across the South to enact a policy of busing if necessary to achieve racial desegregation in public schools. On 3 Nov. 1979 five members of the Communist Workers Party were slain at a Greensboro anti-Klan rally. At a trial in 1980 six Klansmen were cleared of murder charges stemming from the incident. The jury's verdict set off protest demonstrations on several college campuses throughout the state.

In 1981, for the first time in North Carolina history, a county (Moore) was split between congressional districts when the General Assembly turned to the decennial task of redrawing lines for congressional and legislative districts. The state attorney general regarded the redistricting plan as so deficient that he recommended that the General Assembly redraw the lines. Thus began a controversy with strong racial overtones that continued after the next census as well, when North Carolina gained a twelfth U.S. House seat in 1990. In 1992 Melvin L. Watt was elected to represent the new district; he and Eva M. Clayton (elected in the First Congressional District the same year) became the first black congressional representatives from the state since 1900. In 1993 the U.S. Supreme Court ordered further hearings in a case that charged that the gerrymandering of the North Carolina's Twelfth Congressional District violated the rights of white voters. The U.S. Supreme Court upheld the legality of the Twelfth District's boundaries in 2001, but battles over race and representation in the drawing of North Carolina's congressional and legislative boundaries continued to rage in the early 2000s.

In addition to African Americans, other North Carolinians, including Native Americans, women's groups, people with disabilities, gays and lesbians, and AIDS/HIV patients, have fought for and continue to seek civil rights in a variety of legal and social arenas. Civil rights issues lie at the heart of several manufacturing, environmental, and political controversies in the state, as well. In 1982 opposition developed over the selection of sites for hazardous waste disposal, as environmental and civil rights activists tried unsuccessfully to block the deposit of PCB-contaminated soil in a Warren County dump. Some associated the site selection with the high proportion of African Americans in the county. Objections arose, on similar grounds, to a planned waste treatment plant to be privately built in Anson County. Later, residents of Orange, Chatham, and Wake Counties faced "not in my backyard" controversies over unwanted waste disposal sites. National publicity also surrounded a deadly fire at the Imperial Food Products chicken processing plant in Hamlet in 1991, which claimed the lives of 25 employees—19 of them single mothers. Accusations of racial discrimination were raised when it was learned that the Hamlet Fire Chief had refused help during the tragedy from the African American Dobbins Heights Volunteer Fire Department, which was minutes away and offering assistance. The owner of the plant, Emmett J. Roe, was sentenced to 20 years in prison for involuntary manslaughter for having violated numerous safety regulations.

In 1986 Robeson County—long afflicted by triracial controversies involving American Indians, African Americans, and whites—received national attention when, in a bitterly debated referendum, voters narrowly supported the merger of all five of its school systems into one. The murder of Julian T. Pierce, a Lumbee Indian candidate for a judgeship, stirred accusations that he had been assassinated by white political foes. An investigation indicated that he was shot by another Indian, who committed suicide three days later. On 1 Feb. 1988 Eddie Hatcher and Timothy B. Jacobs, calling themselves "Tuscarora Indians," seized the office of the *Robesonian* (a Lumberton newspaper) and held the staff hostage at gunpoint for several hours in an effort to publicize the abuse of Indian civil rights in the county. In a surprise verdict, a federal jury cleared both men on hostage-taking and related charges.

References: David S. Cecelski, *Along Freedom Road: Hyde County, North Carolina, and the Fate of Black Schools in the South* (1994); William H. Chafe, *Civilities and Civil Rights: Greensboro, North Carolina, and the Black Struggle for Freedom* (1980); Jeffrey J. Crow, Paul D. Escott, and Flora J. Hatley, *A History of African Americans in North Carolina* (2002); Jane Elizabeth Dailey, Bryant Simon, and Glenda Elizabeth Gilmore, *Jumpin' Jim Crow: Southern Politics from Civil War to Civil Rights* (2000); Davison M. Douglas, *Reading, Writing, and Race: The Desegregation of the Charlotte Schools* (1995); John Egerton, *Speak Now against the Day: The Generation before the Civil Rights Movement in the South* (1994); Pamela Marie Emerson, *A Newspaper Held Hostage: A Case Study of Terrorism and the Media* (1989); Raymond Gavins, "Behind a Veil: Black North Carolinians in the Age of Jim Crow," in Paul D. Escott, ed., *W. J. Cash and the Minds of the South* (1992); Christina Greene, *Our Separate Ways: Women and the Black Freedom Movement in Durham, North Carolina* (2005); Robert Rodgers Korstad, *Civil Rights Unionism: Tobacco Workers and the Struggle for Democracy in the Mid-Twentieth-Century South* (2003); Waldo E. Martin Jr. and Patricia Sullivan, eds., *Civil Rights in the United States* (2000); Timothy B. Tyson, *Blood Done Sign My Name: A True Story* (2004); Tyson, *Radio Free Dixie: Robert F. Williams and the Roots of Black Power* (1999).

> *William S. Powell*
> *Allyson C. Criner*
> Additional research provided by Scott Matthews, Sally Mullikin, and Wiley J. Williams.

SEE ALSO Black Panther Party; Charlotte Three; Congress of Racial Equality; "Death to the Klan" March; Fourteenth Amendment; Gays and Lesbians; Greensboro Sit-Ins; Ku Klux Klan; Lumbee Indians; National Association for the Advancement of Colored People; Pearsall Plan; Pupil Assignment Act; *Radio Free Dixie*; Student Nonviolent Coordinating Committee; *Swann v. Charlotte-Mecklenburg Board of Education*; Wilmington Ten; Women.

Civil War battles were fought at numerous locations throughout North Carolina, the majority of them in the eastern half of the state. In the western Mountain region, where pro-Union sentiment was strong, the violence tended to be more guerrilla in nature rather than confrontations between opposing armies. During the war, North Carolina suffered a greater number of battle casualties than any other Confederate state. According to available records and estimates, the number of North Carolina soldiers put into the field for state and Confederate service, embracing all classes and categories, was 133,905 men. Because of the incompleteness of the rolls,

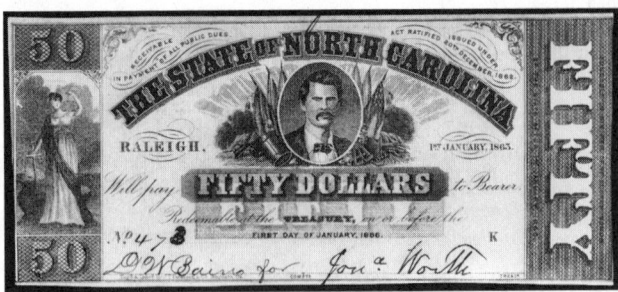

North Carolina $50 note issued in 1863. In the center of the note is a likeness of North Carolina governor Zebulon B. Vance. NCC.

Tintype (with image reversed for correct orientation) of Henry Speck Harris of Bahama, a casualty at the battle of Seven Pines in Virginia, 20 May 1863. NCC.

many historians believe this figure might actually be too low—despite the fact that the 1860 census showed that North Carolina had a white population of 629,932, with only about 115,000 men of voting age. These statistics illustrate how readily the available manpower of the state turned out to serve the Confederacy.

Soldiers from North Carolina represented one-fifth to one-sixth of the troops put into the field by all 11 Confederate states combined. The price paid by North Carolina was similarly disproportionate: 677 officers and 13,845 enlisted men were killed in battle, and 330 officers and 4,821 enlisted men died of wounds, totaling 19,673 battle deaths. This represents 26 percent of the 74,524-man total battle loss suffered by all Confederate forces in the war (South Carolina had the second highest total with 12,922 battle deaths). Death from disease also claimed 541 officers and 20,061 enlisted men from North Carolina, totaling 20,602. Thus, of the 133,905 North Carolina men who fought for the Confederacy, 40,275 (30 percent) did not come home.

In addition, 3,156 white and 5,035 black North Carolinians served in the Union army. Although blacks were not actively recruited into Confederate service for the state, some free blacks were known to have enlisted and served in regular North Carolina regiments.

Secession and First North Carolina Enlistments and Casualties

In North Carolina, the reaction to Abraham Lincoln's election to the presidency was unlike that of the large slaveholding states in the Lower South. Most North Carolinians believed that their state should adopt a wait-and-see policy regarding the new Republican president, and on 28 Feb. 1861 voters rejected a convention to consider secession. The political mood in North Carolina turned in favor of secession only after Lincoln called for troops from the state in April to help suppress the "southern rebellion." Most North Carolinians refused to fight fellow southerners.

The earliest instance of Confederate military service by North Carolinians is that of two young Halifax County friends, Whitmel Hill Anthony and Jacob Higgs. When South Caro-

lina seceded from the Union on 20 Dec. 1860, Anthony, age 17, was the cadet major and Higgs, age 19, a cadet captain at St. Timothy's Hall, a military academy in Catonsville, Md., run by an abolitionist Episcopalian minister but a hotbed of southern sympathies. The two boys traveled by rail to Charleston, where they joined the Palmetto Guard and served on Morris Island training a battery near Fort Sumter. Initially in the service of South Carolina, they became soldiers of the Confederacy in February 1861, when its constitution was ratified in Montgomery, Ala. They served through the bombardment of Fort Sumter on the night of 11–12 April, and when North Carolina began raising regiments soon afterward, they returned to Halifax County to join military companies in their home state. Anthony was elected first lieutenant of the Halifax Light Infantry and later commanded Company B, 1st North Carolina Cavalry. Higgs rose to the rank of sergeant in the Scotland Neck Mounted Riflemen. Both men survived the war.

North Carolinian Henry Lawson Wyatt was the first Confederate soldier killed in action in the Civil War. Wyatt, from Tarboro, was a 19-year-old private in Company A, 1st North Carolina Volunteers, commanded by Col. Daniel Harvey Hill. On 10 June 1861 the regiment fought a battle at Big Bethel Church, Va. Wyatt was one of six soldiers who volunteered to burn a house sheltering Union sharpshooters. As the men ap-

African Americans joining the Union lines near New Bern in early 1863. NCC.

proached the house, Wyatt was shot in the head and died a few hours later. A plaque on the Virginia battlefield and a statue on Union Square in Raleigh commemorate his sacrifice.

Political and Social Turmoil during the War

Wartime relations between Governor Zebulon B. Vance and the central Confederate government in Richmond under President Jefferson Davis were often strained. Vance, along with many North Carolinians, believed that the state was overlooked and unappreciated by the Confederacy. At times Vance publicly defied the Richmond government as he struggled to make North Carolina self-sufficient. Independent North Carolinians were offended by the Conscription Act, and Vance exempted scores of men considered essential for state operations. Increasing taxes also created resentment in a people tired of war. Further, Vance and Davis often clashed over Davis's periodic suspension of the writ of habeas corpus.

Much of the European military supplies delivered by blockade-runners came through Wilmington, and the Wilmington & Weldon Railroad was nicknamed the "lifeline of the Confederacy" because of the vital supplies transported to the Army of Northern Virginia during the final year of the war. All textile production in North Carolina went to the manu-

facture of military uniforms. Since most soldiers were farmers who owned no slaves, the wives and children they left at home faced enormous hardships and responsibilities. The exemption of slaveholders owning 20 or more slaves from military duty also created a class division between nonslaveholders and those who owned slaves. In addition, shortages caused by the blockade coupled with inflation created misery at home and in the army. With no established welfare system, the families of many soldiers literally faced starvation, and women often begged Governor Vance to release husbands and sons from military service. Families also faced the impressment of food supplies and farm animals by Confederate agents. And for the first time, many North Carolina women sought work outside the home in an attempt to support their families.

Unionism and Violence in the Western Counties

The Civil War was especially brutal in the Appalachian Mountains, where numerous residents of Virginia, Tennessee, and North Carolina remained loyal to the Union. Madison County, N.C., suffered greatly from recruiters and raiders. Robberies, murders, and burned-out homes were so commonplace that Confederates considered much of the county, particularly the Laurel Valley, as insurrectionary. Some Unionists became identified with the Heroes of America, or "Red Strings," a secret organization that worked to defeat the Confederacy. Richmond and Raleigh both sent troops to arrest deserters and restore "law and order" in western communities opposed to Confederate rule. When much of eastern North Carolina fell under Federal control, many blacks and some whites enlisted in Union regiments. The lack of food for families and soldiers alike fueled a growing peace movement, led in great part by William W. Holden, editor of the Raleigh-based newspaper, the *North Carolina Standard*.

Military Movements, Battles, and Outcomes in the State

Union victories in the Eastern theater during 1861–62 were largely limited to coastal North Carolina, but these immediately illuminated the Union strategy of controlling the ports and thus limiting supplies to the southern interior. Hatteras fell in a Union amphibious invasion in the late summer of 1861, and on 8 Feb. 1862 Roanoke Island surrendered to Union troops under Gen. Ambrose Burnside. Soon Federal forces held New Bern, Morehead City, Beaufort, and Fort Macon and controlled much of eastern North Carolina.

North Carolinians were appalled over these quick northern victories and furious with the Richmond government, which had left the state largely undefended. For a short time, Lincoln appointee Edward Stanly, headquartered in New Bern, served as military governor of North Carolina. Confederate political and military leaders hoped that newly constructed ironclad vessels would be the key in freeing eastern North Carolina. Although never tested in battle, the CSS *Neuse* was built to liberate New Bern and other coastal towns, while the CSS *Albemarle* played a significant role in the Battle of Plymouth (17–20 Apr. 1864).

In January 1865 Federal forces captured Fort Fisher and a month later the port of Wilmington. Maj. Gen. William T. Sherman entered North Carolina from the south, and the Battle of Bentonville on 19–21 Mar. 1865 was the only major attempt after the Battle of Atlanta to defeat Sherman's army. Federal cavalry under Maj. Gen. George H. Stoneman in late March and April 1865 raided and destroyed property in North Carolina's mountain communities and in the western Piedmont. On 26 Apr. 1865, at the Bennett farmhouse near Durham, Gen. Joseph Johnston surrendered his army to Sherman—the largest Confederate troop surrender of the war. North Carolinians such as Daniel H. Hill, William Dorsey Pender, Stephen Dodson Ramseur, James J. Pettigrew, and Robert F. Hoke proved themselves to be among the most reliable Confederate generals, and Braxton Bragg was among the most controversial.

References: John G. Barrett, *North Carolina as a Civil War Battleground, 1861–1865* (1960); John S. Carbone, *The Civil War in Coastal North Carolina* (2001); Walter Clark, ed., *Histories of the Several Regiments and Battalions from North Carolina in the Great War, 1861–1865* (5 vols., 1901); Paul D. Escott, *Many Excellent People: Power and Privilege in North Carolina, 1850–1900* (1985); John C. Inscoe and Gordon B. McKinney, *The Heart of Confederate Appalachia: Western North Carolina in the Civil War* (2000); William R. Trotter, *The Civil War in North Carolina* (3 vols., 1988–89).

Tom Belton
Paul Branch
Additional research provided by Whitmel M. Joyner, Paul E. Kuhl, and Jo Ann Williford.

SEE ALSO Bentonville, Battle of; Blockade-Running; Fort Fisher, Battle of; Ironclads; Military Installations, Civil War; Peace Movement (Civil War); Secession Movement; Sherman's March; Union Volunteer Regiments.

Civil War Rosters. A *Roster of North Carolina Troops in the War between the States*, by Confederate veteran John Wheeler Moore, was an undertaking by the state of North Carolina in 1881 to publish a list of its Confederate soldiers. The four volumes of Moore's *Roster*, as it came to be called, include the names of 106,498 soldiers—about 70 percent of the state's Confederate troops—and are arranged by military unit. The last volume, after identifying the regiments and separate battalions, lists general and staff officers or North Carolinians in the Confederate navy and elsewhere. For each individual recorded, the roster generally gives rank, date, and county of enlistment. Remarks about promotions, desertions, injuries, capture, and death in battle are sometimes noted.

The North Carolina Civil War Roster Project began in 1961 under the auspices of the North Carolina Confederate Centennial Commission and in 1965 was transferred to the State Department of Archives and History, now the Division of Archives and History of the Department of Cultural Resources. Its purpose is to publish histories of all North Carolina units raised during the war, as well as rosters containing the names and service records of members. When completed, the series, entitled *North Carolina Troops, 1861–1865: A Roster*, will comprise 17 individually indexed volumes, each providing histories and rosters of at least four regiments and service records of approximately 7,500 men. An eighteenth volume, a master index, will give the names of approximately 130,000 North Carolina military personnel listed in *North Carolina Troops* and the volumes and pages on which their service records appear.

Louis H. Manarin headed the Civil War Roster Project from 1961 until February 1970, when Weymouth T. Jordan Jr. took over the editorship. Rosters are arranged numerically by regiment and then alphabetically by company. A field and staff section precedes the company roster for each regiment. Within each company roster, officers and enlisted men, excluding captains, appear alphabetically in separate sections. Captains and field and staff personnel are listed by date of rank. Each

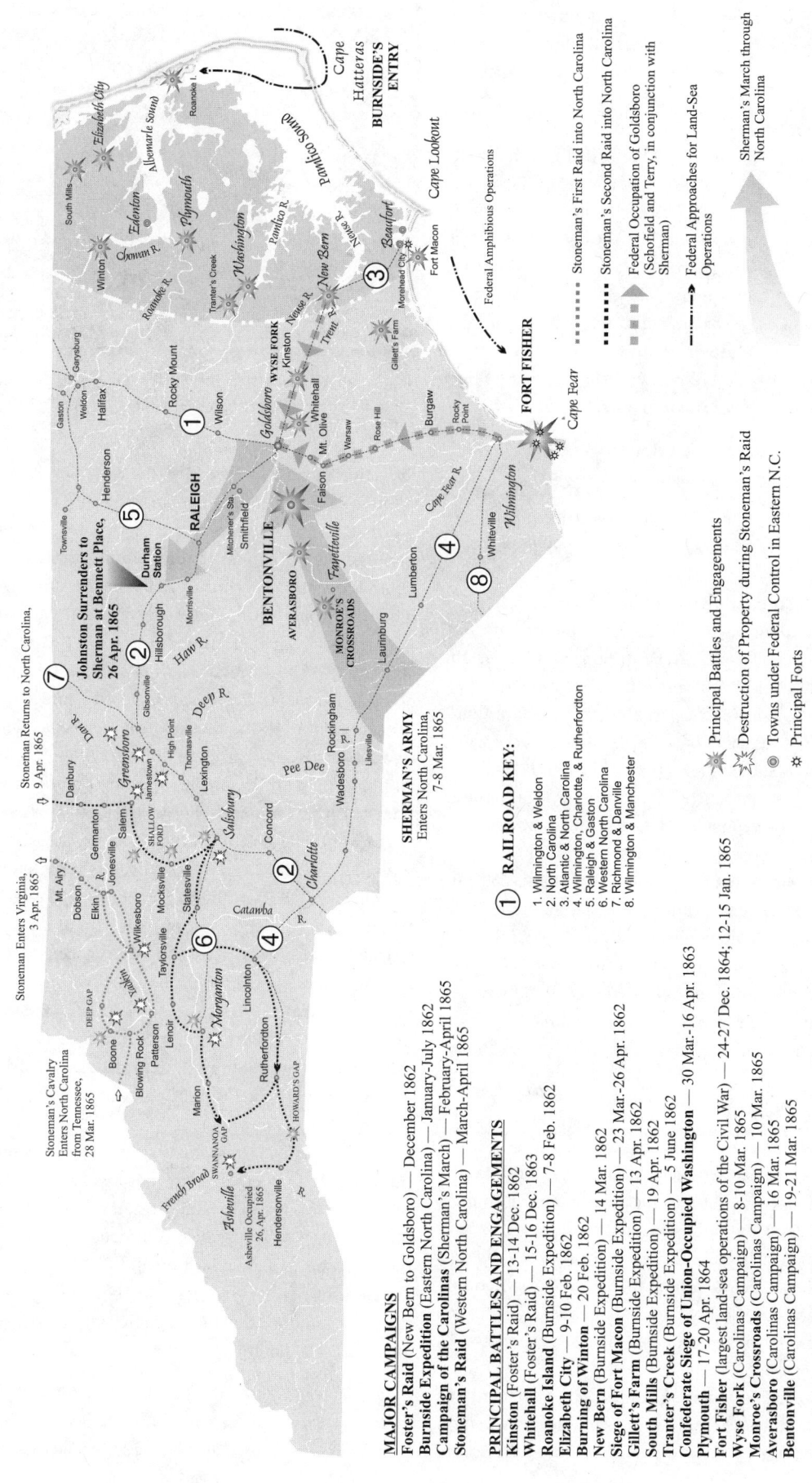

MAJOR CAMPAIGNS

Foster's Raid (New Bern to Goldsboro) — December 1862
Burnside Expedition (Eastern North Carolina) — January–July 1862
Campaign of the Carolinas (Sherman's March) — February–April 1865
Stoneman's Raid (Western North Carolina) — March–April 1865

PRINCIPAL BATTLES AND ENGAGEMENTS

Kinston (Foster's Raid) — 13–14 Dec. 1862
Whitehall (Foster's Raid) — 15–16 Dec. 1862
Roanoke Island (Burnside Expedition) — 7–8 Feb. 1862
Elizabeth City — 9–10 Feb. 1862
Burning of Winton — 20 Feb. 1862
New Bern (Burnside Expedition) — 14 Mar. 1862
Siege of Fort Macon (Burnside Expedition) — 23 Mar.–26 Apr. 1862
Gillett's Farm (Burnside Expedition) — 13 Apr. 1862
South Mills (Burnside Expedition) — 19 Apr. 1862
Tranter's Creek (Burnside Expedition) — 5 June 1862
Confederate Siege of Union-Occupied Washington — 30 Mar.–16 Apr. 1863
Plymouth — 17–20 Apr. 1864
Fort Fisher (largest land-sea operations of the Civil War) — 24–27 Dec. 1864; 12–15 Jan. 1865
Wyse Fork (Carolinas Campaign) — 8–10 Mar. 1865
Monroe's Crossroads (Carolinas Campaign) — 10 Mar. 1865
Averasboro (Carolinas Campaign) — 16 Mar. 1865
Bentonville (Carolinas Campaign) — 19–21 Mar. 1865

RAILROAD KEY:

1. Wilmington & Weldon
2. North Carolina
3. Atlantic & North Carolina
4. Wilmington, Charlotte, & Rutherfordton
5. Raleigh & Gaston
6. Western North Carolina
7. Richmond & Danville
8. Wilmington & Manchester

SHERMAN'S ARMY
Enters North Carolina,
7–8 Mar. 1865

Johnston Surrenders to
Sherman at Bennett Place,
26 Apr. 1865

Stoneman Returns to North Carolina,
9 Apr. 1865

Stoneman Enters Virginia,
3 Apr. 1865

Stoneman's Cavalry
Enters North Carolina
from Tennessee,
28 Mar. 1865

Asheville Occupied
26. Apr. 1865

Federal Amphibious Operations

············· Stoneman's First Raid into North Carolina

▪▪▪▪▪▪▪ Stoneman's Second Raid into North Carolina

⬛ Federal Occupation of Goldsboro
(Schofield and Terry, in conjunction with
Sherman)

– · – · – Federal Approaches for Land-Sea
Operations

⬆ Sherman's March through
North Carolina

✸ Principal Battles and Engagements

✸ Destruction of Property during Stoneman's Raid

◉ Towns under Federal Control in Eastern N.C.

✱ Principal Forts

Civil War campaigns and battles. Map by Mark Anderson Moore, courtesy N COA&H.

name is followed by a service record of approximately 100 words that includes, if known, the soldier's county of birth and residence, his age and occupation at the time of enlistment, his promotion record, whether he was wounded, captured, or killed, and whether he deserted or died of disease.

The Civil War Roster Project had published 15 volumes by 2006. Volumes 1 and 2 cover artillery and cavalry units, respectively; volumes 3–15 contain rosters and histories of infantry units. Volume 16 will present additional Confederate infantry regiments, and volume 17 will contain rosters of miscellaneous Confederate units such as the junior and senior reserves, militia, Home Guard, navy, and marines. It will also include North Carolina Federal troops (four regiments of African American soldiers and four of whites) and many North Carolinians who served in units from other states.

Reference: C. F. W. Coker, *North Carolina Civil War Records: An Introduction to Printed and Manuscript Sources* (1977).

Weymouth T. Jordan Jr.
Wiley J. Williams

Claims Committees were part of both houses of the General Assembly until 1949. North Carolina inherited its fundamental legal system from Great Britain, and under the common law of England, the sovereign was immune from lawsuits. Translated to America, this legal doctrine meant that a state could not be sued in its own courts without its consent. Thus, a citizen who suffered an injury at the hands of a state employee was dependent on the legislature for legal remedy. The claims committees considered the legitimacy of all claims for money damages asserted against the state.

The North Carolina House discontinued its claims committee after 1933 and the Senate, after 1949. The function of the claims committees was made obsolete by the Tort Claims Act (1951), which waived the state's immunity for active negligence up to a specified maximum amount that has been increased from time to time. In the modern day, tort claims against the state are heard and decided by the Industrial Commission.

Joseph Ferrell

The Clansman, a novel recounting the Civil War, Reconstruction, and the so-called redemption of the South by the Ku Klux Klan, was written by North Carolina author Thomas Dixon Jr. (1864–1946) and published by Doubleday, Page and Company in 1905. The book, a sequel to Dixon's *The Leopard's Spots* (1903), was set in Washington, D.C., and the fictional town of Piedmont, S.C. Both volumes expressed the author's outrage at a dramatic presentation of Harriet Beecher Stowe's *Uncle Tom's Cabin*.

With sales exceeding 1 million copies, Dixon adapted *The Clansman* for the stage. The play of the same title opened on 27 Sept. 1905 and was an immediate hit; it toured the South,

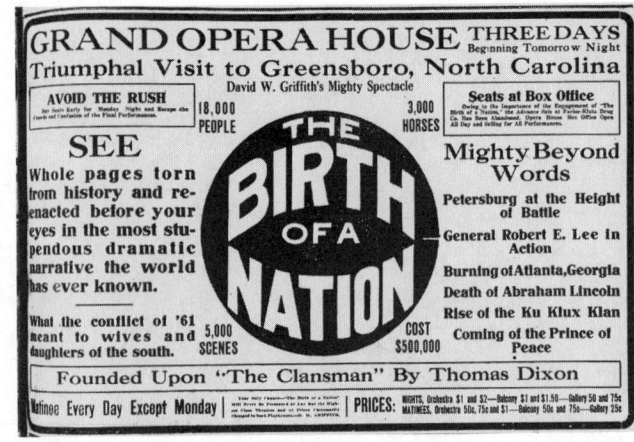

Half-page advertisement for the film *The Birth of a Nation*, based on *The Clansman*, which appeared in the *Greensboro Daily News*, 7 Nov. 1915. NCC.

the Midwest, and ultimately the East. Governor Robert B. Glenn of North Carolina declared that the production would "correct the foul misrepresentation done this beloved section." Although panned by numerous critics and even condemned by the governor of Alabama for stirring racial animosity, the play was a sellout everywhere it appeared.

The novel was then turned into D. W. Griffith's silent film classic *The Birth of a Nation* (1915), starring Lillian Gish. Word of its controversial themes spread rapidly, and it appeared that censors might kill the release. The movie was denounced by Oswald Garrison Villard, editor of the *New York Evening Post*, and Moorfield Storey, president of the American Bar Association. At Dixon's initiative, his good friend President Woodrow Wilson and the cabinet attended a private showing at the White House on 18 Feb. 1915. Wilson is reported to have said the film was "like writing history with lightning." Thereafter Dixon arranged a showing for members of the U.S. Supreme Court and Congress. This squelched a censorship effort in New York City, where the film opened with police protection in March. Despite a riot of 10,000 people in Boston and other protests, as well as the high price of admission ($2.00, versus 15 cents for a typical movie), ticket sales were brisk. Between 1915 and 1927 box office receipts topped $60 million, not including foreign showings.

The Birth of a Nation, the first full-length historical drama translated to film, changed the nature of moviemaking. Use of the production's technical devices of montage, close-up, fade-out, flashback, iris dissolve, soft-focus close-up, and climactic action became standard practice in the genre. Despite its racist overtones, the film has long been recognized as one of the most important technical achievements, as well as profitable works, in American cinema.

References: Roy E. Aitken, The Birth of a Nation *Story* (1965); Raymond A. Cook, *Fire from the Flint: The Amazing Careers of Thomas Dixon* (1968); John C. Inscoe, "The Clansman on Stage and Screen," *NCHR* 64 (April 1987); Fred Silva, ed., *Focus on The Birth of a Nation* (1971).

Ronnie W. Faulkner

Clapp's Mill, Battle of. The Revolutionary War engagement known as the Battle of Clapp's Mill occurred on 2 Mar. 1781 in a wooded area near a gristmill and the intersection of three major roads in present Chatham County. Col. Otho Williams, commander of the newly formed Light Troops of Gen. Nathanael Greene's American army, designed a plan to entrap the British army, hoping to duplicate the results of the Battle of Cowpens in South Carolina. Williams ordered Lt. Col. Henry Lee Jr. and his mounted Partisan Legion, the Botetourt, Va., militia, and a mixture of South Carolina and Salisbury district militia with flanking horse detachments under Capt. Joseph Graham and Capt. Richard Simmons to ford the Alamance River (now Great Alamance Creek) and proceed on the Cross Creek road to the vicinity of the British camp near the mill. In a second line following these troops were detachments of Maryland and Delaware Continentals. At the ford on the Alamance, about a mile from the British camp, Williams positioned Col. William Washington's dragoons and his own Maryland troops in hidden and strategically placed spots.

Lt. Col. Banastre Tarleton, commander of the British Loyal Legion and a favorite of Lord Charles Cornwallis, received intelligence of the approaching Americans and stationed British Light Troops in a cedar woods flanking the road on which the Americans were approaching. Commanding a segment of this force was Capt. Francis Dundas, who later served as the duke of Wellington's strategist in the Napoleonic Wars. Tarleton placed his Loyal Legion in a field by the mill and prepared to sweep around the hill that led down to the mill and turn the Americans' left.

Lee positioned a small detachment of infantry and six Catawba Indians in front of his legion. As these scouts began to enter the woods, they literally smelled the ambush. Heavy firing ensued, taking its toll primarily among the British Guards and Botetourt militia. Having fired several compulsory rounds, the Americans retreated with the militia in some haste and confusion as the British Guards initiated a charge.

The Americans' first line was supported by the Continentals in the second line and rallied by Williams himself; after re-forming at a nearby fort, they waited for Tarleton. Tarleton, believing statements by his prisoners that Greene was waiting at the fort, broke off the chase, evacuated his wounded, buried his dead, and returned past the mill to the British camp. Casualties were variously reported; at least 17 British soldiers were killed on the battlefield, and at least 8 Americans lost their lives. The wounded Americans were transported to the Moravian community at Salem.

As a result of the Battle of Clapp's Mill, Cornwallis, thinking that Greene might be drawn into a wider conflict, attacked him at Wetzell's Mill, New Garden, and Guilford Courthouse. Greene, however, continued to prefer skirmishing actions by small detachments to full-scale battles.

References: John Buchanan, *The Road to Guilford Courthouse: The American Revolution in the Carolinas* (1997); Richard K. Showman and Dennis M. Conrad, eds., *Papers of Nathanael Greene*, vol. 6 (1991).

R. M. Steele
Pat Bailey

Claremont College, founded in Hickory in 1880 as Claremont Female College, was intended to be for young women what Catawba College represented for young men—a school within the Reformed Church's tradition of support for higher education. In 1907 Claremont was accepted by the North Carolina Classis of the Reformed Church in the United States. The school's named was changed to Claremont College in 1909. The institution never achieved financial stability, however, and it closed in 1915. Claremont High School remains on the site of the college.

Reference: Gary R. Freeze, *The Catawbans: Crafters of a North Carolina County, 1747–1900* (1995).

Wiley J. Williams

Clarendon Bridge Company of Cumberland County was established in 1818 by legislative act for the purpose of building and maintaining a bridge across the Cape Fear River near Fayetteville (the company name came from an early name of the river). The General Assembly granted the power and authority for these operations to James Seawell and his associates (not named in the act) and further authorized them to collect tolls for passage over the bridge. As it did for ferries, inns, and taverns, the General Assembly set the rates. The highest toll was 75¢ for a four-wheeled pleasure carriage and the lowest 2.5¢ per head for hogs and sheep.

The Clarendon Bridge Company issued shares to finance the building of the bridge, which was completed in 1820. The largest shareholder, with 53 of the total 74 shares, was Ithiel Town, the illustrious New England engineer and architect, who used his original lattice truss plan (patented in 1820) to build the suspension bridge. Town is better known in North Carolina, however, as senior partner of the pioneer New York architectural firm of Town and Davis, whose work on the North Carolina State Capitol, completed in 1840, helped to create a neoclassical masterpiece.

The Clarendon Bridge, and presumably the company, survived until March 1865, when Gen. William J. Hardee's wing of the Confederate army burned the bridge to delay pursuing Union forces led by Gen. William T. Sherman.

Reference: John A. Oates, *The Story of Fayetteville and the Upper Cape Fear* (1972).

Jean B. Anderson

Clark's Regimental Histories is the popular title for the five-volume *Histories of the Several Regiments and Battalions from North Carolina in the Great War, 1861–1865*, edited by Walter Clark and published by the state in 1901.

In October 1894 the North Carolina Confederate Veterans Association in Raleigh resolved that a history of each regiment or other state organization that served with the Confederate army should be prepared by a member of that unit and printed at state expense. Although this was nearly 30 years after the war ended, men from all but five regiments were found to carry out this assignment. Those not included were the Senior Reserves, who were over age 45 at the time they served, as by 1894 few of them survived.

The General Assembly of 1899 provided funds for publication, but those who prepared the regimental histories did so without compensation. As histories were submitted to the editor and his advisers, they were reviewed and then submitted for publication in newspapers in the community from which the unit originated. This gave veterans of the unit an opportunity to recommend revisions. Among the newspapers that cooperated in this undertaking were the *Raleigh News and Observer*, *Raleigh Morning Post*, *Wilmington Messenger*, *Wilmington Star*, *Charlotte Observer*, *Fayetteville Observer*, *New Bern Journal*, *Asheville Citizen*, and *Waynesville Courier*.

The work is illustrated with wartime pictures, selected by the authors of the regimental histories, of a large number of the men. A few maps also were prepared especially for the work. The final volume contains accounts of numerous battles, many written by the officers in command. There are contributions on various military academies and on the role of the University of North Carolina in the war, the Home Guard, the first soldier from the state to die, the last battle and the last surrender, and other topics. There are indexes to the Appomattox parole list, to illustrations, and to the complete work.

William S. Powell

Classical Music, which includes a wide variety of traditional and contemporary orchestral and choral pieces, symphonies, and operas, enjoys great popularity in North Carolina, especially in larger metropolitan areas such as Charlotte, Winston-Salem, Asheville, Greensboro, and Raleigh. The state's colleges and universities, as well as many public and private high schools, have ongoing "serious" musical programs, men's and women's glee clubs, orchestras, and a variety of instrumental and vocal groups. In addition to enjoying classical music by attending performances of orchestras, bands, instrumentalists, or vocalists, North Carolina en-

thusiasts also turn to radio, television, or sound recordings for entertainment. In the early 2000s numerous FM stations, many of them public radio affiliates, served as classical music outlets for their regions and beyond, including WCQS in Asheville, WTEB in New Bern, WCPE in Raleigh, and WFDD in Winston-Salem.

During North Carolina's colonial and antebellum periods, plantation owners, religious leaders, and professionals in various fields were the primary purveyors of classical music, with the piano being an essential living room furnishing and singing and vocal groups providing musical entertainment at tea and dinner parties. Among the first North Carolinians to place significance on instrumental music were the Moravians, who settled the Piedmont in the mid-eighteenth century. The Moravians of Salem received their first trombones in 1772, and thereafter wind music played a critical role in town life. The Salem Band, which featured flute, clarinet, trumpet, bugle, French horn, bassoon, bass trombone, and bass drum, formally organized in 1831. Brass players from Salem formed the core of the 26th Regimental Band, North Carolina Troops, Confederate States of America. The group performed throughout the Civil War and was present at the Battle of Gettysburg.

Other North Carolina communities encouraged the development of wind bands during the mid-nineteenth century. A special venue for band performances was the North Carolina State Fair. The Agricultural Society hired bands to attract crowds to the inaugural State Fair in 1853. The bands pleased the crowds and became a part of fair tradition for the remainder of the century. The Salisbury Band was a particular favorite in the state fair's early years. Bands from Carthage, Concord, Winston, Raleigh, and Salem performed at later state fairs.

In the postbellum years until the 1890s, North Carolina could be described as culturally unfocused, struggling with the aftereffects of the Civil War, although the construction of "opera houses" in several towns indicated some interest by the middle and lower classes in the shows of traveling actors, bands, and minstrels. Beginning in the 1890s, women began forming groups to promote classical music in their communities. The earliest may have been Greensboro's Coney Club (later the Euterpe Club), organized in 1889. The Reineke Club in Wilmington was organized in 1892, and the Saturday Club in Asheville probably began in 1898. Other such clubs followed, including music clubs in Chapel Hill, Hickory, and Gastonia. Winston-Salem's choral society (renamed the Thursday Morning Music Club) was formed in 1914, as was Raleigh's St. Cecelia Choral Society.

A second and continuing period of the flowering of serious music in North Carolina began in the 1920s. Once again, women's groups, particularly the North Carolina Federation of Music Clubs—which supported classical music by staging performances, training future musicians, and financing research projects—were at the forefront of such efforts. In 1927 the federation's president, Estelle Walker Harper, raised the possibility of a North Carolina orchestra. Returning to the state in 1929, Lamar Stringfield—a North Carolina–born composer, conductor, and flutist who won a Pulitzer Prize in 1928 for his suite, *From the Southern Mountains*—was instrumental in the founding of the Institute of Folk Music at the University of North Carolina at Chapel Hill to link music, drama, and social science research. Soon he was actively advocating a state orchestra, which became the North Carolina Symphony in 1932—believed to be the first state-supported symphony in the country.

North Carolina's appreciation of classical music continued to grow throughout the twentieth century, a fact reflected by the proliferation of musical organizations, bands, orchestras, and companies throughout the state. The Grass Roots Opera Company (later the National Opera Company) was organized in 1948 in Raleigh by Alfred Johnson Fletcher and his wife Elizabeth Utley Fletcher. Since then, the company has taken both light and grand opera in English translation to countless North Carolina towns, with little costuming and without benefit of scenery. The North Carolina Opera Company, founded in 1978, is the educational and touring arm of the Charlotte Opera. Normally limited to in-state tours, its 1980–81 tour of *Porgy and Bess* in four states played to sellout audiences and has been cited as an example of remarkable success in the classical music field, as was its management for "Pavarotti in Concert" on 16 Nov. 2002 at the RBC Center in Raleigh.

North Carolina's largest cities and metropolitan areas are rich in opportunities to enjoy classical music forms. Groups in the Asheville, Winston-Salem, and Greensboro areas are typical of those elsewhere across the state. In addition to the Asheville Symphony Orchestra, music organizations in the Asheville area include the Asheville Chamber Music series, Asheville Choral Society, Brevard Music Center, Land of the Sky Chorus, and the music department of the University of North Carolina at Asheville. Winston-Salem boasts the North Carolina School of the Arts, a unit of the University of North Carolina System. This public institution offers professional training in the performing arts, including music, dance, design and production, drama, filmmaking, visual arts, and general studies. Its Stevens Center, completed in 1983, is used by several organizations, including the Little Symphony of the Winston-Salem Symphony. The city has a chapter of the American Guild of Organists. Forsyth County has two orchestras (Little Symphony and Salem Community Orchestra), the Piedmont Chamber Singers, the Piedmont Opera Theatre, the Winston-Salem Community Band, and the Winston-Salem Piedmont Triad Symphony.

Greensboro's principal classical music organizations include the Bel Canto Company, an adult professional ensemble; the Eastern Music Festival, which presents more than 60 concerts in summer by professionals and talented students from around the world at the Guilford College Campus and other locations; and the Greensboro Opera Company, which offers opera in the original language with English subtitles performed by local and professional artists. Other Greensboro groups include the Greensboro Oratorio Society, the Greensboro Symphony Orchestra, the Greensboro Concert Band, the Choral Society of Greensboro, the Philharmonia of Greensboro, the Greensboro Big Band, and We Are One Youth Choir.

A number of symphony orchestras exist in other cities and regions throughout North Carolina, such as the Salisbury Symphony Orchestra, the Charlotte Repertory Orchestra, the Charlotte Philharmonic Orchestra, and the Wilmington Symphony Orchestra. Instruction in the playing of stringed instruments beginning in grade schools is common in North Carolina. Several youth orchestras, such as the Charlotte Symphony Youth Orchestra and Junior Youth Orchestra, the Greensboro Symphony Youth Orchestra, the Triangle Youth Orchestra, the Winston-Salem Youth Symphony, and the Wilmington Symphony Youth Orchestra, offer young instrumentalists the opportunity to perform classical music. Since 1992, the three ensembles of the Piedmont Youth Orchestra have been a resident company at Chapel Hill Arts and Music in Progress, which has since 1991 included the Durham String Ensemble.

Community bands have flourished throughout the state, including the Gaston Community Concert Band, the Durham Community Concert Band, the Tar River Community Band, and the Raleigh Concert Band. Founded in the 1970s, the Raleigh Concert Band comprises approximately 60 brass, woodwind, and percussion players, all volunteers with various musical backgrounds. The Raleigh Concert Band gives a number of concerts each year and participates in civic events such as Memorial Day and Independence Day celebrations. The Cary Town Band performs a turn-of-the-century repertory of music by John Philip Sousa and his contemporaries. The Triangle Brass Band, its members drawn from the Research Triangle Park area, consists entirely of brass and percussion players. All of these bands strengthen community ties through the joy of performing spirited music for wind ensembles.

Several divisions of the North Carolina government support classical music in various ways. Included in these is the North Carolina Museum of History, whose Music of the Carolinas series offers regular free concerts. North Carolina Arts Council programs in literary, visual, and performing arts provide financial support, information resources, and organizational development assistance to symphonies, opera companies, and summer music festivals. Grants from the National Endowment for the Arts, in-state foundations and businesses such as Belk, Duke Energy, and the Z. Smith Reynolds Foundation, and fund-raising events all help support the state's abundant classical music offerings.

References: North Carolina Federation of Music Clubs, *Enthusiasts All: A Story of the Impact Made by the North Carolina Federation of*

Music Clubs upon the State of North Carolina, 1917–1974 (1974); Benjamin Swalin, *Hard-Circus Road: The Odyssey of the North Carolina Symphony* (1987); David H. Witherspoon, *With a Song in His Heart: The Story of the Grass Roots Opera* (1992).

Margaret Foote
Wiley J. Williams
Additional research provided by Miriam Boyer and Mary Bates Sherwood.

SEE ALSO Brevard Music Center; Eastern Music Festival; North Carolina Symphony; Opera Houses.

Clay-Bank is a Mountain designation for a horse whose color resembles that of the substratum of clay that storm waters uncover in the narrow valleys of western North Carolina.

William S. Powell

Clay County, located in the Mountain region of southwestern North Carolina, was formed from Cherokee County in 1861 and named for Henry Clay, a U.S. congressional leader and presidential candidate from Kentucky. It partially borders the state of Georgia. Early inhabitants of the area included the Cherokee Indians, followed by Scotch-Irish and English settlers. Hayesville, the county seat, was incorporated in 1891 and named for George W. Hayes, a member of the North Carolina General Assembly who worked for the formation of Clay County. The Nantahala National Forest covers a section of Clay County, and other notable physical features include the Hiwassee River, Jack Rabbit Mountain, Chunky Gal Mountain, Yellow Mountain, the Pinnacle, and Standing Indian Mountain.

Clay County prospers from a thriving tourism trade due to its rugged mountains, trout fishing, and crafts industry, centered on the John C. Campbell Folk School in Brasstown, founded in 1925. The school weds a Danish model of study with the cultural traditions of the region. The county's farms produce grain, tomatoes, vegetables, hay, poultry, swine, and beef and dairy cattle. Manufactured products include coaxial cables, textiles, trusses, and resistors for light fixtures.

Clay County has a number of historic landmarks, including the Pioneer Village in Tusquitee and the Clay County Courthouse (1889). Cultural institutions include the Clay County Art and Historical Museum and the Peacock Playhouse. The county also hosts several annual festivals and events, such as the Campbell Folk School Fall Festival and the Blacksmith Auction. In 2004 Clay County's population was estimated to be 9,600.

Reference: J. Guy Padgett, *History of Clay County* (1977).

Jay Mazzocchi

SEE ALSO John C. Campbell Folk School.

Clerk of Court in North Carolina is responsible for the day-to-day operation of courts. Appointed by the Crown clerk or secretary of the province, his duties in 1669 included recording deeds, leases, judgments, and mortgages. Later he was also responsible for reading charges in court, taking minutes, administering oaths, entering appeals, recording marks or bonds, and dismissing suits.

The clerk of the General Court served in multiple capacities. Among them, he kept the court calendar, dispatched constables, handled arrangements, and drew juries. The clerk also attended special courts, swore in the evidence, collected fines, drew up indictments, and recorded court proceedings.

Louis P. Towles

Cleveland County, located in the Piedmont region of southwestern North Carolina, was formed in 1841 from Rutherford and Lincoln Counties; it was named for Col. Benjamin Cleveland, a hero at the Revolutionary War battle of King's Mountain (7 Oct. 1780). Cleveland County partially borders the state of South Carolina. Early inhabitants of the region included the Cherokee and Catawba Indians, followed by German, Scotch-Irish, English, and French settlers. The county seat, Shelby, was incorporated in 1843 and named for Col. Isaac Shelby, a Revolutionary War commander. Other communities in the county include Belwood, Boiling Springs, Mooresboro, Grover, and Earl. Notable physical features include John H. Moss Lake, Benn Knob, the Broad River, and Buffalo and Suck Creeks.

Just across the South Carolina border from Cleveland County is Kings Mountain National Military Park. Gardner-Webb University in Boiling Springs was established in 1905. The county also spawned the "Shelby Dynasty," a generation of twentieth-century politicians that included Governors O. Max Gardner and Clyde Hoey. Author Thomas Dixon Jr., whose 1905 novel, *The Clansman*, became the source of the controversial epic film *The Birth of a Nation* (1915), was a native of Shelby. Cleveland County is home to Rogers' Theatre Block (ca. 1930s) and Shelby City Hall (1939). Cultural and historical institutions include the King's Mountain Fire Museum and the Cleveland County Arts Council. Cleveland County hosts popular annual festivals such as the Ham Fest, the Belwood Antique Tractor and Engine Show, and King's Mountain July Fourth.

Cleveland County agricultural products include soybeans, alfalfa, apples, peaches, cotton, hay, swine, sheep, poultry, and beef and dairy cattle. Manufactured products include textiles, fiberglass, truck cabs, commercial refrigerator systems, and the rescue apparatus known as the "jaws of life." Minerals such as quartz crystal, iron, corundum, beryl, and graphite are also mined in the county. The population of Cleveland County was estimated to be slightly more than 97,000 in 2004.

Jay Mazzocchi

SEE ALSO Gardner-Webb University; King's Mountain, Battle of; Shelby Dynasty.

Climate and Weather in North Carolina are as varied as that of any state, with four distinct seasons and a wide variety of conditions and storms, from paralyzing snowstorms in winter to major hurricanes in late summer and fall. Because the state's geography ranges from Atlantic coastline in the east to western mountains reaching several thousand feet in height, temperature extremes in North Carolina vary greatly from place to place and from season to season. The overall climate is relatively warm; even in the mountains, North Carolina's coldest region, the average temperature in January remains above freezing. The state's record low is −25°, recorded at Grandfather Mountain in Avery County on 30 Jan. 1966. North Carolina's highest recorded temperature, 110°, occurred at Fayetteville on 22 Aug. 1983. The frost-free season in the state ranges from an average of 170 days in the west to 280 days in the east.

Climatic Factors, Precipitation Patterns, and Seasonal Trends

North Carolina is one of only three states in which a major mountain range is adjacent to a warm current of water. The proximity of the Atlantic Ocean's Gulf Stream and the Appalachian Mountains in the west is a primary causative factor in the state's climate and weather. Any time the wind blows from the east, moisture is transported inland from the Atlantic. This damp air is then forced to rise over higher terrain. Rising motion leads to cooling and eventual condensation, resulting in clouds and precipitation. The higher the mountains, the more dramatic the effect. When high pressure exists to the north and low pressure to the south, the combined circulation of these two systems creates an easterly flow of moist air and the possibility of heavy precipitation in the mountains.

The mountains also play a prominent role in the so-called sinking motion, which promotes warming and drying of the atmosphere. The same easterly winds that cause heavy precipitation on the western side of the Appalachians can lead to sunshine on the eastern side. This phenomenon occurs in central and eastern North Carolina when the wind emanates from the west, creating some of the hottest days in the piedmont region of the state. Air starting at the top of the mountains sinks on its way to lower elevations, breaking up the clouds and allowing temperatures to rise.

During the winter months, cold, dense air pushes into North Carolina from the north and west, becoming trapped east of the mountains. If precipitation is falling, the result can be snow and/or ice for the central and western regions of the state. Snowstorms happen with some regularity only in the higher mountains, where the precipitation coming out of a cloud base does not have a chance to melt. In the piedmont and coastal plain regions, the precipitation may be snow when it leaves the base of the cloud but often becomes rain by the time it reaches the ground. Eastern North Carolina usually escapes frozen precipitation as a result of its proximity to the relatively warm ocean waters of the Gulf Stream; longtime residents are aware of a consistent line between Roxboro and Durham that regularly separates snow from rain. Exceptions occur from time to time. A fast-moving depression coming in from the southwest may be sufficiently vigorous to suck cold air from the north. The low level of this cold stops the falling snow from melting, and the eastern part of the state may get a deep snowstorm.

The Gulf Stream is also important because of the tremendous temperature differences, zones of which are called fronts, that it can create between land and sea; even in the dead of winter, water temperatures just off of the North Carolina coast can be as warm as 70°. Because areas of low pressure originate in fronts, this natural phenomenon along North Carolina's coast provides a notorious breeding ground for the famous nor'easters, storms that then move northward and paralyze major metropolitan areas such as Washington, D.C., New York City, and Boston with heavy snow. If these storms develop quickly enough, snow can fall in North Carolina as well.

Thunderstorms occur frequently in North Carolina, especially in the spring and summer. They are created when warm, moist air in the lower levels of the atmosphere collides with cooler air at the higher levels. During the day in the mountains, the sun warms the elevated terrain more rapidly than the surrounding air. The result is a rising motion over the mountains and, with enough instability, the appearance of thunderstorms. Once in place, these storms can move eastward and affect other sections of North Carolina. The Atlantic breeze may also create thunderstorms. They develop when the land heats up more rapidly than the adjacent water, resulting in a cool breeze blowing from the water toward the land. While this airflow can be refreshing and peaceful at the beach, it can produce thunderstorms just inland, where the sea breeze converges with a different wind flow. Tornadoes can develop from powerful thunderstorms, particularly in the spring.

Spring is often a fairly short season in North Carolina. Warm, humid, and cloudy days become more frequent, and cold spells grow less intense. Depressions still pass through the state, bringing periods of continuous rain or drizzle, but the possibility of thunderstorms—and, late in the season, tornadoes—increases. Commonly in spring the soil is full of water ready for the start of the growing season, although in years when the winter depressions are less active than usual, soil water may be in short supply. It is not unusual in early spring for an almost continuous series of rain-bearing depressions to pass over the state, removing problems with water supply but making it difficult for farmers to begin planting in their saturated fields. Some springs mimic summer, bringing high temperatures and little rain. Often these warm, dry springs have bursts of unusually high winds. Late frost, varying from early March to mid-April on the southern coast and from late April to early June in the western mountains, can also create agricultural problems.

When summer comes to the state, precipitation becomes unreliable and temperatures much less variable, changing by only a few degrees from day to day. The most characteristic feature of North Carolina summers is undoubtedly the almost continuous series of high temperature, high humidity days. While some steady rain may come from depressions, in many years North Carolinians rely on isolated thunderstorms, which may provide too much rain (and even floods) in one place while barely affecting another. Forest fires, commonly started by lightning, also reach their peak in summer. Maximum temperatures occur in the coastal plain, but sea breezes keep the coast itself relatively cool.

North Carolina's fall represents the peak hurricane season; the Outer Banks are the most vulnerable coastal areas in the United States due to their eastward projection into the Atlantic Ocean. In years when hurricanes visit the state, fall is also the wettest season. In other years, however, it is often the driest season. The major depressions are still passing mainly to the north while the land surface is becoming cooler and less prone to creating the intense thunderstorms that could cause significant rainfalls. Occasional days still display summer heat, but they become rarer. By the beginning of November, practically all of the state has had at least one cold spell indicative of oncoming winter.

Droughts and Floods in North Carolina

Droughts occur in the state fairly regularly, although long-term, serious droughts are rare. With the volatile nature of summer storms in North Carolina, a summer drought may be short lived and very localized: one farmer may be watching his crops wilt while his neighbor sees his being washed away in an intense thunderstorm. Urban water suppliers are unlikely to be worried by a short dry period whenever it occurs but will be greatly concerned by several months of below-average rainfall for a wide area. In North Carolina, where more than 40 inches of rain a year is normal, an annual total of less than 30 inches probably means a massive drought and economic disruption.

A series of droughts has occurred in North Carolina over the last 100-plus years since the start of routine weather observations. During the first quarter of the twentieth century, droughts affected a relatively small portion of the state or lasted only a couple of months. Droughts became more frequent and more severe in the mid- to late 1920s. Between July 1925 and September 1927, three consecutive growing seasons were almost completely wiped out by drought. Though not affected as severely as a few years earlier, North Carolinians certainly did not escape the catastrophic weather that punished

the "dust bowl" of the early 1930s, suffering through periods of widespread drought every year between 1930 and 1934. Only in 1932, however, did a drought last for a whole growing season, so the state tended to avoid the severity of the problems that plagued the Midwest.

After the early 1940s and apart from a short period in the middle 1950s, when the whole of North Carolina was affected, there were only a few isolated drought areas and months until the 1980s. In July 1988 a catastrophic drought occurred in the state, leaving whole fields of crops wilted and reservoirs reduced to mud puddles. Midwestern farmers, not affected by a drought, organized a massive shipment of hay to feed starving animals and help their North Carolina brethren survive the deadly weather. Since that year, some growing seasons in the state have been affected by dry weather, but there have been no major back-to-back droughts, and government crop support programs have helped farmers survive the vagaries of the weather.

Floods in North Carolina can be divided into two types: those associated with the massive rains and high tides of hurricanes and so-called flash floods, those connected with locally heavy rainstorms, especially thunderstorms. In the western mountains, rapidly developing (and often equally rapidly disappearing) flash floods are one of the major weather-related hazards. A single heavy storm over a small mountain watershed can cause a stream to overflow its banks in a matter of minutes. A few such storms will occur in almost any summer over most watersheds. Fortunately, most are relatively mild affairs; streams may rise to the top of their banks or may overtop their banks for a short period, but relatively little harm is done. However, nearly every summer brings a few heavy thunderstorms that seem to sit over a particular watershed for hours and lead to major flooding.

Once out of the mountains, the concern about floods changes somewhat. The floodwaters coming out of the mountain valleys increase the flow of piedmont rivers, but these rivers can usually absorb the effect of several swollen mountain streams without problems. Major flooding in the piedmont is most likely when the area is already saturated from previous rains. These rains themselves may not have caused flooding, but the saturated ground ensures that when the next rain comes (even though it may not be exceptionally heavy) it has nowhere to go but overland to the rivers, causing them to rise and flood rapidly. If this situation is combined with excess input from mountain streams, major flooding is possible. For instance, a rather weak depression in the exceedingly wet summer of 1963 triggered floods on virtually all piedmont rivers early in July, and severe stormy weather on 25 July sent rivers from Greensboro to Southern Pines back into flood stage. Three days later, thunderstorms in the mountains added to high flows there, causing further piedmont flooding.

Damage to bridges and other structures on a floodplain

Men standing on a railroad bridge in McDowell County after its center supports had been washed away during the great western North Carolina floods of July 1916. NCC.

does occur, with landslides being a possibility and personal injury a major threat. Most flood-related deaths, though there have been mercifully few, happen when people are swept away while attempting to cross swollen, deceptively shallow-looking creeks. In August 1961, when ten inches of rain fell in 24 hours from a stalled cold front west of Asheville, five bridges were destroyed and one person was killed. Fortunately, advances in technology have led to more rapid communications and the greater success of flash flood warnings, both in the mountains and in the piedmont.

References: Jay Barnes, *North Carolina's Hurricane History* (3rd ed., 2001); Charles B. Carney and Albert V. Hardy, *Weather and Climate in North Carolina* (1963); William S. Powell, *North Carolina: The Story of a Special Kind of Place* (1987).

Peter J. Robinson
Gregory B. Fishel

SEE ALSO Hurricanes; Tornadoes; Wet Year; Year without a Summer.

Clinchfield Railroad is a transmountain line connecting the Chesapeake & Ohio at Elkhorn City, Ky., and the Atlantic Coast Line Railroad in Spartanburg, S.C., to serve the bitumi-

nous coalfields of Kentucky and Virginia. It represents the last major railroad constructed in the eastern United States and is unusual in that it has been a profitable venture since 1915. The line totals 290 miles of track, with 117 miles located in North Carolina. Traversing the eastern United States' most rugged terrain, the Clinchfield has 54 tunnels representing 3.5 percent of its total length, an amount greater than any other railroad in the country.

The line was built in ten segments between 1890 and 1909, with construction on each end and in the middle occurring simultaneously. The first trip of the (nearly) completed line took place on 22 Aug. 1908. The line merged with the Seaboard Coast Line in 1967 and became part of CSX Corporation on 1 July 1986.

The Clinchfield was famous for the "Santa Claus Special," a special train that ran the Saturday after Thanksgiving to distribute Christmas presents to children of Appalachia who lived along the line. This tradition has continued under CSX.

References: John Gilbert and Grady Jefferys, *Crossties through Carolina: The Story of North Carolina's Early Day Railroads* (1969); Lou Harshaw, *Trains, Trestles, and Tunnels: Railroads of the Southern Appalachians* (1977).

Donald W. Kern

Clio's Nursery, established by pioneer Presbyterian minister James Hall, was a successful eighteenth-century classical academy located in what is now east-central Iredell County, about ten miles north of Statesville. Although the exact date that the school opened is uncertain, a certificate given to a student in 1780 confirms that it was in operation by August 1778. After the first building was destroyed by a fire, the second schoolhouse was built on top of an adjacent hill.

Hall maintained an active interest in the academy while leaving the teaching to others. During the Revolution, he served both as captain of a militia company and as regimental chaplain. When Hall's militia unit was called to active service, classes continued at Clio's Nursery under the supervision of Hall's brother-in-law, James McEwen. McEwen died a short time after his appointment, and he was succeeded in November 1779 by Francis Cummins. Cummins, who later became a Presbyterian minister, had been born in Pennsylvania and moved to Mecklenburg County with his family.

Because of the invasion of the British army, Clio's Nursery was closed from May 1780 to April 1782, when it was reopened under the direction of John Newton. The last teacher at the school was Charles Caldwell, who began teaching there in 1785 or 1786. The school apparently never reopened after Caldwell left in 1787 to reestablish Crowfield Academy in the bounds of Centre Presbyterian Church in Mecklenburg County.

In the short history of Clio's Nursery, an unusually large number of prominent individuals attended the school. A sketch of the academy published in 1858 listed as alumni George W. Campbell of Tennessee, who served as secretary of the treasury in the James Madison administration; Moses Waddell, who later became president of the University of Georgia; a U.S. congressman; three judges; and eight ministers.

References: William Henry Foote, *Sketches of North Carolina, Historical and Biographical* (1846); Genealogical Society of Iredell County, *The Heritage of Iredell County* (1890); E. F. Rockwell, "The Second Classical School in Iredell County," *North Carolina Journal of Education* 1 (September 1858).

George W. Troxler

Clocks. During the eighteenth and early nineteenth centuries, while clock makers in New England and the mid-Atlantic hand-crafted brass clock movements for tall case and other clocks, few North Carolinians made clocks because the state had not developed cities large enough to support the trade. Thomas Emond, a clock maker known to have worked in Raleigh from 1806 to around 1820, signed an eight-day tall case clock he created for William Boylan. Johann Ludwig Eberhardt (1758–1839), who moved to the Moravian town of Salem in 1799, made more than 30 tall case and shelf clocks, some of which are in the collection of Old Salem, Inc. Other Moravians made clocks, though not on this scale.

The pioneering work of Eli Terry of Connecticut during the first two decades of the nineteenth century led to the mass production of wooden clock movements—first for tall case clocks and later for shelf clocks. Demand for inexpensive shelf clocks manufactured by Terry, Seth Thomas, and other Connecticut makers resulted in the demise of the tall case clock and the widespread practice of clock peddling. The North Carolina General Assembly enacted legislation in 1822 that required those who wished to peddle clocks and other products not manufactured in the state to obtain a license annually from a county sheriff, paying a tax of $20 on each wagon or cart used to transport goods. This legislation, with some modifications, remained in effect at least until October 1858.

Enterprising manufacturers, dealers, and peddlers tried to circumvent the legislation in various ways. Some obtained clocks manufactured in Connecticut (often by Thomas) and pasted their own printed labels inside the cases, while others pasted over the manufacturer's name on the original labels with the name of a fictitious manufacturer in North Carolina. A few wily entrepreneurs in the state may have established assembly shops for clock components manufactured in Connecticut. Early examples with wooden movements, and later examples with brass movements, include North Carolina clocks "made" by J. R. McElever, Oliver & Co., Reeves & Huson, Reeves, Saunders & Co., H. Wright & Co., and Wright & McKee. Such clocks are owned by the North Carolina Museum of History and the North Carolina Collection at the University of North Carolina at Chapel Hill.

During the late nineteenth century, several North Carolinians obtained clock-related patents. On 11 May 1875, George W. White and Walter I. Leary of Edenton obtained one for an "improvement in clock-escapements." Four years later, Robert S. Abernethy, a mathematics professor at Rutherford College and a resident of Happy Home in Burke County, obtained a patent for another improvement in escapements.

References: Frank P. Albright, *Johann Ludwig Eberhardt and His Salem Clocks* (1978); James H. Craig, *The Arts and Crafts in North Carolina, 1699–1840* (1965); George Barton Cutten and Mary Reynolds Peacock, *Silversmiths of North Carolina, 1696–1860* (1984).

Maurice C. York

Clogging is a form of traditional solo step dancing to traditional string music common in western North Carolina and growing in popularity across the state and nation. The term has been used to describe the dance only since about 1930. Clogging differs from flatfooting in that flatfoot dancers rest on their heels and keep their steps low to the floor, whereas cloggers come down on the toes or balls of the feet and incorporate high kicks of the feet. Unlike buck dancing, where dancers also use the toes, clogging also incorporates heel strikes on the floor. Since the 1930s, teams of cloggers have

The Daniel Boone Cloggers from Boone perform on Capitol Square in Raleigh, 1973. Courtesy of NCOA&H.

performed for audiences, and performance has been a powerful engine of change in clogging. Most cloggers use taps to amplify the sound of the rhythms made by their feet, while most flatfoot and buck dancers use regular shoes. Many clogging teams do primarily "precision clogging," which is a choreographed dance incorporating traditional steps in a preestablished pattern which is performed in unison by all the dancers. In North Carolina, clogging has been popularized by Bascom Lamar Lunsford's Mountain Dance and Folk Festival and the Stompin' Ground in Maggie Valley.

Reference: Mike Seeger and Ruth Pershing, *Talking Feet: Buck, Flatfoot, and Tap: Solo Southern Dance of the Appalachian, Piedmont, and Blue Ridge Mountain Regions* (1992).

Bruce E. Baker

Clothing and Fashion styles during the colonial through pre–Civil War eras in North Carolina did not change as quickly as in modern times, but North Carolinians were undoubtedly aware of what was "in style" and what was "old-fashioned." The concern for clothing and fashion was greatest in the wealthier classes of society, while the lower classes, generally occupied with making a living, had less interest in and opportunity for keeping up with new clothing fashions and designs. Wealthy women and men often attired themselves in clothing of British and French styles. As in the modern era, Paris often dictated the latest fashions. Upper-class colonial women wore very large hoop skirts of imported silk or satin, wooden stays or corsets to slim their waistlines, and high-heeled shoes. The gentleman's wardrobe might have included red velvet coats and tight doeskin knee breeches, ruffled silk shirts, silk stockings, silver-buckled shoes, and possibly a small sword or sword cane. Children of aristocrats sought to duplicate adult fashion, even if that meant the girls wore uncomfortable stays.

People of lower economic status usually relied on homespun materials—a cotton-flax mixture (fustian cloth) and flax and wool (linsey-woolsey)—for their clothing requirements. Small farmers often wore homemade jackets and pants, wool socks, heavy boots, and flax-wool shirts. Farm wives made do with a shapeless dress of fustian. Homemade garments, including dresses made from bleached and dyed cotton sacks, were still in style in some places through the Great Depression. Slaves typically were issued a yearly "ration" of clothing by their masters: men might receive a suit and pants of coarse wool or cotton, two pairs of shoes, several shirts, and a hat, while women were given one or two dresses, several shifts or field gowns, and two pairs of shoes. Brightly colored handkerchiefs were worn by both black men and black women.

Beginning in the post-Reconstruction period, North Carolina and other southern states increasingly began adopting national standards of dress. The influence of the mass media of the late 1800s and early 1900s in hastening this nationalization of the South was profound, particularly the role of women's magazines, some of which began prior to 1870 and spread knowledge of clothing and fashion. *Godey's Lady's Book* (1830–92) was a pioneer of such publications, especially under the editorship of Sarah Josepha Hale (1837–77), who included hand-colored plates and pictures of ladies and gentlemen in stylish costumes. *Godey's* was the supreme arbiter in matters of fashion and standards of propriety, and it was the model for later magazines such as *Ladies' Home Journal* (1853–), *Good Housekeeping* (1885–), and *Vogue* (1892–).

The impact of industrialization, the increased availability of ready-made items, higher quality sewing machines, and inexpensive patterns all combined to eradicate sharp class distinctions in fashion. In the mid-1800s manufacturers began to make inexpensive, ready-to-wear clothes, which saved customers both the time it would take to make clothes themselves and the money they would spend on clothes made by a dressmaker or tailor. New fibers also began to be developed, and North Carolinians and other Americans increasingly began to dress for comfort as well as style. In general, North Carolina women have experienced the trends in fashion that have characterized the entire nation: hemlines have risen and fallen; waistlines have shifted, disappeared, and reappeared; and the areas of focus have moved from head to bosom to legs and back again. In the state, as elsewhere, the leading department stores employ buyers whose business it is to keep in touch with fashion design and to attend fashion shows in New York, California, and elsewhere with an eye to upcoming styles, colors, and fabrics that will appeal to their stores' clientele.

The best-known fashion designer with a North Carolina connection is unquestionably Alexander Julian. Born in Chapel Hill, Julian operated Alexander's Ambition, a menswear specialty store in Chapel Hill, before moving first to Philadelphia and later to New York City, where he became president and chief executive officer of Alexander Julian, Inc. He has won several Coty fashion awards and was elected to the Coty Hall of Fame in 1980. He also won the Cutty Sark Award in 1980 and 1985 as outstanding U.S. designer. Unlike many designers, Julian created his own fabrics, working with mills in England, Scotland, Italy, and the United States.

The manufacturing of fabric apparel is a huge, often volatile industry in the state. A large variety of women's, men's, children's, and misses' apparel is produced in the state, including men's and women's suits, coats, overcoats, shirts, underwear, neckwear, dress and work gloves, robes and dressing gowns, and belts.

References: "Fashion Trend-Setting Tar Heels," *Spectator* (8 Mar. 1984); Guion G. Johnson, *Ante-Bellum North Carolina: A Social History* (1937); Steve Levin, "Over the Rainbow: Alex Julian Left Chapel Hill for the Big Apple to Seek His Future in the World of High Fashion," *Carolina Lifestyle* (September 1982).

Wiley J. Williams

Coal in North Carolina is limited to two belts of Triassic sediment: the sporadic Dan River belt and the larger Deep River belt, which runs along the Deep River in Lee, Moore, and Chatham Counties. Metamorphosed from deposits of vegetable matter into hard, long-burning fuel, coal was utilized in forges in the Carolina colony before the American Revolution. During that war, coal from the Horton Mine, near Cumnock, was used by John Wilcox, who operated an ironworks at Gulf in Chatham County.

The Deep River coalfield is the only area in the state known to contain beds of commercial significance. Approximately 35 miles long and between 5 and 10 miles wide, the field contains medium volatile bituminous coal and is centered around 10 miles northwest of Sanford in the Cumnock Formation. Although the Egypt and Coal Glen Mines, using deep shafts and served by two rail lines—the Cape Fear & Yadkin Valley Railway at Cumnock and the Seaboard Air Line at Colon (by means of the Raleigh & Western Railway)—produced coal from this seam only intermittently from 1854 to 1953, significant periods of operation did occur. Because of the Civil War, production, especially from the Egypt Mine (in present-day Lee County), was extremely important, as coal was supplied to the Confederate arsenal in Fayetteville and the Charlotte Navy Yard; though it was often used by blockade-runners, its poor quality produced dark smoke easily detected by Union ships.

Coal production retained the war's boost until 1873; other noteworthy periods were 1889–1905 and 1918–30, both mines operating during the latter interval. Although Coal Glen Mine produced about 14,000 tons of coal in 1949, averaging 100 tons per day, production on the Deep River seam ceased in 1953 because of the depth and the many dissecting faults that broke up the field. For these reasons, the area has proven to be uneconomical to mine, even though reserves are estimated to be 110 million tons.

References: Daniel Andrew Textoris and Eleanora I. Robbins, *Coal Resources of the Triassic Deep River Basin, North Carolina* (1988); Charles Wilkes, *Report on the Examination of the Deep River District, North Carolina* (1859).

Charles H. McArver
Additional research provided by Jean H. Seaman.

Coastal Area Management Act was introduced in the 1973 session of the North Carolina General Assembly in response to the 1972 federal Coastal Zone Management Act, which demanded solutions to mounting problems in coastal areas. A great deal of very vocal opposition caused the bill to be held over for another term while a joint Senate-House legislative committee toured the coastal area and held public hearings on the controversial subject. The revised Coastal Area Management Act (CAMA) of 1975 gave policy-making authority to a 15-member Coastal Resources Commission (CRC), made up primarily of coastal residents nominated by local governments and appointed by the governor. Backing up the commission was a Coastal Resources Advisory Council with representation from each of the state's coastal counties and from coastal municipalities, boards of health, and councils of government.

The basic goal of CAMA was to provide a program for the protection, preservation, orderly development, and management of North Carolina's coastal resources. The law covered the 20 coastal counties between Virginia and South Carolina, the adjacent ocean waters within the limits of North Carolina's jurisdiction, the Outer Banks and other barrier islands, and the inlets, sounds, and other estuarine waters within the state.

CAMA called for immediate action in three areas. The CRC was to develop state guidelines under which each coastal county, town, or city desiring to do so was to prepare its own land-use plan, taking into special consideration the desires of the citizens as to the future of their area as well as the carrying capacity of the land and water resources to sustain the proposed growth. In developing its plan, each governmental unit was to divide its land area into five classifications: developed, transition, community, rural, and conservation. The CRC would also conduct continuing studies (and make periodic reports to the General Assembly) on the development of a better-coordinated, more unified system of environmental and land-use permits in the coastal area. Finally, the CRC was to identify all critical areas in need of protection or preservation and designate them as Areas of Environmental Concern, in which no development activity would be undertaken without a special permit.

From the beginning of the CAMA debate, the law has been considered too restrictive by most prodevelopment interests and too lenient by most environmentalists. In the first two decades after its passage, all efforts to repeal or make major amendments to CAMA failed. A specially created state Office of Coastal Management provides the staff to enforce management policies adopted by the CRC.

David Stick

Coastal Plain. SEE Geography.

Coast Guard, U.S. The U.S. Coast Guard has figured prominently in North Carolina's maritime history; it has long been traditional in many coastal communities for young men to follow their fathers and grandfathers in a Coast Guard career. For more than 40 years local seafaring men served with distinction in the chain of U.S. Lifesaving Service stations running the length of the North Carolina coast from Wash Woods to Oak Island prior to the 1915 formation of the U.S. Coast Guard from the union of the Lifesaving Service with the Revenue Cutter Service. By that time most of the original lifeboat stations had been replaced by larger structures designed to accommodate crews on call throughout the year. Just as steam was gradually replacing sail on the merchant vessels plying shipping lanes off the coast, motors replaced oars in the Coast Guard.

In World War I, Coast Guardsmen responded to distress calls from ships attacked by German submarines, even as the U-boats cruised nearby. After the war the Coast Guard maintained its shore stations, the choice of names most often dictated by prominent geographic features. There were the inlet stations (Caffeys Inlet, Oregon Inlet, New Inlet, Hatteras Inlet, and Bogue Inlet), the cape stations (Cape Hatteras, Cape Lookout, and Cape Fear), and the hill stations (Pennys Hill, Poyners Hill, Paul Gamiels Hill, Kill Devil Hills, and Creeds Hill). Some were named for nearby communities, such as Wash Woods, Kitty Hawk, Nags Head, Chicamacomico, Little Kinnakeet, Big Kinnakeet, Ocracoke, and Portsmouth, or for islands, such as Bodie Island, Pea Island, and Oak Island. Even those fitting into no particular category received distinctive names (Gull Shoal, Durants, Core Banks, and Fort Macon). By the late 1930s local men no longer exclusively manned the area stations, and North Carolina Coast Guardsmen were widely dispersed throughout the country.

The Fort Macon Coast Guard Station originated in 1904, when the U.S. Treasury Department, attempting to close gaps in the Lifesaving Service's coverage of the North Carolina coast, built a station on the old Fort Macon Military Reservation. It was situated on Bogue Banks to protect Beaufort Inlet. Although Fort Macon State Park was created when the state acquired the land by congressional act in 1924, 22.6 acres remained in the hands of the Treasury Department to maintain the Coast Guard station. Since World War II the station has acquired base status by expanding its facilities and providing services beyond its original lifesaving role, such as aid to navigation, marine law enforcement, and drug interdiction. In the early 2000s it employed about 200 active personnel and many others.

During World War II native North Carolinians in the Coast Guard performed a wide range of duties, including serving as coxswain on landing craft used to deposit troops and tanks on the beaches of Anzio and Iwo Jima. Meanwhile, a major Coast Guard air base was established at Elizabeth City in the northeastern part of the state. Throughout the war this new air wing regularly joined with personnel from the shore stations in response to crews of tankers and freighters sunk by German submarines.

The World War II experience, combined with a decline in coastal shipping and the introduction of radar, loran, sonar, and other sophisticated warning systems, resulted in a total restructuring of Coast Guard facilities along the North Carolina coast. One by one, the old shore stations were decommissioned, with only those near the inlets left in service. At the beginning of the twenty-first century Coast Guard cutters operating from the remaining stations as well as Coast Guard aircraft from the Elizabeth City base, which employed about 900 active members and many civilians, were able to respond more quickly to disasters at sea.

References: Karl Baarslag, *Coast Guard to the Rescue* (1937); Joe A. Mobley, *Ship Ashore! The U.S. Lifesavers of Coastal North Carolina* (1994); David Stick, *Graveyard of the Atlantic: Shipwrecks of the North Carolina Coast* (1952); Nell Wise Wechter, *Mighty Midgetts of Chicamacomico* (1974).

David Stick
Additional research provided by Paul Branch.

SEE ALSO Lifesaving Service, U.S.; Submarine Attacks.

Cobb's Point, Battle of. SEE Elizabeth City, Battle of.

Cockfighting in North Carolina dates from the colonial period. A cockfight involves two specially bred gamecocks equipped with steel gaffs attached to each leg fighting until one is disabled. The loser frequently dies from his injuries. The nineteenth century was the heyday of cockfighting in the state. During this period, North Carolinians of high social standing bred and fought birds, frequently winning or losing large amounts of money in the process. By the 1850s written rules were distributed and a regular schedule of fights was held, making the bloody activity one of the state's first organized "sports."

The most successful breeder of gamecocks was Nash County planter Nick Arrington, whose birds, according to legend, were victorious over the birds of Mexican president Santa Ana in a series of contests fought aboard two steamboats in the Gulf of Mexico. One visitor to the Arrington plantation wrote that he "was greeted by such crowing of cocks as he had never heard in all his life before. . . . The air was resonant

Cockfight in eastern North Carolina, ca. 1857. NCC.

with their shrill notes, challenging and replying in fierce and eager tone." George Means of Concord developed a successful fighting breed known as the Red Cuban in the 1890s. James Norwood of Hillsborough, W. S. Church of Boonville, and Ike Rhodes of Wilmington were other successful breeders of fighting birds.

Even at the height of its popularity, cockfighting was controversial. Most North Carolina newspapers refused to take fight-related advertising by about 1820. Although outlawed in the twentieth century, it survived in isolated places on the periphery of legitimate sporting society for many years.

References: Paul B. Barringer, *The Natural Bent: The Memories of Dr. Paul B. Barringer* (1949); B. W. C. Roberts, "Cockfighting: An Early Entertainment in North Carolina," *NCHR* 42 (July 1965).

Jim L. Sumner

Coffee Pot (Old Salem). In 1859 Julius Mickey advertised his tin shop in Old Salem (part of modern Winston-Salem) by placing a large tin coffee pot on a pole in front of his business at the corner of Belews and South Main Streets. This extraordinary coffee pot measured 7 feet 3 inches from top to bottom, 2 feet 3 inches in diameter at the top, and 5 feet 4 inches in diameter at the bottom, with a capacity of approximately 740½ gallons.

The coffee pot remained intact, despite neighborhood youths' knocking it off its pole during many Halloweens, until the construction of Interstate 40 forced its removal. For several years William N. and Eugene Vogler stored the pot. By 1960 officials of Old Salem wanted to display the coffee pot, but the Voglers and the town could not agree on a location. In 1962 James A. Gray suggested placing it on a small grassy island of land formed where Brookstown Avenue joins South Main Street. The coffee pot stands today on a concrete pole, no longer the object of Halloween pranks.

Tradition maintains that a Confederate soldier hid inside the Salem coffee pot to escape from Union soldiers. This possibly occurred in April 1865, when a band of Stoneman's Brigade under Gen. W. J. Palmer came through the town.

References: David Bailey, "The Restless Coffeepot," *Winston-Salem Journal*, 21 Mar. 1976; Adelaide L. Fries, ed., *Forsyth: A County on the March* (1949).

Anna Withers Bair

Coharie Indians in North Carolina have been recognized as an official tribe by the state legislature since 1971 and are represented on the North Carolina Commission of Indian Affairs. The tribal name is derived from the two Coharie Creeks and the Coharie River, all of which flow through Sampson County. The Coharie's history is similar to that of the Lumbee Indians, with whom they have many ties. Community members built the first Indian school in Sampson County in 1859. State funds were used for a separate Indian school in 1911, but for the most part their Indian schools were supported by private subscriptions from the community.

Despite a long history of group unity, Coharie tribal structure developed relatively late. The Sampson County Indian Organization, formed in 1969, was the forerunner of the modern-day Coharie tribe, which was established in 1971. The tribe sponsors an annual powwow and administers both educational and housing programs. There were approximately 1,500 Indians, most of them Coharies, living in Sampson and Harnett Counties in the early 2000s.

References: George E. Butler, *The Croatan Indians of Sampson County, North Carolina: Their Origin and Racial Status. A Plea for Separate Schools* (1916); Ruth Y. Wetmore, *First on the Land: The North Carolina Indians* (1975).

Ruth Y. Wetmore

Coker Arboretum on the campus of the University of North Carolina at Chapel Hill is a five-acre showplace that highlights plants of the temperate Southeast, their East Asian counterparts, gymnosperms, and seasonal plant and color displays. Established by William Chambers Coker, the university's first professor of botany, at the suggestion of President Francis P. Venable in 1903, the area was formerly a damp pasture that for decades had been used as a home for campus animals, most notably President David L. Swain's white mule, Old Cuddy. Coker transformed the five acres into a botanical laboratory planted with more than 400 species of ornamental flowers, trees, and shrubs. Despite its small size, it is one of the most complete botanical gardens in America. Laced with pathways, this parklike area is especially inviting when spring flowers are blooming and is a favorite study or relaxation spot for UNC's students. One of its most notable features is the purple wisteria and sweet-smelling yellow jessamine covering the trellis running along Cameron Avenue. Their perfume will long remain in a visitor's memory.

The main entrance of Coker Arboretum was reconstructed in 1998 as a gift by UNC's class of 1997. The arboretum is administered by the staff of the 329-acre North Carolina Botanical Garden, located south of the central Chapel Hill campus.

References: Lawrence S. Earley, "One Hundred Years of Semi-Solitude," *Carolina Alumni Review* 92 (January–February 2003); William S. Powell, *The First State University: A Pictorial History of the University of North Carolina* (3rd rev. ed., 1992); Marguerite E. Schumann, *The First State University: A Walking Guide* (1972).

Wiley J. Williams

Cokesbury School, the first Methodist-sponsored school in North Carolina, was built near Aquila Phelps's horse ford on the Yadkin River in eastern Rowan (now Davie) County in about 1790. It was named for the first two Methodist bishops, Thomas Coke and Francis Asbury. Asbury wrote in 1793 that the school stood "on a beautiful eminence and overlooked the low-lands and river Yadkin." He described the building as "twenty feet square, two stories and well set out with doors and windows." Minister and teacher James Parks was the school's principal. Asbury visited the school again in 1794, but in 1799, when he preached there, he noted in his journal that the schoolhouse was "now a house for God." The exact date of the closing or removal of the school is unknown.

References: Elmer T. Clark, *Methodism in Western North Carolina* (1966); James W. Wall, *History of Davie County* (1969).

James W. Wall

Coleman Manufacturing Company in Concord was the first black-owned cotton mill in the United States. Warren C. Coleman was born a slave in Cabarrus County on 25 Mar. 1849. At the age of 18, only a few years after the abolition of slavery, he began a career as a merchant and businessman, investing early in real estate in Concord. By the 1890s, Coleman was the wealthiest African American in North Carolina. He turned his attention toward establishing a cotton mill that would break the color line that kept blacks from enjoying the economic benefits of mill employment. Beginning in 1896, Coleman lined up financing for the enterprise, and in February 1897 he announced the project to the public at the Cabarrus County Courthouse.

The cornerstone of the mill was laid on 8 Feb. 1898. Coleman had difficulty securing adequate capital, however, and the completion of the mill was delayed. Coleman Manufacturing finally began production in June 1901, but in 1902 the entire textile industry took a downturn, and the effects were felt severely by Coleman's fledgling enterprise. Further difficulties

in 1903 led Coleman to resign his position as director in December of that year. Three months later, on 31 Mar. 1904, he died in Concord. The next month, Durham financier Benjamin N. Duke foreclosed on a $10,000 mortgage he held on the mill. He sold the property to Concord textile magnate James William Cannon in March 1906. The structure of the Coleman Manufacturing Company was operated for many years afterward as Cannon Plant Number Nine.

References: Allen E. Burgess, "Tar Heel Blacks and the New South Dream: The Coleman Manufacturing Company, 1896–1904" (Ph.D. diss., Duke University, 1977); Jordan K. Rouse, *The Noble Experiment of Warren C. Coleman* (1972); Ernie Wood, "Ex-Slave Is One of Many Who Are Lost to History," *Raleigh News and Observer*, 23 Mar. 1975.

Bruce E. Baker

Cole Manufacturing Company was founded by brothers E. M. and E. A. Cole in Charlotte in January 1900 to manufacture seed planters invented and patented by E. M. Cole. Brightly painted farm implements bearing the Cole Manufacturing Company label were a common sight on North Carolina farms during the first half of the twentieth century. By the mid-1920s, the company was the world's largest factory devoted solely to making seed planters and fertilizer distributors.

Cole Manufacturing, which operated its own foundry, made the transition from mule-drawn implements to multi-row tractor-drawn implements and had sold more than 2 million seed planters, fertilizer distributors, and grain drills in the domestic and export markets by 1961. By the mid-1970s, the company had introduced a line of hand-pushed equipment to capitalize on the interest in home gardening. Jean Cole Hatcher succeeded her father, E. A. Cole, as president of the company, and she was followed by her son John Cole Hatcher. The company ceased operations in the early 1980s.

References: LeGette Blythe and Charles Raven Brockman, *Hornet's Nest: The Story of Charlotte and Mecklenburg County* (1961); Edgar T. Thompson, *Agricultural Mecklenburg and Industrial Charlotte, Social and Economic* (1926).

Douglas Helms

Collards, also called collard greens or simply "greens," grow throughout the South and probably as much as any food delineate the culinary boundaries of the Mason-Dixon Line. Sometimes defined as headless cabbages, collards are best when picked and prepared just after the first frost, although they are eaten year-round. Although collards are grown throughout the South and Southwest (one Indian word for them means "qualities"), they are most prevalent in the Deep South and the eastern plains of North Carolina and South Carolina. The exporting of fresh collards to displaced southerners in the Northeast is big business for several farms in Duplin and Sampson Counties, where over 1,700 acres of greens are harvested twice a year. Because they look fresher, all the collards shipped north and most sold commercially in North Carolina are hybrids, which are a deeper green than the tastier cabbage-like greens that have a slight yellow coloring.

The traditional preparation of collards follows a simple recipe. First, they are "crapped" (cut at the base of a stalk), then "looked" (searched for worms), then cooked on a low boil until tender, usually with fatback, neck, or backbone added. The resultant "mess o' greens," topped with a generous helping of vinegar, can easily make a meal in itself. Pot liquor, or "likker," the juice left in the pot after the greens are gone, is a southern version of nectar from the gods and is valued both as a delicacy—particularly when sopped with cornbread—and for its alleged powers as an aphrodisiac.

Southern childhood memories often include images of collard greens, perhaps the jarring first whiff of the unmistakable odor for which greens are renowned, or, more likely, the pleasant, loving connection of grandma's iron pot and steaming pot liquor. Particularly among rural and poor southerners, collard greens have endured as a dietary staple. Some southerners claim collards kept Union general William T. Sherman's scorched-earth policy from totally starving the South into submission; many North Carolina families in the early 2000s are living testament to surviving Great Depression winters with greens, fatback, and cornbread.

Collards are usually grown for culinary purposes, but southerners have been known to decorate a particularly brilliant plant as a Christmas tree. Thelonious Monk, the great jazz musician from Rocky Mount, wore a collard leaf in his lapel while playing New York City club dates. Collards were first officially celebrated in 1950, when playwright Paul Green led a "Collards and Culture" symposium in Dunn and other North Carolina cities.

Alex Albright

College of Design. In 1946 the consolidated University of North Carolina trustees created the School of Architecture and Landscape Design at North Carolina State University in Raleigh, combining the landscape architecture program from the College of Agriculture and Life Sciences with the architecture program from the College of Engineering. Leaders in North Carolina saw the school as a way of serving the people in the state and helping it move into the modern age. A committee of deans recommended the appointment of Henry L. Kamphoefner as dean of the new school. Upon his arrival, Kamphoefner hired several outstanding architects, including George Matsumoto, James Fitzgibbons, Matthew Nowicki, Eduardo Catalano, and Edward Waugh. He also initiated a guest lecture program that brought prominent architects to campus as visiting professors, among them Lewis Mumford, Frank Lloyd Wright, Ludwig Mies van der Rohe, and Buckminster Fuller. An advocate of modern architecture, Kamphoefner had an enormous impact on the architecture of North Carolina and the Southeast.

In September 1948 the School of Architecture and Landscape Design was renamed the School of Design. The school made a rapid and often favorable impression on architecture in the state. Eschewing traditional styles, it sought to create a new modern style for North Carolina and the South with structures such as Raleigh's Dorton Arena, designed by Nowicki. In 1950 the school's Department of Architecture received accreditation, as did its Department of Design in 1951. Students began to win national design competitions including the Paris Prize, the highest student honor in academic architecture. Student work was also included in exhibitions sponsored by New York's Museum of Modern Art and the American Institute of Architects. The school was one of the top design schools in the country, and by 1952 leaders in the field considered it the most progressive southern school of architecture and allied arts. In 1958 Kamphoefner created a third program in product design.

After 1967 the five-year degrees in the architecture and landscape departments were abolished and were replaced by four-year undergraduate programs and two years of graduate work. The name of the degree was changed to Bachelor of Environmental Design to reflect the School of Design's continuing philosophy of designing structures that harmonized with their setting. In an effort to meet the growing problems of urban areas in the state, a master's degree in urban design was approved in 1969, in conjunction with the Department of City and Regional Planning at the University of North Carolina at Chapel Hill.

The School of Design underwent a controversial and major change in 1973, when Claude McKinney replaced Kamphoefner as dean. McKinney abolished the traditional departmental structure within the school and placed more emphasis on interdisciplinary study. He also encouraged more interaction between students on all levels of the program through the development of a series of core courses. McKinney later went on to oversee construction of N.C. State's Centennial Campus.

Marvin J. Malecha became dean of the school in 1994, which was renamed the College of Design in 2000. The college currently offers undergraduate degrees in architecture, art and design, graphic design, industrial design, and landscape architecture, as well as master's programs in various professional disciplines and a doctoral program in design with concentrations in community and environmental design and information design. The school also engages in community outreach through its Design Camp for high school students and its Design Research and Extension Program.

Wiley J. Williams

Colonial Agents were authorized individuals in London representing the interests of the North American provinces. They conducted business for their respective colonial governments and passed important public information back and forth across the Atlantic Ocean. Agents were either provincials or influential Britons, possibly London merchants or members of Parliament, and they functioned as paid lobbyists seeking legislation, endeavoring to block unpopular bills, and presenting petitions. Prior to the eighteenth century, colonial agents normally were engaged in temporary endeavors. Soon after the Glorious Revolution of 1688–89, which peacefully put William and Mary on the throne, provincial leaders saw the value of a permanent resident in London. Such visible Britons as Edmund Burke, Charles Garth, and Richard Jackson were colonial agents. Benjamin Franklin, the most famous provincial to hold the post, spent many years in that capacity, representing not only his own Pennsylvania but at times other colonies as well.

The tenure of James Abercromby as North Carolina agent (1749–57) illustrates that there were internal as well as imperial problems with the agency. A veteran British administrator, Abercromby was well qualified to assist North Carolina in London; but for a time the Albemarle counties, in the midst of their long-running representation controversy with the Cape Fear region, refused to recognize Abercromby and sent their own spokesman to the metropolis. In 1757 his third term ended on a sour note when he was not reappointed and had trouble collecting his back salary. The following year the Lower House of the Assembly appointed him again; he served another two years, but without the approval of the Upper House and the governor. Fighting over control of the agency seems to have been almost the rule rather than the exception in North Carolina during the 25 years before independence.

References: Samuel J. Ervin, "The Provincial Agents of North Carolina," *Sprunt Historical Publications* 15 (1919); John C. Van Horne and George Reese, eds., *The Letterbook of James Abercromby: Colonial Agent, 1751–1773* (1991).

Don Higginbotham

Colonial and State Records. The basic documents of North Carolina's history from 1662 to 1790 were reproduced in two state-sponsored publications, the *Colonial Records of North Carolina* and the *State Records of North Carolina*. The *Colonial Records*, issued in ten volumes from 1886 to 1890, was edited by William L. Saunders, Confederate veteran, reputed leader of the Ku Klux Klan, and secretary of state of North Carolina from 1879 to 1891. It contains copies of documents located both in the state and in England. Saunders kept numerous documents in his office, as the secretary of state was then responsible for safekeeping the records of the General Assembly and other government units. Some records were located in the courthouses of older counties such as Perquimans and Chowan. Original documents in England were housed mostly in the Public Record Office in London and were transcribed under the direction of W. Noel Sainsbury, keeper of the records and an editor of the documentary series *Calendar of State Papers, Colonial*.

The documents included in the *State Records*, published in 16 volumes between 1895 and 1905, were compiled and edited by Walter Clark, justice of the North Carolina Supreme Court. Many of them were in state offices, and Clark traveled outside North Carolina to Pennsylvania, Maryland, Wisconsin, and Washington, D.C., in search of others. As in the case of the *Colonial Records*, repositories in England, particularly the Public Record Office, furnished a number of important documents. Stephen B. Weeks, a former professor at Trinity College and collaborator with Clark in the collection of material to be printed, prepared a four-volume index to both series, which was published between 1909 and 1914.

Legislative authorization for publication of the records had come in 1881 in the form of a resolution prepared by Saunders and endorsed by Governor Thomas J. Jarvis. The resolution permitted the publication of documents dated to 1 Jan. 1781 "belonging to the state of North Carolina" and entrusted the task to the trustees of the State Library, two of whose three members were Saunders and Jarvis. In 1883 another resolution allowed the procurement and publication of any documents of the colonial era that were "missing from the archives of the state." In 1895 and 1901 the General Assembly extended the terminal date for published material from 1781 to 1790 and 1791, respectively.

Publication of the 28,840 pages comprising the multiple volumes of these records for the first time permitted the critical writing of the early history of the state, and the series remains as an indispensable source for any serious scholarship of the period before 1790. The first volume of the *Colonial Records of North Carolina* [*Second Series*] appeared in 1963, and a second major effort to collect copies of North Carolina–related documents in British repositories took place from 1969 to 1993. Both of the more recent efforts constitute the Colonial Records Project of the North Carolina Division of Archives and History.

Robert J. Cain

Colonization Societies were organized in the early nineteenth century to promote the relocation of African Americans, particularly free blacks, to places such as Haiti, Liberia, the American Midwest, and South America. After the American Revolution the number of freedmen and freedwomen had increased dramatically, due to the gradual emancipation in the North and extensive manumission between the Revolution and the early 1800s. Added to this population were the many slaves who had escaped during the confusion of war and thereafter passed for free.

Colonization societies were numerous in North Carolina, especially in the Guilford-Randolph-Chatham County area heavily populated by Quakers. Although not remarkably antiracist, the Society of Friends opposed slavery; perhaps as a consequence, by 1827, 50 of the 106 antislavery societies in the slave states were concentrated in North Carolina. The American Colonization Society, which was formed in 1816 in Washington, D.C., and established Liberia in Africa, had "auxiliaries," or local chapters, throughout the South. The Raleigh Auxiliary Society for Colonizing the Free People of Colour of the United States was organized in 1819. By 1829 there were 11 auxiliaries of the American Colonization Society in North Carolina, located in communities as far west as Rowan County and as far east as Edenton and Murfreesboro. These early organizations were partly funded by the federal government under the 1819 Slave Trade Act.

Individuals in many areas of North Carolina emancipated their slaves, usually by provisions in their wills, and arranged for their transportation to Liberia. Free blacks and emancipated slaves from Craven, Pasquotank, Chowan, Bertie, Camden, Perquimans, Cabarrus, Iredell, Bladen, Hertford, Franklin, Edgecombe, Orange, Mecklenburg, Guilford, Forsyth, and Wake Counties were among the more than 1,200 who left the state under the auspices of the American Colonization Society. After the Civil War, the society focused on emigration, transporting more than 15,000 individuals from the United States to Africa by 1899. Well-known citizens such as Governor John Branch, Col. William Polk, *Raleigh Register* editor Joseph Gales Sr., Chief Justice John L. Taylor, and University of North Carolina president Joseph Caldwell lent their names to the cause.

Secular groups largely consisting of Quakers, the Meeting of Suffrages, and the North Carolina Manumission Society attempted to work with Colonization Society auxiliaries, composed of prominent non-Quaker North Carolinians (such as Governor James Iredell, who led the the Edenton Auxiliary) dedicated to gradual emancipation and removal of blacks, whom they viewed as a menace to white society. Quakers most committed to abolitionism, however, had long viewed colonization as a betrayal of their principles. As early as 1816, the New Garden (Guilford County) chapter had withdrawn from the Manumission Society because its members did not support the larger body's decision that colonization was an acceptable expression of the society's principles. An early sign of irreconcilable differences within the antislavery movement, this action of the New Garden Friends presaged the demise of the whole colonization enterprise by the 1830s. Supporters of manumission were divided between those who did not nec-

essarily oppose slavery but desired the removal of free blacks and those who called for total emancipation. During the 1820s —a period of relative sectional peace between the Missouri Compromise and South Carolina's attempt to disallow a federal tariff unfavorable to the South—both of these positions managed to coexist.

Given the natural increase of the slave population, the removal of small numbers of free blacks availed little. This was true even in North Carolina, which contributed 10 percent of the 4,000 blacks who were colonized in Liberia between 1820 and 1837. Without substantial government funding, colonization was doomed to fail. Additionally, the more conservative sympathizers seemed to regard colonization as merely shoring up the institution of slavery by creating a society free of slave rebellion (free blacks were often wrongly suspected of encouraging slave revolts).

By 1830 the colonization movement had lost its momentum. Whites friendly to abolition often found themselves forced to move to the North, while those unwilling to embrace black freedom gave up the enterprise altogether. The emergence of a movement for immediate emancipation in the free states, the bloody Nat Turner Rebellion (1831), and other events and issues had destroyed the uneasy alliance among the various groups wrestling with the problem of slavery, and the colonization movement was effectively dead.

References: Memory F. Mitchell, "Off to Africa—with Judicial Blessing," *NCHR* 53 (July 1976); Mitchell and Thornton W. Mitchell, "The Philanthropic Bequests of John Rex of Raleigh," *NCHR* 49 (July 1972); P. J. Staudenraus, *The African Colonization Movement, 1816–1865* (1961).

Jeremy T. Canipe
Memory F. Mitchell

SEE ALSO Manumission Societies.

Colored Farmers' Alliance

Colored Farmers' Alliance was created when an agricultural depression hit the South around 1870 and farmers began to organize themselves into radical political groups. It paralleled the white Southern Farmers' Alliance, whose membership was closed to blacks. Originating in Arkansas and spreading to 20 states, mostly in the South, the Colored Farmers' Alliance had more than 1.12 million members by 1891. At that time it became overtly political, rather than remaining the nominally political labor organization that it had been earlier. As a result of the Fusion movement, in which primarily black Republicans and white Populists cooperated politically, blacks were elected to office at both the state and national levels. Fusion in North Carolina reached its peak in 1894, when these groups gained control of the state government. It was not long, however, before black-white cooperation ended, as Democrats united in successful white supremacy campaigns to oust the Fusionists and discontinue "Negro rule."

References: Lerone Bennett Jr., *Before the Mayflower: A History of Black America* (1993); John Hope Franklin, *From Slavery to Freedom: A History of African Americans* (1994); Hugh T. Lefler and Albert R. Newsome, *North Carolina: The History of a Southern State* (3rd ed., 1973).

Helen Losse

Colson's Supply Depot was a fortified Revolutionary War post located in southwestern Montgomery County on the east side of the Pee Dee River, near Mount Gilead (Montgomery County). Constructed in 1781 and designed to safeguard supplies and provisions gathered for the troops under Gen. Nathanael Greene, it was actually the second supply depot on the lands of John and William Colson. The first stood in the vicinity of William Colson's Mill on Rocky River about three miles west of the Pee Dee where, on 21 July 1780, Col. William Lee Davidson's Whig militia had defeated Col. Samuel Bryan's Tories and captured his ammunition and supply wagons. A guard was posted, but no records indicate additional fortification. William Colson supported the American cause, but any role for his mill beyond its basic function cannot be determined.

Records indicate that the second depot may have featured a stockade surrounded by trenches and redoubts, but details of its structure are unknown. Located on a steep hill, it commanded views of the main road (Montgomery–Richmond County Line Road), Colson's Ferry across the Pee Dee, and any approaches from the west across the expanse known as Colson's Low Grounds. Detachments were sent out daily to look for any signs of enemy activity, and anyone traveling the road or attempting to ferry across the river was stopped and questioned.

Jerry L. Cross

Columbus County, located in the Coastal Plain region of southeastern North Carolina, was formed in 1808 from Brunswick and Bladen Counties and named for explorer Christopher Columbus. It partially borders the state of South Carolina. Early inhabitants of Columbus County include the Waccamaw Indians, followed by English, French, and Scottish settlers. The county seat, Whiteville, was incorporated in 1832 and named for James B. White, who was the first state senator from Columbus County; he also donated the land for the county courthouse in 1808. Other communities in Columbus County are Acme-Delco, Brunswick, Fair Bluff, and Tabor City.

Among Columbus County agricultural products are corn, soybeans, sweet potatoes and Irish potatoes, catfish, pecans, peanuts, beef and dairy cattle, and poultry. Manufactured products include textiles, plywood, doors, windows, furniture, and a variety of tools.

Lake Waccamaw State Park is Columbus County's premier natural attraction. Naturalists John and William Bartram made extensive visits to the Lake Waccamaw area in the eighteenth century and recorded their experiences. Green Swamp is another important natural landmark, representing a unique environment with many animal and plant species. Historic sites in the county include the Robert E. Lee Brown House, built in 1910, and the Snowden Singletary House, dating from the early nineteenth century. Cultural institutions include the Columbus County Theatre Association, the Cultural Arts Center, and the Fair Bluff Historical Society. Whiteville is also home to the North Carolina Museum of Forestry. Popular annual events include the North Carolina Yam Festival, the Strawberry Festival, and the Columbus Chorus Christmas Concert. About 1,800 members of the Waccamaw-Siouan tribe continue to live in Columbus and Bladen Counties. The total population of Columbus County was estimated to be 54,500 in 2004.

Jay Mazzocchi

SEE ALSO Waccamaw Indians.

Commission Merchants. SEE Factors.

Commission of Indian Affairs. The North Carolina Commission of Indian Affairs was created by the 1971 General Assembly as a response to requests of concerned Indian citizens. Among the important concerns of the commission were coordinating federal, state, and local resources to support various programs relating to the state's Indian population; providing aid and protection to Indians and their cultural and religious traditions; furthering the economic and social development of Indian communities; and protecting the rights of Indians in the state as well as making the general population aware of these rights.

Commission membership as established in the 1971 act consisted of 12 North Carolinians of Indian ancestry commissioned by the governor following selection by their tribal communities. Certain state officials also served as ex officio members. During its early years, the commission operated as an independent agency, with its budget and personnel matters being handled generally by the Department of Administration. In 1977 the state legislature reformed the commission and formally transferred it to the Department of Administration, placing it under the direction and supervision of the department's assistant secretary for advocacy programs. By the early 2000s the commission consisted of 19 representatives of the Indian community, 2 persons appointed by the General Assembly, the secretary of health and human services, the director of the State Employment Security Commission, the secretaries of the Department of Administration and the Department of Environment and Natural Resources, and the commissioner of labor.

At times friction has developed between a particular tribe and the Commission of Indian Affairs. For example, in August 2001 the North Carolina Court of Appeals overturned the recommended decision of an administrative law judge in 1999 that the Occaneechi had met the criteria to be recognized by the state as an Indian tribe. In September 2001 the commission decided that it was not ready to accept the tribe into its fold and asked the North Carolina Supreme Court to consider hearing the case. This case was later decided in favor of the Occaneechi, who officially became the Occaneechi Band of Saponi Nation. Other tribes and Indian organizations represented on the Commission of Indian Affairs are the Eastern Band of Cherokee Indians, the Coharie, the Haliwa-Saponi, the Guilford Native American Association, the Lumbee, the Meherrin, the Waccamaw-Siouan tribe, the Triangle Native American Society, the Sappony, the Cumberland County Association for Indian People, and the Metrolina Native American Association.

Reference: North Carolina Commission of Indian Affairs, "A Historical Perspective about the Indians of North Carolina and an Overview of the Commission of Indian Affairs," *NCHR* 56 (April 1979).

Wiley J. Williams

Commission on Interracial Cooperation (CIC), founded in 1919 with support from the Julius Rosenwald Fund and based in Atlanta, was dedicated to the improvement of race relations in the South. In response to racial violence plaguing the region after World War I, Will Winton Alexander, a white Methodist minister, and other whites established the CIC, whose membership soon included black men and black and white women. Under Alexander, the executive director (1919–44), the commission organized some 800 state and local interracial committees throughout the South. By the early 1920s, a CIC press service was sending releases on black achievements and race relations to about 1,200 newspapers and magazines. Through its committees and press service, the CIC worked to combat the Ku Klux Klan and lynching.

Among the commission's most prominent members were North Carolinians E. McNeill Poteat Jr., a Baptist minister who was the CIC's fifth president (1933–37), and Howard W. Odum, an internationally renowned sociologist at the University of North Carolina at Chapel Hill and the CIC's sixth and last president. By the late 1930s Alexander and other leaders, especially Odum, concluded that the commission needed to adopt a new strategy and perhaps a new organization to confront the

inequities of segregation, and the CIC ceased to exist in 1944. Thanks largely to Alexander, the commission had secured the participation of African Americans in various programs of President Franklin D. Roosevelt's New Deal and persuaded government agencies to hire black advisers on minority affairs. The CIC also was influential in bringing about passage of the Bankhead-Jones Farm Tenancy Act (1937), which established the Farm Security Administration.

Reference: Ann Wells Ellis, *The Commission on Interracial Cooperation, 1919–1944: Its Activities and Results* (1976).

Wiley J. Williams

Commission on the Future of North Carolina, also called NC 2000, was created in June 1981 by Governor James B. Hunt Jr. Chaired by William C. Friday, then president of the consolidated University of North Carolina System, with Elizabeth D. Koontz of Salisbury as vice chair, the commission embarked on a long-range planning process, with extensive assistance from professionals and broad-based public participation that reached into each of the state's 100 counties. NC 2000 sought to determine where North Carolina stood in a variety of categories, describe where it was headed, and set goals for the state on its entry into the twenty-first century and recommend ways to meet these goals. The commission's report, transmitted to the governor in March 1983, contained 44 goals and 107 recommendations concerning the state's citizenry, economy, natural resources, and community.

Reaction to the commission's report was mixed and its usefulness debated. The General Assembly's initial response was a bland joint resolution encouraging continuation of the NC 2000 process. The 1983 legislature produced nothing of real substance in reaction to the report, although some of the recommendations were later implemented. Interstate 40 was completed, and the state was successful in stimulating economic growth, especially in the Charlotte, Triad, and Research Triangle Park areas. In 1997 the General Assembly appointed a 23-member Commission on the Future of Electric Service in North Carolina—another step recommended by NC 2000.

Wiley J. Williams

Committee for Economic and Racial Justice was established in February 1934 by a group of like-minded social activists following their resignation from the Fellowship of Reconciliation, a pacifist organization. Reinhold Niebuhr, a Protestant theologian and liberal sociopolitical philosopher, served as chair, with socialist Elisabeth Gilman as treasurer and Howard Anderson "Buck" Kester as southern field secretary based in Nashville, Tenn. Kester and his family moved to Black Mountain, N.C., in 1939.

Kester proposed an agenda to encourage interracial understanding among students, promote the Socialist Party, develop educational programs for agricultural and industrial workers, investigate instances of racial and economic injustice (including lynchings and riots) for the National Association for the Advancement of Colored People and the American Civil Liberties Union, and generally champion the cause of the South's disinherited peoples. Over time, key committee members, including Niebuhr and Gilman, began to feel that Kester had strayed too far from the committee's original goals and that they now had too little information about and control over his activities to warrant their continued support. By 1941 the Committee for Economic and Racial Justice had been dissolved and its programs transferred to the Fellowship of Southern Churchmen, with Kester acting in a similar role.

References: Robert F. Martin, *Howard Kester and the Struggle for Social Justice in the South, 1904–1977* (1991); John A. Salmond, "The Fellowship of Southern Churchmen and Interracial Changes in the South," NCHR 69 (April 1992).

Wiley J. Williams

Committee of One Hundred. Between 1922 and 1926 the North Carolina Conference for Social Service devoted much attention to crime and prison conditions. A citizens' committee consisting of 100 people was composed to study these issues, largely through the efforts of A. W. McAlister of the Men's Club of the Church-by-the-Side-of-the-Road in Greensboro. A paper McAlister presented to the conference in 1922 produced a resolution to form the group. Known as the Citizens' Committee of One Hundred on Prison Legislation, it included Roy Brown and J. F. Steiner, both faculty members at the University of North Carolina in Chapel Hill and later coauthors of a study of chain gangs in North Carolina; Kate Burr Johnson, commissioner of public welfare; and George Ross Pou, superintendent of prisons.

The committee's various subgroups delivered their reports on 22 Nov. 1922. These reports were later drafted into policy proposals and were introduced as legislative measures in 1923. Three of the bills passed that year abolished the criminally insane division at the state prison, established a colony for tuberculosis prisoners, and placed the prison system under the state treasury. Although later proposals were also implemented, the committee ceased to exist after 1923.

Reference: Virginia W. Gulledge, *The North Carolina Conference for Social Service: A Study of Its Development and Methods* (1942).

Robert E. Ireland

Committees of Correspondence were among the first institutions established by the American colonies to maintain communication with each other. In December 1773 the North Carolina Assembly organized its first Committee of Correspondence, consisting of John Harvey, Robert Howe, Richard Caswell, Edward Vail, John Ashe, Joseph Hewes, Samuel Johnston, Cornelius Harnett, and William Hooper. The committee had instructions to gather early information about acts of the British government regarding the colonies, to correspond with the committees of the other colonies about plans for resistance, and to report their proceedings to the Assembly. The intercolonial cooperation of the Committees of Correspondence was the beginning of the American union, as the First Continental Congress, which met in September 1774, evolved from the intercolonial communication established and maintained by the Committees of Correspondence.

References: Lindley S. Butler, *North Carolina and the Coming of the Revolution, 1763–1776* (1976); Hugh T. Lefler and William S. Powell, *Colonial North Carolina: A History* (1973).

Carmen Miner Smith

Committees of Observation existed as a part of the preliminary political and military activity at the beginning of the American Revolution. Citizens who were reluctant to support the movement for independence were often watched closely by those who favored it. As chairman of the Committee of Observation of Halifax County in June 1775, Willie Jones noted that Andrew Miller, a local merchant, had refused to sign an agreement not to engage in trade with British subjects. Committee members Egbert Haywood and Thomas Haynes were directed to call on Miller and inquire why he refused to sign "the Association," as the document was called. Miller explained that he was holding property that belonged to someone in England and could not refuse to return it. Therefore the committee declared that it would not purchase "any goods, wares, or merchandise, of any kind whatever, from the said Miller."

William S. Powell

Committees of Safety were a network of committees authorized by the Continental Congress, endorsed by the Second Provincial Congress of North Carolina and the North Carolina Assembly, and established in late 1774 and early 1775 to enforce the Continental Association banning all trade with Britain. The committees, located in 18 counties and 4 towns throughout North Carolina, performed such duties as spreading Whig propaganda, making military preparations, enforcing price ceilings on strategic items, seizing and selling imported goods, reshipping slaves and other imports, punishing violators of the Continental Association with boycotts, and regulating public morals. The Committees of Safety, particularly the Wilmington–New Hanover committee, one of the most active, contributed to the breakdown of the royal government in North Carolina by causing Governor Josiah Martin to flee in fear in June 1775 to Fort Johnston, on the mouth of the Cape Fear River, and then to the British warship *Cruizer*.

The Assembly, dissolved by Martin on 8 Apr. 1775 for its endorsement of the Committees of Safety, was replaced by the Third Provincial Congress of North Carolina on 20 Aug. 1775. The congress proceeded to declare itself the temporary government and created the Provincial Council to oversee security in the colony and direct the activities of the Committees of Safety.

References: Lindley S. Butler, *North Carolina and the Coming of the Revolution, 1763–1776* (1976); Leora H. McEachern and Isabel M. Williams, eds., *Wilmington–New Hanover Safety Committee Minutes, 1774–1776* (1974).

Carmen Miner Smith

Common Law is the system of legal rules developed over the centuries by English judges in their decisions on cases. Being familiar to the early settlers of North Carolina, the common law was naturally applied during the colonial period; a statute of 1715 required it. After American independence, legislation was passed making the common law the rule in the state unless specifically altered; the North Carolina Supreme Court has consistently defined the "common law" referred to in this statute as that which was in force in England on 4 July 1776. This interpretation remains valid in the state. Undoubtedly, the best source for eighteenth-century common law is Sir William Blackstone's four-volume *Commentaries on the Laws of England*, first published between 1765 and 1769.

John V. Orth

Communism. Following the Bolshevik Revolution in Russia in 1917, American sympathizers founded several communist parties. The two largest ones merged in 1921 to form what came to be called the Communist Party of the United States (CPUSA). There was no organized body of communists in North Carolina for a number of years to come. In 1920, however, during the "Red Scare" after World War I, an army officer in Greensboro informed the director of U.S. Military Intelligence that authorities were making an effort to deport an unnamed, jailed member of the Communist Labor Party. The same report alleged that the U.S. Department of Justice had several prominent North Carolinians "under consideration" for possibly "flirting with radicalism."

In 1929 the National Textile Workers Union, an affiliate of the CPUSA, organized a violent but unsuccessful strike at the Loray Mill in Gastonia. The fruitlessness of this initial foray of the CPUSA into the South was, in the words of one of the strike's organizers, due in large part to the party's failure to recognize and exploit the region's "peculiar conditions."

The CPUSA maintained only a meager presence in North Carolina after the Loray Mill strike, although for several years in the early 1930s Charlotte was the headquarters for the party district comprising North Carolina, South Carolina, Virginia, and Georgia. Army intelligence reports credited the Charlotte headquarters with fomenting industrial unrest in the Carolinas, and in 1934 a strike by textile workers in Burlington, N.C., led to the direct involvement of the party's legal arm, International Labor Defense, in defending strikers accused of plotting dynamite bombings.

Despite its role in the Gastonia and Burlington strikes, the CPUSA realized scant success in the organization of labor in North Carolina. Nor did it make notable progress in increasing its numbers in either white or African American communities, although blacks were especially targeted for recruitment. An army intelligence report of 1940 related that the state headquarters of the CPUSA was in Greensboro, that party membership was divided mainly into textile workers and "agrarians," that little had come of efforts to control textile unions, and that a recent attempt had been made to "enlist the Negro population." In 1945, when membership in the Carolinas district numbered only 53, the party was beginning to make progress in several unions, primarily one representing tobacco workers at the R. J. Reynolds plant in Winston-Salem.

In the immediate postwar period, the party gained some members among students and faculty at the University of North Carolina at Chapel Hill. This growth was due mainly to the efforts of Junius Irving Scales, a Greensboro native, chairman of the Chapel Hill branch of the CPUSA, and later (1948–56) head of the party's organization in North Carolina and South Carolina. But as Cold War tensions began to intensify, party membership sharply declined. In 1955 Scales was tried and convicted under the Smith Act of 1940, which made it a crime to be a member of any group advocating the violent overthrow of the U.S. government. Scales served 14 months before President John F. Kennedy commuted his sentence.

The CPUSA in North Carolina, as elsewhere, was essentially moribund for decades following the Soviet invasion of Hungary and revelations of Joseph Stalin's crimes, events that led Junius Scales to resign from the party in disillusionment in 1957. Although such groups as the Communist Workers Party (which achieved notoriety in 1979 when five members were killed in a confrontation with the Ku Klux Klan in Greensboro) maintained a presence in the state, the CPUSA was virtually extinct. In the mid-1990s the party began to rebuild its organization in the Southeast, including in North Carolina. By that time, communist regimes had fallen in the Soviet Union and throughout Eastern Europe, and communism was perceived by most Americans as no longer constituting a serious threat. In addition, the CPUSA sought to increase its appeal by abandoning its traditional antipathy toward organized religion, as well as maintaining a publication and a website called the *People's Weekly World*. Even so, progress in recruitment was slow; in the early 2000s there were only about 100 members in the Carolinas district.

References: William J. Billingsley, *Communists on Campus: Race, Politics, and the Public University in Sixties North Carolina* (1999); John A. Salmond, *Gastonia, 1929: The Story of the Loray Mill Strike* (1995); Junius Irving Scales and Richard Nickson, *Cause at Heart: A Former Communist Remembers* (1987); Elizabeth Wheaton, *Codename Greenkil: The 1979 Greensboro Killings* (1987).

Robert J. Cain

SEE ALSO Communist Workers Party; "Death to the Klan" March; Gastonia Strike; Scales Trial.

Communist Workers Party (CWP) was a small, Leninist-Maoist organization founded in October 1979 through a reorganization of the Workers Viewpoint Organization (WVO). As it advocated the wholesale overthrow of the U.S. government, the CWP was hardly in the mainstream of more traditional North Carolina activism. However, it did seek to rally a small African American constituency by marrying opposition to both racial and class oppression. WVO and CWP organizers, including veteran Greensboro Black Power activist Nelson Johnson, began their drive to educate working-class North Carolinians by union organizing in textile mills and among Duke University service employees.

The CWP is best known for its ill-fated "Death to the Klan" march in Greensboro in November 1979. In the hope of rallying more working-class African Americans, CWP organizers planned the march to begin at a public housing project to demonstrate against the North Carolina Ku Klux Klan (KKK). While protesters shouted "death to the Klan," the KKK and allied Nazi Party members brought death to their opponents, gunning down five demonstrators. The incident shook the city and the state, belying the image of a placid, progressive North Carolina that had solved the turbulent racial and political unrest of a bygone era.

References: William J. Billingsley, *Communists on Campus: Race, Politics, and the Public University in Sixties North Carolina* (1999); Elizabeth Wheaton, *Codename Greenkil: The 1979 Greensboro Killings* (1987).

J. Christopher Schutz

SEE ALSO "Death to the Klan" March.

Community Colleges. In 1957, in an effort to address the educational needs created by the rapid shift from an agricultural to an industrial economy, the North Carolina General Assembly provided funds for a tax-supported community college system and initiated a statewide system of industrial education centers. A report titled *Community Colleges for North Carolina: A Study of Need, Location, and Service Areas* (1962), popularly known as the Hamilton Report, subsequently documented the need for such a system. It was prepared by Professor C. Horace Hamilton of the Department of Rural Sociology at North Carolina State College (modern North Carolina State University) at the request of the North Carolina Board of Higher Education and the Governor's Commission on Education beyond the High School. The study projected the populations of county high schools and colleges, considered the potential impact of proposed community colleges on existing public and private colleges, verified the low college attendance rate in North Carolina compared to other states, and noted the low income constraints on many college-age citizens. It concluded that a community college system should be established and recommended locations for the institutions.

The Department of Community Colleges, which was to be supervised by the State Board of Education and local boards of trustees, was established in 1963. At that time there were 6 community colleges, 20 industrial education centers, and 5 extension units in the state. Fifteen years later—by 1978—a total of 58 community colleges brought higher education within commuting distance of practically every North Carolinian.

In 1981 control of the community college system was transferred to the new State Board of Community Colleges, whose 20 members were appointed by the governor, State Senate, and State House of Representatives. The board's central responsibility has been to ensure the equitable distribution of funds, maintain state priorities, and approve programs to be offered by the schools. Each college has a board of 12 trustees who are elected by the local school board, county commissioners, and governor. The trustees determine local policy, under which the school's president may make various personnel and administrative decisions.

The 58 constituent colleges of the North Carolina Community College System maintain academic and technical programs organized under several broad categories. Many colleges provide training in business and office skills, agriculture, nursing, allied health skills, and engineering technologies, while others offer courses paralleling the first two years of liberal arts instruction at universities. Several schools emphasize programs for adult basic education, general education development, and continuing education. An additional school, the North Carolina Center for Applied Textile Technology in Belmont, came under the management of the North Carolina State Board of Community Colleges in 1991. The state's community college system is the nation's third largest, with an annual enrollment of more than 800,000 students on campuses that are within 30 miles of 99.9 percent of the population.

North Carolina Community Colleges (2005)

Name	Main Campus Location	Year Established	Selected Programs
Alamance Community College	Graham	1964	Business; human services; humanities and public services; industrial technology
Anson Community College	Ansonville	1962	General education; practical nursing; welding; automotive diesel mechanics
Asheville-Buncombe Technical Community College	Asheville	1964	Allied health; hospitality (tourism); engineering technology; international program in painting and decorating
Beaufort County Community College	Washington	1967	Allied health; business; college transfer courses/general education; industrial trades
Bladen Community College	Dublin	1967	Technical studies; extension and adult education
Blue Ridge Community College	Flat Rock	1969	Horticulture; elder care; travel and tourism technology; automotive restoration
Brunswick Community College	Supply	1979	Business and continuing education; automotive mechanics; industrial maintenance; law enforcement
Caldwell Community College	Hudson	1964	Furniture, hosiery, paper, and metals manufacturing technology; tourism
Cape Fear Community College	Wilmington	1959	Marine studies; nursing; electronic and instrumentation technologies

Name	Main Campus Location	Year Established	Selected Programs
Carteret Community College	Morehead City	1963	Marine engine technology; continuing education
Catawba Valley Community College	Hickory	1960	Automation/robotics; allied health; nursing; recreation/leisure facilities management; business administration
Central Carolina Community College	Sanford	1958	Laser and electro-optics training; automotive mechanics; law enforcement; cosmetology; computer-aided drafting
Central Piedmont Community College	Charlotte	1963	College transfer, high school completion, advancement studies, and continuing education programs
Cleveland Community College	Shelby	1967	College transfer courses; high school completion; television production
Coastal Carolina Community College	Jacksonville	1963	Dental assistance; nursing; operating room technology
College of the Albemarle	Elizabeth City	1961	Vocational, technical, college transfer programs; adult literacy
Craven Community College	New Bern	1965	Data processing; drafting; cosmetology; carpentry; masonry
Davidson County Community College	Lexington	1963	Liberal arts; fine arts; applied sciences; basic skills development

Name	Main Campus Location	Year Established	Selected Programs	Name	Main Campus Location	Year Established	Selected Programs
Durham Technical Community College	Durham	1961	Business; health care; applied science; optometry; microelectronics technology; dental lab technology	James Sprunt Community College	Kenansville	1966	College transfer courses; technical skills; general education; vocational training
Edgecombe Community College	Tarboro	1967	Electronics; nursing; imaging technology; surgical technology	Johnston Community College	Smithfield	1969	Fire and rescue training; electronics engineering technology; truck driver training
Fayetteville Technical Community College	Fayetteville	1963	Applied science, general education, and college transfer programs	Lenoir Community College	Kinston	1960	Broadcasting; aviation; welding technology; cosmetology; horticulture; electronics engineering; marketing
Forsyth Technical Community College	Winston-Salem	1960	Computer engineering; electromechanical technology; women's entrepreneurship; adult literacy	Martin Community College	Williamston	1967	Equine management; physical therapy assistance; automotive technology; commercial refrigeration
Gaston College	Dallas	1963	Engineering technology; business; human resources	Mayland Community College	Spruce Pine	1972	General education; technical programs
Guilford Technical Community College	Jamestown	1965	Computer science; dental assistance; furniture manufacturing; aviation	McDowell Technical Community College	Marion	1964	Machine and tool skills; commercial graphics; photography; firefighting
Halifax Community College	Weldon	1967	Emergency medical services; criminal justice; business; accounting; phlebotomy	Mitchell Community College	Statesville	1959	Occupational skills; adult education; college transfer courses
				Montgomery Community College	Troy	1967	Adult basic education; high school education
Haywood Community College	Clyde	1965	Horticulture; production crafts; fish and wildlife; sawmill trades; forestry; manufacturing engineering	Nash Community College	Rocky Mount	1967	Nursing; welding; electronic engineering; cosmetology; real estate
Isothermal Community College	Spindale	1964	Nursing; fire and rescue training; recreation/fitness; unemployment counseling; human resources	Pamlico Community College	Grantsboro	1967	Cosmetology; practical nursing
				Piedmont Community College	Roxboro	1970	Adult education; technical training

Name	Main Campus Location	Year Established	Selected Programs	Name	Main Campus Location	Year Established	Selected Programs
Pitt Community College	Greenville	1964	Business computer programming; diesel mechanics; electronic engineering technology; nursing; architectural drafting technology	Southwestern Community College	Sylva	1964	Allied health; college transfer courses; general education
Randolph Community College	Asheboro	1963	Floriculture; interior design; commercial graphics; photographic technology	Stanly Community College	Albemarle	1971	Law enforcement; emergency service training; firefighting; nursing assistance
Richmond Community College	Hamlet	1964	Applied science; college transfer courses; adult continuing education	Surry Community College	Dobson	1964	Agriculture; electronics; computer science; drafting
Roanoke-Chowan Community College	Ahoskie	1967	Cosmetology; criminal justice; nursing; radiologic technology; handicapped training	Tri-County Community College	Murphy	1967	Accounting; administrative office technology; business administration; nursing; medical assistance; cosmetology
Robeson Community College	Lumberton	1968	Adult education; technical training	Vance-Granville Community College	Vance County	1969	Business management; computer/information sciences; criminal justice; engineering technology; allied health
Rockingham Community College	Wentworth	1963	College transfer courses; continuing education; adult education	Wake Technical Community College	Raleigh	1963	Foreign languages; law enforcement; emergency medical training; computer technology
Rowan-Cabarrus Community College	Salisbury	1964	Business; human services; engineering technologies	Wayne Community College	Goldsboro	1962	Business; dental assistance; nursing; engineering; welding; diesel vehicle maintenance
Sampson Community College	Clinton	1965	Business and industry training; emergency medical services training; adult literacy	Western Piedmont Community College	Morganton	1964	College transfer courses; adult continuing education; technical training
Sandhills Community College	Pinehurst	1963	Landscape gardening; manufacturing systems technology; computer engineering applications technology	Wilkes Community College	Wilkesboro	1965	College transfer courses; nursing; business technology; dental assistance; criminal justice
Southeastern Community College	Whiteville	1964	Computer/information sciences; health sciences; engineering technologies; criminal justice	Wilson Technical Community College	Wilson	1964	Nursing; business technology; heavy equipment operator training

References: *A Matter of Facts: The North Carolina Community College System Fact Book* (1991); Kenyon Bertel Segner III, *A History of the Community College Movement in North Carolina, 1927–1963* (1974); Jon Lee Wiggs, *The Community College System in North Carolina: A Silver Anniversary History, 1963–1988* (1989).

Edwin R. Andrews
Benjamin Eagles Fountain Jr.

Company Shops was the name given to the community that developed around the array of repair shops built for the maintenance and construction of the North Carolina Railroad's rolling stock. The shops were built between 1855 and 1859 on land purchased by the railroad in Alamance County, between Graham and Gibsonville. In an attempt to promote the sale of town lots, the directors of the railroad changed the village's rather unromantic name to "Vance" for a period between 1863 and 1864, though in July 1864 they voted to resume calling it Company Shops.

Chartered in 1849 and completed in 1856, the North Carolina Railroad followed a crescent-shaped route from Goldsboro through Raleigh, Durham, Hillsborough, Greensboro, and Salisbury to Charlotte. In August 1853 its directors voted to construct shops within five miles of the railway center, and the following May the company bought eight tracts of land totaling approximately 632 acres. The directors were committed to the concept of a company town characteristic of nineteenth-century industrial development; although the railway's construction covered less than 30 acres, the directors wanted the additional land to control development and ensure adequate police oversight of the community where their workers lived.

Construction began in the summer of 1855, and by 1859 there were 57 buildings in the village. Seven shop structures were built: two engine or machine shops, a blacksmith shop, a foundry, a carpentry shop, an engine shed, and a car shed. Workmen in the shops were capable of completely rebuilding engines, constructing boxcars, and repairing all of the railroad's equipment. In addition to the shops, the workers erected a passenger and freight station, a two-story hotel, houses for workers, and three larger houses for railway officials, one of which served as company headquarters.

During the Civil War, Company Shops remained a rustic village without churches or schools. Not until 1863 did stockholders approve the layout of streets and the sale of lots for private homes (lots to be used for commercial purposes could only be leased). The railroad placed a clause in all deeds and leases prohibiting the operation of "any house of ill fame, or house for the sale of spirituous or fermented liquors or for any species of gaming on said lot." The village was incorporated in 1866.

In 1871 the railroad was leased to the Richmond & Danville Railroad, which was acting as a proxy for the Pennsylvania Railroad; the latter company was rapidly building a system to link the Northeast with the Deep South. By 1893 the North Carolina Railroad was part of the Southern Railway system, which would build massive new shops at Spencer.

After the lease to the Richmond & Danville, employment at Company Shops declined as jobs and workers were transferred to Richmond and Manchester. The inappropriateness of the name "Company Shops" and resentment toward the railroad led to a mass meeting on 1 Feb. 1887, when a committee was appointed to choose a new name for the town. A week later the state legislature acted on the request of the residents and changed the municipal charter to read "Burlington." The North Carolina Railroad sold the last of the shop area not used by the Southern Railway in 1921. Four shop buildings, modified by renovations and additions, have survived and are used for commercial purposes.

References: Durward T. Stokes, *Company Shops: The Town Built by a Railroad* (1981); Allen W. Trelease, *The North Carolina Railroad, 1849–1871, and the Modernization of North Carolina* (1991).

George W. Troxler

Computers. SEE Information Technology.

Concessions and Agreement was a document issued by the Lords Proprietors of Carolina on 7 Jan. 1665 to a group of Barbadian planters represented by Maj. William Yeamans. Although the Barbadians intended to settle in the Cape Fear region, the Concessions and Agreement applied to Carolina in its entirety. As such, it was Carolina's first written constitution. The Concessions and Agreement also provided for a method of land distribution and guaranteed settlers freedom of conscience in religion.

From the existing records, it appears that some aspects of the Concessions and Agreement were operative by mid-1665. The document remained in effect until early 1672, when it was superseded by the Fundamental Constitutions of Carolina.

Reference: Mattie Erma Edwards Parker, ed., *North Carolina Charters and Constitutions, 1578–1698* (1963).

John Paden

SEE ALSO Fundamental Constitutions.

Concordia College was established in Conover in 1877 as Concordia High School by the Lutherans of the Tennessee Synod. It was converted into a college in 1881. The college began as a ministerial training school, although by 1919 it also offered programs in French, "mental science," "moral science," and pedagogy. The Depression years brought a gradual decline in enrollment, which had peaked at slightly over 100. On 16 Apr. 1935 the school's administration building burned, and later that year the Lutheran Church voted to close the college.

Cloth inspection section of a Cone Mills textile plant in Greensboro, 1940s. Photograph by Bayard Wootten. NCC.

Reference: Gary R. Freeze, *The Catawbans: Crafters of a North Carolina County, 1747–1900* (1995).

Wiley J. Williams

Cone Mills Corporation was established in 1891 when brothers Moses and Caesar Cone decided to enter the textile business in the South, where for more than a decade they had been wholesale grocery and tobacco distributors. Finding that the bolts of cloth from local mills they often received as payment sold easily, the Cones saw the potential for textile production and bought an interest in cotton mills in Asheville, Salisbury, and Gibsonville. They perceived the need for a better product than the loosely woven fabric they had been receiving in trade as well as for a strong marketing organization in a glutted industry suffering from cutthroat competition.

The Cones obtained a New Jersey charter for the Cone Export and Commission Company, which was first headquar-tered in New York City but later moved to Greensboro because of communications facilities and proximity to producers. By the mid-1890s, the Cones' company was serving approximately 90 percent of the South's mill owners. It saved a number of mills from going under in the hard times of the 1890s and helped manufacturers improve product quality. In 1941 the company's headquarters returned to New York City as its operations broadened.

During the decade between 1895 and 1905, the Cones entered direct manufacturing of denim—their giant White Oak plant near Greensboro opened in 1905—and helped build the South's first cotton flannel mill, the Revolution Mill, which operated until 1982. They would subsequently diversify into printing and other textiles and processes, buy controlling interest in several mills, and build several mill villages.

The corporation remained profitable throughout the Great Depression. World War II saw the production of a variety of fabrics for the armed forces, leading Cone Mills to be honored with the coveted Army and Navy "E" Award. During the war a Cone subsidiary leased 512 acres of its property in the northeast section of Greensboro to the U.S. Army for construction of Basic Training Center No. 10, later called the Overseas Replacement Depot. The army's presence bolstered Greensboro's economy and later aided the city's adjustment to peacetime.

A publicly traded company for more than 30 years, Cone Mills went private in 1984 after threats of a hostile takeover. In 1991 the company celebrated its centennial. Although the challenge of imports and economic recession led to continuous restructuring and changes in operations, in 2002 the company remained one of the nation's largest manufacturers of textiles and related products and a world leader in denim manufacture. A 2002 ranking listed Cone Mills Corporation at number 70 among the state's top 100 companies, with an estimated market worth of $78.9 million. The company was purchased in 2004 by New York financier Wilbur Ross and became, along with Burlington Industries, part of the giant International Textile Group, headquartered in Greensboro.

Reference: Carolyn R. Hines, ed., *A Century of Excellence: The History of Cone Mills, 1891 to 1991* (1991).

Alexander R. Stoesen

Confederate Congress, North Carolina
Members of. A total of 34 delegates from North Carolina served in the Confederate Congress: 29 in the House of Representatives and 5 in the Senate. The following table lists the delegates and the three terms of the Congress in which they served.

Provisional Congress (4 Feb. 1861 to 17 Feb. 1862)

Francis B. Craige	Richard C. Puryear
Allen T. Davidson	Thomas Ruffin
George Davis	William N. H. Smith
Thomas D. S. McDowell	Abraham W. Venable
John M. Morehead	

First Congress (18 Feb. 1862 to 17 Feb. 1864)

SENATORS	Allen T. Davidson
George Davis	Burgess S. Gaither
William T. Dortch	Owen R. Kenan
Edwin G. Reade	William Lander
REPRESENTATIVES	Thomas D. S. McDowell
Archibald H. Arrington	James R. McLean
Thomas S. Ashe	William N. H. Smith
Robert R. Bridgers	

Second Congress (2 May 1864 to 18 Mar. 1865)

SENATORS	REPRESENTATIVES
William T. Dortch	Robert R. Bridgers
William A. Graham	Thomas C. Fuller
Burgess S. Gaither	George W. Logan
John A. Gilmer	James G. Ramsey
James M. Leach	William N. H. Smith
James T. Leach	Josiah Turner Jr.

References: Thomas B. Alexander and Richard E. Beringer, *The Anatomy of the Confederate Congress* (1972); Ezra J. Warner and W. Buck Yearns, *Biographical Register of the Confederate Congress* (1975).

William T. Auman

Confederate Imprints. During the Civil War, printing in North Carolina, as well as in the other Confederate states, was severely restricted by the shortage of manpower and supplies. North Carolina had 74 newspapers in 1860 but fewer than half that number by 1864. The state printed legislative, executive, and supreme court documents, as well as recruiting broadsides. Some private printing dealt with politics in the form of pamphlets or campaign broadsides. Religious works counted for a great percentage of North Carolina's Confederate imprints.

Blum's Farmers' and Planters' Almanac, published by L. V.

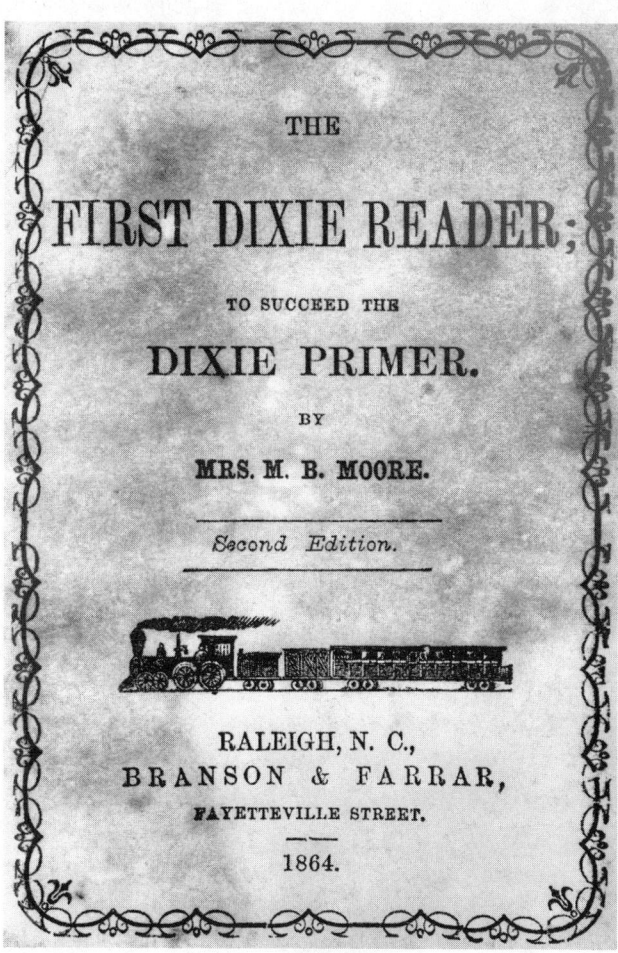

Front cover of *The First Dixie Reader* by Mrs. M. B. Moore, 1864. NCC.

Confederate Memorial Day ceremony at Woodington Universalist Church in Lenoir County, 1920. The event was staged on the bed of a truck parked at the church entrance. NCC.

and E. T. Blum of Salem, and *Turner's North Carolina Almanac*, published by Henry D. Turner at the *Raleigh Register* printing plant, managed to continue throughout the war years. Other surviving imprints relate to hospitals and medicine.

The Greensboro firm of Sterling, Campbell, and Albright printed numerous schoolbooks, as did the Raleigh firm of Branson and Farrar, but only a few works of new fiction appeared in the state. *Hester and Other Poems* (1861), by Theophilus H. Hill (1836–1901) of North Carolina, was the first book published under the Confederate states' newly established copyright law.

Some sheet music and a few music books, or "songsters," were also produced in North Carolina.

References: Karen C. Carroll, "Sterling, Campbell, and Albright, Textbook Publishers, 1861–1865," *NCHR* 63 (April 1986); H. G. Jones and Julius H. Avant, *Union List of North Carolina Newspapers, 1751–1900* (1963); T. Michael Parrish and Robert M. Willingham Jr., *Confederate Imprints: A Bibliography of Southern Publications from Secession to Surrender* (1984).

David A. Norris

Confederate Laboratory, located two miles south of Lincolnton in Lincoln County, was one of at least five laboratories established by the Confederate States of America to manufacture drugs from indigenous plants. The other known facilities

were located in Tyler, Tex.; Augusta and Macon, Ga.; and Columbia, S.C. Although the actual date of construction is unknown, the Lincoln County laboratory was in operation by 24 Aug. 1863. The original building was an oblong brick structure that stood on the banks of the South Fork River.

Strict secrecy was maintained at the facility, and an aura of mystery surrounded it. Lt. A. P. James and the men of Company A, McCorkle's Battalion, North Carolina Senior Reserves, were assigned to provide security for the site. Because of the tight security and the local availability of saltpeter and charcoal, some historians have speculated that the Lincoln County laboratory may also have been used for the production of gunpowder.

Laboratory, a small community south of Lincolnton, took its name from the facility.

References: L. A. Crowell, "Historic Medicine," *Southern Medicine and Surgery* (June 1933); John R. Friday, "Dr. A. Snowden Piggott and the Laboratory Facility," *Carolina Confederate* 8 (1993).

Daniel W. Barefoot

Confederate Memorial Day has been observed in North Carolina and throughout the South on different days and under various names since 1866. In that first year after the close of the Civil War, communities across the South hosted ceremonies at grave sites, on courthouse lawns, and at state

Unveiling ceremony for Confederate monument at Salisbury, 1909. NCC.

capitols. That was the beginning of an annual tradition observed with memorial addresses by dignitaries, band concerts, the laying of wreaths and flowers, picnics, and community meals. Through the years, some southern states began to neglect this custom, but in many places it has continued.

In North Carolina 10 May, the date of the death of Gen. Thomas J. "Stonewall" Jackson, was originally named by the members of the Wake County Ladies' Memorial Association as the day of remembrance. On that first Confederate Memorial Day, the citizens of Wake County secretly made their way to Raleigh's Oakwood Cemetery, since the Reconstruction military governor had threatened to shoot anyone who gathered for such a purpose. Nevertheless, Raleigh citizens assembled then, as they have every year since, to honor North Carolinians who wore the Confederate uniform.

By the end of the twentieth century, two Confederate Memorial Days had come to be observed in North Carolina. The 10 May date remains the official Confederate Memorial Day in North Carolina, when Confederate descendants fly their flags and join in a variety of events to mark the occasion. Depending upon personal and political loyalties, the governor sometimes takes note of the day through an official proclamation. A second memorial is held during the first weekend in May, when the Sons of Confederate Veterans and the Military Order of the Stars and Bars hold their annual conventions. During that weekend, besides the two convening organizations, members of the United Daughters of the Confederacy, the Order of Confederate Rose, the Children of the Confederacy, and other historically minded citizens gather for memorial services at Oakwood Cemetery, at the State Capitol, and elsewhere. Solemn services, as well as dances, balls, and picnics, are also traditionally held in many towns and communities across the state.

Charles C. Davis

Confederate Monuments began to appear in North Carolina and throughout the South almost simultaneously with the departure of the last of the Reconstruction government's occupation forces in the late 1870s. Confederate and state leaders and soldiers were recognized by means of statues, memorial plaques, buildings, and the naming of streets and parks, among other ways. The sites of battles and other places of historical importance were marked a little later; the whole movement reached a climax early in the twentieth century, as economic recovery made funds more plentiful, but it continued throughout the century.

In the beginning, the funding and building of Confederate monuments in the state was the work of monument committees and associations under the guidance of the Southern Monumental Association, the United Daughters of the Confederacy, and the United Confederate Veterans. Their efforts resulted in the raising of most of the monuments placed on courthouse lawns and around the State Capitol. With the passing of time this work was taken up by the Sons of Confederate Veterans, the Military Order of the Stars and Bars, and the Order of the Confederate Rose. The state legislature of North Carolina (and those of other states) also assisted in the funding of monuments at many national battlefield parks.

Capitol Square (officially called Union Square) in Raleigh is the location of some of the state's most widely recognized Confederate monuments. Erected in 1895 on the west side of the State Capitol at the head of Hillsborough Street is the tall, striking monument to all Confederates from North Carolina. A statue of Pvt. Henry Lawson Wyatt of the 1st North Carolina State Troops, the first Confederate soldier to give his life in the war, was completed in 1909. On the east lawn of the square is the statue of Zebulon B. Vance, brigadier general and one of three men who served as governor of the state during the war. On the southern lawn beside Morgan Street is the beautiful statue honoring the women of North Carolina at the time of the war.

Throughout the state are likenesses of Confederate soldiers portrayed in bronze and granite. Notable among them are those in Asheville, Chapel Hill, Goldsboro, Louisburg, New Bern, Salisbury, Smithfield, Warrenton, Washington, and Wilmington. Many of these monuments consist of a single armed soldier in granite atop a tall shaft, facing north as if to defend his home from invaders.

Charles C. Davis

Confederate Negro is a term that was used in North Carolina and other southern states to refer to blacks who made significant contributions to the Confederacy during the Civil War. Some slaves served in noncombatant roles, such as nurses in government hospitals, supply wagon and ambulance drivers, and cooks. They also helped to construct fortifications around cities and strategic military sites such as rivers and railroads. At times slaves carried news from home and delivered supplies and food to their masters on the battlefield, or they brought home the wounded and dead.

As Confederate military fortunes continued to fall, more and more southern whites began to contemplate changes in the slave system, including sending black men—the last source of troops—to fight. In the waning months of 1864 and early 1865, whites debated in the press, the pulpit, and political forums the wisdom of using black soldiers, and Gen. Robert E. Lee announced his plan for arming and freeing the slaves. Yet the Confederate Congress delayed. On 13 Mar. 1865 the southern lawmakers finally authorized President Jefferson Davis to recruit up to 300,000 black troops, but Lee's surrender at Appomattox on 9 April ended the war before they took to the field.

Wiley J. Williams

Confederate Party was active in political battles in North Carolina during the Civil War. In a real sense, the party was created by its opponents, who eventually called themselves "Conservatives." At the beginning of the war, a façade of unity existed in the state, with all prominent political leaders supporting secession from the Union. This surface unity could not hide the fact that virtually all of the state's political leaders still aligned themselves with organizations similar to the antebellum political parties.

The first indications of the survival of partisanship came with the appointment of officers in the North Carolina regiments of the Confederate army. Former Whig congressman Zebulon B. Vance of Buncombe County estimated that 90 percent of the generals from North Carolina were former Democrats. During the election for president of the Confederacy, dissatisfied former Whigs ran an opposition Jefferson Davis ticket that won approximately 40 percent of the vote against the regular slate. In an effort to head off the dissatisfied opposition, the incumbent group nominated former Whig William Johnston of Mecklenburg County for governor in the early spring of 1862. The leaders of the opposition group, now calling it the "Conservative Party," met later in 1862 and chose Vance as their candidate. Led by William W. Holden and William A. Graham, the Conservatives attacked their opposition, which they labeled the "Confederate Party." It is unclear whether the name was selected in an attempt to associate the party with the unpopular Jefferson Davis administration or because an anti-Conservative newspaper in Raleigh called itself the *Confederate*.

The Confederates failed to organize effectively for the 1862 gubernatorial election, and Vance overwhelmed Johnston in the popular vote for governor. From then on, the party rarely offered candidates. It is uncertain whether the party ever existed as a formal organization or whether the title was simply a convenience adopted for the vestige of the Democratic Party that survived into the Civil War.

References: Robin E. Baker, "Class Conflict and Political Upheaval: The Transformation of North Carolina Politics during the Civil

War," *NCHR* 69 (April 1992); John G. Barrett, "North Carolina," in W. Buck Yearns, ed., *The Confederate Governors* (1985); William C. Harris, *William Woods Holden: Firebrand of North Carolina Politics* (1987); Marc W. Kruman, *Parties and Politics in North Carolina, 1836–1865* (1983).

Gordon B. McKinney

Confederate Pensions. Although the Civil War injured or killed tens of thousands of North Carolinians, not until after Reconstruction did the state begin to pass broad pension laws to provide for crippled ex-Confederate soldiers and the widows of deceased veterans. In 1879 the legislature passed a law granting $60 per year to Civil War veterans who had lost both arms or both legs or were totally blind. Only a dozen individuals applied for this pension. An 1885 statute expanded the program by creating a $30,000-per-year fund to pay pensions to soldiers who were at least "three-fourths incapacitated by wounds" and to Confederate widows whose husbands had died during the war. As a result, from 1879 to 1900 approximately 4,500 North Carolinians applied for benefits under the new law.

Although there was an extensive verification process, approximately three-fourths of all veterans' applications were approved in the first year. The most common reason for rejection—which could be appealed—was that the disability was not severe enough to warrant a pension. In 1887 the legislature extended pensions to widows whose husbands had died from disease, not just from wounds. However, the North Carolina pension system was poorly funded; pensioners still received approximately $60 annually, in contrast with Tennessee's system, which provided $100 a year.

At the beginning of the twentieth century, state lawmakers decided that veterans were entitled to pensions simply for suffering the infirmities of old age. In 1901 fixed pensions ranged from $30 to $72 annually, based on the extent of incapacitation, with total pension expenditures not to exceed $200,000 for veterans and widows. This amount was increased during most succeeding legislative sessions, reaching $650,000 in 1919. In addition, in 1909 the lawmakers authorized counties to levy special taxes to benefit veterans residing within their borders. Moreover, veterans' petitions were now approved for reasons that earlier would have resulted in rejection, and applications were simplified.

The most important change after 1900 was that a widow could apply for a pension even if her husband had died after the war, as long as he had never deserted. Furthermore, in 1909 the legislature allowed applications from widows who had married Confederate veterans as late as 1 Jan. 1868—two and a half years after the war ended. In the ensuing years this date was gradually moved forward; by the 1920s widows received pensions even when they had married Confederate veterans

in the 1880s. Another change granted pensions to women who had remarried since the death of their veteran husbands.

Before 1901 about twice as many widows as veterans applied for pensions, as few men believed that they could meet the strict eligibility requirements of the 1885 law. After 1901, with the aging of many former Confederate soldiers, the state received roughly equal numbers of applications from veterans and widows. A total of 35,000 pension applications were filed from 1901 to 1946.

Garett Jones
Robert C. Kenzer

Confederate Postal Service. According to the Confederate Provisional Constitution that was adopted on 8 Feb. 1861, the postal service was to support itself from its own revenue. The Confederate Post Office Department was established on 21 February, and John Henninger Reagan was appointed the first postmaster general. On 27 May North Carolina entered the Confederacy, and on 1 June the Federal postal system was ordered to cease operations in the southern states. Reagan's first actions were to ask existing postmasters and route agents to stay on at old U.S. contracts. He negotiated a 50 percent reduction in the railroad rates for carrying the mail, and, most important, he increased the postal rates from three cents to five cents per half-ounce letter sent less than 500 miles and ten cents if sent farther than 500 miles. It was October 1861 before the first postage stamps were available for use by southern citizens.

In its first year of operation the post office sold $692,067 in postage stamps and in the second year, $2,392,332. The discrepancy can largely be explained by the fact that stamps were unavailable during much of the first year and the postal rate was increased to ten cents for any distance on 1 July 1862. However, postage stamps began to play another important role in the community, as many were used as small change in lieu of available coins.

Mail was carried on the rail lines in specially built mail cars. Route agents traveled in these cars to sort and process the mail along the way, a most unpleasant job. On a good day the route from Goldsboro to Charlotte made 23 stops and took 15 hours. Mail carriers worked seven days a week. Most mail cars had no heat, and the War Department frequently used them to ship dead soldiers home. Complaints were the norm for many route agents. By the end of the war, when almost all materials were in short supply, letters and envelopes turned inside out were reused. It was not uncommon to see a letter written in one direction, turned sideways, and written in the other direction to conserve paper.

Confederate postal operations made a profit every year—something that the U.S. postal system had never done. In the process, however, the Post Office Department sacrificed service for efficiency and economy. By the end of the war, mi-

The Confederate Prison at Salisbury as depicted in an 1886 lithograph. NCC.

grating Confederate soldiers were carrying more mail than the postal system. Postmaster General Reagan had accomplished his goal of profitability, but at the expense of the citizenry.

References: August Dietz, *The Postal Service of the Confederate States of America* (1929); Richard Ridgway, *Self-Sufficiency at All Costs: Confederate Post Office Operations in North Carolina, 1861–1865* (1988).

Tony L. Crumbley

Confederate Prison (Salisbury). On 9 July 1861, six weeks after North Carolina seceded from the Union, the Confederate government asked Governor Henry T. Clark if the state could provide a place to hold prisoners of war (POWS). The 20-year-old Maxwell Chambers textile mill in Salisbury, then vacant, was hurriedly fitted for that purpose. On 9 December 120 prisoners transferred from the Raleigh State Fairgrounds were the first prisoners to enter the Salisbury Prison, the first and only Civil War prison in North Carolina.

The prison population increased to about 1,400 by late May 1862, when the inmates were paroled and returned to the Union. These POWS lived in relative comfort, passing the time by making trinkets, playing baseball, and even engaging in theatrical productions. After their departure, POWS at Salisbury Prison were outnumbered by Yankee deserters and dissident Confederates. This period of "normalcy" suddenly ended in early October 1864, when 10,000 prisoners began arriving at a facility that was intended to hold only 2,500. This huge increase, which resulted from the fall of Atlanta and the ongoing siege of Richmond, made it easier for the Union army to rescue its POWS. Salisbury received some of the Richmond prisoners, and after October 1864, the majority of newly captured Union POWS.

The most painful period for the Salisbury prisoners was from October 1864 until their release in February 1865. Accounts from POW diaries indicate that the prisoners took in about 1,600 calories per day, whereas 2,000 calories was considered the minimum for survival under the adverse conditions that existed at Salisbury. It is not surprising that diarrhea was the most common disease as well as the most deadly, due in large part to the overcrowding and unsanitary conditions.

From December 1861, when it opened, through September 1864, Salisbury Prison experienced a 2 percent death rate (about 100 deaths). But between October 1864 and 15 February 1865, the rate soared to 28 percent. An estimated 4,000 prisoners died at the prison during its existence, for an overall death rate of 26 percent. Bodies were collected daily at the "dead house" and hauled in a one-horse wagon to trenches in a nearby "old cornfield." A visitor to the cemetery today finds these 18 trenches to be the most somber, painful, and shocking part of the Salisbury National Cemetery. The total death rate in Union and Confederate prisons is considered to have been about the same at 12 percent.

In the fall of 1864 escape from Salisbury Prison was considered almost necessary to save one's life. Many POWs escaped, but only about 300 reached Union lines. During an attempted mass escape on 25 Nov. 1864, none got away and about 200 prisoners lost their lives. Tunneling became popular with the POWs. The most famous tunnel escape took place in mid-January 1865, when an estimated 100 managed to flee the prison. According to one prisoner, the easiest way to get "out of this cursed place" was to defect to the Confederacy. Although about 2,100 POWs reportedly defected, these soldiers contributed little to the Confederate cause.

The morale of the prisoners was usually very low. Muggers plagued all Civil War prisons. Prisoners' diaries often mention their faith in God, and Christian services were held at the prison in the fall of 1864. Occasionally, Salisbury residents would hear the sound of a familiar hymn coming from the prison; as one citizen recalled, it was like "a thought of heaven from a field of graves." Fraternal organizations such as the Masons and Oddfellows provided some moral support for the prisoners.

All POWs were transferred from Salisbury in February 1865, about six weeks before Maj. Gen. George H. Stoneman, on 12–13 Apr. 1865, destroyed the prison and other Confederate installations collectively known as the Salisbury Arsenal. In May Federal troops occupied the town, but in early September 1865 the Union commander turned over civil control of Salisbury to duly elected town officials. At the end of the war all Confederate property fell into Union hands and in September 1866 was sold at auction by the Freedmen's Bureau to the Holmes brothers for $1,600.

In 1866 a U.S. military commission charged Maj. John H. Gee, commandant of the Salisbury Prison during late 1864, with murder and "violation of the laws and customs of war." After a lengthy trial, Gee was acquitted of both charges.

References: Louis A. Brown, *The Salisbury Prison: A Case Study of Confederate Military Prisons, 1861–1865* (1992); Annette Gee Ford, *The Captive: Major John H. Gee, Commandant of the Confederate Prison at Salisbury, North Carolina, 1864–1865* (2000).

Louis A. Brown

Confederate Soldiers' Home in Raleigh was first conceived in October 1881, when a number of veterans meeting at the State Fairgrounds in Raleigh formed the Society of Ex-Confederate Soldiers and Sailors of North Carolina (soon renamed the Confederate Survivors' Association of North Carolina). The movement to build a home in North Carolina officially began on 20 May 1884, when a number of prominent Confederate veterans, headed by Senator Zebulon B. Vance, convened at the courthouse in Charlotte and organized the North Carolina Confederate Home Association to solicit and accept donations for "the accommodation" of "maimed, disabled and indigent heroes" and "unfortunate victims of the Lost Cause."

It was not until 1889 that the Confederate Veterans Association of North Carolina was formed and incorporated by the state legislature; the new organization presented as one of its goals the founding and the maintenance of a "home or homes for indigent, infirm and invalid Confederate soldiers and sailors, or their widows and orphans." By September 1890 the Confederate Veterans Association of North Carolina, aided by the Wake County Ladies Memorial Association and the Daughters of the Confederacy, succeeded in raising enough funds to begin leasing an eight-room house located on Polk and Bloodworth Streets, near downtown Raleigh. Within a month, as many as a half-dozen veterans were enrolled in the home, which served, technically, as the first Confederate soldiers' home in North Carolina, though only for a brief time.

A permanent home, complete with medical facilities, was finally established in an act ratified on 14 Feb. 1891, when the state deeded property near Raleigh known as Camp Russell to the newly constituted Soldiers' Home Association—an administrative body consisting of three members of the Confederate Veterans Association of North Carolina, four appointees by the governor, and an advisory board of nine "lady managers." The North Carolina Confederate Soldiers' Home formally opened its doors in May 1891, becoming the fifth state-supported Confederate home in the nation (preceded only by those in Louisiana, Virginia, Maryland, and Texas). Eligible for admission to the home were veterans of either the Confederate army or navy who had served honorably in North Carolina commands until the end of the war and who had "borne a good character since" the war. As many as 1,459 individual Confederate veterans are known to have resided at the Confederate Soldiers' Home from its opening in 1891 to 1926, when the last reliable enrollment figures were kept. Approximately 90 percent of all admissions occurred before 1920, when the average Confederate veteran was well in his eighties. Roughly one-third of these men had been wounded in the war or had suffered from a service-related disability or ailment following the war, and an overwhelming majority had worked as farmers or as nonprofessionals.

During its 47-plus years of existence, the North Carolina Confederate Soldiers' Home accommodated an average of no more than 90 veterans at any one time; enrollment figures exceeded 200 in 1917, although the number who were actually present then at the home was considerably lower. Once admitted to the home, the veteran remained on the roll until he died or was officially discharged or expelled for disciplinary reasons. The average tenure (time in residence) of a North Carolina Confederate Soldiers' Home guest was less than four years.

After the last veteran, Walter Barfield, age 94, left the home in August 1938, the North Carolina Confederate Soldiers' Home officially closed its doors. Soon the property was reoccupied and repaired by the National Youth Association, and the hospital was renovated and reopened as the Raleigh Recreation Center. By 1948 the building was abandoned; today, the intersection of Tarboro Road and New Bern Avenue, where the home formerly stood, is occupied by the North Carolina Division of Motor Vehicles.

References: Fred A. Olds, "History of Soldiers' Home at Raleigh," *The Orphans' Friend and Masonic Journal* (23 Dec. 1926); Herbert Poole, "Final Encampment: The North Carolina Soldiers' Home," *Confederate Veteran* (July–August 1987); Randall B. Rosenburg, *Living Monuments: Confederate Soldiers' Homes in the New South* (1993).

Randall B. Rosenburg

Confederate Women's Home, which opened in Fayetteville in 1915, was established for the benefit of widows and daughters of North Carolina's Confederate veterans. At the 1908 convention of the North Carolina Division of the United Daughters of the Confederacy, Mrs. Hunter G. Smith proposed establishment of such a facility. Five years later the legislature appropriated $10,000 for building purposes and $5,000 per year for maintenance. Smith, who died in 1929, was the first superintendent of the home.

Originally the home was scheduled to close in 1950, but twice it received reprieves. By 1981 only seven women lived in the home, and the North Carolina Department of Human Resources, together with the board of directors, decided it was not practical to keep it in operation. The property was sold to the Fayetteville City Board of Education. In 1982 the two-story brick building was razed and the land used as a parking lot for Terry Sanford High School. Sixty-five women are buried in a cemetery that remains. In 1986 a state highway historical marker was erected at the site.

Michael Hill

Confiscation Acts were passed by the North Carolina General Assembly from 1776 through the 1780s to confiscate the property of Loyalists. This was done to punish and control the Loyalists as well as to obtain income for the state. Most of the confiscated real estate was sold in 1786 and 1787 and netted the North Carolina about £600,000. The Treaty of Paris in 1783 had provided that Congress would recommend to state legislatures the restitution of confiscated property. It also

stipulated that there would be no future confiscations. The states virtually ignored both provisions. The judicial case of *Bayard v. Singleton* arose over the issue of confiscation and established the principle of judicial review in North Carolina.

Reference: Carole Watterson Troxler, *The Loyalist Experience in North Carolina* (1976).

John L. Bell

Congressional Districts in North Carolina, as in other states, have varied widely in size, shape, and number since the state ratified the U.S. Constitution in 1789. The number of congressional districts, reflecting the state's share of representatives in the U.S. House based on the decennial federal census, has ranged from as few as 7 (1865–72) to as many as 13 (1812–43, 2002–).

Drawing the boundaries of congressional districts has been the duty of the North Carolina legislature since 1789. The first districts were named after five geographic divisions: Western (now Tennessee), Yadkin, Roanoke, Edenton and New Bern, and Cape Fear. In 1790 these five were realigned, becoming the Yadkin, Centre, Roanoke, Albemarle, and Cape Fear Districts. After the first U.S. census in 1790, numbers were assigned to districts in 1792, ranging from the First District (Buncombe and four western counties) to the Tenth (Johnston County eastward to Hyde); the west-to-east pattern was reversed in 1802, then reimposed in 1852. These districts remained contiguous geographically, although both the number and exact grouping of counties often changed markedly from one census to the next.

County boundaries were long considered sacrosanct dividing lines by the General Assembly's map drawers because of the legal priorities set out in Article II, sections 3(3) and 5(3), of the North Carolina Constitution. Consequently, juggling the counties to create a reasonable population balance was often complicated. In some instances, redistricting involved both political and demographic factors, such as in 1872, when the Democratic General Assembly attempted to group most of the state's Republicans into one eastern district, the so-called Black Second. Knowing a Democratic candidate could never win the district, the General Assembly selected the counties of the Black Second to isolate and neutralize eastern Republican voters, many of whom were former slaves. From 1872 to 1901 the redrawn district's African American population, nearly 66 percent of the total, elected black congressmen seven times. George White was the last of these early black congressmen in the state, representing the Second District before African American voters were largely disfranchised around 1900. Drawing district lines in favor of Democratic incumbents whenever possible was another device often employed by the General Assembly, since Democrats controlled the legislature during every postcensus session between 1872 and 1991.

After federal pressure to create two predominantly black districts in the state prompted the General Assembly to undertake a cumbersome and complicated redistricting process, the county-boundary rule was seemingly discarded in 1991. Electoral boundaries were adjusted, at least in part, to provide minorities a reasonable opportunity to elect their candidates to Congress, in compliance with the Voting Rights Act of 1965. The results were oddly shaped, long, narrow connectors between centers of black populations: a redrawn First District encompassing 9 eastern counties and parts of 19 more, stretching from Virginia to South Carolina, and a completely new Twelfth District in the Piedmont, which snaked from Durham County west and south to Mecklenburg County, mostly along the narrow "Urban Crescent" of Interstate Highway 85. The process affected adjacent districts as well; almost half of the state's 100 counties were divided, including Cumberland County, which was distributed among the First, Seventh, and Eighth Districts.

In 1992, for the first time in nearly a century, North Carolina voters elected two black members of Congress: Melvin Watt from the new Twelfth District and Eva M. Clayton from the First District. Both Watt and Clayton were reelected several times. But the redistricting that helped lead to their election sparked a number of court battles in the 1990s. Disputes over the districts found their way to the U.S. Supreme Court four times in eight years. At the center of the conflict was Watt's Twelfth District, which was struck down as unconstitutional in 1993 and 1996. In response to these decisions, the state redrew the district twice more, in 1997 and 1998. Finally, in 2001 the Supreme Court upheld its boundaries in a narrow 5–4 decision—just in time for another round of redistricting following the 2000 U.S. census.

The census in 2000 qualified North Carolina for an additional congressional seat, bringing the total number of its congressional districts to 13 for the first time since the early nineteenth century. The new district, located in the northern Piedmont along the North Carolina–Virginia border, encompasses all of Person and Caldwell Counties and parts of Wake, Alamance, Granville, Guilford, and Rockingham Counties. Stretching from Raleigh to Greensboro, the Thirteenth District is primarily urban/suburban, with only about one-third of its voters living in rural settings or small towns. In 2002 Democrat Brad Miller was elected the first U.S. representative from the new Thirteenth District.

References: Eric Anderson, *Race and Politics in North Carolina, 1872–1901: The Black Second* (1981); John L. Cheney Jr., ed., *North Carolina Government, 1585–1979: A Narrative and Statistical History* (1981); Benjamin R. Justesen, *George Henry White: An Even Chance in the Race of Life* (2001); Eric Rise, ed., *Congressional Redistricting in North Carolina: Reconsidering Traditional Criteria* (2002).

Benjamin R. Justesen

Congress of Racial Equality (CORE), founded in Chicago in 1942, crusaded for equality through nonviolence and integration. It came to North Carolina on a 1947 southern bus during a "Journey of Reconciliation," when an interracial group that included North Carolinians faced arrest for not riding in segregated seats. By 1963 CORE had nine chapters in the state, hundreds of members (many of them student activists), and leaders such as black attorney Floyd B. McKissick (1922–91), who became chairman and later national director of CORE. Like its 1961 Freedom Ride, CORE's voter education projects and sit-in campaigns helped energize the struggle for civil rights in North Carolina. In 1966 the organization embraced Black Power, emphasizing self-determination over nonviolent direct action.

References: Jeffrey J. Crow, Paul D. Escott, and Flora J. Hatley, *A History of African Americans in North Carolina* (2002); Floyd B. McKissick, *Three-Fifths of a Man* (1969); August Meier and Elliott Rudwick, CORE: *A Study in the Civil Rights Movement, 1942–1968* (1975); Capus M. Waynick, John C. Brooks, and Elsie W. Pitts, eds., *North Carolina and the Negro* (1964).

Raymond Gavins

Conjure is based on the belief that psychical and magical powers can be exercised in such a way that spells may be cast, enchantments made, bad or good luck established, the future foretold, lost items found or thieves detected, sickness and death induced, or healing performed. Among American Indians and African slaves in North Carolina, the ability to perform these acts was inherent from birth in the practitioner, rather than gained by a compact with Satan as in the European tradition.

In 1767, when Johnston County slaves wished to influence the actions and attitudes of their masters, they traveled to Dobbs County to consult a man named Quash belonging to the Croom family. In 1779 they consulted two other practitioners of conjure in the Smithfield area: Old Bristow, belonging to Col. Samuel Smith, and Frank, belonging to the firm of Mallette, Tolar, and Estes. All three conjure doctors supplied them with mixtures to be added to the food cooked for their masters' families. In 1768 and again in 1779, the conjure was discovered when the white families fell deathly ill from their food, and the slaves involved were sentenced to have their ears cut off at the pillory and to receive public whippings. In 1780, when Lewis Bryan was poisoned to death by his cook, Jennie, she was tried and convicted of murder and sentenced to be burned at the stake.

Though sickness and death resulted from the use of conjure doctors' mixtures in these cases, it is clear that the object was not sinister. In this respect the intent of conjure reflects a departure from the original dark aims of obeah, a system of magic and sorcery originating in the West Indies and popular among slaves in the American South. The effort to invoke the destructive powers of obeah remained a part of the conjure doctor's stock in trade. However, generations of exposure to European tradition introduced elements common to European witchcraft and herbal lore, thus producing the syncretic, or combined, form of conjure that has, as a subcultural belief and practice, survived in North Carolina's African American community for three centuries.

It is not known when conjure achieved its full syncretic form, but it appears to have done so by the first half of the nineteenth century. Writer Charles Waddell Chesnutt, in his famed work *The Conjure Woman* (1899), drew on a tradition of an antebellum syncretism centered in a free black settlement south of Fayetteville. His conjurers appear to be based on actual, though unidentified, free black persons.

Few names of North Carolina practitioners of conjure are known. Joe Sorrell of Bertie County, celebrated during the late antebellum period for his powers, achieved notoriety after the discovery that many harmful spells he was paid to lift were actually cast by him. Murphy Harshaw of Cherokee County, feared by other blacks in his community for his reputation as a conjurer, was brutally murdered by them in 1875. William H. Moore, state representative from New Hanover County in 1874–75 and state senator in 1876–77, was widely known as a practitioner of conjure in both its harmful and helpful aspects. William Anderson, who maintained his practice on the Morgan Farm in Nash County until his death around World War II, and "Doctor" Jim Jordan of Maneys Neck in Hertford County, who practiced until his death in 1962, enjoyed a reputation as helpers and healers and drew clients from several states along the eastern seaboard.

References: Paul Green, "Witchcraft in Chapel Hill," *North Carolina Folklore Journal* 4 (July 1956); F. Roy Johnston, *The Fabled Doctor Jim Jordan* (1963); Patricia S. McLean, "Conjure Doctors in Eastern North Carolina," *North Carolina Folklore Journal* 20 (February 1972).

George Stevenson

SEE ALSO Root Doctors.

Connemara, located in Flat Rock, was the last home of famed poet and historian Carl Sandburg. Christopher Gustavus Memminger of Charleston, S.C., former Confederate secretary of the treasury, built the property as a summer house in 1838. Memminger called the property Rock Hill, but a later owner, Capt. Ellison Smythe, renamed it Connemara. Sandburg bought the property in 1945, seeking peace and solitude for his writing as well as a place for his wife Lilian to raise champion dairy goats. He wrote almost one-third of his works during his 22 years at Connemara. On 17 Oct. 1968, Congress established Connemara as the Carl Sandburg Home National Historic Site to be administered by the National Park

Connemara, late 1930s. Photograph by Bayard Wootten. NCC.

Service. The historic site consists of the antebellum house, a dairy goat barn complex and a representative goat herd, sheds, rolling pastures, mountainside woods, walking/hiking trails, two small lakes, ponds, flower and vegetable gardens, and an orchard.

Jo Ann Williford

Conscientious Objection, the refusal to bear arms based on moral or religious principles, has existed in North Carolina since its formation as a colony. From the colonial period into the twentieth century, authorities recognized only members of certain pacifist sects—Quakers, Mennonites, Dunkards, and Moravians—as conscientious objectors (COs). In recent decades the federal government has extended the right to conscientious objection to anyone with a demonstrable moral aversion to killing.

As the largest and most established pacifist sect, the religious Society of Friends (Quakers) produced the majority of North Carolina's COs. Among the first white inhabitants of the region, Quakers brought their pacifist beliefs with them. In frontier settlements, always threatened by Indian raids or the New World aspirations of European powers, pacifism was not just an academic debate. As early as 1680, nine Quakers endured six months in jail for refusing to bear arms, but such punishment proved the exception in colonial North Carolina.

As early as October 1775, North Carolina Friends attempted to stake out a position of neutrality in the coming conflict with England. The Yearly Meeting reminded its members that "the Setting up and Putting down [of] Kings and Government is God's Peculiar Prerogative." Quaker neutrality bred suspicion of loyalty to the Crown, but, in fact, the society was as split on the issue as most other colonists. Most North Carolina Friends managed to avoid Revolutionary War service, although scattered reports of Quaker troops exist.

The Moravians of North Carolina were exempt from military duty under British law before their first settlement in the colony in 1753, and they adopted a more ambiguous position toward the Revolution. Despite the sect's official pacifist stance, some members voluntarily attended militia musters and sold goods to the contending armies. Moravians steadily abandoned pacifism in the late eighteenth and early nineteenth centuries. With an increasing number of members openly serving in the military, the sect lost its exemption from duty on 4 July 1831 but apparently did not protest the government action.

On the eve of the Civil War in 1861, the state legislature continued the exemption for religious COs established 80 years earlier, but the following year it added a $100 commutation fee. Knowing that many Quakers would refuse to pay a tax on religious liberty, state senator (later governor) Jonathan Worth, himself a former Quaker, formulated a plan to allow objectors to labor at his saltworks in Wilmington in lieu of paying the fee. This marked the first attempt in American history to provide alternative service under civil direction for COs.

The federal Selective Service and Training Act of 1940 included provisions for both noncombatant service in the military (classification I-A-O) and "work of national importance" under civilian direction (IV-E). Given the mechanics of the law, draft boards sought other categories for deferment (such as occupational necessity or family hardship) before granting CO status, so the true number of men who opposed service on conscientious grounds is unknown. In North Carolina, 719 registrants (or 0.7 percent of the total) were classified as COs, split almost evenly between the two categories.

In 1962 the U.S. Defense Department began allowing COs to serve in noncombatant roles or, in certain cases, to be discharged. During the Vietnam War, draft laws recognized conscientious objection based on ethical, in addition to purely religious, principles. The draft law called for a series of individualized work projects for COs. In North Carolina, the projects involved work in government agencies and private charities. The suspension of conscription in 1973 ended involuntary service for pacifists.

References: Peter Brock, *Pacifism in the United States: From the Colonial Era to the First World War* (1968); Spencer B. King, *Selective Service in North Carolina in World War II* (1949); Mulford Q. Sibley and Philip E. Jacob, *Conscription of Conscience: The American State and the Conscientious Objector, 1940–1947* (1952); Edward N. Wright, *Conscientious Objectors in the Civil War* (1931).

Daniel J. Salemson

Conscription of male citizens to supply North Carolina's military forces began early in the colonial era. Enacted first as a frontier necessity, the principle of universal service became enshrined in American tradition. Prior to the Civil War a weak central government relied on the states for soldiers. Despite national conscription laws in both North and South during the Civil War, the federal government did not assume total control over the nation's military until the twentieth century. Conscription played a large role in America's transformation into a global superpower, but the bitter legacy of the Vietnam War effectively ended the draft.

The earliest written authority for conscription appeared in the Carolina charter, issued to the Lords Proprietors by Charles II in 1663. The charter empowered the Proprietors to "levy, muster, and train up all sorts of men . . . and to make war." The near catastrophe of the Tuscarora War (1711–13) resulted in the Militia Act of 1715 establishing the principle of universal service for all "freemen" between the ages of 16 and 60. The act remained largely unchanged during the colonial period, although additional measures were occasionally required. Between 1712 and 1776, when North Carolina enjoyed a period of extended peace, broken only by the French and Indian War and the Regulator uprising, militia service was sometimes neglected.

After the Declaration of Independence in 1776, the new state of North Carolina reorganized the militia system enacted under British rule. Throughout the Revolution the state militia remained separate from the standing army of the Continental Line. A growing list of exemptions spared many citizens from service, and those not exempted could hire a substitute or pay a commutation fee. Following the war and a period of relative tranquility, North Carolina sent 14,000 troops, about half of them conscripted, to fight in the War of 1812. Although the militia was not directly involved in the regulation of slaves, it did mobilize during slave uprisings, such as the Nat Turner Rebellion (1831).

The secession of the Lower South in 1860–61 placed North Carolina in a precarious situation; despite strong Unionist sentiment, the state felt close ties to other slaveholding states. Anticipating the need for defense in the spring of 1861, the General Assembly strengthened the militia law to include all white males between the ages of 18 and 45, except members of the clergy. It further provided for the creation of volunteer companies. Volunteers, expecting quick victory and martial glory, fought the first battles of the Civil War.

By the spring of 1862 the Confederate army faced a probable shortage of troops, and on 16 April the Confederate Congress enacted the first national draft law in American history; the North did not implement a full-scale draft until 1863. The sweeping legislation extended the service of all volunteers for three more years and enrolled all white males between 18 and 35 into the Confederate army. Measures in August and October 1862 increased the ages of eligible men to 45 but added further exemptions.

Conscription only delayed defeat, as dissatisfaction with the Confederacy grew and the Rebel grasp slipped from the southern states. North Carolina, bearing an increasing brunt of the demand for men and matériel, supplied the Confederacy with the highest number of troops and lost the largest number to battlefield death and disease; it also led the new nation with nearly 25,000 deserters, feeding the political war in Unionist counties. Confederate conscription ultimately failed for a number of reasons, including the military's poor control of the system, the attempt to bypass the authority of the states, and the uneven application of the law.

A period of prosperity and peace, briefly interrupted by the Spanish-American War in 1898, followed, and conscription gradually became a national prerogative. In 1873 Congress reiterated the principle of universal service, declaring that every male citizen between 18 and 45 (with several exceptions) was eligible for militia duty in his home state. In 1903 Congress renamed the militia the National Guard and created a separate state Reserve system.

On 18 May 1917, five weeks after declaring war on Germany, President Woodrow Wilson signed into law the Selective Draft Act. The act established the most comprehensive national conscription system to date, with a national organization and more than 4,650 civilian local draft, appeal, and advisory boards. In North Carolina, as in other states, the governor administered the draft through the office of the state adjutant general. Nearly 87,000 North Carolinians served in the military during World War I.

The onset of World War II in Europe and Asia shook America from its isolationism and consequent military weakness. In 1940, at the urging of President Franklin D. Roosevelt, Congress instituted the first peacetime draft in U.S. history. North Carolina members of Congress voted unanimously for the Burke-Wadsworth Bill, signed into law on 16 September as the Selective Service and Training Act of 1940. (North Carolina led the nation in the rate of volunteerism during the six-month period prior to enactment of the law.)

During World War II more than 1.1 million men appeared before the state draft boards. Almost 370,000 North Carolinians served in the military, about two-thirds through conscription; another 1,000-plus North Carolina women served voluntarily. High rejection rates—up to 50 percent in some areas—revealed poor health and educational conditions in the state.

Conscription ended in 1947, only to be reinstated by Congress two years later with the onset of the Cold War. North Carolina sent 177,461 men into the military during the Korean War, although the percentage conscripted is unknown. Throughout the 1950s and early 1960s, volunteerism remained high and inductions low, but the demand for manpower exceeded the number of volunteers as U.S. involvement in Southeast Asia increased. The Vietnam War proved increasingly unpopular among a large portion of the populace, especially with younger people who faced conscription. About 216,000 North Carolina citizens served in the military during the Vietnam era, but a relatively small fraction saw actual combat.

Conscription was discontinued in 1973 with the withdrawal of U.S. troops from Vietnam, and the state office of Selective Service closed in 1976. Thereafter America relied on an all-volunteer military, though a debate raged in the early 2000s over whether to reinstate the draft.

References: Spencer B. King Jr., *Selective Service in North Carolina in World War II* (1949); Memory F. Mitchell, *Legal Aspects of Conscription and Exemption in North Carolina, 1861–1865* (1965); E. Milton Wheeler, "Development and Organization of the North Carolina Militia," NCHR 41 (1964).

Daniel J. Salemson

SEE ALSO Desertion, Civil War; World War II.

Conservation Movement.

North Carolina's cities and towns, natural areas, and public lands have benefited greatly from conservation initiatives starting as early as the eighteenth century, but efforts to control pollution and save natural areas remain controversial as the state faces serious environmental issues and intense competition for available land. Despite the progress made during the last quarter of the twentieth century, several factors—such as urban growth, a proliferation of new highways, extensive development of resorts and vacation homes in the Coastal Plain and Mountain regions, the advent of large-scale industrial livestock operations, the clearance of natural forest habitats for huge pine plantations, mounting soil erosion, and polluted water flowing into streams and estuaries—continue to threaten North Carolina's rural landscapes, natural habitats, and environmental resources.

Initial Water Conservation, Forestry Regulation, and Antipollution Policies

The conservation movement in North Carolina began with methods of maintaining the timber supply and restrictions on wasteful colonial hunting practices. Some eighteenth-century North Carolinians noted the effects of wasteful practices upon wildlife and timber; consequently, North Carolina lawmakers established a closed hunting season on deer in 1738, and in 1768 they restricted deer hunting to owners of large tracts of land. The early exploitative timber harvests in North Carolina began with the domestic need to clear land. The naval stores industry found a center in the abundant longleaf pine forests of eastern North Carolina. After the War of 1812, the state became the center of the turpentine industry. North Carolina was the largest resin gum producer in the South in 1880, producing 6.3 million gallons of turpentine and more than 650,000 barrels of tar. The wasteful turpentine harvest stunted the growth and quality of thousands of square miles of young pines.

Before the late nineteenth century, most North Carolinians had not worried about their impact upon the environment as they remade the landscape to meet their needs. However, the Industrial Revolution introduced the problem of serious pollution to the state. Government officials began to take direct action regarding water pollution, condemning such practices as the mishandling of untreated sewage, the dumping of dead animals in streams and rivers, and the release of sawdust into the water by waterpowered lumber mills. In 1889 the General Assembly began to enact laws to prevent such abuses. In that same year, the legislature prohibited the placement of hazardous waste upstream from the water supply intakes of Mecklenburg County's municipalities and Greensboro. In 1893 the State Board of Health assumed responsibility for the general oversight of inland water. Officials were charged with examining domestic water supplies and consulting with towns, corporations, and institutions.

North Carolina began to intensify efforts to protect water supplies from pollutants during the early twentieth century. In 1903 the General Assembly passed an act to protect watersheds of public water supplies. In 1904 the U.S. Geological Survey issued a report that reviewed all state antipollution laws relating to inland waters and concluded that North Carolina had recognized the importance of and applied general laws for preserving clean water for drinking and domestic use. The General Assembly rewrote public health laws in 1911 to give the State Board of Health more regulatory authority in the disposal of waste, also passing legislation to curb the dumping of mining wastes into two creeks in Burke County. In the 1910s and 1920s, North Carolina made an effort to protect fish with the creation of the Fisheries Commission Board and the Department of Conservation and Development. The State Board of Health also assigned a sanitary engineer to work with the Fisheries Commission. In 1945 the General Assembly created the Stream Sanitation and Conservation Committee to oversee pollution-control work.

In spite of its massive timber harvests, North Carolina developed scientific management of forestry for multiple uses. By the late 1880s, George Washington Vanderbilt had acquired more than 100,000 acres of mountain forest and brought in managers to supervise it. Gifford Pinchot managed Vanderbilt's Biltmore forests with the idea of multiple use, a way of balancing preservation with harvesting. After Pinchot left to head the Forestry Division in the U.S. Department of Agriculture, Carl A. Schenck took over management of the Biltmore forests. Schenck, a German forester, also adhered to the concept of multiple use, and by 1898 he was supervising a forestry school in the Biltmore forests that became highly influential. The school helped establish the concept of professional scientific forestry in the United States.

One of Schenck's coworkers, W. W. Ashe of Raleigh, introduced selective cutting of mature trees and more conservative logging procedures. Ashe also helped secure passage of the Weeks Act (also known as the Appalachian Act), introduced by Senator George Pritchard of North Carolina. The bill, passed in 1911, allowed the federal government to purchase threatened watersheds and timber stands. The Weeks Act led to the National Forest Service's purchase of 5.8 million acres of lands in the South between 1911 and 1933 and the eventual creation of the Great Smoky Mountains National Park.

The wave of conservation that began in the early twentieth century also created concerns over North Carolina's wildlife population. In much of the state, male and female deer could be shot year-round. Quail and wild turkeys had no protection in several counties; shorebirds had little protection; and game wardens were nonexistent. T. Gilbert Pearson of the Audubon Society lobbied for more wildlife protection in North Carolina and influenced a state law in 1903 that protected nongame birds and established hunting seasons and nonresident license fees. Proceeds from the license fees paid the Audubon Society to hire game wardens.

Air pollution in North Carolina began to gradually increase when textile mills switched from waterpower to coal-powered steam engines. In 1880 only 16 percent of the state's cotton mills were steam powered; by 1900 the number had increased to 64 percent. Though the General Assembly had in 1917 permitted municipalities to regulate smoke emissions, amending the law in 1949 to allow for the exception of coal-burning locomotives, years elapsed before harmful air gained greater attention from the government.

By the 1930s concern for the environment focused on farmland. Much of the agricultural lands in the United States had suffered the ravages of overproduction and dependence on soil-exhaustive practices. President Franklin D. Roosevelt's New Deal increased the role of the federal government and scientific managers in conservation concerns. The New Deal created programs and agencies designed to improve the quality of land while also providing Depression-era employment. The Soil Conservation Service, for example, supervised a voluntary plan to pay farmers to plant soil-enriching crops and to take soil-depleting crops, including tobacco, out of production. The Resettlement Administration removed submarginal land from farming through its land-use program. Families were removed from unproductive areas, and the land was adapted for forestation, recreation, and wildlife reserves. North Carolina had five land retirement projects, totaling 152,925 acres.

The Soil Conservation Service, National Forest Service, and National Park Service worked with the majority of the camps of the Civilian Conservation Corps (CCC), a New Deal program that employed young men in conservation projects. From 1933 to 1939, the CCC spent $57.2 million in North Carolina, employing 46,940 workers. Their tree planting and seeding projects covered 18.2 million square yards, and their soil conservation work included 500,000 acres of farmland.

Development of the Modern Environmental Movement

The 1960s marked the beginning of a new focus on the environment in North Carolina and throughout the United States. Residents of the state became more concerned with preserving land for ethical reasons and for the sheer aesthetics of scenic areas. In 1966 the National Park Service conducted in North Carolina and Tennessee the first public hearings on wilderness designation for the national parks. A park service plan called for the construction of a transmountain road through the Great Smoky Mountains National Park and served as a test to see if wilderness designation could include development. More than 300 residents spoke in opposition to the road, and the park service received thousands of letters during the public hearings.

In 1960 the State Board of Health issued a report that blamed air pollution for causing damage to health, property, and animals in one-third of North Carolina's counties. By 1963 state and federal health authorities were conducting studies of air. However, the state allotted no money for air pollution improvement, instead offering assistance to local governments. A few private land trusts—nonprofit, public-interest charities created for local and regional land conservation—were established in North Carolina in the 1960s by visionary conservationists, most notably the Eno River Association by Margaret Nygard and the Southern Appalachian Highlands Conservancy by Stan Murray.

Public concerns and political initiatives regarding environmental protection blossomed nationwide in the early 1970s. Until that time, most of the state's publicly protected natural lands were owned and managed as units of the national forests, national parks, or national wildlife refuges, along with a scattering of state parks and wildlife game lands. Less than 5 percent of the state's total of nearly 34 million acres was in public ownership. In North Carolina an "Environmental Bill of Rights" was adopted by public referendum as Article 18 of the State Constitution, and the legislature enacted several landmark public policies, most notably the State Environmental Policy Act and Coastal Area Management Act.

The first state regulations on air pollution went into effect on 1 July 1970. From 1972 to 1976, there were major additions and creations of new units of the state parks system, including acquisition of small nature preserves. The next few years saw the establishment of several modestly funded state programs in separate agencies for the inventory and protection of unique natural areas and endangered species: the Natural Heritage Program, the Plant Conservation Program, and the Nongame and Endangered Wildlife Program. Most environmental protection programs were administered by what is today called the Department of Environment and Natural Resources. In the 1980s the state legislature enacted a few statutory programs that promoted natural resource conservation—including the Nature Preserves Act, the nation's first state income tax credits for gifts of land for conservation purposes, and improvements in air and water pollution control programs. Generally, however, the governmental responses to environmental threats were small-scale and reactive.

The state field office of the Nature Conservancy opened in 1976, and over the next 25 years it acted on recommendations of the North Carolina Natural Heritage Program to acquire and protect more than 750,000 acres of natural habitats. Acquisitions in the 1980s by the Nature Conservancy and the Conservation Fund of huge areas of wetlands and formerly converted "superfarms" established new wildlife refuges nearly a half-million acres in size located on the peninsula along the Albemarle-Pamlico estuary. Other preserves were established by universities and local conservation groups.

New Programs, Legal Initiatives, and Continuing Environmental Threats

A phenomenal growth of land trusts, or conservancies, similar in focus to the Nature Conservancy began to occur statewide beginning in the mid-1980s. For instance, the Triangle Land Conservancy was established in 1983 to support native wildlife and biological diversity, maintain water quality, preserve cultural heritage, increase recreational opportunities, and expand parks and greenway systems for the region that includes Chatham, Durham, Johnston, Lee, Orange, and Wake Counties. Land registered with or owned by the conservancy is put to only restricted use in order to preserve important natural areas. The dramatic growth of private, not-for-profit land trusts in North Carolina reflected similar trends nationwide.

The 1980s featured several major cases in the state where grassroots activism opposed federal and state plans. In 1982 mass marches against toxic waste disposal in a landfill in Warren County resulted in 523 arrests. On the coast between 1982 and 1986, fishermen and environmentalists stopped plans in Hyde County to strip-mine peat from wetlands and development plans on Permudas Island. An alliance between Bladen, Cumberland, and Robeson Counties pressured state officials into denying a permit request for a radioactive waste incinerator. In the mountains, the U.S. Forest Service's plan for expanded clear-cutting drew fire from environmentalists, and the selection of Haywood County as a potential site for high-level radioactive waste brought widespread opposition, causing the federal government to withdraw the proposal.

In the Haywood County town of Canton, Champion International Paper Company's discharging of toxic waste into the Pigeon River became the center of an intense debate between Tennessee and North Carolina during the 1980s. People claimed that the river's poor condition contributed to economic distress in Cocke County, Tenn. Furthermore, evidence indicated that the river's waters increased cancer rates. In December 1997 Champion accepted an agreement to greatly reduce the amount of pollutants released into the river. The agreement was signed by both states, the U.S. Environmental Protection Agency, local governments in Tennessee, and environmental groups.

During the 1990s, the state confronted the issue of hog waste. As one of the nation's top pork-producing states, North Carolina was the site of large hog farms that dotted the landscape in the eastern section. The waste was sprayed on fields; run-off from these fields polluted nearby waters. Farmers also stored the manure in lagoons, prone to leak or to burst from heavy rains, that caused rank odor, created sickness, and attracted flies. The state reached an agreement with hog producers to reduce waste, but the problem remains serious.

In the 1990s there was also a wave of legislative action in response to growing public concern over the deterioration of environmental quality and increased public health dangers from pollution. Governor James B. Hunt elevated his priority for environmental protection and restoration in public programs. The General Assembly created new funding mechanisms to acquire more public lands, provide increased outdoor recreational opportunities, and clean up polluted waterways and estuaries through establishment of the Natural Heritage Trust Fund, the Parks and Recreation Trust Fund, and the Clean Water Management Trust Fund. State income tax credits were increased to encourage donations of land for conservation purposes. By the early 2000s the amount of public parklands and wildlife refuges, as well as nature preserves managed by private land trusts or conservancies, had increased markedly.

North Carolina's air pollution problem continues to gain attention. The state's major metropolitan areas experienced tremendous growth during the 1990s that resulted in more vehicular traffic. Because of emissions from tailpipes and smokestacks, the American Lung Association in 2005 ranked the Charlotte metro area twelfth among particle-polluted urban areas in the United States. However, some areas in the state have improved their status, and several North Carolina counties, such as Chatham, New Hanover, and Robeson, are among the clearest for short-term particle pollution. The North Carolina Division of Air Quality has established a code system indicating the current state of air quality. The Mountain region in particular suffers from air pollution that comes from power plants, factories, and vehicles, reducing visibility and making the air unhealthy for people to breathe. The Great Smoky Mountains National Park is consistently ranked among the most polluted national parks in the country.

Radioactive waste, produced by nuclear power plants and by medical and research facilities, has also presented a problem for North Carolina since the last decades of the twentieth century. In the summer of 1978, for example, the state experienced an environmental nightmare when 30,000 gallons of cancer-causing polychlorinated biphenyl (PCB) were dumped along 210 miles of the state's roads. In 1982 the state moved 40,000 cubic tons of contaminated soil to a landfill in predominantly black and poor Warren County, leading to charges of racial discrimination. Over 500 people were arrested in their attempt to prevent trucks from delivering the soil to the specially constructed facility. Nineteen years later the state announced a plan to remove the PCB from the soil with high-tech cookers and filters.

The Environmental Protection Agency and the Nuclear Regulatory Commission regulate all types of waste, and various federal laws also govern waste management, though states have an important role as well. High-level waste, such as the spent fuel from nuclear reactors including Duke Power's McGuire Station near Lake Norman, Progress Energy's Shearon Harris plant in Wake County, and the Brunswick reactors at the coast, must be stored at reactor sites, in water pools that provide cooling and radiation protection, or in large, sealed casks. North Carolina has endorsed the plan of developing a permanent national underground repository, possibly opening by 2013, at Yucca Mountain in Nevada.

Low-level waste (LLW), generally less hazardous than high-level waste, may also originate at reactors or may come from hospitals and research centers such as Duke, UNC, and Bowman Gray as a byproduct of medical diagnosis and disease treatment or the study of biological and physical processes by pharmaceutical companies. The Low-Level Radioactive Waste Policy Act, enacted by Congress in 1980, placed responsibility for disposal on the states. In 1983 eight states formed the Southeast Interstate Low-Level Radioactive Waste Management Compact, which chose North Carolina as a future host state for LLW disposal. In 1987 the North Carolina General Assembly created the North Carolina Low-Level Radioactive Waste Management Authority, assigned to establish a new near-surface burial facility. Chem-Nuclear Systems was selected to design, build, and operate the facility, proposed for Wake County. LLW can be given a near-surface burial in a geologically suitable area within protective layers; for a number of years North Carolina utilized another designated facility at Barnwell, S.C., until South Carolina, angered by North Carolina delays—due to financial and other concerns—in creating the chosen site, closed its facility to North Carolina reactors and withdrew from the Southeast Compact in 1995. In 1999, having never begun its facility, North Carolina also withdrew from the compact, leading to a lawsuit in the early 2000s from the remaining members.

Aided by the Conservation Trust for North Carolina, a statewide land trust and service center, the network of local and regional land trusts are active in almost all parts of the state. These groups acquire natural lands and urban green spaces and arrange voluntary conservation agreements with private owners of natural habitats and rural landscapes. Through these grassroots local responses, more of North Carolina's woodlands, greenways, farmlands, and waterways are being safeguarded by private conservation actions. Private conservation initiatives are augmenting and stimulating more conservation actions by governmental agencies.

References: Richard A. Bartlett, *Troubled Waters: Champion International and the Pigeon River Controversy* (1995); Thomas Clark, *The Greening of the South: The Recovery of Land and Forest* (rev. ed., 2004); Albert Cowdrey, *This Land, This South: An Environmental History* (1983); David H. Howells, *Quest for Clean Streams: An Historical Account of Stream Pollution Control in North Carolina* (1990); Raymond L. Murray, *Understanding Radioactive Waste* (1994); Neil R. Sampson, *For Love of the Land: A History of the National Association of Conservation Districts* (1985); Thomas Schoenbaum, *The New River Controversy* (1979).

Charles E. Roe
Karl Rohr

Additional research provided by Dennis F. Daniels, Joan E. Freeman, Raymond L. Murray, and Nancy P. Shires.

SEE ALSO Biltmore Forest School; Environment and Natural Resources, Department of; Forests; Nature Conservancy; Soil Conservation; State Parks.

Conservatism is a school of thought emphasizing the need to maintain traditional order and institutions in the face of radical change. Although its usage has evolved with North Carolina's changing political identity, conservatism is typically viewed as being in opposition to another school of thought known as liberalism or progressivism. These terms have been intimately connected with one another, often serving as the principal rationale for a number of political movements and events occurring in North Carolina—both within the state's long-dominant Democratic Party and in the modern-day divide between national Democratic and Republican agendas. In reality, many North Carolina politicians have embodied both traditions simultaneously, acting on conservative or progressive views depending on the issue.

Political conservatism in the United States is rooted in the Anti-Federalist opposition to the U.S. Constitution and in the faction that evolved from that opposition, the Jeffersonian Republican Party. One such Republican was Nathaniel Macon (1758–1837) of Warren County, regarded as the state's first spokesman of the conservative tradition. Macon, a U.S. representative, senator, and strong Anti-Federalist, became a leading political figure in the early nineteenth century. He had all of the philosophical predispositions that were to become characteristic of two centuries of North Carolina conservatism: he was an advocate of state rights, a believer in strict construction of the U.S. Constitution, a proponent of laissez faire and maximum individual liberty, and a supporter of limited government and low taxes. As a southern planter, he was also a

defender of slavery. Because of his opposition to most appropriations and innovations of the time, Macon was dubbed a "negative radical."

The conservative pattern was well established in North Carolina politics by the mid-nineteenth century, with Zebulon B. Vance, a Civil War governor, emerging as a major advocate of state rights. He was a leader in the postwar effort to organize the state Conservatives to challenge the Radicals (i.e., Republicans). Later, as a Democratic U.S. senator, he stressed the importance of government economy and opposed the expansion of federal power in almost every sphere. Although Vance grudgingly accepted the role of African Americans in state politics, he supported strict segregation of the races. This was typical of nearly all white North Carolina leaders at the time; even Charles B. Aycock, known for his progressive-minded promotion of public school development and "universal education" during his 1901–5 term as governor, was an unabashed advocate of white supremacy.

Vance was succeeded as leader of the conservative forces within the Democratic Party by the even more conservative Senator Furnifold M. Simmons, who played a key role in crushing the "Fusion" of Republicans and Populists in 1898 and in disfranchising blacks in 1900. Simmons was the primary political mover in the state in the first 30 years of the twentieth century; however, his refusal to support Al Smith for president in 1928, largely because of Smith's opposition to Prohibition, led to his political downfall in 1930.

While the hardships of the Great Depression and the perceived benefits of the New Deal produced an even greater Democratic monopoly in North Carolina from 1930 to 1959, they also established cracks in the southern Democrats' conservative armor. Many North Carolinians slowly awakened to the benefits of strong, centralized government—such as the development of the public university system and the construction of roads—although traditional pro-business attitudes and the concurrent opposition to organized labor remained. One recent historian has maintained that much of the state's leadership during this period "used progressive rhetoric to mask a staunch conservatism."

By the 1960s, the traditional conservative and progressive factions within the Democratic Party had grown increasingly combative. This was largely due to domination of the national party by the northeastern states and its liberal stance on labor unions, women's rights, sexual morality, abortion rights, the welfare state, national defense, and—most important—civil rights and the desegregation of schools. Although early in the decade both Democratic and Republican politicians in North Carolina ran on segregationist platforms to secure statewide and national positions, far-reaching federal civil rights measures soon prompted Democrats to abandon either their conservatism or their party. Many—including longtime North Carolina senator Jesse Helms—chose the latter option;

much of what had been the traditional political turf of conservative Democrats relocated to the Republican Party, which became a bastion of conservatism on several key issues. As a result, Republican strength grew in the state. In 1972 James E. Holshouser Jr. became the first Republican elected governor of North Carolina in the twentieth century. In the same year Helms won his first election to the U.S. Senate, becoming the first North Carolina conservative who was in every sense a national figure, with a following and an organization that stretched far beyond the state.

Helms's career was emblematic of the break between the conservative and progressive factions within the state Democratic Party, and his conversion to Republicanism was a bellwether of the mass exodus of the state's conservative voters from the liberal Democratic camp during the second half of the twentieth century. Although conservatism continues to exist in both major parties—many North Carolina Democrats are pro-business, advocate a strong military, and consider themselves "fiscal conservatives" while maintaining more liberal stances on other issues—it is the modern-day Republicans who are viewed as the primary inheritors of the state's conservative traditions.

References: Douglas C. Abrams, *Conservative Constraints: North Carolina and the New Deal* (1992); William E. Dodd, *Life of Nathaniel Macon* (1909, rpr. 1970); Clement Dowd, *Life of Zebulon B. Vance* (1897); Ernest B. Furgurson, *Hard Right: The Rise of Jesse Helms* (1986); J. Fred Rippy, ed., *F. M. Simmons: Statesman of the New South* (1936); Roy Thompson, *Before Liberty: Their New World Made the North Carolinians Different* (1976).

Ronnie W. Faulkner
Robert Blair Vocci

SEE ALSO Conservative Party; Democratic Party; Progressivism; Republican Party.

Conservative Party was the name commonly applied to a loose political organization that first developed in North Carolina during the Civil War, when the old Whig and Democratic Parties ceased to function as separate political entities. A Whig-Unionist coalition evolved in opposition to a Democratic-Secessionist group that came to be called the Confederate Party. After the war there was a further realignment of old-line Whigs with Democrats, called Conservatives to distinguish them from the Radical or Republican Party.

North Carolina was a late adherent to the cause of secession, and its Unionist Whigs remained strong. In 1862 the Confederate Party candidate for governor, William J. Johnston of Charlotte, was easily defeated by the Conservative nominee, former Whig congressman Zebulon B. Vance of Buncombe County. The vote of 55,282 to 20,813 was a notable repudiation of the secession Democrats. During the campaign, William W. Holden, Democratic editor of the *North Carolina Standard*, was a Vance partisan. Despite Holden's endorsement, the Conservative Party was dominated by former Whigs, including former senator William A. Graham, Senator George E. Badger, state treasurer and future governor Jonathan Worth, and others. Two years later Vance beat back a challenge by Holden, who ran as the "peace candidate," by a vote of 58,070 to 14,491. Vance's party, while supporting the war effort, basically advocated state rights and vigorously opposed encroachments on civil liberties by the Confederate government in Richmond.

In May 1865 the first incarnation of Conservatives in North Carolina effectively ended when Vance was arrested by Federal troops. Under the presidential plan of Reconstruction, President Andrew Johnson then appointed Holden provisional governor on 29 May. Holden was soon turned out of office by a Conservative coalition supporting Worth. A Conservative-dominated constitutional convention held in October 1865 and May–June 1866 nullified the ordinance of secession, abolished slavery, and repudiated the Confederate debt but declined to give blacks the vote. The proposed constitution failed to win voter approval. In 1866 the General Assembly adopted a "black code" expanding the civil rights of blacks but refusing to give them political rights. In 1867 the U.S. Congress took over Reconstruction with the passage of a series of Reconstruction Acts, and the state Republican Party was organized around support for Congressional Reconstruction. The confused and discouraged Conservatives, some disfranchised by Congress, were united only by their opposition to Radical Republicanism.

At a new convention election in November 1867, the Republicans prevailed with 107 delegates, as opposed to only 13 for the poorly organized Conservatives. The constitution drawn up by the convention in February 1868 was a liberal document modeled after northern state constitutions. At the same time, the Conservative Party held its own convention; chaired by William A. Graham, it denounced Radical Reconstruction. In April 1868 the new constitution was ratified by a vote of 93,084 to 74,015, and William W. Holden was elected the first Republican governor. The legislature was solidly Republican.

Over the next two years the Conservative Party, which to that point had been more of a coalition than a party, organized to defeat the Republicans. The party campaigned on three major issues: white supremacy, economy in government, and opposition to the Constitution of 1868. In the legislative elections of 1870, the Conservatives were swept into power. They impeached Holden, who had been overly vigorous in his pursuit of the Ku Klux Klan. They scaled back state expenditures, including education, and set up the Shipp Commission to investigate Republican frauds. In 1876, with the likely victory of their nominee for governor, Zebulon B. Vance, and the possible election of Democratic presidential candidate Samuel J. Tilden, they dropped the term "Conservative" to officially become the Democratic Party of North Carolina.

Between 1870 and 1879 the Conservatives achieved most of their main goals. They reduced state expenditures by scaling back the state debt, closing the University of North Carolina (1871–75), and reducing the budget in general. Through a constitutional convention in 1875, they revised the existing state constitution to eliminate Republican and black county officials and strengthen the electoral stranglehold of the Democratic Party. Because of its pro-business attitude, the party was backed by emerging southern business interests. The impact of the Conservative Party on North Carolina politics was significant and long lasting.

References: John L. Cheney, ed., *North Carolina Government, 1585–1979: A Narrative and Statistical History* (1981); Paul D. Escott, *Many Excellent People: Power and Privilege in North Carolina, 1850–1900* (1985); J. G. de Roulhac Hamilton, *Reconstruction in North Carolina* (1914); Marc W. Kruman, *Parties and Politics in North Carolina, 1836–1865* (1983).

Ronnie W. Faulkner

Constable was envisioned in the Fundamental Constitutions of Carolina (1669–98) as one of the seven chief officers of the colony and having his own court. Although this role never materialized, the constable appeared as a servant of the Court of Albemarle as early as 1680 and of the precinct courts by 1696. Modeled on a British official, the constable was generally selected from the planter class for a one-year term. He was expected to keep the peace and maintain the laws and statutes of the Kingdom of Great Britain, including all acts of the local Assembly. The constable was to be armed and to arrest anyone who made "contest, riot, strife or affray in breaking of the said peace."

In return, the constable was exempted from all taxes and excused from roadwork during his year in office. Serving warrants and summons or making arrests or attachments of property earned him one to two shillings per action. However, a constable was not allowed to succeed himself for five years or to hold any other colonial or legislative office concurrently. He could be fined for not fully executing the orders of a justice, forced to forfeit at least 20 pounds for not returning tithable lists, and fined 50 shillings for failing to be sworn into office within a given period.

References: Robert J. Cain, ed., *Records of the Executive Council, 1664–1734* (1984); Mattie Erma Edwards Parker, ed., *North Carolina Charters and Constitutions, 1578–1698* (1963).

Louis P. Towles

Constitution, State. North Carolinians have lived under three state constitutions—the Constitution of 1776, which created the government for the new state and was substantially amended in 1835; the Constitution of 1868, which brought the state back into the Union after the Civil War but was later amended to discriminate against African Americans in a variety of ways; and the Constitution of 1971, which reorganized the entire state government in light of the requirements of the modern economy and society. In general, each constitution expanded the rights and privileges of the citizenry as well as sections of the government. The countless struggles, successes, and failures experienced in the years between the American colonial period and the end of the twentieth century have been reflected in the development of North Carolina's constitution. Since 1971, important amendments have included setting the voting age at 18 and allowing the governor and lieutenant governor to be elected to two consecutive terms.

The Carolina Charter and the Constitution of 1776
Before North Carolina became a state, its people were subjects of the English Crown and lived in accordance with English law. The Carolina charter of 1663, which many colonists referred to as their "constitution," assigned governance of the colony to the Lords Proprietors and clarified the relationship between the residents and their home country. The charter guaranteed them specific liberties and protections—their "rights as Englishmen" established by the Magna Carta of 1215. When some of these guarantees were violated by conflicting instructions from London, the people protested, contributing to the growing movement for independence.

In December 1776 North Carolina's Fifth Provincial Congress, under the leadership of Speaker Richard Caswell, created a state constitution to reaffirm the rights of the people and establish a government compatible with the ongoing struggle for American independence. In drafting this document, North Carolina leaders sought advice and examples provided by John Adams of Massachusetts. They also consulted the newly adopted constitutions of Virginia, Pennsylvania, Delaware, and New Jersey and received specific instructions from the North Carolina counties of Halifax, Mecklenburg, and Rowan. The final version of the constitution was adopted by the legislature without further input from the people of the state.

The 1776 constitution explicitly affirmed the principle of the separation of powers and identified the familiar three branches of government (executive, legislative, and judicial). It gave the greatest power to the General Assembly, which would make the laws as well as appoint all state executives and judges. The governor, serving a one-year term, would exercise little power—the result of grave conflicts with previous royal governors. Even his modest opportunity for personal leadership was hedged in many instances by the requirement that he receive the concurrence of a seven-member Council of State, also chosen by the legislature, for any initiative he might want to exercise. Local officials established by this constitution also included the sheriff, coroner, constable, and justice of the peace.

In 1789, for the first time ever, the General Assembly amended the constitution to add Fayetteville to the list of borough towns permitted to elect a senator. (The constitution would not be revised for another 46 years.) Another change substituted the word "Christian" for "Protestant" to remove any doubt about the eligibility for office of a popular judge. The possibility of relocating the constitutionally designated state capital after a destructive fire was considered, but the idea was dropped and a new capitol was built in Raleigh.

Popular representation in the legislature was inadequately addressed by the Constitution of 1776. Local representation was based on units of local government. Voters of each county elected one senator and two members of the House of Commons regardless of area or population. Six constitutionally designated towns were permitted to elect an additional member of the House. The system gave preference to landowners and afforded little political voice to most of the population. As a result of these shortcomings, over time the constitution came under attack. The convention of 1835, with its substantial constitutional amendments, was an attempt to strengthen the 1776 constitution and improve the political system it created. The number of members of the House and Senate were fixed at 120 and 50, respectively (these figures remained the same in the early 2000s). More populous counties received more representatives. Among other important amendments adopted by the convention, the governor's position was strengthened by providing for his popular election for a two-year term.

The Constitution of 1868

After two state conventions (1861–62 and 1865–66) dealt with North Carolina's secession from the Union and subsequent reentry after the Civil War, a new national authority obliged the state to make its laws conform to terms dictated by the occupying Federal forces. At the time, many former leaders had been disfranchised, and a number of newcomers or otherwise inexperienced men, as well as appointed or otherwise installed civil officials, were in positions of authority. At the direction of the U.S. Congress, in which North Carolina was not then represented, delegates to a constitutional convention were duly elected in April 1868 to consider certain subjects mandated by the national government.

The Constitution of 1868, ratified by North Carolinians by a vote of 93,086 to 74,016, was a relatively progressive document that borrowed from the previous state constitutions and added new provisions. It abolished slavery and provided for universal male suffrage. The power of the people to elect representatives and other officeholders—including key officials in the executive branch, judges, and county officials—was greatly expanded. Voters' rights were increased, with male citizens no longer required to own property or meet specific religious qualifications in order to vote. The position of gov-

ernor was again strengthened with increased powers and a four-year term. A constitutionally based court system was established, county and town governments and a public school system were outlined, and the legislature's methods of raising revenue by taxation were codified. Amendments in 1873 and 1875 weakened the progressive nature of the 1868 constitution. They also clarified the hierarchy of the court system and gave the General Assembly jurisdiction over the courts as well as county and town governments. In 1900 the universal suffrage established in 1868 was diminished by the requirement of a literacy test and poll tax—effectively disfranchising many blacks, Indians, and others.

The Constitution of 1971

After nearly 70 constitutional amendments between 1869 and 1968 and a growing desire for a new constitution in the 1950s and 1960s, the North Carolina State Constitution Study Commission, composed of lawyers and public leaders, was formed to evaluate the need for and outline substantial revisions. The General Assembly endorsed 6 of the 28 amendments proposed by the commission. At a general election on 3 Nov. 1970, citizens approved 5 of the 6 measures, rejecting repeal of the literacy test for voting.

The North Carolina Constitution of 1971 clarified the purpose and operations of state government. Ambiguities and sections seemingly in conflict with the U.S. Constitution were either dropped or rewritten. The document consolidated the governor's duties and powers, expanded the Council of State, and increased the office's budgetary authority. It required the General Assembly to reduce the more than 300 state administrative departments to 25 principal departments and authorized the governor to organize them subject to legislative approval. It provided that extra sessions of the legislature be convened by action of three-fifths of its members rather than by the governor alone. And it revised portions of the previous constitution dealing with state and local finance.

Other provisions permitted the levying of additional county taxes to support law enforcement, jails, elections, and other functions; enabled the General Assembly, rather than the state constitution or the courts, to decide what were necessary local services for taxing and borrowing purposes; abolished the poll tax, which for many years had not been a condition for voting; and authorized the General Assembly to permit local governments to create special taxing districts to provide more services and to fix personal exemptions for income taxes. In addition, the new constitution addressed the ongoing needs of public education, especially regarding funding, school attendance, and organization of the State Board of Education. The legislature's responsibility to support higher education, not just among the campuses of the consolidated University of North Carolina, was also affirmed.

References: John L. Cheney Jr., ed., *North Carolina Government, 1585–1979: A Narrative and Statistical History* (1981); Fletcher M. Green, *Constitutional Development in the South Atlantic States, 1776–1860: A Study in the Evolution of Democracy* (1966); John V. Orth, *The North Carolina State Constitution: A Reference Guide* (1993); Orth, *The North Carolina State Constitution with History and Commentary* (1995).

John V. Orth
Additional research provided by William S. Powell.

SEE ALSO Black and Tan Constitution; Convention of 1835; Convention of 1868; Convention of 1875; Governor.

Constitution, U.S., North Carolina Signers of. The U.S. Constitution, completed on 17 Sept. 1787, was signed on behalf of North Carolina by William Blount, a native of Bertie County; Richard Dobbs Spaight, a native of New Bern; and Hugh Williamson, a native of Pennsylvania. The North Carolina legislature of 1786–87 without enthusiasm had approved the call for a revision of the Articles of Confederation. On 6 Jan. 1787, the final day of the session, it chose Governor Richard Caswell, William R. Davie, Willie Jones, Alexander Martin, and Spaight to be its delegates to the Constitutional Convention, scheduled to meet in Philadelphia. Jones opposed the idea of a central government any stronger than that provided by the Articles of Confederation and declined the appointment. Caswell was not well and did not attend, but he named Williamson on 14 March and Blount on 24 April to fill the two vacancies.

With the exception of Martin, each of these men was strongly Federalist and favored a more powerful national government. Williamson proved to be the most active member of the North Carolina delegates, speaking frequently and serving on several committees. Williamson and Spaight were present from the time they reached Philadelphia until the convention adjourned, but Davie and Martin left early and did not sign the Constitution. Blount was present at the end but had been absent much of the time because he was also a member of the Continental Congress, then in session in New York City.

William S. Powell

Contrabands were slaves who escaped to Union lines during the Civil War. When the conflict began, the North's aim was primarily to preserve the Union, not to end slavery. Slaves who escaped to Union lines early in the war were often returned to their masters. However, Maj. Gen. Benjamin Butler, commanding Union forces at Fort Monroe, Va., refused to return three runaway slaves who reached his lines on 23 May 1861. Butler reasoned that since their former owner was in revolt against the United States, his slaves could be considered "contraband of war" and were not subject to return. Butler's opinion on this issue eventually became Union policy. According to the Confiscation Acts passed by the U.S. Congress during 1861 and 1862, all slaves used by the Confederate military for transportation or construction work would be freed if captured by Union forces. The term "contraband" remained in use throughout the war.

In North Carolina, the Union-held enclaves around Plymouth, Washington, Beaufort, Morehead City, Roanoke Island, and especially New Bern attracted large populations of contrabands. Some made their way to the Union towns singly or in small groups; larger numbers returned with Union raiding parties. Many of these black refugees found employment with the Federals as laborers, teamsters, servants, laundresses, or skilled craftsmen, as well as serving as scouts, spies, soldiers, or sailors. Many of the more than 5,000 black North Carolinians who joined the Union army or navy had been contrabands.

Faced with a huge influx of contrabands, the Union commander in North Carolina during early 1862, Maj. Gen. Ambrose E. Burnside, appointed Vincent Colyer, a New York abolitionist, artist, and former official of the YMCA, to be superintendent of the poor. Beginning on Roanoke Island, where by late spring there were about 1,000 contrabands, Colyer offered the able-bodied men among them jobs as laborers at $8.00 a month plus clothing.

By late spring 1863, recruitment of black soldiers from the contraband population in eastern North Carolina was well under way. Governor John Andrew of Massachusetts and army officers from that state stationed in New Bern were instrumental in raising such regiments in North Carolina. At this time black recruits from the state were organized into three regiments of infantry and one regiment of artillery. On a few occasions, when Union-occupied towns were under threat of Confederate attack, contraband laborers were issued weapons and ordered into auxiliary military companies. In January 1864 approximately 600 contrabands were placed under arms in New Bern. By the end of the war, the contraband population around New Bern was estimated as high as 15,000. A small number of contrabands lived on Hatteras Island, and more than 3,000 were located in and around Union-occupied Beaufort and Morehead City. Many of them made a living on the water fishing, oystering, or carrying freight and passengers around the area.

Roanoke Island was another important center of contraband life during the war. By the beginning of 1865, it was estimated that more than 3,000 blacks occupied nearly 600 houses on the island; these contrabands spent their time farming, fishing, splitting shingles, or working as federal government laborers. Many healthy men of military age served in the Union army, so the colony had a high percentage of children, women, and older men. At the war's end, the contrabands on Roanoke disbanded, as much of the land was returned to secessionist owners who had been pardoned by the Union.

References: Patricia C. Click, *Time Full of Trial: The Roanoke Island Freedmen's Colony, 1862–1867* (2001); Vincent Colyer, *A Report of the Services Rendered by the Freed People to the United States Army, in North Carolina, in the Spring of 1862, after the Battle of Newbern* (1864); Joe A. Mobley, *James City: A Black Community in North Carolina, 1863–1900* (1980); David Stick, *The Outer Banks of North Carolina, 1584–1958* (1958).

David A. Norris

SEE ALSO Maroons.

Controller, Office of.

The General Assembly established the office of controller (originally spelled "comptroller") in 1782 to oversee all "public accounts of the state" and to keep the legislature informed about budgetary facts and issues. The controller's duties included directing the mode of stating, checking, and controlling all public accounts and entering these in special books for inspection. The state's financial accounts continued to be handled by the controller until 1862, when the legislature created the office of auditor of public accounts, to be elected biennially by the General Assembly. The same act provided that the auditor of public accounts was to receive, audit, and adjust all accounts or claims against the state, certifying the amounts and balances and filing these in the controller's office. When the Constitution of 1868 was implemented, the auditor of public accounts was replaced by the state auditor, and the position of controller was abolished.

The office of state controller was reinstated in 1985 and in the early 2000s maintained records regarding the "appropriations, allotments, expenditures, and revenues" of the entire state government. The controller, along with the state auditor, was involved in every phase of the fiscal life of North Carolina, including overseeing the accounting system, keeping financial records of all state transactions, running the payroll system, and reconciling on a monthly basis the financial statements prepared by the state treasurer.

Wiley J. Williams

SEE ALSO Auditor, State.

Convention of 1788.

In the summer of 1788, North Carolina faced the momentous decision of whether to ratify the newly proposed U.S. Constitution drafted at Philadelphia the previous year. The question emerged at a state ratification convention in Hillsborough, a center of political activity since colonial times. At St. Matthews Church between 21 July and 4 August, more than 270 delegates assembled, representing 7 boroughs and 58 counties in the state and its western territories.

These delegates had won their seats the previous March through special elections mandated by the General Assembly in 1787. By a margin of two to one, the Anti-Federalist candidates outpolled their Federalist adversaries, and the guardians of state rights and individual liberties prevailed over the proponents of a strengthened, unified central government. Despite a particularly vigorous Federalist campaign, the election outcome probably surprised no one, as North Carolinians had enjoyed virtual self-government under the decentralized Articles of Confederation since 1781. Even during decades of British colonial rule and eventual independence, citizens traditionally resisted any distant authority perceived to threaten their sovereignty or limit their freedoms. The federal scheme of government in the new Constitution aroused just such suspicions.

Anti-Federalist leader Willie Jones and his followers felt obligated to protect the liberties guaranteed under the state bill of rights in the Constitution of 1776. The Federalists for their part considered it not only "incongruous, but dangerous" to enumerate individual rights. Because the number might be limitless, Federalists reasoned, attempts to specify some rights and not others would provoke needless controversy and deprive the central government of essential authority.

When the convention opened on 21 July, the outnumbered Federalist delegates had a well-prepared strategy. Although they realized that the superior debating skills of their leaders, James Iredell, William R. Davie, Archibald Maclaine, and Governor Samuel Johnston, would likely not alter the predictable outcome at Hillsborough, the Federalists brought a stenographer to record their arguments for eventual publication, hoping to produce a "salutary change" in future public opinion. For days a fiercely partisan debate ensued, one that initially put the Federalists on the defensive and threatened to dissolve the convention. The Federalists so skillfully countered their critics' objections to many issues—including direct taxes, paper money, war debts, western lands, standing armies, and the national judiciary—that the Anti-Federalists became distinctly uncomfortable. When the Federalists doggedly argued for a federal Bill of Rights, their preponderate strength finally moved the convention to recommend that a Declaration of Rights and 26 amendments be submitted to Congress. But only after other states incorporated these "great principles" into the Constitution would North Carolina embrace it.

By a vote of 184 to 84, the Anti-Federalist majority decided on 1 August neither to ratify nor reject the document; and after two more days of procedural business, the convention adjourned. The decisions reached at Hillsborough did not block the formation of the new federal government, and by then few delegates intended that they should. The North Carolinians did, however, significantly influence the eventual decision to frame and ratify a national Bill of Rights and to bring North Carolina into the Union.

References: Michael Lienesch, "North Carolina: Preserving Rights," in Michael A. Gillespie and Michael Lienesch, eds.,

Ratifying the Constitution (1989); Louise I. Trenholme, *The Ratification of the Federal Constitution in North Carolina* (1932).

John C. Cavanagh

Convention of 1789. North Carolina held a ratification convention in Fayetteville during 16–23 Nov. 1789 to debate for the second time whether to accept the U.S. Constitution and join the new federal Union. After the previous state convention at Hillsborough had decided in 1788 neither to ratify nor reject the Constitution, its staunch Federalist defenders pressured the General Assembly into resubmitting the question to the electorate. The Federalists waged such an effective campaign prior to the 1789 elections that their Anti-Federalist opponents secured less than one-third of the 272 seats at the Fayetteville convention. The Federalist triumph marked a rapid reversal of fortune for a group so badly outnumbered the previous year at Hillsborough.

Many factors contributed to this dramatic shift in public opinion. When the popular George Washington was unanimously elected president of an apparently ordered, stable government in early 1789, many Anti-Federalist fears about unbridled federal power were effectively dispelled. Influential Federalists controlled most of the state's newspapers, which they now used vigorously to support ratification and discredit their opponents. Moreover, Anti-Federalist opposition declined rapidly in May 1789, when James Madison, distinguished architect of the U.S. Constitution, handed Congress a proposed Bill of Rights in the form of constitutional amendments. These amendments neutralized the strongest objections of the opponents of ratification, who had long sought such guarantees of individual liberties as a condition for their support.

By the time the ratification convention opened on 16 November in Fayetteville, the major positions on ratification had already been thoroughly explored, and the outcome of the convention was assured. The Federalists now saw it as their task to negotiate a few compromises and "backstairs bargains," hoping to maximize support behind them. The opposing parties agreed to lay before Congress five mutually acceptable amendments, not covered under the proposed Bill of Rights, that would placate lingering demands for further limits on congressional taxing power and on the enlistment terms for soldiers, among other issues.

On 21 November, after five days of deliberations, William R. Davie finally put the ratification question before the convention. Supporters predictably overwhelmed opponents by a margin of 194 to 77. John Huske of Wilmington then led a previously planned walkout of about 68 Anti-Federalists from the chamber in a last defiant gesture. The convention adjourned on 23 November, having made North Carolina the twelfth state to embrace the United States and its Constitution.

References: John C. Cavanagh, *Decision at Fayetteville; The North Carolina Ratification Convention and General Assembly of 1789* (1989); Alan D. Watson, "North Carolina: States' Rights and Agrarianism Ascendant," in Patrick T. Conley and John P. Kaminski, eds., *The Constitution and the States: The Role of the Original Thirteen in the Framing and Adoption of the Federal Constitution* (1988).

John C. Cavanagh

Convention of 1835. The constitutional convention of 1835 was convened to modify the North Carolina Constitution of 1776. Some provisions of the 1776 document were rooted in the colonial experience, and a growing segment of the population came to consider them impediments to an emerging nineteenth-century democratic society, with its developing systems of education, economy, and internal improvements. Efforts to revise the 1776 constitution began shortly after the Revolutionary War and continued periodically until a convention was convened in 1835, when the strong east-west sectionalism over the issues was finally overcome.

The principal changes effected by the 1835 convention involved the election process, including voter qualifications and rules for legislative apportionment. One modification was a shift from annual to biennial elections and sessions of the General Assembly. The composition of the State House of Representatives continued to be based on the county unit system, which guaranteed each county at least 1 representative and permitted a maximum of 120 throughout the state. The 1776 voter qualification of taxpaying "freemen," which still excluded women, was retained to elect state representatives. However, free blacks who had been previously allowed to vote were now disfranchised. The "federal population," which included three-fifths of the former slaves, was used to calculate the apportionment of the remaining representatives beyond the one-per-county guarantee. "Borough" representation, a remnant of the English system, which granted a special representative to towns of commercial importance, was eliminated. Edenton, New Bern, Wilmington, Salisbury, Hillsborough, Halifax, and Fayetteville, previously designated as "borough towns," no longer enjoyed this privilege.

The basis of representation for the North Carolina Senate was changed from a county to a district unit formulated according to the state tax base. A maximum of 50 senators was prescribed, but property ownership was retained as a qualification to vote. None of the existing 65 counties was to be divided in forming the senatorial districts.

The governor, previously elected annually by the legislature, would now be chosen biennially by the same voters who elected the state representatives. This marked the beginning of modern political campaigning, as gubernatorial candidates sought the statewide support of the voting public for the first time. The change also removed the governor's office from a position of almost total subservience to the General Assembly.

The 1835 constitutional convention also extended the religious qualification for holding state office to include not only Protestants but also all other Christians, instituted an impeachment process for state officers, imposed some limitations on the General Assembly in passing private legislation, and developed a procedure for amending the state constitution in the future.

References: Henry Groves Connor, "The Convention of 1835," *North Carolina Booklet* 8 (October 1908); Harold J. Counihan, "The North Carolina Constitutional Convention of 1835: A Study in Jacksonian Democracy," NCHR 46 (October 1969); Fletcher M. Green, *Constitutional Development in the South Atlantic States, 1776–1860* (1930); John V. Orth, *The North Carolina State Constitution with History and Commentary* (1993).

John L. Humber

Convention of 1865.

Convention of 1865. On 29 May 1865 President Andrew Johnson unveiled two proclamations designed to bring North Carolina back into the Union after the Civil War. (Similar announcements affecting most of the other southern states soon followed.) The Proclamation of Amnesty and Pardon granted pardons and the "restoration of all rights of property, except as to slaves" to all citizens who took an oath of allegiance to support the United States, its laws, and its decrees, including Abraham Lincoln's Emancipation Proclamation. The proclamation did not cover 14 classes of former Confederates, who had to apply for special pardons. These classes included those above the rank of colonel in the Confederate army, those who had held office in the Confederate government, those who had left federal judicial posts to aid the Confederate cause, and those who had participated in the rebellion and owned over $20,000 of taxable property.

Johnson's second proclamation appointed William W. Holden provisional governor of North Carolina and outlined the procedure by which the state could establish its loyalty, reorganize its government, and eventually return to the Union. Holden was to convene a state convention, composed of those "loyal to the United States, and no others, for the purpose of altering and amending the Constitution." Only citizens who had taken the loyalty oath or had received a special pardon could vote for or serve as delegates. If necessary, the military would assist Holden in implementing this decree. Privately and publicly, Johnson made it clear that the delegates to this convention were to eliminate slavery in North Carolina, as well as acknowledge that secession had been illegal and that the states were subordinate to the central government. Finally, they were expected to repudiate any debt contracted to aid the rebellion.

Holden waited until 9 August to issue a third proclamation on matters related to timing: the election of delegates would be held on 21 September and the convention would begin on 2 October. At the meeting, delegates focused on determining the absolute minimum requirements the president considered necessary for reunion and then debated the exact ways they would implement them. The ordinance that prohibited slavery in North Carolina engendered little argument. Although a few opposed the inclusion of "forever" in the document, it passed unanimously on 7 October. The proposal to declare the 1861 secession ordinance "null and void" faced more opposition. After a three-day dispute over whether to simply repeal the edict or declare it null and void, the delegates finally passed the original proposal by a vote of 105 to 9.

The longest debate centered around the ordinance "prohibiting the payment of all debts created or incurred in aid of the late rebellion." Many argued that such a repudiation would ruin the state financially and that it was unnecessary for restoration. Not until President Johnson, in response to a Holden telegram, wired the convention that "every dollar of the debt created to aid the rebellion . . . should be repudiated finally and forever," did the delegates, on 19 October, the last day of the convention, enact the ordinance.

The convention achieved little else. It appointed a committee to receive an address from the state's Freedmen's Convention, which recommended the creation of a commission to prepare a code of laws for former slaves. The constitutional convention also resolved to seek the removal of all black troops from the state. Through its debates and resolutions, then, the 1865 convention set the stage for North Carolina's struggle over the transition from slavery to freedom.

References: Roberta Sue Alexander, *North Carolina Faces the Freedmen: Race Relations during Presidential Reconstruction, 1865–67* (1985); Eric Foner, *Reconstruction: America's Unfinished Revolution, 1863–1877* (1988); Eric L. McKitrick, *Andrew Johnson and Reconstruction* (1960).

Roberta Sue Alexander

Convention of 1868

Convention of 1868 was a direct result of the Radical Congressional Reconstruction Acts passed in 1867 overturning post–Civil War Presidential Reconstruction. Gen. Edward R. S. Canby, commander of the Second Military District of the Carolinas, in compliance with the directives of the U.S. Congress, set the vote for a convention for 19–20 Nov. 1867. The poorly organized Conservative Party did not mount an effective opposition, while the newly formed Republican Party successfully promoted the planned convention. The registration for the election included 106,721 whites and 72,932 blacks. In the first statewide vote involving African Americans, the vote stood at 93,006 for a convention and 32,961 against. Of the 120 delegates elected, 107 were Republicans, including 18 men of northern birth (known as "carpetbaggers") and 15 blacks.

The delegates gathered in Raleigh on 14 Jan. 1868. On the second day of the meeting Calvin J. Cowles, a future son-in-law of Governor William W. Holden, was elected president of the convention. The delegates were overwhelmingly sympathetic to Congressional Reconstruction, even passing a resolution commending Congress for the impeachment proceedings against President Andrew Johnson. In the Conservative press much was made of the fact that the convention cost more than $90,000, making it the most expensive constitutional convention in North Carolina history.

The constitution framed at the 1868 convention and submitted to the people on 21–23 April departed significantly from North Carolina's conservative tradition. Based in large part on the constitution of Ohio and other northern states, it was later viewed as "modern, progressive, liberal, and democratic." The new document abolished slavery, provided for universal male suffrage, eliminated property and religious qualifications for voting and office holding, organized a new superior court system, adopted the northern township–county commission form of local government, and authorized the establishment of a "general and uniform system of Public Schools." The term of the governor was extended to four years. County and executive officers were to be elected by the people, as superior and supreme court justices already were.

The 1868 state constitution was ratified by a vote of 93,086 to 74,016. Conservatives, who referred to the document as the "Canby constitution" or the "black and tan constitution," opposed many of its provisions. Objecting to black suffrage, the lack of property qualifications to vote for state senators, and the direct election of judges and many executive officers, they immediately launched a campaign to repeal or revise the document. Despite their adoption, in an 1875 convention, of many amendments that weakened the constitution's democratic aspects, as well as a number of revisions since then, North Carolina's present constitution retains much of the character and wording of the 1868 document.

References: Stephen Marc Appell, "The Fight for the Constitutional Convention: The Development of Political Parties in North Carolina during 1867" (M.A. thesis, UNC-Chapel Hill, 1969); Hugh T. Lefler, ed., *North Carolina History Told by Contemporaries* (1956); John V. Orth, *The North Carolina State Constitution with History and Commentary* (1993).

Ronnie W. Faulkner

SEE ALSO Black and Tan Constitution.

Convention of 1875 resulted from legislation passed on 19 Mar. 1875 providing for the election of convention delegates in August. Since the adoption of the Constitution of 1868, the North Carolina Democratic Party had wanted to eliminate, or at least modify, the "radical" Reconstruction constitution, which they viewed as the product of blacks, northern carpetbaggers, and Unionist scalawags. Early returns from the August ballot did not favor the Democrats, and a Republican victory seemed likely. As election results in Robeson County appeared to be decisive, William R. Cox, chairman of the Democratic Conservative Executive Committee, telegraphed the county's returning board with the message: "As you love the state, hold Robeson." The Democrat-dominated returning board certified the Conservative delegates as elected without waiting for returns from four Republican precincts, and the Democrats won a majority of delegates by a razor-thin margin.

Soon after the election, Democratic delegate William A. Graham of Orange County died. When the convention met on 6 September, the delegation stood at 58 Democrats, 58 Republicans, and 3 independents, one of whom favored the Democrats and one of whom supported the Republicans. Control of the convention rested with Edward D. Ransom of Tyrrell County, who, according to Republican leader Albion W. Tourgée, was "a fool, who in my opinion wants to be bought up." Nominated by the Democrats, Ransom was elected convention president after numerous ballots when he cast a vote for himself.

An attempt by Robeson's Republican delegates to be seated ended in failure. A loud uproar erupted from the Republicans on 30 September, when the Conservative delegates from Robeson, Duncan Sinclair and C. A. McEachin, were permitted to vote for themselves. But for this move by the Democratic Conservatives, the convention would have been under Republican control. The narrow Democratic majority meant that all of the party's delegates had to be present for every vote to prevent the Republicans from adjourning the gathering.

Because of the questionable nature of their mandate, the Democrats were restrained from completely revising the constitution. All measures were agreed upon in party caucus before presentation to the full convention. When the convention adjourned on 11 October, it had adopted 30 amendments, which were presented to the people on a single ballot on 7 Nov. 1876 and passed by a vote of 120,159 to 106,554.

The amendments accomplished a variety of objectives, including prohibiting secret political societies, creating a Department of Agriculture, reducing the state supreme court from five to three members, abandoning the uniform court system in favor of legislative control over a system of inferior courts, denying the vote to those convicted of certain crimes, implementing a one-year residency requirement for voting, requiring "non-discriminatory" segregated public schools, prohibiting interracial marriages, giving the legislature control over county and township government, and simplifying the method of amending the state constitution. The amendment giving the General Assembly the power to modify or abolish county and township government had the most far-reaching effects, as it led to the County Government Act of 1877. This essentially undemocratic law—although it allowed the popular election of county treasurers, registers of deeds, and surveyors—provided that the legislature would appoint justices of the peace and these justices would in turn select county commissioners. The statute was heralded as a bulwark of Anglo-Saxon civilization, for it kept both blacks and white Republicans from holding office.

The convention of 1875 gave the Democrats majority control of political offices across the state that was not justified by their actual electoral numbers. For decades they were able to effectively squelch opposition. The County Government Act was not overturned until the advent of the Populist-Republican Fusion legislature of 1895. Even that reform was short-lived, for when the Democrats returned to power in 1898 they crushed the Republican Party by amending the constitution to disfranchise African Americans.

References: William Durham Harris, "The Movement for Constitutional Change in North Carolina, 1868–1876" (M.A. thesis, UNC-Chapel Hill, 1932); John V. Orth, *The North Carolina State Constitution: A Reference Guide* (1993); Orth, *The North Carolina State Constitution with History and Commentary* (1995).

Ronnie W. Faulkner

Convention of Westerners was held on 10 Nov. 1823 in Raleigh in response to a call by western legislators in the final days of the previous General Assembly. These lawmakers wished to reform the state constitution and to provide for public schools and internal improvements. Delegates from 24 western counties attended the convention and formulated constitutional amendments to be laid before the legislature when it convened the following week. Disputes arising on the convention floor over minor questions on several amendments divided the delegates and prevented unanimous action. This harmless division among the reformers gave eastern legislators an excuse to kill the convention bill. A constitutional convention was not held until 1835.

William S. Powell

Conversion Narratives. From colonial times, many North Carolinians have felt compelled to record the events and emotions surrounding their religious journeys. Most conversion narratives, autobiographical accounts of often powerful spiritual transformations, follow a pattern that traces an individual's experiences through three distinct phases: a previous, often wayward, life; a highly emotional and dramatic conversion; and a reoriented life in the "new light" of faith. Authors may have various reasons for writing down their experiences—to evangelize, to pass on their faith to their children, or to help others understand their own problems and find spiritual solutions—but all desire somehow to publicize a personal crisis that they consider to be the most important point of their lives.

While spiritual conversion is not the possession of any one religion, most North Carolina conversion narratives describe transformations that have taken place within the context of the Christian faith. Herbert Northup, a student at the Greensboro Bible Training School, writes in an undated narrative that he is publishing his experiences "in order that it may help somebody else." Northup describes his life before his conversion as one of tough jobs, constant chewing tobacco use, drunkenness, and jail time. In 1905, after living through the deaths of several friends and acquaintances and feeling as if "God was after me all the time," he went to a mission in Newport, R.I., and "was saved." From that day forward, Northup devoted his life to helping others with similar problems, moving to North Carolina to study the Bible and continue his ministry.

In *A Narrative of a Most Extraordinary Work of Religion* (1802), James Hall of Cabarrus County describes how an undesired visit to a Christian revival led to his surprising religious awakening. After admitting his cynicism about the event, Hall, "struck in the forehead, as if by the end of a person's finger," felt the Holy Spirit descend on him and set his emotions ablaze. "Oh God," he writes, "I am afraid of high professions, but am constrained to acknowledge, from my present feelings, that if the world in all its glory was in my offer I would not receive it as an inducement to exchange my present state for that in which I was yesterday."

Blum H. Vestal, a North Carolinian writing in the early twentieth century, described his life before his conversion as one of poverty and ignorance. After many failed attempts at reform, he visited a church where he listened to young children reading aloud. He began to "hunger to read" himself: "I went to the woods and sat down on a log and began to cry and talk to the Lord the best I knew how. . . . I told him I wanted to read like those little children, and the Lord promised me there that I would live to read and also preach the Word and I have never doubted the call from that moment."

Vestal stayed with the congregation he had visited, attending "church and Sabbath-school for something near twelve months." After hearing a sermon on the "New Birth" and what it was to be "born again," he "went forward, knelt at the altar, made a full confession, accepted Christ in the presence of the people and told them that I was going to live for the Lord." His narrative, titled *From the Saloon to the Pulpit: The Life of Blum H. Vestal* (1911), goes on to describe the many good works Vestal subsequently performed and how his understanding of God and of himself increased during the years following his conversion.

Reference: James Craig Holte, *The Conversion Experience in America* (1992).

Jay Mazzocchi

Convict Labor and convict leasing, the practice of using convicts for work in the public or private sector, was common throughout the South after the Civil War. Its history in North Carolina was complicated by the state's confusing prison system, a patchwork of penitentiaries and work camps whose supervision was constantly in dispute between county and state officials. Unlike some states, North Carolina built a state penitentiary in 1870, and the great majority of its prison labor—an average of 65 percent between 1870 and 1890—was absorbed by construction of the Western North Carolina Railroad, a state-owned enterprise. Indeed, North Carolina's nineteenth-century rail network was largely an achievement of convict labor. These prisoners endured terrible conditions, usually living in filthy railroad cars that had been converted into rolling jailhouses by the addition of bunks, a kitchen stove, and iron rings to accommodate the convicts' chains.

By the late 1800s, when the construction phase of railroad development had concluded, two other industries began to compete for convict labor: road building and farming. In 1887 the legislature authorized counties to establish chain gangs at their own discretion. Equally significant was the state's purchase or lease of extensive farmland in the 1890s. By 1898, 90 percent of the state's prisoners (that is, virtually all able-bodied men) farmed over 8,000 acres. The largest farm, the 4,100-acre Caledonia, bought in 1893 for $67,000, yielded the state $1,000 a week in profits by the mid-1920s.

The state of North Carolina and its counties competed fiercely for custody of sentenced felons, and soon the state opened its own chain gang camps. Because of this unique state-county tug-of-war that masqueraded as prison management, the state did not secure responsibility for all convict operations until 1933. After that, the state simply took over existing county highway camps, and the prison system itself was placed under the jurisdiction of the State Highway Commission.

References: Darnell F. Hawkins, "State versus County: Prison Policy and Conflicts of Interest in North Carolina," *Criminal Justice History* 5 (1984); Matthew J. Mancini, *One Dies, Get Another: Convict Leasing in the American South, 1866–1928* (1996); Jesse F. Steiner and Roy M. Brown, *The North Carolina Chain Gang: A Study of County Convict Road Work* (1969).

Matthew J. Mancini

SEE ALSO Chain Gang.

Cooleemee Plantation

is located in Davie County on the Yadkin River. William Giles, a speculator, purchased the property and sold it to Zachariah Haden, who subsequently deeded it to Richmond Pearson, an in-law. In 1804 Pearson's son, Gen. Jesse Pearson, was given the land as a wedding present. He gave it the name Cooleemee, apparently the name of an Indian village in Alabama, where Pearson served in the Creek War. The name is believed to mean, "place where the white oaks grow."

In 1817 Maj. Peter Hairston bought the 2,300-acre plantation from Pearson. The major's grandson, Peter Wilson Hairston, inherited the plantation in 1832. By 1860 he had increased Cooleemee to 4,200 acres, with 300 slaves raising tobacco, corn, cotton, and hogs. Hairston sold only one of his slaves, and only one ever fled the plantation. Notable among Cooleemee's slaves was coachman John Goolsby, self-described descendant of an African king. When Peter W. Hairston left to serve the Confederacy, Goolsby accompanied him.

The plantation home was built from 1853 to 1855 and is in the shape of a Greek cross. More than 300,000 bricks made on the plantation were used in its construction. Inside is a winding stairway, largely self-supporting. In 1850, *Godey's Ladies Book* carried the house plan and a picture of the proposed building. In 1854 J. E. B. Stuart visited Cooleemee to call on his sister Columbia, wife of Peter W. Hairston and mistress of the plantation. Columbia died in 1857 while giving birth to a daughter. Peter Hairston married again in 1859, to Fanny Caldwell of Salisbury. When the Civil War broke out, Hairston volunteered as an aide for Stuart, who had risen to the rank of general. Later he served as an aide for Gen. Jubal Early in the Shenandoah Valley near the war's end.

After the war, the Hairstons moved to Baltimore, Md. In 1886 Peter died and the family returned to Cooleemee. The plantation remained in the Hairston family throughout the twentieth century. Descendants of the slaves at Cooleemee founded the Hairston Clan, holding their first reunion in 1974. In August 1979, when the U.S. Department of the Interior designated Cooleemee as a National Historic Landmark, Squire Hairston of the Hairston Clan delivered the principle address. A few other notables in the group included Jester Hairston, actor, composer, and musician; Guy E. Hairston Jr., U.S. Air Force general; William Hairston, playwright; Nelson G. Hairston, animal ecologist and Kenan Professor at the University of North Carolina at Chapel Hill; and Happy Hairston, former member of the Harlem Globetrotters basketball team.

References: Peter W. Hairston, *Cooleemee Plantation and Its People* (1986); James W. Wall, *History of Davie County* (1969).

Steve Suther

Coolmore

is a striking antebellum mansion four miles west of Tarboro on U.S. 64. A lantern cupola atop its roof distinguishes this Italianate villa, built between 1859 and 1861 for planter-physician Joseph J. W. Powell. Outbuildings, including a dairy, smokehouse, slave quarters, gas house, and stable, feature cupolas as well. Architect Edmund G. Lind of Baltimore built Coolmore, and Russian émigré painter Ernst Dreyer decorated the interior plaster walls. Visitors marvel over these frescoes, the ornate plasterwork and marbling, and a hand-carved spiral stair leading to the cupola. Family and local lore maintains that the house was spared destruction

Coolmore. Photograph by Tim Buchman. Courtesy of Preservation North Carolina.

Stair in the rotunda of Coolmore. Photograph by Tim Buchman. Courtesy of Preservation North Carolina.

by Union troops in April 1865 because one of the soldiers, an artisan from Maryland who had helped build it, saluted Coolmore.

Reference: Catherine W. Bishir and Michael T. Southern, *A Guide to the Historic Architecture of Eastern North Carolina* (1996).

Bland Simpson

Cool Pool. On 9 July 1933 the Tarboro Town Council voted to ask Frick and Company of Waynesboro, Pa., to design and install a refrigerating unit for its new municipal swimming pool. After operating for only three months, the olympic-design pool, containing 300,000 gallons of water and with a constant flow of 400 gallons per minute, had become uncomfortably warm from the summer's record heat and the activity of swimmers. By mid-August Frick had installed the refrigerating device at a cost of $2,592, making the Tarboro pool what is believed to have been the first and perhaps only refrigerated outdoor pool in the country.

Tarboro's "cool pool" drew crowds of swimmers and swimming meets throughout the 1930s. In 1943 the national Amateur Athletic Union was held there, with Governor J. Melville Broughton as the honored guest. Native Tarboro swimmers won blue ribbons all over the country during this period, as the town's unique pool helped put it firmly in the national swimming picture.

Jaquelin Drane Nash

Copyhold was a form of land tenancy that was never effective in North Carolina, although the term is sometimes encountered in records of landholdings. References to it grew out of the feudal provisions for manors in the Fundamental Constitutions (1669). In England, it applied to tenants bound to lords to whom the land belonged; they were not freemen, being obligated to the landholder, from whom they received a copy of the manor roll specifying their obligation.

William S. Powell

Coree Indians, when first encountered by Europeans arriving in what is now North Carolina, were living south of the Neuse River along the Atlantic Coast. Like other Indians of the Coastal Plain, the Coree (or Core) lived in villages, reportedly three in number, and depended for their livelihood on both agriculture and the ocean. Sharply reduced in numbers by epidemic disease and warfare, they totaled perhaps 100 persons by 1701. Scholars debate whether the Coree spoke an Algonquian or an Iroquoian language. They seem to have been closely associated with the nearby Tuscarora, who spoke an Iroquoian language. At any rate, the Coree allied with the Tuscarora during the Tuscarora War of 1711–13 and were nearly obliterated. Presumably some Coree survivors joined the Tuscarora after the war and may have moved north to the Iroquois country in New York with them. Most, however, joined together with the remnants of other coastal tribes and settled on a reservation at Lake Mattamuskeet. Core Banks and Core Sound on the North Carolina coast were both named for the Coree Indians.

References: Maurice A. Mook, "Algonkian Ethnohistory of the Carolina Sound," *Journal of the Washington Academy of Sciences*

34 (15 June, 15 July 1944); Ruth Y. Wetmore, *First on the Land: The North Carolina Indians* (1975).

Michael D. Green

Corporation Commission.

The North Carolina Corporation Commission was the principal state agency for the regulation of railroads, banks, and electric utilities from 1899 to 1933. Created by the General Assembly of 1899, it replaced the Railroad Commission (1891–99). The move represented one of many efforts by state Democrats to secure their hold on political and economic power in the early twentieth century. It allowed them to wrest authority over banking, as well as railroads, from the non-Democrats in the state treasurer's and auditor's offices.

The most significant additions to Corporation Commission authority after 1900 resulted from the introduction of urban electric, gas, and sewer services, as well as the development of motor vehicle transportation. In 1913 the legislature required the commission to fix rates for electric, gas, and sewer services, except for providers owned by municipal governments. In 1925 the commission was also directed to set rates and service conditions for new motor vehicle carrier operations, both passenger and freight. In the same year, it had to supervise the state's Capital Issues Act, which regulated the sale of many investment securities, including stocks and bonds. Despite its new responsibilities, between 1901 and 1930 railroad rate issues dominated the commission's work.

Both the growth in regulated businesses and the shocks of the Great Depression, including public dissatisfaction with the regulation of utilities and a desire to cut costs, led to the demise of the Corporation Commission. In 1931 legislators stripped the commission of its authority over banks—in large part as a result of criticism of the commission's role in the increasing number of bank failures. In 1933 the General Assembly abolished the Corporation Commission altogether and replaced it with the office of utilities commissioner, a post held by one elected official. Two associate commissioners, appointed by the governor, served at the commissioner's request. The 1933 legislature also rewrote many of the former commission's powers over utilities, particularly regarding the issuance of securities.

References: J. C. D. Blaine, *Rate-Making and the North Carolina Utilities Commission: A Study in Public Policy* (1962); Annie Sabra Ramsey, "Utility Regulation in North Carolina, 1891–1941: Fifty Years of History and Progress," *NCHR* 22 (April 1945).

James L. Hunt

Cotton Balls

were a prominent feature of social life in eastern and central North Carolina beginning in the late seventeenth and early eighteenth centuries. These dances celebrated special events, such as the harvesting of a cotton crop, or otherwise acknowledged the importance of the cotton economy in Piedmont cities such as Charlotte and Greensboro. Although there were instances of people declining to dance with someone regarded as beneath their social class, cotton balls often served as a democratizing element in the state's cultural life, bringing people of all social classes together.

Sometimes the balls were preceded by a dinner, with wine, whiskey, brandy, and fruit punch being served during dinner and the dance itself. At first, the music was provided by one or more African American musicians, but in time bands were likely to be racially mixed. By the 1820s, the balls were being held in prominent hotels, such as the Lafayette Hotel in Raleigh. Charlotte's Mansion House, which became the Central Hotel, was also a favorite site for cotton balls. By about 1920, the Hotel Charlotte, the King Cotton Hotel, and the O. Henry Hotel in Greensboro and the Sir Walter Hotel in Raleigh were competing to host cotton balls and other events.

Reference: A. H. Frank, *Social Dance: A History* (1963).

Wiley J. Williams

Cotton Mills.

The earliest cotton mills in North Carolina, with a few exceptions, operated along rivers and streams in buildings that resembled gristmills or large residential structures. The Schenck-Warlick Mill in Lincoln County (1814), the first Holt factory on Alamance Creek (1837), and the Logan Manufacturing Company in Guilford County (1865) all occupied buildings that had served another manufacturing function. These mill buildings as well as those built to be cotton mills were usually of frame and sometimes log construction. Most were two-story with shingled, gabled roofs. Space just under the roof provided room for storage and for line shafting to run the production machinery. Flooring consisted of rough-lumber boards much like those found in a typical farmhouse of the period. Additions often were haphazard, architecture was stark, and fire walls between sections were rare until late in the century.

The number of cotton mills in North Carolina remained small throughout most of the nineteenth century. In 1884 there were only 75 mills in operation. Within the next 20 years, more than 200 were constructed. The next great wave of mill building occurred during the World War I era, as the number rose from 293 in 1914 to 343 in 1921. During this period, most cotton mills shifted from steam and waterpower to electricity. The growth of the Duke Power Company in Charlotte contributed to this transition. In order to promote the use of electricity furnished by their power plants, James B. Duke and his brother Benjamin often financed the construction of new mills and became part owners of many others. They built the Piedmont & Northern Railway, an electric-powered line that extended for 150 miles through the textile region of North Carolina and South Carolina. The railway, completed in 1914,

Reeling yarn at a cotton mill, ca. 1925. NCC.

provided interurban passenger service and delivered freight to the numerous industrial facilities located along the line.

The main effect of electricity on mill construction was to eliminate the line shafting and belt-driven machinery that often contributed to accidents and shut-downs whenever a problem occurred along the production line. A "better equipment campaign" in the 1920s led to rapid technological change inside most cotton mills. By the mid-1930s these plants were better integrated, requiring fewer interruptions and fewer intermittent processes. Most spinning and roving departments, for example, featured "long drafting" equipment that allowed production steps to be cut by half or a third. In the weaving process, the improved efficiency of looms increased production and allowed a single worker to operate more looms. Weaving machinery was faster, sturdier, and larger. Weave rooms featured better lighting and humidity control. Above all, the uniform speed of motors individually mounted on each set of looms offered consistent operation and minimal disruption.

Further important improvement in cotton mills came after World War II. Survival in this highly competitive industry depended upon cutting costs and increasing production, and the major companies in North Carolina constantly reinvested in their mills and equipment. Burlington Industries, for example, embarked on a far-reaching $50 million campaign in the 1940s and 1950s to replace old equipment, enlarge plants, build new power plants, and install new lighting, flooring, and humidity-control systems. In the 1980s the effort to increase production through technological change continued. In 1984 alone, the industry spent $1.9 billion on new mill equipment ranging from accordion-armed robots, which automatically load and unload pallets of yarn and cotton, to high-speed weaving machines that replace shuttles with jets of water or air.

By the early 2000s the National Cotton Council of America counted 386 textile mills, 47 gins, and 25 warehouses in North Carolina, employing more than 63,300 people in cotton-related work.

References: Brent D. Glass, *The Textile Industry in North Carolina: A History* (1992); Boris Stern, "Mechanical Changes in the Cotton-Textile Industry, 1910 to 1936," *Monthly Labor Review* 45 (August 1937).

Brent D. Glass

SEE ALSO Schenck-Warlick Mill.

Cottonseed. Before the Civil War, most cottonseed left behind after cotton ginning went unused in North Carolina. Some was saved for the next planting, and a few enterprising farmers recognized the seed's value as fertilizer and cattle feed. Generally, though, North Carolina farmers regarded the large piles of seed as ill-smelling, possibly harmful nuisances. By 1835 Lancelot Johnson of Edgecombe County had invented one of several cottonseed hullers, although it did not become the standard design of the antebellum period. Improved machinery designed after the Civil War made the separation of cottonseed oil, meal or cake, hulls, and linters (fibers adhering to the seeds) profitable. Oil and meal were the most valuable of these products; from the oil, processors produced lard compound, salad oil, and margarine. During the latter part of the nineteenth century, the use of cottonseed meal for fertilizer predominated over its use as cattle feed. Feed later became the more profitable product.

Despite the increasing use of cottonseed meal, many farmers still argued that it caused blindness, stiffness of gait, joint swelling, and appetite loss in cattle. In the early twentieth century, W. A. Withers and F. E. Carruth of the North Carolina Agricultural Experiment Station isolated the compound gossypol, discovered in 1899, from cottonseed meal. The purified compound proved toxic to small laboratory animals, although the researchers believed that cooking or other processing inactivated the gossypol and left cottonseed meal safe for cattle. J. O. Halverson and F. W. Sherwood, also of the North Carolina Agricultural Experiment Station, showed that cottonseed meal mixed with roughage could be safely fed continuously to lactating dairy cows.

Historically, farmers have tried to recoup the cost of ginning through the sale of the remaining cottonseed. Currently, selling seed more than compensates for ginning. Domestically, cottonseed oil is used in edible products including salad and cooking oil, baking and frying fats, and margarine. Cottonseed meal and cake, as well as cottonseed hulls, are still used as animal feed, and hulls are used to a lesser degree as a soil conditioner. The once-neglected linters are now used in products such as high-quality writing paper, currency, absorbent medical supplies, automotive upholstery, and felt.

Reference: Lynette Boney Wrenn, *Cinderella of the New South: A History of the Cottonseed Industry, 1855–1955* (1995).

Douglas Helms

Council Extraordinary was a committee established by the General Assembly to exercise executive powers jointly with the governor in revolutionary North Carolina. Under the emergency conditions caused by the British invasion of the state in 1780 and 1781, the governor had little power and was unable to act effectively. Governor Abner Nash had urged the creation of a three-member Board of War to assist him on military matters when the Assembly was not in session. The board was established by the Assembly on 12 Sept. 1780, but Nash soon turned against it because he felt that it was encroaching on his powers. Nevertheless, he still believed that an advisory board with executive authority was necessary.

Accordingly, the Assembly abolished the Board of War in January 1781 and replaced it with another three-member board, called the Council Extraordinary, whose members were to be "elected by joint ballot of both houses." The Council Extraordinary was to last only until the end of the next session of the Assembly, and it had the powers once held by the Board of War and the Council of State. Like the Board of War, the Council Extraordinary divided executive power, which reduced efficiency and caused squabbles over responsibilities and duties in state government. If there was any intention of extending the existence of the council, it was quickly squelched by the next governor, Thomas Burke. In June 1781 Burke pointedly called for the elimination of the Council Extraordinary, as the existence of such a board served to "divide the supreme military command."

Reference: Hugh F. Rankin, *The North Carolina Continentals* (1971).

David A. Norris

Council of Safety was created as an interim government by North Carolina's Fourth Provincial Congress, which met at Halifax in April and May 1776. In the absence of a permanent government created by a state constitution—which the congress had, as yet, failed to adopt—the Council of Safety would execute "full power and authority" over the defense, judiciary, and taxation of the province and lay the foundation for the Fifth Provincial Congress, which would be expected to draft a constitution.

The Council of Safety was staffed by a number of North Carolina's most respected political figures, including Cornelius Harnett, Samuel Ashe, Willie Jones, Samuel Johnston, Whitmill Hill, Thomas Eaton, Thomas Person, John Rand, Hezekiah Alexander, and William Sharpe. These men overcame their political differences in order to work together to handle the immediate crisis and to prepare the way for a new form of government. Harnett was elected unanimously as the first president of the council, and Ashe and Jones followed in succession. To make the councilmen accessible to as many people as possible, meetings took place at different sites, including the towns of Wilmington, Halifax, and Salisbury and Wake County.

Much of the Council of Safety's time was devoted to defense matters. British warships off the coast, aggressive Loyalists, former Regulators, and warring Cherokee Indians all threatened to overwhelm the nascent government. Other problems sapped the strength of the councilmen and took valuable time from the more important work of fielding and supplying military units. In general, the council successfully managed most conflicts and maintained order in the state.

Louis P. Towles

Council of State comprises North Carolina's executive branch of government. Under the North Carolina Constitution, it is composed of ten elected officers: the governor, lieutenant governor, secretary of state, state auditor, treasurer, superintendent of public instruction, attorney general, and commissioners of agriculture, labor, and insurance. The locus of considerable power in the antebellum period, the modern Council of State is assigned little power directly by the state constitution. It is given an important role by statute in certain decisions, particularly in the purchase of property by the state.

John V. Orth

SEE ALSO Governor's Council.

Counterfeiting plagued North Carolina throughout its early history, with criminals making and passing fraudulent coins even before the colony issued its own money. North Carolina distributed its first paper currency in 1712, and by 1714 forging paper money was a felony punishable by death. In colonial times counterfeiters often worked in large organizations that operated in more than one colony, and money from other colonies, especially Virginia and South Carolina, was frequently printed in North Carolina. The legislatures of several colonies soon cooperated and passed laws against forging the currency of other colonies.

The British encouraged the counterfeiting of Continental money during the Revolutionary War to weaken the American war effort. A 1779 law passed by the General Assembly criminalized the reproduction of currency or lottery tickets issued by the Continental Congress or any other state. It also imposed up to a year's imprisonment and branding of the letter *C* on the left cheek of the offender, in addition to the required flogging and pillory time for a first offense.

During the Civil War, Confederate money circulated in North Carolina to replace U.S. coinage. Counterfeiters were particularly active during this time, especially in the early years of the war before inflation destroyed the value of Confederate currency. North Carolina's newspapers often warned the public about new counterfeit notes and advised readers how to detect them. Some forgeries were skillfully made, but others were evidently quite amateurish. In 1863 a batch of bogus three-dollar notes quickly aroused suspicion, as the state was not issuing three-dollar bills at that time.

Many counterfeiters altered genuine notes by pasting numbers clipped from worthless older notes onto new bills to raise their value. In 1862 forgers in Raleigh used this method to transform a number of 2-dollar state bills into 10-dollar notes. Other bills were altered with a pencil, such as a batch of 5-cent notes that were changed to 50-cent notes and circulated in Wilmington.

The National Bank Act of 1863 made the federal government the sole source of U.S. currency and prohibited states, banks, and businesses from issuing their own money. Although laws against counterfeiting remained on the books in North Carolina, detecting and punishing such forgers became a federal matter.

References: Kenneth Scott, "Counterfeiting in Colonial North Carolina," *NCHR* 34 (October 1955); Alan D. Watson, *Money and Monetary Problems in Early North Carolina* (1980).

David A. Norris

Counties. The formation of counties was one of the first matters attended to by the Lords Proprietors after they received their charter in 1663 from King Charles II for the vast tract of land in America he called the province of Carolina. In 1664 the Proprietors formed "all that parte of the province which lyeth on the north east side or starboard side entering of the river Chowan now named by us Albemarle River together with the Islands and Isletts within tenn leagues thereof" into a county that they named Albemarle County for George Monck, the duke of Albemarle, himself one of the Proprietors. This was the site of the first permanent settlement in Carolina. They then divided the new county into four precincts: Currituck, Perquimans, Pasquotank, and Chowan. Albemarle County was subsequently enlarged, and in 1696 the area south of Albemarle Sound was removed from Albemarle and made into a new county, named Bath, which in turn was divided into the precincts of Beaufort, Hyde, Craven and Carteret.

The primary reason for establishing counties (or precincts) was to provide local seats of government where citizens could record documents, such as deeds or wills, and participate in court proceedings. At the same time, the sheriff was provided with a home base from which to fulfill his basic responsibilities of collecting taxes and maintaining law and order.

By 1738 Albemarle and Bath Counties had been dissolved and the 14 precincts then in existence became counties, a designation that has remained since the seventeenth century. Throughout the remainder of the colonial period, as settle-

ment spread westward and population increased, older counties were divided and new ones formed. With statehood came an even greater rate of growth, and by 1800 the number had risen to 59 counties covering all of the state. In many cases, the dividing of counties caused heated political controversy, as eastern counties were often divided to maintain that region's majority in the state legislature against expanding representation from the piedmont and mountain regions. Shifts in population continued throughout the nineteenth century and into the twentieth century, resulting in even more counties. Larger counties were divided, and those in turn were sometimes divided yet again, until the seemingly magical figure of 100 was reached in 1911. (For a time, the number of counties was actually greater than 100, but some of these were ceded to Tennessee in 1789 and others were absorbed into other counties or never fully developed.) The number remained at 100, although in 1933 the General Assembly authorized the consolidation of existing counties subject to approval of the electorate. This could have resulted for the first time in a decrease from the 100 county figure, but as of the early 2000s there had been no such consolidations.

Initially, county government and judicial matters were in the hands of justices of the peace, who formed a body known as the Court of Pleas and Quarter Sessions. The justices were appointed by the governor, with strong input from the members of the colonial Assembly from the affected county, leaving the average citizen with no say as to who would run the government of the county in which he lived. At first the Court of Pleas and Quarter Sessions met wherever it was convenient to assemble a quorum, usually in a private home. A 1722 act of the Assembly instructed the justices to pick a site for a permanent seat of government for each precinct, where they were to buy an acre of land and build a courthouse. Whether in the early precinct days, or after the name of the local government entity was changed from precinct to county, the justices had the support of a sheriff for law enforcement, as well as a clerk of court and a register of deeds. Of the three, both the clerk of court and the register of deeds needed to remain in their offices in the courthouse, which left only the sheriff free to travel about the county. Accordingly, he was also designated tax collector, a position sheriffs continued to hold until the latter part of the twentieth century.

The general system of county government of the early colonial period, with the appointed members of the Court of Pleas and Quarter Sessions running things, was carried over into statehood, and little changed until the adoption of the North Carolina Constitution of 1868. The system called for by the new constitution, known as the Township and County Commissioner Plan, gave control of county government to five commissioners, to be elected at large by the county's voters. In addition, each county was divided into townships whose residents elected two justices to serve as the township's governing

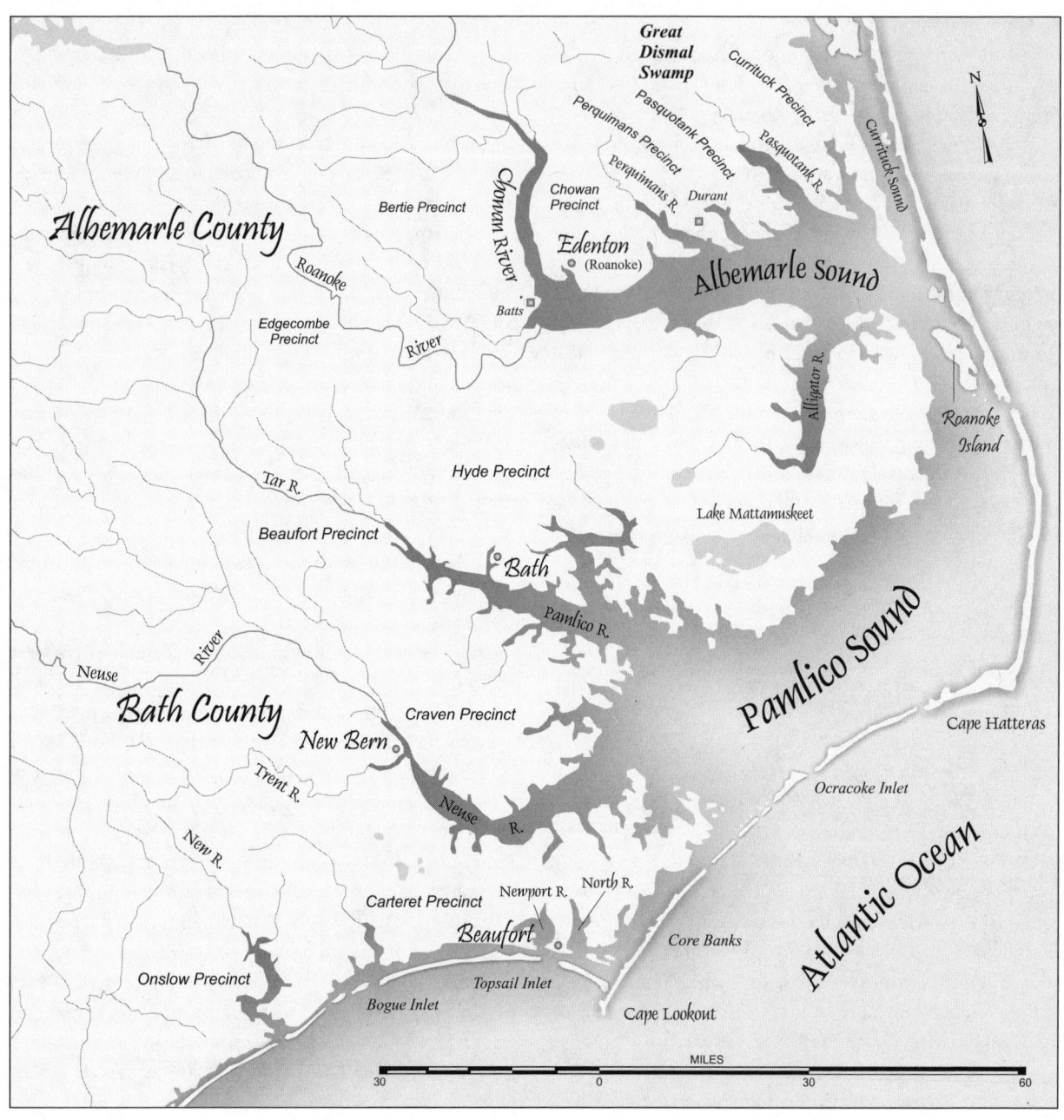

Great
Dismal
Swamp

Currituck Precinct

Pasquotank Precinct

Perquimans Precinct

Pasquotank R.

Currituck Sound

Bertie Precinct

Chowan
Precinct

Perquimans R.

Durant

Chowan River

Albemarle County

Edenton
(Roanoke)

Albemarle Sound

Roanoke

Batts

Alligator R.

Roanoke
Island

Edgecombe
Precinct

River

Tar R.

Hyde Precinct

Lake Mattamuskeet

Pamlico Sound

Beaufort Precinct

Bath

Pamlico R.

Cape Hatteras

Neuse

River

Bath County

Craven Precinct

New Bern

Ocracoke Inlet

Trent R.

Neuse

R.

Atlantic Ocean

New R.

Carteret Precinct

Newport R.

North R.

Core Banks

Beaufort

Onslow Precinct

Topsail Inlet

Cape Lookout

Bogue Inlet

N

MILES

30   0   30   60

Colonial counties and precincts, ca. 1730. Map by Mark Anderson Moore, courtesy NCOA&H.

North Carolina's 100 counties. Map by Mark Anderson Moore, courtesy NCOA&H.

body, as well as a three-member school committee and a constable. The new system significantly reduced the General Assembly's control of county government, since the legislators no longer appointed the justices of the peace who made up the county court.

The Township and County Commissioner Plan, patterned after one previously adopted in Pennsylvania, did not prove universally popular in North Carolina and lasted less than a decade. At a constitutional convention in 1875, the General Assembly was authorized to change the system, and in the session of 1877 townships were reduced to little more than geographic and administrative subdivisions of the counties. This seriously reduced the authority of county commissioners.

The modern system of county government, in which an elected board of commissioners is responsible for managing a county's affairs, including setting the rate and collecting taxes and determining where funds should be expended, dates to the early twentieth century. Periodically after that, the General Assembly conferred additional authority and responsibility on the county commissioners, until at the end of the century they had been provided with such a wide range of "home-rule" statutes that many counties found it impossible to run their greatly expanded business without professional help. This led to the adoption by many counties of the County Manager Plan. Under this plan, commissioners employ a county manager to serve as a sort of chief executive of the county business—in some instances, the largest business in the county—with the manager having certain independent authority, including that of hiring and firing employees.

As with other matters, the state determines what sources the counties may tap for income. Traditionally, the real estate tax has been the primary revenue source for North Carolina counties. However, especially in the last half of the twentieth century, counties were able to prevail on the General Assembly to let them collect from a variety of other sources, among those favored being local sales taxes, land transfer taxes, meals taxes, and occupancy taxes.

References: A. Fleming Bell, ed., *County Government in North Carolina* (3rd ed., 1989); David LeRoy Corbitt, *The Formation of the North Carolina Counties, 1663–1943* (1969).

David Stick

Country Clubs became a part of American life during the last quarter of the nineteenth century with the rise in popularity of golf. Having evolved from city clubs with the influence of resort hotels, hunt clubs, and spas, country clubs, first found in the Northeast, offered their members private social, dining, and outdoor recreational facilities. Although golf clubs appeared more slowly in the South than in the Northeast and Midwest, the original Asheville Country Club golf course may have existed as early as 1893, which would make it the state's first country club and golf course.

Dates for the opening of facilities are far easier to obtain than for the actual founding of the clubs as legal entities. Newly formed clubs issued bonds to their members in order to raise capital to purchase land and build facilities. Although an extant account book demonstrates that the Chapel Hill Country Club existed by 1907 and had purchased golf equipment before 1919, their nine-hole course southeast of the University of North Carolina campus apparently did not open until 1923. Other early North Carolina country club golf courses included Raleigh's Carolina Country Club (1912), Greensboro Country Club (1911), and Forsyth Country Club (1911) in Winston-Salem. In Pinehurst, the Tufts family from Massachusetts developed full-service winter resort facilities, including golf after 1897. It eventually combined a membership country club (currently based on where one lives within the Village of Pinehurst) with a commercial resort.

Country clubs sprang up rapidly during the 1920s, as the middle class desired a way to pool resources to enjoy the affluent lifestyle communally. Charlotte built three country club courses and Asheville and Greensboro two each during the decade, while Rocky Mount (1922) and Salisbury (1927) each welcomed one. When Hope Valley Country Club opened in Durham in 1926, George Watts Hill donated the nine-hole Durham Country Club course to the city for what would become the municipal Hillandale Golf Club. Even smaller, more rural towns gained country clubs during this era, including Morganton (1928), Mount Airy (1928), Roanoke Rapids (1923), and Blowing Rock (1922). Barely in North Carolina, Alleghany County's Roaring Gap Club (1926) features a secluded Donald Ross course 3,700 feet above sea level along the edge of the Blue Ridge Mountains.

Roughly one country club in seven went under between 1929 and 1939 as a result of the Great Depression, and countless new and expansion clubhouse and golf course projects were canceled. Even the survivors experienced hard times, resorting to membership discounts, benefit dances, and other money makers. By the 1950s, as the polio threat subsided and desegregation came to public facilities, pools became as much a staple of the clubs as golf and tennis facilities. Eventually, country clubs sorted themselves into three broad types: fully private clubs open only to members and their guests; semiprivate clubs that permitted some use of the golf or swimming facilities by nonmembers for a daily fee; and those such as Pinehurst or Linville that afforded privileges to guests of specific resort properties in addition to their members.

Country clubs have served as a means of establishing status and separating members from the larger community, often for reasons based on race discrimination. Whereas Jewish patrons had been allowed to join city clubs, most country clubs generally excluded them. Racist, classist, and nativist impulses have undeniably attracted some to private clubs populated solely by "people like us." Barriers to African Americans remained common among country clubs throughout the United States until 1990, when the Shoal Creek (Alabama) affair generated sufficient public pressure to force the governing bodies of both professional and amateur golf to denounce such practices. Many country club rules also excluded women from joining or playing golf at various "heavy traffic" times, such as Saturdays and Sundays.

A group of African Americans in Greensboro organized Forest Lake Country Club during the late 1950s, although it apparently did not offer golf. Opened for golf during the crest of the civil rights movement in 1965, Garner's semiprivate Meadowbrook Country Club became the first country club for blacks south of Maryland. Businessmen M. Grant Batey, James J. Samson Jr., and Paul Jervay founded Meadowbrook in 1958 by purchasing 140 acres of tobacco land. For many years a fully private club with 150 members, Meadowbrook eventually became semiprivate due to financial pressures. In 1960 Charlie Sifford, born in a racially mixed Charlotte neighborhood in 1922, broke the color barrier on the PGA tour after the courts overturned the organization's "Caucasian only" clause.

The boom years between the end of World War II and 1970 brought even further expansion of country clubs in North Carolina than during the 1920s. Twenty new country clubs appeared between 1945 and 1952 alone. Cities added second private clubs, including Raleigh Country Club (1948), Wilmington's Pine Valley (1956), and Willowhaven (1957) near Durham. Smaller communities established their first country clubs, such as Reidsville (1945), Burlington (1946), Washington (1949), Siler City (1954), Wilkesboro (1958), and Robersonville (1965). In 1963 the original 40 members of the Country Club of North Carolina in Southern Pines contained an assortment of the state's elites. Joining members included businessmen J. Gregory Poole and Karl Hudson Jr. and Democratic politicians Richardson Preyer, Voit Gilmore, and Kenneth Royall, as well as Hargrove "Skipper" Bowles.

During the last decades of the twentieth century, both golf courses and country clubs became linked to real estate developments. Some communities—frequently gated ones such as Carolina Trace (1968), south of Sanford; Bald Head Island (1975); Treyburn (1988), north of Durham; and Governors Club (1989), south of Chapel Hill—used exclusive country clubs with marquee golf course architects (Robert Trent Jones, George Cobb, Tom Fazio, and Jack Nicklaus, respectively) to attract residents to high-end developments.

By the end of the twentieth century, however, country clubs accounted for less than 10 percent of new golf course construction. Elitism and discriminatory practices caused many North Carolinians to take a dim view of country clubs. Citizens of Boone rejected the idea of a country club as inappropriate for their community in 1957. The Carolinas Golf Association reported in 1999 that while the number of courses had increased 20 percent during the previous decade, the number of country club courses had decreased 13 percent. Economic and social changes, along with the development of high-end daily fee courses that promised better golf than the private clubs, took their toll on country clubs. Some changed to semiprivate status or accepted more outside play through tournaments and privilege cards. Others turned to real estate tie-ins and aggressive membership campaigns.

While these factors greatly increased access by nonwhites, they also signaled problems for the country club as an institution by the early 2000s. As new country clubs became arms of real estate ventures, the private courses continued to decrease in relative significance as venues for golf. Meanwhile, private clubs similarly lost their near monopolies in North Carolina towns on fine dining, tennis, and swimming.

References: Diane Cashman, *A History of the Cape Fear Country Club* (1984); James M. Mayo, *The American Country Club: Its Origin and Development* (1998); Pete McDaniel, *Uneven Lies: The Heroic Story of African-Americans in Golf* (2000); Calvin H. Sinnette, *Forbidden Fairways: African-Americans and the Game of Golf* (1998).

Arthur Menius

Country Ham—cured for around 40 days with salt, a pinch of saltpeter, and individual spices; aged at least 25 days; and often smoked—was a popular export of North Carolina to England during colonial times as well as a versatile delicacy that came to define and enhance important family gatherings and holidays. Today, many North Carolinians strongly identify country ham with idyllic memories of home and family and an ancestry rooted in an agricultural existence. In North Carolina and other southern states, the easily preserved meat is eaten in various forms, whether as the main dish at dinner or for leftover snacking. Ham biscuits, ham and eggs, ham with red eye gravy, ham and grits, ham-seasoned vegetables, and ham bits sprinkled over a salad, for example, have been commonplace for decades.

Country ham differs from modern "city" ham—which is soaked in brine for tenderness—in the depth and strength of its salty flavor and its dry texture. Since World War II, the popularity of country hams has waned as the meat has been replaced by a variety of easy-to-prepare store-bought hams. The country hams of Smithfield, N.C., and Smithfield, Va., however, have traditionally vied for the title of best ham in the region. The Ham and Yam Festival in Smithfield, N.C., began in 1986 as a contest between these hams, but after the North Carolina hams took first place eight years in a row, the competition (although not the festival) was discontinued.

Country hams may still be purchased at most North Carolina grocery stores, although better selection is available through a variety of mail-order and Internet merchants. Johnston County Hams of Smithfield is one of the leading producers of country hams in the state. Phillips Brothers Coun-

Processing country ham at a plant in Smithfield.
Photograph by Corey Lowenstein. *Raleigh News and Observer.*

try Ham, Inc., of Asheboro is a family-owned business dating to 1947. One of the state's largest pork retailers, the company was awarded the National Country Ham Association's grand champion award in 2004.

References: Randall Chase, "Country Ham: Where Southern Food, Culture Meet," *Charlotte Observer*, 23 Jan. 2000; John Parris, "Roaming the Mountains: Slow Fire for Curing Hams," *Asheville Citizen*, 9 Feb. 1962; Jeanne Voltz and Elaine J. Harvell, *The Country Ham Book* (1999).

Wiley J. Williams

SEE ALSO Hog Killing.

Country Music is a distinctively American form of popular music based on traditional, southern, Anglo-American folk music and influenced to some extent by the blues. North Carolinians played a significant role in the development of this music, particularly in the 1930s, and its popularity has continued in the state. Dozens of the state's radio stations feature country music programming, and concerts featuring both lo-

cal and national acts frequent North Carolina venues throughout the year. Modern-day country stars George Hamilton IV and Randy Travis are both from North Carolina.

The traditional Anglo-American music of North Carolina at the turn of the century encompassed a cappella ballad singing, fiddle and banjo duos, and sacred music. Settlers from the British Isles brought with them ballads of love and death as well as a style of fiddle music played for dances that combined a fast tempo, complex melodies, and a steady rhythm. By the middle of the nineteenth century, African American banjo players from the Piedmont began to teach white musicians how to play, and banjo-fiddle duos, the core of the later string band, appeared among both African Americans and whites. A strong folk hymn tradition also existed among various denominations in North Carolina, especially Baptists. In the early nineteenth century, the shape-note singing movement introduced harmony singing to churches across America. At the start of the twentieth century, blues music took form among the state's African American musicians. The pieces were in place for the development of a new musical style.

Country music in the early days centered around solo vocalists backed by guitar and string bands. The string band, usually a fiddle and banjo with rhythm guitar, was an ensemble rooted in folk tradition, and in the 1920s audiences came to appreciate the music through the new media of radio, records, and concerts. The textile mills of the Southeast played an important role in the history of early country music, providing a meeting place and a supply of steady work for musicians in between musical gigs. The most influential string band to arise from North Carolina's mill communities was Charlie Poole and his North Carolina Ramblers. The Ramblers' tightly arranged sound set them apart from other string bands of the day and had a strong influence on later musicians, particularly in bluegrass.

Several radio stations in North Carolina played country music, but none was more influential than WBT in Charlotte. Founded in 1922, the station played classical and "high culture" music for several years, but by 1929 it was featuring country music as part of its programming. In 1934 the Crazy Water Crystals Company, a laxative manufacturer, sponsored a Saturday night show called the *Crazy Barn Dance*, similar in format to Nashville's well-known *Grand Ole Opry*. Another popular country music show on WBT was *Briarhopper Time*, named for the band the Briarhoppers. In the late 1940s, the Briarhoppers, featuring Roy "Whitey" Grant and "Arval" Hogan, was one of the most well-known radio bands. One of their most popular songs was a version of "Jesse James," which they recorded in 1949 with a small recording company out of Pennsylvania called Cowboy Records.

The WBT programs also attracted a number of other country bands and performers, including Fisher Hendley and his Carolina Tarheels, Claude Casey, Homer "Pappy" Sherrill and

Arthur Smith (right) with the Dixie Liners, ca. 1938. John Edwards Memorial Collection, Southern Folklife Collection, Wilson Library, UNC-Chapel Hill.

DeWitt "Snuffy" Jenkins, and Mainer's Crazy Mountaineers, featuring brothers J. E. and Wade Mainer of Concord. Raised in Weaverville in Buncombe County, the Mainer brothers worked in the cotton mills until 1932, when J. E. started playing fiddle on a radio station in Gastonia. Perhaps the most influential old-time string band of the 1930s, Mainer's Crazy Mountaineers took their name from their first sponsor, the Crazy Water Crystals Company. The group recorded old-time fiddle tunes, such as "Johnson's Old Grey Mule," for Bluebird Records beginning in 1935. The band influenced the singing and playing of other musicians, particularly Clyde Moody, known as the "Carolina Wood-chopper." Wiley and Zeke Morris, members at one time of the Crazy Mountaineers, introduced "Salty Dog Blues," one of the most popular songs in a style that would later be known as bluegrass.

Other popular brother duets emerged in the country music scene. Although born in South Carolina, Dorsey and Howard Dixon eventually settled in East Rockingham, N.C., and began playing publicly in 1932. By 1934 the Dixon Brothers appeared on WBT as part of the *Crazy Water Crystals Saturday Night Jamboree*. With Dorsey playing guitar and Howard on dobro, the pair recorded more than 60 songs for record companies in the 1930s. Dorsey was an accomplished songwriter and the author of the classic "Wreck on the Highway." The brothers' lifelong work in cotton mills inspired mill songs such as "Weave Room Blues," an important part of their repertoire. Howard died in 1961, while Dorsey came back into national prominence during the folk revival of the early 1960s before dying in 1965.

Deriving their moniker from the fact that North Carolina's Blue Ridge Mountains are sometimes referred to as the Land of the Sky, the Blue Sky Boys (Bill and Earl Bolick) launched their successful musical careers in 1935 at WWNC in Asheville and earned great popularity during the 1930s and 1940s. Influenced by Kentucky's Monroe Brothers, the Blue Sky Boys featured Earl singing lead and playing guitar and Bill singing tenor and playing mandolin. Their music influenced many traditional country music duos, particularly the Louvin Brothers, Jim and Jesse McReynolds, Carter and Ralph Stanley, and the Everly Brothers. The band recorded some of their most popular songs on 16 June 1936 in an RCA Victor recording studio in Charlotte for the Bluebird label. Songs coming from that session included "I'm Just Here to Get My Baby Out of Jail," "Sunny Side of Life," "Down on the Banks of the Ohio," and "Where the Soul Never Dies."

Not only was country music played and broadcast in North Carolina, but after the mid-1930s, much of it was recorded in the state as well. RCA Victor made the first country recordings in Charlotte in 1927. The onset of the Great Depression diminished record sales nationwide and recording decreased. In 1936, however, RCA began making records in Charlotte, eventually turning the top three floors of the Hotel Charlotte into a recording studio. Many WBT acts recorded there, including Mainer's Crazy Mountaineers and the Monroe Brothers. By the 1940s, the golden age of country music recording in Charlotte was over, although a few companies made brief stops during this decade. Guitarist Arthur Smith opened a recording studio in Charlotte in 1959, and in 1977 he cofounded CMH Records, a leading bluegrass record label. Sugar Hill Records, founded in 1978 by Barry Poss and located in Durham, occupies a strong independent niche in country, bluegrass, and other traditional roots genres. Sugar Hill artists, who in 2005 included Dolly Parton, Willie Nelson, and Ricky Skaggs, have won ten Grammy Awards and maintain a stature in the country music scene that is rare outside of Nashville.

References: George Holt, ed., *The Charlotte Country Music Story* (1985); Bill C. Malone, *Country Music, U.S.A.* (1983); Kinney Rorrer, *Rambling Blues: The Life and Songs of Charlie Poole* (1982).

Bruce E. Baker
Shelby Stephenson

Country Stores emerged in great numbers in North Carolina's rural, agricultural society following the Civil War, although some had appeared in the early 1800s. Person County, for example, had more than a dozen scattered stores by 1835. These commercial establishments grew out of farmers' need to obtain supplies beyond what they could produce themselves without making a daylong trip to town by wagon over rough roads. Farmers also needed a market for surplus produce. The number of stores in Wake County grew from 11 in 1867–68 to more than 80 by 1872, partially as a result of the 1867 crop lien law that allowed farmers to buy goods on credit, using a future cash crop as collateral.

Usually located at a crossroads, country stores had more than a commercial function, often serving as a post office,

Lamreth-Crutchfield store at Moncure in Chatham County, ca. 1918. NCC.

polling place, or militia muster site. Storekeeper Ben Wilder, at Mitchiner's Crossroads (Franklin County), also made mechanical repairs, barbered, pulled teeth, and, as a justice of the peace, performed marriages. John Allen Gunn's store in Oak Forest (Iredell County) boasted the first telephone switchboard in the vicinity. In whatever location, the country store became a place to exchange news, tell stories, read broadsides heralding upcoming events in the area, play checkers on an upended barrel, register complaints about politics and the weather, and perhaps drink whiskey.

Unlike stores in towns, which tended to specialize, country stores offered a wide range of merchandise related to everyday life, from straight razors to plows, timepieces to guns, eggs to overalls, fiddle strings to fishing tackle, seed to sorghum, and calico to coffee pots. Stocks were necessarily small because of the investment needed to maintain a deep inventory, and often merchants ran out of the most popular items. While the

Cary Durham store in Bynum, 1952. People have gathered to watch one of the first television sets in the community. Photograph by Roland Giduz. NCC.

country storekeeper carried the risk of a large, wide-ranging inventory to meet the needs of farm families and sometimes experienced low sales, profits were generally good, about 35¢ on the dollar.

A gristmill, cotton gin, doctor's office, or blacksmith's shop often would be adjacent to a country store. In Graham County a store that began as a trading post in the 1840s expanded to include the post office and, with a cluster of other buildings, formed the nucleus of what became the town of Robbinsville. A Stokes County community took its name from a country store, Wilson's Store, and in Wayne County, Adams' Store at the crossroads became the name of a community that grew into the town of Adamsville.

When automobiles and paved roads began to cover the landscape, country stores fell into decline. By the end of the twentieth century, few had survived. A. D. Gibsons's store in Scotland County near Snead's Grove operated continuously from 1879 into the middle of the twentieth century. It changed from a place to tie up and water horses to a place with gasoline pumps for automobiles. Another store, dating from 1900 and operated since 1924 by the Bowman family, stands at the juncture of Highway 150 and Brown Summit Road in northern Guilford County. The plank road that once ran by its door and the railroad depot that stood across the road are gone, but the old pot-bellied stove remains inside. The Mast General Store in Valle Crucis, dating from the early 1880s, retains the atmosphere of an old country store and sells some of the same goods but has added such merchandise as ski boots and camping equipment. The country store has been elevated to museum status near Chapel Hill, where Patterson's Mill Country Store displays genuine artifacts and replicates the look and feel of stores that were once important fixtures in North Carolina's rural landscape.

References: Thomas D. Clark, *Pills, Petticoats, and Plows: The Southern Country Store* (1944); Sydney Nathans, *The Quest for Progress: The Way We Lived in North Carolina, 1870–1920* (1983).

Virginia Gunn Fick

County Fairs began in North Carolina nearly 200 years before the first state fair was held in Raleigh in 1853. Early North Carolina counties such as Albemarle, Clarendon, and Craven were authorized by the Great Deed of Grant in 1663 to have fairs for the sale of various "products and commodities." The eighteenth century, both before and after statehood, saw fairs brought to other localities. The General Assembly, in an act of 1750 for "laying out a town" on Samuel Jordan's plantation in Northampton County, provided for establishing two fairs annually. Another act, in 1753, established two fairs annually in a town ordered to be laid out on John Jenkins's land in Anson County. Hillsborough's charter (1770) gave the town power to

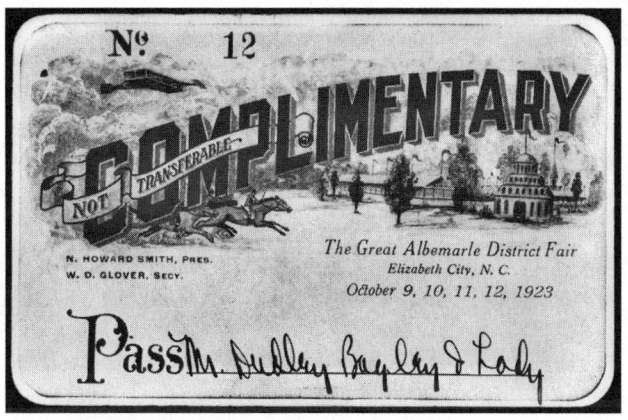

A free pass for the 1923 Great Albemarle District Fair in Elizabeth City. NCC.

hold a market each Saturday and two annual fairs at the courthouse on the first Tuesdays in May and November for the sale and vending of "Black Cattle, Provisions, Goods, Wares and Merchandise whatsoever." Fairs were also established at Wilmington and Halifax in 1777 and at Edenton in 1779, and in 1792 the legislature chartered fairs at places such as Laurel Hill (Richmond County), Brown Marsh (Bladen County), and the James Campbell Plantation (Cumberland County).

Carnival attractions such as sideshows and gambling tents were a sideline at these early fairs, while the emphasis remained on trade, barter, and various competitions for blue ribbons, such as best farmers, best livestock, best counterpanes, and best baking and canning products. The complexion of these fairs, however, gradually changed through the years as gambling, drinking, and fighting began to overshadow the socializing and trading that had been the original intent. Legislation affecting the hours and content of fairs followed.

Between 1813 and 1860, several counties established agricultural societies, and some of them, such as the Beaufort County Society in 1824, held fairs. Some fairs were sponsored by women's charitable societies such as the New Bern Female Charitable Society, the Raleigh Female Benevolent Society, and the Fayetteville Female Society of Industry.

In 2006 the North Carolina Association of Agricultural Fairs listed nearly 50 local or county fairs that were held in the state each year, emphasizing agricultural or other themes. These fairs included the Bethware Community Fair in King's Mountain, the Central Carolina Fair in Greensboro, the Cherokee Indian Fair in Cherokee, the North Carolina Mountain State Fair in Fletcher, and fairs in Burke, Caldwell, Chowan, Haywood, Lenoir, Onslow, Stanly, and many other North Carolina counties.

Wiley J. Williams

SEE ALSO State Fair.

Courthouse Ring refers to a group of politicians and government officials who, by controlling local appointments, increased their power and profits through the collection of fees and the awarding of contracts and jobs. In North Carolina, courthouse rings were most notorious in the late colonial period, although they were also a problem after Reconstruction.

In 1767 royal governor William Tryon believed that the colony's sheriffs stole over half of the poll tax money they collected. An audit in 1770 showed that every county in the colony had at least one defaulting sheriff, and the sheriffs owed the colony more than £64,000 in taxes they had failed to turn over. This excessive embezzlement made it imperative to continue the poll tax far longer than should have been necessary.

The greed of the courthouse rings in the Piedmont, and the failure of the royal government to address their wrongs, greatly contributed to the disaffection of the backcountry settlers that led to the Regulator Movement. Edmund Fanning (1737–1818), a leading figure in Orange County's courthouse ring, perhaps symbolized the abuses of courthouse rings more than any other man. Fanning, who concurrently served as a member of the Assembly, registrar of deeds, superior court judge, and militia colonel, grew wealthy on his fees at the expense of the common people, whom he treated with great contempt. His offenses were so blatant that he was convicted of extortion in 1768, although the court reserved judgment and he escaped punishment. In September 1770, when a mob of Regulators seized the courthouse in Hillsborough, they also assaulted Fanning and destroyed his house.

Reforms to eliminate the power of courthouse rings were implemented very slowly in North Carolina. After the War of the Regulation, there were minor improvements: lawyers' fees were better regulated, some county officers were placed under bond, and some abuses in the handling of tax money and the collection of small debts were curbed. The Constitution of 1776 changed little involving county government. Multiple office holding was restricted by legislation in 1808 and 1809, but sheriffs were not elected by popular vote until after 1829. Throughout the antebellum period, justices of the peace were appointed by the governor on the recommendation of legislators from their counties. Justices of the peace still wielded executive and judicial power through the old county courts until the Constitution of 1868 created a county commission system.

When the Conservatives regained control of the General Assembly after Reconstruction, they passed legislation in 1877 that eliminated the popular election of county commissioners and once again placed the direction of county governments in the hands of the justices of the peace. These measures were made to return the governance of counties with large black or Republican populations to the Conservatives of the Democratic Party; but by placing county authority in the hands of small groups of influential officials, they also permitted courthouse rings to flourish. The right of voters to elect their own county commissioners was restored in all counties by 1905.

References: Robert L. Ganyard, *The Emergence of North Carolina's Revolutionary State Government* (1978); Guion G. Johnson, *Ante-Bellum North Carolina: A Social History* (1937); Hugh T. Lefler and Albert R. Newsome, *North Carolina: The History of a Southern State* (1963); William S. Powell, *North Carolina through Four Centuries* (1989).

David A. Norris

Court of Pleas and Quarter Sessions served as the civil, administrative, and judicial arms of North Carolina county government beginning in the Proprietary period (1663–1729). Staffed by justices of the peace and appointed by the governor, the court heard cases in which the amount of litigation was between 40 shillings and 20 pounds, as well as a variety of minor civil and criminal actions. The Court of Pleas and Quarter Sessions played an important role in the daily administration of county life, as it oversaw the construction and maintenance of roads, bridges, and public buildings; the distribution of licenses for ferries, mills, and taverns; and the apportionment and collection of taxes by the sheriff. Justices also acted as an Orphans' Court for the county and supervised the settling of estates. At the close of the colonial period, the county Courts of Pleas and Quarter Sessions remained virtually intact, but the state legislature now appointed all officers of the court. Following the Civil War, the new state constitution replaced the justices of the peace with a county commissioner form of government in 1868.

References: Paul M. McCain, "Magistrates Courts in Early North Carolina," NCHR 48 (January 1971); William S. Powell, *North Carolina through Four Centuries* (1989).

Johanna Miller Lewis

Courtship Customs in North Carolina have generally followed the same trends evident in the rest of the United States, with slight differences owing to the historically agrarian and rural nature of the state. Activities deemed appropriate and conducive to courting were influenced by the leisure activities of the general population, such as barn raisings, county fairs, and hayrides. Other early leisure activities where couples could exchange glances and perhaps become acquainted were religious revival and camp meetings; school talent exhibitions; ball games; bicycle, horseback, and buggy rides; ice skating outings; strolls or promenades; and church "dinners on the grounds." Any social occasion was an opportunity for couples to get to know each other, and North Carolinians have not lacked for dinners, dances, balls, plays, pageants, ice cream socials, church homecomings, parades, weddings, christenings, guitar "picking" sessions, and sing-alongs on the front porch or around the piano in the parlor.

A custom that flourished in the New England states and that may have been practiced in rural North Carolina areas was "bundling," or allowing a fully clothed couple to "laugh and whisper together in bed, under supervision." Bundling may have developed because homes were small and had no separate place for couples to be alone together, fuel was scarce and could be used sparingly in the house if the couple was warmed under blankets and quilts, and working hours were long, necessitating that most courting opportunities occurred at night. The practice died out in the early 1800s as bigger houses with front parlors became the norm. Disdain from outsiders and pressures from clergy also hastened bundling's demise.

Two innovations that dramatically changed courtship practices in the state and nation were automobiles and the movies. With the appearance of the automobile, particularly closed cars, a couple's "mobile parlor" enabled them to attend parties and dances in towns miles away. Driving became a favorite pastime and, coupled with a leisurely picnic, an ideal courting activity. The automobile provided the means to conduct the private act of courtship in the public world. Going to the movies was "buying dark and privacy in a crowd." Keeping company in the parlor was replaced with Coke dates, movies, and "parking." Going to the movies on Saturday night became a standard date, and drive-in movies and lovers' lanes provided places for couples to nurture their relationships.

During war times, couples courted their loved ones with letters and messages sent through friends and acquaintances. Women wore lockets containing the hair of their beloved, while men carried pictures of their loved one close to their hearts. World War I fueled the pen pal courtship; girls felt it was their patriotic duty to write to lonely soldiers. Broadcast messages of love were sent from overseas back to sweethearts in North Carolina. During World War II, canteens and USOs sprang up around military bases to provide a haven where dancing and socializing were encouraged and opportunities to meet people from different backgrounds flourished.

With North Carolina's economy booming after World War II, roller skating gained in popularity, and swimming pools also became a popular hangout. Dances, or sock hops, were the rage of the 1950s, much like discos would become in the 1970s. Courtship for North Carolinians after the turbulent 1960s has been most affected by a relaxation of sexual mores. While couples may become acquainted by participating in many of the same leisure activities as previous generations, they also may live together openly without marriage ties and for the most part without negative social stigma. The emergence of computers, and particularly the Internet, into everyday lives has opened up the entire world as a meeting place for potential couples. For many, "computer dating" is the courtship practice of the day. Courtship customs for North Carolinians continue to mirror the trends of the national culture

and borrow from international influences as modern means of communication make the world a smaller place.

References: Beth L. Bailey, *From Front Porch to Back Seat: Courtship in Twentieth-Century America* (1988); William J. Fielding, *Strange Customs of Courtship and Marriage* (1942); Henry Reed Stiles, *Bundling: Its Origins, Progress, and Decline in America* (1934).

Taylor Shaw

Covered Bridges. In the low, flat, marshy eastern region of North Carolina, mill dams at water-powered mill ponds became bridges facilitating travel across these wet areas. Traveling through these mill houses was much quicker than following alternate routes, which were often many miles longer. Bridge building at county expense did not begin until 1756; prior to that time, the mill pond owners had borne the cost. Coverings for these bridges were initially built to protect vital machinery and facilitate the unloading of grain in bad weather, making possible the loading of meal and flour as a finished product. In the late 1700s and early 1800s coverings were also adopted to preserve the bridges' timber, planking, and rails (which were vulnerable to rot) as well as their adjacent structures. "Kissing Bridges," as covered bridges have sometimes been called, were once desirable spots for young couples, who could steal a kiss inside the dark, protective walls of the bridge houses.

By the early 2000s, only a small number of covered bridges remained in North Carolina, three of which were located in the east in Bertie County. Hoggard's Mill pond north of Windsor had a gristmill covered bridge and a sawmill covered bridge, both authorized by the County Court in 1736; the Rascoe Mill covered bridge was authorized much later and encompasses a gristmill. Covered bridges in western North Carolina were not mill-related but simply bridges with covering to provide shelter. Two of these—located on Lyle Creek east of Claremont

Pisgah Bridge in Randolph County, ca. 1970s. The bridge still stands in the early 2000s. Photograph by Jerry Cotten. NCC.

Skeen Mill Bridge in Randolph County, ca. 1970s. The bridge is no longer standing. Photograph by Jerry Cotten. NCC.

and at Lake Lure in Rutherford County—remained standing; a third bridge, crossing the West Fork Little River south of Asheboro, was washed away by flood in the summer of 2003.

References: Harry L. Thompson, *The Lost Town of "Cashy"* (1967); Alan D. Watson, "Regulation and Administration of Roads and Bridges," *NCHR* 45 (Autumn 1968).

Harry L. Thompson

Cowan's Ford, Battle of. The Battle of Cowan's Ford, which took place in northwestern Mecklenburg County, was a Revolutionary War action by the Continental forces to delay the British crossing of the Catawba River. The battle was an important part of the fight-and-retreat strategy of Gen. Nathanael Greene, commander of the American army in the South. Although it was unclear to Greene exactly where Lord Charles Cornwallis, leader of the British forces, would cross the river, Cornwallis's line of march in late January 1781 indicated that he planned to cross at either Beattie's Ford or Cowan's Ford. Greene hoped that a substantial delay of the advance would give him the opportunity to select the time and place of a major battle that he saw as inevitable. He left Gen. William Lee Davidson with a relatively small force to carry out his plan after warning his younger compatriot that the wily Cornwallis would probably feign an effort at one ford and attempt to cross at the other.

Greene knew his opponent well: on 31 January Cornwallis sent a detachment to Beattie's Ford, giving all indications that it was the point of entry while the main army crossed at Cowan's Ford. Davidson saw through the ruse, however, and moved the bulk of his troops to the lower crossing during the night, which surprised the British when they arrived on the west bank just before daybreak on 1 February.

The Catawba River near Cowan's Ford was about 400 yards wide, with a rocky and irregular bottom that caused fluctuations in depth. Regular travelers had established two lines of direction for crossing. A wagon ford went directly across to the east bank, and a longer, shallower horse ford started at the same point but turned right about two-thirds of the way across, ran over the end of a large island, and headed toward a rocky hill about a quarter of a mile from the exit of the wagon ford. Recent rains had swollen the river, creating a swirling current, and a misty fog shrouded the area, but Cornwallis wasted no time in ordering his men to cross the wagon ford. They waded in, four to a column, with bayoneted muskets and long staffs to steady them in the rough current. Not until considerable progress had been made did the splashing waters alert American sentries, who sounded the alarm and began firing.

Davidson, expecting the British to cross via the horse ford, had deployed most of his men there. Quickly responding to the sounds of battle, he led the remainder of his force to the scene, but by the time he arrived, the first British troops had reached the shore and cannons brought to the British front on the west bank had begun to pound the American defenses. Davidson ordered his men to fall back to the woods and dense undergrowth to regroup, but while trying to rally a particularly hesitant unit, a ball pierced his chest and he died instantly. With their general down, the Americans broke ranks and fled, turning the battle into a rout for the British.

Greene had hoped to stall Cornwallis at the Catawba River long enough to put a safe distance between their armies. The quick British victory, however, disrupted his plan and forced him to make an uncertain race to the Dan River to cross into Virginia, where he rested his troops, secured reinforcements, and procured much-needed supplies. In a strange twist of fate, the defeat at Cowan's Ford created the revised American strategy that led to the Battle of Guilford Courthouse, which severely weakened Cornwallis's army and facilitated the surrender at Yorktown.

Reference: Hugh F. Rankin, *Greene and Cornwallis: The Campaign of the Carolinas* (1976).

Jerry L. Cross

Cowpens, Battle of. The Battle of Cowpens took place on 17 Jan. 1781 near Spartanburg, S.C. To reverse the appalling pattern of defeat in the South during the American Revolution, Gen. George Washington appointed Gen. Nathanael Greene, an energetic and trusted lieutenant, as southern commander. Greene assumed the post in North Carolina on 2 Dec. 1780 and promptly and audaciously divided his meager force (2,300 infantry, 1,500 present and fit for duty), sending Brig. Gen. Daniel Morgan with about 1,000 men into western South Carolina to possibly draw Cornwallis's forces there. Cornwallis countered by dividing his own army, sending Lt. Col. Banastre Tarleton to find and crush Morgan. Tarleton, the "Red Raider," whose name was synonymous with ruthlessness, set out with about 1,100 troops, most of whom were experienced and disciplined regulars. Tarleton pushed his men hard, intending to catch Morgan's apparently ragtag column before it could receive reinforcements or cross the Broad River.

As Tarleton closed in, Morgan had little choice but to stand and fight. On 16 Jan. 1781 he carefully chose his battleground and arrayed his troops, placing sharpshooters in a "skirmishing line" in front and his remaining forces behind in "progressively stronger" lines. The ensuing battle the next day featured both ferocious fighting by the Americans and tactical brilliance by their leader Morgan, whose creative deployment of his troops surprised and withered the British assault. By battle's end, Tarleton saw his force soundly defeated. Casualty figures vary among sources, but reasonable estimates of British losses include more than 850 soldiers and officers killed, wounded, or captured—a devastating percentage of Tarleton's total forces. American casualty numbers also vary but were undoubtedly far fewer, with estimates as low as 12 killed and 60 wounded.

The fight at Cowpens was truly a disaster for Cornwallis, depriving him of his best light infantry and cavalry and thus seriously weakening the force with which he intended to invade North Carolina. Daniel Morgan became an instant American hero and was awarded a gold medal by the U.S. Congress. His victory at Cowpens breathed confidence into the Carolinas and provided the first link in what would become a final chain of events leading to Cornwallis's ultimate defeat at Yorktown, Va.

References: Lawrence E. Babits, *A Devil of a Whipping: The Battle of Cowpens* (1998); John S. Pancake, *This Destructive War: The British Campaign in the Carolinas, 1780–1782* (1985).

Nathaniel C. Hughes Jr.

Cradle of Forestry. SEE Biltmore Forest School.

Cragmont Assembly. Interest in developing a summer retreat center for North Carolina Free Will Baptists began in the 1930s, but at that time limited resources prohibited any formal action toward the acquisition of such a facility. In 1941 a campaign to raise funds for this project was initiated by Free Will Baptist organizations in the state, and in 1944 a committee representing these organizations was charged with the task of finding a suitable site. Possible sites were evaluated, but no decision was made until the summer of 1945, when the committee found suitable property near Black Mountain. A campaign was begun to raise the balance of the purchase price by 1 Nov. 1945. Once the property was purchased, Cragmont Assembly was incorporated, and a board of directors representing the sponsoring organizations was chosen to make policies governing the assembly and to choose the manager responsible for day-to-day operations.

The first summer retreats and conferences were held at Cragmont Assembly in 1946. The main building, a three-story, multipurpose structure, continued to be used until 1978, when it was replaced by a more modern facility. Meanwhile, other buildings were constructed, including a motel, two dormitories, and a dining hall. Each summer, Cragmont Assembly serves as host for several youth conferences, a ministers' conference, and women's retreats. In addition, weekend retreats for church groups and recreational and inspirational events are held each year to accommodate the many hundreds of people who visit this beautiful spot in the Blue Ridge Mountains.

Reference: Michael R. Pelt, *A History of Original Free Will Baptists* (1996).

Michael R. Pelt

Cranberry Iron Mine is located on an immense subterranean stretch of titaniferous magnetite (titanium, iron oxide) centered around Cranberry in Avery County. Said to have been used by Indians before their contact with whites, it came to be worked mainly from surface ore by 1829 and was opened to systematic production around 1880. In 1882 a railroad facilitated movement of the ore to the furnace (see photograph, p. 310). The ore, low in silica and phosphorus, was characterized as the largest deposit of Bessemer ore in the South. By 1974 it was the only active iron mine left in North Carolina.

Reference: W. F. Wilson and others, *North Carolina Geology and Mineral Resources: A Foundation for Progress*, North Carolina Geological Survey Educational Series no. 4 (1976).

Jean H. Seaman

Craven County, located in the Coastal Plain region of eastern North Carolina, lies within one of early North Carolina's most important regions. Formed in 1705, it was originally called Archdale Precinct of Bath County; in 1712 the name was changed to Craven County in honor of the earl of Craven, one of the Lords Proprietors. New Bern, the county seat, was settled in 1710 and incorporated in 1723. The town was founded by Baron Christoph von Graffenried and named for the city of Bern, Switzerland. New Bern served as the primary seat of colonial government in the 1740s and later as the state capital of North Carolina until the establishment of Raleigh in 1792. Other Craven County communities include Bridgeton, Cove City, Trent Woods, Vanceboro, Havelock, and Dover. Notable physical features include the Neuse River, Catfish Lake, Palmetto Swamp, Hog Island, and Johnson Point.

Eighteenth-century Craven County was home to North Carolina's first newspaper, the *North-Carolina Gazette* (New Bern, 1751), as well as its first chartered school, New Bern Academy (1764). New Bern continues to be the economic cen-

Employees stand in front of the furnace of the Cranberry Iron Mine, ca. 1895. NCC.

ter of the county, with a thriving commercial environment and an important historic district, centered around the restored 1770 colonial capital. The Tryon Palace Historic Sites and Gardens is one of the state's most popular historic attractions. Among the county's other important landmarks and historic sites are the Harvey Mansion (1798), the James Riggs House (ca. 1830), and St. John's Masonic Lodge and Theater (1801). The former pharmacy where Caleb Bradham invented Pepsi-Cola in the 1890s is a point of interest in New Bern. Cultural institutions in Craven County include the Fireman's Museum, New Bern Civic Theater, Atlantic Dance Theater, Union Point Park, and Craven Concerts. The county hosts annual events such as the Chrysanthemum Festival, North Carolina Festival, Bridgeton Blueberry Festival, and Festival of Colonial Life.

Craven County's agricultural products include horticultural crops, soybeans, tobacco, corn, cotton, peanuts, swine, beef cattle, and chickens. Manufactured products include textiles, computer components, plumbing products, furniture, and power tools. Minerals such as lime and shell stone are also mined in the county. In 2004 Craven County's population was estimated to be 92,000.

Reference: Peter B. Sandbeck, *The Historic Architecture of New Bern and Craven County, North Carolina* (1988).

William S. Powell

SEE ALSO Capitals, Colonial and State; *North-Carolina Gazette*; Tryon Palace.

Crazy Water Crystals, a laxative made by the Crazy Water Crystals Company of Mineral Wells, Tex., became known to many rural and working-class North Carolinians during the Great Depression through the company's sponsorship of "hillbilly" music programs on radio stations such as WBT in Charlotte. The crystals—also advertised and sold under such names as Crazy Mineral Water and Crazy Fiz—were produced by the evaporation of mineral water drawn from "world-renowned Crazy Wells." When reconstituted, they were said to aid in the treatment of a variety of intestinal disorders resulting from "faulty elimination."

WBT's salesman-announcer Grady Cole (at the station from 1930 to 1961 and well known as "Mr. Dixie") advertised the product as "the crystals in the bright green box." Popular radio shows featuring local musicians—such as Charles Crutchfield's Briarhoppers, Dick Hartman's Crazy Tennessee Ramblers, Mainer's Crazy Mountaineers, and Fisher Hendley and his Carolina Tarheels—were frequently interspersed with commercials for Crazy Water Crystals. The willingness to spend large amounts of money on radio advertising in the midst of the Depression reflected both radio's selling power and the popularity of the music used to push the product. A mix of homespun humor, flamboyant salesmanship, and extravagant health claims made up the Crazy Water image. Print ads included pictures of a large, modern processing facility in Mineral Wells as well as strings of refrigerated cars painted with the Crazy Water logo. Drugstores often displayed prominent arrangements of the trademark green boxes, augmented by green and white streamers.

The relationship between Crazy Water Crystals and WBT lasted until about 1937, when J. W. Fincher, Crazy Water's North Carolina representative, severed it, apparently over financial disagreements. The product continued to be advertised over other Piedmont stations, however, until a drop in demand forced cutbacks. The company's subsequent demise by the late 1930s has been attributed to investigations by the Food and Drug Administration and the Federal Trade Commission, both concluding that the outlandish claims of Crazy Water's effectiveness were clearly exaggerated.

References: Pamela Grundy, "From *Il Trovatore* to the Crazy Mountaineers: WBT-Charlotte and Changing Music Culture in the Carolina Piedmont, 1922–1935" (M.A. thesis, UNC-Chapel Hill, 1991); Grundy, *"We Always Tried to Be Good People": Respectability, Crazy Water Crystals, and Hillbilly Music on the Air, 1933–1935* (1995).

Wiley J. Williams

Credit Unions. Practical cooperative credit was developed in Germany in the mid-1800s. In 1913 John Sprunt Hill, a wealthy Duplin County businessman and chairman of North Carolina's banking commission, was a member of an American delegation to Europe to study successful systems of cooperative finance, production, and marketing in seven countries. Hill was moved by a statue in Germany memorializing Raiffeisen and depicting the farmers' plight before the creation of credit unions and their prosperity through credit unions. Upon his return to North Carolina, Hill worked to gain farmers' support for the passage of the McRae Credit Union Bill, enacted in 1915. Because of this original rural focus, North Carolina was the only state to place its Credit Union Division

under the Department of Agriculture, where it stayed until it was transferred in 1971 to the Department of Commerce.

Lowe's Grove Credit Union, organized in 1915 after the legislature passed the McRae bill, was the first rural credit union in North Carolina and perhaps the first in the nation. The credit union started with a membership of 24 local farmers and businessmen and a program of 6 percent loans, cooperative buying, and thrifty management. With greater prosperity, the community obtained a charter of incorporation in 1919 that allowed a local government to levy taxes and issue bonds for public services.

In 1923 the Raleigh Post Office Employees Credit Union, which is the oldest credit union still operating in the state, became the first urban credit union. In 1934 the Credit Union National Association was formed, and the North Carolina Credit Union League was formed and admitted to membership that year. The State Employees' Credit Union is the largest state-chartered credit union in the United States and is also a model for minority and community credit unions. At the beginning of the twenty-first century, credit unions in the North Carolina Credit Union League boasted $9.9 billion in assets and 1.9 million members in 182 credit unions.

References: Fran Gariglio, ed., *The North Carolina Credit Union League at Fifty* (1984); J. Carroll Moody and Gilbert C. Fite, *The Credit Union Movement: Origins and Development, 1850–1970* (1971).

Sanford L. Boswell
Additional research provided by Phillip W. Evans.

"Creed of a Rioter" was a political essay penned by James Iredell in the fall of 1776. Iredell's earlier essays had attacked Britain's wrongdoings in dealing with the American colonies. The colonies, including North Carolina, had already entered the war for their independence from Great Britain when internal Whig politics intruded briefly on the effort. Samuel Johnston, Iredell's law teacher and brother-in-law and a strong revolutionary leader, had lost his bid for a seat in North Carolina's Fifth Provincial Congress (November–December 1776) by political opponents who had labeled him a Tory.

Johnston's defeat led to what is considered the most caustic script ever to drip from Iredell's busy quill. Writing under the pseudonym of "A Rioter," Iredell flayed Johnston's extremist detractors even more harshly than he had the British government. They were sworn enemies to all gentlemen, he claimed, possessing neither honor nor virtue. Neglect of mental prowess, in their view, was the surest route to understanding; and the most ignorant in appearance were in fact the most knowledgeable. Iredell argued that these fanatics found the public interest too troublesome to attend to, considered the property of others theirs if at all useful to them, and confidently viewed their own opinions as beyond reproach. The thought that a person might function from virtue alone was so foreign to them, Iredell asserted, that they would consider one so acting a madman.

Figuratively donning the garb of such a "rioter," Iredell concluded: "I think that man alone a Whig, who has sagacity enough to mind his own interest, resolution enough to plunder his neighbors, who views the storm coolly at a distance, and discovers his principles by getting honestly drunk and abusing gentlemen."

The episode reflected the way American political fervor sometimes diverted its citizens from the fight for independence. Iredell soon refocused on that struggle with his essay "To His Majesty George the Third, King of Great Britain, & c.," which contains copious facts and arguments vindicating the American Revolution.

References: Don Higginbotham, ed., *The Papers of James Iredell* (1976); Gordon S. Wood, *The Creation of the American Republic, 1776–1787* (1969).

Willis P. Whichard

Crime Control and Public Safety, Department of.

The 1977 General Assembly passed legislation to restructure and rename the Department of Military and Veterans Affairs (DMVA) as the Department of Crime Control and Public Safety. The new department received the powers and responsibilities of a number of state agencies. From the old DMVA were transferred the National Guard and the Adjutant General, the Civil Preparedness Agency, and the Civil Air Patrol. The State Highway Patrol was transferred from the Division of Motor Vehicles of the Department of Transportation. The State Board of Alcoholic Control's Enforcement Division was transferred from the Department of Commerce. The Governor's Crime Commission (created in 1967 as the Governor's Committee on Law and Order), the Division of Crime Control, the Criminal Justice Information System Board, and the Criminal Justice Information Security and Privacy Board all became part of the new department.

In 1981 the Butner Public Safety Office was transferred to the department as the division responsible for police and fire protection for the state hospital facilities at Butner. Two years later the Victim and Justice Service Division was established to administer community service programs as alternative punishments to prison. This division also operated the North Carolina Center for Missing Persons and the Rape Victim Assistance Program. In 1987 the state legislature established the North Carolina Crime Victims Compensation Fund and Commission and placed it under the department's authority.

The modern Department of Crime Control and Public Safety, headed by a gubernatorially appointed secretary, oversees the many governmental areas involving the safety and well-being of North Carolinians, including response to terrorism, civil unrest, natural disasters, and other emergencies.

Among its several boards and commissions are the Governor's Advisory Commission on Military Affairs, the Juvenile Law Study Commission, and the Office of Homeland Security.

Wiley J. Williams

Crime Rates. The frequency of major crimes in North Carolina—including murder, rape, robbery, aggravated assault, burglary, and larceny—generally has increased with the size of the state's population. Statistics of violent crimes over four centuries, particularly murder and rape, are difficult to track. One of the earliest surviving records of a person charged with murder in North Carolina dates from October 1685, when a young slave named Exeter pleaded guilty of killing his master, Richard Bentley. For his crime, Exeter was "Hanged by the Neck till he be dead." Petty arguments, personal insults, or simply intoxication often caused people to fight and sometimes kill others. However, a person who was tried for murder during the early nineteenth century was often acquitted; between 1811 and 1815, 64 courts tried 89 people but convicted only 26 of them.

Many instances of rape have gone unreported, and the private nature of the crime has made convictions problematic. In the colonial era, English law defined rape as a felony, as it has remained throughout history. A survey of North Carolina records from 1663 to 1776 showed that only 9 cases of rape were brought to trial, and of the 7 known outcomes, none ended in a conviction. A document of 1728 states that although a bill of indictment was presented by a grand jury "against David Oliver for ravishing Elizabeth Hassell," Oliver was "discharg'd by proclamation" and spared even the court costs. The paucity of statistics for rape also applies to antebellum North Carolina. The state prison's annual report for 1871–72 listed 8 prisoners incarcerated for rape and 6 confined for attempted rape. In 1899–1900 the prison took in 5 persons convicted of assault with intent to rape, 16 of attempted rape, and 8 of actual rape. In 1950–52—50 years later—prison authorities listed only 18 prisoners incarcerated for rape.

The Reconstruction era, plagued by economic woes, heated racial discord, and political unrest, was a particularly violent time in North Carolina. After the 1868 killing of a black man in Warren County, Governor William W. Holden declared: "The habit which some of our people have of taking their guns, to be used against colored people, for offences or supposed offences which inflame their passions must be put down." The state prison's annual report for 1871–72 indicates that it held 39 prisoners confined for murder, manslaughter, or felonious slaying; but of the 150 individuals who entered that year, only 7 had been convicted of killing another person.

Violent crime continued to rise in twentieth-century North Carolina. In 1899–1900 the state prison took in 5 offenders for felonious slaying, 24 for manslaughter, 37 for first-degree murder, and 8 for second-degree murder. Between 1909 and 1928,

395 people were charged with first-degree murder, and by 1951 North Carolina ranked seventh in the United States for non-negligent manslaughter, with 110 deaths. In 1965 the Charlotte metropolitan area recorded the highest per capita murder rate in the nation, with 58 murders, or 15.9 killings per 100,000 people. In 1973 the state counted 630 murders—a monthly average of 53, or approximately 1 murder every 14 hours. About 25 percent of these killings were by a family member.

In the second half of the twentieth century, as the crime of rape began to receive more attention through various legislative and social initiatives, statistics began to give a more accurate picture of the incidence of rape in North Carolina. In 1966, 523 cases were reported; in 1967, 551; and in 1973, 805. By the 1990s the number of reported rapes or attempted rapes had skyrocketed.

By 2000, with a population of about 8 million, North Carolina ranked ninth in the total number of crimes reported in the United States, with 4,919.3 crimes per 100,000 people, and eighteenth in the number of violent crimes, with 497.6 per 100,000 people. The state actually led the nation in burglaries, with 1,216 per 100,000 people. North Carolina's national rankings in other major categories included tenth in murder (7 per 100,000 people), twelfth in robbery (156.5 per 100,000 people), thirteenth in larceny (2,891.8 per 100,000 people), twenty-second in aggravated assault (307 per 100,000 people), and thirty-fourth in rape (27.1 per 100,000 people).

References: Guion G. Johnson, *Ante-Bellum North Carolina: A Social History* (1937); Donna J. Spindel, *Crime and Society in North Carolina, 1663–1776* (1989); *State of North Carolina Uniform Crime Report: 2003 Annual Report* (2003).

Dennis F. Daniels

Crittenden Award. The Christopher Crittenden Memorial Award was established in 1969 by the North Carolina Literary and Historical Association in memory of C. Christopher Crittenden, longtime secretary-treasurer of the association and director of the State Department of Archives and History from 1935 to 1968. The annual award is presented to a person, organization, institution, or corporate body engaged in the study, writing, teaching, publication, preservation, restoration, or dissemination of knowledge pertaining to North Carolina history. The major criterion for the award is "adjudged performance in the advancement of North Carolina history."

The Crittenden Award committee consists of the president and immediate past president of the North Carolina Literary and Historical Association, as well as one member elected by the executive committee of the association. The director of the Office of Archives and History serves as an ex officio member.

Crittenden Award Recipients

1970	Hugh T. Lefler
1971	Gertrude S. Carraway
1972	William S. Powell
1973	John E. Tyler
1974	Old Salem
1975	Fletcher M. Green
1976	Joye Jordan
1977	H. G. Jones
1978	John Fries Blair
1979	no award given
1980	Hugh F. Rankin
1981	Memory F. Mitchell and Thornton W. Mitchell
1982	Henry Stroupe
1983	T. Harry Gatton
1984	David Stick
1985	Harley E. Jolley
1986	Guion Griffis Johnson
1987	Lindsay C. Warren Jr.
1988	Robert F. Durden
1989	Robert D. Douglas Jr.
1990	Mattie Erma Edwards Parker
1991	George E. London
1992	William N. Still
1993	Burton F. Beers
1994	Max R. Williams
1995	William S. Price Jr.
1996	Joseph F. Steelman and Lala Carr Steelman
1997	John L. Sanders
1998	Alan D. Watson
1999	Jerry C. Cashion
2000	Alexander R. Stoesen
2001	W. Keats Sparrow
2002	Willis P. Whichard
2003	Catherine Bishir and Michael Southern
2004	Holley Mack Bell and Clara Bond Bell
2005	Lindley S. Butler

Jerry C. Cashion

Croatan National Forest. In July 1936, under the authority granted by the 1911 Weeks Act, President Franklin D. Roosevelt designated as a national forest the 77,000 acres the federal government already owned in North Carolina's Craven, Carteret, and Jones Counties. The forest was named Croatan after the Indian tribe living in the region at the time of the so-called Lost Colony (1587). The federal government had originally acquired this land in 1933, 1934, and 1935 to use for reforestation experiments. The area, about one-half of which was pocosin, or raised bog, and the other half pine forest, had by then lost most of its timber either to forest fires or to lumbermen with little concern for conservation. The only profitable industry associated with that rugged terrain in recent years had been the manufacture of bootleg whiskey, large quantities of which were sold around Havelock and Stella during Prohibition.

Before Europeans arrived in North Carolina, Native American tribes had used this land to hunt and fish. They, like the Europeans and enslaved Africans who came later, found much of the area ill-suited for agriculture. During the colonial and early national periods, enterprising farmers built canals to drain Catfish Lake, Long Lake, and Lake Ellis in hopes of turning these spring-fed lakes into rice and cranberry plantations. Rice did better than cranberries, but neither prospered as well as the native vegetation (everything from 1,000-year-old cypress trees to five kinds of insect-eating plants) and wildlife, including American alligators, rare species of birds such as the peregrine falcon, half a dozen poisonous reptiles, and hundreds of varieties of fish.

By the early 2000s, Croatan National Forest incorporated more than 159,000 acres, including 30,000 acres designated by Congress in 1984 as official wilderness areas. Surrounded by Bogue Sound, the White Oak River, and the Neuse River and its tributary, the Trent, Croatan National Forest, with its unique estuaries and pocosins, continues to remind visitors of the scene many early European settlers must have encountered upon first reaching North Carolina's coast.

References: Sharyn Kane and Richard Keaton, *Southern National Forests* (1993); Marguerite Schumann, *The Living Land: An Outdoor Guide to North Carolina* (1977).

Thomas J. Farnham

CROATOAN was the sole complete word found on Roanoke Island by John White on 18 Aug. 1590 in his search for the English colonists, including his granddaughter Virginia Dare, whom he had left there three years earlier. White reported that the word in "fayre Capitall letters was graven" on one of the chief trees or posts of a palisade or stockade structure that had been built on Roanoke Island. Earlier in the day's search, White had seen the three Roman letters "CRO" carved into a tree on the bluff of the sound shore. In neither place did he discover a cross, the secretly agreed upon sign that the colony, now known as the Lost Colony, was in distress.

White's statements about the word and the absence of a cross indicate that he was comforted to find the word because he thought it was a "certaine token" or sign that the colonists had relocated to Croatan, the principal town of the Croatan (or Hatteras) Indians near Cape Hatteras. White recounted that the colonists had discussed leaving just such a message for him in 1587, although they had then considered moving 50 miles into the mainland rather than about 60 miles south to an isolated barrier island. White recognized Croatan as the native town of the Indian Manteo, who made two trips to England in the 1580s and seemingly had embraced the English colonial efforts. (It is believed that Manteo's mother was a tribal monarch of the Croatoans.)

Ethnologists and anthropologists believe that the word "Croatoan" may have been a combination of two Algonquian words meaning "talk town" or "council town."

References: David B. Quinn, *The Roanoke Voyages, 1584–1590* (2 vols., 1955); Quinn, *Set Fair for Roanoke: Voyages and Colonies, 1584–1606* (1985); David Stick, *Roanoke Island: The Beginnings of English America* (1983).

Phillip W. Evans

Croatoan Indians were a tribal group of Carolina Algonquians who probably inhabited both present-day Hatteras and Ocracoke Islands at the time of the arrival of the English explorers and colonists sent by Sir Walter Raleigh in the 1580s. Also called the Croatan, and later known as the Hatteras Indians, they were recognized as a distinct tribal group until the second half of the eighteenth century. Although they hunted and fished all along the northern Outer Banks and in its surrounding waters, their fields and towns were originally located on the forested sound side of Hatteras Island between modern-day Buxton and Hatteras. Theodore de Bry's 1590 map of Raleigh's Virginia showed three village symbols on Croatoan Island, now roughly the part of Hatteras Island that runs east to west. It is possible that the Croatoan also had a small habitation in the vicinity of present-day Ocracoke, then called "Wococon."

A scholar of Algonquian linguistics has suggested that the word "Croatoan" means "council town" or "talk town," which likely indicates the residence of an important leader and a place where councils were held. Archaeological remains of at least two other Croatoan villages have been located elsewhere on Hatteras Island. The Croatoan are best remembered today because the word "CROATOAN," carved in a post, was found by John White in 1590 in his search for the famous Lost Colony.

The Croatoan's principal town, Croatoan, was possibly located at a site on Cape Creek that has been identified and partially excavated by archaeologists. Undoubtedly, some modern-day residents of coastal North Carolina can claim with considerable justification to be the descendants of the Croatoan/Hatteras and other Algonquians of over two and three centuries ago, but no recognizable tribal entities survive. The remains of a sizable Indian village on Cape Creek and Pamlico Sound near Cape Hatteras have been discovered and to some extent explored by archaeologists under David Phelps of East Carolina University. In addition to artifacts of Indian manufacture, European trade goods have been recovered, giving added credibility to the recorded history of the Croatoan.

References: F. Roy Johnson, *The Algonquians: Indians of That Part of the New World First Visited by the English* (2 vols., 1972); David B. Quinn, *Set Fair for Roanoke: Voyages and Colonies, 1584–1606* (1985); David Stick, ed., *An Outer Banks Reader* (1998).

Phillip W. Evans

Crofter Immigration. The failed immigration of tenant farmers, or crofters, from the Scottish Highlands to the Sandhills region of eastern North Carolina in 1884 is one of the most peculiar instances of European immigration in the state's history. Scottish Americans residing in the area of present-day Scotland, Richmond, Hoke, Moore, Robeson, and Cumberland Counties were inspired to organize a scheme to introduce up to 350 Scottish Highland crofters into the old Highland settlement in the early 1880s. They launched the scheme after hearing of the extreme oppression experienced by these small landholders at the hands of their landlords and factors in their homeland and the organized resistance and rent strikes that began on the Isle of Skye in 1882. Worldwide attention was drawn to that region by a small skirmish between tenants and police known as the Battle of the Braes, which served as the beginning of popular uprisings throughout the Highlands against oppressive land tenure policies. Several of the crofters prominently involved in this event were among the parties that settled for a short time in North Carolina.

The plan, organized by Highlander Margaret MacLeod and others in Scotland, aimed to remove groups of crofters from their holdings on the Isles of Skye and Lewis, as well as other regions of the Scottish Highlands, and relocate them to the established Highland settlement of North Carolina. North Carolina's Highland settlement was thought to be an ideal home for these immigrants as it was expected that the established Scottish American families would foster the successful assimilation of the newly arrived Highland crofters. Private funds were collected for the scheme on both sides of the Atlantic; the North Carolina Bureau of Immigration, under the leadership of John T. Patrick, and the Seaboard Air Line Railway also contributed substantially to the effort. Local efforts were steered by James L. Cooley of Wagram. Unknown to the immigrants, Lord MacDonald and other prominent Highland landlords secretly contributed to the efforts as a means of ridding themselves of some of the land reform agitators and superfluous tenants.

The first group of crofters, numbering 73, arrived in North Carolina via Norfolk in March 1884 and was transported to Laurinburg under the care of Cooley and D. P. McEachern. From there the crofters dispersed throughout the community, as arranged by their sponsors. A second group arrived in May, and its 65 members were transported to the vicinity of Cameron under the care of Cooley and Frank W. Clark of the Seaboard Railway. Additional small parties arrived in Richmond County throughout the spring. Newspaper accounts touted the success of the immigration and spoke of the possibility of additional large parties that would arrive in coming months.

Upon arrival, however, the immigrants found that the promises of free land and employment held forth by MacLeod and others were not true. By July some newspapers reported dissatisfaction and unemployment among the crofters. It became apparent that many of these immigrants lacked the skills necessary to integrate into agricultural pursuits immediately and that many of the families were further handicapped by the fact that they spoke only Gaelic. There is also evidence that the host families had taken advantage of the opportunity for an ethnically attractive labor force, and that their sponsorship of the crofters had not been entirely humanitarian. Two of the crofters returned to Scotland in early July and reported to newspapers that "where work was obtained the only wages given was the bare food, and the houses provided were the small one-roomed huts formerly occupied by slaves."

By the fall of 1884 most of the crofters had made efforts to return to Scotland or relocate to other areas in the United States. Most of the immigrants eventually did return to their homeland, feeling deceived by the organizers and dissatisfied with their experiences in North Carolina. Newspapers of the day show that the crofters themselves were forced to bear most of the blame for the failure of the plan, although the reputation of state immigration agent John T. Patrick was severely tarnished by his association with the affair. As a result, the state did not engage in any further recruitment schemes for foreign immigrants in the late nineteenth century.

Only a handful of crofters remained in North Carolina, most being young men employed as farm overseers or in similar pursuits. One of the most notable families that remained was that of Alexander MacRae. After failing at agricultural efforts in Moore and Robeson Counties, MacRae was employed by businessman Hugh MacRae of Wilmington, who sent him to present-day Avery County to serve as foreman in building the Yonahlossee Turnpike between the new resort village of Linville and the town of Blowing Rock. MacRae and his family operated a guest house for tourists on what is now known as MacRae Meadow near Linville. This site would later become the location of one of the world's largest Scottish gatherings—the Highland Games at Grandfather Mountain.

Reference: Rowland T. Berthoff, *British Immigrants in Industrial America* (1953).

William S. Caudill

Crop Lien System was inaugurated in North Carolina in March 1867, when the General Assembly passed an Act to Secure Advances for Agricultural Purposes. Most former Confederate states passed similar laws during this time. They were made necessary by a post–Civil War cash shortage among both landowning and nonlandowning farmers, who found it difficult to purchase provisions for their families. Under the crop lien system, farmers could get fertilizer, farming equipment, groceries, and other goods by giving merchants a lien on their cash crops, the most desirable being cotton and tobacco. By providing credit until crops were harvested, merchants were allowed to charge higher prices for such purchases—usually adding a markup of 20 to 50 percent, but in some cases much higher. A rapid proliferation of country stores across North Carolina and the South was the result.

Abuses in the crop lien system reduced many tenant farmers to a state of economic slavery, as their debts to landlords and merchants carried over from one year to the next. Many landowners joined the ranks of farm tenants when excessive indebtedness led to foreclosure. An 1887 report of the state's Bureau of Labor Statistics stated that the crop lien system had proven "a worse curse to North Carolina than droughts, floods, cyclones, storms, rust, caterpillars, and every other evil that attends the farmer."

North Carolina leaders of the Farmers Union, which flourished from 1908 until the end of World War I, sought to abolish the crop lien system. Although ultimately not successful, they were able to see a bill go into effect in 1918 making it unlawful for merchants to accept more than 10 percent security above cash prices when goods were bought on time.

A rapid decline in farm tenancy after 1940 brought a corresponding decline in the number of crop liens, especially those signed over to supply-merchants. Landlords and farm lending institutions still use crops as debt security on a regular basis, although under more stringent protective legislation.

References: Hugh T. Lefler and Albert Ray Newsome, *North Carolina: The History of a Southern State* (1973); Charles P. Loomis, "Activities of the North Carolina Farmers' Union," *NCHR* 7 (October 1930); Stuart Noblin, *Leonidas LaFayette Polk: Agrarian Crusader* (1949).

K. Todd Johnson

Man being fitted with used clothes at the "ongoing yard sale" sponsored by Crossnore School as a way to raise money. Photograph by Bayard Wootten. NCC.

Crops. SEE Agriculture; Tobacco.

Crossnore School, a nondenominational Christian home for children located in the town of Crossnore in the Linville Valley of Avery County, was founded by two doctors, Mary Martin Sloop, of Davidson, and her husband, Eustace Sloop. The Sloops came to the mountains as medical missionaries. While Eustace devoted much of his time to the medical needs of the local people, Mary undertook what became a lifelong effort to provide educational opportunities to the region's children, among the poorest in the state. She believed strongly that young women needed to break the cycles of poverty and ignorance perpetuated by a tradition of early marriage and motherhood.

Mary Sloop solicited contributions of used clothing, which she organized into an "ongoing yard sale." Proceeds from this, plus individual gifts and, beginning in the 1920s, financial assistance from the Daughters of the American Revolution (DAR), provided the needed funds to start and expand Crossnore School. What began as a one-room schoolhouse in dreadful condition eventually became a complex of 20 buildings on more than 72 acres, including boarding facilities opened in 1913 for orphans and other children who lived too far to commute to the school. Improvements to schools and roads, modern methods of farming, and a hospital and dental clinic were also part of the Sloop legacy. Crossnore School continues to be privately supported by the DAR, civic groups, foundations, and individuals. Self-support also comes from a working farm and from the Weaving Room, begun as part of vocational training in the high school in 1923 and continuing today. Crossnore School still follows the original purpose of its founding, "to give aid, comfort, and improvement to the lives of poor or troubled children."

References: "The Angels of Avery County," *The State* (March 1996); Horton Cooper, *History of Avery County* (1964); Mary T. Martin Sloop with LeGette Blythe, *Miracle in the Hills* (1953); "They Help Us Learn to Be Happy," *The State* (October 1996).

Bryna R. Coonin

Crowfield Academy, a classical school in what is today Iredell County, was operated by Presbyterians from about 1760 to 1788. Although the school trained many prominent men, records pertaining to its operation are scattered and thin. The first published mention appears in W. H. Foote's 1846 history: "Dr. [James] McRee, in his manuscripts, tells us that there was a flourishing classical school in the bounds of Centre [Presbyterian Church] at a very early period, and after continuing about twenty years was broken up by the invasion." E. F. Rockwell, who taught at Davidson College, provided a fuller account of Crowfield in 1858 and suggested 1760 as the year of the school's opening. The American Revolution apparently interrupted studies at Crowfield, but in 1787 Charles Caldwell moved from nearby Clio's Nursery, a similar school, to reestablish it. Shortly thereafter the academy closed.

Writers have cited Crowfield as the germ out of which Davidson College grew and noted its influence on the University of North Carolina through providing early education to many of its first teachers and students. R. D. W. Connor made such claims in an address to the Daughters of the American Revolution upon the occasion of the placement of a plaque commemorating the school in 1931. Commonly cited as graduates of Crowfield are such important figures in North Carolina history as Samuel McCorkle, James Hall, Adlai Osborne, Ephraim Brevard, Andrew King, William Houston, and Charles Harris. Some sources indicate that David Caldwell taught at Crowfield briefly before moving in 1767 to Guilford County to open his own school. Others count future president of the University of North Carolina David Kerr among the instructors. E. F. Rockwell placed the site of Crowfield at an "old field" near the home of Alexander Osborne in southern Iredell County.

References: Homer M. Keever, *Iredell: Piedmont County* (1976); E. F. Rockwell, "The First Classical School in Western North Carolina," *North Carolina Journal of Education* 1 (July 1858).

Michael Hill

Crown was the term ordinarily used in the colonial period in speaking or writing of the king or queen of England as monarch; it also applied to the authority that position represented. The jeweled crown worn by the monarch on state occasions was the symbol of office, rank, and power; hence the use of the word "Crown" in this impersonal sense. The Lords Proprietors of Carolina constituted the earliest source of authority for the colony in England, and it was to them that leaders in Carolina usually turned for advice and guidance.

Negotiations between the Crown and the Proprietors to make Carolina a royal colony were concluded on or about 11 July 1728. It was only a short time before that date that Crown officials began to demonstrate serious interest in the colony. Even after North Carolina became a royal colony, however, many officials appointed by the Lords Proprietors continued in office for a time.

William S. Powell

CSX Corporation was formed in 1980 from the merger of the Chessie System Railway and the Seaboard Coast Line Railroad. Many of the company's North Carolina lines can be traced to the 1967 merger of the Atlantic Coast Line Railroad and the Seaboard Air Line Railway, which were subsequently absorbed by CSX; the Clinchfield Railroad was added in January 1983. CSX lines incorporated many previously important North Carolina lines, including the Virginia & Carolina Railroad; Seaboard & Roanoke Railroad; Raleigh & Gaston Railroad; High Point, Thomasville, and Denton Railroad; and Durham & Southern Railroad.

Headquartered in Jacksonville, Fla., CSX, by the early 2000s, operated the largest rail network in the eastern United States, a vast system of subsidiaries reaching Philadelphia, Miami, New Orleans, St. Louis, Chicago, Detroit, and Buffalo. In all, its routes covered 23,000 miles in 23 states, the District of Columbia, and parts of Canada. CSX operated 1,142 miles, or 34 percent, of North Carolina's railway system, with 1,400 employees in the state.

Operations were concentrated over three major and two additional routes. One north-south CSX main line connected the Northeast and Florida via Rocky Mount, Wilson, Fayetteville, and Pembroke. An east-west main line linked Wilmington and Charlotte with Atlanta and New Orleans. A second north-south main line (previously the Clinchfield) connected Detroit to Atlanta via Marion. A CSX local route also ran from Rocky Mount eastward, serving Greenville and Plymouth; another operated as a local service route between Norlina and Hamlet by way of Raleigh.

CSX's major North Carolina facilities included freight classification yards at Hamlet, Rocky Mount, Charlotte, and Wilmington; locomotive servicing at Hamlet and Rocky Mount; an intermodal terminal at Charlotte; and bulk-intermodal terminals at Charlotte, Winston-Salem, Apex, and Wilmington. The railroad maintained an industrial development office in Charlotte.

George A. Kennedy

SEE ALSO Atlantic Coast Line Railroad; Seaboard Air Line Railway.

Culpeper's Rebellion in 1677–78 was the most significant of the many rebellions and coups of the Proprietary period in Albemarle County. A variety of problems led to the unrest in the colony that finally resulted in the overthrow of the provincial government. The Albemarle colony was a geographically isolated backwater frontier settlement that fostered self-government and individual initiative. Showing greater interest in their economically more promising colony of Charles Towne (now Charleston, S.C.) in southern Carolina, the Lords Proprietors paid little heed to the growing problems in Albemarle. By the mid-1670s the colony's government was on shaky ground from long-term internal power struggles, an uncertain land policy, rumors that the Proprietors might relinquish the colony to Governor Sir William Berkeley of Virginia, the institution of the more structured semifeudal Fundamental Constitutions, and the lack of commissioned officials. The economy was dealt a severe blow by the Plantation Duty Act of 1673, which imposed a burdensome duty on tobacco to ensure its export to England. If enforced, this duty would curtail the New England intercoastal traders, who were willing to brave the treacherous waters of North Carolina. Another factor that may have inspired the upheaval was that some of the rebels fled into Albemarle after Bacon's Rebellion in Virginia in 1676.

The last commissioned governor of Albemarle, Peter Carteret, left for England in 1672 to air the colony's grievances with the Lords Proprietors, appointing John Jenkins to be president of the council (acting governor). As the years passed with no relief and the commissions of Jenkins and the council ran out, there was increasing discontent in the colony among the political opposition. Jenkins was briefly deposed by Thomas Eastchurch and then returned to power. Eastchurch, appealing to the Proprietors, was commissioned governor in 1676. On the return voyage he tarried in the West Indies to court a new wife, sending his assistant Thomas Miller on to Albemarle as the deputy governor. Although Eastchurch had no legal authority to make this appointment, Miller was initially accepted by most of the colony's settlers on his arrival in July 1677. Miller's political enemies increased, however, when he began collecting the customs duties, seizing cargoes and ships, and making arbitrary arrests.

On 1 Dec. 1677 Miller arrested a popular New England trader named Zachariah Gillam, who had brought arms in his ship, and George Durant, a key leader in the opposition faction. By 3 December John Culpeper, who had earlier been involved in unrest in Charles Towne, had organized armed parties to release Gillam and Durant, arrest Miller and council member John Nixon, and seize the county records and seal. Culpeper's "Remonstrance" became the call for revolt throughout the colony, and the deputy customs collectors, Henry Hudson and Timothy Biggs, also were captured. At a rebel assembly on 24–25 December, Miller was to be tried, but a proclamation condemning the revolt from Governor Eastchurch, who had arrived in Virginia, broke up the meeting. Miller and Biggs were committed to a temporary prison. A rebel council with Jenkins as the acting president took over the government, and John Culpeper was elected customs collector. Eastchurch's untimely death ended the threat to suppress the rebellion from Virginia.

Early in 1678 Biggs escaped to England and was rewarded by the Lords Proprietors with appointment as comptroller of customs. To bring order to the colony, the Proprietors named one of their own, Seth Sothel, as governor. On the voyage to the colony, however, Sothel was captured and held for ransom

by North African pirates. John Harvey, a respected planter of Albemarle, was appointed governor, receiving his commission in the summer of 1679. When Miller escaped to England, his account led to the arrest and trial for treason of Culpeper, who also had gone to England to explain his actions to the Proprietors. To circumvent the voiding of their charter, the Proprietors chose to defend Culpeper and were able to achieve an acquittal. This trial apparently is the reason the rebellion bears his name.

References: Lindley S. Butler and Alan D. Watson, eds., *The North Carolina Experience: An Interpretive and Documentary History* (1984); Mattie Erma Edwards Parker, "Legal Aspects of 'Culpeper's Rebellion,'" NCHR 45 (April 1968); Hugh F. Rankin, *Upheaval in Albemarle: The Story of Culpeper's Rebellion, 1675–1689* (1962).

Lindley S. Butler

Cultural Resources, Department of. The Department of Art, Culture, and History was created by the Executive Organization Act of 1971 and activated in 1972. By this statute, various commissions, boards, and independent state agencies were consolidated and placed under the new department. The formerly independent agencies included the North Carolina State Library, founded in 1812; the Department of Archives and History, formed in 1943 from the North Carolina Historical Commission, which dates from 1903; the North Carolina Museum of Art, established in 1965 as an outgrowth of the North Carolina State Art Society, Inc. (1979); and the North Carolina Symphony, organized in 1932. While these agencies retained their statutory functions and authority, managerial and executive responsibilities were transferred to the head of the new department, a cabinet-level secretary appointed by the governor.

The department was replaced by the Executive Organization Act of 1973 with the Department of Cultural Resources (DCR), whose secretary continues to have administrative responsibility for the department, including such culture-related boards and commissions as the Edenton Historical Commission; the Bath, Hillsborough, Murfreesboro, North Carolina, and Tryon Palace Commissions; and the USS *North Carolina* Battleship and First Flight Centennial Commissions.

The modern DCR attempts to fulfill its mission of enhancing the cultural life of citizens and visitors through the preservation, development, promotion, and dissemination of artistic, historical, and informational resources; the exploration and interpretation of the state's collective culture; and the provision of access to that culture through its various programs. Administratively, the DCR is divided into the Office of Archives and History and the Office of Arts and Libraries. Within these offices are numerous divisions, including the Division of State Historic Sites, the Division of State History Museums, the State Archives, the State Historic Preservation

Office, the Office of State Archaeology, the Historic Publications Section, the State Library, the Arts Council, and the North Carolina Symphony.

Wiley J. Williams

SEE ALSO Archives and History, Office of; Library, State; State Historic Sites Program.

Culture Week brought together annually an unusual assemblage of North Carolina historical and cultural organizations from the late 1930s to around 1970. Under the supervision of the State Literary and Historical Association, some of the state's cultural elite went to Raleigh and spent the entire week at the Sir Walter Hotel, usually the headquarters for the participating groups. Art and historical exhibitions, poetry readings, musical concerts, performances, recitations, addresses, and presentation of art, history, literary, and other cultural awards filled the week. With tongue in cheek, Jonathan Daniels, then the editor of the *Raleigh News and Observer*, accused fellow North Carolinians of trying to imbibe all of their culture in one week so they could ignore it the remainder of the year. Rather than taking offense, C. Christopher Crittenden, secretary of the Literary and Historical Association from 1935 through 1967 and thus chief coordinator of the various meetings, appropriated Daniels's term "Culture Week" as the unofficial designation of the annual assemblage.

H. G. Jones

Cumberland County, located in North Carolina's Coastal Plain region, was formed from Bladen County in 1754. Its name is derived from the title of Prince William Augustus, the duke of Cumberland, the son of King George II who was the victorious commander at the Battle of Culloden in 1746. In 1778 Campbellton, consolidated with nearby Cross Creek, was designated the county seat, and in 1783 the town was renamed Fayetteville in honor of the Marquis de Lafayette, the French general who fought for American independence during the Revolutionary War. Other communities in the county include Falcon, Godwin, Hope Mills, Linden, Spring Lake, Stedman, and Wade.

The area that became Cumberland County was first settled by Highland Scots in the late 1720s. It remained largely undeveloped, however, through the early twentieth century, when construction began on a U.S. military training camp in the northwest corner of the county. Upon its completion in early 1919, Camp (later Fort) Bragg, named after native North Carolinian and Confederate general Braxton Bragg, quickly established close ties with the nearby Fayetteville community. As the base swelled to become one of the largest military installations in the country, Fayetteville experienced significant growth and commercialization to accommodate the military personnel and their families; in the process, Cumberland County rose to become the fifth-most-populous county in North Carolina, with a population estimated at nearly 311,000 in 2004.

Cumberland County's historic landmarks and institutions include the Averasboro Battlefield and Museum, site of the Civil War battle of March 1865; and Fayetteville's Museum of the Cape Fear, Airborne and Special Operations Museum, 82nd Airborne Division War Memorial Museum, and Fayetteville Museum of Art. County agricultural products include tobacco, corn, soybeans, cotton, peanuts, beef cattle, and chickens. Cumberland County facilities manufacture textiles, brick and concrete products, metal products, plastics, power tools, and other items.

Reference: Roy Parker Jr., *Cumberland County: A Brief History* (1990).

Robert Blair Vocci

SEE ALSO Averasboro, Battle of; Fayetteville; Fort Bragg; Museum of the Cape Fear.

Cupola House, a two-and-one-half-story frame house located at 408 South Broad Street in Historic Edenton, is one of the most architecturally significant structures in North Carolina. A unique blend of architectural styles and construction methods, it illustrates both sophisticated and naive vernacular craftsmanship. Noted for its richly detailed interior woodwork, including what many consider the finest early stairway in North Carolina, the house incorporates Jacobean, colonial New England, and early Southern Georgian influences. The house, named for its striking octagonal cupola, was designated a National Historic Landmark in 1970.

Located on lot 1 of the 1722 plan for Edenton, the house initially commanded an expanse that extended to the wharves along nearby Edenton Bay. In subsequent years, outbuildings and commercial structures were also built on the lot. Several owners altered the house itself during the nineteenth century.

Architectural historians long debated the construction history of the Cupola House. Some argued that the core structure was built as early as 1726, when records indicate a residence existed on the site. Dendrochronology tests in 1991, however, support the belief that the present-day house was built in 1758–59 for Francis Corbin, land agent for Lord Granville and prominent colonial official. In 1777 Samuel Dickinson, a prominent Edenton physician, bought the property. He and his descendants owned it for the next 141 years.

Long admired by architectural and decorative arts experts, the Cupola House in 1918 came to the attention of representatives of the Brooklyn Museum in New York, who were seeking colonial and early American antiques and house interiors in the Southeast to incorporate in the museum's American Rooms exhibit. Within three weeks of their initial visit, they arranged to purchase all the interior woodwork and some of the

Cupola House. Photograph by Tim Buchman. Courtesy of Preservation North Carolina.

antique furnishings of the Cupola House. Removal of the first floor woodwork began almost immediately. Installed in the Brooklyn Museum in 1927–28, the materials remain on display there in the Department of Decorative Arts.

The impending loss of the Cupola House outraged much of Edenton. Ten prominent citizens quickly met and formed the Cupola House Library and Museum Association in an effort to save the house. The group bought the second-floor woodwork and staircase back from the Brooklyn Museum representatives and made plans to buy the house and convert it into a museum and public library.

The Cupola House Library and Museum Association was the first community organization specifically established to save a particular historic building in North Carolina. In addition to acquiring the Cupola House, association members established the Shepard-Pruden Memorial (Public) Library, which occupied the building's first floor from 1921 until 1963. The association developed a museum on the second floor. In 1965–66, master artisans created and installed in the house

careful reproductions of the original downstairs woodwork removed to the Brooklyn Museum. Today, the Cupola House is maintained as a historic house museum.

References: Bruce S. Cheeseman, "The History of the Cupola House, 1724–1777," *Journal of Early Southern Decorative Arts* 15 (May 1989); Cheeseman, "The Survival of the Cupola House: 'A Venerable Old Mansion,'" *NCHR* 63 (January 1986); Mary A. Coffey and Murphy Moss, *Deliverance of a Treasure: The Cupola House Association and Its Mission* (1995).

Robert G. Anthony Jr.

Curfew is a term derived from the words "cover fire," a command issued by officials directing retirement for the night or restricting movement to a designated area or period. Authority to order this action in North Carolina was sustained by law or was provided for in a town charter. It was broadly applied on standing order; it also might be enforced when special needs prevailed to ensure public safety, to prevent looting, or for other reasons. In 1807 Edenton had an ordinance requiring that town streets be cleared by a set time. However, free blacks with proper identification could remain out until 10:00 P.M. Many towns had curfews that applied to all blacks, free or slave. Free blacks could not be in the house of a slave without the owner's permission. It was customary for plantation overseers to ring a curfew bell at 9:30 P.M. and soon afterward to make rounds to see that occupants had retired. In 1807 children in Salisbury and Raleigh became so rowdy at night that the town commissioners were asked to restrain them.

During the Union occupation of New Bern in 1862 and 1863, a curfew was established for the men in uniform, and sentinels were posted in three sections of the town to enforce it. Curfews have been authorized during disasters such as fires, hurricanes, and floods to protect life and property.

References: John R. Barden, ed., *Letters to the Home Circle* (1998); Guion G. Johnson, *Ante-Bellum North Carolina: A Social History* (1937); Alan D. Watson, "Slavery in the Lower Cape Fear," *Waves and Currents* 19 (January 1999).

William S. Powell

Currency

Currency problems in various forms troubled North Carolinians until well into the twentieth century. During the eighteenth century, most North Carolinians rarely saw specie (gold or silver coins) at all, and even paper money was in short supply or considered unreliable. The American Revolution created new monetary demands, and the state of North Carolina authorized approximately nine separate issues of paper money to defray the costs of the war and the state administration from 1775 through 1785. The U.S. Constitution, which, among other things, prohibited the states from issuing paper money, was adopted in 1789 and ended the long history of North Carolina provincial and state paper money.

Diverse Currency and Severe Money Shortages in Colonial North Carolina

The Carolina colony's monetary unit was the British pound or pound sterling, and paper currency was valued in pounds, shillings, and pence. Pence (the plural of "penny") were valued at 240 pence to the pound. In 1755 Governor Arthur Dobbs suggested that the mint in England consider producing copper coins for use in North Carolina in denominations of half pence, pence, and two-penny pieces, using copper supplied by the colony. Although Dobbs submitted calculations demonstrating the advantages such a step would have on the colony's financial condition, the idea was rejected.

During the colonial period, the various British Navigation Acts were perhaps the foremost cause of North Carolina's currency problems. Under the acts, provinces such as North Carolina were expected to provide cheap raw materials and in turn furnish a captive market for Britain's more costly manufac-

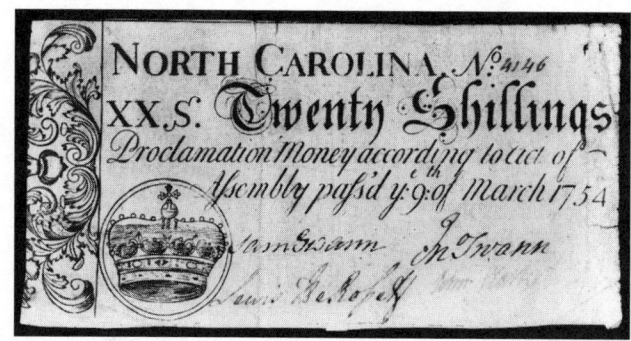

A North Carolina twenty-shilling note of 1754. Images in the lower left (in this case a crown) varied by denomination so as to enable those who could not read to distinguish between the various denominations of currency. NCC.

tured goods. This resulted in a flow of specie out of the colony to Britain, since North Carolina farmers and planters received relatively low prices for their agricultural products and raw materials and paid high cash or credit prices for imported finished goods.

To supplement the relatively small amount of English coins in circulation, coins from other countries were widely circulated. The most popular was the Spanish milled dollar, a large piece usually valued at four shillings sixpence in British currency. The French écu, the Portuguese crusado, and the rixdollars of the Holy Roman Empire, Denmark, and the Netherlands, as well as other coins also circulated in the American colonies. Strands of seashell beads were one other type of money used by colonists, who adopted this medium of exchange—generally known as wampum—from Native Americans. Indians in this region made two distinct types of wampum: disk-shaped beads called "roanoke" and longer, tube-shaped beads known as "peak." In 1709 explorer and surveyor John Lawson recorded the common values of wampum in the Carolina colony.

A persistent lack of money prompted North Carolina and other colonies to print their own paper currencies and to rely on barter. In 1715 North Carolina's provincial government sanctioned a form of barter to sustain economic growth, approving the use of "the chief Produce of the Country" to pay public and private debts. Known as commodity money, this multitiered system had been used informally as early as 1694. In lieu of money, set quantities of tobacco, butter, tar, pitch, feathers, deer skins, beef, pork, whale oil, wheat, and other commodities could be used by citizens to pay their taxes and rents and to satisfy other expenses.

The North Carolina colony tried other means of increasing the supply of currency, or circulating medium. The legislature tried to increase the supply of coins, but North Carolina had no known supplies of gold or silver (until the discovery of gold near Charlotte in the 1830s), and Britain forbade the colonies to coin their own money. An available solution was to try to encourage the flow of coins into the province. As early as 1715, the North Carolina General Assembly declared the official value of British, Spanish, and other European silver and gold coins to be higher than their intrinsic bullion value in the hope that these coins would flow into the colony. This was not successful, however, since many British colonies were engaged in the same pursuit, and the British parliament subsequently made it illegal to rate coins at over one-third of their bullion value.

The most common and more successful solution, however, was the issue of fiat paper money, or "proclamation" money. Proclamation money was essentially a way of setting consistent values for the wide variety of currencies and commodities that served as money in the colony. To standardize this bewildering variety of currencies, the General Assembly would "proclaim" what the relative values of these kinds of money would be in North Carolina. In addition, proclamation money notes issued by North Carolina were essentially IOUs to cover the cost of necessary public works, such as fortifications. They were to be withdrawn from circulation when they were returned to the colony in payment of taxes, and the government would burn the bills they took in each year.

The need for funds to wage war against the Tuscarora Indians prompted North Carolina's government to issue its first paper money in 1712 (£4,000 in bills of credit) and more the following year. Since there was no printer in North Carolina at the time, all of these bills and others issued in 1715, 1722, and 1729 were handwritten. Thereafter, printed bills were used by the provincial government to pay its growing expenses, many of which related to the colony's defense. Appropriations of paper money were made by the General Assembly in 1748 to build two forts—one at Cape Fear, another at Ocracoke—to protect the coastal region from repeated attacks by the Spanish. The outbreak of the French and Indian War in 1754 prompted North Carolina again to issue £40,000 in bills to fund the construction of more forts and equip its troops.

The overissue and counterfeiting of paper money eroded public confidence in colonial currency issues. The disorderly effects of these paper currencies became so severe that Parliament's passage of the Currency Act of 1764 and further legislation in London in 1773 forbade nearly all forms of colonial money. By that time North Carolina had already issued more than £350,000 in paper.

Revolution-Era Currency and the Importance of North Carolina Gold Production

During the American Revolution, monetary instability proved to be as much of a threat to the American cause as British muskets. In North Carolina, the provisional government had an empty treasury and no credit. Money was still needed to govern and equip troops, so North Carolina officials resorted once again to printing currency. In Philadelphia, to help finance America's war effort, the Continental Congress authorized the printing of Continental currency in dollars. Between 1775 and 1779, North Carolina and the other colonies were flooded with over $241 million in this money. Since little or no hard money supported this currency, it depreciated until it became virtually worthless.

The American dollar took its name from the large Spanish coin known to British colonists as the Spanish milled dollar, which was similar in size to the German Joachimsthaler, or thaler. The German thaler was eventually Anglicized into dollar. Small value Continental bills were in fractions of dollars. The current system of using 100 cents to equal 1 dollar was introduced in 1792 at the urging of Thomas Jefferson.

Most of North Carolina's revolutionary currencies were printed by James Davis, the colony's first printer, in New Bern and Hugh Walker in Wilmington. During the Revolution, Davis was entirely responsible for North Carolina's 1778 and 1780 money issues. His colleague, Walker, produced the intervening 1779 currency.

The values of North Carolina's wartime currencies had nearly collapsed by 1780, and after the Revolution all of the Continental currency and other moneys issued during the conflict were discredited. Since sizable deposits of gold or silver had not yet been found in the United States, and the supply of coins minted by the new national government remained insufficient, North Carolina found it necessary to print its own currency in 1783 and again in 1785. To distinguish these issues from the worthless Continental dollars, this new money carried values in British denominations: pounds, shillings, and pence.

When North Carolina joined the Union in 1789, the state government was forbidden by the U.S. Constitution to print money or mint coins. Although the U.S. Mint in Philadelphia began operation in 1792, it was many years before it and subsequent branches could strike and circulate enough coins to satisfy the needs of the states. Foreign coins remained legal tender until 1857. The central government did not specifically forbid the production of money in the private sector by individuals or businesses; as a result, until the Civil War most of North Carolina's paper money was issued by private commercial banks.

Gold from North Carolina mines began to add to the supply of coinage in the 1830s. German jewelers Christopher and Augustus Bechtler operated a private mint in Rutherford County from 1831 to about 1849, using gold from nearby mines. North Carolina gold also served the federal government. Prior to 1829, the state furnished all of the native gold coined in Philadelphia at the U.S. Mint. A branch of the federal mint was established in Charlotte in 1837, and it produced gold coins for the federal government until the Civil War, when it was seized by Confederate forces. Combined, the public operation in Charlotte and the Bechtlers' private mint produced almost $9 million in coinage before 1861.

The Civil War and the Nationalization of the Monetary System

By 1860 there were 36 banks in North Carolina, issuing many millions of dollars in bank notes. Nearly all of the currency by the 1850s was being printed for the banks by engraving firms in New York and Philadelphia. These currencies were far more elaborate in design than earlier varieties. Their detailed images and overlays of color challenged even the most skillful counterfeiters.

North Carolina joined the Confederacy in 1861, and the Confederate Constitution, like its federal counterpart, reserved the coining of money for the South's central government. It did not, however, specifically restrict the states from producing money in other forms. Since the Confederacy's national government lacked adequate metal reserves to produce coinage, it was forced to rely on paper currency to finance the war against the North. Authorities in each of the Confederate states also printed their own notes. As a result, the South's overall monetary system included a wide assortment of paper currencies.

Between 1861 and 1865, North Carolina authorized the printing of over $16 million in treasury notes. This amount was small when compared to the monstrous sums issued by the Confederate government, but for North Carolina it proved to be too much. The strains of war made it impossible for the state's currency to hold its value. In the closing months of the Civil War, runaway inflation and the advancing Union armies led to the frantic production and distribution of southern currency. Clothing and basic foodstuffs by then were commanding huge prices, and gold or other personal valuables, not paper money, were required to buy them. By early 1865, a North Carolinian needed as much as $600 to buy a pair of shoes and $1,500 to purchase an overcoat.

The federal financing of the Civil War led to the nationalization of all U.S. currency. In 1863 the United States began issuing national bank notes. These notes were printed by the authority of the federal government, but they were issued through private banks in the North and, after the war, throughout the entire country. Thousands of private banks were eventually granted national banking charters and were allowed to issue bank notes. In 1865, soon after the fall of the Confederacy, the National Bank of Charlotte became the first of 147 banks in North Carolina that received such a charter.

Since 1887 all U.S. paper currency has been made by the Bureau of Engraving and Printing in Washington, D.C. In an effort to further centralize the nation's monetary system, the U.S. government in 1913 established the Federal Reserve System. This system continues to be the means by which the flow of U.S. currency is controlled, credit is regulated, and cash is introduced into the economy. The paper currencies now used in the United States are Federal Reserve notes. North Carolina is located in the Fifth Federal Reserve District, an area served financially by the Federal Reserve Bank in Richmond, Va.

References: Grover C. Criswell, Douglas B. Ball, and Hugh Shull, *Comprehensive Catalog of Confederate Paper Money* (1996); John J. McCusker, *Money and Exchange in Europe and America, 1600–1775: A Handbook* (1978); Mattie Erma Edwards Parker, *Money Problems of Early Tar Heels* (1957); Alan D. Watson, *Money and Monetary Problems in Early North Carolina* (1980).

John R. deTreville
R. Neil Fulghum
Additional research provided by David A. Norris, John Paden, and Louis P. Towles.

SEE ALSO Bechtler Mint; Counterfeiting.

Currituck County, located in the Coastal Plain region of northeastern North Carolina, was formed in 1668, with its name taken from an Indian word meaning "land of the wild geese." It partially borders the state of Virginia and Currituck Sound, Albemarle Sound, and the Atlantic Ocean. The early inhabitants of the county were the Pasquotank Indians, followed by English and French Huguenot settlers. Currituck, the county seat, is named for the county. The town has never officially been incorporated, although it is mentioned in records dated as early as 1755. Other communities in Currituck County —all, like Currituck, unincorporated—include Corolla, Tulls Creek, Coinjock, Knotts Island, and Sligo.

Currituck County encompasses the northernmost section of the Outer Banks and is largely surrounded by bodies of water, which dominate its culture and economy. The county was home to one of North Carolina's first ports. It contains several wildlife sanctuaries, including the Currituck National Wildlife Refuge. It is also home to the largest population of "Banker" ponies, descendants of a breed of Spanish mustangs left by early explorers.

Currituck County agricultural products include potatoes, wheat, corn, strawberries, peanuts, soybeans, hay, swine, beef cattle, and chickens. It boasts a number of landmarks and historic sites, such as the Haywood Bell House, dating from before the American Revolution, and the Currituck Beach Lighthouse, constructed in 1875. The Albemarle and Chesapeake Canal, built between 1855 and 1859, bisects the county at its midpoint. County cultural institutions include the Currituck County Library. The county hosts several annual events, such as the Currituck Wildlife Festival, the Corolla Seafood Festival, and the Currituck County Resource Fair. In 2004 the population of Currituck County was estimated to be just under 22,000.

Jay Mazzocchi

SEE ALSO Wild Horses.

D

Daily Tar Heel, the student newspaper of the University of North Carolina at Chapel Hill (UNC) and the oldest college daily in the South, commenced publication as a weekly on 23 Feb. 1893. Titled the *Tar Heel*, the paper appeared under the auspices of the University Athletic Association until 1929, when its name was changed to the *Daily Tar Heel* and UNC's Publications Union took over operations. Early on, the newspaper briefly encountered competition from the *White and Blue*, a weekly that objected to the *Tar Heel*'s excessive coverage of sports events and fraternity interests to the exclusion of other campus activities. When the *Tar Heel* agreed to broaden its coverage of campus events, the *White and Blue* ceased publication and its editors agreed to help improve the *Tar Heel*, which soon established itself as one of the finest college newspapers in the nation.

While flourishing on campus and in the Chapel Hill community, the *Daily Tar Heel* was not immune to controversy. In the 1950s the paper voiced its opposition to athletics and the hiring of Jim Tatum as varsity football coach, prompting campuswide furor and an election to recall the editors. In the fall of 1969 a controversy emerged over the financial support of the campus newspaper through mandatory student fees. The Committee for a Free Press, composed of nine UNC students, declared that such fees were unconstitutional. In September 1974 U.S. District Court judge Eugene A. Gordon ruled in the paper's favor; the plaintiffs then appealed to the U.S. Fourth Circuit Court, which upheld the lower court's ruling. On 23 Feb. 1976 the U.S. Supreme Court, by refusing to hear the case, upheld the constitutionality of the fees. The funding decision was upheld for a second time by Judge Gordon and in April 1983 by the Fourth Circuit Court of Appeals. In February 1990 UNC students voted to allow the paper to return student fees over a three-year period, after the publishers determined that the paper could operate by using only advertising revenues. On that basis, some consider 1993, the paper's centennial year, to signal the beginning of true editorial freedom for the *Daily Tar Heel*.

One of the *Daily Tar Heel*'s proudest legacies is the memorable careers of many of its editors and writers through the years. This list includes Edward Kidder Graham and Frank Porter Graham, UNC presidents; J. C. B. Ehringhaus, state legislator and governor; C. Phillips Russell, Oscar J. Coffin, and Walter Spearman, professors at UNC's journalism school; Charles N. Hauser, publisher of the *Providence Journal* (Rhode Island); Orville B. Campbell, longtime editor and publisher of the *Chapel Hill Weekly*; Charles Kuralt, CBS news correspondent; Thomas Wolfe, Pulitzer Prize–winning author; Edwin M. Yoder, *Washington Post* columnist; Jonathan Worth Daniels, longtime editor of the *Raleigh News and Observer*; R. D. W. Connor, UNC librarian, history professor, and the first archivist of the United States; Rolfe Neill, publisher of the *Charlotte Observer*; and Jeff MacNelly, Pulitzer Prize–winning cartoonist and creator of the comic strip *Shoe*, named for legendary newspaperman and UNC journalism professor Jim Shumaker.

Wiley J. Williams

Dairy Industry. Until commercial dairies became commonplace in the early years of the twentieth century, milking dairy cows was a daily chore on North Carolina farms, providing families with fresh milk, cream, and butter. In 1914 John A. Arey of Iredell County was named to the dairy division of the U.S. Department of Agriculture and began assisting North Carolina farmers in good dairy management. Arey was a pioneer in farm extension work and helped establish high standards for dairy farming in the state.

After 1900, in areas of North Carolina where farms were changing from row crops to livestock (primarily the Piedmont and western regions), some farmers with milk surpluses started regular dairy routes. These routes gave farmers ready cash each month rather than forcing them to wait for the annual row crop harvest. Small dairies, or creameries, usually served nearby geographic areas, selling fresh milk, butter, and ice cream to local families. By the early 1940s, such creameries were delivering milk to homes and grocery stores daily. These creameries often developed their own brand names in direct competition with some of the larger processors such as Pet and Sealtest.

The year 1938 marked the beginning of a growth trend in North Carolina dairy herds and an improvement in the overall quality of milk in the state. In 1944, for the first time in North Carolina's history, the state produced enough milk for both home consumption and export to other states. North Carolina continued to appropriate funds specifically for dairy industry support in the annual budget from that time to the present. Dairy farmers were able to get more milk from each cow through better nutrition, care, and facilities. Eventually this success resulted in overproduction, and some dairy herds were sold off.

In 1936 the Carnation Company of Wisconsin established a new facility in Statesville to produce condensed milk. By 1940 the Carnation factory was in full operation. Fresh milk was delivered to Statesville from initial receiving plants across the state at Albemarle, Shelby, Spruce Pine, and other areas as well as from nearby dairy farms. During the 1950s and 1960s, more than 35,000 gallons of milk were being received each day at the Carnation plant at Statesville.

By 1953 more than 300 dairies existed in Iredell County, which has been the leading dairy county in North Carolina since records were officially kept. (Randolph, Allegheny, Alexander, and Rowan Counties have also maintained substantial numbers of dairy cows.) The state's dairy farmers sold their Grade A milk (a designation that signifies wholesomeness, not quality) to major processors in their region and across the state. Lower-grade milk went to Carnation in Statesville, along with surplus Grade A milk.

As grocery chains grew larger they developed their own in-store brands, which were often sold at a lower price. This forced many dairies to merge with larger companies such as Dairymen Cooperative, which processed the dairy products for major grocery chains.

The N.C. Department of Agriculture reported that in 1947 there were 350,000 dairy cows on North Carolina farms; that year these cows produced 175 million gallons of milk. Milk output per dairy cow continued to improve over the next half century, although the number of dairy cows in the state dropped drastically. By 1995 the average output per cow had increased to 1,894 gallons of milk. There were more than 400 commercial dairies in North Carolina at the start of the twenty-first century, maintaining approximately 69,000 dairy cows. Few of the small and medium-size creameries remained. A handful of specialty ice cream companies were exceptions and continued successful operations, such as Mooresville Ice Cream Company in the town of Mooresville.

Chester Paul Middlesworth

SEE ALSO Town Milk.

Dance as a religious ritual, community pastime, and performing art has existed throughout North Carolina history. From the ritual dances of the region's Native Americans, particularly the Cherokee, to the shag dancing popular in beach parties of the 1950s, the state's residents adapted their various ethnic dance traditions and added movements and variations to develop new styles. Some of these dance forms, handed down through generations of families, are familiar features of dance festivals and organizations. Such forms as buck dancing, clogging, square dancing, and step dancing all reflect the state's Native American, European, and African heritage. Dance as a performing art is widely supported by North Carolinians as well, and the state is home to numerous ballet, modern, jazz, and ethnic dance companies and to organizations dedicated to preserving traditional dance forms.

In the twentieth century, some North Carolinians initiated efforts to preserve and revive indigenous dance as part of preserving a group's culture and heritage. An interest in Appalachian mountain culture in the 1920s and 1930s inspired folklife festivals and dance groups to preserve and present indigenous square dancing, clogging, and other variations on traditional mountain dances. Similarly, the Eastern Band of Cherokee Indians and other North Carolina Native American tribes have worked to revive their dance heritage at different times, drawing on memory and anthropologists' records to document and preserve the dances that were once part of religious ceremonies and community celebrations.

Organized ballet companies in North Carolina date to 1959, when the Area Ballet Company formed in Raleigh. The founding of the dance program at the North Carolina School of the Arts (NCSA) in 1965 encouraged more groups to organize. The North Carolina Dance Theatre (NCDT) was created in 1970 as a professional affiliate to the NCSA by Robert Lindgren with a grant from the Rockefeller Foundation. Lindgren, a former leading dancer with the Ballet Russe de Monte Carlo and the New York City Ballet, had extensive touring experience before beginning a teaching career. In 1965 he was appointed dean of the School of Dance at NCSA, a position he held at the time of the creation of the North Carolina Dance Theatre.

The NCDT moved from Winston-Salem to Charlotte in 1992 and is housed in the Blumenthal Center for Performing Arts. DancePlace, the official school for the NCDT, offers classes in various dance techniques to students of all ages and interests, summer intensives, and the opportunity for students to audition for NCDT's annual production of *The Nutcracker*.

In 1997 North Carolina established a new "state" ballet company, which was named the Carolina Ballet. Located in Raleigh, the Carolina Ballet is a professional company that emerged from the vision of Ward Purrington, a Raleigh lawyer, and the work of Ann Vorus, who founded the Raleigh Dance Theatre in 1985. That company became the Carolina Ballet Theatre, and Purrington approached Vorus and Mary LeGere, artistic director since 1994, about taking the company to professional status. Both declined the offer, preferring to concentrate on the Raleigh School of Ballet, and Purrington became board chairman of the Carolina Ballet.

Following an extensive search, Robert Weiss was hired as artistic director of the Carolina Ballet. A former principal dancer with the New York City Ballet, Weiss also brought eight years of experience and success as artistic director of the Pennsylvania Ballet. The Carolina Ballet's inaugural season began in October 1998 at Raleigh's Memorial Auditorium with an all-Balanchine program. Led by Weiss, the Carolina Ballet has surged forward in its goal to be a nationally recognized company. The company has attracted quality dancers and choreographers from across the nation. Performing both traditional ballets and original works by Weiss and local choreographers, the Carolina Ballet's quality and innovation have attracted much attention to North Carolina's ballet community.

Other dance companies, focusing on ballet, modern, and other forms, thrive in the state. The Area Ballet Company settled at East Carolina University in 1965, becoming a resident company for that school's dance program. Since 1984 Durham's African American Dance Ensemble has performed high-quality African and American dance for both local and international audiences. The North Carolina Dance Alliance (NCDA) was established in 1982 with assistance from the North Carolina Arts Council. It is a nonprofit service organization that supports dance activity in North Carolina, provides a statewide network of communication within the dance community, and acts as an advocate for dance in North Carolina. The NCDA represents individuals and organizations who are involved in all areas of dance, including choreography and performance, dance therapy, administration, dance education, dance patronage, and modern, ballet, jazz, tap, folk, ethnic, social, and theatrical dance forms.

References: Mike Seeger and Ruth Pershing, *Talking Feet: Buck, Flatfoot, and Tap: Solo Southern Dance of the Appalachian, Piedmont, and Blue Ridge Mountain Regions* (1992); Susan Eike Spalding and Jane Harris Woodside, eds., *Communities in Motion: Dance, Community and Tradition in America's Southeast and Beyond* (1995); Frank G. Speck and Leonard Broom, *Cherokee Dance and Drama*.

Emily Koos
Patricia L. Pertalion
Additional research provided by Robin Conley and Cecelia Moore.

SEE ALSO African American Dance Ensemble; American Dance Festival; Buck Dancing; Clogging; Shag Dancing; Square Dancing; Step Dancing.

Dan River Steam Navigation Company

Dan River Steam Navigation Company was incorporated by the state legislature in 1855 for the purpose of operating steamboats on the Dan River from Clarksville, Va., to the head of navigation in Rockingham County, N.C. Brothers Marshall and John W. Parks, of Norfolk, Va., both engineers, proposed a design for a shallow-draft steamboat that could tow up to a dozen bateaux through the rapid currents and narrow sluices of the Dan River. Although it is unknown whether this company actually succeeded in navigation on the Dan, there is evidence of at least one privately owned steamboat based in Danville sailing on the upper river in the 1880s.

Reference: Thomas H. Sloan, *Inland Steam Navigation in North Carolina, 1818–1900* (1971).

Lindley S. Butler

Dare County

Dare County, located in northeastern North Carolina along the Atlantic seaboard, was formed from Currituck, Tyrrell, and Hyde Counties in 1870. It was named in honor of Virginia Dare, the first English child born in America. The county contains Roanoke Island, much of North Carolina's Outer Banks, and approximately 85 miles of continuous coastline (the longest of any North Carolina county). Communities in the county include Kill Devil Hills, Kitty Hawk, Nags Head, Southern Shores, and Wanchese. The county seat, Manteo, was named for a local Indian chief who aided the Roanoke Island colony and was taken to England in 1584 by men in the service of Sir Walter Raleigh.

Dare County was originally inhabited by Native Americans of the Croatoan, or Hatteras, tribe. The first English attempts to establish a colony in the New World took place on Roanoke Island in the 1580s. The island was the site of several failed attempts by the English, the last and largest being the so-called Lost Colony of 1587. English colonists eventually were able to settle the region, but the population remained small throughout the eighteenth century.

The county is the site of the first heavier-than-air flight, which took place on 17 Dec. 1903. Ohio natives Orville and Wilbur Wright first flew at what is now known as Kill Devil Hills, though newspapers mistakenly reported that the flight took place at Kitty Hawk, from which Orville Wright had dispatched a telegram home. The centennial celebration in 2003 was a landmark event for Dare County and the entire state.

Nags Head gained a reputation in the nineteenth century as a resort area, and tourism has since continued to be the primary industry of the county. Oceanside towns and resort areas have attracted tourists for decades, resulting in a large seasonal population that surges from June through August. Among Dare County's natural and cultural attractions are the Cape Hatteras National Seashore, the Wright Brothers National Memorial, the Fort Raleigh National Historic Site, Roanoke Island Festival Park (and the reconstructed ship *Elizabeth II*), the Alligator River National Wildlife Refuge, the Pea Island National Wildlife Refuge, Jockey's Ridge State Park, the North Carolina Aquarium, and the celebration of Old Christmas in Rodanthe on 5 January. The population of Dare County in 2004 was estimated to be slightly more than 34,000.

Allyson C. Criner

SEE ALSO Airplane, First Flight of; Cape Hatteras National Seashore; Croatoan Indians; *Elizabeth II*; Fort Raleigh National Historic Site; Lost Colony; Roanoke Voyages.

Daughters of the American Revolution

Daughters of the American Revolution (DAR) is comprised of women who have traced their families back at least to the time of the American Revolution and have found a forefather or foremother who served the revolutionary cause. The North Carolina chapter of the DAR, like its parent organization, is committed to the group's historical, educational, and patriotic ideals.

During the late 1800s, when a patriotic fervor swept the country, the national DAR was formed. In 1898 Mrs. E. D. Latta from Charlotte agreed to become state regent, or president, for the North Carolina Daughters of the American Revolution (NCDAR), organizing the Mecklenburg Chapter. Mrs. Stonewall Jackson, widow of the famed Civil War general, was regent of that chapter for its first two years. By July 1901, when the first state conference was held in Waynesville, Latta had started five chapters in the Piedmont and Mountain regions of the state. Since then, the NCDAR has formed 109 chapters with over 6,000 members. The different chapters are usually named for native sons and daughters who were patriots during the Revolutionary War. Two examples are the Elizabeth Maxwell Steele Chapter, named for a Salisbury woman who gave two bags of gold to Gen. Nathanael Greene as he and his hungry troops passed through her town in 1781; and the David Williams Chapter in Goldsboro, named for the man who helped capture Maj. John Andre in 1780 just after he had finished planning the betrayal of West Point with Benedict Arnold.

Throughout its existence, the NCDAR has undertaken projects of historical or cultural importance to North Carolina. Many monuments and markers have been placed throughout the state to identify sites and remind citizens of the rich historical bounty available to explore. These include monuments at Chief Junaluska's grave site in Cherokee County and at Andrew Jackson's birthplace in Waxhaw; a granite seat on the campus of the University of North Carolina at Chapel Hill as a memorial to Gen. William Richardson Davie, one of the school's founders; and markers at the graves of the three North Carolina signers of the Declaration of Independence, William Hooper, Joseph Hewes, and John Penn. The graves of many Revolutionary War soldiers have also been identified and marked.

During both World War I and World War II, the ladies of the NCDAR bought and sold wartime bonds; provided plasma and whole blood to the Red Cross; provided a bus, a mobile unit, money, surgical dressings, garments, socks, and garment bags to the Red Cross; worked with the USO; and organized home front wartime activities. In addition to these and other statewide projects, the NCDAR has also done its share to rebuild Memorial Continental Hall, the headquarters of the National Society Daughters of the American Revolution (NSDAR) in Washington, D.C. It has raised money for various projects in the hall and furnished the North Carolina room as a colonial dining room. The organization continues to contribute to the upkeep of Memorial Continental Hall. Several pamphlets, books, and a video also have been published to aid in genealogical research, to record the history of the NCDAR, and to note some of the history of North Carolina.

In years past several organizations for children were formed by both the NCDAR and the NSDAR. In 1938 the North Carolina State Society of Children of the American Revolution was organized. The Junior Group was designed to reach young women over 18 years old. Clubs of Sons and Daughters of the Republic were also sponsored by the NCDAR. The organization still sponsors an essay contest each February for high school seniors, with the local winner competing against other students in the state. The state winner receives recognition, money for tuition to the postsecondary school he or she wishes to attend, and a plaque. Every year, each chapter also gives an award to a high school ROTC student who best exemplifies the patriotic criteria of the contest.

References: Ann Arnold Hunter, *A Century of Service: The Story of the DAR* (1991); Lou Rogers, "The North Carolina Society of the Daughters of the American Revolution," *We the People of North Carolina* (March 1946).

Lee Plummer Templeton

Davenport College was established in Lenoir in 1855 by the Methodist Episcopal Church, South, as an institution of higher learning for women. It was named for William Davenport, the largest contributor to the enterprise. William A. Lenoir offered land overlooking the town for the campus, on which a classroom building, a chapel, and a dormitory were erected. The school held its first classes in 1857 and was incorporated as Davenport Female College in 1859, when enrollment stood at 56 students, all from North Carolina and South Carolina. Despite hardships, the college stayed open during the Civil War only to burn to the ground in 1877, without insurance to cover the $25,000 loss. Davenport reopened in 1884, serving primarily as a local high school. By the early twentieth century, Davenport had elevated its academic standing and met the qualifications for accreditation as a two-year college, admitting both women and men. It held this status until 1933, when it succumbed to the economic chaos created by the Great Depression. Five years later, all remaining assets and personal properties belonging to the school were merged with Greensboro College. The buildings were transferred to the town of Lenoir for use as an elementary school.

References: Nancy Alexander, *Here Will I Dwell: The Story of Caldwell County* (1956); E. Carl Anderson, ed., *Heritage of Caldwell County, North Carolina* (ca. 1983); Edmund Jones, "'The Fountain' and Its Builder [William Davenport]," *North Carolina Booklet* 16 (1916).

Jerry L. Cross

Davidson College, located in the town of Davidson, opened its doors in 1837 under the auspices of the Concord (western North Carolina) and Bethel (upcountry South Carolina) Presbyteries as a manual training school. Davidson was the namesake of Gen. William Lee Davidson, a Pennsylvania native who was killed at the Revolutionary War battle of Cowan's Ford near Charlotte. His son, also named William, provided the 469 acres upon which the college now stands, as well as a number of substantive monetary gifts. Also integral to Davidson's founding were Robert Hall Morrison of Charlotte, French-born Stephen Frontis (who later taught languages at the college), and P. J. Sparrow of Salisbury, who was instrumental in securing $30,000 for the college's inception.

An oil painting by Kentucky muralist Frank Long depicts the original quadrangle at Davidson College as it looked during the second half of the nineteenth century. Photograph courtesy of Davidson College.

Davidson's buildings, constructed under the guidance of Samuel Lemly of Salisbury, were situated in a quadrangle pattern: Elm Row, Eumeanean Society Hall, Oak Row, "Old Chapel" (later Shearer Biblical Hall), and Philanthropic Society Hall. Robert Morrison was the college's first president, and the first class consisted of 65 students studying under 3 faculty members. In 1841, within five years after Davidson's founding, the faculty substituted a classical course for its manual one. The college struggled until 1856, when, as a stipulation of the will of Salisbury cotton planter Maxwell Chambers, it received $250,000. The gift made Davidson the most heavily endowed institution south of Princeton. In 1857 the $90,000 Chambers Building, designed by Andrew Jackson Davis of New York, was erected; Chambers also endowed chairs in science and philosophy.

As a result of Chambers's gifts, Davidson's future grew secure. The institution was one of two men's schools in North Carolina to remain open during the Civil War, in part because of efforts of president John Lycan Kirkpatrick to integrate a preparatory course into the curriculum; still, when the conflict ended, Davidson enrolled only 24 students. Academic progress continued, however. Future U.S. president Woodrow Wilson attended Davidson in 1873 before transferring to Princeton. In 1896 future school president Henry Louis Smith and some of his students produced some of the nation's earliest X-ray images. In 1903 Wilson P. Mills received a Rhodes scholarship, the first in Davidson history. During the 1920s the college expanded its curriculum to include both classical and modern languages as well as Bachelor of Science degrees. In 1921 the original Chambers Building burned and was replaced, thanks in part to the Rockefellers, by a $600,000 edifice eight years later. In 1923 Phi Beta Kappa installed its Gamma of North Carolina Chapter at Davidson, and business and music classes were added to the curriculum.

The 1960s witnessed the introduction of the flexible Blue Sky Curriculum, and in 1972 Davidson began admitting women. The 1980s saw the construction of six residence facilities and a new sports complex, and the Visual Arts Building was added in 1993.

Davidson's mascot is the Wildcat; the school seal, with its motto, *Alenda Lux Ubi Orta Libertas* (Let Learning Be Cherished Where Liberty Has Arisen), was designed by Peter Stuart Ney, alleged by some to have been Napoleonic general Marshal Ney. Davidson's alumni, in addition to President Wilson, include former U.S. secretary of state and Rhodes scholar Dean Rusk and North Carolina governors Robert Brodnax Glenn, James E. Holshouser, and James G. Martin. Robert "Bobby" Frederick Vagt, a 1969 Davidson graduate and Duke Divinity School alumnus who built his career in the energy industry, became the school's president in 1997. In the early 2000s Davidson had a student body of approximately 1,600, served by 156 full-time faculty members.

References: Mary D. Beaty, *Davidson: A History of the Town from 1835 until 1937* (1979); Beaty, *A History of Davidson College* (1988);

Bailey Troy Groome, "Davidson College: Living Monument to General William Lee Davidson," in *Mecklenburg in the Revolution, 1740–1783* (1931); George Raynor, *Religion and Education in Piedmont North Carolina* (1991); Cornelia R. Shaw, *Davidson College* (1923).

James I. Martin Sr.

Davidson County, located in the Piedmont region of central North Carolina, was formed in 1822 from Rowan County. It was named after William Lee Davidson, a Revolutionary War general killed in the Battle of Cowan's Ford on the Catawba River in 1781. The county seat, Lexington, was named by its early residents in honor of the 1775 Battle of Lexington, which marked the start of the American Revolution. Other Davidson County communities include Midway, Denton, Thomasville, and Wallburg.

Prior to its settlement by Europeans, the area along the Yadkin River that became Davidson County was inhabited primarily by Saponi Indians. The Saponi, like other native groups in the region, were confronted with major social and economic transformations as European settlers began to arrive in the North Carolina backcountry. By the time English, Scotch-Irish, and German settlers arrived in significant numbers toward the middle of the eighteenth century, many Saponis had been pushed from the area by settlers and other Indian tribes or had coalesced with larger tribes. European settlers generally formed farming communities that remained small through the early nineteenth century, with German Lutheran, Moravian, and Reformed churches and communities clustered in the northern part of the county and English and Scotch-Irish enclaves in the south. Gold, silver, copper, and lead mining sparked further development in the first decades of the nineteenth century. In 1855 the arrival of the North Carolina Railroad laid the foundation for growth of the county's industrial economy after the Civil War. Lexington and Thomasville, both along the railroad's route, grew rapidly and became centers for the state's textile and furniture industries, which remained robust well into the twentieth century.

In the early 2000s, Davidson County remained internationally known for its furniture production. Thomasville, home to Thomasville Furniture Industries, boasts that it is home to the world's largest chair. Proponents of western North Carolina–style barbecue (hickory-smoked pork shoulders with a tomato-laced sauce) refer to Lexington as North Carolina's barbecue capital. While lovers of eastern North Carolina barbecue strenuously dispute this claim, the Lexington Barbecue Festival is the state's largest food festival, drawing more than 100,000 people each year.

Agricultural products of Davidson County include beef cattle, hogs, chickens, tobacco, soybeans, and corn. The county has several cultural and recreational attractions and parks, including High Rock Lake, Boone's Cave Park, the Davidson

County Historical Museum, Childree Vineyards, and the Richard Childress Racing Museum. The North Carolina Vietnam Veterans Memorial, located between Lexington and Thomasville, honors the state's 1,620 soldiers killed or declared missing in action during the Vietnam War. In 2004 Davidson County's population was estimated at just over 153,000.

References: Bob Lasley and Sallie Holt, eds., *Hometown Memories —It Always Rains When Old Folks Die and Other Davidson and Randolph County Tales: A Treasury of 20th Century Memories* (2001); Paul Baker Touart, *Building the Backcountry: An Architectural History of Davidson County, North Carolina* (1987).

Allyson C. Criner

Davie County, located in the western part of North Carolina's Piedmont region, was formed in 1836 from Rowan County. It was named for William R. Davie, governor from 1798 to 1799 and founder of the University of North Carolina. Saponi Indians were the original inhabitants of the region. The county seat, Mocksville, was known as "Mocks Old Field" before it was incorporated in 1839. Other communities in the county include Bermuda Run, Cooleemee, and Farmington.

British soldiers under Lord Charles Cornwallis came through Davie County during the American Revolution, and Stoneman's Raiders came to the county near the end of the Civil War. The county boasts several historic sites, including three historic districts. Cooleemee Plantation and the Hinton Rowan Helper House are designated as National Historic Landmarks. (Helper penned *The Impending Crisis of the South*, a scathing denunciation of slavery published in 1857.) The Cooleemee Textile Heritage Center interprets the mill heritage of the region. Davie County is home to one of North Carolina's oldest annual festivals, the Mocksville Masonic Picnic, held each August since 1878. Agriculture is the dominant industry in Davie County, which in many years ranks as the top dairy-producing county in the state. The county also produces tobacco, corn, wheat, chickens, and beef cattle. The population of Davie County was estimated to be 38,000 in 2004.

Reference: James W. Wall, *History of Davie County in the Forks of the Yadkin* (1985).

Allyson C. Criner

SEE ALSO Cooleemee Plantation.

Davie Poplar is a landmark tree located in McCorkle Place on the campus of the University of North Carolina at Chapel Hill. Originally known as the "Old Poplar," the tree predates the university and has been a source of many legends and tales about the founding of the nation's first state university in Chapel Hill. The area adjacent to the tree has traditionally been considered the site where a committee of men appointed by the Board of Trustees came to a decision on where to locate the university's buildings. In the late 1800s, Cornelia Phillips Spencer gave the tree its widely recognized name in honor of the father of the university, William Richardson Davie. The area beneath the Davie Poplar has been used as a rallying point for university events as well as the site of many graduation ceremonies—including the 1859 commencement, which was attended by President James Buchanan and his secretary of interior and UNC alumnus Jacob Thompson. The tree is incorrectly referred to as a poplar tree, as it is actually a specie of *Liriodendron tulipifera*, a relative of the magnolia. However, southerners typically call such a tree a "yellow poplar" because of its flowers.

The Davie Poplar has been damaged by many storms, which have taken away much of the tree's symmetry. The UNC class of 1918, fearing the demise of the tree, planted a grafted cutting of the Davie Poplar that soon became known as the Davie Poplar Jr. In 1953 a steel band was installed around the upper part of the original tree to attach support cables to nearby younger, stronger trees. The southward-leaning tree has also been strengthened by concrete reinforcements to its hollowed interior, and, during the 1960s, pruned to relieve some of the stress on its trunk.

The Davie Poplar received special recognition during the university's bicentennial celebration in 1993, when 104 sixth-grade students from each of North Carolina's 100 counties (representing the high school class of 2000) were invited to a ceremony held at the tree's base. Each student was given a 20-inch cutting taken from the tree to be planted in their home county as a symbol of the continual link between the university and the public school system of North Carolina.

References: William S. Powell, *The First State University: A Pictorial History of the University of North Carolina* (rev. ed., 1992); Marguerite Schumann, *The First State University: A Walking Guide* (rev. ed., 1985).

Kyle S. Kendrick

Davis School in Lenoir County, a boarding school for boys and young men, was established in LaGrange in 1880 by Adam Clark Davis Jr., reportedly the great-great-grandson of James Davis, the first printer in North Carolina. Adam C. Davis Sr., was doctor-in-residence at the school, which stressed the classics, penmanship, military science, mathematics, history, and English literature and offered commercial courses and training in telegraphy. The school's annual enrollment averaged 200, but at its peak there were 300 students—many from other states and several foreign countries.

The Washington and Jefferson Literary Societies published the school's monthly literary and educational newspaper, the *Davis Cadet*. In 1889 an outbreak of meningitis forced the academy to close, whereupon a number of residents of the

flourishing town of Winston gave the school land and pledged $20,000 to enable it to move there. In 1909, however, the Davis School's buildings and grounds were acquired by the Methodist Children's Home, which occupied the site in 1910.

References: Mary Elizabeth Gray, *LaGrange: Its Origin and History* (1997); Frank V. Tursi, *Winston-Salem: A History* (1994).

Wiley J. Williams

"Dawn of a New Day" was a slogan used by North Carolina Democrats on the eve of the twentieth century in their effort to seize the mantle of reform and innovation from Republicans and Populists. According to Charles B. Aycock, elected governor in 1900, this "new day" centered on the promise of universal education and improved schools for all citizens. Despite the progressive tone of Aycock's platform, however, and the educational and other beneficial programs that emerged from his administration, for Democrats this "new day" also represented a return to white supremacy that had been threatened by Reconstruction, the enfranchisement of blacks, and the increased political power of Republicans in the late nineteenth century. Aycock was himself an advocate of white supremacy, and his enthusiasm for education was based in part on his desire to create more literate white voters.

With the support of business leaders who believed that Aycock's educational initiatives would improve the state's economy and maintain their own power, Aycock found some success in launching his programs. The period of his governorship saw a sharp rise in state expenditures on public education and an increase in the length of the school year. Although white schools received the lion's share of these new moneys, Aycock also increased spending for black education. But the "new day" did not prevent blacks and poor, illiterate whites from losing ground, disfranchised by a 1900 amendment to the state constitution that required all voters to be literate.

References: Hugh T. Lefler and Albert Ray Newsome, *North Carolina: The History of a Southern State* (1954); Paul Luebke, *Tar Heel Politics 2000* (1998); William S. Powell, *North Carolina: A Bicentennial History* (1977).

Alex Coffin

"Death to the Klan" March, which took place in Greensboro in late 1979, involved a violent showdown between members of the Communist Workers Party (CWP), the Ku Klux Klan (KKK), and a neo-Nazi group. Similar clashes had occurred that year in April at Winston-Salem and in July at China Grove, although neither of them had resulted in gunfire. Before the confrontation, a leaflet campaign begun by the Workers Viewpoint Organization had intensified the hostility between the groups. An open letter described the KKK as "a bunch of two-bit cowards" and challenged the Klansmen to come to a "Death to the Klan" march and conference on 3 November, a Saturday.

Only four police officers were assigned to accompany the demonstrators, as authorities assumed that a "low profile" would avoid trouble. However, because the parade was scheduled to start at noon, the police were not present when several vehicles packed with Klansmen arrived early. The shooting began at 11:23 A.M. and resulted in the death of five CWP members. The local media, in response to provocative CWP press conferences, were on the scene to cover the march; their reports and TV cameras provided a graphic record of the violence. Although the CWP and other groups characterized the episode as a "massacre," many Greensboro residents referred to it as a "shootout," thus blaming both sides.

Despite the introduction of TV footage in the courtroom, the 1980 state trial of the KKK and Nazi Party assailants brought an acquittal from the local all-white jury. Three years later, following an extensive investigation by the Federal Bureau of Investigation (FBI) with the code name GREENKIL, a federal grand jury indicted nine of the KKK and Nazi suspects for conspiracy to violate the marchers' civil rights. The 1984 federal trial jury also found them not guilty. But in 1985 the CWP survivors won a $48 million civil suit against the KKK and Nazi Party, the Greensboro Police Department, the FBI, and the U.S. Bureau of Alcohol, Tobacco, and Firearms. In addition to allegations of assault against members of the KKK and Nazi Party, the suit charged the named law enforcement officers for negligence in the shooting, due to an FBI informant's foreknowledge of Klan and Nazi plans to arm themselves and confront the CWP marchers. Even this victory was muted, as the jury awarded only $400,000 of the $48 million requested and found only 7 of 65 individuals guilty as charged.

The Greensboro police were heavily criticized for not doing more to avert the tragedy. The issue of race quickly became the center of the story, especially since the police apparently were unable to prevent the shootings, which had taken place in a black neighborhood. Afterward, several studies of human and race relations were undertaken to improve conditions and communications in the city. Many citizens believed that local officials were insensitive to civil rights. The official report stated that the "Death to the Klan" march had "clearly dispelled the notion that all was well in Greensboro's human relations." Later a Citizens Review Committee proposed 13 ways to improve race relations. Most of these were implemented in the early 1980s, particularly one that urged a greater police presence at confrontational events to ensure the safety of citizens. In the 2000s the Greensboro Truth and Reconciliation Commission was formed to continue fostering better race relations and community healing in the city in the aftermath of the 1979 tragedy.

References: Paul C. Bermanzohn and Sally A. Bermanzohn, *The True Story of the Greensboro Massacre* (1980); Elizabeth Wheaton, *Codename GREENKIL: The 1979 Greensboro Killings* (1987).

J. Christopher Schutz
Alexander R. Stoesen

Debt, Imprisonment for. From the time of the earliest colonial settlements until the mid-nineteenth century, imprisonment for debt was common in North Carolina and throughout British North America. Legal procedures for imprisoning a debtor in default were introduced into the American colonies from Great Britain, where English law generally held borrowers strictly accountable for their financial obligations and allowed individuals to be jailed at their own expense in the event of default. The purpose of the law was to provide creditors a forceful means of collecting payment on a debt.

During the early colonial period, North Carolina was burdened with an unsavory reputation as a haven for irresponsible debtors and runaway indentured servants, in part because of a 1669 law that protected new settlers from foreign creditors for a period of five years. (Virginia and South Carolina particularly berated North Carolina for harboring debtors, although those neighboring colonies enacted laws granting similar protections during the 1600s.) Despite the 1669 law and North Carolina's reputation as a haven for idle debtors, early colonial North Carolina generally adhered to traditional English law in holding borrowers fully responsible for debts and making them subject to imprisonment for default.

Imprisonment for debt (except in cases of fraud) was abolished by the North Carolina General Assembly in 1867. The legislative ban was confirmed the following year under the North Carolina Constitution of 1868. Developments in the law leading to the eventual abolition of imprisonment for debt did not follow a gradual and consistent trend favoring more lenient treatment of defaulters on loans. Instead, changes in the law occurred in a series of sporadic legislative measures and court decisions that reflected changing economic conditions, regional political differences within the state, and an awareness of practical considerations as well as moral and humanitarian concerns.

References: George Philip Bauer, "The Movement against Imprisonment for Debt in the United States" (Ph.D. diss., Harvard University, 1935); Peter J. Coleman, *Debtors and Creditors in America: Insolvency, Imprisonment for Debt, and Bankruptcy, 1607–1900* (1974); Kenneth Edson St. Clair, "Debtor Relief in North Carolina during Reconstruction," NCHR 18 (July 1941).

Robert C. Voigt

Declaration of Rights. The first North Carolina Declaration of Rights, modeled in part on comparable declarations in Virginia, Maryland, and Pennsylvania, was adopted on behalf of the state by the Fifth Provincial Congress on 17 Dec. 1776. The declaration was adopted one day prior to the adoption of the new state's constitution and was specifically incorporated into that document to emphasize the strong commitment of North Carolinians to individual freedoms. The Declaration of Rights proclaimed popular sovereignty and separation of powers as well as basic civil rights, such as freedom of religion and guarantees of a fair trial, many of which were later restated in the federal Bill of Rights. The original Declaration of Rights, largely unchanged—plus a few provisions made necessary by defeat in the Civil War, such as the abolition of slavery and the prohibition of secession—became Article I of the 1868 North Carolina Constitution. With only minor changes, the Declaration of Rights remains the primary article of the state's 1971 constitution.

Reference: John V. Orth, *The North Carolina State Constitution: A Reference Guide* (1993).

John V. Orth

Decoration Day in North Carolina is the name used to describe a variety of ceremonies held in tribute to God, deceased loved ones, country, or community history. The date of a decoration day depends on the type of ceremony. Fixed dates usually accompany tributes to military dead, but many individual churches schedule their own ceremonies to coincide with reunions and other special events.

Honoring the dead after burial has roots in ancient Europe and Asia. Similar Christian traditions can be traced to the Roman Catholic All Souls' Day, a time to decorate graves with flowers and wreaths. African American forms of decoration day appeared in the coastal colonial South with similarities to ceremonies performed in West Africa and the Caribbean. Slaves sometimes held second burial ceremonies months after the original burial. Ceremonies involved music and dance around the grave sites of persons honored, and evidence exists of some slaves commemorating dead ancestors annually.

Official decoration day services in America probably date from the Civil War, as the practice of decorating the graves of dead soldiers became commonplace in many states. In 1865 Adj. Gen. Norton P. Chipman and Gen. John A. Logan recommended that a date be set for an annual decoration of the graves of Union dead. The veterans' organization, headed by Logan and Chipman, supervised a 30 May "Decoration Day" beginning in 1868. The American Legion took over its duties after World War I. On 28 June 1968, President Lyndon B. Johnson designated the last Monday in May as an official Memorial Day, a federal holiday and a time of honoring military dead.

Southern states designated different dates for a similar day to honor the Confederate dead. In North Carolina and South Carolina, the official Confederate Memorial Day is on 10 May, the date of the death of Gen. Thomas J. "Stonewall" Jackson. Confederate Memorial Day celebrations have traditionally included speeches, decoration of graves with Confederate flags, and playing of Confederate anthems. Widespread observance of the day has declined, but the United Daughters of the Confederacy and the Sons of Confederate Veterans continue ceremonies and decoration of Confederate cemeteries.

The religious events known as decoration days in many North Carolina churches sometimes occur on Memorial Day weekend, but they are usually held on a Sunday between late spring and early fall to accompany revivals and reunions. Decoration days in rural cemeteries replace the perpetual care found in larger urban areas and allow graves that would otherwise remain neglected to be decorated. Most of the grave maintenance takes place the weekend before decoration day, and includes clearing of brush, removal of old flowers, straightening of tombstones, and mounding of earth atop the grave sites. Actual decoration day ceremonies start with a church service followed by placement of wreaths and flowers on the graves.

Decoration ceremonies in the Great Smoky Mountains National Park of North Carolina reflect the way some communities continue to venerate a particular locale that is important to their history. The Little Cataloochee Baptist Church and the Methodist Palmer's Chapel in Big Cataloochee hold annual decoration ceremonies, church services, and dinners to honor ancestors who were forced to leave the area to make way for the park. The road to the Little Cataloochee church is only open once a year for the reunion to enable participants to bring grave decorations and food. Road access to cemeteries in the Hazel Creek area of the park in Swain County was flooded with the creation of Fontana Dam in the 1940s. Family members of persons buried in the cemeteries often rely on boat transportation to bring wreaths and flowers for grave decorations.

References: James K. Crissman, *Death and Dying in Central Appalachia: Changing Attitudes and Practices* (1994); Sylvia R. Frey and Betty Wood, *Come Shouting to Zion: African American Protestantism in the American South and British Caribbean to 1830* (1998); Deborah V. McCauley, *Appalachian Mountain Religion: A History* (1995).

Karl Rohr

Decoys. Wild waterfowl provided an abundant source of food for settlers of the North Carolina coastal regions, and early residents often made decoys to lure the birds within range of their guns. Not until the late nineteenth century, however, did decoy making became a serious occupation, when market hunters and wealthy sportsmen exploited the huge flocks of migratory waterfowl wintering in the sounds and bays of North Carolina.

During bad weather, fishermen and farmers produced thousands of gunning decoys for the hunting camps that sprang up from Currituck to Core Sound. The early artisans worked with little more than a hatchet and a knife, and visitors used to the delicate and decorative decoys common around the Chesapeake Bay sometimes greeted the rough-hewn products with derision. Most North Carolina carvers believed fooling the birds was all that mattered. Their decoys worked well and endured rough handling, while fragile beaks and necks could hardly survive such treatment.

Carvers used any available wood along the North Carolina coast for decoys, usually indigenous and plentiful juniper, cedar, or pine. Any material found in the jetsam of the beaches was also used regularly. Carvers produced decoys of a large variety of ducks, geese, swans, and shorebirds, representative of their numbers in the wild or their popularity with hunters. Most were solid and carved from a single block of wood or cork, though some consisted of a wire frame fastened to a board and covered with canvas. Carvers made heads and necks separately and fastened them to the body with dowels or nails. Battered and damaged decoys were often repainted or had new heads attached to prolong use, so it is rare today to find a decoy with original paint or all parts made by a single carver. Hunting decoys were weighted, usually with lead, for adequate performance. Their paint was sometimes abraded to prevent reflectivity that could frighten birds away. Initials of the carver and sometimes the owner were branded or carved into the base.

Restrictions on hunting gradually led to the decline of hunting camps and reduced demand for decoys. By 1950 few decoys were carved in North Carolina except for the personal use of residents. During the last half of the twentieth century, collectors sought out the remaining work of the early decoy makers, and connoisseurs of folk art acquired any they could find. Considered art objects, decoys were now found in living rooms and on fireplace mantels throughout the United States.

The diminished availability of antique decoys led to the rebirth of decoy carving in North Carolina, as experienced carvers worked again and novices took up the craft to help meet the expanding market. Today, decoy collectors pay hundreds or thousands of dollars for an antique decoy in good condition reflecting the handiwork of a well-known carver. Even damaged antique decoys are in demand. Although some gunning decoys are still made and used, the trend is toward realism and decorative pieces. The band saw and the electric grinding tool have replaced original carving methods. Artists use wood burning tools to etch reproductions of individual feathers, and airbrushing and acrylic paint provide delicate work with elegant detail. Tupelo gum is the most popular wood for carvers today, though some still use juniper. Others make reproductions of the old Outer Banks–style decoys of canvas and wire.

Antique decoys reside in museums and private collections, and a large number of modern decorative decoys are available in craft shops and shows. Decoys reflect a tradition that has achieved new recognition in the state and enjoys an increasing number of advocates as an art form.

References: William Neal Conoley Jr., *Waterfowl Heritage: North Carolina Decoys and Gunning Lore* (1982); Henry A. Fleckenstein Jr., *Southern Decoys of Virginia and the Carolinas* (1983); Archie Johnson and Bud Coppedge, *Gun Clubs and Decoys of Back Bay and Currituck Sound* (1991).

Dawson V. Carr

Deep and Haw River Navigation Company. In 1796, as part of a growing effort to improve the navigability of rivers and streams, the General Assembly incorporated the Deep and Haw River Navigation Company. Capitalized at $8,000, it was authorized to clear the Cape Fear River from Averasboro to the junction of the Deep and Haw Rivers and as far up those rivers as possible. Although the company was vested for 99 years, the legislature reserved the right to take over the works after 1830, paying the company for all money expended plus 25 percent of future profits.

In 1809 the legislature authorized a $10,000 "Cape Fear Lottery" to raise additional funds for the company, which ran a second lottery in 1811 and even contemplated a third. In 1815 the legislature increased the company's capitalization to $100,000 and promised $15,000 in state support. The company could now determine its own toll rates on the condition that annual collections not exceed 15 percent of the capital stock. In addition, the legislature gave the firm control of all the tributaries of the Cape Fear River from their sources to the river's mouth. Upon acceptance of the terms of the 1815 statute by the stockholders, the Deep and Haw River Company became the Cape Fear Navigation Company.

Reference: Charles C. Weaver, *Internal Improvements in North Carolina Previous to 1860* (1903).

Alan D. Watson

Deep Creek, Battle of. The Battle of Deep Creek, also called the Battle of Quallatown, was a Civil War engagement that occurred on 2 Feb. 1864. Union troops from the 14th Illinois Cavalry under Maj. Francis M. Davidson attempted to destroy the forces of Cherokee chief William Holland Thomas (called Thomas's Legion) by surprising the Indians and Highlanders at Deep Creek ten miles west of Quallatown. After an hour of fighting, Davidson reported that he killed nearly 200 Confederates, although southern records reported the loss of only 2. The northerners claimed that the Battle of Deep Creek was a great victory in which they had wiped out Thomas's Indian companies. They escorted their Cherokee captives to Knoxville, where they flattered the Indians and promised them substantial rewards if they would abandon the Confederacy. The Cherokee prisoners were also told that they would receive their freedom and $5,000 in gold in return for Thomas's scalp. When the Cherokees agreed to that condition, the Union forces released them. But on reaching their camp, the Indians joked about their promises and promptly returned to Confederate service.

References: Vernon H. Crow, *Storm in the Mountains: Thomas' Confederate Legion of Cherokee Indians and Mountaineers* (1982); E. Stanly Godbold Jr. and Mattie U. Russell, *Confederate Colonel and Cherokee Chief: The Life of William Holland Thomas* (1990).

William L. Anderson

Deertongue, also called dog-tongue and vanilla plant (*Trilisa odoratissima*), is native to the U.S. coastal region from North Carolina to Florida. It is characterized by basal clusters of dog- or deer-tongue shaped leaves followed by a three-to-five-foot central flower stalk with purple flowers in late summer. It inhabits the poor, sandy soil near Carolina Bays or pocosins and flat pine lands and is found as far inland as Sampson and Wayne Counties.

The deciduous leaves of this perennial herb were the focus of its value to people. Deertongue leaves were harvested from June to the first frost, sun dried on blankets, and sold to buyers that baled the dry leaves and in turn sold them to large buying centers. Two of the largest of these centers were in Brunswick, Ga., and Richmond, Va. Most of the dried leaves were then sold to tobacco companies, ground up, and placed in tobacco products to give a pleasant, vanilla-like aroma. Tobacco companies did not make this practice public, but it persisted until at least the 1970s, when supplies of deertongue began dwindling and substitute ingredients were found.

In early homesteads, deertongue leaves were placed in bureaus to impart a pleasant smell to clothing or hung in bundles in rooms to freshen the air. Deertongue also has medicinal properties; Native Americans and the earliest settlers made a tea that was believed to be an all-purpose cure and tonic. Deertongue concoctions were also used as stimulants and sweat-inducing agents.

References: William S. Justice, C. Ritchie Bell, and Anne H. Lindsey, *Wild Flowers of North Carolina* (2nd ed., 2005); Frank A. Montgomery, "Deer Tongue—Unique Carolina Product," *Raleigh News and Observer*, 18 Sept. 1966.

A. J. Bullard

Delco Lights, invented in 1912 by C. F. Kettering in Kokomo, Ind., were used by many North Carolinians before the federal government's efforts to electrify the rural South during the Great Depression. The Delco Light system consisted of a generator that ran on kerosene and was hooked to a series of batteries such as those found in a car. The system produced and stored 32 volts of current without the noise or nuisance of a constantly running generator. The Domestic Engineering Co. of Dayton, Ohio, began producing Delco Lights in 1916, and by autumn 1919 Delco products were advertised for sale in the state in Raleigh, Rocky Mount, and Oxford. These products, together with products from major competitors Kohler, Cooper-Hewitt, and Westinghouse, offered a reliable source of electric lighting and power. Luxuries enjoyed by city dwellers, such as late-night reading, sewing, or working by lamp light, became available to whomever could afford the Delco system.

The Delco system had drawbacks, however. The generator fuel was considered dangerous and poisonous if mishandled. To hold the electric charge, the batteries required a mixture of acid and water—a highly corrosive fluid containing lead that could contaminate the surrounding environment. Those who experienced the life-changing effects of Delco Lights regarded such risks as negligible, though, and the novelty of electric lighting in the countryside resonated in North Carolina. In the tiny Columbus County community of Pershing, a new high school was built with a Delco system installed. Patrons were so awed and proud of their school and its lights that in 1918 they changed the town's name to Delco.

Reference: Glen Banner, *Delco Electronics: A Story of Progress* (1983).

Joanne G. Carpenter

Demesne Land, a term that originated in medieval law, was rarely used in North Carolina and apparently not used at all after about 1730. It applied to land owned or otherwise available to a person but worked by laborers hired by him. After land came to be granted to individual owners, demesne land was restricted to that adjacent to or surrounding the landowner's house. The General Court of North Carolina in March 1716 heard a case concerning William Tyrrell, who on 22 February 1716 "did Demise Grant and to farm left to John [Grey]" a plantation of 177 acres in Perquimans Precinct.

William S. Powell

Democratic Party has wielded great political power in North Carolina. The state's politics have largely been defined by periods of unchallenged, one-party Democratic rule interrupted by other successful movements that have competed against and helped shape Democratic policies. Democrats trace their roots to the Democratic-Republican Party, or Jeffersonian Republican Party, of the early 1790s. Jeffersonian Republicans believed in a strict interpretation of the U.S. Constitution and the advancement of state rights over a powerful national government. North Carolina was strongly Republican in both national and state politics throughout the late eighteenth and early nineteenth centuries.

Andrew Jackson's defeat in the presidential campaign of 1824 resulted in the dissolution of the Jeffersonian Republican Party and the emergence of the modern Democratic Party, which formed with Jackson as its national leader. Four years later North Carolina's eastern politicians, who had dominated state government since 1776, and leaders from the west and sound regions all supported Jackson over John Quincy Adams. But after his election in 1828, Jackson's clear opposition to internal improvements, favored by the North Carolinians who had voted for him, caused a split in the state Democratic Party.

A new national coalition, the Whig Party, was formed around 1832 to oppose the policies of Jackson and the Democrats. Formally organized in North Carolina in 1835, the Whigs quickly attracted considerable support statewide. The party adopted the agenda of Archibald D. Murphey, a forward-looking state senator from Orange County who championed constitutional reform, a system of public education, and internal improvements—issues immensely popular in the west and parts of the east but opposed by the Democrats. The 1835 amendments to the North Carolina Constitution, which changed the state's election process, put further pressure on Democrats to become more "democratic."

When the national Whig Party collapsed in the early 1850s, around the time the Republican Party formed, the balance of power in North Carolina again swung to the Democratic Party. After the Civil War, the southern Democratic wing (sometimes called the Conservative Party) became the primary political alternative to Republican Reconstruction policies. In North Carolina, Democratic leaders branded Republicans as callous outsiders who represented northern and black interests at the expense of the native-born white population. The Ku Klux Klan served as an unofficial but effective tool of political terrorism for these conservative Democrats, often preventing Republicans of both races from voting. By 1876, when Zebulon B. Vance was reelected governor more than a decade after his previous term had ended, the Conservatives had clearly emerged as the state's dominant political force and reclaimed leadership of the Democratic Party.

The success of the Populist Party among small farmers led to a Populist-Republican "Fusion" that was able to win control of both houses of the legislature in 1894 and elect a Republican governor in 1896. However, intense Democratic campaigning based on a doctrine of white supremacy succeeded in returning the Democrats to power in 1898. One of their first actions back in office was to amend the state constitution to effectively disfranchise black voters through a poll tax, literacy test, and grandfather clause. Disfranchisement gave Democrats firm control of state politics, a one-party domination not seriously challenged until the 1960s and 1970s. Democratic

"gangs" such as the Red Shirts and the Ku Klux Klan controlled virtually all of the state by unchallenged force.

The ideology of the North Carolina Democratic Party during the first half of the twentieth century was a mix of economic progressivism and conservative retrenchment, particularly on issues of race. The 1900 election of Governor Charles B. Aycock, who ran on a strong public education platform, embodied the two sides of the emerging Democratic agenda: Aycock was progressive in his desire for markedly better education for white citizens while remaining a steadfast advocate of white supremacy and less-than-equal educational opportunities for African Americans. North Carolina Democrats were less ambiguous when it came to economic goals. In the 1920s Governor Cameron Morrison's policies dramatically increased the quality of state roads, leading to improved economic development. Governor O. Max Gardner instituted programs to attract industry to the state, pushed a worker's compensation law through the General Assembly, and increased spending for higher education. After World War II, the Democratic-controlled legislature funded extensive school construction, forced utilities to expand services in rural areas, and initiated other progressive measures.

The Democratic senatorial primary campaign of 1950 illustrated the ongoing conflict over racial politics and commitment to economic and social progress within the party. In 1949 Governor Kerr Scott, a Democrat, had appointed Frank Porter Graham, president of the University of North Carolina and a noted liberal, to fill the term of the recently deceased Senator J. Melville Broughton. In the subsequent Democratic primaries, his opponent was conservative Willis Smith, who accused Graham of supporting everything from integration to communism. Racial politics inflamed the electorate, and Smith won the Democratic seat.

But as the conservative wing of the party continued to dominate state affairs, the national Democratic Party was growing more liberal. The election of John F. Kennedy and his running mate Lyndon B. Johnson, as well as national party support of civil rights measures, social welfare programs, and a variety of liberal social causes, resulted in dissent among southern Democrats. By the late 1960s, the Republican Party was becoming a competitive force in North Carolina politics, culminating in the state's support of Richard M. Nixon in the 1968 presidential election and the 1972 election of James E. Holshouser Jr. and Jesse Helms, respectively, as the first Republican governor and the first Republican U.S. senator from North Carolina in the twentieth century. As the national Democratic Party continued to court black voters and embrace a more progressive social agenda, conservative Democrats became increasingly willing to vote for Republicans who shared their views, and many ultimately changed their political affiliation.

By the end of the twentieth century, the state's one-party political system, which had been so influential in shaping

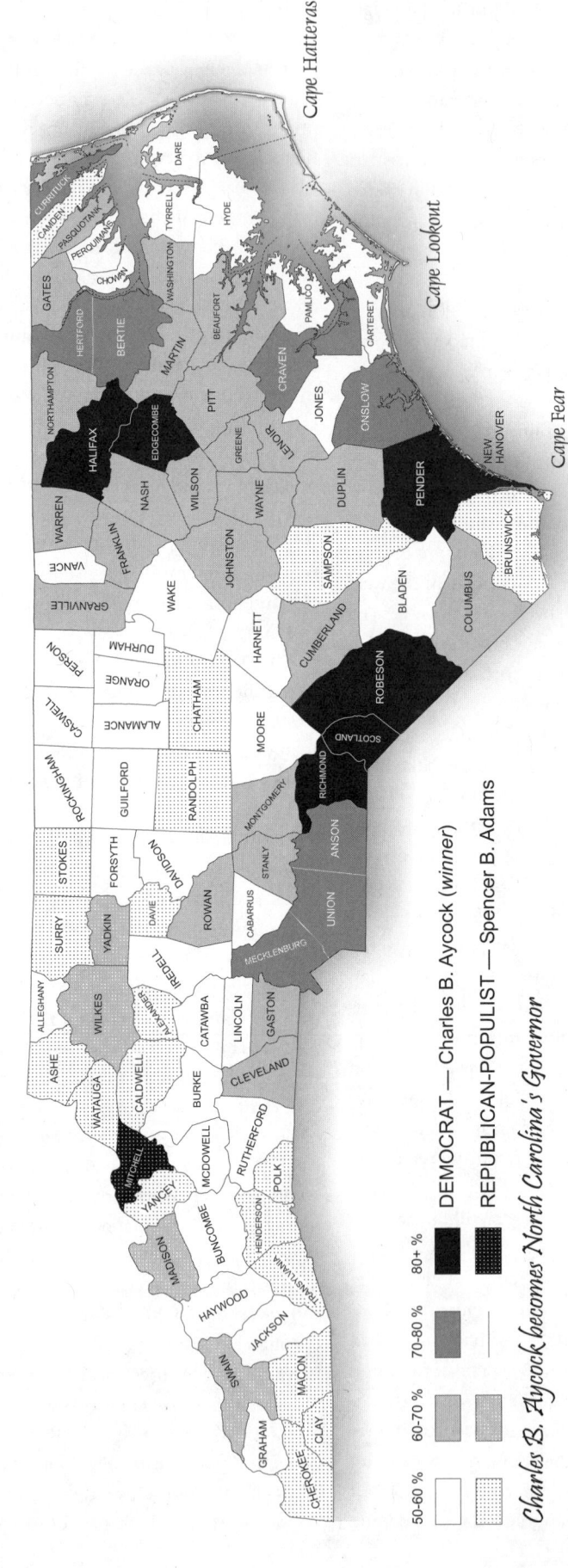

Charles B. Aycock becomes North Carolina's Governor

50-60 %   60-70 %   70-80 %   80+ %

DEMOCRAT — Charles B. Aycock (*winner*)

REPUBLICAN-POPULIST — Spencer B. Adams

Gubernatorial election of 1900, showing winning candidate and vote percentage by county. Map by Mark Anderson Moore, courtesy NCOA&H.

North Carolina's history since the Civil War, had vanished. The Republican Party had significantly boosted its numbers by absorbing the traditionalism abandoned by the Democratic Party's progressive wing, leaving state Democrats struggling to redefine themselves in this new ideological climate. Most Democrats refashioned themselves as moderates, adopting liberal positions on social issues such as racial equality and women's rights to appease the party's new base while continuing their traditional promotion of the state's economic development, even as businesses increasingly turned to the Republican Party. This balancing act proved crucial to the Democrats' survival, for although it seemed that North Carolinians preferred Republicans as their U.S. representatives, senators, and presidents, in 2005 Democrats still outnumbered Republicans in the General Assembly and occupied most of the top state offices, including the governorship. Furthermore, about 2.5 million North Carolinians were registered as Democrats, whereas Republicans, despite their gains, claimed only 1.8 million.

References: Roberta Sue Alexander, *Race and Politics in North Carolina, 1872–1901* (1981); Vanessa Goodman and Jack Betts, *The Two-Party System in North Carolina* (1987); Paul Luebke, *Tar Heel Politics 2000* (1998); Mebane Rash Whitman, "The Evolution of Party Politics: The March of the GOP Continues in North Carolina," *North Carolina Insight* 16 (September 1995).

Richard D. Starnes
Additional research provided by Robert Blair Vocci.

SEE ALSO Disfranchisement; Helms-Hunt Senate Race; Progressivism; Red Shirts; Smith-Graham Senate Race.

Demography. North Carolina has grown from a collection of diverse Indian communities and the first small European settlements of the seventeenth century to the eleventh most-populous U.S. state in the early 2000s. By the 1660s, the first permanent settlers in what is now North Carolina had migrated from Virginia into the Albemarle Sound region. Subsequently, the colony of Carolina (which originally included modern-day North Carolina and South Carolina and all or parts of 14 other states) was granted to eight Lords Proprietors in 1663. The population of the colony grew very slowly under Proprietary rule. In 1689 a government was set up to administer the area located "north and east of Cape Fear." This was the beginning of North Carolina's history as a separate colony.

In 1729 North Carolina became a royal colony under the king of England. As a royal colony (until 1775), North Carolina experienced rapid population growth, particularly during the last half of the period. The colony's population grew from 100,000 in 1752 to 200,000 in 1765, and by 1776 the count was approximately 300,000. North Carolina was then fourth among the 13 colonies in population, with only Virginia, Pennsylvania, and Massachusetts more populous. The tremendous increase in North Carolina's population during this period can be attributed to a large influx of newcomers, most notably Germans, Scotch-Irish, Highland Scots, and African slaves.

After the U.S. Constitution was ratified in 1789, Congress passed legislation the following year requiring that a census be taken every ten years beginning in 1790. According to the first census, North Carolina, with approximately 394,000 people, was the third-most-populous state behind Virginia and Pennsylvania. During the next three decades, North Carolina was ranked fourth among the states. That ranking, however, began to change dramatically when the state dropped from fourth in 1820 to twelfth in 1860. Poor economic conditions led to a steady exodus of North Carolinians, particularly to points west. Although the state's total population increased between 1830 and 1840, 32 out of 68 counties lost population. The 1850 census revealed that some 405,000 North Carolina natives were living in other states.

Following the Civil War, North Carolina experienced steady growth but showed relatively little movement in the state rankings from 1870 to 1920, remaining fourteenth. The decade of the 1920s, however, marked a change. The economy in general expanded dramatically, with help from improved modes of transportation, an ambitious road construction program, and the development of hydroelectric power. The 1930 census revealed that North Carolina had moved from fourteenth to twelfth in the rankings and was the most populous state in the Southeast, having surpassed Georgia in the 1920s and Kentucky, Virginia, and Tennessee in previous decades.

North Carolina continued to grow steadily in the succeeding decades, although not as rapidly as during the 1920s. The state was ranked eleventh in 1940, surpassing Indiana, and tenth in 1950, moving ahead of Missouri. In 1960, however, North Carolina dropped to twelfth place due to a phenomenal population increase in Florida and a growth spurt in Indiana. The state remained in twelfth place until 1980, when it moved back into tenth place ahead of Massachusetts and Indiana (a ranking that was maintained in the 1990 census).

Historically, North Carolina has been a predominately rural state. In 1860 only 2.5 percent of the population was classified as urban. Even as late as 1900, the state's urban population was only about 10 percent. During the first two decades of the twentieth century, however, there was a trend toward urbanization, with the proportion increasing to 19 percent. The trend continued in the decades that followed, and according to 2004 estimates, about 68 percent of North Carolina's population was considered urban.

In 1990 North Carolina was sixth among the states in attracting people from other states. As many as 10,000 retirees alone were migrating to North Carolina each year by the late 1980s and 1990s, and these figures remain on the increase. One definitive phenomenon has been the increase of the Latino population in the state, which rose 26 percent during the decade of the 1980s (from 56,667 to 76,726). The Latino population has continued to rise dramatically, topping 600,000 early in the twenty-first century.

The 2000 U.S. census revealed growth beyond all expectations in North Carolina. State demographers had estimated the growth during the decade of the 1990s at approximately 16 percent, but when the official count was completed, the accurate figure turned out to be an impressive rate of 21.4 percent. In spite of this extraordinary growth, North Carolina dropped from tenth to eleventh in the national rankings because of an even greater increase in population in the state of Georgia —primarily attributed to growth in the Atlanta metropolitan area.

North Carolina Population

(U.S. Census, 1790–2000)

1790	393,751	1900	1,893,810
1800	478,103	1910	2,206,287
1810	555,500	1920	2,559,123
1820	638,829	1930	3,170,276
1830	737,987	1940	3,571,623
1840	753,419	1950	4,061,929
1850	869,039	1960	4,556,155
1860	992,622	1970	5,082,059
1870	1,071,361	1980	5,881,766
1880	1,399,750	1990	6,628,637
1890	1,617,949	2000	8,049,313

References: William S. Powell, *North Carolina through Four Centuries* (1989); *Statistical Abstract of the United States, 1991* (1991); U.S. Department of Commerce, Bureau of the Census (1990 and 2000).

Ron Holland

Dentistry, like medicine, has changed dramatically throughout history. From colonial times through the first decades of the nineteenth century, dental procedures were merely an additional service offered by men in the barber trade or occasionally by an individual with some medical education. Parents usually played the role of "dentist" for their children, pulling out decayed teeth with a variety of crude methods. In North Carolina no formal dental training was available, and consequently there was no way of gauging who was qualified to perform dental surgery. A New Bern shoemaker named E. R. Hubbard, for example, was purported to have occasionally abandoned his cobbler's bench to work on the sore tooth of a complaining customer.

Some early North Carolinians actually called themselves dentists, took their work seriously, and maintained successful practices that often led them from region to region in search of patients. The *Hillsborough Recorder* of 22 Aug. 1821 carried an advertisement by a Mr. Hurley, who "operated for all ill-nesses of teeth and gums, freed the teeth from tartar, filled and plugged decayed teeth, straightened children's teeth, and inserted artificial teeth after the most approved manner and in a style so nearly approaching nature as to bid defiance from detection." Clearly, some form of dental standards had begun to take shape.

In 1835 approximately 15 dentists practiced statewide, and probably countless others occasionally performed dental procedures. Five years later, in 1840, the world's first dental school opened in Baltimore, Md., and schools soon followed in Ohio, Massachusetts, Michigan, and Pennsylvania. W. R. Scott, of Raleigh, who received a degree from the Baltimore College of Dental Surgery in 1842, became the first North Carolinian to graduate from a school of dentistry and practice in the state. As educational opportunities grew, a broader range of people chose to become dentists, and dentistry evolved from a trade into a profession. The dental community created a system of standards and ethics to safeguard its professional gains and ensure that patients received the best care possible.

In October 1856 a group of college-trained dentists met in Raleigh to organize the first North Carolina Dental Society, whose stated goals were the "elevation of the dignity of the profession and the advancement of the science" of dentistry. At the time, it was the only such organization in the United States to require its members to have dental degrees. W. F. Bason of Haw River, who was known as "the merciful dentist" because of the great care he took to reduce pain during dental procedures, served as the society's first president.

Disruptions caused by the Civil War led to the temporary dissolution of the Dental Society. Officially reorganized in 1875 with approximately 200 active members, it began to lobby the General Assembly to bar anyone without a degree from an accredited dental college from practicing in the state. In 1879, after much political wrangling, the legislature passed a law mandating that all future dentists either be graduates of a dental school or prove their competency to the newly established Board of Dental Examiners. The law was amended in 1905 to direct that an individual could not take the state examinations without having first been graduated from a dental school.

The dental profession in North Carolina continued to expand and change throughout the early twentieth century. Cities such as Asheville, Winston-Salem, and Raleigh formed their own local dental societies. With the increase of high-quality instruments and medicines, procedures became less and less barbaric. Before this time, a painless extraction was all but impossible. Fillings made of gold and tin were put into place by chisel and mallet. Anesthesia and sterilization procedures for instruments were not yet perfected. In the early decades of the twentieth century, new advances in preventive dentistry led to a revolution in dental care. The focus shifted from merely pulling and filling teeth and making crude den-tures to informing patients about oral hygiene and keeping their teeth healthy and strong.

In 1918 North Carolina was the first state in the nation to found a statewide dental health program under the auspices of the State Board of Health. During this period, support for the establishment of a dental school in the state began to grow. In 1947 Claude M. Parks, president of the Forsyth County Dental Society, led a committee researching the need for such a school. Facts gathered were alarming: North Carolina ranked a lowly 45th in the nation in dental care, with 1 dentist for every 3,778 citizens; an estimated 42 new dentists every year would be needed even for this low ratio to be maintained. Many North Carolinians who desired to practice dentistry were unable to get into the crowded out-of-state schools or did not return to the state after graduation.

The Forsyth County Dental Society proposed the idea of an in-state dental school to the North Carolina Dental Society, which successfully lobbied the state legislature for funds in 1949. By 1950 dental students at the University of North Carolina at Chapel Hill were studying in Quonset huts while the school was under construction, and in 1954 the first class of 34 students was graduated. The creation of a dental school and subsequent increases in class size did not eliminate the shortage of dentists in the state, however, as the dentist-population ratio continued to hover near the nation's lowest. The situation was worsened by the fact that many dentists preferred to practice in urban areas, leaving many rural regions gravely underserved.

During the last decades of the twentieth century, the dental profession in North Carolina made great strides in educating the citizenry about the importance of dental hygiene. During the 1970s the state initiated pilot programs in several counties to take this message to the public schools, creating manuals for teachers as well as students. New decay-fighting substances and procedures, the fluoridation of water supplies, and a myriad of technical advances—some preventive and others aesthetic—led to greater dental health in populations served by sufficient dental personnel.

Overall, statistics relating to dental health in North Carolina have remained steady. By the early 2000s there were approximately 3,400 dentists and 4,000 dental hygienists, representing a dentist-population ratio of about 1:2,470. Four counties—Jones, Tyrrell, Camden, and Hyde—had no practicing dentists, and Bertie, Currituck, and Gates Counties had only one each. The counties with the most dentists were Mecklenburg (453), Wake (433), Guilford (231), and Forsyth (176). Children's dental health was monitored and enhanced by the Oral Health Section of the North Carolina Department of Health and Human Services.

References: Richard A. Glenner, *The American Dentist: A Pictorial History* (1990); Kermit Knudtzon and Clifton E. Crandell, eds.,

From Quonset Hut to Number One and Beyond: A History of the UNC *School of Dentistry* (1982); Roy Thompson, "N.C. Dental Society Is 100 Years of Age," *Winston-Salem Journal and Sentinel*, 6 May 1956.

Jay Mazzocchi

Desertion, Civil War. Civil War desertion by North Carolina troops remains a controversial topic. Owing to the fragmentary nature of surviving records, researchers have arrived at different conclusions as to how many North Carolina soldiers actually deserted the Confederate army. Soon after the conflict, the U.S. Army's provost marshal general officially estimated that 23,000 North Carolina troops deserted between 1861 and 1865, nearly one-quarter of the total for the entire Confederacy and significantly more than for any other state. Historians have challenged this estimate, one suggesting that a more accurate figure, based on his quantitative analysis of compiled service records, would be about 14,000 desertions.

Although debate continues over exact numbers, undoubtedly the absence of North Carolina troops without leave represented a serious problem for the Confederate army. Gen. Robert E. Lee complained about North Carolina's desertion rate. Many North Carolinians bitterly resented these charges, seeing them as yet another example of the Confederate government's alleged discrimination against their state. Virginia newspapers routinely impugned the effectiveness of North Carolina troops.

Nevertheless, the state did have an unusually high rate of desertion. Several factors contributed to this exodus. Many men left the army after they became aware of the hardships and danger encountered by their families back home. As the ravages of war worsened, wives increasingly wrote letters encouraging their soldier-husbands to desert. Desertion generally increased in a unit when the region from which it had been recruited fell into enemy hands, as did several coastal counties. Desertions also occurred in areas where civilians experienced extreme suffering and law and order broke down, as in several western counties.

The state's 1864 peace movement, led by *Raleigh Standard* editor William W. Holden, may also have contributed to poor morale and desertion among North Carolina soldiers, although Holden publicly condemned this practice. The rulings of North Carolina Supreme Court chief justice Richmond Pearson against the legality of conscription also led many deserters to believe that if they reached their home state, its legal authorities would shield them from punishment. Although some deserters were conscripts who saw little or no active service and some were members of the Unionist secret society called the Heroes of America, many more were relatively devoted Confederates. More than half the state's deserters had served in the army for more than 18 months and almost 70 percent for more than a year. These men apparently felt a greater loyalty to their families, who desperately needed their assistance, or perhaps they recognized the futility of the Confederate cause, particularly in the last, hopeless days of the war.

References: Richard Bardolph, "Inconstant Rebels: Desertion of North Carolina Troops in the Civil War," *NCHR* 41 (April 1964); James M. McPherson, *Battle Cry of Freedom: The Civil War Era* (1988); Richard Reid, "A Test Case of the 'Crying Evil': Desertion among North Carolina Troops during the Civil War," *NCHR* 58 (July 1981).

Michael Thomas Smith

De Soto Expedition. Hernando De Soto traveled through the region that would become the southeastern United States from 1539 to 1543 with an army of more than 600 men in an attempt to discover riches comparable to those found in Mexico and Peru. Highly ambitious, De Soto had been granted the right to oversee the conquest of La Florida (the name given to peninsular Florida and the land between the Gulf and Atlantic Coasts) for the Spanish Crown. Although he traveled almost 4,000 miles and found many bountiful lands, he discovered no gold or silver and very few gems. During his passage, he wreaked havoc on the indigenous chiefdoms of southeastern Indians. Relying on Indian guides and commandeering all available food supplies, he and his army practiced what was in some cases a "scorched-earth" policy. He died on the banks of the Mississippi River on 21 May 1542. The remnants of his army (just over 300 men) ultimately fled La Florida and sailed from the mouth of the Mississippi along the Gulf Coast until they reached Spanish settlements in Mexico.

The actual route that De Soto followed through the Southeast has been the source of much scholarly inquiry. In 1935 the U.S. Congress authorized a comprehensive study of the De Soto expedition to identify and mark his route. The U.S. De Soto Expedition Commission, led by ethnologist John Swanton, published its findings in 1939. According to the commission's report, De Soto's army entered the far western part of present-day North Carolina and passed through what would become Macon, Clay, and Cherokee Counties. More recent research by Charles Hudson and his colleagues suggests a somewhat different route that includes a larger area of western North Carolina. According to this research, De Soto and his army reached the Chiefdom of Cofitachequi, located in the vicinity of present-day Camden, S.C.

De Soto, taking an Indian woman known as the Lady of Cofitachequi as a hostage, departed Cofitachequi on 12 May 1540. His force traveled north following the Wateree/Catawba River Valley. Within two days they encountered villages referred to as being in the territory of Chalaque. This region, described as unimpressive with little corn available, is thought to have been just southwest of Charlotte. Continuing north, De Soto and his men reached the town of Guaquili, possibly in the vicinity of Hickory. From Guaquili, they headed west and arrived at Xuala or Joara, thought to be the principal town of the Chiefdom of Joara. Archaeological evidence suggests that this town was located just north of Morganton. After two days at Joara, the army marched north into the Blue Ridge. Perhaps following the Toe River, they reached the Nolichucky River and the town of Guasili on 30 May 1540. Guasili may have been located near present-day Embreeville, Tenn.

It is believed that De Soto met with ancestors of both Catawba and Cherokee Indians as he crossed through western North Carolina. His journey is significant to historians, anthropologists, and archaeologists for the written accounts that provide the first historical glimpses of the often large and complex chiefdom societies of southeastern Indians.

References: Charles Hudson, *Knights of Spain, Warriors of the Sun: Hernando De Soto and the South's Ancient Chiefdoms* (1997); John R. Swanton, *Final Report of the United States De Soto Expedition Commission* (1939).

David G. Moore

Destructives, the nickname of the original supporters of North Carolina's secession from the Union and involvement in the Civil War, received their unflattering designation from their opponents, the members of the Conservative Party. Although the Destructives briefly held the upper hand in North Carolina politics after the firing on Fort Sumter and Abraham Lincoln's call for troops in April 1861, their period of dominance was short-lived. The Federal occupation of much of coastal North Carolina early in the war and unpopular policies by the Confederate government in Richmond increasingly alienated much of the public. The election of Conservative governor Zebulon B. Vance in 1862, an opponent of secession until the last moment, signified the repudiation of the leadership of the Destructives. Although Vance was often at odds with Jefferson Davis's government, his prowar policies increasingly won him the support of the Destructives—particularly in his 1864 reelection campaign against William W. Holden, the leader of the state's peace movement.

Following the war, the Destructives again supported a successful gubernatorial candidate in opposition to Holden. Their backing of prewar Unionist Jonathan Worth in 1865 contributed significantly to his election and heralded a party realignment made possible by the increasing cooperation between Destructives and Conservatives of Vance's pro-Confederate faction. During Reconstruction, these disparate elements merged into the reconstituted Democratic Party.

Reference: Paul D. Escott, *Many Excellent People: Power and Privilege in North Carolina, 1850–1900* (1985).

Michael Thomas Smith

Devil's Horse's Hoof Prints near Bath are a series of small, saucer-shaped depressions reportedly in existence since 1813. Measuring four to five inches deep with sloping sides from six to ten inches, the holes remain the source of one of North Carolina's most famous and enduring mysteries.

Legend relates that on a Sunday morning about church time, Jesse Elliott and some companions planned to race their horses along the main street of Bath. Elliott mounted and spurred his horse, and as it raced off, he leaned forward shouting in its ear: "Take me in a winner or take me to Hell." Promptly the horse dug its hooves into the soft earth, throwing Elliot against a tree and killing him instantly. Some believe that the horse was actually the devil in the form of a horse.

Tradition maintains that the holes, located just off N.C. 1334, about 3.3 miles west of Bath, have survived every known attempt to permanently eradicate or alter them. Although the holes are located at the edge of a forested area, no vegetation grows inside them. None of the pine needles from the thick mat surrounding the holes ever remains in the earthen saucers. On their way to school, children have deposited various kinds of debris in the depressions only to find that the holes are empty upon their return from school. Countless visitors to the site have experienced the same phenomena.

Scientists have conducted studies at the site to provide an objective explanation of the intriguing holes. Among the most popular theories are that the depressions are vents for a subterranean water pocket or the result of salt veins.

References: Daniel W. Barefoot, *Touring the Backroads of North Carolina's Upper Coast* (1995); John Harden, *The Devil's Tramping Ground and Other North Carolina Mystery Stories* (1949); Nancy Roberts, *North Carolina Ghosts and Legends* (1991).

Daniel W. Barefoot

Devil's Tramping Ground, located ten miles from Siler City in western Chatham County, is a foot-wide bare path forming a perfect circle 40 feet in diameter. Regional legend maintains that Satan frequents this area on his nightly walks, pacing the circle as he contemplates his evil deeds. Normal vegetation surrounds the circle, but only a wiry grass grows inside it, and no plant life of any kind can be found on the path itself. Locals have been unsuccessful in trying to transplant the wiry grass to other soils. Visitors have attempted to anchor sticks and other obstacles in the barren area, but morning always finds these obstacles cleared away.

In addition to the devil-centered explanation, numerous other theories have arisen to account for this strange North Carolina landmark. Some people believe the spot was an ancient meeting place for local Native American tribes, who made the bare circle with their ceremonial dances. Another explanation links the area to the legend of the Lost Colony of Roanoke Island. This story holds that the Tramping Ground was an area called Croatan, named for a fallen tribal chief buried there after a battle, and the word "Croatoan" carved in the tree on Roanoke Island referred to this battle site. In both of these stories, the tribal gods purportedly preserved the barren circle as a memorial to their followers' loyalty.

Scientific explanations for the characteristics of the Devil's Tramping Ground have been offered as well. Some say horses used in the operations of an old molasses mill created the spot with their constant circular treading. However, comparisons to the paths formed at similar mills do not support this theory. Possibly the most plausible explanation came from soil studies once conducted by the North Carolina Department of Agriculture. Samples of earth taken from the bare path proved to be sterile due to an extremely high salt content. The remains of natural salt licks were also found in the area.

References: John Harden, *The Devil's Tramping Ground and Other North Carolina Mystery Stories* (1949); Richard Walser, *North Carolina Legends* (1980).

Kimberly Hewitt

Dinner on the Grounds, a quintessential North Carolina and southern ritual, is a covered-dish meal following the last Sunday morning worship service of many Christian congregations. "Grounds" refers to the church grounds. These events are often held in honor of a church member, to greet or bid farewell to a preacher, as a homecoming, or in connection with a family reunion.

In earlier times, the majority of food was prepared prior to the Sabbath and taken to the church before the morning worship service. In most cases, it was consumed between the morning and afternoon services. This arrangement was not only a pleasant way to socialize with fellow church members but a necessity: the condition of the roads and the common means of transportation generally left inadequate time for most members of the congregation to dine at home between services. Thus, "dinner on the grounds" was a logical as well as edifying experience for countless North Carolina churchgoers.

O. C. Stonestreet III

Dinosaurs. SEE Fossils.

Dirt Eaters, also called "clay eaters," "sandlappers," and other names, are individuals who regularly eat soil as part of their diet. It has been generally accepted that the practice of soil eating (technically known as "geophagy") was brought to America through the slave trade with Africa and the West Indies. The medical records of colonial and antebellum physicians who treated ailing blacks on plantations indicate that some of their maladies, described as debilitating sluggishness and pale skin coloration, were brought on by habitual and excessive clay eating. The condition was treated as a bad habit that needed to be ended, although some physicians surmised that clay eating was the result of iron deficiency in the body. Dirt eating was also observed among Indians in the region. In general, however, the phrase "dirt eater" in North Carolina referred to poor whites who engaged in the practice.

Scientific and medical studies of dirt eating began only in the twentieth century. In 1909 the Rockefeller Sanitation Commission for the Eradication of Hookworm Disease brought its crusade to the rural South. For five years clay and dirt eaters, among others, were surveyed, examined and treated, and educated about the insidious hookworm that enters the body mainly through contact with contaminated soils. One of the many conclusions drawn by the commission was that dirt eating possibly was a reaction to hookworm infestation and that it could be stopped by curing the individual of hookworms. Although many dirt eaters were indeed found to be infested with hookworms, many were not, and though the practice of dirt eating became less frequent after treatment for hookworms, it was not eradicated.

Subsequent studies by sociologists, medical researchers, anthropologists, psychologists, nutritionists, and chemists produced a mass of scientific theories and conclusions. Many studies confirmed that geophagy is a consequence of iron deficiency. A 1997 publication by a team of Canadian scientists, analyzing three geophagic soils from three different continents, reported that the clay in North Carolina's Stokes County had mineral content that supports the theory that the stimulus for earth eating may lie in soil's value as both a nutritional supplement and an aid in easing minor digestive disorders. Scientists have also concluded that dirt eating is a behavior with a history that goes back thousands of years. The practice is often handed down from generation to generation; this appears to be the heritage of the dirt eater, whose ancestors over the centuries survived famine, years of scarcity, and stomach ailments by eating soil for sustenance.

The population continuing to engage in geophagy includes poor women and children in parts of North Carolina and the South. Many individuals still visit specific soil sites, while some have turned to substitutes such as packaged laundry starch and baking soda, which have texture and taste similar to the region's finer clays. Many health professionals consider these substitutes worse nutritionally than edible soils.

References: John M. Hunter, "Geophagy in Africa and the United States: A Culture-Nutrition Hypothesis," *Geographical Review* 63 (April 1973); Robert W. Twyman, "The Clay Eater: A New Look at an Old Southern Enigma," *Journal of Southern History* 37 (August 1971); Donald E. Vermeer and Dennis Frate, "Geophagia in Rural Mississippi: Environmental and Cultural Contexts and Nutritional Implications," *American Journal of Clinical Nutrition* 32 (October 1979).

Carmena B. Zimmerman

Disciples of Christ

Disciples of Christ in North Carolina belonged to the Stone-Campbell movement of primitive Christianity that spread rapidly in Kentucky and Tennessee in the three decades following the famous Cane Ridge Revival of 1801. The Campbellites had been followers of the frontier Scotch-Irish Presbyterian minister Thomas Campbell and his precocious, charismatic, and Scottish-educated son, Alexander. The Campbells, especially Alexander, brought to frontier religion the best elements of European pietism and eighteenth-century mainstream Christianity. They sought to purge the trans-Appalachian West of sectarian differences between Baptists, Methodists, and Presbyterians by blending together evangelical elements common to all Protestants.

Barton Warren Stone, a Presbyterian minister involved in the Cane Ridge Revival, brought his former Presbyterian followers into alliance with the Campbellites in the 1830s. Stone was the first link between the Disciples of Christ and North Carolina. In 1790–91 he had studied at David Caldwell's Academy in Guilford County, and he experienced conversion during a revival led by James McCready in 1791. Stone's friend and protégé, Joseph Thomas, famous for his flowing white robe and known as the "white pilgrim," was an itinerant preacher in North Carolina between 1811 and 1815, influencing several future Disciples preachers. Between 1815 and 1820 Thomas preached in southwestern Virginia in churches that later became affiliated with the Disciples. By 1828 he was living in central Ohio, where his son-in-law became a Disciples minister.

Several circumstances opened North Carolina as a Disciples mission field. The Stone-Campbell newspaper, the *Millennial Harbinger* (which replaced an earlier publication, the *Christian Baptist*, in 1830), attracted a growing number of North Carolina subscribers. In 1833 the Dover Baptist Association in eastern Virginia expelled several churches for espousing Campbellite views. Encouraged by a visit from the Disciples' patriarch, Thomas Campbell, B. F. Hall, one of the expelled Virginia Baptists, began preaching Campbellite doctrine in the Edenton area. Hall condemned the use of creeds, church constitutions and covenants, systems of discipline, qualifications for church membership, and, according to a Baptist critic, preached that "any person is properly qualified for baptism who will say that he believes in Christ, loves God, and is desirous of the ordinance." This set of beliefs attracted many former O'Kellyites, members of another nondenominational primitive movement in the South. The North Carolina Campbellites also attracted adherents from the Free Will Baptists who had broken away from the Regular Baptists over the issue of predestination.

From the 1840s onward, Disciples of Christ churches in North Carolina struggled to resolve the paradox of New Testament primitive Christianity—how to be both otherworldly, unencumbered with denominational trappings, and also truly biblical, to teach a complex sacred text with scholarly and theological integrity. The preeminent Disciples intellectual was John Tomline Walsh (1816–86), a Virginia physician and former Methodist who responded to an invitation in 1852 to evangelize eastern North Carolina. He found the existing Disciples churches in the state isolated from each other and uninformed about the theology of primitive Christianity. Based in Kinston, he founded in 1853 the journal *Christian Friend* (later the *Watch Tower*) to raise the intellectual level of religious discourse, emphasizing the legitimacy of interpreting scripture by recognizing that "literal and figurative" scriptural language "are often mingled together in the same prophesies and require great care and discrimination to understand."

In the face of strenuous opposition—one Baptist writer accused Walsh of "big-headism"—Walsh and his followers advocated, and in 1877 finally achieved, creation of the North Carolina Christian Missionary Convention as the governing body of the Disciples of Christ in the state, with Walsh as the convention's first president. John J. Harper, ordained in 1862, succeeded Walsh after 1886 as the most influential Disciples minister and educator. He became the first president of the church's Atlantic Christian College (modern-day Barton College) in Wilson, incorporated in 1902. The region between Kinston, Wilson, and Rocky Mount has remained the center of Disciples of Christ activity. In the early 2000s, 106 of the 138 Disciples of Christ congregations in North Carolina were in the eastern part of the state.

References: Griffith Askew Hamlin, "Educational Efforts among the Disciples of Christ in North Carolina during the Years 1852–1902" (Th.D. diss., Bethany College and Divinity School, 1947); David E. Harrell Jr., *The Social Sources of Division in the Disciples of Christ* (1973); C. C. Ware, *A History of the Disciples of Christ in North Carolina* (1927).

Robert M. Calhoon

Disfranchisement refers to a constitutional amendment drafted by the 1899 North Carolina General Assembly and approved in the general election in 1900 severely limiting African Americans' right to vote. The intent of disfranchisement was to repudiate the principle of universal male suffrage, especially black suffrage, and to replace it with laws that ensured that only literate white males could vote.

Federal and state constitutional measures adopted during Reconstruction had prohibited the denial of voting rights on the basis of race. The Fifteenth Amendment to the U.S. Constitution, ratified in 1870, banned any infringement on a citizen's right to vote "on account of race, color, or previous condition of servitude," thus giving the federal government domain over voting qualifications. Throughout the 1870s and 1880s, however, access to the ballot in North Carolina was a matter of contention. The Democratic-controlled legislature passed laws that enabled it to control the registration and vote-counting

processes. Under this system, bribery, intimidation, and fraud were common. Yet in 1894 the Democratic election machinery was overthrown by the new Populist-Republican "Fusion" government. Fusionist laws passed by the General Assembly in 1895 and 1897 made it easier for illiterates and blacks to vote and reduced the likelihood of fraud.

By the election campaign of 1898, Democratic leaders, particularly Furnifold M. Simmons of New Bern, had decided that a dramatic restriction of the franchise would eliminate the complexities of voting in the post–Civil War era and ensure Democratic rule. Recognizing the sensitivity of poorer whites to curbs on voting, Democratic candidates naturally denied they would enact such legislation if elected. Using violence and intimidation against Populist and Republican opponents, the Democratic Party regained control of the General Assembly, which in 1899 approved a constitutional amendment restricting the right to vote. The lawmakers then scheduled a special election to be held on 2 Aug. 1900 for public consideration of the amendment.

The disfranchisement amendment was worded in such a way that it circumvented the federal prohibition of overt racial discrimination in voting procedures. Neutral on its face, it merely required prospective voters to pay a poll tax and to pass a literacy test. However, the poll tax was costly to the poor and, of course, applied only to those intending to vote. In addition, in 1900 almost 30 percent of all voting-age males were illiterate, a disproportionate percentage of whom were poor African Americans. Further, the proposed amendment would operate in conjunction with new registration laws passed in 1899 that gave Democrats control of deciding which persons had properly registered. Finally, to appeal to some whites, the amendment included a grandfather clause that allowed an illiterate to qualify if he or a lineal ancestor had been a registered voter before 1867—that is, prior to Congressional Reconstruction—provided he registered by 1908. The grandfather clause indicated that the short-term purpose of disfranchisement was to eliminate black voters.

The debate over the amendment reached its climax in the summer of 1900. Generally, Republicans and Populists opposed the measure, while Democrats, including gubernatorial candidate Charles B. Aycock, supported it. The greatest concern of Republicans and Populists was the potential disfranchisement of poor whites, not African Americans, yet many supported the amendment. In an election characterized by registration abuses by Democratic officials, more violence and intimidation on the part of Democratic ruffians and groups such as the Red Shirts, and elaborate demonstrations of white supremacists, the disfranchisement amendment passed easily.

The effect of the disfranchisement amendment on North Carolina elections was revolutionary. Between 1900 and 1902, white turnout plummeted and black turnout was almost non-

A view of the Dismal Swamp Canal at South Mills, ca. 1900. NCC.

existent. Not until the 1960s, with the passage of strong federal voting rights legislation, did its continuing impact begin to dissipate.

References: Jerry W. Cotten, "Negro Disfranchisement in North Carolina: The Politics of Race in a Southern State" (M.A. thesis, UNC-Greensboro, 1973); Jeffrey J. Crow and Robert F. Durden, *Maverick Republican in the Old North State: A Political Biography of Daniel L. Russell* (1977); Helen G. Edmonds, *The Negro and Fusion Politics in North Carolina, 1894–1901* (1951); James L. Hunt, "Marion Butler and the Populist Ideal, 1863–1938" (Ph.D. diss., University of Wisconsin, 1990); J. Morgan Kousser, *The Shaping of Southern Politics: Suffrage Restriction and the Establishment of the One-Party South, 1880–1910* (1974).

James L. Hunt

SEE ALSO Grandfather Clause; Poll Tax.

Dismal Swamp Canal, believed to be the oldest existing excavated waterway in America, runs generally north and south for 22 miles between Deep Creek, Va., and South Mills, N.C. The canal connects the Elizabeth and Pasquotank Rivers, thereby affording water communication between the Chesapeake Bay and the Albemarle Sound. Proposed as early as about 1730 by William Byrd II, the idea of such a waterway found late-eighteenth-century champions in Hugh Williamson of North Carolina and Virginians Patrick Henry, Thomas Jefferson, and George Washington. Although both states had

approved the canal by 1790, work did not begin until 1793; workers dug from both ends toward the middle, and the two ditches were finally connected in 1805. When completed, however, the canal was "little more than a muddy ditch," according to historian A. C. Brown. After years of shingle flats, the first real ship (a 20-ton craft bearing bacon and brandy from the Roanoke River to Norfolk) finally made passage through the Dismal Swamp Canal in June 1814.

Railroads gave the canal competition in the 1840s and 1850s, and by 1859 a new thoroughfare to the east, the Albemarle and Chesapeake Canal connecting the Elizabeth River with the Currituck Sound, began to steal water traffic away from the Dismal Swamp Canal. The Civil War nearly ruined the canal, which could not service its debt in the 1870s and which by the early 1890s could no longer float a boat of three-foot draft. A major reconstruction took place between 1896 and 1899, and for a time the canal carried more freight than the rival Albemarle and Chesapeake. The federal government subsequently bought the Albemarle and Chesapeake and abolished tolls on it, adversely affecting the renovated Dismal Swamp Canal, which also fell to federal purchase in 1929. Useful strategically during the Atlantic Coast submarine threat of World War II, the canal has since shifted its service as a shipping lane from commercial vessels to pleasure craft. Since the 1950s, there have been efforts by the Army Corps of Engineers to close it altogether.

The history of the Dismal Swamp Canal and the road that

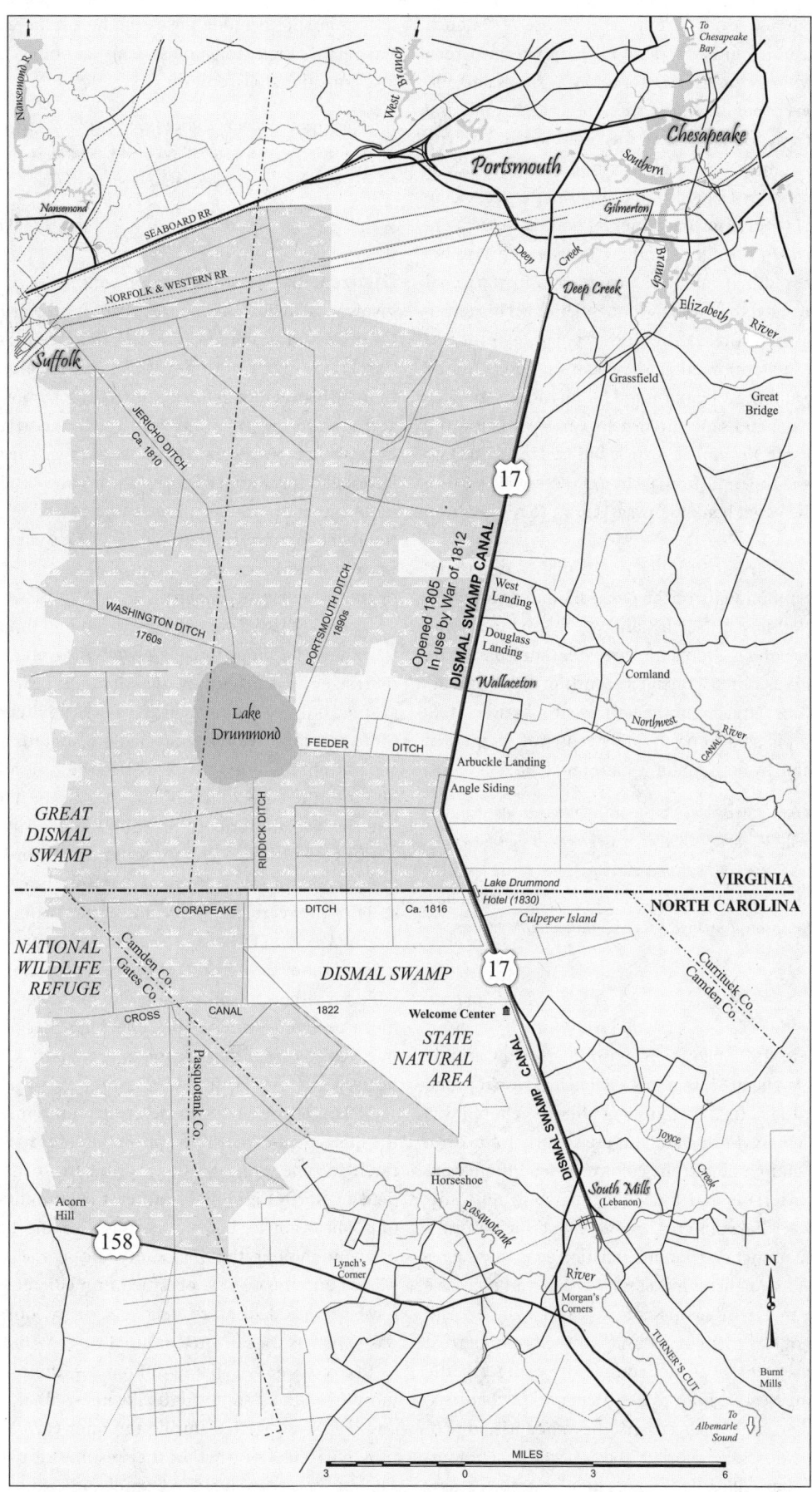

Dismal Swamp Canal. Map by Mark Anderson Moore, courtesy NCOA&H.

parallels it is rich and vivid, particularly because of Camden County's nineteenth-century reputation as a Gretna Green and the swamp's history as a haven for runaway slaves and outlaws. One famous canal bank structure, the Lake Drummond Hotel (or "Half-way House," as it was notoriously known), straddled the Virginia–North Carolina boundary and advertised itself in the 1830s as being "in a superior degree, calculated to render facilities for matrimonial and duelistical engagements." In 1829 President Andrew Jackson ate Virginia ham off a cypress shingle along the canal, and in 1894 poet Robert Frost traversed the canal by foot and boat on his unfulfilled suicide trip to the Great Dismal Swamp. The *James Adams Floating Theatre*, a warm-weather showboat that once toured the Chesapeake and the Albemarle and lay up winters in Elizabeth City, hit snags and sank in Turner's Cut (just below the South Mills locks) in November 1929; it suffered the same fate at another point in the canal in 1937. In 1940 editor W. O. Saunders drove off the canal bank highway, U.S. 17, to his death in the canal.

For most of its course in Virginia, the Dismal Swamp Canal forms the eastern boundary of the Great Dismal Swamp National Wildlife Refuge. In North Carolina, it constitutes the eastern boundary of a 14,000-acre Dismal Swamp park. The North Carolina Welcome Center just south of the Virginia–North Carolina line, situated in the narrow strip between U.S. 17 and the canal, is said to be the only center of its kind in America accessible by both motor vehicle and boat.

References: Edmund Berkeley and Dorothy Berkeley, "Man and the Great Dismal," *Virginia Journal of Science* 27 (Fall 1976); Alexander Crosby Brown, *The Dismal Swamp Canal* (1970); Jesse F. Pugh and Frank T. Williams, *The Hotel in the Great Dismal Swamp* (1964); Bland Simpson, *The Great Dismal: A Carolinian's Swamp Memoir* (1990).

Bland Simpson

Dissenters were those people living in the North Carolina colony after the Anglican Church was established who rejected its beliefs and rituals. In 1711, ten years after the church was established by law in North Carolina, missionary John Urmston found few churchmen in the colony. Instead there were numerous Presbyterians and Independents, "but most anythingarians." Nevertheless, in that same year acting governor Edward Hyde recommended harsh legislation against dissenters. James Reed, an Anglican missionary but not an objective observer, wrote in 1760 that dissenters "can hardly be said to be members of any particular Christian society, and great numbers of dissenters of all denominations come & settle amongst us from New Eng[lan]d[,] Particularly, Anabaptists, Methodist, Quakers and Presbyterians, the Anabaptist are obstinate, illiterate & grossly ignorant, the Methodist, ignorant, censorious & uncharitable, the Quakers Rigid, but the Presby-

terians are pretty moderate except here & there a bigot or rigid Calvinist." Huguenots and Roman Catholics, of course, were also considered dissenters.

References: William S. Price Jr., ed., *North Carolina Higher-Court Records, 1702–1708* (1974); William L. Saunders, ed., *Colonial Records of North Carolina* (10 vols., 1886–90).

William S. Powell

Divorce, like marriage, is a civil contract between the parties involved. Religious and social attitudes toward marriage and property rights made divorce in nineteenth-century North Carolina rare but not impossible. In the colonial period the General Court occasionally ordered separate maintenance, and it often called for alimony. For the marriage contract to be broken, certain conditions had to exist. The marriage must have been legal under North Carolina law and the cause for its termination adultery, cruelty, or desertion (desertion was the most commonly cited). These causes were often cited by women seeking release from restrictions on their right to own or control separate property.

There are two forms of legal divorce in modern-day North Carolina. The older form is absolute divorce, rendering the marriage nonexistent by dissolving it; this was formerly granted only for serious causes, such as adultery or impotence. More recently, divorce from bed and board, a state of legal separation, became possible. After the American Revolution and into the early nineteenth century, the General Assembly had the sole authority to grant both types. After 1827 the superior court in each county could also award divorces, and after a constitutional reform in 1835 only the court could do so.

Over the years, it has become easier to obtain a divorce in North Carolina. Either husband or wife may be granted a divorce without the consent of the other spouse, making it possible for either person to leave the marriage. North Carolina has a no-fault divorce policy, meaning that plaintiffs do not have to prove that they are the injured party. Children cannot be used as grounds for divorce.

North Carolina has two technical requirements for divorce: the husband and wife must prove that they have resided separately for one year, and the plaintiff must have been a resident of North Carolina for at least six months. In instances of spousal abuse, being turned out of the home, adultery, or abandonment, the mandatory one-year separation can be waived and the divorce obtained immediately. All other laws have been added, as deemed necessary, on a case-by-case basis. Just as with divorce, mutual agreement is not required to become legally separated; however, the plaintiff may not move from the state until the divorce is final. If the husband and wife live together during the one-year period of separation, regardless of whether they resume sexual relations, the separation is considered to be null and void.

Divorces involving children must address the issue of child custody. As in other states, custody in North Carolina is determined through a mediation process. Child support and alimony are considered on a need-basis system. The amount of child support, awarded to the parent who has sole custody of the child or children, is determined by the other spouse's ability to pay and the amount needed by the child or children to maintain a "normal" lifestyle. Alimony is decided by the same standards.

References: Helen F. M. Leary, *North Carolina Research, Genealogy, and Local History* (1996); Michael H. McGee, *Separation and Divorce in North Carolina* (1984).

Melissa Semcer

Dixiecrats, officially members of the States' Rights Democratic Party, formed after the 1947 publication of President Harry S Truman's Committee on Civil Rights report, *To Secure These Rights*. This report, reflecting one of the most aggressively pro–civil rights positions taken by the federal government since Reconstruction, mobilized conservative southern Democrats to block civil rights legislation and contest Truman's nomination for a second term. When the Democratic National Convention of 1948 voted for a stronger civil rights platform than even Truman supported, disgruntled southerners bolted. They reconvened in Birmingham, Ala., under the name States' Rights Democratic Party and nominated South Carolina governor J. Strom Thurmond for president and Mississippi governor Fielding Wright for vice president. Citing southern tradition, the Dixiecrats combined a belief in decentralized government with a passionate defense of their racially hierarchical, segregated society.

The Dixiecrats gained a following of varying sizes in each of the former Confederate states, carrying South Carolina, Mississippi, Alabama, and Louisiana in the presidential election. In North Carolina, however, the Dixiecrat campaign failed to generate much enthusiasm for two reasons. First, the powerful *Raleigh News and Observer* doggedly and vociferously opposed the Dixiecrats, describing their leaders on one occasion as possessing "an arrogance that has been rivaled only by their stupidity." Throughout the summer of 1948 the newspaper informed its readers at every opportunity that North Carolinians were not interested in abandoning the national Democratic Party and joining the "rebels."

Judging from the apparent lack of participation by North Carolinians in the Dixiecrat conventions in Birmingham and Houston, it seems that the *News and Observer* was largely correct. At the Birmingham convention, reference to North Carolina came in the form of a Texas state senator castigating the liberal "pinks" in Chapel Hill. A second explanation for the failure of the Dixiecrats in North Carolina was dissension within the state party ranks. Lacking a full roster of candidates for state offices, North Carolina Dixiecrats awkwardly supported regular party Democrats for local election while still opposing Truman at the national level.

Whether arguing for or against the Dixiecrats, North Carolinians revealed the intimate connection white southerners made between issues of governance and race in the mid-twentieth century. The *Asheville Citizen* criticized the Dixiecrats' third-party efforts as futile, yet at the same time it pronounced the national Democratic Party's support of civil rights the result of "the whipsawing of extremists" in the North. Although the *Citizen* recommended avoiding the "hot-headed leaders" of the Dixiecrats, it chided national Democrats for forcing on the South a civil rights position that many whites found repugnant. Ultimately, while many white North Carolinians shared similar concerns over the increasing centralization of power in Washington, D.C., and the growing threats to racial segregation, the institutional strength of the national Democratic Party carried the day and the state. North Carolinians were also swayed by Democratic support of various farm programs and by Truman's leadership in defeating the Axis powers in World War II. Thurmond and the Dixiecrats garnered approximately 54,000 ballots, or 8 percent of the vote, in North Carolina. With Truman's stunning election over Thomas Dewey, the Dixiecrat Party dissolved.

Reference: Robert A. Garson, *The Democratic Party and the Politics of Sectionalism, 1941–1948* (1974).

Charles J. Holden

Dixie Dynamo, the nickname given North Carolina in a 1962 article in *National Geographic* magazine, was widely adopted by the state's political leaders, businesspeople, and journalists as a way of advertising the state's newly prospering economic environment. The article by that title, touting an image of the state based largely on industrial gains over the preceding decade, was a public relations dream come true. Not since 1949 when political scientist V. O. Key termed North Carolina's political culture "progressive" had the state received such widely distributed favorable comment. Malcolm Ross, the author of the 44-page illustrated feature, was a newspaperman and New Jersey native but frequent visitor to North Carolina. "There is something inspiring about the State at this point in the twentieth century," he wrote, "something exciting, dynamic and somehow youthful."

Ross visited with leaders such as Research Triangle Park executive George Herbert, North Carolina State University dean Henry Kamphoefner, journalist Jonathan Daniels, and University of North Carolina president William C. Friday. He found particular promise in the Research Triangle, which he believed typified the "forward-looking, eagerly progressive state." Beyond its recent economic gains, Ross was entranced by the "varied resources and geography" of the state. His travels took him from the coast to the mountains, to practically every major tourist destination, and he "loved every minute of it."

Most of the industrial advances cited by Ross had come about under Governor Luther Hodges, whose term of office extended from 1954 to 1961. During Hodges's administration, investments by business in the state increased by $256 million. Also in those years more than 1,000 new industries located in North Carolina, and an additional 1,400 enlarged their facilities in the state. Not since the 1840s had North Carolina experienced such an era of expansion.

North Carolinians, who had long sought to establish an identity separate from other southern states that were struggling with economic hardship and racial discord, welcomed the publicity. Governor Terry Sanford, in a February 1963 speech to the Sales Executives Club of New York, contrasted North Carolina's "Dixie Dynamo" image with its onetime reputation as the "Rip Van Winkle State." Journalists and cultural leaders adopted the moniker. The North Carolina Museum of History for years thereafter captioned the exhibit covering the modern period of the state's history with the phrase.

References: Memory F. Mitchell, ed., *Messages, Addresses, and Public Papers of Terry Sanford, Governor of North Carolina, 1961–1965* (1966); Malcolm Ross, "North Carolina: Dixie Dynamo," *National Geographic* (February 1962).

Michael Hill

Dog Breeds. Several types of dogs are believed to have originated in North Carolina and South Carolina and have been bred in these states for decades or even centuries, although they have generally gone unrecognized by official dog registries. Most of these breeds were developed during the colonial period to perform very special and necessary functions, such as driving flocks of turkeys to market or livestock to pasture. Like certain tools and weapons, dogs were developed to meet specialized needs in different locales or times.

The Plott hound, the state dog of North Carolina, is probably the best known of these "hidden" dog breeds. It was recognized in western North Carolina in the 1750s and reportedly named for Johannes Plott, who developed it as a hunting dog. The Carolina dog, on the other hand, is classified by experts as being of the ancient pariah type, descended from the original Native American canine breeds. It can still be found in the wild in South Carolina and along the Yadkin River near Salisbury, N.C. Carolina dogs are good hunters and, if properly socialized, can become wonderful companions.

The Boykin spaniel is another example of a dog breed unique to the Carolinas. It was developed in South Carolina for the challenges of turkey hunting, to fit into very small watercraft when the hunters were after waterbirds, or for other specific needs. The black mouth cur, also known as the southern cur or the yellow black mouth cur, is bred to hunt boar, rac-coon, bear, and deer. It is a powerful dog with a deep bay and is excellent in treeing its quarry. The black mouth cur is also protective of children, and the males prefer women to men as companions. The leopard cur also has North Carolina roots. A big hound, it weighs from 45 to 77 pounds and has been used as a watchdog and for hunting game. It is usually a leopard-spotted merle color, although it can also be black and tan, dark brindled, or yellow. The leopard cur is a very hard worker and tends to be one-person dog.

Another "hidden" dog, recognized as the "dog of the Hunt Club of Pender County," was developed by the foxhunters of the Cape Fear region of eastern North Carolina to meet the challenges of the sport there. It is an excellent dog, and its antecedents go back to the late nineteenth or early twentieth centuries. Mention has been found of "scratch hall dogs" from the Dismal Swamp area of North Carolina, but very little can presently be verified concerning their heritage.

Joseph C. Porter

SEE ALSO Plott Hound.

Dog Racing and the pari-mutuel betting that came along with it had a short life in North Carolina, extending only from the late 1940s to the mid-1950s. In the period of rapid growth after World War II, promoters of tourism in coastal counties saw dog racing as a means of attracting more visitors to resort communities while providing a new source of money to supplement the property tax. Following passage of the necessary legislation by the General Assembly, two dog tracks were built, one in Carteret County at Morehead City and the other in Currituck County just south of the border between Virginia and North Carolina.

Opposition to dog racing, fragmented at first, became increasingly organized once the tracks were actually in operation. After little more than a trial run, the General Assembly repealed the law authorizing pari-mutuel betting, dog racing was discontinued, and the two tracks were closed.

David Stick

Dogwood. In 1941 the North Carolina General Assembly designated the flower of the dogwood tree (*Cornaceae*) as the official state flower. In actuality, three species of dogwoods exist in North Carolina. The alternate-leaf dogwood (*Cornus alternifolia*), which is common in the mountains and rare in the northern piedmont, has leaves that are simple and elliptical but are alternate on their stems (hence the name). It has small white flowers that are in loose, flat-topped clusters. Various animals eat its small, deep-blue or black fruit; the plant is usually a shrub or a small tree up to 30 feet tall and eight inches in diameter with a broad, flattened crown.

The gray dogwood (*Cornus racemosa*) is a bush that has simple, elliptical, and opposite leaves. Its gray-to-white fruits and gray twigs give it its name. This dogwood grows in thickets in damp meadows in the mountains of the northwestern corner of North Carolina.

The flowering dogwood (*Cornus florida*), common in the wild and popular as an ornamental, is a tree that enchants people every spring. A relatively short tree, its four white (or sometimes pink) petal-like bracts circle the tiny greenish white flowers in the center. The bracts have dark indentations at their tips. The tree has simple, opposite, elliptical leaves that in fall turn from green to red to maroon, and its red berries are a favorite of birds. The flowering dogwood is found in deciduous woodlands throughout the state up to elevations of 4,500 feet.

In years past the hard, shock-resistant wood of dogwood trees was used to make farm implements, wedges for rail splitting, shuttles for spinning mills, tool handles, and other things. The bark, flowers, berries, and roots of the flowering dogwood also had many medicinal purposes. The bark and sometimes the roots were used as a substitute for Peruvian bark in treating intermittent fevers and malaria. The bark was also employed as an antiseptic and a cathartic. The flowers (not the bracts) made a good substitute for chamomile tea, and the berries, when soaked in brandy, also made a serviceable bitter.

Several legends surrounding the dogwood are still repeated in North Carolina. One popular story holds that 2,000 years ago the flowering dogwood tree stood straight, proud, and tall. Because the tree had such strong wood, the Roman soldiers under Pontius Pilate chose to make the cross of Jesus Christ out of dogwood trunks. The dogwood tree was horrified but had no choice. In order never to serve as a cross again, the dogwood became a slender, twisted tree. In addition, to help people remember Jesus' sacrifice, the dogwood flowers bloom in the spring in the shape of a cross with nail holes at the ends.

References: C. Ritchie Bell and Anne H. Lindsey, *Fall Color and Woodland Harvests: A Guide to the More Colorful Fall Leaves and Fruits of the Eastern Forests* (1990); C. Wilbur H. Duncan and Marion B. Duncan, *Trees of the Southeastern United States* (1988).

Lee Plummer Templeton

Dogwood Festivals

Dogwood Festivals are held in five North Carolina cities: Farmville (Pitt County), Fayetteville (Cumberland County), Lake Lure (Rutherford County), Mebane (Alamance and Orange Counties), and Statesville (Iredell County). All of the festivals, which celebrate North Carolina's state flower, the dogwood, are held in the month of April, when the trees typically bloom. The Farmville Dogwood Festival started in 1988, when Mayor Edna Earle Baker sought a replacement for the discontinued Farmer's Day. The Farmville festival features 35 to 40 musical groups performing all types of music, from bluegrass to reggae. The three-and-a-half-day, family-oriented event attracts up to 40,000 people and functions as a town reunion. Other attractions have included celebrity storytelling, a petting zoo, arts and crafts shows, mounted drill team and antique car exhibitions, and a Civil War reenactment. Activity centers around the gazebo on the Town Common.

The Fayetteville Dogwood Festival began in 1982 when Mayor Bill Hurley declared Fayetteville "The City of Dogwoods." This followed many years of local civic activity promoting the planting of dogwoods. The festival attempts to enlighten, entertain, and educate attendees as well as support and foster the natural beauty of the area. Attendance reaches 100,000 over the ten-day festival period. Some 35 festival-related events have included a golf tournament, a fashion show, a 10K run, a chili cook-off, a rodeo, and a parade. The festival showcase is an 18-mile driving trail called the Dogwood Trail, which winds through the city's most beautiful and historic neighborhoods with their Federal, Greek Revival, and Victorian architecture.

Through the efforts of Jimmy Hook and the Lions Club, Lake Lure began its dogwood festival in 1991. The mountainsides full of blooming dogwood trees are reflected in the lake, creating an especially beautiful natural scene. Attendance runs from 5,000 to 8,000 people. Events have typically included a parade, crafts, music, food, and free health tests such as glaucoma screening.

Sponsored by the Mebane Business Association, the Mebane Dogwood Festival began in 1989. Between 10,000 and 15,000 people attend the weekend festival, which typically includes major musical entertainment, arts, crafts, food, and a golf tournament. Local businesspeople, along with Jim Calabrese, director of the Statesville High School Grenadier Band, founded Statesville's Carolina Dogwood Festival in 1969 to promote high school bands, with a competition that attracts entries from many states. Past events, spread out over a week or more, have also included a parade, an auto show, beauty pageants, golf and softball tournaments, and a beach band concert.

Reference: Gary Sherrill, "Carolina Dogwood Festival History," in Ginny Turner, ed., *North Carolina Traveler: A Vacationer's Guide to the Mountains, Coast, and Piedmont* (1997).

Nancy P. Shires

Doodlebugs

Doodlebugs, or ant lions, belong to the order of insects *Neuroptera* and are found in many parts of the world, including much of North Carolina. They came to be called doodlebugs about 1866. The winged adult has been described as graceful and elegant. The insect lays its eggs in dry sand in sheltered places, such as under the edge of a building, a cliff, or a road embankment. The larvae, requiring as long as three years to attain maturity, construct pits two to three inches in diameter in the sand or dry dust and dirt. The pits resemble funnels or inverted cones, into which ants fall. Concealed in the bottom, the larvae use caliper-like pincers to grab an invading ant. Injected with a digestive enzyme, the ant is then sucked dry.

Doodlebugs have also played a role in North Carolina folk history. They are often "called up" by children, who use a straw or pine needle to stir the pit in imitation of an ant struggling to escape. Children traditionally sing a ditty such as "Doodlebug, doodlebug, your house is on fire," or, "Doodlebug, doodlebug, come get your bread and butter," while attempting to catch the insect. When the doodlebug reveals itself it may be lifted out of its hiding place and held in the palm of the hand. Since it moves backward better than forward, it often backs off the hand quickly and falls to the ground.

References: Harry Ellis, "Lion in a Pit," *Wildlife in North Carolina* 54 (June 1990); Mary Alice Hancoch, "Sing to the Doodlebug," *Pageant* 14 (September 1958).

William S. Powell

Dope Wagons were carts laden with snacks and soft drinks that circulated through North Carolina and other southern textile mills to provide workers with food and beverages. The dope wagon's name was derived from the nickname of one of its most commonly sold products—a "dope," or a bottle of Coca-Cola. With the advent of soda pop and packaged foods, the dope wagon was introduced into the cotton mill setting sometime during the first two decades of the twentieth century. It certainly was a fixture in the mills by the late 1920s. Because it allowed workers to remain on the job while they ate and drank, the dope wagon was suited ideally to the needs of owners determined to increase production in the era of the "speed-up" and the "stretch-out." The dope wagon gradually disappeared, replaced by the canteen and snack bar of modern textile factories.

Richard Rankin

Dorland-Bell School was established in Hot Springs (Madison County) in 1887 under the auspices of the Presbyterian Church. Called at first the Mission School at Hot Springs, the rapidly growing institution was named Dorland Institute in 1893, then in 1918 renamed the Dorland-Bell School following consolidation with Bell Institute. The school was founded by Luke Dorland and his wife, who had retired to the mountain health resort of Hot Springs after a lifetime of Presbyterian mission work. Located six miles from the Tennessee border, the school primarily drew students from North Carolina and the neighboring states of Kentucky, South Carolina, Tennessee, Virginia, and West Virginia. Students ranged in age from 5 to 28, with annual enrollment numbering 100 to 200 annually. Although for its first 40 years, Dorland offered no grade higher than eighth, its graduates were considered exceptionally trained and were certified to teach in most schools.

Maintaining dormitories for both girls and boys, Dorland-Bell was the only coeducational boarding school in the Presbyterians' southern Appalachian network. A large farmstead two miles from the school campus in town was home to more than 50 boys who walked the distance twice daily, regardless of the weather, carrying their books and meager lunches. Surrounding the Boys' Home were 600 acres of fertile river bottom, pasture, and forest. Named the "Willows," the farm became a demonstration model, using its own resources to make substantial improvements—including treating the acid soil with lime and constructing a silo, the first in the region. Another Dorland-Bell innovation, the "practice cottage system," offered girls six weeks of domestic science training as they took turns running a household. The school became known as the pioneer in this teaching method.

In addition to the farmstead's dozen or more buildings, the campus on Bridge Street in town covered a large block of property, supporting a dormitory, a classroom building, a hospital, and seven other buildings, as well as the church. Under supervision, the boarding pupils performed all the work of school and farm. Bible study and church attendance were mandatory, as were uniforms and weekly letters to parents.

The school's identity further changed in 1926 when the New York mission board closed the boys' department. By 1932 grades had been added for high school accreditation, only to be moved a decade later to Asheville Farm School at Swannanoa (a merger that led to what became Warren Wilson College).

References: Jacqueline Burgin Painter, *The Season of Dorland-Bell: History of an Appalachian Mission School* (1996); Manly Wade Wellman, *The Kingdom of Madison* (1973).

Jacqueline Burgin Painter

Dorothea Dix Hospital. SEE Psychiatric Hospitals.

Dorton Arena. The North Carolina State Fair Arena, completed in Raleigh in 1953, was dedicated as the J. S. "Doc" Dorton Arena on 16 Oct. 1961. Dorton, a retired veterinarian, served as State Fair manager from 1937 until his death in 1961. The arena was built to serve agriculture, industry, commerce, and the public as a year-round center for educational, inspirational, and recreational events. In addition to its use during the State Fair each autumn, the arena functions as a statewide exhibit center for trade shows and accommodates conventions, meetings, banquets and exhibitions, and circuses and other entertainment attractions.

The elliptical arena is 300 feet in diameter, with a central concrete floor 221 feet long and 127 feet wide at the widest part of the ellipse. It contains 4,750 permanent opera-type chairs and 360 box seats for a capacity of 5,110. About 4,400 portable seats can be installed on the floor when a stage is used, in-

Dorton Arena shortly after its completion in 1953. Courtesy of NCOA&H.

creasing the total capacity to 9,150. The metal-asbestos, saddle-shaped roof is suspended in a network of cables extending crosswise from the 90-foot parabolic arches. Fourteen-foot-wide arches, reaching a maximum height of 90 feet, cross each other at about 26 feet above the ground and extend into a tunnel below the surface of the east and west ends. Tension cables equalize the weight of the roof, with 14 two-inch strands connecting each end of the parabola through the stress tunnel. The roof, so suspended, eliminates any necessity for structural steel supports and presents no visual obstructions from any seat. The exterior walls consist of translucent heat- and glare-reducing glass above the two ground-level lobby areas. These and two lower-level concourses provide about 25,000 square feet on the arena floor.

Matthew Nowicki conceived the distinctive structure, a daring exercise in architectural design, while head of the Department of Architecture of North Carolina State University. Shortly after accepting the arena commission, Nowicki died in an airplane accident near Cairo, Egypt. His friend, architect William Henley Deitrick of Raleigh, took over the project. The arena, it has been said, serves as a memorial to a potentially spectacular career cut short. At the centennial celebration of the American Institute of Architects in 1957, it was named one of the ten buildings of the twentieth century most likely to influence future architects.

References: Catherine W. Bishir and others, *Architects and Builders in North Carolina: A History of the Practice of Building* (1990); James Vickers, *Raleigh: City of Oaks* (1982).

Wiley J. Williams

Dramatic Arts. Theater productions have been a vital part of the culture and entertainment of North Carolinians since colonial times. Much of the success of North Carolina's theater tradition can be attributed to innovative statewide service organizations. The Institute of Outdoor Drama, the North Carolina Arts Council, and the North Carolina Theater Conference support new and evolving groups, assist in organizational growth, act as a clearinghouse for information, and represent the theater community as a collective voice. The Arts Council, part of the Department of Cultural Resources, has been a state

agency since 1967. The section that deals with theater operated separately as N.C. Theater Arts from 1972 until 1981. The North Carolina Theater Conference, founded in 1970, offers support and a conduit for communication to all levels of theater, both to theater companies and individual practitioners. At the local level, the state boasts more than 100 arts councils, including one of the country's oldest, the Arts Council of Winston-Salem/Forsyth County, founded in 1949. By the early 2000s there were at least 780 theater providers (organizations and individuals) in North Carolina, with at least one in almost every county.

Early Productions and Important Playwrights

The first drama written by an American and produced by a professional company was completed in Wilmington sometime in late 1759. Playwright Thomas Godfrey died before his play, *The Prince of Parthia*, was published in 1765 and produced in Philadelphia in 1767. The next known production to come from the pen of a North Carolinian was former governor Alexander Martin's *A New Scene Interesting to the Citizens of the United States*. This short play, written in 1798 in an effort to engender patriotism, was presented in Philadelphia. The first play that could be considered entirely a product of North Carolina was Lemuel Sawyer's *Blackbeard: A Comedy, in Four Acts;. Founded on Fact*, written and published in 1824. Sawyer, a native of Camden County, wrote the play using characters, settings, and situations based in North Carolina.

In the eighteenth and nineteenth centuries, North Carolinians were entertained by both professional and amateur thespians. Professional touring companies performed standard popular British plays and occasionally inspired North Carolinians to form amateur companies. The state's first firmly established community-based amateur company was the Thalian Association in Wilmington. Organized in 1788 and interrupted by occasional lapses, the association's activities have ranged from producing plays to managing Thalian Hall, which opened in the 1850s to serve as a town hall, library, theater, and home to the association. The tradition in North Carolina of operating a theater in a multipurpose building goes back to the 1700s and early 1800s, with Masonic temples, school buildings, and even the State Capitol hosting theatrical performances.

At the turn of the twentieth century, Christian Reid wrote a play about the Civil War era for production by the United Daughters of the Confederacy. But her *Under the Southern Cross* (1900) was an isolated effort, as was *Esther Wake; or, The Spirit of the Regulators* (1913), a historical play about revolutionary North Carolina by Adolph Vermont of Smithfield. In 1905 Cleveland County lawyer, politician, minister, lecturer, and writer Thomas Dixon Jr. published his play *The Clansman*, a revision of an earlier novel. In 1913 the successful play caught the attention of D. W. Griffith, then an aspiring filmmaker, who

Members of the Carolina Playmakers load a bus with props before leaving on a tour in the fall of 1941. The company, based at the University of North Carolina in Chapel Hill, played an important role in the development of American folk drama and nurtured several generations of North Carolina theater artists. NCC.

convinced Dixon to allow him to create a motion picture adaptation. The movie, *The Birth of a Nation* (1915), is considered a landmark motion picture in terms of technical and artistic achievement. However, its white supremacist theme and racist depiction of African Americans sparked criticism at its debut and remains highly controversial.

Frederick H. Koch, one of the greatest influences on drama and theater in North Carolina, arrived at the University of North Carolina in Chapel Hill in 1918 to teach a new course in writing plays in the English Department. Seventeen-year-old Thomas Wolfe was a member of Koch's first class in Chapel Hill, and Paul Green followed in 1919. Koch encouraged his students to write "folk" plays about the common people, their lives, and their legends. To give his students an outlet for their work, in 1919 he organized the Carolina Playmakers, whose tours brought the folk play productions to the far reaches of North Carolina and beyond. The enthusiasm for amateur the-

atrics encouraged Koch, with the help of the university's Extension Division, to open the Bureau of Community Drama. The bureau encouraged and advised in the writing and production of original plays in North Carolina communities. Koch taught at the university and remained active in North Carolina theater for 26 years until his death in 1944.

While fledgling playwrights worked under Koch, a number of other North Carolina writers worked independently. *What Price Glory?* (1924), coauthored by Lawrence Stallings of Yanceyville, who had served in World War I, rendered a faithful image of the war. Lula Vollmer of Addor, after visiting the lumber camps in the mountains, wrote several plays with a North Carolina setting. Her most famous play, *Sun-Up* (1924), was about a rugged mountain woman who fought the "guv'ment" and did not want her son to go off to World War I.

Paul Green won the Pulitzer Prize for his play, *In Abraham's Bosom*, in 1927. Born near Lillington, Green grew up on his father's farm and became a schoolteacher to save money to attend the University of North Carolina. Green's student days were interrupted when he served in World War I, but after the war he returned to the writing of plays. Among his most famous plays are *Tread the Green Grass* (1931), *Roll Sweet Chariot* (1931), *Shroud My Body Down* (1935), and *Johnny Johnson* (1937). Green was also the author of several outdoors dramas, including the first and most famous, *The Lost Colony* (1937).

Counted among the various plays by Howard Richardson of Black Mountain is his poetic fantasy-drama *Dark of the Moon*, which sustained a long New York run after its premiere in 1945 and has been frequently revived by amateur and professional groups. Richardson, another Koch disciple, based *Dark of the Moon* on the Scottish ballad, "Barbara Allen." The play relates the love of John the witch-boy for bonny Barbara Allen of Buck Creek.

Playwright Romulus Linney, descendant of a prestigious family from the mountain counties of Alexander, Wilkes, and Watauga, spent his youth in Boone. After writing a number of full-length plays set variously in Germany, Hawaii, and Washington, D.C., Linney delved into the North Carolina mountains and hills for his *Holy Ghosts* (1974). *Appalachia Sounding* (1975), Linney's play for the bicentennial celebration, details a mountain family's experiences through 200 years of enduring vitality. *Old Man Joseph and His Family* (1979) is a biblical play dramatizing the boyhood of Jesus.

Pender County's Samm-Art Williams grew up near Burgaw. After graduating from Morgan State University in Baltimore, Williams went to New York to attempt a career in drama. By 1974 he had become a member of the Negro Ensemble Company as dramatist, director, and actor. One of his first plays, *Welcome to Black River* (1975), described North Carolina sharecroppers in 1958. However, it was *Home* (1979) that brought him national recognition. Over the course of his career, Williams has penned many dramas about the black experience in North Carolina.

Community Theaters and School-Related Programs

Community theaters in North Carolina have continued to thrive since Koch's time. With the Little Theatre of Charlotte, now known as Theatre Charlotte, opening in 1927, and theaters in Winston-Salem, Brevard, and Raleigh opening in the 1930s, the state has some of the longest-running community theaters in the nation. Perhaps one of the most notable figures to emerge from the community theater scene was Charlton Heston, who, with his wife Lydia, began directing at the Asheville Community Theater in 1947, its second year in operation. According to the North Carolina Theater Conference, by the early 2000s there were at least 117 community theaters serving various cities, counties, and regions in North Carolina.

There are numerous college and university theater programs contributing to theatrical education in the state, with the oldest, the Belmont Abbey Players, having been in continuous production since 1884. Outdoor dramas and summer theaters such as Mars Hill's Southern Appalachian Repertory Theater, started in 1975, provide both college students and potential professional theater stock an opportunity for quality theatrical experiences. In addition, secondary school theater programs and privately run youth theaters serve as foundations for developing and training the future performers and technical crews of the state's community and professional theaters.

Professional Companies and Festivals

The lively theater scene at the community level has fed the growth of professional theater in North Carolina. The state was in the early 2000s home to more than 70 professional theater organizations. The theater industry generates in excess of $22 million annually and provides annual or seasonal employment to more than 6,500 people. Big-budget Broadway shows, featuring a combination of national stars and local casts, are staged regularly at theaters such as the North Carolina Theatre in Raleigh. Among the oldest professional theaters in the state, the Flat Rock Playhouse, established in the early 1940s, was designated as the State Theater of North Carolina by the 1961 General Assembly. Ranked one of the top ten summer theaters in the nation, it has also branched out into fall and winter holiday productions. Started by Robroy Farquhar, who moved to the North Carolina mountains from New York with his Vagabond Players, and now run by his son Robin, Flat Rock Playhouse remains a vital part of the North Carolina theater scene.

North Carolina has two professional theater companies that are members of the League of Resident Theatres and work with Actors Equity contracts. Founded in 1976, Charlotte Repertory Theatre was originally called Actors Contemporary Ensemble. The resident theater of the city's Blumenthal Performing Arts Center, Charlotte Rep produces five plays each season, including new works, musicals, and world classics, and hosts an annual New Play Festival. PlayMakers Repertory Company in Chapel Hill, established as a professional theater in 1975, grew out of Koch's Carolina Playmakers. The company works closely with the University of North Carolina's Department of Dramatic Art and produces five plays each season in both classic and contemporary genres. Both companies have been recognized nationally for their outstanding efforts.

The National Black Theater Festival is a biennial professional festival held in Winston-Salem since 1989. Founded by Larry Leon Hamlin in an effort to unite black theater companies and ensure their perpetuity, this event now draws international attention. Theater performances, celebrity appearances, workshops, and seminars bring more than 50,000 people to the city for six days of activities.

The North Carolina Shakespeare Festival, founded in 1977

and based in High Point, was started by Mark Woods and Stuart Brooks and drew on the talent of the nearby North Carolina School of the Arts for actors and theater craftsmen. The festival is concentrated on a repertory season that usually consists of two Shakespeare plays and one other classical production. In addition to regular performances in the High Point Theater, the festival travels to Greensboro, Winston-Salem, and other cities. The company also tours performances and workshops to middle schools and high schools throughout North Carolina, with some trips into South Carolina and Virginia.

References: James H. Dormon Jr., *Theater in the Ante-Bellum South* (1967); Philip C. Kolin, ed., *Shakespeare in the South: Essays on Performance* (1983); Harry Gene Lominac, *The Carolina Dramatic Association: Its History, 1922–1962* (1962); Hugh F. Rankin, *The Theater in Colonial America* (1965); Richard Walser, ed., *North Carolina Drama* (1956); Charles S. Watson, *The History of Southern Drama* (1997).

Ansley Herring Wegner
Ted Mitchell
Additional research provided by Cecelia Moore.

SEE ALSO Opera Houses; Outdoor Dramas; Strolling Players; Thalian Association.

Drawbridges were built in North Carolina prior to the American Revolution for the purpose of crossing large rivers. At that time, ferries enabled colonial travelers and tourists to traverse deep water instead of traveling many miles inland looking for a shallow ford, and a floating bridge or barge—which could be swung aside to allow the passage of ships to plantations above—could be used on narrow streams. Larger rivers, though, presented a greater problem.

The state's first drawbridge was built by Benjamin Herron across the Cape Fear River at Wilmington. In 1774 a second bridge was constructed across the Cashie River at Windsor in Bertie County. Drawbridges of that era were typically made of cypress timber, with the drawing mechanism consisting of "3 large iron hinges on each side"; the bridge was opened by "four iron chains and weights with iron sheaves and rollers at the heads of the posts." A few modern navigable waterways in North Carolina, notably the Intracoastal Waterway, are spanned at some point by a drawbridge.

Reference: Alan D. Watson, *Bertie County: A Brief History* (1982).

Harry L. Thompson

Dred, published in 1856, was Harriet Beecher Stowe's much-anticipated sequel to *Uncle Tom's Cabin* (1852) in which she sought to further fan the flames of antislavery sentiment. The book was a response to the violence in Kansas between free-state settlers and pro-slavery voters from Missouri and the caning of Massachusetts senator Charles Sumner by South Carolinian Preston Brook, an incident that greatly incensed northerners (including Stowe, an acquaintance of Sumner). The book is an anomaly in several respects: it was inspired by events then taking place in "Bleeding Kansas," yet the title character is heavily modeled on slave rebellion leaders Nat Turner and Denmark Vesey. Despite inspirations from Kansas, Virginia, and South Carolina, Stowe chose to set her tale in North Carolina, a state she had never visited.

Stowe subtitled the novel *A Tale of the Great Dismal Swamp*, a reference to the vast wasteland that straddled the easternmost border of Virginia and North Carolina. She knew of the area primarily from the descriptions of landscape architect Frederick Law Olmsted, who moved through the Great Dismal during his extensive southern tour of 1853. Olmsted wrote vividly of the slaveholding regimes he had observed in the region, both in his *Journey in the Seaboard Slave States* (also published in 1856) and in correspondence with Stowe.

As literature, *Dred* was considered much inferior to *Uncle Tom's Cabin*; some critics cited the sheer speed with which Stowe wrote it as an obvious reason for its structural and stylistic weaknesses. The novel is far darker and ultimately far more pessimistic than its predecessor in terms of Stowe's hopes of abolishing or reforming the "peculiar institution" of slavery. According to one assessment of the two books, "If *Uncle Tom's Cabin* stands as a war cry to a divided society, *Dred* is a prophecy of disintegration."

Although the appeal of *Dred* proved much more fleeting than that of Stowe's classic first novel, and few people remembered it or read it after the Civil War, President Abraham Lincoln probably had *Dred* as much as *Uncle Tom's Cabin* in mind when in 1863 he proclaimed Stowe as "the little lady who made this big war."

References: Joan D. Hedrick, *Harriet Beecher Stowe: A Life* (1994); Victor A. Kramer, "Harriet Beecher Stowe's Imagination and Frederick Law Olmsted's Travels: The Literary Presentation of Fact," in Dana F. White and Kramer, eds., *Olmsted South: Old South Critic, New South Planner* (1979).

John C. Inscoe

Drexel Furniture Company was incorporated on 10 Nov. 1903 and began making fine furniture in a small factory near Morganton in the foothills of the Appalachian Mountains. In time, the company acquired other furniture plants, including the Table Rock Furniture Company in 1951 and the Heritage Furniture Company and Morganton Furniture Company in 1956. On 1 Dec. 1960 Drexel Furniture became Drexel Enterprises, Inc., and the following year it acquired the Southern Desk Company, manufacturer of a broad line of institutional furniture and equipment for laboratories, libraries, classrooms, dormitories, and churches.

In 1968 U.S. Plywood-Champion Papers bought Drexel Enterprises. As a subsidiary of Champion, the company became Drexel Heritage Furnishings, Inc. Champion sold Drexel Heritage to Dominick International Corporation, a private New York brokerage and investment banking firm, in August 1977. In 1986 Drexel Heritage became a wholly owned subsidiary of Masco Corporation, which, by buying several other leading North Carolina furniture makers, became by the late 1980s the largest U.S. furniture manufacturer.

Drexel for many years sold home and institutional furniture both domestically and abroad. Many of the best-known hotels in the world purchased Drexel furniture, and contracts with the U.S. State Department and the General Services Administration placed Drexel furniture in American embassies and government offices all over the world. In 2004 Drexel Heritage Furniture Industries, Inc., as part of Furniture Brands International, was based in High Point and had 1,300 employees working at several facilities in North Carolina. It remained one of the nation's leading residential furniture manufacturers, producing a variety of wooden and upholstered furniture under several brand names.

References: Allen C. Irvine, *Sixty Years of Progress in the Making of Fine Furniture: Drexel Enterprises, Inc., 1903–1963* [1963?]; Edward W. Phifer, *Burke: The History of a North Carolina County, 1777–1920* (1977).

Wiley J. Williams

Driver's Licenses became mandatory in North Carolina with the passage of the Uniform Driver's License Act, introduced in the General Assembly in January 1935 by Senator Carroll B. Weathers after a thousand deaths had occurred on state roads. The act was ratified on 28 Feb. 1935. Applicants were required to be at least 16 years old and to pay a fee of $1.00. Initially, no test or examination was required; a license was issued on the word of the applicant that he or she was an experienced and careful driver. The program was administered by the Department of Revenue through its newly created Division of Highway Safety. It was not until 1 Jan. 1948 that examinations for a license were required, but those already holding a license and having a safe record were licensed without an examination. Youth in modern North Carolina learn to drive while holding graded licenses that allow them greater driving freedom as they gain experience.

William S. Powell

Drovers were individuals who oversaw the movement of livestock herds from one place to another. From the early 1800s until railroads reached the mountains in the 1880s, livestock droves were a major industry in North Carolina. The chief thoroughfare for moving livestock from eastern Tennessee and western North Carolina to markets in South Carolina followed the French Broad River eastward to Asheville and then south. Overseen by drovers, livestock such as hogs, cattle, mules, horses, and poultry (primarily turkeys) traveled "on the hoof" for 8 to 10 miles per day on what was often a 200-mile journey. Droves were usually made from October to December. A series of toll roads, such as the Buncombe Turnpike from Greenville, Tenn., to Asheville and the Little River Turnpike, which ran southward from Mills River, were built and maintained locally by revenues from toll gates at 10- or 15-mile intervals. "Stands," taverns or inns along the way, provided food and shelter. Stand proprietors were also merchants, selling goods to local farmers in return for corn at harvest time and taking payment from drovers in the form of lame animals or cash after the herds were sold.

References: Wilma Dykeman, *The French Broad* (1955); Foster Sondley, *A History of Buncombe County, North Carolina* (2 vols., 1930).

Ruth Y. Wetmore

Drugstores, or apothecary shops, were scarce in eighteenth-century North Carolina. Solomon Halling and Henry Tooley advertised their New Bern shops in the *North-Carolina Gazette* in 1784 and 1793, respectively. Their ads listed drugs ranging from the innocuous (chamomile) or useful ("Peruvian bark," or cinchona bark, the source of quinine) to the toxic ("sugar of lead," mercury, and arsenic). They also sold spices such as cinnamon and cloves and patent medicines such as Godfrey's Cordials, Bateman's Drops, Stoughton's Bitters, and Daffy's Elixir. The Moravian settlement at Salem had an apothecary shop at least by the 1780s.

In the nineteenth century, drugstores added a great variety of sidelines or "sundries," a practice that continues. A Wilmington shop in 1839 offered drugs, "medicine chests . . . for family and ship's use," as well as "paints, window glass, shop furniture, and . . . perfumery." By 1850 Wilmington's drugstores also sold chemicals; oil, white lead, and a large selection of pigments for making paint; dye stuffs; "fancy soaps," "fancy rouge," hair tonic, cold cream, shaving cream, and shaving brushes; and stationery, pencils, wallets, and garden seeds. Experienced at making medicines from raw ingredients, pharmacists could also concoct cosmetics and paint.

As late as 1851, there were only 17 drugstores in North Carolina, compared with 110 in Virginia. By 1875 the numbers had grown to include 9 in Wilmington; 6 in New Bern; 5 each in Charlotte and Greensboro; 4 in Raleigh; 3 in Fayetteville; and 1 in Durham. The Greensboro stores included W. C. Porter & Company, owned by the uncle of writer William Sydney Porter, better known as O. Henry. Young Porter was an apprentice druggist in his uncle's shop from 1879 to 1881.

When carbonated soft drinks became popular in the 1800s, drugstores capitalized by building attractive fountains of fancy

E. B. Marston's Drugstore in Kinston, ca. 1915. NCC.

ironwork, polished wood, mirrors, and marble. Many drugstores were also ice cream parlors, and pharmacists often turned their talents to preparing their own soft drinks or medicines. Pepsi-Cola was invented by New Bern pharmacist Caleb Bradham. Famous North Carolina medicines include Durham pharmacist Germain Bernard's BC Powder; Vicks VapoRub, invented by Lunsford Richardson of Greensboro; and Salisbury pharmacist Tom Stanback's eponymous headache remedy. To circumvent liquor laws, many people took advantage of drugstores, which could sell liquor if prescribed by a doctor.

Drugstores added many new sidelines in the twentieth century. White's Drug Store in Greenville listed "Huyler's chocolates and bon-bons and a full line of Eastman Kodak supplies" in a 1911 flyer. Davis Pharmacy in Marion advertised a huge list of "holiday suggestions" that included games, books, toy trains, shaving sets, fountain pens, box cigars, electrical toys, flashlights, photo albums, music rolls, cut glass, and handpainted china. Around this time, Williams Pharmacy in Canton began selling gasoline to local automobile drivers.

Established druggists, especially in the post–World War II years, faced competition from new "discount" or "cut-rate" stores as well as growing regional or national chains. By the start of the twenty-first century, North Carolina had more than 500 independent retail drugstores and nearly 1,000 chain stores, plus a few hundred more pharmacies in hospitals, clinics, nursing homes, and other facilities.

Kerr Drug, which began when Banks Kerr opened a drug-store in 1951 in Raleigh's Cameron Village, is the only drugstore chain based in the Carolinas. After being sold to JC Penney in 1995, the Kerr name and 154 stores were bought the following year by former Thrift Drug, Inc., executives. Florida-based Eckerd and Rhode Island–based CVS are among the major national chains with many stores in North Carolina.

References: Sydney Nathans, *The Quest for Progress: The Way We Lived in North Carolina, 1870–1920* (1983); Alice Noble, *The School of Pharmacy of the University of North Carolina: A History* (1961); Waynesville Historical Society, *A Heritage of Healing: The Medical History of Haywood County* (1994).

David A. Norris

Duck Hunting. SEE Waterfowl.

Dueling was a ritual of violence practiced by gentlemen who followed the so-called code of honor in the antebellum South. A perceived insult to the manliness, integrity, or reputation of a gentleman often led to a duel. The offended party challenged his antagonist in order to protect his "honor" in the eyes of the community. Though dueling was uncommon in the colonial South, British and French officers made the practice more popular in the region during the Revolution. The first record of a duel on North Carolina soil involved two British naval officers, Alexander Simpson and Thomas Whitehurst. The two men, rival suitors for the affections of a local woman, fought at Brunswick on 18 Mar. 1765. An American officer from Maryland killed a British colonel in a duel with swords during the Battle of Guilford Courthouse (15 Mar. 1781). Samuel Swann and John Bradley of Wilmington fought possibly the first duel between native North Carolinians behind the Episcopal church in that town on 11 July 1787. Bradley killed Swann and was charged with murder, but he was pardoned by the governor on recommendation of the Assembly.

The heyday of dueling was after the turn of the century. On 5 Sept. 1802, John Stanly killed former governor Richard Dobbs Spaight behind the Masonic hall in New Bern in one of the most famous duels in state history. Although the legislature outlawed dueling in the wake of Spaight's death, North Carolina society condoned affairs of honor, and the law was not enforced. Political rivalries alone account for at least 27 duels in the state between 1800 and 1860; the combatants included legislators, governors, and U.S. senators. If the complete list of all the principals and seconds who participated in duels in antebellum North Carolina could be compiled, it would include many of the state's most prominent males.

In North Carolina dueling began to disappear in the years just before and after the Civil War. In the last recorded duel between native North Carolinians, Joseph Flanner killed fellow Wilmingtonian William Crawford Wilkings in a contest that took place across the state line in South Carolina on 3 May 1856. A prominent Buncombe County citizen sent two challenges as late as 1885, but the duels were not consummated. The demise of dueling indicates that public opinion finally supported legislation that outlawed the practice.

References: W. Conard Gass, "'Misfortune of a High Minded and Honorable Gentleman': W. W. Avery and the Southern Code of Honor," *NCHR* 56 (July 1979); Barbara Holland, *Gentlemen's Blood: A History of Dueling from Swords at Dawn to Pistols at Dusk* (2003); Jack K. Williams, *Dueling in the Old South: Vignettes of Social History* (1980).

Richard Rankin

Duke Endowment, established in December 1924 by tobacco magnate and industrialist James B. Duke, is a perpetual trust for philanthropic purposes in North Carolina and South Carolina. In creating the endowment, Duke systematized for posterity—on a princely scale—a pattern of giving that his father, Washington Duke, had begun in the late nineteenth century and for which his older brother, Benjamin N. Duke, had been primarily responsible from about 1890 onward.

Duke originally placed in the trust securities worth $40 million, mostly stock in the Duke Power Company. He died in October 1925, and by his will added approximately $67 million more to the trust, thus making it one of the largest philanthropies in the nation at that time. Under the terms of the indenture creating the trust, Duke specified that nearly one-third of the annual income from the trust was to go to a new research university, Duke University, that was to be organized around Trinity College, an existing liberal arts college in Durham. Thirty-two percent was to go for the building and support of nonprofit community hospitals for white and African American people in North Carolina and South Carolina. The remainder of the income was to be divided, according to ratios spelled out in the indenture, among Davidson College, Furman University, Johnson C. Smith University, child-care institutions for children of both races in the Carolinas, and certain Methodist purposes in North Carolina (the building and support of rural Methodist churches and assistance to retired Methodist preachers and their dependents).

Headquartered in Charlotte, the Duke Endowment is overseen by a self-perpetuating board of 12 trustees. In the early 2000s it had assets of approximately $2.5 billion, making it by the far the largest private foundation in North Carolina and among the largest in the United States. Duke Endowment grants since 1924 have surpassed $1.6 billion.

References: Duke Endowment, *Annual Report* (2002); Robert F. Durden, *The Dukes of Durham, 1865–1929* (1975).

Robert F. Durden

Duke Homestead. As a nonslaveholding, hard-working yeoman farmer, Washington Duke (1820–1905) typified the great majority of white, male North Carolinians—indeed, white male southerners in general—before the Civil War. In the early 1850s he built a modest frame house on his farm, which was located in what was then Orange County about three miles outside of what would soon become Durham's Station on the new North Carolina Railroad. After his first wife died, Duke married Artelia Roney in 1852. A daughter, Mary Elizabeth, was born to the couple in 1853. A son, Benjamin Newton, followed in 1855, and another son, James Buchanan, was born in 1856. Benjamin's and James's subsequent business successes led to the creation of such important North Carolina institutions as the American Tobacco Company, Duke University, and the Duke Power Company.

Although Washington Duke, like many other North Carolinians, opposed secession, the Confederate draft reached him in 1864 and he served until the end of the war. Returning penniless to his children and farm, he began, with the help of his family, the home manufacture of smoking tobacco, which he carried by wagon to peddle in the more populous eastern part of the state. In 1874, inspired in part by the earlier move of his surviving son by his first wife, Brodie L. Duke, Washington Duke sold the homeplace and moved with his family to the new town of Durham, which was growing rapidly, along with the tobacco and textile industries.

In the early 1930s Washington Duke's granddaughter, Mary Duke Biddle, purchased the old homestead and gave it to Duke

University. In 1974 the university, in turn, gave the house and 37 surrounding acres to the state, which added Duke Homestead to its list of North Carolina State Historic Sites. In 1977 a tobacco history museum opened near the original farmhouse and early "factories." Both the museum and the Duke Homestead are open to the public without charge.

References: *The Duke Homestead Guidebook* (1978); Robert F. Durden, *The Dukes of Durham, 1865–1902* (1975); Richard F. Knapp, ed., *North Carolina's State Historic Sites: A Brief History and Status Report* (1995).

Robert F. Durden

Duke Power Company,

Duke Power Company, since 1997 a subsidiary of Duke Energy Corporation, is an electric utility company with headquarters in Charlotte and a service area in the Piedmont region of North Carolina and South Carolina. The company was the brainchild of James B. Duke and his older brother Benjamin N. Duke. Heavily involved in both tobacco and textile manufacturing, the Duke brothers began to explore the possibilities of hydroelectric power as early as the 1890s. Meanwhile, in 1900 Walker Gill Wylie and his brother Robert H. Wylie established the Catawba Power Company to supply electricity to textile mills near Rock Hill, S.C. The power station they completed on the Catawba River four years later was subsequently purchased by the Dukes and became the first station in the Duke Power system. In 1905 the Duke brothers launched the Southern Power Company (which in 1924 became the Duke Power Company) and began a long, close association with William States Lee, a brilliant electrical engineer. Lee played a key role in building the company and its vast network of dams and power stations.

In the company's early history, the Dukes, Lee, Walker Gill Wylie, and their associates had to work hard to build a market for electric power. As part of this process, the Dukes invested heavily in a number of textile mills in both Carolinas. Built prior to World War I, the Piedmont & Northern Electric Railway Company, an electric interurban line for passengers and freight, also played a large role in the economic development of the area between Charlotte and the cities of piedmont South Carolina.

Aiming from the first at a comprehensive development of the waterpower of a region rather than the random development of isolated sites, the Duke brothers, Lee, and their associates pioneered in developing power technology, in conserving natural resources, and in connecting their own vast power grid with a number of smaller networks (even prior to World War I)—playing an important role in the creation of what has been called the largest "system of systems" attempted in the world up to that time. Coal-burning steam plants such as Southern Power Company's Greenville, S.C., and Greensboro stations, both constructed in 1911, were originally used as standby auxiliaries to the hydroelectric stations. Floods and droughts, such as the devastating 1916 flood of the Catawba River and the record-breaking summer drought of 1925, highlighted the limitations of hydroelectric generation. For this reason, shortly before his death in October 1925, James B. Duke authorized the construction of the Buck Steam Station, the first large-scale central steam station in the south. The station was built in record time on the Yadkin River near Salisbury.

Subsequent large-scale steam stations on the Duke system —Dan River, Riverbend, Cliffside, Lee, Allen, Marshall, and Belews Creek—saw the increasing predominance of steam over hydroelectric generation. Duke Power entered the nuclear age in March 1963, when the Parr Nuclear Station, an experimental reactor built in Fairfield County, S.C., and operated by a regional consortium of electric utilities including Duke Power, began generating electricity. Duke Power later built the Oconee (1973), McGuire (1981), and Catawba (1985) nuclear stations.

Through the final decades of the twentieth century, the company diversified and grew into a Fortune 500 corporate giant. The 1997 merger of Duke Power and PanEnergy Corporation—the first between an electric utility and a gas pipeline company—led to the creation of Duke Energy Corporation, of which Duke Power became a wholly owned subsidiary. Other Duke Energy companies include Duke Energy Merchants, Duke Energy Gas Transmission, DukeNet Communications, Crescent Resources, and Duke/Fluor Daniel. In March 1999 Duke Energy purchased Union Pacific Resources Group, solidifying the company as one of the largest natural gas gatherers and distributors in the world. In 2006 Duke Energy employed more than 23,000 people worldwide.

References: Robert F. Durden, *The Dukes of Durham, 1865–1929* (1975); Durden, *Electrifying the Piedmont Carolinas: The Duke Power Company, 1904–1997* (2001); Carl F. Horn Jr., *The Duke Power Story, 1904–1973* (1973).

Robert F. Durden
Additional research provided by Dennis R. Lawson.

SEE ALSO Southern Power Company.

Duke University.

Duke University. In December 1924, James B. Duke provided the money for a new research university to be created in connection with Trinity College in Durham. The idea and plan, however, came from the president of Trinity, William P. Few, who served for 15 years as Duke University's first president. Eager to see North Carolina and the South begin to catch up with other sections of the nation in the realm of higher education, Few had high ambitions for the university and, before he died in 1940, had the satisfaction of seeing some of them achieved. Recognizing the opportunity to establish a

West Campus of Duke University, with Duke Chapel in the upper center of this aerial view. Photograph courtesy of North Carolina Division of Tourism, Film, and Sports Development.

the School of Medicine and the hospital, which opened in 1930, did not. Under the leadership of Dean Wilburt C. Davison, the medical center, which also included a School of Nursing and other specialized training programs, quickly gained national recognition and proved to be of great service to the state and region. Duke's medical school was for a period the only four-year medical program in North Carolina. Schools of Engineering, Forestry, and, much later, Business were gradually established. In 1972 the Woman's College, as a separate administrative entity, was abolished, and both men and women began to be housed on East and West Campus.

Despite being a nondenominational university with no religious tests for either faculty or students, Duke retains a long relationship with the Methodist Church. This relationship is reflected in the university's motto, chosen by school president Braxton Craven in 1859, *Eruditio et Religio* (Erudition and Religion). The school's famous mascot, the Blue Devil, has no religious connotations, however. The student body selected the name in the 1920s in recognition of a then well-known French military unit, the Chasseurs Alpins. Nicknamed "les Diables Bleus" for their distinctive blue uniform with flowing capes and berets, the French Blue Devils toured the United States during World War I to help raise money for the war effort.

In the early 2000s, under the leadership of its ninth president, Richard H. Brodhead, Duke University enrolled approximately 6,300 undergraduate and 4,500 graduate students representing almost every state and about 75 foreign countries. The curriculum has grown to include studies in fields as diverse as biomedical engineering, public policy, microelectronics, and black church affairs. The Medical Center, through its educational, research, and patient care missions, is a regional and national leader in health care and biomedicine. Duke University consistently ranks in the top ten in academic excellence among the nation's universities, both private and public.

References: Robert F. Durden, *The Launching of Duke University, 1924–1949* (1993); William E. King, *If Gargoyles Could Talk: Sketches of Duke University* (1997).

Robert F. Durden

SEE ALSO Trinity College.

new, unique name for the institution, Few proposed that it be called Duke University, and James B. Duke agreed on condition that it be considered a memorial to his father and family.

Through the Duke Endowment, James B. Duke provided not only long-term support for the new university but also approximately $19 million to construct an elaborate and extensive physical plant. The plan called for constructing 11 new buildings in the classical or Georgian style of architecture, both on the existing Trinity campus and on a new site a mile and a half away. As that construction proceeded from 1925 through 1927, the university operated in cramped quarters on the old campus. In September 1930—when Tudor Gothic buildings made of native stone from a quarry near Hillsborough were completed on the new West Campus—the old or East Campus became the site of the Woman's College of Duke University. Some 5,000 acres of adjoining land (later expanded to around 8,000 acres) became the Duke Forest, also the gift of James B. Duke.

While both Duke Law School and the School of Religion (later the Divinity School) had antecedents in Trinity College,

Dulcimer. Settlement schools in the southern Appalachian Mountains at the start of the twentieth century nurtured elements of mountain culture they believed "native" and "pure." Their favored musical instrument was a quiet zither bearing the name dulcimer, Greek and Latin for "sweet tune" and alternately pronounced "delcimer," "delcimore," or "dulcimore." While a few dulcimers are straight-sided, most have curved sides, either single-bouted or double-bouted. In common usage, the single-bouted is called the "Virginia" shape and the double-bouted the "Cumberland" or "Kentucky" shape, terminology reflecting what is known about the loca-

Don Pedi of Marshall with his dulcimer. Ed Pedi Photography.

tions of early makers. Both styles were made in North Carolina, but among the known makers in the state, the single bout was more common.

The dulcimer is played by pressing a noter, usually made of hardwood, cane, bone, or quill, against either a single string or two strings identically tuned, while strumming a rhythm pattern across all strings. The left hand holds the noter while the right hand strums, using either a flexible pick (quill, switch, or thin wood) or the fingers. This produces a melody accompanied by a harmonizing drone similar to that of the various small bagpipes used in all parts of the British Isles.

Among the existing dulcimers made in North Carolina, the oldest is a single-bouted instrument made by William Thompson in Ashe County in the 1850s. A major variation of the single-bouted type was developed in the late nineteenth century in southwestern Virginia; known as the Galax dulcimer, it is similar to the single-bouted dulcimers made in nearby Surry County, N.C. The double-bouted, or hourglass, style influenced early dulcimer making in North Carolina when a dulcimer of that type entered Watauga County in the 1880s and served as the model for local craftsmen.

References: L. Allen Smith, *A Catalogue of Pre-Revival Appalachian Dulcimers* (1983); Ralph Lee Smith, *The Story of the Dulcimer* (1986).

Carole Watterson Troxler

Dunmore's Ethiopian Regiment consisted of runaway slaves who served as English troops under the last royal governor of Virginia, Lord John Dunmore. In November 1775 Dunmore, who had wearied of tensions with the colony's ruling elite, offered freedom to Virginia slaves who would take up arms against the colonists. In short order, 300 runaways joined him and became known as "Dunmore's Ethiopian Regiment."

Concern over Dunmore's actions to free slaves spread into North Carolina, sparking the colony's first military engagement. Robert Howe led the 2nd Regiment of North Carolinians to Hampton Roads to assist the Virginia Continentals in repelling Dunmore's attacks on Norfolk area houses and plantations. En route, Dunmore's Loyalist troops, including the Ethiopian Regiment, attacked the colonials at Great Bridge, Va., on 9 Dec. 1775. Dunmore's troops lost the battle and were forced to evacuate to English warships in the port at Norfolk.

The British fleet sailed south from Norfolk and eventually anchored off the Cape Fear coast in early 1776. Once they learned of the English ship's arrival, North Carolina slaves began to desert their masters. Capt. George Martin, under Sir Henry Clinton, organized a North Carolina company called the "Black Pioneers," whose main duties were to relieve the British troops of the worst chores of military life: building fortifications, laundering clothes, cooking, and managing the horses and carts. The Black Pioneers also provided valuable intelligence on roads and waterways.

By the summer of 1776 Dunmore had disbanded his black troops and left southern waters, sailing for New York. In the end, few runaway slaves earned their freedom.

References: Jeffrey J. Crow, *The Black Experience in Revolutionary North Carolina* (1977); Allan Kulikoff, *Tobacco and Slaves: The Development of Southern Cultures in the Chesapeake, 1680–1800* (1986); Robert A. Selig, "The Revolution's Black Soldiers," *Colonial Williamsburg* (Summer 1997).

Ellen Fitzgibbons Causey

Duplin County, located in the Coastal Plain region of North Carolina, was formed in 1750 from New Hanover County and named for Thomas Hay, Lord Duplin, a member of the English Board of Trade and Plantations. Early inhabitants of the area included the Tuscarora and Siouan Indians, followed by English, Swiss, Scotch-Irish, and German settlers. Kenansville, the county seat, was incorporated in 1852 and named for James Kenan, one of the town's founders. Other communities in the county include Beulaville, Calypso, Magnolia, Rose Hill, Wallace, and Warsaw. Notable physical features of the county include the Northeast Cape Fear River, Muddy Creek, Bear Swamp, Maxwell Mill Pond, and Picadilly Bay.

Duplin County boasts several historic attractions, among them the Kenansville Historic District, with notable examples of Greek Revival architecture, and the Dickson Farm, dating from the early nineteenth century. Kenansville is the site of Liberty Hall Plantation, ancestral home of the Kenan family. County cultural institutions include the Cowan Museum (a collection of unusual American artifacts), the William Rand Kenan Memorial Amphitheatre, and the Tar Heel Fine Arts Society. The Duplin Winery is the oldest winery in North Carolina, established in the 1960s. The county also hosts many annual festivals and events, such as the Warsaw Veterans Day Celebration (the nation's oldest continuously celebrated Veterans Day event), the North Carolina Pickle Festival, the North Carolina Poultry Jubilee, and Beach Music at the Winery.

Agriculture is a key part of the Duplin County economy, and goods produced include tobacco, cotton, cucumbers, strawberries, corn, soybeans, wheat, barley, sweet potatoes, Christmas trees, turkeys and other poultry, hogs, and beef and dairy cattle. Manufactured products include textiles, pickles, apparel, and frozen foods. Duplin County's population was estimated to be 51,500 in 2004.

Reference: Leon H. Sikes, *Duplin County Places, Past and Present: A Guide to Duplin County, North Carolina* (1984).

Jay Mazzocchi

Durant Bible, printed in London in 1599, is considered to be the book that has been in North Carolina longer than any other. It was owned by George Durant (1632–94), a pioneer settler in the Albemarle section of the colony and a colonial official. The Bible has a dark brown leather binding that is probably not the original one; it measures 6 inches wide, 8½ inches long, and about 3 inches thick. It contains many marginal notes of births, deaths, marriages, and other events. Some entries have been torn out, however.

The Bible was apparently passed down, through marriage, to the Reed (or Reid) family. Members of the Reed family gave the Bible to Professor Charles Force Deems of the University of North Carolina faculty when he requested it sometime between 1844 and 1857, and it later came into the possession of the Historical Society of North Carolina at UNC. It is now held in the UNC Library's North Carolina Collection.

References: Samuel A. Ashe, "George Durant," *North Carolina Booklet* 9 (April 1910); Richard B. Creecy, "Stray Leaves of Our History," *University of North Carolina Magazine* 23 (January 1906).

William S. Powell

Durham, often called the "City of Medicine" for its outstanding medical facilities, was incorporated in 1869. The city was named for Bartlett Snipes Durham, who donated land to build a railroad station. In 1881 the General Assembly created Durham County out of Orange and Wake Counties, and Durham became the county seat. Previous to that, Durham had begun to develop as the site of thriving tobacco manufacturing facili-

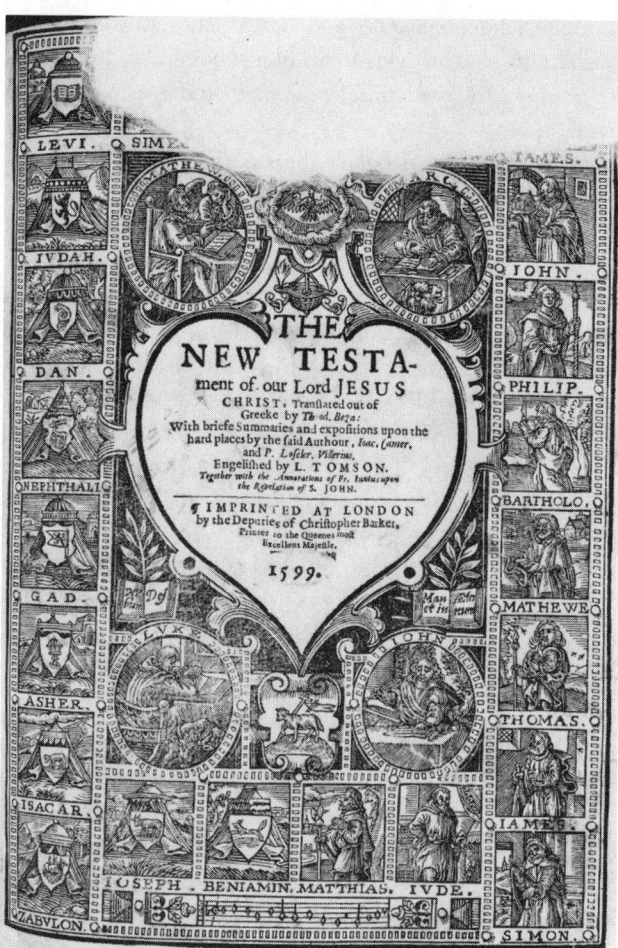

Title page from the New Testament in the Durant Bible, 1599. The upper part of the page was torn by an early reader of the book. NCC.

ties. Tobacco, in fact, drove the economy of Durham, home of the Duke-controlled American Tobacco Company and its successor enterprises, for nearly a century. Beginning in the 1950s, the city's tobacco economy began to falter, as automation reduced the need for employees to prepare, blend, and flavor tobacco or tend machines. Medical findings about the health hazards connected to smoking also played a part in the weakening of Durham's tobacco industry.

In addition to tobacco production, some other types of manufacturing have contributed to Durham's economy, including the making of textiles, pants, boots, hosiery, and soap. Banking and finance also rose to prominence in the city. The North Carolina Mutual Life Insurance Company, the first black-owned insurance company in the state, has been an important Durham business concern since its founding in 1899. The emergence of Duke University (whose precursor was Trinity College) as one of the nation's leading institutions of higher learning, complete with its world-renowned Duke Hospital facilities, greatly enhanced Durham's reputation and economy. Durham is also home to North Carolina Central University and Durham Technical Community College. The North

Carolina School of Science and Mathematics was founded in Durham in 1980 as the nation's first state-funded residential high school for academically talented students in scientific fields.

Durham has been one of the state's cultural, as well as educational, medical, and commercial, centers. In the 1920s and 1930s, the city gained renown with a strain of the blues known as Piedmont blues, distinguished by its ragtime rhythmic rapping of a washboard and punctuated by the whoops and calls of the harmonies. Today, many organizations are supported by the very active Durham Arts Council, which in September 1988 celebrated the completion of a $5 million renovation of the former Durham High School into the Royal Center for the Arts. Another renovated performance center, the Carolina Theatre, in addition to screening classic, foreign, and critically acclaimed films, hosts concerts, operas, dramatic productions, film festivals, and other special events. The American Dance Festival is held each summer on the Duke University campus. The North Carolina Museum of Life and Science features numerous exhibits, devoted to everything from prehistory to space exploration, and offers interactive, hands-on displays of science and technology, many specifically directed toward children.

Important historic sites in or near Durham include Historic Stagville (on what was once one of the South's largest plantations), the Duke Homestead and Tobacco Museum, and Brightleaf Square and the American Tobacco Historic District —former tobacco warehouses that have been turned into office, shopping, and dining complexes. In 2005 Durham was North Carolina's fourth-largest city, with a population in excess of 200,000.

References: Wyatt T. Dixon, *How Times Do Change: A Series of Sketches of Durham and Her Citizens* (1987); Joel A. and Frank A. Kostyn, *Durham: A Pictorial History* (1978); George E. Lougee, *Durham, My Hometown* (1990).

Wiley J. Williams

SEE ALSO American Tobacco Company; Duke Homestead; Duke University; North Carolina Central University; North Carolina Museum of Life and Science; North Carolina School of Science and Mathematics.

Durham Academy,

Durham Academy, a private, independent day school in Durham, was begun in 1933 by Mrs. George Watts Hill for the education of her children and the children of her friends. The school initially included only a kindergarten and a few lower grades, but it gradually grew until all 12 grades were offered in 1972. In its early years the school used the method of instruction devised by the successful Calvert School of Baltimore, Md., and was called the Calvert Method School. The first headmistress was Margaret McGary, previously principal of the public Morehead School in Durham. Initially, classes were held in the Forest Hills neighborhood clubhouse, but with the addition of grades and students, more space was required. The Hills provided the former John Sprunt Hill residence on Duke Street, where the school remained until 1965.

In 1957 the school broke its ties with the Calvert School, and two years later its name was changed to Durham Academy. In 1965 it moved into new buildings on a larger tract of land, and in 1972 it moved the high school grades to an even larger campus in a semirural setting. The first high school class graduated in 1975. George Watts Hill and Frank Kenan made generous donations for endowment and other needs, including a program for children with learning disabilities, open to all schoolchildren. By the early 2000s Durham Academy enrolled approximately 1,100 students in grades prekindergarten through 12 on three campuses and operated the Hill Center for children with learning disabilities.

Reference: Jean B. Anderson, *Durham County: A History of Durham County, North Carolina* (1990).

Jean B. Anderson

Durham & South Carolina Railroad

Durham & South Carolina Railroad (D&SC) was one of six rail lines that reached into Durham's prospering tobacco business in the early twentieth century. Beginning in 1905, the D&SC ran 30 miles south from Durham, generally following New Hope Creek and River, to the Wake County town of Bonsal, where it interchanged with the Seaboard Air Line Railway. By 1917 it had extended south to Duncan in Harnett County, where it connected with the Norfolk Southern Railroad (NS).

The D&SC was moderately successful, at one point owning as many as three locomotives and considerable rolling stock. In 1920 it was leased for operation by the NS, which bought it outright in 1957. In 1982 the NS was acquired by the Southern Railway Company, which operated D&SC's line until it was largely dismantled in 1985.

The East Carolina Chapter of the National Railway Historical Society then purchased the surviving remnant of the line for purposes of historical preservation and public recreation. The name of the railway became the New Hope Valley Railway (NHV), a standard-gauge railroad with about five miles of track and headquarters and shops in Bonsal. The line runs northward, touching Chatham County and returning to its terminus in Wake County near New Hill. The NHV provides regular passenger service throughout the year, as well as special seasonal events, and supports the North Carolina Railroad Museum at Bonsal. The railway's name honors a D&SC predecessor line that was incorporated in 1904 but never built.

References: S. David Carriker, *North Carolina Railroads* (1989); Richard E. Prince, *Norfolk Southern Railroad, Old Dominion Line, and Connections* (1972).

Whitmel M. Joyner

Durham County, located in the Piedmont region of central North Carolina, was formed in 1881 from Orange and Wake Counties and was named after the town of Durham, which had already been established in the area. The early inhabitants of the region included the Occaneechi and Eno Indians, followed by English, Scotch-Irish, and German settlers. Durham, the county seat, was incorporated in 1869. Other communities in Durham County include Bahama and Rougemont (and parts of Chapel Hill spill over from neighboring Orange County). Notable physical features include the Eno and Neuse Rivers, New Hope and Mountain Creeks, and Lake Michie.

Several landmarks and historic sites are situated in Durham County, including Bennett Place, scene of Confederate general Joseph E. Johnston's surrender to Union general William T. Sherman at the close of the Civil War; the Duke Homestead; Historic Stagville Plantation (1857); downtown Durham's Carolina Theatre; and West Point on the Eno, a popular 388-acre park. Duke University, established in Randolph County as Trinity College, moved to Durham in 1892; it is one of the nation's premier institutions of higher learning and a cultural and economic force within Durham County. Parrish Street in downtown Durham was the site of African American entrepreneurial activity ca. 1900 and the focal point of what became known as "Black Wall Street." North Carolina Central University (1909) is also located in the city of Durham. Other cultural institutions in the county include the Durham Arts Council, the Durham Symphony, Duke Art Museum, the Hayti Heritage Center, and the North Carolina Museum of Life and Science. Durham County hosts many annual festivals and events such as the American Dance Festival, the Festival for the Eno, the Bull City Blues Festival, the North Carolina International Jazz Festival, the North Carolina Gay and Lesbian Film Festival, and the Durham Festival of Trees.

The Research Triangle Park, home to many high-tech businesses and institutions, is located in southern Durham County and northern Wake County. The county produces agricultural goods such as tobacco, corn, soybeans, hay, wheat, barley, oats, strawberries, beef and dairy cattle, chickens, and swine, and its manufactured products include telecommunications equipment, electronic integrated circuits, fiber optics, drapes, bedspreads, and surgical instruments. The county also produces minerals such as petrified wood, hematite, pyrite, and hornblende. Durham County's population was estimated to be just under 239,000 in 2004.

Reference: Jean Bradley Anderson, *Durham County: A History of Durham County, North Carolina* (1990).

William S. Powell

SEE ALSO Bennett Place; Duke Homestead; Duke University; Durham; Festival for the Eno; North Carolina Central University; Research Triangle Park; Stagville.

Durham Herald-Sun traces its roots to 1894, when three staff members of the struggling *Durham Daily Globe*—Zeb Council, W. W. Thompson, and a printer named Gates—started a new paper called the *Durham Globe-Herald*, releasing the first issue on 15 Oct. 1894. A few weeks later the men bought a printing outfit from W. Whitaker, from whom they previously had rented a press. The small operation was fragile and, to give it some financial stability, a flat weekly price of five cents was suggested by Joe H. King, who actively joined the operation on 13 Nov. 1894 (although he had advised the original trio from the beginning of the project). The collection of that fee kept the paper afloat when many other newspapers succumbed to the tumultuous economic times.

In January 1895 the paper became a morning daily and the name was changed from the *Durham Globe-Herald* to the *Morning Herald*, as it remained until 1919. On 8 Feb. 1895 Thompson sold his interest to Edward Tyler Rollins, and the newly formed King and Rollins Company assumed direction of the paper. In the partnership, Rollins primarily handled finances and King attended to editorial and journalistic matters. As coverage broadened and circulation increased, the paper's operations were repeatedly moved to more suitable locations. Eventually a building specifically designed to meet the needs of the *Morning Herald* was completed in 1906.

The budding publication likely could find no better locale than Durham at the beginning of the twentieth century. Circulation grew with the vast influx of people to the area, stemming from the Duke family's relocation of Trinity College to Durham in 1892 and the expansion of local businesses, be it the flourishing tobacco industry or successful companies like the North Carolina Mutual Life Insurance Corporation, founded in 1899. As the future paper of record for a county on the rise, the *Morning Herald* acquired a vital social and political voice in the community. Technological advances also accounted for the escalating readership. As the paper grew, opportunities developed for the purchase of more advanced equipment, such as the Linotype. The Linotype, which could set an entire line of print on a metal slug and was operated by a keyboard that resembled a typewriter, so increased efficiency that it made the employment of full-time workers a necessity.

In 1917, a few months before his death, King retired and sold his shares in King and Rollins to Edward Rollins and Carl C. Council, who had started in the *Herald* as a courier and eventually rose through the ranks to the position of circulation manager in 1921. In April 1918 the King and Rollins Company formed a corporation. In August 1919 it obtained an Associated Press franchise, and on 5 Oct. 1919 the *Morning Herald* became the *Durham Morning Herald*.

The *Durham Morning Herald* obtained its local rival, the *Durham Sun*, in 1929. The *Sun* moved to the *Herald*'s headquarters and began to use the name *Herald-Sun*. Although the two papers were published and managed in the same building, they maintained separate editorial staffs. The work of the *Herald* and the *Sun* remained a significant factor in promoting the continued growth of Durham, which, with the presence of Duke University and Duke Hospital, became known as the "City of Medicine." The papers became central news and information sources for Durham, Orange, and Chatham Counties, which would enjoy substantial growth in population later in the century.

On 22 July 1931 Rollins died and left his three-fourths interest in the *Herald* and the *Sun* in trust and the positions of publisher and president to Carl Council. The papers continued to expand, purchasing Durham's primary news radio outlet WDNC in 1936 and maintaining it for almost two decades. Despite its diversified business dealings, the newspaper remained a family institution. At Council's death on 29 Jan. 1964, Steed Rollins, son of the late Edward Rollins, became publisher and president.

In December 1981 Steed Rollins announced his retirement and turned over his positions to his brother Edward T. Rollins Jr., but Steed remained chairman of the board until his death in November 1985. Edward retired in 1988, passing his duties as publisher and president on to Richard J. Kaspar, who had taken a vice presidential position in the organization in November 1987. On 1 Jan. 1991 the *Durham Morning Herald* and the *Durham Sun* merged to form the *Durham Herald-Sun*. William E. N. Hawkins remained executive editor, and Carlton Harrell, editor of the *Sun* before the papers merged, became associate editor of the *Herald-Sun*. Kaspar oversaw the merger and continued as publisher and president until his death in 1995.

The *Durham Herald-Sun* has occupied an odd niche in the state's communications market. Although in the early 2000s it boasted a daily circulation of more than 50,000, it barely made the top ten highest circulating newspapers in North Carolina. Durham's proximity to Raleigh puts the *Herald-Sun* in direct competition with its powerful neighbor, the *Raleigh News and Observer*—a geographic factor not present in Charlotte, Greensboro, Fayetteville, or any other relatively insulated towns with major papers. As a result of this proximity, the 150,000-plus circulating *News and Observer* tallies numerous subscriptions in Wake, Durham, and Orange Counties. Nevertheless, the *Herald-Sun* maintains a significant readership by focusing on local interest stories, especially in Durham and Orange Counties, including regular coverage of popular competitive sports at Duke University and the University of North Carolina at Chapel Hill.

The *Durham Herald-Sun* was one of the few remaining independent dailies in the state until December 2004, when the Rollins family sold the paper to the Paxton Media Group, a Kentucky company started in 1896. The *Herald-Sun* and its approximately 350 employees became Paxton's 29th paper, as well as its largest.

References: L. S. Laprade, "Morning Herald Had Modest Start," *Durham Morning Herald*, 15 Oct. 1934; "Rollins Retiring from Newspaper," *Durham Morning Herald*, 5 Dec. 1981; Thad Stem Jr., *The Tar Heel Press* (1973).

Maie El-Souraidy
Additional research provided by Philip McFee.

Durham Life Insurance Company was founded in Durham in December 1906 as Durham Mutual Protective Association with A. M. Moise as president. The name became Durham Mutual Life Insurance Company in March 1912. Having acquired both Durham Mutual Life and Catawba Mutual Insurance Company, Durham Life was incorporated in December 1913, with Moise serving as president until 1916. He was succeeded by Silas B. Coley that September. Following other acquisitions beginning in 1914, corporate headquarters were moved to Raleigh in June 1920.

Originally, Durham Life wrote industrial insurance to provide low-income people with limited protection in the event of sickness, accident, or death. As the company name suggests, the firm also sold industrial life insurance with somewhat larger premiums than for accident and health policies, including credit and group insurance. As the company grew, it added a wide range of life and accident and health policies.

In 1927 Durham Life purchased radio station WPTF, originally owned by Will A. Wayne. Its call letters stood for "We Protect the Family," which the company had adopted as a slogan in 1914. In 1929 the company established a policy—still in effect—to have WPTF broadcast a live church service every Sunday. Beginning in 1933 the station operated as WPTF Radio Company (later Durham Life Broadcasting, a Durham Life subsidiary). In 1972 the broadcasting company changed the call letters of its FM station to WQDR-FM, and in 1977 that company acquired WRDU-TV and renamed it WPTF-TV.

Corporate changes would eventually take Durham Life out of broadcasting. In 1979 Durham Corporation, a holding company based in Raleigh, was incorporated, and effective 31 December of that year Durham Life became its wholly owned subsidiary. In July 1991 FSF Acquisition Corporation became the new owners of WPTF-TV and the call letters became WRDC (in 1995 they were again changed to WNCN). Durham Corporation merged into Capital Holding Corporation (Raleigh) in 1991. In 1996 Providian Corporation, formerly Capital Holding, sold its Durham insurance operations to the major Dutch firm Aegon.

References: "Durham Corporation: It's a New Holding Company for Mature and Honored Firms," *We the People of North Carolina* 39 (November 1981); Carl Goerch, *Durham Life, 1906–1963* (1963).

Wiley J. Williams

Dyes and Dyeing. Some knowledge of dyeing techniques and materials arrived in the region that would become North

Carolina with the earliest European settlers, but since all dyes were from natural sources until the late 1850s, it was necessary to employ new sources and techniques utilizing the minerals, flora, and fauna of a new and unfamiliar environment. Local Indian tribes had a long history of successful dyeing of leather, feathers, and fibers, and they likely shared much of their knowledge with the settlers.

Dyes were extracted from the leaves, bark, and roots of trees; from the leaves, flowers, fruit, and stalks of weeds, shrubs, and vegetables; and from nuts and nut hulls, coffee, teas, onion skins, and herbs such as turmeric and cinnamon. The range of colors available from these humble sources is quite remarkable, and the aesthetic beauty of the colors makes them useful to the most discerning craftsmen. Recipes for dye baths and ink were as precious as those for medicines and mince pies. Such recipes may still be found in craft books and are still used by artisans throughout North Carolina, particularly in basketry, doll making, knitting, weaving, crocheting, and embroidery.

The major applications of dyeing techniques in the settlement period and early statehood were fabrics, thread, and yarns for clothing, as well as quilts, blankets, embroidery threads, rugs, and other materials of home manufacture such as baskets, paper, and leather. Modern, synthetic dyes were introduced in 1857 and are now used exclusively in commercial dyeing because of their uniformity and dependability.

Reference: Bobbi A. McRae, *Colors from Nature: Growing, Collecting, and Using Natural Dyes* (1993).

Jean Snow

E

Eagles. While the presence of bald eagles has been noted in all U.S. states except Hawaii, their existence in North Carolina, until late in the twentieth century, has seldom been recorded far from the larger rivers and bays of the Coastal Plain. At the time of the first European settlements in the region, the only large bodies of water capable of providing the predominately fish diet of the bald eagle were confined to the eastern part of the state. John Lawson made the first mention of the bald eagle in *A New Voyage to Carolina* (1709), reporting that "they prey on any living thing that they can catch." Naturalist William Bartram, writing in the 1770s, described the bald eagle as a coastal bird in the Carolinas. Alexander Wilson, the "father" of North American ornithology, did the same in the 1820s. In the eras of these men, eagles probably nested every mile or so along the North Carolina sounds and coasts.

Early sightings of golden eagles in North Carolina were largely confined to the western mountains. The eagles of Cherokee Indian legend and lore were most likely golden eagles, whose distribution includes all of the northern hemisphere. However, Native Americans may have seen some migrating bald eagles following the mountain ridges south in the fall.

Over time, several factors contributed to the decrease in eagle populations in the state. By the mid-twentieth century most of the wild, watery habitats and large ancient trees needed by eagles to support their huge nests (up to 10 feet in diameter, 15 feet deep, and two tons in weight) had been supplanted in North Carolina by farms and young woods springing up in abandoned fields. Many eagles were and still are targets of hunters despite federal and state laws protecting them. Lead shot, used by duck hunters, also poisoned eagles feeding on dead and dying lead-contaminated ducks. Most deadly of all, greater use of pesticides such as DDT—used extensively on cotton, tobacco, and a variety of food crops—after World War II had a devastating effect on birds and other wildlife, particularly those high on aquatic food chains such as pelicans, osprey ("fish hawks"), peregrine falcons ("duck hawks"), and bald eagles. Derivatives of DDT caused the birds' eggshells to thin and break during incubation.

In North Carolina only one active bald eagle nest remained by 1970, and between 1973 and 1983, no eagles nested in the state. DDT was banned throughout the United States in 1973, and the persistent poison slowly diminished its impact on the North American environment. In 1983 ten Alaskan eaglets were raised and released at Lake Mattamuskeet in Hyde County in an attempt to reestablish a North Carolina population. Within weeks seven died of avian malaria carried by Carolina mosquitoes (Alaskan eagles had no resistance to this southern disease). Attempts at reintroduction were terminated.

Meanwhile, many new reservoirs had been built throughout the Piedmont to provide drinking water, flood control, power, and recreation for the rapidly growing cities of central North Carolina. At the same time, Florida and Chesapeake Bay eagles were beginning to hatch healthy eaglets again. Occasionally adult and immature eagles appeared at Kerr Lake, Lake Norman, and then Jordan Lake when it was filled in 1982. In 1984 a new nest near Lake Mattamuskeet fledged two eagles, the first successful nesting in North Carolina since 1973.

Early one April morning in 1985, a lone kayaker spotted seven bald eagles roosting in a single tree on Jordan Lake. Monthly counts organized by the New Hope Audubon Society documented a summer roost concentration of about 35 bald eagles on Jordan Lake. Five to ten more were noted on simultaneous counts at nearby Falls Lake every summer. The summer count numbers on Jordan Lake twice rose to more than 60, with 15 to 20 staying on the lake through December. North Carolina had won the honor of hosting the largest summer population of bald eagles in eastern North America. Even in the winter, ten or so eagles remained on Jordan Lake. A new high of 69 wintering eagles was recorded for all of North Carolina in 1992.

The number of attempted nests in North Carolina grew from one nest in 1984 to eight nests in 1990, including two unsuccessful Piedmont nests, one of which was built on Jordan Lake. By the early 2000s it had become clear that bald eagles had not only returned to their ancestral nesting grounds of the Coastal Plain, but they had also established, with help from human beings, new territories in the rapidly developing North Carolina Piedmont.

Jim Keighton

Earle's Ford, Battle of. The Revolutionary War battle of Earle's Ford occurred on 15 July 1780 in western South Carolina adjacent to the far southern end of present-day Polk County. On 13 July 1780 Col. John Jones of Georgia successfully ambushed a party of Loyalists at Gowen's Old Fort near the South Pacolet River in South Carolina. Following the raid, Jones and his men fled north to join a large contingent of Whigs operating nearby under Col. Charles McDowell. Jones crossed the North Pacolet River at Baylis Earle's Ford and made camp near McDowell's troops. Meanwhile, British colonel Alexander Innes dispatched a force of 70 dra-

Harper's Weekly illustration from 11 Apr. 1874 showing terrified settlers outside their home on Bald Mountain in Rutherford County during one of the earthquakes that struck the area during the first half of that year. NCC.

goons under Maj. James Dunlap to overtake the raiders. They reached Earle's Ford late on the night of 15 July 1780 and, unaware that McDowell's larger contingent was encamped nearby, launched a surprise attack.

Fording the river in relative silence, Dunlap's men descended on the sleeping Georgians, killing 8 and wounding 30. Jones himself received eight saber blows to the head. Some Georgians managed to fall back to a fence line about 100 meters behind their camp. Soon, McDowell's troops formed into a line of battle alongside them. Discovering that his enemies had been reinforced, Dunlap called off further attacks and ordered his dragoons back across the North Pacolet River.

The next morning, 52 men under Capt. Edward Hampton rode out to intercept Dunlap. They overtook his force approximately 15 miles away on Old Blackstock Road. The surprise was successful: eight British soldiers were killed in the initial attack, and the rest beat a hasty retreat to a nearby British outpost known as Prince's Fort, which stood near the present town of Inman, S.C.

Reference: John S. Pancake, *This Destructive War: The British Campaign in the Carolinas, 1780–1782* (1985).

John Hairr

Earthquakes are not considered a serious threat by many North Carolinians, although dozens of earthquakes have been recorded in the state since 1755. An earthquake may be defined as a shaking or trembling of the earth's crust. The modern theory of plate tectonics holds that the surface of the earth, or lithosphere, is composed of a dozen or so rigid plates moving slowly on a much softer layer of mantle, known as the asthenosphere. The friction between these plates is immense, and as they move against one another they sometimes get stuck; stress builds up, and when the plates are finally released an earthquake results.

Interestingly, North Carolina falls within an "intraplate zone," an area that should, according to the theory of plate tectonics, remain relatively free of earthquakes. As a consequence, the more than two centuries of earthquake activity observed in North Carolina (more than 80 events by most accounts) are not easy for students of the plate tectonics theory to explain. Certain areas of the state, such as the Blue Ridge escarpment, are apparently more seismic than others, although active faults have proven difficult to identify.

Fortunately, most of the state's earthquakes have been fairly mild, causing little if any damage. Had they been measured, they likely would have registered somewhere between

2.0 and 3.0 on the Richter scale. The most serious quake to affect North Carolina in modern times was the great Charleston, S.C., quake of 31 Aug. 1886. Estimates have placed it at 7.7 on the Richter scale, although it would have registered much more weakly in North Carolina. It was felt throughout the state, toppling numerous chimneys and cracking walls but causing no deaths or injuries. The very strong New Madrid, Mo., quakes of 1811 and 1812 were also felt throughout North Carolina.

The most important earthquakes to have epicenters within the borders of North Carolina were those of 21 Feb. 1916, 20 Oct. 1924, and 2 Nov. 1928. Their effects were concentrated in western North Carolina, and no significant damage was reported. North Carolina's most notorious earthquakes also took place in the western part of the state. From February through June 1874 the present-day Lake Lure area was rocked by a series of as many as 100 mild shocks. Their epicenter was a mountain that later came to be known as Rumbling Bald Mountain. Although mild in intensity, the quakes received national attention. Some even speculated that North Carolina had an active volcano on its hands, although nothing materialized.

A seismograph has been in place at the University of North Carolina at Chapel Hill since 1953, and earthquake activity in the state has been continuously recorded ever since. Research continues on the seismicity of the region, especially as pertains to the Charleston events of 1886. The current understanding of earthquake phenomena in North Carolina does not preclude the possibility of a severe and unprecedented event causing serious damage and great loss of life. In 1988 Robert Ketter, director of the National Center for Earthquake Engineering Research at the State University of New York at Buffalo, predicted that a major earthquake would occur in the eastern United States by the year 2010, though little attention has been paid to earthquake-resistant buildings and preparedness in this area.

References: Gerald R. MacCarthy, "An Annotated List of North Carolina Earthquakes," *Elisha Mitchell Scientific Society Journal* 73 (1957); L. Seeber and J. G. Armbruster, "The 1886–1889 Aftershocks of the Charleston, South Carolina, Earthquake: A Widespread Burst of Seismicity," *Journal of Geophysical Research* 92 (1987).

J. Timothy Cole

East Carolina University, located in Greenville, traces its origins to the East Carolina Teachers Training School, which came into existence amid substantial controversy in 1907. After competing with seven other localities, Greenville was chosen as the site for the campus, largely because of Pitt County's offer of 243 acres and $100,000 for a new facility. Much of the success of East Carolina during its initial years can be attributed to the dynamism of school president Robert Herring Wright. A Sampson County native who had studied at the University of North Carolina, Johns Hopkins, and Columbia University, Wright led East Carolina from 1909 to 1934. He inaugurated the institution's first four-year curriculum in 1920, and East Carolina Teachers Training School changed its name to East Carolina Teachers College the following year. In 1922 the first Bachelor of Arts degrees were awarded, and seven years later the first Master of Arts program came into existence.

Leo Warren Jenkins, a New Jersey native and chief executive of East Carolina from 1960 through 1978, oversaw the period of greatest expansion for the institution. More than any other individual, he was responsible for its metamorphosis from a provincial college to a doctorate-granting university of national stature. The student body virtually tripled in size during his tenure. In the fall of 1963, East Carolina's first African American student, Laura Marie Leary of Vanceboro, matriculated. The 1960s also witnessed the creation of the Schools of Business, Art, Music, Education, Arts and Sciences (with 19 departments), and Nursing. The East Carolina Manuscript Collection was opened to scholars in 1965, and the Schools of Allied Health and Social Professions, Home Economics, and Technology came into being during the last years of the decade. In 1967, thanks to the General Assembly's Henley Bill, which reorganized higher education in North Carolina, East Carolina College achieved university status. The School of Medicine, a dream that started with the establishment of the Health Affairs Division, received funding to establish a four-year program in 1974 and enrolled its first class in 1977.

By the early 2000s East Carolina University was the third-largest institution in the consolidated University of North Carolina System, with a total enrollment of nearly 20,000 students, 102 undergraduate degree programs, and 85 graduate degree programs. The School of Medicine, while addressing the health care concerns of the region, is also a pioneer in robotic surgery and telemedicine.

Reference: Mary Jo Jackson Bratton, *East Carolina University: The Formative Years, 1907–1982* (1986).

James I. Martin Sr.

East Coast Bible College, affiliated with the Church of God, was founded in 1976 on a 100-acre campus west of downtown Charlotte. The college began offering a four-year degree in 1978. By the late 1990s about one-third of its more than 300 students lived on campus, and the faculty numbered about 20. Each student graduated, whether with a bachelor's or an associate degree, with a major in Bible studies in addition to another major. From its inception, East Coast Bible College trained ministers, missionaries, teachers, and lay workers who served across the United States and in countries around the world. The college educated students from 40 states and 31 foreign countries. In 1999 East Coast Bible College became an extension of Lee University of Cleveland, Tenn., and is now known as Lee University at Charlotte.

T. David Sustar

Easter Monday Holiday. The Monday after Easter, rather than Good Friday as in every other state, was a legal holiday in North Carolina for 52 years. The bill establishing the holiday was introduced by Senator Paul Davis Grady of Johnston County and was ratified on 19 Apr. 1935. Although no written documents support the claim, oral tradition has long maintained that the reason North Carolina celebrated Easter Monday was to afford fans a greater opportunity to attend the North Carolina State–Wake Forest baseball game, which for many years was played the Monday after Easter. The law was amended in 1987 to observe the holiday on Good Friday rather than Easter Monday.

Jo Ann Williford

Eastern Belt. SEE Tobacco Belts.

Eastern Music Festival (EMF), established on the Guilford College campus in Greensboro in 1962, is one of the most acclaimed music educational camps and festivals in the United States. Originally called the Guilford Musical Arts Camp by its founder, Sheldon Morgenstern, then a faculty member at Guilford College, the camp was conceived as a place where talented students could receive professional musical instruction and where students of similar ability and training could perform together.

From the first class of 75 students, the EMF has grown to a student enrollment of approximately 200 each year, with competitive auditions for the coveted positions held throughout the United States and several parts of the world. World-class master teachers and trained musician-teachers provide intensive one-on-one and small group sessions for six weeks from late June until early August each year. Students are housed in residence halls on the Guilford College campus, and it is not unusual to hear music emanating from dorm rooms or the shelter of a tall oak at almost any hour.

EMF student orchestras offer full classical concerts twice weekly in Guilford's Dana Auditorium, often with internationally known guest soloists. The Eastern Philharmonic Orchestra (EPO), comprised of professional musicians whose winter affiliations include numerous orchestras and schools of music throughout the nation and the world, performs a classical concert every Saturday night of the season. Maestro Morgenstern, who retired as music and education director in early 1998, led the professional orchestra from its founding; he continued to conduct orchestras in major cities in western and eastern Europe as well as North and South America. Edmon Colomer

of Spain is the current principal guest conductor, and every season other international conductors are guest maestros of the EPO.

Each year, the Eastern Music Festival performs in High Point and Winston-Salem as well as in Greensboro, and it has traveled in the past to other North Carolina locations as well. Project Listen, a program begun in the 1960s, has brought music to people throughout Guilford County otherwise unable to attend the regular EMF season; locales include hospitals, manufacturing plants, and schools. In all, the EMF provides Piedmont North Carolina with about 100 musical events each year, from solo performances to the popular Tuesday night Eastern Chamber Players concerts and the full orchestra concerts.

The students remain the central focus of each season of the Eastern Music Festival. Over the years, scholarship and financial aid programs have been established to assure places for the best students that can be found. In 1985 a gift from Ralph and Janie Price of Greensboro established the International Scholarship Program, bringing students from Japan, Germany, and other locations around the globe; the program continues to be underwritten by Leonard and Tobee Kaplan. Minority and other special scholarships have also been funded by patrons and musicians alike.

Alumni of the EMF have been coming back as performers, teachers, and special guest artists for years. They include classical and jazz trumpeter Wynton Marsalis, perhaps the festival's most widely known alumnus; concert pianists Randall Hodgkinson and Gustavo Romero; composer/conductor Carl Roskott; and classical quartet violist Chauncey Patterson. During the months other than the summer season, thousands of the 4,500 EMF alumni hold major positions with orchestras or chamber music groups; teach at music conservatories, universities, and schools; or tour as guest soloists throughout the world.

References: Abe D. Jones Jr., *Thirty Gleaming Summers: A Celebration of the Eastern Music Festival* (1991); Leslie Mizell, "The Music Man," *Business Life* (June 1994).

Jeaneane Williams

East-West Rivalry is the name for a particularly potent form of sectionalism that has been a major factor in the political, social, and economic development of North Carolina. The state's varied geography shaped the character of incoming European settlements, and there soon emerged distinct regions reflecting differences in nationalities, languages, and religions. Conflict rooted in regional identity was strong, usually developing around political or economic issues and events, the collection and distribution of taxes, and representation in colonial or state government.

Initial rivalries and jealousies existed between the northern and southern parts of the colony, but these were soon followed by those between east and west. The conflicts stemmed primarily from cultural differences born of economic realities and self-interests. Western settlers owned mostly small farms and businesses, while those in the east often had large plantations and commercial enterprises that afforded them more wealth and power. Additionally, westerners usually had few slaves or none at all, whereas many leaders in the east were large slaveholders. The east had wide, shallow, slow-moving rivers and streams suited for river transportation, while the West's narrow, fast-flowing streams limited river traffic but promoted the development of mills and waterpower.

In the years after the Revolution, North Carolinians in the Piedmont and the west prospered and their political aspirations grew. By 1830 more than half of the state's population lived west of Raleigh; the state government, however, remained in the control of the eastern elite, empowered by its advanced political organization and economic status. The 1776 state constitution had mandated equal county representation and included strict property qualifications for officeholders, which put the westerners at a disadvantage. The constitution also contained no provision for amendment, so only a constitutional convention called by the legislature could revise the document.

The climax of this sectional dispute came in the 1830s, when many westerners embraced the Whig Party as their vehicle to gain political power. Using the new campaign tactics of the time, North Carolina Whigs, led by canny politicians such as David Swain, swept to ascendancy in the state government and engineered a constitutional convention in 1835 that equalized representation in the General Assembly. Provisions were adopted and later ratified by the people for reapportionment of the legislature, including abolition of borough representation and partial removal of religious qualifications for voting and office holding. The 50-acre requirement to vote for state senator was retained, but all adult white male taxpayers could vote for governors and representatives in the legislature. The Whig era was a period of reform and modernization, especially in the areas of government-subsidized public education and internal improvement, a source of special concern to those residing in the undeveloped interior of the state.

The Civil War, like the Revolution, often fostered in North Carolinians a tendency toward social polarization and occasional violence. Again, westward communities were more apt to be antigovernment—in this era, consequently, pro-Union —although even the west was home to several Confederate strongholds. At times, however, this social division assumed more of a class conflict than a true regional dispute. Increased settlement in rural areas, by people of varying economic status and political allegiances, had begun to blur sectional lines that in earlier times had been more readily apparent.

The distinctly east-west friction subsided greatly in the twentieth century, as differences between North Carolina's geographical and cultural identities diminished while new divisions arose. A kind of informal rotation pattern occurred for a time, leading to the election of governors, U.S. senators, and other political leaders from both east and west. A new brand of sectionalism emerged in the state during the mid-twentieth century. No longer based on an east-west axis, modern sectionalism is grounded in rural-urban differences. In the 1960s the state's expanding cities demanded a stronger political voice, which resulted in the creation of new voting districts that gave Piedmont and Mountain citizens greater representation in the legislature. The one-person-one-vote rule established by the U.S. Supreme Court in 1962, which emphasized the population size of particular voting districts, also greatly increased the political power of urban areas. In addition, the success of the civil rights movement during this period caused the delineation of some districts to be based on racial demography. This new sectionalism also exhibited class divisions as urban "modernists," rooted primarily in the so-called Piedmont Urban Crescent, clashed with rural "traditionalists" in their quest for political and economic equality.

Many remnants of North Carolina's sometimes volatile east-west rivalry remain. For example, the eighteenth-century conflict and eventual compromise between the eastern and western regions determined the locations of both the state's capital and its first major university. The site for the capital city of Raleigh was arrived at through much east-west political wrangling; it was ultimately selected, according to both legend and historical research, by its proximity to a tavern that served an excellent rum punch. The location of the University of North Carolina in Chapel Hill was likewise a compromise between eastern and western discourse.

References: Hugh T. Lefler and Albert R. Newsome, *North Carolina: The History of a Southern State* (3rd ed., 1973); Paul Luebke, *Tar Heel Politics: Myths and Realities* (1990); William S. Powell, *North Carolina through Four Centuries* (1989).

David L. Cockrell
Additional research provided by Wiley J. Williams.

Ecce Homo (Behold the Man), a famous oil painting by Francisco Pacheco measuring about 30 by 40 inches in size and depicting Christ wearing a crown of thorns, hangs in St. James Episcopal Church in Wilmington. Three Spanish ships attacked and occupied the town of Brunswick in 1747, driving out the inhabitants. Three days later, men of the area gathered to drive out the Spanish. A carefully aimed or unusually lucky shot lobbed a shell onto the Spanish privateer *Fortuna*, still anchored in the Cape Fear River beside the town. The *Fortuna* exploded and the other two ships sailed down river, where they paused to exchange prisoners. *Ecce Homo* was among the goods removed from the sinking ship. The colonial assem-

Ecce Homo. NCC.

bly in May 1751 voted to present the painting to St. Philip's Church in Brunswick. When Brunswick was abandoned after the American Revolution, the painting was moved to St. James Church.

Reference: Louis T. Moore, "Ecce Homo," *Uplift* 32 (4 Mar. 1944).

William S. Powell

Economy of North Carolina has changed dramatically since its establishment as an English colony in the seventeenth century. From its almost entirely agricultural origins, the state has moved steadily toward what has been described as a "dual economy," characterized by growing, economically strong urban centers and depressed rural areas. While agricultural products continued to represent a large percentage of North Carolina's economy, by 2004 North Carolina was also the fifth most industrialized state and among the national leaders in banking, manufacturing, health services, technology, and other industries.

During the colonial period and through early statehood, about 95 percent of North Carolinians engaged in farming and related industries. The abundance and fertility of the land, the demand for exports such as naval stores and lumber, and the desire of the people to be self-sufficient all created an environment conducive to a simple, agrarian lifestyle. While some planters owned large tracts of land, North Carolinians pri-marily maintained small farms and cultivated crops such as tobacco, corn, peas, beans, wheat, rice, and a variety of fruits. Those not reliant on agriculture for their living included merchants, lawyers, doctors, public officials, teachers, and other professionals.

The nineteenth and early twentieth centuries saw the tremendous growth of the aptly named "Big Three" North Carolina industries—tobacco, textiles, and furniture. The manufacture of the many products related to these industries grew naturally from the availability of raw materials in the state. Textile mills of all kinds, factories making a variety of tobacco products, and dozens of high-quality furniture manufacturers were established, creating employment for thousands of North Carolinians. The majority of people still lived in rural areas and often worked both the land and a factory job to make ends meet.

After 1900, the infrastructure for greater economic progress began to appear in the state, as vast improvements were made in transportation facilities, educational initiatives, urban and rural electrification, and modernization of agricultural and factory production. Personal income rose steadily in the first half of the twentieth century, moving from only 47 percent of the national average in 1930 to nearly 67 percent by 1945. (Per capita income reached about 91 percent of the national average by 2000.)

Despite the cultural and financial malaise of the Great Depression, North Carolina emerged during the World War II era with a great deal of economic promise. The state remained the nation's largest producer of textiles, tobacco products, and furniture during the mid-1900s, and new industries began to develop. Shifts occurred from labor-intensive industries to more automated but capital-intensive industries; from manufacturing jobs to jobs in trade, insurance, tourism, finance, transportation, high tech, government, and other service industries; and from small tobacco-dependent family farms to large, often corporate-owned farms producing diverse products such as hogs, dairy products, and poultry.

Beginning in the 1960s, with the founding and success of modern, technology-oriented facilities such as Research Triangle Park in the Raleigh-Durham area and similar complexes in Charlotte, Greensboro, and Rocky Mount, the state's economy was transformed from a predominately rural culture dependent upon agriculture and low-wage industries to an increasingly urban economy. Most economic growth took place in the so-called Piedmont Urban Crescent, represented by booming regions such as the Triangle area (Raleigh, Durham, and Chapel Hill), the Triad (Greensboro, Winston-Salem, and High Point), and the greater Charlotte area. But while the economies of the state's urban counties (Wake, Durham, Orange, Alamance, Guilford, Forsyth, Davidson, Rowan, Cabarrus, Mecklenburg, Gaston, Catawba, Buncombe, Cumberland, and New Hanover) were expanding, the gap between rural and urban workforces continued to widen.

The national economic woes that followed the 11 Sept. 2001 terrorist attacks on New York City and Washington, D.C., affected North Carolina's economy greatly. In 2001 there were 63,222 total layoffs in the state, with 11,695 in textiles and 42,521 in manufacturing. The state's unemployment rate in March 2002 stood at 6.6 percent. Rural areas were hit particularly hard: 87 percent of job losses in rural counties were due to manufacturing layoffs, and those counties' unemployment rate averaged 2 percent higher than the unemployment rate in urban counties.

By 2004 the state's leading industries by gross annual production included finance, insurance, and real estate ($54.9 billion); government ($34.2 billion); retail trade ($24.1 billion); transportation and utilities ($18.7 billion); construction ($13.9 billion); health services ($13.2 billion); chemicals ($11.4 billion); and tobacco products ($10.6 billion). One-fourth of the workforce was employed in manufacturing, with textiles leading the way and the state's approximately 70,000 furniture workers still producing a large percentage of the furniture made in the United States. Charlotte was the second-largest banking center in the United States, and the Research Triangle area was an increasingly important technology and medical research center.

References: Douglas M. Orr Jr. and Alfred W. Stuart, eds., *North Carolina Atlas: Portrait for a New Century* (2000); U.S. Bureau of Economic Analysis, *State Personal Income 1929–97* (1999).

Lisa Coston Hall
Wiley J. Williams

SEE ALSO Agriculture; Banking; Exports; Furniture; Information Technology; Manufacturing; Textiles.

Edenton, incorporated in 1722 and located at the head of Albemarle Sound in Chowan County, was the first colonial capital of North Carolina as well as a significant commercial center. The town was the home of James Iredell, who began his distinguished career as deputy collector for the Port of Roanoke. He became attorney general of North Carolina at the age of 28, worked for ratification of the new constitution in the state, and in 1790 was appointed by George Washington to the first U.S. Supreme Court. He was an exponent of judicial review, and with his friend, Justice James Wilson, laid the foundation for the Eleventh Amendment to the Constitution.

The Daughters of the American Revolution purchased the Iredell House in 1948 and saved it from demolition; in 1951 the North Carolina General Assembly authorized the Department of Conservation and Development to assume title to the property by paying off the debt. Four years later the homesite was transferred to the Department of Archives and History and deemed a North Carolina State Historic Site. The modern-day Historic Edenton State Historic Site features the James Iredell Homesite and the 1767 Chowan County Courthouse. Three

additional historic properties, although not held by the state, are open during conducted tours: St. Paul's Episcopal Church (1736), the Cupola House (1758), and the Barker House (1782).

References: Thomas R. Butchko, *Edenton: An Architectural Portrait* (1992); Don Higginbotham, ed., *Papers of James Iredell* (2 vols., 1976); Richard F. Knapp, ed., *North Carolina's State Historic Sites: A Brief History and Status Report* (1995).

William B. Strong

SEE ALSO Chowan County Courthouse; Cupola House.

Edenton Tea Party. On 25 Oct. 1774, at the home of Mrs. Elizabeth King, 51 women from Edenton, including reputed leader Penelope Barker, drew up a resolution to uphold the "particular resolves" drafted by the First Provincial Congress at New Bern exactly two months before. In light of the celebrated Boston Tea Party, which had taken place less than a year before, it was perhaps inevitable that this later occasion would be called the "Edenton Tea Party"—although tea drinking was not mentioned in the ladies' patriotic statement. Their spirited meeting and declaration might have passed unnoticed had not word of it reached London, where the *Morning Chronicle and London Advertiser* published an account of the event on 16 Jan. 1775. Over the years a satirical cartoon accompanying the article has achieved near-icon status.

The 51 signatures to the resolution published by the London paper were long thought to be an authentic list of the signers. Later research, however, has shown some discrepancies in the list. There is little doubt that the meeting did take place, as contemporary letters mentioned it. Some historians consider it probably the "earliest instance of political activity on the part of women" in the American colonies and one of the colorful events that heralded the coming American Revolution. A colonial teapot mounted on a revolutionary cannon marks the site of the Edenton Tea Party.

References: Elizabeth Vann Moore, *Guide Book to Historic Edenton and Chowan County* (1977); Thomas C. Parramore, *Cradle of the Colony: The History of Chowan County and Edenton, North Carolina* (1967).

Jaquelin Drane Nash

Edgecombe County, located in the Coastal Plain region of eastern North Carolina, was formed in 1741 from Bertie County. It was named for Baron Richard Edgecombe, English member of Parliament and lord of the treasury. Aside from minor boundary adjustments, the county's present dimensions are the result of geographical divisions in 1746, 1758, 1777, and 1855 to form parts of Granville, Halifax, Nash, and Wilson Counties, respectively. In 1746 the county seat was moved from Edgecombe Court House to Tarboro. Other Edgecombe County communities include Conetoe, Leggett, Macclesfield, Pinetops, Princeville, Sharpsburg, Speed, Whitakers, and parts of Rocky Mount (which straddles the Edgecombe-Nash county border).

Tuscarora Indians originally inhabited the lands of Edgecombe County, and the English settlers who followed represented some of the first families of colonial North Carolina. The town of Princeville is also notable among Edgecombe County "firsts": established in 1865 by former slaves, it was the first all-black incorporated town in North Carolina. It and other Edgecombe County communities were devastated by the flooding of the Tar River following Hurricane Floyd in 1999. The first New Deal–era electrical cooperative began generating in Tarboro in 1937. The Tarboro Town Commons is today the only known example of a colonial common remaining in North Carolina.

Edgecombe County natural and cultural attractions include Riverfront Park in Tarboro and Battle Park in Rocky Mount; the Tar River Reservoir; Coolmore, an antebellum mansion built ca. 1860; and the Rocky Mount Arts Center. The Down East Festival of the Arts is held each October in Rocky Mount. Edgecombe County farms produce tobacco, cotton, corn, wheat, chickens, beef and dairy cattle, and peanuts, among other goods. County industrial products include furniture, farm machinery, electric transformers, and fabrics. In 2004 Edgecombe County's population was estimated to be 54,000.

Reference: Sarah Veith Jenkins, *The Edgecombe Story* (1976).

Allyson C. Criner

Education, Adult. The history, purposes, and philosophy of adult education in North Carolina generally parallel those of adult education elsewhere in the United States, while manifesting some significant regional differences. Continuing education, literacy, adult basic education, higher education, professional for-profit business training, and workplace training are all important forms of adult education in the state. Prior to the Industrial Revolution, such adult education as there was occurred mostly at home or in church. White male landowners in North Carolina were much more likely than women, the indigenous population, or slaves to read, write, and compute. In 1816 the American Bible Society began a nationwide literacy campaign to place a Bible in every home: the Bible was frequently the only printed material in a household, and early literacy efforts were designed to equip at least one household member with the skills to read the text.

Native Americans in North Carolina, such as the Lumbees and Cherokees, relied largely on the oral tradition as a lifelong learning process. Storytelling, active modeling, and learning by doing fostered the education of youth, who in their adulthood would become teachers of the next generation. Slaves, for whom literacy was at times outlawed, drew on their African heritage of oral instruction: storytelling, song, and call-and-response (especially among field workers) were richly employed as means of instruction, community building, and survival in a new land. These traditions continue to serve North Carolinians of all races.

The Civil War, which drew thousands of the state's men into service, drained local resources and damaged both physical and social infrastructures. The church and the military were critical agents of adult education throughout the war years. Interestingly, the U.S. Congress used the context of the war to enact the Morrill Land Grant Act in 1862. Under this legislation, acreage was deeded to each state for the purpose of establishing an institution of higher education that would be equal to any in the private sector. This was the first time that federal resources were allocated to higher education. Southern states, including North Carolina, were deeded their land after the war, and the North Carolina College of Agriculture and Mechanic Arts, precursor to modern-day North Carolina State University, was founded in 1887. In the South, land grant universities mirrored the larger society in that they were segregated by race. In response to this situation, Congress passed the Second Morrill Act in 1890, conferring federal funds for agricultural and technical colleges for blacks. North Carolina Agricultural and Technical State University in Greensboro had its beginnings in this second piece of legislation.

At the start of the twentieth century, adult literacy needs were addressed in various ways throughout the state. In many mill villages, basic educational opportunities were made available to workers and their families, often through village libraries. It was believed that illiteracy was worse in rural areas, where population was sparse and there was little communication. Many night schools, also called "moonlight" schools, were established, including those operated under the Community Schools Adult Education Program of Buncombe County, started in 1919 and used as a model in North Carolina as well as nationally. The main purpose of the community schools was to teach adults who could not read or write. Education was achieved through study of normal adult interests, such as reading the newspaper and the Bible, and through writing letters. The program was committed to helping adults who had "missed their chance" at education during childhood. Basic homemaking and nutrition principles and the ideal of community participation were also taught, and basic physical and medical needs were addressed. It was not uncommon for adults to walk several miles to get to a community school, and many pupils never missed a lesson. One 65-year-old woman walked two and a half miles each way to get to class, according to the records of her night school.

Since its inception in 1909, the North Carolina Agricultural (Cooperative) Extension Service has been the mechanism by which the educational needs of many of the state's people have been identified and addressed by the state universities—particularly the land grant universities, which are integrally tied to cooperative extension. Empowered by the federal government under the Smith-Lever Act of 1914, the Cooperative Extension Service provides services and offers programs through a network of higher education departments and faculty, experiment stations, and extension agents located throughout North Carolina. The system is a successful model of federal, state, and local cooperation that is often overlooked in basic education. Agriculture, small and medium business enterprise, homemaking, child care, and nutrition are among the areas in which cooperative extension plays a vital role in adult education.

In 1963 the Department of Extension Personnel was created under the College of Agricultural and Life Sciences at North Carolina State University. Renamed the Department of Adult Education in 1965 and the Department of Adult and Community College Education in 1970, this department offers short courses as well as master's and doctoral degrees in the field of adult education.

North Carolina's community college system originated in the 1950s and was strengthened considerably during the 1960s and 1970s. It is a 58-member system that complements the Cooperative Extension Service by offering both vocational and liberal arts programs. Located so that a community college is within reasonable driving distance of every North Carolinian, the institutions offer a variety of programs designed to address the needs of local communities as well as a standardized liberal arts curriculum similar to that of the state's public four-year institutions. Two-year degree programs, noncredit courses, adult basic education, vocational education, and industry-supported job training complement the liberal arts curriculum of community colleges in the state.

The U.S. military plays a key, if often overlooked, role in adult education in North Carolina. Its six installations, particularly the army's Fort Bragg, are complexes wherein continual training and education are essential. Federal funding and commitment, while varying throughout the twentieth century, ensured the continuance of the military presence in North Carolina and the ongoing education of all service members.

In the last decades of the twentieth century, the state's economy, led by the high-tech and pharmaceutical industries, diversified tremendously. On-site training became a common means of adult education. With the tremendous growth of the Research Triangle Park, which has attracted multinational corporations and big businesses since its creation in the late 1950s, companies such as IBM, Nortel, and SAS have come to be leaders in human resource development and training.

Governors and other government officials, chambers of commerce, the YMCA and YWCA, and agencies such as teacher organizations and parent-teacher associations, as well as private individuals, have addressed adult literacy in North Caro-

lina in a number of ways. In 1987 Governor James G. Martin created the Governor's Commission on Literacy, chaired by William C. Friday, former president of the University of North Carolina System. The commission's report noted programs and institutions already in place to address literacy and basic-skills needs, such as community colleges, county literacy councils, community action groups, private industry councils, and public libraries.

In the 1980s and 1990s North Carolina saw a large influx of residents attracted to the state by its beauty, its strong job market, and its relatively low cost of living. Newcomers tended to be workers from other regions of the country in search of enhanced employment opportunities or retirees seeking a new lifestyle in the Sun Belt. Many had advanced degrees and arrived with expectations for further educational opportunities and enrichment. A second wave of new residents speak Spanish as their first language: between 1990 and 2003, the state's Latino population more than doubled. A significant number of these residents arrived with limited English-language and -literacy skills, creating new demands and challenges for adult education. Responses slowly emerged from the traditional sources of adult education in the state: the church, nonprofits, the community college system, and the Cooperative Extension Service. Nevertheless, and despite much progress, in the early 2000s North Carolina ranked forty-first in the nation in literacy.

References: Bertie Edwards Fearing, *A History of the Department of Adult and Community College Education at North Carolina State University* (1978); Nancy E. Hagan, *Readings in Adult Education* (1991); Sharan B. Merriam and Phyllis M. Cunningham, eds., *Handbook of Adult and Continuing Education* (1989).

Nancy E. Hagan
Additional research provided by
Zoe Rhine and Wiley J. Williams.

SEE ALSO Community Colleges; Extension Service.

Education, Private. Private education has had a long, diverse, and distinguished history in North Carolina. The state's private schools, both on the preparatory and college levels, have grown from the initial efforts of a few individual teachers during settlement and the early colonial period to more than 600 academies and 36 colleges and universities. The success or failure of the earliest schools often reflected changing social and economic trends, with most surviving only a short time and a few serving as the first incarnation of some of the state's modern-day institutes of higher learning. In 2006 North Carolina had 36 private liberal arts colleges and universities, enrolling more than 75,000 students. The North Carolina Association of Independent Colleges and Universities represents these institutions in legal and professional matters at both the state and federal levels.

Private Academies in Colonial North Carolina and Early Statehood

Prior to 1800, young children generally were taught at home by parents, tutors, or governesses. Neighboring children often traveled to share in instruction. A relatively small number of private schools were established during the colonial period. In the absence of government funding, churches and communities coalesced to provide schooling for local white children. Eighteenth-century academies and other schools were organized and supported by a few individuals, particularly those associated with the Anglican Church. In 1709 lay reader Charles Griffin established in Pasquotank County the earliest known school in the colony. A few years later he moved to Edenton, leaving his first school in the hands of the Reverend James Adams, and ultimately joined the faculty of the College of William and Mary in Williamsburg, Va. A school for both Indian and white children was run by Edward Mashborne at Sarum, a site now in Gates County. These schools are the only ones known to have existed in North Carolina in the Proprietary period.

Daniel Earl in 1763 was teaching Latin, Greek, English, and mathematics near Edenton. The schoolhouse he is believed to have used was still standing in 2006, though not on the original site. In 1764 the colonial Assembly provided for the building of a school on church property in New Bern intended to serve more than the local community. Financial support from the church as well as from a provincial tax made it available to a wider range of pupils. With Thomas Thomlinson, the son and grandson of teachers in England, as its first teacher, the New Bern Academy opened in 1764. It continued until 1899, when it was incorporated into the public school system.

James Tate, a Presbyterian minister in Wilmington, established Tate's School as the first classical academy in the colony; it prepared young men for college until the American Revolution. Other Presbyterian clergymen soon followed. Crowfield Academy opened in Rowan County, and David Caldwell began a school in Guilford County in 1767 that served as an academy, a college, and a theological seminary. Before Caldwell died in 1824, many of his "Log College" graduates entered the junior classes at Princeton and the University of North Carolina in Chapel Hill.

In 1771 the Assembly proposed that Queen's College be established in Charlotte as the colony's first degree-granting school, but because of political and religious resentment it was not approved. Instead, an institution called Queen's Museum was organized and may have granted degrees; the approaching American Revolution halted all progress and efforts were transferred to Salisbury, where Liberty Hall Academy replaced it. Following the Revolution, with royal opposition no longer a factor, higher private education began to make headway in North Carolina. Article 41 of the first state constitution, adopted in 1776, provided for schools and one or more universities. Between 1777 and 1789 the legislature chartered 18 academies, 12 of which were warned by their charters not to expect to become one of the universities anticipated in the constitution. After 1795, when the University of North Carolina became the first such state-supported institution in the United States, private institutions of higher learning began to appear with the avowed purpose of preparing young men for the new university.

Antebellum Growth, the Civil War, and the First African American Colleges

By the start of the nineteenth century, 40 private academies existed in the state, including Salem Female Academy (founded in 1772). All of these schools catered primarily to wealthy white students—no private schools accepted black children, free or slave, and few poor white families could spare the time or expense to send children to private schools. It was not until the nineteenth century that religious organizations such as the Society of Friends (Quakers) began to offer African American children any formal education.

In the first six decades of the new century, 287 academies were chartered by the General Assembly. A few flourished, but many closed after a short time. When the legislature did not respond quickly enough in establishing an institution to more conveniently serve the western counties, the Presbyterian Church took the initiative, founding Davidson College in 1837. Other churches soon followed its lead. In Wake County, Baptists opened the Wake Forest Manual Labor Institute (modern Wake Forest University) in 1834, and in Randolph County, Quakers and Methodists organized Union Institute (later Trinity College and eventually Duke University). In 1851 the German Reformed Church founded Catawba College in Newton. These institutions trained men as ministers for the growing congregations across the South.

Female education progressed much more slowly: it was not deemed necessary to train young women in anything but the domestic arts, with a little French, music, dancing, and drawing sometimes added. Before there were female academies in the state, classes for girls were sometimes provided in the boys' schools by women teachers. Salem Female Academy, the state's oldest girls' school, was still open in 2006, having never moved from its original site. At first a "day-school," Salem became a boarding school in 1802. Salem College was developed later, but the academy has retained its identity as a female preparatory school.

The Public School Law of 1839 initiated a gradual shift of primary education to public jurisdiction, although many private schools continued to flourish. Some children of poorer families began to enjoy the same educational opportunities as their wealthier neighbors. Virtually all educational institutions in the state suffered during and immediately following the Civil War. Endowments vanished, buildings and resources were damaged or destroyed, and for a brief period even the University of North Carolina was closed. Soon after the war, however, newly emancipated blacks and progressive whites led the charge for universal, state-supported public education, while wealthy families continued to send their children to private alternatives. Several black schools were established by Roman Catholic, Presbyterian, Episcopal, Methodist, and Baptist churches in the postwar era. Raleigh Institute (modern Shaw University), opened in 1865 as the South's first black institution of higher learning. Other important church-supported African American schools dating from this era include Biddle Memorial Institute (modern Johnson C. Smith University) in Charlotte (1867), Saint Augustine's Normal School and Collegiate Institute (modern Saint Augustine's University) in Raleigh (1867), Bennett Seminary (modern Bennett College) in Greensboro (1873), and Zion Wesley Institute (modern Livingstone College) in Salisbury (1879).

Private academies during the late nineteenth and early twentieth century took many different forms. Many were modeled on the New England ideal—a secluded, exclusive institution providing intensive training in classics, religion, and other traditional subjects. (Several of these schools, including the Asheville School [1900] and Ravenscroft in Raleigh [1937], remain open today.) Other schools, such as Oak Ridge Military Academy (1853), emphasized military discipline and regimentation. Although the vast majority of private schools served white children, black parents also sought the perceived advantages of private education and, often with the aid of northern missionary societies, established private black institutions.

Decline, Desegregation, and the Private School Boom

In the early twentieth century, as the state's public school system began to emerge in earnest, the Roman Catholic Church became a major influence in private education in North Carolina. Often shunned by their Protestant neighbors, Catholics developed a strong alternative educational system that emphasized religious doctrine and discipline, eschewing public schools' perceived secular, or Protestant, orientation. As Catholics grew in number and influence across the South, they built schools to provide their children with a common cultural base. Many schools founded in this period remain in operation, including Charlotte's St. Patrick's Catholic School (originally organized in the late 1800s as O'Donoghue Catholic School), Raleigh's Cardinal Gibbons High School (1909), Hendersonville's Immaculata School (1926), and Burlington's Blessed Sacrament School (1930).

Despite the development of many notable institutions, by the mid-twentieth century private education in North Carolina and the rest of the South lagged far behind the national average. Most citizens were unable to afford any alternative to public schools; furthermore, most people believed that the public schools could provide quality education, reducing the need for private schooling. For many white North Carolinians, this faith in the public schools was undermined by the U.S. Supreme Court's 1954 decision in *Brown v. Board of Education of Topeka, Kansas* outlawing segregation in public education. The state's white leadership, with widespread white support, sought to stop integration with the Pearsall Plan, which gave local citizens the right to close down public schools if faced with desegregation and provided state tuition credits for any white child to attend private schools. The plan also authorized the state to set minimum standards for private schools in terms of teacher certification, curriculum, class size, safety and health requirements, and length of school day and year.

Over the next 20 years, the growth of private education in North Carolina correlated directly with the progress of desegregation and the percentage of blacks in a particular area. For ten years following the *Brown* ruling, few public schools were integrated, and the number of private schools remained relatively constant. In the 1964–65 school year, fewer than 9,500 students attended 83 private schools. But beginning in that year, the U.S. Department of Health, Education, and Welfare began aggressively to enforce the 1964 Civil Rights Act, which prohibited segregation in any program that accepted federal funds. As desegregation progressed, white private schools sprang up across the state, especially in eastern North Carolina's Black Belt, where blacks constituted a majority or near-majority of the population. In the three years between 1968 (when the U.S. Supreme Court demanded immediate public school integration) and 1971, the number of students attending private schools in the state more than doubled, from less than 20,000 to more than 47,000; the number of private schools ballooned from 108 to 235.

Contemporary critics dubbed these new private schools "segregation academies" and "the schools that fear built" because they appeared to be motivated by white disdain for school integration. Not all private schools, of course, were the products of racial fear. Many older ones voluntarily agreed to integrate. Other private institutions, such as the Carolina Friends School in Durham, were established specifically to provide quality education in an integrated setting. Yet the majority of white families that supported these private schools were reacting to perceived changes in American life that they found disturbing, including race relations, the increasingly secular nature of public discourse, the permissive culture encouraged by 1960s liberalism, and impersonal economic and social relationships. In the face of such upheaval, parents sought to create cultural buffer zones around their children via private schools.

As the 1970s wore on, the growth of private education in North Carolina stabilized, and the new academies became entrenched in their communities. Many new schools were "Christian academies" that emphasized evangelical Christian doctrine as part of their curricula. Like their Roman Catholic counterparts earlier in the century, these Protestant schools sought to provide a moral and religious foundation for children growing up in an increasingly secular world.

The 1990s witnessed tremendous growth in private education in North Carolina. At the beginning of the decade, about 53,000 students attended 463 private preparatory schools in the state; by 2001–2, 91,817 students attended 653 schools, 71 percent of which were classified as "religious" by the North Carolina Division of Non-Public Education, part of the Department of Administration. This growth can be traced both to the continuing dissatisfaction with public education as well as North Carolina's increasing economic prosperity.

Other significant movements in private education have been the growing number of children who are homeschooled in the state and the debate over the implementation of a school voucher system to help parents pay for private schooling if their public school alternatives are lacking. Advocates of vouchers claim they would increase the educational choices of poorer children in "troubled" schools, while opponents argue they would severely damage the public school system and essentially use public funds to benefit private, often religious, institutions.

References: R. D. W. Connor, "Genesis of Higher Education in North Carolina," *NCHR* 28 (January 1951); Charles L. Coon, *North Carolina Schools and Academies, 1790–1840* (1915); Calvin Criner, "Non-Public Schools in North Carolina," *Popular Government* 42 (Spring 1977); Rebecca Webster Graves, "Nonpublic Schools Revisited: A Comparative Study of Nonpublic Education in North Carolina from 1975 to 1985" (Ph.D. diss., UNC-Greensboro, 1988); Eugene D. Owens, "Secondary Education in North Carolina in the Eighteenth Century" (Ph.D. diss., George Washington University, 1934); William S. Powell, *North Carolina through Four Centuries* (1989).

Chris Myers
Jaquelin Drane Nash
Additional research provided by William S. Powell and Robert D. Weaver.

SEE ALSO Bennett College; Bingham School; Caldwell School; Clio's Nursery; Davidson College; Duke University; Liberty Hall; North Carolina Association of Independent Colleges and Universities; Queen's College; Saint Augustine's College; Salem Academy and Salem College; Wake Forest University.

Education, Public. The history of public education in North Carolina reflects the state's development from its primarily rural, agrarian beginnings to its position in the early 2000s as a national leader in agriculture, technology, and industry. Turning points in the growth of the public school system include the establishment of common schools in the early nineteenth century and of the first graded schools in the Civil War and Reconstruction eras, actions taken in the early twentieth century to improve schools through the use of public funds and to fully extend public education to African American children, integration of schools during the civil rights movement of the 1950s and 1960s, and introduction of numerous educational reforms and programs that formed the basis of the modern North Carolina public school system. In the realm of higher education, North Carolina's 16-campus University of North Carolina System and 58-campus community college system represent some of the finest such institutions in the nation, serving a huge number of the state's children and adults.

The Literary Fund, the Education Act, and the Growth of Common Schools

Although the North Carolina Constitution of 1776 referred to the education of the new state's youth, it essentially provided for only the establishment of the University of North Carolina in Chapel Hill (which did not open until 1795). All existing schools and academies during this period were privately supported, often by churches and generally for the purpose of educating the children of affluent parents. A statewide system of public schools was first proposed around 1817 by state senator Archibald D. Murphey of Orange County. In 1825 the State Literary Fund was created to support such a system, but the fund was inadequate until supplemented in 1836 by a federal surplus of $1.5 million—the bulk of which went toward the Literary Fund and public education.

The Education Act passed by the General Assembly in 1839 and revised in 1841 created North Carolina's earliest public school system, which lacked statewide standards and at first produced widely varying results. The state's first "common" school opened in Rockingham County in January 1840. Over the next decade thousands of other schools opened across the state after a statewide referendum on public schools in August 1839 won the approval of voters in 61 counties; the remaining 7 counties joined the statewide movement by 1846. Initial funds for common schools were provided from the Literary Fund and a mandatory local tax. These moneys generally paid the salary of a schoolteacher for no longer than two to three months a year, although some districts operated schools for up to nine months. Children of all ages were educated simultaneously. Each school district was initially entitled to an allocation of $40 per annum from the Literary Fund if it agreed to provide a school building for 50 students and raise an additional $20 in local taxes. But political pressures almost immediately made the local tax voluntary and changed the formula to favor eastern counties with large slave populations.

After 1841 the Literary Fund's proceeds were distributed to counties on the basis of the federal population, in which slaves were counted as three-fifths of a white person. Although slaves were not entitled to public education, their sheer numbers inflated allocations to eastern counties at the expense of western counties with far fewer slaves; this formula remained in effect until the 1850s. Some districts chose not to impose a local tax, while others failed to spend all of their Literary Fund appropriations. Public apathy and the unpopularity of the local tax threatened to undermine the school system in many counties.

By 1850, 2,657 common schools employing approximately 1,500 teachers offered primary education to more than 100,000 white schoolchildren in North Carolina. In the antebellum era, educational opportunities for slaves and free blacks were severely limited. It was illegal to teach blacks to read and write, though some learned basic reading skills through illicit lessons by whites or by managing to gain the knowledge on their own. In some instances, private organizations, such as those run by the Society of Friends (Quakers), were established for the education of former slaves and free blacks.

Public schools received a boost in 1852, when the Democratic General Assembly created the post of state superintendent of common schools to head the Department of Public Instruction. Calvin H. Wiley, a Guilford County lawyer and legislator, served as the first superintendent from 1853 to 1865. Under Wiley's energetic leadership, the common schools quickly improved. His notable accomplishments included establishment of the first system of examinations and certification for teachers; formation of county institutes to train teachers; standardization of textbooks, including his own *North Carolina Reader* (1851); and enforcement of the state law requiring regular reports from local school districts. North Carolina's common schools are considered to have been among the best in the South in 1860.

The First Graded Schools, the State Constitution of 1868, and Legal Segregation

North Carolina's system of graded public schools dates from the Civil War era, when the General Assembly authorized expansion of ungraded common schools at Wiley's urging. The advent of war in 1861 slowed the process, but Wiley and his colleagues were undeterred. In 1862 the State Educational Association enthusiastically endorsed a comprehensive system of primary, grammar, and secondary instruction, "embracing the complete curriculum from the lowest primary to preparation for college entrance." It took more than two years for Wiley's proposal to pass both houses of the legislature. The authorizing act of December 1864 envisioned a voluntary network of graded primary and high schools in every county, open to all white children between the ages of 6 and 21. The progressive system also admitted all white female residents under age 27 who wished to teach, as well as disabled male war veterans under age 36. No additional state funding was provided for the new schools beyond the traditional Literary Fund distributions, as public donations were expected to fund additional operating expenses.

After nearly four years of a brutal, expensive Civil War and spiraling inflation, the prospects for adequate school funding proved elusive. The General Assembly voted, in effect, to dismantle the public school system by declining to appropriate funds for its operation after December 1865. In a direct attack on Wiley's progressive policies, the legislature also voted to abolish the position of state superintendent of common schools.

The outlook for public education in North Carolina became more hopeful with the adoption of the state's so-called radical Constitution of 1868, a relatively progressive document that provided for a "general and uniform" public school system, free to children aged 6 to 21 and funded by "taxation and otherwise," to be administered by an elected superintendent of public instruction and a State Board of Education. The 1869 General Assembly was empowered to implement the constitution's provisions, but funding remained sporadic and insufficient, given the high cost of providing adequate instruction for more than 100,000 children of former slaves. Moreover, there was little support from child labor laws or recognition by the general public of the need for improvement.

A significant trend, however, was the growing emphasis on teacher training with the organization of 13 "normal" schools across the state—8 for blacks and 5 for whites, reflecting the need for black educators to catch up with their white counterparts, who often had the advantage of a complete or ongoing college experience to prepare them to teach. Although the legislature of 1869 had established the basis for educating black children, most of the focus remained on whites. Since school funding was primarily a local endeavor, poorer rural communities of African Americans often could not support adequate facilities. Most black normal schools and teachers' institutes were small and poor; their growth and success often depended on funding from black self-help groups, churches, and white northern philanthropy.

The Greensboro Graded School, approved by voters in May 1870, became the first public graded system in North Carolina. It was followed by authorizing acts for local elections in Charlotte (1873), Fayetteville (1878), Asheville (1879), Wilson and Goldsboro (1880–81), and Durham (1881). The 1876–77 General Assembly enacted a graded school law applicable to larger towns and cities, a concept gradually extended to smaller towns. The 1883 legislature then passed the Dortch Act, allowing city voters to divide tax revenues along racial lines, a provision ultimately ruled unconstitutional by the North Carolina Supreme Court.

Economic recovery after the Civil War required an educated population, even in a largely rural state, and by the end of the century, every county had a graded school system for all students. Social and political prejudices were acknowledged, even during Reconstruction. Legal racial segregation, established by constitutional amendment in 1875 and accepted by

Students and teacher in front of their log school, Davidson County, late nineteenth century. NCC.

the two major political parties, led to the creation of "separate-but-equal" schools for white and black students, with facilities and resources for blacks comparatively inadequate by most measures. Native American children attended their own schools, which were also generally substandard.

Expansion, Consolidation, and the School Machinery Act

At the turn of the twentieth century, the Democratic government in Raleigh launched a series of educational initiatives to improve public schools in the state. Appalled by the number of children younger than 14 employed in cotton mills, Governor Charles B. Aycock emphasized the importance of education for all North Carolinians in his inaugural address of January 1901 (Aycock's actual policies reflected his desire for a better-educated white population to keep the Democrats in power). The new governor soon formed the Central Campaign Committee for the Promotion of Public Education, which began operations in 1902 from its headquarters in the office of Superintendent of Public Instruction James Y. Joyner. The committee's stated purpose was to advance public education through all possible legal means, such as campaigning

for local school taxes, consolidation of school districts, better school buildings and equipment, longer school terms, and better-trained and higher-paid teachers.

Also in 1901, the General Assembly under Aycock's leadership directly appropriated tax funds for public schools for the first time in the state's history. Legislation in 1905 provided that every county school board require all children between ages 8 and 16 to attend school for a 16-week term annually. The Rural High School Act (1907) and consolidation of rural school districts, as well as a program of "equalization" in the distribution of funds for education, led to the gradual improvement of free public education. By 1911, 200 public rural high schools were distributed among the state's 100 counties.

In 1907 Asheville city schools became the first school system in North Carolina to finance public kindergarten, but decades passed before kindergarten became a permanent grade in public schools statewide. The General Assembly of 1913 enacted the first statewide law compelling school attendance. The Compulsory Attendance Act required that all children, both black and white, between the ages of 8 and 12 attend school continuously for four months a year, allowing reasonable exemptions and providing reasonable penalties and adequate but inexpensive machinery for its enforcement. Increasingly, the state's child labor laws supported compulsory school attendance by raising the minimum age at which a child could begin to work.

The legislature began to fund public elementary schools for African Americans in 1910 and established the Division of Negro Education in 1921 to oversee the education of black children in many rural schools. High schools for blacks became available only after 1918, when the state's first black secondary school was built. Except in the more progressive (and urbanized) counties of Durham, Forsyth, Guilford, Mecklenburg, and Wake, secondary education for blacks progressed slowly.

In reality, and despite occasional legislative initiatives and the continued efforts of various black advocacy groups and philanthropic organizations, the public education of the state's African American children under Jim Crow remained strikingly inferior to that of white children. The separate-but-equal doctrine adopted by the state in 1875 and subsequent Jim Crow statutes passed in the early 1900s—for example, the 1903 law clarifying that no North Carolina child with "Negro blood in its veins, however remote the strain, shall attend a school for the white race, and no such child shall be considered a white child"—solidified the second-class status of publicly supported black schools.

As civil rights advocate and author Pauli Murray describes in her autobiography, *Proud Shoes: The Story of an American Family* (1956), the North Carolina educational system during the early decades of the twentieth century was focused almost exclusively on the progress of whites, with little regard for black success. Growing up in Durham in a mixed-race family, Murray experienced not only the pain of segregation and the squalor of black facilities but also the pride and determination of many black teachers and students. Murray poignantly remembers the "beautiful red-and-white brick building" that served as the whites' school, in contrast to the blacks' run-down wooden building with "bare and splintery" floors. Such inequities would not be addressed by political leaders in North Carolina for decades, and then only after federal intervention.

Busing of students to and from public schools was initially authorized by the General Assembly in 1911. Craven County schools were the first to transport schoolchildren under this new measure, and in 1917 Pamlico County became the first to purchase a "school truck" for that purpose. By 1928 every county in the state provided pupil transportation, albeit limited in some areas.

After World War I, the strategy of school consolidation—with the goal of improving the quality of the state's rural public schools—began to gain momentum in the North Carolina legislature and among local school boards. The one- and two-teacher schools serving rural districts were incapable of competing economically with the larger facilities of towns and cities, and rural children were suffering the consequences. Consolidating several small districts into one pooled available resources and afforded less-populated areas the advantages of better-funded urban schools. The initiative saw many positive results, as school curricula expanded to include several new subjects and vocational opportunities, and many rural districts began offering high school courses for the first time. An ever-increasing number of students would come to be served more effectively by new facilities born of the consolidation movement.

Severe economic conditions during the Great Depression greatly slowed the progress of public education in the state and nation. To eliminate some of these hardships in North Carolina counties, which were primarily responsible for funding local schools, the 1931 and 1933 sessions of the General Assembly enacted the School Machinery Act. This statute essentially transferred financial support and control of public schools from the counties to the state, established a new sales tax as the source of funding, and designated counties as the "basic governmental unit" responsible for building and maintaining public school facilities and providing additional funds for specific programs and improvements. At this time, the state assumed the cost of textbooks, school supplies, and other necessities.

Throughout the 1940s, North Carolina's public school system continued to grow and change. In 1942 a twelfth grade was added to high school. The following year saw the introduction of school lunches and the lengthening of the school term to nine months. In 1946 the compulsory attendance age increased from 14 to 16. Voters in 1949 approved a $50 million state bond for construction of public schools, the first of its kind in the state. The State Textbook Commission, originating in the early twentieth-century initiatives of Aycock and other progressives, in 1945 gained jurisdiction over the selection and use of textbooks at both the elementary and secondary levels.

Desegregation and Equality in Public Education

Civil rights—particularly those of African Americans—was the locus of change in public schools throughout the 1950s and 1960s. School desegregation in North Carolina, as in other southern states, was a long and arduous process. Absent, however, were the strident pronouncements of detractors such as Mississippi's Theodore Bilbo and Alabama's George Wallace. In contrast, North Carolina presented itself as a voice of moderation, although the state by no means escaped the influence of Jim Crow. As integration loomed, North Carolinians were divided between the desire to maintain the racial status quo and to comply with judicial orders to desegregate.

The integration of the University of North Carolina at Chapel Hill was an early instance of judicially mandated desegregation and foreshadowed the U.S. Supreme Court's decision in *Brown v. Board of Education of Topeka, Kansas*. In March 1951 a U.S. District Court of Appeals overturned a ruling by the state's Middle District Court and ordered the university to desegregate. The black students admitted to the law, medical, and graduate schools had sued for equal treatment as citizens and taxpayers. Their enrollment, and that of three African American men as undergraduates four years later, was uneventful and did not precipitate the violence that occurred on some other southern campuses.

Three years after the integration of UNC-Chapel Hill, the Supreme Court ruled in *Brown* that "separate education facilities are inherently unequal." North Carolina's initial reaction to the decision was to delay implementation of the federal directive. The problem rested with Governor Luther H. Hodges, who was torn between his desire to adhere to the Court's ruling and his need to appease the portion of his white constituency that remained steadfastly segregationist. In the summer of 1955, during a radio and TV broadcast, Hodges urged black residents to accept "voluntary" segregation as an alternative to the unrest that integration would produce. He warned that "the white citizens of the state will resist integration strenuously, resourcefully, and with growing bitterness."

The resourcefulness that Hodges referred to manifested itself in the Pearsall Plan, which sought to legally circumvent full-scale integration. According to the plan—named for Thomas J. Pearsall, chairman of the state's Special Advisory Committee on Education, and enacted by the General Assembly in 1956—education expense grants, financed by public funds, would be provided for the private education of children assigned to integrated schools against the wishes of their parents. Further, local communities, with a majority vote, could suspend the operation of public schools if integration proved to be unmanageable. Opponents viewed the plan as an insidious maneuver by whites to delay implementing the Supreme Court's order while exonerating themselves of obstructing justice.

In time, however, it became evident that continued resistance to integration of the public school system would leave the state vulnerable to a legal challenge. In 1957, when schools opened in Charlotte, Greensboro, and Winston-Salem, a dozen black students entered previously all-white schools. With this token integration, North Carolina became one of only four southern states, along with Arkansas, Texas, and Tennessee, to allow integrated schools. Not until two years later did integration move beyond the three cities. In the fall of 1959, a small number of black students integrated schools in Craven County, Wayne County, Durham, and High Point. The Craven County and Wayne County schools, however, were located in areas housing large military bases and were attended primarily by children of military personnel, many of whom were not from the South. During the 1959–60 school year, more black students attended schools in those two counties than in all other districts combined. To speed integration, the U.S. Civil Rights Act of 1964 contained provisions to deny federal funds to school districts still practicing segregation.

Even that historic legislation was unable to create a truly integrated school system in North Carolina. In 1969 the NAACP Legal Defense Fund filed numerous lawsuits across the state charging discrimination. In a case heard in Mecklenburg County (Charlotte), Judge James B. McMillan ordered the local school system to use "any and all known ways of desegregation, including busing." He determined that the racial proportion of each school should be equal to that of the entire district, which was 71 percent white and 29 percent black. The order was appealed to the U.S. Supreme Court in 1970. In 1971, after long deliberation, the Court in *Swann v. Charlotte-Mecklenburg Board of Education* affirmed McMillan's ruling, and busing became the means to achieve integration in North Carolina and across the nation.

North Carolina's public school system saw other changes throughout the 1950s and 1960s, notably the establishment of the Governor's School for gifted students; more attention to children with learning disabilities; the creation of a Comprehensive School Improvement Program, which subsequently upgraded early childhood education; and free textbooks for all students, from elementary school through high school. Increases in federal funding marked the era and shaped many reforms introduced by North Carolina's educational leaders.

Reform, Innovation, and the Modernization of Public Schools

North Carolina's public schools continued to expand in the final decades of the twentieth century. The 1960s and 1970s saw a greater focus on early childhood education, with the statewide establishment of full kindergarten for all five-year-olds by 1977. Emphasis was increasingly placed on reform, improvements, and accountability of individual schools and county districts. In 1985 the General Assembly established, through the State Board of Education, the Basic Education Program (BEP). The BEP allocated funds for summer school, additional teachers, textbooks, and other vital needs. Under the program, a standardized curriculum, called the Standard Course of Study, was created to clearly outline grade-appropriate achievement levels in all subject areas, including the arts, grammar, mathematics, languages, science, communication skills, physical education and personal health, social studies, and technology.

The public education of Native American children was energized in 1988, when the State Board of Education determined to explore the problems faced by Indian students in grades K–12. The State Advisory Council on Indian Education works with tribal organizations; advises the State Board of Education; coordinates the administration of federal, state, and local educational programs; and advocates on behalf of Indian students, often designing new initiatives to lower the dropout rate and increase academic achievement. The advisory council has recommended the statewide adoption of textbooks that portray American Indians more fairly and accurately, the elimination of school mascots and logos that de-

Wake County classroom, 2002. Photograph by Robert Willett.
Raleigh News and Observer.

mean the Indian population, and the creation of an American Indian Studies elective in North Carolina high schools, especially in districts that serve a large Indian population.

In 1979 the General Assembly reorganized the North Carolina Department of Public Instruction and passed the School Improvement and Accountability Act, which gave flexibility and added responsibility to local schools in the development of improvement plans and the attainment of measurable goals. The grassroots paradigm, in which the greatest advances come from the efforts of the entire community (especially parents), drove many school reforms beginning in the early 1990s. Local schools also began to be "graded" by a State Report Card, issued annually since 1990. Various end-of-grade and other standardized tests were initiated to measure student progress in basic subjects such as writing, mathematics, and reading.

Other programs created in the 1990s included Smart Start (1992), to improve and increase the availability of childcare programs statewide, and the ABCs of Public Education (1996), to strengthen local control of schools, improve school accountability, and facilitate the teaching of the basic "ABCs" of education: reading, writing, and mathematics. The ABCs program, which has covered all North Carolina public schools from kindergarten to twelfth grade beginning in the 1997–98 school year, offers schools financial incentives for ensuring student achievement, measured by end-of-year tests. The staff and teacher assistants at successful schools receive financial bonuses for their efforts.

In 1993 the North Carolina A+ Schools Program was initiated by the Thomas S. Kenan Institute for the Arts (an affiliate organization of the North Carolina School of the Arts) to provide a unique educational experience employing interdisciplinary studies and consistent exposure to the arts. The program, sponsored by private foundations and corporations, such as the Z. Smith Reynolds Foundation, the Wachovia Foundation, and Philip Morris Companies, Inc., was con-

ducted by school personnel and arts professionals. A+ schools covered the Standard Course of Study through an integrated, experiential approach to learning that relied heavily on drama, dance, music, and the visual arts. The program has the advantage of allowing motivated students to learn at their own pace and in ways suited to their individual talents and goals. In 2001 the state's original 25 A+ schools reported that many students had shown improved focus, discipline, academic growth, and achievement since their enrollment in the program. In 2003 the A+ program was moved from the Kenan Institute to the University of North Carolina at Greensboro.

State funding of public schools remains controversial in North Carolina. In 1997 the state supreme court ruled in *Leandro v. North Carolina* that "every child of this state" is constitutionally entitled to "a sound basic education in our public schools." The case was originally filed by the school boards of Cumberland, Halifax, Hoke, Robeson, and Vance Counties and some resident families. The plaintiffs maintained that inadequate state funding of poorer school districts denied their children the same quality of education enjoyed by children in wealthier districts. The court's rulings in *Leandro* continue to inform state decisions on the equitable funding of public school districts.

The General Assembly passed the Excellent Schools Act of 1997 to improve the quality of school personnel and administrators by raising salaries, upgrading training, and increasing the accountability of individual teachers. Student achievement was specifically addressed in 1999, when the State Board of Education established Student Accountability Standards, applied through end-of-year tests to determine a student's readiness to move on to the next grade. This was the first time elementary school, middle school, and high school students in North Carolina were required to meet statewide measurements for promotion. These tests also provide specific data on the so-called achievement gap between white students and minority students (African American, Latino, and American Indian). In 2000 the Advisory Commission on Raising Achievement and Closing Gaps was formed to address the gap between the highest and the lowest achievers. The 2002 No Child Left Behind Act increased the federal role in public education nationwide. Programs resulting from this legislation emphasize closing the achievement gaps among various social and ethnic groups and increasing the accountability of individual schools that may not be adequately serving minority populations.

Greater school choice within the public school system—particularly in the case of poorer, less successful schools and school districts—became the battle cry of many North Carolinians in the 1990s and early 2000s. The General Assembly joined a national movement when it passed the Charter Schools Act of 1996, which authorized up to 100 new charter schools. Such schools offer parental choice with open enrollment; they have more flexibility than public schools but must comply with federal and state guidelines. Although they can be established by any individual, group, or nonprofit corporation, they must remain nonsectarian and employ at least three teachers. Charter schools, which average fewer than 150 students, often focus on a particular theme (e.g., math and science, the arts, character education, or specific teaching methodologies) or on at-risk or other special populations. Magnet schools—public schools that have a special focus, such as art, technology, or language, or use a unique teaching paradigm —also saw dramatic growth in North Carolina, as did homeschooling, in which parents are required to follow state and national standards.

In 2003–4, according to the North Carolina Department of Public Instruction, the state had 115 public school districts, in which 2,171 public schools enrolled 1.33 million students and 93 charter schools enrolled 21,903. The racial composition of students included about 416,000 African Americans, 19,000 American Indians, and 88,355 Latinos. Of graduating high school seniors in 2003, 48 percent reported plans to enroll in four-year colleges or universities; 34 percent, to enroll in two-year colleges; 9 percent, to enter the workforce; and 4 percent, to enter the military. North Carolina public schools had a total operating budget of approximately $8.8 billion, about 93 percent of which came from the state and local governments. The public school system lagged behind the national average in some categories, including SAT scores (1,007 vs. 1,026 nationwide) and teacher salaries ($43,076 vs. $45,891 nationwide).

References: Roberta Sue Alexander, "Hostility and Hope: Black Education in North Carolina during Presidential Reconstruction, 1865–1867," NCHR 53 (April 1976); Hugh Victor Brown, A History of the Education of Negroes in North Carolina (1961); Lindley S. Butler and Alan D. Watson, eds., The North Carolina Experience: An Interpretive and Documentary History (1984); William H. Chafe, Civilities and Civil Rights: Greensboro, North Carolina, and the Black Struggle for Freedom (1980); Davison M. Douglas, Reading and Writing Race: The Desegregation of the Charlotte Schools (1995); Linda Flowers, Thrown Away: Failures of Progress in North Carolina (1990); Hugh T. Lefler, North Carolina History Told by Contemporaries (1956); James L. Leloudis, Schooling the New South: Pedagogy, Self, and Society in North Carolina, 1880–1920 (1996); Marcus C. S. Noble, A History of the Public Schools of North Carolina (1930).

Benjamin R. Justesen
Scott Matthews
Additional research provided by Nayda Swonger Colomb, K. Todd Johnson, E. Michael Latta, and Jay Mazzocchi.

SEE ALSO Community Colleges; Literary Fund; Pearsall Plan; Public Instruction, Department of; Pupil Assignment Act; School Consolidation; *Swann v. Charlotte-Mecklenburg Board of Education*; Textbook Commission; University of North Carolina System.

Education, Special. Special education, also known as "education of exceptional children," has had a long history in North Carolina. Exceptional children are those "who deviate from what is supposed to be average in physical, mental, emotional or social characteristics to such an extent that they require special educational services in order to develop their maximum capacity." From as early as 1816, people pushed for an institution for deaf and blind students. In 1845 Governor John Motley Morehead finally convinced the legislature to establish and fund in Raleigh a school for poor, white, blind and deaf students. The first school for African American deaf and blind students in America opened in 1869 in Raleigh. In 1892 Edward McKee Goodwin convinced the state legislature to separate the school for blind and deaf students into two— one for the blind, to remain in Raleigh, and one for the deaf, to be located in Morganton. All three schools emphasized vocational training over academic training. In 1963 they were integrated.

Other residential schools serving individuals with various handicaps sprang up across the state to help children who needed more care than could be supplied at home or in the public schools. The Stonewall Jackson Manual Training and Industrial School opened in 1908 for juvenile delinquents, and in 1911 the Caswell Training School was opened for youngsters who were severely mentally retarded. Eventually, a number of state-supported institutions were established, housing children with various disabilities too severe for them to be adequately served in the public schools.

By 1947 the General Assembly passed Chapter 818 of the Public School Laws, which founded statewide programs for special education in North Carolina. In 1948 the Division of Exceptional Children was established in the Department of Public Instruction. Funding for exceptional children was begun in the school year 1949–50, with 25 teaching positions in public schools spread across the state. From 1949 until 1974, special education teachers worked to serve as many exceptional students as possible using several methods, including classes within public schools, special schools, guided home instruction, and state institutions. In 1974 the federal government passed the Education of All Handicapped Children Act, which changed the way North Carolina and all other states served exceptional students. The act gave federal money to the local education agencies that followed their rules and provided a free, appropriate education to all children by September 1978.

In the 1990s the categories of exceptional students served in the public schools included specific learning disabled; educable mentally handicapped; trainable mentally handicapped; severely/profoundly mentally handicapped; orthopedically impaired; other health·impaired; visually impaired;

hearing impaired; speech impaired; behaviorally-emotionally handicapped; autistic; multihandicapped; deaf-blind; preschool developmentally delayed; and traumatic brain injured. In 1997 the federal Individuals with Disabilities Education Act was signed into law. The act's requirements include that all students take part in state or district testing, that exceptional children have greater participation in their required individualized education programs, that parents participate in placement decisions, that children are not to be automatically retested every three years, and that discipline for misbehavior involves educating students in alternative settings, if necessary.

References: Katherine Crichton Alston Edsall, *State School for the Blind and the Deaf: A Century of Growth* (1945); North Carolina School for the Deaf at Morganton, *The Education of the Deaf in North Carolina: 1894–1969* (1997); State Department of Public Instruction, *Exceptional Children in North Carolina* (1959); H. Rutherford Turnbull III, "Recent Federal Legislation on Educating the Handicapped," *School Law Bulletin* (July 1977).

Lee Plummer Templeton

SEE ALSO Governor Morehead School.

Education, State Board of.

The North Carolina Constitution of 1868 established the State Board of Education to provide overall policy direction for programs and services offered through the state's public schools. The board's membership and specific powers and duties have been changed by both constitutional amendments and legislative enactments over the years. In 1943 an act by the state legislature changed the membership of the State Board of Education to the lieutenant governor, the state treasurer, the state superintendent of public instruction, and one member from each congressional district to be appointed by the governor. After years of change and seemingly diminished powers, the board was reaffirmed in its role of overseer of the state's public school system by the 1971 North Carolina Constitution.

In 1986 the General Assembly made another change in the statutes relative to the State Board of Education, authorizing the governor to appoint two student advisers to the board. The fiscal control that the State Board of Education had maintained since 1943 was repealed on 1 Feb. 1989, with those duties transferred to the elected state superintendent of public instruction, who had been the board's administrative officer. This 1988 state statute made it clear, however, that the board would continue to establish the policies controlling the public school system. It remained in the early 2000s the most powerful governmental education board in North Carolina. The modern board consists of the state lieutenant governor, the treasurer, and 11 other members appointed by the governor with General Assembly approval.

Reference: E. Michael Latta, *The Constitutional and Statutory Development of the State Board of Education and the State Superintendent of Public Instruction* (1989).

E. Michael Latta

Education, Vocational.

Vocational education—sometimes referred to as occupational or technical education—is an organized educational program that trains individuals for paid or unpaid employment or for additional preparation for a career that does not require a baccalaureate or advanced degree. The federal Smith-Hughes Act of 1917 made funds available to North Carolina and other states that supported vocational education; these funds, subsequently controlled by the State Board of Education, helped facilitate the growth of occupational training programs throughout the state. In 1963 North Carolina's community college system was created, establishing a statewide system of institutions that offer adults technical, vocational, and adult education programs in a variety of fields. In 1977 the General Assembly passed a law that formally recognized the importance of vocational education in the state's public education system. Vocational education is available in the public secondary schools, community colleges, and teacher education programs within the university system.

References: Governor's Study Commission on the Public School System of North Carolina, *Occupational Education for the Public Schools of North Carolina* (1968); E. Michael Latta, *The North Carolina Story* (1989).

E. Michael Latta

Efird's Department Stores.

In 1902 Hugh Martin Efird, with the cooperation of Charles A. Williams of the Williams & Shelton Company, opened a small dry goods store on East Trade Street in Charlotte, operating as the Beehive but formally known as Charlotte Mercantile Company. Soon Efird's brother Joseph Bevins Efird joined the firm, as did brothers Jasper W., John Ray, Paul, and Edmund Lilly. The name Beehive was dropped in 1907 and the firm became Efird's Department Store.

On 7 Sept. 1923 Efird's opened a second Charlotte store on Tryon Street, the Carolinas' most prestigious retail location. The store—across the street from Ivey's, Charlotte's most fashionable store—featured the Southeast's first escalator, beating even Macy's in New York City. Efird's, with Joseph Efird as president, competed aggressively with Belk department stores for middle-income shoppers who also patronized national stores such as JC Penney, Sears, and W. T. Grant. Under Joseph Efird's tutelage, the firm was a pioneer in central office purchasing, one-price cash sales, and insurance and pension benefits for employees. The Efird's chain, which in 1956 was purchased by Belk, at its peak included more than 50 stores in the Carolinas as well as one in Danville, Va. The last Efird's store closed in Smithfield in 1979.

References: LeGette Blythe and Charles R. Brockmann, *Hornets' Nest: The Story of Charlotte and Mecklenburg County* (1961); Howard E. Covington Jr., *Belk: A Century of Retail Leadership* (1988).

Wiley J. Williams

Eighty-second Airborne Division. SEE Fort Bragg.

Election Law in North Carolina has seen significant changes over the years. During early statehood, the governor and two U.S. senators were appointed by the General Assembly, while the other major political officers were popularly elected by white male North Carolinians. Excluded from voting were Jews and other non-Christians, who could not cast a ballot in the state until 1860, as well as women, who gained suffrage with ratification of the Nineteenth Amendment to the U.S. Constitution in 1920. Free men of color participated in North Carolina elections until county representatives resolved to deny them the vote at the 1835 constitutional convention.

That convention also determined that the governor would henceforth be chosen by the people. Edward B. Dudley, a Whig, won the first popular gubernatorial election, held in 1836. With ratification in 1913 of the Seventeenth Amendment to the U.S. Constitution, providing for the popular election of U.S. senators, the General Assembly relinquished its appointment authority.

The next major change in North Carolina election law was made in 1915, when the Democratic legislature passed the Primary Elections Act. In primary elections, citizens select candidates to run against one another within a particular party; the winner becomes that party's official candidate in the general election. The 1915 statute provided for a "primary election for the purpose of nominating candidates of each and every political party in the state" if more than one person aspired to a given office. Until then Republicans had rarely used primaries, but Democrats had introduced primary elections in the 1870s, during Reconstruction, to minimize minority voter strength, originally allowing only white males to vote. After the U.S. Supreme Court struck down the "whites-only" restriction, and following the political success garnered by white and black Republicans and Progressives during the Fusionist era of the 1890s, Democrats modified the primary system to suit their needs. The party also launched a systematic campaign to diminish the turnout of black voters through fear and intimidation, as well as by passing a suffrage amendment that required an individual to be able to read before he could register to vote. Democrats also strategically used race-baiting to separate white voters from black Republicans and thus reduce the number of white Republican voters.

As a result of these efforts, a one-party system emerged, with the Democratic primary becoming the principal statewide forum in which to select officeholders. From 1900 through 1970, most of North Carolina's legislative and other state leaders, as well as the vast majority of its representatives to Congress, were chosen in the Democratic primary. But with the 1972 election of James E. Holshouser Jr.—the state's first Republican governor of the twentieth century—and the emerging strength of the GOP, the importance of primary elections declined and general elections became more significant.

Ironically, the party primary was originally intended to eliminate black votes and return Democrats to office, but by the 1970s it impeded the candidacy of African Americans who had become a crucial element of the Democratic coalition. With their growing role in the Democratic Party, numerous black politicians made unsuccessful bids for major offices, including former Chapel Hill mayor Howard N. Lee for lieutenant governor in 1976 and state representative H. Mickey Michaux for Congress in 1982. When both men garnered a plurality, but not a majority, of votes cast during the first primary and lost to white opponents in the second, many called for reform of the primary system. This change, which finally passed the legislature in 1989, allows candidates who receive more than 40 percent of the votes cast to be their party's nominee. The reform has brought success to black candidates, such as former Charlotte mayor Harvey Gantt, who won the Democratic primary for the U.S. Senate in 1990, and Raleigh city councilman Ralph Campbell Jr., another Democrat, who became the party's nominee for state auditor in 1992. In the general election Gantt lost to the incumbent, Republican Jesse Helms, by a vote of 52 to 48 percent, but Campbell became the first African American ever elected to statewide office in North Carolina.

Most aspects of North Carolina's modern election laws, found in their entirety in the General Statutes, Section 163, parallel those of other states. In 2006 North Carolina had 13 representatives and 2 senators in the U.S. Congress, 10 major statewide elected offices, 120 representatives and 50 senators in the General Assembly, and numerous local officials and judges. Primaries and general elections are administered by the five members of the State Board of Elections, appointed by the governor, and their staffs in Raleigh. The board appoints three members to each County Board of Elections, who are responsible for conducting the primaries and elections in accordance with state law. Every county is divided into election precincts of roughly equal numbers of voters. The County Board appoints election officials, consisting of a chief judge, a Republican judge, and a Democratic judge. Assistants may be named as needed to conduct the elections. The staff of the County Board keeps all records on voter registration and residential addresses and prepares approved voter registration lists for each precinct. These lists determine approval of citizens who arrive to vote on election day, which, by state law, is the Tuesday following the first Monday in November.

To nominate the candidates of each political party, a primary election is held on Tuesday after the first Monday in May preceding the general election. North Carolina polls are open on election day from 6:30 A.M. to 7:30 P.M. Absentee ballots may be cast if a registered voter is sick or will be away from the precinct on election day, or if it is a religious holiday. Some ballots are counted by hand, but the trend has been toward the automated or computerized tabulation of results.

To be qualified to vote in North Carolina, an individual must be a legal citizen of the United States and at least 18 years of age; be resident in his or her precinct for the 30 days prior to the election; and be properly registered with the County Board of Elections.

References: Cortland F. Bishop, *History of Elections in the American Colonies* (1893); John L. Cheney Jr., ed., *North Carolina Government, 1585–1979: A Narrative and Statistical History* (1981); *Election Laws of North Carolina* (1996).

> *Will M. Heiser*
> Additional research provided by Allyson C. Criner and David C. Smith.

SEE ALSO Congressional Districts; Disfranchisement; Free Suffrage; General Assembly; Women Suffrage.

Electric Power, at the start of the twentieth century, was a novelty and a luxury in North Carolina. The first electric lighting in the state came from the arc lamps installed in the Arista Cotton Mill in Salem in 1881. Arc lamps ran off a generator, a device consisting of a rotor inside a magnetic field. Cutting the magnetic flux produced electricity. Thomas Edison and his associates developed a practical incandescent lamp in 1879 so that houses could have electric lighting, but the dream of available, affordable power was years away.

Raleigh's board of aldermen authorized an electric lighting system for the city's streets in October 1885. The Thomson-Houston Electric Light Company supplied the power for arc lights that were turned on in December of that year. Durham Electric Light Company illuminated that city's streets a few weeks later, and Thomson-Houston switched Charlotte's streetlights from gas to electricity in 1886. Arc lights arrived in Winston (which later became Winston-Salem) in 1887, in Asheville and New Bern in 1888, in Goldsboro and Henderson in 1890, in Wilmington in 1891, in Fayetteville in 1895, and in Asheboro in 1900.

The state legislature chartered two electric companies in 1881, four in 1889, six in 1891, and three in 1905. Early companies typically produced steam to run a generator. Interruptions were frequent, and the voltage fluctuated. Small power plants often only operated from dusk until midnight. On nights when the moon was bright, streetlights were sometimes switched off to save fuel. Hydroelectric plants could utilize the power of moving water to produce large quantities of electricity, but construction costs were enormous. Mills, especially sawmills, increased production by lighting their facilities with a steam engine and a generator.

The first electric railway system in North Carolina opened in Asheville on 6 Feb. 1889, running from the public square to the railroad station. Raleigh's railway system switched to electricity in 1891, and other cities added streetcars, which ran until they were replaced by buses in the 1930s. Supplementary census figures for 1902 listed 38 private and municipal North Carolina power stations and 488 miles of power lines. Revenues came to $84,196 for arc lighting, $141,460 for incandescent lighting, and $95,527 for other electric services.

In 1905 James B. Duke, Walker Gill Wylie, and William States Lee organized the Southern Power Company (which later became Duke Power Company), building a string of textile mills and hydroelectric plants along the Catawba River. As the North Carolina textile industry expanded, many mill owners, before signing on with the power company, bargained for electricity for their employees' homes. Lee went on to design and build 32 hydroelectric stations and 7 steam-electric stations, and he also became a pioneer in wire-transmission systems.

In 1908 the Raleigh Electric Company, the Central Carolina Power Company, and the Consumer Light and Power Company merged to form the Carolina Power & Light Company (CP&L). The advent of the electric utilities propelled North Carolina's evolution from an agricultural state into a manufacturing one. Wiring a house or business was expensive, so utilities sent out traveling salesmen to stir up interest in electricity. The utilities sold electric appliances and offered free maintenance.

In 1913 the General Assembly placed electric power companies under the regulation of the Corporation Commission. The North Carolina Utilities Commission took over in 1941, eventually becoming a seven-member body, appointed by the governor, serving as part of the Department of Commerce.

The federal government created the Tennessee Valley Authority (TVA) in 1933 and the Rural Electrification Administration (REA) in 1935. As part of the Roosevelt Administration's New Deal, the TVA built dams in western North Carolina on the Hiwassee and Little Tennessee Rivers, bringing hydroelectric power to several counties. Serving under the U.S. Department of Agriculture, the REA provided farms with electricity and big power companies with wholesale customers. The North Carolina legislature had created a state REA and passed the Electric Membership Corporation (EMC) Act just before the federal agency's appointment. Electricity was not available to all rural residents until well after World War II. EMCs were cooperatives owned by their members. With low-cost loans from the REA, EMCs strung lines and supplied power to rural areas.

During the war years of the 1940s, the utilities supplied power outside of their territories to the defense industry. CP&L

stock became available for public trade on the New York Stock Exchange in 1946, and Duke Power followed in 1961. The possibility of producing electricity from nuclear fission prompted Duke and CP&L in 1956 to form the Carolinas-Virginia Nuclear Power Associates, Inc. Another member was Virginia Electric & Power Company, which supplied electricity as North Carolina Power to residents of the northeastern part of the state. The new nuclear organization pooled information and built an experimental station to run tests. CP&L's Brunswick Plant, the first nuclear-fueled electric generating station in North Carolina, began commercial operation in 1975.

By the beginning of the twenty-first century, North Carolinians received electricity either from one of the three major power companies, municipal systems, or EMCs. Power generation came from nuclear reactors, coal- or oil-fired units, hydroelectric and pumped storage plants, and combustion turbine generators. North Carolina has had a history of receiving electricity at costs below the national average. Probably for this reason, per capita usage in the state typically has run above that of other states.

References: D. Clayton Brown, "North Carolina Rural Electrification: Precedent of the REA," *NCHR* 59 (Spring 1982); Robert F. Durden, *Electrifying the Piedmont Carolinas: The Duke Power Company, 1904–1997* (2001); Jack Riley, *Carolina Power & Light Company, 1908–1958: A Corporate Biography* (1958).

Barry McGee

SEE ALSO Carolina Power & Light Company; Duke Power Company; Nuclear Energy; Rural Electrification.

Elephant Tokens were unique circulating coins created in limited numbers in the early Carolina colony. In general, Carolina Elephant Tokens are more expertly crafted and heavier in composition than any of the standard merchant tokens issued by English tradesmen in the seventeenth century. Carolina pieces are also far more rare than the vast majority of tokens that survive from that era. Such characteristics imply that only small numbers of Carolina tokens were produced and that they were used for a special, perhaps singular purpose.

The Carolina Elephant Token's name, which dates from 1694, derives from the coin's most eye-catching design element: dominating its obverse (front) side is a full tusk-to-tail image of an elephant standing on a slightly textured plain. The animal is portrayed in left profile, with a slightly bowed head, its trunk tightly curling backward, and "an ear that in form resembles a withered tulip." Aside from this image, the only other decoration on original Carolina tokens is a simple, often off-center beaded border that garnishes the rim of their obverses and reverses. Although some specimens of the Carolina token and of other types of "elephant tokens" found their way to North America, likely nestled among the possessions of English immigrants, there is no evidence that the pieces were ever intended for widespread commercial use or employed on the continent for purchases of prescribed goods or services.

The year 1694 and a nearly identical seven-word inscription are struck in relief on the reverses of all Carolina Elephant Tokens: "God Preserve Carolina and the Lords Proprietors." The final word in this inscription at times appears spelled as "Proprieters." Historic studies have proposed that these tokens may have served foremost as promotional devices for drawing much-needed public attention and investments to the Lords Proprietors' struggling "American plantation." With regard to the tokens' production, their physical properties and circumstantial evidence indicate that they were struck during the latter half of 1694 at the Royal Mint, which operated behind the high stone walls of the Tower of London. Records show that during June and July in 1694 the Lords Proprietors held meetings in London on Tower Hill, only a short walking distance from the historic fortress. Since those meetings are the only documented times when the Proprietors convened in 1694, it is probable that arrangements for the token's production at the tower were finalized then and there.

Those who acquire Carolina tokens should take considerable caution, since many specimens thought to be original or marketed as genuine in the past have proven to be fakes. Since the 1860s, assorted reproductions of the token have been made, including struck copies, cast specimens, and high-quality electrotypes. There are electrotypes of the "PROPRIETOR" variety that have fooled both inexperienced and veteran collectors.

References: R. Neil Fulghum, "The Hunt for Carolina Elephants: Questions Regarding Genuine Specimens and Reproductions of the 1694 Token," *Colonial Newsletter* 43 (April 2003); C. Wilson Peck, *English Copper, Tin and Bronze Coins in the British Museum, 1558–1958* (1960).

R. Neil Fulghum

Elise Academy and High School was located in northern Moore County in what became the town of Robbins. Lacking funds, Moore County was unable to build a high school in the area in the 1890s. Local citizens, including William Graham Carter, N. J. Carter, Daniel Horner, and George Horner, organized an effort to construct a private academy. This effort got underway in 1899, and the school opened by 1904. It was named for the daughter of John B. Lenning, a Philadelphia capitalist who was living in the area while overseeing the construction of a section of the new Durham & Charlotte Railroad.

After unsuccessfully seeking assistance from the Methodist Church, organizers of the school were able to acquire necessary additional support through the Fayetteville Presbytery of the Presbyterian Church. This association proved successful, and Elise Academy, like many private/church high schools of the early 1900s, became a rather large boarding school with several buildings and dormitories. Elise offered courses in agriculture, algebra, biology, general science, history, civics, home economics, English, geometry, Latin, French, and Bible studies. Besides its importance to the residents of upper Moore County, the school attracted students from across Fayetteville Presbytery and North Carolina. A number of students attended from Cuba. In 1940 the Presbytery sold Elise Academy to the Moore County Board of Education, which converted it to a public high school.

References: Manly Wade Wellman, *County of Moore, 1847–1947* (1962); Edwin Arthur West, *Elise High School and Upper Moore County* (1974).

Robert L. Remsburg III

Elisha Mitchell Scientific Society,

founded in Chapel Hill in 1883 by Francis Preston Venable and other University of North Carolina scientists, served as a forerunner of the modern North Carolina Academy of Science. Scientists throughout the post–Civil War South, employed largely by underfunded colleges and universities, found themselves unable to travel to national disciplinary meetings and thus isolated from the spirit of professionalism that was sweeping the nation. Well educated and determined to pursue careers as professional scientists, Venable and his colleagues sought to establish the camaraderie they deemed essential to their intellectual growth and research efforts.

During 1883–84 the society, named for UNC scientist and educator Elisha Mitchell (1793–1857), convened seven times, offered a total of 67 papers, and attracted 82 regular members, including UNC faculty, educators from other colleges throughout the state, and members of the community. But despite the organization's apparently successful beginning, it declined steadily thereafter. Given the difficulty of travel even over relatively short distances, few out-of-town members attended meetings. Meanwhile, local citizens lost interest in the technical presentations, and a series of more general public lectures did little to boost interest. By 1888 membership had declined to 66 persons, 41 of whom lived less than 60 miles from Chapel Hill.

In effect, the Elisha Mitchell Scientific Society had become a local organization and in 1892 chose to limit its membership to UNC faculty and students. A decade later North Carolina scientists formed the North Carolina Academy of Science to meet their professional needs. Meanwhile, the Mitchell Society met sporadically until 1983, when it officially "passed its torch" to the larger, statewide academy.

References: Nancy Smith Midgette, *To Foster the Spirit of Professionalism: Southern Scientists and State Academies of Science* (1991); Midgette, "Vanguard of a New Generation: The Elisha Mitchell Scientific Society and the Scientific Profession in the South," *Journal of the Elisha Mitchell Scientific Society* 100 (Summer 1984).

Nancy Smith Midgette

Elizabethan Gardens,

adjoining the Fort Raleigh National Historic Site and the Waterside Theatre on Roanoke Island, are a memorial to the English colonists who settled on the island between 1585 and 1587. Conceived and developed as a project of the Garden Club of North Carolina, Inc., in 1951, the site is maintained as an authentic example of a sixteenth-century Elizabethan pleasure garden.

The idea for reproducing a garden of the Elizabethan Age evolved from a fortuitous meeting between renowned author Inglis Fletcher and Mrs. Charles A. Cannon, the founder of the Society for Preservation of Antiques. Some 500 garden clubs with 15,000 members across North Carolina accepted the challenge in 1951 and worked diligently to make the vision a reality. A ten-acre wilderness park on the island shore was donated by

The Virginia Dare statue by Maria Louisa Lander in the Elizabethan Gardens on Roanoke Island. Photograph courtesy of North Carolina Division of Tourism, Film, and Sports Development.

the Roanoke Island Historical Association to the state garden club for the garden site.

From the outset, the project benefited from the planning and expertise of two of America's foremost landscape architects, M. Umberto Innocenti and Richard Webel. Actual construction commenced on the day of Elizabeth II's coronation as queen of England. Four years of work culminated in the formal dedication of the gardens on 18 Aug. 1955, the 368th birthday of Virginia Dare. The keynote speaker at the dedication ceremonies was educator Frank Porter Graham, and other speakers included Fletcher and playwright Paul Green. Two magnolia trees, representing "mother" England and "daughter" United States, were planted during the festivities.

Several acres of the Elizabethan Gardens have been developed into formal gardens, and the remaining acreage has been preserved in its natural state. The perforated wall enclosing the gardens is constructed of handmade brick salvaged from old structures ranging from churches to tobacco flues throughout North Carolina. The ivy-covered Great Gate once adorned the French Embassy in Washington, D.C. Growing within the garden is a rose bush contributed by Queen Elizabeth II from the Royal Gardens at Windsor Castle. Near the wildflower garden an ancient live oak, believed to have been living when the first Roanoke colonists arrived in 1585, shades the winding path. Numerous pieces of statuary are located throughout the gardens. Of particular interest are the Virginia Dare statue, a gift of Paul Green, and the ancient pool and fountain, which were originally intended as a gift to the Metropolitan Museum of Art by John Hay Whitney, the former U.S. ambassador to Great Britain.

Selected as the most outstanding garden club project in the United States in 1961, the Elizabethan Gardens attracts more than 70,000 visitors annually and hosts historical celebrations, educational workshops, and theater and musical performances. Special events are regularly held, such as the one-woman show *Elizabeth R* and various programs marking the anniversary of the birth of Virginia Dare.

Reference: Daniel W. Barefoot, *Touring the Backroads of North Carolina's Upper Coast* (1995).

Daniel W. Barefoot

Elizabeth City, Battle of. The Battle of Elizabeth City, also known as the Battle of Cobb's Point, was a Civil War engagement between Union and Confederate gunboats on the Pasquotank River in February 1862. Flag Officer William F. Lynch commanded a flotilla of small Confederate gunboats, formerly comprising the North Carolina Navy, which was charged with defending the sounds of eastern North Carolina. The vessels—small river steamers and tugs, each armed with one or two heavy cannons—were derisively dubbed the "Mosquito Fleet."

On 7 Feb. 1862 Lynch's fleet participated in a day-long artillery engagement with Union gunboats that were attacking Roanoke Island's defenses. After his largest ship was sunk, another disabled by mechanical problems, and most of his ammunition expended, Lynch took his fleet to Elizabeth City that night, and the Union captured the island the next day. Lynch remained to defend the city and the entrance to the important Dismal Swamp Canal leading to Norfolk, Va.

Meanwhile, on the afternoon of 9 February, Cdr. Stephen C. Rowan led a flotilla of 14 Union navy gunboats, fresh from their victory at Roanoke Island, across Albemarle Sound to seek and destroy the Confederate flotilla. Lynch prepared his ships for battle less than two miles below Elizabeth City, where on the west bank of the river at Cobb's Point, a small earthen fort mounting four 32-pounders had been built. With the fort as his chief reliance for defense, Lynch deployed five vessels (*Seabird*, *Ellis*, *Fanny*, *Appomattox*, and *Beaufort*) across the river. In addition, a schooner named *Black Warrior*, armed with two 32-pounders, was anchored near the east bank of the river as a floating battery opposite the fort at Cobb's Point.

Rowan's 14 gunboats carried a total of 40 guns, compared to the 11 on Lynch's 6 ships. Lynch went ashore to inspect the fort, only to discover insufficient troops to work the guns. He was forced to bring ashore most of the crew from the gunboat *Beaufort* to man the fort's guns and send the *Beaufort* back to Norfolk with a skeleton crew.

Early on the morning of 10 February, Rowan ascended the river with his fleet. But Rowan's vessels, low on ammunition, did not stop to engage the fort. Instead, they steadily approached the Confederate fleet, withholding their fire until within ¾ mile of the Confederates. Rowan advanced rapidly, opening fire for the first time. The Union gunboats easily passed the fort and the schooner *Black Warrior*, firing into the schooner and forcing the crew to abandon and then set fire to the vessel to prevent its capture. In the river the Union *Commodore Perry* rammed the Confederate *Seabird*, capturing its crew of 42 and leaving it sinking in the river. The Confederate *Ellis* was boarded by Union sailors from the *Ceres*, and its commander ordered his crew to escape over the side while he personally fought the boarders with his cutlass. The commander was wounded and the *Ellis* was taken intact by Union sailors. Several of the *Ellis*'s crew were shot in the water.

The Confederate *Fanny* was disabled by cannon fire and run ashore, where its crew set it afire and escaped. The Confederate *Appomattox* alone managed to escape upriver in a running fight and attempted to enter the Dismal Swamp Canal to reach Norfolk. Incredibly, as the vessel tried to enter the mouth of the canal, it was found to be two inches too wide to enter; the ship was destroyed by its crew to prevent capture. At Elizabeth City the Confederate gunboat *Forrest*, on its way for repairs, was also destroyed to prevent capture. Meanwhile Lynch, who had been unable to get back out to his flagship *Seabird* before the attack began, abandoned the fort at Cobb's Point and retreated with his men overland to Norfolk.

Rowan's vessels continued up the river and took possession of Elizabeth City, having made short work of the Confederate flotilla. Union forces now had complete control of the northeast sounds of North Carolina. The losses in the unequal battle were light: two Union sailors killed and seven wounded; four Confederates killed and at least seven wounded.

References: John G. Barrett, *The Civil War in North Carolina* (1963); Daniel H. Hill, *Bethel to Sharpsburg*, vol. 1 (1926); W. H. Parker, *Recollections of a Naval Officer, 1841–1865* (1883).

Paul Branch

Elizabeth City State University

Elizabeth City State University in Elizabeth City was founded in 1891 as the Normal and Industrial School when the General Assembly passed a bill introduced by Hugh Cale, an African American legislator from Pasquotank County. The institution was established for the specific purpose of "teaching and training teachers of the colored race to teach in the common schools of North Carolina." Under the school's first principal and later president, Peter Weddick Moore, the institute grew both academically and physically in its first years.

In 1937 the school became a four-year teachers college, and the name was changed to Elizabeth City State Teachers College. The expanded school granted its first bachelor's degrees in 1939 in elementary education. In 1972 it became a constituent institution of the consolidated University of North Carolina System, and its current name was formally adopted.

By the early 2000s Elizabeth City State University offered 34 baccalaureate degree programs in the basic arts and sciences, selected professional and preprofessional areas, and an Advanced Master's Degree in Elementary Education through four schools—the School of Arts and Humanities, the School of Business and Economics, the School of Education and Psychology, and the School of Mathematics, Science and Technology. The institution also maintains a nursery school and kindergarten and offers degrees in such fields as geology, physics, accounting, criminal justice, industrial technology, political science, music, merchandising, computer science, and middle grades education. Elizabeth City State has an interracial, international faculty teaching more than 2,000 students from a wide range of geographic and ethnic origins.

References: Evelyn Johnson, *History of Elizabeth City State University: A Story of Survival* (1980); William S. Powell, *Higher Education in North Carolina* (1970).

Charles W. Wadelington

Elizabeth College, a four-year college for women, opened in Charlotte in 1897 under the auspices of the Evangelical Lutheran Church. The aim of the institution was "to afford a broad and liberal culture for women; to furnish to young women an education in the classics, mathematics and sciences." Seeking a site for a Lutheran college for women, Lutheran Synod trustees Charles Banks King and C. L. Fisher sought bids from Columbia, S.C., and Charlotte. Charlotte offered 20 acres of land known as the old Torrence homestead on a hill overlooking the city. Against Charlotte's pledge of $12,800 in cash, the trustees of the institution agreed to spend between $50,000 and $75,000 toward the improvement of the property. King named the new campus Elizabeth College, in honor of his mother-in-law, Ann Elizabeth Watts, wife of Gerard Snowden Watts of Baltimore, Md. Later, the Gerard Conservatory of Music was given by Charles King's brother-in-law, Durham tobacco magnate George W. Watts, in memory of his father. The Watts family provided most of the money for the college.

In 1915, King, suffering from ill health, moved the college to Salem, Va., where it was consolidated with Virginia's Roanoke College for Women. At the time of the merger, each institution enrolled about 200 students. In 1921 the Virginia institution burned to the ground, and most of Elizabeth College's records were lost. The college property in Charlotte at Elizabeth and Hawthorne Avenues was purchased by Presbyterian Hospital, which moved into the main brick building. This building continued to serve the hospital and the School of Nursing until it was torn down in 1980 to make room for a major building expansion. As late as the 1950s, the Elizabeth College Alumnae Association continued to meet in Charlotte.

References: LeGette Blythe, *Hornets' Nest: The Story of Charlotte and Mecklenburg County* (1961); Mildred M. McEwen, *Queens College: Yesterday and Today* (1980).

Stewart Lillard

Elizabethtown, Battle of. The Battle of Elizabethtown, which took place on or around 27 Aug. 1781 and essentially crushed the Tories' sway in the North Carolina's Cape Fear region, involved one of the great ruses in the state's Revolutionary War history. Bladen County was firmly in the hands of the Tories, or Loyalists, and British forces numbering between 300 and 400 men were headquartered in Elizabethtown. The Patriots, about 60 or 70 men, had been driven from their homes and seen their estates ravaged and their houses plundered or burned. Led by Cols. Thomas Brown and Thomas Robeson, the Patriots knew they would need to rely on cunning and strategy against the militarily superior Tories.

Brown and Robeson devised a scheme in which the inferiority of their forces would be masked by false commands to "phantom" soldiers, intended to be heard by the enemy, to make the Patriot numbers appear greater than they were. Once the battle started, the Patriots went on the offensive, crossing the Cape Fear River and surprising the Tories into a disorganized retreat. The Tory commanders, John Slingsby and David Godden, were both fatally wounded, and their troops scattered into the darkness. Many of them plunged headlong into a deep ravine near the river, which has been known ever since as "Tory Hole." When the smoke of battle cleared, 17 Tories were either dead or mortally wounded. Not one Patriot was killed, and only 4 were wounded. In 1939 the state of North Carolina erected a historical marker on Main Street in Elizabethtown, memorializing the battle and the famous Tory Hole.

References: R. F. Beasley, *The Battle of Elizabethtown* (1901); Bladen County Historical Society, *Battle of Elizabethtown* (1957).

Beverly Tetterton

Elizabeth II, a historic attraction on Roanoke Island, is a 69-foot, square-rigged sailing ship representative of the Elizabethan vessels used to carry the first English colonists to the New World. Sir Walter Raleigh sponsored three voyages to Roanoke Island between 1584 and 1587, and the *Elizabeth II* is named for one of the seven vessels that sailed in Raleigh's second expedition in 1585. The original 50-ton *Elizabeth* was captained by Thomas Cavendish and probably carried mariners, colonists, and supplies to be used in establishing a military garrison to support England's claim to the New World.

The twentieth-century *Elizabeth II* was constructed as part of America's Four Hundredth Anniversary, which, between 1984 and 1987, commemorated the anniversary of the Roanoke Voyages. Constructed on the waterfront in the town of Manteo, the ship was permanently berthed a few hundred yards from the construction site.

With historian H. G. Jones as chairman, the America's Four Hundredth Anniversary Committee, which had been appointed by North Carolina's governor in 1978, created the nonprofit American Quadricentennial Corporation to assist in and finance various programs, with special emphasis on the ship.

Elizabeth II at anchor in Manteo. Photograph courtesy of North Carolina Division of Tourism, Film, and Sports Development.

The corporation raised $650,000 privately to build the ship, and the General Assembly in 1982 provided $1.4 million to develop facilities for visitors to the site. Historical ship designer William Baker prepared the initial plans, and naval architect Stanley Potter completed the design for the 50-ton ship. Constructed almost entirely by hand, the ship was launched in 1983 and finished in the water by early 1984. Princess Anne of Great Britain christened it on 13 July 1984.

The ship—which sometimes sails to nearby coastal sites—is part of the 27-acre Roanoke Island Festival Park across from the Manteo waterfront. The park, billed as a celebration of the birthplace of English-speaking America, features the interactive Roanoke Adventure Museum, a settlement site, living history programs, and extensive visual and performing arts activities. An Outer Banks History Center houses an extensive library of resource material. The heavily visited *Elizabeth II* and Roanoke Island Festival Park—like Tryon Palace, the USS *North Carolina* Battleship Memorial, and the State Capitol—is a separate section of the Department of Cultural Resources's Division of State Historic Sites, which also includes the State Historic Sites Program.

References: H. G. Jones, "Genesis of the Quadricentennial," *Carolina Comments* 33 (September 1985); John D. Neville, ed., *America's Four Hundredth Anniversary Committee: Final Report* [1988?].

David W. Latham

Elon University was founded near Burlington in 1889 by the Christian Church (later part of the United Church of Christ). Two denominational junior colleges were forerunners of Elon: Graham Normal College in Graham and the Suffolk Collegiate Institute, established in 1872 in Suffolk, Va. In 1882 the Southern Christian Conference adopted a resolution committing the church to establish a college. Six years later the provisional board of the proposed college accepted an offer of 50 acres of land at Mill Point, a freight loading station on the North Carolina Railroad (later the Norfolk Southern) five miles west of Burlington. The school was named Elon, the Hebrew word for oak, because the site was covered with a variety of massive oaks. Three students were graduated at the first commencement exercises on 2 June 1891.

In order to raise funds for the school, streets were laid out around the site and commercial and residential lots were sold. The community was incorporated in 1893 as the town of Elon College. On 18 June 1923 a fire destroyed the school's main building, which housed the library, classrooms, the chapel, and faculty and administrative offices. Construction of five new buildings—three classroom and office buildings, a library, and an auditorium—began the same year. These five buildings remain at the heart of the central campus.

Elon began offering graduate degrees (in business administration and education) in the 1980s, and by the early 2000s it was the third-largest private school in North Carolina. Elon is one of two private colleges in the state selected to offer the North Carolina Teaching Fellows Program. Enrollment totals about 5,000, including 250 graduate students. In 2000 the Elon board of trustees approved a name change from Elon College to Elon University, marking the institution's successful growth into a comprehensive undergraduate university.

Reference: Durward T. Stokes, *Elon College: Its History and Traditions* (1982).

George W. Troxler

Emancipation of all enslaved African Americans in the South became official on 1 Jan. 1863, when President Abraham Lincoln issued the Emancipation Proclamation freeing the slaves in areas of armed rebellion against the U.S. government, including North Carolina. Although the proclamation marked Lincoln's attempt to end slavery, many slaves in North Carolina had engaged in actions toward the same end from the outset of the Civil War. African American men constituted a large portion of the Confederate labor force working on the fortifications of Pamlico and Albemarle Sounds, as well as along North Carolina's coastal rivers prior to open hostilities between North and South. But this new use of slaves separated black men from their families and subjected them to military overseers, both of which alienated many slaves from the Confederacy. As the war progressed, they fled not only military labor but also Confederate impressment and their owners' actions to move them away from Union lines. Despite the efforts of North Carolina slaveholders, thousands of slaves crossed Union lines to freedom.

When Union commander Maj. Gen. Ambrose E. Burnside launched his expedition into northeastern North Carolina in February 1862, he unknowingly provided slaves with a new sanctuary. Initially, Burnside hoped not to become involved in the slavery issue, but on 21 March he reported to the U.S. secretary of war that "it would be utterly impossible if we were so disposed to keep [slaves] outside of our lines, as they find their way to us through woods & swamps from every side." The massive influx of fugitive slaves created tension between Burnside and Edward Stanly, whom Lincoln appointed military governor of North Carolina in April 1862. Stanly believed it his duty to protect North Carolina law in order to promote Unionism in the state. This conviction led him to disband schools for African Americans in New Bern, to return a local Unionist planter's young female slave, and to protest the Emancipation Proclamation. Ultimately, it was his government's emancipation policy that prompted Stanly to resign on 15 Jan. 1863 because he feared that it would needlessly lengthen the war.

Perhaps there was some truth in Stanly's protests. Despite Lincoln's cautious path to emancipation, his acceptance of it

as a military necessity in July 1862 rattled North Carolinians. Burnside—like other Union commanders already inundated with fugitive slaves when Lincoln issued the preliminary proclamation following the Battle of Antietam (Sharpsburg) in September 1862—encountered swelling numbers afterward. The Emancipation Proclamation exacerbated rising class tensions in North Carolina. In the wake of the Confederacy's April 1862 Conscription Act exempting 1 white male per farm with 20 or more slaves, nonslaveholders' commitment to the southern cause waned.

The North Carolina press viewed the preliminary proclamation as an indication of the Union's intention to abolish slavery and subjugate white men and predicted that southerners would further rally behind the Confederacy. Yet the opposite occurred in North Carolina: class conflict between nonslaveholders and slave owners increased, as did desertion from the Confederate armies. After January 1863, yeoman farmers could no longer conceive of sacrifice for an institution in which they possessed only a "casual interest."

References: Ira Berlin and others, eds., *Freedom: A Documentary History of Emancipation, 1861–1867*, ser. 1, vol. 1 (1985); William C. Harris, "Lincoln and Wartime Reconstruction in North Carolina, 1861–1863," NCHR 63 (April 1986); Harold D. Moser, "Reaction in North Carolina to the Emancipation Proclamation," NCHR 44 (January 1967); Mark E. Neely Jr., *The Last Best Hope of Earth: Abraham Lincoln and the Promise of America* (1993).

Steven E. Nash

SEE ALSO Contrabands.

Emancipation Day in North Carolina was initiated on 1 Jan. 1865 at Union-occupied New Bern. It was conceived as a day of celebration and commemoration of President Abraham Lincoln's 1863 New Year's Emancipation Proclamation that freed all slaves of "persons [who] shall then be in rebellion against the United States." The day of observance included a parade through the main streets of the city with a band and an escort by the North Carolina Heavy Artillery. The procession halted at the army's parade field, where the Emancipation Proclamation was read and Lincoln was eulogized. This was followed by speeches of prominent black leaders and by meetings and dinners at local churches. The format—which became, with modifications, the model for future celebrations —was based on a similar observance held the previous year (1864) by the Federal army in Beaufort, S.C., in conjunction with local freedpeople.

Although Union forces assisted and coordinated these early celebrations to encourage southern slave defections and promote a black/poor-white alliance, the impetus of the movement was soon assumed by the newly freed blacks, who had a purposeful strategy of their own: prosperity through frugality, temperance, industry, and education. By 1878 the Emancipation Day celebration had gained respectability statewide, and politicians such as Zebulon B. Vance, who continued to oppose emancipation until the end of his life, agreed to act as the orator of the day in order to compete for the votes of those gathered. Within 20 years it was generally accepted that key state and national officials and members of both races would attend the ceremonies. On 1 Jan. 1898, for instance, black former congressman H. P. Cheatham addressed an audience that included the governor, secretary of state, other North Carolina officials, numerous news reporters, and "quite a large number of ladies and gentlemen."

Reference: Kathleen Ann Clark, *Defining Moments: African American Political Commemoration in the South, 1863–1913* (2005).

Louis P. Towles

Employment Security Commission. In response to federal initiatives and requirements, the North Carolina General Assembly called a special session in December 1936 and established the state Unemployment Compensation Commission. Its primary function was to aid citizens who were out of work due to circumstances beyond their control and to continue to fund such assistance in consonance with federal directives. In 1939 the legislature extended the commission's quasi-judicial powers, stipulating that its decisions, when docketed by a clerk of court, carried the same force as judgments of a superior court.

Following the nation's entry into World War II, President Franklin D. Roosevelt requested that the states' separate employment services be centralized into one federal agency responsive to the demands of national defense. Effective 1 Jan. 1942, the records of the North Carolina State Employment Division and various other personnel under the Unemployment Compensation Commission were transferred to the U.S. Employment Service under the Social Security Board. The next year the General Assembly empowered the commission to cooperate with other unemployment compensation agencies and make reciprocal agreements with agencies of the federal and other state governments.

In November 1946 the State Employment Division was returned to the Unemployment Compensation Commission, and in 1947 the legislature changed the agency name to the Employment Security Commission. Under the Executive Organization Act of 1971, the Employment Security Commission was placed within the Department of Commerce for administrative purposes, although the commission retained its previously granted powers and duties and was not subject to the authority of the cabinet-level departmental secretary.

The modern commission offers a variety of services and programs, yet its organizational structure is based on its original divisions of Employment Service, Unemployment Insurance Compensation, Labor Market Information (formerly the Bureau of Research and Statistics), and the Office of the General Counsel. In addition to providing job referral and training, the Division of Employment Service offers services to special groups, such as migrant and seasonal workers, veterans, youth, senior citizens, and the handicapped. It also directs federal programs in the state, including the Work Incentive Program, Veterans Employment Service, and the Job Training Partnership Act.

Wiley J. Williams

Endangered Species are a topic of great interest and ongoing research in North Carolina. From the Coastal Plain in the east to the forested Mountain region in the west, the state contains a variety of habitats allowing for a rich and diverse flora and fauna. North Carolina is home to roughly 5,700 species of plants, over 700 species of vertebrates, and invertebrate species numbering well into the thousands. Loss of, or damage to, habitat is the major factor affecting the state's flora and fauna, reducing their diversity and numbers. The draw of North Carolina's natural beauty, coupled with economic opportunity and prosperity, has led to a rapid increase in population density and in the amount of land development over the past few decades. These and other factors such

An endangered male red wolf and pup in the Alligator River National Wildlife Refuge in Dare and Hyde Counties. Image copyright Greg Koch, 2003.

The rare and endangered Yadkin River goldenrod, *Solidago plumosa*, was first described in the 1890s and then lost to science and presumed extinct until rediscovered in 1994 by botanists Alan Weakley and Steve Leonard, working independently of each other. The plant is endemic to North Carolina and grows in rock crevices along a quarter-mile stretch in the Yadkin River Gorge. Photograph by Johnny Randall.

as drainage of bogs and wetlands, contamination by pollutants, suppression of natural fires, introduction of aggressive, nonnative species, and exploitation of economically valuable species have all played a part in impacting the landscapes and ecosystems that support North Carolina's wildlife.

Scientists have stated that mastodons, saber-toothed tigers, musk oxen, wooly mammoths, and other beasts walked the fields and forests of North Carolina approximately 15,000 years ago. Why these animals became extinct is not fully known, but, for other animals that used to live in North Carolina, it is known that humanity is the main culprit. Overhunting by humans wiped out the passenger pigeon and the Carolina parakeet as well as the woods bison, gray wolf, elk, and other species from North Carolina. The fisher, a northern member of the weasel family that was acclimated to spruce fir forests, was limited to the habitats of the mountaintops. Their small numbers and desirable fur guaranteed that fishers

would be trapped out of existence in the Mountains by the 1840s. Other animals succumbed to extinction because they provided food and/or pelts or feathers for the settlers.

Other animals, including eastern cougars, pileated woodpeckers, fox squirrels, and northern flying squirrels are rare-to-extinct in North Carolina because of human destruction of their habitat. Many of the animal species in the state are placed at risk by human carelessness, aggression, or population expansion. When fields and forests are developed for purposes such as housing subdivisions and shopping centers, animals are crowded into smaller spaces or are eliminated. Those that are left also have to deal with polluted runoff waters, human trash, and increased competition for food and shelter, which put greater stresses on the animals and lower their chances for survival.

The North Carolina Wildlife Resources Commission, the National Park Service, and the U.S. Fish and Wildlife Department have worked together to reintroduce some animal species into North Carolina. In the 1930s beavers were reintroduced successfully in a limited area and have since spread throughout the state. Other species such as the peregrine falcon, spotfin chub, yellowfin madtom, river otter, and smoky madtom have also been given another chance in North Carolina. In 1987 red wolves were released into the Alligator River National Wildlife Refuge near the coast, and in 1991 they were set free in Great Smoky Mountains National Park, the largest and most species-rich wilderness in the eastern United States. The brook trout, out-competed in some mountain streams by the nonnative, more aggressive rainbow and brown trout, has been put back after the streams were cleaned of the other trout. Reintroduction of animal species is a controversial, as well as expensive, issue. However, state and federal agencies continue to work to restore as much diversity of animal life to North Carolina as they can.

By the early 2000s in North Carolina there were about 60 species of plants and animals included on federal lists as endangered (in danger of extinction) or threatened (may become endangered in the foreseeable future). At the federal level, these species receive protection from the U.S. Fish and Wildlife Service under the amended Endangered Species Act of 1973. At the state level, North Carolina has additional laws to protect plants and animals under the jurisdictions of the Plant Conservation Program, a unit of the Department of Agriculture, and the Wildlife Resources Commission, part of the Department of Environment, Health, and Natural Resources. In addition, the state extends its legal protection beyond endangered and threatened status to include species determined to be of "special concern" (requiring close monitoring). At present, 159 plant species and 194 animal species have legally protected status at the state level. North Carolina currently has a number of different funding initiatives and mechanisms in place, such as the tax check-off and license plate programs, to enable the public to contribute to its conservation and management efforts.

References: James L. Amoroso, *Natural Heritage Program List of the Rare Plants of North Carolina* (1999); Harry E. LeGrand and Stephen P. Hall, *Natural Heritage Program List of the Rare Animal Species of North Carolina* (1999).

Rebecca Dotterer
Lee Plummer Templeton

SEE ALSO Beavers; Carolina Panther; Carolina Parakeet; Eagles.

Endor Furnace, a large smelting furnace near Cumnock in Lee County, provided iron to the Confederacy from 1862 to 1865 and thereafter operated periodically through the end of the nineteenth century. Two months after chartering the company in 1862, the investors purchased the Deep River plantation of Alexander McIver and constructed the furnace on the site. The furnace probably supplied the Confederate arsenal at Fayetteville in addition to small nearby arms factories. In 1864 the Wilmington businessmen who composed the company sold their interests to local buyers. These individuals emerged from the war heavily in debt, and in 1870 their holdings were sold at auction. George Lobdell of Delaware, a manufacturer of railroad car wheels, bought Endor Furnace, paying $1,000. With his partner J. M. Heck of Raleigh, Lobdell formed the Cape Fear Iron and Steel Company and invested more than $500,000. By 1872 there was in place at the site one of the South's largest and best-equipped iron furnaces along with a rolling mill and foundry.

Two years later the operators discovered that the local mineral deposits were smaller than had been estimated. In addition, the system of dams and locks necessary to reach the port at Wilmington were never satisfactorily completed. By 1876 the operation had ceased and most of the machinery was dismantled and removed. The furnace continued to operate until

The furnace opening at Endor Furnace, ca. 1970. Courtesy of NCOA&H.

1896 on a much smaller scale but served only local manufacturers. Its structure, built of reddish-gray rough-cut stones and standing 35 feet tall, was still standing at the end of the twentieth century.

References: Lester J. Cappon, "Iron-Making: A Forgotten Industry of North Carolina," *NCHR* 9 (October 1932); Malcolm Fowler, "The Endor Iron Furnace," *The State* (19 Apr. 1941); Brent D. Glass, ed., *North Carolina: An Inventory of Historic Engineering and Industrial Sites* (1975).

Michael Hill

Enfield Riots were the culmination of protests in eighteenth-century Edgecombe, Halifax, and Granville Counties against land agents in the Granville District. While the Crown governed the territory as part of the province of North Carolina, Robert Earl Granville, heir of John Lord Carteret, second Earl Granville, possessed land rights in the district. From the creation of the district until the American Revolution, the Granville District was plagued by controversy over corrupt agents, land grants, titles, and the collection of quitrents. During the 1750s protests were centered in Edgecombe and Granville Counties, demonstrating North Carolinians' growing dissatisfaction with the royal government.

A December 1758 report of a committee of the North Carolina Assembly that investigated complaints from settlers confirmed numerous fraudulent acts by Proprietary surveyors but absolved Granville's principal agent, Francis Corbin, of guilt. Many residents of the district no doubt shared Governor Arthur Dobbs's belief that Corbin had influenced the committee's report. Determined to secure redress of their grievances, a party of 20 to 25 men from Edgecombe, Halifax, and Granville Counties went to Edenton and, on the night of 25 Jan. 1759, kidnapped Corbin and his coagent, Joshua Bodley. They took the two men to Enfield, located in the southern part of the newly created Halifax County. Corbin and Bodley were held for four days and forced to agree to open all land records for public inspection. The captors also demanded that Corbin give bond to appear at the spring term of superior court and sign an agreement promising to refund moneys taken illegally by his agents.

The Enfield rioters were not impoverished tenants; those who have been identified were planters and officeholders. The kidnappers' leader probably was Alexander McCulloh, agent and nephew of Henry McCulloh, whose claim to over 300,000 acres in the Granville District preceded the creation and survey of the earl's Proprietary grant. Although Henry McCulloh and Granville had reached an agreement resolving their conflicting claims, Corbin had issued patents for land reserved for McCulloh.

During a second "riot" in Enfield on 14 May 1759, some participants in the kidnappings who had been arrested and jailed were freed by a mob who broke open the jail. As soon as Earl Granville learned of the kidnapping of Corbin and Bodley, he suspended both men. Although Corbin had strong support in the Assembly, he failed to obtain the conviction of the rioters. The Assembly, already conspiring to secure Dobbs's dismissal, charged that the governor had abetted the rioters and had failed to suppress the violence in the Granville District. Corbin's successor, Thomas Child, quickly allied himself with the Assembly and avoided conflict with local settlers and with McCulloh, who negotiated a new accord with Granville in 1761.

References: E. Merton Coulter, *The Granville District* (1913); A. Roger Ekirch, *"Poor Carolina": Politics and Society in Colonial North Carolina, 1729–1776* (1981); Alan D. Watson, *Edgecombe County: A Brief History* (1979).

George W. Troxler

English Dialects. The English language in North Carolina has been growing and evolving since 1584, when the first English explorers to visit North America came to the Outer Banks, making it the first place in the New World where English was spoken. Over the next four centuries, as those first explorations led to the arrival of the colonists who would begin populating the state, the various forms or dialects of English they brought with them became the basis for the English language as it is written and spoken in North Carolina today.

Although there are a number of recognizable English dialects spoken in the state, three predominate. First is the dialect referred to as Lower Southern, which is common in eastern and central North Carolina in a broad swath stretching from the coast through the Piedmont. This southern dialect is what many people think of when they hear the term "southern" or "plantation" English, and it is spoken by people in the Coastal Plain and Piedmont regions of Virginia, North Carolina, and South Carolina and in the Coastal Plain of Georgia. A second southern dialect, known as Upper Southern, is commonly spoken in the western part of the state and in the Mountain regions of West Virginia, Virginia, Kentucky, and Tennessee. The third important dialect in North Carolina is African American English, known more recently as Ebonics, which is spoken by large numbers of African Americans who were born and raised in the state or other parts of the South. Despite the difficulty in pinpointing the origins of African American English, recent scholarship theorizes that it is the linguistic product of interactions between English as it was spoken in the South in the eighteenth century and the West African languages spoken by newly arrived slaves.

Although there are no great differences between the dialects spoken by North Carolinians living near the coast and those living in the western parts of the state, the subtle differences that do exist are traceable to immigration patterns, the history of the state's settlement, and the economic and social differences—both real and perceived—between eastern and western North Carolina. Most of those who settled in the Coastal Plain and Piedmont regions of the state arrived directly from England, bringing with them various dialects of what can be called Modern English. Because settlers coming from diverse regions in England (where there are easily recognizable differences between regional and class dialects) often commingled after coming to North Carolina, the distinctions between the dialects gradually blurred to form the distinctive eastern North Carolina dialect.

The settlement patterns of the western parts of the state differ greatly from those of the east. The primary settlers of the Mountains were Scotch-Irish rather than English, and many of them migrated from Europe to Pennsylvania and then moved southward to the North Carolina Mountains. As a result of the migration pattern and their meetings with pockets of German settlers, the hardy souls who first populated western North Carolina developed a slightly different dialect from the one that is heard in the Piedmont or Coastal Plain. One distinctive feature of the language as it is spoken in the western parts of the state lies in the more widespread use of folk and colloquial expressions.

In addition to the three primary dialects, linguists working with North Carolina State University's North Carolina Language and Life program have identified several others that, while they are not spoken by large numbers of people, comprise linguistically distinct dialects and offer some insight into the state's history. These include the dialect spoken by the "Hoi Toiders," longtime residents of Ocracoke Island and Harkers Island, which, until recently, had remained somewhat isolated from the rest of the state because of their inaccessibility. In addition, linguists have identified and begun to measure and record the distinctive dialects spoken by the Lumbee Indians, who live primarily in the southeastern part of the state, and the Cherokee Indians, who live on and near the reservation in the state's westernmost corner. Furthermore, recent immigration to North Carolina by large numbers of Hispanic and Vietnamese (Hmong) immigrants have sparked two new variations of English.

References: Norman E. Eliason, *Tarheel Talk: A Historical Study of the English Language in North Carolina to 1860* (1956); Walt Wolfram and Natalie Shilling-Estes, *Hoi Toide on the Outer Banks: The Story of the Ocracoke Brogue* (1997).

Matthew C. Porter

SEE ALSO Hoi Toiders.

Eno Indians were likely one of the loosely related tribes of Siouan-speaking Native Americans living in the Piedmont of what is now North Carolina at the time of European exploration. Little is known about them, and their existence is recorded primarily in seventeenth- and early eighteenth-century Virginia and North Carolina documents. Although their villages of Eno Town and Adshusheer in what is now Durham County have not been located, some information about related Siouan-speaking peoples in the region has been found through the long-term Siouan Project of the Research Laboratories of Archaeology at the University of North Carolina at Chapel Hill.

Governor George Yeardley of Virginia first mentioned the Eno Indians (whom he called Haynokes) in connection with their resistance to Spanish explorers. In 1670 John Lederer, a German explorer, gave a somewhat detailed description of the tribe he called the Oenock Indians, who commonly hired themselves out as porters and carriers to neighboring tribes. A few years later, traders' accounts located Aeno- or Eno-Town as a two-days' journey from the Occaneechi village (then located on the Roanoke River) and close to the Great Trading Path that ran roughly from present-day Petersburg, Va., to the Catawba Indian communities in South Carolina.

John Lawson, surveyor general of the colony of Carolina, tells of meeting with Eno-Will, a leader of the Eno Indians and related tribes, in his 1701 exploration. He was entertained at Occaneechi, then located on the Eno River near Hillsborough, and Adshusheer, a combined Eno, Shakori, and Adshusheer village 14 miles east of Occaneechi. Lawson's is the only extended description of the culture of these related tribes.

The combined tribes at Adshusheer suggest the decline in numbers that the individual tribes had already suffered. In 1716 Governor Alexander Spotswood of Virginia tried to settle their remnant permanently at Eno-Town to act as protection from more hostile tribes, but the governors of North Carolina and South Carolina opposed the plan. From this time on, the Eno tribe disappears from the historical record. They were possibly incorporated into the Catawba Nation. William Byrd's history of the survey of the dividing line between Virginia and North Carolina in 1729 presents an elderly, demoralized Shacco-Will, who is almost unrecognizable as Lawson's earlier dignified, respected, and responsible Eno-Will.

References: Douglas L. Rights, *The American Indian in North Carolina* (1957); H. Trawick Ward and R. P. Stephen Davis Jr., *Indian Communities on the North Carolina Piedmont, A.D. 1000 to 1700* (1993).

Jean B. Anderson

Entails were legal arrangements by which ownership of land was confined within a single family, passing at death from generation to generation. Known in legal jargon as a "fee tail," an entailed estate was limited to a person and his biological heirs. Developed in medieval England, entails were well known in colonial North Carolina. The state's first constitution directed the General Assembly to legislate against entails, and a law was passed in 1784 that has remained in force.

Reference: John V. Orth, "Does the Fee Tail Exist in North Carolina?" *Wake Forest Law Review* 23 (1988).

John V. Orth

Environmentalism. SEE Conservation Movement.

Environmental Protection Agency. Following the example of the U.S. Forest Service, the National Center for Health Statistics, and the National Institute of Environmental Health Sciences, the U.S. Environmental Protection Agency (EPA) established its Environmental Research Center in Research Triangle Park (RTP) in the Raleigh-Durham area in 1971. The center's main focus has been the research and assessment of various environmental pollutants, especially their risk to humans and their ecological effects.

Employing more than 1,400 people, North Carolina's EPA facilities include the National Exposure Research Laboratory, National Health and Environmental Effects Research Laboratory, National Risk Management Laboratory/Air Pollution Prevention and Control Division, and National Center for Environmental Assessment. The EPA Office of Administration and Resources Management, Human Resources Management Division, and Office of Air Quality Planning and Standards are also located at RTP; a Clinical Research Facility and a Human Studies Division are at the University of North Carolina at Chapel Hill.

Wiley J. Williams

Environment and Natural Resources, Department of. The origins of what came to be known as the North Carolina Department of Environment and Natural Resources date as far back as 1823, when the state sponsored a geological survey. Later, state research activities were expanded to include forestry, and in 1891 these and other varied functions were combined in a single agency, the North Carolina Geological Survey. The name was changed to the North Carolina Geological and Economic Survey in 1905, and between then and its replacement by the Department of Conservation and Development in 1925 the agency took on still more responsibilities. From the outset, the Department of Conservation and Development was one of the more important divisions of North Carolina state government, and membership on its board was a widely sought political plum.

In addition to geology, mineral resources, and forestry, the divisions of the Department of Conservation and Development included marine fisheries, coastal resources, water resources, tourism, advertising, and state parks. By the time it was replaced by the Department of Natural Resources and Community Development with adoption of the Executive Organization Act of 1971, the new department included 18 different agencies, boards, and commissions. Other name changes followed, and by 1998 the state's catchall agency was known as the Department of Environment and Natural Resources. In the early 2000s, the department worked to protect water quality, air quality, and public health through various programs designed to do everything from encouraging respect for the environment to assisting businesses, local governments, and the public with technical matters related to its divisions.

David Stick

Episcopal Church. Beginning in 1785 with the organization of the Protestant Episcopal Church, the Episcopal Church in the United States emerged from the remnants of the Church of England (Anglican Church) and soon became an influential part of North Carolina's religious culture. Beyond establishing the church in North Carolina and organizing individual congregations, the Episcopal Church, as other denominations, played an important role in education and adopted numerous other social causes in the state.

At the Tarboro Convention in May 1794, a constitution for the Diocese of North Carolina was approved, and Charles Pettigrew was elected bishop of the diocese. (He was never consecrated but remained bishop-elect until his death in 1807.) Formal organization of the Protestant Episcopal Church in North Carolina took place in New Bern in April 1817, and John Stark Ravenscroft became the diocese's first official bishop in 1823. He served until his death in 1830 and was followed by Levi Silliman Ives (1831–53). Ives's episcopate saw the establishment of the Episcopal School (1833) and Saint Mary's School (1842) in Raleigh and Valle Crucis Mission (1842) in Watauga County. However, Ives's leanings toward Roman Catholicism created dissension within the church, and in May 1853, in a letter written from Rome, he renounced his commission and became a Roman Catholic.

During the tenure of the state's third Episcopal bishop, Thomas Atkinson (1853–81), the separation of the southern dioceses from the national church led to formation of the Protestant Episcopal Church in the Confederate States of America, which the North Carolina church joined in May 1862. Atkinson's term also saw the founding of the Ravenscroft School for Boys at Asheville (1856), the Protestant Episcopal Church Publishing Association in Charlotte (1864), St. Augustine's Normal School and Collegiate Institute at Raleigh (1867), St. Peter's Home and Hospital in Charlotte (1876), and John's Guild of the Church of the Good Shepherd, Raleigh's first public hospital (1878).

Conflicts over theological, social, and ecclesiastical issues informed the Episcopal Church in North Carolina and nationwide during the twentieth century. An extensive revision of the 1928 Book of Common Prayer, begun in the 1960s, gained full approval of the national church in 1979 but distressed many traditionalists. Opponents of the change still hoped to retain the conservatism of Anglican worship; some members left the Episcopal Church and joined Anglican parishes that continued to use the 1928 prayer book. In North Carolina, most of these Anglican churches are located in the Piedmont, including St. Benedict's Anglican Catholic Church in Chapel Hill; St. Michael's Anglican Church, St. Peter's Anglican Church, and St. Margaret's Episcopal Church in Charlotte; and St. George's Anglican Church, All Saints Anglican Parish, and St. Timothy's Episcopal Church in Raleigh.

Also in the 1960s the Episcopal Church took a strong stand against the Vietnam War and promoted civil rights and feminism. The ordination of women as Episcopal priests, starting in 1976, caused further rifts within the church. In 1989 in Massachusetts, Barbara Harris, an African American, became the first woman bishop, breaking a 400-year tradition of the worldwide Anglican Communion. Meanwhile, the church increasingly reached out to blacks and Native Americans and later to Latino and Asian minorities. In 1998 the national Episcopal Church launched a campaign to double church membership by the year 2020.

Still another divisive element was the church's growing acceptance of homosexuality, which by the early 2000s had reached a crisis point: some dissenting members reduced or withheld their financial contributions, while others moved to like-minded congregations or left the Episcopal Church entirely. Much of the dissidence was fueled by the 5 Aug. 2003 vote by the church's General Convention to confirm as bishop V. Gene Robinson, an openly practicing homosexual. The same convention also voted to allow individual Episcopal dioceses to continue deciding whether to bless same-sex unions. These actions represented a shift away from traditional Episcopal Church policy, which had deemed homosexual behavior a sin. Bishop Michael B. Curry of the North Carolina Diocese, who in July 2004 authorized same-sex blessings in the state as "one way our community can live the Gospel through faithful and loving pastoral care and spiritual support for each other," was among the bishops who voted for Robinson's confirmation.

Despite these internal conflicts, the Episcopal Church has joined other Anglican churches in the movement for church unity for over 100 years. This movement has been predicated on a return to the "principles of Unity exemplified by the undivided Catholic Church during the first period" of its existence. To this end, the Lambeth conferences, worldwide meetings of Anglican and Episcopalian bishops, are held from time to time at Lambeth Palace, the London residence of Great Britain's archbishop of Canterbury.

By the early 2000s there were approximately 43,000 communicants of the Episcopal Church in North Carolina, divided into the Eastern, North Carolina, and Western Dioceses. A large percentage of the state's Episcopalians lived in the northeastern counties, the Piedmont cities of Raleigh, Durham, Greensboro, Winston-Salem, and Charlotte, and in the greater

Wilmington area. Each of the three dioceses in North Carolina published a diocesan newspaper.

References: Don S. Armentrout, "The Ordination of Episcopal Women in the South," *Sewanee Theological Review* 43 (2000); Lawrence Fay Brewster, *A Short History of the Diocese of East Carolina, 1883–1971* (1975); Robert J. Cain, ed., *The Church of England in North Carolina Documents, 1699–1741*, vol. 1 (1999); Sarah McCulloh Lemmon, "The Genesis of the Protestant Episcopal Diocese of North Carolina, 1701–1823," *NCHR* 28 (October 1951); Lawrence Foushee London and Lemmon, eds., *The Episcopal Church in North Carolina, 1701–1959* (1987).

Wiley J. Williams

Louis P. Towles

SEE ALSO Christ School; Episcopal School for Boys (Raleigh); Episcopal School for Boys (Salisbury); Missionary District of Asheville; Ravenscroft School; Saint Augustine's College; Saint Mary's School.

Episcopal School for Boys (Raleigh)

Episcopal School for Boys (Raleigh) was begun in 1833 by the Episcopal Dioceses of North Carolina under the direction of Bishop Levi S. Ives. Built on a 160-acre tract of land, at that time one mile west of the city, it was intended to improve the quality of religious education in the dioceses and to provide a quality preparatory school in the classics and Christian thought. Students were to be recruited from within the church and from among friends of the denomination, but it was understood that all pupils were to be grounded, as Ives put it, in "the doctrines, discipline, and worship of the Church."

The school was modeled on similar institutions in Round Hill, Mass., and Flushing, N.Y. It was controlled by a committee of clergymen and laity, or trustees, appointed yearly by the convention. This body, presided over by the bishop, employed a rector and several teachers to instruct and mold the young men, generally ages 14 to 19. Students were expected to rise at 5:00 A.M. and to work, with little recreation, until bedtime at 10:00 P.M. Smoking, forays into the capital, and insubordination were strictly forbidden and could result in immediate expulsion. In addition, the rector's word was law and could not be overruled, even by the trustees.

The course of study was both classical and theological. Students were trained in the essentials of English (writing, speaking, spelling, and grammar) as well as in Greek, Latin, French, Spanish, and Italian. Arithmetic, basic algebra, geography, and history were required, and as in most schools of the period, there were classes in the Bible and ethics. Between 1834 and 1835, the student body grew from 36 to more than 100, and the physical plant was increased from one building to five. In 1836 the Episcopal Church's North Carolina General Convention gave $21,500 for the school's support, and ministers in New York subscribed an additional $10,000 a year later.

Progress, however, proved an illusion. The Episcopal School's rapid growth led to the incursion of greater debt than could be retired in the time allowed, and periodic student unrest made it difficult to maintain discipline and public support. Finally, the economic depression of 1836–45 rendered recovery all but impossible. The academy closed in 1838, and for the next three years Bishop Ives used the facility for the training of ministers. In 1842 the diocese recovered part of its investment by converting the academy into Saint Mary's girls' school.

Reference: Lawrence Foushee London and Sarah McCulloh Lemmon, *The Episcopal Church in North Carolina, 1701–1959* (1987).

Louis P. Towles

Episcopal School for Boys (Salisbury)

Episcopal School for Boys (Salisbury) was the third attempt by the Episcopal dioceses of North Carolina to locate a boys' academy within the state. The effort was spearheaded by the Reverend Francis J. Murdock of St. Luke's Church in Salisbury, who sought support from the religious community of western North Carolina at large. It was his dream to help educate youth, particularly those ministerial candidates unable to pay for a quality Christian instruction. To this end and in addition to his regular duties as rector of St. Luke's, he served as a teacher, a fund-raiser, and the treasurer for the Episcopal School in Salisbury.

The institution opened in 1891 with 30 pupils. Enrollment remained constant, between 30 and 40, but funding for the small academy was precarious from the beginning; this problem, together with improvements in the local public school system, forced the Episcopal School to close after only eight years.

Reference: Lawrence Foushee London and Sarah McCulloh Lemmon, *The Episcopal Church in North Carolina, 1701–1959* (1987).

Louis P. Towles

Equal Rights Amendment

Equal Rights Amendment (ERA), the proposed Twenty-seventh Amendment to the U.S. Constitution prohibiting gender discrimination, was passed by Congress on 22 Mar. 1972 and then forwarded to the states for ratification. Before the end of the year, the ERA was ratified by 22 states, but in several states, including North Carolina, disagreement over the amendment's implications led to many years of highly charged debate.

With North Carolina's Republican governor James E. Holshouser Jr. and Democratic lieutenant governor James B. Hunt Jr. initially voicing their approval of the ERA, several organizations were formed in the state to support or oppose the amendment. In January 1973, 1,000 ERA backers gathered at Duke University in Durham to launch North Carolinians United for ERA; Martha McKay of the North Carolina Women's

Former U.S. senator Sam J. Ervin Jr. speaks against the Equal Rights Amendment at Dorton Arena in Raleigh, 1977. *Raleigh News and Observer.*

Political Caucus was a major organizer of the event. Opponents in the ERA debate were led by U.S. Democratic senator Sam J. Ervin Jr., who, after being approached by conservative activist Phyllis Schlafly of Illinois, allowed Schlafly's Stop-ERA group to use his name in its mailings. Schlafly recruited Dorothy "Dot" Malone Slade of Reidsville, a member of the John Birch Society and the National Federation of Republican Women, to lead the statewide organization, North Carolinians against ERA.

After the ERA was formally introduced into the North Carolina legislature in February 1973, many proponents were surprised by the opposition's forceful arguments that outlawing gender discrimination would have detrimental consequences. Robert E. Lee, a Wake Forest University law professor, told the Senate Constitutional Amendments Committee that the simple text of the ERA would be open to interpretation by judges, inviting what he viewed as increasing court interference in public life. Perhaps most unsettling to proponents was the organized opposition from conservative women who feared that civil society would fall into chaos if the amendment passed. While ERA supporters concentrated their efforts on lobbying the General Assembly, opponents were more successful in reaching out to North Carolina women and fueling concerns that the rights and privileges they currently enjoyed, such as maternity leave and basic courtesies, would be eliminated by the ERA. Although they may have lacked the political expertise of ERA supporters, anti-ERA activists found champions in Ervin and North Carolina Supreme Court justice Susie Marshall Sharp, a highly respected Democrat who publicly agreed with Ervin's opposition and made personal calls to legislators.

In 1973 the ERA was defeated in the State Senate by a vote of 27 to 23; it failed again in 1975. The amendment came close to passage in 1977, when Hunt became governor and it sailed through the State House by a vote of 61 to 55. This development prompted 1,500 opponents to stage a rally at Dorton Arena in

Supporters of the Equal Rights Amendment surround a statue of Andrew Jackson on the capitol grounds in Raleigh, 1981. *Raleigh News and Observer.*

Raleigh a week before the scheduled Senate vote; the gathering, at which Schlafly and Ervin spoke, was described by one observer as "a cross between a political rally and a church revival." Opponents found success in lobbying senators, and the ERA was again defeated in the Senate by a vote of 26 to 24.

In 1978, as the expiration date for the ERA neared without ratification from the required 38 states, Congress proposed an extension of the consideration period to 1982. Ervin's successor in the U.S. Senate, ERA backer Robert B. Morgan, maintained that an extension should in fairness also provide for a right to rescind, although his proposal was not accepted. Even though the extension was granted, the ERA failed again in the North Carolina legislature in 1979, 1981, and 1982 before it was ultimately rejected nationally.

References: Margaret A. Blanchard, *Woman's Suffrage, the Equal Rights Amendment, Equal Pay for Equal Work, and Other Such Revolutionary Ideas* (1974); Albert Coates, *By Her Own Bootstraps: A Saga of Women in North Carolina* (1975); Donald G. Mathews and Jane S. De Hart, *Sex, Gender, and the Politics of ERA: A State and the Nation* (1990); Howard F. Twiggs, ed., *Before and After the Equal*

Rights Amendment: The Current Status of Women and the Expected Effects of ERA Ratification in North Carolina (1975).

Ronnie W. Faulkner
Additional research provided by Robert Blair Vocci.

Equal Rights League. The North Carolina State Equal Rights League, founded in 1865, grew out of the state's first freedmen's convention, held in Raleigh on 29 Sept. 1865. Although the state was ruled by Presidential Reconstruction (and effectively under military occupation), African Americans remained politically powerless. Led by provisional governor William W. Holden, North Carolina's white politicians had agreed a week earlier to hold a state convention in October to deal with the political actions required for reentry into the Union; they were prepared to repeal the Ordinance of Secession but would not consider granting the vote to freed slaves.

The convention of September 1865 was a clear attempt by black leaders to press for full political rights for African Americans, including the right to vote. The call for the meeting had originated in New Bern, which also produced the convention's first president, Pennsylvania native James W. Hood, an African Methodist Episcopal minister who had moved to New Bern as a church missionary in 1864. In his acceptance speech, Hood endorsed voting rights for all black males, but some of the 150 delegates disagreed, including James H. Harris of Raleigh.

Harris, a teacher, initially favored "moderation, reconciliation with whites, and education for blacks." He and Abraham H. Galloway of Wilmington engineered the passage of compromise resolutions to be presented at the state convention using "moderate and well-chosen language" supporting the protection and education of freedpeople and the elimination of racial discrimination in order to neutralize the original demand for black suffrage. Harris's personal charisma and shrewd leadership of the moderate wing quickly elevated him to prominence. When delegates voted to establish the Equal Rights League as the convention's vehicle for lobbying state and federal political leaders afterward, Harris was elected its first president.

By 1866 Harris was calling for full political rights for black men, including the right to vote and to hold office. His short-lived moderation on the issue was due, at least in part, to the intransigence of white Democrats, who allowed only limited civil and political rights to freedpeople under a new black code enacted by the 1866 General Assembly. In North Carolina, as in most southern states, Democrats and Conservatives still remained adamantly opposed to black suffrage; the legislature grudgingly accepted the Thirteenth Amendment abolishing slavery but denied that it gave Congress the power to rule on civil and political rights for freed slaves.

Only federal action, in fact, succeeded in forcing the issue; congressional passage of the 1867 Reconstruction Act extended voting rights to black males, who immediately registered as Republicans. By early 1868, the Republican Party suddenly controlled a majority of delegates to North Carolina's constitutional convention, thanks to the registration of more than 70,000 black voters. Among those chosen to write the state's new constitution was Harris, who soon became one of more than a dozen black members of the 1868 North Carolina General Assembly. With the onset of black male suffrage, the North Carolina chapter of the Equal Rights League had all but vanished by early 1868.

References: W. E. B. Du Bois, *Black Reconstruction in America, 1860–1880* (1992); Philip S. Foner and George E. Walker, eds., *Proceedings of the Black National and State Conventions, 1865–1900* (1986).

Benjamin R. Justesen

Escheats are items of property owned by a person who dies without leaving a will or known heirs, which therefore pass to the state. Technically limited to real estate, the term is commonly applied to personal property and has been extended to include unclaimed or abandoned property as well. From the time of its chartering in 1789, the University of North Carolina in Chapel Hill was assigned the benefits of escheats. The North Carolina Constitution now stipulates that escheats be used to provide scholarships for needy state residents enrolled in public institutions of higher education in North Carolina.

Reference: Blackwell Robinson, *The History of Escheats* (1955).

John V. Orth

Esse Quam Videri, the state motto of North Carolina, is a Latin phrase meaning "to be rather than to seem." Its origins are traced to Cicero's essay titled "Friendship." Distinguished jurist and historian Walter Clark selected the state motto and drafted the bill for its adoption in 1893. Senator Jacob Battle of Nash County introduced the bill in the General Assembly, and upon its passage the legislature directed that the motto be engraved on the great seal and coat of arms of the state. Prior to that time, the independent state of North Carolina had never adopted a motto. It was one of the very few American states and the last of the original 13 without one. Until North Carolina declared its independence, the colony maintained on its great seal the Latin phrase *Quae Sera Tamen Respexit*. Referring to the figure of Liberty on the seal, these words meant "Which, though late, looked upon me."

References: Walter Clark, "Our State Motto and Its Origin," *North Carolina Booklet* 9, no. 3 (January 1910); J. Bryan Grimes, *The History of the Great Seal of the State of North Carolina* (1909).

Daniel W. Barefoot

Estates Records are the documents generated by the disposition of a deceased person's property. They are created by executors (named in wills) or administrators (appointed by the court or an officer of the court when the deceased died intestate) whose job it is to settle the estate. Throughout its history North Carolina has seen significant changes in the laws regarding the settlement of estates. From 1777 to 1868 authority to oversee the affairs of executors, administrators, and guardians was held by the county court. After 1868 authority for probate became the function of the clerk of superior court.

Estates records are helpful resources for historians and genealogists. As a group they can reveal the details of social and economic life in a particular time and place. For family historians, they provide a unique look into the everyday lives of their ancestors and often assist in proving blood relationships. Modern estates records are kept in the offices of the clerk of superior court. Since 1966, estates records have been created as loose papers and placed in a decedent's individual estate file. Earlier estates records can be found in the North Carolina Archives. Counties send their older records to the Archives 60 years after probate. There, the loose papers are grouped together and filed alphabetically under the decedent's surname. They are placed in the records of the county of legal residence at the time of death. Early estates records, prior to 1777, can also be found in the Secretary of State Records or the Colonial Court Records, both of which are housed in the Archives.

References: William S. Price Jr., "Historical Origins of Wills and Estates Papers," *North Carolina Genealogical Society Journal* 3 (1977); Raymond A. Winslow Jr., "Estates Records," in Helen F. M. Leary, ed., *North Carolina Research, Genealogy, and Local History* (2nd ed., 1995).

Beverly Tetterton

Estatoe Path was a long-established Indian trail that linked the eighteenth-century Cherokee Lower Towns of northwestern South Carolina and northeastern Georgia with the French Broad River Valley in western North Carolina. It may have originated at the site of Old Estatoe, located on a branch of the Upper Tugalo River near Clayton, Ga. However, it is more often described as originating with the cluster of Lower Towns, including Keowee and a different town of Estatoe on the Upper Keowee River in South Carolina. This path headed north, crossing into North Carolina's present-day Transylvania County to the vicinity of Rosman, where a large Cherokee town was apparently located. The path then followed the French Broad River Valley and ultimately reached the Toe River Valley. It is possible that the Mitchell County community of Estatoe derived its name from the nearby path.

David G. Moore

Etchoe, Battle of. The Battle of Etchoe took place during the Cherokee War of 1760–61 between the Cherokee and the English. That war, a subconflict within the French and Indian War, began when whites murdered a number of Cherokees who were returning home from aiding the Virginians in their contest with the French. These murders, in addition to the mistreatment of some Cherokee women by the commander of Fort Prince George, led Cherokee warriors to attack whites on the Carolina frontier. A delegation of chiefs went to Charles Towne (Charleston, S.C.) to prevent the outbreak of a formal war, but Governor William Henry Lyttleton took the delegation hostage and returned them to Fort Prince George. There he demanded that the Cherokees turn in 24 warriors involved in the frontier killings before he would release the hostages.

Oconostota (Great Warrior), who had been a recent delegation hostage, led an attack on the fort to obtain the release of the Cherokees. The commander of the fort was killed, leading the soldiers to massacre the hostages. Col. Archibald Montgomery subsequently led 1,600 men in an attack on the Cherokees. After relieving Fort Prince George, Montgomery marched toward the Cherokee Middle Towns in western North Carolina.

On 27 June 1761, about eight miles south of Etchoe (near the present-day town of Otto at the deserted Cherokee town of Tessante Old Town), the first Battle of Etchoe took place. Oconostota ambushed Montgomery, killing 20 of his men and wounding 70, including Montgomery himself. Montgomery returned to Charles Towne to begin a new assignment, but meanwhile the Cherokees captured Fort Loudoun in present-day Tennessee. In response, Col. James Grant, a member of Montgomery's earlier expedition, led 2,400 men in a decisive blow against the Indians.

On 10 June 1761, about two miles south of Tessante Old Town and the site of the earlier battle, a second Battle of Etchoe took place. After nearly six hours of fighting, the Cherokees retreated and Grant went on to attack the Middle Towns, which had never been invaded before. Grant's expedition destroyed 15 towns and 15,000 acres of crops and drove 5,000 Cherokees into the remote mountains. Peace was signed with the Cherokees in September 1761.

Reference: David H. Corkran, *The Cherokee Frontier: Conflict and Survival, 1740–1762* (1962).

William L. Anderson

Eugenics Board. The North Carolina Eugenics Board, operating under the theories of the science of eugenics, or racial improvement through selective breeding, began its work in 1933 after the General Assembly passed a sterilization law. The new ordinance replaced a 1929 statute that had been declared unconstitutional. North Carolina was one of several states that created eugenics boards in the 1930s. Between 1929 and 1974, the North Carolina Eugenics Board approved the sterilization of more than 7,600 people, the third-highest figure in the nation behind California and Virginia. The vast majority of individuals sterilized were women who had been diagnosed as "feeble-minded" by various tests.

In 1883 English scientist Sir Frances Galton, a cousin of Charles Darwin, had proposed the science of eugenics, believing that humankind could only reach its full potential by increasing breeding among "desirable stock" and decreasing breeding among "undesirable stock." Sterilization was one of the methods adopted to restrict the increase of undesirable human beings. Many welfare proponents and lawmakers regarded sterilization as an acceptable solution in eliminating poverty and mental defectiveness.

The North Carolina Eugenics Board was composed of five members of state government: the commissioner of public welfare, the secretary of the state board of health, the chief medical officer of the state hospital at Raleigh (Dorothea Dix Hospital), the chief medical officer of a state mental institution outside Raleigh (this position rotated among the different institutions), and the attorney general. Well into the 1950s, white women comprised over three-fourths of those sterilized. This one-sided representation was probably because few African Americans received early welfare assistance and they remained unidentified. In addition, many of those sterilized were inmates of state mental institutions, and of the ten state-operated institutions, only three housed black inmates. When welfare benefits became available to minorities, the number of sterilizations performed on them increased.

Since the eugenics programs only touched people with little public influence, there was almost no local or national opposition to sterilization. Not until eugenics programs came under fire from civil rights and women's rights groups in the 1960s and 1970s did states discontinue sterilization and dissolve the boards. The North Carolina Eugenics Board, which had been one of the most active, was abolished in 1977.

In 2003 a movement to compensate those who had been sterilized began to gain strength in North Carolina. That April Governor Michael Easley—influenced greatly by "Against Their Will: North Carolina's Sterilization Program," a 2002 investigative series in the Winston-Salem Journal chronicling the history and effects of the state's eugenics program—officially apologized on behalf of the state government, appointed a Eugenics Study Committee, and signed legislation that removed all laws that sanctioned involuntary sterilization. Easley and the committee subsequently proposed granting sterilization victims, at state expense, a variety of benefits, including educational support, counseling, health care, and cash payments. The issue of reparations remained controversial, however. In April 2005 Forsyth County representative Larry Womble submitted legislation to the General Assembly that would set payment at $20,000 for every individual victimized by the state's eugenics program, but its future passage was unclear. Approximately 3,400 victims of sterilization were believed to still be alive in 2005.

References: Kevin Begos and David Ingram, "Bill Would Offer Cash Reparations to Victims of Eugenics Sterilization," Winston-Salem Journal, 24 Apr. 2005; Bonnie Rochman, "Sterilized by State Order," Raleigh News and Observer, 15 Apr. 2001; Robert Rollins and Ann Wolfe, "Eugenic Sterilization in North Carolina," North Carolina Medical Journal 12 (December 1973); Johanna Schoen, Choice and Coercion: Birth Control, Sterilization, and Abortion in Public Health and Welfare (2005); Moya Woodside, Sterilization in North Carolina: A Sociological and Psychological Study (1950).

Tom Belton

Eureka College was established by the North Carolina Free Will Baptists in 1898 as the Free Will Baptist Theological College in Pitt County. A building large enough to accommodate the school was erected on Lee Street in Ayden. The school enrolled pupils in a primary department and offered several curricula for students in the "higher branches"—including a theological department for the training of future ministers. The institution was coeducational from the beginning and educated hundreds of students between 1898 and 1925. In addition to the courses of study offered, there was an emphasis on spiritual and moral instruction and on character development.

By 1918 enrollment at the school was declining, in part because of the rapid growth of high schools in rural eastern North Carolina, which led to the establishment of a college curriculum by 1925. In 1926 the board gave a new name to the institution—Eureka College. Enrollment remained low, however, and continuing economic troubles caused it to close in 1931.

Reference: Michael R. Pelt, A History of Original Free Will Baptists (1996).

Michael R. Pelt

Evangelical and Reformed Church was the result of a 1934 merger of two historically German-American Protestant churches, the Evangelical Synod of North America and the Reformed Church in the United States. Virtually all of the resulting Evangelical and Reformed churches in North Carolina had been part of the Reformed Church in the United States.

The Reformed Church in the United States had its origin among the Pennsylvania Dutch in the early eighteenth century. These people came to America from German-speaking areas of Europe and included Protestant groups from both Lutheran and Reformed traditions. By the end of the century, the Reformed groups felt the need to create a formal, American church organization, founding the Synod of the Reformed (High) German Church in the United States of America in 1793. This tradition came to North Carolina largely through the migration of Pennsylvania Dutch families, beginning in the middle of the eighteenth century, to what are now Catawba, Lincoln, Rowan, Cabarrus, Davidson, Forsyth, Guilford, and Alamance Counties. In 1831 members of 16 congregations organized the North Carolina Classis of the German Reformed Church, bringing local governance to the churches that until then had been governed from Pennsylvania. The classis founded Catawba College in Newton in 1851. The college moved to Salisbury in 1925.

The Evangelical Synod of North America also traced its origins back to German-speaking immigrants, those immigrating to the Midwest in the middle of the nineteenth century. These people left Germany after the 1817 Evangelical Union in Germany, which had united the Reformed and Lutheran churches into the Evangelical Church. These immigrants formed a number of synods that eventually joined together into the German Evangelical Synod of North America in 1877.

Although the Evangelical and Reformed Church was created in 1934, it was not until 1939 that North Carolina churches were fully integrated into the new denomination by the formation of the Southern Synod of the church. The Southern Synod was initially made up of 62 congregations with 11,000 members, mostly in North Carolina. These churches were concentrated in the same areas where the Pennsylvania Dutch had settled almost 200 years earlier, and there are still concentrations of former Reformed churches around Hickory, Lexington, and Burlington. The Evangelical and Reformed Church merged with the Congregational Christian Church in 1957 to form the United Church of Christ.

References: Robert T. Fauth, ed., *The Evangelical Synod: One Hundred and Fifty Years, 1840–1990* (1990); Jacob Calvin Leonard, *The Southern Synod of the Evangelical and Reformed Church* (1940).

Thomas K. Tiemann

Evolution, Teaching of. Conflicts involving the teaching of the theory of evolution in North Carolina schools came to the state in 1920 when T. T. Martin, a Mississippi native, criticized William Louis Poteat for teaching evolution in biology classes at Wake Forest College. Poteat, a biology professor and president of the college—as well as past president of both the North Carolina Academy of Science and the State Baptist Convention (SBC)—was placed in a difficult position. The SBC, which controlled Wake Forest College, was more theologically conservative than the college faculty, and the issue of teaching evolutionary theory was to be settled by a simple majority vote on a resolution at the SBC's annual meeting.

Martin and other antievolutionists accused Poteat of undermining biblical faith, thinking like a German militarist, and misappropriating school funds. They further held that the idea of evolution was responsible for virtually everything that was wrong with contemporary culture, from secularism, heresy, and sexual immorality to juvenile delinquency, atheism, and

the "disintegration of the family." Poteat faced his detractors at the state convention in December 1922, when he argued for academic freedom in general instead of defending evolution specifically. The result was the passage of a resolution supporting Poteat and his values. Fundamentalist Baptists tried a second time in 1925 to have the state convention condemn the theory of evolution and Poteat, but they again failed.

A second front for antievolutionary sentiment in the state arose in the General Assembly after David Scott Poole, running on a platform of opposition to Darwinism, was elected to the House of Representatives. His bill to prohibit the teaching of evolution in all tax-supported schools, including state universities, was passed by the Education Committee in January 1925. Sam J. Ervin Jr., then a first-year representative, later recalled the floor debate on the Poole Bill as the most interesting debate of his entire career. The Poole Bill failed, thanks to legislators who were alumni of the University of North Carolina or Wake Forest. A second Poole Bill also failed in 1927.

The curriculum guides for science education in North Carolina's public schools, revised occasionally by the Department of Public Instruction, have been consistently supportive of evolutionary principles. The guides of 1930 and 1935 endorsed the teaching of evolution and recommended certain facts to illustrate it. The 1941 guide was nothing less than an explicit, adamant, and detailed statement of evolutionary science. The 1953 and 1958 guides reaffirmed those policies.

Anecdotal evidence suggests that some North Carolina schools suppressed the teaching of evolution, some presented it as scientific fact, and many found middle-of-the-road compromises, balancing explicit teaching of evolution with religious tolerance for those who could not accept its assumptions. In one notable incident in November 1971, the Gaston County Board of Education fired a substitute teacher for raising the topic of evolution and for offering incendiary opinions about the Bible in a junior high school history class. The teacher, George I. Moore III, sued in federal district court to regain his job, appealing to principles of academic freedom and the separation of church and state. The court ruled in Moore's favor.

While antievolutionary sentiment persisted across many decades, it lay dormant as a major public issue in North Carolina from 1927 until the early 1980s. Creationist successes in California, Arkansas, and Louisiana, and the rise of a powerful evangelical "Christian Right" in national politics, had again made the teaching of evolution a heated issue, and debate over the topic rekindled in the state. Jack Cavanagh, a first-year Republican senator from Forsyth County, introduced a bill in the General Assembly in 1981 to require that North Carolina's public schools teach evolution and creationism on equal terms in their science classes. The antievolution bills of the 1920s (including Tennessee's Butler Act and North Carolina's Poole Bills) had been intended to outlaw the teaching of evolution

Did Not Come From HIM 👉
NEITHER DID YOU!
I May Look Like Him, But
I Refuse to Claim Kin
On This I Stand!

J. Sherwood Upchurch

They are Going to Talk About Him in the Next
LEGISLATURE
So They Say
I WANT TO BE THERE!

J. Sherwood Upchurch, an opponent of the teaching of evolution in North Carolina schools, used this political broadside in his 1926 campaign for the state legislature. He lost the election, but he ran again two years later and won. NCC.

on the grounds that it contradicted the Bible. But those of the 1980s, including Cavanagh's, had a different goal; namely, inserting creationism into the public school science curriculum without trying to ban the teaching of evolution. Cavanagh's bill died in committee without attracting a single cosponsor, either Democrat or Republican.

Conservative Christians again tried to influence the status of evolution in the public school science curriculum in 1985, when they lobbied against the Standard Course of Study, a comprehensive curriculum for grades K–12 prepared by the Department of Public Instruction that emphasized critical reasoning. Ann Frazier, one of the Standard Course of Study's most vocal critics, accused it of being humanistic, anti-Christian, antifamily, and anti-God. (Actually, this document tiptoed around the creation-evolution controversy by never using the word "evolution" explicitly, although it certainly espoused evolutionary principles throughout its section on science.) The State Board of Education endorsed the Standard Course of Study in 1985. Also that year, the General Assembly approved a plan to finance it. Thus ended legislative efforts either to diminish evolution or to elevate creationism in the public school science curriculum.

However, creationist sentiment remained vibrant in many places throughout the state into the 2000s. North Carolina's creationists work through several local organizations, the most visible of which is perhaps the Triangle Association for Scientific Creationism. Creationist views are nurtured by a subculture of conservative Protestantism, and their principal source of inspiration, both spiritual and scientific, is the Institute for Creation Research in California. On the other side of the debate are groups such as the North Carolina Science Teachers Association, which defends evolution as unequivocal scientific fact and essential to a proper understanding of human life and civilization.

References: Willard B. Gatewood, *Preachers, Pedagogues, and Politicians: The Evolution Controversy in North Carolina, 1920–1927* (1966); Suzanne Linder, "William Louis Poteat and the Evolution Controversy," *NCHR* 40 (April 1963); Christopher P. Toumey, *God's Own Scientists: Creationists in a Secular World* (1994).

Christopher P. Toumey

SEE ALSO Poole Bills.

Executive Organization Acts. The General Assembly of 1969 approved seven amendments to the state constitution to be submitted to the North Carolina electorate. On 3 Nov. 1970 voters accepted six of these amendments, one of which required the legislature to reduce the more than 300 administrative departments, agencies, and offices to no more than 25 principal departments by 1 July 1975. To make the administrative structure more manageable and more efficient, the General Assembly in 1971 passed the first of two Executive Organization Acts. This law created 19 principal offices or departments, 10 of which—governor, lieutenant governor, secretary of state, state auditor, state treasurer, superintendent of public instruction, attorney general, and commissioners of agriculture, labor, and insurance—were to be popularly elected. The other 9 departments, including those covering transportation, commerce, cultural and natural resources, and military affairs, were to be headed by gubernatorial appointees.

This reorganization was favorably received by the majority of legislators and influential state newspapers. In a speech to the General Assembly two months before the measure was passed, Governor Robert W. Scott asserted that "through a consolidation of departments, agencies, and boards performing the same or similar functions, we will be in a position to demand that the units of governmental management get in step with one another." Scott left office in January 1973 convinced that his plan for reorganization would be implemented by his successor, and that subsequent administrations would complete it.

The second phase of reorganization, the Executive Organization Act of 1973, was passed early in the administration of Governor James E. Holshouser Jr., the first Republican governor elected in twentieth-century North Carolina. This law affected only the Department of Cultural Resources (the new name, effective 1 July 1973, of the Department of Art, Culture, and History), the Department of Human Resources, and the Department of Revenue. This reorganization and others of later years received less attention than had the 1971 law. A flurry of media attention did occur following the announcement in December 1973 that H. G. Jones, director of the Division of Archives and History of the Department of Cultural Resources (and its predecessor, the Department of Archives and History), intended to resign in protest of the reorganization. Within two years, other critics had joined Jones in declaring that the state reorganization was a failure. Some argued that the state government had become more remote and costly rather than more efficient and responsive, citing the creation of hundreds of middle-management jobs, with many employees drawing executive salaries for jobs once done by lower-level employees. In many cases department heads were given salaries double the original salary, and numerous lower-level bureaucrats were suddenly elevated to deputy or assistant department heads with their salaries increased accordingly.

In 1979—more than six years after he had left office—former governor Scott charged that the Holshouser and James B. Hunt administrations had not been "serious enough about government to make . . . reorganization of state government

work effectively." Although their success is debatable, the acts of 1971 and 1973 permanently changed the structure of North Carolina state government.

Reference: Jack D. Fleer, *North Carolina Government and Politics* (1994).

Wiley J. Williams

Exodusters were African Americans who fled North Carolina because of economic and political grievances after the Reconstruction era. Although there was a steady trickle of black emigrants from the state before 1900, the outflow assumed such immense proportions during two periods that it was labeled an "exodus." The first mass departure took place from 1877 to 1880, peaking in 1879. It resulted in part from an amendment of the 1876 Landlord and Tenant Act that required a tenant to pay for supplies and rent before he received any part of his crop. Blacks were also troubled by the county government system, under which the legislature chose justices of the peace who, in turn, appointed commissioners to administer county government. The white commissioners in eastern counties with dense black populations prevented African Americans from gaining a foothold.

In the late 1870s, whereas most blacks from other southern states mainly migrated to Kansas, many black North Carolinians went to Indiana. One black, Sam L. Perry, was credited with masterminding this exodus. Eastern newspapers, including the *Wilmington Morning Star*, *Tarboro Southerner*, and *Kinston Journal*, charged that Perry and other leaders hoped to pack Indiana with African American Republicans before the 1880 presidential election. Many whites also blamed emigrant agents for luring blacks away with false claims. The movement gradually subsided, although some North Carolina blacks continued to migrate to South Carolina, Georgia, and Alabama.

In the second large migration, approximately 50,000 blacks left the state in a 15-month period during 1889–90. The exodus began in March 1889 after passage of the Payne Election Law, which threatened to restrict the voting rights of blacks. It required a prospective voter to give "as near as may be" his age, occupation, place of birth, full name, residence, and township from which he had moved (if applicable). The law gave broad powers to registrars, who could warn an individual to give correct information or allow him to be imprecise—for example, give his initials rather than his full name—and risk being subsequently disqualified. The mortgage and crop lien system, as well as the agricultural recession caused by low cotton prices and short crops, also contributed to the large migration.

The General Assembly of 1891, labeled the "Farmers' Alliance" legislature, passed a law that required an emigrant agent—defined as one who hired blacks for employment outside the state—to purchase an annual license in each county in which the agent operated for $1,000. Violation of the act constituted a misdemeanor punishable by a fine of $500–$5,000 or 4–24 months' imprisonment for each offense. The statute applied only to specified counties. In 1893 the North Carolina Supreme Court declared it unconstitutional on the grounds that an occupation was taxed inconsistently (in some but not all counties). Meanwhile, the out-migration had begun to subside. The exodusters of 1877–80 and 1889–90 moved from rural to rural areas, whereas the mass departures of blacks during the twentieth century were often rural-to-urban migrations.

References: Frenise A. Logan, *The Negro in North Carolina, 1876–1894* (1964); Nell Irvin Painter, *Exodusters: Black Migration to Kansas after Reconstruction* (1977); Joseph F. Steelman, "The Progressive Era in North Carolina, 1884–1917" (Ph.D. diss., UNC-Chapel Hill, 1955).

Lala Carr Steelman

"Experimental Railroad" usually refers to the mile-and-a-quarter road built by the Experimental Railroad Company of Raleigh in 1832–33 (at a cost of $2,700) to allow horse-drawn cars to transport stone needed for rebuilding the State Capitol, which had burned in June 1831. On Sunday afternoons, ladies and gentlemen desiring to take a railroad airing would travel from adjoining counties to ride on the road's "handsome car," as would legislators when they were in town. The railroad, considered by some historians to be the first in the state, proved to be a great success and stimulated considerable interest in railroad construction. Subsequently, two Internal Improvement Commissions, meeting in Raleigh in July and November 1833, urged the General Assembly to assist private capital in building railroads.

Wiley J. Williams

Exploration, European. Beginning in the fifteenth century, the European powers of France, Spain, Portugal, and England launched several voyages to explore the New World, including the region that would become North Carolina. Their initial motivation was primarily economic: after the "discovery" of America by Christopher Columbus in 1492, several navigators followed in his wake searching for the riches of the Orient. National rivalries soon began to fuel the quest to discover and acquire the treasures of new lands and create colonies that would serve as financial boons to the mother country. Spain and France became early leaders in the race to explore and colonize the New World. England, by contrast, did not develop a significant interest in exploration and settlement until the reign of Queen Elizabeth I in the second half of the sixteenth century.

Initial European Expeditions

The exact identity of the first European to make landfall along the coast of present-day North Carolina is a matter of much speculation and debate. Some historians maintain that various navigators in classical antiquity visited North America, but there is no tangible proof that they set foot in North Carolina. Others make the case that Norsemen passed through the area, citing among other reasons the similarity of eleventh-century Norse descriptions of Vinland and its grapes and Englishman Arthur Barlowe's sixteenth-century accounts of the profusion of grapes growing wild along the Outer Banks. If any of these ancient mariners did in fact sail along the coast of North America, they would of necessity have been acquainted with the treacherous waters of the Carolina coast.

Explorers such as Giovanni Caboto (John Cabot) and Amerigo Vespucci are reputed to have coasted along the southeastern seaboard of North America, but, as in the case of earlier navigators, there is no proof that these voyagers went as far south as the North Carolina coast. The Cantino map of 1503 is thought to contain a representation of the eastern coastline of North America with many landmarks given Portuguese names. The name of the explorer who gathered this information and the exact date and nature of his voyage are unknown. Many scholars believe that the map does not even represent North America but is instead a chart of a small section of the Yucatan Peninsula misplaced by a careless cartographer.

The first documented exploration of the North Carolina coast may have been a Spanish expedition hunting for slaves along the coast stretching from modern Georgia to North Carolina. Two boats made up this expedition, one ship commanded by Pedro de Quejo, another by Francisco Gordillo. Both men were slavers, the latter employed by Lucas Vasquez de Ayllon. Gordillo received directions on how to reach the land north of the Bahamas from Pedro de Salazar, who had apparently gained firsthand knowledge of the coast from a slave raid he had conducted about 1514. Whether Salazar had raided as far north as the present North Carolina coast is unknown. The Spaniards landed somewhere along the coast of an area the natives called "Chicora" in June 1521. The exact location of the landing site is uncertain, but some historians place it on the present coast of South Carolina.

The first European expedition that is known beyond any doubt to have explored the coast of modern North Carolina was led by Florentine navigator Giovanni da Verrazano. Sailing in the employ of France, Verrazano sighted land near Cape Fear on 21 Mar. 1524. After a cursory examination of the coast to the south, he and his men returned to Cape Fear, where they finally went ashore. Verrazano believed that the Outer Banks was all that separated the Atlantic Ocean from a branch of the Pacific, and a passage through this sandy barrier would thus provide a new route to the riches of the Orient. For years afterward, this "isthmus" appeared on maps of the North American coastline. Verrazano's men put back to sea and continued north, landing along the North Carolina coast two more times.

In 1526 Ayllon personally led a colony of 500 people to a place they called the "Rio Jordan." The exact location of Rio Jordan has been much debated; some scholars place it on Cape Fear, others south of the cape on Winyah Bay. Wherever it was, the Spaniards remained there only long enough to build a ship to replace one that was wrecked at the entrance to this river. The colonists moved down the coast to what they expected would be a more suitable locale.

In May 1539 an expedition under noted conquistador Hernando De Soto dropped anchor in Tampa Bay to begin an extensive exploration of the interior regions of the land the Spaniards called "La Florida." De Soto's party, which originally consisted of 650 men, 12 priests, 300 pigs, bloodhounds, and various other beasts and equipage, spent four years exploring much of what later became the southeastern United States. During its second season in the field, the expedition traveled through the mountains of southwestern North Carolina. The explorers crossed the Little Tennessee River, gaining the distinction of being the first Europeans to cross a tributary of the Mississippi. They encountered, and often harshly treated, various Indian communities, including those that are believed to be the ancestors of the modern Cherokee tribe, but they failed to achieve one of their main objectives—finding gold.

In August 1566 Domingo Fernandez sailed north for Chesapeake Bay with 20 men and some Dominican priests. The travelers experienced strong winds off the North Carolina coast and were forced to seek shelter at an inlet at 36° north latitude. The Spaniards sailed into Currituck Sound, landed, and planted a cross claiming the territory for Spain. They spent time exploring the Currituck Sound region before putting back to sea and resuming their original journey. Due to the strong winds, they never reached Chesapeake Bay.

Also in 1566 a Spanish expedition under Capt. Juan Pardo marched north with 25 men from St. Helena Sound, in modern South Carolina. In the foothills of the Blue Ridge Mountains, Pardo built a fort, where he left Sgt. Hernando Moyano and a few of his men before returning to the coast for the winter. The following spring, Pardo returned to the fort, picked up his men, and continued northward, exploring the mountains of present-day North Carolina and Tennessee before heading in a roundabout fashion back to St. Helena Sound.

Sir Walter Raleigh and the Arrival of the English

Queen Elizabeth and her subjects became troubled by Spain's growing wealth provided by its New World colonies and believed that this advantage would inevitably undermine England's cultural identity (particularly its national Protestant faith) and economic independence. In an effort to slow their enemy's progress, Englishmen such as Francis Drake, Richard Grenville, and Thomas Cavendish captured Spanish treasure ships as well as attacked and destroyed Spain's American outposts. The amazing treasures acquired by these actions—gold, silver, jewels, spices, and lumber—excited people of all classes of English society and inspired in them a deep curiosity and an almost manic desire to see and obtain more of America's riches.

Sir Walter Raleigh assumed leadership of England's colonization movement in 1583 after the death of his half brother Sir Humphrey Gilbert, who had convinced the queen that her only recourse was to defeat Spain by aggressively exploring and settling the New World. Raleigh's determination was rewarded in March 1584, when Elizabeth granted a charter allowing him to organize an expedition for the purpose of finding suitable colonization sites in North America.

On 27 Apr. 1584 Capts. Philip Amadas and Arthur Barlowe set sail from Plymouth to scout for a location for Raleigh's proposed colony. On 4 July 1584 they sighted the North American coast and sailed north for 120 miles before finding a suitable inlet that their ships could enter. After anchoring inside the inlet, they landed on a nearby island and claimed the territory for their queen. On this island, either present-day Ocracoke or Hatteras, they made first contact with the natives and began to trade with them. After several days, Barlowe and seven companions took a trip to these natives' home. Barlowe noted that they traveled "twenty miles into the river that runs toward Skicoak, which river they call Occam; and the evening following we came to an island, which they call Roanoke, distant from the harbor by which we entered seven leagues." At Roanoke they were entertained by the Indians and obtained much information about the country. But this was the extent of their explorations. Returning to their ships, they set sail for England, which they reached in September 1584.

In June 1585 Sir Richard Grenville arrived with 107 colonists aboard two ships off Wocokon (modern Ocracoke). From there, the Croatoan Indian Manteo was dispatched to the mainland to send word of the arrival of the Englishmen to King Wingina. Not wishing to waste time, Grenville and several of his men left Wocokon in two boats for an eight-day exploration of the southern reaches of Pamlico Sound. They visited several Indian towns, including Pomeiok, Aquascogoc, and Secotan; they were "well entertained there [at Secotan]" by the natives. Grenville also discovered a "great lake" that the Indians called "Paquipe."

On their return to Ocracoke, the Englishmen moved up the Outer Banks and anchored off "Hatorask" (modern Hatteras Island). Grenville deposited his colonists on Roanoke Island before setting sail for England on 25 Aug. 1585. Under the command of Ralph Lane, the colonists who remained engaged in extensive explorations over the next year. Their ramblings took them north to the Chesapeake Bay and up the Chowan River to the junction of the Meherrin and Nottoway Rivers.

Perhaps this group's best-known exploration was up the

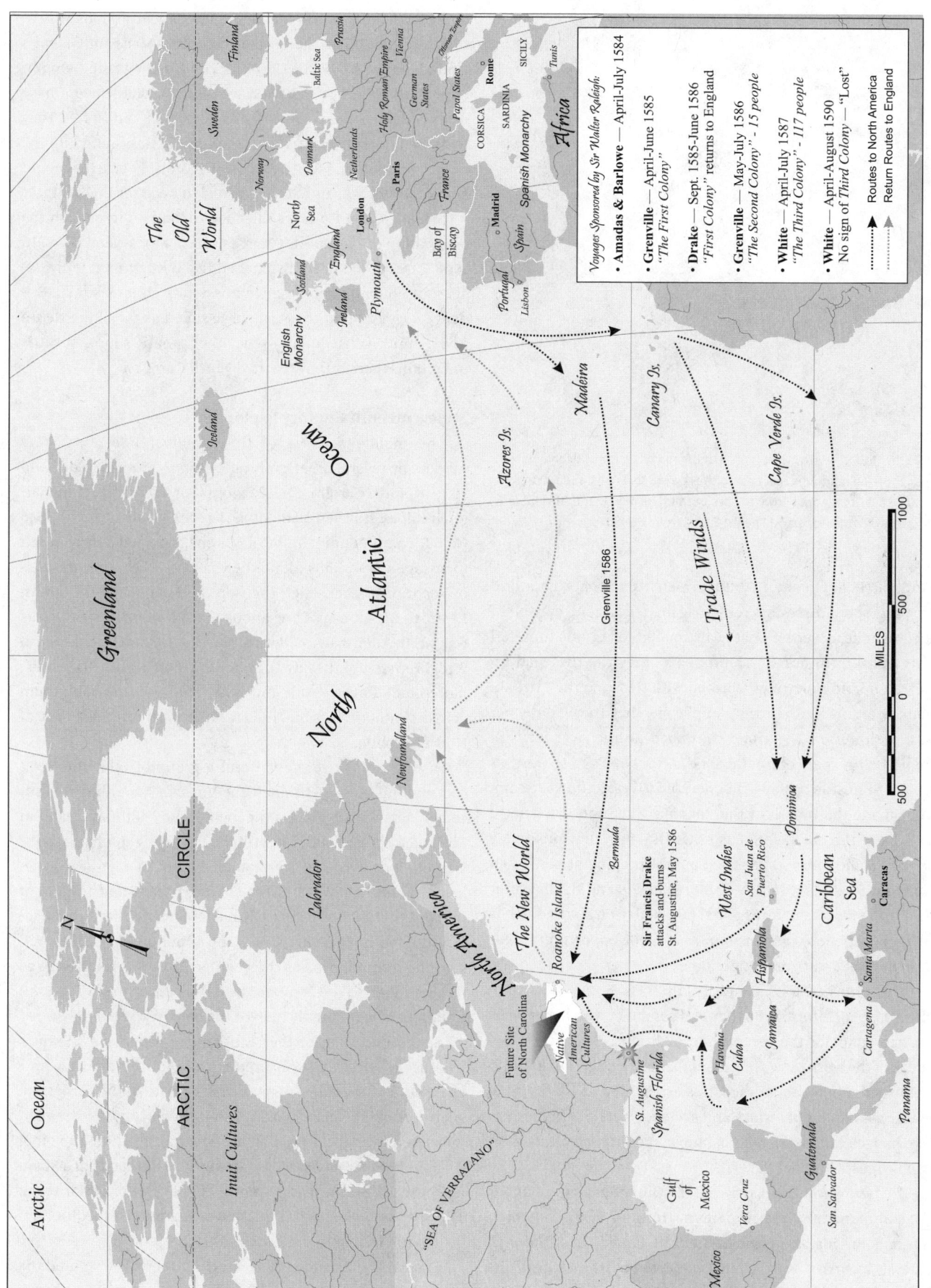

Arctic Ocean

Greenland

ARCTIC CIRCLE

Inuit Cultures

Labrador

Newfoundland

North America

North Atlantic Ocean

The Old World

Finland
Sweden
Norway
Denmark
Prussia
Baltic Sea
Holy Roman Empire
Vienna
German States
Papal States
Rome
Netherlands
Paris
France
England
Scotland
Ireland
Plymouth
London
North Sea
Bay of Biscay
Portugal
Lisbon
Spain
Madrid
Spanish Monarchy
CORSICA
SARDINIA
SICILY
Tunis
Africa

English Monarchy

Ireland

Azores Is.

Madeira

Canary Is.

Cape Verde Is.

Trade Winds

Grenville 1586

Bermuda

The New World

Roanoke Island

Future Site of North Carolina

Native American Cultures

St. Augustine
Spanish Florida

Sir Francis Drake attacks and burns St. Augustine, May 1586

West Indies

San Juan de Puerto Rico

Hispaniola

Havana
Cuba

Jamaica

Caribbean Sea

Cartagena
Santa Marta
Caracas

Dominica

Panama

Guatemala

San Salvador

Gulf of Mexico

Vera Cruz

Mexico

"SEA OF VERRAZANO"

N

MILES
500   0   500   1000

Voyages Sponsored by Sir Walter Raleigh:

- **Amadas & Barlowe** — April-July 1584

- **Grenville** — April-June 1585
  "The First Colony"

- **Drake** — Sept. 1585-June 1586
  "First Colony" returns to England

- **Grenville** — May-July 1586
  "The Second Colony" - 15 people

- **White** — April-July 1587
  "The Third Colony" - 117 people

- **White** — April-August 1590
  No sign of *Third Colony* — "Lost"

········▶ Routes to North America
········▶ Return Routes to England

Roanoke Voyages. Map by Mark Anderson Moore, courtesy NCOA&H.

Gold ring found by archaeologists near Buxton on Hatteras Island in 2005, bearing markings that date to the late 1580s. Englishmen searching for the Lost Colony are known to have been in the region at that time. Courtesy of Professor David Phelps, East Carolina University.

Moratok (Roanoke) River. With 40 men in two boats, Lane and his party spent three days rowing against the strong current of the Roanoke, covering what he estimated to be "one hundred sixty miles from home." The Indians along the river had retreated inland, carrying their food with them, so the Englishmen were unable to obtain supplies as they traveled deeper into the interior. The group continued up the river but still found no prospect of finding food. After Lane's men were attacked by hostile Indians, they decided to return downstream. They made the mouth of the Roanoke after one day's travel and spent the day before Easter waiting for the winds to lay so they could cross Albemarle Sound, stopping at some fish weirs for food. They returned to Roanoke Island the day after Easter in 1586. Then, fearing that they had been abandoned by their countrymen, Lane's colonists took the opportunity of Sir Francis Drake's arrival to sail home.

They returned to England in July 1586. Besides the valuable practical information they had gathered, which appeared on new maps of the area, this expedition is significant because of the work of two of its members: Thomas Harriot, who published a book about the lands explored; and John White, whose watercolor paintings and sketches were the first extensive images of American flora, fauna, and Indian culture seen by Europeans.

The next colonists to arrive on the Outer Banks were under the command of White, who was a strong advocate of settling the region. This group constituted the famed "Lost Colony," and any record of explorations conducted by its members disappeared with them. In 1602 Samuel Mace led an expedition to America financed by Raleigh. One of its missions was to seek information on the missing colonists. Mace and his men landed along the North Carolina coast somewhere between Cape Fear and Cape Lookout, where they established a base from which to search for medicinal plants and herbs. They remained in their camp about a month before sailing up the coast toward Roanoke. A severe storm broke before they could land on Hatorask, and Mace decided to head for England.

Raleigh's Lost Colony continued to have an impact on the exploration of present-day North Carolina for several years. In 1608 Capt. John Smith dispatched two unidentified individuals south on a reconnaissance mission from Jamestown. Evidence suggests that they may have sailed as far as the Neuse River. Smith subsequently sent other groups south, but it is uncertain whether they reached North Carolina.

Seventeenth-Century Explorers

The middle decades of the seventeenth century were marked by several other explorations in the future colony and state of North Carolina. In 1622 John Pory, secretary of the Virginia colony, traveled 60 miles along the Chowan River. In 1646 Gen. Richard Bennett and Col. Thomas Dew led a force south to engage the Indians along the Chowan River. They traveled by sea to Currituck Inlet, then up the Roanoke and Chowan Rivers to the mouth of Weyanook Creek, where the battle was fought. In August 1650 Edward Bland, Abraham Woode, Sackford Brewster, and Elias Pennant left Fort Henry, Va., to explore lands to the south and west. Their journey took them across southern Virginia and into the northern Piedmont of North Carolina.

In July 1653 Roger Green and a group of inhabitants on Nansemond River petitioned the Virginia Assembly to grant 10,000 acres to the first 100 people "who shall first seate on Moratuck or Roanoke river and the land lying upon the south side of Choan river and branches thereof." Green was given 1,000 acres "in reward of his charge, hazard and trouble of first discoverie." The extent of Green's explorations into the interior of North Carolina is unknown, but an old Indian trail running from Virginia to the Pee Dee River was referred to as "Green's Path to the Pee Dee" as late as the 1770s, when John Collet included it on his map of the colony.

At the invitation of the "Emperor of Rhoanoke," Francis Yeardley of Virginia sponsored a group of traders who traveled south in the fall of 1653 to visit the site of the earlier English fort on Roanoke Island. From there, some of the men journeyed overland to the Neuse River area, where they met with the "Emperor of the Tuskarorawes," who spoke of a Spaniard who had been living among his people for seven years. The Spaniard's identity is unknown. Yeardley's expedition returned to Virginia in the spring of 1654.

Capt. William Hilton of Massachusetts twice explored the coasts of North Carolina and South Carolina for potential colonization by fellow New Englanders. His first journey occurred between August and November 1662. Aboard his ship *Adventure*, Hilton and his companions traversed the lower part of the Cape Fear River, which they called the "Charles River," upstream for "15 or 16 leagues." Later Hilton sailed to Barbados and there made the acquaintance of parties interested in establishing a colony on the North American mainland, thus prompting his second visit to North Carolina. In early August 1663 Hilton departed Spikes Bay, Barbados, in the service of "several Gentlemen and Merchants of the island of Barbadoes." For the next two months, he and his crew explored the rivers and tributaries of Lower Cape Fear.

In May 1670 German explorer John Lederer set out overland from the falls of the James River in Virginia on a trek to the south and west. Initially, he was accompanied by a Major Harris and five Indians, but his companions refused to go farther than a branch of the James River. Lederer continued on his own, escorted by one Indian guide. There has been much debate as to Lederer's actual route. Most historians maintain that he made it as far south as the Catawba and Cheraw in the vicinity of modern Charlotte before returning to Virginia through land occupied by the Tuscarora. Though many have ridiculed Lederer's description of a "desert" in the North Carolina interior, it is actually an apt portrayal of the Sandhills region in summer.

With Lederer's travels, one and a half centuries of European exploration drew to a close. Trailblazers had traversed virtually every section of North Carolina. Settlers and colonists followed in their wake, carving homes from the wilderness and adding details to the rough maps supplied by the early pathfinders.

References: Alan V. Briceland, *Westward from Virginia: The Exploration of the Virginia-Carolina Frontier, 1650–1710* (1987); David Corbitt, ed., *Explorations, Descriptions, and Attempted Settlements of Carolina, 1584–1590* (1953); Ivor Noel Hume, *The Virginia Adventure, Roanoke to Jamestown: An Archaeological and Historical Odyssey* (1994); William S. Powell, "Carolana and the Incomparable Roanoke: Explorations and Attempted Settlements, 1620–1663," *NCHR* 51 (January 1974); David B. Quinn, *England and the Discovery of America, 1481–1620* (1974); L. A. Vigneras, "A Spanish Discovery of North Carolina in 1566," *NCHR* 46 (Autumn 1969).

John Hairr

SEE ALSO Amadas and Barlowe Expedition; De Soto Expedition; Lederer Expedition; Lost Colony; Pardo Expeditions; Roanoke Voyages; Verrazano Expedition.

Exports. North Carolina has produced and transported commercial exports since its establishment as an English colony. The primary exports from the colony were products of the forest. By the 1720s naval stores, including turpentine, rosin, tar, and pitch (used for painting, caulking, and preservation of wood and rope), became valuable exports highly sought after by the Royal Navy and the British merchant fleet. Hundreds of thousands of barrels of naval stores worth £50,000 annually and produced from the longleaf pine forests along the Cape Fear River Valley were shipped from Wilmington. Lumber products, primarily cypress shingles and barrel staves, hoops, and headings, were exported by the millions to British colonies in the West Indies and New England as well as to England. Oak bark was also a significant export to England from the colony for use in tanning leather.

Foodstuffs constituted another important category of exports from colonial North Carolina. By the early 1770s, almost 180,000 bushels of corn were being shipped annually to New England via the Albemarle Sound. Much of the wheat crop grown in the colony was destined for export, and beans and peas were shipped to the British West Indies and New England in substantial quantities. Herds of cattle or hogs were driven to markets as far away as Charleston, S.C., Philadelphia, and Lancaster, Pa. Salted meat and fish were also shipped to England and the West Indies. Tobacco was grown mainly in the Albemarle Sound region bordering Virginia. Cured tobacco was packed in 1,000-pound hogsheads and transported to Glasgow by Scottish merchants or to New England in ships owned by Massachusetts or Rhode Island interests.

North Carolina's export trade was severely curtailed by the onset of the Revolutionary War. The colony lost access to its two major markets, England and the British West Indies, as a result of British naval and privateer activity as well as restrictions by the American Continental Congress on trade with the British. Following the war, foreign trade began to revive in the mid-1780s. Naval stores regained their prominence as the most valuable export, but their primary destination became New England. Foodstuffs and lumber products continued to be important export items to the West Indies and northern states. Tobacco exports increased significantly, from 360,000 pounds in 1768 to 6 million pounds in 1788.

In the first decades of the nineteenth century, North Carolina's primitive transportation network and its lack of rich natural resources, a good deepwater seaport, or large-scale manufacturing all hindered the state's economic development. In 1816 only $1.3 million worth of goods were exported from all of the state's ports, mostly carried in New England ships. The northern counties of North Carolina traded primarily with Virginia, while the southern Piedmont and western counties traded with South Carolina and Tennessee.

In the late 1830s, the economic outlook of the state began to improve. The Wilmington & Weldon Railroad steered a greater portion of export goods to Wilmington, at the expense of Norfolk, Va. The North Carolina Railroad, constructed in the 1850s and running from Charlotte to Raleigh and Goldsboro, linked western North Carolina and the Piedmont with the eastern ports and played a critical role in the development of manufacturing and agriculture in the state.

The outbreak of the Civil War dealt another devastating blow to the North Carolina export trade. Wilmington soon became the Confederacy's sole significant outlet to the world in the face of the Union naval blockade. Only about 270 ships, most owned by English and Scottish merchants, successfully ran the blockade in the years before Wilmington was captured in January 1865. The most lucrative outbound cargoes were cotton, tobacco, and turpentine, carried by the blockade-runners to Bermuda and Nassau, then shipped to England and other European destinations.

Beginning in the 1870s, the economy of North Carolina was transformed under the influence of northern capital and the Industrial Revolution. By 1880 textile output in the state had doubled over prewar levels. Many mills spun coarse yarn that was exported to markets in Philadelphia and New York, while others wove and exported various cloths, towels, clothing, and other products. Agricultural products continued to be major exports from North Carolina. After the U.S. Army Corps of Engineers deepened the Cape Fear River channel into Wilmington harbor, cotton exports increased significantly. By 1887, 170,000 bales were being shipped out of the port annually, with about two-thirds going to Liverpool, England, and much of the remainder heading to New York. Peanuts became a significant commercial crop and export after 1900. North Carolina wood products in the form of lumber and shingles continued to be sought after in Boston, New York, Philadelphia, and Baltimore. Naval stores were still exported by Norwegian, German, and British ships to European ports, but demand began to decline toward the end of the nineteenth century with the introduction of iron ships and synthetic substitutes for turpentine.

War once again disrupted North Carolina trade in 1914. Exports out of Wilmington dropped by 50 percent that year due to the loss of the German cotton market, the diversion of merchant ships to wartime needs, and the threat posed by German submarines. However, the war stimulated great demand for textiles in American markets. By the early 1920s, North Carolina had become the nation's leading textile- and tobacco-producing state, and its furniture industry was expanding rapidly. During the decade other companies, including wood pulp and paper producers, fertilizer makers, and cottonseed oil producers, also began to supply exports.

North Carolina exporting was deeply affected by the Great Depression, as annual export tonnage out of Wilmington dropped from 25,000 tons in the late 1920s to about 14,000 tons in 1930 before recovering in the middle of the decade. Tobacco exports increased, but cotton exports fell dramatically due to low crop values caused by overproduction, competition from Texas, depredation by the boll weevil, and development of synthetic fabrics. By the beginning of World War II, Wil-

mington had been reduced to the role of a local port, serving regions of North Carolina, South Carolina, and Tennessee not covered by the ports of Norfolk and Charleston and handling only bulk cargoes, since it lacked facilities for packaged and containerized goods.

World War II brought boom times to North Carolina as the state's industries sold almost $1.4 billion of materials to federal agencies. The state exported substantial quantities of textile products and lumber, all of the tetraethyl lead, and over half of the mica used by the armed forces. Wilmington won a lucrative shipbuilding contract and launched 125 Liberty ships and 117 of the larger Victory cargo ships.

North Carolina's economy experienced considerable diversification in the latter half of the twentieth century, producing a wide range of exports. In agriculture, the state exported tobacco, sweet potatoes, peanuts, and soybeans. Cotton production shrank dramatically as farmers turned to more lucrative crops. The state ranked high in the production and export of turkeys, and U.S. Representative Harold D. Cooley, as chairman of the House Agriculture Committee in the 1960s, helped open European markets for the exporting of North Carolina chickens. North Carolina hogs also became major export products. Shrimp became the state's most valuable seafood catch, while menhaden, a source of oil and protein for animal feed, was the most valuable fish. North Carolina also emerged as a leading brick-producing state in the last decades of the twentieth century, exporting more than 1 billion bricks each year.

By the early 2000s, North Carolina's leading categories of exports included industrial equipment and machinery, tobacco, textiles and knit apparel, chemicals and drug products, plastics, electronic equipment, and transportation equipment. Canada was the leading destination for North Carolina's products, receiving one-quarter of the state's exports. Other destinations included Japan, Mexico, the United Kingdom, Germany, Saudi Arabia, Belgium, the Netherlands, Brazil, and Hong Kong. North Carolina in 2004 was ranked fourteenth nationally in exporting, producing about $19.5 billion in exported products.

References: Brent D. Glass, *The Textile Industry in North Carolina: A History* (1992); North Carolina International Trade Division, *North Carolina Export Facts: North Carolina Trade Balance, 1988–1992* [1993?]; Alan D. Watson, *Wilmington: Port of North Carolina* (1992).

Douglas A. Wait

Express Riders on horseback delivered oral messages, letters, or documents before postal service and other means of communication were available. The term "express messenger" was used in England as early as 1619. Col. John Barnwell on 30 Apr. 1712, during the Tuscarora Indian War in North Carolina, "sent express" to New Bern to have boats and tools brought to him for the campaign against the Indians. On 22 May 1760 the provincial Assembly was directed to "pay the Expences of the Messenger (whilst in Town) which is sent to His Excellency with Express from the Lieutenant Governor of Virginia to this Province and to South Carolina, out of the Tax for Contingencies."

William S. Powell

Extension Service. The North Carolina Cooperative Extension Service, part of a national organization funded by federal, state, and local governments as well as private sources, serves as a link between university agricultural research and the people of North Carolina. The Morrill Acts, passed by Congress in 1862 and 1890, funded North Carolina's land grant colleges (modern-day North Carolina State University in Raleigh and North Carolina A&T University in Greensboro), which were founded to make education available to a greater number of North Carolinians. In the late nineteenth and early twentieth centuries, the idea of wide-ranging agricultural education continued to gain momentum. In 1914 Congress passed the Smith-Lever Act, which established the Cooperative Extension Service. The North Carolina Agricultural Extension Service was soon founded, operating in partnership with the state's land grant colleges. B. W. Kilgore served as its first director.

The Extension Service county agents, home economics agents, and agents who worked with children in what came to be known as 4-H made information available to people who previously had little access to the state's institutions of higher learning. They helped meet the emergencies of two world wars, the Great Depression, and numerous agricultural and financial hard times.

In 1991 the North Carolina Agricultural Extension Service became the North Carolina Cooperative Extension Service, reflecting the national organization. As American society changed, the organization came to serve more urban families than rural. Modern Extension Service agents continue to help with issues concerning agriculture, horticulture, conservation of natural resources, protection of the environment, nutrition, health, and a wide variety of family and economic concerns. They also reach out to youth, mainly through the 4-H Clubs. The mission of the Cooperative Extension Service remains helping North Carolinians improve the quality of their lives through the acquisition of knowledge.

References: James W. Clark Jr., *Clover All Over: North Carolina 4-H in Action* (1984); Wayne D. Rasmussen, *Taking the University to the People: Seventy-Five Years of Cooperative Extension* (1989); I. O. Schaub, *Agricultural Extension Work: A Brief History* (1953).

Barry McGee

SEE ALSO Four-H Clubs; Live-at-Home Program.

F

Factors, also known as "commission merchants," were commercial agents who handled the exchange of goods on behalf of planters. A factor sold cotton or other crops and made the arrangements for finding a buyer, transportation, insurance, and storage in return for a commission. Factors rarely traded on their own account but simply acted as intermediaries. Commission merchants charged planters a fee for arranging the purchase of large quantities of goods from distant sources. Many commission merchants also acted as factors, and the two terms have been used interchangeably by early planters and later historians.

In addition, commission merchant firms operated as auctioneers, wholesale grocers, retail merchants, and in other roles. As early as 1790, the Wilmington firm of Jocelin & D'Herbe advertised the opening of their "coffee-house and tavern" while continuing "their Vendue and Commission business as usual." So-called vertical factors (including Josiah Collins II of Edenton) owned wholesale stores, ships, brick kilns, ropewalks, or other enterprises as well as their commission businesses.

Planters, especially those far from towns, stores, and transportation routes, relied heavily on factors. In addition to selling their crops, factors often loaned them money for seeds, tools, and supplies on the promise of being paid when the crop was ready. Banks and ready cash were scarce in the Old South, and planters were often rich in land and slaves but short on cash or even in debt. The factor's extension of credit supplied necessary help in financing large-scale agriculture in a cash-poor society.

Commission merchants and factors were located in a few of the larger or more developed North Carolina towns with good rail or water connections. Wilmington had a great many commission merchants (three dozen or more in the late nineteenth century). Raleigh, Charlotte, New Bern, Tarboro, Washington, Greensboro, Winston-Salem, and other towns had one or several during much of the nineteenth and early twentieth centuries.

After the Civil War, which disrupted their business, factors were in demand for a time but then began a final decline as large plantations were replaced by farms too small for factors to deal with profitably. Many farmers needed to sell their crops for cash immediately; it took too long for them to ship to a distant factor and wait for the best market conditions. Large cotton mills began to bypass the factors, sending buyers to purchase directly from farmers. Many local merchants also became cotton buyers. Communication and shipping facilities improved to the point where local buyers or farmers could make their own arrangements for the sale and transport of

their cotton or other crops. Eventually, the outright buying of crops replaced selling for commission, and many factors became buyers.

References: Catherine W. Bishir, "'Severe Servitude to House Building': The Construction of Hayes Plantation House, 1814–1817," *NCHR* 68 (October 1991); H. D. Woodman, *King Cotton and His Retainers* (1968).

David A. Norris

Factory Cord is identified as any cord or string not of home manufacture but produced at a factory or mill. The term was used prior to the Civil War in Piedmont North Carolina, where there were early cotton mills. It was perhaps akin to "factory cotton," a term used in 1850 for a manufactured fabric.

William S. Powell

Fairs. SEE County Fairs; State Fair.

Fall Line, or fall zone, in North Carolina is defined in geological terms as the line of erosion between the piedmont and the coastal plain regions at which hard, erosion-resistant rocks descend into softer, eastern rocks. Running through Richmond, Montgomery, Moore, Lee, and other counties, the fall line is particularly apparent in rivers as the place past which boats can no longer navigate because of the occurrence of natural falls or rapids. The fall line has thus greatly influenced transportation, settlement location, population distribution, and industrial development in North Carolina.

Water transportation was the cheapest and most reliable method of moving goods and persons in the early years of the state's development, so it was natural that areas near fall lines in rivers often became population centers. These fall lines also became known as "break-in-bulk points" because at them large shipments coming in on water vessels would be rearranged into smaller lots for further land transportation. Points on rivers adjacent to the fall line also provided a source of energy to run water mills and other important commercial ventures; consequently, the state's early development was concentrated at the fall line along its major eastern rivers. The towns on the fall line of the Tar River were Tarboro, Greenville, and Rocky Mount. On the Neuse River, Kinston, Smithfield, and Goldsboro were developed on the fall line. Weldon was formed on the Roanoke River fall line, Hillsborough on the Eno River fall line, and Alamance on the Alamance Creek fall line.

The fall line remains important in the modern day for the measurement and management of pollution in North Carolina's rivers. The difference in soil types and water flow on either side of the fall line allows scientists to study the effects of pollutants introduced into the rivers, serving, in part, as the basis for various pollution-related regulations.

References: Cordelia Camp, *The Influence of Geography upon Early North Carolina* (1963); J. Wright Horton Jr. and Victor A. Zullo, eds., *The Geology of the Carolinas: Carolina Geological Society Fiftieth Anniversary Volume* (1991); Harry Roy Merrens, *Colonial North Carolina in the Eighteenth Century: A Study in Historical Geography* (1964).

Jim Fowlkes

Family Dollar Stores, a discount general merchandise firm, was founded in Charlotte in 1959 by Leon Levine and his cousin Bernie Levine. Leon's father had founded the Hub, a general department store, in Rockingham in 1908, and his older brother Al had established Pic 'n Pay self-service shoe stores in 1957. The first Family Dollar Store set the pattern for subsequent stores by targeting low- and middle-income families and featuring no merchandise priced over one dollar. The company grew rapidly, opening no-frills, low-overhead stores across North Carolina and in other states. Most Family Dollar stores are located in small communities, with the majority of their merchandise selling for significantly less than the prices paid in chain supermarkets or drugstores. An early emphasis on goods such as clothing, shoes, linens, and towels has over time been complemented by merchandise such as electronics, housewares, health and beauty aids, paper items, and detergents. In 2006 Family Dollar Stores was a multibillion-dollar company with approximately 6,000 stores in 44 states, competing with large firms such as Wal-Mart, Target, and Dollar General.

Wiley J. Williams

Farm Bureau Federation is North Carolina's largest general farm organization, offering a diversity of activities, programs, and services to meet the state's agricultural needs. No record exists of the election of the organization's first board of directors, but on 2 Mar. 1936 chairman J. E. Winslow called the first meeting to order in the county agent's office in Greenville. The Farm Bureau grew quickly by supporting vital issues such as improved farm-to-market roads; cooperative hail and storm insurance; coordination by state and federal agricultural organizations to prevent dual administration; research and extension work; revision of state feed, fertilizer, and seed laws; and the establishment of a maximum interest rate of 3.5 percent on federal farmland loans. Bureau headquarters moved from Greenville to Raleigh in 1938, to Greensboro in 1940, and finally back to Raleigh in 1958. In 1942 farm women became members and gained a voice in affairs by forming

what would become the Women's Committee. The first county offices of the Farm Bureau opened in 1954. Eventually there would be at least one office in all 100 counties.

With a membership that has grown from about 2,000 initially to more than 470,000 by the early 2000s, the North Carolina Farm Bureau Federation has remained the state's "voice of agriculture."

Reference: Bill Critcher, ed., "Fifty Years of Service to Agriculture," *Farm Bureau News* (April 1986).

Barry McGee

Farmers' Alliance, formally known as the North Carolina State Farmers' Alliance and Industrial Union, was a large and influential organization of farmers and rural citizens that was founded in Texas and spread across the South and Middle West in the late 1880s. Its representatives first appeared in North Carolina in 1887; by 1891 more than 100,000 North Carolinians had joined.

This spectacular growth resulted from several factors. Most important, the increasing commercialization of agriculture thrust various classes of the state's farmers into a complex and often-hostile web of trade relationships. Many North Carolina farmers relied on local merchants for credit, materials, and crop marketing. The monopoly of the local merchant resulted in high credit rates and high prices for goods purchased on credit. Market prices for agricultural products were often depressed by harvesttime gluts. Further, loans from the merchant were protected through the crop lien, a legal device that gave the merchant priority rights to crops to satisfy debts. Farmers were also harmed by government policy, including the federal government's protective tariff on purchased goods.

The Farmers' Alliance was a "secret," all-white organization. It permitted men and women farmers, rural mechanics, teachers, preachers, and physicians to join; it expressly excluded lawyers and merchants. The occupational admissions test revealed a Republican-inspired faith in rule by agricultural producers. The North Carolina Alliance included more landowners than tenants or laborers. In fact, leadership tended to be delegated to wealthier planters, as indicated by the high status of the order's two presidents between 1887 and 1891, Sydenham Alexander of Mecklenburg County and Elias Carr of Edgecombe County.

In 1890 the Farmers' Alliance was strong enough to make political demands that would receive a full hearing in the Democratic Party. Most Alliance members, and particularly most Alliance leaders, were Democrats. The two issues of greatest contention in 1890 were the Alliance's Subtreasury Plan and its demand for a state railroad commission. Given the increasingly obvious inability of the order's cooperative devices to thwart the existing credit and marketing system, the Farmers' Alliance proposed that the national government construct warehouses, or subtreasuries, and issue negotiable notes on crops deposited in the warehouses. Combined with the Alliance's more general plan to increase money volume and have all money issued by the federal government, the warehouses would raise the prices for goods received by farmers and reduce the credit and marketing power of merchants.

The Subtreasury Plan was strongly supported by the North Carolina Farmers' Alliance, and considerable pressure was placed on the state's congressional delegation to support the proposal. The state railroad commission idea, which had been defeated in the 1889 General Assembly, was promoted in order to eliminate high intrastate freight rates and low taxation of railroad property.

Political activity by the Farmers' Alliance resulted in the election of a General Assembly dominated by members of the organization. One source estimated that 110 of the 170 representatives in the 1891 assembly belonged to the order.

After early 1891, controversy about the future of the Farmers' Alliance escalated. Division within the North Carolina order developed on such fundamental issues as the Subtreasury Plan, which perhaps one-third of the membership opposed, and a new demand, adopted by the national organization in early 1892, for federal government ownership of railroads. The latter proposal was criticized by many members, including a former president of the North Carolina Alliance, Elias Carr, who favored public regulation instead of ownership.

These disagreements were related to increasing rancor within the Farmers' Alliance about the appropriate political posture of the organization. In particular, members were divided over the duty of the order in national politics. In the summer of 1892 conflict over this issue climaxed, leaving the organization permanently shattered. The formation of Populist parties in other states contributed to the decline. But more significant were the Democrats' nomination of Grover Cleveland in July for president and the growing opposition by some North Carolina Democrats to the influence of the Farmers' Alliance influence within their party.

After 1892 the close connection between Populist and Farmers' Alliance leadership increasingly alienated Democrats from the Alliance. Although the Alliance continued to hold annual meetings in North Carolina through the 1890s, and remnants of the organization persisted until 1941, the order never recovered from the political and ideological battles of 1892. The national Farmers' Alliance organization ceased to exist after 1897.

References: Alan B. Bromberg, "'The Worst Muddle Ever Seen in N.C. Politics': The Farmers' Alliance, the Subtreasury, and Zeb Vance," NCHR 56 (January 1979); John D. Hicks, *The Populist Revolt: A History of the Farmers' Alliance and the People's Party* (1931); Robert C. McMath Jr., *Populist Vanguard: A History of the Southern Farmers' Alliance* (1975); Lala C. Steelman, *The North Carolina Farmers' Alliance: A Political History, 1887–1893* (1985).

James L. Hunt

SEE ALSO *Progressive Farmer;* Subtreasury Plan.

Farmers Union, officially the Farmers Educational and Cooperative Union, was organized in Texas in 1902 to improve the educational, economic, social, and political condition of southern farmers. In 1905 S. H. Colwick of Texas moved to Cleveland County, N.C., and by 1906 he had organized 11 local Farmers Unions, which then formed the Cleveland County Farmers Union. The national union sent organizers into North Carolina in 1907, and growth in membership was sufficiently rapid to spark publication of the *Carolina Union Farmer* in Charlotte that same year. The following year the North Carolina division of the Farmers Union was organized in Charlotte. By 1912, the year of the union's greatest strength, the organization had 33,000 members in the state, numbers it was unable to maintain.

In 1913 the *Carolina Union Farmer* was sold to the *Progressive Farmer*, which in turn promised to publish items of specific interest to the Farmers Union. In 1919 the North Carolina division withdrew its membership from the national union in protest over the amount demanded for national dues ($100). In its heyday, the state union lobbied for the creation of farm-life schools in 1911, organized farmers' cooperatives, and pressed for a system of rural credit. It provided social activities in the form of picnics, rallies, and monthly meetings. The state union was unable, however, to sustain the cooperatives, compete with other farm organizations, or hold onto its local unions and membership. The North Carolina Farmers Union was defunct by the close of 1928.

Reference: John A. Crampton, *The National Farmers Union: Ideology of a Pressure Group* (1965).

George Stevenson

Farm-Life Schools. The establishment of high schools early in the twentieth century, though an important educational advance, benefited only a small fraction of North Carolina's school-age children—most of whom lived in rural settings without access to adequate educational facilities. This fact motivated state superintendent J. Y. Joyner and various farm groups to promote the idea of farm-life schools, which the General Assembly authorized in 1911. If a local governmental unit provided facilities (including dormitories for boys and girls) in the amount of $25,000, then pledged $2,500 for operating expenses each year, the state would match the latter amount. Almost immediately, five counties took advantage of the offer, and by 1916, 21 farm-life schools were in operation.

These schools were required to offer a standard high school

Members of the Farmers Union photographed at Erwin Chapel near Erwin in Harnett County, ca. 1905. NCC.

education in addition to classes and practical experience in vocational agriculture and home economics. In Nash County, local farmer Tom Jones donated 25 acres of land, and the community voted an additional $10,000 in bonds for buildings for the Red Oak Farm-Life High School. Students within walking or horse-riding distances paid no tuition, but boarding students paid $12.50 per month. The boys cut wood for fires, and girls cooked and waited on tables. Crop rotation, contour plowing, selection of nutritious foods, and improved home-making practices were emphasized along with the academic curriculum. A second school—the Rowan Farm-Life School in China Grove, which opened in 1914—was such a success that in 1921 the regular China Grove High School merged with it and shared the farm campus. Academic standards there were high, and the school distinguished itself in scholastic and vocational fields as well as in extracurricular activities at state and regional levels.

In the first quarter of the twentieth century, however, with increased urbanization, the introduction of motorized transportation for students, and the passage of the federal Smith-Hughes Act of 1917 appropriating federal funds for vocational education in public high schools, farm-life schools faded into educational history.

References: "County Farm-Life School Law and Explanations," *North Carolina High School Bulletin* (April 1911); Zeyland G. McKinney, "The County Farm-Life Schools of North Carolina" (M.A. thesis, Appalachian State University, 1953).

H. G. Jones

Farm-to-Market Roads. One of the key arguments of early "good roads" advocates was the need for improved farm-to-market roads. Their position was well stated by men such as Daniel A. Tompkins, a Charlotte cotton mill builder who maintained that building better roadways would not only save farmers on crop and fertilizer delivery costs but also increase church and school attendance and reduce the desire for farm youth to leave their rural homes. Tompkins wrote several pamphlets supporting this position between 1894 and 1909. Other North Carolina spokesmen for this position included state ge-

Kitchen of the Cary Public and Farm-Life School, ca. 1916. Courtesy of NCOA&H.

ologist Joseph A. Holmes and Governor Charles B. Aycock. As the Good Roads campaign spread, it began to focus more on long-distance motor highways built between major cities, and the farm-to-market advocates gradually gave way to their urban counterparts.

References: Robert E. Ireland, *Entering the Auto Age: The Early Automobile in North Carolina, 1900–1930* (1990); G. T. Winston, *A Builder of the New South: Being the Story of the Life of Daniel Augustus Tompkins* (1920).

Robert E. Ireland

Fassifern School, a noted preparatory school for girls, was established in Lincolnton in 1907 by Catherine Cameron Shipp, the daughter of state attorney general William Marcus Shipp. From 1898 to 1902, she and her sister, Anna Shipp McBee, had successfully operated a coeducational preparatory school in Lincolnton. In 1902 Shipp enrolled at Cambridge University in England. Upon her return to North Carolina in

1904, she taught at Saint Mary's until she opened Fassifern, named for an ancestral home that Shipp had visited in the Highlands of Scotland.

Located on the northwestern side of Lincolnton, the original campus consisted of a large frame house nestled in an oak grove near the banks of the South Fork River. The stated mission of Fassifern was "to prepare girls for the best colleges, or to be self-supporting, and to help them become lovers of the best in literature, music, and art." Assisted by her sister and an able faculty, Shipp operated the school much like a Christian home, with a heavy emphasis on academics, religious and physical training, and self-discipline.

Students came from throughout North Carolina as well as other states, and Fassifern gained a reputation as one of the South's best preparatory schools. Despite an addition to the physical plant, the Lincolnton facility quickly became inadequate for an ever-increasing enrollment.

Enticed by an offer from a group of businessmen from Hendersonville, Shipp moved the institution to that mountain town in 1914. On its spacious new campus highlighted by colonial-style architecture, the school continued to grow and prosper under the tutelage of "Miss Kate."

Soon after her sister died in 1924, Shipp sold Fassifern to Joseph R. Sevier, a Presbyterian minister. Sevier and his son John successfully operated the school for a quarter of a century. Fassifern School continued operation on the Hendersonville campus until 1951, when John Sevier moved to Atlanta to accept a position with Southern Airways.

References: Delta Kappa Gamma Society, *Some Pioneer Women Teachers of North Carolina* (1955); William L. Sherrill, *Annals of Lincoln County* (1937).

Daniel W. Barefoot

Fatback, the fatty meat from the back of a hog that is usually dry-cured with salt, has been a staple ingredient in North Carolina and southern cooking since colonial times. Through the years certain synonyms for fatback have arisen, among them salt pork, fat meat, fat pork, (dry) salt meat, salt bacon, seasoning meat, side meat, sowbelly, white bacon, and middling meat. Fatback is used in a dizzying variety of ways: besides being eaten as an entrée in simple meals, it is particularly popular as a seasoning for green beans, new potatoes, turnip and collard greens, fried corn, black-eyed peas, and other dishes. The meat also is believed by some North Carolinians to have value as a folk medicine, curing boils and sore throats and removing warts.

References: William Arnold, "Conventions, Fatback, and Black-Eyed Peas," *The State* 47 (October 1979); "In Defense of Fatback," *The State* 37 (15 June 1969).

Wiley J. Williams

Fayetteville traces its roots to 1755, when John Newberry, a millwright and Quaker immigrant from Pennsylvania, acquired more than 1,400 acres—nearly all of modern-day downtown Fayetteville—in the Upper Cape Fear region and built an overshot waterwheel gristmill on Cross Creek. In the early 1760s the settlement at Cross Creek experienced its first real estate boom. Newberry sold lots for homes, stores, mills, taverns, shops, a tanyard, and a brewery, and by 1762 Cross Creek was a well-established commercial center, although the county courthouse was established in the town of Campbellton, a mile away on the Cape Fear River.

During the American Revolution, except for a few months during the bloody Loyalist-Patriot civil war of 1781–82, Cross Creek was firmly in Patriot hands, serving as a supply depot and occasional military outpost guarding the Cape Fear River Valley against British excursions from Wilmington. For two days in March 1781, Lord Charles Cornwallis's British army, retreating from the Battle of Guilford Courthouse, camped in the village.

After the war, leaders in the growing settlement of Cross Creek hoped for it to become the capital of North Carolina. In 1783 a committee of the state legislature laid out the previously unplanned village with straight streets and squares and renamed it Fayetteville, the first place in North America named in honor of the Marquis de Lafayette, the young French nobleman who fought for American independence. Fayetteville was not destined to become North Carolina's capital, but in 1789 it was host to the Constitutional Convention that ratified the U.S. Constitution and to a legislative session that chartered the University of North Carolina.

For the next 40 years, Fayetteville was the largest inland town in North Carolina. Trade—with goods moving in steamboats along the Cape Fear—was attracted to the town by textile and sawmill operations, stores, taverns, and comfortable inns and hotels. In the 1840s the federal government paid for a handsome military storage armory on Haymount, overlooking the town. During the Civil War, the armory built by the federal government became a gun factory for the Confederate army. In the last days of the war, soldiers of Gen. William T. Sherman's Union army knocked down the armory and burned the offices of the *Fayetteville Observer*.

In the decades following the Civil War, while some other North Carolina towns grew into small cities, Fayetteville did not. In the 1890s railroad lines finally connected Fayetteville with distant places and brought renewed prosperity and growth. Textile factories, sawmills, and turpentine distilleries added economic muscle. In 1918, during the last months of World War I, in what would prove a defining event for Fayetteville, the U.S. Army acquired more than 100,000 acres of nearby pine woods and farmland and established an installation called Camp Bragg. Renamed Fort Bragg, the post was, for its first 20 years, the home of artillery units and Air Corps planes stationed at Pope Field.

In 1940, with war breaking out in Europe, another momentous change occurred: Fort Bragg was enlarged to become the country's largest army training post, and Fayetteville's civilian population grew as a consequence. During World War II, hundreds of thousands of soldiers passed through Fort Bragg on their way to world battlefronts. During the Korean and Vietnam Wars, the post once again became a center for mobilization. The post population reached more than 45,000 soldiers and airmen during the Korean War and has remained constant since.

The wartime booms transformed Fayetteville from a small textile-and-sawmill town to a bustling commercial city. In the 1960s the city attracted new civilian industries making plastics, tires, auto parts, and appliances. Its airport was modernized for more scheduled flights. Retailing and tourist businesses proliferated. By 1970 residential subdivisions sprawled across miles of former cotton fields and pinewoods in a circle around Fayetteville. In the 1970s this suburban growth spurred expansion of retailing into big shopping malls, and by 1980 the mall area near the nineteenth-century McPherson Presbyterian Church ranked among the state's largest retail locations. Population growth and economic development triggered expansion of health care facilities, public schools, cultural opportunities, modern commuter roads, and the campuses of Fayetteville State University, Fayetteville Technical Community College, and Methodist College, a two-year institution that opened in 1960.

In the 1990s this proliferation was capped by the opening of the 12,000-seat Crown Coliseum, a first-class venue for indoor sports and entertainment. Other popular attractions in Fayetteville are the Museum of the Cape Fear, the Airborne and Special Operations Museum, and the Fayetteville Museum of Art. Fayetteville in 2005 was North Carolina's sixth-largest city, with a population approaching 150,000.

References: John A. Oates, *The Story of Fayetteville* (1950); Roy Parker Jr., *Cumberland County: A Brief History* (1990).

Roy Parker Jr.

SEE ALSO Fayetteville State University; Fort Bragg; Museum of the Cape Fear.

Fayetteville Academy

Fayetteville Academy was chartered in 1791 and incorporated in 1799. The school, the first in Fayetteville, was headed by Presbyterian minister David Kerr (later president of the University of North Carolina in Chapel Hill) and enrolled males and females. The school was located on Green Street in downtown Fayetteville until it was destroyed by fire in 1831. It reopened not far away on Hay Street, remaining there until the Civil War. Notable graduates include William Rufus King (U.S. vice president, 1852) and James C. Dobbin (secretary of the navy, 1852).

The modern Fayetteville Academy was incorporated in 1969 and opened for classes in 1970. It is an independent, college preparatory school instructing students in grades prekindergarten through 12. It has no legal charter connection to the original school but was intended by its founders to live up to that predecessor's tradition. The academy emphasizes "academics, competitive athletics, creative fine arts, and a commitment to moral values based upon Judeo-Christian heritage." In the early 2000s the school enrolled approximately 430 students, about 17 percent of whom came from military families.

Jeffrey Allen Howard

Fayetteville Arsenal and Armory. SEE Armories.

Fayetteville Independent Light Infantry Company

Fayetteville Independent Light Infantry Company (FILI) was formed on 23 Aug. 1793, when European countries were involved in a war growing out of the French Revolution. The reason for its organization may have been fear that the Spanish in Louisiana would incite the Indians to attack, but recent scholarship supports the view that alarm over slave rebellions in Haiti was more likely.

In 1825 the company attended the Marquis de Lafayette on his visit to Fayetteville (named in 1784 in honor of the French nobleman who fought with the American revolutionaries). Construction of the U.S. arsenal in Fayetteville in 1838 increased the importance of the company. When the Civil War began, the FILI joined the 1st North Carolina Volunteers, called the "Bethel" Regiment, as Company H. It was the first regiment organized in North Carolina and fought in the Battle of Bethel, the first engagement of the war. Some of its members were among the troops who surrendered at Appomattox.

Although the FILI achieved glory, its history was marked by controversy, such as when it refused to retire the gray uniform of the Confederacy, which prevented its acceptance into the State Guard. During the Spanish-American War, the FILI entered national service as Company A, 2nd Regiment, commanded by Capt. Benjamin R. Huske. Wearing their Confederate uniforms, the enlistees marched into Camp Dan Russell, where "they doffed the grays" and "donned the blues" of the United States. The company trained at Tybee Island, Ga., but did not sail to Cuba. The troops were mustered out at Macon, Ga., on 8 Feb. 1899. In 1917 the company went to Camp Stewart at El Paso, Tex., to help defend the border from raids by Mexican leader Francisco Villa.

During World War I the FILI served as Company F of the 119th Infantry Regiment, part of the Thirtieth Division, and fought in Flanders—its last military service. It has sometimes been confused with the Fayetteville Light Infantry Company, which also fought in a number of wars, including the Civil War.

After World War I, the FILI continued as a fraternal and social organization. It maintained an armory where Fort Bragg soldiers were often entertained, and it established a museum to house records and artifacts from antebellum days and from its World War I service. In the early 2000s the company functioned as a ceremonial unit with a color guard dressed in the uniform of the late antebellum period.

References: James C. MacRae, "The Fayetteville Independent Light Infantry Company," *North Carolina Booklet* (9 Apr. 1908); Roy Parker Jr., *Cumberland County: A Brief History* (1990); Joseph F. Steelman, *North Carolina's Role in the Spanish-American War* (1975).

Lala Carr Steelman

Fayetteville Observer

Fayetteville Observer was founded in 1816 as the *Carolina Observer*. It is considered North Carolina's oldest newspaper, appearing since that date except for the years between 1865 and 1883. (The *Wilmington Star*, founded in 1867, is the state's oldest continuously published paper.) The *Carolina Observer* was evidently launched by several Fayetteville citizens,

This notice from an 1819 issue of the *Carolina Observer* is a humorous but insightful example of the high regard accorded newspapers in local affairs early in the state's history. NCC.

of whom Postmaster John MacRae was the principal. For the next eight years, the newspaper had a succession of at least a dozen owners or editors, with MacRae always in some ownership capacity. In late 1824 the *Observer* was acquired by Edward Jones Hale, a Chatham County native who had apprenticed on newspapers in Raleigh and Washington, N.C. He was the *Observer*'s editor and proprietor from January 1825 to 11 Mar. 1865, when Union soldiers of Gen. William T. Sherman's army destroyed the newspaper's offices.

The *Carolina Observer*'s name was changed to the *Fayetteville Observer* in 1833. Hale, and later his sons, made the newspaper a leading political organ of the Whig Party. In the 1850s it claimed the largest circulation in North Carolina. In addition to political and commercial coverage, the elder Hale encouraged historical writing. He gave many columns to articles by James Banks, a Scottish-born Fayetteville lawyer and amateur historian who traveled widely to historic sites in the state and is credited with a celebration in 1856 that led to the preservation of the Revolutionary War site of the Battle of Moore's Creek Bridge. Hale also started a practice that has immensely enriched historical research in North Carolina: he carefully preserved copies of each edition of the newspaper. Despite fires, invasions, and moves over 180 years, only a handful of editions are missing from the record.

In the months leading up to the Civil War, the *Fayetteville Observer* vehemently opposed secession. Once war began, however, Hale lent his editorial voice to the Confederate cause, breathing defiance even as Sherman's troops marched into North Carolina. Hale played a key role in the election of wartime governor Zebulon B. Vance. During the war years the newspaper was a virtual gazette of news of the conflict, often printing battle accounts and casualty lists from throughout the state.

Hale was joined in the business by his son Peter M. Hale in 1850 and by a younger son, Edward Joseph Hale, in 1860. When Sherman's army destroyed their offices and presses in 1865, the entire family moved to New York. Entering the book pub-

lishing business as E. J. Hale & Sons, they soon recovered their fortune while turning out a notable list of war-related titles.

Edward Joseph Hale returned to Fayetteville in 1883 and restarted the *Observer*. As Fayetteville became a small city in the 1920s, the paper became an afternoon daily. In 1919 a group of local businessmen bought it from the Hale family. It changed hands twice again before W. J. McMurray of New York acquired it in 1923 and incorporated it as the Fayetteville Publishing Company. McMurray's brother-in-law, Charles S. Wilson, became publisher in 1924.

Wilson was deeply involved in the life of the local community. In the tradition of Edward Jones Hale and nearly every other newspaper owner in Fayetteville, he was an inveterate booster of the economy and culture. Wilson was also up-to-date on developments in journalism, beginning his quarter-century tenure as publisher-owner by revamping the paper. He bought new presses and equipment and moved to a modernized building. In the 1920s and 1930s he kept up with advances in technology and newsreel practices, and even during the Depression he tried such innovations as a rotogravure section. The *Observer* published large, special issues, including a sesquicentennial edition in 1939, when the community celebrated the 150th anniversary of the 1789 constitutional convention in Fayetteville.

On his death in 1949, Wilson was succeeded by his son-in-law, Richard M. Lilly, a Fayetteville native and lawyer. Lilly presided over the newspaper's fortunes during a big growth period in the 1960s, when the sleepy courthouse town grew to urban size. The *Fayetteville Observer* kept up with the growth by moving into larger quarters and launching a Sunday edition in 1957.

When Lilly died in 1971, Mrs. Richard Lilly was named chairman of the board, and a son-in-law, Ramon L. Yarborough, became publisher. Under Yarborough's leadership the company established a second newspaper, a morning daily called the *Fayetteville Times*, in 1973. Four years later the firm moved into a large new plant. In the 1970s and 1980s both papers won numerous awards for community service, investigative reporting, sports coverage, editorials, and features. The *Fayetteville Times* was among three finalists for the Pulitzer Prize in 1984.

By the 1980s the *Fayetteville Observer* had the largest circulation of any afternoon daily in the Carolinas. The Fayetteville Publishing Company underwent further technological transformations, installing new computerized production systems. In 1990 the *Times* and the *Observer* were combined into the *Observer-Times*, a morning daily. Charles Broadwell, a grandson of Charles R. Wilson, was named editor. In 1997 the newspaper began a $30 million press modernization project. Two years later the paper reclaimed its former name, the *Fayetteville Observer*, and its status as a morning daily.

References: Roy Parker Jr., *Cumberland County: A Brief History* (1990); Thad Stem Jr., *The Tar Heel Press* (1973).

Roy Parker Jr.

Fayetteville State University

Fayetteville State University had its beginnings in 1867, when seven progressive African American citizens paid $140 for a lot on Fayetteville's Gillespie Street and converted themselves into a self-perpetuating board of trustees to maintain the property as a permanent site for the education of African American children in the area. Gen. O. O. Howard, an early supporter of African American education, erected a building on the site, and the school was named the Howard School in his honor.

In 1877 the state legislature provided for the establishment of a normal school for the education of black teachers. Several areas of the state competed for this first state-supported academy, but the Howard School was selected because of its successful record. It became a teacher training institution known as the State Colored Normal School. In 1929 all high school work was discontinued at the Normal School, and in May 1937 the State Board of Education authorized its designation as a four-year college with authority to grant the bachelor of science degree in elementary education. The name of the institution was changed to Fayetteville State Teachers College in 1939. Under the leadership of James Ward Seabrook, president from 1933 to 1956, the school continued to progress. Another name change, to Fayetteville State College, occurred in 1963 after several additions were made to its physical plant.

In 1969 the school became Fayetteville State University, and three years later it became a constituent institution of the consolidated University of North Carolina System. The facilities have advanced from a single building to a campus of approximately 156 acres and 36 buildings, with an estimated value of over $35 million. By the early 2000s Fayetteville State had a student body of just over 4,000 undergraduates and 231 faculty members. No longer exclusively a teacher training institution, the university offers 11 programs of study leading to the baccalaureate degree in 23 disciplines. Graduate degrees also are offered in education and business administration.

Reference: Ella Louise Murphy, "Origins and Development of Fayetteville State Teachers College, 1867–1959: A Chapter in the History of the Education of Negroes in North Carolina" (Ph.D. diss., New York University, 1960).

Charles W. Wadelington

Federalist Party

Federalist Party, originating in the early 1790s, endured longer in North Carolina than in any other southern state, although it generally achieved only modest success throughout its existence. The party never gained substantial long-term support in large measure because of its obvious disdain for democracy and popular sentiment, its reliance on the well-educated and propertied elite, and its failure to organize effectively. Moreover, the party supported a strong central government while most North Carolinians favored state rights. Only rarely were the Federalists able to balance the state's particular economic interests and political views with their party's ideology and policy agenda.

In the 1790s North Carolina Federalists experienced repeated disappointments at the polls. Only Richard Dobbs Spaight (1792–95), who later deserted the party, and William R. Davie (1798–99) became governors. Jeffersonian Republicans dominated the General Assembly, especially after 1792. The state sent just two Federalists to the U.S. Senate—Samuel Johnston (1789–93), an attorney from Chowan County, and Benjamin Hawkins (1789–95), born in Granville (now Warren) County and previously a North Carolina delegate to the Continental Congress and a U.S. Indian agent. The state's delegation to the U.S. House of Representatives contained a Federalist majority until 1793, but between 1793 and 1799 the only Federalist congressman from the state was William Barry Grove, a prominent Fayetteville attorney. At times the party provided North Carolina with able leaders in the judiciary, where most attorneys were Federalists. In the field of education, Federalists promoted the establishment of the state university—Davie being known as its "father"—and fought to maintain it.

During the presidential administrations of Thomas Jefferson and James Madison (1801–17), Federalist strength steadily eroded. Key party leaders had disappeared from the scene through retirement or death. Four Federalist congressmen—Archibald Henderson, William Grove, John Stanly, and William H. Hill—ignored instructions by the state's Republican legislature to vote for repeal of the Judiciary Act of 1801, and none was reelected. Federalist membership in the General Assembly hovered between 25 and 30 percent, reaching a peak of 40 percent in the Lower House during the War of 1812. Among the distinguished Federalists who served in this body were Archibald Henderson (1807–9, 1814) and William Gaston of New Bern (1807–9). Although the party experienced a brief revival with its opposition to the War of 1812, Federalist William Polk failed in his bid for the governorship in 1814.

The Treaty of Ghent and return of peace struck a mortal blow to Federalists in North Carolina, for they could no longer use the war as a political issue. Moreover, the Hartford Convention of 1814 reflected badly on the party nationwide as well as in North Carolina. The postwar upsurge of nationalism, embraced by Republicans, lured some Federalists away from the party. The election of James Monroe as president, the onset of the so-called Era of Good Feelings, and the lack of major national issues further blurred party lines. Few Federalists saw any reason to keep the party label and themselves stressed the disappearance of partisan differences. Although some old-line Federalists such as Gaston and Henderson kept the faith, by 1817 the party ceased to exist.

References: James H. Broussard, *The Southern Federalists, 1800–1816* (1978); Delbert H. Gilpatrick, *Jeffersonian Democracy in North Carolina, 1789–1816* (1931); Gilbert C. Lycan, "Alexander Hamilton and the North Carolina Federalists," *NCHR* 25 (1948); Wendell Holmes Stephenson and E. Merton Coulter, eds., *A History of the South*, vol. 9 (1961).

Charles H. McArver
Hoyt Doak

Federal Writers' Project (FWP), a New Deal program that from 1935 to 1942 hired unemployed newspapermen, librarians, historians, novelists, and poets, was a component of the Works Progress Administration. From its inception, the FWP in North Carolina had three objectives: to provide jobs for the unemployed, to rehabilitate workers by helping them to maintain and improve their skills, and to produce publications of lasting merit as a contribution to the culture of the state and local communities. At one point as many as 130 North Carolinians were on the rolls of the FWP. About 300 persons were returned to private employment over the life of the project.

The signal achievement of the FWP in North Carolina was the *Guide to the Old North State*, which was published to favorable reviews in 1939 and subsequently appeared in two reprint editions. North Carolinians also contributed to *These Are Our Lives* (1939), a compilation of interviews with ordinary working people in the state.

Several notable North Carolina writers served in the FWP. Novelist Bernice Kelly Harris collected "life histories." James Larkin Pearson, poet laureate of North Carolina from 1953 to 1981, gathered data on Wilkes County for use in the 1939 *Guide*. Manly Wade Wellman, in time a prolific writer of science fiction and mysteries, could not "struggle along" on his own and in January 1936 applied to the FWP. Local consultants such as clerk of court Richard Dillard Dixon in Edenton, newspaperman W. O. Saunders in Elizabeth City, and Moravian archivist Adelaide Fries in Winston-Salem assisted FWP field workers with their research.

A key project planned by the FWP but never finished was the omnibus volume referred to as the "North Carolina Encyclopedia" or the "North Carolina Factbook." National administrators encouraged their state counterparts to undertake such volumes once their state guides were completed. Each volume, it was anticipated, would be about 800,000 words, or 800 pages. Work on the North Carolina encyclopedia proceeded in a haphazard fashion. A four-drawer card index in the State Archives cross-references the planned entries, ranging from golf to the Ku Klux Klan. FWP workers transcribed for inclusion the full texts of documents such as the Halifax Resolves and the state constitutions. They prepared lists of famous North Carolina crimes and trials and of places in the state used as settings for novels, plays, poems, and motion pictures. North Carolina "firsts" rated special attention.

In June 1939 the Federal Writers' Project was renamed the Writers' Program. With this action came a shift in focus, reduction in personnel, and administrative changes. Responding to criticism that the FWP had spent too much public money, officials of the Writers' Program required each state and local unit to line up sponsors to contribute as least 25 percent of the costs. They also encouraged the production of less ambitious but more profitable publications such as recreational guides and pamphlets on scenic attractions.

With the onset of World War II, the Writers' Program devoted increased attention to publications that would assist the war effort, including servicemen's guides. Work proceeded on a map of airfields in North Carolina and a state atlas, but these projects were never finished. In the summer of 1941 the state headquarters in Asheville closed, and the 12 remaining staff members moved to Raleigh. In accelerating the end of the Depression, the war also precluded the need for the Writers' Program and other New Deal relief agencies.

References: Michael Hill, "The Files of the Federal Writers' Project in North Carolina," *Carolina Comments* (September 1991); Jerrold Maury Hirsch, "Portrait of America: The Federal Writers' Project in an Intellectual and Cultural Context" (Ph.D. diss., UNC-Chapel Hill, 1984).

Michael Hill

Fee System, involving the collection of money to cover administrative services and pay government officials, was transported to British America virtually intact by arriving colonists. Proprietary officials in North Carolina relied on fees to compensate them for performing functions such as issuing documents. With the codification of North Carolina law in 1715, fees were set for all provincial and local officials—from governor to deputy marshal. The services covered included surveying land, clearing incoming and outgoing vessels at ports, and issuing writs, warrants, and licenses.

With the advent of royal government, public resentment over fees increased steadily as more efficient government led to the more efficient collection of all revenues. From the first royal governor to the last, clashes between executive and legislative branches over fee rates and methods of payment were a persistent feature of the struggle for power that characterized colonial politics. Government officials realized much of their income from fees. Excessive fee charges by local officials in the backcountry were a major grievance of the Regulators in the 1760s, and at the Fifth Provincial Congress in 1776 delegates from Mecklenburg and Orange Counties (former Regulator strongholds) were instructed to seek lower rates. In 1777 the North Carolina legislature enacted a fee law modeled on the principal colonial act of 1748 but with stiffer penalties for abuse.

Although the establishment of a salary structure for officials generally replaced the fee system in the nineteenth century, vestiges of it remain as payment for the services of various court officers, county officials, and others.

References: Jack P. Greene, *The Quest for Power: The Lower Houses of Assembly in the Southern Royal Colonies, 1689–1776* (1963); William S. Price Jr., "The Fee System in Colonial North Carolina" (M.A. thesis, UNC-Chapel Hill, 1969).

William S. Price Jr.

Fellowship of Southern Churchmen (FSC), organized in 1934 and headquartered in North Carolina, was a loosely affiliated group of prophetic, neo-orthodox southern Christians, both black and white, who worked to eradicate the region's economic and racial problems. Contending that the time had come for radical Christians to lead the way toward a more just society, the FSC attracted such members as Howard Kester, Myles Horton, and Alva Taylor. In 1939 the FSC established headquarters in Black Mountain. From there Kester, the executive secretary, planned meetings and conferences, solicited funds, and sponsored members' activities across the South.

Until 1957, under the leadership of Kester and two other North Carolinians, educator Nelle Morton and the Reverend Charles Johnson, the FSC supported various programs that addressed the South's poverty. During the 1930s and 1940s, fellowship members lent their time and labor to the Southern Tenant Farmers' Union and the Congress of Industrial Organizations. The FSC also served as a clearinghouse for liberal causes in the region. Members distributed pamphlets, speeches, and articles that advocated racial and economic change. After the Supreme Court's 1954 *Brown v. Board of Education* decision, the FSC reprinted and distributed 35,000 copies of Frank Porter Graham's prointegration article, "The Need For Wisdom and Good Faith." They also published the journal *Prophetic Religion*, which espoused their Christian vision of social equality.

While the churchmen blamed the South's problems on greed, power, and ignorance, they also criticized mainstream southern Protestant churches for abdicating their responsibility in the struggles for social justice. They accused churches of catering to the rich and powerful and of neglecting the South's poor blacks and whites. Preaching an updated version of the Social Gospel, the FSC called upon black and white Christians to do good works and to build God's kingdom on earth.

By the 1950s, the FSC had shifted its focus almost entirely to racial justice. Under Kester's leadership, the churchmen vigorously supported the *Brown* decision and sponsored local workshops on school integration. As the civil rights movement gained momentum, however, younger black and white activists flocked to more radical civil rights organizations, and the

FSC—led by older, mostly white southern liberals—lost its appeal. A meeting of southern ministers in the spring of 1957, at which Martin Luther King Jr. spoke, was the FSC's last organized activity. Despite its quiet ending, for more than 20 years the FSC had served as a strong but often lonely voice for economic and racial justice in the South.

References: John Egerton, *Speak Now against the Day: The Generation before the Civil Rights Movement in the South* (1995); Robert F. Martin, "Critique of Southern Society and Vision of a New Order: The Fellowship of Southern Churchmen, 1934–1957," *Church History* 52 (March 1983); Martin, *Howard Kester and the Struggle for Social Justice in the South, 1904–1977* (1991).

Elizabeth Gillespie McRae

Feminism. SEE Women.

Fences. Free range for livestock was the common practice in North Carolina and the rest of the South from earliest settlement until the late nineteenth century. To keep livestock—defined as horses, mules, cattle, goats, sheep, and swine—from ruining crops, farmers customarily kept fences around their fields and garden patches. Free range was most beneficial to landless farmers and small landowners who might otherwise be denied access to waterways and woodlands. Soon after the Civil War ended, however, this system came under attack, since building and maintaining zig-zagging rail fences around crop fields stripped forests and consumed a great deal of farmers' time and energy.

Growth in commercial agriculture in the 1870s and 1880s caused large-scale farmers to seek ways to end this centuries-old practice. In 1873 residents of Alamance, Cabarrus, Mecklenburg, Orange, and Person Counties persuaded the General Assembly to enact the first stock law, or no-fence law, for their counties in the form of enabling legislation. The law, designed to eliminate crop fences and require livestock to be fenced instead, provided for local jurisdiction at either the county or township level. If the measure passed, a fence would be required around the boundary of the entire county or township, financed by a special tax levied on the inhabitants of the stock law territory. Gates were placed across public roads and were often cumbersome to those who traveled frequently in and out of livestock law territory. The responsibility for building and maintaining livestock law fences and gates was assigned to the respective county governments.

By 1880 similar enabling legislation had been passed for Hyde County and about 25 other counties in the Piedmont and western Coastal Plain. After several defeats at the polls, the law was amended so that owners of contiguous tracts could adopt the livestock law even when their neighbors in the same township voted against it. Municipal governments wasted no time in adopting livestock laws and putting up fences and gates

Hannah's Ferry on the Yadkin River between Davie and Rowan Counties, ca. 1900. Courtesy of NCOA&H.

around their boundaries. Children often took turns as unofficial town gatekeepers to ease the flow of traffic and make sure gates were not left open.

In 1901 the legislature passed a measure allowing county commissioners to declare as a lawful fence certain "natural obstructions," such as watercourses and mountain ranges, thereby reducing the burdensome costs of maintaining livestock law fences. A 1917 statute, upheld by the state supreme court in 1918, allowed the responsibility for maintaining fences to be shifted from citizens in stock law territory to those with free range. This law soon ended the practice of free range in most of the state. The livestock law was not adopted along the Outer Banks until 1958, when it became applicable to all livestock except marsh or "Banker" ponies on Ocracoke Island and Shackleford Banks.

K. Todd Johnson

Ferries are an integral part of North Carolina's modern transportation system, with 24 ferries providing regularly scheduled runs on seven different routes across rivers, sounds, and even an ocean access inlet. The capacity of the ferries in the state fleet ranges from 18 to 30 automobiles, and the one-way crossing time runs from 20 minutes on the Neuse River ferry between Minnesott Beach and Cherry Branch to 2 hours and 15 minutes on the voyage across Pamlico Sound from Ocracoke Island to Swan Quarter.

For tourists, a ferry ride is often a pleasant diversion from the routine of highway travel, but the ferries are essential to many coastal residents, providing access to and from work,

school, and shopping centers. The Ocracoke–Swan Quarter ferry offers the only direct access from the isolated barrier island to the county seat on the mainland, and the modest fare charged for the service is considered a bargain. There is also a fee for the Ocracoke-to-Cedar Island run and for the Cape Fear River crossing from Southport to Fort Fisher. The other four routes—Currituck to Knotts Island, Bayview to Aurora, Minnesott Beach to Cherry Branch, and the Hatteras Inlet crossing from Hatteras to Ocracoke Island (the most frequently traveled route)—are free.

North Carolina entered the ferry business after World War II, when it bought out the Thomas A. Baum operations at Alligator River and Croatan Sound, the Toby Tillet ferries at Oregon Inlet, and Frazier Peele's Hatteras Inlet facilities. The current routes have evolved as bridges were built across Alligator River and Croatan Sound, and pressure for improved vehicular access resulted in the establishment of additional runs. The equipment and routes are new, but the use of ferries to enable people to cross the state's immense network of internal waterways dates back to the colonial period. In many instances, the only recourse available to early travelers was to ford the smaller streams in their paths; when it came to the larger watercourses, however, enterprising pioneers responded to the challenge with private ferries. Laws were passed requiring that each ferryman "secure a license from the county court, give bond for the faithful performance of his duty, provide . . . good and sufficient boats, and give constant attendance at the ferry," reported historian C. Christopher Crittenden, adding that "the rates were fixed for each ferry, varying with the length of the passage, the difficulty of crossing, and other similar factors."

A ferryboat design evolved gradually; it called for a craft of flat construction, preferably with sufficient capacity "to take in a carriage and four horses at once." Ferries were often undependable, especially after heavy rains when the freshets pouring down rivers made it impossible to use the cumbersome craft. Storms also affected ferry operations; Governor Arthur Dobbs, returning from a visit to Virginia in 1754, lost a full day at Edenton because the winds were so strong that the ferry could not cross Albemarle Sound. With a maze of rivers, creeks, and runs extending across the entire state, the use of ferries in the piedmont and mountains was just as important as it was in the lowlands. In 1771, while leading his army west, Governor William Tryon encountered Pole Cat Creek, which he described as being "too much swelled to pass over." Tryon had his men cut down a large tree, and they proceeded to cross over the makeshift little bridge "in Indian file."

From the early kunners (vessels made of two or more dugout canoes lashed together) to the modern diesel ships that constitute the current state fleet, there have been many craft of innovative design operating in North Carolina as ferries. One unique craft was the cable ferry, introduced in the nineteenth century for use over narrow waterways; the Sans Souci cable ferry, which crosses the Cashie River in Bertie County, remained in operation in the early 2000s. Most unusual of all was the design Toby Tillet of Wanchese used in 1924 for his 2-car, 45-foot wooden ferry *Oregon Inlet*. Because the channels in the inlet and shoreline were forever in a state of flux, Tillet made no effort to establish any dock or permanent landing place on either the Bodie Island or Hatteras Island side. Instead, he put a landing ramp on the bow that could be raised or lowered by one man with the aid of chains and pulleys. When coming in for a landing, Tillet would ram the bow of his ferry against the shore at whatever he considered the best spot on that particular day, then lower the ramp and guide the drivers as they backed onto the sandy beach. The system proved so successful that Tillet continued to use it in the successively larger ferries he built for the Oregon Inlet run, the 10-car *New Inlet* and 14-car *Barcelona*. In a 1930s hurricane, the original ferry broke loose from its moorings, sailed pilotless out to sea, and was never recovered.

By the early 2000s, according to the North Carolina Department of Transportation's Ferry Division, North Carolina ferries were transporting more than 1.1 million vehicles and more than 2.5 million passengers annually.

References: C. Christopher Crittenden, *The Commerce of North Carolina, 1763–1789* (1936); Bill Sharpe, "Bon Free Voyage," *The State* (5 June 1954).

David Stick

SEE ALSO Blossom's Ferry.

Festival for the Eno, a multiple-day event held annually in northern Durham since 1980 and sponsored by the Eno River Association with the help of local establishments, is considered to be one of the premier folk and arts festivals in North Carolina and the Southeast. The festival is dedicated to conserving and protecting the natural environment, culture, and history of the Eno River basin, with proceeds supporting the association's work in the upkeep of the river and the purchase of land within its watershed. The first festival, a single-day event, was staged on 4 July 1980 by Margaret C. Nygard and a core of 100 volunteers. It featured two stages for performances as well as multiple arts displays, crafts booths, and food stands. The festival drew almost 12,000 people, a number that would steadily rise through the 1980s and 1990s (despite being hindered in some years by record high temperatures and other natural forces, such as a major flood in 1995).

In 1998 the Festival for the Eno first broke the 40,000 attendance mark, bringing more than $100,000 to the Eno River Association. The festival, which continues to be centered around Independence Day, has drawn hundreds of thousands of visitors through the years and, along with numerous local artists and craftsmen, such performers as Doc Watson, Emmylou Harris, and Etta Baker.

Philip McFee

Fiction. Whether by creating historical narratives of important eras and events from the state's past or by portraying the outwardly mundane but emotionally complex realities of small-town, contemporary southern life, North Carolina fiction writers have always been a robust and imaginative voice within American literature. Truly widespread and serious focus on the literature of North Carolina first emerged during the mid-twentieth century, with the publication of three important literary surveys: Walter Spearman's *North Carolina Writers* (1949, revised in 1953); *North Carolina Authors: A Selective Handbook* (1952), by the North Carolina English Teachers Association and the North Carolina Library Association; and *Literary North Carolina* (1970, revised in 1986), by Richard Walser and E. T. Malone Jr. From the founding of numerous literary journals and magazines to the establishment of the annual North Carolina Literary Festival, interest in North Carolina literature, and its fiction in particular, has increased over the decades. General popular and scholarly attention has concentrated on the writings of Civil War–era novelists and poets Charles Waddell Chesnutt and Edwin Wiley Fuller; nineteenth-century historical novelists such as Robert Strange and Calvin Henderson Wiley; early well-known fiction writers such as O. Henry, Wilbur Daniel Steele, and Olive Tilford Dargan; and twentieth-century mass appeal writers such as Thomas Wolfe. From these established icons to still-prolific talents such as Daniel Wallace, Lawrence Naumoff, and Charles Frazier, the state's fiction writers have long since transcended purely regional appeal and become producers of literature that is both brilliantly crafted and highly acclaimed.

Humanizing History: Pioneers of North Carolina Fiction

The first novel written by a resident North Carolinian was *Matilda Berkely; or, Family Anecdotes*, by Winifred Marshall Gales. Published in Raleigh in 1804, the novel weaves a story of the upper class in Russia and England (Gales had already published a novel in her native England). It was not until 1839, however, that a novel with a North Carolina locale was written. In that year, Robert Strange of Fayetteville, a Virginia native but long-time North Carolina resident, published *Eoneguski; or, The Cherokee Chief*, based on materials he collected while serving as a judge in western North Carolina. Strange's characters were thin disguises of white settlers or Indians whom he had met or heard about. His *Eoneguski* is a historical romance in the James Fenimore Cooper tradition, with complex love affairs sharing space with sweeping adventures. Apart from being a potboiler, the novel's secondary, and arguably most valuable function, is as a storehouse of Cherokee legends and customs.

North Carolina's first truly native novelist was the educator Calvin Henderson Wiley, who was born in Guilford County. His *Alamance* (1847) describes gripping Revolutionary War events in and around Alamance Presbyterian Church, southeast of Greensboro. In *Roanoke* (1849), Wiley wrote about the eastern North Carolina towns of New Bern and Wilmington, also through the historical lens of the Revolution. At a time when North Carolina was falling behind other states in literature, Wiley's two novels were a conscientious attempt to recreate some of the most vivid but nearly forgotten episodes in North Carolina history.

Writer, abolitionist, and reformer Harriet Jacobs was born a slave in Edenton in 1813. Her life story, *Incidents in the Life of a Slave Girl, Written by Herself*, published under the pseudonym Linda Brent in 1861, influenced northern attitudes toward emancipation during the Civil War, pulled back the curtain on sexual oppression, and cast an equally critical eye on racial oppression. Jacobs, through her carefully crafted narrative and strategic omissions, maintained a safe distance from her work, giving her insular, sometimes lurid text a distinctively novelistic feel.

While Jacobs broke barriers by integrating the literary community, other authors had success in a specific genre. Mary Ann Bryan Mason's *A Wreath from the Woods of Carolina* (1859) was the first North Carolina book written for young readers. Its ten stories are highly moralistic lessons in which pious children are rewarded and miscreants are punished, usually by death. Mason's novel, *Her Church and Her Mother: A Story of Filial Piety* (1860), is set in Raleigh's Christ Episcopal Church, where her husband was rector.

Essayist, folklorist, short story writer, and novelist Charles Waddell Chesnutt was the first African American writer to receive widespread serious attention during his lifetime as a literary artist and was considered one of the major fiction writers of his era. Born in Ohio in 1858, Chesnutt spent his childhood and early adulthood in Fayetteville. His best-known book, *The Conjure Woman* (1899), is a retelling of seven African American slave folktales from the Cape Fear region. Five of the nine stories in *The Wife of His Youth and Other Stories of the Color Line* (1899) are set in and around Fayetteville, as is the novel *The House behind the Cedars* (1900). Both works deal with the problems confronting people of mixed race, a topic of increasing prevalence made most famous by James Weldon Johnson's 1912 *Autobiography of an Ex-Colored Man*. Other Chesnutt books, *The Marrow of Tradition* (1901), based on the Wilmington race riot of 1898, and *The Colonel's Dream* (1905), set in Reconstruction-era Fayetteville, address the often hopeless situation of blacks in a white society.

Christian Reid of Salisbury was one of nineteenth-century North Carolina's most prolific novelists. The author of 46 books, mostly novels, Reid was representative of the genteel literature of that era. Born Frances Christine Fisher, she chose her pseudonym to delineate the ethical purposes of her writing and to disguise her true identity and gender. In that era it was thought "unladylike" to use one's real name for authorship. Reid's tenth book, *The Land of the Sky* (1876), a travel novel, created a nickname that has ever since denoted the western mountains of North Carolina.

North Carolina Writers in the Early to Mid-Twentieth Century

As the twentieth century dawned, North Carolina fiction writers continued to weave impressive historical narratives, often throwing light on the distressing political, racial, and personal divisions that characterized the state. Thomas Dixon Jr., a native of Cleveland County, wrote *The Leopard's Spots* (1902) and *The Clansman* (1905), novels of the Reconstruction from which the inspiration for D. W. Griffith's epic motion picture *The Birth of a Nation* (1915) was gleaned. A former minister, Dixon was a propagandist for the doctrine of white supremacy. His first two novels became immediate sensations but were imbued with an overly prevailing racism.

Thomas Wolfe has left an indelible mark on the literature of North Carolina and the world. Born in Asheville in 1900, his epic autobiographical novel *Look Homeward, Angel* (1929) has never gone out of print since its publication. Perhaps the most overtly autobiographical of the state's (and the nation's) major novelists, Wolfe's boyhood in his mother's boardinghouse colored his work and influenced the rest of his life. His reflections were so frank and realistic that *Look Homeward, Angel* was banned from Asheville's public library for more than seven years. His second novel, *Of Time and the River* (1935), was a continuation of *Look Homeward, Angel*, and Wolfe's last two major novels (published posthumously), *The Web and the Rock* (1939) and *You Can't Go Home Again* (1940), followed the events of his life in New York City, his wandering travels through Europe, his success as a novelist, and his famous final revelation that "you can't go home again." Wolfe died of brain tuberculosis on 15 Sept. 1938, only 18 days short of his thirty-eighth birthday.

After Robert Strange's *Eoneguski* and Calvin Henderson Wiley's *Alamance* and *Roanoke*, several novels with a background of North Carolina history were published, but few were of major distinction. An exception is James Boyd's *Drums* (1925), a classic of North Carolina literature that determined a new direction for the genre and brought the historical novel out of the commonplace. Boyd had read thoroughly into the documents of the period and his meticulous historical detail permeated *Drums*. The novel is a saga about a North Carolinian's everyday hopes and tribulations during the Revolutionary War. Boyd's Civil War novel, *Marching On* (1927), was also well received.

Another author's careful research continued to strengthen the tradition of the state's fine historical novels. In *Alexandria* (1940), LeGette Blythe of Huntersville rendered the panorama of revolutionary years in North Carolina, focusing on the heroic actions of Whigs in Mecklenburg County. Dozens of celebrated characters from history supplied the background of Blythe's fiction. His *Call Down the Storm* (1958) relates the downfall of a dignified family by interracial marriage in nineteenth-century North Carolina, then moves to the 1950s to relate how history could repeat itself.

Raleigh's Eden (1940) was the first of 12 novels in Inglis Fletcher's "Carolina Series." Like Boyd and Blythe, Fletcher believed that research needed to precede composition. Her work recounts the establishment of a democratic state from an early attempt at colonization up through the ratification of the Constitution. Among novels in her popular series are *Roanoke Hundred* (1948), *The Wind in the Forest* (1957), and *Wicked Lady* (1962).

John Ehle inaugurated his series of historical novels set in western North Carolina by writing a trilogy depicting life in three geographic locations of the state. Ehle began with the Piedmont: In *Move over, Mountain* (1957), he details how a black man in "Leafwood" (Carrboro) succeeds in overcoming obstacles by keeping resolute in his family bonds. (The racial divide in the area would arise decades later in Daphne Athas's Chapel Hill/Carrboro novel *Entering Ephesus*, published in 1971.) The setting of Ehle's second novel, *Kingstree Island* (1958), is actually Ocracoke, where an outsider battles the leader of the island for acceptance. In his third novel, *Lion in the Hearth* (1961), Ehle uses his native Asheville for the story of a sensitive young man in an unfeeling environment. Ehle's other novels include *The Road* (1967), *The Winter People* (1982),

and *The Widow's Trial* (1989). Ehle has also written five books of nonfiction, including *Trail of Tears: The Rise and Fall of the Cherokee Nation* (1988).

North Carolina Fiction Comes of Age

The portrayal of the relationships, perceptions, and struggles of "common" North Carolinians—particularly in small towns ranging from the mountains to the coast—became the focus of the works of many of the state's writers during the second half of the twentieth century, often garnering national and international attention and signaling what may be labeled a literary renaissance. After writing several books of short stories, Statesville-born Doris Betts published her first novel, *Tall Houses in Winter*, in 1957. The central theme of her next work, *The Scarlet Thread* (1965), is a new cotton mill built on the Katsewa (Catawba) River in Stone (Iredell) County and the people whose lives will be changed because of it. Betts's other works of fiction include *Beasts of the Southern Wild* (1973), *Heading West* (1982), *Souls Raised from the Dead* (1994), and *The Sharp Teeth of Love* (1997).

Asheville-born Wilma Dykeman is the author of well over a dozen books, several of them novels, and numerous memoirs. *The Tall Woman* (1962) tells of a courageous mother's attempts to improve life among the primitive inhabitants of the mountains; its sequel, *The Far Family* (1966), continues several generations later. *Return the Innocent Earth* (1973) is based on the fact that Dykeman's husband, James R. Stokely Jr., belonged to the farming family that established the Stokely canning complex. *Explorations* (1984), a collection of essays, reflects many of Dykeman's experiences in nature and with family in western North Carolina as well as many other places, featuring interior as well as outer explorations. Most of her books are influenced by her love of the natural treasures of her region and the variety of the people who live there.

Reynolds Price's first novel, *A Long and Happy Life* (1962), is a fascinating story of pastoral Warren County. Born in Macon, a village near Warrenton, Price graduated from Duke University and in 1955 traveled as a Rhodes Scholar to Merton College, Oxford University, to study English literature. He returned to Duke, where he has stayed the rest of his career. Price has published more than two dozen books, including *The Surface of Earth* (1975) and *The Source of Light* (1981). His novel *Kate Vaiden* (1986) received the National Book Critics Circle Award in 1986, and his *Collected Stories* appeared in 1993. Price has also published volumes of poems, plays, essays, and translations and two volumes of memoirs. He is a member of the American Academy of Arts and Letters, and his books have appeared in 16 languages.

Anne Tyler, brought up in Raleigh and Price's student when he began teaching at Duke, published her first novel, *If Morning Ever Comes*, in 1964. *The Tin Can Tree* (1965) used Tyler's teenage experiences while working in a tobacco warehouse.

The setting of *A Slipping-Down Life* (1970) is the North Carolina towns of Pulqua and Farinia (Fuquay-Varina in Wake County). Tyler's novels include *Dinner at the Homesick Restaurant* (1982), her first best seller, and *The Accidental Tourist* (1985). Her eleventh novel, *Breathing Lessons*, was awarded the Pulitzer Prize in 1988.

Canton native Fred Chappell emerged by 1985 as among the most acclaimed writers in North Carolina. Much of Chappell's work is rooted in his native mountains west of Asheville. *It Is Time, Lord* (1963) tells of a man lost in memories and dreams as he contemplates his grim past. In *The Inkling* (1965) Chappell creates a circular novel, beginning and ending at the same moment. His other novels include *Dagon* (1968), *The Gaudy Place* (1973), and the Kirkman Trilogy—all fictionalized remembrances of Chappell's youth on a mountain farm. In addition to more than 20 books, Chappell has published criticism, essays, and reviews in newspapers and journals.

Lee Smith wrote three novels before moving to North Carolina in 1974. Her first North Carolina novel, *Black Mountain Breakdown*, was published in 1981. In *Oral History* (1983), told in the fashion of a folktale, a young mountain man sets out to find a wife; however, the girl he marries is the witch Red Emmy. Smith also wrote two collections of short stories and was a recipient of the 1991 Robert Penn Warren Prize for Fiction and the John Dos Passos Award. She continues to contribute thoughtful entries to the fiction arena, including 1995's *Fair and Tender Ladies*.

Gail Godwin was born in Alabama but spent her formative years, like so many other literary talents, in Asheville. Although she moved to Woodstock, N.Y., her writing remained distinctly southern. She has taught at Vassar College and Columbia University and has received a Guggenheim Fellowship and the 1981 Award in Literature from the National Institute of Arts and Letters. Her highly praised books include *Violet Clay* (1978), *Mr. Bedford and the Muses* (1983), and *Evensong* (1999). Like Godwin, Asheville native Charles Frazier used his knowledge of the North Carolina mountains to harvest the region's ever-fertile literary themes. A teacher of early American literature at the University of Colorado, Frazier stopped in 1990 to focus on his writing, and his efforts produced the hugely successful Civil War novel *Cold Mountain* (1997), modeled roughly on the geography of his native state. Frazier's work brought him wide critical acclaim, winning a National Book Award and reaching the top of the *New York Times* best seller list.

Beginning with the unique and unsettling twists common to the stories of Greensboro's O. Henry (William Sydney Porter, 1862–1910), North Carolina has been home to a vital community of writers that have gained national acclaim in the mystery and science fiction genres. Lilian Jackson Braun (1916–) and Orson Scott Card (1951–), though born in other states, are long-time North Carolina residents who have been particularly prolific. Beginning in 1966 with the publication of *The Cat Who Could Read Backwards*, Braun has written numerous additions to her series of mysteries featuring the crime-solving Siamese cats Koko and Yum Yum. Card's many popular works have included the seminal science fiction masterpiece *Ender's Game* (1985) and its sequels, as well as other books, plays, stories, and television and film scripts. Raleigh native Margaret Maron has gained a wide following with her Judge Deborah Knott mystery series, beginning with the award-winning *Bootlegger's Daughter* (1992), set in fictional Colleton County, N.C.

Some North Carolina authors have written widely appreciated freshman titles. Rocky Mount–born Allan Gurganus saw his first novel, *Oldest Living Confederate Widow Tells All*, emerge to significant acclaim in 1989. Gurganus followed his debut with the story collection *White People* (1991), and the novel *Plays Well with Others* (1997). His 2001 collection of four novellas, *The Practical Heart*, won a Lambda Literary Award for excellence in gay, lesbian, transgender, and bisexual publishing.

Gurganus represents some of the diverse fiction offerings that continue to emerge from North Carolina writers. Most notably, University of North Carolina at Chapel Hill graduate Randall Kenan's writing explores a broad range of African American life, often reaching back to his childhood in Chinquapin. Kenan's works include the novel *A Visitation of Spirits* (1989); a collection of short stories, *Let the Dead Bury Their Dead* (1992); and the nonfiction *Walking on Water: Black American Lives at the Turn of the Twenty-First Century* (1999), which chronicles a seven-year exploration of the contemporary black experience. Doris Betts protégé at Chapel Hill Sarah Dessen has achieved great success with her young adult selections, including *That Summer* (1996) and *Dreamland* (2000).

References: Joseph M. Flora, Lucinda H. MacKethan, and Todd Taylor, eds., *The Companion to Southern Literature: Themes, Genres, Places, People, Movements, and Motifs* (2002); Robert Gingher, ed., *The Rough Road Home: Stories by North Carolina Writers* (1992); Sarah R. Shaber, ed., *Tar Heel Dead: Tales of Mystery and Mayhem from North Carolina* (2005); Bland Simpson, "Literary North Carolina," *Our State* 70 (November 2002); Walter Spearman, *North Carolina Writers* (rev. ed., 1953); Richard Walser and E. T. Malone Jr., *Literary North Carolina: A Historical Survey* (1986).

Philip McFee
Ted Mitchell
Additional research provided by Michael McFee and Douglas J. McMillan.

SEE ALSO Literary Awards; Literary Journals; *Matilda Berkely; or, Family Anecdotes*; North Carolina Writers Conference; North Carolina Writers' Network; O. Henry Festival; Poetry; Roanoke-Chowan Group; *Sea-Gift*.

Field Names were used in the British Isles to facilitate identification in farm records, to simplify the laying out of tasks, or in the discussion of seasonal plans. They also were used in wills and inventories of estates to designate specific tracts. This practice was continued in the American colonies and has survived to the present time. In North Carolina and elsewhere in the South, many field names are so old that landowners may have no idea of the names' origins. Plantation records, correspondence, and tradition, however, record many of the names. Often the name of a former owner was attached to a tract. Some characteristic of the land—a tree, a boulder, an event that occurred there, or some other source of inspiration—provided a name. Such field names as the Sophia field, the Johnson's old place, the fish pond field, the cypress tree field, the rabbit patch, horse pen ridge, the militia ground, and the like became permanently attached to the land.

William S. Powell

Fifteenth Amendment. SEE Disfranchisement.

Filmmaking. Studio movie production was popular throughout much of North Carolina, especially in the mountains, until the advent of "talkies" in the late 1920s necessitated the more controlled environment of sound stages. In the 1910s several production companies set up summer studios in and around Asheville and Hendersonville to take advantage of both the weather and the exquisite scenery. The eccentric Ned Finley starred in, produced, and directed several successful movies from these locations.

The first in-state studio run by a North Carolinian was probably North State Films, founded by W. S. Scales in Winston-Salem in the first quarter of the twentieth century. Scales, an important and barely documented filmmaker, was one of the few African American film producers of his time. He had been a successful theater owner in Winston-Salem, booking acts from the black vaudeville circuit as well as movies, and the black film industry was still in its infancy when he produced *His Great Chance* and *The Devil's Match* in 1923. At least two other black-owned production companies were formed in North Carolina in the 1920s, but whether they produced any films is not known.

In 1921 North Carolina pioneered the use of motion pictures as an educational tool. Mabel Evans, superintendent of Dare County schools, believed that the story of British efforts to colonize the New World should be told, especially to the state's schoolchildren. Evans received the enthusiastic support of the North Carolina Literary and Historical Association and the State Board of Education. Elizabeth Grimball, the director of the New York School of the Theatre, was selected to direct the picture, and Atlas Film Corporation of Chicago was engaged to do the filming. On 15 Nov. 1921 Governor Cameron Morrison and other state dignitaries gathered in the old Supreme Court Building for the premiere of the five-reel silent motion picture, *The Lost Colony*. This select audience

was pleased with the film, and prints were made for general distribution.

John Warner, founder of Lord-Warner Pictures in Greenville, produced his one theatrical release, *Pitch a Boogie Woogie*, in 1947. Warner, a white man who had entertained local blacks at his Greenville theater with his own versions of "movies of local people" as early as the mid-1930s, was a self-taught filmmaker whose first film experience was freelancing for newsreel companies. He had dreamed of opening a Hollywood-style studio in Greenville, but a combination of factors proved his ruin. Warner also filmed Hurricane Helene (1958) for a local television station, where he worked after his film company folded.

The secretaries of the chambers of commerce of Raleigh, Goldsboro, Wilmington, Charlotte, Morganton, Greensboro, and Asheville met in Raleigh in 1934 and launched an effort to encourage filmmaking in the state. This idea was apparently first voiced by Louis T. Moore, the Wilmington chamber's secretary, prior to the Raleigh meeting. During the 1940s and 1950s, motion picture films and video copies of *North Carolina: Variety Vacationland* were used by the Division of Travel Information of the Department of Conservation and Development to promote the state, its people, and its resources. Feature films such as *Ruby Gentry* (1952), starring Jennifer Jones and Charlton Heston, were also filmed in part in North Carolina during this era.

In 1962, with a grant from the Smith Richardson Foundation, the North Carolina Film Board was created to produce films about the state and to encourage the production of commercial films in the state. The board was dissolved in June 1965

Shooting a scene for the television series *Dawson's Creek* on the campus of the University of North Carolina at Wilmington, 2000. Cast members (left to right) Kerr Smith, Katie Holmes, and James Van Der Beek are seated on the steps. Courtesy of North Carolina Film Office.

after producing 19 films, most of which were historical or educational in nature.

Governor James B. Hunt created the North Carolina Film Office (later the North Carolina Film Commission) by executive order in 1980, and within six years the state had become one of the top three filmmaking states in the nation. It is estimated that between 1980 and 1998, the film business added about $5 billion to the state's economy, more than half of which was spent in Wilmington. This amount reflects direct spending by the film industry, to which is added the income to service companies that support the industry—food catering, equipment companies, and generator and camera companies. Wilmington, sometimes called the "Hollywood of the East," has an estimated crew base of 1,000 professionals, including makeup, wardrobe, and casting personnel. Wilmington's position as the largest filmmaking center in North Carolina (although about three-fourths of the state's 100 counties have been the locale for feature films) has benefited in no small measure by the aggressiveness of the Wilmington Regional Film Commission. In 1998, for instance, the film business generated about $300 million in the state, with about $160 million in the Wilmington area alone.

Other filmmaking centers in the state include Asheville, Charlotte, High Point, Raleigh, and Shelby. Earl Owensby's E. O. Corporation in Shelby, a large independent motion picture complex, owned the state's first independent production studio when it opened in 1973 with the movie *Challenge*. Since then Owensby has produced, directed, or starred in some 40 feature films and television and cable network productions. The Full Frame Documentary Film Festival (previously the DoubleTake Documentary Film Festival) is an international event held annually in Durham. The four-day festival showcases important contemporary regional, national, and international documentaries and facilitates the exploration of their themes, ideas, and filmmaking techniques. The contribution of the North Carolina School of the Arts' school of filmmaking in Winston-Salem has also been substantial. The presence of this state-supported school means that young people seeking film industry work no longer need go to Hollywood or New York City to gain their credentials.

Since 1980, North Carolina has been connected to the production of more than 700 movies and 6 network television series, representing $6 billion in production revenue. Although international competition, particularly from Canada, has caused revenues to slip (by 2002 they were $230 million, less than half of 1993's all-time high of $504.3 million), the state remains home to the largest number of studio facilities (7) and sound stages (30) of any state except California. The long list of successful films made entirely or partially in North Carolina includes *Being There* (1979), *Blue Velvet* (1986), *Bull Durham* (1988), *The Color Purple* (1985), *Dirty Dancing* (1987), *Forrest Gump* (1994), *The Green Mile* (1999), *The Hunt for Red Oc-*

tober (1990), *Lolita* (1998), *Patch Adams* (1998), *The Dangerous Lives of Altar Boys* (2002), and *A Walk to Remember* (2002).

References: Tom Acitelli, "Lights! Camera! North Carolina?," *Spectator* (15–21 May 2002); Alex Albright, "North Carolina's Early Movies," *The State* (July 1986); Billy Arthur, "How the Movies Started in North Carolina," *The State* (December 1963); Jennifer Ann Palcher, "Hollywood East: An Examination of the Film Industry in North Carolina" (M.A. thesis, UNC-Chapel Hill, 1997).

Alex Albright
Additional research provided by Ronnie W. Faulkner and Wiley J. Williams.

SEE ALSO North Carolina Film Board; Town Documentaries.

Fire Departments in North Carolina cities and towns have advanced from sincere but often ineffective community efforts to highly equipped governmental agencies employing numerous professional firefighters. For centuries, North Carolina fires have caused severe damage to property as well as tragic loss of life. The threat of sudden destruction by fire was ever-present in eighteenth- and nineteenth-century towns whose buildings were constructed almost entirely of wood. In these towns, or situated nearby, were businesses highly prone to catching fire, such as naval stores and lumber yards, blacksmith shops, and gristmills. Later in the 1800s, many textile factories, furniture companies, and sprawling warehouses full of dried tobacco proved to be disastrously flammable.

In colonial North Carolina, fear of fire prompted some towns to enact public safety laws and form volunteer firefighting groups. Residents in Edenton were required to keep a ladder at the side of their homes, and in New Bern each household had two leather buckets as well as a ladder to help fight fires. Wilmington even levied a tax on its citizens for fire protection and in 1755 used that revenue to buy its first hand-pumped "water engine." Salem laid one of the South's first public water systems in 1778. Although this system served the convenience of the inhabitants and improved the town's overall hygiene, the wooden water pipes were installed primarily to assist local fire brigades.

Given the predominant use of wood in the construction and heating of buildings and of candles and oil lamps for lighting, as well as the general inadequacies of early water systems, it is understandable that virtually every municipality in North Carolina encountered major fires. Following the charring of about 50 houses and shops in Raleigh in June 1816, many citizens rebuilt with brick and other more flame-resistant materials. Wilmington, too, despite early prevention measures, suffered the ravages of numerous conflagrations; a fire in November 1819 destroyed a large section of the bustling port town.

In 1831 two massive fires occurred in North Carolina. On

29 May in Fayetteville, a small blaze that began on a kitchen roof at the corner of Green and Hay Streets spread rapidly. By day's end more than 600 structures along eight major streets were consumed by flames, including homes, stores, churches, hotels, the Fayetteville Academy, and the town hall where North Carolinians had ratified the U.S. Constitution in 1789. Less than a month later, on 21 June, a fire in Raleigh devastated the old State Capitol. The cause of that disaster was blamed on the carelessness of a workman, who, ironically, started the blaze while installing a fireproof zinc roof. A particularly destructive fire in Greensboro in January 1849 prompted the town to buy an improved fire engine, one manufactured in Baltimore and dubbed "General Greene."

Various volunteer "bucket brigades" and fire departments were formed during the nineteenth century as growing towns began to face ever greater risks from fire. The first fire engine was purchased by the city of Raleigh in 1816. Charlotte's first fire prevention services were authorized by city officials in 1845. The Wilmington Hook and Ladder Company, a volunteer group, was chartered in 1867. Thirty years later Wilmington organized the city's first professional fire department, staffed by 30 men who fought blazes with three steam fire engines and one hook-and-ladder truck.

Before the Civil War, slaves often served as official firemen in their communities. Fayetteville and Wilmington—both ravaged earlier by widespread fires—relied on slave labor to operate the considerable firefighting equipment they had acquired by the late 1840s and 1850s. In 1848, 10 slaves manned Fayetteville's hook-and-ladder company, and 25 others served in the town's two-engine companies. As official firefighters, each slave wore a distinctive cap marked with the number of the engine to which he belonged.

Notable fires in North Carolina have occurred in business and manufacturing settings. In 1923 a raging fire, caused by sawdust that ignited in the factory, wrecked the White Furniture Company's structure in Mebane; no one died, and the business survived. On 28 Jan. 1934 a fire at Wrightsville Beach destroyed the northern end of the island and claimed the celebrated Oceanic Hotel. On 11 Mar. 1948 nine patients perished at Highland Hospital in Asheville; among the dead was Zelda Fitzgerald, the talented yet troubled wife of American author F. Scott Fitzgerald. One of the state's worst industrial disasters occurred at Imperial Food Products, a chicken-processing plant in Hamlet, where on 3 Sept. 1991 a hydraulic line ruptured and started a blaze. Flames and toxic smoke killed 25 workers and injured 56 others. In July 1998 another Asheville fire—attributed to arson—substantially damaged the family home of novelist Thomas Wolfe, author of *Look Homeward, Angel* (1929).

As the twentieth century progressed, fire departments and rescue services came increasingly under the control of local and state governments. The modern-day Office of the State Fire Marshal, a division of the North Carolina Department of Insurance, rose from the state's Firemen's Relief Fund, established by the General Assembly in 1907. The office consists of six divisions: the Engineering Division, Manufactured Buildings Division, State Property Fire Insurance Fund Division, Fire and Rescue Training and Inspections Division, Fire and Rescue Commission Division, and Division of Prevention, Program Development, and Grants. The Engineering Division administers state building codes, and the Fire and Rescue Commission Division regulates city fire departments, rescue squads, and the more than 40,000 certified volunteer firefighters working in the state. Between 1995 and 2005, North Carolina's 1,300-plus fire departments lost 31 professional or volunteer firefighters who were killed on the job.

R. Neil Fulghum
Additional research provided by Jay Mazzocchi.

"First at Bethel, Farthest to the Front at Gettysburg and Chickamauga, and Last at Appomattox"

"First at Bethel, Farthest to the Front at Gettysburg and Chickamauga, and Last at Appomattox" is a traditional saying honoring the role of North Carolina's soldiers in the Civil War. Editor Walter Clark, later chief justice of the Supreme Court of North Carolina, encouraged its use as early as 1901. The initial three words, "First at Bethel," hold a double meaning. The First Regiment of North Carolina Volunteers was instrumental in winning a Confederate victory at Bethel, Va., on 10 June 1861, the first land battle of the war; this engagement took the life of Tarboro resident Henry Lawson Wyatt, the first Confederate soldier to die in action.

During the Battle of Gettysburg, North Carolina infantrymen advanced the greatest distance against withering Union gunfire on 3 July 1863 in an attack commonly known as Pickett's Charge. Some credit the 58th North Carolina Regiment with the deepest penetration of enemy lines on Snodgrass Hill at Chickamauga on 20 Sept. 1863, although at least one historian contends that battle conditions made the claim impossible to substantiate. Finally, the men of Company D, 30th North Carolina Regiment, fired the last shots on federal forces at Appomattox on 9 Apr. 1865, the day Gen. Robert E. Lee surrendered his Army of Northern Virginia to Union general Ulysses S. Grant.

References: Hugh T. Lefler and Albert R. Newsome, *North Carolina: The History of a Southern State* (1973); Greg Mast, *State Troops and Volunteers: A Photographic Record of North Carolina's Civil War Soldiers* (1995).

Jan-Michael Poff

First Citizens Bank & Trust Company began as the Bank of Smithfield, organized in 1898 as Johnston County's first bank and a precursor to the establishment of the Smithfield tobacco market. Founder Allen K. Smith served as president from 1898 until 1906, when Willis Lester ("Less") Woodall assumed the presidency. Under Woodall, the Bank of Smithfield became the First National Bank of Smithfield and was granted membership in the federal reserve system.

Soaring cotton and tobacco prices during and immediately following World War I gave rise to unprecedented growth, and by mid-1919 First National's total assets were over $800,000, with capital stock raised to $100,000. A 1921 merger with Citizens National Bank resulted in the bank taking on another new name, First and Citizens National Bank, which in 1929 was changed to First Citizens Bank & Trust Company. Robert Powell Holding, a Wake Forest native and recent law school graduate, had joined the bank in 1918 as an assistant cashier and was soon promoted to cashier. Considered a financial wizard, Holding succeeded Thomas Ruffin Hood as president in 1935. He continued to enlarge the scope of the bank's operations through the Great Depression, World War II, and the postwar years, building First Citizens into North Carolina's second-largest bank, with more that $200 million in assets and 45 branches serving 31 communities.

Holding's three sons took charge of their father's legacy after his death in 1957. Robert P. Holding Jr. became chairman of the board, Lewis R. Holding became president, and Frank B. Holding became vice president. Within a decade they had further expanded the bank to 114 offices in 51 towns. First Citizens remains one of the largest family-controlled banks in the United States, with a third generation of Holdings in leadership positions. With its headquarters in Raleigh, First Citizens by 2006 had more than 340 branch offices in North Carolina, Virginia, Tennessee, Maryland, and West Virginia, with assets of more than $14 billion.

Reference: Alma W. Jones, "First Citizens Bank & Trust Company," in *Heritage of Johnston County, North Carolina* (1985).

K. Todd Johnson

"First in Freedom"

"First in Freedom" is a slogan referring to the action of an assembly of representatives in colonial North Carolina that adopted a nonimportation agreement on 2 Nov. 1769. This document "took measures for preserving the true and essential interests of the province," according to Assembly Speaker John Harvey. The action was in line with the sentiments of many other colonies, which were resisting such measures as the Stamp Act, an act allowing Parliament the right to levy taxes in the colonies. This was reputedly the first time such a legislative body took action in protest of Parliament's right to tax the colonies. Some historians believe that the slogan "First in Freedom" refers to the Halifax Resolves, the first official state action urging a declaration of independence from England.

References: Hugh T. Lefler and William S. Powell, *Colonial North Carolina: A History* (1973); Powell, *North Carolina through Four Centuries* (1989).

Ginny Orvedahl

First Union Bank Corporation was founded in 1908 by H. M. Victor as the Union National Bank, which developed a strong economic base through innovation. Union National was the first Charlotte bank to open a branch (1947), the first to offer a flat-fee checking account, and the first to offer a bank charge card. In 1958 Union National merged with the First National Bank and Trust Company of Asheville to form the First Union National Bank of North Carolina. Under the leadership of Cliff Cameron and Edward E. Crutchfield, First Union diversified and grew through acquisitions in the 1960s through the 1980s. A 1985 merger with Northwestern Financial Corporation made First Union the state's second-largest bank. Shortly after interstate banking deregulation in 1985, First Union established branches in Florida, Georgia, South Carolina, Tennessee, Virginia, Maryland, and Washington, D.C.

With headquarters in Charlotte, First Union was by the late 1990s the nation's sixth-largest banking company. The bank had 45,000 employees, served 11 million customers, and had nearly 2,000 retail offices nationwide. In 2001 First Union merged with another North Carolina banking giant, Wachovia Corporation of Winston-Salem, and continued under the Wachovia name with headquarters in Charlotte. The new banking corporation became the fourth-largest in the country, with $499 billion in assets and more than 95,000 employees.

Reference: Cliff Cameron, *First Union Corporation: A Bank Holding Company* (1980).

Julian M. Pleasants

Fish. SEE Wildlife.

Fishing, Commercial. Fishing for both finfish and shellfish has long been an important source of income throughout the coastal area of North Carolina. The state's relative isolation from major markets, the absence of efficient transportation systems, and the perishable nature of the product combined to limit the profitability of fishing until the late nineteenth century. In 1890 shad, herring, oysters, mullet, and bluefish accounted for more than 99 percent of the products of the state's fisheries. By 1940, however, nearly half of the commercial catch was in shrimp and hard-shell crabs, and the once-important shad and herring fisheries were on the verge of extinction.

Fishing techniques have varied with species and with advancing technology. The pound net, employed beginning in the nineteenth century in sound fishing, allowed fish to swim into an enclosed area but prevented them from exiting. More

Fisherman poling his boat to a net in Back Sound in Carteret County, 1992. Copyright Edwin Martin, 1992. NCC.

or less permanently set in sound waters, pound nets and their markers were familiar sights. Also common were seine nets, thrown out and drawn around a school of fish by a work crew. For larger species such as sturgeon and red drum heavy tackle has been employed. A disappearing method, which was still used at the end of the twentieth century on the Outer Banks, is "haul net seining" from ocean beaches. In the nineteenth century, this method involved setting a net between two boats just beyond the surf, beaching the boats, and pulling the net to shore by hand. By the mid-1900s, four-wheel drive vehicles provided the pulling power. The technique was favored during seasons when large schools of migrating fish, such as bluefish or sea trout, were likely to swim close to shore.

Although the technology of transporting fresh fish advanced considerably in the late nineteenth century, the preferred method for most food species—such as mullet, mackerel, and shad—was to salt the fish before shipping to extend the life of the product. For sturgeon as well as shad in some seasons, the fishery yielded not the flesh of the species but rather its roe (eggs). An adult female sturgeon in Pamlico Sound, for example, might weigh a half-ton and yield 100 pounds or more of roe, which was salted and sold as caviar. Shad roe was considered a delicacy both locally and in northern urban markets. The emphasis on fish roe as a product for these two fisheries helped lead to declines in numbers and the quick disappearance of mature sturgeon from Pamlico Sound waters.

As the twentieth century progressed, the shrimp fishery declined, but the greatly increased culinary interest in crabmeat —combined with the continuing availability of large quantities of hard-shell crabs in the sounds and an astounding increase in the number of crabbers and crab pots—resulted by 1999 in blue crabs accounting for more than one-third of the total statewide catch of edible finfish and shellfish. Meanwhile, the catch of croaker, bluefish, flounder, king mackerel, spot, and weakfish maintained respectable levels.

Aquaculture, or fish farming, also grew in economic importance in North Carolina during the 1980s and 1990s. The National Fisheries Institute reported that farmed fish production increased at a nationwide average rate of 10.7 percent a year since 1984, as compared to only 2.6 percent for total livestock meat production. By the early 2000s there were approximately 250 individuals in North Carolina licensed for pond and tank aquaculture, with total food-fish aquaculture sales totaling more than $19 million. Trout was the most profitable species, followed by hybrid striped bass, catfish, and softshell crab.

The menhaden fishery developed in the state not to supply food to market but to extract oil and other uses from the menhaden, sometimes known locally as the "fat-back." The processing of menhaden oil and meal has been an important part of the economy of many coastal communities, especially in the Beaufort area. The menhaden fishery was probably the biggest, most profitable fishery in North Carolina from the late nineteenth to the mid-twentieth century. Atlantic menhaden has continued to be plentiful and heavily harvested, although the species is less profitable than such resources as crabs and shrimp. In 1998 fishing crews harvested more than 57 million pounds of menhaden, with a dockside value of $4 million. Culturally, the fishery made a unique contribution to coastal tradition: the work chanteys and lifestyles of early menhaden fishing crews have remained an important and colorful part of the coastal heritage.

References: Barbara Garrity-Blake, *The Fish Factory: Work and Meaning for Black and White Fishermen of the American Menhaden Industry* (1994); N.C. Division of Marine Fisheries, *North Carolina Commercial Landings 1999* (2000); Mark T. Taylor, "Seiners and Tongers: North Carolina Fisheries in the Old and New South," *NCHR* 69 (January 1992).

David Stick
Kathy Carter

Fishing, Recreational. With a primary season stretching from spring through fall and practically no age, gender, or economic barriers to its enjoyment, fishing is one of the most popular outdoor sports in North Carolina. It is estimated that one out of every six citizens in the state either fishes or hunts. Although saltwater fly-fishing is rapidly gaining in popularity, freshwater fishing and deep-sea fishing are the most common types of the sport in the state. Fishing also represents a large part of North Carolina's recreation and tourism economy, with freshwater anglers numbering 1.3 million and spending more than $1 billion each year and saltwater fishermen more than $700 million.

Freshwater fishing takes place throughout North Carolina, as anglers search for particular species in a variety of areas. The eastern part of the state—especially the Roanoke River, which also is home to good-sized populations of large American shad and striped bass—is one of the best locations to find hickory shad in the spring. Cold mountain streams and rivers, such as the Oconaluftee and Nantahala Rivers in Swain and Macon Counties, are the best sources for trout, while largemouth bass may be found in many of the state's rivers, lakes, and ponds. The Neuse River is a particularly good source for hickory shad, blue catfish, American shad, and flathead catfish; Kerr Lake for striped bass; and Falls Lake for largemouth bass and crappie. Many other bodies of water have similar reputations for exceptional fishing of certain species.

Two types of government-designated fishing areas exist in the state, some of which participate in the Fishing Tackle Loaner Program, which lends beginning anglers rods and reels free of charge. Public fishing access areas offer free fishing from cleared banks of many of North Carolina's bodies of water. In some cases these areas are handicapped accessible or provided with amenities such as fish attractors, usually submerged trees and plants that offer habitats to fish. Community Fishing Program locations are primarily situated in parks owned by counties or cities and fished by urban anglers. These sites are intensively managed, being equipped with solar-powered fish feeders and in most locations handicapped-accessible fishing piers. Many are also stocked with good-sized channel catfish from April through September.

Although many North Carolinians fish for relaxation, to spend time with family and friends, or to get away from the busy environment of the state's metropolitan areas, the North Carolina Angler Recognition Program (NCARP) and the State Record Fish Program was established to recognize superior anglers and catches and provide an element of competition to the fishing experience. State records are given to catches with the highest-known weight and length, while the NCARP recognizes fish that do not achieve a state record but are large enough to attain "bragging rights." A "Master Angler" certificate and a complimentary patch are given to anglers who catch six trophy-sized fish of the same species or of six different species. Local ponds—less widely fished and closer to many anglers' homes—actually offer a better chance of landing a trophy-sized catch than the larger venues. Most trophy-sized fish caught in North Carolina are largemouth bass (minimum weight 8 pounds and minimum length 24 inches), with trophy-sized rainbow trout, striped bass, bluegill, and hickory shad following in descending numbers caught. North Carolina is also home to some professional fishing tournaments, such as the CITGO Bassmaster Tour event held at Lake Norman.

Recreational saltwater fishing has increased in popularity since the early 1900s, when records first indicate that fishing moved from a subsistence activity to a more pleasurable one. Saltwater fishing inshore on sounds and tidal rivers and offshore in the Atlantic Ocean became possible before World War II with the development of suitable small craft. After the war, relatively sophisticated surplus boats became more available in addition to the locally built craft, and improvements came in boat design, engine efficiency, speed, and performance as well as in radio communication, navigational aids, and fish-finding electronics. In the 1960s, oil industry crew vessels were introduced, meeting the need for seaworthy craft with high speeds to reach the farthest offshore fishing areas. Later improvements in equipment included VHF and CB radios, radar, side-scan sonar, and other navigation assistance tools.

Thousands of North Carolinians and out-of-state visitors began thronging to the state's tidal creeks and rivers, sounds, and Atlantic coastline in pursuit of their favorite fish, and a charter boat, or head boat, industry arose to meet the needs of those who did not have the resources to invest in expensive fishing equipment or boats. Many potential fishermen also did not have the boating expertise needed to successfully pilot a small boat in changeable weather through dangerous shallow sounds and treacherous inlets to reach suitable fishing grounds close to shore or offshore on the Continental Shelf, Continental Slope, or in the Gulf Stream. Nor did they have the fishing knowledge and experience required to catch certain species of fish.

Head boat operators traditionally have charged a relatively inexpensive fee per person, or per "head," often carrying dozens of people on half-day and one-day trips. Owner/captains provide a seaworthy and speedy small craft as well as their expert knowledge of local weather, sea, and fishing conditions. Fishing equipment, bait, and ice are also often provided as part of the head fee, along with the mates' time, patience, and expertise in baiting hooks, hauling in fish, and stringing fish for the customers. Charter boat operators have always charged by the trip, usually only carrying a party of up to five or six passengers for several hundred dollars. Like head boat operators, captains of charter boats provide the equipment and services, including a personable mate who not only provides expert fishing advice but also baits the lines, lands fish, changes gear, and prepares the fish for transport by filleting, gutting, icing, and arranging for them to be mounted. Charter boat operators leave early for high-speed sprints to far offshore fishing areas or to the Gulf Stream. They rarely seek bottom-dwelling fish and usually troll for king mackerel, bluefish, dolphin, tuna, blue marlin, white marlin, sailfish, amberjack, and cobia.

North Carolina's geography in relation to the Gulf Stream has affected the home ports of head boats and charter boats as well as the species of fish caught. Charter boats and head boats from ports south of Cape Hatteras have occasionally sought fish in the Gulf Stream, but because of the distance of this ocean current from ports such as Morehead City, Sneads Ferry, Carolina Beach, and Southport, few have gone there on day trips. On the other hand, many charter boats are based

Black and white mullet fishermen at a fishing camp on Shackleford Banks, ca. 1880. George Brown Goode, ed.,
The Fisheries and Fishery Industries of the United States, 5 secs. (Washington, D.C.: Commission of Fish and Fisheries, 1884–87), sec. 5, vol. 2.

at Hatteras, Wanchese, or Oregon Inlet and take advantage of the closeness of the Gulf Stream. The cold Labrador Current and the warm Gulf Stream meet off the North Carolina coast, bringing both northern and semitropical fish and making the ocean waters rich in fish and diverse in species.

References: Joel Arrington, "Offshore Bread and Butter," *Wildlife in North Carolina* 4–7 (August 1990); Arrington, "White Marlin Bonanza," *Wildlife in North Carolina* 4–6 (August 1982); North Carolina Division of Marine Fisheries, *Description of North Carolina's Coastal Fishery Resources, 1972–1991* (1993).

Sheila Bumgarner
Additional research provided by Laura Hegyi.

Fishing Camps of primitive design were maintained by crews of commercial fishermen at isolated spots along the North Carolina coast during the last half of the nineteenth century and the early part of the twentieth. Some of the camps were built by shore fishermen who set their nets from the ocean beach at different times of the year to take advantage of the seasonal runs of various species of fish. Others, especially in the vicinity of Core Sound, were the temporary habitations of mullet fishermen who operated in teams. Most men involved in the mullet fishery lived on the mainland and were farmers by occupation, but like many of their descendants still residing in soundside communities, these old-timers probably were drawn to fishing as much by the knowledge that some fishermen make a pile of money in a hurry as they were by a desire to work and live on or near the water.

In 1880 R. Edward Earll described the annual migration of the mullet fishermen, stating that "when the fishing season arrives, they leave their homes and proceed in gangs of four to thirty men to the seashore under the leadership of a 'captain' who controls their movements." The first job when reaching shore was "to build rude huts or cabins in which they eat and sleep until the close of the season." They started out by making a framework of saplings with the butts embedded in the sand and the tops bent over and tied to the ridge pole. These served as studding, to which sticks were attached in horizontal rows a foot and a half to two feet apart. Small piles of rushes, tied together with bear grass, were then laid side by side around the bottom of the structure, with a second tier overlapping the first, in the same manner used when a roof is being shingled. The only openings in the hut, Earll said, were "a small hole at the rear of the gable, to allow the smoke from the campfire to escape, and a square aperture two or three feet in height at the front, which serves as a door."

University of North Carolina geology professor Collier Cobb, in a 1908 *National Geographic* magazine article, provided photographs and descriptions of some of the fishing huts. He said one large hut on Shackleford Banks had been in use for more than 12 years and described it as being 12 feet in diameter and six feet in height, "round at the bottom, with vertical walls" and a roof that was conical in design. On Cedar Island, Cobb said, he had seen a much larger fishing camp consisting of a cluster, or kraal, of conical huts made of woven rush.

Sometimes more permanent fishing camps were built on the western shore of Pamlico Sound or its estuaries, where families would spend the summer months on vacation while the men attended to their fishing. One of these, located on a bluff at the mouth of a Neuse River tributary, was built by a Wanchese resident, "Uncle Lou" Midgett, who returned to the same spot with his family each summer. In 1862, a Federal transport, the *Oriental*, was sunk near Bodie Island across Roanoke Sound from Wanchese. Later, the *Oriental* nameplate was found by Rebecca Midgett, Uncle Lou's wife, who took it to the camp that summer and had it mounted on a tree on the bluff where it could be seen by anyone passing by. The modern-day town of Oriental was established on that site.

Reference: R. Edward Earll, "The Mullet Fishery," in George Brown Goode, ed., *The Fisheries and Fishing Industries of the United States* (1887).

David Stick

Fish Stews are more than eastern North Carolina folk meals; like their cousin the pig pickin', they are highly ritualized and symbolic social events representing a celebration of the cornucopia of a region, a love for Arcadian values and pleasures, and a reverence for democratic ideals. Prepared for a crowd of people—often family members and neighbors who gather and enjoy one another's company while the cooking is underway and during and after the meal—fish stews are festive but informal, "low-down" evening occasions, and the long-standing ritual associated with them reflects the dogged unpretentiousness of a people who value reality over appearances. Thought to have originated with the early English settlers of North Carolina's Coastal Plain, fish stews are often prepared and served by rustic people on weekends, holidays, birthdays, and other special occasions in the fall and winter. Revelry, including music, singing, and the drinking of whiskey and beer, cus-

tomarily accompanies the preparation and serving of stews, even when the meal is hosted by temperance-minded Baptists or Methodists.

Classic fish stews are cooked outdoors under the stars in cast-iron pots suspended from elevated logs or tripods. Typical sites are in backyards and by lean-tos on the sides of barns, but a gala event is sometimes celebrated away from home in a clearing near the edge of a forest or on a riverbank. Heat for cooking comes from a wood fire, or from its modern equivalent, a portable gas burner. While nibbling on snacks and sipping liquid refreshments, cooks and guests are warmed by the burning wood and lighted by its bright flames. Boards held up by sawhorses or chicken wire stretched across wooden frames often function as tables, while tobacco carts, upside-down buckets, and pick-up tailgates can serve as seats.

Perhaps more than any other eastern North Carolina folk custom, the serving protocol for fish stews best reflects the state's motto *Esse Quam Videri* (to be rather than to seem). For example, it is considered a breach of etiquette to ladle the savory stew into fine porcelain bowls; propriety calls for paper bowls, especially those used by butchers to package ground and sliced meats in markets. In a similar vein, it is thought unseemly to use sterling eating utensils; plastic spoons are preferred, although military surplus utensils are acceptable. Elaborate side dishes and condiments are regarded as incorrect and superfluous; instead, fresh, store-bought white bread is held as the perfect accompaniment to the stew, while cornbread and soda crackers are acceptable seconds. Pepsi-Cola, the soft drink of choice because it originated in eastern North Carolina, is served in paper cups, as is the whiskey enjoyed before, during, and after the dinner. It is also proper that beer be drunk directly from the bottle or can.

In many North Carolina counties, custom dictates that the steaming fish stew and its accompanying bread and beverages be the sole entrées for the meal. Accordingly, numerous servings of the main course are usual. To serve anything else would be to mar the delight of the dish and defile the sanctity of the ritual that surrounds it.

Fish stews are known to have health-inducing properties, improving circulation and reviving sagging spirits, especially when enjoyed with liquor made from Tidewater corn. Moreover, the broth, when taken in sufficient quantity, has wide repute as a reliable purgative.

Reference: Karen Baldwin, *Folk Arts and Folklife in and around Pitt County: A Handbook and Resource Guide* (1990).

W. Keats Sparrow

Flag, State. The flag used in colonial North Carolina was the banner of the settlers' mother country, England. In 1777, after the Revolutionary War and American independence, the British flag was replaced by one representing the United States

The state flag of North Carolina. Photograph courtesy of North Carolina Division of Tourism, Film, and Sports Development.

traditional date of the so-called Mecklenburg Declaration of Independence, while 20 May 1861 was the date of North Carolina's secession from the Union. The two May 20th dates symbolized North Carolina's breaking the ties with undesirable governments.

The ordinance establishing the new state flag was ratified on 22 June 1861, and the flag flew over North Carolina until 1885. During the Civil War, the U.S. flag was replaced by the "Bonnie Blue Flag" of the Confederate States of America, which consisted of a blue field with a single white star at its center. North Carolinians recognized this as their national flag, although in some areas other designs of Confederate flags—such as one with a white field, a red canton, and a blue Saint Andrew's cross with white stars—were flown. The familiar Stars and Stripes returned as the national flag when North Carolina was readmitted to the Union in 1868.

In 1885 a new model for the North Carolina state flag was adopted by the legislature, and this version has flown unchanged over the state since that year. The flag features a blue union containing a white star in the center with a gilt *N* on the left and a gilt *C* on the right, the letters' height measuring about one-third the width of the union. The 1885 legislature directed that "the fly of the flag shall consist of two equally proportioned bars; the upper bar to be red, the lower to be white." As to proportions, it directed that "the length of the bars horizontally shall be equal to the perpendicular length of the union, and the total length of the flag shall be one-third more than its width." Above the star in the center of the union is a gilt scroll in semicircular form with the date "May 20th, 1775," and below the star is a similar scroll with the date "April 12th, 1776." The latter date replaced the secession date and commemorates the Halifax Resolves, which represented the first official statement by an American colony calling for a united declaration of independence from British rule.

References: Devereaux D. Cannon Jr., *The Flags of the Confederacy: An Illustrated History* (1988); William R. Edmonds, *The North Carolina State Flag* (rev. ed., 1962).

David C. Smith
Additional research provided by Taylor Shaw.

SEE ALSO Bonnie Blue Flag.

Flogging, or severe physical punishment with the use of a stick, rod, or leather strap, was used in colonial North Carolina for disobedient sailors, servants, or military and political prisoners. Flogging was also employed by schoolmasters seeking to punish or gain the attention of recalcitrant pupils.

In 1694 the Court of Albemarle sentenced a man "to have 30 lashes upon his naked back stript to the wast & severely Whipt." In another case, a man convicted of larceny had already been burned on the hand for that offense when he was sentenced in 1741 to receive 60 lashes on his bare back for a

and consisting of 13 red and white stripes and 13 white stars on a field of blue. North Carolina had no official state flag until the constitutional convention of 1861 took up the subject in connection with the movement to secede from the Union. John D. Whitford, a delegate from Craven County, introduced a resolution to create a flag for the state that "shall be a blue field with a white V thereon, and a star, encircling which shall be the words, 'Surgit astrum, May 20, 1775.'"

Convention delegates created a committee that offered a flag different from that envisioned by Whitford, one probably designed with the aid of William Garl Browne, an artist and resident of Raleigh. The committee's ordinance, adopted by the convention, directed that "the Flag of North Carolina shall consist of a red field with a white star in centre, and with the inscription, above the star, in a semi-circular form, of 'May 20th, 1775,' and below the star, in a semi-circular form, of 'May 20th, 1861.'" There were also to be "two bars of equal width, and the length of the field shall be equal to the bar, the width of the field being equal to both bars; the first bar shall be blue, and the second shall be white, and the length of the flag shall be one-third more than its width." The 1775 date was the second offense. However, because of his "very sick and low condition," the whipping was remitted. Women were not exempt from such punishment. In 1705 an Albemarle County court ordered that "for breach of an Act Entituled an Act agt Fornication & Adultery" a woman was to "be punished by receiving Ten Stripes on her Back well laid on."

During the colonial period a whipping post customarily stood in front of the courthouse of every county. After 1830, reflecting a more humanitarian sentiment, the posts were located behind the building. Yet in 1846, a *Raleigh Register* reader was repulsed after witnessing the humiliating flogging of two men. The 39 lashes they received left each man's skin rough with welts and covered with blood. Public opinion contributed to the gradual amelioration of this cruel punishment, and in 1917 legislation permitted whipping in prison only in the presence of the prison physician. The objections of Frank Murchison, register at the Caledonia Prison Farm in Halifax County, ultimately brought an end to flogging, and the General Assembly abolished it altogether in 1925.

References: Albert Coates, "Crime and Punishment," in *Proceedings of the Thirty-third Annual Session of the North Carolina Bar Association* (1931); Guion G. Johnson, *Ante-Bellum North Carolina: A Social History* (1937).

William S. Powell

Flora MacDonald College in Red Springs originated in 1896 as Red Springs Seminary, a Presbyterian school that was the successor to Floral College (1841–78). In 1903 the college was renamed Southern Presbyterian College and Conservatory of Music, and in 1915 it became Flora MacDonald College—named for the popular Scottish heroine who lived in the Carolina colony for five years beginning in 1774.

In 1952 the Presbyterian Synod of North Carolina authorized a study of seven of the Presbyterian colleges under its jurisdiction and decided to merge Flora MacDonald College with Peace and Presbyterian Junior College to form one coeducational, four-year college to be located at Laurinburg. Chartered in 1958, St. Andrews Presbyterian College opened in September 1961. On 26 Oct. 1961, the Flora MacDonald property was sold to the Red Springs Development Corporation for $50,000.

References: William Richard Bracey, "A History of Flora MacDonald College" (M.A. thesis, Appalachian State University, 1962); William S. Powell, *North Carolina: The Story of a Special Kind of Place* (1987); Dorothy M. Quynn, "Flora MacDonald in History," *NCHR* 18 (1941).

Wiley J. Williams

Flora MacDonald Homesite. The exact location of the home in which Scottish Jacobite heroine and American Loyalist Flora MacDonald lived during her stay in North Carolina has, for decades, been the subject of much debate. With her husband Allan, MacDonald emigrated to North Carolina in 1774 and settled on a plantation purchased from Caleb Touchstone in present-day Montgomery County, not far from where Flora's stepfather, Hugh MacDonald of Armadale, had settled only two years before. The controversy regarding the actual site of the MacDonald homestead has centered on two tracts of land that were owned by Touchstone. One tract was located on Mountain Creek in upper Richmond County and the other on Cheek's Creek in Montgomery County. The two sites are only about five miles apart near the Richmond-Montgomery county border. Historians James Banks and J. P. MacLean reported that the MacDonalds purchased a tract of land on Mountain Creek and named it Killiegray. The site of the Killiegray plantation on Mountain Creek was believed by many to be the site of the MacDonald home; however, the name Killiegray is that of a small island in the Sound of Harris in the lands of the Clan MacLeod in the Scottish Hebrides. The MacDonalds would not have named their plantation after a MacLeod holding with which they had no connection.

Moore County historian and surveyor Rassie Wicker did extensive research on the two tracts of land in question and proved conclusively that the Cheek's Creek tract was the tract that was purchased by Allan MacDonald of Kingsburgh. Wicker's surveys were further supported by the discovery of a document in the Public Record Office in London by Donald MacKinnon. In the July 1775 document, Governor Josiah Martin stated that he was going to deposit some important papers, "with my friend Mr. McDonald of Kingsborough, living upon Cheek's Creek in Anson County." Investigations of the site that were performed in 1952 and 1953 proved that the Cheek's Creek tract was the one owned by the MacDonalds during their brief stay in North Carolina. Later archaeological explorations have shown that there is evidence on the Cheek's Creek site that supports the descriptions made by Allan MacDonald of Kingsburgh in his Loyalist Claims.

The Mountain Creek tract was owned by a Stephen Touchstone in 1756 and was occupied by an Isaac Armstrong from 1772 until 1823. In 1824 the land was passed to a Norman MacLeod and probably received the name "Killiegray" at this time due to the fact that the actual Killiegray in Scotland is located in traditional MacLeod lands. There is no record of that tract being known as "Killiegray" prior to that time, nor is there any evidence of MacDonald connections with the property.

One of the most interesting facets of the stories surrounding the MacDonald residence is that of the mysterious deceased children, whose remains were found at the Killiegray site in 1937. The bodies, who some argued were the children of Flora and Allan MacDonald, were removed from the site and reinterred at Flora MacDonald College in Red Springs. Historians have since disproved the insistent oral tradition regarding the deceased children, especially since Flora was well past her childbearing years when she emigrated to North Carolina and there is no record of any additional children who are not previously accounted for. Nonetheless, these two unknown children still lie in a shrine to Flora MacDonald. The shrine contains MacDonald's original grave marker, erected at Kilmuir cemetery in Skye in 1871 and blown down and broken by a gale in 1873, which was obtained by Charles Vardell, president of Flora MacDonald College in Red Springs, and reassembled at the institution when its name was changed to honor MacDonald in 1922.

References: Hugh Douglas, *Flora MacDonald: The Most Loyal Rebel* (1993); J. P. MacLean, *Flora MacDonald in America* (1909).

William S. Caudill

Flying Squadrons, or motorcades of union picketers, were first used widely in North Carolina by the United Textile Workers of America (UTWA) in the industry's massive General Textile Strike of September 1934. Francis Gorman, vice president of the UTWA and chairman of its strike committee, developed the idea of organizing motorcades of workers who had succeeded in closing their own mills and sending them to mills that were still operating. When the "flying squadron" of picketers arrived at a mill, they would call on its workers to join them. If persuasion failed, they would picket the mill. The workers' ownership of automobiles and trucks made possible the rapid movement of large numbers of union picketers from one community to another, and their arrival often took mill owners and law enforcement officials by surprise.

On 4 Sept. 1934 an estimated 2,500 picketers from Shelby shut down four mills in Spindale, and a flying squadron influenced the closing of the Loray Mill in Gastonia. The same day, 30 members of a flying squadron were arrested in High Point for trespassing. Flying squadrons also managed to stop operations in most of the textile mills in Alamance County. On 5 September workers closed their own mills in Burlington, then made a "motor dash" to mills at Graham, Haw River, Ossipee, and Altamahaw before proceeding to Glen Raven. The local newspaper, sympathetic to management, described how the flying squadron "swooped down" on the Glen Raven Mill, where a handful of anxious employees "were driven from their work after a door had been battered down." Also that month flying squadrons helped spread the strike to mills in Asheville, Black Mountain, Shelby, Kannapolis, Concord, and Charlotte.

Contemporary sources do not present a consistent picture of the flying squadrons' impact, their composition, or their disposition to violence. A University of North Carolina economics professor, speaking at the time of the strike, characterized the use of flying squadrons as an "unfortunate" strategy that had more than anything else alienated public sympathy for the striking workers. Although critics often described strikers as younger males who were prone to violence, women workers also took part in the squadrons, and oral history interviews with former strikers indicate that the squadrons represented a cross section of mill employees. Participation in a flying squadron was an exciting and invigorating experience for many previously unorganized mill workers.

References: Anthony J. Badger, *North Carolina and the New Deal* (1981); Irving Bernstein, *Turbulent Years: A History of the American Worker, 1933–1941* (1970); Jacquelyn Dowd Hall and others, *Like a Family: The Making of a Southern Cotton Mill World* (1987); John M. Kennedy, "The General Strike in the Textile Industry, September 1934" (M.A. thesis, Duke University, 1947).

George W. Troxler

Folk Art. Folk artists thrive in North Carolina, evolving through self-instruction and emulation of the work of others as well as upholding traditional methods of craft passed down through the generations. Folk painting, sculpture, and pottery have strong traditions in the state, from workshop-based potters to painting steered by spirituality and mysticism. A versatile artistic spirit has moved numerous folk artists to create their own aesthetic interpretations of North Carolina, expanding the state's artistic diversity.

While a consensus definition is difficult, folk art generally refers to work done by untrained, nonacademic artists and most often involves a decorative item with minor practical use, made utilizing traditional or family methods with the intent of creating an aesthetically pleasing yet singular artistic piece. The artwork, whether a sculpture, gravestone, or model boat, rises above mere functionality.

Items traditionally produced for practical use are considered crafts, although many items that once served useful purposes are now used almost exclusively as decoration and have consequently become folk art—similar to the now-popular vein of "found" art. For instance, a rag rug woven according to styles and aesthetics passed down through generations and used as a floor covering is a folk craft. The same rug hung on the wall as an object to be viewed, however, becomes folk art through the change in its functional context. This functional change is also seen with quilts, bird decoys, and pottery. Although crafts were often ornamented to some extent, as these objects lose their functional role and become simply works of art, their creators tend to emphasize ornamentation more heavily.

Closely related to folk art is outsider art, sometimes known as naive or visionary art. Outsider art generally refers to the work of self-taught artists who function outside the mainstream of any artistic community, particularly that of an established art academy or educational program. In many cases, outsider artists have experienced economic or social disabilities that have isolated them from the "average" American life-

The Lion of Judah by Minnie Evans, 1960. The work of Evans, a Wilmington native, is regarded highly by critics and art collectors as an example of "outsider art." Photograph courtesy of the North Carolina Museum of Art, Raleigh.

style. Many do not consider themselves artists at all, nor do they typically intend to sell their work. Outsider artists distinguish themselves from folk artists in that while folk art is a tradition, passed on from generation to generation and creating something that is often practical, outsider artists create unique, pure art from a spontaneous inner drive.

Many gifted folk artists working in a variety of media are either native or adopted North Carolinians. Minnie Smith Rinehart of Catawba County was a memory painter who portrayed scenes from the rural life of her childhood. Some artists, such as painter Minnie Evans of Wilmington, are described as visionary painters since the scenes they portray arrive not from memory but from visions, often religious in nature. The images captured in vision and memory painting are impressionistic at their root; rather than a unique interpretation of a physical setting, the artists attempt to recreate the way in which inborn or spiritual forces have shaped their memories or creative consciousness.

Untrained sculptors usually work with wood or metal using skills gained in an occupational context. Clyde Jones of Bynum makes a variety of sculptures but is best known for his "critters," which he carves with a chain saw. Jones often rearranges the display of critters in his yard, frequently cannibalizing finished projects for new works, always attempting to put life into what many would see as nondescript pieces of timber. Jones's methods, and the emphasis on traditional means for most folk artists, demonstrate a tendency in folk sculptors to value process over product. Sculptor and painter James Harold Jennings, who, like fellow folk artist Raymond Coynes, hails from the Pilot Mountain area, created over 4,000 works of art, most of them during the last 15 years of his life. His work, characterized by distinctive, colorful patterns, is a mixture of Appalachian art traditions and a variety of contemporary influences such as comic books and magazines.

In North Carolina cemeteries of the late eighteenth century and early nineteenth century, stone carvers were also folk artists, adding detailed and complex iconography to tombstones. Many of these carvers were not fully professional, making their living instead through farming and carving tombstones only when the need arose. Many stoneworkers, and, indeed, many folk artists themselves, went unnamed or uncredited for their work, either as a function of a workshop environment or a natural lack of vanity. Eugene Gant's father in Thomas Wolfe's *Look Homeward, Angel* is a well-known stone carver. As tombstones are examples of nonacademic art in the public sphere from centuries past, many current efforts—from amateur murals to graffiti—fill the niche of public folk art.

North Carolina continues to be home to a wealth of outsider artists. Vollis Simpson builds large wind-powered sculptures called whirligigs, visible from the road near his home in Lucama. Sculptor Arliss Watford originally began carving to pass the time after his workday, displaying his works outdoors to draw attention to his television repair shop. Many involved in the league of outsider artists are collectors, who feel an affinity to the unprecedented work of artists who operate without technical training.

North Carolina Wesleyan College in Rocky Mount acquired the Robert Lynch Collection of Outsider Art in December 1987. Lynch, born in 1947 in Halifax County, attended the University of North Carolina at Chapel Hill and Harvard Law School. After working for a time as a lawyer in New York City, Lynch returned to rural North Carolina and began collecting mostly African American outsider art in the 1980s. The collection consists of over 400 pieces created by artists of eastern North Carolina. The art is on continuous display at a variety of locations on campus, and portions frequently travel to exhibitions throughout the United States.

Photographer and folklorist Roger Manley, a graduate of the University of North Carolina at Chapel Hill's curriculum in folklore, has been documenting the work of outsider artists in the South since 1970. In 1989 Manley and David Steel were cocurators of an exhibition of North Carolina outsider art at the North Carolina Museum of Art in Raleigh. Conceived to expose these artists to a wider audience, "Signs and Wonders:

Outsider Art Inside North Carolina" displayed works by a small group of artists previously unknown beyond their communities. The accompanying catalog featured over 100 artists from across the state, a testament to the strength of a thriving scene that not only prides itself on its own traditional creations but fosters the creativity of all those who strive to express themselves through art.

In 1989 the folklife section of the North Carolina Arts Council developed the North Carolina Folk Heritage Awards to honor the state's folk artists. Winners range from internationally acclaimed musicians to artists quietly practicing their craft in rural and family settings. Numerous centers and organizations in North Carolina preserve and promote folk arts, including Pocosin Arts in Columbia, the Southern Highland Craft Guild and Folk Art Center on the Blue Ridge Parkway, the Penland School of Crafts in the Blue Ridge Mountains, and the John C. Campbell Folk School in Brasstown.

References: Garry Barker, *The Handicraft Revival in Southern Appalachia, 1930–1990* (1991); John Bivins and Forsyth Alexander, *The Regional Arts of the Early South: A Sampling from the Collection of the Museum of Early Southern Decorative Arts* (1991); Brad Campbell and Jay Fields, *The Craft Heritage Trails of Western North Carolina* (1998); Karekin Goekjian, *Light of the Spirit: Portraits of Southern Outsider Artists* (1998); Robert Isbell, *The Keepers: Mountain Folk Holding on to Old Skills and Talents* (1999); Roger Manley, *Signs and Wonders: Outsider Art in North Carolina* (1989); Daniel W. Patterson and Charles G. Zug III, eds., *Arts in Earnest: North Carolina Folklife* (1990).

Philip McFee
Bruce E. Baker
Additional research provided by Kelly Kress.

SEE ALSO Black Mountain College; Decoys; Fraktur; John C. Campbell Folk School; Pine Needle Art; Pottery; Quilts; Southern Folklife Collection; Southern Highland Craft Guild; Tombstones; Weaving; Woodcarving.

Folk Art Center. SEE Southern Highland Craft Guild.

Folk Festivals and arts festivals are an integral part of North Carolina's cultural and artistic heritage. Held in nearly all 100 counties and ranging from large, highly publicized events to small community gatherings, these lively events define and enhance the strong sense of community, cooperation, and creativity that pervades the state. In many towns, festivals focus on some unique aspect of their locale and identity to both celebrate regional history and boost the economy. Other festivals aim to increase ethnic or environmental awareness or to spread appreciation of regional folklore, folk art, music, or foodways. Regardless of their purpose, all North Carolina festivals share the same essential attributes—a passion for communal gathering, an enthusiasm for regional art and folk achievements, and a desire to advance and enrich the state's artistic life and culture.

Original Folk Festivals and Contemporary Gatherings

The antecedents of contemporary North Carolina folk festivals are traditional events that brought people together in a spirit of celebration. Although centered around necessary labor, communal gatherings such as cornhuskings enabled people to socialize when the work was done. Community dances, usually held in private homes, offered citizens another opportunity to gather for pleasure while enjoying music and dance—two important components of modern folk festivals. Other events, such as fiddling contests, united musicians and listeners and introduced a spirit of competition.

Many early folk festivals were organized by people committed to the continuation and promotion of regional folklore, folk music, and folk art. Beginning in the 1920s, enthusiasts presented these art forms in settings similar to those of public concerts or lectures. In this way, their merits—often disparaged in comparison to "higher culture"—could be made abundantly clear. Reportedly, the first such festival in North Carolina (and the first in the nation) was Bascom Lamar Lunsford's Mountain Dance and Folk Festival, held in Asheville in 1928. In 1948 Lunsford organized the first Carolina Folk Festival at Chapel Hill, a well-attended event that continued into the 1950s.

From these initial gatherings, and as public interest grew, a wide variety of festivals appeared in North Carolina, some developed through local interest and others staged as much for outside visitors as area residents. Many have celebrated the state's agricultural heritage. In 1969 the first National Hollerin' Contest took place at Spivey's Corner in Sampson County to preserve the art of hollering, which farmers once used to communicate across large fields. Mule Day at Benson in Johnston County centers around the long-ago power supply for the state's agriculture industry. Celebrations of the natural environment, such as azalea festivals, dogwood festivals, and harvest festivals, are also common throughout the state.

Festivals centering on music and dance remain among the most popular in the state. The Lake Eden Arts Festival, placing equal emphasis on dance and music, occurs twice a year at Camp Rockmont in Black Mountain. The spring festival coincides with Memorial Day weekend, and the fall event is held in mid-October. The 600-acre property is the former site of historic Black Mountain College. Musical offerings at the festival have included waltz, swing, clogging, Cajun, Zydeco, African, Latin, Celtic, western, and capoeira selections. During the festival the dance schedule for Brookside Pavilion is nonstop, as is the music schedule at Lakeside Stage and Eden Hall. The Poetry Tent features readings by poets as well as activities geared for children and more opportunities for music. In the field next to Lake Eden, juried artists offer their crafts for sale; there is also a place for children to sell their handicrafts.

Some North Carolina folk festivals draw their inspiration from the changing of the seasons or just the simple need to get outside before the arrival of summer's sweltering heat. When spring comes around, the Havelock Spring Festival helps North Carolinians celebrate. Inaugurated in 2005, the family showcase runs in conjunction with the annual Marine Corps Cherry Point Air Show. Started in 2004, Brevard's White Squirrel Festival in late May is a good excuse to get "nutty" during mild spring days. Events include live music, regional artists, and tours to see wild white squirrels. Almost everything at the festival bears the squirrel theme, making it, in the words of the planners, "western North Carolina's squirreliest event."

Durham's Festival for the Eno is one of several events originating from an impulse to conserve and celebrate natural resources, and organizers donate its profits to the preservation and acquisition of land in the Eno River State Park. With multiple stages for a wide range of performers and hundreds of local artists and craftspeople, the festival, now well into its third decade, is the highlight of the outdoor Durham festival scene. Similar to the Eno festival is the Lake Lure Festival of the Arts, held annually on Labor Day. Life-size sculptures, hand-crafted jewelry, and decorative and functional arts pieces are showcased at this "food and fun" festival nestled in the Blue Ridge Mountains. The popular Autumn Leaves Festival in Mount Airy signals the end of summer with an outdoor celebration featuring arts and crafts displays, as well as its biggest draw—the natural grandeur of the changing foliage. The North Carolina Folk Arts Festival in St. Pauls (Robeson County), the Festival in the Park in Charlotte, and MUMfest in New Bern are also representative of gatherings attended by large numbers of North Carolinians and out-of-state visitors.

Ethnic and Holiday Festivals

North Carolina's increasing ethnic and cultural diversity has spawned numerous festivals to promote understanding and community among peoples. Many festivals are held by Native American groups to highlight both traditional and contemporary expressions of Indian culture, including music, drumming, food, and crafts. Since 1996, the Occaneechi-Saponi Cultural Festival has been held annually on the banks of the Eno River in Orange County. It features handmade tribal crafts, dancing, food, and music to raise money and awareness for the preservation of Native American history. Festivals and powwows are also sponsored by the Cherokee, Waccamaw-Siouan, Meherrin, Lumbee, and other tribes in the state. For nine days annually in late June and early July, the Lumbee celebrates Lumbee Homecoming with pageants, sports, gospel singing, an elder's dinner, art shows, and other events. While rooted in a celebration of kinship and community ties, it has also become an opportunity to showcase the causes of tribal recognition and Native American sovereignty.

A number of distinctly African American events are held in North Carolina throughout the year. Some, such as the statewide Kwanzaa celebrations of December and January and numerous church-sponsored festivals, combine cultural and religious features. Others, including the various African American Heritage Festivals, Martin Luther King Jr. celebrations, and black theater festivals, presented by the North Carolina African American Culture Tour, have a greater political or historical focus.

Across the United States, the expanding Latino population is integrating its culture with the American mainstream. Founded in 1994 and boasting an attendance of more than 60,000 in 2006, La Fiesta del Pueblo in Raleigh is billed as the largest Latin American cultural festival in the Carolinas. The two-day event in September presents not only traditional food, music, soccer tournaments, and artwork but also informational exhibits promoting health, housing, employment, and political concerns of the Latino community. Charlotte's Carnaval Carolina, founded in 1998, is another rapidly growing entertainment festival featuring Latino and Caribbean artists.

Perhaps the largest single festival day statewide remains the Fourth of July, when North Carolinians join their counterparts nationally in celebrating the birthday of the United States. One of the largest, Greensboro's Fun Fourth Festival, draws well over 100,000 people annually and provides a major economic boost to Guilford County. The summer months also bring somewhat curious celebrations of the Christmas holiday in several locations around the state; Statesville and Jefferson are among the cities and towns hosting "Christmas in July" celebrations.

Music and Food Festivals

North Carolinians have a wide variety of musical festivals to choose from. Jazz and bluegrass performers appear most often on the festival track, though other types of music fill the calendar. MerleFest, held each April in Wilkesboro, is arguably the most recognized music festival in the state, showcasing dozens of traditional acts each year on numerous stages. Named for Merle Watson, son of North Carolina music legend Arthel "Doc" Watson, MerleFest typically draws top performers from the world of folk, bluegrass, and American roots music. Informal jam sessions in the campgrounds and parking lots surrounding the stages are also a highlight of the event. But North Carolina is also home to countless smaller music festivals that celebrate its musical heritage. Among the oldest and best attended are fiddler's conventions in Jefferson, Union Grove, and Mount Airy.

Each spring brings the Carolina Jazz Festival to the campus of UNC-Chapel Hill. The weekend celebration presents top-billed national artists and student ensembles, as well as a competition for local high school jazz bands. In nearby Durham, Duke University plays host to the North Carolina International Jazz Festival, and the St. Joseph Historic Foundation sponsors the Bull Durham Blues Festival. Both attract top performers from all over the world. Down-tempo and down east is the Cape Fear Blues Festival, which has drawn aficionados to Wilmington for more than a decade. During the multiple-day event, visitors can participate in workshops, take a riverboat Blues Cruise, or listen to a variety of live performers.

North Carolinians flock to many food-based festivals as well; the most popular inevitably feature barbecue. The largest of these events is the Lexington Barbecue Festival, started in 1984 by Joe Sink Jr., publisher of the *Lexington Dispatch*. Festival pitmasters routinely serve more than a dozen tons of barbecue to thousands of guests. Hillsborough Hog Day, founded in 1982 by the Hillsborough/Orange County Chamber of Commerce, features activities ranging from guess-the-weight-of-the-pig to family games and musical performances.

The state also offers numerous nonbarbecue food gatherings. Pamlico County's Croaker Festival started almost 30 years ago when the Oriental United Methodist Church held a fish fry as a fund-raiser. The festivities begin with a street dance on Friday night, followed by fireworks on Saturday evening and worship-themed events on Sunday. The church still holds a fish fry using the croaker variety.

The Sneads Ferry Shrimp Festival has taken place in the small eastern North Carolina town for more than 35 years. Each year a winning dish is selected from the offerings entered in a competition, and a Miss Shrimp Queen and Junior Miss Shrimp Queen are crowned. Other long-established food celebrations include the Winterville Watermelon Festival and Ayden Collard Festival in Pitt County and the Maggie Valley Big Red Chili Cookoff in Haywood County.

References: Garry Barker, *The Handicraft Revival in Southern Appalachia, 1930–1990* (1991); A. P. Hudson, "Carolina Folk Festival," *Journal of American Folklore* 61 (1948); Loyal Jones, *Minstrel of the Appalachians: The Story of Bascom Lamar Lunsford* (1984).

Philip McFee
Bruce E. Baker
Additional research provided by Patricia L. Pertalion.

SEE ALSO Azalea Festival; Eastern Music Festival; Festival for the Eno; Folk Art; Folklore; Folkmoot USA; Folk Music; Hollerin' Contest; MerleFest; Mountain Dance and Folk Festival; Mule Day; Old-Time String Band Music.

Folklore. In North Carolina, a state that puts great emphasis on oral traditions and family customs, the value of folklore and folktales is impossible to overstate. As the collected narrative culture of a group of people through many generations, North Carolina folklore is remarkably complex, representing a huge array of different narrative, traditional, and cultural styles. It may encompass such disparate forms as Cherokee legends, ballad singing among residents of a remote mountain valley, family ghost stories, religious messages on truck dashboards, or even modern-day jokes transmitted on the Internet. Folklore, unlike other cultural forms, usually circulates among members of a group or community in informal ways often not involving printing or other forms of recording. This informality emphasizes the importance of interpersonal relationships within the community, a key to the importance of folklore in creating and maintaining group identity. Sometimes seen as involving only "old-time" customs or stories, folklore is also the constant cultural interplay in the melting-pot environment of modern North Carolina, continuing to produce new folktales and folk customs that will exist for decades to come.

Types of Folklore and the North Carolina Folklore Society

Folklorists and scholars typically consider folklore according to genre and community. Genre refers to the various forms folklore takes, categorized as "oral," "customary," and "material." Oral folklore includes naming, speech, narration, and music. Customary folklore involves traditional actions or behaviors using particular techniques, such as gathering for a festival or acting on a traditional belief. Material folklore consists of the tangible objects that comprise the folk culture of a group, including folk crafts, arts, architecture, and foods.

Folk communities may also be characterized by ethnic and geographic factors. The different histories and lifestyles of communities in the Mountains, the Piedmont, and the Coastal Plain of North Carolina gave rise to different folkways. Likewise, ethnic groups created and continue to maintain distinctive folk traditions. Native American, English, German, and Scotch-Irish groups all contributed items of folklore that became part of the general folklore of North Carolina while remaining identified with the original ethnic groups. African Americans brought foodways and musical styles adopted by many North Carolinians of different backgrounds, and recent immigrants such as Latinos and Southeast Asians continue to contribute new facets to North Carolina's diverse folk culture.

Folklore associated with a particular occupation often arises when people work closely together. Tobacco cultivation and processing exemplifies occupational folk culture in North Carolina. Traditions associated with farming, harvesting, grading, marketing, and processing tobacco pass from one generation to the next; for example, the tobacco auctioneer's style is perfected by listening to and imitating other, more experienced auctioneers. Thus North Carolina possesses a highly symbiotic folklife—trading and advancing traditions by intermingling various folk backgrounds.

Although one locale is generally as rich in folklore as any other, North Carolina has been particularly fortunate to maintain a strong awareness of its folk heritage for many years. The North Carolina Folklore Society is one of the oldest state folklore societies in the country. In 1912 folklorist John A. Lomax, then president of the American Folklore Society, implored folklorists across the country to create state organizations bringing the activities of collecting and preserving American folklore to the local level where they might be more effective. Answering this call, Frank C. Brown of Trinity College (later Duke University) organized the North Carolina Folklore Society. Eighty-five charter members attended its first meeting, held on 24 Mar. 1913, in the North Carolina General Assembly Senate chamber.

The North Carolina Folklore Society worked toward its twin goals of collecting and publishing the state's folklore with the creation of a publishing committee in 1915. Over the next 30 years, Brown continued to amass material but repeatedly delayed its publication. When Brown died in 1943, Newman I. White of Duke University was named general editor of the forthcoming publication. White worked on the mammoth project of sorting Brown's collection, housed in the Duke University archives. Upon White's death in 1948, new general editor Paul F. Baum led the project to fruition. The first three volumes of *The Frank C. Brown Collection of North Carolina Folklore* were published in 1952, and other volumes followed in 1957, 1961, 1962, and 1964. This collection, representing the textually oriented scholarship of its time, is the most comprehensive published collection of folklore from any state in the nation and serves as a benchmark and standard reference work for other collections as well as a rich source for continuing research.

In addition to issuing publications, the North Carolina Folklore Society holds annual meetings combining presentation of folk arts, current scholarship on North Carolina folklore by society members, and organizational business. Meetings were held in Raleigh until 1986, when members decided to convene at various sites throughout the state, usually at a college or an organization involved with folklore. The society initiated a Community Traditions Award in 1992, recognizing organizations and groups contributing to the continuation and appreciation of the state's folklife.

North Carolina Folktales and Storytellers

Among the primary forms of folk narratives, folktales are medium-length stories traditional among a given group. North Carolina enjoys a rich folktale heritage and a wealth of excellent storytellers. Folktales stretch recollections of everyday occurrences into stories of the supernatural. Passed down through generations of storytellers, these tales often reflect the simple farming lifestyle common throughout North Carolina in the nineteenth and twentieth centuries. Isolation and lack of formal education in rural communities led to a reliance on natural signs found in the moon, crops, and livestock to explain everyday events such as births, deaths, and marriages. Folktales capture the spiritual omens, rural traditions, and livelihood of a specific region and may act as historical ref-

erence for future generations. They relay a moral or lesson by involving an ordinary hero, usually the storyteller, in an extraordinary experience. The story's hero often assumes supernatural strength, accuracy, or cunning to overcome an obstacle or accomplish a goal. The storyteller's sincere and straight-faced rendering of the tale often dictates its success.

Native American folktales include animal stories, creation myths, legends, and ghost stories. Indian storytellers, particularly those of the Cherokee Indians of western North Carolina, continue to play a vital role in the state's rich folklife. *Living Stories of the Cherokee* (1998), edited by Barbara R. Duncan, contains stories told by Davey Arch, Robert Bushyhead, Edna Chekelelee, Marie Junaluska, Kathi Smith Littlejohn, and Freeman Owle, Cherokee storytellers who learned their art through familial and community traditions.

Some of the best-known North Carolina folktales, and a prime example of the cultural importing so common in the folk tradition, are the Jack tales, comprising a group of sagas from the southern Appalachian Mountains revolving around the lively deeds and delightful adventures of a young boy named Jack. Although one of these tales, "Jack and the Beanstalk," is extremely well known, less familiar are the 17 other surviving stories. As successive generations passed down the tales by word of mouth, Jack acquired a distinctively mountaineer flavor, but two of the tales preserve elements of Norse mythology that indicate the ancient character of these British-American tales.

In 1927 folklorist Isobel Gordon Carter collected the first three Jack tales from Jane Gentry in Wise, Va., and published them in the *Journal of American Folk-Lore*. Eight years later, folklorist Richard Chase uncovered a dozen more tales as told to him by R. M. Ward and his relatives living near Beech Mountain, N.C. Ultimately, Chase demonstrated that a common ancestor and celebrated storyteller, Council Harmon (1803–96) of Watauga County was the source for all the tales inherited by his Ward and Harmon descendants in North Carolina and his Gentry descendants in Virginia. In the Ward family, the tales functioned practically as a way of entertaining children while they worked at various communal tasks, such as stringing beans. The later discovery of other Jack tales in unrelated families scattered across Appalachia suggests that the tales were once quite common in the region and throughout America. In 1943 Richard Chase edited and published the stories in *The Jack Tales*, which contains a scholarly appendix by folklorist Herbert Halpert.

Jack tales themselves are often referred to as "tall tales," not because of the giant's scope, but because of their aforementioned ability to expand the bounds of reality and belief. In general, tall tales are folk narratives that stretch recollections of everyday occurrences into stories of the supernatural. Tall tales possess all the major characteristics of folklore and also encapsulate an everlasting image of rural innocence.

Beech Mountain storyteller Ray Hicks. *Raleigh News and Observer.*

They relay a moral or lesson through the deeds and commentary of the hero—often the character who provides the audience with the ultimate perspective. All tall tales incorporate elements of the simple life exaggerated to heroic proportions, wherein the simple acts of hunting or fishing might become epic enough to merit timeless status. North Carolina novelist Daniel Wallace, for example, incorporated a strong sense of the southern oral tradition into his sometimes supernatural, folk-infused work *Big Fish* (1998).

North Carolina folklore is, indeed, a cultural crossroads. The communal mode of story crafting has resulted in numerous combinations of popular myths and beliefs to suit particular social or ethnic groups. While the North Carolina folk tradition owes its diversity, in large part, to combining influences, its native storytellers help to boost its popularity within the state. The North Carolina Storytelling Guild supports the state's storytellers through various programs and events centered on the art of oral tradition. The guild's annual storytelling festival, held each November, attracts North Carolina storytellers as well as many participants from outside the state.

North Carolinian Ray Hicks (1922–2003) is widely considered the "grandfather of storytelling" in the United States. His influence extended beyond his Old Beech Mountain roots, annually taking him to Jonesborough, Tenn., where he was the top-billed personality at the National Storytelling Festival since its establishment in 1973. Hicks was credited with reviving the art of American storytelling in the latter part of the twentieth century, a movement he launched from his home in the North Carolina mountains. He strongly believed in the fantastic in everyday life and idolized his family members for their ability to weave stories out of their everyday experiences. Hicks's stories, of which there are thousands, revolved around him but dealt with his alter-ego "Jack"—a nod to the folklore traditions he so deeply revered. The messages in his tales were down-to-earth, gleaned from a hardscrabble life in the mountains living in the house in which he was born.

In a technological age, Hicks insisted on living in his ancestral home, telling his ancestral tales, and acting as a living encyclopedia of natural mountain knowledge. American oral traditions are largely indebted to him—not only for his contributions, but for the profile he set among North Carolinians and storytellers nationwide.

Legends, Animal Tales, and Superstitions

Though threatened by urbanization, the oral tradition of storytelling has been preserved by the tendency for southern men to gather to hunt, fish, and share their stories. And while some stories have proliferated in the region, taking place wherever the tale happens to be told, others are geographically centered and unique to a single significant region. This form of folktale is the local legend. Legends are a form of oral literature in the genre of folk narrative or storytelling closely related to myths, but largely rooted in folk history rather than supernatural occurrence or divine providence. North Carolina legends reflect varied eras and places, precolonial times to the present, and all areas of the state from the mountains to the coast. Local legends often involve the supernatural or important historical events. Stories about the Maco Light in Brunswick County, the Devil's Tramping Ground in Chatham County, and the Brown Mountain Lights in Burke County are some of the better-known local legends of North Carolina. Such stories often become lumped with ghost stories, and though thousands of ghost stories exist in North Carolina, passed from friend to friend or county to county, these tales fall on the typical legend structure. Local legends can also be centered on interesting people, with most towns claiming tales about such "characters." The western village of Murphy was known as *Klausuna* (Large Turtle) according to Cherokee legend because it was the sunning place of a gigantic turtle. On the Outer Banks at Rodanthe, locals tell the legend of Old Buck, a punishing opposite to Santa Claus who appears during the Old Christmas celebration each January.

The most widespread of the state's legends, particularly among high school and college tellers, is the legend often called the Vanishing Hitchhiker. Seen seeking a ride home in every area of the state, the vanishing hitchhiker is a young woman killed in a car accident years ago. She reappears as a human-looking ghost at the scene of her accidental death asking to be taken home by a passing motorist, but she disappears along the way. When the driver proceeds to her home, he or she learns of the woman's death, of which the current day is the anniversary. This oral narrative in countless variations is a past and current favorite legend, not only statewide but throughout the world as well.

Many folklorists consider personal experience narratives, in which a person tells the story of a memorable event in their own lives, to be a form of folktale. Within the tale repertoires of individual storytellers, there is often a continuity of subject matter and theme between personal experience narratives and traditional tales. Legends can be contemporary, and legendary figures still can interact with everyday individuals.

Similar to legends, which often feature natural occurrences or nonhuman characters, animal tales feature animals with human characteristics as heroes and antagonists. The animal characters often appear in pairs and represent opposing human qualities. Animals walk, talk, use tools, and mirror the daily human lifestyle of the storyteller and his or her community. North Carolina's animal tales are rooted in African American, Cherokee, and Appalachian Mountain traditions. Animal tales originating in slave communities were often stories of protest challenging the social order. In the telling of animal tales, many different species come to have specific connotations, or in the annals of folklore, represent specific meanings, omens, or superstitions.

Superstitions are a basic genre of folklore found throughout the world, from ancient times to the present. Because an unnecessarily negative association has come to be attached to the word "superstition," many prefer the somewhat more neutral term "folk belief" to describe the same concepts and sayings. The most extensive collection and analysis of North Carolina–related superstitions is found in *The Frank C. Brown Collection of North Carolina Folklore*, volumes 6 (1961) and 7 (1964). These two North Carolina volumes have become the model for all succeeding attempts at collecting and classifying other American superstitions. Volume 1 (1952) of the same collection also has a brief section on North Carolina superstitions called "Beliefs and Customs," edited by Paul G. Brewster. Almost 9,000 different superstitions, collected in or related to North Carolina, are listed under the general headings "cycle of human life," "the supernatural," "cosmology and the natural world," and "miscellaneous." Examples include: "If a hog's tooth is carried in the pocket, the bearer will never have a toothache," collected from Allie Ann Pearce of Colerain (Bertie County); "An emerald worn in a ring or pin will give the wearer happiness," collected from Lucille Massey of Durham County; and "It is bad luck to start anywhere and forget something," collected from W. J. Hickman of Hudson (Caldwell County).

Though these superstitions were collected from natives or residents of North Carolina or are analogous to items collected in the state, superstitions tend to be lodged in the traditional lore of all Americans and sometimes people all over the world. Some North Carolina superstitions originate with Native Americans, while others come from immigrants of all eras. The people of England, Ireland, Scotland, Africa, and Germany all contributed to North Carolina's superstition tradition.

References: B. A. Botkin, ed., *A Treasury of Southern Folklore* (1949); Robert B. Downs, ed., *The Bear Went over the Mountain: Tall Tales of American Animals* (1964); Robert Isbell, *The Last Chivaree: The Hicks Family of Beech Mountain* (1996); Isbell, *Ray Hicks: Master Storyteller of the Blue Ridge* (2001); Douglas J. McMillan, "The Vanishing Hitchhiker in Eastern North Carolina," *North Carolina Folklore Journal* 20 (August 1972); J. Alexander Mull, *Mountain Yarns, Legends and Lore* (1972); Nancy Roberts, *North Carolina Ghosts and Legends* (1991); Roy Edwin Thomas, coll., *Come Go with Me: Old-Timer Stories from the Southern Mountains* (1994).

> *Bruce E. Baker*
> *Philip McFee*
> Additional research provided by Douglas J. McMillan and Shannon L. Reavis.

SEE ALSO Brown Mountain Lights; Conjure; Devil's Horse's Hoofprints; Devil's Tramping Ground; Folk Music; Ghosts; Maco Light; Madstones; Root Doctors; Southern Folklife Collection; Wampus.

Folkmoot USA, headquartered in Waynesville, is a folk music and dance festival celebrating a diversity of cultures from around the world. Started in 1983, Folkmoot—also known as the North Carolina International Folk Festival—features performance activities in Asheville, Maggie Valley, Mars Hill, Banner Elk, Clyde, and other towns in the western North Carolina mountains. Highlights of the mid-July celebration include an opening parade of nations and an International Festival Day that includes dancers, musicians, and crafters on the last Saturday of the event. Audience participation is invited at some events. An impressive number of countries from all over the world have been represented since Folkmoot began, including China, Cyprus, Latvia, Puerto Rico, Turkey, Egypt, Germany, and others. Organizers also coordinate cultural visits of international youth groups who live with local students and their families in the community, visit schools, and perform during the school year.

> *Patricia L. Pertalion*

Folk Music. North Carolina boasts a strong tradition of folk music dating from the beginnings of settlement to the present day. Folk songs are transmitted primarily through oral and informal means among singers of a given community, with each singer often putting his or her own stamp on the material so that one song usually exists in a number of variant forms. The English scholar and folklorist Cecil Sharp defined a folk song as having been "created by the common people" rather than by the "educated." Sharp theorized an evolution of folk music turning on three factors: continuity, variation, and selection.

Folk songs address every aspect of life. Many ponder personal relationships or express an individual's emotions. Songs of courtship and love as well as the blues fall into this category. Other folk songs convey an individual's relationship with the community and perhaps remark on work or local features, places, or figures. Folk songs also include topics of national significance. In North Carolina, major political and military conflicts such as the Regulator Movement, Revolutionary War, and Civil War inspired folk songs that circulated until at least the beginning of the twentieth century.

Not all folk songs look outward to the world of human endeavors and relationships, however. Many religious songs and hymns are folk songs. In addition, many folk songs are functional in nature, their music and words used for practical purposes. Tunes played for dancing often have many accompanying verses. If instruments are scarce, these tunes can be used alone for dancing. Likewise, some songs, known as "play-party" songs, are associated with particular games, and most lullabies circulate as folk songs. Work songs pace manual labor or pass the time during repetitive tasks. Scholars often consider hollers, wordless but usually tuneful shouts used to communicate across great distances, and auctioneer's chants as quasi-folk songs.

Ballads and Balladists of North Carolina

Different groups popularized different types of folk songs, but the most common distinction made is between narrative folk songs, or ballads, and nonnarrative folk songs. Traditions of balladry existed across most of Europe during the time in which North Carolina was initially settled, so it is not surprising that these traditions were transplanted along with the early settlers. Ballads were learned by listening, and their rhyming schemes and phrase repetitions made them easy to remember. England and Scotland shared a body of ballads, and many of these were carried to Ulster and the Mountains and Piedmont of North Carolina by Scotch-Irish settlers or directly to the coast by English settlers.

The earliest known ballads present in oral tradition are usually identified as "Child ballads" after Francis James Child, a nineteenth-century scholar who published a benchmark collection of these songs. Others entered oral tradition only after publication as broadsides. Many of the Child ballads, such as "The House Carpenter" and "Barbara Allen," were widely sung in North Carolina, but broadside ballads such as "Pretty Polly" were equally popular.

Sharp was surprised to find in 1916 that residents of the southern Appalachians still sang many of the Child ballads. Sharp and his colleague Maud Karpeles collected songs in North Carolina, Kentucky, Virginia, West Virginia, and Tennessee for 46 weeks between 1916 and 1918. Olive Dame Campbell, a student of mountain culture who later founded the John C. Campbell Folk School in Brasstown, collaborated with Sharp and Karpeles and planned their itinerary. Campbell targeted areas along the Great Divide that she considered the least changed since settlement. Sharp and Karpeles specifically sought English folk songs to extend Sharp's earlier collections. Shunning religious music, they learned that asking for "love songs" brought forth the ballads.

With Karpeles recording words and Sharp noting the tunes, the two collected about 500 songs with over 1,600 variant melodies from nearly 300 singers, almost doubling Sharp's previous compilation. Fourteen and one-half weeks in the North Carolina counties of Buncombe, Madison, Jackson, Forsyth, McDowell, and Yancey yielded 559 of the melodies. Most tunes used the pentatonic scale commonly found in the pre-Victorian musical traditions of the British Isles. Sharp's visit and subsequent book alerted many to the ballad-singing traditions of the North Carolina Mountains, and areas such as Madison County became famous for generations as the home of excellent ballad singers.

While ballad singing thrived in the Mountains, strong folk-singing traditions also existed in every other part of North Carolina. Louis Chappell found ballads plentiful in eastern North Carolina, where British settlement was both older and more English than in the Mountains. Meanwhile, George Pullen Jackson studied African American and white religious songs and discovered British ballad tunes woven into the tapestry of the "spiritual."

In addition to ballads brought over from the British Isles, singers found abundant subject matter in North Carolina. Death, in many forms, was the primary theme of Native American ballads. "Naomi Wise," "Nellie Cropsey," and "Tom Dooley" all tell the story of girls murdered by their sweethearts, each in a different part of the state. Other tragic or disastrous events such as train wrecks, floods, lynchings, and fires provided material for many ballads. Unlike the older ballads brought over from the British Isles, it is often possible to identify the composer of North Carolina ballads. Many of these songs circulated only orally, but some were printed and distributed. North Carolina ballads exist from the earliest days of the colony until more recent times, including songs about Revolutionary War skirmishes and the wreck of a smuggler on Harkers Island during Prohibition.

People and Trends in North Carolina Folk Music

Several North Carolinians endeavored to keep traditional music alive in the state. Bascom Lamar Lunsford (1882–1973) remains an important presence in folk music. Remembered by many as the "Minstrel of the Appalachians," Lunsford was an Asheville attorney and an inexhaustible source of southern culture and folklore. He wrote, collected, and performed dozens of ballads, banjo tunes, and sacred songs during the years immediately preceding and following World War II. In 1928 he began the Mountain Dance and Folk Festival in Asheville as a means for people to share the southern Appalachian music and dance traditions handed down through generations in western North Carolina.

Artus Monroe Moser (1894–1992) spent much of his life collecting ballads in and around his home in western North Carolina in an effort to document the folk traditions of Appalachia.

Moser wrote extensively about the folk songs, folklore, and history of Appalachia and recorded the works of numerous Appalachian performers onto acetate discs. In 1945 the Library of Congress provided Moser with the equipment to collect and record more material, which was later placed in the library's Archive of American Folk Song. Dellie Chandler Norton (1899–1993) lived and farmed in Madison County. She was also a ballad singer and storyteller in a tradition passed down for two centuries among the Mountain families. Norton sang the old English and Scottish ballads brought to the Appalachian region by the first settlers. She performed at the Smithsonian's Festival of American Folklife, and Alan Lomax and John Cohen recorded her songs.

North Carolina–born composer, conductor, and flutist Lamar Stringfield (1897–1959) won a Pulitzer Prize for composition in 1928 for his orchestral suite "From the Southern Mountains." Instrumental in founding the North Carolina Symphony, Stringfield was particularly interested in using American folk music in his compositions. Born in Tennessee, Frank Proffitt (1913–65) lived most of his life in Watauga County. In the early 1960s, he became to many a symbol for the newly awakened interest in traditional music and was recognized as the source of "Tom Dooley," the Kingston Trio recording of which sold more than 3 million copies.

Arthel "Doc" Watson, a blind vocalist, guitarist, banjoist, and recording artist, was born in Deep Gap. His professional career took off in the early 1960s when he played to urban folk music audiences at the Newport Folk Festival and on college campuses. His wife, the former Rosa Lee Carlton, coauthored and recorded several love songs with Watson. Their musician son Merle died in a tractor accident in 1985. In his honor, the couple established MerleFest, a yearly festival featuring traditional music held on the campus of Wilkes Community College. Doc Watson has performed at the Smithsonian Institution, the White House, and Carnegie Hall.

Demographic changes have enriched North Carolina's folk and traditional scene with artists from afar or from outside entertainment circles. For example, the Menhaden Chanteymen from Beaufort gained much attention for their performances of the fishing work songs that once were simply a part of their daily lives. Morrisville's Los Peregrinos and the Ricardo Granaldo Group provided the Triangle with two strong Latino ensembles. During the early 1980s, Chapel Hill and Cary provided the home base for Touchstone, an extraordinary Irish outfit. Mickey Mills and Steel and Rolly Gray and Sunfire are two of several North Carolina ensembles specializing in Caribbean folk music.

References: Bertrand Harris Bronson, *The Ballad as Song* (1969); Louis W. Chappell, *Folk-Songs of Roanoke and the Albemarle* (1939); Tristram P. Coffin, *The British Traditional Ballad in North America* (1977); Wayne Erbsen, *Front Porch Old-Time Songs, Jokes and Stories* (1993); Loyal Jones, *Minstrel of the Appalachians: The Story of* Bascom Lamar Lunsford (1984); Dorothy Scarborough, *A Song Catcher in Southern Mountains: American Folk Songs of British Ancestry* (1937).

Bruce E. Baker
Carole Watterson Troxler
Additional research provided by Wiley J. Williams.

SEE ALSO "Ballad of Tom Dooley"; Mountain Dance and Folk Festival; Southern Folklife Collection.

Folktales. SEE Folklore.

Fontana Dam, the largest dam of the Tennessee Valley Authority (TVA) system, is located on the Little Tennessee River in Graham County. Completed in 1945, it is a gravity-type concrete structure 480 feet high, 2,365 feet long, and 376 feet thick at its base. The six-story powerhouse of reinforced concrete with glass walls is located at the base of the dam. Typical of TVA engineering, Fontana is multipurpose, providing electric power, flood control, navigation, and recreation.

Fontana Dam was developed as a part of the war effort. Formerly owned by the Aluminum Company of America, the site had been acquired by the TVA after prolonged negotiations. Because it was situated in a remote, mountainous area about 60 miles from both Knoxville, Tenn., and Asheville, N.C., highways, bridges, and rail lines had to be built to bring in construction equipment, supplies, and workers.

In this wilderness, the TVA built a community for 5,000 workers and their families. The construction camp included 19 dormitories, a cafeteria with a capacity to serve 1,000 people, a community building, a recreation facility, refreshment stands, and a softball field. The permanent village, a mile downstream from the dam site, included nearly 400 houses and 400 trailers. The village featured a 50-bed hospital, a business district, two racially segregated schools, libraries, softball fields, recreation buildings, refreshment stands, and movie theaters.

Fontana's employees maintained three eight-hour shifts, around-the-clock, seven days a week. Because of this accelerated schedule, construction time was slashed almost to half of what it would have been in peacetime. To inspire the workers, military marches and big band music was piped over an intricate public address system that reached the camp, ball fields, cafeteria, and recreation halls. Bright floodlights illuminated the site, and signs everywhere reminded the inhabitants of their patriotic mission in the war effort.

In November 1944 Fontana Lake began to fill, and on 20 Jan. 1945, three years after construction had started, the powerhouse produced electricity for the first time. The project had cost $74.7 million, consumed 2.8 million cubic yards of concrete, and required 34.5 million man-hours to build. The dam created a reservoir of more than 11,000 acres with a 240-

A view of the Fontana Dam and powerhouse, 1950s. NCC.

mile shoreline and a drainage area of more than 1,500 square miles.

By the early 2000s, the three generating units at Fontana Dam had a total productive capacity of 225,000 kilowatts. In addition, the TVA controlled flooding of the Little Tennessee River through a process of storing and releasing water from the reservoir. Recreational activities included fishing, boating, and swimming on Fontana Lake. The Appalachian Trail, which extends over 2,000 miles from Georgia to Maine, crosses the top of Fontana Dam.

References: Carl Condit, *American Building* (1968); Marguerite Owen, *The Tennessee Valley Authority* (1973).

Brent D. Glass

"Fool-Killer." "Jesse Holmes, the Fool-Killer," was the name given by journalist Charles Napoleon Bonaparte Evans to a fictional character well known to Piedmont North Carolini-

ans in the mid-nineteenth century. Evans, editor of the *Milton Chronicle* from 1841 to 1883, created the Fool-Killer as an expression of his own style of folksy humor and social views. A Whig early in his career, Evans shifted to the Democratic Party in the 1850s. But he remained a progressive in politics, a booster of rail and plank roads, agricultural fairs, steamboat lines, and other improvements. He opposed secession until the fact and then, like many other North Carolinians of his generation, became a stalwart advocate of the Confederacy.

The Fool-Killer appeared as the ostensible author of letters to the *Chronicle* discussing the rambles of Jesse Holmes in counties of the northern Piedmont and characters and situations he encountered along the way. Published about once a month, the columns were accompanied by a woodcut of a feisty little character in long-tailed coat and floppy hat carrying a club. The club was for the Fool-Killer's use in bashing various kinds of fools he came across in his journeys. These included overbearing parents, bullying slave patrollers, hard drinkers, faithless lovers, and a variety of others. Not infrequently, the state legislature and other institutions came in for a share of cudgeling. The flavor of a society in the process of moral decay informed the Fool-Killer's letters.

The *Chronicle* reached only a few hundred subscribers, but Fool-Killer columns were often reprinted in other newspapers and enjoyed a wide popularity. Their brand of humor was similar to that of Hamilton C. Jones's "Cousin Sally Dilliard" and Johnson Jones Hooper's "Simon Suggs." A quarter century after Evans's death, the Fool-Killer was resurrected in a story by William Sydney Porter (O. Henry) and in later fiction such as Helen Eustis's 1954 novel of the same title.

References: Thomas C. Parramore, "Discovered: A Sixth Fool-Killer Letter," *North Carolina Folklore Journal* 23 (August 1975); Durward T. Stokes, "Five Letters from Jesse Holmes, the Fool Killer, to the Editor of the *Milton Chronicle*," *NCHR* 50 (Summer 1963).

Thomas C. Parramore

A Fool's Errand, by Albion W. Tourgée, is the most revealing and popular fictional assessment of southern Reconstruction and the reasons it failed. Tourgée, an Ohioan who came to know the South through three different stints in the Union army, moved just after the Civil War to Greensboro, where he opened a plant nursery and law practice. By 1866 he had also entered politics as a Republican fully committed to freedmen's aid and black suffrage and an outspoken critic of Conservatives who opposed both. He served as a delegate to the state constitutional convention in 1868, and a year later he was elected a superior court judge. In both capacities, Tourgée personified what most white North Carolinians found to be the worst in carpetbaggery. Former governor Jonathan Worth once called him "the meanest Yankee who ever settled among us." His bold attempts to prosecute members of the Ku Klux Klan (KKK) made him a frequent target of their harassment.

Conservative government was restored to North Carolina in 1874, but it was only after a serious business setback and a failed bid for Congress in 1878 that Tourgée left the state after 14 years and returned to the North. By the end of the year, while living in New York City, he published two novels, *Figs and Thistles* and *A Fool's Errand*. The latter was a huge best seller, a result of its melodramatic and often suspenseful narrative and the variety of characters and situations that it portrayed. Tourgée entertainingly provided northern readers with a plausible and palatable explanation of the complexities of Reconstruction, as well as the futility of federal efforts to reshape southern society.

The KKK figured prominently in the novel, and Tourgée included vivid, thinly fictionalized accounts of two of its most infamous crimes: the 1870 murder of Union League and Republican leaders John W. Stephens in Yanceyville and Wyatt

Outlaw in Graham. Interest in those cases, and challenges by southern critics to the credibility of Tourgée's portrayal of them, led him to compile a factual supplement recounting testimony (often of victims) of similar KKK atrocities throughout the South. He included this information as an appendix titled "The Invisible Empire" in the 1880 edition of *A Fool's Errand*.

Given the tremendous commercial success of *A Fool's Errand*, its publisher urged Tourgée to write other fictional accounts of the postwar South. The first, *Bricks without Straw*, appearing less than a year after its predecessor, enjoyed nearly as popular a reception. Together, they made Tourgée a celebrity who traveled the country as a lecturer, continued to write novels and essays, and remained a participant in Republican politics—often as an advocate of black rights and public education in the South.

References: Richard Nelson Current, *Those Terrible Carpetbaggers: A Reinterpretation* (1988); Otto H. Olsen, *Carpetbagger's Crusade: The Life of Albion Winegar Tourgée* (1965).

John C. Inscoe

Football is an exceptionally popular sport in North Carolina at the high school, college, and professional level. The first colleges to field football teams in the state were Trinity College (later Duke University), the University of North Carolina in Chapel Hill, and Wake Forest University. The first intercollegiate games were played in 1888. Many of the state's football pioneers, most notably Trinity president John Franklin Crowell, learned the game on northern campuses. North Carolina A&M (now North Carolina State), Davidson College, and other schools started playing football in the 1890s. Livingstone College hosted Biddle Institute (now Johnson C. Smith University) on 27 Dec. 1892 in history's first intercollegiate football game played between black colleges.

From its inception, college football has been controversial. Fears of violent play and professionalism, as well as questions concerning the proper degree of emphasis of football on campus, have plagued the sport. Trinity, Wake Forest, and Guilford all banned intercollegiate football for lengthy periods, although all eventually reinstated the sport. In the 1930s University of North Carolina president Frank Porter Graham unsuccessfully attempted to reform certain aspects of the football culture. Despite these concerns, college football's impact has steadily increased, not just as a form of recreation but also in financial terms. The construction of increasingly larger stadiums, the growth of the alumni and fan base, and the development of radio and television have made the sport a significant campus revenue producer.

North Carolina college football became nationally prominent with the 1931 arrival of Wallace Wade at Duke and the 1934 arrival of Carl Snavely at UNC. Duke hosted the California-based Rose Bowl on 1 Jan. 1942, after fears of possible Japanese attack nearly forced its cancellation. The post–World War II explosion in college enrollment led to something of a golden age in college football, both in North Carolina and across the nation. UNC halfback Charlie "Choo-Choo" Justice, who played from 1946 through 1949, became a North Carolina folk hero for his on-field exploits and later played in the National Football League (NFL). UNC, Duke, Wake Forest, and North Carolina State were charter members of the Atlantic Coast Conference, the dominant college league in the state since its 1953 formation. All four schools have had a mixture of outstanding and less-competitive teams. Most North Carolina college teams became racially integrated in the late 1960s. Smaller colleges such as Lenoir-Rhyne, Elon, Appalachian State, and Western Carolina have been nationally competitive at a lower level. In the 1960s East Carolina University president Leo Jenkins used that school's expanding football program to promote its growth plans.

Since the 1930s, colleges in North Carolina have also produced players who went on to play professionally in the NFL. Former Duke players Clarence "Ace" Parker, George McAfee, and Sonny Jurgensen are members of the Pro Football Hall of Fame, as is former Wake Forest player Bill George. The list of other NFL stars that played at North Carolina colleges includes Lawrence Taylor, Natrone Means, and Julius Peppers (UNC); Earnest Byner and Jeff Blake (East Carolina); Brian Piccolo, Norm Snead, and Ricky Proehl (Wake Forest); and Alex Webster, Roman Gabriel, Randy White, and Torry Holt (N.C. State). Dozens of other professionals hailed from North Carolina towns but played their college football at out-of-state schools.

Not all North Carolina football is played on college campuses. Youth teams abound in the state, and most high schools field football squads. The North Carolina High School Athletic Association has held state football championships since 1913. The organization controls all levels of high school football competition, establishing conferences and placing teams into classifications based on the size of each school's student population (ranging from division 1-A schools, the smallest, to division 4-A schools, the largest).

Several of the state's larger cities have had minor league professional football teams, including the Charlotte Bantams in the 1930s and the Charlotte Clippers in the 1940s. The Charlotte Hornets played in the World Football League, an unsuccessful challenger to the NFL, in 1974 and 1975. Football in North Carolina entered a new era on 26 Oct. 1993, when NFL owners unanimously selected Charlotte as the host city to the 29th NFL franchise and the first expansion team since 1976. Fireworks exploded over the town, where the Carolina Panthers would play in a new 72,300-seat stadium, as jubilant fans gathered to celebrate the end of a bid process that had begun in 1987. Owner and founder Jerry Richardson became the second former NFL player to own an NFL team (after George Halas of the Chicago Bears).

In their inaugural match-up at the preseason 1995 Hall of Fame Game in Canton, Ohio, the Panthers defeated the Jacksonville Jaguars 20 to 14 to become the first expansion team in NFL history to win its initial contest. Their seven first-season wins more than doubled the previous record of three victories by an expansion team in its first year. The Panthers improved dramatically during their second season, advancing to the National Football Conference championship game and moving from their temporary home in Clemson, S.C., to their new stadium in Charlotte. They reached their first Super Bowl during the 2003–4 season, winning their division and three playoff games before losing to the New England Patriots in Super Bowl XXXVIII by a score of 32 to 29.

References: Bill Beezley, *The Wolfpack: Intercollegiate Athletics at North Carolina State University* (1976); Ted Mann, *A Story of Glory: Duke University Football* (1985); Ken Rappoport, *Tar Heel: North Carolina Football* (1976); Jim L. Sumner, *A History of Sports in North Carolina* (1990).

Jim L. Sumner

Footpaths have existed in North Carolina since early colonial days, when roads were not well maintained and traveling by foot was the best way to go from place to place. Long walks were uncommon, although some Moravians actually walked from Bethlehem, Pa., to Wachovia, N.C.—a distance of about 400 miles that usually required more than a month to complete.

There were paths between farms as well as from farms to gristmills, churches, crossroads stores or taverns, racetracks, neighborhood schools, and the nearest villages. Numerous paths to a militia district often led to the muster grounds on which troops regularly drilled. Until the introduction of the railroad, many troops at war generally moved by foot along paths that frequently offered the most direct and secure routes. Streams were crossed by footlogs or, if they were shallow, by boulders at appropriate intervals. Footpaths beside or across a field were not disturbed during plowing. Often the topsoil in fields eroded, while undisturbed paths remained firm and well packed; this resulted in a path sometimes being elevated a foot or more higher than the adjacent field. As late as World War I, it was said that there was a nearly straight footpath from Chapel Hill to Raleigh used by university students for weekend visits home.

Eighteenth-century and early nineteenth-century deeds and wills sometimes mentioned paths by name. John Bryan's will, made in Edgecombe County in 1734, made note of land that he owned "on the Indian path." A Bertie County will from 1751 referred to "Carter's Path" between the homes of William Yeates and Bryan Hare. A journal kept by the Moravians in 1772 indicated that a path from the site of the Battle of Alamance was so poorly marked that a traveler walked a dozen miles in the wrong direction before discovering the error. In 1794 a

View of a foot washing ceremony at the Mount Ronius Free Will Baptist Church at Lake Waccamaw, ca. 1910. NCC.

deed stated that Dr. Charles Pasteur owned 737 acres in Halifax County on "Steel's Path."

Paths were frequently depicted on eighteenth-century maps. Edward Moseley's *A New and Correct Map of the Province of North Carolina* (1722) labeled the trails of the Nansemond and Meherrin Indians in eastern Bertie County. John Collet's *A Complete Map of North Carolina* (1770) included the "Path to the Cherokee Nation," "Crafford Path," "Green's Path," "the Trading Path," and "the Western Path." On his *An Accurate Map of North and South Carolina with Their Indian Frontiers* (1775), Henry Mouzon showed eight distinct paths, several extensive in length. They were labeled "the path from Cahuitta," "Crawford Path," "Lower Path," "Lower Trading Path," "Path from Oalcsoskee," "Old Trading Path," "Trading Path," and "The Western Path." This map was used by both American and British troops in North Carolina during the American Revolution.

William S. Powell

SEE ALSO Great Trading Path; Green's Path.

Foot Washing is an act of worship practiced by various Christian groups in North Carolina and other southern states. The practice involves bathing the feet of a fellow church mem-

ber and is usually followed by words of support and fellowship between those involved. Generally, the washing is performed with males and females gathered in separate rooms after the church's observance of the Lord's Supper. The custom of foot washing among Christians is based on the Gospel of John (13:4–15). In this account of the Last Supper, Jesus got up from the table, took off his outer robe, tied a towel around himself, and began to wash the disciples' feet to emphasize that they were to care for each other as he had cared for them.

In North Carolina, foot washing has been practiced in varying degrees by a variety of Baptist groups, including Primitive, Regular, Old Regular, Free Will, Pentecostal Free Will, and Separate Baptists. The modern-day practice is most evident among the Free Will Baptist groups in the state, although some Roman Catholic, Moravian, and Episcopalian churches are among other congregations that follow the custom.

Reference: H. Leon McBeth, *The Baptist Heritage: Four Centuries of Baptist Witness* (1987).

Glenn Jonas

Fords, areas in streams or rivers that are shallow enough for wading, have been used by North Carolina travelers for centuries to cross certain bodies of water. Suitably shallow and narrow rivers were generally more common in the piedmont and mountains; in the eastern portion of the state first settled, bridges and ferries were required to cross the wide, deep rivers that were often surrounded by swampland. The Moseley map of 1733 shows North Carolina's rudimentary road network and names a number of ferries and bridges while also implying the existence of many fords. As fords were frequently dangerous (and were impassable at high water), they contributed greatly to the hardships and slow speed of travel, which was often restricted to foot or horse.

Fords played a significant role in eighteenth-century colonial conflicts. Governor William Tryon's expedition against the Regulators in 1771 was burdened with several pieces of artillery for assaulting vital fords held by armed Regulators. On the return journey, his forces were delayed by high water at a ford for three days, no doubt due partly to the presence of the cannons. During the Revolutionary War, Lord Charles Cornwallis's pursuit of Gen. Nathanael Greene's battered army during January and February 1781 was frustrated by delays at rain-swollen fords, enabling Greene to escape across the Dan River into Virginia and strengthen his troops for the Battle of Guilford Courthouse in mid-March. Greene's men secured enough boats to allow them to cross the flooded Yadkin and Dan River fords and avoid being trapped there.

A Tar River ford figures in one dubious but popular legend explaining how North Carolinians came to be known as "Tar Heels." To prevent their supplies of tar and turpentine from being captured by the British, so the story goes, Patriots dumped them into the river, where the tar sank to the bottom and stuck to the feet of Cornwallis's troops as they attempted to ford the river. It was claimed that the unfortunate British were still trying to clean their heels when they surrendered at Yorktown.

Although the colonial Assembly passed many laws empowering county courts to oversee the maintenance of state roads, fords were rarely explicitly mentioned until the twentieth century; they seem to have been tacitly accepted as part of the road system with little explanation. But according to a 1901 legislative act, county commissioners (in taking over the administrative functions of the county courts) were placed in charge of a county's "highway, bridges, ferries, and fords." The same act required commissioners to set up guideposts at dangerous fords on highways and public roads.

Most fords in North Carolina were replaced by bridges or ferries in a steady process lasting from colonial days into the automobile age. At the end of the twentieth century, there were still a number of secondary roads with fords in Cherokee, Surry, Swain, Watauga, Wilkes, and Yadkin Counties.

David A. Norris

SEE ALSO Trading Ford.

Forests have played a vital role in virtually all aspects of North Carolina's environmental health and economic development. The first European settlers in the region that would become North Carolina found the majority of the landscape covered with forests. Huge numbers of trees were subsequently cleared away to create farmland or for use—oak being an especially good material—in a variety of essential products, such as planks, casks, barrels, hogsheads, staves, hoops, and shingles. In colonial times, oak barrels were the principal packaging for oceangoing cargo such as tobacco, wine, flour, and pickled deer hides, and oak bark was an important export; it was also essential for tanning and an ingredient in medicines designed to treat such maladies as throat infections, hemorrhages, diarrhea, and consumption. The durability as well as distinctive pattern and coloration of oak lumber were attractive to the makers of furniture, flooring, molding, mantelpieces, wainscoting, and cabinetry. Longleaf pine trees were used to make naval stores such as tar, pitch, and turpentine, with a vast amount of these products being exported to England from the seventeenth century to the Civil War era.

Practically no virgin forest remains in North Carolina; two-thirds of the state is classified as commercial forestland or land capable of producing usable trees, and the state's lumber industry thrives. Pine trees supply local pulp and paper mills as well as some furniture producers. A variety of manufacturers use the state's mixed hardwoods to make flooring, cooperage, veneer, plywood, excelsior, furniture, fixtures, and railroad cross ties.

While matters of economy continue to involve the state's forests and trees, greater emphasis has been placed on their essential role in the quality of North Carolina's natural environment. In 1892 George Washington Vanderbilt, owner of the Biltmore Estate, hired Gifford Pinchot as the nation's first professional forester. Six years later, the first forestry school in the United States began at Biltmore under the direction of Carl A. Schenck, Pinchot's successor. Because of the work of this school and subsequent governmental and private organizations, North Carolina has focused on the importance of forests and forest management for decades.

Before the clearing of land for agriculture began, forests contributed to the development of rich, fertile layers of topsoil through the recycling of nutrients and decomposition of organic matter. In many cases, the topsoil has been mostly destroyed by more than 300 years of land clearing for agriculture and the development of urban areas. Forests have been irreplaceable in maintaining water quality and quantity by lessening erosion and stabilizing the flow of water into streams and rivers. They provide habitats for a number of the state's rare and endangered plants and animals as well as other species such as black bear, squirrel, white-tailed deer, and raccoon. They also have great value for recreational activities such as hunting, fishing, picnicking, hiking, bird watching, horseback riding, and mountain hiking. Finally, many North Carolinians value the state's forests simply for their beauty and for the sense of permanence and solitude they give the landscape.

Important North Carolina Tree Species

North Carolina forests contain the largest diversity of temperate and tropical tree species in the eastern United States. This abundance of species is due in large part to the wide variations in temperature, moisture, and soil that exist in the state's three geographic regions, the coastal plain, the piedmont, and the mountain region. North Carolina's tree population can be divided into two distinct groups. Conifer trees, also called evergreens or softwoods, have needles or scales for foliage and create cone-bearing fruits. Broadleaved trees, or hardwoods, generally lose their foliage each fall. The three regions of the state are rich in a variety of trees, including loblolly, longleaf, shortleaf, and southern pine and upland and lowland hardwoods, especially varieties of oak. Indeed, settlers in the area designated the land either "oakey" or "piney," illustrating the prevalence of these particular types of hardwoods and softwoods.

In the mountains of North Carolina, 90 percent of the timberland belongs to hardwood forests, predominantly oak-hickory forests, although other combination forests such as oak-pine and maple-beech-birch also cover significant acreage. White pine forests dominate the softwood areas in the western part of the state. In the piedmont, over 50 percent of the land has forest cover. Hardwood forest types cover about 74 percent of the timberland, mostly oak-hickory but with notable amounts of oak-pine and oak-gum-cypress combinations. Softwood forests take up about 25 percent of the timberland, with loblolly pine forests being prevalent but Virginia pine and short-leaf pine also being important. Well over half of the coastal plain is forested, hardwoods once again taking up greater acreage with oak-gum-cypress and oak-hickory forests, although pine and oak-pine forests cover about one-fifth of the region's timberland. Softwood forests, chiefly loblolly pines, cover almost 40 percent of the coastal plain.

Eight of the 60 species of pine trees flourish in North Carolina: the loblolly, longleaf, short-leaf, Eastern white, pitch, pond, Virginia, and table mountain pine. Of these, the loblolly and longleaf are the best known. The loblolly, also known as the black pine and the Carolina pine, is the dominant pine of much of the Southeast. The loblolly is extensively used in the production of pulp, paper, plywood, and lumber and is one of the most commercially important trees in the region.

Thirty or so species of oak trees may be found in North Carolina, of which about half are quite common. There is much distribution of species by region; live oaks—often bearded with Spanish moss—are found only in the coastal plain, northern red oak only in the mountains. Turkey oaks seem to thrive mainly in the Sandhills. White oaks and post oaks are found together, as are black oaks and scarlet oaks, and water oaks and blackjacks.

Beech trees are divided into two main types: the American beech and the European beech. These large trees often dominate forests; other plants are unable to grow because of the intense shade produced by dense layers of elliptical, long-pointed leaves, the depth of fallen leaves, and surface roots. Present in North Carolina since 8000 B.C., beech trees are not in the majority today but have maintained a definite forest presence. They are popular ornamentals, often planted in parks, cities, and private yards. Attesting to the tree's long-standing presence are at least 37 North Carolina locations beginning with the word "beech."

American chestnut trees once covered 30 million acres of North Carolina forests as the dominant hardwood tree species in the eastern United States. Native Americans harvested chestnuts and used them in bread, and colonists used them as a stuffing in roasted fowl dishes or in a special sauce made with gravy and thickened with butter. Families gathered bushels of nuts in the fall and ate them raw, boiled, and roasted or sold them for goods. Settlers also used chestnuts to feed hogs and turkeys, and the wood made excellent shingles and fence posts because of its straight grain and high acidity. Commercial uses of the rot-resistant chestnut wood included tannin, lumber, pulpwood, telephone poles, ship masts, railway ties and caskets.

A blight—an Asian fungus from imported nursery stock first appearing on mature chestnuts in the New York Zoological Park—hit American chestnuts in the early 1900s, wiping out nearly the entire species. The fungus killed trees within two or three years by choking the flow of water and sap. The blight moved southward at the rate of 50 miles per year and eventually reached the entire natural range of the chestnut in North Carolina. Despite control efforts, the fungus destroyed nearly every mature chestnut within its natural range in less than 50 years.

American chestnut root systems continue to produce sprouts, but the lifespan of the trees is very short. In an effort to increase the chestnut tree population, plant pathologists spent decades in unsuccessful attempts to cross the American species with the blight-resistant Chinese chestnut. However, the American Chestnut Foundation, founded in 1982, successfully maintains several thousand trees in its experimental farms in southwestern Virginia. Scientists have studied the blight by deliberately injecting trees with the fungus and cross-breeding to create a blight-resistant offspring.

The red mulberry, North Carolina's only native mulberry, is found throughout the state and most of the eastern United States. The reddish fruit—which makes mulberry wine when fermented—is relished by wildlife, swine, and poultry, a fact that led most North Carolina homesteads to keep mulberry orchards up until the early 1900s. Mulberry leaves are the primary food of silkworms and were utilized in North Carolina from colonial times until around 1850 in the silk industry.

The sassafras tree grows throughout the eastern United States, although it is most common in North Carolina in the coastal plain and piedmont. Fossils of sassafras trees dating from the Cretaceous period (125 million to 60 million years ago) have been found in North Carolina, making it one of the first known types of trees in the state. The entire plant is aromatic, but the root bark and its derived oil have been most often used over the centuries as a tea, flavoring, and medicine. Sassafras had an almost magical reputation as a cure for a host of illnesses; a superstition claimed that merely carrying sassafras wood in one's pocket would ward off diseases. The dried, powdered leaves are used to thicken soups and other dishes in Cajun and other cuisines. Federal regulations now prohibit the commercial use of sassafras in food products.

Two species of walnut trees, among the least plentiful hardwoods found in the state's commercial forest land, are native to North Carolina. The black walnut, although most abundant in the piedmont, can be found throughout the state, usually in low-lying areas where the soil is rich and moist. The white walnut grows primarily in the mountains. Native Americans stored and used the sweet, edible nut for food and body oil. During their expedition of 1584 on behalf of Sir Walter Raleigh, Philip Amadas, Arthur Barlowe, and their men received walnuts and other foods from Granganimeo, brother of Wingina, head of the tribe that inhabited Roanoke Island. Because of the wood's durability and resistance to worms, shipbuilders used black walnut on the bottom of boats, and cabinetmakers during the eighteenth and nineteenth centuries favored black walnut over other native hardwoods. Thomas Day, a free black cabinetmaker working in Milton before the Civil War, used walnut as well as maple and mahogany for his pieces.

Efforts to Protect North Carolina Forests and Trees

Forest protection has been undertaken throughout the state in an attempt to prevent and control fires, insects, and disease. Fires, for example, are important ecosystem processes in releasing nitrogen and producing other chemical reactions; consuming debris; and heating, altering, and refreshing the landscape. But fires can also become disastrous for both people and the environment. Some of the most devastating fires have had causes ranging from natural occurrences such as lightning and drought to human accident. The destructive power of forest fires may be seen in the data for a few selected years: 546,000 acres of forest burned in the state in 1879; 1.5 million to 2 million acres burned in 1894; over 1 million acres burned in 1941; over 600,000 acres burned in 1955 (during one of the largest single fires on record in North Carolina); and 23,000 acres burned in Pender County over 10 days in May 1986.

Other problems, perhaps not given the same media at-tention as fires, may have long-ranging, destructive effects on North Carolina forests. Pest outbreaks, including Dutch elm disease, chestnut blights, and gypsy moths, are often unpredictable and cyclic. Forest losses from Hurricane Floyd (September 1999) were estimated by the North Carolina Department of Crime Control and Public Safety's Division of Emergency Management at more than $89 million. On 28 June 2000 Governor James B. Hunt signed legislation that encouraged new public-private partnerships to preserve 1 million acres of farmland, forests, wetlands, and other undeveloped land in the state over the next 10 years. The U.S. Forest Service reported in mid-2000 that trees in Durham and Wake Counties are disappearing faster than in almost any other county in the Southeast. Durham developers are now encouraged to leave some stands of trees intact, in response to a 1999 resource protection ordinance adopted by a group of concerned architects, environmentalists, politicians, and builders.

Various organizations and government initiatives have advocated forest preservation through the years. For instance, for many years the entities that oversee national and state forests in North Carolina and firms in the forest products industry have been practicing forest management techniques such as tree farming, a systematic program of conservation and reforestation designed to ensure continuous commercial production of timber. Many small landowners also use tree farming techniques in an effort to maintain and replenish the state's forests. In addition, the North Carolina Forestry Association consistently works to improve the "health and productivity" of the state's forests. Orange County's Environment and Resource Conservation Department uses a mix of county and state funds and grants to acquire land. Its Land Legacy Program was launched in 2000 with the purchase of 63 acres in Duke Forest near the Eno River and McGowan Creek, west of Hillsborough. Urban forestry was given another boost when the state Department of Environment and Natural Resources awarded a "Tree City USA" designation to 48 cities and towns across the state.

By the early 2000s nearly 62 percent (about 19.9 million acres) of North Carolina was forested, down from 64 percent in 1950 but more than double the 30 percent in the early 1900s —the high point of agriculture in the state. The state's forests slowly continue to repair the enormous soil damage caused by primitive agriculture. In terms of ownership, about 73 percent of the forestland is owned by 300,000 individuals (small farmers) or organizations (such as the Nature Conservancy) not associated with the forest products industry. Eleven percent is owned by the forest products industry, and 16 percent is owned by various levels of government, including four national forests (Croatan, Nantahala, Pisgah, and Uwharrie), six state forests (Clemmons, Holmes, Jordan Lake, Rendezvous Mountain, Turnbull Creek, and Tuttle), and a number of city and county recreation areas with forested acreage.

References: Chris Bolgiano, *The Appalachian Forest: A Search for Roots and Renewal* (1998); William Chambers Coker and Henry Roland Totten, *Trees of the Southeastern States, Including Virginia, North Carolina, South Carolina, Georgia, and Northern Florida* (1934); O. C. Goodwin, *Eight Decades of Forestry Firsts: A History of Forestry in North Carolina, 1889–1969* (1969); J. S. Holmes and North Carolina Department of Environment, Health and Natural Resources, Division of Forest Resources, *Common Forest Trees of North Carolina: How to Know Them* (1995).

Joan E. Freeman
Additional research provided by A. J. Bullard, David A. Norris, Karl Rohr, Jean Snow, David Southern, and Maurice C. York.

SEE ALSO Biltmore Forest School; Logging; Pine Trees; State Parks.

Forest Society is a term applied to the economy of the earliest European settlers of the region that would become North Carolina and other eastern states. It is analogous to "hunters and gatherers" as applied to the native people found in North America by the explorers and colonists sent by Sir Walter Raleigh in the sixteenth century. Both groups—American Indians and settlers—were obliged to live off the land. Early settlers depended on forests for protection from the elements, for warmth in cold weather, for nuts and fruit to supplement their diet, and for furniture for their houses. They also relied on the forests to build boats for transportation and for much of their commerce, as naval stores (tar, pitch, and turpentine), shingles, and lumber became important items in trade.

Reference: Brooke Hindle, ed., *America's Wooden Age: Aspects of Its Early Technology* (1976).

William S. Powell

Forsyth County, located in North Carolina's Piedmont region, was formed from Stokes County in 1849 and took its name from Col. Benjamin Forsyth, a state legislator who fought and died in the War of 1812. The town of Winston, named after Revolutionary War veteran Maj. Joseph Winston, became the county seat in 1851; in 1913 it merged with its older neighbor Salem (a Moravian town named after the Hebrew word for peace) to form Winston-Salem. Other communities in the county include Kernersville, Clemmons, Lewisville, Tobaccoville, Walkertown, Rural Hall, Bethania, Bethabara, and Belews Creek.

The land that became Forsyth County was originally named Wachovia by the Moravians who purchased and settled it in 1753; the name was the Latin form of "Wachau," the Austrian ancestral estate of Moravian Church patron Count Nicholas Ludwig von Zinzendorf. Bethabara ("house of passage") was the first community established in the new land, although Salem (founded in 1766) emerged as the commercial hub of the Moravians' religious haven. Many elements of seventeenth- and eighteenth-century daily life in the town have been preserved in the Old Salem Historic District, which maintains more than 50 restored buildings and features a blacksmith, gunsmith, cobbler, and carpenter in period dress.

From its humble origins, Winston-Salem had emerged by the end of the twentieth century as Forsyth County's economic engine and the fifth-largest city in North Carolina (the county as a whole, with an estimated 321,000 residents in 2004, ranked fourth in population in the state). The city briefly, in 1920, held the title of North Carolina's largest city. In 1875 Richard Joshua Reynolds established his tobacco business in Winston, and the company's growth into one of the nation's largest corporations spurred the development of both the city and Forsyth County. In addition to R. J. Reynolds Corporation, other major businesses with Forsyth County roots include Krispy Kreme Doughnuts and the Wachovia Corporation (although the latter's corporate headquarters were relocated to Charlotte following its 2001 merger with First Union). Important agricultural and industrial products include tobacco, corn, soybeans, furniture, textiles, tractors, and optical fiber.

Winston-Salem, thanks in large part to the philanthropic pursuits of the Reynolds family and the local business community, is also regarded as a major cultural and artistic center in North Carolina. The Reynolds home, known as the Reynolda House, contains a major collection of American art. The city is home to the nation's first local arts council (the Arts Council of Winston-Salem and Forsyth County, established in 1949) as well as the first state-supported arts conservatory (the North Carolina School of the Arts, which opened in 1965). Salem College (1772), Wake Forest University (1834), and Winston-Salem State University (1897) are important academic institutes in the county. Celebrated Forsyth County cultural events include the Dixie Classic Fair, the National Black Theatre Festival (both in Winston-Salem), and the Christmas-themed Festival of Lights at Tanglewood Park (in Clemmons).

Reference: Frank Tursi, *Winston-Salem: A History* (1994).

Robert Blair Vocci

SEE ALSO Moravians; Reynolda House; Salem; Winston-Salem.

Fort Bragg, a 300-square-mile military cantonment and reservation in Hoke and Cumberland Counties, was authorized in August 1918 as a World War I artillery training center for 16,000 soldiers and 5,700 horses and mules but was completed after the armistice. In 1921 the camp was named in honor of North Carolina's Braxton Bragg (1817–76), a U.S. Army captain in the Mexican War and a Confederate general during the Civil War. Pope Air Field, adjacent to the cantonment, was named for Lt. Harley Pope (1879–1919), who, with Sgt. W. W.

Fleming, was killed when his plane crashed in the Cape Fear River.

Fort Bragg's complement of artillerymen included fewer than 3,000 officers and men. Pope Air Field had a small number of pilots whose mission was to observe artillery fire. The field was also a bustling fueling stop for army planes in transit to busier fields to the west and south. In the 1930s the base's dilapidated wooden buildings were mostly replaced by brick and stucco barracks, gun sheds, a chapel, a hospital, a headquarters, and family quarters for both commissioned and noncommissioned officers. This central portion of the cantonment has been preserved as Pope Air Force Base Historic District.

In 1940, when the nation began its military buildup prior to entering World War II, Fort Bragg was expanded by a one-year barracks and hospital construction program to house as many as 60,000 soldiers, making it the largest post in the army. The Ninth Infantry Division and dozens of artillery units trained there. In 1942 Fort Bragg became the home of the 82nd and 101st Airborne Divisions; here the famous parachute and glider divisions trained for their role in the European theater.

The 82nd Airborne had been organized on 25 Aug. 1917 at Camp Gordon, Ga., as the 82nd Infantry Division. Consisting of troops from all 48 states, the division acquired the nickname "All-Americans," which led to its "AA" shoulder patch. After fighting in three major campaigns over five months during World War I, the division was demobilized until 25 Mar. 1942. On 15 Aug. 1942 the 82nd Infantry was redesignated the 82nd Airborne, becoming the first airborne division in the U.S. Army. It participated in campaigns in Italy and Normandy and, for its performance in the occupation of Berlin, gained the further title (from a statement by Gen. George Patton) of "America's Guard of Honor." After the war the 82nd was permanently assigned to Fort Bragg; it was the first division to integrate black soldiers into a white unit when, in 1946, the 555th Parachute Infantry Battalion, the only black paratrooper outfit in the army, was disbanded and became part of the division. The 82nd became a regular army division on 15 Nov. 1948.

Fort Bragg's population shrank to fewer than 20,000 until the Korean War, when it increased to over 40,000. In the 1950s the post was the birthplace and home of the Special Forces (Green Berets). Soldiers from the base took part in missions to Vietnam (1957-75), the Dominican Republic (1965-66), Grenada (1983), Panama (1989), the Persian Gulf (1990-91), Haiti (1995), Afghanistan (2002), and Iraq (2003). By the early 2000s Fort Bragg was one of the largest military bases in the world, housing more than 45,000 soldiers and employing 8,000 civilians on 160,789 acres. The Eighty-second Airborne Division, Eighteenth Airborne Corps, and Seventh Special Forces Group deployed from the post.

Virtually the entire array of U.S. Army activities, other than the training of large armored forces, is displayed at Fort Bragg.

Small post museums depict the history of airborne forces and Special Forces, now known as Special Operations. In recent years the army, in cooperation with the Nature Conservancy, has been involved in extensive protection and preservation of plant and animal habitats at the base.

References: Ruth M. Little, *Fort Bragg Main Post National Register Nomination* (1995-96); Roy Parker Jr., *Cumberland County: A Brief History* (1990).

Roy Parker Jr.

SEE ALSO Pope Air Force Base.

Fort Caswell, named after North Carolina's first governor and Revolutionary War hero Richard Caswell (1729-89), was a permanent masonry garrison built by the U.S. Army Corps of Engineers on the eastern end of Oak Island in Brunswick County between 1826 and 1838. It guarded the mouth of the Cape Fear River as part of a national chain of forts for coastal defense of the United States known as the Third System. Designed by Brig. Gen. Simon Bernard, Fort Caswell was an irregular pentagon with a completely encircling outer wall, or covered way, and an inner main work that was loopholed for defense.

The fort was never fully armed, and until 1861 it was usually occupied only by army caretakers. Following South Carolina's secession from the Union, fears that the Federal government would send troops to occupy North Carolina's forts prompted local secessionist militia troops to seize Fort Caswell on 9 Jan. 1861. But North Carolina had not seceded, and so the fort was returned, only to be retaken on 16 April, after the Civil War began.

Now armed, the fort became one of the main Confederate defenses of the Cape Fear River. The Confederates strengthened it by constructing a massive earthwork defense around the fort and on top of the main work to accommodate 29 heavy guns. However, the fort was never directly attacked; its guns occasionally fired on Union warships in the ocean blockading the Cape Fear entrance. After Union forces captured Fort Fisher on the opposite side of the river on 15 Jan. 1865, retreating Confederate forces detonated gunpowder magazines in Fort Caswell on the morning of 17 January, literally blowing away the southeast face and shattering the west face. After the war, the fort reservation was returned to caretaker status.

In 1885 Secretary of War William C. Endicott's Fortifications Board selected Fort Caswell to receive modern defenses. The work continued from 1894 to 1904, significantly altering the original fortification. The army used the reservation until after World War I, when, in 1923, it was closed by the War Department and listed for sale as surplus property. In 1925 it was purchased by Florida developers. With the onset of World War II, the U.S. Navy bought the reservation in 1941. Sold to the Baptist State Convention in 1949, the reservation has been used as the North Carolina Baptist Assembly.

References: John G. Barrett, *The Civil War in North Carolina* (1963); Ronald B. Hartzer, *To Great and Useful Purpose: A History of the Wilmington District, U.S. Army Corps of Engineers* (1984); Ethel Herring and Carolee Williams, *Fort Caswell in War and Peace* (1999).

Paul Branch

Fort Defiance was the home of William Lenoir (1751–1839), Revolutionary War officer, justice of the peace, state legislator, University of North Carolina trustee, and planter-entrepreneur of Wilkes County (later Caldwell County). Built on the site of a fort once used by British colonists, the two-story frame house was designed by Lenoir and completed in 1790 by local builder Thomas Fields. Located on a 2,000-acre tract south of the Yadkin River, the dwelling measured 40 feet long and 28 feet wide and contained four rooms on each story.

From 1805 to 1880 Fort Defiance served intermittently as a post office. Its postmasters included Edmund Jones (William Lenoir's son-in-law) and Lenoir descendants: Thomas Lenoir, Thomas Isaac Lenoir, and Rufus Theodore Lenoir. William Lenoir enlarged Fort Defiance in 1823 when his son, Thomas, moved into the house with his wife and seven children. William; his wife, Ann; and their unmarried daughter, Mira, occupied the three-room addition.

Including William and Ann Lenoir, seven generations of the Lenoir family made Fort Defiance home. Before William's death in 1839, he distributed more than half of the 2,000-acre tract to his children, who built their own homes on the land. The sociable community of kinfolk near Fort Defiance became known appropriately as "Happy Valley."

By the 1960s, Fort Defiance declined in appearance and in structural maintenance. In 1964 Mildred McDowell Jones, whose husband was a great-great-grandson of William Lenoir, decided to preserve the house as a historic site. With the help of local leaders and the Caldwell County Historical Society, Jones formed the Fort Defiance Project, which raised $15,000 to purchase the dwelling and grounds. In 1965 the project's chairman, Joseph J. Steele, contacted the North Carolina Department of Archives and History (now the Office of Archives and History) in Raleigh for advice.

The restoration of Fort Defiance concluded in 1978, following documentary research by historian Jerry Cashion, acquisition of a $20,000 grant from the state legislature, completion of a successful fund-raising effort, formation of a self-perpetuating board of Fort Defiance, Inc., to oversee the restoration project, and assistance by experts at the Office of Archives and History. It was dedicated later that year as a historic site on the National Register of Historic Places.

Reference: Richard A. Shrader, "William Lenoir, 1751–1839" (Ph.D. diss., UNC-Chapel Hill, 1978).

Richard A. Shrader

Fort Dobbs, located in present-day Statesville, was a defensive fort built in 1756 under the auspices of North Carolina's colonial Assembly during the French and Indian War. The large log fort, deemed necessary for the protection of frontier settlers during the conflict, was constructed by provincial rangers under the command of Hugh Waddell and named for royal governor Arthur Dobbs. Waddell and his rangers manned the fort and used it as a base of operations during the conflict. At times colonists stayed close to the fort's walls for protection. The fort was actually attacked by Cherokee Indians only once, on the night of 27 Feb. 1760, resulting in the deaths of one or two of Waddell's men and as many as 12 Cherokees.

After the Treaty of Paris ended the war, Fort Dobbs was no longer essential to the protection of the colonists, who had seen the boundary of British settlement move farther west through the defeat of the Cherokees. The fort was dismantled, and its buildings eventually fell into disrepair. Archaeologists have determined the exact location of the fort, although its appearance remains unclear. The modern Fort Dobbs State Historic Site allows visitors to view the remains of the fort and also features displays of artifacts, trails, archaeological sites, a gift shop, and recreation facilities.

References: Stephen Israel, *Archaeological Research at Fort Dobbs: A French and Indian War Site on the Carolina Frontier, Iredell County, North Carolina* (1971); Richard F. Knapp, ed., *North Carolina's State Historic Sites: A Brief History and Status Report* (1995).

Paul Branch

Fort Fisher, the largest earthen fortification in the world in 1865, was a Confederate military facility built approximately 18 miles south of Wilmington to defend the New Inlet into the Cape Fear River. Construction began in the spring of 1861, and the fort was expected to be battle ready by the end of September. Work continued under Col. William Lamb for several years. By 1865 Fort Fisher extended across Federal Point, facing north, then turned south 1,900 yards along the sea. Both faces of the fort consisted of sod-covered mounds of sand, inside each of which was a bombproof shelter. Between these were platforms with 44 guns, most of which were smoothbore Columbiads. Three mortars and three Napoleon smoothbores augmented the larger pieces. A sally port midway in the landface allowed access to a palisade of sharpened logs nine feet in height. Two dozen mines outside this could be detonated from inside the fort.

Where the land met the sea was the Northeast Bastion, adjacent to which was a semicircular work known as the Pulpit, in which Lamb had a field headquarters. Underneath this was a bombproof hospital; behind it was the main magazine. A buried telegraph line linked Lamb to Wilmington and the Mound Battery, a 60-foot edifice at the south end of the sea face. Beyond the Mound Battery stood Battery Buchanan. Two stories in height, it boasted five guns. Lamb also had a line of rifle pits from the sea face across to the Cape Fear River.

Because of Fort Fisher's effectiveness, Wilmington remained the last port open to supply Gen. Robert E. Lee's Confederate forces. Supplies reaching the port were shipped by rail across eastern North Carolina to the army protecting Richmond, the Confederate capital. The Union navy, with a very large fleet, bombarded the fort on 24–25 Dec. 1864 and again on 13–15 Jan. 1865. On 15 January, a Union landing force captured the beleaguered fort.

Colonel Lamb tried without success until his death in 1909 to have the fort made into a national military park. The New Hanover County Historical Commission placed a marker there in 1921. Ten years later, the Fort Fisher Preservation Society was formed to try to prevent further beach erosion and to foster public interest but had little to show for its efforts. In World War II a new military post was constructed over part of the old fort and erosion continued at the sea face.

The approach of the centennial of the Civil War aroused interest in Fort Fisher, and in 1958 the state leased 189 acres of federal land. Two years later the North Carolina Department of Archives and History began to develop Fort Fisher as a North Carolina State Historic Site. Work progressed with the assistance of local organizations and individual citizens, and in 1962 the remains of the fort became a National Historic Landmark. The General Assembly appropriated funds for a visitors center, and a local restoration committee raised funds for the purchase of additional land. Before the end of the decade, further land and buildings were added to the site, and steps were taken, insofar as possible, to control erosion. Archaeological research and an underwater archaeology laboratory contributed to the understanding of the site, while exhibits at the visitors center and conducted tours brought more visitors.

The Office of Archives and History controls a majority of the 500 acres of owned and leased land, but the center of the modern Fort Fisher State Historic Site includes only about 30 acres. Special events at the site focus on the role of artillery at the fort. Period reproduction weapons, equipment, and clothing are used in living history demonstrations.

References: Rod Gragg, *Confederate Goliath: The Battle of Fort Fisher* (1991); Richard F. Knapp, ed., *North Carolina's State Historic Sites: A Brief History and Status Report* (1995).

Richard B. McCaslin
Additional research provided by William S. Powell.

Fort Fisher, Battle of.

Fort Fisher, Battle of. The Civil War battle at Fort Fisher consisted of two separate expeditions against the formidable

Confederate fortification near the mouth of the Cape Fear River on 24–27 Dec. 1864 and 12–15 Jan. 1865. Fort Fisher, nicknamed the "Gibraltar of the South," consisted of a huge L-shaped earthwork constructed under the direction of Col. William Lamb, the fort's commander. The fort was located just above New Inlet on the peninsula of Federal Point, with Cape Fear to the west and the Atlantic Ocean to the east. It protected Wilmington, the last major blockade-running port of the Confederacy by late 1864 and the lifeline of Gen. Robert E. Lee's Army of Northern Virginia. Gen. Braxton Bragg was given command of the Department of North Carolina, with Maj. Gen. William H. C. Whiting leading a force at Wilmington.

At the urging of Gideon Welles, secretary of the U.S. navy, plans for a Federal expedition commenced in the fall of 1864. Rear Adm. David Porter was given command of a naval assault force of 48 warships, while Maj. Gen. Benjamin F. Butler was to direct 6,500 men. As planning progressed, Butler devised the notion of floating a ship loaded with gunpowder near Fort Fisher and setting it alight. Although engineers were skeptical of the plan, Porter approved it. An old ship, the *Louisiana*, was loaded with approximately 200 tons of gunpowder and in the predawn hours of 24 December was exploded about 600 yards from shore. The sight and sound were impressive, but one Federal naval officer correctly remarked, "There's a fizzle." Colonel Lamb thought that a Federal ship had accidentally run aground and its magazine had exploded. At 11:30 A.M. Porter opened on the fort with 600 guns. The next day Union troops landed north of Fort Fisher and captured two batteries. However, when Butler drew near the fort and saw its strong defenses, he withdrew on 25–26 December. Butler's departure was so hasty that he left part of a regiment stranded until 27 December. Porter and Lt. Gen. Ulysses S. Grant (the Union army's general in chief) were furious at Butler, and Grant relieved him of command.

Brevet Maj. Gen. Alfred H. Terry replaced Butler as the new army commander with 8,000 more soldiers. Porter's squadron was also reinforced. On 12 Jan. 1865 this new force approached Fort Fisher. General Whiting arrived from Wilmington with an additional 600 men, increasing the garrison defending the fort to 1,950. Bragg had an additional 6,000 troops under Maj. Gen. Robert F. Hoke on the northern end of the peninsula. The Union bombardment started on 12 January and the Federals landed troops the next day. Amazingly, Bragg did not order Hoke up but kept his veteran troops huddled inside their earthworks. The Federal naval bombardment continued until 15 January and constituted the heaviest naval fire in history until that time. That afternoon, Brig. Gen. Adelbert Ames attacked the land face of the fort with 3,000 men, while 2,000 naval personnel assaulted the sea face. The naval column was repulsed, but the land face was captured after desperate hand-to-hand fighting. Whiting led a counterattack, heroically charging into the Union attackers, but he was severely

An 1890 lithograph depicting the capture of Fort Fisher by Union forces on 15 Jan. 1865. NCC.

wounded and his men dragged him to safety. They withdrew southward to Buchanan Battery and surrendered at 10:30 P.M. The port of Wilmington was now closed, but the town did not fall until 22 February.

General Bragg was highly criticized for his handling of the Fort Fisher defense, especially by General Whiting, who wrote two reports from a Federal prison charging Bragg with incompetence. The fall of Fort Fisher hastened the demise of the Confederacy by severing its last lifeline to the outside world.

References: John G. Barrett, *The Civil War in North Carolina* (1963); Chris E. Fonvielle Jr., *The Wilmington Campaign: Last Rays of Departing Hope* (1997); Rod Gragg, *Confederate Goliath: The Battle of Fort Fisher* (1991); Grady McWhiney, *Braxton Bragg and Confederate Defeat*, vol. 2 (1991); Charles L. Price and Claude C. Sturgill, "Shock and Assault in the First Battle of Fort Fisher," *NCHR* 47 (January 1970).

Ronnie W. Faulkner

Fort Hamby in Caldwell County, actually a well-fortified, sturdy house, was located in an isolated region and near the end of the Civil War served as a home for outlaws from both the Confederate and Union armies. Bands of these men roamed Caldwell, Alexander, and Wilkes Counties. A man identified only as Wade, allegedly a former officer in Maj. Gen. George H. Stoneman's cavalry, situated his band on the Yadkin River in Caldwell County.

In need of a base from which to operate, Wade and his men forced themselves on the occupants of a small farm near the road from Wilkesboro to Lenoir. The two-story house of oak logs was perfectly constructed for Wade's criminal purposes. The outlaws converted the cellar into a magazine and vault where they could store munitions and plunder, fortified the first floor, and carved gun ports in the walls upstairs. Wade's men dubbed the farmhouse "Fort Hamby," a reference to the surname of the women who had lived there.

Alternately masquerading in Confederate or Federal uniforms, these outlaws stole articles of every kind, attacked homes and travelers, and indulged in murder at random. After a failed murder attempt, a small contingent of local men, veterans, and boys of the Junior Reserves attacked Fort Hamby. At least two of them were killed, and the others scattered into the woods. Realizing that the "fort" could not be taken with such a small force, they withdrew. But by 14 May 1865, several hundred men from as far away as Salisbury made a second attempt. The fighting continued through the night until, under cover of the early morning darkness and fog, the attackers set one of the outbuildings on fire. The flames quickly spread to the fort, and Wade called out for terms, which he was denied. Eventually the attackers rushed the fort, capturing four men. Wade and some others managed to escape.

Fort Hamby and the majority of its contents burned to the ground, and the four prisoners were executed by firing squad. During the following months Wade was sighted many times, always claiming to be a Federal soldier but never again causing trouble.

Reference: Walter Clark, ed., *Histories of the Several Regiments and Battalions from North Carolina in the Great War, 1861–1865*, vols. 4–5 (1901).

Charles C. Davis

Fort Macon. In the years after the War of 1812, the U.S. military constructed a chain of permanent fortifications to defend its harbors and ports against the threat of foreign invasion. One of the forts was built between 1826 and 1834 on the eastern point of Bogue Banks to guard Old Topsail Inlet (Beaufort Inlet), the entrance to Beaufort Harbor. It was named in honor of Nathaniel Macon (1758–1837), a U.S. congressman, senator, and leading Republican statesman of North Carolina.

Active garrisons occupied Fort Macon in 1834–36, 1842–44, and 1848–49. During the period 1841–46 engineers made structural improvements to the fort's defenses. On 14 Apr. 1861, at the beginning of the Civil War, local militia forces from Morehead City and Beaufort, commanded by Capt. Josiah Pender, occupied Fort Macon in the name of the state without bloodshed. Throughout that year the fort was armed and occupied by North Carolina Confederate soldiers in preparation for an eventual Union attack.

In 1862 the Union army of Maj. Gen. Ambrose E. Burnside launched a campaign on the North Carolina coast, intending to capture Fort Macon and Beaufort Harbor. Forces under Brig. Gen. John G. Parke took possession of Morehead City on 23 March and captured Beaufort three days later without resistance. Five artillery companies of North Carolina troops were garrisoned at Fort Macon. On 23 March, the fort's commander, Col. Moses J. White, who possessed 450 men and 54 heavy guns, refused a demand to surrender.

On 28 March Parke established siege positions within a half mile of the fort. He made a final demand for the fort's surrender, which White rejected on 24 April. Early the next morning Parke's batteries opened fire on Fort Macon, a bombardment that lasted 11 hours. The Union rifled cannons carried the day. This was only the second time in history that rifled artillery had bombarded a masonry fort, and it graphically demonstrated the growing obsolescence of forts as a means of

defense. Parke's rifled cannons required only a few hours to crack Fort Macon's walls and threaten one of its gunpowder magazines.

Colonel White had no choice but to capitulate, which he did at 4:30 P.M. on 25 April. Arrangements for the surrender were completed the following morning, and Union forces formally occupied the badly damaged fort. The Confederates lost 7 killed and 18 wounded; Union losses were 1 killed and 3 wounded. The soldiers in the Confederate garrison were paroled and released.

Union forces repaired the damage to Fort Macon and used it for the remainder of the Civil War. During Reconstruction, the U.S. Army occupied the fort continuously until 1877, using it as a prison. In 1898 the fort was regarrisoned for the Spanish-American War, and in 1903 the U.S. Army abandoned it in the belief that it would never again be needed. It was not used in World War I, and in 1923 the Fort Macon Military Reservation was among several other abandoned forts and military posts that the War Department sold off as surplus property. But as a result of public and political pressure within North Carolina, the reservation was deeded to the state by a congressional act in June 1924 for use as a public park.

Fort Macon was the second area acquired by North Carolina for public use in what has grown into the present system of state parks. During the Great Depression, a Civilian Conservation Corps camp restored the fort and constructed recreational facilities. On 1 May 1936 Fort Macon State Park officially opened as the first developed, functioning park in North Carolina. The park was instantly popular, and the Works Progress Administration established a public beach at the site in the early 1940s.

When the United States entered World War II, the old fort went to war once again. On 21 Dec. 1941 Coast Artillery troops occupied the park for military defense purposes. By November 1944, when German U-boat activities off the North Carolina

Fort Macon. Photograph courtesy of North Carolina Division of Tourism, Film, and Sports Development.

coast had subsided, the fort was deactivated. The army terminated its lease on 1 Oct. 1946, and the property was once again returned to North Carolina and resumed its former role as a state park.

References: Paul Branch, *Fort Macon: A History* (1999); Branch, *The Siege of Fort Macon* (1982); Emanuel R. Lewis, *Seacoast Fortifications of the United States: An Introductory History* (1970).

Paul Branch

Fort Raleigh National Historic Site,

Fort Raleigh National Historic Site, located three miles from Manteo on the north end of Roanoke Island, preserves all the known sites and remains of Sir Walter Raleigh's Roanoke colonies (1584–90), the first English attempts to settle the New World. The Fort Raleigh site is also believed to contain the remains of a Roanoke Indian village, the 1862 Civil War battle of Roanoke Island, a Civil War–era freedmen's colony, the early radio experiments by Reginald Fessenden, and work associated with the nineteenth-century development of North Carolina's state boat, the shad boat. The grounds are also home to the Roanoke Island Historical Association's annual Waterside Theater production of Paul Green's *The Lost Colony* and the Garden Clubs of North Carolina's Elizabethan Gardens.

The Roanoke Colony Memorial Association (predecessor to the present Historical Association) bought and preserved the 16-acre nucleus of the site in 1895. It had previously been protected by the owners of the property, the Dough family. The Doughs farmed and built shadboats near the traditional colony site but did not farm the "fort tract" itself. After purchase by the Memorial Association, the area was marked and soon became the site of increased visits by the public and commemorative events. In the 1920s a silent motion picture about the Raleigh colonies was made there. In the 1930s a conjectural fort and town were constructed and the outdoor drama *The Lost Colony* was first performed. In April 1941 the property was transferred to the U.S. National Park Service.

Archaeological excavations under J. C. Harrington after World War II resulted in the reconstruction in the 1950s of an earthwork fort identified as Ralph Lane's 1585 "New Fort in Virginia." The site was expanded to 122 acres and a handsome, modern visitors center was built in the 1960s. Much of this development was funded by North Carolinians Fred and Emma Neal Morrison. The park also became the headquarters of the National Park Service's Cape Hatteras Group, which includes the Cape Hatteras National Seashore and the Wright Brothers National Memorial at Kill Devil Hills.

Continued archaeological research in 1966 by Harrington and in the early 1980s by John Ehrenhard of the National Park Service led to excavations in the 1990s directed by Ivor Noel Hume. These excavations revealed the remains of what has been called America's first science center—the workshop

of Elizabethans Thomas Harriot and Joachim Gans, who as members of Ralph Lane's 1585–86 colony attempted to assess the natural resources of Raleigh's Virginia. However, these excavations have consequently put in doubt the dating of the earthwork fort to 1585.

In addition to walking trails of the traditional colony site and a Thomas Harriot Nature Trail through the maritime forest, Fort Raleigh's visitors center houses museum exhibits on the region's history and archaeology, a historical film based on the PBS production *Roanoak*, and the oak paneling from an Elizabethan Room removed from Heronden Hall in Kent, England.

References: Paul Hulton, *America 1585: The Complete Drawings of John White* (1984); Ivor Noel Hume, *The Virginia Adventure, Roanoke to James Towne: An Archaeological and Historical Odyssey* (1994); William S. Powell, *Paradise Preserved: A History of the Roanoke Island Historical Association* (1965); David B. Quinn, *Set Fair for Roanoke: Voyages and Colonies, 1584–1606* (1985).

Phillip W. Evans

Fort San Juan de Xualla. SEE Pardo Expeditions.

Fortuna case, decided by U.S. Supreme Court chief justice John Marshall in the U.S. Circuit Court for the District of North Carolina on an appeal from Judge Henry Potter's district court, involved the validity of a maritime prize carried into the port of Wilmington by a commissioned American privateer during the War of 1812. Representative of similar prize cases originating in the District of North Carolina, the case of the *Fortuna* was the only one to receive publication of both the circuit and Supreme Court opinions.

The *Fortuna*'s true nationality, whether Russian and thus a neutral vessel or British and a belligerent ship, would determine the validity of the capture and the ability of a federal court to condemn it as a "good prize." That determination depended on the facts as found by the court. Marshall diligently sought to pierce the confused, if not feigned and deceptive, facts. His tedious opinion delivered at Raleigh construed nearly every word in every piece of paper found aboard the vessel. He concluded that the *Fortuna* was most likely British-owned and therefore a valid American prize. The Supreme Court affirmed the chief justice's circuit court decision in favor of the captors.

References: Herbert A. Johnson, ed., *The Papers of John Marshall*, vol. 8 (1990); John P. Roche and Stanley B. Bernstein, eds., *John Marshall: Major Opinions and Other Writings* (1967).

Peter Graham Fish

Fossils. Fossilized remains of animal and plant life have been discovered at numerous locations in North Carolina, primarily

University of North Carolina at Chapel Hill geology professor Joseph Carter (right) and students examine the remains of an extinct reptile known as a rauisuchian. Carter and his students reassembled the 221 million-year-old skeleton in 1999. Photograph by Dan Sears. UNC-Chapel Hill News Services.

in the sedimentary rock formations of the eastern coastal plain. Fossils often are exposed by erosion along stream and river banks, although some of the richest deposits have been found in commercial rock quarries. Relatively few fossils have been found in the older igneous and metamorphic rock formations of the piedmont and the Blue Ridge Mountains, since the intense heat and pressures of volcanism and metamorphism that occurred during and after the continental plates of Africa and North America collided about one billion years ago obliterated much of the plant and animal remains.

The oldest evidence of life found in North Carolina are impressions of wormlike animals and their burrows dated at about 620 million years old. These were found in rocks of the Carolina Slate Belt north of Durham. Two new species of trilobites living in the Cambrian period (roughly 540 to 500 million years ago) were discovered in the southern piedmont.

Dinosaurs and their reptile cousins of the air and water likely roamed the region that became North Carolina during the Age of Dinosaurs, between 245 and 65 million years ago. Fossil records of their presence have proven elusive, however. Because the region is heavily vegetated, the processes of soil formation often destroy fossils before they can reach the surface. Moreover, the state is somewhat densely populated, and some fossil-producing sediments are buried under cities and suburbs. Still, through careful study of the few fossils that have been found and by making educated guesses based on fossil evidence in other regions, paleontologists have been able to re-create a sketchy history of North Carolina's prehistoric residents.

During the Triassic period 230 million years ago, the earth's continents were joined as one supercontinent known as Pangaea. North Carolina lay nestled against present-day Mauritania on the west coast of Africa. The Atlantic Ocean basin was

just beginning to form a rift between the land masses that eventually would account for the depletion of fossil records in later eras. The only fossilized bones that have been recovered in the state from this period are teeth of a small plant-eating dinosaur called *Pekinosaurus*. These fossils, some of the oldest in the world, were found in Triassic red basins around Pekin.

A mudstone quarry that straddles the Virginia–North Carolina border contains what may be the oldest sets of dinosaur tracks on the East Coast. The tracks, which are located near Leaksville Junction along the Dan River Basin, were made during the Late Triassic period by *Grallator*, a three-toed, bipedal carnivore, and by *Atreipus*, a primitive, quadrupedal dinosaur.

Despite scant evidence of their presence, it is likely that North Carolina hosted the full complement of dinosaurs that inhabited other parts of the East Coast, the American Southwest, and western Africa. All of these areas had similar climates and vegetation. After the finds of the Late Triassic, there is a sizable gap in North Carolina's fossil records. During the Late Triassic and most of the Jurassic periods, the Atlantic coastline was extremely high and eroding rapidly toward the west. As the coastline receded, fossil evidence along the East Coast was swept away with the erosion. Paleontologists believe, however, that until approximately 110 million years ago, dinosaurs of the North Carolina area were similar to those in Africa and on the North American continent.

The famous *Allosaurus*, *Stegosaurus*, and *Apatosaurus* likely made their home in the region, as did an intimidating predator, *Acrocanthosaurus atokensis*. Nicknamed the "Terror of the South," this voracious carnivore stood 12.5 feet tall and 36 feet long. Although no fossil evidence of this creature has been found in North Carolina, paleontologists have hypothesized its presence through fragments located in Maryland. The climate and vegetation in North Carolina during the Late Jurassic and Early Cretaceous periods was similar to that in Texas and Oklahoma, where four *Acrocanthosaurus* skeletons have been discovered. In 1997 the North Carolina Museum of Natural Sciences acquired a rare, nearly complete fossilized skeleton of *Acrocanthosaurus*, one of those unearthed in Oklahoma.

Only in the Late Cretaceous period did North Carolina's prehistoric inhabitants begin to leave a few substantial clues about their existence. At that time the eastern portion of the state consisted of low floodplains and swamps. The rivers in these floodplains deposited massive amounts of sediment along the shore of the Atlantic. Here, carcasses occasionally became bogged down in sediments and eventually were fossilized. Some of these ancient floodplains reach the surface in southeastern North Carolina within the Black River Group geological formation. Sites in this formation have yielded the only Cretaceous dinosaur fossils in the state.

Historically, the most productive site in the Black River Group is in Bladen County at Phoebus Landing on the Cape Fear River, although by the early 2000s it had been heavily mined by both professional and amateur fossil hunters. Identification of the fossils retrieved from this region has been difficult: it appears that no one has ever collected two bones from the same animal. Those that have been found are extremely weathered and worn, including specimens from ostrich and duck-billed dinosaurs, the teeth of small carnivorous dinosaurs, and several marine vertebrates.

Ironically, although the South has relinquished few of its prehistoric secrets, it was North Carolina's second state geologist, Washington Carruthers Kerr, who is credited with the nation's third dinosaur fossil discovery in the late 1860s. Kerr found these bones in a marl pit on Six Runs Creek in Sampson County. His find included an assortment of unidentified bones and a tail vertebra from *Hypsibema crassicauda*, a duck-billed dinosaur about which little is known.

Fossils dating from the current Cenozoic era that have been recovered in North Carolina reflect the rise of mammals following the extinction of the dinosaur about 65 million years ago. Fossils unearthed in a phosphate mine in Aurora include bones of ancestral species of the deer, horse, seal, walrus, and wolf, in addition to fossilized mammoth and mastodon bones. Assemblages scattered throughout the coastal plain in Brunswick, Jones, Onslow, and Pitt Counties contain fossilized remains characteristic of marine and estuarine habitats, including crabs, shellfish, sponges, fish, rays, sharks, turtles, and whales.

References: J. G. Carter and others, *Fossil Collecting in North Carolina* (1988); C. D. Huneycutt, *Dinosaurs of North Carolina* (1998); Margaret Martin, *A Long Look at Nature* (2001); David B. Weishampel and Luther Young, *Dinosaurs of the East Coast* (1996).

Elizabeth Scheld Glynn
Douglas A. Wait

Foster's Raid. In December 1862, with the Civil War in its second year, Brig. Gen. John G. Foster, the Union commander at New Bern, organized a large overland raid to Goldsboro to coincide with Maj. Gen. Ambrose E. Burnside's attack on Gen. Robert E. Lee's position at Fredericksburg, Va. The two Union commanders thus intended to prevent either Confederate force from reinforcing the other. The object of Foster's raid was to destroy the Wilmington & Weldon Railroad bridge over the Neuse River at Goldsboro, thus severing the rail line that was shipping valuable supplies from the port at Wilmington to Virginia.

On 11 Dec. 1862 Foster set out with 10,000 infantrymen, 640 cavalrymen, and 40 artillery pieces. At Kinston, he deployed his force to approach the town from an unanticipated direction on 13 December. A Confederate regiment briefly defended a partially destroyed bridge over a tributary of the Neuse River and then retreated to the main Confederate line two miles south of the bridge. Early on the morning of 14 December, Fos-

ter attacked the well-chosen Confederate position, outnumbering the enemy by more than five to one. The left side of the Confederate line collapsed and retreated across the bridge, mistakenly setting fire to it before the rest of their comrades could cross it. Consequently, 400 southerners were trapped and captured. Foster's men crossed the river and entered Kinston, the defenders retreating before them. Meanwhile, Burnside had met with a bloody repulse at Fredericksburg.

On the morning of 15 December, Foster recrossed the river and advanced westward, stopping for the night four miles outside of Whitehall (now Seven Springs) and sending a reconnaissance party with artillery support toward the town. This force encountered Confederate cavalry crossing the bridge over the Neuse River and setting fire to it. The Union artillery was unlimbered and began shelling the Confederates across the river. Damaged in the bombardment was the incomplete hull of the CSS *Neuse*, which was under construction there. Foster's main force arrived on 16 December and entered the fight, the massed Federal artillery sweeping the north side of the river from a commanding position. But the Confederates fought stubbornly before retreating at nightfall. On the same morning Foster had sent a detachment of New York cavalrymen to Mount Olive Station on the Wilmington & Weldon Railroad, where they dismantled a section of track.

After the Battle of Whitehall, Foster continued toward his main objective, nearing the railroad bridge at Goldsboro early on 17 December. He sent parties to Dudley Station and Everittsville to destroy railroad property in both locations. He also ordered five regiments to burn the railroad bridge at Goldsboro. Sheer firepower and weight of numbers forced the defenders on the south side of the river to retreat over a small span near the railroad bridge. As the Confederates hurried across the river, a Union lieutenant dashed for the bridge to put a torch to it. To prevent any attempt to save it, Foster trained all of his artillery on the bridge. When the vital bridge appeared to be engulfed in flames, the Federal soldiers returned to New Bern, believing that they had accomplished their mission.

Although Foster was satisfied with the success of the operation, damage to the bridge was merely superficial. Within two weeks the railroad was fully operational. The most significant damage from the raid was to personal property, crops, and livestock.

Reference: John G. Barrett, *The Civil War in North Carolina* (1963).

Dan Blair

SEE ALSO Kinston, Battle of; Whitehall, Battle of.

Foundations Bible College is a nondenominational, fundamentalist, separatist Christian institution located in Harnett County near Dunn. The college was founded in 1974 by O. Talmadge Spence, a prolific writer of religious material. It has been associated with the World Congress of Fundamentalists since 1976. It features an undergraduate college, graduate school, and seminary.

John Hairr

Four-H Clubs grew out of efforts by numerous people to improve educational and other opportunities for farm families in America. In the early years of the twentieth century, clubs were organized in several states that were designed to teach improved farming techniques to boys. Seaman A. Knapp worked for the Cooperative Farm Demonstration Service of the U.S. Department of Agriculture (USDA), setting up demonstration farms across the South in an effort to convince farmers to diversify from their absolute reliance on cotton. As part of these efforts, Knapp organized Corn Clubs to teach the latest farming techniques to boys on a one-acre plot. Knapp became convinced of the importance of this youth work, and an agreement was reached between the USDA and the land grant colleges of several states to hire Corn Club agents to oversee this activity. I. O. Schaub, a researcher at North Carolina State College (modern-day North Carolina State University), was the first appointed agent for any state and organized North Carolina's first Corn Club in Ahoskie (Hertford County) in 1909. This was later recognized as the first 4-H Club in North Carolina.

The clubs quickly spread across most of North Carolina, and a demand for clubs for girls developed. In 1911 the first Tomato and Canning Club was organized in Pleasant Garden by Schaub, and Jane S. McKimmon was hired as the state home demonstration agent. Clubs for boys and girls would remain largely separate for some time. Racial segregation was practiced as well. The 4-H Club for African Americans was founded by G. W. Herring in 1914 in Sampson County. The year 1914 saw the passage of the Smith-Lever Act by Congress, which established the Cooperative Extension Service on a more permanent basis. The clubs had expanded to include livestock projects and many crops besides corn. The name 4-H (which stood for head, heart, hands, and health) was officially adopted nationwide in 1911 along with the clover symbol, intended to make goods produced and sold by the youth groups recognizable.

From the inception of the 4-H Clubs, a key purpose of their projects was to make a profit for the boys and girls involved; the funds financed many college educations or farm improvements. The clubs were led by extension agents hired under the Smith-Lever Act. But these agents had many other duties, and in some counties the youth groups languished or did not exist. In 1922 L. R. Harrill was hired in Buncombe County as the first county agent dedicated for 4-H work. The experimental nature of this act is indicated by the fact that his $100 per month salary was paid not by the county or state but by the

Vanderbilt family. In 1926 Harrill was hired by Schaub to be the first state 4-H leader. He remained in this office until his retirement in 1963 and became known across North Carolina as "Mr. 4-H." Under his leadership, boys' and girls' activities were merged and common meetings were held at the state level, although some counties kept the sexes separated until after World War II. 4-H Clubs eventually reached all 100 of North Carolina's counties, with Dare County being the last to form a club in 1937. Racial segregation of the clubs did not end until 1964.

Recreation was felt to be important for farm youth, and 4-H provided a good deal of it for its members. The first recorded 4-H camping trip occurred when Harrill took a group of Buncombe County boys and girls to Chimney Rock in 1922. Under Harrill's statewide leadership, Camp Swannanoa in Buncombe County was built on state land in 1929 primarily from funds raised by the 4-H Clubs. Eventually, five other camps were built. The Betsy-Jeff Penn 4-H center near Reidsville was donated to 4-H in 1964 by Betsy Penn and includes year-round facilities quite different from those used in the early years of the camps.

During World War I, measures to increase food production inspired a rapid rise in 4-H membership. But the 1920s saw a sharp decline until Harrill's leadership emerged. During the Depression, 4-H was an important part of the Live-at-Home program, aimed at making farm families self-sufficient and decreasing the overproduction of cotton and tobacco that further depressed prices for these crops. During World War II, North Carolina 4-H members took part in victory garden programs and other war drives. North Carolina 4-H Clubs raised $3 million for purchase of war bonds and collected over 7 million pounds of scrap iron and steel and over 700,000 pounds of scrap rubber.

Alumni of North Carolina's 4-H Clubs include governors, congressmen, university presidents, and many community leaders. During the 1950s, North Carolina boasted the largest number of 4-H members of any state. However, numbers declined in the 1960s, and the program underwent a change in emphasis to reflect the growing urban population. In addition to the traditional agricultural and home economics programs, bicycle safety, water safety, household chemical safety, automobile mechanics, health and nutrition, pollution, neighborhood crime watch, and other programs were added. Through the years 4-H has provided valuable learning experiences for more than 1 million North Carolinians. The projects of the 4-H Youth Livestock Program are an important feature of the North Carolina State Fair each year.

References: J. W. Clark Jr., *Clover All Over: North Carolina 4-H in Action* (1984); L. R. Harrill, *Memories of 4-H* (1967).

Scott Whisnant

Four-Minute Men gained their nickname because of their four-minute speeches concerning the importance of backing the nation's participation in World War I. In 1917, after a German submarine sank the *Lusitania*, the federal government created the National Four Minute Men's Association to inspire support for the war effort. The association was also called the Flying Squadron. Men with public-speaking experience, who had been approved by local civic and business leaders, were invited to address professional, civic, and other groups on the need to engage in supportive activities, especially investment in the Liberty Loan and Thrift Stamp campaigns and the United War Work Campaign. In North Carolina, the Four-Minute Men were formed under the direction of John Sanford Martin, private secretary to Governor Thomas W. Bickett, with the primary objective of encouraging the purchase of war bonds.

William S. Powell

Fourteenth Amendment, ratified on 28 July 1868 as one of the "Reconstruction amendments," added to the U.S. Constitution such fundamental principles as citizenship and equal protection under the law—rights that had been included in the Civil Rights Act of 1866, which the states of the former Confederacy had resisted. Guaranteeing the rights and privileges of full citizenship for all former slaves, the Fourteenth Amendment continues to serve as the basis of all civil rights claims.

The Fourteenth Amendment was not well received in North Carolina, but given the unusual circumstances of the Reconstruction era, there was nothing the state's former power structure could do about it. Passed by a Congress dominated by Radical Republicans, the amendment was in part a response to the U.S. Supreme Court's pre–Civil War *Dred Scott* decision as well as the South's postwar intransigence regarding black citizenship. The institution by North Carolina and other states of restrictive black codes in the aftermath of the war also prompted Radical leaders to pass the amendment.

The South's resistance to the Fourteenth Amendment only prodded the Radicals to take stronger federal action. Indeed, riding high after their victories in the congressional elections of 1866, they quickly passed the Reconstruction Act of 1867. Under this act, North Carolina and South Carolina became part of Military District Number Two, which was eventually headed by Gen. E. R. S. Canby. The law required that a convention be called to write a new state constitution guaranteeing black suffrage. Provisions for the selection of delegates to the convention allowed for greatly expanded black involvement while limiting that enjoyed by whites. Predictably, the document produced by the delegates featured a liberal Bill of Rights and new guarantees of black rights as well as universal male suffrage for whites and blacks.

The first election under the new North Carolina Constitution took place in April 1868. It was a hard-fought and bitter contest won overwhelmingly by the Republicans. When the new government convened in July, the legislature quickly ratified the Fourteenth Amendment and elected two Republican U.S. senators. Canby turned over control of the government to newly elected governor William W. Holden, a onetime Democratic leader whose views had changed with the times. With the ratification of the Fourteenth Amendment and the approval by Congress of the Constitution of 1868, North Carolina returned with little enthusiasm to the Union it had left seven years before.

References: R. D. W. Connor, *North Carolina: Rebuilding an Ancient Commonwealth*, vol. 2 (1973); J. G. de Roulhac Hamilton, *Reconstruction in North Carolina* (1964).

William H. Pruden III

Fox Grape (*Vitis labrusca*) thrives in North Carolina's piedmont and mountain regions. One variety of fox grape, the Catawba, was apparently first found along the banks of Cane Creek south of Swannanoa in Buncombe County. Catawba wine also became a popular antebellum spirit well outside the South, fortifying Harriet Beecher Stowe in her literary campaign against slavery.

Bland Simpson

Fraktur is a form of folk art imported by Pennsylvania German immigrants to North Carolina in the eighteenth century. Fraktur's central feature is elaborate lettering based on the German gothic typeface of the same name, which has a "fractured" appearance. Watercolor drawings and illuminated manuscripts in the fraktur style combine bright colors and primitive, symbolic figures in a partially abstract border. Most popular during the second half of the eighteenth century and the first quarter of the nineteenth, fraktur is still produced today.

The primary function of fraktur was not decorative but documentary. The most common form of fraktur was the *taufschein*, which recorded the details of a child's birth and baptism. Fraktur first developed as a North American art form around 1740 at the German Seventh Day Baptist Cloister at Ephrata, Pa. It became popular among German immigrants, who brought it to North Carolina. The only known North Carolina fraktur artist was the "Ehre Vater" artist. Probably an itinerant schoolmaster, his work has been associated with the Moravian settlement at Wachovia. Over 35 surviving pieces have been attributed to this prolific artist.

Families often preserved fraktur by pasting it inside the lids of dower chests or keeping it between the leaves of a Bible. Sur-

Fraktur by the artist Ehre Vater commemorating the birth and baptism of George Hege, born at Friedberg on 21 Oct. 1799. The birds are representations of Carolina parakeets. Collection of the Museum of Early Southern Decorative Arts.

viving fraktur is popular among modern collectors of folk art and antiques.

References: John Bivins and Forsyth Alexander, *The Regional Arts of the Early South: A Sampling from the Collection of the Museum of Early Southern Decorative Arts* (1991); Corrine Earnest and Russell Earnest, *Fraktur: Folk Art and Family* (1999); Donald A. Shelley, *The Fraktur-Writings or Illuminated Manuscripts of the Pennsylvania Germans* (1961).

Ruth E. Homrighaus

Frank Johnson's Band was a popular brass ensemble of African American musicians that played frequently at health spas, balls, tournaments, state fairs, and other occasions from the 1830s to about 1870. Organizer and leader Frank Johnson was said to have been born a slave on a Roanoke River plantation in Northampton County in 1774. He appears to have earned enough as a fiddler to purchase his freedom, along with that of his wife and children. Johnson's band included some 15 members, all or most of whom were his sons and nephews. "Old Frank," who conducted in stovepipe hat and spike-tailed coat, could play any instrument and was a fine dancer, sometimes performing at balls in that specialty. He also called the numbers for square dances and reels.

Johnson's group was a favorite among well-to-do planters and was said to perform only for Democrats. The last known appearance of the band seems to have been at a tournament in Halifax in 1866. The band had dispersed by 1871, by which time Old Frank, at the age of 97, was reportedly residing in Tarboro.

Reference: Thomas C. Parramore, "Old Frank Johnson—and the Day the Music Died," *The State* 61 (April 1989).

Thomas C. Parramore

Franklin, State of. In April 1784 the North Carolina legislature ceded the state's western lands to the Continental Con-

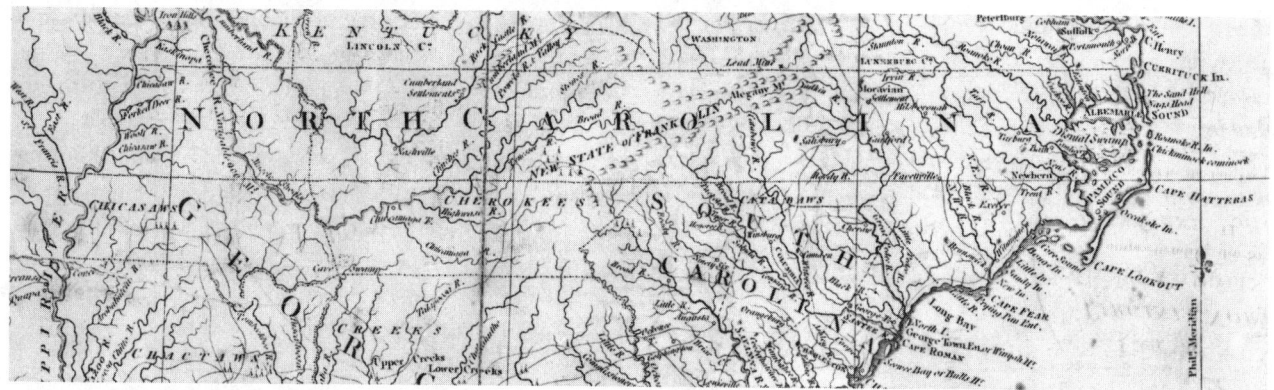

The Joseph Purcell map of 1792 showing the boundaries of North Carolina extending to the Mississippi River. Near the center of the state along the western slopes of the Appalachians the map also locates the "New State of Franklin." NCC.

gress. On 24 August, soon after news of the Cession Act had reached the west, a convention attended by delegates from Washington, Sullivan, and Greene Counties in the northeast corner of modern Tennessee met at Jonesborough, chose John Sevier as president, and moved toward forming a new state. A second convention in December adopted a provisional constitution for the "State of Franklin" and prefaced it with a declaration of independence from North Carolina. Because of slow communications, the December convention was unaware that in November the North Carolina legislature had rescinded the April Cession Act.

Separatists in the western counties decided to proceed with their independence movement, and Franklin's first general assembly met in March 1785. It elected Sevier governor and sent a memorial to the Continental Congress requesting admission to the Union. A motion in Congress to approve the cession that would have paved the way for Franklin's statehood fell short of the required nine votes. The struggle over Franklin coincided with the movement to draft a new federal Constitution, and a provision in Article IV of the Constitution prohibited the formation of a state within the jurisdiction of another state without the latter's consent.

The December 1784 constitution of Franklin did not formally define its boundaries. By implication, jurisdiction was assumed over all of the ceded territory, an area approximating the future state of Tennessee. Franklin leaders also hoped to include portions of western Virginia and northern Georgia in the new state.

Residents of North Carolina's western counties were not unanimous in their support of an independent State of Franklin. Settlers in the Cumberland River Valley in Middle Tennessee, which had been set aside as bounty lands for North Carolina's Revolutionary War soldiers, remained aloof from the Franklin movement.

The attitude of North Carolina politicians toward the separatist movement was influenced by their speculation in western lands. Many citizens had obtained vast tracts under the

1783 "Land Grab Act." This law offered for sale all unappropriated land in the Tennessee country, which was soon to be ceded to the United States. Many North Carolina leaders who opposed the cession had not received grants under the 1783 act. Their opportunity to secure title to eastern Tennessee lands was contingent upon the legislature's continued control of the Tennessee land system.

The short history of the Franklin government is an account of Indian war and attempts to gain title to Indian lands, for much of the land claimed by Franklin was occupied by Creeks and Cherokees. John Sevier and other commissioners appointed by the Franklin assembly negotiated the Treaty of Dumplin Creek with several Cherokee chiefs in June 1785. The chiefs ceded to Franklin a tract of land south of the French Broad River within the "Cherokee Reservation," which the North Carolina legislature had set aside in 1783. This area included the site of Greenville, which was to be the capital of Franklin.

Efforts to infringe on Indian lands were frustrated by the federal government's determination to maintain peace with the western Indians. The Treaty of Hopewell, signed in November 1785 by commissioners of the Confederation Congress and the Cherokees, nullified both the Treaty of Dumplin Creek and the earlier private purchase of the Muscle Shoals region.

After Richard Caswell became governor of North Carolina in 1784, he followed a conciliatory policy toward the Franklin movement. Evan Shelby, who was appointed brigadier general of the Washington district, was a friend of Sevier, and in the spring of 1787 the two men reached an agreement that granted settlers the choice of paying their taxes to North Carolina or to the State of Franklin. In August 1787 the Franklin assembly elected Shelby to succeed Sevier as governor. Shelby refused the offer but soon resigned as brigadier general and recommended that Sevier be his successor. Sevier's term as governor expired on 1 Mar. 1788, and the legislature did not meet again. The Franklin movement was dead except among settlers in the contested lands south of the French Broad River who had received land titles from the Franklin legislature based on the Treaty of Dumplin Creek. Not until January 1789 did these settlers draft "Articles of Association" and petition North Carolina for protection. In February 1789 John Sevier took an oath of allegiance to North Carolina, and in August he was elected to the North Carolina Assembly.

The "lost" State of Franklin is as entangled in historiographical controversy in the twenty-first century as it was in land speculation, Indian affairs, and political intrigue during its four-year history. It remains a subject of debate whether it originated as a western democratic movement, as a land speculators' conspiracy, or as a separatist movement led by westerners who resented subordination of their interests to those of eastern North Carolina.

References: Walter Faw Cannon, "Four Interpretations of the History of the State of Franklin," *East Tennessee Historical Society Publications* 22 (1950); Noel B. Gerson, *Franklin: America's "Lost State"* (1968); Ned Irwin, "The Lost State of Franklin: Sources for Research and Study," *Bulletin of Bibliography* 55 (March 1998); Samuel Cole Williams, *History of the Lost State of Franklin* (rev. ed., 1933).

George W. Troxler

Franklin County,

Franklin County, located in the Piedmont region of northeastern North Carolina, was formed from the southern half of no-longer-extant Bute County in the midst of the American Revolution, in 1779, and named for Benjamin Franklin. Tuscarora Indians were the earliest inhabitants of the Franklin County area, followed by English, Irish, and German settlers. The county seat, Louisburg, originally spelled "Lewisburg," is located in the center of the county. It is home to the oldest junior college in the United States, Louisburg College, first founded as Franklin Academy in 1805. The Person Place, adjacent to the campus, is a restored eighteenth-century home open to the public. Other communities in the county include Bunn, Centerville, Franklinton, and Youngsville.

Franklin has historically been a rural county, and its economy is today based on agriculture, lumber, and textiles. Its growth in recent years is largely attributed to the large number of people who work in the Triangle area but choose to live in more rural settings. The population of Franklin County in 2004 was estimated to be 53,000.

Reference: T. H. Pearce, *Franklin County, 1779–1979* (1979).

Allyson C. Criner

SEE ALSO Louisburg College.

Frank Porter Graham Child Development Center

is a multidisciplinary organization in the Division of Health Affairs at the University of North Carolina at Chapel Hill. It was established in 1966 to study children and families, espe-

cially those children at risk for hindered development due to biological or environmental factors. The center's mission is to "produce scientific work related to children and families, offer services to young children and families in a model child care program and other community settings, provide effective technical assistance, consultation, and materials that use proven knowledge and practices, and educate new professionals through teaching and mentoring." Almost every project at the center focuses on early child development, mainly between birth and age six. Historically, projects have clustered in five areas: child development and intervention studies, family studies, health studies, technical assistance, and professional development. What distinguishes Frank Porter Graham from comparable units at other universities is its broad focus. In addition to concentrating on children reared in poverty, it studies normal development processes and child care services. Its progressive program includes studies that integrate health and behavioral status.

Since its establishment, the center has grown from three trailers on Cameron Avenue to more than 40,000 square feet in three separate Chapel Hill locations. By the early 2000s the center's annual budget was more than $17 million, with most of the funds coming from federal grants issued by the U.S. Department of Education and other national organizations. The center employs about 250 staff members, about 100 of whom are full-time. Of the full-time staff, Environmental Protection Agency nonfaculty serve as primary investigators.

Reference: Frank Porter Graham Child Development Center, *The Frank Porter Graham Child Development Center* (1995).

John Huang

Fraternities and Sororities,

Fraternities and Sororities, officially called National Collegiate Social Greek Letter Societies, have been present in North Carolina since at least 1812 and form a significant presence on the campuses of the state's modern colleges and universities. Greek letter societies incorporate both fraternities and sororities (sororities were originally called "women's fraternities"). Drawing heavily upon Masonic and Phi Beta Kappa Literary Society influences, Kappa Alpha (a different group from the current-day Kappa Alpha Order or Kappa Alpha Society) was founded at the University of North Carolina in Chapel Hill in 1812. Four undergraduate students claiming membership in Phi Beta Kappa used a constitution, a ritual, a badge, and secrets nearly identical to those of Phi Beta Kappa to create Kappa Alpha. This is the first documentation of the founding of a Greek letter social fraternity in the United States.

Kappa Alpha, or Kuklos Adelphon as it was also known, grew popular and spread to more than 21 other college campuses throughout the South. Chapters also existed in county seats and consisted of the "professional and gentry classes," who met for "social and literary purposes." Before its final demise in 1866, Kappa Alpha enlisted many prominent men, including President James K. Polk. Chi Psi, Delta Kappa Epsilon, and Kappa Sigma fraternities absorbed most of the Kappa Alpha chapters after the mother chapter of Kappa Alpha disbanded.

During the 1840s, there was a national backlash against secret societies in general and fraternities specifically. This movement gained mass support and even resulted in the formation of a political party. In North Carolina during this time period, the trustees of the University of North Carolina passed a resolution banning exclusive and secret societies on the grounds that these groups were detrimental to good morals and sound learning. Students were made to take a pledge against joining these societies and were not admitted to the university unless they did so. While some organizations ceased operation because of this edict, others went underground, perhaps becoming even more attractive to rebellious students of the time.

Although the suppression of secret societies worked for a while, by the early 1850s these clubs and fraternities were again operating above ground. Delta Kappa Epsilon, the oldest existing fraternity in North Carolina, was chartered at UNC in 1850. Like most other fraternities, it disbanded briefly during the Civil War. Chi Phi was one of the few fraternities in North Carolina that did not disband. Founded at UNC in 1858, this fraternity expanded chapters to a number of southern states and even formed a chapter in Europe.

By 1885 fraternities and secret societies were so prevalent that the UNC trustees reluctantly granted conditional recognition to the groups, which included the stipulation that the groups had to provide the faculty with membership lists and agree not to have socials with alcohol in Chapel Hill. Despite this recognition, there was still animosity toward the fraternities from some students and faculty members. Fraternities were viewed by some as aloof, "destructive of college spirit," and "hurtful to athletics." Despite these charges, student interest continued, so that by the outbreak of World War I, a diverse fraternity system flourished in North Carolina. In 1923 Chi Tau National Men's Fraternity was formed from the union of Chi Tau local fraternity at Trinity College (present-day Duke University) and Lambda Sigma Delta local fraternity of North Carolina State College (North Carolina State University). Approximately ten chapters spanning four states were chartered before dissension led to the demise of this national fraternity in 1929.

The first women's National Collegiate Social Greek Letter Society in North Carolina was chartered at Elizabeth City Normal and Industrial School (later Elizabeth City State University) in 1902. This chapter of the Kappa Delta sorority survived for only two years, but the movement toward fraternities for women caught on across the state. The first sororities at the University of North Carolina were Chi Omega and Pi Beta Phi, which established chapters in the early 1920s. In 1911 Alpha Delta Pi, the state's oldest existing women's fraternity, was chartered at Trinity College. Others followed, including Tri Delta in 1943.

All sororities have educational as well as social functions, and all are involved with charitable activities. The National Panhellenic Conference, established in 1902, oversees much of the activities of sororities and formulates policies of interfraternity interest and concern; studies changing educational outlooks; and, through discussions, panels, and special programs, contributes to interfraternity understanding and friendship. Each large college campus in North Carolina has a Panhellenic Council, which serves as a unifying force for the sororities.

Defying doomsayers, the majority of fraternities and sororities survived Prohibition, the Great Depression, and both World Wars to see their ranks swell, as veterans and women sought higher education and Greek membership in greater numbers in North Carolina. Though the turmoil of the Vietnam era closed some chapters in North Carolina, by the early twenty-first century the Greek system in the state was continuing to grow in size. Most of the state's major colleges and universities have numerous fraternities and sororities, many with a very specific purpose. For example, Epsilon Chi Nu, the first Native American fraternity in the country, was established at East Carolina University in 1996.

References: Jack L. Anson and Robert F. Marchesani Jr., eds., *Baird's Manual of American College Fraternities* (1991); Albert Coates and Gladys Hall Coates, *The Story of Student Government in the University of North Carolina at Chapel Hill* (1985).

Brian Bullard
Martha Belle Caldwell

Free Bridge, Battle of. The Battle of Free Bridge, a Civil War engagement sometimes called the Battle of Comfort or the Battle of Quaker Bridge, occurred on 6 July 1863. Two days earlier, Gen. C. A. Heckman, commander of the 9th New Jersey, had led his regiment along with other Union companies out of New Bern, then in Union hands, and headed toward Pollocksville. The column arrived there at midday and was joined by additional Union troops. Heckman and his force then began the march to Trenton. At the fork of Comfort and Quaker Bridge Roads, he halted the column and dispatched reconnaissance parties to examine the bridges and fords that crossed the Trent River. His men found that Quaker Bridge had been destroyed, but Wilcox Bridge, on the road from Trenton to Kinston, remained unscathed. On Heckman's orders, the 9th New Jersey demolished it.

After spending the night near Chinquapin Chapel, Heckman sent Lt. Col. John G. Chambers with the 23rd Massachusetts and one section of Belger's Battery to the intersection of Comfort and Free Bridge Roads to hold that location. At the fork, Chambers placed one piece of artillery on Comfort Road and one on Free Bridge Road and then, with several other officers, began to reconnoiter the area. They spotted approximately 50 cavalrymen from the 8th Battalion, North Carolina Partisan Rangers. The Union officers managed to escape to friendly lines, but once there, they and the rest of their men came under a barrage of artillery fire.

About that time, Heckman arrived at the battle scene. He ordered Belger's Battery to move forward and return fire; for a time, the two batteries blazed away at each other. When the defenders' guns fell silent, Heckman did not advance, hoping part of his cavalry, deployed nearby, might encounter the enemy's rear and trap the Confederates between two Union forces. But the cavalry returned by a different route, and Heckman withdrew. He and his troops spent the night at the same burned mill where they had previously bivouacked and were back in New Bern by 6:00 P.M. on 7 July. Two Union soldiers were wounded at Free Bridge; the extent of Confederate casualties was unreported.

References: John G. Barrett, *North Carolina as a Civil War Battleground, 1861–1865* (1960); J. Madison Drake, *The History of the Ninth New Jersey Veteran Volunteers* (1889).

Thomas J. Farnham

Freedman's Savings and Trust Company,

universally known as the Freedman's Bank, was chartered on 3 Mar. 1865. It grew out of two military savings banks established in Norfolk, Va., and Beaufort, S.C., for black Union troops who needed a place to deposit their wages and bounty money. The company was founded by influential Christian philanthropists, humanitarians, and businessmen who convinced the U.S. Congress that former slaves would learn the values of thrift and savings if they had their own bank.

Three branches of the Freedman's Savings and Trust Company were located in North Carolina. A branch at New Bern opened in January 1866, and Raleigh and Wilmington branches were chartered two years later. Charlotte and Salisbury applied for branches in 1868 but never received them. Of the approximately 8,600 depositors for which records survive, the majority were freedmen. Other depositors included a small number of whites, as well as churches, businesses, and social and charitable clubs.

Although the bank was often associated with the Freedmen's Bureau and the American Missionary Association, it was a separate institution. Eventually it opened 37 branches in 17 states and the District of Columbia. Due to high operating costs and low deposits, the bank struggled from 1865 to 1869. In the hope of reversing this decline, it made an effort to encourage more small depositors and to employ more black cashiers and clerks. In addition, the charter was amended to permit the bank to invest in real estate loans. The latter unfortunately spawned corruption in the bank's central offices. The economic panic of 1873 also took its toll on the viability of the bank, which failed in July 1874. Ultimately, 61,100 depositors received 62 percent of the money they had invested.

References: Carl R. Osthaus, *Freedmen, Philanthropy, and Fraud: A History of the Freedman's Savings Bank* (1976); Bill Reaves, *North Carolina Freedman's Savings and Trust Company Records* (1992).

Beverly Tetterton

Freedmen's Bureau,

officially the Bureau of Refugees, Freedmen, and Abandoned Lands, was created by Congress in 1865 after months of debate. The Freedmen's Bureau controlled abandoned and confiscated lands in the South, with authority to divide them into 40-acre plots and rent them to freed blacks and white refugees loyal to the Union. It was also authorized to provide rations and clothing to homeless, sick, and destitute freedmen and refugees. The bureau coordinated educational efforts for freed people, monitored justice in the state courts, and supervised labor relations, overseeing contracts, adjudicating disputes, and providing transportation to jobs. For its time, the grant of such power was revolutionary. Still, the Freedmen's Bureau was a temporary device to help the transition from war to peace and from slavery to freedom; it was authorized to last for one year after the Civil War ended.

Organized geographically, the Freedmen's Bureau was headed by its federal director, Gen. Oliver Otis Howard. Below him, each state had an assistant commissioner. The state was then subdivided into districts administered by a superintendent; assistant superintendents coordinated the activities of subdistricts. Despite this elaborate organization, the bureau was always underfinanced and understaffed; no more than 900 agents served at any one time. Thus, large areas of the South had no bureau supervision.

Throughout the South, the Freedmen's Bureau was widely hated by whites, who believed that it interfered with their efforts to facilitate a return to "normal" relations between the races. White southerners regarded bureau agents as meddlesome, misguided idealists who did not understand the "true nature" of blacks and therefore encouraged them in false hopes and prevented them from settling down to hard labor. Historians, on the other hand, have often criticized the bureau for not promoting true independence and land ownership for the newly emancipated blacks.

When Congress tried to extend the term of the Freedmen's Bureau in 1866, President Andrew Johnson vetoed the bill, creating a political controversy that, along with other factors, eventually led to a split between the president and congressional Republicans. Congress eventually enacted the Freedmen's Bureau Bill, which prolonged the agency's life and increased its powers.

An 1868 engraving of "James's Plantation School" in North Carolina. This freedmen's school is possibly one of those established by Horace James on the Yankee or Avon Hall plantations in Pitt County in 1866. NCC.

In North Carolina, the Freedmen's Bureau, although as understaffed as elsewhere in the South, had a profound impact on both blacks and whites. The state had one assistant commissioner, four superintendents, and several assistant superintendents in charge of between two and four counties. Frequent turnover plagued the state bureau. Between 1865 and 1867 there were five assistant commissioners and two acting assistant commissioners; the same pattern held true for superintendents and assistant superintendents. Despite this problem, the bureau performed a number of important tasks. Initially, it organized camps for destitute freedmen, providing rations, medical care, and work for thousands. It then attempted to establish what it considered to be fair labor relations between the races. While the bureau returned all the abandoned and confiscated land to former owners—following Johnson's orders and his pardon of white southerners—the organization worked to ensure that the contracts signed by freed people did not reenslave them. On the other hand, bureau policies strongly encouraged blacks to work—which meant, for the most part, to do farm labor for white landowners.

The Freedmen's Bureau also arbitrated disputes between white employers and black employees, trying to prevent physical abuse, to ensure payment of wages due, and to stop the most blatant abuses of the apprenticeship system. Bureau officers regularly sat in on sessions of the state courts to prevent discriminatory justice. Finally, the bureau helped promote black education. Most schools for blacks opened immediately after the war were founded by four northern missionary societies: the American Freedmen Union Commission, the National Freedmen's Relief Association, the American Missionary Association, and the Friends' Freedmen's Aid Association. Although the bureau had little money to assist these groups directly, it often provided school buildings or helped find sites for schools. Sometimes, it furnished living accommodations for teachers in the school buildings. F. A. Fiske, a northern

white who served under the Freedmen's Bureau as superintendent of education in North Carolina, dispersed the funds received from the various northern benevolent organizations, coordinated the assignment of teachers, and supervised the curriculum and school schedules.

White North Carolinians generally opposed most bureau activities. They resented agents' "interference" in labor relations. They complained that freedmen were constantly running to the bureau with minor or even fabricated grievances and that agents tended to believe the word of blacks over that of whites. They charged that the bureau impeded the enforcement of state laws, such as those dealing with apprenticeship. Most whites were offended by the establishment of schools for blacks; they felt that the work of the bureau and missionary societies gave blacks ideas about political rights and equality that had no place in the social order. Whites displayed their opposition by drafting petitions and resolutions against the Freedmen's Bureau, by attacking blacks and bureau agents, and by burning schools and generally opposing education for blacks. Many bureau agents faced continual hostility and were ostracized from white society. Blacks, on the other hand, generally trusted the bureau and welcomed its assistance.

References: Roberta Sue Alexander, *North Carolina Faces the Freedmen: Race Relations during Presidential Reconstruction, 1865–1867* (1985); George R. Bentley, *A History of the Freedmen's Bureau* (1955); Patricia C. Click, *Time Full of Trial: The Roanoke Island Freedmen's Colony, 1862–1867* (2001); William McFeely, *Yankee Stepfather: General O. O. Howard and the Freedmen* (1968); Donald G. Nieman, *To Set the Law in Motion: The Freedmen's Bureau and the Legal Rights of Blacks, 1865–1868* (1979).

Roberta Sue Alexander

Freedmen's Conventions in 1865 and 1866 voiced the aspirations of North Carolina blacks, both those previously classified as free and former slaves. The Civil War had been over only five months when more than 100 men, almost all from Piedmont and eastern counties, gathered at the African Methodist Episcopal Church in Raleigh and opened the "Convention of the Freedmen of North Carolina," the first such statewide assembly of black people. Many delegates were newcomers to North Carolina; most of the others were counted among the state's antebellum free blacks, who referred to themselves as "colored men."

The timing of the convention was significant. Under a Reconstruction plan announced by President Andrew Johnson —himself a native of Raleigh—white voters had chosen delegates to a constitutional convention that would be held in the State Capitol on 2 Oct. 1865 to repeal the ordinance of secession, abolish slavery, and prepare for the state's return to the Union. Barred from participation in the election of delegates, the freedmen upstaged the official convention by meeting three days earlier, on 29 September. Emphasizing their seriousness, the black delegates agreed to open each session with devotionals and expel any participant found intoxicated during the sessions.

The largest delegation to the convention was from Craven County (including six members from the black-controlled community of James City). James Walker Hood, a missionary from Connecticut, was elected president of the convention. In his acceptance speech, Hood said: "We and the white people have to live here together. Some people talk of emigration for the black race, some of expatriation, and some of colonization. I regard this as all nonsense. We have been living together for a hundred years and more, and we have got to live together still; and the best way is to harmonize our feelings as much as possible, and to treat all men respectfully." He called for three constitutional rights for blacks: admission of testimony in court, representation in the jury box, and "the right to carry [a] ballot to the ballot box."

Delegates Abraham H. Galloway of Craven County, Isham Sweat of Cumberland County, and James H. Harris of Wake County "made speeches advocating equal rights, and a moderate conservative course in demanding them." Among the messages received from outside the hall, famed New York editor Horace Greeley, who had been married in Warrenton, urged the delegates to be hopeful, patient, peaceful, and diligent, to respect themselves, and to stay in North Carolina, "a noble state, with her resources mainly undeveloped."

All of the speeches were reportedly moderate and respectful; in a formal communication to be delivered to the (white) constitutional convention and the General Assembly, suffrage and judicial reform were not specifically mentioned. Before adjourning on 3 October, the convention resolved itself into the North Carolina State Equal Rights League and adopted a constitution intended to secure "by political and moral means, as far as may be, the repeal of all laws and parts of laws, State and National, that make distinctions on account of color."

At the urging of James H. Harris, president of the State Equal Rights League, a second freedmen's convention was held in the same church sanctuary on 2 Oct. 1866. Again delegates numbered more than 100, but this time several western counties were also represented. Over some objections, Governor Jonathan Worth and former governor William W. Holden were invited to address the participants. Worth, who spoke on morality, education, and religion, was greeted by delegate J. R. Good as a personal friend and one who had voted for Good's emancipation in a previous session of the legislature. The convention then sang a hymn, after which the governor retired "amidst loud and hearty cheers." Two days later Holden lectured on the importance of goodwill between the races. The freedmen needed first to "get homes" and second "to educate their children."

That all was not harmonious in the state was recorded in conflicting reports to the 1866 convention. E. M. Bell of Lenoir County complained that his people had been "outraged" and the Freedmen's Bureau had done little on their behalf. In Bertie County, Charles Harrel charged, "colored men were cheated out of their labor, children were taken and bound without the consent or consultation of their parents," grievances echoed by Charles Carter of Sampson County. Louis Heagie of Forsyth declared that most blacks in his county were in "an abject state of poverty." Conversely, a Guilford County delegate "informed the Convention that the greatest feeling of love and unity existed between both races in his county," and Edmund Bird of Alamance County maintained that "prejudice existing against the negro is only entertained by the lower and ignorant class of whites, whilst the intelligent and better classes are disposed to help the negro."

H. J. Brown, a delegate from Hertford County, appeared before a racially mixed audience to give an evening lecture—described as "one that would have done credit to the most learned person"—on "Phrenology and Ethnology." Arguing that "no two races on the face of the globe were so much alike" as the Caucasian and the Negro, Brown maintained that "the same imitative, moral and intellectual faculties" were found in the brains of both races. Black inferiority, if true, "is owing to the state of slavery under which they have been kept, not allowing the faculties of the mind to be developed; therefore it is the white man's shame." Brown was not as charitable to American Indians, who "will not accept nor can be made to appreciate arts, science, literature and religion . . . showing the negro race superior to the American Indian, and in every respect equal to Caucasian or Anglo Saxon." Brown later donated the $22 he collected for his lecture to help pay for the convention.

The historic freedmen's conventions of 1865 and 1866 were the first meetings where black North Carolinians from across the state openly and collectively expressed their goals. The names of delegates such as James H. Harris, John Hyman, and James E. O'Hara would become familiar in the remaining decades of the century. The convention journals reveal the care with which the freedmen sought to air their complaints without antagonizing whites, whose influence was essential for a realization of their hopes. The conventions were overtly partisan (national Republican policies were repeatedly applauded), but they occurred before developments in 1868 drove a violent political wedge between black and white North Carolinians. The published proceedings thus reflect a period of relative goodwill between the races.

Reference: Roberta Sue Alexander, *North Carolina Faces the Freedmen: Race Relations during Presidential Reconstruction, 1865–1867* (1985).

H. G. Jones

SEE ALSO Equal Rights League.

Freeholders were free persons who owned land. The Fundamental Constitutions of Carolina in 1669 required that, among other things, candidates must be freeholders to qualify for office holding and membership in the colonial Assembly. In some cases the requisite minimum amount of land held was 500 acres. In 1681 instructions to the governor from London directed that five freeholders be elected as representatives in the Assembly.

In 1760, in response to some confusion as to the precise definition of the term, the legislature specified that "freeholder" meant a person in actual possession of real estate for his own lifetime. A person in possession of "an estate of Greater Dignity, fifty acres of Land or a Lot in some Town" in the parish for which an election was held would qualify. A would-be voter also had to be 21 years of age.

William S. Powell

Freemasons. The Ancient Free and Accepted Masons, known as Freemasons or Masons, is a secret fraternal society that has members in all parts of the world. The organization stresses the members' duty to their families, their country, and their fellow men and women, as well as the importance of religious belief. Each Freemason also pledges his allegiance to fellow members. The history of Freemasonry in the British colonies of North America can be traced back to a very early period, and prior to 1735 the group was actively at work in North Carolina. By 1735 enough Masons had assembled in the Cape Fear settlement to form a lodge. Saint John's Lodge of Wilmington, chartered in 1755, is the oldest Masonic lodge in continuous use in North Carolina. Several lodges existed prior to the Revolutionary War throughout North Carolina. Royal White Hart Lodge No. 2. in the town of Halifax was chartered on 21 Aug. 1767 and is also still in existence.

The Grand Masonic Lodge of North Carolina was organized in 1787. For many years the qualifications of the lodge's leader, or Grand Master, were that he should have played a prominent role in the Revolutionary War. The first master of this lodge was Samuel Johnston, a governor of North Carolina. The Grand Masonic Lodge was responsible for building a new Masonic Temple in Raleigh about 1909.

North Carolina Masons continue to meet at lodges in Salisbury, Asheboro, Charlotte, Asheville, Newton, Dunn, Garner, and dozens of other cities in the state. Their work remains charitable in nature, supporting several service projects and facilities, giving scholarships, and helping in times of emergency with disaster relief. The Masonic Home for Children in Oxford and the Masonic and Eastern Star Home in Greensboro are two important Masonic facilities in the state.

Lisa Brantley Kobrin
Monica Moody

Free Produce was the term applied to anything grown, manufactured, or otherwise produced by nonslave labor. The term came into use when abolitionists, particularly Quakers, agreed to avoid buying or using anything even remotely associated with slavery. Preliminary steps in this direction originated in Wilmington, Del., in 1827 and had spread to North Carolina by 1829. One of the free produce movement's aims was to totally eliminate the demand for slave-produced items so as to lead slave owners to abandon the use of slave labor. Several North Carolinians, notably Charles Osborn, Nathan Hunt, and Levi Coffin, supported the boycott. North Carolina proved to be a good source for free labor products. Hunt, in fact, once offered 40 bales of "free labor" cotton for sale in Guilford County. A cotton mill in the state wove cloth by free laborers using cotton grown by whites. Various aspects of the boycott came to be widely discussed and led to dissension among Quakers—and the dismissal of at least one Quaker minister—as well as others. Some pointed out how near parties on the same general side of the boycott came to "war," not necessarily over slavery but over "the form that opposition [to slavery] should take."

In seeking goods free of association with slavery, buyers visited North Carolina to purchase from nonslaveholders. The scarcity of and increased demand for such goods and the expense of importing retail stock from abroad caused prices to rise to such a degree that even Quakers recognized how ineffective the boycott of slave labor was. Free labor advocates were never numerous enough to affect the problem they sought to address. Support dwindled to limited interest among a few Quakers and by the mid-1850s had virtually disappeared throughout the country.

References: Thomas E. Drake, *Quakers and Slavery in America* (1950); Ruth Anna Ketring, *Charles Osborn in the Anti-Slavery Movement* (1937); Ruth K. Nuermberger, "The Free Produce Movement: A Quaker Protest against Slavery," Historical Papers of the Trinity College Historical Society, series 25 (1942).

William S. Powell

Free Soilers were members of an antislavery political party in the years before the Civil War that supported free distribution of government-owned lands. Most North Carolinians probably could have accepted the Free Soilers except for their antislavery stance. Fewer than one-third of the state's whites—mostly planters—owned slaves, but most people opposed abolition and the social revolution it would cause.

During the presidential campaign of 1848, 50 Free Soil delegates met in western Orange (now Alamance) County to support their ticket of former president Martin Van Buren and Charles Francis Adams, son of John Quincy Adams. Retired state Democratic leader William H. Haywood briefly stirred up interest when he endorsed Van Buren, but Haywood and the Free Soil delegates could not entice voters to back their candidate. In the November election, of the more than 80,000 votes cast in North Carolina, Van Buren received only about 60, most of which came from Guilford County. The majority of the state's popular vote and all of its electoral votes went to Whig Zachary Taylor.

The Free Soilers achieved better results nationally, capturing 10.1 percent of the popular vote, although they failed to carry any states. The heavy support the party received in New York took votes away from Democrat Lewis Cass and helped Taylor win that state's crucial electoral votes and the presidency.

The Compromise of 1850 briefly satisfied abolitionists, and the Free Soilers lost much of their enthusiasm. In 1852 John Hale was the party's last presidential candidate, receiving 4.9 percent of the national popular vote and a total of 59 votes in North Carolina. Many Free Soilers later joined the newly formed Republican Party.

References: Archibald Henderson, *North Carolina: The Old North State and the New*, vol. 2 (1941); Seth Beeson Hinshaw, *North Carolina Election Returns, 1790–1866* (1992).

Barry McGee

Free Suffrage was a political concept heatedly discussed among North Carolinians in the mid-nineteenth century. The ownership of 50 acres of property or the payment of taxes had been a prerequisite for voting in certain instances since the colonial period. In the gubernatorial campaign of 1848, however, candidate David S. Reid accepted the proposal of leaders of his Democratic Party that this limitation on the franchise be removed, making free suffrage a key issue in his campaign against Whig candidate Charles Manly. Although Manly won a narrow victory, free suffrage had become important to many North Carolinians. In the 1850 governor's race, Reid won handily over Manly and the Democrats captured control of the state legislature. A free suffrage constitutional amendment continued to be debated in the General Assembly for several sessions until it finally became a reality in 1857, when it won in a popular referendum by a wide majority of 50,007 to 19,397. Estimates from the era indicate that 125,000 North Carolinians gained the right to vote with the state's adoption of free suffrage.

References: Lindley S. Butler, ed., *The Papers of David Settle Reid* (1993); Paul D. Escott, *Many Excellent People: Power and Privilege in North Carolina, 1850–1900* (1985).

William S. Powell

Free Will Baptist is a Christian publication founded in 1873 by the General Conference of Original Free Will Baptists in North Carolina. Up to that time the church had functioned without the benefit of a news medium other than the printed minutes of the annual conferences. Following the distribution of a prospectus, Robert Ellis began to publish weekly issues of the *Free Will Baptist Advocate* at Fremont. After a year, he began publishing the paper at Toisnot (now Elm City) and changed its name to *Toisnot Transcript*, a change that brought dissatisfaction to many, with the result that the publication had to be suspended about 1877. The general conference reactivated it with a new editor and manager who published it under its original name. Because of a lack of support it was again suspended in 1879.

When the conference was convened in 1880, church elder Rufus K. Hearn was asked to submit a plan for successfully publishing a Free Will Baptist newspaper. He urged the conference to obtain full ownership of the printing press, hire an editor, and publish the paper at the expense of the conference with the support of individual subscriptions and contributions from churches. The conference adopted Hearn's plan and hired him as editor, and he began publishing the paper at Fremont, dropping the word "Advocate" from its name. The next year he moved to New Bern and published the paper there. Although the conference was asked to contribute toward expenses, there was never enough money to balance the account. In 1886 a committee recommended that the printing press be loaned to Hearn with the provision that he publish the paper "as a Free Will Baptist organ at his own expense." Hearn continued to publish it on these terms until February 1889. In that year a stock company was formed, and the conference conveyed its interest in the printing press to the Free Will Baptist Publishing Company.

The company assumed the responsibility of publishing the paper, moving its base to the town of Ayden in 1894. From that date until modern times, the *Free Will Baptist* has been published in Ayden. In addition to serving the Free Will Baptists of North Carolina, it has been the church paper for this denomination throughout much of the South from the beginning of the twentieth century. It was instrumental in the formation of the General Conference of Free Will Baptists in the United States in 1921 and later in the merger of this organization with another group to form the National Association of Free Will Baptists in 1935. When the North Carolina Convention withdrew from that organization in 1962, the paper's subscription base was reduced. Because of increased printing costs, in January 1982 the *Free Will Baptist* became a monthly magazine, focusing primarily on the programs and interests of North Carolina Free Will Baptists.

Reference: Michael R. Pelt, *A History of Original Free Will Baptists* (1996).

Michael R. Pelt

Free Will Baptist Children's Home. At the first annual session of the North Carolina Convention of Original Free Will Baptists in 1913, a proposal to establish an orphanage was adopted. During the next two years, possible sites for the location of this facility were discussed. An Orphanage Committee was formed in 1914, and it became the board of trustees for the orphanage in 1915. The board later received a gift of 50 acres of land with a few farm buildings on it from Ben B. Deans of Middlesex. By the end of 1916 construction of the first building, a three-story structure with a full basement, had begun.

In 1920 the orphanage was ready to receive its first children, and on 23 May four children from one family were admitted. During the early decades of operation, most children admitted were either orphans or had only one parent. While the staff endeavored to meet the children's physical and emotional needs and to provide religious training, local physicians provided medical care without charge. The years of the Great Depression in the 1930s were especially difficult times for the staff and the children at the orphanage since they depended upon the generosity of churches and individuals for financial support. During the 1940s better times arrived, and by 1944 the institution had acquired a total of 361 acres of land, much of it suited for agricultural use. Both boys and girls were assigned tasks to perform, either on the farm or around the household.

In 1947 there were 90 children being served by the institution, which was by that time known as the Children's Home. Following World War II, construction of a new chapel was begun, and during the 1950s other buildings were erected to meet the growing needs of the home. Repairs and replacement of old buildings continued during the 1960s and 1970s as the home adapted to cottage-style living with house parents in order to provide an atmosphere that was more like that of a real family. Greater emphasis was placed on counseling parents of children placed at the home, many of whom came from broken or dysfunctional families. A tutorial program was established to help disadvantaged students succeed in school, and a Preparation for Adult Living program was begun in 1983 to assist adolescents in acquiring the skills needed to function successfully in society once they left the home. After much delay in planning, a physical education facility was completed at the home in 1987.

On 18 May 1995, the Free Will Baptist Children's Home celebrated its seventy-fifth anniversary with a luncheon served to hundreds of patrons and supporters, followed by a Founders' Day program. The home has served more than 1,800 children in residential care since it opened at its location near Middlesex in 1920. It is supported by the approximately 250 Free Will Baptist churches in North Carolina, most of which are in the eastern part of the state.

Reference: Michael R. Pelt, *A History of Original Free Will Baptists* (1996).

Michael R. Pelt

Freight Rates in North Carolina, as in most American states, were regulated from the late nineteenth century until the 1970s. In 1890 the Farmers' Alliance elected many members of the N.C. General Assembly, and the resulting 1891 "farmers' legislature" passed the initial bill creating the Board of Railroad Commissioners. The board was charged with fixing reasonable freight and passenger rates, preventing rate discrimination, and supervising express, steamboat, and canal companies as well as railroads.

In 1899 the Republican-controlled legislature abolished the Board of Railroad Commissioners and created the Corporation Commission. By the mid-1920s, trucks were becoming an important mode of freight transport, and in 1925 the General Assembly gave the Corporation Commission jurisdiction over persons and corporations transporting intrastate freight for hire over state highways. The regulation of highway transport was strengthened by the 1947 General Assembly through the North Carolina Truck Act. This act required that highway shippers in North Carolina operate safe equipment, hold insurance, publish rates and charges, collect no more or less than those rates and charges, and serve all shippers.

The name, size, and exact form of the regulatory body changed a number of times after the formation of the Corporation Commission in 1899. Recognizing the importance of utility regulation and the increase it caused in the duties of the commission, the commission was expanded and renamed the Office of Utilities Commissioner in 1933. In 1941 that office was abolished and replaced with the North Carolina Utilities Commission by the General Assembly.

Until the 1980s, state utility regulators dealt with changes in intrastate freight rates charged by both railroad and trucking companies. The last intrastate railroad rate case was decided in 1981; the last motor truck rate case was in 1983, though the Utilities Commission continued to issue certificates for operation after that date. Deregulation of freight rates, both rail and truck, began in earnest in the mid-1970s. The federal Railroad Revitalization and Regulatory Reform Act of 1976 allowed railroads some flexibility in setting interstate rates. The federal Staggers Rail Act and the Motor Carrier Act (both 1980) furthered deregulation of interstate freight rates and established the current system in which rates are generally set by railroads and trucking companies according to the market.

Thomas K. Tiemann

French and Indian War (1754–63) grew out of competition between Great Britain and France for land in North America. As part of the larger Seven Years War in Europe, colonists and Indians were caught up in a bitter struggle that eventually deprived the French of Canada and the Indians of much of their land. North Carolina colonists and the Cherokee fought first as allies, then as enemies. The North Carolina colony raised 2,000 men, half of whom initially fought mostly

A gravestone dating from 1760 in the cemetery at Thyatira Church in Rowan County. Church records from this period offer graphic accounts of white settlers, such as the young man memorialized in the gravestone, killed by Cherokees in the vicinity of Rowan County during the French and Indian War. Photograph courtesy of Claude J. Pickett.

in Virginia and New York. Later the troops concentrated on defending North Carolina against the Cherokee.

The first North Carolina troops, under Col. James Innes, were sent to Virginia, where the governor appointed Innes commander of all colonial forces in Virginia after the death of their leader, Joshua Fry. Innes and 450 North Carolinians arrived in Winchester, Va., in June 1754, but due to a lack of supplies Innes sent most of the men home within the month. On 4 July George Washington surrendered Fort Necessity in southwestern Pennsylvania to the French, leaving the frontier open to attack. In defense, Innes took 40 North Carolinians as part of a larger force of 400 men north into Maryland to join Washington; there they built Fort Cumberland on Wills Creek.

In January 1755 Britain sent Gen. Edward Braddock to America to assume command of the colonial forces in Virginia, including Innes's men holding Fort Cumberland and a new North Carolina company of 100 troops under Capt. Edward Brice Dobbs, son of North Carolina governor Arthur Dobbs. On 9 July the French and Shawnee Indians ambushed part of Braddock's army, killing Braddock, killing or wounding 700 of his men, and routing his army. Dobbs and his North Carolina company, who did not take part in the battle, retreated to Fort Cumberland. There Innes tried to stop the flight of Braddock's remaining men, but they marched on to Philadelphia, leaving 300 to 400 sick or wounded soldiers with Innes. As the army collapsed, half of Dobbs's force at the fort deserted and went home. In 1756 three new North Carolina companies were raised, placed under Dobbs, and attached to the British army in New York. There they participated in three more disasters, including the loss of Fort Oswego in August. By the end of the year most of the North Carolinians had returned home, followed by Dobbs in the spring of 1757.

With the defeat of Braddock's army and the British losses in New York, French and Indian attacks along the western frontier of the English colonies began in earnest. Only the presence of the Cherokee in North Carolina prevented more aggressive Shawnee attacks. In February 1756 Capt. Hugh Waddell helped secure a peace treaty with the Catawba and Cherokee. Under the treaties negotiated by the governors of North Carolina, South Carolina, and Virginia, the Cherokee would send their warriors north to fight the French and the Shawnee in exchange for supplies and forts (to be built by the English) to protect the Indian settlements. That winter a disastrous campaign against the Shawnee left the Cherokee warriors angry and hungry, and on the way home they raided white settlements in Virginia and North Carolina for food and horses. Only the continued negotiations kept them from breaking with the English and siding with the French.

Between 1755 and 1757 North Carolina concentrated on shoring up its frontier defenses. The colony built a fort at the Moravian settlement of Bethabara, Fort Prince George in Lower Cherokee territory, and Fort Loudoun in Upper Cherokee territory. Fort Dobbs, named for Governor Arthur Dobbs, was a small battery on the eastern end of Bogue Banks intended to defend Old Topsail Inlet (modern Beaufort Inlet) and the port of Beaufort. Construction began in 1756 but was not completed; the fort was never armed or used. Another Fort Dobbs, in Iredell County, was built during the same period. Fort Granville, named for John Lord Carteret, Earl Granville, was located on the southern side of Ocracoke Inlet near the new town of Portsmouth to guard both the inlet and the harbor. Work began on Fort Granville in 1755, but it was never finished, although garrisoned and armed with 11 old ship guns. The site was abandoned at the end of the war.

In 1758 refugees from the western frontier and the north streamed into North Carolina to escape the war. Overwhelmed with these emigrants in the winter and spring, the Moravians at Bethabara built an additional fort around its all-important mill and moved refugees there from the village stockade. They also fed hundreds of Cherokee warriors on their way to and from the fighting in Virginia. Maj. Hugh Waddell's men took part in the capture of Fort Duquesne in November 1758. The Cherokee were very dissatisfied with their treatment during the campaign and returned home angry with the colonial forces.

In 1759 a significant number of Cherokees turned against the English. In April and May a raiding party killed as many as 20 settlers along the Catawba and Yadkin Rivers. The forts at Bethabara then filled with 120 refugees, outnumbering the Moravians, who established the town of Bethania to help relieve the overcrowding. That summer typhus broke out in Bethabara, killing many refugees and Moravians.

The South Carolinians forced a peace treaty on the Cherokee in 1759, but it did not last. In January and February 1760 the Indians besieged Fort Prince George and Fort Loudoun and swept through the backcountry settlements, killing everyone they found. Colonial rangers from Fort Dobbs and Betha-bara attempted to rescue settlers and fought the Cherokee. In June Col. Archibald Montgomerie destroyed the Lower Chero-kee settlements and attacked the Middle Cherokees. After a defeat on 27 June, Montgomerie withdrew to Fort Prince George and then to Charles Towne (Charleston, S.C.). The Virginia expedition led by Col. William Byrd to relieve Fort Loudoun failed in July. The fort surrendered to the Upper Cherokees on 7 August, and its commander and much of its garrison were massacred three days later.

In January 1761 Lt. Col. James Grant arrived in Charles Towne with British regulars. By mid-June his army of 2,150 men won a battle near modern Franklin and destroyed 15 Middle Cherokee towns and 1,400 acres of corn. To the north, Waddell's North Carolina troops joined Byrd's Virginians and moved against the Cherokee. Meanwhile, under the threat of additional invasions, the Indians sued for peace; on 18 Dec. 1761 they signed a treaty ending the war.

While the colonists in North Carolina, South Carolina, and Virginia were fighting the Cherokee, the British won the war in Canada against the French. Quebec fell in September 1759, and Canada was surrendered to the English at Montreal in September 1760. On 10 Feb. 1763 the Treaty of Paris officially ended the Seven Years War in Europe and the French and Indian War in North America.

The many hundreds of refugees who fled to North Caro-lina had a significant impact on the colony. Some of them stayed, adding to the population. Yet the French and Indian War slowed the colony's development, ended the migration of German settlers to its backcountry, damaged Anglo-Cherokee relations, and left North Carolina with a huge war debt. The overall cost of the war led Britain to increase taxes on the American colonies, eventually contributing to the American Revolution.

References: Jerry C. Cashion, "North Carolina and the Cherokee: The Quest for Land on the Eve of the American Revolution, 1754–1776" (Ph.D. diss, UNC-Chapel Hill, 1979); Philip M. Hamer, "Anglo-French Rivalry in the Cherokee Country, 1754–1757," *NCHR* 2 (1925); E. Lawrence Lee, *Indian Wars in North Carolina, 1663–1763* (1963); Alfred Moore Waddell, "North Carolina in the French and Indian War," *North Carolina Booklet* 7 (July 1907).

R. Jackson Marshall III
Additional research provided by Paul Branch.

French Broad River is formed by the junction of North Fork and West Fork in southern Transylvania County near the town of Rosman. It flows northeast into Henderson County, where it turns northwest and courses through Buncombe and Madison Counties. The French Broad flows through the city of Asheville, where it picks up the Swannanoa River and con-tinues north into Tennessee. After leaving North Carolina, the French Broad proceeds west for 102 miles, joins the Holston River to form the Tennessee River near the city of Knoxville, and eventually flows into the Mississippi River.

The Cherokee names for the French Broad River vary, but the most common was *Tah-kee-os-tee*, meaning "racing waters." Others, such as *Peo-li-co*, *Agiqua*, and *Zillicoah*, usually referred to only a part of the river. The English originally knew it as the Broad River—the way it was written on a 1766 map of Indian Nations. By 1776, however, the word "French" had been added because much of the territory west of the Blue Ridge, where the river drained, was occupied by the French in the 1700s.

The French Broad River has a North Carolina watershed of 2,830 square miles; its total length in North Carolina is about 70 miles. For much of the twentieth century the river was environmentally threatened, but through several public and private initiatives it has recovered and become an important natural and recreational area. The river basin encompasses 24 municipalities that had a total population of about 400,000 people in the early 2000s. One of two rivers in the United States that flows north, the French Broad is also one of the world's oldest rivers, predated, by some estimations, only by the Nile and New Rivers (the New River is also in the North Carolina mountains).

Reference: Bland Simpson, "The French Broad: On the Road to Wellville," *Wildlife in North Carolina* 63 (November 1999).

Elizabeth Bayley

French Broad Steamboat Company. Although steam-boats operated mainly in coastal North Carolina, they were used for a short time on the French Broad River, high in the mountains. On 3 Feb. 1881 the General Assembly granted a charter to the French Broad Steamboat Company, empower-ing it to operate a steamboat "on the French Broad River and any of its tributaries within the counties of Transylvania, Hen-derson and Buncombe." The president and guiding force of the company was Hendersonville attorney Col. S. V. Pickens, who granted the contract to build a steamboat to Thomas W. Godwin & Company of Norfolk. The contractors sent an experi-enced boatbuilder to Hendersonville to superintend construc-tion of the new boat, which was to be named the *Mountain Lily*.

The *Mountain Lily* was a side-wheeler, powered by two 12-horsepower engines. One account gives its dimensions as "55 feet long and 18 feet wide," with a "draft of more than three feet"; other sources give the boat's draft as 18 inches when loaded. Its capacity was said to be 100 passengers. Congress-man Robert B. Vance, meanwhile, was able to get an appro-priation to blast out rocks and shoals in the river and construct jetties to narrow the channel and deepen the water level.

The owners dreamed of running their boat from a point near Hendersonville to Brevard and even to Asheville. Residents of the area were proud of the little steamboat, claiming that it was "the highest boat line in the world," as it operated at an altitude of 2,200 feet.

The *Mountain Lily* was running by the summer of 1881. The river level was reportedly the lowest it had been in 25 years, though, and its trips were mainly short excursions. The army engineers working on the river began building jetties, but heavy rains that year clogged the jetties and much of the channel with sand and mud. The *Mountain Lily* was left stranded on a sandbar at King's Bridge and was finally abandoned. In 1885 a Captain Farmer reportedly built two small steamboats that were powered by the *Mountain Lily*'s engines. These unprofitable boats were also abandoned, and with them went the dream of steamboat service on the French Broad. The remains of the *Mountain Lily* could be seen in the river as late as the 1930s.

References: Sadie S. Patton, "Steamboat Trips in the Mountains," *The State* (18 May 1940); "Steamboat Once Popular on French Broad River," *Raleigh News and Observer*, 18 May 1940.

David A. Norris

French Gratitude Train was sent to the United States by the citizens of France in appreciation for U.S. military involvement in World War II and American postwar relief efforts. An ocean freighter arrived in New York harbor on 3 Feb. 1949 carrying 49 small French boxcars filled with gifts. These cars, "Hommes 40–Chevaux 8," were French military boxcars designed to carry 40 men or 8 horses. Built between 1872 and 1885, the boxcars had been used in both World Wars as troop and animal carriers. Each car was 29 feet long and weighed approximately 12 tons. They now made up the French "Gratitude Train" and carried gifts from the 40 French provinces. The cars were designated for each of the U.S. state capitals, with one to be shared by the District of Columbia and the Territory of Hawaii.

The tremendous outpouring of U.S. relief sent to the French in the years immediately following World War II culminated with approximately $40 million in relief supplies in the American Friendship Train in 1947. This effort inspired a French rail worker and war veteran named André Picard to suggest that France reciprocate. His original idea was to present one boxcar loaded with gifts representing the country. A local veterans' organization adopted the proposal, and a committee was established to solicit gifts. The response was astounding, and the effort gained national momentum. The National Headquarters of the French War Veterans Association took control and decided to fill 49 cars with gifts. Each car was decorated with the shields of the 40 provinces and other designs.

The boxcar intended for North Carolina arrived in Raleigh on 8 Feb. 1949 and was officially received by Governor W. Kerr Scott. Following the reception ceremony and a parade, the boxcar and the gifts were moved to the state Museum of History for display. Many of the gifts remained with the North Carolina Museum of History, but others were distributed to libraries, schools, and other museums across the state. The car itself was given to the Forty and Eight Society of the American Legion.

In 1981 the Forty and Eight Society loaned the boxcar to the North Carolina Transportation Museum in Spencer. In 1996 the car was repaired and painted, and missing shields were replaced. The car is on exhibit at the museum. Although many of the cars of the French Gratitude Train have been lost, more than half remain on exhibit throughout the United States.

Clare R. Arthur Bass

Fries Manufacturing and Power Company was established in 1897 as a spinoff of the F&H Fries Company, a textile concern founded by Moravian businessman Francis Fries in 1846. Chaired by Francis's son Henry E. Fries, the power company secured a franchise to provide electricity to the towns of Winston and Salem and constructed a dam on the Yadkin River near the community of Idols. When the dam began producing electricity in 1898, it was the first instance of long-distance electrical transmission in the South. Local tradition maintains that the earliest transmissions were carried by barbed wire. The Fries Manufacturing and Power Company was sold to Southern Public Utilities in 1913.

References: Chester A. Davis, "The City's Forgotten Legacy: Frieses Established Industrial Base," *Winston-Salem Journal*, 11 Oct. 1970; Frank Tursi, *Winston-Salem: A History* (1994).

Roger N. Kirkman

Fundamental Constitutions of Carolina, called the "Grand Model," provided the form of government and society for the Carolina colony from 1669 to 1698. The Lords Proprietors of Carolina first issued the constitutions in 1669, then disseminated revisions in 1670, January 1682, August 1682, and 1698. The constitutions were suspended from 1693 to 1698.

The main purposes of the Fundamental Constitutions were to protect Proprietary interests and to avoid the creation of a democracy. The Proprietors used the constitutions to try to establish a feudal government and society, so far as permitted by the Carolina charter of 1663. The feudal government was to be headed by nobles with the titles of palatine, landgrave, and cacique. They were to rule through their own courts, a grand council, and a Parliament. Freemen were to have a voice in government, but slaves and others who were bound were to have none. This government and feudal society were never fully implemented. Only the palatine's (Proprietor's) court operated for a time.

References: Mattie Erma Edwards Parker, ed., *North Carolina Charters and Constitutions, 1578–1698* (1963); Herbert R. Paschal Jr., "Proprietary North Carolina: A Study in English Colonial Government" (Ph.D. diss., UNC-Chapel Hill, 1961).

John L. Bell

Fundamentalism is a religious movement within Protestant Christianity that has deep roots and strong influence in North Carolina. The movement emerged in response to nineteenth-century liberal theology and Darwinism, with an emphasis on preserving certain historic biblical doctrines as constituting the vital minimum of the Christian faith. Common fundamentalist doctrines are the inerrancy of the Bible, the virgin birth, the bodily resurrection of believers, and the second coming and thousand-year reign of Christ (millenarianism). Rooted primarily in the theology of Irish clergyman J. N. Darby, Britain's Charles Haddon Spurgeon, and American evangelist Dwight L. Moody, fundamentalism was eventually codified in 90 articles by 66 interdenominational essayists—one of them a Quaker woman. Published in a dozen booklets between 1910 and 1915, *The Fundamentals* encapsulated conservative biblical scholarship from America, Britain, Canada, Germany, Ireland, and Scotland. Fundamentalists are also referred to as simply "conservative" or "orthodox" Protestants.

The Fundamentals was conceptualized and edited originally by North Carolinian Amzi Clarence Dixon, who promoted the ideology of Darby in his sermons and books and who eventually succeeded to the pulpits of both Spurgeon in London and Moody in Chicago. Before doing so, however, Dixon's North Carolina labors led to the conversions of Charles B. Aycock and Locke Craig, future North Carolina governors; Charles B. Alderman, later the president of North Carolina State University, Tulane, and the University of Virginia; Leonard G. Broughton, founder of the Georgia Baptist Hospital, which became the inspiration for Baptist Hospital in Winston-Salem; J. G. Pulliam, later to be President Warren G. Harding's personal chaplain; and George W. Truett (who converted under Pulliam), later the famed pastor of the First Baptist Church of Dallas, Tex., and a Southern Baptist icon. Upon his death during the Scopes Trial, Dixon was warmly eulogized by no less a source than H. L. Mencken's *Baltimore Sun*. Besides Dixon, other North Carolina–connected contributors and editors associated with *The Fundamentals* were Reuben Archer Torrey, William J. Erdman (a co-founder of the Moody Bible Institute in Chicago) and his son Charles R. Erdman, and Charles Bray Williams.

North Carolina was a fertile field for fundamentalists, beginning in the 1880s with the activities of the "Cotton Mill" revivalist, R. G. Pearson, in Salisbury and those of William J. Erdman in Asheville. Methodist revivalist Sam P. Jones, called the "Moody of the South," was liberally supported by tobacco magnate Gen. Julian Carr of Durham. Jones was almost certainly one of the Methodist revivalists whom James B. Duke credited with prompting his liberal endowment of Trinity College. He also preached in Charlotte, Winston-Salem, and Wilmington. Meanwhile, in Nashville, Tenn., Tom Ryman, a sobered-up riverboat captain, was building a permanent tabernacle—later home of the Grand Ole Opry—in which Jones could preach, using some of the proceeds of Jones's offerings earned in North Carolina. In 1893 Moody himself spoke in Charlotte and Wilmington.

A succession of fundamentalist revivalists roamed North Carolina thereafter until the climactic conversion in 1934 of one-time Presbyterian Billy Graham under the preaching of Southern Baptist Mordecai Ham. Included among them were Dixon, Torrey, W. P. Fife, J. Wilbur Chapman, George Needham (a founder of the Niagara Prophetic Conferences, which became a model for the Montreat Bible Conferences in Black Mountain), Bob Jones, Cyclone Mack, Billy Sunday (supported by James B. Duke and Josephus Daniels, and under whom R. J. Reynolds testified to a conversion experience), "Old Fighting" Bob Shuler, Monroe Parker, Fred Brown, Jimmie Johnson, Gipsy Smith, J. Frank Norris, W. B. Riley, T. T. Martin, John Roach Straton, Napoleon Bonaparte Honeycutt, and Vance Havner. Other contributors to *The Fundamentals* known to have spread its message throughout the state include C. I. Scofield and Arno C. Gaebelein. Though he did not directly contribute to *The Fundamentals*, A. T. Robertson of Statesville emerged from Wake Forest College as a world-class Greek scholar and a participant in fundamentalist Bible conferences nationwide.

In addition to traveling revivalists, some fundamentalists settled down in pastorates throughout North Carolina. These included the Baylor-trained Texan Robert E. Neighbour at the First Baptist Church in Salisbury. Neighbour, along with A. C. Dixon, became one of the founding fathers of the Baptist Bible Union, which would eventually ordain famed Christian radio evangelist Charles E. Fuller. In later years, Neighbour's grandson influenced Paige Patterson to attend New Orleans Baptist Seminary, where he teamed up with Texas judge Paul Pressler to spearhead the historic conservative resurgence in the Southern Baptist Convention in the last third of the twentieth century. Another North Carolinian who figured prominently in the fundamentalist movement was Jasper Cortenus Massee, pastor of Tabernacle Baptist Church in Raleigh.

Although Southern Baptists dominated the fundamentalist movement in North Carolina, Presbyterians such as Burlington's William P. McCorkle and Charlotte's Albert S. Johnson were particularly active in the state's evolution controversy, which preceded the Scopes Trial by only a few weeks and drew the ire of future Watergate prosecutor Sam Ervin Jr. Weston R. Gales, an Episcopalian from the prominent publishing family, was active along with A. C. Dixon and others in the establishment of Montreat and its associated Bible conferences. Some Southern Baptists, such as Charles Stevens in Winston-Salem, found many of their fellow Baptists irredeemably liberal and withdrew from the Southern Baptist Convention altogether, forming the independent Piedmont Bible College. Others, such as James Bulman (East Spencer), Gerald C. Primm (Greensboro), M. O. Owens (Gastonia), Robert Tenery (Morganton), and Calvin Capps (Greensboro) remained within the convention.

Many fundamentalist Christians, seeking to divorce themselves from the "worldliness" of American society, were reluctant to engage in political activity throughout much of the twentieth century. Beginning in about the 1970s, however, a loose association of conservative Christian groups—many avowing fundamentalist theologies—grew into a movement that came to be known as the "new religious right." The movement sought to combat or eliminate "big government," communism, secular humanism, abortion, homosexuality, pornography, illegal drug use, and other forces deemed detrimental to traditional moral and religious values. Prominent leaders of the new religious right included Jerry Falwell, Robert Grant, Beverly and Tim LaHaye, and Pat Robertson, working through organizations such as the Moral Majority, the Christian Voice, Concerned Women for America, the Religious Roundtable, and the American Coalition for Traditional Values. While the national influence of these fundamentalist-rooted groups may have peaked during the 1980s, conservative religious traditions maintain a significant influence in North Carolina worship, culture, and politics. By some estimates, 15 to 20 percent of North Carolinians consider themselves adherents of Christian fundamentalism, practicing their faith in a wide variety of Protestant, nondenominational, and "Bible" churches throughout the state.

References: Willard Gatewood, *Preachers, Pedagogues and Politicians* (1966); James Lutzweiler, *The Revivals of Dwight L. Moody in North Carolina: Charlotte, N.C., March 8–17, 1893 [and] Wilmington, N.C., March 18–25, 1893* (1993); Paul Pressler, *A Hill on Which to Die* (1999); C. Allyn Russell, *Voices of American Fundamentalism* (1976); Ernest Sandeen, *The Roots of Fundamentalism* (1978).

James Lutzweiler
Additional research provided by Jay Mazzocchi.

Funerals in North Carolina have evolved to such an extent that the highly personalized communal rituals of the eighteenth and nineteenth centuries now seem foreign and unfamiliar to many people. Funerals during the colonial period were marked by a group celebration complete with gifts for the attendees, usually rings or gloves, liquor, and a meal. Janet Schaw, a Scottish visitor to North Carolina, described the funeral of Mrs. Jean Corbin of Point Pleasant Plantation near Wilmington in 1775: "Every body of fashion both from town and country were invited," but Schaw felt the occasion "greatly hurt" by a group of "volunteers" who descended on the proceedings just in time for a hearty meal of pork, beef, cornbread, rum, and broth.

During the eighteenth and early nineteenth centuries, the absence of the later practice of embalming made it imperative that bodies be buried immediately, but distances often prevented some family and friends from attending a last-minute funeral service. Therefore, the services were often delayed long past the actual burial, which often occurred without a minister's presence. Martha Thomasson Johnson of Yadkin County, for example, died on 3 Mar. 1859 and was buried the next day. Her funeral service was held on 4 Sept. 1859, when a preacher could be obtained and more people notified to attend the event.

Funeral and mourning customs became much more elaborate during the nineteenth century among the middle and upper classes. Although black, conservative clothing had been worn for mourning since the eighteenth century, nineteenth-century widows were expected to don black crape for at least a year after the death of their spouses. This was followed by another year of wearing combinations of black, gray, lavender or purple, and white. A widow could not return to social activities until after her period of mourning was over. For some this period lasted for the rest of their lives. Mourning etiquette was not as strict for men. They often wore somber, dark suits with a black crape armband or hatband. A man was not expected to remain in mourning as long as a woman. He could return to society before a year passed without incurring social criticism.

In the mountains of North Carolina and other rural regions, services prior to interment were often of the hellfire-and-brimstone variety, sometimes presided over by a circuit-riding minister. Services were held in the home or church. When a funeral service was performed at home, at a church, or at a funeral parlor, a brief committal service was often performed at the graveside prior to interment, and this custom has continued into the modern era. Sometimes handfuls of dirt are sprinkled on the closed coffin, which is usually lowered by ropes, belts, or harness lines into the ground. Funeral practices underwent a transformation during the second half of the nineteenth century. Technological advances in the science of embalming encouraged the development of a professional who would "undertake" all of the funeral arrangements for the family, ushering in the birth of the modern undertaker or funeral director.

One of the most direct and unaltered manifestations of the African influence on the culture of African Americans is found in the social behaviors associated with funerals. Funeral customs were one of the few areas of black life into which white slave owners tended not to intrude. In spite of the conversion of most blacks to Christianity, they retained many of their former rituals associated with the veneration of the dead. They believed, for example, that the spirit of the deceased person might linger for a time before moving to the spirit world. They also believed that the needs of this spirit were similar to those of a living human and that the potential anxiety of a person's spirit could be soothed by presenting it with an item or items the individual had used while alive.

In order to reconnect the dead with the living as well as soothe the soul of the departed, the personal property of the deceased was frequently placed on the grave along with wooden markers and floral arrangements. Sometimes mourners left a single item, perhaps a glass pitcher or a vase; other times mourners deposited a veritable inventory of the deceased's household goods—cups, clocks, toothbrushes, and other items. On some occasions, loved ones laid a patchwork quilt or other article recently used by the deceased upon the grave.

The end of slavery after the Civil War did little to integrate funerals and cemeteries in North Carolina. Well into the twentieth century, blacks were usually buried in graveyards attached to black churches, in private cemeteries owned by black organizations (such as fraternal orders), or in "colored" sections of public cemeteries. Many slave cemeteries have been lost to the ravages of time, weather, desecration, and neglect. In some cases, records have been made of black cemeteries, such as those located in Hertford and Gates Counties.

As the twentieth century progressed, North Carolinians and other Americans accepted the role of the undertaker as the director of all activities surrounding a death of a family member. The funeral home now provides almost all the services that the family and community attended to before, including washing and preparing the body, providing the casket, and arranging the viewing as well as the church and graveside services. By the mid-twentieth century, people were encouraged to rename their home parlors "living rooms" so as to remove all connotations of death from the home. The word "parlor" has become permanently associated with the funeral industry.

References: M. Ruth Little, *Sticks and Stones: Three Centuries of North Carolina Gravemarkers* (1998); Martha V. Pike and Janice Gray Armstrong, *A Time To Mourn: Expressions of Grief in Nineteenth-Century America* (1980); Anne Thatcher Taylor, *Black Cemetery Records, Reunions, and Personality Sketches, Hertford and Gates Counties, North Carolina, 1850–1988* (1988).

Patricia Phillips Marshall
Additional research provided by William G. DiNome and Wiley J. Williams.

SEE ALSO Burial Customs; Decoration Day; Mourning Rings; Tombstones.

Fur and Skin Trade was a significant industry from the earliest permanent settlement of the region that became North Carolina. Pelts shipped to Europe included beaver, bear, deer, raccoon, mink, muskrat, opossum, wolf, and fox. Many were exported to the Middle East, particularly to Turkey, where they were made into clothing. In 1707 Robert Holden wrote to the Board of Trade in London about the varied produce of the Carolina colony. In addition to agricultural crops, he mentioned hides and furs, specifying particularly beaver, otter, fox, wildcat, and bear skins as well as tanned leather. Royal governors for a time were granted a monopoly of the fur trade. In 1736 Henry McCulloh announced his intention to prepare houses for fur storage and employ more than 100 people to carry on the fur trade on tracts of land that he owned in the Cape Fear Valley. Such activity afterward became a significant part of the commerce of the Moravians in the Wachovia settlement on the western frontier, where they had "skin-houses" (warehouses) for that purpose.

Joan E. Freeman

Furniture has been an important product of North Carolina artisans and manufacturers since the early colonial era. The massive success of the industry in the state led to North Carolina's acquiring the nickname "Furniture Capital of the World" during the 1980s, when the state produced approximately one-half of the furniture sold in the United States. While furniture remained a key segment of North Carolina's economy in the early years of the twenty-first century, with more than 600 furniture manufacturers in the state producing in excess of $6 billion in furniture and furnishings and employing nearly 70,000 people, economic and international trade changes in the 1990s and early 2000s resulted in a significant downsizing of the industry.

Furniture as Product and Craft from the Colonial Era to the Civil War

Settlers in colonial North Carolina furnished their dwellings with durable, functional objects that were often self-manufactured or had been brought with them from their previous home. The eastern settlements received a substantial portion of their furniture through the coastal trade from New England, the British Isles, and Europe. Artisans were attracted to the colony as the population increased and could support their work. Most of these cabinetmakers, silversmiths, painters, potters, weavers, and the like were of English ancestry, often immigrating from neighboring colonies, who brought with them knowledge of their respective crafts based on English design. They settled in the Coastal Plain, the Piedmont backcountry, and the Mountains, together with German, Highland Scot, Scotch-Irish, and African immigrants. Each ethnic group made unique contributions to the development of certain furniture design styles that can readily be identified as having originated in North Carolina.

Most of the early furniture was made of woods native to the North Carolina landscape, such as walnut, cherry, cypress,

Exhibit at the Furniture Discovery Center in High Point, a museum interpreting the design, manufacture, and marketing of home furnishings, which also houses the American Furniture Hall of Fame. Photograph courtesy of North Carolina Division of Tourism, Film, and Sports Development.

oak, yellow pine, and poplar. Mahogany was popular but had to be imported. Furniture and furnishings in the seventeenth and early eighteenth centuries were primarily functional. The conservative, simple furniture made by the Moravians and Quakers in the North Carolina Piedmont reflected a utilitarian approach to life on the frontier. The coastal regions were the first to develop and support an artisan class, which grew slowly at first. Most first-generation North Carolinians preferred to accumulate land, agricultural equipment, and slaves rather than tangible personal possessions. Early inventories reveal more detailed descriptions of farming equipment than household goods.

North Carolinians generally sought to emulate their British counterparts in the decoration of their furniture and homes. Cabinetmakers and silversmiths produced wares that imitated the neat and plain styles of the English that many people favored. Trade with England brought a variety of consumer goods into the colony as well as style books and fashionable designs. Furniture took on more decorative and artistic qualities as other specialized forms were being produced to provide for the social customs of the day. Special tables, cupboards, and cabinets for the display and serving of tea wares,

along with silver flatware and imported china, were found in the homes of the upper and middle classes.

Furniture in nineteenth-century North Carolina did not experience noticeable change until the effects of the Industrial Revolution spread into the state. Britain and France continued to establish decorative trends for furniture and home furnishings, which were then adapted to suit American and southern tastes. Popular design styles for furnishings included late Empire, American Restoration, Rococo Revival, Elizabethan Revival or Cottage Style, Gothic Revival, Renaissance Revival, Eastlake, Art Nouveau, Arts and Crafts, and Colonial Revival. Economic class and geography determined the amount and quality of furniture available. Rural North Carolinians continued to purchase locally made objects that were largely utilitarian. They did make and incorporate decorative objects whenever possible using information gathered from local, regional, and national sources.

A substantial North Carolina furniture industry existed before the Civil War. One of the state's most successful furniture operations was owned by Thomas Day, a free black who had moved to Caswell County from southern Virginia in the 1820s. Day became renowned for his finely crafted furniture and other home embellishments, such as mantelpieces and stair railings. In the 1850s, Day invested in steam equipment and woodworking machinery, making him one of the first furniture makers to do so. His business thrived until about 1860, when it succumbed to the economic instability and recession that marked the era. Several of Day's pieces survive under private ownership or in museums.

Furniture Production in the Industrial Age

The 1860 industrial census lists 5 of the 37 cabinet shops in the state as using steam equipment to power operations. The ensuing Civil War and its aftermath effectively put an end to most such enterprises. However, by the late nineteenth century the furniture industry in North Carolina had regained much of its earlier momentum. Piedmont North Carolina was well suited for industrial development at this time. Improved railway transportation in the area, along with large stands of hardwood forests, attracted developers. William H. Snow, a native of Montpelier, Vt., had moved to Greensboro shortly after the war and established a spoke and handle factory with the financial backing of friends. In 1871 he moved to High Point, where he founded a factory that produced shuttle blocks and bobbins from native hardwoods for the northeastern textile mills. His son, Ernest A. Snow, started the Snow Lumber Company in 1881. That year, David A. and William E. White founded a plant in Mebane to produce spindles for the textile industry. The White brothers quickly turned to the manufacturing of furniture. Subsequently, Ernest Snow joined forces with John H. Tate, Thomas F. Wrenn, and M. J. Wrenn to form the High Point Furniture Manufacturing Company in 1889. In 1887 the Goldsboro Furniture Manufacturing Company was chartered in Goldsboro. Soon these and other small factories were producing inexpensive lines of wooden household furniture for a demanding southern market.

The founders of many of the state's first furniture factories sold their interests and started new enterprises with others who had available capital. The early furniture industry was driven primarily by individuals from the business and professional community who pooled together money to erect buildings and install machinery. They hired experienced superintendents (who often had worked in northern furniture factories) to choose and train local workers to operate the facilities. The agricultural depression of the 1890s forced many farm workers out of the country and into developing towns, and North Carolina's early furniture factories took advantage of this relatively inexpensive, unskilled labor force.

By 1900 there were 44 furniture factories in High Point and the surrounding towns of Thomasville, Lexington, Salem, Marion, Mount Airy, Statesville, Hickory, and Greensboro. The central location of the Piedmont made High Point a natural shipping point for southern markets that desired inexpensive, well-made furniture. The industry was also given a boost when several national mail-order companies, including Sears, Roebuck & Co., purchased large lots of North Carolina furniture to market nationwide through their catalogs. Other allied manufacturers set up factories in High Point to provide veneers, plate glass, mirrors, paint, and locks to the furniture companies.

The first decade of the twentieth century was marked by large profits for many North Carolina furniture producers, although by 1910 such prosperity had become more elusive. An increase in the number of factories meant fierce competition for a share in the market and the hiring of competent, experienced workers. Factory operators faced rising labor costs as well as higher costs related to shipping. There were numerous bankruptcies resulting from inexperienced managers who either sold their products well below the cost of production or expanded operations far too quickly. Some companies merged to avoid bankruptcy and actually strengthened their positions. The Standard Chair Company of Thomasville was formed in 1906 from the Lambeth Chair Company, the Cates Chair Company, the Standard Chair Company, and the Thompson Chair Company. It became one of the largest chair-producing firms in the South.

Many manufacturers realized that they could no longer approach furniture making with the simple formula of money, material, and manpower. Several companies began to focus on improving quality and production practices. The White Furniture Company in Mebane developed a solid reputation for quality furniture production. In 1913 it also became the first furniture plant in the South to use electricity to power its machinery. Company officials hired an "efficiency engineer" in 1916 to analyze the factory operations and make recommendations to improve the production process. The Tomlinson Chair Company of High Point was one of the first companies to manufacture quality period reproduction dining and living room suites on a large scale. The company also took an innovative approach in the treatment of its workforce by giving them the opportunity to share in the company profits. Any employee who exceeded their monthly quota would receive a percentage of the profit. In addition to this, Tomlinson provided group life insurance to its workers.

Birth and Development of the Modern Furniture Industry

By 1939 North Carolina was the national leader in total production of wood household furniture. Marketing techniques were an important factor in the phenomenal rise of the North Carolina furniture industry throughout the twentieth century. The American furniture industry created a unique marketing system in which larger cities such as New York and Chicago became national exhibition sites where manufacturers displayed their products and took orders. Furniture dealers and buyers visited these halls at least twice a year, viewing a va-

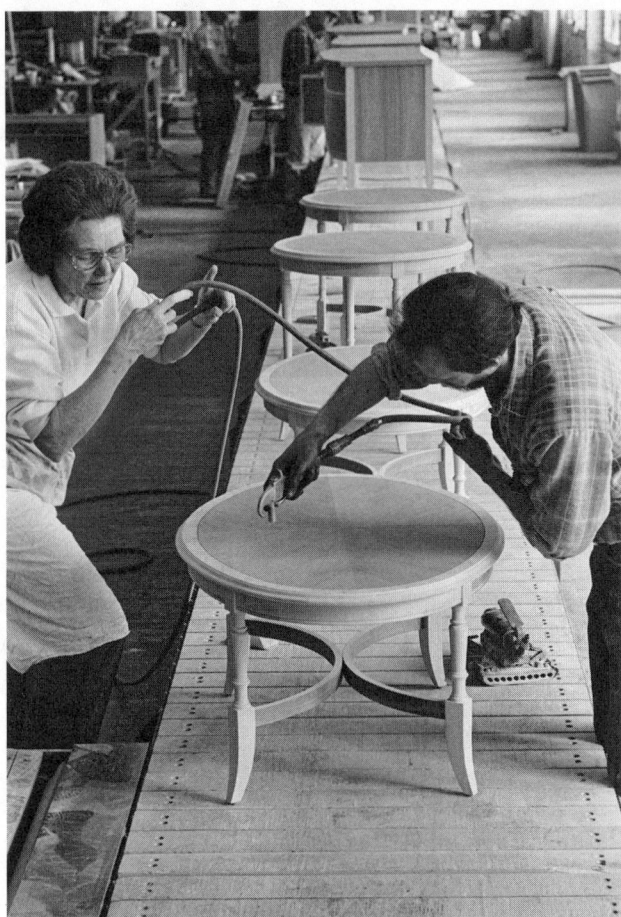

Workers sanding tables at the White Furniture Company in Mebane, 1993. Photograph by Bill Bamberger from *Closing: The Life and Death of an American Factory* (DoubleTake/Norton, 1998).

riety of lines from across the country. North Carolina manufacturers brought the concept home to High Point and eventually created the largest marketing center for home furnishings in the world. On 20 June 1921 the Southern Furniture Exposition, Inc., opened a ten-story building in High Point, complete with 249,600 square feet of exhibition space. Over two weeks, 700 dealers viewed 149 exhibits, and sales came close to $2.25 million. The exposition was held twice a year with increasing numbers and strengthened North Carolina's stature as a national leader in furniture production.

Throughout the second half of the twentieth century, North Carolina continued to lead the nation in production of both upholstered and wooden household furniture. A large number of manufacturers provided relatively stylish and inexpensive furniture for all economic classes. Although many furnishings lost their unique regional quality as North Carolinians became part of a national marketplace, a number of local artisans continued to produce unique, high-quality products.

The 1980s marked the "golden era" of the North Carolina furniture industry, when employment peaked at 90,000 people and the state added nearly 200 new furniture companies to its ranks. However, the boom did not continue. Trouble began in the 1990s with the globalization of the industry and an increase in free trade, resulting in competition from foreign furniture corporations and necessary cost-cutting measures from U.S. firms. The outsourcing of production services to Latin American and Asian countries led to a large decrease in furniture production and employment in North Carolina. China became the North Carolina furniture industry's most effective competitor, producing furniture of equal quality that was available to consumers at a lower price.

North Carolina saw the closing of 47 furniture companies during the 1990s, and the negative trend continued after 2000 with dozens of additional company closings. By 2006 it remained unclear how far the industry would fall before stability was reached, although some believed North Carolina's increasing affluence and urbanization would eventually reverse the economic hardships the industry had experienced.

North Carolina's Largest-Grossing Furniture Companies (2004)

Company	Location	Total Sales (millions)	Number of Employees
Universal Furniture, Ltd.	High Point	$670	12,000
Klaussner Corporation	Asheboro	$621.5	6,064
Thomasville Furniture Industries	Thomasville	$362.8	6,500
Broyhill Furniture Industries, Inc.	Lenoir	$334.9	6,000
Lexington Furniture Industries	Lexington	$167.3	3,000
Bernhardt Industries, Inc.	Lenoir	$122.7	2,200
CV Industries, Inc.	Hickory	$117.1	2,100
Sherrill Furniture Company	Hickory	$105.1	1,650
Carolina Mills, Inc.	Maiden	$96.8	1,500
Henredon Furniture Industries	Morganton	$94.7	1,700
Drexel Heritage Furniture Industries	High Point	$89.2	1,600
Kincaid Furniture Company, Inc.	Hudson	$79.5	1,250
Fairfield Chair Company	Lenoir	$75	700
Cochrane Furniture Company	Lincolnton	$75	600
Clayton Marcus Company, Inc.	Hickory	$49.1	775

References: John Bivins, *The Furniture of Coastal North Carolina, 1700–1820* (1987); John Bivins and Forsyth Alexander, *The Regional Arts of the Early South: A Sampling from the Collection of the Museum of Early Southern Decorative Arts* (1991); Elizabeth Stillinger, *The*

Antiques Guide to Decorative Arts in America, 1600–1875 (1972); Alexander R. Stoesen, *Guilford County: A Brief History* (1993).

Patricia Phillips Marshall
Additional research provided by Michael H. Lewis.

SEE ALSO Broyhill Furniture; Drexel Furniture Company; International Home Furnishings Market; White Furniture Company.

Fusion of Republicans and Populists.

Between 1894 and 1900 the North Carolina Republican and Populist Parties cooperated in state elections and in state government. That cooperation was labeled "Fusion" by its Democratic opponents, although Republicans and Populists maintained separate organizations and did not describe their actions as fusion. In the middle and late 1890s Republican-Populist cooperation resulted in newly configured delegations from North Carolina to the U.S. Congress, Populist-Republican control of the General Assembly, Republicans and Populists in state executive offices, and a non-Democratic state supreme court. A significant number of cooperationist officeholders were African American. Fusion produced the only departure from Democratic Party hegemony after Reconstruction.

The origin of the so-called Fusion was the rise of the People's Party, or Populist Party, after years of economic depression and hardship had motivated small farmers, who suffered the most, to take political action. They formed the Farmers' Alliance, a national organization whose members subsequently became the central component of the Populist Party. North Carolinian Leonidas L. Polk was a primary leader of the Farmers' Alliance in the state, voicing its concerns in his publication, the *Progressive Farmer*, until his sudden death in 1892. During the 1892 election, many Republicans urged cooperation with Populists. Although cooperation as a statewide strategy was eventually rejected, some Republicans and Populists agreed to support joint local candidates. In 1892 the Populist Party attracted roughly 17 percent of North Carolina voters. This was disappointing to the third party, but support for the Democrats fell below 50 percent of the electorate.

There were tensions in the proposed relationship. The organizations disagreed on a wide range of issues, particularly those affecting national economic policy. Populists favored paper currency, government control of money volume, and a federally sponsored system of rural credit. Republicans tended to support a gold standard, a revenue system that discriminated against farmers, and the existing private national banks. Further, Populists were decidedly antirailroad, whereas Republicans supported modest government regulation of railroad rates. Moreover, there were deep cultural differences between the parties' rank and file. Populism was overwhelmingly a coalition of white commercial farmers of modest means from the east and the Piedmont. Republicans were primarily white Mountain anti-Confederates and eastern blacks with a sprinkling of high-tariff manufacturers and urban professionals.

Nonetheless, in 1894 the parties agreed on the need to eliminate laws giving Democrats control of the election process. Both parties were convinced that the election system was fundamentally unfair. Democratic supervision of elections resulted in a range of fraudulent practices, from ballot box stuffing to false counting of votes. The weakness of local government was also a reason for Populist-Republican unity.

With these issues in the forefront, Populists and Republicans in 1894 ran a surprisingly harmonious and spectacularly successful campaign. Their state conventions endorsed the coalition strategy and agreed on who would represent the parties in the few statewide races in contention. Republican and Populist conventions at the county and congressional levels set aside their differences and joined forces against Democrats. The precise methods for local cooperation differed. Sometimes the two parties chose candidates jointly; sometimes they agreed to support the candidate nominated by one of the parties. The results were revolutionary, as the Populists and Republicans won control of the North Carolina Supreme Court, the General Assembly, and most of the state's seats in Congress.

The Republican-Populist General Assembly of 1895 liberalized access to the ballot (especially for blacks), decentralized local government, increased taxes for education, and reduced the legal rate of interest on certain contracts to 6 percent per year. The legislature also sent a Populist, Marion Butler, and a Republican, Jeter Pritchard, to the U.S. Senate.

Despite this initial success, Fusion rule was immediately subjected to intense pressures, most of them related to the substantive differences between the parties and the impending presidential election of 1896. That year, Republican Daniel L. Russell Jr. was elected North Carolina governor with Fusionist support. During his administration the Fusionists began a variety of progressive programs emphasizing public educational reform and enhancement. But divisions soon arose among the factions of Republicans and Populists, accentuating their differences and putting the long-term viability of Fusion in jeopardy. Some Populists, including Butler, wanted to change the direction and scope of cooperation to advance financial reform, in particular the free and unlimited coinage of silver and the elimination of national banks. The rise of black leadership in the state also undermined Fusionist strength. The Russell administration's appointments of many blacks to governmental positions gave the Democrats a stirring political issue with which to energize numerous white citizens.

By the political campaign of 1898, the sole rationale for continued Republican-Populist cooperation was fear of Democratic control. Predictably, the ensuing Fusionist campaign was weakened by the absence of any other reason to win the election. Unable to contest the Democrats' rhetoric and violence, the cooperationists lost control of state government forever. The success of the Democrats and their repeal of the Fusionists' election laws in 1899 reinforced the defensive position of the cooperationists.

The final phase of Populist-Republican Fusion was the state campaign of August 1900, in which the major issue was a proposed Democratic constitutional amendment limiting access to the ballot. Voters would also elect several state-level officials and the next General Assembly. Given the white supremacy intent of the amendment, Populists and Republicans decided that white Populism would lead the opposition and emphasize the amendment's potential effect on poor whites. Republicans officially attacked the proposed disfranchisement as an assault on the federal Constitution. The subsequent triumph of the Democrats destroyed Populism and ensured a dramatic decrease in black Republican votes. Henceforth, Republicans would meet the Democrats alone.

Cooperation between Republicans and Populists was initially an effort to democratize North Carolina politics by giving black and white citizens better access to the ballot and increasing local control of county government. It succeeded to the extent that several groups traditionally excluded by Democratic rule won the right to vote and hold public office. Through the impetus of Populism, Fusion provided a vehicle for the encouragement, adoption, and implementation of laws regulating businesses and benefiting debtors, especially during the General Assembly of 1895. Yet cooperation was also characterized by expedience and fundamental differences as to policy and political strategy; cooperation had occurred partly because Populist and Republican leaders did not believe that their parties could achieve independent pluralities. Ultimately, the experience of Fusion reflected deep conflicts over the meaning of democracy, race, and government in late nineteenth-century North Carolina.

References: Eric Anderson, *Race and Politics in North Carolina, 1872–1901: The Black Second* (1981); Jeffrey J. Crow and Robert F. Durden, *Maverick Republican in the Old North State: A Political Biography of Daniel L. Russell* (1977); Helen G. Edmonds, *The Negro and Fusion Politics in North Carolina, 1894–1901* (1951); Paul D. Escott, *Many Excellent People: Power and Privilege in North Carolina, 1850–1900* (1985); James L. Hunt, *Marion Butler and the Populist Ideal, 1863–1938* (1990).

James L. Hunt

SEE ALSO Farmers' Alliance; Populist Party; Republican Party; Round Knob Hotel Affair; Silver Fusion.

G

Gaelic Language. Beginning in 1739, with the arrival of the Argyll Colony, and continuing through the first decades of the nineteenth century, the Cape Fear River Valley was home to the largest settlement of Highland Scots in North America. A majority of these settlers were fluent speakers of their native Gaelic, and the language was used by these immigrants and their descendants in North Carolina until well into the nineteenth century. Gaelic was the language used in many Scottish homes and, more important, in many of the churches in parts of North Carolina's Highland settlement. Several Gaelic place-names are found in the region, the most obvious being Dundarrach in Hoke County, which in Gaelic means "hill of the oak tree." Some familiar words that have Gaelic origins and usage remain in colloquial speech among older citizens of the region, despite the fact that, as a vital language, Gaelic has long since died out.

The first Gaelic-speaking minister to serve in North Carolina was James Campbell, a native of Argyllshire, who came to the Highland settlement in 1758. Campbell was instrumental in founding the sister churches of Barbecue, Bluff, and Longstreet, all of which had Gaelic-speaking congregations. Campbell was joined just prior to the Revolutionary War by at least two other Gaelic-speaking ministers, John MacLeod and John Bethune, both of Skye. Both of these ministers were Loyalists and did not remain in North Carolina following the American Revolution. Later immigrant ministers, including Angus McDiarmid of Islay, John McIntyre of Argyllshire, and Colin McIver of Lewis, among others, continued to serve the Highland settlement by preaching in both Gaelic and English well into the nineteenth century. Several American-born Gaelic speakers were also ordained in a ceremony at Barbecue Church in 1801.

The size and importance of the Gaelic-speaking population was addressed by the Provincial Congress of North Carolina in 1776, when its members addressed the question of publishing pro-Patriot materials in Gaelic. North Carolina holds the distinction of having the first known Gaelic publication in North America: in 1791 the firm of Sibley, Howard, and Rowlstone of Fayetteville published copies of two Gaelic sermons delivered by Dougald Crawford, a native of Arran and former Loyalist chaplain who remained in the Cape Fear region following the American Revolution. In 1826 a copy of Peter Grant's Gaelic Hymnary was also published. Also worthy of note is the fact that the Gaelic newspaper *An Gaidheal*, of Toronto, had an agency for subscription and correspondence in Lumberton as late as 1871.

In the nineteenth century, many of the Presbyterian churches in what became the Fayetteville Presbytery held two church services, one in English and one in Gaelic, to accommodate their members. This practice was discontinued by many congregations around the time of the Civil War, in part because of cultural assimilation but also because of a decline in newly arriving immigrant Gaelic-speaking Scots. Gaelic services were not completely limited to Presbyterian churches; Daniel White, a converted Baptist from Argyllshire, founded Baptist congregations in Robeson and Scotland Counties in which Gaelic was spoken, and Allan McCorquodale, a Scottish-born Methodist, is also known to have preached in Gaelic to

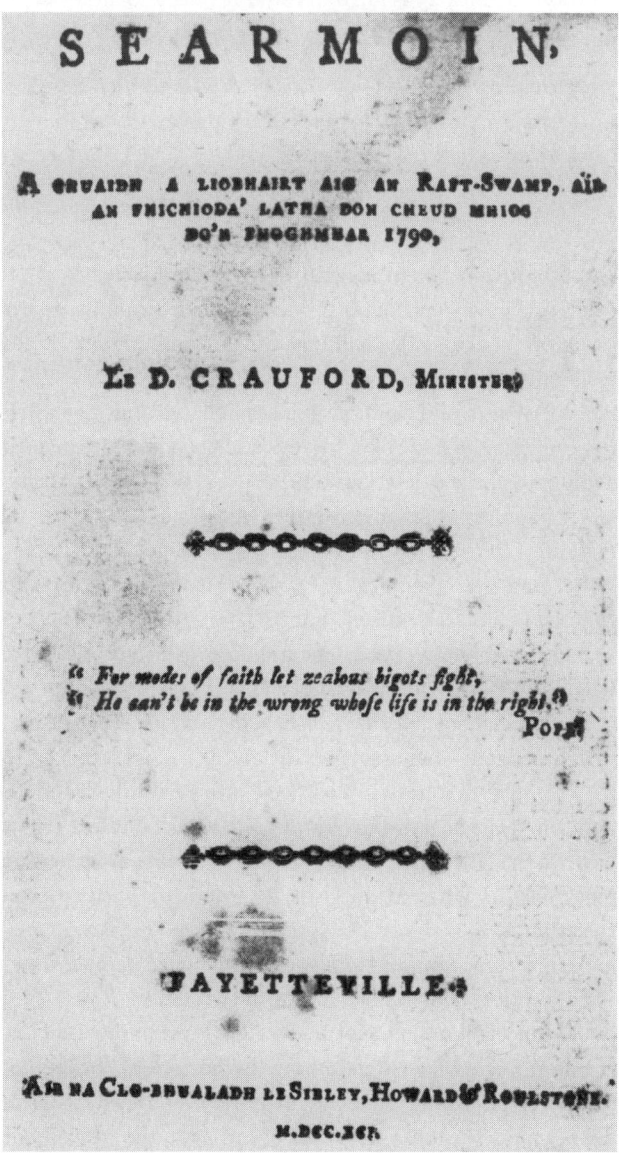

Title page of one of two sermons by the Reverend Dougald Crawford published in Gaelic in Fayetteville in 1791. These sermons are thought to have been the first Gaelic publications in North America. NCC.

several Methodist congregations in the region. There are a few recorded instances of the use of Gaelic in churches after the Civil War. In all, there were at least 30 congregations throughout the Cape Fear region in which Gaelic services were once held.

Among the significant artifacts of the Gaelic language in North Carolina are the songs of John MacRae, the "Kintail bard," who came to North Carolina just prior to the Revolutionary War. MacRae was a Loyalist, and his fate after the war is unknown. However, the songs that he composed in North Carolina, including his best-known song, "Dean Cadalan Samhach" (Sleep Softly, My Darling Beloved), were transmitted through the Gaelic oral tradition, obviously making several transatlantic trips. Folklorists have found MacRae's songs composed in North Carolina to be known in Scotland, Canada, and even as far away as Australia among Gaelic-speaking communities.

References: Charles W. Dunn, *Highland Settler: A Portrait of the Scottish Gael in Nova Scotia* (1953); Duane Meyer, *Highland Scots of North Carolina, 1732–1776* (1961).

William S. Caudill

Gambling. Although illegal in North Carolina since 1764, when a law was enacted limiting personal winnings in any game of chance to five shillings a day, gambling continues to flourish in both legitimate and illegitimate forms. Colonial legislators and opinion makers believed that gambling undermined the value of hard work and encouraged crime. To counteract these deleterious effects, the North Carolina legislature banned public gaming tables (1791), staked card games in public taverns (1799), lotteries (1834), private gaming tables (1835), and slot machines (1939). They also forbade slaves to gamble or play any game of chance (1830).

Worries about the effects of gambling on the citizenry escalated in the late 1970s, when the General Assembly discussed the possibility of legalizing horse racing and pari-mutuel betting, and again when many politicians and citizens began to lobby for a state lottery. Concerned North Carolinians and experts cited the negative effects that legalized gambling might have on the citizenry. Even before pathological gambling was recognized as a mental illness by the American Psychiatric Association in 1980, several chapters of Gambler's Anonymous and GamAnon, support groups for pathological gamblers and their families, were founded in North Carolina.

By the early 2000s, North Carolina's gambling laws remained among the least permissive in the nation. The legislature finally approved a state lottery in 2005 after much political debate about the merits and evils of the institution. Except for the casino run by the Eastern Band of Cherokee Indians in the western mountains, bingo and licensed raffles were the only games of chance permitted by North Carolina law. As a result,

North Carolinians continued to flock to Virginia, Georgia, and South Carolina to place their bets on horses and video poker. Within the state, illegal sports gambling, video poker, off-track betting, and other forms of wagering also continued despite the efforts of law enforcement authorities to stop them.

Ruth E. Homrighaus

SEE ALSO Lotteries.

Gander Pulling. Viewed from the perspective of contemporary Virginians and South Carolinians, North Carolina in the late eighteenth and early nineteenth centuries seemed to exhibit a rough, "backwoods" character with no well-defined culture to smooth the rough edges. The sport of gander pulling, as well as similar rural pastimes such as horse racing, gambling, cockfighting, and "gouging" fist fights, reinforced this image. Gander pulling was particularly popular around Easter time. An old, tough gander (male goose) was hoisted up by his heels with his neck well greased. Each contestant, sufficiently fortified by ample amounts of homemade corn liquor, mounted his horse and galloped by the swinging goose. He reached for the neck and struggled to yank its head from its body. There were frequent failures in this contest. The combination of alcohol, flapping goose, and uneven horse gait easily threw contenders off their mounts.

The event offered a holiday outing for nearly everyone. Female spectators—who seem to have enjoyed gander pulling as much as men—cheered the crude "knights" on their sturdy mounts and encouraged them to "seize the day" (or gander). Each competitor hoped he would tear the prize from the body and nobly present a battered, bloody trophy to the lady of his choice. Although this entertainment seems cruel by modern standards, daily life itself in those days could be quite difficult and barbarous.

Around 1810 many North Carolinians experienced a strong religious revival movement as Evangelical Christians preached to their congregations the need for a disciplined life, free of frivolous entertainment and drunken amusement. Entertainment began to take on a more benevolent form. Corn shucking and barn raising were still acceptable, while gander pulling came to seem a little too brutal for society's new sensibilities. Voting day, however, remained a good excuse for public drunkenness.

References: Hugh T. Lefler, ed., *North Carolina History Told by Contemporaries* (1965); Harry L. Watson, *An Independent People: The Way We Lived in North Carolina, 1770–1820* (1983).

Marilyn Wright

Gaps, often referred to as passes, are breaks or low spots along mountain ranges or ridges. If a gap is particularly precipitous and narrow, it can be designated a gorge. The term "gap" is old, having entered the English language from the Norsemen, gap being the Old Norse word for chasm. It is used mainly in the southeastern United States. Gaps have been important to human advancement on the continent for centuries, representing routes for transportation and communication into or away from areas that would otherwise be cut off from the rest of the world.

Most gaps in North Carolina are named for people (Gillespie Gap, McKinney's Gap) or physical characteristics (Deep Gap, Roaring Gap). Many gaps carry colorful names, such as Maggot Spring Gap, Frying Pan Gap, and Wildcat Gap. Some of the more important gaps in the state are Deep Gap, on the Blue Ridge in Watauga County, a key route for early settlers that is now utilized by U.S. 421; Hickory Nut Gap, on the Buncombe-Henderson County line, a primary route into the Asheville region; Rabun Gap, in Georgia, a route used by settlers coming into the extreme southwestern portion of the state; Soco Gap, an important pass used by the Cherokee Indians to cross the Balsam Mountains; and Swannanoa Gap, on the McDowell-Buncombe County line, a pass for travelers headed into the Asheville area that is now utilized by Interstate 40.

John Hairr

Gardner-Webb University, a coeducational institution associated with the Baptist State Convention of North Carolina, is located near Shelby in Cleveland County. The youngest of North Carolina's Baptist colleges, Gardner-Webb traces its origins to Boiling Springs High School, founded in 1905. Distinguished alumni of Boiling Springs included Wilbur J. Cash, author of *The Mind of the South*, and Dewey Whitaker, president of Lehigh University.

The 1920s witnessed the expansion of public high schools in North Carolina, leading to declining enrollments at sectarian institutions such as Boiling Springs. In response, Boiling Springs High School, along with its sister institutions at Mars Hill and Buies Creek, reorganized as a junior college. The generosity of former North Carolina governor Max Gardner and his wife Faye Webb Gardner led Boiling Springs to change its name to Gardner-Webb Junior College in 1942. In 1947 the North Carolina Baptist Convention began supporting Gardner-Webb. In 1969 the junior college became Gardner-Webb College, and the first four-year class graduated in 1971.

Gardner-Webb's first graduate program, in education, was initiated in 1981. In the 1980s Gardner-Webb also initiated an international study abroad program with Japan's Dhoto University. To the college's graduate education program were added a master of business administration curriculum and a divinity school. In 1993 Gardner-Webb College became Gardner-Webb University. By the early 2000s Gardner-Webb had more than 3,200 students taught by approximately 135 faculty members. The university offers dual degree programs in engineering with Auburn University and the University of

North Carolina at Charlotte. It inaugurated its first doctoral program, a Doctor of Ministry, in 2001.

References: Francis B. Dedmond, *Lengthening Shadows: A History of Gardner-Webb College, 1907–1956* (1957); Lansford Jolley, *Dreaming, Daring, Doing: A History of Gardner-Webb University, 1907–1997* (1997).

James I. Martin Sr.

Gaston County, located in the south central Piedmont region of North Carolina, was formed from Lincoln County in 1846. It partially borders the state of South Carolina. The county was named for William Gaston, member of the U.S. House of Representatives and justice of the Supreme Court of North Carolina. The county seat was originally Dallas but became Gastonia in 1911. Other Gaston County communities include Belmont, Bessemer City, Cherryville, Cramerton, High Shoals, Lowell, McAdenville, Mount Holly, Ranlo, Spencer Mountain, and Stanley.

Catawba and Cherokee Indians originally inhabited the lands of Gaston County, but few remained as European colonists arrived. The first settlers were primarily Scotch-Irish, German (including Pennsylvania Dutch), and English. Small, self-sufficient farms characterized early Gaston County, which did not enjoy the agricultural prosperity of some of the other counties. Corn was one of the more abundant crops and often was quickly converted into whiskey. By 1870 Gaston was known as the "Banner Corn Whiskey County of Carolina." In addition to distilleries, the county's early economy was supported by mines that yielded gold, lime, sulfur, tin, and iron in varying quantities.

Belmont Abbey College was established in Belmont in 1876 by the Roman Catholic Order of Saint Benedict. Gaston County experienced an industrial boom beginning in 1845–48, when the construction of three cotton mills laid the foundation for a textile industry that became vital to the county. A labor dispute at the Loray Mill in Gastonia erupted in violence in 1929. Workers attempting to organize a union were charged with being communists, and the strike was violently suppressed. Textiles continue to dominate Gaston County's industrial structure, although its industrial base has become more diversified. In 2004 the population of Gaston County was estimated at 192,000.

Allyson C. Criner

SEE ALSO Gastonia Strike.

Gastonia Strike, the most notorious textile labor struggle in North Carolina history, occurred in Gastonia in the spring, summer, and early fall of 1929. As in other mill communities of the textile manufacturing region, conditions for confrontation had been ripe in Gastonia throughout the 1920s. The

The children of Ella Mae Wiggins, a union supporter killed during the 1929 Gastonia strike, stand beside their mother's grave on the day of her funeral. NCC.

Loray Mill was particularly vulnerable for two reasons: first, with more than 2,000 workers, it was by far the largest single mill in the state; and second, it was owned by a prominent northern company, Manville-Jencks of Providence, R.I.

In 1927 the company had hired an engineering firm to study ways to reduce labor costs and maintain production levels. The report by the Barnes Textile Service led to a reduction of the workforce at the Loray Mill from 3,500 to 2,200 by the end of 1928. Another factor contributing to the ultimate showdown was the decision of the communist-led National Textile Workers Union to target the mill for a southern organizing drive in the spring of 1929.

On 1 April, within a few weeks of the arrival of union organizers, Loray workers walked off the job. At first the strike enjoyed nearly total participation, but by the end of April many laborers had drifted back to work or the mill had hired replacements. The goals of the strike—a minimum weekly wage of $20, equal pay for women and children, elimination of the stretch-out system (assigning more tasks to fewer workers), and union recognition—were compelling. However, the union persisted in disseminating ideological dogma that alienated and confused some employees. Emphasis on biracial strike committees (despite the small number of black workers at the mill) in the face of strong cultural barriers to racial integration in the state also weakened support for the union.

The union's effort to maintain a headquarters and a tent colony for striking workers who had been removed from their homes by the company became a source of friction with local authorities and a symbol of resistance even after the strike ended. On 7 June violence erupted when Gastonia police confronted guards at the tent colony. The ensuing struggle led to gunfire from both sides, leaving one worker and four police officers wounded. One officer, police chief O. F. Aderholt, died of his injuries the next day.

That summer the community turned its attention to the trial of Aderholt's alleged killers—Fred Beal, a union organizer, and 14 strike leaders. Because of the emotion generated by the case, the presiding judge moved the trial to Charlotte. Nevertheless, Gastonians were riveted on the courtroom proceedings; many hoped for a guilty verdict, which would expel the communists and restore stability to their community. But on 9 Sept. 1929, after the mental breakdown of one of the jurors, the judge declared a mistrial. The community reacted bitterly. Caravans of vigilantes roamed through the mill district of Gastonia harassing former strikers and union supporters. Attempting to regain the initiative for their union campaign, communist leaders called for a mass rally of all textile workers on 14 September. Gastonia police, managers and "loyal employees" from local mills, and deputized citizens tried to stop the rally. They intercepted carloads of workers and sent them away. While pursuing one truck containing strike leaders, they opened fire when the riders attempted to escape. One worker, Ella Mae Wiggins, was shot and killed.

Wiggins, the mother of five children, had been a composer of ballads and a major inspiration during the organizing drive of 1929. Her death caused another wave of violence in Gastonia, and for several days union supporters were beaten and union property was dynamited. By the end of September the communist-led union had abandoned its organizing drive, dismantled its headquarters in Gastonia, and relocated its membership. Five men accused of murdering Wiggins stood trial but were not convicted. The second trial in the Aderholt murder case did produce a conviction of Fred Beal and seven codefendants.

The defeat of the textile unions in Gastonia and other southern towns reaffirmed the authority of the mill owners. To accomplish this victory, the manufacturers needed and received considerable assistance from state and local law enforcement agencies, along with the persuasive and moral power of the local press and religious leadership. For the mill workers, the clash with management was an exhilarating but, in the end, bitter experience. The revolt of these laborers had failed to win concessions from the new order imposed by the industry's high-speed machinery and scientific management.

The dramatic struggle between labor and management in Gastonia ended quickly, but not before the sprawling community had become a national and international symbol for the ailing textile industry in the South. Coverage of the strike, the violence, and the trials was extensive in national newspapers and periodicals. The strike and related legal actions drew the attention of prominent writers such as Sherwood Anderson, John Dos Passos, and Sinclair Lewis. Six novels were published in the 1930s using Gastonia as the backdrop. The Communist Party exploited the tragedies for partisan advantage and, even years later, contributed to the "Gastonia myth." Many Gastonia citizens, for whom the events of 1929 evoke painful memories, have been eager to forget the strike.

References: Brent D. Glass, *The Textile Industry in North Carolina: A History* (1992); Jacquelyn Dowd Hall and others, *Like a Family: The Making of a Southern Cotton Mill World* (1987); Liston Pope, *Millhands and Preachers: A Study of Gastonia* (1942); John A. Salmond, *Gastonia, 1929: The Story of the Loray Mill Strike* (1995).

Brent D. Glass
Michael Hill

Gates County, located in the Coastal Plain region of northeastern North Carolina, was formed in 1779 from parts of Chowan, Hertford, and Perquimans Counties. Its northern border runs along the Virginia–North Carolina state line. It was named for General Horatio Gates, an American brigadier general in the Revolutionary War who led his troops to victory at the Battle of Saratoga in 1777. Gatesville has always been the county seat, although it was until 1831 called Gates Court House. Other Gates County communities include Eure, Hobbsville, Corapeake, and Sunbury.

Beginning in 1660, English colonists settled areas that had originally been inhabited by Nottoway, Meherrin, Chesapeake, Chowanoac, and Nansemond Indians. The economy of the county's rural communities was built around farming and timber. The coming of railroads in the late nineteenth century boosted the economy, as improved transportation made agriculture and lumbering more profitable. In the twentieth century, railroads were eventually superseded by highways, which allowed the cheaper option of truck shipment. Agriculture and lumbering are still the leading commercial enterprises in Gates County.

Gates County encompasses part of the Great Dismal Swamp National Wildlife Refuge, containing thousands of acres of forested wetlands. Other natural attractions in the county include Merchants Millpond State Park and the Chowan Swamp Game Land. Historic sites and cultural events include the Gates County Courthouse (1836) and the Fall Arts and Crafts Festival and the Gates County Swamp Fest. The population of Gates County was estimated to be 11,000 in 2004.

References: Thomas R. Butchko, *Forgotten Gates: The Historical Architecture of a Rural North Carolina County* (1991); Beverly and Glenn Tetterton, *North Carolina County Fact Book* (2 vols., 1998); Paulette Felton Wester, *A Journey in Time: A History of Gates County* (1995).

Allyson C. Criner

Gatling Gun. Inventor Richard Jordan Gatling was born in Hertford County in September 1818. Issued his first patent in 1844 for a rice-seed planter, he soon moved to St. Louis, Mo., and successfully marketed the machine as a wheat-drill. More inventions followed, including a steam plow, a cotton cultivator, and a hemp brake. A Unionist, Gatling was living in India-

A view of the Gatling gun as shown on company letterhead, ca. 1875. Courtesy of NCOA&H.

napolis in 1862 when he patented his first machine gun, employing a cartridge-feeding mechanism adapted from his rice-seed planter. Initial models, built by a Cincinnati firm, had a single barrel fed by a rotary chamber and fired 190 bullets per minute. The Federal Ordnance Department showed no interest, but Gen. Benjamin F. Butler purchased 13 and used them at Bermuda Hundred, near Richmond, in the spring of 1863. As results were inconclusive, the gun saw no further service in the Civil War, although the navy ordered a small number.

Postwar models, using new self-contained brass (rather than paper) cartridges, had six barrels hand-cranked around a central shaft. This design, the first successful machine gun, impressed the army, which bought 100 in 1866. Although Gatling continued to invent mainly agricultural and military machines and implements, he built his career around improving and publicizing his machine gun, manufactured by Colt's Armory in Hartford, Conn., and later by an English firm at Newcastle-on-Tyne. The gun was used by France in the Franco-Prussian War and against Indians in the American West and adopted by Russia, England, Austria-Hungary, Egypt, and other countries. Later models fired up to 3,000 rounds per minute. American Gatling guns saw service in the Spanish-American War, but by this time the weapon had lost ground to the Nordenfeldt and Maxim guns and other machine guns that were based on more advanced principles.

References: F. Roy Johnson and E. Frank Stephenson, *The Gatling Gun and Flying Machine of Richard and Henry Gatling* (1979); Thomas C. Parramore, "The North Carolina Background of Richard Jordan Gatling," *NCHR* 41 (Winter 1964); Paul Wahl and Dan Toppel, *The Gatling Gun* (1965).

Thomas C. Parramore

Gays and Lesbians. Until the final decades of the twentieth century, the personal lives of gay and lesbian people in North Carolina were shrouded in silence. While homosexuality certainly existed in the state, talking about it was gen-

erally taboo. Being a homosexual required caution because North Carolina's statutes contained a prohibition against sodomy. Conviction for a "crime against nature" could result in a fine and possibly a jail sentence. It is likely that the sexual preferences of many gays and lesbians were known to their closest friends and acquaintances, but a brand of the "don't ask, don't tell" rule existed.

While attitudes about sexuality in general and homosexuality in particular began to liberalize slowly in the United States after World War II, little change was evident at first for gay and lesbian people in North Carolina. Acceptance of openly gay and lesbian lifestyles might have been possible in larger cities elsewhere, but in North Carolina's cities, which lacked both size and diversity, accommodation of homosexual communities was slow in developing. Nevertheless, social attitudes and religious mores that marginalized homosexuals and even advocated violence against them surely did not prevent the state's gay and lesbian people from developing significant relationships or expressing their identities. In some cases, these identities were hidden in plain sight; in communities where the terms "gay" or "homosexual" were never spoken or even considered, people may still have whispered about "confirmed bachelors" or unmarried women rumored to be "queer."

Not until the late 1960s and 1970s did a significant number of gays and lesbians in North Carolina find that "coming out" was an option available to them. In time, bolstered by the openness and activism of gay and lesbian communities in cities such as San Francisco and New York—scene of the 1969 Stonewall Riots, which are usually viewed as marking the beginning of the modern gay rights movement in America—southern homosexuals also began to make themselves known. This led to the most significant change in the history of gays and lesbians in the state—open discussion of the subject of homosexuality. One bibliography lists some 6,000 items about homosexuality published in North Carolina newspapers since 1995.

During the 1980s and 1990s, the state's gay and lesbian citizens demanded protection against discrimination in the workplace and elsewhere; insisted that their relationships have equal standing with heterosexual relationships in the areas of family law, taxation, and insurance benefits; and battled legally as well as vocally for other civil rights. While the AIDS epidemic, which first came to light in the state and nation in the 1980s, had a significant impact on North Carolina's public health during this period, the effects of the disease for the state's gay community were particularly profound. While newfound attention has given the average citizen a greater awareness of the presence of gays and lesbians, it has not necessarily led to increased tolerance. Southerners, in general, have been slower than most Americans to accept open homosexuality, and North Carolinians have not deviated from that pattern.

Nevertheless, gays and lesbians in North Carolina continue to press for social acceptance and for civil rights. One key focus is the area of statutory law, where they have sought legal recognition of same-sex unions. Other efforts have focused on modifying the state's laws against consensual sodomy, in light of the U.S. Supreme Court decision in *Lawrence v. Texas* (2003) making such laws unconstitutional, and on passing anti–hate crime legislation that would criminalize violence targeted against victims due to their sexual orientation. A variety of judicial challenges to local and state codes have also been mounted where gay rights advocates view them as discriminatory. Overall, however, the legislative and judicial climate in North Carolina has remained unfavorable for these efforts.

Despite legal obstacles and persistent social and religious opposition, thriving communities of gay and lesbian people now exist in the state's largest cities and many smaller towns. Although relatively few openly gay or lesbian candidates have won political office, in 1995 Michael R. Nelson became North Carolina's first openly gay mayor, when he won election in

Marchers in the North Carolina Lesbian and Gay Pride Parade, Durham, 1986. NCC.

Carrboro. Some businesses and institutions, as well as some of the state's cities and counties, give partners in same-sex unions benefits if they are applied for, but there is no uniformity about conferring such benefits. Same-sex unions may be performed in the Duke Chapel and at Wake Forest University's Wait Chapel for persons connected with those universities, and some of the state's Protestant denominations have also allowed same-sex commitment ceremonies to be held in their churches, following a nationwide trend. While churches have generally refused to ordain openly gay clergy, in the fall of 2000 the new Wake Forest Divinity School in Winston-Salem began to admit homosexuals.

Almost any public announcement about the activities of gays and lesbians generates correspondence on the editorial pages of North Carolina's newspapers. In 2000, for example, a front-page article in the *Greensboro News and Record* about the adoption of twin Vietnamese boys by a homosexual couple led to a jousting match of correspondence in the paper. While one letter stated that "the Bible does condemn homosexuality," a response suggested that "love makes a family [and] families come in all configurations." As such debates suggest, while North Carolinians have begun to speak openly and often about homosexuality, any full reconciliation of opinions will not come easily.

References: Edward Flud Burrows, *Flud: One Southerner's Story* (1989); John Howard, ed., *Carryin' on in the Lesbian and Gay South* (1997); Howard, *Men Like That: A Southern Queer History* (1999); James T. Sears, *Lonely Hunters: An Oral History of Gay and Lesbian Southern Life, 1948–1968* (1997).

Alexander R. Stoesen

Genealogy, the study of family origins and descent, has interested North Carolinians for centuries. Colonial printer James Davis of New Bern printed genealogical information regarding his family, and in the nineteenth century, the historical publications of John H. Wheeler and Samuel A. Ashe contained a great deal of genealogical information. J. R. B. Hathaway of Edenton published the *North Carolina Historical and Genealogical Register* for several years around the beginning of the twentieth century. Several national lineage societies have created chapters in North Carolina, with an emphasis on researching and proving family lines as a basis for membership. These societies have helped raise interest in genealogy even further.

In the early twentieth century, North Carolina secretary of state J. Bryan Grimes published *An Abstract of North Carolina Wills* (1910) and *North Carolina Wills and Inventories* (1912). In 1968 Frederick A. Olds compiled another abstract that supplemented Grimes's works. The twentieth century saw an explosive growth in the genealogical field as more people realized the importance of family research. The building of a new

North Carolina Archives helped to provide better facilities for researchers and genealogists. Manuscript departments at many of the universities and colleges in North Carolina also contain a wealth of genealogical information, and public libraries have expanded their holdings as more genealogical materials have become available. The availability of computers, CD-ROMS, published indexes, the Internet, e-mail, and other recent technological developments have all contributed to the growth of interest in genealogy by making resources more readily available to researchers. The North Carolina Genealogical Society, founded in 1974, and local societies are also important resources for genealogists.

Reference: Helen F. M. Leary, *North Carolina Research Genealogy and Local History* (2nd ed., 1996).

R. S. Spencer Jr.

General Assembly, the lawmaking body of North Carolina, evolved from the colonial legislature established under British rule. That legislature was a bicameral body, with a royal council appointed by the Crown acting as the Upper House and an elected Assembly known as the House of Commons serving as the Lower House. By the end of the colonial period, the Lower House, by controlling the treasury, had become the colony's strongest branch of government.

The North Carolina Constitution of 1776 continued the trend toward a strong legislature and a weak executive. It created a bicameral General Assembly, consisting of a Senate made up of one member from each county and a House of Commons with two members from each county and one from each of several designated towns. Initially only property owners were eligible to serve—House members had to own at least 100 acres and senators at least 300—and the lawmakers were not paid for their services. Early legislative sessions were short, often lasting only a day or two. The governor, who was to be chosen annually by the General Assembly, had no veto power and little control over patronage, nor could he convene, prorogue, or dissolve the Assembly.

Elections to the General Assembly were held annually until the Constitution of 1835, after which they were held every other year except for a brief period of annual elections during Reconstruction. Until the 1835 reforms, the members of the General Assembly were the only state officials elected by popular vote. African Americans were first elected to the Assembly during Reconstruction (1865–77). Henry E. Frye of Guilford County became the first black legislator in modern times when voters sent him to the North Carolina House of Representatives in 1969. After the Twentieth Amendment to the U.S. Constitution passed in 1920, Lillian Exum Clement of Buncombe County in 1921 became the first woman to serve in the North Carolina House of Representatives.

From time to time changes in the state constitution altered the powers and structure of the General Assembly. The sweeping reforms of 1835 provided for the popular election of governors for two-year terms. The 1868 constitution changed the name of the House of Commons to the House of Representatives and created the office of lieutenant governor. The lieutenant governor serves as president of the Senate, standing first in line of succession if the governor dies or becomes incapacitated.

Citizens in western North Carolina resented the early pattern of representation, which, because it was based on the number of counties rather than population, gave control of the General Assembly to the eastern counties. The problem was addressed in the Constitution of 1835, which allotted 50 members to the Senate and 120 to the House. (The number of members remained the same in 2006.) Senators were to be elected from districts based on population. House members were still elected from counties, with each county having at least one representative and the remaining seats parceled out among the more populous counties.

By the early 1960s, urban areas were grossly underrepresented in the General Assembly. In 1963, for instance, the 12 most populous counties had between them 36 House seats representing 1.7 million people, while the 12 least populous held 18 seats representing fewer than 85,000 people. Urban areas were similarly underrepresented by the Senate districts. Under pressure from federal courts, the 1966 General Assembly reapportioned the House and Senate districts. House members were elected from "county districts," which created districts of roughly equal population by combining less populous counties. Senate districts were also reorganized for a fairer distribution of population. Urban districts gained many seats in the legislature at the expense of rural areas.

The General Assembly met in several towns (including Halifax, Hillsborough, New Bern, Fayetteville, Smithfield, and Tarboro) until a permanent capital was established at Raleigh in time for the 1794–95 session. After the original 1796 capitol burned in 1831, the legislature held at least some of its sessions in the governor's "palace" until the current capitol was completed in 1840. By the 1950s the capitol could no longer provide adequate space for legislative sessions, committee meetings, and offices. In 1959 the General Assembly appropriated funds for a new building on Jones Street near the capitol. On 6 Feb. 1963 the lawmakers held their first session in the new Legislative Building. At this time members of both houses, no longer limited by a lack of space, began employing larger professional administrative staffs.

Legislative sessions generally began in November of odd years until 1875, when the opening day shifted to the first Wednesday after the first Monday in January after an election. From 1957 to 1967 sessions were convened in February, but since 1967 they have begun in January. A 1989 law specifies that the General Assembly convenes at noon on "the third

Wednesday after the second Monday in January after the election." From the eighteenth century until well into the twentieth, the "long" sessions held in odd years generally lasted from one to three months, depending on the amount of business pending. In recent years, sessions have lasted for six or seven months. The General Assembly now also holds a "short session" in even-numbered years to adjust the budget and deal with other necessary matters.

All lobbyists, and the "principals" that they represent, must register and maintain a strict record of the expenses and transactions related to their role. Lobbyist registration and regulation is controlled by the Department of the Secretary of State. In 2005 the fee to register as an official lobbyist in North Carolina was $200.

References: Elizabeth Balanoff, "Negro Legislators in the North Carolina General Assembly, July 1868–February 1872," *NCHR* 49 (January 1972); Henson P. Barnes, *Work in Progress: The North Carolina Legislature* (1993); John L. Cheney Jr., ed., *North Carolina Government, 1585–1979: A Narrative and Statistical History* (1981); Allen W. Trelease, "Fusion Legislatures of 1895 and 1897: A Roll-Call Analysis of the North Carolina House of Representatives," *NCHR* 57 (July 1980).

David A. Norris

General Court of North Carolina

General Court of North Carolina was formed as an outgrowth of a grant of powers by the English Crown to the Lords Proprietors of Carolina in 1663 and 1665. The Proprietors were charged by these charters to establish "justice unto courts, sessions, and form of judicature, and manners of procedure therein." In compliance, the Proprietors through their Fundamental Constitutions attempted to establish a system of manorial, precinct, and governmental courts to apply justice, but the lack of population, funding, and order in the early colony delayed implementation.

The General Court, composed of the governor and his deputies, was an extension of the council and operated in the 1600s as the primary law court as well as the high court of the colony. Minor cases from precinct and magistrate courts were carried over to this court, and important criminal and civil actions, including equity, were initiated here. In the 1680s the jurisdiction of the General Court was temporarily eclipsed by the appearance of an intermediary court, the Court of Albemarle, under the governor's direction. This newly appointed body absorbed much of the original prerogative of the General Court, leaving the high court as little more than a court of last appeal.

The General Court, despite its necessity, was unpopular because of the politics sometimes involved in the appointment of its chief justice and the clerkships they controlled. The court was not one of those reaffirmed by the new state of North Carolina in 1777, and the state delayed nearly three decades before finally accepting a supreme court of final jurisdiction.

References: Robert J. Cain, ed., *Records of the Executive Council, 1664–1734* (1984); Mattie Erma Edwards Parker, ed., *North Carolina Higher Court Records, 1670–1696* (1968); William S. Price Jr., ed., *Higher Court Records of North Carolina, 1701–1708* (1974).

Louis P. Towles

General Education Board

General Education Board (GEB) was a philanthropic organization endowed by the Rockefeller family and chartered in 1903 by the U.S. Congress for "the promotion of education in the United States of America, without distinction of race, sex or creed." During its 62-year existence (1902–64) the GEB appropriated more than $325 million, of which about 20 percent was earmarked for African American education. Because rural areas in North Carolina, as in other southern states, were generally without schools, the GEB designated much of its initial support to developing rural schools. It also funded training in agricultural economics and community development on the premise that the southern economy had to improve before educational development could occur.

From the mid-1920s until the Supreme Court's decision in *Brown v. Board of Education* (1954) outlawing segregation, the GEB was increasingly concerned about the weakness of black educational institutions and disenchanted with industrial education as the major tool for black development. This led to an increase in its grants to southern institutions of higher education, its efforts to make southern governments less discriminatory toward blacks in their distribution of public funds, and its support of interracial conferences. The GEB did not directly attack black poverty, segregation, and political powerlessness—the root causes of the problems that plagued the southern black community. Instead, the board sought to aid blacks primarily by grants, fellowships, and programs designed to create a strong, separate black community.

Many GEB grants were given to Duke University, the University of North Carolina at Chapel Hill, North Carolina State University, and Wake Forest University, among others. For instance, the libraries of UNC, Duke, and N.C. State participated in an unusual cooperative enterprise directed by Nathan Carter Newbold, longtime director of the Department of Public Instruction's Division of Negro Education in North Carolina. In 1935 the libraries began, with a GEB grant, to build collections of books by and about African Americans to support study in that field. Over the course of several years, each library added to its collection, with the result that a total of 12,000 volumes was assembled.

References: Ron Chernow, *Titan: The Life of John D. Rockefeller Sr.* (1997); Louis Round Wilson, *Louis Round Wilson's Historical Sketches* (1976).

Wiley J. Williams

Gentry

Gentry, also known as the "planter class," is a term associated with colonial and antebellum North Carolina and other southern states that refers to an upper middle class of wealthy gentlemen farmers who were well educated, politically astute, and generally came from successful families. The gentry in North Carolina were also primarily Anglican in belief and social mores. They owned and ran plantations or large farms, owning slaves, controlling the contracts of indentured servants, and renting land to tenant farmers. Ultimately, the gentry had the responsibilities of patriarchs, with the lives of many relying on their decisions and planning.

In eighteenth-century North Carolina, rural characteristics generally kept the size of land holdings small, but each area had its significant families who built mansions, were well traveled, owned horses and carriages, and wore fine apparel. The women in these families did not labor or cook but closely supervised house and kitchen servants and set elegant tables. The plantations of the gentry were small, self-sufficient cities, where people from skilled artisans to unskilled field hands produced the goods needed for everyday living—from food (including meat, vegetables, and dairy products) to wool and cotton cloth.

Although small in number and reliant on an oppressive economic system based in great part on slavery, the gentry were vital to the economic and cultural growth of eastern North Carolina and the Piedmont. Members of the gentry developed a culture of their own, encouraging religious observances and meeting at least the most basic needs of those for whom they were responsible. They also maintained a strong commitment to local commerce and society, supporting the church, upholding the courts, and helping to keep order. Class lines were not as rigid among Americans as among the British; in the colonies it was possible to move into the gentry class through hard work or marriage.

Reference: Guion G. Johnson, *Ante-Bellum North Carolina: A Social History* (1937).

Joanne G. Carpenter

Geography of North Carolina encompasses distinct regions that are separated by dramatic differences in terrain, natural resources, and history. The Coastal Plain, which also includes the North Carolina Sandhills, is an area roughly comprising the eastern two-fifths of the state, stretching from the counties bordering the Atlantic Ocean to the fall line—a boundary dividing the rich but rock-filled land of the Piedmont from the coastline's sandy soil. The Piedmont, with its rolling hills and farmlands, is located in the central part of the state. The Mountain region, part of a larger area in the Appalachian Mountains called the Blue Ridge Range, contains the state's most rugged terrain. The Mountain region is located west of a line that zigzags through Surry, Wilkes, Caldwell, Burke, Rutherford, and Polk Counties.

The state varies in altitude from sea level along the Atlantic coastline in the east to 6,684 feet at the top of Mount Mitchell in Yancey County on the Tennessee border. Its total area as of 2004 was 52,669 square miles, with 48,843 square miles of land and 3,826 square miles of water. North Carolina's geographic center, as determined by the U.S. Geological Survey, is in Chatham County near the town of Gulf, about 10 miles northwest of Sanford.

The Cradle of North Carolina: Coastal Plain and Sandhills

Twenty or more counties lie in North Carolina's Coastal Plain, which is generally considered to be all of the state's land east of modern-day Interstate 95. Below the rapids of the Roanoke River at Roanoke Rapids and Weldon, and below Raleigh on the Neuse River and Fayetteville on the Cape Fear River, broad terraces nearly 200 miles wide in places drop into enormous stretches of river bottom, swamp, pocosins, and marsh. Bodies of water increase with proximity to the ocean, with greater sounds dominating the northern area and lesser ones in the southern portion. These sounds, the largest of which are the Albemarle Sound and the Pamlico Sound, separate the mainland easternmost Coastal Plain from the barrier islands, or Outer Banks, which include Currituck Banks, Core Banks, Shackleford Banks, Bogue Banks, and a succession of close-in barrier islands stretching down to the South Carolina state line.

Hunted, farmed, and fished by Native Americans for millennia, and settled with difficulty by English, Highland Scots, and other Europeans during the seventeenth and eighteenth centuries, the amazingly fecund Coastal Plain was characterized by daunting problems of transportation. Only two deepwater inlets served the vast coast, and the Coastal Plain presented those traveling by foot, horse, coach, or wagon with no shortage of swamps and sloughs, murky basins, and seemingly impenetrable pocosins. The very southeastern portion of the region early in colonial times supported a rice culture, and between the 1790s and the Civil War some portions of the upper Coastal Plain did see massive land-clearing, drainage, and corn and wheat plantations.

One of the Coastal Plain's chief natural assets was once a vast band of longleaf pine forest, almost all of which was tapped for rosin for tar, pitch, and turpentine by the early twentieth century. Coastal Plain waters offered fishermen considerable bounty, and the Albemarle Sound herring hauls of the nineteenth century were legendarily productive. Much of the Coastal Plain was opened up in the decades after the Civil War by the development of a network of steamship and railroad connections, allowing coastal fish, fowl, and market crops to be shipped quickly and efficiently to northern markets such as Baltimore, Philadelphia, and New York.

Peanuts and Irish potatoes remain important crops in the northern Coastal Plain, while blueberries, strawberries, watermelons, and sweet potatoes grow in the southern portion. Tobacco, though in decline, was still a significant eastern North Carolina crop in the early 2000s. Large livestock operations —involving both poultry and pork producers—have created both employment opportunities and environmental concerns across the region, as has large-scale commercial forestry. Vineyards are also on the rise in the modern era.

With larger cities such as Wilmington and Greenville as exceptions, the Coastal Plain is mainly a web of small towns and crossroads communities. Most of its counties fall under the jurisdiction of the state's Coastal Area Management Act (CAMA), passed in the early 1970s in an attempt to guide planning, manage expected population growth, and preserve and protect the area's rich and diverse natural resources. Numerous national wildlife refuges are in the Coastal Plain, including the Great Dismal Swamp; the Alligator River, Pocosin Lakes, Mattamuskeet, and Swan Quarter National Wildlife Reserves; and the Croatan National Forest.

Against this abiding natural wealth, and owing in part to the decline of small-farm agriculture, many of the Coastal Plain's counties, particularly those in the central and northeastern area, have long been numbered among the poorest in the South and have been further hampered by racial disunity. Significant efforts are also being made—particularly since the floods of Hurricane Floyd in 1999 devastated large sections of the Coastal Plain—to remedy the region's chronic underemployment and impoverishment, with such agencies as the Golden LEAF Foundation, the Rural Prosperity Task Force, and the Fund for a New East taking the lead.

The Sandhills region in the southwest corner of North Carolina's Coastal Plain includes parts of Cumberland, Harnett, Hoke, Lee, Montgomery, Moore, Richmond, and Scotland Counties. The state's peach-growing industry is concentrated in the Sandhills, and cotton and tobacco are also important crops. The region is one of fairly small cities and towns, with Fayetteville in Cumberland County being by far the largest. Each county in the Sandhills contributes to the diverse overall economy of the region. Cumberland County, the home of Fort Bragg and Pope Air Force Base, is also a center for printing and publishing, lumber and wood products, and apparel and textile products from fibers. Lee County, known as the "Brick Capital of America," also manufactures clay and pottery products and fabricated metal products (excluding machinery and transportation equipment). Moore County is famous as a resort and golf destination, centered at Southern Pines, Pinehurst, and the adjoining cities of Aberdeen and Pine Bluff.

Attractions and events in the Sandhills include several museums at or near Fort Bragg, such as the John F. Kennedy Special Warfare Museum and the Airborne and Special Operations Museum, which opened in August 2000. The National Railroad Museum and Hall of Fame is in Hamlet, a railroad town for more than a century. The Weymouth Woods Sandhills Nature Preserve near Southern Pines has more than 600 acres of natural area, hiking trails, and fields of wildflowers, as well as a nature museum to aid visitors in interpreting the flora and fauna of the region.

The Piedmont Region: Economic Center of the State

Rising from the edge of the Coastal Plain just east of Raleigh, the Piedmont, which means "foothills," stretches west some 200 miles to the face of the Blue Ridge Mountains. Piedmont terrain is usually gently rolling, varying from 500 to 1,500 feet in elevation, although there are ancient eroded mountain ranges—the Uwharries, the South Mountains, and the Sauratowns—that are scattered across the region and that rise to elevations of over 2,500 feet.

Originally known as the "backcountry" by early European settlers, the Piedmont was opened to settlement during the mid-eighteenth century primarily by immigrants coming south on the Great Wagon Road from Pennsylvania and Virginia. Chiefly Scotch-Irish and Germans, these new settlers poured into the region by the tens of thousands prior to the American Revolution, acquiring small farms, founding villages, and bringing to the colony a diversity of ethnic backgrounds and religions. Craft and industrial centers such as the Moravian town of Salem developed in the colonial era.

In the nineteenth century, the inexpensive and efficient transportation provided by the North Carolina Railroad, which ran from Goldsboro to Charlotte, brought rapid industrial development to the region that would become known as the Piedmont Urban Crescent. Also located along the rail line were textile, tobacco, and furniture operations, the state's historically dominant industries that became the foundation of the state's economy. By 1900 company-owned mill villages, situated near textile mills and housing families of mill workers, had become commonplace throughout the Piedmont. As the economy of the state changed and many mills closed later in the century, these mill villages were often abandoned, although some towns, such as Kannapolis (Cabarrus County), have survived.

With the exception of the great river systems of the Yadkin, the Catawba, the Neuse, the Cape Fear, and the Roanoke, the narrow, shallow, rocky streams and smaller rivers of the Piedmont provided ideal conduits to be harnessed for water power for grist mills, textile mills, and electricity. Today, hydroelectric and steam generating plants dot the Piedmont landscape, creating great impoundments at Lake Gaston and Kerr Reservoir on the Roanoke River, Jordan Lake on the Haw River, Lake Hickory and Lake Norman on the Catawba River, and Badin Lake and High Rock Lake on the Yadkin River.

The Piedmont consists of 42 counties containing over 22,000 square miles. As of the early 2000s, the majority of the state's population, wealth, and metropolitan business centers, including excellent educational institutions and research centers such as Research Triangle Park (RTP) in the Raleigh-Durham area and Charlotte's University Research Park, were in the Piedmont. Drawing on the resources of three of the state's universities (the University of North Carolina at Chapel Hill, Duke University, and North Carolina State University), RTP has attracted international high technology corporations and has fueled an economic and population boom in that area. Charlotte's development into a national banking and financial center has also stimulated unprecedented growth in the southern region of the Piedmont. North Carolina, particularly in the Piedmont, is rapidly evolving from a rural, small-town environment to an urban landscape, led by these metropolitan areas as well as the Triad of Winston-Salem, Greensboro, and High Point. Consequently, many towns on the outskirts of this growth—textile towns in counties in which manufacturing and other jobs have diminished—have been severely affected, both in economic terms and population.

Rugged Beauty and Age-Old Culture: The Mountain Region

Running roughly northeast to southwest, North Carolina's western Mountain region rises abruptly from the Piedmont plateau along the Blue Ridge escarpment on the east, ending with the Unaka Range on the western boundary, then taking a more gradual decline to the west into Tennessee. As the ancestral home of the Cherokee Indians, the Mountain region was the primary territory for the native people who first settled the rich but rugged mountain terrain. Today, the Eastern Band of the Cherokees live in the Qualla Boundary, a reservation established following the forced removal of the Cherokee to Oklahoma Indian Territory in 1838. At 63,000 acres, it is the largest reservation east of the Mississippi River.

In 1540 Hernando De Soto became the first European to visit North Carolina's Mountain region. In the eighteenth century, Daniel Boone traveled the area, hunting, trapping, and gathering ginseng for sale in northern markets. William Bartram, noted eighteenth-century botanist, explored the region as well. European settlement of the Mountain region began in earnest in the eighteenth century with the arrival of Scotch-Irish, English, and German settlers from Virginia and Piedmont North Carolina.

Geologically, eons of uplifting, folding, and erosion of the earth's surface have shaped the ancient mountains of western North Carolina to their present form. Prominent cross ranges extend between the Blue Ridge and Unaka Mountains, including the Pisgah, Balsam, and Black Mountains. The Pisgah Mountains run to the Tennessee line and include Mount Pisgah at 5,750 feet. The Balsams have an average elevation of 5,500 feet and include 15 summits above 6,000 feet. The Unaka Range also includes the Great Smoky Mountains. Strad-

dling the state line between North Carolina and Tennessee, the Smokies encompass more than 800 square miles of heavily wooded wilderness. The Great Smoky Mountains National Park, with 9 million visitors annually, is the most visited park in the national park system. The highest peak in the Smoky Mountains, Clingman's Dome, is 6,642 feet.

Some Mountain region rivers—among them the Hiwassee, the Little Tennessee, the French Broad, the Nolichucky, the Pigeon, the Elk, and the Watauga—rise west of the Eastern Continental Divide and ultimately drain into the Gulf of Mexico. The New River (not to be confused with the New River of eastern North Carolina) is regarded as the second-oldest river in the world, after the Nile in Egypt.

The Black Mountains, although the smallest mountain range in North Carolina, include the state's highest peaks. Extending a mere 15 miles in length in Yancey County, the Black Mountains boast 6 peaks that are among the 10 highest in the eastern United States, including Mount Mitchell, the highest point east of the Mississippi River at 6,684 feet. The name of the range comes from the thick, dark forests of balsam and fir trees that cover it.

The great variety of flora and fauna in the Black Mountains long inspired scientific interest in the region. Naturalist William Bartram, French botanists André Michaux and his son François, and Englishman John Fraser explored the area in the late eighteenth century. The elder Michaux collected over 2,500 species of plant life during a trip to the area in 1789. Their writings inspired further botanical exploration and collection throughout the antebellum period, most notably by eastern North Carolina naturalist Moses Ashley Curtis.

The range became a popular area of interest for tourists and scientists throughout the rest of the nineteenth century. Concern over the conservation of its forest resources resulted in the creation of Mount Mitchell State Park in 1915, North Carolina and the South's first state park. Mount Mitchell's peak was made more accessible to tourists at that time, when a logging railroad was opened to passengers; by the end of the 1910s it had become one of eastern America's most popular tourist attractions. A motor road completed in 1922 opened the peak to automobile traffic for the first time.

The completion of the Blue Ridge Parkway through the Black Mountains in 1950 dramatically increased the number of tourists to the Mountain region. A campaign in the 1970s by Asheville writer and environmentalist Michael Frome and Congressman Roy Taylor to create a national park in the Black Mountains met considerable resistance from Yancey County residents and was abandoned in 1979.

In addition to its vast forest assets, North Carolina's Mountain region is a major source of mineral resources. The Spruce Pine mining district is renowned around the world for its mineral production; today it is a source for ultrapure quartz used in computer applications. Forestry, mining, agriculture, and tourism provide income to many Mountain residents. Growing cities such as Asheville, Boone, and Hendersonville offer increasingly diverse opportunities for work, education, and cultural enrichment.

References: Ora Blackmun, *Western North Carolina: Its Mountains and Its People to 1880* (1977); David Cecelski, *A Historian's Coast: Adventures into the Tidewater Past* (2000); Chris Florance, *Up from Mount Misery: The Blossoming of North Carolina's Sandhills* (1990); Linda Flowers, *Throwed Away: Failures of Progress in Eastern North Carolina* (1990); Thomas W. Hanchett, *Sorting out the New South City: Race, Class, and Urban Development in Charlotte, 1875–1975* (1998); Douglas M. Orr Jr. and Alfred W. Stuart, eds., *The North Carolina Atlas: Portrait for a New Century* (2000); Timothy Silver, *Mount Mitchell and the Black Mountains: An Environmental History of the Highest Peaks in Eastern America* (2003); Bland Simpson, *Into the Sound Country: A Carolinian's Coastal Plain* (1997); Ina W. Van Noppen and John J. Van Noppen, *Western North Carolina since the Civil War* (1973).

Lindley S. Butler
Bland Simpson
Additional research provided by Stephen C. Compton and John C. Inscoe.

SEE ALSO Backcountry; Cape Fear; Fall Line; Great Dismal Swamp; Mount Mitchell; Outer Banks; Piedmont Urban Crescent.

Geological Survey. The North Carolina Geological Survey (NCGS), which researches all aspects of the state's geology and natural resources, was founded by University of North Carolina professor Denison Olmsted in 1822 under a $250 per year appropriation by the General Assembly. In 1825, on Olmsted's departure for Yale, Dr. Elisha Mitchell assumed the direction of the survey and completed the third volume of Olmsted's report. The legislature failed to fund the survey after 1825 due to an economic panic that gripped the state that year, and it was discontinued in 1828. The survey was revived in 1851 and led by Ebenezer Emmons until 1864.

Beginning in the early 1900s, the NCGS was enlarged in scope to become the Geological and Economic Survey, which geologist Joseph Hyde Pratt controlled until his departure for France in World War I. The survey headquarters, located in Chapel Hill, had become very active in the North Carolina Good Roads Association, and by 1918 both the survey and the association were administered by civic and political activist Harriet Morehead Berry. In 1923 Pratt was politically eliminated from the survey, and in 1925 it was renamed the Department of Conservation and Development.

The modern NCGS, under the administrative control of the Department of Environment and Natural Resources, has grown to encompass broader research goals, such as the creation of geologic and topographic maps, the gathering of mineral resource and geochemical information, and the establishment of environmental and earth science educational programs.

Robert E. Ireland

Geology. North Carolina's rich geologic history and composition are as dramatic as its topography. The collisions of numerous ancient landmasses resulted in majestic mountains, with their blend of diverse rock types, and the state's expansive coast was formed from the eroded sedimentary remnants of those same peaks. Beneath these impressive features lies an immense wealth of mineral resources deposited by regular geologic activity over hundreds of millions of years.

North Carolina's long and often turbulent geologic history reveals the effects of both plate tectonics and weather. The earth's crust is essentially a crude patchwork of continually shifting plates that collide with one another as new crust is generated. On a regional level, these violent collisions have resulted in orogenies, sites where the crust has been pushed upward to form mountain chains (the Appalachians were formed by three such orogenies that raised their height to nearly 30,000 feet). Geologic evidence suggests that parts of North Carolina—including the oldest known rocks in the state (1.8 billion years old), located in the western Blue Ridge Mountains—were once at the boundaries of plates, although the creation of new crust in the Atlantic Ocean has moved the state's position to the middle of the North American plate.

This system of plate tectonics is further transformed by weather. Exposure to the elements has, over time, worn down much of the once-mighty Appalachians. Rain and melting snow carried the eroded rocks and soil downhill to streams and rivers; these waterways then transported the materials to the coastal plain, where they accumulated and formed the state's extensive beaches and barrier islands.

Modern-day North Carolina is typically divided into three geologic regions with distinct properties. The narrow mountain region in the west is dominated by the Blue Ridge Mountains, part of North America's eastern Appalachian chain. The region's assorted sedimentary, volcanic, igneous, and metamorphic rocks—often dating to widely different eras—are a testament to the periodic disturbances that gave rise to the mountains. Although rains and rivers have taken their toll on the Appalachians, in North Carolina this range includes no fewer than 43 peaks with heights above 6,000 feet; Mount Mitchell, at 6,684 feet, is the highest point in the country east of South Dakota's Black Hills. Among the Blue Ridge Mountains are deposits of feldspar, mica, and other raw materials mined for industrial purposes.

The state's central geologic region, known as the Piedmont Plateau, runs from Alabama to New Jersey but is at its widest (150 miles) in North Carolina. This region, composed mainly of metamorphic and igneous rocks, has been greatly worn down over time, although some isolated outcroppings called monadnocks (including Pilot Mountain and the Uwharries) have withstood erosion. The Carolina Slate Belt reveals evidence of ancient volcanic activity. Gneiss, schist, lithium, clay, sand, gravel, and building stone can be found throughout the piedmont, and gold was once mined there in abundance. The region's hard rock meets the soft sediment of its eastern neighbor at an area known as the "fall line," or "fall zone," which is the site of many rapids and waterfalls.

The coastal plain is North Carolina's largest geologic region, accounting for about 45 percent of the state. During the Mesozoic era, the coastal plain was a broad sloping region well above sea level. Its loose soil continually eroded from rains and streams flowing toward the ocean. During the Cenozoic era and occasionally the Mesozoic era, the ocean covered the lowland and then subsided repeatedly, creating terraces each time. In the modern coastal plain, rivers and streams deposit sediments and sedimentary rocks originating in the mountain region; the sediment becomes deeper and denser near the coast. The movement of rivers is also responsible for shaping the coastal plain's gradual downward slope toward sea level. The region is rich with sand (utilized in industries such as glass-making) and clay; limestone and phosphate (North Carolina's most important mineral resource) are also mined in quantities.

References: Fred Beyer, *North Carolina, the Years before Man: A Geologic History* (1991); J. Wright Horton Jr. and Victor A. Zullo, eds., *The Geology of the Carolinas: Carolina Geological Society Fiftieth Anniversary Volume* (1991); Mary-Russell Roberson and Kevin G. Stewart, *The Geologic Story of the Carolinas: A Field Guide* (2006); Jasper Leonidas Stuckey, *North Carolina: Its Geology and Mineral Resources* (1965).

Robert Blair Vocci
Lee Plummer Templeton

SEE ALSO Fall Line; Geological Survey; Granite; Mining; Slate Belt.

German Settlers first came to what is now North Carolina as part of the second expedition sent to the Roanoke area by Sir Walter Raleigh in the 1580s. The largest influx of German people to North Carolina, however, occurred in the eighteenth century, beginning with a joint effort between a Swiss land company and the British Crown to settle 100 families of German Palatines in the town of New Bern on the Neuse and Trent Rivers in 1710. The colony flourished and prospered for 18 months, but in 1711 the colony was virtually destroyed after suffering an attack by Tuscarora Indians.

Despite such setbacks, German settlers continued to come to North Carolina throughout the eighteenth century. As unoccupied land became harder to find in the populous Pennsylvania region where they had originally settled, many Germans migrated south and settled mainly in the backcountry, or modern-day Piedmont, of North Carolina, the first arriving in the colony by 1747. Because they were migrating from Pennsylvania and because their own word meaning German —"Deutsch"—was not translated very well by English settlers, the newcomers into North Carolina were sometimes termed the "Pennsylvania Dutch." There were four primary religious groups among these people: German Protestants, Lutherans, German Reformed, and Moravians. Because of language and cultural barriers, the Germans kept mainly to themselves, and many continued to speak German even into the mid-1800s.

Most of the Germans were farmers who settled near lakes and streams, where the land allowed them to produce successful crops as well as to keep livestock. Because the region was sparsely populated during that era, land was plentiful; farmers could take fresh land each year instead of refertilizing farmed land, a practice that increased the size of farms but also caused damage to forest lands. Most German families lived in traditional pioneer cabins built of logs and consisting of one large room with a smaller loft above. Later, as the colonists became more prosperous and better adjusted, these cabins were replaced with wooden and stone houses.

Some of North Carolina's German settlers, in particular the Moravians, held different views of society from most of their neighbors. According to meticulous records still preserved today, the Moravians arrived in 1753 to settle a piece of land—the Wachovia Tract in what is now Forsyth County—acquired from Earl Granville. All of the land was owned and controlled by the church for use by all residents. Land for homes, farms, and businesses was used by individuals but belonged to the community. The settlement was self-sufficient, and all residents and visitors were welcomed, served, and honored without respect to race or creed. Because their religion condemned the use of military force, the Moravians remained neutral during the Revolutionary War, paying rent to their British landlord Granville as well as taxes to the newly formed U.S. government.

Although the language barrier kept many German settlers relatively isolated from other settlers for their first few decades in North Carolina, the barrier eventually fell away and Germans actively joined the greater society. Until this breakthrough occurred, most Germans found careers in either the schools or churches of their community. Once the language barrier disappeared, however, they were able to find careers in all areas of society. People of German descent participated in the Civil War primarily as common soldiers. Though some Germans did own slaves, most worked their own land and felt removed from the slavery issue. Nonetheless, many Germans did fight and die in the nation's bloody conflict.

Although the German population eventually blended into a common North Carolina culture, German influences have had an important impact in the state that continues even today. The religious influences of Germans are notable, for example, and the Moravian village of Old Salem remains as a reflection of their impact. Education is another arena in which North Carolina's German settlers left their mark, establishing Catawba College in Newton in 1851, the Western Carolina Male Academy (which became North Carolina College) in 1852 in Mount Pleasant, and the Mont Amoena Female Seminary in Cabarrus County in 1859.

References: Carl Hammer Jr., *Rhinelanders on the Yadkin* (1965); Hugh T. Lefler and Albert Ray Newsome, *North Carolina: The History of a Southern State* (1963); William S. Powell, *North Carolina through Four Centuries* (1989).

Laura Young Baxley

SEE ALSO Swiss and Palatine Settlers.

Germanton Academy was established in 1810 as a private school in Germanton, the county seat of what was then Stokes County. (In 1849 the county was divided and the southern part became Forsyth County, with the town of Germanton split by the line.) Money for establishing the school was raised through the sale of lottery tickets. During its early years, the academy offered the standard course of study of that time: grammar, Latin, arithmetic, and geography. In 1890 the school was still functioning, and in 1906 it became more securely grounded when it received a state charter. Stock at five dollars per share was sold to raise $5,000 to erect a building on Salem Street in town. The headmaster was J. C. Brown, who afterward became superintendent of schools in Stokes County. However, in 1923 Germanton Academy closed when public schools replaced many private academies throughout North Carolina.

References: Charles L. Coon, *North Carolina Schools and Academies, 1790–1840* (1915); John R. Woodard Jr., *Heritage of Stokes County, North Carolina* (2 vols., 1982, 1990).

Ken Otterbourg

Gettysburg, Battle of. From the time the first Confederate troops crossed the Potomac River under Brig. Gen. Stephen D. Ramseur, a North Carolinian, until the death of Brig. Gen. James J. Pettigrew, a fellow North Carolinian, during the retreat, North Carolinians played many crucial roles in the Civil War's Gettysburg campaign of 1863. Following the Federal rout at Chancellorsville in May, Gen. Robert E. Lee moved his army north in June to strike the enemy in Maryland and Pennsylvania. He was convinced that southern success there would accelerate the growing peace movement in the North and allow his army to gather provisions in the rich agricultural regions of the two states. The resulting Battle of Gettysburg, during 1–3 July 1863, is widely acknowledged as the greatest land battle fought in North America. At Gettysburg, the Army of Northern Virginia under Lee numbered about 75,000 men, compared to the estimated 93,000 soldiers in Maj. Gen.

George C. Meade's Army of the Potomac. The battle ended with approximately 50,000 Union and Confederate soldiers killed, wounded, or missing.

After Lt. Gen. Thomas J. "Stonewall" Jackson's death at Chancellorsville, Lee reorganized his army into three corps, each containing approximately 20,000 men. Lt. Gens. James Longstreet commanded the First Corps, Richard S. Ewell the Second Corps, and A. P. Hill the Third Corps. Although North Carolinians could be found in all three corps, they were especially prevalent in the commands of Ewell and Hill. The Battle of Gettysburg opened early on the morning of 1 July, when Confederate soldiers from Hill's Corps encountered dismounted Union cavalry outside the town under Brig. Gen. John Buford. After an initial Confederate repulse, the battle resumed with troops from Hill's Corps attacking from the west and Ewell's men from the north. The combined force cracked the Federal line, and Union troops fled in disorder through the streets of Gettysburg. Many of the first day's casualties were North Carolinians, as 7 of the 16 Confederate brigades engaged were from the state. In McPherson's Woods, Col. Henry K. Burgwyn Jr.'s 26th North Carolina Regiment alone lost almost 600 out of 800 officers and men—including Burgwyn, who was killed. Nearby, around 800 North Carolinians out of approximately 1,500 in Brig. Gen. Alfred Iverson's Brigade fell while attacking Union troops behind a stone fence. Although Lee's men pushed the Federals out of Gettysburg, at the end of the day the Union army remained in control of the high ground south of town.

On the morning of 2 July Lee's battle plan called for a strike against the Union left by Gen. Lafayette McLaws's and Maj. Gen. John Bell Hood's Divisions from Longstreet's Corps, with support from Gen. R. H. Anderson's Division of Hill's Corps. In addition, Ewell was ordered to support Longstreet's attack by assaulting the Union right on Culp's Hill and Cemetery Hill. After an exhaustive flanking movement, Longstreet opened the attack with an artillery barrage and then an infantry assault that achieved initial success before being repulsed. Ewell responded with his artillery when he heard Longstreet's guns, and late in the afternoon, he sent troops forward to capture Culp's Hill and Cemetery Hill. North Carolinians in Maj. Gen. Robert F. Hoke's Brigade under Col. Isaac E. Avery charged up East Cemetery Hill in twilight until they were compelled to withdraw due to a lack of support. Other North Carolinians met a similar fate on Culp's Hill. North Carolina's futile efforts that day may best be reflected in the note the dying Avery scribbled at the base of East Cemetery Hill: "Tell my father I died with my face to the enemy." Despite some Confederate successes, 2 July ended with Meade's forces still occupying the high ground south of Gettysburg.

Believing that Meade had weakened his center to meet the attacks on the Federal left and right on 2 July, Lee was determined to strike again the next day. He ordered Longstreet to execute a frontal attack against the Union center on Cemetery Ridge, using Maj. Gen. George E. Pickett's Division from Longstreet's Corps and two divisions from Hill's Corps. Due to wounds suffered by Maj. Gens. Henry Heth and William Dorsey Pender, their divisions were placed under the temporary command of Brig. Gens. Pettigrew and Isaac R. Trimble, respectively. After an extensive artillery bombardment of the Union center, approximately 12,000 Confederate soldiers exited the woods on Seminary Ridge and began the long march toward Cemetery Ridge. Of the 42 southern regiments taking part in the assault, 15 were from North Carolina. The Confederate infantry was in the open, and Union artillery and small arms fire swept their ranks. Braving the devastating blasts of musketry at close range, North Carolinians made the deepest penetration into the Union center, but the survivors had to fall back to the safety of Seminary Ridge. Thenceforth, the phrase "farthest to the front at Gettysburg" became part of North Carolina's proud military heritage.

The battle was a staggering defeat for the Army of Northern Virginia. Lee lost thousands of veteran officers and soldiers whom he could not replace. Indeed, the Gettysburg disaster and the fall of Vicksburg on 4 July were devastating blows to the Confederacy. One-fourth of the Confederate casualties at Gettysburg were North Carolinians, and the state lost more soldiers in the battle than any other southern state. North Carolina's final casualty came with the death of General Pettigrew during the retreat. A few days after the battle, a Richmond newspaper erroneously reported that the great charge had failed because "raw troops" from North Carolina did not support Pickett's Virginians. This story was treated as fact in many postwar accounts of the battle, and only in recent years has North Carolina received due credit for its prominent role in the Battle of Gettysburg.

References: Earl J. Hess, *Pickett's Charge: The Last Attack at Gettysburg* (2001); Harry W. Pfanz, *Gettysburg: Culp's Hill and Cemetery Hill* (1993); Pfanz, *Gettysburg: The First Day* (2001); Pfanz, *Gettysburg: The Second Day* (1987); Jeffry D. Wert, *Gettysburg: Day Three* (2001).

Tom Belton

Gettysburg Monument. The monument to North Carolina soldiers who fought and died at the Battle of Gettysburg (1–3 July 1863) during the Civil War was created by Gutzon Borglum of San Antonio, Tex., at a cost of $50,000. The sculpture was unveiled on the battlefield on 3 July 1929. Sculpted in bronze on a base of North Carolina Balfour pink granite, the monument includes five images of charging Confederates and stands 12 feet in height. It is situated on West Confederate Avenue, where the North Carolinians emerged from the trees to join Pickett's Charge on 3 July. At the end of a flagstone walk from the avenue to the monument are two inscribed Bal-

The North Carolina Memorial on the Gettysburg battlefield. Photograph by Jerry Cotten. NCC.

four pink granite markers provided by the North Carolina Division of the United Daughters of the Confederacy. The main inscription on the larger monolith praises North Carolinians who fought at Gettysburg. The smaller tablet lists the North Carolina regiments that were there. Governor O. Max Gardner presided over the unveiling ceremony, while former governor Angus W. McLean, who just two years earlier had asked the legislature for the funds to build the monument, made the principal address to a crowd of several hundred.

References: "North Carolina at Gettysburg," *Confederate Veteran* 37 (August 1929); "North Carolina Memorial at Gettysburg," *Greensboro News*, 4 July 1929; Mrs. S. L. Smith, comp., *North Carolina's Confederate Monuments and Memorials* (1941); Ralph W. Widener Jr., *Confederate Monuments: Enduring Symbols of the South and the War Between the States* (1982).

Richard B. McCaslin

Ghosts. The literature and lore of North Carolina are filled with stories of haunted islands, houses, churches, mines, trains, bridges, swamps, and mountains. The very shore itself seems from earliest settlement to have been awash with spirits. The ghost deer of Roanoke is a story that mixes early settlement and Native American lore. In this tale, the infant Virginia Dare does not disappear with the famous Lost Colony, but grows to womanhood among the Indians and is then transformed by an old witch doctor, jealous of the warrior Okisko, who loves her, into a white doe. When Okisko hunts the white doe and shoots her with a charmed arrow to her heart, the doe turns back into Virginia Dare for a moment but then dies. Ever since, a white doe is said to roam Roanoke as a ghost.

Since the Outer Banks are well known as the "Graveyard of the Atlantic," it is only fitting that a notorious, long-dead pirate haunts the coastal region. Teach's Light, a ghost light in the Pamlico Sound area, was said by novelist Nell Wise Wechter to be the spirit of the pirate Edward Teach, more famously known as Blackbeard. Blackbeard died at the naval Battle of Ocracoke (1718) from multiple gunshot and stab wounds, after which he was beheaded, his head put upon a bowsprit, and his skull ultimately turned into a drinking mug. A ship believed to be Blackbeard's *Queen Anne's Revenge* was discovered near Beaufort Inlet in 1996, and the clamor between coastal towns over the sunken wreck's artifacts illustrated the haunting hold the old brigand still has upon North Carolina imaginations and dreams.

Diamond Shoals off Cape Hatteras provide the setting for the legend of the "Ghost Ship of Diamond Shoals." The five-masted schooner *Carroll A. Deering* fetched up one winter night in 1921 with all sails set, food on the galley table, no crew aboard, and none ever found. Mountain ghost stories include the Cherokee tale of a mysterious sheet-like ghost on a nighttime trail in Edna Chekelelee's "Santeetlah Ghost Story." A case could even be made that the state's highest mountain, Mount Mitchell, is also haunted, since the discoverer and champion of its primacy, University of North Carolina professor Elisha Mitchell, fell from a precipice to his death in those hills and is buried atop the great peak.

Other famous and long-lived North Carolina ghostly legends include the Maco Light, the Brown Mountain Lights, the Devil's Horse's Hoof Prints, and the Devil's Tramping Ground. North Carolinians take spirit matters seriously enough that ghosts have entered their colorful comparative vernacular. People particularly unpleasant or hideous by nature are capable of making "a ha'nt hug a thornbush," and others are frightening enough to "to haunt a nine-room house." The only thing worse is the person or ghostly being that can "haunt a nine-room house from *across the street*." Also in the North Carolina voice, albeit on a more literary plane, is the spectral apostrophe in the prefatory lyric of Thomas Wolfe's *Look Homeward, Angel*, a ringing line that forever beseeches a haunting: "O lost, and by the wind grieved, ghost, come back again."

References: John Harden, *Tar Heel Ghosts* (1954); Nancy Roberts, *Ghosts from the Coast* (2001); Roberts, *North Carolina Ghosts and Legends* (1991).

Bland Simpson

SEE ALSO Brown Mountain Lights; Devil's Horse's Hoof Prints; Devil's Tramping Ground; Maco Light; Pirates; White Doe, Legend of.

Gibbs's Rebellion in July 1690 was one of several rebellions and attempted coups in North Carolina's turbulent political environment during the Proprietary period. It occurred at the time of King William's War, which was primarily a duel between France and the New England colonies for control of the Upper Hudson River Valley, St. Lawrence River Valley, and Hudson Bay. With the French presence in North America primarily concentrated in Canada and the New England area, North Carolina and the Lower South were spared the ravages of this war. The only serious conflict to affect North Carolina at this time was Gibbs's Rebellion.

Under the Fundamental Constitutions, a governance system established in 1669, the Lords Proprietors created the only American colonial nobility. Using the titles of palatines, landgraves, and caciques, the document allowed a noble to assume the governorship of the colony if neither a governor nor a Proprietor was in residence.

When Governor Seth Sothel was deposed in 1689, Capt. John Gibbs of Pasquotank Precinct, who was related to the late duke of Albemarle and had been a cacique since 1682, claimed the governorship and was accepted. He held at least one Assembly during his tenure. In December 1689 the Lords Proprietors commissioned Col. Philip Ludwell of Virginia as governor of northern Carolina. On Ludwell's arrival in the late spring of 1690, Gibbs challenged his authority and vowed to fight to the death. Having gathered 80 armed supporters, Gibbs descended on a precinct court on 6 July, declared it unauthorized, closed the proceedings, and arrested two magistrates. Ludwell appealed for help to the governor of Virginia, who advised Ludwell and Gibbs to lay their claims before the Proprietors in England. The rebellion was over as soon as the Proprietors chose to support Ludwell. Gibbs apparently did not return to the colony.

References: Mattie Erma Edwards Parker, ed., *North Carolina Higher Court Records, 1670–1696* (1968); William S. Powell, *North Carolina through Four Centuries* (1989).

Lindley S. Butler
Additional research provided by Patrick Morton.

Gideon's Band was the name of a secret political order that purportedly operated in North Carolina between 1892 and 1894. The group, which was said to have only a few hundred adherents, was believed to be headed by S. Otho Wilson, a Wake County member of the Farmers' Alliance and Populist Party leader. There is some debate over whether Gideon's Band actually existed or whether it was simply a fabrication of the Democratic Party. Most of the persons who argued that the organization was real were strong Democrats, including Furnifold M. Simmons, chairman of the Democratic Executive Committee; Samuel A. Ashe, editor of the *Raleigh News and Observer*; and Josephus Daniels, soon-to-be editor of the *News and Observer*. In the final analysis, no evidence of the group's actual operation has ever been found. Nonetheless, the persistent rumors about Gideon's Band did somewhat tarnish the image of the Populist Party, especially in the campaign of 1892.

Simmons, desperate to combat the expected defections to the Populists, obtained letters in October 1892 from persons proclaiming the existence of "an unlawful and dangerous political society" led by Wilson. Simmons intimated that the third-party movement, which had constituted such a mystery to loyal Democrats, was thus explained. Eventually three men gave testimony about the mysterious order. Ashe called for Wilson's prosecution under a state law that prohibited secret political societies. Solicitor Edward W. Pou prosecuted in early 1893. In March, on the advice of attorneys, Wilson pleaded no contest, which the Democrats interpreted as an admission of guilt. The disgruntled Populist attempted to have the plea withdrawn, but the judge would not allow a reversal. Wilson was widely ridiculed in the press over this affair.

References: Josephus Daniels, *Tar Heel Editor* (1939); Ronnie W. Faulkner, "Samuel A'Court Ashe: North Carolina Redeemer and Historian, 1840–1938" (Ph.D. diss., University of South Carolina, 1983); Lala Carr Steelman, *The North Carolina Farmers' Alliance: A Political History, 1887–1893* (1985).

Ronnie W. Faulkner

Gimghoul Castle in Chapel Hill is a large stone building constructed in the style of a medieval castle or fort, situated on Point Prospect (sometimes known as Piney Prospect) in Battle Park. It is the lodge and headquarters of the Order of

Gimghoul Castle. Photograph by the Wootten-Moulton Studio. NCC.

Gimghoul, a student society of secret and exclusive membership at the University of North Carolina. Founded in 1889 and initially occupying a lodge at the corner of Boundary and East Rosemary Streets, the Order of Gimghoul organized around the imaginative speculations of Wray Martin, a student who received his law degree in 1891. Strongly influenced by Sir Thomas Malory and other medieval chroniclers of the Arthurian legends, Martin enjoyed retiring at night to Point Prospect to write his private mythology. Martin created a "City of the Gimghoul," surrounded by a great, island-dotted sea and defended by a castle or fortress on the spot where he indulged in his reveries. The story of Peter Dromgoole inspired him to use the name "Gimghoul." Dromgoole, a student at the university in the 1830s, supposedly fought a duel on the same promontory over the affections of a girl named Fanny, leaving his own or his opponent's blood indelibly splattered on a rock at the site.

In 1915 the Order of Gimghoul began a complicated series of land transactions to acquire Point Prospect and its environs, employing a group of stonemasons from Valdese (descended from the medieval Waldensians of southern France and Italy) to build the castle. Completed in 1926, it retains its aura of mystery and romance while functioning as the social and fraternal center of the order.

References: Phillips Russell, *These Old Stone Walls* (1972); Louis Round Wilson, *Historical Sketches* (1976).

Jerry Leath Mills

Ginseng. American ginseng (*Panax quinquefolium*) grows wild in the deciduous forests of North Carolina's Appalachian Mountains as well as in the upper Piedmont. Often found on the north slopes of heavily shaded coves, distinctive whorls of five leaves, bright red berries, and yellow leaves in the fall make ginseng easily distinguishable from other plants. The mature root, growing up to eight inches long, looks much like a human figure, leading some to call the tuber "man-root." In North Carolina Mountain parlance, ginseng is sometimes called "sang," "seng," or "sangtone."

The native peoples of North America had long utilized the attributes of ginseng when colonists, the first being a Jesuit missionary priest named Joseph Lafitau in 1715, began to value the plant. Highly prized for its purported medicinal and aphrodisiac qualities, nearly 400 tons of ginseng were exported, mostly to Asia, from the United States in 1824. Even the famed fur trader Daniel Boone, whose family once resided in present-day Davie County, collected ginseng. The extraordinary value of ginseng is seen in an advertisement, dated 1 Apr. 1927, for roots and herbs by Statesville's Sig Wallace, who offered 1 to 10 cents per pound for other roots but the relatively phenomenal price of $10 a pound for wild, carefully collected ginseng.

As wild growths of ginseng are diminishing in quantity

throughout North America, attempts at cultivating the plant have been made. Because the North Carolina Mountains remain a significant source of wild ginseng for both domestic and foreign markets, the Plant Industry Division of the North Carolina Department of Agriculture and Consumer Services, working with the U.S. Fish and Wildlife Service, runs the Plant Conservation Program to regulate ginseng's trade within and export from the state. The trade in wild ginseng brings in over $3 million annually to the state; approximately 3,000 ginseng collectors, often Mountain folk who depend on the income to supplement a subsistence lifestyle, receive at least $200 to $300 per pound from the more than 40 permit-holding dealers, who mostly export to places such as Singapore and Hong Kong. As wild ginseng is a legally protected plant, considered by the state to be of "special concern," collection is prohibited during the summer growing season, and only roots at least five years old and with three prongs may be sold. Collection is prohibited in state and national parks.

Stephen C. Compton

Girl Scouts of the U.S.A. (GSUSA) was founded in 1912

in Savannah, Ga., by Juliette Gordon Low, who wanted to provide experiences for girls beyond the usual household confines of the times by arranging opportunities for them to serve their communities and participate in camping trips and other outdoor activities. It appears that the first Girl Scout troop in North Carolina was organized two years later, according to notes in a history of the Girl Scout Council of Coastal Carolina. It is not clear where it existed. Another very early troop was in Southern Pines in 1918; its main purpose, and that of others organized during this period, was to help with the World War I effort by rolling bandages and knitting. The movement spread quickly during the Great Depression of the 1930s since there was little money in the average home for recreation; communities throughout the state recognized that young girls were in need of some interest or activity.

Early Girl Scout troops were organized into many area councils based around urban centers. These small councils gradually merged, until Girl Scouts in the state's 100 counties became divided into eight administrative councils of volunteers and employed staff. From west to east, their names and headquarters are Pisgah Girl Scout Council (Asheville); Pioneer Girl Scout Council (Gastonia); Hornet's Nest Girl Scout Council (Charlotte); Catawba Valley Girl Scout Council (Hickory); Tar Heel Triad Girl Scout Council (Colfax); Pines of Carolina Girl Scout Council (Raleigh); Girl Scout Council of Coastal Carolina (Goldsboro); and Girl Scout Council of the Colonial Coast (Chesapeake, Va.), a council shared with southeastern Virginia counties. The councils maintain their own scenic campsites, each with unique features that allow for a great diversity of activities. The campsites are used for day camps, summertime resident camping sessions, and year-round weekend troop camping and adult training. Each council is governed by an elected board of directors of local adult volunteers, responsive to the membership through a system of elected delegates.

By the early 2000s, more than 50,000 girl scouts, served by thousands of volunteer group leaders, were registered in North Carolina. In each council, member troops are organized by age and grade: Daisy (kindergarten), Brownie (grades 1 to 3), Junior (grades 4 to 5/6), Cadette (grades 6/7 to 8/9), and Senior (grades 9/10 to 12). These levels are flexible to allow for differences among school districts and in girls' maturity, and "sister troop" activities facilitate and encourage advancement upward to the next level. Each level gives special recognition for girls' achievements, the highest recognition being the Girl Scout Gold Award, which can be earned at the Senior Girl Scout level. There are also Campus Girl Scout chapters registered at most North Carolina colleges and universities, where students can continue their involvement with community projects and with local Girl Scout troops.

Some of the troop and individual community service projects North Carolina Girl Scouts have initiated or participated in include making stuffed toys for hospitalized children, working on Habitat for Humanity homes, developing community greenways and parks, planning and constructing playgrounds at homeless shelters, implementing community literacy programs, and doing peer counseling and tutoring. The expanding scope of the Girl Scout program has kept pace with girls' increasing diversity of culture, interests, and needs while maintaining an emphasis on community service and outdoor enjoyment and appreciation. A wide variety of constructive and exciting explorations in the worlds of science, the arts, people, health, and the outdoors are included in the *Girl Scout Handbook* for each age level and in badge and patch activity books. Other publications on arts and crafts, ceremonies, songs and games, physical and emotional development, the sciences, and other areas of interest to today's girls are used; a regular revision cycle keeps these works relevant and appealing.

Volunteer leaders share ideas and lists of local resources at monthly or bimonthly meetings, which are held to plan events and to give leader support. The required Leader Basic Training courses are offered throughout the year, as are optional enrichment opportunities. Whether held at university centers or well-appointed Girl Scout campgrounds, these sessions are always well attended.

Prominent North Carolina women who have been Girl Scouts include Elizabeth Hanford Dole (U.S. senator and past president of the American Red Cross); Maya Angelou (poet, writer, dramatist, and Reynolds Professor of American Studies at Wake Forest University); Gloria Randle Scott (president of Bennett College and past Girl Scout National President); Sandra Thomas (president of Converse College and past vice president of Meredith College); Debra W. Stewart (vice chancellor and dean of graduate studies at North Carolina State University); Elaine F. Marshall (secretary of state of North Carolina); Betsy Justus (executive director of the North Carolina Electronics and Information Technology Association); Gwendolyn C. Chunn (director of the North Carolina Division of Youth Services); and Renee McCoy (TV news anchor).

Grace R. Brashear

Glass House, formerly located on the west side of the old Raleigh & Gaston (later Seaboard Line) Railroad near the town of Kittrell in Vance County, was the popular name of the first winter resort in North Carolina. Not to be confused with the Kittrell Springs Hotel located about one-quarter of a mile away (probably the first summer resort in North Carolina), the Glass House stood outside the perimeter of the springs and retained a distinctively separate history.

Washington Franklin Davis bought the old Collins Hotel in 1870 and began a massive rehabilitation. When completed a year later, the structure stood two stories high and accommodated 100 guests. Glassed-in porches on the east and south sides of both stories displayed potted plants and hanging baskets, giving the building a unique showcase appearance. Officially named the Davis Hotel, the building soon acquired the nickname "Glass House." Originally from Boston, Davis maintained his New England ties by buying supplies and equipment exclusively from northern merchants. His amiable personality, charitable nature, and outgoing manner earned him community respect and the affectionate title "Yankee" Davis.

While the Kittrell Springs Hotel catered almost exclusively to southerners, the Glass House served as a haven for northerners. Hunters brought servants, horses, and dogs, the boarding of which generated additional revenue for the hotel. The sportsmen returned home with stories of the sun-washed openness of Davis's unusual hotel, as well as the picturesque setting, salubrious climate, and abundant pine trees that allegedly gave curative value to the North Carolina air. The hotel also attracted tuberculosis sufferers seeking relief from cold northern winters. Although not strictly a tuberculosis sanitarium, the Glass House offered limited patient care, at one time employing seven French nurses. The large glass windows provided much needed sunlight, the porches afforded exercise areas, and hair mattresses allowed more comfortable sleeping.

The Glass House filled with hunters and tubercular patients annually from October to May. Indoor activities included dances, billiards, bowling, drama, card games, and a reading library, while guests enjoyed horseback riding, hunting, and walks in the sunshine outdoors. Music sometimes came from a traveling orchestra but most often from the talented fingers of Mrs. Joe Person on the piano.

In the early morning of 29 Apr. 1893, the Glass House caught fire and burned; all of its contents were destroyed, but fortunately there was no loss of life. The fire ended the hotel's 22 years of service during the "Golden Age" of spas, healing springs, and health resorts in North Carolina.

Reference: Samuel Thomas Peace, *"Zeb's Black Baby," Vance County, North Carolina: A Short History* (1956).

Jerry L. Cross

Glebes were plots of ground designated for the use of clergymen assigned to a parish in England or the British colonies in America before 1776. The glebe was considered a part of the cleric's stipend, and he could farm, rent out, or otherwise use the land for his maintenance. At a meeting of the vestry of St. Paul's Parish in Chowan County on 5 May 1708, it was agreed that 500 acres that had been purchased was a glebe. In 1762, however, the North Carolina Assembly directed that every parish should have a glebe, and it specified the buildings that each should contain. This law directed that except for normal use, the property should be maintained at public expense.

After the American Revolution, unoccupied glebe land attracted squatters and speculators and in some cases resulted in legal action to settle claims. Some churches, including St. Thomas Church in Bath, still hold title to ancient glebe property.

William S. Powell

Glencoe, named for a Scottish battle, in central Alamance County is the site of Glencoe Mill and Village, one of the best preserved mill communities in the state. Built between 1879 and 1880 by William and James Holt, sons of textile magnate Edwin M. Holt, the 95-acre complex was home to one of many prosperous textile mills in North Carolina. Glencoe Mill produced flannel, plaid, and other cotton cloth for almost 80 years. When the mill ceased production in 1954, the workers abandoned their company-owned homes in search of work.

The village sat virtually untouched for nearly three decades, a stark reminder of a once vibrant textile industry. The site was listed on the National Register of Historic Places in 1979. In 1997 Preservation North Carolina (PNC), an organization dedicated to preserving the state's historic structures, bought the 105-acre property, which had 32 remaining houses (some in very poor condition) and several mill buildings. PNC installed water and sewer lines, upgraded the roads within the property, and began selling the houses to buyers interested in restoring them and living in Glencoe. Several new houses also have been built in the style of the historic houses, and the mill buildings are undergoing renovation.

References: Julian Hughes, *Development of the Textile Industry in Alamance County: Evolution of Warp and Weft in Alamance* (1965);

The company store (left) and houses along a street in Glencoe, 1978. Courtesy of NCOA&H.

Preservation North Carolina, "A New Start for Glencoe Mill and Mill Village," *North Carolina Preservation* 2 (1997).

Sheila Bumgarner

Goals and Policies Board. In 1971 the General Assembly created the Council on State Goals and Policies to work with citizens "to identify the kind of future they want for themselves." In this long-range planning context, the council's task was to present the governor with goals and policy recommendations that would lead to the future that citizens desired. From 1975, when the council was given full board status, until the summer of 1977, the Goals and Policies Board was inactive. It was reactivated in July 1977 by Governor James B. Hunt, who desired the board to serve as his "chief citizen advisory body" in policy matters.

As its first step in the citizen participation process, the board conducted a "North Carolina Tomorrow" survey in the fall of 1977. More than 100,000 responses to a questionnaire of 15 items were received. Concurrent with this effort was a scientific telephone survey, administered by the National Testing Service of Durham, which consisted of a random sample of 1,400 people. About 7 percent of the respondents in this mass survey believed the top four problems in North Carolina to be jobs and the economy, education, welfare, and crime/law enforcement.

In 1980 the Goals and Policies Board issued a report titled "North Carolina Tomorrow: Year Three," which pointed out that the state had acted on about two-thirds of its 1979 recommendations that same year. A March 1987 report by the board called for a major economic initiative to prepare the state for the possible loss of tobacco as a vital income crop, to accelerate the development of additional or alternate crops, and to assist farmers in marketing those crops profitably.

In succeeding years, the Goals and Policies Board received considerably less attention by the citizens and state government officials. It was repealed by the legislature in 1995.

Wiley J. Williams

God's Acre is the name Moravian congregations give their church cemeteries. In this case, "acre" is from the Old High German word for "field"; "der Gottesacker," or God's Field, is where the physical body is planted and rests until it rises as a spiritual body. The area is divided into large squares with paths between them. All of the gravestones are recumbent, made of white marble, and measure 20" × 24" × 4" for adult graves. Their uniformity is symbolic of the Moravian belief that all people, no matter their position in life, are equal in the eyes of God.

The largest North Carolina God's Acre is in Winston-Salem, where members of the Salem Congregation are buried. It is about 40 acres in size and is located 100 yards north of Home Moravian Church and Salem Square. The first burial in Salem's God's Acre was that of John Birkhead on 7 June 1771. His grave can be found by entering under the center arch and looking to the right of the path in the second square. In the first square on the left of the center path is the grave of the first

Members of the Moravian congregation tend to the graves in God's Acre at Home Church in Old Salem, some of which date from the eighteenth century. Photograph by Billy E. Barnes, Chapel Hill.

female buried on this site, Eva Anna Berothin (Beroth), who died on 3 Sept. 1773. Graves are arranged in accordance with the eighteenth-century choir system, with men and boys separated from women and girls. Familial ties are not of concern; God's family, it is believed, includes everyone, making God's Acre one big family plot.

An extension on the eastern side of Salem's God's Acre was opened in 1970, and the second part of the Easter Dawn Service is now held there annually. It is customary for family members or young people of Home Church to clean the white gravestones on Good Friday or the day after (Great Sabbath) and place flowers on the graves in the old section. When the thousands of worshippers enter God's Acre just before the sun rises on Easter morning, the area has the appearance of a vast garden. This new section can be reached by automobile from the road beside Salem Academy and the Salem College Fine Arts Building.

All Moravian churches have a God's Acre near their church building if their grounds are large enough to accommodate one. This is not the case in most urban areas, such as the city of Winston-Salem. Consequently, all 13 Moravian churches that form Salem Congregation use the God's Acre at Home Church. By the early 2000s the cemetery contained more than

6,000 graves. Most God's Acres follow the pattern of the one in Salem, offering a place of quiet beauty and repose in the midst of a world of noise and confusion.

Anna Withers Bair

Go-Forward Program is associated with the election campaign and administration of Governor W. Kerr Scott (1949–53), who used the slogan "go forward" to characterize his platform and accomplishments. The phrase first appeared in his speeches and newspaper advertisements during the months prior to the Democratic primary on 29 May 1948, then more frequently during the runoff primary campaign against state treasurer Charles M. Johnson. In his inaugural address, Scott compared the state treasury surplus to a "deficit in public services" and proposed "to wipe out this deficit" with a 15-point "go-forward program" that included better roads, schools, public health services, rural telephones, and electricity.

In a December 1952 "Report to the People," Scott again used the phrase "go forward" to describe his administration. Among the most important accomplishments mentioned in this document and cited again by Scott when he left office in 1953 were the paving of nearly 15,000 miles of secondary roads, new school construction, a statewide public school health program, new hospital construction and expanded public health programs, new rural electric connections and more than 75,000 rural phone installations, and the completion of port terminal facilities at Morehead City and Wilmington that provided modern ports for ocean-borne commerce.

References: John William Coon, "Kerr Scott, the 'Go-Forward' Governor: His Origins, His Program, and the North Carolina General Assembly" (M.A. thesis, UNC-Chapel Hill, 1968); David Leroy Corbitt, ed., *Public Addresses, Letters, and Papers of William Kerr Scott, Governor of North Carolina, 1949–1953* (1957).

George W. Troxler

Gold Hill Mine is located in the center of a geologic zone known as the Gold Hill Mining District and within the North Carolina village of Gold Hill. The Gold Hill district, in the southeastern portion of Rowan County, contains what was once one of the most significant gold and copper mining facilities in the state. Although gold was first discovered in this district prior to 1824, most of the mines were found between 1842 and 1844 and worked until 1915. Important mines in the Gold Hill district included the Gold Hill Mine, Barnhardt Shaft, Miller Shaft, Honeycutt Mine, Troutman Mine, Union Copper Mine, and Barringer Mine.

Gold production from the Gold Hill Mine through 1915 is estimated at $1.65 million. The Randolph Shaft is one of the deepest in the South, reaching 820 feet. The largest vein in this mine was also the Randolph vein, which varied in width from 2 to 15 feet. The upper levels of the mine were reported to be extremely rich in gold, with samples ranging from ½ ounce to almost 19 ounces per ton in gold and less than 1 percent copper. During the last period of operation in 1914–15, 7,250 tons of ore was milled with a recovery of 3,877 ounces of gold, 6 ounces of silver, and 23,112 pounds of copper. All of this came from Gold Hill Mine's north vein.

References: Brent D. Glass, "King Midas and Old Rip: The Gold Hill Mining District of North Carolina" (Ph.D. diss., UNC-Chapel Hill, 1980); Francis Baker Laney, *The Gold Hill Mining District of North Carolina, North Carolina Geological and Economic Survey* (1910).

Joan E. Freeman

Gold Rush. The precious metal gold is found as grains and nuggets in stream bed deposits, in veins, and as mineralized zones in schists and slates of the middle and western counties of North Carolina. The first authenticated discovery of gold was in 1799 at the farm of John Reed in Cabarrus County; Reed Gold Mine, established in 1803, was said to have yielded $1 million worth of gold between 1804 and 1846 and later became a State Historic Site.

Reed's initial strike and other early finds were celebrated in

An engraving from *Harper's New Monthly Magazine* of August 1857 depicting miners descending the shaft at Gold Hill Mine. NCC.

print across the country and even in Europe, prompting a rush of placer miners eager to sift through North Carolina's stream beds for surface deposits of gold. Many farmers sold their mineral rights and sometimes their entire farms to speculators and entrepreneurs who were hoping to unearth large quantities of gold. In 1824 the first lode deposit was worked on Tobias Barringer's land in Stanly County. Many mines followed in its wake, including Union County's Smart Mine (operational from 1835 to 1911) and Howie Mine (1840 to 1942). In the 1830s and 1840s, the peak years of the North Carolina gold rush, the state was home to about 56 different mining operations, and boom towns were established to support the thriving industry and its 25,000-strong workforce.

North Carolina's gold belt counties—which also included Davidson, Guilford, McDowell, and Randolph—produced the nation's gold supply from 1803 to 1848, when California emerged as the industry leader. Until 1829, North Carolina was also the only state producing domestic gold for the nation's coinage, prompting the U.S. government to open a branch mint in Charlotte in 1835. Mining continued at intervals up to 1971, yielding a total output estimated at $25 million (the vast majority found before 1900). Traces of gold were discovered during excavations for the One First Union Center in downtown Charlotte in 1988 and beneath the NationsBank (Bank of America) Corporate Center in 1992.

References: Richard F. Knapp, "Golden Promise in the Piedmont: The Story of John Reed's Mine," *NCHR* 52 (January 1975); Dennis J. LaPoint, "The Gold Rush in North Carolina," *Geotimes* 44 (December 1999); Bruce Roberts, *The Carolina Gold Rush* (1971); Jasper Leonidas Stuckey and W. G. Steel, *Geology and Mineral Resources of North Carolina*, North Carolina Geological Survey Educational Series no. 3 (1953).

Jean H. Seaman
Additional research provided by Robert Blair Vocci.

SEE ALSO Gold Hill Mine; Portis Gold Mine; Reed Gold Mine.

Goldsboro Female College began in 1854 as Wayne Female College in Goldsboro. The institution started as an academy and made the transition to the public school system after the Civil War. The school's first location was the Borden Hotel. The college moved to a new four-story building on North William Street in 1857. During the Civil War classes were suspended, and the college served as a Confederate hospital until 1865, when Union general William T. Sherman occupied Goldsboro on his way to Raleigh. The building then became a Federal hospital that cared for the wounded from the Battle of Bentonville.

Classes resumed in the fall of 1868 under the new name of Goldsboro Female College, with the school rented alternately to the Methodist and Presbyterian Churches for management.

In 1874 the school became the Goldsboro High School for Boys and Girls, and in 1881 it was absorbed into the new State Public Graded School System. The building was torn down in 1927.

References: Mary Daniels Johnstone, *The Heritage of Wayne County, North Carolina* (1982); Charles S. Norwood and Bob Johnson, *History of Wayne County, North Carolina: A Collection of Historical Stories* (1979).

Rachel Hake
Charles B. Ellis

Golf. North Carolina's mild climate and varied landscape have helped make golf an extremely popular and profitable sport in North Carolina. Early forms of golf were played in colonial North Carolina, but the modern game dates from the 1890s. It was during that decade that a number of golf courses were constructed in the state, including the Asheville Country Club, Fayetteville's Highland Country Club, and the Hot Springs Country Club in Madison County. There is little doubt, however, that the most important golf course construction in the state took place in the Sandhills community of Pinehurst, where, beginning in 1895, James Walker Tufts, a retired Massachusetts businessman, created one of America's premier golfing resorts. Pinehurst's famous Number Two course is the best-known course in the state and is regarded as one of the world's finest. It and several other North Carolina courses were designed by Donald J. Ross, a native Scotsman who settled in Pinehurst around 1898.

Golf courses outside of Pinehurst that have received national acclaim include the Grandfather Mountain Golf Club in Linville, the Quail Hollow course in Charlotte, Tanglewood Golf Park in Clemmons, and Forest Oaks Country Club in Greensboro. Golf initially was an upper-class pastime, but this began to change after World War II, when leisure time and recreational opportunities expanded. President Dwight D. Eisenhower's highly publicized golf outings gave the sport a boost in the 1950s, as did the charisma of dynamic champion and Wake Forest graduate Arnold Palmer. The sport has become wildly popular with a broad cross section of the sporting public.

North Carolina has hosted many professional and amateur tournaments. The Greater Greensboro Open was first held in 1938, making it one of the oldest tournaments on the Professional Golfers Association (PGA) tour. Over the years Pinehurst, Charlotte, Durham, Asheville, Raleigh, Winston-Salem, and Wilmington have all hosted PGA tournaments. The North and South Amateur has been held at Pinehurst since 1900. Golf was one of the first sports in which women competed seriously, and women's tournaments have been held in the state since the turn of the century. Raleigh, High Point, Greensboro, and other cities have all hosted tournaments of the Ladies' Professional Golfers Association tour.

Payne Stewart reacts to his winning shot on the final hole of the 1999 U.S. Open Golf Championship at Pinehurst. *Raleigh News and Observer.*

(NCAA) titles. Haddock's program included such notable future PGA standouts as Curtis Strange and Lanny Wadkins. Duke University's Art Wall and Mike Souchak in the 1950s and the University of North Carolina's Davis Love III in the 1990s all have had considerable success on the PGA tour.

Beginning in the early 1990s, North Carolina underwent a golfing boom that pushed the number of courses in the state to well over the 400 mark. Many residential developments and resorts have been built around golf courses, and the sport has become a major source of tourist income.

References: William Price Fox, *Golfing in the Carolinas* (1990); O. B. Keeler, *Golf in North Carolina* (1938); Charlie Sifford with James Gullo, *Just Let Me Play: The Story of Charlie Sifford* (1992); Richard S. Tufts, *The Scottish Invasion, Being a Brief Review of American Golf in Relation to Pinehurst and the Sixty-second National Amateur* (1962).

Jim L. Sumner

SEE ALSO Country Clubs.

"Goodliest Soile under the Cope of Heaven" is the phrase used by Ralph Lane, leader of one of Sir Walter Raleigh's Roanoke voyages, to describe the coastal region of North Carolina. Lane penned the description in a letter to Richard Hakluyt the elder on 3 Sept. 1585. The oft-quoted phrase, which is sometimes rendered incorrectly as the "Goodliest lande under the cope of heaven," is revered by North Carolinians as a romantic and fitting expression of the natural beauty of the state.

Reference: David B. Quinn, ed., *The Roanoke Voyages, 1584–1590,* vol. 1 (repr., 1967).

William S. Powell

Good Roads Campaign to improve North Carolina's roads and highways was first launched in Asheville in 1899 by the Buncombe County Good Roads Association, ultimately leading to the state earning the nickname the "Good Roads State." In February 1902, after the U.S. Department of Agriculture's Bureau of Public Road Improvement had sponsored a "Good Roads Train" to provide demonstrations of road-building techniques to a number of communities, the North Carolina Good Roads Association (NCGRA) was founded in Raleigh. It was organized by Good Roads Association leaders on the local and county level, and by state geologist Joseph A. Holmes, who invited National Good Roads Association president W. H. Moore to preside over the initial meeting. The purpose of NCGRA was to promote the building and maintenance of the state's roads, which lagged far behind much of the nation's. P. H. Hanes of Winston-Salem was its first president, serving from 1902 to 1910.

As interest in good roads grew during the next decade, several thousand North Carolinians joined local Good Roads

Perhaps the most successful North Carolinian on the PGA tour has been Fayetteville native Raymond Floyd. His 62 professional victories include the 1986 U.S. Open, the 1976 Masters, and the 1969 and 1982 PGA titles. Badin's Johnny Palmer, Charlotte's Clayton Heafner, and Durham's Stewart "Skip" Alexander enjoyed success on the PGA tour in the 1940s and 1950s. More recent standouts include Chip Beck (Fayetteville), Joe Inman (Greensboro), and Scott Hoch (Raleigh). Charlotte native Charlie Sifford overcame years of racial prejudice to become the first African American to win on the PGA tour. Tarboro's Harvie Ward, High Point's Dale Morey, and Morganton's Billy Joe Patton were outstanding amateurs in the 1950s. Chapel Hill's Estelle Lawson Page was a standout amateur player in the 1930s and 1940s. Greensboro's Marge Burns succeeded her as North Carolina's top female amateur, and High Point's Kathy Johnston was a standout at UNC before becoming a professional in the early 1990s.

Most North Carolina colleges and many high schools have golf teams. Wake Forest University has been extremely successful in men's college golf. Besides being Arnold Palmer's alma mater, the school, under coach Jesse Haddock, won the 1974, 1975, and 1986 National Collegiate Athletic Association

Automobiles, thought to be part of a caravan organized to illustrate the need for better roads, pause at Hickory Nut Gap near Asheville, 1916. NCC.

Associations, urging their county governments and the state to finance highway improvements. In 1912 Locke Craig was elected as the state's first "Good Roads Governor," and in 1917 a State Highway Commission was established. Leading figures in the Good Roads movement included University of North Carolina geologist Col. Joseph Hyde Pratt; Lexington publisher Henry B. Varner, who served as NCGRA's second president (1910–18); and Harriet "Hattie" Morehead Berry, who was designated the "Mother of Good Roads" for her successful lobbying on the issue (in 1986 the State Department of Transportation named Orange County's 12-mile segment of Interstate Highway 40 the Harriet Morehead Berry Freeway).

Under the leadership of these individuals, and with the public interest generated by the automobile, the Good Roads campaign prospered. Between 1910 and 1920 Varner published *Southern Good Roads*, a periodical that served as NCGRA's unofficial organ. Presenting testimonials in support of road building, methods for sound road construction, and a variety of advertisements for road machinery, the magazine enjoyed considerable success as the Good Roads movement gained momentum.

By 1915 NCGRA was instrumental in creating the state's first Highway Commission, and by 1921 it had spearheaded a successful lobbying campaign for the General Assembly's passage of a $50 million road-building bond issue. These actions resulted in the modern state highway system.

References: Cecil K. Brown, *The State Highway System of North Carolina: Its Evolution and Present Status* (1931); Robert E. Ireland, *Entering the Auto Age: The Early Automobile in North Carolina, 1900–1930* (1990); Harry Wilson McKown Jr., "Roads and Reform: The Good Roads Movement in North Carolina, 1885–1921" (M.A. thesis, UNC-Chapel Hill, 1972).

Robert E. Ireland
Additional research provided by Wiley J. Williams.

Gospel Music, in both its African American and white traditions, is a very popular and influential musical form in North Carolina. The term "gospel" usually refers to a style of religious music performed by individual artists, quartets, or choirs rooted in late nineteenth-century urban spirituals, blues, and ragtime. Black gospel gained a significant following beginning in the 1930s. White gospel music, emerging in the 1870s and 1880s as a recognizable form, encompasses both formal church music used in regular Sunday services and other forms. In North Carolina, both black and white gospel is performed at church sings, at concerts, on radio and TV programs, and on records.

North Carolina has produced some of the nation's most successful artists in black gospel music. Shirley Caesar, known as the "First Lady of Gospel," was born in Durham in 1938. Her "rock gospel" sound, upbeat and rhythmic with large choral backups, helped propel gospel to the forefront of American music. Caesar won the first of nine Grammy Awards in 1972, received honors from the Gospel Music Association and the National Association for the Advancement of Colored People, and was inducted into the Gospel Music Hall of Fame. In 1999 she received a National Heritage Award from the National Endowment for the Arts. In the 1980s Caesar, an ordained minister, established the Mount Calvary Word of Faith Church, in Raleigh, where she continued to serve as pastor in the early 2000s.

At the end of the twentieth century, Yanceyville's Badgett Sisters ranked among the finest black traditional gospel groups in the country. The a cappella trio was formed by their father, Courtelyou Badgett. After his death in 1978, his three daughters—Celester, Connie, and Cleonia—continued to perform. The group is well known in North Carolina, particularly through performances at the Festival for the Eno in Durham. The sisters received national recognition through appearances in New York City's Carnegie Hall with the North Carolina Black Heritage Tour and the release of several albums. After Cleonia, the group's lead singer, died in 1991, Celester and Connie continued to appear as the Badgett Sisters. They are noted for close harmony and enthusiastic renditions of traditional African American spirituals.

In the white gospel tradition, Canadian-born George Beverly Shea, a longtime resident of Montreat, became an internationally celebrated gospel singer during the mid-twentieth century. Shea, sometimes called "America's Most Beloved Gospel Singer," is best known for his long association with Billy Graham and TV pioneer and performer Arthur Smith. The Johnson Family Singers also sang with Smith. Kenneth M. Johnson of Randolph County, along with his father Jesse ("Pa"), mother Lydia ("Ma"), sister Betty, and twin brothers Bob and Jim, formed the gospel and popular music singing group and performed on WBT radio throughout the 1940s, 1950s, and 1960s. The family, which read music through shape-note notation, also appeared at schools, churches, conventions, sings, and rallies in the Carolinas and recorded for Columbia and RCA Victor. Betty Johnson left the group in 1952 to pursue a solo singing career. She made several television appearances on the *Tonight Show* and the *Ed Sullivan Show*, and her connection with Sullivan led to the family's appearance on his show in 1958.

Between 1948 and mid-1950 the Rangers, including Erman Slater, his wife Nora, and their children, lived in Raleigh and performed on WPTF and WBT. The Swanee River Boys, emphasizing soft harmony that fell somewhere between black and white gospel, sang for about a year with Grady Cole on CBS,

originating from WBT. The Kingsmen's Quartet was both the leading singing group and gospel music promoter in Asheville. The group sang in the city auditorium and on Asheville's WLOS-TV in the 1970s.

Other North Carolina gospel groups, such as the Inspirations, Pine Ridge Boys, Down East Boys, Dixie Melody Boys, Heaven Bound, and Anchormen, often performed in schools and churches. Their routines usually included gospel music in addition to other songs and comedy skits.

References: Horace Clarence Boyer, *How Sweet the Sound: The Golden Age of Gospel* (1995); Mellonee V. Burnim, "The Black Gospel Music Tradition: Symbol of Ethnicity" (Ph.D. diss., Indiana University, 1980); Shirley Caesar, *The Lady, the Melody, and the Word: The Inspirational Story of the First Lady of Gospel* (1998); Bill Carpenter, *Uncloudy Days: The Gospel Music Encyclopedia* (2005); Steve Huffman, "From Carnegie to Caswell: The Badgett Sisters Prepare for Sunday's Homecoming Concert," *Burlington Times-News*, 15 Nov. 1990; Bob Terrell, *The Music Men: The Story of Professional Gospel Quartet Singing* (1990).

Lisa Brantley Kobrin
Additional research provided by Margaret Foote and Wiley J. Williams.

Gouging, also known as "no-holds-barred" or "rough-and-tumble" fighting, was an especially violent form of fighting popular in the antebellum southern backcountry. A mixture of boxing, wrestling, and brawling, gouging prohibited only the use of weapons. A match ended when one of the participants gave up or was unable to continue. Although there are accounts of gouged-out eyeballs littering the ground, most historians think that the loss of an eye or other body part was rare. Still, there is little doubt that a serious gouging contest presented a real possibility of broken bones, scarring, maiming, or even death.

North Carolina was considered a stronghold of gougers. In 1746 Governor Gabriel Johnston criticized the "barbarous and inhuman manner of boxing which so much prevails among the lower sort of people." Although legislators responded by making it illegal to cut out tongues, pull out eyes, or bite off noses or fingers, North Carolina's gougers persevered.

Travelers' accounts up to the time of the Civil War confirm North Carolina's reputation for producing effective gougers. Some told of gougers who sharpened their nails and filed their teeth. A witness named Charles Janson described one match in 1807, when the two combatants were "fast clinched by the hair, and their thumbs endeavoring to force a passage into each other's eyes, while several of the bystanders were betting upon the first eye to be turned out of its socket. At length they fell to the ground and in an instant the uppermost sprung up with his antagonist's eye in his hand! The savage crowd applauded, while, sick with horror, we galloped away from the infernal scene."

Gouging gradually disappeared following the Civil War as backcountry culture absorbed the civilizing influences of towns, schools, churches, and the market economy.

References: Elliott J. Gorn, "Gouge and Bite, Pull Hair and Scratch: The Social Significance of Fighting in the Southern Backcountry," *American Historical Review* 90 (February 1985); Thomas C. Parramore, "Gouging in North Carolina," *North Carolina Folklore* 22 (May 1974).

Jim L. Sumner

Gourd Patch Affair. SEE Llewellyn Conspiracy.

Governor. The office of governor in North Carolina has changed dramatically through the years, emerging from its practically powerless beginnings to a position of immense influence and authority. Ralph Lane, who led Sir Walter Raleigh's colony on Roanoke Island in 1585–86, was the first person to hold the position. Early colonial governors were appointed by the Lords Proprietors, then the Crown (after 1730), and generally did their bidding, maintaining little autonomy in decision-making. Following adoption of the first state constitution in 1776, the governor was elected by the General Assembly for a one-year term with the possibility of serving no more than three years in any six-year period. The office remained relatively weak compared to the legislature. A small increase in executive power occurred after the constitutional convention of 1835, which provided for election of the governor by the people every two years.

The North Carolina Constitution of 1868 increased the governor's term from two to four years and further expanded the office's duties and powers, including the ability to make appointments. Over the years, the governor began to gain more control over the state budget. The administration of Governor Cameron Morrison (1921–25) was instrumental in this development, and Governor O. Max Gardner (1929–33) added to Morrison's accomplishments. Serving during the Great Depression, Gardner oversaw such reforms as the creation of more appointed positions within the government and the reorganization of state agencies, the initiation of the Australian (secret) ballot in statewide elections, the establishment of workman's compensation, the assumption of state responsibility for maintaining public schools and roads, and the consolidation of the University of North Carolina System. Through Gardner's efforts, the office of governor became more powerful and central to the state's governmental system than ever before.

Under Governor Robert W. Scott (1969–73), North Carolina's government was again reorganized and altered in several important ways. Scott directed the adoption of the state's third constitution, which has been in effect since 1971. The document made few changes in the governor's role, although in 1977 the citizens voted to allow the governor and lieutenant governor to run for a second consecutive term. (James B. Hunt Jr. was the first governor elected consecutively, winning office in 1976 and 1980 and again in 1992 and 1996.)

Since the ratification of the new state constitution and the passing of the Executive Organization Act, both in 1971, the office of governor has been one of the 19 departments in the executive branch of state government. The Executive Organization Act charged the governor with preparing and submitting to the General Assembly a comprehensive and balanced budget, then, following enactment by the legislature, administering it. By the early 2000s, the governor was the state's chief executive officer, directing a multibillion-dollar enterprise with about 200,000 employees. The publicly elected members of the Council of State—consisting of the governor, lieutenant governor, attorney general, secretary of state, state treasurer, state auditor, superintendent of public instruction, and commissioners of labor, insurance, and agriculture—serve as the executive advisory board. The heads of the state's other executive departments—including the Departments of Administration, Commerce, Revenue, Correction, Crime Control and Public Safety, Cultural Resources, Environment and Natural Resources, Health and Human Services, and Transportation—are appointed by the governor. The office of state controller is also of primary importance to the work of the executive branch.

There are several principal administrative branches of the governor's office. The executive assistant oversees administrative operations, serves as the governor's link to cabinet members, advises the governor on legislative matters, and represents the governor in matters of state. The legal counsel monitors all legal issues relating to the governor and cabinet, advises the governor when policy developments involve legal issues, and investigates the merits of pardon and extradition requests and those of rewards and payments of legal fees charged by the state. The Office of Budget and Management directs preparation of the budget and advises the governor on policy decisions related to the biennial budget, legislative issues, and the management of state government. The Boards and Commissions Office reviews applications and submits recommendations for appointments to the governor for more than 350 statutory and nonstatutory boards and commissions controlled by the governor. It also researches qualifications and requirements, maintains records, and serves as a liaison with associations, agencies, and interested individuals and groups.

The Office of State Planning compiles and disseminates statistical data to promote sound public policy analysis, planning, and decision-making. As of the early 2000s, it included the Strategic Planning and Analysis Section, the State Data Center, the State Demographics Unit, the Center for Geographic Information and Analysis, the Community Resource

Information System, and the North Carolina Geodetic Survey Section. The Press Office, whose principal official is the press secretary, serves as the voice of the governor's office, coordinating communications efforts (press releases, speeches, and public service announcements) for the administration. The Press Office also plans public events for the governor. The Office of Citizen Affairs works to make state government more responsive to North Carolinians, such as responding to complaints and helping citizens tackle problems with the help of state agencies.

The legislative counsel is responsible for establishing and maintaining a working relationship with members of the General Assembly on all legislative matters of importance to the governor. The Eastern Office (New Bern) and the Western Office (Asheville) serve as regional links between the governor and the residents of 33 eastern and 27 western counties. Finally, North Carolina's Washington, D.C., office is a liaison between the governor, the state's congressional delegation, federal agencies, and the president.

Through most of the state's history, the governor has not had the power to veto the legislation of the General Assembly. The ability to unilaterally block legislation through veto is a product of the constitutional tenet that bills require the signature of the chief executive to become law. Typically, a bill that is vetoed may become law if passed again with a special majority. In 1996 North Carolina became the last state in the Union to grant its governor the veto power. Previously, all bills passed by the legislature became law when signed by the presiding officers of both houses of the General Assembly.

The governor's specific duties and responsibilities are mandated by the state constitution and legislative statutes. They include directing all phases of the state budget, from initial preparation through execution; serving as commander in chief of the state militia; chairing the Council of State; convening special legislative sessions; faithfully executing the laws of the state; granting pardons, commuting prison sentences, and issuing extradition warrants; joining interstate compacts; reorganizing and consolidating state agencies under his or her direct control; exercising final authority over state expenditures and administering funds and loans from the federal government; and delivering the annual state-of-the-state address to a joint session of the legislature.

References: John L. Cheney Jr., ed., *North Carolina Government, 1585–1979: A Narrative and Statistical History* (1981); John V. Orth, *The North Carolina State Constitution with History and Commentary* (1995).

John V. Orth
Additional research provided by Wiley J. Williams.

Governor Morehead School, North Carolina's school for the blind, opened in 1845 as the North Carolina Institution for the Education of the Deaf and Dumb and the Blind. This state-supported, educational program for students with disabilities was one of the first of its kind in the South. William D. Cooke of the Deaf and Dumb Institution at Staunton, Va., wrote to North Carolina governor John Motley Morehead in 1843 suggesting that enough students could be recruited from North Carolina's "deaf-mutes," then estimated to be about 280, and from the overflow at the Staunton school to start a private school in North Carolina. Morehead, already an advocate of educating citizens with disabilities, brought his correspondence with Cooke to the attention of the Presbyterian Synod of North Carolina when it met in Raleigh in 1844 and gained their support. Later in 1844, Morehead sent a message to the General Assembly suggesting the establishment of a public school for the "deaf, dumb, and blind."

On 8 Jan. 1845, the legislature approved an act "to provide for the education of the poor and destitute deaf-mutes and blind persons in this State." This act provided $5,000 annually from the Literary Fund and established that $75 for each handicapped student be paid yearly by the county from which he or she came. A building on Hillsboro Street (modern-day Hillsborough Street) in Raleigh, two blocks west of the capitol building, was rented, four teachers were employed, and the North Carolina Institution for the Education of the Deaf and Dumb and the Blind opened on 1 May 1845. Cooke was elected principal (a title applied to the head of the school until 1918) and opened the school with 23 deaf students between the ages of 8 and 32 who attended classes in reading, writing, arithmetic, history, geography, domestic and industrial arts, and the Bible. With a $15,000 appropriation by the legislature, land for a new school was purchased around 1849 on Caswell Square in Raleigh at the intersection of Jones and McDowell Streets, and a board of directors was established.

Blind students were not enrolled in the school until 1851. Cooke established vocational classes for older students. Blind girls were taught knitting, and deaf girls were taught sewing; blind boys were taught broom making, and deaf boys were taught shoe making and printing. The *Annals for the Deaf* was published at the school for several years, and in 1851 the *Deaf-Mute Casket* appeared under Cooke's editorship. The *Casket* was the first paper printed for and by deaf students in one of their own schools. Books for the blind, using raised letters, were also produced. Printing was done for the public, and some tradespeople in Raleigh complained about the competition. In 1858, the school enrolled 39 deaf and 18 blind students.

In 1867 North Carolina first addressed the need for a school for deaf, dumb, and blind African Americans. The U.S. War Department agreed to pay rent for a suitable building and to supply rations, and the North Carolina Institution for the Education of the Deaf and Dumb and the Blind was asked to provide teachers and supervision. The "Colored School" opened on 4 Jan. 1869 in a building rented from the American Missionary Association in southeastern Raleigh with 21 deaf students and 7 blind students. This was the first school for African American blind students in the United States.

The General Assembly appropriated money for the establishment of a separate school for white deaf students in 1891. When this new school in Morganton opened in 1894, white blind students remained on Caswell Square in Raleigh, and black blind students and black deaf students remained on South Bloodworth Street in Raleigh. John E. Ray became principal of the North Carolina Institution for the Education of the Deaf and Dumb and the Blind in 1896. Enrollment reached 535 in 1912, making the school the largest of its kind in America at the time. Through Ray's efforts, the General Assembly passed a law for the compulsory school attendance of the blind, which now requires blind students between the ages of 7 and 18 to attend school. In 1905 the name of the institution was changed to the State School for the Blind and Deaf, and in 1913 $30,000 was appropriated by the General Assembly to purchase a 75-acre tract adjoining Pullen Park in Raleigh. With an additional $150,000 from the legislature in 1917, plans were made to move the school for white blind students to the current location on Ashe Avenue in Raleigh.

In 1929 the General Assembly appropriated funds to purchase 234 acres on U.S. 70, also called Garner Road, for the school's programs for black deaf students and black blind students. Between 1949 and 1959, the General Assembly appropriated approximately $1 million for additional buildings and development of the Garner Road campus. In 1959 the school's board of directors instructed the superintendent, Egbert Peeler, to consider consolidating the Garner Road and Ashe Avenue campuses. The General Assembly authorized the board in 1963 to change the name of the school to the Governor Morehead School in honor of former governor John Motley Morehead.

In 1967 the General Assembly and the board of directors announced plans for the phasing out of services for black deaf students at the Garner Road campus and for transferring those students to the "two other Schools for the Deaf in North Carolina" (in Morganton and Wilson). During 1968 new superintendent Samuel Cole began his term, and a study published by a private architectural firm indicated that the Ashe Avenue campus was the more desirable location for a one-campus site for black and white blind students. By 1971 the consolidation was complete. The newly formed Governor Morehead School received reaccreditation by the Southern Association of Colleges and Schools in 1972 and conducted its first summer camp in 1974 at the F. B. Simmons Future Farmers of America Camp in Swansboro. In 1979 the board of directors approved the school's seal, which featured a bell, and recommended the school motto be selected by the students and staff. The motto selected was "By Faith, Not By Sight." The modern Governor Morehead School offers complete educational and residential programs for visually impaired students from North Carolina, preschool through age 21.

References: Manuel H. Crockett and Barbara C. Dease, *Through the Years, 1867–1977: Light Out of Darkness: A History of the North Carolina School for the Negro Blind and the Deaf* (1990); William S. Powell, *North Carolina through Four Centuries* (1989).

William G. Apple

Governor Richard Caswell Memorial. SEE *Neuse*, CSS, State Historic Site and Governor Richard Caswell Memorial.

Governor's Commission on Education beyond High School,

commonly referred to as the Carlyle Commission, published a report in 1962 that led to legislation in 1963 establishing the state's community college system and public universities at Asheville, Charlotte, and Wilmington. The commission was appointed in 1961 by Governor Terry Sanford to plan for the higher education of the rapidly increasing baby boom high school graduates and to consider other issues relating to the state's change from an agricultural to a technology-based economy. Irving E. Carlyle, attorney and former legislator from Winston-Salem, was chairman of the 20-member panel of educators and citizens, and W. Lunsford Crew, president pro tem of the North Carolina Senate from Halifax County, served as vice chairman.

The commission's report contained 61 recommendations for higher education on statewide planning and coordination, the University of North Carolina and public senior colleges, comprehensive community colleges, students, faculties, finance, and extension and public service. The commission also initiated a comprehensive demographic study, titled *Community Colleges for North Carolina: A Study of Need, Location, and Service Areas* (1962), led by C. Horace Hamilton of the Department of Rural Sociology at North Carolina State College (modern North Carolina State University). The Hamilton Report documented the great need for additional institutions of higher education in North Carolina.

References: Arnold K. King, *The Multi-Campus University of North Carolina Comes of Age, 1956–1986* (1987); Jon Lee Wiggs, *The Community College System in North Carolina: A Silver Anniversary History, 1963–1988* (1989).

Benjamin Eagles Fountain Jr.

Governor's Council.

During the Proprietary period in North Carolina (before the establishment of royal government in 1731), the "governor's council," precursor to the modern Council of State, was a group of 6 to 12 men appointed by the governor. The council served as the Upper House of the legislature, acted as an advisory board to the governor (similar to the modern gubernatorial cabinet), and sat as the highest court of appeals until about 1712. From then until the American Revolution, the council functioned as the Court of Chancery for the colony. The president of the council served as chief executive in the governor's absence.

With the advent of royal government, the council became even stronger than its Proprietary forebear. When it functioned as a legislative branch, the governor no longer attended its sessions, as had frequently been the case before 1731. The council had an extensive role in shaping executive proclamations and decrees, granting land, and extending patronage, especially the appointments of justices of the peace. Although the Proprietary council had had these powers too, the often muddled authority characterizing the Proprietary years tended to dilute the council's role.

The term "governor's council" is misleading, particularly during the royal period. Although governors nominated councillors, the Privy Council in England was the appointing authority, and it sometimes named its own members. Even in the most favorable circumstances to a governor, a period of 18 to 36 months usually ensued between nomination and swearing in. Furthermore, governors sometimes discovered that their nominees did not vote as expected.

Councillors were usually among the wealthiest citizens of the province and as such were leaders of society. That wealth often provided a measure of independence from the governor. Finally, councillors served at the "king's pleasure," not the governor's, and a new governor would usually face a council with "holdovers" from a prior administration. Current hindsight tends to downplay the importance of the council in light of the rise of the Lower House of the legislature prior to the Revolution, but the council was a powerful political force in colonial North Carolina.

References: Robert J. Cain, ed., *Records of the Executive Council, 1664–1734* (1984); William S. Price Jr., "'Men of Good Estates': Wealth among North Carolina's Royal Councillors," *NCHR* 49 (1972).

William S. Price Jr.

Governor's Mansion, located at 200 North Blount Street in Raleigh, is the official residence of the governor of North Carolina. It is the third structure in Raleigh to serve in that capacity since the city's designation as the state capital. The first, a two-story frame house located at the corner of Fayetteville and Hargett Streets, was initially provided to the governor in 1797. It proved inadequate, and in 1816 an elaborate brick structure with white-columned porticoes was built. Known as the Governor's Palace, it stood at the end of Fayetteville Street, facing the old statehouse. North Carolina governors used it until 1865.

The Governor's Mansion in Raleigh. Photograph courtesy of North Carolina Division of Tourism, Film, and Sports Development.

From 1865 until 1891, the state's chief executive was responsible for securing his own accommodations while in Raleigh. Most governors rented private homes or stayed at the Yarborough House on Fayetteville Street. Although a state commission in 1879 had investigated building a new residence, the General Assembly did not authorize construction of the house to be located on Burke Square until 1883. Samuel Sloan and assistant Adolphus Gustavus Bauer of Philadelphia were selected as architects.

Construction began in the summer of 1883, with extensive use of convict labor from the nearby penitentiary. Bricks and other building materials were also provided by the prison. Sloan died in 1885 before the house was completed, and Bauer assumed direction of the project. Col. William J. Hicks, warden of the prison, supervised construction work.

The Executive Mansion, which is the official name of the house, was completed in 1891. Governor Daniel Fowle moved in on 5 January of that year. The state's chief executives and their families have lived there continuously ever since, except during brief periods when renovations have been undertaken. The house, considered an outstanding example of the Queen Anne Cottage style of Victorian architecture, is noted for its many turrets, bays, and towers, steeply pitched gables, colored textural surfaces, and elaborately turned woodwork. It is open to the public by appointment.

References: William Bushong, *North Carolina's Executive Mansion: The First Hundred Years* (1991); North Carolina Department of Cultural Resources, *The Executive Mansion, Raleigh, North Carolina* (5th ed., 1985).

Robert G. Anthony Jr.

Governor's School of North Carolina is the nation's oldest statewide residential summer program for academically gifted high school students. Founded in 1963 at the urging of Governor Terry Sanford and his adviser John Ehle, the

Governor's School was originally funded by a Carnegie Corporation of New York grant and donations from Winston-Salem businesses. In 1966 the General Assembly decided to continue the school with public funds, and in 1978 Governor James B. Hunt Jr. expanded the school to a second campus. The program is open to rising seniors, with exceptions for rising juniors in the performing/visual arts area. Offering a noncredit, six-week curriculum, the school is located on two campuses with 400 students at each: Governor's School West at Salem College in Winston-Salem and Governor's School East at St. Andrews Presbyterian College in Laurinburg.

The State Board of Education and Department of Public Instruction, through the Exceptional Children Division, administers the Governor's School. A board of governors appointed by the State Board of Education serves the program in an advisory capacity. With an emphasis on the study of twentieth-century theories as they relate to the past and the future, the school's curriculum is divided into three major areas. In Area I, students explore their chosen subject area. Area II relates that chosen subject to other topics and fields of study on the abstract level through an investigation of philosophy, ethics, epistemology, and aesthetics. In Area III, students explore the interaction of self with society, learning about their own values, morals, and thought processes. There are no tests, no grades, and little homework.

Each local school superintendent or private school headmaster submits a quota of student names based upon the school population. The top two students chosen by each superintendent are invited to attend Governor's School, and a selection committee chooses remaining students from the pool of eligible candidates. Students in the performing and visual arts also audition.

References: H. Michael Lewis, *Opening Windows onto the Future: Theory of the Governor's School of North Carolina* (1969); Elizabeth Marshall Murray Thomas, *A Retrospective Evaluation of the Governor's School of North Carolina* (1984).

Kevin Cherry

Graham County, located in western North Carolina along the Tennessee border, was formed in 1872 from the northeastern part of Cherokee County. It was named for William A. Graham, U.S. senator and governor of North Carolina. Communities in the county include Lake Santeetlah, Fontana Village, and the county seat, Nashville, incorporated in 1893. Much of Graham County is covered by the Nantahala National Forest, which includes the Joyce Kilmer Memorial Forest in the western part of the county. The lands of Graham County belonged to the Cherokee until President Andrew Jackson ordered the removal of the Indians in 1838. The grave of Cherokee leader Junaluska is located in Robbinsville.

Tourism is the leading industry in Graham County, in which 90 percent of the land has a slope of 30 degrees or more. Fontana Dam, constructed on the Little Tennessee River between 1942 and 1944, was a major Tennessee Valley Authority initiative and is the highest dam in the eastern United States. Fontana Lake attracts thousands of visitors each year with its enormous recreational opportunities. The Cherohala Skyway is a unique scenic byway passing through breathtaking mountain vistas. The Appalachian Trail also runs through Cherokee County.

Graham County farms produce tobacco, corn, chickens, Christmas trees, and other goods. Industrial manufactures include apparel, lumber, furniture, and cheese. Graham County's population was estimated at 8,000 in 2004.

Reference: Graham County Heritage Book Committee, *Graham County Heritage, North Carolina* (1992).

Allyson C. Criner

SEE ALSO Fontana Dam.

Graham County Railroad Company was one of dozens of logging railways built in North Carolina in the late 1800s and early 1900s. Constructed over steep grades through the Nantahala Mountains between Topton and Robbinsville in 1925, this 12.6-mile line was one of the nation's last railways to use steam locomotives before it shut down in 1970. Bible-quoting, hymn-singing engineer Ed Collins ran the train for almost 40 years. The last run of the Sidewinder, a specially designed geared steam locomotive prized for its strength and agility, was covered by TV newsman Charles Kuralt. The railroad's original locomotive, No. 1925, is preserved at the North Carolina Transportation Museum in Spencer.

James Wrinn

Grand Assembly of Albemarle was the name of the legislative body summoned by North Carolina's first governor, William Drummond (1663–67), to assist in the drafting of temporary laws and to act within the guidelines of the Concessions and Agreement pact (1665) between the Lords Proprietors and existing settlers. Among other powers, the Assembly had control over its own call and dismissal, taxation, and the appointment of county courts and officials. It also gave the body responsibility for the governor's salary and all "necessary" governmental funding, wartime appropriations, and any laws deemed essential for the welfare of the colony.

Although the bulk of the enactments of this period have been lost, usage of the term "Grand Assembly of Albemarle" persisted throughout the Proprietary period, as did "Albemarle County" and the use of the county's seal for the colony as a whole.

References: Robert J. Cain, ed., *Records of the Executive Council, 1664–1734* (1984); Mattie Erma Edwards Parker, ed., *North Carolina Charters and Constitutions, 1578–1698* (1963).

Louis P. Towles

Grandfather Clause was an important component of the 1900 constitutional amendment restricting North Carolina's class of eligible voters. The disfranchisement amendment provided that voters must be able to read and write a section of the state constitution in the English language and to pay a poll tax. Far from attempting to encourage literacy, however, the primary goal of the amendment, as admitted in the Democratic Party's pro-amendment campaign in 1900, was to eliminate African American voters as a factor in North Carolina politics. The large number of poor illiterate black males, as well as the bias of white Democratic registrars, ensured that the literacy test and the poll tax would be used to reduce the electorate.

The drafters of the amendment were aware of the politically unacceptable fact that illiterate whites could also be excluded by the literacy test. The answer to this problem was the grandfather clause, which stated that no one should be denied the right to register and vote because of the literacy requirement if he or a lineal ancestor could vote under the law of his state of residence on 1 Jan. 1867, provided that he registered before 1 Dec. 1908. The 1867 date was important because it preceded any federal prohibition of racial discrimination; therefore very few blacks were eligible to vote. In practical terms, it meant that illiterate whites were absolved of the embarrassment of a literacy requirement and blacks were not, thus enhancing the discretionary power of Democratic registrars.

North Carolina's grandfather clause was modeled on a Louisiana statute, and similar versions appeared at roughly the same time in Alabama and Georgia. By its terms, it expired in 1908. In 1915 the U.S. Supreme Court declared a similar clause in Oklahoma to be an unconstitutional attempt to deny voting rights on the basis of race.

References: Jerry W. Cotten, "Negro Disfranchisement in North Carolina: The Politics of Race in a Southern State" (M.A. thesis, UNC-Greensboro, 1973); Helen G. Edmonds, *The Negro and Fusion Politics in North Carolina, 1894-1901* (1951); James L. Hunt, "Marion Butler and the Populist Ideal, 1863–1938" (Ph.D. diss., University of Wisconsin, 1990); J. Morgan Kousser, *The Shaping of Southern Politics: Suffrage Restriction and the Establishment of the One-Party South, 1880–1910* (1974); Joseph F. Steelman, "The Progressive Era in North Carolina, 1884–1917" (Ph.D. diss., UNC-Chapel Hill, 1955).

James L. Hunt

Grandfather Mountain is one of the most popular tourist destinations in North Carolina and is an invaluable part of the state's natural heritage. The mountain is located in a corner of Avery County near the borders of Caldwell and Watauga

Grandfather Mountain as seen from the Yonahlossee Road between Linville and Blowing Rock, 1919. NCC.

Counties and is the highest point in the Blue Ridge Mountain range, with a peak of 5,964 feet. Formed more than 750 million years ago, Grandfather Mountain contains some of the oldest geological formations on earth and is one of the most readily recognizable mountains in the Blue Ridge. Called *Tanawha* ("fabulous bird" or "eagle") by the Cherokee Indians, the mountain acquired the name "Grandfather" from early settlers who saw the face of an old man's profile in the outline of the peaks against the sky. Well-known early explorers who visited the mountain include Daniel Boone, who reportedly explored the area in the mid-1700s; the French botanist and explorer André Michaux, who climbed the mountain in 1794; and Sierra Club founder John Muir, who visited in 1898.

In the late nineteenth century, Grandfather Mountain was acquired by Donald MacRae of Wilmington, who purchased the mountain and a large tract of land in the area from the descendants of Gen. William Lenoir (the Revolutionary War leader for whom the Caldwell County town of Lenoir is named). MacRae planned to develop the area around Linville, and a development company called the Linville Improvement Company was organized. Eventually, one of Donald MacRae's sons, Hugh MacRae, became head of the company and directed the building of one of the first mountain resorts in the area at Linville. To further encourage tourism, he directed the construction of the Yonahlossee Road, now U.S. 221, between Linville and Blowing Rock.

The natural beauty of Grandfather Mountain would prove to be the area's greatest attraction. Many visitors began to make the climb up the steep slopes to enjoy the mountain scenery from Grandfather's summit. For the first half of the twentieth century, access to the summit was by an old trail that curved up to a point where a wooden platform had been built at an overlook. A small fee was charged to visitors who wished to ascend to the viewing area.

In the early 1950s, Hugh MacRae's grandson, Hugh MacRae Morton, inherited Grandfather Mountain. He proceeded to widen the old trail up the mountain and improve access to the peak. Morton directed the construction of a 228-foot suspension bridge, known today as the Mile High Swinging Bridge, at the summit. As a result, the number of tourists visiting Grandfather Mountain dramatically increased.

Large numbers of visitors have also been drawn to two unique cultural events that are held on the mountain. Each summer since 1924, Singing on the Mountain, one of the country's longest-running "old-time" gospel conventions, has been held at the foot of Grandfather Mountain. In addition, the Grandfather Mountain Highland Games have been staged at the site since the late 1950s. Patterned on centuries-old clan gatherings in Scotland, the Highland Games have become one of the largest and most popular celebrations of Scottish heritage in the United States.

Morton has also actively sought to preserve much of Grandfather Mountain's natural environment. He established a habitat for native wildlife, and, in cooperation with the Nature Conservancy of North Carolina, he set aside large areas of the mountain as a wilderness preserve. In the 1980s, after many years of negotiations between Morton and the U.S. Park Service over possible routes, the final section of the Blue Ridge Parkway was finally completed around Grandfather Mountain. At Morton's insistence this section of the parkway, the Linn Cove Viaduct, was built using special European-style construction techniques and individually preformed sections in order to minimize physical impact on the mountain's fragile environment. In 1992 Grandfather Mountain had the distinction of being selected by the United Nations Educational, Scientific and Cultural Organization (UNESCO) for membership in the international network of Biosphere Reserves.

References: "A Brief History of Grandfather Mountain," *Grandfather Mountain News*, vol. 1 (1995); Ron Fisher, *Blue Ridge Range: The Gentle Mountains* (1992).

Robert D. Weaver

Grand Model. SEE Fundamental Constitutions.

Grange, also known as the Order of the Patrons of Husbandry, is a rural organization that promotes community val-ues and serves as a vehicle for farmers to mold and shape state policies. The Grange began after the Civil War, when cotton yields skyrocketed and prices plummeted. Facing similar economic problems, farmers nationwide formed the National Grange in 1867 to serve as the political and social voice of their interests. Following the precedent set by this national organization, North Carolina farmers established the state's first Subordinate Grange in Guilford County in 1873. The legislature incorporated the North Carolina State Grange on 20 Feb. 1875. Since then, farmers have used the Grange, in both early and modern forms, to shape the state's commitment to agriculture.

The political purpose of the early Grange was twofold. Farmers wanted an organization that would offer them collective power in the market and the strength to force the state legislature to establish a Department of Agriculture, which it did in 1877. With this achievement, Grange chapters dwindled. By the 1890s farmers looked to other political organizations, such as the Farmers' Alliance and the Populist Party, for relief.

By the 1920s high yields, low prices, and railroad monopolies caused farmers to reconsider the older organization. The new North Carolina Grange was organized on 27 Sept. 1929, but its objectives had changed. Although this Grange was committed to many principles of the early Grange, the state's experience with Populist politics afforded farmers a new knowledge of government. Grange members now pressured the legislature to provide rural electrification and telephone service. Grange committees sought to improve highways and education, as well as to promote tax reform and agricultural science. The new Grange again established cooperatives to raise prices.

One of the most significant differences between the old Grange and the new was the change in leadership. Women asserted a public role that was unprecedented in the early Grange. Margaret Caldwell, wife of Harry B. Caldwell, a former state Grange master, held the same post (1946–48, 1963–75). Beginning in the 1930s, she built up the Juvenile Grange to train children in leadership, agricultural science, and community responsibility. Frances Perkins, labor secretary in the Franklin D. Roosevelt administration, appointed Caldwell to the national Advisory Committee on Maternal and Child Welfare. Caldwell, like her forebears, pushed for federal price supports so farmers could make a fair profit; yet her experiences as a wife and mother enabled her to shape the Grange into an organization that supported not only farm families but also rural women and children.

The North Carolina Grange has produced state leaders such as Governors W. Kerr Scott, Robert Scott, and James B. Hunt Jr. and Commissioner of Agriculture Jim Graham. The modern Grange has encouraged youth education and organized the first continuous rural group health insurance program through Blue Cross and Blue Shield of North Carolina.

Italian master carvers were employed at the Mount Airy Granite Company in the early 1900s; here, column capitals they have crafted are loaded on a railroad car. NCC.

Reference: Stuart Noblin and Bill Humphries, *Hold High the Torch: The Grange in North Carolina, 1929–1989* (1990).

Karin Lorene Zipf

Granite is a massive igneous rock with a crystalline texture containing feldspar, quartz, and one or more dark iron silicate or ferromagnesian minerals, usually biotite or hornblende. The granite in North Carolina is described as first in quality in the southeastern states and second in quantity to that of Georgia. In 1980 the state's granite production was sixth in the United States, with ten quarries in five counties: Avery, Mitchell, Rowan, Surry, and Watauga. The earliest recorded granite quarry was in Wake County southeast of Raleigh about 1805 for local use. A second quarry east of Raleigh in a granite gneiss supplied stone for building the State Capitol in 1833–36. Rowan County had quarrying near Salisbury before the Civil War, as did Davidson County near Lexington for the courthouse in 1856 and piers for a railroad bridge. Stone for Davidson College was excavated in Iredell County in the same era.

Modern quarrying methods and improved transportation to markets encouraged expansion of the industry in the late nineteenth century with numerous openings extended or be-

gun. Crushed stone from scrap has been sold for road metal as an important complement to dimension stone production.

Types of granite found in North Carolina include Balfour pink, a rose to pink granite from Rowan County that has been sold as "Salisbury pink" and "Arabian pink" since before 1860; gabbro, dark gray to black granite with dark minerals predominant that was quarried by the Old Consolidated Granite Company in Rowan County as black granite about 1902 and shipped as monument stock to locations up and down the eastern seaboard; orbicular diorite, granite in which dark green nodules of hornblende occur in a white matrix of feldspar, which is unique to Davie County near the Yadkin River; and Mount Airy granite, a white to light gray biotite granite of uniform texture and color found in Surry County northeast of the city of Mount Airy. In 1979 Mount Airy granite was designated as the official state rock.

References: R. J. Councill, *Commercial Granites of North Carolina*, North Carolina Geological Survey Bulletin no. 67 (1954); U.S. Bureau of Mines, *Minerals Yearbook: The Mineral Industry of North Carolina* (1980).

Jean H. Seaman

Granville County, located in the Piedmont region of north central North Carolina and partially bordered by the state of Virginia, was formed in 1746 from Edgecombe County. It was named for John Lord Carteret, second Earl Granville, who was granted the land of the Granville District by King George II. The county reached its present dimensions after being divided in 1752, 1764, and 1881 to form parts of Orange, Bute (no longer extant), and Vance Counties, respectively. Oxford is the county seat, having succeeded Granville Court House in that capacity in 1811. Other communities in Granville County include Butner, Creedmoor, Stem, and Stovall.

Tuscarora and Saponi Indians dominated the many tribes that once inhabited Granville County. Settlers, mostly from Virginia, began to occupy the area after the Tuscarora War of 1711–13. Agriculture, particularly the production of tobacco using slave labor, drove the early economy of Granville County, which, during slavery's peak in the mid-nineteenth century, was one of a handful of North Carolina counties with as many as 10,000 slaves. The county also had a sizable community of free blacks, including dozens of craftsmen such as the masons who helped build the homes of some of the county's more affluent families. The development in the 1850s of bright leaf tobacco, which could be cultivated in the sandy soil of the Piedmont, kept tobacco production strong in the county following the elimination of a slave-based plantation economy.

Granville County is still one of the largest tobacco-producing areas in the state, but with the introduction of manufacturing industries, the county's economy is no longer primarily agricultural. Manufactured products include apparel, tires, telecommunications equipment, cosmetics, and china. Camp Butner, a major World War II military installation, was converted for other uses, including a federal prison and state mental hospital. In 2004 the population of Granville County was estimated to be 53,000.

Reference: Lewis Bowling, *Granville County Revisited* (2003).

Allyson C. Criner

Granville Grant and District. When Charles II granted "Carolina" to the eight Lords Proprietors in 1663 and 1665, he gave them an area that extended, in modern terms, from south of Daytona Beach, Fla., to the Virginia–North Carolina border and from the Atlantic Ocean to the Pacific Ocean. Although the Proprietors provided for an elaborate system of government in the Fundamental Constitutions, many problems arose as shares in Carolina were sold or were the subject of bequests. In 1728 all of the Proprietors except John Lord Carteret, second Earl Granville, who had inherited the share of Carolina originally granted to Sir George Carteret, agreed to sell their interests in the province back to the Crown. In 1729 Parliament approved the purchase of seven undivided parts of Carolina, with Earl Granville's share specifically excluded.

On 15 Sept. 1742 King George II and the Privy Council finally approved the setting off of Granville's one-eighth of Carolina. The Granville District was a wide stretch of land encompassing the area between the present Virginia–North Carolina border and a line about 65 miles south (35°34′ north latitude). With the acceptance of the grant, Granville surrendered any claim on the remainder of Carolina; he also gave up any participation in the government of North Carolina. Governor Gabriel Johnston later complained that Granville not only had more than half the province but that he had the better half.

Earl Granville administered the district from across the Atlantic through agents, the most noteworthy of whom were Edward Moseley, Francis Corbin, and Thomas Child. Further grants of unclaimed land were made in the period beginning in 1748 and ending in 1763, following the death of John Earl Granville. The district was then tied up in chancery litigation. Although his heir, Robert Earl Granville, planned to reactivate the district with Josiah Martin as agent, the Revolutionary War prevented him. Other Granville heirs, to whom the district was bequeathed by Robert Earl, filed unsuccessfully for recovery of the district in 1801.

References: A. Roger Ekirch, *"Poor Carolina": Politics and Society in Colonial North Carolina, 1729–1776* (1981); Helen F. M. Leary, ed., *North Carolina Research: Genealogy and Local History* (1996); Thornton W. Mitchell, "The Granville District and Its Land Records," NCHR 70 (April 1993); W. N. Watt, *The Granville District* (1992).

Thornton W. Mitchell

SEE ALSO Enfield Riots.

Granville's Devisee v. Allen. In 1805 U.S. Supreme Court chief justice John Marshall and district judge Henry Potter, sitting in the U.S. Circuit Court for the District of North Carolina, considered the claim to the Earl Granville estate of about 300,000 acres originally bestowed on loyal Cavaliers and the Lords Proprietors by King Charles II and regranted by King George II. North Carolina's confiscation of this Tory property during the American Revolution and its subsequent grants of the land ignited an ejectment action in 1801 by Granville's devisee, represented by the formidable William Gaston. Marshall removed himself from the proceedings on grounds of bias related to his participation in a Virginia syndicate that purchased portions of the vast Lord Fairfax estate sprawled across Virginia's Northern Neck. His apparent response to local public opinion left Potter to charge the jury in a manner favorable to the state's confiscation and to its grantees.

Gaston's appeal to the Supreme Court foundered in an environment of unpropitious domestic and foreign events. The case lingered on the docket until 1817, when the parties consented to its dismissal. By that time the Court had delivered its landmark opinion in *Fairfax's Devisee v. Hunter's Lessee* (1813), protecting from state destruction the Fairfax title and those holding land under it, including John Marshall. The outcome differed in North Carolina, where withering of the Granville appeal meant extinction of the original title to the benefit of North Carolina grantees whose labors had rendered a wilderness productive and valuable. Nathanial Allen was a member of the Lake Company, which in 1788 completed the draining of 100,000 acres of extremely fertile land in Tyrrell (now Washington) County.

References: Herbert A. Johnson, ed., *The Papers of John Marshall, 1800–1807*, vol. 6 (1990); John P. Roche and Stanley B. Bernstein, eds., *John Marshall: Major Opinions and Other Writings* (1967); W. N. Watt, *The Granville District* (1992).

Peter Graham Fish

Granville Wilt is a bacterial disease that affects the tobacco plant. It was discovered in 1881 in Granville County. By 1910 it would cost tobacco farmers in North Carolina between 25 percent and 100 percent of their crops annually. The U.S. Department of Agriculture tobacco specialists feared that the entire U.S. tobacco crop would be wiped out as a result of Granville wilt. The disease forced many North Carolina farmers to sell their farms and homes in the early twentieth century. Many producers went bankrupt, gave up planting tobacco, and moved away or chose other crops.

Granville wilt thrives under moist and hot conditions. It works its way into the plant through surface wounds then multiplies rapidly into the vascular system, producing a slimy mucous that plugs up the plant's vessels and causes the tobacco to wilt. The bacteria that cause the disease are carried throughout tobacco production on transplants, plow points and other farm equipment, and the feet of humans and animals. In the modern day, successful control of Granville wilt depends on carefully selected methods that include wilt-resistant tobacco varieties, crop rotation, root destruction, and soil treatment.

Reference: Furney A. Todd, *Tobacco in the United States* (rev. ed., 1979).

W. W. Yeargin

Grasses. Because of its moderate climate, well-distributed rainfall, and wide variation of altitude and soil conditions, North Carolina has a relatively large number of grasses—some 360 species and varieties representing nearly all of the 14 or 15 known grass tribes. The largest areas of grasses, many noted by early writers such as Mark Catesby, John Lawson, John Brickell, and Moses Ashley Curtis, are found in coastal brackish marshes, old fields and deforested land, and mountain balds. Gerald McCarthy, a botanist with the North Carolina Agricultural Experiment Station, asserted in a 15 Oct. 1890 bulletin that southern states possess the soils and climate for growing many of the best grasses. Nearly three-fourths of North Carolina's grasses are native.

Of the native grasses in the state, the largest number belongs to the tribe Paniceae. The most abundant coastal grass is smooth cordgrass, though other species such as sea oats and American beach grass also grow on dunes and sandy beaches. Wild rice or wild oats and Carolina canary grass are found along streams in the coastal plain. Broomsedges are the most abundant native grasses in the piedmont. Sedges, the most frequent species being mountain oat grass, dominate North Carolina mountain balds, which are a dense, lush green in summer and burnished gold in autumn. Other examples of grasses found on balds are red fescue and timothy grass.

North Carolina grasses are very important for agriculture and the natural environment. Beyond their obvious agricultural applications as grain and hay and in pastures, grasses are used to provide watershed protection, retain or improve soil fertility and quality, prepare and stabilize soil, conserve soil and water, control erosion and runoff, decrease sedimentation in waterways, hasten dune formation, protect beaches and shorelines, and lessen or prevent pollution by decreasing the movement of pollutants such as pesticides into streams. Grasses are also used for lawns, golf courses, parks, and other recreational or aesthetic purposes.

Researchers from North Carolina State University are studying the use of grass—already proven useful in removing such inorganic pollutants as fertilizers—as buffers near rivers and other bodies of water that may help eliminate contaminants from animal wastes. The fibrous root system of grasses helps to manage the nitrogen in soil and results in better soil tillage and water-holding capacity and healthier soil microorganism populations, including earthworms, rhizobia, and bacteria. After using fescue covers, farmers are able to increase their tobacco and corn crops, and a rye crop planted after a corn crop prevents nitrogen from leaching into water.

Many North Carolina pastures need improvement, partially because farmers tend to keep out weeds and grass, avoiding combinations of grasses that might enrich the soil. The best pasturage is found in the western part of the state, where Kentucky and Canada bluegrass, orchard grass, timothy, red top, fescues, and various species of *Danthonia* grow. The finest pastures of the coastal plain have bermuda, Dallis, and carpet grass.

Hay is made from both wild and cultivated grasses. In mountain valleys it is mowed twice a year and includes red top, orchard grass, timothy, Kentucky and Canada bluegrass, meadow fescue, and tall oatgrass. On fallow land, orchard grass, meadow fescue, timothy, and clovers are used. The best piedmont meadows are cut two or three times a year, and broomsedges are the main grasses there. In the coastal plain, wild grasses for hay are scarce.

Erosion is a serious threat in North Carolina, as it can cause the loss of tons of soil per acre of cropland and pastureland. Annuals such as crabgrasses and fescues and perennials such as bermuda grasses and broomsedges are used to conserve road shoulders. A problem to beaches, shorelines, waterfront property, and dunes, erosion may also be lessened by transplanting salt-marsh grasses, more effective and cheaper than building bulkheads or groins.

References: H. L. Blomquist, *The Grasses of North Carolina* (1948); Douglas S. Chamblee, ed., *The Production and Utilization of Pastures and Forages in North Carolina* (1995); Harry Ellis, "High, Wide, and Handsome," *Wildlife in North Carolina* 61 (May 1997).

Nancy P. Shires

SEE ALSO Soil Conservation.

Graveyard of the Atlantic

Graveyard of the Atlantic refers to the Atlantic Ocean waters along the North Carolina coast, which have been the scene of an unusually large number of shipwrecks. The warm waters of the northbound Gulf Stream meet the cold waters of the Arctic Current off Cape Hatteras at Diamond Shoals, and the entire coast is an area of shifting inlets, bays, and capes, representing a shipping hazard for both coastal and transatlantic vessels.

Remnants of some of the lost vessels are still visible to those on shore; many more are buried in the ever-shifting sands beyond the breakers. They include a fleet of Spanish treasure ships, returning to Europe after successful raids in the Caribbean in 1750 only to encounter a hurricane and end up strewn along the North Carolina coast. There is the coastal steamer *Pulaski*, lost on the Charleston-to-Baltimore run when it wrecked on the beach at Ocracoke in 1838 with the loss of 100 passengers and crewmen. Among other notable remains are those of sleek Civil War blockade-runners that failed in their effort to sneak into the Cape Fear River under the cover of darkness; the little ironclad *Monitor*, the "cheesebox on a raft," sunk off Cape Hatteras while being towed south following her famous battle with the *Merrimac*; and the United States gunboat *Huron*, run aground at Nags Head through navigational error, with the count of lost crewmen reaching 103.

There have been many other recorded shipwrecks in North Carolina's Graveyard of the Atlantic. Modern underwater searching equipment has brought the current estimate to the neighborhood of 2,000. They range from the tanker *Mirlo*, lost off Chicamacomico in 1918 after hitting a German mine, to larger tankers—a total of more than two dozen of them—sunk by Nazi submarines in 1942, including six in the course of one terrible day and night within sight of Cape Hatteras. A large number of doomed ships in the days of sail were schooners, but there was a fair sampling of everything from barks, brigs, and brigantines to a clipper ship and a pilot boat. Among the more modern craft lost were freighters, trawlers, barges, light-ships, and even two battleships sunk by aircraft off Cape Hatteras to prove Gen. Billy Mitchell's claim that airpower would be an important part of future warfare.

Despite the widespread publicity given to North Carolina's deadly coastline, it has competition. The shoreline of Sable Island, off Nova Scotia, is so littered with shipwrecks that it, too, has earned the name "Graveyard of the Atlantic."

Reference: David Stick, *Graveyard of the Atlantic: Shipwrecks of the North Carolina Coast* (1952).

David Stick

SEE ALSO *Huron*, USS; *Mirlo* Rescue; Shipwrecks.

Great Awakening

Great Awakening was one of the earliest Protestant revival movements to sweep through North Carolina. This religious revival, which actually encompassed two parts separated by a few decades, established several new sects of Methodists, Baptists, and Presbyterians in North Carolina in the 1700s and 1800s. The First Great Awakening occurred in the 1730s. After that, the American Revolution effectively halted all religious movements in North Carolina. Religious revivals returned to the state around 1800 with the Second Great Awakening. This movement lasted up until the outbreak of the Civil War.

In the 1730s Methodist missionaries, reformers who had split with the Church of England, came to the American colonies to preach a new way of worship. These missionaries emphasized a personal participation in religion and a new connection to God that allowed freer, more passionate and enthusiastic religious practices. These evangelical expressions differed dramatically from Anglican methods of worship, which often followed dispassionate rituals.

George Whitefield, one of the most famous of the Methodist missionaries, traveled through North Carolina in 1739 and returned to the colony again in 1765. On his 1739 trip he passed through Edenton and stopped at Bath on 22 December before moving farther south through New Bern and into the Cape Fear River region. Whitefield had no success converting North Carolinians, and he quickly moved on to South Carolina to continue his work. Almost 30 years passed before another Methodist minister made an effort to convert the people of North Carolina. Devereux Jarratt, a powerful and convincing speaker, worked in North Carolina from 1763 until 1775, warning listeners to recognize their sin and counseling them that the only remedy for their weaknesses was to rely on Christ for salvation. One of Jarratt's lessons was that the convert needed to develop a personal connection with God. This idea, which Whitefield had taught earlier, became very important to later revival movements.

Baptist Shubal Stearns of Connecticut, a follower of Whitefield and a former Congregationalist, arrived in Orange County in 1754 and established the influential Sandy Creek Baptist Association in 1758. When Stearns died in 1771, the Baptist church lost one of its most important leaders. Baptists were slow to be swept up in the revival movement, and not until after the Revolutionary War did Baptists regain strength in North Carolina.

David Caldwell was a Presbyterian missionary who came to North Carolina in 1765, opening a school to train other ministers. One of his students, James McGready, came to Guilford County in 1778 and later worked as a minister in the Haw River and Stoney Creek congregations. His message attacked the immorality and greed he saw in many Piedmont settlers. In Guilford County, McGready trained several Presbyterian ministers.

McGready and a group of his students traveled to Kentucky, where, in 1800, they organized the first Great Revival, signaling the beginning of the Second Great Awakening. Among the organizers was William McGhee, a Presbyterian, and his brother John, a Methodist. When participants returned to their home churches, the excitement generated by the revivals spread to the other churches. One of those in the crowd listening to McGready and other speakers was Lemuel Burkitt, the pastor at the Sandy Run Baptist Church in Bertie County and an active participant in the Kehukee Association of eastern North Carolina Baptists. His reports to congregations so inspired the Baptists that they began to hold their own revivals. In 1802 and 1803, Baptist revivals drew large crowds. In late March 1802 a Mecklenburg County revival attracted 5,000 people who heard 17 preachers urgently deliver their salvation message. By 1803, the Baptists had gained 1,500 new members. Spreading like a fire, the revival movement swept through the Presbyterian, Methodist, and Baptist faiths throughout the South.

Presbyterian revivals and camp meetings were held at the Cross Roads Church and Hawfields in Orange County. In January 1802, David Caldwell called for a meeting at Bell's Meeting House on the Deep River in Randolph County. He invited all area denominations to the gathering. From that one meeting, waves of revivals spread out across the state. In June 1802 thousands attended a revival at the Rutherford County Courthouse.

The religious fervor continued when the Methodists began to hold revivals at their camp meetings. In 1805 a camp meeting was held at Bethel, where 300 people were converted. Nearby Rock Spring became the location for one of the state's largest religious meetings.

The Second Great Awakening peaked in 1804, but aspects of it continued until the Civil War. After the end of the War of 1812, revivals were often held in cities—including Raleigh, Tarboro, and Fayetteville—rather than the countryside. The *Raleigh Star* reported in 1829 that "a considerable revival has taken place in the Methodist Church in this town, within the last ten days. . . . The preachers and leading members exert themselves in a surprising degree." Later, Greensboro and Charlotte also experienced religious revivals rooted in the Second Great Awakening.

References: John B. Boles, *The Great Revival, 1787–1805* (1972); Robert M. Calhoon, *Religion and the American Revolution in North Carolina* (1976); Bill Cecil-Fronsman, *Common Whites: Class and Culture in Antebellum North Carolina* (1992); Guion G. Johnson, *Ante-Bellum North Carolina: A Social History* (1937).

Ellen Fitzgibbons Causey

SEE ALSO Camp Meetings; Mourner's Bench; Revivals.

Great Deed of Grant (1668) was a petition from the Lords Proprietors of Carolina permitting settlers in Albemarle County to hold land under terms equivalent to those offered settlers in Virginia. The petition was submitted by the Grand Assembly of Albemarle County to the Proprietors to encourage settlement in the county by removing the disparity between the landholding terms of Albemarle and those of Virginia. Virginia landholders were permitted to hold larger tracts than settlers in Albemarle County, and were charged a much lower quitrent (a rent paid in lieu of service by feudal custom) than was the case in Albemarle and which was payable in produce. The granting of this petition on 1 May 1668 removed these formidable barriers to the growth of Albemarle County.

Edward Smith

Great Depression in North Carolina caused immeasurable hardship for a large percentage of citizens and, by way of President Franklin D. Roosevelt's New Deal programs, brought the federal government into the lives of average North Carolinians more than ever before, fundamentally changing the relationship between individuals and government. The Depression was quantitatively the single largest economic downturn the United States and the world had ever experienced. It began in August 1929 and did not effectively end until December 1941 with U.S. involvement in World War II. In 1933, when Roosevelt took office, the nation was plagued by relentless economic depression. Between August 1929 and March 1933 industrial production had fallen by more than 50 percent, deeply damaging the world's economy. The money supply had dropped by more than 30 percent, as had the general level of prices, and the financial system had been decimated by a series of banking crises and panics.

In North Carolina, then primarily an agricultural state, the deflation of crop prices was devastating. In 1933 gross farm income was only 46 percent of its 1929 level. The banking community that was so closely linked to the farming community consequently grew weaker and more desperate, and the absence of credit for farmers compounded an already miserable situation. Mass unemployment had become increasingly widespread across the state and nation. By 1933 in North Carolina, 27 out of every 100 persons were on relief; mountain and coastal regions were hardest hit. As one editor of an eastern North Carolina newspaper put it, "a trail of poverty" ran through Northampton, Martin, Bertie, Gates, and Halifax Counties.

North Carolina industries saw the decline in manufacturing value added by more than 50 percent—from $1.3 billion in 1930 to $878 million in 1933. From 1929 to 1933 North Carolina cotton and textile industry wages declined 25 percent. Falling wages and mass unemployment led to substantial labor unrest across the state.

New Deal Agencies in North Carolina

On becoming president, Roosevelt immediately instituted many reforms that had an instant positive impact in North Carolina and throughout the nation. These expedients included removing the gold standard for U.S. currency, instituting a bank holiday for a three-day period in 1933, and establishing federal deposit insurance and a series of measures to provide financial rehabilitation for the banking community, debtors, and individuals seeking credit. Perhaps most important to North Carolina and other states, the Roosevelt administration established New Deal programs that greatly aided the economy, made needed improvements to North Carolina's transportation and other infrastructures, built numerous public-use and cultural facilities, and created employment opportunities for thousands of citizens.

Few states were willing to wholeheartedly accept the liberalism of the New Deal's revolutionary programs, and North Carolina was no exception. The state's relative poverty, and the allocation of federal welfare and construction funds on a matching basis, made full participation in the programs difficult. Governors John C. B. Ehringhaus and Clyde R. Hoey and the legislature, dominated by farmers and conservative businessmen, were determined to both resist Roosevelt's advanced social agenda and maintain a balanced state budget. Nevertheless, several New Deal initiatives had wide influence in North Carolina.

Agricultural Adjustment Administration (AAA). The the most important New Deal program for North Carolina, the AAA initiated farm production control that proved to be a boon to tobacco, though less to cotton. During the early years of the Depression, tobacco prices plummeted from around 20.0 cents per pound during the end of the 1920s to 8.4 cents in 1931. Cotton prices fell from 22 cents a pound in 1925 to 6 cents in 1931. To improve crop prices, the AAA offered rental and benefit payments to farmers who reduced crop production. County agents of the Agricultural Extension Service worked with local committees of farmers to administer the program.

Agricultural officials focused first on cotton. Because crops for the 1933 season had already been planted, the AAA decided that farmers nationally had to plow up 10 million acres of planted cotton. North Carolina's 150,000 cotton farmers mobilized by signing individual contracts to destroy part of their crop in return for government payments. The plan brought immediate positive results. Cotton prices rose from 7.12 cents per pound in 1932 to 10.80 cents in 1933; cotton income rose 57 percent throughout 1932, and government payments to cotton farmers totaled nearly $3 million. In 1934 Congress enacted compulsory crop control for cotton through the Bankhead Act, taxing the cotton of nonparticipating farmers. Cotton growers, in a referendum on crop control, overwhelmingly approved it. Through 1935 prices inched upward and acres in cultivation declined dramatically.

Crop controls for flue-cured tobacco developed after growers, angry about low opening market prices in 1933, pressured the AAA's Tobacco Section to persuade cigarette manufacturers to pay higher prices. To assure tobacco companies of their seriousness, AAA officials asked tobacco farmers to sign up for a 30 percent acreage reduction for 1934 and 1935. After 95 percent of tobacco growers complied, manufacturers eventually accepted a marketing agreement, promising a set price for the 1933 crop. The results were striking: that year, tobacco sold for 15.3 cents per pound compared to 11.6 cents in 1932. The AAA's tobacco program was successful, as the policy of scarcity drove prices up. For each year between 1934 and 1939, flue-cured tobacco farmers earned three times as much for their crop as they had in 1932.

In 1936 the U.S. Supreme Court declared the AAA unconstitutional. But farmers continued to consent to AAA tenets through referenda and participated in the decentralized, local administration of the program. Businessmen and politicians were enthusiastic allies, and in 1938 Congress reestablished many AAA programs, including marketing quotas. These congressional programs of 1938 brought crop control again to North Carolina tobacco farmers. Financed by general revenues rather than a tax on cigarette manufacturers (as was the first AAA), this scheme proved constitutional and growers overwhelmingly endorsed it.

Federal Emergency Relief Administration (FERA). Created to give direct cash relief for states and local governments to distribute, FERA funds between 1933 and 1935 provided relief payments to about 300,000 North Carolinians per month. Governor Ehringhaus established the North Carolina Emergency Relief Administration (NCERA) to distribute the federal funds, but local state welfare personnel often were FERA officers. Ehringhaus selected Annie Land O'Berry to direct the NCERA. She eventually administered the NCERA with 220 state office employees and about 2,000 county level assistants.

From 1933 to 1935 the NCERA administered relief remarkably free from corruption, spending almost $40 million in federal dollars and about $700,000 in local money. In addition to general relief, it funded public works, rural rehabilitation, education projects, a cattle program, distribution of surplus commodities, a fishing cooperative, and an urban vagrancy program.

In 1935 Congress stopped grants to states for direct relief, ending the NCERA, and in its place created work relief under the Works Progress Administration. From 1933 to 1935 about 10 percent of North Carolina's population was on relief, but these funds proved inadequate in both urban and rural areas, despite the millions of dollars that the FERA poured into the state. Per capita, North Carolina ranked a lowly forty-third nationally in FERA grants.

Public Works Administration (PWA). Created under the National Industrial Recovery Act in June 1933, the PWA sought to stimulate business activity by offering loans to private industry to build public works, also indirectly providing work relief. The PWA spent millions on constructing facilities at Fort Bragg in Fayetteville, improving the navigability of the Cape Fear River, and expanding the Blue Ridge Parkway. In 1934 the PWA allotment for North Carolina, including both federal and nonfederal projects, totaled just over $22 million. Former highway department chairman Frank Page and University of North Carolina engineering dean Herman G. Baity headed the Advisory Committee on Public Works for the state. By the end of the 1930s, the PWA in North Carolina had sponsored 903 projects at an estimated cost of $86.1 million and employed 6,938 workers.

Works Progress Administration (WPA). Intended as a permanent replacement for the FERA, the WPA concentrated on providing jobs for the able-bodied unemployed. Programs ranged from large construction projects to undertakings in social services, public health, conservation, education, the fine arts, and scholarly research. George W. Coan, former mayor of Winston-Salem, was appointed the first state administrator of the WPA in North Carolina in 1935. He was succeeded by Charles C. McGinnis in 1939.

Local conservative opposition to the WPA contributed to a relatively low amount of WPA spending in the state. Despite this, the WPA built 14,500 miles of highways, roads, and streets and about 700 bridges in North Carolina. Road projects concentrated on constructing secondary and "farm-to-market" routes and repairing and straightening existing roads. In towns, the WPA built sidewalks, curbs, gutters, and culverts and removed streetcar tracks. Workers raised nearly 1,000 new public structures, including city halls, municipal office buildings and garages, courthouses, and National Guard armories; they erected, renovated, or upgraded numerous schools, utility plants, water treatment plants, sewage treatment plants, reservoirs, airports, parks, school and municipal stadiums, and hospitals.

WPA North Carolina conservation projects included restoring oyster beds, building sand fences along the Outer Banks, planting more than 633,000 trees, restocking streams with trout and bass, and constructing levees, jetties, and breakwaters. In WPA sewing rooms, North Carolina women made more than 10 million garments and many Christmas presents for the needy. A WPA sewing room provided the first costumes

for the outdoor drama *The Lost Colony* in Manteo. The WPA organized school lunch and breakfast programs, served 54 million school lunches, and organized adult education and literacy classes and nursery schools. WPA workers rebound more than 4 million library books in North Carolina and expanded public library service to 41 additional counties.

The WPA also employed artists, writers, and musicians in North Carolina and established several community arts centers. The WPA's Federal Writers' Project paid writers to conduct oral history interviews and compile a state guidebook. Scholars recorded traditional blues, bluegrass, gospel, and other music indigenous to the state. The Historical Records Survey published the nation's most comprehensive inventory of county records, and WPA workers cataloged manuscript collections at the University of North Carolina at Chapel Hill and Duke University, as well as other public and private collections of records and manuscripts. The WPA Federal Theater Project, started in 1935, hired professional artists to assist in community drama, building on the work of the Carolina Playmakers in Chapel Hill to develop a native drama. The Theater Project aided children's theater in Greensboro and Charlotte and adult community drama in Raleigh, Wilmington, Wilson, and Kinston. Through the Federal Art and Music Projects, hundreds of thousands of North Carolinians experienced art exhibits, took courses, and attended lectures, demonstrations, and performances. The North Carolina Symphony started as a program of the Federal Music Project in 1932.

Civilian Conservation Corps (CCC). One of the most remarkable and innovative New Deal programs, the CCC employed young men between the ages of 18 and 25 on conservation-oriented projects with emphasis on reforestation and erosion control. To expedite immediate enrollment, every state, and every county in that state, was assigned a quota of CCC enrollees based on population. North Carolina's quota ranged from 253 enrollees for Mecklenburg County to 9 for Dare County. The War Department screened enrollees and sent the eligible recruits to a military base, such as Fort Bragg, for a brief period of physical conditioning before assigning them to work projects.

The CCC had at least 66 camps in North Carolina, employing 13,600 men in 47 counties. One of the earliest camps was Camp John Rock, which operated in what is now the Pisgah National Forest from 1933 to 1936. The camp's major projects included a fish hatchery, fawn rearing, road building and maintenance, trail improvement, reforestation, and forest conservation. By the end of the program in July 1942, CCC workers had rehabilitated thousands of acres of ravaged land in North Carolina, including beach fronts. They also had either built or restored many recreational resources that established the state as a leader in tourism, including the Appalachian Trail, Great Smoky Mountains National Park, the Blue Ridge Parkway, national forests (such as Pisgah), state parks (such as

Civilian Conservation Corps workers in front of the barracks in which they were housed at Globe, 1934. Courtesy of NCOA&H.

Hanging Rock and Morrow Mountain), state forests, and the Cape Hatteras National Seashore.

National Youth Administration (NYA). The NYA was a student aid program organized in 1935 to keep young people in school. Initially, Charles E. McIntosh led the agency in North Carolina, but after August 1938 John A. Lang directed it. For the 1935–36 school year, the NYA provided $572,571 to assist an average of 5,907 students per month in 53 North Carolina colleges and 885 public schools. Students received part-time jobs, scholarships, and loans based on need. By 1941 NYA enrollments peaked at 15,000 students per month. North Carolina ranked second nationally in the number of participating schools and colleges. Lang, an energetic and capable director, was responsible for much of this success.

National Recovery Administration (NRA). In June 1933 Congress created the NRA to regulate wages, hours, and production to stimulate business recovery. Most North Carolina employers welcomed the assistance, with cotton textile executives in the forefront. Textile companies had cooperated with each other through a trade association since the 1920s, and the NRA strengthened efforts to bring order to the industry by establishing a textile code calling for a 40-hour work-

week, a two-shift limit, and a minimum wage (lower in the South than in the North). Employers had to accept the right of workers to unionize and eliminate child labor, but they exercised power as principal administrators of the textile code through their trade association. By the end of 1933, use of the NRA textile code had produced only a modest increase in profits and wages. In 1934 opposition to the code mounted. Mill owners continued to take a tough stand against unions, and NRA collective bargaining rights remained illusory to textile workers in the state. By May 1935, when the U.S. Supreme Court declared the NRA unconstitutional, it had fallen short of its major goals for North Carolina's cotton textile industry.

The furniture industry, the state's third-largest commercial enterprise, had a similar relationship with the NRA. Conditions had been bad for the industry since the 1920s, and its leaders were eager for assistance; the NRA and manufacturers created and enforced a code with little difficulty. The program proved so helpful that in May 1935, when the Supreme Court ended the NRA, furniture executives sought its continuance.

The tobacco industry in North Carolina was not nearly as cooperative with the NRA as textile and furniture manufacturers had been. Cigarette companies, prosperous despite the

Depression, did not need the NRA. They signed a temporary agreement in August 1933 but did not begin code hearings until a year later. The code was not completed until a few months before the NRA was invalidated.

Tennessee Valley Authority (TVA). Created by Congress in 1933, the TVA was to be a bold experiment in the use of regional planning to achieve "the unified conservation and development" of the Tennessee River Valley. The Tennessee River, rendered barely navigable by reefs and shoals, flows 650 miles from Knoxville south into Alabama and then northwest to its juncture with the Ohio River at Paducah, Ky. Its entire watershed, comprised of tributaries extending into Alabama, Georgia, Kentucky, Mississippi, North Carolina, and Virginia, came under the TVA's jurisdiction. The primary goals of the TVA were flood control, river navigation, and the generation of hydroelectric power. The authority also sought to enhance the valley's socioeconomic development by creating agricultural programs, such as those to promote soil conservation and improve fertilizers; facilitating the purchase of low-cost electrical appliances; and forming model communities with libraries, schools, and parks.

The TVA's impact in North Carolina can be seen in the far southwestern counties, where the authority built four dams in the 1930s and 1940s—the Hiwassee, Chatuge, and Appalachia Dams on the Hiwassee River and the Fontana Dam on the Little Tennessee River.

Social Security Act (SSA). The SSA, passed by Congress in 1935, not only introduced compulsory old-age and survivors' insurance but also provided federal funding for state unemployment compensation and a variety of state welfare programs. Under the act, when states established qualifying unemployment compensation programs, they would receive 90 percent of the federal payroll taxes collected in the state. States that did not have approved programs would lose the payroll taxes collected after 1 Jan. 1936. Since North Carolina's program did not meet the federal guidelines, a special session of the General Assembly was required to enact the needed legislation. Governor Ehringhaus was reluctant to call the special session and delayed action until December 1936, when the legislature created the state Unemployment Security Commission. The SSA also provided matching funds for state old-age pensions; state programs for blind, dependent children; and vocational rehabilitation. Initially, North Carolina did not contribute sufficient matching funds to receive the maximum payment allowed by the federal program, foreshadowing future problems in state-federal relations.

References: Douglas Carl Abrams, *Conservative Constraints: North Carolina and the New Deal* (1992); Anthony J. Badger, *North Carolina and the New Deal* (1981); Badger, *Prosperity Road: The New Deal, Tobacco, and North Carolina* (1980); John L. Bell Jr., *Hard Times: Beginnings of the Great Depression in North Carolina, 1929–1933* (1982); James S. Fackler and Randall E. Parker, "Accounting for the Great Depression: A Historical Decomposition," *Journal of Macroeconomics* 16 (Spring 1994); Ronald E. Marcello, "The Politics of Relief: The North Carolina WPA and the Tar Heel Elections of 1936," *NCHR* 68 (January 1991).

Douglas Carl Abrams
Randall E. Parker
Additional research provided by H. Tyler Blethen, Michael Hill, Harley E. Jolley, David A. Norris, and George W. Troxler.

SEE ALSO Blue Ridge Parkway; Federal Writers' Project; Fontana Dam; State Planning Board.

Great Dismal Swamp. The mysteriously and formidably named Great Dismal Swamp straddles the North Carolina–Virginia border only a few miles inland from the Atlantic coast. This region was referred to in correspondence as "dismal swamp" as early as 1715, and appears as Great Dismal Swamp on the 1733 Moseley map. The Great Dismal is a relatively young feature on the North American continent. Believed to be only about 10,000 years in age, the Great Dismal is a wet, forested mantle of peat above a Pleistocene-era ocean bed. Once a vast morass over 2,000 square miles in size, it is now a hemmed-in wilderness only a fraction of its original size, with approximately 175 square miles of it preserved as the Great Dismal Swamp National Wildlife Refuge. As such, it is one of the most important black bear sanctuaries in the eastern United States and a breeding paradise for songbirds returning from South America, Central America, and the Caribbean each spring.

Native Americans hunted this area thousands of years before European settlement, when it was a great reach of open marsh. Archaeological digs have discovered countless artifacts —including bola weights, projectile points, tools, and weapons—that the Indians used. Once the Ice Age ended and the climate warmed, the cold weather woods fell in succession to new forests, first of beech and birch, then of oak and hickory, and, finally, a wet stretch of cypress, gum, and juniper (Atlantic white cedar).

The huge wilderness lying between the first two English settlements in the New World, the Great Dismal Swamp long held the attention of American settlers. William Byrd II, one of Virginia's commissioners for the 1728 boundary line survey expedition, wrote memorably of the swamp and its nearby inhabitants in both his official report, *History of the Dividing Line betwixt Virginia and Carolina*, and his rich, ribald daybook, *The Secret History of the Line*. These manuscripts circulated widely among Virginia's eighteenth-century social and business elite and influenced contemporary thinking about swamp drainage and agriculture, as well as the potential for a commercial shipping route through the Dismal Swamp to connect the Chesapeake and the Albemarle.

Young George Washington, who considered reclamation of

the Great Dismal for farming a grand opportunity, successfully organized an agricultural syndicate, "the Adventurers for Draining the Dismal Swamp," in the 1760s. Washington Ditch, the first canal to penetrate the swamp, runs from what was once the "Dismal Town" settlement south of Suffolk down to Lake Drummond, the 3,100-acre natural lake at the swamp's center, discovered by and named for William Drummond, governor of Albemarle in the 1660s and subsequently a participant in Bacon's Rebellion in Virginia.

Rice and corn farming in the Dismal Swamp was only marginally successful, and, as the Dismal Swamp Company, Washington's adventurers moved into what would be an enormously profitable enterprise: timbering, felling cypress and juniper trees, riving shingles in the swamp, and shipping them out by flat boats called lighters. By 1795 the Dismal Swamp Company had cut over 1.5 million shingles in the Great Dismal Swamp. Though wooden shingles would eventually give way to tin and slate as popular roofing materials, vigorous swamp timbering operations employing railroads and, later, trucks would go on from after the Civil War until well into the twentieth century.

Between 1793 and 1814, a combine called the Dismal Swamp Canal Company realized Byrd's dream and dug a major shipping canal between Deep Creek, Va., and South Mills, N.C., connecting the Elizabeth River to the Pasquotank River and, thereby, creating an important water communication between the Chesapeake and the Albemarle. In 1812 the Canal Company dug the Feeder Ditch between Lake Drummond and the Dismal Swamp Canal in order to keep the canal's level at depths sufficient to float large craft, and the first real ship (a 20-ton craft bearing bacon and brandy from the Roanoke River) finally made passage through the Dismal Swamp Canal in June 1814.

Among important literary works set in the Great Dismal Swamp are Thomas Moore's wildly popular 1803 ghost ballad, "The Lake of the Dismal Swamp," a poem that engendered something of a nineteenth-century tourist business for the Great Dismal; Henry Wadsworth Longfellow's 1842 poem, "The Slave in the Dismal Swamp"; and Harriet Beecher Stowe's 1856 novel *Dred: A Tale of the Dismal Swamp*, her best-selling successor to *Uncle Tom's Cabin*. Stowe's work, in which a fictional slave runaway named Dred hides out in the swamp, was inspired by the true story of Southampton, Va., slave rebel Nat Turner and played upon the well-known fact that there was a large runaway-slave population living within the swamp for decades prior to the Civil War. Other noteworthy comments on the Great Dismal's evolving life and lore since Byrd's day include works by Johann David Schoepf, Edmund Ruffin, Frederick Law Olmsted, Porte Crayon (David Hunter Strother), and Alexander Hunter.

On the anniversary of George Washington's birthday in 1973, Union Camp Corporation made a donation of its 49,100-acre holding in the swamp, land that is the core of today's 111,000-acre Great Dismal Swamp National Wildlife Refuge. This grant, made through the Nature Conservancy to the U.S. Department of Interior's Fish and Wildlife Service, was the largest single land donation to that date ever made to the American people for wildlife preservation.

References: Paul W. Kirk Jr., ed., *The Great Dismal Swamp* (1979); Charles Royster, *The Fabulous History of the Dismal Swamp Company* (1999); Bland Simpson, *The Great Dismal: A Carolinian's Swamp Memoir* (1990).

Bland Simpson

SEE ALSO Dismal Swamp Canal.

Great Falls Mills, chartered by the North Carolina General Assembly on 10 Apr. 1869, was located in Rockingham (Richmond County) at the falls of Falling Creek and along railroads lines from Wilmington, Charlotte, and Rutherfordton. The company acquired its property in November 1868 from the Richmond Manufacturing Company, whose textile mill had been burned by Union general William T. Sherman's troops in March 1865 near the end of the Civil War. The superintendents' and workers' houses, storehouses, and a church survived. Walter Francis Leak, John Wall Leak, and Robert Leak Steele rebuilt the textile mill, acquired by Claude Gore in 1901. The mill engaged in the whole manufacturing process, from carding and spinning to dyeing and weaving. When it closed in 1930, the facility included a five-story building, a dye house, 6 warehouses, 2 office buildings, 42 spinning frames, and 205 looms. The mill burned in 1972, but much of the ruins remained.

Reference: James E. and Ida C. Huneycutt, *A History of Richmond County* (1976).

John L. Bell

Great Smoky Mountains National Park. The movement to create national parks in the United States to preserve the environment from human encroachment and development began with the establishment of Yellowstone in 1872. Unlike national forests, which are multiple-use areas and can be commercially exploited, national parks are intended to protect flora and fauna in their natural habitats. Suggestions for creating a park in western North Carolina arose in the 1880s. A serious effort was launched in Asheville in 1899 with the formation of the Appalachian National Park Association, but the lumber industry was opposed and the federal government uninterested.

By 1924 national opinion grew much more favorable toward preserving important wilderness areas. Seventeen national parks existed by then, but only one, Acadia on the coast of Maine, was east of the Mississippi River. In that year U.S.

secretary of the interior Hubert Work appointed a committee to study some 30 proposed sites for an eastern park. Among them were two sites in North Carolina: the Linville Gorge–Grandfather Mountain area and a rugged section of the Great Smoky Mountains straddling the border between North Carolina and Tennessee. Although the latter area was being intensively logged, about one-third of it was still old-growth forest.

In 1924 Work's committee recommended establishing two parks, Shenandoah in the Blue Ridge Mountains of Virginia and the Great Smoky Mountains National Park. The following year, Congress authorized the secretary to determine boundaries for the proposed parks and begin accepting donations of land and money. Unlike the 17 previous parks, which were created by setting aside federal lands, these two new ones were to be formed by purchasing lands from private owners. The proposed area for the Great Smoky Mountains National Park, encompassing 704,000 acres, was controlled by more than 6,600 owners. With strong support from advocates such as David C. Chapman, Carlos C. Campbell, and Willis P. Davis of Knoxville, Tenn., and Horace Kephart, author of the popular *Our Southern Highlanders*, of Bryson City, N.C., a fund-raising campaign began that eventually brought in $1 million. In 1926 President Calvin Coolidge signed a law providing for the official establishment and administration of the park as soon as a minimum of 150,000 acres had been bought and turned over to the federal government. Actual development of the park would only begin when purchases reached 300,000 acres.

Besides raising the needed funds to purchase the land, the park's founders also faced the difficulty of persuading all the owners of land within the proposed boundary to sell. Over 85 percent of the area was owned by 18 timber and pulpwood companies who valued their holdings as a source of hardwoods and southern conifers. Most of them were willing to sell their land, but only after they had harvested the timber. Another 1,200 of the targeted tracts were farms of various sizes, many of them family homesteads passed down from generation to generation whose owners were reluctant to sell. Finally, some 5,000 small lots and summer homes lay inside the park boundary. To deal with these reluctant landowners, the state legislatures invoked the right of condemnation. Many landowners, especially the logging companies, fought condemnation in the courts, so the purchase of land for the park dragged on for more than ten years. The resulting removal of residents from their communities, schools, churches, and cemeteries generated hard feelings that still linger among the people of the area.

In 1930 a road was built through the park connecting Cherokee, N.C., with Gatlinburg, Tenn., and crossing through Newfound Gap. Four years later, enough land had been purchased to convince Congress to authorize full establishment and development of the park. President Franklin D. Roosevelt dedicated it in a ceremony held at Newfound Gap on 2 Sept. 1940.

National parks are administered to achieve two often-conflicting goals: conserving the land and making it available for public use. Advocates of these opposing objectives fought each other over the establishment of the Great Smoky Mountains National Park, and they continue to argue over its administration as more than 9 million people visit the park each year. Land in the park has been conserved. Its approximately 521,000 acres enclose a wildlands sanctuary at its lower elevations that preserves the world's finest example of a temperate deciduous forest. Along the park's mountain crests, more than 6,000 feet high, stretches a conifer forest like those found in central Canada. The park has been designated an International Biosphere Reserve in recognition of the more than 1,500 kinds of flowering plants it contains, and animals such as wolves, elk, and river otters have been reintroduced into its environment.

The desire to conserve this environment led to an unfortunate decision in the park's early days to eradicate all human traces from the land. Consequently, the National Park Service destroyed most of the structures left behind when inhabitants moved out. Only later did park managers change their philosophy to allow the preservation of cultural history. The most significant examples of the amended policy are the restoration of some structures in Cades Cove and in the Cataloochee Valley. As a result of the new policy, the park has been designated a World Heritage Site, unfortunately not before much of its historical and cultural importance was destroyed. Today, the environmental purposes of the Great Smoky Mountains National Park are seriously threatened by air pollution generated outside its borders, and its name, originally a romantic description of the natural haze created by the respiration of its massive forests, is now, ironically, more technically accurate.

H. Tyler Blethen

Great Trading Path, or the Occaneechi Path, was one of many Indian trails in use when the English first explored the North Carolina backcountry during the late seventeenth century. Before recorded history, the trail likely existed as a series of minor, shorter footpaths that linked the many small villages scattered across the Piedmont landscape. However, with the establishment of a fur trade between Virginians and the Catawba, Cherokee, and neighboring Siouan tribes during the 1670s, it quickly became the primary route of travel and commerce across the North Carolina Piedmont. For about 30 years, the trail was traveled by Virginia traders whose lengthy pack trains brought European manufactures such as metal tools, cloth, blankets, trinkets, firearms, ammunition, and rum to the native population. On the return trip, their horses carried deerskins and furs bound for markets in Europe.

Knowledge about the location of the Great Trading Path and the Indian villages along it comes primarily from two sources. First, they are recorded in the journals and accounts of those who actually journeyed along the trail, such as John Lederer in 1670, James Needham and Gabriel Arthur in 1673, and John Lawson in 1701. These accounts provide a firsthand glimpse into the cultural and physical geography of the trail. Second, because of the trail's prominence in the fur trade and the fact that it was later transformed into a wagon road (after the mid-eighteenth-century arrival in the Piedmont of immigrants of English, German, and Scotch-Irish descent), it has been preserved on several colonial maps of North Carolina, such as those by Edward Moseley in 1733, John Collet in 1770, and Henry Mouzon in 1775.

The Great Trading Path ran southwestward from Fort Henry (now Petersburg, Va.) to Occaneechi Island (at Clarksville, Va.), where the Occaneechi tribe resided and acted as middlemen in the trade during the 1670s. From there the trail ran southward into North Carolina, crossing the Tar River near Oxford. After the Occaneechi tribe's defeat during Bacon's Rebellion of 1676, this segment of the trail was abandoned for a more easterly route that crossed the Roanoke River at Moniseep Ford near the North Carolina–Virginia line. From Oxford, the trading path ran southwest toward present-day Charlotte, crossing the Flat and Little Rivers north of Durham, the Eno River at Hillsborough, the Haw River near Swepsonville, the Uwharrie River west of Asheboro, and the Yadkin River at the Trading Ford near Spencer. From the Trading Ford, the trail turned south toward the populous Catawba and Waxhaw villages on the Catawba River below Charlotte. From the Catawba, trails ran both westward toward the Lower Cherokee and southward to the Congaree River (near Columbia, S.C.) and Augusta, Ga., trading posts.

North Carolina Indian tribes whose villages were located along or near the Great Trading Path during the late 1600s and early 1700s include the Saponi and Tutelo (at the Trading Ford), the Keyauwee (on Caraway Creek), the Sissipahaw (along the Haw River), the Occaneechi and Shakori (on the Eno River), and the Eno (on the Little and Flat Rivers).

References: Clarence W. Alvord and Lee Bidgood, *The First Explorations of the Trans-Allegheny Region by the Virginians, 1650–1674* (1912); William P. Cumming, ed., *The Discoveries of John Lederer* (1958); Cumming, *North Carolina in Maps* (1966); Douglas L. Rights, "The Trading Path to the Indians," NCHR 8 (October 1931).

R. P. Stephen Davis Jr.

Great Wagon Road was the most important frontier road in the state's western Piedmont during the eighteenth century. Sometimes called the "Great Philadelphia Wagon Road," it began in Philadelphia, crossed westward to Gettysburg, turned south to Hagerstown, Md., continued south to Winchester, Va., through the Shenandoah Valley to Roanoke, and on to the North Carolina border. There it entered present-day northeastern Stokes County and passed through Walnut Cove, Germanton, Winston-Salem, Salisbury, and Charlotte before continuing into South Carolina and Georgia.

The route that became the Great Wagon Road was originally a Native American hunting, trade, and war trail called the "Warrior's Path." In the mid-1700s European colonists, many arriving from ships in or near Philadelphia, began traveling south along the trail in search of land for new homes. At first the road was so narrow and rough that only travelers on horseback could use it; the farther south it went (from Pennsylvania into the wilderness), the more impassable it became. But as the settlers made their way along the trail, they cut trees, found suitable fords across rivers, and worked around obstacles until wagons could pass. In time the Great Wagon Road improved, by colonial standards.

From the 1750s the Great Wagon Road was critical to the development of North Carolina. Tens of thousands of German and Scotch-Irish immigrants entered the colony from the north along the road and settled in the western Piedmont. The Moravian settlements of Bethabara, Bethania, and Salem, as well as the cities of Salisbury and Charlotte, owe their creation and expansion to the Great Wagon Road. Important as a trade route, it provided a means for transporting frontier goods like deerskins to trade for salt, firearms, iron, and other items. Livestock such as hogs were herded down the road to markets in Virginia or South Carolina. In fact, the road was crucial to the survival of the western fringe of colonial settlement.

During the Revolutionary War, the Great Wagon Road was the key supply line to the American resistance in the western areas of the colonies, especially in the South. For this reason Lord Charles Cornwallis led his English army from Charleston to the Great Wagon Road at Camden, S.C. His troops marched north along the road through Charlotte, and later through Salisbury and Salem, in an attempt to destroy Gen. Nathanael Greene's Continental Army and civilian support in North Carolina. Although unsuccessful in all these efforts, Cornwallis fully understood the importance of the Great Wagon Road during the Revolution.

The road continued to play a significant economic role in North Carolina into the nineteenth century. With the expansion of railroads and the development of new roads in each community, however, it fell into disuse and in many areas disappeared. Much of the original route can still be found in Maryland and Virginia as State Highway 11, but there is no state or federal road that follows it in North Carolina. Parts of the old road can be found in heavily wooded tracts, and often local roads follow a brief stretch of the old route, but the cities that owe their existence to the Great Wagon Road have largely buried it through urban development.

References: Forrest W. Clonts, "Travel and Transportation in Colonial North Carolina," NCHR 3 (January 1926); James M. Cooper, *The Indian Trading Path and Great Wagon Road across*

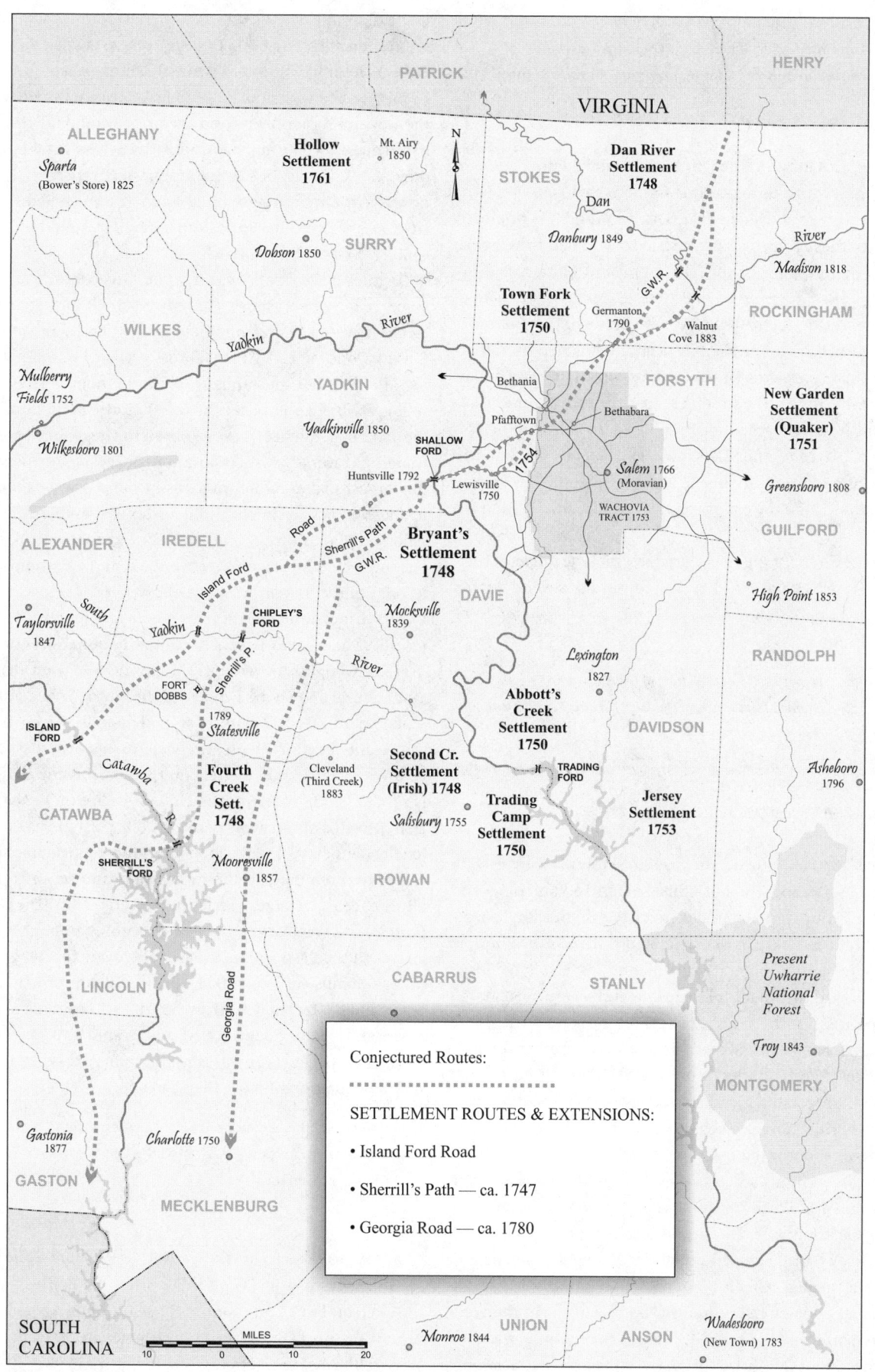

ALLEGHANY

Sparta
(Bower's Store) 1825

PATRICK

HENRY

VIRGINIA

**Hollow
Settlement
1761**

Mt. Airy
1850

N

STOKES

**Dan River
Settlement
1748**

Dan

Danbury 1849

Madison 1818

River

ROCKINGHAM

Dobson 1850

SURRY

**Town Fork
Settlement
1750**

Germanton,
1790

G.W.R.

Walnut
Cove 1883

WILKES

Yadkin

River

YADKIN

Yadkinville 1850

Bethania

FORSYTH

Pfafftown

Bethabara

**New Garden
Settlement
(Quaker)
1751**

*Mulberry
Fields* 1752

SHALLOW
FORD

Huntsville 1792

Lewisville
1750

1754

Salem 1766
(Moravian)

Greensboro 1808

Wilkesboro 1801

Road

Sherrill's Path

**Bryant's
Settlement
1748**

G.W.R.

WACHOVIA
TRACT 1753

GUILFORD

ALEXANDER

IREDELL

Island Ford

Mocksville
1839

DAVIE

High Point 1853

Taylorsville
1847

South

Yadkin

CHIPLEY'S
FORD

Sherrill's P.

Lexington
1827

RANDOLPH

River

**Abbott's
Creek
Settlement
1750**

FORT
DOBBS

1789
Statesville

**Second Cr.
Settlement
(Irish) 1748**

TRADING
FORD

DAVIDSON

Asheboro
1796

**ISLAND
FORD**

Cleveland
(Third Creek)
1883

Salisbury 1755

**Trading
Camp
Settlement
1750**

**Jersey
Settlement
1753**

Catawba R.

**Fourth
Creek
Sett.
1748**

**SHERRILL'S
FORD**

Mooresville
1857

ROWAN

*Present
Uwharrie
National
Forest*

LINCOLN

Georgia Road

CABARRUS

STANLY

Troy 1843

MONTGOMERY

Gastonia
1877

Conjectured Routes:

Charlotte 1750

GASTON

SETTLEMENT ROUTES & EXTENSIONS:

• Island Ford Road

• Sherrill's Path — ca. 1747

• Georgia Road — ca. 1780

MECKLENBURG

SOUTH
CAROLINA

MILES

10   0   10   20

UNION

Monroe 1844

ANSON

Wadesboro
(New Town) 1783

The Great Wagon Road and its offshoots in North Carolina, 1750–1780. Map by Mark Anderson Moore, courtesy NCOA&H.

North Carolina: Highlighting Rowan and Cabarrus Counties (1995); C. Christopher Crittenden, "Overland Travel and Transportation in North Carolina, 1763–1789," *NCHR* 8 (July 1931).

R. Jackson Marshall III

Greene County, located in the Coastal Plain region of east central North Carolina, was formed from Dobbs County (which no longer exists) in 1791. Tuscarora Indians originally inhabited the region, but after a period of conflict with English settlers culminating in the Tuscarora and Yamassee Wars (1711–15), they were forced out. Greene County is the site of Fort Neoheroka, scene of the decisive battle of the Tuscarora War in March 1713. The site has been investigated by archaeologists in recent years. The county was originally named Glasgow County, for North Carolina secretary of state James Glasgow, but it was renamed for Revolutionary War commander Nathanael Greene after Glasgow was indicted for fraud in 1799. Communities in Greene County include Hookerton, Walstonburg, and the county seat, Snow Hill, incorporated in 1828.

Greene County agricultural products include tobacco, corn, soybeans, swine, and chickens. The county has several lumber mills. The population of Greene County was estimated to be 20,000 in 2004.

Reference: James M. Creech, *History of Greene County, North Carolina: Compiled from Legends, Hearsay, Records Found There and Elsewhere* (1979).

Allyson C. Criner

SEE ALSO Tuscarora Indians.

Greensboro and surrounding Guilford County were first inhabited by Occaneechi and other Siouan Indian tribes and later settled by Germans, Quakers of Welsh and English descent, and Scotch-Irish, who migrated to the North Carolina backcountry from the northern colonies, especially Pennsylvania, around the middle of the eighteenth century. In March 1781 the area was the site of a pivotal Revolutionary War battle when Gen. Nathanael Greene made a stand against the British troops of Lord Charles Cornwallis at Guilford Courthouse. Although Cornwallis prevailed, the encounter severely weakened the British force, which was forced to surrender at Yorktown seven months later.

Guilford's county seat was moved from Martinsville (originally named Guilford Courthouse), in the northwestern corner of the county, to the central location of Greensboro in 1808. Greensboro, named in honor of Nathanael Greene and originally spelled "Greensborough," soon achieved a reputation as an educational center. By 1837 Quakers in the community had formed a boarding school for training teachers. Known today as Guilford College, it was the first coeducational institution in the South. In 1838 Greensboro Female College (modern-day Greensboro College) was established. Bennett College, founded in 1873 as Bennett Seminary, has, for most of its history, been a school for African American women. In 1891 the General Assembly passed an act providing for the establishment of the Normal and Industrial School for White Girls (now the University of North Carolina at Greensboro). What is now North Carolina Agricultural and Technical State University was chartered in 1891 as the Agricultural and Mechanical College for the Colored Race.

Textiles have been important in Greensboro's economy since 1828, when Henry Humphreys built the state's first steam-powered cotton mill there. In 1895 brothers Moses and Caesar Cone picked Greensboro for their Southern Finishing and Warehouse Company, the forerunner of Cone Mills. In 1935 a company based in Burlington—Burlington Mills, founded by J. Spencer Love—moved to Greensboro and continued to diversify. VF Corporation, based in Greensboro, is the largest maker of denim jeans in the country. Major nontextile businesses include the insurance and media giant Jefferson-Pilot Corporation; tobacco company P. Lorillard; Lucent Technologies, an AT&T spin-off; and communications leader General Dynamics Advanced Technology Systems.

As the location of the famous Woolworth lunch counter sit-ins in February 1960, Greensboro drew national attention during the civil rights movement. The city has also been an important cultural and sports center. It is home to the headquarters of the Atlantic Coast Conference, and its coliseum hosts many important sporting events. Greensboro has been particularly rich in the field of music. The Euterpe Club, organized in 1889, is said to be the oldest music club in the South. R. Nathaniel Dett, director of music at Bennett College from 1937 to 1942, led the Bennett Women's Choir on annual tours in major cities across the country. The choir made appearances on a nationally broadcast CBS radio series in the early 1940s. The Greensboro Opera Association, the Greensboro Chamber Music Society, and the Eastern Music Festival provide further opportunities for musical enjoyment. Writer William Sydney Porter, better known by his pen name "O. Henry," was a Greensboro native and is memorialized by the city's annual O. Henry Festival. In 2005 Greensboro was North Carolina's third-largest city, with a population of more than 230,000.

References: Ethel Stephens Arnett, *Greensboro, North Carolina: The County Seat of Guilford* (1975); Gayle Hicks Fripp, *Greensboro: A Chosen Center* (2001).

Wiley J. Williams

SEE ALSO Eastern Music Festival; Greensboro College; Greensboro Sit-Ins; Guilford Courthouse, Battle of; Jefferson-Pilot Corporation; North Carolina Agricultural and Technical State University; University of North Carolina at Greensboro.

Greensboro College was chartered in 1838 by the Methodist Church as Greensboro Female College, the first chartered college for women in North Carolina and the third such institution in the United States. The first students entered in 1846 after the completion of a building that stood on the site of the current main building. The original building was destroyed by fire in 1863, forcing the college to close for ten years. In 1873 the college opened its doors in a new building, but by 1903—when Greensboro's Lucy H. Robertson had become the first woman president of a college in North Carolina—the trustees had decided to close Greensboro Female College and sell its assets. However, thanks to the efforts of Robertson and alumna Nannie Lee Smith, $25,000 was raised to keep the college afloat.

In 1912 the school's name was changed to Greensboro College for Women, and in 1913 the first bachelor's degrees were conferred. In 1919 the name was again changed, this time to Greensboro College. By the time of its centennial celebration in 1938, Greensboro College had reached a record enrollment of 400 students. In 1941 another major fire occurred when the main building was hit by lightning and partially destroyed. It was soon restored and remains Greensboro College's primary edifice facing West Market Street near downtown Greensboro, where it serves as an administrative center.

In 1954 Greensboro College began to admit men, making it one of the first women's colleges in the nation to do so. In 1968 Greensboro College joined with Guilford and Bennett Colleges as a part of the Greensboro Tri-College Consortium. Cross-registration enables students to take courses at colleges in other locations in Guilford County as well as at Elon University and Salem College.

By the early 2000s Greensboro College had an enrollment of more than 1,250 students served by 105 faculty members, with majors in 22 areas. The school is also a fully accredited teacher training institution.

References: Luther L. Gobbel, *Greensboro College, 1935–1952: My Seventeen Years as Its President with a Resume of the Years before 1935* (1977); Samuel B. Turrentine, *A Romance of Education: A Narrative Including Recollections and Other Facts Connected with Greensboro College* (1946).

Alexander R. Stoesen

Greensboro News and Record had its genesis in the afternoon *Greensboro Daily Record* and the morning *Greensboro Daily News*, both begun around the beginning of the twentieth century and both successful promoters of Greensboro as a railroad and industrial center. Harper Elam, John Benson, and Joseph Reece, printers who probably worked for the older *Greensboro Patriot*, founded the *Daily Record* on 17 Nov. 1890. After buying the shares of Elam and Benson, Reece continued to publish the newspaper until his death in 1915. It was then acquired by Al Fairbrother, who sold it to Julian Price and associates in 1919. The paper experienced several management changes before its purchase by the Greensboro News Company in 1930. Throughout its early history, the *Daily Record* identified itself with "independent-Democratic" party politics.

The *Greensboro Daily News* grew out of the old *Daily Industrial News*, first published by Carl Duncan in 1905 as an organ of the Republican Party. When the *Daily Industrial News* went bankrupt in 1908, its assets were bought by two Asheville newsmen, Walter A. Hildebrand and George Crater. E. B. Jeffress, also of Asheville, joined them as owners in 1911 and acquired the total assets in 1918. At that time he brought in Earle Godbey of Asheville as editor, A. L. Stockton as managing editor, and A. B. Joyner as business manager, all of whom became stockholders. Hildebrand, from whom the Jeffress associates bought their stock, was a Republican. One stipulation of the sale was that the *Greensboro Daily News* would always be "kind" to Republicans.

The new management of the *Daily News* considered itself "independent" politically but immediately became identified with Democratic politics through the statewide civic activities of Jeffress. He and Godbey attracted outstanding journalistic talent who went on to distinguished careers at other newspapers, including Gerald W. Johnson, *Baltimore Sun* editorialist and historian; Lenoir Chambers, Pulitzer Prize–winning editor of the *Norfolk Virginian-Pilot*; Ernest B. Hunter, managing editor of the *Charlotte Observer*; and Brodie S. Griffith, managing editor of the *Charlotte News*.

After the Greensboro News Company purchased the *Record* in 1930, the two newspapers continued as separate morning and afternoon publications. The *Daily News* had extended its circulation throughout much of the state, and under publisher Carl O. Jeffress and editors H. W. Kendall, Miles Wolff, and William D. Snider it established a national reputation for journalistic and literary excellence. It hired the first book page editor in the 1920s and the first editorial page cartoonist in the 1950s. Among its distinguished staffers in the post–World War II era were cartoonist Hugh Haynie, editor Miles Wolff, editorialist Henry Belk, and Pulitzer Prize winners Edwin M. Yoder Jr. and Jonathan Yardley.

The *Daily News* was also instrumental in the development of college sports in North Carolina, particularly basketball. Legendary sports editor Smith Barrier was an eloquent and tireless advocate during the early years of the Atlantic Coast Conference (ACC), which was formed in 1954. He and his talented staff were among the first to shine a journalistic spotlight on the "Big Four" basketball teams (Wake Forest, University of North Carolina at Chapel Hill, Duke, and North Carolina State), covering the contests and greatly increasing interest in ACC basketball, the state's premier spectator sport. The Greensboro Coliseum and ACC offices are Greensboro institutions largely because of the work of Barrier and the high-quality sports pages of the *Daily News*.

In 1965 Landmark Communications, Inc., of Norfolk, Va., bought the *Record* and the *Daily News*, and in March 1984 they were merged as the *Greensboro News and Record*, a morning publication. In 2006 the paper had a daily circulation of about 90,400 and a Sunday circulation of about 111,000.

Reference: Ethel Stephens Arnett, *Greensboro, North Carolina: The County Seat of Guilford* (1955).

William D. Snider

Greensboro Sit-Ins of February 1960 launched the movement to integrate lunch counters and other eating establishments throughout North Carolina and the rest of the South. Sit-ins had previously occurred in other places, but the Greensboro protests sparked widespread activism and media attention. The sit-ins began when four students from North Carolina Agricultural and Technical State University—Ezell A. Blair (now Jibreel Khazan), Franklin E. McCain, Joseph A. McNeil, and David L. Richmond—sat at the lunch counter of the Woolworth Store on Elm Street in Greensboro late on the afternoon of 1 Feb. 1960. At the time, Woolworth's only served African Americans at a stand-up counter. Instead of having the students arrested for trespassing, the manager closed the lunch counter, intending to leave them stranded at closing time. The Greensboro store, one of the most profitable in the region, had a large black clientele—hence the need for prudence. However, by not filing charges, the manager left an opening for further nonviolent action.

The next day, the number of demonstrators grew rapidly, and in the days and weeks that followed, sit-ins spread to other eating places in Greensboro's central business district. Some managers closed their operations, but by the end of the summer an agreement had been reached to end segregation in public eating places. In the process, Greensboro became an important focal point of the civil rights movement. In addition to the integration of many businesses, a principal outcome of the sit-ins at the national level was the creation of the Student Nonviolent Coordinating Committee, which pushed for the use of direct action to obtain civil rights.

In 1993 several local civic leaders founded an organization called Sit-In Movement, Inc., to purchase the original Woolworth building on Elm Street and create a museum to memorialize the events of 1960 and the years following. The modern-day International Civil Rights Center and Museum features a large auditorium, an art gallery, and 14 informative exhibits, including a popular "lunch counter experience."

References: William H. Chafe, *Civilities and Civil Rights: Greensboro, North Carolina, and the Black Struggle for Freedom* (1980); Miles H. Wolff, *Lunch at the Five and Ten: The Greensboro Sit-Ins, a Contemporary History* (1970).

Alexander R. Stoesen

SEE ALSO Student Nonviolent Coordinating Committee.

Green's Path was one of the principal routes used during the second and third quarters of the eighteenth century by settlers moving south from Virginia into those sections of the Roanoke, Tar, Neuse, and Cape Fear River basins that lay in the inner coastal plain of North Carolina. The path ran southwest between the Western and Eastern (or Tuscarora) Trading Paths, parallel to both. On Collet's 1770 map of the colony (which is essentially the work of William Churton and reflects information that had been current around 1764), Green's Path is shown as a route leading from Surrey and Brunswick Counties in Virginia into North Carolina, crossing the Roanoke River at Eaton's Ferry (now covered by Lake Gaston in northeastern Warren County). From there the path ran south-southwest into modern western Nash County and then into eastern Johnston County, where it shifted to a southwest course, crossing the Lower Little River at the old Cumberland County Courthouse at Chafferington. The path continued to Cross Creek, where it intersected an east-west path connecting the section of the Western Trading Path on the head of the Rocky River with the Eastern Trading Path near Nahunta. It then merged with a road following a south-southeast direction along the western side of the Cape Fear River to settlements in Bladen County.

Edgecombe County court records from the 1730s and 1740s speak of persons using "John Green's Path" to travel from Contentnea Creek to the Tar River and up the Tar to the Western Trading Path. Those records also include testimony reporting the passage of a family that had set off for Green's Path on their departure from Edgecombe County to South

Students from North Carolina Agricultural and Technical College sit in at the whites-only lunch counter at the F. W. Woolworth store in downtown Greensboro on 1 Feb. 1960. Left to right: Ezell Blair, Franklin McCain, David Richmond, and Joseph McNeil. *Greensboro News and Record.*

Yates Mill, a gristmill in Wake County, 1958. Courtesy of NCOA&H.

Carolina and Georgia. Presumably these references are to the same path. If so, the path assumedly took its name from John Green, whose family accompanied him from Virginia to the Roanoke River settlements around 1715, moving down to the Tar River around 1730 and on to Bladen County around 1740. None of the original route of Green's Path appears to have survived in the state's modern road system, but the road leading south-southeast on the west side of the Cape Fear River from Cross Creek (modern Fayetteville) through Elizabethtown before reaching Wilmington appears to have survived in large part as State Highway 87.

Reference: C. Christopher Crittenden, "Overland Travel and Transportation in North Carolina, 1763–1789," *NCHR* 8 (July 1931).

George Stevenson

Gristmills used to grind corn, wheat, and other grains into flour and meal were a common sight in eighteenth- and nineteenth-century North Carolina. The first recorded North American gristmill was built in Jamestown, Va., in 1621. As settlers moved from the Jamestown area into what is now

northeastern North Carolina, they carried their milling techniques with them and began building small mills to grind grain.

Gristmills generally operated by guiding a stream of water into a waterwheel, which provided the power to rotate the series of huge millstones that crushed the grain into progressively smaller pieces. Most early North Carolina gristmills were situated along creeks for a source of waterpower, usually near natural falls. Many gristmills had saws attached, harnessing the waterpower not only to grind flour but also to saw lumber. Power was increased by building dams. On some mills, millraces were built to carry water to the mill, particularly those equipped with an overshot type of wheel.

The demand for grinding grain for use as flour or meal grew as the population of North Carolina increased. In an effort to encourage the settlement of the Carolina backcountry frontier, the legislature in 1715 passed a law granting 50 acres of land and exemption from taxes and service in the state militia to gristmill and sawmill operators. This act contained a provision subjecting all mills to government regulation because of their "public" character. Despite these efforts, the number of mills in the colony remained small until the mid-eighteenth century. A more extensive and detailed law was passed in 1758, giving the colonial government greater supervision over the operation of mills.

Roller mills, an 1876 invention first used in John Sellers's mill in Philadelphia, had a tremendous impact on the milling industry. The roller mill had several advantages over stone mills. Primary among them was a product that was more uniform and had a more appealing appearance to customers. The use of rollers eliminated the need for stone "dressing," the periodic sharpening of millstones, saving the miller money and time. The rollers also extracted more flour from the same amount of wheat as the millstones. Most North Carolina mills built after 1876 were of this variety.

Few of North Carolina's older gristmills remained operational at the beginning of the twenty-first century, having become obsolete in the shadow of the larger, more efficient grain processors of the Midwest. House's Mill near Newton Grove in Sampson County claims to be the oldest continuously operating gristmill in the state, having ground flour and meal since 1812.

Reference: Grimsley Hobbs, *Exploring the Old Mills of North Carolina* (1985).

Joey Powell
Additional research provided by Natalie Popovic.

Grits, a staple in North Carolina homes and restaurants, are a simple, nutritious dish made from the rougher bits of grain and husk left over after the miller grinds corn for meal. Grits have generally been underappreciated, at times even ridiculed, outside the South. Grits are not hominy, though many dictionaries describe grits as "coarse hominy." Well-prepared grits are a flavorful addition to ham and eggs, while poorly prepared grits usually sit in the bowl and turn into a glue-like substance.

Early North Carolina cooks liked grits because they were wholesome and easy to prepare. After an overnight soaking in salted water, the grits were put on the stove top for a slow boil. Frequent stirring was necessary to avoid lumps, but within 20 minutes the chef had produced a pleasing pot of grits. The dish was set at the back of the stove to remain warm and, if necessary, a little more water was added just before serving. Often day-old grits were fried, drizzled with maple syrup, and recycled as another breakfast dish. Grits were a good energy food that prepared the farmer for a hard day in the fields.

Grits remain a ubiquitous side dish in North Carolina kitchens and restaurants and have even become commonplace in meals other than breakfast. North Carolina chef Bill Neal was a pioneer in the creative use of grits, and variations on his famed shrimp and grits recipe, first published in *Bill Neal's Southern Cooking* in 1985, continue to be popular.

References: Cornelius O. Cathey, *Agriculture in North Carolina before the Civil War* (1966); John Egerton, *Southern Food: At Home, on the Road, in History* (1987); Bill Neal and David Perry, *Good Old Grits Cookbook: Have Grits Your Way* (1991).

Marilyn Wright

Grocery Stores. North Carolina is home to one of the nation's largest supermarket chains, Food Lion, as well as major regional chains. One of the state's earliest grocery chains, Pender Stores (forerunner of Colonial Stores and Big Star), was founded in 1900 by David Pender, the nephew of Pender County namesake Maj. Gen. William Dorsey Pender, a Confederate leader slain at Gettysburg. The first Pender Store opened on Monticello Avenue in Norfolk in 1901 and eventually expanded to include a delicatessen, soda fountain, and restaurant under the name Pender's Mammoth Food Department Store. By 1926, when controlling interest in the business was sold to New York investors, the Pender Stores had expanded to 244 locations, many in North Carolina, and employed more than 1,500 people. Pender remained as managing director, and his chain merged with the Rogers chain of stores in Georgia, Alabama, and South Carolina to cover the entire Southeast. In the mid-1930s, they were the first major chains in the South to move into the supermarket business. The larger supermarkets were named Big Star; their smaller counterparts were called Little Star. In 1940 the David Pender Grocery Company became Colonial Stores, Inc., and Rogers Stores ceased to exist. In 1988 Harris Teeter bought out the chain from the Grand Union Company, selling some Big Star stores to other chains while switching most to its brand.

Food Lion, originally called Food Town, was established in 1957 when Ralph Wright Ketner, along with his older brother Clifford Brown Ketner and family friend Wilson Smith, left the large southern supermarket chain Winn-Dixie to start their own store in Salisbury. Other Food Town stores were established, and early in 1968 Ralph Ketner, president and CEO of the company from the start, instituted what has become known as "the Big Change." He transformed the small chain virtually overnight into a food discount store operating under the "everyday low prices" concept, which was emerging at about the same time in general retailers such as Wal-Mart and K-Mart. Ketner cut the prices of thousands of items to levels at or below wholesale. This strategy proved extraordinarily successful, and Food Town grew dramatically over the next two decades from 7 stores and $5.8 million in sales in 1967 to 106 stores and $543 million in sales by 1980.

The name of the company was changed to Food Lion in 1983 after the discovery that another grocery firm owned the Food Town name. (The logo of the Belgium-based Delhaize Group, which acquired the company in the 1970s, featured a lion.) Clifford Brown Ketner left the company in the early 1970s, and Smith retired in 1979. Ralph Ketner held the reins until he stepped down as chairman of the board in 1991. He had gradually relinquished control to Tom E. Smith (no relation to Wilson Smith) from China Grove, who had become president in 1981. Smith, a steady manager who carefully built upon and consolidated his predecessor's successes, added the titles of chief executive officer in 1986 and board chairman in 1991.

Food Lion has remained a tightly run, cost-efficient discount store with a distinct niche in the South's retail food industry. Although the company experienced problems in the 1990s—an overly ambitious effort to expand into the Southwest, labor difficulties, and widely publicized charges that it at times sold tainted food—by 2006 Food Lion operated more than 1,200 stores in 11 southeastern and mid-Atlantic states, with about 70,000 employees and 10 million customers per week.

Another successful North Carolina–based grocery store firm, Ingles Markets, Inc., was established by founder Bob Ingle in Asheville in 1963. In 1978 the company added a large distribution facility there. Its strategy has included locating stores within 250 miles of the facility to boost quality control. In 1982 Ingles acquired the former Sealtest milk processing and packaging plant in Asheville. Operating as Milkco, Inc., the company provides Ingles supermarkets with dairy products, citrus juices, and bottled water and sells more than 60 percent of its products to other retailers, wholesalers, and food service distributors. Annual production grew from 5 million gallons in 1982 to more than 48 million in 1998. Ingles ranked twenty-sixth in the *Raleigh News and Observer*'s 2002 listing of the state's top 100 publicly held companies and operated 201 stores in the Carolinas, Georgia, Tennessee, Alabama, and Virginia, many of them in rural areas and small towns ignored by larger chains.

Based in Matthews, Harris Teeter Stores began in 1936 when W. T. Harris borrowed $1,500 to open a grocery store in Charlotte. The original Harris Super Market opened in 1949 as Mecklenburg County's first air-conditioned supermarket and the first to remain open until 9 P.M. on Fridays. In 1939 Willis L. Teeter and his brother Paul borrowed $1,700 to open Teeter's Food Mart in Mooresville. The two young and prospering companies first worked together in 1958, pooling buying efforts and storage facilities. In February 1960 Harris Super Markets and Teeter's Food Marts officially merged to form Harris Teeter Super Markets, Inc.

Within three years after the merger, 25 Harris Teeter stores were in operation, the first being in Kannapolis. A new, larger warehouse with office facilities was established, and Harris Teeter expanded by purchasing five supermarkets from Tilman's Grocery of Shelby and independent grocery stores in Charlotte and Gastonia. In 1969 Harris Teeter was bought by the Ruddick Corporation of Charlotte, a holding company traded on the New York Stock Exchange. In 1984 Harris Teeter merged with Food World, a successful supermarket chain started in 1917 by George E. Hutchens of High Point operating in central North Carolina and parts of Virginia. The merger added 52 stores, a distribution center, and nearly 3,000 associates to Harris Teeter. The company now covered four states and had 7,000 employees, making it the second-largest grocery chain in the Carolinas.

Between 1988 and 1993, Harris Teeter purchased 52 additional supermarkets operating under the Big Star name; a warehouse from the Grand Union Company; the Borden Dairy Plant, which in conjunction with Harris Teeter's Hunter Dairy greatly increased dairy product production; a 97,000-square-foot building in Matthews for its corporate offices; and five South Carolina Bruno stores. Distribution and transportation facilities for Harris Teeter are located in Greensboro and Indian Trail. By 2006 there were 149 Harris Teeter supermarkets in North Carolina, South Carolina, Virginia, Tennessee, Florida, and Georgia, employing 13,900 people.

Lowes Food Stores began in 1954 with one store in North Wilkesboro, which remained its headquarters until a 1989 move to Winston-Salem. The firm (privately owned since 1983) operates more than 100 stores in North Carolina and Virginia after aggressive expansion beginning in the mid-1980s. Some of its stores are acquisitions of existing stores of other companies, such as its 1997 purchase of the Byrd's Foods chain of Burlington—which gave Lowes a presence statewide—and the 2000 purchase of Hannaford stores in the Raleigh area. Lowes's annual sales were estimated in the early 2000s to be $700 to $800 million. The chain is a division of Alex Lee, Inc., of Hickory.

References: Ralph W. Ketner, *Five Fast Pennies* (1994); J. Tevere MacFadyen, "The Rise of the Supermarket," *American Heritage* 36 (October–November 1985); Richard S. Tedlow, *New and Improved: The Story of Mass Marketing in America* (1990); Mark Wineka and Jason Lesley, *Lion's Share* (1991).

Peter A. Coclanis
Additional research provided by Sonya Elam, Gail B. Joyner, and Wiley J. Williams.

Grove, built in the late eighteenth century, was the home of Willie Jones (1741–1801), a leading North Carolina planter and Anti-Federalist politician. Situated in a grove of native white oaks near the town of Halifax, it is believed to have been the first tripartite, or T-plan, house in North Carolina. This plan, which features a two-story, pedimental central block flanked by one-story wings, was a popular house type among Roanoke River planters. Of particular interest was a large bay window placed so that Jones could view his flower garden and beyond it a private racetrack and his prized horses. The house remained standing, but in dilapidated condition, until early in the twentieth century, when it collapsed completely. In 1969

Postcard showing golfers at the Grove Park Inn, ca. 1915. NCC.

the Daughters of the American Revolution deeded the 3-acre tract of land containing the ruins of the Willie Jones house and the grave of his young daughter to the state of North Carolina, which subsequently sold it to the Historic Halifax Restoration Association, Inc. None of the beloved trees for which the house was named, and that Jones's will stated "are to be held sacred from the ax," remain.

References: Catherine W. Bishir, *North Carolina Architecture* (1990); Mills Lane, *Architecture of the Old South: North Carolina* (1985); Blackwell P. Robinson, "Willie Jones of Halifax, Part One," *NCHR* 18 (January 1941); Robinson, "Willie Jones of Halifax, Part Two," *NCHR* 18 (April 1941).

Terry M. Harper

Grove Park Inn. Edwin W. Grove, a pharmacist and entrepreneur from St. Louis, Mo., built Asheville's Grove Park Inn in 1913. Grove, often considered "the father of modern Asheville," grew enamored of the city after spending summers there in an effort to relieve his chronic insomnia and bronchitis. During his frequent visits, he amassed a large amount of property in and around Asheville, including the slope and foot of Sunset Mountain in the eastern part of town.

Constructed of native granite taken from Grove's surrounding properties, the inn was built in under a year, requiring a crew of 400 laborers and 20 Italian stonemasons working ten-hour days. When it opened on 12 July 1913, U.S. secretary of state William Jennings Bryan delivered the official address, aptly calling the Grove Park Inn a hotel "built for the ages." The original inn contained 156 guest rooms, a dining room, and a lobby 120 feet long and 80 feet wide. Massive fireplaces large enough to hold 12-foot logs stood at both ends of the lobby. The rock chimneys concealed elevators. While Grove provided the capital to finance the inn's construction, the vision of Fred L. Seely, Grove's son-in-law and codeveloper, gave the inn its character. An admirer of the Arts and Crafts movement, Seely sought the finest artisans of the day to furnish the inn with simple pieces that would stand the test of time in both form and function.

Seely leased the inn from Grove in 1914 and managed daily operations, instituting austere policies that appealed to "tired, busy people [seeking] to get away from excitement and all annoyances and rest their nerves." The Grove Park Inn prohibited alcohol and discouraged guests from bringing small children. Guests were not permitted to run water or speak above a whisper during evening quiet hours. Seely sought to offer quality entertainment, modern conveniences, and the comforts of home. The inn originally boasted a 40-foot indoor swimming pool and shower room, a bowling alley, a billiards room, and a movie screen in the Great Hall. Vocalists, lecturers, and musicians performed almost every evening in the Great Hall. Seely's efforts attracted many famous faces to the inn, including presidents and entertainers. Although famous figures such as President Franklin D. Roosevelt; his wife, Eleanor; and writer F. Scott Fitzgerald continued to frequent the Grove Park, its financial state grew precarious.

During and after World War II, the U.S. government leased the Grove Park Inn as temporary housing for various groups affected by the war. In 1942 the inn hosted Axis diplomats and their families awaiting deportation. Later that year, it housed military officers requiring rest and convalescent care. In 1944 exiled Philippine president Manuel L. Quezon arrived with his family and staff and established headquarters for his government-in-exile at the inn.

By the mid-1950s, the Grove Park Inn was suffering from a lack of consistent, competent management. In 1955 Texas businessman Edward Sammons purchased the hotel, immediately investing $100,000 toward its first major restoration. These first changes represented the beginning of Sammons's long-term commitment to restore the Grove Park Inn as a world-class resort. In 1976 Sammons bought the Asheville Country Club and Golf Course. This purchase laid the groundwork for a historic restoration of the Main Inn and construction of the Sports Center and the Sammons and Vanderbilt wings. The $65 million effort, begun in 1982, was guided in large part by Sammons's wife, Elaine, who recognized the important heritage of the inn and encouraged architects and designers to preserve and duplicate the granite walls, oak woodwork, and Arts and Crafts furnishings.

When construction ended in 1988, the Grove Park Inn boasted 140 acres of grounds, 510 guest rooms, 40 meeting rooms, 2 ballrooms, 4 restaurants, 2 swimming pools, an 18-hole golf course, 9 tennis courts, and a full-service sports center. The Grove Park Inn's excellent accommodations continue to attract guests from around the world.

References: Bruce E. Johnson, *Built for the Ages: A History of the Grove Park Inn* (1991); Milton Ready, *Asheville, Land of the Sky: An Illustrated History* (1986).

Elizabeth Scheld Glynn

Guilford College, affiliated with the Society of Friends (Quakers), is the third-oldest coeducational institution in the nation. Located in Greensboro, the school was opened in 1837 by the Quakers as the New Garden Boarding School. Its main building, Founders Hall, was a two-story brick structure that stood in the middle of a vast hardwood forest. Situated in the midst of the state's Quaker population, the school was a station on the Underground Railroad as well as a center of resistance to Confederate conscription during the Civil War. During Reconstruction, the school reorganized with assistance from the Society of Friends and was renamed Guilford College.

Degrees were first conferred in 1889 under a charter issued in 1887. The preparatory department was dropped in 1924, and in 1929 the courses were organized into a "core curriculum."

Although Guilford College has changed over the years, it retains its commitment to basic Quaker principles, including pacifism. It is the only Quaker college in the South. The college in the early 2000s had an enrollment of about 1,200 students, offering 40 academic majors and 5 cooperative preprofessional programs. Guilford College maintains a close relationship with the North Carolina Yearly Meeting of the Society of Friends (the statewide organization), but ownership and ultimate responsibility is held by a self-perpetuating, 36-member board of trustees. Two-thirds of the board members must be recognized as Quakers by the Yearly Meeting based on the recommendations of local monthly meetings.

References: Alexander R. Stoesen, *Guilford College: On the Strength of 150 Years* (1987); Dorothy Gilbert Thorne, *Guilford: A Quaker College* (1937).

Alexander R. Stoesen

Guilford County, located in North Carolina's Piedmont region, was formed from parts of Orange and Rowan Counties in 1771. It was named after Francis North, first earl of Guilford and father of the prime minister of Great Britain at the time. The county seat moved from Martinsville (originally named Guilford Courthouse) to Greensboro, its present location near the geographic center of the county, in 1808. In the early 2000s, Guilford County was the third-most-populous county in the state, with a population estimated at 434,700 in 2004. Greensboro and High Point (the "furniture capital of the world") are its two major cities. Other communities in the county include Jamestown, Stokesdale, Summerfield, Whitsett, and parts of Archdale and Gibsonville.

Guilford County's history and culture have been among the richest of any North Carolina county. The important Revolutionary War battle at Guilford Courthouse, commemorated today by a national military park, took place in March 1781. The city of Greensboro boasts several institutions of higher learning, including Guilford College (1837), Greensboro College (1838), North Carolina Agricultural and Technical State University (1891), and the University of North Carolina at Greensboro (1891). High Point University in High Point was founded in 1924. The sit-ins by four North Carolina A&T students at a downtown Woolworth Store lunch counter in 1960 became a national focal point of the civil rights movement. Institutions dedicated to presenting and interpreting Guilford County history include the Greensboro Historical Museum, the Charlotte Hawkins Brown Museum (a North Carolina State Historic Site), the High Point Museum, and Mendenhall Plantation, a Quaker homestead in Jamestown that dates to 1811.

Throughout its history, Guilford County has depended

upon its role as a commercial transportation hub to spark its economy. Greensboro was connected to seven main roads by 1820, and the arrival of the North Carolina Railroad in the 1850s facilitated the shipping of goods through the area. In the wake of the Civil War, Guilford County's attractive combination of low taxes, inexpensive labor, and abundant raw materials such as cotton, timber, and tobacco promoted rapid industrialization. The county continued to thrive throughout the twentieth century, with many corporations such as Jefferson-Pilot, VF, and Lorillard taking up residence. The local economy, long centered around the manufacture of textiles, apparel, and furniture, has since greatly diversified (though the International Home Furnishings Market in High Point remains a celebrated and lucrative annual event). Agricultural products include tobacco, corn, chickens, swine, and beef and dairy cattle. Guilford County has also been host to a number of recreational and cultural events, including the North Carolina Shakespeare Festival, the Eastern Music Festival, the City Stage street festival, the Greater Greensboro Chrysler Classic golf tournament, and the Atlantic Coast Conference and Southern Conference basketball tournaments.

Reference: Alexander R. Stoesen, *Guilford County: A Brief History* (1993).

Robert Blair Vocci

SEE ALSO Charlotte Hawkins Brown Museum; Greensboro; Greensboro Sit-Ins; Guilford Courthouse, Battle of; High Point.

Guilford Courthouse, Battle of. The Battle of Guilford Courthouse, a decisive engagement of the Revolutionary War that took place north of Greensboro on the afternoon of 15 Mar. 1781, pitted the Patriot forces of Gen. Nathanael Greene against Lord Charles Cornwallis's British army. After 1779 the British military strategy had centered on conquering the South and restoring royal authority, then attempting to take control of the North. Prior to Guilford Courthouse, both Greene and Cornwallis had divided their forces in the hope of quick victories, but the Americans had the best of it. They had defeated the British at King's Mountain (7 Oct. 1780) and Cowpens (17 Jan. 1781) through Greene's ingenuity—because his contingent of regulars did not equal Cornwallis's, he avoided typical eighteenth-century battle lines in favor of violent skirmishes and strategic retreats. After Cowpens, Greene began a withdrawal that ranged as far north as Virginia and wore down his British pursuers. Cornwallis burned his baggage train in the interest of speed but never caught Greene. By early March 1781 Greene was ready with a maximum force to meet Cornwallis at a place of his own choosing.

The place Greene selected was Guilford Courthouse, located on the main north-south road between Petersburg, Va., and Salisbury, N.C. The site consisted of little more than a few log buildings, but it was the ideal backwoods assembly point for the approximately 4,400 soldiers fighting under Greene. Equally important was the terrain around the courthouse, where, from the south, the road passed through mixed woods and fields before reaching a high clearing surrounded by dense timber. Additionally, Greene knew that there were no nearby bodies of water where his troops might be trapped if they left the battlefield. They could simply disappear into the woods and reassemble at a designated point. This had been Greene's tactic since he assumed the southern command in December 1780.

By mid-March 1781, Cornwallis and his approximately 2,000 well-trained, experienced men were a few miles southwest of the courthouse at Deep River Friends Meetinghouse, where he was informed of the growing force of Americans there. In the words of one historian, Cornwallis accepted Greene's "invitation" to battle. Put another way, the British fell for his trap. To strike at the largest American force in the South, Cornwallis had to move his men up New Garden Road and eventually to the clearing and up the incline at the courthouse. Greene followed a simple plan of positioning his troops in three lines, with the first line held by militia from North Carolina, reinforced with sharpshooters. They were expected to get off two or three rounds before retreating. A second line of Virginia militia reinforced with small field pieces was expected to perform in the same manner. Greene reserved his experienced 1,500 Continental regulars for the third line. By the time the remaining British met them, he hoped, they would be heavily depleted.

The attack began in the early afternoon of 15 March. The British force broke through the first and second lines relatively quickly but suffered many casualties. The iron discipline of the British army kept Cornwallis's men moving forward despite their losses and the difficult terrain between the second and third lines. After inflicting further damage to the enemy, Greene withdrew his troops. The British held the field and could claim victory, but in reality the Americans had prevailed: Cornwallis had lost nearly one-quarter of his forces to death or injury, whereas Greene had suffered fewer casualties and left the battle with his vital units of regulars practically unscathed.

Shortly afterward the American army began to reassemble 15 miles away at Troublesome Creek. Although Greene was initially disappointed with his troops' performance, it soon became apparent that they had done irreparable damage to Cornwallis's army. He slowly withdrew to Wilmington to refit and, after a period of rest, carried out a reconquest of the Carolinas using hard-hitting guerrilla tactics. Cornwallis retreated to safety, searching for supplies and a way to mend his shattered force.

Cornwallis's so-called victory in the Battle of Guilford Courthouse was derided in England, where Charles James Fox told the House of Commons that "another such victory would ruin the British Army." The accuracy of his observation was borne out before the end of the year. Cornwallis, still intending to conquer the South, shifted to Virginia, where another American force was assembling. At Yorktown, seven months later, Cornwallis surrendered to Gen. George Washington. Thus, while technically an American defeat, the brief struggle at Guilford Courthouse proved to be a strategic victory for the Americans.

After years of neglect, the Guilford Courthouse Battleground Company was established in Greensboro in 1887 by former superior court judge David Schenck and his associates to preserve the site of this key Revolutionary War battle. Shortly after arriving in Greensboro in 1881, Schenck examined the area and found little to indicate the intense struggle that had taken place on the afternoon of 15 Mar. 1781. Few citizens seemed to know anything about the battle. In October 1886 he wrote in his diary that he was going to "save the battlefield." The Battleground Company was formed and granted a state charter on 7 Mar. 1887 to preserve the site and erect "monuments, tombstones, and other memorials to commemorate the heroic deeds of the American patriots who participated in this battle for liberty and independence."

In the 30 years of its existence, the Battleground Company erected 27 monuments, cleared miles of grounds and trails, and achieved Schenck's goal of preserving the battlefield site. The privately owned and operated park at Guilford Courthouse was one of the earliest efforts to preserve a Revolutionary War site in the United States. In 1917 the federal government assumed control of the site, which became the Guilford Courthouse National Military Park. Located about six miles north of downtown Greensboro, the park features a visitors center, completed in 1976, that includes artifacts, an audiovisual presentation, and publications for sale.

References: Thomas E. Baker, *Another Such Victory: The Story of the American Defeat at Guilford Courthouse That Helped Win the War for Independence* (1981); Baker, *The Monuments at Guilford Courthouse National Military Park* (1980); John Buchanan, *The Road to Guilford Courthouse: The American Revolution in the Carolinas* (1997).

Alexander R. Stoesen

SEE ALSO New Garden, Battle of.

Guilford Courthouse Flag,

Guilford Courthouse Flag, also known as the North Carolina militia flag, is one of several early variations of the U.S. national flag. According to oral history, troops of the North Carolina militia carried the flag at the Battle of Guilford Courthouse on 15 Mar. 1781 during the American Revolution. The flag featured a unique configuration of stars and stripes, with an enlarged white canton displaying 13 blue, 8-pointed stars bordered by alternating red and blue stripes. A partially complete specimen of such a flag can be found in the North Carolina Museum of History.

The Guilford Courthouse Flag. Courtesy of NCOA&H.

The lack of reliable evidence establishing the Guilford Courthouse flag at the time of the Revolution has caused many historians to question its authenticity. Regardless of whether the flag was actually present at the time of the Revolution or was a later creation, its unusual dimensions and color combinations make it one of the more interesting and attractive early American flags.

References: Henry W. Moeller, *Shattering an American Myth: Unfurling the History of the Stars and Stripes* (1995); Margaret Seden, *Star-Spangled Banner: Our Nation and Its Flag* (1993).

Robert C. Voigt

Gulf Stream is a warm current in the Atlantic Ocean that flows out of the Gulf of Mexico along the east coast of the United States and east in the North Atlantic toward Europe. The Gulf Stream affects North Carolina's climate and economy dramatically, particularly along the coast, where it approaches Cape Hatteras and gives that part of the state a milder winter than would otherwise be the case. Winter temperatures of the surface waters there are approximately 63 degrees, while summer temperatures are about 80 degrees. The current, passing between 30 and 50 miles off of North Carolina's coast, has a strong impact upon the economy of the state, as tourists and residents flock to the coast for scuba diving, surfing, birding, and other activities made possible by the temperate climate. Gulf Stream fishing is an especially important industry, attracting thousands of people in need of charter boats to carry them out into the stream to catch the wide variety of deep-sea fish living there.

The Gulf Stream was first described by Benjamin Franklin, and it appears on a map prepared for him in 1770 by Nantucket, Mass., whaler Timothy Folger. Royal Governor Arthur Dobbs of North Carolina on 10 July 1756 wrote to the earl of Loudon urging the construction of a fort to protect trade passing through the "Gulphe stream" off the coast of the colony. Governor William Tryon on 8 Dec. 1764 suggested to the postmaster general in London that by taking advantage of the stream, dispatches passing between North Carolina and the Crown could be received more quickly.

William S. Powell

Gum Swamp, First and Second Battles of. The two Civil War battles at Gum Swamp occurred in April and May 1863. Companies B, D, and F of the 56th North Carolina Regiment were sent down the Lower Trent Road to a picket post on the Trent River about four miles above Trenton. Companies H and K were ordered to Moseley Creek on the Neuse Road, and Companies E, G, and I were dispatched to guard the junction of Dover Road and the Atlantic & North Carolina Railroad, just east of Gum Swamp. There, while managing a vulnerable, zigzag line of "badly constructed" breastworks, four Federal regiments attacked on 28 Apr. 1863 with overwhelming numbers. While Col. Paul Fletcher Faison held his ground awaiting reinforcements, the enemy destroyed the Confederate camp east of Gum Swamp. The parting Confederate volley—despite some Federal assertions of a decisive rout—suggests that the Confederate retreat, at least in parts of its fallback line, was orderly. It seems to be an undisputed fact, as well, that the Confederates were not seriously pursued beyond their fallback position. The retreat was Faison's recognition that his men were in danger of being cut off or destroyed. Federal losses at First Gum Swamp were officially reported as two men killed and five wounded. The 56th North Carolina Regiment lost three men killed, one mortally wounded, four wounded, and one captured.

The Second Battle of Gum Swamp occurred on 22 May 1863 after the 56th North Carolina Regiment under Faison marched back to the swamp and took up a position in the portion of the zigzag breastworks running south from the Atlantic & North Carolina Railroad. There the regiment, with perhaps 500 men, was attacked by about 2,000 Federals under Col. J. Richter Jones. Superior Union numbers, strategy, and timing prompted the Rebel retreat. The Federals closed in on the Confederates from multiple directions. Brig. Gen. Robert Ransom, heading the 25th North Carolina, attempted to reinforce the trapped men but was forced from the field by a shower of Unionist balls.

Union troops remained in the Gum Swamp vicinity until late afternoon, demolishing the Confederate breastworks. Meanwhile, Maj. Gen. Daniel H. Hill mounted a counterattack from Kinston, arriving at Gum Swamp late in the afternoon. After a brief exchange of artillery, Union troops retreated down the Dover road to get out of range. At about midnight, Hill's artillery shelled the Federals, who again retreated.

In the aftermath of Second Gum Swamp, Faison, being severely criticized for his regiment's performance, demanded an inquiry. In July he was brought before a court-martial under charges of "neglect of duty" and "misbehavior in the presence of the enemy." The accusations were questionable because, as the court implied in its findings, General Ransom bore a substantial share of responsibility for the disaster. Ransom was culpable primarily by placing too weak a force at Gum Swamp, thereby leaving Faison with the choice of either inadequately protecting his flank or fatally weakening his main line. In any case, the court stated, Faison could not have been expected to string out pickets from his post at Gum Swamp to the Lower Trent Road without superior orders. The court's decision did not extend to taking a hard look at Ransom's performance. Whatever the truth regarding the 56th North Carolina's performance, it is clear that the men of the regiment blamed Ransom, not Faison, for its defeat. The 56th lost 4 men mortally wounded, 6 wounded, and 144 captured at Second Gum Swamp. Federal losses were recorded as 1 man killed, 1 mortally wounded, 5 wounded, and 1 missing.

Reference: John G. Barrett, *North Carolina as a Civil War Battleground, 1861–1865* (1960).

Wiley J. Williams

Gunboats, Wooden. Wooden gunboats were built in North Carolina during three historical eras: the Revolutionary War, the period of the Thomas Jefferson and James Madison administrations (1803–ca. 1811), and the Confederacy's first year. All of the boats were designed for use in shallow water, propelled by both sails and oars.

The first of these ships used in the Revolutionary War were armed merchantmen intended to protect coastal towns in 1776. Three, the *Pennsylvania Farmer*, *King Tammany*, and *General Washington*, were outfitted as guard vessels. Because they were not totally satisfactory, North Carolina opted to combine resources with Virginia and build two rowing galleys to defend Ocracoke Inlet: the *Caswell* and the *Washington*, the *Caswell* serving at Ocracoke under Capt. Willis Wilson during 1778–79. Neither galley engaged in battle, but both were somewhat effective in protecting trade passing through Ocracoke Inlet. By 1780 the worm-ridden *Caswell* was sunk at its mooring in New Bern and the crew and weaponry were taken aboard the *Washington*.

The Jeffersonian gunboats were designed for coastal defense and for use on the western rivers. Ultimately, several served in the Mediterranean as well. First authorized in 1803, a total of 177 gunboats were built in many port cities of North Carolina until at least as late as 1811. Ranging from about 50 to over 75 feet long, they generally carried from one to three large guns, plus swivels.

At least six gunboats were stationed at Wilmington before and during the War of 1812. Others served at Ocracoke; after the war, these undistinguished vessels were usually laid up or sold out of service. A wreck uncovered on Bodie Island in 1939 may be the remains of Gunboat 140, which exploded, burned, and sank on 23 Sept. 1814 at Ocracoke Inlet. Gunboats 166, 167, 168 were built at Wilmington (in Smithfield) by Amos Perry. Gunboat 166 served during the War of 1812 as the *Alligator*; it sank in Port Royal Sound in July 1814 and was raised and sold in June 1815. Gunboat 168 plied the Atlantic coast and after the war was used as a guard ship between Savannah and Charleston.

Wooden Civil War gunboats took two forms. Some were prewar vessels adapted for military use, many serving in North Carolina's navy, the "Mosquito Fleet," which was destroyed in and after the fighting around Roanoke Island and Elizabeth City in 1862. The other form was custom-built under contract to the Confederate government in various coastal towns, primarily Washington, N.C. Both that town and Elizabeth City fell to Union forces in the spring of 1862, leading to the termination of several plans to build wooden gunboats in the state. One Washington gunboat was apparently taken up the Tar River and hidden in a creek in Pitt County. When it became obvious that the vessel could not be finished, it was burned. The wreck has been studied by underwater archaeologists since 1973.

References: William N. Still Jr., *North Carolina's Revolutionary War Navy* (1976); Spencer C. Tucker, *The Jeffersonian Gunboat Navy* (1993).

Lawrence E. Babits

H

Hackney Brothers Wagon Company. SEE Trucks and Trucking.

Halifax, located in Halifax County, was in colonial times an important political, social, and commercial center in northeastern North Carolina. The town of Halifax was chartered by the General Assembly in 1757 and became the county seat of Halifax County (formed out of Edgecombe County) in 1758. Settlers had come to the surrounding area even earlier, drawn by river transportation and the nearness to trade in Virginia.

With the 1757 legislative act, directors and trustees were ordered to design and plan a town on 100 acres of land owned by James Leslie on the south side of the Roanoke River. In 1769 Claude Joseph Sauthier, cartographer for King George III, drew a map of Halifax that has been invaluable in establishing the location of early residences and public buildings. The town was named to honor the earl of Halifax, and its streets were named for British leaders and the patron saints of the British Isles.

In June 1758 a public sale of town lots was held, with 49 buyers purchasing almost all of them. Halifax grew rapidly until the American Revolution, serving as a trade center for overland and river transportation. As a political and economic center, Halifax also saw an increase in social activities such as elegant dinners and balls and horseracing.

Many wealthy planters from the Roanoke Valley established themselves as leaders in the colony's politics. In 1776, during the American Revolution, Halifax hosted two meetings of the colony's Provincial Congress. During the Fourth Provincial Congress held in Halifax, a resolution now known as the Halifax Resolves was adopted. The resolution, adopted on 12 Apr. 1776, was the first official call for independence by any colony. It was fitting that North Carolina's first public reading of the Declaration of Independence later occurred in Halifax, and today the North Carolina flag bears the date of the Halifax Resolves.

Throughout the war, Halifax served as a military depot and recruiting center for patriot troops. Except for brief occupation by Lord Charles Cornwallis's troops on their march to Virginia, the town saw little action. After independence was won, the Fifth Provincial Congress met in Halifax, adopting the state's first constitution and appointing Richard Caswell as the first governor.

Following the Revolutionary War, Halifax gradually declined as a center of political activity, and its viability as a commercial center waned in the nineteenth century, with the advent of railroads and other improved methods of transportation. Although it continues to be the county seat, with fewer than 400 people living within its corporate limits, modern-day Halifax has a culture and economy that largely revolve around its historic district, now a North Carolina State Historic Site.

Historic Halifax State Historic Site is on U.S. 301, accessible from Interstate 95. A visitors center offers an orientation program and a museum. Conducted scheduled tours of homes and public buildings dating from 1750 to 1835 originate at the center, which also has an herb garden and a formal garden for viewing. In 1970 Historic Halifax became the first National Register Historic District in North Carolina. The 12 April anniversary of the Halifax Resolves is appropriately observed each year, and for a few weeks in the summer an independent company produces an outdoor drama, *First for Freedom*, chronicling the events leading to the signing of the resolves.

References: *Historic Halifax Guidebook* (1976); Richard F. Knapp, ed., *North Carolina's State Historic Sites: A Brief History and Status Report* (1995); Marion P. Sykes, "Profile of Colonial Halifax County, North Carolina" (M.A. thesis, East Carolina University, 1964).

Monica Moody

Halifax County, located in North Carolina's Coastal Plain region (on the fall line between the coastal plain and the piedmont), was formed from Edgecombe County in 1758. Its name is derived from George Montague, second earl of Halifax and president of the British Board of Trade and Plantations. The county seat, also named Halifax, had been established in 1757; other Halifax County communities include Roanoke Rapids, Weldon, Littleton, Enfield, and Scotland Neck.

Constitution-Burgess House in Halifax in the early twentieth century, before it was restored. Tradition holds that North Carolina's first state constitution was framed and adopted in the house. NCC.

Originally home to Tuscarora Indians, the area was settled in the early eighteenth century by English colonists migrating south from Virginia. Slave-driven plantations soon emerged to take advantage of the fertile soil. The town of Halifax developed along the banks of the Roanoke River and established itself as the trading hub for goods passing from settlement to settlement. However, the prosperity Halifax County enjoyed came to an end with the rise of the railroads, which diminished the importance of rivers for freight transportation, and the abolition of slavery, which brought the age of the wealthy plantation owner to an end. Remnants of an antebellum canal and aqueduct can be seen at Roanoke Rapids.

On 12 Apr. 1776, the North Carolina Provincial Congress met in Halifax and unanimously passed a resolution later known as the Halifax Resolves. The first resolution of its kind, the document instructed North Carolina's delegates to the Second Continental Congress in Philadelphia to vote for independence from Great Britain. The date of the Halifax Resolves is commemorated on the state's flag, and 12 April is celebrated each year as Halifax Day in the county, with individuals in period costumes demonstrating colonial-era activities and craftsmanship. The Historic Halifax State Historic Site interprets these events.

Halifax County natural attractions include Medoc Mountain State Park, Lake Gaston, and Roanoke Rapids Lake. The Lakeland Arts Center, the Canal Arts Center, and the Roanoke Valley Players theater group are a few of the county's cultural institutions. Agricultural and manufacturing products include tobacco, peanuts, cotton, corn, textiles, paper, and apparel. In 2004 the estimated population of Halifax County was 56,400.

Reference: W. C. Allen, *History of Halifax County* (1993).

Robert Blair Vocci

SEE ALSO Halifax; Resolves, Prerevolutionary.

Halifax Resolves. SEE Resolves, Prerevolutionary.

Haliwa Indians were recognized as a tribe by the North Carolina legislature in 1965. The tribal name is a combination of Halifax and Warren Counties, where the majority of the Haliwa live. One tradition relates that the present Indian communities in this area were founded by wounded survivors of the Tuscarora War and other colonial conflicts who were unable to rejoin their original tribal groups. In addition to North Carolina coastal tribes, Accomac, Cherokee, Nansemond, Occaneechi, Saponi, Tuscarora, and Tutelo Indians are claimed as Haliwa ancestors. Since 1975, the Haliwa have referred to themselves as the Haliwa-Saponi.

Although Indians were living in this area before the American Revolution and some served as soldiers in that war, the emergence of the Haliwa with a collective Indian identity has been relatively recent. The Haliwa Indian Club was organized in the 1950s, and its membership roll became the arbiter of Indian identity. As they were for other state-recognized tribes in North Carolina, schools and churches were important in strengthening Haliwa group identity, although a separate Haliwa school was not established until 1957.

In 1965, when the Haliwa became a state-recognized Indian tribe, nearly 400 persons successfully brought suit in Halifax County court to change the racial designation on their birth certificates, marriage licenses, and driver's licenses to "Indian." In the early 2000s there were approximately 3,000 Haliwas living in Halifax and Warren Counties. The tribe holds an annual powwow in April and conducts a number of economic and educational programs for its members.

References: J. K. Dane and B. Eugene Griessman, "The Collective Identity of Marginal Peoples: The N.C. Experience," *American Anthropologist* 74 (1972); Alfred Tamarin, *We Have Not Vanished: Eastern Indians of the United States* (1974); Ruth Y. Wetmore, *First on the Land: The North Carolina Indians* (1975).

Ruth Y. Wetmore

Hamilton Report. SEE Community Colleges.

Handicrafts. SEE Basket Making; Biltmore Industries; Decoys; Penland School of Crafts; Pottery; Quilts; Southern Highland Craft Guild; Weaving; Woodcarving.

Hanes Brands. In 1872 Pleasant Henderson Hanes organized P. H. Hanes Tobacco Company in partnership with a younger brother, John Wesley, and a Davie County friend, Maj. Thomas Jethro Brown. When the business burned in 1874, Brown left the organization and was replaced briefly by another of Pleasant's brothers, Benjamin Franklin. Pleasant traveled to promote the tobacco market while John Wesley remained at the plant to attend to the manufacturing process. After the brothers sold the tobacco business to R. J. Reynolds in 1900, they entered the textile business.

In 1901 John Wesley Hanes opened the Shamrock Hosiery Mills to make infants' and men's socks. In 1902 Pleasant Henderson Hanes joined with his sons (Pleasant Huber and William Marvin) to set up the P. H. Hanes Knitting Company to make men's and boy's underwear. Shamrock was renamed Hanes Hosiery Mills in 1910 and soon became recognized as the world's largest producer of women's seamless nylon hosiery. In 1920 Hanes Hosiery began focusing on women's apparel. Hanes Dye & Finishing Company was opened in 1925 to bleach, dye, and finish cotton piece goods. During World War II, Hanes received many War Department contracts.

In 1965 the Hanes Corporation was formed out of the two Hanes companies, with Pleasant Huber Henderson Hanes Jr., as president. On 30 Jan. 1979 the corporation became part of Consolidated Foods Corporation of Chicago. (Consolidated Foods changed its name to Sara Lee Corporation in 1985.) Hanes, with its highly successful men's underwear, L'eggs brand women's hosiery, and Hanes Her Way women's underwear brands, manufactures a significant portion of Sara Lee's diversified consumer product lines, which also include Sara Lee bakery goods, Aqua Velva, Playtex Wonderbra, Ball Park frankfurters, Hillshire Farms and Jimmy Dean sausages, and Kiwi shoe polish. Sara Lee is headquartered in Winston-Salem, and there are Hanes–Sara Lee facilities in Butner, Valdese, Yadkinville, Asheboro, Rockingham, Tarboro, High Point, Kernersville, and Mount Airy. The Hanes name continues in a number of Sara Lee subsidiaries, such as Hanes France, Hanes Italia, Hanes Puerto Rico, and Hanes U.K. Ltd. In 1997 Hanes brands generated more than $2 billion in sales for the first time, and Hanes remained in the early 2000s the world's largest apparel brand.

References: P. H. Hanes Knitting Company, *The Hanes Story* (1960); Jo White Linn, *People Named Hanes* (1980); Frank V. Tursi, *Winston-Salem: A History* (1994).

Wiley J. Williams

Hang Gliding has been associated with the North Carolina coast from the sport's earliest incarnation. Francis Rogallo and his wife and coinventor Gertrude set out in the early 1940s to see if they could design a kite or flexible wing that could be held together in controlled flight by the action of the air itself. The result, patented in 1947, was the Rogallo Wing, which was considered in the early years of the space program as a possible method of returning space capsules to earth. The Rogallos began examining the possibility of developing a man-carrying Rogallo Wing at Southern Shores, just north of Kitty Hawk, in 1967, conducting experiments on the beach in front of their cottage with the help of a daughter and interested neighbors. The couple moved to Southern Shores in 1972, by which time people were building and flying their own Rogallo Wings with modifications that included the addition of tubes on the wings and keel and a crossbar in front. The term "hang gliding" soon came into use, probably when practitioners had difficulty describing their unusual activity as Rogalloing or, even worse, Rogallo Winging. Interest in the new activity spread so rapidly that the first national hang gliding meet was held in the summer of 1973 at Jockey's Ridge.

A Rogallo Wing has no engine, no wheels, no brakes—in fact no moving parts. The rider takes off in the Rogallo Wing running downhill as fast as possible with the wing in front. The position of the nose must be exact, because miscalculating can result in either too much drag or the nose dipping and ramming into the ground. Once in flight, the rider hangs in a prone position, face down, in a harness that hugs his or her hips, with hands holding on to the crossbar in front. To nose

A hang glider at Jockey's Ridge at Nags Head. Photograph courtesy of North Carolina Division of Tourism, Film, and Sports Development.

down, the rider pulls forward a little bit; to nose up, the rider pushes back; and to turn left or right, the rider pushes his or her body to the desired side. The easiest part of all is landing: the rider simply noses way up, causing forward motion to stop, and lands on his or her feet like a bird.

The procedures followed by the first people to experiment with the Rogallo Wing have continued, as fliers using hang gliders the world over have learned to climb and stay aloft for hours by flying back and forth in rising air currents. Thousands of people, men and women, children and seniors, have taken lessons and learned to fly hang gliders at Jockey's Ridge. In fact, the ridge's name has become almost as synonymous with hang gliding as those of nearby Kill Devil Hills and Kitty Hawk are with the first flights by Orville and Wilbur Wright in 1903. Grandfather Mountain and other sites in the western section of North Carolina have also become favorite spots for hang gliding enthusiasts.

Reference: Wolfgang Langewiesche, "The Flyingest Flying There Is," *Reader's Digest* (February 1974).

David Stick

Hardee's Restaurants began in Greenville in September 1960, when Wilber Hardee opened a restaurant featuring a limited menu, fast service, and low prices. Hardee had recently visited the McDonald's restaurant in Greensboro (the first McDonald's in the state) and seen how much money could be made selling 15¢ hamburgers and 10¢ french fries. His restaurant was so successful that it caught the entrepreneurial attention of Rocky Mount businessmen Leonard Rawls, an accountant, and Jim Gardner, then an executive with a dairy processing company. Rawls, Gardner, and Hardee, after brief negotiations, formed a corporation, Hardee's Drive-Ins, Inc. Hardee owned one-half of the new company and Rawls and Gardner the other. No money changed hands; Rawls and Gardner agreed to bear the cost of opening a second Hardee's in

Rocky Mount. This was as successful as the original Greenville operation, and Rawls and Gardner began making plans to open more restaurants. Hardee did not share his associates' enthusiasm for expansion, and in June 1961 he sold his share of the business to them for $20,000.

In August 1963 Hardee's made its first public stock offering and two years later opened its first restaurant outside the United States. It acquired the 200 outlets of the Sandy's hamburger chain in 1972, the same year that Hardee's stock was first listed on the New York Stock Exchange. Rawls, who located the company's headquarters in Rocky Mount, served as Hardee's first chief executive officer until 1975, by which time the business had changed its name to Hardee's Food Systems, Inc. Gardner left the company in 1966 to pursue a career in politics. Both men had realized from the first that franchising would be the most expeditious way to develop their business. In 1961 they sold their first franchise to Jerry Richardson and Charles Bradshaw, who formed Spartan Food Systems, a firm that eventually came to operate 500 Hardee's outlets in ten states. The second franchise went to the parent company of Boddie-Noell Enterprises, which owned more than 300 Hardee's stores in four states by 2006.

The restaurant firm continued to grow, acquiring the 648 units of the Roy Rogers chain from the Marriott Corporation in 1990. By the early 1990s, with headquarters still in Rocky Mount, Hardee's stood as the third-largest fast-food restaurant company in the world, with annual sales in excess of $4 billion. In 1997 Hardee's became a subsidiary of California-based CKE Restaurants, Inc., which operated more than 3,400 restaurants, including other chains such as Carl's Jr. Headquartered in St. Louis, Hardee's in 2006 operated nearly 2,000 company- and franchise-owned restaurants in 31 states and 11 foreign countries. After several years of lagging sales and financial losses, Hardee's has attempted to revitalize its brand image by remodeling its restaurants into "Star Hardee's," returning to its heritage of charbroiled burgers, and offering new products.

References: Jerry Bledsoe, *From Whalebone to Hot House: A Journey along North Carolina's Longest Highway* (1986); Hardee's Food Systems, Inc., *This Is Our Story* (1993).

Thomas J. Farnham

Harkers Island Boats, with their distinctive high, wide, flared bows, are the most easily recognizable traditional watercraft in coastal North Carolina. A shipyard existed on Harkers Island as early as 1752. In the late nineteenth century many flat-bottomed sharpies were produced in the Core Sound area. After conversion to engine power between 1912 and 1920, the sharpies snaked and vibrated, and the machinery obstructed the cockpit. Compensating for these problems, local boatbuilders combined sharpie attributes with power, and the

Boat in the early stages of construction at the Lewis Brothers boat works on Harkers Island, 1992. Copyright Edwin Martin, 1992. NCC.

Harkers Island design was born. This unique boat type was well adapted to the local maritime environment of the Carolina sounds, with an engine allowing much higher speeds in open waters and a flared bow, known as the "Harkers Island flare" or "Carolina flare," that threw water away from the hull at high speeds in the choppy local waters. Credit for the first flared bow went to Brady Lewis, who worked with his father on Bogue Sound overhauling and repairing sailing vessels. After moving to Harkers Island in 1926, they began building boats in their yard.

Handcrafted, "backyard" boat-building remains the typical production method employed by Harkers Island designers and builders. Harkers Island boats are used for trawling, shrimping, dredging, and recreational fishing.

References: Michael B. Alford, *Traditional Work Boats of North Carolina* (1990); Sonny Williamson, *Sailing with Grandpa* (1987).

Lawrence E. Babits

Harmony Hall, a restored late eighteenth-century house on King Street in Kinston, was known for 120 years as the Peebles House. Efforts to save and preserve the structure in the mid-1960s resulted in a change of its name to Harmony Hall, the reasons for which remain unclear. The name has no historical association with the house; none of its occupants referred to the house as Harmony Hall; and, considering the history of those who have lived there, the name seems ironic.

Simon Bright III built the dwelling in the early 1790s. Bright was a one-term state senator and clerk of the Lenoir County Court of Common Pleas and Quarter Sessions. After suffering a mental breakdown in 1799, he shot and killed a slave woman on King Street, acting under the delusion that blacks were stealing all his turkeys. Convicted of murder, he was placed under house arrest instead of jailed. He died in his home shortly after 1800 while appeal of his conviction was pending in the courts.

Jesse Cobb bought the house, and after his death, his widow Elizabeth Heritage Cobb lived there until her death in 1820. Her heirs transferred the house and lot to Abner Pearce in 1824. Abner died at the age of 29, and his daughter Susan, who was born in the house, never reached her seventeenth birthday. Abner's widow, Phoebe, subsequently remarried, but her new husband died a few years later. Phoebe, in her early forties, passed away less than three months after her second husband. In 1846 John Henry Peebles bought the house at public auction. His family resided there for the next 75 years.

Eleven of John and Harriett Peebles's 13 children were born in their new home, but eight of them died before reaching three years of age. Of the other three, only one—a son named Henry—lived past the age of 45. The Civil War claimed virtually all of John Henry Peebles's financial assets. He grew despondent with his and the South's deteriorating situation late in 1864. On 5 October of that year, in an upstairs back room, Peebles ended his despondency with a single gunshot.

Reduced to poverty, Harriett Peebles took in boarders to survive, and only with the help of her Cobb relatives did she manage to keep the house. Her relationship with her only surviving child, Henry, became strained and eventually dissolved completely. She died in 1898 without reconciling with him. Henry married and lived in the home until the early 1920s, when he moved to Massachusetts, ending the long Peebles residency that gave the structure its name.

The Peebles House served as a private residence and rental property until the Kinston Woman's Club bought it to use as a clubhouse and public library. The library remained for 15 years, after which the Women's Club used the structure for special occasions. Preservation efforts began on the rapidly deteriorating house in 1966. Nearly 20 years passed before the house was restored and opened as Harmony Hall in 1984.

Reference: Jerry L. Cross, *The Peebles House in Kinston: A Research Report for the Structure Restored as "Harmony Hall"* (1990).

Jerry L. Cross

Harnett County, located in North Carolina's Coastal Plain region, was formed from Cumberland County in 1855. It is named for Cornelius Harnett, Revolutionary War patriot and delegate to the Continental Congress. The county's communities include Dunn, Coats, Angier, Erwin, Buies Creek, Bunnlevel, and Johnsonville, as well as the county seat, Lillington, incorporated in 1859.

The region was originally inhabited by Tuscarora and Saura (Cheraw) Indians. Among the earliest European settlers in Harnett County were Scottish immigrants, many of whom left their homeland after the 1745 Jacobite Rebellion. Forced to vow that they would never again fight the British, many Scots who adopted a neutral stance during the Revolutionary War were executed as traitors by American Patriots. Harnett

County nevertheless maintained a large Scottish population—Gaelic was spoken in parts of the county well into the late nineteenth century—and even today many families in the area can trace their ancestry back to those early Scots.

Harnett County was the site of one of the last battles of the Civil War, a confrontation between Gens. William T. Sherman and William J. Hardee at Averasboro, near Erwin, on 15–17 Mar. 1865. Historical markers denote major events and a museum interprets the battle.

Harnett County's principal towns developed into important local trading and commercial centers after urban development began in the 1880s, though by the early twenty-first century the county had only recently begun to promote industrial expansion. The primary source of income remained agriculture, which either employed or indirectly sustained a majority of the county's population.

Important agricultural products include tobacco, cotton, sweet potatoes, soybeans, wheat, swine, and beef and dairy cattle. Manufactures include textiles, building materials, furniture, mobile homes, and athletic equipment. Raven Rock State Park, established in 1970, is one of the county's principal natural attractions. In 2004 the population of Harnett County was estimated at 99,600.

Reference: John Hairr, *Harnett County: A History* (2002).

Robert Blair Vocci

SEE ALSO Averasboro, Battle of.

Harriet-Henderson Cotton Mills Strike. In 1895, with the financial assistance of local investors, brothers David Y. and John D. Cooper organized the Henderson Cotton Mill on the north side of Henderson for the production of sheeting. The mill began operations the next year. Its profitability led the Coopers and others to develop a second factory, the Harriet Mill, on the south side of Henderson. This mill, which started up in 1901, spun coarse yarns. In 1909 and 1913 the company opened two new plants at the Harriet Mill site. The Harriet and Henderson cotton mills became major producers of yarns.

Following a national trend, the directors modernized the mills in the late 1930s to increase their efficiency and competitiveness. These efforts caused dissatisfaction among the employees, who in 1943 voted to join the Textile Workers Union of America (TWUA)—a rare occurrence in the South. Unionization resulted in significant improvements in the lives of textile workers in Henderson. However, further modernization in the early 1950s, increased workloads to offset the effects of economic recession, and management's refusal in 1958 to agree to a contract that required arbitration of grievances precipitated a strike at the mills.

Members of TWUA Locals 578 and 584 met on 16 Nov. 1958 and voted to strike. The strikers received strong financial support from the union. Many of Henderson's business and civic leaders viewed the situation as a detriment to the town's economic progress. The mills remained closed until February 1959, when the company decided to operate with nonunion workers. Because the economy was poor and unemployment high, management was able to hire new workers. When this occurred, Henderson experienced incidents of vandalism and rock throwing, shootings, and bombings. At the request of local law enforcement officials, Governor Luther H. Hodges, himself a former textile executive, called in the North Carolina State Highway Patrol to escort workers across picket lines and to maintain law and order. He also authorized the State Bureau of Investigation to investigate the violence.

Hodges met with union and company officials, urging them to agree to a new contract. This was accomplished on 17 Apr. 1959. The agreement stipulated that arbitration would be contingent upon mutual consent of labor and management. The company agreed that workers could strike when the company refused to allow arbitration of disputes. Strikebreakers would retain all first-shift jobs, but most remaining positions would be given to strikers. Soon the strikers learned that management had held only 30 positions for the hundreds of workers who were still on strike; the rest were given to strikebreakers who would work on a second shift. Despite the governor's appeals to mill president John D. Cooper, the company soon hired enough new employees to run a third shift at its plants. Owing to this act of bad faith, the agreement unraveled and more violence erupted.

Bowing to pressure from those who disagreed with his use of the Highway Patrol in Henderson, Hodges ordered the National Guard to take its place at the mills in May 1959. More than 60 union members or sympathizers, including Boyd E. Payton, who had represented the TWUA in Henderson, were tried and convicted in superior court for various acts of violence. (Payton was later paroled and pardoned by Governor Terry Sanford.) Although the union had failed to achieve its goal, it did not officially end the strike until 1 June 1961, after spending more than $1 million to support the strikers. Most of them never worked in the Harriet and Henderson cotton mills again. The divisions in Henderson caused by the labor dispute continued for many years.

References: Daniel J. Clark, *Like Night and Day: Unionization in a Southern Mill Town* (1997); Brent D. Glass, *The Textile Industry in North Carolina: A History* (1992).

Maurice C. York

Hatteras Inlet, Battle of. In late August 1861 the Federal victory in the Civil War battle at Hatteras Inlet deprived the Confederate army of a base for privateering, opened the interior coast to the Union, and served as a model for future combined-arms operations. The success of this mission also provided a needed boost for Union supporters in the North, whose morale suffered after the Union disaster at the First Battle of Manassas (Bull Run) in July 1861.

Maj. Gen. John E. Wool at Fort Monroe on the Virginia coast organized a contingent of troops to assist the navy in an attack on the Confederate fortifications. Commanding these men in the actual engagement would be politician–turned–major general Benjamin F. Butler. The naval squadron, led by Cdre. Silas H. Stringham, comprised seven ships. Two chartered vessels that carried the troops and several smaller ships accompanied the fleet when it weighed anchor from Hampton Roads on 26 Aug. 1861. Guarding Hatteras Inlet were two sand and log forts. Fort Clark, the smaller, stood near the ocean to cover the entrance to the inlet with its five 32-pounder smoothbores. Three-quarters of a mile west of Fort Clark stood Fort Hatteras, which guarded the channel through the inlet. Although incomplete, Fort Hatteras mounted 12 32-pounder smoothbores. Five other cannons, including a 10-inch gun that would have been invaluable in the battle, lay in the sand still unmounted.

The Federal fleet arrived off Hatteras Inlet late in the afternoon of 27 August. Early the next morning, the troops boarded small boats and made for the shore. Meanwhile, four Union gunboats opened fire on Fort Clark, whose guns did not have the range to respond. By noon the first of the Union soldiers hit the beach a short distance up from the fort. In heavy seas, only 318 of the 880 troops actually attempted a landing. They made it to shore, but their gunpowder was soaked and they had no provisions. Their vulnerability was mitigated by the fact that Fort Clark had run out of ammunition. The fort's garrison spiked its guns and retreated to Fort Hatteras.

National Guardsmen face off with townspeople in Henderson after being mobilized by Governor Luther Hodges during the Harriet-Henderson Mills strike in May 1959. Courtesy of NCOA&H. The *Raleigh News and Observer* files.

With Fort Clark abandoned and boats in the sound fleeing the area, General Butler ordered the fleet to cease firing. Commodore Stringham sent the shallow-draft gunboat *Monticello* into the inlet to take possession of Fort Hatteras. The southern-held fort met the approaching warship with a well-aimed volley resulting in several hits. The *Monticello* fled out to sea, and the other Union vessels unleashed a barrage on Fort Hatteras.

Darkness and threatening weather halted firing temporarily. Throughout the night the exhausted garrison of Fort Hatteras received reinforcements from nearby posts, and Cdre. Samuel Barron, commander of coastal defenses in Virginia and North Carolina, arrived at the fort. At dawn the Union fleet steamed in once again and anchored just beyond range of the fort's guns but close enough for its own superior weaponry to do its work. By 11:00 A.M. the Confederates realized that their situation was hopeless, but before they could spike their guns and withdraw, a shell hit and ignited the magazine, forcing Barron to raise a white flag. Butler insisted on unconditional surrender, and Barron's officers and men became prisoners of war.

The original plan had called for the shallow inlet to be obstructed to prevent its further use. At Butler's recommendation, however, the Union held the forts and left the inlet open for the Federals' convenience. This victory represented one of the few highlights of Butler's controversial career and provided the Union with an all-important entrance into the North Carolina sounds.

References: John G. Barrett, *The Civil War in North Carolina* (1963); John S. Carbone, *The Civil War in Coastal North Carolina* (2001); David Stick, *The Outer Banks of North Carolina, 1584–1958* (1958).

Dan Blair

Hatting, or hat making, was a significant craft in North Carolina from the mid-eighteenth century well into the nineteenth. In a letter dated 4 Jan. 1754, Governor Arthur Dobbs informed the Board of Trade that a few hats were being made in the colony. Governor William Tryon in 1767 reported that the colony had five or six hatters but "none of them of any note." Many of North Carolina's hatters were among the settlers who poured through the Shenandoah Valley into the colony beginning in the mid-1700s. These skilled craftsmen from hat-making centers such as Philadelphia, Nantucket, and Danbury, Conn., usually engaged simultaneously in farming, milling, or tanning, with hat making as a profitable and even prestigious sideline. In the state's social hierarchy, hatters and other artisans were just below the level of the gentry.

Early styles, primarily for men, included the felt three-cornered hat, the broad-brimmed Quaker hat, and various high hats. Those who wore high hats paid an annual state tax of four dollars for the privilege. Better quality hats were made of fur, with beaver pelts being most desirable. A high-quality handmade hat could cost more than any other article of clothing, the equivalent of $50 in today's currency. To keep costs down, hatters sometimes substituted raccoon, otter, and muskrat for beaver skins. An inferior grade of felt was made of wool and vegetable fibers.

North Carolina's hat-making industry was most vibrant in the Piedmont and Mountains. Among the few hatters known to operate in the eastern region were Constant Devotion and Samuel Snowden in Edgecombe County. They produced beaver or castor hats, competing with less expensive felt hats imported from England. Because imports were not readily available in interior regions, those with the skills and tools to make hats had a ready market.

Around the mid-eighteenth century, the Beard family, Quakers from the North, began making hats in Guilford County. In 1795 20-year-old David Beard inherited the trade and tools from his father William and thereafter built a profitable business. He also held two patents for blocking and cutting machinery. Salem Village in Forsyth County also boasted several hatmakers.

In Transylvania County in western North Carolina, hat making was a lively industry during the decades leading up to the Civil War. Jimmie Neill's Hattery Shop, located about two miles north of Brevard, was among several places where headgear was fashioned from the pelts of local wild animals. Another Transylvania hatter, Billy Wilson, known far and wide as "Hatter Billy," made hats from his sheep's wool. Wilson sheared the sheep, his wife carded and spun the wool, and then he dyed it using walnut hulls.

The introduction of mass-produced hats during the industrial age of the late nineteenth century led to a decline in the number of hatters in the state. By 1884 only four counties listed a hatter among their tradesmen, as hatters, like other artisans, had shifted from production to retailing.

References: C. Yvonne Bell Thomas, *Roads to Jamestown: A View and Review of the Old Town* (1997); Harry L. Watson, *An Independent People: The Way We Lived in North Carolina, 1770–1820* (1983).

Virginia Gunn Fick

Hayes Plantation is a farm in Chowan County, across Queen Anne's Creek from Edenton. The plantation is known chiefly as the seat of the Johnston family. Samuel Johnston (1733–1816) purchased Hayes in 1765 from David Rieusett and made it his family's home until 1793, when he moved to the Hermitage, a plantation in Martin County. In 1814 Samuel Johnston gave Hayes to his son, James Cathcart Johnston (1782–1865). With the help of the English architect-builder William Nichols, James Cathcart Johnston built a new plantation house at Hayes, and he and his three sisters returned there to live in 1817. The plantation remained in the Johnston family

Hayes Plantation house as seen from the waterfront. Photograph by Tim Buchman. Courtesy of Preservation North Carolina.

until James Cathcart Johnston's death. In his will, Johnston left all his Chowan County property, including Hayes, to a business associate, Edward Wood. The Wood family continues to operate Hayes as a working farm.

The plantation that Samuel Johnston purchased contained 543 acres. It grew modestly during his lifetime to 665 acres, but dramatic growth occurred under the ownership of his son James Cathcart Johnston. The younger Johnston was an energetic manager of his estates, keenly interested in agricultural innovations. He acquired and cleared additional land, so that by 1860 the plantation encompassed 1,374 acres. Corn was the principal crop grown in the antebellum era, but Johnston planted other grains as well and raised livestock.

James Cathcart Johnston also inherited a substantial collection of books from his father. To house those books, he built a special wing for the library in the new plantation house at Hayes. The octagonal, Gothic library is one of many distinctive features of the stately structure. The house, still in use as a private residence, is considered one of the finest antebellum houses in North Carolina. A reproduction of the library, which includes many of the original books and furnishings from the Hayes house, is on display in Wilson Library at the University of North Carolina at Chapel Hill.

Reference: Catherine W. Bishir, "Severe Survitude to House Building: The Construction of Hayes Plantation House, 1814–1817," *NCHR* 68 (October 1991).

Eileen McGrath

Haywood County, located in North Carolina's Mountain region, was formed from Buncombe County in 1808 and took its name from John Haywood, the state treasurer at the time. The Great Smoky Mountains National Park and Pisgah Na-

tional Forest comprise some 40 percent of the county's land area and are key elements in the county's economy and culture. Communities in Haywood County include the county seat of Waynesville, founded in 1810, Canton, Clyde, Maggie Valley, and Hazelwood.

Haywood County was home to a thriving Cherokee culture when Europeans arrived in the sixteenth and seventeenth centuries, but smallpox devastated their numbers in 1715 and the Cherokee were eventually forced westward. In the decades following the Revolutionary War, the area attracted a large number of white settlers, many of Scotch-Irish, German, and Dutch descent. Despite its isolated location, the casualties and ruin brought on by the Civil War, and the loss of land for the formation of other counties, Haywood County continued to draw settlers. The creation of the Western North Carolina Railroad in the 1880s provided a boon to its limited agrarian economy and elevated new industries such as logging and tourism to prominence.

Modernization in Haywood County was slow but steady during the twentieth century, and sluggish population growth was compensated for by the influx of tourists and the expansion of facilities to accommodate them, such as North Carolina's first ski resort at Cataloochee Ranch. The county also hosts several festivals related to mountain heritage and culture, including the annual Singing in the Valley, the Stompin' Ground Clogging Competition, and the Smoky Mountain Folk Festival. The Folkmoot USA festival, a popular multicultural celebration of music and dance, is held in Haywood County each summer. County agricultural products include apples, tomatoes, chickens, and beef and dairy cattle. In 2004 the estimated population of Haywood County was 56,500.

References: *Haywood County Heritage, North Carolina* (1994); W. Clark Medford, *The Early History of Haywood County* (1961); Medford, *The Middle History of Haywood County* (1968).

Robert Blair Vocci

SEE ALSO Cataloochee Ranch and Ski Area; Folkmoot USA.

Headache Powders, usually mixtures of aspirin and caffeine, are a form of pain reliever extremely popular in North Carolina and other southern states. Local pharmacists originally concocted their own painkilling remedies, buying raw ingredients and creating dosages on demand. They often sold this medicine in powder form because creating pills was more difficult and expensive. Hundreds of local headache powder brands, such as B. D. Mint, Speedo, PDQ, Galax, Stop-Ake, and Wink, had grown out of these recipes by the 1920s and 1930s.

Promotion and advertising played a crucial role in the success of headache powders. Perhaps the most successful form of promotion was the earliest: direct sampling at mill and mine gates, where machinery noise and dust created prime

Goody's Headache Powder advertising tag designed to be hung from a string in a store. NCC.

customers for the medicine. As a result, the powders have long been a favorite of southern blue-collar workers. Nicknamed "production powders" by these workers, the remedies were sold on the factory floor from "dope carts," which also carried soft drinks, cigarettes, coffee, and cookies.

The popularity of headache powders increased during the Great Depression, driven by the early use of radio advertisements. Manufacturers have also relied heavily upon point-of-purchase advertising (counter displays), with salesmen carrying the powder out of drugstores and pharmacies and placing it by cash registers in rural service stations and general stores. Headache powder promotion, known for its folksy nature, tied itself to regional pursuits, country music, and sports—especially auto racing and professional baseball.

The three products that came to dominate the headache powder market, B.C., Goody's, and Stanback, all have North Carolina roots. In 1906 Commodore Thomas Council founded B.C. Powders while working in Germain Bernard's Durham drugstore. According to legend, the mixture included crushed aspirin, caffeine, and a secret ingredient from Bernard's not-yet-perfected remedy for sore feet. Durham was then at the start of its tobacco boom, and Council's product was a favorite among the people flocking to work in the factories. In 1910 Council and Bernard named their powder B.C., a combination of their surname initials. They hired their first full-time salesman in 1917, just in time for local doughboys to carry B.C. out of the South. In 1928 B.C. expanded into its own facility. The Block Drug Company of Jersey City, N.J., bought B.C. in 1967 and five years later moved production to Memphis, Tenn.

Pharmacist Thomas M. (Dr. Tom) Stanback created his powder recipe in 1910 while working in a drugstore in Thomasville. Stanback moved to Spencer a year later and began production of his painkiller on a small commercial scale, selling it to workers at that town's railroad repair facility. Although these men spread the fame of Stanback's product along their routes, Stanback's headache powder business remained a sideline to his drugstore until 1924, when he convinced his younger brother Fred to try selling the powder to retail stores. With this beginning of a full-time sales force, Stanback Medicine Company steadily expanded until it occupied a factory in Salisbury in 1931. It remained a family business until 1998, when it was also sold to the Block Drug Company.

Goody's Headache Powder was founded by tobacco and candy wholesaler A. Thad Lewallen in 1932, when he bought Winston-Salem pharmacist Martin C. (Goody) Goodman's pain formula. Lewallen and his first employee, Goodman's former soda jerk Hege Hamilton, set up shop over a bank before moving in 1941 to a renovated clothing factory on Salt Street in Old Salem. Hamilton became president of Goody's in 1945 when Lewallen died. The Lewallen family retained control of the company until December 1995, when the Block Drug Company purchased Goody's. Block soon closed the Winston-Salem facility and moved production to Memphis, Tenn.

References: Tucker Mitchell, "Take a Powder," *The State* (April 1993); "Taking a Powder," *Salisbury Post*, 1 Oct. 1989; Janice Westmoreland, "A Good Sample of How to Build a Business," *Wachovia* (Fall 1992).

Kevin Cherry

Headrights, or landrights, was a term applied in the colonial period to the system of granting unclaimed land to persons who imported new settlers to the Carolina colony. In 1663 the Crown divided territory that included North Carolina among eight Lords Proprietors to dispose of as they chose. As early as 1681 the Proprietors made grants, varying in size, to individuals who brought in settlers. The size of the grant depended on the number of settlers, even though all the land belonged to the importer. The grant usually, but not always, comprised 50 acres per individual, counting the importer himself as well as each individual such as a spouse, child, relative, servant, or slave. William Symons, for example, "proved 5 rights": for himself, Robert Smith, Emanuel Altooy, "Maria a negro transport," and Hannah Symons.

The headrights system required that a certain portion of the issued land be cultivated, and an annual fee (based on acreage and called a quitrent) was levied. After the American Revolution, however, the system of headrights was no longer used.

William S. Powell

Health and Human Services, Department of. The North Carolina Department of Health and Human Services (DHHS) is responsible for the welfare of all North Carolina residents, including children, the elderly, the economically impoverished, and the physically and developmentally disabled. By the early 2000s it was the state's largest government agency, with a 2005 operating budget of over $11 billion—more than 20 percent of the state's total budget.

The modern DHHS is an amalgamation of many previously existing state agencies and departments, including the Department of Public Welfare, Department of Public Health, and Department of Mental Health. In 1971 the General Assembly created the Department of Human Resources, which combined government agencies and free-standing departments performing similar functions. This umbrella organization continued to expand with the addition of the Division of Vocational Rehabilitation in 1973, Office of Rural Health in 1974, and Division of Aging in 1977. The administration of the Medicaid program was reassigned from the Division of Social Services to the newly created Division of Medical Assistance in 1978. In 1989 a Division for the Deaf and Hard of Hearing was formed, and the Division of Public Health was transferred to the Department of Environment, Health, and Natural Resources. In 1997 the Department of Human Resources reacquired the Public Health Division and was renamed the Department of Health and Human Services.

The three largest modern-day DHHS divisions are the Division of Medical Assistance (which accounts for over half of the department's budget), Division of Social Services, and Division of Mental Health, Developmental Disabilities, and Substance Abuse Services. Other DHHS branches include the Division of Child Development (created in 1993) and the Early Intervention and Education Division (established in 1999 and renamed the Office of Education Services in 2001).

Robert Blair Vocci

Heath Patent. Sir Robert Heath (1575–1649), attorney general of England during the reign of King Charles I, in 1629 received from Charles a patent for all lands in America between 31° and 36° north latitude. The territory granted was named "Carolana" in honor of the king and extended from the Atlantic Coast to the South Seas (Pacific Ocean). Within less than a year, a Huguenot refugee in England, the baron de Sancé, was negotiating with Heath to establish a colony somewhere between Cape Fear and Albemarle Sound. No settlement resulted, however, and in 1638 Heath conveyed his interest in Carolana to Henry Frederick Howard, Lord Maltravers. Maltravers and subsequent claimants under the grant also failed to organize any settlements.

Although the Heath patent contained no clause requiring the seating of colonists within Carolana, in 1663 and 1665 King Charles II conveyed the territory, renamed "Carolina," to the eight Lords Proprietors, under the presumption that the Heath patent had lapsed. Claimants continued to contest the grants of the 1660s, however, and in 1768 the Heath title was finally extinguished with the Crown's compensatory grant of 100,000 acres in the colony of New York to the descendant of Daniel Coxe, who had acquired the Heath claim in 1696.

References: Paul E. Kopperman, "Profile of Failure: The Carolana Project, 1629–1640," *NCHR* 59 (January 1982); Mattie Erma Edwards Parker, ed., *North Carolina Charters and Constitutions, 1578–1698* (1963); William S. Powell, "Carolana and the Incomparable Roanoke: Explorations and Attempted Settlements, 1620–1663," *NCHR* 51 (January 1974).

Robert J. Cain

Heilig-Meyers. Brothers-in-law William A. Heilig and J. Max Meyers, both Lithuanian immigrants, opened the first Heilig-Meyers retail home furnishing store in Goldsboro in 1913. This partnership ended in 1946 with the partners dividing up the stores and with Meyers keeping the Heilig-Meyers name. The company moved its headquarters to Richmond, Va., in 1951. Soon thereafter, the firm added stores, first in North Carolina and then throughout the Southeast.

The 1970s, 1980s, and 1990s were years of expansion and financial strength. Heilig-Meyers went public in 1972 to raise money for aggressive expansion plans, and by 1986 the company had 216 stores throughout the South, making it the largest publicly owned home furnishings retailer in the country. Late in 1989 the firm opened its first store in the Midwest. Expansion into other new areas occurred in 1993 with the acquisition of 92 McMahan's Furniture stores in California, Arizona, New Mexico, Texas, Nevada, and Colorado. In 1995 the company ventured outside the United States for the first time, buying 17 furniture stores from Berrios Enterprises, the largest volume furniture retailer in Puerto Rico. The company decided to penetrate the big-city market by buying chains with successful metropolitan formats, and in 1996 it acquired Rhodes, Inc., a 106-store chain based in Atlanta with stores in 15 southern, midwestern, and western states. The next year the retailer added the 10-store, Dallas-area chain Room Stores (which featured the relatively new concept of selling furniture in room-ready packages) and Mattress Discounters' 169 stores.

Late in 1997, however, the firm's restructuring and expansion plans were scaled back, and Heilig-Meyers reported a net loss of more than $55 million for fiscal year 1998. In March 1999 the company sold Rhodes and Mattress Discounters, and in 2000 more stores were closed and Berrios Enterprises was sold. These measures proved inadequate, and on 16 Aug. 2000 Heilig-Meyers filed for bankruptcy protection. In April 2001 the company announced that it would close its remaining Heilig-Meyers stores and concentrate its full attention on its profitable Room Stores chain, located entirely in the metropolitan markets of Texas, Maryland, and Washington, D.C.

Wiley J. Williams

Helms-Hunt Senate Race. The fight for a U.S. Senate seat in 1984, pitting Democratic governor James B. Hunt Jr. against incumbent Republican senator Jesse Helms, is considered one of North Carolina's most infamous political battles. The campaign received unprecedented national and international attention because of the use by both sides of negative media ads and brutal personal attacks. It is seen as a prototype of the no-holds-barred brawls that typify a strand of modern-day partisan politics, polarizing voters along distinct ideological lines. *New York Times*, *Washington Post*, *Los Angeles Times*, *Wall Street Journal*, and *USA Today* reporters consistently followed the campaign, as did print journalists from Canada, Great Britain, Sweden, France, Denmark, Switzerland, and Japan and German and Dutch TV reporters. The tremendous amount of money spent on the campaign (more than $25 million) contributed to this coverage. One ABC News anchor at the time called the race "the closest thing we have ever had to a national race for the U.S. Senate."

Both Hunt and Helms were skilled campaigners who had fervent supporters and detractors in North Carolina. Many of Helms's admirers considered him a courtly, grandfatherly figure as well as a courageous conservative warrior battling the "tax and spend" approach and immoral values of liberal Democrats. Hunt's admirers touted his forward-thinking dedication to educational and economic progress in the state and approved of his pragmatic gubernatorial leadership and open-minded moderation on social issues.

Helms saw his popularity begin to wane in the early 1980s, evidenced by several polls that showed him trailing Hunt by double-digit numbers. In April 1983, a full year and a half before the election, Helms began running radio and newspaper ads attacking Hunt, followed by TV ads over the next several months. These ads characterized Hunt, in highly unflattering terms, as a liberal, valueless, pro-union politician—a theme the Helms campaign continued throughout the race. That fall,

Campaign button from the unsuccessful 1984 U.S. Senate bid of James B. Hunt. NCC.

Helms led a filibuster of a U.S. Senate bill to establish slain African American leader Martin Luther King's birthday as a national holiday. The ads and Helms's position as perhaps the staunchest conservative on the national scene bolstered his numbers in North Carolina, and within months he had pulled even with Hunt in the polls.

Hunt began to fire back with his own inflammatory attack ads beginning in May 1984, linking Helms to the acts of right-wing dictators around the world. With Hunt's entry into the media fray, harsh accusations and bitter rebuttals became the backbone of both campaigns. Among other things, Hunt accused Helms of supporting cuts in popular social programs such as social security and school lunches while backing efforts to provide tax breaks for the rich and oil companies, of trying to "divide our people" along racial lines, and of disrespecting veterans by calling veteran benefits "welfare." Helms accused Hunt of a variety of liberal views and agendas and called his patriotism into question for his lack of military service.

After a long and bitter campaign, the election on 6 Nov. 1984 saw Helms win by a relatively wide margin of 52 to 48 percent. In the end, the election served to bolster the ever-hardening lines between the political right and left. Analysts of the election returns noted that Hunt carried nearly all of the African American vote and much of the college-educated, urban, liberal-to-moderate vote. Helms took a large percentage of the white middle-income, blue-collar worker vote and that of the loose coalition of Evangelical conservative voters who came to be known as the Christian Right. The campaign took a toll on the positive reputations of both men and, for all the national attention it received, temporarily damaged the state's political standing. In addition, the use of attack ads to point out the weaknesses of opponents became ever more commonplace, at least in part because of their effectiveness during the 1984 Helms-Hunt race.

References: Frederick A. Day and Gregory A. Weeks, "The 1984 Helms-Hunt Senate Race: A Spatial Postmortem of Emerging Republican Strength in the South," *Social Science Quarterly* 69 (December 1988); Michael R. McLaughlin, "Hunt Versus Helms: Old Time Politicking in the New South" (M.A. thesis, UNC-Chapel Hill, 1984); William D. Snider, *Helms and Hunt: The North Carolina Senate Race, 1984* (1985).

Jay Mazzocchi

Hemp is the generic term for *Cannabis sativa* (or in its wild form, *Cannabis indica*), an annual herb used for millennia as a source of fiber for rope, cloth, and paper and also as a psychotropic drug. In colonial North Carolina hemp was one of many naval stores exported, and its cultivation was encouraged on both sides of the Atlantic throughout the eighteenth century. In more recent years it has been designated a "controlled substance," for, though the form bred for fiber has little or no psychoactive potential, the species is the raw source of marijuana and its refined derivatives; cannabis cultivation in the United States—excepting the smallest amounts grown with a government license—has been illegal since 1937.

The greatest instance of hemp advocacy in eighteenth-century North Carolina belongs to Governor William Tryon's administration. Tryon pitched the efficacies of the crop before the Assembly in 1760 and again two years later, resulting in a bill that was passed on 2 Dec. 1762. In 1766 the Assembly further passed an "Act for Establishing Public Warehouses in the Towns of Halifax and Campbleton, for the Inspection of Hemp and Flax." These warehouses were to be supplied with bonded inspectors and equipment for weighing and compressing the fiber for exportation. It was directed that they be open from 1 November to 1 January and again from 1 March to 1 May. The inspectors were to label the various batches by point of origin, mark them as dew-retted (or soaked) or water-retted, and issue certificates. There were severe penalties for counterfeiting certificates.

As commodities for export, hemp and flax went the unfortunate way of many other ill-fated colonial endeavors. Though the climate and soil were right for hemp culture, the logistics of transport were prohibitive, meaning that hemp never became a crucial commodity for export. A pandemic of drug use in the second half of the twentieth century brought the plant's cultivation back into favor; marijuana has become a persistent social and legal problem. In some of the more remote reaches of North Carolina, including the hill country, the traditional home of illegal distilleries, marijuana farming has largely replaced moonshining.

Reference: Jack Frazier, *The Great American Hemp Industry* (1991).

David Southern

Henderson County, located in North Carolina's Mountain region, was formed from Buncombe County in 1838. Like its county seat, Hendersonville (incorporated in 1847), the county takes its name from Leonard Henderson, chief justice of the North Carolina Supreme Court from 1829 to 1833. Other Henderson County communities include Fletcher, Laurel Park, and Flat Rock.

Originally inhabited by the Cherokee, the site of modern-day Hendersonville was part of the early land grants west of the Blue Ridge Mountains. Revolutionary War soldier William Mills, who settled his new property in 1787, is credited with establishing the foundations for the county and its principal city. Mills planted hundreds of fruit trees in the area, in addition to more typical crops, and today Henderson County leads the state in apple production. The county's modern economy depends more, however, on its tourist industry and retirement facilities than on agriculture. Visitors can enjoy a full range of outdoor activities—from hiking through the Pisgah National Forest to taking in the panoramic views from scenic overlooks along the Blue Ridge Parkway and other highways—while the county's tranquil setting and mild climate have earned it a place among the nation's top retirement destinations. Literary giant Carl Sandburg spent the last 22 years of his life in Flat Rock, and Connemara, his home and farm, are preserved as a historic site. Flatrock Playhouse, established in the early 1940s, is the official North Carolina State Theater. Henderson County had an estimated population of slightly more than 96,000 in 2004.

References: *The Heritage of Henderson County, North Carolina* (1985–88); Lenoir Ray, *Postmarks: A History of Henderson County, North Carolina, 1787–1968* (1970).

Robert Blair Vocci

SEE ALSO Connemara.

Henry Clay Oak, a venerable white oak of unusually large height and girth, stood in Raleigh near the northwest corner of the intersection of North Blount and East North Streets from a time possibly predating the city's 1792 founding until 1991. The tree grew to a height of more than 100 feet, with a 100-foot spread and a trunk diameter of 6½ feet. It typified the type of tree that early North Carolina settlers used for building homes and other structures, as well as making furniture and farm implements. The bark was equally useful for tanning leather.

The name "Henry Clay Oak" derives from local tradition, which holds that in 1844, under the shade of this tree in the side yard of the residence known as the William Polk House, Whig presidential candidate Henry Clay penned his famous "Raleigh letter," which supposedly cost him the presidential election. On 17 April of that campaign year, he wrote the widely read letter opposing annexation of Texas, an action he predicted would precipitate war with Mexico.

Weather damage and irreversible disease necessitated the tree's destruction on 9 Oct. 1991. A bronze marker that had been erected in 1939 by the Colonel Polk Chapter, Daughters of the American Revolution, marks the former location of the tree. An unofficial count of the rings suggested an age nearer to 200 years than to several earlier estimates varying between 250 and 600 years. The landscape services section of the State Department of Administration germinated seedlings from the tree soon after it was felled and provided one seedling to each of the 100 schools in Wake County, with instructions for planting the seedling on the school grounds. Woodcarvers made Henry Clay Oak souvenirs from the felled tree, including a reproduction acorn fashioned by Darrell Rhudy, a member of the Triangle Woodturners of North Carolina. The acorn was deposited in Raleigh's bicentennial time capsule on New Year's Eve 1992.

References: Elizabeth Reid Murray, *Wake: Capital County of North Carolina*, vol. 1 (1983); Elizabeth Culbertson Waugh, *North Carolina's Capital, Raleigh* (1992).

Elizabeth Reid Murray

Herbs and their use as medicines date back to the earliest recorded history of the region that became North Carolina. Native Americans, under the direction of tribal medicine men, established many herbs as natural remedies and used "medicinal plants" for a wide range of treatments. Modern tribes of Native Americans in North Carolina continue to use herbal remedies for illnesses, although to a lesser degree.

Early European settlers of North America brought herbs with them for medicinal use. They soon found similar and new plants and herbs being used by the local Indians. The marketing of herbs in North Carolina began in colonial times. Druggists, physicians, and medical institutions purchased a variety of herbs from small herb-gathering groups and individuals. As early as 1600, some merchants were buying and selling herbs on a regular basis and druggists were advertising for the specific types needed.

By the middle of the nineteenth century, businesses marketing medicinal roots and herbs were operating in Piedmont North Carolina. The *Statesville Landmark* reported in 1888 that "there were only three herbariums in the United States, those of the Wallace Bros. and L. Pinkus in Statesville and that of Park, Davis & Co. in Charlotte." The Wallace brothers began trading in herbs in the early 1850s in South Carolina before moving to Statesville. They opened their firm in Statesville in 1859 and expanded their herb purchasing and selling rapidly. By 1870 the Wallace Brothers Herbarium had grown so large that the brothers established it as a separate branch from their other businesses. They also hired famed botanist Mordecai E. Hyams as a researcher and manager. Hyams had worked for the Confederate government during the Civil War, buying roots, bark, and plants from which medicine could be made for the Confederate army.

In 1876 the Wallace herbarium entered a botanical display in the Philadelphia Centennial. It included 300 varieties of the fruits from medicinal plants, 125 varieties of mosses, 200 kinds of wood, 400 boxes of the types of roots purchased annually, and 600 medicinal plants in glass frames with the root and flower of each. The display took the gold medal for first place; two years later, a similar exhibit took first place at the world's fair in Paris.

In 1888 the Wallace brothers purchased the herb business of Park, Davis & Co. (which later became a major pharmaceutical firm) and moved that operation from Charlotte to Statesville. The Pinkus firm was a large operation and continued as competition for the Wallaces until after the turn of the century.

The Wallaces continued in the herb business until 1942, helping North Carolina remain a leader in the buying and selling of herbs. The popularity of natural herbs and roots was renewed in the latter part of the twentieth century, when natural food stores were established and many herbal medicines once again came to public attention, even becoming available through major grocery store chains.

References: Anthony Cavender, *Folk Medicine in Southern Appalachia* (2003); Molly Culbertson, *Country Home Book of Herbs* (1994); Frances P. Porcher, *Resources of the Southern Fields and Forests* (repr., 1970); Charles Wilson, *Green Treasures: Adventures in the Discovery of Edible Plants* (1974).

Chester Paul Middlesworth

Heritage Bible College, founded in 1971, is a small, private four-year college operated by the Pentecostal Free Will Baptist Church on an 80-acre campus near Dunn in eastern Harnett County. Heritage awards associate's and bachelor's degrees in theology/religion and religious education certificates, offering biblical higher education training for the denomination's future leaders. Incorporators of the college included J. E. Andrews, R. O. Byrd, and Shelton Weeks.

Benjamin R. Justesen

Heroes of America (HOA), also referred to as the "Red Strings," was an underground, pro-Union organization operating in North Carolina, Virginia, West Virginia, and perhaps other southern states during the Civil War. Its ranks were composed mainly of deserters, draft dodgers, and Unionists as well as some slaves and free blacks, and its purpose was to protect its members from Confederate authorities. Those members engaged in a range of subversive activities, including encouraging disloyalty on the home front and desertion in the Confederate army, providing military intelligence to Federal authorities, maintaining an underground railroad to spirit members to the Union lines, promoting the formation of anti-Confederate guerrilla units, and furthering class conflict by promising the poor a postwar redistribution of the wealth of the planter class.

The HOA likely had its roots in a group of armed Unionists who emerged in central North Carolina in July 1861. Confederate troops quelled the insurgency and charged the men with treason. The best-known organizer and leader of the HOA was John Lewis Johnson, a druggist and physician. The organization's Grand Council, formed in Raleigh, became the center of HOA activity. Johnson eventually inspired the establishment of a National Grand Council in Washington. The HOA strongly supported the peace movement begun in 1863 by William W. Holden, editor of the Raleigh-based *North Carolina Standard*. In 1864, when Holden challenged incumbent Zebulon B. Vance for governor, the leader of the peace movement was publicly accused of being a leader in the disloyal HOA. Fearing reprisals, few of Holden's supporters showed up to vote for him, and Vance won by a landslide. With Holden's defeat, the HOA ceased to play a role in the politics of Confederate North Carolina.

Through the efforts of North Carolina members, however, the HOA had spread to southwestern Virginia. By the winter of 1864, bands of deserters and disloyal county officials, many of whom belonged to the Red Strings, controlled much of the region. During Reconstruction, the HOA protected its members (including numerous Union army veterans from North Carolina) from hostile ex-Confederates. It is ironic that the HOA, a clandestine terrorist organization, served as a model for the Ku Klux Klan, which was purportedly organized in part to counter the power of the Heroes. In the gubernatorial campaign of 1868, the HOA aligned itself predominately with the "scalawag" wing of the Republican Party, supporting the winner of the election, William W. Holden.

During the Civil War and Reconstruction, members of the HOA were prime examples of the "Other South." They were southern whites who, during the war, opposed the Confederacy and, during Reconstruction, supported the Republican Party. Their story challenges the often-held view that the nineteenth-century South was monolithic in its beliefs and attitudes.

Reference: William T. Auman and David D. Scarboro, "The Heroes of America in Civil War North Carolina," *NCHR* 58 (October 1981).

William T. Auman

Hertford County, located in North Carolina's Coastal Plain region and partially bordering the state of Virginia, was formed from Bertie, Chowan, and Northampton Counties in 1759. The county took its name from Francis Seymour Conway, earl and later marquis of Hertford. Communities in the county include the county seat of Winton (originally Wynntown [incorporated in 1766], which replaced Cotton's Ferry), Ahoskie, Murfreesboro, Harrellsville, Como, and Cofield.

Once inhabited by Chowanoac, Meherrin, and Tuscarora Indian tribes, the eastern area of Hertford County was explored by English settlers of the early Roanoke Island and Jamestown colonies and became a British possession known as the Parish of St. Barnabas. Settlers took full advantage of the area's rich farmland as well as the opportunities for fishing offered by the Chowan River. The town of Winton was the first North Carolina town to be burned during the Civil War (20 Feb. 1862).

Though the county later experienced some industrial development and had incorporated manufacturing into its economy by the 1950s, agriculture continued to dominate through the early 2000s, with staples such as tobacco, cotton, peanuts, corn, and soybeans among the leading crops. Chowan College, a Baptist school, was founded in Murfreesboro in 1848. The county also hosts the modern-day Meherrin Indian tribe, which has about 700 members. The overall population of Hertford County was estimated to be 23,700 in 2004.

Robert Blair Vocci

SEE ALSO Meherrin Indians; Winton, Burning of.

Highland Games. The staging of Highland Games in a number of sites throughout North Carolina — home to the largest settlement of Highland Scots outside of Scotland until well into the nineteenth century — has succeeded in creating a renaissance of interest in Scottish history and culture in the state and beyond. The events also serve as favored tourist attractions and colorful reminders of the contributions made by one of North Carolina's most successful immigrant groups. With North Carolina's rich Scottish heritage, there is little wonder that the state is home to several such events, one of which has achieved international stature in its relatively short existence.

Modern-day Scottish Highland Games and gatherings are the offshoot of ancient Celtic tests of strength and fitness, as well as competitive activities that later took place at cattle fairs, or "trysts," in Scotland. Some historians credit the eleventh-century king of Scotland, Malcolm Canmore, with the origination of Highland Games. Typical Highland Games as they are known today include various athletic events such as the tossing of weights and the tossing of the caber, as well as competitions in bagpipe playing, Highland dancing, and other festivities. The concept of the "clan gathering" is an Ameri-

The hammer throw at the Highland Games on Grandfather Mountain. Photograph by Hugh Morton.

can addition to these traditional events, with the atmosphere being somewhat reminiscent of a large family reunion.

The first Highland-type games in North Carolina likely occurred at the "Scotch Fairs" held at various sites in the old Highland settlement of the Cape Fear region, notably at Laurel Hill and Ellerbe. Such events were eventually banned by an act of legislature in the 1870s, as it was reported that they had turned into occasions of gambling and drunkenness. It was not until the middle of the twentieth century that interest in Highland Games in their truest sense was revived.

The Grandfather Mountain Highland Games, the first and largest in the state, were cofounded in 1956 by the late Agnes MacRae Morton of Linville and Wilmington and Donald F. MacDonald, a native of the Highland settlement of the Cape Fear region who was at the time a reporter with the *Charlotte News*. MacDonald, inspired by attending the 1954 Braemar Highland Gathering in Scotland, had returned to North Carolina with the idea of recreating a similar event in the state. He had already been instrumental in founding the Robert Burns Society of Charlotte and the Clan Donald Society of the United States, and it was through publicity for these events that Morton learned of his interest in Highland Games. Morton, who had herself been inspired by a relative's report on the Round Hill (Conn.) Highland Gathering, also shared the vision of creating a Highland gathering to be held on the slopes of Grandfather Mountain. Through a mutual friend, the two met and planned the launch of the first Grandfather Mountain Highland Games, which were held on 19 Aug. 1956 to commemorate the 211th anniversary of the first rising of the Jacobite standard at Glenfinnan and the beginning of the 1745 Jacobite Rebellion in Scotland.

The Grandfather Mountain Highland Games, moved to the second full weekend in July in 1958, have gained international stature, and the standards of competition in athletics, piping and drumming, and dancing are recognized worldwide. Due to the attendance of numerous Scottish clan and family soci-

eties, most of which are affiliated with hereditary clan chiefs in Scotland, the Grandfather Mountain Highland Games boasts of being the largest "clan gathering" in the world, with well over 100 such organizations represented each year. The event has grown into a four-day festival that includes a torchlighting opening ceremony, held on the Thursday evening prior to the commencement of the games, and concerts, sing-alongs, dancing, and other musical events in addition to the games themselves.

The state's second Highland Games, the Flora MacDonald Highland Games and Gathering of Scottish Clans held in Red Springs, is the only such gathering held in an area recognized for its Scottish settlement. Founded by interested citizens in Red Springs, the first Flora MacDonald Highland Games grew out of the success of a 1976 colonial muster and reenactment of two Revolutionary War skirmishes that involved local Scottish Tories. A full spectrum of competitive events in athletics, piping and drumming, and dancing was added the next year, and the event has become an annual event on the Scottish American calendar, occurring on the first full weekend of October. Fittingly, the event is now held on the campus of the old Flora MacDonald College in Red Springs.

Another North Carolina Highland Games was founded in 1979 in Waxhaw, an area settled primarily by Ulster Scots. The idea for these games was conceived in 1978 by interested parties who had been active in Scottish events and who were involved in that year's production of the outdoor drama, *Listen and Remember*, which documented the coming of Ulster Scots to the Waxhaw region. The Waxhaw Scottish Games are held annually on the last weekend in October and are staged by the Scottish Society of the Waxhaws.

The Loch Norman Highland Games, held on the Rural Hill Plantation just north of Charlotte, is the latest outgrowth of the interest created by the Grandfather Mountain Highland Games. By 2004 it was the state's second-largest Highland gathering. Founded in 1992 by numerous members of the Scottish American community in the Charlotte area and deriving its name from nearby Lake Norman, this gathering occurs annually in April and is considered to mark the beginning of the Highland Games season in the South.

References: Emily Ann Donaldson, *The Scottish Highland Games in America* (1986); R. Celeste Ray, *Highland Heritage: Scottish Americans in the American South* (2001).

William S. Caudill

Highland Regiment, North Carolina.

Many Highland Scots, who had immigrated to America (primarily settling in New York and North Carolina) in growing numbers after 1745, generally supported the English Crown during the Revolutionary War. Having been defeated in uprisings backing the Stuart restoration in 1715 and 1745, the Scots were wary of rebelling against the monarchy a third time. Many of them were recently arrived yeoman farmers of modest means or moderately wealthy merchants and officeholders living near the seat of colonial government in Wilmington. This dependent situation in which the Scots found themselves contributed to their Loyalist tendencies, and they had little desire to see their trade as well as capital threatened by rebellion.

With this in mind, Governor Josiah Martin wrote to the earl of Dartmouth in 1775 requesting that his relinquished commission in the British army be restored and that he be allowed to command a regiment of loyal Highland troops. In his response dated 12 July 1775, Dartmouth stated that the king would not allow Martin to be reinstated in the army but approved the raising of a battalion of Highlanders under Lt. Col. Allan MacLean. It was not until 10 Jan. 1776 that Martin finally issued the call to arms that would raise the North Carolina Highlanders. In light of Tory attempts to crush Patriot recruiting, MacLean assured Martin that the loyal Scots were rallying to the king's standard. The majority of these Highlanders came from Anson, Cumberland, and Bladen Counties, locations of heavy Scottish settlement.

British general Thomas Gage sent Brig. Gen. Donald MacDonald and Lt. Col. Donald McLeod to rally the Scots in North Carolina, believing that they would contribute a considerable number to the British ranks. The regiment they were to raise to join the Royal Highland Emigrants was then to march to Wilmington and join the king's troops. At the same time, Martin was creating his own North Carolina Highland Regiment. Although unclear in the *Colonial Records*, it appears that the two groups consolidated into one battalion rather than marching separately to Wilmington. At Wilmington, the emigrants were to join the main body of British troops, while Martin's Highland Regiment was to stay in North Carolina to counter any actions by the Tory militias being formed in the area.

On the march to Wilmington, the massed Highland army under MacDonald engaged Patriot forces at the Battle of Moore's Creek Bridge on 27 Feb. 1776. Despite the ferocity of their attacks, the Scots met defeat at the hands of North Carolina militia under Alexander Lillington, James Moore, and Richard Caswell. With this blow, Scottish resistance all but crumbled, with the victors confiscating Scottish firearms and broadswords and even carrying off the belted plaids of many vanquished Highlanders.

Despite the outcome at Moore's Creek, Martin remained hopeful of leading a Scottish army. Residing in Charles Towne (modern-day Charleston) in late May 1780, he wrote to a Salisbury man named Weickerman that he "would be in Cross Creek [now Fayetteville] within a fortnight" at the head of Loyalist militia. In 1780 Martin raised a two-company battalion, the North Carolina Highland Regiment, for service. Scanty records survive of their activities, which most likely consisted of acting as a part of the Royal Highland Emigrants.

The commander of the Highlanders was Lt. Col. Samuel Bryan. In 1782 the Highlanders were sent to New York to become a brigade in the British army, and in 1783 they were disbanded in Canada.

References: Wallace Brown, *The Good Americans: The Loyalists in the American Revolution* (1969); Stuart Reid, *Eighteenth-Century Highlanders*, Men-at-Arms series no. 261 (1993).

Patrick Morton

Highland Scots. SEE Scottish Settlers.

High Point, in southwest Guilford County, is a center of the wood furniture industry in the United States. The city was founded after the legislature in 1849 approved construction of a plank road from Fayetteville to Salem and a railroad from Goldsboro to Charlotte. The community that developed where the road crossed the rails took its name from the fact that it was the highest point on the rail line. The town was incorporated in 1859, and the first furniture factory opened in 1888. Within 50 years, High Point was home to 160 companies, half of which produced furniture or woodwork.

The first furniture exposition in North Carolina was held in 1905 at High Point, and construction of the Southern Furniture Exposition Building in 1921 allowed High Point to replace Chicago as the site of the nation's most important annual furniture show. The 1920s became the town's first boom era. High Point's population swelled from 14,302 to 36,745 over the decade, while almost $20 million in building permits were issued and more than $26 million was spent on city improvements. The 1950s brought the second boom. The population grew from 39,973 in 1950 to 62,063 in 1960. The furniture industry set the pace, but there was also strong development in textile manufacturing. Growth of the "furniture market," as it is called, mirrored that of the city itself after the 1950s. In 2005 High Point, with a population of about 100,000, was the eighth-largest city in North Carolina.

References: High Point Chamber of Commerce, *The Building and the Builders of a City* (1947); Roy J. Shipman, *High Point: A Pictorial History* (1983).

Richard B. McCaslin

SEE ALSO Furniture; International Home Furnishings Market.

High Point Female College operated under a charter from the North Carolina legislature as a joint-stock enterprise from March 1889, when it relocated to High Point from Thomasville at mid-term, until June 1893, when it closed and was replaced in the building by the High Point Institute and Business College. The college occupied a three-story brick building at the junction of Broad and College Streets, later

Hayden Place, one block west of Main Street. The faculty of High Point Female College, who numbered about a dozen, provided a limited variety of mostly preparatory courses to boys and girls under the supervision of J. N. Stallings, whose wife and three daughters comprised one-third of his teaching staff. According to the catalog, enrollment in March 1889 totaled 20, though other sources claim this increased to at least 40.

Reference: Michael G. Pierce, *History of the High Point Public Schools, 1897–1993* (1993).

Richard B. McCaslin

High Point University, situated in southwestern Guilford County, was founded in 1924 by the Methodist Protestant Church. Led by Joseph F. McCulloch, Methodists desiring to build a college in North Carolina secured a financial commitment from their church and a site from High Point, a growing city with the greatest number of Methodists of any community in the state. Methodists dominated the board of trustees during the college's early years, a period marked by economic struggle and determined development under presidents Robert M. Andrews and Gideon I. Humphreys. The establishment of the United Methodist Church in 1939 brought economic stability and a change in leadership. After the resignation of Humphreys, Dennis H. Cooke assumed the presidency and won national accreditation for the college. He then stepped aside in favor of Wendell M. Patton, who promoted the growth of the institution during a presidency of 21 years.

High Point College became a university in the fall of 1991, offering master's degrees in three areas: business administration, management and international management, and administration of nonprofit organizations. By the early 2000s it had an enrollment of approximately 3,000 students, with some 500 of these enrolled at the school's Madison Park campus in Winston-Salem.

References: William R. Locke, *No Easy Task: The First Fifty Years of High Point College* (1975); Richard B. McCaslin, *Remembered Be Thy Blessings: High Point University—The College Years, 1924–1991* (1995).

Richard B. McCaslin

Highway Commission. The first State Highway Commission, established by Governor Charles B. Aycock in 1901, consisted of the state geologist, the commissioner of agriculture, and a third person selected to act as secretary. This early commission filed only one report (in 1902) during its one-biennium lifespan; it had no budget with which to operate and was expected to serve only in an advisory capacity. It was not until 1915 that another commission was formed during the waning months of Governor Locke Craig's administration, this one

a seven-member panel that included the governor, the state geologist, two road engineers, and three citizens selected by the governor. The result of years of effort by state geologist Joseph Hyde Pratt to create such a body, this second commission was formed in large part to meet the requirements for receiving federal funds for highway construction. A third restructuring of the State Highway Commission occurred in 1919 with passage of the Stacey Bill, which enabled the newly appointed commission to direct the state's increasing involvement in road building. Fueled by a massive $50 million bond issued in 1921, the commission, headed by Frank Page, undertook the construction and maintenance of nearly 6,000 miles of highway.

The State Highway Commission is viewed as the predecessor to the North Carolina Department of Transportation. In 1941 the General Assembly created the Department of Motor Vehicles, consolidating services previously provided by the secretary of state and the Department of Revenue. The Department of Motor Vehicles, in turn, was combined with the State Highway Commission to form the North Carolina Department of Transportation and Highway Safety through the Executive Organization Act of 1971 (which also created the North Carolina Board of Transportation). In 1979 "Highway Safety" was dropped from the department's name when the Highway Patrol Division was transferred to the newly created Department of Crime Control and Public Safety.

References: John Harden, *North Carolina Roads and Their Builders*, vol. 2 (1966); Capus Waynick, *North Carolina Roads and Their Builders*, vol. 1 (1952).

Robert E. Ireland

Highway Patrol. The enormous growth of motorized traffic after World War I created a problem for law enforcement officials in North Carolina. Although more than 100,000 automobiles traveled the expanding highway system, no state agency could enforce traffic laws on intrastate roads; only county and local police patrolled these roads, and then only infrequently. Finally, in 1929 the General Assembly authorized the creation of the North Carolina State Highway Patrol and a patrol training school at Camp Glenn, near Morehead City. Initially, the Highway Patrol, with headquarters in Raleigh and district offices throughout the state, consisted of a captain, 9 lieutenants, and 27 officers; by 1931 the force had grown to 67 officers. Patrolmen pursued offenders on Harley-Davidson motorcycles until 1937, when they were assigned their own cars.

Over the years the Highway Patrol has undergone many administrative changes as the population and highway system has grown, but its mission continues to be making North Carolina highways as safe as possible. The modern patrol is divided into eight troops that cover the state, with head-

A 1935 Highway Patrol car donated to the North Carolina Transportation Museum in 1983. Courtesy of NCOA&H.

quarters at Raleigh, Greenville, Fayetteville, Greensboro, Salisbury, Newton, Asheville, and Monroe. In 2004, 1,445 troopers and 365 motor carrier officers monitored commercial vehicles; they made 26,005 arrests for drunk driving, investigated 1,119 fatal collisions, and seized illegal drugs worth $10 million. North Carolina's state troopers also promote various initiatives for child safety and seat belt use and oversee evacuations due to major emergencies, such as hurricanes and chemical spills.

References: Robert E. Ireland, *Entering the Auto Age: The Early Automobile in North Carolina, 1900–1930* (1990); Thomas C. Parramore, *Express Lanes and Country Roads: The Way We Lived in North Carolina, 1920–1970* (1983).

Robert E. Ireland

Highways. North Carolina's approximately 78,000 miles of paved highways represent one of the largest systems in the United States. Highways were initially a product of the popular Goods Roads campaign of the early twentieth century. Roads across the state had improved little since colonial days and were among the nation's worst, encumbered with steep grades, blind curves, and many dangerous water crossings. Seasonably muddy or choked with dust, they often remained impassable for weeks. In red clay country, thin wagon wheels easily sliced the surface and potholes grew quickly into small ponds. The system of repair and maintenance was little changed from ancient times: under the "road-tax," as it was called locally, land-owning neighbors were obligated for a certain number of days of work per year cutting ditches and filling holes under the eye of a titular boss, usually another neighbor. This was seldom more than a social occasion, and the roadwork achieved was far from scientific.

North Carolina's Highway System Takes Shape

In the early nineteenth century, visionary state leader and jurist Archibald D. Murphey preached a dual vision of state-supported education and infrastructure to elevate North Caro-

lina from its chronic poverty. Some who followed Murphey promoted a system of linked and branching state-owned, east-west railroads designed to connect inland markets with ports. The corridor from Morehead City to Asheville became the path of the first unified "motor-road" in North Carolina. Connected and improved during the administration of Governor Locke Craig (1913–17), it was called at first the "Central Highway," sometimes the "Main Street of North Carolina," later "N.C. 10" or "Old No. 10," and finally, with the advent of a Federal Highway System, "U.S. 70."

In 1921 the General Assembly passed a $50 million bond issue to be paid with a raised license fee and a one-cent-per-gallon tax on gasoline. This bond endowed serious civil engineering and directly financed the pavement of 5,500 miles of roads connecting county seats. In the process many dangerous railroad grade crossings were eliminated, many curves were straightened, and gradients decreased with cuts and fills to an optimal 4 percent. Moreover, the erection of new concrete bridges shortened mileage significantly (the bridge over the Roanoke River cut the distance from Windsor to Williamston from 140 to 17 miles). North Carolina's highway program of the 1920s proved such a conspicuous success that in 1929 Louisiana governor Huey "Kingfish" Long hired away chief engineer Leslie R. Ames and 21 staff members to repeat the miracle in his state.

By the Highway Act of 1921, the state government in Raleigh officially became responsible for the maintenance of North Carolina's highways to "relieve the counties and cities and towns of the state of this burden." In 1931, under the pressure of widespread economic failure of county governments during the Great Depression, the state added to its purview the maintenance of practically all roads in North Carolina. In the early 1920s the principal through highways were N.C. 10, N.C. 15 (now U.S. 21, intertwined with Interstate 77 almost border to border), N.C. 20 (the old Wilmington-Charlotte-Asheville Highway, now U.S. 74), and N.C. 75 (today, parts of U.S. 15 and 64 via Oxford, Durham, Chapel Hill, Pittsboro, Siler City, and Lexington). Also crossing the state were the Capitol-to-Capitol Highway (soon to become U.S. 1 from Calais, Maine, via Washington, D.C., to Key West, Fla.) and the unfinished Bankhead Highway emanating from Washington, D.C., and marked with yellow-and-white-striped telephone poles (the South's answer to the Lincoln Highway).

The Establishment of Federal Highways and the Interstate System

In 1925 the Federal Highway System was created, giving funds to the states for building, improving, and maintaining key through roads. Under this system, nationally uniform engineering standards were established, and uniform route numbers and signage came into use. Routes running east and west were assigned even numbers, with the nine most impor-

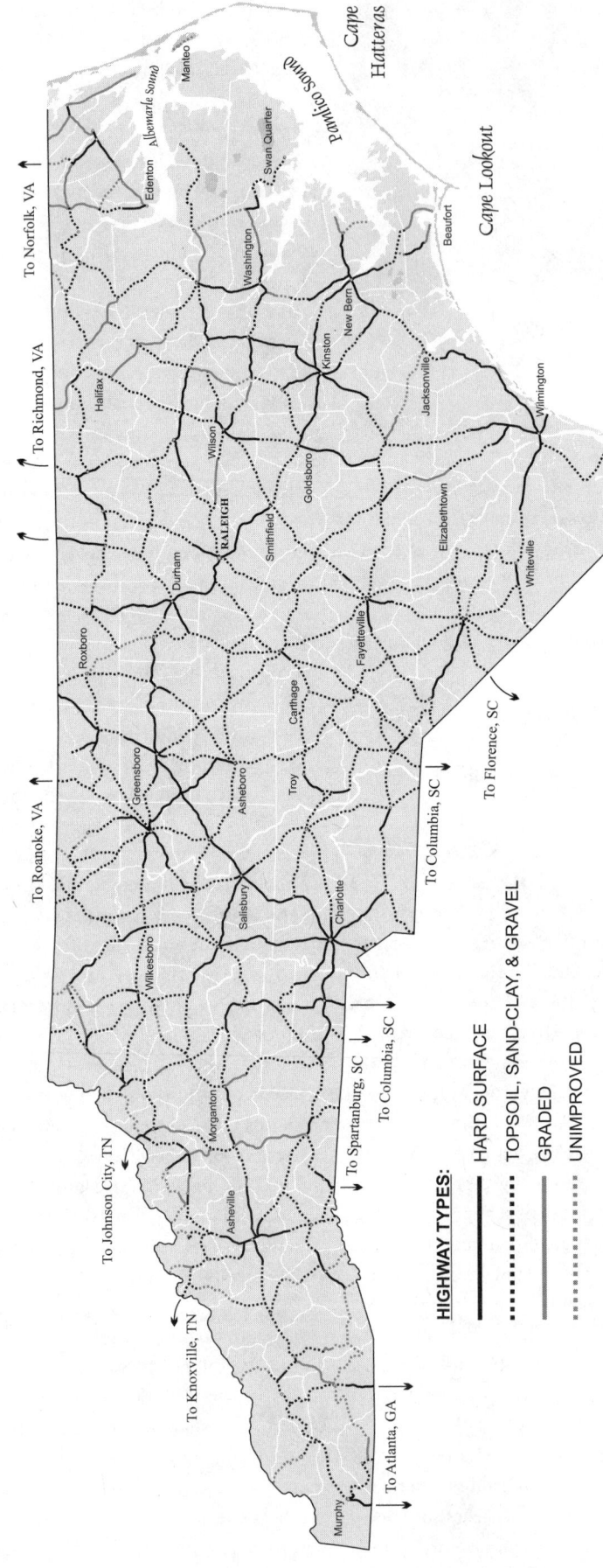

HIGHWAY TYPES:

——— HARD SURFACE

••••••• TOPSOIL, SAND-CLAY, & GRAVEL

——— GRADED

- - - - UNIMPROVED

Highways, ca. 1924. Map by Mark Anderson Moore, courtesy NCOA&H.

tant coast-to-coast routes given numbers ending with zero. Similarly, north and south routes received odd numbers, those most important ending in five, thus completing a major national grid. (Later the interstate system would imitate this number scheme.)

In North Carolina, the primary U.S. highways are numbers 1, 13, 15, 17, 19, 21, 23, 25, 29, 52, 64, 70, and 74. The -01 and -21 series were designed to be feeders or alternates of U.S. 1 and U.S. 21, respectively. For more than 30 years, U.S. 421, passing diagonally through the state by way of Boone, North Wilkesboro, Winston-Salem, Greensboro, Sanford, Dunn, and Wilmington, was the main road connecting North Carolina's most populous cities. U.S. 301 shares the general track of Interstate 95 as far as Richmond, Va. Until the completion of Interstate 40, U.S. 701, by linking U.S. 70 and U.S. 421, served as the most direct route between Raleigh and Wilmington. U.S. 117 is a more inland alternate to U.S. 17, and U.S. 158 and 258 are North Carolina tributaries of U.S. 58, running across southern Virginia.

In 1956, after six years of debate, Congress authorized the National System of Interstate and Defense Highways. Using tax revenues from gasoline, tires, and other auto-related products, it was to provide a nationwide system of 41,000 miles of interconnected "super highways." Each state was to receive 90 percent federal aid for its allocation of highway miles, with the federal government deciding which routes to build. In North Carolina, 769 miles were allocated and five systems were created: I-85, running 233 miles from Virginia to the South Carolina border; I-40, spanning 219 miles from Greensboro to Canton; I-95, stretching 182 miles from Weldon to Lumberton; I-77, linking the 96 miles between Virginia and Charlotte; and I-26, connecting the 40-mile segment separating Asheville from South Carolina. Some highways had already been under construction since 1949, at a cost to the state of $60 million. Perhaps the most difficult area of the original interstates in North Carolina was a 22-mile western stretch near Asheville of I-40—which was later extended east to Raleigh and Wilmington—that cut through the Pigeon River Gorge.

Concurrent with the development of the interstate system was an equally important movement for the hard-surfacing of county roads. The so-called Farm-to-Market drive came in two distinct waves that were the hallmarks of the administrations of Governors W. Kerr Scott (1949–53) and Dan K. Moore (1965–69). Their scope was sufficiently inclusive that, today, the unpaved rural road has become a rarity.

Federal highways comprised the state-of-the-art motor network well into the 1960s, or until the interstate system neared completion. It was on these roads or their newer alternates that such modern improvements as bypasses and four-lane divided highways first appeared, many of them becoming the first sections of the interstates. In this superhighway era, lengthy sections of U.S. Highways 1, 29, 64, 70, 74 and 421 have been rebuilt as limited-access, interstate-style roads. Often given entirely new corridors, they bypass scores of smaller towns like Cameron, Clayton, Creedmoor, Landis, Liberty, Momeyer, and Wake Forest, in which they once formed Main Street.

Many of North Carolina's 30-odd federal highways can claim ancient lineage. U.S. 17 follows essentially the same track as the Post Road or King's Highway from Boston to Charleston. A span of U.S. 311 lies near a part of the Fayetteville-to-Bethania plank road, itself on the track of a very old Indian trail. A Cherokee trail, the Estatoe Path, is ancestral to the part of U.S. 64 that runs through the Blue Ridge. Portions of U.S. 301 from about Wilson north echo an older road used by British commander Lord Charles Cornwallis in his march from Wilmington in 1781. From the Smithfield area to the Cape Fear Valley, this same road runs a route similar to that of "Green's Path," also from the colonial era.

North Carolina's Scenic Byways

From the coast to the mountains, North Carolina highways include a number of scenic byways. Running from the Great Smoky Mountains National Park to Virginia's Shenandoah National Park, the Blue Ridge Parkway forms a narrow, linear preserve for automobile touring along the crest of the Blue Ridge range. With an average elevation of 3,000 feet, the parkway runs 469 miles, offering panoramic views of coves, valleys, and distant ridges. Begun in 1935, the roadway was completed near Grandfather Mountain with the construction of the Linn Cove Viaduct, itself a marvel of modern engineering.

The Cherohala Skyway passes through the Cherokee and Nantahala National Forests (for which it is named), extending 36 miles between the mountains of North Carolina and Tennessee. The dream of what would become North Carolina's most expensive highway at $100 million began in 1958, when hundreds of horseback riders and dozens of covered wagons traveled from Tennessee to Murphy, N.C., in an organized wagon train event that thereafter was celebrated annually. After several setbacks, the highway officially opened in 1996, connecting Tellico Plains, Tenn., and Robbinsville, N.C. The Cherohala Skyway is popular among motorcyclists, car enthusiasts, and tourists in search of breathtaking natural scenery.

North Carolina's more than 40 other scenic routes include the Alligator River Route, running through the swamps and wetlands just inland from the Atlantic Coast (Dare and Tyrrell Counties); the Blue-Gray Scenic Byway, a history-rich tour of Civil War sites and landscapes (Johnston, Wayne, Lenoir, and Jones Counties); the Outer Banks Scenic Byway, running down the state's barrier islands from Whalebone to Beaufort (Dare, Hyde, and Carteret Counties); and the Millbridge Scenic Byway, offering drivers a memorable trip through the rural, small-town North Carolina countryside (Rowan County).

References: Cecil Kenneth Brown: *The State Highway System of North Carolina: Its Evolution and Present Status* (1931); John Harden, *North Carolina's Highways and Their Builders*, vol. 2 (1966); Tom Lewis, *Divided Highways: Building the Interstate Highways, Transforming American Life* (1997); Capus Waynick, *North Carolina Roads and Their Builders*, vol. 1 (1952).

David Southern
Additional research provided by Stephen C. Compton, Laura Hegyi, and Robert E. Ireland.

SEE ALSO Blue Ridge Parkway; Good Roads Campaign; Highway Commission; Powell Bill; Roads.

Hillbillies is a term of derision used to identify the inhabitants of the Appalachian and Ozark Mountains of the South. In North Carolina, the term is usually applied to the economically disadvantaged population of the Mountain counties in the western part of the state. The most recent scholarship indicates that this description of Mountain people, if not the actual word, began to be used in the early nineteenth century. Scholars have identified certain "local color" writers of the last quarter of the nineteenth century as being particularly responsible for the widespread acceptance of the southern mountaineer stereotype. Some of the earliest of the writers of this period wrote about the people who lived in western North Carolina. For example, Rebecca Harding Davis wrote a short story titled "The Yares of Black Mountain," which was published in *Lippincott's Magazine* in 1875. This story offered a contrast between the life of people in the mountains with middle-class urban Americans. While Davis was sympathetic toward the Mountain people she was describing, many writers who followed were not.

In addition to writers, moviemakers and newspaper reporters discovered that sensational stories about negative aspects of Mountain life served their purposes. Starting in 1904, with a film titled *The Moonshiner*, people of the southern mountains were the subject of more than 450 silent films. The addition of sound did not stop the rush of movie portrayals of mountaineers, and the advent of television brought southern mountaineers into virtually every home through such popular programs as *The Dukes of Hazard* and *The Beverly Hillbillies*. Cartoonist Al Capp contributed to the popular stereotype of the Appalachian highlanders for several decades through his nationally syndicated *Li'l Abner*. These portrayals of the people of the southern Appalachians, including western North Carolina, have shown great staying power and seem likely to remain in the popular consciousness for some time to come.

References: Allen Batteau, *The Invention of Appalachia* (1993); Henry D. Shapiro, *Appalachia on Our Mind: The Southern Mountains and Mountaineers in the American Consciousness* (1978); Cratis D. Williams, *The Southern Mountaineer in Fact and Fiction* (1961); J. W.

Williamson, *Hillbillyland: What the Movies Did to the Mountains and What the Mountains Did to the Movies* (1995).

Gordon B. McKinney

Hillsborough Academy was the name given various schools established by prominent citizens of the town of Hillsborough over a period of 80 years. A school chartered in 1779 as Science Hall seems to have evolved into Hillsborough Academy by the time it opened in 1785. Subscriptions were raised among a number of North Carolinians for its establishment and the purchase of confiscated Loyalists' land, but the money was used only to repair the old Anglican church for use as the school building. The first principals of the academy were Benjamin Perkins and Solomon Pinto, both graduates of Yale. Zadoc Squire replaced Pinto as principal in 1787. The board of trustees included such illustrious eighteenth-century figures as William Hooper, Nathaniel Rochester, Thomas Hart, John Kinchen, Thomas Burke, James Hogg, and William Johnston. The curriculum had a practical bent but included classical subjects as well. Never a thriving institution, the school seems to have closed in 1790 after Zadoc's death.

A second classical academy with the same name opened a decade later. In 1801 Hillsborough Academy was advertised as a school for "youth of both sexes" by trustees Walter Alves, William Kirkland, William Whitted, William Cain, and Duncan Cameron. The first principal, Andrew Flinn, was a graduate of the University of North Carolina in Chapel Hill. With an assistant, Flinn taught the classics, English, the "three R's," bookkeeping, and "the plainer branches of mathematics." Little is known of the female department beyond its existence under

Students in front of the brick castlelike school building of Hillsborough Academy, ca. 1870s. NCC.

the direction of Elizabeth Russell in 1812 and a Miss Farly in 1815. The girls were taught needlework, painting, and drawing in addition to the elementary subjects. Thereafter no mention is made of the school's commitment to female education. For more than 25 years, the school for boys had a precarious existence under a series of short-lived principals.

The Hillsborough Academy was again chartered in 1814, and in 1815 a Mr. Graham, not otherwise identified, was principal. In 1818 another Presbyterian minister, John Knox Witherspoon, became headmaster. Strict Presbyterianism assumed a prominent role in the curriculum; boys were required to attend morning and evening worship as well as church on Sunday, on which day they had to refrain from every kind of amusement including riding, walking, visiting, or studying. A new headmaster, John Rogers, served from 1821 through 1824. In 1825 another Presbyterian minister, the Reverend William Hooper, son of the signer of the Declaration of Independence of the same name, took over.

With the arrival in 1827 of William James Bingham, the son of Presbyterian minister William Bingham, however, the school began its upward ascent to fame if not fortune. From 1827 until 1843, under the younger Bingham's direction, the school became synonymous with his name. He showed his mettle in 1839 when a student plot to resist authority was discovered. He accosted the renegades and commanded submission, routing the ringleader after the boy came at him with a pistol. Known as "the Napoleon of schoolmasters," Bingham kept the boys in line and the standards high. Enrollment was more than 100 students.

When Bingham moved to the country to open his own school in 1844, Hillsborough Academy continued under his brother John Archibald Bingham and coprincipal James H. Norwood, both of whom had taught there. The next year they resigned, Norwood opened his own school, and John Witherspoon returned to head the academy. He had as an assistant James H. Horner, a former student and later a noted schoolmaster himself.

Just as the old academy was floundering without a strong principal, it became subsumed in the Caldwell Institute, the creation in 1836 of the Orange Presbytery, under principal Alexander Wilson. A serious epidemic of typhoid fever had prompted Caldwell to leave Greensboro and relocate. Hillsborough citizens paid for the refurbishment of the academy building to accommodate the new school, which at first thrived but by 1849 had declined. Wilson resigned in 1850 and moved to Alamance County to open a school of his own.

In 1851 Hillsborough Academy was resurrected by Benjamin R. Huske and Ralph Henry Graves, former teachers at Caldwell Institute, and again chartered in 1852. It continued under Graves through 1853. Hazell Norwood conducted the school in its last days from 1854 through 1858. The building was occupied in 1859–60 by the Hillsborough Military Academy while its new buildings were being constructed.

References: Ruth Blackwelder, *The Age of Orange* (1961); Charles L. Coon, *North Carolina Schools and Academies, 1790–1840* (1915).

Jean B. Anderson

SEE ALSO Bingham School.

Hill's Ferry, from before the Revolutionary War and into the early twentieth century, was a crossing point on the Roanoke River along the road from the Rocky Mount and Tarboro area northeast to Suffolk and Tidewater Virginia. The 1733 Moseley map shows the road from "Tarburg" crossing the Roanoke at this location, as do the 1770 Collet and 1775 Mouzon maps. Most later maps of this area give the name Hill's Ferry (even into the 1920s), although Solomon Cherry's 1877 map incorrectly locates it several miles upriver.

The ferry was built and operated by wealthy revolutionary Patriot and legislator Whitmel Hill (1743–97) on his lands in what were then Martin and Bertie Counties. It was located at the tip of a large western bend of the Roanoke, about a half mile east of the present-day town of Palmyra and about seven miles from Scotland Neck near the modern boundary between Martin and Halifax Counties. Hill's grandson, Whitmel Hill Anthony (1810–51), owned a large warehouse and shipping business in the area, and for a few years it was called Anthony's Ferry (remains of the warehouse were still visible in the 1930s). There is a written record of army movements at Hill's Ferry during both the Revolution and the Civil War.

The Roanoke River at the site of Hill's Ferry is deep enough for commercial boat traffic. Hill operated a commercial fleet between the coastal plain fall line upstream at Weldon and the Albemarle Sound, and some vessels could even sail on to the West Indies. In 1785 the General Assembly acted to establish the town of Blountville with a public wharf on land east of the Roanoke donated by Hill. The town was named to honor the family of his wife, Winifred Blount, whose roots led back to the Anglo-Saxon King Alfred the Great (871–99). But the settlement never had more than a few structures, and its name is rarely found in written records. Today, the community of Palmyra, named for Hill's plantation there, sits on or near where Blountville was laid out.

There are likely two major reasons why Hill's Ferry and Blountville did not prosper beyond their immediate area. There is no evidence of mail routes crossing the Roanoke there, and no sizable towns arose anywhere to the east of the ferry in Bertie. Most commerce with the Tidewater areas of North Carolina and Virginia passed north of the region, while commerce with Edenton and other North Carolina ports went farther south. With these patterns set by the end of the eighteenth century, the railroad lines that later followed passed the area by. The state's highway system has never found the need to maintain a bridge or road at the site, which today is accessible only by walking through planters' fields.

Whitmel M. Joyner

Historical Collections. Important collections of North Carolina historical documents, books, photographs, and other materials are maintained at many libraries throughout the state. The North Carolina Collection, a department of the library of the University of North Carolina at Chapel Hill, is the largest and most comprehensive repository of published materials relating to any single state. Its origins date to 1844 when David L. Swain, then president of the university, founded the Historical Society of the University of North Carolina. Following Swain's death during Reconstruction, parts of his collection were removed from the university, but the surviving materials were safeguarded by Kemp P. Battle and then by Louis Round Wilson, who became university librarian in 1901. Wilson established the North Carolina Collection as a department within the library, and with funds provided by John Sprunt Hill hired Mary Lindsay Thornton as its first full-time librarian in 1917. William S. Powell succeeded Thornton in 1958, and upon Powell's transfer to the UNC Department of History in 1974, H. G. Jones became curator. Jones retired in 1994, and Robert G. Anthony Jr. assumed the post.

The university's purchase of historian Stephen Beauregard Weeks's library in 1918 approximately doubled the size of the book holdings. History professor Joseph G. deRoulhac Hamilton was so successful in bringing in manuscripts from North Carolina and neighboring states that, in 1930, most of the manuscript materials were transferred from the North Carolina Collection to the newly established Southern Historical Collection at UNC. While not exclusively focused on North Carolina, the Southern Historical Collection began to collect a vast amount of materials relating to the state. Thereafter, except for the Thomas Wolfe Collection and a few other special groups of manuscripts, the North Carolina Collection concentrated on books, pamphlets, periodicals, broadsides, maps, microforms, and university theses and dissertations.

The beneficence of John Sprunt Hill, who earmarked profits from the Carolina Inn and a block of business buildings in downtown Chapel Hill for the support of the collection, as well as endowments established by North Carolinians Bruce Cotten and Archie K. Davis, among others, have continued to supplement library funds. The extra funds allow the North Carolina Collection to continue its policy of acquiring one or more copies of all publications by North Carolinians regardless of subject and language and about North Carolina or North Carolinians regardless of author or language. When the collection commemorated its sesquicentennial in 1994, its cataloged holdings numbered 120,839 books, 78,051 pamphlets, 4,258 broadsides, 4,545 maps, 17,760 microforms, and thousands of other items. The collection's staff identifies, or-

ders, catalogs, maintains, and provides reference services to its impressive holdings. Because the collection is a statewide resource for the benefit of North Carolina citizens, its reading room is open seven days a week, though closed on state holidays.

The North Carolina Collection began the formal development of a photographic archive in 1929. In the early 2000s the collection's photographic holdings totaled more than 400,000 images of North Carolina's people, places, and events, maintaining files for all 100 of the state's counties. During the renovation of Wilson Library in the 1980s, the collection's reading room moved to the west wing and the library converted its former space in the east wing into the North Carolina Collection Gallery. The gallery displays many rare examples of North Caroliniana along with artwork and museum items acquired by the collection over the years.

Unique collections of North Carolina historical materials exist at practically every university library within the University of North Carolina system as well as at libraries of the state's private universities. These include collections of oral histories, music, books, legal documents, wills, and other primary artifacts and materials. The Verona Joyner Langford North Carolina Collection at East Carolina University originated in 1909, when the university's library began to collect materials related to the state's history. In 1962 Mrs. Frankie Cubbedge was hired to oversee the collection, which had grown to require a new library addition and a reading room. In 2000, after further expansion under Marguerite Wiggins, librarian from 1968 to 1991, the collection was renamed for benefactor Verona Joyner Langford. The collection, one of the largest in the state, is the best collection of materials relating to North Carolina's eastern region.

The Southern Historical Collection at UNC-Chapel Hill has continued to expand in both size and service. In the early 1980s, the administrative unit's name changed to the Manuscripts Department, with holdings organized in three separate components: the Southern Historical Collection, the University Archives, and General and Literary Manuscripts. In 1985 the department added the Southern Folklife Collection, established to document the region's expressive traditions, especially in music and folklore. By the early 2000s the Manuscripts Department had grown to more than 20 million manuscripts, 86,000 still images, and 124,000 audio and moving-image recordings.

The Southern Historical Collection continues to acquire eighteenth- and nineteenth-century manuscripts, along with substantial collections of twentieth-century materials. The collection includes documents of people who spent their entire lives in small North Carolina communities and oral history interviews with textile workers and bank presidents. Some collections, such as those of the Cameron family of North Carolina and the senatorial files of Sam J. Ervin Jr., are very large, while others consist of a few letters or a brief diary. Other subject strengths include southern literature, journalism, business history, legal history, and African American life.

There are notable local and regional North Carolina historical collections at many public libraries throughout the state. Some of them, including those in Asheville, Charlotte, Greensboro, New Bern, Salisbury, and Wilmington, have been in existence for many years, are well-maintained, and offer access to historical documents not found elsewhere.

References: H. G. Jones, "Preserving North Carolina's Literary Heritage," *Popular Government* (Winter 1990); J. Carlyle Sitterson, "The Southern Historical Collection, 1930–1980: The Pursuit of History," *Bookmark* (1961); D. A. Yanchisin, "For Carolina's Sake: A Case History of Special Librarianship," *Journal of Library History* (January 1971).

H. G. Jones
Timothy D. Pyatt

Historical Commission. In 1903, at the behest of the North Carolina Literary and Historical Association, the General Assembly established the North Carolina Historical Commission to collect and print "from the files of old newspapers, from court records, church records and elsewhere valuable documents pertaining to the history of the State." Its gubernatorially appointed members served without salary, and its initial annual appropriation was $500. William J. Peele was the commission's first chairman, and R. D. W. Connor served as secretary. During its first four years, the commission's chief accomplishment was publishing *Literary and Historical Activities in North Carolina, 1900–1905.* In 1907 the legislature expanded the commission's authority, and with a tenfold increase in appropriated funds, the commission engaged Connor as its first paid secretary. From that date North Carolina retained a true state archival agency, successfully guided by Connor until 1921, when he resigned to become a history professor at the University of North Carolina at Chapel Hill.

During his tenure, Connor launched an aggressive campaign to acquire private manuscripts and to transfer county and state records to the State Archives. Oversight of the Hall of History, a museum started by Frederick A. Olds, was transferred to the commission in 1914. The entire agency moved into the new State Administration Building (later known as the State Library Building and now the Court of Appeals Building), where it remained until moving to the first floor of the new Education Building in 1939. Meanwhile, from 1915 to 1933 the commission also administered the Legislative Reference Library.

Following Connor's departure, secretaries D. H. Hill (1921–24), Robert B. House (1924–26), Albert Ray Newsome (1926–35), and C. Christopher Crittenden (1935–68) carried on the various programs of the Historical Commission. The distinguished series of documentary publications continued, the quarterly *North Carolina Historical Review* began in 1924, and public records legislation in 1935 gave the commission authority over the disposal of all public records: local, county, and state. During the Depression the commission administered several federal relief projects that inventoried and publicized the state's historical resources, most notably the county records. During both world wars it collected war-related records for future research, and, after 1935 the commission erected highway historical markers throughout the state. Its record has been summarized in *The North Carolina Historical Commission: Forty Years of Public Service, 1903–1943* (1943).

The name of the agency changed in 1943 to the State Department of Archives and History, and two years later the name of the seven-member commission changed to Executive Board and the secretary became the director. After the Department of Archives and History became a division of the new Department of Art, Culture, and History (later renamed the Department of Cultural Resources), however, the name North Carolina Historical Commission was revived in 1973 and applied to a professional body with broad policymaking powers over the Office of Archives and History.

References: Frontis W. Johnston, "The North Carolina Historical Commission, 1903–1978," in Jeffrey J. Crow, ed., *Public History in North Carolina, 1903–1978* (1979); Ansley Herring Wegner, *History for All the People: One Hundred Years of Public History in North Carolina* (2003).

H. G. Jones

Historical Markers in North Carolina are typically freestanding, silver-and-black cast aluminum signs on posts erected along roadsides, but they also include plaques and other forms of commemoration. In 1903 the legislation establishing the North Carolina Historical Commission noted the scarcity of monuments or tablets "commemorating the services of eminent sons of the state, or marking the sites of historic events" and proposed to remedy the situation. The commission assumed its first project in 1910 when it resolved to acquire busts for eight empty niches in the State Capitol rotunda. Between 1903 and 1929, the commission erected approximately 110 bronze tablets across the state in cooperation with local historical and patriotic societies.

C. Christopher Crittenden, secretary of the Historical Commission and the Department of Archives and History from 1935 to 1968, spearheaded the effort to establish a state highway historical marker program. Using a Virginia program begun in 1926 as a model, Crittenden enlisted public support for the project, sought newspaper publicity for the plans, and solicited suggestions from citizens across the state.

The Marker Advisory Committee, a group of college and university professors specializing in North Carolina history, was also established in 1935. The committee weighed the historical authenticity, appropriateness, and relative merit of all subjects proposed for consideration, setting statewide historical significance as the principal eligibility requirement. At their first meetings, the committee members reviewed several proposed models and selected a design resembling the pages of an open book and incorporating the State Seal at the top. The signs are cast aluminum and mounted on concrete posts sheathed in aluminum, with inscriptions limited to five or six lines of about 24 letters and spaces per line. The committee selected the design to enable passing motorists to read the markers. Exceptions are extended text markers using smaller letters, and larger map markers illustrating and describing historic events. The first official state marker, dedicated to one of the state's signers of the Declaration of Independence, John Penn, was erected at Stovall in Granville County on 10 Jan. 1936.

The Department of Conservation and Development initially cosponsored the highway historical marker program. Today the program operates with the cooperation of the Department of Transportation, whose field offices assume responsibility for placement and maintenance. Markers are placed on state-maintained, numbered highways but not on interstate or limited-access routes.

Since 1935, the program has erected more than 1,400 markers, with at least one in each county, and beginning in 1939 administrators issued a continually updated *Guide to North Carolina Highway Historical Markers*. The program was suspended during World War II because of a materials shortage, and in the early 1980s inadequate funding made it impossible to consider new proposals for several years.

Private markers of varying types and designs have also been placed throughout the state. Between 1913 and 1938, Boone Trail Highway and Memorial Association founder J. Hampton Rich constructed a series of monuments along the supposed travel route of Daniel Boone. Some memorials incorporated a stone or concrete arrowhead or a bronze tablet depicting Boone and his dog. After World War II, the Garden Clubs of North Carolina erected a series of "Blue Star Memorial Highway" markers alongside several major state highways to honor veterans. The State Highway Commission participated in the effort by designating the routes. An individual cannot be considered as a subject for a state marker until 25 years after his or her death, though privately sponsored local groups have more quickly erected markers to some individuals. For example, in 1987 the Burke County Historical Society erected a marker at the birthplace of Senator Sam J. Ervin.

The Office of Archives and History regularly advises local groups, church congregations, and individuals on the private purchase of markers and plaques, which cannot bear the State Seal and must be placed outside the highway right-of-way. The rise of the historic preservation movement led local organiza-tions to designate properties listed on the National Register of Historic Places with plaques, and to delineate boundaries of local historic districts with distinctive street markers.

References: Michael Hill, "The Fiftieth Anniversary of the North Carolina Highway Historical Marker Program," *Carolina Comments* (March 1986); Hill, ed., *Guide to North Carolina Highway Historical Markers* (9th ed., 2001); Raymond F. Pisney, *Tombstones on Posts?: A Preview to Historical Marking* (1976).

Michael Hill

Historical Societies. The General Assembly incorporated the first North Carolina Historical Society in 1833 at the behest of Governor David L. Swain. No records exist indicating a meeting of the society, but the act, authorizing the incorporators "to transcribe or cause to be transcribed" public records, presaged future efforts of Swain and others to gather, copy, and print selections from the early records of state government. Swain later moved from the governor's office to the presidency of the University of North Carolina, where he devoted more time to what became his passion: collecting sources of North Carolina history and literature. In 1841 William H. Haywood Jr. wrote that Swain had been named chairman of a committee of "our Lity. & His: Socy" and proposed a meeting which, if held, was not reported in the press.

Finally, however, in January 1844 Swain announced the organization of the Historical Society of the University of North Carolina with himself as president and the entire faculty as members of the executive committee. Among the society's purposes were to obtain copies of Proprietary and colonial records relating to North Carolina in British repositories and to collect, arrange, and preserve at the university "one or more copies of every book, pamphlet and newspaper published in this State . . . and, especially, all the records, documents and papers to be found within the State, that may tend to elucidate the history of the American Revolution." Within a year the society received an impressive number of gifts, including an orderly book kept during the Regulator Movement, a "large collection" of the papers of John Steele and Thomas Burke, and rare printed materials. Although its name remained alive until the Civil War, the society was in fact a one-man operation providing legitimacy for Swain's personal solicitation of materials.

The Historical Society of the University of North Carolina died with Swain in 1868, but two years later a new Historical Society of North Carolina emerged with one central objective: "to procure from Mrs. Eleanor H. Swain the books and manuscripts claimed by the society." During his presidency, Swain had kept the manuscripts in his university office along with personal belongings, and a lengthy controversy followed when his widow claimed them all as private property. This latest organization also disappeared when the university temporarily closed in 1871, but in 1875 the General Assembly chartered another Historical Society of North Carolina with authority to "acquire and hold" the materials collected by Swain. At first this organization was centered in Raleigh, but within a few years it too became associated with the university, with Kemp P. Battle as president. Meanwhile, Mrs. Swain held onto the valuable manuscript collection until her death in 1883. Although some of the papers were sold during settlement of her estate, most were preserved through the diligence of executor Walter Clark and later formed the nucleus of the Southern Historical Collection in Chapel Hill. Clark borrowed others while editing *The State Records of North Carolina* and never returned them to Chapel Hill, giving the papers instead to the North Carolina Historical Commission. These papers remain in the State Archives.

With the only functioning historical society then located at the university, the publication of *The Colonial Records of North Carolina* stirred sentiment for a more active statewide organization. In 1893 the General Assembly memorialized the name of the recently deceased editor of the ten-volume *Colonial Records* series by chartering the William L. Saunders Historical Society of North Carolina. Like several previous efforts, this one perished before it was formally organized. Local organizations soon followed, however, spurred on by these statewide efforts as well as by regional pride and growing interest in local history. An early example, the Historical and Scientific Society of Wilmington, was organized in October 1876 for the purpose of developing the intellectual and physical resources of the Cape Fear region and collecting and publishing the history, traditions, genealogy, and biography of the area's early settlers. The society met monthly, usually in a fraternal hall of one of the large churches in Wilmington. Club members gave most of the lectures, but occasionally speakers were brought in from out of town. By 1883 the society had also begun to collect artifacts, photographs, paintings, music, books, relics, and botanical specimens. The Historical and Scientific Society of Wilmington continued to meet throughout the 1880s but is not mentioned in Wilmington newspapers or city directories after 1890. Except for some published papers, it is not known what happened to the archives and museum artifacts collected by the society.

The Trinity College Historical Society was established in 1892 under the leadership of Stephen B. Weeks, a professor of history and other subjects at Trinity College (later Duke University) in Durham. The society was intended to encourage the study of history and the collection of historical materials. Weeks soon left Trinity, but his successor, John Spencer Bassett, proved equally energetic and resourceful in building up the library, encouraging research in primary sources, and generally promoting historical study through the society. In 1897 Bassett and the society launched a long-running series of *Historical Papers*, the first such scholarly enterprise in the state.

Bassett's student and successor as professor of history, William K. Boyd, also proved to be an enterprising scholar who took a leading role in the society, especially after Duke University was organized around Trinity late in 1924. The Trinity College Historical Society continued well after midcentury to have a vigorous life as a meeting place and forum for graduate students, faculty, and others interested in history. By the last two decades of the twentieth century, however, the society had become moribund.

The Wachovia Historical Society, chartered in March 1895, grew out of the Young Men's Missionary Society, which in 1841 had begun collecting cultural curiosities and examples of natural history from around the world that had been obtained through a network of Moravian missionaries. In 1845 the group opened a small museum to display its artifacts. The museum's location shifted several times but eventually settled in the Boys School on Salem Square in what is now Winston-Salem. Fifty years later the group decided to organize a more formal historical society focusing on Moravian, North Carolina, and local history. Eventually the historical society expanded into historic preservation, acquiring the Adam Spach Rock House in Davidson County, the site of the Hans Wagner Cabin at Bethabara, and Salem Tavern. In 1953 the Wachovia Historical Society and Old Salem, Inc., entered into an "operating agreement," allowing Old Salem to maintain the museum, lease and restore the tavern, and use the society's collections in its exhibit buildings.

As the state continued to emerge from the economic and social turbulence of the late nineteenth century, many North Carolinians pushed ever harder for ways to research and collect information regarding state history. An important manifestation of this historical awakening occurred in 1900 with the founding of the North Carolina Literary and Historical Association by many prominent men and women. The association involved leaders of all three branches of government and within five years could share credit for many major accomplishments, including the establishment of North Carolina Day in the public schools, promotion of public and school libraries, commemoration of the Roanoke colonies, passage of a history textbook act, and, most important, the establishment of the North Carolina Historical Commission to serve as the state's official archival and historical agency. The Historical Commission's first major publication, *Literary and Historical Activities in North Carolina, 1900–1905* (1907), contained an impressive record of activity for a state that so recently had seemed to ignore its past.

During the next century, historical societies formed in most of North Carolina's counties and some of its municipalities, their success depending largely upon the vigor of their volunteer officers. The Western North Carolina Historical Association (WNCHA), incorporated in 1952, was founded by a group of authors, publishers, educators, and collectors of historical information to preserve and encourage the study of western North Carolina history. (The Cherokee Historical Association, which oversees the Oconaluftee Indian Village and the Museum of the Cherokee Indian, emerged at the same time as the WNCHA.) Dean William E. Bird of Western Carolina University (then Western North Carolina Teachers' College) in Cullowhee served as the association's first president. The Smith-McDowell House, the oldest surviving house in Asheville, serves as the WNCHA's headquarters and museum. The association rescued the property from demolition and, after complete renovation, opened it to the public in 1981 as a museum and regional cultural center. The firm of Frederick Law Olmsted, which also landscaped the Biltmore House grounds and Central Park in New York City, designed a landscape plan for the property in 1899. Since its founding, the WNCHA has presented an annual award for achievement in the field of history related to western North Carolina. In addition, the association's Thomas Wolfe Literary Award, a silver cup contributed to the Historical Association by the family of Morris Lipinsky Sr., one of Wolfe's boyhood friends, annually recognizes an outstanding published work about western North Carolina.

For decades, the North Carolina Literary and Historical Association, concerned with all aspects of the state's heritage, was the most influential private organization in the state. Gradually, however, members with more specific interests formed subgroups, including the Folklore Society in 1913, the Art Society in 1926, the Roanoke Island Historical Association in 1932, the Archaeological Society in 1933, the Society for the Preservation of Antiquities in 1939, the Society of County and Local Historians in 1949, the Museums Council in 1964, and the Genealogical Society in 1974. These groups initially maintained close relations with "Lit and Hist," holding their annual meetings during one concentrated Culture Week in Raleigh, but by the 1980s all met separately.

At the end of the twentieth century, the Literary and Historical Association, the Historical Society of North Carolina (founded in 1945 and limited to scholars who published on North Carolina subjects), and the North Caroliniana Society (founded in 1975 and limited to members elected on the basis of their demonstrated commitment to the promotion of the state's history and culture) continued to promote North Carolina's history in its breadth. In addition, dozens of local and regional historical organizations were created to explore and preserve North Carolina history. The Federation of North Carolina Historical Societies, a coalition composed of representatives from local, regional, and statewide historical associations, commissions, and societies, had more than 130 members in 2005.

References: Frontis W. Johnston, "The North Carolina Literary and Historical Association, 1900–1975," NCHR 53 (Spring 1976); H. G. Jones, For History's Sake: The Preservation and Publication of North Carolina History, 1663–1903 (1966); Bradford L. Rauschenberg, The Wachovia Historical Society, 1895–1995 (1995); Nannie M. Tilley, The Trinity College Historical Society, 1892–1941 (1941).

H. G. Jones
Additional research provided by Edwin R. Andrews, Robert F. Durden, Christopher E. Hendricks, and Beverly Tetterton.

SEE ALSO Culture Week; Historical Collections; Historical Commission; Literary and Historical Association; North Caroliniana Society.

Historic Preservation. During the 1930s North Carolina received federal money for historic preservation through the Works Progress Administration, part of President Franklin D. Roosevelt's New Deal. Federal funds permitted the restoration of the John Wright Stanley House in New Bern, as well as Buck Hill, the 1781 home of Nathaniel Macon. Federal money also funded various archaeological excavations across the state and the indexing of archival records.

In 1955 the General Assembly transferred administrative control of state historic sites to the Division (now Office) of Archives and History, which expanded to cover many areas of preservation, including protection of properties on the National Register of Historic Places, aiding historical museums, and evaluating potential state historic properties. The North Carolina Museum of History also expanded to include four locations in Raleigh, Fayetteville, Elizabeth City, and Old Fort, together housing more than 250,000 artifacts. The State Historic Preservation Office aids private citizens and institutions, as well as local, state, and federal groups in identifying and protecting historically significant North Carolina properties and archaeology. The office also nominates eligible properties to the National Register of Historic Places, provides technical assistance to owners in the restoration of historic properties, and aids with state and federal rehabilitation, income tax credits, and grant assistance for the preservation of historic projects.

Maintained by the National Park Service, the National Register of Historic Places is the nation's official list of historic properties worth preserving. It constitutes an important component of a larger preservation program operated as a partnership among federal agencies, states, local governments, American Indian tribes and Alaska natives, and private preservationists. North Carolina made its first nominations to the National Register of Historic Places in 1969; more than 2,100 listings represented all 100 counties by the early 2000s. Of these listings, approximately 300 are historic districts, including residential neighborhoods, commercial districts, prehistoric and historic archaeological districts, industrial complexes, mill villages, and rural farming districts.

Preservation North Carolina (PNC), officially the Historic

Preservation Foundation of North Carolina, Inc., is a private, nonprofit, statewide fund for historic preservation, with a mission to protect and promote buildings, landscapes, and sites important to the heritage of North Carolina. PNC receives little financial support from the state or federal government, relying primarily on private donations and membership fees. Through its revolving fund, the group purchases endangered historic properties, places protective covenants in the deeds, and then sells the properties to private buyers willing to restore them. Once a property sells, PNC uses the proceeds from the sale for another property.

Preservation North Carolina's origins coincide with North Carolina's federally funded preservation projects in the 1930s. A significant private preservation effort began in 1938, when C. Christopher Crittenden, secretary of the North Carolina Historical Commission, invited Margaret Wilmer, president of the Association for the Preservation of Virginia's Antiquities, to speak to the North Carolina Historical Commission on preservation endeavors in Virginia. Mrs. Wilmer's report inspired commission member Ruth Coltrane Cannon and others to call for the formation of a steering committee to establish a similar organization in North Carolina. Through the successful efforts of the steering committee, the North Carolina Society for the Preservation of Antiquities was launched on 5 Oct. 1939.

The Antiquities Society held its first annual meeting on 7 Dec. 1939. The meeting brought to the forefront the need to restore colonial Tryon Palace in New Bern, and the next year the group gave its first grant of $200 to Tryon Palace as well as providing additional grant money for the Clerk's Office in Halifax, Richmond Hill in Yadkin County, and the Andrew Johnson birthplace in Raleigh. World War II temporarily delayed further efforts to restore Tryon Palace, but in 1944 Maude Moore Latham created the Maude Moore Latham Foundation to help purchase the land where Tryon Palace once stood as well as additional money to reconstruct a public museum and park.

Activities of the Antiquities Society quickly accelerated over the next decades. In 1974 the organization's name was changed to the Historic Preservation Society of North Carolina, Inc., and the group hired its first full-time professional staff in 1981. Since its inception, PNC has saved more than 400 endangered historic properties ranging from eighteenth-century houses to twentieth-century schools and factories, generating an estimated $100 million in private investment. PNC also operates the Bellamy Mansion in Wilmington and Ayr Mount in Hillsborough, issues awards, conducts workshops, makes television documentaries, promotes public education, and pushes for legislative acts. By the early 2000s the group had a net worth of more than $5 million and a membership of 5,500.

Although Preservation North Carolina is the largest organization of its kind in the state, many local and regional preservation organizations are active in North Carolina. These include historic preservation commissions in Hickory, Burlington, Greensboro, Washington, Black Mountain, Beaufort, Concord, Snow Hill, Fayetteville, Thomasville, and many other communities, as well as preservation societies in many counties in the state.

North Carolina Private, Nonprofit Historic Preservation Advocacy Organizations (2005)

The Alliance for Historic Hillsborough
Beaufort Historical Association
Capital Area Preservation, Inc. (Raleigh)
Catawba County Historical Association (Newton)
Chapel Hill Preservation Society
Coe Foundation for Archaeological Research (Raleigh)
Gates County Historical Society (Gates)
Hickory Landmarks Society
Historic Burke Foundation (Morganton)
Historic Cabarrus, Inc. (Concord)
Historic Charlotte, Inc.
Historic Preservation Society of Asheville and Buncombe County
Historic Preservation Society of Durham
Historic Shelby Foundation, Inc.
Historic Wilmington Foundation
Murfreesboro Historical Association
New Bern Preservation Foundation
North Carolina African American Network on Historic Preservation (Durham)
North Carolina Archaeological Society (Raleigh)
Ocracoke Preservation Society
Outer Banks Conservationists, Inc. (Corolla)
Piedmont Preservation Foundation, Inc. (Concord)
Preservation Greensboro
Preservation North Carolina (Raleigh)
Rockford Preservation Society
Transylvania County Historical Society (Brevard)
Washington Area Historic Foundation (Washington)

References: David Louis Sterrett Brook, *A Lasting Gift of Heritage: A History of the North Carolina Society for the Preservation of Antiquities, 1939–1974* (1997); State Historic Preservation Office, *Legacy 2000: North Carolina's Comprehensive Historic Preservation Plan, 2000–2005* (2000).

Alan K. Lamm
Joanne G. Carpenter

Histories documenting North Carolina's past and present were written by North Carolinians and others beginning in the early nineteenth century. Through the years, the purpose, focus, and style of historical research has changed, but the commitment of historians to document North Carolina history in informative and relevant terms has remained the same.

The first professional historian trained in the "scientific" or German school of historical investigation to work in North Carolina was Stephen Beauregard Weeks in the early twentieth century. However, several other "historians" (the title was loosely defined in their day) preceded him as researchers, writers, and especially collectors of historical resource materials. Pennsylvania native Hugh Williamson spent only one-fifth of his life in North Carolina, but during that time he served as surgeon general with the state's troops in the Revolution and also held a number of government positions. Williamson authored *The History of North Carolina*, a two-volume narrative based on a few of the scant primary documents available in 1812. He quoted extensively from those sources, not always correctly and often to underscore his political views.

The second printed history of the state was François Xavier Martin's *The History of North Carolina, from the Earliest Period*, published in New Orleans in 1829. A native of France but editor of a New Bern newspaper from 1785 to 1798, Martin published a revisal of the state's laws and served in the House of Commons. He also copied selected state records and some private papers of leading families before accepting appointment as a judge in the Mississippi Delta region. When he learned that Archibald D. Murphey, an assiduous collector of historical documents, intended to write a North Carolina state history, Martin unpacked his materials and rushed into publication his own two-volume work. When identified more than a century later, Martin's collection of sources proved disappointing. Murphey, though he failed to write his own history, amassed a huge and valuable collection of original materials that provided rich fodder for later authors.

In 1834 researcher and collector Joseph Seawell "Shocco" Jones published *A Defence of the Revolutionary History of the State of North Carolina from the Aspersions of Mr. Jefferson*. The book, however, was little more than a diatribe against Thomas Jefferson's refusal to believe that the citizens of Mecklenburg County declared independence on 20 May 1775.

Hertford County native John Hill Wheeler served in the House of Commons before holding a succession of offices. While state treasurer, he published a partial index to documents in London relative to North Carolina and began studying state records in Raleigh and private papers in the possession of prominent families. New England historians George Bancroft and Peter Force also provided him with materials. The result was Wheeler's *Historical Sketches of North Carolina from 1584 to 1851*, published in 1851. Consisting of two volumes bound as one, the book was the first history of the state written by a native-born North Carolinian. Sometimes called the "Democratic Stud Book" because of its favoritism toward members of Wheeler's own political party, *Historical Sketches* was useful especially for its county-by-county essays. For example, in the Cabarrus County sketch was printed for the first time George Barnhardt's account of the first discovery of gold in the United States (by Conrad Reed in 1799). Despite its weaknesses, Wheeler's work represented progress in North Carolina historiography and, with an initial printing of 10,000 copies, led to increased interest in state and local history.

Although he never wrote a history book, David Lowry Swain emerged as North Carolina's most important antebellum collector of historical documents. As a young circuit judge, Swain was embarrassed by North Carolina's reputation as the Rip Van Winkle State and spent his spare time browsing the records of the counties he visited. He believed that North Carolinians had a proud history that simply needed to be told. In 1832 Swain was elected governor, and he organized the state's first historical society during his administration. He left the governor's office for the presidency of the University of North Carolina, a position that permitted him to devote much of his attention to collecting original and printed materials for the next 30 years.

In 1857–58 Francis Lister Hawks, a New Bern–born attorney and priest of the Episcopal Church then living in New York, published his *History of North Carolina*, but the heavily documented two-volume work covered only the exploratory and Proprietary periods. Hawks and Swain planned to collaborate on a monumental documentary history of the state but never carried out the project.

Colonial and State Records and the First Generation of Professional Historians

When William Laurence Saunders took office as North Carolina's secretary of state in 1879 and found a cache of neglected colonial documents in the old arsenal on Capitol Square, he prepared a report that detailed the wretched condition of the public records and proposed gathering the surviving papers and putting selected ones into print. However, remembering the earlier appeals of Swain and Wheeler to procure copies of the colony's records preserved in London, he soon broadened his proposal. Consequently, the General Assembly of 1883 gave him complete discretion to copy and print those records that he judged important. An agent was hired to supervise the copying of records in London, and within five years about 15,000 pages of transcripts had been received. Ten volumes of *The Colonial Records of North Carolina* were printed at state expense under Saunders's editorship from 1886 to 1890. The 10,982 printed pages of documents dating from 1622 through 1776 constituted the most monumental and significant historical enterprise in the state to that time.

Inspired by Saunders's accomplishment, Walter Clark, an associate justice of the state supreme court, volunteered to continue the documentary series. He arranged for the copying of additional records found in state offices, selections from Swain's collection, and records relating to North Carolina located in other repositories. Clark's first volume of *The State Records of North Carolina*, published in 1895, continued Saunders's numbering, but Clark was less careful than Saunders in printing documents in chronological order. He wisely engaged

Stephen B. Weeks to provide a complete three-volume index to the combined series, along with a useful narrative survey of historical activities in the state and an analysis of materials used in the combined series. Clark wrote or edited many other works, including the five-volume *Histories of the Several Regiments and Battalions from North Carolina in the Great War 1861–1865*, published in 1901.

In 1890 Edward Augustus Johnson published the first *School History of the Negro Race in America from 1619 to 1890*. Johnson, born into slavery, in 1917 became the first elected black legislator in New York. Another former slave, William Harvey Quick, wrote *Negro Stars in All Ages of the World*, also published in 1890. The Democratic Party's policy of disfranchising and segregating nonwhites hampered prospects for further literary works by blacks for several decades.

The printing of the state's early records at the end of the nineteenth century coincided with the introduction of professionally trained historians in North Carolina. Weeks, John Spencer Bassett, William K. Boyd, R. D. W. Connor, and J. G. deRoulhac Hamilton were all indoctrinated in a new historical methodology traced to German historian Leopold von Ranke. Weeks, who held the first genuine professorship of history in North Carolina at Trinity College, was also an avid collector, and in 1918 his book collection formed the nucleus of the North Carolina Collection at the University of North Carolina. Connor, Boyd, and Hamilton each wrote a volume in the three-volume *History of North Carolina* (1919), and Connor wrote the two-volume *North Carolina: Rebuilding an Ancient Commonwealth* (1929). Connor helped organize the North Carolina Historical Commission in 1903, became the first Archivist of the United States in 1934, and later returned to Chapel Hill to continue his teaching. Hamilton also wrote the massive *Reconstruction in North Carolina* (1914), which reflected the prevailing "southern point of view."

The availability of published resources also attracted nonhistorians like newspaperman Samuel A. Ashe, whose two-volume *History of North Carolina* (1908, 1925) added flavor to the raw facts of history and was the first work to draw upon the published colonial and state records as a source. He also edited the eight-volume *Biographical History of North Carolina . . .* (1905–17). Mathematician Archibald Henderson wrote history around his own ancestors in his two-volume *North Carolina: The Old North State and the New*, published in 1941. The North Carolina Historical Commission (after 1943 the State Department of Archives and History) produced a remarkable series of documentary volumes of primary sources and also created the *North Carolina Historical Review* in 1924, providing a vehicle for scholarly articles. During the Carolina Charter Tercentenary, a new series of *The Colonial Records of North Carolina* began, and to commemorate the centennial of the Civil War, the multivolume *North Carolina Troops, 1861–1865: A Roster*, also commenced.

Twentieth-Century Achievements and New Historical Approaches

The next generation of historians benefited from an improving methodology that stressed greater objectivity in research. John Hope Franklin began a long and distinguished career as an interpreter of African American history with the 1943 publication of *The Free Negro in North Carolina, 1790–1860*. Albert Ray Newsome and Hugh T. Lefler coauthored *North Carolina: The History of a Southern State* (1954), which served as the standard college-level textbook for three decades. Lefler's *North Carolina History Told by Contemporaries* provided a useful supplementary text. Guion Griffis Johnson's *Ante-Bellum North Carolina: A Social History* (1937) broke new ground with its extensive use of newspaper reports of nonpolitical activities. William S. Powell, combining his training as a librarian and a historian, became the state's most prolific writer and editor of history, publishing the popular *North Carolina Gazetteer* (1968), the college-level textbook *North Carolina through Four Centuries* (1989), the six-volume *Dictionary of North Carolina Biography* (1979–96), and many other works. English professor Richard Walser published widely on the literary history of the state, and H. G. Jones, historian and curator of the North Carolina Collection at the University of North Carolina Library, published *North Carolina Illustrated, 1584–1984* (1983), the first pictorial history of North Carolina.

State and local history underwent another change near the end of the twentieth century, when the writing and teaching of chronological history was largely superseded by the examination of particular aspects of the past. Local records and personal accounts provided fodder for a new cadre of historians emphasizing history of people who may have been previously overlooked. Their subjects, often narrow in scope, combined to broaden the landscape of historical studies by bringing to light vast quantities of information previously buried in county records, local newspapers, obscure manuscripts, and oral tradition. Ethnicity, race, and gender attracted particular attention from adherents of this new social history.

Once incorporated in theses and dissertations, new information found its way into broader studies, enriching and often challenging previous interpretations of the past. While faculty and graduates of the University of North Carolina at Chapel Hill had produced many of the earlier publications on state and local history, interest in the subject spread to other institutions. For example, Duke University historians joined UNC-associated authors in producing a series titled *The Way We Lived in North Carolina* (1983; reissued in 2003). This broadening of the geographical base of researchers was reflected by the Historical Society of North Carolina, which sought institutional diversity among its elected membership.

State and local history, once considered "provincial" by some historians, thus found its way into the mainstream.

Ironically, while both written and visual images of the past were being given increased attention by a new generation of historians, the teaching of courses in North Carolina history was losing ground both in college and in the public schools.

References: Jeffrey J. Crow and Larry E. Tise, eds., *Writing North Carolina History* (1979); H. G. Jones, *For History's Sake: The Preservation and Publication of North Carolina History, 1663–1903* (1966); Jones, *North Carolina History: An Annotated Bibliography* (1995); Ansley Herring Wegner, *History for All the People: One Hundred Years of Public History in North Carolina* (2003).

H. G. Jones

History of the Dividing Line refers to the lively account, written by Virginia commissioner William Byrd II, of the North Carolina–Virginia boundary line that was surveyed by a joint commission in 1728 because the Carolinas were to be sold to the Crown by their Lords Proprietors. The work, whose complete title is *The History of the Dividing Line betwixt Virginia and North Carolina. Run in the Year of our Lord 1728*, has become a classic of southern colonial literature.

The boundary expedition was the first exploration of much of the border region, and the urbane Byrd vividly described the natural wonders, flora, fauna, and Indians of the area. His humorous sketches of the lazy Carolina frontier folk, inhabiting a "Lubberland," have entertained readers since the publication of the narrative in 1841. Byrd was so taken with the beauty and apparent fertility of the Dan River Valley that he acquired 20,000 acres of the region from the North Carolina commissioners and named his tract the "Land of Eden."

Reference: Louis B. Wright, *The Prose Works of William Byrd of Westover* (1966).

Lindley S. Butler

Hog Farming, an important part of North Carolina agriculture since colonial days, has grown into a massive industry with a gross value in excess of $2 billion annually. In the latter years of the twentieth century, it also represented a significant environmental problem, with the dangers of hog lagoons—which store hog waste for later use as fertilizers—consistently threatening water supplies and raising health concerns in several hog-producing counties.

Purebred hog breeds played a major role in upgrading the quality of hogs in the state and have continued through the years to be the primary source of breeding stock. The Berkshire breed appeared in North Carolina in 1881, when John O'Hagan of Wilson brought a boar from Maryland. In the late 1880s Julian S. Carr was declared the first constructive Duroc Jersey breeder in the state. Chester Whites came to North Carolina in 1898, and by 1910 there were Tamworths, Hampshires, and Yorkshires. More than 10 purebred swine

A farmer in Northampton County feeds his hogs, 1939. Photograph by Charles Anderson Farrell. NCC.

breeders have been inducted into the North Carolina State Fair Livestock Hall of Fame, which was established in 1980.

North Carolina has supported its hog farming industry in several ways. In 1918 W. W. Shay moved to Raleigh to head swine extension. During the next 14 years his work with "Result Demonstrations" gained him a reputation as the "father" of the North Carolina commercial swine industry. In 1961 a Swine Evaluation Station was established to encourage producers to collect and use performance data in selecting breeding stock, and in 1962 the North Carolina Pork Producers Association, Inc., was chartered for promotion, research, and education. The Swine Development Center near Rocky Mount was built in 1965 to demonstrate the finer points of swine production. In the late 1970s as many as 200,000 feeder pigs moved through 10 organized quality and graded feeder pig sales annually. By the early 1980s the state gained the distinction of having more large herds than any other state. In 1989 North Carolina had 70 herds with more than 1,000 sows each, and Sampson County was the top-ranked county in the nation for hog production.

After years of fluctuating numbers, hog populations in North Carolina began to increase dramatically during the 1990s, accompanied by a dramatic decrease in the number of hog farms in the state. Most hog farms are in the southeast, especially Sampson, Bladen, Robeson, and Duplin Counties. The growth of "mega farms" owned by large corporations has been a key development of the hog farming industry. Major companies such as Smithfield, Tyson, Swift, and Hormel have massive operations in North Carolina, at times drawing the ire of health professionals for the poor working environments of their employees.

By the 1990s, disposal of waste produced by hog farming became a major issue in the state. The most common practice for disposing of the waste was placing it in lagoons—large basins where it could decompose and wastewater could be filtered and purified before returning to the groundwater system. But there was no uniform standard for these lagoons, and with the growth of large hog farms, area residents increasingly complained about their odor and worried about the danger of contaminants leaking into water supplies for human consumption. A law stipulating the safe location of hog lagoons—at least 1,500 feet from homes and 2,500 feet from schools, hospitals, and churches—was enacted in 1995. The Clean Water Responsibility Act, passed by the General Assembly in 1997, placed a moratorium on the construction of new farms with more than 250 hogs, halting the growth of the industry. But two years later, Hurricane Floyd's heavy rainfall caused the overflow of many North Carolina hog waste lagoons, creating massive contamination of several watersheds. The moratorium on new lagoons was renewed in 1999 and was further extended in 2003 through the efforts of Governor Michael Easley. Today's hog processors, researchers, and environmental engineers continue work on improving methods for waste disposal in the industry.

Despite restrictions on hog production, by the early 2000s North Carolina ranked second nationally in swine production behind Iowa and was the largest swine state outside the traditional Corn Belt. Modern hogs are lean and muscular, and most are raised in confinement. They are sired in a breeding barn, born in a furrowing house, grown in a nursery, and "topped out" in a finish facility. Market weight is 210 to 250 pounds at five to six months of age.

James R. Jones

Hog Killing in rural North Carolina was traditionally initiated on the first autumn or winter day after the weather had turned frigid. Neighbors often shared in the labor, when perhaps as many as 100 hogs had been penned up and fattened on peas, potatoes, or corn gleaned from harvested fields or on mast from the woods. Workers gathered from the neighborhood well before dawn. Large stones were heated in a big, open fire and dropped into barrels to heat water. The hogs were killed with large knives and then bled, scalded, hung on a gambrel, and scraped to remove the hair. They cooled overnight and generally were cut up the next day and salted. The meat was packed in bulk—with hams, sides, shoulders, jaws, and heads separated—on a tight, slightly tilted platform a foot or more from the ground or floor of the smokehouse. Troughs under the lower side caught the dripping brine, which was afterward evaporated and the salt saved for stock.

In the weeks after the hog killing, people enjoyed a variety of pork products, including spare ribs, liver, and sausage. Hams were ready for eating later, a month or two after proper curing.

References: Paul B. Barringer, *The Natural Bent: The Memoirs of Dr. Paul B. Barringer* (1949); Charles S. Powell, "Hog Killing before the War," *Smithfield Herald*, 8 Jan. 1916.

William S. Powell

Slaughtered hogs in Halifax County, 1939. Howard Odum Collection, no. P-3167, Southern Historical Collection, Wilson Library, UNC-Chapel Hill.

Hogshead is a large barrel used primarily to store and/or transport tightly packed, or "prized," leaf tobacco. By the mid-1700s, tradition, convenience, and statutes to discourage smuggling ultimately required tobacco to be shipped in a hogshead rather than by bulk. Hogsheads were transported by water and land, and they often were rolled a mile or more by hand from the plantation to the wharf. So-called tobacco rollers would haul a hogshead to market with the aid of one or two horses.

Over time, loose-leaf tobacco warehouse auction sales replaced the traditional method of selling tobacco in a hogshead. Loose-leaf sales allowed buyers to examine the entire bulk of the tobacco they were bidding for, while those buying by the hogshead could only examine a small sample. Prizing leaf into hogsheads was a way to help protect it during shipping and to economize on shipping space. However, the prizing damaged the leaf, and a planter in the 1870s could get more money for tobacco that was wrapper quality (leaves that were used to wrap tobacco plugs).

The hogshead is no longer the standard means of tobacco shipping or marketing but is chiefly used by manufacturers for storage during the curing process. A uniform size for the hogshead was never successfully established in colonial times or afterward; consequently, its changing size has remained a source of frustration for researchers trying to determine tobacco statistics from colonial and nineteenth-century North Carolina.

Reference: Robert K. Heimann, *Tobacco and Americans* (1960).

John F. Ansley

Hoi Toiders is the commonly used name for the residents of certain sections of the Outer Banks in North Carolina who, because of geographic barriers, have retained a unique dialect unheard in other parts of the state. Many of the early settlers on the Outer Banks were English, Scottish, Irish, and Scotch-Irish; others came from the Albemarle Sound region of North Carolina, Tidewater Virginia, Maryland, and Pennsylvania. Separation from the interior regions of North Carolina, and the uncertainties of the sea and weather, made them fiercely independent, stalwart, and unwilling to accept change. Picturesque villages such as Wanchese, Hatteras, Ocracoke, and Harkers Island remain the homes of these North Carolinians whose culture and dialect are a result of their isolation and seafaring tradition.

The Hoi Toiders' unique speech—labeled by linguists as an Ocracoke brogue—is a combination of many early influences, especially seventeenth-century English regional dialects. The dialect's most characteristic feature is evident in the pronunciation of the phrase "high tide" as "hoi toide" in a way similar to how it is pronounced in parts of southwestern England even today. Usages such as "weren't" in the place of "wasn't" ("she weren't here") and "to" for "at" ("she's to the store now") also mark Hoi Toider speech and appear to have come from eastern England. The word "mommick," meaning to harass or bother, which was used in the time of Shakespeare, remains in the Outer Banks lexicon thanks to the Hoi Toiders.

Hoi Toiders have earned a living as fishermen, pilots, whalers, seamen, and boatbuilders. After the Civil War, many worked in commercial fisheries and menhaden factories. They also were the first members of the U.S. Lifesaving Service. Whatever their occupation, they have been resourceful, as evidenced by the women's using seaweed to stuff mattresses and the men's salvaging shipwrecks to build skiffs, homes, and churches. Regardless of the influence of "dingbatters," or nonnatives of the Outer Banks, Hoi Toiders' culture, and much of their "relic" language, continue to survive in the early 2000s.

References: Rodney Barfield, *Seasoned by Salt: A Historical Album of the Outer Banks* (1995); Walt Wolfram and Natalie Shilling-Estes, *Hoi Toide on the Outer Banks: The Story of the Ocracoke Brogue* (1997).

Amelia Dees-Killette

Hoke County is located in North Carolina's Coastal Plain region in an area originally inhabited by Saura (Cheraw) and Lumbee Indians. The county was formed from Cumberland and Robeson Counties in 1911—the third attempt (after failures in 1907 and 1909) to create a new jurisdiction for disaffected residents of the two counties. Popular support for the successful 1911 campaign hinged on naming the proposed county Hoke in honor of prominent Confederate general and railroad president Robert F. Hoke. Raeford (incorporated in 1901) became the county seat and is the principal city; other communities include Dundarrach and McCain. The Fort Bragg Military Reservation, established and developed in the late 1910s and early 1920s, occupies the northern third of the county.

Near the end of the twentieth century, Hoke County earned distinction as the host of the annual North Carolina Turkey Festival, honoring the state's status as the national leader in turkey production. Originating as the "Hoke Heritage Hobnob" in 1984, the festival was at first a relatively minor one-day affair in Raeford; but in the years following, the event's scope and appeal grew substantially, with up to 60,000 people attending yearly in the early twenty-first century.

Besides turkeys, Hoke County agricultural products include tobacco, corn, soybeans, cotton, hogs, and beef cattle. Manufactured goods include wool and polyester fabrics, beauty aids, and concrete blocks. The county is home to a substantial number of Lumbee Indians. In 2004 the estimated population of Hoke County was 38,600.

Robert Blair Vocci

Hoke v. Henderson, a case decided by the North Carolina Supreme Court in 1834 in an opinion by Chief Justice Thomas Ruffin, held that state offices were a form of property, and that officeholders were therefore protected by the state constitution against arbitrary removal by the legislature. Although the legal argument was eventually rejected by the courts of every other state and by the federal courts, *Hoke* remained the law in North Carolina throughout the nineteenth century, being often reaffirmed. In the late 1890s, as political power shifted from the Democrats to the "Fusion" of Republicans and Populists, then back to the Democrats, *Hoke* was invoked to protect officeholders against ouster. Reliance on that precedent by two justices of the state supreme court became, in fact, one of the grounds for their impeachment in 1901. Although finally overruled in 1903, *Hoke* remains a classic statement of judicial independence.

Reference: Walter F. Pratt Jr., "The Struggle for Judicial Independence in Antebellum North Carolina: The Story of Two Judges," *Law and History Review* 4 (1986).

John V. Orth

Holiness Church in North Carolina was an outgrowth of the Holiness movement within the Methodist Church and the Methodist-related National Camp Meeting Association for the Promotion of Holiness (1867). These two movements, inspired by the works of John Welsey, Adam Clarke, and John Fletcher, sought to encourage not just initial salvation but a second conversion, or "second blessing," known as "entire" or "full" sanctification.

The Holiness Church of North Carolina, as distinguished from a church of the same name in California, was formed from the Methodist Episcopal Church, South, by one of its ministers, Ambrose B. Crumpler (1863–1952). Crumpler, after being inspired in 1889 by Holiness evangelist Beverly Carradine, accepted entire sanctification in his life and became a Holiness evangelist. In 1897 he formed a Holiness association and began conducting revivals that attacked materialism, ornamentation, the use of tobacco and alcohol, and Methodist Church bishops. Two years later, he left the Methodist Episcopal Church to establish the Holiness Church at Goldsboro. He published a denominational newsletter at Fayetteville and served as president of the church for nine years (1900–1909).

One of Crumpler's followers, Gaston B. Cashwell (1826–1916), soon carried Holiness one step further. Cashwell, who left Crumpler's church in 1906 for the new Pentecostal movement, began a series of Pentecostal revivals in eastern North Carolina. Cashwell preached on the imminent second coming of Christ, on faith healing, and on how speaking in tongues was a sign of the "third blessing" in individuals. Wesleyan, Baptist, Presbyterian, and Congregational churches joined Cashwell, and the Holiness Church, in spite of Crumpler's vehement opposition, deserted its founder to become part of the newly formed Pentecostal Holiness Church (1911).

References: Nils Bloch-Hoell, *The Pentecostal Movement* (1964); J. E. Campbell, *The Pentecostal Holiness Church, 1898–1948: Its Background and History* (1951); Melvin E. Dieter, *The Holiness Revival of the Nineteenth Century* (1980); Charles E. Jones, *A Guide to the Study of the Holiness Movement* (1974); Vinson Synan, *The Holiness-Pentecostal Movement in the United States* (1971).

Louis P. Towles

SEE ALSO Pentecostal Holiness Church.

Hollerin' Contest,

Hollerin' Contest, an annual fair established in Spivey's Corner in 1969, celebrates the art of hollering, which, before the telephone, was an essential means of communicating for people in the rural areas of North Carolina. People used a repertoire of hollers to communicate with each other over long distances, from simple "good mornings" to messages alerting neighbors of an ongoing or impending emergency. This essential part of the rural culture of farm families of North Carolina eventually was obscured by the communication technologies of the twentieth century.

The idea for the Hollerin' Contest, which regularly attracts 2,000 to 3,000 people to Spivey's Corner every June, was first discussed on a local radio talk show; organization for the contest began shortly thereafter. The efforts of the local community were rewarded, as the contest drew national attention in its first year. North Carolinian and CBS reporter Charles Kuralt and reporters from *Time* magazine, the Associated Press, and United Press International wrote about the event. The first Hollerin' Contest winner, 70-year-old Dewey Jackson, hollered a rendition of "What a Friend We Have in Jesus." He was sent

H. H. Oliver of Goldsboro delivers his prize-winning holler at the second annual Hollerin' Contest at Spivey's Corner on 20 June 1970. Courtesy of NCOA&H.

a letter of congratulations from President Richard Nixon and also appeared on NBC's *Tonight Show*.

The main goal of the Spivey's Corner Hollerin' Contest continues to be keeping the art of hollering alive in the state and raising funds for the Spivey's Corner Volunteer Fire Department. Since the first contest in 1969, the event has grown into a full day of family-oriented events, including a 10-K Hollerin' Run, a craft show, music, and dancing. The contests are often judged by invited guests, who have included a North Carolina agriculture commissioner, a North Carolina secretary of state, and U.S. congressmen.

Craig Stinson

Home Guard. Although the term "Home Guard" appears in the names of several North Carolina military units raised early in the Civil War, it usually refers to the statewide organization formed by an act of the General Assembly of 7 July 1863. The Home Guard replaced the militia, the ranks of which had been filled, except for officers, by Confederate conscription. The Home Guard included all able-bodied white males between the ages of 18 and 50 who were exempt from Confederate service, excepting only the governor, judges, members of the General Assembly and Congress, clergymen, county sheriffs, registers of deeds, and clerks of court.

The first organization of the Home Guard consisted of approximately 12,500 men. They were arranged mostly in battalions of one to five companies from the same county. Eight regiments were formed from large counties or from combining the battalions of smaller adjacent counties. Four counties that could only muster a few men contributed one company each. While called up for duty, men of the Home Guard were paid by the state at the same rate that their rank would entitle them to in Confederate service. In the fiscal year 1863–64 the state budgeted $100,000 for Home Guard pay.

The duties of the Home Guard were to catch deserters; to guard bridges, supply depots, and other strategic points; to break up armed gangs of deserters that plagued many areas; and to aid in repelling Union invasions of the state. Members also performed guard duty at Salisbury Prison in late 1864. Home Guard units in the Piedmont and the Mountains were often too small and scattered to accomplish much against Union forces and armed deserters. Loyal Union men dodged Home Guard service or performed their duties halfheartedly; many other men were reluctant to leave their homes and families unprotected.

Despite low numbers and poor morale, the Home Guard sometimes performed well, even late in the war. In October 1863 the Home Guard of Cherokee County, with some Confederate cavalry and Cherokee soldiers of Thomas's Legion, pursued and captured most of a Unionist guerrilla band under Goldman Bryson. On 6 Apr. 1865 Asheville's Home Guard helped to drive off a large force of Union cavalry. On 17 Apr. 1865, 80 men of the Burke County Home Guard under Col. T. G. Walton fought two brigades of Union cavalry for some time before being outflanked at Rocky Ford near Morganton.

The occasional brutality of Home Guard activities is graphically depicted in Charles Frazier's National Book Award–winning novel, *Cold Mountain* (1998), and the major motion picture based on the book that was released in 2003.

References: Walter Clark, ed., *Histories of the Several Regiments and Battalions from North Carolina in the Great War, 1861–1865*, vol. 4 (1901); William R. Trotter, *The Civil War in North Carolina* (3 vols., 1988–89).

David A. Norris

Homeland Security. The tragic events of 11 Sept. 2001— during which approximately 3,000 people died when Islamic terrorists hijacked commercial airplanes and used them to strike the World Trade Center in New York City and the Pentagon in Arlington, Va.—led to a variety of changes at the federal level and in North Carolina government. In the days following the attacks, at the request of President George W. Bush, Congress established the Office of Homeland Security, with Pennsylvania governor Tom Ridge as its director. After activating the North Carolina National Guard and placing the State Highway Patrol at vulnerable sites (such as nuclear reactors and airports), Governor Michael Easley initiated several additional measures to increase public safety across the state.

Among other actions, Easley asked the General Assembly for authority to use special state funds for security purposes, established antibioterrorism teams, and signed stricter laws involving possible weapons of mass destruction. He also assembled an Anti-Terrorism Task Force that involved the most critical state agencies, including the Department of Crime Control and Public Safety (Divisions of Highway Patrol, Emergency Management, Alcohol Law Enforcement, and the National Guard), the Department of Health and Human Services (Division of Public Health), the Department of Justice and the State Bureau of Investigation, and the Office of Information Technology Services. Four committees were established: the Threat Assessment and Reduction Committee, to determine the vulnerability of North Carolina facilities and businesses to attack; the Emergency Response Committee, to improve the state and local response to attack; the Training Committee, to increase counterterrorism training statewide; and the Public Information Committee, to keep the public informed of threats and appropriate government resources. Based on the recommendations of these committees, funds, resources, and agencies were realigned to increase governmental effectiveness in case of attacks against North Carolina citizens and facilities.

In November 2002 Congress authorized expanding the Office of Homeland Security and making it a new executive department. The U.S. Department of Homeland Security, which became operational in January 2003, merged 22 federal agencies (excluding the Federal Bureau of Investigation and the Central Intelligence Agency) with shared responsibility for immigration, border and coastal control, customs, transportation security, emergency response, safeguarding the publicly and privately owned infrastructure (including power plants, pipelines, shipyards, chemical plants, water supplies, and storage sites for hazardous materials), stockpiling vaccines and antibiotics, and vaccinating military and emergency personnel against smallpox. The department coordinates responsibility for domestic safety by working with federal, state, and local authorities in the design and implementation of national strategies.

The North Carolina government cooperates with Homeland Security on a variety of security concerns and receives from the department an annual allocation of funds to be used for antiterrorism and other programs. In 2005 the state's allotment of about $46 million supported the State Homeland Security Program (training and equipment for security forces), the Urban Areas Security Initiative (for Mecklenburg and surrounding counties), the Emergency Management Performance Grant Program, and the Law Enforcement Terrorism Prevention Program.

North Carolinians, like citizens of other states, are informed of terrorist threats through Homeland Security's color-coded advisory system. Other statewide programs have been instituted. For example, on 2 Feb. 2004 North Carolina began enforcing stricter requirements for obtaining driver's licenses. George Tatum, commissioner of the Division of Motor Vehicles, claimed that these new procedures, called "Operation Stop Fraud," were among the strongest in the nation and reflected security recommendations from the FBI and the Department of Homeland Security.

Jay Mazzocchi

Honeybees have long played an important role in North Carolina's agricultural economy. Vital as pollinators of several major cash crops in the state (especially cotton, alfalfa, fruits, and vegetables) and useful for their production of honey and wax, European honeybees (*Apis mellifera*) have been a staple of farm life and folk culture for over three centuries.

Native to Europe, Africa, and Asia, honeybees reached North America aboard English vessels as early as 1622. Quickly adapting to the rich flora of the New World, they thrived and spread rapidly. Court records indicate the presence of bees in the Albemarle region as early as 1697. In 1731 the naturalist John Brickell, a resident of Edenton, observed "the Bees are in great Plenty, not only in Hives . . . but are likewise to be met with in several parts of the Woods in hollow Trees, wherein are frequently found vast quantities of Honey, and Wax." Twenty years later the Swedish traveler Peter Kalm, noting the practice of beekeeping among two North Carolina farmers, concluded that "bees succeed very well here."

By the mid-1700s, beeswax, used widely for candles and in cosmetics, became a frequent, if minor, export from North Carolina, while honey generally remained an article of local trade. The colonial government recognized the economic value of beeswax, authorizing its use for taxes under the 1745 Quit Rent and 1768 Tax Acts, at the rate of one shilling per pound.

Requiring little effort and offering high rewards, the practice of beekeeping was well established across the state by 1800. Small farmers and plantation owners alike kept hives, while slaves often foraged for the honey produced by feral bee colonies to supplement their rations. The products of the hive played a prominent role in folk medicine, including the use of honey as a salve on burns and bee stings and to treat arthritis. Beekeeping was so ubiquitous that, despite antiquated practices and the Civil War, North Carolina led the nation in

Beekeepers at work near High Point, 2002. Photograph by Nelson Kepley. *Greensboro News and Record*.

production of beeswax and was one of the major producers of honey throughout the nineteenth century.

The early decades of the twentieth century saw a growing awareness of the importance of beekeeping in North Carolina. The state's honey production reached its peak of 2.5 million pounds per year around the turn of the century. The qualities of North Carolina honey varies depending on the local flora, from the light honeys of the basswood in the west and gallberry in the east to the dark honey of the tulip poplar in the piedmont region. The dense, sweet honey of the sourwood, found in the piedmont and western areas, is widely considered a delicacy and commands a substantially higher price than other varieties. In all, bees forage on more than 25 different types of "honey plants" throughout the state.

Though the honeybee was named North Carolina's state insect in 1973, the future of beekeeping has grown less secure as it enters its fourth century in the state. In the early 1990s beekeepers in several western counties reported sharp losses from Tracheal and Varroa mites, parasites for which honeybees have no natural defense. Spread by bees that drift from one colony to another, the mites soon infested colonies across the state with devastating results. According to federal census data, North Carolina beekeepers experienced a drop of almost 50 percent in the number of recorded hives and in honey production between 1987 and 1992, to a level barely above the nadir of 1969; by the early 2000s almost all feral colonies had disappeared. The cessation of the federal honey price support program in 1992 and increasing international competition have placed additional economic stress on the industry. The potential migration into the state of the more aggressive Africanized honeybee from Central America, as far north as Texas by 1996 but by the early 2000s still not moving eastward, may serve to drive all but the most dedicated of beekeepers out of the business, reducing yields and driving up prices of the state's agricultural products.

References: Joe M. Graham, ed., *The Hive and the Honey Bee* (1992); Harry E. Scott, *Honey Bees in North Carolina* (1976).

Daniel J. Salemson

Hooker, a slang word for prostitute, was used in an 1845 letter written by a student to a classmate at the University of North Carolina. This is the earliest known written usage of the word in this sense. The letter was found in the university library's Southern Historical Collection by noted UNC professor and philologist Norman E. Eliason. The date of his finding undermines the popular notion that the term came into usage in the Civil War era in "honor" of Union general Joseph Hooker's well-documented personal proclivities.

Reference: Norman E. Eliason, *Tar Heel Talk: An Historical Study of the English Language in North Carolina to 1860* (1956).

Whitmel M. Joyner

Horne Creek Living Historical Farm in southeastern Surry County, a North Carolina State Historic Site, grew out of an interest on the part of a broad-based coalition of businesspeople, educators, farmers, and others in the northwest Piedmont who wished to preserve the state's agricultural heritage. The coalition came together in the 1960s, and a legislative appropriation funded a study of the feasibility of creating an agricultural museum. The site chosen for the museum, the Hauser family farm, was considered one of the best-preserved examples of a nineteenth-century, middle-class North Carolina farm. It had begun as a 100-acre tract of land obtained by John Hauser, the great-grandson of Alsatian immigrants, in 1830. Throughout the nineteenth century the farm prospered under the stewardship of Hauser and his youngest son, Thomas. By 1900 Thomas, his wife, and their 12 children (11 boys and 1 girl), together with several hired hands, raised tobacco, fruit, corn, wheat, oats, rye, hay, vegetables, and livestock on 450 acres. The farm continued to thrive through

the first decade of the twentieth century, until the death of Thomas Hauser in 1911.

Rather than focus on this single farm, it was agreed, the museum should be representative of farms throughout the northwest Piedmont. This decision led to the site's being called Horne Creek Living Historical Farm—the name deriving from the creek running through the property. On 17 Oct. 1987 the farm was officially designated a North Carolina State Historic Site.

The staff and volunteers at Horne Creek Living Historical Farm strive to recreate the physical environment and agricultural and domestic activities of the Hauser farm, and others like it, between 1900 and 1910. Using agricultural and household implements, breeds of livestock, and varieties of plants that were available to the Hausers and their neighbors early in the twentieth century, the staff has transformed this site into a "historical laboratory" where it is possible to study traditional methods of constructing buildings, planting and harvesting crops, and preserving foods. Educational programs are offered to teach the making of useful farm and household necessities of the past. Among the structures on the farm are a tobacco barn, fruit house, well house, smokehouse, and corncrib; in addition there is an orchard, a garden, and even a family cemetery.

References: Gilbert C. Fite, *Cotton Fields No More: Southern Agriculture, 1865–1980* (1984); Richard F. Knapp, ed., *North Carolina's State Historic Sites: A Brief History and Status Report* (1995); Linda A. McCurdy, *The Hauser Farm on Horne Creek in Surry County, North Carolina, Circa 1880* (1987).

Lisa R. Turney

Horner School, Horner and Graves's School, and Horner Military Academy were a few of the names given to the secondary school established by James Hunter Horner and his family members over the course of their long teaching careers. An 1844 graduate of the University of North Carolina in Chapel Hill, Horner taught at Hillsborough Academy and Oxford Male Academy before establishing his own Oxford Classical and Mathematical School on the outskirts of Oxford (Granville County) in 1855. The school offered two 20-week sessions a year for $95 a session. The boys were housed in a series of two-room cabins placed along the edge of the Horner homestead.

During the early years of the Civil War, the school closed when Horner served as captain of Company E of the 23rd North Carolina Regiment. In 1863 ill health returned him to civilian life and teaching. In 1873 he took as a partner Ralph H. Graves Sr., another noted teacher, and they were persuaded to move their school to Hillsborough to occupy the impressive brick facilities built in 1860 for Hillsborough Military Academy. The Horner and Graves's School opened in Hillsborough in January 1874. Its letterhead described it as a "Classical,

Members of the class of 1900 at the Horner School in Oxford. NCC.

doomed it. The aging Jerome Horner felt unequal to building up a school on a new campus. Although he continued to teach in other schools for three more years, the Horner School officially closed in 1920.

Jean B. Anderson

Hornet's Nest. SEE Charlotte, Battle of.

Horse Racing was the most popular spectator sport in North Carolina from the colonial period until after the Civil War. As early as the 1730s writer John Brickell noted residents' fondness for it. Early horse racing was crude and often dangerous. It began to become more refined in the last two decades before the Revolution, when planters imported expensive English breeding stock to Virginia and North Carolina. Gradually plantation owners with the financial resources to purchase, breed, train, and race horses dominated the sport, which became a way for North Carolina's financial elite to display their wealth. This group included such prominent North Carolinians as Willie Jones and Jeptha Atherton. Gambling on horse races was widespread among all classes. The Wilmington Jockey Club was established in 1774. The famous

Mathematical, Scientific and Military Academy," but an advertisement of its courses makes no mention of military instruction. In 1875 the partnership between Horner and Graves was dissolved, probably because of Horner's illness; he spent months of 1876 and 1877 in the Insane Asylum of North Carolina. Horner recovered from what was probably a nervous breakdown and taught a few classes each year until his death in 1892.

Meanwhile, aided by Hugh Morson, Graves continued the school in Hillsborough until his death late in the spring of 1876. The buildings of the Horner School in Oxford were occupied by another professional schoolteacher, Fred A. Fetter, during 1874. But James Hunter Horner's family moved back to Oxford, and the Horner School was reestablished there in 1876. It was operated by Thomas J. Horner (a younger brother of James Hunter Horner), Robert H. Marsh, and John Martin. In the spring of 1877 Junius M. Horner, son of Thomas Horner and a future bishop of the Episcopal Church, continued his father's school with the assistance of Frank R. Underwood. In the fall of that year, Jerome C. Horner, an older brother of Junius, took the helm.

Having decided to turn the classical academy into a military academy, Jerome Horner spent 1879 teaching at Cape Fear Military Academy in Wilmington. On his return to Oxford, he built barracks and a large schoolroom on the property and instituted a military program in the 1880 school year. The Horner Military School continued at Oxford with great success for the next 33 years.

When new barracks, built in 1891, were destroyed by fire in 1913, several cities offered Jerome Horner attractive accommodations and promises of support. He chose Charlotte in which to rebuild the institution. The Horner Military Institute operated in the Myers Park suburb from the fall of 1914 until the spring of 1920. The need for city expansion is said to have

The Sparrow Cup, made in London to commemorate the victory of the horse Sparrow in a race at Pembroke Plantation near Edenton in 1754. Courtesy of Rebecca Miles, Greensboro. Photography courtesy of Colonial Williamsburg Foundation.

The Celebrated Horse

SIR ARCHIE

Will stand the ensuing season at my stable, in Northampton county, North-Carolina, about 3 miles from the Court House, 9 miles from the town of Halifax, and 24 miles from Belfield, Va. He will cover mares at 75 dollars the season, payable on the 1st of January next, with one dollar to the groom in all cases. Such of Sir Archie's friends that live at a distance will send their notes with the mares, payable on the first of January; also feeding of the mares to be paid for when taken away. The season will commence on the first February, and terminate on the first of August.

Extensive fields of small grain and clover are sown for the benefit of mares, which may be left with the horse, with the addition of grain feeding, at 33 1-3 cents per day. Separate enclosures are provided for mares with colts. No pains will be spared in taking the best possible care of mares, &c which may be left, but no responsibility for escapes or accidents.

☞ Sir Archie's blood, great size, performance on the turf, and celebrity as a foal getter, are sufficient recommendations.
JOHN D. AMIS.

February 22, 1827.
LAWRENCE & LEMAY, PRINTERS, RALEIGH.

An 1827 broadside produced by John Amis, Sir Archie's owner, advertising the horse at stud. From the Cameron Family Papers, no. 133, Southern Historical Collection, Wilson Library, UNC-Chapel Hill.

race horse Janus was kept in North Carolina during the 1770s, establishing an enviable breed of thoroughbreds.

Horse racing expanded its hold after the American Revolution, as jockey clubs were established in every region, annual races became major social events, and horse breeding became big business. It became necessary to standardize racing weights, distances, and other variables. As a result horse racing became the first sport to become bureaucratized. The preferred distance for the top thoroughbred races was four miles, the so-called "heroic distance."

The center of North Carolina racing in the antebellum era remained the region near the Roanoke River. That area was the home of the state's most famous race horse, Sir Archie (1805–33), a horse so successful that his career ended after only a handful of races because his owner could find no competition. Sir Archie's owner at that time was Warren County native William Ransom Johnson, a well-respected trainer and owner known by the national racing fraternity by his nickname "Napoleon of the Turf." Johnson eventually moved to Virginia but not before selling Sir Archie to former governor William R. Davie. Eventually Northampton County planter William Amis acquired Sir Archie, putting the horse at stud at his Mowfield Plantation. Sir Archie became one of the most successful studs ever, with the careers of his 400 progeny leading to his designation as the "Foundation Sire of the American

Thoroughbred." Many champions trace their line through Sir Archie.

The Civil War ended the plantation system upon which southern horse racing had been established. Despite the disappearance of the jockey clubs, however, horse racing continued to be a popular activity at the North Carolina State Fair in Raleigh and at regional and county fairs. These races were much shorter than those in the antebellum period—usually about one mile—and, at the fairs, were almost evenly divided among flat and harness racing. The advent of the automobile in the early twentieth century further marginalized horse racing, and the sport eventually disappeared from the fair circuit.

But horse racing never completely disappeared. In the early 1950s, steeplechases became popular at Stoneybrook Stables near Southern Pines. The mountain community of Tryon also has hosted successful steeplechase races. In 1992 harness racing was reintroduced at the state fair after an absence of decades. By the late twentieth century, however, big-time horse racing had become closely connected to gambling, an illegal activity in North Carolina. Several attempts have been made to institute pari-mutuel gambling in the state, but by 2006 none had gained legislative approval.

References: Elizabeth Amis Blanchard and Manly Wade Wellman, *The Life and Times of Sir Archie: The Story of America's Greatest Thoroughbred, 1805–1833* (1958); Henry W. Lewis, "Horses and Horsemen in Northampton before 1900," *NCHR* 51 (April 1974); Alexander Mackay-Smith, *The Colonial Quarter Race Horse* (1983); Jim L. Sumner, "The State Fair and the Development of Modern Sports in Late Nineteenth-Century North Carolina," *Journal of Sport History* 15 (Summer 1988).

Jim L. Sumner
Additional research provided by David M. Egner.

Horses. The date of the first appearance of horses in North Carolina is not known. One source suggests that in about 1585 Sir Richard Grenville's ship, en route to Roanoke Island and carrying Spanish mustangs picked up in Puerto Rico, ran aground off Ocracoke Inlet. Many horses were lost overboard or perhaps put overboard to lighten the ship's weight while repairs were being made. Another source tells of horses arriving in the 1500s on Spanish ships, escaping from shipwrecks or being put off deliberately when the ships returned to Spain. However and whenever they first came to North Carolina, the centuries that followed have seen an exciting and sometimes sad history for these wild horses, often called "Banker" ponies. Today, the descendants of these original horses, managed by the National Park Service, can be seen in a 180-acre pen on Ocracoke Island.

Not until around 1700 did horses begin to be kept by North Carolinians in substantial numbers. Before the advent of trains, tractors, and automobiles, horses were used to transport people and goods and to pull plows, stagecoaches, and wagons. The sport of horse racing also enjoyed tremendous popularity in the state from the colonial period until after the Civil War.

Equine populations in North Carolina continued to increase throughout the nineteenth century. By 1915 there were 182,000 horses in the state, with an average value of $130 per head. Although horses were still used for racing, this was more the exception than the rule. Horses primarily were farm animals, pulling plows and helping to grow the food to feed a state. Their numbers started to decrease in 1925, as they were replaced or complemented by tractors and other farm equipment that needed no horse power. The "horseless carriage," or automobile, helped cause this decline. By 1943, with World War II raging, the number of horses in North Carolina had fallen to 80,000 and was continuing to drop. This decrease brought about a plea from then commissioner of agriculture W. Kerr Scott: "If we are to continue to grow feed for meat production and food for our soldiers and for civilian consumption, it is imperative that we produce horses and mules with which to cultivate our crops."

After bottoming out, the North Carolina horse population began to rebound by 1955, thanks to a strengthening interest in recreational riding, racing, and events such as horse shows and rodeos. The equine industry suddenly entered a period of growth powerful enough to induce agriculture commissioner Jim Graham to appoint an advisory committee in March 1971 to help broaden the agency's activities related to the rising horse population, numbering that year at 113,000, mostly pleasure horses. By 1976 the North Carolina horse population was at 150,000. Nearly 200 horse events were staged during that year in the state, and in addition about 100 wagon train associations gathered, most of which used horses. By 1979 North Carolina's reputation as a producer of great horses was growing; in response, horse owners, breeders, and trainers formed the North Carolina Thoroughbred Breeders Association.

The number of horses in the state had increased to 220,000 by 1983. People had begun to look at the animals as more than work or pleasure creatures — they were also being seen as moneymaking investments and tax shelters. The early 1980s also witnessed the beginning of a great migration of horsemen and -women to North Carolina from all over the country, particularly from the North, due in part to the numerous major shows in and around the state and a climate that is hospitable to year-round training.

The Sandhills area of North Carolina is recognized as a leading center of the state's equine industry. For many people in this region, which encompasses Moore County and parts of Cumberland, Richmond, Scotland, and Harnett Counties, life revolves around horses. Southern Pines, the main hub of the Sandhills, is also the home of the Equine Research Cen-

ter, a satellite of North Carolina State University's veterinary program, and the Walthour-Moss Foundation, a 2,500-acre nature preserve established in 1974 to be used by the public for the enjoyment of equine sports and nature hikes. The James B. Hunt Horse Complex, located in Raleigh, opened in 1983 and has been consistently booked with horse activities. It is home to the North Carolina State Fair Horse Show, one of the largest all-breed shows in the nation.

Two other major centers, the Western North Carolina Agricultural Center in Asheville and the Senator Bob Martin Eastern North Carolina Agricultural Center in Williamston, are testaments to the existence of horse-related activities from the coast to the mountains, activities that include polo and fox hunting. All 100 North Carolina counties have some type of horse activities, and in 1999 more than 500 horse shows occurred in the state. All major breeds are represented, and North Carolinians can boast of producing national and international champions.

The need to help disseminate research-based information about horses to North Carolina horse owners led to the creation of the Regional Equine Information Network System in 1995. Established by Bob Mowrey, a specialist on horse husbandry at N.C. State University, this unique program rigorously trains volunteers across the state to assist horse owners in issues concerning horses or horse-related activities.

By the early 2000s there were an estimated 225,000 horses in North Carolina, with an equine industry valued at more than $500 million annually. While issues such as loss of area from development, zoning laws limiting horse ownership, and waste disposal problems in urban areas affect the industry, horses remain a vital part of North Carolina's economy and culture.

Reference: Robert S. Curtis, *The History of Livestock in North Carolina* (1956).

Deborah Raenette Meyer

SEE ALSO Horse Racing; Mules; Wild Horses.

Hospitals. Well into the twentieth century, sick or injured North Carolinians were cared for primarily at home. In colonial times ill persons without families were looked after in almshouses. As contagious illnesses often arrived by ship, groups of private citizens in port communities began to set up facilities to quarantine incoming seamen who were ill and to assist victims of malaria and other coastal scourges. The first of these, Mount Tirzah Hospital, was built in Wilmington in 1835. In 1869 the state established a quarantine station and hospital at Beaufort Harbor.

The development of hospitals in North Carolina rested almost entirely with churches and associations of physicians into the twentieth century. Government played only a small role in this arena. Not until the passage of the federal Hospital Survey and Construction Act, known as the Hill-Burton Act, in 1946 did North Carolina government become involved in hospitals to any substantial extent. Under this legislation, the federal government provided up to 50 percent of construction funds for hospital projects approved by the designated agency in each state, with state and local funds providing the rest. Hill-Burton also introduced regulation, requiring that federally funded hospitals be licensed and meet minimum standards for their maintenance and operation. A total of $200 million in Hill-Burton funds financed 275 construction projects and added 7,486 new beds for medical care in North Carolina.

In 1848 the state established Dorothea Dix Hospital in Raleigh, its first facility for the mentally ill. The North Carolina Constitution of 1868 gave the state responsibility for such patients, and two more facilities were built in Goldsboro and Morganton later in the century. Hospitals providing general medical care, however, were slow in coming. So horrendous were battlefield conditions during the Civil War, and so futile were the well-intentioned attempts at care, that even years later efforts to establish civilian hospitals met with widespread public resistance. This attitude, along with the poverty that bedeviled Reconstruction, delayed the development of hospitals in the state.

St. Peter's Hospital, which opened in Charlotte in 1876, is credited with being North Carolina's first general hospital. Nineteenth-century Charlotte, like many communities throughout the South, lacked adequate medical facilities for poor and working-class citizens. The leading voice behind the new hospital was Jane Renwick Smedburg Wilkes, remembered as the "Godmother of Charlotte Hospitals." St. Peter's, originally called Home and Hospital, occupied two rooms on East Seventh Street. During its first year the facility moved to various locations throughout the city. In 1877 a local organization called the Busy Bee Society raised $273.42 and purchased a lot on modern Poplar Street, where the Home and Hospital of St. Peter's Episcopal Church began operations on 4 June. Fund-raising activities conducted by Jane and John Wilkes, as well as charity balls and monetary gifts from other philanthropists, kept the hospital open during its early years.

From the beginning, St. Peter's Hospital fought the public's fear of such institutions. Conditions in some nineteenth-century hospitals were so horrible that resistance to using them was common. Even though St. Peter's provided the finest medical care available, patients literally had to be forced to enter and local police officers stood guard to prevent rioters from shooting into the building.

Many of Charlotte's leading physicians practiced at St. Peter's, including R. E. M. Brevard and G. W. Pressly, who provided the first X-ray apparatus in a North Carolina hospital.

The facility continued to grow and prosper until the late 1930s, when it became apparent to the board of directors that a larger hospital was needed to serve Charlotte's ever-growing population. St. Peter's Hospital closed on 7 Oct. 1940, when Charlotte Memorial Hospital opened.

Initially, St. Peter's had admitted white patients only, but soon Jane Wilkes and other Charlotte women began to solicit funds for a hospital for African Americans; Trinity Episcopal Church of Southport, Conn., made the first financial contribution for its development in December 1882. The Episcopal Diocese of North Carolina then organized a Chapel of St. Michael for blacks in 1883. Two years later the diocese purchased a lot near the chapel for $400 "to be held for a hospital for colored." Good Samaritan Hospital was completed in 1891 at a cost of $4,400. Other hospitals then serving the African American community were the North Carolina State Hospital at Goldsboro (1880) and Leonard Hospital at Shaw University in Raleigh (1882).

During Good Samaritan's first six months of operation, 13 patients were admitted and treated. In 1893 the hospital provided care for 54 patients, 35 of whom were from Charlotte. Patients also came from outside the city and from South Carolina and Virginia. The institution operated on an annual budget of about $825. Ten years later, its patient list included individuals from North Carolina, South Carolina, Georgia, Virginia, and Martinique (West Indies). In the 1920s and 1930s Good Samaritan continued to expand its services and to build additions to the original building, located at 411 West Hill Street, between South Mint and South Graham Streets.

In the late 1950s Good Samaritan's facilities and professional standards came under scrutiny. The local chapter of the National Association for the Advancement of Colored People demanded that the hospital be closed and its patients be moved to the community-supported Charlotte Memorial Hospital. In the spring of 1960 the Episcopal Diocese donated Good Samaritan to the city of Charlotte. In 1964, after a steady decrease in the number of patients resulting from the desegregation of Charlotte Memorial, the city of Charlotte began operating Good Samaritan as Charlotte Community Hospital. The Community Hospital closed in 1982, following Charlotte Memorial's major expansion; the site was later used for a stadium built and operated by the Richardson Sports Group for the Charlotte Panthers, a franchise of the National Football League.

McCain Sanatorium, named for its longtime, innovative superintendent, Paul P. McCain, was a state-operated hospital established near Raeford in Hoke County in 1907 and first called the North Carolina Sanatorium for the Treatment of Tuberculosis. In addition to treating patients with the respiratory disease, the sanatorium contributed many innovations in health care, including a nurses' home on the site. In 1923 the

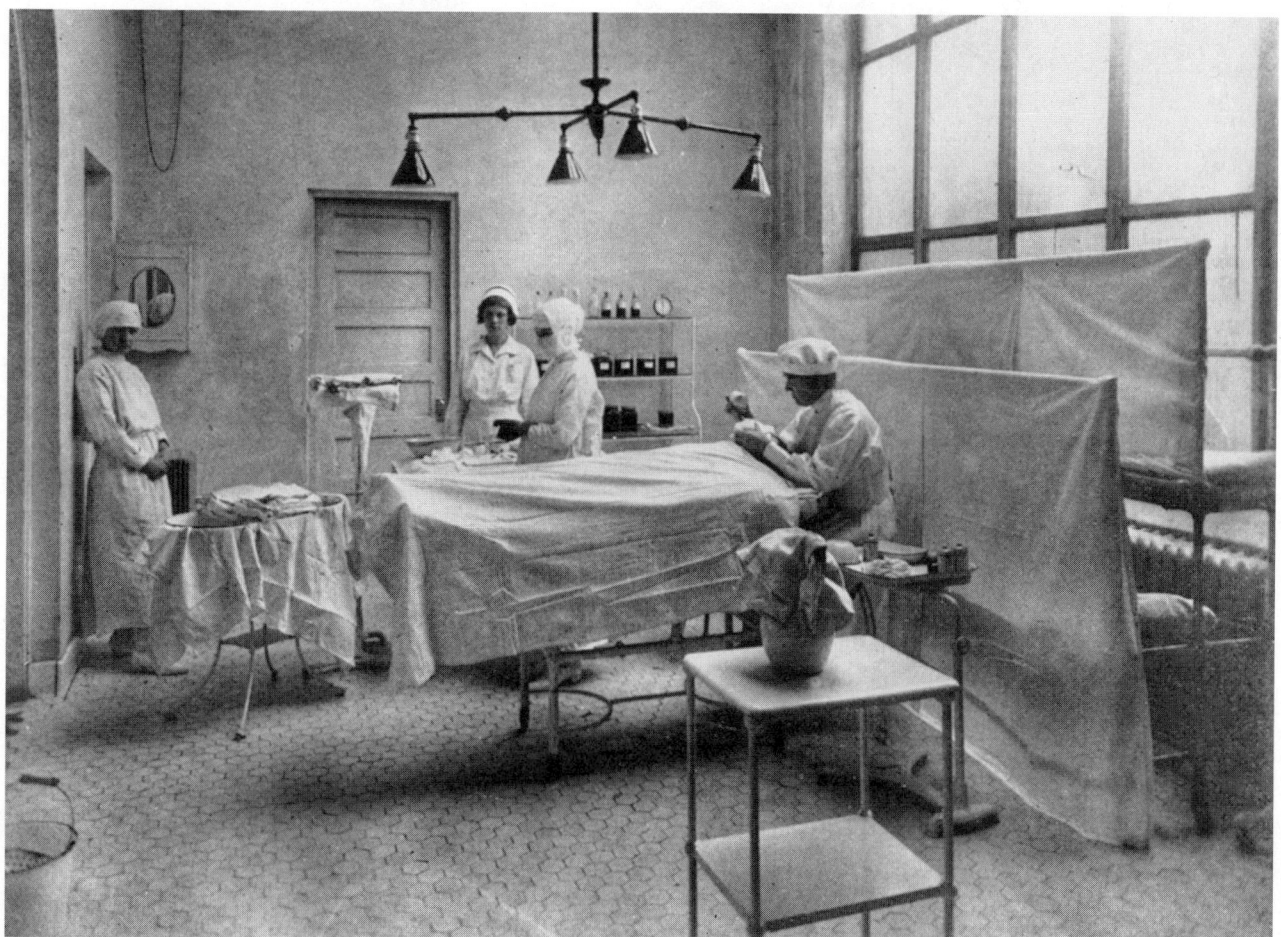

Operating room at Rex Hospital in Raleigh, ca. 1923. NCC.

General Assembly approved the expenditure of $100,000 for the construction of a "Colored Division" at the facility, adding 50 beds for the care of African Americans. After making many strides in the management of tuberculosis, the sanatorium closed in 1950. Taken over by the Division of Prisons in 1983, the structure became the McCain Correctional Hospital for minimum-custody male prisoners.

Rex Hospital, which opened in Raleigh in 1894, was by the early 2000s North Carolina's oldest existing general hospital. Its roots reached back to 1839, when the will of John Rex, a Raleigh tanner, provided for the establishment of a facility "for the sick & afflicted poor belonging to the City of Raleigh." Legislation authorizing the appointment of trustees was ratified in 1841, and five men were named to the board of trustees. As a result of investment problems and the economic turmoil created by the Civil War, however, progress on the hospital was stalled. It was not until 1893 that the board bought a hospital operated by St. John's Guild, an Episcopal organization. Located in the former home of Governor Charles Manly on South Street, Rex Hospital opened on 1 May 1894 and soon became known for its pioneering use of X-rays. Its affiliated school of nursing, the first in North Carolina, was organized by Mary Wyche, head nurse, who joined Rex in July 1894; the school operated until May 1975.

The need for better and larger quarters led to the demolition of the old Rex Hospital and the construction of a new building on the same site. After multiple expansions and moves, Rex by 1980 occupied a massive site on Lake Boone Trail. Additions to the complex in the 1980s and early 1990s included the Rex Cancer Center, Cardiac Catherization Laboratory, Wellness Center, Rex Family Birth Center, and Rex Convalescent Care Center, as well as the capacity to provide same-day surgery and open-heart surgery.

In 1948 Governor Robert Gregg Cherry approved the future site of the University of North Carolina Medical School and Hospital in Chapel Hill, allowing fund-raising and further planning to begin. The goal was to build a 400-bed hospital in addition to expanding the UNC Medical School. The huge expense anticipated for construction caused much political wrangling; in fact, the $5.29 million raised by 1949 barely covered the estimated base value of the project.

As far back as 1922 it had been agreed that a hospital would be a fitting memorial to North Carolinians who died in World War I. With this in mind, the General Assembly decided to call

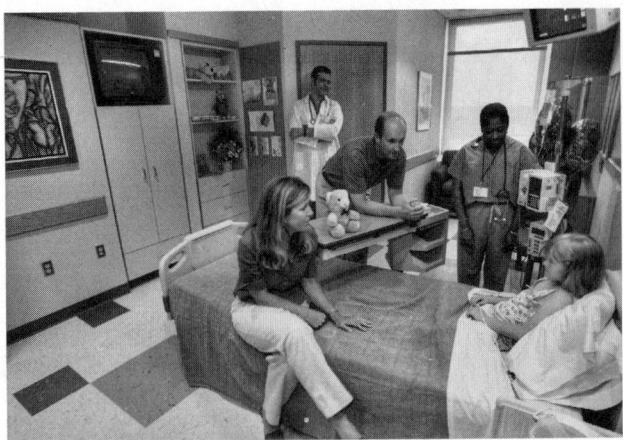

Patient's room in the North Carolina Children's Hospital in Chapel Hill, 2002. Photograph courtesy of UNC Health Care.

the new facility the North Carolina Memorial Hospital to commemorate the dead of all wars. A plaque noting the dedication was placed near the entrance. After construction delays, the hospital opened in September 1952, two months later than planned. But this postponement enabled almost all of the staff to be in place before the start of operations. The medical complex eventually included the North Carolina Neurosciences Hospital, the North Carolina Children's Hospital, and the North Carolina Women's Hospital.

By the early 2000s North Carolina had more than 200 hospitals and medical centers owned by the state, counties, cities, churches, or private companies. The majority of these were general acute-care facilities, with others providing psychiatric, rehabilitation, and specialty care. Most of the hospitals were not-for-profit institutions. Four facilities were teaching hospitals: Baptist Hospital, connected to the medical school of Wake Forest University, Winston-Salem; Duke University Hospital, Durham; Pitt County Hospital, operated jointly by Pitt County and the East Carolina University School of Medicine, Greenville; and the UNC Hospitals, Chapel Hill.

Hospitals in North Carolina were regulated by the Division of Health Services in the Department of Health and Human Services. Most of the these facilities were members of the North Carolina Hospital Association, a private organization working to improve hospital services.

References: John Braun, "Historic Black Hospital Healed Many," *Charlotte Observer*, 18 Feb. 1990; Anne M. Dellinger, "A History of Hospitals in North Carolina," *Hospital Law in North Carolina* (1985); Dorothy Long, ed., *Medicine in North Carolina: Essays in the History of Medical Science and Medical Service, 1524–1960* (1972); Memory F. Mitchell, "A Half-Century of Health Care: Raleigh's Rex Hospital, 1894–1944," *NCHR* 64 (April 1987); North Carolina Hospital Association, *Composite Statistics on North Carolina Hospitals, 1999* (1999).

Margaret Taylor
Memory F. Mitchell
Additional research provided by Robert G. Anthony Jr., Sheila Bumgarner, Ellen Fitzgibbons Causey, Maggie Goloboy, and Stewart Lillard.

SEE ALSO Psychiatric Hospitals.

Hot Springs is a small North Carolina community tucked deep into the Appalachian Mountains of western Madison County. The warm thermal springs after which the town was named, though known to Indians in the area, were first discovered by whites in 1778 near the banks of the French Broad River. A proposed community called Warm Springs Colony was created by the Western North Carolina Cooperative Manufacturing and Agricultural Association of New York City in 1870–71. The stockholders, with Dwight S. Elliott as president and Hinton Rowan Helper as a booster, sought to establish two colonies—one for manufacturing, one for agriculture—on a tract owned by James H. Rumbough on the French Broad River in Madison County. A Raleigh Episcopal rector said he had heard that 1,000 bushels of white potatoes could be grown per acre in the surrounding rich soil, which also was suited for corn, wheat, cranberries, apples, medicinal herbs, and root crops.

Predicting that the area would become the "New England of the South," the organization advertised for hundreds of farmers and workers skilled in wood, iron, and stone, each to own one share in the association. A local hotel was to be used as housing until individual homes could be built. The proposed hotel lease, however, fell through, and little is known about the colonists who actually came to Warm Springs.

The community's name was changed to Hot Springs in 1886 and the town incorporated three years later. The warm, mineral-rich water that rises to the surface from a geologic fault is the linchpin to the past and present of the town of Hot Springs. A tavern built near the springs served drovers and travelers in the late 1700s and was a regular stopping place as early as 1803 for Francis Asbury, the first bishop of the Methodist Church in the United States. The old tavern gave way to the first resort on the site, the Warm Springs Hotel, where a young Zebulon B. Vance, later governor of North Carolina during the Civil War, clerked.

While the development of Hot Springs and the success of the Warm Springs Hotel in the early 1800s were assured by its prime location on a stagecoach line, its status as a resort destination came with the advent of rail service. With new owners, the hotel was renamed the Patton Hotel in the 1830s. By the late 1800s, the Patton Hotel had evolved under the ownership of James Edwin Rumbough into the grand Mountain Park Hotel. Beyond the cool summer temperatures and luxurious accommodations, the hotel offered hot mineral bathing, tennis, equestrian sports, fine dining, dancing, music, and golf

Guests on the portico of the hotel at Hot Springs, ca. 1873. Photograph by Rufus Morgan. NCC.

at the Wana Luna Golf Club, North Carolina's first organized golf club. The hotel and grounds were leased to the United States during World War I at the rate of $1,500 per month. The government converted the hotel, its grounds, and the golf course into a civilian internment camp for German merchant marines. The internees passed the time by constructing a village reminiscent of their Bavarian homes, participating in a band, and building a fully operational carousel, complete with a scene of German merchant ships plying the Atlantic. The structures built by the Germans at Hot Springs were blown up by guards in celebration of the signing of the armistice, and

the Mountain Park Hotel was destroyed by an arsonist in the early 1920s, never to be rebuilt.

The rare geologic features that led to the founding of Hot Springs by early white Americans also drew Native Americans in an earlier time. Prior to discovery by white settlers in the late 1700s, the area was significant in Cherokee Indian culture not only for the rare warm mineral springs but for outcroppings of rock along the banks of the French Broad River. Only a short distance upriver from Hot Springs is a high rock outcropping that commands views of the entire town and surrounding valley. Located in the Pisgah National Forest and on the Appalachian Trail system, the rock outcropping is known as "Lover's Leap." It is there that a Cherokee maiden named Mist-on-the-Mountain, a daughter of Lone Wolf, is purported to have leapt to her death upon hearing the news of the death of her lover Magwa at the hands of the jealous brave Tall Pine, who was soon thereafter killed by a panther.

Only a few miles downstream from Hot Springs is another significant rock outcropping known as Paint Rock, which is only yards away from North Carolina's border with Tennessee. Paint Rock, like Lover's Leap, appears to have been significant in Cherokee culture. Its name is derived from figures painted on the rock face (by Cherokee Indians, early settlers believed), which are now almost indiscernible. Paint Rock was the site of a blockhouse used to protect settlers from Indians and was the location of the former town of Paint Rock, which was incorporated for a brief period in the late 1800s.

While the springs were reopened in the 1980s, Hot Springs is no longer a resort destination; it remains a small community surrounded by a national forest, attracting tourists and campers.

References: Della Hazel Moore, *Hot Springs of North Carolina* (1992); Mary Ellen Wolcott, "Zeb Vance Once Clerked in Hotel in Hot Springs," *Asheville Citizen-Times*, 21 Jan. 1965.

H. G. Jones
David K. Davis

House in the Horseshoe (the Alston House) is located in a "horseshoe" bend of the Deep River in Moore County. Phillip Alston (1745–91) built the house in 1772, and it was one of the first "big" houses in the North Carolina backcountry.

Back door of the Alston House. Note the bullet holes around the door. Courtesy of NCOA&H.

Alston was a colonel in the Whig militia during the American Revolution. On 29 July or 5 Aug. 1781 (the evidence is unclear) a skirmish took place at the house involving Alston's militia and the Tory militia commanded by David Fanning. Numerous bullet holes from this encounter are still visible in the exterior of the house. In 1798 the house and surrounding plantation were acquired by Benjamin Williams, who had served as a colonel under George Washington. A year after buying the plantation he became governor. In addition to serving four one-year terms in that office, Williams was a member of the first Board of Trustees of the University of North Carolina and served in the U.S. Congress in Philadelphia.

In 1954 the Moore County Historical Association purchased the house, outbuildings, and 4.2 acres of land. The next year the state assumed jurisdiction over the property. With local cooperation, the house was restored and more of the surrounding land was purchased. In 1971 the House in the Horseshoe was designated a North Carolina State Historic Site, which by 2005 featured, in addition to the Alston House, a visitors center, outdoor exhibits and monuments, picnic facilities, and a gift shop. Craft demonstrations and reenactments of the famous skirmish are also held at the site.

References: Richard F. Knapp, ed., *North Carolina's State Historic Sites: A Brief History and Status Report* (1995); Stephen E. Massengill, "The House in the Horseshoe," *Research Reports*, Ser. 1, No. 31 (1973); Blackwell P. Robinson, *History of Moore County, North Carolina, 1747–1847* (1956).

William H. Thompson Jr.

Hue and Cry was a term used in English criminal law as early as 1275 and commonly applied in colonial North Carolina. Any person aware of a robbery or felony was required to raise a hue and cry "with horn and voice" to create an alarm for the pursuit and capture of the criminal. The person raising the alarm was expected to describe the offender and tell which way he or she had gone. The constable in the adjoining precinct was to take up the chase, and so on, "till the Offender is apprehended, or pursued to the Sea Side." Goods retaken from thieves were to remain in the custody of the officers who apprehended them "till Restitution is awarded by the Justices."

An example of hue and cry occurred on 9 Oct. 1697, when the provost marshal or his deputy was ordered to search for John Griffen "and to make hue and cry after him from place to place and him being found to apprehend and safely to convey [him] to the provost marshall." Full provisions of hue and cry were set forth in *The Office and Authority of a Justice of Peace*, published in New Bern in 1774 by James Davis, the provincial printer. The system was not always successful, however. In March 1721 the marshal informed the court that he "had pursued [a felon] by Hue and Cry to the Uttmost Limitts of the Government and that he could not be taken within the Same," so the case was dismissed. Even so, in the absence of a faster means of pursuing criminals, the North Carolina Assembly in 1749 reenacted the statute of 17 Elizabeth (1585) concerning the hue and cry law.

References: Mattie Erma Edwards Parker, ed., *North Carolina Higher-Court Records, 1697–1701* (1971); William S. Price Jr., ed., *North Carolina Higher-Court Minutes, 1709–1723* (1977); Price, ed., *North Carolina Higher-Court Records, 1702–1708* (1974).

William S. Powell

Huguenots, persecuted French Protestants, first came to North Carolina around 1690, when a small group settled near the head of the Pamlico Sound at the point where the Tar River widens into the sound just west of Bath. Other French Protestants settled in Bath during the first decade of the eighteenth century, but there is little information on these early settlements. Another group of Huguenots migrated to the Trent River about 1707 from Mannakin Town, a settlement on the James River near present-day Richmond, Va. The Trent River settlement was founded by a French nobleman, Philippe de Richebourg, one of three ministers who had immigrated with other Huguenots to Virginia in 1699–1700.

The original founders of Mannakin—Daniel Coxe, an Englishman, and two Huguenots, the Marquis de la Muce and Charles de Sailly—had planned to sell some of Coxe's land along the North Carolina border to the French settlers. The Virginia Council, however, directed the settlers to colonize land near the falls of the James River and created King William Parish. By 1707 dissension had developed in the parish between Huguenot and English colonists. In that year de Richebourg first petitioned for a separate Huguenot parish and then later led a large part of the Huguenot group south. After leading Huguenots to North Carolina, de Richebourg himself joined another Huguenot colony, St. James Santee, in South Carolina. Early descriptions of the French Huguenot settlements in North Carolina come from the journal of explorer and surveyor John Lawson, *A New Voyage to Carolina* (1709).

Although Huguenots resided in 10 of the original 13 colonies, the number who came to this country was not large. Their absolute numbers were belied, however, by their considerable influence in shaping the new nation where their descendants played an important role in molding attitudes on such important areas of public interest as religious freedom, individual rights and liberties, scholarship, education, and representative government. John Adams, John Hancock, Thomas Jefferson, Paul Revere, and George Washington are but a few of the Huguenot descendants who contributed to the founding of the United States.

A number of early Huguenot settlers are represented by their direct descendants in the Huguenot Society of North Carolina, which was organized in Raleigh on 17 Oct. 1938 as a branch of the Founders of Mannakin in the Colony of Virginia. Mrs. James B. James of Greenville, who helped organize the society, served as the first president and arranged for Governor Clyde R. Hoey to be the speaker at the first annual assembly, held in March 1939 at the Sir Walter Hotel in Raleigh. The Huguenot Society remains an active organization dedicated to perpetuating the memory and preserving the principles and virtues of the Huguenots, commemorating the great events of Huguenot history, and collecting and preserving data and relics illustrative of that history. The society has designated the North Carolina Office of Archives and History as its archival repository.

References: Charles Washington Baird, *History of the Huguenot Emigration to America* (1973); Jon Butler, *The Huguenots in America: A Refugee People in New World Society* (1983); Jane Hawkes Liddell, "Why Huguenots Flocked to the Carolinas," in Peter Steven Gannon, ed., *Huguenot Refugees in the Settling of Colonial America* (1985); George A. Rothrock, *The Huguenots: A Biography of a Minority* (1979).

Carolyn Sparks Whittenburg
W. Keats Sparrow

Humor has played a distinctive role in the lives of North Carolinians from the days of the earliest British explorations to the region. As much as any other aspect of human life, humor can be considered a window into cultures and peoples that have long since disappeared. U.S. senator Sam J. Ervin Jr., an insightful student of North Carolina humor, summarized the state's affinity for the lighter side of life in a speech to members of the North Carolina Literary and Historical Association: "North Carolinians have always loved to laugh. Their own merry hearts and the many humorists abiding among them have always enabled them to indulge this love."

North Carolina humor has been mined from all levels of the human condition, from the most powerful offices of government to the simple lives of poor farmers and tradesmen. Folk humor, by both blacks and whites, has been conveyed between generations primarily through oral means. It is rooted in the mundane details of life, such as work, family, community, religion, and getting along (or not getting along) with one's neighbors.

Englishman John Lawson, after visiting the young colony in 1701, described many amusing sights and experiences in *A New Voyage to Carolina* (1709). His frank, often witty observations concerning the native culture and animals, as well as the Europeans' interaction with local Indians, stand as the first written examples of North Carolina humor. Lawson observed, for example, that "most of the Savages are much addicted to Drunkenness, a Vice they never were acquainted with, till the Christians came amongst them." Such biting humor appears throughout *A New Voyage to Carolina*, making it an insightful and entertaining work for modern readers.

Humor has a way of connecting a generation with its predecessors, whose sophistication the modern mind may tend to underestimate. It may surprise contemporary North Carolinians that the state's first century left many examples of "verbal play" that are often more subtle and urbane than what passes as first-rate humor today. In addition, coarse, raw humor is not a modern invention: shocking and ridiculing people has always been the humorist's fertile ground. Ham Jones, a graduate of the University of North Carolina, became acclaimed for his "Cousin Sally Dilliard" sketches that poked intuitive fun at southern life and culture—particularly its court system (Jones was a lawyer by trade). Charles Napoleon Bonaparte Evans, the editor of the *Milton Chronicle* in Caswell County from 1841 until his death in 1883, found fame through his "Fool Killer" letters, which were allegedly written by a man wielding a club with which he threatened or actually brained those he found annoying or deserving of his wrath. Only five of these brutally hilarious letters remain.

Other nineteenth-century humor exists in the form of news items that strike the modern reader as absurdly funny. The *Carteret County Telephone* (7 Apr. 1882) ran this important news item: "LOCAL. While whittling with his axe, William Weekly chopped off his entire little finger. No trace of the finger has been found and it is assumed that one of his chickens got it."

Zebulon Baird Vance, North Carolina's Civil War governor and later a U.S. senator, was one of the state's most influential figures as well as a seemingly endless source of humorous retorts and observations. His brilliant wit, rooted in a salt-of-the-earth intellect that came from his Buncombe County upbringing, was known throughout the nation. Perhaps the most famous one-liner in North Carolina history—"What did the governor of North Carolina say to the governor of South Carolina? 'It's a damn long time between drinks'"—has even been attributed to him by some historians. Whether or not this was his line, Vance left more than his share of memorable and amusing witticisms.

In the twentieth century, the works of author Thomas Wolfe and playwright Paul Green, although serious art, were nevertheless laced with much humor and wit. Writer and newspaper editor Harry Golden, who moved from New York City to Charlotte in 1941, took on such vital issues as race relations and civil rights with his brand of broad humor. Contemporary author David Sedaris, in his books, on public radio, and onstage, has entertained audiences with stories of his North Carolina childhood in Raleigh.

References: Sam J. Ervin Jr., "Humor, Wise and Otherwise," *NCHR* 59 (April 1982); F. Roy Johnson, *Oral Folk Humor from the Carolina and Virginia Flatlands* (1980); Loyal Jones and Billy Edd Wheeler, *Laughter in Appalachia: A Festival of Southern Mountain Humor* (1987); Charles O. Pitts Jr., ed., *Carteret Fish 'N' Chips: Nineteenth Century Newspaper Humor* (1988); Richard Walser, ed., *Tar Heel Laughter* (1974).

Jay Mazzocchi

SEE ALSO *Carolina Israelite;* "Fool-Killer."

Hunting in North Carolina is a popular and economically significant recreational activity as well as an important focus of the state's governmental agencies in charge of wildlife preservation and control. There are between 300,000 and 400,000 licensed hunters in North Carolina at any one time, generating more than $400 million of sales revenues and taxes in the state each year. It is estimated that outdoor sports activities such as hunting and fishing create 35,000 jobs in the state. A large number of programs and workshops are offered by the North Carolina Wildlife Resources Commission to educate both novice and experienced hunters. While hunting is an activity often shared between generations and connected to both cultural tradition and respect for the state's wildlife populations, it may also be seen as a statistically dangerous sport. Between 1990 and 2004, 61 people were killed and 479 injured as a result of hunting-related accidents.

North Carolina's first European settlers brought their hunting experience with them, including, for the upper classes, a love of fox hunting with hounds. The Native Americans whom the settlers encountered were likewise hunters. At that time, the land was rich in buffalo, elk, deer, bear, rabbit, squirrel, beaver, raccoon, opossum, wild turkey, partridge, and pigeons. In time, with more hunters seeking food or recreation or both, game laws were introduced in the colonial period and were continued by the state following the American Revolution. Until 1903, however, there was no statewide governmental organization to protect wildlife. In that year the General Assembly provided partial state funding to the Audubon Society of North Carolina, which also received "state-like" authority to enforce laws and protect wild birds and animals.

The Audubon Society had only limited success, and in 1927 the legislature ended the arrangement with this private organization and transferred its functions to the office of game warden and to the new State Game Commission. Eventually the powers and duties of this commission, along with the office of game warden, came under the control of the Department of Conservation and Development. That department, created in 1925 to replace the State Geological and Economic Survey (which in this act was abolished), and its Board of Conservation and Development, had been established to consolidate all agencies involved in the conservation and development of the state's resources.

In 1947 the General Assembly established the North Carolina Wildlife Resources Commission as a separate, semi-

Rabbit hunters pose with their game in Chatham County, ca. 1901. NCC.

autonomous agency to manage, protect, regulate, and restore the state's wildlife resources and to administer all applicable laws. The commission absorbed the corresponding functions of all agencies that had previously dealt with wildlife conservation and restoration. In 1997 the Wildlife Resources Commission became a part of the Department of Environment and Natural Resources. It is responsible for the sale of hunting and fishing licenses to residents and nonresidents, setting and implementing qualifications for its agents, promoting boating safety, and the preservation of endangered species in consonance with the federal Endangered Species Act of 1973 as amended. The commission also conducts an extensive environmental education program for school-age children. Its official publication, *Wildlife in North Carolina*, begun in 1937, is dedicated "to the sound conservation of North Carolina's wildlife and other interrelated natural resources and also to the environment we share with them." Each year its September issue includes "North Carolina Hunting Season," a summary of the dates of the hunting season and daily and season limits for each species (dove, deer, black bear, and so forth).

Most of the over 1.8 million acres of public hunting grounds in North Carolina is available for hunting during open seasons by those with Game Lands Use Licenses. Special additional permits may also be required due to quotas in areas with a history of heavy use, for specific hunting methods such as trapping, or because of careful game management, particularly with turkey, waterfowl, deer, and small game. For example, 5,000 permits are granted annually for hunting of the tundra swan (North Carolina has the largest winter swan population on the East Coast). Although squirrels, rabbits, doves, and waterfowl are very popular game animals in the state, deer are by far the most hunted. Other large game animals frequently hunted include wild boar and black bear, whose numbers are higher in North Carolina than in any other southeastern state.

Various hunting seasons extend throughout much of the year, though hunting is not permitted on Sundays except on certain federal military installations. Bear season generally runs from mid-October through late November or the end of December, with certain counties and regions having variations in the dates. Boar season runs for about a month during October and November and likewise closes out the month of December. Wild turkey may be provisionally hunted for about a month between April and May, select counties allowing a few days of hunting around January. Deer season varies based on location and type of hunting (bow and arrow, muzzle-loading weapon, or gun), but any hunting of the species generally be-

A duck hunter crouches inside a blind at Currituck, 1944.
Courtesy of NCOA&H.

gins in mid-September and typically ends by the end of December.

References: Lawrence S. Earley, *The Crisis in Habitat: Protecting Wildlife's Future in North Carolina* (1985); North Carolina Wildlife Resources Commission, *North Carolina Inland Fishing, Hunting, and Trapping Regulations* (selected years).

Wiley J. Williams
Additional research provided by Laura Hegyi.

SEE ALSO Waterfowl.

Huron, USS. The USS *Huron* remains one of the most famous shipwrecks in North Carolina's "Graveyard of the Atlantic." A man-of-war steamer, the *Huron* ran aground off Nags Head in the early morning hours of 24 Nov. 1877 while on a routine survey expedition from New York to the Caribbean via Key West. A failure to adjust course to account for a slight eastward curve of the coastline caused the 541-ton, steam-powered ship to ground on a reef just off the beach. High seas broke apart the barkentine-rigged vessel over the course of the predawn hours. Of 16 officers aboard only 4 survived, and 85 of 115 crewmen perished.

The wreck happened just two miles from one of seven lifesaving stations erected on the Outer Banks in 1874, but it oc-

curred after the lifesaving season of the summer and fall had ended; observers on the beach could do little more than watch the *Huron*'s destruction. Mourned nationally, the tragedy led to reforms in the U.S. Lifesaving Service, including extension of the lifesaving patrol season and construction of additional lifesaving stations along North Carolina's coast and elsewhere. The remains of the vessel lie submerged off Nags Head.

References: Joe A. Mobley, *Ship Ashore!: The U.S. Lifesavers of Coastal North Carolina* (1994); David Stick, *Graveyard of the Atlantic: Shipwrecks of the North Carolina Coast* (1952).

Kathy Carter

Hurricanes are the most spectacular and destructive weather events experienced in North Carolina. Commonly formed off the coast of Africa over the warm tropical waters of the Atlantic Ocean, embryonic hurricanes drift westward across the ocean, slowly drawing energy and moisture from the warm waters. If the storm continues to gain strength, as is typical when it approaches the Caribbean Basin, winds may exceed 74 miles per hour, the threshold for a hurricane. Hurricanes are divided by size and wind speed into five numerical categories, with a category five hurricane being the most intense. Generally, as hurricanes move away from the warm tropics and into the cooler mid-latitudes, they lose energy so that windspeeds slowly decrease. Consequently, many hurricanes will have passed their peak by the time they reach North Carolina. Also, because hurricanes tend to weaken once they move inland, those coming in from the coast may initially be severe, but may rapidly lose power as they track inland. Nevertheless, a number of category four hurricanes have crossed into North Carolina over the past 100 years, and North Carolinians are well aware of the devastating force and impact that hurricanes have had on the state.

Hurricanes in Colonial and Nineteenth-Century North Carolina

Geological evidence along the Outer Banks clearly shows that hurricanes have, for centuries, been frequent visitors to the state. The first severe storm recorded in North Carolina took place on 6 Sept. 1667, when strong winds and rain struck the Outer Banks, destroying corn and tobacco crops and demolishing some buildings. More detailed accounts from Virginia tell of the 12 days of rain that accompanied this storm. Later, in the mid-eighteenth century, severe storms along the North Carolina coast destroyed ships and flooded coastal towns. In one such storm in 1752, the town of Johnston, then the Onslow County seat, built in an area known today as Old Town Point (part of present-day Camp Lejeune), was completely destroyed, as were all of the county's records and deeds. Highly detailed reports of a hurricane that hit North Carolina in September 1769 tell of great destruction in the region from Smithville (present-day Southport) through New Bern. During this storm, the Brunswick County Courthouse was reportedly blown down, and the tide in New Bern rose 12 feet higher than average. Other hurricanes hit the New Bern area again in 1803, 1815, 1821, and 1825. Two major hurricanes in 1842 resulted in the famous "wet year" that saw massive destruction of homes, businesses, and crops. Throughout the nineteenth century, storm damage repeatedly affected areas of the North Carolina coast and sometimes inland as far as Winston-Salem.

In 1896 and 1899, two great hurricanes unleashed their full fury on Shackleford Banks. Most of the residents of Diamond City—the most populous of the five communities that developed on this nine-mile-long strip of the Outer Banks during the eighteenth and nineteenth centuries—had weathered many hurricanes, but these two storms were unlike any that had struck before. After the first of the storms sent seawater into gardens and homes, residents began to discuss openly the possibility of leaving the island. Several families moved, but most decided to stay.

The hurricane that slammed into the central coast of North Carolina in August 1899 was one of the worst ever to hit the area. It produced a storm surge that inundated everything on the island, save the tops of a few of the taller sand dunes. When the great storm waters subsided, Diamond City was a scene of utter devastation: the giant dune that ran through the village was gone; countless homes were either destroyed, washed away, or badly damaged; gardens, fruit trees, and other vegetation were covered with sand and salt water; sheep, horses, cattle, and other livestock had vanished; wells were laced with salt water; and cemeteries revealed uncovered caskets and human bones.

Twentieth-Century Hurricanes

The first severe hurricane of the twentieth century to move across the North Carolina coast was a category three that passed near Hatteras on 13 Nov. 1904. The hurricane brought high tides and heavy rains, and a number of people drowned at New Inlet as a result of the storm surge. In September 1913, a short-lived but intense hurricane crossed over Core Banks into Pamlico Sound. The flooding that resulted in New Bern and Washington damaged crops, homes, and businesses. Reports of extreme damage came from Goldsboro, Tarboro, Wilson, Farmville, and Durham. In total, five lives were lost and an estimated $3 million worth of damage was done. In 1933 North Carolina was hit by two hurricanes in a single season. The first came on 22 August, producing high tides along the Outer Banks and causing crop damage as far inland as Granville County. The second, less than one month later, devastated the coastal cities, leaving 21 dead and damages of over $3 million. A Red Cross survey indicated that 1,166 buildings had been totally destroyed and 7,244 severely damaged.

In 1944 North Carolina once again felt the effects of two hurricanes. The first, a category one, hit Southport on 1 August and brought winds of 80 miles per hour to Oak Island. The most extensive damage occurred at Carolina Beach, where 30-foot waves destroyed the town's boardwalk and a large number of beachfront homes. The total damage from the storm was in excess of $2 million. The second hurricane to hit, the Great Atlantic Hurricane of 1944, neared the Outer Banks on 14 September and passed just east of Cape Hatteras on its way to careening into Long Island, N.Y. While the eye of the hurricane remained offshore, sparing North Carolina's coast a direct hit, serious flooding took place in Avon, and high winds caused extensive damage in Elizabeth City and in the Nags Head area. While only one North Carolinian was killed as a result of the hurricane, the storm took nearly 400 lives as it tracked along the Atlantic Coast.

The second half of the twentieth century saw a number of highly destructive hurricanes wreak havoc in North Carolina. The National Weather Service began naming hurricanes after World War II. In the years 1953 to 1955 alone, seven hurricanes struck the state, one of which, Hazel, has been hailed as one of the worst natural disasters in the state's history. Sweeping inland near the North Carolina–South Carolina border on 15 Oct. 1954, Hazel brought with it winds of up to 150 miles per hour and massive storm surges that flooded the southern beaches. Barreling through the state, Hazel not only demolished buildings and bridges along the coast, but also brought destructive winds and rain in cities such as Wallace (Duplin County) and Parkton (Robeson County). In the city of Raleigh, it was reported that an average of two or three trees per block fell. Perhaps the most destructive hurricane in North Carolina history, Hazel took the lives of 19 people and injured over 200. Fifteen thousand homes and structures were destroyed, 39,000 structures were damaged, and a total of 30 counties received major damage. In all, Hazel caused approximately $136 million in property losses.

Following Hazel, North Carolina was hit by a string of hurricanes throughout the remainder of the 1950s. Hurricane Connie, a category three storm that swept along the North Carolina coast on 12 Aug. 1955, caused large amounts of flooding in the eastern counties. Hurricane Diane swept right through the middle of North Carolina just five days after Connie had hit the coast. Coupled with the large amounts of water left by the earlier storm, Diane furthered the extensive flooding that was occurring along the coast, and, when it swept across the middle of the state, began to produce record amounts of rainfall in the northeastern region of the state. Combined, Connie and Diane accounted for over $80 million in damages in North Carolina.

In September of that year, yet another hurricane struck the state. Hurricane Ione struck the coast just west of Atlantic Beach and brought with it massive amounts of rain that flooded the eastern counties. Nine North Carolinians were killed as a result of the storm, and an estimated $90 million worth of damages was done. In 1960, closing out a decade of destruction for North Carolina, the state became a victim of Hurricane Donna. Hitting on 11 September, Donna was responsible for extensive damage to coastal communities such as Atlantic Beach, Morehead City, and Beaufort. In addition, strong winds moved inland, causing destruction in Goldsboro, Kinston, and Greenville. In the end, Donna was responsible for eight deaths in North Carolina.

From a meteorological standpoint, the 1960s proved to be a peaceful time in the coastal region, with no serious hurricane damage. Even in 1971, when Hurricane Ginger struck the state in late September, the storm lacked the intensity of the hurricanes that had torn through the state in the 1950s. In 1972 Hurricane Agnes swept across the interior of the state, causing damage primarily in the eastern part of the Blue Ridge Mountains. After Agnes, a period of seven years passed before Hurricane David struck the state, following its predecessor's path through the Piedmont region. Fortunately, there were no deaths in North Carolina as a result of the storm. The 1980s saw four major hurricanes sweep through the state: Diana in 1984, Gloria in 1985, Charley in 1986, and Hugo in 1989. Of these, Hugo, a category four hurricane, was by far the most devastating to the state. After first coming inland near Charleston, S.C., Hugo blasted its way up to North Carolina, swerving through Charlotte and Hickory. In Charlotte, strong winds ripped trees from the soil, and forests were destroyed throughout the state; the timber losses alone were valued at $250 million. Overall, Hugo was responsible for seven deaths in North Carolina and cost the state an estimated $1 billion.

Devastating Hurricanes of the 1990s and Early 2000s

In the 1990s, North Carolina experienced another decade marred by powerful hurricanes and destruction throughout the state. The first of the storms to strike the state was Hurricane Emily, a category three that hit Hatteras Island on 31 Aug. 1993. While no lives were lost during the storm, an estimated $13 million of damage was done to the 17-mile stretch that absorbed the brunt of the hurricane force. Three years after Emily hit Hatteras Island, another storm, Bertha, struck the coast in July. The worst of the storm was focused on Topsail Island, and a number of homes were destroyed there. In the eastern counties as a whole, a tremendous amount of overall damage was caused by the storm, with surveys indicating that more than 1,100 homes were destroyed and another 4,000 damaged.

Just a few months after Bertha hit the coast in 1996, North Carolina suffered another, more devastating blow. Hurricane Fran was an enormous, category three storm that carved a destructive path through the center of the state, starting in the southeastern corner and continuing deep inland as far as the Raleigh-Durham-Chapel Hill area. Strong winds and heavy flooding affected much of the state, 24 deaths were reported, and damages were estimated at $5 billion. In 1998 North Carolina was hit again, this time by Hurricane Bonnie, a category two storm that hit Onslow County on 27 August. While floods and heavy rainfall affected some of the eastern part of the state, Bonnie was relatively calm when compared to earlier storms such as Fran. Still, Bonnie was responsible for a few deaths and economic losses estimated at $480 million.

The year 1999 proved to be significant in North Carolina hurricane history. In late August, the state was struck by Hurricane Dennis, a meandering storm that fluctuated between category two strength and tropical storm classification. While not a particularly strong storm, Dennis caused extensive damage to crops and homes in the coastal region of the state. Just two weeks after Dennis first came ashore, Hurricane Floyd began to tear through North Carolina. Touching down at Cape Fear on 16 Sept. 1999, Floyd was a category four storm that would overshadow Hurricane Fran as the state's most devastating disaster in recent memory. After moving along the New Hanover shoreline, Floyd moved inland, crossing over Pender and Onslow Counties. Eventually, Floyd passed over New Bern and Washington as well. While damage was done by wind and the tides that Floyd brought with it, the real danger was a result of the enormous amounts of rainfall that accumulated and eventually flooded a vast majority of the coastal region. In all, a total of 63,000 houses were flooded and 7,300 homes destroyed. In North Carolina alone, 66 counties were declared disaster areas, damages totaled between $5.5 and $6 billion, and the storm claimed a devastating 52 lives.

In September 2003 Hurricane Isabel, a category two storm, cut through North Carolina and other states, causing massive destruction to crops and property and taking 38 lives. North Carolina agricultural concerns were particularly hurt, with more than $152 million in damage caused to crops as well as farm structures and equipment. On 3 Aug. 2004 the center of Hurricane Alex, a category two storm, came within ten miles of the Outer Banks, hitting Hatteras and Ocracoke Island the hardest and causing $5 million in flood and wind damage, $2.4 million of that in Dare County. Hurricane Ivan, which made landfall in Alabama in September 2004, passed over the western portion of North Carolina, leading to eight deaths and causing flood damage to many roads, including the Blue Ridge Parkway and part of Interstate 40 in Haywood County.

Reference: Jay Barnes, *North Carolina's Hurricane History* (3rd ed., 2001).

Peter J. Robinson
Additional research provided by Daniel W. Barefoot, Charles Battle, and Laura Hegyi.

SEE ALSO Wet Year.

Hush Puppies in North Carolina and other southern states are pieces of deep-fried cornbread that may contain egg, leavening, salt, pepper, onion, sugar, or wheat flour. Elsewhere, the term can also signify a cornmeal dumpling, a piece of baked cornbread, a hash patty, white gravy, or a salsa-like relish. Most hush puppies are spheroids formed by dropping a ball of batter into hot fat, but some cooks shape their hush puppies. A popular explanation of how the dish was invented and named is that fishermen in earlier times used hush puppies to quiet their hungry, yelping dogs.

However they originated, hush puppies are a quintessential southern food. The name is English; the main ingredient, native; the method of cooking, West African. Lacking palm oil, slaves and their descendants preserved the ancient tradition of deep-frying by using lard and whatever else was on hand, including surplus cornbread batter. The hush puppy is thus a descendant of the Nigerian *acara*, made of black-eyed peas, and related to Brazilian *acarajé*, Caribbean *acras*, and Creole *calas*. It is also an ancestor of the large, sweet midwestern corn fritter, which often contains kernels of corn and is sometimes served with condiments such as blueberry syrup. Hush puppies are usually served with fried seafood and are a typical accompaniment to barbecue and Brunswick stew.

References: Marion Brown, *Marion Brown's Southern Cookbook* (1968); John Egerton, *Southern Food: At Home, on the Road, in History* (1987).

Wynne Dough

Hyde County, located in North Carolina's Coastal Plain region, was formed from Bath County in 1705. The area was originally inhabited by various Algonquian Indian tribes. The precinct of Wickham, as it was then known, was renamed Hyde in 1712 (taking its name from Lord Proprietor Edward Hyde) and became Hyde County in 1739. Over the course of the following century, the county seat was relocated from Woodstock to Bell's Bay (or Jasper's Creek) to Germantown to Lake Landing to Swan Quarter (settled ca. 1836), where it is today. Other communities in the sparsely populated county include Engelhard, Fairfield, Ocracoke, Sladesville, Panzer, Scranton, Beulah, New Holland, Nebraska, Gull Rock, and Newlands.

The islands and inlets of Hyde County greeted European explorers from the early sixteenth century through the seventeenth, as colonies were first established in the New World. For a time, particularly in the early eighteenth century, the region's port communities and sea vessels were terrorized by pirate raids, including those led by the notorious Blackbeard. In 1845 Ocracoke Island—which, up until that point, had been part of Carteret County—was annexed to Hyde County. Today the island is part of the Cape Hatteras National Seashore.

During the early 1900s, a massive land reclamation and drainage project was undertaken at Lake Mattamuskeet (North Carolina's largest natural lake) in order to pump fresh water from the lakebed out into the Pamlico Sound. With public funds and investments from private individuals (who organized themselves as the Southern Land Reclamation Company), canals were dredged and a pumping plant was built to house the largest centrifugal pumps ever designed. Plans to develop the newly drained lakebed were abandoned, however, and the area instead became a national wildlife refuge. Canals were again dredged through the mainland in the 1920s for the creation of the Intracoastal Waterway. The heretofore isolated Ocracoke Island, meanwhile, began to emerge as a tourist destination with the establishment of a ferry system in the late 1950s.

Other Hyde County natural and cultural attractions include the Swanquarter National Wildlife Refuge, the Ocracoke Lighthouse (1823), and the Ocracoke Museum. Festivals such as Hyde County Farm Days, Swan Days, and the Fairfield Heritage Bass Tournament are held annually in the county. The estimated population of Hyde County in 2004 was 5,600.

References: Morgan H. Harris, *Hyde Yesterdays: A History of Hyde County* (1995); *Hyde County History: A Hyde County Bicentennial Project* (1976).

Robert Blair Vocci

Hymnody. The singing of hymns has long been an integral part of the lives of many North Carolinians. During the colonial period, two denominations, the Anglicans and the Moravians, brought distinctive collections of hymns to North Carolina. The hymns of the Anglican Church were English hymns transplanted to American shores. Following the break with England, this denomination became the Protestant Episcopal Church, but the core of Episcopal hymns remained English. The Moravians, who settled in the Piedmont, were devoted to the singing of hymns with roots in Germany and Eastern Europe. They held *Singstunden*, services completely devoted to hymn singing, and enhanced their singing with instrumental accompaniments ranging from organ to orchestra.

Following the American Revolution, evangelical hymnody, developed by John Wesley, spread throughout the new nation. Wesley, the father of Methodism, believed that hymns could contribute to an individual's personal salvation experience. A well-written text wedded to a simple tune could offer an individual more theology than a lengthy sermon. The Methodist Episcopal Church spread into the Carolinas by the early 1800s and brought with it the fervent hymn singing authorized by Wesley. Participants sang hymns both in the church and at a new phenomenon, the camp meeting. Born of Methodist revivalism upon the frontier, the camp meeting offered the devoted and the lost, both black and white, the chance to hear preaching and to learn and sing hymns. Through camp meetings, revival hymns spread from congregation to congregation.

The singing schools that arose in the nineteenth century provided opportunities to learn hymns. Periodically a singing master arrived in a region and taught hymns to interested members of a community using shape-note songbooks, which provided easy singing instruction for those who could not read music. Singing schools were enjoyed by many for the pleasure of singing hymns, as well as for the pleasure of courtship and other similar social benefits. All-day hymn singings were an outgrowth of the singing schools, a practice that continues in a few communities.

The singing of hymns permeates religious life today in North Carolina. Hymns remain the central musical offering of church services, and they accompany events such as baptisms, weddings, foot washings, revivals, communions, funerals, and decoration days. Instrumental accompaniments to hymns range from organ and piano to electric guitar and tam-bourine, although two denominations, the Primitive Baptists and the Church of Christ, forbid the use of musical instruments. A blending of hymn traditions exists as well. The revival hymn "Amazing Grace," for instance, is sung by members of the Pentecostal Holiness Church as well as members of the Episcopal and Roman Catholic Churches. Black spirituals are sung now by a number of white congregations. The Cherokee, as they adopted Christianity, adopted its hymns.

Reference: Robert Stevenson, *Protestant Church Music in America* (1966).

Margaret Foote

SEE ALSO Gospel Music; Moravian Music; Shape-Note Singing.

I

IBM. SEE Information Technology; Research Triangle Park.

Iceberg. On 30 Jan. 1940 an iceberg as large as a small island and extending six feet above the surface of the water was sighted in the Atlantic Ocean off Salter Path on Bogue Banks (Carteret County). Local resident Rufus Sewell, who had previously made several trips to the Arctic, stated that if the visible ice was six feet above the water, approximately 50 feet of ice was beneath the water. The iceberg was drifting westward.

William S. Powell

Iced Tea, lovingly nicknamed the "Table Wine of the South," is the quintessential southern beverage, enjoyed by North Carolinians and other southerners year-round and served in virtually every restaurant and home as well as at all social events. In North Carolina, those ordering iced tea at a restaurant will usually receive "sweet tea," an extremely sugary version of the beverage, unless they specifically request unsweetened tea. Iced tea in northern states is almost always served unsweetened.

Tea was cultivated in China more than 2,000 years ago, spreading to Japan in about A.D. 800 and shortly thereafter to the West by way of the Persian caravans. Tea arrived in England about 1653 and quickly became the national drink in place of ale. It was the drink of the nobility, which assured its popularity. The East India Company began importing it directly from China by 1689 and held a monopoly on the tea trade from 1721 until 1833.

In 1670 English colonists in Boston began drinking tea, although it was not sold to the public until about 1690. It became a trade commodity between the colonies and England by 1720. A mass meeting in Edenton on 22 Aug. 1774 was held in protest of taxes imposed on tea by the Boston Port Act. Following this meeting, a group of ladies from Edenton joined the protests, and their "Edenton Tea Party" of 25 Oct. 1774 led to a declaration of unity against using British imports, including tea.

Following the American Revolution in 1789, America began trading directly with China, and the drinking of tea in America resumed. Tea began to be grown in Charleston, S.C.; this remains the only tea grown in the United States. Most tea continues to be imported from Asia and India. The introduction of iced tea in the United States followed the St. Louis World's Fair in 1904, at which it was first served during a heat wave. Following World War II, iced tea became a culinary fixture in the South. Many native North Carolinians recall the childhood task of breaking up the block of ice from the ice box to cool their summer tea.

References: Hugh T. Lefler, ed., *North Carolina History Told by Contemporaries* (3rd ed., 1956); Jill Norman and Gwen Edmonds, *Teas and Tisanes: Everyday and Unusual Teas and Tisanes and Dishes Flavored with Them* (1989).

Nayda Swonger Colomb

Ice Hockey, popular in northern states for decades, took many years to take hold in the sports landscape of North Carolina. Hockey first skated into the state in 1957 with the expansion of the Eastern Hockey League to Greensboro and Charlotte. Carson Bain and Stanley Frank paid $2,500 for their expansion team, the Greensboro Generals, which had previously been based in Troy, Ohio. About a dozen local citizens owned 75 percent of the original Greensboro club. Hockey started in Charlotte when the Baltimore Clippers came to town and became the Checkers. The team continued there until 1977, when the Eastern Hockey League folded.

For 11 years after that, hockey seemed to have died in North Carolina. In 1988, however, the newly formed East Coast Hockey League (ECHL), headquartered in Charlotte, established a team in Winston-Salem known as the Carolina Thunderbirds. The ECHL consisted of 21 teams when it first opened, spanning the East Coast from Pennsylvania to Florida. North

Game four of the Stanley Cup finals between the Carolina Hurricanes and the Detroit Red Wings in Raleigh, 10 June 2002. Photograph by Kevin Seifert. *Durham Herald-Sun.*

Carolina's ECHL team in 2005 was the latest incarnation of the Charlotte Checkers, who won the league championship Jack Riley Cup in 1996 and have consistently been a national leader in minor league hockey attendance.

The Raleigh Ice Caps were a successful ECHL franchise from 1991 to 1998. The relocating of the National Hockey League's Hartford Whalers to Raleigh in 1997—where the franchise became the Carolina Hurricanes—resulted in the end of the Ice Caps and the birth of hockey at its highest level in the state. For the first two years, the Hurricanes played in Greensboro while a new arena in Raleigh was being built. After a few difficult years with modest achievements on the ice and low attendance, the team began to find success. The Hurricanes reached the Stanley Cup finals in 2002, ultimately losing to the Detroit Red Wings. Four years later they returned to the finals, this time defeating the Edmonton Oilers in seven games to become the 2006 Stanley Cup champions.

Susan Jelinek Mellage

Immanuel College in Greensboro was a residential high school, junior college, and theological seminary for African Americans operated by the Missouri Synod of the Lutheran Church from 1903 to 1961. Initially located in Concord, the college relocated in 1905 to a 13-acre campus in Greensboro at the corner of East Market and Luther Streets, two blocks from Grace Lutheran Church. Immanuel College trained scores of African American teachers, and the theological department trained most of the African American Lutheran clergymen ordained in the South before the 1960s.

A product of the Jim Crow period of segregation during the first half of the twentieth century, Immanuel College became an early victim of the movement toward school desegregation when the Lutheran Synodical Conference, meeting in 1961 in Milwaukee, abruptly decided to close the school and concentrate denominational resources in Concordia Academy and College in Selma, Ala. Among the college's best-known alumni are James Cheek, former president of Howard University; S. R. McClendon, principal of Florence Elementary School in Guilford County; Jim Wright, director of the Greensboro Human Relations Commission; and Gregg Morris, a television actor who appeared in the show *Mission Impossible* from 1966 to 1973.

References: Richard C. Dickinson, *Roses and Thorns* (1977); Rosa Young, *Light in the Dark Belt: The Story of Rosa Young as Told by Herself* (1950).

Robert M. Calhoon

Immigrant Colonies. Most immigrants to North Carolina came either individually or as part of a family or group of families. A number of them, however, were members of larger groupings, sometimes settling together as a body. The Lost Colony was such an entity, as was the Swiss and German Palatine colony established by Baron Christoph von Graffenried in present-day Craven County in 1710. The so-called Argyll Colony of Scots emigrated as a group in 1739, although they did not settle in a compact community. The other notable "colony" of the eighteenth century was the one established in 1753 at Bethabara in what is now Forsyth County by Moravians from Pennsylvania.

Shortly after the end of the Civil War, North Carolina followed the example of a number of other states of the former Confederacy that sought to encourage inward migration from northern states and from Europe in order to help rebuild their shattered economies. In 1877 the General Assembly established the Department of Agriculture, Immigration, and Statistics; the new department's responsibilities regarding immigration were carried out by the North Carolina Bureau of Immigration. The first agriculture commissioner, Leonidas L. Polk, sent an agent to England to seek immigrants from Britain. In 1881, under the auspices of the Bureau of Immigration, 69 "German Polander" immigrants arrived in Salisbury. Until its abolition in 1905, the bureau also published promotional literature and reports, in addition to establishing a number of agencies in northern states. Unfortunately, the extent of the state's official promotion of immigration is difficult to assess, since the records of the North Carolina Bureau of Immigration are unaccountably missing.

A projected settlement of Scots in the Sandhills in the early 1880s came to nothing, as did the plan of a Scottish land company to establish a colony of Scots in Madison and Haywood Counties. However, a number of immigrant colonies did come into being in various parts of North Carolina in the 1890s and the first decade of the twentieth century. In 1893 a group of Waldensians from northern Italy founded Valdese, a notably successful community in Burke County. Between 1905 and 1908 the Wilmington entrepreneur Hugh MacRae was responsible for the establishment of five settlements of various nationalities in the southeastern section of the state: St. Helena, an Italian colony, in Pender County; Artesia, composed mainly of Dutch and Polish settlers, and New Berlin, of Germans, in Columbus County; and Marathon, settled by Poles, and Castle Hayne, a Dutch and Hungarian colony, in New Hanover County. None of them was as successful as MacRae had hoped. The settlement at St. Helena eventually numbered several hundred, but apparently there were considerably fewer at the other four. Today, only Castle Hayne, St. Helena, and New Berlin (renamed Delco) survive as tiny communities.

Another venture of MacRae's was the Pender County community of Van Eeden. Named for a Dutch visionary, Frederick van Eeden, who in 1909 collaborated with MacRae in purchasing land for the settlement of Dutch immigrants, the projected colony attracted only a handful of farmers. Within a few years Van Eeden had been abandoned. In 1939 MacRae and a friend were instrumental in the formation of a corporation that bought the Van Eeden land as a haven for German Jews. A small number of refugees settled in Van Eeden in the early years of World War II, but within three or four years almost all of them had left.

The idea—if not the reality—of immigrant colonies in North Carolina has proved to be persistent. In 1990 a plan to establish an industrial colony of Soviet Jews in Hyde County was proposed but failed to attract the support necessary for its implementation.

References: Susan Taylor Block, *Van Eeden* (1995); W. Turrentine Jackson, *The Enterprising Scot: Investors in the American West after 1873* (1968).

Robert J. Cain

SEE ALSO Argyll Colony; Crofter Immigration; Moravians; Swiss and Palatine Settlers; Waldensians.

Immigration has been the means by which North Carolina came into existence, steadily grew through decades of changing population trends and expansion, and ultimately emerged as an ethnically diverse modern state in the early twenty-first century. The peak period of immigration to and settlement of the region that became North Carolina lasted from about 1730 until the American Revolution. This period witnessed a virtual flood of English, Scottish, German, Irish, and other immigrants into North Carolina, first into the land immediately adjacent to the Atlantic Coast and then farther west and into the backcountry. Although European settlers could be found in every part of the state by about 1830, the ethnic makeup of North Carolina continued to evolve through the integration of new peoples from practically every country and culture in the world.

Many of the colony's earliest immigrants had first landed in other British colonies, such as Virginia, Maryland, South Carolina, and Pennsylvania. By the 1660s, several hundred settlers had moved from Virginia into the Albemarle region to find farmland and to trade with the Native Americans. French, German, and Swiss people were among these settlers, some of whom (particularly the Swiss) were fleeing religious and social persecution; the Germans were escaping cold winters, poverty, and war. In 1710 the Swiss and Germans settled New Bern, an action that helped spark the colony's first major conflict with native people, the Tuscarora War (1711–13). After the Indians were defeated by local militias with the help of the Virginia colony, white immigration into the Middle Coastal Plain increased because the war had decreased the Indian threat.

The process of becoming a citizen in colonial North Carolina was quite simple. Immigrants signed a statement of allegiance as they came off the ship. The process of naturalization and subsequent granting of citizenship could take place in almost any court. The English Parliamentary Statute of 1740 required a residence of seven years, but immigrants need not live continuously for seven years in the colony where they were to apply for citizenship. The relatively few instances of naturalization recorded in the *Colonial Records of North Carolina* make no mention of a residency requirement, but they routinely note that the persons seeking naturalization "took the oaths and subscribed the test as required by law." Prospective citizens would take an oath of loyalty to the Crown and colony before having citizenship conferred upon them and would receive the Sacrament of the Lord's Supper within three months of taking the oath. For every naturalization, a payment of two shillings was required.

In the 1720s the first permanent settlers arrived in the Lower Cape Fear region. They included colonists from South Carolina who were fleeing economic depression, high taxes, and political unrest, as well as those from New York, Pennsylvania, Maryland, and Massachusetts. In 1739 Welsh and Scotch-Irish immigrants began to arrive. High rents, burdensome taxes, unemployment, and famine in Ireland had driven away the Scotch-Irish in particular. Highland Scots settled in the Upper Cape Fear Valley in present-day Fayetteville and in Cumberland, Bladen, and other nearby counties.

Africans—most of whom were slaves—added greatly to the colonial population, either coming from other American colonies or from abroad. Most slaves lived in the Lower Cape Fear region, where South Carolina and Virginia immigrants often brought their slaves with them and thus began the plantation culture of rice, indigo, and naval stores. Slaves were less common in the Albemarle and Middle Coastal regions, where there were fewer large plantations.

The Piedmont initially was settled by English colonists from the coastal towns. By the 1780s Scotch-Irish and German settlers arrived via the Great Wagon Road from Pennsylvania, Maryland, and Virginia. Germans of Lutheran and German Reformed faiths located near the Yadkin and Catawba Rivers. In 1753 Moravians from Pennsylvania began building a well-planned, tightly controlled congregational community at Salem and other villages in Forsyth County. Salisbury, Hillsborough, and Charlotte were established between 1753 and 1766. The immigrants who populated the Mountain region were primarily of English, Scotch-Irish, and German descent, many of whom had migrated from the Piedmont and the Coastal Plain. By 1830 western North Carolina had more people than the eastern region, which nevertheless continued to control the government.

North Carolina's poor conditions—earning it the nickname the "Rip Van Winkle State"—slowed the number of immigrants throughout the early to mid-nineteenth century and led to significant out-migration from the state. While some reformers and newspapers pointed out the high degree of ignorance and poverty in which people lived, most state leaders failed to address these needs, often opposing spending for schools, roads, agricultural reforms, or scientific advancement. In response, many farmers and other settlers moved west.

The out-migration of North Carolina's African Americans escalated following the Civil War, which brought them freedom but left them to face poverty in an increasingly repressive political climate. With the return of white Democratic rule after the 1876 election, harsh discrimination, a practically nonexistent political voice, inferior housing and schools, and low wages prompted blacks to move elsewhere. In the final quarter of the nineteenth century, about 100,000 blacks left North Carolina, and between 1910 and 1950 about 280,000 blacks moved to cities such as as Washington, D.C., New York, and Detroit.

Not until World War II did the out-migration of North Carolinians, both black and white, begin to wane. The civil rights advances of the 1960s and 1970s, the end of segregation, and a tremendous economic growth began to lure thousands of people to the state. Growth was and remains most pronounced in the Charlotte area, the Piedmont Triad (Winston-Salem/Greensboro/High Point), the Research Triangle (Raleigh/Durham/Chapel Hill), and, more recently, Asheville and Wilmington. These and other areas have attracted people from across the nation and the world in search of jobs, education, and a better way of life.

Beginning in the 1960s and 1970s, the increased diversity of immigrants to North Carolina—including Asians, Indians, and Latinos—has provided new dimensions to the state's modern-day culture. Of the huge numbers of Asians arriving in the United States in the 1970s, particularly in the turbulent aftermath of the Vietnam War, many settled in North Carolina. Just prior to the fall of Saigon on 30 Apr. 1975, President Gerald R. Ford authorized the entry of 125,000 Vietnamese refugees into the country, and by 1980 about 2,400 of them were living in various parts of North Carolina. A "second wave" of these immigrants in the 1980s consisted of "boat people," most of whom were semiliterate farmers and fishermen and small-town merchants.

The Hmong, a highland tribal people thought to have originated in prehistoric central Asia or northern China, began leaving war-torn Laos in 1975 and heading for Thailand and then the United States. A year later, the first Hmong refugees arrived in North Carolina directly from camps in Thailand. Of the approximately 250,000 Laotians who had resettled in the United States by 1990, about 2,000 lived in North Carolina.

Immigration from India and elsewhere in South Asia to North Carolina has occurred almost wholly since the 1960s. Most of these residents live in the Triangle area of Raleigh/Durham/Chapel Hill. Many are engineers and scientists, although physicians, college professors, and members of the business community abound among the ranks of the close-knit, highly educated Indian American population. The Triangle community has grown large enough to support a 700-member Hindu temple in Morrisville, built in 1986. In 1997 the nationwide Indian American Forum for Political Education held its annual convention in Raleigh, as a tribute both to local Hindu Priest Swadesh Chatterjee and to the growing influence of the North Carolina contingent of Indian Americans.

Other Asians, especially Chinese, Japanese, and Koreans, began coming to North Carolina in the last quarter of the twentieth century to study and to start businesses. By the year 2000, North Carolina's Asian-American population included about 26,000 East Indians, 19,000 Chinese, 15,000 Vietnamese, 12,000 Koreans, 9,000 Filipinos, 7,000 Hmong, and 4,000 Pacific Islanders.

By the early 2000s, the fastest growing immigrant group in North Carolina was of Latino descent. More than 600,000 Latinos were believed to be living in the state—many in the Charlotte, Triad, and Triangle areas as well as near military installations. Cubans, who in the 1960s fled the socialist revolution that put Fidel Castro in power, constituted the first wave of Latinos to enter the state. Beginning in the mid-1970s and early 1980s, many thousands of Mexicans arrived in the United States—some illegally—in search of better jobs, lifestyles, and educational opportunities. Some, having heard of employment opportunities through friends and family members already in the state, entered North Carolina as migrant workers to harvest tobacco, cucumbers, tomatoes, sweet potatoes, and other crops. More recently, immigrants in other occupations have come from Central and South America as well as Mexico. Other Latinos in the state fled civil war in countries such as El Salvador, Guatemala, Nicaragua, and Peru or political-economic problems such as those in Colombia and Venezuela.

In 2006 illegal immigration to the United States remained a serious problem, with states and the federal government attempting to develop solutions that were both fair and legally sound.

References: David W. Haines, ed., *Refugees as Immigrants: Cambodians, Laotians, and Vietnamese in America* (1989); David Levinson and Melvin Ember, eds., *American Immigrant Cultures: Builders of a Nation* (1997); James Joseph Maslowski, "North Carolina Migration, 1870–1950" (Ph.D. diss., UNC-Chapel Hill, 1953); Thomas C. Parramore and Douglas C. Wilms, *North Carolina: The History of an American State* (1983); Robert W. Ramsey, *Carolina Cradle: Settlement of the Northwest Carolina Frontier, 1747–1762* (1964).

Ron Holland
Wiley J. Williams
Additional research provided by William G. DiNome, Benjamin R. Justesen, and Jo White Linn.

SEE ALSO Exodusters; German Settlers; Immigrant Colonies; Latinos; Scottish Settlers; Swiss and Palatine Settlers; Welsh Settlers.

Impeachment is a process whereby accusations are brought against a civil official by a legislative body. Legally, the term applies only to an indictment, but in practice it often refers to the actual trial of the accused. Article IV, section 4, of the North Carolina Constitution specifies that the State House of Representatives has the power to impeach and the State Senate serves as the court for impeachment. When the governor or lieutenant governor is impeached, the chief justice of the state supreme court will preside. A two-thirds majority is required to convict.

The only North Carolina governor to be impeached as of the year 2006 is William W. Holden. In 1870, following the murder of a Republican officeholder in Alamance County and a state senator in Caswell County, Holden declared martial law in the two counties and put them under the command of Col. George W. Kirk. A number of individuals were arrested, and both Kirk and Holden refused to recognize writs of habeas corpus issued by state judges. When Josiah Turner Jr., publisher of the *Raleigh Sentinel*, wrote a scathing criticism of the governor in which he dared Holden to arrest him, Holden complied. Soon after, a federal judge issued a writ of habeas corpus requiring that the prisoners be brought before him. President Ulysses S. Grant, who had supported Holden's actions to this point, now ordered him to obey the writ, and the so-called Kirk-Holden War came to an end. When Democrats regained control of the State House in 1870, impeachment proceedings were begun, although the decision to do so was opposed by some Democrats, including U.S. senator Zebulon Vance. Holden faced eight counts of malfeasance; he was convicted of six of the eight and was removed from office. Vance remarked: "It was the longest hunt after the poorest hide I ever saw."

In framing the U.S. Constitution, the procedure for impeachment of government officials was first proposed by Hugh Williamson, one of North Carolina's signers of the Constitution. The terminology and procedures agreed upon were based heavily on English common law. The first person to be indicted under the impeachment clause of the U.S. Constitution was William Blount, another signer of the document from North Carolina. Blount, who at the time of his impeachment was serving as a U.S. senator from Tennessee, was charged with a high misdemeanor when it was discovered that he had written a letter proposing that Indians and frontiersmen attack Louisiana and Spanish Florida. The proceedings were dismissed by the Senate following Blount's expulsion from that body.

Another native North Carolinian impeached on the federal level was Andrew Johnson—the seventeenth president of the United States and a native of Raleigh, although his political career was primarily in Tennessee. Following the Civil War, Johnson found himself at odds with the Radical Republicans in Congress, who wished to impose strict requirements on the southern states for reentry into the Union. Johnson attempted to thwart them through civil and military appointments. When Johnson, in 1868, removed Secretary of War Edwin Stanton from office, Republicans claimed that the president had violated the newly enacted Tenure in Office Act and began impeachment proceedings. The Radicals demanded that all Republicans in the Senate vote for conviction, but six refused to do so. The final vote was 30 in favor of conviction and 19 against it, just one vote shy of the two-thirds majority needed to convict. Johnson was acquitted and remained in office.

Reference: Buckner F. Melton, *The First Impeachment: The Constitution's Framers and the Case of Senator William Blount* (1998).

Jo Ann Williford

The Impending Crisis of the South,

The Impending Crisis of the South, by Rowan County–born abolitionist Hinton Rowan Helper (1829–1909), was published by A. B. Burdick of New York in 1857. The book, along with Harriet Beecher Stowe's *Uncle Tom's Cabin* (1852), stands out as one of the most significant antislavery works preceding the American Civil War. The publication aroused little notice until 1858, when New York editor Horace Greeley undertook publication of an abbreviated compendium, for which he solicited a number of Republican endorsements. In 1859 the Republicans attempted to elect John Sherman, an endorser of the Helper book, as Speaker of the U.S. House of Representatives. After a lengthy and violent debate, during which the book gained significant notoriety, southern representatives managed to defeat Sherman's election.

Helper's *Impending Crisis* compared the South unfavorably with the North by selective use of the censuses of 1790 and 1850. Helper had been careless with statistics before in his *California Land of Gold: Reality vs. Fiction* (1855). *Impending Crisis* aroused even more concern, however, because of its intemperate attacks on the planter class. In fact, Helper's book was so virulent that it had taken him several months to find a publisher. The work urged class agitation against slavery or, failing that, the violent overthrow of the slave system by poorer whites. Helper concluded that slaves would join with nonslaveholders because "the negroes . . . in nine cases out of ten, would be delighted with the opportunity to cut their masters' throat." Despite his abolitionist sentiment, Helper sympathized far more with poor whites and capitalists than with blacks. A racist to the core, he advocated white supremacy.

Helper could not return to North Carolina after the publication of his book, which became an official Republican campaign document. *Impending Crisis* was banned throughout the South, and a number of people were arrested for possessing the volume. Helper's opposition to slavery has been explained by such factors as his German background and his own lack of success in a slave state. Whatever the cause, he produced the most important nonfictional antislavery book ever written.

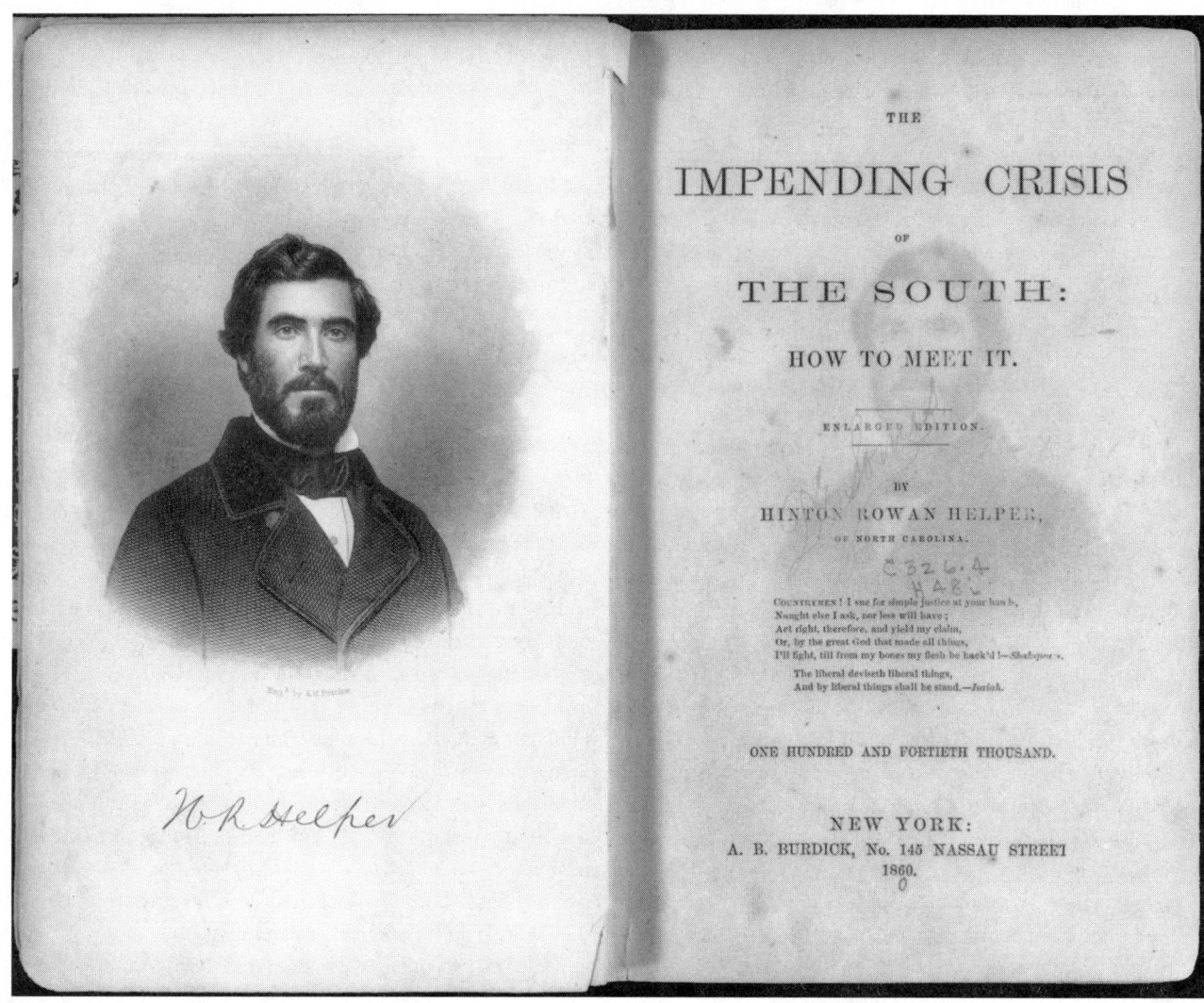

Title page and frontispiece portrait of Hinton Rowan Helper in the 1860 edition of *The Impending Crisis of the South*. NCC.

References: Hugh C. Bailey, *Hinton Rowan Helper: Abolitionist-Racist* (1965); Hugh T. Lefler, *Hinton Rowan Helper: Advocate of a "White America"* (1935); Laurence Shore, *Southern Capitalists: The Ideological Leadership of an Elite, 1832–1885* (1986).

Ronnie W. Faulkner

Incidents in the Life of a Slave Girl. SEE Slave Narratives.

Indentured Servants were white Europeans of modest means who for various reasons wanted to go to the British colonies but could not pay the cost of their passage. During the colonial period, a thriving business developed in Europe in which young men and women agreed to work for a specific time in the New World for a master who paid their way across the Atlantic Ocean. The indenture was the contract they signed and carried with them for the length of their service. A typical servant's contract noted the length (usually four to seven years) and place of service, the master's name, and the minimal food, clothing, and shelter that he or she was to provide.

In the eighteenth century, as the servant population grew (although it never became very large in North Carolina), the North Carolina Assembly found it necessary to enact regulatory laws, particularly since the system lent itself to abuse on the part of both servant and master. According to printer James Davis's legal guide, published in New Bern in 1774, runaway servants who were caught would serve double time after the expiration of their contracted term. Servants who resisted their masters could "suffer corporal Punishment, at the Discretion of a Justice, not exceeding Twenty One Lashes."

For their part, masters had to provide their servants with a "Competent Dyet, Clothing & Lodging," and they could "not exceed the Bounds of moderation in correcting them." By all accounts, life for indentured servants was difficult. Many died of disease before the end of their contracts, and most who survived were poor.

References: A. Roger Ekirch, *Bound for America: The Transportation of British Convicts to the Colonies, 1718–1775* (1986); Ekirch, *"Poor Carolina": Politics and Society in North Carolina, 1729–1776* (1981); Abbot Emerson Smith, *Colonists in Bondage: White Servitude and Convict Labor in America, 1607–1776* (1947).

Donna J. Spindel

Independence Building,

Independence Building, which stood on the northwest corner of "The Square" (the intersection of Trade and Tryon Streets) in uptown Charlotte, was the first steel-frame high-rise building in North Carolina and, at 12 stories, is considered to have been the state's first true "skyscraper." The building was designed by architect Frank Pierce Milburn, completed in 1908, and named the Realty Building—a symbol of Charlotte's "New South" image. The building became known as the Independence Building following the founding of the Independence Trust Company in 1912.

Beginning with the Great Depression and continuing into the 1970s, the Independence Building was faced with considerable tenant turnover, as occupants moved to more modern buildings. On 30 Apr. 1976 all floors above the first were closed off, and two years later the building was placed on the National Register of Historic Places. In July 1981 Faison Associates (headed by Henry Faison) bought the property and announced plans to demolish the structure and build Independence Center—an office, retail, and hotel complex—on the site. On a Sunday morning in September 1981, the Independence Building was imploded in seven seconds.

References: Frank McInnis, "The First N.C. Skyscraper," *The State* (October 1983); Lawrence Wodehouse, "Frank Pierce Milburn (1868–1926), a Major Southern Architect," *NCHR* 50 (July 1973).

Wiley J. Williams

Indian Museum of the Carolinas

Indian Museum of the Carolinas is nestled in a grove of pine, sweet gum, and white oak trees off Turnpike Road in Laurinburg. Opened in 1972 by a group of Scotland County citizens under the leadership of local anthropologist David McLean, this modest building holds treasures from North Carolina Native American communities, from prehistoric artifacts to contemporary arts and crafts. Although emphasis is placed on a nine-county area, the museum collections include items from other tribal groups in North America and South America. The stated mission of the museum includes two major goals: to educate the public through the preservation, exhibition, and interpretation of artifacts from the native peoples of North Carolina and South Carolina, and to further archaeological research in the Carolinas. In addressing these goals, the exhibit area in the museum provides an eclectic but interesting group of displays.

There are two major exhibit areas in the museum: the front room at the entrance focuses on North Carolina Native American history, and a second area includes rotating displays on North Carolina Indians and other tribes. From the exhibits and their interpretations, a visitor can learn about topics ranging from native foods such as nuts, fish, and cattails, to planting corn with digging sticks, playing stickball, and the role of the shaman in religious and healing ceremonies. Reflecting the Indian worldview, displays are arranged in a more circular or topical fashion rather than in a linear, chronological mode (from prehistory to the present). Because McLean was also an archaeologist, a major component of the museum's collection is prehistoric artifacts, including thousands of projectile points, stone tools, and pottery shards. However, the more recent displays depict the contemporary life of local tribes, particularly the Lumbee and the Catawba.

In addition to the exhibits inside, a seasonal Native American garden featuring plants used by the native population for food, medicine, and textiles is located on the perimeter of the museum grounds. The garden, a favorite of local students, not only serves as an instructional tool but is instrumental in research.

Southeastern North Carolina is often overlooked as an area of Native American history and culture, although the Lumbee tribe in Robeson County is the largest Indian tribe east of the Mississippi. Since its creation, the Indian Museum of the Carolinas has taken the challenge of remedying this oversight. By bringing attention to the rich heritage of the Native American peoples of this region, the museum provides the opportunity for North Carolinians to increase their knowledge and enhance their appreciation of one of the diverse cultures of the region and state.

References: Mark A. Mathis and Jeffrey J. Crow, eds., *The Prehistory of North Carolina: An Archaeological Symposium* (1983); Ruth Y. Wetmore, *First on the Land: The North Carolina Indians* (1975).

Linda Oxendine

Indian Trading Paths.

Indian Trading Paths. The oldest paths and trails in the area that became North Carolina were made by animals in search of food, water, and salt; and native Indians adopted these paths for the same purpose. As agriculture evolved, life became more settled for many groups, and paths developed between major settlements and villages. Long before Europeans approached the New World, these paths were traveled by Indian ambassadors, war parties, couriers, traders, families, and even whole communities.

Precisely when trading began among native peoples is not known, but it is clear that the Indians of the area traveled widely. As tribal groups established territories they considered their own, exchanges developed on a more or less regular basis, with traders traveling by foot, carrying those items most in demand. The Coastal Plain, Piedmont, and Mountains each produced items desirable for trade, generating

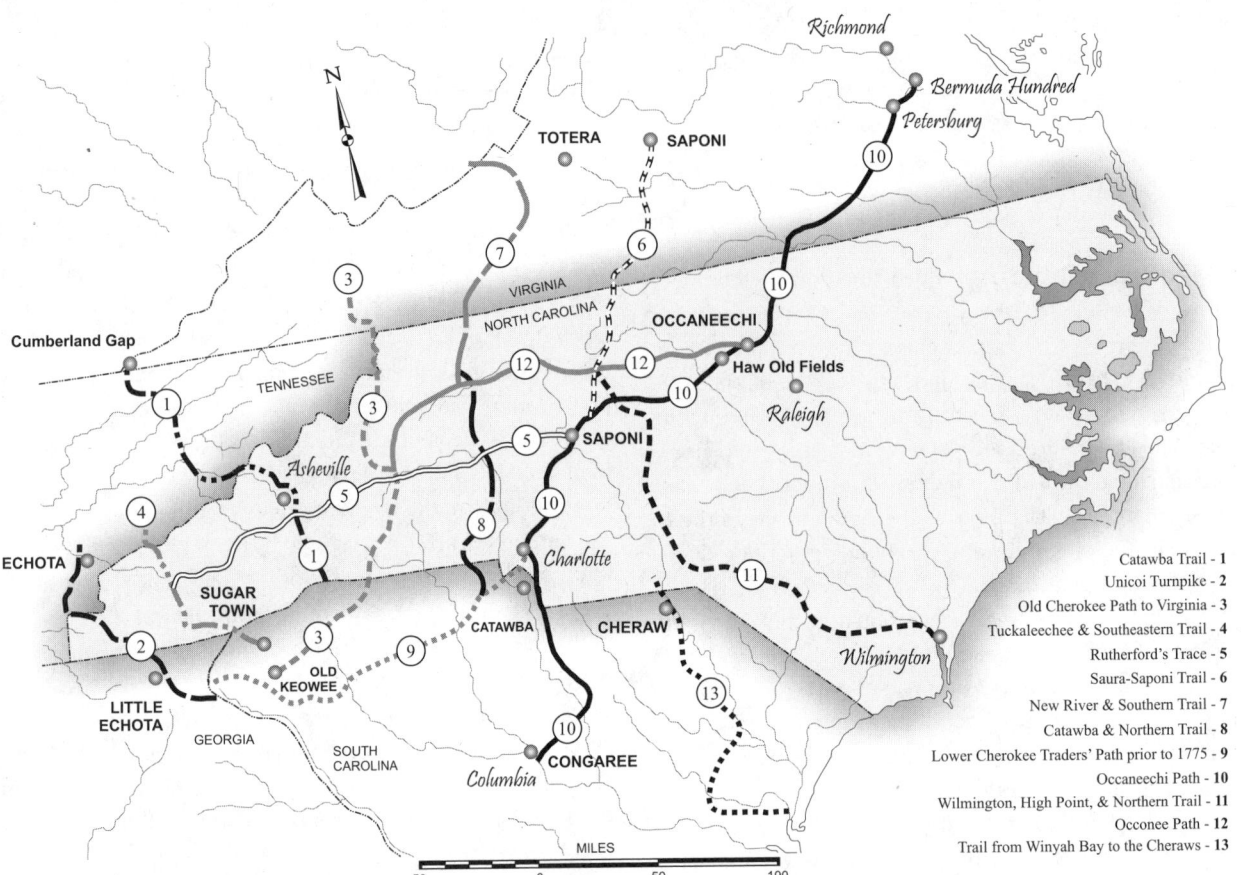

Indian trading paths in North Carolina (conjectured routes). Map based on information in the *Forty-Second Annual Report of the Bureau of American Ethnology to the Secretary of the Smithsonian Institution, 1924–1925* (1928). Map by Mark Anderson Moore, courtesy NCOA&H.

contact among the native peoples of the three regions as they exchanged goods, often at feasts and ceremonies. From the coastal regions, shell beads, especially conch shell beads known as wampum or roanoke, had relatively fixed values and served as a medium of exchange. Leaves of certain hollies found along the coast were a standard trade item, and coastal salt was frequently traded inland. Coastal and piedmont Indians also supplied hardwoods for bows, minerals for paint, and stone for weapons and tools. The Catawba exchanged skins and mica with coastal tribes in return for fish and salt. From the mountains came heavy bear and buffalo skins, copper, and mica. In addition to raw materials, some man-made goods were traded. The Tuscarora, for example, made wooden utensils to exchange with other tribes for uncured deerhides, which they tanned and traded elsewhere. The Cherokee became known for their carved stone pipes.

A new trading era began when Indians were exposed to European goods: guns and ammunition, hatchets, kettles, metal tools, liquor, woolen cloth and blankets, trinkets, and glass beads. In return for these goods, Europeans traders wanted furs and hides from beavers, otters, deer, muskrats, and raccoons. As long as there were plenty of animals, the Indians fared well in bargaining, often trading hides for firearms.

But when animals became scarce, Indians were left without a medium of exchange for the trade goods on which they were increasingly dependent. The historic record makes it apparent that the Europeans often took advantage of the Indians in trade transactions.

English traders often named Indian paths and trails after their destinations. Thus, the primary trails crossing North Carolina along the north-south axis were the Peedee, Catawba, and Cherokee Trails. One part of the Catawba Trail was called the Occaneechi Trail (sometimes referred to as the Great Trading Path), and another was called the Waxhaw Trail. The Peedee, Catawba, and Cherokee Trails generally correspond to portions of modern-day interstate highways 95, 85, and 40, respectively.

Watersheds and river crossings, more than any other factors, dictated the route of Indian trading paths. For travelers who moved north and south—as did most of the English traders, explorers, and adventurers who first encountered the native peoples of North Carolina—rivers were unavoidable barriers. Fording them, the act of crossing streams without bridges, was a daily risk. Some of the river fords employed earned lasting place-names, such as Nations Ford on the Catawba River, Trading Ford and Shallow Ford on the Yadkin

River, Piney Ford on the Haw River, Fish Dam Ford on the Neuse River, and Moniseep or Horse Ford on the Roanoke River.

Many of North Carolina's modern highways lie within mere feet of the ancient Indian trading paths. For example, Highway 158, which runs from Kill Devil Hills on the Outer Banks to the mountains at Mocksville in Davie County, once connected the natives of the Albemarle with the Cherokee and all the tribes in between. East of the Haw River, Highways 10 and 70 run along the course of the Great Central Coast Road, down the watershed between the Neuse and Cape Fear basins; Highways 1, 15, 29, 64, and 74 likewise follow lines forged by people far beyond memory.

Eighteen Indian trading paths have been identified as having lain totally or partially within the present boundaries of North Carolina, including the Unicoi Turnpike, the Catawba Trail, the Saura-Saponi Trail, and the Lower Cherokee Traders' Path prior to 1775. Many of these paths extended into the states of Georgia, South Carolina, Tennessee, Kentucky, and Virginia, knitting the peoples of North Carolina together with those of the rest of the Southeast and North America. Beginning in 1941, the Department of Archives and History erected highway historical markers for many of these paths.

References: William E. Myer, "Indian Trails of the Southeast," in U.S. Bureau of American Ethnology, *42nd Annual Report, 1924, 1925* (1928); Theda Perdue, *Native Carolinians: The Indians of North Carolina* (1985); Douglas L. Rights, *The American Indian in North Carolina* (2nd ed., 1957); Ruth Y. Wetmore, *First on the Land: The North Carolina Indians* (1975).

Tom Magnuson
Additional research provided by Wiley J. Williams.

SEE ALSO Great Trading Path; Trading Ford.

Industrial Commission is the state agency that administers the federal Workers' Compensation Act, which provides compensation benefits for industrial injuries. The purpose of the act is not only to offer a swift and certain remedy for an injured worker, but also to ensure a limited and determinate liability for employers. The Industrial Commission was created by the North Carolina General Assembly in 1929. The governor appoints its members for six-year terms.

Armistead Jones Maupin

Infectious Diseases. Before the widespread distribution of vaccinations, many serious, often deadly contagious diseases were commonplace in North Carolina and other American colonies and states. The Carolina colony initially tried to battle epidemics by restricting imports. Passage of the "Distempered Act" in 1755 also barred from the colony immigrants who suffered from "malignant infectious distempers." But these ac-

tions proved to be detrimental to the commercial interests of those seeking settlers to inhabit their lands, and the act was repealed in 1760. The Revolutionary War brought the new practice of inoculation to the colonies. This entailed the exposure of a potential victim to a mild case of a disease to prevent further infection. Predictably, the general public was wary of this innovation and its inherent risk of unintentionally causing an epidemic. Only in isolated instances were inoculations routinely accepted and used.

The Moravian settlement in Piedmont North Carolina was probably the first to adopt the practice of inoculation against infectious diseases, causing much trepidation in their neighbors. When Continental troops arrived in Salem in 1779, bringing with them several cases of smallpox, the town conducted an inoculation program that drew the wrath of those in the surrounding countryside. Some "ignorant and malicious" individuals, according to Moravian records, threatened to "destroy" the settlement if the inoculations were given. Soon after the war, James R. Alexander, one of the state's first public advocates for preventative infection, began inoculating his patients in Mecklenburg County against smallpox.

By the turn of the century the practice of vaccination was becoming increasingly common in North Carolina, though not without conflict. In 1800 Calvin Jones unsuccessfully attempted to open a vaccination hospital in Smithfield. The physician's failure was due, in part, to his charge of $10 per vaccination (perhaps the result of Continental dollar depreciation) but was no doubt largely the result of the persistent public fear of the procedure. The prevalence of this feeling is illustrated by the reaction of one community to inoculation. When, in 1801, a well-to-do citizen of Fayetteville returned from Europe with smallpox vaccinations for his family, public outcry forced him to halt his treatment and move his kin to a "remote and private situation."

At times the misapplication of inoculations exacerbated this hostility and further damaged the credibility of the procedure. In fact, an event in North Carolina dealt a setback to the national movement toward widespread inoculation. In 1821 James Smith, vaccine agent of the U.S. government, mistakenly sent a packet of actual smallpox tissue, instead of the expected vaccine, to a physician in Tarboro. Unknowingly, the doctor caused an epidemic in using the material. This led to the collapse of the fledgling inoculation campaign in North Carolina and resulted in the ouster of Smith from his position. It was clear that medical science had much progress to make before the general public placed their trust in the inoculation process.

Vaccines to prevent many diseases were developed in the late nineteenth and early twentieth centuries. The General Assembly passed laws to encourage vaccination against smallpox, typhoid fever, and diphtheria, but it was reluctant to enact mandatory legislation. A major campaign against typhoid fever began in North Carolina in 1914, when a state laboratory made and distributed a free antityphoid vaccine. In 1919 third-year medical students, furnished with cars or motorcycles, also administered typhoid vaccines. Thousands of people were immunized by programs run by the North Carolina State Board of Health, which also urged many citizens to ask their own doctors for vaccinations.

The legislature eventually passed laws for compulsory vaccination. A 1939 statute required all schoolchildren to be vaccinated against diphtheria. Of particular concern was poliomyelitis, or polio, which ravaged the state during the 1930s. In 1959 North Carolina became the first state to initiate compulsory inoculation with the Salk vaccine. A 1957 law required children to be vaccinated against diphtheria, tetanus, and whooping cough before their first birthday and against smallpox before enrollment in school.

Despite the availability of vaccines and the mandatory vaccination laws, preventable diseases continued to appear in North Carolina. In 1962 not even one-half of its children were getting the required immunizations before their second birthday. The state's Immunization Activity Project introduced a "birth certificate follow-up program" in 1964. By 1968, 92 percent of the children in North Carolina had begun and 79 percent had completed their vaccinations. The General Assembly passed laws that required children to be vaccinated against red measles in 1971 and rubella in 1979.

Significant Infectious Diseases in North Carolina History

The following infectious diseases caused serious damage to the lives and health of North Carolinians before the discovery of successful inoculations and vaccines.

Ague. An acute form of fever that often damages nerves and is sometimes fatal, ague was present in North Carolina from colonial times until the 1930s. The term was prevalent among early colonists, although ague and malaria shared many symptoms and were often mistaken for one another. In fact, little information exists that relates specifically to ague because the histories of the diseases are so intertwined.

Early colonists coined the term "seasoning" to refer to cases of ague and similar diseases. Ague and malaria began to reach epidemic proportions among white colonists after the arrival of ships carrying infected slaves from Africa between 1682 and 1685. An abundance of marshland and an inadequate water supply exacerbated the problem as mosquitoes, the diseases' primary carrier, thrived in the region.

In the twentieth century, records of ague cases became more accurate. The disease was prevalent on the coast and in the Piedmont, whereas infections were rare in the Mountains. By the 1930s, enhancements in sanitary conditions and better medical treatment began to greatly lessen the threat of ague and similar diseases among North Carolinians.

Diphtheria. One of the dreaded diseases of both children and adults, diphtheria was present in nineteenth-century North Carolina. The disease is of bacterial origin, the toxin from which causes damage to the throat area with possible obstruction to the breathing passages and subsequent suffocation. Many cases described as croup before the germ theory of contagion were no doubt actually diphtheria, since it is one of the several infections that presents with a "croupy" cough.

In 1887 diphtheria was listed in official records as the third most important cause of death in North Carolina. During 1920–24 there were 25,460 reported cases, with 1,864 deaths attributed to this disease. It was not until the early 1920s that an effective vaccine for diphtheria was developed and not until 1939 that compulsory immunization for schoolchildren with the diphtheria vaccine was mandated by the General Assembly. By the early 2000s diphtheria was rare, not only in North Carolina but nationwide, and antibiotics were available for those cases that did occur.

Influenza. An infectious disease of viral origin that is worldwide in distribution, influenza, or "the flu," was first described by Hippocrates, the "Father of Medicine," in 412 B.C. About 29 pandemics were recorded between 1510 and 1918. In the great "Spanish" flu pandemic of 1918–19, after World War I, North Carolina lost 13,644 citizens, including Edward Kidder Graham, the new president of the University of North Carolina.

The causative virus of influenza was first isolated in 1933, and a vaccine was developed in the 1940s. The ability of the virus to shift susceptibility to the vaccine requires an annual change in its composition to ensure the inclusion of protection against the strains most likely to be encountered in that particular year.

Malaria. A major public health problem for decades, malaria was especially prevalent in coastal North Carolina during the early years of settlement. The disease is caused by a protozoan parasite named plasmodium. There are several varieties, all of which are transmitted from person to person by the bite of a female Anopheles mosquito. The year 1889 was a particularly bad one for malaria in North Carolina, probably due to an unusually mild winter with no killing frosts. Control of the disease was slow until 1898, when the mechanism of mosquito transmission was identified. Following this discovery, efforts at mosquito control began to see results.

In 1936 malaria was declared a reportable disease to the State Board of Health; a widespread attempt to obtain blood smears from persons in high-incidence areas was undertaken, and a concerted effort to drain swamps in these areas was intensified. Quinine became available for the treatment of malaria around 1820, although the use of powdered cinchona bark, from which quinine was derived, had been used by the Spanish in Peru as early as 1638 and to some extent in the United States. Since 1946, however, chloroquine has been the drug of choice, supplemented by quinine and related substances in resistant cases. Since 1970 North Carolina has reported only sporadic incidents of malaria, generally contracted by persons during travel to endemic areas in other parts of the world.

Poliomyelitis. A contagious viral infection, polio is manifested by an aseptic meningitis, often with paralytic results that may be permanent or, in the worst cases, fatal. The disease affects both children and adults, but because of its frequent occurrence in small children, it came to be known as "infantile paralysis." Perhaps its most famous victim was President Franklin D. Roosevelt.

Polio epidemics, occurring especially in the summer, struck terror into the hearts of American parents during the first half of the twentieth century. In 1948, an especially bad year for North Carolina, 2,516 cases and 143 deaths were reported. A special emergency polio hospital was set up in the Greensboro area since Guilford was the hardest hit county in the state. The National Foundation for Infantile Paralysis, whose annual fund-raising effort is called the "March of Dimes," was founded on 3 Jan. 1938 to help finance a nationwide campaign of education, research, and relief for victims of epidemics. In 1948 alone, the foundation allotted more than $1.4 million to North Carolina to mitigate the statewide tragedy.

In the prevaccine era, the so-called iron lung machine—a respirator device into which persons unable to breathe for themselves because of the effects of polio were placed and artificially ventilated—became a familiar sight in all hospitals treating polio patients. In 1955 a vaccine named after its developer, Jonas Salk, became available for injection. It was quickly put into general use across North Carolina, resulting in an almost immediate decline both in new cases and deaths from the disease. In 1959 North Carolina was the first state to add the polio vaccine to the list of immunizations mandatory for children. In 1962 the Sabin vaccine, an improved preparation that could be administered orally, was introduced and soon largely replaced the injectable vaccine. The virtual abolishment of this dreaded disease in households across the nation was one of the most dramatic medical success stories of the twentieth century.

Scarlet Fever. Also known as scarlatina, scarlet fever is a febrile illness accompanied by a characteristic red rash and sore throat caused by infection with a toxin-producing strain of Streptococcus bacteria. Before the discovery of penicillin, scarlet fever could only be treated symptomatically and allowed to run its course. To prevent its spread through household contact, strict quarantine was mandated by public health officials. Epidemics of scarlet fever were commonplace in North Carolina until the advent in the 1940s of penicillin, which has been the drug of choice in treatment of this infection.

Smallpox. Also known as variola, smallpox, one of the ancient viral illnesses of epidemic and endemic proportions, was introduced into the North American mainland by the earliest European settlers. By 1711 smallpox had become endemic among the North Carolina population, including the Indians of the region. Primitive efforts of quarantine and isolation were ineffective in preventing its spread, such as the virulent smallpox epidemic in Charlotte in 1770. In 1798 Edward Jenner, an English physician, discovered that an inoculum derived from the cowpox virus, a similar but less potent pathogen, could prevent smallpox in humans. Yet many years elapsed before this type of vaccination became generally acceptable to the public, and many more years passed before it became mandatory.

In 1836 Ashe County alone reported 70 cases of smallpox. Other North Carolina epidemics occurred in Charlotte in 1851, in Salisbury in 1863, and in Wilmington in 1865. Compulsory smallpox vaccination in schools was required in Hyde County and a portion of Washington County in 1905. The State Board of Health, created by the General Assembly in 1877, led a decades-long battle to promote vaccination against smallpox. In 1911, 113 years after Jenner's development of the vaccine, the legislature enacted a statute requiring inoculation against smallpox, and in 1918 the State Board of Health made smallpox a reportable disease. Following these important public health measures, the annual cases dropped to 3,845 by 1924 and continued to decline rapidly. The last death from smallpox reported in North Carolina occurred in 1943, and the last reported case in the state was in 1953. Due to the worldwide promotion of immunization by the World Health Organization, smallpox was eliminated as a health hazard, and consequently the requirement for smallpox vaccination in North Carolina was lifted in 1973.

Tuberculosis. Sometimes referred to as the "Great White Plague" and frequently called "consumption," tuberculosis was also introduced into North Carolina by the earliest English settlers. John Lawson, in *A New Voyage to Carolina* (1709), noted the apparent absence of the disease among the local Indians. By the latter half of the nineteenth century, tuberculosis was the leading cause of death in the United States. Prior to the advent of antituberculosis drugs, the preferred treatment was institutional care in facilities located in a mountainous environment with pure, cool, and dry air. In North Carolina, Asheville became famous for its large number of private sanatoriums and consequently for the many physicians who specialized in the care of tuberculosis patients drawn to the area.

Tuberculosis was made a reportable disease by the State Board of Health in 1913. The first state-supported sanatorium opened near Aberdeen in April 1908; state-supported tuberculosis hospitals were later established at Wilson, Swannanoa, and Chapel Hill to permit full coverage across North Carolina.

In 1947, 1,056 people died from tuberculosis statewide.

There was no effective medicine to treat the disease until the mid-1940s, when streptomycin was discovered and began to be used. Subsequently, a number of other antituberculosis drugs were introduced and usually used in combination for optimum treatment. Following the introduction of these drugs, the number of new cases began to decline. By 1962 all county sanatoriums had been closed and the residual patients transferred to one of the state-supported institutions.

In the early 2000s tuberculosis continued to be a public health problem in North Carolina. The incidence of tuberculosis was again on the increase, especially among AIDS victims. Periodic skin testing as a means of tuberculosis case-finding remained part of careful medical practice.

Typhoid Fever. A bacterial infection depending in large part on contaminated water and food supplies for its transmission, typhoid fever was present in endemic proportions among the earliest settlers in North Carolina. Although the first description of epidemic typhoid fever was penned by Thomas Willis in 1659, it was not until 1880 that the typhoid bacillus—the causative agent of the disease—was discovered. The first inoculations with a killed bacterial suspension began in 1896, and the vaccine had a good measure of success during the World War I years of 1914–18. After that, summertime clinics providing "typhoid shots" were commonplace across the state.

A much more effective method of controlling this disease was the effort by public health departments to clean up water, milk, and food supplies. In the 1880s municipal waterworks began to replace wells and public pumps in Raleigh, Charlotte, Wilmington, and Winston-Salem. By 1894 Charlotte, New Bern, Asheville, Winston-Salem, and Raleigh had sewerage systems. After another half century, the outdoor privy had virtually disappeared.

In 1901 there were still 8,000 to 10,000 cases of typhoid fever in North Carolina annually. In 1918, when large-scale typhoid immunization programs went into effect, the number dropped to 3,461 cases and subsequently declined steadily; after 1953 fewer than 10 cases were reported annually. The first useful antibiotic for typhoid fever, chloramphenicol, was developed in 1948; this drug and new antibiotics were very helpful in controlling the disease.

Typhus. An infection caused by a Rickettsial organism transmitted by the bites of lice that have also infested rats, typhus was endemic among early North Carolina colonists, especially in port cities where ships containing many rats in the holds and among the cargo were coming and going. In 1758, during the French and Indian War, a large number of refugees flocked to the Moravian settlement of Bethabara, resulting in an outbreak of typhus that took the lives of many refugees as well as Moravians. In 1940, when 65 cases of typhus were reported in the state, the disease became a concern of public health authorities. A major effort was directed toward rodent control and rat-proofing of buildings; by 1952, only 12 cases were reported, and none occurred by 1970.

Yaws. Still a major health hazard in many Third World countries, yaws was a crippling disease for many North Carolinians in the late seventeenth and early eighteenth centuries. Yaws is contracted through infection by a spirochete, *treponema pallidum*, associated with primitive living conditions. It is transmitted by skin contact and manifests itself as pimples that, on sloughing off, leave mulberrylike growths of fungi. These tend to develop into malignant ulcers that may cover the body, attacking especially glands of the armpits, groin, throat, palate, and soles of the feet. Believed to have been imported into the American colonies on slave ships from Africa and the West Indies, yaws caused many North Carolina victims to lose their noses and palates.

Physicians treated yaws by the same methods used against venereal syphilis, the symptoms of which were nearly identical. Mercury, a mixture of several kinds of barks and roots (called "papaw's remedy"), "sweating boxes" to dry up ulcers, "yaws houses" to segregate infected slaves, restricted diets, and other remedies had little effect. The disease appears to have largely disappeared by 1750, although a prominent physician claimed to have found it in coastal areas of the state at the beginning of the twentieth century.

Yellow Fever. An acute viral illness characterized by high fever, jaundice, and brain disease, yellow fever is transmitted from person to person by the bite of an Aedes mosquito, which serves as the insect vector for the disease. In colonial North Carolina, yellow fever was frequently encountered in coastal settlements, especially where mosquitoes were found in abundance. For 200 years it was one of the great plagues not only of the United States but also of the entire world.

In September 1862, in the midst of the Civil War, a severe epidemic of yellow fever struck Wilmington after a blockade-running vessel from Nassau in the Bahamas loaded with supplies made its way into the Cape Fear River and docked in the port. In the zeal to off-load much-needed food and other cargo, the quarantine laws were apparently overlooked. A few days later, several Wilmington physicians reported cases suggestive of yellow fever, and it was found that there had been cases aboard the vessel from Nassau. The disease spread rapidly. Deaths numbered as high as 18 in a single day, and at one time as many as 500 cases were being treated. Physicians and nurses from as far away as Charleston, S.C., responded to the call for assistance. The epidemic lasted until 6 Nov. 1862, when a heavy snowstorm occurred. About 1,000 people died. One of the victims was James H. Dickson, a former president of the North Carolina Medical Society. The death of one of their colleagues increased the realization among North Carolina physicians that more had to be done to prevent yellow fever and other deadly contagious diseases in the state.

Progress in controlling yellow fever was slow until 1898,

when it was discovered that the mosquito was the carrier for its transmission. Thereafter, widespread efforts to drain swamps and eradicate the mosquito population helped prevent infection.

There was no satisfactory vaccine against yellow fever prior to 1937. That year a substance utilizing a strain of yellow fever virus called "17D," obtained by prolonged propagation in chick embryo tissue, was found to be effective and safe for humans and used experimentally. The vaccine was available during World War II to protect troops entering areas endemic to yellow fever.

No cases of yellow fever appeared in North Carolina after the advent of modern-day reporting in 1932. In the early 2000s this disease was endemic only in South America and Africa.

References: Thomas J. Farnham and Francis P. King, "'The March of the Destroyer': The New Bern Yellow Fever Epidemic of 1864," *NCHR* 73 (October 1996); Frederick L. Hoffman, *Malaria in Virginia, North Carolina, and South Carolina* (1933); Dorothy Long, ed., *Medicine in North Carolina: Essays in the History of Medical Science and Medical Service, 1524–1960* (1972); Thomas C. Parramore, "The 'Country Distemper' in Colonial North Carolina," *NCHR* 48 (Winter 1971); William S. Powell, *North Carolina through Four Centuries* (1989); Benjamin Earle Washburn, *A History of the North Carolina State Board of Health, 1877–1925* (1966); Jane Zimmerman, "The Formative Years of the North Carolina Board of Health, 1877–1893," *NCHR* 21 (January 1944).

William S. Joyner
Additional research provided by David L. Cockrell, Andrew Hosfeld, David A. Norris, and Thomas C. Parramore.

SEE ALSO Public Health.

Information Technology. North Carolina is home to one of the world's most vibrant information technology (IT) industries, which generally includes businesses and organizations engaged in the electronic storage, transmission, or processing of data through the use of computers. More than 2,300 companies involved in virtually every aspect of the manufacture, development, sales, and servicing of computers and computer-related products are located in the state and employ about 204,000 people. About 37 percent of these companies are located in the Triangle area (Raleigh/Durham/Chapel Hill), 27 percent in metropolitan Charlotte, and 16 percent in the Triad (Greensboro/Winston-Salem/High Point).

A worldwide revolution in information and communications technologies has paved the way toward a new digital economy, and personal computers, mobile phones, and the Internet are altering the way that Americans work, shop, learn, and play. All of these changes have been a result of the growth of the IT industry across the country. The production and application of semiconductors—materials that make up the wide variety of microchips and other components used in computer technologies—represent a key segment of the IT industry and are the focus of several North Carolina firms. Hardware production and assembly relating to personal computers, software development, the manufacture of telecommunications and networking equipment, and a vast array of IT services also contribute to the diversity of the industry in the state.

The steady evolution of computer technology has greatly affected government, businesses, and personal lives in North Carolina. IT applications within state government have been numerous. In the 1990s North Carolina became the first state in the nation to implement a statewide digital network for data and voice communications. It also deployed a broadband network—an advanced communications infrastructure, or "information highway," that in the early 2000s served as a foundation for video and other connectivity across regions.

The genesis of the North Carolina IT industry in the public sector was in the initial application of computers in governmental affairs. Employing his wide experience in business, Governor Luther H. Hodges in the 1950s sought to bring business management strategies to the state government. To this end, he persuaded the General Assembly to create a Department of Administration, which became effective on 1 July 1957. Charged with coordinating fiscal and planning operations, the department soon began developing and operating statewide data processing and computer centers.

Computers entered North Carolina public higher education with much fanfare in March 1960, when the University of North Carolina Computation Center and its 19-ton Remington Rand Univac computer was dedicated in Chapel Hill. In his address marking the occasion, Hodges traced the eight-year effort (1952–59) that led to the establishment of the center. The personalities and groups he credited included UNC presidents Gordon Gray and William Friday, chancellor Robert House, and other UNC officials, as well as executives of Remington Rand, the National Science Foundation, and the U.S. Bureau of the Census.

Arguably Hodges's most important accomplishments as a state leader came through his role in the development of the Research Triangle Park (RTP). Situated squarely between the campuses of UNC-Chapel Hill, Duke University, and North Carolina State University, the RTP subsequently attracted many government agencies and research and technology companies. By the mid-1960s, largely because of the RTP, the state had become a national leader in programs supporting IT and other scientific endeavors. Currently, the RTP is ranked as one of the top technology centers in the world and remains a high-profile example of the progressive application of government-level technology policy for economic development. The Centennial Campus (Raleigh) and the Piedmont Triad Research Park (Winston-Salem) are other examples of successful high-tech facilities in North Carolina.

Hodges's successors, such as Governors Robert W. Scott, James B. Hunt, and James G. Martin, continued to promote the interdependence of business and state government through computer technology. In the private sector, the IT industry underwent massive growth beginning in the late 1990s with the proliferation of "dot-com" companies, only to suffer from the collapse of many of these businesses a few years later. The declining price of hardware products, a result of the trend toward economic globalization, has led to manufacturing declines in the state and the "outsourcing" of skilled jobs abroad. Some North Carolina firms downsized their operations in an effort to remain successful.

International Business Machines (IBM), a giant in the IT industry since the 1950s, moved operations to North Carolina in 1965 as one of the first RTP tenants, becoming one of the state's most important employers. The company manufactured and supplied software for its own computer systems beginning in the 1970s and continued to adjust manufacturing strategies, including deciding to outsource and downsize its workforce by nearly 30 percent in the early 2000s and to stop producing its own computer hardware. Nevertheless, North Carolina remains home to IBM's Global Services Division, which comprises the world's largest number of IBM employees, most of them highly skilled.

Many other major IT companies maintain a presence in North Carolina. RF Micro Devices in Greensboro became one of the world's largest producers of semiconductor analog chips used in wireless communications (including cell phones) and other applications. The company grew remarkably in little more than a decade; by 2004 it employed 1,800 people, earned $650 million in annual sales, and provided its wares to firms such as Nokia, Samsung, Motorola, and Qualcomm. In the same period Red Hat, a leader in software production and computer consulting services, maintained its headquarters in North Carolina, as did another software giant, SAS. The state also boasted the second-largest number of Microsoft and Cisco employees, large operations of telecommunications companies Nortel, Solectron, and Flextronics, and important semiconductor manufacturers Cree, Nitronex, Ziptronix, and the Silicon Wireless Corporation.

References: Information Resource Management Commission, *E-Government: Using Technology to Transform North Carolina's Governmental Services and Operations in the Digital Age* (2001); Albert N. Link, *A Generosity of Spirit: The Early History of the Research Triangle Park* (1995); North Carolina Board of Science and Technology, *Forces for Change: An Economy in Transition* (1999).

Mark Anderson Moore
Additional research provided by Wiley J. Williams.

SEE ALSO Research Triangle Park.

Inlets. Several dozen inlets have existed along North Carolina's Atlantic coastline since European settlers first arrived in the sixteenth century. A few important inlets have remained nearly permanent travel corridors between North Carolina's coastal towns and the open sea, while others, created in the Outer Banks during hurricanes and other severe storms, stayed open for very short periods of time. Throughout the years, hurricanes have also closed a number of the state's inlets, some of which have been reopened at great public expense.

Ocracoke Inlet, just south of Ocracoke Island, is the only inlet that has been open throughout North Carolina's more than 400 years of recorded history. In 1585 the first colonists sent out by Sir Walter Raleigh entered the inlet en route to Roanoke Island. Early settlers and traders, bound for the ports on the Pamlico and Neuse Rivers, found Ocracoke the only deepwater inlet that connected the Atlantic Ocean with the Pamlico Sound. In the early 1700s, the other Outer Banks inlets—Currituck, Roanoke, and old Hatteras—became progressively less reliable, and by the late eighteenth century all three had closed. This left Ocracoke Inlet as the main port of entry for northeastern North Carolina, including the Albemarle Sound, the Pamlico Sound, and all of their estuaries.

Northern Carolina planters continued to be dependent on Ocracoke Inlet both for shipping products abroad and for importing commodities that were not produced there. With the advent of steam power, Ocracoke Inlet was used also by the new passenger-carrying steamships, especially on the route between New York City and New Bern. In a 12-month period in 1836 and 1837, more than 1,400 vessels passed through Ocracoke Inlet. Meanwhile, Portsmouth continued to grow. In 1840 a post office was established there, and in 1846 the federal government opened a marine hospital to take care of sick seamen. In 1850 the official population of the town was 505.

The decline of Ocracoke Inlet began on 7 Sept. 1846, when a powerful hurricane opened two new inlets through the Outer Banks, Oregon Inlet and a new Hatteras Inlet. Within 15 years, when the Civil War spread to coastal North Carolina, Hatteras Inlet had replaced Ocracoke as the most important inlet along the Outer Banks. In late 1861, after the Confederate forts at Hatteras Inlet had been captured by Union forces, several stone-filled vessels were towed south to Ocracoke Inlet and sunk to block the channel. Ocracoke Inlet never regained its prominence, and Portsmouth, the town dependent on its survival, gradually withered away. Ocracoke Inlet remains navigable by small craft and still appears on North Carolina maps and charts. It is identified primarily as the boundary line between Hyde and Carteret Counties and between the Cape Hatteras National Seashore and the Cape Lookout National Seashore.

Hatteras Inlet, which separates Hatteras from Ocracoke, has remained open continuously since its creation in the hurricane of 1846. (The first Hatteras Inlet, open during the colonial period, is reported to have shoaled up and closed prior to the Revolution after a British warship was stranded in the channel.) Prior to that, Ocracoke was a peninsula attached to Hatteras Island, and a solid line of beach extended from above Cape Hatteras to Ocracoke Inlet. The modern Hatteras Inlet is wide and shallow, and consequently able to accommodate only relatively small vessels, but it is used extensively by a large commercial fishing fleet operating out of Hatteras Village and other Pamlico Sound ports. A fleet of state-run ferry boats also cross the inlet between Hatteras and the north end of Ocracoke Island. The ferries are free, and during the summer tourist season the traffic is so heavy that they depart both sides of the inlet every few minutes.

Oregon Inlet, very changeable and less important to commerce than Hatteras and Ocracoke Inlets, served enough shallow-draft vessels to earn attention from the government. In the 1870s the Army Corps of Engineers, yielding to public demands, made the first of many studies of improvements. Use of Oregon Inlet declined with the share of maritime trade borne by small vessels but began to grow again in the 1930s, when roads and bridges revived tourism in Dare County. Acquisition of land on both sides of the inlet for Cape Hatteras National Seashore in 1953 stopped private-sector development in the vicinity. Growth on Hatteras Island led to the construction of the Herbert Bonner Bridge in 1964. This project caused or coincided with the onset of wild changes in depth and a rapid narrowing of the Oregon Inlet from more than 7,700 feet to less than 2,500. Maintaining the channel has since become difficult, and the inlet has nearly closed from hurricanes and other factors several times. Even before the bridge was built, the instability of Oregon Inlet and the violence of its currents led the North Carolina Wildlife Resources Commission to declare it the most dangerous place in the state for boating.

Beaufort Inlet is a deepwater channel that traverses the Outer Banks west of Cape Lookout, connecting Bogue Sound with the Atlantic Ocean. Originally known as Topsail Inlet or Core Sound Inlet, it has served North Carolina as a port of entry since the early days of settlement. Efforts to maintain the natural depth of Beaufort Inlet (15 to 20 feet), or to increase it by stabilizing the channel and reducing its width, were begun by the Army Corps of Engineers in the 1880s with the construction of jetties at Shackleford Point on the north side and Fort Macon Point on the south side. In modern times, with Beaufort Inlet serving as the entranceway to the State Port at Morehead City, the depth of the main channel is maintained at 30 feet.

Bogue Inlet, the southern limit of the Outer Banks, may have been visited by Europeans as early as 1524 when Giovanni da Verrazano, a Florentine explorer employed by the French, sent a small party ashore near the modern boundary between Carteret and Onslow Counties. The inlet remained

largely ignored until the beginning of the eighteenth century, when Queen Anne's War transformed the ongoing rivalry between Spain and England into formal belligerency. During much of the nineteenth century, Bogue Inlet continued to be the site of considerable maritime traffic. Lumber, turpentine, tar, and pickled beef and pork came down the White Oak River and departed through the inlet for other parts of the United States, while fertilizer and manufactured goods arrived through the passage.

After the Civil War, a series of events conspired to reduce Bogue Inlet's significance. Some shippers found that transporting goods through Bogue Sound to Morehead City made more sense than moving them across the open ocean. As if to retaliate for being neglected, the inlet began to fill with silt, eventually providing only about a fathom of water at low tide. Onslow County became connected to Wilmington, a deepwater port, by rail in the 1890s, and the Inland Waterway, as of 1931, provided a vastly superior route than Bogue Inlet did to Swansboro—by then just a quiet fishing village, no longer the busy port it had once been.

Several other inlets have been significant in North Carolina history and have remained important features of the state's coastline. Beginning in the 1720s and throughout the colonial period, New River Inlet, located at the mouth of the New River in Onslow County, served as a significant artery of trade, and in 1758 it was designated as an inspection point for export commodities. Maritime trade through New River Inlet continued during most of the eighteenth and nineteenth centuries, accompanied by sporadic efforts by both the state and federal governments to improve its channels of navigation. This trade declined markedly in the 1890s, however, with the completion of a railroad link between Wilmington and Jacksonville.

Maritime use of New Topsail Inlet, located along the coast of Pender County at the lower end of Topsail Beach, began in the second quarter of the eighteenth century, and for nearly 200 years thereafter the inlet served as a significant artery of coastal trade. In close proximity to ongoing residential and recreational development, the inlet by the late twentieth century was being used primarily by pleasure craft and sport fishing boats. Lockwoods Folly Inlet, situated between Holden Beach and Long Beach in south-central Brunswick County, provides an outlet to the Atlantic Ocean for the Lockwoods Folly River. The inlet was improved by the federal government as early as the 1890s, but its use as an artery of commerce had diminished considerably by the 1930s. Carolina Beach Inlet is a man-made inlet located just north of Carolina Beach. Early plans for an artificial inlet in that area were formulated by 1938 but were not carried into effect for another 14 years. Other North Carolina inlets existing in 2006 were Swash Inlet, Drum Inlet, Bear Inlet, Brown's Inlet, Rich Inlet, Mason Inlet, Masonboro Inlet, Corncake Inlet, and Tubbs Inlet.

References: Gary S. Dunbar, *Historical Geography of the North Carolina Outer Banks* (1958); Robert L. Gray, "Opening an Inlet to the Carolina Sound," *Literary Digest* 7 (March 1925); Jay Langfelder and others, *A Historical Review of Some of North Carolina's Coastal Inlets* (1974); David Stick, *The Outer Banks of North Carolina, 1584–1958* (1958).

Wilson Angley
David Stick
Additional research provided by Wynne Dough and Thomas J. Farnham.

Innes Academy. SEE Thalian Association.

Inns and Taverns played an important role in the economic and geographic development of colonial North Carolina. These establishments—also known as "ordinaries" in eighteenth-century America because they often catered to the full spectrum of social classes—were frequently one of the first businesses to appear in newly designated county seats, offering food and lodging to travelers and visitors to court. Consequently, inns and taverns provided a variety of goods and services, from meals and liquor to overnight accommodations. While colonial law required innkeepers to provide suitable lodgings at a reasonable price, exactly what constituted "suitable" was always in question. Travelers staying the night might find themselves sharing a bed with two or three others, if they were lucky enough to get a bed at all. Not surprisingly, many female travelers avoided sleeping or eating at public inns in favor of private homes.

Various wines, beers, hard ciders, and exotic punches were standard offerings on the drink menus of early North Carolina taverns and public houses. Many well-known eighteenth-century establishments regularly served liquor-based toddies to weary patrons in need of relaxation after a long day of difficult travel. The drinks' potency and warmth, and the addition of nutmeg or other spices, made toddies particularly welcome in colder months. They were also widely considered elixirs with great medicinal value, effective against symptoms of viruses, nervous conditions, and other ailments.

Tavern keepers adhered to strictly enforced laws requiring them to post their rates for meals, beverages (especially liquor and spirits), and some services. With a built-in local customer base, tavern keepers frequently branched out into auxiliary economic endeavors to provide other services for their customers and make a larger profit. Taverns that doubled as ferry (and later, stage) stops and inns that housed general merchandise stores were popular combinations.

Perhaps North Carolina's most famous colonial tavern is Salem Tavern, located in the heart of Old Salem. Its structure, which is currently a museum located next to a full-service restaurant, dates to 1784, when it was reconstructed after an earlier wooden tavern burned to the ground. Person's Or-

dinary, in the present-day town of Littleton, was originally licensed to Thomas Person in 1764 and again to William Person Little in 1820. The small frame building served for several generations as a way-station to travelers on the "high" or "stage-coach" road between Hillsborough and the town of Halifax. Stories of duels surround the early history of the ordinary. One, related by Rebecca Leach Dozier in her history of Littleton and credited to an ex-slave called "Mammy Lissa," describes a Revolution-era duel between a Whig named Drugger and a Tory named Drumghould, wherein Drugger eventually kills his opponent over a political insult.

Pop Castle was a legendary inn and recreation center in colonial Granville County at a site now in Vance County, one mile west of Kittrell. It was reputedly first occupied by an unidentified nobleman, a political refugee from Europe, and later owned by one Captain (Nathaniel?) Pope, a pirate who was said to have buried gold nearby. Known for a time as Popecastle Inn, it was soon altered to Pop Castle by local usage after an adjoining cockfighting pit and tavern began to attract people. A racetrack was laid out during the Revolution. The main building of the inn was finally taken down after the Civil War. The site was marked by a large lone oak tree for many years, but myths of Pop Castle survived into the twentieth century.

Hunter's Tavern in Wake County was established by Isaac Hunter in 1769 on land probably deeded to him by his father, Theophilus Hunter. When the North Carolina legislature convened at Hillsborough during the summer of 1788 to consider ratification of the U.S. Constitution, it also decided the site of the permanent capital of the state. Several places were proposed, including "Mr. Isaac Hunter's in Wake County," which was nominated by James Iredell. On 2 Aug. 1788 it was chosen, and thus the capital of North Carolina was to be erected within ten miles of Hunter's Tavern. Commissioners selected by the General Assembly to select a specific site met at Hunter's Tavern on 20 Mar. 1792. Hunter apparently hoped to sell land for the capital, but the commissioners adjourned to the residence of Joel Lane, from whom they eventually purchased land. Hunter sold the tavern property in 1801 to William Camp, husband of his daughter Elizabeth. The property passed through the hands of several owners, including the late J. Crawford Biggs. The North Raleigh Hilton is currently located on the site of Isaac Hunter's tavern.

Eagle Tavern was a hostelry that welcomed visitors to Hertford, the seat of Perquimans County, from colonial times to the beginning of the twentieth century. From a modest beginning in 1762 in the home of Charles Jordan, the tavern ultimately became a sprawling multistory frame structure of 25 rooms that covered six lots at the corner of Church and Grubb Streets. George Washington purportedly stayed at the Eagle while he was engaged in the survey of the nearby Great Dismal Swamp. Among other famous eighteenth-century guests was

William Hooper, one of North Carolina's three signers of the Declaration of Independence. The old rambling building was razed in 1915.

Casso's Inn was the largest and most popular hostelry in the early years of Raleigh. The inn (sometimes called a tavern) was best known for a traditional association with Andrew Johnson, seventeenth president of the United States. Built between 1790 and 1795 by Peter Casso, who had come to Raleigh from Beaufort County, the inn stood on the northeast corner of Fayetteville Street (Lot 162 in the plan of the city) diagonally across from the statehouse. Its only competitor was the Indian Queen, which it quickly surpassed in patronage and size. Despite the popularity and apparent success of his inn, Peter Casso proved to be an inefficient businessman. By 1799 he had established a pattern of indebtedness from which he would never recover.

Local tradition maintains that Andrew Johnson's mother, Mary "Polly" McDonough, worked at Casso's Inn as a weaver before she married Jacob Johnson, and that Andrew was born in one of the kitchens then serving as the Johnsons' home. Extensive research neither upholds the truth of the story nor proves it false beyond a doubt. In the absence of conclusive evidence to the contrary, the tradition will continue to claim a place in the history of Casso's Inn.

References: Daniel W. Barefoot, *Touring the Backroads of North Carolina's Upper Coast* (1995); Donoh W. Hanks Jr., "Popcastle Inn," *The State* (14 Nov. 1936); Daniel B. Thorp, "Taverns and Tavern Culture on the Southern Colonial Frontier: Rowan County, North Carolina, 1753–1776," *Journal of Southern History* 62 (November 1996).

Johanna Miller Lewis
Additional research provided by Daniel W. Barefoot, Jerry L. Cross, Jerry Leath Mills, and Thornton W. Mitchell.

SEE ALSO Salem Tavern; Travelers' Rooms.

Institute for Research in Social Science

Institute for Research in Social Science (IRSS) at the University of North Carolina at Chapel Hill was founded in 1924 with support from the Laura Spelman Rockefeller Memorial of New York. At first, most of the institute's resources went to support a cadre of talented research assistants assigned to work on faculty-initiated projects. Many went on to distinguished scholarly careers: Guy B. Johnson, T. J. Woofter Jr., and Arthur F. Raper in the study of race relations; Lee M. Brooks in criminology; Rupert B. Vance in demography; Paul W. Wager and Edward J. Woodhouse in the study of local government; and William S. Jenkins, Guion G. Johnson, and Fletcher M. Green in southern history. Two other early research assistants were sociologist Gordon Blackwell, who succeeded Howard W. Odum as IRSS director from 1944 to 1957, and statistician Daniel O. Price, who served as director from 1957 to 1966.

After 1944 the emphasis of the IRSS began to change, shifting away from the regional orientation that had characterized many of the institute's early research projects. Moreover, the nature of social science research was changing: what faculty required in the way of facilities was now computational hardware and support in statistical analysis, the use of computers, and data acquisition. Over the next 25 years, the IRSS gradually took on major responsibilities in these areas. The institute's Social Science Data Library, for example, has become the third-largest repository of social science data in the United States. Its holdings include the public opinion surveys of alumnus Louis D. Harris and the National Network of State Polls, for which IRSS serves as headquarters.

The name of the institute officially became the Howard W. Odum Institute for Research in Social Science in 1999. The IRSS continues to serve a faculty whose interests are more diverse and less regionally oriented than ever. The institute frequently conducts statewide public-opinion surveys and in the 1990s carried out a series of "Southern Focus Polls," national surveys with special attention to matters of regional interest. In 1995 the interdisciplinary quarterly *Southern Cultures*, begun by the institute, was taken over by the University of North Carolina's newly established Center for the Study of the American South. That center was itself initially housed and supported by the IRSS in a process of organizational "incubation," as was the Center for Urban and Regional Studies in the 1960s.

References: Wayne D. Brazil, *Howard W. Odum: The Building Years, 1884–1930* (1988); Guy Benton Johnson and Guion G. Johnson, *Research in Service to Society: The First Fifty Years of the Institute for Research in Social Science at the University of North Carolina* (1980).

John Shelton Reed

Institute of Government

Institute of Government. The concept of the Institute of Government was devised by state official and academician Albert Coates in 1931, when he recognized that many local governments in North Carolina did not have the time, resources, or personnel to stay abreast of legal and political changes taking place at five overlapping governmental levels. He proposed to meet these deficiencies through a series of guidebooks, a clearinghouse of information, and a central meeting place near the University of North Carolina at Chapel Hill. Coates established a steering committee in 1931, held an organizational meeting the next year, distributed 100,000 copies of his plan to the general public, and by September 1932 held the first training program for public officials. His staff produced the publication *Popular Government* for local officials, as well as a legislative service. In 1939 a $100,000 building was dedicated for the use of the Institute of Government, mainly through the generosity of several large contributors. In 1942 the institute became a part of the University of North Carolina.

Now under the umbrella of UNC-Chapel Hill's School of

Government, established in 2001, the Institute of Government continues to provide educational, advisory, and research support for local and state governments. It is the largest university-based local government training, consulting, and research organization in the country, sponsoring more than 200 classes, seminars, schools, and specialized conferences for more than 14,000 public officials annually. The success of the institute is due to a unique relationship with North Carolina's nearly 700 county and municipal governments. Elected officials, city and county managers, finance directors, purchasing agents, information services directors, attorneys, budget directors, school officials, and numerous other public managers and employees have regular contact with faculty and staff. Every year the institute publishes more than 100 books, bulletins, chapters, articles, and other reference works related to state and local government. When the General Assembly is in session, the institute's Legislative Reporting Service puts out the *Daily Bulletin* in print and electronic format for legislators and others.

Reference: Albert Coates, *The Story of the Institute of Government* (1981).

Robert E. Ireland

Instructions to Royal Governors. Every governor of Great Britain's royal colonies received an official commission and a set of instructions from the Board of Trade that were to guide his actions while in office. The instructions detailed the powers of the governor, executive council, and Assembly and touched on nearly all administrative and executive matters. Written in England by officials who were unaware of the colonies' political realities, the instructions often placed the governors in an awkward position. Governors were required to abide by the instructions, which were intended to assert stronger British control of the colonies and make them more profitable for the homeland. This brought the governors time and again into conflict with the Assembly and colonists of the unruly province of North Carolina until the final break with Britain in 1775. British authorities regarded the instructions as having the force of royal commands, whereas the colonists viewed them as no more than guidelines or suggestions and bristled at the thought that they were mandatory.

Governors' commissions were public documents, but the royal instructions were secret documents intended for the governor alone, although occasionally he might make parts of their contents known to the council or Assembly. This secrecy was another source of colonial resentment. Usually, a royal governor's instructions were drawn up by the Board of Trade, sent to the secretary of state and the Privy Council for approval, and finally endorsed by the king. The instructions were cumulative; that is, instructions sent to one governor were binding on his successors unless changed.

The pressure to obey instructions from the Board of Trade made it difficult for a governor to rule in North Carolina. The colonial Assembly, which dated back to the Proprietary charters of 1663 and 1665, was used to operating without much restraint from British authority, but after 1729 the Crown held that the Assembly's authority existed only by royal decree and tried to limit its powers. The colonists believed that the powers of the Crown were still restricted by the Carolina charter, and that rights and privileges granted the colony by the charter were still valid. The Assembly, which retained much control of the colony's finances, reacted to British pressure by refusing to pay the salaries of royal officials and quarreling over the governors' appropriations. Governors often had to disobey parts of their instructions in order to reach compromises with the Assembly to attain at least some of their goals. These compromises sometimes resulted in laws that were rejected by the Crown when news of them reached England.

Josiah Martin, North Carolina's last royal governor, strictly adhered to his instructions, insisted that they required obedience from the Assembly as well as himself, and made little effort to understand the colonists' views. In 1773 the Assembly added to a vital courts bill an attachment clause that permitted the seizure of property of non–North Carolinians who owed a debt in the province. Martin, citing his instructions, refused to allow the bill. The Assembly refused to pass a courts bill without it, and therefore after 1773 there were no courts in the colony except those of the county magistrates. Martin tried to use his authority to create new criminal courts, but the Assembly refused to pay for them. In response to Martin's blind regard to his instructions, the Assembly also established a Committee of Correspondence to keep in touch with the increasingly rebellious representatives of the other colonies.

References: Leonard W. Labaree, ed., *Royal Instructions to British Colonial Governors, 1670–1776* (2 vols., 1935); Charles Lee Raper, *North Carolina: A Study in English Colonial Government* (1904); Blackwell P. Robinson, *The Five Royal Governors of North Carolina, 1729–1775* (1963).

David A. Norris

Insurance. North Carolinians, both white and black, relied on fraternal societies, voluntary assessment associations, and mutual benevolent societies for burial insurance and sick benefits throughout the nineteenth and early twentieth centuries. Slaves organized insurance societies as early as the 1840s to provide for burials. After emancipation, these societies continued to flourish. Wealthier white citizens also organized state-chartered legal reserve companies. These white companies determined that blacks were not profitable customers due to higher death rates at each age, lower life expectancies, and lower policy renewal rates. As a result, the insurance industry remained highly segregated until the

1960s, when black leaders began emphasizing integration of predominantly white institutions rather than strengthening black institutions. The number of black insurance companies nationwide declined from 42 in 1973 to 39 in 1975, 23 in 1993, and a mere 13 by 1998.

North Carolina Mutual Life Insurance Company of Durham was founded in 1899 as a mutual assessment association. In 1913 it was the first black mutual assessment association nationwide to convert to a more financially accountable state-chartered legal reserve status. The company survived the Great Depression, which caused the collapse of many American insurance companies, to emerge in 1939 as the largest black-owned company in the nation.

In 1899 the state legislature established the North Carolina Department of Insurance; before that time, the secretary of state had overseen the licensing and regulation of the state's insurance companies. Over the years, insurance fraud has been a major concern of the industry. The Department of Insurance continually investigates and seeks to thwart fraudulent claims. In 2000, for example, the state achieved approximately 30 criminal convictions, representing more than $17 million in savings for the industry and consumers.

The combined category of insurance, finance, and real estate in the early 2000s employed between 4 and 5 percent of North Carolina workers, with businesses concentrated in Charlotte, Greensboro, and Durham. In addition to Mutual Life of Durham, some of the state's most notable insurance companies in 2006 were Jefferson-Pilot Corporation of Greensboro, a diversified nationwide company; Blue Cross and Blue Shield of North Carolina, a medical service and hospital corporation serving more than 2.9 million members; North Carolina Farm Bureau Mutual of Raleigh, a statewide agricultural insurer; Integon Indemnity and Specialty Insurance Companies of Winston-Salem; and Builder's Mutual Insurance of Raleigh. Most national insurers maintained facilities in North Carolina, including Royal and Sun Alliance and Kemper Insurance, both with major facilities in Charlotte.

References: "The List: P & C Insurance Companies," *Triangle Business Journal* 14 (4 June 1999); Robert E. Weems Jr., "A Crumbling Legacy: The Decline of African-American Insurance Companies in Contemporary America," *Review of Black Political Economy* 23 (1994).

Gordon Neal Diem

SEE ALSO Blue Cross and Blue Shield of North Carolina; Durham Life Insurance Company; Jefferson-Pilot Corporation; North Carolina Mutual Life Insurance Company.

Integral Society was a descriptive term for the objective of royal governor Arthur Dobbs (1754–65) to alleviate the problem of unsatisfactory race relations between the English and the native Indians. When Dobbs arrived in North Carolina in 1754, he proposed that the Indians should be treated fairly and justly, expecting that kindness and honest treatment would ensure peaceful relations. He suggested that soldiers take Indian wives as a step that would lead to the permanent establishment of the British in America.

After living in the colony for a time, however, and gaining experience with the Indians as well as the colonists, Dobbs changed his views. He concluded that a better plan, in war at least, was to kill warriors and enslave women and children. Cruel as this was, it apparently was a scheme that most colonists also favored.

William S. Powell

Internal Improvements was a nineteenth-century term referring to investment in transportation projects such as roads, railroads, canals, harbors, and river navigation projects. These public works are an accepted responsibility of the modern state government, but in earlier times the concept of public funding for such projects was new and controversial. North Carolina was so isolated and poor in the early nineteenth century that it was derisively nicknamed the "Rip Van Winkle State." At alarming rates, emigrants fled its stagnant economy, worn-out farmland, poverty, and lack of opportunity. Among the state's greatest handicaps was inadequate transportation. Only a few rivers in the east were navigable, and even these were shallow and difficult to travel. The coast offered few good harbors, and roads, where they existed, were terrible. Under such conditions transportation was slow, inefficient, and so expensive that farmers could not afford to ship their produce more than a few miles.

Some state leaders, such as Governors Alexander Martin in 1791 and Nathaniel Alexander in 1806, asked the General Assembly for money to finance internal improvements. But many legislators and voters strongly opposed raising taxes or increasing government's involvement in internal improvements; for years, the state's role was limited to granting charters to private companies to operate toll bridges, canals, and navigation projects.

North Carolina's greatest advocate of internal improvements was state legislator and Caswell County native Archibald D. Murphey, who recommended that the government undertake ambitious transportation projects, develop market towns to build the state's economy, and drain swamps in the east to create new, fertile farmland. A revised version of his proposals to the General Assembly from 1815 to 1818 appeared in his 1819 *Memoir on Internal Improvements*. Murphey's plans included providing North Carolina with an extensive network of canals and navigable rivers linked by good roads. The new routes would be funneled into three systems: the Roanoke River and Albemarle Sound; the Tar and Neuse Rivers, which would have ocean access through Ocracoke Inlet; and a linking of the Yadkin and Catawba Rivers with the Cape Fear, to give western North Carolina access to the Atlantic. One of the state's great visionaries, Murphey did much to popularize internal improvements; however, he died before his ideas became reality.

In 1819 the work of Murphey and like-minded leaders persuaded the legislature to create a corporation, called the President and Directors of the Board of Internal Improvements, to manage a Fund for Internal Improvements, which would be a permanent source of revenue to underwrite internal improvements. The Board of Internal Improvements consisted of the governor (as an ex officio member) and six directors elected from each of the state's six judicial districts by a joint ballot of the two houses of the legislature. The duties of the board included appointing civil engineers for the state, subscribing to stock in public works as authorized by the General Assembly, recommending surveys and additional projects for legislative consideration, and reporting on the status of the Fund for Internal Improvements and internal improvements in which the state had an interest.

The General Assembly originally underwrote the Internal Improvements Fund using the proceeds from the sale of land formerly belonging to the Cherokee Indians. Federal treaties had extinguished title to approximately a million acres in the mountains in 1819, and the state proceeded to sell the land. In its 1821–22 session, the legislature, declaring that the fund was "entirely insufficient," augmented land sales with dividends from state-owned stock in the Bank of New Bern and the Bank of the Cape Fear.

From the inception of the Internal Improvements Fund to the mid-1830s, the legislature used its moneys in conjunction with direct appropriations from the state treasury to promote various projects. Of $291,865 spent on internal improvements to 1836, $205,388 came from the fund. Engineering (surveys) amounted to $67,808; stock subscriptions in navigation companies (Roanoke, Cape Fear, Yadkin, Tar, Neuse, Catawba), the Clubfoot and Harlow Creek Canal Company, and turnpike companies (Buncombe and Plymouth), $142,900; direct appropriations for river improvements and highways, $59,157; and loans to support the Clubfoot and Harlow Creek Canal, Old Fort and Asheville Roads, and the Tennessee River Turnpike, $22,000.

Beyond financial assistance to the railroads and the usual expenses of the Board of Internal Improvements (travel for members of the board and salary of a clerk), relatively small sums of money from the fund were used to survey the Nags Head area on the Outer Banks and to finance road building and maintenance in the Mountain region. In 1847 the General Assembly, facing financial difficulties, decided to transfer the balance of the Internal Improvements Fund—$75,840—and all securities and sources of revenue for the fund to the public treasury. Thereafter most internal improvements were underwritten by direct appropriations.

Murphey's was not the only voice promoting reform. In 1828 Joseph Caldwell raised public interest in railroads through a series of newspaper essays, later republished as *The Numbers of Carlton*. The once nearly monolithic Republican Party split over several issues at the federal and state levels, including internal improvements. Progressive Republicans who supported internal improvements and other reforms formed the Whig Party around 1834–35. The Whigs adopted many of Murphey's ideas, making the party popular in western North Carolina, an underdeveloped region that hoped to benefit from new roads. The Albemarle Sound area, dependent on trade with Virginia, also favored the Whig policy of aiding transportation. By the mid-1830s, support for internal improvements was a crucial factor in the Whig ascendancy to the governorship and control of the General Assembly. Whig governors Edward B. Dudley, John Motley Morehead, and William A. Graham strongly advocated internal improvements.

By the advent of the Whig Party, the public was more interested in railroads than in water transportation. Railroads could reach anywhere in the state and did not depend on water flow and constant dredging, as did water routes. The first railroad company in North Carolina, the Wilmington & Raleigh, was founded in 1833, followed by the Raleigh & Gaston Railroad in 1835. The Whigs aided railroad construction by having the state buy railroad stock, and many other railroads were chartered in the antebellum period. Railroads would ultimately be the state's most successful internal improvement.

On regaining control of state government in the 1850s, the Democrats adopted many of the Whigs' progressive policies, including pushing for internal improvements. Newspaper editors like William W. Holden were very influential in getting the party to give up its opposition to state aid for transportation projects. Democratic initiatives in that area included greatly increased aid to railroads, including the east-west North Carolina Railroad, two-thirds of which was owned by the state. At this time Morehead City was founded to serve as an ocean port at the eastern terminus of the state railroad.

North Carolina's growth and prosperity in the 1850s were largely due to the increased ease of transportation and the growing economy produced by the internal improvements movement. Farmers profited by having cheap rail access to distant markets. Cities like Raleigh and New Bern, their growth fueled by railroad links, grew rapidly. This era ended with the outbreak of the Civil War in 1861. When internal improvements again became possible after the war, the state's poverty and conservative leadership prevented much direct state aid. But the public demand for reforms continued. In the late nineteenth century, the state, mainly by holding to a laissez-faire policy that protected business from taxes and regulations, helped railroads and other needed projects. As the twentieth century progressed, significant improvements such as the construction of state ports, reservoirs, highways, and public airports became a primary focus of state and county government. The term "internal improvements" eventually came to refer to these and other projects vital to the infrastructure of modern society.

References: Jeffrey E. Thomas, "Internal Improvements and Political Parties in Antebellum North Carolina, 1836–1860," NCHR 55 (April 1978); Alan D. Watson, "North Carolina and Internal Improvements, 1783–1861: A Case of Inland Navigation," NCHR 74 (January 1997); Harry L. Watson, "Squire Oldway and His Friends: Opposition to Internal Improvements in Antebellum North Carolina," NCHR 54 (January 1977); Charles C. Weaver, *History of Public Improvements in North Carolina Previous to 1860* (1903).

Alan D. Watson
David A. Norris

International Home Furnishings Market

International Home Furnishings Market in High Point and Thomasville is the largest furniture market in the world, drawing more people than the next four largest furniture markets combined (Cologne, Tokyo, Guadalajara, and Milan). An average of 74,000 people come twice a year to High Point and Thomasville to attend the nine-day event, which features 8 million square feet of permanent showroom space displaying all types of furniture, decorative accessories, lighting, rugs, and bedding. There are 2,400 exhibitors, about 105 of whom are international. Attendees hail from all 50 states and include representatives from 106 foreign countries. The market is held in April and October, the dates being set 20 years in advance. Manufacturers, home furnishings retailers, interior designers, architects, suppliers, and news media come in numbers to buy, sell, research, and publicize the latest furniture trends. The event is not open to the public, but its highlights are covered in many national publications.

The International Home Furnishings Market originated in 1909, when a group of manufacturers in High Point and neighboring towns used two buildings to show their wares to buyers from other states. Their efforts prospered, and in June 1921 the ten-story Southern Furniture Exposition Building was opened for two shows a year. Eventually the number of buyers increased, but larger furniture markets continued to be held in Grand Rapids, Mich., Chicago, and New York City. As southern manufacturers began producing more upscale furniture and travel became easier, buyers from other states began to attend the High Point market in larger numbers. More exhibitors soon came as well, and other showrooms were built at many local factory sites. After the International Home Furnishings Market had become the top market in the country, new showrooms were created in the former downtown area of High Point. By 2000 the showroom complex, which after 1988 was officially called the International Home Furnishings Center, had spread into 160 separate buildings.

References: Holt McPherson, *High Pointers of High Point* (1976); F. J. Sizemore, *The Building and Builders of a City* (1947).

Elizabeth H. Conner

Inter-State Farmers' Conference

Inter-State Farmers' Conference, held in Raleigh in August 1888, was the Second Annual Meeting of the Inter-State Farmers' Association. The association had been formally organized by elite southern agriculturalists in Atlanta in 1887. Delegates to the Atlanta meeting were chosen by the governors of several southern states. Leonidas L. Polk, former North Carolina commissioner of agriculture and then editor of the *Progressive Farmer*, became the association's first president.

The three-day Raleigh conference, which began on 21 Aug. 1888, attracted delegates from nine southern states. It was described as the largest convention ever held in the city. Polk was again chosen as president, and Elias Carr, an Edgecombe County planter, was selected as an officer from North Carolina. The delegates heard a speech from Governor Alfred M. Scales, attended the laying of a cornerstone at the new Agricultural and Mechanical College in Raleigh, and spent a day touring Durham tobacco factories. They also adopted resolutions favoring southern manufacturing, a national Department of Agriculture, stronger federal railroad rate regulation, the prevention of trusts, an end to the national banking system, an increased money supply, and diversified farming.

The Inter-State Farmers' Association held its last meeting in Montgomery, Ala., in 1889. By that time the more radical Farmers' Alliance was the stronghold of the rural reform movement in the South.

References: Robert C. McMath Jr., *Populist Vanguard: A History of the Southern Farmers' Alliance* (1975); Lala C. Steelman, *The North Carolina Farmers' Alliance: A Political History, 1887–1893* (1985).

James L. Hunt

Intracoastal Waterway

Intracoastal Waterway, a federally protected and maintained shipping route, extends along the Atlantic seaboard from the St. John's River near Jacksonville, Fla., to Norfolk, Va., and the entrance to the Chesapeake Bay. More broadly defined, the term "intracoastal waterway" is often applied as well to the less-sheltered passages connecting northward to Boston and southward to Key West.

An initial impetus behind the waterway's construction was the need for coastal shipping to avoid the treacherous waters off North Carolina's shores, particularly Cape Hatteras. The waterway enters the state from Virginia by way of two alternative routes—the less-traveled passage through the Dismal Swamp Canal and the more popular Virginia Cut to the east. The waterway's southern exit from the state occurs at Little River Inlet near Calabash. Between these two points, the waterway meanders through more than 300 miles of sounds, rivers, creeks, marshes, and manmade cuts.

Cameron Langston Bridge over the Intracoastal Waterway on N.C. 58, connecting Cape Carteret and Emerald Isle. Photograph by Charles E. Jones. North Carolina Department of Transportation.

Two early surveys of projected waterway routes through North Carolina were undertaken in 1837 and 1875, but systematic construction began only after passage of the federal Rivers and Harbors Act of 1912. Subsequently, major portions of the project were completed during the 1910s and 1920s. The last North Carolina section to be built, extending from the Cape Fear River to the South Carolina line, opened to traffic in 1934.

Once completed, the North Carolina portion of the waterway came under heavy usage by motor vessels, barges, and tugs, with commercial tonnage consisting primarily of seafood, fertilizers, agricultural commodities, petroleum products, and general merchandise. Also making use of the waterway from the time of its completion were yachts and various other pleasure craft. During World War II, the waterway provided a means of transporting vital cargoes through North Carolina waters while avoiding the menace of German submarines offshore.

The North Carolina section of the Atlantic Intracoastal Waterway remains a significant artery of commerce for the movement of heavy, bulky cargoes such as timber, pulpwood, and crushed stone. Although it is still important to commercial and sport fishermen, its use is increasingly associated with pleasure craft. Especially in the spring and fall, the waterway

provides a protected passage for traveling mariners en route to second homes or those in pursuit of adventure, natural beauty, and the society of kindred spirits. Largely in response to such boaters' presence and relative affluence, communities along the waterway such as Elizabeth City, Belhaven, Oriental, Beaufort, Wrightsville Beach, and Southport have become tourist centers and ports of call.

References: Allan C. Fisher Jr., *America's Inland Waterway: Exploring the Atlantic Seaboard* (1973); Ronald B. Hartzer, *To Great and Useful Purpose: A History of the Wilmington District U.S. Army Corps of Engineers* (1984); Bob Simpson and Mary Simpson, "The Big Ditch," *Wildlife in North Carolina* (May 1988); Claiborne S. Young, *Cruising Guide to Coastal North Carolina* (1994).

Wilson Angley

SEE ALSO Dismal Swamp Canal.

Inventions. North Carolinians have produced thousands of inventions—new machines, unique processes, and other original products—in home workshops, factories, and scientific laboratories and on farms. Since 1790 most of these inventions have been recorded at the U.S. Patent Office in Washington, D.C. During the nineteenth century, North Carolinians patented approximately 2,000 inventions. The first North Carolinian issued a federal patent was G. F. Saltonstall of Fayetteville, who in 1801 registered his design for a cotton-cleaning machine. Richard Jordan Gatling, born in Hertford County in 1815, is best known for developing and patenting in 1862 the Gatling gun, a hand-cranked, multibarreled, revolving weapon. He also devised scores of new agricultural machines, tools, and transportation devices.

Other North Carolinians patented early machine guns. Orange County resident Grey Utley patented such a weapon, along with many other inventions. His rapid-fire "Carolina Cannon" was registered in 1858, a full four years before Gatling obtained the patent for his gun. During the Civil War, J. W. Howlett of Greensboro also invented a new breech-loading firearm, recording it with the Confederate States Patent Office in 1862. Yet another inventor in this period was Parker D. Robbins, a free black landowner from Bertie County. In addition to being a soldier in the Union cavalry and a representative in North Carolina's postwar legislature, Robbins was a first-rate mechanic. In the 1870s he registered patents for a new cotton cultivator and a saw sharpener. Greene County's Hardy Spears, also an African American, received a patent in 1870 for a protective device for soldiers, described as a "portable shield with gun slots."

North Carolina women also patented new machines, medicines, and, at least in one case, architectural designs. Harriet Irwin of Mecklenburg County secured a patent in 1869 for her design of a hexagonal house, which supposedly had many advantages over traditional four-sided structures. Irwin built a version of her house on West Fifth Street in Charlotte. Two other female inventors, Mary H. Ramsaur of Lincolnton and Lizzie E. Brady of Gatesville, patented special medicinal formulas around this time.

In North Carolina, as elsewhere in the nation, the rapid industrialization and urban development of the late nineteenth and early twentieth centuries prompted a dramatic rise in the number of patents being issued to inventors. The state at this time was the site of the successful test of a machine that would revolutionize transportation, both military and commercial. On 17 Dec. 1903, on the wind-swept dunes of Kitty Hawk in Dare County, Ohio inventors and aviation pioneers Orville and Wilbur Wright achieved the world's first sustained and controlled flight of an aircraft. The Wright brothers had come to North Carolina to take advantage of Kitty Hawk's steady breezes and unobstructed shoreline.

During World War II, U.S. soldiers relied heavily on the M-1 carbine, a semiautomatic rifle invented by David Marshall Williams of Cumberland County. The army ordered more than 8 million of these famous rifles. Eventually, "Carbine" Williams recorded more than 50 patents for firearm mechanisms, producing innovative gun designs for the Colt, Remington, and Winchester companies from his small workshop in Godwin.

During the last decades of the twentieth century, North Carolina's increasing investment in high-tech industries further inspired the creativity of native sons and daughters in areas such as aerospace design, pharmaceuticals, medicine, nuclear engineering, and computer science. William F. Troxler, for example, saw his small basement workshop grow into a multimillion-dollar international electronics firm. A native of Thomasville and a graduate of North Carolina State University, Troxler in the late 1950s and early 1960s began making highly specialized components for satellites, navigational instruments, and nuclear gauges. Worldwide interest in his products resulted in the establishment of Troxler Electronics and fueled his company's rapid development in the Research Triangle Park during the 1970s and 1980s.

References: R. Neil Fulghum, "Forgotten Genius: North Carolina Inventors of the Nineteenth Century," *Tar Heel Junior Historian* (Winter 1980); Margaret Knox, "Basement Business Now Worldwide," *North Carolina Leader* (9 Nov. 1978); Lloyd Little, "William F. Troxler: Selling Electronics around the World," *Raleigh News and Observer*, 14 Sept. 1969.

R. Neil Fulghum

Iredell County, located in North Carolina's Piedmont region, was formed by the division of Rowan County in 1788. The area was originally inhabited by Cherokee and Catawba Indians. It was named for James Iredell, North Carolina attorney general during the Revolution and delegate to the U.S. Constitutional Convention who was later appointed to the U.S. Supreme Court by President George Washington. Iredell County communities include Statesville (established as the county seat in 1789), Harmony, Love Valley, Mooresville, Troutman, Union Grove, Turnersburg, Mount Mourne, and Barnum Springs. Lake Norman, the largest man-made lake in the state in terms of surface area, has 520 miles of shoreline within Iredell County.

Scotch-Irish and German immigrants seeking good soil, game, and proximity to freshwater had settled the area of modern-day Iredell County by 1753. Fort Dobbs (named for Governor Arthur Dobbs) was erected as a defense facility during the French and Indian War (1754–63). Today it is a North Carolina State Historic Site. The arrival of the Western North Carolina Railroad in 1858, soon followed by the Atlantic, Tennessee, and Ohio Railroad, marked the beginning of a long period of growth that continued through the first half of the twentieth century. Industries producing tobacco, liquor, and herbs (Statesville's Wallace Herbarium was one of the largest such facilities in the world during the late nineteenth and early twentieth centuries) were later supplemented by the production of livestock, dairy products, and breeder chickens, of which the county remains a leading producer. Iredell County hosts a number of recreational and cultural events, including the Ole Time Fiddler's and Bluegrass Festival in Union Grove and the National Balloon Rally in Troutman. The North Carolina Auto Racing Hall of Fame in Mooresville (known as "Race City USA") and Love Valley's western-themed campgrounds also attract numerous visitors. The population of Iredell County was estimated to be 136,000 in 2004.

Reference: Genealogical Society of Iredell County, *The Heritage of Iredell County*, vols. 1 and 2 (1980, 2000).

Robert Blair Vocci

SEE ALSO Fort Dobbs.

Iron and Steel Industry. The search by European settlers for sources of iron in North Carolina began with the earliest explorations. Members of Sir Walter Raleigh's first expedition to Roanoke Island and the Chowan River Valley in 1585 reported two iron ore discoveries. Over time, three localities with substantial iron ore deposits were to play a modest role in the economic history of the state. These were the Deep River deposits in Chatham County, the deposits centered around the Big Ore Bank in Lincoln County, and the substantial magnetite ore deposits in Avery County. However, no significant refining in North Carolina was to occur for almost two centuries after the initial sixteenth-century discoveries.

As part of the effort to maintain the British colonies in North America as economic dependencies unable to compete with home industries, the British Parliament passed an act in 1750 that prohibited the manufacture in the colonies of any iron product except pig iron and bar iron, which had not yet been forged into useful implements. As relations between the Crown and the American colonies deteriorated, the colonial legislature resolved to encourage the development of a native iron industry. In 1775 the North Carolina Provincial Congress offered a bounty for the establishment of the first colonial iron forge. At the end of the same year the Provincial Congress rented the furnaces and iron forges built by John Wilcox at Ore Hill near the Deep River iron ore deposits in Chatham County in order to supply iron cannons and cannonballs for the revolutionary forces. Operations were greatly hindered by the lack of well-trained, experienced workers, and the enterprise collapsed before any substantial armaments were produced. Congress surrendered its interest in the works to Wilcox in 1777. The structures were heavily damaged by a storm in 1780 and were abandoned.

Farther west in Lincoln County, some of the state's most important bloomeries and forges were successfully established. This region possessed all the necessary resources: a rich and substantial iron ore deposit, hardwood trees to produce charcoal fuel, limestone to extract the impurities from the metal, refractory crystalline rock to build the furnaces, and falling water to power the bellows and heavy hammers of the forges. Equally important, this region was settled by Germans

and Ulster Scots, many of them trained craftsmen, who established Lincoln County as a major industrial center in North Carolina during this period by founding the iron and textile industries.

The impetus for the development of iron manufacturing in Lincoln County was the passage in 1788 of "An Act to Encourage the Building of Iron Works in this State" by the North Carolina General Assembly. The act provided a ten-year tax exemption and a grant of 3,000 acres of land (unfit for cultivation, to be used as a source of trees for charcoal) to anyone who built an operating iron forge. Within a decade, a number of family-owned forges were in operation in Lincoln County. In 1789 Peter Forney and several associates obtained the Big Ore Bank property and began to exploit its substantial iron ore deposits. John Fulenwider built and operated forges at two locations beginning in 1804. Pig iron produced in the furnaces was forged into a wide range of products for neighboring towns and farms, including plows, horse shoes, wagon tires, chains, nails, tools, muskets, and kitchen implements. Iron products and bar iron were sometimes used as a medium of exchange. During the War of 1812, cannonballs cast at Fulenwider's High Shoals Iron Works were shipped by flatboats to Charleston.

The peak production of pig iron was achieved in 1830, when 1,800 tons of the metal was refined. The skilled iron workers of Lincoln County used this iron to fabricate items as simple as kitchenware and as sophisticated as clocks, steam engines, and farm machinery.

At the outbreak of the Civil War, 49 ironworks were known to be active in the state, mostly in Lincoln, Cherokee, Cleveland, Surry, and Cumberland Counties. When the Confederacy lost its access to northern iron manufacturers, efforts were made to invigorate the iron industry in North Carolina. In 1861 the Sapona Iron Company built a furnace at Ore Hill (now known as Mount Vernon Springs) in Chatham County on the site of John Wilcox's eighteenth-century ironworks, operating it throughout the war. George Lobdell and J. M. Heck, founders of the Cape Fear Iron and Steel Company, operated the Endor Furnace near the Deep River in Lee County beginning in 1862. Iron ore was transported by boat from nearby mines to the furnace. The resulting iron stock was shipped to Fayetteville, where railroad wheels were fabricated. In February 1865 the Congress of the Confederate States passed a bill to build a foundry and arsenal in the Deep River Valley. Construction began but was ceased when the war ended.

The iron industry in North Carolina fared poorly in the face of northern competition following the end of the Civil War. The maturation of iron-making operations in nearby states such as Virginia and Tennessee, as well as the expansion of works in New York and Pennsylvania, combined to ruin the promise that North Carolina's ironworks had shown during the early and mid-nineteenth century. The disappearance of slave labor dealt a severe blow to the industry. Substantial deforestation also played a role in the decline, particularly in Lincoln County, where the small furnaces operated intermittently or closed down.

Another chapter in the history of the North Carolina iron and steel industry occurred in Avery County. The presence of magnetite iron ore in the western mountains was first noted by Reuben White in about 1780. In 1826 Joshua Perkins and two of his brothers took advantage of the General Assembly's 1778 act to build a forge and a dam at the Cranberry iron deposit. The first underground tunnels were driven into the vein in 1882, and a small blast furnace was constructed at the site to smelt the low-titanium ore. In that same year the East Tennessee & Western North Carolina Railroad began to run ore trains from Cranberry to Johnson City, Tenn., where the Cranberry Furnace Company later operated a larger blast furnace. In the first two decades of the twentieth century, annual iron shipments from Cranberry to Johnson City ranged from 50,000 to 100,000 tons. Mining at Cranberry continued until about 1940.

Since the early years of the twentieth century, numerous metal fabricating businesses have operated in North Carolina, manufacturing a wide range of finished iron and steel products. The starting materials utilized by firms such as Charlotte's Nucor Corporation have been refined iron and steel stock purchased from mills located outside of the state.

References: W. S. Bayley, *Magnetic Iron Ores of East Tennessee and Western North Carolina* (1932); Lester J. Cappon, "Iron-Making: A Forgotten Industry of North Carolina," *NCHR* 9 (October 1932); Robert B. Gordon, *American Iron, 1607–1900* (1996).

Douglas A. Wait

Joshua McKaughan

SEE ALSO Big Ore Bank; Endor Furnace; Nucor Corporation; Troublesome Creek Ironworks.

Ironclads were warships designed to be impervious to enemy shot and shell by virtue of their iron-armored wooden hulls. Other names for these ships include rams, armorclads, iron gophers, iron elephants, iron coffins, turtle-backs, and mud-crushers. Attempts to armor war vessels had been made during the 300 years prior to the American Civil War, but it was not until the mid-nineteenth century that steam-powered warships and the development of large-caliber rifled cannons made armoring practical and indeed necessary. The Civil War clearly demonstrated the superiority of ironclads and revolutionized naval warfare.

The Confederacy concluded in June 1861 that ironclad warships would best suit its needs. With its limited shipbuilding capacity, the Confederate navy found it more advantageous to build a few impregnable warships to combat the numerically superior Union navy. The first Confederate attempt was the CSS *Virginia*, a conversion of the Union frigate *Merrimack* that had been burned at Gosport Navy Yard when Union forces abandoned the Norfolk, Va., area. Although slow and able to operate only in deep water, the *Virginia* proved a resounding success. In March 1862, in Hampton Roads, Va., the brand-new ironclad set out to destroy the entire Union blockading squadron. On the first day of fighting, the *Virginia* handily dispatched two wooden Union vessels. The rest were saved from certain destruction on the second day by the appearance of the Federal ironclad *Monitor*. The two impregnable ships fought to a draw, but the *Virginia*'s defeat of two wooden warships confirmed the preeminence of armorclad vessels.

Construction of a dozen or more Confederate ironclad gunboats, rams, and floating batteries was begun in North Carolina during the war. Most of them were not completed, including the *Wilmington*. There would have been many more had not most of the state's larger coastal towns fallen early in the war. The paucity of Confederate records makes identifying these vessels difficult. However, four ironclad rams were commissioned and finished in North Carolina. They were the *North Carolina* and *Raleigh*, built in Wilmington on the Cape Fear River; the *Neuse*, built at Whitehall and completed at Kinston on the Neuse River; and the *Albemarle*, built at Edwards Ferry and completed at Halifax on the Roanoke River. Considering North Carolina's lack of maritime industries or a major prewar port, the state made a substantial contribution to the Confederate navy's ironclad fleet.

At least two ironclad floating batteries were converted from existing lightships. The Frying Pan Shoals lightship was being converted to a floating battery in the rear of Fort Caswell, near the Western Bar Inlet of the Cape Fear River, when a party from the Union ship *Mount Vernon* burned it in late December 1861. The *Arctic* was converted in 1863 and later used as a receiving ship for the Wilmington Station. In March 1863 and January 1865 the Union navy reported Confederate ironclad sightings, but there is no documentation to confirm either account.

Union ironclads were also associated with North Carolina. The USS *Monitor* sank off Cape Hatteras on 31 Dec. 1862. The following Union ironclad vessels took part in the 24–27 Dec. 1864 and 12–15 Jan. 1865 attacks on Fort Fisher: the single-turreted monitors *Canonicus*, *Dictator*, *Mahopac*, *Saugus*, the double-turreted monitor *Monadnock*, and the ironclad warship *New Ironsides*.

After the Civil War, there was little need for ironclad vessels. Few of the ships were seaworthy, and those only barely so. The majority were scrapped for iron. In the late nineteenth century improvements in the steelmaking process ended the need for ironclad vessels. Rather than using a wooden hull with armor only above and a few feet below the waterline, the entire ship could be made from steel. Nonetheless, ironclads were a crucial innovation in the history of naval warfare.

References: Leslie S. Bright, William H. Rowland, and James C. Bardon, *C.S.S. Neuse: A Question of Iron and Time* (1981); Robert G. Elliott, *Ironclad of the Roanoke: Gilbert Elliott's Albemarle* (1994);

Paul H. Silverstone, *Warships of the Civil War Navies* (1989); William N. Still Jr., *Iron Afloat: The Story of the Confederate Armorclads* (1985).

Henry Harris

SEE ALSO *Albemarle*, CSS; *Neuse*, CSS; *North Carolina*, CSS; *Raleigh*, CSS; *Wilmington*, CSS.

Islam is a small but growing religion in North Carolina. Although controversial because a small percentage of its adherents have engaged in deadly terrorist activities in the United States and around the world, it generally differs little from Christianity and other faiths in relation to North Carolina society. In the antebellum period, a few Muslim slaves from Africa won special privileges from their masters. Some of them were converted to Christianity, as, for instance, Umar ibn Said, who joined the First Presbyterian Church of Fayetteville in 1820. Umar apparently remained a "closet" Muslim, faithful to Allah behind a veneer of Christian homilies and activities. To the end of his life, his writings were as likely to include Muslim prayers and verses from the Koran as Christian sentiments.

Before the influx of Asian, Middle Eastern, and African Muslims in the latter half of the twentieth century, a small number of Islamic black nationalist groups—including several incarnations of the Nation of Islam—gathered a following in North Carolina. These groups experienced the greatest growth and influence in the 1950s and 1960s, although high-profile leaders such as Louis Farrakhan continued to make news in the early 2000s.

Beginning in the 1970s, many Muslim immigrants from the Middle East, North Africa, and Asia arrived in North Carolina (and elsewhere in the United States) to further their education, work in high-tech centers, or improve their quality of life. Many became U.S. citizens and formed their own organizations, such as the Muslim Student Associations at Duke University, East Carolina University, North Carolina State University, the University of North Carolina at Chapel Hill, and the University of North Carolina at Charlotte. These organizations are affiliated with the Muslim Student Association of the United States and Canada.

Deadly Islamic terrorist attacks at the World Trade Center in New York City in February 1993, and, more significantly, on 11 Sept. 2001 placed the Muslim population in North Carolina and throughout the United States in a precarious position. Already a small minority within a predominately Christian nation, many Muslims were forced to convince their fellow Americans that only a tiny fraction of Islamic believers advocated violence and terrorism. After the 11 September attacks, a mosque in Raleigh was desecrated and a Muslim school was forced to close. Other threats to Muslim individuals, organizations, and businesses occurred across the state. Meanwhile, U.S.-based Muslim groups, including the Muslim

American Society Imans Consultative Body of North Carolina, denounced terrorism and spread the message that they were as saddened and outraged by the attacks as the rest of the nation. In an effort to open debate about the issue, in May 2002 UNC-Chapel Hill announced its choice of *Approaching the Qur'an: The Early Revelations* as the mandatory summer reading for incoming freshmen that year. While many considered the selection timely and wise, others viewed it as overtly contentious and inappropriate considering recent events.

In the early 2000s Muslims worshipped in a number of mosques in North Carolina, primarily in the larger Piedmont cities. About half of the state's estimated 50,000 Muslims lived in the Charlotte (7,000), Winston-Salem/Greensboro/High Point (12,000), and Raleigh/Durham (6,000) areas. In addition to mosques, a few Islamic schools have been established in the state.

Wiley J. Williams

Isothermal Belt is a zone in western North Carolina, primarily in Rutherford and Polk Counties, in which temperature inversion resulting in milder temperature contributes to longer growing seasons than in the immediate surrounding region. The phenomenon usually occurs on the southern slopes of mountains and foothills protected from frost and freezing temperatures by higher mountains to the north and northwest. The temperature inversion, possible at any time, usually develops in the early spring. The condition is advantageous for tender plant life and early blooming trees as well as for the cultivation of fruit, especially apples and grapes.

In 1858 Silas McDowell of Franklin coined the name "isothermal belt" based on the concept of the isotherm, a line on a weather map linking all points that have an identical mean temperature for a given time. Since then the term has been widely used and modified by scientists and area residents to sometimes exaggerate the advantages of the area. The names of Thermal City in Rutherford County and Isothermal Community College, which serves Rutherford and Polk Counties, are derived from this term.

Paul L. McCraw

"It's a Damn Long Time between Drinks" is the famous statement allegedly made by North Carolina governor John Motley Morehead during a tense visit from South Carolina governor James H. Hammond in the 1840s. While in the midst of a long and heated argument, Morehead supposedly uttered the phrase, which had the effect of lessening the hostilities and restoring good will between the two men. Another possible origin of the quotation dates to 1838, when North Carolina governor Edward B. Dudley purportedly said it while he and South Carolina governor Pierce Mason Butler were taking refreshments at the Nancy Jones House on a trip between Raleigh and Chapel Hill. North Carolina author Thomas Wolfe's *Of Time and the River* (1935) contains an allusion to the phrase in a scene in which the protagonist sits in an English pub: "Eugene's glass was almost empty and he looked at it, and wondered if he ought to have another. He thought they made them very small, and kept thinking of the governors of North and South Carolina."

The quotation has been used at least since 1891 as a catchphrase for any long and tedious process. It acquired new meaning and renewed popularity after 1933 when, despite the repeal of national Prohibition, selling liquor by the drink remained illegal in both North Carolina and South Carolina. Railway passengers traveling from Washington, D.C., to Atlanta found themselves faced with "a long time between drinks" because of the train's closed bar.

References: Eric Partridge, *A Dictionary of Catch Phrases, British and American, from the Sixteenth Century to the Present Day* (1986); Richard Walser, "Damn Long Time between Drinks," *NCHR* 59 (April 1982).

Jerry Leath Mills

Ivey's Stores. J. B. Ivey & Company was established on 18 Feb. 1900 as a partnership involving Joseph Benjamin Ivey, the principal owner and active head of the firm; his brother George Franks Ivey; and Rev. J. A. Bowles. The first store was located at 231 North Tryon Street in Charlotte and subsequently moved to various addresses on that street. In 1935 Ivey's joined with Keith's, an established department store in Greenville, S.C., and this second store became known as the Ivey-Keith Company. In 1937 Ivey's, Inc., opened in Asheville. More stores followed in other locations in the Carolinas and Florida. Competition with two other Charlotte-based department stores, Belk and Efird's, was quite intense beginning in the 1920s, but by World War II Ivey's had an established reputation as a leader in high-quality merchandise.

On more than one occasion, Joseph Ivey gave much credit for the firm's success to his associates. Among these were David Ovens, who joined Ivey's in 1905 and was second in authority until his death in 1957, and William T. Buice, who joined the firm in 1929 and was second vice president at the time of his death in 1951. Ivey and his associates introduced a one-price system (replacing the practice of selling goods for whatever the merchant could get) and installment buying (buying "on time"), for which customers were apparently willing to pay a small additional charge.

Ivey's was sold to the Chicago-based Marshall Field department stores in 1980, which two years later was purchased by Batus, Inc., the U.S. subsidiary of the London-based B.A.T. Industries. On 4 June 1990 Dillard Department Stores, Inc., acquired the 23 Ivey's stores from Batus.

References: LeGette Blythe and Charles R. Brockmann, *Hornets' Nest: The Story of Charlotte and Mecklenburg County* (1961); J. B. Ivey, *My Memoirs* (1940).

Wiley J. Williams

J

Jackson County, located in North Carolina's Mountain region, was formed from Haywood and Macon Counties in 1851, taking its name from President Andrew Jackson. Webster served as the county seat until 1913, when it was moved to Sylva (incorporated in 1889). Other communities in the county include Dillsboro, Cullowhee, Cashiers, Glenville, Balsam, Tuckasegee, and parts of Highlands, Cherokee, and Sapphire. Jackson County also contains part of the Qualla Boundary, the reservation of the Eastern Band of Cherokee Indians. Natural features important to the area include Judaculla Rock, with Indian markings of ancient origin, and Ellicott Rock, a boundary landmark.

Bordering both South Carolina and Georgia in the extreme southwestern portion of North Carolina, Jackson County's location in the Great Smoky Mountains has ensured a vibrant tourist industry. Skiing and hiking opportunities are available, while the Tuckasegee River is renowned among enthusiasts of whitewater rafting and trout fishing. The Great Smoky Mountains Railroad, operating out of Dillsboro, offers a variety of scenic day trips, and the county also boasts no fewer than 16 waterfalls. Despite significant population growth during the 1990s, Jackson County remains heavily wooded—most of its area lies within the Nantahala National Forest, and lumber and Christmas trees are an important source of revenue. The town of Cullowhee is home to Western Carolina University and the North Carolina Center for the Advancement of Teaching, the first state-funded program in the nation dedicated to the professional development of public school teachers. The estimated population of Jackson County in 2004 was 35,600.

Reference: *The History of Jackson County* (1987).

Robert Blair Vocci

SEE ALSO Cherokee Indians; Judaculla Rock; Western Carolina University.

Jack Tales. SEE Folklore.

James City in Craven County evolved during the Civil War and Reconstruction years and represents attempts by African Americans to establish an independent community in North Carolina. In 1862 Union forces captured New Bern and other towns along the North Carolina coast. While Union troops occupied New Bern, former slaves—who had no place else to go—flooded into the town, which represented the largest refuge in North Carolina for black men and women. Some former slaves joined the U.S. Army, but many others hoped to establish homes and farms of their own in the area. Army officials established a settlement for the refugees along the Trent River, which lay just outside of New Bern. To accommodate so many former slaves, army officials chose to construct the settlement on confiscated lands formerly belonging to Peter G. Evans, a Confederate colonel. The settlement, known at first as the Trent River Settlement, contained 800 houses. By 1865 nearly 3,000 blacks lived in the camp, which was renamed James City in honor of its founder, Horace James, superintendent of Negro affairs and agent for the Bureau of Freedmen, Refugees, and Abandoned Lands.

During Reconstruction the settlement gained township status and began to resemble a city. Teachers from the American Missionary Association and the New England Freedmen's Aid Society established schools in James City; the Freedmen's Bureau established a hospital; and residents built churches, farmed land, and embarked upon business ventures. Many residents deposited their savings in a local branch of the Freedman's Savings and Trust Company. In 1865 James City residents selected delegates such as Joseph Green to represent them at state conventions and appeal for universal male suffrage and homestead rights. Soon after the war ended, James City had transformed itself from a squatter's camp dependent upon military aid to a thriving and independent community. Many black men and women, in fact, preferred to live in James City rather than work for plantation owners in the countryside.

Conditions worsened, however, in the late 1860s. Heavy rains one year and drought the next created poor harvests. The Freedmen's Bureau dramatically reduced aid to the needy, and sanitary conditions declined. In 1867 the federal government restored the land that comprised James City to the family of its former owner. Residents were forced to leave the camp, pay rent to the white owners, or work as sharecroppers. Freedmen and -women who once owned their entire crop before land restoration suddenly had to make do with only one-third of the proceeds from harvests. As a result of their new circumstances, residents of James City faced encroaching poverty.

By the 1880s the population had dwindled to 1,100, and women outnumbered men three to two. Most residents farmed, fished, or worked as laborers and domestics. Though the city's population had decreased, James City's men and women formed a tenacious community that protected itself from white supremacy and the whims of employers and landlords. Religious denominations such as the African Methodist Episcopal Zion Church provided for social and religious needs, and in 1881 James City laborers went on strike to protest low wages and unfair prices. That same year, residents amassed $2,000 and offered to buy James City from its new owners, Mary and James A. Bryan, who refused to sell.

James City, ca. 1910. Photograph by Bayard Wootten. NCC.

In the 1880s and 1890s, the Bryan family embarked upon a bitter campaign to collect rents and evict tenants from James City. Many families argued that they had never paid rent, and others demanded compensation for improvements they had made, such as homes they had built and land that had been made suitable for farming. James Bryan refused to negotiate, and in 1892 the matter landed before the North Carolina Supreme Court, which decided in favor of Bryan and his wife. Some tenants bought tracts of land in nearby Graysville, Meadowsville, Brownsville, or Leesville, where they established a single community and named it the "new" James City. Bryan continued to rent the land in old James City to lumber companies and black women and men who refused to move. When World War II created jobs in industrial areas, many residents left James City, which, at the opening of the twenty-first century, had about 700 residents who owned or rented property there and possessed a strong sense of heritage. Organizations such as Jones Chapel AME Zion Church and the James City Historical Society seek to preserve the community's vibrant history and tradition.

References: Roberta Sue Alexander, *North Carolina Faces the Freedmen: Race Relations during Presidential Reconstruction, 1865–1867* (1985); Mark S. Mitchell, "A History of the Black Population of New Bern, North Carolina" (M.A. thesis, East Carolina University,

1980); Joe A. Mobley, *James City: A Black Community in North Carolina, 1863–1900* (1981); Karin Lorene Zipf, "Promises of Opportunity: The Freedman's Savings and Trust Company in New Bern, North Carolina" (M.A. thesis, University of Georgia, 1994).

Karin Lorene Zipf

James K. Polk Memorial at Pineville in Mecklenburg County, the probable birthplace of the nation's eleventh president, consists of a reconstructed house, kitchen, and barn as well as the relocated Polk family cemetery. Polk was born at the family farm on 2 Nov. 1795, but the family moved to Tennessee when Polk was 11 years old. Although he returned to the state to attend the University of North Carolina in Chapel Hill, Polk achieved fame in Tennessee, and no thought was given to the significance of his birthplace. By 1900 the family's log house at Pineville had fallen to the ground, but four years later the local chapter of the Daughters of the American Revolution erected a stone pyramid and plaque at the site.

Historians in the mid-twentieth century began to conclude that Polk had been one of the most successful American presidents, and thought was given to preserving his birthplace. Under the leadership of James A. Stenhouse, a Charlotte architect and historian, funds were raised locally, grants secured, and legislative support enlisted. In 1964 Polk's birthplace became a North Carolina State Historic Site. A donated log house and other building materials, dating from the time the young Polk lived at the site, were used to reconstruct buildings such as would have been familiar to him. A visitors center at the 21-acre site features a theater and exhibits depicting the life and times of Polk.

References: James J. Horn, "Trends in Historical Interpretation: James K. Polk," *NCHR* 42 (October 1965); Richard F. Knapp, ed., *North Carolina's State Historic Sites: A Brief History and Status Report* (1995); Charles Grier Sellars, "Early Career of James K. Polk, 1795–1839" (Ph.D. diss., UNC-Chapel Hill, 1950).

Joyce White

Jamestown Exposition of 1907 marked the three-hundredth anniversary of England's first permanent American settlement at Jamestown, Va. Held along two miles of the Norfolk, Va., waterfront from 29 April to 1 December 1907, the exhibition's purpose was to educate people on the growth and expansion of the United States since 1607 and to encourage American patriotism. Including North Carolina, 26 states took part in the exposition. An active participant, North Carolina provided exhibits related to agriculture, horticulture, textile manufacturing, mining, tobacco, furniture, lumber, and pottery, as well as contributing the North Carolina Historical Exhibit in the exposition's Palace of History.

Three women curated and maintained the North Carolina Historical Exhibit, one of only two state exhibits organized by women. Mrs. Lindsay Patterson, the North Carolina vice president general of the Daughters of the American Revolution, planned the exhibit. Patterson and two assistants organized a statewide collection campaign, locating numerous artifacts dating from the colonial and revolutionary periods of the state's history. The women used funds allocated from the state legislature and the North Carolina Historical Commission for the project, and representatives in each of the state's major cities helped organize the collection of the "relics." All of the artifacts, including a large exhibit on Moravian life organized by the Wachovia Historical Society, were assembled into an exhibit describing the history of North Carolina's settlement and growth.

The exhibit included many paintings of important historical figures from North Carolina's early history. The walls were hung with images of the state's three signers of the Declaration of Independence (William Hooper, John Penn, and Joseph Hewes), as well as copies of John White's drawings of North Carolina's native peoples. Silver items, pieces of furniture, manuscripts, miniatures, Revolutionary War–era weapons, and clothing and other textiles were packed into the exhibit space. Many of the items were directly associated with notable events, historical places, or important characters in the state's history. The exhibit featured a silver teaspoon owned by William Hooper, a miniature portrait of Judge James Iredell, and a full-size portrait of Winifred Hoskins, secretary of the Edenton Tea Party. Signed letters from the Marquis de Lafayette and the gun owned by Governor Jesse Franklin (who fought at the Battle of Guilford Courthouse in 1781) were displayed as well. The exhibit also represented women as important participants in early North Carolina history by including a china plate owned by Edenton Tea Party participant and tavernkeeper Elizabeth Horniblow, a glass cologne bottle owned by Dolley Payne Madison, and the white satin slippers of the wife of Governor James Turner (1802–6).

For their efforts, the organizers of North Carolina's Historical Exhibit won a silver medal of merit. Many of the "relics" were returned to their owners, but some of the artifacts were preserved in the collection of the North Carolina Museum of History in Raleigh.

References: Mary Hilliard Hinton, *The North Carolina Historical Exhibit at the Jamestown Ter-Centennial Exposition* (Publications of the North Carolina Historical Commission, Bulletin No. 2, 1916); Jamestown Official Photograph Corporation, *The Jamestown Exposition Beautifully Illustrated* (1907).

Ellen Fitzgibbons Causey

Jargon Society, one of the oldest and most prestigious small presses in the country, was founded in 1951 at Black Mountain College by Jonathan Williams, an Asheville native and student at the school. Inspired by Charles Olson, a fellow student at the Chicago Institute of Design and a Black Mountain teacher and poet, Williams began by publishing works of fellow students and teachers. In Williams's words, "Jargon placed itself at the forefront of the avant garde while celebrating and preserving the best of the traditional." It sought out the overlooked and neglected and is credited with saving from obscurity the women modernist poets Lorine Niedecker and Mina Loy; many poets' first, and oftentimes major, works were Jargon titles. The press also championed visionary folk art by publishing books about these artists while working to preserve the fragile art produced by them. Jargon has been noted for the craft of its book making and the talented poets, photographers, designers, and artists who have collaborated on the books.

Jeffery Beam

Jazz. Although the blues captivated many North Carolinians earlier than jazz did, the state nevertheless produced a long and impressive list of jazz musicians throughout the twentieth century. The scarcity of early jazz in North Carolina gave way to the popularity of swing music during the 1930s and 1940s. Several bandleaders were born in the state, while others attended school in North Carolina. The Hal Kemp and Kay Kyser bands began as undergraduate groups at the University

Hamlet-born John Coltrane as seen on the cover of his 1964 album *Black Pearls*. NCC.

of North Carolina in Chapel Hill. John Scott Trotter, who wrote for the Kemp band and later for television, also attended UNC. In Durham, Duke University proved a starting point for bandleaders Les Brown, Johnny Long, and Sonny Burke. Dean Hudson, Freddie Johnson, and Jack Wardlaw are other Swing Era leaders identified with the state, as are drummer and singer Skinnay Ennis and tenor saxophonist Saxie Dowell, two veterans of the Kemp orchestra who later formed their own bands.

Among Swing Era band sidemen, trumpeter Johnny Best, from Shelby, and pianist and arranger Eddie Wilcox, from Method, are the most distinguished. Best worked with Les Brown, Charlie Barnet, Glenn Miller, Artie Shaw, Sam Donahue, and Benny Goodman and later became a studio musician on the West Coast. Wilcox played with and wrote for the Jimmie Lunceford band in the mid-1940s. Judy Ellington, another Raleigh native, sang with the Barnet band. An adopted North Carolinian, Billy Strayhorn, born in Dayton, Ohio, but reared partly in Hillsborough, spent 28 years with the Duke Ellington Orchestra as staff arranger, composer, occasional pianist, and Ellington's indispensable right-hand man. Saxophonist Bud Shank, also born in Dayton, went to high school in Durham and attended the University of North Carolina in Chapel Hill, where he played with John Satterfield's band in the mid-1940s before beginning his career. He later became a much-in-demand studio musician on the West Coast and then a fiery soloist with his own combo.

Big band music declined after World War II, replaced by unique new styles. Pianist and composer Thelonious Monk, born in Rocky Mount in 1917, and drummer Max Roach, born in New Land in 1924, helped create bebop, jazz's new post–

Swing Era language. They, along with tenor and soprano saxophonist John Coltrane, born in Hamlet in 1926, remain certified giants in the history of jazz music. Concurrently, more and more musicians began to idolize and emulate Coltrane, who would become the most influential jazz musician of the last third of the twentieth century.

Jazz pianist Billy Taylor, born in Greenville in 1921, became a purveyor of a smooth, bop-based trio style ca. 1950 and a well-known radio and television host, the latter on Charles Kuralt's *Sunday Morning* series. He also wrote the first bebop instruction book. Other North Carolina jazz pianists include Linton Garner (Greensboro), Frank Kimbrough (Roxboro), Loumell Morgan (Raleigh), Mickey Tucker (Durham), and songwriter Loonis McGlohon (Ayden). Bassist Percy Heath, born in Wilmington, is best known for his 40-year tenure with the Modern Jazz Quartet. Scott Lee, from Greensboro, is another North Carolina bassist.

North Carolina jazz drummers include Freddie Moore (Washington), Dannie Richmond (Greensboro), and Grady Tate (Durham). Moore played in early New Orleans jazzman Joe "King" Oliver's band in 1930, several years after Louis Armstrong began his rise to fame in the same unit. Saxophonist Willis Hargrove, born in Chapel Hill, performed with Oliver in the mid-1930s. Dixieland clarinetist Bill Napier (Asheville) and saxophonists Lou Donaldson (Badin), Harold Vick (Tarboro), Numa "Pee Wee" Moore (Raleigh), and Tab Smith (Kinston) are North Carolina reedmen. The state's jazz trumpeters include Ray Codrington (Dunn), Waymon Reed (Fayetteville), and Woody Shaw (Laurinburg). Among guitarists, the state boasts Skeeter Best (Kinston), Tal Farlow (Greensboro), and Bill Harris (Nashville).

Jazz singers include Nina Simone (Tryon) and Nnenna Freelon, an adopted North Carolinian who lives in Durham and who has recorded several albums for the Columbia and Concord labels since the early 1990s. Vibes players Jon Metzger, who lives in Gibsonville, and Steve Hobbs, from Raleigh, also released albums on nationally distributed labels in the 1990s.

Beginning in the 1960s, high school and college dance bands evolved into stage bands, with music education as an emphasis. This afforded both local and name jazz musicians opportunities to work as artists-in-residence or become full-time faculty members. Mary Lou Williams, revered for her Swing Era arrangements and consistently modern piano style, joined the faculty of Duke University in 1977. After Williams's death in 1981, Paul Jeffrey, a New Yorker who played tenor saxophone with the Thelonious Monk Quartet in the early 1970s, followed. He has been at Duke for more than 20 years. Most of the schools in the University of North Carolina System now include jazz bands and jazz courses in their curricula, as do Elon University, Shaw University, and the North Carolina School of the Arts, among others.

In the 1990s, the formation of the North Carolina Jazz Repertory Orchestra by UNC-Chapel Hill music professor James Ketch signaled a new era in the status of jazz in the state. The group's programs of music by Ellington, Goodman, Stan Kenton, and other famous leaders have reached into the schools as well as concert halls. The state also boasts several jazz festivals throughout the year, including the North Carolina Jazz Festival, held in Wilmington.

References: Kenny Mathieson, *Giant Steps: Bebop and the Creators of Modern Jazz, 1945–65* (1999); Dave Oliphant, *The Early Swing Era, 1930 to 1941* (2002); George T. Simon, *The Big Bands* (1971).

Owen Cordle

Jeanes Fund, the popular name for the Negro Rural School Fund of the Anna T. Jeanes Foundation, was endowed by a Philadelphia Quaker benefactor in 1907 with $1 million. The original board of trustees, which first met on 29 Feb. 1908 in New York City, was an impressive list of educators and other dignitaries that included President William Howard Taft, Booker T. Washington of the Tuskegee Institute, banker and philanthropist George Foster Peabody, industrialist and philanthropist Andrew Carnegie, Jeanes Fund president James H. Dillard (1907–31), and journalist Walter Hines Page (a North Carolina native living in New York). In later years the board included at least two other distinguished North Carolinians: William P. Few, the president of Duke University, and George W. Clinton, a bishop of the African Methodist Episcopal Zion Church.

After exploring several ways to enact Anna Jeanes's wish to promote the training of blacks, the board settled on the sponsorship of teachers. Originally these African American "Jeanes teachers" instructed other teachers in techniques of teaching simple industrial arts, such as mat making, chair caning, and wood working as well as domestic skills. Gradually the Jeanes teachers evolved into academic supervisors and, ultimately, into "unofficial" assistants to school superintendents responsible for directing black schools.

The influence of the Jeanes teachers and supervisors on the lives of the men, women, and children with whom they came in contact was extraordinary. The teachers lived in the homes of those they worked with, worshiped in their churches, and participated in their parent-teacher meetings. In a real sense, they were like members of the family. One Jeanes supervisor, Annie W. Holland of Gates, became the first state supervisor of elementary schools. In 1937 the Jeanes Fund, having contributed some $250,000 to African American education in North Carolina since 1908, was merged with the Slater Fund, other foundations, and the Southern Education Fund.

References: Will W. Alexander, *The Slater and Jeanes Funds* (1934); Hugh V. Brown, *A History of the Education of Negroes in North Carolina* (1961); Lance G. E. Jones, *The Jeanes Teacher in the United States, 1908–1933* (1937); Arthur D. Wright, *The Negro Rural School Fund, Inc. (Anna T. Jeanes Foundation), 1907–1933* (1933).

Wiley J. Williams

SEE ALSO Slater Fund.

Jefferson-Pilot Corporation is one of the largest shareholder-owned life insurance companies in the United States. During the first decade of the twentieth century, ten insurance companies were incorporated in Greensboro, the strongest of which was Security Life Insurance Company. At the same time, Jefferson Standard Life Insurance Company was founded in Raleigh, although by 1912 the company had depleted its surplus by paying excessive commissions to its agents. Security Life acquired the Raleigh firm and the new company created by the merger retained the name Jefferson Standard. Under the leadership of Julian W. Price, the company doubled its capital stock to $1 million by 1926. It survived the Great Depression by issuing policies designed to "meet the times" with a graduated payment scale that enabled people to hold on to their policies. Dividends continued to be paid, and the company continued buying bonds and lending money. It came to be considered one of Greensboro's depression-proof industries.

By 1950 Jefferson Standard's capital stock was valued at $15 million, and its total assets were $265 million. The company became Jefferson-Pilot Corporation in 1968 when a holding company was formed out of Jefferson Standard Life Insurance Company, Pilot Life Insurance Co., and Jefferson Standard Broadcasting Co. By 1980 Jefferson-Pilot's assets topped $1 billion. Despite one record year after another during the next decade, the presidency of W. Roger Soles, which had begun in 1967, was embroiled in controversy as several stockholders led by Julian Price descendant Louise Price Parsons crusaded to oust Soles for "mismanagement." An acrimonious dispute lasted from May 1991 until April 1993 and included a series of bitter courtroom episodes and turbulent stockholders meetings. The dispute was settled with the retirement of Soles, the implementation of a mandatory retirement age of 65 for officers, and a 20 percent reduction in the size of the board.

David Stonecipher of Atlanta took office as president of Jefferson-Pilot in April 1993. Stonecipher called for the company to double its life insurance sales and return to its roots of selling insurance. In a series of mergers, Jefferson-Pilot acquired Kentucky Central Life Insurance Company, Alexander Hamilton Life Insurance Company, Chubb Life Insurance Company, and Guarantee Life Insurance Company. By 1995 it was the second-fastest-growing insurance company and the fifteenth-largest life insurer in the United States. In January 1998 the company adopted Jefferson-Pilot Financial as its brand name to reflect its position as a "national company with financial savvy." By 2002 Jefferson-Pilot had 3,770 employees, and its companies had more than $210 billion of life insurance in force. One of its best-known subsidiaries, Jefferson-Pilot Communications Company, in 2004 owned 3 television stations and 18 radio stations in the Southeast. Jefferson-Pilot Corporation underwent a merger with Lincoln National Corporation in April 2006, with the new company operating under the name Lincoln Financial Group.

Alexander R. Stoesen

Jehovah's Witnesses were started in Pennsylvania in 1870 by Charles Taze Russell (1852–1916) as a result of Bible study among friends and followers that emphasized the second coming of Christ. Russell imparted to his followers that Christ would return to earth spiritually in 1874 in order to prepare for a personal reign in 1914. In the meanwhile, God, or Jehovah, would single out those of goodwill that he wished to save and destroy the wicked. Then, when the time was right, Christ would lead the righteous (i.e., the hosts of heaven and the angels) to destroy the forces of Satan totally at the final battle of Armageddon as the population looked on. The just would then be permitted to reproduce and prosper without dying for a thousand-year reign, and a select group of the just—144,000 Christians—would then ascend to heaven with Christ in order to rule at his side. It was Russell's promise that "millions now living will never die."

Despite controversies, court battles, schisms, and the failure of Russell's predictions regarding 1914 to come true, Jehovah's Witnesses have grown in numbers. By the early 2000s there were more than 1.8 million Witnesses in the United States in nearly 11,000 congregations, or Kingdom Halls. There are nearly 16 million adherents worldwide. North Carolina is ranked in the top 20 among U.S. states in the number of Jehovah's Witnesses, with 0.8 percent of the total population professing the faith.

References: Frank S. Mead and Samuel S. Hill, *Handbook of Denominations in the United States* (10th ed., 1995); M. J. Penton, *Apocalypse Delayed: The Story of Jehovah's Witnesses* (1985).

Louis P. Towles

Jenkins' Ear, War of. The War of Jenkins' Ear (1739–42), a West Indies maritime struggle that was part of the wider Anglo-Spanish War (1739–48), was fought between England and Spain over the control of trade in the Caribbean. To a lesser degree, the war also involved the defense of Great Britain's colonies in the Western Hemisphere and the fear that Spain and France might form an alliance to contain future British expansion in America. Spain sought to prevent Dutch, Danish, English, and French smugglers from trading with its American possessions and to limit the legal transactions of the English-owned South Sea Company with the area.

The unusual name of the war stemmed from an incident in 1731 in which a Spanish gunboat crew boarded the English ship *Rebecca* to confiscate some of its cargo. When the captain of the ship, Robert Jenkins, resisted, the Spanish soldiers tore off his ear and told him to "carry it to his King and tell him they would serve him in the same manner should an opportunity offer." Jenkins took his severed ear to England in a bottle in search of compensation and displayed it to the country, arousing considerable popular indignation.

Between August and mid-December 1740 Governor Gabriel Johnston of North Carolina raised and dispatched 400 men, the same number as Virginia, to fight in the war, admitting that he could have gathered half as many again if he had possessed the resources to feed and deliver them to the West Indies. As it was, he was able to supply the needs of his recruits with £1,200 raised by the colonial Assembly but had to furnish transportation from discretionary funds because shipowners would not accept North Carolina's paper money.

The North Carolina volunteers arrived in Jamaica by 9 Jan. 1741 and joined nearly 9,000 soldiers, both regular troops and provincials, and 15,000 sailors who awaited orders. On 23 March they attacked Cartagena but did not capture the city. Losses for the Cartagena Expedition, from both fighting and yellow fever, were heavy, forcing Adm. Edward Vernon to become less aggressive in future operations. For the remainder of the war, and in the following King George's War (1744–48), Vernon limited his activities to protecting English shipping in the Caribbean and destroying local Spanish trade.

The War of Jenkins' Ear brought no sense of accomplishment to the English colonies in America generally or to North Carolina in particular. Only 600 of the original 3,600 volunteers lived to return to their respective colonies. In North Carolina, 25 out of one company of 100 men returned home; the other three companies probably fared no better. In addition, beginning in 1741 dozens of colonial vessels were lost along the Carolina coast to Spanish privateers, a number of which briefly operated out of the Outer Banks. Cities like Beaufort and Brunswick were raided and forced to pay tribute, and proposed powder magazines and forts (Ocracoke Island, Bear Inlet, Topsail Inlet, and on the Cape Fear River) either were not built or accomplished nothing. The feeling in North Carolina was that colonial interests were sacrificed to broader English objectives.

References: Francis L. Berkeley Jr., "The War of Jenkins' Ear," *Old Dominion* (1964); Hugh T. Lefler and William S. Powell, *Colonial North Carolina: A History* (1973); Franz A. J. Szabo, "The War of the Austrian Succession and the Seven Years War, 1740–1763," in Frank W. Thackeray and John E. Findling, eds., *Events That Changed the World in the Eighteenth Century* (1998).

Louis P. Towles

Jerusalem Oak (*Chenopodium ambrosioides*) is a weedy perennial plant found throughout North Carolina and the United

States. Those with an eastern, rural North Carolina background use the name Jerusalem oak more commonly than the names often recognized elsewhere in the United States—Spanish and Mexican tea and wormseed.

Jerusalem oak seeds and leaves had a number of important uses and were sought by various manufacturers of fragrances and medicines in the late nineteenth and early twentieth century. This demand created a financial opportunity for many rural persons, primarily women and children from the 1800s to the 1940s, who probably would otherwise have been unable to find employment, particularly during the Great Depression years. Gathering the dried seed and selling to local "middle men" earned from 10 to 25 cents per pound. Locals also used the seeds and leaves as a remedy for hookworm, boiling them and drinking the tea. Athlete's foot was treated by soaking the feet in such solutions.

Commercially, the oil (ascaridol) of the Jerusalem oak was used in medicines, primarily as an anthelmintic (remedy for worms) for humans and animals. The Maryland Distillery near Baltimore, dating back to the mid-1800s and the leading distiller of ascaridol as late as the mid-1900s, processed a major portion of the North Carolina harvest. In recent years substitute medications with lower production costs have emerged, and today the major modern use of this plant centers around fragrance components in creams, detergents, lotions, perfumes, and soaps.

A. J. Bullard

Jim Crow Laws. SEE African Americans; Civil Rights Movement; Greensboro Sit-Ins; *Plessy v. Ferguson*.

Joel Lane House in Raleigh, named "Wakefield" by owner Joel Lane in honor of colonial governor William Tryon's wife, Margaret Wake, was built in the 1760s. Lane did major remodeling in the 1790s, including the addition of a front porch and alteration of the roof shape from gable to gambrel. The house is significant as the site of the first session of the Wake County Court, which convened there in 1771. Ten years later, the North Carolina General Assembly also met at Lane's Wakefield. As part of Lane's large plantation holdings known as Bloomsbury, the house originally faced east overlooking the 1,000 acres that were purchased from Lane in 1792 as the planned site of North Carolina's permanent capital, Raleigh. The house, located on West Hargett Street, has been restored to its 1790s appearance and is maintained as a historic house museum.

References: Elizabeth Reid Murray, *Wake: Capital County of North Carolina* (1983); James Vickers, *Raleigh, City of Oaks: An Illustrated History* (1982).

William J. McCrea

John Birch Society was founded in Indianapolis on 9 Dec. 1958 by Robert Henry Winborne Welch Jr., a Fundamentalist Baptist born in Chowan County and a graduate of the University of North Carolina at Chapel Hill. The society was named after Capt. John Birch, a missionary from Macon, Ga., who, while serving as a U.S. intelligence officer, was killed by Chinese communists ten days after V-J Day. At the founding, Welch—a retired Boston candy manufacturer—addressed 11 businessmen from a number of states in a marathon 17-hour speech (over two days), which he later published as *The Blue Book of the John Birch Society*. Birch, according to the society, was the first hero of the Cold War. In setting forth to his captive audience the background, methods, and purposes of the society, it was clear that Welch was obsessed with the political threat to America that he believed communism posed.

In addition to supporting various anticommunist causes and haranguing political leaders who did not share the opinions of its members, the John Birch Society also advocated a return to minimum federal government and repeal of the federal income tax and social security. It opposed federal aid to education, sex education programs in the schools, the civil rights movement, and the Equal Rights Amendment (in North Carolina and the nation).

At its height in the mid-1960s, the John Birch Society's total membership was estimated to be 100,000. In the mid-1970s, the *Raleigh News and Observer* estimated North Carolina's total members at 2,000 to 4,000, many of them in the Rocky Mount area. Other cities around the state, including Charlotte, Greensboro, Raleigh, Asheville, Burlington, and Kinston, had active chapters at one time or another. After the late 1960s, society members grew openly unhappy with Welch's autocratic rule, and since Welch's death in 1985 the John Birch Society has been sinking into obscurity, both in North Carolina and throughout the nation.

References: G. Edward Griffin, *Life and Words of Robert Welch, Founder of the John Birch Society* (1975); Gene Grove, *Inside the John*

This 1887 drawing is perhaps the earliest likeness of the Joel Lane House. NCC.

Birch Society (1961); Gerald Schomp, *Birchism Was My Business* (1970).

Wiley J. Williams

John C. Campbell Folk School is located in Brasstown, near the town of Murphy in western North Carolina (Cherokee County). Named for social worker and writer John C. Campbell, the school was founded after Campbell's death in 1925 by his wife, Olive Dame Campbell, who served as the school's first director until her 1946 retirement, and Marguerite Butler. John Campbell's extensive study of the culture, conditions, and needs of Appalachia served as the basis for the school's work. The curriculum has historically focused on four main areas, each of which has received varying degrees of emphasis during different eras: traditional performing arts, especially folk music and dance; "creative making," which encompasses a wide variety of arts and crafts both native to the local area and from other regions; studies connected to the natural world, including agriculture and forestry; and cultural awareness studies such as history. Students learn in group settings and develop a variety of skills.

The year 1973 signaled a change in the history of the John C. Campbell Folk School and the beginning of its modern structure. Gus and Maggie Masters, who had been heads of the craft department, took over as codirectors and redirected the school's emphasis toward crafts, modeling the program on other craft schools that used resident artists rather than a fixed faculty. They sold the school's dairy herd and began converting farm buildings to crafts studios. An October fall festival was also established during the Masterses' tenure and became the largest annual event in Cherokee County.

Ronald G. Hill, a native of Cherokee County, became the director of the John C. Campbell Folk School in 1985. He brought his experience as Cherokee County manager to bear on the school, developing a more stable fiscal plan and carrying out numerous improvements to the buildings. In 1992 Jan Davidson, a folklorist from Murphy with an interest in the handicraft movement, became the director. The school continues to offer noncompetitive classes in crafts and music to students from all over the United States as well as to local citizens.

References: Pat McNelly, ed., *The First Forty Years: The John C. Campbell Folk School* (1966); David E. Whisnant, *All That Is Native and Fine: The Politics of Culture in an American Region* (1983).

Bruce E. Baker

John F. Blair, Publisher. SEE Book Publishing.

John Kuners (also known as John Kooners, John Canoes, Junkanoes, or Jonkonnu) were troupes of slaves and free blacks, brightly dressed and often masked, who sang and danced on Christmas and New Year's Day in the Wilmington, Lower Cape Fear, and Albemarle Sound areas throughout much of the 1800s. The custom closely paralleled the annual "John Canoe" celebrations that survive today in Jamaica and the Bahamas. In the United States, however, the practice of "Kunering" or "Koonering" was apparently unique to North Carolina, except for isolated observances in Suffolk, Va. (suppressed after Nat Turner's Rebellion in 1831), and in Key West, Fla. All these practices seem to share roots in the West African Gold Coast, although details of their origin and spread are unknown.

James Norcom described an "exhibition of John Cannu" in 1824 at a plantation near Edenton. Other celebrations were reported at Somerset Place Plantation (1829), in Bertie County (1849), and at various times in Southport, New Bern, Hillsboro, Martin County, and as far west as Iredell County.

In Wilmington, where newspapers regularly reported the practice through the 1850s, as many as eight to ten groups of Kuners, some with 20 members each, went from house to house, singing and beating rhythms with rib bones, cow's horns, triangles, and mouth harps. Kuners, who kept their identities secret, wore "tatters," or brightly colored rags sewn to their clothes, and masks, often made of buckram. All Kuners were men, although many dancers wore women's clothing. At each house, Kuners stopped to collect pennies. On plantations, they received small treats, rum, or desserts.

Historian Elizabeth A. Fenn has interpreted the custom as a "safety valve" for slave resentments and "a medium for social change and commentary." Some of the costumes and improvised verses seem to have poked fun at white hypocrisy and pretensions.

Kunering survived the Civil War and Emancipation but seems to have died out in Wilmington by the 1880s. Scholars have attributed its decline to black clergymen who denounced the practice as demeaning. Strict enforcement by white officials of laws relating to the wearing of masks may also have played a role. However, white youths in Wilmington, Fayetteville, Kinston, and other places continued to copy the custom into the early 1900s, dressing up and parading in blackface at Christmastime.

References: Elizabeth A. Fenn, "'A Perfect Equality Seemed to Reign': Slave Society and Jonkonnu," NCHR 65 (April 1988); Dougald MacMillan, "John Kuners," *Journal of American Folk-lore* 39 (January 1926).

Bennett L. Steelman

John Locke Foundation, named for the seventeenth-century English philosopher whose writings are central to American political thought, is a Raleigh-based nonprofit and nonpartisan think tank, incorporated in 1989 for the purpose of shaping public policy in North Carolina. As with other conservative think tanks such as the Heritage Foundation and the

American Enterprise Institute, the foundation's policy agenda centers on the supremacy of individual liberty, limited government, and free market principles.

The John Locke Foundation utilizes a variety of methods to influence state legislators and citizens to support lower taxes, deregulation of business, and other conservative initiatives. The resident scholars who comprise the Research Division study North Carolina policy and offer their recommendations in reports and during appearances before the legislature. The Communications Division acts as chief liaison to the public and the mainstream media and is responsible for distributing the *Carolina Journal*, a monthly newspaper spotlighting current policy issues. Luncheons, receptions, and other public events are organized by the Events and Outreach Division, which has secured leading conservatives such as Dick Cheney and Newt Gingrich as speakers.

As a nonprofit think tank, the John Locke Foundation is funded by private contributions rather than government aid, receiving support from some 1,500 individuals, businesses, and other foundations. Although still quite young compared with its ideological forebears—the American Enterprise Institute (founded in 1943), Heritage Foundation (1973), and Cato Institute (1977)—the John Locke Foundation has quickly become a leading North Carolina think tank by successfully supplementing its policy research with aggressive self-promotion and public relations efforts.

Robert Blair Vocci

Johnson C. Smith University,

Johnson C. Smith University, a historically African American institution associated with the Presbyterian Church, was established in Charlotte in 1867 as a "freedman's school" under the auspices of the Catawba Presbytery. Two white ministers, Samuel C. Alexander, a Pennsylvania native, and Willis L. Miller, a former slaveholder and Confederate soldier, proved instrumental in the school's founding. They were assisted in this endeavor by a gift of $1,400 from Philadelphian Mary Duke Biddle, widow of Union major Henry J. Biddle. The school was situated on eight acres of land in northwest Charlotte donated by former Confederate colonel William R. Myers.

From 1867 through 1923, the school was known first as the Henry J. Biddle Memorial Institute and later as Biddle University. In 1891 Daniel Sanders became the first African American to head Biddle University. Born a slave in South Carolina, Sanders had been educated at Western Theological Seminary in Allegheny, Pa., and as a pastor and public school principal in Wilmington had produced the *African-American Presbyterian*.

The university implemented a teacher training curriculum in English, history, language, music, and science in 1912. During the 1920s, after a tragic fire, Biddle received $720,000 from Jane Berry Smith, widow of prominent Pittsburgh pharmacist

and industrialist Johnson C. Smith. The Smith family's most lasting monument was the University Church, which was built in 1929 and remains a center for religious activities. In 1923, in response to the family's generosity, the trustees changed the name of the university to Johnson C. Smith University. In 1924 tobacco magnate James Buchanan Duke established the multimillion-dollar Duke Endowment, naming Johnson C. Smith University as the recipient of 4 percent of the endowment's income.

In 1925 the university was accredited by the North Carolina Department of Education as a four-year college, and two years later the school's teacher education graduates were certified in every southern state. In 1928 Johnson C. Smith University implemented a two-year premedical curriculum, and the next year the school discontinued its high school curriculum. In 1932 the university witnessed the beginnings of coeducation when, as a result of a reciprocity agreement, Barber-Scotia Junior College, a historically black school for women in Concord, began sending its graduates to Johnson C. Smith to complete their degrees; this arrangement would last until 1941, when Johnson C. Smith began admitting female first-year students.

In 1994 Dorothy Cowser Yancy, a Johnson C. Smith alumna with a Ph.D. in political science from Atlanta University, became the first female president of the university. Her tenure was marked by a successful $50 million fund-raising campaign and by joint research ventures with several leading universities. Johnson C. Smith maintains international studies agreements with Al Akhawayn University and Mohammed V University (Morocco), Moscow State Institute of Public Policy, Moscow State University, Oxford University, the University of Cape Coast (Ghana), and the University of Swinburne (Australia).

Johnson C. Smith has had a number of notable firsts since its founding. Biddle University was the first southern four-year institution to have a black professor and a black president. An 1892 football contest between Biddle and Livingstone College (Salisbury) was the first black intercollegiate football game. Johnson C. Smith was the first historically black institution in North Carolina to construct a gymnasium (1928); it entered the Colored (now Central) Intercollegiate Athletic Association in that year. The school was also the first black college in North Carolina to obtain accreditation from the Southern Association. The school in the early 2000s enrolled approximately 1,400 students and had 80 faculty members.

References: Arthur A. George, *100 Years, 1867–1967: Salient Facts in the Growth and Development of Johnson C. Smith University* (1968); Inez Moore Parker, *The Biddle-Johnson C. Smith Story* (1975).

James I. Martin Sr.

Johnston County, located in North Carolina's Coastal Plain region, was formed from Craven County in 1746, taking its name from Royal Governor of North Carolina Gabriel Johnston. Communities in the county include the county seat of Smithfield (incorporated in 1777), Clayton, Selma, Benson, Kenly, Four Oaks, Pine Level, Princeton, Wilson's Mills, and Micro.

Johnston County was originally inhabited by Tuscarora Indians, most of whom migrated to New York—joining the Iroquois, to whom they were related—when their efforts to resist European settlement in the area ended with their defeat in the Tuscarora War (1711–13). The county's first town, Smithfield, was then established as an early trading post along the banks of the Neuse River at Smith's Ferry. During the nineteenth century, cotton emerged as Johnston County's chief product, while the simultaneous extension of the railroad facilitated its shipping for commercial purposes; Selma, located at the junction of the North Carolina and Atlantic Coast Line railroads, became the county's second commercial center. Fluctuating cotton prices during the late nineteenth century paved the way for a rise in tobacco production, bringing the county a new prosperity that ended only with the onset of the Great Depression. The postwar era, which introduced productivity-boosting highways to the county, brought an increase in manufacturing to compensate for declining job prospects in the agricultural sector. Nevertheless, Johnston County remains heavily dependent upon farming, with more farms than any other North Carolina county and standing as the leading county in the state in terms of total income derived from agricultural crops, such as sweet potatoes, corn, and soybeans. It also continues to be a state leader in the production of flue-cured tobacco.

Johnston County's Bentonville Battleground State Historic Site commemorates the last major battle of the Civil War, also notable as the largest military engagement in North Carolina's history. The county is also home to the Ava Gardner Museum in Smithfield, a tribute to the Johnston County native and screen legend. The town of Benson annually hosts the popular Mule Days festival. The Tobacco Farm Life Museum in Kenly interprets the history of tobacco farming in the state. Growth in the Triangle area has accelerated a modern housing boom in Johnston County, which had an estimated population of 141,300 in 2004.

Reference: Thomas J. and T. Wingate Lassiter, *Johnston County: Its History since 1746* (2004).

Robert Blair Vocci

SEE ALSO Bentonville, Battle of.

Johnston's Riot Act of 1771 was an attempt by members of the royal colonial government to control and punish the Regulators, North Carolinians from the frontier counties who had revolted against them. Particularly in vast, western counties such as Orange, Rowan, and Anson, the sheriffs and other appointed officials proved to be dishonest. Governor William

Tryon wrote in 1767 that "the sheriffs have embezzled more than one-half of the public money ordered to be raised and collected by them." The Regulators formed to oppose the unjust practices. When local authorities ignored and harassed them, the Regulators turned violent. The North Carolina Assembly tried to address the injustices, but legal remedies moved too slowly for the Regulators. In September 1770 a mob stormed into the Hillsborough courthouse, drove the judge from his bench, tormented and brutally whipped attorneys, then rioted through the streets.

When word came that the Regulators were ready to march on New Bern to take over the Assembly, the legislators immediately took action to punish them. Samuel Johnston, of Edenton, an attorney, clerk of court, and Assembly member since 1759, introduced the "Riot Act," which he based on English law. This act gave the attorney general the right for one year to prosecute charges of riot in any court he chose in the province. When summoned by the court, the rioters had to surrender within 60 days or be declared outlaws whose lands and chattels would become the property of the government and who could be killed with impunity. The militia would enforce the law, which the Assembly ratified on 15 Jan. 1771.

Peaceful citizens protested that Johnston's Riot Act violated their rights, and the Regulators sneered at the "riotous act." They vowed to stop courts from meeting and swore that "now we shall be forced to kill all the clerks and lawyers." The ultimate defeat of the Regulators ended the need for Johnston's Riot Act, which expired in early 1772.

Reference: William S. Powell, *The War of the Regulation and the Battle of Alamance, May 16, 1771* (1949).

Barry McGee

John Wesley College. The origins of John Wesley College can be traced to the founding of the People's Bible School in Greensboro in 1932. The school began with 4 teachers and 18 students and an interdenominational board of trustees headed by John R. Church. It was the intent of the founders to maintain the college as an independent institution totally free of any organized financial backing or denominational control. All funding came from tuition and personal offerings. The school's charter stated that it was "an undenominational holiness training school."

For its first ten years, the People's Bible School offered both grade school and high school courses along with the first two years of a Bible college curriculum. It was the publisher of the *People's Herald*, a holiness periodical that later became the *John Wesley College CRUSADER*. Most of the students at the People's Bible School were enrolled in the college-level program. In 1936, 40 acres of land were purchased in a subdivision being developed by J. P. Scales southwest of Greensboro on the "High Point–Greensboro Asphalt Road." Students helped erect a large frame tabernacle building. Female students lived in a nearby rented house, while the males occupied several "hastily constructed cabins." The second building to be built was a dormitory for women. In spite of construction expenses, the People's Bible School avoided any serious debt problems.

During World War II the People's Bible School was approved by the Selective Service System for draft exemption for ministerial students. By 1949 an administration building and a men's dormitory had been completed. That year the name was changed to People's Bible College, and ten years later the name was again changed, to John Wesley College.

John Wesley College is the only interdenominational college in the historic Wesleyan tradition in the southeastern United States that is affiliated with the Christian Holiness Association. The college began its relocation to High Point in 1979 and was accredited in 1982 by the American Association of Bible Colleges. That year the Norman D. Carter Building was dedicated, and classes began on the new campus in September. John Wesley College was reaccredited in 1987 and in 1992 was given a ten-year accreditation. In the mid-1990s a new adult degree-completion program was instituted along with a campus master plan approved by the city of High Point.

Alexander R. Stoesen

Jones County, located in North Carolina's Coastal Plain region, was formed from Craven County in 1779, taking its name from radical Revolutionary War leader and Anti-Federalist Willie Jones. Trenton (originally known as Trent Bridge) was established as the county seat in 1784. Other Jones County communities include Maysville, Pollacksville, Comfort, Pleasant Hill, and Wyse Fork. Large portions of the county are part of the Great Dover Swamp, White Oak Pocosin, Croatan National Forest, and Hofmann Forest, the nation's largest forest laboratory.

Originally inhabited by Tuscarora Indians, the area of modern Jones County was first settled by Europeans in the early eighteenth century; but the early communities formed by German and Swiss immigrants were soon disturbed by Cary's Rebellion and the Tuscarora War (1711–13). Nevertheless, in the wake of the Tuscarora War a thriving agricultural economy soon developed, with the Trent River serving as a source of irrigation and the primary means of transportation. During the following century and a half, the burgeoning county became dominated by plantation life, and on the eve of the Civil War the abundance of slaves and fertile farmland had made Jones County one of the most prosperous in the nation. The devastation of the war and the end of slavery brought the county's prominence to an end, however. Through the end of the twentieth century the economy of the county remained heavily dependent upon crops (principally tobacco) from its farms and lumber from its extensive forest lands. In 2004 the estimated population of Jones County was slightly more than 10,000.

Reference: Julia Pollack Harriett, *History and Genealogy of Jones County, North Carolina* (1987).

Robert Blair Vocci

Journalism Hall of Fame. With individual newspapers serving its many small and medium-sized cities, North Carolina saw the rise of a high-quality and competitive press that, in turn, developed a large community of talented journalists. In 1981 the North Carolina Journalism Hall of Fame was established to honor these journalists. The Hall of Fame is sponsored by the School of Journalism and Mass Communication at the University of North Carolina at Chapel Hill, although honorees need not have a tie to the school. Individuals selected, however, are distinctively identified with North Carolina or have strong ties to the state. Inductions take place during the school's spring "Journalism Days" celebrations. The Hall of Fame's first five inductees were Josephus Daniels of the *Raleigh News and Observer*, Charles Kuralt of CBS News, C. A. "Pete" McKnight of the *Charlotte Observer*, Vermont Royster of the *Wall Street Journal*, and Tom Wicker of the *New York Times*. As of 2004, more than 100 journalists had been inducted, including such luminaries as Harry Golden, Roger Mudd, Jeff MacNelly, Lou Harris, Marjorie Hunter, David Brinkley, and Jonathan Yardley.

Alex Coffin

Judaculla Rock, associated with the Cherokee legend of *Tsu'kalu*, is a large soapstone rock covered with petroglyphs located on Caney Fork Creek off N.C. 107 in Jackson County. According to legend, Judaculla was a great slant-eyed giant who courted and wed his wife at the Cherokee town of Kanuga on the west fork of the Pigeon River near the Bethel School in Haywood County. The newlyweds returned to his residence

Postcard showing petroglyphs on Judaculla Rock, ca. 1940. Photograph by Larry W. Mull. NCC.

(Judaculla Old Fields) on a mountaintop, where he had cleared about 100 acres for farming. The carvings on Judaculla Rock are said to be scratches left by the giant when he jumped from his farm on the mountaintop to the valley below. Some people believe the markings may represent a picture map of the Battle of Taliwa, which was fought between Creeks and Cherokees in 1755. The Creeks lost the battle, which took place near present-day Canton, Ga., and were driven from their settlements in north Georgia.

Reference: Hiram C. Wilburn, "Judaculla Rock," *Southern Indian Studies* 4 (October 1952).

William L. Anderson

Judaism. Jewish religious developments in North Carolina have reflected national trends marked by evolution from a European traditionalism to an American Judaism. Jewish immigrants brought with them the religious culture of their homelands, but in America they progressively liberalized their beliefs and practices.

Jacob Mordecai, who settled in Warrenton in 1792, was a learned and observant Jew who had been a founder and president of Richmond's Orthodox synagogue. Many, though not all, of his children were assimilated into the Christian community through marriage and conversion. Isolated and very few in number, early North Carolina Jews lacked an organized community to sustain their faith.

German Jews, who began arriving in the middle of the nineteenth century, came from religiously Orthodox communities. Jews from southwestern Germany had felt the liberating effects of the Enlightenment and Napoleonic emancipation, while Prussian Jews, whose migration tended to come later, were more firmly rooted in Polish Orthodoxy.

Early North Carolina Jews came mostly from Baltimore, Richmond, Philadelphia, or Charleston. The state's Jewish communities were colonies of these larger centers; North Carolina's Jews took religious direction from them and often returned to them to find spouses, rabbis, and kosher supplies. In turn, Durham, Goldsboro, and Wilmington served as religious centers for rural communities where few Jews resided. Religion, as well as kinship and commercial ties, kept Jews intimately bound as a distinct people.

Since Jews required burial in consecrated ground, the first formal act of local community organization was to form a Cemetery Society. This society was a traditional European institution (a *Chevra Kadisha*, Hebrew for "Holy Fellowship") that not only provided ritual burial but also organized worship and welfare for the poor and transients—the obligation of taking care of one's own being deeply ingrained in Jewish religious culture. Such societies formed in Wilmington in 1852, Raleigh and Charlotte in 1870, and Goldsboro in 1873. Circuit-riding rabbis, most notably Rabbi Edward Calisch of

Wilmington's Temple of Israel, the oldest synagogue in North Carolina. Photograph by Tim Buchman. Courtesy of Preservation North Carolina.

Richmond, traveled through the state organizing worship services and religious schools.

North Carolina Jewry in its early days was, for the most part, traditionalist in its religious orientation. Goldsboro's Jews stated that Sabbath and holiday observance was to be guided by "Biblical injunction, rather than by expediency." Traditionalists held services in Hebrew and maintained kosher dietary laws. Over time, however, local Jews acculturated and liberalized. Like most southern Jews, Jewish North Carolinians aligned themselves with the Reform movement after the founding in Cincinnati of the Union of American Hebrew Congregations in 1873. Dietary laws were typically abandoned. As civic-minded Americans of the Hebrew faith, Reform Jews espoused a universalistic, prophetic Judaism that deemphasized Jewish parochialism. Zebulon Vance, in his "Scattered Nation" lecture of 1874, described American Jews as "simply Unitarians or Deists." Social and economic forces worked against Orthodoxy. The state's Jewry was almost entirely mercantile, and with payday at the mills on Friday night and market day on Saturdays, Sabbath observance became economically difficult. Communities tended to be divided between traditionalists and modernists.

The arrival of East European immigrants after 1880 transformed the Jewish character of the state. They were Yiddish-speaking Jews who came from self-governing East European

Jewish enclaves, urban ghettos, and rural shtetls. Their orientation was traditionalist, if not strictly Orthodox. In larger towns like Durham, they concentrated in a Jewish neighborhood anchored by a synagogue and kosher bakery, grocery, and butcher shop. Orthodox Jews maintained regimens of daily prayer with a quorum of ten men. A local or itinerant ritual slaughterer, a *schochet*, ensured a supply of kosher meat. The early immigrant rabbi was often an unordained, self-proclaimed "reverend" who served as a religious master of all trades. As one Durhamite recalled, "He circumcised you, married you, buried you, and killed your chickens."

If the migration from Eastern Europe to the port cities of Baltimore or New York represented one break from a traditional society, the secondary move to the remote, small Jewish communities of North Carolina represented another. Although some Jews struggled to maintain their Orthodoxy, larger numbers were less scrupulous in their observance of ritual and dietary laws, although they were still pervasively immersed in the East European Jewish ethnicity known as Yiddishkeit.

In larger communities, social and denominational fault lines often existed between the acculturated, native-born Jews of German origin and the newly arrived, Orthodox immigrants from Eastern Europe. Where numbers were small, Jewish unity forced compromise. Historical trends worked in favor of liberal, Reform Judaism. In 1941 Rabbi Robert Jacobs of Asheville wrote that "our membership is an amalgamation of 'Reform' and 'Orthodox,' with the emphasis on Reform Judaism. The Reform group . . . has lost its early rigidity, and the Orthodox group . . . has lost its scrupulous observance of the minutiae of Jewish law. . . . With our Temple, an American type of Judaism is a-borning."

With the Americanizing of the immigrants, religious practices eroded, although ethnic bonds remained strong. Jewish group solidarity was preserved not just by the synagogue but also by such societies as the men's B'nai B'rith and the women's Hadassah. These philanthropic groups linked local Jews to international Jewry. The North Carolina Association of Jewish Women (1921) and the North Carolina Association of Rabbis (ca. 1951) encouraged religious observance and education. Jews, regardless of affiliation, were united locally by federations that provided social services and connected them to a national institutional network.

In the 1930s Orthodoxy began yielding to Conservative Judaism, which sought to accommodate religious law to modernity. Its theological approach was historical rather than fundamentalist, and it also moved hesitatingly toward gender equality. In the post–World War II years, Jewish education became a priority with the rise of an assimilated youth. Conservative Judaism grew ascendant in the immediate postwar years, with Reform Judaism enjoying stronger growth more recently. Many High Point Jews evolved from Orthodoxy, to Conserva-

tism, to Reconstructionism, an innovative offshoot of Conservatism that viewed Judaism as a civilization and not just as a religion. As women have achieved equal liturgical status in the Reform and Conservative movements, they now serve as rabbis, synagogue presidents, and leaders of Jewish federations.

As the Sunbelt drew thousands of Jews southward, North Carolina Jewry became more reflective of national Jewish demography. Mobility, intermarriage, and suburban dispersal have attenuated Jewish bonds and religious difference. Population growth has also made the state's Jewry religiously pluralistic. Durham's Beth El Congregation is led by a Reconstructionist rabbi and holds both Conservative and Orthodox services. The Lubavitcher Hasidim, an ultra-Orthodox sect that combines religious enthusiasm with strict adherence to Jewish law, located emissaries in Raleigh and Charlotte to encourage traditional observance. Though traditionalism has shown renewed life, the overwhelming number of North Carolina Jews are religious liberals, affiliating with the Reform or Conservative movements.

References: Eli Evans, *The Lonely Days Were Sundays: Reflections of a Jewish Southerner* (1993); Evans, *The Provincials: A Personal History of Jews in the South* (1997); Harry Golden, "The Jewish People of North Carolina," NCHR 32 (April 1955); "The Jewish New Year Book," *Southern Jewish Times* (30 Sept. 1932).

Leonard Rogoff

SEE ALSO Temple of Israel.

Judiciary, Federal. The federal judicial system was created with the opening words of Article III of the U.S. Constitution: "The Judicial Power of the United States shall be vested." The framers of the Constitution desired a system of national courts to effectively implement the powers of the national government, as they feared that state courts might not fully enforce federal policies, especially if federal and state interests conflicted. Moreover, federal courts were viewed as important to protect individual liberties. Reacting to these concerns, Congress, through the Judiciary Act of 1789, established lower federal courts in 11 of the original 13 states. A national Supreme Court already had been created directly by Article III.

Early attempts to hold the lower federal courts contemplated by Article III led to a series of mishaps in North Carolina. A convention meeting at Fayetteville ratified the Constitution in November 1789, too late for the state to be included in the organization of the young nation's first federal courts created by the Judiciary Act passed earlier that year. Efforts to fix the location of federal tribunals in North Carolina were not completed until 4 June 1790, when Hugh Williamson, who represented Edenton and New Bern in Congress, shepherded through both houses a bill stating that all courts would meet in New Bern. William Richardson Davie, Revolutionary War hero and a founder of the University of North

Carolina, was President George Washington's first choice for the post of federal district court judge of North Carolina. On 8 June 1790 the Senate confirmed the appointment, but Davie later declined it. Washington then nominated John Stokes of Rowan County, but within two months Stokes was dead, never having mounted the bench. Washington and his successor, John Adams, enjoyed greater success in naming North Carolinians to seats on the U.S. Supreme Court. James Iredell (1790–99) and Alfred Moore (1799–1804), both staunch Federalists, remained as of 2006 the only North Carolinians ever appointed to the Supreme Court.

The federal courts in North Carolina achieved a surer footing with Washington's appointment of John Sitgreaves, a New Bern attorney, to the district court bench on 17 Dec. 1790. Sitgreaves served as the state's federal district judge for 12 years, holding courts in New Bern, Wilmington, and Edenton until his death in 1802. Twice each year, in tandem with a Supreme Court justice, Sitgreaves held the U.S. Circuit Court for the District of North Carolina, first at New Bern and later in Raleigh after the government relocated there. The numerous differences between the respective jurisdictions of the district and circuit courts were set forth in the provisions of the Judiciary Act of 1789, though the subject matter jurisdiction of all federal courts was extremely narrow throughout the nineteenth century. Most of the caseload in North Carolina involved concerns of the admiralty, a small group of federal crimes, and, from 1790 to 1810, claims by British citizens for restoration of property lost or seized during the Revolution. Perhaps as a result of North Carolina's moribund commercial life, none of the important decisions by Chief Justice John Marshall interpreting the Commerce clause of the Constitution emanated from local federal courts.

The most significant case brought before the North Carolina federal circuit court was *Granville's Devisee v. Allen*, a Revolutionary War reparations action heard in 1805. Although most of North Carolina's colonial Lords Proprietors had ceded their landholdings in the New World to the Crown half a century before shots were fired at Lexington and Concord, Earl Granville retained the right to dispose of property in a vast region known as the "Granville District." Occupying much of the northern third of the colony, the Granville District was teeming with settlers and land speculators soon after the 1777 General Assembly enacted statutes vesting title to the whole district in the state. Three decades later, Earl Granville's heirs brought a test case seeking to eject substantial planters William R. Davie (whom Washington had sought to make a federal judge) and Josiah Collins, and by extension, thousands of other settlers, from the land. Chief Justice John Marshall, who in 1805 had been leading the U.S. Supreme Court for four years, was to preside over the circuit court along with federal district judge Henry Potter. On the ground that he had served as counsel and had had a financial interest in a similar Virginia case, Mar-

shall recused himself from the case. Left to hear and decide the dispute on his own, Potter ruled that the defendants could keep their land. Highly popular with the public, this decision may have stanched the flow of North Carolinians migrating to other states as a result of the Granville heirs' claim.

When North Carolina seceded from the Union in 1861, Potter's successor, Asa Biggs, resigned as district judge. No federal court was held in the state for the duration of the Civil War. After Gen. Robert E. Lee surrendered at Appomattox, Chief Justice Salmon P. Chase declined to come to Raleigh to open the U.S. Circuit Court, maintaining that it was inappropriate for a member of the Supreme Court to exercise civil authority in a state still under military occupation. Nevertheless, the first session of the circuit court to be held in the former Confederacy opened in Raleigh in June 1867. Even after North Carolina was readmitted to the Union, federal judges performed their official duties among a resentful and politically hostile people.

By an act of Congress dated 4 June 1872, taken in recognition of the precipitous growth of the state's western counties, North Carolina was divided into two federal judicial districts: the Eastern District and the Western District. In another important structural development, Congress in 1891 created a layer of intermediate appellate courts to relieve the Supreme Court of the duty of considering all appeals in cases originally decided by the federal district courts. The U.S. Court of Appeals for the Fourth Circuit, by which the federal appeals court with jurisdiction over North Carolina came to be known, originally was supplied with three permanent circuit judges.

Although North Carolina was long the largest state in the circuit (which embraces Virginia, Maryland, West Virginia, and the Carolinas), only six North Carolinians have served as judges in the Fourth Circuit. These six, however, have exerted remarkable influence over the course of the court's jurisprudence. Jeter C. Pritchard, appointed to the court in 1904, served until his death in 1921. John Johnston Parker Jr., named to the Fourth Circuit in 1925 by President Calvin Coolidge, quickly garnered praise as one of the most admired federal judges in the country. Although the Senate failed to confirm Parker's nomination to the Supreme Court by President Herbert Hoover in 1930, Parker continued to serve as the Fourth Circuit's chief judge until his death in 1958. His successors, Jesse Spencer Bell (1961–67), James Braxton Craven Jr. (1966–77), James Dickson Phillips Jr. (1978–94), and Samuel James Ervin III (1980–99), are numbered among the Fourth Circuit's most influential judges. Ervin, who became chief judge in 1989 and served until his death in 1999, was the second North Carolinian to lead the Fourth Circuit after Parker.

In 1927 Congress further subdivided North Carolina into three federal districts, carving counties out of the old Eastern and Western Districts to form a new Middle District. Congress also recognized the growing federal caseload in the state by adding judgeships to each district. Beginning in 1994, four active district judges held court in the Eastern and Middle Districts; in the Western District, three presided. Each district also had at least one judge of senior, or semiretired, status who held court according to his inclinations. Counting the state's 2 sitting circuit judges, 2 prospective circuit court appointments, and 15 active and senior district judges, the Article III federal bench sitting in North Carolina numbered nearly 20. In addition, within each judicial district, groups of federal magistrate judges and bankruptcy judges assisted the district judges with decision-making duties in certain statutorily defined categories of cases. Considered as a whole, the federal judicial system in North Carolina by the early 2000s had grown thirtyfold since its creation in 1790.

References: Peter G. Fish, *Federal Justice in the Mid-Atlantic South: United States Courts from Maryland to the Carolinas, 1789–1835* (2002); Kermit L. Hall, ed., *The Oxford Companion to the Supreme Court of the United States* (1992); Crockett W. Hewlett, *The United States Judges of North Carolina* (1978).

Martin H. Brinkley
Peter Graham Fish

Judiciary, State. When North Carolina became a state in 1776, the colonial structure of the court system was retained nearly intact. The Court of Pleas and Quarter Sessions, the county court that existed from about 1670 to 1868, was still held by the assembled justices of the peace in each county. The justices, appointed by the governor on the recommendation of the General Assembly, were paid from fees charged to litigants. On the lowest level of the judicial system, justices of the peace held magistrate courts of limited jurisdiction, singly or in pairs, when the county court was out of term.

The Constitution of 1776 empowered the legislature to appoint judges of the North Carolina Supreme Court. The state judiciary began in 1777 with legislative authorization of three superior court judges and the creation of judicial districts. Sessions were supposed to be held in the court towns of each district twice a year. At that time, the terms "supreme court" and "superior court" were interchangeable. From its inception, the judicial system prompted complaints and demands for reform. Infrequency of sessions, conflicting judicial opinions, an insufficient number of judges, and no means of appeal were some of the problems cited, although the absence of a real supreme court was considered the greatest weakness.

In 1779 the General Assembly required the superior court judges to meet in Raleigh as a court of conference to settle cases the district courts could not resolve. Subsequent legislation directed the justices to put their opinions in writing to be delivered orally in court. The court of conference was changed in name to the supreme court in 1805 and authorized to hear appeals in 1810. In 1818 an independent three-judge supreme

court (raised to five in 1868, reduced to three in 1875, and returned to five through a voter-approved constitutional amendment in November 1888) was created to review cases decided at the superior court level. Meanwhile, semiannual superior court sessions in each county were made mandatory in 1806, and the state was divided into six circuits, with six judges sitting in rotation and two judges constituting a quorum. The county court of justices of the peace continued as the lowest court and as the agency of local government.

The North Carolina Constitution of 1868 implemented major changes to modernize the state judiciary and make it more democratic. The county court's control of local government was abolished. Capital offenses were limited to murder, arson, burglary, and rape, and the constitution stated that punishments were intended not only to satisfy justice but also to reform the offender and thus prevent crime. Appointment of supreme court justices and superior court judges was transferred from the General Assembly to the voters, with vacancies filled by the governor until the next election. The Court of Pleas and Quarter Sessions was eliminated; its responsibilities were divided between the superior court and the individual justices of the peace, who were retained as separate judicial officers with limited jurisdiction. In 1875 the General Assembly was empowered to appoint justices of the peace.

Most of the modernizing changes in the 1868 constitution endured, and the judicial structure continued without systematic modification through most of the twentieth century. During these years legislative enactments resulted in gradual changes and additions to the state court system, which by the 1960s consisted of four levels: the supreme court, with appellate jurisdiction; the superior court, with general trial jurisdiction; the local statutory courts, such as county, municipal, and township recorder's courts, domestic relations courts, and juvenile courts; and justices of the peace and mayors' courts with limited jurisdiction.

The need for a comprehensive evaluation and revision of the court system received the attention and support of Governor Luther H. Hodges in 1957, and he encouraged the leaders of the North Carolina Bar Association to pursue the matter. In late 1958 the Court Study Committee, established as an agency of the association, issued a report proposing reorganization. A legislative Constitutional Commission, working with the Court Study Committee, submitted a similar report in early 1959. Both groups called for the establishment of an all-inclusive court system to be directly state-operated, uniformly organized throughout the state, and centralized in its administration. An important part of the proposal was that the local statutory courts be replaced by a single district court. Further, the office of justice of the peace should be abolished and the new position of magistrate created within the district court.

Constitutional amendments introduced in the legislature of 1959 failed to gain the required three-fifths vote of each house. The proposals were reintroduced and approved by popular vote in 1962, and in 1965 the General Assembly enacted laws to enforce the new system in stages. By 1971 all of the county courts had been incorporated into the new General Court of Justice, established by the Constitution of 1971. This designation of the entire judicial system as a single, statewide court, with components for various types and caseload levels, was adapted from the seventeenth-century General Court of North Carolina.

Also new to the court system was the Administrative Office of the Courts, created by the 1965 General Assembly to maintain an efficient court system and develop a single budget covering the whole judicial system and its employees. The office is responsible for directing the nonjudicial, administrative, and business affairs of the judicial branch. Its functions include fiscal management, purchasing services, personnel services, information and statistical services, appointment of legal guardians, supervision of record keeping in the trial court clerks' offices, liaison with the executive and legislative departments of government, and administration of programs that provide legal representation to indigent persons.

By the early 2000s the North Carolina court system featured a supreme court (a chief justice and 6 associate justices), a court of appeals (15 judges in rotating panels), superior courts (one or more judges for each of 46 districts), district courts (one or more judges for 40 districts), magistrates, district attorneys (one for each of 39 districts), and 100 clerks of superior court (one for each county). Since the 1970s the selection of judges has been controversial. Although judges have continued to be elected by popular vote, lawmakers have proposed constitutional amendments that would have the legislature appoint judges according to merit. The proposed amendments have received a majority backing but not the three-fifths required to submit constitutional amendments to popular vote.

References: Joan G. Brannon, *The Judicial System in North Carolina* (1994); Mebane Rash Whitman and Ran Coble, eds., *North Carolina Focus: An Anthology on State Government, Politics, and Policy* (3rd ed., 1996).

Wiley J. Williams

SEE ALSO Supreme Court of North Carolina.

Judson College was a nineteenth-century academy located in the mountain town of Hendersonville. The school was conceived by the Western Carolina Baptist Association in 1858 and originally named the Western North Carolina Female College. Construction of the college's main building was begun in 1860 under the direction of a board of trustees that included the Reverend Nelson Bowen as president, Daniel King as treasurer, and A. T. Allen as secretary. The Civil War halted

the building process, however, and the incomplete structure housed a variety of ventures until 1879, when a high school was opened on the site.

The Judson College catalog for the academic year 1887–88 shows the curriculum to have included mathematics, English grammar, natural science, "language lessons," North Carolina history, geography, Latin, and Greek. A six-year "common school" course of study was available to students, preparing them for "entrance to high school or academic work." The Preparatory Department was a three-year course for individuals interested in attending the University of North Carolina or another college in the state. Finally, the Normal Department offered its graduates either a teaching certificate or a Bachelor of Divinity degree, depending on the length of the course. Tuition for these courses ranged during the 1890s from 24 cents to $1.00 per week; for students boarding at the school, an additional $2.50 per week was charged.

While Judson College never established itself as an influential academy on a state level, it was an important part of its local educational environment. A number of the college's former students became leaders in Hendersonville and Henderson County, including V. L. Hyman, a mayor of Hendersonville; S. M. King and J. P. Fletcher, clerks of superior court; and F. M. Jordan, a member of the state's Department of Insurance. The school also produced many influential teachers and educational administrators before it was closed in 1899, a victim of two decades of financial struggles.

References: J. T. Fain Jr., "'Old Judson' Is Coming Down," *Hendersonville Times-News*, 11 Aug. 1965; "Old Judson College Marker to Be Unveiled Today," *Asheville Citizen-Times*, 13 June 1954.

Jay Mazzocchi

Jugtown. In nineteenth- and early twentieth-century North Carolina, "jugtown" referred to a number of rural, pottery-producing communities. Jugtowns were known to have existed in Buncombe, Catawba, and Moore Counties, but one particular site came to be considered the premier North Carolina jugtown.

The abundance of clay beds attracted English Staffordshire potters to the area that became Sheffield Township about 1740. Isolation and poverty insured survival of the potters' craft, and local potters produced tableware and other articles for their neighbors. In the nineteenth century, a major source of income for the Moore County potters included production of jugs for the whiskey trade. In 1921 Jacques and Juliana Busbee established Jugtown Pottery near Seagrove in Moore County. By all accounts, the Busbees, who moved to the area from Raleigh, saved the Moore County pottery industry from extinction. Jacques Busbee had studied art and design in New York City. His wife, a photographer and illustrator, had actively pro-

The dining room in the home of Jacques and Juliana Busbee at Jugtown, showing pieces of their pottery. Courtesy of NCOA&H.

moted folk crafts as chair of the art department of the Federation of Women's Clubs of North Carolina. The Busbees collected local pottery and promoted Moore County potteries. They scoured the area, searching for examples of early traditional designs. For several years the Busbees gave orders to local potters, shipped the wares to New York, and marketed the pottery at a tearoom in Greenwich Village operated by Juliana Busbee. To exert greater control over design and finish, the Busbees built the potters' shop known as Jugtown and hired and trained young potters to preserve the traditional shapes and glazes. Several Jugtown trainees later started their own potteries in the Jugtown community.

Jacques Busbee most admired the primitive and early periods of Chinese pottery, and at Jugtown he introduced "translations" of Oriental ceramics and developed a "Chinese Blue" glaze. Under his influence, the Jugtown potters produced a great number of utilitarian and decorative pieces in a wide variety of glazes.

After Jacques Busbee's death in 1947, Juliana Busbee continued to operate Jugtown Pottery with the assistance of master potter Ben Owen, who had worked with the Busbees since 1923. John Mare assumed management of the pottery in April 1959 but closed it after Owen left to establish his own pottery. Mare reopened the pottery with master thrower Vernon Owens, cousin of Ben Owen, in April 1960. Both Mare and Juliana Busbee died in 1962, ending plans for expansion. The pottery was sold in 1968 to Country Roads, Inc., a nonprofit corporation. In 1983 Vernon Owens purchased the pottery and has run it with his wife Pam Owens since then. Jugtown Pottery was listed on the National Register of Historic Places in 1999.

References: Juliana R. Busbee, "Jugtown Comes of Age," *The State* 5 (19 June 1937); Jean Crawford, *Jugtown Pottery: History and Design* (1964).

George W. Troxler

Junebugs, more properly called green June beetles, are common to North Carolina and other southeastern states. The insect emerges in June and July from its larval form into an adult beetle averaging slightly less than an inch in length. A noisy flyer, the junebug is a metallic green with a dusky yellow along its sides. It feeds on pollen, ripening fruits, and a variety of leafy garden and ornamental plants.

Though hated by gardeners and farmers—the larvae are especially destructive of tobacco plants—junebugs were once a source of recreation to North Carolina children, who in bygone days delighted in flying them around on kite strings fastened to the insects' sturdy legs. With several such self-propelled projectiles in flight at the same time, the string-pulling pilots staged aerial dogfights, complete with sound effects worthy of the war movies that inspired their games.

Reference: Lorus and Margery Milne, *National Audubon Society Field Guide to North American Insects and Spiders* (1995).

Jerry Leath Mills

Junior Reserves. SEE Reserve Troops.

Justice, Department of. SEE Attorney General.

Justices of the Peace, or judges of record, were appointed in early colonial North Carolina for certain county or borough districts to preserve the peace and ensure that the law and legal processes were thoroughly and expeditiously observed. Appointments of justices of the peace were made by governors on the recommendation of the Proprietary royal council of the colony, giving the post significant executive power. In colonial North Carolina, at least three justices of the peace had to be present for business to be conducted at the county court, or Court of Pleas and Quarter Sessions, which met quarterly. The proceedings were recorded in the Minutes Books, frequently in great detail.

The justices of the peace exercised wide administrative and executive powers and were often the most visible governmental officials in the lives of North Carolinians prior to the Civil War. Their actions are a matter of record in the counties whose records have survived. When the state's inferior courts were abolished in 1868, the justices of the peace retained their power to appoint county commissioners and oversee taxation; however, their usual duties became trying petty cases and solemnizing marriages. In the modern court system, justices of the peace are minor functionaries, dealing with local cases such as trespass and assault.

References: Paul M. McCain, *The County Court in North Carolina before 1750* (1954); William S. Powell, *North Carolina through Four Centuries* (1989).

Jo White Linn

K

Kaolin is a fine clay mineral used in ceramics and insulators. The Cherokee Nation was issued a patent in 1744 for the production of porcelain from a mixture of kaolin, quartz, and feldspar. In 1767 Thomas Griffiths had five tons of kaolin dug and transported to England from the Cowee section of modern Macon County for use by the Wedgwood potters in making fine medallions. Systematic mining began in 1888 near Webster in Macon County, and by 1900 North Carolina had become a significant producer with tonnage sent to Trenton, N.J. Kaolin has continued to be an important product of North Carolina mining.

References: J. L. Bundy and P. A. Carpenter, *Feldspar Resources of North Carolina*, North Carolina Geological Survey Information Circular 20 (1969); J. C. Olson, *Mica Deposits of the Franklin-Sylva District*, North Carolina Geological Survey Bulletin no. 49 (1946).

Jean H. Seaman

Kate B. Reynolds Charitable Trust is a philanthropic foundation created in 1947 and based in Winston-Salem. By virtue of the intent of its donor, the trust is dedicated to improving health care for the indigent and medically underserved people of North Carolina and to helping the poor and needy residents of Winston-Salem and Forsyth County. The trust was established in 1947 by the will of Kate Gertrude Bitting Reynolds (1867–1946), the wife of William Neal Reynolds, chairman of R. J. Reynolds Tobacco Company.

Kate Reynolds designated that one-fourth of the income from the trust be used for the poor and needy in Winston-Salem and Forsyth County and that three-fourths of the income be used for charity patients in North Carolina hospitals. These designations have become known as the Poor and Needy Division and the Health Care Division, respectively. In 1970 the trust successfully appealed to the North Carolina Supreme Court for the ability to expand the latter designation to include broader health care needs in the state.

In its first 50 years, the Poor and Needy Division of the Reynolds Trust granted more than $39 million. The Health Care Division has made an additional $119 million in grants for programs throughout the state. Programs have included a focus on health care for the elderly, mothers and infants, people with AIDS, and the disabled, among others. The trust has also worked to provide increased access to health care in the state's rural areas and supported health education, including nursing programs at community colleges. It has often worked in collaboration with other foundations dedicated to improving the lives of North Carolinians, including the Duke Endowment and the Z. Smith Reynolds Foundation.

The Kate B. Reynolds Charitable Trust's assets more than doubled in 1989 when the R. J. Reynolds Tobacco Company was sold in a leveraged buyout. In the early 2000s the trust's assets were more than $470 million, and the organization designates about $24 million annually in grants through its two divisions.

Reference: Jan Johnson Yopp, *A Legacy of Caring: The Kate B. Reynolds Charitable Trust* (1997).

Cecelia Moore

Keeley Institute was incorporated in September 1891 and opened the next month in the Central Hotel Building at Elm and Market Streets in the center of Greensboro. It was reincorporated on 20 Mar. 1892, with Col. W. H. Osborn of Greensboro as president and chief stockholder and Benjamin N. Duke and James Buchanan Duke among the other stockholders. The institute's purpose was the rehabilitation of alcoholics and drug addicts through a program developed by Leslie E. Keeley, who founded the original institute in Dwight, Ill., in 1879.

Keeley's literature claimed to "guarantee success" through use of his "Double Chloride of Gold" remedies. Described as rational and scientific, Keeley's method for use of this substance would result in the "restoration of poisoned and narcotized nerve cells to a healthy condition." This meant an end to cravings—six weeks for alcohol and four weeks for drugs. The Keeley treatment began with a thorough physical examination, followed by daily checks by physicians, careful laboratory work, and reconstructive remedies taken under "daily medical direction." Recreational activities also were used to restore patients to a "normal" medical state. In the early years the institute's services were limited to male patients, but later women were admitted. At one time there was a Keeley Institute in every state. The reasons for the institute's demise likely included the rise of Alcoholics Anonymous, the enlargement of state institutions, and the recognition of alcoholism as a disease.

Reference: Carl Goerch, "The Keeley Institute," *The State* (17 Sept. 1938).

Alexander R. Stoesen

Kehukee Baptist Association was formed in the eighteenth century by Baptist churches in eastern North Carolina that had belonged to the Charleston Baptist Convention but decided, because of distance and divergent interests, to form their own association. The actual date of the formation is now

Keeley Institute, ca. 1903, after its move to Blandwood. NCC.

accepted as 1769. These churches were initially considered Regular Baptist, but they gradually moved to a strong Calvinist position under the leadership of Lemuel Burkitt. The association grew to include all eastern North Carolina Baptists until around 1806.

The Kehukee Association was modeled on the Philadelphia Association and adopted the strongly Calvinistic Philadelphia Confession. Members of the Philadelphia Association became known as Particular Baptists, so called because they believed in "limited atonement," holding that only a few people would be saved and those people had already been selected by God. During the Revolutionary War, the Kehukee Association divided into two groups over the question of accepting as church members those who had been baptized "in unbelief." The dissidents, led by Burkitt, who wanted the more restrictive membership requirement, joined in 1789 with churches across the Virginia line to form a new association, which was called the United Baptist Association. The new association contained several Separate Baptist and several Regular Baptist churches

—something new in Baptist history—and claimed a total of 61 churches in North Carolina and Virginia. It adopted a Confession of Faith that was again strongly Calvinistic.

With the growth of the general population, the Kehukee Association grew also. It reached a membership of approximately 37 churches and 2,000 congregants by 1900. During the nineteenth century the antimissionary, or Primitive, Baptists had spread thinly across North Carolina, claiming several associations in the north central part of the state and in the mountains. Primitive Baptist churches nationwide reached about 3,000 in number, with 120,000 members by 1900, but these numbers had declined somewhat by the latter decades of the twentieth century.

References: Maloy A Huggins, *A History of North Carolina Baptists, 1727–1932* (1967); George Washington Paschal, *History of North Carolina Baptists* (2 vols., 1938).

Anne Moore

Kellenberger Foundation. The Kellenberger Historical Foundation (formerly the May Gordon Latham Kellenberger Historical Foundation) was established in 1979 in New Bern, following the donor's death on 1 May 1978. The foundation limits its giving to Craven County and New Bern. It aids and supports projects related to Tryon Palace Historical Sites and Gardens and Historical New Bern, with emphasis on building/renovation, program development, publication, and research. The donor's husband, John Kellenberger, served as treasurer of the Tryon Commission. Besides their work with that organization, the Kellenbergers gave generously to many causes in the Greensboro area.

Wiley J. Williams

Keyauwee Indians, at the beginning of the eighteenth century, were living in a town surrounded by palisades located near the Uwharrie River in present-day Randolph County. Nestled in a valley surrounded by cornfields, their village was vulnerable to attack, and their numbers, according to the chronicles of John Lawson, were minimal. Shortly after Lawson's 1701 visit, the Keyauwee relocated. Joining with the Tutelo, Saponi, Occaneechi, and others in 1714, they briefly found shelter at Fort Christanna, an outpost and reservation established by Virginia's governor Alexander Spotswood. After a few years the Keyauwee left to join with the Saura (Cheraw) and the Peedee on the Pee Dee River in South Carolina, where they carried on a trade in deerskins with Charleston traders. The Keyauwee allied with their Indian neighbors in the 1715 Yamassee War against South Carolina, after which they joined other Siouan-speaking people in the Catawba Nation.

References: James H. Merrell, *The Indians' New World: Catawbas and Their Neighbors from European Contact through the Era of Removal* (1989); Douglas L. Rights, *The American Indian in North Carolina* (1947).

Michael D. Green

Kidney Stone Belt refers to the region in the southeastern United States where the rate of kidney stones, or kidney calculi, is excessive. North Carolina reportedly has the highest incidence of kidney stones in the nation; some research indicates that white males (the highest-risk group) have a 15 percent chance of developing kidney stones versus a much lower risk for the same group in other parts of the country. Sedentary white-collar workers are more likely to form stones than are active blue-collar laborers.

The reasons given for this high occurrence vary. In 1995 it was reported that the wide consumption of iced tea in North Carolina could be a contributing factor, because tea is loaded with calcium oxalate, which is a main ingredient in certain kinds of kidney stones. But more recent studies suggest that the consumption of tea actually reduces the risk of stone formation, in some cases by as much as 14 percent.

Another theory finds a correlation between the high incidence of kidney stone formation and the consumption of hard water. Because much of North Carolina remains rural, many people continue to use wells as their primary or only source of drinking water. The mineral content of water is thought to be a possible source of stone disease. According to some studies, excessive water hardness causes kidney stones to form and people with a history of stones should consider avoiding private wells. Still other studies suggest that water hardness has only a minor impact on stone formation. Some researchers believe that the high incidence of stones in North Carolina and in the South generally is coincidental and that the "kidney stone belt" is actually a myth.

Rusty Rains

Kilpatrick's Shirt-tail Skedaddle. SEE Monroe's Crossroads, Battle of.

King's Bounty (1757) was a grant of £200,000 that England gave its American colonies in repayment for their military assistance during the French and Indian War (1754–63). The portion of this money intended for North Carolina—less than £8,000—became a source of dispute between the colonial Assembly and Governor Arthur Dobbs (1754–65). Both claimed the right to distribute the funds, the Assembly through its acknowledged control of regular colonial funds and the governor by royal prerogative, or executive privilege, because he considered the money a grant rather than traditional income. The two branches of government also divided sharply over their intended use of the funds. The Assembly wished to spend them on church lands and free schools, whereas Dobbs, according to his instructions, sought to prosecute the war, establish a permanent seat of government, and finance governmental buildings.

The issue, however, went further than the distribution of funds. In 1754 London began strengthening the Crown's prerogative by limiting the powers of the Assembly. When he became governor, for instance, Dobbs was instructed to use his royal prerogative for the creation of towns and charters, the naming of representatives to the Assembly, and the designation of court meetings. In addition, he was to establish a seat of government, to reform the mode of paying quitrents and the process of making land grants, and to establish an exchequer court, which would be the final authority in all matters involving governmental funding. Until recently, most of these functions had been handled by the Assembly in conjunction with the governor.

It was the proposed grant of King's Bounty that broke the uneasy truce. The House of Commons, or Lower House, refused to recognize Dobbs's prerogative to choose a capital unless the governor surrendered the funds in question to the House's administration. He refused, on the grounds of prerogative, because his instructions admonished him to personally grant and dispense all public moneys contingent only on the consent of the North Carolina Council, or Upper House. The impasse was fueled by the Board of Trade in London. Although the board knew Dobbs's orders and sympathized with him, they ruled against him, ostensibly because moneys were traditionally controlled by the Lower House; but, more practically, because they wished to avoid colonial controversy. This ruling expanded the conflict between governor and Assembly to other issues, including courts, paper money, and the militia. The conflict did not end until Dobbs was removed and his successor, William Tryon, essentially accepted that the House of Commons would control all funds of whatever origin.

Though neither Dobbs nor Tryon surrendered the King's Bounty, utilizing it as an executive fund, the money proved to be a hollow victory. The prerogatives of the House of Commons were greatly strengthened as those of the Crown correspondingly declined.

References: Samuel A. Ashe, *History of North Carolina* (2 vols., 1908, 1925); William L. Saunders, ed., *Colonial Records of North Carolina*, vols. 5–6 (1888).

Louis P. Towles

King's Daughters and Sons developed out of a new Christian service order, the Silent Sisters of Service, formed in New York City by Margaret Bottome on 13 Jan. 1886. Originally open only to women, it accepted men in 1887 and was incorporated in 1891. Emma G. Williams of Wilmington was in New York when the order was founded. After returning home in 1886, she organized a branch at Wilmington's First Baptist Church, which was soon opened to women of all churches. Its first project was the purchase of a cemetery plot for the "worthy poor." In 1887 a group was formed in Greensboro, and from 1891 to 1893 it operated that city's first hospital. Salisbury, Greenville, and Henderson soon had local orders, and the first state convention in North Carolina was held in Greensboro in 1890.

By 1902 there were 26 active groups of King's Daughters engaged in charitable projects at the local level. At the annual convention that year the president, Margaret Burgwyn, led in uniting them to undertake projects of statewide significance. Chartered by the General Assembly in 1903, they soon offered to donate a 50-acre tract in Moore County for a "reform" school and pledged $1,000 for construction of a carpenter's shop. They failed to secure legislative support, however, and it was not until 1907 that lobbying efforts led to the creation of the Stonewall Jackson Training and Industrial School. Three members of the King's Daughters were named to the board of trustees and the order, joined by the Federation of Women's Clubs and other organizations, lent significant financial support to the new school. A handsome stone memorial chapel erected in 1914 was named for Burgwyn, who served as president of the North Carolina branch of the King's Daughters for 23 years.

In 1911 a retirement home for women was erected by the Durham order, and in 1923 a similar home was dedicated in Raleigh. In 1921, with the help of churches throughout the state, the King's Daughters began to raise funds to construct a chapel for young female offenders housed at Samarcand Manor, a state correctional institution in Moore County. Support of the order in Durham resulted in the construction of the Sara Barker Development Center in Durham to enrich the lives of mentally handicapped children.

Although membership in the North Carolina branch declined near the end of the twentieth century, local orders of the King's Daughters and Sons have continued to support programs of long standing, some nearing the century mark. The group continues to operate as an interdenominational, interracial Christian service organization dedicated to the "development of spiritual life and stimulation of Christian activity." It supports a scholarship program to train leaders for positions of Christian leadership and for health-related careers and to educate North American Indians. It also supports such international projects as Laubach International, World Vision, and Habitat for Humanity. In addition, it places emphasis on the global eradication of leprosy. The group's headquarters is at Lake Chautauqua, N.Y.

References: Sara F. Gugle, *History of the International Order of the King's Daughters and Sons* (1931); Mrs. Charles Sorrels, *History of the North Carolina Branch of the King's Daughters and Sons, 1970–1975* (1975).

Clarence E. Horton Jr.

King's Mountain, Battle of. The stunning victory won by a force of about 1,800 backcountry "Overmountain Men" over approximately 1,000 Tories at King's Mountain on 7 Oct. 1780 has been justly described as a key turning point in the American Revolution. According to British commander Henry Clinton, the American victory "proved the first Link of a Chain of Evils that followed each other in regular Succession until they at last ended in the total loss of America." The Tory force at King's Mountain was commanded by Maj. Patrick Ferguson, the son of a Scottish judge. At the Battle of Brandywine, Ferguson's right arm had been shattered. However, he practiced so assiduously that he learned to wield his sword with his left hand, earning him the nickname "Bulldog" in the process.

A few weeks before King's Mountain, Ferguson, who guarded Lord Charles Cornwallis's left flank, led a foray to the vicinity of Old Fort in North Carolina. At about that time he bluntly warned the local revolutionaries that if they did not cease their rebellion he would march over the mountains, hang their leaders, and lay waste their settlements with fire and sword. This brought an indignant reaction from the back-country forces and a conference between Cols. Isaac Shelby and John Sevier, who agreed that they should take the offensive. They called a rendezvous at Sycamore Shoals (now in Tennessee) for 25 September. On that day Sevier and Shelby arrived with 240 troops each to join Col. Charles McDowell, who was already there with 160 North Carolina riflemen. They were heartened when Col. William Campbell marched in with 400 Virginians.

While the little army was marching over Roan Mountain, two of Sevier's troops, James Crawford and Samuel Chambers, were reported missing. Suspecting that they would warn Ferguson, Sevier changed the march plans. On 30 September the American force reached Quaker Meadows in Burke County, where it was joined by Col. Benjamin Cleveland and 350 North Carolinians. By 1 October the Americans were camped just south of King's Mountain. Rain kept them there a day while the officers elected Campbell commander.

Ferguson was also slowed by rain and never reached Charlotte to join Cornwallis, as was his apparent plan. He had not intended to install his army atop King's Mountain, which had allegedly been named for a farmer who lived at its foot and not for King George III. The mountain, with its short and relatively level summit, must have impressed Ferguson as a good defensive position; he wrote to Cornwallis, asking for reinforcements and boasting that he was on King's Mountain and could not be driven off.

Early on the afternoon of 7 October, the Americans arrived at the foot of King's Mountain, near where it extends into South Carolina. They launched a four-pronged attack, with two columns on each side of the mountain, led by Colonels Campbell and Sevier on the right and Shelby and Cleveland on the left. Ferguson and his men apparently were taken by surprise by the boldness and rapidity of the Overmountain Men's aggression. Over the roar of the battle could be heard intermittently a shrill shriek from the silver whistle Ferguson used to direct his troops. It was soon silenced, however, as Ferguson was killed while leading a desperate sortie by a few of his men to break out of the mountaineers' cordon. Capt. Abraham DePeyster, the second in command, almost immediately raised a white flag. However, several minutes elapsed before the surrender could take effect, and during that period several more Tories were killed. Some Americans kept firing because they did not understand what was going on, and others did so because they recalled that when Col. Abraham Buford, an American, was defeated several weeks before, British colonel Banastre Tarleton had kept on firing, an action Cornwallis had applauded.

Finally the guns fell silent and the American victory was complete. In an hour's time, Ferguson and 119 of his men had been killed, 123 wounded, and 664 captured. The Americans had lost 28 killed and 62 wounded. The Americans were still so angry at their enemies that on their ride home, Campbell found it necessary to issue an order directing the officers to halt the slaughter of prisoners. Finally Campbell convened a court-martial to try some of the prisoners. According to Shelby, 36 men were convicted of "breaking open houses, killing the men, turning the women and children out of doors and burning the houses." Of those convicted, 9 were actually hanged.

The American victory at the Battle of King's Mountain altered the tenor of the American Revolution, disheartening Cornwallis and his army, threatening and eventually altering British military strategy, and adding renewed vigor to the American cause.

References: Lyman C. Draper, *King's Mountain and Its Heroes: History of the Battle of King's Mountain, October 7th 1780 and the Events Which Led to It* (repr., 1967); Phillips Russell, *North Carolina in the Revolutionary War* (1965).

Noel Yancey

SEE ALSO Overmountain Victory National Historic Trail.

Kinston, Battle of. The Civil War battle at Kinston on 13–14 Dec. 1862 was the first major Confederate opposition to the advance of Brig. Gen. John G. Foster to Goldsboro. Foster led a force of about 10,000 infantry, 640 cavalry, and 40 pieces of artillery. The defending Confederates numbered about 2,014 and were commanded by Brig. Gen. Nathan G. "Shank" Evans, who won fame at the First Battle of Manassas (Bull Run).

On 12 Dec. 1862, as his column approached Kinston from New Bern, Foster sent a small party of cavalry on a feint down the main road into Kinston. Meanwhile, the main body detoured to the south and west, intending to attack the town from the southwest, an unanticipated direction. At midmorning on 13 December, the Union army reached Southwest Creek, a small tributary of the Neuse River. Two regiments forced a crossing of the creek, driving back the North Carolina regiment holding the position. When Evans arrived, he withdrew all of his forces to a defensive line two miles from the bridge crossing the Neuse at Kinston and held this strong natural position overnight.

The Union attack resumed at 9:00 A.M. the next day. The inexperienced Federals faced both stiff Confederate resistance and casualties inflicted by their own artillery. Nevertheless, they crossed the swamp in front of the Confederate position and turned its left flank, sending that portion of the troops retreating north across the bridge. Evans, who thought that all of his men were safely across, ordered the bridge burned and turned his artillery on the troops remaining on the right and center of what had been the Confederate line. Shelled by the enemy and their own commander, the remaining Confederate troops made for the bridge. Closely pursued by the Federal advance, the organized retreat fell apart when the men approached the burning span. Nearly 400 of Evans's command were captured in the race for the burning bridge. Confederates north of the river retreated to establish a position two miles beyond Kinston. Foster's men extinguished the flames on the bridge and crossed on the partially destroyed span. Once across the river, Foster entered Kinston and sent a request for Evans's surrender, which was curtly refused. Before Foster could reform his units for another attack, the Confederate commander withdrew once more. The Union forces camped near Kinston that night and recrossed the river the following morning to resume their advance. Foster had lost about 160 killed and wounded in the fight. Confederate casualties were 125 killed and wounded and 400 captured, and Kinston was thoroughly looted by the Federal troops.

References: John G. Barrett, *The Civil War in North Carolina* (1963); Clifford C. Tyndall, "Lenoir County during the Civil War" (M.A. thesis, East Carolina University, 1981).

Dan Blair

Kinston College, a private coeducational college preparatory school, began in 1871 as Kinston Collegiate Institute and retained that name for the next 11 years. Founded by Joseph H. Foy, the school enrolled more than 100 students by the end of its first term. Future North Carolina governor Charles B. Aycock attended the school and delivered its commencement address in June 1879. The school was reorganized in the spring of 1882 when the Kinston College Stock Company was formed by a number of leading citizens. After $3,000 worth of stock was sold, a lot on Kinston's East Street, between King and Caswell Streets, was purchased and a building was begun. In September 1882 the school opened as Kinston College, with Richard H. Lewis as principal.

Apparently experiencing financial difficulties, the institution was reorganized in 1891 by Professors W. B. Lee and J. L. Crowell (brother of Trinity College president J. F. Crowell), who bought the property and served as coprincipals. Kinston College was described as a high-grade school offering intermediate and primary instruction as well as high school courses. The school opened in August 1892 with 74 students; enrollment rose to 102 before the end of the first year. In June 1892, Lee wrote a lengthy article for the local newspaper recounting the school's first year under new management. The article mentioned continued financial difficulties and sought fiscal support from the town to erect accommodations on campus for between 75 and 100 boarding students. There is no evidence that the town provided any money to the college for this purpose.

As of the fall of 1893, the school was again under new management, with D. T. Edwards now the principal. Just how long the school continued to exist is unknown. It is last mentioned in the local newspaper in the spring of 1894. With the growing efforts placed on local public schools at that time, it is likely that Kinston College's demise came soon after.

References: Talmadge C. Johnson and Charles R. Holloman, *The History of Kinston and Lenoir County* (1954); Mike Kohler, *200 Years of Progress: A Report of the History and Achievements of the People of Lenoir County* (1976).

Charles E. Taylor

Kirk-Holden War. SEE Reconstruction.

Kittrell College was established in 1886 in Vance County by the African Methodist Episcopal Church as a normal and industrial school to train African American male youth. Additional support in its early years came from church groups in Virginia and Pennsylvania. The name of the institution changed three times, becoming Kittrell College in 1901. The original wooden buildings of the campus were destroyed by fires, and support to replace the old structures came from Benjamin N. Duke. Duke provided funds for the old buildings of Trinity College (later Duke University's East Campus) in Durham to be dismantled and moved to the Kittrell campus, where they were reassembled.

From its beginning, Kittrell offered work-study programs to enable students of limited financial means to gain a higher education. The college offered a two-year course in either a terminal vocation or in work that could be credited toward a bachelor's degree. In 1975 its enrollment was 396. Soon thereafter, the school experienced severe economic problems and was forced to close.

Reference: William S. Powell, *Higher Education in North Carolina* (1970).

Charles W. Wadelington

Knights of the Golden Circle (KGC) was a secret military organization created in 1859 by George W. L. Bickley in Cincinnati, Ohio. Its stated aim was to sponsor and conduct military expeditions into the Caribbean region (the "Golden Circle") for the purpose of bringing new slave territories into the Union. Jingoistic newspapers that supported American intervention in Mexico and similar initiatives included the *Norfolk Day Book*, which enjoyed some popularity in northeastern North Carolina, especially among subscribers to the *Murfreesboro Citizen*. Maine native Charles Henry Foster, editor of the *Citizen* during 1859 and most of 1860, had been associated with the *Day Book* for a year or two before taking over the *Citizen*. Through him, the KGC was introduced in North Carolina. On a visit to Norfolk in early 1860, Foster was initiated into the KGC by Virginius D. Groner, a Norfolk militia colonel and ardent supporter of the KGC. (Groner later delivered the order to fire the first gun at Fort Sumter at the start of the Civil War in April 1861.)

Foster returned to Murfreesboro and began promoting the KGC through his newspaper and organizing KGC "castles" at Murfreesboro and nearby communities. Bickley held a KGC convention at Raleigh in May and addressed an audience at Murfreesboro in July. A *Citizen* editorial warned that acquisition by the federal government of Cuba, Nicaragua, or parts of Mexico by force, purchase, or other means would be accompanied by abolitionist colonization that would exclude slavery from such territories, as in the case of Kansas. The South, therefore, should support only territorial acquisitions that occurred outside federal authority. Like Texas, only these could be reliably settled as slave regions and presented as such for annexation.

During much of 1860, newspapers devoted considerable attention to KGC preparations in Texas for an invasion of Mexico. Some KGC members and groups traveled to Mexico that summer, but it soon became evident that Bickley's claims were much overstated. The confidence of his followers had been seriously eroded before Abraham Lincoln's election as president in November 1860 diverted the nation's attention to the secession crisis. During the Civil War Gatling gun inventor Richard J. Gatling, a native of Murfreesboro, was suspected of participation in the KGC, but the allegation appears to have been unfounded.

References: Ollinger Crenshaw, "The Knights of the Golden Circle: The Career of George Bickley," *American Historical Review* 47 (1941); Frank L. Klement, *Dark Lanterns: Secret Political Societies, Conspiracies, and Treason Trials in the Civil War* (1984).

Thomas C. Parramore

Know-Nothing Party. SEE American Party.

Korean War. When communist North Korea first invaded its southern neighbor, North Carolina's entire congressional delegation supported President Harry Truman's use of U.S. troops to combat the aggression. On 28 June 1950 Senator Clyde Hoey voiced the general consensus that the president's action was justified. Chatham County's representative was optimistic that with an American show of force, the North Korean offensive would "fizzle."

North Carolina vigorously mobilized for war, deploying state National Guard units to Fort Jackson for additional training by early July. The Air National Guard was also alerted to prepare for active duty. After the federal government ordered the state to open 101 local draft boards immediately and to call up 610 men by mid-September, Raleigh leaped from nineteenth to first place among southern induction centers in monthly recruitment. In addition, the Wilmington shipyard was reactivated with the potential to employ 21,000 men.

More than 177,000 North Carolinians served in the Korean War, with 784 killed and 201 listed as either prisoners of war or missing in action. The Medal of Honor was awarded to Jerry Crump of Charlotte, Charles George of Cherokee, and Bryant Womack of Mill Spring. George was one of three Native Americans to receive the medal for service in the Korean War.

The state was not spared the political upheaval associated with the conflict, which ended in a stalemate and a cease-fire, established on 27 July 1953. While newspapers ran a regular column detailing war casualties, the House Un-American Activities Committee began investigating five North Carolinians for communist affiliations. Some North Carolina veterans also marched on the State Capitol to demand their service bonus, reminiscent of the famous bonus march two decades earlier.

David L. Cockrell

Körner's Folly is the name applied to a house completed in 1880 by Jule Körner (1851–1924) in Kernersville. Noted for its odd exterior appearance as well as for its eccentric and highly decorated interior, the house features high gabled roofs and tall, narrow, irregularly spaced windows. Its many unusual architectural elements reflect the extraordinary imagination of its creator.

Körner was a photographer, sign painter, and portrait painter. Under the pseudonym Reuben Rink, he achieved success designing signs and other advertisements for the Blackwell Tobacco Company, makers of the wildly popular Bull Durham brand of smoking tobacco.

After Körner's death, the house was used for many enterprises, including a funeral home, an antique shop, and an architect's office. Körner's Folly Foundation, a nonprofit organization made up of family members, eventually took over the house. Dedicated to preserving the highly unusual house and opening it for public view, the foundation continues to raise money for the preservation and restoration of the house.

Reference: Catherine W. Bishir, *North Carolina Architecture* (1990).

Jim McPherson

Krispy Kreme Doughnut Corporation was founded in Winston-Salem in 1937 by Vernon Rudolph. A few years earlier Rudolph's uncle, a Paducah, Ky., storeowner, had purchased a secret yeast-raised doughnut recipe and the copyrighted name Krispy Kreme from New Orleans chef Joe LeBeau. The uncle hired Rudolph to sell doughnuts door-to-door, but soon Rudolph was looking for a way to sell on a larger scale. He and various family members subsequently opened shops in Nashville, Tenn., Charleston, W.Va., and Atlanta, Ga.

Rudolph eventually settled in Winston-Salem, where he and two partners began making Krispy Kreme doughnuts and selling them out of a 1936 Pontiac with a delivery rack in the back seat. As demand for his fresh doughnuts grew, Rudolph

![Körner's Folly. Photograph by Tim Buchman. Courtesy of Preservation North Carolina.]

Körner's Folly. Photograph by Tim Buchman. Courtesy of Preservation North Carolina.

converted his doughnut-making facility in the Old Salem area into a retail store by cutting a hole in the wall and installing a sales window. In the 1940s and 1950s, the company standardized its product with central manufacturing of the Krispy Kreme mix, distributed to a growing network of doughnut and coffee shops, and invented and manufactured its own doughnut-making machinery. By the 1960s Krispy Kreme stores were visible throughout the Southeast with recognizable green-tiled roofs and glowing signs touting "Hot Doughnuts Now." After Rudolph died in 1973, the company was reorganized for a 1976 sale to Beatrice Foods. A group of associates, early franchisees, bought the firm in 1982.

Krispy Kreme opened its first store in New York City in 1996 and its first in California in 1999. In April 2000 Krispy Kreme became a publicly traded company, and in December 2001 it opened a store in Toronto, Canada, one of 49 added that year. Despite store closings in Canada and controversy related to the company's bookkeeping methods, by 2006 Krispy Kreme was selling a total of 2.7 billion doughnuts annually at nearly 400 locations.

Doughnuts being processed at a Krispy Kreme factory. Photograph courtesy of Krispy Kreme Doughnut Corporation.

In 1997 Krispy Kreme gained icon status when company artifacts were donated to the Smithsonian Institution's National Museum of American History.

Reference: David A. Taylor, "Ring King," *Smithsonian* vol. 28, no. 12 (March 1998).

Jay Mazzocchi

Kudzu (*Pueraria lobata*), or "kuzu" as it is known in Japan, was introduced to the United States in 1876 as part of the Japanese pavilion at the Philadelphia Centennial Exposition. In Japan it is lauded for its many culinary, textile, and medicinal uses; and it gained popularity in the United States as an ornamental shade plant, well received for its fragrant flowers and adaptability. During the 1920s and 1930s, people all over the South planted kudzu seedlings, available through mail-order catalogs, around their porches and arbors. In addition, the Soil Erosion Service, established in 1933 and renamed the Soil Conservation Service in 1935, chose kudzu as the ideal cover crop to prevent erosion of southern lands. The vine became one of the chief measures for erosion control on the Tennessee Valley Authority projects. However, farmers in the South had their reservations about the difficulty of controlling kudzu and the potential of its overtaking valuable land.

By 1945 it was estimated that 500,000 acres in the Southeast were covered in kudzu; by 1948 the acreage covered in Georgia alone had grown to 480,000 acres. Kudzu could grow anywhere, from the lowlands of Georgia and South Carolina to the mountains of western North Carolina. By 1955 people had grown irritated with the vine's relentless appetite for more space; as one southerner put it, "It was like discovering Ole Blue was a chicken killer." The poet James Dickey called kudzu "a vegetal form of cancer." During the 1960s several programs for eradication were started. By 1970 the estimated area of land covered by kudzu was 85,000 acres, just 17 percent of the estimated 500,000 covered in the years 1945–50. However, kudzu still runs rampant in the forests of the South, including those of North Carolina. The vine invades forests, climbing trees and smothering them by cutting off sunlight.

Kudzu now grows more prolifically in the Deep South than in any other part of the world, and what was once hailed as an "agricultural miracle" is now more widely considered to be a "green menace." While many yearn to eradicate kudzu, others argue that creative uses must be found for the persistent vine. There are still those who praise kudzu for its use in erosion control and as a livestock feed. Others propose that kudzu be planted in barrels on top of buildings so that the vine can grow down, covering the building and serving as a natural coolant. Health food stores sell kudzu powder imported from Japan for culinary and medicinal use. Researchers at Vanderbilt University are looking into using the vines and leaves as a source of fuel and the roots as a fermentation substrate for the production of baker's yeast and ethanol fuel. Alcoholism researchers at the University of North Carolina at Chapel Hill and Research Triangle Park are studying a Chinese hangover remedy that includes kudzu.

Kudzu also gives its names to various pieces of southern culture. For example, the Winston-Salem grassroots organization Carolina Music Ways Music Heritage Resource Group, which seeks to promote the musical traditions of the northwest Piedmont, was originally called Kudzu. In addition, *Kudzu*, a popular, nationally syndicated comic strip created by Greensboro native Doug Marlette, is set in the fictional North Carolina town Bypass and deals with the experiences of the teenage dreamer Kudzu Dubose. Despite the problems it causes, kudzu has gained a permanent place in the southern landscape and culture.

References: William Shurtleff and Akiko Aoyagi, *The Book of Kudzu: A Culinary and Healing Guide* (1977); Angela Spivey, "Sobering Effects from the Lowly Kudzu," *Endeavors* 12 (April 1996).

Brooke Calton

Ku Klux Klan (KKK). There have been three KKK movements in North Carolina and the nation, similar in character but distinct organizationally and chronologically. The first Klan flourished in the Reconstruction era, its name derived from the Greek word *kuklos* for circle or band; it was almost exclusively southern in its membership and mission to perpetuate white supremacy. Beginning as a social fraternity in Pulaski, Tenn., in 1866, the KKK was soon taken over by former Confederate officers, including Gen. Nathan Bedford Forrest, and transformed into a paramilitary force to oppose Republican policies, especially black suffrage, in Tennessee. In 1868 the order quickly spread across the South as other Republican

Ku Klux Klan demonstrators march down Franklin Street in Chapel Hill on 14 June 1987. Photograph by Jerry Cotten. NCC.

state governments were established under the Congressional Reconstruction acts.

The most Klan-ridden areas of North Carolina were Alamance and Caswell Counties in the northern Piedmont in 1869–70 and Rutherford and Cleveland Counties in the southern foothills a year later. Neighboring counties, such as Sampson, Lenoir, and Jones in the southeast, were also affected. In these places, disguised night riders roamed the countryside, dragging people from their homes; lynching, whipping, shooting, or otherwise assaulting them; driving them away, or destroying their property. Most of the victims were black, but white Republicans were also attacked, especially in Rutherford County.

Around the turn of the twentieth century, the KKK, and the Confederate Lost Cause generally, took on for southerners a retrospective romantic appeal that had been lacking amid the suffering immediately after the war. This attraction was greatly stimulated by North Carolinian Thomas Dixon's novel, *The Clansman* (1905), and D. W. Griffith's film based on the novel, *The Birth of a Nation* (1915). The second incarnation of the KKK was born in that environment in Atlanta, Ga., in 1915, encouraging superpatriotism during World War I. After the war, its membership and geographic range expanded dramatically.

During its heyday in the early 1920s, the second KKK numbered about 3 million members nationwide. It gained political power in Indiana, Oklahoma, Oregon, and other states but was comparatively weak in North Carolina. Unlike the first Klan, it was primarily urban, reflecting demographic changes in the country. Its members, drawn chiefly from the lower middle class, were often religious fundamentalists who felt threatened by the drift away from the small-town Protestant culture they had known growing up. They disdained immigrants, especially communists and other radicals, labor unions, Jews, Catholics, and the increasing number of blacks moving into both northern and southern cities. Some Klansmen resorted to the terrorism of earlier days, but the vast majority were nonviolent.

The modern-day KKK emerged in 1946, two years after the second Klan had disbanded as a result of its legal, financial, and political crises. Although this new KKK was fueled by the fear of communism abroad and at home, practically all of its violent activities were directed at undermining efforts to secure the civil rights of African Americans in the South. In North Carolina, one of its banner states, the modern Klan thrived among mill workers and other blue-collar laborers in the Piedmont. One of its greatest embarrassments occurred in 1958, when a prospective KKK rally near Maxton (Robeson County) was broken up by a group of Lumbee Indians. Nationally, the peak in membership came during the civil rights demonstrations of the 1960s, when it may have reached 55,000 (9,800 members in North Carolina). By 1995 the Klan was at its lowest ebb in many years, nationally and locally.

The modern Klan has been chronically fragmented and prone to internal conflicts over policy and leadership. Groups have differed in their readiness to embrace violence. In 1979 Klansmen attacked a Communist Workers Party "Death to the Klan" march in Greensboro, killing five people. They have sometimes forged alliances with like-minded organizations, as when North Carolina Klansmen (also in 1979) briefly formed a United Racist Front with the state's tiny Nazi Party.

For all of its ability to make headlines, the KKK historically has failed to accomplish its major objectives. It did not end southern Reconstruction in the 1870s; that was more nearly the work of organized rioters and Red Shirt campaigners. It did not significantly deflect the nation's progress toward a pluralistic, democratic society in the 1920s. And its major effect on the civil rights movement was to hasten the triumph of that cause when Klan bloodshed mobilized public support for passage of landmark civil rights legislation in the 1960s.

References: W. Fitzhugh Brundage, ed., *Under Sentence of Death: Lynching in the South* (1997); David Chalmers, *Hooded Americanism: The History of the Ku Klux Klan* (3rd ed., 1987); Otto H. Olsen, "The Ku Klux Klan: A Study in Reconstruction Politics and Propaganda," *NCHR* 39 (July 1962); Allen W. Trelease, *White Terror: The Ku Klux Klan Conspiracy and Southern Reconstruction* (1971); Wyn Craig Wade, *The Fiery Cross: The Ku Klux Klan in America* (2nd ed., 1998).

Allen W. Trelease

SEE ALSO *The Clansman*; "Death to the Klan" March; Lynching; Red Shirts.

L

Labor, North Carolina Department of. The Bureau of Labor Statistics, predecessor of the modern North Carolina Department of Labor, was established by the General Assembly in 1887 as an agency within the Department of Agriculture, Immigration, and Statistics. The bureau was headed by a commissioner appointed by the governor, with state senate approval, to a two-year term. The commissioner of labor statistics collected information on work hours, wages, workforce education, and finance, and on ways to promote the "mental, material, social, and moral prosperity" of the state's labor force. The commissioner was aided by a chief clerk and other assistants appointed as needed. A detailed annual report on the bureau's findings was submitted to the legislature and supplied to newspapers around the state. In later years, the commissioner could institute legal proceedings for safety violations, and all violations, accidents, injuries, and deaths were to be recorded by the commissioner's office.

In 1899 the bureau was re-created as the Bureau of Labor and Printing, separate from the Department of Agriculture. In addition to collecting and publishing data relating to labor, the new bureau oversaw all printing and binding for state government. The two-year term of the commissioner, now publicly elected, was extended to four years, and an assistant commissioner with practical printing experience was employed. In 1919 the governor was added to the State Printing Commission (formed in 1901), and the bureau became the Department of Labor and Printing. Finally, in 1931 the General Assembly reorganized the department and changed its name to the Department of Labor. This legislation laid the broad groundwork for the department's gradual development into an agency that administered laws and programs affecting a majority of North Carolina citizens.

The modern Department of Labor's principal regulatory, enforcement, and promotional programs are implemented by various bureaus, each headed by a bureau chief. They include Apprenticeship and Training, Boiler Safety, Elevator and Amusement Devices, Employment Discrimination, Wage and Hour, and Agricultural Safety and Health. Support services are handled by the Budget and Management, Human Resources, and Communications Divisions, a departmental library, and a legal affairs office.

Five statutory boards assist the labor commissioner in policy and program development. The Occupational Safety and Health Review Board is a separate unit, independent of the Department of Labor, which hears appeals of citations and penalties imposed by the department's Occupational Safety and Health Division.

Wiley J. Williams

Laboratory Corporation of America Holdings (LabCorp), with headquarters in Burlington and facilities in Charlotte and Research Triangle Park, is one of the world's largest clinical laboratory companies. It was incorporated in Delaware in 1973 as DCL Health Laboratories. The present name was adopted in 1995 through the merger of Roche Biochemical Laboratories and national Health Laboratories Holdings, Inc. Other acquisitions followed, including Genetic Design of Greensboro (1996), Coastal Medical of Florida (1998), and Pathology Laboratories of San Diego (2000).

LabCorp provides a full range of clinical, anatomical, and substance-abuse tests to individual physicians, managed-care organizations, hospitals, clinics, and long-term care facilities. Medicare and Medicaid account for about 16 percent of LabCorp's revenues. Through a national network of laboratories, LabCorp offers more than 4,400 different clinical laboratory tests. In 2006 the company had annual revenues of more than $3 billion and employed 24,000 people across 20 states.

Wiley J. Williams

Labor Unions. The first labor organizations in North Carolina were formed by skilled workers in the larger towns. One of the earliest was the Raleigh Typographical Union, organized in 1854. By the mid-1880s printers in Wilmington and Charlotte also were working under trade union agreements with their employers. A second and broader labor movement came to the state in 1884, when the first North Carolina assembly of the Knights of Labor (originally organized by Philadelphia garment workers in 1869) met in Raleigh. Three years later the Knights claimed assemblies in most counties and a membership that included whites, blacks, men, and women from diverse skilled occupations (no employees of furniture, textile, or tobacco factories participated). Although by 1887 the Knights of Labor began to decline in importance, it had acquainted blue-collar workers with the advantages that might be gained through organization.

Early Labor Movements and Conflicts in the Textile Industry

The American Federation of Labor (AFL) began organizing efforts in North Carolina in 1898, specifically targeting the growing textile industry. Women and children as well as men worked in textile mills, often under dangerous and unhealthy conditions. The AFL's goals were compulsory education for children, child labor laws, use of the strike as a bargaining weapon, a national eight-hour workday, and a protective tariff. The AFL made little progress organizing workers due to opposition by manufacturers and negative attitudes among laborers.

In 1887 a state Bureau of Labor Statistics, precursor of the Department of Labor, was created to compile statistics, issue reports, and make recommendations on labor issues. A permanent labor organization, the North Carolina State Federation of Labor, was formed by about 1,000 delegates from local unions statewide in Raleigh's Odd Fellows Hall on 18 Oct. 1905. The Raleigh Central Labor Union (CLU), formed on 7 Aug. 1900 by representatives from locals for the printing trades, machinists, and bookbinders, appears to have been the main force behind this federation. Within its first year, the CLU had organized retail clerks, painters, musicians, and cigar makers in the state. The CLU and other organizations such as the Charlotte Building Trades Council, the Allied Printing Trades Council in Raleigh, and trade union locals of skilled workers were thus in a position to take the lead in the formation of a statewide federation.

From 1905 to World War I, there were no major unionizing activities in the state. The war spurred efforts to organize southern industrial laborers in the tobacco, furniture, and textile industries. In 1919 the United Textile Workers Union (UTW), an affiliate of the AFL, organized thousands of workers in a series of strikes, the largest of which took place at the Highland Park plant in Charlotte. After three months, Governor Thomas W. Bickett intervened to pressure both management and the union to negotiate a settlement that restored wages, reduced hours, and secured a promise that the mill owners would not "discriminate against any person on account of organization affiliation." For the next two years, management and striking workers engaged in a tense confrontation, with mill owners determined not to recognize collective bargaining and workers desperately trying to sustain economic gains made during the war years. The economic woes of 1921 quickly ended the strikes and lockouts. The mills restored wage levels, and workers dropped their demands for bargaining rights.

Significant labor activity returned to North Carolina in 1929, when many textile workers in the Gastonia-Marion area, discontented with lagging wages and unsatisfactory working conditions, responded to the organizing efforts of Fred E. Beal of the radical National Textile Workers Union (NTWU). Several NTWU unions were formed and organized the notorious Gastonia strike at Loray Mill. The violence associated with the strike left two people dead and drew international attention. The ultimate failure of the unionization attempt amounted to a major setback for the labor movement and sparked rampant opposition to organizing efforts across the South.

The General Strike of 1934 and the Battle for Union Leadership

A surge in union membership coincided with the widespread recognition in the summer of 1934 that national recovery had not taken hold and that violations of National Recovery Administration (NRA) standards had become commonplace. The stage for a great confrontation had been set in May, when the NRA's textile board announced a reduction in hours of operation that resulted in the closing of many mills for one week each month. In mid-August at a national UTW convention, southern representatives called for a general strike. On 1 September organized car caravans known as "flying squadrons" moved through the Carolinas, shutting down mills with remarkable speed. Within a week, about 400,000 textile workers nationwide had left the mills, and the industry had virtually closed down in every state, including North Carolina.

The General Strike of 1934, the largest in American history, ended abruptly in failure. The UTW had rested its hopes for winning concessions from manufacturers on the intervention of the federal government. But the Roosevelt administration went only so far as endorsing the findings of a mediation panel that called for further study and general recognition of legitimate grievances by workers. The union, fearing the loss of federal support if it did not comply with the recommendations of the mediation panel, ended the strike after only 22 days.

Never again would textile workers in any region or state demonstrate such broad solidarity as they did in September 1934. Nor did the UTW regain the strength it had enjoyed during that period; it gradually lost membership and influence to the Textile Workers Union of America (TWUA), an affiliate of the Congress of Industrial Organizations (CIO) founded in Philadelphia in May 1939. During its formative years, the TWUA met resistance from both manufacturers and rival unions. In North Carolina several mills voted to accept the union, including 10 Fieldcrest mills in Rockingham County (in 1939 and 1941) and the Harriet and Henderson mills in Henderson County (1943). By the end of World War II, membership in the TWUA stood at 450,000.

Civil Rights Unionism, "Operation Dixie," and the Birth of the ACTWU

In the 1940s a poignant chapter in North Carolina labor union and civil rights history was written in Winston-Salem, where 10,000 tobacco manufacturing workers, the majority of them African American, used their union to challenge the severe racial discrimination, economic injustice, and political oppression that they experienced as employees of the massive R. J. Reynolds Tobacco Company and as citizens of the city. Operating through Local 22 of the Food, Tobacco, Agricultural, and Allied Workers–Congress of Industrial Organizations (FTA-CIO), these workers, many of them women, fought not only for fair labor conditions but also for civil rights legislation and increased control of their social and political lives, registering thousands of African American voters and in the process revitalizing the local moribund chapter of the National

Association for the Advancement of Colored People. Although many of their efforts ultimately failed, the blending of unionist and civil rights objectives attracted national and international attention and raised awareness of the acute racial inequities and flawed democratic system so prevalent in the mid-twentieth-century South.

In May 1946 the CIO launched a drive in the South known as "Operation Dixie." Its purpose was to preserve the gains made by organized labor in the previous decade and, more important, to protect its members from the textile industry's tendency to leave organized regions such as New England and the Midwest for locations in the traditionally nonunionized South. The organizing strategy of Operation Dixie called for a major campaign by the TWUA, since the textile industry was the region's largest industrial employer, with a special effort in North Carolina as the leading textile-manufacturing state.

From its headquarters in Atlanta, the TWUA dispatched teams of organizers to the Carolinas, Georgia, Alabama, and Virginia. It became immediately clear, however, that southerners were not prepared to accept the CIO concept of "one big union" of industrial workers. The effort to unionize southern textile plants failed for several reasons. A postwar mood of conservatism marked by fears of worldwide communism dampened the enthusiasm for collective action. Opposition from the AFL and factionalism within the CIO itself further undermined Operation Dixie. Finally, the unique political and social culture of management and labor relations in the South proved a powerful obstacle to traditional appeals by organizers for class solidarity.

Operation Dixie officially ended in 1953. Defeat in the bellwether textile industry proved a devastating, though not fatal, blow to the CIO and TWUA. In November 1958 the TWUA called a strike against North Carolina's Harriet and Henderson mills when the company refused to sign a new contract. The strike became violent with rock throwing, vandalism, shootings, and bombings after the company tried to hire new workers to replace the strikers. Governor Luther H. Hodges attempted to intervene without success and called up the state police and National Guard to protect the mills and their new employees. The mills resumed operations, and by May 1959 the workforce was at full complement.

The defeat of the Harriet-Henderson strike did not lessen the determination of union leaders to gain recognition by the textile industry and to negotiate for rank-and-file workers. In the 1960s and 1970s the TWUA conducted a major campaign to organize workers at the J. P. Stevens Company plants in Roanoke Rapids. After a decade of organizing and litigating, the TWUA scored a victory in 1974 by carrying 54 percent of more than 3,000 votes cast by workers in Roanoke Rapids. The vote reflected the impact of black workers, who by that time represented 30 to 40 percent of the workforce. In June 1976 the TWUA merged with the Amalgamated Clothing Workers

Union to form the Amalgamated Clothing and Textile Workers Union (ACTWU), thus creating a major new labor organization with half a million members. The ACTWU's efforts against J. P. Stevens gained international attention with the 1979 release of the film *Norma Rae*, starring Sally Field, which was based in part on the true-life experiences of Crystal Lee Sutton, a Roanoke Rapids textile worker who was fired by J. P. Stevens for her organizing activities.

North Carolina Organized Labor: The Modern Era

Although the ACTWU eventually won a contract and preserved its right to bargain for the Roanoke Rapids workers, this hard-fought victory did not translate into greater influence at other plants in North Carolina. In 1985 workers at the Cannon mills overwhelmingly refused to support union representation, and two subsequent elections in 1991 and 1997 were thrown out by the National Labor Relations Board. In 1999, however, the Union of Needletrades, Industrial, and Textile Employees, a successor to the ACTWU, won a narrow election held at the Fieldcrest Cannon mills in Kannapolis. Labor experts cited the uncertainty caused by shifts in ownership, the increased demands of modern production, and the growing number of immigrants in the workforce who tended to support unions as reasons for the stunning union victory. Nevertheless, some experts have deemed the Kannapolis election the most important labor victory in the South's history.

While organized labor made some headway in the second half of the twentieth century, a major setback was the failure of the national unions and the State Federation of Labor to prevent North Carolina from becoming a right-to-work state in 1947. Since the 1970s, a decline in employment and union membership in manufacturing industries has been partially offset by union growth among public employees (including police and fire personnel) and service employees. By the early twenty-first century, organizing activities increasingly focused on the state's agricultural and food-processing workers. A 1995 strike and union election by largely Guatemalan poultry processors at Morganton's Case Farms was one such effort that garnered regional and national attention. While workers voted to affiliate with the Laborers International Union of North America, Case Farms management refused to negotiate with the union, sparking labor strife that lasted through the end of the 1990s.

In the early 2000s, North Carolina remained among the least-unionized states in the nation. Total union membership at times has been estimated to be no more than 8 percent of the state's nonagricultural workforce, although the U.S. Department of Labor reported North Carolina union membership at only about 3.2 percent in the early twenty-first century.

References: Daniel J. Clark, *Like Night and Day: Unionization in a Southern Mill Town* (1997); Leon Fink, *The Maya of Morganton: Work and Community in the Nuevo New South* (2003); David Firestone,

"Victory for Union at Plant in South Is Labor Milestone," *New York Times*, 25 June 1999; Brent D. Glass, *The Textile Industry in North Carolina: A History* (1992); Jacquelyn Dowd Hall and others, *Like a Family: The Making of a Southern Cotton Mill World* (1987); Harley E. Jolley, "The Labor Movement in North Carolina, 1880–1922," *NCHR* 30 (July 1953); Robert R. Korstad, *Civil Rights Unionism: Tobacco Workers and the Struggle for Democracy in the Mid-Twentieth-Century South* (2003); Robert H. Zieger, ed., *Organized Labor in the Twentieth-Century South* (1991).

Brent D. Glass
Wiley J. Williams

SEE ALSO Child Labor; Flying Squadrons; Gastonia Strike; Harriet-Henderson Cotton Mills Strike; Right-to-Work Law.

Lafayette's Visit. As an official guest of the United States in 1824 and 1825, the Marquis de Lafayette, at age 68, planned to remain in the northern and middle Atlantic states, avoiding extensive travel. But after being repeatedly pressed by southern legislatures and governors, including those of North Carolina, the French general yielded in early 1825 and agreed to make a 5,000-mile tour of the South.

As the foremost living symbol of America's success in the Revolution, Lafayette could expect to be feted extravagantly at every stop. It would nevertheless be a harrowing journey since most of the time he would travel by carriage over poor roads. In particular, the road from Richmond, Va., to Raleigh was "so broken" that he was obliged, as he wrote to Thomas Jefferson, "to take the sandy Lower Road by Suffolk and Halifax." Raleigh had received such late notice of the general's trip that no official welcoming party reached him until he was at Northampton Courthouse (modern Jackson). After appropriate salutations, the party, including seven carriages of delegates from Raleigh under Attorney General Beverly Daniel and Chief Justice John Louis Taylor, proceeded to Halifax. Lafayette spent the evening at the Eagle Hotel and, before leaving town the next morning, visited about an hour at the home of Mrs. Willie Jones (widow of the former governor), who was attended by her daughter, the wife of Governor Hutchings Burton.

The route from Halifax continued through the village of Enfield, across Falls of Tar River near Tarboro, and to Col. Allen Rogers's Tavern at Rogers Crossroads in eastern Wake County. Here the party spent the night of 28 Feb. 1825 before moving on to Raleigh. Lafayette was met at Crabtree Bridge and conducted by military escort to the Governor's Mansion. Highlights of the overnight sojourn included a viewing of Canova's statue of George Washington at the capitol, which the general pronounced a good likeness, and a ball with 150 ladies present. Leaving Raleigh on the morning of 1 March, Lafayette and his entourage reached his namesake town Fayetteville that afternoon. He was feted at a ball at the Lafayette Hotel in the evening and was an overnight guest of merchant and postmaster Duncan MacRae. After an afternoon banquet the next day, he left for South Carolina.

No event in the state's history had received such newspaper coverage or universal outpouring of public adoration as Lafayette's visit. Huge crowds greeted him everywhere, packed his reception rooms, and trooped along with him wherever he rode or walked. Reams of poetry were written, songs composed, commemorative knickknacks sold, and Revolutionary War episodes recounted. Military units came from coastal points and from as far west as Charlotte to form part of the general's escort at Raleigh and elsewhere. There appeared to be a palpable awareness that this would be the last direct link Americans could hope to experience with the leadership of the struggle for independence.

References: Auguste Levasseur, *Lafayette in America, in 1824 and 1825; or, Journal of Travels in the United States* (1829); Thomas C. Parramore, "Lafayette, You Were Here," in F. Roy Johnson and Parramore, *The Daily Roanoke–Chowan News' Roanoke-Chowan Story* (1962–).

Thomas C. Parramore

Lake Lure Rest and Redistribution Center was established in the town of Lake Lure (Rutherford County) by the Army Air Force (AAF) in July 1943 to provide 10 to 20 days of rest and relaxation for combat aviators and their wives. It was the first center of its kind in the nation. The AAF found that rest centers helped to deter combat fatigue and prepare aviators for future assignments. During their stay, the pilots were examined by surgeons and psychiatrists to determine their fitness for further combat.

The center occupied the former Lake Lure Inn, Rocky Broad Inn, and adjacent tracts, with additional barracks completed just before VJ Day. The Rutherford County Chapter of the American Red Cross and the Rutherford County Library provided equipment, services, and books for the approximately 5,000 returnees processed during the center's two-year life. The last returnees left the camp on 15 Oct. 1945; permanent personnel vacated on 26 October. The center was officially closed on 1 Nov. 1945, and the buildings were returned to the original owners.

References: Clarence W. Griffin, *The History of Rutherford County, 1937–1951* (1952); J. J. Lichman, "AAF Shangri-La: Lake Lure Rest Center, North Carolina," *Flying* 35 (July 1944); Sidney Shalett, "'Repair Stations' for the Battle-Weary," *New York Times Magazine* (23 Jan. 1944).

John L. Bell

Lakes can be found in virtually every part of North Carolina, although all of the state's natural freshwater lakes of consequence are located in the eastern region of the state. Most North Carolina lakes are relatively shallow bodies of water. Several of the lakes in the southeastern part of the state are examples of the unusual geographic features known as Carolina Bays. Used primarily for sports and recreation, the five largest natural freshwater lakes in North Carolina are Lake Mattamuskeet (30,000 acres), Scuppernong Lake (16,600 acres), Lake Waccamaw (8,938 acres), Alligator Lake (6,000 acres), and Pungo Lake (2,700 acres).

Lake Mattamuskeet in central Hyde County, the largest of North Carolina's natural lakes, is shallow, with a maximum depth of five feet, and sits at an elevation of three feet below sea level. Efforts to drain Mattamuskeet for farming date as far back as 1789, and the Southern Land Reclamation Company built an enormous pumping station, with a 125-foot smokestack, at the lake's western end between 1909 and 1916. Southern Land failed, though, selling out to North Carolina Farms in 1918; that firm in turn sold out to New Holland Corporation in 1923. Four enormous steam engines of nearly 1,000 horsepower apiece, in league with attendant drainage canals, finally succeeded, and 12,000 acres of Lake Mattamuskeet's bottom was under cultivation—with rice, wheat, rye, and the biggest soybean crop in the world—when Franklin D. Roosevelt was elected president in 1932. But rainfall, pestilence, and mud caused the New Holland farmers to decide that keeping the water out of the lake bed was too difficult to continue.

Lake Mattamuskeet took little time to refill its shallow declivity and has long been one of North Carolina's favorite hunting and fishing grounds. In 1934 its swampy land became a wildlife refuge (with controlled hunts). Waterfowl populations vary from year to year, with the annual December count of geese, swans, and ducks reaching the tens of thousands.

West of the fall line, most large bodies of water in North Carolina are man-made, created when several of the state's rivers were dammed for either drinking water, flood control, or hydroelectric power. The five largest artificial lakes lying entirely within the borders of North Carolina—all popular tourist destinations—are Lake Norman, High Rock Lake, B. Everett Jordan Lake, Falls Lake, and Fontana Lake. Located northwest of Charlotte and created in the 1960s, Lake Norman is the state's largest man-made lake, covering 32,510 acres. High Rock Lake, nine miles from Lexington, stretches across 18,000 acres and has often been the site of one of the world's most prestigious fishing competitions, the BASS Master's Classic. With 13,942 acres, B. Everett Jordan Lake, originally New Hope Lake but renamed in 1973 in honor of the former North Carolina senator, stands mostly in Chatham County. Jordan Lake has several beaches and is popular among waterskiing enthusiasts. Falls Lake, spreading over 11,310 acres, was created from the 1981 damming of the Neuse River to minimize flooding problems in the area just north of Raleigh. Fontana Lake, created in the 1940s and located along the southern border of Great Smoky Mountains National Park, spans 10,530 acres and boasts the highest dam east of the Rocky Mountains.

References: Jim Dean, "Mattamuskeet Memories," in Dean and Lawrence S. Earley, eds., *Wildlife in North Carolina* (1987); Phillip Manning, *Afoot in the South: Walks in the Natural Areas of North Carolina* (1993); Bland Simpson, *Into the Sound Country: A Carolinian's Coastal Plain* (1997).

Bland Simpson
John Hairr

Lance, Inc., a major producer of packaged crackers, potato chips, cookies, nuts, and other snacks, started in 1913 when Philip L. Lance, a Charlotte coffee salesman, purchased 500 pounds of Virginia peanuts for a customer who subsequently decided he could not use them. Reluctant to return the peanuts to the farmer, Lance took them home, roasted them, and sold them for a nickel a bag.

Lance and one of his associates in the food brokerage business, his son-in-law Salem Van Every, founded the Lance Packing Co. The peanut-roasting business outgrew the Lance home and moved to College Street in Charlotte. A mechanical roaster was installed, leading to the manufacture of peanut butter. To demonstrate the quality of his new product, Lance, with the help of his wife and daughter, spread it on crackers, creating the first commercially sold peanut butter cracker. These became very popular with soldiers at Charlotte's Camp Greene during World War I.

Sales of Lance's peanut butter products increased, along with the growth of its mail-order business. The company moved its facilities to Ninth Street and then to South Boulevard in 1926, the same year in which Philip Lance was killed in an automobile accident. A corporation was formed subsequent to Lance's death.

Lance Packing began making its own crackers in 1938, and the firm name was changed to Lance, Inc., the next year. When Van Every died in 1943, his son Philip took over as president and reorganized sales and distribution on a district basis with sales managers in key areas. Lance became a publicly traded company in 1961. In 1962 the company moved its facilities farther out South Boulevard to a 275-acre tract.

In 1988 Lance began producing a number of products low in saturated fats and cholesterol, and in 2004 the company removed all trans fats from its cracker and cookie selections. Lance vending machines can be found at more than 60,000 locations in 40 states from the Atlantic Coast to the Rocky Mountains. The company maintains manufacturing facilities in Charlotte as well as Burlington, Iowa; Hyannis, Mass.; and Ontario, Canada. It has approximately 4,200 employees and $600 million in yearly sales. Marketing efforts have included new packaging, the introduction of new cookies and other products, and an amusing radio advertising campaign featuring the phrase, "I've got Lance in my pants!"

References: Doug Mayes and Nancy Stanfield, *Charlotte: Nothing Could Be Finer* (1996); Philip Lance Van Every, *The History of Lance* (1974).

Alex Coffin

Land Grant Colleges were the brainchild of Jonathan Baldwin Turner, a Yale-educated newspaper editor from Illinois who, in 1850, espoused a "Plan for a State University for the Industrial Classes." The idea did not take hold until Justin Smith Morrill, a member of the U.S. House of Representatives from Vermont, introduced the plan to Congress in 1857 with the intention of building universities of this type for the working men in his and other states. The schools' purpose was to provide a "liberal and practical education" with particular emphasis upon the then-growing need for agricultural and technical studies, subjects generally ignored or underemphasized in the curriculum of existing colleges and universities. The bill was not approved, but it passed four years later when reintroduced with emphasis upon military tactics—necessary in the ongoing Civil War. The measure, known as the Morrill Act, allocated up to 30,000 acres for each state that was willing to teach agriculture, military science, and mechanical arts, "without excluding other scientific and classical studies." Further endowment was provided in a second Morrill Act (1890), part of which went to provide African American land grant colleges.

North Carolina was quick to avail itself of land from the Morrill Act but slow to establish a college of agriculture and technology. In the early 1870s the state received and sold 127,000 acres of public land and contributed the sum to the University of North Carolina, with the intent of making the university fit the Turner/Morrill model. The effort failed; public outcry, particularly from the Farmers' Alliance and state businessmen, forced the creation of two new schools—the first, the North Carolina College of Agriculture and Mechanic Arts in Raleigh, in 1887, and the second, the North Carolina Agricultural and Mechanical College for the Colored Race in Raleigh (and soon thereafter, Greensboro), in 1891.

Neither school was an immediate success. In part, this was due to the educational monopoly exercised in the state by the University of North Carolina, but a lack of available funds also held the new schools back. Simply put, North Carolina remained a poor state until after World War II, and education on any level was not a prime concern. Citizens saw the agricultural and technical colleges as adjuncts to the state and federal departments of agriculture. As such, the schools were expected to teach agricultural techniques, crop production, and the eradication of plant and animal diseases. Few people envisioned these colleges as degree-granting institutions.

The State College of Agriculture and Mechanic Arts grew steadily from its first graduating class of 19 in 1893. In 1963 the reputation of State College was such that it was awarded university status, and its name was changed to North Carolina State University two years later. The Agricultural and Mechanical College began operating in Raleigh in 1891 in cooperation with Shaw University but moved to Greensboro in 1893, when its campus was completed. In 1915 the college was renamed North Carolina Agricultural and Technical College, and ten years later it became a four-year school. Regional accreditation was not achieved until 1936, with graduate approval coming in 1939. Then, as now, the strength of the school lay primarily in its farm and community outreach programs, as well as in its educational and nursing curriculums. In 1971 it was elevated to the status of a state university.

References: Henry S. Brunner, *Land-Grant Colleges and Universities, 1862–1962* (1962); Ralph D. Christy, *A Century of Service: Land Grant Colleges and Universities, 1890–1990* (1992); Ian Carl Madfie, *Southern Land Grant Universities* (1991); National Association of State Universities and Land Grant Colleges, *The Land Grant Tradition* (1995).

Louis P. Towles

SEE ALSO North Carolina Agricultural and Technical State University; North Carolina State University.

Land Grants, or gifts of land to individuals in perpetuity, were instrumental in the growth and development of North Carolina beginning in 1663 with the granting of the first Carolina charter by King Charles II. That charter endowed a great theoretical swath of land from the neighborhood of St. Augustine, Florida, to what became the Virginia line, and westward from the Atlantic Ocean—disregarding French and Spanish claims and the homelands of indigenous nations—all the way to the South Seas (Pacific Ocean). The grantees, the eight Lords Proprietors who had helped restore the Stuarts to the throne of England, shared equal control over the land but were generally ineffectual speculators.

Important Land Speculators of the Seventeenth and Eighteenth Centuries

Among the first land speculators to receive grants were Richard Averitt, Maj. George Pollock, William Little, John Lovick, and Edward Moseley. Averitt was in fact Sir Richard Everard, the last Proprietary governor, and Major Pollock was of the powerful Pollock family of the Albemarle. Little, Lovick, and Moseley were, with Christopher Gale, the North Carolina commissioners of the line dividing the colony from Virginia. They are familiar figures in William Byrd's two histories of that endeavor, and in the ribald version called *Secret History of the Line* they appear as Puzzlecause, Shoebrush, Plausible, and Judge Jumble, respectively.

In 1729 the English Crown repurchased Carolina from the heirs of seven of the eight Lords Proprietors. John Carteret—the future Earl Granville—demurred, and his one-eighth share was declared and situated in a strip parallel to the Virginia line from which English mathematician Samuel Warner calculated latitudes for a depth of 60 miles. But the grant became mired in paperwork, and 15 years would pass before the Granville District was established with a granting office, surveyors, and collectors of quitrents. The *Unitas Fratrum*, the Moravian colony led by Bishop Augustus Gottlieb Spangenberg, bought the largest tract from Granville's agents, the 98,985 acres called Wachovia. Vestiges of the old Granville line may be discerned in the lateral borders of several counties in the middle of the state.

When North Carolina became a royal colony, George Burrington was named governor a second time. During his brief term as royal governor he managed to secure for himself much of the Hawfields—an area of red clay old fields of incomparable fertility, mostly in present Alamance County—which he still retained on returning to England after the installation of his replacement, Gabriel Johnston. Johnston also was aware of the value of the Hawfields, or soon was made so by William Byrd. Johnston arrived at his post in 1734 much indebted to a cartel of London investors, including his agent, the wily merchant Henry McCulloh, and even more to his mentor and principal employer, Spencer Compton, Lord Wilmington.

Next to Granville, McCulloh was North Carolina's greatest land speculator, controlling at one time well over 1 million acres in the Piedmont. His investments seem to have begun with a pair of grants on the northeast and northwest branches of the Cape Fear River. Of the latter, 60,000 acres adjacent to the Hawfields, it has been found that he was holding it in trust and that Lord Wilmington had earmarked it for Gabriel Johnston so that he might profit from the settling of it and thus repay some of his London creditors.

No correspondence exists between Johnston and McCulloh from this time, but evidence points to a vicious falling-out between these former allies. Their feud was apparently lifelong, and each party suppressed the other's grants of land, with Johnston getting his 60,000 acres on the Upper Eno only after he finally applied his signature and seal to the 1.2 million-acre McCulloh grant. By the time of that accommodation, in 1745, the Granville District was in place, seriously compromising between one-third and one-half of McCulloh's claim and all of Johnston's.

From Lord Granville, Johnston finally received in 1751 a tract of 8,929 acres on the Upper Eno, the center cut of his abortive 60,000-acre grant, and he had the surveyor William Churton subdivide it immediately. Whereas he had imagined his clientele to be French and Italian Protestants (Huguenots and Waldensians), his eventual customers were mostly Irish Quakers from Pennsylvania. Johnston had scarcely begun to sell the lots when he died, in July 1752, and John Rutherfurd (who married Frances, Johnston's widow) enjoyed most of the profits of the sales.

From the beginning, McCulloh had parlayed portions of his vast holdings to a second echelon of speculators, among them future governor Arthur Dobbs, George Selwyn, John Frohock, and John Campbell. Lord Granville died in 1763, and no more grants were issued from the Granville office. Ultimately, the unsold Granville and McCulloh holdings were confiscated by the new state of North Carolina and regranted. But for many years afterward, indeed long after the Revolution, the English heirs sought compensation for their losses in American courts.

Land Grants and the Recruitment of Settlers to the Carolina Colony

Land grants were also given to individuals on a much more modest scale. A recipient, in exchange for a land grant, was obliged to pay each year an established rent (called a quitrent), either nominal, such as peppercorn or Indian arrows, or real in the form of sterling (coin) or produce. Beginning in 1667, every free person who came to the province was eligible to receive 40 acres under the system. Each servant entitled the owner to 20 additional acres, and rents were to be remitted for a period of three to five years to allow the settlers to establish themselves.

Since the recruitment of people was often difficult, grants were gradually increased to 100 acres for a freeman with a gun and powder who could come on his own and 50 acres for a person who had to be transported. Although it was possible to receive sizable grants—such as 6,000 acres to Sir John Yeamans in 1665 to assist him in subsidizing a settlement and 1,500 acres to Captain William Merrick that same year to help him undertake a voyage—such gifts were unusual and could only be assigned directly by the Proprietors in London. As rule, less than 700 acres was the maximum amount of land allowed to be granted or regranted in the province.

Grants were awarded by a process in which a recipient first received a warrant, then a survey of land, or plat, and finally the grant itself. Each part of the process was to be checked by the appropriate provincial official before the grant was finally approved, and if the procedure was not followed completely, the property would revert to the granter, with the grantee often subject to a fine. In addition, if a person failed to properly "seat" his grant—that is, clear and work the requisite number of acres within three years—died without heirs, or failed to pay quitrents, the land could be lost and regranted to someone else.

By 1715, through the intervention of the Proprietors and the North Carolina Assembly, grantees had received certain important rights. By decree from London, an impoverished family that could not pay its rent was not to be deprived of the land, and those that had been were to have property restored. In addition, by action of the Assembly and the agreement of the governor in council, all existing grants were declared valid, and all claims based on seven years' occupancy of the land were considered legal.

The price of the perpetual lease in the land grant system began under the Proprietors as a farthing per acre in 1663 and gradually rose to a penny per acre by 1669. In the early 1700s these payments varied widely. Settlers came to resent the arbitrary and permanent nature of the quitrents, particularly since the Proprietors often refused to accept payment in produce or proclamation money as they had promised to, demanding payment in sterling instead.

The purchase of North Carolina by the English Crown in 1729 failed to noticeably improve either the process of granting land or the collection of quitrents. Payment rates were stabilized under the Crown, but they also became more expensive. Land was still surveyed but not recorded, or it was claimed through blank grants circulated among the elite. While the continued lack of accurate rent rolls made taxation difficult, the reluctance of the Crown to accept produce or proclamation money in lieu of sterling made payment at times impossible. As a result, on the eve of the American Revolution, many quitrents were thousands of pounds in arrears.

References: Margaret M. Hofmann, "Land Grants," in Helen F. M. Leary, ed., *North Carolina Research: Geneology and Local History* (1996); A. B. Pruitt, *Colonial Land Entries in North Carolina* (1994); W. N. Watt, *The Granville District* (1992).

David Southern
Louis P. Towles

SEE ALSO Granville Grant and District; Sugar Creek, War of.

Land of Eden

Land of Eden was the name William Byrd II gave to his 20,000-acre grant in the Dan River Valley in North Carolina. Byrd acquired the land as a result of surveying the North Carolina–Virginia boundary line in 1728. He made a second expedition to the region in 1733 to survey his vast tract, describing this trip to the Carolina backcountry in *A Journey to the Land of Eden*. As surveyed, the tract lay in present-day Caswell and Rockingham Counties, the bulk located in the northeast corner of the latter. In 1742 Byrd purchased 6,000 additional acres adjoining the southwest side of the grant. Although he hoped to attract settlers to his Carolina lands and continually sought to promote them, his efforts never succeeded. Byrd's son William Byrd III inherited the estate, but to satisfy debts he sold it in 1755 to Francis and Simon Farley, merchants from Antigua. Francis's son, James Parke Farley, came to the Dan River in 1769 to manage the plantation. Two years later he married Elizabeth, the daughter of William Byrd III. The Farleys returned to Virginia on the eve of the American Revolution. After Farley's death, the estate was in litigation, and the plantation was divided into seventeen tracts and sold in 1803. The name is perpetuated by the city of Eden, which is located in Rockingham County on the western border of the original grant.

References: Lindley S. Butler, *Rockingham County: A Brief History* (1982); Louis B. Wright, ed., *The Prose Works of William Byrd of Westover* (1966).

Lindley S. Butler

Land of the Sky

Land of the Sky is a slogan applied to the Mountain region of western North Carolina. It was adopted from the title of a novel, *"The Land of the Sky"; or, Adventures in Mountain By-Ways* (1876), written by Frances Christine Fisher Tiernan (1846–1920), a native of Salisbury, under the pen name Christian Reid. The story describes the activities of summer travelers who enjoy the scenery of North Carolina's mountainous west while engaging in mild flirtations.

Wiley J. Williams

The Land We Love

The Land We Love was a magazine published monthly in Charlotte from May 1866 to March 1869. Founded and edited by ex-Confederate general Daniel H. Hill, it reflected his interests, tastes, and beliefs as a military man, a southerner, and an academician. The magazine had a distinct emphasis on the South. Included in its issues were essays on history, agriculture, literature, politics, and military topics. It also presented book reviews of literary and other publications on a regular basis and included new poetry and fiction (despite the fact that Hill did not like fiction). The magazine's creation by Hill and two partners (James P. Irwin and J. G. Morrison) was the first literary event of any magnitude in Charlotte, and the publication served as a literary catalyst there and across the South. In 1867 it claimed 12,000 subscribers in 32 states, including many northern readers. The variety of its interests are suggested by its ads for farm machinery and for Tiffany's (in both New York City and Paris). In March 1869 *The Land We Love* was absorbed by the *New Eclectic* of Baltimore. Some of its former printers went into business together, buying an old press and discarded typefaces to start their own newspaper and print shop. Their venture was the first incarnation of the *Charlotte Observer*.

Although its other subjects were important to many readers, *The Land We Love*'s greatest significance was literary. Its contents and editorial positions highlighted the southern point of view and heritage, and its authors were primarily from the South. Nevertheless, the magazine did not totally ignore northern writers and past and contemporary English authors such as John Milton, William Cowper, Lord Tennyson, and Charles Dickens. Especially interesting are three long and informative essays about Dickens's 1867–68 American reading tour, written by southerner Thomas Cooper De Leon, who was then living in New York City.

The magazine especially encouraged southern writers. It reprinted poems by Edgar Allan Poe, Washington Allston, and Charlotte's Philo Henderson and published new poems by

Paul Hamilton Hayne, Henry Timrod, and Charlotte's Fanny M. Downing. In addition to at least 22 poems by Downing, the magazine published her novel *Perfect through Suffering*, which was serialized over 15 months in 1867–68. She also provided the magazine some editorial and reviewing assistance. Her first published poem (July 1866) reflected Hill's theme of southern vindication. The poem, titled "The Land We Love" and dedicated to Hill, began:

> The land we love—a queen of lands,
> No prouder one the world has known,
> Though now uncrowned, upon her throne
> She sits with fetters on her hands.

References: Ray M. Atchison, "*The Land We Love*: A Southern Post-Bellum Magazine of Agriculture, Literature, and Military History," NCHR 37 (1960); Julian Mason, "Charles Dickens in *The Land We Love*," *Dickens Studies Annual* 16 (1987).

Julian Mason

Last Signal Message (Civil War).

The last signal message of the Civil War in North Carolina was sent by Lt. George C. Round of the U.S. Signal Corps from atop the State Capitol in Raleigh. Round was among the first Federal occupation troops to arrive in Raleigh on 13 Apr. 1865. As a Union signal officer, he established his station on the top of the capitol. Having received word of Gen. Joseph E. Johnston's surrender to Maj. Gen. William T. Sherman at the Bennett House near Durham on 26 April, Round obtained permission to proclaim the news using signal rockets. He spelled out the word "peace" and lit a rocket indicating the end of the word. When it failed to fire, Round went back to relight it. As he leaned over the rocket, it exploded in his face, singeing off his eyebrows and eyelashes. But after an extended pause, Round resumed his message, which read: "Peace on earth, goodwill to men."

Reference: George C. Round, "The Last Signal," *The State* (June, July 1980).

Jo Ann Williford

Latimer v. Poteat.

The case of *Lessees of Margaret Latimer & Others v. William Poteat* was heard by Supreme Court chief justice John Marshall and district judge Henry Potter at the May 1833 term of the U.S. Circuit Court for the District of North Carolina. An ejectment action by Pennsylvanian Latimer and her North Carolina lessees for removal of William Poteat from 49,920 acres in western North Carolina raised two issues. One questioned the validity of a 1783 law enacted by the then–sovereign state reserving specified lands "to the Cherokee Indians and their nation forever." The other questioned whether the involved land granted by the state to William Cathcart in 1796, and subsequently transferred to Latimer, fell within the boundaries of that reserved to the Cherokees as determined

by a series of treaties, made supreme by the U.S. Constitution (Article VI) to state laws, and related surveys.

Acting against a backdrop of massive forced migration authorized by the Indian Removal Act signed by President Andrew Jackson in 1830, Marshall refused to charge the jury that North Carolina had repealed by implication the 1783 law. An exhaustive analysis of the treaties of Hopewell (1785), Holston (1791), and Tellico (1798) led him to endorse the boundary lines thus fixed. His doubts about the accuracy of the Hawkins-Pickens survey line embodied in the Tellico Treaty failed to dissuade the jury from giving judgment in favor of the possessor-defendant Poteat, who asserted title under the Cherokee claim. The Supreme Court hesitatingly affirmed the circuit court's decision five years after Marshall's death.

Reference: John P. Roche and Stanley B. Bernstein, eds., *John Marshall: Major Opinions and Other Writings* (1967).

Peter Graham Fish

Latinos, also referred to as Hispanics, lived in North Carolina in relatively small numbers until the 1980s, when many people of Mexican and Central American descent began coming to the state in search of seasonal farm work. By the end of the twentieth century, Latinos had become the fastest-growing minority group in the state, their numbers increasing by 35 percent annually. Overall, the number of North Carolina Latinos rose from 76,726 in 1990 to an estimated 600,000 by the early 2000s, with ever-increasing political, cultural, and economic influence attending that growth.

During this surge of immigration, some Latinos came to North Carolina directly from Mexico and Central American countries, but most arrived from California, Texas, Florida, or New York. In 1990, 69 percent of the state's Latinos were born in the United States, Puerto Rico, or other U.S. territories. Latino immigrants tend to be younger than the rest of the population, with 37 percent under the age of 18, compared with 25 percent for other North Carolinians. Forty percent of Latinos in the state are between the ages of 18 and 35, as compared with 27 percent of the rest of the population. A younger population usually means more children, which held true for the state's Latinos: in 1997, for example, when Latinos accounted for 2 percent of North Carolina's population, they produced 5.7 percent of all births in the state. In 1990, 43 percent of the state's Latinos had less than a high school education, but that trend was changing by the end of the decade. By the 1997–98 school year, for example, the North Carolina Department of Public Instruction reported that 33,000 Hispanic children were enrolled, a 250 percent increase from the previous year.

In the 1990s, North Carolina Latinos began to branch out into fields of work other than farming. Many found jobs and settled along the state's urbanized I-85 corridor, placing Wake, Mecklenburg, Forsyth, Guilford, and Durham Counties among

Venezuelan dancers perform at the 2005 Fiesta del Pueblo, an annual festival celebrating Latino culture in North Carolina. Photograph courtesy of El Pueblo, Inc.

the 30 U.S. counties with the highest rates of Latino population growth. Other Latinos settled in and around military bases such as Fort Bragg and Camp Lejeune or in smaller farming communities in the eastern part of the state. Latino workers were concentrated in agricultural, military, and service industries, including food and hotel service, construction, landscaping, and livestock slaughterhouses during the 1990s. By the early 2000s, a growing Latino middle class developed, with a more widely diversified place in the state's workforce and economy.

Groups such as Student Action with Farmworkers, based in Durham, have been important allies for Latinos as they grapple with problems of health and safety, educational barriers, immigration policies, and discrimination in the workplace. Some employers are trying to meet the needs of their Latino workers, such as Carolina Turkeys of Mount Olive, which has created affordable housing for its workers near the plant. But Latino workers have also found themselves at the center of labor struggles, most notably perhaps a group of Guatemalan poultry workers at Morganton's Case Farms, who went on strike in 1995, seeking improved work conditions.

As the number of Latinos in North Carolina rose, their political impact grew as well. In the year 2000, there were 52,300 North Carolina Latinos who were U.S. citizens of voting age. The state's political parties have become more interested in Latinos, as evidenced by the formation of groups such as Hispanic Democrats of North Carolina. Congressman Bob Etheridge was among the first elected representatives to create a Latino advisory committee to learn more about the needs of his Latino constituents. In May 2002 the state Board of Elections approved permitting counties to print voter registration forms in Spanish.

Several Spanish-language radio stations began operations in North Carolina in the 1990s, and by the early 2000s nine Hispanic newspapers and magazines were being published in the state. In addition, Latino-run grocery stores, video stores, nightclubs, and other businesses continue to multiply. Regional Mexican and Central American restaurants and foodways are also increasingly evident in the state, as they are elsewhere in the Southeast and the nation. Government and nonprofit organizations are increasingly producing bilingual materials to serve the state's Spanish-speaking population. And numerous Latino associations and provider groups have emerged across the state. El Pueblo, Inc., a Raleigh-based nonprofit, has been an early leader in this area, offering statewide advocacy and promoting Latino cultural traditions through such events as La Fiesta del Pueblo, an annual festival held at the North Carolina State Fairgrounds and boasting some 60,000 attendees each year. Other service groups include the Hispanic/Latino Resource Center in Durham, the Latin American Association of North Carolina in Raleigh, and the Latin American Coalition in Charlotte.

Churches have also sought to reach out to the growing Hispanic community. Because a significant number of Latinos have come to North Carolina as active participants in the Roman Catholic Church, Catholic charities and other organizations have been particularly prominent in these outreach efforts. Many Protestant denominations also sponsor aid organizations for Latinos, however, and offer Spanish-language worship services.

In an effort to improve service to the state's Latino population, in September 1998 Governor James B. Hunt Jr. appointed H. Nolo Martinez as North Carolina's first director of Hispanic/Latino affairs. The director's job is to assist and coordinate various state programs intended to meet the needs of the Latino community. Some of these state efforts include Migrant Health Programs, Interpreter Training, Cultural Diversity Training, Bilingual Materials, Project Esperanza (which works with battered Latina women), Immigrants Legal Assistance Project, Legal Services of North Carolina, and Migrant Unit. Hunt also appointed a Hispanic/Latino Advisory Council made up of 25 members, with 15 voting members and 10 ex-officio members, most of whom are representatives of various state departments. The council's mission is to advise the governor on issues affecting the Latino community in the state, provide a forum for discussion, and promote state efforts to improve relations between Latinos and other North Carolinians. The council is divided into seven working committees that focus on issues in the areas of education, health and human resources, workers' rights, immigration, documentation and licensing, political involvement, and crime control and public safety.

References: Ned Glascock, "Latinos' Political Leverage Growing," *Raleigh News and Observer*, 16 July 2000; James H. Johnson Jr., Karen D. Johnson-Webb, and Walter C. Farrell Jr., "A Profile of Hispanic Newcomers," *Popular Government* (Fall 1999).

Alan K. Lamm

Laurel Creek Massacre. In April 1864 a Union brigade from Tennessee, commanded by Col. George Washington Kirk, entered Madison County to recruit "home Yankees" for the 2nd and 3rd North Carolina Mounted Volunteers, defeat Confederate forces, and chastise Confederate sympathizers. Kirk's Brigade arrived unopposed and scoured the Laurel Valley, where Shelton Laurel Creek flows into Big Laurel Creek. Madison County was defended only by Home Guard units from Yancey County under Brig. Gen. John W. McElroy, who was ensconced at Mars Hill bracing himself for an attack.

Kirk's Mounted Volunteers encountered the home of a 40-year-old widow, Nance "Granny" Franklin. They characterized Granny Franklin's four sons as Confederate sympathizers who had fought alongside Confederate forces and bushwhacked Union troops moving through the area. Only three sons were present that day, George Franklin being away. When troops surrounded the house, Granny Franklin urged her sons to defend themselves. Balus, James, and Josiah emerged from the cabin shooting. A return volley killed Balus and James. Fifteen-year-old Josiah crawled under the house and killed two soldiers who tried to capture him. Granny Franklin was trying to prevent the soldiers from burning the cabin when one of them shot off a lock of her hair. On emerging from under the burning building, Josiah was killed immediately. As Kirk's Brigade left Granny Franklin with her three dead sons, they rode off shouting, "Bloody Madison!"

This and the earlier Shelton Laurel Massacre were the most notorious incidents of western North Carolina's own civil war within the Civil War.

References: James O. Hall, "The Shelton Laurel Massacre: Murder in the North Carolina Mountains," *Blue & Gray* (February 1991); Phillip Shaw Paludan, *Victims: A True Story of the Civil War* (repr., 2004); Manly Wade Wellman, *The Kingdom of Madison: A Southern Mountain Fastness and Its People* (1973).

Paul E. Kuhl

Laurinburg & Southern Railroad was incorporated on 4 Mar. 1909 in response to protests from three industries in Laurinburg that were dissatisfied with the service of the railroad on which they were located. N. G. Wade, D. M. Flynn, J. F. McNair, J. Blue, A. L. Jones, and J. A. Jones were the incorporators, with McNair serving as president. Construction from Johns to East Laurinburg was completed on 2 July 1909, and soon the railroad made its first shipment of freight, a carload of finished cotton goods. Within a year the line was completed to Wagram, and on 12 Nov. 1921 a section from Wagram to Raeford was purchased from the Aberdeen & Rockfish Railroad. Passenger service began on 11 June 1910 and later that year was expanded to include through service with the Atlantic Coast Line Railroad.

In the early 2000s the 28-mile Laurinburg & Southern was owned by the Gulf & Ohio Railways of Knoxville, Tenn., which also owned the Nash County Railroad and the Yadkin Valley Railroad and connected with CSX and the Aberdeen & Rockfish Railroad. Its chief traffic included grain, fertilizer, soda ash, coal, and lime. The company also performed contract track construction and crossing maintenance.

Reference: Bill Robertson, *Eighty Years of Laurinburg and Southern History* (1989).

Donald W. Kern

Laurinburg Normal and Industrial Institute was established in 1904 by Emanuel Montee McDuffie and his wife, Tiny, educators who had traveled from Alabama in response to a request by the African American citizens of Scotland County to build a school in their community. Initially, the school had only one teacher, seven students, and assets of 15 cents. By 1915 Laurinburg Institute was providing valuable leadership and opportunity for blacks throughout Scotland County and beyond. Although a private institution, the school cooperated with state and county educational agents in establishing curriculum and standards. Academics were divided into primary, intermediate, and high school departments.

Ever mindful of the need to develop the economic independence of its students, the school also offered courses in housekeeping, dressmaking, laundering, wheelwrighting, blacksmithing, and printing. In this regard, the school embraced the philosophy and political position of black educator and leader Booker T. Washington. His belief in the "green ballot"—learning skills and trades that would provide blacks with economic self-sufficiency—was sometimes sharply criticized by other black leaders, but the policy helped pave the way for community acceptance of and support for the institute. In 1909 Washington visited Laurinburg as a guest of the McDuffies, and his public speeches there were well attended by the community's citizens, both black and white.

By 1932 Laurinburg Institute had been transformed from a single building to a thriving school complex. On former swampland stood 14 buildings that, together with the school's livestock, were estimated to represent up to $250,000 in assets. Twenty-seven teachers instructed 684 enrolled students; graduates operated the Hallowell-Wellington Kindergarten for black children. In 1915 former students also organized the Colored Civic League, an organization that promoted temperance, thrift, and industry and worked to improve sanitary conditions in the community.

Laurinburg Institute influenced life in Scotland County in several other ways. The school published a newspaper and circulars for the black community, and citizens used its printing facilities to produce opera house tickets, bulletins, and announcements. Laurinburg Institute's orchestra also enjoyed considerable success, as its members spent many hours on the road fulfilling requests for performances and bringing needed income to the school. A spin-off band formed by members of the orchestra featured famous trumpeter Dizzy Gillespie for two years, during which time he reputedly developed his well-known "bebop" style. Charlie Scott, the first African American to play varsity basketball at the University of North Carolina at Chapel Hill, attended Laurinburg for one year. Laurinburg Institute in the early 2000s remained a thriving private high school and two-year college under the direction of Emanuel McDuffie's grandson, Frank H. "Bishop" McDuffie.

Reference: Marilyn Wright, ed., *A Sense of Place* (1991).

Marilyn Wright

Law Schools. In the eighteenth and early nineteenth century, legal education in North Carolina was a haphazard undertaking. A young law student studied on his own or under the tutelage of a licensed lawyer, reading books owned by an attorney and picking up information from his mentor. Such noteworthy early attorneys and public figures as Thomas Ruffin, David L. Swain, Robert Strange, William Gaston, David F. Caldwell, and Archibald D. Murphey instructed students in their offices.

In due time, private law schools were organized. The first to be advertised was that of John Louis Taylor, whose school opened in Raleigh in 1822. Other private schools were conducted by outstanding lawyers such as Murphey, Leonard Henderson, and Frederick Nash. Two teachers of note were Richmond M. Pearson, who had law schools in Mocksville and later at Richmond Hill, and William Horn Battle of Chapel Hill. Battle's was the first law school to be affiliated with an established institution of higher learning. He and James Iredell Jr. had taught law in Raleigh in 1841, prior to Battle's 1843 move to Chapel Hill. In Chapel Hill he began teaching in his office; by 1845 he was professor of law at the University of North Carolina. The university offered the bachelor of law degree beginning at that time.

Four other university-level law schools were subsequently established in North Carolina, forever replacing the small private schools of the antebellum period. Wake Forest University's School of Law was established in 1894. Duke University was founded in 1924, and immediate efforts to provide legal education led to the establishment of a law school in 1930. Trinity College, out of which Duke University grew, had offered an undergraduate class in law in 1868 and set up a school of law in 1904. Raleigh's Shaw University established a law school for African American students in 1888, but it was closed in 1914. North Carolina Central University's School of Law was opened in 1939. It immediately closed for lack of students but reopened the next year and continues to operate successfully. Finally, Campbell University established a law school in 1976.

References: Robert F. Durden, "The Rebuilding of Duke University's School of Law, 1925–1947," *NCHR* 66 (July 1984); Fannie Memory Farmer, "Legal Education in North Carolina, 1820–1860," *NCHR* 28 (July 1951); Harold R. Washington, "History and Role of Black Law Schools," *North Carolina Central Law Journal* 5 (Spring 1974).

Memory F. Mitchell

SEE ALSO Richmond Hill Law School.

League of Women Voters of North Carolina was founded in 1920 by leaders of the movement for women suffrage to inform and encourage active participation by citizens in public policy issues. As a nonpartisan organization, the league does not support or oppose any candidate or political party. It encourages citizen participation and education through voter registration drives, public debate, and forums, and it fosters change through advocate lobbying efforts at all levels. It also studies and promotes a wide range of issues, such as universal voter registration and effective election laws; fair, honest, and open campaign practices; protection of natural resources; responsible local, state, and federal fiscal policies; safe, affordable housing; child care and women's issues; an effective criminal justice system; and fair and equitable taxes.

The North Carolina league is a three-tiered organization with a national office in Washington, D.C., a state office in Raleigh, and a state board of directors that serves as an administrative unit for 27 local leagues representing 23 counties in the state.

References: *Celebrating a Quarter Century of Political Participation in North Carolina: A History of the League of Women Voters in North Carolina, 1951–1976* (1976); Kathryn L. Nasstrom, "'More Was Expected of Us': The League of Women Voters and the Feminist Movement in the 1920s" (M.A. thesis, UNC-Chapel Hill, 1988).

Marian Dodd

Lederer Expedition. John Lederer's expedition of 20 May 1670 to 18 July 1670, the second of three journeys by the German explorer, was the first extensive exploration of the Carolina Piedmont and provided the first description of the backcountry American Indian tribes. Virginia governor Sir William Berkeley, one of the Lords Proprietors of Carolina, commissioned young Lederer, a recent arrival from Germany, to explore the South and West in preparation for opening the region to trade and future settlement. The Hamburg native, who had studied medicine, had a scientific interest in the area's natural resources and the Native Americans.

Leaving from the falls of the James River, Lederer returned to the Appomattox River in Virginia nearly 60 days later, claiming to have traveled hundreds of miles and seen fantastic sights, including strange native customs, a large inland sea, and a vast desert. Although his account was discredited in his own day, scholars have been divided over Lederer's credibility and the interpretation of his confusing record. A recent study based on geographic analysis has established a plausible route for Lederer through the North Carolina Piedmont. His description and map, though containing faulty information, provided the first topographic glimpse of the interior and appeared on the earliest maps of the Proprietary province of Carolina. Shortly after returning to Virginia, Lederer left for Maryland and later went to Connecticut. He returned to Germany in 1675.

References: Alan V. Briceland, *Westward from Virginia: The Exploration of the Virginia-Carolina Frontier, 1650–1710* (1987); William P. Cumming, ed., *The Discoveries of John Lederer* (1958).

Lindley S. Butler

Lee County, located in North Carolina's Piedmont region, was formed from Moore and Chatham Counties in 1907 and took its name from Confederate general Robert E. Lee. Sanford (incorporated in 1874) became the county seat; other Lee County communities include Broadway, Northview, Cumnock, Tramway, Lemon Springs, Swann, and Colon.

Although it was one of the last of North Carolina's counties to be established, the area that became Lee County had long since demonstrated its importance to the state's economy and well-being. During the American Revolution, the Wilcox Iron Works supplied iron goods for North Carolina's war effort. In 1855 the first commercial coal mine in the state, Egypt Mine, was opened in the county; it too served the state's needs in time of conflict, supplying coal to blockade-runners during the Civil War. Lee County's most important manufactured products, today as well as historically, are bricks. Sanford has traditionally been regarded as the nation's "brick making capital," having produced more bricks than any other city in the United States. In 2002 the city also hosted the first Sanford Pottery Festival to celebrate the state's pottery-making heritage. While the Seagrove Pottery Festival in neighboring Randolph County is older, the Sanford festival quickly established itself as the largest pottery festival in the state. In 2004 Lee County's estimated population was slightly more than 50,000.

Reference: J. Daniel Pezzoni, *The History and Architecture of Lee County, North Carolina* (1995).

Robert Blair Vocci

SEE ALSO Brick Making.

Lees-McRae College, located in Banner Elk, is an independent, coeducational institution affiliated with the Presbyterian Church (U.S.A.). It was founded in 1900 by Edgar Tufts as part of an Appalachian ministry of service and education.

Known as the "Campus in the Clouds" (the school is 4,000 feet above sea level), Lees-McRae emphasizes personal religious values and vocational guidance that contributes to each student's welfare and growth.

Tufts, a newly ordained minister in the Southern Presbyterian Church, came to Banner Elk in 1897 with the intention of founding a congregation in the remote mountains of western North Carolina. Upon his arrival he found no church, no school, and no doctor. When he died in 1923, Tuft's vision had led to the founding of a college, the 20-bed Grace Hospital, and an orphanage caring for 100 children. Tufts named his fledgling school the Elizabeth McRae Institute for Girls in honor of a dedicated teacher from South Carolina. In 1905 Tufts created a boys department and amended the name of the school to honor benefactor Mrs. S. P. Lees of Kentucky and New York. The boys and girls schools were chartered by the state in 1907 as Lees-McRae Institute. In 1914 a high school was set up; in 1927 the school became coeducational; and in 1931 the institute became Lees-McRae College, a fully accredited junior college with 225 students. The Southern Association of Colleges and Schools in 1990 granted Lees-McRae status as a senior (four-year) institution.

From the beginning, the college combined the theoretical with the practical, emphasizing the training of its students in a useful occupation. In the early years there was a gristmill, a cannery, a farm, and a woodworking shop. The students built roads, laid power lines, and made furniture. They received classroom instruction in math, physics, and chemistry, which paralleled the physical labor they were doing. In the summer, the college became the Pinnacle Inn, an attractive summer resort where students learned hotel management and earned funds to pay for their schooling. By 1941 Lees-McRae had sent 40 percent of its graduates on to a university, while other graduates returned to their mountain area as agricultural experts or nurses or opened businesses.

Over the years Lees-McRae expanded its curriculum to include new majors in math, computer science, and business administration. The college in the early 2000s had approximately 780 students served by 80 faculty members. The school continues to pursue its purpose of nurturing and graduating students who have developed a sense of integrity and social responsibility.

References: "Campus in the Clouds," *Reader's Digest* (November 1941); Lees-McRae College, *Handbook* (1999); "Life Goes On in the School," *Progressive Education* 18 (November 1941).

Julian M. Pleasants

Legends. SEE Folklore.

Lenoir County, located in North Carolina's Coastal Plain region, was formed from no-longer-extant Dobbs County in

1791. It was named for General William Lenoir, a prominent Revolutionary War hero, Speaker of the State Senate, and trustee of the University of North Carolina. The new county retained Dobbs County's seat, Kinston, which was incorporated in 1762 as Kingston (in honor of King George III). Other communities in Lenoir County include La Grange, Pink Hill, Graingers, Deep Run, Institute, Dawson, and part of Grifton. The county's estimated population was 58,500 in 2004.

Although it continues to produce traditional agricultural commodities such as tobacco, Lenoir County has also been on the cutting edge of new business ventures. In 1954 the DuPont Company established its first polyester manufacturing plant in the county. During the 1990s, the county again made history with the construction of the Global TransPark, an innovative, fully integrated business and transportation complex (although it has been plagued by tenancy and financing problems).

Among Lenoir County's many attractions are the Kinston Indians Class-A baseball team—Kinston is the smallest city in the nation with a professional team—and the CSS *Neuse* State Historic Site and Governor Richard Caswell Memorial, where visitors can view a Confederate ironclad gunboat, the CSS *Neuse*. The ship, which was deliberately sunk by its captain in 1865 to prevent it from falling into Union hands, was found to be in remarkably good condition when it was recovered nearly a century later. Nearly 15,000 associated artifacts were recovered along with the ship. Lenoir County was also the scene of two major Civil War engagements, the 1862 Battle of Kinston and the 1865 Battle of Wyse Fork, second only (among actions fought in North Carolina) to the Battle of Bentonville in the number of troops engaged.

Reference: *Heritage of Lenoir County, 1981* (1981).

Robert Blair Vocci

SEE ALSO Kinston, Battle of; *Neuse*, CSS, State Historic Site and Governor Richard Caswell Memorial; Wyse Fork, Battle of.

Lenoir-Rhyne College

Lenoir-Rhyne College opened in Hickory as Highland College (successor to Highland Academy) in 1891. Its founders were four Lutheran pastors and educators—Andrew L. Crouse, Robert A. Yoder, William P. Cline, and Jason C. Moser—who had dreamed of establishing a Christian college in the town. The school stood on 56 acres originally owned by Wilkes County lawyer Walter Waightstill Lenoir, who donated the land in his will for the purpose of establishing a school. The school opened as Highland College, but changed its name four months later to Lenoir College in memory of its benefactor. In 1895 the school established a sponsorship with the North Carolina Synod of the Evangelical Lutheran Church in America that remains in place. The institution's name was changed to Lenoir-Rhyne College in 1923 in recognition of textile manufacturer, banker, and philanthropist Daniel Efird Rhyne, who made a generous donation to the college in 1922.

Founded on a dedication to a "liberal culture upon Christian principles," Lenoir-Rhyne enrolled more than 1,400 students by the early 2000s. The college's liberal arts core curriculum features 60 majors in the liberal arts, the sciences, and preprofessional programs. Lenoir-Rhyne created an Institute for Multi-cultural Education and Training in 1989 and a center for women's studies in 1991.

References: Jeff L. Norris and Ellis G. Boatman, *Fair Star: A Centennial History of Lenoir-Rhyne College* (1990); Charles J. Preslar Jr., ed., *A History of Catawba County* (1954); John E. Trainer Jr., *Celebrating a Century of Excellence in Education* (1990).

Wiley J. Williams

Leonard Medical School

Leonard Medical School, established in Raleigh by Shaw University in 1880, trained more than 400 African American physicians during the nearly 40 years of its existence. Soon after Henry Martin Tupper of Massachusetts, a missionary representing the American Baptist Home Mission Society, founded Shaw in 1865, he cited the need for educating black physicians. Stressing the absence of any institution for their training between Washington, D.C., and New Orleans, he finally persuaded Shaw's trustees to organize a medical department on the Raleigh campus. Partial funding came from the American Baptist Home Mission Society and other northern philanthropists, primarily Judson Wade Leonard, of Hampden, Mass., the brother of Tupper's wife. In his honor the new department was named Leonard Medical School. The site, a square acre at the southeast corner of the antebellum governor's mansion lot, then occupied by Raleigh's Centen-

Faculty of Leonard Medical School, ca. 1902. NCC.

nial Graded School, was donated by the North Carolina General Assembly.

The Leonard Medical Building, or Leonard Hall, was under construction by the spring of 1881 and opened on 1 November with a faculty of two white Raleigh physicians. Dr. James McKee held the chair of physiology and medical principles and practices, while continuing his own medical practice, and Dr. F. A. Spafford, already a classics professor at Shaw, taught anatomy. As enrollment increased, as many as 23 other members of Raleigh's white medical profession acted as part-time faculty over the life of the school.

Tuition for the initial student body was partially financed by a small endowment and later by the John F. Slater Fund. The students helped reduce their expenses by performing some of the maintenance work in Leonard Hall. Their first-year curriculum of necessity included some preparatory science classes as well as medical courses. By the first graduation, in 1886, Leonard offered a graded program requiring a full four years, thus becoming one of the first four-year medical schools in the nation.

Leonard's first graduates included six doctors, all of whom passed their licensing board examinations. Two of them were North Carolinians, and the others were from Georgia, South Carolina, Virginia, and West Virginia. Two of the six began their medical practice in the state. One of these, class valedictorian Lawson Andrew Scruggs, was resident physician at Leonard Hospital for several years.

Although Leonard continued to graduate well-trained, successful physicians, its limited endowment made it increasingly difficult to expand and keep pace with other black medical schools. Meharry Medical College in Nashville, Tenn., and Howard Medical College in Washington, D.C., received much more funding. In Raleigh, Saint Augustine's College completed a massive new three-story building for its St. Agnes Hospital during the 1908–9 academic year.

In 1914 the Shaw trustees shortened the medical curriculum to two years, with the expectation that graduates with bachelor of science in medicine degrees would go on to Meharry or Howard, which were by then receiving considerable Rockefeller funding. Finally, the decision was made to close the school, with the last classes apparently held during 1918–19.

Two structures built for the Leonard Medical School are extant, both on the west side of the 700 block of South Wilmington Street—Leonard Hall and the adjacent Tyler Hall (1910). After the medical school and hospital closed, these structures were used for a variety of purposes. Both buildings are within Raleigh's East Raleigh–South Park Historic District, which was entered in the National Register of Historic Places in 1990.

References: Wilmoth A. Carter, *Shaw's Universe: A Monument to Educational Innovation* (1973); Dorothy Long, ed., *Medicine in North Carolina: Essays in the History of Medical Science and Medical Service, 1524–1950* (2 vols., 1972); Todd L. Savitt, "The Education of Black Physicians at Shaw University, 1882–1918," in Jeffrey J. Crow and Flora J. Hatley, eds., *Black Americans in North Carolina and the South* (1984).

Elizabeth Reid Murray

Levine Museum of the New South is a private, non-profit museum dedicated to preserving and presenting the history of Charlotte and the surrounding Carolina Piedmont. Recognizing the momentous transformation of the Charlotte area since the Civil War, the museum focuses on the historical period known as the "New South," which it defines as encompassing the post-Reconstruction era to the present day. Located at the heart of Charlotte's uptown cultural district, the institution features exhibits, tours, lectures, and programming for all ages.

In the summer of 1990, members of the Mecklenburg Historical Association developed the idea of the Museum of the New South and approached Sally Robinson, a community leader and cultural advocate, about organizing the institution. Robinson formed a working group of local historians, university professors, and community leaders to consider the museum proposal. The organizing group settled on the name "Museum of the New South" as a reflection of Charlotte residents' belief that the city exemplifies much of the history signified by that term. The museum was incorporated in April 1991, and a diverse board of trustees was assembled. The board decided that the museum should look at history on a regional scope and distinguish itself from other local history museums by focusing on the "New South" period, that it should rely on current scholarship and be closely associated with area educational institutions, and that it should begin its existence without a building of its own.

The decision to operate without a building was made for financial and philosophical reasons. At the time, there was little support in the community for building another cultural facility, and the board felt that operating without a permanent structure would offer tremendous flexibility in developing exhibitions and programs. As a result, for the first four years, the museum was a "museum without walls," mounting exhibits in public places and organizing numerous outreach programs in the community. Among the museum's projects during this period were the exhibitions The Most Democratic Sport: Basketball and Culture in the Central Piedmont, 1893–1994; When Southern Women Went to College, 1880–1930; and Charlotte and the New South: A Region at Work, the latter taking the form of a traveling interactive kiosk.

In the spring of 1994, the Museum of the New South engaged in a long-term planning process that identified developing collections and installing a core exhibit as priorities. As a result, with the help of the state of North Carolina and private funding, the museum purchased a building at 324 North College Street in Charlotte's cultural district. After building renovations, the museum opened in January 1996 with the exhibit New South: A to Z. The museum subsequently mounted exhibits about Billy Graham, women reformers, African American churches, and World War II.

In 1997 the museum received a $200,000 implementation grant from the National Endowment for the Humanities to prepare its core exhibit. In 2001 the Levine Museum of the New South—renamed in honor of museum patrons Leon Levine, founder of the Family Dollar Stores retail chain, and his wife Sandra—opened in a 40,000-square-foot, state-of-the-art building located at 200 East Seventh Street in Charlotte. Its 8,000-square-foot permanent exhibit, Cotton Fields to Skyscrapers: Charlotte and the Carolina Piedmont in the New South, explores the social history of the economic transformation of the Piedmont from a rural, agriculture-based society to the major financial, business, and industrial center that it is today.

Reference: Mary Norton Kratt, *Charlotte: Spirit of the New South* (1992).

Brenden Martin

Liberty Hall, an eighteenth-century academy of higher learning in Mecklenburg County located in the former Queen's Museum building in Charlotte, was the product of Hezekiah Alexander and Waightstill Avery's efforts in the Halifax Convention (1776) to provide for the instruction of youth through direct public support. North Carolina's constitution committed the state to the public support of education. The General Assembly's May 1777 term saw the approval of a bill to create Liberty Hall, but the fledgling state government was unable to provide funds for public education during the Revolutionary War.

Of the trustees who met in Charlotte on 3 Jan. 1778 for their first organizational session, five had served as trustees of the earlier Queen's College (1771–73): Thomas Polk, Abraham Alexander, Thomas Neal, John McKnitt Alexander, and Waightstill Avery. Isaac V. Alexander served as president; additional trustees were Ephraim Brevard, John Simpson, Adlai Osborn, James Edmonds, Thomas Reese, Samuel E. McCorkle, Thomas H. McCaule, James Hall, and David Caldwell. The trustees elected a local scholar, Robert Brownfield, as the school's first president for one year. The president's salary was set at £195, and additional town lots in Charlotte belonging to Col. Thomas Polk were sought for expansion. At first, Liberty Hall provided education for men too young for combat and for older men whose service was no longer needed.

During 1779 Alexander MacWhorter, an "eminent preacher of the gospel" and "ardent patriot," was persuaded to relocate from New Jersey to the dissenter stronghold in Mecklenburg County and serve as pastor of Sugar Creek Church and president of Liberty Hall. Liberty Hall closed its doors as an academy in September 1780 when Lord Charles Cornwallis moved troops into Charlotte. After the British withdrew, the institution, which had been used as a hospital during the occupation of the city, did not reopen. In 1784 trustees reported that the buildings were in ruin and decay. The trustees petitioned the legislature to move the academy to Salisbury and change its name to Salisbury Academy.

References: Norris W. Preyer, *Hezekiah Alexander and the Revolution in the Backcountry* (1987); D. A. Tompkins, *History of Mecklenburg County*, vol. 1 (1903).

Stewart Lillard

Liberty Ships, a number of which were built in Wilmington, carried two-thirds of U.S. cargo during World War II, thus playing a significant role in the Allied cause as merchant vessels. According to standards developed by the U.S. Maritime Commission in 1940, Liberty ships were 440 feet long, 66 feet wide, and, with 2,500 horsepower, capable of cruising at 11 knots. Some were armed. These ships were the first vessels to be mass-produced using welding instead of riveting; welding was faster, cheaper, and lighter, and it took less time to train welders than riveters. Consequently, the ships became known for their rapid production. Nationally, over 2,700 Liberty ships were built and about 200 were sunk by the enemy.

Between 1941 and 1946 the North Carolina Shipbuilding Corporation in Wilmington produced 243 vessels, of which 125 were Liberty ships. In 1943, 20,000 workers were involved in this effort. Many of these Liberty ships were named for famous North Carolinians and for cities and counties that conducted war bond drives. On 6 Dec. 1941 the USS *Zebulon B. Vance* was the first Liberty ship launched in Wilmington, just hours before the attack on Pearl Harbor. The *Vance* made several successful runs to London before being damaged by a mine on a return trip; it was repaired and rejoined the Liberty fleet. Later the *Vance* was converted to a hospital ship and renamed the USS *John J. Meany*. Finally, it was reconverted back to the *Vance* to transport "war-bride" dependents of American military personnel to the United States.

After the war, a number of Liberty ships became merchant vessels and others were stored for future use. Most were subsequently scrapped. In the early 2000s two restored and functioning Liberty ships remained: the USS *Jeremiah O'Brien* on the West Coast and the USS *John W. Brown*, moored in Baltimore, which visited Wilmington in 1996. As part of the North Carolina artificial reef program, the Liberty ship USS *Theodore Parker* was sunk in 50 feet of water just off Fort Macon near

Ships lined up at outfitting piers of the North Carolina Shipbuilding Company in Wilmington. NCC.

Morehead City and became a popular site for scuba divers and fishermen.

References: Roderick M. Farb, *Shipwrecks: Diving the Graveyard of the Atlantic* (1985); Sarah McCulloh Lemmon, *North Carolina's Role in World War II* (1964); Alan D. Watson, *Wilmington: Port of North Carolina* (1992).

Jim Fowlkes

SEE ALSO *Zebulon B. Vance*, USS.

Library, State. The North Carolina General Assembly established the State Library in 1812 as a collection of public documents—chiefly laws and legislative journals—for use by legislators and other state government officials. In authorizing the secretary of state to collect and maintain these publications, legislators placed North Carolina in the midst of a national trend. Although such states as Pennsylvania, South Carolina, and Virginia had established collections of public documents in the colonial period, formal development of state libraries did not begin until the early nineteenth century. In North Carolina, legislative committees established policies for the library that were carried out by Secretary of State William Hill.

Although in its early years the State Library of North Carolina grew chiefly through exchange of documents with other states and the federal government, the collection quickly evolved into more than a legal reference collection. In 1816 the General Assembly authorized an annual expenditure of $250 for the purchase of books for the "public library." Legislators doubled this sum in 1821. Although appropriations were not always expended, these funds allowed the State Library

to develop a collection much broader in scope than originally intended. By 1827 its 1,200 volumes included works of agriculture, biography, geography, history, literature, science, and travel. Since the libraries housed at the University of North Carolina in Chapel Hill were perhaps the only other significant collections in a public institution in the state, legislators appear to have viewed the State Library as a statewide literary resource.

Virtually all of the State Library collection was destroyed in 1831 when the State Capitol building burned. Three Whig governors laid the foundation for a new collection during the 1830s and 1840s. Beginning in 1834, the Literary Board carried out a legislative mandate to develop a new collection. Governor David Lowry Swain, acting on behalf of the board, acquired the extensive library of visionary state leader and jurist Archibald D. Murphey; with the assistance of William Gaston, a member of the North Carolina Supreme Court, he also purchased basic legal works.

State librarians discharged various duties in North Carolina. Like their colleagues in other states, they compiled and published catalogs of the collection. In addition to acquiring books approved by the trustees, they oversaw the binding of newspapers and books in poor condition. Until 1871, they managed the library of the state supreme court. In 1859 the General Assembly instructed the state librarian to establish and manage libraries for both of its houses.

During the late nineteenth and early twentieth centuries, the State Library made improvements in collection organization, placed increasing emphasis on historical work, and served a variety of clients. In 1901 the General Assembly appointed a committee to author a plan for developing the State Library's collection. The committee chose to emphasize works pertaining to North Carolina or by North Carolinians. Although fiction by North Carolinians would be acquired, the State Library was to become strictly a reference collection. The facility was heavily used by local residents, including college students and schoolchildren, whose educational standards were being raised by a vigorous statewide plan of improvement.

Legislation passed during the 1970s affected the State Library in significant ways. As a result of Governor Robert Scott's reorganization of state government, the library in 1971 lost its status as an independent agency, becoming an office of the Department of Art, Culture, and History (later renamed the Department of Cultural Resources). Its governing board was replaced first by the State Library Committee, then, in 1981, by the State Library Commission. Through the leadership of state librarian David N. McKay, the General Assembly in 1977 authorized the State Library to take a lead role in promoting cooperative endeavors among libraries of all types in North Carolina, as well as with national or regional entities.

Although the State Library continued to fulfill many of its traditional functions during the next 20 years and took on new responsibilities such as the Summer Reading Program for children in public libraries, it also carried out this legislative mandate. In the early 1980s it assisted libraries in developing "zones of cooperation." It was instrumental in the development of the North Carolina Online Union Catalog and administered the North Carolina Information Network, which by the end of the 1990s was providing widespread access to electronic bulletin boards and the library's online catalog. In 1987 the General Assembly passed the North Carolina Documents Depository Act, which designated the State Library as the official repository for all published state documents and as a clearinghouse for the distribution of documents to depository libraries statewide.

Beginning in 1989, the library played a major role in administering the United States Newspaper Program, a federally funded project to identify, microfilm, and catalog historic newspapers. The State Library has also provided much current information about the state through its FTP, Gopher, and World Wide Web servers, and has assumed a leadership role in the development of NC LIVE, a cooperative effort to provide important electronic databases to libraries of all types throughout the state.

References: Charles R. McClure, ed., *State Library Services and Issues: Facing Future Challenges* (1986); Thornton W. Mitchell, *The State Library and Library Development in North Carolina* (1983); Maurice C. York, "A History of the North Carolina State Library, 1812–1888" (M.A. thesis, UNC-Chapel Hill, 1978).

Maurice C. York

Lifesaving Service, U.S.

Established as a federal agency in 1872 and operating in North Carolina by 1874, the U.S. Lifesaving Service (USLSS) was an integral part of coastal life in North Carolina, as it was elsewhere in the nation. Originally an arm of the U.S. Treasury Department, the USLSS was combined with the Revenue Cutter Service in 1915 to form the U.S. Coast Guard.

As originally conceived, the USLSS operated out of a series of stations, each constructed within view of the waters offshore. The stations were to be manned from late spring to early fall, when hurricanes threatened and commercial sea traffic was at its busiest. A keeper and a crew of six lifesavers served at each station. After the wreck of the USS *Huron* in 1877, the lifesaving season was extended, and keepers eventually became year-round federal employees. The crews remained seasonal, although they could be called up for emergencies out of season. By the founding of the Coast Guard, stations were manned year-round. In North Carolina, the service began with the construction of seven stations—at Jones Hill, Caffeys Inlet, Kitty Hawk, Nags Head, Bodie Island, Chicamacomico, and Little Kinnakeet—starting in 1874. Eventually a total of 29 stations created a chain of vigilance along the coast. Each station's crew was responsible for patrolling a stretch of beach in search of grounded or foundering vessels. This patrol was conducted on foot in all weather conditions.

From the 1870s to World War I, the USLSS on the Outer Banks in particular performed many rescues. The Pea Island Station under Capt. Richard Etheridge, for instance, was manned by the only all-black crew in North Carolina; despite racial prejudice and segregation, the men served heroically in many rescue operations. The captain and crew of the Chicamacomico station distinguished themselves in the rescue of the crew of the *Mirlo*, a British tanker torpedoed off Hatteras Island in 1918.

Rescue operations were extremely hazardous and required regular drill training. At first, crews rowed a small dory through crashing waves and high seas to the site of a wreck as many times as necessary to carry survivors to safety. After 1878 the use of the Lyle gun—a small cannon positioned on the beach that fired the breeches buoy (in which survivors sat with their legs dangling through the buoy as though they were wearing a pair of breeches)—made rescues safer. Using a secured line, the breeches buoy carried survivors to shore one at a time. By the early twentieth century, motor-driven boats had become more common at lifesaving stations. The modern Coast Guard serves as the legacy of the lifesaving captains and crews of earlier days.

References: Joe A. Mobley, *Ship Ashore!: The U.S. Lifesavers of Coastal North Carolina* (1994); David Stick, *Graveyard of the Atlantic: Shipwrecks of the North Carolina Coast* (1952).

Kathy Carter

SEE ALSO *Mirlo* Rescue.

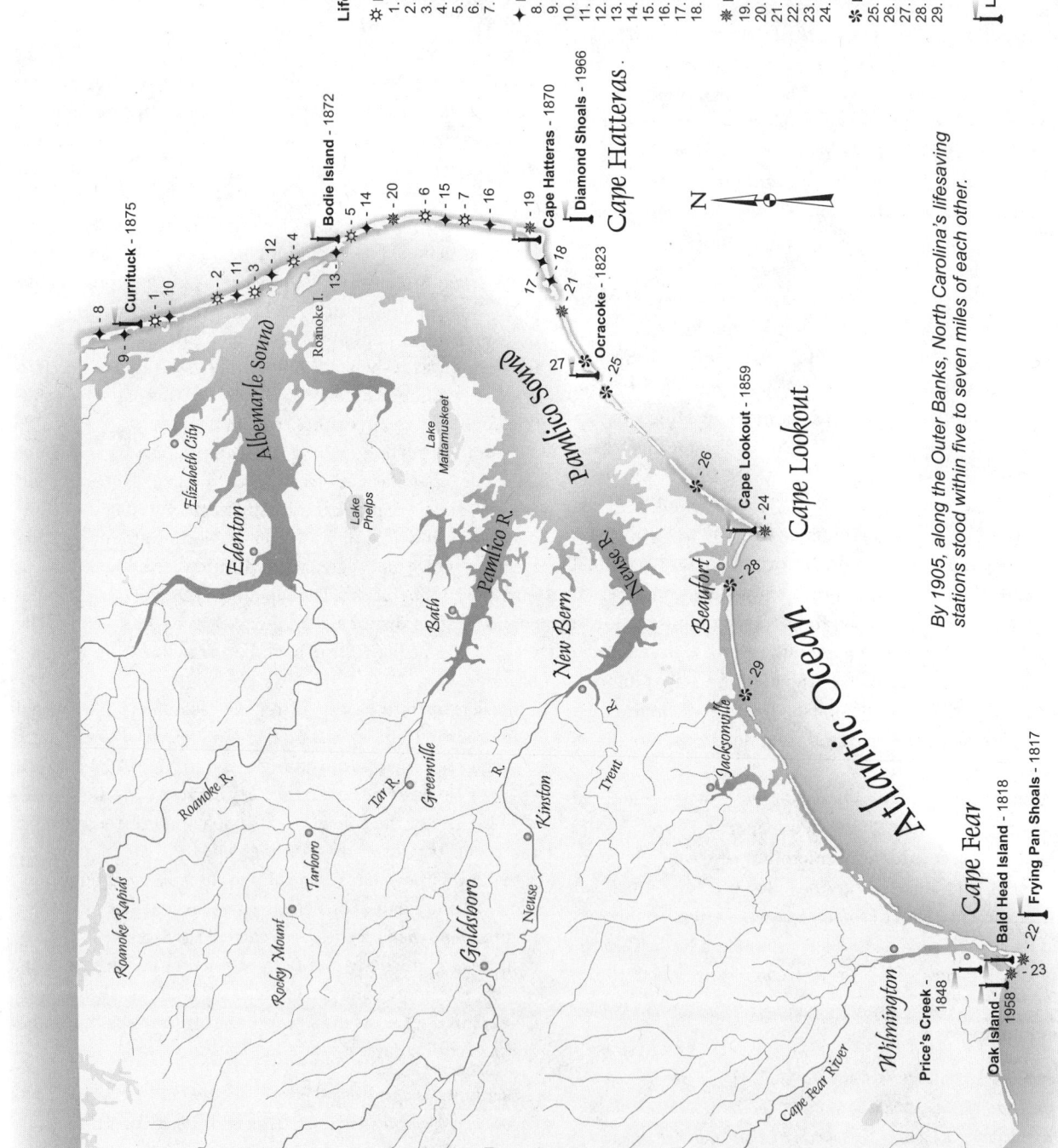

Lifesaving Stations:

☀ **BUILT 1874**
1. Jones Hill (Whale Head/Currituck Beach)
2. Caffeys Inlet
3. Kitty Hawk
4. Nags Head
5. Bodie Island (Oregon Inlet)
6. Chicamacomico
7. Little Kinnakeet

◆ **BUILT 1878**
8. Deals Island (Wash Woods)
9. Old Currituck Inlet (Pennys Hill)
10. Poyners Hill
11. Paul Gamiels Hill
12. Kill Devil Hills
13. Tommys Hummock (Bodie Island)
14. Pea Island
15. Cedar Hummock (Gull Shoal)
16. Big Kinnakeet
17. Creeds Hill
18. Hatteras (Durants)

✺ **BUILT 1880-1888**
19. Cape Hatteras - 1880
20. New Inlet - 1882
21. Ocracoke - 1883 (Hatteras Inlet)
22. Cape Fear - 1883
23. Oak Island - 1886
24. Cape Lookout - 1888

✳ **BUILT 1894-1905**
25. Portsmouth - 1894
26. Core Banks - 1896 (Atlantic)
27. Ocracoke - 1904
28. Fort Macon - 1904
29. Bogue Inlet - 1905

I **Lighthouse** - Date Constructed

By 1905, along the Outer Banks, North Carolina's lifesaving stations stood within five to seven miles of each other.

Lifesaving stations and lighthouses. Map by Mark Anderson Moore, courtesy NCOA&H.

Bodie Island Lighthouse and keeper's quarters. Photograph courtesy of North Carolina Division of Tourism, Film, and Sports Development.

Lighthouses did not appear on the North Carolina coastal horizon until the last years of the eighteenth century, even though North Carolina, of all the coastal colonies, clearly was in need of navigational aids. The barrier islands that parallel the mainland are particularly prone to shoal waters, shifting sand bars, and disappearing inlets. Dangerous underwater shoals are especially prominent off Cape Hatteras, Cape Lookout, and Cape Fear.

The state's first lighthouse was built at Bald Head on Smith's Island just off Southport (Smithville). The U.S. Congress took on responsibility for lighthouse construction and maintenance in 1784, but it was 1792 before funds were appropriated for the Bald Head Light. Three additional appropriations were required to cover cost overruns before the tower was finally lighted in 1795. Its beacon guided mariners around the treacherous Frying Pan Shoals that obstructed clear sailing into the mouth of the Cape Fear River. Wilmington, 20 miles upriver, was the state's only deepwater port facility. The light lasted a mere 25 years, replaced in 1818 by a 109-foot facility farther from the water and the effects of erosion. This light still stands as the state's oldest.

North Carolina's second lighthouse in the state was constructed at Shell Castle Island, a lightering and warehousing complex built on an oyster rock inside Ocracoke Inlet by John Gray Blount and John Wallace. The light was a pyramid-shaped wood-frame structure with a shingled exterior that stood 55 feet tall. It guided mariners through Ocracoke Inlet and into Wallace's Channel. The light was struck by lightning and destroyed in 1818, a final humiliation for the complex, which by that time had already been deserted due to the shoaling of the channel.

The congressional act of 1794 that authorized the Shell Castle Island light also provided for construction of a light at Cape Hatteras, the easternmost point in North Carolina and the home of some notoriously treacherous waters. Diamond Shoals stretches 14 miles into the Atlantic from Cape Hatteras, a meandering clutch of sandbars and shoals that have grounded hundreds of ships. Moreover, the northward flow of the warm Gulf Stream collides with the southward thrust of a cold Labrador Current off Diamond Shoals, creating a maritime corridor so turbulent it has been nicknamed the Graveyard of the Atlantic.

Despite an obvious need, Cape Hatteras was not lighted until 1803, when what has been described as a sandstone structure some 100 feet in height was built. This light proved inadequate, and in 1852 Congress appropriated funds to ele-

Currituck Beach Lighthouse and keeper's residence at Corolla. Photograph courtesy of North Carolina Division of Tourism, Film, and Sports Development.

vate the tower and install a new and modern Fresnel lens. The work was completed in 1854. The existing Cape Hatteras Lighthouse was constructed between 1868 and 1870 at a cost of $155,000. The massive structure, requiring 1.25 million bricks and featuring solid masonry walls 14 feet thick at the base, for more than 100 years has served as a vital warning sign to sailors venturing into the waters of Diamond Shoals. At 198 feet in height, it remains the nation's tallest masonry lighthouse and perhaps the most famous and photographed lighthouse in the world, with its unique black-and-white spiral design recognizable to millions. In 1999 the Cape Hatteras Lighthouse was moved 2,900 feet to avoid destruction by the encroaching Atlantic, the shoreline at the time of the move being only 120 feet from the light.

Cape Lookout, at the southern end of the Outer Banks, did not have a light until about 1812. The light constructed then had two towers, a brick tower 93 feet high inside a wooded, shingled tower painted in red and white horizontal stripes. It was replaced in 1859 with a new tower of 150 feet. During the Civil War, Confederate troops tried to render it inoperable—as they did for other lights along the Federally occupied coast—but did not manage to destroy the structure. It stands today, its black-and-white diamond design a signal to mariners that they are nearing Shackleford Banks and Beaufort Inlet. The lost nineteenth-century town of Diamond City on Shackleford Banks took its name from the Lookout light.

Ocracoke was the state's busiest inlet during the eighteenth and nineteenth centuries. The inlet often drew oceangoing ships into the Pamlico Sound, the vast barrier bay mistaken by explorer Giovanni da Verrazano for the western route to the Orient. The destruction of the Shell Castle Light necessitated a new light for Ocracoke Inlet, and in 1823 the present-day light went into operation. Though slightly newer than the state's oldest light on Bald Head, it is the oldest light on the Outer Banks. In the late 1830s and 1840s, in a concerted effort to

render the Cape Fear River safe for navigation up to Wilmington, a series of small lighthouses was erected from Oak Island at Caswell Beach to the very outskirts of the port city. Lights were also situated at Price's Creek, Horse Shoe, Orton's Point, Campbell's Island, and Upper Jettee.

The 1850s were boom years for lighthouse proponents. A congressional review that year led to efforts to upgrade and standardize lighthouse operations. A Light House Board was established to oversee management and improvements. Bodie Island and Beacon Island were already scheduled to receive lights and did so in 1852. Ocracoke Channel also got a light that year. Old Topsail (Beaufort) Inlet received two lights in 1855, both of which were destroyed a few years later by Confederate troops from Fort Macon. In 1859 a second Bodie Island Light went up, a 90-foot brick structure painted white and topped with a Fresnel lens, but Confederate troops destroyed the tower during the war. A final light of 150 feet was erected in 1872 and remains standing.

The first Currituck Lighthouse was lighted in 1875. It was left in its natural red brick to distinguish it from the other lights. The newest and brightest light in North Carolina was erected at Oak Island in 1958.

The expense of lighthouse construction inspired Congress to look at alternatives for navigational aids. One answer was lightships. These bulky tankers had no function other than to anchor near shoal waters and shine their lamps brightly for passing maritime traffic. Another alternative to land-based lighthouses were "screw-pile" lighthouses mounted on pilings over the water. Frame houses built onto pilings with lights on their roofs, these screw-pile lights withstood wind and high water better than lightships, which they replaced after the Civil War. At least six screw-pile lighthouses hovered over North Carolina's sound waters in the second half of the nineteenth century. By the beginning of the twenty-first century, there were seven lighthouses still standing in North Carolina: Currituck, Bodie Island, Hatteras, Ocracoke, Cape Lookout, Oak Island, and Bald Head Island. All except Bald Head, which is privately owned, are electronically operated and under the jurisdiction of the U.S. Coast Guard.

References: Cheryl Shelton-Roberts and Bruce Roberts, *North Carolina Lighthouses: A Tribute of History and Hope* (2004); David Stick, *North Carolina Lighthouses* (1980).

Rodney D. Barfield

SEE ALSO Lightships.

Lightships, beginning in the early nineteenth century, were anchored off the North Carolina coast to alert seagoing vessels to the proximity of hazards. Designed to supplement lighthouses and mark sandbars and channels, these ungraceful but sturdy ships were placed in locations that could not be marked with fixed structures. Ships and crews remained on station in all weather conditions, warning sailors of treacherous waters. Operation of lightships was overseen by the U.S. Treasury Department until 1852, when the Lighthouse Board assumed control. The U.S. Lighthouse Service replaced the Lighthouse Board in 1910 and was superseded by the U.S. Coast Guard in 1939.

Lightships had official designations such as "LV," "WAL," or "WVL" and were numbered sequentially according to the order of their construction, though when on duty each ship temporarily received the name of the hazardous region it protected. Vessels could be identified by color codes, lights, foghorn and radio signals, and large letters painted on their sides. These ships were built to sustain the severe pounding of the fierce storms and agitated waters of North Carolina's most feared shoals. Although some were sunk by weather and others by collision or Civil War engagements, most of the craft and their crews survived.

Many channels and shoals marked by the lightships gradually moved, and the need for these vessels subsequently diminished. Diamond Shoal and Frying Pan Shoal lightships were replaced by Texas-type light towers, and other areas were marked by buoys or fixed lights. These and other forms of technology eliminated the usefulness of lightships, and by the end of the twentieth century none were operating in North Carolina waters.

**North Carolina Lightship Locations
(with years of operation)**
Brant Island (1831–63)
Cape Lookout Shoal (1905–33)
Diamond Shoal (1824–27 and 1897–1966)
Frying Pan Shoal (1854–1964)
Harbor Island (1836–61 and 1863–67)
Horseshoe Shoal (1851–70)
Long Shoal (1825–61 and 1864–67)
Neuse River (1828–62)
Nine Foot Shoal (1827–59)
Ocracoke Channel (1852–59)
Roanoke Island (1835–61)
Roanoke River (1835–61 and 1863–66)
Royal Shoal (1826–67)
Wades Point Shoal (1826–55)

References: Willard Flint, *Lightships of the United States Government* (1989); Mina Lewiton, *Lighthouses of America* (1964); David Stick, *Graveyard of the Atlantic: Shipwrecks of the North Carolina Coast* (1952); Stick, *North Carolina Lighthouses* (1980).

Dawson V. Carr

Lightwood (pronounced "lite'ood"), also called "rich pine" or "fat pine," is wood that generally comes from the stump, roots, or heart of long-dead pine trees in which rosin has accumulated. It is highly flammable and is used as kindling or as a torch for light. The term seems to have been used in Barbados in the late seventeenth century and in Virginia by 1705. John Lawson's *A New Voyage to Carolina* (1709) refers to its use by Indians. The will of Thomas Boyd of Bath County in 1725 directed that his slaves "be constantly kept at Work on Lightwood." John Boone of Bertie County willed his wife and son-in-law his "Light wood" in 1733. Several owners spoke of their "lightwood land" as if it were regularly productive. In 1774 Scottish visitor Janet Schaw observed that the poorer people of North Carolina burned lightwood while "people of fashion use only Spermaceti [candles]." The production of lightwood was profitable, and small bundles of it have long been available in markets.

"The Light'ood Fire" by John Henry Boner was published on the front page of the *North Carolina Review* on 7 Nov. 1909:

When wintry days are dark and drear
And all the forest ways grow still,
When gray snow-laden clouds appear
Along the bleak horizon hill,
When cattle all are snugly penned
And sheep go huddling close together
When steady streams of smoke ascend
From farm-house chimneys—in such weather
Give me old Carolina's own,
A great log house, a great hearthstone,
A cheering pipe of cob or briar
And a red, leaping light'ood fire.
When dreary days draw to a close
And all the silent land is dark,
When Boreas down the chimney blows
And sparks fly from the crackling bark,
When limbs are bent with snow and sleet
And owls hoot from the hollow tree,
With hounds asleep about your feet,
Give me old Carolina's own,
A hospitable wide hearthstone,
A cheering pipe of cob or briar
And a red, rousing light'ood fire.

William S. Powell

Lily-White Politics was a term popularly used from the 1890s until the 1930s to describe the views of advocates of an all-white Republican Party in the South. Formed in the 1850s as an antislavery organization, the Republican Party had come to power in North Carolina and other southern states after the Civil War with the help of the votes of newly enfranchised former slaves. By the 1890s, however, the party was losing ground to Democrats under the relentless attack of white supremacists. Only North Carolina, which elected a Republican governor and a Fusion legislature dominated by Republicans and Populists in 1896, remained truly competitive, although its presidential vote was consistently Democratic. North Carolinian Jeter C. Pritchard, the region's only Republican U.S. senator, indirectly owed his two elections to black support, since more than half of the state's Republican Party membership was African American. The South's last black legislators served in the North Carolina General Assembly until 1901; the nation's last black congressman of the nineteenth century, George Henry White, served the state's Second District from 1897 to 1901.

As the number of eligible black voters dwindled across the South, lily-white factions in southern states began to battle the traditional "black and tan," or biracial, wing of the Republican Party. After his first election in 1896, Republican president William McKinley unsuccessfully attempted to increase his party's standing in the region by reaching out to white voters during two southern tours. As lily whites became more powerful, national pressure mounted to end the party's dependence on black votes; this was particularly true in North Carolina, which in 1900 was preparing to follow the example of Louisiana, Mississippi, and South Carolina by disfranchising illiterate black voters.

In 1900 Pritchard reversed his previous stand and publicly opposed black officeholders. North Carolina's delegation to the national convention in June contained just two black delegates (George White and Henry Hagans). Voters soon overwhelmingly approved the suffrage amendment to the state constitution, which would take effect in 1902, and Republicans lost every major statewide race in the 1900 elections.

Pritchard now led the lily-white wing of North Carolina Republicans and became an important adviser to President Theodore Roosevelt. Roosevelt dealt pragmatically with both factions, allowing local conditions to dictate the racial makeup of a state's party. After lily whites gained control of the North Carolina Republican Party in 1902, for instance, Pritchard successfully recommended that Roosevelt appoint a white replacement for the town of Wilson's black postmaster, Samuel H. Vick. After Pritchard left the Senate in March 1903, Roosevelt appointed him to the District of Columbia Supreme Court, and later to the Fourth Circuit U.S. Court of Appeals.

In other states, the struggle between lily whites and traditional black and tans continued until the 1930s, by which time almost all black voters had shifted their support to the Democratic Party.

References: Eric Anderson, *Race and Politics in North Carolina, 1872–1901: The Black Second* (1981); Edward L. Ayers, *The Promise of the New South: Life after Reconstruction* (1992); Helen Edmonds, *The Negro and Fusion Politics in North Carolina, 1850–1900* (1954); Richard B. Sherman, *The Republican Party and Black America: From McKinley to Hoover, 1896–1933* (1972).

Benjamin R. Justesen

SEE ALSO Black and Tan Constitution.

Lincoln County, located in North Carolina's Piedmont region, was formed in 1779 from Tryon County, which was subsequently eliminated in an effort to erase the memory of oppressive royal governor William Tryon. Like its seat, Lincolnton (incorporated in 1785), the county takes its name from Revolutionary War general Benjamin Lincoln, who was appointed by George Washington to receive Lord Charles Cornwallis's sword when the British commander surrendered at Yorktown. Other Lincoln County communities include Denver, Triangle, Lowesville, Iron Station, Boger City, Godsonville, Crouse, Reepsville, Vale, and Toluca.

Cherokee and Catawba Indians were the first inhabitants of the area that became Lincoln County. With the westward migration of many North Carolina settlers in the early nineteenth century, the county became one of the most populous and prosperous counties in the state. With ten forges and four furnaces (several of which are still standing), it led the state in the production of iron, and in the early part of the century the Schenk-Warlick Mill, the first textile mill in the South, was established within its borders. Farming was also important in the county, with wheat and dairy products among the most lucrative commodities. During the 1840s, however, Lincoln County was greatly reduced in size to form Cleveland, Catawba, and Gaston Counties; the loss of factories and farmland halted further growth until the establishment of new textile mills and other local businesses during the twentieth century revived the local economy. In the late 1950s and early 1960s, part of Lincoln County's Catawba River was dammed to produce Lake Norman, the largest man-made lake in the state, which provides a steady source of electricity as well as recreational activities. In 2004 Lincoln County's population was estimated to be 68,000.

Reference: David C. Heavner, *Lincoln County, North Carolina, 1779–1979: Past, Present, Future* (1979).

Robert Blair Vocci

Lindley's Mill, Battle of. The Battle of Lindley's Mill on 13 Sept. 1781 was the largest engagement of North Carolina's so-called Tory War, a prolonged civil conflict following Lord Charles Cornwallis's invasion of the state during the American Revolution. After Loyalist David Fanning's surprising victory on 1 September over superior forces at Bettis's Bridge, the Loyalists were encouraged to rally in large numbers. Fanning, a leader of the Loyalist militia, had received approval from Maj. James H. Craig, the British commander at Wilmington, for a raid on the state capital, then located at Hillsborough.

Fanning rendezvoused with troops commanded by Cols. Archibald McDugald of Cumberland County and Hector McNeil of Bladen County; the combined command totaled 1,200 men. The Whigs were led to believe that the Loyalists would attack Gen. John Butler's militia camp on Deep River. Instead,

Fanning's army was able to enter Hillsborough undetected in the foggy dawn of 12 September and, following a brief skirmish, quickly secured the town, capturing over 200 prisoners, including Governor Thomas Burke. While plundering the state capital, Fanning's men opened its liquor stores, but by noon the long, somewhat unruly column left Hillsborough on the Cape Fear road bound for Wilmington.

Receiving news of the disaster at Hillsborough, Butler rode immediately to intercept the Loyalist force where the Wilmington road crossed Cane Creek at the ford at Lindley's Mill in present-day southern Alamance County. On a plateau overlooking Stafford's Branch, Butler and Col. Robert Mebane laid an ambush to stop the Loyalists and possibly recover the prisoners.

On the morning of 13 September, as the unsuspecting vanguard of the straggling Loyalists crossed the branch, a volley tore into their ranks, instantly killing McNeil and pinning down Capt. Archibald McKay's company of Highlanders. After securing the prisoners in the rear at Spring Friends Meetinghouse, Fanning rode forward to organize a flanking attack on the Whig position. Under assault from both front and rear, the Whigs stubbornly held their ground for several hours but were finally driven from the field. When he was seriously wounded in the arm late in the battle, Fanning gave the command to McDugald, who safely reached Wilmington with the prisoners. The killed and wounded, more than 250 men on both sides, were buried and cared for by Quakers in the surrounding community. The hard-fought battle was the bloodiest of the war in North Carolina, with more casualties for the numbers engaged than at the Battle of Guilford Courthouse.

The raid on Hillsborough and the subsequent battle proved to be a turning point. The Loyalists expected the Whigs to succumb to this double blow, but the effect was quite the opposite: incensed by the audacity of the raid and the loss of the battle, the Whigs redoubled their efforts to suppress the Loyalists and win the war.

References: Lindley S. Butler, ed., *The Narrative of Colonel David Fanning* (1981); Algie I. Newlin, *The Battle of Lindley's Mill* (1975).

Lindley S. Butler

Linen, woven from fibers obtained from the flax plant, was an important fabric in many European areas, especially in the northern Irish province of Ulster. Flax and linen products were initially brought to America by immigrants from these and other regions. While pure linen cloth was preferred for home furnishings, linen warp threads had been joined with woolen weft threads since the Middle Ages, resulting in a mixed fabric known as "linsey-woolsey." In the late eighteenth century, linen faced increasing competition from cotton, which was easier to weave, more comfortable to wear, and more profitable for those wishing to sell cloth. Cotton provided another option for spinners, and the term "linsey-woolsey" expanded to include cotton and linen mixtures. Cotton's popularity caused flax production to decline dramatically in the United States in the nineteenth century. North Carolina, the fifth-largest producer of flax in 1850 with 593,796 pounds, dropped to sixth place in 1860 with a crop that had plummeted to 216,490 pounds. By 1880 North Carolina produced only 9,621 pounds of flax. Changing consumer preferences removed linen from its common place in everyday clothing, relegating it to expensive home furnishings brought out for special occasions.

H. Tyler Blethen

Linn Cove Viaduct is a 1,243-foot curved bridge that carries the Blue Ridge Parkway around one of the most environmentally sensitive areas of Grandfather Mountain in Avery County. The viaduct opened to traffic on 11 Sept. 1987, exactly 52 years after construction of the parkway began. Completion of the 469-mile scenic highway was delayed for many years while the National Park Service and Grandfather Mountain, Inc., considered various routes around the eastern slopes of the mountain. The design of the viaduct provided the long-awaited solution to traversing the Linn Cove boulder field, the most problematic area from an environmental standpoint to be crossed by the parkway. Construction of the viaduct redefined expectations for modern bridge-building design by proving that structures could be utilitarian in function and still preserve the environment.

The viaduct was designed by Figg and Mueller Engineers, Inc., of Tallahassee, Fla., and the general contractor on the project, whose cost totaled $10 million, was Jasper Construction, Inc., of Plymouth, Minn. The S-curve roadbed rests on seven vertical piers spaced 180 feet apart and consists of 153 precast concrete segments cemented together with epoxy glue and held in place by tension cables that run through the center of the span. Each of the 100,000-pound segments is a different shape, and only segment No. 93 is square and straight. The road served as the building platform from which workers erected the bridge one segment at a time, moving their equipment out along the span to begin the next section. This method eliminated any need to scar the landscape with access roads or to compact fragile soils with heavy machinery.

The Linn Cove Viaduct has received more than a dozen national design awards, including a Presidential Design Award in 1984 and the American Consulting Engineers Council Award for Engineering Excellence in 1985. Its distinctive S-shape is recognizable in numerous national automobile TV commercials. In response to the public's interest in the viaduct, the National Park Service has built a visitors center

Linn Cove Viaduct on the Blue Ridge Parkway at Grandfather Mountain. Photograph courtesy of North Carolina Division of Tourism, Film, and Sports Development.

nearby with interpretive exhibits as well as a system of trails that winds under and around the bridge.

Reference: "Viaduct Designer Revisits Landmark," *Avery Journal*, 16 Sept. 1993.

Renné Vance

Linville Caverns. SEE Caves and Caverns.

Linville Gorge is among the most spectacular and ecologically important natural areas in North Carolina. Located in Burke and McDowell Counties, the gorge was carved by the Linville River, which arises on the slopes of nearby Grandfather Mountain and runs for 12 miles in a 2,000-foot descent through the Blue Ridge before joining the Catawba River on the piedmont below. The gorge is formed by two parallel ridges, Jonas Ridge on the east and Linville Mountain on the west, which average about 3,400 feet in elevation along their rims. The riverbed is about 1,500 to 2,000 feet below the surrounding ridges, but in a few spots the gorge is almost 2,800 feet deep.

Bold outcroppings, jagged spires, chimney-like formations, and steep cliffs protrude from the dark green mantle of forests that cloak much of the region. Perched high on the gorge rim, Wiseman's View and Table Rock Mountain provide dramatic vistas of the gorge and nearby mountains and piedmont. The dramatically rugged scenery is due to the resistant Precambrian granitic quartzites that were solidified more than a billion years ago from molten rock. Considered to be the deepest chasm in the eastern United States, Linville Gorge's terrain was largely unsuitable for logging, so that extensive tracts of virgin timber have survived.

The gorge was named for William Linville, who, along with his son John, was killed by Indians just above the main waterfall in 1766 during a hunting and exploring expedition. Subsequently, the waterfall and gorge were named in memory of Linville. The region was a popular collecting site for many pioneer botanists such as André Michaux, John Fraser, and Thomas Nuttall. In more recent years, the upper section of the gorge was preserved through the generosity of John D. Rockefeller as the Linville Falls Recreation Area, and 10,975 acres of the gorge were incorporated into the Linville Gorge Wilderness, part of the original national wilderness system established in the 1960s.

A hiker surveys the horizon from the edge of Linville Gorge. Photograph courtesy of North Carolina Division of Tourism, Film, and Sports Development.

References: Kay Scott, "The Land Nobody Wanted," *Wildlife in North Carolina* 52 (1988); Marcus B. Simpson Jr., *Birds of the Blue Ridge Mountains* (1992).

Marcus B. Simpson Jr.

Literacy. SEE Education, Adult; Education, Public.

Literary and Historical Association. The North Carolina Literary and Historical Association was formed on 23 Oct. 1900 for the purposes of the "collection, preservation, production, and dissemination" of North Carolina literature and history and the "encouragement of public and school libraries; the establishment of an historical museum; the inculcation of a literary spirit among our people; the correction of printed misrepresentations concerning North Carolina; and the engendering of an intelligent, healthy State pride in the rising generations." North Carolina Supreme Court Justice Walter Clark was elected president, and the association's membership included the historical, political, and social elite of the state.

Although several historical organizations already existed, none had a statewide focus. Consequently, the new association launched an ambitious program for arousing public sup-

port. In its first year, members wrote and shepherded through the General Assembly an act establishing a North Carolina Day in the public schools and another encouraging the establishment of rural libraries. In its second year, it sponsored at Manteo a celebration of the Roanoke voyages of the 1580s, and in its third year, the association created the North Carolina Historical Commission (later the Department of Archives and History). The period was so vibrant that the Historical Commission's first major publication, *Literary and Historical Activities in North Carolina, 1900–1905* (1907), contained 623 pages.

The North Carolina Historical Commission was so poorly funded that "Lit and Hist," as the association was affectionately called, served as lobbyist and drumbeater for historical and literary interests both in the legislature and among the public. Its annual meetings featured advocates of cultural literacy, including visiting speakers such as Thomas Nelson Page, Edwin Markham, William E. Dodd, Henry Cabot Lodge, Lord James Bryce, and former presidents William Howard Taft and Harry S Truman. From the "mother" association, more specialized organizations gradually emerged, such as the North Carolina Folklore Society (1913) and the North Carolina Federation of Music Clubs (1917). As these younger groups developed, they scheduled their meetings in connection with those of the Historical Association, during a period called "Culture Week."

Beginning in 1905, the association presented the Patterson Award to the North Carolina author of a book—fiction, poetry, or nonfiction—judged to be the best published the previous year. President Theodore Roosevelt presented the first award to John Charles McNeill in the Senate Chamber of the State Capitol, but the award was discontinued after 1922 when space ran out on the original cup. In 1930 the Society of Mayflower Descendants in North Carolina presented the Mayflower Society Cup to the Literary and Historical Association. A small replica of the cup, which is silver with an image of the *Mayflower* standing on a base of Belgian marble, was given annually to the author of an "original nonfiction work of outstanding excellence." The awarding of the Mayflower Cup ceased in 2002 because of the high expense of the program.

Subsequently, affiliated organizations established other literary awards that are presented during the annual meetings of the Literary and Historical Association: the Sir Walter Raleigh Award for fiction by the Historical Book Club of North Carolina, the AAUW Award for juvenile literature by the North Carolina Chapter of the American Association of University Women, the Roanoke-Chowan Award for poetry by the Roanoke-Chowan Writers Group, and the R. D. W. Connor Award for the best article in the *North Carolina Historical Review* and the Hugh T. Lefler Undergraduate Award, both by the Historical Society of North Carolina. The Literary and Historical Association also created the Christopher Crittenden Memorial Award, given first in 1970, for extraordinary contributions to the promotion of North Carolina history, and the R. Hunt Parker Memorial Award, first given in 1987, for significant contributions to the literature of the state.

In the early 2000s the North Carolina Literary and Historical Association continued to serve as the state's central organization dedicated to the promotion of history and literature. Much of North Carolina's progress in both state-supported and private activities can be traced to discussions and recommendations emanating from association meetings and committees. This progress can be seen both in North Carolina's ranking in historical, literary, and cultural activities among other states and in the vibrancy of younger organizations whose founders received their inspiration while participating in the association.

References: William Burlie Brown, "The State Literary and Historical Association: 1900–1950," *NCHR* 28 (April 1951); W. J. Peele, ed., *Literary and Historical Activities in North Carolina, 1900–1905* (1907).

H. G. Jones

SEE ALSO Crittenden Award; Culture Week; Literary Awards.

Literary Awards. A number of literary awards have been established to honor the achievements of North Carolina writers. The first award for such a purpose in the state was probably the Patterson Cup, established in 1905 by J. Lindsay Patterson of Winston-Salem in memory of her husband, William Houston Patterson. The Patterson Cup recognized an eminent North Carolinian whose poetry or prose demonstrated "the greatest excellence and the highest literary skill and genius." If any one author won the award three times, it was stipulated that the ornate cup would become his or hers forever, but the award never found a permanent owner before it was retired in 1922.

The Patterson Cup was replaced by the Mayflower Cup, born of the Society of Mayflower Descendants in the State of North Carolina, a group founded in 1924. Five years later, the North Carolina Literary and Historical Association determined the need for an annual award for the best published literary or historical work by a resident North Carolinian, and, the following year, accepted a cup and small replicas from the Society of Mayflower Descendants. Designed to stimulate interest in North Carolina literature, the award was presented annually to an author who had produced an outstanding work of literature that year.

Past winners of the Mayflower Cup include W. J. Cash, Max Steele, John Ehle, Louis Rubin, Tim McLaurin, and numerous others. In 2002 the North Carolina Society of Mayflower Descendants ceased awarding the Mayflower Cup because of the difficulty of obtaining new cups and the high cost of the program. Since the creation of the Sir Walter Raleigh Award for Fiction in 1952, the Mayflower Cup competition had been limited to works of nonfiction. The Raleigh Award remains the premier award for fiction writing in the state.

Another literary prize still awarded within the state is the R. Hunt Parker Award, which also was conceived by the North Carolina Literary and Historical Association. First awarded in 1987, the prize is named for Robert Hunt Parker (1892–1969), a justice for the North Carolina Supreme Court. Winners include a number of familiar names from the popular canon of North Carolina authors, including Sam Ragan, Elizabeth Spencer, Lee Smith, and James Applewhite.

In North Carolina, where many authors demonstrate a fluid ability to excel in both prose and poetry, several individuals have been awarded prizes for work in different genres. This trend likely will continue for generations to come. The state's premier poetry prize, the Roanoke-Chowan Award, is sponsored by the Roanoke-Chowan Group of Writers and Allied Artists, an association that began as a country gathering at the home of baker Gilbert T. Stephenson in 1948. The award is presented with other state literary awards at the annual meeting of the association. Stephenson, who was to serve as president of the association in 1956, wanted to prove that "material for literature as well as art is to be found in every nook and cranny of our state." Over the decades, winners have included Carl Sandburg, Randall Jarrell, Guy Owen, Reynolds Price, and Fred Chappell.

References: Sturgis E. Leavitt, *A History of The Society of Mayflower Descendants in the State of North Carolina* (1966); Gilbert T. Stephenson and Grace Stephenson, *We Came Home to Warren Place* (1959).

Martha Belle Caldwell
Roy Parker Jr.

SEE ALSO Roanoke-Chowan Group.

Literary Fund was a term used in the nineteenth century to denote a financial account created to establish and maintain a rudimentary educational system. Each of the original colonies had such a fund, with those of Virginia, Massachusetts, New York, and North Carolina being the most notable. Although schools and education were mentioned in the General Assembly occasionally after 1802, it was not until 1815 that a joint committee under the chairmanship of Archibald D. Murphey issued a report on education in the state. In 1825 provision was made for the creation of a fund to support schools and a Literary Board to administer the money. Money in the fund came from stock owned by the state in two banks, navigation companies, the sale of public land (particularly swampland), and direct appropriation. Yet no precise provision was made for the creation of a system of schools.

The Literary Fund was used for purposes other than education, including loans to individuals, current state expenses in anticipation of tax receipts, and the purchase of a library for the state following the burning of the capitol building in 1831. Surplus revenue from the federal treasury in 1836 and 1838 brought additional income to the Literary Fund and a reorganization of the Literary Board.

On 8 Jan. 1839 the General Assembly enacted North Carolina's first public school law. Local funds were to be employed, but money from the Literary Fund was also to be granted each school district. The Literary Fund remained a significant part of the system until after the end of the Civil War, when the Literary Board was dissolved by the legislature effective in May 1868.

Reference: Elmer Lawson, "History of the North Carolina Literary Fund, 1776–1868" (Ph.D. diss., UNC-Chapel Hill, 1956).

Elmer Lawson

Literary Journals. North Carolina writers and scholars support a number of literary publications in the state and have for decades. The *Carolina Quarterly*, one of the oldest and most influential university literary publications in the United States, traces its origins to the *University Magazine*, founded by a committee of senior students at the University of North Carolina at Chapel Hill in 1844. Financial difficulties ended the *University Magazine*'s initial run after only ten issues, but the publication was revived largely under the influence of university president David Lowry Swain in 1852. It came to be filled with short histories, poetry, literary criticism, occasional commencement addresses, and reflections upon social issues of the day. Of particular value are short histories and biographies of North Carolinians and events contributed by UNC professors and other state leaders. Despite Swain's support, the magazine continued to face financial difficulties until 1859, when the university's two student literary societies became financial backers.

Difficulties linked to the Civil War caused the *University Magazine* to fold again in 1861. It was revived in 1882 through the efforts of student leaders. Fifteen years later, the two campus literary societies again began to back the publication. The year 1923 saw it receive direct funding from the student body through the creation of a Publications Union; in 1929, under the new *North Carolina Magazine* moniker, it became a supplement to the student newspaper by campus vote. In 1941 editor Henry Moll refashioned the magazine in the image of that day's popular press with features, interviews, and reviews of a nonliterary bent. The following year it merged with the cam-

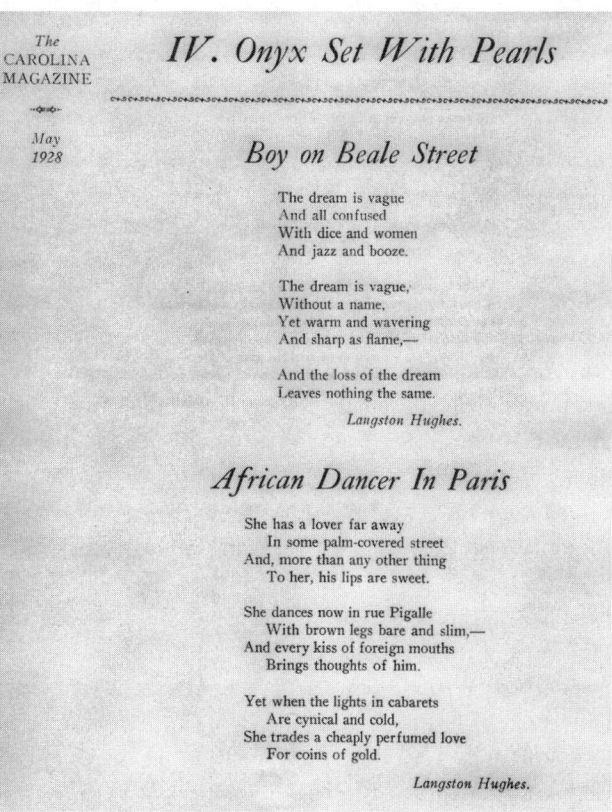

Langston Hughes poems featured in the May 1928 issue of the *Carolina Magazine*, one of the several incarnations of the modern-day *Carolina Quarterly*. NCC.

pus humor magazine, *Tar 'N' Feathers*, causing a clash between the publication's humor and serious literary endeavors. Student pressure for a full-fledged humor publication led to a student referendum on the content of the magazine in 1948, and the *University Magazine* lost to the humor magazine *Tarnation* by four votes.

After the split, however, there was an immediate student outcry, and a petition was started for the creation of a campus literary magazine, the result of which was the founding of the *Carolina Quarterly*. During the early twentieth century, student writers such as Josephus Daniels, Phillips Russell, Jonathan Daniels, Paul Green, Thomas Wolfe, LeGette Blythe, Walker Percy, Joseph Mitchell, Walter Spearman, and Frances Gray Patton had exhibited their work in the pages of the *University Magazine* and the *North Carolina Magazine*. After the establishment of the *Carolina Quarterly*, the tradition of publishing new and emergent writers continued, although contributors were no longer limited to university students or even North Carolinians. The many fine writers and poets who have had their work published in the *Carolina Quarterly* include Richard Ford, Charles Wright, Fred Chappell, Lewis Nordan, Robert Morgan, and Cathy Song. The publication continues to be edited by students of the university.

Now more than a century old, the *South Atlantic Quarterly*, from the time of its first publication in 1902, has sought to inspire, enlighten, and even outrage its readers. The journal was the creation of its first editor, John Spencer Bassett, a Trinity College (now Duke University) history professor who represented a new generation of southern intellectuals. Born and raised in the post–Civil War South, this generation sought to move their native region into a brighter future through education and the free exchange of ideas. Bassett himself trained to become a historian at Johns Hopkins University in the 1880s, which was at that time an enviable position in the most innovative graduate program, a veritable haven for aspiring southern scholars. Bassett came to Trinity College in the mid-1890s, a time when North Carolina's political situation was filled with animosity and division that ran along both racial and social lines.

Following the Wilmington race riot of 1898 and the white supremacy political campaign of 1900, a campaign noted for its inflammatory use of antiblack rhetoric, Bassett was disgusted at the political and social scene in the state. True to his generation's outlook and professional training, Bassett became convinced that North Carolina and the South needed a literary magazine that would both educate its readers and provide intellectuals a means of escape from the tension-filled world of politics. The *South Atlantic Quarterly* was established in Durham to fill that need.

The journal offered a variety of articles on history and social commentary. Its contributors were some of the bright-

est minds of the new generation of southern scholars, including U. B. Phillips, William E. Dodd, Samuel Chiles Mitchell, and Edwin Mims, as well as Bassett himself. The *South Atlantic Quarterly* captured regional and national attention in 1903, when Bassett published the article "Stirring up the Fires of Race Antipathies," in which he criticized the white South for appealing to emotion rather than principle during its ascension back into political power. While that point itself would not have won many friends, Bassett worsened the negative reaction by daring to list Booker T. Washington alongside Robert E. Lee as the two greatest southerners born in the nineteenth century. The reaction was fast and furious, testing the extent of the journal's devotion to free speech and the open exchange of ideas—a test the *South Atlantic Quarterly* passed by virtue of its continued support for its besieged editor.

Successive editors during the mid-1900s maintained the journal's commitment to social commentary and the advocacy of education. The *South Atlantic Quarterly* also continued its explorations into the ever-changing world of literature, poetry, and historical interpretation while persisting in its cautious support of civil rights for African Americans. The journal expanded its interests during these years to include foreign affairs, featuring articles that examined the rise of fascism, Nazism, and communism before these were widely known and feared by the American public. The *South Atlantic Quarterly* continues to provoke, inform, and startle. In the last two decades of the twentieth century, entire issues were devoted to one theme, such as the works of Ezra Pound, the rise of maternalist feminism, and analyses of country music.

Throughout the twentieth century, North Carolina continued to spawn literary journals and critical reviews. Such publications include the *Southern Literary Journal*, founded in 1968 and published by the Department of English at the University of North Carolina at Chapel Hill, and the *North Carolina Literary Review*, founded in 1992 and published jointly by the Department of English at East Carolina University and the North Carolina Literary and Historical Association. The *Appalachian Journal*, founded in 1972, is an interdisciplinary, peer-reviewed quarterly featuring research studies, interviews, scholarly studies in various fields, and a variety of other items, as well as poetry and reviews of books, films, and recordings focusing on the Appalachian region. Started in the mid-1990s, the *Asheville Poetry Review* is a literary journal that publishes poems, interviews, translations, essays, historical perspectives, and book reviews. Many journals also exist in small publication, including various regional reviews and campus literary magazines, representing the entrance to a world of academic or literary publication within the state.

References: Martha Miller Brandis, "History of the University of North Carolina Magazine, 1844–1948" (M.A. thesis, UNC-Chapel Hill, 1964); Bruce Clayton, *The Savage Ideal: Intolerance and*

Students and faculty at Littleton Female College, 1892. NCC.

Intellectual Leadership in the South, 1890–1914 (1972); William Baskerville Hamilton, ed., *Fifty Years of the South Atlantic Quarterly* (1952).

Kevin Cherry
Charles J. Holden
Additional research provided by Philip McFee.

Literary Lantern was a column by Addison Hibbard published in several North Carolina newspapers beginning in 1923. An English professor and dean of the College of Liberal Arts at the University of North Carolina, Hibbard signed his columns "Telfair, Jr." The Literary Lantern was a weekly column "intended to throw light on writing around and about the South." At its peak in the 1920s, it was syndicated in 15 southern newspapers in the Carolinas, Virginia, and Tennessee, with a combined circulation of 450,000. Those early columns, which usually featured an extended review or two, lots of notices and news, and an original poem, were important vehicles for redefining southern literature during the twentieth century. Several poems originally published in it were selected for inclusion in Braithwaite's annual anthologies of periodical verse.

The Literary Lantern's authorship changed often. Hibbard turned it over to Raymond William Adams, although Hibbard continued to write occasional columns at least as late as 1927, when several were also signed by "The Book-keeper."

Over the next two decades, the column was written by Howard Mumford Jones, Elizabeth Lay Green, Paul Green, Phillips Russell, Cara Mae Russell, and Jessie Rehder. The Green-Russell-Rehder years were dominated first by Elizabeth Lay Green, who took over the column from Jones, and Cara Mae Russell, who wrote it almost continuously from 1935 to 1942.

Walter Spearman began writing the column in 1946, continuing to do so until his death in 1987. Ted Malone then wrote it until 1990, when Guy Munger took it over. After more than 75 years of continuous publication, the Literary Lantern ceased to appear in newspapers at the beginning of the twenty-first century.

Alex Albright

Littleton College, a Methodist institution of higher learning in Littleton, opened in 1882. Founded as Central Institute and subsequently renamed Littleton Female College and, finally, Littleton College, the school was housed in several substantial three-story buildings. In 1905 it claimed 22 teachers. Though privately owned, Littleton was regarded as a Methodist college. Accounts of its progress were included in the church's annual *North Carolina Conference Journal*. The college offered courses in chemistry, physics, physiology, and psychology, among other disciplines. More then 200 students were enrolled yearly. In 1907 enrollment stood at 274 students.

Methodist minister and educator James Manly Rhodes

(1850–1941) was, except for a two-year period, Littleton's president throughout its existence. The school operated until 1919 when a fire destroyed its buildings; it was never reopened.

References: Michael Hill, *Guide to North Carolina Highway Historical Markers* (1990); O. Kelly Ingram, *Methodism Alive in North Carolina* (1976); William S. Powell, *Higher Education in North Carolina* (1970).

Grady L. E. Carroll Sr.

Live-at-Home Program, inaugurated in December 1929, had as its goal the complete agricultural self-sufficiency of North Carolina. Sponsored by Governor O. Max Gardner in conjunction with North Carolina State University, the Department of Agriculture, and the Agricultural Extension Service, the program encouraged farmers to lessen their emphasis on commodities and increase the production of food, feedstuffs, and livestock products necessary for year-round family and farm consumption. As rural people became self-sufficient, they would take any surpluses to local towns and cities—selling at "logical markets" rather than growing for export. Gardner argued that North Carolinians wasted money to import agricultural goods that might have been produced at home. Ultimately, he sought "ways of improving farm conditions and rural life in North Carolina" in the wake of impending economic disaster attributed to ever-increasing tobacco and cotton acreage and steadily declining prices.

In December 1929 Gardner invited about 200 editors from newspapers across the state to a Live-at-Home dinner. The dinner proved successful as daily and weekly papers subsequently made a great effort to publish Extension Service material on the Live-at-Home campaign. North Carolina agricultural agencies further promoted the program statewide and locally. Extension Service county agents demonstrated methods of increasing corn yields to feed livestock and organized livestock clubs for breed improvement and community meat sharing. Women extension agents, through Home Demonstration, encouraged farmwives to grow vegetables and fruit and can them for home use.

In a 1932 circular titled "North Carolina's Live-at-Home Program Worth Fifty-five Million Dollars," which reviewed the program's three years of operation, Charles Sheffield, assistant director of the Agricultural Extension Service, pronounced it an overwhelming success. According to the evaluation, farmers working under the Live-at-Home program were closer to satisfying the food needs of the state than in any other year since World War I. But the Extension Service stopped short of claiming total victory; it cautioned farmers not to overlook their "first duty—to make a living, and then grow a combination of cash crops"—should the price of tobacco and cotton gradually return to a respectable level.

References: Jack Temple Kirby, *Rural Worlds Lost: The American South, 1920–1960* (1987); Hugh T. Lefler, *North Carolina History Told by Contemporaries* (1956).

Michael D. Thompson

Livestock is a term generally synonymous with "farm animals"—domesticated animals raised by humans for food, fiber, draft, and pleasure. In America this category of animal includes cattle, sheep, pigs, goats, horses, donkeys, mules, and, by some accounts, poultry (fowl such as chickens, ducks, geese, and turkeys). Historically, domesticated animals were kept on nearly every farm and plantation. Cattle, hogs, oxen, horses, sheep, and poultry in varying numbers and combinations contributed to the subsistence of their owners.

Until after the Civil War, virtually all livestock in North Carolina was so-called native stock that was of no specific pure breed. Breeding to achieve a certain physical characteristic was simply not done. Consequently, much of the livestock had a certain nondescript look. Furthermore, some livestock were often used for dual purposes. The same cow used as a source of milk one year was driven to market the next year as beef. Its male offspring may have been castrated and trained as draft animals. This haphazardness contributed to inferior commodities, but it also produced livestock well adapted to a particular environment and suited for a wide range of purposes.

Many North Carolina farmers, like many other farmers throughout the United States, considered it unnecessary to provide shelter for or supplement the diet of their livestock. Consequently, little attention was paid to the development of meadows for hay; the sowing of oats, buckwheat, and other grain crops for feed; and the construction of barns. Because of this treatment large numbers of livestock perished during the winter. Predators, thieves, and diseases such as tick fever, carried by the cattle tick, accounted for additional losses. The tick fever problem, which killed thousands of cattle each year, was not eradicated until the 1920s.

Despite this seemingly callous attitude toward the welfare of livestock, early accounts of North Carolina claimed that many farmers owned hundreds, even thousands, of cattle, hogs, and sheep. Estate records and inventories, however, suggest that most North Carolinians owned far less livestock, probably between 6 and 16 animals. Accurately counting livestock was tricky. Until the mid-nineteenth century, most livestock roamed free, unenclosed by fences. Farmers built fences to keep livestock out of fields and gardens, not to keep them in pastures. Fencing in or corralling livestock only occurred at "cow pens" in which local cattle were collected, identified, and marked before being driven to market. There is some dispute as to whether these early pens were actually enclosures or merely open spaces where livestock could be collected and watched by herders.

Many early North Carolinians are depicted as self-sufficient yeoman farmers, little interested or able to engage in the larger market economy. In reality, many early North Carolinians purposefully raised livestock for the market. While data are inconsistent and at times suspect, it is apparent that North Carolina exported large numbers of livestock to other colonies (and later, states) as well as abroad. In 1733 North Carolina's governor wrote that some "fifty thousand fatt hoggs are supposed to be driven into Virginia from this Province & almost the whole number of fatted Oxen in Albemarle County with many Horses, Cows and Calves, much barreled Pork is carried into Virginia." Livestock, especially hogs and cattle, was commonly driven to cities outside of North Carolina for market. Charleston, Camden, Savannah, Petersburg, and Norfolk were regional market destinations. Between 1810 and the Civil War, tens of thousands of animals each year were driven from the state's western counties to the South Carolina and Georgia lowcountry. Livestock was also frequently driven as far north as Baltimore and Philadelphia. Although the extent of this trade is unknown it is likely that hundreds of thousands of animals were driven out of state for sale. Livestock drives continued until the 1870s, when access to railroads made them unnecessary.

North Carolina farmers and planters were slow in importing improved or pure livestock breeds into the state. Mules were one exception. These animals were virtually nonexistent in North Carolina in 1800, but by 1860 there were more than 51,000 in the state. Mules remained many farmers' primary source of farm power until after World War II. During the late antebellum period some planters did import breeding stock to begin improving extant livestock populations. Around 1841 the first shorthorn bull was introduced, but it was not until the 1870s that other breeds such as jersey and Guernsey cattle, Berkshire swine, and Shropshire sheep came into the state in any number.

After the Civil War, livestock continued to be an important aspect of agriculture in North Carolina. However, as the state's farmers increasingly turned their attention to the more profitable tobacco and cotton and improved transportation increased access to commercially available food products and textiles, fewer North Carolinians raised sheep and dairy and beef cattle. Hogs, however, continued to flourish across the state, serving as many people's only source of meat.

At the beginning of the twentieth century, interest in improving breed stock was increasing, although few North Carolina farmers had either the money or the desire to acquire purebred animals. To combat this apathy, organizations formed across the South to promote the improvement of livestock breeds. In 1911 the Animal Husbandry Section of the Association of Southern Agricultural Workers was formed, and in 1913 the Southern Cattlemen's Association organized. Breed improvement was slow; it was not until after the Depression that purebred stock began to be common around the state.

For much of the 1900s, North Carolina was known for its tobacco and cotton production. By the end of the century, however, livestock had become North Carolina's primary source of agricultural revenue. In 1964 livestock and poultry accounted for less than 30 percent of total cash receipts of all agricultural commodities. By 1994 that percentage had climbed to almost 53 percent. Much of that change was due to the meteoric rise in hog and poultry production. These two commodities, efficiently raised indoors in factory-like operations, alone accounted for 45 percent of all cash receipts. Most major hog operations are concentrated in a belt of 22 eastern counties. Broiler production is centered in the southern Piedmont, with turkeys in the southeast and chickens in general across the central portion of the state. Although serious attempts were made to promote beef and dairy production in the state during the first half of the twentieth century, they have never been a major aspect of North Carolina agriculture. In 1994 dairy products and cattle each accounted for a mere 3 percent of all agricultural cash receipts.

Livestock farming in the 1990s was in a very different position than it was at the beginning of the century. Nontraditional livestock such as catfish, trout, and emus were introduced to North Carolina and quickly began to contribute to the state's agricultural economy. Other efforts are focused on preserving breeds formerly common in this state and others. The American Livestock Breed Conservancy, centered in Pittsboro, is an international organization attempting to educate the public and agriculturists about the need to preserve livestock biodiversity.

Livestock plays a major role in North Carolina's modern-day agriculture but plays little or no role in most North Carolinian's daily lives: less than 3 percent of all North Carolinians make their living from agriculture, and few of these even have contact with animals. At one time, virtually all North Carolinians had daily contact with livestock on the farm or on the streets of cities. The role of livestock has also changed and has become more focused with time. Most livestock in the early 2000s was raised entirely for human consumption, and horses had become primarily recreational animals.

References: Cornelius O. Cathey, *Agriculture in North Carolina before the Civil War* (1966); Robert S. Curtis, *The History of Livestock in North Carolina* (1956).

Charles LeCount

SEE ALSO Cattle Drives; Hog Farming; Horses; Mules; Poultry.

Livingstone College in Salisbury was founded by the African Methodist Episcopal Zion Church in 1879. Its two previous names were Zion Wesley Institute and Zion Wesley College. The institute was named in 1887 in honor of the great Christian missionary to Africa, philanthropist, and explorer David

Livingstone. Its first president, Charles Joseph Price, was a noted scholar, preacher, and orator who attracted students and funding to the college until his death in 1893. Beginning with a single building and 40 acres of land, the campus has grown to over 300 acres containing more than 18 brick buildings.

Livingstone consists of two schools: an undergraduate College of Arts and Science and Hood Theological Seminary, a graduate school of theology. The college supports high intellectual, cultural, and moral standards based upon sustaining values emanating from the Judeo-Christian ideal. To provide this, the college offers a coordinated program of liberal arts and career-oriented curricula with cocurricular activities through which the student may acquire competencies and skills necessary to function responsibly in society. Livingstone remains under the auspices of the African Methodist Episcopal Zion Church. By the early 2000s it had approximately 867 undergraduates served by 81 faculty members.

References: Irving Boone, "An Appraisal: Livingstone Occupies Unique Position among Institutions of Higher Education," *Church School Herald Journal* 34 (July 1956); William J. Campbell, "Origin and Development of Livingstone College and Hood Theological Seminary of the A.M.E. Zion Church and the Progressive Administration of President William Johnson Trent" (M.A. thesis, Hood Theological Seminary, 1950); Louise Marie Rountree, "Livingstone College," *A Brief Chronological History of Black Salisbury-Rowan* (1976).

Charles W. Wadelington

Llewelyn Conspiracy. Between the destruction of the Tory, or Loyalist, forces at Moore's Creek Bridge on 27 Feb. 1776 and the arrival of the British army of Lord Charles Cornwallis in September 1780, there was only scattered overt Tory resistance to the revolutionary government of North Carolina. One exception during those years was a clandestine plot known as the Llewelyn Conspiracy (also called the "Gourd Patch Affair" or "Tory Plot"), which involved a group of people opposed to the American cause on the grounds that Anglican dominance of North Carolina's affairs would be undermined in a revolution. The conspirators knew that the 1776 state constitution removed the privileges that the Anglican Church had held as the colony's established church. Further, in their distrust of the revolutionaries' intentions, they thought that an alliance with France would result in the imposition of Catholicism and the destruction of Protestant congregations throughout the colonies. The conspirators had also heard about the deistic position of some revolutionary leaders and questioned their intentions regarding Christianity in general.

The central figure in the conspiracy was John Llewelyn, a Martin County planter and justice of the peace. By March 1777 Llewelyn, his son William, and James Rawlins, an Anglican lay reader, had written a "constitution" (now lost) that outlined the aims of their organization and had begun looking for recruits to join their underground group. Most of the plotters planned to aid deserters and draft resisters, secretly obtain and store small amounts of gunpowder and lead, and wait to join the British troops that were sure to reach North Carolina in good time. Llewelyn himself had a more ambitious, and violent, agenda. He planned the assassinations of prominent Whig leaders in the region, including several acquaintances, and wanted to make a raid on Halifax to capture Governor Richard Caswell and the state magazine. To draw American troops away from Halifax, he intended to spark a slave revolt with the aid of a Loyalist slave patroller.

Instead, on 4 June 1777, the slave patroller gave revolutionary leaders important, if incomplete, information about Llewelyn's plans that seems to have provided their first knowledge of the conspiracy. Two weeks later another conspirator, William May Jr., came forth with more information, naming William Tyler, who was arrested the next day carrying papers regarding the more violent plans. That night at the gourd patch, Llewelyn's group laid plans to free May and Tyler from jail using powder they had obtained from Daniel Southerland, a Loyalist merchant in Tarboro.

In July about 30 conspirators were caught and disarmed while attempting to attack Tarboro and release May from jail. This failure was the high-water mark of the conspiracy. Most of the other known conspirators were arrested or gave themselves up. In all, about 90 people were implicated in the plot, most of whom were from Martin, Tyrrell, Hyde, Edgecombe, or Bertie Counties.

In the trials at Edenton, the revolutionary government was lenient with the conspirators. Most of them made depositions to the court, agreed to take the state loyalty oath and submit to militia service, and were never charged with a crime. Charges were dropped against most of the 18 who were tried. But Llewelyn was convicted of treason in September 1777 and sentenced to be hanged. Numerous requests for clemency came from friends, relatives, and even the presiding judge in his trial. Governor Caswell later pardoned him, and Llewelyn lived peacefully until his death in 1794.

References: Jeffrey J. Crow, "Tory Plots and Anglican Loyalty: The Llewelyn Conspiracy of 1777," *NCHR* 55 (January 1978); Carole Watterson Troxler, *The Loyalist Experience in North Carolina* (1976).

Carole Watterson Troxler
David A. Norris

Local Government Commission was created by the General Assembly in 1931 after the funds invested in banks by many local governments had been lost in the stock market crash of 1929. Previously, North Carolina counties, cities, and other local taxing units had been given broad authority to bor-

Logging operation in western North Carolina (date unknown). Horses were used to move logs to a staging area where they were picked up by a tractor on rails. NCC.

row money and issue bonds. There were no limitations on the amount of bond indebtedness for which local governmental units could be obligated or on how these public funds could be invested. As a result, in many instances small, local, and often poorly managed banks were the depositories of choice for counties and cities, and often they were among the first to fail. As for bonds, in some cases county bonds, sold in the 1920s, were finally paid off in the 1930s at the rate of ten cents on the dollar.

The specific responsibility given the Local Government Commission was to approve, sell, and deliver all North Carolina bonds and notes. It was designated as the agency whose approval was required for certain types of financial agreements involving local governments, while at the same time it was to help counties, cities, and other local taxing units set up and maintain their financial and accounting systems. The commission was even called on to provide educational programs on finance and cash management for local officials. Adding extra clout in fulfilling these assignments was the commission's high-level membership. It consisted of nine members: four state officials serving ex officio, including the state treasurer, state auditor, secretary of state, and secretary of revenue; three members appointed by the governor, one of

whom was required to be, or to have been, the mayor or member of the governing body of a city and the other a member of a county board of commissioners); and two members selected by the lieutenant governor and the Speaker of the North Carolina House. With these important officials and the state treasurer, who served as chairman, the authority of the commission was established from the outset.

As an early result of the legislative decision to provide the new agency with the supervisory powers needed to correct the costly mistakes of the 1920s, the Local Government Commission soon became, and remains, a bulwark of North Carolina government. One important consequence is that the state and many of its counties and cities consistently maintain credit ratings well above the average for other states.

David Stick

Logging. For more than four centuries, North Carolinians have benefited from the commercial use of the state's timber resources. As early as the seventeenth century, the Carolina colony's rich forests gave rise to a lucrative naval stores industry that found ready markets as far away as England and the West Indies. Despite profits derived from pitch, tar, and other naval stores, logging soon became the most profitable use of North Carolina's forests.

Commercial logging operations and sawmills sprang up during the late seventeenth century. These were mostly local concerns serving construction demands in fairly small localities. By the early eighteenth century, improvements in transportation made sawed lumber an important export. Ships sailing from New England arrived bearing rum, cloth, and other goods and filled their hulls with North Carolina lumber for the return trip. Eventually, North Carolina timber found its way to European and Caribbean markets.

Logging supported westward development throughout the antebellum period. Rich timber resources in the Mountain and Piedmont regions made logging and sawmilling a lucrative, though largely localized, business. As railroad lines progressed westward in the years before the Civil War, the market for timber increased. The completion of the Western North Carolina Railroad after the war gave unprecedented access to rich mountain timberland. This opened new markets to North Carolina timber, increasing the potential for profits. At the same time, northern capitalists financed the acquisition of vast tracts of timberland and numerous commercial sawmills, making logging one of the state's most important New South industries. The development of large-scale commercial logging fueled the development of North Carolina's furniture industry, providing a ready supply of quality hardwood for factories in High Point, Hickory, and elsewhere. After 1900, logging also provided raw materials for the state's emerging pulp paper industry.

Although the pay was often good, logging was extremely dangerous work. Harvesting trees, particularly on steep mountainsides, required focus, skill, and experience. Sawmill operators often carried the results of a moment's inattention around in the form of lost eyes or amputated limbs. Log flumes, wooden troughs filled with running water, were used to transport logs in steep, mountainous terrain. Flumes were usually used by lumbermen only when other modes of transport were found to be impracticable. Most flumes were built by nailing two boards together at a 90-degree angle, producing a trough that was V-shaped. In North Carolina, flumes are known to have been in operation near Robbinsville, Sylva, and Wilkesboro. The most extensive log flume constructed in North Carolina was built in Wilkes County by the Giant Lumber Company ca. 1907. The flume stretched for 19 miles from the company's extensive timber holdings along the Blue Ridge to the railroad at North Wilkesboro. The structure was destroyed during a flood in 1916 and never rebuilt.

Like other extractive industries, logging often came to define a rural community. Logging companies would build a town adjacent to the sawmill, complete with a school, a general store, and worker housing. Despite its dangers, logging often represented the best-paying occupation for uneducated workers in rural areas, and there were seldom labor shortages.

By the 1890s the expansion of logging threatened the future of North Carolina's forests. George Vanderbilt, owner of the lavish Biltmore Estate near Asheville, decided to take action. In 1895 Vanderbilt brought German forester Carl Schenck to Biltmore to form the first forestry school in the United States, allowing Schenck to use Biltmore's extensive forests as a laboratory for the latest techniques in scientific forest management. By the 1920s, the state and federal governments began acquiring land for forest management. Loggers and the industries they supported often opposed these state and national forests on the grounds that limits on timber harvesting stymied North Carolina's industrial potential. Proponents of forest management countered that such methods were the only way to guarantee a supply of timber for future uses. More efficient methods of harvesting made this issue more divisive. Logging companies, often because of regulatory oversight, eventually adopted more environmentally sound practices, but the controversies surrounding logging continued. Despite such divisions, logging has had a tremendous influence in North Carolina's social and economic history.

References: Edward L. Ayers, *Promise of the New South: Life after Reconstruction* (1992); Ronald D. Eller, *Miners, Millhands, and Mountaineers: Industrialization of the Appalachian South, 1965–1920* (1979).

Richard D. Starnes
Additional research provided by John Hairr.

Longleaf Pine. SEE Forests; Pine Trees.

Long Street Presbyterian Church, originally known as McKay's Meeting House, was established in 1756 on land that is now part of the Fort Bragg military reservation to serve a community of Scottish settlers. In 1758 the Reverend James Campbell, a Scotsman, established three "preaching stations": Long Street, Bluff, and Barbecue Churches. These are among the oldest Presbyterian churches in North Carolina. The third building to house the Long Street congregation, a Greek Revival derivation, was constructed in 1847 and still stands on the military reservation amid firing ranges and training fields not generally accessible to the public. Elise Academy, a boarding school, was once located near the church. In 1921 the federal government purchased the church building and six acres surrounding it for addition to the Fort Bragg; it now maintains the building, the cemetery, and the grounds.

Many gravestones in the cemetery bear the inscription "Born in Scotland," and a large monument commemorates the burial at the site of a number of Civil War dead, including 30 Confederate casualties from a nearby battle. On the last Sunday in June each year, descendants of former members of Long Street congregation gather at the church for a worship service, a picnic lunch, and a program to recount their Scottish Highlands heritage.

References: William C. Field, *A Guide to Historic Sites in Fayetteville and Cumberland County, North Carolina* (1993); R. A. McLeod, *Long Street Presbyterian Church* (1923); John A. Oates, *The Story of Fayetteville and the Upper Cape Fear* (1972).

Mary Keene Remsburg

Loray Mill Strike. SEE Gastonia Strike.

Lord's Acre Plan, calling for farmers to devote some portion of their crops or livestock to God, was set forth by the Religious Affairs Division of the Farmer's Federation in 1930. James McClure, who headed the Farmer's Federation, developed the plan for the federation, which was based in the mountain counties of North Carolina. The Lord's Acre Plan had a twofold purpose. First, profits of these crops were to be given to the church, either in place of or as a supplement to a personal tithe. This plan aided farmers by allowing them to pay their tithe during the Great Depression, a time when currency was scarce, and provided struggling churches with the necessary funds to meet their budgets and stay in operation in addition to making improvements to church structures. The Farmer's Federation also saw this as an opportunity for farmers to put to better use the new farming techniques that had been provided by the federation.

The Lord's Acre Plan proved to be a great success, quickly spreading across North Carolina and throughout the United States. Countries all over the world had adopted the Lord's Acre Plan by 1950, and its use continued for several years thereafter, until economic conditions made it obsolete.

Reference: John Curtis Ager, *We Plow God's Fields: The Life of James G. K. McClure* (1991).

Marc Sanders

Lords Proprietors were the eight Englishmen to whom King Charles II granted, by the Carolina charters of 1663 and 1665, the joint ownership of a tract of land in the New World called "Carolina." All of these men either had remained loyal to the Crown or had aided Charles's restoration to the English throne. Two of them—William Berkeley, former governor of Virginia, and John Colleton, a West Indies planter—actually had some personal knowledge of the New World. The other six Proprietors were Edward Hyde, earl of Clarendon; George Monck, duke of Albemarle; William, Earl Craven; John, Lord Berkeley; Anthony Ashley Cooper; and Sir George Carteret.

Although the king retained full sovereignty over Carolina, he granted the Lords Proprietors extensive powers, mainly to establish civil structures, to collect taxes and duties, and to maintain order, as well as to have certain game and min-

eral ownership. Through a combination of problems—mostly their tentative and inefficient governance of the huge area—the Proprietors failed to attract and keep settlers and to avail those that came a secure and orderly life. Moreover, the Proprietorship endured disruption through troubles with the Tuscarora Indians and pirates along the coast. By January 1712 the vast tract was separated into northern and southern parts in hopes of improving civic conditions. With their venture so lacking in success, the Proprietors were feeling pressure from the Crown to return the land. In 1719 South Carolina was set apart as a royal colony, and in 1729 George II made cash payments to all but one of the Proprietors that ended their or their heirs' roles as grantees of the former Carolina. Only the heir of George Carteret, John Lord Carteret (later second Earl Granville), refused to sell his one-eighth share and was eventually granted a large tract known as the Granville District.

Many North Carolina districts, counties, settlements, bodies of water, and landforms once bore the names of the original Lords Proprietors, and several still do. Included in these are Hyde County and two small communities named Clarendon; Albemarle Sound and Albemarle Beach (Washington County); two townships and the city of Albemarle in Stanly County; Craven and Carteret Counties; and Dare County's Colington (a version of Colleton) Island, with its small community of Colington and the nearby Colington Creek.

Reference: William S. Powell, *North Carolina through Four Centuries* (1989).

Whitmel M. Joyner

Lost Cause. Immediately following the Civil War, many southerners began paying nostalgic tribute in print and in public to the Old South and the Confederacy, which became popularly known as the "Lost Cause." Through magazines and monuments, reference to the Lost Cause eased the sting of defeat, providing a source of pride through its tales of Confederate military bravery. The Lost Cause, however, also served as a vehicle for easing the South forward into a new, unknown era. Leaders of the New South paid tribute to the Lost Cause to assure their reluctant fellow southerners that the region could accommodate change within "traditional" southern values. In both uses of the Lost Cause, whether easing the hurt or escorting the present into an uncertain future, North Carolinians played prominent roles.

In 1866 former Confederate general Daniel H. Hill began publishing a journal, the *Land We Love*, from Charlotte. In its initial editions, the *Land We Love* tread difficult waters, honoring the Old South yet offering a critique of its shortcomings. But the publication became more defiant as Reconstruction-era policies disenchanted an increasing number of white southerners. Another publication, *Our Living and Our Dead*, appeared out of New Bern and then Raleigh between 1873 and

1876. It fit the more commonly understood role of a Lost Cause magazine by focusing on military matters to prove that the North did not so much win the war as the South ran out of men and matériel. The magazine also accused northern authors of partisanship and urged southerners to read only southern authors and teach only the southern view of the prewar crisis and the war itself.

The Lost Cause can still be seen in the hundreds of statues commemorating Confederate soldiers on the town squares and college campuses of North Carolina. Often funded by groups such as the Sons of Confederate Veterans and the United Daughters of the Confederacy, most of these statues were erected in the late 1800s and early 1900s. Appearing during a bleak period in the state's race relations, the statues were both celebrations of the reestablishment of white supremacy and tributes to Confederate heroes whose living representatives were steadily dwindling. These monuments continue to spark discussion and, at times, controversy among North Carolinians. Those disturbed by their presence view them as highly objectionable symbols honoring slavery and racial discrimination, whereas the monuments' defenders prefer to see in the often nameless image of the common soldier themes of bravery and a willingness to defend one's home from invasion. The Lost Cause continues to generate strong passions arising from North Carolina's complex heritage of bravery and slavery, defeat and emancipation. As the war itself was a hotly contested struggle, so too remains its memory and its meaning.

References: Catherine W. Bishir, "Landmarks of Power: Building a Southern Past, 1885–1915," *Southern Cultures* (1993); Gaines Foster, *Ghosts of the Confederacy: Defeat, the Lost Cause, and the Emergence of the New South, 1865 to 1913* (1987); Charles Reagan Wilson, *Baptized in Blood: The Religion of the Lost Cause, 1865–1920* (1980).

Charles J. Holden

Lost Colony is the popular name given to the English colony of approximately 150 men, women, and boys that settled on Roanoke Island in July 1587 under the leadership of artist John White. The colony was one of Sir Walter Raleigh's efforts to establish an English settlement on the coast of the New World in what is now North Carolina. Like previous voyagers, White and his crew sailed through the West Indies, but they did not trade there. Although they had expected to settle on the Chesapeake, their pilot, Simon Fernándes, refused to transport them after they stopped to look for a handful of men presumably left on Roanoke Island by Sir Richard Grenville the previous year. These new colonists found no sign of Grenville's men. Reluctantly, White ordered the settlers to establish themselves in the abandoned town. There, on 13 Aug. 1587, Manteo, a friendly Croatoan Indian, was baptized and made Lord of Roanoke and Dasamunkepeuc by order of Raleigh. On 18 August Virginia Dare was born to White's daughter Eleanor

Roanoke colonists leave Fort Raleigh at the climax of Paul Green's dramatic recreation of their story in *The Lost Colony*. Photograph by Aycock Brown. NCC.

and her husband, colony leader Ananias Dare, becoming the first English child born in the New World. A few days after his granddaughter's christening, White sailed back to England to hasten and encourage efforts to resupply and reinforce the colony. His departure marked the last known contact between the English and their colony in America.

The Spanish Armada of 1588 disrupted efforts to send voyages to Virginia. White was able to get away to sea that year in two small vessels with 15 new settlers, but these ships were beset by calamities common in this age of privateering and returned home. On 7 Mar. 1589 Raleigh reached an agreement with White and numerous merchants of London to put the colonizing effort on firmer financial ground in exchange for Raleigh's grant of certain trading rights to the investors.

In 1590 White was finally able to secure passage back to Roanoke Island aboard another privateer. He reached the Virginia coast in mid-August. On 18 August, the third birthday of his granddaughter, colonist Virginia Dare, White once again landed on Roanoke and began a search for the colonists he had planted there. He soon discovered that the colony was deserted and the houses of their settlement had been dismantled. His primary clue to the potential whereabouts was the word "CROATOAN" cut into a tree or post of a palisade built sometime after his departure in 1587. White took this as a sign that the colonists had abandoned the Roanoke Island settlement without immediate distress. He also found ruined articles from chests he had left with the colonists, which they had buried and the Indians had excavated. Stormy seas and lack of cooperation on the part of the sailing masters prohibited White from any further search for the colony in 1590.

Raleigh claimed to have sent other expeditions to regain contact with the colonists, but none was successful. The eventual fate of the Lost Colony has both fascinated and puzzled even casual students of early American history for centuries. English explorers and settlers at Jamestown in present-day Virginia searched for the colonists in the early seventeenth century but found none of them, coming eventually to believe that most, if not all, of the Roanoke settlers had died at the hands of belligerent Indians. Since then, others have speculated that the colonists may have intermixed with the Indians of the North Carolina Coastal Plain, one theory advancing the idea that they are among the ancestors of the modern Lumbee Indians. Other theories suggest natural disaster as the reason for the colony's disappearance. Despite the abundance of speculation, imagination, and even outright fabrication on the part of various theorists, the fate of the Lost Colony remains as much a mystery today as it was in the sixteenth century.

References: David B. Quinn, *Set Fair for Roanoke: Voyages and Colonies, 1584–1606* (1985); Thomas Schouweiler, *The Lost Colony of Roanoke: Opposing Viewpoints* (1991); David Stick, *Roanoke Island: The Beginnings of English America* (1983).

Phillip W. Evans

SEE ALSO CROATOAN; Fort Raleigh National Historic Site.

Lost Colony Symphonic Drama. SEE Outdoor Dramas.

Lost Provinces was a term applied to the region of North Carolina consisting of the counties of Currituck, Camden, Pasquotank, Perquimans, Chowan, and Gates. Because of their location north of the Albemarle Sound and the presence of rivers and swamps, they were isolated and difficult to reach except through Virginia.

William S. Powell

Lotteries enjoyed widespread favor in colonial America and the early United States, including North Carolina. Before they were sanctioned by public authority, lotteries prevailed in the form of private raffles, also a popular mode of raising money in England. North Carolinians raffled horses, shoe buckles, and land, but the practice in all of the colonies eventually met opposition by the English authorities, who felt that such activities ought to be approved by the government to prevent fraud. The North Carolina Assembly authorized only two lotteries before the Revolution.

Once freed from the dominion of Great Britain, the new states and the national government frequently resorted to lotteries, including the Continental Congress to obtain money to prosecute the Revolution. Although in 1780 North Carolina banned private lotteries except for those intended to support schools, many individuals continued the practice on their own initiative. The General Assembly authorized at least three lotteries during the 1780s. The advent of the new nation in 1789 witnessed a heightened appreciation of lotteries throughout the United States.

Lotteries were used to fund educational institutions, internal improvements, religious bodies, fraternal societies, private projects, and enterprises of local and county government. The average sum of money that North Carolina lotteries intended to raise was $5,555, though an obvious trend after 1814 pointed to fewer but more remunerative drawings. However, with so many lotteries both in and beyond the state pursuing so little available cash, drawings were often delayed or never held.

The popularity of lotteries in North Carolina began to wane after 1815. Some opposition was in reaction to the frauds that seemed to inhere in lotteries, reflecting a similar aversion nationwide. Reinforcing that sentiment was an antipathy to gambling and its ill consequences, spurred in part by the evangelicals of the revival movement in the early nineteenth century. The antilottery forces gradually gained ascendance. In 1827–28 the General Assembly forbade the sale in North Carolina of lottery tickets authorized by another state. And effective 1 Apr. 1835, the legislature banned all lotteries, public and private, in the state.

In 2000 the election of Michael Easley as governor set off another lottery controversy. The first governor to endorse a lottery in recent history, Easley had made a state lottery one of the pillars of his campaign; once in office, he hoped to have one in place by 2002. The slowing economy had diminished the state's finances, and Easley wanted a lottery to fund improvements in education, such as reducing class sizes in public schools and instituting a prekindergarten program for at-risk children. A bill introduced in the General Assembly calling for a binding referendum of the voters generated a fierce debate over whether a lottery was in the best interest of the state; the bill was defeated in the referendum in September 2002. Supporters of the referendum, including the North Carolina Association of Educators, anticipated the extra education funding; they pointed out that the money North Carolinians spent on games in neighboring Virginia and Georgia could then be kept in the state. The bill's major opponent was a coalition of liberals and conservatives called Citizens United against the Lottery. Among other concerns, the group contended that the lottery would prey on the poor with promises of quick wealth, erode the work ethic, and wrongly put government in the gambling business. Despite these arguments, a state lottery was established by the North Carolina legislature in August 2005, ending years of speculation and controversy if not political debate.

References: John Samuel Ezell, *Fortune's Merry Wheel: The Lottery in America* (1960); Jennifer Strom, "Lining 'Em Up: The Forces Holding Off a Lottery," *Independent Weekly* (July 24, 2002); Alan D. Watson, "The Lottery in Early North Carolina," NCHR 69 (October 1992).

Alan D. Watson

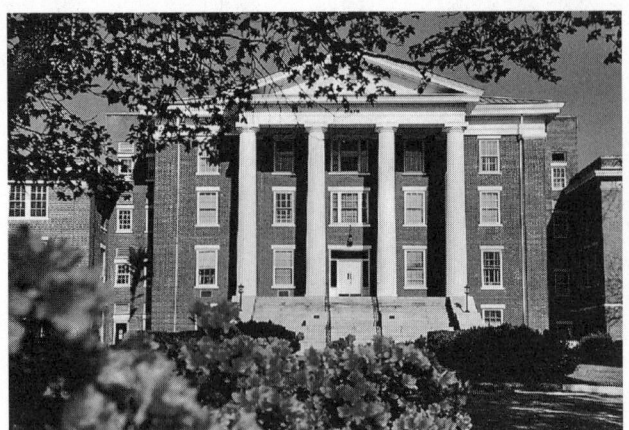

Main Building, Louisburg College.
Photograph courtesy Publications and Media Relations, Louisburg College.

Louisburg College in Louisburg is recognized as the oldest chartered two-year, church-related coeducational college in the United States. The institution evolved from three earlier institutions. The Franklin Male Academy, which opened to students in 1805, was located on the east side of the Louisburg town commons, now part of the east side of the present college campus. In 1814 Louisburg Female Academy was chartered and was located on the west side of the town commons. By the 1850s, the school was a highly respected female seminary under the direction of Asher H. Ray and his wife, Jane Curtis Ray. The success and reputation of the Rays' seminary resulted in a movement to establish a female college in Louisburg. In January 1855, the state legislature authorized the transfer of property by the trustees of Louisburg Female Academy to the directors of Louisburg Female College Company. A four-story, 50-room brick Greek Revival building was constructed in 1857 to serve as the student dormitory, faculty living quarters, classrooms, library, dining hall, and administrative offices. Located on the west side of the current campus, "Old Main" is still in use as the administrative building of Louisburg College.

During the 1870s and 1880s, the college opened and closed a number of times. A period of relative stability and growth was experienced during the presidencies of Matthew S. Davis (1896–1906) and his daughter Mary Davis Allen (1906–17). At the beginning of the twentieth century, the institution became known as Louisburg College and became officially linked to the Methodist Church. Although Louisburg College offered a four-year course and awarded A.B. degrees, after affiliation with the Methodist Church the college was reorganized into an institution with a junior college rating (1914–15).

Louisburg College became coeducational in 1931, and in 1952 it received accreditation from the Southern Association of Colleges and Secondary Schools. In 1956, when the North Carolina Conference of the Methodist Church decided to au-

thorize establishment of two new senior colleges, an active campaign by college alumni and Franklin County citizens influenced the decision of the conference to maintain Louisburg College as an accredited junior college. Louisburg College has the distinction of being the only institution in North Carolina still functioning as a private two-year college. It has extensive transfer agreements with many public and private universities, including the 16-campus University of North Carolina System, allowing qualified students to enter the four-year institutions as juniors.

Reference: George-Anne Willard, *Louisburg College Echoes: Voices from the Formative Years, 1787–1917, with a Summary of the Expansion Years, 1917–1987* (1988).

George-Anne Willard

Louisburg Female Academy, located on the west side of what was then the center of Louisburg, was chartered by the North Carolina General Assembly on 27 Dec. 1814 and opened with 23 students on 23 Aug. 1815. The first principal of Louisburg Female Academy was Harriet Partridge Bobbitt, who served from 1815 to 1820 and again from 1832 to 1842. A newspaper notice of the school's opening indicated tuition as follows: "for spelling, reading, writing and plain needle work, $4 per quarter; English grammar, Arithmetic and Geography, $5 per quarter; Painting, drawing and embroidery, $6 per quarter."

Asher H. Ray and his wife, Jane Curtis Ray, took charge of the academy in 1843, and from 1851 to 1857 they advertised the institution as Louisburg Female Seminary. The four-year regular course at the seminary consisted of English grammar, arithmetic, geography, history, physiology, chemistry, moral philosophy, geometry, logic, "Elements Criticism," "Geography of Heavens," geology, mental philosophy, and "Evidences of Christianity." Students paid extra for classes in piano, guitar, drawing, painting, French, Latin, and Greek. For $40 per session, they could room in the Rays' spacious home adjacent to the academy.

The female seminary prospered, and steps were taken between 1855 and 1857 to transform it into Louisburg Female College. Although Asher Ray owned stock in the Louisburg Female College Company, he died prior to its opening in the fall of 1857. Moved to a location south of the new college building, the old female academy building survived until 1927, when it was destroyed by fire. The Ray home, known as the "Person Place," is a preservation project located on the Louisburg College campus.

Reference: George-Anne Willard, *Louisburg College Echoes: Voices from the Formative Years, 1787–1917, with a Summary of the Expansion Years, 1917–1987* (1988).

George-Anne Willard

Louisburg Male Academy, known as Franklin Male Academy until the late 1820s, was chartered by the North Carolina General Assembly on 6 Jan. 1787 and rechartered on 18 Dec. 1802. Located on the east side of the original town commons of Louisburg, the academy opened to students on 1 Jan. 1805 as the first school in Franklin County.

The first advertisement for the academy indicated that students would be taught subjects that included writing, arithmetic, English grammar, geography, Latin, Greek, Hebrew, French, and philosophy. The first principal (1805–8) was Connecticut native and Yale graduate Matthew Dickinson. The principals with the longest tenures included Franklin County natives and University of North Carolina graduates John B. Bobbitt (1816–20, 1832–44) and Matthew S. Davis (1856–80). Over the years, the academy prepared numerous students for admission to the University of North Carolina in Chapel Hill; in its most successful years, enrollment probably did not exceed 100 students. In 1905 the academy property was conveyed to the Louisburg graded school and in 1961 was acquired by Louisburg College. Somewhat to the northeast of its original location, the old academy building remains on Louisburg's campus.

Reference: George-Anne Willard, *Louisburg College Echoes: Voices from the Formative Years, 1787–1917, with a Summary of the Expansion Years, 1917–1987* (1988).

George-Anne Willard

Louise Wells Cameron Art Museum opened in 1962 in St. John's Masonic Lodge at 114 Orange Street in Wilmington as the St. John's Museum of Art. The building had been designed to house St. John's Lodge No. 1 of Ancient York Masons and the Grand and Royal Chapter of Jerusalem, commonly called the Royal Arch. Between 1825 and 1943 the building —Georgian style with Federal modifications—was the private residence of Thomas W. Brown and his heirs. The most striking interior decoration was an allegorical overmantel of Masonic emblems. The restoration of this mural was carried out by Claude Howell, a local artist and one of the founders of the museum. By the 1990s, the St. John's Museum complex actually included St. John's Lodge (1804), the oldest lodge in North Carolina, which housed a permanent collection including 13 Mary Cassatt prints and a shop selling the works of 80 North Carolina artists; the Burch-Cowan House Studio (1830), formerly one of the state's oldest public schools, which featured educational programs and art classes; and St. Nicholas Greek Orthodox Church (1943), named the Samuel H. Hughes Gallery, which housed changing exhibitions.

A drive for a new facility began in September 1997, when the Bruce B. Cameron Foundation, Inc., gave St. John's Museum of Art a $4 million grant—the largest grant given to a cultural organization in Wilmington's history—toward a project expected to cost about $11 million. The children of Bruce Cameron and the late Louise Wells Cameron at the same time donated land valued at more than $2 million to the museum in memory of their mother, whose name the museum now bears. Charles Gwathmey, of Gwathmey Siegel & Associates Architects in New York and a Charlotte native, was chosen as architect for the project. Gwathmey is perhaps most noted for his renovation and addition to the Solomon R. Guggenheim Museum in New York, as well as three projects in North Carolina: the Thomas I. Storrs College of Architecture at UNC-Charlotte, the Center for Jewish Life at Duke University, and the IBM Office Building and Distribution Center in Greensboro.

The Louise Wells Cameron Art Museum—which opened in new quarters at the intersection of Independence Boulevard and 17th Street in April 2002, two years after groundbreaking —is dedicated primarily to collecting, preserving, and exhibiting the art of North Carolina. The museum contains more than 700 works, representing a unique collection of work by the state's artists, from visionary painter Minnie Evans to Howell. The 42,000-square-foot, state-of-the-art facility features a permanent collection of North Carolina and American art from the eighteenth century to the present, color prints by Mary Cassatt, and a sculpture garden. The museum offers temporary exhibitions, educational and outreach programs, and invitational exhibitions for the Cape Fear region's artists. Its 9.6-acre campus also features recently restored Confederate defensive mounds built by Clingman's Brigade during the Battle of Forks Road, which preceded the fall of Wilmington in the last days of the Civil War.

References: Victoria Cherrie, "New Museum to Be Named for Louise Wells Cameron," *Wilmington-Star News*, 11 May 1999; Linda C. Grattifiori, "St. John's Museum of Art," *Our State* (January 1999); Tony P. Wrenn, *Wilmington, North Carolina: An Architectural and Historical Portrait* (1984).

W. Lee Johnston Jr.

Louis Orr Etchings were 51 etchings by world-class artist Louis Orr, portraying public school buildings, churches, private residences, and scenic views around North Carolina selected for their historic, architectural, or geological significance. A native of Hartford, Conn., Orr lived and worked for most of his life in Paris, where he gained a reputation as one of the foremost etchers of his time. Attorney and businessman Robert Lee Humber, who hailed from Greenville, lived in Paris during the 1920s and 1930s. In 1927 Humber and Orr met and developed a close friendship.

During the 1930s, Humber proposed that Orr execute a series of etchings reflecting some of the finest examples of North Carolina's architecture and historical sites. Humber hoped to preserve North Carolina's heritage through the work of a recognized master of the art and to provide affordable, original artwork to schools, colleges, public libraries, and institutions as well as individuals throughout the state.

Meeting in New York City in 1939, Orr and Humber agreed that Orr would produce 50 etchings of a uniform size, plus a larger one of the State Capitol. Humber would underwrite the cost of the project. They refined the final list of subjects in consultation with North Carolina historians and other authorities on the state's history, including C. Christopher Crittenden, R. D. W. Connor, and Archibald Henderson.

Orr began the series in 1939 and completed it in 1952. He made several tours of the state to sketch his subjects, returning to his Hartford studio to execute the copper plates. In 1953 Orr returned to Paris, where he continued to work until his death in 1966.

Reference: Robert Lee Humber, "History of the Etchings on North Carolina by Louis Orr," *North Carolina Libraries* 23 (Summer–Fall 1975).

John L. Humber

Love Feasts, or "agape meals," are simple communal meals and services that are intended to promote fellowship, brotherhood, unity, and Christian love among participants. Love feasts originated in the first century among early Christians and are similar to the more widely known Lord's Supper, or Eucharist. The ceremony utilizes the love feast as a memorial of the death of Christ and may include foot washing—one church member washing the feet of another, as a sign of Jesus's humility and servitude—singing, and informal speaking or preaching.

The love feast as a service did not achieve prominence until the late 1600s, when it was adopted by German and Czech Pietists. Through them it spread to Mennonites, the Church of the Brethren, and Moravians, who continue to make it part of their worship. Other denominations, including Roman Catholics, Pentecostals, Seventh Day Adventists, and some Southern Baptists, have a form of love feast in their rites, with a heavy emphasis upon foot washing.

References: D. F. Burnbaugh, *The Church of the Brethren, Yesterday and Today* (1971); J. Gordon Melton, *Encyclopedia of American Religions* (4th ed., 1993); J. Taylor and Kenneth G. Hamilton, *History of the Moravian Church in America* (1967).

Louis P. Towles

Lovejoy Academy was established in 1842, when Jefferson Madison Lovejoy decided to open his Classical and English School in Raleigh. Lovejoy's school occupied an existing school building on Burke Square a few blocks northwest of the State Capitol building, the site of the present-day Governor's Mansion. Although the school operated under a variety of names before becoming known as Lovejoy Academy in 1852,

it soon became known as one of the state's best private boys' schools.

Students of Jefferson Lovejoy recalled his passionate devotion to Greek, Latin, and English literature. Virgil's *Aeneid* and Samuel Augustus Mitchell's *Ancient Geography* were among his favorite texts. Teaching by having students read lessons aloud from their books while he corrected their mistakes, Lovejoy had "a formidable reputation for severity," especially on occasions when he encountered the "three vices of slothfulness, deception, and intemperance." One of his former pupils, Kemp Plummer Battle (later president of the University of North Carolina), recalled that Lovejoy was quick to deliver hard swats to the hand to any student caught breaking his rules.

The Civil War dealt a severe blow to Lovejoy Academy, as a number of the older boys joined the military and hard economic times prevented some parents from continuing their sons' enrollment. Despite these problems, the school remained open until near the end of the war. When Lovejoy died in 1877, a Raleigh newspaper noted that few other men had done as much for the cause of education in North Carolina.

References: Moses N. Amis, *Historical Raleigh with Sketches of Wake County and Its Important Towns* (1913); Elizabeth Reid Murray, *Wake: Capital County of North Carolina* (1983).

David McGee

Lowe's Companies, Inc., headquartered in Mooresville, is a North Carolina–based building supply and home improvement firm that has grown into one of the nation's largest retailers. Lowe's was founded in 1921 in North Wilkesboro by I. S. Lowe as a single hardware store. Lowe soon brought his son and a son-in-law, Carl Buchan, into the business. Buchan became sole owner of Lowe's in 1952 and oversaw its expansion to a chain of 15 stores by 1960. Lowe's experienced rapid growth in the 1960s and 1970s, becoming a publicly held company beginning in 1961 after Buchan's death. At about the same time, a profit-sharing plan was instituted for employees. In 1979 Lowe's was listed on the New York Stock Exchange.

During its early years, Lowe's sold its products mainly to professional contractors, and its store design resembled that of small local hardware stores. When Robert Strickland became chairman of the company in 1978, he implemented a marketing plan to target do-it-yourself homeowners. By the mid-1980s, following a national trend, more than one-half of Lowe's sales were to nonprofessionals in the general public. Competing with Atlanta-based Home Depot, Lowe's stores became huge, warehouse-style buildings. The company's product line was also expanded beyond its large tool and building supply inventory to include appliances, home decorations, and garden products. By 2006 Lowe's was the nation's second-largest home improvement retailer behind Home Depot, with more than $43 billion in sales and 1,250 stores in 49 states.

Lisa Brantley Kobrin

Lowe's Grove Credit Union. SEE Credit Unions.

Lowry Band. During the Civil War many Lumbee Indians of Robeson County banded together under the leadership of Allen Lowry and hid in swamps along the Lumber River to avoid forced labor in the building of Confederate fortifications along the Cape Fear River. After the war, former Confederates under the name of Conservatives dominated the county government and began to retaliate against the Native Americans. With Lowry as leader, the new band of refugees started raiding the plantations of the Conservatives. In 1865 Allen Lowry and his oldest son, William, were executed as bandits, and leadership of the band passed to Henry Berry Lowry, Allen's youngest son.

Governor William W. Holden proclaimed Henry Berry Lowry an outlaw on 10 Nov. 1868. Lowry surrendered and was jailed in Lumberton but escaped. Eight members of the band were captured in the winter of 1869–70; two were tried and found guilty but escaped from the Wilmington jail where they were imprisoned, and the band continued its raids and killings. On 12 Nov. 1870 a federal artillery battery was sent to Robeson County to subdue the Lowry Band but failed to contain the raids. In 1871 the General Assembly offered a bounty on Henry Berry Lowry. Col. Francis Marion Wishart organized a militia unit in an effort to capture Lowry but only managed to seize several members of the band.

On 15 Oct. 1871 federal troops withdrew from the county, and early in 1872 the Lowry Band conducted a lucrative raid on Lumberton, after which Lowry apparently disappeared. It is not known whether he was killed, either accidentally or intentionally, or vanished with the money obtained in the Lumberton raid, but his disappearance marked the end of the Lowry Band. By the close of 1872 its remaining members had been killed. Whatever his fate, in the years since 1872 Henry Berry Lowry has become a folk hero to the Lumbee Indians.

Reference: W. McKee Evans, *To Die Game: The Story of the Lowry Band, Indian Guerrillas of Reconstruction* (1971).

Thornton W. Mitchell

An imagined likeness of Henry Berry Lowry from the cover of a pamphlet published in New York, ca. 1872. NCC.

Loyalists, or Tories, were residents of the colonies who supported the British during the American Revolution. Popular imagery has created the Loyalist stereotype as the local rogue —the drunkard, the miser, the wild man in the woods, the robber, or the sly trader in any line of work. Although some North Carolina Loyalists might be classed as rogues, most belonged to segments of society that would be expected to remain attached to the British government, including merchants whose businesses were seated in Scottish trading centers, English officeholders serving their time in colonial administration (and on the side making property investments in America for their extended families), and immigrants recently arrived from various parts of Europe (but largely from the British Isles). Others declared their allegiances as a result of personal rivalries and experiences or issues faced in their immediate setting.

North Carolina's Loyalists were as varied in their interests, occupations, origins, education, ambitions, and expectations for the future as those who believed in and fought for American independence. Most of them had a deep love for North Carolina and the social ties that they enjoyed there, and they were undoubtedly troubled by the divide between them and many of their fellow citizens. However, they were willing to fight for a principle. Loyalist Jonas Bedford, who was born in

1735 in Elizabethtown but later lived in the western part of the colony, expressed the sentiment of many Loyalists in his response to a Patriot officer urging him to sign an oath: "I have been Sworn as an Officer and Magistrate under my lawful Sovereign. I never will turn my back to my King's cause and perjure myself. I shall remain a loyal Honest Subject during my life and to my King and Country." For five years Bedford lived quietly and unmolested—until the British arrived in the neighborhood in 1781. It was then that his insecure neighbors burned his house. He was forced to flee, leaving his wife and eight children behind.

Loyalists who could afford to do so often left the colony. Many officeholders who owed their position to the royal government simply packed their possessions and went into exile. Large numbers of Highland Scots who had been in North Carolina for a generation or less moved to Nova Scotia or Florida, neither of which was involved in the American Revolution.

Some historians have argued that there was a higher proportion of Loyalists among North Carolina residents than in any other colony, but this appears to be false. North Carolina's proportion seems to have been greater than that of Pennsylvania and Connecticut, but the colony seems to have lagged behind New York's and Georgia's Loyalist population. The excellent port facilities at New York Harbor, New York City's concentration of wealth, and the fact that it offered refuge to Loyalists from elsewhere may explain its large number. Georgia, as the youngest English colony in America, was not as completely weaned from the mother country as the older colonies had been.

Loyalists' Role in the War

In the weeks before the Battle of Moore's Creek Bridge in February 1776, Loyalists responded to Governor Josiah Martin's call to arms to oppose the "illegal" actions being taken by revolutionaries. The British troops that the government had promised to Martin failed to arrive, and the Loyalists who still remained in the rendezvous area (predominantly Scottish Highlanders) were dramatically defeated and humiliated. As a result, for some time thereafter men whose positive response to the governor's call was known or suspected found it unsafe to remain in their homes. Ethnic resentments against "Scotch" people in various areas worsened their position.

During the time between the Declaration of Independence in July 1776 and the arrival of British forces in Charles Towne (now Charleston, S.C.) in May 1780, many men who later would take a Loyalist stand served in the new state militia as it evolved from the colonial militia. Some militia leaders and their followers arranged compromises by which they agreed to fight Native Americans but not the British government. Others refused to swear an oath of allegiance to the state, which during these years became a requirement for participation in the

militia. Service in the militia was required from every able-bodied man, except Quakers, Moravians, Dunkards, and Mennonites, who paid higher taxes instead. So refusal to take the oath of allegiance generally meant that a man would have to hide in the woods to evade capture or else leave the area.

The years 1780, 1781, and even much of 1782 saw bitter civil war, sometimes called the "Tory War," led by men such as infamous Loyalist leader David Fanning. There was also much side-switching among Loyalists and Patriots. In 1781 it was said that British commander Lord Charles Cornwallis and American general Nathanael Greene fought each other with armies composed largely of the other's deserters. For prisoners of war, service in the captor's forces was a working option, and men were still joining the Continental Army in 1782 after having been captured as Loyalists in battle or its aftermath.

African American Loyalists

For black slaves, the presence of British forces presented an opportunity for independence and a new life as Loyalists. At the start of the conflict, British commanders offered freedom to enslaved blacks who would join them. Such proclamations were pragmatic efforts to weaken the rebels. They were framed by military and political considerations, not humanitarian ones. Even so, during and after the war philanthropists and advocates of emancipation in Britain provided practical assistance to former slaves who had managed to leave with the British and maintain their freedom. For black North Carolinians, the chief opportunities to escape slavery in this way came near the beginning and the end of the war, when British forces were nearby. The pro-British Black Pioneers originated with the 1776 exodus. Black sergeants Thomas Peters and Murphy Steel were crucial leaders in this corps, although their commanding officer was a white North Carolinian, Allen Stewart. For larger numbers of African Americans, however, the British installations at Wilmington and Charles Towne were magnets during 1781 and 1782.

For a self-emancipated black Loyalist, serving in the British war effort did not guarantee either personal liberty or eventual economic independence. For one thing, white Loyalists might claim them as property, legally or not. In addition, once the war's outcome became clear, victorious revolutionaries tried to bargain with the departing British and Loyalists for the return of former slaves. The fact that revolutionaries and Loyalists had stolen slaves from each other throughout the war increased confusion and complicated official efforts to sort out ownership.

Black Loyalists served in many capacities: as artillery workers, laborers for myriad tasks of construction and military engineering, trumpeters, drummers, guides, sailors, laundresses, cooks, personal servants for privileged officers, foragers, and pilots for other fugitives. A few black men ended the war as privates in the Royal North Carolina Regiment. From Charles Towne and New York, black North Carolina Loyalists dispersed as free people largely to East Florida and Nova Scotia, where they faced further threats to their independence.

Loyalist Fate at War's End

Historians have described North Carolina's treatment of Loyalists as "light." There were many trials and imprisonments, but large numbers of Loyalists were merely paroled to their neighborhoods. Serious offenders against the trend to independence, or those who continued to wage attacks in the state after the war had officially ended, had their property confiscated, but as often as not provision was made for wives and dependent children to continue in possession of adequate resources. Individuals who were potentially dangerous, however, were rounded up and transported out of North Carolina to an area that was more securely in American hands.

When Cornwallis went into Virginia, a number of North Carolinians, mainly militia, accompanied him. Some of them were captured after Yorktown, and they were exchanged for transport to the British post at New York and went from there to Nova Scotia. Similarly, other North Carolina Loyalists who happened to be with British forces at the time of their departure went with them to East Florida, England, Scotland, Ireland, British North America, the Bahamas, the West Indies, and the Mosquito Coast. Many of them returned to North Carolina; probably far more Loyalists remained in North Carolina than left it. On the other hand, in the early 1790s a few Loyalists moved from Rowan and Orange Counties to present-day Ontario, Canada.

In general, the perception and treatment of Loyalists in North Carolina depended on local relationships and circumstances. This was as true after the war as it was during the conflict. Wartime legislation gave authority to district commissioners to sell property owned by persons named in the Confiscation Acts. Later, those named in the acts were specifically excluded from the pardon that the 1783 Act of Pardon and Oblivion provided. The law also denied pardon to anyone who had held a British commission.

After the war, American Loyalists could have their claims concerning lost land, property, money, and salary reviewed by a special committee in England. A great many whose losses were only moderate probably made no effort to recoup anything. There were 243 people, however, who took the time and trouble to obtain the evidence necessary to support their claims. The majority of the claims were rejected, and the claimants who were paid received only about 10 percent of the value of their losses.

The final arbiter of property owned by Loyalists seems to have been the district and county courts. Particularly on the county level, persons accused of Loyalism stood to lose their property by debt suits and resulting sheriffs' sales unless they were protected by friends and family with local authority. Several wives petitioned the legislature for ownership of their departed husbands' property. A wife's ownership was not a protection against debt suits, however. On the other hand, some Loyalists returned to their home areas and resumed peaceful lives, and many never left their North Carolina homes.

References: Wallace Brown, *The King's Friends: The Composition and Motives of the American Loyalist Claimants* (1965); Jeffrey J. Crow, *The Black Experience in Revolutionary North Carolina* (1977); Robert O. DeMond, *The Loyalists in North Carolina during the Revolution* (1964); John Hairr, *Colonel David Fanning: The Adventures of a Carolina Loyalist* (2000); Carole Watterson Troxler, *The Loyalist Experience in North Carolina* (1976).

Carole Watterson Troxler
Additional research provided by Laura Morgan.

SEE ALSO Act of Pardon and Oblivion; Brown's Marsh, Battle of; Highland Regiment, North Carolina; Lindley's Mill, Battle of; Llewelyn Conspiracy; Moore's Creek Bridge, Battle of.

Lumbee Indians. The Lumbee tribe, with 53,800 enrolled members, was in the early 2000s the largest of North Carolina's American Indian groups and the ninth-largest tribe in the United States. The Lumbee have been identified by a number of names during the history of their official relationship with the state of North Carolina. Native historians believe that the modern tribal name originates from the Lumber River, which traverses Robeson County and is an important historical, cultural, and spiritual symbol for many tribal members. Most Lumbees live in Robeson County and the adjacent counties of Cumberland, Hoke, and Scotland, and these counties are considered by the Lumbee Tribal Council to be the tribe's home territory, although there are also sizable communities of Lumbee people in Greensboro and elsewhere. Some Lumbees resided in the Bulloch County, Ga., area from 1890 through 1920. The Robeson County communities of Pembroke, Prospect, Union Chapel, Fairgrove, and Magnolia have long been predominantly Lumbee.

Theories of Lumbee Origins

The earliest and perhaps most famous theory of the Lumbee tribe's origins is the so-called Lost Colony theory, proposed in 1885 by Robeson County legislator and local historian Hamilton McMillan and later expanded upon by North Carolina historian Stephen B. Weeks. The theory holds that the Lumbee are descendants of Sir Walter Raleigh's Roanoke Island colonists. The colonists left their settlement, according to the theory, sometime after Governor John White had returned to England in 1587, moving south to an island or mainland location called "Croatan"—the sole word White and his men found carved in a wooden post upon returning to

Elementary school children visit a Native American museum at Lumberton, ca. 1989. Photograph by Billy Barnes. NCC.

the island in 1590. There the English colonists settled among and intermarried with the friendly Croatan Indians, and by 1650 they migrated to the area of present-day Robeson County. The Lost Colony theory gained considerable credence among Lumbee people as well as non-Indians when Lumbee historian and author Adolph Dial argued in favor of it during the latter half of the twentieth century.

John R. Swanton, an anthropologist with the Smithsonian Institution, wrote a report for the U.S. Department of the Interior in 1933 on the probable origins of the Lumbee. His research concluded that the tribe descended mainly from Siouan tribes, primarily the Saura (Cheraw) and Keyauwee. The Saura theory of origin has also been supported by Jack Campisi, an ethnohistorian who was the primary author of the tribe's massive 1987 petition to the Bureau of Indian Affairs seeking full federal tribal recognition, and by William Sturtevant, editor of the Smithsonian Institution's *Handbook of North American Indians*.

Several other theories have been advanced, including the Cherokee theory, which states that during the Tuscarora War of 1711–13, Cherokees joined Col. John Barnwell in fighting the Tuscarora and marched home through Robeson County. Some Cherokees may have remained there and intermarried with local residents. Angus Wilton McLean, a Robesonian who served as governor, advocated this theory before Congress in 1913. Mary W. Norment, in an 1875 book, also proposed descent from the Tuscarora. Lumbee oral tradition reveals no fewer than four other migration theories, documented by anthropologist Robert K. Thomas in an unpublished 1976 report.

Archaeological research reported by Stanley Knick in 1988 established that the land that makes up Robeson County has been inhabited by native peoples continuously from 12,000 B.C. (the early Paleo-Indian period), through the Archaic period (8000–1000 B.C.) and Woodland period (1000 B.C.–1600 A.D.), and up to the present day. In addition, Robeson County was a zone of cultural contact from the Middle Archaic period through the Woodland period and into colonial times. Knick argues that Indians from tribes of three eastern Carolina language families (Algonquian, Iroquoian, and Eastern Siouan) interacted with the Indians already living in the area. Early in the colonial period, European diseases and Indian wars began to decimate the southeastern tribes. As these processes unfolded, remnants of tribes from the three Eastern Carolina language families—primarily Saura and Siouan-speaking Indians—coalesced with the Indians already living in geographically isolated Robeson County. The area, dominated by swamps and other marginal lands for settlement and agriculture, did not generally interest whites, so the Indians' chance of survival was increased. Evidence suggests that the amalgamated tribe that became the Lumbee was in place in Robeson County by 1750.

Discrimination and Injustice in the Nineteenth Century

Like most of North Carolina's American Indian people, the Lumbee lived in relative obscurity for much of the eighteenth and nineteenth centuries. Any sense of difference was likely tempered by the fact that Lumbee people spoke English, followed the same agricultural practices as white settlers, attended Christian churches, and in many other ways blended in with the rest of the sparse population of the marginal lands in and around Robeson County. For political and other purposes, prior to the revised state constitution of 1835, the Lumbee were classified as "free persons of color." But the 1835 constitution decreed that "no free Negro, free mulatto, or free person of mixed blood, descended from ancestors to the fourth generation inclusive" could vote for state legislators. Under this constitution, Lumbee people, like other American Indians in the state, lost many of their civil rights. Later, the Lumbee and other free nonwhites were also stripped of their rights to serve in the militia or to own or carry firearms or other weapons without a license. Some Lumbees used the courts to challenge their classification as free persons of color. The June 1837 court case *State v. Oxendine*, the 1853 case *State v. Noel Locklear*, and an 1857 case against William Chavers for carrying a shotgun are examples in which the challenge proved successful.

The Lumbee endured many privations and injustices during the Civil War, including forced conscription to serve as laborers building fortifications at Fort Fisher near Wilmington, starvation, and harsh treatment by the Home Guard. One such incident led to the rise of perhaps the most famous figure in tribal history, Henry Berry Lowry. Due to a complex series of accusations and incidents involving thefts and conscription, the Home Guard shot Lowry's father and brother while he watched from hiding. He and a triracial band of supporters then began an eight-year (1865–72) "war" to avenge those deaths and, indirectly, other injustices suffered by the Lumbee people. The Lowry Band, outlawed in 1868, killed 18 men and was pursued by local, state, and federal militia, detectives, and bounty hunters. The reward for Lowry rose from $300 in 1866 to $12,000 in 1871–72. Lowry was arrested twice, escaped from pursuers many times (and from jail on the two occasions when he was arrested), and was never tried. He disappeared mysteriously in February 1872, and today he remains an important symbol of Lumbee pride and the tribe's authentic Indian identity.

Lumbee Pursuit of Education, Civil Rights, and Self-Governance

A desire for education has traditionally been a central concern of the Lumbee. Amendments to the state constitution in 1875 provided for segregated public schools but made no mention of Indians. Lumbees were disallowed from attending white schools and, consistent with their resistance of having laws restricting blacks applied to them, they would not attend schools for African Americans. Progress began with an 1885 state law, sponsored by Rep. Hamilton McMillan, that designated the tribe as "Croatan Indians" and provided for them separate schools, their own school committees, and the right to select their own teachers. McMillan sponsored a second law, enacted in 1887, that provided for the establishment of a normal (or teacher-training) school for the Croatans and set aside $500 for instructor salaries. Public school education began to improve in the 1920s, when the normal school had graduated several teachers. Thirty-one subscription schools (one-room wooden buildings) were built by Indians in Indian communities. By 1924 Robeson County Indian schools had a total enrollment of 3,400 students.

The growth of the University of North Carolina at Pembroke, which began as a school for the Lumbee in the late 1800s, is an important example of Lumbee educational efforts. The Lumbee have also worked for educational rights through legal activism. In the 1940s many Lumbees attempted to gain admission to colleges within North Carolina other than the school in Pembroke, and in 1972 tribal members fought to preserve Old Main, the building on the Pembroke campus that, for them, symbolized Indian education and progress. By the 1960s Robeson County had five school systems—four town systems, attended by whites and blacks, and a county system, attended mainly by Indians and blacks. Under the county's "double-voting" arrangement, residents of the towns could vote for both the town and the county school boards, but county residents could vote only for the county school board. In 1972–73 the county school system had 80 percent nonwhite enrollment, but the 12-member school board was 75 percent white. After Lumbee leaders were unable to change the situation through appeals to the state legislature, they sued under the Voting Rights Act in federal court. The court denied relief, but in 1975, in *Janie Maynor Locklear v. North Carolina State*

A Lumbee father and son watching a parade during the annual Lumbee Homecoming. Photograph by Billy Barnes. NCC.

Board of Elections, the U.S. Circuit Court of Appeals reversed the lower court, saying that town residents could no longer vote for county school board members.

The most famous case of Lumbee activism occurred on 18 Jan. 1958 at a field near Hayes Pond, west of Maxton, provoked by two cross-burnings a few days earlier—one at the home of an Indian family in an all-white Lumberton neighborhood and the other at the home of a white woman who was involved with an Indian man. A planned Ku Klux Klan rally, announced by Klan grand wizard James W. "Catfish" Cole of Marion, S.C., received heavy advance publicity. The Lumbee made known their plans to disrupt the event.

The rally was attended by about 40 armed Klansmen, the county sheriff and several deputies, many newspaper and wire service reporters, and 1,500 or more Indians armed with rifles and shotguns. In preparation, the Klan put up a large banner, a sound system, and a naked light bulb atop a tall pole. While Cole was talking to the sheriff and deliberating on whether to begin his speech, one Lumbee grabbed the light pole while another broke the light bulb. A burst of shooting began. In twenty minutes, the shooting had ended, the Klan members had run off, and the field was cleared. There were no deaths, and the only injury was to a photographer whose face was grazed by shotgun pellets. The incident received widespread publicity, with coverage in *Life* magazine and the *New York Times*.

Other violent incidents have occurred in Robeson County. During the 1980s, drug trafficking and racial violence were the cause of several unsolved murders in the county. Poor economic and educational conditions were widespread, and reports documented unfair treatment of Native Americans by the criminal justice system. Large numbers of Native Americans, blacks, and whites held mass political meetings to address these and other concerns. A coalition, Concerned Citizens for Better Government, was formed and turned out 1,500 people for a protest march on Easter Monday 1987. The group supported the candidacy of Lumbee lawyer Julian Pierce for superior court judge. When Pierce was murdered in March 1988, local law enforcement officials proclaimed the case solved as a domestic dispute four days later.

On 1 Feb. 1988 Eddie Hatcher and Timothy Jacobs, both Tuscarora Indians, held the employees of the *Robesonian* newspaper hostage for ten hours in order to draw attention to the county's drug trafficking, violence, and corruption. As a condition of their release of the hostages, Hatcher and Jacobs obtained an agreement from the governor that a task force of state officials would be formed to investigate the problems. The incident brought national attention to Robeson County (although much of it was viewed by residents as unfavorable rather than sympathetic), and many positive changes resulted. The county appointed a triracial Human Relations and Unity Commission. A second Superior Court judgeship was created, and Lumbee Dexter Brooks was appointed to the position. A plan was developed to balance election districts for the County Commission according to the county's racial percentages, and the county's crime rate dropped. Lumbee people also attained new leadership positions. In 1992, for example, Lumbee Purnell Swett was offered the position of superintendent of the merged public schools of Robeson County. In 1994 Glenn Maynor was elected as the county's first Native American sheriff. The Lumbee tribe has had formal governance since 2001, when it installed its first elected tribal council, adopted a constitution, and appointed a supreme court.

The Fight for Federal Recognition

The Lumbee have never received funding through the U.S. Bureau of Indian Affairs or the Indian Health Service, although the tribe has been working to obtain true federal recognition since 1888. By virtue of state recognition, they have received aid from other federal programs for Indians. In 1935 the Lumbee received a memo from the U.S. Department of the Interior stating that those who were of one-half or more Indian blood could organize under the Wheeler-Howard Indian Reorganization Act to receive employment, education, or reservation benefits. To determine who was eligible, Harvard anthropologist Carl C. Seltzer was sent to Robeson County to test the 209

A July 1978 performance of the outdoor drama *Strike at the Wind!*, presented each summer at the North Carolina Indian Cultural Center in Robeson County. Photograph by Billy Barnes. NCC.

Lumbees who were applying for recognition. According to his anthropometric measurements, only 22 qualified. Although Seltzer's methods fit the theories of race at that time, they later came to be viewed as invalid.

Several other bills representing various strategies for obtaining support for the Lumbee were introduced in Congress, but all were unsuccessful until the 1956 Lumbee Act. It designated the Indians living in Robeson and adjoining counties as "Lumbee Indians of North Carolina" (the state of North Carolina had recognized the Lumbee name three years earlier). The final sentence declared that the act did not make them eligible for any federal services offered to Indians, however, and that federal laws affecting Indians did not apply to the Lumbee.

In 1978 a set of seven mandatory criteria for federal acknowledgment of tribes was published in an attempt to make the process of recognizing additional tribes uniform, rigorous, and systematic. Tribes are required to prepare a detailed petition addressing all of these criteria, and the petition is then evaluated by the Bureau of Indian Affairs' Office of Federal Acknowledgment. The Lumbee spent seven years preparing their three-volume petition and submitted it in 1987. Two years later, the Bureau of Indian Affairs' Office of the Solicitor issued a ruling that the language of the 1956 Lumbee Act forbade a relationship between the Lumbee and the federal government through the bureau. Therefore, the petition could not be considered unless Congress amended the last sentence of the Lumbee Act. This action prompted the Lumbee to continue seeking federal recognition by asking Congress to pass a new recognition bill, rather than asking that the 1956 act be amended and probably waiting many more years for their petition to be evaluated. From 1988 through 2003, the Lumbee introduced 12 bills asking for complete federal recognition. Two practically identical bills seeking Lumbee recognition were introduced in 2004 by Senator Elizabeth Dole and Congressman Mike McIntyre; Dole introduced another bill, the Lumbee Recognition Act, in March 2005.

Lumbee Language and Culture

The North Carolina Language and Life Project at North Carolina State University has conducted extensive research on Lumbee speech beginning in 1994. Researchers have found that Lumbee Vernacular English is much like other southern dialects, especially Appalachian English. It does, however, have its own distinctive features. Some of its unusual vocabulary words include "cuz" (a greeting for a fellow Lumbee) and "toten" (a smell, sound, or vision indicating the presence of a spirit). Linguistic features of Lumbee Vernacular English include perfective "I'm" ("I'm got to do it"), finite "bes" ("sometimes it bes that way"), and consonant cluster reduction ("ol'" for "old," for example). Some of the ways in which Lumbee speakers combine and pronounce words distinguish them from African American or white speakers in Robeson County.

The writings of anthropologists, Lumbee scholars, and a diverse array of "ordinary" Lumbee people illustrate several aspects of tribal culture. Placing great value on family is one key characteristic of the Lumbee, who typically maintain frequent (often daily) contact with extended family members. Children often live near their parents or on their parents' land. Most Lumbees marry within the tribe; a sampling of the tribal roll in 2002 showed that 70 percent of Lumbees were married to another tribal member. Many Lumbee people also have extensive knowledge of their personal genealogy.

Faith, church attendance, and love of church and gospel music are also central to Lumbee culture. According to one estimate, Robeson County has some 130 Lumbee churches (the majority of them Methodist and Baptist). The church serves a strong social function in Lumbee culture, involving members in a variety of activities beyond the Sunday worship service. Churches have also served as training grounds for Lumbee political, educational, and business leaders.

The Lumbee have always had a deep love for Robeson County and the Lumber River—often calling it the "Lumbee" —and a desire to own and hold onto their land. In the early 2000s, 64.6 percent of tribal members lived in seven primarily Lumbee communities in Robeson County, and another 30 percent lived elsewhere within North Carolina. Most Lumbees who have moved away (usually to find work) still consider Robeson County their home and return frequently to visit family, for the Lumbee Homecoming (a large festival held since 1970 around 4 July), and when retirement or job availability makes it feasible.

References: Karen I. Blu, *The Lumbee Problem: The Making of an American Indian People* (1980; rev. ed., 2001); Adolph L. Dial, *The Lumbee* (1993); Dial and David K. Eliades, *The Only Land I Know: A History of the Lumbee Indians* (rev. ed., 1996); Stanley Knick, *The Lumbee in Context: Toward an Understanding* (2000); Gerald M. Sider, *Living Indian Histories: Lumbee and Tuscarora People in North Carolina* (2003); Glenn Ellen Starr Stilling, *The Lumbee Indians: An Annotated Bibliography Supplement* (2002); Walt Wolfram and others, *Fine in the World: Lumbee Language in Time and Place* (2002).

Glenn Ellen Starr Stilling

SEE ALSO Lowry Band; University of North Carolina at Pembroke.

Lumber Room was a term applied to a room in a home or an out-building in which seldom-used objects were stored if it seemed they might be of use in the future. A North Carolina law enacted in 1715 required that "Household Stuffs & Lumber" being held for a minor orphan, should, if the goods might deteriorate with age, be "sold at Publick Outcry" and the money held for the orphan until he came of age. In the epilogue to his three-act comedy, *Nolens Volens; or, The Bitter Bit*, published in New Bern in 1809, playwright Everard Hall took little pride in his work and conceded that "his play may rank with useless lumber."

William S. Powell

Lutheran Church in North Carolina and throughout the United States has experienced several schisms, mergers, and other organizational changes that have resulted in a number of bodies adhering to related but theologically distinct beliefs. Lutheranism is rooted in the teachings of sixteenth-century German reformer Martin Luther, whose central theology is based on the premise that salvation comes from God's grace alone rather than through human effort. A wide disparity in doctrinal interpretation, particularly in relation to church hierarchy and authority, as well as ethnic differences among immigrant groups, especially those from Germany and Scandinavia, impeded Lutheran unity in North Carolina and across the United States for much of the nineteenth and twentieth centuries.

Among the immigrants that came to America to build a new life following economic reversals and religious persecutions in the late 1600s and early 1700s were German Lutherans, who first went to New York and Pennsylvania and then migrated south through Virginia into North Carolina. The state's oldest existing Lutheran congregations are in Guilford and Rowan Counties, with official organization dates of 1745. (There is evidence of a Lutheran congregation of Swiss in New Bern as early as 1710, but they were wiped out in an Indian attack shortly afterward.)

Most of the early congregations in North Carolina depended on lay leadership and a small number of pastors coming down from Pennsylvania. In 1772 Zion (now Organ) congregation in Rowan County and St. John's in Cabarrus County sent delegates to Germany in search of a pastor, returning with Pastor Adolphus Nussmann and Johann Gottfried Arends, a schoolteacher who was later ordained. With increasing numbers of congregations came the need for organization, and in 1803 the North Carolina Lutheran Synod, the first such body in the South, was established, with headquarters in Salisbury. In 1820—as a consequence of theological differences between advocates of "old" Lutheranism and "American," progressive Lutheranism—several North Carolina congregations and pastors joined with others in South Carolina, Tennessee, and Virginia to form the more conservative Evangelical Lutheran Tennessee Synod. That same year the General Synod, the first national organization of American Lutherans, was formed in Hagerstown, Md. Representatives from both the North Carolina and Tennessee Synods participated.

Over the course of the nineteenth century, North Carolina's Lutherans encountered further divisions. During the Civil War, synods in North Carolina, Tennessee, and elsewhere in the South withdrew from the national General Synod over political differences. Following the war, several Lutheran pastors in Rowan and Cabarrus Counties encouraged the black members of their churches to form their own congregations and trained four African American men as ministers. The new ministers subsequently formed an all-black synod known as the Alpha Synod, but owing to economic factors and the death of one of its leading pastors, the synod had a short life. The black congregations asked for help from the North Carolina Synod, but it could provide none given the strain on its postwar resources. At one time there were several African American congregations in Rowan, Cabarrus, and Guilford Counties and a Lutheran college for blacks in Greensboro. Most of these congregations no longer exist, although mergers among them have enabled a few to survive.

In 1880 the North Carolina Synod established a college in Conover. In 1891 the question of where the college should be located was revisited, however, and the school was moved to Hickory, where it was opened with the name of Highland College. This institution was the precursor of modern-day Lenoir-Rhyne College. The establishment of numerous church-supported schools for elementary-age children followed during the next few decades.

Lutherans in North Carolina and other southern states remained organizationally isolated from their northern brethren until the early twentieth century, when a series of mergers began to take place at both the national and regional levels. In 1921 the North Carolina Synod, with 77 congregations, merged with the Tennessee Synod, with 119 congregations, to form the United Evangelical Synod of North Carolina. This synod in turn became part of the newly formed United Lutheran Church in America (ULCA), which also had incorporated the General Synod.

In 1962 the ULCA and other Lutheran bodies merged to form the Lutheran Church in America (LCA). Further unification efforts led in 1988 to the formation of the Evangelical Lutheran Church in America (ELCA), a massive organization that incorporated the more than 5 million members of the LCA (including those in the North Carolina Synod), the American Lutheran Church, and the Association of Evangelical Lutheran Churches. By the early 2000s, most of North Carolina's 300-plus Lutheran congregations were under the jurisdiction of the ELCA, although some remained part of the Lutheran Church, Missouri Synod or of minor bodies that reflected continuing historic, cultural, or theological distinctions. Lenoir-Rhyne College in Hickory remained one of the 28 ELCA-controlled colleges and universities in the United States and the only Lutheran institution of higher learning operating in North Carolina.

References: H. George Anderson, *The North Carolina Synod through 175 Years* (1978); Raymond M. Bost and Jeff L. Norris, *All One Body: The Story of the North Carolina Lutheran Synod, 1803–1993* (1994); Bernard W. Cruse, *Foundations of Lutheranism in North Carolina* (1973); Jacob L. Morgan, Bachman S. Brown Jr., and John Hall, eds., *History of the Lutheran Church in North Carolina* (1953).

Karl M. Park
Robert M. Calhoon

SEE ALSO Lenoir-Rhyne College.

Lutheran Schools of Mount Pleasant. By the middle of the nineteenth century, the North Carolina Synod of the Lutheran Church had become concerned about the lack of schools that could prepare the young men of North Carolina for a career in the ministry. At a special meeting of the Lutheran Synod in Concord on 21 July 1852, Western Carolina Male Academy was established at nearby Mount Pleasant. Col. William A. Weddington was awarded a contract to construct a three-story brick building on a tract of 16-plus acres purchased for $81.25 from Matthias Barrier. Weddington also built a home on the site for the school's first president (and first professor), William Gerhardt, who was inaugurated on 24 May 1853. The school prospered to the extent that in 1859 a charter was secured from the General Assembly converting the academy into North Carolina College. Mount Pleasant itself was incorporated by an act of the same legislature. Two additional buildings, Philaethian and Pi Sigma Phi Literary Halls, were erected on campus in 1859. All students over age 14 were required to join one of those two societies, which stressed public speaking and debating. Classes were interrupted in 1861 by the Civil War and did not resume until 1867.

The first postwar class graduated in 1871. During the 1873–74 school year, there were 115 students enrolled—95 students of high school age at the academy level and 20 at the college level. A Theological Department was added for aspiring ministers unable to attend a regular seminary. A Commercial Department was added in the 1890s. At its zenith, the college offered the B.A., B.S., and Ph.D. degrees. During the next 29 years, 66 men graduated from North Carolina College, and most entered the learned professions. At least 28 of them became Lutheran ministers. By 1900 enrollment at North Carolina College had dropped to 56 students, and financial problems worsened. The class of 1901 was the last to graduate from the college.

In 1859 a Lutheran school for young women was established in Mount Pleasant, with Mrs. D. H. Bittle, the wife of a Lutheran minister, as principal. Her husband was then serving as president of North Carolina College. The school was first known as Mount Pleasant Female Seminary. In 1892 school officials changed its name to Mont Amoena Seminary, using the Latin version of the town's name. In 1868 G. D. Bernheim, who was then in charge of the school, offered to transfer it to the synod on favorable terms. The transfer was completed in 1869, and the first board of trustees of the school was elected. Mont Amoena had 112 students by 1897.

In 1903 a school named Mount Pleasant Collegiate Institute began operating on the campus of the then-defunct North Carolina College. The Lutheran Synod resumed sponsorship of the institute, which retained the original purpose of preparing young men for the seminary and other professional careers. During the 1903–4 school year, 3 teachers taught 52 students at the institute; by 1923 there were 8 teachers, 173 students, and some 200 alumni.

At the Mount Pleasant Female Seminary, the financial situation was more stable. The seminary burned on 30 Nov. 1911, but a large, new brick structure soon replaced the burned frame building. The school was quite successful for about half a century, but after a time it became increasingly difficult for it to compete with newer facilities such as Elizabeth College in Charlotte. Public high schools also began duplicating the work of the seminary, and Mont Amoena finally closed its doors in 1927. Thereafter, the first female students were allowed on the campus of Mount Pleasant Collegiate Institute as day students.

Prior to the merger of the North Carolina and Tennessee Lutheran Synods in 1921, the Mount Pleasant Collegiate Institute could depend on some funding from the synod and from individual Lutheran congregations. After the merger, however, it became even more difficult to obtain adequate funding, as the institute had to compete with more successful institutions such as Lenoir-Rhyne College. Fees and tuition alone were simply not adequate to fund the school's continued operation. Economic necessity finally forced the school's permanent closing in 1935.

References: Raymond M. Bost and Jeff L. Norris, *All One Body: The Story of the North Carolina Lutheran Synod, 1803–1993* (1994); Jacob L. Morgan, Bachman S. Brown Jr., and John Hall, eds., *History of the Lutheran Church in North Carolina* (1953).

Clarence E. Horton Jr.

Lynching, the unlawful killing of a person by a mob and one of the most extreme forms of community sanction, has occurred in North Carolina on numerous occasions throughout its history. The term originally referred to whipping, but by the beginning of post–Civil War Reconstruction it had come to mean killing almost exclusively. Although lynchings were carried out by a variety of means, hanging, followed by shooting, was the most common method in North Carolina; unlike in parts of the Deep South, it appears that no one in the state was burned to death. A few white Republicans were killed by mobs, but the overwhelming majority of victims in North Carolina were black.

The turmoil of Reconstruction incited several dozen lynchings in the state, most of them carried out by the Ku Klux Klan (KKK) in Chatham, Orange, Alamance, Caswell, and Rockingham Counties. On 26 Feb. 1870, for example, Wyatt Outlaw, a black councilman in Graham and founder/president of the local Union League, was taken from his home by Klansmen and hanged from a tree in the town square. Because the killing followed a year-long KKK rampage across many parts of the state, the public outcry was vehement. It was also one of the events that helped to ignite the so-called Kirk-Holden War later that year.

In December 1883 and July 1885, two gruesome murders occurred in Chatham County south of Pittsboro. The fact that axes were used and the motive seemed to be robbery for both crimes led authorities to conclude that the same party was responsible. Two months after the second murder, a coroner's jury determined that Jerry Finch, his wife Harriet, and Lee Tyson—all African Americans—were responsible. They were arrested and confined in the Pittsboro jail, where another black man, John Pattishall, was already being held on suspicion that he also was involved. On the night of 30 Sept. 1885, a mob of 75 to 100 men overwhelmed the elderly jailer and seized the Finches, Tyson, and Pattishall. About a mile south of town, all four were hanged from a large oak tree. A coroner's inquest determined that the victims "came to their deaths at the hands of persons unknown to the jurors," which was typical phrasing for such findings. Harriet Finch's murder was one of only four lynchings of women to occur in North Carolina.

After 1892, two things about lynching changed in the South. First, there was a marked increase in the number of blacks killed and a marked decrease in the number of whites. Second, a five-year wave of antilynching statutes were enacted, due in part to the efforts of activist Ida Wells of Memphis, Tenn. North Carolina passed such a law in 1893, but it was not used for over a decade. During the same period, Jim Crow laws and disfranchisement were put in place to control blacks' social and political ambitions. Over the next 15 years, lynching took more than 25 lives in North Carolina. A vigorous legal assault on the practice occurred during the term of Governor Robert Glenn (1905–9), which saw a new emphasis on identifying and prosecuting lynch mobs.

Over the next decade the number of lynchings declined sharply (11 people between 1908 and 1918), but then they increased again (11 blacks were lynched between 1919 and 1923). After 1923, death by mob action became increasingly rare in North Carolina, with some years passing without a single incidence and no more than one between 1926 and 1941.

In 1941 Robert Melker, a 23-year-old black man living near Cherryville in Gaston County, was driving with his wife when four young white men in a passing car yelled at him. The whites then chased them home and into their house. Melker's mother stepped outside and fired a shotgun to frighten the attackers away, slightly wounding one. The four returned with shotguns of their own, called Melker to the door, and shot him down. At their trial Graham Dellinger, Haywood Dellinger,

Robert Sellers, and Fred Hudson all pled guilty to second-degree murder and received sentences of 14 to 25 years.

In modern times, the term "hate crime" has generally replaced "lynching" when race or other factors have led to an individual's murder by a group of people. A well-known example in North Carolina is the 1970 killing in Oxford of Henry "Dickie" Marrow, a 23-year-old black veteran, by Robert Teel, a white man with KKK connections, and his sons. Teel's acquittal, and the subsequent racially motivated violence that engulfed the town, became the subject of historian Timothy B. Tyson's much-praised book, *Blood Done Sign My Name: A True Story* (2004).

References: Bruce E. Baker, *Lynching Ballads in North Carolina* (1995); W. Fitzhugh Brundage, ed., *Under Sentence of Death: Lynching in the South* (1997); James H. Chadbourn, *Lynching and the Law* (1933); W. S. Lockhart, *Lynching in North Carolina, 1888–1906* (1972); Allen Trelease, *White Terror: The Ku Klux Klan Conspiracy and Southern Reconstruction* (1971).

Bruce E. Baker

M

Mace was a club or staff used in the Middle Ages as a defensive weapon. It had a spiked head that could penetrate a suit of armor and could be used against a foe in hand-to-hand combat. Later the mace, often made of precious metal and decorated with jewels, came to be merely symbolic of power or authority. It was carried by a mace bearer in procession before a public official or laid on a table before a legislative body. Governors of some of the American colonies seemed to have considered use of the mace to be significant in reflecting their position as a representative of the Crown.

The earliest mace bearer noted in North Carolina records was Daniel Dupree (or Dupee), recommended for the post by the colonial Assembly in October 1756 and commissioned by Governor Arthur Dobbs. Whether North Carolina acted before its southern neighbor to acquire a mace is not known, but the South Carolina mace, which it still owns, was made in that year by a London goldsmith, Magdelene Feline. In 1760 the North Carolina Assembly was one member short of having a quorum present when an important vote was about to be taken. The member was at home ill, so the Speaker, accompanied by the mace bearer, went to the bedside of the absent member to record his vote. With the beginning of the American Revolution, the mace ceased to be used in any official way.

References: Walter Clark, ed., *State Records of North Carolina*, vol. 22 (1907); William S. Powell, ed., *Correspondence of William Tryon and Other Selected Papers* (1980–81).

William S. Powell

Maco Light, also called the Ghost at Maco Station, is one of North Carolina's most well-known and enduring supernatural phenomena. It dates to a fatal train wreck in 1867 at a small rural station then called Farmer's Turnout, 14 miles west of Wilmington on the line serving Wilmington, Florence, S.C., and Augusta, Ga. Conductor Joe Baldwin, riding in the last car of a wood-burning train, discovered that his car had come uncoupled. He died waving a lantern from the rear of that car in a failed attempt to signal and stop a second train coming from behind. One witness saw Baldwin's lantern fly clear of the train wreck, land and right itself in the adjacent swamp, and burn on.

Shortly afterward and for over a century since, a flickering light has appeared regularly along the railroad tracks in the vicinity of the 1867 collision. Legend attributes this light to the ghost of Joe Baldwin, who was decapitated in the wreck; the ghost is said to be looking for its head. From 1873 until after an 1886 earthquake, railroad workers reported a pair of Maco lights that would appear together. Over the years, the Maco Light has been bright enough to fool many railroad workers into stopping their trains. To remedy the ghost's schedule-thwarting attempts, signalmen at Maco used two lights, one red, and one green. While President Grover Cleveland's train was wooding and watering up at Maco in 1889, the president saw the two signal lights, asked about them, and got the full story of Old Joe Baldwin.

In the spring of 1964, the South Eastern North Carolina Beach Association contacted parapsychologist and ghost-hunter Hans Holzer to come to Maco and investigate the mysterious light. After his visit, Holzer gave an apparent certification of the phantom conductor, citing the consistency of his return appearances. Since the railroad tracks were removed around 1980, sightings of the Maco Light have "greatly diminished, if not completely disappeared," according to Cape Fear Museum historian Harry Warren. In its time the Maco Light has been the object of many a dark vigil at Maco Station, where anywhere from a few to dozens of people would frequently gather at night. It has also been the subject of numerous newspaper stories and at least one narrative ballad, "The Maco Light," which sums up the tale:

> They found Joe's body,
> They found Joe's head!
> They buried 'em both,
> But he's not dead!
> On a dismal night in a dismal swamp,
> You can see his lantern shine!

References: John Harden, *Tar Heel Ghosts* (1954); Bland Simpson and Jim Wann, *King Mackerel and the Blues Are Running: Songs and Stories of the Carolina Coast* (1986).

Bland Simpson

Macon County, located in North Carolina's Mountain region, was formed from Haywood County in 1828 and named for Nathaniel Macon, an early nineteenth-century North Carolina political leader who served as both a U.S. senator and the Speaker of the House of Representatives. Franklin (incorporated in 1855) is the county seat, and other communities include Highlands, Gneiss, Cullasaja, Otto, Norton, Rainbow Springs, Aquone, Scaly Mountain, Nantahala, Cartoogechaye, Burningtown, Ellijay, and Cowee.

The area of Macon County, in the southwestern portion of North Carolina above Georgia, traditionally was thought to have been first explored by Spaniards, including Hernando De Soto. Modern scholarship, however, places the explorers in the Catawba Valley. The land was ceded to European settlers in 1819 by the Cherokee, who had previously flourished there. The capital of the Middle Cherokees, Cowee, was in what is now Macon County, and the preserved Nikwasi Indian Mound in Franklin (*Nikwasi* meaning "center of activity") marks what was an important Cherokee ceremonial center.

The Nantahala National Forest, the largest of the state's four national forests, comprises almost half of Macon County, offering an array of outdoor activities, including fishing and whitewater rafting on the Nantahala River and Nantahala Lake and hiking along the Appalachian Trail. The county's land is also rich with minerals and gemstones—including rubies, sapphires, amethyst, moonstone, and garnets—and no fewer than three major gem shows are offered annually, drawing thousands of amateur mineralogists and gem enthusiasts. The natural history of the area has long been studied, from the visit of naturalist William Bartram in the 1770s to the modern establishment of a biological station at Highlands. Macon County's population was estimated to be 31,700 in 2004.

Reference: *The Heritage of Macon County, North Carolina* (1987–1998).

Robert Blair Vocci

Macon's Bill Number Two was one of a succession of economic retaliatory measures enacted in the years preceding the War of 1812. Determined to avoid war with Great Britain yet desirous of defending the nation's threatened neutrality rights, the Republican administrations of Thomas Jefferson and James Madison sought to alter the oppressive commercial restrictions imposed by both Great Britain and France after the Napoleonic Wars escalated again in 1803. The Republican-dominated Congress sought an alternative that would shift the burden of commercial retaliation from Americans to the British and the French.

Much of the responsibility for fashioning a new policy fell to Nathaniel Macon, chairman of the House Foreign Relations Committee. A North Carolina tobacco planter from Warren County and an old Jeffersonian, Macon was the acknowledged dean of his state's congressional delegation, having served on Capitol Hill since 1791 and as Speaker of the House of Representatives for the Seventh, Eighth, and Ninth Congresses.

In April 1810 Macon reported a new measure out of his committee. The bill proposed reopening free commercial relations with Great Britain and France. However, it also provided that if one of the warring parties adopted a more favorable position toward the United States, Washington would immediately reimpose trade restrictions on the other country.

Macon's Bill Number Two satisfied neither house, and efforts to strengthen it failed. Passed by a divided session on 1 May 1810, it marked the virtual abandonment of the Republicans' experiment with economic coercion. In September

1810 an opportunistic Napoleon revoked the Berlin and Milan Decrees, which had been objectionable to the United States. When Britain did not follow suit within three months, an embargo automatically went into effect against it in early 1811. This embargo ultimately persuaded Britain to lift its blockade of Europe in mid-June 1812, but the action came too late to prevent war.

References: Delbert Harold Gilpatrick, *Jeffersonian Democracy in North Carolina, 1789–1816* (1931); Ronald L. Hatzenbuehler and Robert L. Ivie, *Congress Declares War: Rhetoric, Leadership, and Partisanship in the Early Republic* (1983).

Caroline Pruden

Madison County, located in North Carolina's Mountain region, was formed from Buncombe and Yancey Counties in 1851 and was named for President James Madison. Communities include the county seat of Marshall (incorporated in 1863), Mars Hill, Faust, Hot Springs, Spring Creek, Joe, Trust, Luck, Walnut, and Whiterock.

Located along North Carolina's border with Tennessee, the area that became Madison County was, like many of the state's Mountain counties, originally inhabited by the Cherokee and then settled by immigrants from Scotland and Ireland. The Shelton Laurel Massacre, the execution of several men and boys suspected of Unionist sympathies in 1863, led to the moniker "Bloody Madison." Due in part to its geographic isolation, the county has preserved a vibrant folk tradition that has incorporated the customs of these Scotch-Irish pioneers. English folklorist Cecil Sharp collected ballads in the region in 1916. The mountains also yield a wide variety of outdoor recreational opportunities, including skiing, hiking, and mountain biking, while the French Broad River is a popular destination for whitewater rafting as well as canoeing, kayaking, and fishing. In addition, Madison County is home to Hot Springs, a resort named for its warm mineral waters, which flourished in the nineteenth century (and for a brief period during World War I held German prisoners of war). Mars Hill College, a Baptist school, was established in 1856. As vital as tourism is to Madison County's economy, its farms and forests—principally tobacco but also Christmas trees and other products—remain its driving force. The estimated population of Madison County was 20,000 in 2004.

Robert Blair Vocci

SEE ALSO Hot Springs; Shelton Laurel Massacre.

Madstones have existed from antiquity in the realms of magic and have appeared at various times in North Carolina folklore. Akin to precious and semiprecious stones, to which fortune or healing were always attributed, madstones supposedly cured hydrophobia, or rabies, but also bites of poisonous creatures such as snakes and spiders. Madstones traditionally have been animal, vegetable, or mineral in origin and are usually described as porous. In Wales and England, they were white and pink alabaster. In the Orient, *tabasheer*, which function as madstones, are the opals of a siliceous white or translucent substance occasionally found in bamboo joints. In the Orient, Europe, and America, bezoars (gall stones or stomach growths of hair, fiber, or calculi) found in ruminant animals such as deer, buffalo, and cattle were used for medicinal purposes.

People used madstones in two different ways. By far the most common usage in North Carolina was the application of the stone to a wound, where it adhered, exerting some suction, until it absorbed all the poison in the wound or all the poison it could hold. Then it fell off and was cleansed in milk or warm water, and, if necessary, reapplied. A less common method, used among Native Americans, was to scrape off portions of the stone and give it to the patient in milk.

The source of these stones in North Carolina was usually traveling strangers who gave them to local families. Joseph Blount Cheshire Jr., a bishop of the Episcopal Church in North Carolina, collected much information about the madstone used by the Pointer family. His close friend Benjamin F. Thorp used the Pointer stone before he inherited his own madstone and witnessed many cures by their use. Cheshire was hard put to understand the phenomenon, for though dubious of the folklore, he had complete confidence in his friend's integrity.

References: Joseph D. Clark, "Madstones in North Carolina," *North Carolina Folklore Journal* 24 (1976); C. J. S. Thompson, *Magic and Healing* (repr., 1973).

Jean B. Anderson

Malcolm X Liberation University (MXLU), an experimental institution of higher education focusing on African American history and life, opened in Durham in October 1969. Named for slain black leader Malcolm X (Malcolm Little), the school was established after black students at Duke University protested the absence of a black studies program. MXLU moved to Greensboro in 1970.

The leader of MXLU was Howard Fuller, a controversial black activist who later changed his name to Owusu Sadaukai. Sadaukai, who went by the title "Head Nigger in Charge," said the purpose of MXLU was "to provide a framework within which black education can become relevant to the needs of the black community and the struggle for black liberation." In Durham, a two-story building on Pettigrew Street—in the heart of the black community—housed MXLU. The school began with a staff of about 12 members and 40 students, all of whom were black. Its two-year program aimed to help all in-

terested blacks, from those who never finished their secondary education to those who already had attended institutions of higher education. Students in their first year at MXLU studied subjects such as African civilization, slavery, and colonialism. Second-year students received technical training in order to enter a profession that involved "working with black people" to help them become liberated.

MXLU's funding sparked controversy, since a sizable portion—about $45,000—came from the Episcopal Church's Urban Crisis Program. The money, which drew both support and fire from Episcopal leaders, was investigated by a federal grand jury in 1969. In 1973, three years after moving to Greensboro, MXLU was forced to close due to the lack of funding. Afterward, Sadaukai stated that the school had been hampered by its overemphasis on Africa as an important factor in the lives of blacks in the United States.

Nahal Toosi

Mangum Terrace. Priestly H. Mangum, a Wake County farmer, is generally acknowledged as the inventor of the Mangum terrace, a system of hillside ridges used to increase cultivatable land, conserve soil moisture, and minimize erosion, and a feature that came to dominate the agricultural landscape of the cotton South. Mangum's inspiration came from his desire to find a substitute for the hillside ditches then used for drainage in fields, which hindered the operation of a newly bought wheat binder, then very rare in his area. In 1885 he constructed his first terrace on his farm near Wake Forest. The terraces were made about two feet high and six feet deep, creating a flat depression about ten feet wide on the upslope side. The attribute of the terrace most enticing to farmers was that the whole terrace surface area could be cultivated and used for crops.

Contemporaneously, the Agricultural Experiment Station at North Carolina State College (now North Carolina State University) had been experimenting with similar ideas. As early as 1888 the station was calling for broad, cultivatable "hillside ditches." In 1896 the experiment station published a set of instructions for making the Mangum-type terrace, and their endorsement helped spread its use on farms across the state.

Other state experiment stations and the U.S. Department of Agriculture (USDA) promoted the Mangum terrace as well. In 1912 the USDA published instructions for constructing the terrace, stating that it "admirably meets the requirements of the farm for modern machinery equipment." As late as 1920, the Mangum terrace, long in use in the South, was being promoted in Missouri and others states where terracing was just beginning to be tried. The historical geographer Arthur Hall, in his study of soil erosion, found the southern piedmont to be the incubator for indigenous inventions in soil conservation such as the hillside ditch, contouring, and terraces, with little

Mangum terraces near Raleigh, ca. 1912. NCC.

borrowing from foreign practices. To Hall, developments such as the Mangum terrace "represent distinctive contributions to the art of agriculture on the part of the region."

References: J. S. Cates, *The Mangum Terrace in Its Relation to Efficient Farm Management* (1912); E. W. Lehmann and F. L. Duley, *The Mangum Terrace* (1920).

Douglas Helms

Manors in England after the Norman conquest were organized estates held by a knight, a religious body, or a certain corporation. Eventually manors were headed by feudal lords who were recognized as owners of the land and who could have tenants of varying degrees of obligation. In the provisions of the Carolina charter of 1663, the Lords Proprietors envisioned a feudal society based on a hereditary order of titled holders of manors and tenants. They drew up an elaborate scheme of government outlining these provisions, but preexisting conditions in Carolina and the independent spirit of the people already living there hindered its implementation. The word "manor," however, was employed for a time to define the hold-

ings of some landowners, many of whom later probably had little understanding of the origin or meaning of the term.

In his 1728 will, Francis Leydon of Albemarle County directed that when his son, William, came into possession of the "manor," he should pay £10 to each of his three younger brothers who inherited parcels of land. It was Leydon's intention that this estate would remain in the family forever. Over the decades, countless other wills and inventories of estates used the term "manor" in one form or another. John Maule of Beaufort County used the form "mannor plantation" in his will dated 11 Dec. 1773—110 years after the Carolina charter employed the term.

References: J. Bryan Grimes, ed., *North Carolina Wills and Inventories* (1912); Mattie Erma Edwards Parker, ed., *North Carolina Charters and Constitutions, 1578–1698* (1963).

William S. Powell

"Manteo to Murphy" is a phrase often used in reference to the entire east-west width of North Carolina, particularly when describing a phenomenon that touches all regions of the state. The phrase was famously applied to the 1876 gubernatorial campaign between Zebulon B. Vance and Supreme Court Justice Thomas Settle Jr., in which Vance's victory set off "rejoicing by Democrats 'from Manteo to Murphy.'" This followed from the fact that Vance and Settle had toured the state in a series of debates that resulted in the largest Democratic majority (over 13,000) in any election between 1868 and 1900. The phrase is actually a symbolic and not literal rendering of the extreme east-west width of North Carolina, since neither Manteo (Dare County) nor Murphy (Cherokee County) is situated precisely at the state's borders.

Wiley J. Williams

Manual Labor Schools were the forerunner of the North Carolina Community College System. They were created to provide an education that would help young people become working members of their communities. Practical in nature, these schools put less emphasis on academics than traditional schools in their attempt to develop a skilled work force essential to the state's economic development.

Manual labor schools were begun in the 1830s in the United States, but they did not become popular in the South until after the Civil War. Prior to this time, manual labor was looked down upon by the upper class, and poor white boys generally worked on their families' farms. As society changed following the Civil War, manual labor schools evolved to offer trade skills for females as well as males. The schools could be public, private, or church-run and were variously operated for the poor and orphaned on the elementary, secondary, and more advanced levels.

The current North Carolina Community College System does not include the manual labor component of the earlier schools, and the system is much expanded to include a two-year college program. But the emphasis on providing a wide base of training for the citizens of North Carolina to fill jobs in the community continues to be a main emphasis of the current system.

References: Charles William Dabney, *Universal Education in the South*, vol. 2 (1936); Ben E. Fountain Jr., *The Community College System in North Carolina: A Brief History* (1990).

Jim Fowlkes

Manufactured Homes, frequently called mobile homes, are single-section or multisection dwelling units made in factories and sold fully built. Such units are also used for schoolrooms, bank branches, construction site offices, and similar commercial applications. North Carolina's manufactured home industry received a tremendous boost during World War II, when it was necessary to provide housing for the military and for civilians working in war production factories (often quite far from their previous homes). This need continued in the postwar years, although the speed with which manufactured homes were produced often led to a lack of quality and safety. The industry was thus faced with the challenge of dispelling the "trailer park" image, which it accomplished to some extent.

Demand for manufactured homes grew through the decades, and financing options for buyers of these homes became closer to those for buyers of conventional housing. The industry continued to encounter zoning restrictions, which virtually deny the use of these homes unless they are placed in a manufactured housing park or community.

Greensboro's Oakwood Homes became one of the nation's most successful manufactured homes companies, designing, manufacturing, and marketing single-section and modular (multisection) houses and financing the majority of its sales. The company operated manufacturing plants in Texas, Georgia, Indiana, Arizona, and several other states before its acquisition in 2004 by Tennessee-based Clayton Homes, Inc.

Wiley J. Williams

Manufacturing has been a diverse and vital component of North Carolina's economy since the early nineteenth century. Initially, farming or planting was widely seen as the most profitable business opportunity, and industrial investment and interest tended to arise only during periods of agricultural depression. Early manufacturing activity was meager, the result of the state's few easily exploited deposits of minerals such as iron and coal, its modest and somewhat inconstant waterpower sources, and its lack of capital. North Carolina soon became an industrial force, however, with much of its industry centered around furniture, textiles, and tobacco. Despite troubling economic trends affecting its industries, and seemingly in contrast to the predominately rural character of many of its counties, North Carolina in the early 2000s remained one of the nation's ten most industrialized states.

Manufacturing in the Colonial and Antebellum Eras

In colonial North Carolina, the British mercantile system, and acts such as the Iron Act designed to support it, discouraged significant manufacturing. The very purpose of colonies under the British Empire was to provide raw materials to Britain's factories and a market for British manufactured goods. Nonetheless, craftsmen, farmers, and planters with access to waterfalls engaged in limited manufacturing. Millers, tinsmiths, wheelwrights, blacksmiths, and other artisans produced goods for strictly local markets. Free farmers and planters' slaves also engaged in home manufacturing, cutting lumber, tanning leather, spinning yarn, throwing pottery, weaving cloth, and making candles, furniture, and bricks. Many small iron deposits were exploited in the colonial period. The iron was most often used locally, although some raw iron was shipped to England by the 1720s and 1730s.

The American Revolution cut off most British imports, leaving North Carolinians primarily to their own resources. The war spurred iron production along the Deep River in Chatham County. The state government provided subsidies to those producing textiles (using the "put-out" system of home looms rather than factories), but once the war was over it offered little encouragement. In about 1790 Michael Schenck arrived from Pennsylvania and subsequently established a gristmill, a sawmill, a small ironworks, and an early textile mill on the south fork of the Catawba River in Lincoln County.

The War of 1812 was the main impetus for the beginning of the Industrial Revolution in New England, which continued rapidly after that conflict. However, North Carolina and other southern states lacked the large sums of capital available to New England investors, and most new manufacturing enterprises in the South failed in the face of postwar competition, lack of business experience, and the flow of the region's limited capital to more certain profits in agriculture. Nonetheless, interest in manufacturing grew again in the South in the late 1820s. The North Carolina General Assembly issued a report in 1828 encouraging manufacturing, and it chartered 15 textile corporations in the late 1820s and early 1830s (though the simultaneous interest in railroads siphoned off much of the available capital after 1834).

Factories, especially labor-intensive textile mills, were employment options for ordinary people as well as investment opportunities for the wealthy. Farm families (suffering as a result of low cotton prices), widows, and orphans could find work and a certain amount of security in the mills, though often in exchange for long hours and low wages. Indeed, supplying work for poor whites was often proffered as an added rationale for the establishment of cotton mills from the antebellum period through the end of the nineteenth century, though profits remained the primary motive for investors. Slaves were sometimes employed, but mill owners generally found them to be too costly, especially after increases in prices for slaves in the 1850s. By 1843 the *Greensboro Patriot* reported that North Carolina was home to 25 textile mills capitalized at more than $1 million. These mills had 50,000 spindles, employed 1,200 to 1,500 workers, and consumed 15,000 bales of cotton. Seven years later, North Carolina investments in all kinds of manufacture totaled $7.5 million in nearly 2,700 mills, shops, processing plants, and factories.

Decline of Iron Production and the Effects of the Civil War

By 1860 North Carolina was one of the South's leading industrial states, with nearly 3,700 manufacturing plants of all types capitalized at $9.7 million and producing products valued at $16.7 million. Many of these comprised a number of small operations. Turpentine manufacture was the largest industry (North Carolina produced two-thirds of the U.S. supply),

but the state's manufacturing establishments also included 640 gristmills and 100 tobacco products factories. There were also 39 textile mills, more than in any other southern state. The state's leading industries were almost all related to agricultural products. Some analysts have seen this close connection as a weakness and a result of planter design. More likely, however, it reflected the scarce nonagricultural resources of the state.

North Carolina's iron industry declined rapidly after the discovery of the process of making cheap, reliable iron from anthracite coal in Pennsylvania. The dearth of iron production would prove costly, especially during the Civil War. The state's poor iron supplies account for the fact that North Carolina and Florida were the only Confederate states east of the Mississippi that did not produce a significant number of cannons for the war. Propellers, shafts, and anchors, as well as parts for engines and boilers, were produced at the Confederate Navy Yard in Charlotte, however. In the production of small arms, the state fared better. Privately owned factories near Jamestown and Greensboro manufactured modest quantities of rifles, pistols, and carbines. Following the capture of the Federal arsenal at Harpers Ferry, Va. (now West Virginia), by Gen. Stonewall Jackson, the Confederate government moved much of the arsenal's machinery to Fayetteville, where quantities of small arms were produced.

With severe shortages of consumer goods brought on by a Union naval blockade, there was considerable interest in increasing domestic manufacturing. However, limited natural resources and machinery, as well as military priority for all available resources, prevented many new factories from being built. Most production increases came at factories that existed before the war. During the war, many textile mills that had previously spun only yarn began to make cloth as well. Even so, most of the cloth produced went to the military, where it was used for uniforms and tents and as substitute for scarcer materials (horse bridles and rifle slings, for example, were often made of cloth to conserve leather for army shoes). Most civilian manufacturing needs went begging as North Carolinians often had to return to the pioneer days of home manufacture. The state government helped as it could. It purchased blockade-runners to bring in goods, including cotton cards (pairs of wire-toothed brushes that straighten fibers) so that soldiers' wives and widows could use the state's abundant raw cotton to spin yarn and knit or weave their own cloth.

Postwar Struggles and the Growth of the Milling, Tobacco, and Textile Industries

With the end of the Civil War, times seemed propitious for North Carolina finally to attain the diversified economy it had so long expected and sought. The end of slavery would, in theory, create a strong domestic market for manufactured goods, and the weakening of the planter class would allow less emphasis on agriculture. But there were massive obstacles. Factories and shops that survived the war were often worn out from constant activity and a lack of replacement parts. A domestic market would be many decades away, as the collapse of the price of cotton after about 1874 impoverished both white and black farmers. Capital, always in short supply, was even harder to come by after the war. Most North Carolinians' savings and investments had been in Confederate currency, made worthless by the Reconstruction acts and the Fourteenth Amendment. Almost every bank in North Carolina was bankrupt as a result of the war. After the passage of the federal National Banking Acts in 1863 and 1864 and the move toward a gold standard, the entire nation suffered from deflation until at least 1900. Most cash was concentrated in northeastern cities, and would-be entrepreneurs in North Carolina often had to seek capital there, ceding at least partial ownership and control to northern lenders.

By about 1880, however, it was obvious that any gains in manufacturing would have to revolve around the resources that North Carolina possessed; namely, agricultural and forest products and cheap labor. By the late 1870s, tobacco processing was a major industry in Durham, Winston-Salem, and Reidsville, with the Bull Durham factory in Durham being the largest producer of smoking tobacco in the United States. Indeed, until it was dissolved by an antitrust suit in 1911, James B. Duke's American Tobacco Company controlled 80 percent of the U.S. market.

Lumbering operations and sawmills increased in importance in the state, especially in the Sandhills region, as lumber railways were built to open more pine forests to exploitation. North Carolina's furniture industry also began to expand during this period. Based primarily in High Point, Thomasville, Lexington, Hickory, Salisbury, and Statesville, the industry first provided unfinished hardwood to northern factories and wooden spindles, bobbins, and shuttles to local textile mills, but it soon established a reputation for its finished furniture as well. Related industries producing veneer, plywood, and varnish grew as they provided materials to the furniture manufacturers.

Textile production received a great deal of investor attention for several reasons. From an economic standpoint, industrial revolutions, whether in Britain, the northern United States, or North Carolina, almost always began with textiles. It was a labor-intensive industry in which low-wage, inexperienced, unskilled workers (including women and children) could serve as a major resource. From the standpoint of the state's cotton planter or merchant facing the decline of his current business, textiles provided a new but related outlet with a positive potential. To local communities dependent on the failing cotton trade, it promised economic salvation in the form of work for bankrupted or failing farmers or their families, business for local retail establishments, increased property values, and economic growth.

Surviving antebellum mills carried on, and experienced mill owners rebuilt or modernized their mills. But many more new mills were established, especially under the precepts advanced by Daniel Augustus Tompkins. Tompkins, who settled in the Charlotte area in 1883, owned his own foundry and design firm and also represented several northern manufacturers of textile machinery. He helped local communities organize grassroots drives to "bring the cotton mill to the cotton fields" through newspaper and publicity campaigns. Local economic leaders would pledge what they could to capitalize a factory, but the less wealthy were also urged to contribute as much as they could afford, subscribing to stock in monthly installments. In this way, many local factories were established in the "cotton mill campaign" of the 1880s. In 1877 there had been fewer than 40 mills in North Carolina, most survivors of the Civil War. By 1884 75 mills existed. Two decades later, there were estimated to be 318 factories capitalized at $3.9 million, operating more than 67,000 looms and providing employment to 51,000 North Carolinians, many of them women and children.

Twentieth-Century Labor Problems, the Great Depression, and Economic Recovery

In the severe deflation of the Gilded Age (1870s to 1890s), workers were grateful for any work, and the long hours (11 to 12 hours on weekdays, plus half a day on Saturday) were not so different from those experienced on the farm. But between 1900 and 1920, people's attitudes toward mills began to change, as did conditions in which the mills operated. Most mills were controlled by major stockholders, including absentee shareholders, rather than the local community; consequently, workers felt less beholden to the owners. In addition, by about the 1920s changes in the style of women's apparel had reduced the amount of cloth needed for its manufacture. More important, competition from Europe, now recovering from World War I, and from new mills in Japan increased pressure on owners to keep wages down. Ironically, the number of textile mills in North Carolina was increasing as New England factories, hurt even more by imports, moved mills south to take advantage of the state's prevailing low wages. Labor strife was inevitable. Major strikes erupted at Charlotte in 1919 and Gastonia in 1929, and a 22-day statewide general strike was staged in 1934. On the eve of the Great Depression, industrial workers in North Carolina totaled 209,000.

The Great Depression—which began in 1929, reached its nadir in 1933, and endured until 1941—affected all North Carolina industries. The New Deal of Franklin D. Roosevelt's administration halted the decline, but not before many factories had scaled back or failed altogether. Government programs seemed unable to restore the situation to even the levels of 1929. For those workers who still held jobs, however, New Deal legislation brought a reduced work week with a minimum wage as well as an end to child labor (once 24 percent of the textile industry workforce plus a large portion of that of the tobacco industry). But it took World War II to restore the nation's industrial economy.

World War II brought $2 billion in federal military contracts to North Carolina. Most went to shipyards in Elizabeth City, New Bern, and Wilmington, where submarine chasers, minesweepers, and Liberty ships were built and launched. Other industries boosted by wartime spending included the manufacture of ammunition and radar components. Traditional industries such as textiles and lumber returned to prosperity.

New Industries, Increased Competition, and Diversification in the Modern Era

The postwar era found North Carolina and other southern states ready to take on even more industrial development, as high wages, strong union influence, and declining protective tariffs reduced northern industries' ability to meet increasing foreign competition. Eventually, foreign competition would undercut even North Carolina's lower costs, but in the interim the state benefited as companies closed their plants in the North and moved them south. By 1976 nearly three-fourths of American textile production was concentrated in the South. Tobacco production also remained important through much of the early postwar period. By 1969 North Carolina was growing 51 percent of U.S. tobacco, and this gave the state a similar lead in tobacco manufacture. The state's furniture production flourished as North Carolina surpassed New York as the national leader, producing about 20 percent of the nation's total furniture products.

As the end of the twentieth century approached, North Carolina manufacturing faced several new challenges. Free trade agreements were instituted with various foreign countries, particularly those in Latin America and Asia, giving North Carolina textile mills tremendous competition, and corporations moved many operations abroad, closing all but the most efficient plants. Between January 1990 and December 2001, the state lost more than 155,000 manufacturing jobs, nearly 100,000 of them in the textile industry. Environmental concerns brought accusations against many industries for polluting water and air resources, most notably in western North Carolina along the Pigeon River. Health concerns and legal action dealt the tobacco industry heavy blows, and tobacco manufacture dropped to sixteenth place among North Carolina manufacturing industries.

North Carolina industries faced not only increased competition but also changes in the business climate. With most corporate stocks owned by institutions such as mutual funds and pension plans rather than individual investors, there was less interest in manufacturing itself and more interest in its profitability. Formerly, investors were willing to accept lower profits in stable industries, but institutional investors demand universally high profits from all businesses. To increase the bottom line, corporations downsized, often closing otherwise successful plants that were seen as relatively unprofitable. The 1990s were characterized by mergers of large businesses into even larger, more diversified corporations. In the process, more marginally profitable plants were closed and management functions consolidated, resulting in large layoffs among white-collar, middle-management executives in the 1990s. In addition, the state lost a number of corporate headquarters.

Rising worldwide lumber prices and environmental concerns spawned wood chip processing plants that made more efficient use of valuable forest resources. Hog and poultry processing plants made North Carolina a major national supplier of hogs, chickens, and turkeys by 2000. Despite some economic struggles, the furniture industry was still strong, remaining the second-largest employer in the state, with approximately 70,000 workers.

Companies specializing in telecommunications, pharmaceuticals, biotechnology, and other industries became important contributors to North Carolina's manufacturing economy. University Research Park in Charlotte and Research Triangle Park (RTP) in the Raleigh-Durham-Chapel Hill area brought to the state not only research endeavors but also light manufacture of electronic components and development of computer software and other telecommunications equipment. In 2006 IBM, Nortel Networks, Cisco Systems, and Sony Ericsson all maintained significant operations in RTP. RTP and the university research hospitals at Duke and the University of North Carolina at Chapel Hill also attracted major drug-manufacturing companies, including GlaxoSmithKline and Bayer Corporation, to the Triangle area.

In 2006 the production of fabricated metal products, electrical and transportation equipment, chemicals, paper, rubber, plastics, stone, clay, and glass were all significant in the state. Major Charlotte manufacturers included Goodrich Corporation, a Fortune 500 company that produces aerospace components, systems, and services; SPX Corporation, makers of products as diverse as fire detection systems and freezer units for blood banks; Nucor Corporation, makers of a wide variety of steel products; and Sonic Automotive, Inc., one of the nation's largest automotive retailers. Other large North Carolina manufacturers included Greensboro-based VF Corporation (clothing and apparel), Winston-Salem–based Reynolds American, Inc. (consumer goods), and Raleigh-based Martin Marietta Materials, Inc. (stone aggregates for roadways and other construction) and Red Hat, Inc. (technology).

References: Brent D. Glass, *The Textile Industry in North Carolina: A History* (1992); Douglass C. North, *The Economic Growth of the United States, 1790–1860* (1961); North Carolina Dept. of Commerce and Harris Publishing Co., *North Carolina*

Manufacturers Directory (2002); George B. Tindall, *The Emergence of the New South, 1913–1945* (1967).

John R. deTreville
Additional research provided by Lisa Coston Hall.

SEE ALSO Exports; Furniture; Information Technology; Iron and Steel Industry; Textiles; Tobacco.

Manumission Societies began as an eighteenth-century movement to abolish slavery through voluntary emancipation. The undertaking was initiated primarily by the Society of Friends (Quakers) on grounds that slavery was immoral and against Christian teaching. In North Carolina the first major step was taken in 1776, when owning or trading slaves was added to the list of practices punishable by banishment (called "disowning") from the Quaker meeting. As the egalitarian ideals of the American Revolution became popular in the Federalist era, Quakers attempted to convince non-Quakers to manumit, or free, their slaves.

By 1800 North Carolina's Quaker population was the largest of any state, with its members residing mostly in Randolph and Guilford Counties. Seeking legal advice, the Friends found a novel, if temporary, solution to their slavery concerns. As a legal entity, the Yearly Meeting (the central body of Quakers in North Carolina) could own slaves. Beginning in 1808, persons wishing to manumit their slaves could do so by transferring them to the Yearly Meeting. Consequently, within a few years the Society of Friends became one of the largest slaveholders in the state—to Quakers, a perplexing and ironic situation, for the remedy was only a stopgap.

In this environment, a few small manumission societies were organized at the urging of Charles Osborne, a Quaker minister from Tennessee. Four of these groups formed a larger Manumission Society, which held its first meeting in 1816. Osborne then attempted to persuade Baptists, Methodists, Presbyterians, and Moravians to join the movement, and at this point some Methodists and Presbyterians agreed. The Manumission Society grew rapidly, welcoming all petitioners. Among the new members were slaveholders who obviously had joined merely to disrupt the proceedings, but a large faction urged the membership to affiliate with the American Colonization Society. This faction was successful in appending "and Colonization" to the society's name. Over the next few years, the Quakers continued to deal with these fractious elements, but in 1823 the Manumission and Colonization Society ceased to exist as a formal body.

In 1824 Benjamin Lundy, a New Jersey Quaker, revived the society from the original membership, calling it the Manumission Society of North Carolina. This organization was more pragmatic than its predecessor and took steps to give it more structure. By 1826 the North Carolina Manumission Society acquired, from a core of 14 individual societies, more than 45 af-filiates; its approximately 3,000 members represented almost half of the antislavery societies in the nation. In the same year one of its members was elected to the North Carolina legislature, demonstrating its growing influence. Moreover, the new society expanded its base to include Baptists, Methodists, and other religious groups across the state.

A major task of the North Carolina society was to equitably resolve the situation of the 600 slaves nominally owned by the Quakers' Yearly Meeting. A poll of these blacks revealed that half of them wanted to go to Liberia, whereas two other sizable voting blocs desired to either "go West" or "stay at home." Wishing to respect these requests, the society collected $2,000 to relocate the largest group. A boat with 40 freed slaves sailed for Liberia in 1826, followed by a boat with 120 bound for Haiti, accompanied by two Quakers. Another vessel left for Liberia a little later. In Haiti, however, the African Americans met with extreme resistance, and most of them returned to North Carolina. Moreover, the society discovered that one boat bound for Liberia actually docked in New Orleans, where the freed slaves were auctioned off and returned to bondage.

The North Carolina Manumission Society continued to promote emancipation by various means, but increasingly its efforts were blocked by legislation and judicial rulings. In 1831 anti-education acts effectively closed the black schools operated by the society. In the aftermath of the Nat Turner Rebellion, which occurred in Southampton County, Va., in August 1831, the organization's activities were barred at virtually every avenue; it became risky for followers even to continue their membership. As President Andrew Jackson contained the Nullifiers (radical advocates of state rights) in South Carolina in 1832, interest in the society somewhat revived, but by 1834 member organizations had dwindled to only a few affiliates, convening for the last time at Marlborough Meeting in Randolph County. Thereafter, those elements still in North Carolina existed only as depots on the Underground Railroad.

Whether by trepidation or frustration, many manumission supporters went west, largely to Indiana and Illinois. There, reportedly, they helped found the Free Soil movement and ultimately drew all antislavery parties into the Republican Party.

References: Jeffrey Brooke Allen, "The Racial Thought of North Carolina Opponents of Slavery, 1789–1876," *NCHR* 54 (January 1982); Seth B. Hinshaw, *The Carolina Quaker Experience, 1685–1985: An Interpretation* (1984); Patrick Sowle, "The North Carolina Manumission Society, 1816–1834," *NCHR* 42 (January 1965).

Roger N. Kirkman
David A. Norris

Man Will Never Fly Memorial Society was formed in 1959 with the motto, "Birds Fly—Men Drink." Each year the society holds a party beginning the afternoon of 16 December and ending at 10:45 A.M. on 17 December, the exact time of what the society refers to as "the Wright Brothers alleged first flight." During the evening program—which one writer described as the break between the cocktail party and the drinking that follows—the group has, on occasion, presented anti-aviation awards to groups or individuals who the members feel have done the most to deter the advance of aviation. Many of the society members are pilots.

Reference: Jack Aulis, "Never-Fly Group Proves Members Can Fly High," *Raleigh News and Observer*, 17 Dec. 1971.

Jo Ann Williford

Maple Syrup and maple sugar, usually associated with Vermont and other parts of New England, began to be produced by Moravian settlers in Piedmont North Carolina soon after they arrived in the region. A daily journal for 3 Jan. 1754 recorded that the settlers boiled sap from maple trees (*Acer saccharum*) growing around them to make syrup. Ten years later, they noted that the sap was "so sweet that some sugar can be boiled from it, and so plentiful that some use it for a drink at the time it is rising. It flows best on clear, cool nights in spring." Early settlers discovered the Indians using maple sap in this manner.

Reference: Adelaide L. Fries, ed., *Records of the Moravians in North Carolina*, vols. 1 and 2 (1922).

William S. Powell

Maps. The story of cartography, or mapmaking, in the North Carolina region may have begun with the Vinland map of 1440. Although its authenticity has been questioned, the map gives ample evidence, as tested by renowned scholars, that the East Coast of the New World from Newfoundland to Cuba was visited by Europeans well before Columbus. This was when North Carolina, as it is defined today, was known as "Nova Albion."

The early maps of the area that was to become North Carolina resulted from the mapping and compilation of information of the coast by ancient mariners and explorers. Mapping and recording observations from the deck of a bouncing ship were not easy tasks. The early maps were generally nothing more than rough sketches of the coastline with latitudinal measurements taken with a backstaff, distances measured with an alidade, and depths taken with a lead line. Surveying by the more modern method of triangulation came into practice with Thomas Harriot on the second of the Raleigh voyages in 1585–86, although triangulation was used to make maps as early as 1535 by Gerhard Mercator. Early maps did not usually have longitude, nor were they very accurate, sometimes intentionally so. Still, some of the maps were quite good (especially John Smith's map of 1612).

Much of the exploration and discovery of America in the late fifteenth century and the sixteenth century was undertaken to find a shorter route to the Far East, and many maps were used to market that theme. Indeed, often a map's accuracy was secondary to its elaborate beauty. Such are the maps of the Thames School. In particular, Nicholas Comberford's map of 1657 shows a very generalized North Carolina coastline with scattered trees inland and Pamlico Sound described as a broad bay or inland sea. The Comberford map contains the earliest evidence of permanent European settlement of the region that became North Carolina. This colored manuscript map on vellum in the National Maritime Museum, Greenwich, England, is titled "The South Part of Virginia." Another one in the New York Public Library, otherwise virtually identical, has added in a later hand, "now the north part of Carolina." Shown between the Roanoke River and Salmon Creek is "Batts House," the trading post/home of Nathaniell Batts, believed to have been the first permanent settler of the colony.

By the mid-seventeenth century, maps were used to describe the virtues of America and other places of the New World. John Ogilby's atlas of America in 1671 and John Speed's map and description in 1676 are wonderful examples of early marketing. The early settlement of North Carolina, known as "Virginia" in 1675, began in the Albemarle Sound area and continued into the early 1700s. William Hack's map of 1684 shows the Appalachian Mountains, as more was being learned about the interior of America. Exploration of the interior portion of North Carolina was soon followed by settlement inland. John Lawson's map of 1709 and his surveying commentary attest to the acclimation of explorers to the landscape. More and more place names were being mapped and recorded. Place names began to appear on the maps in vastly greater density, and the descriptions on the maps were in much better detail.

In colonial times, as settlements were located more inland, explorers established trails, most of which were borrowed from the Indians. Surveyors following by foot or on horseback trotted across the frontier to divide up the land established by the king. Edward Moseley's map of 1733 added greatly to the understanding of the interior of North Carolina, as did James Wimble's 1738 map of the coast. John Collet's map of 1770 gives the names of settlers, and details such as shoals, swamps, and roads appear on the 1775 map of Henry Mouzon. Joshua Fry and Peter Jefferson's map of the same year shows the name and location of stores, ferries, and roads. The North Carolina area was finally becoming settled.

As the United States became more spatially and politically organized after the American Revolution, the government took on the responsibility of mapmaking. Surveying and mapping by the government began by act of the Continental Congress on 20 May 1785, and the Board of Engineers was created in the early 1800s. The mapping of the coasts, harbors, and rivers became very important to the government. Thus, the need for individual surveyors, mapmakers, and the like became practically obsolete in the private sector, and they moved on to do mapping in the western United States, Canada, South America, Africa, and Pacific Coast.

Mapping programs by government agencies, particularly the U.S. Geological Survey, continued throughout the twentieth century and into the twenty-first century. The U.S. Coast and Geodetic Survey had a continuous chart-updating program, and the U.S. Corps of Engineers continued its reconnaissance survey work. Major oil companies began to produce state road maps, and the North Carolina Highway Commission started its county road map series. Using these maps, Garland P. Stout researched old maps, deeds, and other records and recorded information on the North Carolina county maps. Each county map shows the location of post offices, schools, churches, gristmills, mine sites, and abandoned settlements.

Efforts to map soils began after World War I and continued throughout the century. The U.S. Soil Conservation Service, the North Carolina Soil Conservation Service, and the North Carolina Department of Natural Resources and Community Development completed the mapping program by 1978. North Carolina was also covered by U.S. Geological Survey topographic maps with the assistance of the North Carolina Department of Natural Resources and Community Development.

With the advent of satellite imagery and computerized databases, mapping in North Carolina became permanently altered by the technical revolution. Mapping is now accomplished with a computer using a geographic information system (GIS), and place names are found in the geographic names information system (GNIS).

Cartographers or Publishers of Maps of the North Carolina Area

EARLY MAPS

1440?	Vinland
1500	Juan de la Cosa (sailed with Columbus)
1507	Martin Waldseemuller
1526	Juan Vespucci (nephew of Amerigo Vespucci)
1529	Diego Ribero (or Diogo Ribeiro)
1529	Giovanni da Verrazano (from voyage in 1524)
1538	Gerhard Mercator
1542	John Rotz
1550	Pierre Desceliers
1558	Diogo Homem
1560	Baptista Agnese (Portolan Atlas)
1562	Diego Gutierez
1567	Alonso de Santa Cruz
1569	Gerhard Mercator
1580	John Dee
1582	Michael Lok
1584	Ortelius-Chives

ELIZABETHAN-ERA MAPS

1585	John White (watercolor drawing)
1587	John White (probably drawn by Thomas Harriot and published in 1590 by Theodor de Bry)
1590	Ortelius
1590	John White (published by de Bry, probably compiled from earlier maps)
1591	Theodor de Bry (probably drawn by Jacques le Moyne de Morgues)
1597	Cornely Van Wytfliet (used White as a partial source)
1605	Willem Janszoon Blaeu
1606	Gerhard Mercator–Jodocus Hondius
1608	John Smith
1611	Velasco
1612	Grauen B. Wm. Hole (probably from Smith)
1615	Cornely Van Wytfliet
1624	John Smith
1630	Gerhard Mercator
1640	Blaeu (based on Mercator-Hondius map of 1606)
1646	Robert Dudley
1647	Johannes Jansonius
1651	John (or Nicholas?) Farrer (or Ferrar?)
1651	John Goddard (or Gaddard) (possibly used Farrer's map as source)
1653	Juan Jansonio (or Jansonius)
1656	Sanson (or Janson)
1657	Nicholas Comberford (Thames School)
1660	Jan Jannsson
1662	John Locke

PROPRIETARY PERIOD MAPS

1666	Horne (compilation of explorations published by Hilton)
1667	John Farrer
1670	Augustine Herman (very near North Carolina area)
1671	John Locke (from Spanish sources)
1671	John Ogilby (used Locke's map and Lederer's information)
1672	Blome and John Ogilby
1672	John Lederer (shows first town "Sapon" on Roanoke River)
1672	John Ogilby–James Moxon (Lords Proprietors order)
1673	Robert Morden and William Berry
1676	Lamb (probably from John Speed)
1676	John Speed (similar to Ogilby's map of 1671)
1676	Capt. John Wood (used Morden and Berry as source)
1677	Joel Lancaster (Thames style)
1679	Joel or James Lancaster
1682	Joel Gascoyne (Gascoigne)
1682	Joseph (or James?) Moxon
1684	William (or John) Hack
1684	Maurice Mathews

1685? John Thornton, Morden and Lea
1686? John Thornton and Fisher
1687 John Thornton
1695 John Thornton and Morden
1695 Willdey
1696 Guillaume De Lisle
1696 John Sanson (Pierre Mortier was probably publisher
     using Thorton and Morden under Sanson's name)
1709 John Lawson
1715 Moll
1718 Guillaume De Lisle
1720 Moll
1720 Van Kenlen

ROYAL COLONY PERIOD, REVOLUTIONARY,
AND POSTREVOLUTIONARY MAPS

1729 Pierre or Peter Vander Aa
1732 Hinder
1733 Edward Moseley
1733 James Wimble
1736? Moll
1737 Brickell
1738 Edward Moseley
1738 James Wimble
1751 Joshua Fry and Peter Jefferson (two maps)
1755 Dalrymple (revised from Fry and Jefferson)
1768 Thomas Jefferies (or Jefferys)
1770 John Collet
1775 Henry Mouzon
1777 John Gascoigne
1792 Dubibin (from a map dated 1756)
1794 Henry Mouzon and others
1795 Henry Mouzon

NINETEENTH-CENTURY MAPS

1808 Jonathan Price–John Strother
1820 Hamilton Fulton
1833 John MacRae (or Mac Rae)–Robert H. B. Brazier
1843 John Calvin Smith
1856 Adam and Charles Black
1861 Bachmann
1861 J. H. Colton
1882 Kerr-Cain

References: William P. Cumming, *The Southeast in Early Maps* (1962); David B. Quinn and Alison M. Quinn, *The First Colonists: Documents on the Planting of the First English Settlements in North America, 1584–1590* (1982); Richard A. Stephenson, "Comparative Cartography and Coastal Processes: Four Hundred Years of Change on the Outer Banks of North Carolina," *Terrae Incognitae* 22 (1990).

Richard A. Stephenson
William S. Powell

Market Houses. Markets in colonial North Carolina were a part of the English tradition brought by early settlers. As early as the thirteenth century town markets in England offered opportunities to buy and sell. North Carolina's first town, Bath (chartered in 1705), had a town common where fairs and markets were held. In the 1720s the colonial Assembly passed acts to create marketplaces in towns, and in 1731 Governor George Burrington's commission empowered him to establish fairs and markets.

Some courthouses and, occasionally, municipal buildings had open space underneath them for public markets. Early market houses existed in Charlotte, Edenton, Fayetteville, New Bern, Raleigh, Salem, and Wilmington. Maps, plans, and documents for other places contain references to streets named "Market," clear evidence that they were common. Wilmington and New Bern had separate fish markets, and Salem by 1803 had a meat market that was open twice a week. The *Kinston Journal* on 30 Dec. 1878 announced the pending opening of a large town hall built over a market house. Municipal, county, and state governments continue to provide market space to the benefit of both producer and consumer.

References: Adelaide L. Fries, ed., *Records of the Moravians in North Carolina*, vols. 4–5 (1930, 1943); Guion G. Johnson, *Ante-Bellum North Carolina: A Social History* (1937).

William S. Powell

Marl Beds are found along the eastern and southeastern coastline of the United States and on land across the world that was once covered by the sea. Such beds, referred to by Roman writer Marcus Varro as "white fossil clay," were formed by the breakdown of rock and the buildup of seashell, animal, and plant remains. The result was a varying mixture of sand, clay, azote, magnesium, iron, and limestone that was used by the Greeks, Romans, Gauls, Britons, and others to add lime, a natural fertilizer, to the soil.

In North Carolina, marl has been found in most of the counties that make up the coastal plain. This marl area, which consists of more than 20,000 square miles, extends west from the fall line and is in places nearly 200 miles from the Atlantic shore. North Carolina's natural limestone was far less valuable and accessible than that of neighboring states. The blue/gray and green marls, found chiefly in Pitt, Columbus, Wayne, Lenoir, Craven, Duplin, and Onslow Counties, were generally suitable only for supplemental side-dressing of the lighter and poorer state soils. Since the effect lasted for little more than a season, few farmers availed themselves of local "white fossil clay." By the early 2000s, marl beds in the state were lying dormant.

References: F. Willard Berry, *Marls and Limestones of Eastern North Carolina* (1947); Gerald F. Loughlin, *Limestones and Marls of North Carolina* (1921).

Louis P. Towles

Maroons were escaped slaves who lived in swamps and forests, although the term "Maroon" was far more prevalent in the West Indies than in North Carolina. The vast Great Dismal Swamp, in particular, was long a hiding place for Maroons. Taking advantage of its size, fertility, and natural abundance, residents of the swamp were more likely to subsist in the Great Dismal than elsewhere in the state. Prior to the Tuscarora War in 1711, many fugitive slaves were given refuge in the Indian towns, and at least a few Maroons fought with the Indians in that conflict.

In the first half of the nineteenth century, fugitive slaves formed Maroon bands at various locations in the state, raiding the surrounding community for food and other supplies. From Wake County in 1818 it was reported that the governor had offered a reward of $250 for the capture of seven named outlaws, including $100 for their leader, Billy James. Onslow, Carteret, and Bladen Counties were the scenes of other incidents involving marauding bands of fugitive slaves.

William S. Smith

SEE ALSO African Americans; Great Dismal Swamp; Slave Rebellions; Slavery.

Marriage in North Carolina, until 1868, could be either by license or by banns (public announcement) in the county where the bride lived. It is estimated that in North Carolina two-thirds of all marriages prior to 1868 were by banns, as they were quicker and cheaper than licenses. If a marriage by license was desired, a marriage bond, which was free of charge, was procured to ensure that there was no legal impediment to the union. The bond was not proof of marriage but only of the intent to marry. The consent of parents or guardians was required if either party was under age 15 and had not previously been married. Those not wishing to bother with licenses and bonds could publish the banns on three successive Sundays and then be married by a clergyman or magistrate. No public record was made of this procedure. An act of 1868 transferred the power to issue marriage licenses to the registers of deeds and made the license the only legal public record of the nuptials.

After 1851 all justices and clergy were required to return licenses for marriages they had performed to the clerk of court; these marriages were recorded chronologically in the Marriage Registers of each county, few of which have been published. Therefore, the absence of a marriage bond in North Carolina does not indicate that the couple was not married in the state, but only that there is no extant civil record of it. The percentage of extant records of marriages performed in North Carolina prior to 1868 would be generously set at 20 percent. The counties with the largest number of extant marriage bonds are Rowan and Orange.

In general, marriage severely limited the rights of women.

Although a single woman or a widow could buy and sell land, a married woman could not unless she held the legal status of a single woman. Additionally, from 1784 until 1868, a widow was entitled to only a life estate of one-third of the real property her husband held at his death.

In 1866 the state legislature passed an Act Concerning Negroes and Persons of Color or of Mixed Blood, according to which slaves who had been living together as man and wife during slavery were now "deemed to have been lawfully married . . . at the time of the commencement of such cohabitation." Such couples could go before the clerk of court in the county where they resided, or before a justice of the peace, and legalize their union through the purchase (for 25 cents) of a marriage bond. Cohabitation bonds were also filed with the register of deeds and were retroactive, legitimizing the marriages of former slaves who had lived together as husband and wife. These bonds provided the name and age of the bride and groom, the length of time they had been married "in the eyes of God," and the names of their previous masters. The statute required that cohabitation bonds be registered prior to 1 Sept. 1866, and most were. These records are enormously important to persons searching black or mixed races. North Carolina prohibited marriages of mixed race from 1715 until 1976.

Common-law marriages, in which couples are considered to be legally married merely through a long-term commitment and without a license or any ceremony whatsoever, are not recognized in North Carolina.

Jo White Linn

SEE ALSO Divorce.

Marshals, U.S. The Office of U.S. Marshal was created by the Judiciary Act of 1789, the same legislation that established the U.S. Supreme Court and the federal judicial system. President George Washington appointed the first 13 U.S. marshals to represent each of the original colonies. These marshals were given extensive authority to support the federal courts within their judicial districts and to carry out all lawful orders issued by judges, Congress, or the president.

On 4 June 1790 Congress created the District of North Carolina, and four days later the U.S. Senate confirmed Washington's appointment of John Skinner of Perquimans County as North Carolina's first U.S. marshal. During the 82 years of its existence, the original District of North Carolina had 12 marshals. Beverly Daniel holds the record for serving the longest term in state history at 32 years (1808–40). In 1872 Congress divided the original district into the Eastern and Western Districts of North Carolina. Samuel T. Carrow and Robert M. Douglass became the first marshals of the Eastern District and Western District, respectively. In 1927 Congress added the Middle District of North Carolina, whose first marshal was Charles G. Bryant.

The U.S. Marshal Service retains the responsibility for the custody, care, and transportation of federal offenders; apprehension of federal criminals who jump bail, violate parole, or escape from prison; protection of the courts, judges, attorneys, and witnesses; enforcement of court orders; management of assets seized or forfeited as a result of being acquired from the profits of criminal activities; and provision of a swift law enforcement response to significant national emergencies requiring federal intervention.

References: Frederick S. Calhoun, *The Lawmen: United States Marshals and Their Deputies* (1989); U.S. Department of Justice, *United States Marshals, 1789 to Present* (1996).

William Irwin Berryhill Jr.

Mars Hill College,

a Baptist institution located 18 miles north of Asheville, traces its origins to the French Broad Baptist Academy, which opened its doors in 1856 on land donated by Edward Carter. According to contemporary accounts, a slave named Joe Anderson was employed as collateral by the academy's contractor until the contractor was remunerated for his work. Among other early benefactors of the academy were J. W. Anderson (Joe Anderson's owner), T. S. Deaver, Berry Duyck, William Keith, Thomas Ray, and J. C. Sams. In 1859 the North Carolina General Assembly granted the academy the name suggested by trustee Lewis Palmer, Mars Hill College, from the Bible's Acts 17:22: "Then Paul stood in the midst of Mars Hill."

During the Civil War, which split the region around Mars Hill along Unionist and Confederate lines both during and after the conflict, the school was closed for two years (1863–65). Fourteen school presidents served between 1865 and 1897, reflecting the instability of the institution. From 1872 to 1878 the college was closed; its building functioned as a branch of the Oxford Masonic Orphanage under John Robert Sams and J. H. Moore from 1872 to 1876 and as a "subscription school" under James Bassett Lunsford from 1876 to 1878.

Mars Hill College reopened in 1878 but continued to struggle throughout the remainder of the nineteenth century. It was the accession of Wake Forest alumnus Robert Lee Moore as president of the college in 1897 that precipitated an era of growth. In 1921 Mars Hill obtained junior college status, and in 1937 its high school division was eliminated. Moore retired in 1938 and was succeeded by South Carolinian Hoyt Blackwell, a Latin and Greek professor. During Blackwell's tenure, Mars Hill achieved four-year status and awarded its first baccalaureate degrees in 1964. The college began admitting African American students in 1961; notably, the first black student to enroll was Oralene Graves, the great-great-granddaughter of Joe Anderson.

The modern Mars Hill College occupies over 200 acres of land with 32 buildings. In the early 2000s it enrolled nearly 1,000 students and offered bachelor's degrees in 30 majors.

References: Edward Jennings Carter, "A History of Mars Hill College" (M.A. thesis, UNC-Chapel Hill, 1940); Clarence Dixon Creasman, *Moore of Mars Hill* (1950); John Angus McLeod, *From These Stones: Mars Hill College, 1856–1968* (1968).

James I. Martin Sr.

Martin Academy.

On 9 May 1783 the North Carolina General Assembly granted a charter authorizing John Causon, Hezekiah Balch, Samuel Doak, and others to organize Martin Academy in Washington County (now in Tennessee) in honor of Governor Alexander Martin. The legislators made quite clear, however, that the state would not support the school in any way. The bill enabled the small school—previously founded in Salem in 1780 by Doak, a Princeton graduate and Presbyterian minister—to become North Carolina's "first organized school west of the mountains." Two years later the State of Franklin also granted a charter to Martin Academy, and in 1795 the academy attained college status. At this time the institution's name was changed to Washington College to honor the nation's first president.

With the exception of the Civil War years, Washington College Academy has been in continuous operation since its founding by Doak, evolving from a modest academy to a college to a privately owned secondary school. It is located near Jonesborough, Tenn.

Nathaniel C. Hughes Jr.

Martin County,

located in North Carolina's Coastal Plain region, was formed from Halifax and Tyrrell Counties in 1774. It was named for Josiah Martin, the last royal governor of North Carolina. The county seat of Williamston (originally Squhawky or Skewarky) was incorporated in 1779; other communities include Oak City, Jamesville, Hamilton, Hassell, Gold Point, Parmele, Everetts, Robersonville, Bear Grass, and Darden.

The area that became Martin County was settled by English colonists early in the eighteenth century, supplanting the land's original Tuscarora Indian inhabitants. Williamston, the county's first incorporated town, developed along the banks of the Roanoke River as an important shipping hub for tar, turpentine, and other local products. Although later towns such as Jamesville and Hamilton were established along the river to participate in the thriving shipping business, Williamston continued to flourish as a trade center throughout the nineteenth century and well into the twentieth with its integration into a network of railroads and highways.

The Confederate outpost Fort Branch is one of Martin County's popular tourist attractions, and the Roanoke River and its surrounding lowlands provide an abundance of opportunities for hunting and fishing. Tobacco, peanuts, corn, soybeans, and cotton are produced in Martin County, and its manufactured products include paper, farm machinery, and textiles. In 2004 Martin County's estimated population was 24,700.

Reference: *Martin County Heritage* (1980).

Robert Blair Vocci

Mary Duke Biddle Foundation, established in 1956 in New York City and now headquartered in Durham, provides support for private higher and secondary education, specified churches, cultural programs (particularly in music, dance, and theater), projects in the arts, and aid to the community and the handicapped. Giving is limited to North Carolina and New York City, with half of the grants committed to Duke University in the form of support for program development, conferences and seminars, fellowships, and scholarships. By the early 2000s, the foundation had awarded grants totaling more than $28 million.

References: Mary Duke Biddle Foundation, *Fifteen Year Report, 1956–1970* (1970); Charles W. Stanford, *Art for Humanity's Sake: The Story of the Mary Duke Biddle Gallery for the Blind* (1976).

Wiley J. Williams

Massachusetts Circular Letter was written by Samuel Adams on behalf of the Massachusetts legislature in reaction to the unpopular Townshend Acts passed by Parliament in 1767. Dated 11 Feb. 1768, the letter asserted that Parliament had no right to tax Americans, as they were not represented by that legislative body. Further, as Parliament was separated from the colonies by 3,000 miles of ocean and could never properly represent them, legislative power was vested in a "subordinate legislature" in each colony, which alone had the right to tax the colonists. Objections were also raised to the Crown's appointment of governors, judges, and other officers at the expense of the colonies without their consent. The letter ended with professions of loyalty to the Crown and the hope that the "united & dutifull Supplications" of the colonists would be granted by the king. Copies of the letter were sent to the legislatures of most North American colonies.

The circular letter was received in North Carolina on 1 Apr. 1768 by John Harvey, Speaker of the House. The British government was quite concerned at the prospect of the American colonies uniting to resist their directives. The Massachusetts Assembly had been ordered to withdraw the letter, and the other colonial legislatures were directed to ignore it or face "an immediate prorogation or dissolution." The earl of Hillsborough, secretary of state for the colonies, instructed Governor William Tryon to end the present session of the Assembly if he thought that it was likely to act on the letter from Massachusetts; he did so at the end of April, before the legislature took any action.

When the Assembly reconvened in November, Harvey presented the Massachusetts Circular Letter to the delegates. Harvey and some others advocated a strong response, but the majority of the delegates voted for moderation. They verbally directed the Speaker to answer the letter and appointed a committee to compose "an humble, dutiful and loyal address" to the king. The rather mild response angered Samuel Johnston and Joseph Hewes, who refused to serve on the committee. The address to the king, while polite, firmly stated the Assembly's belief that the Townshend Acts were illegal because "free men cannot be legally taxed but by themselves or their representatives." The Assembly also instructed the colony's agent, Henry Eustace McCulloh, to work with the agents of the other colonies to try to persuade Parliament to repeal the Townshend Acts.

Speaker Harvey's answer to the Massachusetts legislature was dated 11 Feb. 1769, a year after the date of the Massachusetts Circular Letter. Harvey called for a stronger friendship between North Carolina and the other colonies, especially Massachusetts. He wrote that "the Assembly of this Colony will at all Times receive with Pleasure the Opinion of your House in Matters of general Concern to America, and be equally willing on every such Occasion to communicate their Sentiments," and he promised that North Carolina would "ever be ready, firmly to unite with their sister colonies, in pursuing every constitutional measure for redress of the grievances so justly complained of." After Harvey's letter was received in Massachusetts, the *Boston Evening Post* wrote: "The colonies, no longer disconnected, form one body." The Massachusetts Circular Letter forged an early link between North Carolina and the other colonies in their united resistance to Britain's policies.

Reference: Henry Steele Commager, ed., *Documents of American History* (1968).

David A. Norris

Matilda Berkely; or, Family Anecdotes, by British-born Winifred Marshall Gales (1761–1839), is considered the first novel published in North Carolina written by a resident of the state. The author's husband, *Raleigh Register* founder Joseph Gales, printed the book in 1804 on his press in Raleigh. Instead of listing the novelist's name, the title page revealed only that the work was "By the Author of the History of Lady Emma Melcombe and her Family, &c." This earlier novel was published in 1787 in England, where the couple lived before moving to the United States in 1795.

The youngest daughter of a Newark-on-Trent family, Winifred Marshall began writing poems and stories as a child and by 17 had published her first novel. After Marshall's marriage in 1784 to Joseph Gales, the couple settled in Sheffield. There they opened a bookshop and published the liberal *Shef-*

field Register until 1794, when Gales's activism in the Constitutional Reform movement necessitated his leaving England. They eventually immigrated to America, settling in Raleigh in 1799. That year Gales issued the first number of his long-lived *Raleigh Register*. He soon opened a bookshop, importing a large part of its stock from England. Biographer Robert N. Elliott characterizes the Galeses' home as a center of social activity, noted for good conversation, quoting one of their visitors as crediting a large part of its attractiveness to Gales's "brilliant wife."

In Winifred Marshall Gales's written recollections of her parents, her description of her own English mother parallels some of the qualities with which she endows the fictional Matilda. The "strength of a sensible mind" saw her through "many trials," including separation by a great distance from part of her family; namely, daughter Winifred's removal from England to America. Twentieth-century reviewers described the book as typical of the English novels of the last half of the eighteenth century, "concerned with incidents of the *haut-monde* who looked down on the governesses and companions from the upper middle class."

References: Grady Lee Ernest Carroll Sr., *The Gales Family in Raleigh and Washington* (1978); Richard Walser and E. T. Malone Jr., *Literary North Carolina* (1986).

Elizabeth Reid Murray

Mattamuskeet Apples are named for Lake Mattamuskeet, in North Carolina's coastal Hyde County, where the apples originated. Ranging from medium to large in size, the apples have a yellow flesh covered by a rusty red peel coated with white dots. They are hard when first picked, but after being stored in a dry place they become mellow while retaining their firmness. The apples are noted for their ability to remain fresh for a long period and are good for cooking. Their shape differs from other apples in that the apple tends to be slightly flattened when sitting on the stem end. Legend tells that the seeds for the first Mattamuskeet apple trees were brought to the area in the gizzard of a goose. Hyde County old-timers call them "Skeet apples." A small number of Mattamuskeet apple trees existed in 2006, especially on the old plantation homesteads.

R. S. Spencer Jr.

Mattamuskeet Indians, also known as the Machapunga or Marimiskeet Indians, inhabited the region of present-day Hyde County at the time of the attempted settlements on Roanoke Island in the 1580s. According to explorer John Lawson, by 1701 the Mattamuskeet/Machapunga were reduced to a single village, called Mattamuskeet, and numbered about 30 warriors (representing a probable total of less than 100 people). The Mattamuskeet were known as expert watermen.

They likely became dependent on European trade, as did their neighbors, and in the years prior to the Tuscarora War (1711–13) they undoubtedly witnessed their share of the clashes that were becoming frequent between natives and European settlers. Along with the Bay River Indians and the Pamlico Indians, the Mattamuskeet joined the lower Tuscarora, the Coree, the Woccon, and possibly other tribes, in fighting against European settlers in the Tuscarora War.

Following the war, several remnant Indian bands, comprised mainly of Mattamuskeets and Corees, were relegated to a Mattamuskeet reservation, an isolated tract of about 36 square miles of marsh and low ridges bordering Lake Mattamuskeet in Hyde County. The Coree evidently did not remain long on the reservation. The Indians occupying the reservation began selling off their land to white settlers as early as 1731, and the final sale, dissolving the reservation, occurred in 1761. Sporadic references to surnames common among these Indians continued to be recorded through the 1800s, and some surnames survive in Hyde County today.

The Mattamuskeet apparently faced constant pressure from white settlers, and in 1724 Mattamuskeet "kings" John Squires and John Mackey petitioned the Colonial Council for their lands to be surveyed and conveyed as a formal grant. The grant was approved in 1727, but the actual survey seems never to have occurred. The Indians had been given 10,240 acres, but in reality they received a considerably larger number of acres in exchange for two buckskins and an annual quitrent of one shilling per 100 acres.

Squires served as chief of the Mattamuskeet from 1718 until his death in the 1740s, apparently residing on a 150-acre tract at the mouth of Mattamuskeet Creek, later renamed Middle Creek. After Squires's death, a leadership struggle appears to have occurred, with power split between several individuals.

Alexander Stewart reported after his 1761 trip to the area that the Roanoke and Hatteras Indians had joined the Mattamuskeet and were residing with them at that time. Stewart baptized more than 25 Indians during his visits in 1761 and 1763. The Mattamuskeet Indians declined in number, and in 1792 the entire reservation was sold for £50 to a white settler. That deed was signed by four adult females and three children.

By the early 1800s, apprentice bonds revealed that Mattamuskeet Indian youth were being taught trades by white masters. Afterward the remaining individuals with Mattamuskeet Indian surnames were frequently referred to as "free persons of color" and apprenticed as such and also listed in the Hyde County census records under that classification. Even in the late twentieth century, some Hyde County families—including the Collins, Barber, Chance, Clayton, and Bryant families—can trace their Indian heritage back to the Mattamuskeet.

References: Patrick H. Garrow, *The Mattamuskeet Documents: A Study in Social History* (1975); Douglas L. Rights, *The American Indian in North Carolina* (1947); John Reed Swanton, *The Indians of the Southeastern United States* (1946); Ruth Y. Wetmore, *First on the Land: The North Carolina Indians* (1975).

R. S. Spencer Jr.
William G. DiNome

McDowell County, located in North Carolina's Mountain region, was formed from Rutherford and Burke Counties in 1842 and took its name from Revolutionary War colonel Joseph McDowell. The county seat of Marion (incorporated in 1844) was named for Gen. Francis Marion, the "Swamp Fox" of the Revolution; other communities include Old Fort, Ashford, Little Switzerland, Nebo, Pleasant Gardens, Glenwood, Woodlawn, Dysartville, and Sugar Hill.

Originally Cherokee and Catawba Indian territory, the land later organized as McDowell County was settled in the eighteenth century by Scotch-Irish immigrants. To protect the settlers, a series of forts was constructed along the frontier, and it became known as the "Gateway to the Mountains" for westward-bound pioneers. Although its deposits of gold helped North Carolina become, in the early nineteenth century, the nation's leading gold producer, McDowell County has been largely untouched by urban development. Roughly 75 percent of the county remains forested and boasts a wide array of wildlife, waterfalls, and scenic vistas. One of the Mountain region's most well-known natural attractions, the spectacular Linville Caverns, lies beneath the McDowell County–Avery County line. The town of Old Fort is also home to Mountain Gateway Museum and the Arrowhead Monument, a 15-foot-tall arrowhead carved from pink granite in the 1930s as a tribute to the county's original Native American inhabitants. Andrews Geyser, west of Old Fort, was built in 1885 as a unique attraction for railway patrons. Carson House, a home dating to the late eighteenth century, served as a courthouse and home to a prominent local family. McDowell County produces many goods, including Christmas trees, livestock, textiles, furniture, and pharmaceuticals. The population of the county was estimated to be just over 43,000 in 2004.

Reference: Mildred B. Fossett, *History of McDowell County* (1976).

Robert Blair Vocci

McIntyre's Farm, Battle of. Also known as the Battle of the Bees, the Battle of McIntyre's Farm was a Revolutionary War skirmish fought on 3 October 1780 in Mecklenburg County. When British commander Lord Charles Cornwallis left Charlotte on 12 Oct. 1780 after a 16-day occupation, he was heard to say that the defiant and rebellious town was a "damned hornet's nest." Although the British were figuratively stung by unrelenting hostility and violent ambushes, one foraging party was stung both literally and figuratively (by Patriots and by bees) in the skirmish at McIntyre's Farm.

Cornwallis's supplies at Charlotte were running low, so he ordered Maj. John Doyle to lead a foraging expedition into the surrounding countryside. The British were prepared for trouble; their 40 wagons were accompanied by 450 foot soldiers and a cavalry detachment. As Doyle's force marched up Beattie's Ford Road, they were trailed by 13 Patriots under the command of Capt. James Thompson. Thompson's men kept out of sight as the British halted seven miles from town at McIntyre's farm. There, some of the British remained behind to plunder the farm while Doyle and the rest of the party began to march on.

As some Redcoats loaded wagons with farm produce, other soldiers and their dogs made a great commotion chasing chickens. A British captain in the doorway of the farm's log cabin laughed loudly at the lively scene as his men accidentally turned over a beehive and ran from the enraged bees. As the disorganized British tried to elude the bees, the Patriots fired into them. The laughing British captain, nine men, and two horses were said to have been shot down by the first volley. Because the Patriots fired from cover with great accuracy and constantly shifted their positions, it seemed to the startled Redcoats that they were under attack from a much larger force.

Believing that they were outnumbered, Doyle ordered his men to retreat. Rebel fire killed some of the horses drawing the supply wagons, which blocked the road and added to the confusion. Some British soldiers cut loose uninjured animals and escaped on them. Patriots from the neighborhood sniped at the retreating troops. It seemed to the survivors that "every bush along the road concealed a rebel." Many years later, historian Joseph Graham numbered the British losses as 8 men dead and 12 wounded.

The Battle of McIntyre's Farm was only one of several sharp clashes fought between Cornwallis and local Patriots around Charlotte. The McIntyre cabin, one of the oldest buildings in Mecklenburg County, still bore bullet holes from the battle when it was demolished in the 1960s. A county historical site, opened in 1976, commemorates the spot.

References: Daniel W. Barefoot, *Touring North Carolina's Revolutionary War Sites* (1998); Dolores A. Blythe, "Hornets at Work," *The State* (November 1978); C. L. Hunter, *Sketches of Western North Carolina, Historical and Biographical, Illustrating Principally the Revolutionary Period* (1877).

David A. Norris

McLean Trucking Company. In 1931, when Malcolm P. McLean began working at a service station, North Carolina was rapidly becoming a major east-west transport route. Recognizing the potential for motor freight carrying, the Maxton native bought his first truck in 1934 and began hauling dirt for WPA road construction projects. Later, he transported textiles to New York. By the mid-1960s, the McLean Trucking

Company had become the fifth-largest trucking company in America, with a fleet of 5,000 trucks and trailers and 65 terminals scattered throughout 20 states. The Winston-Salem terminal was considered the largest in the world when it was constructed in 1954.

McLean (who died in 2001 at age 87) sold his company in 1955 for $6 million and bought a small tanker firm, which he renamed Sea-Land. After becoming a pioneer in container shipping, he cashed in those shares for $160 million in 1969.

Reference: Thomas C. Parramore, *Express Lanes and Country Roads: The Way We Lived in North Carolina, 1920–1970* (1983).

Robert E. Ireland

Mealtimes in North Carolina were long set to accommodate those engaged in manual labor, particularly field workers in planting and harvesting. Farms and plantations generally had a large bell mounted on a tall post; it would be rung before meals and in case of emergencies. The first meal of the day was called breakfast, as it broke the night's fast. The principal meal of the day, eaten about midday, was called dinner. On 15 Mar. 1779, the Moravians at Salem, for example, noted that a woodshed fell under a heavy snow just as the sisters were sitting down to dinner at noon. The name dinner occasionally was dropped in favor of lunch or luncheon by mid-twentieth century. Yet when the Marquis de Lafayette, for whom Fayetteville was named, visited the town in 1825, the banquet served at 3 P.M. was called dinner. The evening meal was supper, and it was usually served long enough before dark to permit work in the kitchen to be completed while it was still light.

The ritual of taking tea in the afternoon was never widely adopted in North Carolina, although there are accounts of special occasions on which it was served. When Governor and Mrs. William Tryon visited the Moravians at Bethabara in September 1767, they had afternoon tea. Tea parties were mentioned in letters in the nineteenth century, and a Confederate soldier at home on leave during the Civil War appreciated the tea and cake served by the belles of his neighborhood.

Following the practice of the New England states, some North Carolinians, and other southerners of the fashionable or professional classes, began to drop the word dinner for their midday meal and speak of "lunch," or on a more formal occasion, of "luncheon." While the main meal was still called dinner, it was served at the end of the day. Many people, nevertheless, still stick to the accustomed name and hour for dinner even into the twenty-first century, sometimes simply as a matter of pride in their heritage.

Reference: Guion G. Johnson, *Ante-Bellum North Carolina: A Social History* (1937).

William S. Powell

Mechanics and Farmers Bank, North Carolina's oldest African American–owned bank, was established in 1908 in Durham under the auspices of the North Carolina Mutual and Provident Association (renamed the North Carolina Mutual Life Insurance Company in 1919). The original charter members included Richard Fitzgerald, John Merrick, Aaron M. Moore, William G. Pearson, J. C. Scarborough, Charles C. Spaulding, J. A. Dodson, and Stanford L. Warren. The bank first operated from space in the building of the North Carolina Mutual and Provident Association, later moving to a building on West Parrish Street.

Mechanics and Farmers became an important source of financing in the 1920s, saving more than 500 African American farms and residences, when its loan department provided $200,000 in individual loans. The bank's policy stated its intent to provide "no large loans . . . to a few profiteers, but rather conservative sums to needy farmers and laborers." The bank was one of about a dozen African American banks to survive the Great Depression and holds the distinction of being the first lending institution in North Carolina to receive a Certificate of Authority from the Federal Housing Administration (1935).

In 1999 Mechanics and Farmers shareholders approved the creation of M&F Bancorp, Inc., a holding company of which the bank became a wholly owned subsidiary. Julia Wheeler Taylor served as chair of Mechanics and Farmers from 1983 to 2000, following in the footsteps of her father John H. Wheeler, chief executive from 1952 to 1978, and her grandfather Stanford L. Warren, a cofounder and early president. In addition to its corporate headquarters and branches in Durham, the bank in 2006 had two branches in Charlotte, two in Raleigh, and one in Winston-Salem.

References: Jean B. Anderson, *Durham County: A History of Durham County, North Carolina* (1990); Wyatt T. Dixon, *How Times Do Change: A Series of Sketches of Durham and Her Citizens* (1987); Walter B. Weare, *Black Business in the New South: A Social History of the North Carolina Mutual Life Insurance Company* (rev. ed., 1993).

Wiley J. Williams

Mecklenburg County, located in North Carolina's Piedmont region, was formed from Anson County in 1762 and took its name from the German duchy of Mecklenburg-Strelitz, home of the wife of King George III, Charlotte Sophia. The county seat, Charlotte (incorporated in 1768 and originally called Charlotte Town), was named after the queen as well. Today Mecklenburg County is the most populous county in the state (with an estimated population of 769,000 in 2004) and Charlotte the largest city; the communities of Davidson, Cornelius, Huntersville, Mint Hill, Matthews, Pineville, Newell, Allen, Paw Creek, and Caldwell are also in Mecklenburg County.

Catawba, Waxhaw, and Saponi Indians originally inhabited the region. In the mid-1700s, Scotch-Irish settlers established what would later become Charlotte at the intersection of two Indian trading routes near the Catawba River. Despite the allegiance to the king demonstrated by the city's chosen name, Charlotteans in time earned the moniker "Hornet's Nest" for patriotic fervor during the Revolution. The date of 20 May 1775 is featured on North Carolina's state flag in commemoration of the "Mecklenburg Declaration of Independence," a disputed chapter in North Carolina history.

In 1799 a 17-pound gold nugget was unearthed in Mecklenburg County (in what is now Cabarrus County)—the first such discovery in the new nation—prompting a gold rush and the establishment of a branch of the U.S. Mint in Charlotte. The city grew into its role as a financial hub; by the early 2000s it was home to two of the largest banking chains in the country, the Bank of America and Wachovia Corporation, and had emerged as the nation's second-largest banking center (trailing only New York City). Today Charlotte is one of the most populous metropolises in the southeastern United States. The city is home to the Charlotte Bobcats of the National Basketball Association, the Carolina Panthers of the National Football League, and NASCAR's Lowe's Motor Speedway. Among its natives sons are President James K. Polk (celebrated by a State Historic Site) and evangelist Billy Graham.

Other Mecklenburg County cultural and historic attractions include the Hezekiah Alexander House, the Charlotte Museum of History, and the Latta Plantation. The Levine Museum of the New South focuses on broader issues of the North Carolina Piedmont. The Mint Museum of Art, the Charlotte Repertory Theater, the Charlotte Symphony Orchestra, and Opera Carolina add to the cultural fabric of Mecklenburg County. Institutions of higher learning in the county include the University of North Carolina at Charlotte, Queens University of Charlotte, Johnson C. Smith University, and Davidson College.

References: Legette Blythe and Charles Raven Brockmann, *Hornet's Nest: The Story of Charlotte and Mecklenburg County* (1961); Mary Norton Kratt, *Charlotte, Spirit of the New South* (1991).

Robert Blair Vocci

SEE ALSO Charlotte; Charlotte, Battle of; Levine Museum of the New South; University of North Carolina at Charlotte.

Mecklenburg Declaration of Independence is the

name given to a document that was allegedly produced on 20 May 1775, when the residents of Mecklenburg County declared themselves "free and independent people." The so-called declaration did not surface until 1819, 44 years after the event, when it was published in the *Raleigh Register* at the behest of U.S. senator Nathaniel Macon. The original document

was supposedly destroyed in a fire in 1800, and the published text was reconstructed from memory by John McKnitt Alexander and given to Macon by his son, William Alexander. William Polk, the son of the organizer of the Charlotte meeting, gathered testimony from several elderly men who claimed to have been present. Mecklenburgers immediately started celebrating the date.

The authenticity of the document was not seriously questioned until the posthumous publication of the works of Thomas Jefferson in 1829. In a letter of 9 July 1819 to John Adams, Jefferson dismissed the Mecklenburg Declaration as a hoax. The North Carolina legislature in 1830–31 was so aroused by this development that it established a committee to investigate. As committee chairman Thomas G. Polk organized the fiftieth anniversary celebration of the Mecklenburg Declaration, it is not surprising that his committee gathered evidence to support the contention that the declaration was authentic.

Despite North Carolina's efforts, a number of scholars outside the state maintained that the Mecklenburg document was a fraud. The ultimate scholarly blow came in 1907 with the publication of William Henry Hoyt's *The Mecklenburg Declaration of Independence: A Study of Evidence Showing That the Alleged Declaration of Mecklenburg County, North Carolina, on May 20th, 1775, Is Spurious*. Using the latest methods of scientific history and internal criticism, Hoyt maintained that the evidence was overwhelming that the reconstructed declaration was a misconstruction of the Mecklenburg Resolves of 31 May 1775, which contemporary newspapers proved had been written. Most North Carolinians ignored Hoyt's work, but not Samuel A. Ashe, editor, historian, and descendant of one of the state's most prominent families. The first volume of Ashe's *History of North Carolina* (1908) presented both sides of the issue but ultimately agreed with the naysayers.

A bitter fight broke out in the North Carolina General Assembly over a bill authorizing the purchase of Ashe's book for the public schools. House Speaker Augustus W. Graham, the son of a governor and descendant of a "signer" of the Mecklenburg Declaration, took the floor and defeated the authorization bill. Opponents of the measure, appealing to patriotism, noted that the date of 20 May was enshrined on the state flag and seal. However, the difference in the old style (Julian) and new style (Gregorian) calendars was 11 days at the time the British adopted the new style in 1752. Even in 1775, Charlotte was in a remote area, and some persons still may have been using the old calendar. This fact could have contributed to a misapplication of the 20 May date to the authentic Mecklenburg Resolves of 31 May 1775.

The negative opinions of professional historians toward the Mecklenburg Declaration, including such luminaries as Stephen B. Weeks, John Spencer Bassett, and R. D. W. Connor, remained intact. The one academic who did support the

Mecklenburg legend was Archibald Henderson, a mathematics professor at the University of North Carolina at Chapel Hill. Although modern scholars no longer accept the Mecklenburg Declaration as authentic, it has long been maintained and celebrated. The document emerged at a time when North Carolina was the sleeping and backward "Rip Van Winkle State" and thus appealed to pride by establishing that the state was not only progressive but also in the vanguard of the independence movement.

References: Richard N. Current, "That Other Declaration: May 20, 1775–May 20, 1975," *NCHR* 54 (April 1977); Ronnie W. Faulkner, "Samuel A'Court Ashe: North Carolina Redeemer and Historian, 1840–1938" (Ph.D. diss., University of South Carolina, 1983).

Ronnie W. Faulkner

Mecklenburg Resolves. SEE Resolves, Prerevolutionary.

Medical Board. The modern North Carolina Medical Board (NCMB) began as the North Carolina State Board of Medical Examiners, created by the General Assembly in 1859 "in order to properly regulate the practice of medicine and surgery for the benefit and protection of the people of North Carolina." The board originally consisted of seven members, all of whom were physicians whose names were provided by the North Carolina Medical Society. The board selected its own officers, met annually, kept its records open for public inspection, and published the names of newly licensed physicians in Raleigh newspapers.

From the beginning, a major duty of the NCMB has been the examination of applicants for a license to practice medicine in the state. In the mid-1800s any person at least 21 years of age and of good moral character could apply to be examined. Physicians who had practiced prior to 1859 were in most cases automatically licensed. The board had the right to rescind the licenses of persons guilty of immoral conduct. Any individual practicing medicine without a license was prohibited from suing to recover charges for medical services rendered, but there was no legal penalty. The first medical license issued by the NCMB was received by Lucius C. Coke of Palmyra (Martin County) on 6 June 1859. Annie Lowrie Alexander of Charlotte became the first woman to be a licensed practicing physician in the state in 1887, having been certified by the Maryland Board of Medical Examiners two years earlier.

In 1921 the General Assembly passed a law specifying that only licensees of the NCMB were allowed to register and practice in the state. The legislature also defined what legally constituted the practice of medicine, repealed the statute permitting unlicensed individuals to practice by registering with a clerk of a superior court under oath of having practiced in the state before 1885, and detailed specific reasons and procedures for the revocation of licenses. Among the reasons for revocation were engaging in grossly immoral conduct, performing criminal abortions, obtaining a medical license by fraudulent means, using narcotics, misrepresenting medical skills or practice, violating the rules and regulations of the state board, and any other unprofessional conduct. Only the board could revoke or restore a license, although persons affected could appeal the board's decision to the superior court.

In the final decades of the twentieth century, minor additions to the law involving the NCMB were made, including charging fees for licenses, requiring the biennial registration of physicians, and regulating the use of physician assistants. The NCMB also kept up with changing medical law, such as the monumental 1973 U.S. Supreme Court decision in *Roe v. Wade* legalizing abortion. In 1981 the board was reorganized to consist of eight members, seven of them licensed physicians chosen by the North Carolina Medical Society and named by the governor. The eighth member, from outside the health profession, was appointed directly by the governor. In 1993 four more board members were added—two public members, one at-large member, and one physician assistant or nurse practitioner. All four were selected by the governor.

In 2000 the NCMB's proposal for increased medical education was adopted, requiring licensed physicians to accrue 150 hours of continuing education over a three-year period beginning in 2001. The board has also been a significant contributor to medical licensure on a national scale, with four members serving as president of the Federation of State Medical Boards of the United States. The NCMB newsletter has been a leading professional publication since its establishment in 1996, featuring timely articles, essays, and reports on medical issues. The board's website, also begun in 1996, has earned high marks as one of the most informative medical licensure sites in the nation.

Reference: Ivan M. Procter and Dorothy Long, *One Hundred Year History of the North Carolina State Board of Medical Examiners, 1859–1959* (1959).

Wiley J. Williams

Medical Care. SEE Hospitals; Infectious Diseases; Medical Schools; Medical Society; Public Health.

Medical Schools. Medical education for North Carolinians who desired to become physicians in the eighteenth or nineteenth century was generally obtained through a program of apprenticeship. In the absence of formal medical schools, experienced physicians, usually of advanced age, often accepted a single pupil or sometimes a small number of pupils. Among physicians active in the colony or state who accepted apprentices were men who had been educated in the medical center in London, Edinburgh, Basle, Utrecht, or Berlin, or in one of the pioneer American medical schools in Philadelphia, New

York City, Louisville, Ky., or Charleston, S.C. Those in training to become doctors "read medicine," as it was expressed, and worked closely with their instructor until they were deemed qualified to practice alone.

The Moravian community in mid-eighteenth–century North Carolina was home to a number of highly qualified physicians who provided apprenticeships, including Samuel Vierling and Jacob Bonn. In the Wilmington area were Nathaniel Hill and John Fergus, the latter having served on Gen. George Washington's staff. When the State Medical Society of North Carolina was formed in 1849, 91 of the first 172 members had been trained at the University of Pennsylvania, the school most often chosen by North Carolinians before formal medical training became available at the University of North Carolina in Chapel Hill in 1879.

Edenborough Medical College, possibly the first chartered medical school in North Carolina, opened in 1867 near the modern town of Raeford. Its founder, Hector McLean, was born in Robeson County and purportedly received a medical degree from the University of Louisville, although no records exist to verify this claim. The General Assembly granted McLean a charter to open the school because of the state's dire need of doctors.

Not long after it opened, the Edenborough Medical College ran into trouble with the Medical Society of North Carolina. In 1876 the society appointed a committee to investigate the school, and a year later the committee issued a report condemning the school's academic quality. Since no records of graduates from Edenborough exist, it is difficult to evaluate the charges. The committee's report was adopted, but there is no record of further action. McLean died in 1877, and the school subsequently closed. The college's accountability was never resolved.

Although African American residents of North Carolina undoubtedly employed traditional folk remedies in the treatment of family and friends, often very effectively, they were not licensed to practice medicine until 1886. Six years earlier, in 1880, Leonard Medical School was established on the campus of Shaw University in Raleigh with a white faculty and a student body of black males. A small hospital was built nearby, and a four-year curriculum, unusual for its time, was begun. In 1894 Lucy Hughes Brown became the first African American woman to be licensed to practice medicine in the state.

Two of the earliest distinguished woman physicians in the United States each had firm North Carolina connections. Susan Dimock (1847–76) was a native of Beaufort County, and Annie Lowrie Alexander (1864–1929) was a native of Mecklenburg County. Their careers, Dimock's abroad and Alexander's in North Carolina, are recounted in various histories of medicine. Dimock was introduced to medicine when she accompanied a neighbor, S. S. Satchwell, on his visits to ill neighbors in the countryside; Alexander studied under a private tutor and received medical training under her father, a physician.

The School of Medicine of the University of North Carolina at Chapel Hill began in 1879, with Thomas W. Harris as dean and professor of anatomy. After the school closed for five years following Harris's resignation in 1885, Richard H. Whitehead became dean and promptly helped raise the school's academic reputation. The two-year medical program continued to grow in stature, and many graduates, after completing their medical education at the country's finest schools, returned to North Carolina to practice.

North Carolina Medical College was founded in 1902 in Raleigh to offer the last two years of medical instruction, supplementing the first two years provided by the UNC School of Medicine. Hubert A. Royster was dean of faculty and professor of gynecology throughout the school's eight-year history. The college gave training in general medicine, surgery, obstetrics, clinical pathology, orthopedic surgery, and other areas. Although technically a department of the university, the college was funded solely through student fees, with faculty members drawing no regular salaries. Inadequate facilities and funding eventually led to an unfavorable appraisal by the Carnegie Foundation and the American Medical Association. Between 1903 and 1910, the school graduated 76 doctors, the majority of whom set up practices in North Carolina.

The UNC School of Medicine became a four-year program in 1954, two years after North Carolina Memorial Hospital (part of the modern UNC Hospitals) opened and became the medical school's primary teaching facility. Both the medical school and the hospital expanded throughout the last half of the twentieth century, when many new buildings, departments, and facilities were established. The school's student body grew to about 640 by 1980 and remained at that number in the early 2000s. The UNC Health Care System was organized in 1998, consolidating the UNC Hospitals and the clinical programs of the medical school.

Wake Forest School of Medicine, originally the Bowman Gray School of Medicine, began as a two-year medical program at Wake Forest College in 1902. The school became a four-year program in 1941, the same year it moved to its new location in Winston-Salem (15 years ahead of the rest of the college). In the early 2000s the Wake Forest Medical Center encompassed the school and several other facilities. Wake Forest researchers have been involved in many firsts in medical history, such as the first medical center in North Carolina to treat cancer using cobalt (1957), the first hand implantation in the United States (1964), the first use of ultrasound to detect prostate cancer in the United States (1969), and the first in the world to successfully use magnetic resonance imaging to locate blood vessel blockages.

Both the Duke University School of Medicine and Duke Hospital were organized in the late 1920s, with classes beginning in August 1930 and Wilburt Cornell Davison as dean. Duke's reputation for cutting-edge medical procedures and education spread throughout the century. In 1957 the school and hospital became part of the Duke University Medical Center, a national and international leader in the research and treatment of cancer, AIDS, Parkinson's disease, schizophrenia, diabetes, Alzheimer's disease, arthritis, and heart disease as well as a world-renowned center for the study of human genetics and medical ethics.

North Carolina's youngest medical school, the Brody School of Medicine at East Carolina University in Greenville, enrolled its first class in 1977 after years of strong support by local leaders who believed that the state's eastern region did not have access to sufficient medical care. After East Carolina presented a successful one-year program for students who went on to complete their medical studies at UNC-Chapel Hill, the General Assembly in 1974 appropriated funds for a four-year institution to be called the East Carolina School of Medicine. Since then the school (which was renamed for the Brody family in 1999), with its connection to regional physicians and University Health Systems of Eastern Carolina, has become a leading medical center in North Carolina.

References: Guion G. Johnson, *Ante-Bellum North Carolina: A Social History* (1937); Dorothy Long, ed., *Medicine in North Carolina: Essays in the History of Medical Science and Medical Service, 1524–1960* (2 vols., 1972); William W. McLendon, "Medical Practice and Medical Education in North Carolina: A 400-Year Overview," *North Carolina Medical Journal* 40 (June 1979).

William S. Powell
Additional research provided by K. Todd Johnson and Marilyn Wright.

SEE ALSO Leonard Medical School.

Medical Society.

The North Carolina Medical Society was founded in 1849 "to unite, serve, and represent physicians, in order to enhance physician advocacy for their patients, and improve the health of the people of North Carolina." As early as 1790, some state leaders had attempted to organize the medical profession in North Carolina. The idea languished until the General Assembly created a corporation called the North Carolina Medical Society in 1799. According to the *Raleigh Register*, the new organization would enable the community "to distinguish the true physician from the ignorant pretender" and possibly to suppress "the fatal and criminal practices of quacks." The society remained active until the early 1800s, when it ceased to exist. North Carolina was consequently not represented at the first American Medical Association Convention in 1847.

That situation was rectified in 1849 with the founding of the modern North Carolina Medical Society, which, as of the early 2000s, has held meetings every year except for three years during the Civil War and one year during World War II. The modern society has approximately 10,000 members, comprising physicians and physician assistants throughout the state. An executive vice president and professional staff directs the society's operation from its headquarters in Raleigh.

Despite significant growth, the Medical Society's basic objectives have remained constant since 1849. These include improving all areas of the medical profession to increase its effectiveness, giving the state's medical personnel the opportunity to practice in a dedicated and advanced professional environment, and publicizing and eliminating problems where they may occur. The society also stresses the importance of national organization, particularly through its membership in the American Medical Association.

Reference: Dorothy Long, ed., *Medicine in North Carolina: Essays in the History of Medical Science and Medical Service, 1524–1960* (2 vols., 1972).

Susan Tucker Hatcher

Medicine Shows,

from roughly the end of the Civil War through the 1940s, provided a frequent and vital form of rural entertainment throughout North Carolina and the South. Medicine shows also served as the training ground for hundreds of blues and "hillbilly" musicians and comedians, who lacked few alternate venues until the development of radio after World War I.

During the era before mass entertainment, medicine shows encountered little competition for audiences. Small-town residents flocked to see the free, touring shows with little regard to their quality. The announcement of a free show usually preceded the beginning of the musical presentation. The show's "doctor" generally served as master of ceremonies. Once the musicians had drawn a sufficient crowd, the doctor began pitching a cure-all product that rarely consisted of much more than a healthy dose of grain alcohol. The entertainers usually

Singer and storyteller Arthur "Peg Leg Sam" Jackson (left) is interviewed by students from the University of North Carolina during a medicine show at the 1972 Chatham County Fair. NCC.

worked the crowd, actually handling the sales while the doctor told of the nostrum's wondrous powers. Sometimes medicine shows were led by an American Indian entertainer. A famous example is Leo Kahdot, a Potawatomie Indian from Oklahoma. As "Chief Thundercloud," Kahdot had begun his career as a vaudeville piano and trumpet player and became a fixture, along with other musicians, on the medicine show circuit.

The concept of professional rural entertainers, whether white or black, developed in the twentieth century. Touring medicine shows provided the first outlet for these performers other than local dances. Nationally, Roy Acuff, Jimmie Rodgers, and Sonny Terry remain the best-known names to have worked the medicine shows. Besides Terry and Rodgers, artists with North Carolina connections who worked the medicine shows included Homer "Pappy" Sherrill, Dewitt "Snuffy" Jenkins, "Greasy" Medlin, Arthur "Peg Leg Sam" Jackson, Clarence "Tom" Ashley, Pink Anderson, Curley Sechler, and Doc Tommy Scott.

Besides developing several generations of entertainers and spreading songs throughout the rural South before radio and phonograph recordings, medicine shows also shaped the early days of radio. Large-scale patent medicine companies, such as Crazy Water Crystals, transferred the medicine show concept to the broadcast medium by sponsoring live radio shows by "hillbilly" performers. In North Carolina, the Monroe Brothers on WBT in Charlotte and WPTF in Raleigh proved the most popular Crazy Water Crystals act.

A few medicine shows continued to tour increasingly smaller towns until about 1970. Pete Lowry recorded Peg Leg Sam and Chief Thundercloud in Pittsboro in 1972. The UNC Center for Public Television documented a number of medicine show veterans for its "Last Free Show" special in 1981.

References: Bill C. Malone, *Country Music, U.S.A.* (rev. ed., 2002); Charles Reagan Wilson, "Traveling Shows," in Wilson and William Ferris, eds., *Encyclopedia of Southern Culture* (1989).

Arthur Menius

SEE ALSO Crazy Water Crystals.

Meherrin Indians,

Meherrin Indians, in the mid-seventeenth century, were living in two settlements on the north side of the Meherrin River in the eastern part of present-day North Carolina. The Meherrin spoke an Iroquoian language and were related to the Nottoway north of them and the Tuscarora to the south. In 1669 they were reported as having "50 fighting men," suggesting a population of about 160 persons.

Like the Nottoway, the Meherrin supported the Virginia government in Bacon's Rebellion and were subsequently considered "tributary" Indians of that colony. By 1691 they had moved southeast to the mouth of the Meherrin River. In 1705 Virginia opened new lands for colonial settlement by eliminating the former Indian boundary on the Blackwater River. While the Meherrin were assigned land equal to the area within a circle six miles in diameter, this change allowed settlers to expand around the Indian lands so that they were incorporated into the Virginia colony. Subsequent land disputes between Indians and colonists were complicated by a lack of agreement on the location of the Virginia–North Carolina boundary and the failure of North Carolina citizens to recognize Virginia's treaty obligations to the Meherrin.

Although the Meherrin sided with the colonists against the hostile Tuscarora during the Tuscarora War (1711–13), colonial records contain few references to them after that time. In 1731 fewer than 20 Meherrin families had taken refuge near the Chowan River settlements in North Carolina for protection against their Indian enemies. Between 1755 and 1761, the Meherrin were living on the Roanoke River in Northampton County together with remnants of the Tuscarora, Saponi, and Mattamuskeet tribes. The number of Meherrin "fighting men" increased from 8 in 1755 to 20 in 1761, which may indicate the incorporation of additional refugees.

It is not known when the Meherrin ceased to exist as a group, although some scholars believe they went north with the Tuscarora in 1802. Just as likely is that members of the tribe became acculturated, intermarried, and continued to live in North Carolina. There is some indication that unsuccessful attempts to reestablish their Indian identity were made in the late 1800s and early 1900s.

A Meherrin tribal group was chartered in 1977. Nine years later, the Meherrin Tribe of Hertford County became the sixth Indian tribe recognized by the state of North Carolina. In the early 2000s approximately 700 Meherrin Indians lived along the lower Meherrin River near Winton.

References: Lewis Binford, "An Ethnohistory of the Nottoway, Meherrin, and Weanock Indians of Southwestern Virginia," *Ethnohistory* 14 (1967); Douglas W. Boyce, "Iroquoian Tribes of the Virginia–North Carolina Coastal Plain," in Bruce B. Trigger, ed., *Handbook of North American Indians*, vol. 15 (1978).

Ruth Y. Wetmore

Melungeons

Melungeons are descendants of people of mixed ethnic ancestry who, before the end of the eighteenth century, were discovered living in limited areas of what is now the southeastern United States, notably in the Appalachian Mountains near the point where Tennessee, Virginia, and North Carolina converge. Earlier they may have lived near the Atlantic coast but, preferring a more secluded setting and seeking refuge from persecution, chose to move west as the coastal region became more densely populated by newcomers from Virginia and elsewhere.

The origin and early history of Melungeons remain relatively unknown. They have been identified at various times as having Portuguese, Spanish, French, Welsh, and Turkish ancestry; some theories even claim that they are descendants of members of Roanoke Island's Lost Colony of 1587. Most modern researchers have concluded that their ethnicity is triracial, with European, Native American, and African lineage. Their earliest ancestors may have been explorers, seamen, or colonists stranded along the Atlantic coast before permanent settlement had begun who later intermarried with Indians and Africans.

Melungeon skin tones varied from dark to light, reflecting their mixed heritage. In time, the U.S. Census Bureau classified them as "free persons of color." Because of their unique appearance, Melungeons faced extensive racial and social prejudice throughout much of their history. Although rarely subject to legal restrictions such as those imposed on blacks and Native Americans, they were often ostracized socially because of their nonwhite heritage. The term "Melungeon" itself was created and used as an insult by whites. Most researchers believe that it derived from the French word *mélange*, which means "mixture." Other possible linguistic roots include *melon can*, Turkish for "cursed soul"; the Italian word *melongena*, technically meaning "eggplant" but used in reference to someone with dark skin; and *melan*, the Greek word for "black." In any case, "Melungeon" came to signify a person of low social status and "impure" bloodlines, who was ignorant or possessed other negative traits.

The mystery surrounding Melungeons also led to a variety of folk beliefs, some of which portrayed them as frightening mythical creatures capable of evil deeds, including kidnapping children who misbehaved. While Melungeon ancestry is not uncommon in North Carolina Mountain counties such as Alleghany, Mitchell, and Ashe, the majority of Melungeons eventually settled in urban areas throughout the Southeast and became practically indistinguishable as a separate ethnic group. For generations, many people, seeking to avoid being stigmatized, ignored or denied their Melungeon ancestry. By the late twentieth century, however, several organizations were celebrating and seeking information about possible Melungeon family histories. In addition, researchers continue to examine Melungeon origins, at times employing such advanced technologies as DNA testing to trace previously undetectable bloodlines.

References: Bonnie Ball, *The Melungeons: Notes on the Origin of a Race* (1992); Jim Callahan, *Lest We Forget: The Melungeon Colony of Newman's Ridge* (2000); Elizabeth C. Hirschman, *Melungeons: The Last Lost Tribe in America* (2005); Wayne Winkler, *Walking toward the Sunset: Melungeons of Appalachia* (2004).

William S. Powell

Menhaden Chanteymen are a group of retired African American fishermen who previously worked off the coast near Beaufort. The group, during their working years, used singing to synchronize the pulling of their nets of menhaden, or shad. A leader sang out the first line of the song alone, to be answered with another line sung in harmony by the rest of the crew. The songs derived from many sources, including hymns and gospel songs, blues, and barbershop quartet songs, and they were often improvised.

In 1988 folklorists Michael and Deborah Luster, hired by the North Carolina Arts Council to survey the folk culture of Carteret County, arranged a gathering of about a dozen retired coastal fishermen. Beaufort blues singer and guitarist Richard "Big Boy" Henry, who worked for a time as a menhaden fisherman, helped the Lusters organize the event. Although they had not sung together in more than 30 years, the men recollected their songs almost effortlessly when they began to pantomime the action of working the net.

That year the ex-fishermen performed at a public event sponsored by the North Carolina Maritime Museum in Beaufort. Since then the group, officially named the Menhaden Chanteymen, has performed for the North Carolina General Assembly and the National Council on the Arts. They have also appeared at New York City's Carnegie Hall and on national television and radio. In 1990 the Menhaden Chanteymen recorded a collection of maritime work songs, *Won't You Help Me to Raise 'Em: Authentic Net Hauling Songs from an African-American Fishery*, for Global Village Music.

Kelly Kress
Additional research provided by Margaret Foote.

Mennonites are a Protestant group whose origins can be traced to Zürich, Switzerland, during the Reformation. Their name is taken from Menno Simons, one of their early leaders. Mennonites suffered religious persecution from both Roman Catholic and Protestant church authorities in Europe, and, as a result, many immigrated to North America starting in the 1600s. At the end of the twentieth century there were approximately 100,000 Mennonites in the United States, with the greatest numbers being in Pennsylvania, Ohio, and Indiana. The Mennonite population in North Carolina has always been small.

The early history of Mennonites in North Carolina has never been comprehensively studied, but evidence suggests that scattered groups were present in the state by the late eighteenth century. Their presence can be inferred from the *Records of the Moravians in North Carolina*, which contain numerous references to Mennonites and other Anabaptist groups (which advocate adult, not infant, baptism). Often these references are in relation to legislation in the colonial Assembly concerning church groups and military service. It appears that the early Mennonites never established a congregation and lost contact with other North American Mennonite groups by the early 1800s.

If present at all, Mennonites in North Carolina in the early years of the nineteenth century were disorganized and few in number. The Moravian records mention that in 1843 a Mennonite preacher was in the state, although it is not clear whether he was from North Carolina or merely passing through. During the Civil War, a Virginia Mennonite met a soldier from North Carolina who reported the existence of a Mennonite church near his home. Nevertheless, when J. S. Coffman of Elkhart, Ind., tried to visit the North Carolina Mennonites in the early 1880s, he could not find a group recognizable as Mennonites.

Congregations of the church began to be formed in North Carolina in 1899 with the arrival of missionaries from the Krimmer Mennonite Brethren Conference. Along with their churches, the Mennonites built schools and orphanages. Most North Carolina Mennonite congregations became part of the General Conference of the Mennonite Brethren Church of North America in 1960 and later joined the Virginia Conference of the Mennonite Church U.S.A. At the beginning of the twenty-first century, there were Mennonite congregations in Asheville, Chapel Hill, Durham, Greensboro, Hickory, Raleigh, Rocky Mount, and other locations throughout the state.

References: H. S. Bender, "Mennonites in North Carolina," *Mennonite Quarterly Review* (July 1927); Adelaide L. Fries, ed., *Records of the Moravians in North Carolina*, vols. 3–4, 7 (1926, 1930, 1947); Minnie J. Smith, ed., *Records of the Moravians in North Carolina*, vol. 9 (1964).

Stephen Moyer

Mental Illness. SEE Psychiatric Hospitals.

Mental Retardation Centers.
North Carolina has five state-run facilities under the control of the Division of Mental Health, Developmental Disabilities, and Substance Abuse Services for mentally handicapped residents. The Caswell Developmental Center in Kinston, the state's oldest facility, opened in 1914 as the North Carolina School for the Feebleminded; the next year its name was changed to the Caswell Training School (now the Caswell Center) in honor of Richard Caswell, Revolutionary War hero and first governor of the state. Assisting thousands of residents of eastern North Carolina, the school emphasized medical treatment until the 1970s, when education, individual treatment plans, and vocational training of mentally handicapped citizens were introduced. By 2006 the center served about 450 resident clients and hundreds of other individuals in less restrictive settings in the eastern counties.

In 1957 the Goldsboro Training School became the first facility in the nation dedicated to the support and treatment of mentally handicapped African Americans. The school accepted 150 patients from the psychiatric department of nearby Cherry Hospital, offering education and vocational training for the mildly retarded. In 1966, with the desegregation of state facilities, Goldsboro Training School became a regional center for 23 counties in south-central North Carolina. By 2006 the facility, under the name O'Berry Developmental Center, served more than 400 clients, offering real-life job training, self-help direction, and other skills to help them lead independent, fulfilling lives.

In 1947 Butner Training School for the mentally retarded was set up in an abandoned army barracks. The school received transfer clients from the Caswell Center in Kinston and in 1957 moved into a modern facility, eventually serving about 700 severely mentally retarded citizens from 16 counties. Its name was changed to the Murdoch Developmental Center in honor of James Murdoch, a leader of mental health reform in North Carolina.

The J. Iverson Riddle Developmental Center (originally, the Western Carolina Center) opened in Morganton on 16 Dec. 1963 to provide residential care for the mentally handicapped from the state's western counties—people who otherwise would have had to travel hundreds of miles for assistance. State representatives John W. Umstead Jr., of Orange County, who had a mentally retarded grandchild, and Joe K. Byrd, of Burke County, introduced and secured passage of a bill in 1959 providing $4 million to build a center in western North Carolina. In a subsequent meeting of the North Carolina State Hospital Board of Control, of which Umstead was chair, the decision was made to locate the unit in Burke County rather than Rowan County because the town of Morganton had agreed to furnish sewage treatment service at no cost to the state.

From the beginning, the center's philosophy has been to provide care only after the exhaustion of all other community resources. It has used an interdisciplinary approach toward meeting the needs of profoundly and severely handicapped people while respecting their rights and their due process. The center is believed to be one of the first facilities in the country to develop an aggressive patient advocacy program, a Foster Grandparent Program, and an extensive fine arts program, as well as to stress parental training and early intervention with the families of mentally handicapped infants. The center's name was changed in honor of longtime director J. Iverson Riddle.

The Black Mountain Developmental Center began as an offshoot of the Western Carolina Center in 1977 and became an autonomous facility in 1982. Six years later Black Mountain was funded as a treatment and care facility for patients with severe Alzheimer's disease, which is sometimes accompanied by violent behavior. A program to assist the aged with special medical needs was instituted in 2004.

Wiley J. Williams

Mercantilism
dominated economic thought in the West between roughly 1500 and 1800. In the mercantilist system, a

colony such as North Carolina was intended to contribute to the economic and political strength of the metropolitan power that undertook or authorized its establishment. A colony supplied the mother country—in North Carolina's case, Great Britain—with important raw materials, commodities, or products. It also served as a market or "vent" for commodities, goods, and services supplied by the mother country. North Carolina's imports were largely processed, finished, or semifinished goods. Moreover, almost all of North Carolina's trade was conducted according to British mercantile guidelines regarding venues, carriers, and personnel.

Some of North Carolina's exports, however, received monetary encouragement in the form of bounties or subsidies from the mother country, without which they would have been much less competitive. When one factors in the relatively high living standards in colonial North Carolina, the superior quality and low price of most imported goods, and the relatively inexpensive military protection provided by Britain, it seems clear that on balance the mercantilist relationship was not particularly burdensome to North Carolina's economic development.

References: C. Christopher Crittenden, *The Commerce of North Carolina, 1763–1789* (1936); Justin Williams, "English Mercantilism and Carolina Naval Stores, 1705–1776," *Journal of Southern History* 1 (1935).

Peter A. Coclanis

Meredith College, the largest private college for women in the Southeast, is a four-year, liberal arts institution located in Raleigh. It owes its origins to Thomas Meredith, who in 1838, along with other North Carolina Baptists, called for the establishment of a "female seminary of high order." It was not until 1889 that the Baptist Convention authorized such a seminary. In 1891 the Baptist Female University was founded under the auspices of the Southern Baptist State Convention, accepting its first students eight years later. The first graduating class of 1902 consisted of ten students. The school's name was changed to Baptist University for Women in 1904 and finally to Meredith College, in honor of Thomas Meredith, in 1909. The original campus was situated in downtown Raleigh in a building designed by architect A. G. Bauer. Continued growth in enrollment resulted in the building of a new campus, opened in 1925, at its modern site in west Raleigh.

In Meredith's early years, its curriculum included graduate and undergraduate degrees as well as a preparatory school that taught students from first grade through high school. The graduate degrees were discontinued in 1911, and the preparatory school was phased out by 1918. In 1983 graduate programs in music, education, and business were established. In 2000 Meredith College marked a significant occasion in its history, electing Maureen Hartford as the college's first woman president. Meredith in the early 2000s enrolled more than 2,400 students from 26 states and 20 countries. While continuing its commitment to the education of women, the college enrolls men in its graduate programs, which include business, elementary education, and music.

References: Suzanne Britt, *Images: A Centennial Journey* (1991); Mary Lynch Johnson, *History of Meredith College* (1956; rev. ed., 1972).

Jo Ann Williford

MerleFest, a huge American roots and folk music festival that yearly draws nearly 80,000 people to Wilkes Community College and its surrounding area, stands as a musical homage to its namesake, the late Merle Watson (son of legendary musician and Deep Gap native Arthel "Doc" Watson). MerleFest's lineup of more than 100 diverse musicians performing on the festival's 13 stages provided a boost to the regional economy in excess of $15 million in 2004.

With the assistance of Ralph Rinzler, the first MerleFest took place in late April 1988, touting a relatively small number of acoustic artists playing on stage in Wilkes Community College's John A. Walker Center and on the deck of two flatbed trucks to a crowd of 4,000 people. The idea behind the festival was for musicians, with the help of the Watson family, to converge and celebrate the life of Merle, who died in 1985, through music. Over the years, guest performers have included Mary Chapin Carpenter, Natalie McMaster, Earl Scruggs, Alison Krauss, Willie Nelson, and others.

In the early 1990s, North Carolina Public Television created an eight-part series, *Pickin' for Merle*, which showcased numerous acts over MerleFest's four-day span. The series has been shown on public television stations nationwide. MerleFest continues to grow in popularity, adding stages and performers and constantly shifting its artistic influences. Regardless of changes, the festival remains committed to two things: promoting true "Americana" music by celebrating the lives of Doc and Merle Watson and supporting the numerous facets of the Wilkesboro community through fund-raising.

Philip McFee

Messuage was a term not widely used in North Carolina, although it appears occasionally in deeds and wills. It refers to the residence or dwelling house, outbuildings, supporting structures, garden, and lawn—but not the forest or farmland —of a property owner.

William S. Powell

Methodist Church. Methodism originated in 1738 in Oxford, England, as a reform movement led by John Wesley and other young laymen and members of the clergy of the Anglican Church, or Church of England. In time, it became the last of the major reform movements among Protestant denominations to gain a foothold in North Carolina. The earliest Methodists to visit the colony came as part of a reform movement in the Church of England rather than as representatives of a new or unfamiliar church. Perhaps the most eminent of these was George Whitefield, who in 1739 made the first of several trips to North Carolina. He was always welcomed by the people as well as by the Anglican clergy and colonial officials since he had remained a communicant of the Church of England and made no effort to establish a new denomination. It was not until 1772, when Joseph Pilmore arrived in America, that a new denomination was recognized, and not until 1773 that the first Methodist Society in the American colonies was formed.

Early Methodist pioneers met with remarkable success in North Carolina. In 1775, in connection with their preaching, a great revival swept over the northern section of the colony and brought 683 new converts. A conference held in Baltimore in 1776 established a North Carolina circuit and assigned three preachers to serve the state. Their field of labor was unrestricted, and they covered large portions of the state, laying firm foundations for Methodism. In the wake of the American Revolution, Methodism's ties to the Anglican Church were severed, and at a meeting held in Baltimore in 1784 the Methodist Episcopal Church in the United States was organized. The next year the first Annual Conference of the Methodist Episcopal Church in America convened at Louisburg. Green Hill House, at which the 20 delegates gathered, still stands.

Much of the early appeal of Methodism in America came from the fact that it could serve the needs of worshippers more directly than could the Anglican Church, which had no bishops in the colonies to provide services such as ordaining new ministers or performing confirmations. Methodist clergy could provide such services without disruption in the lives of the faithful since, in essentials such as ritual, Methodism continued to be Anglican-based. Methodism flourished under the guidance of newly designated bishops, the expanding work of the laity, and the labor of circuit riders who carried its doctrine into the expanding frontier. The Methodist Episcopal Church grew quickly in North Carolina as well as other states.

With this growth, however, came division. The African Methodist Episcopal Church, founded in Philadelphia in 1816, and the African Methodist Episcopal Zion Church, chartered in New York City in 1801, both grew out of the desire of blacks to escape racial discrimination from within the Methodist Episcopal Church. The white Methodist Protestant Church emerged in Baltimore in 1830 after disgruntled members of the Methodist Episcopal Church left that body in protest over the perceived lack of ecclesiastical power of the laity. The greatest challenge for American Methodism, however, came during the turbulent times leading to the Civil War. As the issue of slavery divided the nation, so it became a catalyst for divisions in the Methodist Episcopal Church. The pro-slavery Methodist Episcopal Church, South, was officially formed in 1845. The presence of both the Methodist Episcopal Church and the Methodist Episcopal Church, South, in North Carolina—often churches of both denominations could be found in close proximity—was a visible reflection of mixed attitudes toward slavery among the state's citizens.

Although the national split caused by the Civil War ended in 1865, the major division in American Methodism was not healed until 1939. The Methodist Church was officially formed at the General Conference of that year in Kansas City, Mo., with the merger of the Methodist Protestant Church, the Methodist Episcopal Church, and the Methodist Episcopal Church, South. The United Methodist Church, the largest Methodist body in the United States, was created in 1968 through the merger of the Methodist Church and the Evangelical United Brethren Church. The United Methodist Church in North Carolina is divided into two conferences: the North Carolina Conference and the Western North Carolina Conference. Together they form the second-largest Protestant body in the state, behind Baptists, representing 10 percent of the overall population.

United Methodists in North Carolina have a long tradition of support for church-related institutions of higher education, including Duke University (formerly Trinity College), Bennett College, Brevard College, Greensboro College, High Point University, Louisburg College, Methodist College, North Carolina Wesleyan College, and Pfeiffer College. They have also supported children's homes and retirement communities in each conference. Their official organ, the *North Carolina Christian Advocate*, is published in Greensboro.

The World Methodist Museum is located in North Carolina at the International Headquarters Building of the World Methodist Council on the grounds of Lake Junaluska Assembly. Central to the museum's collection are extensive holdings related to the life and ministry of John Wesley. The museum possesses what is probably the world's largest collection of Staffordshire pottery commemorating Wesley's life. The 4,000-square-foot facility includes a library of rare books, manuscripts, and print materials that are available for public use.

References: Elmer T. Clark, *Methodism in Western North Carolina* (1966); Howard D. Gregg, *History of the African Methodist Episcopal Church* (1980); Mack Stokes, *Our Methodist Heritage* (1963).

Lynne S. Lepley

SEE ALSO African Methodist Episcopal (AME) Church; African Methodist Episcopal Zion Church; Camp Meetings; Circuit Riders; *North Carolina Christian Advocate*.

Methodist College, a four-year liberal arts college affiliated with the North Carolina Conference of the United Methodist Church, was chartered in Fayetteville in 1956 and first opened its doors in September 1960. The school was established in response to several factors. The end of World War II triggered a tremendous surge in undergraduate enrollment at schools across the nation and a similar increase in low interest federal loans for college expansion. At the same time, the national governing body of the Methodist Church began to emphasize undergraduate education. This emphasis encouraged the North Carolina Conference, led by presiding bishop Paul N. Garber, to propose at least one new college to augment Duke University and Louisburg College. Such proposals counted on the willingness of Methodist communities across the nation to provide cash and land incentives to new colleges. Intense competition between North Carolina communities in the 1950s led to the creation of two schools: North Carolina Wesleyan College in Rocky Mount and Methodist College in Fayetteville. Fayetteville and Cumberland County offered $2 million to match the North Carolina Conference's capital contribution; the community also promised $50,000 in annual support.

Methodist College has drawn students primarily from North Carolina. The number of these students grew from 154 in 1960–61 to more than 1,000 by 1967. By the early 2000s, the school served approximately 2,000 students who were pursuing either associate or bachelor's degrees through the college's full-time program or its evening/weekend program.

Richard A. Jenkins

Methodist Home for Children (MHC) in Raleigh developed from the Methodist Orphanage, which was founded in 1899. The number of children enrolled at the orphanage jumped from 28 in 1901 to 340 by 1931; and as the numbers grew, so did the scope of the institution. Its main purpose expanded from simply caring for disadvantaged children to encouraging and strengthening family systems. This evolution to a central focus on the family was a response to dynamic pressures in society, such as those produced by the Great Depression. Family life specialists offered family, parenting, and marital counseling services to help those dealing with stress. In addition, seminars, workshops, and retreats were presented in churches and the community. The new name for the orphanage, Methodist Home for Children, was adopted in 1955.

As of the early 2000s, the MHC served more than 1,000 children and families in various facilities. Originally housing children in dormitories or cottages on its 60-acre base site, the MHC now utilizes youth homes and family-centered outreach programs across the eastern part of North Carolina. The MHC operates 11 residential youth homes and 5 juvenile homes. These homes are staffed by live-in married couples called teaching-parents. These couples are trained to work out individualized programs of care and treatment while providing a safe and healthy environment for the children. Foster care is available for children under the age of 18 who have special medical or emotional needs.

The juvenile homes offer a positive and secure alternative to detention placement for troubled teens, helping build respect among the youths themselves and their families. Skills are also taught to help adolescents successfully re-integrate into their families and the community. The MHC helps similar types of agencies get started nationwide and assists local churches in the development of family services. Although fiscally independent, the MHC has close ties to the North Carolina Conference of the United Methodist Church and depends on the support of its member churches. It is accredited by the Council on Accreditation of Services for Families and Children, Inc.

Virginia Renna Deaton

Mexican War. North Carolina–born President James K. Polk declared war on Mexico on 13 May 1846 after disputes regarding the admittance of the former Mexican province of Texas into the Union in 1845 and the location of the Texas-Mexico border boiled over. Two weeks later, on 22 May, Governor William A. Graham of North Carolina called for volunteers. Early in the war the state raised 32 companies, all but 1 of which were rejected because they enlisted for only 12 months. The state issued a new call for volunteers in December, but by then war fever had cooled considerably. Even with a ten-dollar enlistment bounty, it took until February 1847 to enlist 10 companies for the state regiment, and those never reached full strength. Desertion and death from disease whittled the unit's numbers even before it left for Mexico.

Most volunteer soldiers, including those from North Carolina, belonged to Polk's Democratic Party, which generally supported the war. Problems arose when Governor Graham, a member of the Whig Party, which opposed the war, appointed three fellow Whigs to lead the regiment: Robert A. Paine as colonel, John A. Fagg as lieutenant colonel, and Montford Sidney Stokes as major. The unit's existing officers strongly objected to these appointments, having expected to elect their own regimental commanders as was traditional in the state militia. The company from Mecklenburg County, refusing to serve under Paine, asked permission to join a regular army regiment and was transferred to the Third U.S. Dragoons. Two other North Carolina infantry companies were formed and added to the 12th U.S. Infantry, under Col. Louis D. Wilson of Tarboro—the original choice of the officers of the North Carolina regiment.

Most of the regiment's officers and men considered Paine incompetent. Matters came to a head when the troops turned on Paine in August 1847. Control was asserted over the regiment only when Gen. John Wool posted regular troops as guards at the camp and temporarily relieved Paine. Although Paine had lost the confidence of most of the unit, a court

North Carolina's "first class of law controlled and class instructed midwives" on the steps of the Beaufort County Courthouse, 1925. Several of the women hold signs printed with lessons they have learned, such as "The New Midwife Must Be Clean" and "We Must Report the Baby's Birth." NCC.

of inquiry in early 1848 upheld his actions, and he remained in command until the regiment mustered out at the end of the war. The controversy spilled over into the North Carolina press, with Whig newspapers supporting Paine and Democratic papers taking the part of the disaffected men and officers.

By the summer of 1847 the North Carolina regiment was protecting supply trains in Mexico; the unit never saw combat, although 172 troops died of disease. Another 62 men received medical discharges, but three-quarters of them died before arriving home. Interestingly, despite the mutiny against Paine, the North Carolina regiment had a very low desertion rate for a Mexican War unit. The companies of the North Carolina regiment returned home to muster out in July and August 1848. Even with the stain of the mutiny, the men were welcomed back with patriotic celebrations.

The North Carolina companies of the 12th Infantry and the Third Dragoons saw action in the final battles of the war as the U.S. Army fought its way to Mexico City. The North Carolinians of Company G particularly distinguished themselves at the Battle of the National Bridge on 12 Aug. 1847. Outnumbered by enemy troops, the Americans were pushed back and forced to abandon their two cannons on the bridge itself. Led by Lts. H. B. Sears and Édward Cantwell, a dozen men from Company G dashed forward under fire and recovered one of the cannons left on the bridge. After this action, the tide of the battle turned and it ended in a U.S. victory. The popular commander of the 12th Infantry, Colonel Wilson, died of disease before the war ended. Wilson County and the town of Wilson were named after him.

A peace treaty was signed in February 1848 after the fall of Mexico City. About one-third of Mexico's territory was ceded to the United States, creating its modern borders, except for the Gadsden Purchase (1852) lands, Alaska, and Hawaii. Although limited, the military experiences of the Mexican War gave a handful of North Carolinians some firsthand combat training that would be put to use in the Civil War. Several North Carolina officers in the regular army, including future Confederate generals Daniel H. Hill, Braxton Bragg, and James G. Martin, distinguished themselves during the fighting in Mexico.

References: William S. Hoffmann, *North Carolina in the Mexican War, 1846–1848* (1959); Lee A. Wallace Jr., "Raising a Volunteer Regiment for Mexico, 1846–1847," *NCHR* 35 (January 1958).

David A. Norris

Midwives, who help expectant mothers through the labor process, lend emotional support, and attend the delivery, have been present in North Carolina since the arrival of the first English settlers. Most midwives in the colonial period received no formal training but learned through apprenticeship (often under their own mothers) and experience. Until the beginning of the nineteenth century, midwives were the primary birth attendants in North Carolina. Physicians became more involved in infant births during the 1850s; before then, a man's presence in the delivery room was prohibited due to modesty and moral taboos.

Initially, rural landowners used midwives to help with family and tenant births. As medical care evolved, wealthy North Carolinians began using professional medical personnel and traveling to hospitals to give birth. As a result, midwives serviced mainly poor, often black, mothers who could not afford a doctor. A midwife was often seen hurrying across town, toting a leather or cloth bag filled with birthing supplies (cotton pads, sewn sheets, clean newspapers, and a large knife or scissors).

In 1917, the year midwives were first licensed in North Carolina, 9,000 women were registered. In the 1930s the state government launched an effort to regulate midwifery, which resulted in a steady decline of registered midwives. This trend continued through the 1970s as medical professionals voiced their concern that the combination of poor, high-risk patients with minimally trained caretakers was dangerous to the patients' health.

A resurgence in the popularity of at-home births in the early 1980s led to a revival of the midwife profession in the state and nation. In 1983 North Carolina legalized nurse-midwifery and created a Midwifery Joint Committee to regulate midwives. It also approved Certified Nurse-Midwives (CNMs) to practice. Unregistered or lay midwives were not included in the legislation, although some continued to practice illegally.

By the early 2000s, 176 CNMs practiced in hospitals, university medical centers, clinics, birth centers, and homes across the state. Many expectant mothers preferred to use nurse-midwives because they spent more time with patients and did not administer drugs, making labor a more natural and holistic experience. The Charlotte area had the largest number of CNMs with 22, followed by Asheville/Henderson, 13; Durham/Chapel Hill and Greenville, 12 each; and Greensboro, 10. If problems or difficulties arose during labor, CNMs were required to call in their supervising physician, although the profession was trying to move away from such restrictions. Midwives rarely performed cesarean sections.

East Carolina University in Greenville offers a master's degree in nurse-midwifery. Although it remains a female-dominated profession, some men have become CNMs.

References: Michael Cory, "Midwives Still Labor under Misconceptions," *Business North Carolina* (January 1999); *Manual for Midwife Practice in North Carolina* (1969); Patrick R. Ninneman, "Midwives in North Carolina" (M.A. thesis, UNC-Chapel Hill, 1996); P. Radochl, "Midwives in the United States: Past and Present," *Population Research and Policy Review* (1986).

Sarah Mobley

Migrant Workers have been a mainstay of North Carolina's agricultural economy since around 1900. Before that time, the farm labor population had generally been made up of indentured servants, African slaves, sharecroppers, and tenant farmers, with any excess demand for seasonal labor supplied by workers hired from the local area.

Beginning in the early twentieth century, the mechanization and improved technology of farming operations altered labor requirements in North Carolina and other states. Many farms planted and cultivated more acres than the local workforce could harvest. An urgent need developed for seasonal labor during the harvest period for cotton, tobacco, cucumbers, potatoes, sweet potatoes, string beans, tomatoes, apples, peaches, and other crops. Workers who could not find sufficient employment near their homes became increasingly mobile with the introduction of the automobile and the development of a better highway system. They (and often their families) could follow the crops as they matured, working only a short time on each farm.

As the twentieth century progressed, many of North Carolina's migrant workers, especially Latinos, moved north from the warmer climate in Florida. The presence of large populations of migrant workers has, since the late 1940s, given rise to a number of problems in the state, including matching labor supply and demand and addressing workers' needs in a broad range of areas from health care and housing to child care and education.

A number of public agencies at the federal, state, and local levels, as well as private agencies, have put considerable energy and funding into the effort to solve these problems. Federally, the Office of Economic Opportunity and the Departments of Agriculture, Education, Health and Human Services, and Labor are most actively involved. At the state level, the Departments of Agriculture, Commerce, Environment and Natural Resources, Health and Human Resources, Labor, and Public Instruction provide valuable services and programs for migrant workers. A 1983 report by the Legislative Research Commission to the North Carolina General Assembly outlined the state's responsibility for ensuring safe housing and working environments, as well as adequate health insurance, for migrant workers.

At the local level, county departments of social services are often willing to help migrant workers and their families but usually have limited resources at their command. Various organizations in the private sector have tried to aid migrant workers. The North Carolina Council of Churches, for example, has sponsored several committees to address the plight of these laborers and their families. Individual churches and ministerial associations have also lent their help. The Farmworkers Legal Services of North Carolina offers legal assistance to workers, and the North Carolina Farmworkers Project has visited and reported on conditions in agricultural labor camps.

The controversial North Carolina Growers Association (NCGA), headquartered in Vass, is the state's largest supplier of legal immigrant agricultural laborers. Led by Stan Eury, the NCGA contracts out thousands of Mexican and other Latino men and women to farmers who need fieldworkers, especially those growing cucumbers for Wayne County–based Mt. Olive Pickle Company. Complaints that NCGA, which operates under a little-known federal visa program, has abused its workers in a variety of ways—such as refusing them water in the fields and denying them medical care after exposure to pesticides—have persisted. In September 2004 a five-year boycott of Mt. Olive Pickle Company—supported by some 60 organizations, including the Roman Catholic Diocese of Raleigh—was ended when 8,000 NCGA workers were allowed union representation for the first time.

Some migrant workers, wishing to stay in the United States, have moved on to service jobs and, with additional education and experience, to white-collar and professional positions. This pattern has been successfully followed in recent decades by immigrants from Asian countries as well as immigrants from Mexico and other Latin American countries.

References: Tracey Jean Maxwell, "Plant, Pick, and Pressure: The Migrant Experience in North Carolina" (M.A. thesis, UNC-Chapel Hill, 1989); Sandra C. Nonini, "Uprooting Justice: Gains for Farmworkers Show That Solidarity Matters," *Southern Exposure* 30 (Fall 2002); North Carolina General Assembly, Legislative Research Commission, *Migrant Workers: A Report to the 1983 General Assembly of North Carolina* (1983); Barry Yeoman, "Silence in the Fields," *Mother Jones* 26 (January–February 2001).

Wiley J. Williams

SEE ALSO Latinos.

Military Installations, Civil War.

North Carolina was home to more than 100 Confederate and Union military installations during the Civil War. Dozens of camps—some serving as temporary bases and others as long-lived training facilities—were established across the state, often in close proximity to one another. Many so-called camps of instruction were created so that individuals could be passed through the muster process and supplied with uniforms and arms. Basic training was begun while the new recruits were formed into companies, battalions, batteries, and regiments. Instructors for these camps came from the cadet corps of the state's various military academies and from the ranks of professional officers formerly in the service of the United States. The most regularly recognized instruction facilities were located at Asheville, Carolina Beach, Company Shops (now Burlington), Fort Caswell (Brunswick County), Garysburg, Halifax, High Point, Kittrell, Raleigh, Ridgeway, Warrenton, and Weldon.

Many Civil War forts and batteries were built in defense of towns and other strategically important locations throughout North Carolina. These installations varied greatly in size and design and were rarely intended to be permanent. They ranged in sophistication from simple earthen mounds and felled trees to well-engineered systems of trenches, bombproof enclosures, and magazines. Only a few of the defenses that came to be called forts match the popular image of substantial stone or wood structures with massive gates, elevated walkways and firing positions, and enclosed gun emplacements. Batteries, many little more than hastily entrenched artillery units used as the outermost defense for larger forts or cities, were often named for men of local prominence or for distinguished soldiers known to the defenders.

(See table of military installations, pp. 738–46.)

References: Walter Clark, ed., *Histories of the Several Regiments and Battalions from North Carolina in the Great War, 1861–1865* (5 vols., 1901); Chris E. Fonvielle Jr., *The Wilmington Campaign: Last Rays of Departing Hope* (2001).

Paul Branch
Charles C. Davis
Additional research provided by Daniel W. Barefoot, John G. Barrett, Dan Blair, Millie Hart, Whitmel M. Joyner, L. J. Kimball, Richard B. McCaslin, David McGee, Gene Purcell, Alexander R. Stoesen, Beverly Tetterton, and Rich Weidman.

SEE ALSO Fort Caswell; Fort Fisher; Fort Macon.

Military Ocean Terminal at Sunny Point

is situated on the west bank of the Cape Fear River, 26 miles south of Wilmington, in Brunswick County. It occupies approximately 8,500 acres between the ruins of the Brunswick Town State Historic Site and Walden Creek. Built in 1951, the terminal serves as a transfer point between rail cars, trucks, and ships during the import or export of weapons, ammunition, explosives, tanks, and military equipment for the U.S. Army. As the world's largest military terminal, Sunny Point ships more explosive cargo and equipment to the nation's armed forces and allies than any other facility.

The terminal was located in Brunswick County because of its proximity to rail, highway, and sea traffic and because it was isolated, tree-covered, and uninhabited. Governor George Burrington built the earliest plantation on the property in 1725. It became known as Snow's Point when rice planter Robert Snow acquired the property in the 1750s. During the Civil War the area was the site of a minor battery in the Cape Fear defense system, and a locally run saltworks. Around the turn of the twentieth century, the name "Reaves Point" was changed to "Sunny Point." By the 1950s the land was agricultural and contained few structures. It was considered an ideal location for ammunition storage and exchange.

Despite its isolation, Sunny Point is an impressive facility. Its three huge docks or concrete wharves can handle several ships at one time. Large cranes and a massive railroad system with 62 miles of tracks within the terminal move military supplies and explosive cargo. During the Vietnam War (1957–75) Sunny Point bristled with activity, loading as many as six ships at once with armaments. More than 466,000 measured tons of cargo used in the Persian Gulf War (1991) passed through the port.

In the early 2000s security at Sunny Point was tight. Visitors entered by appointment and were asked to surrender any matches or lighters. Safety was emphasized. Plexiglas was used instead of glass in all buildings to eliminate the scattering of glass fragments during accidental explosions, and cargo waiting to be loaded into ships was temporarily stored be-

North Carolina Civil War Military Installations

CAMPS

Name	Location	Description
Camp Advance	Near Weldon (Halifax County)	Confederate training ground for Company H, 40th North Carolina Regiment (Heavy Artillery).
Camp Alamance	Company Shops (now Burlington, Alamance County)	Confederate organization point for Company F (Hawfield River Boys), 6th North Carolina Regiment.
Camp Ashe	12 miles east of Wilmington (now Scotts Hill, Pender County)	Established by the 8th Regiment May 1863; part of the Confederate defense system protecting the port of Wilmington from northeast land invasion and the sound areas from Union warships.
Camp Baker	Near Hamilton (Martin County)	Primary headquarters of the 70th North Carolina Regiment (1st Junior Reserves), which defended several eastern counties from further Union invasion. Named for Brig. Gen. Lawrence S. Baker.
Camp Beauregard	Ridgeway (Warren County)	Established in May 1861 by Governor John W. Ellis as the first Confederate cavalry training ground in the state. The 1st North Carolina Cavalry Regiment (9th North Carolina Regiment) trained here, later winning one of the first cavalry encounters of the war in Vienna, Va. Named for Gen. P. G. T. Beauregard, who had earlier directed the capture of Fort Sumter.
Camp Black Jack	Near Moseley Hall (now LaGrange, Lenoir County)	Temporary Confederate camp established in June 1862 by the 52nd North Carolina Regiment to protect the Atlantic & North Carolina Railroad.
Camp Boylan	Raleigh (Wake County)	Confederate training ground of the Ellis Light Infantry and later (1862) the 49th North Carolina Regiment, commanded by Maj. Stephen D. Ramseur. Named for William Boylan, who provided the land.
Camp Campbell	Near Cork Creek, south of Kinston (Lenoir County)	One of several Confederate camps and picket posts guarding the area between Kinston and New Bern, occupied in the fall of 1862 by the 8th Regiment.
Camp Canal	Near the Carteret County–Craven County line (north of Morehead City)	Established in October 1861 by William A. Herring's Confederate artillery company (1st Company I, 36th North Carolina Regiment) to guard the Clubfoot and Harlow Creek Canal and the road between Beaufort and Adams Creek.
Camp Clarendon	Garysburg (Northampton County)	One of several unofficial names for the Confederate camp of instruction where the 3rd North Carolina Regiment formed and trained, June 1861.
Camp Clingman	Asheville (Buncombe County)	Confederate organization and training ground of the Twentieth Battalion, Junior Reserves. Named for Gen. Thomas L. Clingman, an antebellum political leader and Civil War officer.
Camp Cobb	Near Wilmington (New Hanover County)	Confederate camp that provided housing for recruits and troops stationed in batteries and forts defending Wilmington, the Cape Fear River, and Fort Fisher. Likely named for Gen. Howell Cobb, secretary of the treasury under President James Buchanan.

CAMPS

Name	Location	Description
Camp Collier	Near Goldsboro (Wayne County)	Confederate camp briefly used by the 61st North Carolina Regiment en route to Kinston from the Wilmington area, October 1862.
Camp Crabtree	Near Raleigh (Wake County)	Confederate training ground (also known as Camp Carolina) established in July 1861 and commanded by Maj. Henry K. Burgwyn Jr.
Camp Daniel	Near Garysburg (Northampton County)	Confederate camp of instruction used by the First Battalion of Junior Reserves in preparation for joining the Sixth Battalion of Junior Reserves to form the 70th North Carolina Regiment (1st Junior Reserves). Named for Brig. Gen. Junius Daniel of Halifax County.
Camp Davis	Near Wilmington (New Hanover County)	Confederate camp that provided housing for recruits and troops stationed in batteries and forts defending Wilmington, the Cape Fear River, and Fort Fisher.
Camp Fisher	High Point (Guilford County)	Established in the fall of 1861 as one of two Confederate infantry training camps in the county. Companies organized here include the 28th, 34th, and 37th North Carolina Regiments (1861) and the 11th North Carolina Regiment (1862). Named for Col. Charles F. Fisher, the second president of the North Carolina Railroad and a casualty at the First Battle of Manassas (Bull Run).
Camp Floyd	Near Weldon (Halifax County)	Confederate camp of instruction that was the temporary base of the 38th North Carolina Regiment in February 1862. Likely named for Maj. Gen. John B. Floyd, secretary of war under President James Buchanan.
Camp Hill	Near Asheville (Buncombe County)	Confederate camp that was the temporary base of the 39th North Carolina Regiment between November 1861 and February 1862. Named for Maj. Gen. Daniel H. Hill.
Camp Hill	Near Garysburg (Northampton County)	One of several unofficial names for the Confederate camp of instruction where the 4th North Carolina Regiment formed and trained in May 1861. The 42nd North Carolina Regiment was also stationed here in 1863. Named for Maj. Gen. Daniel H. Hill.
Camp Holmes	Near Raleigh (Wake County)	Confederate camp of instruction, training ground of the 72nd Regiment (3rd Junior Reserves). Likely named for Lt. Gen. Theophilus H. Holmes.
Camp Hopkins	Near Wilmington (New Hanover County)	Confederate camp that provided housing for recruits and troops stationed in batteries and forts defending Wilmington, the Cape Fear River, and Fort Fisher.
Camp Johnston	Near Kinston (Lenoir County)	Confederate camp occupied by the 52nd North Carolina Regiment in April 1862.
Camp Lamb	Near Wilmington (New Hanover County)	Confederate camp that provided housing for recruits and troops stationed in batteries and forts defending Wilmington, the Cape Fear River, and Fort Fisher. Named for Col. William Lamb, commander of Fort Fisher.

Name	Location	Description
Camp Leventhorpe	Near Garysburg (Northampton County)	One of several unofficial names for the Confederate camp of instruction where the 38th North Carolina Regiment formed and trained in February 1862. Named for Brig. Gen. Collett Leventhorpe.
Camp Long	Near Garysburg (Northampton County)	One of several unofficial names for the Confederate camp of instruction where the 5th North Carolina Cavalry (63rd North Carolina Regiment) formed and trained in the fall of 1862. Named for Lt. Col. John O. Long.
Camp McLean	Near Goldsboro (Wayne County)	Temporary base of many Confederate units, including the 72nd North Carolina Regiment (3rd Junior Reserves), guarding rail and river approaches to Goldsboro. Likely named for Gen. A. D. McLean of Cumberland County.
Camp Macon	Near Warrenton (Warren County)	Confederate camp and site of organization of the 8th North Carolina Regiment. Likely named for Nathaniel Macon of Warren County.
Camp Mangum	Raleigh (Wake County)	Primary Confederate camp of instruction in North Carolina. Its commanders included Maj. Gens. Daniel H. Hill and Stephen D. Ramseur.
Camp Mason	Near Graham (Alamance County)	First military base of the 7th North Carolina Regiment, organized and mustered in August 1861.
Camp Mason	Near Goldsboro (Wayne County)	Temporary base of many Confederate units guarding rail and river approaches to Goldsboro.
Camp Patton	Near Asheville (Buncombe County)	Confederate camp of instruction where Capt. Robert B. Vance, commander of Company A, Buncombe Life Guards, stationed his company in the summer of 1861 before they joined the 29th North Carolina Regiment.
Camp Radcliffe	Near Smithville (Brunswick County)	Confederate camp established and occupied by the 61st North Carolina Regiment in the fall of 1862. Named for Col. James D. Radcliffe.
Camp Ransom	Near Garysburg (Northampton County)	One of several unofficial names for the Confederate camp of instruction used by the Sixth Battalion, Junior Reserves, while the unit joined the First Battalion, Junior Reserves, to form the 70th North Carolina Regiment (1st Junior Reserves). Likely named for Brig. Gen. Matthew W. Ransom.
Camp Vance	Near Sulphur Springs (Buncombe County)	Temporary duty station of the 29th North Carolina Regiment. Likely named in honor of Col. Zebulon B. Vance, the commander of the 26th North Carolina Regiment and later governor of North Carolina.
Camp Vance	Berry's Mill Pond (6 miles from Morganton, Burke County)	Training base for various regiments of Confederate Junior and Senior Reserves. Captured and destroyed in June 1864 by Col. George W. Kirk's 3rd North Carolina Mounted Infantry (Union).
Camp Vance	Near Goldsboro (Wayne County)	Temporary base of many Confederate units guarding rail and river approaches to Goldsboro.
Camp White	Near Kinston (Lenoir County)	Temporary base of the 7th North Carolina Regiment during the 1863 campaigns of Maj. Gen. Daniel H. Hill. Possibly named for Dr. W. E. White, the regiment's assistant surgeon.

CAMPS

Name	Location	Description
Camp Whiting	Near Wilmington (New Hanover County)	Confederate camp that provided housing for recruits and troops stationed in batteries and forts defending Wilmington, the Cape Fear River, and Fort Fisher. Occupied by the 8th North Carolina Regiment, November–December 1862. Likely named for Maj. Gen. William H. C. Whiting.
Camp Winslow	Near Wilmington (New Hanover County)	Confederate camp that provided housing for recruits and troops stationed in batteries and forts defending Wilmington, the Cape Fear River, and Fort Fisher. Named for North Carolina governor Warren Winslow (died 1862).
Camp Woodfin	Near Asheville (Buncombe County)	First Confederate camp of instruction in western North Carolina. The 69th North Carolina Regiment, 8th Cavalry (Woodfin's Fourteenth Battalion) was raised here. Last camp in which the 64th North Carolina Regiment was stationed, April 1865. Named for John W. and Nicholas Woodfin, political and military leaders who donated the land.
Camp Wyatt	South of Wilmington (New Hanover County)	Temporary base of the 2nd North Carolina Regiment in the spring of 1862. Served as a hospital and supply point between Fort Fisher and Wilmington. Named for Pvt. Henry L. Wyatt of the 1st North Carolina (Bethel) Regiment, believed to have been the first Confederate soldier killed in action.

FORTS

Name	Location	Description
Fort Allen	Near New Bern (Craven County)	Built in 1862 by Confederate forces on the west bank of the Neuse River to defend New Bern. Manned by Company B, 1st Maryland Regiment.
Fort Amory	Near New Bern (Craven County)	One of a series of Federal forts built in 1862–63 to enable Union forces to hold New Bern. Mounted three 32-pounder cannons. Named for Col. Thomas J. C. Amory of the 17th Massachusetts Regiment.
Fort Anderson	Near New Bern (Craven County)	One of a series of Federal forts built in 1862–63 to enable Union forces to hold New Bern. Mounted four 32-pounder carronades, a 24-pounder howitzer, and a 12-pounder howitzer. Named for Lt. Col. Hiram Anderson of the 92nd New York Regiment, which comprised the fort's garrison.
Fort Anderson	South of Wilmington (near the mouth of the Cape Fear River, New Hanover County)	One of six major Confederate forts built to secure the port of Wilmington and the Wilmington & Weldon Railroad. Large earthwork fort armed with nine 32-pounder cannons, three 24-pounder cannons, and at least one Whitworth gun. Named for Col. George B. Anderson.
Fort Bartow	Western Roanoke Island (Dare County)	Confederate earthwork fort built to defend southern approaches to Roanoke Island through Croatan Sound. Mounted nine 32-pounder cannons (one rifled) and manned by Companies I and L, 17th North Carolina Regiment. Named for Brig. Gen. Francis Bartow, killed in the First Battle of Manassas (Bull Run).

FORTS

Name	Location	Description
Fort Benjamin	Near Newport (Carteret County)	Large earthwork Union fort built to guard a railroad bridge over the Newport River and a large permanent troop encampment called Newport Barracks. Captured by Confederate forces in February 1864 but subsequently abandoned and reoccupied by Federal forces.
Fort Blanchard	Western Roanoke Island (Dare County)	Small Confederate earthwork fort built to defend approaches to Roanoke Island through Croatan Sound. Mounted four 32-pounder cannons and garrisoned by Company G, 31st North Carolina Regiment. Named for Brig. Gen. A. G. Blanchard.
Fort Branch	Near Hamilton (Martin County)	Confederate fort built on a 70-foot bluff known as Rainbow Banks on the south side of the Roanoke River. Protected vital railroad bridge at Weldon and naval facilities at Halifax and Edward's Ferry. Mounted 11 guns by 1864. Named for Brig. Gen. Lawrence O. Branch, killed at the Battle of Sharpsburg (Antietam).
Fort Campbell	Oak Island (Brunswick County)	Confederate earthwork fort that guarded the western approaches to the Western Bar Channel of the Cape Fear River and helped protect Confederate blockade-runners leaving the mouth of the river. Garrisoned by Company F, 3rd North Carolina Artillery, and Company B, First North Carolina Heavy Artillery Battalion. Named for Col. Reuben P. Campbell, killed at the Battle of Gaines's Mill.
Fort Campbell	South of Wilmington (New Hanover County)	One of several Confederate earthwork forts on the east side of the Cape Fear River. Guarded a series of defensive river obstructions near the junction of the Cape Fear and Brunswick Rivers. Mounted one eight-inch Columbiad, one 18-pounder cannon, one 24-pounder cannon, two 32-pounder cannons, two 9-inch Dahlgrens, and one 30-pounder Parrott rifle.
Fort Caswell	Near the mouth of the Cape Fear River (Brunswick County)	Permanent masonry fort on the west bank of the Cape Fear River completed in 1838 for coastal defense. Seized by Confederate troops in April 1861, it became a mainstay in the Confederate defense of the river and Wilmington. Named for Richard Caswell, North Carolina's first governor and a Revolutionary War hero.
Fort Chase	Near New Bern (Craven County)	One of a series of Federal forts built in 1862–63 to enable Union forces to hold New Bern. Located on the north side of the Neuse River, it mounted three 24-pounder cannons.
Fort Clark	Southwest end of Hatteras Island (Dare County)	Confederate earthwork fort guarding the entrance to Hatteras Inlet. Irregular square fort with an 18-foot-thick parapet, mounting five Navy 32-pounder cannons and three 6-pounder cannons and manned by Capt. J. C. Lamb's company of the 17th North Carolina Regiment. Named for Governor Henry T. Clark.
Fort Comfort	Plymouth (Washington County)	One of many Federal installations built in defense of Union-held Plymouth. Located on the east side of the city. Captured during Brig. Gen. Robert F. Hoke's attack in April 1864 by the 35th North Carolina Regiment.
Fort Croatan	Near New Bern (Craven County)	One of a series of Federal forts built in 1862–63 to enable Union forces to hold New Bern. Manned by a garrison of Rhode Island troops until its capture in 1864 by the 65th North Carolina Regiment.

Name	Location	Description
Fort Davis	South of Wilmington (New Hanover County)	One of several Confederate forts comprising the defense of the Cape Fear River approaches to Wilmington. Constructed early in the war and continually improved.
Fort Dixie	6 miles south of New Bern (Craven County)	Confederate earthwork fort on the west bank of the Neuse River serving as part of the defenses of New Bern. Mounted four 24-pounder cannons and four 32-pounder cannons (one rifled) and garrisoned by Company G, 36th North Carolina Regiment.
Fort Dutton	Northwest of New Bern (Craven County)	One of a series of Federal forts built in 1862–63 to enable Union forces to hold New Bern. Small redoubt mounting a 100-pounder Parrott rifle and two 32-pounder cannons. Also known as Fort Union.
Fort Ellis	4 miles south of New Bern (Craven County)	Confederate earthwork fort built as part of the defenses of New Bern. Mounted one 8-inch Columbiad and seven 32-pounder cannons and was garrisoned by Company E, 36th North Carolina Regiment. Named for Governor John W. Ellis.
Fort Fisher	18 miles south of Wilmington (New Hanover County)	Confederate fort that was the world's largest earthwork fortification in 1865. Defended the New Inlet into the Cape Fear River. Mounted 44 guns (mostly smoothbore Columbiads) and assorted mortars, mines, and peripheral batteries. Featured a bombproof hospital. Named for Col. Charles F. Fisher, killed in the First Battle of Manassas (Bull Run).
Fort Forrest	Redstone Point (west side of Croatan Sound, opposite Roanoke Island, Dare County)	Confederate floating battery built as part of the defenses of Roanoke Island. Mounted seven 32-pounder cannons and garrisoned by Company E, 17th North Carolina Regiment, and Company A, 31st North Carolina Regiment. Named for Confederate Cdre. French Forrest.
Fort Gaston	2 miles south of New Bern (Craven County)	One of a series of Federal forts built in 1862–63 to enable Union forces to hold New Bern. Located on the south bank of the Trent River. Mounted seven 32-pounder cannons and guarded the point at which the main county road to Beaufort crossed the Trent River at Clermont Bridge to enter New Bern.
Fort Gray	North of Plymouth (Washington County)	One of many Federal installations built in defense of Union-held Plymouth. Overlooked the Roanoke River at Warren's Neck. Mounted one 100-pounder Parrott rifle and two smoothbore 32-pounder cannons. Named for Col. Charles Gray, 96th New York Infantry, killed at the First Battle of Kinston.
Fort Hal	Near Plymouth (Washington County)	One of many Federal installations built in defense of Union-held Plymouth. Located on the west bank of the Roanoke River, it protected both land and water approaches to the town. Mounted one 200-pounder cannon.
Fort Hatteras	South end of Hatteras Island (Dare County)	Confederate earthwork fort guarding Hatteras Inlet. Mounted several 32-pounder cannons, two 8-inch seacoast howitzers, and one 10-inch Columbiad. Garrisoned by companies of the 17th North Carolina Regiment. Captured in August 1861 by a Union fleet commanded by Cdre. Silas H. Stringham.

Name	Location	Description
Fort Heckman	Near Morehead City (Carteret County)	Federal earthwork fort built in 1863 as part of the landward defenses of Morehead City. Mounted one 24-pounder flank howitzer, two smoothbore 32-pounder cannons, and one rifled 32-pounder cannon. Named for Brig. Gen. Charles P. Heckman.
Fort Hill	6 miles southeast of Washington (Beaufort County)	Confederate earthwork fort built in 1861 in defense of the Pamlico River. Mounted two rifled 32-pounder cannons, three smoothbore 32-pounder cannons, and two 24-pounder cannons. Garrisoned by Companies B and I, 3rd North Carolina Artillery. Named for Maj. Gen. Daniel H. Hill.
Fort Holmes	South of Wilmington (New Hanover County)	One of several Confederate forts comprising the defense of the Cape Fear River approaches to Wilmington. Constructed early in the war and continually improved.
Fort Huger	West end of Roanoke Island (Dare County)	Largest of the Confederate defenses of Roanoke Island. Situated on Weir Point overlooking Croatan Sound. Mounted twelve 32-pounder cannons (two of them rifled) and garrisoned by a company of the 8th North Carolina Regiment. Named for Maj. Gen. Benjamin Huger.
Huggins Island Fort	Huggins Island (Onslow County)	Confederate earthwork fort built in 1861 in defense of Swansboro and Bogue Inlet. Mounted six 32-pounder cannons and garrisoned by Company B, 36th North Carolina Regiment.
Fort Johnston (Fort Pender)	Southport (Brunswick County)	Federal fort seized early in the war by Wilmington militia troops. Became part of the Confederate defenses of the lower Cape Fear. Renamed Fort Pender in 1863 in honor of Maj. Gen. William D. Pender.
Fort Lane	3 miles south of New Bern (Craven County)	Confederate earthwork fort built as part of the defenses of New Bern. Manned by Company A, 3rd North Carolina Artillery (40th Regiment). Named for New Bern mayor Frederick Lane.
Fort Macon	East of Atlantic Beach (Carteret County)	Federal masonry fort seized early in the war by local militia forces commanded by Capt. Josiah Pender. Guarded Beaufort Inlet. Captured by Union forces on 25 Apr. 1862 after heavy bombardment.
Fort Ocracoke (Fort Morgan)	Near Ocracoke (Beacon Island, Hyde County)	Confederate earthwork fort built early in the war to guard Ocracoke Inlet from Union warships. Garrisoned by Companies B and K, 17th North Carolina Regiment. Abandoned 30 Aug. 1861 after Union forces captured Hatteras Inlet.
Fort Oregon	North end of Hatteras Island (Dare County)	Confederate earthwork fort on the south side of Oregon Inlet. Garrisoned by Companies I and L, 17th North Carolina Regiment. Abandoned 31 Aug. 1861 after Union forces captured Forts Hatteras and Clark at Hatteras Inlet.
Fort Rollins	Blowing Rock (Watauga County)	Union stockade built in 1865 by forces commanded by Maj. W. W. Rollins.
Fort Rowan	Northwest of New Bern (Craven County)	One of a series of Federal forts built in 1862–63 to enable Union forces to hold New Bern. Guarded the point at which the Atlantic & North Carolina Railroad passed through Union works on the way from Kinston. Mounted a 100-pounder Parrott rifle, two 32-pounder

FORTS

Name	Location	Description
		cannons, two 3-inch rifles, and two 8-inch mortars. Named for navy commander S. C. Rowan.
Fort Spinola	1 mile south of New Bern (Craven County)	One of a series of Federal forts built in 1862–63 to enable Union forces to hold New Bern. Anchored a line of earthwork forts running along Scott's (or Greenspring) Creek down to Fort Amory on the south bank of the Trent River. Mounted eight 32-pounder cannons. Named after Brig. Gen. Francis B. Spinola.
Fort Stevenson	1 mile northwest of New Bern (Craven County)	One of a series of Federal forts built in 1862–63 to enable Union forces to hold New Bern. Secured the flank of a strong earthwork defensive line encircling New Bern on its western side. Mounted five 32-pounder cannons. Named for Brig. Gen. Thomas G. Stevenson.
Fort Strong	South of Wilmington (New Hanover County)	Largest of the region's Confederate Cape Fear River defenses. Fell to the Federal forces in 1865 prior to the fall of Wilmington.
Fort Thompson	Near New Bern (Craven County)	Confederate earthwork fort built in 1861 as part of the Neuse River defenses of New Bern. Mounted thirteen 32-pounder cannons and garrisoned by Company I, 10th North Carolina Regiment, and Company G, 40th North Carolina Regiment. Fell to Maj. Gen. Ambrose E. Burnside's forces in March 1862 during the Battle of New Bern.
Fort Totten	Western edge of New Bern (Craven County)	Largest of the Union forts built in 1862–63 to enable Union forces to hold New Bern. Its lines of entrenchments extended on either side to the Neuse and Trent Rivers. Named for the U.S. Army's chief engineer, Brig. Gen. Joseph G. Totten.
Fort Wessels	Southwest of Plymouth (Washington County)	One of many Federal installations built in defense of Union-held Plymouth. Named for Brig. Gen. Henry W. Wessels, Federal commander of the Plymouth garrison.
Fort Williams	Near Plymouth (Washington County)	One of many Federal installations built in defense of Union-held Plymouth. Earthwork fort anchoring the center of a line of earthworks enclosing the town's eastern side. Named for Brig. Gen. Thomas Williams.

BATTERIES

Name	Location	Description
Battery Anderson	About 15 miles south of Wilmington (New Hanover County)	One of several Confederate outlying works of the Fort Fisher complex and Cape Fear River defenses. Roughly seven miles north of Fort Fisher. Garrisoned by Company A, Thirteenth Battalion.
Battery Bolles	About 15 miles south of Wilmington (New Hanover County)	One of several Confederate outlying works of the Fort Fisher complex and Cape Fear River defenses. Garrisoned by Company D, Thirteenth North Carolina Battalion.
Battery Buchanan	About 15 miles south of Wilmington (New Hanover County)	One of several Confederate outlying works of the Fort Fisher complex and Cape Fear River defenses. Massive two-tiered, oval-shaped earthwork fort located one mile south of Fort Fisher. Named in honor of Adm. Franklin Buchanan.

Name	Location	Description
Battery Gatling	About 15 miles south of Wilmington (New Hanover County)	One of several Confederate outlying works of the Fort Fisher complex and Cape Fear River defenses. About seven miles north of Fort Fisher. Garrisoned by Company A, Thirteenth North Carolina Battalion.
Half Moon Battery	About 15 miles south of Wilmington (New Hanover County)	Small Confederate gun emplacement located four miles north of Fort Fisher. Mounted one or two smoothbore field pieces. So named by Union soldiers because of its crescent shape.
Battery Huger	West side of Roanoke Island (Dare County)	Small Confederate gun emplacement captured in February 1862 by forces commanded by Maj. Gen. Ambrose E. Burnside.
Battery Lamb	About 17 miles south of Wilmington (Reeve's Point, Brunswick County)	Two-gun Confederate emplacement constructed to protect both water and land approaches to the port of Wilmington from the west.
Pond Battery	About 15 miles south of Wilmington (New Hanover County)	One of several Confederate outlying works of the Fort Fisher complex and Cape Fear River defenses. Located north of Fort Fisher, it housed one or two smoothbore field pieces.
Battery Purdie	About 15 miles south of Wilmington (New Hanover County)	One of several Confederate outlying works of the Fort Fisher complex and Cape Fear River defenses. Garrisoned by Company D, Thirteenth North Carolina Battalion.
Battery Shaw	Oak Island (Brunswick County)	One-gun Confederate emplacement that was part of the defenses protecting the entrance to the Cape Fear River known as Old Inlet.
Battery Worth	Western edge of Plymouth (Washington County)	One of many batteries and redoubts comprising the Federal works at Plymouth. Mounted one 200-pounder gun. Fell to Confederate forces under Brig. Gen. Robert F. Hoke in April 1864.
Zeke's Island Battery	South of Wilmington (New Hanover County)	Confederate sand emplacement located across New Inlet Channel from Fort Fisher. Garrisoned by Company K, 18th North Carolina Regiment, and mounted two 32-pounder cannons.

tween earthen barricades to localize such incidents. To prevent harm to the surrounding community, there was a 2,100-acre buffer zone on Pleasure Island (Carolina, Kure, Wilmington, and Fort Fisher Beaches) and a 4,300-acre buffer in Brunswick County. The two most controversial cargoes shipped through the terminal were World War II nerve gas in 1970 and European spent nuclear fuel rods in 1994.

Beverly Tetterton

Militias, Colonial. Settlers in North Carolina in the 1660s were required to own musket, powder, and shot in order to claim land grants, and as early as 1667 Governor Samuel Stephens was ordered to "trayne bands and companies" of soldiers "to suppress all intrigues and rebellions [and] to make war offensive and defensive with all Indyans, Strangers, and Foreigners." To this end the colonial Assembly was to "nominate, place and commissionate all Military Officers under the Governor" with instructions to said governor "to take, to mus-

ter and trayne all the soldiers . . . and to exercise the whole militia." Implicit in this arrangement was the establishment of a muster ground, a central or an acceptable field or fields, to perform the training and review the militia.

Whether a militia was actually organized, trained, and fielded at that time is unclear, as the Fundamental Constitutions of 1669 only required that men aged 17 to 60 be summoned to serve as soldiers "whenever the grand council shall find it necessary." Since there was no mention of an active militia in the 1600s and early 1700s—probably because of a large Quaker population and others who refused service—it can be presumed that North Carolina was among a number of colonies that, as pointed out to Queen Anne in 1706, lacked a "regular militia" establishment.

In 1711 the Assembly, in response to attacks by the Tuscarora Indians, required that all men aged 16 to 60 either fight or pay £5 in lieu of service. The Quakers' refusal to do either, as well as insubordination in the ranks of those being trained, hampered the implementation of the law but indicated that the training of companies under captains was taking place. Four years later a second law, similar to the first, enlisted men and strengthened the fines of those who would not serve. The act also required each company captain to create a list of eligible freemen, update it every October, and send one copy to the governor and a second to the colonel of the regiment. Regular training sessions, or musters, were not mandated, with the assumption that a muster would be called in response to a crisis. This act, with modifications, was reissued in 1740.

Governor Arthur Dobbs (1754–65) found the implementation of these laws inconsistent with the defense obligations of his office, because the militia regiments were understaffed, ill-equipped, and poorly trained. In addition, they lacked leadership, had no muster rolls, and were unable to take the field if needed. Accordingly, in 1758 Dobbs fashioned a stronger militia bill that increased fines for derelict behavior, improved record keeping, and required at least eight musters per year — four for each company and four general musters per regiment. Successive militia laws in 1764, 1766, 1773, and 1774 sustained Dobbs's work but reduced training for each unit. By 1774 companies and regiments were expected to drill only twice a year. Companies were permitted, as was traditional, to train at a site chosen by their captain, but regiments were for the first time in 1774 required to muster at the courthouse.

Even with these reforms, the system functioned little better. During the American Revolution, most militia units were, in the words of Gen. George Washington, "totally unacquainted with every kind of military skill" and were unreliable in combat. Although commanders like Washington and Nathanael Greene increasingly called for professionally trained soldiers, or Continentals, postwar economic restraints forced a return to a militia system.

In an effort to coordinate and improve the quality of these citizen soldiers, the newly established federal government implemented a militia act in 1792. According to this law, companies made up battalions that created regiments that composed the brigades and divisions of a national militia. Companies were to muster six times a year, whereas regiments and battalions met biannually. Brigades and divisions came together only annually. The 1792 measure signaled the end of local militias, although problems in the militia system were not unknown. By the 1820s it was reported that drunkenness, lawlessness, and insubordination among militia troops was common, and where this did not occur the muster was likely to become a holiday with weapons intentionally left at home. In the words of one militia colonel, "Our militia are worse than useless."

References: R. D. W. Connor, *North Carolina: An Ancient Commonwealth* (1929); Jean M. Flynn, *The Militia in Ante-bellum South Carolina* (1991); Guion Griffis Johnson, *Ante-Bellum North Carolina: A Social History* (1937).

Louis P. Towles

Milk Sickness, also called "milk sick fever" and "sick stomach," is caused by the excretion of tremetol or tremetone, the toxin in white snakeroot and rayless goldenrod, when these common plants are consumed by herbivorous animals. The human poisonings resulting from the consumption of contaminated meat and milk products were a serious problem in North Carolina from colonial days through the nineteenth century. Milk sickness seldom troubled populated areas but frequently devastated frontier communities of Appalachia and other regions where medical information was scarce. For that reason milk sickness was not widely understood until the early twentieth century and was frequently confused with other diseases and attributed to contaminated water, various insects, metals, and a variety of plants. Physician Thomas Barbee first published an account of the malady in 1809, and fellow doctor Daniel Drake began to study it the following year. It was Drake who observed in 1835 that the disease had been known in North Carolina for more than 60 years.

Milk sickness appeared annually from July until the onset of winter. In especially hot, dry summers, some communities lost one-quarter to one-half of their inhabitants. Settlers soon learned to recognize signs of the ailment in their cattle, a general weakness known as the "trembles," especially noticeable after the animals had run for a few minutes. Similar symptoms of weakness, accompanied by nausea, vomiting, and constipation afflicted humans. Death occurred in two to ten days. The victim might recover only to relapse and die after exertion or survive but remain weakened for months or years.

By the 1820s researchers had identified a connection between cattle that were allowed to run freely in the woods and the increased frequency of milk sickness and noted that cultivated pastures virtually eliminated it. In 1828 an Illinois woman, Anna Pierce, correctly identified the cause of the sickness with the advice of a Shawnee woman, but her discovery remained little known. In 1840 Drake argued to a wider audience that herbivorous animals got milk sickness by eating an unidentified plant and then transmitted it to humans through the consumption of meat, milk, and butter. Unfortunately, he incorrectly identified poison oak and poison ivy as the culprits. It was not until 1906 that white snakeroot and rayless goldenrod were proved to be the sources of the toxin. Gradually, improved knowledge of the causes led to an abatement of the illness.

References: "Deadly Milk Sickness," *Greensboro Patriot*, 25 Nov. 1903; David Cameron Duffy, "Land of Milk and Poison," *Natural History* 99 (July 1990); Reida E. Niederhofer, "The Milk Sickness: Drake on Medical Interpretation," *Journal of the American Medical Association* 254 (October 1985).

Curtis W. Wood

Millstones of large diameter used for grinding cereals, ores for paint, fertilizers, and other products have been quarried from a variety of rocks in North Carolina since colonial times. In Moore County a quartz conglomerate from Parkwood was an important source. The Smith granite quarry near Charlotte was worked for millstones that were used in early ore mills. Triassic sandstones were used for millstones and whetstones. During the twentieth century, most millstones were from Rowan County granite, and as recently as 1953 they continued to be used in the preparation of paints, fertilizer, and feldspar.

Jean H. Seaman

Mill Villages. SEE Textiles.

Mining. A variety of minerals, gems, and rocks have been excavated in North Carolina since the precolonial era. Mining was known to the region's Indians before European settlement, and evidence of mica mining and trade with other tribes may be seen at the Baird Mine in Macon County and the Sink Hole Mine in Mitchell County. It appears that Indians also used talc and soapstone for making utensils. Other resources exploited early were clay and kaolin. The colonial period saw mainly local use of these materials as well as the burning of shell marls for cement and small-scale iron making from the most accessible deposits.

This engraving from an 1880 issue of *Harper's New Monthly Magazine* shows mica being mined, split, and cut near Waynesville. The accompanying text noted that the "flakes are cut in oblong squares by enormous shears, packed, and sent north. Heaps of broken wafer-like waste sheets littered the whole side of the mountain, sparkling like silver in the sun." NCC.

In the nineteenth century there was an abundance of mining activity as the state surveyed its mineral assets. As early as 1822, Professor Denison Olmsted at the University of North Carolina submitted a descriptive list of rocks and minerals to the *American Journal of Science*, some of which he had collected himself and others that had been sent to him. In 1871 C. E. Jenks began to mine gem corundum in Macon County, but this evolved into the more profitable abrasive business with gemstones an erratic by-product. Around 1874 J. Adlai D. Stephenson of Statesville offered rewards to anyone finding minerals of interest and was the first collector reported to have the then-unknown hiddenite in his collection. Gen. Thomas L. Clingman, William E. Hidden, and George F. Kunz were also active mineral collectors of the late nineteenth century.

North Carolina's small but unique gemstone supply—the state has the greatest variety and quantity of gemstones in the East—became attractive to collectors. From 1881 to 1919 the production of all gemstones, including aquamarines, rhodolite garnets, golden beryl, emeralds and hiddenite, and gem corundum (rubies and sapphires), was a minor but colorful industry. As the twentieth century progressed, lithium and tungsten mines and phosphate deposits were opened. New industrial applications were found, while the market for old reliables such as feldspar and mica, along with new beneficiation techniques, increased their rate of recovery. Gemstones in the late twentieth century remained a factor in the state's economy, with numerous mines open to amateur collectors and annual production averaging about $50,000. Several of these commercial mines, such as the Cherokee Ruby Mine, Cowee Mountain Ruby Mine, and Jackson Hole Mine, were located in Franklin (Macon County), which is also the site of the Franklin Gem and Mineral Museum.

Important Minerals, Gems, and Rocks Mined in North Carolina

Amethyst. Violet quartz gemstone colored by inclusions of hematite or other minerals, found in Stokes, Burke, Lincoln, Iredell, Moore, Warren, and Franklin Counties. Southeast Macon County's Tessentee Creek was originally operated by Tiffany and Company of New York around 1900. Other mines such as the Connally and Rhodes Mines also operated in Macon County.

Argillite. Fine-grained, gray-to-dark colored sedimentary rock. By the 1980s argillite (such as that quarried in Davidson County) was becoming widely used in the hearths of manufactured homes and in prefabricated fireplaces.

Asbestos. Silky, fibrous form of silicate minerals first discovered in 1871. Its nonflammable character found applications in insulation (shingles and siding) and served other heat-resistant needs (firefighters' products). Though asbestos was reported in Wilkes and Polk Counties by 1900, production in Yancey County in 1919 was among the highest in the nation that year. The mining of anthophyllite (used as asbestos) remained a minor industry in Yancey through the late 1970s.

Beryl. Very hard mineral (beryllium aluminum silicate) found in granitic rocks and pegmatites. Discovered in Macon County in 1871, aquamarine (blue beryl) and golden beryl were mined in Mitchell County in the early 1900s; by the end of the century, Macon County's Littlefield Mine and Yancey County's Ray Mine continued to produce modest amounts for amateur collectors.

Chromium. Found as chromite (chromium oxide) in olivine-rich rock called "dunite." Known to exist since 1870, chromite is found in Yancey County's Day Book Mine and in Buncombe County's Democrat Mine, as well as in deposits in Iredell, Macon, and Jackson Counties. After mining between 1880 and 1900 and during both world wars, chromite came to be considered a reserve mineral.

Copper. Element found as sulfides such as chalcocite, chalcopyrite, and bornite in the mountain belt (Ashe, Jackson, Swain, and Haywood Counties), Guilford, Granville, and Person Counties, and other areas throughout the state. Exploited as early as 1585, when Roanoke Island explorers reported its use by Indians, copper was first mined commercially in Granville County in 1852 (one of the first such mines in the nation). The industry, though never flourishing, continued until 1962.

Corundum. A form of aluminum oxide, second only to the diamond in hardness, found in Madison County in 1846. Mining began in 1871 in Macon County, where corundum soon found greater application as an abrasive than a gemstone. By 1895 nearly all of the corundum produced and used in the United States came from the counties west of the Blue Ridge, though the use of artificial abrasives after 1900 brought an end to the industry.

Diamond. The hardest known mineral, found only rarely in western North Carolina. Thirteen diamonds have been reported from the region, beginning in 1843 with a 1.33 carat octahedral crystal from Brindletown Creek Ford in Burke County. The largest, discovered in 1886, was a 4.33 carat green-gray crystal from Dysartville in McDowell County (now in the American Museum of Natural History in New York). The last North Carolina diamond was found in 1893 at King's Mountain.

Emerald. Green gem variety of beryl, first found in Alexander County in 1874 and later in Mitchell County in 1894–95. The 1880s saw the largest emerald at that time, an eight-and-one-half-inch crystal. In 1969 the

Rist Mine yielded the largest crystal seen in North America, a 1,438 carat piece; a 13.14 carat "Carolina Emerald" also was acquired by Tiffany and Company of New York. In 1973 the emerald was adopted as the state's official gemstone.

Feldspar. Abundant group of aluminum silicates found commercially in pegmatites and feldspar-rich granitic rocks called "alaskite." Important in the glass and ceramics industries, the first feldspar was mined as early as 1744 in present-day Macon County; systematic exploitation began late in the nineteenth century. The Spruce Pine area mines of Deer Park and Chalk Mountain helped North Carolina become the nation's leading feldspar producer, a position held since 1917.

Gold. Precious metal found as grains and nuggets in the middle and western counties. With the first authenticated discovery in 1799 in Cabarrus County (followed by finds in Stanly, Union, Davidson, Guilford, and Randolph Counties), North Carolina produced the nation's gold supply from 1803 to 1848. Mining continued up to 1971, although little gold was found after 1900.

Hiddenite. Grass-green gemstone and variety of spodumene unique to Alexander County, where it was discovered in 1880. A novel gem that sold well above its real value, hidden (later hiddenite) was exhibited at the Charleston Exposition in 1901–2. The community of Salem Church changed its name to Hiddenite in its honor and is now home to the Hiddenite Center, an important folk and cultural arts center.

Kyanite. Aluminum silicate, often in flattened blue crystals, found in metamorphic rock and some pegmatites. It was commercially produced in the Spruce Pine district southeast of Burnsville from 1934 to 1944 for use as a refractory. Kyanite has continued to interest mineral collectors, and occasionally gem-grade material is found.

Lithium. Element used in aluminum making, glass, ceramics, greases, and other products, mined from pegmatites as spodumene in Cleveland, Gaston, and Lincoln Counties. Major production began in 1942 near King's Mountain in Cleveland County. Together, Gaston and Cleveland Counties contain more than 80 percent of the known reserves in the nation, and in 1980 North Carolina produced over 50 percent of the world's estimated output.

Marble. Crystalline form of limestone, found in a narrow belt centered on Murphy in Cherokee County. Much of it is too broken by jointing to be good as a dimension stone, but in 1902 the National Marble Company was in operation at Regal, shipping blocks to Canton, Ga., for finishing work. In 1980 three active companies were reported in Cherokee County.

Mica. Group of aluminum silicates occurring in the Blue Ridge Mountains and western piedmont, notable for its perfect cleavage into thin, elastic sheets. Used early on as a form of window glass (called isinglass), mica was first mined in Mitchell County in 1858 and in Jackson County in 1867. North Carolina produces two-thirds of the nation's scrap mica, which found numerous industrial uses in the late nineteenth and early twentieth centuries.

Olivine. Pale green igneous rock with a sandy texture. Found in the mountains, deposits of olivine rock were known as early as 1875 as "crysolytic sandstone" and later as "olivine" or "dunite." Beginning in the 1930s olivine has been used as a basic refractory in the steel industry and as a molding sand in foundry work. North Carolina is the nation's major olivine producer, with mines in Jackson, Mitchell, and Yancey Counties.

Phosphate. Dark, nodular mineral found in the coastal counties. Castle Hayne north of Wilmington has produced phosphate rock commercially since about 1900, when the mineral was manufactured into fertilizer. In 1958 a vast deposit was discovered in Beaufort County and christened the "Pungo River Formation" in 1964. Since then North Carolina has become the second-highest phosphate producer in the nation (the state's sole producer is Texasgulf, Inc.).

Pyrophyllite. Soft white silicate associated with the metavolcanic sedimentary rock of the Carolina slate belt. Used in ceramics, insecticides, and other products, pyrophyllite was first identified in 1856 in Moore County. In 1921 a processing plant was built near Robbins on what proved to be the largest deposit in the state and the only underground workings. North Carolina is the nation's largest domestic producer, with mines in Moore and Orange Counties.

Quartz. One of the most widespread minerals, found in all classes of rock. Quartz (silicon dioxide) comes in many varieties, such as milky quartz. Rock crystal, a glass-clear variety, is sought by collectors in the western counties; one Ashe County piece (now in New York's Metropolitan Museum of Art) was displayed at the 1900 Paris Exposition. Avery, Mitchell, Yancey, and Cleveland Counties produce quartz sand for industrial use.

Rhodolite. Pink variety of garnet unique in North America to North Carolina. Pale pink rhodolite was reported in Asheville in 1893 and discovered in 1895 during mining for ruby corundum in the Cowee Valley. A mixture of ⅔ pyrope garnet to ⅓ almandine garnet, it was named for its color's resemblance to the blooms of rhododendron. Between 1900 and 1926 rhodolite was mined on Sugarloaf Mountain in Jackson County for use as an abrasive.

Ruby. Blood-red gem variety of corundum. The Cowee Valley in Macon County, site of the first efforts to recover the gemstone from gravel in 1895, yielded only flawed rubies. Though the ruby industry never enjoyed the success of corundum, tourists can still purchase buckets of gravel with sluices and sieves to search the contents for rubies.

Sandstone. Sedimentary rock formed mainly of quartz grains, quarried for dimension stone beginning in the late nineteenth century (when "brownstone" was popular) in counties such as Anson, Lee, Montgomery, Stokes, Burke, and Wilkes. The Wilmington Post Office, Moore County Courthouse, and early buildings on the campus of North Carolina State University in Raleigh all contain sandstone.

Sapphire. Gem corundum of any color except blood-red (reserved for the ruby). Sapphires were first mined regularly at the Corundum Hill Mine in Macon County in 1871, then in Jackson County in 1892 (400 tons yielded 25 percent nearly pure crystals). Notable sapphires, such as a 1,025 carat blue star sapphire found near Canton in 1888, have been found on occasion, and tourists still enjoy searching through buckets from old sapphire mines with screens and sluices.

Silver. Precious metal mined in North Carolina as a secondary product to gold and copper. The modern-day Silver Hill Mine opened as the Kings Mine in 1838 in Davidson County near Lexington and later operated as the Washington Silver Mine between 1840 and 1855. During the Civil War it produced lead for bullets and was worked intermittently for silver, lead, and zinc until 1898. Some silver production was reported from 1954 to 1963, but the metal is of minor importance to the state.

Soapstone. Soft, slippery rock containing talc (a hydrous magnesium silicate). The Indians used soapstone, or talc, to carve utensils; early settlers shaped it into sills and wainscoting. The stone was also used to line the fireplaces in the State Capitol and many private homes because of its ability to hold heat for a considerable time. Soapstone has been found in about a third of the counties, but deposits have generally been too small and erratic for commercialization.

Thorium. Derived from the rare mineral monazite (thorium phosphate) and found in alluvial deposits called black sands. Mined from sediments in a belt covering Alexander, Burke, Catawba, Cleveland, Iredell, Lincoln, and Rutherford Counties from 1886 to 1910, thorium enjoyed a period of demand as a necessary component of the Welsbach incandescent gaslight.

Tin. Mined as cassiterite (tin oxide), occurring in pegmatites and as alluvial deposits. Discovered in 1883 near King's Mountain, cassiterite remains a widespread but uneconomical reserve throughout the Cleveland-Gaston-Lincoln Counties area. In 1982 three companies—Texasgulf, Billiton (Royal Dutch/Shell subsidiary), and ASARCO Inc.—were all engaged in explorations for cassiterite in southern Rutherford County.

Tungsten. Hard, malleable metal (found as tungstates) with great tensile strength. It was recognized in gold mines as early as 1875 in Cabarrus County and reevaluated there in 1956 by the Carolina Tungsten Company. A large deposit in Vance County (first reported in 1890) prompted the building of the Tungsten Queen Mine in 1942. Considerable reserves remain.

Unakite. Igneous rock found in Madison and Mitchell Counties as narrow veins of green epidote with red feldspar and quartz in schistose granite. It is chiefly of interest to collectors, since it makes a colorful polished stone.

Uranium. Element essential to the production of nuclear energy, existing in potential reserves of 5–10 million pounds in the Wilson Creek gneiss and Grandfather Mountain Formation in the western counties of Avery and Caldwell. Rare minerals containing uranium (torbernite, gummite, autunite, and uraninite) can be found in Mitchell County.

Vermiculite. Alteration product of hydrothermal activity on magnesium and iron mica. Closely associated with olivine, it can be found in the western counties, particularly Macon and the Swannanoa area of Buncombe. Used for its insulating properties and as a packing material, vermiculite was of little interest before 1933, when a small industry developed in the state.

Zircon. Mineral found as a silicate of the rare element zirconium. First discovered in 1869, zircon was rediscovered in the 1880s as a component in gas mantles and electric lighting, but deposits are of no commercial importance. Zircon is often flawed by the radioactivity of trace elements, but some crystals are heat-treated to gain bright, desirable colors. Cubic zirconia, from zirconium dioxide, has a brilliance that challenges natural diamonds.

References: P. A. Carpenter III, *Metallic Mineral Deposits of North Carolina*, North Carolina Department of Natural Resources and Community Development Bulletin no. 84 (1976); Jasper Leonidas Stuckey, *North Carolina: Its Geology and Mineral Resources* (1965); W. F. Wilson and B. J. McKenzie, *Mineral Collecting Sites in North Carolina*, North Carolina Department of Natural Resources and Community Development, Information Circular 24 (1978).

Jean H. Seaman

SEE ALSO Bechtler Mint; Big Ore Bank; Cabinet of Minerals; Gold Hill Mine; Gold Rush.

Carolina Shout by African American artist and Charlotte native Romare Bearden on display at the Mint Museum of Art. Photograph by Sean Busher. Courtesy of the Mint Museum of Art.

Mint Museum of Art is located in Charlotte in a building that once served as the first branch of the U.S. Mint outside Philadelphia. Gold was discovered in the Charlotte area in 1799, and by the 1830s there was enough gold production to warrant the creation of a branch of the U.S. Mint in Charlotte. The building, originally uptown, was designed by William A. Strickland, and the mint began operating in 1836. During the Civil War, the building was used as a Confederate headquarters and hospital; it later was an assay office.

In 1933, when adjacent construction and expansion threatened its existence, the building was bought for $950 by a group of preservationists led by Mrs. Harold C. Dwelle and moved to its current site on Randolph Road, where it was reconstructed from 1934 to 1936. In 1936 the Mint Museum of Art opened as the first art museum in North Carolina. Expansion programs in 1967 and 1983 increased the size of the facility.

The museum has diverse collections of American and European paintings and sculpture; pre-Columbian, African, and Spanish colonial art; historic costumes; and one of the premier collections of European and American porcelain and pottery in the nation. The museum also hosts touring exhibits and supports two research libraries.

The Mint Museum of Craft and Design opened in a former department store building nearby in January 1999 to house the museum's growing collections of decorative arts and regional crafts, including North Carolina pottery and turned wood. The Mint Museum of Art had begun its crafts collection in earnest in 1964 with the acquisition of John Acorn's brazed steel sculpture *Growth Form* and the first in a series of juried Piedmont Craft Exhibitions. By 2006, the Mint Museums, as they became called collectively, had approved further expansion plans, which include a new 145,000-square-foot facility for the Craft and Design Museum on Tryon Road.

Bruce E. Baker

"Miracle of Hickory" refers to an emergency hospital established in Hickory during the summer of 1944 to treat infantile paralysis (polio). The descriptive name comes from the title of a pamphlet issued by the National Foundation for Infantile Paralysis (March of Dimes) later that year. The hospital was started in response to a serious epidemic that developed in June and was centered in the Catawba Valley. When the facilities at Charlotte Memorial Hospital and an orthopedic hospital in Gastonia were filled, it became necessary to treat patients at Hickory. The "miracle" was the speed with which the hospital was conceived and put into operation. The decision to open a hospital was made on a Wednesday at noon, and the first patients were admitted on Saturday morning, a mere 54 hours later. The initial building was a stone structure that was already occupied as a summer camp. Army hospital tents were used throughout the summer, and several additional frame structures were built. Much of the construction and other work at the hospital was accomplished by a massive local volunteer effort.

The March of Dimes provided doctors and contributed more than $500,000 for the hospital. The American Red Cross recruited several hundred nurses, most of whom were housed at the Hotel Hickory. Numerous other specialized medical personnel came from throughout the country. Several leading medical schools, including Yale, Johns Hopkins, and Bowman Gray, had research teams at the hospital.

Treatments at the facility were a vindication of the methods of Sister Elizabeth Kenny, who had been fighting the medical establishment for several years to substitute heat treatments, massage, and hydrotherapy for the conventional splinting and immobilization. Over 500 patients received treatment.

Almost from the time it was built, the hospital was controversial. It received national publicity, particularly in *Life* magazine, and Hickory became known as "the polio city." Some parents left town with their children, and shoppers and visitors were afraid to enter the area. A quarantine was in effect for several weeks. One faction wanted to keep the hospital and another group wanted to get rid of it. By December, the National Foundation for Infantile Paralysis believed that it should be closed. An arrangement was finally made to transfer the remaining patients to Charlotte Memorial Hospital. The last patients were moved from Hickory to Charlotte in a highly publicized motorcade on 5 Mar. 1945.

Richard L. Zuber

Mirlo Rescue, conducted by the Chicamacomico Coast Guard Station (originally part of the U.S. Lifesaving Service) on 16 Aug. 1918, is considered one of the most dramatic operations in U.S. Coast Guard history. The British tanker *Mirlo*, a 6,679-ton vessel with a crew of 52, was transporting a full load of gasoline from New Orleans to Norfolk when it struck a German mine off of Wimble Shoals early in the afternoon. The initial explosion rendered its engine room and wireless inoperative, and a second blast set the cargo of gasoline ablaze. With no hope of saving the vessel, the captain and crew boarded the *Mirlo*'s three lifeboats. The first capsized, throwing its 16 passengers into the sea. Only 6 of the men clinging to the overturned lifeboat survived a third explosion, which split the *Mirlo* in two and set the sea on fire with burning gasoline. The second lifeboat, with 19 men on board including the first mate, drifted aimlessly in the sea of fire. The third, carrying the captain and 16 crewmen, soon cleared the mass of flames and headed toward shore.

From the Chicamacomico Coast Guard Station, Capt. John Allen Midgett, with a handpicked crew of 6 surfmen, launched his power surfboat. The men passed the captain's lifeboat on its way to shore and proceeded toward the cloud of black smoke masking the scene of the disaster. Midgett and his crew, cutting the motor and relying on oars, were soon able to maneuver to the overturned lifeboat and haul the 6 seamen aboard the Coast Guard craft. Even as one of his own crewmen collapsed from exhaustion and exposure to the intense heat, Midgett, using motor power again, began searching for the mate's lifeboat, whose crew was both bailing water and beating at flames on the boat. Just before dusk the Coast Guardsmen sighted the lifeboat, put a line on board, and towed the boat and its 19 survivors toward Chicamacomico and safety. Releasing the mate's craft, Midgett left it and the captain's boat offshore while he off-loaded the 6 survivors he rescued first onto the beach. He then returned twice in the darkness until all 42 survivors were safely ashore.

For their exceptional bravery, each member of the Coast Guard crew was awarded a Gold Lifesaving Medal from the United States and a Victory Medal from the British government.

The seven remaining buildings of the Chicamacomico Station in Rodanthe were decommissioned by the Coast Guard in 1954. Listed on the National Register of Historic Places, the buildings are the finest extant examples of early U.S. Lifesaving Service facilities in the nation. The Gothic architecture of the original building, which dates to 1874, is itself unique, and many artifacts related to the history of the Lifesaving Service and shipwrecks are on display in the main station (1911) and adjacent buildings.

References: Edwin C. Bearss, "The *Mirlo* Rescue," NCHR 45 (October 1968); David Stick, *Graveyard of the Atlantic: Shipwrecks of the North Carolina Coast* (1952).

David Stick
Kathy Carter

Missionary District of Asheville, formed in October 1895, was the precursor of the Episcopal Diocese of Western North Carolina. It consisted of approximately the western

Chicamacomico Lifesaving Station, late 1980s. Photograph by Tim Buchman. Courtesy of Preservation North Carolina.

third of the state. Within the polity of the Episcopal Church, a missionary district is a geographical region large enough in land area to constitute a separate diocese but with too few churches and church members to be financially self-supporting. When the Episcopal Diocese of North Carolina was organized in 1817, it included the entire state, but as population gradually increased during the nineteenth century, it became difficult for the bishop to visit each congregation annually. In 1883 the eastern third of the state became a separate diocese, the Episcopal Diocese of East Carolina, and elected its own bishop, locating his office in Wilmington.

The western part of the state, however, remained part of the Diocese of North Carolina, which had its headquarters in Raleigh. After Bishop Joseph Blount Cheshire Jr. took office in 1893, it became clear to him that a new strategy was needed in the west, where outside of the city of Asheville there were few communities large or prosperous enough to support congregations. Cheshire, noting the small proportion of his time that he was able to give to the western counties, requested and received approval of his own North Carolina diocesan convention in May 1895 to establish the district, to which six missionaries were then assigned. The General Convention of the Epis-

copal Church, meeting later in 1895, approved the anticipated constitutional change and ceding of this particular territory in North Carolina. Cheshire provided episcopal services for the new district for the following three years, until it had its own bishop.

Oxford native Junius M. Horner, a member of the diocesan Missionary Council and priest-in-charge of two small churches in Goshen and Stovall, was elected by the General Convention as bishop of the Missionary District of Asheville in 1898. He served in this capacity until 1922, when the district became the Diocese of Western North Carolina. The new diocese chose Horner as its first bishop, and he continued to serve in that capacity until his death in 1933.

Reference: Norvin C. Duncan, *Pictorial History of the Episcopal Church in North Carolina, 1701–1964* (1965).

E. T. Malone Jr.

Mississippi Navigation Crisis of 1786–88 was the first serious North-South political quarrel in U.S. history. Some of the most outspoken and vociferous opponents to Secretary of State John Jay's proposed treaty with Spain—the conditions of which threatened to trade away the southern states' interest in western lands and the navigation of the Mississippi River for northern fishing, shipping, and commercial privileges—were political leaders from North Carolina. They included Timothy Bloodworth, Richard Caswell, Hugh Williamson, Benjamin Hawkins, and William Blount.

From the end of May 1786 until September 1788, Jay of New York, Rufus King of Massachusetts, and other northern congressmen argued that the critical situation of American trade and foreign relations warranted forbearing navigation of the Mississippi River for 25 years. In exchange for exclusive control of the river, Spain promised to open ports on the Spanish mainland and its Mediterranean islands, as well as in the Canary Islands and the Azores, to U.S. ships and their merchandise. The northern states, which controlled American shipping and freighting, stood to benefit most from the proposed treaty. In addition, many northern political leaders believed that a closed Mississippi River would slow western expansion and thereby maintain eastern land values, free labor supplies, and the political dominance of the seven northern states. Delegates from Virginia and North Carolina stood their ground in Congress, even when numerous northern representatives met secretly to discuss forming a separate confederacy.

The Mississippi Navigation Crisis was one of the most significant precipitating events of the constitutional convention. During the convention, the subject was fully discussed and was one of the southerners' strongest justifications for requiring in Article II, section 2, clause 2, of the Constitution that no treaty be signed with a foreign nation without the consent of two-thirds of the Senate. By requiring a two-thirds majority, they ensured that a southern bloc could obstruct the passage of any treaty injurious to the South. The Navigation Crisis was also an important bargaining point in the three-fifths slavery compromise.

Delegates from North Carolina urged the motion in the Continental Congress that finally put an end to the proposed treaty with Spain. On 16 Sept. 1788 Congress passed the North Carolina motion that declared Mississippi navigation an "essential right of the United States." The issue was deferred to the "new Government." Americans did not formally gain navigation rights to the Mississippi until the signing of Pinckney's Treaty in 1795; they did not enjoy a completely free and uninterrupted commerce on the river until the Louisiana Purchase in 1803.

References: Michael Allen, "The Mississippi River Debate, 1785–87," *Tennessee Historical Quarterly* 36 (Winter 1977); Samuel Flagg Bemis, *Pinckney's Treaty* (1960); Eli F. Merritt, "Secret Conflict and Sectional Compromise: The Mississippi River Question and the United States Constitution," *American Journal of Legal History* 35 (April 1991); Arthur Preston Whitaker, *The Mississippi Question, 1795–1803* (1934).

Eli F. Merritt

Deneen Z. Graham of North Wilkesboro after being crowned Miss North Carolina on 25 June 1983. She was the first African American to win the title. Courtesy of NCOA&H.

Miss North Carolina Scholarship Pageant. Each year in late June, local pageant winners from across North Carolina convene in Raleigh to compete for the title of Miss North Carolina and the right to represent North Carolina in the Miss America Pageant in Atlantic City, N.J., in September. The Miss North Carolina Scholarship Pageant celebrated its 69th anniversary in 2006, although there is disagreement about when the first pageant was actually held. According to pageant records, the event has been held annually since 1937 except for one year during World War II. The *Wilmington Star* reported that there was a pageant held in 1933 in Wrightsville Beach, which was won by Miss Sanford, Leola Councilman. Miss America Pageant records, however, do not include a mention of a 1933 Miss North Carolina.

The last time a Miss North Carolina reigned as Miss America was in 1962, when Maria Beale Fletcher, Miss Asheville, won the honor. By the early 2000s the Miss North Carolina Scholarship Pageant had begun emphasizing academic, philanthropic, and other accomplishments rather than mere beauty. In addition to being judged during the pageant in talent, interview, swimsuit, and evening wear categories, modern contestants must have previously chosen a social cause and performed community service. The winner and the runners-up are awarded scholarships and prizes. The reigning Miss North Carolina not only represents the state in the prestigious Miss America Pageant but also maintains a busy schedule, presiding over local pageants, charity events, and festivals.

Angelyn H. Patteson

Mitchell County, located in the Mountain region of western North Carolina, was formed in 1861 from Yancey, Watauga, Caldwell, Burke, and McDowell Counties; it was named for University of North Carolina professor Elisha Mitchell, who died exploring the famous mountain peak in western North Carolina that now bears his name (Mount Mitchell, Yancey County). Mitchell County partially borders the state of Tennessee. Early inhabitants of the area included the Cherokee Indians, followed by German and Scotch-Irish settlers. The county seat, Bakersville, was incorporated in 1868, although it had been established for more than 10 years prior to that time. The town was named for David Baker, who received a land grant and settled in the area in 1797. Other Mitchell County communities include Spruce Pine, Bandana, Red Hill, Penland, and Poplar. The acreage of Mitchell County comprises a large section of the Pisgah National Forest. Notable physical features include the North Toe River, Big Yellow Mountain, Chalk Mountain, and Roan Mountain.

Mitchell County's Penland School of Crafts, established in the late nineteenth century, is one of America's oldest and most successful handicraft schools. Other historic places include the English Inn, dating from the early nineteenth century, and the Lunday footbridge, constructed in the mid-twentieth century. Mitchell County cultural institutions include the North Carolina Mineral Museum and Twisted Laurel Gallery. Popular annual events held in the county include the Rhododendron Festival, Fall Festival of the Arts, Music in the Mountains Folk Festival, and North Carolina Mineral and Gem Festival at Spruce Pine.

Mitchell County has one of the richest mineral deposits in the United States. Fifty-seven different minerals are mined there, including mica, emerald, aquamarine, quartz, garnet, sapphire, kaolin, and feldspar. The county's agricultural products include burley tobacco, horticultural crops, Christmas trees, and beef cattle, and its leading manufacture is furniture. Mitchell County's estimated population was 16,000 in 2004.

Jay Mazzocchi

SEE ALSO Penland School of Crafts.

Modern Greece was a screw steam freighter used as a blockade-runner by Confederate forces during the Civil War.

Weighing 753 tons and spanning 210 feet in length, the ship was originally built by Richardson's of Stockton, England, for use in the Hull-Baltic timber trade in 1859. The *Modern Greece*'s movements and activities were kept secret until it mysteriously appeared near land approximately three miles north of Fort Fisher and New Inlet at 4:15 A.M. on 27 June 1862. This was only one day after an article appeared in the *Wilmington Journal* (26 June 1862) stating that "the steamer *Modern Greece*, fitted out at Hull, sailed from Falmouth 28th April ostensibly for Tampico." The Union blockader USS *Cambridge* fired on the *Modern Greece*, which sped parallel to shore to reach the protection of Fort Fisher's big guns. Under heavy fire, it ran hard aground about one-half mile north of the fort. There is some speculation that the heavily laden, deep-draft vessel may not have succeeded in entering New Inlet, whose channel depth was only 12 feet.

Once the *Modern Greece* was aground, the USS *Cambridge* and the USS *Stars and Stripes* shelled the ship, striking it several times before being driven back by cannon fire from Fort Fisher. Solid shot was fired from the fort into the *Modern Greece* to prevent Union forces from pulling it off and salvaging it and to prevent gunpowder thought to be on board from exploding. Confederates at Fort Fisher immediately began salvage efforts, which continued for some time. Intelligence reports from both Union and Confederate sources vary widely, but they indicate that at least four 12-pounder Whitworth rifled cannons were salvaged, along with 5,000 small arms, powder, whiskey, bales of clothing, and a large assortment of household goods.

The remains of the *Modern Greece* gradually settled on the ocean floor and were forgotten for 100 years. Divers discovered them after a storm uncovered the site in 1962. That find, early in the celebration of the Civil War Centennial, sparked renewed interest in the vessel, which prompted the state of North Carolina and the U.S. Navy to salvage more than 10,000 artifacts from the *Modern Greece* along with its anchors and capstans. These were preserved for study and display at a nearby museum/visitors center built at the Fort Fisher State Historic Site. Now protected by North Carolina shipwreck salvage laws, the wreck remains where the ship sank, about 300 yards offshore in about 25 feet of water near Fort Fisher.

References: Leslie S. Bright, *The Blockade Runner* Modern Greece *and Her Cargo* (1977); Stephen R. Wise, *Lifeline of the Confederacy: Blockade Running during the Civil War* (1988).

Leslie S. Bright

Monitor, USS. The USS *Monitor*, lying in 230 feet of water off Cape Hatteras, is probably the most famous victim of the infamous "Graveyard of the Atlantic" off the North Carolina coast. The *Monitor* was the third Union ironclad approved for construction during the Civil War and the first to be completed

An illustration from the 24 Jan. 1863 issue of *Harper's Weekly* showing crewmen being rescued from the ironclad *Monitor* as it sinks in a storm off Cape Hatteras in December 1862. NCC.

for the Union navy. The two previously contracted ironclads were comparable to the growing number of European ironclads. Swedish designer John Ericsson's *Monitor*, however, was unlike any previous warship. The *Monitor* was a 776-ton vessel measuring 172 feet long and 41 feet in beam. The freeboard of the ship was just over 1 foot, so even in a light sea its deck was awash. The ship was well protected, with the entire upper portion of its hull encased in iron armor. Amidships, a short cylindrical tower 20 feet in diameter housed the *Monitor*'s two guns. Steam power enabled the turret to rotate 360°, allowing the guns to be trained in any direction without maneuvering the ship. The wall of the turret was 8 inches thick, composed of 8 layers of 1-inch-thick iron plate. Designed by Rear Adm. John Dahlgren, the guns were 11-inch smoothbores.

On 6 Mar. 1862 the *Monitor* left New York Harbor for Hampton Roads, Va., towed by the tug *Seth Low* and accompanied by two escort ships. There, the new Rebel ironclad *Virginia* (converted from the old USS *Merrimack*) was expected to make its first appearance in a strike at Union blockaders. The trip

to Hampton Roads became dangerous for the *Monitor* when, on 7 March, it encountered a squall that sent waves crashing through air vents on the deck and over the smokestack, nearly drowning the boiler fires. Only fair weather the next day saved the ship from foundering. That night the *Monitor* steamed into Hampton Roads, only to find a Union naval disaster.

The CSS *Virginia* had left Norfolk on 8 March to meet the Federal fleet. The wooden Union ships were thoroughly outmatched. The armored *Virginia* had rammed and sunk the USS *Cumberland* and destroyed the USS *Congress* with gunfire. The USS *Minnesota*, only lightly damaged, had run hard aground during the battle and would be helpless if the *Virginia* returned. Capt. John Worden anchored his *Monitor* near the *Minnesota* to protect it and awaited the reappearance of the Confederate ironclad.

Early on 9 Mar. 1862 the 270-foot, well-armed *Virginia* approached the still-stranded *Minnesota* and the strange-looking ship guarding it. At first the *Virginia* ignored the new Union vessel, concentrating fire on the *Minnesota*, but then the *Moni-*

tor opened fire with its two big guns. For several hours the two ironclads pounded each other. The more maneuverable and lighter draft *Monitor* circled its opponent, constantly rotating the turret to protect the guns except when ready to fire—thus managing to withstand intense enemy shelling. Conversely, the *Monitor* failed to damage the *Virginia*. Eventually the two ships broke off the fight, each believing the other had withdrawn first.

Two months later, Confederate forces abandoned Norfolk and scuttled the *Virginia*, which enabled the Union fleet to operate up the York and James Rivers. In mid-May the *Monitor* participated in its final engagement, battling southern shore defenses at Drewry's Bluff. In the fall of 1862 it was overhauled in Washington and at the end of December headed south to participate in an attack on the defenses of Charleston, S.C. Under tow by the USS *Rhode Island*, the two vessels ran into foul weather off Cape Hatteras. The stormy seas proved too much for the ironclad, as rushing water eventually drowned the boiler fires and cut off power to the engines and pumps. The *Rhode Island* was able to rescue many of the sailors, but on 31 Dec. 1862 the *Monitor* sank, taking 16 of its crew to the bottom of the sea.

In August 1973 an expedition sponsored by the National Science Foundation and the National Geographic Society located the remains of the *Monitor*, whose identification was confirmed in May 1974. On 30 Jan. 1975 the site became the nation's first National Marine Sanctuary, to be administered by the National Oceanographic and Atmospheric Administration (NOAA). The *Monitor* was in an advanced state of deterioration, and NOAA instituted a stabilization and recovery program for the wreck. In August 2002 the *Monitor*'s 235-ton gun turret was recovered and installed at the Mariners' Museum in a conservation tank on full public display. It joined hundreds of other *Monitor* artifacts, including the steam engine, propeller, condenser, propeller shaft, and engine room floor. But the hull of the vessel remains upside down 16 miles southeast of Cape Hatteras.

References: George E. Bass, ed., *Ships and Shipwrecks of the Americas: A History Based on Underwater Archaeology* (1988); William C. Davis, *Duel between the First Ironclads* (1975); Gordon P. Watts Jr., *Investigating the Remains of the USS Monitor: A Final Report on 1979 Site Testing in the* Monitor *National Marine Sanctuary* (1982).

Dan Blair

Monroe's Crossroads, Battle of.

Monroe's Crossroads, west of Fayetteville and situated within the present Fort Bragg, was the site of one of the last battles of the Civil War, fought on 10 Mar. 1865. Lt. Gen. Wade Hampton led the Confederates and Brevet Maj. Gen. Judson Kilpatrick commanded the Union forces in the cavalry engagement. On 4 Mar. 1865 Maj. Gen.

William T. Sherman's Union army entered North Carolina, headed for Goldsboro. Riding ahead of Sherman's infantry was the cavalry under the controversial Kilpatrick. Known as "Kill Cavalry" to his hard-driven men, Kilpatrick was a small, brave, cocky, and often unpredictable officer. General Hampton, at 46, was an aristocrat without formal military training, but by 1865 he had emerged as perhaps the finest cavalry commander in the Confederate army.

Having learned that Hampton was headed east toward Fayetteville, Kilpatrick decided to block his route. On the night of 9 March his men encamped at Monroe's Crossroads, squarely in Hampton's path. Kilpatrick himself occupied the deserted home of the Charles Monroe family and retired for the night. Meanwhile, Hampton and his officers rode out into the damp darkness to observe the Federal camp. They planned to attack at daylight. Throughout the night, the Confederates deployed and then waited quietly in a chilly rain.

At dawn on 10 March, the Confederates overran the Union camp, capturing cannons, freeing Confederate prisoners, and driving back the bewildered Federal horsemen. Kilpatrick was only half-dressed when a Confederate captain asked for his whereabouts. He obliged by pointing to a cavalryman fleeing on horseback. Kilpatrick thus escaped and began rallying his men, many of whom had fled to a swamp at the edge of their camp.

Meanwhile, the tide of the battle had turned against the Confederates. Most of the Federals had the presence of mind to grab their carbines or rifles before they fled. Their firepower exacted a heavy toll. The resurgent Union forces recaptured their cannons and turned them against the Confederates. By 8:00 A.M., the brief but bloody fight was over.

Kilpatrick claimed victory because his men had retaken their camp. He put his losses at 19 killed, 68 wounded, and 103 captured, but he was known for his fanciful battle reports, so these numbers are probably low. He also claimed to have found the bodies of 80 enemy soldiers. The Confederates, who reported capturing 500 Federals, claimed victory because they had accomplished their goal of clearing the road to Fayetteville.

At the Bennett Place near Durham Station, where Johnston surrendered to Sherman on 26 Apr. 1865, Kilpatrick and Hampton were both present. Hampton reminded the stillsmarting Kilpatrick of his surprise attack one month earlier. Because of Kilpatrick's unceremonious flight into the swamp, Union foot soldiers dubbed the fight, "Kilpatrick's Shirt-tail Skedaddle."

References: John G. Barrett, *Sherman's March through the Carolinas* (1956); Mark L. Bradley, *Last Stand in the Carolinas: The Battle of Bentonville* (1996); William R. Trotter, *Silk Flags and Cold Steel: The Piedmont* (1988).

Steve Suther

Montagnards, or Dega as they call themselves, are a tribal people of the Malayo-Polynesian and Mon Khmer language groups, some 30 tribes of which live in the central highlands of Vietnam. Between 1962 and 1972, the Montagnards' mountain domain was the scene of some of the most intense fighting in the Vietnam War, and members of the U.S. Army Special Forces (Green Berets) fighting there often bonded with the Montagnard militia, who were regarded as courageous fighters and fiercely loyal friends.

With the collapse of the South Vietnamese government in 1975, Montagnards who had cooperated with the Americans were viewed with suspicion by officials of the new Socialist Republic of Vietnam, often being subjected to persecution, imprisonment, or death. Many fled to Cambodia, where they organized a resistance to communist rule but were ultimately persecuted by the Khmer Rouge.

By 1985 Americans had become aware of the dire circumstances of the Montagnards, and arrangements were made the following year for Montagnard refugees to enter the United States. In 1992 another band of Montagnards, located in eastern Cambodia, was evacuated under threat of annihilation by the Khmer Rouge and Vietnamese. Through the efforts of Lutheran Family Services and Catholic Social Services, a majority of the approximately 3,000 Montagnard refugees now living in the United States have been successfully resettled in the North Carolina cities of Charlotte, Greensboro, and Raleigh. Although many Montagnards hold to their traditional belief in spirits associated with the forces of nature, most are now Christians. Those who remain in Southeast Asia continue to face severe persecution.

References: Gerald Cannon Hickey, *Shattered World: Adaptation and Survival among Vietnam's Highland Peoples during the Vietnam War* (1993); Hickey, *Sons of the Mountains: Ethnohistory of the Vietnamese Central Highlands to 1954* (1982); Roy C. Russell III, *The Montagnards of Vietnam: Endgame of Cultural Survival* (1994).

Surry Roberts

Mont Amoena Seminary in Cabarrus County was founded by Mrs. D. H. Bittle in 1859, under the name Mount Pleasant Female Seminary, as a private liberal arts academy for girls of high school age. It first consisted of one two-story frame building. The school was acquired by the North Carolina Lutheran Synod in 1869 and continued to educate both day students and boarders in fields including English, Latin, mathematics, and music. Many of its headmasters were Lutheran ministers. After the Civil War, it became popular with parents in Concord, and according to one source "was an island of culture in the difficult years" that followed the war.

In 1892 the school's name was changed to Mont Amoena Seminary, the name being the Latin equivalent of Mount Pleasant, the location of the school. The school's original multipurpose frame building was destroyed by fire in November 1911, and a new three-story brick building with white columns and modern amenities was constructed on seven acres near the old site at a cost of $30,000.

In 1927, after more than 65 years of educating young women, Mont Amoena Seminary was closed, largely because of worsening school finances and improvements in the local public schools. Several years thereafter, its male equivalent academy, Mount Pleasant Collegiate Institute, also closed its doors.

Reference: Raymond M. Bost and Jeff L. Norris, *All One Body: The Story of the North Carolina Lutheran Synod, 1803–1993* (1994).

Lisa Brantley Kobrin

Montgomery County, located in the Piedmont region of south central North Carolina, was formed in 1779 from Anson County and named for Gen. Richard Montgomery, a Revolutionary War brigadier who was killed at the Battle of Quebec. The early inhabitants of the region were Keyauwee and Saura (Cheraw) Indians, followed by German and Scottish settlers. The county seat, Troy, was incorporated in 1852 and named for either the ancient city of Troy, North Carolina General Assembly member John B. Troy, or Robert Troy, a member of the North Carolina State House. Other communities in the county include Steeds, Ether, Star, Pekin, Wadeville, Uwharrie, Eldorado, and Mount Gilead.

A large section of Montgomery County is covered by the Uwharrie National Forest, which dominates much of the region's character and economy. Other notable physical features include Badin Lake, sections of the Yadkin–Pee Dee River, Lick Fork, Shelter Mountain, Horse Trough Mountain, Cheek Creek, and Drowning Creek. The county's farms produce cotton, tobacco, livestock, poultry, dairy products, and a variety of vegetables. Manufactured products include textiles, furniture, lumber, clay products, rugs, and shoes. Montgomery County has minerals such as clay, gold, silver, and copper.

Montgomery County historic attractions include the Town Creek Indian Mound State Historic Site, the location of a 600-year-old Native American ceremonial center, which is still being excavated. The Montgomery Arts Council, the Montgomery Community Theater, and the Roller Mill Historical Museum are a few of the county's cultural institutions. Montgomery County hosts annual festivals and events such as the Indian Heritage Festival, the Troy Fest, the Mount Gilead Christmas Parade, and the Star Christmas Parade. Montgomery County's population was estimated at just over 27,000 in 2004.

William S. Powell

SEE ALSO Town Creek Indian Mound.

Montreat. In 1897 the Mountain Retreat Association formed one of the earliest mountain religious resorts in North Carolina. John C. Collins, a Congregational minister from New England, wanted to create a religious retreat for church members in the North Carolina mountains. He formed the Mountain Retreat Association in 1897 and purchased 4,000 acres east of Asheville near Black Mountain. Over the next ten years, the new retreat called Montreat (a name derived from the association's name) saw the construction of several cabins and the Montreat Hotel. Montreat hosted a series of conferences but was always on the edge of financial collapse.

In 1906 the Presbyterian Synod of North Carolina, led by Charlotte minister James R. Howerton, purchased the property for use as a retreat for Presbyterian Church members in North Carolina and from across the South. Despite some improvements in infrastructure, Montreat's financial prospects continued to decline. In 1911 fortunes began to change with the appointment of Robert Campbell Anderson to run the resort. The former pastor of First Presbyterian Church in Gastonia, Anderson initiated a highly successful capital campaign, a building program, and a promotional program designed to attract more visitors to Montreat. He also wanted the conference center to play a larger role in mission work, a goal he accomplished through numerous training conferences and the establishment of Montreat Normal School.

Apart from its institutional role, Montreat has had an important place in the church life of southern Presbyterians. The retreat has served as a testing ground for new doctrinal ideas and hosted integrated meetings that fostered racial justice within the Presbyterian Church. Women also have found increased roles in church life through participation in events at Montreat. In 1934 Montreat Normal School became Montreat College, a four-year institution providing instruction to future generations of Presbyterian leaders. As early as the 1920s, Montreat served as a repository for archival materials related to southern Presbyterianism. Now called the Presbyterian Church (USA) Department of History (Montreat), the archive assists churches in record preservation and encourages scholarly research in Presbyterian history and theology. Montreat has also become a retirement community for Presbyterian leaders, a reflection of the important place the retreat has in the hearts of the faithful.

References: Robert C. Anderson, *The Story of Montreat from Its Beginning, 1897–1947* (1949); William Bean Kennedy, "Montreat: Education Center of the Presbyterian Church," *American Presbyterians: Journal of Presbyterian History* 74 (Summer 1996); Mary-Ruth Marshall, "Handling Dynamite: Young People, Race, and Montreat," *American Presbyterians: Journal of Presbyterian History* 74 (Summer 1996).

Richard D. Starnes

Montreat College, located 15 miles east of Asheville in Montreat, began in 1916 as Montreat Normal School, an in-

stitution founded by the Presbyterian Church (USA) to prepare young women to become Christian teachers. In 1933 the school was renamed Montreat College and became a junior college for women, and from 1945 to 1959 it was a four-year college for women. In 1959 Montreat became coeducational. In 1986, responding to both the needs of its students and the needs of the church at large, the college began offering baccalaureate degrees in human services and liberal arts.

Montreat's founders established the college for the purpose of teaching the "biblical view of the nature of man and the meaning of life." This commitment to a faith-centered education continues. The school seeks to integrate faith and learning in a caring Christian community. Montreat College is a liberal arts college, awarding both associate and bachelor's degrees. By the early 2000s the school's enrollment was approximately 1,000, including students enrolled through the School of Professional and Adult Studies.

References: Asheville Presbytery, *Our Mountain Work*, vol. 1 (1939); Montreat College, *Catalogue* (2002).

Ted Mitchell

Mooning means to expose the bare buttocks as a challenge or a taunt. Although it was undoubtedly used previously in some settings, the word first came to national attention after it appeared in a report in the Chester, S.C., *News and Reporter* on 23 Apr. 1974. It was picked up and included in the 1989 edition of the *Oxford English Dictionary*, where it was defined and described as a slang word.

The act of mooning, although at the time not named as such, was reported to have occurred in eighteenth-century North Carolina. The journal kept by Benjamin Elledge of Wilkes County recorded that on 8 Sept. 1776, the local militia under Brig. Gen. Griffith Rutherford was on an expedition against the Cherokee Indians. "Some of Our troops saw 7 or Eight Indians this day," Elledge wrote. "One Indian flung up his Arse Clout & Smack't his arse at Our Men Tho [they] took Care to be On a Mt too far for Bullitting."

This early episode was brought to light on 26 Aug. 1997, after an incident of mooning reported by a resident of Charlotte was publicized. Walking up the stairs to her condominium early one morning in July 1995, the woman encountered the bare backside of a man bent over at the waist and wearing no underwear. He was charged with indecent exposure, and the case languished for three years as it made its way through a lengthy appeal procedure. Finally found guilty, the accused appealed again, and this time mooning was ruled not to be indecent. The case ultimately went to the North Carolina Supreme Court, where the defendant's conviction was restored.

William S. Powell

Moonshine, illegal, untaxed whiskey distilled by the "light of the moon," has been a part of North Carolina lore and culture for centuries. From the state's eastern swamps and pocosins to its remote mountain coves, no small number of North Carolinians have engaged in the manufacture of unbonded whiskey, which has also been called mountain dew, blockade, white liquor, white lightning, corn liquor, popskull, stumphole whiskey, forty-rod, and shine.

Moonshining in the United States dates back to colonial days, but the industry's most infamous period began with Prohibition in the 1920s and 1930s and continued after its repeal and the establishment of the alcohol tax. As time progressed, a vocabulary evolved around moonshining. The term "bootlegger" is said to have originated with the mandate against the sale of alcohol to Indians, when traders often concealed flasks of liquor in their boots to avoid detection. By the early twentieth century, a bootlegger was technically the seller of illegal alcohol, the moonshiner was the producer, and those who transported the product were called "runners" or "blockaders." But often these duties overlapped, with moonshiners delivering their own products or runners selling some as well. Law enforcement officials attempting to stop moonshiners were nicknamed "revenuers."

Despite the ban on the production and sale of liquor, there was a great deal of demand for it, and moonshiners did their best to meet that demand. Before Prohibition became law with the ratification of the Eighteenth Amendment in 1919, bootleggers traveled regular routes like milkmen, going door to door delivering whiskey in saddlebags and hot water bottles. During the Prohibition era, Chicago was considered the center of illegal liquor activity. But the secluded stills of the rural South produced the life and legend most associated with moonshine, rising out of places such as Dawson County, Ga.; Cocke County, Tenn.; Franklin County, Va.; and Wilkes County, N.C.—once the self-proclaimed "Moonshine Capital of the World."

The key to any successful moonshine operation, besides a quality product, was a good car. Bootleggers modified their vehicles to get the best possible smuggling space and driving performance. Back seats were removed to make room for cases of liquor which, when loaded, would be covered with blankets. The 1929 Chevy touring cars could be refurbished with box-like traps underneath and a false back seat with a built-in door. These contraptions held 125 to 135 gallon jars of moonshine—all completely hidden. A few mechanics even converted their fuel tanks to "shine tanks," hiding up to 35 gallons of whiskey in a false tank with the real fuel tank hidden under the floorboards. By the 1930s, space had given way to a preference for speed, and Fords became the vehicles of choice.

Moonshining was a highly profitable industry. If a bootlegger rounded a curve and spotted a revenuer roadblock, he might just jump from the car, leaving the agents to deal with

Law enforcement officers test the evidence during a raid on an illegal liquor distillery in the Eno Township of Orange County in 1958. Photograph by Roland Giduz. NCC.

the run-away auto and its illegal cargo. Moonshiners could lose every third car and shipment and still turn a profit. Federal agents, besides combing the countryside for moonshine stills, were forced to create new ways to combat the runners. Often the agents themselves drove cars they had confiscated from bootleggers. One inventive roadblock tactic was known as "spiking." Several large nails would be embedded in a two-by-six board, and the agents would throw the "spikes" onto the road in the path of a moonshine car, shredding the tires and forcing the driver to stop.

Despite the constant battle between the two, however, most moonshiners and revenuers were traditionally quite civil, even friendly, toward one another. Amos Owens, a resident of Cherry Mountain and legendary creator of the wildly popular "Cherry Bounce," purportedly remained a gentleman despite being perhaps the most notorious moonshiner in the state. As legend has it, he once was discovered by revenuers (which he called "red-legged grasshoppers") while preparing a shipment of his brew—three parts whiskey, one part cherry juice, one part sugar—and offered his captors breakfast. When they declined, he offered them some Cherry Bounce, which they drank happily. After several drinks, one officer staggered into the woods and disappeared for a few hours, while the other passed out in Owens's house. Owens made no attempt to escape and waited patiently for the agents to regain their sobriety. When they did, they arrested Owens and took him to South Carolina, where he served six months in jail. The day after his release, Owens was back on Cherry Mountain, making whiskey and entertaining friends from miles around.

A law enforcement officer pauses after a raid on an illegal liquor distillery in the Eno Township of Orange County in 1958. Photograph by Roland Giduz. NCC.

The lore surrounding moonshine eventually made its way into popular culture. North Carolina's tradition of auto racing developed in the garages of bootleggers, particularly on the roads between North Wilkesboro and Charlotte. Legendary auto racers Junior Johnson and Curtis Turner were well-known bootleggers in the 1950s. Many of the winning entries at local Saturday night race events would be hauling illegal whiskey the following morning. Movies such as *Thunder Road* (1958), starring Robert Mitchum, and television series such as *The Dukes of Hazzard* offered both factual and fictional accounts of the exploits of moonshiners in the rural South. Moonshine Kate became wildly successful in Georgia in the late 1910s with songs such as "The Drinker's Child," paving the way for a niche industry of bootlegger songsters. The most famous was hard-drinking, three-fingered banjo player and renowned bootlegger Charlie Poole, who, with his North Carolina Ramblers, recorded a string of massively successful albums in the late 1920s, touting hits including "Take a Drink On Me" and "Good-bye Booze." Poole died young, however, fittingly expiring in 1931 at the end of an epic bender.

There is a large body of literature regarding moonshine, one that is likely to increase in the twenty-first century as the actual practice of moonshining is supplanted by trafficking in other contraband and bootlegging recedes into the realms of romantic nostalgia. In reality, much illegal liquor was virtual poison, high in lead salts, although some excellent distillers undoubtedly came up through the moonshine ranks. Even by the early 2000s, Stokes County white liquor had found favor in the nonbackwoods, supposedly sophisticated Research Triangle area of central North Carolina.

References: Joseph Earl Dabney, *Mountain Spirits: A Chronicle of Corn Whiskey from King James' Ulster Plantation to America's Appalachians and the Moonshine Life* (1974); Wilbur R. Miller, *Revenuers and Moonshiners: Enforcing Federal Liquor Law in the Mountain South, 1865–1900* (1991); Bland Simpson, *The Great Dismal: A Carolinian's Swamp Memoir* (1990); Alec Wilkinson, *Moonshine: A Life in Pursuit of White Liquor* (1985).

Bland Simpson
Additional research provided by Kimberly Hewitt and Noel Yancey.

Moore County, located in the Sandhills on the border between North Carolina's Piedmont and Coastal Plain regions, was formed in 1784 from Cumberland County and named for Alfred Moore, a Revolutionary War captain who later served as a U.S. Supreme Court justice. Early inhabitants of the area included the Saura (Cheraw) and other Siouan Indians, followed by Highland Scot, German, English, and Scotch-Irish settlers. Carthage, the county seat, was incorporated in 1796 and named after the ancient North African city. Other communities in the county include Aberdeen, Cameron, Robbins, Seven Lakes, Eastwood, Hill Crest, Eagle Springs, and Parkwood. Notable physical features of the county include Pine Lake and Drowning, Herds, Sugar, Big Juniper, and Little Crane Creeks.

The Moore County economy benefits greatly from a thriving tourism and recreation industry centered on the resort towns of Pinehurst and Southern Pines—home to some of the nation's finest golf courses. The Pinehurst Golf Club, with its world-famous Number Two course, was established in 1903. Pinehurst hosted the 2005 U.S. Open Championship and annually hosts the Pinehurst Men's North/South Amateur Golf Tournament. Pottery is a vital part of the local economy; Jugtown is in Randolph County, but many of the craft's pioneering families lived and worked in Moore County. The health care and retirement industry in the county also has grown significantly over the years. Agricultural goods produced on Moore County farms include tobacco, peaches, strawberries, and poultry. Machine tools and furniture are manufactured in the county, and amethyst, zircon, copper, and quartz crystals are mined there.

Moore County landmarks and historic sites include the House in the Horseshoe State Historic Site, scene of a 1781 Patriot-Loyalist skirmish; Aberdeen Historic District, featuring 96 historic buildings; and the stately Carolina Hotel (1901), today part of the Pinehurst resort complex. Cultural institutions include the Campbell House Galleries, Sandhills Council Garden Clubs, and the Tufts Archives, located within the Given Memorial Library. Festivals and annual events held in

Moore County include the Moore County Agricultural Fair, the Carthage Buggy Festival, the Pet Parade and Bark-in-the-Park Festival, and the North Carolina Playwright Festival. Moore County had an estimated population of 79,300 in 2004.

Reference: Manly Wade Wellman, *Story of Moore County: Two Centuries of a North Carolina Region* (1974).

Jay Mazzocchi

SEE ALSO Carolina Hotel; Golf; House in the Horseshoe; Resorts.

Moore General Hospital,

Moore General Hospital, located between Swannanoa and Black Mountain on U.S. 70, was built as a general army hospital for the treatment of sick and wounded soldiers during World War II. Named for Samuel Preston Moore, a native of Charleston, S.C., and surgeon general of the Confederacy, the hospital complex was designed to include numerous buildings, 1,520 beds, and a full-time staff of 1,500 people. Government engineers envisioned it as the "Walter Reed of the South." Supervised by a private firm from Asheville, construction of the hospital began in May 1942, and the first patients began arriving the following November. Col. Frank W. Wilson was the hospital's first commanding officer. In addition to the buildings for patients and staff, the site also included 36 structures to house men in training for service with the medical corps; the first training unit assigned there was the 28th General Hospital.

A rehabilitation center, which officially opened in June 1944, was added when the hospital took over the new Sand Hill High School building in West Asheville. In September 1944 the facility expanded to include a Tropical Disease Center capable of treating an additional 1,400 patients. In May 1945 German prisoners of war were brought in to provide maintenance and other labor services; they were housed in a separate camp on the north section of the hospital grounds.

In September 1946 the U.S. War Department declared Moore General Hospital a surplus facility, and it was taken over by the Veterans Administration. For several years it was known as the Swannanoa Rehabilitation Center, an annex of the Oteen Veterans Hospital, and served as a tuberculosis rehabilitation center. In 1960 the Veterans Administration consolidated its operation at a central location in Oteen, and the Moore General Hospital property was deeded to the state of North Carolina for use as a juvenile evaluation center.

Ann S. Wright

Moore's Creek Bridge, Battle of.

Moore's Creek Bridge, Battle of. Fought in present southwestern Pender County on 27 Feb. 1776, the engagement at Moore's Creek Bridge was the first battle of the American Revolution to take place in North Carolina. In early January 1776 exiled Governor Josiah Martin received notification from

London that his plan to restore royal authority in North Carolina had been approved. Two commands of British regulars, one composed of seven regiments under Lord Charles Cornwallis and the other made up of 2,000 troops led by Sir Henry Clinton, would sail from Ireland and New England, respectively, and converge on the Lower Cape Fear River near Brunswick Town. There they would be joined by an army of Loyalists who would assist in putting down the rebellion.

On 10 Jan. 1776 Martin issued a call for loyal subjects to serve as troops and a proclamation ordering the Royal Standard to be raised in North Carolina. By mid-February approximately 1,600 Highland Scots and other Loyalists had assembled at Cross Creek (now Fayetteville). Commanding the troops was Brig. Gen. Donald MacDonald, a veteran of the Battle of Bunker Hill.

As the Loyalist forces finalized preparations for their march toward Wilmington, Col. James Moore, commander of the Patriot army in southeastern North Carolina, masterminded a strategy to foil MacDonald's rendezvous with the British regulars. When MacDonald began his advance on 21 February, Moore was able to block the initial route taken by the Highlanders. MacDonald altered his movement by crossing the Cape Fear River en route to Corbett's Ferry on the Black River. There he anticipated slipping past the militiamen of Col. Richard Caswell; his army would then proceed over the bridge at Moore's Creek and hasten on to Wilmington.

When Moore learned that MacDonald had won the race to Corbett's Ferry, he ordered Caswell's force to Moore's Creek, where they were joined by additional Patriot troops under Col. Alexander Lillington. Caswell and Lillington found that the narrow bridge, located on a sand bar, offered an excellent defensive position. Situated at the highest elevation in the area, the bridge crossed the dark, swampy creek at a place where the waterway was 50 feet wide and 3 feet deep. Also known at the time as Widow Moore's Creek because it flowed past land owned by widow Elizabeth Moore, the creek flowed into the Black River about ten miles above the river's confluence with the Cape Fear.

On the night of 26 February, Caswell manned the west bank of the creek with 800 soldiers while Lillington stationed 150 men near a slightly elevated knoll on the east bank. Moore positioned his 1,000 troops between Moore's Creek and Wilmington. While the Patriot forces assumed their defensive positions, MacDonald convened a council of war with his officers at his camp about six miles from Caswell on the same side of the creek. The decision was made to attack, but MacDonald fell ill, and command of the Highlanders devolved to Lt. Col. Donald McLeod.

At 1:00 A.M. on 27 February McLeod put his 1,500-man army on the march through the swamps in bone-chilling temperatures. After struggling through the wilderness for hours, the Highlanders caught sight of Caswell's camp, which had been abandoned during the night. To deceive the enemy, Caswell had left his campfires burning while he moved his force to the east bank. Following the night crossing, the Patriots had removed the planks from the bridge, greased the girders, and positioned artillery to cover the road and bridge.

At Caswell's abandoned camp, McLeod's troops regrouped and waited for daybreak to pursue the rebel army, which they thought was in retreat. But to the contrary, nearly 1,000 Whig soldiers were waiting across the bridge. The stillness of the swamp was broken at sunrise when 500 Highlanders, broadswords in hand, stormed toward the bridge. Bagpipes played in the background as the attackers shouted, "King George and broadswords!" Only a few Highlanders managed to make their way over the slippery remnants of the bridge, and they fell rapidly from the heavy fire coming from the Patriot breastworks. Within three minutes, the battle was over. About 70 Highlanders were killed or wounded. Among the dead was McLeod, a bridegroom of only a few weeks. The officer's body was riddled with 9 bullets and 24 swan shot. About 850 soldiers were taken prisoner, including General MacDonald, who was captured in his tent. The booty claimed by the victorious Patriots was substantial: 150 swords, 1,500 rifles, and £15,000. In the battle, the Whigs lost only one man, John Grady, who died four days later.

Called the "Lexington and Concord of the South," the Battle of Moore's Creek Bridge was significant for several reasons: it marked the permanent end of royal authority in North Carolina, it prompted the Provincial Congress meeting at Halifax on 12 Apr. 1776 to instruct North Carolina's delegation to the Continental Congress in Philadelphia to vote for independence, and it prevented the British from seizing control of the South at the onset of the war. The site of the battle, including the reconstructed bridge, has been preserved within Moore's Creek National Military Park. The 86-acre complex, operated by the federal government since 1926, is located one mile southwest of Currie.

References: Daniel W. Barefoot, *Touring the Backroads of North Carolina's Lower Coast* (1995); Dan L. Morrill, *Southern Campaigns of the American Revolution* (1992); Hugh F. Rankin, "The Moore's Creek Bridge Campaign, 1776," *NCHR* 30 (January 1953); Phillips Russell, *North Carolina in the Revolutionary War* (1965).

Daniel W. Barefoot

SEE ALSO Highland Regiment, North Carolina.

Moore's *Roster*. SEE Civil War Rosters.

Moravian Music is one of North Carolina's most striking and significant contributions to the heritage of the fine arts in the United States. In the late eighteenth and early nineteenth centuries, Salem and the other Moravian communities of the Wachovia tract in modern Forsyth County reached a level of musical composition and performance matched in North America only by that in the Moravian settlements in Pennsylvania.

Although a small body of secular music, particularly chamber music, exists by Moravian composers, most of their works were sacred in character, written to express or enhance the spirituality of these intensely devout communities. Music was an essential part of formal Moravian worship, but it was also used to punctuate the ordinary routines of communal life and commemorate special occasions. Births, deaths, marriages, worship services, and festivals were announced in a Moravian settlement through hymns or chorales played from the church steeple by a trombone ensemble. Congregational singing was an important part of nearly every service. Arias for soloists, choral anthems, and instrumental works were also in great demand. While some of these were taken from the works of non-Moravians, the large majority were written by a series of accomplished Moravian musicians, many of whom were ministers who considered themselves musical amateurs, between the mid-eighteenth and late nineteenth centuries.

In larger Moravian centers such as Salem, the *collegium musicum*, or civic orchestra, was dedicated to maintaining high musical standards through teaching, performance, instrument making, and music acquisition. The roots of the Moravian Church in both its original and renewed forms were sunk deep in Bohemia and Germany, some of the most musically fertile parts of Europe. Moravians in Saxony drew on both the rich musical heritage of German Protestantism and the proximity of many prominent composers of the late baroque, classical, and early romantic eras. Because the various Moravian groups in Europe, England, Pennsylvania, and North Carolina were in constant contact with each other, these composers' styles, techniques, and works spread rapidly throughout the Moravian community. As a result, the inhabitants of Salem in the revolutionary and early national eras sang, played, and sometimes wrote music similar to what might have been heard or written at the same time in Vienna, Prague, Leipzig, or London.

Three men with connections to Salem illustrate aspects of the town's musical life. Johannes Herbst (1735–1812), a native of Swabia, served his church in Germany and England before coming to America in 1786, bringing with him a library of well over 1,000 choral and vocal works, mostly copied in his hand and including more than 300 compositions of his own. After many years in Pennsylvania, he was sent in 1811 to minister to the congregation at Salem. He died eight months later, leaving his great collection. Johann Friedrich Peter (1746–1813) was born in Holland, arrived in Pennsylvania in 1770, and served as pastor in Salem from 1780 to 1790, where he composed, in addition to many anthems and solo songs, six string quintets which are the earliest-known chamber music written in America. Finally, Edward William Leinbach (1823–1901), a native of Salem, was one of the relatively rare professional musicians among the Moravian composers. After study in Boston he returned home to life as a church organist, choirmaster, and teacher in the Salem Female Academy, in the course of which he composed a number of anthems and hymn tunes.

Leinbach reached maturity as the distinctions between the Moravians in Salem and the surrounding non-Moravian culture were diminishing. Existing only in manuscript copies, most Moravian music was never widely known outside Moravian circles, and by the time Leinbach died in 1901, much of it was forgotten. Still, thousands of pieces rested in the Moravian archives in Bethlehem, Pa., and Winston-Salem. In 1950 the first Moravian Music Festival began modern performance of these works, and in 1956 the Moravian Music Foundation was established in Winston-Salem to foster research and publication in line with current scholarly and editorial standards.

References: Donald M. McCorkle, *The Moravian Contribution to American Music* (1956); Daniel B. Thorp, *The Moravian Community in Colonial North Carolina* (1989).

John A. Hutcheson Jr.

Moravians are members of a church—officially called the *Unitas Fratrum*, or Unity of Brethren—that, by the time of their arrival in North Carolina in the middle of the eighteenth century, had already seen almost three centuries of rich religious life. They are spiritual descendants of the Czech priest Jan Hus, who for his attempts at reform was martyred in 1415. In 1457 some of his followers founded a church body consecrated to following Christ in simplicity and a life dedicated to God. This new church developed a productive and orderly ecclesiastical life in the fifteenth and sixteenth centuries.

By 1732 the Moravian Church began sending missionaries from Herrnhut to all corners of the world. After establishing themselves in England, the Moravians sent colonists to America in 1735, but this initial settlement, in Georgia, proved unsuccessful, partly because of disruptions caused by war between Protestant England and Catholic Spain to the south in Florida. The Moravians established themselves more permanently in Pennsylvania in 1741, with the town of Bethlehem as their chief center.

In part to facilitate the Moravians' settlement in the New World, the British Parliament in 1749 recognized the Moravian Church as "an ancient Protestant Episcopal Church." That vote of approbation brought several offers by English noblemen seeking solid, hard-working settlers for their lands in various parts of the world, including an offer by John Lord Carteret, second Earl Granville, who had chosen to retain his holdings in Carolina after the other Lords Proprietors had surrendered their lands to the Crown in 1729.

A survey expedition was sent to North Carolina late in 1752, and a tract of nearly 100,000 acres, subsequently named Wachovia, was selected as the site for a new Moravian settlement. The first settlers arrived in November 1753. Over the next dozen years, this initial community (Bethabara) gave rise to four others (Bethania, Salem, Friedberg, and Friedland), in what is now Forsyth County. From the very beginning, the Moravians kept and preserved meticulous records of their church, community, and commercial life. Along with this emphasis on record keeping, the Moravians maintained active communication with other Moravian centers in Europe and throughout the world. This dedication to sharing and receiving information continues today throughout the worldwide Moravian Unity.

During the American Revolution the Moravians were officially neutral, which caused them to be viewed with suspicion by those seeking independence and those loyal to the king alike. The North Carolina legislature, however, continued the Moravians' exemption from bearing arms and confirmed the title to their land, which had been threatened with confiscation. At the close of the conflict, the Moravians held the only known official celebration in obedience to Governor Alexander Martin's proclamation that 4 July 1783 should be observed as a day of thanksgiving for the return of peace.

Once independence was won, the Moravians quickly affirmed their allegiance to the new state and national governments. Increasing experience with "American freedom" also encouraged North Carolina Moravians to seek more independence from their church's centralized authorities in Germany and led individual members to call for less church regulation of marriages and the trades.

The Moravian communities, especially Salem, had developed into major trade and commercial centers in the western part of the state. They had also developed a rich cultural life, especially in their music. Education was important to the Moravians. From the beginning, their first settlements provided schools for both boys and girls. In Salem, their central administrative center, the boys' school, throughout the nineteenth century and into the opening decade of the twentieth, educated local youths, including many non-Moravians who offered valuable contributions to the state. A local girls' school was begun in 1772, and in 1804 a girls' boarding school, the Salem Female Academy, was added, attracting young women from throughout the South. This institution continues today as Salem Academy and College.

As part of the worldwide Moravian Church, North Carolina Moravians have helped support that denomination's extensive missionary work in Greenland, the Caribbean, and southern Africa. They also had direct responsibility for a mission to the Cherokee in northern Georgia, begun in 1802. This mission followed the Cherokee to Oklahoma after the Trail of Tears in 1838. An abortive mission to African slaves in northern Florida was also begun in 1847. Closer to home, work among African Americans around Salem led to the establishment of a congregation for them in 1822. A new building, erected in 1860 and used until the 1950s, is believed to be the oldest surviving African American house of worship in North Carolina.

For more than a century after the Moravians' initial settlements in North Carolina, all their civic and commercial activities were under the direct control of the church; thus their early records document not only ecclesiastical concerns, but the total life of the community and its relation to its neighbors. Control of trades in Salem was given up in the 1840s, and land was provided north of Salem for Winston, the seat of the new county of Forsyth, in 1849. Salem itself was incorporated with a secular town administration in 1857.

By the time of the Civil War, the Moravians had lost their exemption from military service. Many of them served in the Confederate army, and several of them formed the musical bands of local regiments. The best known of these is the 26th North Carolina Regiment band, though Moravians served as band members in the 11th and other regiments also. In Salem, the Fries Woolen Mill provided cloth for many of the uniforms worn by North Carolina troops throughout the war.

In 1877 Edward Rondthaler (made a bishop in 1891) arrived in North Carolina to provide more than 50 years of leadership in rebuilding and expanding the church's life and work. Several new congregations were established, and the Moravians emerged as a small but "mainstream" denomination in America, though ties with the worldwide Moravian Church remained intact.

Throughout the twentieth century the Moravian Church in North Carolina cooperated with other denominations in ecumenical discussions and joint programming in response to the needs of the day. At the same time, it expanded to have congregations in many of the major cities of North Carolina, and new churches were established in Virginia, Georgia, and Florida as part of the Southern Province of the Moravian Church. Total membership in North Carolina at the beginning of the twenty-first century stood at just over 20,000.

References: J. H. Clewell, *History of Wachovia in North Carolina* (1902); C. Daniel Crews, *My Name Shall Be There: The Founding of Salem* (1995); Crews, *Through Fiery Trials: Moravians and the Revolution* (1996); Crews, *Villages of the Lord: The Moravians Come to Carolina* (1995); Adelaide L. Fries and others, eds., *Records of the Moravians in North Carolina* (11 vols., 1922–68); Kenneth G. Hamilton, *History of the Moravian Church* (1967).

C. Daniel Crews

SEE ALSO Bethabara; Salem; Wachovia.

Morehead Foundation. The John Motley Morehead Foundation was established by businessman, industrial scientist, and philanthropist John Motley Morehead III in 1945 to sustain and enhance the excellence of the University of North Carolina at Chapel Hill. The foundation set out to accomplish this through two avenues: the construction of the Morehead Planetarium Building on campus and the creation of the Morehead Scholarship Program. The planetarium, one of the largest and most advanced in the nation at the time of its completion, was given to the university in 1949. Begun in 1951 as the first nonathletic merit scholarship program in the country, the Morehead Scholarship Program was designed to draw gifted student leaders from across the state to UNC. The program employed a unique, intensely competitive selection process that included several levels of interviews designed to discern candidates' qualifications in four distinct areas: academic ability, moral force of character, physical vigor, and the capacity to lead and motivate peers as evidenced by extracurricular achievement.

Former UNC track coach and athletic director Robert A. Fetzer was named as the Morehead Program's first executive director. He was followed in 1958 by Roy Armstrong, who had been the university's director of admissions. Mebane M. Pritchett, a Morehead alumnus, became the executive director in 1972 and served until 1987, when he was succeeded by Morehead alumnus Charles E. Lovelace Jr.

Initially, only high school seniors from North Carolina, nominated by their school administrations, were eligible to enter the Morehead selection process. In 1954 selected out-of-state schools became eligible to nominate Morehead candidates, and in 1969 the first British Morehead scholars came to Chapel Hill. Women became eligible for the program in 1974. The selection process has continued to expand and grow in response to various academic trends; by the early 2000s, it included direct applications from North Carolina students and nominations from the UNC admissions office and eligible affiliate programs. The Morehead nominee pool also included direct or sponsored applicants from any secondary school or *cégep* in Canada and any secondary school in the United Kingdom.

From its inception, the Morehead Scholarship Program has provided more than 2,600 students with a four-year scholarship to the University of North Carolina at Chapel Hill and, since 1974, opportunities for international travel and internships through the Morehead Summer Enrichment Program. Approximately 50 scholarships are offered each year, resulting in about 200 Morehead scholars on campus at any one time.

Morehead scholars have held a wide array of leadership positions both on and off campus. They have served as student body presidents and vice presidents; editors-in-chief of the UNC student newspaper, the *Daily Tar Heel*; student attorney generals; chairs and vice chairs of the undergraduate honor court; chief justices of the student supreme court; student congress speakers; Phi Beta Kappa presidents; presidents of the Black Student Movement, Asian Students Association, and Carolina Hispanic Association; and presidents of the Campus Y, Carolina Union, APPLES Service-Learning Program, and the Carolina Athletic Association. When they have seen a need or had a special interest that was not represented among existing campus organizations, Morehead scholars have often founded new ones. More than 80 campus organizations and publications were founded by Morehead scholars, including campus a cappella groups the Clef Hangers and the Loreleis; campus publications the *Cellar Door*, the *Phoenix*, the *Blue & White*, and *Bounce*; athletic programs such as women's varsity lacrosse and women's varsity crew; and the UNC Dance Marathon, the university's largest student-run fund-raiser. Among the honors received by Morehead scholars are Chancellor's Awards for distinguished campus service and departmental awards for best honors theses. As of 2006, 21 of UNC's 24 Rhodes scholarship recipients were Morehead scholars. Moreheads are often recipients of other major awards, such as Luce, Truman, Marshall, and Fulbright scholarships as well as Mellon, Ford Foundation, Woodrow Wilson, National Science Foundation, and MacArthur fellowships

Approximately three-quarters of all Morehead alumni have advanced degrees from leading universities such as Columbia, Duke, Harvard, Princeton, Stanford, UNC, the University of Virginia, Vanderbilt, Yale, and Oxford University. A few of the many distinguished Morehead alumni and their accomplishments include Anthony Harrington, U.S. ambassador to Brazil; Taylor Branch, author of the Pulitzer Prize–winning *Parting the Waters: America in the King Years, 1954–1963* (1988) and *Pillar of Fire: America in the King Years, 1963–65* (1998); U.S. congressmen David Price, Jim Cooper, and Mike McIntyre; Sallie Krawcheck, chairwoman and CEO of Citicorp; record-setting track-and-field athlete Tony Waldrop; Jim Exum, chief justice of the Supreme Court of North Carolina; Francis Collins, director of the Human Genome Project; Ann Livermore, president of Hewlett-Packard Services; Alan Murray, Washington Bureau Chief of CNBC; and Bill Swofford, 1960s pop singer known as "Oliver," whose songs "Good Morning, Starshine" and "Jean" became top-three *Billboard* hits.

References: John Motley Morehead Foundation, *Annual Report* (1996); Richard Moll, *The Public Ivys* (1985); William D. Snider, *Light on the Hill* (1992).

Amy Curtin Pini
Additional research provided by Alex Coffin.

Mormon Church, or the Church of Jesus Christ of Latter-day Saints, was founded by Joseph Smith in New York in 1830 and based on his doctrinal teachings. Jedediah M. Grant introduced the Mormon Church to North Carolina in May 1838 as the first missionary to enter the state. Traveling alone, he preached in Surry, Stokes, Patrick, and Rockingham Counties, baptizing four people. Shortly after June 1838, two other Mormon leaders joined Grant. In addition to baptizing eight more people, Francis Gladden Bishop published a pamphlet for the purpose of correcting the misrepresentations that had, in his view, prejudiced the public against the Latter-day Saints. In late 1839, Joshua Grant Jr. joined his brother Jedediah, further expanding the missionary effort in North Carolina.

Although the Mormon missionaries concentrated their efforts mostly in northwestern North Carolina, the church was also introduced to other sections of the state. A letter written by John Eldridge dated 2 Jan. 1844 reveals that he "traveled through NC to Raleigh (Wake County)," where members of the legislature invited him, as their guest, into their respective boardinghouses. From Raleigh, Eldridge traveled to Fayetteville, then on to Wilmington. On the coast he "baptized some in the sea" before heading for the North Carolina mountains, where he found "some saints raised up by Jedediah M. Grant." He started holding meetings with them.

After Latter-day Saints leader Joseph Smith was killed at a Carthage, Ill., jail on 24 June 1844, most missionary activity in the church was curtailed; however, R. H. Kinnamon, Joshua Grant, Henry G. Boyle, and others continued their proselytizing in North Carolina and Virginia. In October 1875, the Southern States Mission was officially organized. It included North Carolina and 12 other states. After a 1928 division, North Carolina became part of the newly created East Central States Mission.

A list of Mormon Church members baptized in North Carolina between 1868 and 1895 reveals that 28 percent of them moved westward out of the state. On 29 Oct. 1887 the western counties of North Carolina were transferred to the East Tennessee Conference, decreasing the number of traveling missionaries in the North Carolina Conference from 19 at the end of August 1887 to 8 by August 1888. By 1891, from the total of 195 North Carolina Mormon Church members, 35 had emigrated west, 17 had died, and 15 had been excommunicated, leaving 128 members in the North Carolina Conference in 1894. Later, newly converted members were encouraged by church leaders to stay in the state and build branches; however, according to the year-end report dated 24 Dec. 1893, there was only one branch of the church in the North Carolina Conference.

The Southern States Mission was only one of 19 missionary fields in the Mormon Church at the close of the nineteenth century. At that time, almost all the missionaries came from the main body of Mormons in the intermountain West. They depended on their fellow Mormons for the support of their families; they also depended on daily North Carolina contacts for food and lodging. Some Mormon doctrines, particularly the practice of polygamy, raised alarm among many North Carolinians and made the work of Mormon missionaries difficult. Even though the church submitted to the U.S. law against polygamy passed in 1890, the notoriety associated with the practice plagued Mormons for years to come.

The Mormon Church experienced exponential growth in North Carolina in the twentieth century. Primarily college-aged men and women have converted many thousands of the state's residents. In the early twenty-first century, North Carolina Mormons numbered more than 53,000, and two missions existed in the state.

References: Wallace R. Draughon, *History of the Church of Jesus Christ of LDS in North Carolina* (1992); W. W. Hatch, *There Is No Law: A History of Mormon Civil Relations in the Southern States, 1865–1905* (1968); Joseph Smith, *History of the Church of Jesus Christ of Latter-day Saints* (1948).

Joan S. Boudreaux

Morris Field was conceived in 1936 as a New Deal Works Project Administration program in Charlotte. In April 1941 the Army Air Corps identified a site on the outskirts of downtown, and over the next few months a small airstrip with two runways was constructed. Work crews composed of civilian and military personnel tore up the surrounding countryside in preparation for more buildings if the need arose. On 15 Sept. 1941 a chapel was erected for the few men stationed at the base, officially called Charlotte Airbase. The first commanding officer of the facility was Col. C. W. Howard.

During the turbulent years of World War II, Charlotte was transformed into a military zone of men and matériel. Inside the city was a massive Quartermaster Corps Depot, and just across the border in South Carolina was a plant that made artillery shells for the navy. The attack on Pearl Harbor sparked an extension and renovation of Charlotte Airbase. In January 1942 the post was renamed Morris Field in honor of Maj. William C. Morris from Harrisburg, Pa. Throughout the war the base changed as new units rotated through, becoming a repair base for flights in transit along the East Coast. This conversion led to problems such as the crash of a B-17 bomber in October 1943 costing more than $300,000 in damages. But operations at Morris Field were generally successful. Stationed there were the 29th Air Group, 40th Matériel Group, 56th Pursuit Squadron, and 62nd Pursuit Squadron. The 29th Air Group eventually went to the Pacific Theater, where many of its pilots died fighting the Japanese.

In May 1946 the Air Corps vacated Morris Field. To relieve the postwar housing shortage, Charlotte officials converted many structures that once held airplanes and brave young soldiers into apartment buildings. The city purchased the rights to the airstrip, and Morris Field became the precursor to Charlotte's Douglas International Airport. The air base where so many men trained to fight eventually became home to the North Carolina Air National Guard. In September 1998 the guard observed its 50th anniversary, dedicating a granite memorial during the ceremonies. The monument was placed close to Morris Field's original location, southwest of Charlotte, near the Charlotte Douglas International Airport.

Joshua Howard

Mosquito Fleet was the whimsical nickname for the four small steamers that comprised the North Carolina Navy at the beginning of the Civil War. The ships were under orders not only to defend sounds and rivers but also to seize Union ships moving along the coast. The side-wheeled steamer *Winslow* was the first ship to be commissioned, followed by the *Beaufort*, *Raleigh*, and *Ellis*—all propeller-driven, small river boats originally designed for canal use. The latter three mounted only one gun apiece. Instead of veteran sailors, this diminutive fleet of small boats was manned primarily by soldiers and farmers with no seagoing experience. Nonetheless, the success of these vessels, especially the *Winslow*, along with that of the Confederate privateers, drew Union strikes at the North Carolina coast in 1861 and 1862. Even though the small gunboats were no match for the enemy ships, Union authorities maintained that landing on the North Carolina mainland first required absolute control of the sounds, an impossibility until the state's navy was destroyed.

With the capture of Roanoke Island by Union forces in February 1862, Confederate commander W. F. Lynch, in an effort to save his vessels (now six in number), moved them to Elizabeth City on the Pasquotank River, but to no avail. At Cobb's Point a short distance downriver, a Union flotilla under Cdr. S. C. Rowan disposed of the mosquito fleet except for the *Beaufort*, which escaped to Norfolk.

References: John G. Barrett, *The Civil War in North Carolina* (1963); John S. Carbone, *The Civil War in Coastal North Carolina* (2001); William N. Still Jr., ed., *The Confederate Navy: The Ships, Men, and Organization, 1861–65* (1997).

John G. Barrett

Mothball Fleet, the nickname for the U.S. Maritime Commission's reserve fleet, was located on the Brunswick River across from the city of Wilmington. Following World War II, Congress made the Maritime Commission responsible for determining the number and type of vessels to be placed in reserve in case of future expansion; the southeastern North Carolina site was one of four in the country. The lay-up basin for the reserve fleet was operational when the first ship arrived in August 1946. The ships placed in "mothballs" had their hulls scaled, coated with oil, scaled again, and finally coated with red oxide paint, which stopped the rusting of metal surfaces. The internal system of "mothballing" consisted of draining all of the various systems and pumping in oil under pressure. All turbines, engines, and gears were also coated with an oily film.

A total of 648 ships were, at varying times, moored in the reserve fleet. The majority of vessels stored in the facility were of the Liberty class, some of them built in Wilmington. Over the years many were scrapped, sold to private concerns, sunk for artificial reefs, or recommissioned. The last ship to be removed from the mothball fleet was the uss *Dwight W. Morrow*, which was scrapped in February 1970.

Reference: Alan D. Watson, *Wilmington: Port of North Carolina* (1992).

Beverly Tetterton

Mother Vineyard is a community on the north end of Roanoke Island in Dare County where an ancient and famous scuppernong grapevine grows. Known at times as the "Sir Walter Raleigh Vine" and the "Mother Vine," it is the subject of much legend and lore. The vine is reputed to be the oldest grapevine in the United States, as well as the original vine from which all subsequent scuppernong grapes descended. In 1909 horticulturalist F. C. Reimer refuted these claims, showing that the oldest vines in the state grew in Tyrrell County. As for the scuppernong vines of Roanoke Island, he found five old vines growing "in two straight rows." North Carolina grape authority Clarence Gohdes called this statement "sure evidence that they are survivors of a modern vineyard" and placed their origins back to the 1850s.

"Old Mother Vineyard" was established on Roanoke Island ca. 1930 and supplied grapes to winemaker Paul Garrett. Mother Vineyard became a trademark for a popular brand of scuppernong wine originally produced from grapes of Old Mother Vineyard on Roanoke Island. The rights to the name were subsequently sold to a company in Petersburg, Va., in 1956, which claimed to use North Carolina grapes in its wine but not specifically those grown on Roanoke Island.

References: Clarence Gohdes, *Scuppernong* (1982); Roger Payne, *Place Names of the Outer Banks* (1985); F. C. Reimer, *Scuppernong and Other Muscadine Grapes* (1909).

John Hairr

Motto, State. SEE *Esse Quam Videri.*

Mountain Dance and Folk Festival has been held, traditionally on the first weekend in August, in Asheville since 1928. That year, Bascom Lamar Lunsford, a passionate lover of mountain music and culture and an active collector of folk music, organized a contest for musicians and dancers in conjunction with the Rhododendron Festival. This first festival was held on 6 June 1928 in Pack Square in the center of Asheville. In 1930 Lunsford's festival separated from the Rhododendron Festival and became known as the Mountain Dance and Folk Festival. It served as the model for several other important folk festivals that began in the 1930s across the country.

What distinguished the Mountain Dance and Folk Festival from other commercial presentations of mountain music in the budding country music industry and in some other folk festivals of the time was Lunsford's commitment to presenting the musicians and dancers with dignity. The contestants in the festival, who have included some of western North Carolina's finest musicians and dancers for decades, were invited by Lunsford, and he discouraged, for at least the first several years of the festival, the use of "hillbilly" costumes. Although traditional music continued to evolve, especially with the popularity of bluegrass after World War II, Lunsford emphasized the older forms and styles of mountain music while he directed the festival. On the other hand, he encouraged some changes in dance, such as using clog steps in square dancing and using shoes with steel taps, in order to increase the program's appeal to a widening audience. According to some scholars, the festival also had the effect of moving square dancing from private and informal contexts to public and formal settings and introducing an element of competition. The festival declined in popularity somewhat by the early 1960s, but it experienced a resurgence of interest later in the decade and into the 1970s as interest in mountain music grew nationwide.

Although Lunsford died in 1973, the Mountain Dance and Folk Festival has continued to gain in popularity. During the 1980s, the festival was the subject of three documentary films. It remains a leading attraction for both local residents and tourists.

References: Loyal Jones, *Minstrel of the Appalachians: The Story of Bascom Lamar Lunsford* (1984); David E. Whisnant, "Finding the Way between the Old and the New: The Mountain Dance and Folk Festival and Bascom Lamar Lunsford's Work as a Citizen," *Appalachian Journal* 6 (1979).

Bruce E. Baker

Mountain Heritage Center, located at Western Carolina University in Cullowhee, is a museum focusing on the natural and cultural history and heritage of western North Carolina and the southern Appalachian region. The museum houses one permanent exhibit, Migration of the Scotch-Irish People. It produces a variety of temporary exhibits that illustrate the natural world and mountain societies, past and present. Themes have included blacksmithing traditions in the mountains, Cherokee myths and legends, mountain trout, the natural and cultural history of an Appalachian watershed, baskets and their makers, and the enduring popularity of hand-woven coverlets and the southern Appalachian handicraft movement.

The Mountain Heritage Center also offers educational programs to the public, presents concerts and lectures, and produces books, tapes, and other materials. The center's largest annual event is Mountain Heritage Day, which is held on the last Saturday in September and boasts a full schedule of traditional music, dance, and craft demonstrations. A midway fea-

Observation Tower,
Mt. Mitchell—6711 feet,
Top. of Eastern America,
Asheville, N. C.—25
"Where life is worth while."

Postcard from 1920 showing the observation tower on the summit of Mount Mitchell and incorrectly listing its elevation as 6,711 feet. The exact height of Mount Mitchell was not established until well into the twentieth century. NCC.

tures some 200 craft booths offering handmade items ranging from woodwork and pottery to quilts and stained glass along with food booths offering traditional treats such as cider, barbecue, and Cherokee fry bread.

Bruce E. Baker

Mountains. SEE Geography.

Mount Mitchell, at 6,684 feet above sea level, is the highest point in the eastern United States. Located in the Black Mountain range of the Southern Appalachians, it is part of an intricate mountain system featuring some of the oldest and most complex geological formations on earth. Although the Black Mountains are only about 15 miles in length, the major peaks average well above 6,000 feet in elevation.

Anthropologists believe the earliest inhabitants in the vicinity of Mount Mitchell settled there some 13,000 years ago. At the time the first white explorers and settlers arrived, the area was a hunting ground for the Cherokee Indians. Following the American Revolution, however, the Indians were pushed westward from the area by a relentless tide of white settlers.

Perhaps the first European to ascend Mount Mitchell was French botanist André Michaux, who collected plant specimens in the Black Mountains in 1789. Michaux also ascended

Grandfather Mountain, mistakenly proclaiming it to be the highest peak in the Appalachians. Another botanist who explored the area was John Fraser, for whom the Fraser fir was named. The Fraser fir grows naturally along the Black Mountain summits.

The first person to scientifically study Mount Mitchell and the Black Mountains from the standpoint of physical geography was Professor Elisha Mitchell of the University of North Carolina. In 1835 Mitchell took barometric pressure readings from the major peaks of the Black Mountain range to determine their altitudes. From his observations Mitchell determined that the highest point in eastern America was in the Black Mountains rather than in the White Mountains of New Hampshire, as was previously believed. Mitchell returned to the Black Mountains in 1838 and again in 1844 for further study.

In the mid-1850s, Mitchell became embroiled in a bitter dispute with a former student, Congressman Thomas Lanier Clingman, over whether or not Mitchell had correctly identified the highest peak in the Black Mountains. The dispute escalated until the summer of 1857, when Mitchell returned to the Black Mountains to try to verify his earlier scientific findings. In the process of trying to obtain corroborative evidence, Mitchell was hiking across the northwest side of Mount Mitchell when he slipped and fell from a cliff near a 40-foot waterfall, hitting his head and drowning. The location of his death is known today as Mitchell Falls.

The controversy, which did not die with Mitchell, subsequently became entangled further in the politics of the day. Zebulon B. Vance was one of Mitchell's most vocal defenders. Clingman may have won the public debate while Mitchell lived; however, after the tragic accident, the beloved professor was vindicated as far as Clingman's political enemies and the people in general were concerned. Mitchell's body, having been interred in Asheville, was reinterred a year later at the summit of the mountain that continues to bear his name.

In 1939 the Blue Ridge Parkway was completed from N.C. 80 to Black Mountain Gap. The following year the state acquired and improved the toll road from the parkway to Camp Alice. As a result, the public was given toll-free motor road access to Mount Mitchell for the first time. A new road (present-day N.C. 128) from the parkway was constructed to within a short walk of the summit in 1948. Two years later, the Blue Ridge Parkway was completed to Asheville, resulting in more than 200,000 people making their way to Mount Mitchell in 1950. A new observation tower was completed in 1960 to accommodate the increase in visitation.

In the 1970s legislation proposing to make Mount Mitchell a national park was passed by Congress; however, there was considerable local opposition and the idea was dropped in 1979. In the 1980s and 1990s, an environmental problem developed that threatened Mount Mitchell State Park as well as other peaks in the Southern Appalachians approximately 6,000 feet elevation and above. The balsam forests at the mountain summit were attacked by an insect called the balsam woolly aphid. Acid rain and other atmospheric pollution from industrial activities in other areas of the country began taking a toll on the balsams also. By the mid-1990s practically all of the trees at the summit had died. A number of scientists set forth the theory that the trees were weakened by pollution, therefore making them susceptible to insect attack. Although young seedlings on the summit appeared to be healthy, it was questionable as to whether the balsam forests on Mount Mitchell and the other Black Mountain summits would return or not.

In 1993 Mount Mitchell was designated as an International Biosphere Reserve by the United Nations Educational, Scientific, and Cultural Organization (UNESCO). This designation added Mount Mitchell to an elite group of sites throughout the world that are protected for the purpose of discovering the solutions to problems of conservation, sustainable development, and other issues.

References: Thomas E. Jeffrey, "'A Whole Torrent of Mean and Malevolent Abuse': Party Politics and the Clingman-Mitchell Controversy, Part 1," *NCHR* 70 (July 1993); Jeffrey, "'A Whole Torrent of Mean and Malevolent Abuse': Party Politics and the Clingman-Mitchell Controversy, Part 2," *NCHR* 70 (October 1993);

Timothy Silver, *Mount Mitchell and the Black Mountains: An Environmental History of the Highest Peaks in Eastern America* (2003).

Ron Holland

SEE ALSO Mount Mitchell Railroad.

Mount Mitchell Railroad, although fully operational for only four years, was among the most popular and successful tourist attractions in North Carolina in the early twentieth century. Originally created as a logging enterprise by lumbermen Fred A. Perley and W. H. Crockett, the narrow-gauge line originated near Black Mountain in the Swannanoa Valley and over some 21 miles ascended more than 3,500 feet to Camp Alice, just below the summit of Mount Mitchell. The railroad had been established to transport spruce and other commercial timber, but by 1914 the owners had built passenger cars for use on their logging railroad. Perley and Crockett subsequently hired Col. Sandford H. Cohen, a leading booster of tourism in western North Carolina; under his aggressive promotion, the Mount Mitchell Railroad officially opened for general passenger traffic in July 1915.

Sharing the railbed with the logging trains, the Mount Mitchell Railroad expanded its service and in 1916 carried more than 10,000 passengers to Camp Alice, which had been constructed in 1914 or 1915 specifically for tourists. The camp included a large rustic dining hall and platform tents for overnight campers, and a moderate one-mile trail ascended to Mount Mitchell's summit, the highest elevation in the United States east of the Rocky Mountains. Despite the popularity of the enterprise, the passenger service was terminated in June 1919 so the railroad could be devoted exclusively to timber removal.

By 1921 logging operations had ceased due to the depletion of timber resources. The tracks and ties were pulled up and the old railroad bed was used to create the Mount Mitchell Motor Road, which opened for automobiles in June 1922.

Reference: Timothy Silver, *Mount Mitchell and the Black Mountains: An Environmental History of the Highest Peaks in Eastern America* (2003).

Marcus B. Simpson Jr.

Mount Olive College. In 1951 the Convention of Original Free Will Baptists authorized the establishment of a junior college that opened in 1952 at Cragmont Assembly near Black Mountain as Mount Allen Junior College. In 1953 the school was moved to the town of Mount Olive and began a liberal arts program with a Christian emphasis, with W. Burkette Raper serving as president. In 1956 the school's name was changed to Mount Olive Junior College. In 1958 the college was accredited by the North Carolina College Conference and in

1960 achieved full accreditation by the Southern Association of Colleges and Schools. The decision to establish Mount Olive as a liberal arts school raised some criticism from Baptists who favored the idea of a Bible college committed to a fundamentalist philosophy of education, but friends of the college rallied to its support.

The school continued to expand, and in 1965 the first buildings were completed and occupied on land located on the outskirts of Mount Olive that by 2000 consisted of 138 acres. In 1979 the sponsoring convention endorsed a decision by the board of trustees to make Mount Olive a fully accredited senior college as soon as possible. Thus, the junior and senior classes were added in 1984 and 1985, and in December 1986 the Commission on Colleges of the Southern Association granted full accreditation to Mount Olive as a four-year institution awarding associate and baccalaureate degrees.

In 1975 Mount Olive College began an educational program at Seymour Johnson Air Force Base in Goldsboro, which has served both military and civilian students. Recognizing the need to provide special degree programs for nontraditional students at other locations, Mount Olive began to offer such programs in New Bern (1993), Wilmington (1995), and Durham (1997). In the early 2000s roughly 1,400 of Mount Olive's nearly 2,000 students were nontraditional students enrolled through the college's offsite locations.

References: Mount Olive College, *Catalogue* (2003); Michael R. Pelt, *A History of Original Free Will Baptists* (1996).

Michael R. Pelt

Mourner's Bench, also called an anxious bench, was a ritualized prayer technique used extensively by nineteenth-century Christian revivalists. Aimed at securing the immediate and dramatic conversion of sinners, the technique originated as part of the "New Measures" conceived by New York's Charles G. Finney—perhaps the most influential revivalist of the so-called Second Great Awakening. Beginning in the 1820s, Finney traveled to large New York cities and towns, successfully spreading his own brand of aggressive, high-energy revivalism. Finney's strategies, unique at the time, included direct and powerful sermons; long, intense prayer meetings; greater female involvement in public services; the calling of individuals in need of repentance by name; overtly familiar references to God; and the insistence upon obvious, often physical "proof" of conversion. The mourner's bench, and later the altar call, helped carry the conversion process to a climax.

Finney's New Measures, although controversial among many traditional Protestant churches, became a model for rural revivals and camp meetings throughout the 1800s and early 1900s. In North Carolina, widely attended camp meetings such as those at Town Creek near Wilmington, Wesley

Chapel Camp Ground and Balls Creek Camp Meeting in Catawba County, and Shepherds Crossroads in Iredell County all featured a mourner's bench in one form or another.

At such gatherings, the mourner's bench was usually placed in the center of the congregation, adjacent to the pulpit and in plain view of everyone present. The "bench" might be several plain wooden benches, a few chairs, or perhaps just an enclosed area without seats. People went to the mourner's bench when they considered themselves finally ready to abandon a life of sin and step unfalteringly toward eternal salvation. Intense praying, exhortations by the preacher and other previously converted Christians, crying, singing, proclamations of guilt and shame by the "convicted," and occasional spiritual exercises (such as the "jerks" and speaking in tongues) often accompanied the transformation. In the end, the experience was both a personal journey from unbelief to faith and a public declaration of a commitment to change one's life.

Whether the result of intense psychological coercion, as some suggest, or evidence of a real spiritual conversion, the drama elicited by the mourner's bench was an essential part of the nineteenth-century revival experience.

References: Guion G. Johnson, "The Camp Meeting in Antebellum North Carolina," *NCHR* 10 (April 1933); Thad Stem Jr., "Those Revivalists of Another Era," *Raleigh News and Observer*, 4 Sept. 1966.

Jay Mazzocchi

Mourning Rings, worn as a memorial of a deceased person, were mentioned as early as 1703 in England. In his will in 1716, James Blunt of Chowan County left each of his five daughters a gold ring, although the rings were not described as mourning rings. The inventory made in 1753 of the estate of Henry Snoad of Beaufort County, however, specifically mentioned a gold mourning ring; the estate of Governor Gabriel Johnston in 1756 included two gold mourning rings. Such rings were advertised for sale in Williamsburg, Va., in the *Virginia Gazette* of 4 June 1772. At her death in Edenton in 1775, Mrs. Jean Corbin owned two gold mourning rings. Richard Blackledge of Craven County, in his will of 20 Feb. 1776, left £10 each to his daughter and to Betsey Baker to buy mourning rings. Numerous wills survive in the records of North Carolina in which bequests for this purpose are mentioned, and Earl G. Swem's *Virginia Historical Index* includes an even larger number of such bequests.

William S. Powell

Mule Day is an annual celebration drawing tens of thousands of visitors to the small Johnston County town of Benson. Held in late September, the event was started in 1949 by Nowell Smith Jr., with the assistance of local livestock dealer Willis McLamb and a group of merchants, to recognize farmers and the area's major draft animal, the mule—the sterile offspring of a male donkey and a female horse. The first celebration featured more than 300 mules, and every float was pulled by the ornery beasts. Over the years this annual "exercise in nostalgia" has grown larger, while the number of mules participating has shrunk: despite the name of the celebration, the number of horses involved has often surpassed the number of mules.

It was fitting that Benson should be the site for an extravaganza recognizing the mule, since the town was once the location of a thriving mule trade—so much so that if one said he was from Benson the response would inevitably be, "You're from mule town." One publication on the annual celebration reminded visitors that the mule was a noble animal, and "that a relative of his mother is cheered to victory each year at the Kentucky Derby, and that a kinsman of his father walked through Jerusalem on Sunday 2,000 years ago, with palms beneath his feet."

The three to four days of festivities include swine judging, hog calling, a parade, a concert, beauty contests, political speeches, a street dance, a rodeo, a fiddler's convention, and fireworks. There are also a variety of mule-judging events, including awards for racing, pulling, youngest, oldest, ugliest, and largest. These culminate in the selection of a "grand champion mule." With recent social changes in the area have come added events, such as the Mule Day "Tee Off" golf tournament at Reedy Creek, arts and crafts shows, barbecues, and children's rides.

References: Spencer Carter, "Stepping out in Muletown," *The State* (August 1975); Annis W. Jackson, "Mule Days Again," *The State* (September 1981).

Ronnie W. Faulkner

Mules were common features of the North Carolina landscape until the mid-twentieth century. From a census number of 125,608 in 1940, mules have declined so precipitously in the state—beaten out by mechanized farming and in many cases sold for dog food—that even to see one in the early 2000s may require a trip to the town of Benson's annual Mule Day festival or to a place of amusement such as the E-Z Ride Ass and Mule Farm near Liberty.

The mule's ancestry is specified in its taxonomical designation, *Equus caballus x asinus*, a creature born of a mare and sired by a jackass (in the rare cases in which the female parent is the donkey, the offspring is called a "henny"). Its tenure in the United States is almost coextensive with the Republic itself: George Washington founded the American line, breeding his Virginia mares to a jack named Royal Gift, a present from the King of Spain, as early as the 1780s. Washington, an astute and innovative farmer, foresaw an almost infinite expansion of agriculture in the new nation and recognized the appropriateness of the mule's many virtues to that awesome demand.

Mules, as the future president discovered, possess wonderful stamina and can easily work 12 hours a day on just over half the rations demanded by a horse. Their dietary needs can be met with cracked corn supplemented by browse of the animal's own choice—a choice famously unfinicky, as the phrase "grinning like a mule eating briars" acknowledges. Mules are steady, sure-footed, and cautious, able to walk between rows without trampling crops and to negotiate treacherous terrain without much danger of disabling injury—even at night, when serving as the coon hunter's mount as he follows the hounds through woods and across streams. Mules are extremely hardy and disease resistant (a proverb in the British army declares that "one never sees a dead mule") and considerably longer lived than the average horse (a mule in Vance County attained a documented age of 50 years).

Along with these virtues come some problematic qualities. An annoyed mule will kick with deadly force, and mules seem to nourish grudges. As William Faulkner observed, a mule will work for you for many years for the opportunity to kick you just once, and it is wisely stated that if you have anything to say to a mule you had better say it to his face. There is a folk tradition that a mule will willingly follow a white horse; but the truth is that he will follow anything if he wants to and nothing if he does not. Among the many stories of the stubbornness of mules is an anecdote about a man who, infuriated by his mule's refusal to pull an overloaded wagon, built a fire under the animal in order to make it move, whereupon the mule simply took a few steps forward to position the wagon over the fire.

Such stories abound in southern literature, wherein mules both living and dead make numerous appearances. Among North Carolina writers who have dealt with mules in fiction are Doris Betts, Clyde Edgerton, Kaye Gibbons, Bernice Kelly Harris, Ovid Pierce, Flora Ann Scearce, and Thomas Wolfe. North Carolina oral tradition is also rich in mule material. Such literary and subliterary matter formed the theme of the Dead Mule Club, a restaurant and bar in Chapel Hill whose walls boasted mule-related artifacts of various kinds, including an authentic mule skull above the fireplace.

References: Harry Crews, "The Mythic Mule," *Southern Magazine* (October 1986); Pete Daniel, *Breaking the Land* (1985); Jerry Leath Mills, "Equine Gothic: The Dead Mule as Generic Signifier in Southern Literature of the Twentieth Century," *Southern Literary Journal* 19 (1996).

Jerry Leath Mills

"Mummy Letters," four articles written from 1 Feb. to 6 Mar. 1886 by journalist Walter Hines Page for Josephus Daniels's *State Chronicle* (Raleigh), stridently called for changes in North Carolina's political, educational, and economic status quo. Page, a transplanted former editor of the *Chronicle*, was living in New York when he penned the epistles. With biting sarcasm, he argued that the reactionaries and Confederate veterans who controlled North Carolina were like the mummies of ancient Egypt—though "dead" and hopelessly out of touch, they held the state in their grip. "Our great lawyers, great judges, great editors," Page wrote, "are all of the past. . . . In the general intelligence of the people, in intellectual force and in cultivation, we are doing nothing." To reform itself, Page suggested, North Carolina needed "a few first-class funerals."

Page's first "Mummy Letter" aroused a storm of criticism. The *Chatham Record* declared that "if such men as [Senator Zebulon B.] Vance, [Senator Matt W.] Ransom, [Governor Alfred M.] Scales and the other leading men of North Carolina are 'mummies' and Mr. Page is a LIVE man, then please give us some more 'Mummies.'" The outraged Vance canceled his subscription to the *State Chronicle*.

Page's assault appears to have had little immediate impact on the state's provincialism, but his views influenced several progressive leaders, including Daniels, Judge Walter Clark, and Charles B. Aycock. While in Raleigh, Page had been the center of the Watauga Club, a group of forward-thinking North Carolinians who met regularly to discuss ways to improve conditions in the state. Although the Watauga Club was short-lived, the ideas it generated later became commonly accepted, and the efforts of Page and his peers are credited with the 1887 establishment of the North Carolina College of Agriculture and Mechanic Arts (present-day North Carolina State University) in Raleigh. Aycock, who was elected governor in 1900, told Page "that fully three-fourths of the people are with you and wish you Godspeed in your effort to arouse better work, greater thought and activity, and freer opinions in the State." The "Mummy Letters" played a significant role in forming North Carolina's more progressive reputation after 1900.

References: Burton J. Hendrick, *The Training of an American: The Earlier Life and Letters of Walter Hines Page, 1855–1913* (1928); Oliver H. Orr Jr., *Charles Brantley Aycock* (1961).

Ronnie W. Faulkner

Museum of Early Southern Decorative Arts (MESDA),

founded in Winston-Salem in 1965 by Frank L. Horton, is dedicated to exhibiting and researching the regional decorative arts of the South before 1821. Building on a core collection that belonged to Horton and his mother, Theo Liipfert Horton Taliaferro, the holdings of MESDA include furniture, paintings, textiles, ceramics, silver, and other metalware made and used in Maryland, Virginia, the Carolinas, Georgia, Kentucky, and Tennessee. The museum is a collection of 19 room-settings and 6 galleries built into what was once a grocery store in Old Salem. Exhibits include a seventeenth-century Virginia great hall, a one-room Maryland plantation dwelling, a back-

country North Carolina log house, and a parlor from Charleston, S.C. MESDA's interpretation and education programs reflect the fundamental divisions and sharp cultural contrasts found in the South between the Chesapeake region, the lowcountry, and the backcountry (Piedmont).

MESDA includes a research center, open to scholars and the general public, with a photographic catalog of approximately 15,000 objects and a comprehensive listing of documentary information on more than 60,000 artisans in the South working in 125 different trades. A library with more than 5,000 volumes on subjects related to the decorative arts is supplemented by extensive microform holdings of primary documents. Publications from MESDA include the *Journal of Early Southern Decorative Arts* and a newsletter, *The Luminary*, both published twice a year. The museum has also published several books on early southern decorative arts.

References: John Bivins and Forsyth Alexander, *The Regional Arts of the Early South: A Sampling from the Collection of the Museum of Early Southern Decorative Arts* (1991); "Frank's Place," *The Luminary* 9 (Winter 1988); "MESDA's Silver Jubilee," *The Luminary* 11 (Winter 1990).

Martha Belle Caldwell

Museum of the Albemarle

Museum of the Albemarle in Elizabeth City chronicles the story of the people of the first region of North Carolina opened to European settlement through permanent and changing exhibits, presentations, and programs. This state museum is operated by the North Carolina Museum of History as one of its three regional branches. In addition to interpreting the history and culture of northeastern North Carolina, the museum furnishes technical assistance and services to local historical agencies and museums in the ten-county Albemarle Sound region.

The Pasquotank Historical Society conceived the idea for the Museum of the Albemarle in the 1950s, but the facility did not open until 1967, when the county donated the old highway patrol building south of Elizabeth City to function as its home. Susan Stitt served as its first director. A twenty-fifth anniversary celebration in 1992 featured a gala event sponsored by the North Carolina Museum of History Associates and the installation of a remodeled permanent gallery. The museum moved to a new 50,000-square-foot facility on the Elizabeth City waterfront in 2006. Visitors to the museum can enjoy permanent exhibits that include "Inez," a steam-pump fire engine from the 1880s, the museum's signature artifact; rotating exhibits on specialized topics; "Hands on History" presentations; lectures; audiovisuals; and a gift shop.

Reference: Museum of the Albemarle, *Marking Time* (1994).

Angelyn H. Patteson

Museum of the Cape Fear in Fayetteville is the third regional branch of the North Carolina Museum of History and the only one that began as a branch museum. (The other two regional branches, the Museum of the Albemarle in Elizabeth City and the Gateway Museum in Old Fort, operated independently before coming under the Museum of History's umbrella.) The free-admission Museum of the Cape Fear opened in 1987 with funding assistance from the Historic Fayetteville Foundation and with Rodney Barfield as its first curator. It introduces visitors to the history and culture of southeastern North Carolina through exhibits, lectures, and workshops and, as part of its mission as a regional branch, offers expertise to the nonstate historical museums, sites, and agencies in its 20-county service area.

The museum features permanent exhibits on the history of the Piedmont and the lower North Carolina coast from early Native American settlements through the Civil War period. Exhibits on transportation in the region, Fayetteville history (including the devastating 1831 fire), and an 1890 potter's shop are of particular interest. Visitors and school groups are drawn to the temporary exhibit gallery, where changing exhibits have highlighted, among other subjects, African American women in the Cape Fear, traditional crafts of the region, and the region's archaeology. A meeting room provides space for programs, lectures, and films.

References: Angela Fracaro, "A Fast Start at Looking Back," *The State* 57 (June 1989); Karen Rosalinde Zimmer, "An Audience Development Plan for the Museum of the Cape Fear in Fayetteville" (M.A. thesis, UNC-Chapel Hill, 1989).

Angelyn H. Patteson

Museum of the Cherokee Indian, established in 1948, was originally housed in a log building on the Qualla Boundary of the Eastern Band of Cherokee Indians. The initial collection of the museum was comprised of artifacts donated by Samuel E. Beck, a local Cherokee businessman who had profited during the early days of tourism and had long been interested in preserving the Cherokee heritage. Later the museum added the Kirksey collection of Union Mills, N.C., the Weatherly Collection of Grant, Va., and the artifacts of noted ethnologist Frank Speck. In addition, thousands of Cherokees made individual contributions. Tom Underwood originally ran the museum, while Mose Owle served as curator and chief lecturer.

In 1958 a fire destroyed the old building, but the museum artifacts had been in storage in a separate building and were consequently spared. While plans were being made for the lengthy task of raising funds to build a new facility, the museum reopened in a building belonging to the Cherokee Historical Association, which had purchased the museum in 1952. In 1976, after many years of work—and with the financial help of the Economic Development Foundation, a North Carolina Legislative Grant, the Cherokee Historical Association, the Z. Smith Reynolds Foundation, the Percy B. Ferebee Endowment, and the Hillsdale Fund of Greensboro—the new building opened its doors.

The new Museum of the Cherokee Indian, enlarged and renovated in 1998, is one of the most modern facilities of its kind in the United States and houses the greatest collection of Cherokee artifacts in existence. Through audio-visual exhibits that rely heavily on computer-generated graphics and other special effects, visitors can learn about the sacred myths and legends of the Cherokee, hear the Cherokee language spoken, and follow the story of the Cherokee people from their prehistoric origins to the Trail of Tears and the subsequent history of the Eastern Band of Cherokee Indians.

References: Barbara R. Duncan and Brett H. Riggs, *Cherokee Heritage Trails Guidebook* (2003); Duane H. King, comp., *Cherokee Heritage* (1976).

William L. Anderson

N

Nags Head Woods Ecological Preserve. Hammocks —unique fertile areas along coastal regions characterized by hardwood vegetation and higher elevations than their surroundings—grew up along the shore of Roanoke Sound and are today protected as Nags Head Woods Ecological Preserve, a forest of beeches, oaks, hollies, pines, maples, sweet gum, and hickories located in Dare County. Some of the trees there are more than 300 years old. In addition to a well-developed maritime forest, the 1,092-acre ecological preserve has ancient dunes, freshwater ponds, and saltwater and freshwater marshes. Elevations in Nags Head Woods rise to heights of 60 feet.

The ecologically diverse forest is home to more than 100 species of birds and 65 species of reptiles, amphibians, and mammals. Rare and endangered birds, including the Cooper's hawk, the swallow-tailed kite, the osprey, and the pileated woodpecker, can be found there.

Various Native American tribes first explored this forest, hunting for game and gathering berries, nuts, and plants. Italian explorer Giovanni da Verrazano discovered the forest in 1524 and called it Arcadia. A small community of about 40 families was established there in the mid-1700s, but the settlers soon migrated to the beach side of the Outer Banks. During the eighteenth and nineteenth centuries, loggers cleared trees from the forest to build ships and, later, cottages. Faced with the threat of growing development in the early 1970s, the area was designated as a National Natural Landmark in 1974. With the help of the North Carolina Nature Conservancy, Nags Head Woods now encompasses more than 1,000 acres between Jockey's Ridge State Park and the Wright Brothers National Memorial. A visitors center on the site offers interpretive programs, guided canoe tours, and nature walks.

References: Jim Dean and Lawrence S. Earley, eds., *Wildlife in North Carolina* (1987); Dirk Frankenberg, *The Nature of the Outer Banks: Environmental Processes, Field Sites, and Development Issues, Corolla to Ocracoke* (1995); North Carolina Wildlife Resources Commission, *North Carolina Wild Places* (1993).

Rich Weidman

Nancy Jones House, located in Wake County on what was once the main stage road between Raleigh and Chapel Hill, was possibly built around 1803 by Nathaniel Jones, father-in-law of Nancy Jones. Nancy's husband, Henry, inherited the property. The two of them operated a stagecoach stop and tavern out of the house, although Henry was primarily a farmer who left the running of the tavern to his wife. The house is purported to have served as the setting for one of the state's favorite legends. Tradition holds that in 1838 Governor Edward B. Dudley of North Carolina and Governor Pierce Mason Butler of South Carolina stopped at the house during a trip between Raleigh and Chapel Hill. The governors consumed servings of apple and peach brandy, and between rounds Dudley reportedly said to his colleague, "It's a damn long time between drinks." The quote has also been ascribed to Governor John Motley Morehead, who supposedly said it during a tense meeting with South Carolina governor James H. Hammond in the 1840s.

President James K. Polk, a North Carolina native, stopped at the Nancy Jones House on his way to Chapel Hill in May 1847 to deliver the commencement address at the University of North Carolina. Governor William Alexander Graham and former governor Morehead joined him at the house. Union general William T. Sherman and his troops bivouacked in the vicinity in April 1865, but no damage was done to the property. There is some indication that Nancy's son, Adolphus, operated a school out of the house following the Civil War. The Nancy Jones House still stands as a private residence.

Reference: Richard Walser, "Damn Long Time between Drinks," *NCHR* 59 (April 1982).

Jo Ann Williford

Nantahala National Forest, established in 1920, is located in the most southern portion of the Appalachian Mountains in North Carolina. Covering thousands of acres in parts of Macon, Jackson, Transylvania, Graham, and Swain Counties and managed by the U.S. Forest Service, it is the largest of North Carolina's four national forests. Named for the Indian word meaning "land of the noonday sun," Nantahala is publicly held and managed for numerous purposes, including timber production, agriculture, wildlife management and preservation, and recreation. The Nantahala region features a number of mountain streams with cascades and waterfalls, deep pools, and rivers as well as many ponds and lakes, some very large. At 3,013 feet, Nantahala Lake, created when a dam was built across the Nantahala River, has the highest elevation of any lake in North Carolina. The river itself is found in the Nantahala Gorge, which follows along a fracture zone called Murphy's fault. The river then flows northeast and drops 900 feet into Fontana Lake.

The 3,800-acre Joyce Kilmer Memorial Forest, part of the Nantahala National Forest and the Joyce Kilmer–Slickrock Wilderness, is one of the largest areas of old-growth trees, or virgin forest, in the eastern United States. It was dedicated in 1936 in honor of poet Joyce Kilmer. Famous for his poem "Trees," Kilmer was killed in action during World War I. A two-mile National Recreation Trail allows visitors to walk among towering trees such as poplars, hemlocks, and oaks, many of which are hundreds of years old.

References: James Bannon, *North Carolina: A Guide to Backcountry Travel and Adventure* (1996); Sharyn Kane and Richard Keaton, *Southern National Forests* (1993); George Scheer, *North Carolina: A Guide to the Old North State* (1982).

Elizabeth Hardin

Nantahala Power and Light Company.

SEE Aluminum Company of America.

NASCAR. SEE Auto Racing.

Nash County, located on the border of the Coastal Plain and Piedmont regions of North Carolina, was formed in 1777 from Edgecombe County and named for Revolutionary War general Francis Nash, who died at the Battle of Germantown. Early inhabitants of the area included the Tuscarora Indians, followed by English and Irish settlers. The county seat, Nashville, was named for the county and incorporated in 1815. Nash County shares the towns of Rocky Mount, Whitakers, and Sharpsburg with adjacent counties; communities wholly within Nash County include Spring Hope, Bailey, Stanhope, Castalia, and Momeyer. The county's notable physical features include the Tar River, White Oak Swamp, and Moccasin, Swift, and Deer Branch Creeks.

Nash County farmers produce agricultural commodities such as tobacco, sweet potatoes, cucumbers, soybeans, corn, peanuts, cotton, beef and dairy cattle, and poultry. The county's manufactured products include diesel engines, electronic fuel control systems, textiles, apparel, and pharmaceuticals. The second textile mill in the state, Rocky Mount Mills, was established in 1818 and operated until the end of the twentieth century. Minerals such as gold and iron are mined in the county.

North Carolina Wesleyan College was incorporated in Rocky Mount in 1956 and opened in 1960. Nash County landmarks include the first Hardee's restaurant (1960) and the China American Tobacco Company Factory, built in 1919. Cultural institutions include the Country Doctor Museum, the Playhouse Community Theatre, the Tank Theatre, and the Nash County Historical Association. Nash County hosts several festivals and annual events, including the Outdoor Art Show, the Nashville Blooming Festival, the Spring Hope Pumpkin Festival, and the Freedom Celebration. Nash County's population stood at an estimated 90,700 in 2004.

Reference: Richard L. Mattson, *History and Architecture of Nash County, North Carolina* (1987).

Jay Mazzocchi

SEE ALSO North Carolina Wesleyan College.

Nash-Hooper House, located on West Tryon Street in Hillsborough, was constructed in 1772 by Francis Nash on land purchased from Isaac Edwards, secretary to Governor William Tryon. Nash, a prominent political and revolutionary military leader, was killed at the Battle of Germantown in Pennsylvania. The house was purchased in 1782 by William Hooper (1742–90), a Patriot leader and a signer of the Declaration of Independence. He died in the house and was buried on the property. Ownership was retained by the Hooper heirs until 1853, and significant additions were made to the structure during that time.

William A. Graham (1804–75), governor, U.S. secretary of the navy, and Confederate senator, acquired the house around 1870. Graham also was buried in the adjacent cemetery. The Graham family kept the property until 1906. Alfred G. and Mary Claire Randolph Engstrom purchased the estate in 1959. In 1971 the Engstroms sold the house to Cecil Leroy Sanford, a retired career diplomat. Listed in the National Register of Historic Places and designated a National Historic Landmark, the Nash-Hooper House is privately owned and not open to the public.

Reference: Mary Claire Engstrom, "Nash-Hooper House," Research Branch, North Carolina Division of Archives and History (1975).

Jerry C. Cashion

National Association for the Advancement of Colored People

(NAACP) is the nation's oldest civil rights organization, founded in 1909 in New York City by black and white activists seeking to influence the progress of social justice in the United States. Its primary focus has been the advocacy of ethnic minorities in their quest to gain equal rights under the law.

In 1917 the first three North Carolina branches of the NAACP were established and immediately began waging antilynching, fair employment, voter registration, and equal education campaigns. Over the next 25 years, the number of branches increased sevenfold, and in 1943 a State Conference of NAACP Branches was formed to serve the state's (primarily black) membership of 5,700. Five years later the leadership of the state conference was assumed by Kelly M. Alexander, who had previously revived his native Charlotte's NAACP branch in 1940. During Alexander's 36-year presidency (he relinquished the post only months before his death in early 1985), the North Carolina State Conference of NAACP Branches became the largest in the nation; it eventually included more than 120 branches with a membership of 30,000. In 1955, in the wake of the U.S. Supreme Court's *Brown v. Board of Education of Topeka, Kansas* decision, Alexander led the NAACP fight to desegregate North Carolina schools. A dominant figure within the national organization as well, he was elected to the NAACP

Board of Directors in 1950; he became vice chair in 1976 and chair in 1984.

Robert F. Williams was another native North Carolinian recognized by the national NAACP, although he was cast in a less favorable light. Formerly the president of the NAACP branch for his hometown of Monroe, Williams was removed from office and denounced by the organization's leadership in the late 1950s for encouraging "armed self-reliance" among his Ku Klux Klan–terrorized black membership. Williams's defense—he had advocated self-defense, not aggression—inspired a national debate among civil rights groups over violent versus nonviolent tactics; his 1962 book *Negroes with Guns* had a profound influence on Black Panther Party founder Huey P. Newton. The 1960 Greensboro sit-ins and their imitators, while essentially nonviolent in nature, presented another challenge to the national NAACP's courts-oriented approach to activism, and the organization only hesitantly expressed its support for these student protests.

Although its methods may have appeared mild to some civil rights activists, North Carolina's NAACP remained a highly visible and controversial force in state politics throughout the second half of the twentieth century. It was a favorite target of traditionalist groups that opposed the goals of integration and racial equality and conservative politicians who stressed the close ties (both real and imagined) between the NAACP and allegedly communist-driven organized labor. In the post–Cold War era, red-baiting has been largely replaced by accusations of reverse discrimination and excessive political correctness. Racial tension and other animosities between the NAACP and its detractors continue to run deep. Nevertheless, state and local NAACP leaders have amassed an impressive list of civil rights victories on behalf of North Carolina's African American population and remain vigilant against any and all attempts to disfranchise them. As of 2006, there were 101 NAACP branches in the state.

References: Wyllisa R. Bennett, "The Alexanders: NAACP Family Affair," *Southeast Perspective Magazine*, vol. 2, no. 3 (1996); Jeffrey J. Crow, Paul D. Escott, and Flora J. Hatley, *A History of African Americans in North Carolina* (2002); Raymond Gavins, "The NAACP in North Carolina during the Age of Segregation," in Armstead L. Robinson and Patricia Sullivan, eds., *New Directions in Civil Rights Studies* (1991).

Raymond Gavins
Additional research provided by Robert Blair Vocci.

National Congressional Club (NCC), originally the Congressional Club of North Carolina and later renamed the Conservative Club, was a political action committee formed by Tom Ellis in 1973 to help retire the campaign debts of U.S. senator Jesse Helms. The club rapidly became a formidable fund-raising and media organization closely identified with

Helms and his conservative agenda. It also was noteworthy for what critics called "attack ads"—television ads that emphasized presumably negative aspects of an opponent's record.

Under Ellis's leadership and with Carter Wrenn as executive director, the NCC successfully managed a number of campaigns for the U.S. Senate, including Helms's runs in 1978, 1984, and 1990, as well as John East's campaign in 1980 and Lauch Faircloth's in 1992. It is also credited with Ronald Reagan's victory in the 1976 North Carolina GOP primary against incumbent President Gerald Ford and raised an estimated $10 million during Reagan's successful 1980 campaign for the presidency.

In the mid-1980s Fairness in Media, a committee of NCC members and allies of Helms, initiated a very public fight to take over the Columbia Broadcasting System in order to promote their political goals. The takeover bid failed but gained a great deal of publicity for Helms and the Congressional Club. In 1993 the NCC supported the first successful twentieth-century Republican candidate for mayor of Raleigh, Tom Fetzer, a former staffer for the organization. It was not as successful in other races, notably those for Congress and the governorship.

The NCC had a falling out with Helms in 1993 and had to lay off some staff members and relocate its offices from Raleigh to Franklin County. In 1996, calling itself the Conservative Club, it was revitalized and gave a brief boost to the presidential aspirations of millionaire businessman Steve Forbes, a proponent of the flat tax. Forbes won a few early GOP primaries and did some early damage to front-runner Bob Dole of Kansas, but the legendary attack ads of the Congressional Club did not have national staying power, and even Forbes started to take a more positive tone before his campaign collapsed.

References: Rob Christensen, "Forbes' Fabulous Rise Is Conservative Club's Comeback," *Raleigh News and Observer*, 29 Jan. 1996; Michael Crowley, "Under a Rock," *New Republic* (29 Jan. 1996); Ernest B. Furgurson, *Hard Right: The Rise of Jesse Helms* (1986); William D. Snider, *Helms and Hunt: The North Carolina Senate Race, 1984* (1985); John F. Stacks, "The Machine That Jesse Built," *Time* (14 Sept. 1981).

Ronnie W. Faulkner

National Guard. North Carolina has maintained a military force since the Revolutionary War. In 1877 its original militia was restructured into the North Carolina State Guard, headed by the adjutant general. This active militia consisted of volunteers who were regularly enlisted, uniformed, and equipped and could be called up at any time. During the Spanish-American War (1898), the State Guard was not subject to the president's call for troops, but the adjutant general supervised its reorganization to provide volunteers for the war effort. In 1903 the General Assembly changed the name of the State

Guard to the National Guard in conformity with a 1903 act of Congress.

On 3 June 1916 the power to mobilize the guard shifted from the governor to the president, and the National Guard was sent to the Mexican border under the command of Gen. John J. Pershing. In August 1917, with the U.S. entry into World War I, National Guard units nationwide were drafted into federal service in preparation for combat duty overseas. North Carolina governor Thomas W. Bickett, recognizing the need for a home military force to maintain peace and order, issued a proclamation on 23 Sept. 1917 calling up 5,000 persons from the unorganized militia. (Only in Winston-Salem, where a lynching was threatened, were the services of these troops actually required.) On the return of the National Guardsmen, the reserve militia was disbanded in 1918.

Camp Glenn, located in Carteret County about three miles west of Morehead City, was the permanent site of the Annual Encampment of the North Carolina National Guard from 1911 until the end of World War I. Named for Governor Robert B. Glenn, the facility was transferred to the U.S. Navy in 1918 and expanded into a regular naval air station. The camp was then turned over to the Coast Guard and became operational on 24 Mar. 1920 as the first Coast Guard Air Station in the nation. Camp Glenn was again occupied by the North Carolina National Guard from 1921 to 1941, when the U.S. Navy purchased part of the land for use as a section base during the war.

When the National Guard was called into active service during World War II, the General Assembly reestablished the State Guard to provide state militia. In June 1947, when the National Guard was released from federal service, the State Guard was deactivated.

In the early 2000s state and federal funds supported the National Guard in its mission to assist state and local authorities in disaster management and, in extreme cases, law enforcement. The guard could also be called up by the president to preserve national security. After 1947, when the Army Air Corps became the U.S. Air Force, the National Guard was divided into two components: the Army National Guard and the Air National Guard. In the early 2000s well over 11,000 people were members of the North Carolina National Guard, and many on active duty had served in Afghanistan and Iraq. On 29 Jan. 1988 Executive Order 65, issued by Governor James G. Martin, established the North Carolina State Defense Militia, within the Department of Crime Control and Public Safety, to assume the state functions of the North Carolina National Guard in the guard's absence.

References: F. Wilson Angley, *A Brief History of the North Carolina Militia and National Guard* (1985); E. Milton Wheeler, "Development and Organization of the North Carolina Militia," *NCHR* 41 (July 1964).

Wiley J. Williams
Additional research provided by Paul Branch and Jeffrey Allen Howard.

National Humanities Center. In September 1978, the National Humanities Center at Research Triangle Park admitted its first class of fellows. In keeping with its stated purpose—"to encourage scholarship in the humanities and to enhance the influence of the humanities in the United States"—the Humanities Center since that time has supported advanced study in history, languages and literature, philosophy, and other fields of the humanities. Each year, the Humanities Center selects about 40 fellows who are chosen in an open competition by a jury of scholars. Up to one-third of the fellowships go to scholars who are no more than ten years beyond receipt of their Ph.D. The center provides stipends, and each fellow has a study in which to write. The center also encourages the exchange of ideas at conversation over lunch or coffee, at conferences, and at interdisciplinary seminars, most of which have been conceived and organized by fellows. A library staff secures books for fellows from neighboring university libraries and other institutions and maintains a reference library. A 35-member board of trustees supervises the work of the National Humanities Center, which is carried on under the aegis of a director.

The National Humanities Center also produces a range of information. *Ideas*, a semiannual periodical, features essays by fellows; *Soundings*, the center's weekly radio interview program, is heard on more than 300 stations nationwide; and public lectures are given by fellows and visiting scholars. The center also sponsors summer institutes for faculty from 33 liberal arts colleges and for secondary school teachers from across the United States, and it has developed a pilot program for teachers at North Carolina high schools.

The idea for the National Humanities Center emerged from the experience of three distinguished humanists, Meyer Abrams of Cornell, Morton Bloomfield of Harvard, and Gregory Vlastos of Princeton, who were working together at the Center for Advanced Study in the Behavioral Sciences at Palo Alto during 1967–68. Impressed by the fruitful interchanges among scholars that took place at that institution, which largely catered to social scientists, they contemplated creating a similar center for humanists modeled on the one in California and on the Institute for Advanced Studies at Princeton. When the American Academy of Arts and Sciences approved the idea, a number of institutions aspired to become the site of the new center; but after considering 15 potential locations, the academy determined that the most attractive bid was from the Triangle Universities Center for Advanced Studies, Inc., a consortium of Duke University, the University of North Carolina at Chapel Hill, and North Carolina State University. This organization provided a valuable 15-acre site in Research Triangle Park and nearly $3 million for the construction of a building and toward the first five years of operation.

North Carolinians who played significant roles in launching the National Humanities Center included John Caldwell, William Friday, Dan Lacy, C. Hugh Holman, Vermont Royster, Terry Sanford, and, above all, Archie K. Davis. Davis, a Winston-Salem banker, made a major contribution in raising funds at the outset, within a month raising $1.5 million in pledges. In recognition of his role, the Humanities Center's building bears his name. Another North Carolinian, Claude McKinney, the dean of the College of Design at N.C. State, chaired the committee that supervised construction of the building, a much-admired edifice of white brick and glass designed by Hartman-Cox of Washington.

In the ensuing years, the main sources of funds for the Humanities Center have been foundations, especially the Andrew W. Mellon Foundation and the National Endowment for the Humanities. Money has also come from a number of other foundations, including the Research Triangle Foundation, as well as from corporations, the three area universities, and individual donors. The Rockefeller Foundation, the Delta Century Fund, the Ford Foundation, the MacArthur Foundation, the Olin Foundation, and the Jessie Ball duPont Foundation have also been important benefactors.

William E. Leuchtenburg

National Negro Business League was created by Booker T. Washington in 1900 to encourage black entrepreneurs in the United States. While one of the most visible aspects of the league was its national leadership and structure, its foundation actually was based on local chapters at the municipal level that came together to form state organizations. By 1915 there were local chapters in 24 North Carolina communities, most of which had more than 1,000 residents.

The league primarily attracted the elite among North Carolina black businessmen. The cost of individual membership in the league, and the fact that participation in black fraternal societies such as the Masons may have been more advantageous for black entrepreneurs, possibly discouraged many businessmen from joining. Prominent black businessmen who were leaders of the National Negro Business League in North Carolina included Richard Fitzgerald, owner of one of the state's largest brick-making firms; Berry O'Kelly, probably North Carolina's wealthiest black businessman during the early twentieth century; and Charles C. Spaulding, a director of the North Carolina Mutual Life Insurance Company.

Robert C. Kenzer

National Society of the Colonial Dames of America in the State of North Carolina, formerly called the North Carolina Society of the Colonial Dames, was the fourteenth state society added to the national organization founded in 1891. Membership is for women of lineal descent from residents of the American colonies before 1750 who rendered service to their country before 5 July 1776, including the signers of the Declaration of Independence. Forty states have these societies.

The North Carolina Society of the Colonial Dames was organized in 1894. Florence Wilson Hill Kidder was the founder and first president of the organization. The charter members were all residents of Wilmington. During the first decade of the twentieth century, other areas of North Carolina organized their own county or town committees of the North Carolina Society of Colonial Dames. Early on, marking historic sites became a primary goal of the statewide group. Under the leadership of Luola Murchison Sprunt, president from 1906 to 1912, the Colonial Dames compiled a list of 77 important sites in North Carolina, an early attempt to designate or register such places. Bronze tablets and granite markers commemorating important historical events began to appear throughout the state.

Gabrielle Moore deRosset Waddell, a society officer for 39 years, served as president from 1916 to 1935. During her tenure, the society began to award medals, loans, grants, and scholarships to worthy students of North Carolina history. It also began to generously support the publication of scholarly books, essays, and research concerning the history of the state. A sampling of books that have been supported by the Colonial Dames include *Journal of a Lady of Quality; Being the Narrative of a Journey from Scotland to the West Indies, North Carolina, and Portugal in the Years 1774 to 1776*, by Janet Schaw (1921); a reprint of *The Journal of Thomas Lawson—Gentleman* (1936); *The Early Architecture of North Carolina*, by Thomas T. Waterman (1941); and *The North Carolina Portrait Index, 1700–1860* (1963).

The society has also been actively involved in the historic preservation movement in North Carolina, giving generously to various restoration projects. Colonial Dames have preserved four important early North Carolina buildings. The Joel Lane House, built ca. 1760 and located in Raleigh, was acquired by the Colonial Dames in 1926. The Fourth House, built in 1772 and located in Winston-Salem, was purchased for preservation by the Colonial Dames in 1935. In 1937 they acquired the Burgwin-Wright House in Wilmington for their state headquarters. Built around 1770, it is one of the finest examples of Georgian architecture in the state. Haywood Hall, built around 1799 and located in Raleigh, was inherited by the Colonial Dames in 1977. The society continues to support the preservation of these buildings and makes them open for public tours.

Other activities of the Society of Colonial Dames include war relief efforts during both of the world wars; help for the needy during the Great Depression; assistance to the Red Cross; support of libraries, museums, and night schools; nursing scholarships for Native American women; scholarships and loans for gifted college students; and support of various social services. Members of the North Carolina society also support the activities of the National Society of the Colonial Dames, including the preservation of Dumbarton House, the national headquarters located in Washington, D.C.

Reference: Frances Sutherland Lee, *A History of The National Society of the Colonial Dames of America in the State of North Carolina, 1961–1994* (1994).

Beverly Tetterton

Nativism, or support for anti-immigrant discrimination, briefly emerged as a major political force in North Carolina and nationwide in the early 1850s. A lengthy economic depression in the previous decade reduced the number of available jobs and increased the intense economic competition between native-born workers and immigrant laborers who were often willing to work for lower wages. At the same time, the number of immigrants, especially from Ireland and the German states, rose sharply. During an era of intense anti-Catholicism in the United States, many Americans also suspected the existence of a plot, led by the pope and supported by largely Catholic immigrants, to undermine American democracy. Also, the newcomers tended to support the Democratic Party instead of the Whig Party, which was closely associated with Protestant reform movements. In addition to doubting whether the country could assimilate large numbers of immigrants and preserve its culture and institutions, many Whigs resented the newcomers as a source of strength to their political opponents. Although private nativist organizations had existed in the United States for some time, they began to grow and become more active due to these factors.

As the national Whig Party disintegrated in the early 1850s, the new nativist American (or Know-Nothing) Party formed and briefly threatened to constitute a legitimate second party in opposition to the Democrats. Former Whig leader Kenneth Rayner took the lead in organizing North Carolina's American Party in late 1854. Although members won several statewide offices and congressional seats, in 1858 divisions within the party and lackluster electoral results led North Carolina Know-Nothings to merge with Whigs into the short-lived Opposition Party. Nativism had run its course as a political force and would not again become a major public issue in North Carolina.

References: Gregg Cantrell, *Kenneth and John B. Rayner and the Limits of Southern Dissent* (1993); Michael F. Holt, *The Rise and Fall of the American Whig Party* (1999); W. Darrell Overdyke, *The Know-Nothing Party in the South* (1950).

Michael Thomas Smith

SEE ALSO American Party.

Natural Gardens of North Carolina (1932) was written by Bertram Whittier Wells, chair of the Department of Botany at North Carolina State College (modern-day North Carolina State University) from 1919 to 1949. Wells was a passionate conservationist and a pioneer in ecology, and his work significantly altered the study of wildflowers and native plants by looking at them within "natural gardens," or communities of plants located in certain areas. This approach, in which Wells describes the habitats of the gardens and then details the wildflowers growing there, was designed to support the idea of conservation of the plant communities. There are 11 major natural gardens in North Carolina mentioned in the book, designated the sand dune, the salt marsh, the freshwater marsh, the swamp forest, the aquatic vegetation, the evergreen shrub bog/pocosin, the grass-sedge bog/savanna, the sandhill, the old-field community, the upland forest, and the high mountain spruce-fir forest. A revised edition of *The Natural Gardens of North Carolina* was published by UNC Press in 2002.

Laura Hegyi

Natural Gas is an odorless, colorless mixture composed largely of methane that became in the twentieth century one of North Carolina's most important energy sources. The U.S. Department of Energy lists North Carolina as one of the states with no producing natural gas wells, and no proved underground reserves. The Southwest, primarily Texas and Louisiana, including the Gulf of Mexico, holds vast reserves. By 1900 natural gas had been discovered in 17 states, but without means of transportation, its use was limited. When found with oil or coal, the gas was often simply vented.

Some North Carolina cities acquired manufactured gas in the 1850s. Organization of the Wilmington Gas Light Company in 1854 brought gas streetlights to that city. Charlotte added gas streetlights in 1858, and that same year the Raleigh Gas Light Company lit the capital's streets. Gas fixtures went into buildings under construction, such as the Dorothea Dix Hospital. In January 1859 the General Assembly voted to install gas lights in the executive mansion.

In 1949 the Transcontinental Gas Pipeline Company (Transco) began constructing a 1,832-mile pipeline from production and storage fields in Texas to New York City. The pipeline ran through Piedmont North Carolina. When operation began in early 1951, vast quantities of natural gas became available for utilities to offer customers. In 1998 the Transco pipeline carried 957,525 million cubic feet of natural gas into North Carolina. Including 5,019 million cubic feet supplied from Virginia, a total of 240,980 million cubic feet went to North Carolina companies and families for power production, heating, cooling, cooking, and water heating. As a source of primary energy, natural gas ranked fourth in North Carolina, after petroleum, coal, and nuclear fuel. The state's average price for natural gas was higher than the national average, since all supplies were imported.

By the early 2000s, eight of the state's cities maintained a municipal gas system. Large distributors in the state included Duke Energy; Piedmont Natural Gas; Public Service Company of North Carolina, incorporated in 1938 and later a part of Scana Corporation; North Carolina Natural Gas Corporation, a subsidiary of Progress Energy; NUI–North Carolina Gas Service Division; and Frontier Utilities of North Carolina, Inc.

Barry McGee

Natural History of North-Carolina. First published in Dublin in 1737, John Brickell's *Natural History of North-Carolina* was ostensibly written from firsthand observations made by Brickell during his sojourn in North Carolina. The 408-page book contains abundant information on the flora, fauna, history, medical practices, and human cultures of the region, and many scholars have relied on it as an important primary source for the colonial period in North Carolina. As early as 1826, however, historians were warned that much of the content of Brickell's *Natural History* was a bold plagiarism, in which Brickell used a first-person account to relate observations and events taken from other publications.

The most important source of plagiarized material was John Lawson's *A New Voyage to Carolina* (1709), initially printed in London as part of John Stevens's *A New Collection of Voyages and Travels*. *A New Voyage* provided an estimated 85 percent of the text for Brickell's *Natural History*; not only was the organization of the *Natural History* copied from Lawson, but whole sections of text were lifted out of *A New Voyage* and transposed, often verbatim, into Brickell's work. Additional important sources included John Clayton's "Letters" to the Royal Society of London, which appeared in the *Philosophical Transactions* in 1693–94; Thomas Harriot's *A Briefe and True Report of the New Found Land of Virginia* (1588); and John Ray's *Ornithology of Francis Willughby*, produced by the Royal Society in 1678.

Brickell also borrowed from multiple sources for the copperplate illustrations of animals and plants that graced his book as well as for the state map, the latter being a version of Edward Moseley's "A New and Correct Map of the Province of North Carolina" (1733). Most of the bird and fish plates were taken from John Ray's *Ornithology of Francis Willughby* and *Historia Piscium*, respectively, while many other animal plates were borrowed from Edward Topsell's *The Historie of Fourefooted Beasts* and *The Historie of Serpents*. Plant illustrations were derived from John Gerard's *Herball* and Nicholás Monardes's *Primera y Segunda y Tercera*.

Although Brickell's plagiarisms have been extensively delineated, few substantiated details have emerged about his life. His family background, dates and places of birth and death, and circumstances of his medical training remain un-known. Brickell apparently lived in North Carolina at least from 1729 to 1731, served as physician to Governor Richard Everard, was a member of the North Carolina Grand Jury, and testified before a committee of the Irish House of Commons in 1735–36 after his return to Ireland.

References: Marcus B. Simpson Jr., "Copperplate Illustrations in Dr. John Brickell's *Natural History of North-Carolina* (1737): Sources for the Provincial Map, Flora, and Fauna," *NCHR* 62 (April 1985); Simpson, "Dr. John Brickell's *Catalogue of American Trees and Shrubs* (1739): A Bibliographic Misadventure," *Archives of Natural History* 21 (1994).

Marcus B. Simpson Jr.

Natural Walls in Rowan County, freshly exposed from subterranean sites by heavy rains in the summer of 1794, sparked widespread interest at home and abroad. They were discovered near Second Creek and South Yadkin River at several places ranging between three and nine miles east of the town of Salisbury. They appeared to be laid in a straight line. The top of the most fully exposed wall seemed to be made of stones carefully cut into blocks, fitted and held together by mortar of various colors. The wall measured about 22 inches wide at the top, slightly wider at the bottom, and 12 to 14 feet high. Locally, the material was called "black whin," and people who saw portions of the wall concluded that it had been laid by prehistoric people whom they called mound builders.

By 1881 the true nature of the wall was known, although at various times throughout the next century newspapers continued to repeat the old beliefs. The wall was formed naturally of traprock, which is found in a dozen North Carolina counties. It originated as magma of volcanic origin and consists of basalt, diabase, and gabbro, identified by Jasper L. Stuckey, state geologist, as including "dense, dark-colored, and fine-grained igneous rocks" that form distinctive joints on cooling.

References: Jethro Rumple, *A History of Rowan County, North Carolina* (1881); Jasper L. Stuckey, *North Carolina: Its Geology and Mineral Resources* (1965).

William S. Powell

Nature Conservancy, with headquarters in Arlington, Va., is a national organization working for land conservation and the preservation of biodiversity. North Carolina's chapter, the North Carolina Nature Conservancy, was started in 1977. Headquartered in Durham, the organization had 27,000 members by the early 2000s. Well known for its purchases of ecologically important areas, the Nature Conservancy uses a wide array of conservation tools, from conservation easements that allow private landowners to protect their property to the negotiation of innovative agreements with private companies and government agencies. The conservancy's work has led to the

The Black River in Pender County, home to 1,700-year-old cypress trees identified as the oldest living trees east of the Rocky Mountains, is among the North Carolina habitats protected by the Nature Conservancy. This 1986 photograph shows one of the old-growth trees. Photograph by Frederick W. Annand.

the Sandhills, the lower Cape Fear River valley, the upper Tar River, the Roanoke River valley, and the Green Swamp–Boiling Springs Wetlands.

Reference: Ida Phillips Lynch, *North Carolina Afield: A Guide to Nature Conservancy Projects in North Carolina* (2002).

Bland Simpson

Nature's Sample Case has long been a term applied to North Carolina because of its more than 300 native rocks and minerals, such as iron, limestone, gold, emeralds, sapphires, and moonstones. More than 70 have economic value and about 50 have been mined or quarried in commercial quantities. The North Carolina Geological and Economic Survey published a series of bulletins—begun in 1893 and continuing into the twenty-first century—about geology, mineralogy, and geography, including significant reports on the sources, quality, and conservation of water.

The state proved to be a valuable source of scarce and important natural resources during World War II. With the assistance of the U.S. Bureau of Mines, both tungsten and manganese were discovered, and more than 400 mines of various kinds were opened and operated. A research library was established at North Carolina State University to be of use in identifying, planning for, and preserving the state's mineral resources.

References: North Carolina Department of Conservation and Development, Information Bulletin No. 137, *North Carolina, Nature's "Sample Case" of Gems* (1964); William S. Powell, *North Carolina through Four Centuries* (1989).

Alex Coffin

Naval Section Bases were small naval bases established by the U.S. Navy on the North Carolina coast prior to and during World War II for coastal patrol and antisubmarine defense. In 1940–41, when it became increasingly evident that the United States would be forced to enter the conflict, the federal government initiated massive programs of military buildup and preparedness. Among these programs, the section base was to function as part of the navy's Inshore Patrol, providing the administrative and operational facilities for small naval or Coast Guard vessels engaged in local harbor defense, coastal patrol, and minesweeping. In 1941 two section bases were authorized, for Morehead City and Southport; in 1942 a third was approved for Ocracoke.

The site for the Morehead Naval Section Base was a 58-acre tract, purchased by the navy in 1941 for $15,000, within Camp Glenn on Bogue Sound just west of Morehead City. Construction began on 14 November. The base consisted of a two-story, multiwinged building housing the administrative offices, mess hall, and barracks; additional barracks; ma-

creation of more than 1,400 nature preserves nationwide, enjoyed by many thousands of visitors each year. The preserve system includes over 100,000 acres in North Carolina, with Bat Cave, Bluff Mountain, and the Roanoke River being among the state's most popular preserves.

By 2004 the North Carolina Nature Conservancy had protected and preserved over 545,000 acres of critical lands in the state. Some of its most prized projects to date include Bluff Mountain in Ashe County, Green Swamp in Brunswick and Columbus Counties, the Black River corridor, Alligator River National Wildlife Refuge, the longleaf pine stand at Weymouth Woods, the hardwood swamps of the Roanoke River bottomlands, and the maritime forest and dunes at Nags Head Woods in Dare County. The North Carolina Nature Conservancy's campaign, Forever Wild: A Campaign to Save the Last Great Places in North Carolina, initiated in the early 2000s, has sought $25 million toward purchasing large acreage in the New River's mountain headwaters, Hickory Nut Gorge, chine and repair shops; a medical facility; a heating plant; and other buildings. In a remote area north of the post were eight concrete magazines for the storage of ammunition, depth charges, and explosives. A pier with two extensions accommodated up to eight patrol vessels and subchasers. The base, costing more than $1 million, was located about five miles from the entrance to Beaufort Inlet and the Atlantic Ocean.

Although incomplete, the Morehead base was formally commissioned on 17 Mar. 1942, with the German U-boat offensive along the North Carolina coast well under way. It quickly became the most important reception and processing center on the North Carolina coast for the survivors of sunken or damaged merchant ships. Over the course of the war, both U.S. Navy and Coast Guard personnel used the base, whose primary duty was to serve the vessels patrolling the coast for German U-boats. Navy patrol craft, Coast Guard cutters, and other boats operated from the base in conjunction with larger vessels at the State Port in Morehead City and the Fort Macon Coast Guard Station on Bogue Banks. They aided in minesweeping and in maintaining a submarine net across the entrance to the ship channel in Beaufort Inlet. The base was also available to supply ammunition, make small-scale repairs, and provide refitting.

The need for the base diminished after the summer of 1942, when U-boat attacks off the North Carolina coast became infrequent. It was designated a Naval Frontier Base on 15 Mar. 1944 and was disestablished on 30 June 1944. After the war, the base was declared surplus property and authorized for disposal. In the fall of 1946 North Carolina bought the property on which to build a marine fisheries research institute through its Division of Commercial Fisheries of the Department of Conservation and Development. By the early 2000s, the North Carolina Institute of Marine Sciences occupied the land.

On 17 Nov. 1941 the U.S. Navy also purchased the old Fort Caswell Military Reservation near Southport for use as a section base for the Inshore Patrol. Almost $1 million was appropriated to make the Fort Caswell Naval Section Base operational, build docking facilities, and adapt the reservation's original buildings. Operations began in early 1942. From the base's docks in the Cape Fear River, various patrol boats, Coast Guard vessels, armed yachts and fishing boats, and minesweepers guarded the coast off Cape Fear and Frying Pan Shoals from German U-boats. At the end of the war the Navy Department retained the base for several years with the intention of adapting it for other uses. It sold the property to the North Carolina Baptist State Convention in 1949.

The U.S. Naval Section Base at Ocracoke began operations in May–June 1942 with construction of the Hatteras Minefield, a ring of contact mines laid in an irregular arc offshore from Cape Hatteras to Ocracoke enclosing a protected anchorage for merchant ships. The base itself consisted of a large, two-story administrative building and barracks, a hospital, and various support facilities. Three large piers were built into Silver Lake, which was dredged to shelter Coast Guard and navy patrol craft. By the time the base was formally commissioned on 9 Oct. 1942, its original purpose had ceased to exist, as the Hatteras Minefield proved too difficult to maintain. When five friendly ships were sunk or damaged after entering the minefield by mistake, it was discontinued.

The Ocracoke facility continued to operate as a base for navy and Coast Guard vessels on antisubmarine patrol. In 16 Jan. 1944, with the U-boat menace significantly diminished, it became an Amphibious Training Base, and in 1945 it operated as a Combat Information Center. The base was decommissioned at the end of the war, and eventually most of the buildings were torn down, although the adjacent Coast Guard station remained open. On 31 Mar. 1952, by congressional act (HR 4974), the land containing the base was transferred to the National Park Service as part of the Cape Hatteras National Seashore.

References: Paolo E. Coletta, *United States Navy and Marine Corps Bases—Domestic* (1985); Ethel Herring and Carolee Williams, *Fort Caswell in War and Peace* (1983).

Paul Branch

SEE ALSO National Guard.

Naval Stores. North Carolina's production of naval stores —tar, pitch, and turpentine, all products of the pine tree— began in the 1720s and declined as a major industry by the Civil War. The abundance of pine trees in North Carolina and England's dependence on seagoing vessels made naval stores an essential commodity in the colony's economy. Great Britain even offered a bounty for naval stores, encouraging the growth of the industry. With a multitude of longleaf pines, the Cape Fear Valley, especially the region made up of present-day Harnett and Cumberland Counties, was the location of most naval stores production. Settlers in this region extracted sap from pine trees, collecting it in barrels. These barrels were placed on flatboats made of logs and transported down the Cape Fear River to Wilmington. By 1768 North Carolina accounted for 60 percent of the naval stores produced in the colonies.

The nineteenth century saw further expansion in the industry, with a resurgence beginning in the 1830s and continuing through the 1850s. In 1840 North Carolina produced 95.9 percent of all naval stores in the United States. In 1847 *De Bow's Review* reported that the state produced 800,000 barrels of turpentine, with an estimated market value of $1.7 to $2 million. The industry employed almost 5,000 laborers and had 150 processing stills. By the late 1850s naval stores became the South's third-largest export crop. This growth was further spurred by the completion of the Wilmington & Weldon Railroad in 1840

North Carolina turpentine distillery, 1884. NCC.

and the North Carolina Railroad, running from Goldsboro to Charlotte, in 1856, which extended transportation routes into the interior of the pine forest regions.

Because naval stores production was labor intensive, slave labor was crucial to its success. Slaves were used especially in the winter months, and conditions tended to be much harsher than in plantation agriculture because of the solitary and migratory nature of the work. On occasion slaves resisted their harsh treatment by running away or by setting fires in the forest so that turpentine could not be collected.

After the Civil War, the naval stores industry declined in North Carolina. This decline is attributed to several factors: the burning of some large pine forests by Union general William T. Sherman's troops decreased the amount of turpentine produced for a time; iron vessels eventually replaced wooden sailing ships, causing a reduction in demand for the industry's products; and, finally, synthetic solvents began to be used to thin paints, diminishing the need for turpentine.

The phrase "Tar Heel," the nickname for North Carolinians and the state itself, possibly originated from the fact that people working around turpentine stills often got tar on the soles of their shoes, allegedly helping them "stick" to their assigned jobs.

References: Robert B. Outland III, "Slavery, Work, and the Geography of the North Carolina Naval Stores Industry, 1835–1860," *Journal of Southern History* 62 (February 1996); Veronica Bever Platt, "Tar, Slaves, and New England Rum: The Trade of Aaron Lopez of Newport, Rhode Island, with Colonial North Carolina," NCHR 48 (January 1971); Justin Williams, "English Mercantilism and Carolina Naval Stores, 1705–1776," *Journal of Southern History* 1 (May 1935).

Lloyd Johnson

Navigation Acts (1651, 1660) were acts of Parliament intended to promote the self-sufficiency of the British Empire by restricting colonial trade to England and decreasing dependence on foreign imported goods. The Navigation Act of 1651, aimed primarily at the Dutch, required all trade between England and the colonies to be carried in English or colonial vessels, resulting in the Anglo-Dutch War in 1652. The Navigation Act of 1660 continued the policies set forth in the 1651 act and enumerated certain articles—sugar, tobacco, cotton, wool, indigo, and ginger—that were to be shipped only to England or an English province. In effect, these acts created serious reductions in the trade of many North Carolina planters and merchants. To continue intercolonial trade, the colonies resorted to smuggling, particularly Albemarle County in North Carolina, the chief producer and exporter of tobacco, which carried on a profitable trade with the Massachusetts and Rhode Island colonies. The violations of the Navigation Acts led to passage of the Plantation Duty Act of 1673, one of the factors that led to Culpeper's Rebellion.

Barrels filled with pine resin being loaded on a German ship at the port of Wilmington in the early 1870s. NCC.

References: Oscar T. Barck and Hugh T. Lefler, *Colonial America* (1965); Lefler and William S. Powell, *Colonial North Carolina: A History* (1973); Hugh F. Rankin, *Upheaval in Albemarle: The Story of Culpeper's Rebellion, 1675–1689* (1962).

Carmen Miner Smith

Navigation Companies. SEE Albemarle Steam Navigation Company; Cape Fear and Deep River Steam Navigation Company; Deep and Haw River Navigation Company; Neuse River Navigation Company; North Carolina Catawba Company; Tar River Navigation Company; Yadkin River Navigation Company.

Negro Head Road was originally the colonial stage road that ran from Point Peter in New Hanover County to Duplin County. It began at the junction of the Cape Fear River and the Northeast Cape Fear River, just opposite the city of Wilmington. It followed the west side of the Northeast Cape Fear, through present-day Pender County, and into Duplin County. Point Peter was also known as Negro Head Point as early as 1760.

Shortly after the Nat Turner Rebellion in Southampton County, Va., in August 1831, a similar slave revolt was suspected in southeastern North Carolina. In Duplin County a slave called Dave, who belonged to Sheriff Thomas K. Morrisey, was tortured until he confessed to being a ringleader of a planned slave revolt. A report issued by the Duplin justices of the peace on 13 Sept. 1831 claimed that Dave and his coconspirators planned to march to Wilmington, killing white landowners on the way. In Wilmington they planned to rendezvous with an armed force of 2,000 more slaves and free blacks. Fearful whites reacted by seizing Dave and his alleged accomplice Jim. The two men were killed and their heads stuck on poles as a warning to other slaves.

In Wilmington, 15 blacks were arrested. The 6 who were tried and convicted were killed; their heads, too, wound up on poles at several entrances to the city. One was placed at Point Peter at the beginning of Negro Head Road. As late as 1940, the *WPA Guide to North Carolina* referred to U.S. 117 as "Negro Head Road."

Reference: Charles Edward Morris, "Panic and Reprisal: Reaction in North Carolina to the Nat Turner Insurrection, 1831," *NCHR* 62 (January 1985).

Beverly Tetterton

Neuse, css. In October 1862 the Confederate navy commissioned the building of the ironclad gunboat css *Neuse* to strengthen southern defenses and prevent Union occupation of the sounds and rivers of North Carolina. One of 22 ironclad warships commissioned by the Confederacy, the *Neuse* was designed by naval contractor John L. Porter and built by Howard and Ellis, shipbuilders of New Bern. It was constructed near the town of Whitehall (now Seven Springs) on the Neuse River, for which it was named. A sister ship, the css *Albemarle*, was built simultaneously on the Roanoke River. The ironclad concept had been proven in the battle between the uss *Monitor*

and css *Virginia* at Hampton Roads in the spring of 1862. Construction of these superior, armored floating batteries with a built-on ram was intended to reduce the advantage of the much larger U.S. Navy's fleet of warships.

On 22 Apr. 1864, in an attempt to navigate downstream and retake the town of New Bern from Union forces, the recently completed *Neuse* ran aground on a sandbar one-half mile below Kinston. It remained stuck there for almost a month. During this period, its support troops were transferred from Kinston to Virginia, preventing a second attempt to retake New Bern when the *Neuse* was finally freed. On 12 Mar. 1865, as the Confederacy was collapsing, Cdr. Joseph Price, on orders from Gen. Braxton Bragg, ordered his crew to shell advancing enemy cavalry and then burn the *Neuse* to prevent its capture. Before fire consumed the vessel, a loaded gun discharged and blew a hole in the *Neuse*, which sank rapidly. Shortly after the war, machinery and armor were salvaged from the *Neuse*. After settling on the river bottom, it lay undisturbed except for shifting sands and slight exposure during periods of low water until 1961.

Driven by curiosity and a rumor that a barrel of gold could be found on the old gunboat, three Kinston men began a salvage project that lasted until June 1963. By the time the *Neuse* was cut into three sections and transported five miles to Governor Caswell Park in Kinston, a great number of citizens, groups, clubs, and political leaders, including the governor of North Carolina, had contributed in some way to the recovery of the *Neuse*. Artifacts and hull remains are on display at the css *Neuse* State Historic Site and Governor Richard Caswell Memorial in Kinston.

References: Leslie S. Bright, William H. Rowland, and James C. Bardon, *C.S.S. Neuse: A Question of Iron and Time* (1981); William N. Still Jr., *Confederate Shipbuilding* (1987); Still, *Iron Afloat: The Story of the Confederate Armorclads* (1985).

Leslie S. Bright

Neuse, css, State Historic Site and Governor Richard Caswell Memorial. The css *Neuse* State Historic Site and Governor Richard Caswell Memorial, located on U.S. Business 70 in Kinston, is administered as a single 46-acre tract, although it commemorates two unrelated historical events from different centuries. One features the hulk of the css *Neuse*, a Civil War gunboat constructed by the Confederacy in 1865 in a vain effort to recapture New Bern from Union forces. The ironclad gunboat, built alongside the Neuse River, failed in its objective because it was too large, the river was too shallow at the time, and the enemy threatened to capture it. Scuttled by its builders, the *Neuse* sank to the bottom of the river, from which it was recovered in 1963. Now located beside the river and protected by an overhead shelter, the keel is preserved as an interesting relic. Adjacent at this historic site is a visitors center with informative displays and artifacts from the boat.

Remains of the hull of the ironclad css *Neuse* on display at the css *Neuse* State Historic Site in Kinston. North Carolina Department of Cultural Resources, Historic Sites Division.

Nearby is the other featured portion of this site: the family cemetery in which Governor Richard Caswell (1729–89) is buried. In a separate building there are exhibits on Caswell as a colonial official, a Revolutionary War officer, and the first governor of North Carolina as an independent state.

References: Clayton Brown Alexander, "Public Career of Richard Caswell" (Ph.D. diss., UNC-Chapel Hill, 1930); Leslie S. Bright, William H. Rowland, and James C. Barden, *C.S.S. Neuse: A Question of Iron and Time* (1981); Richard F. Knapp, ed., *North Carolina's State Historic Sites: A Brief History and Status Report* (1995).

G. Eugene Brown

Neuse River is formed in western Durham County by the junction of the Eno and Flat Rivers. It flows southeast along the Durham County–Granville County and Durham County–Wake County lines, eventually passing through Wake, Johnston, Wayne, Lenoir, and Craven Counties. The river then flows along the border between Craven and Pamlico Counties and Carteret and Pamlico Counties before draining into Pamlico Sound.

The Neuse River was named by English explorer Arthur Barlowe in 1584 for the Neusiok (meaning "peace") Indians; the Tuscarora Indians called it *Gow-ta-no*, or "pine in water." The river's entire 195-mile length is encompassed by North Carolina; the size of its watershed measures 6,235 square miles. In addition to flowing through seven counties, the Neuse River Basin encompasses 73 municipalities, including Durham, Kinston, Goldsboro, Smithfield, Raleigh, and New Bern. In the early 2000s the region had a population of more than 1.2 million.

The Neuse River has faced various environmental threats, most notably hog waste. Groups such as the Neuse River Foundation continue to work with government and other private groups to ensure the health of the river. Many ancient artifacts have been discovered on the shores and in the waters of the Neuse River, the most notable being the CSS *Neuse*, built by the Confederate navy, which was burned and sunk in 1865. The remains of the ship were raised in 1963 and are now on display at the Governor Caswell Memorial in Kinston, a North Carolina State Historic Site.

Reference: Chris Powell, "The Fight for the River of Peace," *Wildlife in North Carolina* 63 (November 1999).

Elizabeth Bayley

Neuse River Navigation Company, incorporated by statute in 1812 and capitalized at $50,000, superseded several previous organizations and had the right to clear the Neuse River from the head of navigation to Crabtree Creek and to charge a toll for its efforts. The company began to sell stock in 1813, elected former governor and U.S. senator David Stone as its president, and mapped the river in 1814. An 1816 amendment to the earlier law offered a state stock subscription of $6,000 and permitted the company to clear the river from its source to Fort Barnwell near New Bern and to construct a toll road from the river to Raleigh.

From the beginning, Neuse River Navigation suffered setbacks, including Stone's death in 1818. The following year John D. DeLacy, who had been hired to open the Neuse from Stone's Mill above Smithfield to New Bern within six months for boats of 7 tons (and within three years for boats of 14 tons), apparently defaulted on his contract. Even with a new president—federal district court judge Henry Potter—and efforts in 1819 by Hamilton Fulton, the state's civil engineer, and his assistant Robert H. B. Brazier to examine and survey the Neuse and by stockholders to determine the best building plans and estimate costs, little progress was made.

In 1823 the General Assembly ended the state's subscription to stock in the company until it could determine the legality of its organization and until the company agreed to place its operations under the management of the Board of Internal Improvements—a stipulation that the firm would not accept. As a result, the state bought only $1,800 worth of stock. In 1825 the legislature reduced the scope of the company's operations, and by 1834 the Board of Internal Improvements reported that Neuse River Navigation "has long since ceased to act as a corporation and there appears to be no disposition to revive its existence."

The incorporation of the North Carolina Railroad in 1849 prompted the General Assembly in 1851 to incorporate another Neuse Navigation Company, giving it control of the river from Watson's Landing above Smithfield to New Bern and promising to invest in stock. The town of New Bern was particularly enthusiastic, subscribing in 1852 to $50,000 worth of stock in the company. After undertaking some work toward improving the navigability of the river, the company exhausted its funds and looked to the town to pay its promised subscription.

In 1854, however, New Bern offered bonds worth $15,000 rather than cash, and the company divided, with the majority of the stockholders in favor of rejecting the bonds. Later improvement plans in New Bern and Craven County also included subscriptions worth $150,000 in bonds to the Atlantic & North Carolina Railroad, but the majority of the stockholders in the navigation company again rejected any New Bern subscription not paid in full and in cash. The Neuse Navigation Company subsequently ceased to exist.

References: William B. Thompson, *Report upon the Survey of the Neuse River: Together with Plans and Estimates for the Improvement of the Same* (1852); Charles C. Weaver, *Internal Improvements in North Carolina Previous to 1860* (1903).

Alan D. Watson

New Bern, Battle of. The Civil War battle at New Bern occurred on 14 Mar. 1862 between the Union forces of Maj. Gen. Ambrose E. Burnside and Confederate troops under Brig. Gen. Lawrence O. Branch. In February 1862 Burnside had swept across the northeastern sound region of the North Carolina coast with a powerful amphibious force of about 13,000 soldiers on transports, supported by army and navy gunboats, in a campaign that has become known as the "Burnside Expedition." On 12 March his fleet advanced up the Neuse River, carrying about 11,000 soldiers, with the intention of capturing New Bern, an important coastal trade center and the second largest town in North Carolina.

On 13 March Burnside's troops landed on the riverbank at Slocum's Creek, near Havelock, and began their advance. At New Bern, General Branch had no more than 4,000 soldiers at his disposal to man a series of prepared defenses. The town's river defenses included lines of river obstructions and a chain of forts (Lane, Ellis, Allen, Thompson, and Dixie) on the west bank of the Neuse extending six miles below the town. Two lines of entrenchments protected the land approaches along the west bank: the Croatan Works and the Thompson Works. Branch concentrated his limited forces at the Thompson Works, the least exposed of the two. This strong entrenched line was anchored on the river bank by Fort Thompson (mounting 13 guns) and extended west one mile to the Atlantic & North Carolina Railroad. However, the Confederates were unable to fill a 150-yard gap in the line before the Union attack.

Branch placed in the trenches between Fort Thompson and the railroad, from left to right, the 27th, 37th, 7th, and 35th North Carolina Regiments and a local militia battalion—all supported by two field batteries. The 26th North Carolina extended the line westward beyond the railroad, and the 33rd North Carolina was held in reserve.

At about 7:30 A.M. on 14 March, Burnside's advancing Union forces, supported by gunboats on the river, moved in front of the Confederate lines to begin the battle. Burnside placed his First Brigade on the right between the river and the railroad, the Second Brigade west of the railroad, and the Third Brigade in reserve behind the two. The First and Second Brigades made little progress against the Confederate works, but part of the Second Brigade soon found the gap in the Confederate line and promptly broke through east of the railroad into the rear of the Confederate trenches, surprising the green battalion of North Carolina militia. The militiamen broke in confusion, taking with them the next regiment, the 35th North Carolina.

As Federals charged down behind the Confederate trenches, the next Confederate regiment, the 7th North Carolina, recoiled and counterattacked with a portion of the 37th North Carolina. This force drove out the Union troops and briefly reestablished the Confederate line. Meanwhile, Burn-side's Third Brigade had formed for battle. Its attack broke through the same gap in the Confederate line just recently reestablished. The assault of these fresh troops overwhelmed the Confederates, who abandoned the works and retreated toward New Bern, evacuating the river forts as they went. Unaware of the retreat, the 26th and 33rd North Carolina were almost cut off. They only escaped by crossing the swamps to the west, leaving a portion of the 33rd North Carolina and its commander in Federal hands.

New Bern was evacuated, and the pursuing Union forces took possession. Union losses were 90 killed, 380 wounded, and 1 missing, whereas the Confederates lost 64 killed, 101 wounded, and 413 captured or missing. Held by the Union for the remainder of the war, New Bern became the largest Federal stronghold in eastern North Carolina. Confederate forces made three unsuccessful attempts to retake the town.

References: John G. Barrett, *The Civil War in North Carolina* (1963); John S. Carbone, *The Civil War in Coastal North Carolina* (2001); William Marvel, *Burnside* (1991).

Paul Branch

New Bern, Confederate Expeditions against. The Union capture of New Bern in March 1862 was a severe blow to the Confederacy. The second-largest town in North Carolina and an important railroad and river trade center, New Bern became a base for Union raids against railroads and communications in the interior. The Confederates attempted to recover the town three times: in March 1863, February 1864, and May 1864.

The first expedition was in concert with operations in southeastern Virginia intended to put Union forces on the defensive in eastern North Carolina. The goal was to recapture New Bern or at least contain its Union defenders in order to gather supplies and provisions from adjacent areas. In March 1863 Maj. Gen. Daniel H. Hill attacked New Bern with 13,000 Confederate troops. Maj. Gen. John G. Foster, commanding at New Bern, held the town with a greatly reduced force. Hill's plan included a siege of heavy cannon firing from the north, an infantry assault from the southwest, and a cavalry advance to cut the Atlantic & North Carolina Railroad in order to isolate the New Bern garrison.

On the afternoon of 13 March, Hill's men overran a Union outpost at Deep Gully, eight miles southwest of New Bern. The next morning, Brig. Gen. James J. Pettigrew's cannons opened fire on both Fort Anderson and Union gunboats in the river. But the Confederates could neither significantly damage the fort nor drive off the gunboats, which bombarded them from far out on the river. Accordingly, Pettigrew abandoned the attempt and retired along the same route on which he had advanced. Because Pettigrew's success was essential to the operation, Hill had no choice but to withdraw. Despite his failure to recapture New Bern, Hill turned his attention to a similar operation against Washington, N.C., two weeks later.

Command of the second expedition to recapture New Bern was given to Maj. Gen. George E. Pickett, who assembled 13,000 Confederates at Kinston in late January 1864. Pickett divided his force into three columns, which were to converge on the town from three directions: from the north bank of the Neuse River to capture Fort Anderson, from the south bank of the Neuse to seize the Union works there, and directly from Kinston. Meanwhile, Confederate troops would prevent the arrival of Union reinforcements from Morehead City and capture Union gunboats on the Neuse. Approximately 5,500 Union soldiers, led by Brig. Gen. Innis N. Palmer, defended New Bern, sheltering behind formidable earthworks and forts ringing the town.

When the attack was launched on 1 February, Confederate forces dispatched to the north and south banks of the Neuse found the Union defenses impregnable. Advancing from Kinston, Pickett halted before the powerful line of defensive forts and works ringing the city's western side. His column was not strong enough to carry the works alone, and he was unable to bring another column around to join him in time for a frontal assault. Pickett was thus compelled to abandon the entire operation and return to Kinston. Although the prize of New Bern eluded them, the Confederates captured and destroyed the Union gunboat *Underwriter* and destroyed the Union base at Newport Barracks before their advance on Morehead City was interrupted.

The third and final Confederate assault on New Bern, in May 1864, was commanded by Maj. Gen. Robert F. Hoke. He planned to attack the town's defenses from both land and water with the cooperation of the Confederate ironclad rams *Albemarle* and *Neuse*. Although the *Neuse* was still unfinished, it was thought that the mere presence of the rams would neutralize any threat from Union naval vessels defending the town.

On 4–5 May 1864 Hoke's forces overran Union outposts on the north and south banks of the Trent River and cut the Atlantic & North Carolina Railroad. Hoke then demanded that New Bern surrender, but the Union commander, General Palmer, refused. Further, Hoke's naval support failed to materialize. The *Neuse* hopelessly ran aground a short distance from its berth at Kinston, and the *Albemarle* was severely damaged by Union gunboats in Albemarle Sound on 5 May and had to return to Plymouth for repairs.

Soon afterward, Hoke received orders to abandon operations against New Bern immediately and transfer his command by rail to Virginia, where various Union forces had begun offensives against Richmond and other targets.

References: John G. Barrett, *The Civil War in North Carolina* (1963); John S. Carbone, *The Civil War in Coastal North Carolina* (2001).

Paul Branch

New Bern Academy was established in March 1764 when the North Carolina legislature authorized the town of New Bern to build "a House for a school and Residence for the School Master" and appointed seven men as trustees. Work on the new building began in 1765, and by April 1767 John Whiting, a visitor from Newport, R.I., reported that New Bern had "a very large & handsome school house." Closely tied to the Anglican Church, though not a parochial school, "the Public School in New Bern" quickly earned a reputation as "one of the best regulated schools of the kind in America."

The school suffered a period of decline, however, and in 1784 it was reorganized by the legislature. The new plan, which included the first specific use of the name "Newbern Academy," did not refer to the institution as a public school, open without charge to poor students, nor did it mention any connection with the Anglican Church. The legislature did provide the academy with several lots in New Bern, the income from which functioned as an endowment. When its original frame building was destroyed by fire in 1795, the school was moved to temporary quarters. Leaders convinced the legislature to authorize the raising of money for a new schoolhouse, and in 1810 the academy moved into a handsome new brick building. John Alonzo Attmore introduced the Lancasterian system of education to New Bern Academy in 1814; this system, which required older pupils to tutor younger ones, remained a feature of the academy until the 1850s, when the school once again fell into decline. The Civil War and Reconstruction prolonged the school's hard times.

Financial problems continued to plague New Bern Academy until 1882, when it was reestablished as a graded school —an approach then new in the United States—and began receiving funds from Craven County. The following year the legislature recognized this new form of school organization and allowed the imposition of specific taxes to support schools divided into grades. Attendance increased to the point that additional space was required. In 1885 a second building joined the 1810 structure. Two others were later added.

Just as the academy's problems appeared to be resolved, the North Carolina Supreme Court declared, in *Riggsbee v. the Town of Durham*, that the levying of municipal taxes to support private graded schools was unconstitutional. In 1899 New Bern Academy ceased to function independently and became part of the city school system. All the academy buildings continued to serve as schools until 1971, when the New Bern school board decommissioned the 1810 building. By 1977 none of the original New Bern Academy structures were used as schools.

Because of the academy's rich past and because the 1810 building was such an impressive structure, in 1975 the legislature created the New Bern Academy Historical Commission and charged it with preserving the school's history and original building. The building's restoration was completed

New Bern Academy, ca. 1864. NCC.

in 1985, and in December 1991 it opened as the New Bern Academy Museum. The Tryon Palace Commission operates the museum.

References: Mary Ellen Gadski, *The History of the New Bern Academy* (1986); Alan D. Watson, *A History of New Bern and Craven County* (1987).

Thomas J. Farnham

New Bern Benevolent Society traces its roots to the 1812 founding of the New Bern Female Charitable Society, the first benevolent society incorporated in North Carolina. The society was formed to offer relief to the poor and to educate poor female children. According to an 1823 financial report, the society brought in $324.50 that year, earning most of the money from the sale of manufactured articles. Expenditures amounted to $240.31, with the majority of that used to employ poor women.

The society reorganized in 1837 and was chartered in 1854,

changing its name to the New Bern Female Benevolent Society. The name of the organization eventually evolved into the New Bern Benevolent Society. In 1953 the New Bern Benevolent Society built the Enoch Wadsworth Memorial Home to provide a home for elderly women on limited incomes. Funds for the building of the Wadsworth Home came in part from a trust fund left by Mrs. Enoch Wadsworth in her will. By the early 2000s the New Bern Benevolent Society had decreased to fewer than 20 members, mostly representatives from local Catholic, Protestant, and Jewish groups.

Victor T. Jones Jr.

Newbold-White House, located near Hertford in Perquimans County on the west bank of the Perquimans River adjacent to the Albemarle Sound, is one of North Carolina's oldest examples of colonial architecture. The house served as an important meeting place for the state's Quaker congregations as well as a center for governmental courts and assemblies. It stands as a unique link to North Carolina's Proprietary period.

Newbold-White House. Photograph by Tim Buchman. Courtesy of Preservation North Carolina.

A construction date of 1730 has been given to the brick house based on dendrochronology tests of the rafter timbers. The pre-Georgian architecture of the building and available deed records indicated that a late seventeenth-century occupation period is plausible. While the extant house dates to the early eighteenth century, archaeological features and land records suggest a previous dwelling on the tract. A land grant from the Lords Proprietors to Joseph Scott for 640 acres included this tract of land and house site. Personal journals of Quaker missionary George Fox describe a meeting with Joseph Scott and his neighbors at his home in 1672. Later Scott, along with his family and neighbors, established their own Quaker congregation.

Following the death of his first wife, Scott married Mary Hudson in 1683. Until her death in 1692, Mary Hudson Scott opened her home as a meeting place for Quaker congregations and for sessions of the county precinct court and assembly. James Coles and his wife, Mary, bought the land in 1703 and continued to hold court sessions at the farm. The property was sold at auction in 1726 and was bought by Abraham Saunders, a Quaker and planter. Saunders most likely built the one-and-one-half-story brick dwelling that later came to be known as the Newbold-White House. The name Newbold-White derived from its last two private owners, Jim Woodward White and John Henry Newbold. The Perquimans County Restoration As-

sociation, Inc., purchased the house in 1973 with the intention of preserving it as a historic site.

Archaeological research on the Newbold-White House began in 1970 and continued intermittently until 1994. Findings include a cemetery, cellar, outbuildings, and thousands of domestic-related artifacts dating from the seventeenth to nineteenth centuries. For archaeologists, the site offers valuable information into the material culture of early English settlement in North Carolina.

For architects and historians, the house is an interpretative jewel of the early eighteenth century. A simple, rectangular structure, the house measures 20 by 40 feet, with a steep gabled roof framed by common rafters and end chimneys. Oriented lengthwise to the river, it has central doors on each front and small, segmented-arched windows. It conforms to a hall-parlor plan, having two rooms of unequal dimensions with a central hallway. Originally visitors entered the hall, where most cooking, socializing, and public events occurred, then passed into the parlor, or the more private portion of the house. During the middle to late eighteenth century, a partition was installed to create the central passage, equalizing the size of each room. The exterior walls of the house are laid in Flemish bond with glazed headers, forming a checkerboard pattern. Architectural restoration of the house took place in the 1970s, at which time all modifications were removed and the house restored to its original eighteenth-century appearance.

References: Catherine W. Bishir, *North Carolina Architecture* (1990); Dru G. Haley and Raymond A. Winslow, *The Historic Architecture of Perquimans County, North Carolina* (1982); Norman Penney, ed., *The Journal of George Fox* (1911).

Linda F. Carnes-McNaughton

New Deal Agencies. SEE Great Depression.

New Garden, Battle of. The Battle of New Garden was a series of Revolutionary War clashes that took place on the morning of 15 Mar. 1781 immediately preceding the Battle of Guilford Courthouse. The battle began just after sunrise at New Garden Friends Meetinghouse west of Greensboro and extended along New Garden Road north of the Crossroads over the next three hours. Involving both cavalry and infantry, the hostilities opened with a brief skirmish at the meetinghouse. There, Lt. Col. Banastre Tarleton's British scouts discovered the American pickets, who promptly retreated toward Lt. Col. Henry Lee's vanguard. Tarleton's force, numbering nearly 600, came from his Loyalist cavalry legion, the German Yagers and Bose Regiment, and a later reinforcement of the Welsh Fusiliers. Lee's command, comparable in size, consisted of his cavalry, Col. William Campbell's veteran riflemen, and Virginia militia.

The first of the three "sharp encounters" was a cavalry assault on New Garden Road, where Lee's troops drove off Tarleton's dragoons in some confusion. Tarleton's retreat ended at the meetinghouse, where he was joined by the German infantry, which stood firm against Lee's advance. Among the several casualties was Tarleton himself; he was seriously wounded in the hand but remained in the action for the rest of the day. The approach of Lord Charles Cornwallis's main army forced Lee to retire north to the Crossroads, where he took up a strong position in a wooded area. Another general action ended finally with the commitment of the Welsh Fusiliers, which dislodged the stubbornly resisting Americans who now retreated the three miles to Gen. Nathanael Greene's position just south of the county seat.

The spirited actions, including a brief skirmish, a swirling cavalry clash, and two general engagements, inflicted a number of casualties on the British, led to a significant delay, and contributed to the fatigue of an already weary army that had set out on a predawn advance without breakfast. That day a significant portion of the British army endured two battles, involving some five hours of combat. New Garden was preliminary to the main action at Guilford Courthouse that afternoon, but it has been established that in time elapsed, numbers involved, casualties, and complexity of maneuver, the conflicts near New Garden Friends Meetinghouse deserve to be considered apart from the greater battle that day that has in history so overshadowed the events of the morning.

References: John Buchanan, *The Road to Guilford Courthouse: The American Revolution in the Carolinas* (1997); Algie I. Newlin, *The Battle of New Garden* (1977).

Lindley S. Butler

New Hanover County, located in the Coastal Plain region of southeastern North Carolina, was formed in 1729 from Craven County and named in honor of England's King George I of the House of Hanover. Original inhabitants of the area included the Cape Fear, Waccamaw, and other Siouan Indians, followed by English, Welsh, Irish, French Huguenot, and Highland Scot settlers. Wilmington, the county seat, was originally called New Carthage; it was incorporated in 1739–40 and named for Spencer Compton, earl of Wilmington.

New Hanover County is located in a primarily maritime region, bordered by the Atlantic Ocean to the east and the Cape Fear River to the west. The county benefits from a thriving tourist industry based in some of North Carolina's most popular beach towns, including Carolina Beach, Wrightsville Beach, and Kure Beach. The Fort Fisher State Historic Site, an important Civil War fort, is situated at the southernmost tip of the county, near the mouth of the Cape Fear River. The North Carolina Aquarium at Fort Fisher is also located nearby.

Wilmington is the ninth-largest city in the state and has many important businesses and institutions. The Wilmington Race Riot (10 Nov. 1898), in which racial violence led to the overthrow of the city government, constituted a dark chapter in North Carolina history. The completion of I-40 to Wilmington in the early 1990s greatly boosted the local economy. Wilmington since the 1980s has hosted a film and television studio and for a time was considered the "Hollywood of the East." The city is the berthing place of the USS *North Carolina* Battleship Memorial. Other communities in New Hanover County include Castle Hayne and Seabreeze.

New Hanover County cultural institutions include the Cape Fear Museum, the Wilmington Children's Museum, Thalian Hall, the Wrightsville Beach Museum of History, and Cape Fear Shakespeare. Annual events held in the county include the popular North Carolina Azalea Festival, the Cape Fear Marlin Tournament in Wrightsville Beach, the Festival of Trees, Old Wilmington by Candlelight, and Countdown on Cape Fear.

New Hanover County agricultural products include nursery and horticultural plants, flowers, fruits, and vegetables. Manufactured products include optical fibers, nuclear fuel components, chemicals, molded plastic parts, nails, fabricated and stock steel, and computer software. In 2004 New Hanover County had an estimated population of 174,300.

References: Lawrence Lee, *A Brief History of New Hanover County, North Carolina* (1971); Beverly and Glenn Tetterton, *North Carolina County Fact Book* (2 vols., 1998).

Jay Mazzocchi

SEE ALSO Azalea Festival; Cape Fear Museum; Fort Fisher; *North Carolina*, USS; Wilmington; Wilmington Race Riot.

New Lights refers to a specific sect of Baptists that emerged during the Great Awakening of the 1730s and the Second Great Awakening of the early 1800s. During these revivals, some converted Baptists were named "New Lights" because they believed that God had brought new light into their lives through their emotional conversion experiences. These New Light Baptists were also known as Separate Baptists for their belief in conversions, which set them apart from other Baptists, who preached Calvinistic ideas of predestination. These differences in beliefs caused the Baptist Church in North Carolina to develop slowly during the colonial period.

The General Baptists had moved into North Carolina from the beginning of settlement. The first permanent General Baptist church was organized in Camden County in 1729, the same year North Carolina became a Crown colony. While the General Baptists were getting settled in the colony, the Great Awakening brought other missionaries to North Carolina to preach their evangelical messages. In 1739 George Whitefield traveled from Connecticut and stopped in Edenton to preach the Methodist faith. Many people listened to Whitefield's sermons, but few converted.

One of Whitefield's New England converts was Shubal Stearns, who traveled to North Carolina on a mission of conversion. In 1754, Stearns, a former Congregationalist who had converted to the Baptist faith, arrived from Connecticut in present-day Randolph County. With a small group under his leadership, Stearns founded the Sandy Creek Association four years later. It was his Sandy Creek Association churches that subsequently became known as New Light Baptist churches.

The cultural impact of New Light Baptists on North Carolina is widespread. The Baptists settled in communities all over the state and left their names behind. In northwestern Wake County, the New Light District was settled by Baptists. The New Light Meeting House in that community was founded in 1775. Within that settlement, two gristmills and three general stores were established and thrived until the 1880s. In modern times, that section of Wake County is still known as the New Light community.

References: John B. Boles, *The Great Revival, 1787–1805* (1972); Robert M. Calhoon, *Religion and the American Revolution in North Carolina* (1976); Guion G. Johnson, *Ante-Bellum North Carolina: A Social History* (1937).

Ellen Fitzgibbons Causey

New River in western North Carolina is formed by the convergence of two smaller rivers, the North Fork New River (43 miles long) and the South Fork New River (72 miles long), which flow out of the Blue Ridge Mountains of Watauga and Ashe Counties. It flows north from the Ashe-Alleghany County line into Virginia and West Virginia, entering the Kanawha River at Charleston, W.Va. The New River is unique among North Carolina rivers for several reasons. It is believed to be the only major river in the United States to flow north. In addition, and in contradiction to its name—the result of its discovery in 1749 in "new" sections of North Carolina and Virginia—the New River is one of North America's oldest rivers, created between 10 million and 360 million years ago. Some geologists believe the New to be the second-oldest river in the world, behind the Nile River in Egypt.

The New River is one of the state's least-industrialized rivers, populated by relatively small towns and flowing practically untouched through many miles of bucolic highland terrain. In 1976, 26 miles of the South Fork New River was declared a National Scenic River by the federal government, and the following year the state of North Carolina established the New River State Park in an effort to protect the river's natural beauty and resources. The New was named an American Heritage River in 1998. Conservation groups, including the National Committee for the New River, continue to work to protect the river from possibly harmful development projects and to improve the environment of its more than 765 squares miles of watershed in the state.

Reference: John Manuel, "New River Rhythm," *Wildlife in North Carolina* 63 (November 1999).

Jay Mazzocchi

New River, Battle of. The Civil War engagement called the Battle of New River occurred in Onslow County over a three-day period beginning 23 Nov. 1862. In preparation for the action, Lt. William B. Cushing of the Union navy took his iron-hulled gunboat, the converted side-wheel tug *Ellis*, up the New River. His mission was to capture Jacksonville, the seat of Onslow County, 20 miles from the river inlet; destroy any saltworks he encountered; and seize any blockade-runners found in the river. The blockaders sought sanctuary from Union cruisers in the smaller, less accessible havens of the New River. Saltworks had materialized along the inlets and sounds to produce the increasingly scarce but always vital commodity.

On the morning of 23 November, Cushing arrived at the Jacksonville dock before Confederate pickets could warn the inhabitants of his approach, and a landing party quickly occupied the public buildings. After raising the U.S. flag above the courthouse and capturing two schooners, a store of clothing, numerous small arms, and several contraband slaves, Cushing withdrew. But the local Confederate authorities were now determined to have their revenge.

Two companies from the 2nd North Carolina Cavalry harassed the *Ellis* as it attempted to reach the inlet before dark. Cushing, impeded by the slower-moving schooners and engaging the cavalry on both banks, was compelled to anchor in midstream when darkness arrived. Meanwhile, the Confederates constructed an ambush on the west bank of the river. The next morning Cushing managed to avoid the ambush and drive off the Confederates, but he ran aground within easy range of the temporarily abandoned positions.

Unable to free the stranded gunboat, Cushing used the time to strike ashore and burn a nearby saltworks. Then, uncertain that the next morning's tide would free his ship, he lightened the vessel, leaving one gun, and sent the schooners downstream with all but six volunteers. During the night, the Confederates moved back into their positions overlooking the river.

At first light on 25 November, the Confederates opened fire and rapidly overwhelmed the *Ellis*'s depleted crew and single gun. Unable to escape with the ship, Cushing set it afire and manned the remaining ship's boat to make for the awaiting schooners. The exultant Confederates attempted pursuit but were deterred by the thunderous explosion of the *Ellis*'s magazine, and Cushing safely reached the Atlantic.

References: L. J. Kimball, *The Battle of New River, 23–25 November 1862* (1997); Ralph J. Roske and Charles Van Doren, *Lincoln's Commando: The Biography of Commander William B. Cushing, U.S.N.* (1957).

L. J. Kimball

New River Navigation Company, incorporated by the General Assembly in 1855, superseded several companies whose efforts had been directed mainly at removing an oyster shoal, or obstruction, at the mouth of the New River in Onslow County. In the late 1830s Congress had appropriated moneys to eliminate the barrier, but the attempts had been unsuccessful. When an 1850 petition by Onslow residents resulted in another appropriation to resurvey the lower New River, it was found that the stubborn oyster bed remained. The legislature now directed the New River Navigation Company to clear the river from its mouth to Sneads Ferry, obligated the state to purchase as much as $20,000 worth of stock in the venture, and permitted the company to charge a toll on river traffic to reward its stockholders.

In November 1855 New River Navigation convened its first meeting, at which the president reported that contracts had already been let to hire a surveyor and secure a dredging machine. Work progressed slowly in 1856 due to a paucity of laborers, sickness of the available men, frequent breakdowns of the dredging machine, and the lack of a dumping boat to carry off spoilage. Nevertheless, by May 1857 the company had opened a 25- to 60-foot channel, 7 feet deep at low tide and 1,975 yards in length. Despite the state's infusion of $20,000 and an attempt by the General Assembly in 1858 to enlarge the powers of the New River Navigation Company, work apparently ceased by 1859, at which time the company's dredge and dumping boat lay on the bottom of the river.

Reference: Charles C. Weaver, *Internal Improvements in North Carolina Previous to 1860* (1903).

Alan D. Watson

Newspapers, although appearing later in North Carolina than in the other original British colonies, over time became a vibrant social and political force that helped shape the state's enduring reputation as a progressive southern state. Thanks in part to strong competition among newspapers in the many small towns and medium-sized cities that were characteristic of the state until the late twentieth century, the North Carolina press produced several generations of talented journalists, some of whom moved on to national prominence as reporters, editors, cartoonists, or commentators. Following a widespread trend, over time ownership and management of the state's newspapers moved from initial control by smaller, local printers to wealthy family publishers and ultimately to powerful corporate conglomerates. These stages reflect the increasing costs of recruiting talent, gathering news, and printing and distributing papers in a media market with tastes and interests that have become increasingly national and international. As costs have risen and conglomerates have gained greater control, the number of newspapers has declined, leaving them (like radio and television) in the hands of fewer owners. Although it has been argued that these developments have adversely affected quality and uniqueness, the press in North Carolina continues to maintain a central position in the dissemination of news, information, and editorial opinion.

North Carolina's First Newspapers

By the time the first newspaper was published in North Carolina in the mid-eighteenth century, 11 other colonies already had publications. Because it was a frontier colony, its population was widely scattered on farms and plantations; there were no large towns or well-defined community centers. Illiteracy on the frontier also delayed the demand for printed matter. But by midcentury, New Bern, the unofficial capital, had become a town of some size and the colonial Assembly urgently needed a printer to distribute newly revised laws. In 1749 the lawmakers found one in Virginian James Davis, who accepted their five-year contract and moved his printing press to New Bern to reproduce the colony's legal paper and currency. Two years later, on 9 Aug. 1751, he published the first issue of the *North-Carolina Gazette*. Four other versions of this newspaper would appear before 1798.

At the start of the Revolutionary War, five different newspapers were in circulation, including Adam Boyd's *Cape-Fear Mercury* (1769–76), but they all eventually failed, leaving the state without a single paper between 1778 and 1783. Soon, however, a minor renaissance began with the introduction of new printed matter, including Hillsborough's *North Carolina Gazette* in 1785, the *Edenton Intelligencer* in 1788, the *Fayetteville Gazette* in 1789, the *Halifax North Carolina Journal* in 1792, and Salisbury's *North Carolina Mercury and Salisbury Advertiser* in 1797.

Most of these early newspapers consisted of foreign dispatches from several weeks to several months old, poetry, farming tips, and items copied from other publications. Local news was largely confined to obituaries and wedding announcements; horse races and cockfights—both popular sports of the time—were also widely covered. In small-town colonial North Carolina, everyone already knew the local news before a newspaper was printed. Appearing only weekly, early papers were sidelines to other businesses such as printing, book selling, and retail sales of various imported merchandise.

Advertisements during this era were mostly legal notices and announcements of the arrival of new merchandise. Seldom did a display ad appear; many merchants, as well as lawyers and physicians, had their business cards printed in the newspaper. Subscription rates and postage costs were extremely high, and most readers picked up their copies of the news at the printing shop. High costs and scattered populations in small communities led to low circulation rates. Indeed, circulation of the various versions of New Bern's *North-Carolina Gazette* seldom reached 150 copies.

Political Affiliations of
Nineteenth-Century Newspapers

The promotion of political causes and parties by North Carolina's newspapers began in earnest in the late 1780s, when debate over the ratification of the U.S. Constitution was at its peak. In the succeeding decades, numerous papers were founded to serve as organs for political, economic, and religious interests, becoming primary participants in the state's public life. Because many newspapers were subsidized by political parties or by partisan organizations, they experienced an enormous turnover in ownership. Moreover, it was not unusual for publications to fail once their political cause had become obsolete. After about 1820, newspapers began to change and expand, putting less emphasis on foreign affairs and focusing on timely state and national news, which was obtained mainly through the mail. Expansion of the federal postal system, in fact, greatly aided newspaper circulation. In 1832 about 75,000 copies of North Carolina papers were published every week, and several editors also served as postmasters.

One of the first politically significant newspapers in the state was the *Raleigh Register and North Carolina Weekly Advertiser*, founded in 1799 by Joseph Gales, who had moved to North Carolina from Pennsylvania. The *Raleigh Register* became known as a leading political voice, first for the Republican Party and later for the Whig Party, as well as for its publishing innovations. It became the state's first semiweekly in 1823 and its first daily in 1850; it ceased publication in 1868.

The newspapers that were started to espouse Whig politics during the early to mid-1800s included the *Fayetteville Observer* (1816), established by several Fayetteville citizens and later acquired by Edward Jones Hale, who used it as an organ of the Whig Party; the *North Carolina Whig* (Charlotte, 1852–63); and the *North State Whig* (Washington, N.C., 1843–54). Influential Democratic newspapers from this era were the *North Carolinian* (Fayetteville, 1841–63); the *Raleigh Standard* (1834–70), founded by Philo White and later acquired by William Woods Holden, who used it as a powerful organ of the Democratic Party and later the Conservative Party; the *Western Sentinel* (Winston, 1852–1926); and the *Daily Journal* (Wilmington, 1844–95).

Some papers began to publish more articles of general interest to families, such as agriculture, homemaking, literature, and local happenings. A leader among these "family" papers was the *Western Democrat* (Charlotte, 1852–97), founded by Rufus M. Herron and Robert P. Waring. Other papers were created to support specific causes, such as the *Spirit of the Age* (Raleigh, 1849–71), a temperance organ established by Alexander M. Gorman for the North Carolina Sons of Temperance chapter, and the *Western Carolinian* (Salisbury, 1820–44), which advocated equal representation for western counties in the General Assembly.

As the number of newspapers increased and higher circulation rates were achieved, North Carolinians began to rely on the press for information and editorial opinion on a wide variety of statewide and community issues. In 1827 the first railroad in the state was proposed, for example, in a series of columns titled "Numbers of Carlton," which appeared in local newspapers before being published as a book in 1828. Through continuing newspaper promotion and agitation, the idea came to fruition in 1849 with the formation of the North Carolina Railroad, built with $2 million in state money and $1 million in private funds. Construction was completed in 1856. When telegraph poles appeared beside the tracks, communication within the state was greatly enhanced. The development of a state system of public education (for white males only), changes in the court system, and mill labor reform were among other ideas promulgated in newspaper editorials during this period.

Until the mid-nineteenth century, slavery was not a frequent topic in most North Carolina papers. The majority of editors viewed it as a regional matter and avoided taking a position. But as secession became more probable, the issue bitterly divided North Carolinians, including newspaper editors. Their opinions essentially split along party lines, with most Democratic editors favoring secession and most Whig editors opposing it.

An Expanding Press Champions Economic
and Social Progress

With the Civil War, predictably, most North Carolina newspapers suspended publication, as many editors and printers entered military service, printing supplies became increasingly scarce, and the economy worsened. Papers in Wilmington, Fayetteville, and Raleigh continued to appear sporadically. After the war, the state's larger papers resumed regular publication, as did weeklies in many small towns. As the postwar recovery took hold, additional newspapers were founded, several of them becoming the leading lights of North Carolina journalism throughout the twentieth century. The *Raleigh News and Observer* (1865), *Wilmington Morning Star* (1867), *Charlotte Observer* (1869), *Asheville Citizen-Times* (1870), *Statesville Record and Landmark* (1874), *Raleigh Times* (1879), *Watauga Democrat* (1888), *Greensboro News and Record* (1890), *Durham Herald-Sun* (1894), and *Winston-Salem Journal* (1897) all trace back to this period.

Changes in newspapers that had begun in northern cities during the war slowly began to take root in North Carolina and other southern states. Among these changes were the increased use of professional reporters to gather the news; the use of the telegraph to speed news transmissions; the appearance of one-column, multiple-deck headlines on the front page; and more editorials and advertisements. There were technological developments in the printing process as well. In 1866 a paper-making technique that used wood pulp instead of rags was introduced in the United States. Linotype machines began to appear, along with cutting, folding, and collecting devices. There was some primitive photoengraving in the early 1870s, but sketch artists remained prevalent.

By 1873 journalism had acquired the status of a profession, represented by the founding of the North Carolina Press Association in Goldsboro in May. Representatives from 28 newspapers were present at the "convention," which established a central depository for information about each paper's ownership and passed resolutions relating to subscription practices, editorial staff, advertising rates, and mechanical specifications. The organization's executive committee was instructed to research the character and reliability of advertising agencies, which were distrusted by most newspaper executives.

Some papers, such as the staunchly Democratic *Fayetteville Eagle* (1868–75), published racist editorials during the 1890s and afterward. A white supremacy political movement at the time, along with rumors of race riots, made the issue of race a controversial but intriguing topic for newspaper readers. A lack of respect for, or outright animosity toward, blacks was a common failing of many editors, who were often reticent when it came to reporting on lynchings or condemning lynch mobs. African American newspapers fought against racism and injustice whenever possible. The *Wilmington Daily Record* (1892–98), founded by Alexander L. Manly as the "Only Negro Daily in the World," supported progressive causes in Wilmington's black community. Racial tensions forced the paper to cease publication and Manly to leave Wilmington shortly before the printing plant and offices were destroyed in the Wilmington race riot of 1898.

Despite their relative silence on race issues during this era, many editors of the late nineteenth and early twentieth centuries began to promote social causes and uncover rampant political corruption, helping North Carolina to achieve a reputation as a progressive southern state. Some journalists began to call attention to environmental issues, such as the need for flood control legislation and protection of North Carolina's oyster interests. Newspapers like the *Charlotte News* (1888)—for decades the largest and most successful afternoon daily in North Carolina—emerged as a strong liberal force, uncovering public fraud and corruption and pushing to improve local government.

One of the state's most influential journalistic crusaders was Josephus Daniels, the legendary editor of the *Raleigh News and Observer*, who turned that newspaper into arguably the most powerful political voice in North Carolina. After buying the paper in 1894, Daniels conducted a campaign to curb railroad power and make railroads pay taxes like other corporations. He distrusted all "big business" and fought the "tobacco trust," advocating antitrust legislation, free coinage of silver, a graduated income tax, and the direct election of senators. Daniels was also an early supporter of women suffrage, workmen's compensation laws, and the regulation of child labor.

Daniels's reputation fares less well in the area of race relations, however. In the "white supremacy" campaign of 1898, the *News and Observer* warned readers of "Negro domination"; it later supported an amendment to the state constitution that effectively disfranchised most black voters. (In 1944, while opposing southern efforts to write a white supremacy plank in the Democratic platform, he wrote that he was ashamed of his earlier racism.)

A progressive and competitive press helped the state move forward economically, politically, and socially during the twentieth century. With improved transportation came increased circulation and influence for many papers, especially large city dailies such as the *Charlotte Observer*, *Greensboro Daily News*, and *Raleigh News and Observer*. One of the important causes was the building and maintenance of quality roads and highways. Promoted by editors as early as 1911, the idea led to the formation of the State Highway Commission in 1915, a year before passage of a Federal Highway Act. As a result of this movement, North Carolina ultimately became known as the "Good Roads State." The *Elizabeth City Independent*, led by William O. Saunders, took on problems of racial hatred and the actions of the Ku Klux Klan. Over the decades the press across the state spoke out on a variety of other issues, including educational reform, industrial development, internal improvements, conservation initiatives, civil rights, and improved race relations.

Changing Technologies, New Voices, and the Trend toward Corporate Ownership

In the late nineteenth century many editors of the larger papers began to correspond with their counterparts around the state. Much of their correspondence related to news items, but often it consisted of gossip, small talk, or jokes. Some newspapers belonged to the Southern Associated Press, one of seven regional groups that exchanged news with the original New York Associated Press. In 1915 the Associated Press (AP) opened its first branch office in North Carolina, just in time to provide coverage of the country's entry into World War I. The AP wire service soon became essential to the 15 or so newspapers that subscribed to it.

The dominance of newspapers as the main source of information for the average North Carolinian began to be challenged soon after the turn of the century. Advertising revenues had contributed greatly to the growth of the newspaper industry and enabled papers to afford such new technology as Linotype, photo engravings, and wire press services. But by 1914, as society grew more technologically advanced and the means of communication were becoming institutionalized, a transition in newspaper publishing was under way. Newsreels in movie theaters had started to become popular about 1910. When radio appeared in 1920, it initially had little effect on newspapers, but as its appeal increased, it began to drain some advertising dollars from the press. In North Carolina, as elsewhere, the rise of television in the 1950s caused great attrition of individual newspapers. The economic impact of advertising losses from both TV and radio was heavy. As people increasingly turned to TV for their news, afternoon papers ceased publication, and by 1998 not a single city in the state could claim two daily newspapers.

Improved technologies helped surviving papers serve their readers with ever greater speed and accuracy, given the rapid changes in news gathering, editing, production, and distribution. Electronics made the most impact through the facsimile transmission of news, computerized editing systems, photocomposition machines, offset presses, and digital color in what, for many decades, had been a black-and-white medium. Numerous local papers began to carry syndicated columns from successful large city newspapers across the country even as many editors began to focus on local news, "human-interest" stories, and other articles aimed more at entertainment than education.

Throughout its history, the North Carolina press has produced a number of journalists who became leaders in their profession and have been recognized by induction into the North Carolina Journalism Hall of Fame. The long list of these individuals includes Harriet Doar, pioneering literary journalist of the *Charlotte Observer*; Beatrice Cobb, widely quoted columnist and publisher of the *Morganton News Herald* from 1916 to 1959; Jack Claiborne, author and longtime correspondent and columnist for the *Charlotte Observer*; and Harry Golden, civil rights advocate and publisher of the nationally recognized *Carolina Israelite* from 1941 to 1968. Among the journalists who worked on a North Carolina paper before going on to national prominence, either in print, TV, or radio journalism, are Vermont Royster, Edward R. Murrow, Tom Wicker, David Brinkley, Clifton Daniel, Charles Kuralt, and Charlie Rose.

In addition to some of the larger papers, the *Tabor City Tribune* (1946–91), *Whiteville News Reporter* (1904–), and *Washington Daily News* (1909–) have all been awarded the Pulitzer Prize. Several newspapers were created specifically for North Carolina's African American communities. In 1927 Louis E. Austin (1898–1971) became majority shareholder and editor of the *Standard Advertiser*, Durham's only black paper. He renamed it the *Carolina Times*, adopted "The Truth Unbridled" as its motto, and built his weekly into one of the state's most important African American newspapers. The *Times* preached racial pride and protest throughout the segregation era, exhorting blacks to buy from each other, to educate their children, to oppose injustices like police brutality, and to vote. Its outspoken editorials inspired many civil rights struggles and successes in the 1960s.

The *Carolinian* in Raleigh, another prominent black paper, was founded in 1940 by Paul R. Jervay Sr. as a politically independent weekly, publishing news of importance to the black community. The mission of Greensboro's *Carolina Peacemaker*, established in 1967 by John Marshall Stevenson, has been to unify African Americans and provide a journalistic outlet for expressing ideas and issues relevant to black life in the modern world, including civil rights, politics, religion, local government, and economics. Other black papers continuing to publish in the early 2000s were the *Winston-Salem Chronicle* and the *Wilmington Journal*. With a growing Latino population, North Carolinians also gained access to several newspapers catering to Spanish-speaking citizens and immigrants. These included *El Sol* and *La Noticia* in Charlotte, *Nuestro Pueblo* in Durham, and *La Conexión* in Raleigh.

Mergers and acquisitions by powerful conglomerates marked the newspaper industry in both the state and the nation by the 1990s and early 2000s. The trend toward corporate ownership, as well as the rise of nonprint media such as the Internet, has led to a decline in the number of local newspapers. By 2006 several North Carolina papers were owned by large conglomerates, including the *Lexington Dispatch*, *Hendersonville Times-News*, and *Wilmington Star-News* (New York Times Company); the *Jacksonville Daily News*, *Burlington Times-News*, *Gaston Gazette*, *New Bern Sun Journal*, and *Shelby Star* (Freedom Newspapers); and the *Asheville Citizen-Times* (Gannett Company). This ownership paradigm is believed to have undermined attention to local affairs and the relative balance that the North Carolina press has traditionally achieved. But it has also been argued that the rise of the Internet—which has seen individual websites become part of the daily operations of most newspapers—has increased reader access to news, information, and opinion.

References: Thomas D. Clark, *The Southern Country Editor* (1948); Carol Sue Humphrey, *The Press of the Young Republic* (1996); Robert F. Karolevitz, *From Quill to Computer: The Story of America's Community Newspapers* (1985); Hugh M. Morton and Edward L. Rankin Jr., *Making a Difference in North Carolina* (1988); Thad Stem Jr., *The Tar Heel Press* (1973); Henry Lewis Suggs, ed., *The Black Press in the South, 1865–1979* (1983); Stephen B. Weeks, *The Press of North Carolina* (1891).

Edwin H. Mammen
Additional research provided by Raymond Gavins, Sarah Mobley, and Roy Parker Jr.

SEE ALSO *Carolina Peacemaker*; *Charlotte Observer*; *Fayetteville Observer*; *Greensboro News and Record*; North

Carolina Press Association; *Raleigh News and Observer*; *Wilmington Star*; *Winston-Salem Journal*.

A New Voyage to Carolina. John Lawson's *A New Voyage to Carolina*, published for the first time in 1709, is among the most comprehensive accounts of North American Indian culture and natural history written during the American colonial period. A London native, Lawson arrived in Charles Towne (present-day Charleston, S.C.) in August 1700 and soon set off on a 550-mile trek through the wilderness backcountry of the Carolina colony. He settled near the site of present-day New Bern and extended his explorations to Roanoke Island, the "Ledges of Mountains," and into Virginia. A keen observer, Lawson spent much of his time surveying eastern Carolina, and in 1708 he was appointed official surveyor for the Lords Proprietors.

In addition to his detailed journal of the 1700–1701 expedition, Lawson compiled extensive notes on Native Americans and on the flora, fauna, geology, geography, agriculture, and climate of the region. Early in 1709 he returned to England, where in April the renowned editor John Stevens published the first installment of Lawson's account of Carolina in *A New Collection of Voyages and Travels*. The entire series was subsequently issued as *A New Voyage to Carolina; Containing the Exact Description and Natural History of that Country: Together with the Present State thereof. And a Journal of a Thousand miles travel'd thro' several Nations of Indians. Giving a particular Account of their Customs, Manners, &c.* In 1711 Lawson's work was included in Stevens's two-volume *New Collection of Voyages and Travels*, and in 1714 and 1718 the work was reissued with new title pages as *The History of Carolina*.

Lawson returned to North Carolina in April 1710 and resumed his explorations and natural history research, which included gathering botanical specimens for James Petiver, a London apothecary and avid collector of "natural curiosities." Lawson's continued surveying activities aroused the resentment of the local Indians, and in September 1711 he was captured, tortured, and executed by the Tuscarora tribe during its widespread uprising against the white settlements along the North Carolina coast.

Most of the accounts in Lawson's *New Voyage* are rich in detail, succinct, and crafted in an engaging literary style. His zoological and botanical observations permit ready identification of most species mentioned. His sympathetic descriptions of the Indians provide one of the most thoroughly documented accounts of any native culture inhabiting the eastern coast of North America, a complex civilization that was destroyed by European settlement long before most observers thought it worthwhile to study or record any of its details. The value of Lawson's work was well recognized in the 1730s by authors who plagiarized extensive portions of the *New Voyage*. These thefts included *The Natural History of North-Carolina* (1737) by John Brickell and the *Neu-gefundenes Eden* (1737) by Samuel Jenner.

Reference: Michael P. Branch, ed., *Reading the Roots: American Nature Writing before Walden* (2004).

Marcus B. Simpson Jr.

Ney Myth, propagated by several North Carolina writers as fact but dismissed by historians as spurious, held that Rowan County teacher Peter Stuart Ney, who died on 15 Nov. 1846, was the assumed identity of Napoleon's trusted lieutenant Marshal Michel Ney, who was rumored to have escaped execution in 1815 and fled to America. This romantic legend held evident appeal for several generations of North Carolinians but, like many legends, had little basis in documented fact. Extensive research by William Henry Hoyt and others resulted in conclusive evidence that Marshal Ney did not escape the firing squad. The grave of Peter Stuart Ney at Third Creek Presbyterian Church in the town of Cleveland is located near the session house at which he taught classes.

References: James Edward Smoot, comp., *Marshal Ney before and after Execution* (1929); George V. Taylor, "Scholarship and Legend: William Henry Hoyt's Research on the Ney Controversy," *South Atlantic Quarterly* 61 (Summer 1960).

Michael Hill

Nickels for Know-How was the title of a program created following World War II to support scientific research to improve crop production and farming methods. Established by legislative action in 1951, it permitted farmers to cooperate in encouraging agricultural research and the dissemination of research findings. For this purpose farmers and other growers of agricultural commodities voted an assessment on themselves not to exceed five cents per ton on commercial feed and fertilizer.

In North Carolina the Farm Bureau Federation, the State Grange, and the North Carolina Agricultural Foundation held the referendum that approved the Nickels for Know-How program in the state. Collected levies are paid to the state commissioner of agriculture, who remits them to the Agricultural Foundation to be disbursed for the foundation's purposes. In 1991 the law was amended to create the Tobacco Research Commission and to provide for a levy of 10 cents per 100 pounds of tobacco marketed to support tobacco research. By the early 2000s, the program yielded $650,000 annually for its work.

Thomas L. Norris Jr.

Nissen Wagon Works, located in Forsyth County, was one of the largest wagon makers in the South during the nineteenth century. In 1834 John Philip Nissen opened a wheel-

A Nissen wagon as shown in an advertisement that appeared in the *Southern Tobacco Journal*, 17 June 1919. Courtesy of NCOA&H.

wright shop on Waughtown Hill, four miles south of the Moravian town of Salem. The son of a Broadbay farmer, the younger Nissen breathed new life into an industry that had withered among the Moravian settlements following the death of his Danish-born grandfather, wagon maker Tycho Nissen, in 1789. From 1834 through 1837 (when Salem wheelwright Ernst Henry Meinung expanded his small carriage-making business) Nissen, operating without competition, thrived by meeting the emigrants' need for wagons.

By 1850 Nissen and his six employees were producing 65 wagons annually, far more than his competitors such as Meinung, whose six-man work force managed to turn out a mere 12 carriages on a yearly basis. The good years that followed found Nissen tripling the amount of capital invested in his business as he purchased steam- and horse-powered machinery to double his production capacity. Increased competition also accompanied the 1850s in the form of William E. Spach's nearby wagon works, which opened in 1854 and supplied wagons whose quality rivaled those made by Nissen. Together, the two firms would dominate Forsyth's wagon-making industry through the second half of the nineteenth century and well into the twentieth. Following Nissen's death, his sons, George E. and William M. Nissen, assumed control of the business and guided it until 1925, when it was sold for nearly $1 million.

References: Chester Davis, "Locally Built Wagons Changed Face of the U.S.," *Winston-Salem Journal and Sentinel*, 10 Apr. 1966; Adelaide L. Fries, Stuart T. Wright, and J. Edwin Hendricks, eds., *Forsyth: The History of a County on the March* (rev. ed., 1976).

Joshua McKaughan

Nobility. SEE Peerage.

Nonimportation Agreement (1768), which required the American colonies to purchase English goods over those from foreign lands, was a result of Britain's attempt to find new sources of revenue for colonial defense and administration. Prominent among these sources were the Townshend Acts—imposing duties on glass, lead, paper, tea, and paint —that passed Parliament in June 1767 and went into effect four months later. Most colonials found hard times during the 1760s, with money in short supply, reduced trade, and an increased cost of living. With conditions such as these, merchants and consumers alike were reluctant to become involved in a new campaign against Britain's colonial policies, and those who were willing sought more conservative means to protest the duties.

In North Carolina, attitudes toward the measures were affected by serious internal problems. The sectional quarrels of nearly three decades escalated into an east-west struggle known as the Regulator Movement in 1768 at the same time as the Townshend Acts were introduced. Before the confrontation was over in 1771, 40 people were dead, several hundred were wounded, and thousands had permanently departed the colony. To add to this human suffering and economic and political turmoil, one of the worst hurricanes in North Carolina's history struck the Cape Fear region in September 1769, leaving vast damage to crops, homes, and shipping.

It was, therefore, not surprising that little was done in North Carolina to fight the Nonimportation Agreement. Governor William Tryon dismissed the House of Commons before it could vote on nonimportation. Although the members later pledged themselves to purchase English goods, it was clear that most merchants abstained from backing the measure. Ultimately, American, and North Carolina's, imports from Britain and customs payments to the mother country declined, and the Nonimportation Agreement was largely ineffectual.

Reference: Hugh T. Lefler and Albert Ray Newsome, *North Carolina: The History of a Southern State* (1954).

Louis P. Towles

Norfolk Southern Railroad was founded on New Year's Day 1883, with its original road running from Norfolk, Va., to Elizabeth City, N.C. Its predecessor, the Elizabeth City & Norfolk Railroad, chartered in 1870, had completed tracks south to Edenton on the Albemarle Sound in 1881. This was a continuation of a commercial connection between these points dating back to the Dismal Swamp Canal efforts of the late 1700s. In 1891 the road was reorganized as the Norfolk & Southern Railroad, but after 1900 consolidations brought back the name Norfolk Southern and the system was extended to New Bern, Raleigh, and Charlotte.

In 1907 work commenced on a five-mile trestle to cross the sound, which by January 1910 cost more than $1 million. The railroad lacked sufficient funds to adequately maintain the trestle, which perhaps led to its collapse in 1957—an accident that dropped a train into the sound and killed two crew members. But the trestle opened the way to connect with points in Piedmont North Carolina. Several of the state's smaller lines became part of the Norfolk Southern, including the Winston-Salem Southbound Railway, Raleigh & Western Railway (originally the Egypt Railway), Raleigh & Cape Fear Railway, North Carolina Midland Railroad, and Charlotte, Columbia, and Augusta Railroad. The line eventually ran from Norfolk to both Charlotte and Greensboro via Raleigh. In 1961 the company offices were moved from Norfolk to Raleigh.

The Norfolk Southern was noted for transporting agricultural and lumber products, and it aided in industrial development, especially in the rural counties of eastern North Carolina. At times the railroad offered passenger service, but after 1948 it was completely a freight road. Never strong financially, the company went into receivership on several occasions. On 1 Jan. 1974 the Norfolk Southern united with the Southern Railway System but continued to operate under its own name. At the time of the merger, the Norfolk Southern consisted of nearly 1,000 cars and engines and 624 miles of track. In 1982, when Southern Railway merged with the Norfolk & Western Railroad, the railroad became a part of the massive Norfolk Southern Corporation.

In 1990 the Norfolk Southern Corporation leased the old Elizabeth City & Norfolk line between Chesapeake, Va., and Edenton, N.C., to RailTex, Inc., a short-line company based in Texas that began operating the line as the Chesapeake & Albemarle Railroad (C&A) under Norfolk Southern's "Thoroughbred Shortline Program." The 73-mile C&A was a member of the RailAmerica, Inc., family of railroads headquartered in Boca Raton, Fla., which also included the North Carolina & Virginia Railroad. The C&A linked up with the Norfolk Southern and another giant transportation company, CSX Corporation, at Norfolk.

By the early 2000s the Norfolk Southern Corporation was a holding company headquartered in Norfolk that owned and managed the Norfolk Southern Railway as well as a telecommunications firm and a natural-resource company. The railroad system, which began operating about 7,200 miles of Conrail routes in 1999, extended approximately 21,800 miles across 22 states, the District of Columbia, and Canada. The Norfolk Southern operated 1,450 miles, or 43 percent, of North Carolina's rail system. One of its north-south main lines connected the Northeast and Midwest with Atlanta via Danville, Va., Greensboro, and Charlotte. A second north-south main line linked Tennessee with Spartanburg, S.C., through Asheville, while an east-west main line connected Salisbury and Asheville. Seven other routes, either owned or leased by the Norfolk Southern, served eastern and central North Carolina. The Norfolk Southern Corporation also employed nearly 1,500 people in North Carolina and carried 593,712 carloads for 723 North Carolina industries.

References: Burke Davis, *The Southern Railway: Road of the Innovators* (1985); George H. Drury, *The Historical Guide to North American Railroads* (1985); Edward A. Lewis, *American Shortline Railway Guide* (1996); Robert Reisweber, "The Norfolk Southern Railroad," *Green Light* (April 1976).

Warren L. Bingham
Wingate Lassiter

SEE ALSO Southern Railway System.

Northampton County, located along the fall line between the Coastal Plain and Piedmont regions of North Carolina, was formed in 1741 from Bertie County and named for James Compton, earl of Northampton. It is bordered in part by the state of Virginia. Early inhabitants of the county were the Tuscarora and Meherrin Indians, followed by Scottish, Scotch-Irish, French Huguenot, and English settlers. The county seat, Jackson, was established in 1742 as Northampton Courthouse; the name was changed in 1823 in honor of U.S. president Andrew Jackson. Other communities in Northampton County include Gaston, Garysburg, Rich Square, Seaboard, Vultare, Severn, Margarettsville, and Milwaukee. Notable physical features of the county include the Roanoke River, Roanoke Rapids, Occoneechee Neck, Taylors Mill Pond, and Gumberry and Panther Swamps.

The Peebles House (nineteenth century), Lee-Grant Farm (ca. 1830), Cedar Grove Quaker Meetinghouse (1868), and Duke-Lawrence House (mid-eighteenth century) are a few of Northampton County's historic attractions. The region hosted an active horse racing scene in the early nineteenth century, which predated that in Kentucky. Sir Archie, a noted thoroughbred, died in 1833 and is buried at Mowfields. Cultural institutions include the Jackson Museum and Northampton Memorial Library. Northampton County also hosts annual events such as the Northampton County Farm Festival June Jubilee.

Important agricultural products of Northampton County include peanuts, soybeans, corn, cotton, broilers, and hogs. Manufactured goods such as chemicals, foodstuffs, farm machinery, lumber and other wood products, and apparel are also produced in the county. In 2004 Northampton County's estimated population was 21,500.

Jay Mazzocchi

North Carolina, CSS. The CSS *North Carolina* was a steam-powered ironclad ram, one of two *Richmond*-class ironclads built for the Confederate navy in Wilmington during the Civil War. Six *Richmond*-class ships were laid down in Richmond, Wilmington, Charleston, and Savannah during the spring of 1862. Naval shipbuilder John L. Porter designed these vessels for harbor defense, adapting plans he had originally conceived in 1846. The new vessels were 174 feet long, 150 feet between perpendiculars with an extreme beam of 45 feet; they carried four rifled guns housed in a sloping rectangular casemate placed amidships. For protection, four inches of iron plating covered the casemate and two inches of armor blanketed the decks. The *Richmond* ironclads had an elliptical shape, coming to a point at both ends. At the stem, a formidable ram added another weapon to the ships' battery; at the stern, an overhang protected the propeller.

The *North Carolina*'s career was brief and uneventful. The ship was usually stationed near the mouth of the Cape Fear River opposite the town of Smithville, where it maintained a defensive position in cooperation with nearby forts. But navigation on Cape Fear was almost impossible for the ironclad. Its weak engines could not stem the river current, and its deep draft frequently caused it to run aground. As a result, the underpowered ironclad had to be towed almost everywhere it went.

Although the *North Carolina* was poorly built and unfit for combat, it did achieve limited success in the defense of Cape Fear. The ironclad's presence on the river helped deter Union attacks on Wilmington and the Cape Fear region until December 1864. Union intelligence was unaware of the ship's decrepit condition until late summer 1864, and Federal naval commanders did not want to attack unless their squadron included monitors to combat the *North Carolina* and any other ironclads the Confederates might have in commission. The deterrence provided by the *North Carolina* against Union attack was the defective ironclad's most important service during its short career.

References: William N. Still Jr., *Confederate Shipbuilding* (1987); Still, *Iron Afloat: The Story of the Confederate Armorclads* (1985).

Edwin L. Combs

North Carolina, USS.

When commissioned at the New York Naval Shipyard on 9 Apr. 1941, the USS *North Carolina* was considered the "greatest sea weapon in the world." Built at a cost of $70 million, the new "super-dreadnought" was as long as two city blocks, as tall as a 15-story building, and 35,000 tons in weight. It held nine 16-inch guns and carried 1,800 officers and sailors. For 40 months, the ship took part in every major offensive in the South Pacific, including Guadalcanal, the Philippines Sea, Iwo Jima, and Tokyo Bay. During a battle in August 1942, an observer from another U.S. ship wrote that the *North Carolina*'s gunfire was so heavy, "she look[ed] to be ablaze throughout." The Japanese reported on several occasions that the vessel had been sunk; this misinformation was probably due to the tactic of repainting the ship different colors. The *North Carolina* earned 12 battle stars and the nickname "Showboat," supposedly received when the crew of the USS *Washington* played the Broadway tune "Here Comes the Showboat" as a joke.

In 1960 the USS *North Carolina* was destined for the scrap

The USS *North Carolina* at its berth in Wilmington. Photograph by Charles E. Jones. North Carolina Department of Transportation.

heap, sparking a statewide fund-raising campaign to save it. Citizens raised $345,000 and purchased the ship from the U.S. government. Restored to its wartime appearance, the *North Carolina* was permanently docked across the Cape Fear River from the city of Wilmington, opening on 14 Oct. 1962 as a memorial to North Carolinians who had died in World War II. As of the early 2000s, tours of the ship were conducted and a museum was open every day of the year. During the summer a 70-minute outdoor drama, titled *The Immortal Showboat*, artfully portrayed the ship's role in American naval history. In March 1986 the USS *North Carolina* became one of 22 ships to be registered as a National Historic Landmark.

Craig M. Stinson

North Carolina Academy of Science

is a significant part of the professional lives of the state's scientists. Organized in 1902, the academy sought to fill the need for collegiality among scientists who, as faculty members of underfunded colleges and universities, often could not attend national disciplinary meetings. State academies of science had proliferated in other regions of the country during the late nineteenth century, an outgrowth of the emerging spirit of professionalism among the nation's scientists. In addition to sponsoring annual meetings, these organizations endeavored to publish modest journals and to provide an avenue whereby scientists could offer their expertise for the public good.

The idea for the North Carolina Academy of Science originated with William Willard Ashe, who, as forester for the North Carolina Geological Survey, did not benefit from even the limited professional contact within a university community. A group of Raleigh biologists, including Herbert Hutchinson Brimley, Franklin Sherman, and F. L. Stevens, quickly turned the idea into reality by soliciting support among their colleagues throughout the state and calling an organizational meeting in March 1902.

The academy limped along until 1909, when minor changes in membership requirements and the meeting format, as well as a membership drive, brought in 45 new associates. By 1920 membership totaled 112 persons; ten years later that figure had climbed to 305 persons. Membership declined a bit during the Great Depression, but following World War II it skyrocketed, reflecting primarily the expansion of institutions of higher education.

Although the North Carolina Academy of Science has always sought a broad membership, welcoming high school science teachers, industrial scientists, and state government employees, most members have come from colleges and universities. Consequently, the goals of the organization have reflected the professional needs of this group of scientists, including an opportunity to meet to discuss their research, a forum for the formal presentation of research results, and a publication outlet.

The academy achieved the first two of these goals; since 1909 annual meetings have attracted broad participation and offered wide-ranging programs. Prior to World War II, these meetings were often the only professional conventions that scientists attended. After the war, established scientists began to use the forum to announce research that they would flesh out in future publications, and young scholars, having discovered the difficulty of accessing the programs of national meetings, were able to find a place on the agenda of the state academy and thus enter the professional world.

The academy was less successful in publishing a journal. In 1904 it teamed up with the Elisha Mitchell Scientific Society to sponsor a joint publication and was able to produce a quarterly journal fairly regularly. The volumes, though, were often small and frequently appeared late. With minimum funding, editors who had academic responsibilities as well, and a membership that preferred to submit their most promising scholarship to a national journal first, the *Journal of the Elisha Mitchell Scientific Society* was regarded as a secondary but nonetheless creditable professional publication.

Beginning in the 1920s, the North Carolina Academy of Science expressed concern over environmental issues and the quality of public education and made a number of efforts to influence legislation in these areas. These issues continued in the post–World War II era, culminating in such actions as the sponsorship of a Junior Academy of Science and high school science fairs (funded to a considerable extent by National Science Foundation grants). With the decline of federal funds in the early 1970s, the outreach programs contracted. In the early 2000s the academy continued to maintain both education and conservation committees that served a watchdog function, reacting when some aspect of their area of interest seemed threatened.

References: Nancy Smith Midgette, "In Search of Professional Identity: Southern Scientists, 1883–1940," *Journal of Southern History* 54 (November 1988); Midgette, *To Foster the Spirit of Professionalism: Southern Scientists and State Academies of Science* (1991).

Nancy Smith Midgette

SEE ALSO Elisha Mitchell Scientific Society.

North Carolina Agricultural and Technical State University

North Carolina Agricultural and Technical State University (North Carolina A&T) in Greensboro was created as the Agricultural and Mechanical College for the Colored Race by the General Assembly in March 1891. The college really began operation the previous year as a result of the Morrill Act (1890), which furnished federal funds to be allocated in biracial school systems. The North Carolina College of Agriculture and Mechanic Arts for whites in Raleigh had been created by the General Assembly in 1887 and was ready to receive its share of funds by the fall of 1890. First, however, it was necessary to provide for a school of the same type for African American students. The board of trustees of the white school was empowered to make temporary arrangements to satisfy this requirement, and a plan was worked out whereby the college for African Americans was operated as an annex to Shaw University in Raleigh from 1890 through 1893.

Lacking a state-supported educational institution for African Americans in central Piedmont North Carolina, a group of interested citizens in Greensboro asked to have the college moved there. The group donated a 14-acre site for the school and $11,000 to aid in constructing buildings. This amount was supplemented by $2,500 from the General Assembly. The first building was completed in 1893, and the college opened on its own campus that fall.

In 1915 the name of the school was officially changed to the Agricultural and Technical College of North Carolina. In 1967 the General Assembly designated the college a regional university, and North Carolina A&T joined the consolidated University of North Carolina System in 1972. It is the largest of the historically African American colleges in North Carolina and is home to one of the state's three engineering colleges. Nearly 90 percent of the state's African American professionals and paraprofessionals in agriculture are graduates. Moreover, more than half of the state's black teachers and principals are among its alumni.

By the early 2000s, North Carolina A&T was a thriving public university with a student body of approximately 8,500. The school is comprised of a college of arts and sciences, a college of engineering, and six professional schools. It maintains extensive research programs in engineering, transportation, and agriculture. The school's physical plant occupies a 200-acre main campus near downtown Greensboro and a 600-acre research farm.

References: Warmoth T. Gibbs, *History of North Carolina Agricultural and Technical College: Greensboro, North Carolina*

(1966); Frenise A. Logan, "The Movement in North Carolina to Establish a State Supported College for Negroes," *NCHR* 35 (April 1958).

Charles W. Wadelington

North Carolina Arts Council. Governor Terry Sanford created the North Carolina Arts Council in 1964 to survey the status and needs of the arts and to advance the interests of the arts in the state. The Arts Council became a state agency in 1967 and is now a division of the Department of Cultural Resources, providing technical assistance and more than 1,300 grants each year to artists and nonprofit organizations throughout the state. By the early 2000s, North Carolina had a network of more than 100 local arts councils, more than 2,000 arts organizations operating in the state, and over 34,000 artists in all disciplines.

The Arts Council is governed by a 24-member board appointed by the governor to serve three-year terms. The board includes members from urban and rural areas across the state and from diverse racial, economic, and cultural backgrounds. Members set policy for the council and serve on panels that recommend grant awards. They also work with community organizations to help them expand and develop, targeting rural areas, urban organizations in communities with limited resources, and established organizations going through transition. Through their programs, the Arts Council gives grants, organizational assistance, and guidance to the groups and individuals that make up North Carolina's arts community. The Arts Council also recognizes North Carolina's eminent folk artists through the Folk Heritage Awards, given to a wide range of artists throughout the state.

In 1977 the General Assembly initiated the Grassroots Arts Program, the first such program in the country, to fund local arts initiatives on a per capita basis and allow decision making for the spending of the funds to remain at the local level. The money is administered by the Arts Council, matched at least dollar for dollar by local funds and used for projects in schools, community colleges, and libraries as well as other programs selected by local community groups. A Visiting Artist Program was introduced in 1971–72 as a joint project with the North Carolina Department of Community Colleges, with artists becoming active participants in community colleges, technical institutes, and the community itself.

The Arts Council also established the Artists-in-Schools Program in 1971–72. While the Visiting Artists Program provided residencies at community colleges, the Artists-in-Schools Program sent artists in all disciplines into the public schools in grades K–12 to teach, perform, and encourage creative expression in students during their formative years. The council was also instrumental in funding two arts-based curriculum experiments at Sunset Park Elementary School in Wilmington and Southport Elementary in Southport. The success of these programs and others has led to the development of North Carolina's A+ Schools, public elementary and secondary schools that have agreed to integrate arts with core curriculum instruction.

The General Assembly ratified legislation providing funds for commissioned artworks for installation in state buildings in 1982. From 1989 to 1995, the General Assembly designated 0.5 percent of any new or renovated state building's construction costs for artwork. Each of the artworks was selected through an open process involving users of the agency, design and arts professionals, and other citizens. Selection criteria included artistic excellence and relevance to the use, history, or character of the site, as well as safety and maintenance considerations. The Arts Council currently administers the 63-piece collection. While the Artworks for State Buildings Program no longer exists, public art sponsored by cities, counties, and private corporations can be found in parks, office buildings, and municipal facilities around the state.

The North Carolina Arts Council works closely with North Carolina's network of local arts councils across the state. The Arts Council of Winston-Salem/Forsyth County, established in 1949, is one of the oldest such organizations in the country.

Marianne B. Hayworth

North Carolina Association of Colleges and Universities traces its origins to October 1921 at a meeting of the state's college presidents and delegates in Greensboro. The meeting represented the birth of the North Carolina College Conference, which continued to meet until November 1965. At that time the conference's name was changed to the North Carolina Association of Colleges and Universities. It is the only statewide organization that brings together the University of North Carolina General Administration and its 16 public universities; the state's independent and church-related colleges and universities, including senior institutions and junior private colleges; the North Carolina Association of Independent Colleges and Universities; the State Department of Community Colleges and many of its community colleges, technical colleges, and technical institutes; and other related groups. The association provides a forum for the exchange of ideas and the sharing of solutions to mutual problems. Its African American counterpart, the North Carolina Negro College Conference, merged into the association in 1962.

Reference: J. Braxton Harris and Richard D. Howe, *North Carolina Association of Colleges and Universities, 1921–1986: A Short History of the Association and its Leaders and Honorees* (1986).

Wiley J. Williams

North Carolina Association of Educators (NCAE) was formed in 1970 with the union of the white North Carolina Education Association and the black North Carolina Teachers

Association. Its earliest origins can to traced to 1857, when the Education Association of North Carolina was formed by white teachers under the leadership of Calvin H. Wiley, the state's first superintendent of common schools. Only loosely organized, it sponsored Chautauquas, or adult educational events, in the summer for a number of years. By 1922 the association had grown and strengthened, with a full-time staff and headquarters in Raleigh.

During its first ten years, with the assistance of the four incumbent governors of North Carolina, the NCAE was instrumental in obtaining implementation of the Fair Employment and Dismissal Act of 1971, maternity leave, salary increases, kindergarten expansion, longevity pay, and student competency tests.

The joining of the black and white associations, involving 13,000 blacks and 50,000 whites, created some tension, since a biracial cooperative venture of this type had never been attempted in the state. The NCAE lent formidable support to the Equal Rights Amendment movement, and through its mouthpiece, *North Carolina Education*, opposed segregated academies, school vouchers, state tuition grants to private colleges, and the National Teachers Examination. Through its political action committee, the organization has sought to channel more state revenue toward teacher salaries and benefits and has concerned itself with issues such as school prayer, school violence, and gender discrimination. The NCAE has also taken an adamant stand against merit pay, a proposed career ladder system, and teacher dress codes, mainly on the grounds that decisions regarding these issues would be made subjectively by administrators.

References: Mary C. Cridlebaugh, "The North Carolina Education Association: An Interest Group Attempting to Influence State Policies in Education" (M.A. thesis, UNC-Chapel Hill, 1966); Percy Murray, *History of the North Carolina Teachers Association* (1984).

James I. Martin Sr.

SEE ALSO North Carolina Teachers Association.

North Carolina Association of Independent Colleges and Universities

was established in 1969 by North Carolina's regionally accredited private four-year colleges and universities as an advocate for private higher education in the state. The establishment of this organization was critical to the survival of North Carolina's private institutions of higher learning, which faced 5,000 vacancies at a time when enrollment in the state's public university system expanded. To shore up this imbalance, the Association of Independent Colleges and Universities successfully lobbied the General Assembly in 1971 to pass a law offering North Carolina residents enrolled in private institutions the opportunity to receive legislative tuition grants of $200 a year. Over the years these grants have made tuition for North Carolinians more af-

fordable, enabling more students to enroll in private schools. Full-time North Carolina residents are eligible for a Legislative Tuition Grant, and financially needy state residents can receive funds through the State Contractual Scholarship Fund.

The North Carolina Association of Independent Colleges and Universities represents all of the state's 36 independent institutions, providing information and research for its member schools in areas including public policy and government activities. A sister organization, the North Carolina Center for Independent Higher Education, promotes independent institutions to prospective students and others.

Lloyd Johnson

North Carolina Awards

are the highest civilian honor given by the state. Established by the General Assembly in 1961, they were first conferred in May 1964 and have been granted annually since then. State senator Robert Lee Humber of Pitt County (1898–1970) conceived the awards to recognize the superior achievements of North Carolinians in science, literature, the fine arts, and public service, as well as of one North Carolinian living outside the state who had been distinguished in one of the areas. Humber hoped that the awards would inspire others to excel in their chosen fields.

Shortly before his death, eminent American sculptor Paul Manship produced the design for the 2¾-inch diameter 14-caret gold medal presented to every recipient. Sculpted on the front in bas-relief is the Great Seal of North Carolina with the words "State of North Carolina Award" around the border. On the reverse are two scrolls, the first located in the center of the medal, inscribed with the name of the recipient and the date of the award and surrounded by a wreath. The second scroll is on the lower margin below the wreath and inscribed with the field for which the recipient is recognized. Encircling the central scroll and wreath along the outer margin is the motto Humber penned for this medal: "Achievement Is Man's Mark of Greatness."

The North Carolina Department of Cultural Resources, through a five-member North Carolina Awards Commission appointed by the governor, administers the North Carolina Awards. The commission works through committees of knowledgeable persons in the four fields from which nominees are considered. Anyone can submit nominations to the Awards Commission for consideration. By the early 2000s more than 200 individuals had received the award, including Hiram Houston Merritt (science, 1967), Samuel J. Ervin (public service, 1973), Andy Griffith (fine arts, 1984), Maya Angelou (literature, 1987), David Brinkley (public service, 1988), John Hope Franklin (literature, 1993), and LeRoy T. Walker (public service, 2004).

John L. Humber

Members of the North Carolina Bankers Association at the Atlantic Hotel in Morehead City, June 1908. NCC.

North Carolina Bankers Association (NCBA), a trade group acting as a legislative liaison at the state and federal level, was formed in July 1897 at a meeting held by the leaders of 22 North Carolina banks. Rocky Mount banker Thomas Hall Battle (son of Kemp P. Battle, president of the University of North Carolina and state treasurer) was the principal organizer. Battle was elected the first president of the NCBA, and Samuel Fox Mordecai, dean of the Trinity Law School, served as the association's first general counsel. In 1922 the office of NCBA secretary was made a full-time position, and Raleigh was designated the site of the association's headquarters. The title later was changed to executive secretary, then to executive vice president, and still later to president. The list of those filling this position includes Paul P. Brown (1923–40), Fred W. Greene (1944–50), Jesse A. Helms (1953–60), T. Harry Gatton (1960–81), Alvah D. Fuqua Jr. (1981–86), and Thad Woodard (1997–).

The NCBA began a unique banking education experience in 1937 at the University of North Carolina in Chapel Hill. The first state banking school in the nation, it was widely copied by other banking associations. The North Carolina School of Banking was followed in 1970 by successful efforts to cooperate in establishing the Southeastern Trust School at Campbell University in Buies Creek. In 1997 the Community Bankers Association of North Carolina merged with the NCBA; the new organization continued to be known as the NCBA and operated under its original charter. The NCBA offers educational and training programs and other services to its member institutions. The organization also publishes *Carolina Banker* magazine and operates the Community Investment Corporation of North Carolina, which provides long-term, low-cost financing for low- to moderate-income, multifamily developments in the state.

Reference: T. Harry Gatton, *Banking in North Carolina: A Narrative History* (1987).

T. Harry Gatton

North Carolina Baptist Historical Collection at Wake Forest University in Winston-Salem grew out of the work of the North Carolina Baptist Historical Society, established in 1885. The society began the collection and preservation of Baptist newspapers and other periodicals, college catalogs, minutes of Baptist associations and conventions, and other publications of historical value to North Carolina Baptists. Much valuable material originally was collected and kept in Raleigh under the supervision of the general secretary of the Baptist State Convention. By 1922 the collection had far outgrown the space that could be devoted to it, and negotiations were begun to move it to Wake Forest (then Wake Forest College, in Wake County), under special provisions that did not surrender the claim of the convention to the material. The removal was begun at that time but was not completed until a fireproof extension to the library was built in 1926.

Through the work of several prominent faculty members, most notably George W. Paschal and Charles C. Pearson, the collection continued to expand. But it was through the efforts of Ethel Taylor Crittenden, Wake Forest's librarian from 1915 to 1946, that the North Carolina Baptist Historical Collection became officially designated by the Baptist State Convention as the repository for all North Carolina Baptist historical materials and records. The daughter of the college's sixth president, Charles E. Taylor (1884–1905), Crittenden collected her father's papers and received donations from the North Carolina Baptist Historical Society and the state convention. In 1970 the North Carolina Baptist Historical Collection was renamed in her honor. The modern Ethel Taylor Crittenden Collection in Baptist History contains a vast amount of materials dating from the 1770s to the present, including more than 16,000 books and other publications and hundreds of biographical and autobiographical materials relating to Southern, Missionary, Primitive, African American, and other Baptist churches in the state. The collection, located in a wing of the Z. Smith Reynolds Library, is now almost exclusively supported by Wake Forest University, with its connection to the North Carolina Baptist State Convention diminished.

Reference: George Washington Paschal, *History of North Carolina Baptists* (2 vols., 1938).

Wiley J. Williams

North Carolina Bar Association dates to 1899, although a short-lived organization of lawyers had been formed in 1885. The first group had only two meetings and was formally disbanded after the 1899 association formed. On 10 Feb. 1899 lawyers met in Raleigh to establish a statewide association for the purpose of fostering goodwill among attorneys and improving the legal system, including codification of the laws. As president, the group named Platt D. Walker of Charlotte, and as secretary-treasurer, J. Crawford Biggs, professor of law at the

University of North Carolina and a prime mover in the effort to organize the state's lawyers. A charter of incorporation was obtained from the General Assembly.

By 1915 the legislature had granted the Bar Association the authority to create a board of legal examiners composed of the chief justice and two associate justices of the North Carolina Supreme Court. The board was responsible for testing and licensing applicants for the bar as well as for disbarring lawyers should the need arise, but by 1932 the Bar Association agreed that an incorporated bar should handle those functions. The following year the North Carolina State Bar came into being as a legal entity.

The modern voluntary bar is made up of two closely related organizations: the North Carolina Bar Association and the North Carolina Bar Foundation, Inc. The Bar Association is a trade organization concerned with substantive and procedural law and needed legislation. The Bar Foundation functions as a charitable and educational organization; it sponsors continuing education programs, encourages lawyers to provide legal assistance to the poor and disadvantaged, and works to improve the administration of justice in the state. By the early 2000s there were more than 12,500 members of the North Carolina Bar Association. In June 1991 Rhoda Billings, professor of law at Wake Forest University and former state supreme court justice, became its first woman president.

Reference: Fannie Memory Blackwelder, "Organization and Early Years of the North Carolina Bar Association," NCHR 34 (January 1957).

Memory F. Mitchell

North Carolina Booklet was a numbered and dated series of pamphlets published in Raleigh by the North Carolina Daughters of the American Revolution. Begun under the leadership of the society's founder, Mrs. Spier Whitaker, the *Booklet* was intended to develop and preserve North Carolina history by chronicling important events in a monthly publication. From 1901 to 1905 the *Booklet* appeared monthly, but in 1905 it changed to a quarterly. It continued as a quarterly until 1920, appeared for a year as a semiquarterly, and then was published annually, with one interruption, until 1926, when it ceased operations.

Raleigh native Mary Hilliard Hinton, educated at St. Mary's School and Peace Institute, was the *Booklet*'s editor throughout most of its life. Hinton's editorial assistants demonstrated great skill in historical and biographical research and writing, and the publication earned the respect of many of their contemporaries, including highly regarded educators of both men's and women's colleges, and from the general public. Civic and military leaders of the late nineteenth and early twentieth centuries wrote for the series, and businesspeople, jurists, and literary figures were among its contributors as well. The *Booklet* also published contributions by many noted historians of the state, including Samuel A. Ashe, Kemp P. Battle, R. D. W. Connor, J. Bryan Grimes, Marshall DeLancey Haywood, and Stephen B. Weeks.

William S. Powell

North Carolina Botanical Garden, a unit of the University of North Carolina at Chapel Hill, is a center for the study, display, interpretation, and conservation of plants and the natural areas of which those plants are a part. The botanical garden is among the nation's leading conservation gardens through its programs of reintroduction, plant rescue, conservation through propagation (in order to eliminate collection in the wild as a threat to wild populations), natural area management, and promotion of native plants combined with policies that prevent the release of exotic pest organisms. The botanical garden is responsible for the development, maintenance, and management of plant displays and natural plant communities. Known for rich displays of native plants and many species of endangered plants, the garden's collections also include highly valued and unique natural areas as well as seven nature preserves located across the state. Recent additions to the garden include the UNC Herbarium, and a Visitor Education Center has been proposed.

In 1903 William Chambers Coker, UNC's first professor of botany, began planting a teaching collection of trees and shrubs adjacent to the campus; this area became the Coker Arboretum, the first of the three units administered by the North Carolina Botanical Garden. Starting in the late 1920s, Coker and Henry Roland Totten proposed to build a more complete botanical garden south of the main campus. Although some plantings were made in the 1930s and 1940s, in 1952 the UNC trustees dedicated 70 forested acres for botanical garden development. To this tract were added 103 acres of dramatic creek gorge and rhododendron bluffs, donated by William Lanier Hunt, a horticulturist and a former student of Coker and Totten.

In 1961 C. Ritchie Bell was appointed the garden's first director; he was succeeded by Peter S. White in 1986. The garden's first public offering, the nature trails, opened on Arbor Day in 1966. In 1971 the first permanent employees were hired, the first display gardens were created, and the garden's volunteer program was initiated. One group of volunteers, lead by Mercer Reeves Hubbard, began the Herb Garden in 1973, creating a garden for the interpretation of human dependence on plant diversity. In 1976 the Totten Garden Center, named for Henry Roland Totten and his wife Addie, opened. In 1985 more than 15 years of work on the propagation of native plants was summarized in the popular book *Growing and Propagating Wild Flowers*, written and illustrated by the garden staff. The 1960s also saw the initiation of field research on a contiguous 367-acre tract of UNC land dedicated by the UNC trustees in 1984 as the Mason Farm Biological Reserve. Based on work at Mason Farm, John K. Terres, a noted ornithologist, published *From Laurel Hill to Siler's Bog* in 1969.

The main display area of the North Carolina Botanical Garden houses eight major collections: the Southeastern Habitat Collection, which includes the Mountain Collection, the Sandhills Collection, and the Coastal Plain Collection; the Plant Families Garden; the Carnivorous Plant Collection; the Rare Plant Collection; the Southeastern Fern Collection; Native Perennial Borders; the Aquatic Collection; and the Mercer Reeves Hubbard Herb Garden. In addition to the cultivated collections, a nature trail system provides access to 165 acres of natural Piedmont woodlands, including stands of mature hardwoods that surpass 200 years of age. Adjacent to the nature trails is the William Lanier Hunt Arboretum. The garden is also the home of the historic Paul Green Cabin. Used by the playwright as a retreat for creative inspiration, the cabin was rescued, moved, and restored on the site.

The North Carolina Botanical Garden's Rare Plant Collection is being developed in cooperation with the Center for Plant Conservation as a national resource for the protection of critically endangered species over a multistate region of the southeastern Piedmont. This collection is critical to conservation agencies for the restoration of wild populations.

Peter S. White

SEE ALSO Coker Arboretum.

North Carolina Catawba Company. The Catawba River rises in McDowell County and flows through several western counties for approximately 150 miles before entering South Carolina west of Charlotte. Along with the Wateree River, it was set to be cleared from the South Carolina line as far as might be feasible by North Carolina's first toll navigation company, incorporated by the General Assembly in 1788 but abandoned in 1796. The following year the legislature chartered the Catawba Company, which would be funded by private subscriptions and use local labor; the company was authorized to appoint overseers for the river and call upon men living within four miles to work on the watercourse. Replacing the Catawba Company in 1801 was the North Carolina Catawba Company, capitalized at $15,000, which was similarly permitted to clear the river from the South Carolina line as far as navigation might be "practicable."

The North Carolina Catawba Company experienced a lackluster existence for three decades, although by 1808 it had complied with its act of incorporation by making progress in rendering the river navigable. In 1809 the General Assembly authorized the company to conduct a lottery to obtain an additional $5,000 and in 1816 agreed that the state would subscribe to $6,000 worth of stock, grant the company control over all tributaries, and permit it to erect toll bridges across the river.

Notwithstanding the generosity of the state, attempts to collect installments on stock subscriptions and to undertake improvements proceeded slowly; one excuse was that the most formidable obstructions to navigation lay in South Carolina and thus prosecution of the work in North Carolina was inexpedient until its neighbor to the south finished its improvements. In 1824 the assistant state civil engineer completed a survey of the river that proved to be of little advantage. Legislative amendments to the company charter in 1821 and 1825 created confusion and additional headaches when the statutes referred to the Catawba Navigation Company and the North Carolina Catawba Navigation Company, respectively, rather than the North Carolina Catawba Company. Although the firm held a stockholders' meeting in 1830, interest had dissipated. In 1834 the Board of Internal Improvements, which had assumed responsibility for supervising the work on the river, reported that it had been so long since it had heard from the company that it despaired of receiving any communication. The board then recommended that the public would be best served if the company surrendered its charter.

Reference: Charles C. Weaver, *Internal Improvements in North Carolina Previous to 1860* (1903).

Alan D. Watson

North Carolina Central University in Durham was the first state-supported liberal arts college for African American students in North Carolina. It was chartered as a private institution in 1909 and opened its doors to students in July 1910. Its founder, James E. Shepard, served as its first president. In the beginning the college was known as the National Religious Training School and Chautauqua. Its purpose was the development of young African American men and women into citizens with fine character and sound academic training.

In 1915 the school was sold and reorganized as the National Training School. During this period Mrs. Russell Sage, a wealthy New York philanthropist, was a generous contributor to the school. In 1923 the General Assembly appropriated funds for the purchase and maintenance of the school, making it a publicly supported institution that operated as the Durham State Normal School. Two years later the legislature again renamed the college, and it became the North Carolina College for Negroes. Its mission was to offer African American youth of the region a liberal arts education and prepare graduates to become future teachers and principals of secondary schools.

The school graduated its first class as a four-year college in 1929 as a result of the sincere interest of Governor Angus W. McLean, generous gifts from Durham industrialist and philanthropist Benjamin N. Duke, and contributions from Durham citizens. In 1930 state appropriations made it possible for the school to expand its physical plant and improve its educa-

tional facilities. By 1939 the General Assembly authorized the establishment of graduate work in liberal arts and the professions. The School of Law began operation in 1940, and the School of Library Science was created in 1941. Because of this growth and expansion, the legislature changed the name of the institution to North Carolina College at Durham.

In 1969 the legislature again changed the name of the college to reflect its new university status. In 1972 North Carolina Central University became a constituent institution of the University of North Carolina System. The university in the early 2000s enrolled nearly 6,000 students earning degrees in a wide variety of undergraduate and graduate programs on its 100-acre campus.

References: William S. Powell, *Higher Education in North Carolina* (1970); Elizabeth J. Seay, "A History of North Carolina College for Negroes" (M.A. thesis, Duke University, 1941).

Charles W. Wadelington

North Carolina Christian Advocate. At a meeting of the Eastern North Carolina Conference of the Methodist Episcopal Church, South, in Pittsboro in December 1854, the idea for the publication of a paper as an official church organ was discussed and adopted. The first issue of the *Raleigh Christian Advocate*, as the paper was called, appeared on 4 Jan. 1856. The *Advocate* was suspended during the Civil War, reappearing as the *Episcopal Methodist* on 16 Jan. 1867, with H. T. Hudson as managing editor. After several years of leadership changes at the paper and only sporadic success, church leaders proposed the merging of the *Episcopal Methodist* with the *Western Carolina Advocate*, the official organ of the Western North Carolina Conference of the Methodist Episcopal Church, South. The merger was not finalized until 1919, when church leaders decided that having one paper would strengthen the bonds of fraternity and brotherhood between North Carolina's two Methodist conferences. Under a new charter providing for a joint publication board to be known as the Methodist Board of Publication, with its principal office in Greensboro, the *North Carolina Christian Advocate* became the official organ of the state's Methodists.

Since the merger, the *Advocate* has consistently publicized the work of the Methodist Church in the state, offering church members news and information regarding Methodist agencies and programs, missions, and disaster relief initiatives.

Reference: Henry S. Stroupe, "Beginnings of Religious Journalism in North Carolina, 1823–1865," *NCHR* 30 (January 1953).

Wiley J. Williams

North Carolina Classical, English, and Mathematical School—at times also called North Carolina Literary, Scientific, and Military Academy or Raleigh Institute—was a preparatory school for boys in Raleigh in the 1840s led by Robert Gray. The school opened in one of the buildings that had previously housed the Episcopal School for Boys on the Hillsborough Street site that became the campus of Saint Mary's School. In addition to "the regular Preparatory Classical Course," the school offered instruction in French, music, painting, and drawing. Gray's specialties were the classics and English, and his assistant principal Charles Doratt's were the visual arts.

The school moved in its second year into a remodeled school building in Baptist Grove (Moore Square), and later to an unidentified campus described only as "in the suburbs." In mid-1844, as the nation was involved in events leading to the Mexican War, the faculty and curriculum were enlarged to include military training. The former principal of the Portsmouth, Va., Military Academy, Oel A. Buck, became coprincipal and taught military tactics, including infantry and artillery practice, and introduced civil engineering and surveying. After Buck's departure in 1846 for service in the Mexican War, Simon Preston took over the mathematics and military department. The school apparently closed that year or early the next.

References: Elizabeth Reid Murray, *Wake: Capital County of North Carolina* (1983); Martha Stoops, *The Heritage: The Education of Women at St. Mary's College, Raleigh, North Carolina, 1842–1982* (1984).

Elizabeth Reid Murray

North Carolina Collection. SEE Historical Collections.

North Carolina College was opened in 1852 in Mount Pleasant as Western Carolina Male Academy. The school was organized by the North Carolina Synod of the Lutheran Church as "a high school of collegiate character." It consisted of a three-story brick building and a president's home, with William Gerhardt of Pennsylvania as president and professor. In 1859 the synod decided to have the charter amended in order to change the academy to a degree-granting college, and the institution became known as North Carolina College.

The college's prospects for many years of service seemed bright until its work was interrupted by the Civil War and many of its students entered the army, its professors resigned, and the school closed. In 1866 the college reopened with Louis A. Bikle as president. The first class was graduated in 1871. Many of the graduates entered the ministry, and some became leaders in church and state affairs. North Carolina College never recovered from its troubles during the Civil War and the loss of its endowment, however. In 1901 the synod, in a decision agreed to by the college's board of trustees, decided to suspend operations at the end of the 1901–2 academic year. From 1902 to 1933 Mount Pleasant Collegiate Institute, a secondary school, operated on the grounds that once housed North Carolina College.

Reference: Annie Hoover, "Two Fine Old Schools," *Uplift* 31 (June 1943).

Wiley J. Williams

North Carolina Conference for Social Service was formed in 1912, when a body of socially conscious men and women recognized that little attention was being paid to many disadvantaged North Carolinians. At that time, not a single county welfare department existed in the state, nor was there a probation plan for boys and girls or separate prison facilities for youthful offenders. The state did not offer aid to destitute widowed mothers or reparation for injured workers, and there were no effective child labor or minimum wage laws. Only the barest provisions existed for public assistance to the needy, aged, and blind.

The first conferences considered areas of greatest concern, which included illiteracy and compulsory school attendance, the need for reformatories and orphanages, procedures for dealing with youthful offenders, improvements to rural life, child labor laws, care of the mentally ill, and associated charities. In 1916 the conference drafted a bill to create county welfare offices, and the next year the General Assembly approved it—establishing the first system of its kind in the nation. Prisons, juvenile court reform, and protection for adopted children were among other issues soon addressed by the Assembly.

For many years the Conference for Social Service met in the spring to identify a topic for the year. Committees, forums, seminars, and publications were employed to bring subjects to public attention; resolutions, lobbying, and pronouncement of findings then followed. By fall the members had refined the subject, and it was subsequently presented to the General Assembly for action. Ellen Winston led the conference for many years and personally provided much of its financial support. Her death in 1984 brought a decline in the conference's resources. After a final meeting in September 1997, its remaining limited funds were used to establish a scholarship in the name of Winston and of Friends of Residents in Long Term Care, a group that had grown out of one of the conference committees.

W. W. Finlator

North Carolina Cotton Growers Association was founded as the North Carolina Cotton Growers Co-operative Association in 1922 to help cotton farmers gain greater control over the way their crops were marketed. The association was formed after the state's delegation to the American Cotton Association's convention in Alabama returned with favorable reports of the organizational plans proposed by California lawyer Aaron Sapiro. In 1920 cotton was one of the most important crops in North Carolina, accounting for 25 percent of the state's agricultural acreage and total crop value. When cotton prices dipped after World War I, falling from 40 to 10 cents per pound, North Carolina growers were desperate for some help. Cooperative marketing strategies were seen by many as the only solution to the industry's faltering stability. Through the efforts of B. W. Kilgore, director of the Extension Service of North Carolina State College (later North Carolina State University), and Clarence Poe, editor of the *Progressive Farmer* and *How Farmers Cooperate and Double Profits*, and with the cooperation of Governor Cameron Morrison, a coalition of bankers, politicians, cotton farmers, and extension workers incorporated the cooperative on 8 Feb. 1922.

The organization began as a means for individual farmers to achieve group bargaining power with textile mills, warehouses, and other markets. This allowed farmers who belonged to the association to work together to negotiate better prices for their crops. In 1964 the organization became the Carolinas Cotton Growers Cooperative; by the early 2000s, it included 1,500 cotton producers from North Carolina, South Carolina, Virginia, and Georgia. The group's mission has grown; the modern-day Carolinas Cotton Growers Cooperative assists planters with all aspects of growing, harvesting, and marketing their cotton crops. In order to help farmers plant and maintain a healthy crop, the cooperative serves as a clearinghouse for information concerning seed, seed treatments, plant growth, weed and pest control, and other related subjects. To assist with the harvest, the cooperative informs farmers of the latest technological advances in tractors, pickers, and other farm equipment. In addition, farmers can also turn to the cooperative for information concerning ginning and warehousing. Most importantly, the cooperative provides farmers with information and advice concerning a variety of marketing options to ensure that farmers get the best price for their crops.

Matthew C. Porter

North Carolina Council of Churches, founded in 1935, preceded the National Council of Churches, with which it nevertheless has a spiritual affiliation. The state council owes its origin to some remarkable North Carolinians, chief among them Greensboro-born H. Shelton Smith. Smith, after serving as professor of religious education at Columbia and Yale Universities, felt called to return home because of, in his words, "the ecumenical concern, the racial concern, and the concern for academic excellence in a region that sold down the river in a terrible war its best people and suffered for a century as a result of it." While teaching at Duke Divinity School, he gathered together leaders such as Episcopal bishop Edwin A. Penick, Methodist bishop Paul Kern, Moravian bishop Kenneth Pfohl, and the Reverend Trela Collins, executive secretary of the Baptist Sunday School Association.

They envisioned the council as a way to promote fellowship and joint service among Christian denominations. The acting secretary for the council's preliminary forum was Christian novelist and educator Liston Pope. Prominent black leaders such as Harold L. Trigg also worked with the North Carolina Council of Churches in the early years. From the beginning, the North Carolina Council of Churches sought to balance theological concerns with social action. Its programs have addressed such matters as "spiritual awakening," outreach to the unchurched, religious education, foreign missions, greed and society, promotion of the annual Week of Prayer for Christian Unity, and ecumenism.

The council has garnered public attention and even controversy mostly because of its stands on issues related to race, peace, labor, criminal justice, migrant farm workers, gays and lesbians, and other social concerns. For its first 20 years, it was the state's only interracial religious assembly. Its 1977 hearings and follow-up document questioning the immorality of the tobacco industry attracted national attention. Since the 1970s, the North Carolina Council of Churches has maintained a legislative liaison at the General Assembly and publishes a legislative newsletter as well as a general-purpose one.

All the mainline denominations, including Roman Catholics, whose dioceses joined the organization in 1977, belong to the North Carolina Council of Churches. Despite the early involvement of Baptist leaders, the Baptist State Convention declined to join, though some individual Baptist churches have remained active.

Sixteen member denominations provide financial support for the council and are represented on a governing board in proportion to their denomination's number in North Carolina. Delegates and denominational leaders occasionally issue joint statements and position papers, but most council work is practical and program oriented, conducted through working committees made up of volunteers or through special projects that attract outside funding. Such projects have included an Office of Economic Opportunity program that grew into a multistate organization for migrant and seasonal farmworkers, a refugee resettlement program, an interfaith disaster recovery committee, a program providing health care for low-income children, a program to train church members for ministry to persons with AIDS, People of Faith against the Death Penalty, and the JUBILEE project, which convenes churches to assist with and monitor welfare reform.

Reference: Sister Evelyn Mattern, SFCC, *We Come Together by Working Together: The First Fifty Years of the North Carolina Council of Churches* (1985).

Sister Evelyn Mattern

North Carolina Crop Improvement Association, designated by state law as the official agency for seed certification in North Carolina, had its origin in the North Carolina

Purebred Crop Seed Program that was conceived in the Crops and Plant Breeding Department of North Carolina College of Agriculture and Mechanic Arts (modern-day North Carolina State University) in 1928. At that time a study was made of crop improvement associations in 15 states. A certification plan was then presented to Ira Obed Schaub, dean of the college's School of Agriculture and the first full-time director of the college's Agricultural Extension Services, and Governor O. Max Gardner. The plan formed the basis of the crop seed program, which was enacted into law in 1929. The association, formed in July 1929, became a member of the International Crop Inspection Association (today the Association of Official Seed Certifying Agencies), whose members are responsible for seed certification in their respective states and Canada. The association's principal office is on the N.C. State campus in Raleigh.

Wiley J. Williams

North Carolina Day was a program presented in North Carolina's public schools during the early years of the twentieth century that was designed to "awaken a proper pride in the history of the state." The state's educational system had been ruined in the financial collapse following the Civil War. During Reconstruction, the Republican government passed the Constitution of 1868, which mandated that the state provide uniform, free public schools for all children between the ages of 6 and 21. These schools were also required to be operated for four months out of the year. Despite the intentions of the 1868 constitution, North Carolinians were disinterested in public education. Taxes were not levied and four-month sessions were ignored. As a result, illiteracy in the state rose and the quality of education worsened. When economic conditions in the state improved in the 1890s, new interest in the improvement of the public schools gained support.

By 1900, state officials began to emphasize education in North Carolina, sparking other cultural interests among North Carolinians. In September 1900, a group of citizens met in Raleigh to form the Literary and Historical Association, an organization devoted to the stimulation of literary and historical activity in North Carolina. The following year, the association began to sponsor North Carolina Day in the statewide public school system, and it continued to be celebrated for the next 25 years.

The purpose of this initiative was to set aside one day out of the school year to focus on one aspect of the state's history. The Literary and Historical Association created booklets on each year's topic for the schools. During the first years of the program, the topics covered broad concepts, such as the first English settlements in America and North Carolina. The 1904 North Carolina Day focused on the Pamlico section of the state. The day's program opened with a prayer and the singing of "My Country, 'Tis of Thee." Readings and recitations covered various topics related to the Pamlico area, all of which the students were to have read and studied in preparation for the day. Topics included De Graffenreid's colony at New Bern, the Cary Rebellion, the death of John Lawson, early education in the region, and fishing in eastern North Carolina. Questions were posed of the students, and the whole program concluded with the singing of "The Old North State."

Ellen Fitzgibbons Causey

North Carolina Debutante Ball. Debutante balls, or cotillions—social events in which parents formally present their teenage daughters to adult society—have been a feature of U.S. culture since the late nineteenth century. These balls, some of them all-white affairs, continue to be held in small numbers in North Carolina and other states. They remain controversial because of their unconcealed exclusivity, which is often based on economic and racial distinctions. The private, closed nature of some of the clubs that sponsor debutante balls has raised concern among those who view them as anachronistic and disturbing remnants of a racially segregated past. Supporters of debutante balls, however, argue that the events are important cultural institutions rooted in honorable traditions of personal and family pride, women's stature, and social responsibility, as well as a constitutional right to form private organizations.

The oldest and perhaps most influential ball still held in the state is the North Carolina Debutante Ball, sponsored annually by the Terpsichorean Club of Raleigh. Long considered the premier social event in the state, it originated in 1923 as the "Raleigh Fall Festival," sponsored by the merchants of the city. Prominent young white ladies from throughout the state were presented as candidates for Queen of the Festival before a queen was crowned by the governor. In 1927 the Terpsichorean Club was formed and held the first North Carolina Debutante Ball. The purpose of the club, which derived its name from the Greek mythological muse, Terpsichore, the goddess of dancing and choral song, was to "sponsor annually a ball for the presentation of North Carolina Debutantes to be held in Raleigh on the first weekend after Labor Day."

As the debutantes' activities grew from a one-night ball to a weekend of parties, teas, luncheons, and a second big dance, the ritual of having the debutantes formally presented was established. Each participant originally chose one chief marshal and four assistants. In 1956 the number of assistant marshals was reduced to two, and in 1963 the selection of fathers as chief marshals was encouraged, a change that greatly enhanced the dignity and significance of the occasion for the debutantes and their families.

The North Carolina Debutante Ball has been held every year since 1923, except during World War II. Because of the polio epidemic in 1948 it was postponed until a few days after

The debutante ball at Memorial Auditorium in Raleigh, 11 Sept. 1938. Courtesy of NCOA&H.

Christmas, and it was postponed for the same period in 1996 because of the damage wrought across the state by Hurricane Fran.

Hart Huffines

North Carolina Equal Suffrage Association

was formed in 1894 in Asheville but had little activity until November 1913, when it met in Charlotte and elected Barbara Henderson of Chapel Hill as president. Membership extended only to white men and women. On 1 Dec. 1913 the North Carolina organization was formally recognized by and became affiliated with the National American Woman Suffrage Association. Within a year, statewide membership had reached 210, and by the end of 1917 the association boasted 1,000 members. Its early efforts were devoted to promoting suffrage at the grassroots level, while members worked to present a non-militant organization that offered no threat to the stability of either home or society.

After years of controversy, the Nineteenth Amendment passed the U.S. Congress in 1919. By March 1920, 35 of the 36 states needed for ratification had approved it. North Carolina suffragists hoped that their state would cast the deciding vote but were bitterly disappointed when state senator Lindsay Warren of Beaufort County managed to have the issue tabled until the following year. When Tennessee voted for ratification in 1920, the suffrage amendment became federal law without North Carolina's vote. Eventually many former suffragettes joined the newly formed League of Women Voters. The North Carolina General Assembly finally ratified the Nineteenth Amendment in 1971.

References: Sara M. Evans, *Born for Liberty: A History of Women in America* (1989); Anne Firor Scott, *The Southern Lady: From Pedestal to Politics, 1830–1930* (1970); Elizabeth Taylor, "The Woman Suffrage Movement in North Carolina," NCHR 38 (January and April 1961).

Tom Belton

North Carolina Exposition of 1884,

promoting the agricultural and mechanical arts, was an important step in the progress of the state's industrial growth. The aim of the exposition was to boost North Carolina's industrial development and propel the state to a leadership position in the New South. The event was also designed in part to demonstrate to residents and outsiders alike that the state had recovered from the Civil War.

The exposition was held in October 1884 on a 55-acre tract on the north side of Hillsborough Street in Raleigh (the site of the North Carolina State Fair from 1873 to 1925). The exposition's history is linked to the development of its neighbor on the south side of Hillsborough Street, the North Carolina College of Agriculture and Mechanic Arts (present-day North Carolina State University). Exposition president William S. Primrose, a Raleigh insurance executive, served as the first chairman of the trustees of that land grant college, chartered in 1887.

In 1884 Primrose organized the state's business elite behind his idea of a large exposition. Such exhibitions were then in vogue, with the 1876 Philadelphia Exposition counted as a major success. The date of the North Carolina Exposition was selected to coincide with the 300th anniversary of the first of the Roanoke voyages. The organizational meeting took place on 30 January at the State Capitol, where Primrose took the leadership role and Salem businessman Henry E. Fries was elected secretary. In the weeks following, Primrose and Fries scoured the state, drumming up interest in the exposition. They had the assistance of nine vice presidents representing each of the state's congressional districts. Fries also made out-of-state visits to population centers along the East Coast, in time visiting more than 350 companies to promote the event.

A massive, square exhibition building, measuring 336 feet on each side with a 100-foot-square courtyard in each quadrant, was constructed over the course of the summer. The exposition operated from 1 Oct. to 1 Nov. 1884, with the traditional North Carolina State Fair and the state fair for blacks as adjuncts. On display were the finest products of the state's forests, farms, mines, and factories. Counties competed for the best exhibit, with those representing Durham and Forsyth generally judged to be the best. Many North Carolinians gained their first introduction to electric lights at the exposition. It all constituted one of the most impressive displays in North Carolina history.

Attendance, however, estimated at 60,000 over the course of four weeks, failed to meet the expectations of organizers. Even more disappointingly, no large-scale northern investment resulted from the event despite the best hopes of the planners. Fries in 1912 wrote to state leaders to inquire about the 1884 exposition's impact. All agreed that the exposition had boosted commerce and had inspired numerous North Carolinians, who returned to their communities with new enthusiasm for industrial development.

Reference: Jim L. Sumner, "'Let Us Have a Big Fair': The North Carolina Exposition of 1884," *NCHR* 69 (January 1992).

Michael Hill

North Carolina Farmer, a publication that referred to itself as a "journal of Agriculture, Horticulture and Domestic Economy," was established in June 1876 in Raleigh. Published monthly by James H. Enniss & Company, the journal cost one dollar per year or 10 cents per issue. In a three-column, 8 1/2″ by 11 1/2″ format on newsprint, the first issues had 14 pages. Regular departments included Soils and Fertilizers, Grasses and Grains, Rules and Tables, Cotton and Tobacco, Birds and Insects, and a Farm Calendar detailing chores for each month. Over the years, the *North Carolina Farmer* became a more general farm family publication, introducing departments including Family Fun, Hygiene, Poetry, Popular Science, and House-wifery. Contents also expanded to include short stories and market information.

In 1878 the masthead changed to include an illustration of the state capitol building, and the publication referred to itself as the "Organ of the Farmers of North Carolina." Also that year,

front-page news was eliminated in favor of an illustration department, with drawings each month of a different crop, animal, or bird along with descriptive material. Advertising included insurance, farm supplies, Bibles, and home remedies.

By February 1882 the *North Carolina Farmer* had expanded to 24 pages. It is not known exactly when the *Farmer* ceased publication. The last issue available is dated May 1888.

Edwin H. Mammen

North Carolina Farmers' Association evolved out of two meetings, the first of which took place in Raleigh on 18 Jan. 1887. Creation of the organization was inspired by a network of farmers' clubs organized under the leadership of Leonidas L. Polk, editor of the agrarian newspaper the *Progressive Farmer*. These clubs were for farmers with a desire to improve their conditions, especially through industrial education. The Morrill Land Grant Act of 1862 had donated public lands or land scrip to the states for education in agriculture and mechanical arts. North Carolina's land scrip fund, with an annual interest of $7,500, was awarded to the University of North Carolina, and its president, Kemp Plummer Battle, wanted to retain the funding. Polk and other agrarian leaders saw the need to establish an agricultural college.

Governor Alfred Moore Scales, an ally of Battle, invited the farmers to meet with the Board of Agriculture in Raleigh on the night of 18 Jan. 1887. Polk regarded this invitation as an attempt to sabotage the organizational efforts of farmers, who had already scheduled a mass meeting in Greensboro on the following day. Some farmers attended the meeting with the Board of Agriculture and forced the adoption of two resolutions. The first advocated creation of an agricultural college; the second demanded reorganization of the Department of Agriculture so as to place it under the control of practical farmers. Both resolutions were adopted.

The mass meeting was rescheduled and held in Raleigh on 26 Jan. 1887, with 243 delegates in attendance. Called to order by Polk, the delegates drew up a constitution that established the North Carolina Farmers' Association. It provided for a president, one vice president from each congressional district, a secretary, assistant secretaries, a treasurer, and an executive committee of five, all to be elected at the regular annual meeting for one-year terms. The constitution authorized the president to appoint standing committees of five on several matters, including industrial education, commercial fertilizers, and crop rotation. The delegates elected Elias Carr, an Edgecombe County planter, as president of the association.

The convention petitioned the legislature to establish an agricultural college, to which would be transferred the land scrip fund authorized by the Morrill Act. A second resolution demanded that the Department of Agriculture direct the college and be placed under the control of practical farmers and relieved of nonagricultural functions, such as immigration activities. The president was authorized to appoint a committee to lobby for the enactment of the resolutions and to formulate a plan for the college. Primarily concerned about industrial education, the delegates nevertheless pressed for other demands, such as the repeal of crop lien laws and the employment of convict labor on public roads in lieu of its lease to corporations. The philosophy of the order emphasized the farmer's individual responsibility for his success; nevertheless, it mobilized farmers for political action to achieve moderate goals.

A bill passed the legislature in March 1887 to establish the North Carolina College of Agriculture and Mechanic Arts. The institution would receive funding from the land scrip fund, grants from the Department of Agriculture, labor from the penitentiary, and private gifts of land. The Hatch Act passed by Congress in March 1887 authorized a federal grant of about $5,000 to help fund the college. Passage of the agricultural college bill was the outstanding achievement of the association.

The second meeting of the organization was held in Greensboro in January 1888 with more than 200 delegates in attendance. Carr and other incumbents were reelected. The delegates endorsed establishment of the agricultural college and again demanded reform of the Department of Agriculture. Committee reports were made on such subjects as drainage, crop rotation, use of improved seeds, stock breeding, and public roads. A farmers' institute was conducted during two days of the session. The body agreed to receive a delegation from the Farmers' Alliance, an organization that spread from Texas to North Carolina, in April 1887. The delegation explained the purposes of the order. The assemblage passed a resolution to "commend" the Farmers' Alliance to the public. The association agreed to meet in Raleigh one year later. That meeting never took place. The organization merged with the Farmers' Alliance in spite of some objection by executive committee members.

References: Stuart Noblin, *Leonidas LaFayette Polk: Agrarian Crusader* (1949); Lala Carr Steelman, *The North Carolina Farmers' Alliance: A Political History, 1887–1893* (1985).

Lala Carr Steelman

SEE ALSO Farmers' Alliance.

North Carolina Film Board

North Carolina Film Board (NCFB), the first state-sponsored documentary film unit in the United States, existed from 1962 to 1965 under Governor Terry Sanford. According to Sanford, the purpose of the board was to "produce films for use in North Carolina." The idea for the agency was brought to Sanford's attention by John Ehle, an associate professor in the Radio, Television, and Motion Pictures Department at the University of North Carolina in Chapel Hill. James Beveridge, head of the National Film Board of Canada, was chosen as director of the board. Members of the original NCFB advisory committee included playwright Paul Green, North Carolina A&T University chancellor Lewis Dowdy, and *Raleigh News and Observer* executive editor Sam Ragan.

The NCFB received ideas and requests for films from members of Sanford's staff, departments of state government, and historical organizations in North Carolina. Sanford himself asked that a film be made documenting the workings of the state legislature. In all, the board produced 19 films, each running an average of 30 minutes and costing approximately $30,000. Films were produced by a variety of filmmakers on a contract basis, although the board's staff often scripted the works.

Among films credited to the NCFB are *Land of Beginnings*, an exploration of the state's historic sites through the eyes of one North Carolina family; *Mirror of the Past*, a cinematic tour of Tryon Palace in New Bern; *Road to Carolina*, a historical journey through the state's first century; and *North Carolina's Tribute to President John F. Kennedy*, which covers the ceremony held on 17 May 1964 at Kenan Stadium in Chapel Hill honoring the late president and acknowledging the state's donation of $230,000 to the Kennedy Memorial Library Fund. Films about economy and labor—including *The Goodliest Land*, *Big Fish, Little Fish*, and *Food and the Future*—were also produced by the board, as was *The Search for Excellence*, a film about school consolidation.

The NCFB's most controversial project was a series of films requested by Sanford under the title *Minority Report*. These films, produced in conjunction with WUNC Television, were close examinations of the civil rights movement through personal interviews with young blacks—many of whom were taking part in the demonstrations that then defined college life on black college campuses throughout the state. The progressive nature of the films did not suit the political agenda of many state legislators, including Senator Tom White, chairman of both the Advisory Budget Commission and the Senate Appropriations Committee. When Sanford was defeated in the 1964 gubernatorial race by Dan Moore, support for the film board—considered by White and other legislators to be primarily the outgoing governor's "pet project"—all but died. In June 1965 the NCFB was terminated after only three years in existence.

References: Susan E. Ferrara, "The Demise of the North Carolina Film Board" (M.A. thesis, UNC-Chapel Hill, 1981); "Films Tell Tar Heel Stories," *Winston-Salem Journal*, 7 Feb. 1965; "Negro Youths to Discuss Discontent on TV Series," *Charlotte Observer*, 17 Mar. 1964; Elmer Oettinger, "The North Carolina Film Board: A Unique Program in Documentary and Educational Film Making," *Journal of the Society of Cinematologists* 5 (June 1965).

Jay Mazzocchi

North Carolina Folklore Society. SEE Folklore.

North Carolina Fund, a statewide antipoverty program for rural and urban communities, operated from 1963 to 1968. In those five years, the fund received and spent more than $13 million in what director George Esser described as a "quest for new ways to enable the poor to become productive citizens, to encourage self-reliance, and to foster institutional, political, economic, and social change designed to strengthen the functioning of democratic society." Inspired by Governor Terry Sanford and his assistant, John Ehle, the Ford Foundation provided initial funds for a demonstration program that would be dissolved after five years. Additional money from North Carolina foundations and the federal government enabled the fund to expand its support for education, community action, manpower development, research and planning, training and leadership development, and other efforts to fight poverty.

The largest of the fund's worker development programs was Manpower Improvement through Community Effort, which established field offices in eastern North Carolina to assist unemployed workers and their families using local resources. Mobility, the other major manpower effort, recruited unemployed rural people, developed jobs in industrial areas, and helped families to move and adapt to new jobs and homes.

Other programs sponsored by the North Carolina Fund included a summer volunteer project for college students, training for community leaders and workers, training for members of the federal VISTA (Volunteers in Service to America), and internships and curriculum development programs in colleges. Some organizations and programs established by the North Carolina Fund continued after the fund's termination, including the Learning Institute of North Carolina to improve public education, the Foundation for Community Development to facilitate economic development and leadership training, and the Low-Income Housing Development Corporation to assist communities in developing private, low-income housing and explore home ownership for low-income citizens.

Linda Sellars

North-Carolina Gazette, established by printer James Davis in New Bern, was North Carolina's first newspaper. Judging from the earliest extant copy—volume 1, number 15—the first issue was published on 9 Aug. 1751. Davis had emigrated from Virginia at the behest of the colonial Assembly, which urgently needed a printer to disseminate revised laws. North Carolina and Georgia were the last original colonies to acquire a printing press; many North Carolinians depended on the *Virginia Gazette* for news and for business and legal advertising. In many ways that paper served as North Carolina's newspaper. James Davis may even have been associated with the Virginia paper before emigrating south.

The *North-Carolina Gazette* had neither headlines nor column rules. It mostly provided international news, with emphasis on the arrivals and departures of ships. It thus presented little local or state news and offered no editorials. Periodically, the paper carried advertising, mainly notices from local merchants about new stocks of goods, some legal advertisements, and rewards for runaway slaves. Although it was supposed to be a weekly newspaper, the *Gazette* had no regular day of publication during its early years. The day of publication was altered or stopped temporarily many times and ultimately suspended in about 1759.

After four years of experimenting with the state's first magazine, the *North Carolina Magazine*, Davis revived the *North-Carolina Gazette* on 27 May 1768 with a larger page size and a new volume 1. But a violent storm in September 1769 destroyed his printing shop and buried the type in sand. A few months later he resumed operations but only intermittently. Due to the great difficulty in obtaining paper during the Revolutionary War, no other newspaper had appeared in North Carolina since 1775. In 1778 Davis was also forced to suspend publication when his son and assistant, Thomas Davis, was conscripted into the colonial army.

James Davis subsequently made another attempt to revive the *North-Carolina Gazette*, this time with Pennsylvanian Robert Keith. The first issue was dated 28 Aug. 1783, two years before Davis's death. With Davis in ill health, Keith took charge, naming the paper the *North Carolina Gazette; or, Impartial Intelligencer and Weekly General Advertiser*. The paper still had no headlines or column rules and offered little local news. The last known issue is that of 2 Sept. 1784. Another version of the newspaper was published from 1786 to 1798 by François X. Martin, who used the paper to support the Bill of Rights and other causes.

A community worker for the North Carolina Fund teaches math to two children on the front porch of their home near Boone in 1964. Photograph by Billy Barnes. NCC.

References: Clarence S. Brigham, *History and Bibliography of American Newspapers, 1690–1820*, vol. 2 (1947); Guion G. Johnson, *Ante-Bellum North Carolina: A Social History* (1937); Thad Stem Jr.,

JULY 4, 1777.   THE   NUMBER 363.

NORTH-CAROLINA GAZETTE.

With the latest ADVICES, FOREIGN and DOMESTIC.

SEMPER PRO LIBERTATE, ET BONO PUBLICO.

LONDON, *March* 20.

A N hundred men have been draughted from the artillery at Dublin, who are now on their march to Corke, to embark there for America.

Extract of a letter from Lisbon, *Feb.* 25.

"On the 21st instant the prince of Beira was married to his aunt, the princess Maria Teresa; and on the 23d departed this life Joseph I. king of Portugal. The prince of Brasil was proclaimed king, and the prisoners in all the prisons, as usual on accession of a new king, were set at liberty. The new monarch is said to be a true son of the Roman Catholick church, and a favourer of the Jesuits.

March 21. Yesterday a great number of officers, who are appointed to go to America, took leave of his majesty at St. James's, and received orders to repair to their different stations immediately.

A draught of 20 men is ordered to be made from every regiment in Ireland to reinforce the king's forces in America, which are to be replaced by recruits to be raised immediately for that purpose.

Extract of a letter from Plymouth, *March* 16.

"It is said his majesty's ships Somerset and Nonsuch have orders to sail the first fair wind, but their destination is a secret. The Blenheim of 90 guns is put into commission, and the command is given to capt. Hartwell, so that there are in commission, at Hamoaze, the Prince of Wales of 74 guns, Bienfaisant of 64, Foudroyant of 80, Queen of 90, Ocean of 90, and Boyne of 70, with the Blenheim as before, the Experiment of 50 guns, and Thetis frigate."

March 22. Saturday 100 of Burgoyne's light horse embarked at Gosport for America, and the same day his majesty's ship Romney sailed for Spithead.

General Clinton and lord T. P. Clinton are to embark the week after next for America.

quay gate to the common, after which he proceeded through the ropehouse where the fire happened; that he might himself be a witness to the devastation it had occasioned. He seemed very penitent, but had no clergyman with him, which gave reason to many to think him a Roman Catholick. He made a long harangue to the people, the particulars of which I have not been able to collect. His body, after hanging the usual time, was taken down and affixed into another gibbet on the beach, at the entrance of the harbour, near Blockhouse fort."

HOUSE of COMMONS, *March* 21. The House met at 2 o'clock, and read several private and publick bills. As soon as the current business was finished, the House went into a committee of supply, and came to the following resolutions, which were ordered to be reported on Monday. That 36,928 l. be granted for the pay of the Hessian chasseurs for the year 1777, pursuant to treaty; that 16,326l. be granted for Hanau chasseurs, ditto; that 39,588l be granted for 1282 Brandenburg Anspach, including artillery; that 3398l. be granted for Hessian deficiencies of the year 1776, and that 295,852l. surplus of the sinking fund be granted towards making good the supply.

PHILADELPHIA, June 5.

WE can with pleasure inform our readers, that general Washington has now received such supplies of men, &c. that he has removed his head quarters from Morristown to Middle Brook, on the east side of the Rariton, within seven miles and a half of Brunswick, where his army (which is not composed of soldiers whose times of service are continually expiring, but of those enlisted for the war) are encamped, and make a show that must please every person who is not a Tory.

From our posts near Middle Brook we are able to see and watch the movements of the enemy, who are encamped on Brunswick hills, the west side of the Rariton.

A portion of the front page of the *North-Carolina Gazette* for 4 July 1777. A news item with the byline "Philadelphia, June 5" describes the movements of George Washington and his army. NCC.

The Tar Heel Press (1973); Isaiah Thomas, *History of Printing in America: With a Biography of Printers and an Account of Newspapers* (1970).

Edwin H. Mammen

North Carolina Genealogical Society was established in 1974 to raise the standards of genealogical research; to encourage and instruct members in the area of genealogical research; to acquaint members with sources of genealogical material; to serve those interested in genealogy through its publications and workshops; and to promote the collection, preservation, and utilization of manuscripts, documents, and other material of genealogical or historical value. The society is served by an elected president, first vice president, second vice president, secretary, treasurer, a past president, and six directors representing all sections of the state. The society issues a quarterly journal and a quarterly newsletter, holds at least two workshops each year, and has various genealogical publications for sale. Its 2,200 members reside all over the United States and in several foreign countries.

In 1973 the North Carolina Literary and Historical Association appointed an exploratory committee to determine the feasibility of creating a genealogical section within that organization. In November of that year, a group of interested parties voted instead to form an independent genealogical society; a steering committee was appointed with Adm. A. M. Patterson serving as chairman.

The formal organization of the society occurred on 22 June 1974 in Raleigh after articles of incorporation and bylaws had been established by the steering committee earlier that year. Charles R. Holloman was elected the first president of the North Carolina Genealogical Society. In late 1974 a publications committee was authorized to plan for a quarterly journal of the society. Guidelines were adopted and the first journal, edited by George Stevenson (alias Haywood Roebuck), was issued in early 1975. In 1987 the society hosted the annual National Genealogical Society Conference in Raleigh. Over the years, the board of directors of the society has met at locations all over North Carolina in an attempt to involve members in its work. An annual meeting is held in Raleigh in late October each year consisting of a workshop featuring noted genealogical speakers and a society business meeting.

Reference: Jo White Linn, *History of the North Carolina Genealogical Society, 1974–1984* (1984).

R. S. Spencer Jr.

North Carolina High School Athletic Association,

which traces its origin to 1913, is a voluntary nonprofit corporation that administers the state's interscholastic athletic program. Any public or nonboarding parochial high school in the state is eligible for membership, provided it is accredited by the state Department of Public Instruction and as long as the school adopts and maintains a prescribed code designed to guarantee wholesome athletic competition. Each of the more than 300 member schools has pledged to put the best interests of the student athletes above any other athletic purpose.

In 1913 University of North Carolina librarian-professor Louis Round Wilson spearheaded the founding of a state high school athletic association as a part of the university's Extension Division, of which he was director. The first statewide high school athletic contest—a track meet at UNC on 11 Apr. 1913—was conducted by the Greater Council, a UNC student organization composed of the president of the student body, class presidents, and other student leaders. As a result of this track meet, the General Alumni Athletic Association of UNC, seeing the possibilities of conducting a statewide program of interscholastic high school athletics, appointed a committee on high school athletics (part of the Extension Division), which until 1924 exercised general supervision of the various championship contests.

The athletic association, which has offices in Chapel Hill, recognizes athletic activities as an integral part of a child's educational experience. By uniting in a cooperative manner,

member schools are better able to promote the growth of interscholastic athletics, to maintain a high and uniform standard for all high school sports activities, to enact as well as enforce rules and practices that afford equitable competition, and to protect the athletes from exploitation by special interests whose purpose is not educational in nature. Other services rendered by the organization include certifying the eligibility of more than 90,000 students in various sports; providing catastrophe insurance coverage for athletes, cheerleaders, managers, and coaches; maintaining financial records and distributing funds to the schools; investigating incidents of unsportsmanlike conduct and levying prescribed penalties as appropriate; recruiting, organizing, and training game officials; and working with the news media and the public to promote interscholastic athletics.

References: Ernest M. Allen, "A Study of the North Carolina High School Athletic Association" (M.A. thesis, UNC-Chapel Hill, 1940); *Facts about the North Carolina High School Athletic Association* (1978).

Wiley J. Williams

North Carolina Historical Review was founded in 1924 under the aegis of the North Carolina Historical Commission. Trinity College history professor William K. Boyd proposed the quarterly journal in 1922, and the following year the legislature provided the funding to launch it. The first editor was Robert B. House, who had worked for the Historical Commission since 1919 and attempted to fashion the *North Carolina Historical Review* after the *American Historical Review*. He appointed the first three-member editorial board and solicited articles from scholars of North Carolina and southern history. Beginning as an editorial assistant with the second issue, David Leroy Corbitt inaugurated a 37-year career with the *Review*. For seven years he edited a "Historical Notes" section and later became managing editor of the *Review* until his retirement in 1961. Though House was the *Review*'s first editor, R. D. W. Connor, the first secretary of the historical commission and by 1924 Kenan Professor of History at the University of North Carolina in Chapel Hill, was in many respects the guiding influence behind the new quarterly. Consulting closely with House, Connor suggested two regular features that were eventually adopted: a "Historical News" section and a bibliography of recent articles on North Carolina history. Connor also chose the publication's title.

In 1952 members of the North Carolina Literary and Historical Association began to receive the *North Carolina Historical Review* as a benefit of membership. Also in that year, the North Carolina Department of Archives and History launched the bimonthly newsletter *Carolina Comments* as a companion to the *Review*. Although a Historical News section continued in the *Review* through 1966, *Carolina Comments* absorbed much of its content. In 1953 the Historical Society of North Carolina established the annual R. D. W. Connor Award for the best article to appear in the *Review*.

In 1934 the *North Carolina Historical Review* began printing an annual bibliography of recently published books about North Carolina, and it added an annual bibliography of theses and dissertations about the state in 1979. For many years the *Review* published papers delivered at the annual meeting of the North Carolina Literary and Historical Association during "Culture Week," but that practice was discontinued during the 1980s.

Over the course of its history, the *North Carolina Historical Review* has published more than 800 articles and thousands of book reviews. While the articles have focused primarily on North Carolina, articles on adjacent states and on the South in general have also appeared. In addition, the *Review* has published many thoroughly annotated original documents. Two comprehensive indexes to the *Review* have been published: one covering the journal's first 50 years (1924–73) and one covering the following ten years (1974–83). An Advisory Editorial Committee, today consisting of five members who specialize in the history of North Carolina and the South, assists the editors in appraising articles submitted for publication. Members of the committee serve five-year, staggered terms, with annual rotation.

The *Review* is a scholarly journal that insists upon high standards of research, writing, and presentation. Fully illustrated and indexed, each volume (4 issues, published in January, April, July, and October) runs between 500 and 600 pages. A typical issue includes 3 articles, a review essay or bibliography, 25 to 30 book reviews, and 5 to 10 book notes. Approximately 1,500 people and institutions subscribe to the *North Carolina Historical Review*. It is widely regarded as one of the best state historical journals in the nation. Many of its articles are cited in scholarly works, reprinted in anthologies, and assigned as readings in state, regional, and national history courses.

References: Willard B. Gatewood Jr., "'Rendering Striking Historical Service': North Carolina's Historical Publications Program, 1903–1978," in Jeffrey J. Crow, ed., *Public History in North Carolina, 1903–1978* (1979); Paul Murray, "Thirty Years of the New History: A Study of the *North Carolina Historical Review*," *NCHR* 32 (April 1955); Thomas C. Parramore, "Forging the Tremulous Link: The First Half-Century of the *North Carolina Historical Review*," *NCHR* 51 (October 1974).

Jeffrey J. Crow

North Carolina Humanities Council (NCHC). In 1970 the National Endowment for the Humanities (NEH), a federal agency established in the mid-1960s to promote research and education in the humanities, was authorized by Congress to organize and fund state-based humanities councils. These councils were charged with making the fields of the humanities more a part of the civic discourse by shifting humanities scholars from colleges and universities into local communities. In June 1971 a small group of North Carolinians—including John Caldwell, chancellor of North Carolina State University; H. G. Jones, director of the North Carolina Department of Archives and History; and George Bair, director of Educational Television at the University of North Carolina—organized the North Carolina Committee for Continuing Education in the Humanities. This committee, subsequently renamed the North Carolina Humanities Committee and later still the North Carolina Humanities Council, received funds each year from the NEH, which in turn "regranted" the money to public libraries, colleges, and community groups that applied for financial assistance to sponsor public programs.

In the early 1970s the NCHC solicited proposals that focused on public policy issues arising from North Carolina's transition from a rural, agricultural society to an urban, industrial one. Dozens of projects—community forum series, discussion groups, films, lectures, and plays—were funded in communities across the state, and thousands of people participated. In 1976 the NEH began encouraging state councils to fund projects dealing with a wider variety of issues, and the NCHC broadened the scope of the proposals it solicited.

By the mid-1990s, more than 1 million North Carolinians had taken part in a program funded by the NCHC, and the council's budget had grown to more than half a million dollars annually. Every year, hundreds of humanities scholars—historians, poets, philosophers, and others—crisscrossed the state participating in public programs that explored topics ranging from the history of the blues to medical ethics and U.S. foreign policy.

By the early 1990s the council's primary funding source, the NEH, along with its sister agency, the National Endowment for the Arts, had come under steady attack by conservative critics in Congress and the media for its alleged promotion of "indecent" artistic works. Funding cuts and even the elimination of both agencies were proposed. Two former heads of the NEH joined the critics and recommended that the agency they had once led be dismantled. In response to this challenge, the council began, in the mid-1990s, to solicit more funding from private sources and to pursue funding from the state government. This strategy began bearing fruit as private contributions rose, and in 1997 the North Carolina General Assembly approved an appropriation of $100,000 for the NCHC. By 2006 the council had an annual budget of more than $1 million and had recorded more than $13 million in total grants since its founding.

John J. Beck

North Carolina Industrial Association (NCIA), an organization of African American civic leaders formed in 1879,

was known primarily for its presentation of the annual North Carolina Industrial Fair from 1879 to 1930. The central purpose of the NCIA, as stated in its charter granted on 14 Mar. 1879 by the General Assembly, was "to encourage and promote the development of the industrial and educational resources of the colored people of North Carolina." The NCIA secured permission from federal government officials to hold the first fair in 1879 in the barracks buildings and grounds of Camp Russell near the site of the 1853–72 state fairs, east of Raleigh. Successive fairs continued there through 1890; the Confederate Soldiers Home acquired the site that year. Afterward, the fair was held on North Carolina's official State Fairgrounds, beginning in most years during the week immediately following the "white" state fair each October.

The New York pictorial publication *Frank Leslie's Illustrated Newspaper* sent two men to North Carolina to cover the first fair. The 6 December issue featured a full page of sketches by the illustrator and the reporter's detailed description of the parade, competitions, educational exhibits, and entertainment features. Parades from Fayetteville Street to the grounds inaugurated opening day of the fair each year, and balls frequently closed the annual festivity. Some additional social events were fund-raisers for charities, the beneficiaries one year being St. Agnes and Leonard Hospitals in Raleigh. It became a custom for the state's governor to make a short opening address. Featured speakers over the years were other North Carolina officials, U.S. congressmen, African American leaders, and such widely known public figures as Frederick Douglass in 1880, Booker T. Washington in 1903, and black bank president Maggie L. Walker of Virginia in 1915.

The final North Carolina Industrial Fair took place in October 1930, under the management of educator Charles N. Hunter, one of the founders of the association and the fair. Although preparations were partially under way for a 1931 fair, it did not materialize; Hunter died in Raleigh on 4 Sept. 1931. His biographer notes that the *Raleigh News and Observer*'s report on the cancellation of the black fair included the statement that "Professor Hunter's death put a stop to the arrangements."

References: John H. Haley, *Charles N. Hunter and Race Relations in North Carolina* (1987); Frenise A. Logan, "The Colored Industrial Association of North Carolina and Its Fair of 1886," NCHR 36 (January 1959).

Elizabeth Reid Murray

North-Carolina Magazine; or, Universal Intelligencer,

was the first magazine in North Carolina. It was published by printer James Davis in New Bern during a period when his *North-Carolina Gazette*, the state's first newspaper, was suspended. The first issue, dated 1–8 June 1764, was eight pages, printed without column rules and two col-

umns to the page. The magazine was meant to be bound annually; pages were numbered consecutively from the first issue until the last, four years later.

The lack of regular mail greatly limited the amount of news in the *North-Carolina Magazine*. Instead, it was filled with long extracts from the works of religious writers and historians or selections from British magazines. In the fifth issue, dated 6–13 July 1764, a long history of the Roman Empire was begun and continued through several succeeding installments. A page and a half was given to advertisements, including several offering rewards for the return of runaway slaves and one from Davis presenting for sale a "Collection of All the Acts of Assembly of the Province of North Carolina." A notice to the freeholders of Christ-Church Parish of an election to be held for new vestrymen advised: "There is a fine of Twenty Shillings on every Freeholder in the Parish who fails to attend, and give his vote."

Initially, the price for the magazine was four pence; with the issue of 28 Dec. 1764, the size was reduced to four pages without any change in price. On 27 May 1768 the *North-Carolina Magazine* was succeeded by another version of the *North-Carolina Gazette*, James Davis's original imprint.

References: Clarence S. Brigham, *History and Bibliography of American Newspapers, 1690–1820*, vol. 2 (1947); Thad Stem Jr., *The Tar Heel Press* (1973); Stephen B. Weeks, *The Press of North Carolina* (1891).

Edwin H. Mammen

North Carolina Manual was first published in 1874 by the North Carolina secretary of state as a volume of nearly 400 pages entitled *Legislative Manual and Political Register of the State of North Carolina*. Another edition was printed in 1903, and thereafter it appeared biennially. The title *North Carolina Manual* was first used in the 1917 edition.

Athough always intended to provide information for state legislators, the manual also has been useful to the general public, especially the news media, historians, and government officials. With the exception of the three editions between 1903 and 1907, the manual has contained biographical sketches of North Carolina's members of Congress, state legislators, state executive and administrative officials, and state and federal court judges. Most of the early volumes included retrospective material; the 1905 issue, for example, listed the governors since 1663 and the secretaries of state since 1777. The 1913 edition, compiled by R. D. W. Connor, secretary of the North Carolina Historical Commission, contained more than 1,000 pages and for the first time presented a substantial amount of information about North Carolina's political history in one volume. This edition also gave election returns for presidents and governors from 1836 to 1912, as well as the votes on various conventions and constitutional amendments. Information found in the 1913 *Manual* was verified, updated, extended, and expanded in *North Carolina Government, 1585–1974*, edited by John L. Cheney Jr.

Subsequent editions of the *North Carolina Manual* have been expanded to include state symbols, election statistics, maps and charts, information on higher education, historical perspectives of the counties, photographs (both color and black and white), census figures, and other information.

Wiley J. Williams

North Carolina Maritime Museum began under the auspices of the U.S. Fish and Wildlife Service and the North Carolina Department of Conservation and Development in the 1930s. Local citizens donated valuable marine life specimens and maritime artifacts that held memories and represented the life and work of coastal natives. Roy Hampton of Conservation and Development was de facto curator of the collection in Morehead City, which was located on the site of the present-day civic center.

Exhibits at the North Carolina Maritime Museum in Beaufort. Photograph courtesy of North Carolina Division of Tourism, Film, and Sports Development.

In 1950 the collection was taken over by the North Carolina Department of Agriculture as an extension of the North Carolina Museum of Natural History. Ruth Deyo of Morehead City became manager of the collection and tended it on an unpaid, seasonal, part-time basis much as Hampton had done. In 1975 Charles McNeill was named curator of the collection by Agriculture Commissioner James A. Graham and became its first paid employee. The museum moved to a storefront location on Turner Street in Beaufort, and McNeill began the process of building a staff.

The modern Maritime Museum features an eclectic collection of maritime artifacts and natural history specimens. The former include navigational instruments, boat models, boatbuilding tools, nautical paintings and prints, and traditional wooden boats of North Carolina origins. The museum's natural history collection includes animal and reptile mounts representative of the coastal plain and one of the largest shell collections on the East Coast. It also includes a small aquarium supplied from sea life captured locally by staff members. The museum researches and publishes works on topics pertinent to its mission of preserving the state's maritime and natural coastal history. Works on traditional boats, coastal flora, boat models, and maritime history are written by members of the museum staff, produced by the museum, and sold in the museum bookstore. Coastal folklife was added to the museum's areas of research in 1988.

One of the museum's strong suits has been its high-quality, imaginative public programs, led by curators with appropriate academic backgrounds. The programs include offshore trawl and dredge trips, where participants get firsthand looks at whatever the net has captured; tours to capture sea life at nearby jetties; searches for shells on Bird Shoal and for fossils at Aurora; bird stalking on the Outer Banks; and talks with local boat builders on Harkers Island. The former U.S. Coast Guard station at Cape Lookout serves as a program facility for studying dolphin behavior and for the barrier island conservation curriculum.

Since the museum opened a 20,000-square-foot facility in 1985, it has attracted about 200,000 visitors annually. Reminiscent of the old Outer Banks lifesaving stations in style, the building has a gray cypress shingle exterior; the interior is post-and-beam, all-wood construction of warm, unpainted yellow pine. Property for the museum and its boat building center added in 1990 on the waterfront was donated by Harvey and Evelyn Smith.

Rodney D. Barfield

North Carolina Military Academy, also called the Hillsborough Military Academy, was established in Hillsborough in 1859 by Charles C. Tew, a graduate of The Citadel, and chartered in 1861. While its buildings were being constructed west of town on a high ridge close to the railroad, the school was conducted in the old Hillsborough Academy building in town. Assisting Tew was W. D. Gaillard. Both entered the Confederate forces during the Civil War, and Tew was killed at Sharpsburg in 1862. Throughout the war the school was run by Maj. William H. Gordon and continued to supply officers and enlisted men to the forces.

In 1867 the legislature changed the school's name to the North Carolina Military and Polytechnic Academy and stipulated that eight students a year receive free tuition in return for two years' teaching in the state upon graduation. Apparently a failure, the school was discontinued in 1868.

The massive three-story, crenellated barracks that held 125 cadets, the uncompleted matching headquarters, and a half-dozen smaller structures were purchased by Paul C. Cameron in 1872, and in 1874 he persuaded the principals of the noted Horner and Graves School at Oxford to relocate to Hillsborough and occupy the buildings. The illness of one principal and death of the other within two years again left the buildings empty, and Cameron was unable to persuade another organization to take over the facility permanently. His heirs sold the 42 acres with the existing buildings to the Farmers' Alliance in 1895. In 1919 that organization sold the tract to a developer. The barracks and frame service buildings slowly decayed, or the bricks were appropriated for other construction. The headquarters building, a National Register structure, remains a private residence.

Reference: Ruth Blackwelder, *The Age of Orange* (1961).

Jean B. Anderson
Additional research provided by Robert E. Ireland.

North Carolina Military Institute,

a state-supported military school, opened in Charlotte in 1859. North Carolina by that time had established itself as a leader in private military education, which became popular throughout the South. After Virginia, South Carolina, and other southern states subsequently experimented with publicly supported military schools, North Carolina followed suit. Due to the efforts of future Confederate general Daniel H. Hill, the cornerstone for the institute was laid in 1858. The school received a charter from the state legislature in 1859 and opened its doors that fall with 40 cadets. The first instructors included Hill and future Confederate generals James H. Lane and Charles C. Lee. Within a year the school had more than 100 cadets, and that number had grown to 150 by April 1861.

The coming of the Civil War closed the institute in 1861. Governor John W. Ellis ordered the entire corps of cadets to duty as drillmasters in Raleigh, and many later served in the 1st North Carolina under Hill, their former superintendent. The school was revived briefly in 1873 by Col. John P. Thomas, later superintendent of The Citadel. After a few years, it functioned as a graded school only.

References: John Hope Franklin, *The Militant South, 1860–1861* (1956); Edgar W. Knight Jr., *A Documentary History of Education in the South before 1860*, vol. 4 (1952).

Rod Andrew Jr.

North-Carolina Museum

was one of the names associated with a short-lived effort in Raleigh in the 1810s to gather and display an assemblage of natural and manufactured objects, curiosities, and works of art. It was also referred to as the Raleigh Museum, and sometimes in newspaper notices simply as "the Museum." Later writers have called it Marling's Museum, because the name of artist Jacob Marling (1774–1833) is most often associated with the effort. In 1818 Marling constructed a building to house his collection on the north side of East Martin Street, some 80 feet east of Fayetteville Street. Marling had advertised in May 1815 his intention of opening a "Museum and Gallery," for which he had "commenced collecting whatever is rare and curious, in the production of nature," as well as art and literature.

Associated with the museum during part of its short existence was a public reading room and library. Marling had extended an invitation for people to deposit in the museum collection "articles worthy of notice" that they might have found "in their excursions." Gen. Calvin Jones of Raleigh was one of those who some months later "transferred the whole of his collection to this institution." Meanwhile, Marling began constructing on the Martin Street lot a building designed for exhibiting the collections. In August 1818 he pronounced the North-Carolina Museum open. The admission price was 25 cents and tickets for the year cost $5. Marling again invited individuals to contribute "natural and artificial curiosities, sketches, maps, drawings and paintings, rare coins and books," promising to append to those exhibited "the name of the liberal donor."

It is unclear why or when Marling closed or lost the museum, but transfer of the loaned collections to another location and to other proprietors may have begun as early as 1819 based on newspaper accounts and advertisements. The reading room apparently continued for a while after that date.

References: Charles L. Coon, *North Carolina Schools and Academies, 1790–1840* (1915); Marshall DeLancey Haywood, "Jacob Marling: An Early North Carolina Artist," *North Carolina Booklet* (April 1911); Ben F. Williams, "Jacob Marling, Early North Carolina Artist," Retrospective Exhibition Catalogue, North Carolina Museum of Art (1964).

Elizabeth Reid Murray

North Carolina Museum of Art

was established in Raleigh in 1947 when the General Assembly appropriated $1 million for the purchase of Old Master paintings. By that action, North Carolina became the first state in the nation to use pub-

Exhibit areas of the North Carolina Museum of Art. Photograph courtesy of the North Carolina Museum of Art, Raleigh.

lic funds to create an art collection for its citizens. Although the State Art Society had begun in 1924 to promote the foundation of an art museum for the state, it was not until 1943 that Robert Lee Humber, international lawyer and state legislator, went to New York to search for sources of support. Through his efforts, the Samuel H. Kress Foundation matched the General Assembly's appropriation, and the purchase of paintings began.

In 1953 the General Assembly authorized the expenditure of additional funds to renovate the former State Highway Building in Raleigh as a facility for the display of the collection. The museum in 1961 separated from the State Art Society, and in 1967 the General Assembly authorized the creation of a State Art Museum Building Commission charged with the construction of a new museum building. In 1983 the museum left downtown Raleigh for new facilities on Blue Ridge Road in western Raleigh. The modern museum includes exhibition galleries, a conservation laboratory, educational facilities, an auditorium, technical workshops, offices, a reference library, and a gift shop.

The function of the North Carolina Museum of Art is to acquire, preserve, and exhibit works of art for the education and enjoyment of the people of the state and to conduct programs of education, research, and publication designed to encourage an interest in and an appreciation of art. The museum

now houses a collection spanning more than 5,000 years of the history of art, from ancient Egypt to the present, making it a major cultural resource for the state and the region.

In the 1990s, officials began working to develop outdoor portions of the museum's 100-acre site, which now includes several art installations and the Joseph M. Bryan Jr. Theater in the Museum Park. The outdoor theater, opened in 1997 with seating for 500 and a large lawn that can accommodate 2,000 additional guests, hosts films and musical performances. A clever feature of the museum's grounds is a massive representation of the phrase "Picture This" in 80-foot-long letters built of natural and man-made materials, readable only from the air.

While continuing to build its contemporary art collection as well as one of the Southeast's finest collections of Old Master paintings, the museum in 1999 began a series of blockbuster shows highlighted by Monet to Moore: The Millennium Gift of Sara Lee Corporation, and Rodin: Sculpture from the Iris and B. Gerald Cantor Collection and Additional Works. The Rodin show drew 300,000 visitors and was accompanied by a number of related events under the name Festival Rodin, which became the largest-ever marketing effort for the arts in North Carolina. A major renovation of the Museum's European Galleries was completed in 2002. In 2003–4 a major observance of the centennial of the Wright Brothers flight at

Kitty Hawk took place at the museum, centered on the special exhibit Defying Gravity: Contemporary Art and Flight. Between October 2004 and January 2005 the museum hosted another hugely popular exhibit, Matisse, Picasso and the School of Paris: Masterpieces from the Baltimore Museum of Art, which featured works by Van Gogh, Gauguin, Cézanne, Monet, Rodin, and Degas, as well as Matisse and Picasso.

Reference: Edgar Peters Bowron, ed., *The North Carolina Museum of Art: Introduction to the Collections* (1983).

Armistead Jones Maupin

North Carolina Museum of History.

"A ponderous key" was the seed that eventually grew into the North Carolina Museum of History, located in Raleigh. The key's owner, a Mr. Kruester, presented it to the *Raleigh News and Observer* in 1883, claiming the key unlocked a door in North Carolina's first capitol building, which had been destroyed by fire in 1831. The gift spurred the newspaper's city editor, Frederick Augustus Olds, known as "Colonel" Olds because of his service in the State Guard, to write an editorial titled "Some Old Relics." Olds's editorial urged readers to notify him of any "curiosities" they might possess, and the artifacts that he amassed over the next half century ultimately became the North Carolina History Museum's core collection.

Olds became known statewide as an insatiable collector. He left the *News and Observer* in 1886 but continued to accumulate artifacts during the 1880s and 1890s. In 1900 the State Literary and Historical Association appointed him chairman of the Committee on Historical Museums. But the state had no history museum. The State Museum, housed in the agricultural building, did provide space for a few historic objects. The museum had exhibited since 1893 a musket from the Sharpsburg (Antietam) battlefield and the smokestack of the CSS *Albemarle*. A precedent set, the State Museum appeared to be the logical place to include room for such objects.

The North Carolina History Museum's birth became official in December 1902, when the State Museum opened "a small room" called the "Hall of History." Olds, in becoming the museum's director, commented: "For fully twenty years the writer has hoped for such a hall, a place to show what the State has done; . . . pleasing and instructive . . . only limited by space." Exhibits included "the skeleton of an Indian found in Wilkes County" and "two minie balls taken from General Toom's body."

Olds soon solicited the newly created North Carolina Historical Commission for support. In November 1903, three days before the commission held its first meeting in Warsaw, he requested and received $50 to reproduce photographs. A productive relationship developed quickly between Olds and the commission's secretary, R. D. W. Connor. They worked together on various projects, such as the Jamestown Tercentennial Exhibition, and the commission later became the Hall of History's administrative overseer.

Collecting with unbridled enthusiasm, Olds traveled the state, visiting each county on numerous occasions as he created an important but often undocumented collection. Early acquisitions included a tea caddy from the Edenton Tea Party; Confederate battle flags, weapons, and uniforms; a whiskey still "captured in Scotland by Robert Burns, the poet"; and a wine bottle found at Bath, from which Olds speculated that "that roistering devil" Blackbeard had drunk deeply. Soon the Hall of History's collection outgrew its room in the State Museum.

Olds and Connor lobbied the General Assembly for money to build what Olds called a "fireproof building" with "ample room" where the work of the commission could "be greatly extended." The state responded by giving the commission's archive collection and the Hall of History's artifacts quarters in the new State Administration Building. The new Hall of History was opened to the public on 14 Mar. 1914. Spurred by the new accommodations, Olds visited each county at least three times between 1914 and 1924 to speak and to obtain artifacts. Finally, slowed by age and poor health, he was compelled to leave his position in 1934.

Joseph Carlyle Sitterson became director and immediately began to compile a "scientific catalogue" to inventory and document the museum's thousands of items. The never-ending need for space necessitated a move to the first floor of the Education Building in 1939. The Historical Commission began to employ professionally trained curators and administrators, who focused on classifying and organizing the materials collected.

The 1940s through the 1970s saw an increase in educational programs and professional services offered by the museum. The Tar Heel Junior Historian Association was established in 1953 to promote history at the junior high school level. The North Carolina Museum of History Associates, Inc., a private, nonprofit support group, was formed in 1975. A succession of capable and forward-thinking administrators—among them Mattie Erma Edwards Parker, Joye Jordan, and John Ellington—guided the museum as it grew into a modern facility.

In July 1965 the Hall of History was renamed the North Carolina Museum of History. Three years later the museum moved more than 90,000 artifacts into a new $3 million building at 109 East Jones Street, sharing space with the North Carolina Archives and History and the State Library. The museum finally received a home of its own in April 1994, when a $29 million, 55,000-square-foot facility, complete with classrooms, a research library, and an auditorium, opened at One East Edenton Street. Over the years, satellite museums were established in Fayetteville (Museum of the Cape Fear), Elizabeth City (Museum of the Albemarle), and Old Fort (Mountain Gateway Museum).

The North Carolina Museum of History, started as a haphazard collection of historic odds and ends managed by one person, entered the twenty-first century with a staff of more than 100—curators, conservators, registrars, artifact handlers, research assistants, and others—and more than 250,000 items relating to the state's history. The artifacts are broadly categorized as pertaining to agriculture and industry, community history, costumes and textiles, folklife, furnishings and decorative arts, military history, or political and socioeconomic history. In addition to standing exhibits such as the North Carolina Sports Hall of Fame, the museum mounts shorter-term exhibits with themes such as "health and healing" and the Civil War.

References: Valerie Howell, "The People Museum: Alive with the Past," in *North Carolina Stories: The Grand Opening Celebration of the New North Carolina Museum of History Building* (1994); "North Carolina's New Hall of History," *Raleigh News and Observer*, 28 Dec. 1902; W. J. Peele, ed., *Literary and Historical Activities in North Carolina, 1900–1905* (1907); Harry S. Warren, "Colonel Frederick August Olds and the Founding of the North Carolina Museum of History" (M.A. thesis, East Carolina University, 1988).

Harry S. Warren

SEE ALSO Museum of the Albemarle; Museum of the Cape Fear; North Carolina Sports Hall of Fame.

North Carolina Museum of Life and Science

in Durham was founded in 1946 as the Children's Nature Museum. The original facility was a small trailside nature center adjacent to Northgate Park (then the Northgate Bird Sanctuary) that offered natural history exhibits and classes. In 1949 the museum incorporated and moved to an old white house on Georgia Avenue. In 1961 its Board of Directors secured a long-term lease from the city of Durham for a site on Murray Avenue and started construction of buildings on the south side of the campus. At the time, the museum was distinguished by a "Pre-History Trail," which opened in 1967, followed by an outstanding aerospace exhibit, which opened in 1975. The Ellerbee Creek Special, a replica of the famous C. P. Huntington train of the Southern Pacific running along a mile-long course, opened in 1977.

The development of the museum paralleled the growth and change of the region it served. Though the north central region of North Carolina retains a rural tradition, it became home to the Research Triangle Park, encompassing many high-technology, science-based companies doing research and manufacturing in such diverse fields as biotechnology, pharmaceuticals, computer electronics, medicine, and communications. The museum kept pace with this evolution while remaining rooted in a community-service tradition. Its unique dual focus on the natural and physical sciences came to reflect both the traditional and emerging needs of the regional community.

The late 1980s marked the beginning of a second major period of growth in the museum's history. Phase I included the construction of an indoor Nature Center featuring live North Carolina animals. Phase II, completed in 1991, included a new auditorium, temporary exhibit gallery, expanded lobby and gift shop, a new tree house discovery room, and 6,000 square feet of exhibition space. In 1993 Phase III included the completion of a 50,000-square-foot building for new exhibits and the physical science discovery room, Scientifica, increasing the range of programs in the natural and physical sciences. During this period recognition of the museum's commitment to hands-on exhibits came in the form of full membership in the prestigious Association of Science-Technology Centers; only 34 other museums worldwide have been accorded this status.

The third period of growth featured Bio*Quest* as a plan to utilize the museum's full 70-acre campus by expanding its north side with outdoor environmental and animal interactive exhibits, including a permanent Magic Wings Butterfly House and Insectarium, an updated dinosaur trail and dig, and exhibits on flight and large terrestrial animal communication. With the completion of Bio*Quest*, the museum made the "great outdoors" a resource of learning and enjoyment and became a model for museums, zoos, and botanical gardens internationally.

One of the most popular year-round visitor attractions in the Triangle, the North Carolina Museum of Life and Science by the beginning of the twenty-first century attracted 300,000 persons annually, including 100,000 students from North Carolina, Virginia, West Virginia, and Maryland. The main facility is 53,000 square feet, including 25,300 square feet of exhibit space and 3,600 square feet of program space. An additional 15,000 square feet of program space is available in other buildings on the museum campus.

Martha Bethea

North Carolina Mutual Life Insurance Company,

the first black-owned insurance company in the state and the largest in the nation, was incorporated on 28 Feb. 1899 as the North Carolina Mutual and Provident Association. The bill of incorporation was introduced in the N.C. General Assembly by legislator Thomas Fuller, who was among the organizers of the association. Its stated purpose was "the relief of the distress of Negroes" in North Carolina. The association, led by Clinton native John H. Merrick, opened in the office of Aaron M. Moore, its medical director and treasurer, in the Kempner Corner Building at Main and Church Streets in Durham. Merrick was elected president and D. T. Watson handled daily activities as secretary and general manager. A spiritual descendant of the Free African Society founded in Philadelphia in 1787, North Carolina Mutual followed a tradition of mutual benefit associations as instruments of social welfare. Merrick had been an agent for a fraternal aid society, the Grand United Order of the True Reformers in Richmond, Va. The associa-

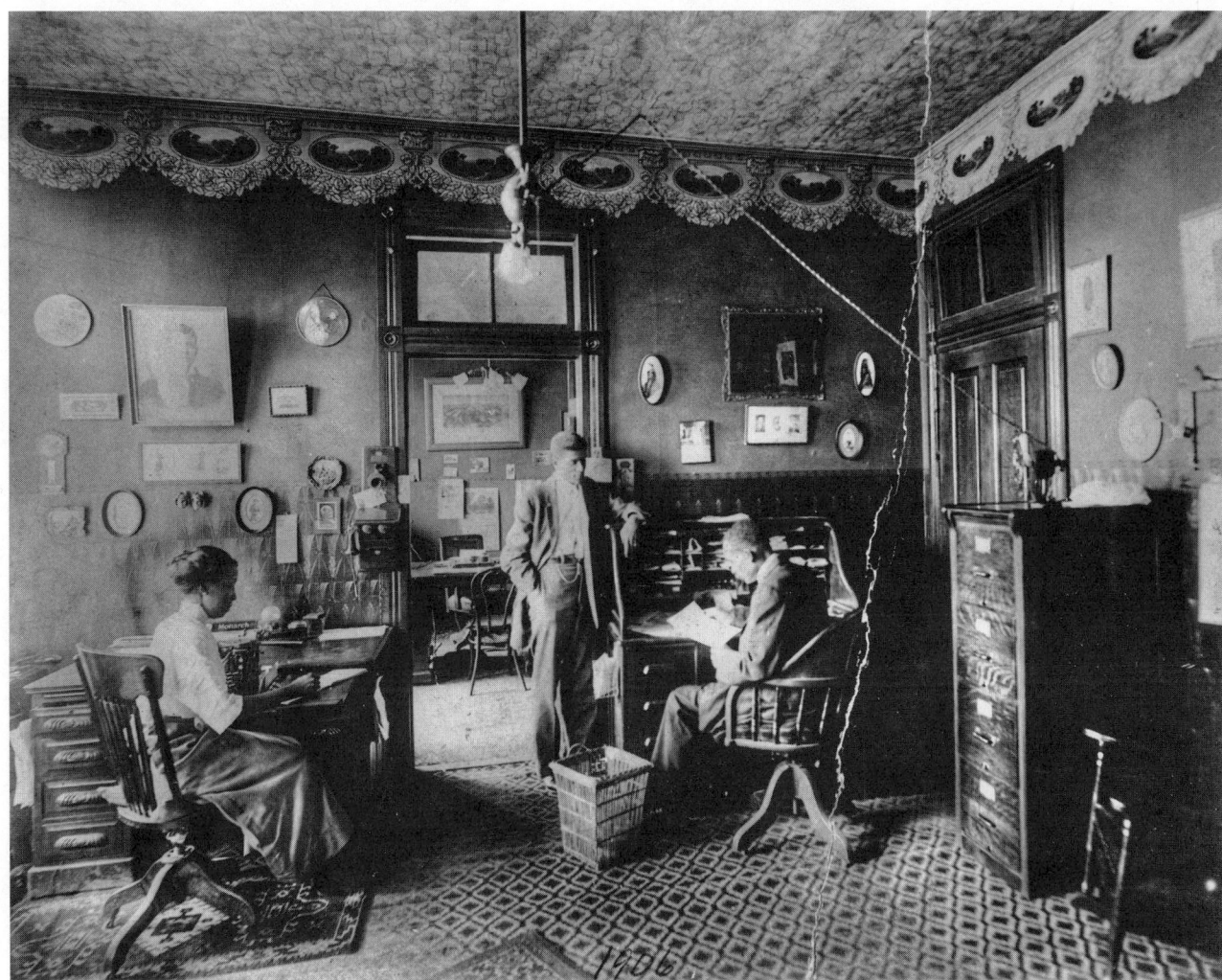

Employees of the North Carolina Mutual Life Insurance Company in 1906.
Left to right: Susan V. Gille Norfleet, C. C. Spaulding Sr., and John Merrick. NCC.

tion grew from such roots and assumed its social welfare philosophy, becoming a catalyst for minority social and economic
development through jobs, investments, loans, contributions,
and support of social programs.

In the first year, all of the original organizers left except
Merrick and Moore. Charles C. Spaulding was hired as general manager and the company moved into two rooms at 121 ½
East Main Street. These three men, known as the "Triumvi-
rate," carried the company to unprecedented success. Merrick
and Moore personally financed North Carolina Mutual for several years until 1903, when they were able to hire their first full-
time agent. In 1904 the association hired its first out-of-state
agent and moved into a new two-story building at 114 Parrish
Street in the heart of Durham's banking and business district.

North Carolina Mutual expanded by absorbing other failing
insurance companies and bought into Mechanics and Farmers Bank, another local black-owned business. The founders'
business philosophy was compatible with the self-help advo-

cacy of Booker T. Washington, a personal friend of Merrick and
Moore, and the association was often touted as vindicating the
principles promoted at Washington's Tuskegee Institute. The
executives were ardent supporters of the National Negro Business League and faithful to the creed of mutual aid. During
the early 1900s the three principals founded Lincoln Hospital (1901), the National Religious Training School and Chautauqua (1909), Durham Colored Library (1913), and the Rural
Extension Department of the N.C. Teachers Association (1914).
They served on the boards of a host of civic organizations, including Oxford Orphanage and Shaw University.

In 1919, after Merrick died, Moore was named president
and the firm's name was changed to North Carolina Mutual
Life Insurance Company. Viola Thompson was elected the
board's first female member; Sadie Tanner Mossell, the first
black female Ph.D. in America, was a member of Thompson's
staff from 1921 to 1923. The company extended its reach in
the 1920s to promote North Carolina College, the YMCA and

YWCA, the Boy Scouts, White Rock Baptist Church, and St. Joseph's AME Church. After Moore died in 1923, Spaulding assumed the presidency, holding it until his death in 1952.

North Carolina Mutual became a clearinghouse for black politics, education, and philanthropy in the Upper South, and by 1937 it was one of the state's largest companies. Spaulding was a member of President Herbert Hoover's Federal Relief Committee and of the National Urban League, he supported the early efforts of the NAACP, and he was active in the influential Durham Committee on Negro Affairs. In the 1940s North Carolina Mutual wrote group insurance for such industrial concerns as Ford Motor Company. By 1945 it was worth $14 million and declared a dividend to policyholders from a $1 million surplus. It invested $4.45 million in U.S. Government Bonds during World War II, and officials watched with pride as the Liberty ship SS *John Merrick* was christened at Wilmington. North Carolina Mutual proclaimed itself the largest black-owned insurance business in the world.

Asa T. Spaulding guided North Carolina Mutual through the social upheavals of the 1960s and presided over the 1966 opening of the Mutual Plaza Building, one of the tallest buildings in Durham, erected on the soil of former Duke Tobacco holdings. Joseph W. Goodloe succeeded Spaulding in 1968 and steered the company to its $1 billion insurance-in-force level in 1971, making it the first black-managed company in America to achieve the distinction. James H. Speed Jr. assumed the company presidency in 2004. North Carolina Mutual in 2006 operated in 23 states and the District of Columbia and had assets of $151 million and $12.5 billion worth of insurance in force.

References: William Kenneth Boyd, *The Story of Durham: City of the New South* (1927); William Jesse Kennedy Jr., *The North Carolina Mutual Story* (1970); Walter B. Weare, *Black Business in the New South: A Social History of the North Carolina Mutual Life Insurance Company* (rev. ed., 1993).

Rodney D. Barfield
John F. Ansley

North Carolina National Bank. SEE Bank of America.

North Carolina Press Association (NCPA) was established on 14 May 1873 in Goldsboro, making it one of the oldest such organizations in the United States. J. A. Engelhard, of the *Wilmington Journal*, who was elected president, is regarded as "the father of the association." Concerns over the deluge of advertising for quack medicines and other questionable products as well as a need for professional fraternity were motivating forces behind its formation.

A resolution that came out of the 1873 founding meeting urged the legislature to obtain and disseminate accurate information about the state's resources, such as minerals. Other early concerns of the association included improving education, the post office system, and roads. In 1875 the NCPA met in Wilmington and decided that the ports of Wilmington, Morehead City, and New Bern needed to be developed. In 1881, at the yearly meeting in Winston, former governor William W. Holden urged participants: "But above all, gentlemen, let us be true to the welfare and glory of North Carolina. Let our chief attention be given to our home interests." In 1883 the association held its annual meeting in conjunction with the Boston Exposition and invited Governor Thomas J. Jarvis to address the group. In 1885 "journalism as a profession" and the poor reading habits of the public were major topics of discussion at the meeting held in Smithville (present-day Southport).

In the 1920s the NCPA established an annual contest in news, feature, and editorial writing that helped raise journalistic standards across the state and led to greater professionalism in the North Carolina press. In 1949 the association organized the nonprofit School of Journalism Foundation, Inc., to aid the journalism program at the University of North Carolina at Chapel Hill and encourage excellence in its graduates. In the third quarter of the twentieth century the NCPA began a continuing battle for press freedom and against government secrecy. It opposed an American Bar Association report that recommended considerable secrecy in criminal cases. In the late 1990s, the NCPA stated that its purposes were to protect First Amendment freedoms, to keep public meetings and public records open, to ensure the public's accessibility to the entire state government process, to facilitate communication among members and growth of the membership, to maintain high industry standards, to represent the business interests of newspapers, and to promote literacy.

A 12-member board of directors leads the NCPA, located in Raleigh. The organization maintains a legislative committee as well as committees on the future of newspapers, professional development, finance, member services, and membership. The NCPA also retains a lobbyist.

For its 125th anniversary the NCPA established, with the North Carolina Museum of History, a permanent traveling exhibit on the history of the press in the state. The association continues to give awards in various categories to encourage high standards. By 2006 membership amounted to 202 newspapers, and services to members included a legal hotline, a home page on the World Wide Web, an annual directory and conference, a monthly newsletter titled the *North Carolina Press*, a press release service, and a marketing subsidiary to simplify classified advertising.

References: "Legal Victories for the N.C. Press," *Editor and Publisher* 128 (30 Sept. 1995); "NCPA Honors Past Presidents," *Raleigh News and Observer*, 3 Aug. 1963; Thad Stem Jr., *The Tar Heel Press* (1973).

Nancy P. Shires

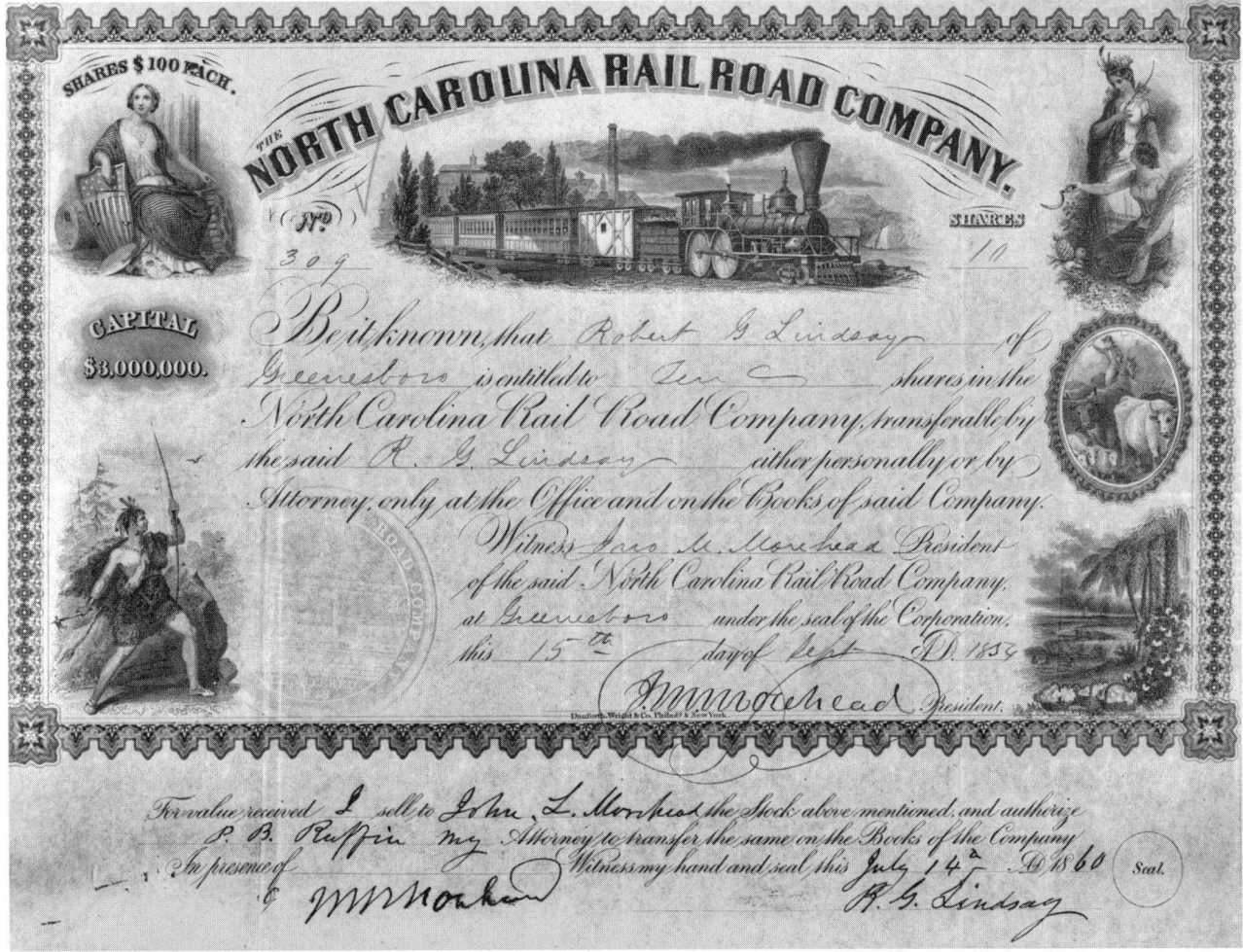

Stock certificate for the North Carolina Railroad issued in 1859 and signed by NCR president John Motley Morehead. Courtesy of NCOA&H.

North Carolina Railroad (NCRR), under lease since 1999 to the Norfolk Southern Corporation, was chartered in 1849 and completed in 1856 from Goldsboro through Raleigh, Greensboro, and Salisbury to Charlotte, a distance of 223 miles. The railroad was largely responsible for the Piedmont Urban Crescent that developed along its route, contributing to the growth of its towns and bringing into existence others, including Durham, Burlington (originally Company Shops, the site of its repair shops from the 1850s to the 1870s), High Point (at the road's highest elevation), and Thomasville.

The NCRR was for many years the longest railroad and the largest corporation in North Carolina. Since the state heavily subsidized its construction, receiving three-fourths of its stock in return, the NCRR was also for a time the state's largest single source of revenue. A state proxy appointed by the governor continues to vote that stock and the governor appoints two-thirds of the board of directors.

The NCRR was intended to be the centerpiece of an east-west rail line linking the state's seaports with the mountains and, through other rail connections, with a point on the Pacific Coast. To that end, the Atlantic & North Carolina and Western North Carolina Railroads were built a few years later, running east from Goldsboro and west from Salisbury, respectively. From the beginning, however, the main flow of rail traffic ran north and south, not east and west. Thus the NCRR became a vital link in one of the main north-south trunk lines connecting the urban Northeast with the Deep South. Its immediate connection to the south (albeit with a gauge difference that required unloading and reloading every train) was the Charlotte & South Carolina Railroad; to the north its connections were the Raleigh & Gaston at Raleigh and the Wilmington & Weldon at Goldsboro—both of which ran north to Weldon, where they connected with railroads into Virginia. In 1864, under wartime duress, a more direct northern connector, the Piedmont Railroad, was built from Greensboro to Danville, Va., where it met the Richmond & Danville Railroad.

The NCRR played a vital, if precarious, role in supporting the Confederacy in Virginia. This was especially true toward the end of the Civil War, when it was part of the only line left open to connect the Lower South with Gen. Robert E.

Lee's army and the Confederate government at Richmond. In 1871 the NCRR fell prey to the consolidation movement then forging a national rail network out of the local and regional lines that marked the early years of railroading.

Leased for 30 years to the Richmond & Danville (itself under northern control by then), the NCRR was leased again in 1895 to J. P. Morgan's new Southern Railway (now the Norfolk Southern). In 1989 the road gained an additional 94 miles from Goldsboro to Morehead City by absorbing the similarly state-controlled Atlantic & North Carolina Railroad. In 1998 the state of North Carolina bought all remaining private shares of the company's stock and the following year reached an agreement with Norfolk Southern allowing that line exclusive maintenance and freight operations on the NCRR line, now totaling 317 miles, for 15 years. Millions of dollars continue to be spent upgrading the line; in 2001, $10 million worth of improvements to the corridor between Goldsboro and Morehead City were completed, followed by repair work on the Neuse River Bridge in Kinston. In addition to freight trains operated by the Norfolk Southern, in the early 2000s Amtrak ran two passenger trains, the Piedmont and the Carolinian, along the NCRR corridor; CSX used a small portion of the route. Plans also existed for regional mass transit operations along NCRR's rails in Charlotte, the Triangle area (Raleigh, Durham, and Chapel Hill), and the Triad (Winston-Salem, Greensboro, and High Point). High-speed rail transit connecting the northeastern United States with Charlotte and Atlanta was also under consideration.

References: Cecil K. Brown, *A State Movement in Railroad Development: The Story of North Carolina's First Effort to Establish an East and West Trunk Line Railroad* (1928); Allen W. Trelease, *The North Carolina Railroad, 1849–1871, and the Modernization of North Carolina* (1991).

Allen W. Trelease

SEE ALSO Company Shops; Norfolk Southern Railroad; Western North Carolina Railroad.

North Carolina Reader, published in 1851 by Calvin H. Wiley, the state's first superintendent of public schools, was the first in a series of textbooks prepared for use in the pub-

lic school system. The book was "a work designed to familiarize the minds of the young with the character, history, and resources of their own well-favored father-land." It contained a brief history of the discovery, settlement, and progress of the state; political and oratorical exercises, some written by North Carolinians; and chronological and historical tables.

Wiley published the *Reader* at his own expense. Upon becoming the superintendent of public schools in 1853, he disposed of his copyright, sold all copies and the plates of the book at cost, and refused to accept further remuneration for his work, which became a standard school text. Wiley turned over his textbook work to a University of North Carolina professor, who edited two additional volumes in the series.

Reference: Guion G. Johnson, *Ante-Bellum North Carolina: A Social History* (1937).

Edwin H. Mammen

North Carolina Rural Electrification Authority

(NCREA) was created by the General Assembly in April 1935 to secure electric service for rural communities. Composed of six members appointed by the governor, the NCREA was empowered to survey needs of farm communities, assist communities in organizing "Electric Membership Corporations," help these organizations obtain financing, and assist privately owned power companies in extending service to rural areas or provide power to consumer-owned cooperatives. One month later, in May 1935, President Franklin D. Roosevelt, under authority of the Emergency Relief Administration, established the Rural Electrification Administration (REA), which acquired permanent status as a federal lending agency after passage of the REA Act in 1936.

In North Carolina, as in most of the other 14 states with rural electric agencies, controversy developed between the federal REA and the state organization. Critics in the 1930s, including *Raleigh News and Observer* editor Josephus Daniels, accused the NCREA of undermining the work of the federal agency and releasing information to private power companies before approving nonprofit farmer cooperatives. Private utilities were charged with constructing "spite lines" that "skimmed the cream" by providing power to the most densely populated section in a proposed cooperative's area, thereby thwarting formation of the cooperative.

In 1935, 3.2 percent of North Carolina farms had electricity, compared to 10.9 percent of farms nationally. Unquestionably, the NCREA promoted the extension of electric service to rural areas. Privately owned utilities played a larger role in electrification in the state than the REA. By the end of 1940, private utilities and municipalities had built or authorized 15,700 miles of power line and were serving 103,500 customers; REA-supported membership cooperatives had installed 11,200 miles of lines serving 37,500 customers; and

PRONOUNCING VOCABULARY OF GEOGRAPHICAL AND PROPER NAMES.

Albemarle (Al'-be-marle).   Name of a sound.
Algonquin (Al-gong'-kwin).   Name of a race of Indians.
Beaufort (Bo'-fort).   Name of a county and town.
Bertie (Bur-tee').   Name of a county.
Bogue (Bo'g).   Name of a sound.
Buncombe (Bun'-kum).   Name of a county.

Entries from the 1851 edition of the *North Carolina Reader*. NCC.

25.9 percent of North Carolina farms had electricity, compared to 30.4 percent of farms nationally.

Those who defended the NCREA cited the low percentage of rural electrification in 1935, the relative isolation of North Carolina farms, and the extent of rural poverty throughout the South. Conservative North Carolina politicians emphasized close cooperation with business interests while the federal agency relied on loans to membership cooperatives to achieve similar ends. Both the availability of federal REA loans and the work of the NCREA forced private utilities and municipalities to extend service to rural customers. Nevertheless, S. H. Hobbs, whose analysis of the NCREA was more favorable than many, acknowledged that the friction between the federal and state organizations "tended to retard rural electrification progress in North Carolina."

Operating under legislation last revised in 1979, the modern NCREA is part of the Department of Commerce. The governor appoints five board members for four-year terms and two staffers in the state office, including the state REA administrator, who serves as secretary to the board. Although electric and telephone service is generally available to all areas of the state, the NCREA continues to review and approve loan applications to the federal REA from electric membership corporations and telephone membership corporations who wish to increase their generating capacity or update their equipment. The NCREA hears complaints and reviews service of the 28 electric membership cooperatives and 9 telephone cooperatives operating in the state.

References: Douglas Carl Abrams, *Conservative Constraints: North Carolina and the New Deal* (1992); D. Clayton Brown, "North Carolina Rural Electrification: Precedent of the R.E.A.," *NCHR* 59 (April 1982); Samuel Huntington Hobbs, *A Brief History of Rural Electrification in North Carolina* (1963).

George W. Troxler

North Carolina School of Science and Mathematics

opened in Durham in 1980. Governor Terry Sanford had first proposed the concept of a public residential science and mathematics school in the 1960s. Through the comprehensive efforts of Governor James B. Hunt Jr., the concept gained momentum in 1977, and on 16 June 1978 the legislature committed itself to establishing the school. Durham was selected as the site based on its central location within the state and proximity to three major research universities: the University of North Carolina at Chapel Hill, Duke University, and North Carolina State University. The city also provided, at no charge, the former Watts Hospital as a campus site. The hospital design (easily converted to classrooms and dormitories) and ample room for growth appealed to the development committee. As of the early 2000s, the campus covered 27 acres and included 16 buildings, with an $8 million complex under construction. High school juniors and seniors enroll after an admissions process.

The school achieves its goal of providing an enhanced science and mathematics program to advanced students through innovative teaching methods and curriculum materials. To that end, all full-time teaching staff members hold master's degrees in their assigned area, and approximately one-third hold doctorates. Additionally, the School of Science and Mathematics requires teaching experience with advanced secondary students, ability to use educational technology, and a commitment to innovative curriculum design. Consequently, instructors and students enjoy flexibility in the presentation of course work. The staff also works to improve the teaching of science and mathematics throughout the state to the benefit of all North Carolina students. More than 99 percent of graduates attend college.

Among the nation's first residential science and mathematics schools, the North Carolina School of Science and Mathematics continues to be an educational model for similar schools. Since its inception, the school has gained national and international attention. *Newsweek* magazine featured the school on its cover in 1983 and, in an article titled "Saving Our Schools," profiled it as an alternative to less effective math and science programs. In 1986 the Royal Kingdom of Jordan asked the School of Science and Mathematics for assistance in starting a similar school. The school's numerous achievements and distinguished reputation as an innovator in education continues to draw the state's top science and mathematics students and a highly motivated faculty.

Alesia K. Stevenson

North Carolina School of the Arts

in Winston-Salem was established in 1963 by the North Carolina General Assembly as the nation's first state-supported residential school of the arts. A constituent institution in the University of North Carolina System, the school trains students for professional careers in the fields of dance, drama, filmmaking, music, the visual arts, and production and design. Study at the School of the Arts qualifies students to receive high school, college arts, bachelor's, and master's degree diplomas. All programs of instruction emphasize first-hand experience and performance; the audition/interview is therefore the most important portion of the application for admission. Collectively, members of the school's community offer more than 350 performances to the public each year.

In accordance with state legislative requirements, at least 50 percent of the students enrolled at the School of the Arts must be North Carolina residents; the remaining one-half come from 40 other states as well as more than a dozen other nations. In the early 2000s the school enrolled about 1,100 students—more than 700 of them college undergraduates—on its 67-acre campus in Winston-Salem. Tuition that year was

Members of the North Carolina Society of New York gathered for a dinner at the Hotel Astor, 3 Dec. 1909. NCC.

free for in-state high school students and $1,900 for out-of-state students. Undergraduates paid $733 and $4,265, respectively, and graduates, $768 and $4,367. Scholarships are available to all students based on financial need, talent, or both.

The North Carolina School of the Arts has produced a significant number of prominent alumni, including Tony Award nominee Terrence Mann; Metropolitan Opera bass-baritone John Cheek; Mary Cochran of the Paul Taylor Dance Company; and film/theater art director Tony Fanning.

References: Leslie Banner, *A Passionate Preference: The Story of the North Carolina School of the Arts* (1987); North Carolina School of the Arts, *Bulletin* (1994); Frank V. Tursi, *Winston-Salem: A History* (1994).

Catherine A. Whittenburg

North Carolina Society of New York is the oldest surviving state society in New York City. The society was founded in 1898 by five New York residents who were North Carolina natives and who were prominent in the business and professional community of New York in their day: George Gordon Battle, a well-known attorney and founding partner in the firm of Battle and Marshall (later Battle Fowler); George Garland Allen, then an employee of the American Tobacco Company and later chairman of the board of the Duke Endowment; James Buchanan Duke, founder of the American

Tobacco Company; Judge Amasa Junius Parker, a New York State Court judge who received the Democratic nomination for governor of New York in 1856 and 1859; and William Whitehead Fuller, who served as general counsel of the American Tobacco Company. Augustus Van Wyck, a justice of the Supreme Court of New York, who ran as the Democratic candidate for governor of New York against Theodore Roosevelt in 1898, was named the society's first president.

The constitution of the society, drawn by its founding members, stated that the society was established "to cultivate social interest among its members, to promote their common interests and to contribute to the welfare of the State of North Carolina." A requirement for membership was that the applicant be a native of North Carolina, although the husbands of North Carolina–born women were also eligible for membership. Membership in the society was originally restricted to men, but it was later extended to include women and graduates of North Carolina universities and colleges.

The society's principal organizer and promoter during the period of the 1950s through the mid-1990s was J. Sadler Hayes, a prominent New York insurance executive who was described by the *Raleigh News and Observer* at the time of his death in 1997 as "Mr. North Carolina of New York." The North Carolina Society of New York in the early 2000s had approximately 500 active members. In addition to informal gatherings throughout the year, the society hosts a formal annual dinner dance in New York City to honor distinguished North Carolinians. By tradition, the annual dinner dance is scheduled for the first Friday in December and in recent years has been held at the Union League Club on Park Avenue and 37th Street. Honorees have included such distinguished North Carolinians as William Friday, former president of the University of North Carolina system; Bob Timberlake, a well-known North Carolina artist; Richard Jenrette, a prominent investor and insurance executive in New York; and Charles Kuralt and Tom Wicker, national journalists.

Thomas Woodbury

North Carolina Sorosis, organized in Wilmington on 4 Dec. 1895, was the first federated woman's club in North Carolina. Begun by 15 community-minded women, the organization's name comes from the well-known New York woman's club, Sorosis, a Greek word that means a cluster of flowers on one stem. Highlighting the group's endeavors was a circulating library begun in 1897. The original collection and a 1906 donation of 1,700 books formed the nucleus of the present New Hanover County Public Library. In the early 1900s, North Carolina Sorosis actively promoted better sanitary conditions —assisting housewives in complying with city sanitary ordinances, promoting the use of garbage cans with lids, and protesting the use of the common drinking cup found at every neighborhood water pump. Members helped organize the Young Women's Christian Association in 1913 and in the early 1920s began a night school for the residents of the Delgado Mill community. In 1925 Sorosis was instrumental in the city of Wilmington's purchase of Greenfield Lake as a recreational park.

Sorosis members were committed to home front activities during both world wars, selling war bonds, making bandages, and canning fruit. In the 1950s Sorosis first awarded a scholarship for a girl to attend Wilmington College and financially assisted Girls Club (today known as Girls, Inc.). The organization, with its younger associates, Junior Sorosis, looking on, celebrated its 100th anniversary on 21 May 1995.

Reference: Gertrude Jenkins Howell, *A History of the North Carolina Sorosis, 1895–1957* (1957).

Barbara Rowe

North Carolina Sports Hall of Fame (NCSHF), which honors coaches, administrators, journalists, and other sports-related professionals in addition to athletes, was established in 1963 through the efforts of Jack Wood, a Charlotte merchant, and Lloyd Caudle, a Charlotte attorney, with support of the Charlotte Chamber of Commerce. The first five inductees were runner Jim Beatty, baseball pitcher Wes Ferrell, football players Charlie Justice and Ace Parker, and golfer Estelle Law-

son Page. Each was officially inducted into the NCSHF at a banquet in Charlotte in December 1963.

All subsequent NCSHF members have been elected annually and required to attend an induction banquet, where they provide the Hall of Fame with mementos of their career, including uniforms worn and equipment used. In 1969 the Charlotte Coliseum agreed to display the mementos in trophy cases in the corridors of the building. The memorabilia was later transferred to the North Carolina Museum of History in Raleigh, where it has become a permanent exhibit. In April 1994 the NCSHF moved into a new 4,000-foot wing of the museum.

As of 2006, there were 236 members of the NCSHF, about half of whom were still living. Members include golfers Peggy Kirk Bell (inducted in 1976), Raymond Floyd (1981), and Arnold Palmer (1988); football players Christian "Sonny" Jurgensen (1971), Dwight Clark (1997), and Jethro Pugh (1980); track-and-field athletes Tony Waldrop (1977) and Betty Springs Geiger (2003); baseball players Gaylord Perry (1973) and Jim "Catfish" Hunter (1974); auto drivers Dale Earnhardt (1994) and Richard Petty (1973); sports journalists Marvin "Skeeter" Francis (1993) and Billy Packer (1996); swimmers Sue Walsh (2003) and Peggy Pate Chappell (1993); basketball players Phil Ford (1991), David Thompson (1982), and Mike Gminski (2003); and basketball coaches Dean Smith (1981), Jim Valvano (1995), Kay Yow (1989), Mike Krzyzewski (2000), and Norm Sloan (1994).

Alex Coffin

North Carolina State Bar was created by the General Assembly in 1933 as an agency of the state. Its purpose is to render more effective service and improve administrative justice, particularly in matters pertaining to bar admission as well as disciplining and disbarring attorneys-at-law. No person other than a member of the State Bar may participate in the proceedings of any North Carolina court or otherwise engage in the practice of law.

The government of the State Bar is vested in a council, which is elected by the bar members from the state's various judicial districts. The council, in turn, elects the officers of the State Bar. To practice law in North Carolina, applicants must pass an examination, then be licensed by the Board of Law Examiners, which is appointed by the council. The council also promulgates and enforces rules of professional conduct.

Armistead Jones Maupin

North Carolina State University (NCSU) began in 1887 in West Raleigh as the North Carolina College of Agriculture and Mechanic Arts. Its creation by the General Assembly was due primarily to the efforts of the Watauga Club, a group of New South promoters, and the North Carolina Farmers' Alliance, led by Leonidas L. Polk. Founded as the state's first land grant college, the school opened its doors to students in October 1889. The faculty consisted of six members, including school president Alexander Quarles Holladay. The purpose of the college was to provide theoretical and practical education in agriculture and mechanic arts (engineering) while maintaining a basic curriculum in classical (liberal arts) studies. In 1894 military science was added to the curriculum, and for several years it was an important part of student activities.

Though short on financial support and physical facilities, the college had enrolled 250 students by 1900, few of whom were agricultural students. The Agricultural Experiment Station, however, which was connected to the college in 1889, soon conducted valuable research for farmers and related companies in the state. In 1909 a Department of Agricultural Extension was established to distribute the latest information in scientific farming and home economics. When the Smith-Lever Act of 1914 provided federal funds for demonstration activities, agricultural extension became an integral part of the college's mission.

The college's name was changed in 1917 to North Carolina State College of Agriculture and Engineering, and the School of Agriculture was established. During the first three decades of the twentieth century, State College, as it was known, grew at a modest rate. Though engineering continued to be its centerpiece, programs in forestry, textiles, business, and education were added during this period. The Great Depression slowed the college's expansion. In 1931 the General Assembly established a consolidated University of North Carolina System, with State College as one of the three member institutions.

World War II proved a watershed in the history of the college. During the war the institution converted its technological and scientific resources to the training of thousands of military personnel. After the war former servicemen, financed mainly by the GI Bill of Rights, flooded the campus, requiring the rapid construction of facilities and the expansion of faculty and staff. Graduate and research programs were also expanded. In 1947 more than 5,000 students, twice the prewar figure, registered for classes. The number of women admitted to the college increased significantly during and after the war.

A doctoral student and faculty adviser look over equipment in the Physics Department's nanotribology laboratory. Photograph by Roger Winstead. Courtesy of North Carolina State University.

The school's greatest growth occurred during the administration of John Tyler Caldwell, who served as chancellor from 1959 to 1975. By the time of Caldwell's retirement, 12,800 undergraduates and 2,600 graduate students matriculated on the campus. In 1963 a school of liberal arts was created, offering an array of degrees in the humanities and the social sciences. Two years later the General Assembly approved North Carolina State University as the official name of the institution. The new name reflected its emergence as a comprehensive and nationally recognized center of learning and research with overseas scientific and technological programs. The quiet racial integration of the institution during the 1950s and 1960s also contributed to its growing national and international stature.

Modern-day North Carolina State University is an acclaimed research university with a student body of nearly

Students beside the "Brickyard" at North Carolina State University, with Harrelson Hall in the background. Photograph by Roger Winstead. Courtesy of North Carolina State University.

The North Carolina Symphony, with Gerhardt Zimmermann, music director and conductor from 1982 to 2003. Photograph by Michael Zirkle. Courtesy of the North Carolina Symphony.

30,000 and a faculty of more than 1,500. In addition to its 1,800-acre campus in Raleigh, NCSU operates more than 100,000 acres in research and extension farms, forests, and facilities throughout the state. It is a national leader in science, engineering, veterinary medicine, design, and technology, ranking in the top ten institutions for industry-sponsored research and in the top 20 for licensing revenues and patents. Centennial Campus, a model of university-industry collaboration, provides opportunities for students to work with government and business partners. Expanding the institution's extension mission, every college at the university has an outreach function, working with various groups in every county of the state.

References: Murray Scott Downs and Burton F. Beers, *North Carolina State University: A Pictorial History* (1986); Alice Elizabeth Reagan, *North Carolina State University: A Narrative History* (1987).

William C. Harris

SEE ALSO Agricultural Experiment Stations; College of Design.

North Carolina Symphony had its origins in Chapel Hill as a work relief project as part of President Franklin D. Roosevelt's New Deal agencies in 1932. The first conductor was Lamar Stringfield, who directed the orchestra from 1932 to 1938. Benjamin Swalin became the director in 1939, and under his leadership the North Carolina Symphony became the first symphony to receive state aid. The "horn-tooter" bill passed by the General Assembly in 1943 provided $2,000 for each year of the 1943–45 biennium. From the beginning, the orchestra had an active, supportive Symphony Society and strong business leadership. Martha Maxine Swalin also was a partner in building the symphony.

The North Carolina Symphony's mission has always been to be a "people's orchestra" and to take its music to the masses. Its music education program has been shared by more than 3 million people since 1945, when the children's

concert division of the North Carolina Symphony was organized by Ben and Maxine Swalin and director of education Adeline McCall. The symphony still performs about 55 music education programs a year in 30 to 40 communities across the state. Students in the fourth, fifth, and sixth grades attend these concerts. Three generations of North Carolinians have shared the experience of seeing and hearing the symphony when they were children.

Today, the North Carolina Symphony is a fully professional orchestra with 65 members, playing in Meymandi Concert Hall in Raleigh's Memorial Auditorium. It performs for 100,000 children and more than 275,000 adults a year. In addition to traditional classical concerts, the symphony has a pops series of lighter music, a ballet series, and a Saturday morning young people's series. The orchestra has been able to attract world-renowned guest artists such as pianist André Watts for its classical series and singer Mel Tormé for its pops series.

The symphony's annual budget of more than $8.5 million comes from a grant-in-aid from the North Carolina General Assembly and the North Carolina Department of Cultural Resources and from ticket sales, contract sales, individual contributions, corporate sponsorships, and grants from Cary, Raleigh, Wake County, and the National Endowment for the Arts. There are more than 20 endowed chairs and more than 25 endowed Special Funds.

Reference: Benjamin Swalin, *Hard-Circus Road: The Odyssey of the North Carolina Symphony* (1987).

Mary Bates Sherwood

North Carolina Tax Relief Association (NCTRA) was formed in Raleigh in March 1930 to address the dire economic issues stemming from the Great Depression. As farm prices fell and businesses closed, tax revenues at the state, county, and municipal level fell precipitously. Local and county governments cut back salaries and services, and citizens began to call for tax relief. Under the sponsorship of the Buncombe

County Association for Property Tax Relief, representatives from 44 counties, the majority of whom were farmers, created the NCTRA to address these issues. The association promptly passed a series of resolutions demanding state support of the constitutional six-month school term and state maintenance of public roads and bridges. It also called for state, county, and municipal economy in government; reduction of land valuation on county tax books; complete reform in the method of land value appraisal; and a tax reduction pledge from every member of the General Assembly and all state and county officers.

In response to NCTRA resolutions, Governor O. Max Gardner commissioned a study by the Brookings Institution analyzing state and county government organization. The Brookings Institution report, delivered in December 1930, formed the basis for significant reforms. The state government assumed the responsibility for constructing and maintaining roads and for operating the six-month school term, established the consolidated University of North Carolina System, and assigned the Local Government Commission to supervise the borrowing practices of county and municipal governments. A general sales tax was defeated, and the state left ad valorem taxes to the use of local governments, but corporation taxes were increased.

References: Josephine Lane Doughton, "Passage of the Sales Tax Law in North Carolina, 1931–1933" (M.A. thesis, UNC-Chapel Hill, 1949); William S. Powell, *North Carolina through Four Centuries* (1989).

Wiley J. Williams

North Carolina Teachers Association

North Carolina Teachers Association (NCTA) served as the statewide organization for African American educators for nearly a century after the post-Reconstruction era, ending with the desegregation of the state's public schools of the 1960s. Although many African Americans, including such illustrious teachers as James H. Harris, James E. O'Hara, Charles W. Chesnutt, and Joseph C. Price, had been active educators in North Carolina since the end of the Civil War, more than a decade passed before they successfully united under the statewide banner of the NCTA in the early 1880s.

Although most historical accounts list 1881 as the year of the NCTA's founding, one contemporary journalistic account suggests the organization did not formally adopt its constitution until 1882. Its precursor was the State Colored Education Convention, at which 140 delegates from 40 counties met in Raleigh, probably in 1880. Officers included a cross section of college-educated African Americans, such as former legislators James H. Harris of Raleigh (president) and George L. Mabson of Wilmington (vice president), future Livingstone College president Joseph C. Price of New Bern, and John C. Dancy of Tarboro. By the time of its fourth meeting in Raleigh in 1885, the NCTA boasted two future members of Congress—Henry P. Cheatham of Henderson (1889–93) and George H. White of New Bern (1897–1901)—on its executive committee. Beginning their careers as teachers, both politicians had served as normal school principals, Cheatham at Plymouth and White at New Bern.

The NCTA continued to meet annually in Raleigh until the 1890s, when it moved to Kittrell College in Vance County. After about 1900, the association began to meet at alternate locations each year, beginning on the Raleigh campus of Shaw University. No more than 200 teachers and other leaders gathered for the two-week summer sessions until a change to two-day meetings during the Thanksgiving period enabled more than 800 to attend in 1922 alone.

Although nearly 3,000 African Americans worked as educators in North Carolina by 1921, fewer than 10 percent were members of the NCTA that year. During the 1920s, however, membership grew rapidly. Leaders during this period included Scotia Seminary president Luke Dorland; Simon G. Atkins, head of the Winston-Salem State Normal School; and James E. Shepard of Durham, founder of North Carolina College for Negroes (precursor of modern-day North Carolina Central University). Other notable early leaders included Charles N. Hunter and C. H. Moore, whose early occasional journal, the *Progressive Educator*, grew into the permanent *North Carolina Teachers Record* in 1930, published quarterly after 1932.

Shepard served as NCTA president during the early 1920s, succeeded by S. G. Atkins in 1926. As the NCTA grew in membership, it hired future Barber-Scotia College dean and president Leland S. Cozart as its first executive secretary in 1930; Cozart's successors in this post included G. E. Davis and W. L. Greene. In 1936, under the leadership of president Charlotte Hawkins Brown, the NCTA voted to create its first district associations, beginning with four—the Western, Piedmont, Southeastern, and Northeastern—and increasing to eight by 1960.

At the same time, local NCTA units began to appear across the state, swelling membership to nearly 8,000 by 1950. The NCTA set up its first permanent offices in the old Lightner Building on Raleigh's East Hargett Street in 1946, acquiring the building a year later. The NCTA eventually merged in 1970 with its all-white predecessor, the North Carolina Education Association, to form the North Carolina Association of Educators (NCAE). By the time of its merger into the NCAE in 1970, the NCTA had become one of the nation's strongest teachers organizations.

References: Hugh Victor Brown, *A History of the Education of Negroes in North Carolina* (1956); Jeffrey J. Crow, Paul D. Escott, and Flora J. Hatley, *A History of African Americans in North Carolina* (1992); Percy E. Murray, *History of the N.C. Teachers Association* (1971).

Benjamin R. Justesen

Private railroad dining car that belonged to James B. Duke and was named "Doris" for his only child. The car was donated to the North Carolina Transportation Museum in 1980. Courtesy of NCOA&H.

North Carolina Transportation Museum

North Carolina Transportation Museum at Spencer is a North Carolina State Historic Site occupying the buildings of the Southern Railway's central repair facility, begun in 1896. Approximately halfway between Washington, D.C., and Atlanta, it was the company's largest steam locomotive servicing facility. Both Spencer Shops and the town of Spencer that grew up around it were named for Samuel Spencer, the first president of Southern Railway. By 1932 the shops performed daily light repairs on 75 steam locomotives and turned out a completely rebuilt locomotive each day. The company also established its largest freight transfer facility at Spencer, where more than 40 trains set out every day. At its peak the company retained 2,500 workers and was the largest employer in the area.

In the late 1940s and the 1950s diesel locomotives replaced trains driven by steam, and the need for the kind of service delivered at Spencer declined. In 1960 the main shops closed, and only a few employees remained to make light repairs and refuel diesel locomotives and freight cars. All work stopped in 1979, when the Southern Railway moved to a modern complex across the Yadkin River at Linwood, site of the new freight switching yard.

When it became known that Spencer Shops would be closing, preservationists and local legislators took actions to pre-

serve the historic buildings as a Transportation Museum. Funds were appropriated for a feasibility study, and Southern Railway was approached about selling or donating the property and buildings. In September 1977 railway president L. Stanley Crane presented a deed to nearly 4 acres on the site as a gift to the people of North Carolina. In 1979 the company donated 53 more acres of land and several historic buildings. Funds from the General Assembly made it possible to begin to stabilize and restore the buildings.

The first exhibit area opened in 1983. Others followed as restoration and repair of buildings and equipment could be completed; next to open were the master mechanic's office, flue shop, roundhouse, and a narrated on-site train ride for visitors. The North Carolina Transportation History Corporation was chartered in 1977 as a nonprofit support group to assist in fund-raising and in the acquisition and restoration of artifacts. Numerous former employees of the Southern Railway, retired but still living in the vicinity, spent countless hours restoring and maintaining equipment as well as operating locomotives to pull rolling stock to give visitors a true feel for rail transportation.

In addition to railroads, the Transportation Museum features canoes, automobiles, fire trucks, the state's first highway patrol car, airplanes, motorcycles, wagons, and other means of moving people and goods in North Carolina.

References: Burke Davis, *Southern Railway: Road of the Innovators* (1985); Duane Galloway and Jim Wrinn, *Southern Railway's Spencer Shops, 1896–1996* (1996); Richard F. Knapp, *North Carolina's State Historic Sites: A Brief History and Status Report* (1995).

William S. Powell

North Carolina Troops, 1861–1865: A Roster.

SEE Civil War Rosters.

North Carolina Wesleyan College

North Carolina Wesleyan College, chartered in October 1956 and opened in 1960, is a four-year, coeducational, liberal arts college in Rocky Mount. It was established by citizens of Nash and Edgecombe Counties in cooperation with officials of the North Carolina Conference of the United Methodist Church; Bishop Paul Neff Garber and the Reverend Leon Russell were among its founders. The school was named for Englishmen John and Charles Wesley, considered the founders of modern Methodism.

The main campus in Rocky Mount is on a 200-acre wooded site. In addition to bachelor of arts and bachelor of science curricula, the college offers a master's degree program in business administration in cooperation with Campbell University of Buies Creek. There are also off-campus facilities in Goldsboro, Raleigh (at Athens Drive Senior High School), Research Triangle Park, and New Bern. In 1987 the North Carolina Wesleyan College Press was established with the objective of making writings from regional authors and poets more widely available; it closed in 1995. In the early 2000s Wesleyan enrolled nearly 2,000 students through its programs.

References: Roger W. Ireson, *Handbook of United Methodist–Related Schools, Universities and Theological Schools* (1992); North Carolina Wesleyan College, *Catalog* (1995).

Grady L. E. Carroll Sr.

North Carolina Writers Conference (NCWC), the oldest general organization of writers in the state, was inspired by a suggestion by novelist Inglis Fletcher and an invitation from publisher Lambert Davis for writers "to meet informally and discuss the problems we share," following a performance of Paul Green's outdoor drama *The Lost Colony* in Manteo on 8 Aug. 1950. Attending the first meeting, and therefore eligible to be called founders, were important North Carolina literary leaders Fletcher, Davis, Green, Paul Ader, Huntington Cairns, Chalmers G. Davidson, Brennan Fagan, John Harden, Gerald Johnson, Josephine Niggli, John Parris, William T. Polk, William Meade Prince, Marian Sims, Betty Smith, and James Street. Others, such as Walter Spearman and Richard Walser, were involved in the planning but were unable to attend the initial meeting. Davis reported that the discussion covered shoptalk, craft talk, and true confessions.

Although the group voted to meet again, it was adamant in wanting neither a formal organization nor an apostrophe in its name. Deciding which North Carolina writers merited an invitation to join the group proved difficult, and Davis, Fletcher, Parris, and Spearman were charged with preparing a list of invitees; under no circumstances were they to call themselves a committee, however. The group's rejection of a bureaucratic structure has remained one of its guiding principles. It has never had a constitution, bylaws, an annual report, or a president. Inevitably, however, someone had to mail invitations and make local arrangements. Accordingly, a chair, a vice chair, and a secretary-treasurer were eventually chosen. The group has shied away from publicizing itself, and except for two issues of a newsletter duplicated by Doris Betts in 1956, the conference produced no publications of its own. The membership selection process was always shadowy, but keen observers in the 1960s began to credit anointment by Sam Ragan, who by then was called the "godfather" of the conference. In the early years, meetings often were held alternately in the western and eastern parts of the state, but as attendance increased, Raleigh, Chapel Hill, and Southern Pines frequently hosted the meetings.

Beginning in 1977, NCWC honored a North Carolina writer every year at its annual banquet (except for 1999, when the conference returned to Manteo for a special fiftieth meeting.) Recipients of this honor have included Green, Jonathan and Lucy Daniels, Thad Stem, Reynolds Price, Fred Chappell, Burke Davis, Wilma Dykeman, John Ehle, H. G. Jones,

John Foster West, Daphne Athas, John Hope Franklin, Shelby Stephenson, and Roy Parker Jr. Speeches made during these award banquets usually were published in *Pembroke Magazine*. A current membership roster of the NCWC is maintained by the curator of the North Carolina Collection at UNC-Chapel Hill. *Fifty Splendid Summers: A Short History of the North Carolina Writers Conference, 1950–1999*, compiled by Charles Blackburn Jr. and Robert G. Anthony Jr., was copublished in 1999 by the NCWC and the North Carolina Collection, with financial support from the Paul Green Foundation.

Reference: Bernadette Woodlieff Hoyle, *North Carolina Writers Conference: A Little Write-up* (1967).

H. G. Jones

North Carolina Writers' Network (NCWN), founded in 1985, is a nonprofit organization with some 1,800 members, making it one of the nation's largest independent literary organization. NCWN's mission is to serve writers at every stage of development through programs offering opportunities for professional growth. The network provides information and instructional services to its members and to others interested in the literary arts, promotes and maintains the tradition of writing by North Carolina authors, and provides readings, network opportunities, workshops, and a critiquing service. NCWN also includes the Center for Business and Technical Writing, which administers workshops and individual instruction for state businesses in technical writing and business English. The network sponsors five writing competitions each year, and in 2003 it inaugurated the Elizabeth Daniels Squire Writers-in-Residence Program at Peace College in Raleigh. In cooperation with the Weymouth Center for the Arts and Humanities, NCWN oversees the North Carolina Literary Hall of Fame in Southern Pines.

Writers' Network News is sent bimonthly to current members of the NCWN. The publication features articles about NCWN programs, North Carolina writers, and literary news and events across the state and beyond, as well as information on workshops, classes, conferences, competitions, and publishing opportunities. NCWN also publishes *North Carolina's Literary Resource Guide*, a comprehensive guide to opportunities for writers, and offers a library and resource center, an annual conference, and outreach programs in prisons, homeless shelters, and hospitals. Located in Carrboro, the resource center is open weekdays and Saturdays by appointment.

Wiley J. Williams

North Carolina Zoological Park, located in Asheboro, was the first American zoo originally designed to display its animals in situations as close to their natural habitats as possible. Zoos were not designed as such until relatively recently; instead, animals, alone or in limited numbers, were displayed as curiosities or as educational objects in what were called menageries. North Carolinians kept some native animals (deer, squirrels, or rabbits) as family pets; a large portrait of the children of John Hawks in New Bern included their pet deer. Occasionally, some shop owners—such as an early twentieth-century merchant in Hillsborough—kept a small monkey on a leash before their shop to attract customers. Public zoos did not become widely appreciated until the nineteenth century, the first notable one in the United States opening in 1894 in Philadelphia.

Beginning early in the twentieth century, a few animals such as an occasional buffalo, bear, monkey, tiger, lion, or even an elephant, perhaps aging and abandoned by a previous owner, could be found in municipal parks in Asheville, Charlotte, Greensboro, Raleigh, and elsewhere. A small privately maintained zoo in the town of Windsor had, in addition to animals, such exotic fowls as rhea, both blue and white peacocks, and Royal Palm turkeys.

A group of civic-minded North Carolinians in Raleigh in the late 1960s concluded that there ought to be a zoo in the state. There followed a campaign to convince the people of the state of a zoo's benefits for their own education and enjoyment as well as in saving many species of animals that were nearing extinction. The idea was convincing, and a North Carolina Zoological Society was formed; a site selection committee devoted two years to considering possible locations and ultimately accepted the gift of 1,371 acres from the society. Voters passed a $2 million bond referendum. The site was in Randolph County in the Uwharrie Mountain Range near the geographic center of the state, and Governor Robert W. Scott dedicated it in the spring of 1972. The Z. Smith Reynolds Foundation granted $1 million toward permanent construction, and the General Assembly appropriated $11.8 million for construction of the first geographic exhibition area, devoted to Africa. The zoo opened in 1979 with a 3.5-acre Forest Edge Habitat for zebras, ostriches, and giraffes. It was soon enlarged, however, with new habitats for elephants, rhinoceros, lions, chimpanzees, and baboons. In 1982 a forest aviary became the zoo's first indoor exhibit. With the creation of North American habitats in 1993 and the opening of the Australian Walkabout in 2004, the North Carolina Zoo became even more positively identified as a natural habitat zoo.

As the large area devoted to animals was developed, attention was also paid to plants. The North Carolina Zoological Park maintains both rare and ordinary plants common to the regions reproduced in the displays. Among the objectives of the state zoo are information, education, and enjoyment for visitors as well as the welfare and maintenance of the species. Facilities are available for study and research, and the zoo participates in the protection and restoration of threatened animals and plants.

William S. Powell

North Caroliniana Society

North Caroliniana Society was founded in 1975 by H. G. Jones, William S. Powell, and Louis M. Connor Jr. for the promotion of knowledge and appreciation of North Carolina's historical, cultural, and literary heritage. A nonprofit corporation under provisions of the General Statutes of North Carolina, the society elects to membership individuals meeting a strict criterion of "adjudged performance" in service to the state—that is, those who have demonstrated a continuing interest in and support of North Carolina's historical, literary, and cultural strengths. Membership is limited, and there are no dues. The major beneficiary of the society is the North Carolina Collection at the University of North Carolina at Chapel Hill, where the society's office is located, but assistance is also given to other agencies and organizations with kindred objectives. The society also sponsors or cosponsors conferences and symposiums, such as the International Sir Walter Raleigh Conference in 1987 during the quadricentennial of the Roanoke voyages, For History's Sake: State Historical Collections in the Early Republic in 1994 during the sesquicentennial of the North Carolina Collection, and Lawson's Legacy: Nature Writing and North Carolina, 1701–2001 in 2001. From 1992 to 2002, the North Caroliniana Society cosponsored the Second Sunday Readings Series with the North Carolina Collection and the Creative Writing Program in UNC's Department of English. Free and open to the public, the series hosted 122 North Carolina writers of fiction, nonfiction, and poetry during its ten-year history.

Dating from 1978, the North Caroliniana Society Award annually recognizes distinguished service in the encouragement, production, and preservation of North Caroliniana. Recipients through 2006 have included Doris Betts, Archie K. Davis, Wilma Dykeman, Sam J. Ervin Jr., William and Ida Friday, Paul Green, Frank B. Hanes Sr., Richard H. Jenrette, Frank H. Kenan, Charles Kuralt, William S. Powell, Reynolds Price, W. Trent Ragland Jr., and J. LeRoy T. Walker. In its first 20 years, the society published 25 numbers in its *North Caroliniana Society Imprints* series and five *North Caroliniana Society Keepsakes*. Beginning in 1976, the annual reports of the society and the North Carolina Collection were published together.

In 1987 the Research Triangle Foundation gave the society an endowment fund of $250,000, the income from which during the following 15 years assisted more than 100 scholars in gaining access to original source materials on North Carolina history through Archie K. Davis Fellowships, named for the foundation's retiring chairman. In 2002 the North Caroliniana Society created a $25,000 endowment in the names of Alice and Jerry Cotten, longtime employees of the North Carolina Collection at Wilson Library, who retired that year. Interest from the endowment will be used to promote the study of novelist, playwright, and Asheville native Thomas Wolfe and to preserve photographs related to the state.

H. G. Jones

Northern Lights, or the aurora borealis, are a rare, spectacular display of multicolored lights in the sky associated with solar flare activity. Usually seen waving—sometimes suggesting blowing curtains—at high latitudes across the northern sky from the horizon, the lights are mostly yellow-green with areas of red, purple, and white. They have occasionally been seen in areas such as Pennsylvania and Virginia and have at times been witnessed in North Carolina. Moravians in Wachovia observed the phenomenon on 6 Aug. 1772 and also reported in their daily journal for 14 Nov. 1789 that "at night the North Lights were very red with fiery beams spreading over the heavens."

In October 1865 a "most wonderful electrical display" was seen in the skies over Mecklenburg County, disturbing "the serenity of many of the people . . . who witnessed the gorgeous display in the after part of the night." Two late deserters from the Confederate army became alarmed and approached E. A. McAuley to know what the strange sight meant. His reply: "It was the devil uncapping hell to take in all deserters of the Confederate Cause."

William S. Powell

Nuclear Energy first came to North Carolina in 1950 with the construction of a reactor for training and research at North Carolina State College (now North Carolina State University) in Raleigh. Faculty members of the physics department designed and built a ten-kilowatt "water boiler," adapted from a design by the laboratory at Los Alamos, N.M. This Raleigh Reactor and its several successors have been used ever since for education in the field of nuclear engineering and for radiation research and services.

In response to the U.S. Atomic Energy Commission's challenge to American industry to demonstrate the possibility of commercial nuclear power, a consortium of southeastern energy companies was formed in 1956. The Carolinas-Virginia Nuclear Power Associates (CVNPA) included the three electric power companies that served North Carolina—Carolina Power & Light Company, Duke Power Company, and Virginia Electric & Power Company—as well as South Carolina Electric & Gas Company. Between 1963 and 1967 the group built and operated at Parr, S.C., a 17,000-kilowatt, heavy-water moderated pressure-tube type reactor, similar to those operating in Canada. This prototype provided knowledge and experience on the new energy source for management and for design and operating engineers. Subsequently, CP&L built two large, multimegawatt light-water moderated reactors of the boiling-water type (BWR) in Southport (1975 and 1977); Duke Power built two larger reactors of the pressurized-water type (PWR) in Cornelius (1981 and 1983); and CP&L built an additional PWR in New Hill (1987).

Plans for several additional nuclear units were canceled in the 1970s owing to the energy crisis and an unfavorable economic climate. The 1979 accident at the Three Mile Island nuclear plant in Pennsylvania prompted a number of changes in equipment and procedures to enhance safety. The utilities became closely associated with two national organizations, the Institute of Nuclear Power Operations and the Electric Power Research Institute.

By 2006 about one-third of all electric power in North Carolina came from nuclear power plants. One of the major supporting facilities for the state's BWRs was General Electric's Nuclear Fuels Plant near Wilmington. Electric power for 19 cities was provided by North Carolina Municipal Power Agency No. 1, using its part ownership of a reactor.

References: Robert F. Durden, *Electrifying the Piedmont Carolinas: The Duke Power Company, 1904–1997* (2001); Raymond L. Murray, *Nuclear Energy* (1993).

Raymond L. Murray

Nucor Corporation, headquartered in Charlotte, is the second-largest U.S. steel producer after United States Steel LLC (formerly the USX-U.S. Steel Group). Nucor grew out of the Nuclear Corporation of America, a descendant company of Reo Motor Company, the second automobile venture of Ransom Olds of the Oldsmobile car line. Olds had built his first gasoline-powered car in 1897 and later sold his company to General Motors. In 1962 Nuclear Corporation bought Vulcraft, a maker of steel joists, gaining at the same time the services of Kenneth Iverson, who became its chief executive officer in 1965. Iverson moved the administrative headquarters to Charlotte, shut down or sold about half of the company's business, and focused on its profitable steel joist operations. By 1968 Nuclear was the leading builder of steel joists in the country, with 20 percent of the market.

At that time, the firm depended on imports for 80 percent of its steel needs, so Iverson decided to move into steel production. Nuclear built its first "minimill" in 1969. Unlike traditional steel mills, minimills use highly efficient electric arc furnaces to melt scrap metal, which is then rolled into products such as steel decks, joists, girders, beams, and fasteners. The company, which was renamed Nucor Corporation in 1972, came to dominate the minimill industry.

Nucor continued to expand its mills, add new facilities, and pursue acquisition opportunities. In 1998 the company announced plans to build its first steel plate mill, which became operational in 2000. Nucor employed 11,000 people and had estimated sales of $12.9 billion by 2006. Besides its North Carolina facilities, the company operated in Alabama, Arkansas, South Carolina, Texas, and other states.

References: Ken Iverson, *Plain Talk: Lessons from a Business Maverick* (1998); Jeffrey L. Rodengen, *The Legend of Nucor Corporation* (1997).

Wiley J. Williams

Nullification Crisis of 1832 found North Carolina generally opposed to the position of other southern states, particularly South Carolina, regarding a federal tariff on agricultural goods. The "tariff of abominations" that they found so harsh did not radically affect North Carolina's diversified agricultural economy. In 1830 early indications of South Carolina's bold stand against the federal government produced scattered demonstrations throughout North Carolina denouncing such action. At year's end, the General Assembly passed a resolution declaring that, although the tariff was "unwise" and "oppressive," it was not constitutional for "an individual state of this Union to nullify a law of the United States." In the words of Judge William Gaston, "the people [of North Carolina] may disapprove of the tariff but they love the Union more."

South Carolina's adoption of its nullification ordinances in November 1832 sparked renewed criticism from vocal North Carolinians. The editors of the *Raleigh Register*, one of the state's most prominent newspapers, called these ordinances "revolutionary" and warned that their passage could only lead to "dissolution" of the Union. While a resolution moved through the General Assembly condemning the South Carolinians for their actions, a few moderates, such as Richard Dobbs Spaight Jr., offered to mediate the crisis. Ominously, during the resolution's final passage several lawmakers declined to support the motion. A few editorialists echoed these sentiments, asserting that, despite the fact that South Carolina was in the wrong, any "tyrannical act of oppression would be apt to enlist North Carolina in the cause of her sister state."

Reference: Archibald Henderson, *North Carolina: The Old North State and the New*, vols. 1–2 (1941).

David L. Cockrell

"Numbers of Carlton" were 22 essays "addressed to the People of North Carolina on a Central Rail-road through the State" written by Joseph Caldwell, the first president of the University of North Carolina, using the pseudonym "Carlton." Dated and signed weekly beginning on 8 Sept. 1827 and compiled as a book in 1828, the essays were probably columns or letters sent to local newspapers.

Caldwell, a mathematician, was very detailed in his writings. After two essays extolling the advantages of a railroad versus a canal, he estimated the costs and timetable of building a railway from Beaufort, on the coast, to the mountains. A column from 22 Oct. 1827 included tables of mileage from 82 towns to the proposed railroad line, the most distant being 52 miles, "which could be covered in two or three days with a double team and wagon."

Caldwell's writings probably had wider circulation and more influence than any pamphlet published during the period. On 1 Aug. 1828 news of a meeting in Chatham County drew 200 people representing four counties. The gathering ended with a resolution that "a committee be appointed to address the citizens on the importance and necessity of a Central Rail-road."

Two recommendations in "Numbers of Carlton" seem a bit idealistic and impractical today. The writer urged "rail-ways of wood rather than iron" in a state with many forests and suggested that there would be little engineering cost "since the State already has engineers in employment."

Reference: Thad Stem Jr., *The Tar Heel Press* (1973).

Edwin H. Mammen

Nutbush Address. Discontent began to develop in the newly created North Carolina counties of Granville, Orange, and Rowan around 1760. This unhappiness was based, in part, on dissatisfaction with the Granville District and its agents as well as on the activities of provincial and county officials, especially the fees they charged and collected. These issues later developed into the primary motivations behind the Regulator Movement.

On 6 June 1765 George Sims, a resident of Nutbush in Granville County, spoke to the citizens of Granville about these complaints. Sims, who dedicated his address to Thomas Person, was concerned with the "recovery of native rights and privileges" and with clearing the "country of those public nuisances which predominate with such tyrannical sway." He also wanted to "resume our ancient liberties and privileges as free subjects" and complained of lawyers' excessive fees, which were as much as double the amount allowed by law. Sims also was troubled by the ease with which real and personal property could be seized and sold for a fraction of its value to satisfy the exorbitant fees that were charged.

In the later-named Nutbush Address, Sims stopped short of raising the specter of public violence in response to these concerns. Although he was quoted extensively in Herman Husband's *A Fan for Fanning and a Touchstone to Tryon* (1771), a history and justification of the Regulator Movement, Sims did not express a lack of faith in the British system as did the Regulators. He urged the citizens of Granville County to act with deliberation and to do nothing against the law. He also voiced support for the king, the royal governor, and the colonial Assembly.

References: William K. Boyd, ed., *Some Eighteenth Century Tracts Concerning North Carolina* (1927); William S. Powell, James K. Huhta, and Thomas J. Farnham, eds., *The Regulators in North Carolina: A Documentary History, 1759–1776* (1971).

Thornton W. Mitchell

Oak Ridge Military Academy traces its origins to 7 Apr. 1850, when local citizens "desirous of promoting the cause of education" met and appointed a board of trustees to secure funds to erect a schoolhouse. Virtually everyone in the northwestern Guilford County community of Oak Ridge contributed to the total of $629. The school, originally named Oak Ridge Institute, opened on 3 Mar. 1853, with a classical curriculum of 18 courses and 63 students from North Carolina and Virginia. By 1856 it had 85 students, roughly three-quarters of whom were from places other than Oak Ridge.

The entire Oak Ridge Institute student body volunteered in 1862 for service in the Confederate army, which necessitated the school's temporary closing. Shortly after the end of the Civil War, the school faced extinction when the main building burned to the ground the day before classes were to begin in September 1865. Classes were held in a nearby log cabin while supporters rallied to keep the school open. By 1875 J. Allen Holt had become principal and began an expansion program.

In 1899 Oak Ridge Institute became the first secondary school in North Carolina to be accredited by the Southern Association of Colleges and Secondary Schools. By 1901 it had 259 boarding students and claimed to be the largest "preparatory and fitting" school in the South. A junior unit of Army ROTC was established at Oak Ridge in 1926, making the U.S. Army the only organization with which the school has had any official affiliation. Since that time it has become in essence a military school that has repeatedly received high marks from army inspectors.

In 1971 the school's name was changed to Oak Ridge Military Academy. That year it also became one of the first military academies in the United States to admit females. (Women had been in attendance earlier, prior to its becoming a military school.) The goal of the academy, which enrolled students in grades 7 through 12, became preparing students for college, and at the end of the twentieth century Oak Ridge offered a guarantee that "every cadet who graduates from Oak Ridge is accepted to college."

The General Assembly designated Oak Ridge Military Academy the "official military academy" of North Carolina in 1991. Its 101-acre campus is a National Historic District. Virtually all of its 11 major buildings, some of which date from the 1914 reconstruction of the school, were remodeled in the early 1990s. The exceptions were Linville Chapel, built in 1914, and the Holt infirmary, built in 1938.

Reference: William P. Pope, "The Spirit of '66," *The State* (15 Aug. 1970).

Alexander R. Stoesen

Oakwood Cemetery in Raleigh was established by the Raleigh Cemetery Association in 1869, making it Raleigh's oldest private, nonprofit cemetery. The cemetery is located on gently rolling hills adjacent to downtown Raleigh, its numerous monuments and markers set off by the natural topography, featuring oaks, cedars, and flowering trees and a meandering stream. Seven North Carolina governors, five United States senators, eight chief justices of the North Carolina Supreme Court, and Raleigh's first mayor are buried in Oakwood. A Jewish cemetery and a Confederate Cemetery, containing the graves of 2,800 Confederate dead, also lie within Oakwood Cemetery's boundaries.

The Confederate Cemetery was established directly after the close of the Civil War, in 1866. A group of Raleigh women conceived the idea of establishing a permanent burial place for Confederate soldiers who at that time were buried on the location of the present Federal Cemetery on Rock Quarry Road. Using land donated by Henry Mordecai, the Wake County Ladies' Memorial Association began the preparation of a graveyard on the new site. In 1867 a federal agent was sent to Raleigh to find a cemetery site for Union soldiers. He chose the Rock Quarry Road location and gave local citizens three days to move their Confederate dead from that cemetery. More than 500 bodies were hurriedly exhumed and relocated on the Mordecai property.

The graves within the Confederate Cemetery were originally marked with small granite posts bearing only a number. In 1989 the U.S. government furnished larger monuments identical to those used in federal cemeteries throughout the country. A House of Memory commemorating American veterans of all wars stands adjacent to the Confederate graves. The Confederate Cemetery is improved and cared for by the Sons of Confederate Veterans.

Armistead Jones Maupin

Occaneechi Indians were a tribe of American Indians who lived in the Piedmont region of what are now North Carolina and southern Virginia prior to European settlement. They are first mentioned in historical records in 1650, when an Appomattox Indian guide told the English explorer Edward Bland that there was an island in the Roanoke River near present-day Clarksville, Va., where "some of the *Occonacheans* lived." The Occaneechi reached their greatest prominence as middlemen in the fur and deerskin trade that flourished between the Virginians and the Piedmont Indians during the 1660s and 1670s. Although no written accounts of the Occaneechi language have survived, the tribe is thought to have spoken an eastern Siouan dialect like many of their Piedmont neighbors, and the early Virginia historian Robert Beverley noted in 1705 that the Occaneechi's was the general language used by other Indians in the trade.

John Lederer, a German explorer and doctor, visited and described the tribe's island village in 1670. A subsequent visit by James Needham and Gabriel Arthur in 1673 was described in a letter written by the Virginia trader Abraham Wood. The Occaneechi's control of the trade resulted in part from their strategic location astride the Great Trading Path that led from the Virginia Colony to the Catawba and Cherokee. This situation came to an end in 1676, when the Occaneechi were attacked by a frontier militia led by Nathaniel Bacon. Following their defeat, the Occaneechi abandoned their island home on the Roanoke and moved south to the Eno River at present-day Hillsborough in Orange County. English explorer John Lawson visited and briefly described their village there in 1701. He noted that "their Cabins were hung with a good sort of Tapestry, as fat Bear, and Barbakued or dried Venison; no *Indians* having greater Plenty of Provisions than these."

Lawson's "Achonechy" Town was excavated by archaeologists from the University of North Carolina at Chapel Hill between 1983 and 1986. These excavations revealed a small, briefly inhabited village that consisted of about a dozen wigwamlike houses that formed a circle surrounding an open plaza. At the center of the village was a large sweat lodge. The houses were surrounded by a defensive stockade, and a cemetery containing numerous graves was located just outside the village. Artifacts found at the site included fragments of Occaneechi-made clay pots and stone tools and numerous European-made items acquired through trade, such as axes, hoes, knives, scissors, bottles, and glass beads. Food refuse, consisting of animal bones and charred plant remains, reflects a subsistence economy based primarily on growing corn, beans, and squash and hunting deer. Relative to the small size of the village and the brief time it was occupied, a large number of graves were found, attesting to the devastating impact that Iroquois war parties and European-introduced diseases had on the Occaneechi in the early eighteenth century.

By 1712 the Occaneechi had left the Eno River Valley and moved to the northeast, seeking the protection of the Virginia colonial government at Fort Christanna on the Meherrin River. There they joined the Saponi, Tutelo, Stenkenock, and Meipontsky, gradually losing their identity as a distinct tribe. They are last mentioned in the historical record in 1728 by William Byrd II, who observed that the Fort Christanna Indians were "now made up of the remnant of several other nations, of which the most considerable are the Saponis, the Occaneechis, and Stoukenhocks, who, not finding themselves separately numerous enough for their defense, have agreed to unite into one body, and all of them now go under the name of the Saponis." Although circumstantial evidence suggests that at least some of the remaining Occaneechi may have migrated northward with the Tutelo and Saponi to Pennsylvania and New York, a small community of Indians in North Carolina's Orange and Alamance Counties, known as the Occaneechi Band of Saponi Nation, claim descent from the eighteenth-century Occaneechi and were officially recognized by the state of North Carolina in 2001.

References: Clarence W. Alvord and Lee Bidgood, *The First Explorations of the Trans-Allegheny Region by the Virginians, 1650–1674* (1912); H. Trawick Ward and R. P. Stephen Davis Jr., "Archaeology of the Historic Occaneechi Indians," *Southern Indian Studies* 37 (1988); Robert Beverley, *The History and Present State of Virginia*, ed. Louis B. Wright (1947).

R. P. Stephen Davis Jr.

Oconaluftee Indian Village. On 16 Aug. 1950 the board of trustees of the Cherokee Historical Association in Cherokee—sponsor of the popular outdoor drama *Unto These Hills*—approved the idea of constructing a replica of an eighteenth-century Cherokee village. The research necessary for creating an accurate replica was to be performed by the Tsali Institute for Cherokee Research, established by the board in May 1951. Noted archaeologists and anthropologists working on the village project and serving as members of the Tsali Institute included Joffre Coe (University of North Carolina at Chapel Hill), A. R. Kelly and W. H. Sears (University of Georgia), T. M. N. Lewis and Madeline Kneberg (University of Tennessee), and John Whittoft (Pennsylvania State Museum). P. A. Willett supervised construction of what became Oconaluftee Indian Village on a wooded, 40-acre tract in Cherokee near the Mountainside Theater, where *Unto These Hills* is performed each summer. The village opened to the public in August 1952, with Walter Jackson serving as the first manager.

Oconaluftee Indian Village was designed to depict life in an eighteenth-century Cherokee community. Cherokee men and women, in traditional attire, perform ancient rites and provide traditional craft demonstrations (see photograph, p. 842). The village also features replicas of a seven-sided council house and homes and other structures from the 1700s. Guides in native attire interpret for visitors the social structure of Cherokee society. A botanical garden and nature trail became a part of the village in 1954. Total paid attendance at the village had topped 6 million by 2000.

Reference: William P. Connor Jr., *History of Cherokee Historical Association, 1946–1982* (1982).

Ron Holland

Odd Fellows Home and School for the Orphaned Children of North Carolina was built on East Ash Street at the corner of Herman Street in Goldsboro by the Grand Lodge of the North Carolina Odd Fellows. It was located on a 20-acre tract

Basket weavers demonstrate their craft at the Oconaluftee Indian Village in Cherokee.
Photograph courtesy of North Carolina Division of Tourism, Film, and Sports Development.

of land donated in 1891 by W. A. Peacock, a member of the local Odd Fellows lodge, and his wife, Hattie. The first child was admitted to the home on 9 May 1892. The home provided for 960 children before closing in 1971. The property was sold to the city of Goldsboro in the late 1970s and became part of a city park. The Wayne County Public Library was built on a portion of the land.

Ted Powell

Odd Fellows Lodge is a benevolent and fraternal organization whose stated goal is to visit the sick, relieve the distressed, bury the dead, educate the orphans, and protect the widows. The group was organized in the United States in 1805, and a lodge was formed in Baltimore in 1819. Some time afterward a lodge was organized in Portsmouth, Va., and in March 1841 one was begun in Weldon, N.C., with a second lodge formed in Wilmington soon after. A Grand Lodge was organized in North Carolina in 1843. During the Civil War the Odd Fellows in Wilmington provided service for the sick and wounded. A witness reported that members "walked amidst the terrors of those hours undaunted, and soothed many a dying pillow with sweet words of love."

From 1819 until 1981 headquarters for the national organi-

zation were located in Baltimore, but since that time Winston-Salem has had that distinction. In January 1991 the Grand Lodge of North Carolina established the archives of the state group in a historic building at Goldsboro. In the 2000s Odd Fellows support an arthritis foundation, a world eye bank and visual research foundation, a world hunger and disaster fund, an international youth exchange program, and a variety of local causes including Boy Scouts, Little League Baseball, both senior and youth programs, orphan homes, and the Red Cross.

William S. Powell

Ogden v. Witherspoon (Blackledge) was heard before circuit justice John Marshall and resident district judge Henry Potter in 1802. The judges sharply disagreed about the meaning of several eighteenth-century statutes affecting creditors' rights asserted in this case by British citizens seeking payment of debts contracted by North Carolinians prior to the American Revolution. Potter, in an opaque opinion, interpreted the ambiguous statutes as favorable to the local debtors, whereas Marshall construed them in light of the 1783 peace treaty with Great Britain barring impediments to debt recovery by British creditors. He denied that the statute of limitations had taken effect and concluded that the state had retrospectively impaired vested property rights protected by Article I, section 10, of the U.S. Constitution. The judges' disagreement resulted in certification of the case to the U.S. Supreme Court, the first case of its kind argued in that forum. The Supreme Court affirmed Marshall's decision, but on statutory grounds alone.

Reference: John P. Roche and Stanley B. Bernstein, eds., *John Marshall: Major Opinions and Other Writings* (1967).

Peter Graham Fish

O. Henry Festival, held annually in Greensboro in April, was founded in 1985 to commemorate the life and works of native son William Sydney Porter (1862–1910), who became world famous for writing short stories under the pen name O. Henry. Porter's gentle and ironic stories, often ending with a surprise that has become known throughout the world as an "O. Henry ending," remain favorites that are still anthologized today. As the seventy-fifth anniversary of Porter's death neared, Marvin L. Skaggs, a retired Greensboro College history professor, convinced a group of citizens of the community that the city needed a visual link to its great writer. A steering committee, spearheaded by Seth C. Macon, a senior vice president at Jefferson-Pilot Insurance, and Bruce B. Stewart, provost of Guilford College, broadened the idea for a sculpture into what eventually became a week-long festival in April.

During the first festival, a sculpture designed by Maria Kirby Smith, who had been awarded the commission following a national competition, was unveiled in downtown Greensboro. It stands on North Elm Street across from the site where the O. Henry Hotel stood until it was demolished in 1979, one block from the Greensboro Historical Museum. The completed sculpture, in three parts, depicts a 7½-foot-high open book with a readable copy of one of O. Henry's most famous stories, "The Ransom of Red Chief," as well as a bas-relief sculpted picture of the couple from another famous story, "The Gift of the Magi," in their New York City flat. Nearby a small boy peeps from behind the book; a free-standing sculpture of a dog, based on an illustration from another well-known O. Henry story, "Memoirs of a Yellow Dog," stands nearby. To the side stands a life-size sculpture of O. Henry himself, modeled on a photograph of Porter, holding an open notebook in one hand and a pencil in the other.

In addition to the sculpture unveiling, the 1985 festival included expansion of the O. Henry exhibit at the Greensboro Historical Museum. The permanent exhibit incorporates part of the downtown Greensboro drugstore in which Porter worked as a young man, as well as a schoolroom that was part of the schoolhouse his aunt Lina Porter operated and where the young Porter was educated. In addition, an original musical drama by Joseph Hoesl, based on O. Henry's works, was premiered by the Community Theatre of Greensboro; a special exhibit, "O. Henry Replayed," at the Greensboro Public Library

displayed original manuscripts, first editions, and films; and a memorabilia exhibit was shown at Brock Museum at Greensboro College. The week-long festival ended with a gala that included an original work by the Frank Holder Dance Company and a pops concert by the Greensboro Symphony.

Most of the festival events are sited at Greensboro College, now the official home of the festival, although the Greensboro Historical Museum continues to present "5 by O. Henry," a series of dramatic sketches, every other year around Porter's birthday (11 September).

References: Abe D. Jones Jr., "An O. Henry Extravaganza" and "Greensboro Honors a Very Private Man," *Greensboro News and Record*, 31 Mar. 1985; Seth C. Macon, *From the Boiler Room to the Board Room* (1996).

Jeaneane Williams

Oil. Geologists for many years have recognized that North Carolina is "dry hole country" with almost no potential for hydrocarbon reserves. Despite this fact, several individuals and companies have drilled for oil within the borders of the state. The search for oil in North Carolina began in 1924, when a well was drilled to a depth of 2,404 feet in Craven County. The well found no indications of hydrocarbons and was the first of 126 dry holes drilled in the state.

Almost all of the exploratory wells have been drilled along North Carolina's coastline in hopes of reaching marine sediments. Five counties—Brunswick, Carteret, Dare, Hyde, and Onslow—account for 79 of the wildcat locations. The rest of the wells were drilled primarily in other coastal counties. Seven wells have been drilled inland in Lee County near Sanford. Most of the wells were drilled to relatively shallow depths: 105 wells are shallower than 5,000 feet and 75 of these are less than 2,500 feet. Only 1 well, drilled by Exxon in Dare County, was deeper than 10,000 feet.

Chevron (now ChevronTexaco Corporation) during the mid- and late 1990s attempted to gain permission to drill a deep test well offshore from the Outer Banks, about 40 miles from Cape Hatteras. The target of this well, which was to be drilled in nearly 2,700 feet of water, was a reef structure on the continental shelf that was believed to contain 3 to 4 trillion cubic feet of natural gas. The project was delayed by legal and environmental concerns as well as regulatory difficulties.

William G. Fick Jr.

Okra, a popular vegetable of the mallow family grown in North Carolina and elsewhere in the South, is believed to be named for the town of Accra, Ghana, in West Africa. From there in the eighteenth century, okra was taken by Africans or slave traders by way of the West Indies into what became the southern United States. It promptly became popular in the re-

A rider tumbles off "Old Buck" during an Old Christmas celebration at Rodanthe in the 1950s. Photograph by Ben Dixon MacNeill. NCC.

gion, where the climate favored its growth. In North Carolina and other southern states, the young seed pods of okra, a mucilaginous plant, are boiled or fried or used in combination with tomatoes in soups and stews. With the shortage of coffee during the Civil War, parched okra seeds were found to be an acceptable substitute, but the shortage of even this source led to the realization that roasted grains of rye were more palatable.

William S. Powell

Old Christmas, or "Little Christmas," celebrated by some eighteenth- and nineteenth-century North Carolinians around 5 January each year, resulted from the adoption of the Gregorian calendar by the British Empire in 1752. Scattered parts of the American colonies refused to celebrate Christmas on the new date (25 December) and eventually merged Old Christmas into the new Epiphany (6 January), creating a joint observance not seen in the West since the fourth century. A few communities in coastal North Carolina became a minority within a mi-

nority by maintaining the distinction. In time, 25 December became the focus of religious sentiment, and Old Christmas turned secular.

In some communities, it was customary to bless fruit trees on Old Christmas or to go outdoors in the early morning hours to watch livestock kneel in remembrance of the Nativity, but dancing, feasting, exchanging gifts, and other common practices had no special Christian meaning. In Stumpy Point (Dare County) and elsewhere, girls and unmarried women sometimes set out a meal at a "dumb table" on the eve of Old Christmas, hoping to glimpse the apparitions of their future husbands hovering over the empty places. On Hatteras Island, loose bands went from house to house, often in disguise, soliciting food and drink and making raucous music. Leaders of such processions sometimes carried a pole topped with the head of a cow or steer, a mascot that evolved into Old Buck — one or more revelers in a roughly bovine costume.

Wynne Dough

East Building on the campus of the University of North Carolina at Chapel Hill, sketched by a student, John Pettigrew, in 1797. NCC.

Old East, on the campus of the University of North Carolina at Chapel Hill, is the oldest state university building in the nation. Except during short periods of extensive renovation in 1922–23 and 1991–93, it has been in constant use for more than two centuries. Old East, originally called the "East Building," sits at the crest of McCorkle Place. On 12 Oct. 1793, the cornerstone was laid in a ceremony led by North Carolina's Grand Master Mason and later governor William Richardson Davie. A bronze plate placed in the stone states, in English and in Latin, that the event occurred at "New Hope Chapel Hill . . . [i]n the year of Masonry 5793 and in the 18th year of American Independence." Old East became home for the university's first student, Hinton James, when he arrived in February 1795.

Originally built in two stories, Old East acquired a third level in 1823 to mirror Old West, constructed opposite it. The "north towers" were added to both buildings in 1848, extending them and bringing them to their present dimensions. Most of the new areas served as library and debating chambers for the university's literary societies, with the Philanthropic

Society (the "Phi") located in Old East and the Dialectic Society (the "Di") across the way. This reflected how the societies traditionally determined memberships, as the Phi claimed students from eastern North Carolina and the Di held their western counterparts.

Although used mostly as a men's dormitory, Old East has also held classrooms and offices, and it contained the University Library from 1853 through 1869. Among the thousands who have lived in Old East was James K. Polk, the eleventh president of the United States.

In 1922 the building was condemned as unsafe, after which it was completely gutted and refurbished. A second renovation of Old East in the early 1990s included the installation of air conditioning and elevators and asbestos removal but also returned the lime-washed building to an earlier appearance, reinstalling skylights, mantels, and (nonworking) fireplaces. The building was designated a National Historic Landmark in 1965. In 2000 female students were allowed to live in Old East for the first time.

The Thirtieth Infantry Division overseeing the movement of German prisoners of war. Courtesy of NCOA&H.

References: William James Battle, ed., *Memories of an Old-time Tar Heel* (1945); "Renewing Old East," *University Report* 38 (August 1991); Louis Round Wilson, *The Library of Our First State University* (1960).

Whitmel M. Joyner

Old Field Schools.

The state of North Carolina did not take an active role in establishing a statewide system of public schools until the General Assembly passed a public school law in 1839. Before that time, there were two alternatives: private academies and local subscription schools. The subscription schools were often called "old field schools" because many were built on worn-out farm fields.

Old field schools were set up on a local basis, sometimes by parents and sometimes by teachers. The school term usually ran for about three months in the winter. Accommodations and educational materials were minimal, as was the pay for teachers. Qualified teachers were hard to find. The *Raleigh Register* dismissed the typical old field school teacher as "a man, who is distinguished alike for his ridiculous ignorance and vulgarity" and who was "too indolent to obtain support in active employment." Educational reform proceeded slowly in the decade following the 1839 public school law, but as state efforts to establish a school system intensified, the old field schools were gradually replaced by public schools.

References: Thomas H. Clayton, *Close to the Land: The Way We Lived in North Carolina, 1820–1870* (1983); Charles L. Coon, *Publications of the North Carolina Historical Commission: Public Education in North Carolina: A Documentary History, 1790–1840* (1908).

David A. Norris

Old Hickory Division,

a World War I unit, initially consisted of National Guard units from North Carolina, South Carolina, and Tennessee. Officially the Thirtieth Division, it was nicknamed in honor of general and seventh U.S. president Andrew "Old Hickory" Jackson, who had connections with all three states. The division was formed on 18 July 1917 at Camp Sevier near Greenville, S.C.; later the state National Guard distinctions were eliminated. In October 1917 additional draftees from North Carolina, South Carolina, Tennessee, Kentucky, Indiana, Illinois, Iowa, Minnesota, and North Dakota increased the Old Hickory's ranks to full wartime strength of approximately 27,000 men. Ninety-five percent of its original members had American-born parents, a rarity when compared to other U.S. divisions in World War I. Further, Old Hickory contained more North Carolinians, and its soldiers were awarded more Congressional Medals of Honor, than any other division.

In April 1918 the Old Hickory Division prepared for transfer to Europe. On arrival in France, the Fifty-fifth Field Artillery Brigade, including the 113th Artillery Regiment, was detached and assigned to the American Expeditionary Force. The rest of the division went with the American Second Corps, attached to the British Army in northern France. In July 1918 Old Hickory joined the British Second Army in Belgium, where it received additional training for combat. On 16 August the division was sent to the trenches in the canal sector between Ypres and Voormezeele in anticipation of the British Ypres-Lys offensive. On 1 September, following a British artillery barrage, both regiments advanced. During the next two days of fighting, they captured all of their objectives, including Lock No. 8 on the Ypres Canal, Lankhof Farm, and the village of Voormezeele. The North Carolinians in the two regiments inflicted about 300 enemy casualties in the 1,500-yard advance, with a loss of 37 dead and 128 wounded.

On 20 Sept. 1918 the American Second Corps (composed of the Twenty-seventh and Thirtieth Divisions) was transferred to the British Fourth Army, and by 25 September the U.S. divisions were in position opposite the Hindenburg Line's St. Quentin trench complex in preparation for a massive assault on the German lines. Under cover of darkness, U.S. divisions captured the German outpost line, and the British bombarded the enemy with artillery fire for two days. North Carolinians ventured into no-man's-land to run barbed wire and to prepare paths through the wire for the attacking infantry. At 5:50 A.M. on 29 September, the corps attacked. Due to high casualties, barbed wire entanglements, and smoke from shellfire, the advancing lines lost all sense of organization. Despite the confusion and losses, the North Carolinians of Old Hickory broke through the Hindenburg Line by 7:30 A.M. Nauroy, the objective of the attack, was won by midday. The next day, 30 September, the Americans were pulled out of battle and sent to the rear. Old Hickory's attack was a huge success, and the division was later credited as the first to break the Hindenburg Line. The Thirtieth suffered approximately 3,000 casualties, many of them North Carolinians.

On the night of 5 October, infantry regiments went back into the line. In the first two days of fighting, Old Hickory advanced more than six miles, often leaving behind the British troops on both flanks. The enemy at Vaux-Andigny, near the La Selle River, stopped this advance. In the five days of combat, the Thirtieth Division lost another 1,108 men. From July to October the division's casualties were 1,641 killed or dead from wounds, 6,774 wounded, 198 missing, and 27 taken prisoner—for a total of 8,415 losses.

For the remainder of October and until the armistice on 11 Nov. 1918, Old Hickory was not engaged. In March 1919 the division sailed homeward from St. Nazaire. After the units took part in parades throughout North Carolina, South Carolina, and Tennessee, the men were discharged. Demobilization was completed by the end of April 1919.

References: Sam J. Royall, *History of the 118th Infantry, American Expeditionary Force, France* (1919); John O. Walker, *Official History of the 120th Infantry, "3rd North Carolina," 30th Division, from August 5, 1917, to April 17, 1919* (1919).

R. Jackson Marshall III

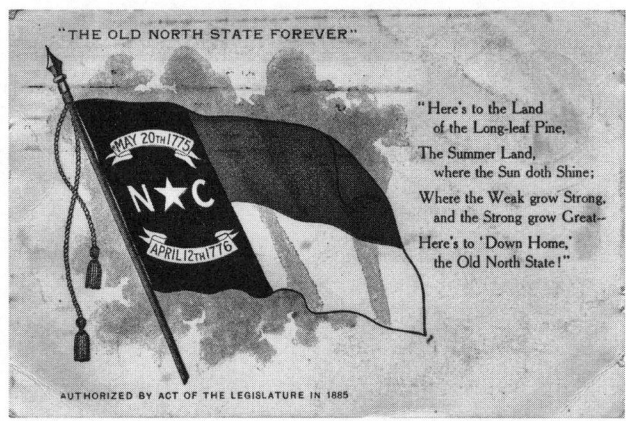

A postcard dating from the early 1900s showing the state flag and the state toast. NCC.

Old North State is a nickname for North Carolina as well as the title of the state song and state toast. The moniker dates back to 1710, when the Carolina colony was effectively divided into two colonies, South Carolina and the earlier-settled North Carolina. The first written reference to the Old North State is credited to Joseph Seawell "Shocco" Jones in the introduction to his *Defence of the Revolutionary History of the State of North Carolina from the Aspersions of Mr. Jefferson*, published in 1834 in Boston and Raleigh. The book included a history of the state from the Regulator Movement to 4 July 1776 and a defense of the so-called Mecklenburg Declaration of Independence of 20 May 1775.

The song "The Old North State" was written in 1835 by William Gaston, a North Carolina Supreme Court justice. The words were adapted to a tune played by a troupe of Swiss bell ringers during a visit to Raleigh. Gaston was staying at the home of his sister, Mrs. John Louis Taylor. The first public performance of "The Old North State" was at a mass meeting of the Whig Party on 5–6 Oct. 1840. The song was first published in 1851 in the *North Carolina Reader* by Calvin H. Wiley and was adopted by the General Assembly as the official state song in 1927. The lyrics are as follows:

Carolina! Carolina! Heav'n's blessings attend her,
While we live we will cherish protect and defend her;
Tho' the scorner may sneer at, and witling defame her,
Our hearts swell with gladness whenever we name her.
Hurrah! Hurrah! The Old North State forever!
Hurrah! Hurrah! The good Old North State!

Tho' she envies not others their merited glory,
Say, whose name stands the foremost in Liberty's story!
Tho' too true to herself e'er to crouch to oppression,
Who can yield to just rule a more loyal submission.
Hurrah! Hurrah! The Old North State forever!
Hurrah! Hurrah! The good Old North State!

Plain and artless her Sons, but whose doors open faster
At the knock of the stranger or tale of disaster;
How like to the rudeness of their dear native mountains,
With rich ore in their bosoms and life in their fountains.
Hurrah! Hurrah! The Old North State forever!
Hurrah! Hurrah! The good Old North State!

And her daughters, the Queen of the Forest resembling—
So graceful, so constant, yet in gentlest breath trembling;
And true lightwood at heart, let the match be applied
    them,
How they kindle and flame! Oh! none know the land that
    we live in
(As happy a region on this side of Heaven).
Where Plenty and Freedom, Love and Peace smile
    before us,
Raise aloud, raise together, the heart-thrilling chorus!
Hurrah! Hurrah! The Old North State forever!
Hurrah! Hurrah! The good Old North State!

The state toast, also called "The Old North State," was written by Leonora Monteiro Martin of Raleigh for a banquet of the North Carolina Society of Richmond, Va., on 20 May 1904. The verses immediately found favor in North Carolina and were widely copied, memorized, and recited. Very modest changes were made in five words, not affecting the sentiment, between 1910 and 1933. Printed on a heavy, high-quality paper and decorated with boughs of longleaf pine, sprigs of dogwood blossoms, and the state flag, the toast was framed and hung in schools, homes, and offices. In 1932 Mary Burke Kerr of Clinton composed music for the toast at the request of Susan Fulgham, Wayne County school supervisor. On 21 May 1957 the General Assembly passed Senate Bill 305, making this piece the official state toast.

Here's to the land of the Long Leaf Pine,
The Summer Land, where the sun doth shine;
Where the weak grow strong and the strong grow great—
Here's to "Down Home," the Old North State!

Here's to the land of the cotton bloom white,
Where the scuppernong perfumes the breeze at night,
Where the soft Southern moss and jessamine mate,
'Neath the murmuring pines of the Old North State!

Here's to the land where the galax grows,
Where the rhododendron's rosette glows;
Where soars Mount Mitchell's summit great,
In the "Land of the Sky," in the Old North State!

Here's to the land where maidens are fair,
Where friends are true, and cold hearts are rare,
The near land, the dear land, whatever fate,
The blest land, the best land, the Old North State!

References: Sturgis Lee Hedrick, "How North Carolina Got a 'Toast,'" *New East* 4 (January–February 1976); H. G. Jones, *North Carolina History: An Annotated Bibliography* (1995).

William S. Powell
Additional research provided by Robert L. Remsburg III and Wiley J. Williams.

Old Quawk's Day, by long-standing tradition, is a day when residents of Ocracoke Island on North Carolina's Outer Banks are advised not to wander far from home. It was on that day many years ago that an unsociable, eccentric man who had been shipwrecked on Ocracoke and decided to take up residence there is said to have shoved off in his small fishing boat at the height of a tempest, all the while shouting blasphemous threats toward heaven. He was never seen or heard from again. Ever since then, according to the legend, there have been an unseemly number of shipwrecks and lost lives on that date.

Nobody knew the man's name, but because of his strange, guttural voice they called him Old Quawk (or Quork, or Quoke). In modern times, there is a point on Ocracoke Island with that name, and nearby a creek and hammock. Although the story figures prominently in Ocracoke Island folklore, there is little uniformity in the way it is told. In his 1956 book *Ocracoke*, Carl Goerch listed Old Quawk's Day as 16 March and traced the event back to the early part of the nineteenth century. Yet in his *Legends of the Outer Banks and Tar Heel Tidewater* (1966), folklorist Charles Harry Whedbee gave the date as 6 Feb. 1788. Goerch stated that the name came from the resemblance of the man's voice, particularly when he was excited, to the cry of the coastal night heron, which is nicknamed "the qwak." Whedbee, however, attributed the name to the sound made by the croaker, a common coastal fish. All seem to agree, though, that Old Quawk was a strange and disagreeable man who lived apart from others on the island and made contact with fellow Ocracokers only when he had fish to sell or supplies to buy. To this day, many old-timers agree that it is prudent not to venture out on the water on Old Quawk's Day.

David Stick

Old Salem. SEE Salem.

Old-Time String Band Music. Among North Carolina rural whites and blacks at the turn of the century, a "string band" meant a fiddler and banjo player who would perform for dances held in private homes. The fiddle is the classical violin played in a folk fashion, the most popular and recognizable of which in North Carolina and across the South are the fiddle styles of old-time country music and bluegrass music. In old-time music playing, the fiddle is likely to have an edgier presentation than in bluegrass, where a smoother, long-stroke style generally predominates. There is much overlap, however,

The Red Clay Ramblers practice in Tommy Thompson's basement in Chapel Hill, ca. 1974. Left to right: Jim Watson, Mike Craver, Tommy Thompson, and Bill Hicks. Thompson's son, Tom Ashley, is in the foreground. Photograph by John Rosenthal.

and fiddle players in both styles use the instrument to create hoedown dance music such as jigs, reels, and polkas as well as to lend a weeping quality to sentimental country waltzes.

Only after 1900 did the guitar become common, adding more stable rhythm and greater volume to the earlier banjo-fiddle duet. Country guitar players tended to use a plectrum, or pick, to brush the strings to play chords in accompaniment to instrumental tunes. Blues and ragtime influences led to more complex bass lines added to the simple chordal accompaniment, and the guitar gradually became a more important rhythm instrument in string band music.

After World War I, fiddlers' conventions served to draw together musicians from different communities, and dances began going public. The heavy investment in school infrastructure after 1900 in North Carolina provided hundreds of potential dance venues. Dance organizers, often the musicians themselves, could charge a nickel or a dime admission fee, which usually paid for the dance band.

Charlie Poole (1892–1931) and the North Carolina Ramblers stand among the earliest and best-known of the state's hillbilly string bands. Consisting of such artists as banjoist Poole, fiddlers Posey Rorrer and Lonnie Austin, and guitarists Norman Woodlief and Roy Harvey, the North Carolina Ramblers began recording for Columbia Records in 1925, selling more than 100,000 copies of "Don't Let Your Deal Go Down." That song and several others, including "If I Lose," "White House Blues," and "Sweet Sunny South," entered the folk tradition and remain popular with bluegrass and old-time musicians to this day. Many other North Carolina string bands made records and achieved varied degrees of fame. The most memorable included Al Hoplins' Hill Billies, the Piedmont Log Rollers, the Carolina Tarheels with Clarence "Tom" Ashley, and the Carolina Buddies. Other musicians from mountains to coast provided dance music until jukeboxes put them out of work toward the end of the Great Depression.

The string band sound, called old-time music since the 1920s, survived in parts of North Carolina through the enthusiastic support of musicians and fans. WPAQ-AM, founded by Ralph Epperson and broadcasting from Mount Airy in Surry County beginning in 1948, became a principal advocate of the genre, presenting countless live performances by local and professional bands on its popular *Merry-Go-Round* weekly show and other programs. Old-time music gained an even wider following when it was rediscovered by young musicians in the 1960s and 1970s. Groups such as the Camp Creek Boys from Surry County finally recorded during that period, while artists from the prewar era began new careers. Formed in 1966 in Durham, the Hollow Rock String Band took its name from the large and unusual stretch of undercut rock formations along New Hope Creek in eastern Orange County, near the country home of Bobbie and Tommy Thompson. The band's original members included fiddler Alan Jabbour, mandolinist Bertram Levy, Bobbie Thompson on guitar, and Tommy Thompson on banjo. Jabbour made numerous tape recordings of "old-timers" in the mountains of North Carolina and Virginia, and Hollow Rock's replication of their distinct old-time country playing styles and, in many cases, their nearly extinct tunes, became the mission of the band, with the Thompsons' home becoming the site of a regular Friday night musicale for years.

In North Carolina, unlike some other southern states, the older African American string band tradition coexisted with the newer blues style. The Chapel Hillbillies, a black band active from the 1930s through the 1950s, could move from

Radio station founder and owner Ralph Epperson, a well-known champion of North Carolina's folk music traditions, in the studios of WPAQ 740 AM in Mount Airy in the early 1990s. Photograph by Cedric N. Chatterly. Courtesy of the North Carolina Arts Council.

string band to blues to pseudo–big band music to suit their differing audiences. Cousins Joe and Odell Thompson, from Cedar Grove, performed African American banjo and fiddle music until Odell was killed in a 1994 automobile accident.

The Fuzzy Mountain String Band was a so-called urban revival string band, ca. 1967–73, which grew out of the Hollow Rock String Band. Following the philosophy of the Hollow Rock String Band, the Fuzzy Mountain String Band also strived to learn actual tunes from specific old-time players and to play them accurately and with care. As one of the first "young old-time" bands, or "young fogies," the Fuzzy Mountain String Band proved very important as a model for other bands and a source for tunes. The tunes on the band's records, for the most part melodies known only in tiny regions of the Appalachians when the band "discovered" them, are now known by thousands of players all over the world, wherever old-time Appalachian music is played.

The Red Clay Ramblers, a string band from Chapel Hill, was founded in 1972 by Tommy Thompson (banjo), Bill Hicks (fiddle), and Jim Watson (guitar, mandolin), originally to recreate the repertoire and playing style of old-time bands. With the addition of pianist Michael Craver in 1973, the Ramblers' participation in Bland Simpson and Jim Wann's hybrid musical *Diamond Studs* (which opened in Chapel Hill in 1974 and New York City in 1975), and the arrival of Jack Herrick (trumpet, bass, pennywhistle) in 1975–76, the band's sound became an eclectic mix of southern mountain fiddle tunes, bluegrass, swing, gospel (both black and white), stomp blues, and original songs of all sorts. Over two decades, the Ramblers' participation in the development of "musicians' theatre," musical shows incorporating the band on stage with the rest of the performers, distinguished the group from virtually all other acoustic, folk, and bluegrass acts. These shows have included *Life on the Mississippi* (Chapel Hill, 1982), *A Lie of the Mind* (New York, 1985–86), *The Merry Wives of Windsor, Texas* (Houston, 1988; St. Louis, Columbus, Durham, 1989; Cincinnati, 1994), and *Fool Moon* (New York, 1993; Los Angeles, Vienna, and Munich, 1994; and New York, 1995).

North Carolina continued to host a number of thriving fiddlers' conventions at the end of the 1990s and early 2000s, featuring dozens of bands consisting of younger musicians such as the Piedmont Hepcats and the Old Hollow String Band. The Ole Time Fiddler's and Bluegrass Festival, held each Memorial Day weekend at Fiddler's Grove Campground in Union Grove, is the state's longest-running fiddlers' convention, with roots stretching back to 1924. The event has been featured on a PBS documentary, *Fiddler's Grove: A Celebration of Old-Time Music*, and has received other national and international acclaim. The Bluegrass and Old-time Fiddlers Convention in Mount Airy features about 150 bands competing in several musical categories, including bluegrass and old-time band music, folk music, and various forms of banjo, guitar, dobro, dulci-

mer, autoharp, mandolin, and bass playing. The Toast String Stretchers from Mount Airy, one of many old-time bands active in the 1990s, served as the host band for the Cultural Olympiad in Atlanta during July 1996.

References: Bruce Bastin, *Red River Blues: The Blues Tradition in the Southeast* (1986); Bill C. Malone, *Country Music, U.S.A.* (1985); Kinney Rorrer, *Rambling Blues: The Life and Songs of Charlie Poole* (1982).

Bland Simpson
William Hicks
Additional research provided by Kelly Kress and Art Menius.

SEE ALSO Bluegrass Music; Country Music; Square Dancing.

One-Party Politics. SEE Democratic Party; Political Parties.

Onslow County, located in the Coastal Plain region of southeastern North Carolina, was formed in 1734 from New Hanover County and named for Arthur Onslow, Speaker of the House of Commons in the British Parliament. The county is bordered in part by the Atlantic Ocean. Early inhabitants of the region included Siouan Indians, followed by English, Welsh, French, Swiss, Scottish, and German settlers. Jacksonville, the county seat, was established and incorporated in 1843 and named for President Andrew Jackson; formerly, the county seat had been Onslow Courthouse. Other communities in Onslow County include Swansboro, Sneads Ferry, Midway Park, Hubert, Dixon, Folkstone, and Petersburg. Notable physical features of the county, in addition to the extensive coastline, include the New River, Onslow Bay, Stones Creek, Catherine Lake, Onslow Beach, and Wolf and Bachelors Delight Swamps.

Camp Lejeune Marine Base is in many ways a dominant factor in the life and economy of Onslow County. The base, established during the World War II era, is home to the Second Marine Expeditionary Force, making Jacksonville—like Fayetteville in Cumberland County—one of the United States' principal military cities. The county's economy is also strengthened by its coastal location; Topsail Island, situated along the Atlantic coast, brings in thousands of vacationers and tourists each year (the northeastern end of the island, including the community of North Topsail Beach, lies in Onslow County, while the southwestern end is in adjacent Pender County).

Otway Burns, a privateer in the War of 1812, built the first steamboat in Onslow County in 1818. The county has several historic attractions, such as Historic Swansboro, Mumfort Historic Cemetery, and the Beirut Memorial, erected to honor all servicemen who died in Lebanon and Grenada in 1983. The Montford Point Marine Museum presents the history of the

World War II recruit training depot for African American marines. County cultural institutions include Opera Carolina and the Onslow County Crafts Guild. The county hosts popular annual events such as the Onslow County Fair, the Sneads Ferry Shrimp Festival, Swansboro Arts-by-the-Sea, the Topsail Island Kite Festival, and the Coastal Storytelling Festival.

Onslow County agricultural products include tobacco, fruits and vegetables, cattle, swine, and poultry. Fishing and forestry contribute significantly to the county's economy as well. Manufactures from Onslow County include textiles, plywood, fuel injectors, meat products, and yachts. In 2004 the population of Onslow County was estimated to be 159,700.

Jay Mazzocchi

SEE ALSO Camp Lejeune.

Opera. SEE Classical Music.

Opera Houses. From the mid-1870s until World War I, any building used for presenting entertainment on stage was popularly called an "opera house." The term was something of a euphemism: despite the popularity of live theater during the period, an antitheatrical prejudice was still in evidence; calling a hall an opera house lent an air of respectability to the act of play-going. Except in larger North Carolina cities such as Charlotte, Raleigh, and Wilmington, very little grand opera was actually presented. Other terms used to describe theaters included academy of music, auditorium, or town hall.

The oldest surviving opera house in North Carolina, New Bern's Masonic Temple Theatre, was built between 1801 and 1804 as part of the Masonic Lodge. Most early halls were converted out of available space in the upper floors of existing buildings: Raleigh's Tucker Hall and Fayetteville's Williams Hall were in commercial buildings, and Greensboro's Benbow Hall and High Point's Jarrell's Hall were in hotels. Some were built as part of a city hall or other municipal structure; certainly North Carolina's most famous opera house, Wilmington's Thalian Hall, comes under this heading, but there were also opera houses as part of municipal buildings in Apex, Belhaven, Dunn, Durham, Greensboro, High Point, King's Mountain, Oxford, Raleigh, Randleman, Smithfield, Tarboro, Warrenton, and Washington.

The typical opera house manager was a local businessman for whom running a theater was a sideline. Managers were jewelers, grocers, carpet dealers, pharmacists, lawyers, bankers, physicians, or even railroad agents. When the hall was associated with a lodge such as the Masons or the Elks or one of the local militias such as the Fayetteville Independent Light Infantry, management was one of the responsibilities of being an officer. If the hall was located in a municipal building, the manager might be a city official.

One profession that did have a direct relation to opera house management was that of bill poster. A bill poster was responsible for putting up the posters that were the primary advertising medium for touring theatrical troupes, particularly in towns that had no daily newspapers. These bill-posting companies developed into the modern outdoor advertising industry.

The most significant figure in theatrical management in North Carolina during this period was Wilmington's S. A. Schloss, as he was the first, and for many years the only, manager to devote his energies primarily to running a theater. Starting with the Wilmington Opera House (Thalian Hall) in 1895, Schloss acquired leases on opera houses in Raleigh (1898), Greensboro (1901), Charlotte (1903), Winston-Salem (1905), Asheville (Grand Opera House, 1906), and Monroe (1907); Tarboro, Goldsboro, and Wilson (1908); Concord (1909); and again in Asheville (the Asheville Auditorium, 1910). At the height of its success, the Schloss Theatres Circuit controlled 14 opera houses in North Carolina, South Carolina, and Virginia.

A major factor in Schloss's operations and the operations of every opera house manager was the so-called Theatrical Syndicate. This organization, whose booking office in New York City was run by Marc Klaw and Abraham Erlanger, controlled most of the major touring attractions that might play a larger town and all of the smaller attractions that would play the smaller towns. Klaw and Erlanger controlled the bookings of every opera house in North Carolina, either directly, through lessees such as Schloss, or indirectly, since managers who refused to deal with the syndicate or whose towns were too small for the syndicate to be interested in could not get even second-rate attractions.

The term "attraction" was used to cover a wide variety of presentations, including plays, musicals, minstrel shows, vaudeville, motion pictures, lectures, or concerts. A company that produced a single play or musical comedy (a recent New York success), carried its own star, supporting cast, and scenery, and played one-night stands was called a combination company. Troupes that played a week in each town (six nights with two matinees, no Sundays), had a selection of plays (non-royalty plays or old chestnuts that had long since lost their value to the combination companies), and used the stock scenery provided by each opera house were called repertoire companies. The straight plays were generally melodramas such as *East Lynne* or *Ten Nights in a Bar Room*, though farces like Charles Hoyt's *A Trip to Chinatown* (one of the sources for *Hello, Dolly*) were nearly as popular.

Minstrel shows reached their peak of popularity in the 1870s but were still part of an opera house season as late as the 1920s. Vaudeville, a descendant of the minstrel shows, was part of the program for many touring repertoire companies, though by the years immediately preceding World War I there were specific opera houses in North Carolina that ran vaudeville exclusively. The motion picture as an attraction had made its debut in North Carolina as early as 1900, usually as part of a vaudeville bill. By 1910 there were halls in the larger North Carolina towns devoted exclusively to movies, and by the end of World War I movies had become the primary source of popular entertainment. Some halls in the larger cities continued to present live theater into the 1920s, but by then "the road" was dead and the era of the opera house was over.

References: Gus Hill, *Gus Hill's National Theatrical Directory* (1914); J. B. Jeffery, ed., *Guide and Directory to the Opera Houses, Theatres, Public Halls, Bill Posters, etc., of the Cities and Towns of America* (11 vols., 1878–90).

Paul F. Wilson

SEE ALSO Thalian Association.

Opossums (from the Powhatan Indian word *aposoun*) are the only marsupials indigenous to North Carolina and the United States. Formerly trapped in great numbers for their fur, which was used for various inexpensive items, they were once confined to the southeastern and south-central United States but are now common from southern Canada to Argentina, even in cities, often becoming agricultural and household pests. The night-roaming opossum eats carrion and deals with threats by displaying its 50 sharp teeth or slipping into fear-induced catatonia ("playing 'possum").

North Carolinians of all races have shunned the opossum as unsanitary, celebrated its comas and illusory cleverness, and considered its meat to be a requisite of gracious living. The opossum hunt, customarily held under a waning autumn moon by groups of men with dogs, artificial lights, and strong drink, was once an important social event in rural areas. Some epicures still consider opossum a delicacy when the animal is taken alive, given clean food to improve its flavor, and baked with sweet potatoes. "'Possum 'n' 'taters" reached the height of respectability in North Carolina during the gubernatorial administrations of William Kerr Scott (1949–53) and his son Robert Walter Scott (1969–73). From 1970 to 1973 the National Hollerin' Contest in Spivey's Corner included a "Prettiest Possum" competition. Public outcry saved the first winner, Slowpoke, from the gubernatorial table.

North Carolina place names inspired by the opossum include Opossum Swamp (Sampson County); two Possum Branches (Macon County); Possum Quarter (Pasquotank County); Possum Neck Swamp (Craven County); Possum Swamp (Pamlico County); Possumquarter (Warren County), the estate of Governor Gabriel Johnston (1699–1751), and its probable namesake, Possumquarter Creek; Possumtown, now Bethany (Davidson County); and Possumtrot Community and Creek (Yancey County).

Reference: William David Webster, James F. Parnell, and Walter C. Biggs Jr., *Mammals of the Carolinas, Virginia, and Maryland* (1985).

Wynne Dough

Opposition Party was the name temporarily adopted in 1860 by North Carolina members of the Whig Party, which had practically dissolved over the slavery issue. Its supporters nominated John Pool for governor on a platform of union and an end to sectional agitation. Pool lost to John W. Ellis, the Southern Rights candidate.

William C. Harris

Orange County, located in the Piedmont region of North Carolina, was formed in 1752 from Johnston, Bladen, and Granville Counties and named for William V of Orange, the infant grandson of King George III of England. Early inhabitants of the area included the Eno, Occaneechi, and Haw Indians. English, German, Scotch-Irish, and Welsh settlers later populated the region. The village of Occaneechi on the Great Trading Path was visited by explorer John Lawson in 1701. Hillsborough, the county seat, was incorporated in 1759 as Childsburgh, named after Attorney General Thomas Childs; in 1766, the name was changed to Hillsborough in honor of Wills Hill, earl of Hillsborough. The town had a central role in the War of the Regulation (1764–71). Hillsborough maintains a substantial historic district with many important properties. Other communities in the county include Chapel Hill, Carrboro, Cedar Grover, Efland, Caldwell, Carr, and part of Mebane. Notable physical features of Orange County include the Eno River, Couch Mountain, Lake Michael, Turkey Hill Creek, Blackwood Mountain, and Chestnut Ridge.

Orange County is home to the University of North Carolina at Chapel Hill, which was chartered in 1789 and is the nation's oldest state university. Many cultural, historic, and educational institutions are associated with the university, including several libraries housing important historical collections, the Carolina Playmakers and Paul Green Theater, the Morehead Planetarium, and the Ackland Art Museum. Apart from campus buildings, Chapel Hill's historic structures include the Horace Williams House and the Episcopal Chapel of the Cross. Non-university-related cultural institutions in Orange County include the ArtsCenter in Carrboro and the Jewish Heritage Foundation. Orange County hosts several popular annual events, such as the Festifall street fair in Chapel Hill, Hillsborough Hog Day, the Hillsborough Candlelight Christmas Tour, and the Occaneechi-Saponi Spring Festival and Pow Wow.

Orange County agricultural commodities include corn, tobacco, dairy products, berries, horses, sheep, and swine. Manufactured goods from the county include food products, tobacco products, rubber, chemicals, paper, apparel, and fur-

Shaft at the Ore Knob Copper Mine in Ashe County (date unknown). Courtesy of NCOA&H.

niture. Topaz, hematite, granite, and clay are mined in the county. As part of the thriving Triangle area, Orange County continues to move toward greater urbanization. The county's estimated population in 2004 was 120,900.

William S. Powell

SEE ALSO University of North Carolina at Chapel Hill.

Orchestras. SEE Classical Music.

Ore Knob Copper Mine in Ashe County was first conceived in the spring of 1854, when John Mason Lillard of Decatur, Meigs County, Tenn., channeled his resources into the organization of the Meigs County & Virginia Mining Company and the Decatur Mining Company. Lillard managed the original opening of the Ore Knob Copper Mine in 1855, when "four shafts were sunk on the property to depths of 90, 40, 30 and 40 feet and enough ore that assayed 19 percent copper was mined to make a profit of $9,400." But the distance of 63 miles over "poor mountain roads" to the nearest railroad prevented the mine from being profitable, and it was closed in 1856.

S. S. and J. E. Clayton of Baltimore reopened the mine in 1873, and that July "about 1,400 tons of ore" were raised, "averaging more than 25 percent of copper." Other periods of operation included 1896, 1913, 1917–18, 1927, 1942–43, and 1953–62, when the mine was "completely worked out" and abandoned.

In January 1982 two bodies were found in the abandoned Ore Knob Copper Mine; Johnny Sands, known as the "Nashville Flame," wrote a popular ballad about the incident. The large, gaping entrance to the mine remains a forbidding reminder of the dangers—both physical and financial—of mining.

References: Eben E. Olcott, "The Ore Knob Copper Mine and Reduction Works, Ashe County, N.C.," *American Institute of Mining Engineers Transactions* 3 (1874); Thomas J. Schoenbaum, *The New*

River Controversy (1979); Jasper Leonidas Stuckey, *North Carolina: Its Geology and Mineral Resources* (1965).

Stewart Lillard

Organs. Moravians first brought the organ into North Carolina for use in worship services. Joseph Ferdinand Bulitschek, a Salem cabinetmaker and millwright, built two early organs for Moravian congregations in the Wachovia settlement. Bulitschek's organ for Bethania, built in 1773, was in use until destroyed by fire in 1942. Other eighteenth-century organ builders included Jacob Loesch of Bethania and a Mr. Stirewalt of Rowan County.

Two of ten surviving organs by the renowned Moravian organ builder David Tannenberg of Pennsylvania are housed at Old Salem. The first was installed in 1798. New York's Henry Erben, touted as America's premier organ builder of the nineteenth century, built five organs in North Carolina by the mid-1840s. Christ Episcopal Church in Elizabeth City purchased one of Erben's organs in 1845.

Theater organs, pipe organs with tremulant and percussion sounds made by wooden pipes, were manufactured in the early twentieth century for use in accompanying silent movies. Robert Morton built theater organs for Lumberton's Carolina Civic Center and Greensboro's Carolina Theater. A Barton organ from Milwaukee's Upton Theatre is in a private Raleigh residence. The enormous Moller organ in Charlotte's Calvary Church, which includes theater organ pipes, is the thirteenth-largest organ in the world.

Duke University Chapel boasts three organs. The Aeolian, built in 1932, was the last organ the Aeolian Organ Company built before merging with the E. M. Skinner Organ Company. Recently renovated, its pipes number around 6,900. In 1976, the organ now installed over the chapel entrance was com-

Tannenberg organ in Home Church in Old Salem, 1890s. Courtesy of Old Salem, Inc.

pleted in the shop of the famous D. A. Flentrop in Zaandam, Holland. The tones of its 5,033 pipes reflect Dutch and French organs of the early eighteenth century, considered the "golden age of organs." In 1997 John Brombaugh and Associates of Eugene, Ore., installed an organ with 960 pipes in a swallows nest gallery on the middle north wall of Duke Chapel for use during weekly worship services. Since then, the Flentrop is used primarily for processionals and recessionals at larger worship services, university events, and recitals. A Flentrop organ also was installed at Reynolda Presbyterian Church in Winston-Salem in 1961.

Two pipe organ builders, the Knowlton Pipe Organ Company in Davidson and Cornel Zimmer in Denver, currently work in North Carolina. Zimmer also manufactures digital organs. Allen Organ Company, based in Macungie, Pa., made electronic and digital organs in Rocky Mount for some 30 years until closing the plant in March 1999.

Reference: Orpha Ochse, *The History of the Organ in the United States* (1975).

K. Todd Johnson

Orphans were an important part of colonial North Carolina society because of high mortality rates and the large number of children present in the population. As early as 1665, William Drummond, the colony's first governor, complained that something needed to be done "to save the rights of orphans." This warning would become one of the guiding standards of the colony.

Orphans were primarily treated according to their "rank and degree," with wealthy individuals being granted more attention by the law. A guardian, often a relative, was appointed to competently maintain the minor's estates—land, animals, buildings, and physical wealth such as slaves, money, and plate—and to support him or her from the interest produced. Each year this trustee was required to report on the progress of the estate, his disbursements, and the well-being of his charge. A guardian was not permitted to abuse the orphan, to neglect care or education, to misuse the legacy, or to marry the child if it was female. In the event that a court—superior, inferior, the General Court, or the more specialized Orphans' Court—suspected wrongdoing, it had the power to immediately intervene, investigate and displace the guardian, and, if necessary, take charge of the estate.

Orphans with insufficient inheritance or with none at all were represented yearly as a group before the Orphans' Court by the church wardens of each parish. The very young were appointed guardians, with the parish usually supplying an annual sum of money to maintain them. Older youths were assigned to "some tradesman, merchant, mariner, or other person" until a male reached age 21 or a female, 18. The youths were expected to be fed, clothed, taught to read and write, and educated in a trade. In return they contributed labor, a commodity always in short supply. If the bargain was incomplete at the time the apprenticeship ended, the apprentice was expected to continue to pay on his contract; but if the tradesman failed to do his part, he was subject to prosecution.

During the twentieth century, the care of orphans and other disadvantaged children increasingly became the focus of various state and federal agencies. Today, the North Carolina Division of Social Services maintains a number of programs for children in need, with private organizations such as the Methodist Home for Children in Raleigh providing additional resources.

Louis P. Towles

Orthodox Church has 225 million members worldwide and 6 million members in North America. In North Carolina, the church is represented by the Greek Orthodox Church and, to a lesser extent, the Russian Orthodox Church. From 1900 until about 1920—paralleling the nation's "third wave" of immigration—the number of Greek and Russian immigrants to the state increased. Orthodox churches were subsequently established, beginning in about 1905 with a Greek Orthodox Church in Asheville. Some 30 years later, the number of Greek Orthodox churches in the state had grown to three, with a total membership of about 400 communicants. By the early 2000s there were about 1,000 members altogether in Greek Orthodox churches in several metropolitan areas, including Asheville, Burlington, Charlotte, Durham (which traces the Parish of Saint Barbara from 1945), Fayetteville, Greensboro, Raleigh, Wilmington, and Winston-Salem.

North Carolina was, for many years, home to the only Russian Orthodox Church in the South—Saints Peter and Paul, formed in 1932 in St. Helena, a small Pender County community. In that year, on land acquired from Wilmington real estate promoter Hugh MacRae, the tiny red brick church began with 15 charter members and their families. By 2006 Russian Orthodox congregations could be found in the Piedmont and Mountains as well as the Coastal Plain, in the form of Holy Trinity Orthodox Church in Durham and St. Nicholas Orthodox Church in Fletcher.

Reference: Paula Maria Stathakis, "Development of a Greek-American Community in the South: Charlotte, North Carolina, 1900–1940" (M.A. thesis, UNC-Charlotte, 1988).

Wiley J. Williams

Ould Virginia as a term enjoyed brief currency in the seventeenth century as a name for territory south of the Chesapeake Bay covered by Sir Walter Raleigh's 1584 patent of discovery. John Smith may have coined the name, and Robert Vaughan's map of "Ould Virginia" in Smith's *General History of Virginia* (1624) accelerated its spread. William Strachey had used *South Virginia* in the same sense around 1612. While the two names were interchangeable, confusion sometimes occurred because "South Virginia" also referred to the land holdings of the Virginia Company of London (34°–41° N). By midcentury the use of both names was in decline. North Virginia, the holdings of the Virginia Company of Plymouth (38°–45° N), had come to be known as New England (perhaps another of Smith's coinages), so there was no further need for a South Virginia to balance it. Meanwhile, the most populous part of South Virginia had been partitioned into Virginia and Maryland, and the Royal grants of 1629 and 1663 officially named the sparsely settled area below the 36th parallel "Carolana" and "Carolina," respectively. Virginia's nickname of "Old Dominion" refers to the predominant royalism of Virginia in the Commonwealth Period and has nothing to with Ould Virginia.

References: Matthew Page Andrews, *Virginia: The Old Dominion* (1949); John Fiske, *Old Virginia and Her Neighbours* (1897); William S. Powell, *North Carolina through Four Centuries* (1989).

Wynne Dough

Our Living and Our Dead was a literary-historical periodical first published in New Bern on 2 July 1873. Stephen D. Pool, the editor of the weekly folio, declared that its purpose was "to make a fair and impartial record of my native State, and of her gallant sons,—of the living, maimed or able-bodied, as well as the dead, whose remains filled every cemetery, reposed beneath the sod of almost every battle-ground, or in the enclosure of every hospital and Confederate cemetery, and of every prison pen at the North." *Our Living and Our Dead* contained miscellaneous sketches, correspondence, state news, war diaries, war reminiscences, registers of North Carolina troops, and selected verse, as well as reprints from other southern periodicals. While most of the material in the publication focused on North Carolina's role in the Civil War, articles on other subjects also appeared. For example, the periodical published a number of articles defending the authenticity of the Mecklenburg Declaration of Independence of 20 May 1775.

In October 1873, *Our Living and Our Dead* became the official publication of the North Carolina Branch of the Southern Historical Society. In 1874 it was moved to Raleigh, became a single-column monthly, and continued regular publication until March 1876. Theodore B. Kingsbury and James H. Pool (the editor's brother) became associate editors. Kingsbury, a North Carolina author and literary critic, wrote many essays for the magazine and became the publication's most prolific contributor. He prepared historical and biographical sketches, as well as articles on education, southern textbooks, poetry, and plagiarism.

The circulation of *Our Living and Our Dead* ranged from about 1,500 to 2,000 readers. This proved to be an inadequate subscriber base, and the periodical ceased publication in

Title page of the last issue of *Our Living and Our Dead*, 1876. NCC.

March 1876. The magazine stands out as the most provincial of the South's postwar literary-historical periodicals. In addition to being a major source for the work and ideas of Kingsbury, the publication remains a resource for the history of the state, especially in relation to North Carolinians' involvement in the Civil War.

References: Ray M. Atchison, "*Our Living and Our Dead*: A Post-Bellum North Carolina Magazine of Literature and History," *NCHR* 40 (October 1963); Atchison, "Southern Literary Magazines, 1865–1887" (Ph.D. diss., Duke University, 1956).

Ronnie W. Faulkner

Our State magazine's name and subtitle, *Down Home in North Carolina*, capture its mission of describing the state's people, places, history, and folklore. Newspaperman and radio broadcaster Carl Goerch set out in 1933 to publish "a weekly survey of North Carolina, dedicated to cause people to be more appreciative of their state by becoming better acquainted with it." Goerch was supremely confident in launching a magazine during the Depression, and his good name and salesmanship drew the backing of business leaders. Early advertisers included R. J. Reynolds, Liggett & Myers, the American Tobacco Company, Jefferson Standard Life Insurance, Wachovia Bank, and Carolina Power & Light.

Goerch first published his magazine on 3 June 1933 under the banner *The State*, a title that was used for 63 years. He called his job "a picnic and a vacation," as he crisscrossed the state promoting his magazine, gathering material, and selling subscriptions. He also filled the publication with his own humorous observations on life in North Carolina. A native New Yorker, Goerch noted the difference between North Carolinians and his Empire State brethren: "We folks down here get more pleasure out of five years of living than those damn Yankees get in a lifetime." Longtime contributor Billy Arthur compared *The State* to a small-town newspaper, given its chatty bits of statewide news, editorials, quizzes, and humorous columns.

In 1951 Goerch sold the magazine to Bill Sharpe, also a former newspaperman and a former state advertising director. Sharpe added features but switched from weekly to monthly publication. In strident editorials he took on communists, integrationists, and others on the national and international scene, making for a curious editorial mix, but he also knew his beat. Sharpe won the Mayflower Cup, at the time the state's top literary award, for *A New Geography of North Carolina*, a four-volume collection of his feature stories on North Carolina counties.

W. B. Wright, publisher from 1965 to 1987, brought to the job newspaper experience, a degree in creative writing, and a 16-year apprenticeship at the magazine. Wright gave additional play to historical and business stories and published the work of leading North Carolina writers.

For many years *The State* was a fixture in homes from Cherokee to Chicamacomico. It was dependable, informative, and entertaining. It was also quaint. Its appearance changed little over a half century, remaining resolutely black and white through the technicolor and psychedelic eras.

In 1987 Shaw Publishing in Charlotte bought the magazine, adding color and updating its graphic design. In 1996 Shaw sold it to Bernard Mann, a publisher and former radio executive who moved *The State* to Greensboro. With the August 1996 issue, Mann changed the name to *Our State*, explaining that the new name was warmer, more inclusive, and more suited to the publication. Mann also increased the use of color photographs and improved the magazine's design but retained its editorial focus.

Our State readers are fiercely loyal. Mann's initial marketing research revealed a subscription renewal rate of 87 percent, measured against the industry standard of 35 to 37 percent. By 2004 circulation had grown to 120,000, which included paid subscriptions, newsstand sales, and complimentary copies. Approximately 85 percent of the paying subscribers lived in North Carolina.

Reference: Steve Huffman, "Magazine Gets New Look, Keeps Distinctive Content," *Raleigh News and Observer*, 16 Feb. 1997.

Speed Hallman

Outdoor Dramas, sometimes called symphonic dramas, are a type of theatrical production that takes its story from local history and augments it with music, dance, and spectacle. The style evolved from pageant dramas, popular in the United States in the late nineteenth and early twentieth century, which were spectacles that presented historical events in a tableaux manner. The symphonic drama differed in that it used plot and character to tell a historical story on a grand scale. Both as popular entertainment and as tourist attractions, outdoor dramas have become key to the economic vitality of many North Carolina communities, drawing thousands of visitors each summer and providing a training ground for young actors and theater technicians. These dramas are produced for the most part by nonprofit community collaborations. In the early 2000s there were 11 outdoor dramas in production in North Carolina, more than in any other state.

The outdoor drama movement had its genesis in North Carolina with the successful production of *The Lost Colony*, written by Pulitzer Prize–winning author and Harnett County native Paul Green. Intended as a single season celebration of the 350th anniversary of the first English settlers' arrival on the continent, Green's drama has remained in continuous production on Roanoke Island every summer since 1937, with the exception of the World War II years. Green himself coined the term "symphonic drama" to describe his new production because it involved "all the elements of the theatre working together—one for all and all for one, a true democracy." The play relates in dramatic form the experiences of John White's ill-fated 1587 colony, one of the earliest English attempts to establish a settlement in the New World. The White settlement has gone down in history as the "Lost Colony" because the colonists vanished after White's departure for supplies in August 1587.

Green was inspired by the folk drama work of Frederick Koch, who encouraged writers to use the local stories of a community for plays. Koch and the group he founded at the University of North Carolina in Chapel Hill, the Carolina Playmakers, participated in the production of *The Lost Colony* and other outdoor dramas. As interest in the genre grew, Green wrote other dramas, including *The Highland Call* for Fayetteville, *The Common Glory* for Williamsburg, Va., *Wilderness Road* for Berea, Ky., *Cross and Sword* for St. Augustine, Fla., and *Texas* for Canyon, Texas.

Another outdoor drama, *Unto These Hills*, was first per-

Scene from the outdoor drama *Unto These Hills*, staged each summer in Mountainside Theater in Cherokee. Cherokee Historical Association.

formed in the summer of 1950 in the village of Cherokee on the Cherokee Indian Reservation in the North Carolina mountains. The production was sponsored by the Cherokee Historical Association, which had been established in 1948 by the Western North Carolina Associated Communities. *Unto These Hills* traces Cherokee history from the arrival of Hernando De Soto's expedition in 1540 to later contact with whites in the American Revolution, the War of 1812, and the forced removal to Oklahoma Territory in 1838. All but a small number of Cherokees were removed; it was this remnant, along with some who returned from Oklahoma, that became the nucleus of the Eastern Band of Cherokee Indians.

Samuel Selden, director of the Carolina Playmakers at the University of North Carolina at Chapel Hill, was involved in the early planning and production of *Unto These Hills*. Kermit Hunter, a playwright and graduate student at UNC, agreed to write the drama. Harry Davis, also with the Carolina Playmakers, became the first director (1950–67) and was followed by William Hardy, who served in that capacity for more than three decades. The musical score was composed by Jack F. Kilpatrick.

A 2,800-seat amphitheater, called the Mountainside Theater, was completed in 1990. *Unto These Hills* has been credited with having an impact on the establishment of outdoor dramas throughout the country. By the time of its fiftieth anniversary season in 1999, approximately 5.5 million people had seen the production, making it one of the most successful outdoor dramas in America.

Horn in the West is an outdoor drama that was established in Boone in 1952 and has been performed every year in July and August since that time. The idea developed from the success of a centennial pageant called *Echoes of the Blue Ridge*, which was performed in 1949 and repeated in 1950. Realizing the possibilities that presumably would be derived from a permanent outdoor drama, local leaders established a nonprofit organization called the Southern Appalachian Historical Association (SAHA).

After visiting a performance of *Unto These Hills*, leaders of the SAHA commissioned Kermit Hunter to write a play about the frontier, the American Revolution, and Daniel Boone. An architect from Charlotte and design students from North Carolina State College designed the amphitheater and grounds. Perry Greene Construction Company built the theater between April and June of 1952, barely completing the work in time for the 27 June opening. That first season attracted more than 50,000 people.

Hunter rewrote the play at least four times, but the plot remained basically the same. Aristocratic Loyalist Geoffrey Stuart has to remove to the western mountains after his son Jack is involved in the Regulator Movement. The play focuses primarily on the elder Stuart's transition from Loyalist to Patriot as he sees the insidious Col. McKenzie arm the Cherokee Indians and turn them against the settlers. The culminating event of the play is the Battle of King's Mountain, in which Jack is killed. Daniel Boone was a minor character in the original play, but the role became more and more prominent over the years. One actor, Glenn Causey, played the Boone role for 40 years.

Randolph Umberger has been another influential voice in the outdoor drama movement, authoring the North Carolina plays *The Liberty Cart*, in Duplin County, and *Strike at the Wind!*, a story of the Lumbee Indians presented in Pembroke.

In 1963 UNC-Chapel Hill established the Institute of Outdoor Drama to encourage productions and provide advice. The institute currently serves over 100 outdoor dramas around the country (including historical dramas, Shakespeare festivals, and religious dramas), as well as communities considering their own productions (of which there are generally 30 to 40 at any given time).

References: Laurence G. Avery, ed., *A Paul Green Reader* (1998); William P. Connor Jr., *History of Cherokee Historical Association, 1946–1982* (1982); William J. Free and Charles B. Lower, *History into Drama* (1963); Vincent Kinney, *Paul Green* (1971); Walter Spearman, *The Carolina Playmakers: The First Fifty Years* (1970).

Cecelia Moore
Additional research provided by Ronnie W. Faulkner, Ron Holland, and Richard L. Zuber.

Outer Banks are a chain of barrier islands that skirt the coast of North Carolina from the Virginia border to Cape Lookout through Currituck, Dare, Hyde, and Carteret Counties. More than 175 miles long, they are separated as much as 30 miles from the mainland by a series of shallow sounds. Pamlico Sound, the largest sound on the East Coast of the United States (and some say the world's largest), is 80 miles long and 15 to 30 miles wide. It is separated from the Atlantic Ocean by a part of the Outer Banks and drains into the Atlantic Ocean through Hatteras and Ocracoke Inlets. Albemarle Sound, the second largest (some 50 miles long and 5 to 14 miles wide), was named after George Monck, duke of Albemarle, one of the Lords Proprietors of the Carolina colony. The state's first permanent settlements were made along its northern shore. Other North Carolina sounds include Core Sound, Croatan Sound, Currituck Sound, and Roanoke Sound.

The topography of the Outer Banks is constantly changing, as inlets open and close and beaches narrow and widen. Windswept and remote, the islands were sparsely populated until the paving of roads, the construction of bridges such as the Herbert Bonner Bridge in the 1960s, and the institution of large-scale ferry service between Ocracoke and the mainland and Ocracoke and Hatteras islands. Once largely uninhabited except for small villages, the Outer Banks are now a popular tourist destination and the permanent home of increasing numbers of residents.

The first inhabitants of the Outer Banks were Native Americans. Many place names, such as Hatteras, Ocracoke, Kinnakeet, Chicamacomico, Manteo, and Wanchese, bear testimony to these early residents. Native Americans on Hatteras Island befriended explorers Philip Amadas and Arthur Barlowe in their reconnaissance mission for Sir Walter Raleigh. Conflicts with Europeans, combined most likely with disease, led to the virtual disappearance of Native American tribes on the Outer Banks by the seventeenth century.

During the colonial period, European settlement on most of the Outer Banks was sparse. After the English failed to establish a permanent settlement at Roanoke Island in the 1580s, few Europeans showed interest in the Outer Banks for the next century and more. In the eighteenth century, probably the most strategic and most heavily populated area of the Outer Banks centered around the islands of Ocracoke and Portsmouth, where colonial shipping found entrance into the southern Pamlico Sound and on to coastal towns like Bath. The inlets and isolation made the Banks attractive to pirates and smugglers; famed pirate Blackbeard (Edward Teach) met his death in the sound waters off Ocracoke, one of his bases of operation. The importance of this part of the Outer Banks to shipping and travel can be seen later as well, in the construction during the early national period of the Ocracoke Lighthouse, operational in 1819.

During the nineteenth century, the Outer Banks remained remote, physically and culturally isolated from mainland North Carolina. Generally removed from the mainstream, Outer Bankers lived a subsistence lifestyle that combined fishing, the salvaging of shipwrecks, piloting of vessels through inlets, and waterfowl hunting. A distinctive English dialect, called the Ocracoke brogue—featuring the unusual pronunciation of the vowel "i" as "oy," leading to the nickname "Hoi Toiders" for those who speak it—developed and remains as a reminder of the remoteness of past Outer Banks communities. Among the affluent planters of the Albemarle, the custom evolved of vacationing in summer at locations such as Nags Head. Nevertheless, the islands remained largely untouched by outside influences.

During the Civil War, occupation of the various inlets along the Outer Banks made the remote islands strategically important to both the Confederacy and the Union. The latter succeeded in occupying the islands throughout most of the war.

Changes in technology, transportation, and economy began to affect the Outer Banks in the late nineteenth century. The construction of the Albemarle and Chesapeake Canal by 1859 connected the upper banks with the mouth of the Chesapeake Bay. After the Civil War, the canal became integral in the development of new economies on the Outer Banks. A shift from subsistence living to commercial fishing and oystering occurred, as the lives of people on the Outer Banks became intertwined with regional and national market needs and trends. The increasing presence of summer visitors at places such as Nags Head and the arrival of sport waterfowl hunters each fall along the length of the Outer Banks also marked the latter part of the nineteenth century.

In the early twentieth century, the Outer Banks began to feel the pull of mainstream life, and their windswept beaches and dunes earned them a place in history. From January 1901 to August 1902, Reginald A. Fessenden succeeded in sending wireless messages from a tower on Roanoke Island to Cape Hatteras and to Cape Henry, Va. He also received musical notes transmitted from Cape Hatteras. On 17 Dec. 1903, Wilbur and Orville Wright flew an experimental motor-driven airplane for 12 seconds at Kitty Hawk, changing transportation forever. Two world wars brought submarine warfare to the coast of the Outer Banks, especially in the waters off Hatteras Island.

The advent of the affordable automobile combined with the paving of roads, especially U.S. 12 on Bodie, Hatteras, and Ocracoke Islands, began to transform the Outer Banks in the 1920s and 1930s. Federal New Deal funds allowed for road paving and dune stabilization, and large tracts of land were designated in 1937 for the creation of the Cape Hatteras National Seashore. This was followed just before World War II by the creation of the Pea Island National Wildlife Refuge.

Although regions of the Outer Banks have remained among the least developed stretches of seashore on the Atlantic coast of the United States, increasing tourism and contact with the outside world has led to tremendous development in the area. Approximately 7 million visitors from around the world stay for short or extended periods in the Outer Banks, enjoying ocean activities such as swimming, hang gliding, fishing, windsurfing, and bird watching as well as cultural activities. The Outer Banks History Center in Manteo has thousands of manuscripts, pamphlets, photographs, maps, paintings, and other items related to the history of the area. Population growth in the Outer Banks has been approximately double the North Carolina average. By 2004 the year-round population of the banks had increased to more than 45,000 people, creating great demand for new housing, particularly in the northern areas.

References: John Alexander and James Lazell, *Ribbon of Sand: The Amazing Convergence of the Ocean and the Outer Banks* (2000); Rodney Barfield, *Seasoned by Salt: A Historical Album of the Outer Banks* (1995); Dirk Frankenberg, *The Nature of the Outer Banks: Environmental Processes, Field Sites, and Development Issues, Corolla to Ocracoke* (1995); Thomas J. Schoenbaum, *Islands, Capes, and Sounds: The North Carolina Coast* (repr., 1988); David Stick, *The Outer Banks of North Carolina, 1584–1958* (1958); Stick, *An Outer Banks Reader* (1998).

Kathy Carter
Additional research provided by Wiley J. Williams.

SEE ALSO Cape Hatteras National Seashore; Cape Lookout National Seashore; Hoi Toiders; Inlets.

Outlawry, involving declarations issued by the courts against fleeing felons, came to North Carolina as part of English common law. During the Regulator crisis in 1764, a statute replacing common-law outlawry was enacted. It permitted any person, not just an officer of the court, to "kill and destroy such offender" without the threat of prosecution. The law was revised in 1866 in response to the acts of violence committed in Robeson County by the infamous Lowry Band, led by Lumbee Indian Henry Berry Lowry.

Under the 1866 statute, the judges of North Carolina were required to outlaw any person charged with a felony if an affidavit showed that the accused person had fled or evaded arrest. Anyone could file the affidavit, and the judge could unilaterally determine whether the affidavit was valid, whether the felon was dangerous to others, or whether such an extreme measure was inappropriate and unnecessary. Under the proclamation, the public had license to kill an accused felon if the person tried to escape after being ordered to surrender. This law still appears in the General Statutes of North Carolina, although it was declared unconstitutional by a federal court in 1976 and has not been enforced since then.

Reference: Bobby G. Deaver, "Outlawry: Another 'Gothic Column' in North Carolina," *North Carolina Law Review* 41 (1963).

M. Keith Kapp

Outlyers were people with Loyalist, or Tory, sympathies on the eve of the American Revolution who hid in the countryside to avoid being impressed into the Patriot ranks. The Moravians noted that living along the Yadkin River were "many who sided with the King [and] were driven from house and home by persecution." They asserted that these individuals were "the first Outlyers, as they were later called." In passing through Salem some of them, when questioned, replied that they "were on their way to join the King's Standard and do their duty."

William S. Powell

Outsider Art. SEE Folk Art.

Outward Bound School. In 1965 Joshua L. Miner III, president of Outward Bound in the United States, came to North Carolina to encourage the founding of a new school based on his philosophy that young people needed authentic adventure and challenges in order to break out of the "cult of comfort and conformity" in which they were raised. In January 1966 a group of prominent citizens officially incorporated the North Carolina Outward Bound School and began the process of raising $300,000 to construct the necessary facilities. Early supporters included Governor Terry Sanford; Lieutenant Governor Robert Scott; Watts Hill Jr., chairman of the State Board of Higher Education; and Waldo Beach, head of the graduate school of religion at Duke University. L. Richardson Preyer, a former federal judge and candidate for governor in 1964, was elected chairman of the board. Preyer praised the Outward Bound idea—which has its roots in Great Britain in the 1940s—as an effort to "fulfill the need to preserve an undefeatable spirit and drive of youth by kindling the joy of exploration and adventure."

Marjorie Calloway and Jack Mansfield, director of special projects for the North Carolina Fund, selected the Linville Gorge area of the Pisgah National Forest as the site of the Outward Bound School. Designed by founder Kurt Hahn, the original plan called for a year-round school that would hire about 30 instructors and accommodate 1,000 students per year. The emphasis was on young people ages 16 to 23. The group would undergo a 26-day training program with a progressively more rigorous series of physical challenges. The training was based on the concept that "experience in encountering physical and intellectual danger leads to a self-comprehension that enables one to persevere when confronted with challenge." The climax to the training was a three-day "solo" experience in which the students were left to survive in the wilderness with minimum supplies and no outside assistance. The school drew students from all economic, social, and geographic backgrounds. Half were required to pay the full tuition of $350, and the rest attended on scholarships provided by various civic and business organizations.

By 1980 the Outward Bound School had expanded its curriculum and service components. The school emphasized environmental awareness from the beginning and began partnering with the U.S. Forest Service to collect litter (the "leave no trace" camping technique) and maintain the extensive trail system in Pisgah National Forest. Students and staff work at the Wildlife Care Center for injured animals and volunteer at the Signature Home in Morganton for developmentally disabled adults. Each course of instruction incorporates a day of service, and staff and students complete more than 4,300 days of service each year.

By the early 2000s the private, nonprofit, nonsectarian North Carolina Outward Bound School had adventure courses in western North Carolina, the North Carolina Outer Banks, the Florida Everglades, the Bahamas, Costa Rica, and northern Patagonia (Argentina). The school offers a variety of courses, from backpacking, rock climbing, and mountain biking to white-water canoeing. The emphasis remains on challenge and personal growth. Courses are geared toward youth ages 14 to 21, but there are courses for women only, educators, parents and teens, as well as an instructor training course and a Going Beyond course designed for adults age 50 and older. The school also offers professional development programs for businesses with an emphasis on leadership, team building, and communication as well as semester courses offered for college and high school credit. Outward Bound provides nearly $200,000 annually in scholarships.

References: Martin Flavin, *Kurt Hahn: Schools and Legacy* (1996); Dan Meyer, *To Know by Experience: Outward Bound, N.C.* (1979); Joanna Richardson, "Adventures in Learning," *Education Week* 14 (9 Nov. 1994).

Julian M. Pleasants

Overmountain Men. SEE King's Mountain, Battle of.

Overmountain Victory National Historic Trail runs

from Abingdon, Va., to the Kings Mountain National Military Park in South Carolina, crossing parts of Tennessee and North Carolina. A separate branch stretches from Elkin to Morganton in North Carolina, where it joins the main trail. The trail commemorates the route used by Patriot forces that marched across the mountains and defeated an army of Loyalists under Maj. Patrick Ferguson at the Battle of King's Mountain on 7 Oct. 1780. There are three different routes in the Overmountain Victory National Historic Trail: a motor route along public highways; the original, often inaccessible route of the Patriot army; and the route utilized in modern times by the Overmountain Victory Trail Association in their annual reenactment of the historic march.

The idea for the reestablishment of the trail began in 1975, when a group of reenactors and grassroots activists, with the help of the Appalachian Consortium, organized the first march over the old route. The next year Harry Smith of Abingdon led a group along the entire route. In 1977 the effort gained momentum, thanks to the work of Lenoir residents Bill Stronach, director of the Lenoir Parks and Recreation Department, and Congressman James T. Broyhill of North Carolina. The latter pushed legislation through Congress for a feasibility study of the route's designation as part of the National Trails System. In September 1980 the route was designated a National Historic Trail.

References: Robert Collins, "The Overmountain Men March Again," *The State* (August 1979); National Park Service, *Overmountain Victory National Historic Trail* (n.d.).

John Hairr

Overseas Replacement Depot. Between March 1943 and

September 1946 Greensboro was home to the country's largest military base within the limits of any American city; more than 330,000 soldiers passed through its gates. Built on 652 acres on the city's east side, the eventual Overseas Replacement Depot began as the Army Air Force's (AAF) Basic Training Center No. 10. It was conceived by the AAF's Technical Training Command, at that time operating out of the Pilot Life complex in Sedgefield; the command's plans called for a facility large enough to train and mobilize the tens of thousands of crewmen needed for the air war in Europe and Asia. Strategically located, surrounded by the necessary transportation and support facilities, and willing to develop the large tracts necessary for the project, Greensboro was awarded the base in 1942.

Basic Training Center No. 10 opened on 1 Mar. 1943. Trainees endured from four to eight weeks of intensive training in weapons, drill, physical fitness, and chemical warfare. Airmen then left for advanced training at other bases prior to assignment in combat theaters around the world. Among the 87,500 trainees who passed through the facility were members of the Women's Air Corps, whose six-week stints trained them in a variety of administrative and support fields. The center also trained African American airmen, a fact that displeased some of Greensboro's citizens. Black servicemen were segregated, and despite their repeated requests for equal treatment as military personnel, their training was restricted to support services and labor battalions.

The focus of the center shifted in 1944, when it became the AAF's principal Overseas Replacement Depot (ORD) on the East Coast; it served in this capacity until the end of the war. By 1 May, with trained airmen available in sufficient numbers, ORD processed personnel for rotation to overseas combat operations. In August 1945 the ORD was also designated AAF Redistribution Station No. 5 and assumed responsibility for reassigning returning soldiers to other posts in the United States.

In September 1945, the ORD became a major discharge center and processed thousands of returning veterans. When it closed in September 1946, the Bessemer Improvement Company bought 433 acres of the ORD land, along with nearly half of the buildings, and opened the area to residential development.

Reference: J. Stephen Catlett, *Army Town: Greensboro, 1943–1946* (1994).

Clyde Ellis

Overseers is a term referring to employees of plantation owners before 1865 who served as general managers of routine farming operations. They sometimes were former indentured servants themselves, liberated and in search of a better life. Others had been unsuccessful small farmers or the sons of small farmers who sought a more reliable source of income. Often lacking formal education, they generally were knowledgeable in the fields of agriculture, planting, harvesting, and husbandry and in the care and management of servants, slaves, and other laborers. Overseers routinely were entrusted with the care of property valued at thousands of dollars.

Although generally treated with courtesy, and despite the critical role he played in the life of the plantation, the overseer and his family were rarely accepted into the society of the planter class. In addition, he was typically despised by the black population for his role as disciplinarian on the plantation. The overseer could absent himself from the plantation only with the permission of the planter and had to be present whenever the owner was away. Although slaves usually worked no more than nine hours a day, an overseer's workday was frequently longer. He arose early to prepare for the day's tasks and remained late to attend to the needs of the workers. He had to see to the security of all property, often making rounds at night to do this. Attempting to maintain order and peaceful relations among the workers and enforcing the directives of the owner were also among the overseer's duties.

Reference: John Spencer Bassett, ed., *The Southern Plantation Overseer as Revealed in His Letters* (1925).

Charles C. Davis

Oxford College (originally Oxford Female College) was a female academy established in Oxford, the Granville County seat, in 1850. The school's first president was Samuel Wait, a Baptist minister and educator. He served as president until 1857, when he was succeeded by John H. Mills. The school continued to operate during the Civil War, unlike many similar academies throughout the South. When Mills left in 1868, the school passed through a series of management changes until 1880, when F. P. Hobgood became president.

Hobgood had for the previous ten years operated the Raleigh Female Seminary, and soon Oxford College was transformed by his administrative skill and personal charisma. The school's course of study was divided into "preparatory" and "collegiate" departments; its curriculum included classes in English language, literature, mathematics, history, science, Latin, French, and German. Students were also required to en-gage in daily physical activities, many of which were based on "the Swedish system of physical culture" that promoted their "gracefulness of bearing and movement." All students wore the same uniform "for the sake of economy and appearance and to prevent rivalry." Students were also required to attend "chapel service every morning and [to take] part in suitable devotional exercises that consist of singing hymns, reading of Scripture in concert, and prayer." On Sundays, students could attend any church they desired.

The success and popularity of Oxford College during the Hobgood administration, as well as its importance to the region, was evidenced in January 1904 following a fire that destroyed the school's buildings. Without solicitation, a group of Oxford citizens established a corporation that succeeded in raising money to rebuild the college "on a larger and more enduring basis."

Tuition and board expenses for Oxford students early in the twentieth century were $142.50 per year. Additional courses of instruction, such as piano, typewriting, or stenography, required additional fees. Financial assistance was available, as was a discount to daughters of Baptist ministers. Oxford College was closed in 1925.

Reference: Ross Scott, "The Hushed Halls of Oxford," *Durham Morning Herald*, 26 Sept. 1971.

Jay Mazzocchi

Oyster War. In 1891 North Carolina declared "war" on the oyster fishermen who had drifted down from the north. By the 1880s overfishing had dangerously depleted the seemingly inexhaustible oyster beds of Maryland and Virginia. Armed oyster pirates were destroying what remained with dredges that gathered seed oysters and mature oysters indiscriminately. In 1888 the governor of Maryland armed the state's patrol vessels with cannon and ordered them to return fire, ram dredges, and oust the pirates from Chesapeake Bay at all costs. Consequently, the pirates moved their dredging operations to North Carolina. Also in 1888, seven armed pirate vessels from Virginia were reported plying the waters of Hyde County, gathering and transporting 7,000 bushels of oysters weekly through the Albemarle and Chesapeake Canal and the Dismal Swamp Canal to Virginia. During the 1890 season Carteret, Hyde, and Pamlico Counties dispatched patrol boats to drive off the pirates, but individual confrontations locally proved ineffectual.

In the first week of 1891, 150 Maryland dredge boats were reported in Pamlico Sound while Virginia pirates, said to be armed with Winchester rifles and 36-pounders, were said to have taken possession of all of the beds off of Dare and Hyde Counties. Governor Daniel G. Fowle immediately pushed through the General Assembly legislation strong enough to put the dredgers out of business and to prevent the shipping of North Carolina oysters to out-of-state markets. Fowle then hired a vessel, called out Company E, 1st Regiment, of the National Guard to man it, and armed the men as an oyster patrol. On 21 January he sent a copy of the newly enacted oyster law to Col. J. E. Wood with orders to cruise the oyster beds in Pamlico Sound, serving notice on all boats and ships and arresting any that persisted in dredging or other illegal operations. Within a week, the foreign vessels had departed and all was quiet in North Carolina waters. To keep it so, Fowle hired another boat, the *Nellie B. Dey*, outfitted it with a howitzer, and deputized Capt. Adam Warren as sheriff to patrol Pamlico Sound and arrest any dredgers. From 31 Jan. to 20 Apr. 1891 the *Dey* seized only one vessel, the schooner *Sailor's Return*. Its dredges were impounded and its captain and crew charged and tried in the Pamlico County Superior Court, thus ending the oyster war.

George Stevenson

P

Pacifism. SEE Conscientious Objection.

Painting. SEE Visual Arts.

Palatine Court. "Palatine" was the title applied to the senior ("eldest") member of the Lords Proprietors (and his successors), to whom the colony of Carolina was granted by the English Crown in 1663. The Palatine Court, headed by the palatine, was designed to be the executive body of colonial North Carolina under Proprietary rule. The court existed in two parts: one in England and the other in the New World. In England, the palatine and the seven other Proprietors formed an administration that controlled the activities of North Carolina and South Carolina from afar. The provincial Palatine Court, like its namesake in England, was essentially a governing board that was intended to carry out the wishes of the Proprietors on the local level. It was to create courts; appoint justices, sheriffs, and other officials; call and dissolve Parliament; and, if necessary, veto acts and judgments of that body. The Palatine Court was also empowered to establish new towns, recognize titles of nobility, review cases (particularly questions of admiralty law), and grant pardons.

The Palatine Court could grant land, and it could call out and control the militia, but its powers were limited by the Fundamental Constitutions and decrees of the Proprietors in England. Although the court met in North Carolina from the 1670s through the 1720s, little is known of its activities. In all likelihood, considering the Carolinians' disdain for the Fundamental Constitutions, this court may have functioned largely as an appeals court, with much of its power falling to the governor and his council. It ceased to exist in 1729, when the Crown purchased the Proprietors' shares in Carolina.

References: Robert J. Cain, ed., *Records of the Executive Council, 1664–1674* (1984); Mattie Erma Edwards Parker, ed., *North Carolina Charters and Constitutions, 1578–1698* (1963).

Louis P. Towles

Palmer-Marsh House in Bath is one of North Carolina's most notable eighteenth-century homes. Famous for its massive chimney, the two-story home was built for Michael Coutanche, a merchant and colonial official, around 1751. Coutanche had moved to Bath from Boston in 1739, setting himself up in the naval stores trade. Coutanche may have used the main room downstairs as a store or office for his business. Michael Coutanche died in 1761, and his daughter and son-in-law sold the house and property to brothers Lillington and James Lockhart in 1763.

In 1764 Robert Palmer purchased the house from the Lockhart brothers. Palmer had come to North Carolina from Scotland in 1753 as surveyor general of the state and, upon his arrival, also became collector for the port of Bath. The property remained in the Palmer family for the next 38 years, but the Palmer children eventually sold their shares. By 1802 the house and lot belonged to Jonathan Marsh, who had moved to North Carolina from Rhode Island with his brother Daniel. Both were merchants, with ships plying the waters between Beaufort County, the West Indies, and ports along the eastern seaboard. The property remained in the Marsh family until 1915. In 1918 Henry Ormond bought the Palmer-Marsh House and turned it into a hotel.

Eventually, the heirs of Henry Ormond sold the property to the Beaufort County Historical Society. The house was restored to its colonial appearance in 1959 and opened to the public for tours in 1962. Exposed on the interior, the house frame includes a large summer beam over 50 feet in length supporting the second story. The stairway in the central hall is original, Georgian-style woodwork. Near the Palmer-Marsh House is a small cemetery, which contains graves of the Coutanche and Marsh families. In 1964 ownership of the Palmer-Marsh House and lot was transferred to the state of North Carolina, under the jurisdiction of the Department of Archives and History. The house was designated a National Historic Landmark in 1970.

On 10 Dec. 1989 a fire broke out in the attic of the house, destroying the roof and attic and closing the home to tours for more than three years. Renovations from 1989 to 1993 allowed researchers to accurately determine the age of the house. Historians previously estimated the house's construction date as around 1744, but dendrochronology reports stated the house was built from timber cut during the winter of 1751–52.

References: Catherine Bishir and Michael T. Southern, *A Guide to the Historic Architecture of Eastern North Carolina* (1996); Jerry L. Cross, *Historical Research Report for the Palmer-Marsh House, Bath, North Carolina* (1976); Kenneth Marsh and Blanche Marsh, *Colonial Bath: North Carolina's Oldest Town* (1966).

Victor T. Jones Jr.

Palmer Memorial Institute, located between Greensboro and Burlington, was founded in 1902 by educator Charlotte Hawkins Brown as the Alice Freeman Palmer Memorial Institute. Brown served as the school's president for 50 years. The school for African American youth was named in honor of educator Alice Freeman Palmer, Brown's friend and benefactor. It originally began operating in an old, run-down blacksmith shed, providing education for local rural black youth. From the beginning, Palmer emphasized both an academic and an industrial education. The school also ran a farm that provided agricultural training. The farm made it possible for students unable to pay tuition to work their way through school.

Palmer Memorial Institute was fully accredited by the Southern Association of Colleges and Secondary Schools (1922) at a time when few African American high schools were. By that time Brown had built Palmer into the only finishing school of its kind in America. It had evolved into an institution with a national reputation. At its height, the campus consisted of more than 300 acres of land and 14 buildings.

Starting in the late 1920s and early 1930s, the school abandoned an attempt to develop a junior college, changed from its original emphasis on industrial education, discontinued its elementary department, and limited its focus to college preparatory work. The changes proved successful, and by the end of the 1950s Palmer had an enrollment of more than 200.

For decades, over 90 percent of Palmer's graduating students attended college, and 64 percent pursued postgraduate degrees. Several years after Brown's death in 1961, the school began to decline. This was partly a result of integration, which made it possible for African Americans to be admitted to white public schools, and partly because of increasing costs associated with private education. Because of this and other factors, Palmer Institute experienced tremendous financial difficulties and was finally forced to close after a disastrous fire destroyed the school's administration and classroom building in 1971. The former campus is part of the Charlotte Hawkins Brown Museum, a State Historic Site.

References: Lucinda Saunders, "An Idea That Grew into a Million," *Abbott's Monthly* (November 1930); Sandra N. Smith and Earle H. West, "Charlotte Hawkins Brown," *Journal of Negro Education* 51 (Summer 1982); Charles W. Wadelington and Richard F. Knapp, *Charlotte Hawkins Brown and Palmer Memorial Institute: What One Young African American Woman Could Do* (1999).

Charles W. Wadelington

SEE ALSO Charlotte Hawkins Brown Museum.

Pamlico County, located in the Coastal Plain region of North Carolina, was formed in 1872 from Craven and Beaufort Counties and named for the Pamlico Sound, which, in turn, was named for the Pamlico Indians. It partially borders the sound and the Neuse River. Early inhabitants of the area included Algonquian Indians, followed by English, Welsh, Swiss, German, and French settlers. Bayboro, the county seat, was incorporated in 1881 and named for the Bay River (itself named for the bay tree, which abounds in the area). Other Pamlico County communities include Arapahoe, Minnesott Beach, Stonewall, Vandemere, Mesic, Hobucken, Olympia, Oriental,

and Pamlico. Notable physical features of the county, other than its coastline, include Cedar Island, Deep Run, Dawson Creek, and Bay City Pocosin.

Pamlico County's economy is based on tourism and recreation, especially fishing, owing to its coastal location. Oriental, which is known as the "Sailing Capital of North Carolina," holds many sailing regattas, including the Oriental Regatta. The county also produces agricultural commodities such as cotton, tobacco, corn, potatoes, and soybeans.

Landmarks and historic sites in Pamlico County include the Grist Mill (ca. 1915) and Reel Cotton Gin (ca. 1905). The county is home to such cultural attractions as the Silver Hill Heritage Museum, Pamlico County Drama Clubs, and the Candycane Theatre, and notable among its annual festivals and events is the Pamlico County Croaker Festival. Camp Sea Gull and Camp Seafarer, summer camps run by the YMCA of the Triangle Area, Inc., have been hosted by Pamlico County since the mid-twentieth century. The county's estimated population was 13,000 in 2004.

Jay Mazzocchi

Pamlico Indians lived south of the Pamlico River in present-day Beaufort and Pamlico Counties and were known as the Pomouik by members of the 1585–86 Raleigh expeditions. A smallpox epidemic in 1696 nearly destroyed the tribe. By 1709 John Lawson found the survivors living in a single village with 15 "fighting men." Lawson recorded a small vocabulary from their language, which confirms their Algonquian affiliation.

During the Tuscarora War (1711–13), the Pamlico were one of the smaller tribes that joined the Tuscarora faction. After the Barnwell expedition against Tuscarora strongholds in 1712, the smaller tribes (Coree, Bay River, and Pamlico) continued to attack settlers along the Neuse and Pamlico Rivers. In the treaty that ended the war, the Tuscarora agreed to destroy their former allies, including the Pamlicos, whom the colonists still considered dangerous. Any Pamlico Indians who survived were probably enslaved or incorporated into the Tuscarora tribe.

References: Christian F. Feest, "North Carolina Algonquians," in Bruce Trigger, ed., *Handbook of North American Indians*, vol. 15 (1978); Hugh T. Lefler, ed., *A New Voyage to Carolina by John Lawson* (1967).

Ruth Y. Wetmore

Panics, Economic. Financial panics and other economic disruptions have had varied effects on the North Carolina economy. The panic of 1786 was an economic slump following the end of the American Revolution. Its most acute cause lay in the new national government's lack of power. The fledgling nation did not have a strong central government with a financial scheme to tax the populace, run the country, or pay the nation's debts. Without the English market or the British pound as backing, the former colonies had a very unstable currency. North Carolina's war debt loomed large, its paper money was worthless, and the market for the state's principal products of naval stores, pitch, tar, and rosin, as well as timber, was gone. In spite of this, the recession did not affect North Carolina as severely as it did other states.

In contrast, the panic of 1819 followed a period that abounded in overspeculation in land, commodities, and stocks. High cotton prices encouraged southerners to buy land at exorbitant prices; westerners were buying land for more cattle; and northerners were building new factories at a brisk rate—all with worthless collateral or no collateral at all. In North Carolina, the three state banks had made excessive loans and could not meet the request for payments to the Bank of the United States in gold, silver, or national bank notes. Low crop prices and hard times hit North Carolina as land values plummeted. Not only were many North Carolinians poverty stricken, they were further distressed by the depletion of the fertility of their soil. Cotton production, the main activity of the state, began moving to the Southwest. North Carolinians blamed deflation and falling land values on the banks. The state came out of the panic with a growing bitterness and a negative attitude toward bankers, a conflict between the creditor and the debtor class that lasted long after the panic.

The panic of 1837 triggered a severe national depression blamed in part on the economic policies of President Andrew Jackson's administration. After months of growing uneasiness in the financial world, the banks in New York City, followed by most others in the country, halted specie payments on 10 May 1837. Economic chaos spread, causing widespread bankruptcies and unemployment. The *Raleigh Register* reported on 2 May 1837 that "great embarrassment" was already being felt in New Bern, Fayetteville, and Wilmington "on account of the Northern failures." The Bank of North Carolina suspended specie payments on 18 May. Falling prices and high emigration lowered the value of farm property in North Carolina and other southeastern states. Farmers forced to sell their property for debts recovered only a fraction of their pre-1837 value; some North Carolinians reportedly got as little as 2 percent of the former value of their farms. The depression sparked by the panic of 1837 lasted well into the 1840s.

The panic of 1857 halted a national economic boom that had lasted since the Mexican War (1846–48), but North Carolina and other southern states were not seriously affected. Similarly, the panic of 1873, triggered by the collapse of several New York financial firms, most severely affected the northern states, which were more dependent on industry and financial institutions than the agrarian South. The economies of North Carolina and its southern neighbors were already in such serious trouble after the ravages of the Civil War, mounting interest on war debts, and high taxes and spending by Reconstruction governments that the panic seemed to have little direct effect on most people.

North Carolina was hard hit by the panic of 1893 and the subsequent economic depression, from which the United States did not fully recover until 1897. Many factors contributed to the severity of the panic, including the trade contraction caused by the high rates of the McKinley Tariff and the fear of investment in the nation resulting from the collapse of Baring Brothers, an English banking firm. As a result, several political and economic changes, at both the national and state level, were instituted. In North Carolina, the state Democratic Party joined the national movement for free coinage of silver. The economic situation did not improve significantly until 1897, when poor European crops stimulated American exports and gold importation.

The panic of 1907 was one of the most severe economic downturns in the history of the U.S. business cycle, ranking second only to the Great Depression in how sharply output fell during any twentieth-century recession. Although severe, the downturn was short lived, with the panic ending and the economy getting back on track quickly in 1908. The panic of 1907 was the final episode of financial instability that convinced legislators of the need for a central government monetary authority.

The panic of 1929, which began in October, is usually regarded as the beginning of the Great Depression, although the business cycle began its downturn in August of that year. In the latter part of the 1920s, the Federal Reserve became concerned that the stock market was overvaluing assets and that these asset values were not reflective of true market fundamentals. The combination of tight money and a weakened economy took its toll on the stock market on 23 Oct. 1929. The result was, in percentage terms, the second-largest one-day fall in the market as panic selling hit Wall Street. The panic had left the banking system vulnerable to a continued weak economy as depositors liquidated assets, and the economic uncertainty generated by the crash of the stock market further weakened consumer and business spending and accelerated the economic slide. North Carolinians, along with millions of other Americans, were hit hard by the economic and social woes brought on by the panic of 1929 and the subsequent Great Depression.

The introduction of bank deposit insurance in 1933, along with changes in the Federal Reserve system and a better understanding of the root causes of financial panics, helped to eliminate these events from the U.S. economic system.

References: John L. Bell Jr., *Hard Times: Beginnings of the Great Depression in North Carolina, 1929–1933* (1982); James L. Huston, *The Panic of 1857 and the Coming of the Civil War* (1987); Samuel Rezneck, "The Depression of 1819–1822," *American Historical*

Review 39 (October 1933); Robert Sobel, *Panic on Wall Street: A History of America's Financial Disasters* (1968).

Randall E. Parker
Additional research provided by Joanne G. Carpenter, Ronnie W. Faulkner, and David A. Norris.

SEE ALSO Bank Holiday of 1933; Great Depression.

Paper Mills. The earliest North Carolina paper mill, erected in 1777 in Orange County by John Hulgan, was equipped with a water-powered stamper to pound rags to fiber. From 1777 to 1896, there were ten water-powered paper mills (many of them under a succession of owners) at work at various times in six North Carolina counties, all of which made paper from rags and cotton waste. Besides the original mill in Orange County, there was the Buffalo Paper Mill, in operation in Cleveland County from 1851 to 1883. Cumberland County had two mills: David Anderson's mill on Cross Creek (1808–20s) and David Murphy's mill on Rockfish Creek (1850–65). Forsyth County's only paper mill was built by Gottlieb Shober in 1790, when the area was still part of Stokes County, and lasted until 1873. Lincoln County's two paper mills were the Long Shoals Paper Mill (1832–83) and the Lincolnton Paper Mill (1856–91). Wake County had three paper mills: Raleigh Paper Mill (1808–65), Neuse Manufacturing Company (1843–65), and a mill at the falls of Neuse River (1854–96). The primary products of these mills were printing paper and wrapping paper, but some also manufactured writing, blotting, and manila hemp paper.

Just prior to the Civil War, paper manufactured in North Carolina was said to have brought approximately $145,000 annually from northern markets into the state's economy. Some of the state's paper mills did not survive the war, and of the five that did, none outlasted the nineteenth century. Had any mills survived into the twentieth century, only an enormous infusion of fresh capital and a complete reequipping of their plants would have permitted them to compete in an industry undergoing dramatic technological changes. In 1867 the Pagenstecher brothers of Interlaken, Mass., imported from Germany two Voelter grinders specifically designed to grind wood into pulp, set up the first ground wood mill in the United States, and began selling ground wood pulp to paper manufacturers.

Some North Carolinians discerned that the production of wood pulp for papermaking was a development of great economic importance. In 1901 the General Assembly made a deliberate effort to attract the wood pulp industry to the state by passing an act to encourage the building of pulp mills and paper mills. The act granted to firms spending $100,000 in establishing a pulp mill in Haywood and Swain Counties an exemption from criminal prosecution for polluting any watercourse on which they should build. The natural resources of plentiful rivers and great virgin stands of suitable hardwoods in the area, as well as the provisions of the act of 1901, proved irresistible. In 1906 the Champion Paper and Fibre Company began erecting a plant at Canton to supply pulp made by the soda and sulfite processes to the company's parent paper mill in Hamilton, Ohio. At the same time, the Halifax Paper Company began the production of kraft paper in Roanoke Rapids.

In 1939, the Ecusta Paper Corporation at Pisgah Forest in Transylvania County perfected a method of making fine Oxford India paper direct from the cellulose of the flax plant without having first to spin the retted and braked fiber into linen. The Ecusta mill remains a major supplier of tobacco papers for the United States and world markets, with a daily production capacity of 300 tons of paper. The company's line of specialty papers include those used to produce bibles, hymnals, dictionaries, reference books, and catalogs. In 2002, after its purchase by PURICO Corp., Ecusta employed about 1,000 people at the Pisgah Forest plant.

By the middle of the twentieth century, North Carolina paper production totaled $26 million annually. Twenty years later, the value was $431 million. By the early twenty-first century, there were eight paper mills operating in North Carolina. The annual value of paper and related products manufactured in the state was in excess of $2 billion; nearly 21,000 people were employed in their manufacture, with a payroll of $372 million a year.

References: Arthur V. Goyette Jr., "Factors Influencing the Location of Paper Mills in the South: The Example of North Carolina Mills" (M.A. thesis, UNC-Chapel Hill, 1967); Dard Hunter, *Papermaking: The History and Technique of an Ancient Craft* (1978); Lyman H. Weeks, *History of Paper Manufacturing in the United States, 1690–1916* (1916; repr., 1969).

George Stevenson
Additional research provided by Lynn Roundtree and Wiley J. Williams.

SEE ALSO Champion Paper and Fibre Company.

Pardo Expeditions were significant for the information their records provide on the locations of mid-sixteenth-century Native American towns and villages in South Carolina, North Carolina, and Tennessee. Juan Pardo served in the Spanish Indies fleet under Capt. General Pedro Menendez de Aviles, who in April 1566 founded the town of Santa Elena at modern Parris Island, S.C. At Santa Elena, which was to be the capital town of the Spanish territories in North America, Menendez ordered Pardo to explore the interior, subdue the Indians, and find a route to Zacatecas, Mexico, over which the Spanish could transport their silver without threat from French and English ships in the Gulf of Mexico and along the Atlantic Coast of Florida. This ill-conceived order resulted from the Spaniards' poor understanding of the geography of the lands north of the Gulf of Mexico; they vastly underestimated the overland distance from the Atlantic Coast to northern Mexico.

Pardo and 125 soldiers left Santa Elena on 1 Dec. 1566, headed north, and several days later arrived at the Indian town of Guiomae on the Congaree River. Continuing north along the Wateree, they arrived at Cofitachequi (near present-day Camden, S.C.), apparently the same town visited in 1540 by the Spaniard Hernando De Soto. From Cofitachequi they followed the Wateree/Catawba River north, reaching the Indian towns of Tagaya, Tagaya the Lesser, Yssa, and finally, Joara, believed to be located in present-day Burke County, N.C., near the foot of the Blue Ridge Mountains.

Pardo and his men were unable to enter the mountains because of heavy snow. They stayed at Joara for two weeks while the soldiers built a small fort, Fort San Juan de Xualla, which Pardo left garrisoned with 30 men under Sgt. Hernando Moyano de Morales. The fort, believed to be situated on the modern Cherokee Indian Qualla Boundary in Swain County, consisted of a blockhouse and presumably a stockade. Pardo and his remaining troops traveled east along the Catawba River to Quinahaqui, near present-day Catawba. From Quinahaqui, they appear to have moved east, leaving the Catawba River, and two days later arrived at Guatari, possibly near present-day Salisbury.

At Quinahaqui, Pardo had received word that Santa Elena was threatened with a French attack. He left for Santa Elena immediately (leaving one chaplain and four soldiers garrisoned at Quinahaqui), traveling south to Otariyatiqui (believed to be near Charlotte) and Aracuchi, then meeting his original trail north at Tagaya the Lesser. He arrived in Santa Elena with about 90 men on 7 Mar. 1567.

Pleased with Pardo's report of excellent lands, Menendez ordered Pardo to undertake a second expedition to locate the best road to Zacatecas and to take possession of all the lands for the king of Spain. Pardo left Santa Elena to return to the interior on 1 Sept. 1567. The record of the towns visited and chiefs met is much more detailed than for the first expedition. The route seems to have differed slightly from the earlier expedition, but Pardo and his men once again traveled into the Catawba Valley and met Indians at the towns of Otari, Quinahaqui, and Guaquiri (now near Hickory). On 24 September they arrived at Joara, where Pardo received word that Moyano was besieged by Indians at Chiaha. Pardo then traveled into the mountains to the town of Cauchi and then on to Chiaha, which he reached on 7 October.

Finding Moyano safe, Pardo returned to Fort San Juan, arriving on 6 Nov. 1567. After resting with his men for two weeks, he left 31 of them garrisoned at San Juan and began his return to Santa Elena, building two more forts—Santiago and Santo Tomás—along the way. They finally arrived at Santa Elena on 2 Mar. 1568. Pardo never returned to the interior, nor were other expeditions sent out from Santa Elena. It is believed that the forts were soon abandoned.

References: Robin A. Beck Jr., "From Joara to Chiaha: Spanish Exploration of the Appalachian Summit Area, 1540–1568," *Southeastern Archaeology* 16, no. 2 (1997); Charles Hudson, *The Juan Pardo Expeditions* (1990); David G. Moore, "Late Prehistoric and Early Historic Period Aboriginal Settlement in the Catawba Valley, North Carolina" (Ph.D. diss., UNC-Chapel Hill, 1999).

David G. Moore

Parent-Teacher Associations in North Carolina were an outgrowth of the National Congress of Parents and Teachers, organized in Washington, D.C., on 17 Feb. 1897 as the National Congress of Mothers. Later broadened to include fathers, teachers, and others, this organization promoted the educational, social, and economic well-being of children. In 1902 citizens meeting in Greensboro formed the Woman's Association for the Betterment of Public Schoolhouses and Grounds. Later, some local units of the Parent-Teacher Association (PTA) in the state grew out of local branches of this association.

Some communities in North Carolina formed parent-teacher groups prior to the creation of a statewide organization. At the call of Edith Will Yates of Charlotte, the first president of the Charlotte Federation of Parent-Teacher Associations, representatives of local groups met in Charlotte in November 1919 to form a North Carolina branch of the National Congress of Mothers and Parent-Teacher Associations. In 1924 the name was changed to the North Carolina Congress of Parents and Teachers.

Dedicated to giving children opportunities for physical, mental, moral, and spiritual growth, the North Carolina Congress of Parents and Teachers organized local groups into districts, held annual meetings, published the *Parent-Teachers Association Bulletin* beginning in 1922, sponsored regional workshops, and, in 1923, hired its first field secretary, Catherine Albertson of Elizabeth City. The state organization also tried to influence legislation that would benefit public education and child welfare. A Summer Round-up, begun in 1926, grew out of a desire to ensure that children were healthy at the beginning of each school year. The first of many summer institutes was held in 1928 to teach the fundamentals of PTA work. The University of North Carolina Extension Division cooperated with the congress by publishing several editions of a *Parent-Teacher Handbook for North Carolina*. By 1930 more than 22,000 men and women from 361 units belonged to the organization.

Meanwhile, African Americans had become involved in PTA work. The General Assembly in 1921 authorized the Negro Division of the Department of Public Instruction. During the 1923–24 school year, following her appointment as supervisor of elementary education within this division, Annie Wealthy Holland began organizing local parent-teacher associations. On 2 Apr. 1927, a year after a national parent-teacher organization for African Americans had been founded, local representatives called to Shaw University by Holland formed the North Carolina Congress of Colored Parents and Teachers, with Holland as president. Organized in much the same way as its counterpart for whites, the North Carolina Congress of Colored Parents and Teachers worked to improve school attendance, promote the health of children, and lengthen the school year. Local units raised money to purchase land for schools, to beautify school grounds, and to acquire musical instruments and other equipment. By the early 1930s, more than 20,000 members participated in approximately 1,000 local units organized within four districts. Later that decade, the organization began publishing its newsletter

Responding to changing economic, educational, and social conditions, both organizations continued to work within their respective national organizations to improve public schools and the lives of schoolchildren. During the 1950s and 1960s the North Carolina Congress of Parents and Teachers employed radio and television advertising to further its goals. Its growing membership, which in 1960 stood at around 373,000, led to the completion that year of a headquarters building in Raleigh. Among other activities, the North Carolina Congress of Colored Parents and Teachers held annual summer camps for children and workshops for adults in Franklinton.

The two organizations merged in 1969 to become the North Carolina Congress of Parents and Teachers, known also as the North Carolina PTA. Subsequently the organization addressed such issues as early childhood education, day care, vocational education, sex education, drug and alcohol abuse, AIDS, school violence, and online pornography. The group does not seek to direct the administrative activities of the schools. In a growing number of middle and high schools, the local groups are called Parent-Teacher-Student Associations (PTSAS), as students are given a role that has included helping develop new methods of instruction and pushing for more minority participation in school activities.

References: Hugh Victor Brown, *A History of the Education of Negroes in North Carolina* (1961); N. C. Newbold, *Five North Carolina Negro Educators* (1939); North Carolina Congress of Parents and Teachers, *Yearbook and Convention Proceedings* (selected years); Thad Stem Jr., *PTA Impact: 50 Years in North Carolina, 1919–1969* (1969).

Maurice C. York
Additional research provided by Wiley J. Williams.

Parole in North Carolina began shortly after the Civil War, when the Constitution of 1868 allowed the governor to release prisoners before they had served their full sentences. The first major step toward institutionalizing early release was taken in 1930, when Governor O. Max Gardner, responding to concerns about prison crowding, appointed a commission to study the prison system. In its report, the commission strongly recommended "the adoption of a system of parole and probation with adequate machinery for its proper administration," maintaining that such a system would be vital for "prison management to more economically handle the prisoners."

In 1975 the North Carolina Commission on Sentencing, Criminal Punishment, and Rehabilitation, charged with finding a solution to increasingly crowded prisons that did not require new construction, reconfirmed the recommendations of the 1930 report. Four years later the General Assembly instituted "re-entry parole," which mandated that prisoners be released 90 days before the end of their sentences so they would have time to readjust to life outside of prison. "Community service parole," which allowed prisoners early release if they performed a community service, became an option in 1984. Prisoners were eligible for community service parole if they were sentenced prior to the Fair Sentencing Act of 1980 and had served at least half of their minimum terms, or if they were sentenced after the Fair Sentencing Act and served at least one-fourth of their terms. Those convicted of crimes including sex offenses, kidnapping, abduction of children, and drug trafficking were ineligible for community service parole.

By 1987, despite the construction of thousands of new cells and the release of thousands of prisoners, North Carolina's prisons were still overcrowded. That year, the General Assembly enacted the Prison Population Stabilization Act, which limited the number of prisoners who could be held in state facilities, as part of the settlement of a federal lawsuit relating to overcrowding in North Carolina's prisons. When the number of prisoners exceeded the "cap" for 15 consecutive days, the state released enough individuals to drop the number of inmates to 97 percent of the cap.

From 1960 to 1991 the crime rate increased 212 percent in the United States and 399 percent in North Carolina. In 1994 Governor James B. Hunt Jr. called a special legislative session on crime, and the General Assembly passed its most serious attempt at criminal justice reform since the Fair Sentencing Act of 1980. The new law, called Structured Sentencing, was touted as the solution to the state's crime problem, as it was intended to increase the time served and keep more violent offenders behind bars. Structured Sentencing abolished parole for anyone convicted after 1 Oct. 1995 to ensure that later convicts would serve their full sentences. This reform actually decreased the length of many sentences, however, and completely phased out prison terms for numerous "nonviolent" crimes. Although it abolished parole for subsequent offenders, every prisoner convicted before 1 Oct. 1995 was still subject to the law as it was written at the time of conviction.

References: Stevens H. Clarke, *Law of Probation and Parole in North Carolina* (1979); Clarke, *Law of Sentencing, Probation, and Parole in North Carolina* (2nd ed., 1997).

Andrew Cline

Pasquotank County, located in the Coastal Plain region of North Carolina, was formed in 1681 as the Pasquotank Precinct of Albemarle County. It was named after the Pasquotank Indians; the Indian word *pāsk-e'tan-ki* means "where the current divides or forks." The county is bordered in part by the Albemarle Sound. Early inhabitants of the area included the Pasquotank Indians, followed by English settlers. The initial land grant in what is now North Carolina was acquired by Nathaniell Batts in 1660 at the Pasquotank County Courthouse. Elizabeth City, the county seat, was incorporated in 1793 as Redding; the name was changed to Elizabeth Town in 1794 and then to Elizabeth City in 1801, after the wife of Adam Tooley, on whose land the town was built. Other communities in the county include Morgans Corner, Nixonton, and Weeksville. Notable physical features of the county, in addition to the Albemarle Sound, include the Little River, Big Flatty Creek, Wade Point, Cobb Point, and Goat Island.

The U.S. Coast Guard Air Station is a significant part of Elizabeth City's heritage and economy. Elizabeth City State University was established in 1891 as a normal school for African Americans and is now part of the 16-campus consolidated University of North Carolina. The Elizabeth City Historic District covers a 30-block area and includes the McMullen Building (1891) and the Virginia Dare Hotel and Arcade (1917). Other county cultural attractions include the Museum of the Albemarle, which is a branch of the North Carolina Museum of History, and the Elizabeth City State University Planetarium. Annual events hosted by the county include the Albemarle Craftsman's Fair, the Taste of Summer Festival, Jazz by Candlelight, and the Holiday Celebration and Lighted Boat Parade.

Pasquotank County's major industry is lumbering. The county's farmers produce potatoes, soybeans, wheat, corn, cabbage, and broccoli. The first commercial processing of soybeans in North Carolina took place in Elizabeth City in 1915. In 2004 Pasquotank County's estimated population was 37,600.

Jay Mazzocchi

SEE ALSO Elizabeth City State University; Museum of the Albemarle.

Pasquotank Indians, also known as the Paspatank, were last identified in the early eighteenth century on the Pasquotank River north of Albemarle Sound. They were probably part of the Weapemeoc group. An Algonquian-speaking people, the Pasquotank farmed, hunted, fished, and lived in villages often surrounded by palisades made of logs. They were not mentioned in the documents of the Roanoke Colony, but in the early eighteenth century Englishman John Lawson described them as a tiny tribe numbering 10 warriors, suggesting a total population of less than 50.

References: Christian F. Feest, "North Carolina Algonquians," in Bruce Trigger, ed., *Handbook of North American Indians*, vol. 15

(1978); Maurice A. Mook, "Algonkian Ethnohistory of the Carolina Sound," *Journal of the Washington Academy of Sciences* 34 (15 June, 15 July 1944).

Michael D. Green

Patent Medicines were proprietary drugs, often containing alcohol, narcotics, or opiates, that enjoyed their greatest popularity in America between the 1870s and the 1930s prior to the era of modern medicine and federal pure food and drug laws. During this period, there were no laws requiring drug manufacturers to prove that their preparations were safe and effective, that ingredients be divulged on the container, or that their producers have any medical or scientific training. Because of this, many hucksters bottled their nostrums under unsanitary conditions and made exaggerated claims that their products would cure a number of widely divergent maladies. Many patent medicines had formulas that were never actually patented, but their manufacturers relied on trademark protection for their distinctive advertising and packaging.

One example of a patent medicine produced in North Carolina is the syrup bottled by Mrs. Joe Person of Franklinton in the 1880s for the prevention of scrofula. Scrofula was a type of lymph node disease that today is known to have resulted from the drinking of tainted milk before the advent of pasteurization. Like many other patent medicine manufacturers, Person used testimonial advertising in newspapers to promote her product. Also typical was her claim that the formula was based on an old Indian recipe so it would have more credibility with people who believed in the curative powers of Native American herbal medicine. On the bottle Person's remedy was said to "purify the blood" and cure rheumatism, skin eruptions, eczema, and stomach troubles, among other ailments.

Some patent medicine makers went on the road in horse-

A potential customer sniffs a bottle of patent medicine offered by a street salesman in Mebane, 1939. Howard Odum Collection, no. P-3167, Southern Historical Collection, Wilson Library, UNC-Chapel Hill.

drawn wagons to promote their concoctions by staging showy demonstrations in which mostly spurious "miracle" cures were performed by application or ingestion of their products. In the late nineteenth century these "traveling medicine shows" were an immensely popular form of entertainment throughout the nation.

Because of the exaggerated curative powers of many patent medicines, their potential for harm from some ingredients, and their widespread availability, the North Carolina Pharmaceutical Association tried to have sales restricted in general stores as early as 1876. But the public demand for the products and the strong lobbying of local merchants' associations prevented state legislation. A further attempt was made to curb over-the-counter sales of patent medicines in 1923, when elements of the North Carolina temperance movement allied with druggists to introduce legislation prohibiting groceries and general merchandise stores within five miles of a pharmacy from selling patent medicines.

Many prohibitionists in North Carolina felt that patent medicines were a threat to sobriety because they represented a loophole by which the public could legally buy products with a high alcohol content. Five years into Prohibition, an official of the North Carolina Anti-Saloon League denounced "the enormous sale of bottled concoctions carried in the stock of grocery stores and general merchandise establishments which in truth is largely ethyl alcohol colored."

State legislation continued to be weak and did little to restrain the deceptive business practices of the patent medicine industry. Not until 1938, when the labeling laws of the federal Pure Food and Drug Act of 1906 were strengthened by passage of the Food, Drug, and Cosmetic Act, did many medicine makers become more accountable for the safety and effectiveness of their products.

References: David Armstrong and Elizabeth M. Armstrong, *The Great American Medicine Show: Being an Illustrated History of Hucksters, Healers, Health Evangelists, and Heroes from Plymouth Rock to the Present* (1991); "Big Convention of the Anti-Saloon League," *Greensboro Patriot*, 18 Jan. 1923; "The Persistence of Mrs. Joe Person," *The State*, vol. 54 (October 1986).

Lisa Brantley Kobrin

SEE ALSO Medicine Shows.

Paternalism, the controlling of all aspects of an employee's life by the employer, was characteristic of many nineteenth- and early twentieth-century North Carolina mills and factories. The roots of paternalism were evident in an earlier era, when southern slaveholders came to regard taking good care of their slaves as of primary importance. Although partly a humanitarian concern, this focus on slaves' welfare derived mostly from business considerations; sufficient food, housing, medical care, and clothing kept slaves at least outwardly con-

tent and enabled them to work more efficiently. This understanding of the importance of the quality of life of one's workforce continued to motivate owners in the tenancy system and later in the creation of mill villages.

Paternalism was the philosophical and fiscal underpinning of many North Carolina cotton mill villages, which were organized as "company towns" to keep workers and their families satisfied and thus loyal and more productive. Paternalistic mill owners also claimed the right to discipline employees. Violators of specific rules and laws were first warned, then fired and made to vacate their house after a second offense. Drunkenness, spouse abuse, sexual immorality, and stealing were some of the most serious offenses, and only a small legal force, usually one man, was needed for the entire village.

World War II essentially brought an end to paternalism, as most North Carolina mill villages and all of their homes, hospitals, libraries, and even community buildings were incorporated into neighboring towns.

References: Jacquelyn Dowd Hall and others, *Like a Family: The Making of a Southern Cotton Mill World* (1987); Harriet L. Herring, *Passing of the Mill Village: Revolution in a Southern Institution* (1949).

Gene Purcell

Peace College was founded as Peace Institute in Raleigh in 1857 by the Presbyterian Synod of North Carolina. It was named for a significant benefactor, William Peace, an elder at Raleigh's First Presbyterian Church who contributed $10,000 and land for the college. The Civil War delayed the opening of the school and completion of its original edifice, Main Building. The unfinished building served as a Confederate hospital during the war and as an office of the U.S. government's Freedmen's Bureau afterward. Finally in 1872, Peace Institute

Students take a spring stroll at Peace College, 1947. Courtesy of NCOA&H.

was opened, and Main Building received students for the first time.

The school was a pioneer in several areas of instruction. In 1875 it established the South's first school of art and painting. By 1880 it was operating the South's first kindergarten and the region's first school of cooking. Though offering instruction for women of various ages for much of its history, by 1969 the school had evolved into a two-year junior college and awarded associate of arts degrees. In 1995 the college moved to baccalaureate status and began offering four-year degrees. There have been several variations of the official college name, but it has been known as Peace College since 1943.

Throughout its history, Peace has been controlled by individuals or groups closely associated with the Presbyterian Church. The modern school is governed by an independent board of trustees but remains affiliated with the Presbyterian Church (U.S.A.) and the Raleigh First Presbyterian Church. However, students from all church denominations are welcome. The school, which is noted for its liberal arts and sciences instruction, remains exclusively female and occupies the original site. Enrollment in the early 2000s stood at about 700. The 15-acre campus near the State Capitol has won state and national recognition for its attractively designed landscape.

Warren L. Bingham

Peace Movement (Civil War). Various peace movements that occurred in the North and South during the Civil War had a strong impact on the political climate of both sections. In the Confederacy, North Carolina produced the largest and most aggressive peace movement, which developed in three phases: a protest against the state draft in March 1862, the establishment of the Peace Party in the summer of 1863, and a convention movement in 1864.

Initial Demonstrations for Peace

The first political rallies for peace in the Confederacy occurred during the summer of 1861 in the central North Carolina counties of Randolph and Davidson. Protesting a draft of one-third of the state militia into the Confederate army, some 50 members of the Randolph County militia marched under a white flag and prayed for peace. At a "Union meeting" in neighboring Davidson County, leaders denounced the Confederacy and advocated reunion. Hundreds of troops were sent into the Randolph/Davidson area during this period to quell an uprising of armed militant Unionists. The peace and anti-draft demonstrators of 1862 met the same fate: scores of dissidents were arrested by Confederate troops and forced into the ranks or sent to prison for disloyalty.

In January 1863 northern Peace Democrats launched a peace movement that precipitated a southern peace drive, especially in North Carolina, where strong peace sentiment already existed. In May 1863 James T. Leach, a planter and owner of 150 slaves, wrote a letter to the *Raleigh Weekly Standard* suggesting that the South consider returning to the Union on the basis offered by the northern Democrats. Leach was willing to cede Confederate independence for reunion based on an "honorable peace," a position considered disloyal by many southerners. That fall, peace candidate Leach was elected to the Confederate House, where, until war's end, he remained the most outspoken advocate for peace in the Confederate Congress.

The Peace Party, William W. Holden, and the Election of 1864

Leach's letter signaled the beginning of the 1863 phase of the peace movement in North Carolina, marked by the development of the Peace Party. Between July and September, about 100 political rallies were held across the state at which speakers expressed their discontent with Confederate rule and advocated various proposals for peace. Two-thirds of the peace meetings were held in the central Piedmont, where independent yeoman farmers were common and support for slavery was weak. At a few of these meetings ardent Unionists hoisted the U.S. flag. Some peace advocates called for Richmond to arrange a peace based on Confederate independence. One faction urged that a convention of all the Confederate states convene and negotiate a peace with the North, while another called for reunion with all constitutional rights guaranteed, including the right of slave ownership.

William W. Holden, editor of Raleigh's *North Carolina Standard*, emerged as the leader of the state's peace movement. He printed accounts of its meetings and supported it editorially. In the 1850s Holden had been an ardent secessionist, but during the secession crisis of 1860–61, he became a Unionist. When North Carolina seceded, he supported the new Confederacy and became Governor Zebulon B. Vance's chief spokesman in the press. Unable to prevent Holden from endorsing the peace cause, which he regarded as likely to lead to a civil war within the Civil War, Vance broke his political ties with Holden and denounced the peace movement as dangerous and subversive. On 8 Sept. 1863 rioting Confederate troops, believing Holden a traitor, sacked his newspaper office. The next day, Vance issued a proclamation denouncing the peace meetings. These acts marked the end of the 1863 phase of the peace movement.

The peace movement emboldened deserters, draft dodgers, and militant Unionists, hundreds of whom congregated and organized into bands in the central Piedmont in the summer of 1863. By August, these armed bands roamed the central counties at will, defying both state and national authorities. Faced with an insurrection, Vance sought aid from Richmond, and Gen. Robert E. Lee ordered a brigade of Confederate troops led by Brig. Gen. Robert F. Hoke into central

North Carolina. On 8 Sept. 1863 Hoke's troops arrived by train at High Point, a railhead in southwestern Guilford County, the heart of "deserter country." What followed was one of the largest deserter hunts carried out in the Confederacy. Vance ordered out hundreds of state Home Guard and militia troops to support Hoke's force. For five months these Confederate and state troops scoured the central Piedmont from Wilkes County in the west to Chatham County in the east. Thousands of deserters and draft dodgers were captured and forced into the ranks.

Meanwhile, in the fall of 1863 six of the ten congressmen seated from North Carolina had campaigned on a peace platform. Although only three of them were allied with Holden, all advocated an "honorable peace." Believing that the election results reflected strong grassroots support for his peace policy, Holden reactivated the Peace Party in January 1864. He knew that Jefferson Davis would never assent to any peace short of Confederate independence. But by 1864, Holden and many others had become convinced that the South could no longer hope to "conquer" a peace. They concluded that the only way to overcome Richmond's intransigence and prevent defeat, emancipation, and Federal military rule was to call a convention of all the Confederate states or, failing that, hold a state convention to consider peace negotiations. Thus began the third phase of the peace movement.

Alarmed at the rebirth of the Peace Party in North Carolina and the determined drive by its adherents for a state convention to supersede the Confederate president and Congress in negotiating a peace with the Federals, Davis asked the Congress to grant him authority to suspend the writ of habeas corpus. In February 1864 the Confederate Congress passed a law giving him the power to do so in 13 instances. The instance pertaining to the peace advocates denied the writ to any person arrested for "advising or inciting others to abandon the Confederate cause, or to resist the Confederate states, or to adhere to the enemy."

Suspension of the writ spread terror through the ranks of peace advocates, and an intimidated Holden ceased publication of his newspaper. But the editor soon regained his courage and announced on 3 Mar. 1864 that he would run against Vance in the August election. If elected governor, Holden promised, he would "do everything in my power . . . to secure an honorable peace." A gifted and popular orator, Vance largely preempted Holden's position, which championed state rights, civil liberties, and peace, by strongly advocating the same principles. But Vance made it clear that the peace he spoke of must be based on southern independence. Due to Vance's appeal to the common man, the suspension of the writ, the stationing of troops at polling places on election day, the use of color-coded ballots, and other forms of intimidation, the incumbent won by a landslide.

The Final Defeat of the Peace Movement

Infuriated by Vance's strong-arm tactics and his use of war conservatives to defeat Holden, many of Holden's supporters in the army deserted and returned home after the election. By mid-August, powerful bands of deserters again roamed the central Piedmont, robbing, terrorizing, and killing loyal Confederate citizens, especially Home Guard and militia officers. With Maj. Gen. William T. Sherman approaching from the south and Federal naval and army forces threatening Fort Fisher at the mouth of the Cape Fear River, Vance took strong measures to suppress the deserter uprising. He mobilized all of his Home Guard and militia forces in the western part of the state and ordered most of them into the disaffected counties. Skirmishes between the opposing forces resulted in the killing or wounding of numerous men on both sides. Vance ordered his troops to ignore the civil law and to arrest the wives, children, parents, and siblings of deserters and hold them captive at ad hoc prison camps in the field. The ploy worked—deserters surrendered in droves. By October, the deserter hunt was over and Vance's state forces were free to be deployed in the defense of the Cape Fear region.

Holden's 1864 convention movement and gubernatorial campaign comprised his second attempt to circumvent Richmond and lead North Carolina and the South back into the Union, thereby avoiding defeat, military occupation, and emancipation. Perhaps the movement was also intended to increase peace sentiment in the North and promote the election of a Democrat to the White House in the fall. Holden's defeat in the 1864 gubernatorial election in August, as well as the military repression of his supporters in the central Piedmont that followed, delivered the death blow to the peace movement in Confederate North Carolina.

References: William T. Auman, "Bryan Tyson: Southern Unionist and American Patriot," NCHR 62 (July 1985); William C. Harris, *William Woods Holden: Firebrand of North Carolina Politics* (1987); Marc W. Kruman, *Parties and Politics in North Carolina, 1836–1865* (1983); Joel H. Silbey, *A Respectable Minority: The Democratic Party in the Civil War Era, 1860–1868* (1977).

William T. Auman

SEE ALSO Heroes of America.

Pearls. In modern times, no oyster species native to North Carolina's coastal region creates pearls of any value. Pearls were long gathered, however, by coastal Indians and used as ornaments or bartered for skins and other articles in the region that became North Carolina. English explorer Philip Amadas, who visited Roanoke Island in 1584, presented black pearls to Queen Elizabeth I. Members of the 1585 colonization venture also took pearls to sell in England to help cover the expenses of the voyage, but the queen seized them all for herself. Some had been acquired by Ralph Lane and Sir Francis

Drake in trade with the natives. Lane mentioned a rope of black pearls that he had lost overboard in returning to the ship in a storm. One member of the colony reported amassing a collection of 5,000 pearls, some of which he used to make "a fayre chaine" that he intended as gift for the queen, but it, too, was lost in the storm.

The Indians valued their oyster beds as a source of pearls and prohibited "strangers" from visiting them. Black pearls, they noted, came from oysters in shallow waters, whereas the choice "white, great, and round" ones were found in deeper water. John Lawson, who visited one of the sandy islands on the Carolina coast in 1709, reported that he had found the kind of oyster shells in which pearls developed.

William S. Powell

Pearsall Plan. On 17 May 1954, the U.S. Supreme Court declared in *Brown v. Board of Education* that racial segregation in public schools was unconstitutional. In the years that followed, the southern states individually passed legislation designed to resist *Brown*. North Carolina's Pearsall Plan of 1956 did not in theory preclude the formation of integrated schools, but it did offer parents and local school boards new tools for avoiding desegregation.

The Pearsall Plan evolved from earlier legislative measures that decentralized public school authority and gave local districts wide discretion in making student assignment plans. In August 1954 Governor William B. Umstead had named 16 whites and 3 blacks to an Advisory Committee on Education, whose task was to craft the state's legislative response to *Brown*. Thomas J. Pearsall, a Rocky Mount businessman and former Speaker of the House in the North Carolina General Assembly, chaired this group. Umstead died later that fall, but his successor, Luther H. Hodges, endorsed the committee's conclusion that integration lacked widespread public support and therefore "should not be attempted." In order to provide communities with ready means for delaying desegregation, the committee proposed giving local districts total control over the assignment of students to schools. In the spring of 1955, the General Assembly enacted that recommendation with the passage of the Pupil Assignment Act, which established a broad array of seemingly race-neutral criteria that local districts could use in making student assignments. In practice, local officials used those criteria to thwart black students wishing to transfer to white schools.

The Pearsall Plan took the idea of local control several steps further. Governor Hodges named in the summer of 1955 a new committee to discuss the school situation. This seven-member group, also chaired by Pearsall, included no African Americans. In April 1956 the Pearsall committee submitted its recommendations, which officials crafted into a legislative package known as the Pearsall Plan. The plan included an amendment to the Compulsory School Attendance Law that excused students from attendance requirements if they were assigned against their wishes to an integrated school and could claim no other public or private school options. The Pearsall Plan also contained a constitutional amendment with two components. First, the state pledged to pay, upon special application, private school tuition grants to parents whose children were assigned to integrated public schools. In addition, a local option clause declared that each school district contained multiple "local option units," roughly corresponding to the territory surrounding any given school. Under the new amendment, each of those units, if faced with pressure to integrate, could hold a public referendum on whether to close its schools. Finally, the Pearsall Plan included a "resolution of condemnation and protest" against the Supreme Court's decision.

The Pearsall Plan had the support of Hodges, who convened a special session of the General Assembly in July 1956. Legislators passed the Pearsall Plan with only two dissenting votes, but its enactment remained contingent on the outcome of a public referendum. Prior to voting on the Pearsall proposals, citizens voiced a wide spectrum of opinion in the press and in public forums. Many black leaders and a small number of white opponents assailed the plan as a direct violation of *Brown*, while other critics attacked the plan primarily as a threat to the state's public schools. A different voice of protest came from staunch segregationists who warned that the Pearsall Plan did not do enough to prevent integration. A broad spectrum of proponents hailed the plan both as a "safety valve" against interracial unrest and as an effective means of preserving segregated schools. In the end, the proponents claimed victory. On 8 Sept. 1956, voters approved the proposals by a margin of more than four to one.

Over the next decade, no districts in North Carolina used the Pearsall measures to shut down their schools. Likewise, local districts did not provide any private school tuition grants to parents seeking to avoid desegregated schools. Integration opponents ultimately had little reason to use the Pearsall Plan, as the Pupil Assignment Act and later "freedom of choice" plans effectively stalled change. In 1964, one decade after *Brown*, less than 1 percent of the state's black children attended school with whites.

In 1966 three African American families from Charlotte, represented by civil rights attorney Julius Chambers, challenged the Pearsall Plan in federal court, where a three-judge panel declared it unconstitutional. Integration, however, did not become an accomplished fact in North Carolina until several years later, when the federal courts declared in a series of cases that local districts had an obligation not only to remove any race-based attendance plans but also to create racially balanced schools. Those rulings climaxed with *Swann v. Charlotte-Mecklenburg Board of Education* (1971), in which the U.S. Supreme Court upheld the use of busing plans for achieving integration. North Carolina's schools rapidly desegregated following *Swann*. The Pearsall Plan ultimately failed to block public school integration. Yet in legitimating white fears of desegregation, it contributed to the larger southern resistance movement that delayed *Brown*'s implementation for well over a decade.

References: William H. Chafe, *Civilities and Civil Rights: Greensboro, North Carolina, and the Black Struggle for Freedom* (1980); Davison Douglas, *Reading, Writing and Race: The Desegregation of the Charlotte Schools* (1995).

Sarah C. Thuesen

SEE ALSO Pupil Assignment Act; *Swann v. Charlotte-Mecklenburg Board of Education.*

Peddlers in southern business history and lore are usually associated with antebellum northern entrepreneurs who sold clocks, tinware, and other items, but itinerant merchants were familiar figures in North Carolina until the twentieth century. In a rural state where many residents remained distant from general stores, peddlers linked country dwellers to a world of manufactured goods that expanded briskly after the Civil War. Besides the wares that filled their packs or festooned their wagons, peddlers arrived with another valuable commodity: news from beyond the neighborhood. They turned backyards and front rooms into merchandise showrooms and accepted payment in trade, practices that made them especially welcomed by rural women whose trips to town or country stores often were rare.

In nineteenth-century American folklore, peddlers aroused a mixture of fascination, fear, and fantasy. They heralded a new consumer culture and symbolized the apprehension and ambivalence generated by the spread of a market economy. In popular imagination, peddlers aroused suspicion as outsiders and shrewd tricksters who found women, in particular, vulnerable to verbally seductive sales pitches. In the antebellum South, race-based anxieties compounded such suspicions. Planters feared that peddlers trafficked with slaves who bartered for goods with pilfered livestock. Slave owners, moreover, worried that itinerant merchants were abolitionists in disguise, sowing seeds of rebellion.

After the Civil War, Jews who had recently emigrated from eastern Europe got a foothold in business by peddling in North Carolina and other southern states. With little capital themselves, immigrant peddlers often catered to poor whites and blacks whose access to store credit was limited; some peddlers managed to accumulate enough cash to start their own permanent stores.

Although stereotyped as shady dealers, in reality peddlers were vulnerable travelers who could be easy crime targets. Such was the fate of Samuel Tucker, a Jewish peddler from Richmond who sought overnight lodgings in Franklin County in 1892 only to be robbed and murdered. The culprits tossed Tucker's body into a vine-covered ravine, where it went undetected for months.

Determining the precise number of peddlers who sold their wares in North Carolina at any given time is difficult. What is clear, however, is that this ancient form of selling remained an important part of the state's commerce into the twentieth century, when more sophisticated traveling salesmen replaced peddlers and improved transportation made getting to the store easier for consumers.

References: David Jaffee, "Peddlers of Progress and the Transformation of the Rural North," *Journal of American History* 78 (September 1991); Lu Ann Jones, "Re-visioning the Countryside: Southern Women, Rural Reform, and the Farm Economy in the Twentieth Century" (Ph.D. diss., UNC-Chapel Hill, 1996).

Lu Ann Jones

Peerage. The Fundamental Constitutions of Carolina of 1669 outlined an idealistic version of feudalism as the intended form of government for the colony under Proprietary rule. The Lords Proprietors had the power to create a hereditary peerage in Carolina. Forbidden to use the same ranks of nobility that were used in England, the Proprietors chose the title of "landgrave" (a German designation, approximately equal to a count) as the highest rank and the title of "cacique" (sometimes spelled and pronounced "cassick") as the lower rank. The latter term derives from a West Indian aboriginal word meaning "chief" or "headman." In addition, the eldest Proprietor was to have the title of "palatine" and would preside over governmental meetings.

The title "baronet" was a rank of honor or dignity created in England by James I in 1611. It was not an order of the peerage but ranked below a baron and above a knight and was the lowest inheritable order in Great Britain. Held by commoners, it was "intended to give rank, precedence, and title without privilege." In colonial North Carolina there were several baronets, among whom were Sir Nathaniel Duckenfield, Sir Richard Everard, and Sir John Yeamans.

In the settling of Carolina, landgraves were to be granted four "baronies" (48,000 acres) and caciques two baronies (24,000 acres) in each county as it was created, and they were strictly limited in their right to dispose of the land other than by lease. Originally, there was to be one landgrave for each county, and twice as many caciques as landgraves. In practice, more landgraves than caciques were appointed.

Under the Fundamental Constitutions, the nobles were intended to have legislative and judicial powers in Carolina; however, this system was never really implemented and the powers and titles of the nobles were mainly on paper. South Carolina had 26 landgraves and 13 caciques, whereas North Carolina had only a few of each. Most landgraves and caciques apparently remained in England; of those who immigrated to the New World, few settled permanently in North Carolina. Among Carolina nobles, Sir John Colleton, Robert Daniel, Charles Eden, Christoph von Graffenreid, and Sir John Yeamans were landgraves; John Gibbs, who unsuccessfully claimed to be governor of North Carolina, was a cacique. Of "upwards of 800,000 acres" granted to landgraves and caciques in South Carolina, less than 10,000 acres had been "taken up or ascertained" when that province became a royal colony in 1719. The lack of nobles in Carolina was one of the reasons that the plan of government under the Fundamental Constitutions failed. After several revisions, the Fundamental Constitutions were abandoned, leaving the Carolina nobility without an official role in government.

As late as 1726, a warrant for a landgraveship was granted to Col. Samuel Horsey; it was never taken up "by reason of the unsettled state of the province." References to caciques and landgraves are scarce in North Carolina after it became a royal colony in 1729, when seven of the eight Proprietors sold their shares to the Crown. Records are somewhat fuller for South Carolina, where the heirs of some of the original landgraves and caciques were embroiled in legal disputes over their old land grants for several years after South Carolina became a royal colony.

It is unclear what happened legally to the hereditary titles of Carolina's landgraves and caciques. The land rights of some were lost individually. In 1730 the grant of Sir Nathaniel Johnson, who became a cacique in 1686, was declared void by the attorney and solicitor general on the grounds that his grant from the Proprietors was so vague that it gave no description of the location of his lands and did not even state that they were to be in Carolina. Other grants lapsed when their holders died without heirs.

Aside from the potential rights to large land grants, the old titles of landgrave and cacique otherwise seem to have had little meaning or prestige as the eighteenth century progressed. At any rate, the 1776 state constitution forbade the granting or holding of titles of nobility by citizens of North Carolina, and the U.S. Constitution repeated this restriction on the federal level.

References: Mattie Erma Edwards Parker, ed., *North Carolina Charters and Constitutions, 1578–1698* (1963); William S. Powell, *North Carolina through Four Centuries* (1989); Waddy Thompson and Joseph McLean, "Orders of Nobility in North Carolina," *North Carolina Historical and Genealogical Register* 1 (October 1900).

David A. Norris
Robert J. Cain

Pender County, located in the Coastal Plain region of North Carolina, was formed in 1875 from New Hanover County and named for Confederate general William D. Pender, who died at the Battle of Gettysburg in 1863. It is bordered in part by the Atlantic Ocean. Early inhabitants of the area included the Burgaw Indians, followed by English, German, Welsh, and French settlers. When establishment of the county seat was authorized in 1875, its name was to be Cowan; in 1877, however, the name was changed to Stanford and then, in 1879, changed again to Burgaw—which it has remained—when the city was officially incorporated. Beach communities important in the county's recreational and tourist trade are Topsail Beach and Surf City, and other communities include Hampstead, Scotts Hill, Penderlea, and Rocky Point. Notable physical features, in addition to the shoreline, include the Cape Fear River, Topsail Island (shared with Onslow County), Roan Island, and Beasley's, Rock Fish, and Colvins Creeks.

The Battle of Moore's Creek Bridge, the first southern battle and Patriot victory in the Revolutionary War, took place in what is now Pender County on 27 Feb. 1776. The battlefield is now a national historic site. Pender County's other historic sites include Sloop Point Plantation (1726), North Carolina's oldest house. Cultural institutions include Topsail Island Missiles and More Museum, commemorating the rocketry experiments of the late 1940s, the Penderlea Homestead Museum, and the Poplar Grove Plantation Museum House and Cultural Arts Center. The county hosts annual events such as Autumn with Topsail, Burgaw Pumpkin Day, the Atkinson Christmas Jubilee, and the Grape Festival.

Pender County's agricultural products include strawberries, blueberries, grapes, tobacco, sweet potatoes, soybeans, swine, and poultry, and its manufactures include apparel, crushed stone, and pressure sensitive labels. The rare Venus flytrap grows in the wild in Pender County. In 2004 the population of the county was estimated at slightly more than 45,000.

Jay Mazzocchi

SEE ALSO Moore's Creek Bridge, Battle of; Penderlea Homesteads; Rocketry Experiments; Sloop Point Plantation.

Penderlea Homesteads, a model farm community in Pender County planned by Hugh MacRae and operated by the federal government after 1934, drew its inspiration from resettlement projects founded by MacRae in the early twentieth century. Beginning in 1905, MacRae recruited European immigrants to come to southeastern North Carolina for resettlement in six cooperatively organized farm colonies along the railroad 40 miles north and west of his business operations in Wilmington. By 1908, 800 immigrants had settled in his six colonies. Initially the settlers were grouped by nationality; in time the groups became mixed. The colonies ignored traditional crops such as corn, tobacco, and cotton, concentrating instead on dairy products, fruits and vegetables, and flowers. Three of the six colonies were successes.

Dutch settler working the land at Van Eeden, 1913. NCC.

Castle Hayne was the most successful of MacRae's experiments. The site selected in New Hanover and Pender Counties was once a colonial plantation belonging to Roger Haynes. The settlers were principally Dutch. Their main industry was flower growing, including the cultivation of daffodils, irises, and gladioli. St. Helena, located four miles south of Burgaw in Pender County, was settled initially by Italians but populated in time by Poles, Hungarians, Austrians, Belgians, Danes, and settlers of other nationalities. A Russian Orthodox community continues to thrive and annually celebrates "Old Christmas." Marathon, settled initially by Greeks, benefited from its proximity to Castle Hayne before eventually losing its own identity and being absorbed by the latter community.

New Berlin, among the more ambitious of MacRae's homesteading projects, was nevertheless unsuccessful. MacRae plotted 193 farms and 23 town blocks to be settled by German and Hungarian immigrants. Remnants of the colony survive as the community of Delco in Columbus County. Van Eeden was settled by Dutch newcomers in Pender County, but the colony suffered from drainage problems; all evidence of the community was gone by 1939. Artesia, a Polish community between Lake Waccamaw and Whiteville in Columbus County, was also not successful.

MacRae's experience with the farm colonies benefited him almost 30 years later when he sought to develop Penderlea Homesteads. MacRae decided, during the depths of the Great Depression, to create on a grand scale a model farm community at Penderlea. As manager of the Penderlea Homesteads corporation, he was assisted by a board of directors from North Carolina State College (later North Carolina State University), Princeton, and Harvard. Their intention was to build, with government assistance, the "best planned rural community in the world." A tract of 10,000 acres was set aside, land was cleared, and homes and a community center were built. MacRae differed with Interior Secretary Harold Ickes over how Penderlea should be managed, and on 12 May 1934 the entire program was federalized under the New Deal. MacRae appealed to President Franklin D. Roosevelt without success, and a few months later he resigned as manager. First Lady Eleanor Roosevelt visited the project on 11 June 1935.

Control of Penderlea Homesteads passed from the Division of Subsistence Homesteads to the Resettlement Administration to the Farm Security Administration, each with a new set of policies and requirements. The original goal of 500 20-acre farms was never met. A total of 142 units were leased, but by the onset of World War II few of the original homesteaders remained. Liquidation followed, and by 1947 all of the farms had been sold, most to their tenants with low-interest loans. Today many homes, the large community center, and other structures associated with the project remain.

References: Paul Conkin, *Tomorrow a New World: The New Deal Community Program* (1959); John Faris Corey, "The Colonization and Contributions of Emigrants Brought to Southeastern North Carolina by Hugh MacRae" (M.A. thesis, UNC-Chapel Hill, 1957); Marcia G. Synnott, "Hugh MacRae, Penderlea, and the Model Farm Communities Movement," in *Proceedings of the South Carolina Historical Association* (1988).

Michael Hill

Penland School of Crafts is one of the oldest and most prestigious handicraft schools in America. Located in the western mountains of Mitchell County, the school was established in the late 1920s by Lucy Morgan, director of the Appalachian School in the village of Penland. While visiting Berea College in Kentucky, Morgan learned weaving techniques and returned home with modern looms and the idea of reintroducing the art of weaving cloth to her community. The Penland School originally served as a training ground and social center for area women. Eventually, Morgan also assisted local craftspeople in selling their finished products to tourists. A small cabin on the grounds of the Appalachian School served as Penland's first home. In 1928 Penland advocate Edward F. Worst of Chicago wrote an article in the *Handicrafter*. Soon Morgan received applications from people from outside the community interested in studying handicrafts at Penland. During the next 33 years, people from around the world found their way to Penland to learn traditional crafts such as pottery, basket weaving, silversmithing, and metalworking.

In 1962 Morgan retired, and Bill Brown, former assistant director of the Haystack Mountain School of Crafts in Deer Isle, Maine, became Penland's second director. Under his leadership, Penland moved from a school devoted to teaching traditional crafts to a school focused on advancing the professional aspects of handicrafts and exploring innovative craft techniques. Brown hired the best teachers in their respective fields and added woodworking and glassblowing to the curriculum. Penland was one of the first schools in the country to teach the art of glassblowing, a pursuit that has attracted such artists as Harvey K. Littleton, Mark Peiser, and John Nygren. Many students continue to pursue their craft on a professional level and have achieved critical acclaim after leaving Penland. The Resident Craftsman's Program enables artists to enjoy their own studio space. Resident artists are full-time, self-supporting craftspeople who live and work at the school for three years. Developed by Brown, the program provides participating artists with the time to develop their techniques and explore the marketability of their work and provides students with models for a life in craft.

The Penland School of Crafts continues to attract people from around the world, and the school remains a popular haven for artists. From the original cabin, the school has expanded to include 41 structures on its 400-acre campus,

An instructor demonstrates glassblowing techniques at Penland School, ca. 1995. Photograph by Robin Dreyer.

hosting more than 1,200 people each year. The school offers one- and two-week classes in the summer and and eight-week sessions in the spring and fall. Most classes are a mix of demonstrations, lectures, individual studio work, and field trips. The school features courses in book- and papermaking, clay, drawing, glassblowing, metalsmithing, photography, printmaking, textiles, and woodworking. The Penland Gallery is the information and display area of the school. Attracting over 14,000 visitors each year, the gallery displays and sells work by Penland instructors, resident artists, students, and neighbors. A knowledgeable staff provides information about craft processes, the school program, the artists, and studios in the area.

Shelia Bumgarner

Penmanship as a deliberate manner of writing was scarcely practiced in North Carolina until the nineteenth century and, with the rise of computers by the end of the twentieth century, was in danger of becoming an educational relic. The rise of private academies in the state early in the nineteenth century coincided with the availability of copybooks that were designed and published by acknowledged writing masters in the North. Copybooks contained engraved specimens of capital and small letters and were published as aids to the teaching of a variety of hands. Most popular was the current (or running) hand in which the letters were usually slanted to the right and the words formed without lifting the pen from letter to letter. In round (or copperplate) hand, the slope also inclined to the right, but the letters were round, bold, and full.

In most North Carolina academies, boys and girls were given the same kinds of primary copybooks in which to copy short letters, short and long letters combined, and short words commencing with capitals. While girls were expected to master the techniques to a degree higher than boys, both might have examples of their penmanship separately scrutinized in a public examination at the close of the school year.

Few copybooks survive to reveal either the designer of the hand that was taught or the method of teaching it in the antebellum academies and private schools in the state. An examination of surviving letters and exercise books written by students suggests that a variety of models and methods were taught. The great majority of antebellum students, whose education was limited to the common schools, were taught the basic shapes of the letters and the rudiments of a cursive hand. The schools generally had terms of only three to four months in the year, and no effort was made to train the students in a highly finished hand. The common school system collapsed at the end of the Civil War, and after the public schools were reopened in 1870, the system remained moribund for most of the century. Nevertheless, many of the towns and counties that were able to sustain their public schools in the postbellum period began to furnish their students with copybooks that had been approved by the State Board of Education. In this era, a wide variety of copybooks were used, most notably ones that focused on the Spencerian hand, a system of penmanship developed about 1855 by Platt Rogers Spencer (1800–64) of Ohio.

Two men from the world of classical writing masters dominated penmanship in the state's public schools during the first half of the twentieth century. Charles Paxton Zaner (1864–1918) of Ohio and Austin Norman Palmer (1860–1927) of Iowa both had been influenced by Spencerian forms, but both, in their specimen alphabets for schools, abandoned elongated loops, flourishes, and shading of letters. Palmer's method of moving particular muscles in writing while resting the fleshy part of the forearm on the desk was of advantage to commercial writers. Beginning in 1916, texts and writing books of the Zaner-Boser Company and the Palmer Company were used exclusively in the primary and commercial writing classes in the state's public schools.

With an ever-increasing reliance on home computers for homework and other assignments, penmanship has become systematically de-emphasized in North Carolina school systems. By the early 2000s, schools often required assignments to be typed rather than handwritten, and many students simply have never been made to learn the basics of modern cursive techniques, such as the D'Nealian method. With keyboards replacing pens and pencils, the future of penmanship in the state remains unclear.

References: William E. Henning, *An Elegant Hand: The Golden Age of American Penmanship and Calligraphy* (2002); Ray Nash, *American Penmanship, 1800–1850* (1969).

George Stevenson

Pennsylvania Farmer was the most well known of three vessels obtained for the North Carolina Navy in early 1776

for service in the American Revolution. The North Carolina Provincial Council, meeting at the Johnston County Courthouse in December 1775, authorized the purchase of three ships to protect the state's maritime trade. In February 1776 the state paid £1,000 for the *Pennsylvania Farmer* at New Bern. A board of eight commissioners was appointed to find a crew and obtain provisions for the ship. The approximately 120-ton vessel was armed with 16 four-pounder and six-pounder carriage guns and 10 small swivel guns; some of the guns were sent from Philadelphia, and others were purchased overseas. Its crew ranged from 80 to 110 officers and men, including a marine detachment. Perhaps the name of the vessel was inspired by *Letters from a Pennsylvania Farmer*, a series of pro-independence writings by John Dickinson.

When the *Pennsylvania Farmer* at last left port in December 1776, it was for a trading voyage to bring back salt, guns, and ammunition for the state of North Carolina from the West Indies. The captain, Joshua Hampstead, sold the cargo when the ship returned and disappeared with the money. He was apparently never heard from again. Soon afterward, smallpox was detected on board, and the ship and crew had to be quarantined for a time at Cape Lookout.

In September 1777 two British brigs, "one a very large one," captured several vessels in the North Carolina sounds. The *Pennsylvania Farmer* and two other rebel ships were reported to be "preparing to sail . . . in quest of the English pirates," but ostensibly the vessels never confronted the British.

By late 1777 the General Assembly was considering the sale of the *Pennsylvania Farmer* and the other two brigs of the North Carolina Navy, as they had been of little use in protecting the state's maritime trade. In May 1778 the *Pennsylvania Farmer* was put up for sale but a buyer could not be found. Later, the ship mysteriously sank at its moorings; the sinking was blamed on a saboteur. In June 1779 the ship was again offered for sale at Edenton "as she now lies"; after that, there appears to be no further record of the *Pennsylvania Farmer*.

Reference: William N. Still Jr., *North Carolina's Revolutionary War Navy* (1976).

David A. Norris

Pentecostal Holiness Church evolved from two religious traditions that spread rapidly among North Carolina evangelical Christians during the nineteenth and early twentieth centuries. The Holiness movement began with a series of Methodist revivals that occurred in 1867. In the eighteenth century, John Wesley had first introduced the doctrine that salvation required two "blessings," or religious experiences. The first, justification, represents a believer's conversion; the second, sanctification, signifies an individual's purification. In this stage, the individual reaches a state of "holiness" that enables him or her to lead a pure life, free from sin. In the twentieth century some Holiness churches began to advocate a third blessing, the Pentecostal experience, which included speaking in tongues (glossalalia) to indicate an individual's "baptism by the Holy Spirit."

Ambrose B. Crumpler, a Methodist preacher, was the first to spread the Holiness doctrine in North Carolina. In 1896 a Holiness revival took place in Dunn, and Crumpler encouraged his adherents to find the second blessing, sanctification. The doctrine spread quickly throughout eastern North Carolina towns such as Elizabeth City and Goldsboro. In 1899 Crumpler withdrew from the Methodist Church and joined the newly formed Pentecostal Holiness Church in Goldsboro.

Crumpler preached his revelations without contest until an auspicious revival in 1906 presented him with a major doctrinal challenge. That year brought the Azusa Street Revival in Los Angeles, the first revival that preached the baptism of the Holy Spirit, which led to speaking in tongues. To be sure, some North Carolinians had experienced speaking in unknown languages upon conversion; but not until Gaston B. Cashwell returned from Los Angeles in 1908 preaching the doctrine of baptism of the Holy Spirit did North Carolinian Pentecostal Holiness Churches embrace the notion that an individual must speak in tongues upon receiving the Holy Spirit. Converts not only spoke in tongues but also practiced other traditional evangelical signs of conversion, such as making strange movements, jumping, falling into trances, and lying rigid on the floor.

Crumpler and many other congregants refused to acknowledge this "third blessing" of Pentecostalism. Between 1908 and 1911, Pentecostal and Holiness churches of North Carolina splintered into many groups. Some churches had Methodist origins and others had Freewill Baptist origins. For example, the Fire-Baptized Holiness Church became dominant in southeastern North Carolina.

Holiness and Pentecostal traditions have attracted the interests of many groups throughout North Carolina, with both black and white congregants embracing the doctrines of sanctification and speaking in tongues. The United Holy Church, located near Wilmington in Method and founded in 1886, represented one of the first holiness denominations organized by African Americans. The largest African American Pentecostal denomination, the Church of God in Christ, was formed in 1897. Some early congregations were interracial, such as the Pentecostal Assemblies of the World, the Church of God, the Fire-Baptized Holiness Church, and the Pentecostal Holiness Church. But these denominations split in the 1920s as African American churches gained independence and whites desired segregated services. African Americans turned to the Church of God in Christ and whites established the Assemblies of God.

The Pentecostal Holiness Church, the Assemblies of God, and the Church of God in Christ came to represent the three largest Pentecostal and Holiness denominations in the na-

tion. In 1973 the Pentecostal Holiness Church became the International Pentecostal Holiness Church. It represents a fundamentalist religion that believes in Christ's resurrection, truth in the scriptures, justification, sanctification, baptism of the Holy Ghost, divine healing, and the premillennial return of Christ to earth. Most congregations follow these doctrines consistently, although customs vary somewhat among African American, white, and Native American members. By the early 2000s, the International Pentecostal Holiness Church had approximately 2.5 million adherents spread throughout 35 states and more than 70 foreign countries. More than 300 affiliated churches are in North Carolina. The denomination, headquartered in Oklahoma City, also manages three colleges—one in Oklahoma, a second in Georgia, and a third in South Carolina.

References: C. Eric Lincoln and Lawrence H. Mamiya, *The Black Church in the African American Experience* (1995); W. Eddie Morris, *The Vine and Branches: Holiness and Pentecostal Movements* (1981); Vinson Synan, *The Holiness-Pentecostal Movement in the United States* (1971).

Karin Lorene Zipf

People's Ticket of Andrew Jackson for president and John C. Calhoun for vice president won the popular vote of North Carolina in the 1824 election despite the overwhelming support of the Democratic-Republican Party caucus for William H. Crawford of Georgia. Following the election of 1820, state Republican leaders began to solicit backing for Crawford, whose views were more compatible with their political philosophy than those of John Quincy Adams of Massachusetts. By 1824 key individuals in the party who made up the state's caucus had pledged their support and the implied vote of their state to Crawford for president. Many North Carolinians, particularly those in the west and along Albemarle Sound, were angry. The depression of 1819 had drained their resources and made money scarce. Most of them had endorsed the failed campaign of Archibald D. Murphey for increased state public education, internal improvements, and political reapportionment in the west. When Crawford's nomination was announced, the dissidents joined with Murphey, William Polk, and Charles Fisher to form the People's Ticket, with John C. Calhoun, a prominent advocate of education and internal improvements, as their candidate.

Popular support for Calhoun proved insufficient, but Andrew Jackson quickly caught the public fancy. An alliance of Jackson for president and Calhoun for vice president was accordingly concluded, and the two politicians carried the election in North Carolina, although they lost the national vote. In 1828, this time with the state caucus behind them, Jackson and Calhoun won North Carolina by an even larger margin on their way to the presidency and vice presidency.

C. D. Bradham's drugstore in New Bern in the 1910s, with Pepsi-Cola advertisement painted on a mirror behind the soda fountain. Photograph by Bayard Wootten. NCC.

References: R. D. W. Connor, *A History of North Carolina* (1919); Robert C. Jeffrey, *The Thought of John C. Calhoun* (1985); David Lindsay, *Andrew Jackson and John C. Calhoun* (1973).

Louis P. Towles

Pepsi-Cola, advertised as the "Taste Born in the Carolinas," is one of many carbonated soft drinks invented in the South between the Civil War and World War I, when the temperance movement, poverty, and the relatively high prices of coffee and tea conspired with the climate to create a regional market for inexpensive, nonalcoholic social beverages. Caleb Bradham (1867–1934) first concocted Pepsi-Cola as a fountain drink at a pharmacy at Pollock and Middle Streets in New Bern in 1893. Three years later he formally gave "Brad's Drink" a new name—Pepsin Cola. He began bottling and marketing Pepsi under its present name in 1898 and founded the Pepsi-Cola Company in 1903. By World War I Pepsi was sold in 24 states.

During the war, Bradham invested heavily in sugar in order to ensure a reliable supply, and the glut of 1920 abruptly ended his prosperity and his ownership of the company. Pepsi-Cola changed hands repeatedly over the next decade, but bottlers who had large stocks of syrup kept some Pepsi drinkers satisfied without interruption.

Unable to get a high-volume discount from Coca-Cola, Loft's, a chain that sold fountain Coke in more than 100 candy stores, bought Pepsi-Cola (then headquartered in Richmond) in 1931 for $14,000. After its chemists had removed pepsin from the recipe and made other changes probably still in effect, the firm began to sell Pepsi at its fountains, then in bottles. In 1934 Loft's fired the first accurate shot in the "cola wars" when it introduced a 12-ounce Pepsi that sold for the same price as the 6.5-ounce Coke. Pepsi-Cola turned handsome profits ($2 million in one year) through a struggle for control that financier Walter Mack won in 1939.

Mack was new to the soft drink industry, but he seems to have realized quickly that Pepsi is hard to distinguish from other cola drinks. (The similarities may not be accidental; the Coke recipe was not guarded closely during the first few years of its existence.) One way to inspire brand loyalty to such products is to price them competitively, as Loft's did. Another is to drum imaginary or unimportant distinctions into consumers' heads. Under Mack, Pepsi-Cola (now based in New York) began to advertise aggressively, hiring skywriters, saturating the airwaves with its jingle "Pepsi-Cola hits the spot," and placing countless ads in national magazines.

During World War II, Pepsi-Cola circumvented some freezes and shortages by building a syrup factory in Mexico. Ignoring the lesson of Bradham's ruin, the company agreed to buy all the excess sugar produced by that country. The gamble succeeded, enabling Pepsi-Cola to meet the burgeoning demand for soft drinks at defense plants and military bases and lay the foundation for later growth. Wartime hardships and the postwar multiplication of supermarket chains, which preferred national brands, forced many small competitors out of business. Pepsi-Cola and Coca-Cola profited accordingly.

In 1965 PepsiCo, Inc., was founded by the merger of Pepsi-Cola and Frito-Lay Corporation. Herman Lay became chairman of the board of directors of the new company, and Donald M. Kendall became its president and chief executive officer. That year PepsiCo reported sales of $510 million and had 19,000 employees. Since the late 1960s, both PepsiCo and Coca-Cola—huge multinational corporations—have followed strategies based on diversification, new brands (36 between 1970 and 1988), and lavish advertising. Both changed the recipes of their flagship brands. In 1985 Coca-Cola unveiled New Coke, formulated to taste more like Pepsi, but bowed to public pressure and hastily restored old Coke under the name Coke Classic. Pepsi introduced huge national advertising campaigns and giveaways beginning in the 1980s under the theme "Pepsi: The Choice of a New Generation." In the late 1990s and early 2000s, PepsiCo offered a variety of new soft drink brands as well as the original Pepsi-Cola. These included vanilla-, cherry-, and lemon-flavored Pepsi, Diet Pepsi, Mug Root Beer, Mountain Dew, Lipton Iced Tea, Aquafina bottled water, and Sierra Mist.

References: J. C. Louis and Harvey Z. Yazijian, *The Cola Wars* (1980); William Poundstone, *Big Secrets: The Uncensored Truth about All Sorts of Stuff You Are Never Supposed to Know* (1983); John J. Riley, *A History of the American Soft Drink Industry: Bottled Carbonated Beverages, 1807–1957* (1958).

Wynne Dough

Periauger was a wooden boat created by digging out a log, then splitting it longitudinally and adding at least one keel plank between the halves. The keel plank improved stability and increased cargo capacity without increasing draft. Unlike in other places, the term in North Carolina refers to a hull type rather than a rig and was first noted as a distinct North Carolina boat style by John Lawson in 1701. Powered by oars or sails and featuring two unstayed masts without headsails, it was a popular vessel throughout Tidewater North Carolina and Virginia until around 1880, when it was replaced by the sharpie and the V-shaped deadrise shad boat. A replica was completed in Beaufort in 2004 and sailed to Hertford in the "Periauger Odyssey."

References: William C. Fleetwood Jr., *Tidecraft* (1995); Harry Pecorelli, Michael Alford, and Lawrence E. Babits, *A Working Definition of "Periauger"* (1996).

Lawrence E. Babits

Perquimans County, located in the Coastal Plain region of North Carolina, was formed in 1679 and originally called Berkeley Precinct of Albemarle County; it was later renamed for the Perquimans Indians of the area. It is partially bordered by the Albemarle Sound. The Weapemeoc as well as Perquimans Indians were early inhabitants of the county, followed by English and Welsh settlers. Hertford, the county seat, was incorporated in 1758 and named after Hertford, England; the town was originally called Phelps Point after a local landowner named Jonathon Phelps. Other communities in Perquimans County include Winfall, Belvidere, Durants Neck, Chapanoke, and Snug Harbor. Notable physical features, in addition to the Albemarle Sound, include the Perquimans, Little, and Yeopim Rivers, Harvey and Grassy Points, and Godwin and Sutton Creeks.

Among Perquimans County's landmarks and historic sites are the brick Newbold-White House (ca. 1730), the Alfred Moore House (ca. 1825), the Thomas Nixon Plantation (1848), and Piney Woods Friends Meetinghouse (1854). The county hosts several popular festivals and annual events, including the Perquimans County Indian Summer Festival, the Hearth and Harvest Festival, and the Spring Fling and Old-Timers Game.

Perquimans County, with 100 miles of shoreline, is a haven for boaters, fishers, and hunters. The county has more than 65,000 acres of active farmland producing soybeans, corn, peanuts, cotton, vegetables, poultry, swine, and beef cattle. The county's primary manufactured product is apparel. The estimated population of Perquimans County in 2004 was slightly less than 12,000.

William S. Powell

SEE ALSO Newbold-White House.

Persian Gulf War. The immediate effect on North Carolina of Iraq's invasion of Kuwait in August 1990 was the deployment of the 82nd Airborne Division from Fort Bragg to Saudi Arabia. Although the army cloaked the movement in secrecy, the absence of thousands of men from Fort Bragg could not be hidden. Units from the 82nd had taken part in previous operations, but this time the entire division disappeared almost overnight.

Although the state had long taken pride in being the home of the 82nd, some negative aspects emerged within weeks of the deployment. The economy of Cumberland County slumped, and businesses dependent on military trade suffered; some failed and others came close to collapse. These problems were compounded by the mobilization of reserve and National Guard units, leaving hospitals, fire departments, and other public services shorthanded.

The possibility of a peaceful solution to the crisis disappeared by November, leading to demonstrations by both antiwar groups and those favoring Iraq's forced withdrawal from Kuwait. The prospect of war influenced the senatorial campaigns of Jesse Helms and Harvey Gantt: Republican incumbent Helms reminded voters that, earlier, Gantt had spoken in favor of a reduction in military expenditures, while Gantt insisted that he supported the troops in the field. For his part, Senator Terry Sanford announced that he favored letting the United Nations resolve the conflict through negotiation.

Nearly every week, additional reserve and National Guard units were called up. After processing at Fort Bragg, units were promptly sent to the Persian Gulf, where their accommodations were uncertain. The 139th Rear Area Operations Center camped in the sand, whereas the 382nd Public Affairs Detachment was housed in a hotel with chandeliers and waiters. In December 1990 a ceremonial sendoff was held at Camp Lejeune for the departure of 24,000 men for the Gulf. It was the marines' largest troop review in the twentieth century. The soldiers spent Christmas at sea.

In mid-January, believing that war was not inevitable, a group of "peace pilgrims" traveled from Raleigh to Baghdad in an ultimately futile attempt to confer with Iraqi dictator Saddam Hussein. That month, the state's U.S. representatives split 10 to 3 along party lines in favor of debate over the president's war powers, but all voted to give President George H. W. Bush the authority to wage war.

The war began on 17 Jan. 1991 as massive air strikes targeted Iraq. Many North Carolinians demonstrated their support for the troops and displayed the flag every day. High Point University canceled an appearance by antiwar activist Daniel Berrigan, and schools throughout the state adopted service personnel as pen pals.

Ground operations began on 24 February, with the 82nd Airborne Division first over the line. On 27 February President Bush declared Kuwait liberated. By 9 March some of the 82nd's troopers were back at Fort Bragg, and by the end of May most North Carolina reserve and National Guard units

had returned home. A total of 25,000 North Carolina soldiers had participated in the Persian Gulf War. Among the war's 306 American casualties were 12 North Carolinians. A parade in Raleigh on 29 June 1991 officially commemorated the end of the war.

Alexander R. Stoesen

Personal Names. While naming traditions vary widely in history and among North Carolina's diverse cultural and ethnic groups, personal names in families are often used for many generations. Out of the 393,000 people in the state by 1790, only 71 people among the heads of families had more than a single given or Christian name. A large majority of the people had biblical names. Such names as Aaron, Abraham, Benjamin, Daniel, David, Emmanuel, Isaac, Jacob, James, Jeremiah, John, Joseph, Lazarus, Luke, Mark, Moses, Peter, Reuben, Shadrack, Solomon, Stephen, Thomas, Timothy, and numerous others appear over and over in the census lists. Christian also was a popular name for males. Biblical names were equally as common for women. Mary and Elizabeth probably were the most popular, but Anne, Esther, Martha, Rachel, Ruth, Sarah, Susanna, and others appeared frequently. Eliza, Jane, Jenny, Leanah, Lucy, Margaret, Patty, and other nonbiblical names are also found in the historical record. Perhaps the popularity of Patience and Prudence as given names suggests the hopes of parents that the traits they denoted might mark their daughters.

On the other hand, records reveal some unusual names that later generations were likely to avoid even though they had belonged to ancestors. Some interesting examples of eighteenth-century North Carolina names are Onisephorus Dameron, Melchazedick Nordan, Indignation Flowers (Bladen County), Sorrowful Hendrixson (Carteret County), Anthorite Martin (Caswell County), Karonhappuck Moore (Perquimans County), Lamentation Oneal (Edgecombe County), Leannerday Canneday (Wake County), and Sarcenet Roach (Wayne County). It was not his given name, Richard, that may have caused a lad of Granville County some concern, but his surname—Ornerry. On the other hand, Noble Ladd of Stokes County may have taken pride in his interesting combination of names, while Over Jordan of Northampton County undoubtedly had a different reaction to his, as perhaps also did Justin Corn of Wake County.

In the absence of a middle name, it was sometimes necessary to devise a means for distinguishing between people of the same name. In Moore County there were two men named John Overton. After his name, one of them added "(Bigg)" while the other wrote "(Little)." In Burke County the two Dennis Tramels faced the same dilemma; one called himself Big Dennis Tramel and the other was known as Little Dennis Tramel. They wrote their names as if Big and Little were their first names.

William S. Powell

Person County, located in the Piedmont region of northern North Carolina, was formed in 1791 from Caswell County and named for Revolutionary War general Thomas Person. It is partially bordered by the state of Virginia. Early inhabitants of the area included the Occaneechi Indians, followed by English and German settlers. The county seat, Roxboro, was incorporated in 1855 and named for the town of Roxburgh, Scotland. Person County's other communities include Hurdle Mills, Gordonton, Bushy Fork, Brooksdale, Moriah, Bethel Hill, and Concord. Notable physical features of the county include Hyco Lake, constructed by Carolina Power & Light Company in the early 1960s as a cooling reservoir for a steam electric-generating plant, Flat River, Castle Creek, and the Tar River.

Person County historic sites include Webb House, built in the early 1800s, and Hall House, built ca. 1900 and considered the oldest brick house in Roxboro. Cultural institutions include the Roxboro Little Theatre, the Person County Museum of History, the Person Players, Timberlake Art Gallery, and the Person County Nature Society. Person County hosts several annual events and festivals, including the Person County Agricultural Fair, the Person-ality Festival, and Pops in Person.

Agricultural crops grown in Person County include tobacco, wheat, corn, and soybeans. Manufactured products include parachutes, aluminum siding, textiles, and auto parts. Minerals such as pyrite, limonite, kyanite, malachite, and azurite are mined in the county. In 2004 Person County's population was estimated to be 37,000.

Reference: Stuart T. Wright, *Historical Sketch of Person County* (1974).

Jay Mazzocchi

Pfeiffer University is a comprehensive, United Methodist–related university located on 330 wooded acres at Misenheimer in Stanly County. It was founded as Oberlin Home and School near Lenoir in 1885 by Emily Prudden, a Congregationalist from New England and a pioneer in education. Prudden originated at least 15 home schools in the Carolinas from 1885 to 1909, setting up each institution and deeding its care to a church mission.

The Oberlin Home and School began at Lick Mountain, near Hudson in Caldwell County. The Women's Home Missionary Society of the Methodist Episcopal Church assumed responsibility for it in 1903. The school has had several other names and was moved to its present location in 1910. In 1935 it was renamed Pfeiffer Junior College for benefactors Henry and Annie Merner Pfeiffer of New York, who provided funds to construct four brick buildings and the president's house in 1935; additional philanthropy by Henry Pfeiffer's brother in 1954 allowed the school to become a senior college, renamed Pfeiffer College. In 1958 a black student registered as a transfer at Pfeiffer, becoming what is believed to be the first African American in the state to matriculate at a private four-year college.

Pfeiffer College became affiliated with the Western North Carolina Conference of the United Methodist Church in 1961. The Woman's Division of the General Board of Global Ministries and the United Methodist Women of the conference pledged annual amounts of $35,000 and $428,000, respectively, for the following decade. The college opened a campus in Charlotte in 1977 and began offering graduate programs in 1985. In 1996, to better reflect the school's growing graduate programs and national and international student body, the trustees voted to reorganize its structure to university status, renaming the school Pfeiffer University. The university has experienced growing enrollment through all of its programs, with approximately 1,000 full- or part-time students on the main campus at Misenheimer in 2006.

References: G. W. Bumgarner and James Elwood Carroll, *The Flowering of Methodism in Western North Carolina* (1984); Roger W. Ireson, *Handbook of United Methodist–Related Schools, Colleges, Universities, and Theological Schools* (1992); William S. Powell, *Higher Education in North Carolina* (1970).

Grady L. E. Carroll Sr.

Photography. SEE Visual Arts.

Pianos were ubiquitous in North Carolina homes, churches, and schools from the late eighteenth century to the middle of the twentieth century. By the late 1700s, pianos were imported to America by affluent families, including those living in North Carolina's coastal towns and on the large plantations of the eastern plain.

Antebellum North Carolina families could purchase a piano for between $200 and $300. Many homes had at least one instrument, and music became a focus of life, especially under the influence of German immigrants and the Moravians of Old Salem. In the antebellum period, piano playing was considered an important skill for women to learn, as it bestowed grace on the household. The piano was not associated with the fine arts during the period of its greatest popularity but was the centerpiece of home entertainment.

Through most of the nineteenth century, students learned piano playing mostly through private instructors. At least one institution offered piano instruction as early as 1800, after Moravian families requested it for their daughters enrolled in the girls' school at Salem. Raleigh's Peace College employed a German piano instructor in the 1880s, and the State Normal and Industrial School in Greensboro (later the University of North Carolina at Greensboro) offered lessons in piano playing and the playing of other stringed instruments in 1899 in order to train musicians for schools, churches, and other community groups. In 1920 State Normal was likely the first college in the South to offer a major in public school music. That year the college started the Annual High School Music Contest, further boosting interest in the piano. The contest featured 13 elite high school piano students from around the state. As an outgrowth of this contest, the North Carolina Music Teachers Association organized in 1959 at the Woman's College of the University of North Carolina (formerly State Normal). Since 1961 this organization has continued sponsoring student auditions and workshops for piano teachers.

While the earliest pianos in North Carolina were imported from Europe, by the early nineteenth century pianos were being manufactured in North Carolina and other states. Beginning in 1958, Sam Westbrook produced pianos in Marion until he sold his business in the 1970s. That manufacturing operation continued until 1982 under the name Currier. Kohler & Campbell, a New York company founded in 1896, manufactured pianos in Granite Falls, N.C., from 1954 to 1985, selling them under the names Kohler and Brambach. The Marantz Piano Company of Morganton built pianos under the names Marantz, Grand, Kincaid, and Jesse French until 1984.

North Carolina's involvement with the piano is reflected in many of its major music festivals, which feature a number of piano events. Since 1936 the Brevard Music Center and festival, held from late June to mid-August, hosts as many as 70,000 people a season. The Eastern Music Festival, resident for six weeks each summer at Guilford College in Greensboro, began in 1962 as a music camp. Over four decades it has built a reputation that draws students and faculty from most of the 50 states and a dozen foreign countries.

References: Alfred Dolge, *Pianos and Their Makers* (1972); Arthur Loesser, *Men, Women, and Pianos* (1954).

Virginia Gunn Fick

Picket, USS. The USS *Picket* was a small Union gunboat that fought during the Civil War in the sounds and rivers of North Carolina until September 1862, when it was sunk in the Tar River at Washington, N.C. The Union had purchased this civilian vessel for use in an expedition along the coast of North Carolina led by Maj. Gen. Ambrose E. Burnside. The exact origin of the *Picket* was obscured by the existence of a larger, side-wheel steamer of the same name that also served during the war. The two vessels are sometimes confused in existing records.

The smaller *Picket* was one of seven armed propellers accompanying the Burnside expedition when it sailed for North Carolina in January 1862. The ships were collected in haste and formed a motley fleet that inspired skepticism among Burnside's officers and men as to their seaworthiness. Therefore, to demonstrate his own confidence in the vessels, Burnside chose the *Picket* (the smallest ship in the fleet) as his flagship for the voyage. After the Burnside expedition began operations in North Carolina waters, the *Picket*, with its shallow draft, proved to be particularly valuable for covering the landing of Union troops at Roanoke Island, New Bern, and Fort Macon.

On the morning of 6 Sept. 1862, as the *Picket* lay with the navy gunboat *Louisiana* in the Tar River at Washington, N.C., a Confederate force made a surprise attack on the town. Both gunboats went into action to shell the advancing Confederates, but the *Picket* was able to fire only one gun before it exploded and sank in the river, killing its captain, Sylvester D. Nicoll, along with 18 crewmen and leaving 6 others wounded.

References: John S. Carbone, *The Civil War in Coastal North Carolina* (2001); Robert U. Johnson and Clarence C. Buel, eds., *Battles and Leaders of the Civil War*, vol. 1 (1887–88).

Paul Branch

Piedmont. SEE Geography.

Piedmont Airlines. SEE Aviation.

Piedmont Urban Crescent is a semicircular band of cities and towns extending from Raleigh to Charlotte, including Durham, Burlington, Greensboro, Winston-Salem, High Point, Salisbury, and many smaller communities. It owes its origin in large part to the North Carolina Railroad (NCRR), which was built in the 1850s. Of the cities named, only Winston-Salem does not lie immediately on the line of the NCRR. Although the railroad was deliberately routed to join the existing towns of Raleigh, Hillsborough, Greensboro, Salisbury, and Charlotte, they were at the time little more than villages and were widely separated. Within a generation they grew in size as the new towns of Durham, Burlington, High Point, Thomasville, and others were called into existence by the railroad. The Urban Crescent was clearly apparent by 1910.

With advancing technology, the cities attracted newer forms of transportation, following essentially the same route and contributing further to urban growth. U.S. 70 follows the Urban Crescent from Raleigh to Salisbury, and Interstate 85 runs from Durham to Charlotte. The three airports at Raleigh/Durham, Greensboro/Winston-Salem/High Point, and Charlotte are by far the largest in the state.

The NCRR penetrated the post–Civil War tobacco and cotton belts and the Piedmont hardwood forest; consequently, the towns that grew up alongside it were well placed to develop the state's three major manufacturing industries of the late nineteenth century and afterward: tobacco, textiles, and furniture. The Urban Crescent became the most urbanized and industrialized region of the state. In 1980 its 10 counties from Wake (Raleigh) to Mecklenburg (Charlotte) contained 32 percent of the state's population on just 10 percent of its land. In 1955 these counties employed about 45 percent of the state's industrial workers and accounted for over half of the value added by manufacturing; about 37 percent of the state's retail sales volume and 60 percent of its wholesale trade were centered there.

Further, the state's most influential newspapers and television stations are located in the Urban Crescent, as are the leading institutions of higher education and the high technology industries that depend on them. The Research Triangle lies near its eastern end, between Raleigh, Durham, and Chapel Hill. The proportion of college graduates (and high school graduates) in the Urban Crescent far exceeds that in the state at large. The region has also enjoyed comparably greater economic growth and higher per capita incomes.

Population growth, in large part due to in-migration— though recently out-migration has increased around the state —demonstrates a strong urban shift. In the early 2000s, nearly 83 percent of the state's net growth occurred in the larger urban areas, known as Metropolitan Statistical Areas (MSAS). The Raleigh-Cary MSA grew by 14.8 percent, the Wilmington MSA by 10.4 percent, and the Charlotte-Gastonia-Concord MSA by 11 percent between 2000 and 2004. By 2004 the so-called Combined Areas of Charlotte-Gastonia-Salisbury and Raleigh-Durham-Cary held almost 38 percent of the state's population, accounting for nearly 62 percent of North Carolina's net gain in this period.

As they grow larger, North Carolina's cities are also growing together. Raleigh, Durham, and Chapel Hill are coalescing around the Research Triangle; Greensboro and High Point now touch and are approaching closer to the expanding city limits of Burlington and Winston-Salem. Taken as a whole, the Piedmont Urban Crescent represents a miniature version of the megalopolis of the Northeast.

References: Ole Gade and H. Daniel Stillwell, *North Carolina: People and Environments* (1986); Paul Luebke, *Tar Heel Politics: Myths and Realities* (1990); Coy T. Phillips, "North Carolina's Rich Crescent," *Journal of Geography* 54 (April 1955); Allen W. Trelease, *The North Carolina Railroad, 1849–1871, and the Modernization of North Carolina* (1991).

Allen W. Trelease

Piedmont Wagon Company was founded in 1878 outside of Hickory by George G. Bonniwell, a mechanical engineer, architect, and builder, and A. L. (Andy) Ramseur, operator of a gristmill, an iron forge, and a sawmill. They formed a partnership and began small-scale construction of wagons, becoming one of the area's first industrial enterprises. Two years later the firm moved to the western part of Hickory for access to a railroad and to obtain additional capital. By 1890 it had an investment of more than $100,000 in land, machinery, and raw materials, and demand for its wagons was so great that the company inaugurated a night shift (probably Hickory's first).

Under the direction of G. Harvey Geitner, plant superintendent from 1887 to 1918, Piedmont's primary market was extended throughout the southern states from Virginia to Texas and eventually to Great Britain. By World War I the company received a contract for all-metal carts for the French army. It was said that Piedmont rivaled the work of leading wagon companies in St. Louis, the center for the industry.

Following a series of ownership changes, Piedmont Wagon Company became involved in a tax controversy and subsequent lawsuit stemming from its failure to pay income taxes from 1917 to 1919. The firm was sold to Henry Leonard in the 1940s, the era that production ground to a halt. The tax problems did not end, and a series of tax liens were placed on the property beginning in 1948. The Hickory Development Corporation bought it, intending new industrial and business sites. In August 1960 the site, which a local paper called a "rat-infested jungle," was bulldozed. Overshadowed perhaps by the tax problems was the fact that Piedmont Wagon Company was a victim of its owners' apparent failure to foresee the automobile's impact on horse-drawn wagons and carriages.

References: Gary R. Freeze, *The Catawbans: Crafters of a North Carolina County, 1747–1900* (1995); Lucille M. Fulbright, ed., *Heritage of Catawba County* (1986).

Wiley J. Williams

Pig Pickin'. SEE Barbecue.

Pilot Mountain, located in southeastern Surry County, is one of North Carolina's most recognizable geologic features. Rising more than 1,400 feet above the surrounding landscape, it consists of Big Pinnacle, a white quartzite monadnock with sheer rock walls and a rounded, vegetation-covered top, and Little Pinnacle, a lower section that is comprised of metamorphic rock not usually found in the region. Geologists believe that the 200-foot-high Big Pinnacle was formed by the compression of sand from a beach that existed in western North Carolina approximately 1 billion years ago. The sand was first compressed into sandstone and later became quartzite through heat and pressure. The metamorphic rock of the mountain's base is believed to have developed from a deep marine environment.

The mountain's unmistakable shape, visible from great distances, has been a guidepost for travelers for centuries. The Saponi and Tutelo Indians who lived in the area called the peak *Jomeokee*, the "great guide" or "pilot." The Great Wagon Road, which brought settlers into the Piedmont from

Pilot Mountain. Photograph courtesy of North Carolina Division of Tourism, Film, and Sports Development.

the Northeast, skirted the base of Pilot Mountain. Catching a glimpse of the solitary mountain was a boost to the spirit of the people who were embarking on new lives in the Carolinas. An entry in the diaries of Moravian settlers in 1753, 37 days into their journey from Pennsylvania, suggests the joy that settlers found in spotting the peak: we "saw the Pilot Mountain, and rejoiced to think that we would soon see the boundary of Carolina, and set foot in our own dear land." In 1968, primarily through the efforts of local citizens, Pilot Mountain became North Carolina's fourteenth state park.

References: Adelaide L. Fries, Stuart Thurman Wright, and J. Edwin Hendricks, *Forsyth: The History of a County on the March* (1976); J. Wright Horton Jr. and Victor A. Zullo, eds., *The Geology of the Carolinas: Carolina Geological Society Fiftieth Anniversary Volume* (1991).

Ken Otterbourg

Pine Bark Beetles. Three species of pine bark beetles—ips beetles, black turpentine beetles, and southern pine beetles—destroy significant numbers of North Carolina's extensive pine tree population each year. Of these pests, the southern pine beetle, characterized by a short, dark reddish brown winged body, is the most serious threat to North Carolina pines. These beetles breed in all species of yellow, white, red, and spruce pines, preferring shortleaf, loblolly, Virginia, and pitch pines. Southern pine beetles will attack healthy trees and can kill several hundred acres during a single outbreak. Affected trees are characterized by browned tree crowns and S-shaped galleries under the bark. Southern pine beetle infestation usually kills trees by attracting a blue stain fungus that weakens the connective tissue of the tree and renders it useless for timber. Each year, southern pine beetles destroy North Carolina timber worth hundreds of millions of dollars; good forestry management practices are the best defense against all three varieties, as weak or damaged trees are always attractive hosts.

References: James A. Beal and Calvin L. Massey, *Bark Beetles and Ambrosia Beetles (Coleoptera: Scolytoidea): With Special Reference to Species Occurring in North Carolina* (1945); Eric Day, "Bark Beetles," Virginia Cooperative Extension Publication No. 444-216 (1996).

Lisa D. Smith

Pine Needle Art is an outgrowth of an ancient material culture tradition in North Carolina. For several millennia, the Native Americans living in the region that became North Carolina fashioned utilitarian and decorative objects from the trees and plants surrounding them. The abundance of pine trees in the region led to the use of pine needles to make baskets and other objects. Pine needle objects made with coiled techniques have European, African, and Native American origins.

Pine needle art uses the leaf of the pine tree. After boiling, drying, and removing the caps from the pine needles, the artist bundles together the needles. Coiling them in tight spirals, the artist builds each new row upon the preceding one, and binds the rows together with strong raffia, nylon, or rayon threads. The artist often adds a coating of shellac or clear acrylic to protect the finished object.

Pine needle art includes a variety of utilitarian and decorative forms and functions. These include trays, baskets, bowls, coasters, mats, and wall hangings.

References: Judy Mofield Mallow, *Pine Needle and Nut Crafting*, vol. 1 (1984); Linda L. Millikin, *Pine Needle Baskets* (1920); Veronica T. Walsh, *The Book of Pine Needle Craft* (1977).

Dennis W. Cross

Pine Trees were virtually the trademark of North Carolina and the Southeast in the colonial period and remain a significant feature and symbol of the state. One or more species, including the loblolly, the longleaf, the eastern white, the Virginia, and the table mountain pine, still grows naturally in each of the state's 100 counties. Conifers, or evergreens, pine trees perpetually contribute to the state's pleasant natural atmosphere, except perhaps during the spring season when clouds of pine pollen fill the air and cover the countryside with a layer of yellow powder. Pine trees have for centuries supplied many important wood products; from the early colonial years until well into the eighteenth century, the longleaf pine was a primary source of naval stores—tar, pitch, and turpentine—which were essential in the construction and maintenance of sailing ships and also gave rise to the state's "Tar Heel" nickname.

Pine forests, or "barrens," were mentioned in nearly all diaries and travel accounts of those who passed through the region during the colonial period. In September 1752 Bishop August Gottlieb Spangenberg, scouting for a place for a Moravian settlement, wrote in his diary: "In Chowan and Bertie Counties one can ride for three hours without seeing anything except Pine Barrens, that is white sand grown up in pine trees." In 1791 George Washington described a similar pine-dominated landscape as he traveled south through the state along the "King's Highway," an ancient colonial route (now largely U.S. 17).

Also known by names such as longstraw and pitch, the longleaf pine formed an ecosystem that once may have covered 90 million acres in the Southeast, though fewer than 3 million acres remain in the region. There are currently many efforts to restore the endangered longleaf ecosystem, including projects and programs of the U.S. Fish and Wildlife Service. In addition, the Longleaf Alliance, located at Auburn University's Solon Dixon Forestry Education Center in southern Alabama, was formed in 1995 to coordinate the efforts of various conservation groups and agencies seeking to reestablish the longleaf and some of the habitat it provided.

In 1963 the North Carolina General Assembly designated the pine as the official state tree. Though enthusiasts debate whether the assembly meant the loblolly or the longleaf pine, the latter is generally assumed to have been intended because of its appearance in North Carolina art and poetry as well as its mention in the first line of the state toast: "Here's to the Land of the Long Leaf Pine."

References: Linda C. Askey, "Kissed by Fire," *Southern Living* (November 1999); H. J. Green, *Common Forest Trees of North Carolina* (1983); James W. Patton, "Glimpses of North Carolina in the Writings of Foreign Travelers, 1783–1860," *NCHR* 45 (1968).

William S. Powell

Pirates who frequented coastal North Carolina during the early colonial period were involved in enough nefarious activities to emerge as the subjects of at least a dozen books and numerous articles and short stories. Yet the bulk of this history centers around two men, Edward Teach and Stede Bonnet, both of whom appeared off the Carolina coast in 1717 and departed before the end of the following year, one beheaded and the other hanged.

Teach, better known as Blackbeard, was the very personification of a pirate, a man of frightening appearance and brutal action who had terrorized the citizenry of Charles Towne (Charleston, S.C.) and coastal South Carolina before moving his freebooting activities to the sounds and rivers of North Carolina. Bonnet, who sometimes employed the surname Thomas, was just the opposite. He was described as the master of a plentiful fortune, the possessor of a liberal education, and a gentleman of good reputation in the island of Barbados; reportedly, he turned to piracy because he could not get along with his wife. His may be the only case on record of a man using his own money to buy and outfit a vessel for the specific purpose of pursuing piracy.

There were other differences between the two thieves. Whereas Blackbeard was a man of considerable maritime experience, Bonnet had a military rather than a naval background. And while Blackbeard began his career as a pirate under a captain experienced in privateering and piracy, Bonnet simply set sail with a crew he recruited on the docks at Barbados.

For a brief period in early 1718 the two pirates joined forces off the Carolina coast, but Blackbeard quickly took advantage of his new partner and they soon parted company. In time both

A nineteenth-century engraving of Edward Teach, also known as Blackbeard. NCC.

21 Nov. 1718 Maynard caught up with Blackbeard, in a small sloop named *Adventure*, near Ocracoke Inlet. In a ferocious battle the next day, all of Blackbeard's crew were either killed or captured and the pirate himself was beheaded. Ten days later, in Charles Towne, the onetime Barbados gentleman, Stede Bonnet, was hanged in the public square, thus bringing to an end what has been called the golden age of piracy in North Carolina.

Though the brief careers of Blackbeard and Bonnet dominate the history of piracy in North Carolina, they were not the only buccaneers who operated along the colony's coast. As early as the 1690s it was reported that pirates had "flocked into Carolina from every quarter." Some of them were onetime Red Sea bandits seeking a place to retire in the American colonies far from their base of operations, but they seemed to prefer the busy port of Charles Towne to the less inhabited areas of North Carolina.

The single year 1718 saw more piratical activity in Carolina than any other time in its recorded history. A number of pirates who accepted the king's offer of clemency at New Providence in the Bahamas made their way to the American mainland and resumed their freebooting ventures. Again, they concentrated on the Charles Towne area, harassing vessels entering and leaving the busy port, and leaving periodically to cruise elsewhere, including along the North Carolina coast.

Almost three centuries after his death, Blackbeard made new headlines in North Carolina and around the world. In June 1718 Blackbeard's flagship, the *Queen Anne's Revenge*, had run aground approximately one mile off the North Carolina coast and eventually sank. The site of a wreck was discovered in November 1996, and the North Carolina Division of Archives and History began underwater archaeological investigations, believing the remains to be those of the notorious pirate's ship. Recovered artifacts include a brass blunderbuss barrel and a bronze bell dated 1705. Still submerged, the shipwreck features, among other items, cannons, anchors, a grapple hook, numerous barrel hoops, navigational instruments, pewter ware, lead shot, small arms, and gold dust.

Reference: Lindley S. Butler, *Pirates, Privateers, and Rebel Raiders of the Carolina Coast* (2000).

David Stick

accepted the king's offer of clemency and were given certificates of pardon by North Carolina governor Charles Eden; they then quickly resumed their piratical activities. Bonnet headed north, capturing several prizes off the Virginia coast before returning to the Cape Fear River to repair and refit his new flagship, the *Royal James*. When word reached Charles Towne that Bonnet was back, South Carolina's governor sent out two sloops commanded by Col. William Rhett to track him down. In late September 1718 Rhett captured Bonnet and his crew near Cape Fear and returned them to Charles Towne for trial.

Meanwhile, Blackbeard had established his base of operations in the North Carolina town of Bath, where he is reputed to have taken a teenaged girl as his fourteenth wife while establishing a working relationship with Tobias Knight, the governor's secretary, and even with Governor Eden himself. Alternating between capturing cargo vessels at sea and harassing traders on the Pamlico River and nearby sounds, Blackbeard seemed to have no fear of retribution because of his close relationship with Knight and Eden. Distressed by these activities, the responsible planters of the region finally appealed to Governor Alexander Spotswood of Virginia for help in ridding the provinces of the pirate.

Spotswood responded by sending Lt. Robert Maynard in pursuit of Blackbeard with two sloops. Late in the evening of

Pisgah National Forest was the first of North Carolina's national forests. It derived its name from Buncombe County's Mount Pisgah, named in 1776 by the Reverend James Hall during Gen. Griffith Rutherford's expedition against the Cherokee. The biblical "Pisgah" was the peak from which Moses, though not allowed to enter, could view the promised land.

The genesis of the Pisgah National Forest was directly related to the forest holdings of George W. Vanderbilt, whose

Biltmore estate near Asheville was completed in the 1890s. For a time, experienced forestry experts such as Carl Alwin Schenck and Gifford Pinchot managed Vanderbilt's extensive lands, but Schenck's Biltmore Forest School, established in 1898 as the first professional forestry field school in the United States, closed in 1913. The Weeks Act was passed by Congress on 1 Mar. 1911, authorizing the federal purchase of eastern lands for conservation purposes. In 1915 the widowed Mrs. George Vanderbilt sold approximately 500,000 acres to the federal government at a nominal price. Despite the chance for vast material benefit, Vanderbilt realized that only the federal government could preserve the forest, which became the Pisgah National Forest and remains roughly the same size today.

Currently the Pisgah National Forest lies in 15 North Carolina counties. The forest is divided into three separate ranger districts according to geographic features. The Grandfather District includes Avery, Burke, Caldwell, Watauga, and McDowell Counties. The Appalachian District manages land in Haywood, Madison, Avery, Buncombe, Mitchell, and Yancey Counties. Finally, the Pisgah District covers parts of Buncombe, Haywood, Henderson, and Transylvania Counties. The total land amount in the early 2000s was over 510,000 acres.

References: Thomas Clark, *The Greening of the South: The Recovery of Land and Forest* (1984); Sharyn Kane and Richard Keaton, *Southern National Forests* (1993); Carl Alwin Schenck, *The Birth of Forestry in America: Biltmore Forest School, 1898–1913* (1955).

Michael Bonner

Pitt Academy in Greenville was first granted a charter by the North Carolina General Assembly in 1786, but there is no evidence that the school opened until 1814. That year the General Assembly granted a charter to the trustees of a school to be known as Greenville Academy. The 1814 act made no mention of any previous charter, although some historians believe that the two charters were essentially for the same school under different names. The board of trustees for the original Pitt Academy included Governor Richard Caswell and two signers of the U.S. Constitution, William Blount and Hugh Williamson. The names Robert Williams and Arthur Forbes appear as trustees of both institutions, furthering the belief that the schools were connected.

Greenville Academy was housed in a two-story frame building at Second and Greene Streets; the trustees purchased the lot on 20 Apr. 1815. In 1821 the school was reorganized and renamed Pitt Academy. In later years, it was also known as Greenville Male Academy. The academy eventually moved to a new location on Evans Street. The school closed before the end of the nineteenth century, and in 1903 the academy building was torn down to make room for a new public school.

References: Alice Barnwell Keith, ed., *The John Gray Blount Papers*, vol. 1 (1952); Henry King, *Sketches of Pitt County: A Brief History of Pitt County, 1704–1910* (1911).

David A. Norris

Pitt County, located in the Coastal Plain region of eastern North Carolina, was formed in 1760 from Beaufort County and named for William Pitt, earl of Chatham. Early inhabitants of the area included the Tuscarora Indians, followed by English and Welsh settlers. The site of Catechna, a fortified Tuscarora town and the site of a siege by Col. John "Jack" Barnwell and his troops in April 1712, is north of Grifton. Greenville, the county seat, was incorporated in 1771 as Martinsborough, named for North Carolina's last royal governor, Josiah Martin; in 1786, the name was changed to Greenville in honor of Revolutionary general Nathanael Greene. Other Pitt County communities include Ayden, Bethel, Simpson, Black Jack, Calico, and Toddy. Notable among the physical features of the county are the Tar River, Clayroot Swamp, Pinelog Branch, Grindle Creek, Pea Branch, and Lake Kristi.

East Carolina University (founded in 1907 as the East Carolina Teachers Training School), located in Greenville, has a tremendous cultural and economic influence on the county. Pitt County historic structures include several buildings on the East Carolina campus as well as the Pitt County Courthouse (1910–11). Non-university-related cultural institutions include the Greenville Museum of Art, the Nature Science Center, Ayden's Art and Recreation Center, the Dance Arts Theatre, and the Adventures in Health Children's Museum. The county hosts annual events and festivals such as Winterville Watermelon Festival, the Farmville Dogwood Festival, and the Ayden Collard Festival.

Pitt County is a producer of tobacco, soybeans, grain, peanuts, vegetables, eggs, and swine and other livestock. County manufactures include textiles, pharmaceuticals, concrete products, and furnaces. Flooding of the Tar River as a result of Hurricane Floyd in 1999 caused more than $1.5 billion in damages to Pitt County communities and businesses. In 2004 the county's estimated population was 141,500.

Jay Mazzocchi

SEE ALSO East Carolina University.

Plank Roads. SEE Roads.

Plantation Duty Act of 1673 was an act of Parliament intended to eliminate the smuggling of articles enumerated in the Navigation Act of 1660 and to induce the colonists to export those articles directly to England by allowing them to be traded to other colonies with the payment of the usual English import duty. Colonists in Albemarle County, the chief producer and exporter of tobacco—an enumerated article—

considered the Plantation Duty Act a threat to their profitable trade with the Massachusetts and Rhode Island colonies and refused to comply. The noncompliance of Albemarle County was one of the factors leading to Culpeper's Rebellion, one of the first popular uprisings in the American colonies.

References: Oscar T. Barck and Hugh T. Lefler, *Colonial America* (1965); Wesley F. Craven, *The Colonies in Transition, 1660–1713* (1968); Hugh F. Rankin, *Upheaval in Albemarle: The Story of Culpeper's Rebellion, 1675–1689* (1962).

Carmen Miner Smith

Plantation Names began to be used in the North Carolina area in the seventeenth century as a means of identifying specific tracts of land. The eight original Lords Proprietors of Carolina spoke of their large grant of land from the Atlantic Ocean to the Pacific through the middle of North America as their "Plantation of Carolina." With an increasing population as well as a growing area of settlement, individual owners of smaller tracts within the expansive Carolina grant also sometimes referred to their personal grants as plantations.

Names were adopted as means of defining places of residence. These names often provide clues to the origin or descent of a family. Sometimes they also offer clues to the political or religious attachment of the owner or some natural feature of the site, or they even offer a bit of humor. In some cases, a name became so familiar or closely associated with a place or family that it was retained for generations and became that of the local community, a post office, or a nearby town.

There was no requirement that a plantation name be registered, nor was a name necessarily considered to be permanently associated with a site—an heir or a new owner, for example, might change the name or use no name at all. Although an owner might ask the county court or other local office to record his choice in county records, such a request carried no advantage. Nevertheless, hundreds of such names were adopted, although only a fraction of these are still known. Orton, Cooleemee, and Hope are among the plantation names still in use.

J. Bryan Grimes, North Carolina secretary of state in the early twentieth century, compiled and published two volumes —*Abstract of North Carolina Wills* (1910) and *North Carolina Wills and Inventories* (1912)—that contain information that often includes the names of plantations and farms dating from the seventeenth and eighteenth centuries. His information was drawn from records then in the office of the secretary of state but more recently in the Office of Archives and History in Raleigh. Grimes's volumes contain names of 329 plantations that can be reasonably identified as well as many not fully cited in the records; plantation names also occur in works on architecture, local history, and genealogy.

A Sampling of Eighteenth-Century North Carolina Plantation Names

Name of Plantation	Family	County	Date Established
Abington	Upton	Pasquotank Precinct	1715
Alden of the Hill	Moseley	Edgecomb	1745
Batts Grave	Crisp	Chowan	1727
Beach Ridge	Poyner	Currituck	1758
Blew Water	Early	Albemarle	1732
Conahoe	Johnston	Tyrrell	1751
Forck of the Duckinstool	Thomas	Chowan	1738
Frog Hall	Chesher	Bertie Precinct	1728
Haltons Lodge	Halton	New Hanover	1748
Ludlow Castle	Bridgen	New Hanover	1757
Middle Plantation	Blount	Albemarle	1706
Mount Pleasant	Shepard	Carteret	1774
New Abbey	Low	Pasquotank	1726
Point Pleasant	Innes	New Hanover	1759
Rich Level	Turnbull	Tyrrell	1753
Rose-Field	Pollock	Chowan	1721
Sand Hills	Porter	Bath	1733
Springfield	Heritage	Craven	1769
Walnut Hill	Caswell	Dobbs	1787

William S. Powell

Playwrights. SEE Dramatic Arts.

Plessy v. Ferguson. In 1896 the U.S. Supreme Court upheld the so-called separate-but-equal segregation of whites and blacks in public facilities in its decision on *Plessy v. Ferguson.* Homer Plessy, a Louisianian who was seven-eighths Caucasian, bought a first-class ticket and sat in the "whites only" car of a train leaving New Orleans. When asked to move, he refused, and he was subsequently arrested. The Court ruled that "laws permitting, and even requiring [the two races'] separation in places where they are liable to be brought into contact do not necessarily imply the inferiority of either race to the other." Enforced separation of the races—what Justice John Marshall Harlan called "the thin disguise of equal accommodations" in his dissent in *Plessy*—remained the law of the land until several decisions on segregation in public accommodations by the Court in the 1950s. In *Brown v. Board of Education of Topeka, Kansas* (1954), the Supreme Court specifically overruled *Plessy.*

Two North Carolinians stood as steadfast opponents of the separate-but-equal doctrine at its outset. Both Judge Albion W. Tourgée, a state superior court judge during Reconstruction and an equal rights advocate, and Samuel Field Phillips, a leading North Carolina lawyer and former solicitor general of the United States, acted as counsel for the plaintiffs in *Plessy* and argued the case orally before the Supreme Court.

The virulent white supremacy campaigns at the beginning of the twentieth century brought to power public officials ready and willing to pass laws, statutes, and ordinances requiring separate—and often patently inferior—public facilities. For more than half a century, North Carolina blacks, living under Jim Crow laws, were physically segregated from whites, denied the right to vote, and severely limited economically.

References: Jeffrey J. Crow, Paul D. Escott, and Flora J. Hatley, *A History of African Americans in North Carolina* (2002); Otto H. Olsen, ed., *The Thin Disguise: Turning Point in Negro History; Plessy v. Ferguson: A Documentary Presentation, 1864–1896* (1967); Joel Williamson, *The Crucible of Race* (1984).

Lynn Roundtree

Plott Hound became the state dog by legislative decree on 12 Aug. 1989. It is the only dog breed that is officially recognized as having originated in North Carolina and one of only four breeds that began in the United States. Ancestors of the modern Plott hound were among the dogs brought to America by Johannes Plott, a German gamekeeper, when he immigrated to Cabarrus County in 1750. The Plott family and other Germans used these European cur dogs with traces of mastiff to protect their employers' shooting preserves from large predators such as bear, boar, and wolves. The Plotts continued to develop the breed through careful culling and rare but productive outcrossing to hound stock such as the black-and-tan coonhound. In 1800 Johannes's son John moved the family to a large tract in Haywood County near Waynesville, where an abundant population of bear and (after 1908) imported European boar kept the dogs in high demand, as they have remained.

The Plott hound is a medium-to-large dog, averaging 50 to 60 pounds, of somewhat stockier build and with shorter ears than typical hound breeds. Its head tends to be more massive and its jaws more imposing, and, although it trails as well as the best of hounds, its voice tends to be less melodious. It is a powerful and tenacious fighter, held in high esteem wherever large game is hunted with dogs, such as in the mountains of North Carolina and Tennessee. Most specimens of Plott hounds are of a dark brindle color, but black and buckskin color phases are not uncommon.

Reference: Curtis Wooten, "Johannes Plott's Famous Hunting Dogs," in Jim Dean and Lawrence S. Earley, eds., *Wildlife in North Carolina* (1987).

Jerry Leath Mills

Plymouth, Battle of. The Battle of Plymouth, the most effective Confederate combined-arms operation of the Civil War, was waged in April 1864. Two years earlier, in May 1862, Union forces had occupied Plymouth, near the mouth of the Roanoke River. From their bases in Plymouth, Washington, N.C., and New Bern, the Federals conducted frequent raids in eastern North Carolina. Meanwhile, by the spring of 1862, two Confederate ironclads under construction at Edward's Ferry on the Roanoke River and at Kinston on the Neuse River were nearing completion. The assistance of these vessels, the *Albemarle* and the *Neuse*, was essential to the success of any attempt to recapture the coastal towns. Brig. Gen. Robert F. Hoke, acting with Cdr. James Cooke of the *Albemarle*, concentrated first on Plymouth.

By late afternoon on 17 Apr. 1864, three brigades of infantry—about 10,000 troops—commanded by Hoke was within five miles of Plymouth. Defending the town was a Union garrison of 2,834 men. Although badly outnumbered, the Federals had strongly fortified the post and repulsed the first Confederate attacks. But the next day, 18 April, saw heavy shelling, with Union vessels in the river sunk or damaged and forced to retreat to Plymouth. Meanwhile, U.S. Navy gunboats provided artillery support against the Confederates, but their success was short-lived.

During the night the *Albemarle*, taking advantage of an abnormally high river level, safely passed over the obstructions and slipped undamaged past Fort Gray, west of Plymouth. In the predawn hours of 19 April, Cooke's ship encountered the USS *Southfield* and USS *Miami*, the most powerful Union vessels on the Roanoke. The *Albemarle* promptly sank the first and heavily damaged the second, forcing the *Miami* and two other gunboats to retreat. Late that afternoon, Hoke launched a double envelopment attack against both the east and west sides of the town. The *Albemarle*, having returned to Plymouth, furnished supporting fire on the east side of town.

On 20 April Hoke renewed the attack on each flank, capturing forts from both directions. But the Union commander, Brig. Gen. Henry Wessels, refused to surrender and gathered the remainder of his forces inside Fort Williams, the Federals' last remaining stronghold, near the center of Plymouth. Hoke unleashed his artillery on the bastion, and the *Albemarle* added its two large rifled cannons to the bombardment. Heavily shelled from all sides, Wessels unconditionally surrendered his entire command. In addition to the Union garrison, Hoke captured 25 artillery pieces, at a cost of only 50 Confederates killed and wounded. His victory provided a badly needed morale boost for the Confederacy.

Following the fall of Plymouth, Federal forces abandoned Washington, N.C., as well. The Confederates held the town until the *Albemarle* was sunk by Union raiders in late October 1864. With the ironclad gone, the southern troops abandoned Plymouth, which remained in Federal hands for the duration of the war.

References: John G. Barrett, *The Civil War in North Carolina* (1963); Hardy Z. Brogue, "Confederate Victory at Plymouth," *Confederate Veteran* (November–December 1991).

Dan Blair

Pocosins are naturally occurring freshwater evergreen shrub bogs or wetlands of the southeastern coastal plains. In 1962 pocosins still covered nearly 2.25 million acres in North Carolina—accounting for almost three-quarters of the pocosin ecosystems in the United States—but by 1979 forestry and farming operations had totally or partially altered all but about 700,000 of these acres. In 1985 the Environmental Protection Agency described North Carolina's pocosins as one of the most critically endangered of the nation's many wetland types.

The word "pocosin" is Algonquian in origin and is variously spelled "poquosin," "pequessen," "poccoson," and "percoarson." The generally accepted meaning of the word is "swamp on a hill." John Lawson made a number of references to pocosins in his book, *A New Voyage to Carolina* (1709), but ecologists, differentiating these often impenetrable formations from river bottomlands, wooded swamps, and marshes, have labored well into the twentieth century to arrive at a good, general definition. Pocosins have been described as "occurring in broad, shallow basins, in drainage basin heads, and on broad, flat uplands" and having "soils of sandy humus, muck or peat."

Some of the state's better-known pocosin areas include many of the Carolina Bays; the Green Swamp; Holly Shelter Swamp and Angola Bay; the Croatan National Forest; the Open Ground in Carteret County; the Alligator River National Wildlife Refuge; and, as of 1990, the Pocosin Lakes National Wildlife Refuge in Tyrrell and Washington Counties, said to feature some of the best remaining large pocosins in eastern North Carolina.

References: Jack Temple Kirby, *Poquosin: A Study of Rural Landscape and Society* (1995); Douglas Neil Rader, *Carolina Wetlands: Our Vanishing Resource* (1989); Curtis J. Richardson, ed., *Pocosin Wetlands: An Integrated Analysis of Coastal Plain Freshwater Bogs in North Carolina* (1981); Vic Venters, "A Look at Our Newest Refuge," *Wildlife in North Carolina* 55 (August 1991).

Bland Simpson

Poet Laureate. On 11 May 1935 the General Assembly of North Carolina passed a resolution empowering the governor to appoint a poet laureate for the state. The position remained empty until 1948, when outgoing governor Gregg Cherry chose Arthur Talmadge Abernethy (1872–1956) to serve as poet laureate of North Carolina. Cherry's choice was never publicly announced, but in 1949 Governor William Kerr Scott reappointed Abernethy to the position. Abernethy, son of the founder of Rutherford College, was educated at Rutherford and completed graduate work at Trinity College (now Duke University) and Johns Hopkins University in Baltimore. He was a noted classical scholar who began teaching Latin at Rutherford at age 17. During his lifetime, Abernethy wrote for several newspapers and published numerous works of theology. Since his literary reputation was based more on his journalism and theological writing than on his poetry, Abernethy's appointment was somewhat controversial.

Wilkes County poet James Larkin Pearson (1879–1981) was appointed to take over the post of poet laureate in 1953. Pearson was a nationally respected poet and rumored favorite of Upton Sinclair. In sharp contrast with Abernethy's intellectual upbringing, Pearson was born in a log cabin and claimed to have only 12 months of formal schooling. After working in the newspaper business for a while, Pearson opened a printing press in the basement of his farmhouse. From this location, he published several volumes of his own poetry and two original periodicals, *The Fool Killer* and *The Literary South*. Pearson balanced literature with agriculture and even claimed to have composed most of his early poems while plowing his family's fields. Pearson held the office of poet laureate until his death at age 102.

After Pearson's death in 1981, journalist and poet Sam Ragan was appointed to fill the post of North Carolina poet laureate. Ragan, an award-winning poet, was also a veteran of 50 years of newspaper work and a well-known patron of the arts. In 1965 Ragan was chosen to direct the North Carolina Arts Council, and in 1972 he helped establish the State Department of Cultural Resources. Ragan was also among the founders of the North Carolina School of the Arts (1963). Ragan's 1996 death left the office of poet laureate unfilled. In December 1997, Governor James B. Hunt appointed Fred Chappell North Carolina's poet laureate. Born in Canton and a graduate of Duke University, Chappell has written numerous books of verse, stories, and criticism as well as several novels. One of his first duties as poet laureate was to write and read a poem in August 1998, when President Bill Clinton visited the state to designate the New River as an American Heritage River. On 24 Feb. 2005 Kathryn Stripling Byer of Cullowhee was appointed by Governor Michael Easley to succeed Chappell as poet laureate of North Carolina.

Lillian Craton

Poetry. Although their acclaim has varied and their notability fluctuated, North Carolina poets have always been active, and the poetic drive has always been present in the state. Like its prose counterpart, creative verse underwent a veritable renaissance in the late twentieth and early twenty-first centuries. The days of luminaries such as Carl Sandburg, where only a single name was worthy of notoriety or critique, are gone, replaced by a widespread and successful group of poets working in many different social and academic settings.

North Carolina Poets of the Nineteenth and Twentieth Centuries

George Moses Horton (ca. 1797–1883) was probably North Carolina's first professional poet. Born into slavery in Chatham County, Horton taught himself to read using an old speller and a Methodist hymnal. His master, James Horton, often sent him to Chapel Hill to sell produce, where his advanced vocabulary impressed university students. He began to sell poems for students to send to their sweethearts and published a collection, *The Hope of Liberty* (1829), the first book published in the South by a black man. His other books include *Poetical Works of George M. Horton* (1845) and *Naked Genius* (1865). Today Horton's elegant, structured verse stands out not only as the state's prime poetic expression of the nineteenth century but also as one of the most memorable literary testaments to the muted anger and intense yearning of African Americans in the South before the Civil War.

The late nineteenth through early twentieth centuries saw a number of poets make somewhat minor marks on the literary history of the state. Among the contributors were Windsor's William Henry Rhodes (1822–76), whose work includes *Caxton's Book: A Collection of Essays, Poems, Tales and Sketches* (1876) and *The Indian Gallow and Other Poems* (1946). Benjamin F. Sledd (1864–1940), who was born in Bedford County, Va., but later taught at Wake Forest University, was the author of *From Cliff and Scaur: A Collection of Verse* (1897), *Watchers of the Hearth* (1902), and *A Young Man's Visions; an Old Man's Dreams: A Collection of Poems* (1957).

Native Kentuckian Olive Tilford Dargan (1869–1968) fell in love with North Carolina on a college camping trip and later had homes on the Nantahala River in Swain County and in Asheville. Widely considered one of the best writers from the southern Appalachians, her books of verse include *Lute and Furrow* (1922), *Pathflower and Other Verses* (1914), and *The Spotted Hawk* (1958). John Charles McNeill (1874–1907) had a brief life but secured for himself an impressive reputation. As a student, he contributed poems to and edited the literary journal at Wake Forest University while taking law courses. He practiced law while continuing to write poetry until 1904, when *Charlotte Observer* editor Joseph P. Caldwell hired him to write "whenever and whatever he pleases." His well-known columns included anecdotes, fables, reports on fires and funerals, book reviews, and special events in North Carolina and South Carolina. McNeill's books include *Songs, Merry and Sad* (1906) and various volumes of collected works. Arthur Talmadge Abernethy (1872–1956) of Rutherford College also chose to publish his poems via newspaper submissions—tallying hundreds in his lifetime. For his accomplishments, Gover-

nor Robert Cherry named Abernethy the first poet laureate of North Carolina in 1948.

Born in Galesburg, Ill., Carl Sandburg (1876–1967) moved to a Flat Rock, N.C., farm in 1945 searching for peace and quiet. Though already an acclaimed writer, Sandburg published more than one-third of his works during his time in North Carolina. His books of verse include *Complete Poems* (1950), *Harvest Poems, 1910–1960* (1960), *Wind Song* (1960), *Plowed Ground: Humorous and Dialect Poems* (1969), and *Early Harvest: The First Experimental Poems of a Self-Taught Farm Boy* (1953).

Helen Smith Bevington (1906–2001) was born and raised in New York but moved to Durham when her husband accepted a teaching position at Duke University. Bevington attributed her interest in writing to "the particular pleasure of living in North Carolina" and was best known for her light, witty verse, a torch later taken up by fellow North Carolinians A. R. Ammons and Jonathan Williams. Books by Bevington include *Dr. Johnson's Waterfall* (1946), *Nineteen Million Elephants* (1950), *A Change of Sky* (1956), and *When Found, Make a Verse of* (1961).

Randall Jarrell (1914–65) attended Vanderbilt University and studied under southern literary magnate Robert Penn Warren. After graduation he eventually settled in Greensboro to teach at Woman's College (which later became the University of North Carolina at Greensboro). Jarrell was a tireless author and erudite literary commentator, tallying nine books of poetry, four books of literary criticism, four children's books, five anthologies, a best-selling academic novel, a translation of Goethe's *Faust, Part I*, and a translation of Chekhov's *The Three Sisters*, produced on Broadway. Jarrell served as the consultant in poetry to the Library of Congress from 1956 to 1958. His most notable collections of verse include *The Woman at the Washington Zoo* (1960) and *Randall Jarrell: The Complete Poems* (1969).

While Jarrell's work commanded a sizable audience, other poets worked through the decades of the mid-twentieth century to less public acclaim. Charles Edward Eaton (1916–) was born in Winston-Salem and graduated from the University of North Carolina in Chapel Hill in 1936. After attending graduate school at Harvard, where he worked with Robert Frost, Eaton returned to Chapel Hill to teach creative writing from 1946 to 1952. His books of poetry include *The Bright Plain* (1942), *The Shadow of the Swimmer* (1951), *The Man in the Green Chair* (1977), and *New and Selected Poems, 1942–1987* (1987). Thad Stem Jr. (1916–80) lived his entire life in Oxford and began writing poetry in the mid-1940s. Rooted in love for his home, his work described the town of Oxford and the people of Granville County, with volumes including *Picture Poems* (1949), *The Jackknife Horse* (1954), and *Penny Whistles and Wild Plums* (1962). Born on a tobacco farm in Bladen County, literary polymath Guy Owen (1925–81) also received more focused acclaim within the state, producing collections such as *Cape Fear Coun-*

try and Other Poems (1958), The Guilty and Other Poems (1964), and The White Stallion and Other Poems (1969).

Modern-Day North Carolina Poets

Sam Ragan (1915–96) was North Carolina's first secretary of the Department of Cultural Resources and first chair of the North Carolina Arts Council. Over the course of almost half a century, he helped lead North Carolina poetry into the contemporary period while bolstering the state's arts community in the process. Ragan also held the job of state editor for the *Raleigh News and Observer*, where he began writing his trademark column, Southern Accent, in 1948, becoming a household name through the newspaper, as had McNeil and Abernethy. Named poet laureate by Governor James B. Hunt in 1982, Ragan was the author of books including *Collected Poems of Sam Ragan, Poet Laureate of North Carolina* (1980), *Journey into Morning* (1981), *A Walk into April: Poems* (1986), and *Listening for the Wind: Poems* (1995).

A. R. (Archie Randolph) Ammons (1926–2001) grew up on a farm in Whiteville and began writing poetry while with the navy during World War II. His science studies at Wake Forest University later influenced his unique style, and his work was concerned with people's relationship to their environment; the problems of identity, permanence, and change; and the processes of nature. Ammons's books include *Collected Poems, 1951–1971* (1972), *Garbage* (1993), *Glare* (1997), *The North Carolina Poems* (1994), *The Really Short Poems* (1990), and *Selected Longer Poems* (1980).

A like-minded verse stylist, Asheville's Jonathan Williams (1929–) has spent much of his life on Skywinding Farm near Highlands. In college, Williams identified with the rebellious and experimental works that characterized Beat poetry, drawing influence from music, painting, a love for the brilliantly quirky, and a piercing social eye. Williams calls on his association with the Black Mountain group of poets, who experiment with poetic presentation, and on Mountain speech and traditions, frequently quoting hill folk in his poems and essays. His books include *Blues and Roots* (1971; 1985), *An Ear in Bartram's Tree: Selected Poems, 1957–1967* (1969), *Elite/Elate Poems: Selected Poems, 1971–75* (1979), *Get Hot or Get Out: A Selection of Poems, 1957–1981* (1982) and *No-Nonse-Nse* (1993).

Born in St. Louis and raised in segregated rural Arkansas, poet, civil rights activist, and memoirist Maya Angelou (1928–) came to North Carolina to teach at Wake Forest University in 1981. While best known for novels such as *I Know Why the Caged Bird Sings* (1969) and *Heart of a Woman* (1981), Angelou has also written several books of poetry, including *And Still I Rise* (1978), *Just Give Me a Cool Drink of Water 'Fore I Diiie* (1971), and *Phenomenal Woman: Four Poems Celebrating Women* (1994). Angelou also wrote "On the Pulse of Morning," composed for and read at President Bill Clinton's first inauguration on 20 Jan. 1993.

Ronald H. Bayes (1932–) was born in Freewater, Ore., and educated at Eastern Oregon State College and the University of Pennsylvania. He taught at Eastern Oregon State College and the University of Maryland before accepting the position of writer-in-residence at St. Andrews Presbyterian College in Laurinburg, N.C. Bayes founded and became executive editor of the *St. Andrews Review* and the St. Andrews Press and established the St. Andrews Writers Forum, a weekly event that brought outside writers and poets to the college for readings. Among his 16 books of poetry are *6 × 2: Six Poems* (1966), *Fram* (1976), *A Beast in View: Selected Shorter Poems* (1985), and *Guises: A Chainsong for the Muse: New and Selected Poems, 1970–1990* (1992).

Gerald W. Barrax (1933–) was born in Attalla, Ala., but spent much of his youth in Pittsburgh. He received his B.A. from Duquesne University in 1963 and earned a master's degree in English from the University of Pittsburgh before moving to North Carolina to join the English department of North Carolina State University. Barrax's interest in the experimental and political passions of the Black Arts Movement are apparent in his early poems, though he emphasized issues of family and community in later works. His poetry includes *Another Kind of Rain* (1970), *An Audience of One* (1980), *The Deaths of Animals and Lesser Gods* (1984), and *Leaning Against the Sun* (1992).

James Applewhite (1935–), from Stantonsburg, teaches poetry and creative writing at Duke Univeristy and has published essays on American poetry and southern literature. He is the author of many books of poetry, including *Ode to the Chinaberry Tree and Other Poems* (1986), *River Writing: An Eno Journal* (1988), and *Daytime and Starlight* (1997). Jim Wayne Miller (1936–96), born in Buncombe County, wrote extensively about Appalachian literature and the Appalachian experience. In 1980 he won the Thomas Wolfe Literary Award for his poetry collection *The Mountains Have Come Closer*. Other Miller works include *Copperhead Cane* (1964), *Brier: His Book* (1988), and *The Brier Poems* (1997).

Betty Adcock (1938–) is the author of five poetry collections, including *Beholdings* (1988), *The Difficult Wheel* (1995), and *Intervale: New and Selected Poems*, which was awarded the 2002 Poets Prize and named Distinguished Book of the Year by the Dictionary of Literary Biography Yearbook. She is the Kenan Writer-in-Residence at Meredith College. William Harmon (1938–) is the James Gordon Hanes Professor of English at the University of North Carolina at Chapel Hill. He is the editor of *The Top 500 Poems* (1992) and *The Oxford Book of American Light Verse* (1979) and the author of several volumes of poetry, including *The Intussusception of Miss Mary America* (1976) and *Mutatis Mutandis* (1985), for which he won the William Carlos Williams Award.

Shelby Stephenson (1938–) was born on a farm near Benson. He began to publish his own poetry in the spring of 1973, drawing on his youth in rural Johnston County for inspiration.

His first book, *Middle Creek Poems* (1979), was the cowinner of the Zoe Kincaid Brockman Memorial Award. His other books include *Carolina Shout!* (1985); *Finch's Mash* (1990); *The Persimmon Tree Carol* (1990); *Plankhouse* (1993), a poetic documentary with photographs by Roger Manley; and *Poor People* (1998).

James Seay (1939–) was born in Panola County, Miss. He has taught creative writing at UNC-Chapel Hill since 1974, serving as director of the writing program from 1987 to 1997. His four poetry collections include *Let Not Your Hart* (1970), *Where Our Voices Broke Off* (1978), *The Light as They Found It* (1990), and *Open Field, Understory* (1997).

Current North Carolina poet laureate Kathryn Stripling Byer's (1944–) four books of poetry are *Catching Light* (2002); *Black Shawl* (1998); *Wildwood Flower*, the 1992 Lamont Selection of the Academy of American Poets; and *The Girl in the Midst of the Harvest* (1986). Byer grew up in southwest Georgia and earned her master of fine arts from the University of North Carolina at Greensboro. Past poet-in-residence at Western Carolina University and Lenoir Rhyne College, Byer lives in Cullowhee. Community activist and poet Jaki Shelton Green (1953–) was born in Efland. Her poetry collections, which include *Dead on Arrival* (1983) and *Conjure Blues* (1996), focus on the experiences of African American women.

Michael McFee (1954–) was born in Asheville and received both his B.A. and M.A. from the University of North Carolina at Chapel Hill. He is currently Bowman and Gordon Gray Distinguished Professor of English at UNC-Chapel Hill, where he teaches poetry writing and contemporary North Carolina literature. McFee has published six collections of poetry, including *Earthly* (2001), *Colander* (1996), and *Sad Girl Sitting on a Running Board* (1991). He is also the editor of *The Language They Speak Is Things to Eat: Poems by Fifteen Contemporary North Carolina Poets* (1994).

While known primarily as a novelist, Duke University's Reynolds Price (1933–) has also written numerous volumes of poetry, including *The Laws of Ice* (1986), *The Use of Fire* (1990), and *Vital Provisions* (1982). Several North Carolina authors, among them successful Hendersonville-born novelist Robert Morgan (1944–), have published both verse and prose. Although Morgan has achieved more prominence as a novelist, his enthralling verse shines in poetry collections such as *Zirconia Poems* (1969), *Bronze Age* (1981), *At the Edge of the Orchard Country* (1987), *Sigodlin* (1990), and *Green River* (1991). Morgan is currently Kappa Alpha Professor of English at Cornell University. Born in Albemarle in 1939, Heather Ross Miller writes collections of short stories and poems as well as novels. She currently teaches creative writing and literature at Washington and Lee University in Lexington, Va., where she is the Thomas H. Broadus Professor of English, Emeritus. Her poetry collections include *Adam's First Wife* (1983), *Hard Evidence* (1990), and *Friends and Assassins: Poems* (1992).

Perhaps the most well-known crossover talent in the state is former North Carolina poet laureate and UNC-Greensboro professor Fred Chappell (1936–). Born in Canton and a graduate of Duke University, Chappell has written numerous collections of poetry, including *The World between the Eyes* (1971), *C: Poems* (1993), and *Spring Garden: New and Selected Poems* (1995). Chappell also writes a monthly poetry column for the *Raleigh News and Observer*. In 1987 he received the O. Max Gardner Award, the highest teaching award given by the University of North Carolina System. In 1988 Chappell was named the Burlington Industries Professor of English at UNC-Greensboro.

References: Robert Bain and Joseph M. Flora, eds., *Contemporary Poets, Dramatists, Essayists and Novelists of the South* (1994); Robert Bain, Joseph M. Flora, and Louis D. Rubin Jr., eds., *Southern Writers: A Biographical Dictionary* (1979); Ronald H. Bayes, ed., *North Carolina's 400 Years: An Anthology of Poems by North Carolina Poets to Celebrate America's 400th Anniversary* (1986); Guy Owen and Mary C. Williams, eds., *Contemporary Poetry of North Carolina* (1977); Louis D. Rubin Jr., ed., *History of Southern Literature* (1985); Richard G. Walser, *Poets of North Carolina* (1963).

Kelly Kress
Philip McFee

SEE ALSO Literary Awards; Roanoke-Chowan Group.

Political Parties of all kinds have vied for control of North Carolina's government from the earliest years of the republic, although most of the time only the Democrats and Republicans have achieved meaningful success. In 1787 the state's first parties clashed over the adoption of the federal Constitution. The Anti-Federalists, believers in state rights who feared that a strong central government would threaten individual liberties, prevailed over the Federalists, who argued that a powerful national government would bring order and prosperity. Due to the strength of the Anti-Federalists, North Carolina did not ratify the U.S. Constitution until November 1787, being the next-to-last of the 13 original colonies to do so. This victory heralded the ascendancy of the Federalists, led by William R. Davie, James Iredell, and Hugh Williamson. In the late 1790s, however, the Federalists became the minority party in North Carolina, giving way to Jeffersonian Republicans (later known as Democrats). After the War of 1812, the Federalist Party collapsed. Under the direction of Nathaniel Macon, North Carolina Jeffersonian Republicans, with their economic focus on agriculture rather than industry and their emphasis on limited federal power and expenditures, dominated state politics well into the 1830s.

Between 1833 and 1837, during Andrew Jackson's second term as president, a new Whig Party formed to oppose Jackson's antibanking and other policies. Adopting a program emphasizing internal improvements and economic development, conceived by state legislator Archibald D. Murphey, the

Whigs soon gained a narrow edge over the Democrats in North Carolina, an edge they generally maintained into the early 1850s. Under such leaders as William A. Graham and Willie P. Mangum, the Whig Party even convinced the Democrats to drop their opposition to the increasingly popular program of state-funded internal improvements such as railroads, turnpikes, and canals. After the collapse of their national organization in the early 1850s, North Carolina Whigs vainly tried to reorganize under labels such as the American and Constitutional Union Parties but could not regain their former dominance. Democrats again garnered the balance of power in the state.

The coming of the Civil War led to a period of one-party rule, as enthusiasm for secession and North Carolina's entry into the Confederacy temporarily erased old party differences. The pro-war Democrats, or "Destructives," as their opponents labeled them, did not hold power for long. Party differences soon reemerged, as opponents of the original supporters of secession formed a new, loosely organized Conservative Party. Led by popular former Whig Zebulon B. Vance, the Conservatives gained control of the state government in 1862 and retained it for the duration of the war. During Reconstruction, Vance's pro-Confederate Conservative supporters increasingly cooperated with the Democrats, eventually uniting under the old Democratic banner. Their new opponents were northern-backed Republicans, whose ranks included recently enfranchised African Americans as well as northern carpetbaggers and native white scalawags, mostly former Unionists. The Republicans, led by Governor William W. Holden, briefly controlled the state after the party's formation in 1867 until they lost control of the General Assembly in 1870. Holden was impeached and removed from office the following year, and the Conservative/Democratic Party, determined to restore white supremacy in the state, clearly asserted its power.

Except for a brief period in the 1890s when a "Fusion" of Republican and Populists temporarily wrested control away from them, Democrats would essentially rule the state for a full century. North Carolina's long-interrupted tradition of two-party politics returned at the end of the twentieth century. In the 1970s North Carolinians elected James E. Holshouser, the state's first Republican governor of the century, as well as Republican U.S. senator Jesse Helms, who would go on to win reelection four times. The Democratic Party, under the leadership of four-term governor James B. Hunt Jr., remained a primary political force in the state, although the majority of voters supported Republican presidential candidates in every election but one from 1972 to the mid-2000s. This trend was also observed in other states of the once staunchly Democratic "Solid South."

In addition to Democrats and Republicans, other parties and movements have influenced North Carolina politics, including the Progressives of Theodore Roosevelt in 1912, the States' Rights Party (Dixiecrats) of 1948, and the American-Independents of George Wallace in the 1960s. By the early 2000s several "non-mainstream" political parties attracted adherents—among them, the Communist Party, the Green Party, the Libertarian Party, the Natural Law Party, the Southern Party, and the Reform Party.

References: Vanessa Goodman and Jack Betts, *The Two-Party System in North Carolina* (1987); Marc W. Kruman, *Parties and Politics in North Carolina, 1836–1865* (1983); Alexander P. Lamis, *The Two-Party South* (1990); Paul Luebke, *Tar Heel Politics 2000* (1998); William S. Powell, *North Carolina through Four Centuries* (1989).

Michael Thomas Smith

SEE ALSO Anti-Federalists; Democratic Party; Dixiecrats; Federalist Party; Fusion of Republicans and Populists; Populist Party; Republican Party; Whig Party.

Polk County, located in the Mountain region of western North Carolina, was formed in 1855 from Henderson and Rutherford Counties and was named for Revolutionary War colonel William Polk. It is partially bordered by the state of South Carolina. Cherokee Indians originally inhabited the area, followed by Scotch-Irish and German settlers. The county seat, Columbus, was incorporated in 1857 and named for Columbus Mills, a member of the General Assembly who was instrumental in the county's formation. Other Polk County communities include Tryon, Saluda, and Mill Spring. Notable among physical features of the county are the Green River, White Oak, Panther, and Walnut Creeks, Tryon Mountain, White Oak Mountain, and Brushy Mountain.

Polk County has unusually temperate weather due to its location in the "thermal belt," a southern slope of the Blue Ridge Mountains, making it a popular tourist and retirement destination. County landmarks and historic sites include the Green River Plantation, established in the early 1800s, and the Mills-Screven Plantation, established ca. 1820. The Saluda Grade, the steepest standard-gauge, mainline rail line in the nation, opened in 1878 in the county. Cultural institutions include the Polk County Historical Museum, the Polk County Community Arts Council, and the Tryon Little Theater. Polk County farms produce corn, hay, soybeans, apples, and peaches, and the county's manufactured products include synthetic fibers, yarns, knits, crafts, glass, golf carts, and diamond dies. Minerals such as epidote and hornblende crystals are mined in the county. The estimated population of Polk County was 19,000 in 2004.

Jay Mazzocchi

SEE ALSO Isothermal Belt.

Poll Tax, ordinarily a flat rate of one or two dollars that was to be paid before a voter was allowed to cast his ballot, was just one of several means devised in North Carolina and other states to disfranchise blacks and other would-be voters. ("Poll" is an old English term for "head.") A poll tax was sometimes regarded as a revenue measure, primarily in the colonial period. Together with the poll tax there might also have been a literacy test to determine whether the applicant voter could read and interpret the U.S. Constitution. Early in the twentieth century in certain sections of the United States, a poll tax was sometimes levied on each taxpayer at the same rate without regard to property owned or personal status. By state constitutional amendment in 1919, payment of the poll tax in North Carolina was eliminated as a qualification for voting. As a revenue measure, the poll tax continued in use until prohibited by the North Carolina Constitution of 1971.

Reference: Frederic Ogden, *The Poll Tax in the South* (1958).

John V. Orth

Pollution. SEE Conservation Movement.

Pontiac's Conspiracy. SEE Proclamation of 1763.

Poole Bills, also called "Poole Monkey Bills," were a series of attempts in the 1920s by General Assembly member D. Scott Poole to outlaw the teaching of evolution in state-supported schools. Inspired by actions of the Tennessee legislature that precipitated the infamous Scopes Trial of 1920, and backed by fundamentalist forces centered around a committee of 100 churchmen of the North Carolina Presbyterian Synod, Poole introduced his first bill in 1925 and saw it defeated by a narrow margin. In February 1927 Poole's bill was reintroduced and defeated in committee by a margin of 25 to 11 after a rousing speech by Paul J. Ryan, a law student at the University of North Carolina in Chapel Hill. Victory for the bill's opponents was widely attributed to some presentations and debates in Charlotte sponsored by former students of Horace Williams (1858–1940), the controversial philosophy professor at UNC-Chapel Hill.

Jerry Leath Mills

Pope Air Force Base was established in 1919 as Pope Field, named for 1st Lt. Harley Halbert Pope (1879–1919), who was killed when his JN-4 Jenny crashed into the Cape Fear River near Fayetteville. The base is located on 1,885 acres next to Fort Bragg in Cumberland County. From 1919 to 1927 the base was used for observation balloon training. In 1927 Maj. Carl Spaatz conducted bombing training there, and in 1929 the base was used for joint air-ground training. The runways were paved in 1940. The base was used in World War II and afterward for training crews in airborne drops and resupply missions. The first fighter unit was stationed at Pope in 1954.

In 1970 the base was modified to accept the heavy transport plane C-5A. Personnel and aircraft from the base have been involved in humanitarian disaster relief and White House–directed combat actions such as Operation Urgent Fury in Grenada (1983–85), Operation Just Cause in Panama (1989–90), Operation Desert Shield/Desert Storm in Kuwait and Iraq (1991), Operation Enduring Freedom in Afghanistan (2002), and Operation Iraqi Freedom (2003). Pope also has supported Fort Bragg's Airborne and Special Operations paratroopers. In the early 2000s the base was home to the Forty-third Airlift Wing of C-130 Hercules cargo airplanes; the 23rd Fighter Group, an Air Combat Command unit, flying A/OA-10 Thunderbolt II close air support aircraft; and the 18th Air Support Operations Group, which worked with U.S. Army units worldwide to coordinate air and ground operations.

John L. Bell

Populist Party, also called the People's Party, led a dramatic and temporarily successful revolt against Democratic Party rule in North Carolina during the 1890s. Its origins can be traced to the growth of the Farmers' Alliance and the rise of anti-Alliance sentiment within the state Democratic Party. Prior to the spring of 1892 the Farmers' Alliance, led in North Carolina by Leonidas L. Polk and his *Progressive Farmer*, worked primarily within the Democratic Party to advance its agenda, including regulation of railroad rates, fairer taxation of railroads, and increased aid to public education. Thwarted attempts by the Farmers' Alliance to dominate the state Democratic convention in May 1892, however, proved disappointing to many Alliance members. Their failure prompted the first manifestation of organized Populism in North Carolina: on 18 May 1892, at a meeting in Raleigh, adherents selected delegates to the upcoming national Populist convention.

In July, after a national convention of Democrats nominated Grover Cleveland for president, some North Carolina Alliancemen who did not participate in the earliest meetings of the party declared their intention to vote for the Populist presidential nominee, James B. Weaver. However, these men planned to remain Democrats for political purposes. Their plan collapsed in early August, when the state Democratic Party chairman, Furnifold M. Simmons, banned Cleveland's opponents from receiving nominations for state and local offices. With support for Cleveland as the measure of Democratic loyalty, the bond between the party and many former Alliance members, sorely tested since May, was broken.

North Carolina Populists held their first nominating conventions in early and mid-August 1892 and developed a full slate of candidates for state office. They adopted national Populism's Omaha Platform, which endorsed government ownership of railroads and a federally controlled money supply. On state matters, the party demanded a 6 percent limit on contract interest rates, full taxation of railroad property, and encouragement to education, agriculture, and manufacturing. Together, financial, transportation, and educational reforms—the leading tenets of Alliance ideology—became the rallying cry of North Carolina Populists.

The Populists' first campaign ended in disappointment. The party captured fewer than 50,000 votes, about 17 percent of the total, and won more than 35 percent of the vote in only six counties, all in the east or eastern Piedmont. This setback resulted from two factors: the decision by many Alliance members to remain in the Democratic Party and the failure of the state's strong Republican Party, the overwhelming majority of whose members were black, to support the Populists. Although the first problem proved impossible to reverse entirely, the balance of power in state politics shifted in early 1893, when Populist and Republican leaders began to plan a cooperative strategy for the next election. The goals of the union were to forge a new majority with Populist votes, repeal Democratic laws restricting access to the ballot, and give the General Assembly control over local government.

The leading Populist behind "Fusion," as Democrats termed the Republican-Populist agreement, was Marion Butler of Sampson County. In 1893 and 1894 Butler conducted repeated negotiations for cooperation. By the 1894 Populist nominating convention, practically all party members endorsed cooperation with Republicans for legislative offices and continued support of traditional Populist reforms. The so-called Fusion was successful, as the 1894 election sent 60 Populists, 56 Republicans, and 54 Democrats to the 1895 General Assembly. Three Populists won election to Congress. During the 1895 session Butler and Jeter Pritchard, a Republican, were elected to the U.S. Senate. The Populist state representatives also achieved demonstrable change. Various Populist-inspired reforms were enacted, including a new election law, local government democratization, and a 6 percent interest law. The 1895 General Assembly was the legislative high–water mark of Populism.

After 1896 the party began to decline. A major reason was growing internal factionalism between Populists and Republicans, which was exacerbated in the 1897 General Assembly and undermined much of the Fusionist administration of Republican governor Daniel L. Russell Jr. According to the party's 1896 platform, all Populists stood for financial reform, public control of railroads, free elections, and better schools. However, some lawmakers, who were very attached to Republican allies, failed to use their power in the General Assembly to achieve their party's goals. The Fusionist legislature of 1897 was an unmitigated disaster, as Populist members split into pro-Republican and anti-Republican camps.

In addition, Populists were not ideologically or politically prepared to meet the violence of the Democrats' white supremacy campaign. Although Populists had always claimed that Democrats used racist rhetoric to stifle reform, the party was composed primarily of former Democrats committed to white supremacy. Many eastern Populists were uncomfortable cooperating with black men and left the party because of the issue. Although Populists managed a respectable campaign in 1898, it was overshadowed by the well-orchestrated brutality of their opponents. Democrats, partly through the employment of terrorist groups known as Red Shirts, physically assaulted and intimidated Populists before and on election day. Their strategy worked, ending Populist-Republican rule in the General Assembly.

In 1900 Democrats resurrected the violence of 1898, passed the disfranchisement amendment, and once again gained control of state government. The state Populist organization collapsed immediately, although some local units persisted for a short time. Bitterness toward Democrats among Populists was so strong that a large faction of the party faithful, partly attracted by the reform rhetoric of Theodore Roosevelt, defected to the Republican Party after 1901. Many former Populists became third-party members again in 1912, joining Roosevelt's Progressives. These ex-Populists were always a minority among North Carolina Republicans in the first decades of the twentieth century, and they never fully controlled party policy. Some historians believe that a form of Populism endured in Randolph County, Sampson County, and other places, evidenced by "islands" of strong Republican support throughout much of the Democrat-controlled twentieth century.

References: Jeffrey J. Crow and Robert F. Durden, *Maverick Republican in the Old North State: A Political Biography of Daniel L. Russell* (1977); Durden, *The Climax of Populism: The Election of 1896* (1965); Helen G. Edmonds, *The Negro and Fusion Politics in North Carolina* (1951); James L. Hunt, *Marion Butler and American Populism* (2003); Lala Carr Steelman, *The North Carolina Farmers' Alliance: A Political History, 1887–1893* (1985).

James L. Hunt

SEE ALSO Farmers' Alliance; Fusion of Republicans and Populists; Gideon's Band; Red Shirts; *South Dakota v. North Carolina*.

Portis Gold Mine, located in the northeastern corner of Franklin County, was the first mine in the Eastern Carolina Belt (composed of Warren, Halifax, Franklin, and Nash Counties) and operated intermittently from about 1835 to 1936. The Portis gold deposit was in the rocks of the Spring Hope Formation in the eastern slate belt. The primary mining method has been identified as "hydraulicking" 15 to 30 feet of surface material, but recovery was hampered by the region's sticky clay. The total amount of gold mined is unknown. In 1884 the estimate was more than $1 million, and in 1972 one geologist projected that up to $7 million worth of gold was mined in that area.

By the end of the nineteenth century, gold in the Portis mine was difficult to find and there were no profits to be had. The final attempts to extract gold were by the Norlina Mining Company, which brought in heavy mining equipment and constructed an assay lab, a main building for the crushing equipment, a dormitory, a superintendent's house, a blacksmith and machine shop, and a six-million-gallon reservoir for the water required by the gold recovery process. The cost of the mining operation exceeded by one-third the value of the gold recovered, and the mine was closed in 1936.

References: P. Albert Carpenter III, *Gold Resources of North Carolina* (1972); Richard F. Knapp, *North Carolina Gold: A Selected Bibliography of Mining History, Technology, and the Reed Gold Mine* (1978); Thilbert H. Pearce, "The Portis Diggings," *The State* (1 Apr. 1972); Bruce Roberts, *The Carolina Gold Rush* (1971).

George-Anne Willard

Ports and Harbors. Beginning in the colonial period, North Carolina's ports of entry were settlements where a vessel's cargo could be checked by a government inspector and import fees collected. The ports were essential elements in developing the early commerce of the colony. From the time the first permanent residents started settling in the area north of Albemarle Sound, there were ongoing efforts by the successive governments—first the Lords Proprietors, then the British Crown, and finally the state of North Carolina—to provide aids to navigation throughout the region's vast network of inlets, sounds, and rivers.

Initially, most of the ships entering or leaving the new colony passed through Roanoke Inlet opposite Roanoke Island. Consequently, in 1676 the Lords Proprietors issued instructions to their representatives there to establish three towns, which were to be "the port towns of your county of Albemarle." The first of these, on Roanoke Island, was to be "the Cheife towne and the place where the Councell assemble should meete." The second was to be located on the Perquimans side of Little River and the third at the western end of Albemarle Sound between the Roanoke and Chowan Rivers.

These instructions appear not to have been followed, but for most of the colonial period there were five official ports of entry, although they were of varying degrees of importance. The ports were designed to serve maritime traffic throughout the colony, from Virginia to South Carolina.

Port Brunswick covered the Cape Fear River area, with the port collector located in the town of Brunswick below Wilmington. Port Beaufort handled the commerce through Topsail Inlet near Cape Lookout. Port Bath, situated in the town of Bath on a tributary of the Pamlico River, was where boats entering through Ocracoke Inlet were supposed to go for clearance, while the collector's office for Port Roanoke, which served most of the Albemarle settlement, was actually located in Edenton. Finally, Port Currituck, established to serve commerce through Currituck Inlet, was a port in little more than name, for by the time it was established the inlet had shoaled so seriously that only small vessels could navigate the ever-changing channel. Even then it was difficult to find the port inspector, since his office was wherever he happened to be at the time.

By the early nineteenth century, both Roanoke Inlet and Currituck Inlet had closed, and although Port Currituck no longer existed, there was as much business as ever at the office of the collector for Port Roanoke in Edenton. By that time the only navigable inlet through the Outer Banks was Ocracoke Inlet, located between Ocracoke Island and Core Banks. This meant that all vessels bound to or from the Pamlico or Albemarle Sounds and their tributaries had to pass through Ocracok Inlet. There was an unsuccessful effort to do away with the port collectors' offices at Edenton and Bath and establish a

A cargo-laden barge moves up the Cape Fear River to the port of Wilmington. Photograph by Charles E. Jones. North Carolina Department of Transportation.

new one at Ocracoke Inlet to serve all of northern North Carolina.

Although the importance of the ports lessened with the gradual shift from maritime traffic to railroads and highways, North Carolina continued to maintain and improve its ports. In 1923 Governor Cameron Morrison became interested in developing a state port facility. He was instrumental in the creation of the State Ship and Water Transportation Commission (SSWTC), whose purpose was to study the possibility of establishing docks, wharves, terminals, and other facilities to promote waterborne commerce. The SSWTC reported that development of such facilities was not only possible, but also would be beneficial. The Ports Commission, which replaced the SSWTC in 1924, was given the task of establishing port facilities for seagoing vessels. A statewide bond referendum for $8.7 million to develop the facilities was placed on the ballot in November 1924 but failed to pass. Lacking funding to accomplish its task, the Ports Commission ceased to exist.

Despite the absence of a state port program, Wilmington and Morehead City continued efforts to improve their respective facilities. To boost these local movements, the General Assembly created the Morehead City Port Commission in 1933 and the Wilmington Port Commission in 1935. In 1945 it established the North Carolina State Ports Authority, with responsibility for developing and improving harbors at Wilmington, Morehead City, Southport, and anywhere else that would benefit waterborne commerce. Construction of state port facilities at Morehead City and Wilmington began in 1949 with the appropriation of $7.5 million and was completed in 1952. Located along the Newport River and Bogue Sound, the original facilities at Morehead City included a 2,500-foot wharf, two transit sheds totaling 92,000 square feet, two storage warehouses with a capacity of 176,000 feet, and a paved open storage area of 60,000 square feet. The State Port at Morehead City was officially dedicated on 14 Aug. 1952.

Historically, the State Port at Morehead City has handled a wide variety of cargoes, but it is best known for moving unmanufactured tobacco, phosphate, and wood chips. As a result of extensive dredging, Morehead City has the distinction of possessing one of the deepest harbors along the Atlantic Coast.

The State Port at Wilmington, located 26 miles up the Cape Fear River from the Atlantic Ocean, saw its original facilities dedicated on 16 Sept. 1952. They consisted of a 1,510-foot wharf, two transit sheds with a capacity of 158,000 square feet, and a storage warehouse of 86,100 square feet. There were three acres of paved, open storage. The port has experienced steady growth, and its primary exports have been forest-related products.

In addition to the facilities along the coast, North Carolina's Ports Authority operates the Charlotte Intermodal Terminal and the Piedmont Triad Intermodal Terminal. Since 1996 these two facilities in Piedmont North Carolina have helped businesses and industries in the interior utilize the growing port facilities operated by the state government.

References: Hugh T. Lefler and Albert R. Newsome, *North Carolina: The History of a Southern State* (1963); William S. Powell, *North Carolina through Four Centuries* (1989); Alan D. Watson, *Wilmington: Port of North Carolina* (1992).

David Stick
John Hairr

Postal Service. When the first colonists landed on Roanoke Island in 1587, they likely wrote letters to friends and relatives back home in England. For a small fee, the ship's captain would then transport the letters to Europe. A transaction such as this represented the birth of postal operations in America and North Carolina. In 1710 the British Parliament passed an act that specifically provided for the management of a postal system in the colonies; by the 1730s Deputy Postmaster General Alexander Spotswood had extended delivery through North Carolina to Charles Towne (Charleston, S.C.). Mail coach service arrived in 1744.

In 1789 North Carolina had 4 post offices, operating in Edenton, New Bern, Washington, and Wilmington; by 1851 it had 785. Railroads, which came to the state in 1836, soon became the chief means of carrying mail, employing special cars to pick up mail at railway stations and process it on the train for delivery farther down the line. Regular use of postage stamps began in the late 1840s; the first U.S. postage stamps of 5-cent and 10-cent denominations were delivered to Elizabeth City on 13 Mar. 1848.

By 1861 North Carolinians had become accustomed to regular and timely mail delivery. The Civil War and Reconstruction disrupted the postal service and forced staffing changes. Indi-

A Rural Free Delivery mail carrier at Chadbourn, early 1900s. NCC.

viduals who had a formal role in the Confederacy could not serve in a formal capacity for the Union, so Confederate postmasters were not eligible to fulfill their duties after the war. As a result, the number of female postmasters in North Carolina increased significantly.

During this time most post offices consisted of a table in a prominent citizen's home or in the local general store or tavern. Mail was delivered and placed on the table, though a few offices in larger cities had pigeonholes for sorting the mail. Citizens were responsible for collecting their mail at the post office, and unclaimed mail was advertised in the local newspaper, for which an additional two cents would be charged. A major change in postal operations occurred in 1899 with the beginning of the rural free delivery experiment. In North Carolina, China Grove was one of the first towns to test the system, in which mail carriers would deliver and pick up mail in rural areas for no additional charge. It took months, however, for the China Grove carriers to convince residents to try this new system. North Carolina's first airmail was carried from Wilmington in 1912, but it was not until 1928 that regular airmail service was flown over the state on a route from New York to Miami. A 1948 postal experiment utilized trucks to carry and process the mail, and these highway post offices, as they were called, lasted until 1972. The last mail was carried by train in the 1970s. Today most mail going any distance travels by air, while local mail is carried by truck.

In 1892 the U.S. postal system began issuing stamps to commemorate people, places, or events, and in 1937 North Carolina celebrated publication of the state's first historical stamp, which depicted Virginia Dare. Eight days later a special souvenir sheet was issued in Asheville in honor of the Great Smoky Mountains. Since then, additional stamps have been issued in North Carolina to honor the Roanoke voyages, the Wright Brothers, the Carolina charter, and North Carolina statehood. Six postal cards have also been issued in the state, honoring the University of North Carolina at Chapel Hill, North Carolina beaches, and the Battle of King's Mountain, among other landmarks.

References: Richard Ridgway, *Self-Sufficiency at All Costs: Confederate Post Office Operations in North Carolina, 1861–1865* (1988); Alex ter Braake, *The Posted Letter in Colonial and Revolutionary America, 1628–1790* (1975).

Tony L. Crumbley

SEE ALSO Airmail Service.

Post Roads were routes created to facilitate correspondence between America's European settlers and their home countries. The earliest record of an attempt to set up a post road in North Carolina is a letter written by William Farris, dated 27 Jan. 1739. Farris, who identified himself as "postmaster of North Carolina," petitioned the South Carolina Common House of Assembly to contribute money to establish a post road from Georgetown to Eden Town, "from whence they have a regular Post once a month to Virginia." This post was established, as records indicate that Farris was paid £200 for his services—although the post apparently was short-lived, as no appropriation was made after the first year. In October 1755 a message was read during a session of the North Carolina legislature clearly stating that "there is no established post thru this Province."

Until 1792 post roads through North Carolina, such as they were, served only a few coastal towns; anyone who lived in the interior had to depend on travelers or private mail carriers to carry their letters to and from the coastal post offices. In 1792 Congress authorized a change in the location of the main post road, moving it back to pass through Halifax, Tarboro, Smithfield, Fayetteville, and Lumberton, with cross posts to the coastal offices. In 1794 the main north-south post road was moved even farther inland, so that it passed through Warrenton, Louisburg, the new state capital at Raleigh, Averasboro, and Fayetteville. By 1795 cross posts had been established for all but the most westerly counties, and by 1801 an extensive network of post roads stretched across the entire state.

Robert J. Stets

Potecasi Creek, Battle of. The Battle of Potecasi Creek, also called the Battle of Mount Tabor Church, was a Civil War skirmish in Hertford County that occurred on 26 July 1863, while elements of Maj. Gen. John G. Foster's Union expedition made their way toward the Confederate rail junction at Weldon. Advancing up the Chowan River from Roanoke Island, a Federal force landed at Winton and set out for Murfreesboro, ten miles north. Three miles outside of Winton, the advanced guard was ambushed as it approached Hill's Bridge on Potecasi Creek. The attackers were members of the dismounted Fourth North Carolina Cavalry Battalion, recently recruited in Hertford and Northampton Counties and led by Maj. Samuel J. Wheeler of Murfreesboro. Wheeler's men fired from wooded cover on both sides of the road before retreating across the bridge to a prepared entrenchment 100 yards long on the northern side of the creek. Union troops found the planking thrown from the bridge floor, but, under the cover of friendly fire, they were able to cross on the stringers and take a dozen or so Confederate prisoners.

At least one Confederate was killed and several men on both sides were wounded, with the remaining defenders scattering. Two days later the Union advance was turned back at the Battle of Boon's Mill by Col. Matt W. Ransom's 34th North Carolina Regiment.

Reference: Thomas C. Parramore, "Five Days in July, 1863," in F. Roy Johnson and Parramore, eds., *The Roanoke-Chowan Story* (1959–61).

Thomas C. Parramore

Pottery. North Carolina's internationally renowned pottery tradition reaches back centuries—to the time native inhabitants formed local clay into functional pots and ceremonial vessels. Archaeologists have documented nearly complete pots crafted by Cherokee and other native makers that date from the early 1500s. Later, as Europeans settled the region in the eighteenth century, folk potters satisfied the demand of local people who could not afford or had no access to imported ceramics. Adapting techniques from their native England, Germany, and elsewhere, these potters took local clay, glazed their pieces with lead, wood ash, or salt, and fired them in wooden kilns to produce functional vessels for daily use.

Specific characteristics and methods evolved among North Carolina potters in various parts of the state. Through the nineteenth century, although functional use of folk pottery declined, the state's master potters continued to practice and refine their craft, passing it to subsequent generations. In time, folklorists, collectors, and others came to appreciate the distinctive forms of North Carolina pottery as artistic expressions. Potters once again adapted, producing wares to meet this new demand. In the second half of the twentieth century, rising interest in the folk arts helped reinvigorate the potter's craft, prompting contemporary potters to expand traditional techniques and forms in yet other new directions. Today, North Carolina pottery is among the most highly prized in the world. As Chatham County potter Mark Hewitt has written, "As theater is to Broadway, pottery is a treasured manifestation of North Carolina."

Among North Carolina folk potters, three principal regions of pottery production are generally recognized: the eastern Piedmont (Chatham County and the Seagrove area of Randolph, Moore, and Montgomery Counties), the Catawba Valley (Catawba, Lincoln, and Union Counties), and Buncombe County. Potters in these regions produced both earthenware (pieces made of clay with a high content of impurities, fired at a relatively low temperature) and stoneware (pieces made of higher-quality clay, fired at much higher temperatures for greater durability). But in each region, the backgrounds and traditions of potters who settled and worked there influenced the evolution of their wares. The availability of local clays and materials for glazes also helped create regional variations.

The primary earthenware period in North Carolina lasted from the 1750s to the 1840s, slightly longer than in most northern states. A later production period compared to that of the North is due largely to later settlement patterns, a less-developed trade network, and the slower introduction of technological advancements. As a vessel, earthenware exhibits brittle and porous characteristics; it was often coated on the interior or around handles with a dull, lustrous, lead-based glaze ranging from browns and oranges to green-blues. The danger of lead glazing was widely known in the Northeast by the third quarter of the eighteenth century. However, North

Ben Owen at work in Jugtown, ca. 1930s. Photograph by Bayard Wootten. NCC.

Carolina potters fired with lead glazes up to the mid-nineteenth century and even use some for nonutilitarian pieces today.

Moravians produced some of the earliest earthenware in North Carolina. Folk potters ordinarily worked part-time with clay, training and employing predominantly male family members and neighbors to make pottery. Traditional gender roles combined with the strength necessary to turn a 5-, 10-, or 20-gallon jar or jug called for male potters. Women occasionally turned smaller pieces, helped with glazing, and performed other chores in pottery production. The familial method of teaching helps explain the over 200-year continuous tradition and multiple generations of folk potter families in the state.

The successor to earthenware was the more durable and vitreous stoneware. The earliest verifiable stoneware producer in North Carolina was Gurdon Robins & Co., established in Fayetteville by 1820. Edward Webster, a member of a prominent family of potters from Hartford, Conn., later operated the pottery under his own name. His brothers, Timothy and Chester, also helped and later moved the pottery to Randolph County, a primary location of stoneware production today. E. A. Poe

& Co. in Fayetteville in 1880 typified another North Carolina pottery method. For Poe, a large brickmaking operation, pottery was a side venture, as was common throughout the United States. Unlike Gurdon Robins, who had to import some of his potters in 1820, Poe used North Carolina turners, chiefly William Henry Hancock, who had worked with J. Dorris Craven, and Manley William Owen, from northern Moore County.

Folk potters primarily focused on practical shapes such as jugs, churns, crocks, bowls, pipes, pitchers, and pots of all kinds. Nineteenth-century vessels usually had little decoration, and potters rarely signed their work. Distinctive coggle marks, size inscriptions, handle attachments, general shapes, and other subtle decorative characteristics can identify nineteenth-century pieces. By contrast, early twentieth-century potters embraced the arts and crafts movement in response to customer demand. They discovered a new range of colors and were more explorative with forms. In North Carolina, whimsical pieces such as face jugs or ugly jugs are almost purely twentieth century in popularity. Face jugs show influences from African, German, English, and American Indian precedents.

Well-known potters in western North Carolina in the early twentieth century included Hilton Pottery, Pisgah Forest Pottery, Omar Khayyam Pottery, and Brown's Pottery. The Hiltons produced one of the first pottery catalogs in North Carolina around 1920. Walter Benjamin Stephens at Pisgah Forest became famous for his Wedgwood-style pots depicting frontier scenes in cameo relief. Oscar Louis Bachelder explored unique forms derived from the art pottery movement. The Brown family produced utilitarian ware, which Charles Brown continued to make in the early 2000s. In 1925 Davis and Javan Brown turned one of the largest pots ever made in North Carolina. The six-foot-tall vase remains on display at Brown's Pottery in Arden.

In contrast to selling pottery from a shop or hauling pots by wagon to customers, J. B. Cole, C. C. Cole, A. R. Cole, Rainbow, and North State Potteries made North Carolina's Seagrove area (near Asheboro) known throughout the eastern United States by publishing catalogs of their wares. Pottery catalogs offered customers a chance to select wares without visiting the shop. The Coles received some of their inspiration from the most famous shop in the state, Jugtown Pottery, opened by Jacques and Juliana Busbee in 1921. The Busbees hired local potters Charlie Teague and Ben Owen to turn wares, which were sold locally as well as shipped to Juliana's Village Shop in New York's Greenwich Village. In the early twenty-first century, descendants of the Cole, Teague, and Owen families and Jugtown Pottery continued to produce traditional folk pottery in the Seagrove area and around the state.

The growing interest in traditional arts and crafts that encouraged folk potters of European descent to advertise their wares in catalogs and experiment with new forms and methods also influenced the state's Native American potters, particularly among the Cherokee. While European potters typically turned their pieces on wheels and fired them in closed kilns, Cherokee potters traditionally manufactured coil and pinch pots by hand and, it is believed, fired them in open pits of wood coals. Until the late nineteenth century, native potters concentrated on producing earthenware for their own use, including large jars for hominy and a variety of smaller cooking pots and vessels. These pots were not glazed like European earthenware or stoneware; rather, they were sealed with soot from burned corncobs that allowed the vessels to hold liquids. Some were stamped with paddles, producing a distinctive design.

By the twentieth century, Cherokee and other native potters in the state found an emerging tourist market for their work, prompting many to produce more polished pieces. As anthropologists and other scholars worked with Cherokee potters and recovered older pieces that could serve as models, however, interest in returning to traditional forms and methods grew as part of a larger Native American cultural renaissance in the late twentieth century. Today, such work can be seen and purchased at such locations as the Qualla Arts and Crafts Mutual and the Museum of the Cherokee Indian in Cherokee.

In the early 2000s more than 2,000 potters were active statewide, creating forms of all types—from eighteenth-century traditional shapes and modern utilitarian ware to abstract wall-mounted sculptures. Only a handful of turners created pots in the "traditional folk manner." In the Seagrove area, more than 70 pottery shops produced wares on a small commercial scale. A few traditional folk potters were working in Lincoln County near Charlotte and in Buncombe County near Asheville. Many turners adhered to forms produced in North Carolina for over 80 years. Some potters strived to develop unique shapes and glazes. The majority, however, as exemplified by potters such as Burlon B. Craig, Vernon Owens, Ben Owen III, Charles Brown, and Bob Armfield, were combining the turning arts of the past with fresh perspectives, enriching the storied folk pottery tradition in North Carolina.

References: John Bivins Jr., *The Moravian Potters in North Carolina* (1972); James H. Craig, *The Arts and Crafts in North Carolina, 1699–1840* (1965); Jean Crawford, *Jugtown Pottery: History and Design* (1964); Mark Hewitt and Nancy Sweezy, *The Potter's Eye: Arts and Tradition in North Carolina Pottery* (2005); Robert C. Lock, *The Traditional Potters of North Carolina* (1994); Barbara Stone Perry, *North Carolina Pottery: The Collection of the Mint Museums* (2004); Quincy J. Scarborough Jr., *North Carolina Decorated Stoneware: The Webster School of Folk Potters* (1986); Sweezy, *Raised in Clay: The Southern Pottery Tradition* (1984); Charles G. Zug III, *Turners and Burners: The Folk Potters of North Carolina* (1986).

David M. Egner
Additional research provided by Mark Simpson-Vos.

SEE ALSO Jugtown.

Poultry. Once ubiquitous on North Carolina farms, the practice of keeping domesticated birds for eggs or meat evolved into a specialized billion-dollar industry in the latter half of the twentieth century. In the early twentieth century, the tasks of raising chickens and turkeys and gathering eggs fell primarily to North Carolina's farm women. Their small flocks required little capital, and caring for poultry fit easily into women's round of duties in house and field. Eggs and live fowl provided a ready medium of exchange, and women found buyers in any number of ways. Storekeepers in country and town alike accepted poultry products in trade. At the Wayne County home of Roy Taylor, the son of tenant farmers, the Saturday arrival of the "fish man" selling a fresh catch from eastern North Carolina rivers signaled that his mother's cache of eggs would be raided. "Go see if your Mammy has any extra eggs," Taylor's father would instruct him. "If she's got three dozen or so eggs, the dollar added to the egg money will be enough for the speckled trout."

Although farm educators championed increased poultry production as a new source of income, poultry raising remained underdeveloped, in part because it carried the stigma of being "women's work." Compared to other regions of the country, poultry production in the South lagged far behind. In 1900, for example, nearly 88 percent of North Carolina farms had poultry flocks, but they averaged just 22 birds each. Farms in the upper Midwest, by comparison, kept flocks that averaged 61 birds, earning the region the moniker of the nation's "egg basket." But several technological advances—such as artificially heated incubators, mechanical brooders, ventilated railroad freight cars, and mechanical refrigeration—set the stage for expanded poultry production.

During the first four decades of the twentieth century, women formed the vanguard of a quiet revolution in the poultry industry. They took advantage of increasing demand for eggs and fowl, experimented with new ways to raise and market chickens, and proved that poultry could turn profits. The state played a crucial role. Agricultural extension agents promoted poultry-raising innovations, and professors at North Carolina State College (modern-day North Carolina State University) conducted research on poultry feed, housing, and diseases. In the 1920s the state Department of Agriculture and commission merchants organized marketing cooperatives that shipped railroad car lots of eggs and live chickens to buyers in New York and other distant cities. At the same time, enthusiasm for poultry quickened when boll weevils invaded fields and profits from cotton and tobacco withered during the Great Depression. In 1929, for example, the 5.8 million chickens sold off of North Carolina farms brought in nearly $4.4 million, and the 240 million eggs sold reaped some $6.3 million.

These economic lessons were not lost on farmers, especially those who lived in the foothills, where poultry growers started raising larger flocks in the 1920s and 1930s. Looking back on the development of the Wilkes County broiler industry, pioneer entrepreneur Charles O. Lovette credited much of its early inspiration to farm women who already understood the economics and care of poultry. Lovette himself got his start in the 1920s as a huckster who bought chickens, eggs, and vegetables from Wilkes County farms and country stores and then peddled the products in Charlotte and Winston-Salem. In 1942 Lovette's son Fred joined his father's huckstering business, and two years later he expanded the poultry buying and selling enterprise. In less than a decade, Fred had purchased a chicken processing plant, and what would become North Carolina's premier poultry agribusiness, Holly Farms, was born.

Fred Lovette entered the family business just as demand for eggs and chickens soared during World War II, as the federal government bought large quantities to serve in military mess halls. By 1943 North Carolina farmers had shattered all previous poultry records; growers, for example, sold 15.5 million chickens and grossed $15.7 million. Wartime demand accelerated the evolution of the industry and floated North Carolina and other southern states to the top of poultry production charts.

By the early 2000s, poultry was the largest food industry in North Carolina, with production of chickens, turkey, and eggs approaching $2.2 billion annually. Wilkes County led the way in broiler production, while Duplin County growers raised the most turkeys in the state. The nearly 3 billion eggs produced gave North Carolina a ranking of ninth in the nation. More than 4,300 farmers were involved in the poultry industry, employing more than 22,000 people in hatcheries, feed mills, and processing plants.

Increased production, however, exacted a toll. As poultry raising grew in scale and required more capital investment for houses the length of a football field and feed laden with growth stimulants and antibiotics, farm men usually assumed the position of managers, while women and children performed much of the actual work. As the industry underwent vertical integration, with companies such as Holly Farms controlling the operation from hatchery and feed mill to processing, agribusinesses closely supervised the operations of contractors, made key managerial decisions, and eventually reduced growers to little more than wage laborers. In 1991 a fatal fire at the Imperial Food Products plant in Hamlet demonstrated that workers who processed poultry often endured hazardous circumstances.

In their separate ways, contract growers and poultry factory workers have organized in efforts to improve these conditions. While consumers enjoyed an abundance of meat that was once reserved for Sunday dinner, many mourned the loss of the old-time taste of free-range chickens that factory farming destroyed. Changes in the poultry industry have created mixed blessings: consumers enjoy an abundant supply of inexpensive meat, but it is produced and processed under conditions that are open to criticism.

References: Lu Ann Jones, "Re-Visioning the Countryside: Southern Women, Rural Reform, and the Farm Economy in the Twentieth Century" (Ph.D. diss., UNC-Chapel Hill, 1996); Tom Morris, *Poultry Can Crow at NCSU: A History of Poultry at North Carolina State University* (1980); Gordon Sawyer, *The Agribusiness Poultry Industry: A History of Its Development* (1971); Hope Shand, "Billions of Chickens: The Business of the South," *Southern Exposure* 11 (November/December 1983); Roy G. Taylor, *Sharecroppers: The Way We Really Were* (1984).

Lu Ann Jones

Poverty. Programs and initiatives to alleviate poverty and aid the needy have been undertaken in North Carolina since colonial times. In addition to private organizations and churches, government at various levels has attempted to address poverty issues, with mixed results. There is a direct correlation between poverty and poor health, reduced access to cultural and recreational opportunities, increased crime victimization, and below-average academic achievement. Even with the state's overall economic prosperity, poverty remains a persistent and disturbing feature of North Carolina's landscape, particularly in the rural Coastal Plain. According to the U.S. Census Bureau, in 2005, 23 North Carolina counties—19 of which were located in the east—experienced poverty rates of over 18 percent. Twenty of these poorer counties had held similarly high rates since data collection began in 1960. More than half a million rural North Carolinians were living in poverty, with children and minority groups suffering disproportionately higher rates.

Public Charity in the Colonial Era through the Nineteenth Century

Attempts by the North Carolina government to alleviate poverty and assist the poor can be traced as far back as 1777. That year, the colonial Assembly provided for the election of county officials as "overseers of the poor," positions that previously had been held by local Anglican Church wardens, who, in addition to their other parish responsibilities, performed this duty under a statute based on the poor laws of England. Known after 1783 as "wardens of the poor," these officials were empowered to levy poll and property taxes for the benefit of the poor, who could be given small cash allowances or "let out under contract"—given room and board by private individuals (though county reimbursement often went to the lowest bidders). Although the amount of work and low pay made warden of the poor an unpopular job, later necessitating state laws to compel appointees to serve or face fines, these positions persisted into the late eighteenth century.

Specially constructed facilities for the poor, popularly (and officially) called "poorhouses," were first authorized under a bill passed by the state legislature in 1785. The law applied only to Northampton, Nash, Halifax, Chowan, Carteret, Wayne, and Onslow Counties, but within a few years other counties would adopt similar laws. In 1793 the General Assembly enacted a general law giving county wardens authority to erect poorhouses, although years or even decades would pass before some counties actually built them, probably deterred by fear that the system would not pay for itself. To assist in raising funds for poorhouses, the Assembly also passed a measure empowering newly appointed county wardens to collect any poor-tax revenues owed by former sheriffs, clerks of court, and others.

New enabling legislation in 1831 authorized the Court of Pleas and Quarter Sessions in each county to order the building of poorhouses when necessary. By that time, the practice of requiring inmates to perform farm labor and domestic work was gaining popularity among taxpayers and, coupled with the new legislation, led to a greater number of poorhouses.

Living conditions in poorhouses varied greatly from county to county, as indicated by Dorothea Dix's 1848 survey of 30 facilities housing many mentally ill citizens. Although Dix characterized the Iredell County facility as "a model of neatness, comfort, and good order, having a most efficient master and mistress," few others received similarly high ratings. She recalled a man in the Granville County poorhouse who had been chained to the floor for years, his "flesh and bones . . . crushed out of shape by the unyielding irons." To end such injustices, a state asylum for the mentally ill was opened in 1853.

Records of the Johnston County facility—called the "Poor House" or "Home of Aged and Infirm"—during 1890–95 indicate that residents usually numbered between 10 and 20, and separate houses were maintained for whites and blacks. Superintendent George S. Wilson was a local farmer who hired laborers to help run both the poorhouse and his own farming operation. The lack of paid cooking and laundry staff implies that able-bodied inmates performed such chores.

To reduce costs, some counties in the 1920s began to close their homes for the poor and board inmates in adjoining counties. According to a 1936 report, only 86 counties maintained homes for the poor, 49 of which did not meet the state's standards. By 1954 the number of counties with below-standard homes was down to 38. By the early 2000s, Beaufort was the only North Carolina county to operate a home for the poor. Privately owned and operated group care homes, licensed by the state, now serve the function of former county homes and poorhouses.

Statewide Public Welfare Initiatives and the Modern Division of Social Services

The North Carolina Constitution of 1868 established a five-member Board of Public Charities to reform the state's treatment of the poor. Inadequate funding hampered the board until Governor Daniel G. Fowle reorganized it in 1889. After securing extra funding from the General Assembly in 1891, the board introduced uniform registration books for county home superintendents, abolished the practice of awarding care of the poor to the lowest bidder, required quarterly visits to the poor by a committee that included a member of the board of county commissioners, and established a juvenile correctional school.

The Board of Public Charities made great strides in social welfare reform in the 1890s and 1910s, obtaining its first regular office space in the State Capitol in 1904. In 1917 the board was reorganized as the Board of Charities and Public Welfare. Its primary function continued to be the supervision and investigation of the entire system of penal and charitable institutions, and it was given greater fiscal and legal resources to accomplish its mission. The board was authorized to hire a commissioner of public welfare and other employees and to spend appropriated funds. Charitable institutions for children, such as private orphanages, were required to submit to the board an annual statement of moneys received and expended and work performed. They were also to be licensed annually by the board before soliciting funds from the public.

In subsequent years the General Assembly gradually broadened the state welfare program. In 1925, for instance, the Bureau of Work among Negroes was created to study the social problems of blacks and to coordinate community-based programs. Also in 1925 the Board of Charities and Public Welfare began close cooperation with the newly established School of Public Welfare at the University of North Carolina in the training of social workers. (The school became the School of Social Work in 1950.)

In 1937, as a result of the Great Depression and federal remedial legislation, the General Assembly created the Division of Public Assistance within the state board to coordinate assistance for the aged and dependent children. The State Old Age Assistance Fund and the State Aid to Dependent Children Fund were established to administer both federal Social Security funds and state and county funds set aside to assist these groups. In 1945 the legislature changed the name of the state welfare agency to the State Board of Public Welfare, and the various county boards incorporated the term "public" in their titles. This subtle change brought North Carolina into accord with a modern social understanding of social service as genuinely public welfare, not charity.

By an act of the General Assembly in 1969, the state and county boards were changed to boards of "social services." The commissioner of social services served as the chief administrator of the State Department of Social Services, which in the 1971 reorganization of state government was transferred to the Department of Human Resources. The modern-day Division of Social Services is part of the massive Department of Health and Human Services.

Public housing for North Carolina's low-income families has traditionally been provided by city housing authorities, which were established under state laws that permit their participation in federally aided programs. These housing authorities may either build new housing or purchase it from a developer, buy existing housing and restore it, or lease existing homes. Despite the efforts of a variety of private agencies—including church-related rescue missions, organizations like Habitat for Humanity, and government agencies—homelessness, lack of affordable housing, and substandard housing remain.

By the early 2000s, the Division of Social Services, operating under the North Carolina Department of Health and Human Resources, existed to help children and adults in need of various kinds of assistance, including shelter from abusive environments, economic hardship, and disabling physical or mental problems. North Carolina's Temporary Assistance for Needy Families program, called "Work First," reflected contemporary approaches to public welfare by emphasizing individual responsibility and accountability, job training, literacy and education, and other measures to help people on welfare become self-supporting as quickly as possible. In addition, about 40,000 North Carolinians were enrolled in the federal Food Stamp Program, aimed at temporarily helping individuals in the areas of nutrition and health.

References: A. Laurance Aydlett, "The North Carolina State Board of Public Welfare," *NCHR* 24 (January 1947); Guion G. Johnson, *Ante-Bellum North Carolina: A Social History* (1937); Robert S. Rankin, *The Government and Administration of North Carolina* (1955).

David A. Norris
Additional research provided by K. Todd Johnson, Jay Mazzocchi, and Wiley J. Williams.

Powell Bill was the successful product of a 15-year fight by the League of Municipalities to have the state of North Carolina fund the building and maintenance of major city streets. Senate Bill 120, as it was known to legislators, was introduced on 30 Jan. 1951 by Junius K. Powell of Whiteville and 37 other state senators. After Governor William Kerr Scott recommended an additional one-cent gasoline tax to fund the proposed measure, the Powell Bill became Chapter 260 of the 1951 General Statutes of North Carolina on 15 Mar. 1951.

Section 1 asserted that city and town streets were part of the state public roads system and would be constructed, reconstructed, and maintained by the State Highway and Public Works Commission from state highway funds. Section 2 provided additional money (taken from a half-cent gas tax) directly to municipalities—based on their population and street mileage—to maintain, repair, and construct city streets that were not part of the state highway system. Since the Powell Bill's ratification in 1951, minor changes have been made, generally increasing allocation to cities under Section 2.

Reference: John Alexander McMahon, "Roads and Streets in North Carolina: Report to the State-Municipal Road Commission," *Popular Government* (September 1950).

W. Lee Johnston Jr.

Precincts exist in North Carolina as voting district subdivisions of both cities and counties. In the Proprietary province of Carolina, however, precincts were administrative and judicial districts of the counties or colonies. Corresponding to the modern county, each Proprietary precinct—governed by a court of justices chaired by a steward—had a sheriff as its chief law officer. The precincts also were used in determining representation in the Assembly and organizing the militia. Since the colonial Assembly first met in 1665, precincts may have been established at that time, but the earliest documentation is a 1668 commission that confirms that Pasquotank Precinct was in existence. It is likely that Chowan, Currituck, and Perquimans Precincts were created at the same time. These four governmental units are North Carolina's oldest extant counties.

Lindley S. Butler

Presbyterian Church, rooted in Calvinist theology, was founded by sixteenth-century Scottish reformer John Knox. The first Presbyterian minister to conduct services in North Carolina was Francis Makemie, who is regarded as the father of the Presbyterian Church in America. Makemie arrived in the colonies in 1683 and before his death in 1708 organized numerous churches in Pennsylvania, Maryland, and Virginia. Makemie made his home on the Eastern Shore of Virginia and on his travels preached in most of the American colonies, including North Carolina.

Immigrants from Ireland, Scotland, and Wales who began arriving in North Carolina in the 1730s and 1740s organized the first Presbyterian congregations in the colony. The first Scotch-Irish immigrants settled in present-day Duplin, Pender, and New Hanover Counties in the 1730s. A few hundred colonists from Ulster settled on the lands of Henry McCulloh and Arthur Dobbs in Duplin County and formed the nucleus of the Grove Church approximately three miles southwest of present-day Kenansville. Presbyterians from Wales settled in what is now Pender County and eventually formed the Rockfish congregation near Wallace.

The larger migration of Scotch-Irish via the Great Wagon Road began coming into the backcountry in the 1740s. The earliest congregations in old Orange County included Hawfields, Eno, Little River, Redhouse, Hyco Red House, Bethesda,

and Grier's. The Buffalo and Alamance churches in present-day Guilford County and the Speedwell Church in what is now Rockingham County were organized by 1764. In addition, at least 13 congregations had been organized along the tributaries of the Yadkin and Catawba Rivers before 1770. There were three meeting places in Rowan County: Fourth Creek, now the First Presbyterian Church of Statesville; Cathey's Meeting House, later Thyatira; and Osborne's Meeting House or Centre. In the part of Anson County that was set off as Mecklenburg County in 1763, Steele Creek, Goshen, Sugaw Creek, Rocky River, Coddle Creek, Unity, Hopewell, Philadelphia, and Providence congregations were formed. Poplar Tent congregation was centered west of present-day Concord in Cabarrus County.

The Highland Scots who settled on the Cape Fear River around Cross Creek brought their Presbyterian faith with them to North Carolina. However, many of the first settlers in the Cape Fear Valley were Scotch-Irish. James Campbell, the first regular minister, was called in 1758 to the three congregations in the Highland settlement. He preached twice each Sunday, first in Gaelic and then in English.

Governing authority in the Presbyterian Church is divided between church sessions and higher "courts"—presbyteries, synods, and a general assembly. In 1741 the Presbyterian Church was divided by issues growing out of the Great Awakening. The Synod of Philadelphia or the "Old Side" opposed the revival and generally did not ordain anyone who had not been educated in a Scottish university. The "New Lights" or the "New Side" Synod of New York emphasized the more emotional approach to the faith and were willing to ordain ministers who had received a "private education" by studying under another minister. Although the two synods were reunited in 1758, the debate over these matters remained an issue in the early church. The first North Carolina congregations, which were organized during this period of internal division, were most often served by New Side clergy trained in the American colonies.

The first New Side ministers in North Carolina became members of Hanover Presbytery in Virginia. In March 1770 the six ministers who were serving churches in North Carolina requested that the Carolina churches be organized as a separate presbytery. The following May the synod created Orange Presbytery (so named because two of the ministers lived in Orange County), which included all of the congregations in the Carolinas.

A South Carolina Presbytery was set off from Orange in 1784, and in 1785 the synod created Abingdon Presbytery, consisting of all of the churches west of the Appalachian Mountains. The General Assembly set off the two Carolina presbyteries and Abingdon as the Synod of the Carolinas in 1788, and in 1813 it established a Synod of North Carolina. In 1996 the Synod of North Carolina included eight presbyteries east of the Appalachian divide. The western portion of the state is a part of the Synod of Appalachia.

Disagreement over church government and doctrine led to a division between the "old school" and "new school" Presbyterians in 1837; the great majority of southern congregations were within the old school, which stressed biblical inerrancy. In December 1861 commissioners from 47 old school presbyteries, including those in North Carolina, met in Augusta, Ga., and organized the Presbyterian Church in the Confederate States of America. In 1864 the new school United Synod of the South was absorbed into the Southern Presbyterian Church, which, following the Civil War, took the title of Presbyterian Church in the United States.

Not until 1983 did the Presbyterian Church in the United States (or Southern Presbyterian Church) unite with the United Presbyterian Church in the U.S.A. (or Northern Presbyterian Church); the resulting Presbyterian Church U.S.A. represents the largest body of Presbyterians in North Carolina, with more than 200,000 members in the early 2000s. Other Presbyterian groups with relatively large congregations in North Carolina are the Associated Reformed Presbyterian Church, the Presbyterian Church in America (about 74 churches and over 17,000 communicants), and the Evangelical Presbyterian Church. St. Andrews Presbyterian College in Laurinburg continues to be affiliated with the Presbyterian Church and supported by individual North Carolina congregations.

References: Lefferts A. Loetscher, *A Brief History of Presbyterians* (3rd ed., 1978); Robert Hamlin Stone, *A History of Orange Presbytery, 1770–1970* (1970); Ernest Trice Thompson, *Presbyterians in the South* (3 vols., 1963–73); George Wesley Troxler, "The Establishment of Presbyterianism in North Carolina" (M.A. Thesis, UNC-Chapel Hill, 1966).

George W. Troxler

SEE ALSO Peace College; St. Andrews Presbyterian College; Thyatira Church and Community.

Presbyterian Junior College for Men

Presbyterian Junior College for Men was established in 1927 by the Presbyterian Synod of North Carolina and Fayetteville Presbytery. In 1928 the trustees acquired the campus and properties of Carolina College for Women in Maxton, and the school was opened on 11 Sept. 1929 with 84 students. The first president was R. A. McLeod, former superintendent of Elise Academy in Elise (now Robbins). McLeod died in 1932. He was succeeded by R. G. Matheson Jr., and later by Cary Adams. By rigid economy and local support, the school survived the Great Depression, and a strong curriculum in business training was established.

In 1938 Louis C. LaMotte became president and served for the next 23 years. A challenge gift of $20,000 in 1939 by W. H. Belk of Charlotte and R. L. McLeod of Maxton, and matching funds from the synod, placed the school on a sound financial basis, and it continued to grow. In 1939 the Civil Aeronautics Authority established a Civilian Pilot Training Program at the school, which later became part of the War Training Service as World War II approached. This brought students from across the United States to the school. Elise Academy was merged with Presbyterian Junior College in 1940.

The college reached its peak enrollment of 503 students in the years immediately following World War II. It continued to operate until 1961, when it and Flora MacDonald College were merged into the newly created St. Andrews's College at Laurinburg by the Synod of North Carolina. Carolina Military Academy operated on the campus from 1962 to 1969, and the main building burned in 1973.

Reference: Maud Thomas, *Away Down Home: A History of Robeson County, North Carolina* (1982).

Henry A. McKinnon Jr.

Preservation North Carolina. SEE Historic Preservation.

Presidents, U.S. Three North Carolina natives have served as president of the United States. Andrew Jackson, the seventh

Andrew Jackson. Lithograph by Nathaniel Currier. NCC.

James K. Polk. Painting by Thomas Sully. Original owned by the Dialectic and Philanthropic Literary Society, UNC-Chapel Hill. Dialectic and Philanthropic Societies Foundation, UNC-Chapel Hill.

Andrew Johnson. NCC.

president, was reputedly born in a log cabin south of the town of Waxhaw in 1767. This claim continues to be disputed by many who maintain that Jackson was actually born in South Carolina. After a distinguished military and political career, he was elected president in 1828 and again in 1832. His larger-than-life personality and political savvy while in office increased the power of the presidency and inspired the development of a truly unified national identity.

James K. Polk, the eleventh president, was born in Mecklenburg County near the town of Pineville in 1795. Polk was elected in 1844 and served one term, the highlight of which was the acquisition of the western one-third of the modern United States after war with Mexico.

Andrew Johnson, the nation's seventeenth president, was born in Raleigh in 1808 but lived most of his life in Tennessee, from which his political career was launched. He was the only southern U.S. senator to remain loyal to the Union during the Civil War. Johnson was chosen as Abraham Lincoln's running mate in 1864 and assumed the presidency after Lincoln's assassination the following year. His administration was marred by his 1867 impeachment by the Radical Republican–led House of Representatives, which vigorously disagreed with his handling of southern Reconstruction after the war. He was acquitted in the Senate by one vote.

References: Burke Davis, *Old Hickory: A Life of Andrew Jackson* (1977); Thomas M. Leonard, *James K. Polk: A Clear and Unquestionable Destiny* (2001); Milton Meltzer, *Andrew Jackson and His America* (1993); Hans L. Trefousse, *Andrew Johnson: A Biography* (1989).

Sion Dayson

Primogeniture was the name for the English law that made the oldest son heir to a family estate if the head of the family died without a will or without providing for some disposition of his or her property. This practice was intended to preserve large estates in aristocratic England. For a number of reasons, including their greater desire to duplicate the English way of life, the southern American colonies adhered more closely to the practice of primogeniture than did the colonies in the North. As early as 1762, however, the North Carolina Assembly provided that, in cases of intestacy, a wife was to receive one-third of landed property with "all the rest by equal Portions, to and amongst the Children." After the Revolution, the state legislature also ended primogeniture with a bill in 1784 requiring that land be divided equally among all children in cases where no will existed. By the end of the eighteenth century, primogeniture had been abolished everywhere in the United States.

References: Richard B. Morris, *Studies in the History of American Law* (1958); Marylynn Salmon, *Women and the Law of Property in Early America* (1986).

Donna J. Spindel

Princeville, an Edgecombe County town incorporated in 1885, originated in 1865 as a resettlement community for ex-slaves. At the close of the Civil War, when Union troops occupied the area around Tarboro, many of the former slaves in surrounding counties left their plantations and came to the Federals' encampment seeking freedom and protection. The future faced by the mostly illiterate, unskilled, penniless freed-persons was uncertain and unpromising.

The ex-slaves congregated around the Union troops biv-ouacked on the south side of the Tar River below Tarboro. Although the soldiers advised them to return to the plantations and work for their old masters, a sizable number of freedmen and -women remained encamped at the site after the troops had departed. They called their new village Freedom Hill (or sometimes Liberty Hill), a name adopted from a nearby hill or knoll where northern soldiers had addressed the former slaves, telling them that the Union victory in the war had made them free. The knoll where the soldiers made their speeches was on the west side of Old Sparta Road near what is now the intersection of U.S. 64 and U.S. 258.

The ex-slaves who remained encamped on the river soon erected makeshift shelters. White landowners made no effort to evict them from the land, which was so swampy that it was otherwise useless. In fact there is some evidence that the "squatters" were encouraged to remain at the site and thus keep their distance from the white community in Tarboro. In the 1870s the landowners began selling lots to blacks. One of the buyers was Turner Prince (1843–1912), a carpenter for whom the community was renamed upon its incorporation in 1885. James City, located across the Trent River from New Bern, had origins similar to those of Princeville but remained unincorporated.

Princeville's economy grew in the late nineteenth and early twentieth centuries, as black-owned businesses proliferated, but the rise of white supremacy brought a serious threat to Princeville's continued existence as a black town. Despite mounting calls for the town's dissolution, residents resisted, and today the town remains a cohesive black community. In 1999 the town's struggle to survive the devastating flooding caused by Hurricane Floyd became national news, leading to a number of public and private relief efforts. In 2006 the restoration of Princeville was ongoing.

Princeville's history is often compared to that of Eatonville, Fla., another "all-black" southern town that was incorporated in 1887. Being two years older, Princeville lays claim to being the "oldest city chartered by blacks in America."

Reference: Joe A. Mobley, "In the Shadow of White Society: Princeville, a Black Town in North Carolina, 1865–1915," NCHR 63 (July 1986).

Michael Hill

SEE ALSO James City.

Printing. In 1749 North Carolina's provincial government brought James Davis from Virginia to become the colony's public printer and establish the first printing press in the then-capital city of New Bern. Prior to Davis's arrival, printing jobs had been sent to Williamsburg, Va., or Charleston, S.C. While North Carolina was the ninth of the 13 colonies to establish a printing operation, it did so 110 years after the colonies' first press appeared in Massachusetts. A number of factors contributed to North Carolina's relatively late entrance into the world of type. The lack of a press had helped the provincial government control the distribution of information. As late as 1671, Lord Proprietor Sir William Berkeley expressed his relief that North Carolina had "no free schools and no printing, and I hope we shall have none these hundred years." Also, many of the American colonies' earliest presses had started in large urban centers such as Boston (1639), Philadelphia (1685), and New York (1693). North Carolina, a primarily agricultural province, did not have the population density of large cities to help support a printer. The province's closest neighbors, Virginia and South Carolina, only established presses a decade before North Carolina.

The N.C. Assembly brought Davis to New Bern to help with the distribution of their proceedings and laws. Prior to his establishment as the public printer, multiple copies of such documents were made by hand for key officials. Davis's first New Bern publication was the *Journal of the House of Burgesses of the Province of North Carolina*, printed in 1749. He also issued the first collection of public laws printed in North Carolina as authorized by the Assembly of 1747, titled *A Collection of All the Public Acts of Assembly, of the Province of North Carolina: now in Force and Use, etc.* (1751). Davis published later editions of the acts of the Assembly and also started North Carolina's first newspaper, the *North-Carolina Gazette*, in New Bern in 1751. He remained active as a printer until his death in 1785.

Other printers made significant contributions to the early history of North Carolina. Andrew Steuart, a native of Ireland, established the second printing operation in North Carolina in Wilmington near the end of 1763 (or possibly in early 1764). Steuart supported himself by establishing the colony's second newspaper, also called the *North-Carolina Gazette*. Adam

Boyd, a native of Pennsylvania, purchased Steuart's press and type after Steuart's death in 1769 and established himself as a printer in Wilmington. That year he started the *Cape-Fear Mercury*, which proved to be successful. Abraham Hodge, a native of New York, worked as a printer for Samuel Loudon during the American Revolution. Around 1785, Hodge moved to Halifax to establish a printing office. He was appointed North Carolina state printer in 1785, after Davis's death. Hodge worked in partnership with a number of different printers and established printing offices in Edenton, Fayetteville, and New Bern in addition to Halifax. He served as public printer for 15 years, started three newspapers, and printed almanacs. His career helped establish a broader publication base within North Carolina. Other early luminaries in the North Carolina printing industry include Joseph Gales, François-Xavier Martin, and John Christian Blum.

From Johann Gutenberg's printed Bible to colonial newspapers, the art of printing had made little progress. Impressions were made from the inked type onto paper by a slow process dating back several centuries. Ink was made of linseed oil and lampblack. The process of hand-setting the type letter by letter was tedious and limited printers in styles and sizes. In 1820, however, the all-metal "Washington" press came on the market. It was still operated by hand but was much faster than the ancient "screw-style" press. North Carolina's larger cities got the first of these presses for newspaper and circular printing.

In the last quarter of the nineteenth century printers were still composing type by hand. This changed in 1890 with the invention of the Mergenthaler Linotype. This metal casting machine produced type in a solid lead casting, one line at a time. When the type was no longer needed the line of type was remelted to form new lines. A milestone development for North Carolina printers, although not as obvious as the new presses or Linotype, was the publication of the *Franklin Price Book*, a cost-setting reference guide that assured a profit from each printing job. Developed in the 1920s, this book remains a vital tool for public printers.

The technology of printing once again changed dramatically as new offset printing presses and related electronic typesetting came on the market in the early 1950s. Soon afterward, the introduction of computers revolutionized the printing industry. Even a one-person print shop could produce very professional work through computer imagery and specialized programs. North Carolina printing companies grew to serve the needs of a variety of customers, with firms such as Edwards & Broughton and Seeman among the leaders. One of the largest commercial printing firms in the nation, Meredith-Burda, established a large plant in Newton in the 1960s. This firm prints *Better Homes & Gardens* magazine and many advertising tabloids with press runs in the millions of copies.

References: Robert F. Karolevitz, *From Quill to Computer: The Story of America's Community Newspapers* (1985); Douglas C. McMurtrie, *Eighteenth-Century North Carolina Imprints, 1749–1800* (1938); George Washington Paschal, *A History of Printing in North Carolina* (1946); Mary L. Thornton, *Official Publications of the Colony and State of North Carolina, 1749–1939: A Bibliography* (1954).

Timothy D. Pyatt
Chester Paul Middlesworth

Prisoner of War Camps. SEE World War II.

Prisons. SEE Central Prison; Confederate Prison (Salisbury).

Privateers were privately owned and manned ships authorized by their governments during wartime to attack and capture enemy shipping vessels. Documents called "letters of marque" officially spelled out their authority to equip a ship with arms and seize another nation's citizens or goods. Originally known as "Private Men of War," such vessels came to be called privateers in the seventeenth century, possibly as a shortened version of the words "private" and "volunteer."

Privateers have operated in North Carolina waters and off its coast since at least Elizabethan times. After the initial colonization of the East Coast, both American and foreign privateers were involved in the intermittent wars and battles between Great Britain, France, and Spain. They played a significant role in the American Revolution, when North Carolina merchants fitted out their own privateers. Probably the most widely known and most successful commander was Otway Burns of Swansboro. During the War of 1812, he fitted out a fast Baltimore clipper as a privateer named *Snap Dragon*, armed it with four 12-pound guns plus a pivot gun, and ranged from Newfoundland to the Caribbean. In the first seven months after sailing with a letter of marque, Burns exacted a staggering toll on British shipping, capturing 10 vessels, 250 prisoners, and cargo valued at approximately $1 million.

In 1856 all of the major European powers except Spain signed the Declaration of Paris, which made privateering illegal. The United States was not a signatory to the declaration, maintaining that its fledgling navy was inadequate to defend its extensive seacoast. Thus, when the Civil War broke out, both sides fitted out private vessels to attack enemy shipping. In North Carolina, a number of ships were outfitted at Wilmington and operated effectively out of the Cape Fear and Hatteras Inlets. Including everything from schooners to former tugs, pilot boats, and steam packets, they were in constant conflict with the vessels of the Union fleet that were trying to maintain a blockade of the North Carolina ports.

American privateering finally ended in 1907, when the U.S. government subscribed to the terms of the Second Hague

Grave of Otway Burns at the Old Burying Ground in Beaufort, ornamented with a cannon from his ship, the *Snap Dragon*. Photograph (taken ca. 1898) by Collier Cobb Sr. NCC.

Conference making privateering illegal. Spain, the last of the major powers to end privateering formally, did so in 1908.

David Stick

SEE ALSO *Snap Dragon*; *Wasp*.

Privies—also known as latrines, loos, johns, outhouses, ajaxes, toilets, or necessaries—were typically small, separate structures associated with a larger domestic, commercial, or industrial building. Although the privy's function has remained constant as a receptacle for human waste, its location, specific architecture, and subsequent furnishings vary. Archaeologically, at least six historic sites have been identified with privy features. One early privy associated with the second jail in historic Halifax was excavated in 1970. Built between 1759 and 1762, this brick-lined privy pit measured six by eight feet and was almost three feet deep. It likely served as the latrine for colonial prisoners as well as visitors to the town and courthouse. At a private residence in historic Edenton, two privies were excavated in the rear yard. Both pits were lined with hewn timbers at the bottom and bricks at the top; they were filled with domestic-related trash from the late eighteenth and early nineteenth century. A third site located in Old

Salem provided evidence of an early tub or barrel privy typically associated with a Piedmont house. This privy, also filled with old domestic trash, was once attached to the side of a barn located in the rear yard. At the E. A. Poe House in Fayetteville, archaeologists uncovered the circular pits of five backyard privies.

Many extant privies from the eighteenth and nineteenth centuries are associated with individual houses, but others have been discovered on the sites of a schoolhouse, hunt clubs, commercial properties, churches, and a large camp meeting ground. The latter, located in Lincoln County, was described as having 288 individual family cabins, each with its own privy. The school had two privies, one for women and one for men. Examples of early privies also exist at plantation or historically significant sites such as the James Iredell House in Edenton and Bellamy Mansion in Wilmington.

North Carolina privies began to be regulated by the State Board of Health beginning in 1877. Primary issues of concern included the safety of drinking water, disease prevention, control of infectious diseases, and proper water and sewage disposal. By 1879 more than half of the state's counties had organized health boards addressing these issues. In February 1919 North Carolina's General Assembly passed a statewide privy

References: Jacob Stohler, "Outhouses Left out of State's Progress," *Raleigh News and Observer*, 3 Sept. 1996; Benjamin Earle Washburn, *A History of the North Carolina State Board of Health, 1877–1925* (1966).

Linda F. Carnes-McNaughton

Proclamation of 1763 is intimately tied to the history of English–Native American relations during the colonial era. The purpose of the proclamation was to stop white settlers or traders from exploiting American Indians. Although that relationship varied from one colony to another, by the eighteenth century most coastal tribes had already been decimated by disease or war or had moved westward. But even those who migrated to the interior came to rely on European trade, a fact that led to destructive competition among the tribes. Determined to preserve their way of life before the European advance, several northern tribes led by Pontiac, an Ottawa chief, launched a major offensive against English forts in the west. This episode, known as Pontiac's Conspiracy, prompted the English government to issue the Proclamation of 1763.

This decree established the governments of East and West Florida and Quebec, reserved the enormous western lands outside of these areas to Native Americans, imposed strict regulations on the fur trade, and required the approval of royal officials of any land purchases in the future. If the proclamation was to preserve peace on the frontier, it was also designed to limit the areas of white settlement and thereby keep the growing rebellious attitude of the colonists under close scrutiny. The line of 1763, beyond which white settlers could not advance, extended across the western border of North Carolina. At this time, however, England's new policy had minimal impact on the colony since white settlement there had not extended to the western line.

Reference: Ian K. Steele, *Warpaths: Invasions of North America* (1994).

Donna J. Spindel

SEE ALSO Tryon's Line.

Profanity. The existence of profanity in North Carolina, as in other states, can be attributed to the English-speaking settlers who established themselves in the New World. Their newly attained political independence from the mother country greatly affected both their linguistic freedom and their observance of the constricting correctness of British models for language.

Profane language can be divided into seven categories: names of deities, angels, and devils; names connected with the sacred matters of religion; names of saints, holy persons, or biblical characters; names of sacred places; words relating

Sampson County privy (showing a new seat before it was installed), ca. 1915. Courtesy of NCOA&H.

law mandating strict health and safety requirements, scheduled inspections, and prosecution of violators.

By the late 1920s, advancements in sanitary engineering fostered construction and installation of underground sewage disposal. Indoor plumbing and flush toilets replaced outdoor privies in most areas, but wooden privies remain a feature of the rural landscape. A 1996 newspaper article revealed that 3.4 percent of Chatham County residences lacked modern toilets, and nearly 50,000 homes within the greater Triangle area (Raleigh, Durham, and Chapel Hill) lacked indoor plumbing. The author cited building code restrictions and the inability to equip houses with piping or appliances as primary reasons for this deficiency.

to the future life; vulgar words, or words and phrases unusual or forbidden by polite usage; and expletives, including words or phrases having unusual force for various reasons. Although some of these categories are related to the need to vent emotionally through vocalization, most involve religion.

The federal government provides guidelines regarding the use of profanity. The primary responsibility of the Federal Communications Commission (FCC) is to authorize and regulate interstate communications services, including the Internet. The FCC's 1996 Communications Decency Act, which criminalized profanity by equating it to harassment, affected all computers in homes, libraries, and schools connected to the Internet. In 1997 the U.S. Supreme Court declared the act unconstitutional, observing that the Internet was a unique medium entitled to the highest protection of free speech under the First Amendment to the U.S. Constitution.

In 2001 the North Carolina State Senate, amending a law governing embalmers and funeral directors, passed a bill regulating the for-profit transportation of bodies. This bill prohibits the use of "profanity, indecent, or obscene language in the presence of a dead human body." The Clean Language clause was already law in funeral homes and was extended to the transportation of bodies out of respect for the dead and their loved ones.

References: Lars Andersson and Peter Trudgill, *Bad Language* (1990); Geoffrey Hughes, *Swearing* (1991).

Sean Kenniff

Progress Energy Carolinas. SEE Carolina Power & Light Company.

Progressive Farmer is among the oldest and most widely read of the nation's agricultural periodicals. The history of the publication reflects dramatic changes in southern rural life and journalism. The paper was founded in Winston (now Winston-Salem) in February 1886 by Leonidas L. Polk, a former Confederate officer and North Carolina commissioner of agriculture. Initially, it appeared in a weekly newspaper format. The *Progressive Farmer* promoted more efficient agricultural practices and improved farm life. Polk also used the paper to stimulate organization among farmers, in particular the Farmers' Alliance and Industrial Union, or Southern Farmers' Alliance, for which the paper served as the official state organ.

After Polk moved his publishing enterprise to West Hargett Street in Raleigh in 1887, the *Progressive Farmer* was increasingly involved in political controversy. In the late 1880s and early 1890s the paper championed a wide range of reform causes, including the establishment of an agricultural college in Raleigh, railroad rate regulation, and the Subtreasury Plan. Although its editorials first maintained that these reforms could be achieved through legislation supported by the Demo-

cratic Party, just before Polk's sudden death in June 1892 the *Progressive Farmer* announced its endorsement of the newly formed People's, or Populist, Party. At that time, the circulation of the paper exceeded 20,000, making it one of the leading Farmers' Alliance–Populist papers in the nation.

After Polk's death, editorial control of the *Progressive Farmer* passed to James L. Ramsey. Ownership of the company remained in the hands of Polk's daughter, Juanita Polk Denmark, whose husband, James W. Denmark, was business manager. Ramsey's tenure, which lasted until 1899, was shaped by the turbulence of Populism, Fusion, and Democratic white supremacy politics. During the 1890s the paper continued to portray itself as the friend of farmers. It endorsed all of the Populist platforms and supported Populist-Republican candidates. In 1896, the newspaper supported the Democratic-Populist nominee for president, William Jennings Bryan.

The demise of Populism required a new political and journalistic strategy. This different direction was conceived and executed by Clarence Poe, a native of Chatham County. Although only 18 years old, Poe became editor-in-chief of the *Progressive Farmer* in July 1899. Poe had written for the newspaper since 1897, and he was deeply interested in rural problems. Poe had been approved for the editorship by the Denmarks and by Ramsey. Yet Poe was not committed to third-party politics. He immediately made peace with North Carolina Democrats, disengaged the *Progressive Farmer* from Populism, and

Front page of the Thanksgiving issue of the *Progressive Farmer*, 1906. NCC.

supported the Democrats' disfranchisement legislation of 1900.

In 1903, with the help of borrowed money, Poe completed the transition by purchasing Polk's Progressive Farmer Company for slightly more than $7,000. He then formed a new company with the same name, buying almost 47 percent of the stock. The other owners of the new *Progressive Farmer* were B. W. Kilgore, later dean of agriculture at North Carolina State College (modern-day North Carolina State University); Charles W. Burkett, then head of the Agriculture Department at the School; T. B. Parker, a prominent member of the North Carolina Farmers' Alliance; and the Baptist editor Josiah W. Bailey of Raleigh. Impressed by the failures of Populism, Poe declared that the new *Progressive Farmer* would be free from "all partisan politics and political scheming" but would remain dedicated to "everything that makes for the uplift or betterment of farm life." This strategy, as well as high-quality writing and production, proved an immediate success. Subscriptions grew from 6,000 in 1903 to more than 35,000 by 1908.

Poe served as president of the *Progressive Farmer* until 1956. Under his leadership the publication experienced continued transformations. Growth in readership was exponential, reaching well over 1 million by the mid-1950s. But because of its aggressive search for new subscribers, the publication's primary connection with North Carolina was destroyed. An increasingly regional focus and mergers with rural papers from outside North Carolina resulted in a decision to move the headquarters and printing plant from Raleigh to Birmingham, Ala., in 1911. Raleigh became a regional office, and additional offices were later added in Memphis and Dallas. The regional system permitted local editions with attention to different agricultural conditions. In 1932 the weekly newspaper format was dropped in favor of a monthly magazine with color illustrations.

Although generally directed to self-help and private forms of improvement, Poe's *Progressive Farmer* endorsed many causes, including better rural health, improved farm roads, equal railroad freight rates for the South, mechanization of farms, and better public education. Poe also used the *Progressive Farmer* to promote rural racial segregation. Unlike the first *Progressive Farmer*, however, the *Progressive Farmer* of the twentieth century steadfastly kept Poe's initial promise by supporting agricultural programs within the context of Democratic political control.

In the early 2000s, the *Progressive Farmer* reached more than 1.5 million readers 20 times a year. The Progressive Farmer Company ran several other operations from its Birmingham, Ala., headquarters, including the monthly magazine *Southern Living* and a popular website on the Internet.

References: Emory Cunningham, *Eighty-Nine Years of Service in the South: The Story of the Progressive Farmer Company* (1975); Stuart Noblin, *Leonidas LaFayette Polk: Agrarian Crusader* (1949); Clarence Poe, *My First Eighty Years* (1963).

James L. Hunt

Progressivism, like its ideological counterpoise, conservatism, has taken different forms in North Carolina. Progressivism generally refers to a political philosophy that promotes measures leading to the state's educational, economic, or social development. Although the term has come to be associated with aspects of social liberalism, from the earliest years of statehood leaders of all political parties have encouraged business, educational, transportation, and other initiatives to help the citizenry move forward. In numerous instances, however, to be forward looking on one issue did not guarantee a similar approach to others.

The modern understanding of progressivism evolved during the Progressive Era of the early twentieth century and was subsequently embodied in the presidential administrations of Theodore Roosevelt, Woodrow Wilson, and Franklin D. Roosevelt. True progressivism in North Carolina began with the election of Democratic governor Charles B. Aycock in 1900. Aycock's emphasis on public support for education was forward looking indeed, whereas his view on equal access to education for African Americans was decidedly the opposite. Nevertheless, the achievements of his administration and those of the next generation of Democratic leaders could be considered monumental and essential to the state's development throughout the century.

One far-reaching result of North Carolina's progressive thinking was the growth of the public health movement. Between 1909 and 1915 the work of the Rockefeller Sanitary Commission for the Elimination of Hookworm, in cooperation with the North Carolina State Board of Health, led to the widespread treatment of the parasitic infestation, improved the health of citizens by increasing their knowledge of modern medicine, and paved the way for later public health initiatives. North Carolina, still predominately rural, had much to gain by improved sanitary practices. Under the guidance of public health director Watson S. Rankin, the state's public health system emerged as one of the best in the nation. Primarily because of the efforts of Democratic governor Cameron Morrison in the 1920s, North Carolina also became known as the "Good Roads State."

North Carolina's Democratic leaders, operating in what was basically a one-party system until the 1970s, retained wholly nonprogressive stances toward several issues. As a result of their opposition to the women suffrage movement, North Carolina was one of a handful of states that failed to ratify the Nineteenth Amendment in 1920. Political leaders also revealed their basic conservatism by their lukewarm acceptance of numerous New Deal programs of the 1930s, although many farming and working-class citizens welcomed the support.

The Progressive Party was formed in North Carolina in 1948, but its candidacy of Henry Wallace was short-lived.

In the latter half of the twentieth century, North Carolina progressivism took a new shape while retaining familiar elements. Moving decidedly left, progressives took the lead in issues of racial equality, demanding that the state live up to the tenets and legal requirements of the federal civil rights laws of the 1950s and 1960s. As the national Democratic Party embraced an array of liberal causes during the 1960s and 1970s, the modern-day definition of North Carolina progressivism came to include everything from abortion rights to environmentalism.

Yet room remained for "old-fashioned," pro-business attitudes among North Carolina progressives. Governors and other state leaders of both major political parties have promoted the state's tremendous economic growth, the expansion of its community college and university systems, the upgrading and modernization of its public schools, and other achievements. While distinct differences between conservatives and progressives continue to exist on a variety of issues, perhaps an equal number of similarities lead to the perpetual "gray area" that has typified North Carolina politics from its beginnings.

References: David L. Cockrell, "A Blessing in Disguise: The Influenza Pandemic of 1918 and North Carolina's Medical and Public Health Communities," NCHR 73 (July 1996); William A. Link, The Paradox of Southern Progressivism, 1880–1930 (1992); Paul Luebke, Tar Heel Politics 2000 (1998); William S. Powell, North Carolina through Four Centuries (1989).

David L. Cockrell
Additional research provided by Allyson C. Criner.

Prohibition of the manufacture and sale of intoxicating liquors in North Carolina was in effect statewide between 1909 and 1935. As early as 1852 a petition seeking prohibition was presented to the General Assembly, but no legislative action was taken. Antiliquor forces did gain enough influence in the Democratic Party in 1881 to win the legislature's approval of a popular referendum on the measure, but it was overwhelmingly defeated by a vote of 166,325 to 48,370.

In the late nineteenth and early twentieth centuries, many municipalities were allowed to regulate the sale of alcohol through dispensaries controlled by town commissioners. In 1903, at the urging of a newly organized Anti-Saloon League, the Democratic-controlled legislature passed the Watts Act, prohibiting the manufacture and sale of spirituous liquors except in incorporated towns. According to historians Hugh T. Lefler and Albert Ray Newsome, the law was designed "to get rid of the county distilleries," which Democratic Party leader Furnifold M. Simmons called "Republican recruiting stations." In 1905 the Ward Law extended Prohibition to incor-

porated towns of fewer than 1,000 inhabitants, meaning that 68 of the 98 counties in the state had Prohibition.

The Anti-Saloon League and Governor Robert B. Glenn finally convinced the General Assembly to authorize a statewide referendum on Prohibition, which was scheduled for 26 May 1908. The measure passed by a vote of 113,612 to 69,416, with 21 counties voting against it. Statewide Prohibition became effective in January 1909. In 1913 Congress passed a law making it illegal to transport liquor from wet states into North Carolina and other dry states; six years later, the Eighteenth Amendment of the U.S. Constitution established Prohibition as federal law.

Prohibition was slowly phased out in North Carolina after national Prohibition was repealed in 1933. "Light" wine and beer sales were allowed soon afterward, and a county-option liquor law in 1937 established the Alcoholic Beverage Control system.

K. Todd Johnson

SEE ALSO Alcoholic Beverage Control Commission; Anti-Saloon League; Temperance Movement; Turlington Act.

Prostitution was not a crime in seventeenth-century North Carolina since there were no laws pertaining to it. Fornication, or illicit sexual activity, was viewed as a matter of morals rather than a rule of state; until the colony adopted the Anglican faith in 1701, prostitution and other sexual deviance was not an issue in the public forum. Marriage, adultery, cohabitation, and divorce, however, were treated more seriously, because children, legitimate or otherwise, might be affected, and the state could be required to support them or to arbitrate property disputes regarding their rights.

Not until the Sabbath Observance Act of January 1715 did the state legislature come out forcefully against vice, including drunkenness, profanity, adultery, and prostitution. Under the new law, any male or female convicted of the crime of prostitution would be fined 50 shillings, one-half being paid to the informer and the other half to the local church. For those without the means to pay the fine, the penalty was 21 lashes with a whip, delivered publicly. Both sentences were commuted in 1741 to 20 shillings proclamation money for each offense, or less than 10 shillings sterling.

The nineteenth century saw little change in the law, because many men, even those in high office, including legislators, were involved with the prostitution trade. Although the 1741 statute regarding vice was amended in 1805, this revision further obscured the issue by placing prostitution in the category of adultery and cohabitation. The practice of "drinking and pandering to the lustful passions of . . . men" was either ignored for gentlemen, as it had been in colonial times, or charged only against poor whites and blacks. Prostitutes and gamblers were handled through vagrancy statutes; women were arrested and either fined or imprisoned. In 1822 the city of Raleigh began jailing convicted prostitutes for ten days. After completing the sentence, the women were then required to repay the city for arresting and incarcerating them by working the streets once more.

Prosecution for prostitution changed in the twentieth century partly because of clearer statutes, which explained the crime, why it was unlawful, the procedure of prosecution, the degrees of guilt, and the stages of punishment. Prostitution was clearly defined as "offering or receiving of the body for sexual intercourse with or without hire." Yet, although it was possible to convict and imprison a person for violating prostitution laws, there remained the centuries-old problem of enforcement. At the beginning of the twenty-first century, as in years past, only the prostitutes themselves—not their wealthier clientele—appeared to be the most readily available targets for arrest.

References: Guion G. Johnson, *Ante-Bellum North Carolina: A Social History* (1937); William W. Sanger, *The History of Prostitution* (1937).

Louis P. Towles

Protestant Episcopal Church Publishing Association

was founded in Charlotte in 1864 by John Wilkes, a businessman and prominent Episcopal layman. The likely catalyst for the establishment of the association was the need to find a way to revive publication of the *Church Intelligencer*, a Raleigh-based weekly newspaper that had served the Episcopal denomination throughout the southern states since 1860. As the territory controlled by the Confederacy shrank and economic conditions deteriorated, the number of subscribers declined, and the paper was forced to suspend operations with the 8 Apr. 1864 issue.

Five months later, on 14 September, the *Church Intelligencer* reappeared under the proprietorship of the Protestant Episcopal Church Publishing Association, of which Wilkes was treasurer and chief financial backer. In addition to publishing the newspaper, the association proposed to help fill "the great need of suitable Tracts for the army, and Sunday School Literature and Prayer Books for the Church at large." During the next three months, the association published 21 tracts, ranging in length from 4 to 55 pages. Of their six named authors, three were Episcopal bishops, while the others were the rector of Saint Mary's School in Raleigh, a Methodist clergyman from Tennessee, and a former Unitarian minister who had become an Episcopal priest (and was the only northerner among the named authors).

Despite a seemingly promising beginning, the association was soon forced to curtail its tract program. Although December issues of the *Church Intelligencer* announced the impending availability of two additional tracts and four Sunday School

books, no copies of these works with the association's imprint can be found today, and it is doubtful that they were ever published.

In spite of this retrenchment, the association carried on with the newspaper until 3 May 1865, when it was forced to suspend all operations temporarily. Publication resumed on 31 August, but Wilkes replaced the association as proprietor in February 1866. The newspaper ceased publication with the issue of 7 Mar. 1867.

References: Joseph Blount Cheshire, *The Church in the Confederate States: A History of the Protestant Episcopal Church in the Confederate States* (1912); T. Michael Parrish and Robert M. Willingham, *Confederate Imprints: A Bibliography of Southern Publications from Secession to Surrender* (1984).

Robin Brabham

Provincial Congresses.

From the summer of 1774 through 1776, five extralegal representative assemblies patterned after the colonial Lower House led the transition from royal to state government in North Carolina. In the process, these Provincial Congresses created a revolutionary governmental structure, issued bills of credit to finance the movement, organized an army for provincial defense, and wrote the bill of rights and the constitution that established the state.

Despite the opposition of royal governor Josiah Martin, John Harvey, Speaker of the Lower House of the Assembly, conspired with William Hooper in proposing an election of delegates for a provincial meeting to select representatives for the forthcoming Continental Congress to be held in Philadelphia in September. With a majority of the towns and counties represented, the First Provincial Congress convened in the capital of New Bern on 25 Aug. 1774 with Harvey as moderator. In three days the delegates selected delegates to the Continental Congress and approved a trade boycott as a response to the punitive measures that Great Britain had imposed on Boston. As royal authority deteriorated, town and county committees had emerged as the de facto local government, and the First Provincial Congress charged these committees with the enforcement of the proposed boycott.

The Second Provincial Congress, of 3–7 Apr. 1775, also held in New Bern with Harvey as moderator, approved the Continental Association, an economic boycott that had been authorized by the Continental Congress. Just a month later the news reached North Carolina of the bloody clash at Lexington and Concord in Massachusetts; soon Governor Martin fled the capital to the safety of British warships in the Cape Fear River, ending royal government in the province. Overt military action began on 18 July, when the Cape Fear militia burned Fort Johnston.

As a result of the recent events, the atmosphere was more revolutionary when the Third Provincial Congress met during 20 Aug.–10 Sept. 1775 at Hillsborough. Because of the recent death of Harvey, Samuel Johnston was elected to preside. This congress established the Provincial Council, an executive committee, to conduct the affairs of the province when the Provincial Congress was not in session. Representation on the council was based on the six military districts, which were also used for organization of the province's militia and minutemen units. Bills of credit, which were used as currency, were issued to fund defense and the government. Two regiments of Continental troops (regulars) were raised and in the coming months sent to aid both South Carolina and Virginia.

The Loyalist uprising early in 1776, and the ensuing Moore's Creek Bridge conflict and British incursion on Cape Fear, radicalized the Fourth Provincial Congress, held at Halifax during 4 Apr.–15 May 1776. With Johnston again presiding, the congress reorganized the militia for more efficient administration and raised an additional four regiments of regulars. Preliminary steps were begun on a state constitution, and more bills of credit were authorized. The important accomplishment was the passage on 12 April of the Halifax Resolves, which was the first official action toward independence by any province.

Coming after the signing of the national Declaration of Independence, the Fifth Provincial Congress convened during 12 Nov.–23 Dec. 1776 also at Halifax, to draft a state constitution. Richard Caswell, one of the heroes of the Battle of Moore's Creek Bridge, was elected congress president. By 18 December a "Declaration of Rights" and state constitution were adopted, and two days later Caswell was elected the first governor of the new state of North Carolina.

References: Robert L. Ganyard, *The Emergence of North Carolina's Revolutionary State Government* (1978); Hugh T. Lefler and William S. Powell, *Colonial North Carolina: A History* (1973).

Lindley S. Butler

Pseudonyms have been used by North Carolinians since the eighteenth century to conceal identities for many reasons. Among those who used pseudonyms were creative writers and authors in various fields, men who wrote poetry in an age and place when that was considered an effeminate occupation, politicians and public officials, lovers, the shy or modest, and women who lived in a time when they were deemed by many to be incapable of literary accomplishments.

It is reasonable to assume that only a small portion of pseudonyms can ever be identified or that their secret can be discovered without a good clue or other information. The following is a list of some known North Carolina pseudonyms.

True Name	Pseudonym
Arrington, Alfred	Charles Summerfield
Badger, J. Lawrence	Jemmy Critus
Baker, Emma	Eugene Hall
Brown, William	Hill Columbus
Bruckner, Margaretta	Margaret Howe
Bryant, H. E. C.	Red Buck
Byrd, William, II	Inamorato L'Oiseaux
Caldwell, Joseph	Carlton
Chapman, John & Mary	Maristan Chapman
Clark, Charles Dunning	W. J. Hamilton
Clarke, Mary Bayard	Tenella
Craven, Braxton	Charlie Vernon
Daniels, Jonathan	Nicholas Worth
Daniels, Josephus	Rhamkatte Rooster
Dargan, Olive Tilford	Fielding Burke
Deal, Borden	Lee Borden
Downing, Fanny Murdaugh	Viola
Evans, Charles Napoleon Bonaparte	Fool Killer
Fosdick, Charles Austin	Harry Castlemon
Frayser, Lou H.	Zillah Raymond
Fulton, David Bryant	Jack Thorne
Gale, Christopher	Judge Jumble
Gaston, William	Anon. (1808)
Gifford, James Noble	Carol Holliston
Gilmore, James R.	Edmund Kirke
Glascock, Harold	Robert Winfield
Harwood, Dr. Edward	Spectator
Hass, Ben	John Benteen, Ben Elliott, John M. Elliott
Holman, Clarence Hugh	Clarence Hunt
Hooper, Johnson Jones	Simon Suggs
Housekeeper, Mrs. William G.	Rose Batterham
Iredell, James	A Man Who Despises Your Pardons, Marcus, A Planter, A Rioter
Jackson, Andrew	Anon. (1801)
Jones, Calvin	Anon. (1807)
Jones, Joseph Seawell	Schocco Jones
Kaler, James Otis	James Otis
Kelly, Jonathan F.	Falconbridge
Korner, Jule Gilmer	Reuben Rink
Little, William	Puzzlecause
Long, Virginia Love	Mariposa
Lovick, John	Shoebrush
MacLaine, Archibald	Publico
Martin, Alexander	Anon. (1798)
Martin, John Sanford	Santford Martin
McCora, Patrick William	Daly Wise
McEachern, Daniel Purcell	Synder
McNair, Colin	Eddie McLean
Miller, Helen Hill	Helen Hill
Mitchell, Elisha	"N"
Moore, Bertha Belle	Brenda Cannon, Betsy McCurry

Moore, Maurice	Atticus
Moseley, Edward	Judge Jumble
Murfree, Mary Noailles	Charles Egbert Craddock
Murphey, Archibald D.	Florian, Philo-Florian
Nelms, Henning	Hake Talbot
Newell, Robert Henry	Orpheus C. Kerr
Page, Walter Hines	Nicholas Worth
Parham, James A.	General Mecklenburg
Petch, Allan J., Colonel	Jeremy North
Pettigrew, Charles	Flagillator Scurvarum
Pettigrew, James Johnston	A Carolinian
Pollock, John Alfred	Ronleigh de Conval
Porter, William Sydney	O. Henry
Powell, Talmage	Jack McCready
Pritchard, John W.	Ian Wallace
Raymond, Rene	James JH. Chase
Rhodes, William Henry	Caxton
Rivenbark, Mrs. Robert W.	Mita Leon
Schaw, Janet	Lady of Quality
Simms, William Gilmore	Bachelor Knight
Smith, Charles Henry	Bill Arp
Smith, Leverette	Arthur Mann Kaye
Spencer, Cornelia Philips	Magnus
Spencer, DeLeon G.	Jo Jo
Steuart, Andrew	Philanthropes
Stickland, William Herman	Emmitt Lookabee
Strange, Robert	An American
Strother, David Hunter	Porte Crayon
Swann, Samuel	Bo-otes
Taliaferro, Hardin E.	Skitt
Thompson, William	Major Jones
Throop, George Higby	Gregory Seaworthy
Tiernan, Frances Christina Fisher	Christian Reid
Tourgée, Albion W.	"C," Henry Churton
Vail, Abner	Viator
Walz, Audrey	Francis Connamy
Wellman, Frances	Frances Garfield
Wicker, Tom	Paul Connolly
Williamson, Hugh	Sylvius
Witherspoon, John Knox	Knox
Wright, Watkins Eppes	Allen Eppes

William S. Powell

Additional research provided by Wilson Angley, Jerry C. Cashion, Jerry L. Cross, Michael Hill, Michael R. McVaugh, W. Keats Sparrow, Shelby Stephenson, and Willis P. Whichard.

Psychiatric Hospitals. By the early 2000s the North Carolina Division of Mental Health, Disabilities, and Substance Abuse Services operated four psychiatric hospitals for care of the mentally ill, each serving a specific region of the state. Dorothea Dix Hospital, in Raleigh, the state's oldest psychiatric institution, served residents of North Carolina's south-central region; John Umstead Hospital, in Butner, the north-central region; Cherry Hospital, in Goldsboro, the eastern region; and Broughton Hospital, in Morganton, the western region. Before these hospitals appeared beginning in the mid-1800s, North Carolinians suffering from many forms of mental illness were kept at home, sent to private out-of-state facilities, or held in local jails. Many people had a superstitious fear of the insane, and although the state authorized the courts to appoint guardians who would protect the property of the mentally ill, their care remained the responsibility of individual families.

In the nineteenth century, state psychiatric hospitals offered little more than beds and food for the mentally ill, alcoholics, and the mentally retarded. In 1909 former asylum patient Clifford Beers (1876–1943) established the National Committee for Mental Hygiene (now the National Association for Mental Health) as part of his crusade to improve the care of people with mental illness. The North Carolina branch of the foundation was formed in 1914, and the advent of modern mental health care in North Carolina can be traced from this date. After state legislators changed commitment law in 1973 to permit the involuntary hospitalization of people imminently dangerous to themselves or others, psychiatric hospitals began to treat more involuntary patients with a history of violence.

Although the General Assembly considered building an asylum for the mentally ill in 1825, 1838–39, and 1844, it was only when nurse and social reformer Dorothea Lynde Dix (1802–87) addressed the lawmakers in 1848 that funding for a hospital was set aside. By 1851 a tract of 182 acres just west of Raleigh had been acquired, and planning for the Dix facility was begun. State appropriations and several bonds funded construction of the first building, a Romanesque structure with a large central section and two wings designed by prominent New York architect Alexander T. Davis. A second building, containing a kitchen, bakery, and apartments for staff, was soon added. This was the first public building in Raleigh to have steam heat and gas lighting. Dorothea Dix refused to have the hospital named after her but agreed to the designation of the site on which it was located as "Dix Hill," in memory of her physician grandfather, Elijah Dix.

The hospital began admitting patients in 1856. Over the years, its mental heath services expanded and additional buildings were constructed. In 1902 the Dorothea Dix School of Nursing was established. By the mid-twentieth century, the hospital occupied 1,248 acres, much of them left as forest. In 1959 the name of the facility was changed to Dorothea Dix Hospital, in memory of the woman who had been essential to its founding.

By 1974 the Dix complex had grown to 282 buildings on 2,354 acres, plus 1,300 acres of farmland; patient capacity was 2,756. Over the next several decades, however, demand for long-term hospitalization of the mentally ill declined as out-patient care was emphasized. In addition, other state hospitals and private institutions offered mental health services that were closer and more convenient for many citizens. By the early 2000s, Dix Hospital had 120 buildings and occupied a 425-acre tract, accommodating a maximum of 682 patients. The hospital's approximately $60 million annual budget was supported by state and federal funds as well as patient fees.

By 1875 it was recognized that mentally ill citizens in western North Carolina were underserved, and in March of that year the General Assembly provided funds to build a second state hospital, the Western North Carolina Insane Asylum, in Morganton. Patients began to be admitted in 1883, with about 100 individuals transported by railroad from the overcrowded Raleigh facility. The hospital grew, with many buildings added through the late nineteenth and early twentieth centuries, and various new therapies became available to patients. The name of the hospital, which had been changed in 1890 to the State Hospital at Morganton, officially became Broughton Hospital in 1959 in honor of Governor J. Melville Broughton. In the early 2000s the facility served about 3,600 patients.

In 1877 the General Assembly appointed a committee to recommend the selection of a site for a facility that would serve African American mentally ill citizens statewide. On 11 Apr. 1878, 171 acres were purchased two miles west of Goldsboro. On 1 Aug. 1880 the first patient was admitted to the new Asylum for Colored Insane; in 1959 the name was changed to Cherry Hospital in honor of Governor Gregg Cherry. Cherry Hospital was the only facility in the state for mentally ill blacks until 1965, when the hospital was desegregated following the 1964 Civil Rights Act. As of the early 2000s Cherry Hospital cared for hundreds of patients from 33 counties in eastern North Carolina.

John Umstead Hospital, built on the site of an old prisoner-of-war compound, began admitting patients in 1947. Its mission has been to treat mentally ill persons efficiently and successfully and help them return to their homes and communities. By the early 2000s Umstead Hospital maintained a research and educational program to promote knowledge of mental health issues.

In the 1960s and 1970s North Carolina used federal funds to open a number of community mental health clinics to relieve the overcrowded state psychiatric hospitals. Part of the national "deinstitutionalization" trend, the state's goal became treating the majority of patients within their communities rather than in long-term institutions. By the late 1980s, however, it had become clear that many local facilities were either inadequate or nonexistent, funding was unevenly distributed, and several areas relied on rest homes for the elderly to absorb the deinstitutionalized population. As a result of these trends, a reevaluation and downsizing of the state mental health programs was undertaken. The populations of the four state psychiatric hospitals decreased from approximately 10,000 in 1964 to 2,700 by 1989. As patient populations continued to shrink at state hospitals, physicians began to offer more sophisticated treatments. By 2006, in addition to the state psychiatric hospitals, several area programs provided a variety of services for North Carolinians with mental illness. These services included assessment, diagnosis, and treatment plans, individual and group therapy, help with financial or housing problems, daytime social or employment programs, and crisis intervention. Dorothea Dix Hospital, once the cornerstone of psychiatric care in the state, was scheduled to be closed in 2007.

References: Clark R. Cahow, *People, Patients, and Politics: The History of the North Carolina Mental Hospitals, 1848–1960* (1980); Guion G. Johnson, *Ante-Bellum North Carolina: A Social History* (1937); Ethel M. Speas, *History of the Voluntary Mental Health Movement in North Carolina* (1961); Lloyd J. Thompson, "History of Mental Health in North Carolina," in Dorothy Long, ed., *Medicine in North Carolina: Essays in the History of Medical Science and Medical Service, 1524–1960*, vol. 2 (1972).

Robert G. Anthony Jr.

Ruth E. Homrighaus

Additional research provided by J. Field Montgomery Jr.

Public Health. From the colonial era to the present day, North Carolina has made major strides in decreasing health risks and improving the medical care of its citizenry, although compared to the rest of the country the state ranks relatively low in several public health categories. By the early 2000s North Carolina was among the national leaders in immunization rates and low infant mortality, but it was consistently average in per capita physicians, hospital beds, and other medical care facilities. Moreover, a significant percentage of North Carolinians had no health insurance. Although epidemics of typhoid fever, malaria, hookworm, pellagra, and other grave diseases are no longer a health problem in North Carolina, the state still contends with a prevalence of heart disease, cancer, diabetes, Acquired Immune Deficiency Syndrome (AIDS) and other sexually transmitted diseases, and mental illness. The health of minorities, particularly African Americans, who have higher mortality rates than whites, is a recurring concern. Similarly, since a large proportion of medical practitioners live and work in urban areas, access to quality health care remains a serious problem for many citizens in rural settings.

The State Board of Health and Other Early Public Initiatives

The first public health regulation in North Carolina was a maritime quarantine law of 1712 to prevent individuals with contagious diseases from entering the province. From then until the late nineteenth century, a few rules addressed specific health problems at the local level. In 1877 the General Assembly established the North Carolina State Board of Health and made every member of the Medical Society of North Carolina a member of the board. The lawmakers approved a less-than-adequate appropriation of $100 and appointed Thomas F. Wood of Wilmington health officer on a part-time basis.

In 1893, at the urging of private physicians and county health superintendents, the legislature authorized county commissioners to establish health care systems operated by a county health superintendent who either charged a fee for his services or received a subsidy from the county of $100 to $1,000 per year. At the same time, incorporated towns were empowered to raise taxes for public health, but most continued to view health matters as a county responsibility. Over time, the State Board of Health's authority was expanded. In 1893 the board was authorized to check inland waters to ensure their safety as water supplies, to advise managers of institutions and towns on their water supply and sewage disposal systems, to inspect the sanitation of public institutions annually, and to regulate the transportation of human remains on common carriers to prevent the spread of disease. By 1915 the board was supervising these activities through its bureaus on education and engineering, vital statistics, quarantine, school inspection, and county health work.

The first training school for nurses was organized by Mary Wyche at Raleigh's Rex Hospital in October 1894, with five student nurses in the first class. Classes were held in a part of the hospital where patients' bells could be heard, and, if necessary, the students left the classroom to answer them. By the early 2000s, North Carolina offered 84 nursing programs that encompassed four possible educational patterns for entering the nursing profession. Five universities in the state offered courses leading to the Master of Science in Nursing degree; nurses with this credential were most often employed in advanced clinical positions or in education, administration, or research.

In 1909, under the impulse of progressive reform, the General Assembly appropriated $10,500 for the state's first full-time health director, a position filled by Watson S. Rankin. Two years later it authorized counties to create their own health departments. Guilford County (1911) and Robeson County (1912) had among the first such health departments in the United States. Over the next few decades all of the municipal departments were dismantled, and public health became solely a county responsibility. The duties of county boards included quarantining, confining, or isolating patients with dangerous diseases, administering vaccinations, gathering vital statistics, and performing postmortem examinations for coroners.

Expansion of Government Health Agencies and Major Health Issues in the State

The public health community in North Carolina received support in the first half of the twentieth century from private philanthropy and the federal government. From 1909 to 1915 the Rockefeller Sanitary Commission for the Elimination of Hookworm Disease, in cooperation with the State Board of Health, worked to control hookworm. Federal grants were provided under the Social Security Act of 1935 to assist states and other political subdivisions in the delivery of public health services. The Duke Endowment, established in 1929, helped build and equip more than 250 nonprofit hospitals in the Carolinas. As North Carolina recovered from the Great Depression, private charity again aided progress in the public health arena.

Major health issues in early twentieth-century North Carolina included high infant mortality rates, childhood diseases, hookworm, typhoid fever, smallpox, and some cases of malaria and typhus. After a state vital statistics law was passed in 1913, it was discovered that the median age of North Carolinians at death was 28. (By the mid-1990s it was 72.) Hookworm was gradually brought under control with help from the Rockefeller Commission, and typhoid fever and smallpox were practically eliminated by vaccination programs. In 1916 a nationwide study praised the state for its "progressive attitude" toward the health of its citizens. That year approximately $61,000 was budgeted for public health and another

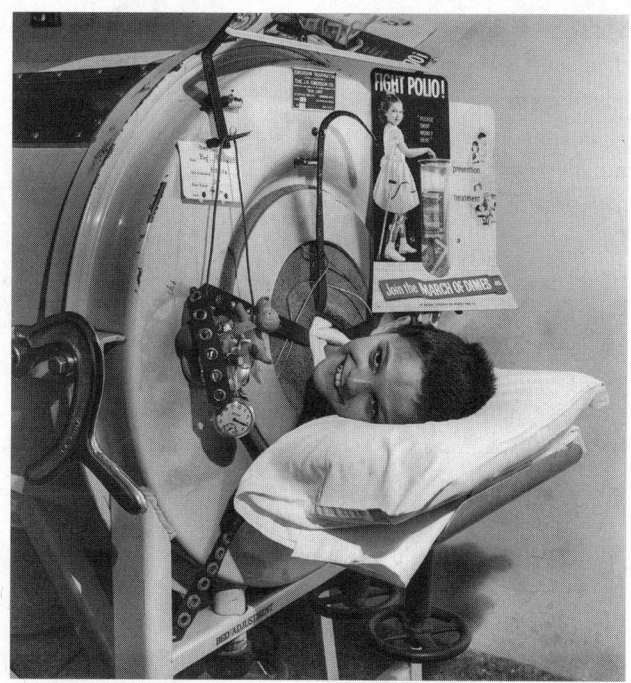

An eight-year-old polio victim in an "iron lung" respirator at North Carolina Memorial Hospital in Chapel Hill, ca. 1954. The March of Dimes poster and receptacle for contributions suggest that this may have been a promotional photograph to encourage donations to the campaign against polio. NCC.

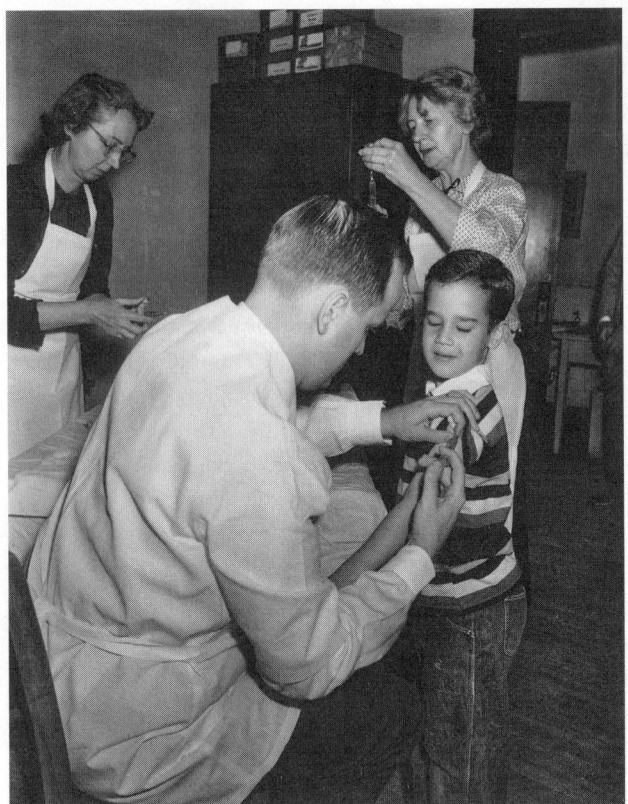

A student receives a polio vaccination on the first day they were administered in North Carolina schools, 18 Apr. 1955. Photograph by Roland Giduz. NCC.

$52,000 for tuberculosis sanitariums, making North Carolina thirteenth in the country and fourth in the South in per capita spending in these areas.

In the following decades the state's development of many programs paralleled that of the rest of the nation, although occasionally North Carolina led the way. In 1916 it introduced free vaccinations against typhoid and in 1917, free dental clinics for schoolchildren. A School of Public Health was opened as a division of the University of North Carolina School of Medicine in Chapel Hill in 1936. The vitamin deficiency disease pellagra, popularly known as Black Tongue, which was pervasive in some localities, was finally contained in the 1940s. By 1945 immunization against whooping cough and smallpox were compulsory, and in 1959 North Carolina was the first state to require immunization against polio.

In 1945, at the urging of Governor R. Gregg Cherry, the General Assembly created the North Carolina Medical Care Commission, with a board of 20 directors. Allocated responsibilities, following the governor's suggestions, provided for a statewide program of hospital and medical care through assessment, development, enhancement, and encouragement of existing plans. Aside from its statutory duties, the Medical Care Commission developed facilities for the care of chronically ill patients, for the rehabilitation of disabled persons,

and for more nursing homes offering medically supervised care. In 1947 the legislature expanded the commission's powers to include the licensing of hospitals according to standards set by the commission, the right to inspect hospitals, and approval of all new construction and renovations. The Health Care Facilities Act of 1975, which authorized the commission to update health care facilities through purchase and contract, also allowed the issuance of tax-exempt bonds and notes to municipalities for health facility construction, subject to approval by the Local Government Commission.

Sexually transmitted diseases have been and remain a significant challenge to public health officials in the state. The incidence of syphilis skyrocketed from 4,365 reported cases in 1932 to 21,333 cases in 1940. Progress in the effort to detect and treat syphilis received a huge boost in 1937, when the Z. Smith Reynolds Foundation provided a large grant to the State Board of Health. By 1952 the number of cases had dropped to 3,709 and by 1970 to 1,363—no doubt a result of the development in the 1940s of penicillin, the drug used most effectively against this disease. By the 1990s, however, North Carolina and the entire nation began to report syphilis cases at numbers rivaling those of the 1950s. Similar statistics exist for gonorrhea: by the early 2000s, cases reported in North Carolina ran between 30,000 and 35,000 annually.

In 1982 a sexually transmitted viral agent, which came to be known as the HIV (human immunodeficiency) virus, appeared in the United States. This virus is the causative agent for AIDS, a devastating disease that attacks the body's immune system, which is relied on to repel infections. By 1988, 629 cases of AIDS were reported in North Carolina, a number that seems to have doubled every 15 months. HIV/AIDS remains a leading cause of death for North Carolinians between the ages of 15 and 44, with minorities most severely affected. From 1981 to September 1995, a total of 5,981 AIDS cases were reported in the state. After a temporary decrease in reported cases, by the early 2000s the number of North Carolinians contracting the disease jumped to about 1,000 per year. The high incidence of AIDS continues to place an ever-increasing burden on health care facilities and providers.

At least since the 1930s, a range of government agencies have been concerned with birth control, including the Department of Public Welfare, State Health Department, UNC School of Public Health, Carolina Population Center at UNC-Chapel Hill, Department of Health and Human Services (DHHS), and county health agencies. North Carolina was the first state to establish a state-supported birth control program, and North Carolina women could get tax-supported advice on the subject from maternity clinics as early as 1959. For decades the controversial Eugenics Board, created by the legislature in 1933, oversaw the sterilization of hundreds of mentally ill, "feeble-minded," or epileptic patients, inmates, and noninstitutionalized individuals. State offices of the U.S. Office of Economic Opportunity began increasing their efforts to give family planning advice in 1969. North Carolina and South Carolina have been recognized as the first states to consider family planning as fundamental to any public health program.

The U.S. Supreme Court in 1973 decreed a constitutional right to abortion, with several minor qualifications. Federal funding of elective abortions for women in poverty was available from 1975 to 1977, and its elimination prompted the North Carolina General Assembly, with the support of Governor James B. Hunt, to establish the State Abortion Fund to provide abortion services to low-income women. The annual legislative appropriation ranged from $424,000 to $1.374 million until fiscal year 1995–96, when opponents of the fund succeeded in having it reduced to $50,000. Between 1973 and the early 2000s, the total number of reported abortions performed in the state annually increased from about 12,000 to 37,000. State funds are provided for abortions in cases of rape, incest, or life endangerment.

North Carolina's Modern Health Care System

The Executive Organization Act, passed by the General Assembly in 1971, restructured the North Carolina state government into large departments that included agencies with a related focus. In 1997 the health branch of state government, the Division of Public Health, was placed within the newly named DHHS. Led by the state health director, the Division of Public Health maintains a number of programs and services affecting public health policies in the state.

North Carolina's Area Health Education Centers (AHEC) program was developed in the early 1970s to address the unequal distribution of medical personnel within the state. It trains, recruits, and retains health professionals, thereby serving students, health practitioners, and communities. In 1973 federal money enabled the UNC School of Medicine to open AHEC facilities in Wilmington, Charlotte, and Rocky Mount, and the following year the General Assembly appropriated $24.5 million to build six more centers. Using the state's academic medical centers—UNC-Chapel Hill School of Medicine, Duke University Medical Center, Wake Forest University School of Medicine, and Brody School of Medicine at East Carolina University—as hubs, AHECs developed a regionalized network that links communities in every county in the state to a major hospital or administrative center. All North Carolina medical students complete a clinical rotation in one of the AHEC regions. In 2006 the state's 10 AHECS were located in Asheville, Charlotte, Durham, Fayetteville, Greensboro, Greenville, Raleigh, Rocky Mount, Wilmington, and Winston-Salem.

In the last 30 or more years, public health professionals concentrated on providing education, analyzing vital statistics, and reacting to various health emergencies, such as influenza outbreaks in winter. Immunization of children against diseases also became a major focus. Tuberculosis, though curable, has remained a rare but serious health concern.

A myriad of studies and statistics offer insights into the status of public health in North Carolina in the early 2000s. The state has received praise for its "healthy habits" and "healthy environment." In 2004 a national child health "report card" gave North Carolina high-to-acceptable marks in reducing infant and child mortality and teenage pregnancy, providing necessary immunization, and ensuring adequacy of medical insurance across groups, but the state earned exceedingly low marks in child abuse and neglect, obesity among low-income children, asthma, and the use of alcohol, tobacco, and illegal drugs. In addressing these problems, a task force was appointed to reach future objectives, such as ending disparities between rich and poor North Carolinians and giving further emphasis to preventive services.

The complexity of the state's modern health care system is demonstrated by its many different types of medical facilities, such as acute-care, rehabilitation, and psychiatric hospitals; nursing homes; assisted-living facilities; home health care services; and hospice centers. Administration of health care continues to be a joint responsibility of public agencies at the federal, state, and local levels and private organizations. The DHHS oversees several health-related agencies and state facilities, including the Division of Public Health (encompassing the Departments of Epidemiology, Health Statistics, Women's and Children's Health, and other agencies); the Division of Medical Assistance; the Division of Mental Health, Developmental Disabilities, and Substance Abuse Services; the Division of Aging; and the Office of Research, Demonstrations, and Rural Health Development. The North Carolina Office of the Chief Medical Examiner manages a statewide network of 600 physicians who serve as volunteer investigators in deaths involving unusual circumstances.

Among the private health care organizations are state chapters of national groups, such as the Alzheimer's Association, American Parkinson's Disease Association, Arthritis Foundation, and Alliance of AIDS Societies. Groups founded in the state include the Mental Health Association of North Carolina, North Carolina Dental Society, North Carolina Hospital Association, North Carolina Nurses Association, and North Carolina Psychiatric Association.

Federal Medicare and Medicaid legislation in 1965, and subsequent amendments, ushered in many changes in the health care industry. Medicare assistance for Alzheimer's patients was announced by President George W. Bush in April 2002. By assuming the responsibility of financing health care services for the elderly and the poor, the federal and state governments have become a major force in shaping the way the health care system will continue to operate. The Center for Medicare and Medicaid Services (formerly the Health Care Financing Administration) predicts that government sources will fund about 56 percent of the projected $3.2 trillion in domestic health care expenditures by 2008 as the population continues to age and the baby boom generation enters the Medicare program.

References: Mary Agnes Carey, "Analysts See a Seismic Shift in Health Policy Debate," *CQ Weekly Report* (23 Mar. 2002); Dorothy Long, ed., *Medicine in North Carolina: Essays in the History of Medical Science and Medical Service, 1524–1960* (1972); Kathleen Ann McMorrow, "AHEC: Bridge between the Health Sciences University and the Community" (M.A. thesis, UNC-Chapel Hill, 1990); North Carolina Progress Board, *Measuring for Progress* (1997); Benjamin Earle Washburn, *A History of the North Carolina State Board of Health, 1877–1925* (1966).

Jay Mazzocchi
Additional research provided by Robert J. Cain, Jerry L. Cross, Gail B. Joyner, and Alexander R. Stoesen.

SEE ALSO Black Tongue; Eugenics Board; Health and Human Services, Department of; Hospitals; Infectious Diseases; Medical Board; Medical Schools; Psychiatric Hospitals.

Public Instruction, Department of. In 1817 Archibald D. Murphey, a state senator from Orange County, submitted to the General Assembly his report advocating a publicly financed system of education in North Carolina. Though this proposal was largely ignored by his fellow legislators, Murphey is nevertheless regarded as the "Father of the Common School" because he envisioned a state-operated public education system.

In January 1839 the North Carolina legislature passed the state's first common school law, establishing the principle of combined state and local funds to support schools. In 1852 the legislature created the Department of Public Instruction with the superintendent of common schools as its head. Calvin H. Wiley was chosen to fill this position. Wiley served in that capacity from 1 Jan. 1853 to 26 Apr. 1865, when all state offices were declared vacant after the surrender of the Confederacy. As superintendent, Wiley worked tirelessly for the establishment of common schools and the improvement of education throughout the state.

The position of North Carolina superintendent of public instruction was created by the Constitution of 1868. It is the only constitutional office in the state assigned duties related exclusively to public schools. Although the duties and powers of the position have been altered many times by the General Assembly, the superintendent of public instruction remains the secretary and chief administrative officer of the State Board of Education.

While the Department of Public Instruction's administrative structure has undergone certain changes since the department's formation in 1852, its primary mission—to ensure that a "general and uniform system of free public schools shall be provided throughout the state, wherein equal opportunities shall be provided to all students"—remains constant. Under the leadership of the State Board of Education, the department establishes and administers overall policy concerning educational curriculum and instruction, teacher training, budget decisions, and other areas. The superintendent of public instruction manages the department and administers the policies set by the board. The board—which includes the lieutenant governor, the state treasurer, and 11 gubernatorial appointees subject to confirmation by the General Assembly in joint session—adopts rules and regulations for the schools that are consistent with other laws enacted by the General Assembly. The superintendent of public instruction serves as secretary to the board. The department is organized under the state superintendent into three program areas: Instructional and Accountability Services, Information and Technology Services, and Financial and Personnel Services. Each area is headed by an associate state superintendent.

References: E. Michael Latta, *The Constitutional and Statutory Development of the State Board of Education and the State Superintendent of Public Instruction* (1989); William W. Peek, *The History of Education in North Carolina* (1993); William S. Powell, *North Carolina through Four Centuries* (1989).

E. Michael Latta
Additional research provided by Wiley J. Williams.

Public Libraries. Anglican clergyman Thomas Bray is commonly credited with establishing the first public library in North Carolina. Bray arrived in the colony to recruit clergy to return to Maryland but found the population mostly poor and uneducated. In response, he joined with the Society for the Propagation of the Gospel in Foreign Parts to send, on 2 Dec. 1700, 36 titles for a layman's library and 148 titles for a parochial library. It was not until after the American Revolution that several additional private, parochial, and associated libraries were founded in North Carolina. Between 1794 and 1848, 32 library societies were incorporated by the General Assembly.

In the mid-nineteenth century, the census declared that North Carolina had the highest illiteracy rate in the nation. In response, Charles C. Jewett, librarian of the Smithsonian Institution, decided to donate several thousand volumes to various North Carolina libraries. At the same time, the North Carolina secretary of state began building a collection of books in his office that evolved into the State Library; formally established in 1812, this State Library was the only tax-supported library existing in North Carolina before the twentieth century. The Library Commission, an advisory body to the secretary of the Department of Cultural Resources regarding State Library operations and programs, traces its origin to the 1871 legislation creating a board of trustees for the State Library and to the late nineteenth-century movement for expanded public libraries.

In 1867 North Carolina's first free library, named the Good-Will Free Library, was opened by Charles Hallet Wing in Ledger (Mitchell County). This library, which remained in existence until 1926, opened with 12,000 volumes. By 1886 there were 22 libraries of more than 300 volumes each in the state. All but four—the library at the Insane Asylum, the State Library, the State Law Library, and the Library Association in Wilmington—were located at schools, colleges, and universities. In the late 1890s, the growth of industrialization resulted in an increase in leisure time, allowing Americans to indulge in more intellectual pursuits. Consequently, more libraries were called for on a national level. In addition, a new school of thought had evolved that claimed the best means of preventing social disorder was the development of formal public institutions. Rooted in an agrarian culture, North Carolina was affected by such ideas later than the rest of the country. On 9 Mar. 1897 the General Assembly ratified an act requiring any town of more than 1,000 people to provide for the establishment of a public library. By 1900 North Carolina had 57 libraries. Grants from industrialist Andrew Carnegie and the Carnegie Corporation supported the building of ten more libraries, located in Greensboro, Charlotte, Winston-Salem, Andrews, Durham, Hendersonville, Hickory, Murphy, and Rutherford College.

The Durham Public Library, the first free, tax-supported public library in North Carolina, began as an idea discussed by Professor Edwin Mims of Trinity College (now Duke University) with the Canterbury Club, a local literary club, in June 1895. Lalla Ruth Carr and her father, industrialist and philanthropist Julian Shakespeare Carr, solicited support for the establishment of the library. Julian Carr, along with Mrs. Thomas H. Martin, donated the land for the library. On 5 Mar. 1897, an act incorporating the Durham Public Library was passed by the North Carolina General Assembly. The library was finished in January 1898 and opened its doors to the public in early February of that year. Prior to 1900, fewer than 2 percent of all of the nation's tax-supported public libraries were located in the Southeast. Other public libraries in North Carolina began as subscription libraries. These lending libraries charged borrowers a membership fee instead of, or in addition to, a specific charge for books borrowed. Many subscription libraries became tax-supported in the early 1900s.

In Greensboro a small group of citizens banded together to form the Library Association on 4 May 1904. This association later spurred the passage of a 1909 legislative act that established an official North Carolina Library Commission to open and give assistance to libraries, including the establishment of traveling libraries. Traveling libraries consisted of collections of books loaned to smaller towns and rural areas where no library facilities existed. Each traveling library contained 30 to 40 volumes, equally divided between fiction, nonfiction, and children's books. The books were placed in special wooden cases that, when opened, doubled as display shelves. Each traveling library was loaned to a town or rural area for three months at a time then returned and replaced by another collection. Supported by the North Carolina Federation of Women's Clubs, eight traveling libraries circulated in 15 North Carolina counties beginning in 1909. By the mid-1920s, there were 1,275 traveling libraries consisting of at least 40 books sent to over 865 locations in North Carolina. As regular library service expanded, traveling libraries dwindled to only 260 by 1944.

Despite the increased availability of libraries and books, by 1926 only 32 percent of the state had ready access to public libraries. Under President Franklin D. Roosevelt, the New Deal Works Project Administration approved a statewide library project in North Carolina with Julius Amis as the head. By 1942 the percentage of North Carolinians with library access had increased to 85 percent. President Dwight Eisenhower's 1956 Library Services Act helped extend services to the remaining rural parts of North Carolina that were without services. The Library Services and Construction Act a decade later served to promote interlibrary cooperation and provide library services to the elderly.

The Citizens Library Movement of the 1960s was a widespread effort to further improve North Carolina's public libraries through the coordinated actions of support groups in each of the state's 100 counties. It began in early 1964, when Governor Terry Sanford appointed 39 educators, bankers, editors, authors, librarians, and other library supporters to a Governor's Commission on Library Resources. The commission's charge was to make a comprehensive survey of all types of library resources in the state, measure these resources against present and future needs, and produce recommendations to point the way "for all citizens and agencies to take steps toward meeting the state's growing and changing library needs." A key finding of the commission, stated in its 1965 report, was that average expenditures for public libraries in North Carolina fell far below the national average. To a large extent this was due to the fact that the methods employed in financing public libraries in the state had evolved throughout the years on a piecemeal basis with no clear-cut and understandable statewide financing plan. The commission's primary recommendation was for the formation of a Statewide Citizens Committee for Better Libraries.

At its biennial meeting on 5 Nov. 1965, the North Carolina Association of Library Trustees took up the challenge issued by the Governor's Commission on Library Resources. A steering committee was named, and by early 1966 an organization known as North Carolinians for Better Libraries (NCBL) had been formed with the goal to "help local libraries help themselves." Soon a state headquarters had been established in Raleigh, and members were being recruited in every county. By the spring of 1967, there was an NCBL representative in each county and active local library support groups in many of them, all coordinating their actions through the Raleigh office. One of the major accomplishments of this unified effort was the creation of the Legislative Commission to Study Library Support in the State of North Carolina. The emphasis of this five-member commission (made up of two state senators, two state representatives, and a chairman appointed by the governor) was to study the pattern of library financing in the state. The commission was to report back to the General Assembly in 1969 with recommendations for more equitable and adequate financing of public libraries.

The governmental reorganization acts of 1971 and 1973 ultimately transferred the Library Certification Board, which holds the power to establish libraries, to the Department of Cultural Resources. Interest in library development diminished as the majority of the state gained access to adequate library resources. At the beginning of the twenty-first century, the State Library had become a leader in the improvement of library services on a national level.

References: Robert G. Anthony Jr., "History of Tar Heel Libraries and Librarianship as Found in *North Carolina Libraries and North Carolina Library Bulletin*: A Bibliography," *North Carolina Libraries* 50 (Spring 1992); Thornton W. Mitchell, *The State Library and Library Development in North Carolina* (1983); Wendell Smiley, *Library Development in North Carolina before 1930* (1971).

David Stick
Jerry L. Cross
Additional research provided by Anne M. Berkley, Faye Terres Blalock, Rusty Rains, and Katherine Zeisel.

SEE ALSO Carnegie Libraries; Library, State.

Pupil Assignment Act was North Carolina's first and most effective legislative response to the U.S. Supreme Court's ruling in *Brown v. Board of Education*. On 17 May 1954 the Court declared that racially segregated schools were inherently unequal, overturning the "separate-but-equal" principle it had established almost 60 years earlier. North Carolina's strategy to resist school desegregation, later nicknamed "the North Carolina way," did not rely on overt racist demagoguery or direct defiance of federal authority—tactics practiced unsuccessfully in other states such as Virginia, Arkansas, and Alabama. Instead, it used a legalistic defense of racial segregation that proved to be far more formidable.

In August 1954, Governor William B. Umstead created the Governor's Special Advisory Committee on Education to study *Brown* and recommend a course of action. The committee of 19 was headed by Thomas J. Pearsall, a businessman and politician from Rocky Mount, and included three blacks, all of whom were state employees. That December the committee's report suggested that the mixing of the races in public schools

"cannot be accomplished and should not be attempted," and it recommended that the state enact a series of measures designed to delay racial integration by turning control of public education over to local school districts. Governor Luther H. Hodges, who had replaced Umstead after Umstead's untimely death, endorsed the committee's plan. The General Assembly quickly approved it.

The Pupil Assignment Act became law in March 1955. It removed all references to race in the state's school laws and transferred responsibility for pupil assignment, enrollment, and transportation from the State Department of Education to the individual county and city boards of education. The act created vague criteria to govern the transfer of students between schools, including previous schools attended, residence, and even "local conditions." A complicated appeals process intended to discourage parents from challenging a school board's decision also was included.

In spite of North Carolina's insistence that the Pupil Assignment Act complied with *Brown* by removing racial criteria from public school policy, the measure was clearly designed to delay the implementation of the Supreme Court's desegregation order. Enough obstacles that were not specifically race based had been created that even the most qualified African American student could be turned away from a white school on nonracial grounds. According to one report, a school district rejected one black family's request to transfer their son to an all-white school because he was a C student and therefore too academically weak, but disqualified another black family's petition because their son was an A student and should not have his academic success disrupted.

A related legislative initiative, the Pearsall Plan (1956), further expanded North Carolina's shift toward local control of schools. Token integration proceeded in North Carolina at a snail's pace for over a decade. While the state could correctly claim by the end of 1965 that most of its school districts had been desegregated, in 1966 only 6 percent of its black children were actually attending schools with whites. It was not until the late 1960s and early 1970s, when the federal courts ruled in a series of cases that the state not only had to stop segregating students by race but also had an obligation to integrate schools, that Jim Crow education came to an end in North Carolina.

References: David S. Cecelski, *Along Freedom Road: Hyde County, North Carolina, and the Fate of Black Schools in the South* (1994); William H. Chafe, *Civilities and Civil Rights: Greensboro, North Carolina, and the Black Struggle for Freedom* (1980); Jeffrey J. Crow, Paul D. Escott, and Flora J. Hatley, *A History of African Americans in North Carolina* (1992).

Karl E. Campbell

Q

Quakers, or the Religious Society of Friends, are the oldest organized Christian church in North Carolina. Founded in England through the prophetic insights and evangelical ministry of George Fox, the sect expanded rapidly after the mid-seventeenth century. Self-described as "children of light," the Friends eschewed both creed and ritual to live a sacramental life that followed the leading of the Holy Spirit, which they sought in open worship and meditation. Their core belief in the sacredness of human life was the basis for their testimonies on the human family, gender equality, pacifism, and the abolition of slavery. Their vigorous public witness against political, social, and religious discrimination led to their persecution in England and the eventual establishment by William Penn of a colonial refuge in Pennsylvania.

North Carolina Quakers originated as a result of a missionary band that George Fox led to the Caribbean and North America in 1671. Leaving Fox and the others, the Irish evangelist William Edmundson visited the Albemarle region in March 1672 for three days, holding the first religious services in the colony and laying a foundation that would result in North Carolina's becoming in its early years virtually a Quaker province. That November, George Fox spent nearly three weeks in the settlement leading numerous worship services, meeting with the governor and other officials, and preaching to the local Indians. When Edmundson returned to the colony in 1676, he reported that Friends were "finely settled." Tradition has it that the earliest meeting for worship was established in present Perquimans County at the home of Francis Toms, which was also the site of the first meeting in 1698 of North Carolina Yearly Meeting, the oldest extant religious organization in the state. The earliest existing meeting records, which date from 1680, are from Perquimans Monthly Meeting. By the end of the century there were two monthly meetings in Perquimans and another in Pasquotank. Strong believers in the importance of education, Quakers apparently sponsored the first school in the colony, which was begun in 1705 adjacent to the Pasquotank (later Symons Creek) Monthly Meeting.

Quakers exerted an important influence in the political life of the Proprietary colony. Among the many Quaker government officials and Assembly representatives was John Archdale, who was not only a Proprietor but was also governor of Carolina (1694–96). Friends are on record as protesting the unrest generated by Culpeper's Rebellion, and in 1680 nine Friends were imprisoned for refusing militia service. Following the Cary Rebellion of 1711, Friends were effectively excluded from colonial politics and thereafter seldom held office in the state until modern times.

From a base of well-established meetings in the Albemarle region, Friends gradually spread into the counties south of the sound. By the mid-eighteenth century, the backcountry was growing rapidly because of a large influx of settlers from Pennsylvania and Virginia, some of whom were Quakers who formed meetings for worship in the Cane Creek valley and to the west in modern Guilford County. These meetings would draw some of the Albemarle Quakers west to the Piedmont. By 1751 Cane Creek Monthly Meeting was established, followed in 1754 by New Garden.

North Carolina Friends entered a century-long period of decline during the civil strife that began with the War of the Regulation and continued into the American Revolution. The pacifist Quakers were particularly affected by the military operations and the protracted violence of the internal conflict between the Whigs and Loyalists. The key factor, however, in the diaspora of southern Quakers was their witness against slavery, which began in the late eighteenth century and intensified in the nineteenth century. Quakers organized manumission and African colonization societies and gradually began to advocate abolition of slavery. Levi Coffin of Guilford County was a founder of the Underground Railroad, which enabled thousands of slaves to escape to freedom. The southern community met the Quaker antislavery stance with escalating hostility, precipitating mass migrations of Quakers to the free states of Ohio and Indiana.

A major accomplishment of North Carolina Friends in this period was the opening in 1837, under the guidance of Nathan Hunt, of New Garden Boarding School, the oldest coeducational school in the South. By 1888, from this small beginning, evolved Guilford College, which has achieved a national reputation for excellence as a liberal arts college. At the college are the Quaker Center, which has an important role in interpreting the beliefs and practices of the denomination, and the Quaker Historical Collection, which is the archival repository for southern Friends.

During the Civil War North Carolina Friends were persecuted by Confederate authorities for their radical views on slavery as well as their refusal to support the war effort. By the end of the war there were few Friends left in the state, and without the aid of northern Quakers, particularly the support of Francis King and the Baltimore Association, the church might have disappeared from North Carolina. The Baltimore Association established schools for both whites and freedmen, formed new meetings, and set up a model farm near High Point to teach improved agricultural methods. A significant contribution to minority education was the High Point Normal and Industrial Institute, which was founded in 1891 and eventually was incorporated into the public school system as William Penn High School.

In the nineteenth century Friends were divided by the effect of the spiritual fervor of evangelical revivals that swept the country in the Second Great Awakening. New converts, with little appreciation for traditional Quaker beliefs, readily accepted the theology and practices of other Protestant churches, especially the use of professional pastors. The new ideas were more evident in North Carolina after the Civil War when out-of-state evangelists began to hold revivals. From an 1887 conference in Richmond, Ind., emerged both a uniform discipline and eventually the Friends United Meeting, first called the Five Years Meeting. Although most yearly meetings had been divided along the previously noted lines, North Carolina did not experience a separation until 1904, when the North Carolina Yearly Meeting (Conservative) was established by a small minority. Presently there is extensive cooperation among all major branches of the Society of Friends—the Friends United Meeting, the Conservative, Evangelical Friends Alliance, and the Friends General Conference. North Carolina Yearly Meeting (Friends United Meeting) has grown to become one of the largest yearly meetings in the country. North Carolina Quakers are centered in Greensboro, where the denomination's major institutions are located: the yearly meeting office, Guilford College, and Friends Homes, Inc., a nationally recognized retirement community. Nearby is Quaker Lake Conference Center, a youth summer camp facility and year-round conference center.

References: Hiram H. Hilty, *By Land and by Sea: Quakers Confront Slavery and Its Aftermath in North Carolina* (1993); Hilty, *New Garden Friends Meeting: The Christian People Called Quakers* (1983); Seth B. Hinshaw, *The Carolina Quaker Experience 1665–1985: An Interpretation* (1984).

Lindley S. Butler

SEE ALSO Cane Creek Connection; Manumission Societies.

Qualla Boundary. SEE Cherokee Indians.

Quallatown, Battle of. SEE Deep Creek, Battle of.

Queen Anne's Revenge. SEE Pirates.

Queen Anne's War,

known in Europe as the War of Spanish Succession, was another attempt by King Louis XIV of France at territorial expansion in Europe. The majority of military activity in the American colonies took place in the New England area, but with the French occupation of the Lower Mississippi Valley in 1699, North Carolina and the southern colonies were directly threatened by England's Bourbon enemy. With war declared in 1702, French officer Pierre Lemoyne, Sieur d'Iberville, had already concluded an alliance between France and the Choctaw and Chickasaw nations in the lower Mississippi. With this support, d'Iberville was ready to implement his own plan for the French pacification of the English colony of Carolina.

D'Iberville's "Project sur la Caroline" of 1702 called for a Franco-Spanish alliance to proceed in a joint expedition to capture Carolina. Six hundred Spanish troops from Havana, St. Augustine, and Vera Cruz would be joined by 300 French, 100 Canadians, and 1,500 Indians, making a force of 2,500. This army would then sweep northward through Carolina toward Virginia. With this proposed conquest of Carolina, the stage would be set for an alliance with the Creek, Cherokee, and Tuscarora tribes located in and around the colony. This new Indian alliance would give the Franco-Spanish army the manpower to conquer Virginia and drive north, easily taking the other English seaboard colonies. Although clearly defined in terms of goals, the project was opposed by the French ministry and never carried out.

D'Iberville's machinations, coupled with an unsuccessful attack on Charles Towne (Charleston, S.C.) by Spanish governor Zúñiga in 1702, prompted Carolina to plan a counterattack. In September 1702, Governor James Moore of South Carolina led a force of 500 Carolinians and 300 Indians against the Spanish city of St. Augustine. Arriving on 27 October, Moore's fleet of eight ships found St. Augustine deserted and its inhabitants fortified in the Castillo de San Marcos, located just north of the city. Unable to breach the walls of the fort, Moore lay siege to it for eight weeks; however, without siege weapons, Moore's four cannons were useless. Mid-December saw Spanish reinforcements arrive from Havana to lift the siege. Burning their ships and the town of St. Augustine to avoid capture, Moore's Carolinians fled northward on foot to Charles Towne.

With Moore's return, the emphasis of the war in the South now turned toward southern Carolina and the destruction of the Apalachee Indians, allies of the Spanish. By 1704 Moore had totally subjugated the Apalachee and eliminated Spanish influence in the region. As a result, Carolina no longer stood in danger of invasion from Spanish troops from the south. The fighting moved northward, and the South was left relatively calm for the rest of this conflict.

References: Verner Crane, *The Southern Frontier, 1670–1732* (1928); Douglas Edward Leach, *Arms for Empire: A Military History of the British Colonies in North America, 1607–1762* (1973).

Patrick Morton

Queen's College

in Charlotte was the first institution of higher learning in North Carolina, although it was never officially recognized by the British administrative system and was disallowed by King George III. In 1770 the Colonial Assembly passed a bill for the "founding, establishing, and endowing of Queen's College, in the Town of Charlotte," which was ratified by Governor William Tryon in 1771. The act called for the endowment of the institution to be collected from a "duty of six pence per gallon on all rum or other spirituous liquors brought into and disposed of in Mecklenburg County . . . during a space of ten years."

Col. Edmund Fanning of Hillsborough, with a B.A. degree from Yale College (1757) and an M.A. degree from Harvard College (1764), was chosen as president of the institution out of deference to his scholarship, patriotism, and membership in the established Anglican Church. Abner Nash was the only other member of the established church appointed a trustee. Dissenter members included Thomas Polk, Robert Harris Jr., Abraham Alexander, and Hezekiah Alexander.

The 35 volumes of books that Waightstill Avery purchased from Matthew Troy of Salisbury between 1771 and 14 July 1772, titled "Mecklenburg Library," were likely used by the tutors of this original college. The library collection included several biblical harmonies and commentaries, histories, the poems of Edward Young, and Henry Fielding's *The Adventures of Joseph Andrews*.

The college opened in a building that had been erected by Thomas Polk at what became the southeast corner of South Tryon and Third Streets in Charlotte. Advertisements for the college first appeared in the *New London (Conn.) Gazette* on 5 July 1771 and the *Gazette* (Mass.) for 3 Mar. 1772. These references suggest that the college operated during 1771 and 1772 without final approval from the British government.

Fanning probably never assumed the position of president, as he was actively suppressing a second Regulator Movement in Orange (now Alamance) County in the spring of 1771. Subsequently, Governor Tryon and Fanning departed the Carolina colony in the summer for a post in the New York colony. As the colonial Assembly gathered for the 19 Nov. 1771 session, an amended proposal was drawn up by Thomas Polk and others for the modification of the original charter to permit the trustees' choosing of a vice president in the absence of the president. This amendment was approved by the Lower House and the Council and given assent prematurely by Governor Josiah Martin on 23 Dec. 1771.

The great distance and the slowness of sea passage between New Bern Palace and the colonial offices in London's Whitehall contributed to the incongruity of the situation. It was not until February 1772 that His Majesty's Commissioners for Trade and Plantations took under deliberation the acts passed during the 1770–71 session of the colonial Assembly. They recommended "Royal disallowance of this Act" establishing Queen's College, and George III agreed.

A second effort to establish the college was begun in January 1773 when John Phifer presented a petition from the inhabitants of Rowan and Mecklenburg Counties concerning the establishing of a "public Seminary of Learning in the West-

ern part of this Province." Little was to come of this second effort, for news of the king's displeasure with the original effort reached New Bern in June 1773.

References: Norris W. Preyer, *Hezekiah Alexander and the Revolution in the Backcountry* (1987); William L. Saunders, ed., *Colonial Records of North Carolina*, vols. 8–9 (1886–90).

Stewart Lillard

Queens University of Charlotte was founded in 1857 as the Charlotte Female Institute in a building on College Street facing Ninth Street. The Reverend Robert Burwell and his wife Margaret Anna Burwell moved from Hillsborough to Charlotte to open the institute, which operated under an older charter for Charlotte Female Academy. From 1891 to 1896, the school operated as Long's Seminary under the direction of Elizabeth Webb Long. In 1896 it became affiliated with the Presbyterian Synod of North Carolina and became known as the Presbyterian College for Women. In 1912 the college moved from its College Street location to 50 acres in Myers Park. To inspire renewed interest in the school, the trustees changed the name to Queens College in commemoration of the first institution in North Carolina to carry the name, begun in 1771 but disallowed by the British Crown in 1772. Chicora College in Columbia, S.C., merged with Queens in the fall of 1930, and for almost a decade the college went by the hyphenated name of Queens-Chicora.

With the return of the soldiers from World War II, Queens College began to admit male students in 1946 as day students and became fully coeducational in 1987. The college began offering graduate degrees in business administration in 1980 and steadily added graduate programs over the next 20 years. In 2001 the trustees agreed to change the institution's name to reflect its enhanced educational programs, adopting the name Queens University of Charlotte in 2002. The modern-day Queens University has approximately 1,200 students and 91 faculty members.

Reference: Mildred Morse McEwen, *Queens College Yesterday and Today* (1980).

Stewart Lillard

Quids, or Tertium Quids (meaning "a third way"), were a splinter political group organized by members of the early Republican Party. Beginning in the 1790s, the Republicans and their principal leader, Thomas Jefferson, opposed the policies of Federalists like John Jay and Alexander Hamilton, who advocated a loose interpretation of the U.S. Constitution that threatened to grant the federal government broad powers. Republicans such as Jefferson and James Madison believed in a strict interpretation of the basic law that emphasized state sovereignty and local control. Resolutions of Virginia and Kentucky laid out the party's ideology and outlined its geographic appeal. While Federalists dominated affairs in New England, Republican ranks swelled in southern states, especially North Carolina.

Jefferson's presidential election in 1800 was a great triumph for Republicans nationally, but once in office he began to modify his views on the power of the federal government. In the minds of some party faithful, Jefferson began to stray from the fundamentals of Republican ideology. The Louisiana Purchase, although praised by the majority of Republicans, led some citizens to conclude that Jefferson was exercising executive powers not mentioned in the Constitution. In 1805 these dissenters formed a group they called the Tertium Quids, who sought to remain true to the principles of strict constitutional construction and state sovereignty. The Quids' national leader was Virginia representative John Randolph of Roanoke, who remained a political thorn for the administration throughout Jefferson's term. His chief deputy was Speaker of the House Nathaniel Macon of North Carolina. Although the Quids hailed from across the South, Macon's leadership made the faction especially popular in North Carolina.

Macon was an agrarian who strongly believed that the strength of American society lay in the rural, agricultural existence of the majority of the people. In addition to state rights, Macon supported limited taxes and annual elections and criticized the emerging influence of the commercial classes in politics. Although from a prominent family and educated at the College of New Jersey, his outspoken endorsement of the cause of common North Carolinians, his esteemed reputation, and his generally accepted positions helped popularize the Quid faction in North Carolina.

Nevertheless, the Quids never enjoyed a majority of Republican support on the state or national level. But their eloquent advocacy of traditional Republican principles, especially state rights, remained an important challenge to the political status quo.

References: Noble E. Cunningham, *In Pursuit of Reason: The Life of Thomas Jefferson* (1987); Harry L. Watson, *An Independent People: The Way We Lived in North Carolina, 1770–1820* (1983).

Richard D. Starnes

Quilts, in textile terminology, consist of two layers of fabric, frequently with some form of batting or stuffing sandwiched between them, held together by ties or stitched designs. In early North Carolina, quilts usually served as bed coverings, though sometimes they were made into clothes. As the twentieth century progressed, people came to admire quilts both for their decorative stitch work, which incorporated motifs including scrolls, flowers, and fruit, and for the beauty of the quilt tops, with their appliquéd designs or pat-

Northampton County quilters, 1939. Photograph by Charles Anderson Farrell. NCC.

terns rendered from geometric blocks of fabric. One quilt design popular among the Scotch-Irish settlers in North Carolina's Coastal Plain was the counterpane (sometimes called "white work"), a white, whole-cloth quilt with light batting and sometimes cording, intricately quilted so that a range of details and subtleties were revealed in different levels of light. A wonderful example made ca. 1812 by Salem Academy student Frances Lewis Graves features a center medallion framed by a leaf-formed oval, with a neoclassical vase of flowers inside.

"Quilting bees" or gatherings, during which groups of women assembled quilts, became special social events for women in nineteenth-century North Carolina. The numerous creative possibilities inherent in combining varieties of fabrics, quilting patterns, and patchwork tops gave women of all classes an important artistic arena in which to express themselves. Quilts served an economic purpose, as well, as women who could not afford to purchase wool blankets saved scraps of material to make patchwork quilts.

Unfortunately, the humid North Carolina climate, the presence of insects, and the wear and tear incurred by use resulted in the loss of most quilts made in the state in the eighteenth, nineteenth, and early twentieth centuries. North Carolina Quilters is a statewide organization dedicated to the promotion of the craft and the education of quilters interested in learning new or traditional techniques. In addition, a large number of quilt guilds exist in individual cities and towns across the state.

References: John Bivins and Forsyth Alexander, *The Regional Arts of the Early South* (1994); Bivins and Paula Welshimer, *Moravian Decorative Arts in North Carolina* (1981); North Carolina Museum of Art, *Two Hundred Years of Visual Arts in North Carolina* (1976).

Johanna Miller Lewis

Quitrents were small annual fees paid by a landowner in colonial North Carolina to the proprietor (or granter) who had conferred the holding. Rooted in the feudal system, quitrents were more closely related to a tithe than a tax since they released the subject from any further obligation of service to the proprietor. The privilege to collect quitrents—paid to the king in the case of a royal colony—was established in Pennsylvania, Maryland, New Jersey, Virginia, South Carolina, and Georgia as well as in North Carolina. The fee was not based on the value of the land or the ability of the holder to pay but rather on the acreage in the land grant. Although established by charter, the fee could be set aside or manipulated at the will of the receiver.

In North Carolina, quitrents originally had to be paid in cash rather than in crops or products. In a society with little ready money, this fee, as well as taxes in general, was always considered odious. Consequently, quitrents were often inefficiently collected.

References: Beverley W. Bond Jr., *The Quit-rent System in the American Colonies* (1965); William S. Powell, James K. Huhta, and Thomas J. Farnham, eds., *The Regulators in North Carolina: A Documentary History, 1759–1776* (1971).

Joanne G. Carpenter

R

Racket Stores were individually owned and operated retail businesses carrying a large assortment of merchandise not unlike that of a country store or, later, a five-and-dime store. Racket stores offered shoes, dry goods, groceries, hardware, tableware, pots and pans, washtubs, ladies' and men's ready-to-wear clothing, and other merchandise at low prices. The earliest known use of the term was in Asheville, where an establishment called the Racket Store opened in 1887. In May 1888 William Henry Belk opened a store in Monroe called the New York Racket. "New York" was included in the name apparently to suggest class. There were also racket stores in Charlotte and Statesville; these stores apparently closed before 1929, but the one in Asheville was in operation as late as 1937. Racket stores appeared elsewhere in the South, but there seem to have been none in the North.

William S. Powell

Radio Broadcasting, since its inception in the early twentieth century, has brought an ever-changing variety of programming into the homes of North Carolinians. Growing from amateur rigs on kitchen tables to 1,000-foot towers within just a few decades, radio has evolved from a niche industry into a thriving business with substantial impact on social and economic life. Broadcasting, once the pet project of like-minded businessmen, became a source of entertainment in the prewar era, a catalyst for social change during the civil rights movement, and a lucrative business network in the commercial push of the late 1990s. From amplitude modulation (AM) to frequency modulation (FM) to the Internet, radio has shaped and steered the state for almost 100 years.

North Carolina's First Radio Stations

North Carolina radio began in 1920 with the partnership of Fred W. Laxton of General Electric, Frank L. Bunker of Westinghouse Electric, and Earle J. Gluck with the Charlotte office of Southern Bell; all three were trained in electronics and wished to launch the new technology in the state. Using various rooms of Laxton's house and a receiver in a former chicken coop, these pioneers broadcast their amateur signal to an extremely limited range of potential listeners. In 1921, via the U.S. Department of Commerce, they secured the call letters "4XD" under an "experimental" license. With a commercial license and a new location—the eigthth floor of the Independence Building in downtown Charlotte—the trio signed on WBT radio in April 1922, broadcasting four hours a day with a 100-watt signal.

Also in 1922 a noncommercial station, WLAC 600 AM, went on the air from North Carolina State College in Raleigh—the culmination of a joint project by engineering students and professors. It shut down in less than a year, but WBT continued to prosper. Selling radio parts under the moniker of the Southern Radio Corporation, the Charlotte station's founders secured the future "Colossus of the Carolinas" a lasting place on the dial. Not long after the birth of commercial radio, however, corporate broadcasters began scrambling to tap into the newfound commercial options. Fledgling networks such as NBC and CBS began calling for government protection of the airwaves, and as a result many small stations opted for the security and additional programming of the larger corporations. WBT joined CBS in 1929, which, by 1933, increased its power to 50,000 watts, the legal limit at the time. WPTF—whose call letters stood for "We Protect the Family," the motto of the station's owner, the Durham Life Insurance Company—joined NBC only five years after its small-scale commercial launch as WFBQ. Becoming part of the larger networks gave the stations increased financial security, particularly in the 1930s, when the twin blows of the Great Depression and the Communications Act of 1934—which threw noncommercial stations off the AM band in exchange for mild cooperation by larger entities—crippled a number of smaller broadcasters.

Radio Enters Its "Golden Age" in North Carolina

The segue from the 1920s into the 1930s saw not only increases in the number of stations and their respective broadcast strengths, but programming changes as well. In the 1920s the newly forming airwaves had been dominated by local news and talk. By the early 1930s, North Carolina stations carried a wider variety of programs and the medium truly began to affect communities in significant ways. The proliferation of the technology and its increased cultural importance led the prewar era to be dubbed the first "Golden Age of Radio Broadcasting." In the difficult years of the Great Depression, President Franklin D. Roosevelt's "Fireside Chats"—nationwide evening radio addresses—harnessed the airwaves to promote a sense of national unity, although many southerners deeply resented his and his wife Eleanor's views on civil rights. Using special programming, live broadcasts, and raffles in which radios were the prize, numerous churches and organizations also launched successful fund-raising drives. And many politicians, such as Charlotte reform mayor Ben E. Douglas (1935–41) and Governor Clyde Hoey (1937–41), used the improved signals for political campaigning.

Radio's real significance for the majority of southerners, however, came from the entertainment it offered, especially

In 1931 Raleigh radio station WPTF broadcast the marriage of Felton Williams and Peggy Fussell, shown here looking out of the car window. Courtesy of NCOA&H.

improved coverage of sporting events and musical programs. Better technology permitted easy access to live broadcasts of college football, Joe Louis's boxing matches, and baseball's World Series. Jefferson Standard Broadcasting Company, a subsidiary of Jefferson-Pilot, used its resources to pioneer spot news, entertainment, and sports programming on its stations, among them Greensboro's WBIG and the newly overhauled WBT. WPTF presented some radio "firsts" for the Piedmont, including coverage of football games, basketball games, political events, and the state fair.

Radio also played an essential part in the increased popularity of many musical performers and genres in North Carolina. WSJS in Winston-Salem specialized in hillbilly and church music, a growing trend with the advent of technology needed to provide live musical broadcasts. In 1939 seminal bluegrass musician and Shelby native Earl Scruggs, then only 15 years old, first played on North Carolina radio. A year later Kay Kyser, a Rocky Mount native who earlier had achieved national success with his big band variety show *Kay Kyser's Kollege of Musical Knowledge*, made $1 million with his nationally syndicated program that reached an estimated 20 million listeners. Legendary banjo player Bill Monroe also delivered numerous live performances from WBT in the late 1930s and early 1940s, as did fellow bluegrass favorites Lester Flatt and Charlie Poole. For enthusiasts of classical music, WPTF also provided broadcasts of the Metropolitan Opera from New York City on selected nights.

National Networks and Popular Local Shows and Personalities

With the Japanese attack on Pearl Harbor in December 1941 came a temporary freeze on radio station applications, which hampered smaller carriers. Through the 1940s, the airwaves were dominated by the four major broadcast networks: NBC, ABC, CBS, and the now-defunct Mutual Broadcasting System. In addition to war-related news, the networks provided a wealth of block programming—from serialized dramas to live performances. Comedy shows featuring Fred Allen, Jack Benny, George Burns, and Gracie Allen, along with dramas such as the *Lux Radio Theater*, *Orson Welles's Mercury Theatre on the Air*, and *The Guiding Light*, made radio the centerpiece of family entertainment. Kay Kyser joined the ranks of big band leaders like Benny Goodman, Glenn Miller, and Duke Ellington on nationally broadcast shows.

Despite the networks' seeming monopoly of radio real estate, small stations still managed to spring up across North Carolina. Mount Airy's WPAQ, after its birth in 1948, began broadcasting live string band performances at 10,000 watts while also amassing a sizable catalog of traditional and folk music. In 1947 the North Carolina Association of Broadcasters was founded to provide support and information to state radio talent. Recognizable on-air personalities carved out reputations in the region. Greensboro native Edward R. Murrow moved on to a national audience, but local color ruled the state's airwaves. Commentators such as WBT's fiery, pulpit-

Kay Kyser (in cap and gown) and his band entertain U.S. Navy personnel during a live NBC radio broadcast of *Kay Kyser's Kollege of Musical Knowledge*, ca. 1943. NCC.

tested J. S. Nathaniel Tross and WRAL's Fred Fletcher, known for his children's programming and traffic reports, were radio fixtures for years. Although by the 1950s television replaced radio as America's "everyday" medium, local radio fought the advance of network TV by filling spots on the airwaves normally overlooked by larger corporations, such as early morning time slots. For 30 years Grady Cole, beloved as "Mr. Dixie," was the voice of WBT's sunrise schedule, providing farm reports, community announcements, weather reports, and more into the early 1960s.

Devotion to certain broadcasters induced listeners to continue tuning in, either for a chance of catching the "Voice of the Duke Blue Devils," announcer Lee Kirby, or the sweet sounds of Crackerjacks bandleader Arthur Smith. In addition to Grady Cole, WBT helped bring Charles H. Crutchfield, a station program director and the eventual president of Jefferson-Pilot Broadcasting, to prominence in the postwar years.

Radio Broadcasting and the Civil Rights Movement

While many working in radio were content to entertain in their designated time slots, Crutchfield and others became part of a bigger change largely made possible by the support of the airwaves. By the late 1950s a new ethnic diversity had arisen to complement the programming diversity made possible in the previous decade. Charlotte stations WBT and WGIV were starting to aim a majority of their programming at a black audience. In Winston-Salem, the first black-oriented AM station, WAAA, hooked listeners with its popular features like Oscar "Daddy-Oh" Alexander's hit program *Daddy-Oh on the Patio*. By this point, the opinionated Nathaniel Tross, under Crutchfield's guidance, was delivering blistering editorials calling for radical action against segregation. At WGIV disc jockeys such as Eugene "Genial Gene" Potts used a more family-oriented tack to advocate patience and tolerance, while drawing on their connections with the minority community to defuse tensions rather than to accentuate them.

But tensions did flare. Following the 1957 desegregation of the schools, North Carolina's Lumbee Indian and black populations launched a huge campaign against the Ku Klux Klan. Crutchfield, along with the powerful minority voice in the Charlotte Chamber of Commerce, staged a number of events focusing on empowerment and education. Of these, the landmark race relations-themed "Project '60," broadcast on WBT in November 1959—an event attended by thousands that far exceeded its allotted time slot—arguably was the most crucial in establishing radio as a medium for a new and growing voice in southern social discourse.

Growth of FM Stations and Increasing Corporate Ownership

The 1960s ushered in a change in broadcasting, less in its content than in its manner of presentation. Due to the continuing success of television, radio stations began to leave behind serials and soap operas in favor of format broadcasting more suitable to the medium. This change was hastened by the Federal Communications Commission (FCC) ruling that stations no longer could simulcast on both AM and FM bands, necessitating a split in content. The 1960s comprised the era of the Top-40 giants, and new start-up stations, such as the jazz-gospel WSHA at Shaw University (the first black college in America to own a radio station), emphasized genre-based programming. Talk radio, which had regained its popularity in the 1950s, continued to flourish, with stations including NPR-affiliate WUNC rallying behind esteemed commentators like Carl Kassel and Charles Kuralt. Rekindling the torch of its earlier station WLAC, college station WKNC resumed broadcasting from North Carolina State, where it remained into the twenty-first century.

With the dissolution of the right to simulcast and the refocusing of content on individual stations, the 1970s harkened the close of the second Golden Age of Radio Broadcasting, said to have begun in the mid-1950s. The FM band, with its possibilities for taste-specific commercial programming and increased sound integrity, became immensely popular in the state at the beginning of the decade. By 1971 eight FM stations were on the air in the Triangle area alone. AM still carried on, and in 1970 the North Carolina Association of Broadcasters created its Hall of Fame, which that same year inducted Charles Crutchfield, among others. By 2005 the hall boasted more than 80 members, including inductee Woody Durham—the "Voice of the Tar Heels"—whose career had begun in the 1970s.

North Carolina radio in the 1980s was much more independent than it had been in decades past. Broadcast power increased, giving 1970s start-ups such as WDCG, "Durham's Country Giant" (1974), and classical broadcaster WCPE (1978)

a chance to thrive. The FCC relaxed its rules, permitting "big stick" antennas—potent arrays rising more than 1,000 feet and capable of surpassing 100,000-watt signals—to power their way, at times, into other parts of the country. This free-market mind frame also saw format stations going head-to-head on the dial, as genres were no longer exclusive to a single station. In 1994 the University of North Carolina at Chapel Hill's WXYC found a new way to broadcast its signal, becoming the first station ever to launch a streaming Internet broadcast.

By 2006 North Carolina hosted more than 400 radio stations representing innumerable genres. As the industry diversifies, however, the need for strength in conglomeration once again becomes prevalent beyond regional suppliers such as Jefferson-Pilot. San Antonio's Clear Channel Communications, Inc., is the front-runner of the new corporate consolidation mode of radio management. In 2006 the company owned more than 1,200 radio stations in the United States, 22 of which were in North Carolina. Infinity Radio, a subsidiary of the massive Viacom Corporation, also owned 9 radio stations in the state. Some independents still thrive, but consolidation comes with the promise of more protection against government regulation.

References: Pamela Grundy, "From 'Il Trovatore' to the Crazy Mountaineers: WBT-Charlotte and Changing Musical Culture in the Carolina Piedmont, 1922–1935" (M.A. thesis, UNC-Chapel Hill, 1991); Mary Norton Kratt, *Charlotte: Spirit of the New South* (1992); Wesley H. Wallace, "The Development of Broadcasting in North Carolina, 1922–1948" (Ph.D. diss., Duke University, 1962); Brian Ward, *Radio and the Struggle for Civil Rights in the South* (2004).

Philip McFee
Wiley J. Williams

SEE ALSO Durham Life Insurance Company; Jefferson-Pilot Corporation.

Radio Free Dixie was an African American, English-language radio program broadcast from Radio Havana from 1962 to 1965 that called upon "oppressed Negroes to rise and free themselves." Narrated by Monroe native Robert Franklin Williams, a civil rights and political activist, the show was directed at southern blacks but was heard by listeners all over the United States and Canada. At first Cuban dictator Fidel Castro befriended Williams and his program, which included jazz, blues, and "the new music of freedom," as well as the activist's increasingly revolutionary rhetoric castigating the U.S. government for its tepid pro–civil rights stance and weak protection of African Americans. Williams left Cuba for Beijing in 1965 after the political climate in Cuba began to turn against him. In addition to his radio program, Williams published a civil rights reader, *Negroes with Guns* (1962), and a Cuban edition of the *Crusader*, a monthly newsletter.

Reference: Timothy B. Tyson, *Radio Free Dixie: Robert F. Williams and the Roots of Black Power* (1999).

Wiley J. Williams

Raft Swamp, Engagement at. Raft Swamp was a notorious Loyalist refuge during the American Revolution and the site of the most important action of the Wilmington campaign. On 15 Oct. 1781, in the course of Gen. Griffith Rutherford's expedition against Wilmington, the Whig cavalry vanguard commanded by Maj. Joseph Graham clashed briefly with some mounted Loyalists of Col. Hector McNeil on Rockfish Creek. The Loyalists fled and were tracked by Graham, who was reinforced with mounted infantry of Col. Thomas Owen. The Loyalists were brought to bay several miles south of McPhaul's Mill near a causeway in Raft Swamp. A spirited charge by Graham's command broke the Loyalist cavalry and led to a melee on the narrow causeway, as well as another clash on a second causeway. A series of charges and confused engagements was resulting in the disintegration of the Loyalist force when darkness ended the action.

The Whigs committed 150 men and suffered no losses. The Loyalists, apparently with 200 men in the battle, lost 16 dead and 50 wounded. The Loyalists did not further contest Rutherford's march to Wilmington. As Graham described it, the Raft Swamp defeat "completely broke their spirit."

References: John Hairr, *Colonel David Fanning: The Adventures of a Carolina Loyalist* (1998); William Henry Hoyt, ed., *The Papers of Archibald D. Murphey*, vol. 2 (1914).

Lindley S. Butler

Railroad Commission, or Board of Railroad Commissioners, was North Carolina's first attempt to regulate businesses through a bureaucratic state agency. The commission was established by the Farmers' Alliance-dominated legislature of 1891 primarily to reduce freight and passenger rates on intrastate railroads and to increase the taxable value of railroad property.

The statute creating the commission, drafted by the Farmers' Alliance caucus and its leader, Marion Butler of Sampson County, was modeled on similar laws in Georgia as well as the federal Interstate Commerce Act of 1887. The 1891 act provided for three commissioners, chosen by the General Assembly to serve six-year terms, whose major responsibility was to set or approve maximum passenger and freight rates for the state's railroads. Standard rates were generally derived from a comparative process in which the commission attempted to keep profits in North Carolina similar to those of railroad companies in other southern states.

The 1891 General Assembly also empowered the Railroad Commission to prevent discrimination in rates or service, to require information from railroad companies, to promulgate administrative rules for passenger and freight business, to hold hearings on complaints about service or rates, to appraise railroad property for taxation purposes, and to act as a court of record in resolving disputes. Moreover, the commission's rate-setting powers extended to intrastate steamboat, canal, express, and telegraph companies. Its orders were subject to review in state courts.

After the Democratic Party's successful white supremacy campaign of 1898, the 1899 General Assembly abolished the Railroad Commission and promptly established in its place a nearly identical Corporation Commission, whose membership the party could control.

Despite its short life, the Railroad Commission signaled the beginning of a transformation in state government. The idea advanced by its agrarian founders—that the state should control the rates and services of certain transportation and communications companies through administrative action—was a radical step toward modern public administrative authority. The agrarian idea did not, however, produce radical results. In its greatest moment of political conflict, in 1897 and 1898, the commission deferred to railroad claims that especially low rates would drive the lines out of business. The experience of the Railroad Commission reflected the limitations of control that sought to sustain the interests of both the regulated businesses and the public.

References: J. C. D. Blaine, *Rate-Making and the North Carolina Utilities Commission: A Study in Public Policy* (1962); Martha Frances Bowditch, "The North Carolina Railroad Commission, 1891–1899" (M.A. thesis, UNC, 1943); Annie S. Ramsey, "Utility Regulation in North Carolina, 1891–1941: Fifty Years of History and Progress," NCHR 22 (April 1945).

James L. Hunt

Railroads. The development of railroad lines in North Carolina was initially energized in 1835 by state constitutional changes that gave greater representation to the population in the west and by the rise of the Whig Party, which advocated government support for public improvements and economic development. In the beginning, passenger traffic provided significant revenue to the railroads, but by the 1850s freight shipments became the most important source of income. The railroad industry was a central component of the Confederacy's transportation system during the Civil War, and in the postwar decades it became a cornerstone of the state's economic recovery. World wars, the Great Depression, and increased competition from the trucking and airline industries in the twentieth century led to countless changes in railroad names, routes, and affiliations. By the 2000s railroads, though diminished in number and significance compared to earlier decades, were still an important part of North Carolina's transportation industry as well as a compelling link to the state's cultural and economic heritage.

First Rail Lines and the Birth of the North Carolina Railroad

The Wilmington & Raleigh Railroad, which changed its route and its name to the Wilmington & Weldon Railroad when the citizens of Raleigh failed to show sufficient interest, was founded in 1833. To encourage construction, the state government purchased 40 percent of the railroad's stock. The 161-mile route, at that time the longest railroad line in the world, was completed in 1840. The state also bought two-thirds of the Atlantic & North Carolina Railroad, running between Goldsboro and Morehead City, as well as one-half of the Western North Carolina Railroad.

In 1849 the General Assembly chartered the North Carolina Railroad, which was to be constructed from Charlotte to Goldsboro via Salisbury and Raleigh. The chosen route was a compromise between eastern and western economic interests. Easterners wanted an east-west route to connect ports with western markets via the conjunction of the North Carolina Railroad terminus and the Wilmington & Weldon Railroad at Goldsboro. Westerners wanted to expand their existing north-south trade with Virginia via the Danville & Richmond Railroad and with South Carolina, utilizing the Charlotte & South Carolina Railroad. Of the estimated $3 million needed to build the North Carolina Railroad, the state provided 75 percent in the form of purchased stock. Construction of the 223-mile route began in 1851 and was completed in 1856. Slaves owned by shareholding landowners along the route, who were paid half in cash and half in railroad stock, did much of the work. The iron rails were imported from Wales. The first steam locomotives were the sturdy engines built by William Norris of Philadelphia.

Eastbound freight prior to the Civil War consisted primarily of agricultural and forest commodities, including wheat, flour, dried fruit, lumber, and naval stores (turpentine, tar, and pitch). Westbound freight included guano fertilizer, bacon, tobacco, and manufactured goods from the more industrialized northeastern states. The most dramatic effect of railroad construction was the connection of the Piedmont to the ports of eastern North Carolina and the industrial Northeast, as well as to other cities and markets in the South. The resulting cash-crop agriculture and industrialization shifted economic dominance in North Carolina from trade and agricultural interests in the east to those in the central part of the state. Cities like Burlington, Durham, Goldsboro, High Point, Mebane, Selma, and Thomasville owed their existence to the railroad, which also significantly enhanced the economic fortunes of municipalities such as Charlotte, Greensboro, and Salisbury.

The Civil War, Postwar Struggles, and the Transportation of Agricultural Products

The outbreak of the Civil War produced an unprecedented increase in railroad traffic. Railroads in North Carolina provided a vital north-south link to the Confederacy, moving men and supplies for Gen. Robert E. Lee's Army of Northern Virginia and connecting the army with the vital port of Wilmington. In 1860–61 the North Carolina Railroad carried 90,000 passengers; in 1864–65, 506,000 passengers, mostly soldiers, rode the line. Freight volume eventually exceeded carrier capacity and piled up at stations along the line. The industry that shouldered this burden had lost many skilled railroad crews and unskilled maintenance workers to the army and was totally cut off from its sources of iron rails, locomotives, and spare parts. Replacement rails were cannibalized from little-used lines. Replacement locomotives were acquired primarily from orphaned Virginia lines taken over by Union forces. The result was a crippling deterioration of track, roadbed, equipment, and service. The invasion of North Carolina by Union general William T. Sherman's army in the last months of the war led to considerable destruction, mostly by retreating Confederate troops, of bridges, track, and rolling stock on the Wilmington & Weldon Railroad and on the North Carolina Railroad between Goldsboro and Raleigh. Union forces, equally dependent on the railroad for supplies, repaired the damage almost as quickly.

At the end of the conflict, the state's railroads were in a shabby condition, due more to lack of maintenance and overuse than wartime destruction. Recovery occurred relatively rapidly with the assistance of the federal government, which sold off captured rolling stock on easy terms, and the repairs made by the Union army. From 1865 to 1875 the state government issued almost $18 million in bonds to 13 different railroads. But during the inept administration of Governor William W. Holden, most of these funds were lost to corruption and extravagant spending at the hands of North Carolinians like George W. Swepson, the first president of the Western North Carolina Railroad, and northern carpetbaggers such as the infamous Milton S. Littlefield. Nevertheless, the state witnessed the roads' expansion from 984 miles to 1,356 miles of track in the first postwar decade.

The national economy experienced numerous booms and depressions in the last quarter of the nineteenth century, and railroads often were forced to file for bankruptcy during economic downturns. The entire industry began a period of consolidation that continued throughout the next century. Southern rail companies, which tended to be capital-poor, were frequently takeover targets. In 1871 the Pennsylvania Railroad established a holding company, the Southern Railway Security Company, to gain control of strategic southern railroads and build a network connecting major southern cities, including Richmond and Atlanta, with its northern rail lines. When it took over the Richmond & Danville Railroad, to which the state of North Carolina had leased the North Carolina Railroad for 30 years for $260,000 per year, the Pennsylvania Railroad acquired access to the strategic Charlotte-Greensboro

An 1874 engraving shows the roundhouse and machine shops of the Raleigh & Gaston Railroad in Raleigh. NCC.

route. But rail traffic never met expectations, and the holding company collapsed in the aftermath of the financial panic of 1873.

With the revival of the economy in the mid-1880s, the state's railroad companies embarked on a new round of track-laying, with mileage doubling to 3,128 between 1881 and 1891. Dozens of short-line railways were constructed in the 1880s. Passenger traffic continued to decline, but freight revenue accelerated. The port of Norfolk, Va., became a prime destination for agricultural commodities heading to the industrial Northeast by ship. Cotton production increased rapidly after the Civil War, while wheat and flour shipments declined as grains from midwestern states took over the market. The railroads carried guano fertilizer—arriving by ship in Norfolk from South America—into the Piedmont at reduced rates to encourage the development of commercial agriculture. Substantial quantities of manufactured goods from the Northeast also entered North Carolina by rail, as did Virginia tobacco being transported to Durham and other destinations. Overall, the railroad perpetuated the state's economic role as a producer and exporter of commodities and an importer of manufactured goods. Although the return of depression and railroad defaults in the 1890s slowed construction of

new track, company reorganizations and consolidations continued apace.

Passenger and Tourist Train Services

Although originally built for commerce, North Carolina's railroads from the beginning tried to offer passenger service as a matter of pride and as a "bonus" to bring in more profits. The railroads became a critical means of transportation for North Carolinians of all economic levels, but in the early days amenities were few. There were no dining cars, and schedules were planned with stops for meals at stations and hotels along the route. Cars were poorly heated; in the summer, open windows let in smoke, ash, and cinders along with air. Nevertheless, wooden cars were often elegantly fitted out with gilt scroll work and gleaming coats of varnish.

Steel cars with central heating (and later air-conditioning) arrived on the major lines after the turn of the century, and passenger trains remained the major form of long-distance travel through the 1920s. However, the convenience of the automobile in the late 1920s and the onset of the Great Depression of the 1930s started the decline of passenger traffic. Local service suffered the most; on main lines across the state the railroads responded with sleek stainless steel and

The Seaboard Air Line Depot at Hamlet was built in 1900, at the site where north-south lines between the Northeast and Florida crossed the east-west Wilmington-Charlotte route. Photograph by Tim Buchman. Courtesy of Preservation North Carolina.

aluminum streamliners pulled by cleaner diesel engines. The gas and tire shortages of World War II temporarily restored ridership, but the early 1950s saw another decline that ended with the discontinuance of all local passenger trains and most long-distance ones.

Tourists had constituted a major part of passenger traffic. Some of the first trains on the Raleigh & Gaston in the 1840s were designed for residents on the line to take their first ride, and a number of lines, such as the Western North Carolina Railroad in 1878, ran excursions to watch the railroad being built through the scenic mountains. As the novelty wore off, railroads increased passenger traffic by running special trains to the beaches and to the mountains. To further encourage ridership, they often built hotels at vacation spots and offered special package rates. The Atlantic & North Carolina Railroad owned the Atlantic Hotel at Morehead City from 1880 until it burned in 1933 and promoted it as a summer resort. The railroads opened still-prominent resorts in Southern Pines and Asheville as well as many others, almost forgotten, such as those around medicinal springs. Railways also were critical in the opening of religious assembly retreats, in particular the ones at Ridgecrest, Lake Junaluska, and Montreat.

Twentieth-Century Trends and Decline

At the beginning of the twentieth century, North Carolina was served by about 30 short lines and three major railway systems: J. P. Morgan's Southern Railway Company, which controlled the Western North Carolina Railroad Company and had signed a 99-year lease of the North Carolina Railroad in 1895; the Atlantic Coast Line Railroad, the result of the consolidation of more than 100 railroad companies from Virginia to Florida, including the Wilmington & Weldon Railroad; and the Seaboard Air Line system, which absorbed the Raleigh & Gaston and the Central Carolina Railroads. The most significant new tracklaying of the era was the construction of what came to be known as the Carolina, Clinchfield, and Ohio Railroad from Kentucky across the Appalachian Mountains into North Carolina, thereby connecting the state and the Atlantic Coast with the Ohio River Valley and the valuable coal and iron ore deposits along its route.

In 1920 North Carolina reached a peak of 5,522 miles of track. As the twentieth century progressed, the importance of the railroad industry to the state's economy began to decline as a result of growing competition from the trucking and, eventually, airline industries. By the 1920s truck traffic had

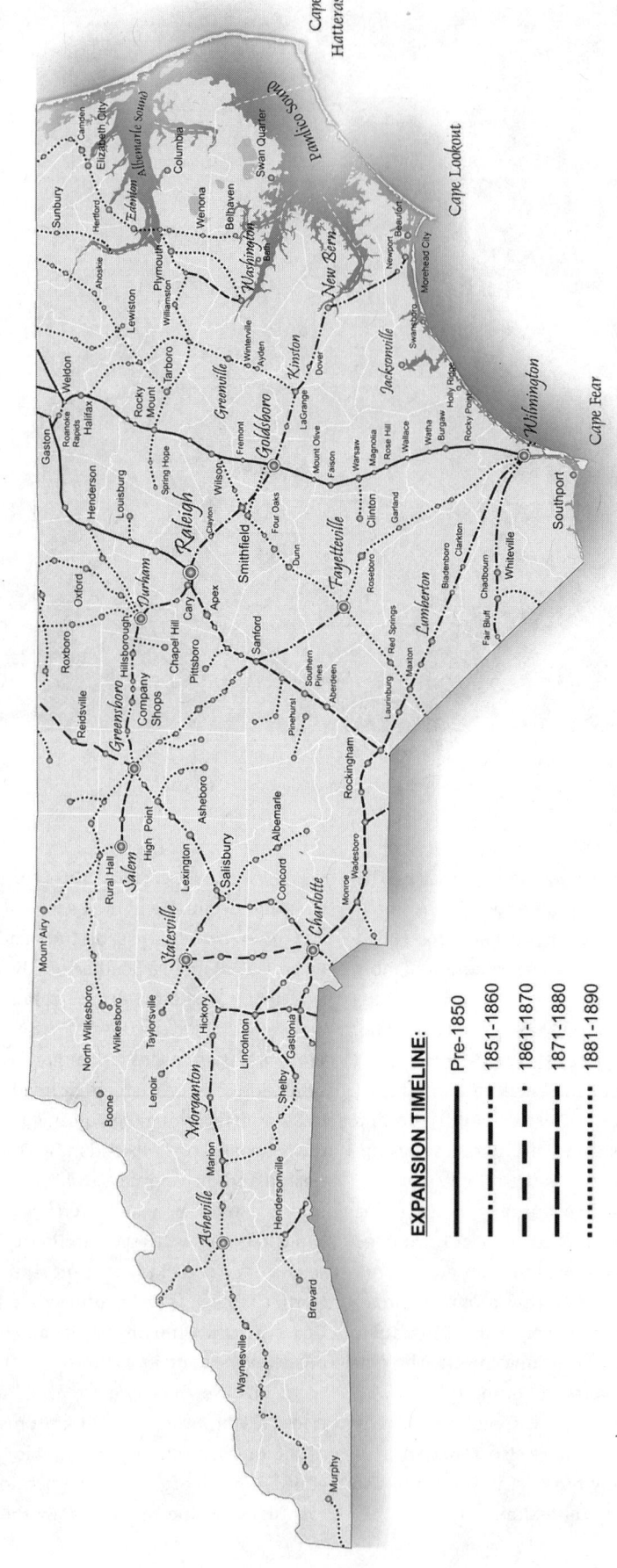

EXPANSION TIMELINE:

Pre-1850
1851–1860
1861–1870
1871–1880
1881–1890

Principal railroad lines, 1890. Map by Mark Anderson Moore, courtesy NCOA&H.

begun to take away much of the railroads' business in small ("less than a car load") lots. Government regulation, originally intended to prevent the gouging of farmers and small business people by the all-powerful railroads, came to discourage innovation and modernization of the freight system and to favor trucks for many commodities formerly carried by rail.

After World War II, the steady loss of passenger traffic to the automobile led many railway companies to abandon money-losing passenger service. By the 1970s, railroads both in the state and throughout the nation were doing poorly financially. With deregulation, they were free to turn away small lots, most of which went to trucks anyway, and concentrate on carrying bulk loads. In 1970 the federal government attempted to restore passenger service by instituting the National Rail Passenger System, or Amtrak.

By 1970 railroad track in the state had dropped to 4,349 miles and consolidation continued to shrink the roster of railroad companies. In 1967 the Atlantic Coast Line and the Seaboard Air Line had merged to form the Seaboard Coast Line Railroad. In the 1970s the Clinchfield Railroad and the Seaboard Coast Line became part of the CSX Transportation Company. In 1982 the Southern Railway merged with the Norfolk & Western to become the Norfolk Southern Corporation. The State Utilities Commission estimated that in 1993 the railroad industry in North Carolina possessed almost $17 billion in assets, with revenues of $450 million. In 1998 private shareholders of the North Carolina Railroad agreed to sell their shares to the state after dissatisfaction arose with the terms of the renewal of the road's lease to the Norfolk Southern Corporation in 1995. By the early 2000s, North Carolina was still served by the Norfolk Southern and CSX as well as more than 20 independent short lines using more than 3,500 miles of track.

After 1971 the federal government had gained control over almost all passenger traffic. Amtrak continued to run a number of famous "name" trains through North Carolina, such as the Crescent from New York City to New Orleans (passing through Greensboro and Charlotte), and trains between Florida and the North, such as the Silver Star, Silver Palm, and Silver Meteor. Except for the state-owned Piedmont (Raleigh to Charlotte) and the state-supported Amtrak Carolinian (New York to Charlotte), however, stops and schedules were based on the needs of the northern origination points and their destinations. Tourist trains for the general public were provided by the Great Smoky Mountains Railway in western Carolina, the Tweetsie Railroad near Blowing Rock, Spencer Shops (part of the North Carolina Transportation Museum), and the New Hope Valley Railroad near Raleigh. The National Railroad Museum and Hall of Fame is located in Hamlet.

Light rail systems—using single- or double-car trains operating on fixed rails running in already-existing railroad rights-of-way—are under consideration in Charlotte and the Triangle area (Raleigh, Durham, and Chapel Hill). Charlotte's South Corridor Light Rail Project, the first light rail plan in the state, will feature a ten-mile stretch of track operating within the Norfolk Southern right-of-way between Interstate 485 and uptown Charlotte. The Raleigh area's Regional Rail Transit System plan would employ diesel-powered, rather than electric, trains operating on new tracks in existing North Carolina Railroad and CSX Railroad rights-of-way. There are plans for 12 rail stations and 28 miles of track, linking the Triangle cities, the Research Triangle Park, North Carolina State University, the University of North Carolina at Chapel Hill, Duke University, and other locations.

Freight has continued to be the major source of revenue for railroads in North Carolina, but its nature has changed. In the first century of rail freight, cars were small and railroads had stations in every small community along the line. Incoming and outgoing freight could be shipped in small quantities. Indeed, dairy farmers could transport individual milk cans to creameries in the larger cities. Individuals could send packages by way of express companies that operated their own railway cars, such as Adams Express, the Southern Express Company, and later the Railway Express Agency.

In much of the United States, even greater efficiency in bulk freight shipments comes from the use of containerized shipping, in which a sealed container leaves its point of origin on a truck trailer and is lifted off the vehicle at special "intermodal facilities" or transfer yards, such as those at Charlotte or Greensboro, and onto train cars. The container is then offloaded at its destination to another truck or directly into a container ship at ports like Wilmington or Morehead City. North Carolina has not seen extensive use of containers, since most of that shipping originates on the West Coast or in the Northeast, but the 1998 acquisition of Conrail, the primary railroad of the Northeast, by the two major railroads that serve North Carolina, CSX and Norfolk Southern, has led to some increase in this practice.

References: John Gilbert and Grady Jeffreys, *Crossties through Carolina: The Story of North Carolina's Early Day Railroads* (1969); John F. Stover, *The Railroads of the South, 1865–1900* (1955); Allen W. Trelease, *The North Carolina Railroad, 1849–1871, and the Modernization of North Carolina* (1991).

Douglas A. Wait
John R. deTreville

SEE ALSO Atlantic Coast Line Railroad; Carolina Central Railway; CSX Corporation; Norfolk Southern Railroad; North Carolina Railroad; Seaboard Air Line Railway; Southern Railway System; Western North Carolina Railroad; Wilmington & Weldon Railroad.

Raleigh, the capital city of North Carolina, named for Roanoke voyages sponsor Sir Walter Raleigh, was created by an act of the legislature in 1792. Joel Lane sold the state 1,000 acres in the vicinity of Wake Court House on which to build a town. Raleigh was planned by state senator William Christmas of Franklin County. The original plan consisted of 400 acres and included five public squares. The largest lot, known as Union Square and located in the center of the plan, was designated as the site of the statehouse. Another of the squares was suggested as the location of a governor's residence, although it would be another 100 years before one was actually built there.

Raleigh grew very slowly and experienced several devastating fires in the early nineteenth century. The arrival of the railroad in 1840 spurred some development, and the city limits were expanded for the first time in 1857. A new capitol building to replace the statehouse that had burned in an 1831 fire opened the same year the railroad was completed.

The Civil War brought an end to Raleigh's midcentury economic boom. In April 1865 the city was occupied by Union forces after surrendering peacefully, avoiding the destruction suffered by many other southern cities. Like the rest of the postwar South, however, Raleigh—and all of North Carolina—struggled to overcome the economic devastation of the war. Important in the city's later development were several colleges established in the second half of the nineteenth century, including Shaw University (1865), Meredith College (1891), and modern-day North Carolina State University (1887). A new governor's residence was completed in downtown Raleigh in 1891.

A second expansion of the Raleigh city limits came in 1907. A number of suburbs, reached by trolley lines, sprang up outside of the original boundaries. The city experienced significant growth during the First and Second World Wars, and in the second half of the twentieth century, the expansion of state government and the development of the Research Triangle Park brought an influx of people and businesses to the area. Cary, directly adjacent to Raleigh, became one of North Carolina's most populous cities. Many new state buildings were constructed, including a new Legislative Building completed in 1963.

Raleigh has numerous cultural attractions, partly by virtue of being the seat of state government. The publicly funded North Carolina Museum of Art, North Carolina Museum of History, and North Carolina Museum of Natural Sciences are flagships in the state's historical, cultural, and educational offerings. The State Fair is held in Raleigh each October. The city's Progress Energy Center for the Performing Arts features Raleigh Memorial Auditorium, the Fletcher Opera Theater, the Kennedy Theatre, and the Meymandi Concert Hall, the latter serving as home to the North Carolina Symphony. In addition to hosting major college sporting events and touring shows, Raleigh's RBC Center is home to the Carolina Hurricanes of the National Hockey League. Raleigh's population was more than 325,000 in 2005, making it North Carolina's third-largest city.

References: Candy Lee Metz Beal, *Raleigh: The First 200 Years* (1992); Elizabeth Reid Murray, *Wake: Capital County of North Carolina* (1983).

Jo Ann Williford

SEE ALSO Capitals, Colonial and State; Joel Lane House; Meredith College; North Carolina Museum of History; North Carolina Museum of Art; North Carolina State University; Shaw University; State Capitol.

Raleigh, CSS. The CSS *Raleigh* was a steam-powered ironclad ram, one of two *Richmond*-class ironclads built for the Confederate navy in Wilmington during the Civil War. Six *Richmond*-class vessels were laid down in Richmond, Wilmington, Charleston, and Savannah in the spring of 1862. Naval shipbuilder John L. Porter designed these ships for harbor defense, adapting plans that he had originally conceived in 1846. On 20 Apr. 1864 the newly completed *Raleigh* steamed down the Cape Fear River and joined the ironclad *North Carolina*, which was already in service at Smithville.

The *Raleigh* drew 13 feet of water, 6 inches less than the waterlogged *North Carolina*, and Flag Officer William F. Lynch quickly decided to take the new ironclad over the bar at New Inlet and attack the Union blockading squadron. The plan was ill conceived because the *Richmond*-class ironclads, intended for harbor defense, were unseaworthy. Nonetheless, the officers and men prepared the ship for combat. On the night of 6 May the *Raleigh*, accompanied by two small steamers, stood out into the Atlantic. The ensuing engagement was shrouded in darkness and marked by confusion. The *Raleigh* made contact with several Union vessels, but because of its slow speed, it was unable to close with them. Flares and gunfire alerted the rest of the blockading squadron, but most commanders, unaware of the ironclad's presence, assumed a blockade-runner had been cornered. For the rest of the night, the *Raleigh* steamed blindly through the blockading squadron, unnoticed by the Federals. At daybreak, the ironclad returned to New Inlet and crossed the bar at 7:15 A.M. The "battle" was over, neither side sustaining serious damage.

After entering Cape Fear, the *Raleigh* turned south and soon ran aground on a bar known as "the Rip." As the tide went out, the weight of the casemate, guns, and machinery bore down on the stern of the ship. Unable to sustain the added weight, the *Raleigh* "broke her back," resulting in a total loss. Salvage crews saved the iron plating and guns and sent the boilers to the CSS *Chattahoochee*, then being repaired at Columbus, Ga.

References: William N. Still Jr., *Confederate Shipbuilding* (1987); Still, *Iron Afloat: The Story of the Confederate Armorclads* (1985).

Edwin L. Combs

Raleigh Academy was established when the North Carolina General Assembly, responding to an 1801 petition from prominent citizens, passed an act to establish a school for both boys and girls and named 14 trustees. Funds for building were slow to come, and not until late 1803 did John M. Goodloe complete a structure two stories high, 40 feet long, and 24 feet wide, with a brick chimney at each end. The new academy was located near the center of Burke Square with doors facing north and south.

The first four men to serve as principal of the academy averaged only one session each, and student enrollment stood at 60. Not until William Turner arrived in the fall of 1806 did the institution make real progress. He established a uniform textbook, formalized the curriculum, expanded the faculty, and enhanced the school's reputation. The number of students tripled to 180 during his three-year tenure, requiring the construction of a second building in 1807. William McPheeters accepted the call to succeed Turner at the academy in late 1809. During his 16-year administration, he further expanded the curriculum, specialized the faculty, built a new structure for a preparatory school, and introduced the Lancasterian system of education at the academy (requiring older students to teach younger ones).

Jonathan Otis Freeman took charge of the Raleigh Academy in 1827. Freeman had spent 30 years as an educator, but even that wealth of experience proved no match for an ever increasing number of private schools and academies competing for a limited amount of funds. The last closing ceremonies of the institution were held in November 1828. With financial resources drained, the trustees could no longer guarantee faculty salaries. Instead, they permitted individual teachers to rent classrooms for private instruction and to keep tuition payments. The fate of the Raleigh Academy for the next half century was to serve as rental space for a series of private schools, including one conducted by Freeman himself. In February 1830, Peter Le Messurier announced that he "would commence a school for gentleman only in the Raleigh Male Academy." This was the first time any structure on Burke Square had been called the Raleigh Male Academy, the name the school would bear in years to come.

Jefferson Madison Lovejoy, formerly of the Pittsborough Academy in Chatham County, moved his Classical and English School into the old building in 1843, which shortly thereafter became known as the Lovejoy Academy. The Civil War apparently forced the closing of the school. In 1870 S. G. Ryan reopened "the well-known Raleigh Academy on Burke Square." Seven years later, Capt. John J. Fray took over the Raleigh Male Academy and hired a University of Virginia graduate, Hugh Morson, later honored by having a Raleigh high school named for him. In 1878 Morson became a coprincipal with Fray; together they ran the Raleigh Male Academy until 1883, when plans for a new Executive Mansion demanded that Burke Square be cleared of existing structures. The educational function of the lot ceased after eight decades of service, excluding the war years.

References: Kemp Plummer Battle, *Memories of an Old-Time Tar Heel* (1945); Hope Summerell Chamberlain, *History of Wake County, North Carolina* (1922); Charles L. Coon, *North Carolina Schools and Academies, 1790–1840* (1915); Elizabeth Reid Murray, *Wake: Capital County of North Carolina* (1983).

Jerry L. Cross

Raleigh-Durham Army Air Field, an auxiliary training base for Army Air Corps (AAC) pilots during World War II, was located at the modern site of Raleigh-Durham International Airport. Air service in the area began in September 1929 with commercial flights at Curtiss Field (later Raleigh Municipal Airport) just south of Raleigh. Eastern Air Transport (later Eastern Airlines) introduced regularly scheduled commercial flights in April 1931, focusing on air mail service. With war looming on the horizon, Curtiss Field began to see a strong military presence. The AAC commandeered aircraft and painted them in camouflage. Airlines became an essential part of the military effort, moving cargo and passengers based on a wartime priority system. This system threatened the continuation of air services in Raleigh because Curtiss Field was hemmed in by a railroad, highways, and a cemetery, leaving no room for expansion.

In 1938 Capt. Eddie Rickenbacker, famous aviator, World War I ace, and president of Eastern Airlines, became a strong advocate for a new, modern airport. In 1940 the state acquired 891.7 acres with encouragement from the Civil Aeronautics Administration. Soon after ground was broken for the Raleigh-Durham Airport, the Japanese bombed Pearl Harbor, and the need for AAC training facilities became pressing. Aided by good flying weather, favorable terrain, and large open tracts, the property acquired for the Raleigh-Durham airfield project was considered highly suitable for that purpose. The secretary of war and the secretary of the navy each declared that the planned facility was necessary to the national defense.

Nine days after the Japanese attack on Pearl Harbor, construction began on the training facility. In January 1943 the War Department designated it the Raleigh-Durham Army Air Field. On 1 May 1943 the airport became operational with three runways, barracks, and an air traffic control tower. But the airfield was used sparingly by the military, becoming one of many such bases that were essentially kept on standby. This situation proved fortunate for the Raleigh-Durham Aeronautical Authority (later the Raleigh-Durham Airport Authority), which persuaded the federal government to allow commercial airline service to continue. Eastern Airlines agreed to build a small terminal in return for prepaid rent.

On 1 Jan. 1948 the military officially deeded the air base to the Raleigh-Durham Airport Authority, which, for the initial investment of $65,000 by local governments to establish a commercial airport, now owned a 1,283-acre property valued at $2.23 million. By the early 2000s the Raleigh-Durham International Airport was a major hub for air transportation in North Carolina.

Rusty Rains

Raleigh News and Observer, dating to 1865, has been one of North Carolina's most influential newspapers for more than a century, particularly regarding state and national politics. Before wire services became the norm, news reports from the *News and Observer* were routinely clipped and reprinted in other North Carolina dailies and often made the subject of editorial comment. As the daily paper in the state capital, it has served as a constant gadfly, tormenting inattentive or incompetent government officials at every level. Through the exuberance and vision of its longtime owner Josephus Daniels and his descendants, the *News and Observer* became the primary source of news and information for North Carolinians as well as a state leader in the technological advances in journalism. Its staff has boasted some of North Carolina's most outstanding journalists, including Sam Ragan, Herb O'Keefe, Nell Battle Lewis, Woodrow Price, Simmons Fentress, Dick Herbert, and Bob Brooks.

In 1865 the Reverend William E. Pell founded the *Sentinel* in Raleigh, using the newspaper to fight against the domination of carpetbaggers and other forces during Congressional Reconstruction. This journalistic battle was carried on even more effectively after Josiah Turner Jr. acquired the paper in 1868. Turner's crusade is considered to have been largely responsible for the recapture of the state legislature by the Democrats (then called Conservatives) and for the overthrow of Governor William W. Holden in 1870 and his impeachment in 1871.

But Turner was no financial wizard, and on 16 June 1876 the *Sentinel* was sold by the sheriff to George A. Smith and W. P. Batchelor. In 1877 Smith and Batchelor sold it to Peter M. Hale and William L. Saunders, who had established the *Raleigh Observer* on 18 Nov. 1876. The *Sentinel* ceased publication in March 1877. The *Observer* advocated the development of the state's natural resources and supported a strong program of internal improvements, including extension of a railroad to the western counties. In 1879 Samuel A. Ashe withdrew from a law partnership and acquired the paper. A year later Ashe merged the *Observer* with the *Raleigh News*, publishing the first issue of the *Raleigh News and Observer* in September 1880 as the city's only morning daily.

Ashe was financially successful from 1880 to 1885 because he secured the state printing contract from the legislature's Democratic caucus, which controlled state government. By the mid-1880s, however, Ashe increasingly lost favor with the Democratic Party and the *News and Observer* was financially distressed. Josephus Daniels, who, through his work at various newspapers, especially the *State Chronicle*, had become widely recognized as the dominant political editor of the state, purchased the bankrupt *News and Observer* in 1894 with the back-

ing of his former patron, Julian S. Carr, and other Democratic friends. From 1894 to 1948, the year of his death, Daniels was editor and publisher of the Raleigh paper, tirelessly supporting the state Democratic Party and a variety of other causes.

Under Daniels's guidance, the *News and Observer* was updated technologically (it was the first paper in the state to own a Linotype) and regularly fought against special interests, exposed corruption, condemned vice and the liquor traffic, and fought for better public schools—including Daniels's special concern, the University of North Carolina in Chapel Hill (UNC), where he served on the board of trustees from 1901 to 1948. He supported women suffrage and workers' compensation, state industrialization, better roads, and crop rotation. His paper played a leading role in the disfranchisement of blacks in 1900, a "reform" Daniels believed was necessary to remove a corrupt element from state politics and incidentally to ensure the ascendancy of the Democratic Party. Well into the twentieth century the newspaper continued to champion white supremacy and the perpetuation of "the white man's party." Although he was later ashamed of the racism that had inspired him in 1898 and 1900, Daniels continued to favor what he considered to be Governor Charles B. Aycock's approach of solving racial problems through education.

After Daniels's death in 1948, leadership of the *News and Observer* passed to his four sons: Josephus Jr., Frank A., Worth, and Jonathan. As owners of the paper, they all were active in its operation in some important way for the next several decades. Jonathan had served as editor from 1933 to 1941 (when his father was ambassador to Mexico) and then from 1948 to 1968. Under his direction, the *News and Observer* followed an increasingly progressive agenda, urging the South to accept school desegregation and to improve its race relations, especially in providing educational and economic opportunities for all citizens. During his tenure as editor, the publishing company bought the afternoon *Raleigh Times* in 1955. (The *Times* continued to publish until 30 Nov. 1989.) In 1956 both papers moved into a new building on South McDowell Street.

With Jonathan Daniels approaching retirement, the *News and Observer* hired Claude Sitton as editorial director in 1968. Sitton, a Georgian, had established his reputation as a reporter (especially on civil rights) and editor at the *New York Times*. As editor and a vice president of the *News and Observer* (1971–90), he continued to enlarge the paper's reputation as a moderate-to-liberal voice on civil rights and a government watchdog—trying, it was said, to keep "honest people" in positions of public trust. In 1983 Sitton received the Pulitzer Prize for ten editorials during the previous year. Sitton's was the first Pulitzer Prize for the *News and Observer*; it was followed by a second award in 1989 for criticism (Michael Skube's book reviews) and a third award in 1995 for public service (a series on the impact of agricultural corporations, including hog farming and hog waste, on North Carolina towns).

Frank A. Daniels Jr. served as president and publisher of the paper from 1971 to 1996, when he was succeeded by Fred D. Crisp Jr. Under Frank Jr., the company increased the staff, circulation, and advertising revenues; expanded into other markets (such as Hilton Head and Rock Hill, S.C.); and bought several other papers, such as the *Waynesville Mountaineer* (1979), *Smithfield Herald* (1980), and *Chapel Hill News* (1993). The staffs of the *News and Observer* and *Raleigh Times* merged in 1987. The *News and Observer* also began using computers in 1973, well ahead of most newspapers. In 1994 NandO.net was established as one of the nation's earliest online providers and NandO Times as one of the first electronic newspapers. The paper also added a weekly section, "Connect," covering technology and computer issues.

In a sale completed in August 1995, McClatchy Newspapers of Sacramento, Calif., bought the News and Observer Publishing Company for $373 million, ending the Daniels family's ownership after 101 years. Before his retirement in 2000 and the naming of Orage Quarles III as president and publisher of the *News and Observer*, Crisp oversaw its transition from a family-owned newspaper to one operating as part of a large conglomerate. Beginning at this time, the paper began to focus its circulation (167,000 weekday subscribers in 2006) on the Triangle area, pulling back home delivery from much of eastern North Carolina and greatly expanding staffing and coverage of Durham and Chapel Hill.

References: Josephus Daniels, *Editor in Politics* (1941); Daniels, *Tar Heel Editor* (1939).

Wiley J. Williams

Ramps (*Allium tricoccum*) are wild leeks or onions found in eastern North America. They grow wild high in the Great Smoky Mountains. Related to the ramson, a kind of garlic with broad leaves, the ramp has an edible and strongly flavored root. Besides eating them, Native Americans, in particular the Cherokee, used wild ramps in treatments for coughs and colds and in a poultice applied to bee stings. They were also valuable to early settlers because they offered variation in a relatively limited diet and were even thought to cleanse the blood.

Some modern North Carolinians chop ramps up and add them to dishes such as scrambled eggs, while others prefer them raw. Mountain folk, nicknamed "ramp-eaters," have long enjoyed gathering ramps in springtime. During the early 1930s these gatherings evolved into the Haywood County Ramp Convention, a tradition that has become a present-day local festival. The convention, which also features picnicking, music, singing, and traditional Mountain activities, is possibly North Carolina's most odorous festival. The Rainbow and Ramps Festival in Cherokee is also held each March.

Beverly Tetterton

Ramsgate Road, afterward corrupted into "Ramcat Road," was constructed by militiamen from Johnston and Wake Counties in about one week in May 1771 as a military road following an older Indian trail. Its purpose was to expedite the movement of equipment from Granville County to Hillsborough to suppress the Regulators. Its construction in so short a time was regarded as a remarkable accomplishment. The road was named for the one followed by Canterbury Pilgrims in England's County of Kent; it had been rehabilitated in 1749 leading to Ramsgate, a Harbor of Refuge for the Downs, a region similar to the North Carolina coast. North Carolinians undoubtedly felt that they had done the same with one of their old roads.

The Indian trail is shown on the John Collet map of 1770 and the Henry Mouzon map of 1775. Ramsgate Road is designated in an illustration of the Mouzon map in the *North Carolina Booklet* (1926).

Reference: Collier Cobb, "The Ramsgate Road," *North Carolina Booklet* 13 (1926).

William S. Powell

Ramsour's Mill, Battle of. The Revolutionary War battle at Ramsour's Mill in Lincoln County took place on 20 June 1780. With the American surrender of Charles Towne (present-day Charleston, S.C.) on 12 May 1780, British military control of South Carolina and Georgia was virtually complete. North Carolina, which had been spared warfare since the Battle of Moore's Creek Bridge four years earlier, appeared to be the next objective of British commander Lord Charles Cornwallis and his 8,345-man army.

While Cornwallis was content to spend the summer in Charles Towne, giving his troops an opportunity to rest and resupply, two of his American officers, Lt. Col. John Moore and Maj. Nicholas Welch, were anxious to pave the way for the invasion of their home state. In early June Moore and Welch returned from service in South Carolina and promptly set about organizing a band of Loyalists, or Tories, to aid in the British conquest of North Carolina.

On 13 June the Loyalists recruited by the two officers began to assemble in Lincoln County at Ramsour's Mill on the north side of present-day Lincolnton, about seven miles west of the homes of Moore and Welch. On receiving the news of the massing Loyalists, Gen. Griffith Rutherford sent word to Col. Francis Locke of Rowan County and Maj. Robert Wilson of Mecklenburg County to gather a force to disperse the Loyalists. On the night of 19 June, with 400 poorly trained, ill-equipped militiamen from Rowan, Mecklenburg, and Lincoln Counties, Locke set out from his camp on Mountain Creek for Ramsour's Mill, some 15 miles away. Meanwhile, the number of Tories camped on the wooded hill 300 yards from the mill had grown to 1,300, although one-fourth of them had no weapons.

As he neared the site of the Tory encampment in the pre-dawn hours of 20 June, Locke was greeted by Adam Reep, a local Patriot who had scouted and monitored the Loyalists' activities. Once Reep had supplied him with information about enemy troop strength and local terrain, Locke decided to launch an attack against the unsuspecting Tories.

With cavalrymen out front, the Patriots began their ascent of the east side of the hill at first light. Fog limited visibility to 50 feet. Although momentarily caught off guard, the Tories rallied, and a savage battle raged for almost two hours. Brother against brother, neighbor against neighbor, the men fought in mortal hand-to-hand combat. In this civil war, there were no uniforms. To identify themselves, the Patriots pinned white paper on their hats while the Tories stuck green twigs in theirs.

Although they outnumbered the Patriots by more than three to one, the Tories were routed and fled down the west side of the hill toward the mill. When the fog lifted and the smoke cleared, the battlefield revealed more than 70 dead and 200 wounded, equally divided between the two sides. The unclaimed dead were buried in a mass grave on the hill.

The Battle of Ramsour's Mill effectively disrupted Tory support for the British war effort in the region. Not only did it rob Cornwallis of badly needed Loyalist assistance when he crossed into North Carolina; it also provided the impetus and inspiration for the crucial Patriot victory that was to follow less than 30 miles away at the Battle of King's Mountain on 7 Oct. 1780.

Although much of the battlefield is now covered with public school buildings, the mass grave site and the graves of several of the officers who fell in the battle have been marked through the efforts of historical groups and individuals.

References: William A. Graham, "The Battle of Ramsour's Mill," *North Carolina Booklet* 4 (June 1904); William Sherrill, *Annals of Lincoln County* (1937).

Daniel W. Barefoot

Randolph County, located in the Piedmont region of North Carolina, was formed in 1779 from Guilford County and named for Peyton Randolph, the first president of the Continental Congress. Early inhabitants of the area included the Saponi, Keyauwee, and other Siouan Indians, followed by German, Scotch-Irish, and English settlers. Quakers and Moravians also migrated to the area in the eighteenth century. Asheboro, the county seat, was incorporated in 1796 and named for Samuel Ashe, a former governor of North Carolina. It is the location of the North Carolina Zoological Park, which attracts thousands of visitors each year and has spurred a great deal of growth in the town and county. Other Randolph County communities include Archdale, Ramseur, Liberty, Seagrove, Franklinville, Coleridge, Whynot, Trinity, and Worthville. Randolph County is covered in part by the Uwharrie National Forest. Other notable physical features of the county include the Uwharrie River, Purgatory Mountain, Squirrel Creek, the Little River, and Needhams Mountain.

Several important participants in the War of the Regulation (1764–71) lived in what is now Randolph County. Trinity College, established in 1838, moved to Durham in 1892 and became Duke University. Randolph County is home to a number of historic sites and landmarks, such as the Sunset Theatre, built in 1929; the Asheboro City Cemetery, in use since 1827; and Skeen's Mill Covered Bridge, built in the 1890s. Cultural institutions include the Museum of North Carolina Traditional Pottery, the American Classic Motorcycle Museum, the Richard Petty Museum, and the North Carolina Pottery Center. The Seagrove region is a very important center of North Carolina pottery production. The county hosts festivals and annual events that include the Spring Kiln Opening in Seagrove, Festival of the Dogs in Franklinville, and Christmas parades in several towns.

Randolph County produces agricultural goods such as eggs, tobacco, corn, soybeans, hay, vegetables, fruit, and poultry. Manufactured products include furniture, dry batteries, hospital supplies, cushions and pillows, shoes, fabrics, apparel, and industrial components. The county's estimated population in 2004 was 135,800.

Jay Mazzocchi

SEE ALSO North Carolina Zoological Park; Pottery.

Rangers were county officers in North Carolina from the colonial period until 1868. The post was a survival of British officialdom when royal parks and forests were patrolled against intruders and poachers. Their specific duties in North Carolina were defined by law at various times during the eighteenth century. Although rangers were expected to serve "for the Protection and Defense of the Frontier," it is unclear from the term whether some of them were engaged in the War of the Regulation to quell the uprising.

Rangers were appointed by the justices of the county court for a term of one year. One of their main county duties was to watch for stray livestock and to return it to its owner, for which they received specific compensation. They were also instructed to see that hunters did not leave deer that they had killed in the woods to attract vermin. In 1764, following the French and Indian War, any ranger operating at his own expense was entitled to be paid £30 from the treasury for each enemy Native American killed or captured. On 30 July 1776, during the American Revolution, the Council of Safety spoke of keeping in the ranger's custody anyone who was regarded as "an Enemy of the Colony."

References: Robert J. Cain, ed., *North Carolina Higher-Court Minutes, 1724–1730* (1981); Clarence W. Griffin, *Essays on North Carolina History* (1951).

William S. Powell

Ravenscroft School in Raleigh is believed to have grown from an Episcopal parochial school begun in 1868. Befitting its association with Christ Church, the school was originally housed in the Sunday school rooms of a newly constructed building on the church grounds facing Capitol Square in downtown Raleigh. This school was, in part, a product of a bequest from Josiah Ogden West, who had died in 1852 but whose will provided a fund to employ a teacher for a parish school for Christ Church Raleigh. This parochial school continued operation at the site until at least 1891, after which it appears to have closed.

A school named Ravenscroft—named in honor of John Stark Ravenscroft, first bishop of the Episcopal Diocese of North Carolina as well as the first rector of Christ Church—opened in the fall of 1937 using funds provided by West's will. Ravenscroft was an immediate success, part of its attraction being its nine-month school year versus the eight-month calendar of Raleigh's public schools. The Tucker Street school established the foundation for the modern institution as it implemented its philosophy of educating the whole child. Emphasis on the fine arts and athletics complemented academic pursuits, which were offered in small classes that featured much individual attention. The school prospered and expanded, with sixth and seventh grades being added by 1940.

The 1960s saw continued growth for Ravenscroft School, but Christ Church began to have internal financial troubles that would impact the school's future significantly. In 1966, seeking to avoid abandonment of the school by the financially troubled church, a group known as the Friends of Ravenscroft developed a plan that guaranteed the school's continued operation. The agreement provided for the transfer of the property at Tucker Street to the group while ending the church's responsibility.

Recognizing the changing nature of Raleigh occasioned by the development of Research Triangle Park, Ravenscroft's new board of trustees and its leader Robert Holding sought to implement a developing vision of a better, if costlier, school, whose expansion would necessitate relocation. In July 1968 Holding detailed a plan that called for Ravenscroft to become a top-quality college preparatory school, something he believed was needed in Raleigh. Later that year, responding to Holding's vision, the trustees purchased 115 acres of land on Falls of the Neuse Road, a spot that at the time was just at the northern end of the city's water and sewer lines.

Construction of the new temporary facility began in June 1969, and groundbreaking for the first permanent facility, the Middle School, took place in March 1970. That building, Edward N. Richards Hall, named for a long-time school supporter, was officially dedicated on 9 Jan. 1971. A torrent of construction projects followed. Upper and lower schools were followed by a sixth grade center and the A. E. Finley Activity Center, which included two gymnasiums as well as a swim-ming pool. The Robert P. Holding Jr. Memorial Garden, a gift from Holding's brother Lewis, was dedicated in 1988. Ravenscroft School, finally free of the debt incurred as a result of the move to the new campus, was a modern, first-rate academic institution in the early 2000s, with a student body of approximately 1,000.

William H. Pruden III

Ravenscroft School for Boys opened in Asheville in 1856 on land purchased by the Episcopal Diocese of North Carolina. The Diocesan Convention of 1854 had agreed to establish a church school for boys in memory of John Stark Ravenscroft, the first bishop of the Episcopal Church in North Carolina, and selected Pittsboro as the site. Jarvis Buxton, pastor of Trinity Church in Asheville, was appointed principal. Buxton's parishioners, however, were so reluctant for him to leave that they offered to build the school in Asheville. The school operated in Asheville until 1864, when it was forced to close because of the Civil War. In 1868 Bishop Thomas Atkinson, along with Buxton, abandoned the idea of a boys school and organized the Ravenscroft Associate Mission and Training, an effort to educate local young men for the ministry. On Sundays, the students went to surrounding areas to conduct services and do missionary work.

In 1887 the Diocesan Convention voted to reestablish the boys' high school. Henry A. Prince was appointed headmaster, and a new building, Schoenberger Hall, was constructed on the grounds to house the training school. Prince was soon succeeded as headmaster by his assistant, Haywood Parker. From 1889 until 1894, Ronald McDonald, son of well-known English writer George McDonald, directed the school as a private enterprise under contract with the church. Despite its excellent reputation, the school was unable to attract enough students to make it a financial success. The high cost of tuition, along with advances in the public school system, brought about the close of the school in the late 1890s. Schoenberger Hall became the bishop's residence for western North Carolina and the rest of the property was sold. The old Ravenscroft School building remains as one of the oldest buildings in Asheville.

References: Marshall DeLancey Haywood, *Lives of the Bishops of North Carolina from the Establishment of the Episcopate in that State to the Division of the Diocese* (1910); Lawrence Foushee London and Sarah McCulloh Lemmon, eds., *The Episcopal Church in North Carolina, 1701–1959* (1987).

Ann S. Wright

Rawls's Mill, Battle of. The Civil War battle at Rawls's Mill in Martin County took place on 2 Nov. 1862. Maj. Gen. John G. Foster, commander of Union forces in North Carolina, was leading his 5,000 soldiers from Washington, N.C., to Wilmington when attacked by Confederates under Col. Henry "Harry" King Burgwyn Jr. At Rawls's Mill, approximately six miles south of Williamston, Foster's infantry, artillery, and cavalry fought a spirited half-hour battle with Burgwyn's troops, which had far fewer men and neither artillery nor cavalry. The Confederates were driven from their works and across a bridge, burning it to prevent pursuit. Nevertheless, this encounter was a trying ordeal for the green Union recruits of such regiments as the 44th Massachusetts, which had been organized only 60 days previously.

About noon on 3 November, Foster's army arrived at Williamston. They expected another fight, but the town was nearly deserted. The troops plundered the town, destroying everything that could not be taken.

References: John G. Barrett, *The Civil War in North Carolina* (1963); Louis H. Manarin, comp., *North Carolina Troops, 1861–1865: A Roster*, vol. 7 (1979); Francis M. Manning and W. H. Booker, *Martin County History*, vol. 2 (1979).

Wiley J. Williams

Real Estate is one of the largest industries in North Carolina, representing billions of dollars of the state's economy and touching the lives of millions of North Carolinians, from first-time homeowners to large corporations such as Charlotte's Summit Properties, owners of some 50 apartment complexes in the Southeast. In North Carolina law, real estate, as distinguished from personal property, is land; anything permanently attached to land, such as buildings, fences, trees, grass, shrubs, minerals, and other substances beneath the surface; and the airspace above land. The real estate industry in the state is made up of real estate brokers and salespersons, who market real property on behalf of owners. Many more people work in appraisal, architecture, building, contracting, mortgage finance, market analysis, and related fields.

In 1927 the General Assembly created the first North Carolina Real Estate Commission, whose major responsibility was to issue licenses that were renewable annually. However, it was not until 1957 that the state attempted comprehensive regulation and licensing of the profession. The act, applicable statewide, defined a real estate broker as a person, corporation, or firm who for compensation sold, auctioned, exchanged, bought, leased, or rented real estate; and a real estate salesperson as any person who for compensation was engaged on behalf of a broker to perform any of these tasks. As amended in 1967, a real estate licensing board was required to maintain a current roster of brokers and salespersons. The General Assembly in 1979 reenacted the board and established the Real Estate Recovery Fund, whereby the board was to set aside $100,000 to be used for payment of unsatisfied judgments where an aggrieved party suffered a direct monetary loss by reason of acts committed by licensed brokers or sales

personnel. (Additional legislation about the fund was enacted in 1987.) The second session of the 1979 legislature added the regulation and licensing of real estate schools to the board's responsibilities. In 1983 the General Assembly changed the board's name to the Real Estate Commission, with the position of executive director replacing that of secretary-treasurer as the chief administrative officer. In 1989 the General Assembly established the North Carolina Real Estate Appraisal Board as an advisory agency to the Real Estate Commission, and four years later this board was made independent.

A few years before the state first attempted real estate regulation, real estate–related organizations began to appear in the private sector. Most prominent was the North Carolina Association of Realtors (NCAR), which was founded in 1921 and became "the voice of real estate in North Carolina." The association offers members such special services as contract forms, legislative and regulatory representation, and continuing education workshops and seminars. Its political action committee (RPAC) is active in lobbying the state legislature and other state agencies, and it maintains a monthly publication, *Tar Heel Realtor*. NCAR is one of 54 state and territorial associations affiliated with the National Association of Realtors, founded in 1908. Other real estate–related organizations have established state or regional offices, principally in Charlotte, Greensboro, and Raleigh.

A state business directory in 2002 listed more than 6,300 North Carolina real estate firms of all sizes, with thousands of separate listings for such related occupations and fields as appraisers, auctioneers, consultants, developers, environmental assessment services, inspection services, investment services, loan officers, property managers, rental services, real estate schools, time-sharing (i.e., vacation) rentals, and title specialists.

References: Fillmore W. Galaty, Wellington J. Allaway, and Robert C. Kyle, *Modern Real Estate Practice in North Carolina* (3rd ed., 1998); David A. Hagen and Ralph A. Palmer, *North Carolina Real Estate: Principles and Practices* (1991).

Wiley J. Williams

Receiver General of colonial North Carolina was responsible until 1776 for the collection of land rents (called quitrents), the sale of land, and the management of forfeitures. The office was not mentioned by name in either the Concessions and Agreement of January 1665 or the Fundamental Constitutions (1669–98), but the need for such a position was clearly understood by the Lords Proprietors of Carolina, who laid down procedures for granting, selling, and renting land. Although the Proprietary board, as early as 1670, considered appointing precinct sheriffs to manage their property and rents and to construct towns, storehouses, prisons, churches, and a statehouse, the board accepted that one director—until

1711, the governor—was the most logical repository of their trust. Accordingly, from 1670 until 1712 North Carolina's governors appointed "a person or persons to collect the quit rents of land due" who were generally permitted to expend these moneys for the benefit of the colony. Implicit in this arrangement was that each governor would furnish in time "a true and just account" of all funds that were amassed and disbursed and as accurate a rent roll (the names of all landholders, the amount of individual acreage held, and the number of years an account might be in arrears) as was possible to collect.

From the revenues collected, the receiver general was responsible for covering the salaries of the colony's leadership. In 1715, for instance, Daniel Richardson paid the chief justice, the secretary, the attorney general, the governor, the president of the Provincial Council, and his own expenses for collecting quitrents in each precinct. Eleven years later, William Little was obliged to find funds for these same positions as well as for a provost marshal, three deputy marshals, and six deputy receivers.

References: Beverley W. Bond Jr., *The Quit-rent System in the American Colonies* (1965); Robert J. Cain, ed., *Records of the Executive Council, 1664–1734* (1984); Alan D. Watson, "The Quitrent System of Royal South Carolina" (M.A. thesis, University of South Carolina, 1971).

Louis P. Towles

Reconstruction. At the close of the Civil War, Presidents Abraham Lincoln and Andrew Johnson successively urged a quick and lenient restoration of the South to the Union, demanding only its renunciation of secession and slavery. To that end, they appointed Unionist provisional governors in each southern state (Lincoln in Union-occupied states during the war, Johnson in the remainder after the war) to reorganize their states and prepare them for readmission. Accordingly, new governments were organized in the southern states, including North Carolina. But the radical and moderate Republicans controlling Congress feared that such a quick restoration would bring to power a coalition of northern Democrats and former Confederates that would perpetuate slavery in substance if not in name and restore the conditions that had led to war. Hence they insisted on stricter conditions for southern readmission and refused to seat the new senators- and representatives-elect from the South.

The Fourteenth Amendment and the Beginning of Congressional Reconstruction

In 1866 Congress proposed the Fourteenth Amendment to the Constitution, embracing a compromise Reconstruction formula. It would guarantee equal legal rights (but not the vote) for blacks and give every state representation in Congress and the Electoral College based on whatever propor-

tion of the adult male population it allowed to vote. When every southern state except Tennessee rejected this amendment, Congress, on the advice of President Johnson, assumed control of Reconstruction in 1867. It required the states to adopt new constitutions that provided for black suffrage and then to ratify the Fourteenth Amendment. Blacks and white Unionists, it was hoped, would form a loyal body politic controlling some of if not the entire Confederacy. To that end, most former Confederate officials—civilian and military alike—were temporarily forbidden to hold political office. A year later Congress approved the Fifteenth Amendment, extending African American suffrage throughout the country.

Meanwhile, in May 1865 Johnson had appointed *Raleigh Standard* editor William W. Holden provisional governor of North Carolina and charged him with implementing the president's lenient restoration plan. Holden had organized and led a peace movement in the state during the Civil War. He now made the prior support of that movement a litmus test of postwar loyalty and thereby antagonized many moderates who were ready in 1865 (as they had not been during the war) to accept the lenient peace terms offered by Washington, D.C. As a result, one of those persons, former Confederate state treasurer Jonathan Worth, defeated Holden for governor in the first postwar election in 1865. Worth was reelected in 1866. As in the South at large, North Carolina's newly freed blacks played no part in these elections and governments. The new legislature's black code relegated them to a second-class citizenship patterned after that of free blacks before the war. Such measures contributed strongly to Republican concerns in Washington and the North.

With the advent of Congressional Reconstruction in 1867, Republican Parties formed in every southern state to support the new policy. Holden and his allies, forsaking the discredited President Johnson, took the lead in North Carolina, where the party consisted of three groups: black freedmen, who supported the party that had freed and enfranchised them; a minority of whites, more numerous in the western part of the state, who (like Holden) had opposed secession and the Confederate war effort; and a small number of northerners who had settled in the state during and immediately after the war, more important in the east than in the west. The latter two groups were quickly labeled by their enemies "scalawags" and "carpetbaggers," respectively. The majority of whites, supporting the Conservative, or Democratic, Party, rejected Congressional Reconstruction, sometimes to the point of armed resistance.

Statewide Changes and Achievements during Reconstruction

Republicans dominated the elections of 1867 and the state constitutional convention that followed. The resulting Constitution of 1868 endured for more than a century, albeit with many amendments. It provided for universal manhood suffrage and basic legal rights for whites and blacks alike (complying with congressional mandates) and introduced locally elected county government and a public school system for both races. In April 1868 voters ratified the constitution and elected Republicans to all statewide offices, including Holden as governor and a Republican legislative majority. Blacks won no statewide offices but were elected to many local positions, especially in the east. Northerners were also elected to offices in predominantly black counties in the east, filling a partial vacuum of talent left by the legacy of slavery. Statewide and in most localities, especially in the west, the great majority of Republican officeholders were native whites (scalawags to their enemies).

In office, the Republicans compiled a notable and generally positive record of achievement. The new legislature ratified the Fourteenth Amendment, as Congress required. It elected to the U.S. Senate John Pool, of Elizabeth City, a recent Whig Party gubernatorial candidate, and Joseph C. Abbott, of Wilmington, a former Union army general. The legislature created (but did not adequately fund) the state's first public school system for blacks as well as for whites, adopted a progressive civil law code, reaffirmed the legal and political equality of the races and ratified the Fifteenth Amendment, established the state's first penitentiary, abolished flogging as a punishment for crime, took steps to alleviate economic distress, and dealt as best it could with Democratic terrorism operating through the Ku Klux Klan (KKK). The legislature was a more democratic body than any of its predecessors and, for many years after, its successors. On the other hand, it went beyond the limits of prudence and legality in voting money for railroad construction, most of which never took place; a year later the same legislators had second thoughts and withdrew most of the state aid. A few members took bribes in return for pro-railroad votes, the money emanating from a pair of promoters, George W. Swepson and Milton S. Littlefield. But North Carolina saw less corruption than many other states, North and South.

In terms of legislative voting, blacks and northerners compiled a more radical (or egalitarian) record than native white Republicans. All were more radical than the Conservative (Democratic) minority, but in North Carolina, as in the Upper South generally, radical egalitarianism never extended far beyond the ballot box. (Radical rule was more a Conservative campaign slogan than a reality.) Blacks remained poor, undereducated, and relatively dependent on whites. Few whites of either party favored racial integration; segregation remained the norm in the schools, on the railroads, and in most places of public accommodation. But in contrast to previous regimes, which had excluded blacks from most state institutions and services, Republicans made an effort to provide equal facilities.

The End of Reconstruction and the Return of Democratic Control

Conservative opposition took many forms during the Reconstruction period. In addition to legitimate political activity, Democrats frequently ostracized white Republicans and threatened economic sanctions against dependent black laborers who voted Republican. Intimidation and violence were more successful against Republican officials and voters of both races. This took the form of parading by extralegal military companies, rioting, and, most spectacularly, night riding in disguise by the KKK. In 1870, after the Klan virtually took over Alamance and Caswell Counties, Governor Holden declared a state of insurrection and sent in militia under Col. George W. Kirk. The resultant military occupation and arrests in the two counties have sometimes been called the "Kirk-Holden War," although no battles actually took place.

Whether in reaction to the militia campaign or the Republican political record, or because of the intimidation of black voters, Democrats captured control of the legislature in the fall of 1870. In apparent retribution for Holden's actions in the Kirk-Holden War, the new Democratic legislature, partially controlled by KKK members, impeached the governor for "high crimes and misdemeanors" and removed him from office. Holden was the first state governor in American history to be so treated. His successor, Republican lieutenant governor Tod R. Caldwell, was elected to a term in his own right in 1872. Following Caldwell's death two years later, Republican Curtis H. Brogden became the last Reconstruction governor of the state. Democrats regained the governorship with Zebulon B. Vance in 1876. Their domination for the next generation was assured by a series of constitutional amendments they pushed through in 1873 and 1875, offered in the name of white supremacy and small government. The most important amendment transferred control of county government from locally elected commissioners—who in some counties were black as well as Republican—to justices of the peace chosen by the legislature.

The oft-recited horrors of Reconstruction took two main forms in North Carolina and the South as a whole. Economic suffering was widespread, the result almost entirely of the ravages of the war. Reconstruction policy had comparatively little to do with this problem, except that higher taxation may have added to it. The second form of suffering, more psychological and political in nature, was that experienced by whites—especially the prewar ruling elite—when they found themselves replaced in power by people they regarded as social and racial inferiors. In truth, Reconstruction wrought only half a revolution. By the Compromise of 1877 and the withdrawal of federal troops from the South, conservative Democrats had reestablished most of their economic and social force. Before long an acquiescent North permitted them to regain political mastery as well. By disfranchising their opponents in the years that followed, they maintained power, with the exception of the Fusionist period, for almost a century.

References: Eric Foner, *Reconstruction: America's Unfinished Revolution, 1863–1877* (1988); Foner and Olivia Mahoney, *America's Reconstruction: People and Politics after the Civil War* (1995); J. G. de Roulhac Hamilton, *Reconstruction in North Carolina* (1914); William C. Harris, *William Woods Holden: Firebrand of North Carolina Politics* (1987).

Allen W. Trelease

SEE ALSO Black and Tan Constitution; Redeemer Democrats; Scalawag; Union League.

Recording Industry and record labels in North Carolina, beginning in the 1930s, featured an impressive array of talented producers and helped gain exposure for North Carolina musicians and songwriters with diverse musical styles. During the industry's infancy, the bulk and expense of recording equipment prohibited widespread independent record production, causing most of the recording of North Carolina music to be done by the major American labels until after World War II. The second half of the twentieth century saw an increase in independent studios and labels as new artists came onto the scene and unique markets grew. By the early 2000s the state was home to a vibrant recording industry, with most labels—representing rock, jazz, Christian, hip-hop, and other genres—located primarily in the major urban areas of Charlotte, Winston-Salem, and the Raleigh–Durham–Chapel Hill Triangle.

North Carolina Recording Pioneers

The 1923 success of Georgia native Fiddlin' John Carson's recording of "Little Old Log Cabin in the Lane" proved the public's fascination with authentic rural string band music and launched the so-called hillbilly industry. Many rural North Carolina artists and string bands were recorded by the major labels (mainly RCA Victor and Columbia) during the 1920s, though most of these artists traveled to major cities to make the actual recordings while maintaining a home base in the state. Charlie Poole and the North Carolina Ramblers, Bascom Lamar Lunsford, the Carolina Tar Heels, and Ernest Thompson became exclusive recording artists and their records were distributed nationally. In 1937 RCA Victor set up a semipermanent recording studio in the Hotel Charlotte, although the major labels had previously made field records of southern artists in several strategic southern locations. Until 1945 many North Carolina country acts recorded in the Charlotte studio, including Wade Mainer, the Blue Sky Boys, the Dixon Brothers, the Tobacco Tags, and J. E. Mainer and the Crazy Mountaineers. Although not North Carolina natives, Bill Monroe and his brother Charlie were based out of the state during that time, and their 1936 recording of "What Would You Give in Ex-

change for Your Soul" (made in Charlotte) became one of the largest selling records of that decade. Some consider it to be the first bluegrass recording.

Black blues and gospel acts from North Carolina were also recorded by the major labels, mainly through the efforts of businessman J. B. Long. While managing the United Dollar Store in Kinston, Long scouted the local area for talent, leading to successful records by the Cauley Family, Lake Howard, and Mitchell's Christian Singers for the A.R.C. labels group. After being transferred to Durham, Long hit pay dirt with his discovery of blues men playing in the East Coast Piedmont style: Sonny Terry, Gary Davis, and Blind Boy Fuller. Fuller, who was probably the most popular and influential of the East Coast blues performers, recorded 130 sides for Columbia Records until his premature death in 1941. Long acted as his personal manager, lining up recording sessions, taking him to recording locations in New York or Chicago, and writing songs and rehearsing Fuller for these sessions.

Independent Labels Find Success

World War II and the 1940s brought many changes to the recording industry. Early in 1942 the government restricted the use of shellac needed for 78 rpm record production. That July J. C. Petrillo, president of the American Federation of Musicians, announced a ban on all recording and closed down the studios for two years. The major labels, after resuming recording activities, gave up the field trips and temporary recording locations and concentrated their work in three major cities: New York, Los Angeles, and Nashville. Their lack of interest in regional musical styles opened the door for independent record production, which began in North Carolina in the late 1940s and early 1950s.

The rural string band tradition underwent some changes in the 1940s with the development of bluegrass music by Bill Monroe and his original Blue Grass Boys band. This style of music, as well as the older string band styles, gained popularity in certain regions of North Carolina. Blue Ridge Records, run by Drusilla Adams of North Wilkesboro, was an early independent label to feature this style of acoustic music in the state. The label recorded its acts locally, on several occasions using the facilities at radio station WPAQ in Mount Airy. "Missing in Action" by "Smilin" Jim Eanes was a big seller for Blue Ridge Records, reportedly moving over 400,000 units.

Colonial Records of Chapel Hill was undoubtedly the most successful of the independent record companies in North Carolina. Its owner, Orville Campbell, kept the label in business from 1948 to 1965, releasing a wide variety of recordings from bluegrass and country to pop, novelty, comedy, folk, and early rock 'n' roll. Colonial launched the careers of several personalities who later prospered in the entertainment field, including Andy Griffith, John D. Loudermilk, George Hamilton IV, and Billy "Crash" Craddock. As with Blue Ridge Records, Colonial usually recorded its acts locally using existing facilities after school hours—in this case, the recording lab of the University of North Carolina at Chapel Hill (UNC) located in Swain Hall.

Most of the early Colonial releases were novelty affairs, including a version of "Wabash Cannonball" by renowned ex-pitcher–sports announcer Dizzy Dean. In 1953 Campbell produced a live recording by "Deacon" Andy Griffith, a down-home comedy monologue titled "What It Was Was Football." This release by the then-unknown North Carolina high school teacher became so popular that Campbell could not distribute the record properly, so he sold the master to Capitol Records in Los Angeles. Wisely, he kept the publishing rights to the performance, thus exposing Griffith to national prominence and gaining wealth for his own small recording operation. Colonial continued to make records covering a wide variety of musical styles until 1965, but it never regained the success it had enjoyed during the mid- to late 1950s.

A similar North Carolina label was Brooke Records from Asheboro. Brooke, like Colonial, presented a variety of musical styles—including pop, country, and rock 'n' roll—and shared the same recording facilities on the UNC campus. "I Don't Know What It Is" by the Bluenotes (who also recorded on Colonial) became popular regionally and gained some national exposure through a deal with a midwestern distributor.

Renown Records based out of Durham seems to have been a vehicle for artists associated with Jim Thornton from Johnston County. Thornton was a colorful country music performer and businessman whose musical career began in the 1940s when he performed with the Johnston County Ramblers over radio station WPTF in Raleigh. His late-night TV program *Saturday Night Country Style* reached many viewers and featured Thornton, usually barefooted and dressed in overalls, with local country music guests. The most successful Renown releases, however, were by Wayne Handy, a rock 'n' roller who performed both up-tempo numbers and Elvis-type ballads. His initial single, "Say Yeah," was popular regionally, but subsequent records ("Betcha Didn't Know" and "Seminole Rock 'n' Roll") gained national exposure after they were leased to the more established Trend label after showing signs of promise locally. Handy was last heard on the Parkway label out of Philadelphia, which brought the world "The Twist" by Chubby Checker.

With the increased number of recording studios in North Carolina in the 1960s, the average performer had greater opportunities to have a record released. A practice that seemed to flourish was the manufacture of custom releases in which the musician paid for studio time and record production expenses to secure copies for self-distribution. Many gospel acts, country groups, and fledgling rock bands chose this route, with the Arthur Smith studios in Charlotte providing guidance for independent record production. Many groups found a manager who was willing to assist with investments and promotion through established connections in the entertainment field. The most affordable form was 45 rpm singles, but custom long-playing albums were seen more frequently and were produced by acts with a larger budget.

Beach music and its attendant shag dancing was long a staple of North Carolina culture. This good-time, horn-driven dance music, based on 1950s black rhythm and blues, developed a regional cult following with the Carolina beaches as a focal point. The Embers, the premier North Carolina beach band, began its career in the 1960s. Its early releases were produced by Jimmy Capps, a popular Raleigh disc jockey who operated his own JCP record label. The band later switched to self-production, scoring big in 1979 with "I Love Beach Music" (Ripete EEE 1001)—regarded by many as the anthem of the beach music scene. In 1968 the O'Kaysions of Kenly recorded a single at the Pitt Sound studio in Greenville that reached the national top ten that year after being sold to ABC Paramount Records in New York. "Girl Watcher" brought national attention to the Carolina beach sound and reportedly sold over a million copies. Other regional best sellers included "Hey I Know You" by the Monzas, "If I Only Had a Dime" by Bob Collins and the Fabulous Five, "Summertime's Calling Me" by the Catalinas, and "Myrtle Beach Days" by the Fantastic Shakers. Doug Clark and the Hot Nuts gained a reputation on college campuses along the East Coast with their racy fraternity house shows featuring adults-only humor. The group ran its own label, Gross Records, out of Chapel Hill, recording six albums during the 1960s. Unlike most other North Carolina beach bands, the Hot Nuts was an all-black unit that performed for mainly white audiences.

Record Production since the 1970s

With the exception of beach music, the 1970s saw a decline in regional hit records with the advent of FM radio and formatted radio programming and the decline of the jukebox as a promotional tool. Local recording studios, independent labels, and custom recording remained in high gear, with cassette releases replacing the once-popular 45 singles by the early 1980s. Later local studios were forced to update their equipment for compatibility with new digital formats. Portable and easily affordable home-recording units began to allow both amateur and professional musicians to make quality recordings at home, lessening the need for studio time except for professional projects. Independent studios and record labels continued to thrive in North Carolina, including Reflection studio in Charlotte, the Drive-In studio in Winston-Salem, TGF, Sound Wave studios and Merge Records in Chapel Hill, and Jag studio in Raleigh. Independent record labels such as Sugar Hill Records in Durham and the World Music label based in Hillsborough released recordings that were distributed internationally, while several hip-hop labels in Charlotte and elsewhere gained attention in the industry.

References: Bruce Bastin, *Crying for the Carolinas* (1971); Robert M. W. Dixon and John Godrich, *Recording the Blues* (1970); Lew Herman, *Recording at the Hotel Charlotte* (1989); Bill C. Malone, *Country Music USA: A Fifty Year History* (1968).

Michael L. Wells

SEE ALSO Bluegrass Music; Blues; Country Music; Gospel Music; Old-Time String Band Music; Rock Music.

Red Cross. The American Red Cross, a nonprofit humanitarian organization dedicated to helping citizens prepare for and respond to large-scale emergencies, was formed in 1881, modeled on humanitarian work by volunteers in the Crimean War (1854–56) and the later Austrian-Italian War (1859). In North Carolina, women often took the lead in organizing Red Cross chapters. Some of the state's first chapters were formed in Buncombe, Rowan, and New Hanover Counties. A Wilmington chapter was organized on 10 Nov. 1908 and an Asheville chapter on 17 Apr. 1911. These early chapters were formed to help meet the needs of individual families affected by crises such as natural disasters or fires. The Salisbury chapter dates to the beginning of World War I and later played a leading role in the establishment of the blood donor program.

An American Red Cross chapter was organized by local women in Raleigh in 1916; the following year it founded a "colored auxiliary" for African Americans. Chapters were organized in Durham and Greensboro in 1917. Among the North Carolina Red Cross's early projects were the opening of a tuberculosis sanitarium near Wilmington just prior to World War I, the operation of canteens at railroad stations for World War I servicemen, and aid in the influenza epidemic of 1918. First aid and lifesaving classes were also offered. In some communities around the state, the Red Cross in the early years provided public health nurses, home classes in infant care and nutrition, and care for disabled veterans. It provided notable assistance during a hurricane in 1933 and in railroad accidents in 1943.

Many Red Cross chapters were formed in North Carolina during the World War II era and afterward. By the early 2000s there were more than 50 chapters in the state, with service districts covering all 100 counties. The Greater Carolinas Chapter is North Carolina's largest Red Cross chapter, serving nearly 1 million people in Charlotte and surrounding towns. The Red Cross has been irreplaceable during North Carolina's most horrific natural disasters, particularly major hurricanes. Probably the most visible Red Cross–sponsored events, blood drives, are often carried out by volunteers in churches, on university campuses, and in several other settings. The Rowan County Red Cross Chapter was renamed the Elizabeth Hanford Dole Chapter in 1995 to honor the Salisbury native who was then the president of the American Red Cross and who was elected a U.S. senator from North Carolina in 2002.

Reference: Foster R. Dulles, *The American Red Cross: A History* (1950).

John B. Dysart

Redeemer Democrats was a self-imposed term used by nineteenth-century southern Democrats fond of talking about "redeeming" their states from the alleged "misrule and corruption" wrought by Republican carpetbaggers, scalawags, and their black allies who assumed control as Congressional Reconstruction began in 1867–68. The Ku Klux Klan and similar domestic terrorist organizations played an important role in helping the Democrats reach their goal, which was done at different times between 1869 and 1877 in various southern states. Many Redeemer Democrats, or Redeemers, such as Zebulon B. Vance of North Carolina and Wade Hampton of South Carolina, had been Whigs before the Civil War. During Reconstruction, Democrats (temporarily also called "Conservatives") sought to bring as many voters as possible into "the white man's party." By the 1890s the Redeemers lost control of the southern Democratic Party, and more rabid racists, intent on disfranchising black voters, gained control of the party and of the governments of southern states.

Reference: C. Vann Woodward, *Origins of the New South, 1877–1913* (repr., 1971).

Robert F. Durden

Red Shirts were armed gangs of white men acting as a terrorist and intimidation wing of the Democratic Party in the state elections of 1898 and 1900. The Red Shirts received their name from loose red tunics worn as uniforms. The costumes, in turn, derived from the South Carolina Red Shirts, another white supremacy group that sought to end Republican Reconstruction in that state in the 1870s.

In 1898 the political strategy of the North Carolina Democratic Party, which had lost power to Populist and Republican Fusionists in 1894, was to regain control of the General Assembly by emphasizing the danger of African American office holding and voting. Early in the campaign, Democratic leaders recognized that success would depend on more than logical persuasion. As a result, they used Red Shirts to threaten and intimidate black and white Populists and Republicans.

The Red Shirts played a substantial role in the 1898 election, which produced the first Democratic General Assembly since 1893. Red Shirts were organized as groups of mounted men, often masked, who carried pistols, rifles, and shotguns. Centered in the eastern part of the state, they made threats of death and physical or economic harm to political opponents. Red Shirts broke up anti-Democratic meetings and prevented Fusionist candidates from speaking. They also engaged in direct forms of violence: beatings and whippings of African Americans, assaults on candidates, and murder. While roaming in rural areas, they shot into opponents' residences. On election day 1898, Red Shirts prevented non-Democrats from getting to polls. One gang mobbed the train of Republican governor Daniel L. Russell Jr. at Hamlet, while others paraded in front of the governor's mansion. The Red Shirts appear to have attracted men from various economic classes; well-known ministers, for example, led their processions. Prominent Red Shirts included future congressman Claude Kitchin and future governor Cameron Morrison.

In 1899 Democratic legislators planned to guarantee the party's continued rule by formally disfranchising its opponents. The device for this grip on state government was a constitutional amendment limiting the right to vote, for which an election was to be held in August 1900.

Once again Red Shirts were called upon for violence and intimidation. In Smithfield, they attacked a Populist speaker's platform. Red Shirts beat and threatened Populists, dragged African Americans from their homes and whipped them, and threatened opposition voters with death if they appeared at polls. In 1900 they collected large stores of arms, harassed opposition orators, and stole Fusionist mail. Populist U.S. senator Marion Butler was assaulted by Red Shirts when he tried to leave a train in eastern North Carolina. In contrast, Red Shirts escorted their Democratic heroes, including future governor Charles B. Aycock. Advertising the muscle of white supremacy, they appeared frequently at Aycock's rallies in the eastern part of the state. Rather than an accidental by-product of white supremacy fervor, Red Shirt violence was planned by Democratic officials. It is likely, for instance, that campaign funds raised by the state party were used to hire Red Shirts and to buy alcohol for them.

The bloody campaigns of intimidation were successful. Voting results indicate fraud and massive declines in black turnout. Democrats, including Josephus Daniels, Furnifold M. Simmons, and Aycock, justified the admittedly criminal acts of 1898 and 1900 as necessary given the "evil" of black political participation. Red Shirts' activities demonstrated the expediency of the politics of white supremacy, the limited appeal of universal democracy among North Carolina's early twentieth-century leaders, and the persistence of violence as a political tactic.

References: Helen G. Edmonds, *The Negro and Fusion Politics in North Carolina, 1894–1901* (1951); James L. Hunt, "Marion Butler and the Populist Ideal, 1863–1938" (Ph.D. diss., University of Wisconsin, 1990); J. Morgan Kousser, *The Shaping of Southern Politics: Suffrage Restriction and the Establishment of the One-Party South, 1880–1910* (1974); Robert W. Wooley, "Race and Politics: The Evolution of the White Supremacy Campaign of 1898 in North Carolina" (Ph.D. diss., UNC-Chapel Hill, 1977).

James L. Hunt

Red Strings. SEE Heroes of America.

Reed Gold Mine State Historic Site. Photograph courtesy of North Carolina Division of Tourism, Film, and Sports Development.

Reed Gold Mine, located in Midland, 12 miles southeast of Concord, is the site at which the first authenticated discovery of gold in the United States occurred. In 1799 Conrad Reed, the 12-year-old son of German immigrant John Reed, uncovered a 17-pound gold nugget while fishing in Little Meadow Creek. Within four years, the first gold mine in the country had been established, starting as a placer mine and later expanding to vein or lode mining. As mining spread, North Carolina experienced a gold rush that made it the largest domestic producer of the precious metal until the California rush of the 1850s. Reed Gold Mine was one of the richest mines in the South and was noted for its large nuggets, weighing up to 28 pounds.

The most impressive physical work at the mine occurred in about 1854, when miners greatly expanded the underground workings and built a substantial engine millhouse with a stone chimney and a steam engine. The Reed mine's success was sporadic, and like many other mines in the state, after the Civil War it operated intermittently. In 1895 the Kelly family of Springfield, Ohio, purchased almost exactly the undivided acreage that John Reed had owned. They did not operate the mine profitably but instead kept the property for nearly eight decades as a southern retreat. The site was recognized as a National Historic Landmark in 1966, and the North Carolina Department of Archives and History three years later consulted the heirs of Armin L. Kelly about acquiring it. In December 1971 the Kellys sold 760 acres at a very reasonable price and donated 70 acres for the establishment of Reed Gold Mine State Historic Site.

The National Park Service prepared a master plan for the site, and Geological Resources, Inc., of Raleigh prepared a study of the underground workings at the mine. Further planning and historical research were undertaken, and a support group, the Gold History Corporation, was formed. In 1971 the General Assembly appropriated funds for development, and a staff began work at the site. Artifacts were collected; a visitors center was built; 400 feet of underground tunnel was restored;

roads, bridges, and walking trails were laid out; and the site was opened to the public in April 1977. In the ensuing years, mining machinery and equipment reclaimed from other abandoned mines were displayed at the Reed Gold Mine site. The staff at the site provides interpretive programs, special events, and educational work, and a panning area allows visitors to try panning for gold.

References: P. Albert Carpenter III, *Gold in North Carolina* (1993); Linda Funk, *Reed Gold Mine Guidebook* (1979); Richard F. Knapp, "Golden Promise in the Piedmont: The Story of John Reed's Mine," *NCHR* 52 (January 1975); Knapp, ed., *North Carolina's State Historic Sites: A Brief History and Status Report* (1995); M. A. Schwalm, *A Hessian Immigrant Finds Gold: The Story of John Reed* (1996).

Robert L. Remsburg III

Reformed Church. Because of doctrinal differences, two movements developed from the Protestant Reformation of the sixteenth century: followers of Martin Luther formed Lutheran congregations in Germany, the Scandinavian countries, and Iceland; and adherents of John Calvin and Ulrich Zwingli established churches in parts of Germany, Switzerland, the Netherlands, France, and Scotland. The pressures of religious persecution, wars, and famine soon forced many persons of both the Lutheran and Reformed traditions to seek out the broad lands of the New World.

In 1690 French Protestants fleeing Catholic persecution migrated to the Pamlico Sound region of North Carolina. They settled in Bath but never organized a congregation. Christoph Graffenreid (later, Baron von Graffenreid) led a contingent of Swiss and German Reformed settlers to the Carolina coast in 1710. They founded a town on the Neuse River, naming it New Berne in honor of Berne, Switzerland. Indian attacks destroyed the colony, however, and the survivors joined the Scottish Reformed (Presbyterian) Church.

In the 1730s land-hungry Scotch-Irish Presbyterians from Pennsylvania turned their eyes south to the fertile lands of the Valley of Virginia. Some, after stopping for a season in Virginia, continued down the Great Wagon Road to the Carolina backcountry. German settlers, both Lutheran and Reformed, followed them a decade later, settling in the rolling lands at the foot of the North Carolina mountains, from the present county of Guilford south to old Mecklenburg County. Their Moravian cousins settled in the area around present-day Winston-Salem. The Germans of both traditions tended to settle in the same neighborhoods, so they could share their common language and heritage. Many of the earliest churches they built were union churches, in which both Lutheran and Reformed believers worshipped in harmony on alternate Sundays.

There were no resident Reformed ministers for many years, but early German settlers met together for worship in pri-vate homes and later began to build log churches. Although they could not participate in the sacraments without a minister, they felt the need to come together to pray, sing, have an educated member read a sermon, and share common concerns. The first Reformed people in North Carolina were aided by occasional missionary visits from Christian Theus, a Reformed minister who lived in South Carolina. A Swiss minister, James Martin, came among them in 1759, followed by a French Reformed minister, Richard Du Pert (Dupert) in 1764.

North Carolina's earliest German Reformed churches included Grace (Lowerstone) Evangelical and Reformed Church in Rowan County. It claims an organization date of 1745, when the church was known as "Hickory Church." Pilgrim (Leonard's) Church in Davidson County was organized about 1757, and a membership list for Cold Water Church in present-day Cabarrus County dates from 1766. Although the list of members for Cold Water is of uncertain origin, the legendary Reformed minister Samuel Suther preached there for Governor William Tryon when he visited the region in 1768. Suther brought cohesion to the Reformed churches of central North Carolina, preaching throughout the Piedmont region. He moved to the Orangeburg District of South Carolina in 1786, and died there.

Mt. Zion (Savitz) Church in Rowan County was built about 1770, closely followed by St. Paul's Church in Catawba County in 1771. During the Revolution, members of the historic Brick (Clapp's) Church in Guilford County built a large schoolhouse to use as a church. Prior to that time, the Reformed people in Guilford County had worshipped with the Lutherans in Low's Church. Beck's Church in Davidson County is another pre-revolutionary Reformed congregation, although the deed for its property dates from 1787. The faithful of Stanly County held worship services at Beck's Church long before they built the Bethel (Bear Creek) Church in 1806.

During the years following the Revolutionary War, German immigration declined and church membership suffered. Much of the credit for the survival of the Reformed Church during that period goes to the Reverend Andrew Loretz, a Swiss minister who preached throughout the German communities of North Carolina and South Carolina.

In 1831, the 17 North Carolina Reformed congregations formed the North Carolina Classis. By 1843 all of the congregations had a regular pastor. The classis withdrew from the Synod of the Potomac in 1853, due to disagreement with the theological doctrines taught at the Mercerburg Seminary, but rejoined the synod in 1866.

The Classis started a "high school" in Newton in 1851 and also supported Claremont Female College near Hickory. The school in Newton grew into Catawba College; in 1925, it moved to a new location in Salisbury and has prospered there. Nazareth Orphans' Home in Rowan County was opened in 1906.

In 1934, the Reformed Church merged with the Evangelical

Synod of North America to form the Evangelical and Reformed Church. Despite organizational differences, the Evangelical and Reformed Church merged with the Congregational Christian Churches in 1957 to form the United Church of Christ.

References: James I. Good, *History of the Reformed Church in the U.S. in the Nineteenth Century* (1911); Jacob Calvin Leonard, *The Southern Synod of the Evangelical and Reformed Church* (1940).

Clarence E. Horton Jr.

SEE ALSO Evangelical and Reformed Church; United Church of Christ.

Refugees (World War II).

The European refugees who came to North Carolina in the years of Hitler's ascendancy in Germany added significantly to the state's academic institutions and enriched its cultural life in general. Notwithstanding the plight of the Jewish population and all those who opposed Hitler's National Socialism, the United States was not ready in the 1930s to admit many of those persecuted in Europe. Unemployment remained high as the Great Depression continued, and new laws restricted sharply the number of immigrants who could come to America. Refugees from Germany faced often insurmountable barriers to leaving their homeland, so that only 100,987 of the 211,895 quota spaces for immigration to the United States could be used in 1939–40. Predictably, the flow of immigrants declined drastically after the beginning of World War II.

Relatively few European refugees settled in the American South at first. Leaders at the University of North Carolina at Chapel Hill advocated an open-door policy for admission of new immigrants in 1938, arguing that, because of the South's stagnant economy, "an infusion of new blood would be one of the greatest blessings" in the region. North Carolina thus became foremost among the southern states in offering opportunities to European refugees. In 1933 the experimental Black Mountain College was established near Asheville and invited a host of artists and scientists from all over Europe to join its faculty.

Duke University's president, William P. Few, took advantage of the list of persons in need of appointments circulated by the Emergency Committee in Aid of Displaced German Scholars in 1938 (the German was changed to "Foreign" later on) and brought as many as seven scholars to the university, including Raphael Lemkin, from Poland, who coined the word "genocide"; physicist Fritz London; and psychologist William Stern. During the administration of President Frank Porter Graham, UNC-Chapel Hill also attracted a number of refugees. One of these was Edward Danziger, a confectioner from Vienna who opened what would become a highly successful candy and coffee shop—and later a number of restaurants—in Chapel Hill.

The Chapel Hill members of the Society of Friends (Quakers) were also actively involved in the settlement of refugees in the state. J. Curt Victorius, who became a professor at Guilford College, decided to come to North Carolina after he read an advertisement in the *New York Times* (placed there by President Graham in the spring of 1938) inviting refugees to the state. Ernst Moritz Manasse in 1938 became the first nonblack faculty member at the North Carolina College for Negroes (now North Carolina Central University). Many nonacademic refugees undoubtedly came to North Carolina as well, although a record of their lives is harder to uncover. One example is Fritz Stern, who arrived in Charlotte via Richmond, Va., in 1943 and founded Southern Knitwear Mills.

References: Gabrielle Simon Edgcomb, *From Swastika to Jim Crow: Refugee Scholars at Black Colleges* (1993); Donald Fleming and Bernard Bailyn, eds., *The Intellectual Migration: Europe and America, 1930–1960* (1969).

Christoph E. Schweitzer

Regionalism.

After the Civil War ended and Reconstruction had run its course, many southerners looked ahead to a brighter future. In the late 1920s and early 1930s, there emerged two disparate views on how the region could reconnect with the rest of the Union while maintaining its unique identity. One view, centered at Vanderbilt University in Nashville, Tenn., advocated agrarianism—a culture "of the soil" based on the old order and critical of those who would lead the South down the path of modernity, especially by displacing agriculture with industrialization. In *I'll Take My Stand* (1930), a book of 12 essays, the Vanderbilt agrarians issued a clarion call for the region to hold on to the social, moral, and economic ways of the past and not surrender its distinct historical and sectional identity.

At the University of North Carolina in Chapel Hill, sociologists Rupert B. Vance and Howard W. Odum, and other social scientists, advanced a second way to integrate the South into the nation. Their doctrine of regionalism acknowledged the differences between the South and the rest of the country, encouraging diversity while advocating the treatment of the region's problems in relation to the national welfare. In *Human Geography of the South* (1932), Vance declared that "the purpose of regionalism was to use the American South as a test of human adequacy to master the resources of a given region and to develop thereon a distinctive and component subculture." The task, as Vance perceived it, was to bring about a new southern "cultural and material renaissance." Odum's magnum opus, *Southern Regions* (1936), criticized the South's shortcomings while seeing hope in a future based on planned development.

As applied specifically to North Carolina, regionalism has allowed the state to embrace its role not only as a southern state but also as a state of the South Atlantic, the Southeast, and the mid-South region. Politically, these regional constructs have enabled North Carolinians to make common cause with other states in expressing educational, economic, environmental, and other concerns. One early manifestation of this regional cooperation in conjunction with the federal government was the Tennessee Valley Authority, created in 1933 to bring economic and social improvements to a region hard hit by the Great Depression. After World War II, a variety of regional organizations and associations developed to address particular issues. State leaders now participate in such organizations as the Southern Governors' Association (formerly Conference), the Southern Regional Education Board, and the Southern Growth Policies Board.

By the early 2000s North Carolina retained many demographic, economic, and cultural characteristics associated with the South, yet a variety of technological advances, changes in patterns of migration, and other factors have complicated the state's place within the region. The increasing urbanization and suburbanization of the state along the I-85 and I-40 corridors have been a significant factor in this transformation of the state's regional identity. North Carolina's cities and suburbs increasingly resemble those in other parts of the United States, and the diversified economy and social opportunities provided in these cities draw people from all over the country and the world, changing the ways North Carolinians understand themselves and their relationship to the greater South. Nevertheless, institutions such as the Center for the Study of the American South, based at the University of North Carolina at Chapel Hill, still play an important role in locating a distinct regional identity.

Wiley J. Williams

Register of Deeds. The office of register of deeds in North Carolina can be traced to the Concessions and Agreement of 1665 issued by the Lords Proprietors, which provided for the appointment of "chiefe Registers or Secretarys" to record public business as well as land grants, conveyances, and leases. The colonial Assembly of 1715 directed that a register of deeds be appointed for each county, and in 1777 the General Assembly made the same stipulation. The North Carolina Constitution of 1868 provided for the election of a register of deeds, and since then it has been an elective office. The 1971 constitution does not mention the position but leaves it to the General Assembly, which provides for the election of a register of deeds in each county. The term of office is four years.

The primary purpose of the office of register of deeds is to maintain records of real property to enable the owner to give notice of that ownership and to produce and preserve satisfactory evidence of the transfer of an interest in real property. Under North Carolina law, it is the general rule that actual notice of an interest in real property is insufficient unless the instrument creating that interest is registered. Deeds, mort-

gages, deeds of trust, maps, leases for more than three years, easements, contracts, and other instruments that create an interest in real property or affect title to it are recorded in the office of the register of deeds of the county in which the real property (or any part thereof) is situated. An examination of these records generally takes place when the title to real property is being transferred to a new owner or is encumbered by a mortgage or deed of trust.

The register of deeds also maintains records of certain transactions under the Uniform Commercial Code relating primarily to security interests in personal property. Miscellaneous records maintained by the register of deeds include birth and death certificates, records of marriages, armed forces discharges, and a list of notaries public.

References: William A. Campbell, *North Carolina Guidebook for Registers of Deeds* (1994); Patrick K. Hetrick and James B. McLaughlin Jr., *Webster's Real Estate Law in North Carolina* (1988).

William W. Smith

Regulator Movement in mid-eighteenth-century North Carolina was a rebellion initiated by residents of the colony's inland region, or backcountry, who believed that royal government officials were charging them excessive fees, falsifying records, and engaging in other mistreatments. The movement's name refers to the desire of these citizens to regulate their own affairs. An unfair system of taxation prevailed under which less productive land, such as that in the western and Mountain regions, was taxed at the same rate as the more fertile, level soil of the Coastal Plain. These and other hardships contributed to the Regulators' feelings of sectional discrimination and deep distrust of authorities rooted in eastern North Carolina. Led by men such as Rednap Howell, James Hunter, and Herman Husband—considered the movement's chief spokesman—the Regulators organized a resistance to these abuses, first through protest and ultimately through violence.

Modern scholarship has focused on the role that evangelical Christianity may have played in shaping the social and political ethos underpinning the Regulator rebellion. The religion of Husband and other Regulators—frontier Protestants who were members of Baptist, Presbyterian, Quaker, Moravian, and other evangelical or pietistic sects—emphasized an individualistic approach to church, salvation, and personal morality that profoundly influenced their understanding of public relationships and economic issues. Ultimately, it has been argued, this fervent brand of Christian faith bonded the Regulators together and fueled their antiauthoritarian stance toward what they believed to be an unjust, essentially "evil" governmental structure. Women, although not officially recorded as participants in the movement, undoubtedly played essential roles as supportive and influential partners in the

Edmund Fanning, a superior court judge and colonel of the militia headquartered at Hillsborough, became a focal point of Regulator anger. Miniature attributed to Thomas Goddard. Photograph courtesy of Andrew C. Wickham for the Wickham Family Trust.

spiritual development of the Regulators as well as advocates of their cause.

Residents of the frontier counties of Anson, Orange, and Granville (much larger then than today) began to protest publicly in 1764. Many appointed, rather than elected, officials became targets of numerous threats and violence, including sheriffs, tax collectors, registrars, court clerks, and judges. Royal governor Arthur Dobbs issued a proclamation against the taking of illegal fees, but that directive was ignored. Dissatisfaction grew and unrest spread among the people. A new governor, William Tryon, arrived in 1765; he was a veteran army colonel and became the cause of renewed unrest, in part after he occupied a large new building—"Tryon's Palace," designed as both governor's home and capitol, which he constructed in New Bern at public expense.

Officials grew concerned for their own safety in 1770 after a mob seized a county officer against whom it held grievances —the much-despised Edmund Fanning, a corrupt multiple-office holder in Orange County—grabbed his heels, and pulled him down the stairs, banging his head on each step. The home

of another official was entered and his personal possessions were thrown out the window.

When a special term of court was called in Hillsborough in 1771, the judges hesitated to attend and Tryon called out the militia to protect them. The Regulators sought a public meeting with colonial officials to discover "whether the free men of this [Orange] county labor under any abuses of power or not." The officials ignored the call for a discussion as well as a request for an explanation of other recent events. Their failure to respond precipitated further determination and closer bonding among the Regulators. As a governor appointed by the Crown as well as a trained and experienced army officer, Tryon would brook no such action as he anticipated from the men of North Carolina. With the approval of the colonial Assembly, the governor called out the militia, and at its head led his army from New Bern, the capital, to the western frontier intent on settling the question of authority in his colony.

West of Hillsborough where they were camped, the Regulators on 16 May 1771 tried once again to confer with Tryon. They could do so, he replied, only if they dispersed and laid down their arms within the hour. This infuriated the Regulators. When they made no response, Tryon sent an officer to say that unless they disbanded promptly he would fire on them. "Fire and be damned" was their answer, and orders were issued. Training and adequate supplies contributed to the militia victory in the famous two-hour engagement known as the Battle of Alamance. Tryon's men lost 9 killed and 61 wounded. Largely untrained frontiersmen, the Regulators took cover behind large rocks and trees and removed their casualties promptly, so there is no reliable count of their losses.

The militia took a few prisoners, one of whom was hanged without even the show of a military court. Although the execution was reported to have occurred on the battlefield, Tryon noted that it took place at Great Alamance Camp the next morning. Of the 14 captives tried at a special term of the superior court, 12 were convicted of treason and sentenced to death. Altogether 6 were hanged, but on Tryon's recommendation the remainder were pardoned by King George III.

Tryon issued an offer to pardon, with few exceptions, anyone who swore an oath of allegiance to the royal government. The Regulators generally took advantage of this offer, and within six weeks 6,409 had complied with its terms. The governor actually was more generous to the Regulators than the legislature was. When the British government suggested that the Assembly enact a general amnesty, the two Houses could not agree on its terms and the proposal failed to pass.

By then, most of the leaders of the Regulator Movement were either dead, in exile, or in hiding, and the rebellion's ordinary soldiers were scattered and disheartened. Many simply returned to their former way of life, but a few moved away. Some formed a settlement on the banks of the Mississippi River near the site of Memphis, but later, when some of

Tryon's former militiamen appeared in their midst, they packed up and moved farther away. The coming of the American Revolution soon erased the differences between the two groups of Carolinians. Many men from both sides joined in the fight for independence from Britain and served together in a common cause.

References: Marjoleine Kars, *Breaking Loose Together: The Regulator Rebellion in Pre-Revolutionary North Carolina* (2002); William S. Powell, *North Carolina through Four Centuries* (1989); Powell, James K. Huhta, and Thomas J. Farnham, eds., *The Regulators in North Carolina: A Documentary History, 1769–1776* (1971).

William S. Powell

SEE ALSO Alamance, Battle of; Cabarrus Black Boys; Courthouse Ring; Johnston's Riot Act.

Religion is what people believe about the meaning of existence, how they conceive of the holy and the source and end of life, and how they define personal obligation. Believers come to understand these things from a particular perspective within communities of faith, which give each generation the mental and emotional tools with which to encounter the daily tasks and momentous events that affect every human life. Native peoples living in what is now North Carolina shared religious ideas and experiences across the generations for hundreds of years before European discovery and settlement took place in the sixteenth and seventeenth centuries. With the Europeans came a greater complexity in the religious makeup of the region, and different ways of Christian worship were added to native variations. North Carolina's Christian faithful have not always agreed on what the Bible means or how they are required to practice their faith. The resulting conflicts created long-lasting conversations among different faith communities and birthed a pluralism that was made more complex by the immigration of non-Christians in subsequent eras. By the beginning of the twenty-first century, North Carolina Christians practiced their faith alongside Jews, Buddhists, Muslims, Hindus, and other groups.

Native Beliefs and the Arrival and Spread of Christianity

Long before Europeans settled the Coastal Plain and moved into the Piedmont during the seventeenth and eighteenth centuries, native peoples had already developed communal beliefs about the origins of their people, how the world had nurtured them, and where sacred places existed. They took their cues about the sacred from the natural world around them and from the holy men and women who they believed had a special openness to the spirit world. Cherokee religious myth, for example, proposed that the earth was the creation of higher beings that left the sun and moon to watch over and control it and all human life. Springing from this essential creation story was a system of worship and ceremonies that touched every aspect of Cherokee life and activity, including marriage, child rearing, communal obligation, arts and crafts, hunting, and agriculture.

Religious life changed drastically for Native Americans, however, as Europeans invaded from the east and north and began to lay claim to Indian lands in the late sixteenth century. European Christianity was profoundly different from the religion of Native Americans. The faith was centered on a book, the Bible, and instead of living in harmony with nature, the settlers claimed dominion over it as they and their successors changed the landscape through new farming techniques and the building of towns.

The first Christians to settle and remain in North Carolina were Quakers who migrated over the boundary with Virginia in the 1670s. After North Carolina was separated from South Carolina in about 1712, the North Carolina Assembly passed several ineffectual vestry acts that required citizens to pay taxes for the support of Anglican priests. (The vestry is a group of church members who manage the everyday affairs of the church.) Quakers, joined by Presbyterians, Baptists, and even some Anglicans—called "dissenters" because of their desire to separate themselves from the Church of England—were angered by these taxes. They were further dismayed when, beginning in 1704, they were required to take an oath to the English monarch and the Church of England, despite the fact that in the past Quakers had enjoyed the right of affirmation rather than taking an oath, which was condemned by their religion. This meant that unless they swore an oath they could not legally hold office. An act of 1765 established support for a weak Church of England, which was subsequently disestablished by the American Revolution.

The majority of North Carolina's Christians of this era belonged to Protestant sects outside of the Church of England. Organized Presbyterian activity came to the North Carolina Piedmont during the 1730s to 1770s and to eastern counties (Duplin and New Hanover) as early as 1736. The first large group of Presbyterian Highlanders from Scotland made their way up the Cape Fear River and settled at Cross Creek (now Fayetteville) in 1746. The Presbyterians were the first group to attempt to establish a college, with the founding of short-lived Queen's College in the 1770s in Charlotte. Baptists date from at least 1714, although their first church—to which both Free Will and Separate (Missionary) Baptists trace their beginning—was not established until 1722 in Chowan County.

The first North Carolina Lutherans were wiped out by the Indians in 1711. Permanent Lutheran congregational life dates from the mid-eighteenth century with the coming of German immigrants from Pennsylvania into the Piedmont. Initial members of the Reformed tradition of Protestantism came into the Pamlico section of North Carolina from Virginia in

1690. Many of the members also were killed by the Indians in 1711, and their survivors went into the Presbyterian Church.

By the 1750s Moravians had settled in the Piedmont. During and after the Revolution, Methodists came into the region as well. Catholic immigrants first settled in the Pamlico Sound region as early as 1737. The first Jewish settlers came into the colony from Barbados and were of Spanish-Portuguese origin. Wilmington seems to have had a Jewish community as early as 1738. Jews who came into the state in the second half of the nineteenth century were mostly immigrants from Germany. Gradually, the colony and state attracted a variety of settlers who expressed themselves in a number of faiths, while many African slaves came in chains and bereft of the social solidarity of either religious or ethnic identity. By the end of the 1820s, immigrants of both African and European descent were brought under the discipline of Baptist, Methodist, Moravian, Episcopal, Lutheran, Campbellite, and Presbyterian Churches; in Baptist and Methodist groups, African American men were even allowed to preach.

The Ascent and Influence of Evangelical Christianity in North Carolina Culture

The character and style of North Carolina's Protestantism was primarily evangelical. Evangelical faith emphasized biblical authority, commitment to proselytizing, sympathy for revivals, suspicion of liturgical formalism (such as in Roman Catholicism), and a subjective assurance of personal conversion—having been "born again" in Christ. Most Christian groups adhered to these beliefs, although some Quakers and Moravians, and a few Baptists, Presbyterians, Lutherans, and Episcopalians, resisted. Each denomination of Christians created periodicals, schools, colleges, and networks of churches, so that by the Civil War, although there were different kinds of Protestants, evangelical values dominated formal as well as informal religion and exercised considerable cultural influence beyond the churches.

In the 1750s, as the religious fervor of the First Great Awakening swept through the colonies, ministers came to North Carolina hoping to ignite stronger Christian faith among the people. These preachers, mostly Presbyterians and Baptists, started a number of churches in the Coastal Plain and the Piedmont. This revival movement declined in the years just before and during the Revolution. The spark, however, was kept alive by isolated groups of Moravians, Quakers, Lutherans, and others. But the war ended any influence that the Church of England might have had, for in 1817 its successor, the Episcopal Church, was established, although it did not get its first bishop until 1823.

The Second Great Awakening—a revival movement featuring large outdoor meetings, fiery preaching, singing, and confession of personal sin—came to the state around 1800. Soon the churches were displaying their interest in the area of edu-

cation by opening church-sponsored colleges, such as Wake Forest College begun by the Baptists (1834), Davidson by the Presbyterians (1837), Trinity (later Duke University) by the Methodists (1839), and New Garden (later Guilford College) by the Quakers (1837). The latter was the only one of these schools that from the start educated men and women together. The education of women was, however, of special concern to several churches. The Methodists established Greensboro Female College (later Greensboro College) in 1838; Episcopalians established Saint Mary's in Raleigh in 1842; and the Baptists started Chowan Baptist Female Institute (now Chowan College) in Murfreesboro in 1848. Some denominations established hospitals during this era, to which Duke University Hospital (Methodist) and North Carolina Baptist Hospitals at Winston-Salem date their origins.

Evangelical Christianity was complex in North Carolina, affecting people differently according to their race, class, and gender. A key element was the undeniable democratic effect the spread of evangelical Calvinism (mostly among Baptists but among a few remarkable Presbyterians as well) and Anglicanism (Methodism) had on North Carolina society—not in making elites soften their sense of entitlement but in encouraging those without rank to think of themselves as important and precious to God. The proof of this was a sensible experience of the presence of God in worship and interpreting the promises of the Bible under the rubric that "God was no respecter of persons." Women, especially among Methodists, and African Americans, together with relatively powerless white men, believed, through evangelical doctrine, that they were as valuable to God as were white male elites.

For a generation or two after the American Revolution, this democratic leaven encouraged black preachers and a few religious virtuosi among women to strengthen the communal life of African American communities and the bonds of womanhood. Between the Revolution and the 1820s, some religious activists—especially under the influence of radical republicanism and Quakers—toyed with opposing African slavery; but the institution was too entrenched, and the traditional elites were too covetous of their privileges to surrender them easily. The issue of slavery led to deep schisms among Protestant churches. The three major denominations fell out with their northern colleagues and acted to form separate regional denominations. The Methodist Episcopal Church, South was organized in 1845. The next year saw the birth of the Southern Baptist Convention. The Presbyterian Church in the United States came into formal existence in 1864–65 after three decades of strained relations with northern Presbyterians.

North Carolina's white elites soon discovered that evangelical Protestantism could be more supportive of traditional power structures than subversive of them. As elite men converted to evangelical Christianity, they found that neither the Bible nor the Holy Spirit that settled on revived communities demanded gender or racial democracy. Being reborn in Christ and conversant with the scriptures could make white men as convinced of their rectitude as were their dependents and slaves. Confederates could come to terms with their defeat in the Civil War through interpreting their suffering as similar to that of Christian martyrs and their Lord before them; their "Lost Cause" could be sanctified through hope strengthened by the Christian doctrine of Resurrection.

African Americans, who saw their own suffering transformed through the biblical Jubilee of emancipation, could celebrate their vindication by God's "terrible swift sword" but be forced by suffering under white supremacy and segregation (supported by evangelical whites) once again to "wait upon the Lord." During the antebellum years in North Carolina, blacks and whites had often worshipped as one body in a white church. After the war was over, northern-based black denominations began to prosper in the South, including the African Methodist Episcopal Zion Church (founded in 1801), the African Methodist Episcopal Church (founded in 1816), and the Colored (now Christian) Methodist Episcopal Church (founded in 1870).

Religious Trends and Conflicts of the Twentieth Century

Religious life in twentieth-century North Carolina was conflicted on a range of issues created by scientific discovery, U.S. Supreme Court decisions, and changes in personal and public life. A key aspect of these conflicts was their roots in evangelical views of authority, personal independence, and revelation. Ultimately, differences in biblical interpretation and the meaning of subjective confirmation of faith—the twin bases of evangelical authority—continued to prevent Christian harmony regarding many issues.

In the 1920s, as high school textbooks began exposing students to explanations of biological evolution through natural selection, some concerned believers tried to prevent this aspect of modern science from being taught; but North Carolina state legislators refused to acquiesce. In the early 1960s, the U.S. Supreme Court forbade prayer in public school assemblies (although the practice persists in defiance of the ban), and this led white conservative Christians to establish private academies—some of which were founded to avoid racial integration of schooling as much as to resist secularism.

Less radical attempts to resist secular trends were continued by Christians fighting to restrict public school students' access to knowledge about birth control devices and frequently to dictate specified lesson plans on sexual behavior even beyond health classes. When the Equal Rights Amendment was introduced to extend constitutional rights to women during the 1970s, a group that included conservative Christians rallied to defeat it as a referendum on feminism. Christian denominations in North Carolina also continue to wrestle with the ordination of women, homosexuality, abortion, capital punishment, and ethnic differences. These issues and others emphasize the continued presence of conservative, moderate, and liberal factions within denominations.

The religious style, cadences, music, and sensibility of the civil rights movement of the 1960s demonstrated the immense power of religion among North Carolinians. But religion, meaning, and obligation—what people held sacred and how they behaved in responding to the holy—was so affected by gender, race, class, and power that it could not meld North Carolinians into a cultural consensus. Sharing the same Bible and believing themselves responsible to the same God —sometimes even singing the same hymns—allowed the religious of both races to make common cause only in rare instances. Yet by the end of the twentieth century, blacks and whites were beginning to share more readily across the racial divide, relying on the religion they shared to struggle toward mutual understanding.

Religious Pluralism in Modern-Day North Carolina

Sectarian differences have always meant that believers would disagree on certain practices and beliefs. Many Protestants have traditionally been suspicious of Roman Catholicism, yet by the end of the twentieth century, this wariness was weakening as evangelicals and Catholics found they agreed on certain issues such as abortion and the importance of Christian faith even if not on worship, church structure, and the primacy of the Eucharist.

Beyond the din of public conflict, however, North Carolina believers find solace, meaning, and reassurance within their communities of faith. Immigrants from Mexico, as well as from India, Vietnam, Pakistan, and African countries, have created a more richly diverse population in the state. These new North Carolinians, like those who preceded them, find in their worship and community religious life a reminder of ancient truths, the meaning of life and death, and the personal and familial satisfaction of celebrating values that reward them with certitude as well as hope. This has meant a more complex patchwork of faiths, to be sure; but new North Carolinians agree with those whose families have been here for hundreds of years: religion is essential to personal and social life and is to be honored and embraced.

In the future, North Carolinians can expect to find among the faithful not only Korean-speaking Presbyterians, nondenominational fundamentalist churches, bilingual Roman Catholic parishes, and many different kinds of Baptist congregations, but also many more Jewish temples, Buddhist and Hindu societies, and Islamic centers. There will continue to be differences and conflict among the faithful as long as there is religious freedom—which is, after all, one of the principles North Carolinians insisted on for the new U.S. Constitution before they ratified it in 1789.

References: Catherine L. Albanese, *Nature Religion in America from the Algonkian Indians to the New Age* (1990); Mary Best, ed., *North Carolina Churches: Portraits of Grace* (2004); Diana L. Eck, *A New Religious America: How a "Christian Country" Has Become the World's Most Religiously Diverse Nation* (2001); C. Eric Lincoln and Lawrence H. Mamiya, *The Black Church in the African American Experience* (1995); Donald G. Mathews, *Religion in the Old South* (1977); Mathews, "'Spiritual Warfare': Cultural Fundamentalism and the Equal Rights Amendment," *Religion and American Culture* 3 (Summer 1993); Amanda Porterfield, *The Transformation of American Religion* (2001); Anne Russell, Marjorie Megivern, and Kevin Coughlin, *North Carolina Portraits of Faith: A Pictorial History of Religions* (1986); Frederick W. Schmidt Jr., *A Still Small Voice: Women, Ordination and the Church* (1996).

Donald G. Mathews

SEE ALSO Baptists; Church of England; Episcopal Church; Evolution, Teaching of; Fundamentalism; Great Awakening; Islam; Judaism; Lutheran Church; Methodist Church; Moravians; Pentecostal Holiness Church; Presbyterian Church; Quakers; Reformed Church; Roman Catholic Church.

Rent Rolls were lists of landowners showing whether they had paid the annual quitrents owed the receiver general or were in arrears (behind in their payments). Since money from quitrents was under the exclusive control of the English Crown (unlike taxes, which were controlled by the colonial Assembly) —and since the governor's contingent expenses and the salaries of the principal civil officers of the Crown in the colony were paid from it—it was desirable that the Crown have a current rent roll. The Lords Proprietors were never able to obtain an up-to-date rent roll during the period they owned Carolina. When Governor Gabriel Johnston in 1735 ordered the preparation of a rent roll, it was revealed that half a million acres were held by people who paid no quitrent and great tracts of land were lying dormant.

Settlers, whenever possible, evaded payment of the quitrents, which were not collected by sheriffs as taxes were. As a result, there was almost perpetual tension between the desire of landowners to avoid the rent and the desire of Crown officials to collect it. In 1732 the Crown authorized the establishment of a Court of Exchequer to compel payment of quitrents, but the court sat only briefly between 1735 and 1737. Rent rolls and quitrents were abandoned at the time of the American Revolution, and a land tax was set by the General Assembly as a substitute for the payments formerly owed to the king or the Proprietors.

References: William L. Saunders, ed., *Colonial Records of North Carolina*, vols. 4–5 (1895); W. N. Watt, *The Granville District* (1992).

George Stevenson

Republican Party in North Carolina has progressed through several discrete periods of strength and weakness to become a prominent political organization in the state, on a nearly equal competitive footing with the long-dominant Democratic Party. Shortly after President George Washington's inauguration in April 1789, a two-party national political system began to take shape. Secretary of the Treasury Alexander Hamilton led the Federalists, who believed that the U.S. Constitution should be loosely interpreted and advocated a strong national government in the hands of a "rich and well-born" minority. Hamiltonians also pushed for a large peacetime army and navy as well as a stable financial system, and they tended to favor the interests of commerce and manufacturing over agriculture.

Secretary of State Thomas Jefferson led the Republicans, or Anti-Federalists, who preferred (as most modern Republicans still do) a stricter interpretation of the Constitution by which powers not delegated to the central government were reserved for the states. Despite the fact that North Carolina was predominantly a state of small farmers (a source of Republican strength in the South), most members of its congressional delegation between 1789 and 1793 were Federalists, although they were reluctant to support such Hamiltonian policies as tariffs and the national bank.

For the remainder of the eighteenth century, most of the state's governors were Jeffersonian Republicans, and after 1792 the party dominated the legislature. Under the leadership of Willie Jones of Halifax and, later, Nathaniel Macon of Warren County, the state became a bulwark of Republicanism. As the Federalists weakened after 1800, disappearing as an organized party by 1815, Republican state leaders and local patrons developed a strong political machine in North Carolina. The contentious presidential campaign of 1828, however, split the national Republican Party (or the Democratic-Republican Party, as it was called then) into several groups. Andrew Jackson emerged as the candidate of one of these groups, whose supporters would come to be known as Democrats.

In 1854 a new national Republican Party was organized in opposition to the ruling Democrats. Not until after the Civil War (1867) was its North Carolina counterpart formally launched, supported by the loyalty of three main groups: resettled northerners (derisively known as "carpetbaggers"); blacks, logically attracted to the party of Abraham Lincoln, which had given them their freedom and the right to vote; and native whites (or "scalawags"), who had grown tired of life under the planter class. Former Democrat William W. Holden, editor-publisher of the influential *North Carolina Standard* from 1842 to 1868 and provisional governor in 1865, became the Republican Party's chief advocate.

With Holden reelected governor and a large legislative majority, the Republican Party held power from 1868 to 1870. Its positive contributions—support of public education and extension of the right to vote by adopting the Fifteenth Amendment of the U.S. Constitution—were offset by tax and debt increases and irregularities in the sale of legislatively authorized railroad bonds. In the election of 1870, North Carolina's conservative Democrats regained control of the legislature, although the state continued to elect Republican governors (Tod R. Caldwell in 1870 and Curtis H. Brogden in 1874). The Democrats then won a resounding victory in 1876, taking control of the governor's office, the legislature, and most of the congressional seats. Not until 1896, when the Populists and Republicans joined together in political "Fusion," was a Republican again elected governor; Fusionists also took over the legislature and the judiciary. However, the return to power was short lived. In 1898 the Democrats unleashed a fierce white supremacy campaign, underscored with violence, that ended Republican-Populist rule. Two years later, Democrats further solidified their power through the disfranchisement of African Americans and other measures, ushering in a long and troubled era of segregation.

Cracks in the Democratic one-party domination of twentieth-century North Carolina politics did not appear again until the 1920s, when some Republicans began to portray themselves successfully as the "lily-white" party. Republicans carried the state in the 1928 presidential election, as many Democrats opposed Al Smith's candidacy, which they dubbed "rum and Romanism" in reference to his anti-Prohibition views and Catholic faith. That year Charles A. Jonas became the first Republican elected to Congress from North Carolina (his son Charles R. Jonas became the second Republican congressman in 1952 and was reelected to nine successive terms). Dwight D. Eisenhower's popularity in the state in his 1952 and 1956 presidential runs were further examples of Republican success during this era.

After 1960 an ideological battle began to take shape that polarized Democrats and Republicans even further, both within the state and nationally. GOP candidates generally came to oppose many liberal causes that occupied the national Democratic Party. Issues of race became a central factor in how North Carolinians voted. Increasing Democratic support of federally mandated integration and civil rights laws—as well as feminism, abortion rights, gay rights, government entitlements, the antiwar movement, and other liberal causes—alienated the party from many southerners and opened the door for the election of more conservative, "traditional" Republicans. Richard M. Nixon's "Southern Strategy," capitalizing on the race theme, was successfully implemented in his 1972 presidential run. That same year, Jesse Helms and James E. Holshouser Jr. became, respectively, North Carolina's first Republican senator and governor elected in the twentieth century.

Although the Republican presence in the North Carolina General Assembly was severely diminished in the wake of the Watergate scandal of 1974, Republicans continued to make political gains with the election of James G. Martin to two terms as governor in 1984 and 1988, as well as a steady increase in the number of Republican-controlled local offices. In the 1980s the rise of the Christian Right—evangelical conservative Christians organized in a political coalition to fight against what they perceived as the "godless" ideologies of the liberals—swept through North Carolina and the South, leading to further GOP gains. Political Action Committees, such as the ardently conservative, Helms-controlled Congressional Club, gained in status and potency. After the 1962 election, the state's U.S. House representatives included 2 Republicans and 9 Democrats; by 1984, 5 of 11 North Carolina congressmen were Republicans, with the split remaining more or less equal in the years following. While Republican rolls increased from 541,916 in 1972 to more than 1.6 million by 2000, many registered Democrats voted for GOP candidates, particularly for national seats. Republican presidential candidates handily carried North Carolina and much of the South in every election between 1968 and 2004, except for the post-Watergate election in 1976 of southerner Jimmy Carter.

In 1994 Republicans took control of the North Carolina General Assembly as part of a GOP national landslide that also resulted in Republican control of the U.S. Senate. Since that year, although the 1996 and 1998 elections saw the scales tip back in favor of the Democrats, the state has seen more-or-less equal competition between partisans of both parties. By the early 2000s, the Republican Party in North Carolina continued to maintain a strong presence in a state so thoroughly Democratic for much of its history. GOP rolls have increased further through spectacular Republican growth in the suburbs of the state's largest cities and the continued influx of conservative retirees and professionals. While actually sharing a number of socially and fiscally conservative policies with many North Carolina Democrats, the state's Republicans were seen as the strongest conservative voice in local and national elections, touting the benefits of a healthy business environment, strong national defense in the face of terrorist and other threats, limited governmental regulation, traditional social values, and other views.

References: Earl Black and Merle Black, *The Rise of Southern Republicans* (2002); Vanessa Goodman and Jack Betts, *The Two-Party System in North Carolina* (1987); Jonathan T. Y. Houghton, "The North Carolina Republican Party: From Reconstruction to the Radical Right" (Ph.D. thesis, UNC-Chapel Hill, 1993); Paul Luebke, *Tar Heel Politics 2000* (1998); Mebane Rush Whitman, "The Evolution of Party Politics: The March of the GOP Continues in North Carolina," *North Carolina Insight* 16 (September 1995).

Robert Blair Vocci

SEE ALSO Conservatism; Fusion of Republicans and Populists; Helms-Hunt Senate Race; Lily-White Politics.

Research Triangle Park, the largest planned research center in the United States, was created in 1959 through the efforts of Governor Luther Hodges and hundreds of scientists, politicians, and business leaders. Located between Raleigh and Durham and the Triangle's three acclaimed universities—the University of North Carolina at Chapel Hill, Duke University, and North Carolina State University—Research Triangle Park (RTP) in 2006 encompassed 7,000 acres and was home to more than 100 research and development organizations employing 38,000 North Carolinians. Smaller but highly successful research parks also existed in Charlotte, Greensboro, Rocky Mount, and elsewhere, playing an important role in the diversification of the state's economy.

The need for a redirection of economic development away from traditional products such as textiles, tobacco, and furniture was envisioned in the early 1950s by some of North Carolina's more progressive leaders. In 1952 Howard Odum, a renowned UNC-Chapel Hill sociologist and founder of the university's Institute for Research in Social Science, voiced a number of ideas about cooperative research centers that could benefit the state by combining the strengths of its three research universities. State leaders considered how these institutions could become a foundation for economic development.

In the mid-1950s Greensboro construction company executive Romeo Guest, state treasurer Brandon P. Hodges (no relation to Governor Hodges), and Walter Harper of the State Board of Conservation and Development were recruiting industry to North Carolina from other states. Guest, who had studied at the Massachusetts Institute of Technology, had seen firsthand the growth of university-related industry along Boston's Route 128. Hoping that the phenomenon could be duplicated in North Carolina, Guest coined the term "Research Triangle" after noticing the triangular relationship on a map of Chapel Hill, Durham, and Raleigh. He discussed the idea with business and academic leaders around the state throughout 1954. Prominent among the business leaders was Robert M. Hanes, president of Wachovia Bank. The group decided that government participation would be needed, and members approached Governor Hodges. Over time, Hodges agreed with the concept and soon became one of its strongest proponents.

In September 1956 the Research Triangle Committee (changed in 1958 to the Research Triangle Foundation) was formally incorporated. Members included Hodges in his capacity as chairman of the Board of Trustees of the consolidated University of North Carolina, President William C. Friday of the consolidated University of North Carolina System, President A. Hollis Edens of Duke University, and Norman A. Cooke, chairman of Duke's Board of Trustees. The foundation hired George L. Simpson, a sociology professor at UNC, as its executive director. He and Elizabeth Johnson Aycock, his office

Futuristic-looking office and research building completed in 1968 by the Burroughs Wellcome Company (and now owned by GlaxoSmithKline) during a period of rapid expansion in the Research Triangle Park. Photograph courtesy of the Research Triangle Foundation of North Carolina.

manager and secretary, were the first two full-time employees of the committee.

In 1957 Hodges and Simpson approached Karl Robbins, who had sold off extensive textile holdings in North Carolina and retired to New York, and asked him to begin to create a development suitable for the RTP. Robbins agreed and authorized Guest to purchase or buy options in the middle of the Raleigh-Durham area. The land was primarily infertile farm acreage and young pines. Robbins incorporated a company called Pinelands, of which Guest was president. However, few people bought stock in the company; moreover, by 1958 several state leaders began to feel uneasy about using the resources of the state universities to promote a for-profit endeavor.

In August 1958 Hodges met with Archibald "Archie" K. Davis, Hanes's successor at Wachovia, to consider the next step, and Davis suggested that the enterprise be turned into a nonprofit venture. Hanes and Hodges agreed, and Davis embarked on a whirlwind tour to raise money to buy out Pinelands and fund the creation of the Research Triangle Institute (RTI), an independent nonprofit contract research corporation established by the three universities but operating under separate management with separate facilities, staff, and board of governors. By the end of the year Davis had raised nearly $1.5 million, and by early 1959 the creation of the RTP, under the control of the nonprofit Research Triangle Foundation, was announced. George Herbert, lured from Stanford Industrial Park in Palo Alto, Calif., was named head of RTI, which began operating on 2 Mar. 1959.

By year's end, five organizations were either located in the RTP or were constructing facilities to move there. In 1962 the U.S. Forest Service became the first federal tenant. Any doubts about the park's success were dispelled beginning in 1965,

Computer under construction at an IBM production facility in Research Triangle Park, 1984. Photograph by Billy Barnes. NCC.

when International Business Machines (IBM) and the National Institute of Environmental Health Sciences announced plans to establish operations in the RTP. In time, professional associations such as the American Association of Textile Chemists and Colorists, Instrument Society of America, and International Union of Pure and Applied Chemistry and Underwriters Laboratories, as well as banks, restaurants, and other service organizations, joined a growing list of organizations settling in the RTP.

RTP industries have remained remarkably diverse, with several large, long-term occupants representing the health and pharmaceutical sciences, information technology, microelectronics, biotechnology, and environmental sciences. By the 2000s several foreign firms had operations in the RTP. Other federal agencies such as the National Center for Health Statistics and the U.S. Environmental Protection Agency also had RTP facilities. The UNC Center for Public Television moved into the park in 1989. A prominent occupant of the RTP since 1978, the National Humanities Center—created by a special committee of the American Academy of Arts and Sciences and the Triangle Universities Center for Advanced Studies—attracted some of the world's most distinguished scholars, leading to important books in the fields of history, biography, literature, sociology, politics, and other related areas. In the early 2000s RTP's largest employers were IBM (13,300), GlaxoSmithKline (5,000), Nortel Networks (3,000), and Cisco Systems (2,500).

References: "As RTP Turns 40, the Big Picture Is to Think Small," *Raleigh News and Observer*, 10 Jan. 1999; Albert N. Link, *A Generosity of Spirit: The Early History of the Research Triangle Park* (1995); "Research Triangle Park 40th Anniversary—Special Report," *Triangle Business Journal*, 15 Jan. 1999.

Wiley J. Williams

Reserve Troops, by the spring of 1864, were regarded as essential to North Carolina's ongoing contribution to the Confederacy. Heavy losses due to combat, disease, and desertion took a toll on manpower. Faced with a looming crisis, on 17 Feb. 1864 the Confederate Congress had extended the age of military conscription (with only limited exceptions) to males from 17 to 50 (originally 18 to 45). Initially slated for rear-echelon duty, some reserve units served on the front line during the final months of the war. In North Carolina, three regiments composed largely of 17-year-olds were raised and organized as the Junior Reserves Brigade. In March 1865 the Junior Reserves fought in the Battles of Wyse Fork and Bentonville. At Bentonville, the Junior Reserves comprised the largest brigade in Gen. Joseph E. Johnston's Army of the South. At the other end of the age spectrum were the five regiments of reserves between 45 and 50—the Senior Reserves. The 7th Senior Reserves participated in the Battles of Averasboro and Bentonville.

Among Junior Reserves recruits was Fabius Busbee, just a few days past his seventeenth birthday when he was mustered in. Soon afterward, Busbee was promoted to second lieutenant, making him one of the youngest commissioned officers in the Confederate army. One of the Junior Reserves' field officers was Maj. Walter Clark, the future chief justice of the North Carolina Supreme Court. Clark was just 18 years old in March 1865 when he commanded the Junior Reserves' skirmishers at Bentonville, yet he was a veteran of the 1862 Battles of Sharpsburg (Antietam) and Fredericksburg.

William S. Powell

Resolves, Prerevolutionary. As North Carolina chafed at British rule and edged toward independence during 1774 and 1775, the former colony was governed largely by a new Provincial Congress and, at the county level, by local Committees of Safety. News of resistance in other colonies was spread by local Committees of Correspondence. As events unfolded, several local committees published documents, known as "resolves" or "associations," that stated the position of the delegates on loyalty to the Crown and to the emerging American republic. The early resolves usually carefully pointed out that the rebellious colonists were actually loyal to the Crown but objected to certain policies of Parliament that they believed to be unfair. Gradually, the professed loyalty to the Crown became conditional upon the colonies receiving fair treatment and justice from the king. From that point, without meaningful overtures from the Crown, it was a short step to calls for complete independence.

An early series of resolves in North Carolina date from the summer of 1774, when county Committees of Safety were selecting delegates to the First Provincial Congress, held in New Bern from 25–27 August. The North Carolina resolves of 1774 affirmed loyalty to the Crown while also declaring that the colonists could not be taxed without their consent or the consent of their elected representatives. Most of these documents specified that the colonial Assembly, not Parliament, had the right to tax them, that the colonists should have the same rights as British citizens, that recent Parliamentary acts to punish Boston for radical activities were cruel and unlawful, that the colonies should unite to resist unfair British policies, and that a boycott of British goods by the colonies should be imposed if Parliament did not institute more favorable policies. Each set of the surviving 1774 county resolves also named delegates to the upcoming Provincial Congress. The resolutions passed by the First Provincial Congress closely echoed the resolves enacted by the counties.

Another series of resolves, more emphatic and advocating complete independence from Great Britain, was passed after the 19 Apr. 1775 Battles of Lexington and Concord, in Massachusetts, which marked the beginning of armed conflict with Britain. On 31 May the New Bern Committee of Safety passed a strongly worded set of resolves calling for support for the armed struggle against England, because the "*British* Ministry mean no longer to receive the peaceable addresses of the much injured People of *America*."

Also on 31 May 1775, the Mecklenburg County Committee of Safety met in Charlotte and passed the Mecklenburg Resolves. Far more radical than the New Bern document, the Mecklenburg Resolves denied the authority of Parliament and specifically rejected the authority of the king—the first time any colonial committee had done so. The document declared all laws passed under royal authority to be void, condemned all holders of royal commissions as enemies, and called for a temporary local government to run affairs until a Provincial Congress could meet and pass new laws.

Following the Mecklenburg Resolves, the New Hanover County Committee of Safety drew up an "association" that was "unanimously agreed to, by the inhabitants" on 19 June 1775. Although holding out hope for "a reconciliation" with Britain, the New Hanover committee stated that "under our present circumstances, we shall be justified . . . in resisting force by force." In Cumberland County, 54 men signed a similar document at Liberty Point on 30 June 1775, using wording much like that of the New Hanover Association.

On 1 July 1775 the Pitt County Committee of Safety produced a set of resolves at Martinborough. This committee still professed loyalty to the Crown but pledged to follow the directives of the Continental Congress to resist "the several arbitrary Illegale acts of Parliament." The Tryon Resolves were passed by the short-lived Tryon County's Committee of Safety on 14 August. All of the resolves penned in 1775 declared that British provocation had driven the people of North Carolina to armed resistance, that they should unite in resistance with the other colonies, and that they would follow the directives of the Provincial and Continental Congresses.

The Halifax Resolves, signed on 12 Apr. 1776 by the delegates of the Fourth Provincial Congress, ended the series of resolves with a bold call for independence not only for North Carolina but also for all of the American colonies. The dates of the Halifax Resolves and the 20 May 1775 Mecklenburg Declaration of Independence (a legendary document that is most likely a distorted echo of the Mecklenburg Resolves) are inscribed on the state flag of North Carolina.

Reference: Robert L. Ganyard, *The Emergence of North Carolina's Revolutionary State Government* (1978).

David A. Norris

Resorts and resort towns in North Carolina grew naturally out of the state's varied landscape and geographic features. The cool mountain air and the restorative waters of the mineral springs, or the sea breezes and salty surf of the Atlantic Ocean, promised relief to those threatened by malaria and yellow fever and remedy for those suffering from bronchial problems, dyspepsia, or rheumatism. Consequently, North Carolina's resort towns were primarily health spas from the 1830s to the 1920s. The state's geographical assets amply qualified it for resort status, but development of resort towns depended on investment capital (much of it from beyond the state's borders) and the building of railroads in the nineteenth century and roads in the twentieth century. Beginning in the 1920s, resort growth was fed by the coming of the automobile age, by post–World War II prosperity, and by the modern belief that vacations are beneficial even if one is not plagued by health problems. By 1930 resorts had become an important component of the state economy and a major social and cultural force in local communities.

Resorts of Western North Carolina

The Sulphur Springs Hotel near Asheville was typical of North Carolina's antebellum resorts. Its chief attraction was a mineral spring of purported medicinal value, but the hotel also offered guests gourmet food and drink, carriage rides to take in mountain scenery, a grand ballroom, and an orchestra of free black musicians. Slaves served as cooks, bellmen, waiters, and laundresses. Perhaps the most important attraction was the company of other elites. Early resorts became seasonal centers of high culture where the gentry interacted, providing a social outlet that women, who often felt isolated on family plantations, particularly appreciated. Similar resorts developed at Shocco Springs in Warren County, Kittrell Springs in Vance County, and other locations.

After the Civil War, the size and number of North Carolina's resorts grew. An expanded rail network and the burgeoning Victorian consumer culture created the access and the means for new visitors to enjoy the state's resorts. Asheville became the largest of North Carolina's mountain resort towns. The

75-mile Buncombe Turnpike, completed in 1828, linked Asheville to South Carolina and Tennessee, but not until the long-awaited penetration of the mountains by the railroad in 1880 did the city begin to develop as a resort. A 24-hour train trip brought guests from such faraway points as New York, Chicago, or New Orleans.

Asheville reportedly was visited by 30,000 tourists in 1886, and in 1893 it was given top honors in George H. Chapin's book, *Health Resorts of the South*. An 1892 promotional brochure for the city listed such hotels as the Hotel Belmont, the Oakland Heights, the Swannanoa, the Grand Central, the Oaks, and the Glen Rock, plus boardinghouses for the less affluent. The Kenilworth Inn, completed in 1890, stood in the middle of a 160-acre park that looked down on the rapids of the Swannanoa River and across at some of the area's highest peaks. Even grander and catering to the well-to-do was the Battery Park Hotel, built in 1886 by Col. Frank Coxe of Pennsylvania. It offered such luxuries as an elevator, room bells connected to the desk, public and private baths, a telegraph office, a ten-pin alley, a movable stage for theatricals, billiard rooms, and even a dark room for photographers. Later Asheville hotels included the grandly rustic Grove Park Inn, built in 1913 at the foot of Sunset Mountain by E. W. Grove of St. Louis, using some of the fortune he had made selling the popular tonic Bromo-Quinine. Among those who stayed at the Grove Park in the early years were businessmen Thomas Edison, Henry Ford, and Harvey Firestone; Presidents Herbert Hoover and Woodrow Wilson; and writer F. Scott Fitzgerald.

West and south of Asheville, despite the hazards of stagecoach travel over rough roads before the Civil War, other resort towns were established. One was Warm Springs (later Hot Springs), 37 miles west of Asheville by way of the Buncombe Turnpike. The springs were discovered in 1785 by members of the Tennessee militia skirmishing with Cherokee warriors. Word spread, and those suffering from gout, rheumatism, sciatica, or neuralgia came for the benefits of the warm mineral water. In the 1830s, James Washington Patton built the hotel that bore his name. The Patton Hotel had a porch with 13 columns representing the original colonies. After the Patton burned in 1884, a group of northern businessmen built the Mountain Park Hotel, which featured bowling, billiards, tennis, a swimming pool, riding stables, theatrical performances, a ballroom, and a golf course that may have been among the first in the Southeast.

Another antebellum resort town, also situated on the Buncombe Turnpike, was Flat Rock in Henderson County. Because of accessibility from the south, Flat Rock was developed by wealthy families from Charleston and Savannah seeking respite from the heat and diseases of the lowlands. The town became known as Little-Charleston-of-the-Mountains. Highlands, about 50 miles to the west, was like Flat Rock in two respects: it was equally accessible from the south and it was founded by people from outside the state. A decade after the Civil War, Samuel Truman Kelsey of New York and Clinton Carter Hutchinson of Kansas came to the area after traveling several weeks from Atlanta. The original name of the site was Kelsey's Plateau, which was changed to Highlands in 1875. To accommodate visitors, Central House (later Old Edwards Inn) opened in 1878. It was followed in 1880 by the Highlands Inn, a three-story hotel with 30 rooms and a double piazza extending the length of the building.

One of the grandest of the post–Civil War mountain resorts outside Asheville was the Haywood White Sulphur Springs Hotel in Waynesville. In 1878 Colonel and Mrs. W. W. Stringfield converted a large home, built before 1830 by the Love family, into a hotel. Though the hotel burned in 1892, it was rebuilt as a three-story brick building with 45 rooms, situated in a landscaped park of around 50 acres. It featured wraparound verandas and an observation tower on the roof so that guests could take in the view.

Lake Lure is a spectacular 1,500-acre man-made lake in Rutherford County. With Chimney Rock nearby, the Lake Lure region became one of North Carolina's most popular resorts of the 1920s and 1930s. A century earlier, the area was already well known. In Hickory Nut Gap in the shadow of old Bald Mountain, the rustic and romantic Esmeralda Inn had been built around 1840 as a stagecoach stop on the trail from Asheville to Rutherfordton. The inn became the setting for several silent films, including *The Heart of the Blue Ridge* (1915), starring Clara Kimball Young. Its celebrity guests included movie stars Mary Pickford, Douglas Fairbanks, Clark Gable, and Lew Wallace, author of *Ben Hur*, who finished the novel while occupying Room 9 at the inn. Destroyed by fire in 1917 and again in 1997, the inn was rebuilt both times, and in 1987 the site was the location for the shooting of the film *Dirty Dancing*. Tryon, located in the thermal belt due south of Lake Lure, also drew celebrities such as Sidney Lanier, Margaret Culkin Banning, and F. Scott Fitzgerald, as well as other notables such as David Niven, Mrs. George Marshall, Mrs. Calvin Coolidge, and Lady Astor.

Up the Blue Ridge, nearly 100 miles north of Asheville, is Blowing Rock, a residential resort whose name derives from a legend that tells of two Indian warriors who fought over the chief's beautiful daughter. The stronger of the two threw the other one over the edge of the rock. The maiden, realizing that the vanquished was the one she truly loved, prayed to the God of the Winds to spare him. In answer to her prayer, he was caught by the wind and lifted to safety. From that day forward, according to the legend, a wind always blows up onto the rock from the valley below, returning objects thrown from it and even causing the snow to fall "upside down." The Green Park Inn, dating from the late nineteenth century, became the first "grand" hotel in Blowing Rock and in 2006 was still in operation. By the mid-1930s, Blowing Rock had become a fashionable resort town.

The Esseeola Inn and Golf Club was established in Linville by Hugh MacRae in 1888. Located at the foot of Grandfather Mountain, the inn offered guests not only golf but also cool weather, beautiful scenery, ox races, and dancing by cloggers. The original inn burned in 1936 and was replaced by the Esseeola Lodge, which remains one of the region's most popular resorts. Farther north and east on the Appalachian chain is Roaring Gap, developed as a summer resort by Hugh Gwyn Chatham, who said his father had discovered the site while riding through the mountains to buy wool for his mill in Elkin. The Roaring Gap Hotel, with 30 rooms and four nearby cottages, opened in 1894.

Not all mountain resorts sprang from a desire to enjoy better health or worldly diversions. North Carolina became an important center for religious resorts during the last decade of the nineteenth century. By the 1920s, the state was home to the summer retreats of the southern Presbyterians (Montreat); the Methodist Episcopal Church, South (Lake Junaluska); and the Southern Baptists (Ridgecrest); and several others would emerge in subsequent decades. These resorts became centers of missionary activity, ecclesiastical training, civil rights reform, and other church-related training.

Although stricter land-use regulations have been established to preserve the natural beauty of the region, North Carolina's man-made and natural mountain attractions continue to draw thousands of tourists each year. A number of hotels, bed and breakfasts, golf resorts, and other establishments have been developed, affording a wide variety of services and easy access to spectacular vistas, hiking trails, cultural events, craft shopping, and other mountain activities.

Piedmont and Coastal Resorts

While the Atlantic Coast is undoubtedly a primary attraction for both in-state and out-of-state travelers, the rolling hills and pine forests of the Piedmont and Sandhills regions of North Carolina boast some of the state's finest resorts. In 1890 James Tufts of Boston began construction on the Carolina Hotel in Pinehurst, and soon the town had gained an international reputation as a world-class golf resort with a mild climate. The many other hotels, resorts, and golf courses located in and around Pinehurst and Southern Pines have led to the claim that Moore County is the "Golf Capital of the World." Newer golf resorts, such as Greensboro's Grandover Resort and the Ballantyne Resort in Charlotte, also have begun to attract both out-of-state and in-state visitors to the North Carolina Piedmont.

North Carolina's Atlantic beaches were attracting people at least as far back as the early part of the nineteenth century and soon spawned a major tourism industry, providing the primary economic base for many coastal communities. Hotels are believed to have been at Nags Head since 1838, and some documents indicate that people had gone there in the summer well before the 1830s. Of the distinctive architecture of early twentieth-century coastal resort hotels, one example remains at Nags Head: the First Colony Inn, with its unpainted, weathered shingle siding, third-floor dormers, and bi-level wraparound porches. It was built in 1932 as LeRoy's Seaside Inn and was relocated and refurbished in the 1980s.

Ocracoke appears to have been the first of North Carolina's ocean resorts, though it has remained among the least developed. There are recorded visits to Ocracoke and nearby Portsmouth for sea bathing as early as the 1750s and 1760s, and in 1795 Jonathan Price said of Ocracoke, "this healthy spot is in autumn the resort of many of the inhabitants of the main." The village of Ocracoke is limited in its potential growth by virtue of being surrounded by the lands of one federal park (Cape Hatteras National Seashore) and being next door to another (Cape Lookout National Seashore).

The establishment of the nation's first national seashore in the 1950s (centered at world-famous Cape Hatteras), the construction of the Oregon Inlet bridge, and the paving of a road the length of Hatteras Island in the 1960s opened up more than one-fifth of North Carolina's total ocean shoreline for development. All seven of the Hatteras Island villages were transformed into thriving ocean resorts. Meanwhile, after the construction of a state highway north from Duck to Corolla in the 1970s, the last of the privately owned ocean frontage in the northern part of the state was subjected to development, and the old Currituck Banks area has since experienced a veritable building boom.

Development of ocean resorts along North Carolina's central coast has followed a pattern similar to that on the northern Outer Banks. There are references from the late colonial period to people at Beaufort going on excursions to the nearby seashore, but the emergence of the area as a widely known resort did not come until the 1850s. At that time, former governor John Motley Morehead, an official of the Atlantic & North Carolina Railroad, announced plans for a large development on Bogue Sound north of Beaufort called Morehead City. On the railroad by 1858, boasting a three-story hotel called Macon House built in 1860, and incorporated as a town in 1861, Morehead City did not gain widespread publicity until 1880, when the 300-room New Atlantic Hotel was built at a choice location overlooking Bogue Sound.

In the 1920s, a bridge was constructed across Bogue Sound to the banks, where a resort town known as Atlantic Beach was already being developed. A large oceanfront hotel and pavilion at Atlantic Beach served the public through the 1940s, gradually siphoning off tourist business from Morehead City. Following the war, most of the remainder of Bogue Banks was developed, and the ocean resorts of Pine Knoll Shores, Indian Beach, and Emerald Isle now share popularity with Atlantic Beach—though many people continue to refer to the Carteret County resorts as "Morehead." Beginning in the late

Lumina pavilion at Wrightsville Beach, as seen in a postcard, ca. 1907. NCC.

1940s, development was initiated farther down the coast on Topsail Island, resulting in still more ocean resorts known as North Topsail Beach, West Onslow Beach, Surf City, and Topsail Beach.

Hugh MacRae, who had previously established the Esseeola Inn and Golf Course at Linville in western North Carolina, was instrumental in the development of the barrier islands east of Wilmington, which up to that time were accessible only by boat. In 1853 the Carolina Yacht Club, said to be the oldest in the United States, built a clubhouse on what was later to become Wrightsville Beach. By 1899, when the town of Wrightsville Beach was incorporated, there were several hotels and more than 50 cottages there. In 1905 MacRae built the centerpiece of Wrightsville, the famous Lumina, a three-story, 25,000-square-foot pavilion on the oceanfront that was elaborately illuminated at night with several thousand incandescent light bulbs. On the second floor was a 50-by-120-foot dance floor surrounded by wide promenades. A balcony for spectators formed the third floor. During the big band era the most outstanding bands in the country played the Lumina, including those headed by Paul Whiteman, Hal Kemp, Guy Lombardo, Cab Calloway, Benny Goodman, Tommy Dorsey, Jimmy Dorsey, and North Carolina's own Kay Kyser. Some claim the shag, a popular dance, was invented at the Lumina.

Although Carolina Beach, located nearer to Cape Fear, was developed at about the same time as Wrightsville Beach, all of the New Hanover County ocean resorts—including Wrightsville Beach, Carolina Beach (sometimes called "Little Coney Island of the South"), and Kure Beach—are often referred to collectively as "Wrightsville." The newest ocean resort in New Hanover and Pender Counties is Figure Eight Island. The remaining Cape Fear–area resorts (some public and some private, gated communities) are in Brunswick County, and most of them—including Sunset Beach, Ocean Isle Beach, Holden Beach, Oak Island, Caswell Beach, and the famously exclu-

sive Bald Head on Smith Island—are the result of post–World War II development activity.

Located across Snow's Cut from Carolina Beach was Sea Breeze, a thriving resort for African Americans built on a 2,500-acre tract previously owned by black businessman Robert Bruce Freeman. The first building on the beach was constructed in 1922. Eventually Sea Breeze had its own hotels, restaurants, amusement park, fishing pier, and night spots, drawing African Americans from neighboring counties and becoming known as the "National Negro Playground." It became a site for major conventions and housed black musicians during the time when Wilmington hotels would not give rooms to these traveling band members. Whites as well as blacks were drawn to the music showcased at the resort, which became the basis of beach music. During World War II, Sea Breeze was a popular recreational spot for black service people from nearby military bases. Destruction by Hurricane Hazel and the demise of segregated beaches put an end to this all-black beach resort by the early 1970s.

The building of the Blue Ridge Parkway and the creation of the Great Smoky Mountains National Park in the mountains, as well as the natural beauty of North Carolina's beaches and national seashores, have continued to make tourism one of the state's major industries. After World War II, the travel industry's focus shifted from wealthy leisure travelers to more mobile, less affluent middle-class tourists. Second-home developments also sprang up in all three resort regions. In the early 2000s, in places such as Beech Mountain, Pinehurst, and Caswell Beach, affluent second-home owners enjoy the same attractions as earlier visitors in exclusive planned communities rather than exclusive hotels. Families visit season after season, often as property owners or cottage renters rather than as hotel guests.

References: Virginia Pou Doughton, *Tales of the New Atlantic Hotel, 1880–1933* (1994); Guion G. Johnson, *Ante-Bellum North Carolina: A Social History* (1937); Sydney Nathans, *The Quest for Progress: The Way We Lived in North Carolina, 1870–1920* (1983); Alan D. Watson, *Wilmington: Port of North Carolina* (1992).

Virginia Gunn Fick
Richard D. Starnes
Additional research provided by David Stick.

SEE ALSO Andrews Geyser; Carolina Hotel; Grove Park Inn; Hot Springs; Outer Banks.

Revenue Cutter Service, which employed federal cutters to enforce maritime laws, was established in 1790 to collect much-needed revenue for a post–Revolutionary War U.S. Treasury and to terminate well-established smuggling activities along the Atlantic Coast. The newly elected first president, George Washington, gave the task of organizing the cutter service to Alexander Hamilton, the nation's first secretary of the

Treasury. Hamilton enlisted the help of customs collectors by inquiring in two Treasury Department circulars, dated 2 Oct. 1789 and 23 Sept. 1790, whether smuggling existed in their districts and if they needed boats to secure revenue. Overwhelmingly, the collectors replied that smuggling was rampant. Armed with collectors' correspondence, Hamilton presented Congress with a bill on 22 Apr. 1790 calling for establishment of a Revenue Cutter Service. Congress passed Hamilton's bill on 4 Aug. 1790, empowering the president to build and equip ten boats for the service. North Carolina received one of these boats.

By 1837 the Revenue Cutter Service was participating in the rescue of and aid to vessels in distress, and by 1871–72 the service was involved in the organization of lifesaving stations along the Atlantic Coast. In 1878 the Treasury Department formally established the U.S. Lifesaving Service, and Revenue Cutter Service officers acted as inspectors of lifesaving stations. Vessels that have operated in North Carolina include the cutters *Diligence, Gallatin, James C. Dobbin, George M. Bibb, W. H. Crawford, Colfax, Morrill,* and *Seminole.* In 1915 Congress combined the Revenue Cutter Service and the Lifesaving Service to form the U.S. Coast Guard.

Reference: Irving H. King, *The Coast Guard under Sail: The U.S. Revenue Cutter Service, 1789–1865* (1989).

Beverly Tetterton

Revision of 1751. SEE Swann's Revisal.

Revivals. The term "revival" has been used to describe what happens in local congregations when people manifest a deep religious fervor that may be accompanied by a large number of religious conversions. Early revivals often took place in the woods, near a river or a stream. People brought tents and food and slept outdoors during the event. These gatherings were also social events, when people saw friends and family members they might not have seen for a long time. Revivals usually began with singing, followed by a powerful and emotional sermon. Charismatic ministers preached a message of personal salvation, or a new birth. The minister then would walk among the people, which was something ministers had never done before. These very emotional meetings lasted for hours. People were taken over by what was called "the exercises." As part of their conversion experience, people would sometimes dance, shake, laugh, bark, or fall to the ground.

Such revivals occurred in New England and the Middle Atlantic colonies during the period known as the First Great Awakening (1730–60). Among such groups as Separate Baptists in New England, local revivals continued in scattered communities long after this period. Several families of these Separate Baptists, led by Shubal Stearns and Daniel Marshall, migrated south and finally settled on Sandy Creek in Guil-

ford (now Randolph) County in 1755. There they organized a church, and soon they also began to preach in their exuberant style in other communities over a wide area, winning converts and organizing more churches. In the 1770s and 1780s, Methodist itinerants made inroads into North Carolina, bringing their own brand of evangelical religion to the backwoods and hamlets of the state. Presbyterians, who had earlier moved into the Piedmont, were sometimes visited with revivals like the one sparked by James McCready in Guilford County prior to his removal to Logan County, Ky., in 1797.

Prior to 1800 there was growing concern among Baptists, Methodists, and Presbyterians about a general decline in the religious and moral climate of the South and the entire nation. The popular press was disseminating the views of deists like Thomas Paine; people were migrating in large numbers west of the mountains in search of cheap land and quick wealth; and the churches in the East were losing members and could not keep up with the rapidly growing population on the frontier of America.

In 1800 the first wave of the Second Great Awakening began on the frontier in Kentucky and Tennessee with the tried and proven method of revivalist preaching by James McGready, who was soon joined by others, including Presbyterians and Methodists. The revival soon spread into Virginia and the Carolinas as ministers who had longed to see revival in their own churches journeyed to the frontier to witness for themselves the remarkable effects of this revival. Using the same technique in the churches back east, revivalists soon discovered that similar results could be expected though they would not always be accompanied by the unusual physical manifestations seen in the frontier revivals. This Great Revival, as it became known in the South, was to have a lasting impact on the shape of religion in the region.

Revivals continued to be a characteristic feature of North Carolina churches throughout the nineteenth century and well into the twentieth. These revivals, unlike the more spontaneous revivals during the First Great Awakening, became a technique for winning converts and giving new life to the churches. More and more preachers sought to bring about a revival by utilizing means that had demonstrated their effectiveness in attracting crowds and persuading many to "make a decision for Christ," all of which was possible because of a shift in the underlying theology of the churches. On the frontier, camp meetings became the vehicle for revivals, especially among the Methodists, who placed great emphasis on the religion of the heart and were inclined to impose few restraints on emotions. Baptists and Presbyterians also made use of camp meetings but more often preferred to stage revivals either in church buildings or auditoriums that could accommodate large numbers.

Although more popular revivalists such as Dwight L. Moody and Billy Sunday were to be found in the North, the South had its share of effective though lesser-known figures as well as some famed preachers. Beginning in the late 1940s Billy Graham, a native of North Carolina who was to become perhaps the best-known evangelist of the twentieth century, burst upon the scene, using the latest means of communicating the gospel. His evangelistic work in this country and abroad won him recognition beyond that enjoyed by any of his peers.

References: John B. Boles, *The Great Revival, 1787–1805* (1972); William G. McLoughlin, *Revivals, Awakenings, and Reform* (1978).

Michael R. Pelt
Additional research provided by Ellen Fitzgibbons Causey.

SEE ALSO Camp Meetings; Mourner's Bench.

Reynolda House. In 1914 Richard J. Reynolds, founder and president of Reynolds Tobacco Company, and his wife, Katharine Smith Reynolds, hired Philadelphia architect Charles Barton Keen to draw up plans for an English-style village and manor house to be located on 1,067 acres that Reynolds purchased on the outskirts of Winston-Salem. Reynolds planned the village to be self-sustaining for the needs of his family and estate workers, most of whom would live on the grounds. The village included a church, post office, greenhouse, blacksmith shop, dairy, school, administrative offices, barn, and a formal garden designed by Thomas Sears of Philadelphia. All buildings and homes were constructed of white stucco with green tile roofs.

Much of the original acreage was later sold, and 300 acres of the estate were given to Wake Forest College in 1951. The college, now Wake Forest University, opened its Winston-Salem campus in the summer of 1956. The village buildings and some of the cottages have become specialty shops and restaurants, but all retain their white stucco facades and green tile roofs. The main house and 20 acres around it were not included in the gift to Wake Forest.

The manor house was built in the unpretentious bungalow style popular in the first quarter of the twentieth century rather than the extravagant showplace architecture customary for great estates. Like the village buildings, it is white stucco with a green tile roof and consists of 40,000 square feet and 100 rooms. R. J. Reynolds's daughter Mary Reynolds Babcock and her family lived in the manor house until 1964, when her husband, Charles Babcock Sr., donated the property for use as a nonprofit art and education museum. Their daughter, Barbara Babcock Millhouse, granddaughter of R. J. Reynolds, was instrumental in collecting an important group of representative American paintings, including work by John Singleton Copley, Thomas Eakins, Mary Cassatt, and Georgia O'Keeffe. The collection, which opened to the public in 1967, has been called "the finest concentration of American art in a public collection south of Washington, D.C."

Reynolda House is furnished as it was when the Reynolds family lived there, and visitors can sit in easy chairs or on sofas while viewing the paintings on the first two floors of the house. The museum acquires new paintings occasionally, and special exhibits are loaned from other museums. Other collections include Doughty birds and American art pottery, and on the third floor of the house, a costume collection includes dresses and accessories dating from Mrs. R. J. Reynolds's 1905 wedding suit to clothes worn by the Reynolds children in the 1920s.

Education programs relating American art of different periods to literature and music of the same periods are an important part of the year-round offerings of Reynolda House. They are geared to different age groups from kindergarten to senior citizens, as well as to groups with special needs. Reynolda House is included in the National Register of Historic Places and accredited by the American Association of Museums.

Barbara Mayer, *Reynolda: A History of an American Country House* (1997); Margaret Supplee Smith, "Reynolda: A Rural Vision in an Industrializing South," *NCHR* 65 (July 1988).

Anna Withers Bair

Rhine Research Center, located in Durham, studies telepathy, clairvoyance, precognition, and other paranormal experiences. The center traces its roots to 1928, when William McDougall left Harvard University to head the psychology department of Duke University in Durham. Notoriously sympathetic to nonbehavioristic approaches to psychology and a past president of the British Society for Psychical Research, McDougall, before leaving Harvard, had encouraged a young biologist named Joseph Banks Rhine to move to Durham to conduct experimental research into postmortem survival. Rhine did so, and in 1929 McDougall found him a position in the psychology department of Duke University. Rhine soon shifted the focus of his experiments from postmortem survival to psychic phenomena such as telepathy and clairvoyance, believing that these had to be understood first. He used Duke students as his subjects, asking them to guess target cards whose simple designs—star, cross, circle, square, wavy lines—had been suggested by psychologist Karl Zener, a colleague at Duke.

Rhine achieved astonishing success with these card-guessing experiments, which he reported in his work *Extra-Sensory Perception* (1934). His assertion that telepathy and clairvoyance were common, easily demonstrable human abilities attracted enormous attention to his work and to Duke in the 1930s. Journalists found him an ideal subject for articles, and he returned their interest, actively courting popular science writers and in 1937 taking part in a series of national radio broadcasts sponsored by the Zenith Radio Corporation. His account of the Duke studies, *New Frontiers of the Mind* (1937), sold widely, and his research began to receive financial support from people anxious for him to extend his investigations to the possibility of life after death.

Rhine's newly named Parapsychology Laboratory (he adapted the word "parapsychology" from a German term) soon disposed of more money for research and graduate student support than did most other branches of the university. It also began to publish the *Journal of Parapsychology*, which Rhine hoped would be a nucleus of communication within a new branch of science. But many psychologists were unhappy with what they interpreted as Rhine's unprofessional, publicity-seeking behavior, especially since his first successes seemed not to be replicable. Indeed, Rhine himself was dismayed to find after 1934 that only he himself could achieve statistically significant indications of success at extrasensory card-guessing.

These issues continued to affect the field of parapsychology during the 1940s and 1950s. Rhine, then a professor of psychology at Duke, and his assistants continued their research in new directions. They announced experimental confirmation of two other extrasensory faculties—precognition (predicting future events) in 1938 and psychokinesis (moving or affecting objects with the mind) in 1943. In 1948 Rhine's wife Louisa began to collect and analyze reports of "spontaneous extrasensory perception." Through these initiatives, Duke and the Rhines continued to generate considerable positive publicity. In 1950 the Parapsychology Laboratory left the psychology department and became a separate entity at Duke.

In 1965, at age 70, Rhine retired from the Duke faculty. He chose to take the laboratory's endowment and redirect it as a private research institute, unassociated with Duke and renamed the Institute for Parapsychology. He set up the facility within his newly created Foundation for Research on the Nature of Man (FRNM) in buildings on Buchanan Avenue, immediately across the street from Duke's East Campus. Rhine continued trying to identify good subjects, establishing a foolproof experimental procedure that could not be challenged by skeptics, expanding the application of statistics to their work, and carrying the research into new fields.

Rhine finally resigned as director in 1973, but neither his resignation nor his death in 1980 materially affected the work of his institute. The FRNM remained a center of research into parapsychology, with a small permanent staff and a contingent of visiting students—although the automatic association of North Carolina and Duke with parapsychological research was no longer as strong in the public consciousness as it had been in Rhine's day. The FRNM was renamed the Rhine Research Center in 1995, on the centenary of J. B. Rhine's birth. In 2002 the center sold its property on Buchanan Avenue to Duke and relocated to a new facility on Campus Walk Avenue. The center continued to be a world leader in psychic research, studying unusual and unexplored areas of human perception.

References: Seymour Mauskopf and Michael R. McVaugh, *The Elusive Science: Origins of Experimental Psychical Research* (1980); "The Rhine Research Center," *Southern Living* (October 2000).

Michael R. McVaugh

Rice Diet. In 1939 Walter Kempner of the Duke University Medical Center in Durham began to prescribe a short-term diet based almost entirely on rice—high in fiber, low in protein and fat, and salt-free—to patients with kidney disease and hypertensive vascular disease. Within a few years he concluded that his diet was of general benefit in reducing blood pressure and other heart conditions, and in 1944 he presented some of his pioneering conclusions at a meeting of the American Medical Association.

By the late 1950s this diet had also become popular as a way to drastically reduce weight. Over the next few decades Kempner began to attract patients from all over the country who were seeking to lose weight. At first they lived in private homes in Durham, where the diet would be specially prepared for them and where Kempner and his staff could monitor their progress. As their numbers increased, patients lived in motels or rented apartments, and a Rice Diet Center was created with a common room and a common kitchen. In the first weeks their diet consisted of nothing but fruit and small amounts of rice; tomatoes were then added and gradually a few other vegetables, as patients came closer and closer to their target weight. Walks were prescribed between meals.

Medical examinations, tests, and living expenses made treatment at the Rice Center expensive—around $4,200 a month by 2002—but it drew many people who testified happily to its effectiveness, including several celebrities. Popular books praising Durham as the "Diet Capital of the World" increased the rice diet's fame. After Kempner retired in 1991, the Rice Diet Program continued under Robert Rosati's direction along much the same lines, although a number of educational programs were arranged to help participants change their eating behavior and a few spices were introduced into what was originally an intentionally bland (and therefore unappetizing) diet. Tai Chi, yoga, meditation, and other forms of mental and physical development were also available to rice diet participants.

References: Jean Renfro Anspaugh, *Fat Like Us* (2001); Eda J. LeShan, *Winning the Losing Battle: Why I Will Never Be Fat Again* (1979); Judy Moscovitz, *The Rice Diet Report* (1986).

Michael R. McVaugh

Richmond County, located in the Piedmont region in southern North Carolina, was formed in 1779 from Anson County and was named after Charles Lennox, the third duke of Richmond. Early inhabitants of the area included the Saura (Cheraw) Indians, followed by Highland Scot, German, Scotch-

Irish, and English settlers. Rockingham, the county seat, was established in 1779 as Richmond Court House; the name was changed in 1785 to honor Charles Watson Wentworth, the marquis of Rockingham, who maintained friendly relations with the American colonies during the Revolution. Other communities in the county include Hamlet, Ellerbe, Ghio, Cordova, and Hoffman. Notable physical features of the county include several lakes, as well as the Pee Dee River, Seaburn Spring, and Naked, Hamer, and Buffalo Creeks.

The North Carolina Motor Speedway in Rockingham, known locally as "the Rock," was an important center for auto racing for decades, hosting NASCAR's AC Delco 200 Busch Grand National Race and the AC Delco 400 Winston Cup Race and bringing thousands of visitors annually to the county. The track held its last race in February 2004. County cultural institutions include the National Railroad Museum and Hall of Fame, the Rankin Museum of American and Natural History, the Richmond County Community Theatre, and Richmond County Community Concert. Hamlet and Ellerbe have historic districts with many historic houses. The county also hosts a number of annual events, such as Seaboard Festival Day and the Rankin Museum Festival.

Richmond County produces agricultural goods such as cotton, peaches and other fruits, corn, tobacco, vegetables, and soybeans. Manufactured products include textiles and apparel, wood moldings, furniture, plastic closures, poultry processing, and steel fabricators. In 2004 Richmond County's population was estimated to be 46,400.

Reference: John Hutchinson, *No Ordinary Lives: A History of Richmond County, North Carolina, 1750–1900* (1998).

Jay Mazzocchi

Richmond Hill Law School in what became Yadkin County was established about 1846 by Judge (later Chief Justice) Richmond M. Pearson, who had conducted an earlier school in nearby Mocksville. Until Pearson's death in 1878, the school was one of the preeminent law schools in the state, its only true rival being Judge William Horn Battle's school in Chapel Hill. Instruction at Richmond Hill was offered both to students studying for their county court licenses and to more advanced students preparing for practice in the superior courts. The mode of instruction was rigorously Socratic, involving intensive discussion of both the law and its underlying principles. Pearson himself claimed to have instructed "more than a thousand law students" at Mocksville and Richmond Hill, many of whom achieved distinction in the legal and political life of North Carolina and the nation.

References: Wilson Angley, *Richmond M. Pearson and the Richmond Hill Law School* (1978); Fannie M. Farmer, "Legal Education in North Carolina, 1820–1860," *NCHR* 28 (July 1951); Council S.

Wooten, "A Famous Old Time North Carolina Law School," *North Carolina Journal of Law* 2 (1905).

Wilson Angley

Rights as Englishmen was a phrase used frequently on the eve of the American Revolution by people in North Carolina and other colonies who understood and wanted to assert their position under the English Crown. The phrase referred to the rights and privileges granted specifically to colonists in Carolina by the 1663 charter from King Charles II. These basic rights were recognized to be the same as those enjoyed in England by subjects of the Crown. In the colonists' minds, their rights were being violated in several dire ways, particularly through "taxation without representation." Other rights were also considered essential, among them freedom of worship and the right to share in the fish and mineral bounty of the New World.

Reference: Hugh T. Lefler and Albert Ray Newsome, *North Carolina: The History of a Southern State* (1963).

William S. Powell

Right-to-Work Law. North Carolina's right-to-work law, ratified on 18 Mar. 1947, greatly limits the power of labor unions in the state. The statute makes illegal the closed shop, by which union membership is a condition of being hired as well as of continued employment. The union shop, whereby union membership is made a condition of employment but in which the employer may hire nonunion workers provided they become members within a stated period, is also illegal. Finally, the law prohibits the mandatory collection of union dues by employers through deduction from workers' wages.

Section 14(b) of the Labor-Management Relations Act of 1947, popularly known as the Taft-Hartley Act, passed by Congress on 23 June 1947, provided that if a state law was more restrictive on union membership than the federal law, the state law prevailed. Labor organizations at both state and national levels promptly denounced right-to-work laws as disguised union busting and sought repeal of both section 14(b) of the Taft-Hartley Act and all state legislation based on it. Unions declared that North Carolina agencies were using the state's anti-union climate as a selling point to recruit industry. The AFL-CIO's confrontation in 1958 with the National Right-to-Work Committee's efforts to extend right-to-work laws to six more states resulted in the defeat of such laws in five of the six states, but it had no effect on the North Carolina law. In 1965 organized labor again tried to get Congress to repeal Taft-Hartley section 14(b), but there was no change in North Carolina. Since then, state and national campaigns to repeal right-to-work legislation have declined sharply, and the number of states with these laws has stabilized. By the early 2000s there were 20 southern and western states with such legislation.

Wiley J. Williams

Ring Tournaments were relics of the medieval sport of jousting, dating from the eleventh until the fifteenth century. Rather than trying to knock another rider down, as in jousting, a ring tournament participant negotiated a course ranging between 80 and 125 feet long on horseback, attempting to spear a series of small ($\frac{1}{2}$- to 2-inch) rings suspended overhead using an $8\frac{1}{2}$-foot lance. This sport spread from France to England and to the American colonies. Participants often dressed in colorful medieval garb, assumed titles, and presumed to honor certain ladies. Judges observed the contest and declared as victor the one who took the greatest number of rings. Chivalry, honor, and the virtues of womanhood were the consistent themes. At a tournament held at Bellevue Plantation in Beaufort County on 4 Jan. 1867, men were implored to be courteous, amiable, and polite, while maintaining their personal honor and self-respect and recognizing the principles of "a sound, moral, and religious government in all the secular interests of the world."

The earliest ring tournament noted in North Carolina was held at Shocco Springs on 15 Sept. 1857. The pageantry was contagious, and several other tournaments followed in various towns. Following the hiatus occasioned by the Civil War, a schedule of tournaments at Wilmington on 1 Feb. 1866 drew large gatherings. On 1 Jan. 1867 nearly 3,000 people—including former governors Zebulon B. Vance and Thomas Bragg, and Gen. Robert F. Hoke as speaker—attended tournaments on the banks of the Neuse River at New Bern with several inches of snow on the ground. The popularity of ring tournaments continued unabated into the next decade. In February 1867 a modified version for children, described as "chivalry in pantelets," was staged. Of even more significance was the organization in early 1871 of the Wilmington Tournament Association by the young black men of the city and the ensuing parade and successful tilt on 1 May.

Interest in the sport dwindled after 1876, especially in the towns of Wilmington and New Bern, where there was more interest in the social aspects of the tournaments. In New Bern on 1 Jan. 1895, only the Queen of Love and her court, not the tilt, merited the attention of the local press.

References: Alberta Ratliffe Craig, "Old Wentworth Sketches," NCHR 11 (July 1934); Esther J. Crooks and Ruth W. Crooks, *The Ring Tournament in the United States* (1936); Guion G. Johnson, *Ante-Bellum North Carolina: A Social History* (1937).

Louis P. Towles

Rip Van Winkle State was the derogatory nickname given North Carolina in the early decades of the nineteenth century. From 1815 to 1835, the state was deemed to be so undeveloped, backward, and indifferent to its condition that it appeared to be as comatose as Rip Van Winkle. In 1830 a legislative committee reported that North Carolina was "a state without foreign commerce, for want of seaports or a staple; without internal communication by rivers, roads, or canals; without a cash market for any article of agricultural product; without manufactures; in short, without any object to which native industry and active enterprise could be directed." In addition to all of these handicaps, there was general political apathy under the state's Democrat-controlled one-party system, which resulted in widespread indifference to all economic, social, and cultural improvements. A letter writer to the *North Carolina Farmer* in 1845 voiced his frustration: "O! that our State, . . . would wake up from her Rip Van Winkle agricultural sleep! and, for her own best interests, would become a reader and extensive patronizer of the North Carolina Farmer and other agricultural periodicals!"

Fortunately, North Carolina's "Rip Van Winkle" period was relatively short-lived. The constitutional reforms of 1835 paved the way for a quarter-century of remarkable development in the state, carried out for 15 years under Whig leadership and for 10 years under Democratic leadership. This development included the building of a state system of railroads and plank roads; support for a statewide system of public schools; the establishment of institutions for the care of the blind, deaf, and mentally ill; a reformed tax system; changes in the legal status of women; the improvement of agricultural and manufacturing conditions; and the growth of the University of North Carolina and other colleges, academies, and religious agencies.

References: Hugh T. Lefler and Albert R. Newsome, *North Carolina: The History of a Southern State* (3rd ed., 1973); William S. Powell, *North Carolina through Four Centuries* (1989).

Wiley J. Williams

River Navigation. In the centuries before railroad and motor transportation, North Carolina's rivers provided valuable travel routes. But accidents of geography severely limited the potential of river travel in the region. Sandbars and sunken logs obstructed many coastal plain rivers, and piedmont rivers contained not only these obstacles but also rocks, rapids, and waterfalls. The Outer Banks, pierced only by shifting and shallow inlets, blocked the sounds from the ocean. This lack of direct access to the ocean limited the value of even the most navigable stretches of coastal rivers. Of these, the Chowan and the Roanoke Rivers empty into the Albemarle Sound, and the Tar-Pamlico and Neuse Rivers empty into the Pamlico Sound. The White Oak and New Rivers flow into the Atlantic, but they are small and offer little access to the interior. The Cape Fear River, formed by the Deep and

Haw Rivers in the piedmont, empties directly into the Atlantic and has given the state access from much of the interior to the ocean. Navigation was made more difficult by wild fluctuations in water level, as rivers were vulnerable to prolonged droughts as well as floods. From colonial days until the steamboat era, river travel was easiest when water levels were high during the winter and often was halted completely during dry summers.

Despite less-than-ideal conditions, early explorers and settlers managed to use rivers to great advantage. English explorers pressed deep into North Carolina by way of the Roanoke and Chowan Rivers in 1586. The Cape Fear River gave passage to Spanish settlers under Lucas Vasquez de Ayllon in 1526 and English settlers in the 1660s, although neither colony was successful. Virginian settlers observed Saura (Cheraw) Indian tribes on the Dan River in the late 1600s, later finding others on Drowning Creek, which would become the Lumber River in Robeson County. (The Lumbee Indians remain centered around the Lumber, now a national Wild and Scenic River noted for animal life.) Other settlers from western Virginia staked out lands along rivers that flowed into Albemarle Sound beginning in the 1650s; others later followed the Neuse, Pamlico, Tar, and Cape Fear Rivers. The long navigable stretches of the Cape Fear and its tributaries encouraged a thriving trade in produce and naval stores through the ports of Brunswick and Wilmington.

Because they gave access to transportation, lands along navigable rivers were usually the first to be settled. Colonial laws provided for a number of public landings to allow residents entry to rivers. North Carolina's early towns—Bath, Beaufort, New Bern, Edenton, Brunswick, Wilmington, and others—were located by navigable streams. In addition, rivers divided the state into small regions based on river valleys. Because of poor road conditions, these valleys offered no easy access to other regions of the state, and rapids and waterfalls at the fall line, where the level of the land drops between piedmont and coastal plain, divided inhabitants into eastern and western factions. The limited usefulness of rivers as trade routes retarded agricultural, industrial, economic, and cultural growth; encouraged isolation and sectionalism; and contributed to the backwardness of the state and the high rates of emigration during the early nineteenth century.

Early settlers in the piedmont found their rivers to be more barriers than highways. Most rivers in this region are relatively small, and many are interrupted by rocks and rapids or waterfalls. Of the major rivers in the piedmont, the Dan flows into Virginia before uniting with the Roanoke and winding back into North Carolina, and the Catawba and the Yadkin–Pee Dee begin in the mountains and flow into South Carolina. Although of limited use for navigation, the piedmont rivers became valuable sources of waterpower—first in running gristmills, then in operating cotton mills and other facto-

ries, and finally in powering hydroelectric projects. Although often grand and beautiful, the mountain rivers were too shallow and rocky to be of much use as travel routes. Many of them also have been harnessed to provide electric power.

Following the American Revolution, particularly in the first half of the nineteenth century, North Carolina undertook a program of internal improvements to enhance its economy, an important facet of which was to improve the navigability of watercourses. During and after the colonial era, the legislature empowered the county courts to order the clearing of navigable rivers and streams within their jurisdictions. From the Revolution to the Civil War, however, the General Assembly often addressed specific waterways, mandating the county courts to require mill owners to provide slips for the passage of boats and occasionally appointing individuals to clear streams. Generally those efforts were unproductive.

Beginning in 1815, the General Assembly deemed the promotion of internal improvements so important that it instituted the practice of buying stock in several companies on behalf of the state. In the 1840s it renewed its attempts to improve river navigability by chartering more companies and investing additional state funds in these organizations. The state acquired stock in reincorporated Neuse and Yadkin companies and in the New River Navigation Company in Onslow County. The legislature reserved its major investment for the Cape Fear and Deep River Navigation Company, eventually buying the company, which proved to be a disappointment. The Roanoke and the Cape Fear remained the only successful navigation companies, at least to the extent that they remained afloat and paid dividends throughout the antebellum era. The difficulty of the undertakings, lack of engineering expertise, scarcity of labor, adverse weather conditions, and damaging freshets generated by heavy rains undermined many promising operations.

Ferries have carried passengers across North Carolina's rivers since at least 1699. Early ferries were wooden flats usually guided across a stream by a cable. The cable could be lowered into the stream to permit other boats to pass. Today, the state maintains free ferry service across several rivers, ranging from large ferries that cross the Neuse, Pamlico, and Cape Fear Rivers to small, two-car ferries, such as the one at Sans Souci on the Cashie River in Bertie County.

By the late nineteenth century, boats powered by gasoline or diesel engines began to replace steamboats. Commercial river travel in North Carolina declined significantly, pressed by competition from railroads and later from automobiles and trucks on the expanding network of paved roads in the state. Half a century later, passenger service on the rivers (except for ferries) was long a thing of the past. Commercial river business consisted of hauling bulk cargoes such as logs, fertilizer, oil, farm products, pulpwood, and fish. Barges towed by motor vessels still carry bulk cargoes on some rivers in the coastal plain, and Wilmington, 30 miles up the Cape Fear River from the Atlantic, remains the state's major port. North Carolina's rivers are now seen less as highways than as an important part of the environment, crucial for their role in supporting wildlife and providing drinking water. Many residents and tourists seek out these rivers for recreation, fishing, or simply to appreciate their natural beauty and their role in history.

References: Michael B. Alford, "The Ferry from Trent: Researching Colonial River Ferries," *Tributaries* (October 1991); Lindley S. Butler, "The Forgotten Boatmen: Navigation on the Dan River, 1792–1892," *Tributaries* (October 1993); Alan D. Watson, "North Carolina and Internal Improvements, 1783–1861: The Case of Inland Navigation," NCHR 74 (January 1997).

Alan D. Watson
David A. Norris

SEE ALSO Blossom's Ferry; Cape Fear and Deep River Steam Navigation Company; Ferries; Steamboats.

Rivers. SEE Cape Fear River; Catawba River; French Broad River; Neuse River; Roanoke River; Yadkin–Pee Dee River.

Riverside Cemetery, on rolling, tree-covered grounds in the historic Montford District of Asheville, was established in 1885 by the Asheville Cemetery Company. The property overlooks the French Broad River and contains 87 acres of beautifully landscaped grounds on five terraced levels with more than three miles of roads. The natural beauty of ancient and massive oaks, poplars, evergreens, dogwoods, mimosas, azaleas, rhododendrons, and laurels complement unusual monuments and mausoleums.

Riverside Cemetery contains the graves of many people important to the history of Asheville and western North Carolina, as well as other North Carolina notables. Some prominent North Carolinians buried there include authors Thomas Wolfe and William Sydney Porter (O. Henry); Confederate generals Robert Brank Vance and Thomas L. Clingman; North Carolina governors Zebulon B. Vance and Locke Craig; U.S. senator Jeter C. Pritchard; George T. Winston, an educator and the president of the University of North Carolina; Lillian Exum Clement Stafford, the first woman to serve in the North Carolina legislature; diplomat Richmond Pearson; English-born botanist John Lyon; architect Richard Sharp Smith; and Japanese-born photographer George Masa. Unique burial plots include the Beth Ha-Tephila Jewish cemetery, a plot for 18 German seamen who died while interned as aliens during World War I, a plot with more than 175 veterans of World War I and World War II who died while patients in the Oteen Veterans Administration Hospital, and a stone monument to the graves of six English stonecutters who worked on the Biltmore Estate.

When the cemetery was established, graves were moved from earlier burial grounds, including three church cemeteries on Church Street. By the middle of the twentieth century, the Asheville Cemetery Company was having financial problems. In 1952 the cemetery was taken over by the city of Asheville, and it is still maintained by the City Parks and Recreation Department. There are approximately 13,000 graves, and grave sites remain available. The cemetery is listed on the National Register of Historic Places.

Zoe Rhine

R. J. Reynolds Tobacco Company began as Reynolds Industries, a small tobacco company in what is now Winston-Salem. Twenty-four-year-old Richard Joshua Reynolds moved from Virginia to Winston—population about 400—in 1874 and immediately recognized two commercial advantages: the town was the center of the new flue-cured tobacco market and was on a newly constructed railroad line. Reynolds bought a lot next to the tracks and built the "Little Red Factory," a two-story building that covered less area than a tennis court. In the spring of 1875 he hired a few workers and produced 150,000 pounds of chewing tobacco that year.

As his company rapidly grew, Reynolds experimented with using saccharin as a sweetener, although publicly he said that only the area around Winston could grow tobacco so "naturally sweet." He established a large sales force and almost continually brought in new, modern machinery to increase production. Reynolds used his capital wisely to expand his facilities and buy out competitors. He incorporated the R. J. Reynolds Tobacco Company in North Carolina in 1890. In 1899 Reynolds Tobacco became part of James B. Duke's tobacco trust, but it went independent again when the trust was broken up in 1911. After the turn of the century, Reynolds Tobacco produced one-fourth of the nation's flat plug chewing tobacco.

Anticipating an increase in the popularity of smoking tobacco, Reynolds introduced several new brands, including Prince Albert pipe tobacco in 1907. Prince Albert was an instant success: production in the first four years went from 250,000 pounds annually to more than 14 million pounds. In that era most smokers rolled their own cigarettes, but Reynolds introduced four manufactured brands in 1913. Camel, a blend of burley and bright leaf tobaccos, with a touch of Turkish leaf for aroma and taste and a healthy amount of sweetener, became an astounding success. The public bought 425 million Camel cigarettes that first year, and four years later Camel was the most popular cigarette in the United States. The label, drawn from a photograph of Old Joe, a dromedary from the Barnum & Bailey Circus, was famous throughout the nation. By 1925 more than one-half of the cigarettes smoked in the United States were Camels.

Richard Joshua Reynolds died in 1918. That year his company employed 10,000 people who worked in 121 buildings in Winston-Salem (the two towns had merged in 1913). In 1929

Inspecting cartons of Camel cigarettes at R. J. Reynolds Tobacco Company. NCC.

the company's headquarters moved into the Reynolds Building, which was cited as the best new building of the year by the National Association of Architects. A larger replica, the Empire State Building, was later built in New York City.

Over the years Reynolds Tobacco produced other successful cigarette brands, including Winston, Salem, Vantage, and Doral. When television took over American entertainment, Reynolds used this new advertising medium to reach a nationwide audience. In 1948 Camel cigarettes sponsored the *Camel News Caravan* with John Cameron Swayze, one of the first national news programs. Reynolds diversified its international tobacco operations, and in 1956 the company amended its charter to permit investment in nontobacco enterprises. Archer Aluminum, originally formed to produce foil for tobacco products, began making other consumer packaging products. Reynolds purchased Hawaiian Punch fruit drink, Vermont Maid syrup, Chun King oriental foods, Patio Mexican foods, and other brands that were placed under subsidiary RJR Foods. In 1969 Reynolds acquired Sea-Land Service, Inc., the world's first and largest containerized freight operation. In 1970 Reynolds entered the energy business by acquiring American Independent Oil Company. Also in 1970 the company became R. J. Reynolds Industries, Inc. (RJR).

Acquisitions continued throughout the 1970s and 1980s, with RJR obtaining Burmah Oil and Gas Company and Burmah Oil Development, Inc. (1976); Del Monte, the huge processor of fruits and vegetables (1979); Heublein, Inc., a worldwide marketer of distilled spirits (including its flagship product, Smirnoff Vodka), wines, fast foods, and grocery products (1982); and Canada Dry and Sunkist soft drinks (1984). RJR spun off its Sea-Land Service and sold its energy business before acquiring Nabisco Brands, Inc., in 1985. The parent company became RJR Nabisco, Inc., and management moved the corporate headquarters from Winston-Salem to Atlanta.

In the late 1980s, a wild bidding war raged for the huge company. The investment firm Kohlberg, Kravis, Roberts & Company won with a $25 billion leveraged bid. The buyout was said to symbolize the economic climate of the 1980s and was the subject of Bryan Burrough's best-selling book *Barbarians at the Gate: The Fall of RJR Nabisco* (1990). Saddled with the huge debt, RJR Nabisco sold off assets and in the early 1990s became a publicly traded company again. Headquarters were subsequently moved to New York City.

In 1985 RJR Nabisco was challenged by critics of the tobacco industry for introducing the character of "Joe Cool Camel" in advertisements for Camel cigarettes. Although the company denied that the advertising campaign targeted underage smokers, the character was immensely popular, and Camel's share of the under-18 market increased from 0.5 percent to 32.8 percent in the two years following Joe Camel's appearance. In July 1997 RJR Nabisco decided to retire the controversial figure and replace him with other advertising themes targeting "mature" consumers.

Faced with tobacco's massive legal liability, in March 1999 RJR Nabisco announced the sale of its international tobacco business and its plans to split the domestic tobacco and food businesses into two independent companies. That June R. J. Reynolds Tobacco Company became the wholly owned subsidiary of R. J. Reynolds Tobacco Holdings, Inc., and corporate headquarters returned to Winston-Salem. In January 2002 R. J. Reynolds Tobacco Holdings, Inc. acquired Santa Fe Natural Tobacco Company, Inc., and two years later merged with Brown & Williamson Tobacco Company to form Reynolds American, Inc.

Reference: Nannie M. Tilley, *The R. J. Reynolds Tobacco Company* (1985).

Barry McGee

Roads made of several different materials have been common in North Carolina during various eras of its history. One of the earliest attempts at road building in the state was the construction of corduroy roads leading from Albemarle Sound in present-day Perquimans and Pasquotank Counties. The roads were created by laying logs lengthwise along the roadway, crossing them with small cuttings, and adding sandy soil to hold them in place. Although this method was common in swampy areas of northeastern North Carolina, it failed to become widespread elsewhere in the state. One of these early "floating roads" between Elizabeth City and the Camden County line was used until 1922, when it was replaced with a more modern surface.

Between 1836, when a successful Canadian experiment with plank roads became known, and 1860, when the Civil War ended their support and maintenance, North Carolina roads were commonly made of wood. During this period, so-

A section of the Western Plank Road discovered by archaeologists in 1984 during street excavations in Fayetteville. Photograph courtesy of Kenneth W. Robinson.

called plank road fever accounted for 84 chartered roadways, of which some 500 miles were constructed using state and private funds estimated from $300,000 to $800,000.

The concept of the plank road was especially popular in areas where forests were abundant and wood was relatively inexpensive. The roadways were constructed of pine and oak sills six to eight inches thick placed on an adequately drained roadbed and covered crosswise with planks eight inches wide and at least three inches thick. The planks were then covered with gravel or sand, which was hardened by horse droppings into a firm surface. The Fayetteville & Western Plank Road, a toll route between Fayetteville and Bethania in Forsyth County covering 129 miles, has the distinction of being the longest wooden highway ever constructed. Built of oak and pine between 1849 and 1854, it was abandoned in 1862. Although plank roads served the purpose of rising above the mud in many places, they ultimately fell into disuse and disrepair due to insufficient maintenance.

Macadam roads, which gained popularity at the end of the nineteenth century, were an integral part of the state's mod-

ern attempts to improve roadways. Named for their inventor, Scottish engineer John L. McAdam, macadam (or macadamized) roads helped North Carolina rebuild its state and local highway system after nearly 40 years of neglect caused by the destruction and loss of capital that followed the Civil War and Reconstruction.

Before the advent of macadam roads, many North Carolina roadways were little more than wide clay paths. Rutted and dusty when dry and nearly impassable when wet, clay roads made travel very difficult and hindered the movement of goods to market and to rail stations. The macadam process helped to change all that because it required roadways to be graded so that they drained properly. More important, the graded roadway was covered with five to nine inches of crushed stone, creating a solid, stable base that was then rolled with a steam-powered roller, sprinkled with water, covered with dust, and rolled again. The addition of the dust served to repel water and helped to bind the stones together by filling the spaces between them. Later, a "bituminous" or liquid asphalt binder replaced the water binder. In many cases, macadam roads, covered with asphalt, became the foundations of new roadways.

Although in 1838 an internal improvements committee meeting in Raleigh had sought to gain state financial support for the construction of North Carolina's first macadam road, few if any were built until around 1880, when Charlotte mayor William Johnston implemented a plan to macadamize the Queen City's clay roads. After Charlotte covered five miles of road with stone pavement (at a cost of approximately $25,000), Mecklenburg County moved to improve roads outside the city. Several years later, Capt. S. B. Alexander influenced the State Senate to pass the Mecklenburg Road Law of 1885, which called for the use of convict labor and the implementation of a local property tax to help pay for road construction and improvement. With the money raised from the new tax and cheap labor supplied by inmates, Mecklenburg County was able to complete 30 miles of macadam road by 1894 and 75 miles by 1900.

Many other counties, including Forsyth, Iredell, Cabarrus, Alamance, and Wake, soon enacted improved road laws. With a few exceptions, such as New Hanover County's experiments with building roads of oyster shells, almost every new road project in North Carolina called for macadam. By 1910, however, many of the roads had deteriorated due to increased automobile traffic and damage from freezing water. Because macadam roads were so expensive to build and maintain, most counties stopped building them. In 1912 the state boasted 1,232 miles of macadam roads, but by 1929 the figure had plummeted to 313 miles. Many of these roads were in mountain counties where stone was more plentiful than sand. The macadam roads are at least partially responsible for three important advances: improved travel and communication, the advent of Rural Home Delivery, and far greater mobility to move agricultural and manufactured products around the state.

Sand-clay roads became a cheap and popular alternative to paved roads in much of North Carolina early in the twentieth century, especially starting around 1910. They were made by mixing sand with clay, proportioned so there was just enough clay to act as a binder for the sand. The related topsoil road was made of earth found near the road already naturally mixed in usable proportions of sand and clay. Sand-clay roads were most often found in the South, particularly in Georgia, North Carolina, South Carolina, and Texas. In North Carolina, there were 4,313.5 miles of county sand-clay roads in 1914—double the mileage of 1912. These roads held up well under horse-drawn vehicles and light automobile traffic. The sand-clay road has remained useful for certain routes, mostly rural secondary roads where asphalt is not needed.

Asphalt came into widespread use later in the century, with great improvements developed for military purposes during World War II. State road construction was given a boost by the federal government in 1956, when Congress passed the State Highway Act, designating billions of dollars for highway construction. North Carolina has one of the largest highway systems in the nation, with 78,000 miles of paved roads.

References: Cecil Kenneth Brown, *The State Highway System of North Carolina: Its Evolution and Present Status* (1931); Robert E. Ireland, *Entering the Auto Age: The Early Automobile in North Carolina, 1900–1930* (1990); Harry Wilson McKown Jr., "Roads and Reform: The Good Roads Movement in North Carolina, 1885–1921" (M.A. thesis, UNC-Chapel Hill, 1972); Capus Waynick, *North Carolina Roads and Their Builders*, vol. 1 (1952).

David A. Norris
Robert E. Ireland
Additional research provided by John Hairr and Matthew C. Porter.

SEE ALSO Appian Way; Great Wagon Road.

"Road to Nowhere" is the droll nickname of an unfinished six-mile stretch of highway that is the result of an unfulfilled promise by the U.S. government to a small community in Swain County. The genesis of the road began in the 1930s and 1940s, when the federal government and the Tennessee Valley Authority took over 67,800 acres of public and private land in Graham and Swain Counties to build Fontana Dam, creating Fontana Lake and part of the Great Smoky Mountains National Park. In compensation for the land, which had been owned by many families for generations, the government promised to reimburse Swain County for the loss of flooded Highway 288, which had provided access to the area. Another assurance was the construction of a road approximately 30 miles long that would follow the northern shore of the lake and help substitute for the highway and allow the displaced residents access to their family cemeteries.

Begun in the 1940s, this road, called Lakeview Drive, extended about six miles by 1969 but was stalled by environmental issues. Although Congressman Charles Taylor and Senator Jesse Helms obtained $16 million in federal funding for the North Shore Road Project in October 2000, the road was never completed, partly because of the projected costs of construction. It remains a sensitive issue for area residents, who continue to view the "Road to Nowhere" as a broken promise.

Despite the difficult social and political issues surrounding the road, it offers some of the least-crowded views of Great Smoky Mountains National Park. Beginning about three miles outside of Bryson City, the drive provides views of Fontana Lake and the Tuckasegee River as well as encounters with woodlands and many small streams. Several hiking trails, like the approximately 44-mile Lakeshore Trail, lead from the road to some of the highlights of the park, including its highest peak, Clingman's Dome, reached by Noland Creek Trail.

Laura Hegyi

Road Wagons, or freight wagons, were large horse-drawn wagons used primarily before the advent of the railroad to haul produce to market and carry other goods and supplies. Often operated as a business by two or more men, these wagons followed trails or roads from the backcountry to such centers of commerce as Fayetteville, Wilmington, Petersburg, Va., or Charleston, S.C., and later to the railroad. Some occasionally took passengers. On 6 Dec. 1815 one couple traveled from Bethabara to Salem to attend a meeting, but the onset of rain, snow, and sleet compelled them to return home "in a freight-wagon" that they encountered in Salem "and which was coming this way."

Bennehan Cameron recalled a black man named George, born in 1790 on the plantation of Cameron's grandfather, who "had all his life charge of the road wagons to Petersburg . . . and then to Henderson after the completion of the old Raleigh and Gaston Railroad, so that he knew everybody along the road and everybody knew him." In Salisbury, the *Yadkin and Catawba Journal* (25 Feb. 1829 and 26 Nov. 1832) advertised road wagons for sale from the estates of the late Nicholas Filhowar and John Pool, respectively; the estate of Abel Cowan of the same county (1844) also included a road wagon.

William S. Powell

Roanoke Canal. The Roanoke River, by far the largest river in terms of water flow in North Carolina, was for centuries a path of commerce and travel, first by American Indians and later by European settlers. In 1812 North Carolina lawmakers directed the subscription of shares in the new Roanoke Navigation Company, formed to build and maintain internal improvements that would promote commercial navigation on the Roanoke and its tributaries. Although the company was chartered in 1812 by the state legislature, the cooperation of Virginia would be needed to secure the benefits of a commercial waterway reaching deeply into the interior. In December 1815 Col. William Lewis traveled in a bateau from Greenhill, Va., on the Staunton River, to Norfolk. His successful journey convinced the Virginia General Assembly of the practicality of commercial navigation on the Roanoke River system, and a charter was approved. Later, Virginia investors gained control through stock acquisitions. Almost all of the stockholders were businessmen with interests nearby or upriver.

The Roanoke River system consisted of three major components: the lower 100-mile portion of the Roanoke River between Weldon and the Albemarle Sound; a nine-mile network of locks, basins, and a canal at the falls at Weldon; and the upper 300-mile stretch of rivers that reached to the foot of the Blue Ridge Mountains. The canal itself was to be about 15 feet deep and 40 feet wide, with a 10-foot-wide towpath alongside it.

By 1828 the lower Roanoke was improved to allow navigation by steam-powered vessels, and the steamer *Petersburg* was placed in service carrying cargo from Weldon to Norfolk. The same year it was possible to traverse the Staunton as far as Salem, Va. The Dan River could be navigated by bateau as far as Leaksville in 1828, although it remained impeded until 1834. The Dan was improved and eventually made navigable as far as Madison. The Staunton was opened to Clark's Landing, Va.

For over a decade, the Roanoke Canal prospered, transporting vessels powered by tow animals, sail, and steam. The legislatures of North Carolina and Virginia contributed funds and bought bonds in the company, viewing the canal as part of a project to complete and improve both it and a canal through the Dismal Swamp to Norfolk. Beginning in 1831, fairly steady annual dividends enabled the company to finance waterway improvements extending over 244 miles of river above the canal, as far as Rockingham County on the Dan and Salem, Va., on the Roanoke.

When the Petersburg Railroad in Virginia reached the Roanoke just across from Weldon in 1833, the "iron horse," free from rivers and almost never halted as canals were, cast the die against the Roanoke Navigation Company and similar operations. As other rail lines were built, the canal's revenues plummeted, and the Roanoke Navigation Company produced its last detailed annual report in 1855. As traffic disappeared, the property fell into disrepair. In 1875 the North Carolina General Assembly ordered that Roanoke Navigation be dissolved and its property sold. The canal would never again play a role in transportation. The company was one of only three such public improvement companies in North Carolina that ever returned money to its investors, paying over its lifetime 57.25 percent of stock prices in dividends.

In 1885 several wealthy businessmen, many from Petersburg, Va., purchased the Roanoke Canal property for $19,525. The new company, the Roanoke Navigation and Water Power Company, sought manufacturing, milling, and foundry operations to use the canal's water. After some success, company directors announced in 1890 a much more notable goal: using the canal to generate electricity. By 1892 generators were in place at both Weldon and the middle locks, and the Roanoke Canal was supplying the first electric power to Weldon and its environs. Weldon soon boasted new cottonseed, corn, and peanut mills, cotton yarn and fabric mills, and a large winery and bottling plant. As a result of Roanoke Canal electricity, the hamlets of Rosemary and Roanoke Junction developed, near the middle locks, into present-day Roanoke Rapids.

Physical evidence of the Roanoke Canal remains, largely because of the work of preservationists. Weldon, laid out in 1820, is the only surviving municipality created primarily by the canal's construction. The beautiful, impressive stone aqueduct in Weldon that carried the canal over Chockoyotte Creek has been preserved, as have the walls of the combined locks in Roanoke Rapids.

References: Peggy Jo Cobb Braswell, *The Roanoke Canal: A History of the Old Navigation and Water Power Canal of Halifax County, North Carolina* (1987); Philip M. Rice, "The Early Development of the Roanoke Waterway: A Study in Interstate Relations," NCHR 31 (January 1954); William E. Trout III, "The Roanoke Navigation: Taming the River of Death," *Journal of Rockingham County History and Genealogy* 3 (October 1978).

Whitmel M. Joyner
Fred Moore

Roanoke-Chowan Group. The Roanoke-Chowan Group of Writers and Allied Artists began in 1948 as an informal gathering of writers, musicians, painters, and patrons of the arts called together by retired banker Gilbert T. Stephenson and his wife, Grace, at their Northampton County country home, known as Warren Place. In 1953 the organization established and endowed the Roanoke-Chowan Award, since given annually to the best book of poetry by a North Carolinian that year. The endowment for the award was subsequently transferred to the North Carolina Literary and Historical Association, which names judges. The award is presented with other state literary awards at the annual meeting of the association.

Stephenson, who served as president of the North Carolina Literary and Historical Association in 1956, wanted to prove that "material for literature as well as art is to be found in every nook and cranny of our state." The original Roanoke-Chowan Group included 14 authors, 5 painters, and several musicians. Among its early and enthusiastic luminaries were authors Bernice Kelly Harris of Seaboard, Mebane Holoman Burgwyn of Northampton County, Inglis Fletcher of Chowan County, and Ovid Pierce of Halifax County; painters Francis Speight of Bertie County and Frith Winslow of Plymouth; church historian Henry Lewis of Jackson and Chapel Hill; and journalists Holley Mack Bell of Windsor and Roy Parker Jr. of Jackson and Ahoskie.

For several years in the 1950s, members of the group met annually, usually in summer at a member's home, where they shared a typical eastern North Carolina feast of fried chicken, ham biscuits, watermelon rind pickles, and summer vegetables. Into the 1960s, some members would meet together at annual meetings of the North Carolina Literary and Historical Association during "culture week" in Raleigh. Roanoke-Chowan Award winners have included Frank Borden Hanes for *Abel Anders* (1953), Carl Sandburg for *Wind Song* (1961), Fred Chappell for *The World between the Eyes* (1972), Reynolds Price for *Vital Provisions* (1983), Kathryn Stripling Byer for *Black Shawl* (1998), and Michael McFee for *Earthly* (2001).

Reference: Gilbert T. Stephenson and Grace Stephenson, *We Came Home to Warren Place* (1959).

Roy Parker Jr.

Roanoke Institution was established in 1829 in Littleton, between Warrenton and Halifax in what was then Warren County. The institution was under the general direction of Capt. Alden Partridge of Norwich, Vt., and under the immediate superintendency of Daniel H. Bingham. Prior to this, Bingham had operated a military school at Williamsboro beginning in January 1827. The aim of the Roanoke Institution was to give each student "a good practical scientific education, to prepare him for the correct and efficient discharge of the duties of any situation in life." Three courses of study—classical, mathematical, and English, plus physical education (including some military training)—were planned.

In September 1829 the school moved to Oxford, the next year opening under Bingham as the North Carolina Literary, Scientific, and Military Institution. Soon thereafter the school was moved to Raleigh, apparently to no success: by late 1832 Bingham had become an engineer on an experimental railroad that Joseph Gales Sr.—in his role as mayor of Raleigh and secretary of the Internal Improvements Board—perceived as a way to convince the General Assembly to rebuild the State Capitol (which had burned in 1831) in Raleigh. In 1833 the *Raleigh Star* announced that Bingham had moved to Alabama to accept a position as rail engineer, and the school presumably ceased to exist.

References: Charles Lee Coon, *North Carolina Schools and Academies, 1790–1840: A Documentary History* (1915); Guion G. Johnson, *Ante-Bellum North Carolina: A Social History* (1937); Elizabeth Reid Murray, *Wake: Capital County of North Carolina* (1983).

Wiley J. Williams

Roanoke Island, Battle of. In February 1862 a Civil War battle was fought at Roanoke Island, situated in the narrow passage of water between Pamlico and Albemarle Sounds. With Union forces in possession of Hatteras Inlet since August 1861, the island was a critical link in North Carolina's defenses, denying Union access to Albemarle Sound, the canals leading to Norfolk, and the upper third of the state's coast. In January 1862 Maj. Gen. Ambrose E. Burnside had arrived at Hatteras Inlet with a Union fleet, intending to sweep through and secure the rivers and sounds of North Carolina. On 5 February he headed north up the sound to attack Roanoke Island.

To defend the island, Brig. Gen. Henry A. Wise commanded less than 2,500 Confederates, most of whom were poorly armed and equipped. Wise himself lay sick in bed at Nags Head, leaving Col. H. M. Shaw of the 8th North Carolina in charge of the island's defense. Reaching Roanoke Island on the morning of 7 February, Burnside's gunboats kept up a long-range bombardment from midmorning until dark. After dark, his ordnance expended, Flag Officer William F. Lynch took his Confederate "mosquito fleet" to Elizabeth City in search of more ammunition and was unable to return for the remainder of the battle. Meanwhile, Burnside landed about 10,000 soldiers on the lower end of Roanoke Island unopposed and prepared to attack the next day.

Shaw's only hope of resisting the Union forces lay in a three-gun battery and a line of entrenchments built across the island, but the works were so narrow that only 400 men could fit into them. Early on 8 February Burnside's First Brigade, under Brig. Gen. John G. Foster, led the advance up the island's road, reaching the Confederate battery and works at about 8:00 A.M. When Foster failed to drive the Confederates from the works, he sent troops through the swamps to flank them.

Assailed simultaneously from all sides, the Confederates were forced to abandon the works and retreat up the island. Shaw, having no second line of defense, surrendered the island, its defenders, and defenses to Burnside. Along with their forts, artillery, and most of their weapons, 2,488 troops capitulated. A handful of Confederates managed to escape from the island to Nags Head and join General Wise as he retreated up the Outer Banks with the remnant of his command.

The Union army's losses at Roanoke Island were 37 killed, 214 wounded, and 13 missing; its navy suffered 1 killed and 13 wounded. In addition to those captured, Confederate losses were 23 killed, 58 wounded, and 62 missing. Six Confederate naval personnel were also wounded. General Burnside now had achieved his first objective—the key to the northeast sounds of North Carolina. His next objective was New Bern.

References: John G. Barrett, *The Civil War in North Carolina* (1963); John S. Carbone, *The Civil War in Coastal North Carolina* (2001); Daniel H. Hill, *Bethel to Sharpsburg*, vol. 1 (1926).

Paul Branch

Theodor de Bry included this plate made from a drawing by John White in his volume *America*, published in 1590. The illustration shows the island of Roanoac, but the only human habitation depicted is an Indian village surrounded by palisades and fields. NCC.

Roanoke Island Festival Park. SEE *Elizabeth II*.

Roanoke River is formed in the Blue Ridge Mountains in Montgomery County, Va., north of the city of Roanoke, by the junction of North Fork and South Fork; it then flows southeast into Warren County, N.C., north of Roanoke Rapids. From there it travels along the Halifax-Northampton, Halifax-Bertie, Bertie-Martin, and Bertie-Washington County lines into Batchelor Bay in the Albemarle Sound. The Roanoke River has appeared under a variety of names in North Carolina history, including Morattico River in 1657 and Noratake River in 1671, but Edward Moseley wrote the name "Roanoke River" on his map of 1733. The river was a source of water for the early settlements in Virginia, North Carolina, and South Carolina.

The Roanoke is dammed several times along its course to form a series of reservoirs. In northeastern North Carolina, the river is impounded to constitute the Lake Gaston reservoir, which stretches north and reaches the John H. Kerr Dam in Virginia, which forms Kerr Lake. Other reservoirs include the Smith Mountain Lake and Leesville Lake. The size of the Roanoke's North Carolina watershed is 3,600 square miles;

the total length of the river is about 410 miles. The river basin encompasses 37 municipalities in the state, including Henderson, Halifax, and Williamston. In the early 2000s the region had a population of more than 275,000. The Roanoke has benefited from conservation efforts by the Nature Conservancy, the North Carolina Wildlife Resources Commission, and other agencies and private organizations. It remains a vital habitat for large numbers of fish, birds, and mammals as well as a principal recreational area for North Carolinians and visitors to the state.

Reference: Garnet Bass, "Roanoke's Dazzling Diversity," *Wildlife in North Carolina* 63 (November 1999).

Elizabeth Bayley

Roanoke Voyages were attempts by Sir Walter Raleigh, under his 1584 patent from Queen Elizabeth I, to establish an English colony in the New World on the coast of present-day North Carolina between 1584 and 1590. The first of these voyages was led by two explorers in Raleigh's employ, Philip Amadas and Arthur Barlowe. On 25 Mar. 1584 Raleigh received a charter from the queen to explore and settle "remote heathen and barbarous lands." Less than a month later, on 27 April, Amadas and Barlowe set out on two ships for the coast of America. They surveyed the Outer Banks and sounds, learning from the local Indians they met that the area was known as "Wingandacoa." After approximately six weeks of discovery and trade, they returned to England with two of the inhabitants of Wingandacoa, the Roanoke Wanchese and the Croatoan Manteo. Barlowe's glowing report of the newly explored land encouraged Raleigh to attempt a settlement the next year.

In January 1585 Raleigh was knighted by Queen Elizabeth and his American possession of Wingandacoa was renamed "Virginia" in honor of the "virgin queen." In April Raleigh sent a seven-vessel fleet commanded by his cousin, Sir Richard Grenville, to establish an English colony in this new region. Grenville explored the Indian towns of Pamlico Sound before deciding to plant an English settlement under Ralph Lane on Roanoke Island. Lane's men built a fort and dwellings on the island, where they remained for almost 11 months. During their sojourn in Virginia, these colonists advanced English explorations to the southern part of the Chesapeake Bay and up the Roanoke and Chowan Rivers. They also cataloged and scientifically tested the commodities of the Native Americans and the natural resources of the region, although they did not discover any source of valuable metals in the Coastal Plain before returning to England in the spring of 1586.

In 1587 John White, an artist in the Grenville expedition of 1585–86, led approximately 150 men, women, and boys to establish a colony in Virginia under a charter from Raleigh. Reluctantly, White ordered the settlers to establish themselves in the town abandoned by Lane. There, on 13 Aug. 1587, the friendly Croatoan Indian Manteo was baptized and made Lord of Roanoke and Dasamunkepeuc by order of Raleigh. On 18 August the colony noted the birth of Virginia Dare, the daughter of colony leader Ananias Dare and his wife Eleanor (the daughter of John White) and the first English child born in the New World. A few days after Virginia's christening, White sailed back to England to encourage and accelerate plans to resupply and reinforce the colony. His departure marked the last known contact between the English and the famous "Lost Colony." When White returned three years later, he found no colonists and only remnants of the structures they had built.

Although Raleigh was unable to establish successful English colonies in America under his 1584 charter, the Roanoke voyages and colonies were valuable precursors to the eventual formation of a permanent English colony at Jamestown, Va., in 1607. The experience and knowledge gained by the English in the 1580s served as an important foundation for later efforts to establish colonies along the coast of North America.

References: Ivor Noel Hume, *The Virginia Adventure, Roanoke to Jamestown: An Archaeological and Historical Odyssey* (1994);

David B. Quinn, *The Roanoke Voyages, 1584–1590* (2 vols., 1955);

Quinn, *Set Fair for Roanoke: Voyages and Colonies, 1584–1606* (1985);

David Stick, *Roanoke Island: The Beginnings of English America* (1983).

Phillip W. Evans

SEE ALSO Amadas and Barlowe Expedition; Lost Colony.

Robeson County,

located in the Coastal Plain region of North Carolina, was formed in 1787 from Bladen County and was named for Revolutionary War colonel Thomas Robeson. The Saura (Cheraw) and Lumbee were the area's earliest inhabitants, followed by Scottish, English, Welsh, and French settlers. Lumberton, the county seat, was incorporated in 1788 and named after the Lumber River. Other communities in the county include Pembroke, Rowland, Maxton, Red Springs, Parkton, Lumber Bridge, Allenton, Alma, and Shannon. Notable physical features of the county, in addition to the Lumber River, include Panther and Horse Pen Branches, Gum Swamp Canal, and Currie and Bear Bays.

Much of Robeson County's history has involved the trials and accomplishments of the Lumbee Indians, North Carolina's largest tribe, who populate the region. One of their most famous tribal members, Henry Berry Lowry, led a band of outlaws in the state during and after the Civil War, at times using violence to bring attention to the plight of the Lumbee. His story is the subject of the long-running outdoor drama *Strike at the Wind!*, performed in Pembroke during the summer months. Lowry's restored cabin is on display at an adjacent recreational area.

Robeson County has a number of historic sites and landmarks, including the Luther Henry Caldwell House, built around 1903; the Carolina Theatre, built in 1927; and the Archie Buie House, built in 1902. Cultural institutions include Robeson Little Theatre, the North Carolina Indian Cultural Center, the Border Belt Farmer's Museum, and the Robeson County Showcase Museum. Robeson County is also home to the University of North Carolina at Pembroke, which was established in 1887 as the Croatan Normal School and became a campus of the consolidated University of North Carolina in 1972. The county hosts festivals such as St. Paul's Annual Festival, Fairmont Farmers Festival, the Native American Wild Game Festival, and the Lumbee Spring Pow Wow.

Agricultural commodities raised in Robeson County include tobacco, cotton, soybeans, vegetables, poultry, hogs, and beef cattle, and manufactures include transformers, water pipes and valves, speakers, textiles, wood products, and manufactured homes. The estimated population of Robeson County in 2004 was 126,500.

Reference: Adolph L. Dial, *The Lumbee* (1993).

Jay Mazzocchi

SEE ALSO Lowry Band; Lumbee Indians; University of North Carolina at Pembroke.

Rocketry Experiments were conducted in two locations along the North Carolina coast from the 1940s to the 1970s. After World War II, the U.S. Navy leased much of Topsail Island (Pender County) as a test range for multistage rockets and ramjet engines. The Kellet Corporation operated the range under navy contract, with assistance from the Johns Hopkins University Applied Physics Laboratory, until 1948, when the navy moved its testing activities to White Sands, N.Mex., and Cape Canaveral, Fla.

From 1962 to 1971 the Atlantic Research Corporation occasionally tested propellants for the Air Force Systems Command and other agencies by firing rocket engines attached to concrete pads at several sites along eight miles of the Currituck Banks. The road that the company desired was not built until after the tests were completed, and the expected flood of new jobs did not materialize. In addition, the task of determining how much of what substances entered the local groundwater from buried steel drums was still unfinished by the early 2000s. Concrete towers built north of Oregon Inlet (Dare County) in 1962 were used not for launching rockets, as rumors insisted, but for monitoring launches by the National Aeronautics and Space Agency from Wallops Island, Va., and Cape Canaveral.

Reference: David A. Stallman, *Operation Bumblebee, 1946–1948, Topsail Island, N.C.* (1992).

Wynne Dough

Rockfish, Battle of. The Revolutionary War engagement called the Battle of Rockfish took place on 2 Aug. 1781 at Rockfish Creek, about one mile south of the present town of Wallace in Duplin County. Earlier that year, on 28 January, a British force led by Maj. James H. Craig had taken possession of the nearby port and town of Wilmington. Under his command were 18 vessels with a full supply of provisions and munitions and 400 regular troops, artillery, and dragoons. Craig used Wilmington as a base from which to foray into the countryside, arresting Whigs and enlisting Loyalists. In the early summer, he issued a proclamation that all men in the surrounding counties were British subjects and must enroll as Loyalist militia. Those who did not do so by 1 August would be harassed and their property seized and sold. On the last day of grace, Craig began to march through the eastern counties.

At Rockfish Creek, he encountered a Whig militia that was ready to contest his passage. Craig advanced with approximately 500 troops and attacked. Sources tell conflicting stories of the battle, although clearly the British prevailed. Craig, with 60 horses and 2 infantry companies, probably was able to encircle the Patriots and surprise them. Half of the Patriots fled before they had a chance to fire their weapons, which apparently were in short supply. It was reported that approximately 30 or 40 Patriots were taken prisoner.

Although the victor at Rockfish, Craig was forced to retreat after 17 Oct. 1781, when Lord Charles Cornwallis surrendered to Gen. George Washington at Yorktown, Va. Craig destroyed any guns, munitions, and supplies that he could not take with him and sailed with his troops to Charles Towne (Charleston, S.C.).

References: Dan L. Morrill, *Southern Campaigns of the American Revolution* (1992); John S. Pancake, *This Destructive War: The British Campaign in the Carolinas, 1780–1782* (1985).

Beverly Tetterton

Rockingham County, located in the Piedmont region of North Carolina, was formed in 1785 from Guilford County and named for Charles Watson-Wentworth, second marquis of Rockingham, the British prime minister at the time of the repeal of the Stamp Act and a supporter of American Independence. It is partially bordered by the state of Virginia. Early inhabitants of the area included the Saura (Cheraw) Indians, followed by English, Scotch-Irish, and German settlers. Wentworth, the county seat, has the same namesake as the county and was incorporated in 1799. Other communities in Rockingham County include Reidsville, Eden (formed in 1967 by the merger of Leaksville, Draper, and Spray), Madison, Ellisboro, Williamsburg, and Ruffin. The Dan and Mayo Rivers flow through the county, as do Beaver, Matrimony, Quaqua, and Lovelace Creeks, among others.

Rockingham County farms produce agricultural goods such as tobacco, corn, peaches, blueberries, apples, blackberries, strawberries, tomatoes, Christmas trees, beef cattle, swine, and horses. Manufactures include textiles, furniture, food products, bricks, carpets, draperies, tobacco products, and plastics.

Among Rockingham County historic sites are the Penn House, built in 1932; the D. F. King House, built in 1875; the Tallula A. Richardson House, built in 1890; the Wright Tavern, erected in 1816; and the Troublesome Creek Ironworks, a Revolutionary War facility. Cultural attractions include the Dan River Arts Market, the Community Concert Series, the Rockingham Community Theatre Guild, and the Rockingham Theatre, the first theater in the state that was built to show sound films. The county also hosts festivals such as Gatsby Day at Chinqua-Penn Plantation, Shiloh Air Show, Mayodan Homecoming Festival, Eden Apple Festival, and the Madison Fair. Rockingham County's 2004 population was estimated to be slightly more than 92,000.

Reference: Lindley S. Butler, *Rockingham County: A Brief History* (1982).

William S. Powell

Rock Music in North Carolina has always been marked by a "do-it-yourself" streak—meaning that some of the state's

Ryan Adams (right) performs with the band Whiskeytown at the Brewery in Raleigh, 1996. Photograph by Marc Kawanishi. *Raleigh News and Observer.*

most notable musicians have practiced their craft while holding down day jobs. In this regard, many local rock artists are not far removed from the Depression-era bluesmen who farmed or worked in textile mills and tobacco warehouses during the week, then picked a little guitar at Saturday night house parties. Clearly there is a historical context for the modern-day underground rock band putting out its own record.

North Carolina has boasted a fair number of rock acts who were bigger and better known elsewhere than at home. Some of the state's key musical exports include Corrosion of Conformity, a Raleigh band that helped pioneer the speed-metal genre in the 1980s; Southern Culture on the Skids, Chapel Hill's aptly named roots-rock band; Petey Pablo, a hip-hop star from Greenville who came to prominence as a protégé of New Orleans rapper Mystikal; and the Connells, a Raleigh pop-rock group who scored a No. 1 hit in Europe and won that continent's equivalent of a Grammy Award in 1995. Several North Carolina natives have also gained fame after leaving the state, including James Taylor, George Clinton, John Coltrane, Loudon Wainwright III, Roberta Flack, former Whiskeytown frontman Ryan Adams, and *American Idol* stars Clay Aiken and Fantasia Barrino.

During the 1970s and 1980s, alternative-leaning groups such as Chapel Hill's Arrogance, Winston-Salem's dB's and Let's Active, and Charlotte's Fetchin' Bones received attention from the national media. A large part of that was due to North Carolina's connection to the Athens, Ga.–based supergroup R.E.M., whose first out-of-state booking was in Carrboro and whose first two albums were recorded in Charlotte and co-produced by Arrogance bassist Don Dixon and Let's Active guitarist Mitch Easter. However, the most commercially successful North Carolina band of this era was Nantucket, a Raleigh-based rock band in the mode of straight-ahead 1970s southern rock acts such as the Allman Brothers and Lynyrd Skynyrd.

During the early 1990s, Superchunk, Archers of Loaf, and other Chapel Hill punk bands received widespread national coverage far out of proportion to their relatively modest sales. At the time, the music industry was desperately seeking another hard-edged, alternative-leaning band with commercial potential. To the amusement of the locals, pundits dubbed Chapel Hill "the next Seattle [home of 1980s and 1990s grunge rock]," a prediction that did not come true.

North Carolina's best-selling bands at the time were actually headquartered halfway across the state in Charlotte—the mainstream pop-metal band Firehouse, whose 1991 debut album sold more than 2 million copies, and gospel-gone-secular rhythm-and-blues quartet Jodeci, which scored three multimillion-selling albums during the first half of the decade with frankly sexual, bump-and-grind seduction ballads.

Chapel Hill finally yielded a couple of surprising million-selling acts in the late 1990s. One was Ben Folds Five, a piano-pop trio with almost no connection to Chapel Hill's underground rock scene (which bandleader Folds sardonically referred to as "40 delusional scenesters"). That did not stop Ben Folds Five's 1997 single "Brick" from turning into a big radio hit, earning the group a coveted performance slot on NBC's *Saturday Night Live* in early 1998. Chapel Hill's other breakout act was the Squirrel Nut Zippers, whose 1930s-style hot jazz produced a left-field hit with "Hell" in 1997 and unwittingly helped launch the short-lived "swing revival."

References: David Menconi, "Marking Time: Durham Rediscovers Its Past as a True House of Blues," *Raleigh News and Observer*, 2 Sept. 2001; Menconi, "North Carolina's Big Musical Bang Explained," *Raleigh News and Observer*, 24 Mar. 1995.

David Menconi

SEE ALSO Blues.

Rocky Mount Mills was founded in Rocky Mount by Joel Battle and two partners in 1818. Its original facility was the second cotton mill built in North Carolina, following the 1814 Schenck-Warlick Mill near Lincolnton. By 1825 Battle was the sole owner of the mills, which were built on a 20-acre tract at the falls of the Tar River. After Battle's death in 1829, the mills were owned by Battle and Brothers, a firm headed by his eldest son, William H. Battle. The *Wilmington Journal* of 19 Feb. 1869 described the original mill as built "of rock—granite—with which the spot so abounds, and three stories high with a basement." The mill was powered by a large dam, which also powered a gristmill.

The mills were run by slave labor until hired workers, most of them girls and women, replaced the slaves in 1852. The Battles usually employed 50 to 60 mill hands, who were paid approximately $2.50 a week during the late 1860s. Many lived near the mill in what were described as "neat white cottages, sufficiently numerous to have the appearance of a village."

As one of the biggest industrial complexes in North Carolina, Rocky Mount Mills became the target of a Union cavalry raid during the Civil War. On 20 July 1863, Brig. Gen. Edward E. Potter's forces raided Rocky Mount and Tarboro, and six cavalry companies were sent to destroy the mills. They burned the cotton mills and gristmill, along with the other buildings and vast amounts of cotton, yarn, flour, and hardtack. According to local tradition, the nearby Battle home was spared because the mill's superintendent persuaded a fellow Mason among the Union officers not to burn the house.

After the Civil War, William S. Battle rebuilt the destroyed Rocky Mount Mills, raising a brick building on the original stone foundations. The rebuilt mill could consume 700 pounds of cotton a day, turning out 500 pounds of cotton yarn and 1,200 yards of shirting. Battle erected another brick building after fire again devastated the mill in 1869. In 1883 financial problems forced him to give up control of the mill, which was reorganized by a board of trustees. Thomas A. Battle, Joel Battle's great-grandson, was elected secretary, and later president, of the new company. The business flourished, and new mill buildings were added in 1889 and 1894.

A combination of increased competition, high cotton prices, and falling demand forced Rocky Mount Mills to close in June 1996, resulting in the loss of 320 jobs. At the time of its closing, Rocky Mount Mills was believed to be the oldest operating cotton mill in the South. The mill and mill village property and buildings have been designated a local historic district and are undergoing extensive redevelopment.

References: Richard L. Mattson, *The History and Architecture of Nash County, North Carolina* (1987); *Rocky Mount Mills: A Case History of Industrial Development, 1818–1943* (1943).

David A. Norris

Rogue's Harbor was an insulting nickname assigned to the Albemarle region of the colony of North Carolina by Virginia officials. The nickname, along with other derogatory labels, suggested that the North Carolina colony was inhabited primarily by debtors, pirates, and other criminals—an image that was associated with the colony for years to come.

Reference: Hugh T. Lefler and Albert Ray Newsome, *North Carolina: The History of a Southern State* (1954).

Laura Young Baxley

Roman Catholic Church is a comparatively small but rapidly growing religious force in North Carolina. A few Catholics, the majority of them English, lived in the region during the colonial period. In *The Natural History of North-Carolina* (1737), John Brickell states that Catholics lived in various places throughout the colony, but "mostly in and about Bath-Town." The first recorded appearance of a priest in the state was in 1784, when Irishman Patrick Cleary settled in New Bern.

The Vatican established an American bishopric at Baltimore in 1789, with John Carroll as the nation's first Catholic bishop. In 1820 southern Catholics were given their own bishop with the appointment of John England as the first bishop of Charleston. England visited North Carolina's scattered flock for the first time in 1821, encountering small numbers of Catholics in various congregations throughout the state—many of them immigrants from diverse countries who were finding it practically impossible to maintain the practice of their faith. England's evangelical efforts during this trip resulted in the conversion of 13 adults and 27 children, several of whom were African American slaves.

A steady influx of Catholic immigrants increased the ranks of the church in North Carolina and throughout the South during the early and mid-nineteenth century. A unique American Catholic identity, born of economic, theological, and cultural struggle, began to develop. Bishop England, acknowledging the lack of religious leadership so vital to Catholic ecclesiology, attempted to encourage lay people to create suitable worship services "so that even when there is no clergyman they may assemble together on the Lord's day" and pray. England's personal charisma and intelligence, and his widely expressed love for the United States and its people, helped North Carolina Catholics avoid much of the animosity experienced by many other Catholics in an overwhelmingly Protestant nation. However, as the number of Catholics grew, a tide of anti-Catholic nativism began to spread, leading to a series of legal and cultural conflicts.

North Carolina's most prominent early Catholic was New Bern lawyer William Gaston, who, after serving in the state legislature from 1813 to 1817, became a member of the North Carolina Supreme Court. In that capacity, he championed religious freedom and argued against the state constitutional ban on Catholics holding public office. The state's first Catholic church was built in Washington in 1828. Churches were also erected before the Civil War in Raleigh (1834), Gaston County (two in 1843), and Charlotte (1852). In 1860 there were 350 Catholics in seven parishes in North Carolina.

A large migration of Catholics from the North and Midwest, relocating primarily for economic reasons, resulted in remarkable growth in the South's Catholic population during the twentieth century, particularly after 1960. As church rolls continued to swell, many new parishes and schools were established in North Carolina. In 1972 the Diocese of Charlotte was formed out of the Diocese of Raleigh, with jurisdiction over 46 of the state's western counties. During the 1970s, the number of Catholics in the state increased by 37 percent, although they continued to make up less than 2 percent of the state's total population (one of the smallest percentages in the nation).

North Carolina's Catholic population during the 1990s continued to be characterized by rapid growth, strained resources, and a sometimes critical dearth of priests. Two diocesan newspapers, *NC Catholics* in Raleigh and the *Catholic News and Herald* in Charlotte, cover local issues and events as well as national and international news. The church has been further transformed by the arrival in the state of a huge number of Latinos, most of whom are Catholic and many of whom have turned to the church for social and financial support as well as religious instruction. By the early 2000s, there were approximately 325,000 registered Catholics in North Carolina parishes, with a nearly equal number of unregistered but active Latino Catholics in the state.

References: Jeremiah Joseph O'Connell, *Catholicity in the Carolinas and Georgia: Leaves of Its History, A.D. 1820–A.D. 1878* (1972); William F. Powers, *Tar Heel Catholics: A History of Catholicism in North Carolina* (2003); Yonat Shimron and Angela Paik, "Tradition, Modern Trends Meld: Face of Catholic Priesthood Is Changing as the Church Grows," *Raleigh News and Observer*, 28 June 1998; Stephen C. Worsley, "Catholicism in Antebellum North Carolina," *NCHR* 60 (1983).

Jay Mazzocchi

Root Doctors are the traditional healers and conjurers of the rural, black South. They use herbs, roots, potions, and spells to help and sometimes to hurt recipients of their ministrations. Root doctors are still common in the region and found in many rural areas of North Carolina. The practice of "working roots" is familiar to many African Americans living in the South, though apparently not as commonly known today among whites. Voodoo is a more widely known version of the conjuring tradition most associated in the popular imagination with New Orleans, although the term "voodoo" or "hoodoo doctor" was commonly applied to root doctors in other parts of the South.

The ideas and practices that came to define the root doctor undoubtedly had their origins in the folk beliefs of West Africa, the region of origin of many of the people brought to the South as slaves in the seventeenth and eighteenth centuries. The root doctor traditionally treats natural ailments with various remedies made from such plants as mint, jimson weed, sassafras, and milkweed. Some remedies have genuine medicinal properties, while others are at least soothing, and the psychosomatic effect of any remedy cannot be underestimated. Treating a victim of a spell is more complicated. The individual might be sick, inexplicably drawn to someone, or experiencing profound anxiety. The doctor must first discover if conjuring is the cause of the problem. The severity and suddenness with which the symptoms appeared may provide a clue, or sometimes physical evidence of the spell exists. A powder, often known as "goofer dust," may be found. Once the doctor determines that the problem is a spell, he or she must prescribe the proper rituals and potions to restore harmony to the patient's life.

Root doctors may also be asked to "put a root" on someone, a process that often involves concocting goofer dust from such elements as graveyard dirt and powdered snake or lizard. A wife may ask a root doctor to put a root on her husband to stop him from seeing other women, while a man pining for a woman might ask the doctor to work a spell on the object of his affection. Finally, root doctors may also prescribe a "mojo" to ward off spells. One North Carolina mojo described in several sources is a dime worn around the ankle. A small bag filled with a preparation made of various plant and animal ingredients and worn around the neck has also been a popular mojo. In an often hostile and capricious world, the mojos, spells, and herbal preparations of the root doctor have provided believers with treatment of their ills, protection, a way of hurting enemies and attracting lovers, and, importantly, a sense that they need not be passive victims of circumstance or fate.

References: Wayland D. Hand, ed., *Popular Beliefs and Superstitions from North Carolina*, vols. 6 and 7 (1961, 1964); Lawrence W. Levine, *Black Culture and Black Consciousness* (1978); Holly Matthews, "Doctors and Root Doctors: Patients Who Use Both," in James Kirkland and others, eds., *Herbal and Magical Medicine: Traditional Healing Today* (1992).

John J. Beck

Ropewalks were sites where hemp fiber was spun into yarn and then twine, cord, and rope of various dimensions. The name derived from the fact that production required the artisan, called the spinner, literally to walk backward many feet, carrying the hemp yarn and gradually feeding out lengths of it as it was twisted into rope by a turning wheel. Colonial American shipbuilders and merchants initially depended on British ropewalks for supplying cordage and cables, but soon colonists began making these products themselves.

The earliest and best-known ropewalk in North Carolina was established at Edenton in 1783 by Josiah Collins Sr. and Samuel Johnston (as silent partner and one-third owner). The site, located on a 131-acre tract on the east side of town parallel with Oakum Street, included the ropewalk, a wheelhouse, and two yarn houses. While the shipbuilding industry continued to boom, the Collins ropewalk manufactured hawsers, cables, and cordage of all kinds necessary for rigging ships. Its products in 1795 were said to be superior to any imported ones. At the turn of the century, the decline in local shipbuilding coincided with the rise of seine fisheries in the Albemarle Sound area; from that time forward, the Collins ropewalk produced seine twine, hanging twine, leading line, sinking line, ratline, rope up to three inches in circumference, and other products.

The Collins ropewalk remained in operation until 1839. A rival ropewalk specializing in cordage and seine twine had been established at New Bern by the early nineteenth century. Although its range of products was not so extensive as the Collins ropewalk, the New Bern ropewalk made sewing and whipping twine and bed cords as well as the usual seine cordage. A third ropewalk was erected at Plymouth in about 1818.

Rope making appears to have been a craft practiced at times by slaves in North Carolina. During the eighteenth century, when ropewalks specialized in supplying shipbuilders' needs, as many as 18 skilled male slave artisans were constantly employed. During the nineteenth century, when the output was primarily cordage and twine for commercial seine fisheries, ropewalks employed about a dozen male and female slaves.

Reference: Carl Bridenbaugh, *The Colonial Craftsman* (1950).

George Stevenson

Rosedale, a handsome plantation house about three miles from downtown Charlotte, is considered one of the finest examples of Federal architecture in North Carolina. Particularly notable is the original woodwork in the parlors, done in the classical style of eighteenth-century English architect Robert Adam. When Rosedale was built around 1815, its elegant Palladian style contrasted sharply with that of the log-and-plank homes common to the area. The neighbors called it "Frew's Folly," after its owner Archibald Frew, a local merchant and tax collector. Frew's business is said to have carried him often to the coastal cities of the state, where Federal architecture was fashionable. This may explain the superior detail of the house. He is also said to have purchased furnishings for it while traveling in Europe. The original French-style wallpaper in an upstairs bedroom seems to verify this claim.

In 1818 Frew encountered financial difficulties and sold the house and 911 acres to satisfy warrants issued by the comptroller of the treasury of the United States. William Davidson, whose sister was married to Frew, bought the property through agents. Davidson was a wealthy and prominent citizen of Mecklenburg County, who served as a state senator and U.S. congressman.

The house remained in the Davidson family until 1986, when sisters Mary Louise Davidson and Alice Davidson Abel sold Rosedale and its eight remaining acres to the Historic Preservation Foundation of North Carolina. In 1987 the Colonial Dames raised enough money to enable the newly formed Historic Rosedale Foundation to purchase the house and begin restoration. Rosedale is open to the public on Sunday afternoons. Its grounds contain trees designated by Mecklenburg County as official "treasure trees" for their age and size.

References: Pat Borden Gubbins, "Christmas at Rosedale," *Charlotte Observer*, 1 Dec. 1996; Mary Norton Kratt, *Charlotte: Spirit of the New South* (1992).

Rosemary Clifford Neill

Rosenwald Fund. From the 1910s through the 1930s, the philanthropic Julius Rosenwald Fund was a major force in North Carolina education. Its matching grants aided in the construction of more than 800 public school buildings for African American children and helped found the University of North Carolina Press in Chapel Hill.

Soon after becoming president of Sears, Roebuck and Company in 1909, Julius Rosenwald of Chicago became interested in black education, influenced in part by the book *Up from Slavery*, by African American educator Booker T. Washington of Alabama's Tuskegee Institute. Rosenwald met Washington in 1911 and soon became a trustee of Tuskegee. When Rosenwald earmarked his first $25,000 in 1912 for black colleges and preparatory academies, Washington asked to use a small sum for grants to black communities near Tuskegee for building rural elementary schools. Rosenwald consented, with the stipulation that each community must match the gift.

By Washington's death in 1915, Rosenwald had given matching funds to around 80 schools in a three-state area. One of these was a two-teacher school in North Carolina's Chowan County, completed in October 1915. The black community contributed $486, the white community and school system added $836, and Rosenwald gave $300. Such results spurred him to formally establish the Julius Rosenwald Fund two years later. The Tuskegee staff administered the fund until 1920, when the volume of applications and school-building projects led Rosenwald to set up an office in Nashville, Tenn. To run the program, he hired Samuel Leonard Smith, a school administrator who also had expertise in country schoolhouse design.

Public funds generally covered about half the cost of a school building, with the remainder divided equally between local, private contributions and the Rosenwald Fund. North Carolina led the South in the number of Rosenwald school buildings erected (813 of the 5,300 total), largely due to the efforts of leaders such as Nathan Carter Newbold, the state's director of black education. With 46 schools, Halifax County had by far the greatest number of schools in a single county built with Rosenwald funds.

In the late 1920s, Rosenwald Fund administrators began to expand their efforts, financing projects such as hospitals, libraries, and publishers of reports and texts on southern social and educational problems. Rosenwald funding helped establish the University of North Carolina Press in Chapel Hill, the South's first academic press.

Most Rosenwald schools continued to operate across the state until consolidation and racial desegregation in the 1960s closed their doors. A few, such as those in Zebulon and Wilkesboro, were still operational schools in the early 2000s, while most of these remaining historic landmarks serve as community centers, homes, and businesses. Extant Rosenwald schools adapted to other purposes include senior citizens' housing in Asheboro, the Raleigh Catholic Diocese offices near Smithfield, and the Town Hall at Princeville.

References: Edwin R. Embree and Julia Waxman, *Investment in People: The Story of the Julius Rosenwald Fund* (1949); Thomas W. Hanchett, "The Rosenwald Schools and Black Education in North Carolina," *NCHR* 65 (October 1988); James L. Leloudis, *Schooling the New South: Pedagogy, Self, and Society in North Carolina, 1880–1920* (1996).

K. Todd Johnson

Rose's Stores. In 1915 Paul Howard Rose purchased a stock of merchandise from a failing firm (United Stores) in Henderson and opened a five-and-dime store. With the success of that first store, Rose subsequently opened more stores. In May 1927 the firm was incorporated in Delaware as Rose's 5, 10 and 25 Cents Stores. The name was changed to Rose's, Inc., in 1962. By the late 1980s the chain had some 280 stores in 11 southeastern and border states.

At the height of its success, Rose's had three distribution warehouses, a fixture manufacturing plant, a New York buying office, and a fleet of trucks. Beginning in the late 1980s, however, the company experienced serious problems stemming from a failed merchandising strategy, unstable top management, and an inability to compete with Wal-Mart, K-Mart, and other large national chains. In September 1993 the company filed for Chapter 11 Bankruptcy protection from creditors. By May 1995 the firm, now named Rose's Stores, Inc., had successfully emerged from bankruptcy.

In December 1997 Art and John Pope, owners of Variety Wholesalers, Inc., of Raleigh, one of the largest family-run companies in North Carolina and owner of other discount retailers such as Maxway and Bargain Town, bought the 106 remaining Rose's stores for $15.3 million. Some key Rose's executives were retained, including Ed Anderson, who became president and chief financial officer of Variety Wholesalers. Rose's, based in Henderson, continued to streamline operations and cut prices in an effort to win back customers lost during the days of the bankruptcy protection.

Reference: George T. Blackburn, *Heritage of Vance County* (1984).

Wiley J. Williams

Round Knob Hotel Affair was a major political event in North Carolina in the late 1890s, pitting the Fusionist administration of Governor Daniel L. Russell Jr. against the state's Railroad Commission in a contest over the reduction of rates. The three-person Railroad Commission, created in 1891, was authorized to set passenger and freight rates for state railroads and to determine the valuation of railroad property for tax purposes. In the 1890s railroad rates constituted a significant political issue, largely because their reform was demanded by organized agricultural shippers in the state Farmers' Alliance and Populist Party.

After the triumph of Populist-Republican Fusion in the election of 1896, the new Republican governor Russell encouraged the Railroad Commission to reduce rates and increase taxes on railroads. Yet the commission did not dramatically lower rates in 1897. Russell, supported by influential reformers, including Populist U.S. senator Marion Butler and North Carolina Supreme Court justice Walter Clark, did not accept this defeat quietly. Russell wanted to ensure that in the future the commission would be vigorously antirailroad.

Conveniently, even before the failure of rate reduction, Russell's attention had been drawn to a possible breach of public trust by two railroad commissioners, James W. Wilson and S. Otho Wilson (no relation). The governor's concerns focused on the Round Knob Hotel, a resting and eating place on a branch of J. P. Morgan's Southern Railway Company between Hickory and Asheville. James Wilson had built the Round Knob in 1881 in partnership with A. B. Andrews, the North Carolina lobbyist for the Southern Railway. In the 1890s James Wilson leased the Round Knob to Otho Wilson's mother, and it was used as a dinner station for Southern Railway passenger trains.

On 24 Aug. 1897 Governor Russell, acting pursuant to a section in the Railroad Commission law allowing him to remove from office any commissioner having an interest in a railroad, demanded that the Wilsons show cause why they should not be removed. Although James immediately replied that he had sold his interest in the Round Knob because of concerns raised by Russell's order, and Otho tried to distance himself from his mother's business, Russell suspended the Wilsons on 23 September. Initially the two commissioners refused to vacate their offices, but after a legal battle the Fusionist state supreme court, with the vote of Walter Clark, upheld Russell's right to remove them.

The Round Knob Hotel affair highlighted the aggressiveness of Russell, the sensitivity of the more radical Fusionist reformers to the corruptive power of the railroads, and the increasing importance of the regulatory authority of North Carolina government. Ironically, the incident helped splinter Fusionist ranks by further isolating Russell from some Republicans, tainted Fusionist rule with scandal, and raised serious ethical questions about the political activities of Justice Clark. Because the 1899 Democratic legislature abolished the Railroad Commission, the affair also confirmed the commission's limitations, North Carolina's first extensive experiment with administrative government.

References: Francis Bowditch, "The North Carolina Railroad Commission, 1891–1899" (M.A. thesis, UNC-Chapel Hill, 1943); Jeffrey J. Crow and Robert F. Durden, *Maverick Republican in the Old North State: A Political Biography of Daniel L. Russell* (1977).

James L. Hunt

SEE ALSO Railroad Commission.

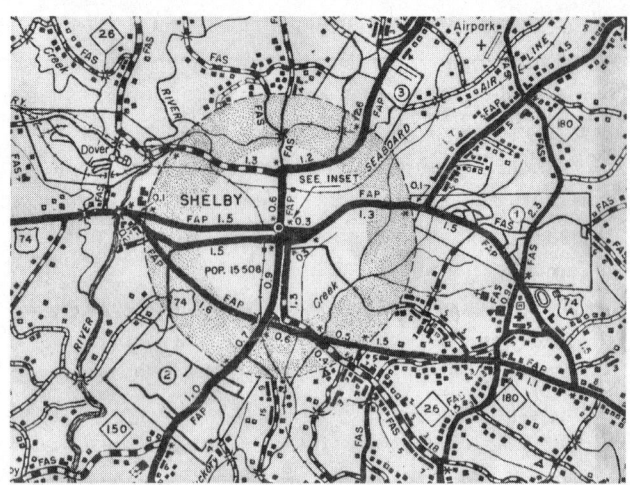

Map of Shelby, a round town until 1957. NCC.

Round Towns are incorporated towns in which the boundaries are fixed at a certain distance from a central landmark, forming a circle. In North Carolina round towns first arose in the early nineteenth century, when many new towns were incorporated. The state had 34 "true" round towns in 1968, along with several other former round towns that had altered their circular shapes by annexation; the number in 1990 had fallen to 27. In 1990 Cleveland County was home to the largest number of round towns in one county, with seven: Waco, Lattimore, Earl, Mooresboro, Polkville, Casar, and Belwood, the last of which is shared with Lincoln County.

The boundaries of each round town are detailed in town charters in the various volumes of North Carolina laws. For instance, the boundaries of the Chatham County town of Goldston, incorporated in 1907, were "a radius of one-half mile from the depot of the Southern Railway Company at Goldston." The town limits of Newland, incorporated in 1913, were "120 rods" from the Avery County Courthouse. The Northampton County town of Milwaukee, incorporated in 1915, fixed its town limits at a one-mile radius from the center of the crossroads in the town.

Other landmarks used by round towns to set boundaries include a railroad bridge (Waco, incorporated in 1907) and the center of the local high school building (Boiling Springs, in Cleveland County, incorporated in 1911 but no longer a round town). The town limits of Bear Grass, incorporated in Martin County in 1909, were "all that territory within a radius of five hundred yards from a certain white oak on the east side of the public road, near a well at the stores of Rogers Brothers and Cowing Brothers."

One of North Carolina's early round towns was the Cleveland County seat of Shelby, incorporated by an act of the General Assembly in 1843. The original town boundary formed a circle with a quarter-mile radius, beginning at the courthouse. In 1901 the town limits were increased to a radius

of three-quarters of a mile from the courthouse and in 1928 increased again to a radius of a mile and a half. Shelby remained a round town until the annexation of a development in 1957, which altered its circular shape. Several later annexations added more "bumps" to the town limits. By 1976 the city council had begun changing the town limits to conform with property lines, but Shelby's boundaries still contained traces of its days as a round town.

Round towns are also found in Indiana, Georgia, and Mississippi, states to which many North Carolinians emigrated in antebellum times.

David A. Norris

Rowan County, located in the Piedmont region of North Carolina, was formed in 1753 from Anson County and was named for Matthew Rowan, the governor of North Carolina at the time of the county's establishment. Early inhabitants of the area included the Catawba and Saponi Indians, followed by German and Scotch-Irish settlers. Salisbury, the county seat, was incorporated in 1755 and was named after the cathedral town in England; during much of the nineteenth century, it was the largest city in western North Carolina and served as a major center of trade and politics. Other communities in the county include Spencer, East Spencer, China Grove, Bear Poplar, Mount Ulla, Millbridge, Faith, Craven, and part of Kannapolis, extending up from Cabarrus County. Notable physical features of the county include the Yadkin River, High Rock Lake, Dunn Mountain, and Panther and Beaverdam Creeks.

Catawba College (1851) and Livingstone College (1879) are located in Rowan County, which also is home to several landmarks and historic sites, such as Old Stone House, the county's oldest building, constructed around 1766. This and other sites are run by Rowan Museum, Inc. Other significant landmarks include the Confederate Prison and the Gold Hill Mining District. Cultural institutions in Rowan County include the North Carolina Transportation Museum at Spencer Shops, Waterworks Visual Arts Center, Catawba College's Shuford School of Performing Arts, and the Catawba Community Children's Chorus. The county hosts festivals and annual events such as the Rowan County Agricultural Fair, the National Sportscaster and Sportswriters Hall of Fame Awards, the Old Miners Jubilee, Santa Claus Special, the Rockwell Craft Festival, and Take Pride in Granite Day.

Rowan County produces agricultural goods such as horticultural crops and livestock. Manufactured products include polyester fiber, trucks, textiles, yarn, furnaces, furniture, and mobile homes. The population of Rowan County was estimated to be 133,000 in 2004.

Reference: James S. Brawley, *Rowan County: A Brief History* (1977).

Jay Mazzocchi

SEE ALSO Confederate Prison (Salisbury).

Royal Cake Company, one of the oldest and largest bakeries in the United States, was established in Winston-Salem in 1925 as Easley Cookie Company, with David W. Easley as owner. Gray G. Welch and Henry Hicks bought the company in 1926. With Welch as president and Hicks as secretary-treasurer, the firm became Royal Cake Company in the mid-1930s. By the 1950s, Royal Cake's cream-filled oatmeal cookies (the firm's best seller) and 20 other types of pastries—including chocolate chip cream-filled cookies, banana marshmallow pies, Swiss rolls, brownie rounds, and fruit-filled cereal bars—were available in convenience stores, grocery chains, vending machines, and other venues in all states east of the Mississippi River. In the early 2000s Royal Cake Company, headed by CEO James B. Whitney, had 200 full-time employees and more than $30 million in annual sales.

Reference: Lynn Jessup, "Royal Cake Company: Creme-Filled Creations," *Our State* 69 (May 2002).

Wiley J. Williams

Royal Knights of King David was an organization formed in 1883 by John Merrick, modeled after a similar group in Georgia. Merrick, a black Durham businessman who owned a chain of five barbershops, incorporated the North Carolina body in his own name, with W. G. Pearson as president. Organized as a fraternal and social group with religious overtones, the Royal Knights also provided insurance for members; indeed, providing insurance was one of the primary objectives Merrick envisioned for the organization.

A "Lady Knights Department" was formed in order "to unite fraternally all acceptable colored women of any reputable profession, business or organization" to assist one another. Membership included provisions for life insurance coverage and burial expenses. The constitution of the Durham unit permitted as many as six men to join the Lady Knights, but they were not allowed to vote or hold office, and their primary purpose was to act as pallbearers at the funerals of members.

In 1898 Merrick built upon the insurance activities of the Royal Knights to organize the business that became the North Carolina Mutual Life Insurance Company.

References: R. McCants Andrews, *John Merrick: A Biographical Sketch* (1920); Walter B. Weare, *Black Business in the New South* (1973).

William S. Powell

SEE ALSO North Carolina Mutual Life Insurance Company.

Royal North Carolina Regiment was the premier provincial corps of Loyalist North Carolinians during the Revolutionary War. Provincial corps were regiments that served with British forces; their organization and procedures mirrored those of the British regular troops, but their actual status was somewhere between the British regulars and the Loyalist militia. In issues regarding rank, provincial officers were counted as one rank lower than their regular counterparts. This and other indications of a lesser, "colonial" status rankled provincial officers, particularly those of the Royal North Carolina Regiment, most of whom were Scots. Following the suppression of the 1745 Jacobite Revolt, Scotsmen had been encouraged to join the royal service, with the promise of honorable treatment and equal opportunity for advancement.

The regiment's origins lay in some of the commissions with which Governor Josiah Martin prepared for the Loyalist uprising that met defeat at the Battle of Moore's Creek Bridge in February 1776. Martin called his unit the North Carolina Highland Regiment. The force that Martin coordinated consisted largely of Scottish Highlanders in the Upper Cape Fear area and former Regulators from deeper in the interior. They intended to assist British troops who were expected to land in the Cape Fear estuary early in 1776. The troops did not arrive as scheduled, and with the British rout at the Battle of Moore's Creek Bridge, many North Carolina Highlanders were captured or fled the area, making their way to British forces wherever they could reach them over the next four years.

Meanwhile, in 1777 North Carolina Loyalist John Hamilton refused the state oath of allegiance in Halifax County, where most of his property was located, before leaving for the British installation at New York. In New York, Hamilton offered his services and his armed brig *Britannia* for the imminent invasion of the South. The expedition commander, Lt. Col. Archibald Campbell, authorized a new provincial corps, the North Carolina Volunteers, with Hamilton as commander. About 30 men of the new corps, most or all of them officers, were aboard the *Britannia* when Campbell's forces landed in Georgia during the final days of 1778, thus opening the Southern campaign.

Hamilton's North Carolina Volunteers helped defend Savannah against Adm. Count Charles Hector d'Estaing's attack and then fought at Briar Creek, Kettle Creek, Stone Ferry, Moncks Corner, and Guilford Courthouse. When Lord Charles Cornwallis left Wilmington, at least 114 of them accompanied him into Virginia and defeat at Yorktown, while others were transferred from Wilmington back to Charles Towne (present-day Charleston, S.C.) in November 1781.

When exchanged to the British in New York, the North Carolina Volunteers were grouped with a unit of the New York Volunteers and traveled with them to New Brunswick, Canada, where they settled. Allen Stewart was the spokesman for this group, which included a number of his relatives and some African Americans who had served in a company of Black Pioneers under Stewart's supervision. Thomas Peters, a former resident of the Cape Fear area and the leading spokesmen for black Loyalist settlers in Nova Scotia, was a sergeant in this unit.

The North Carolina Highlanders were reactivated in 1781 during the Southern campaign, with recruiters going from the British-held areas of South Carolina to North Carolina and acting under Martin's 1776 commissions. In 1782 the companies that had remained in South Carolina were joined by the North Carolina Highlanders and John Hamilton's North Carolina Volunteers to constitute the Royal North Carolina Regiment. Hamilton, now a lieutenant colonel, was named commander of the consolidated corps, which embodied more than 1,100 men in the course of the war, with a peak strength of about 750 men. Its losses were heaviest at Hanging Rock and Camden.

After the British evacuated Charles Towne in the fall of 1782, the Royal North Carolina Regiment transferred to St. Mark's garrison fort in St. Augustine, Fla., along with the South Carolina Royalists and the King's Carolina Rangers (a largely Georgia corps). Hamilton led them as the senior provincial officer under the garrison commander, Gen. Archibald McArthur. In February there were rumbles of mutiny in outrage over the British cession of East Florida and West Florida to Spain, but Hamilton's decisive leadership thwarted it. In June 1783 the Royal North Carolina Regiment numbered 496 men in East Florida, with 156 men still listed as "prisoners with the enemy."

When the British pulled out of East Florida, they offered members of the Royal North Carolina Regiment transportation to Britain, the Bahamas, or Nova Scotia, but about one-quarter of the corpsmen did not go. About 30 officers of the regiment went to Britain, and a few men accompanied McArthur to the Bahamas. Approximately 45 percent of the regiment went to Nova Scotia, along with smaller proportions of the King's Carolina Rangers and South Carolina royalists. They settled together at Country Harbour, about 100 miles east of Halifax. Some of the former corpsmen moved to other parts of Nova Scotia, to New Brunswick, to Scotland, to the Bahamas, and also back to North Carolina. Hamilton, after an unsuccessful bid for the governorship of the Bahamas, became British consul at Norfolk.

References: John S. Pancake, *This Destructive War: The British Campaign in the Carolinas, 1780–1782* (1985); Hugh F. Rankin, *North Carolina in the American Revolution* (1959); Carole Watterson Troxler, "'The Great Man of the Settlement': North Carolina's John Legett at Country Harbour, Nova Scotia, 1783–1812," *NCHR* 67 (July 1990).

Carole Watterson Troxler

Rule of Three (or Rule of Proportion) was the term for the mathematical formula used to find a fourth, unknown number from three given numbers, when the first is in the same proportion to the second as the third is to the unknown fourth. In the eighteenth century, masters of apprentices were sometimes required to teach them to write and decipher to the rule of three. Among the apprentices to whom this applied were tailors, house carpenters, cordwainers, and others; girls who were apprenticed to learn to spin, weave, or other domestic arts were not required to be so taught. In their last wills, fathers sometimes inserted the stipulation that sons be taught arithmetic to this point. In 1816 North Carolina Quakers opened a school where black males could be taught to read and decipher to the rule of three but females would only be taught to write.

Reference: John Hope Franklin, "Slaves Virtually Free in North Carolina," *Journal of Negro History* 28 (July 1943).

William S. Powell

Rural Electrification. Although electric generation began in North Carolina in the 1880s, for most of the next 50 years electric service was primarily available only in the state's cities and towns. Extension to rural areas in the late nineteenth and early twentieth centuries was slow. The development of electric cooperatives, particularly between 1935 and 1960, radically changed rural life in North Carolina.

The onset of rural economic depression and a change in political climate led to increased awareness of the need for rural electric service during the 1930s. In April 1935 the General Assembly created the North Carolina Rural Electrification Authority (NCREA). Alone, however, the potential of this organization was not great. It had no independent power to set rates or to order the construction of new lines but merely worked with the state's existing electric companies to expand service or petition the North Carolina Utilities Commission. Nonetheless, North Carolina was among the first states to attempt to implement its own rural electrification program.

The role of the NCREA was transformed when, beginning in May 1935, President Franklin D. Roosevelt's New Deal provided money for the extension of electric lines to rural areas through the federal Rural Electrification Authority (REA). The REA subsequently established electric membership corporations (EMCs) as the local mechanism for the extension of electricity to farmers. Nonprofit corporations with authority to own and construct facilities to provide electricity to unserved areas, EMCs were composed of member-customers who paid dues and elected a local board of directors. In North Carolina, the authority for organizing and providing electric service was the North Carolina Electric Membership Corporation Act of 1935. Under state law, EMCs were created upon application to the NCREA. EMCs could not get direct loans from the federal government but had to apply through the NCREA.

The effect of federal dollars and state and local organization was dramatic. In 1935 roughly 3 percent of North Carolina farmers had electricity. The NCREA sent power through its first distribution line in May 1936. By 1940 about 24 percent, or 70,000 of the state's 278,000 farms, had electricity. Only 15 years later, in the mid-1950s, more than 95 percent of North Carolina's farms were electrified. Electricity changed not only personal living conditions on farms, providing light and the possibility of new appliances, but it allowed the use of refrigeration and other electric production devices.

In 1958 EMCS in western and eastern North Carolina merged into the North Carolina Electric Membership Corporation. By 2006, North Carolina's 27 electric membership corporations were serving approximately 2.4 million customers. The corporations' service and territorial boundaries are regulated by the North Carolina Utilities Commission.

References: D. Clayton Brown, "North Carolina Rural Electrification: Precedent of the REA," NCHR 59 (Spring 1982); Ken Soo, "Marking a Powerful Milestone: 50 Years Ago, Advent of Electricity Co-ops Began Brightening the Lives of Farm Families," Charlotte Observer, 12 May 1985.

James L. Hunt

SEE ALSO North Carolina Rural Electrification Authority.

Rutherford College,

Rutherford College, a forerunner of Brevard College, was established in 1853 by the Reverend Robert Laban Abernethy as a private school known as Owl Hollow Schoolhouse in Burke County. It was built on 600 acres of forestland given by John Rutherford. In 1858 the school was chartered as Rutherford Seminary; Brantley York served as a professor on its faculty in later years. In 1900 the school came under control of the Methodist Church. It was a coeducational institution, and one-fourth of the students were admitted tuition-free. Reportedly, more than 4,000 students matriculated at Rutherford College throughout its existence. In the early 1930s, Rutherford College and Weaver College merged with Brevard Institute at Brevard to become Brevard College.

References: George W. Bumgarner and James Elwood Carroll, *The Flowering of Methodism in Western North Carolina* (1984); Elmer T. Clark, *Methodism in Western North Carolina* (1966).

Grady L. E. Carroll Sr.

Rutherford County, located on the border of the Piedmont and Mountain regions of North Carolina, was formed in 1770 and named after Revolutionary War general Griffith Rutherford, a member of the North Carolina Provincial Congress. Early inhabitants of the area included the Cherokee Indians, followed by Scotch-Irish, German, French, Swiss, and English settlers. Rutherfordton, the county seat, was incorporated in 1787 and has the same namesake as the county. Other Rutherford County communities include Forest City, Harris, Ellenboro, Union Mills, Sunshine, Thermal City, and Chimney Rock. The Bechtler Mint, established in 1831 near Rutherfordton, minted more than $2 million in gold coins from 1831 until the late 1840s.

The Lake Lure region, including Chimney Rock, is an important tourist area, adding revenue to the county's economy. Filmmaking has also been important to Rutherford County, which was the site of the filming, at least in part, of the popular movies *Last of the Mohicans* (1992), *Dirty Dancing* (1987), and *Firestarter* (1984). Rutherford County is also home to historic sites and landmarks such as the Carrier-McBrayer House (ca. 1835) and the Lake Lure Inn and Resort (1920s). Cultural institutions include the Forest City Performing Arts Guild, Isothermal Community College Players and Singers, Shakespeare's Globe Theatre, and Gem Hill Ruby Mine. The county hosts festivals and annual events such as the Easter Sunrise Service in Chimney Rock Park, Chimney Rock Sports Car Hill Climb, and Lake Lure Dogwood Festival.

Rutherford County produces timber and forest products and its farms raise soybeans, wheat, corn, cotton, pumpkins, Christmas trees, watermelons, strawberries, beef cattle, poultry, and hogs. Manufactures include textiles, apparel, furniture, bricks, concrete products, and bronze castings. The county is also home to minerals such as garnet, granite, gneiss, beryl, quartz, galena, fuchsite, corundum, and diamonds. In 2004 Rutherford County's population was estimated at 63,200.

Jay Mazzocchi

SEE ALSO Chimney Rock.

Rutherford's Campaign was North Carolina's contribution to a multistate military effort, planned early in the Revolutionary War, to break the power of the Cherokee before they could combine with the British against the rebels. Cherokee leaders such as Dragging Canoe saw the outbreak of the Revolution as a chance to reclaim lands taken by the settlers of the Carolinas and Georgia. British Indian agents John Stuart and Alexander Cameron, interested in gaining full advantage from the Cherokee force in the fight against the American independence movement, tried unsuccessfully to prevent the Cherokee from going to war until they could coordinate their attacks with the arrival of regular British forces. Between April and July 1776, several dozen frontier settlers were killed; hundreds were besieged in frontier forts, and Cherokee raiders reached the western banks of the Catawba River across from Mecklenburg County.

Brig. Gen. Griffith Rutherford, commander of the militia in the Salisbury District, wrote the North Carolina Council of Safety on 5 June 1776 for permission to strike deep into Cherokee territory. He also proposed that South Carolina and Virginia participate in the attack. At the same time, unknown to Rutherford, Gen. Charles Lee, commander of the Continental troops in the South, and John Rutledge, president of the South Carolina Council of Safety, were asking North Carolina and Virginia to join such a campaign.

North Carolina's forces, under Rutherford, were to besiege the Middle and Valley Cherokee towns in western North Carolina, while forces from other states would assault the Cherokees in other areas. Despite consenting to the ambitious plans, the three state governments could not launch their attacks at the same time. Communication between each state was slow, and the need for action compelled each one to strike as soon as their troops were assembled. South Carolina moved first, sending 1,100 men under Col. Andrew Williamson against the Lower Cherokee towns at the end of July.

At Davidson's Fort at the head of the Catawba, Rutherford gathered his forces. On 1 Sept. 1776 he marched toward the mountains with about 1,700 troops, leaving about 400 men to protect forts in Tryon, Rowan, and Surry Counties. Rutherford crossed the Blue Ridge at Swannanoa Gap and followed portions of the Swannanoa River, Hominy Creek, the Pigeon River, and Richland Creek. They saw no Indians until reaching the latter stream on 6 September. Later that day, at Scott's Creek (a tributary of the Tuckasegee River), the first blood of the campaign was shed. A slave belonging to John Scott, an Indian trader, was mistaken for an Indian and was shot by the Reverend James Hall, chaplain of the expedition.

Over the next few days Rutherford's troops destroyed several mostly deserted Cherokee towns, including the Indians' cornfields and food supplies. On 16 September Rutherford and 1,200 men left Nuquassee to attack the Valley towns, leaving his remaining troops to wait for Williamson. When Williamson arrived at Nuquassee on 18 September, the South Carolinians marched after Rutherford. At Wayah Gap, they were ambushed by Cherokees and lost 12 men killed and 20 wounded in a two-hour battle before driving off the Indians.

On 26 September Williamson and Rutherford linked forces on the Hiwassee. They decided against continuing the campaign to the Overhill towns, expecting that the Cherokee would block the mountain passes. On 27 September they began their return march.

The Rutherford and Williamson expeditions had burned 36 Cherokee towns. They recorded 12 Cherokees killed and 9 taken prisoner by Rutherford. Seven white men and 4 slaves were captured in the Cherokee towns, along with horses, livestock, and much plunder, including £2,500 worth of deerskins, powder, and lead. Although few Cherokees were killed, the campaign cost them dearly in the loss of their towns and food for the winter. In mid-October 1776 Virginia forces brought the war to the still-unaffected Overhill settlements. After burning five towns, the Virginians negotiated a peace and returned home.

The defeat of the Cherokee in 1776 sharply reduced the Indian threat to the frontiers of North Carolina and the other southern states. Many refugees from the towns destroyed by Rutherford and Williamson were scattered throughout the mountains; others found shelter with the Overhill Cherokee, and as many as 500 went as far as Florida, where they were aided by the British. Cherokee strength and morale were shattered, and the credibility of the British as Indian allies was damaged. Had the Cherokee been able to mount a serious attack on the frontier country in 1780 and 1781, the outcome of the British Southern Campaign and the American Revolution itself might have been different.

References: Samuel A. Ashe, "Rutherford's Expedition against the Indians, 1776," *North Carolina Booklet* 4 (December 1904); Roy S. Dickens Jr., "The Route of Rutherford's Expedition against the North Carolina Cherokees," *Southern Indian Studies* 19 (October 1967); Robert L. Ganyard, "Threat from the West: North Carolina and the Cherokee, 1776–1778," NCHR 45 (January 1968); Tom Hatley, *The Dividing Paths: Cherokees and South Carolinians through the Era of Revolution* (1993).

David A. Norris

S

Sacred Heart College, a Roman Catholic liberal arts college for women in Belmont, was founded in 1892 at the request of Leo Haid, bishop and vicar apostolic of North Carolina. The college, operated by the Sisters of Mercy, offered elementary and secondary courses. In 1935 Sacred Heart College was accredited as a junior college and academy, and in 1966 it became a four-year liberal arts institution. Throughout the 1970s and 1980s, enrollment fluctuated. It closed in 1987, citing financial troubles and the declining success of small Catholic women's schools.

Wiley J. Williams

Sailing has been a popular form of outdoor recreation on the sounds, lakes, and rivers of North Carolina since the days when handmade log canoes were the most common boats in use. Initially, the canoes were hollowed out from single logs of native juniper or cypress in much the same manner as that employed by the native Indians. As boat builders became more proficient, they experimented by splitting a log down the middle and adding timbers to make their canoes wider and lighter, with more stability and capacity. After sawmills were introduced to colonial North Carolina, sailboats made with milled lumber replaced the log canoes, sometimes known as "kunners." As late as the early part of the twentieth century, however, watermen were still using the log canoes. It appears that it was not unusual for such old-timers to be challenged to race against the more modern craft that plied North Carolina waters: sharpies, spritsail skiffs, and even shad boats.

People who spend most of their lives on the water tend to develop the same kind of attachment for their boats—especially those they designed or built themselves—as cowboys do for their horses. Traditionally, their bragging and challenging has often resulted in spirited sailboat races. In his 1975 book, *The Kinnakeeter,* Charles T. Williams II said the fishermen of Avon "were always arguing who had the fastest skiff," which often resulted in Saturday sail skiff races on Pamlico Sound that drew crowds of onlookers. Williams traced this back to the 1890s, as did others who told of similar races in the Beaufort area, often with native watermen competing against seasonal visitors.

Elizabeth City and the Pasquotank River became a center of sailboat racing in the 1930s after a waterman named Joel Van Sant, the captain of a yacht stopping off there for repairs, designed what was described as "a small, cheap, easy to build boat that could be designed and built by amateurs and . . . used for sailing in shallow and shoal bodies of water where other types of sail boats could not be adapted." This was the moth boat, and interest in the new design grew rapidly. Only three years after Van Sant built the first one, a National Moth Boat Association was formed in Elizabeth City to take care of the hundreds of inquiries that were pouring in regarding plans, specifications, and measurements for the popular new boat. Soon moth boat regattas were being held annually in Elizabeth City. Moth boat clubs were formed in Florida, Atlantic City, and elsewhere, and by 1938 there were more than 1,500 registered moth boats worldwide, including several owned by the Greensboro Boy Scouts and a fleet in Charlotte.

The Pamlico County town of Oriental developed sailing fever in the early 1960s, and its Oriental Sailing Social was so successful that it became an annual affair. More recent sailing races and regattas in the large man-made lakes created in this century, as well as in the more traditional coastal area rivers and sounds, involve boats that are quite different from the old log canoes. Many are modern sailing yachts, 30 to 40 feet in length, though a few have been designed especially for racing. With the tremendous increase in the use of North Carolina waters by sailboats, there still is spirited competition between owners of a wide variety of new types of small craft.

Most sailboats used for recreational purposes until fairly recent times were built as workboats, though many were also used for transportation or family outings. Even before the Civil War, popular forms of recreation at the sound-side resort of Nags Head included sailing to Roanoke Island or fishing expeditions to Oregon Inlet. When the 300-room New Atlantic Hotel was built at Morehead City in 1880, one of its advertised attractions was moonlight sailing on Bogue Sound and sailboat excursions to Cape Lookout. Today, nearly all of the many thousands of sailboats in North Carolina waters were built solely for recreational use.

David Stick

St. Andrews Presbyterian College in Laurinburg was preceded by a number of institutions with ties to the Presbyterian Church. They include Donaldson Academy and Labor School, which was founded in Fayetteville in 1833 and existed in some capacity until 1883; Floral College; and Flora MacDonald College, previously called Red Springs Seminary (1896–1903) and Southern Presbyterian College and Conservatory of Music (1903–14). Other predecessors to St. Andrews included Elise Academy in Robbins, which came under the jurisdiction of the Fayetteville Presbytery in 1904 and remained open until 1940; and Presbyterian Junior College for Men (1929), an offshoot of Elise Academy located at Maxton.

Flora MacDonald and Presbyterian Junior College merged in 1958 to form what would become St. Andrews Presbyterian College, named for the University of St. Andrews (founded in

1411), the premier Christian university of Scotland. The new institution, briefly called the Consolidated Presbyterian College, was situated on 800 acres of land south of Laurinburg. St. Andrews formally opened in 1961 and soon acquired a reputation for innovative curricula and facilities. Its Christianity and Culture Program included courses in European history, non-Western cultures, American studies, and futurism. The late 1970s witnessed the implementation of the St. Andrews General Education Program, which sought to integrate elements of the Christianity and Culture Program with more consideration of world affairs. The college augmented its preprofessional offerings as well as majors in business administration, mathematics, natural sciences, and psychology. In 1978 the North Carolina Department of Public Instruction designated St. Andrews as the campus for the Governor's School East.

In 1985 St. Andrews began conducting overseas programs in Beijing, China; Cuenca, Ecuador; and Brunnenburg Castle, Italy; the school also has exchange arrangements with Kansai Gaidai University in Japan and Han Nam University in Korea. In 1989 the Scottish Heritage Center was established in the school's DeTamble Library. In the early 2000s curricular offerings included Equine Business Management and Therapeutic Riding. Enrollment was approximately 700 students served by 83 faculty members. The college boasts an award-winning pipe band, a four-time national champion equestrian team, and St. Andrews College Press, the first undergraduate college press in the country.

References: Robert F. Davidson, *Adventures in Ideas and Values* (1984); Roy Parker Jr., *Cumberland County: A Brief History* (1990); Ruth J. Trivette, *The Merging of the Gaels: A History of the Fayetteville Presbytery, 1813–1983* (1987).

James I. Martin Sr.

SEE ALSO Elise Academy and High School; Flora MacDonald College.

Saint Augustine's College

Saint Augustine's College in Raleigh was founded in 1867 as Saint Augustine's Normal School and Collegiate Institute for blacks. The school was created through the joint efforts of the Freedman's Commission of the Protestant Episcopal Church and a group of clergy and laymen of the Diocese of North Carolina. The normal school began operations early in 1868 in a facility lent to them by the U.S. Freedman's Bureau. However, before the year was over a new structure had been built on land owned by the institute.

The school began to receive regular support from the national Episcopal Church by 1907. By 1928 it had evolved into a full four-year college, which graduated it first class in 1932. Harold L. Trigg was named the college's first African American president in 1947.

Saint Augustine's College has remained committed to providing the highest quality education possible for its more than 1,800 students. The college continues to be closely associated with the Protestant Episcopal Church and seeks to develop the highest ethical and moral values in its undergraduates. The modern-day school offers degrees in 31 distinct disciplines and emphasizes student preparation for graduate studies and careers. Courses also include computer science, radio broadcast journalism, and physical therapy. Students come from 31 states, the District of Columbia, and 22 foreign countries. Saint Augustine's was the first historically black college to develop on-campus commercial radio (WAUG-AM 750) and television (WAUG-TV 68) stations.

References: Cecil Durelle Halliburton, *A History of Saint Augustine's College, 1867–1937* (1937); William S. Powell, *Higher Education in North Carolina* (1970); Thelma Johnson Roundtree, *Strengthening Ties That Bind: A History of Saint Augustine's College* (2002).

Charles W. Wadelington

St. John's Church

St. John's Church in Williamsboro, built in 1757, is the oldest frame church in North Carolina. St. John's Parish was created by the provincial Assembly of North Carolina in 1746. The church was built by the Lewis family of Granville County near Nut Bush Creek, and throughout the colonial period it was commonly called Nut Bush Creek Church. In 1772 Judge John Williams moved the church to its present location, which is about one-half mile from the original site. The community that grew up around the church was incorporated in 1787 and called Williamsboro in honor of Judge Williams.

Nut Bush was a church of the Anglican faith under British rule. The clergy, including the Reverend James McCartney, appointed rector by Governor William Tryon in 1769, were all educated in England. It is therefore not surprising that most rectors had Tory sympathies. The transition from the Anglican to the Episcopal Church in America in the revolutionary period was a slow and difficult process.

From 1800 to 1821 St. John's had no minister. The congregation was first officially recognized as a parish of the Episcopal faith in the newly formed Diocese of North Carolina in 1819. In 1821 William Mercer Green, later the first bishop of Mississippi, took charge of the church, and through his tireless efforts it was revived both spiritually and physically. Since the building had been used occasionally for secular meetings and entertainments, the congregation felt that it should be reconsecrated. Accordingly, on 16 Oct. 1875, Bishop John Stark Ravenscroft, the first Episcopal bishop of the state, consecrated the building, which was officially given the name of St. John's. From 1830 to 1900, St. John's had several rectors, the last of whom—William Shepard Pettigrew, son of bishop-elect Charles Pettigrew—served until his death in 1900. Following his death, the congregation steadily declined. Many families moved away, while other parishioners were buried in the graveyard surrounding the church.

In 1947 a movement to restore the old building was begun by a group called the Friends of St. John's. Bishop Edwin A. Penick appointed a restoration committee; the restoration itself was done under the direction of Milton L. Grigg of Charlottesville, Va., one of the country's leading architects specializing in work of the colonial period. The architectural importance of St. John's was also recognized by Thomas T. Waterman, one of America's foremost authorities on colonial architecture. In his detailed study of the church for the restoration committee, Waterman noted that the church was important "both as an example of colonial church building in North Carolina and as a historic monument."

The restoration was completed in 1956, and the church was rededicated by Edwin A. Penick, bishop of the Episcopal Diocese of North Carolina, on 30 September. St. John's Church is listed in the National Register of Historic Places.

References: Catherine W. Bishir, *North Carolina Architecture* (1990); Lawrence Foushee London and Sarah McCulloh Lemmon, eds., *The Episcopal Church in North Carolina, 1701–1959* (1987).

Wiley J. Williams

Saint Mary's School in Raleigh has been in continuous operation since 1842 as a school for young women. The Reverend Aldert Smedes and his wife opened Saint Mary's in May of that year at the request of the Levi Silliman Ives, bishop of the Episcopal Diocese of North Carolina. Smedes held a law degree, had served as the successful rector of St. George's Church in Schenectady, N.Y., and had owned a school for young ladies in New York City. He came to Raleigh because Judge Duncan Cameron was willing to rent the campus of the defunct Episcopal School for Boys, which he had bought from the diocese at auction. From the beginning, Saint Mary's was considered a diocesan school even though there was no official connection until an 1897 act of incorporation. Because of the tutoring that was available in advanced subjects, historians usually list the school among the nineteenth-century institutions of higher learning in the state.

Over the years, the configuration of academic levels and courses at Saint Mary's has changed to meet contemporary demographic demands. In 1997, for example, the Saint Mary's trustees voted unanimously to focus all of the institution's efforts on a boarding and day preparatory program for girls in grades 9 through 12, with an additional postgraduate year. The trustees saw this new focus as a direction that met the needs of the times and that continued the long tradition of preparing young women for success in college and life.

The Saint Mary's campus remains at its original location off of Hillsborough Street, in an oak grove not far from the State Capitol. The entire campus is listed in the National Register of Historic Places. The 1857 Gothic Revival chapel designed by Richard Upjohn, the two buildings erected from stone left over

from the capitol (1834–35), and Smedes Hall (1837) are especially striking. The student body (about one-third of whom are Episcopalians) numbers 400 and hails from across the nation and from several foreign countries.

References: Katherine Batts Salley, ed., *Life at Saint Mary's* (1942); Martha Stoops, *The Heritage: The Education of Women at St. Mary's College, Raleigh, North Carolina, 1842–1982* (1984).

Martha Stoops

St. Peter AME Zion Church, a brick Gothic Revival church in New Bern, traces its origins to St. Andrew's Chapel, built in 1802. In 1863 James W. Hood, an African Methodist Episcopal Zion (AME Zion) missionary—later a bishop and, from 1868 to 1871, the assistant North Carolina state superintendent of public instruction, with the major responsibility of founding and supervising schools for blacks—came to New Bern and Beaufort, both of which were under Union control and had a considerable population of African American Methodists. Under his leadership, St. Andrew's Chapel and Purvis Chapel in Beaufort affiliated in 1864 with the AME Zion Church, which initially had been formed in 1796 and chartered five years later by a group of blacks who withdrew from the biracial John Street Methodist Church in New York City. St. Andrew's Chapel was the first church in the state and in the South to join the AME Zion Church. In 1879 the congregation changed its name to St. Peter and built a new frame church. After the church burned in 1922, it was rebuilt in stages from 1923 until 1940.

References: Catherine W. Bishir and Michael T. Southern, *A Guide to the Historic Architecture of Eastern North Carolina* (1996); Peter B. Sandbeck, *The Historic Architecture of New Bern and Craven County, North Carolina* (1988).

Wiley J. Williams

St. Philip's Church in Brunswick Town, which survives today as a ruin, was begun in 1754 and consecrated in 1768. It was the largest church in North Carolina at the time and among the finest in colonial America. Built of brick, the church was more than 76 feet long and 53 feet wide. Its walls, which still stand, were nearly 3 feet thick, and surviving portions stand more than 24 feet high. They once supported an arched wooden ceiling and a belfry above the roof. A large arched window and two smaller, rectangular chancel windows open the east wall. A massive arched door opened the west wall, and similar doors opened each of the side walls, along with pairs of arched windows.

Funding for construction of the church was provided by a 1745 act of the Assembly designed to encourage people to settle in Brunswick Town, which was then losing economic ground to the rival port of Wilmington. Construction was repeatedly interrupted, slowed by the tax burden of the war against the French and by the destruction of the roof by lightning in 1760. Governor Arthur Dobbs was buried within the church walls in 1765; his remains have not been located. St. Philip's Parish had been created out of St. James Parish in 1741 by an act of the General Assembly. The remains of St. Philip's Church are preserved as part of Brunswick Town State Historic Site. St. Philip's Church in Southport (erected in 1843) was ushered into the diocese as "Old St. Philips" in 1850 in memory of the original St. Philip's Church at Brunswick.

Reference: Lawrence Lee, *The Lower Cape Fear in Colonial Days* (1965).

William G. DiNome

St. Thomas Episcopal Church in Bath, North Carolina's oldest existing church, was begun in 1734 under John Garzia, the first permanent minister to serve St. Thomas Parish. As early as 1701, however, the parish had received a library of more than 1,000 books and pamphlets as part of the overseas mission work of the Society for the Propagation of the Gospel in Foreign Parts. The church seems to have been used for services from 1735 onward but apparently required extensive repairs in the 1750s, during the long and fruitful rectorship of the Reverend Alexander Stewart.

The simple but dignified church features brick walls two feet thick, laid in Flemish bond. Its floor plan is basically rectangular, several feet out of square. It appears to have been erected by mistake some 50 feet north of its intended location, and in the middle of what was supposed to be a public street.

Severely damaged by a storm in about 1840, St. Thomas was not completely repaired until after the Civil War. Extensive renovations followed in the 1880s. Subsequent efforts to restore St. Thomas began in the 1920s, but it was not until after the Great Depression that this was finally accomplished through the efforts and dedication of the Reverend A. C. D. Noe. Noe served as full-time rector of the church from 1936

St. Thomas Episcopal Church at Bath, ca. 1923. NCC.

until 1953 and maintained an active interest in its welfare until his death in 1978. A treasured and familiar landmark in North Carolina's oldest town, St. Thomas Episcopal Church continues today as an active house of worship.

References: Wilson Angley, "A History of St. Thomas Episcopal Church, Bath, North Carolina," Research Branch, North Carolina Division of Archives and History (1981); Joseph Blount Cheshire, *Sketches of Church History in North Carolina* (1892); Herbert R. Paschal, *A History of Colonial Bath* (1955).

Wilson Angley

Salem was officially established in 1772 as the main town on the Wachovia Tract, the 99,000-acre tract of land the Moravians purchased from Lord Granville in 1753. While the highly organized Moravians originally intended to build their "town of trade and manufacture" shortly after arriving in Wachovia in 1753, construction on Salem did not begin until 1766, when the first residents moved to the still-unfinished town in the wilderness. Spurning the circular town plans drawn by Count Nicholas von Zinzendorf, Wachovia administrator John Frederich Marshall opted for a grid plan that placed the main buildings of the town (the *Gemein Haus* and later Home Moravian Church, the Single Brothers House, the Single Sisters House, and the general store) on the central square. Establishments such as Salem Tavern, which would be frequented by "strangers" or non-Moravians who could be disruptive or negative influences on town residents, were removed from the square.

By offering a full complement of German artisans and their wares and services, as well as a general store and tavern, Salem became the economic center of the North Carolina backcountry shortly after its founding. Even though the Moravians abandoned their semicommunal lifestyle when moving from Bethabara to Salem, church boards still tightly controlled all economic and social aspects of life in Salem through a lease system. As business prospered, however, the Moravians gradually relaxed their grip on Salem's economy and society, allowing a more typical American capitalism to have freer rein. Business moved from individual shop production by artisans to production in manufactories, such as those for textiles. The church ended the lease system in 1856 and, some three years later, ended all pretense of control, so that Moravian businesspeople operated in the same manner as their non-Moravian neighbors.

Freedom from all church restrictions meant that business in Salem continued to succeed and, in the process, expand the town's geographical boundaries. By 1849 the local population had grown to the point that a new county, Forsyth, was created, although its courthouse was situated not in Salem but in the newly created town of Winston. Political differences kept Salem and Winston (which became a manufacturing cen-

Single Brothers House at Old Salem, restored in 1964 to its 1769 condition (brick addition, 1786). Photograph by Tim Buchman. Courtesy of Preservation North Carolina.

ter for tobacco) separate until well after the Civil War. An ill-fated attempt by Salem's political leaders to consolidate the two towns under the name of Salem failed in 1879. But an 1888 chamber of commerce pamphlet championed Winston-Salem as "the Twin City"; by 1899 residents got their mail addressed to "Winston-Salem"; and in 1913 the towns officially consolidated as the city of Winston-Salem.

The idea for the preservation and restoration of historic Salem, or Old Salem, originated in the late 1930s, but the work did not begin in earnest until after World War II. Postwar prosperity brought a boom in construction to Winston-Salem and Forsyth County, which led to the creation of a joint city-county temporary planning commission to try to bring order to the rapid growth that was taking place. By the spring of 1947 a permanent planning commission was in place. This came just as a proposal to build a grocery store in what is now the center of Old Salem appeared. Plans for the store threatened the oldest remaining building in Old Salem, which, even though it was very run down, was known to be of historic significance. The proposal put the commission to its first test, and it was decided to move beyond zoning into the preservation of large areas, something new to North Carolina.

The Citizens Committee for the Preservation of Historic Salem was created, with the aim of developing a careful study of the structures in Old Salem. This, and the work of professional planners, including Russell Van Nest Black, culminated in the development of a citywide zoning plan that included the Old and Historic Salem District. The plan was placed in effect in 1948. In the meantime, a ban had been enforced on any new construction in the old area, which made some property owners uneasy.

The concept of a historic district was on shaky legal ground in North Carolina at the time, since the establishment of such districts had never been attempted before. The leaders of the Winston-Salem preservation effort knew that the key to their situation was to avoid a court case challenging their work. Fortunately, the idea of preservation was taking hold and spreading around the state. By the 1960s the General Assembly began to approve preservation legislation for other areas, and it looked to what had been done in Winston-Salem as a way to create laws that would stand the test of time.

The first project to be completed in Old Salem was the Eberhardt House, along with several of its dependencies, which dated from 1832. This project was completed in 1951 and depicted the 1832 condition of the structures. By 1985 a total of 63 projects had been completed, although work continued on other projects. The most popular place is Salem Tavern, with its dining rooms that were restored to their original 1816 condition in 1968. Other popular buildings are the Miksch Tobacco Shop, restored to its original 1771 condition in 1960, and the Winkler Bakery, which dates from 1800 and was restored to its 1818 condition in 1968. Perhaps the most memorable building is the Single Brothers House, which was restored to its condition of 1769 (the half-timbered original) and 1786 (a brick addition) in 1964. The Single Brothers House is the first stop in Old Salem after the visitors center and is the central point for obtaining information from appropriately garbed guides and living history demonstrations of the arts and crafts of people who lived in Salem in colonial times.

A number of Salem's houses are either privately owned or owned by Old Salem, Inc., the corporation that oversees the historic district, and rented out to individuals, which makes Old Salem a viable residential enclave in Winston-Salem. This is the result of restoration and reconstruction projects in which work on privately owned buildings has been carefully controlled so that the appearance of each conforms strictly to the exact requirements of the historic district. The fact that the Moravians kept careful and exact records of the buildings that comprised the town has enabled the corporation to carry out this work. Some private homes are open to the public on special occasions.

In order to provide continuity and financing, a charter was obtained from the state creating Old Salem, Inc. This enabled a board of trustees to acquire property and to develop long-range plans for financing the projects that have been undertaken at Old Salem. Relying at first on contributions from wealthy benefactors, the corporation has since developed more sophisticated and stable methods of financing. Today, the largest part of the corporation's funding comes from income generated by admissions, while endowment income and a combination of enterprises also contribute to funding. Old Salem has received allocations from state and local governments, as well as grants from federal agencies.

References: C. Daniel Crews, *Villages of the Lord: The Moravians Come to Carolina* (1995); Frances Griffin, *Old Salem: An Adventure*

Salem Female Academy, ca. 1869. NCC.

in *Historic Preservation* (1985); Johanna Miller Lewis, *Artisans in the North Carolina Backcountry* (1995); Daniel B. Thorp, "The City That Never Was: Count von Zinzendorf's Original Plan for Salem," *NCHR* 56 (Summer 1984); Thorp, *The Moravian Community in North Carolina: Pluralism on the Southern Frontier* (1989).

Johanna Miller Lewis
Additional research provided by Alexander R. Stoesen.

Salem Academy and Salem College trace their origins to 1772, when the Moravian community in North Carolina started a school for the education of young girls. This first school met in one room of the *Gemein Haus* (congregation house) in the Salem community with one teacher and three young students. In 1804 the school was opened to those outside the Moravian community, and the first boarding students were admitted. Classes were taught in German and English, and girls arrived from across North Carolina, South Carolina, Tennessee, and Georgia.

In 1866 Salem Female Academy sought and was granted an act of incorporation from the North Carolina General Assembly. Besides clarifying taxation status, incorporation enabled a measure of identity separate from the church and prepared the academy for its evolution into separate academy and college programs with appropriate courses and degrees. By 1890

the first bachelor of arts degrees were awarded, and Salem Female Academy became Salem Academy and College.

In 1912 the academy and the college separated academically. Fulfilling the hopes of thousands of Salem students and alumnae, Salem inaugurated its first woman president, Julianne Still Thrift in 1991. The thirteenth-oldest college in the nation and the first to be founded for women, Salem College in the early 2000s enrolled more than 1,000 women in its liberal arts and professional programs. Salem Academy, a college preparatory/boarding school for girls in grades 9 through 12, shares the 57-acre campus. The academy has an enrollment of approximately 200 girls, both boarding and day students. Both institutions continue to reflect the Moravians' commitment to the education of women.

Reference: Frances Griffin, *Less Time for Meddling: A History of Salem Academy and College, 1772–1866* (1979).

Martha Walker Fullington

Salem Tavern, established in Salem in 1772 and today part of the Old Salem Historic District in Winston-Salem, likely offered the finest hospitality available in backcountry North Carolina for nearly a century. It provided fine accommodations, quality food, and honest dealings to both the ordinary traveler and the distinguished visitor, including George Washington, who visited the establishment in 1791. The tavern was an integral part of the town of Salem's plan and purpose. The Moravians who founded Salem intended the town to be a commercial center for the North Carolina backcountry, providing both a market for products of the interior and a place where necessary items of a high quality could be purchased by the area population.

Those who came to Salem to trade frequently needed a place of refreshment. The tavern was, therefore, a primary point of contact between Moravians and the outside world. It was located on the southern periphery of the town so as not to interfere with the primary mission of a community in which evangelical religion was a central feature. The first tavern structure was half-timber, but it burned in 1784 in Salem's first major fire. It was rebuilt immediately, all brick construction, with an English architectural influence. Its two stories surmounted a full cellar whose vaulted ceilings were finished with plaster. The kitchen, with stone floors and massive cooking fireplaces, adjoined the rear of the building. Outbuildings, stables, gardens, and pasturage completed the complex.

The interior of the tavern provided two levels of entertainment. One dining hall served meals at a common table at designated times, while a second room featured smaller tables and individual service. Upstairs, guests could sleep in small private rooms or opt for the less expensive alternative of renting a space in a bed. Extant inventories reveal furnishings of simple beauty and high utility.

Salem Tavern served an important political purpose as well. On its spacious front porch, citizens listed their taxable property with the sheriff and paid their county levies. On election day, the tavern yard served as a polling place. From tavern walls echoed the political opinions of Patriots and Tories during the heated days of the American Revolution. Often words led to blows and rough-and-tumble fights, which raised Moravian fears of a disorderly establishment. For these reasons, the tavern was exclusively for the use and convenience of "strangers," that is, non-Moravians who were passing through. On several occasions, community leaders admonished the tavernkeeper that Salem citizens should not be served from the bar or be allowed to linger around the guests.

The variety of events at Salem Tavern brought Salem Moravians in touch with the secular world and undoubtedly contributed to fundamental change in the town. But time itself created the greatest transformations, as Salem's first generation passed away and a new generation of town leaders emerged. By the 1840s, most of Salem's communal enterprises were in financial difficulty. Economic individualism increased in Salem, and gradually the community divested itself of unprofitable businesses. The gristmill, the tannery, the pottery, the store, and finally the tavern were sold to individual Moravians. When the new county of Forsyth was established in 1849 with its seat in Winston, immediately adjacent to Salem's northern border, the entire nature of the community shifted. The tavern was sold to Adam Butner in 1850. He soon recovered his investment and operated a profitable hostelry for several years.

The old Salem Tavern building passed through a number of owners and finally ceased operating as a hotel about 1890. When the restoration of Old Salem began in the 1950s, the tavern building was given to the Wachovia Historical Society. They leased it to Old Salem, Inc., for careful, authentic restoration to its eighteenth-century character. It is currently open to visitors with guided tours.

References: Frances Griffin, *Old Salem: An Adventure in Historic Preservation* (1985); Hunter James, "A Tavern in the Town," *Three Forks of Muddy Creek* 4 (1977).

Jerry L. Surratt

Salisbury Academy had its origins in Liberty Hall, an institution established by the Presbyterian Church in Charlotte in about 1771. In 1784 Liberty Hall moved to Salisbury and was renamed Salisbury Academy. Its trustees included John McKnitt Alexander of Charlotte as well as Adlai Osborne, Samuel McCorkle, James Hall, David Caldwell, Thomas Polk, and Maxwell Chambers. Among the teachers were McCorkle and Carl August Gottlieb Storch. After years of decline, the school was revived on 21 May 1807 when the trustees of Salisbury Academy (with Maxwell Chambers as chairman) announced in the *Raleigh Minerva* that Chambers had "a pile of buildings containing twelve rooms where Latin, Greek, and Science would be taught to both males and females" (separately) by John Brown, formerly a teacher in Wadesborough and later president of Columbia College in South Carolina.

In January 1815 a new main building for the Salisbury Academy was constructed on the Great North Square, across from what would later become the Frank B. John School and was then known as Academy Square. In 1825 the academy received $10,000 from a state lottery, and in 1834 the North Carolina state lottery sold tickets at the Mansion House on the corner of Main and Innes Streets for the benefit of Salisbury Academy. Tickets were sold also in Fayetteville, Asheboro, Wentworth, Hillsborough, Raleigh, Bethania, Mocksville, Pittsboro, and New Bern. The Salisbury Academy lottery met with great success, and one newspaper reported that it "has assumed a truly statewide character and has become a multi-million dollar affair."

In 1838 a new building was constructed on property that faced Jackson Street and was located behind the Presbyterian church. Known as the Wrenn Building—named for Jimmie and Mollie Wrenn, faithful and much-loved members of the church—the tin-roofed structure, plain but substantial, housed the Salisbury Academy and various other Presbyterian schools through the years. Many of Salisbury's future leaders and candidates for the Presbyterian ministry received their secondary school education at the Salisbury Academy before its closing sometime before the Civil War. The Wrenn Building remained standing in the early 2000s.

References: Charles L. Coon, *North Carolina Schools and Academies, 1790–1840: A Documentary History* (1915); Neill Roderick McGeachy, *Confronted by Challenge: A History of the Presbytery of Concord, 1795–1973* (1985).

Jo White Linn

Salisbury Arsenal. The Confederate Arsenal at Salisbury was functional as early as 1863. By that time a foundry, built by Nathaniel Boyden for the manufacture of agricultural machinery, had been converted to produce war munitions such as cannons, guns, and other arms. In the spring of 1863, the Confederate Medical Department added to the arsenal by purchasing a distillery at Salisbury that consisted of 25 acres, a 60-horsepower steam engine, a three-story rectifying house, a malt house, and a cooper shop along with three comfortable dwelling houses.

By 1864 the original foundry was producing horseshoes and shells for Parrott guns, and in February the Confederacy established a Niter and Mining Bureau at Salisbury. In August 1864 the Confederate Congress officially named the buildings the Confederate Arsenal at Salisbury. The arsenal was destroyed by Maj. Gen. George H. Stoneman and his Union troops on 12–13 Apr. 1865.

Reference: Louis A. Brown, *The Salisbury Prison: A Case Study of Confederate Military Prisons, 1861–1865* (1980).

Louis A. Brown

Salisbury Post was launched as the *Salisbury Evening Post* on 9 Jan. 1905 by J. B. Doub, E. C. Arey, and Gabe M. Royal from their Royal Printing Company in Salisbury, with John M. Julian as editor, Doub as business manager, and W. Thomas Bost as assistant editor. In May 1912 James Franklin Hurley, who had founded the *Concord Daily Tribune* in Concord, moved to Salisbury and in July 1912 acquired the controlling interest in the *Post* through a stock company composed of A. H. Boyden, M. L. Jackson, C. D. Rose, F. N. McCubbins, and Stahle Linn. The *Post* was the smallest newspaper in the state to publish seven days a week, starting in 1924, and the first to have its own engraving plant; it was also the first to use offset printing. In the early 2000s it remained one of the few papers in the state with a circulation exceeding the population of its hometown. It has consistently won state awards for excellence.

By 1955 the *Salisbury Post* was owned entirely by the Hurley family. At his father's death, James Franklin Hurley Jr. took over operations. By the time of his own death in 1986, he had been either manager, publisher, or chairman of the board of the Post Publishing Company for 66 years. Hurley family members owned the paper until its sale in 1997 to the Evening Post Publishing Company, based in Charleston, S.C.

The *Salisbury Post*'s commitment to providing the best for Salisbury and Rowan County has motivated its endorsement of many progressive causes. These have included the purchase in 1928 (from a prize herd in California) of a purebred Guernsey bull, which was offered for stud to local farmers to upgrade their herds; the building of the Veterans' Administration Medical Center Hospital in Salisbury; and direct support for Livingstone and Catawba Colleges to ensure educational opportunities for the citizenry.

Jo White Linn

Salmon Creek, the site of several historically significant developments in precolonial North Carolina, lies in southeastern Bertie County, where it empties into Albemarle Sound just south of the mouth of the Chowan River. In 1586 Ralph Lane's colonists found a Weapemeoc Indian village called Metakquam (also Metocuuem), apparently on the south bank of the Salmon Creek's mouth. Nicholas Comberford's 1657 map depicts a structure at the same location labeled "Batts House," referring to the trading post built in 1653 for fur trader Nathaniell Batts of Lynnhaven River, Va. Batts appears to have made his home at the site of present-day Edenton, occupying the trading post only seasonally. Evidence indicates that a small refugee settlement of Chuckatuck, Va., Quakers occupied the site for about six years before being driven off by the Tuscarora Indians in 1667. The trading post appears to have continued to function under a succession of operators until the early eighteenth century.

John Lawson visited Salmon Creek prior to 1710 and described the then-existing structure as "a log house such as the Swedes in America very often make, and are very strong." The area had been designated by the Lords Proprietors in 1676 as a site for one of three towns they wished to be established "where the shipps shall lade and unlaid." In the 1680s and 1690s Proprietor Seth Sothel, perhaps with that end in mind, built a considerable establishment at the site with a two-story manor house, ship's landing, dairy house, and stock of cattle. Throughout most of the eighteenth century it was owned by William Dukinfield and his descendants. At Dukinfield's death in 1721 the property went to his nephew, Nathaniel Dukinfield, who also later inherited the baronetcy of his father, Sir Robert Dukinfield. The Dukinfields built a gristmill on Salmon Creek by 1721 and a "pitch landing" for the naval stores business by 1738. Governors Edward Hyde and Thomas Pollock also lived at the site, and the main engagement of the Cary Rebellion was fought at the creek's mouth in June 1711.

Salmon Creek was the principal setting for George Higby Throop's novel, *Bertie; or, Life in the Old Field* (1851). The Capehart family operated a highly successful herring fishery at Avoca, with its plantation on Salmon Creek, during most of the nineteenth century and into the twentieth century.

References: Robert J. Cain, ed., *Records of the Executive Council, 1664–1734* (1984); Mattie Erma Edwards Parker, ed., *North Carolina Higher-Court Records, 1670–1696* (1968); Parker, ed., *North Carolina Higher-Court Records, 1697–1701* (1971).

Thomas C. Parramore

Salt Licks are places on the ground where salt appears naturally or has been deposited by humans and where birds and animals congregate to savor the taste. Parts of the modern-day highway system were originally animal trails and later Native American trails that led to salt access—either salt licks or the ocean. Rest stops and both temporary and permanent villages were established along these trails, which were used and improved upon by early explorers to permit horse and wagon traffic.

American Indians, and later European settlers, held salt in high esteem. Since the region lacked natural salt, even the salt "waste" from preserving hides and meats was put to use. The Indians carefully saved the salt remnants and placed them strategically on their hunting grounds to attract wild animals and birds. These recycled salt licks were enhanced at every opportunity with additional salt scraps. They became tribal property, not to be infringed upon by neighbors, although they were often discovered and seized by settlers. Local names such as "Big Lick," "Licking Creek," and "White Lick" appear in various parts of the state. These salted areas lasted for centuries, perhaps with some assistance by later settlers who dumped their salt scraps on the old salt licks.

A modern-day salt lick, located on Boy Scout property near Hickory, provides a "wildlife observation" area. The site had served as a dairy farm "cow lick" 50 years earlier, when the farmer provided the salt in block form. Wildlife officers in the western half of the state continually deal with poachers who hunt deer over salt licks, which is illegal. For some reason, deer in the east are not attracted to salt licks, but rabbit, raccoon, skunks, small rodents, and birds are. Occasionally, rogue hunters will unlawfully pursue dove over salt.

John R. Kennedy

Saluda Grade, the steepest standard-gauge main line railway grade in the United States, crests in the center of the Polk County town of Saluda. Since it opened in 1878, the three-mile-long stretch of track has earned a prominent place in railroad lore, owing chiefly to the wild train runaways that have taken place there over the years.

Rising an average of 4.7 feet per every 100 feet in length, the Saluda grade far outdistances its nearest rival, the 3.5 percent Santa Fe grade in New Mexico. Construction of the line in the 1870s marked the first use of state convict labor on a large scale, although the high casualties among the workforce prompted a special legislative investigation. The first train made its passage up the mountain on 4 July 1878. Originally built as part of the Asheville & Spartanburg Railroad, the grade was taken over by the Southern Railway (later Norfolk Southern) in 1895.

Both during and after construction, the grade was the scene of numerous accidents, many resulting in death or injury to train crews. In 1880 alone, 14 men were killed on the Saluda grade; in 1886 a runaway train killed 6 convicts, 2 guards, and a foreman. The summer of 1903 saw no less than three separate crashes. Most train derailments took place at Slaughter Pen Cut near Melrose about halfway down the mountain, where trains would often skip the tracks. The last major incident occurred in 1964.

References: Frank Clodfelter, "Saluda," *Trains* (November 1984); John Gilbert and Grady Jeffreys, *Crossties through Carolina: The Story of North Carolina's Early Day Railroads* (1969).

Michael Hill

Salvation Army, an international Christian religious and charitable organization founded in England in 1865, came to the United States in 1879. The basic unit of the Salvation Army is the corps community center, which is the local congregational expression of the organization. The corps provides religious activities in the Wesleyan-Holiness tradition and administers social services.

In January 1879 a pioneer Salvation Army officer visited Raleigh to conduct meetings in the chapel of the state penitentiary. At that time the first North Carolina corps was established in Raleigh. In 1887 the Salvation Army in the Carolinas "declared war on the devil and claimed people for God, parading up and down the streets with fiddles and tambourines." Crowds gathered wherever they appeared, and they generated much excitement. Sometimes they were misunderstood, however, and even jailed; occasionally they were obliged to cease their activities. In addition to the pioneer corps in Raleigh, others were opened before 1900 in Wilmington, Durham, New Bern, Goldsboro, Fayetteville, Kinston, and Asheville. By the early 2000s there were Salvation Army corps in 41 North Carolina cities and towns.

In addition to providing religious services, the Salvation Army in North Carolina operates a variety of institutions, including drug and alcohol rehabilitation centers, camps, homes for transients, and day care centers, and it also offers family assistance programs.

References: Allen Satterlee, *Sweeping through the Land: A History of the Salvation Army in the Southern United States* (1989).

William W. Smith

Samarcand Manor, officially the State Home and Industrial School for Girls, was a humane correctional institution for young women established near Eagle Springs by the North Carolina state legislature in 1918. The purpose of the school was to reclaim and train delinquent girls by providing a "homelike place where those who have fallen may find temporary shelter, and under a firm yet kind discipline, begin to live morally." The school, built on 230 acres in Samarcand (named for the Muslim city conquered by Alexander the Great that served as his empire's seat of learning and culture), was one of the first institutions of its type in the South. The original clients were young girls or women who had been convicted of being prostitutes, vagrants, or habitual drunkards or who were guilty of any misdemeanor suggesting that they were "not virtuous." There were no definite terms, but the clients could not be held more than three years and were to be released on good behavior.

Agnes B. MacNaughton became Samarcand's first superintendent, and by 1919 more than 200 women between the ages of 10 and 30 had arrived. In the 1920s the daily program emphasized Bible study, manners, cleanliness, music, nature, and sports in addition to the regular academic subjects. The girls also received vocational training in sewing, weaving, canning, laundry work, and poultry and dairying activities. The program stressed self-reliance and pride in one's work. Between 1928 and 1930 a total of 296 girls were admitted, most between the ages of 12 and 16. By 1930 Samarcand had a hospital and an accredited high school.

In 1931, 16 Samarcand inmates set fire to two dorms and were charged with arson, then a capital crime. While awaiting trial, the girls burned their jail cells. Eight of the 12 involved were eventually sent to prison. Samarcand survived this notorious 1931 incident and other difficulties but was unable to withstand the financial strains of the Great Depression and the siphoning off of staff during World War II. In 1974 the state changed the name of the institution to Samarcand Manor and placed it under the purview of the North Carolina Department of Human Resources, Youth Division. Samarcand became one of five state training schools designed to rehabilitate delinquent children (both male and female) between the ages of 10 and 17. The school shifted its emphasis to treatment and therapy. In the early 2000s Samarcand had approximately 190 clients (40 females and 150 males) and 210 staff members.

References: Ida Briggs Henderson, "The Work at Samarcand," *The State* (4 Apr. 1936); Lisbeth Parrott, "Samarcand Opens Door of Hope to 1,000th Girl in Tenth Year," *Raleigh News and Observer*, 7 Oct. 1928; *Samarcand Manor: 50th Anniversary, 1918–1968* (1968).

Julian M. Pleasants

Sampson County, located in the Coastal Plain region of North Carolina, was formed in 1784 from Duplin County and was named for Col. John Sampson, a member of the North Carolina House of Commons. Early inhabitants of the area included the Coharie Indians, followed by English, Welsh, and Scottish settlers. Clinton, the county seat, was incorporated in 1852 and was named after Richard Clinton, the foster son of John Sampson, the original owner of the land on which the town was built. Other communities in the county include Newton Grove, Suttontown, Turkey, Elliott, Harrells, Tomahawk, Parkersburg, Garland, and Keener. The Black River, Warrens Pond, Mingo and Starling Swamps, Dismal Bay, and Turkey and Wild Cat Creeks are a few of the county's significant physical features.

Notable among Sampson County's historic sites and landmarks are the Clinton Depot and Freight Station (ca. 1920); the Graves-Stuart House, built in the 1840s; the Archibald Monk House, built around 1824; and Thirteen Oaks, built in 1902. Cultural institutions include the Community Theatre Group, the Dr. Victor R. Small Cultural Arts Center, and the Sampson County History Museum. The county hosts festivals and annual events such as the National Hollerin' Contest in Spivey's Corner, the Fireman's Day Parade and Festival, the Sweet Potato Festival, and the Rotary Fair and Parade.

Sampson County produces agricultural goods such as tobacco, vegetables, cotton, corn, soybeans, swine, and poultry. Manufactured goods include lumber and lumber products, furniture, apparel, and animal feeds. The estimated population of Sampson County was 62,600 in 2004.

Reference: Tom Butchko, *An Inventory of Architecture of Sampson County, North Carolina* (1979).

Jay Mazzocchi

SEE ALSO Hollerin' Contest.

Sand Dunes along the North Carolina coast are an integral part of the ecosystem immediately adjacent to the sea. The dunes are formed when sand particles that have been washed ashore are picked up by the wind and blown inland until an obstruction is encountered. The obstruction usually consists of some form of jetsam that has been deposited high up on the beach during a storm, though it can also be types of vegetation. Eventually the dune itself becomes enough of an obstruction to block the windblown sand.

Normally, along the North Carolina coast the dunes are located less than 100 yards from the average high-tide line. Experienced observers cite a general rule: the finer the sand, the more gradual the slope of the beach, and the more coarse the sand, the steeper the slope of the beach. An ideal oceanfront sand dune is considered by many coastal residents as one where the beach slopes up gradually until the crest of the dune is reached. In such areas, even during storms, the waves tend to flow up the beach and then drain back again, causing no damage until the dune is breached and the seawater floods

Sand dunes at Cape Hatteras National Seashore covered with stabilizing plants.
Photograph courtesy of North Carolina Division of Tourism, Film, and Sports Development.

the area behind it, known as the "back beach." On the other hand, when the sand dunes are located too close to the water, the seaward side is often cut away, especially during larger storms, leaving a sand cliff that can be higher than the height of a man. Under such circumstances, the wave action in subsequent storms is liable to intensify the erosion, eating away at the sand cliff until the dune disappears.

Once the oceanfront dunes are eroded away on the barrier islands, especially in areas where the islands are narrow and the beach is low, each successive storm brings water from ocean to sound, or, under certain conditions, from sound to ocean. At such times forest growth and other vegetation is destroyed, wide areas of low, flat beach appear, and in extreme cases new inlets are formed. In the days of sailing vessels, these low, denuded areas were used for hauling small craft between the sound and the ocean, and therefore were called "haulovers."

By the 1930s, large parts of the coastal islands were so denuded of vegetation that steps were taken to restore the oceanfront dune system. In preparation, the North Carolina General Assembly enacted legislation prohibiting further use of the coastal area as an open range for livestock. Concurrently, a massive beach restoration program was begun, with Depression-era transient workers and Civilian Conservation Corps teams doing the bulk of the work. In the process, hundreds of miles of sand fences were constructed and tons of beach grass seedlings were planted, providing a man-made obstruction to catch windblown sand.

Later, with the growth of oceanfront development, it became a common practice for property owners, seeking the best view of the ocean, to bulldoze the sand dune or build their cottage on top of the dune and as close to the ocean as possible. Subsequently, many of these homes have fallen down in severe storms or hurricanes, almost always resulting in widespread TV, radio, and newspaper coverage of their loss.

Oceanfront sand dunes, seldom reaching a size of more than 15 feet or so in height and a couple of hundred feet in width, should not be confused with the massive migratory sand hills along the upper North Carolina coast. Technically, these also are sand dunes; however, they have been formed over a period of hundreds of years and traditionally have been known as sand hills and not as sand dunes. The best known of these was the site of the Wright brothers' early experiments with man-carrying kites and gliders. It was always known as Kill Devil Hill, and never as Kill Devil Dune.

David Stick

Sandhills. SEE Geography.

Sandy Creek Baptist Association was North Carolina's first Baptist association and one of the most influential in the South. Shubal Stearns, a Separate Baptist and pastor of the Sandy Creek Baptist Church in Randolph County, was instrumental in its formation. His influence led to the organization of the association in 1758 with member churches Sandy Creek, Deep River, Abbott's Creek, Little River, Dan River, Grassy Creek, New River, and Black River in North Carolina, and Pittsylvania City and Lunenburg City in Virginia. Within a few years of its organization, the Sandy Creek Association extended from the Potomac River to Georgia and rivaled the older Charleston Association, which had been formed in 1751.

Being composed of Separate Baptists, the churches of the Sandy Creek Association had some practices that might be considered peculiar to many modern North Carolina Baptists. These practices included the so-called nine Christian rites, namely, baptism, the Lord's Supper, love feasts, the laying-on of hands, the washing of feet, the anointing of the sick, the right hand of fellowship, the kiss of charity, and the devoting of children. The churches also had ruling elders and deacons that were both male and female.

In 1770 the Sandy Creek Association divided over regional differences among the churches. The divisions may also have been the result of the dictatorial influence of Stearns. The association was divided into three new associations: the Virginia churches organized into the Rapidan Association, and the South Carolina churches formed the Congaree Association, while the North Carolina churches retained the Sandy Creek name.

The defeat of the Regulators at the Battle of Alamance in 1771 caused an exodus to Tennessee, South Carolina, and Georgia of many Baptists sympathetic with the Regulator Movement. This loss greatly decreased the size of the Sandy Creek Baptist Association. The association continues to exist, but it is composed of churches now affiliated with the Baptist State Convention of North Carolina.

References: Maloy A. Huggins, *A History of North Carolina Baptists, 1727–1932* (1967); H. Leon McBeth, *The Baptist Heritage* (1987); George W. Paschal, *History of North Carolina Baptists* (1930).

Glenn Jonas

Saponi Indians were a Siouan-speaking people who lived in the Virginia Piedmont near present-day Charlottesville. John Smith found them there, in a region he broadly labeled Monacan, in 1607. Sometime during the next several decades they moved south, seldom remaining stationary until the mid-eighteenth century. A small group of corn farmers and hunters, the Saponi moved to find protection from more powerful enemies.

In 1670 German explorer John Lederer found the Saponi among the Nahyssan on the Staunton River in Virginia. In the 1680s, they were on the upper Roanoke River, living adjacent to the Occaneechi. When John Lawson visited them in 1701, the Saponi were on the Yadkin River near present-day Salisbury, along with the Tutelo and Keyauwee. The Saponi chief told Lawson that the three tribes were planning to join and move again. In 1714 the Saponi, Occaneechi, Tutelo, and other small tribes concluded a treaty with Virginia governor Alexander Spotswood to return to that colony and settle on a six-mile-square reservation laid out on the Meherrin River. Named Fort Christanna, the reservation was to be a refuge for Piedmont Indians willing to serve the Virginia settlements as frontier scouts. In 1729 the Saponi and their friends abandoned the fort and headed for the Catawba River, where the Catawba Nation offered sanctuary.

In 1731 growing dissatisfaction with their situation caused the Saponi to fragment. A few remained with the Catawba, but most left. Some moved north to join those Tuscaroras who remained in North Carolina after the Tuscarora War (1711–13); others migrated to New York, where the Cayuga, one of the Six Nations of Iroquois, adopted them. Still others drifted toward the English settlements, where they were ultimately absorbed into the general population. By the early 2000s the Haliwa-Saponi tribe was a small, state-recognized tribe with headquarters in the town of Hollister in Halifax County.

References: James H. Merrell, *The Indians' New World: Catawbas and Their Neighbors from European Contact through the Era of Removal* (1989); Douglas L. Rights, *The American Indian in North Carolina* (2nd ed., 1957).

Michael D. Green

Sarah P. Duke Gardens occupy 55 acres close to the center of Duke University's West Campus. They were begun in 1934 when Frederic M. Hanes, an avid gardener and iris lover as well as important figure in Duke's medical center, persuaded Benjamin N. Duke's widow, Sarah P. Duke, to pay $20,000 for a garden featuring irises. Hanes then hired a well-known landscape architect, Ellen B. Shipman, to design a terraced garden, the gift of Mary Duke Biddle as a memorial to her mother, Sarah P. Duke. Opened to the public in 1939, this portion of Duke Gardens, with a rock garden on the opposite hillside, is the oldest and best-known feature. In subsequent years the Hugo L. Blomquist Garden of Native Plants—containing several thousand specimens indigenous to the Southeast—the Doris Duke Center Garden, and the extensive Culberson Asiatic Arboretum, dedicated to plants of eastern Asia, were developed. The Sarah P. Duke Gardens are open to the public every day of the year without charge and each year attract over 300,000 visitors.

Reference: Marcus Embry, "Watching the Gardens Grow," *Duke: A Magazine for Alumni and Friends* (July–August 1989).

Robert F. Durden

Saura Indians, also known as the Cheraw, were one of a number of small Siouan tribes in the colonial backcountry (the modern-day Piedmont) of North Carolina. The ancestors of the Saura are believed to have migrated to the region many centuries prior to European contact, which first occurred with the sixteenth-century Spanish incursions into the Southeast. Hernando De Soto's expedition entered Saura country in 1540, and in 1566 Juan Pardo left a garrison commanded by Hernando Moyano in the Indian town of Joara, which may have been located on the upper Catawba River. Probably because of the Spanish intrusions, the Saura moved northeast across the Piedmont to settle in the Dan River Valley on the Virginia line by the early seventeenth century, establishing at least two large village complexes, Upper Sauratown and Lower Sauratown.

Upper Sauratown was on the west bank of the Dan River north of Town Fork Creek, and Lower Sauratown was on the south bank just below the confluence of the Dan and Smith Rivers. The towns were occupied in the second quarter of the seventeenth century and were abandoned in the early eighteenth century. While surveying his "Land of Eden" grant in North Carolina in 1733, William Byrd of Virginia visited the location of the former Lower Sauratown. The towns' names appear on the 1751 Fry-Jefferson map of Virginia and on the 1770 John Collet map of North Carolina. In the late eighteenth century, Lower Sauratown was a small frontier settlement and a plantation site. In the twentieth century the two town sites became important sources of archaeological information, with excavations beginning in 1938 and continuing into the 1970s and 1980s.

German explorer John Lederer, moving south from Virginia, visited the Saura in 1670. Three years later the Saura were encountered by Virginia Indian traders James Needham and Gabriel Arthur, the latter of whom returned to a Saura village in 1674. By the early eighteenth century the dwindling tribe, decimated by epidemic diseases, moved south to unite with the Keyauwee in the Yadkin–Pee Dee River Valley in South Carolina. Their village was situated near the present town of Wallace, S.C.

Some Sauras joined Col. John Barnwell's expedition against the Tuscarora in 1711–12 but did not complete the campaign. After the close of the Yamassee War, a 1715 South Carolina census numbered the Saura at 510 people settled near the North Carolina–South Carolina border (adjacent to modern-day Anson and Richmond Counties). That same year the Saura, who were trading with Virginians, were involved in raids against settlers, but by 1718 it appears they were at peace with the South Carolinians. Approximately three-quarters of the greatly reduced Saura, now known as the Cheraw, eventually went west to join the Catawba Nation, although they maintained much autonomy and political independence. The Cheraws who remained on settlements in the east along Drowning Creek (the modern-day Lumber River) are believed by some historians to have given rise to the Lumbee tribe.

After devastating smallpox epidemics struck the Catawba and their satellites in the late eighteenth century, the Cheraw as a separate tribe disappeared from history. Their name is perpetuated in the Sauratown Mountains of Stokes County and in the town of Cheraw, S.C.

References: Lindley S. Butler, *Rockingham County: A Brief History* (1982); Richard A. Seybert, "'Curiosities Worthy a Nice Observation': Archaeological Investigations of Siouan Village Sites in the Dan River Drainage," *Journal of Rockingham County History and Genealogy* 15 (June 1990); Seybert, "A History Unwritten: The Colonial Period Saura Indians of the Carolina Piedmont," *Journal of Rockingham County History and Genealogy* 13 (December 1988); Ruth Y. Wetmore, *First on the Land: The North Carolina Indians* (1975).

Lindley S. Butler

Sauthier Maps. Between 1768 and 1771 Claude Joseph Sauthier, a French surveyor and cartographer, was commissioned by royal governor William Tryon to create a set of detailed maps for North Carolina's chief (principally political or commercial) colonial towns and one battlefield. The towns that Sauthier mapped, in order, were Hillsborough (October 1768), Brunswick Town (April 1769), Bath and New Bern (May 1769), Edenton and Halifax (June 1769), Wilmington (December 1769), Cross Creek (Fayetteville) and Salisbury (March 1770), and Beaufort (August 1770). In 1771 Sauthier also mapped the Alamance Battleground, the scene of the decisive battle of the Regulator uprising against Tryon's militia prior to the American Revolution.

Sauthier delineated key buildings or areas—such as churches, courthouses, markets, jails, mills, tanyards (or "tann yards"), flagstaffs, schools, breweries, still houses, and some residences—by an alphabetical letter in descending order of importance, with churches usually listed as *A*, courthouses as *B*, jails as *C*, and so on. Major roads leading to neighboring or important distant towns were carefully marked. Geographic features such as rivers, creeks, mountains or marshes, dams, canals, and even racetracks were usually identified.

Buildings were indicated by small rectangles with heavy outlines on two sides—usually the right angle and the lower side. These two heavy lines have been interpreted as indicating a shadow cast by the bulk of the building, a convention used by Sauthier to illustrate mass. The idealized "formal gardens" behind many town residences also reveal this convention, suggesting a mass of green foliage rising above the surrounding paths. The homes shown on the maps were all built near the street and were typically rectangular in shape, with fields or gardens located adjacent or behind the structures. The *X* inscribed within the perimeter of a structure has been interpreted to mean that it was a single-story building. On the originals some buildings were shown in color highlight (red), which may indicate dwellings.

Sauthier's maps have offered valuable two-dimensional guidance into town plans and features of eighteenth-century North Carolina. His map of New Bern was used by architectural restorationists in the reconstruction of Tryon Palace. For decades archaeologists have consulted his maps of Halifax, Brunswick Town, Hillsborough, Edenton, and Bath to investigate subsurface ruins of the old towns. Historians have also used these maps to re-create historic towns and battlefield layouts for public visitation and education.

As research tools, Sauthier's maps have provided archaeologists, architects, historians, and cartographers with colonial period templates of urban lot arrangements, which are often camouflaged by later nineteenth- and twentieth-century alterations. Thus, they offer a glimpse into what otherwise would never be visible in its entirety—the towns and battlefields as they once were. The originals of most of these maps became the property of the British Museum in London.

Linda F. Carnes-McNaughton

Savings and Loan Associations (S&LS) in North Carolina were an outgrowth of the original building and loan associations, which were unregulated financial cooperatives owned by members who generally used funds they had borrowed and/or accumulated to build houses or purchase homesteads. While legislative involvement with building and loan associations began in 1870, it was not until 1915 that the General Assembly changed the name of credit unions and general cooperative associations to S&LS, which for a time were regulated by the Department of Agriculture. In 1937 the legislature permitted federally chartered S&LS to convert to state-chartered building and loan associations under a plan approved by the state commissioner of insurance and a designated federal authority. The same General Assembly also authorized these associations to invest in mortgages of the Federal Housing Administration, pending approval for credit insurance by FHA.

In 1967 the state legislature created the Savings and Loan Advisory Board within the Department of Insurance. The board was charged with reviewing rules and regulations promulgated by the commissioner. In the same year the legislature granted the state's S&LS certain powers held by federal S&LS, including authority to invest in capital stock or other securities of service cooperatives operating under state laws.

In 1971 the General Assembly made changes that again affected North Carolina S&LS. Under one law, they were made subject to audit by the commissioner of insurance and were required to engage in activities approved by the commissioner and the Federal Home Loan Bank Board. In a separate action, the legislature endorsed the Executive Organization Act of 1971, including provisions for reorganization of the Department of Insurance and creation of the Department of Commerce. The commerce department absorbed various regulatory agencies, boards, and their administrative divisions, including the Savings and Loan Advisory Board and the Savings and Loan Division, both of which retained their previous statutory powers and duties. The name of the Savings and Loan Advisory Board was subsequently changed to the State Savings and Loan Commission.

In the late 1980s, during a period marked by the failure of many federal S&LS, the North Carolina legislature made changes to the application process for new associations and specified that failure of any institution to maintain the requisite level and type of regulatory capital could result in supervisory action by the administrator. In special legislation in 1989, the General Assembly authorized the administrator of the Savings Institutions Division to promulgate rules and regulations governing conversion of state associations to federal institutions with requirements equal to or greater than those required under federal charters. In 1991 the General Assembly specified a new procedure requiring the administrator to present recommendations regarding the establishment of a proposed savings bank to the Savings Institutions Commission during a public hearing, whereupon the commission was to decide whether the bank would be chartered. The legislative body also established procedures for mergers of banks and former S&LS and guidelines for conversion of S&LS to state-chartered banks.

References: Savings and Loan Study Commission, *Report to the Governor and the 1981 General Assembly* (1980); "Thrift Industry: State S&LS Feel the Pinch but Are Better Off than Most," *We the People of North Carolina* 40 (August 1982).

Wiley J. Williams

Sawtooth Center for Visual Art, an arts education facility located in downtown Winston-Salem in a renovated 1910 textile mill with a distinctive jagged roofline, serves the Triad community (Winston-Salem, High Point, and Greensboro) as a place for people to learn about and work creatively in painting, ceramics, fibers, glass, graphics, photography, metals, and wood. The building also has three art galleries featuring presentations by local artists, traveling exhibitions, and national juried shows. Founded in 1945 as one of the country's first community visual arts schools, the center was purchased by the R. J. Reynolds Tobacco Company and donated to the Arts Council of Winston-Salem and Forsyth County for adaptation to community use. Formal opening of the center in 1945 included such divergent attractions as Zsa Zsa Gabor, the Glenn Miller Band, Preservation Hall musicians from New Orleans, and the Ink Spots. The Sawtooth Center for Visual Art is part of a cultural complex designed to revitalize downtown Winston-Salem.

Kelly Kress

Scalawag was the derogatory nickname used by conservative southern whites to describe other southern whites who were active members of the Republican Party during Reconstruction. In North Carolina, the latter group was quite large and contained a significant number of outstanding leaders. The native-born white Republicans were primarily concentrated in two parts of the state: the "Quaker belt" in the Piedmont, including Randolph, Moore, and Guilford Counties; and the Mountain areas of the west, especially Mitchell and Wilkes Counties.

Most native white Republicans had come to oppose the Confederacy at some point during the Civil War. *Raleigh Standard* editor William W. Holden became their leader during the last stages of the conflict and the early part of Reconstruction, when President Andrew Johnson appointed him provisional governor of the state. After he was defeated for a full term by Conservative Party candidate Jonathan Worth in 1865, Holden and many other white Republicans endorsed the congressional Republicans and African American male suffrage. In 1868 the native white Republicans dominated a constitutional convention that created the most democratic state charter in North Carolina's history. Under the new document, Holden was elected governor and Tod R. Caldwell, of Burke County, lieutenant governor. Other white Republicans, including Alexander H. Jones of Henderson County, were sent to Congress.

When white supporters of the Conservative Party resorted to violence during the 1870 legislative campaign, Holden created and used a state militia composed of partisans from western North Carolina and eastern Tennessee. This so-called Kirk-Holden War dominated the 1870 elections, which the Conservatives won decisively. When the General Assembly impeached and turned Holden out of office, Caldwell became governor. Caldwell was elected to a full term in 1872; he died in 1874 and was succeeded in office by Curtis Brogden.

The revived and renamed Conservatives—now calling themselves Democrats—nominated Zebulon B. Vance for governor in 1876 and defeated the Republicans despite a strong run by Thomas Settle Jr. of Rockingham County. Settle, a former North Carolina Supreme Court justice and U.S. ambassador to Peru, was widely respected by opponents and allies alike. His aggressive campaign provided the impetus for a strong white presence in the North Carolina Republican Party throughout the post-Reconstruction period, when whites deserted the party in many other states of the former Confederacy.

References: William C. Harris, *William Woods Holden: Firebrand of North Carolina Politics* (1987); Gordon B. McKinney, *Southern Mountain Republicans, 1865–1900: Politics and the Appalachian Community* (1978); Richard L. Zuber, *North Carolina during Reconstruction* (1969).

Gordon B. McKinney

Scales Trial. Junius Irving Scales, from a prominent Greensboro family that included his great-uncle, Governor Alfred Moore Scales, in 1939 joined the Communist Party of the United States while enrolled at the University of North Carolina in Chapel Hill. He soon became state president of the communist-affiliated American Student Union. In 1946, after serving four years in the U.S. Army, Scales entered UNC as a graduate student and assumed the chairmanship of the Chapel Hill Communist Party. By 1951 he was chairman of the party's Carolinas District, going underground to evade arrest.

In 1954 Scales was apprehended and charged with violating the Alien Registration Act (commonly known as the Smith Act) of 1940, which made it illegal to advocate the violent overthrow of the U.S. government or to organize or become a member of any group espousing such doctrine. At his 1955 trial in

Junius Scales, 1946. NCC.

the Greensboro federal court, Scales was convicted and sentenced to six years in prison. The conviction was upheld by the Fourth Circuit Court of Appeals but reversed by the U.S. Supreme Court in 1957, shortly after Scales had resigned from the Communist Party. The basis for the reversal was that the government had not provided to the defense the notes and other material of prosecution witnesses. Retried in Greensboro the next year, Scales was represented by Telford Taylor, a nationally recognized expert on the Smith Act, and by McNeill Smith, a prominent local attorney. Scales again maintained that he had never advocated the violent overthrow of the government, but he was again convicted and sentenced to six years' imprisonment. This time the conviction was upheld by the Supreme Court in a five-to-four decision. In October 1961 Scales entered the federal penitentiary in Lewisburg, Penn.; he served 15 months before his sentence was commuted by President John F. Kennedy.

Reference: Junius Irving Scales and Richard Nickson, *Cause at Heart: A Former Communist Remembers* (1987).

Robert J. Cain

Schenck-Warlick Mill,

erected about 1814, was the first cotton mill built in North Carolina and an important factor in the emergence of the southern textile industry. Michael Schenck, a Pennsylvania native, arrived in Lincoln County in about 1790 and established the small cotton-spinning mill on a fork of the Catawba River located about one mile east of Lincolnton. Some pieces of the machinery for the facility were purchased in Providence, R.I., while others were crafted locally by Absalom Warlick, a skilled iron worker and a relative of Schenck's wife. The mill operated profitably and emerged as

The Schenck-Warlick cotton mill, the first cotton mill in North Carolina. David Schenck Papers, no. 652, Southern Historical Collection, Wilson Library, UNC-Chapel Hill.

the first successful textile mill erected south of the Potomac River.

A flood destroyed the mill and the nearby dam in 1816, but Schenck promptly joined with Warlick to rebuild. Within 12 months, a larger mill was in operation on Warlick's land below the original site. In 1819 Schenck teamed with two other local men, James Bivens and Col. John Hoke, to erect the larger Lincolnton Cotton Mill on the South Fork River some two miles south of Lincolnton. The 3,000-spindle factory continued in operation until it was destroyed by fire in 1863.

References: Marvin A. Brown and Maurice C. York, *Our Enduring Past: A Survey of 235 Years of Life and Architecture in Lincoln County* (1986); Brent D. Glass, *The Textile Industry in North Carolina: A History* (1992); Bill Sharpe, "Patriots, Iron, and Spindles," *The State* 30 (April 1960).

Daniel W. Barefoot

School Commission.

The General Assembly of 1933 created the State School Commission to be the fiscal agency for the state's public school fund, succeeding the State Board of Equalization. Membership on the commission was composed of the governor as ex officio chairman, the lieutenant governor, the state treasurer, the state superintendent of public instruction, and one member appointed by the governor from each of what were then North Carolina's 11 congressional districts—for a total of 15 persons. The commission was given broad and plenary powers over the administration of the public schools and the distribution of state funds to schools. The State School Commission continued until 1943, when the General Assembly abolished it and reassigned its powers and duties to the State Board of Education.

Reference: E. Michael Latta, *The Constitutional and Statutory Development of the State Board of Education and the State Superintendent of Public Instruction* (1989).

E. Michael Latta

School Consolidation

was a trend that developed in North Carolina immediately following World War I as state and local leaders sought to improve the quality of rural public schools. Parents of children in rural districts served by one- and two-teacher schools began to demand educational advantages more comparable to those in towns and cities. Leaders tried to accomplish this in many cases by consolidating several small districts into one, financed by a special school tax that a majority of voters in the respective districts imposed on themselves.

People in rural communities often resisted efforts to close small neighborhood schools in exchange for larger and better-equipped facilities, however. Higher taxes, loss of local autonomy, and less personal rapport between students and teachers were among the leading reasons for opposition to school consolidation. In many instances, local taxes required to finance consolidated schools were defeated at the polls several times before winning voter approval.

Proponents of the consolidation movement were successful in convincing voters of the benefits of home economics, agriculture, and other vocational courses not found in the smaller schools. Larger facilities also allowed rural communities to have high schools for the first time, as well as teachers with specialized training in academic subjects such as English, history, mathematics, science, and foreign languages. Moreover, larger schools meant more competitive athletic teams, which had an undeniable influence on school and community spirit. North Carolina's good roads were paramount to the success of consolidation, since students had to be bused several miles to larger facilities. The purchase and maintenance of school "trucks," and keeping a driver behind each steering wheel, became major expenses in school system budgets.

There were still one- and two-teacher schools in half of North Carolina's counties as late as the 1960s, but the success of the consolidation movement of the 1920s is clear. In 1900 there were 7,166 schools in the state, serving a population of 1.9 million, with buildings and equipment valued at $1.7 million. By 1930, when North Carolina's population had reached 3.2 million, there were only 6,340 schools, with buildings and equipment valued at $110 million.

K. Todd Johnson

Scotch Bonnet is the official state shell of North Carolina. The shell's inhabitant (*Phalium granulatum*) is a member of the helmet family, marine snails whose shells are characterized by short spires, large body whorls, and thickened outer lips. The scotch bonnet is found from North Carolina to Brazil and is distinguished by its pattern of small orange squares, which give it a plaid appearance (hence its name). The shell usually reaches 3 to 3½ inches in length when fully grown.

In the mid-1960s, state representative Moncie Daniels of coastal Dare County introduced the legislation naming the scotch bonnet as the official state shell and promised a keepsake shell to any of the 170 legislators who supported him. When he was able to find only two scotch bonnets, his colleagues grew hesitant to select such a rare shell. State senator Jimmy Johnson of Iredell County stated that inlanders "don't want to spend their time . . . horsing around for something that's extinct." Johnson suggested naming the chicken eggshell the official shell of Iredell County. Governor Dan K. Moore avoided the question and recommended the decision be left to those who knew more about shells. The bill passed in the Senate on 21 May 1965 and consequently became law after weeks of campaigning by Daniels and the bill's sponsor in the Senate, Ashley Futrell of Beaufort, who had acquired a box full of scotch bonnets and handed them out to his fellow senators.

Reference: William K. Emmerson and Morris K. Jacobson, *The American Museum of Natural History Guide to Shells* (1976).

Sarah Spink Downing

Scotch Fair. In the early 1800s, the Sandhills region of North Carolina faced considerable obstacles to economic prosperity. There was only one river of any consequence in the area, the Cape Fear, which ran along the region's northern border and emptied directly into the Atlantic Ocean. The Lumber River, which flowed through the middle of the Sandhills, was slow moving, encumbered with cypress trees, and flowed south into the Pee Dee River of South Carolina. There were no convenient waterways that made transportation of goods and people convenient or economical or connected the area with other parts of the state. Resourceful Scottish settlers in the region, however, devised a solution to their dilemma.

In 1792 a Scotch Fair was chartered, to be held in May and October of each year. The site selected for this event was approximately half the distance between Fayetteville, N.C., and Cheraw, S.C., placing the location one-quarter mile from Laurel Hill Church (the modern-day Old Laurel Hill Church). The fair appears to have been well advertised, since by the early 1800s it was attracting large crowds of people from as far away as the mountains. Merchants of Fayetteville, Cheraw, Wilmington, and Charlotte, along with peddlers of all sorts, sold or bartered their merchandise. Covered wagons from the mountains, loaded with apples, potatoes, and other produce, actually made the journey to this attraction. People brought their chickens, baked goods, handicrafts, and extra horses to sell during Scotch Fair week.

The excitement of athletic competition and horse races also attracted large crowds. Poker games and horse trading caused tempers to flare, but apparently only one man was killed during the history of the fair. Fighting events were popular, and those with overblown confidence fueled by whiskey consumption bet large sums of money on the outcomes. The winner of these savage fights walked away with a handsome purse, but he may also have left with an empty eye socket, an earlobe chewed in half, or the tip of his nose bitten off. One famous visitor to the Scotch Fair was a scruffy fighter known as "one-eyed Hector McNeill," who had had an eye gouged out during a previous match.

In the mid-1830s a number of Laurel Hill citizens were concerned about the drinking, fighting, and gambling that took place at the Scotch Fair. State statutes made efforts to regulate these unsavory activities but seemed to have little effect in controlling the raucous behavior. By the 1840s, members of the Laurel Hill community and Laurel Hill Church were petitioning the state legislature to abolish the Scotch Fair.

The Civil War put fair activity into a period of dormancy for several years. The Scotch Fair apparently was revived after the war, because complaints about it reappeared in the late 1860s. Finally, in 1873 Senator Richard Long presented a petition to the General Assembly on behalf of the citizens of Richmond County. The petition was granted and the Scotch Fair officially came to an end.

References: Joyce Gibson, *Scotland County Emerging: 1750–1900* (1995); Ruth Jane Trivette, *Legacy of the Committed* (1982); Marilyn Wright, *A Sense of Place* (1991).

Marilyn Wright

Scotch Merchants. Often intended as an insult, the term "Scotch merchant" referred to men, by no means all of them Scots, who functioned as factors and agents for large mercantile companies headquartered along the American coast, in England, or in Scotland. They purchased crops of any size and extended credit to even small-time planters, encouraging the extension of tobacco production far into the interior of Virginia and North Carolina. Hamilton and Company was the most important so-called Scotch merchant firm in North Carolina. In 1761 this company opened a store just outside of Halifax, about 60 miles inland from Edenton, the region's principal port. From that base of operations the company supplied credit, slaves, and consumer items to planters as far west as Granville and Orange Counties and dispatched the tobacco it acquired to Virginia warehouses in carts and wagons.

In times of economic distress, many colonial merchants called in the credit extended to planters, employed lawyers to bring debt suits against those who could not or would not pay, and had court clerks produce the writs that led to the attachment and ultimate public auction of the debtor's property. Although the image of such greedy merchants reducing honest planters to poverty was surely an overreaction to an economic crisis over which neither had much control, the Scotch merchant consequently became an icon of villainy in the popular culture of the late colonial era.

References: Harry Roy Merrens, *Colonial North Carolina in the Eighteenth Century: A Study in Historical Geography* (1964); James P. Whittenburg, "Planters, Merchants, and Lawyers: Social Change and the Origins of the North Carolina Regulation, 1765–1777," *William and Mary Quarterly* 34 (April 1977).

James P. Whittenburg

Scotland County, located at the border of the Piedmont and Coastal Plain regions of North Carolina, was formed in 1899 from Richmond County and named for the ancestral home of many of its inhabitants. It partially borders the state of South Carolina. Early inhabitants of the area included the Saura (Cheraw) Indians, followed by Highland Scots and En-

glish settlers. Groups of Quakers also migrated to the area in the eighteenth century. The county seat, Laurinburg, was incorporated in 1877 and named for the McLaurin family, prominent among the county's early Scottish settlers. Other communities in the county include East Laurinburg, Gibson, Old Hundred, Laurel Hill, Hasty, and Johns. Notable physical features of the county include the Lumber River, Shoe Heel and Jordan Creeks, Big Muddy Lake, Juniper Swamp, and McNair Pond.

Scotland County's heritage as a destination for thousands of Scottish settlers during the eighteenth century greatly influenced its growth and development. St. Andrews Presbyterian College, the successor of a number of Presbyterian educational institutions dating back to the nineteenth century, was established in Laurinburg in 1958. It houses the Scottish Heritage Center. The county is home to several historic sites and landmarks, including Camp Mackall Military Reservation (1943), the Richmond Temperance and Literary Society Hall (1860), and the Jesse Mason House (1895). Cultural institutions include the Indian Museum of the Carolinas in Laurinburg, and the Vardell Art Gallery. The county hosts festivals and annual events such as the John Blue Cotton Festival, ScotchFest, and the Laurinburg Christmas Parade.

Scotland County generates forest products and agricultural goods such as cotton, corn, soybeans, tobacco, and swine. Manufactured products include textiles and apparel, hospital equipment, cabinet accessories, and mobile homes. The population of Scotland County was estimated to be 36,800 in 2004.

Jay Mazzocchi

SEE ALSO Indian Museum of the Carolinas; St. Andrews Presbyterian College; Scottish Settlers.

Scottish Settlers. Scots—as individuals and in families—have been in North Carolina since the beginning of permanent settlement. The first Proprietary governor of Albemarle, William Drummond, was born in Scotland, and later Scots—such as the Glaswegian Thomas Pollock, who came to North Carolina in 1683—achieved prominence in the mercantile and political life of the colony. The earliest surviving court and land grant records reveal modest numbers of distinctively Scottish names.

The first sizable group of Scots to arrive in North Carolina in a body was the so-called Argyll Colony of 1739, which came from the Highland county of Argyll and settled on the Cape Fear River between Cross Creek and the Lower Little River. Numbering some 350 men, women, and children, the group was led by Highland gentry who provided much of the financing for the venture and received the largest grants of land. Gabriel Johnston, a Lowland Scot and North Carolina governor from 1734 to 1752, was accused of showing favoritism to his compatriots, and the General Assembly exempted the newcomers from taxation for ten years after their arrival.

The second large wave of Highland immigrants began in the late 1760s and reached its peak in 1774. It is not known exactly how many Highlanders came to North Carolina, but in 1784 James Knox estimated that 20,000 Highlanders migrated to America during this second wave. Most of the Highlanders who came as part of the second wave settled in the Upper Cape Fear region that includes modern-day Cumberland, Harnett, Hoke, and Moore Counties. Many Highlanders lived in the rural areas on the roads leading to the town of Cross Creek (later Fayetteville), which was chartered by the General Assembly in 1760. The abundance of pine trees in the Sandhills enabled these settlers to make their living in naval stores, extracting the sap and processing it into tar, pitch, and turpentine, which they sent down the Cape Fear River to Wilmington on flatboats made of logs. Many Highlanders were also small farmers growing crops and raising horses, cattle, and hogs.

Other individuals and families found their way directly from the Scottish Highlands to North Carolina during the remainder of the colonial era, mainly through the ports of Brunswick and Wilmington. The colony, in fact, came to be extolled as "the best poor man's country" as promotional tracts and letters home praised its climate and soil and the ease with which land could be acquired. Lowland Scots also immigrated individually or in small groups to North Carolina and other colonies throughout the seventeenth and eighteenth centuries. Because Lowland Scots were widely dispersed and more readily assimilated in the colonies, their story is less easily told than that of their Highland compatriots. While there were far fewer Lowland Scots than Highland Scots in North Carolina, some Lowlanders filled important roles as merchants, high-ranking officials, or military officers. Others ranged from poor immigrants and indentured servants to well-educated teachers, physicians, and clergymen.

The migration of Scotch-Irish settlers to America began in the 1680s but did not occur in large numbers until the 1720s. Pennsylvania was the most popular destination, but Scotch-Irish immigrants also settled in South Carolina, New Jersey, and Maryland. The Scotch-Irish, or Ulster Scots, were descendants of the Lowland Scots, whom James I of England had settled in Ulster, the northern and most isolated and conservative part of Ireland. During the reign of Elizabeth I, the native aristocracy of Ulster had rebelled against the English government and its newly established Anglican Church. The earliest concentrated settlement of Scotch-Irish immigrants in North Carolina was in Duplin and New Hanover Counties around 1740. The Scotch-Irish were also the largest ethnic group among the settlers in the Carolina backcountry in the eighteenth century, and they were the largest group among the pioneers who crossed the Blue Ridge and Allegheny Mountains and settled in southwestern North Carolina in the late eighteenth and early nineteenth centuries.

Although the Scottish emigrants, in coming to America, were assured freedom to exercise their Presbyterian religion at a time when the Stuart monarchy favored spreading the Anglican Church throughout the British Isles, the most important motivation for Scottish emigration was economic. Profound changes in agricultural organization following the Jacobite insurrection of 1745 raised rents to unprecedented heights and resulted in large numbers of evictions. Entire communities often emigrated, with the enterprise many times being organized by "tacksmen"—leaseholders who traditionally held long leases from the landowner and in turn rented to tenants.

Several North Carolina Scots gained prominence in the colony, with Governor Johnston, Royal Council member John Rutherfurd, and official and planter James Murray being examples. Scots were also important in the religious life of the colony, being well represented among both Presbyterian and Anglican clergy. A Scottish immigrant, James Innes, was a notable military leader in the French and Indian War (1754–63). The military prowess of North Carolina Loyalist Scots was put to the test at the Battle of Moore's Creek Bridge in February 1776. Although they suffered a bloody defeat in that contest, Scots constituted the backbone of North Carolina Loyalism throughout the war, and with the establishment of independence many of them sought refuge in the British colonies of Nova Scotia and New Brunswick.

After the Revolutionary War, Scottish immigration to North Carolina gradually resumed and continued until the War of 1812. The number of immigrants who came to the state during this period is unknown, but Scottish port records of the 1790s and the opening years of the nineteenth century list several dozen emigrant vessels clearing for North Carolina, mainly Wilmington. After the War of 1812, at least a trickle of immigration resumed: in 1820, for example, a ship carrying migrants was cleared from Campbelltown to Wilmington. The U.S. Census of 1850 listed some 1,200 Scottish-born citizens in North Carolina, most of them residing in the counties of Cumberland, Moore, Robeson, and Richmond. In the census of 1880 the number was down to some 400. A Scottish corporation in the 1880s purchased land in Madison and Haywood Counties with a view to bringing in Scottish settlers. The venture was unsuccessful, as was the effort to bring Highland crofters (tenant farmers) to the Sandhills at about the same time. A similar attempt of the early 1890s to attract Scots to the lands of J. Bryan Grimes in Pitt County fared little better.

Immigrants from the Scottish Highlands often retained distinctive elements of their culture. The Gaelic language was spoken by some to at least a limited extent until the mid-nineteenth century. Presbyterianism continues to flourish in the areas of Scottish settlement, and Scottish music influenced the development of local musical forms. Clan societies and the Highland Games at Grandfather Mountain and elsewhere in North Carolina continue to help keep alive a sense of the importance of the state's Scottish heritage.

References: Tyler Blethen and Curtis Wood Jr., *From Ulster to Carolina: The Migration of the Scotch-Irish to Southwestern North Carolina* (1986); David Dobson, *Scottish Emigration to America, 1607–1785* (1994); Ian C. C. Graham, *Colonists from Scotland: Emigration to Scotland in the Eighteenth Century* (1956); Duane Meyer, *The Highland Scots of North Carolina, 1732–1776* (1961).

Robert J. Cain
Additional research provided by Lloyd Johnson, David A. Norris, and George W. Troxler.

SEE ALSO Argyll Colony; Crofter Immigration; Gaelic Language; Highland Games.

Sculpture. SEE Folk Art; Washington, Statues of.

Scuppernong Grape, named the state fruit of North Carolina in 2001, is a bronze-green variety of the muscadine grape (*Vitis rotundifolia*). It is one of the best-known names in North Carolina's (and the nation's) viticulture, being the first grape actively cultivated in the United States. Once also called the white grape, the big white grape, and the Roanoke grape, the scuppernong gained popularity and noteworthiness as a wine grape on the south side of Albemarle Sound. In 1811 it was named after Scuppernong River, Scuppernong Lake (now Lake Phelps), and the settlement of Scuppernong, all around Washington and Tyrrell Counties. The word "scuppernong" comes from the Algonquian *askuponong*, meaning "place of the askupo," which is the sweet bay tree (*Magnolia virginiana*). Old, variant spellings of the word include scoponum, coscoponum, cuetupcaning, skoupernong, and cascepunong.

Samuel Huntington Perkins, a Yale graduate on his way to Lake Landing Plantation on the southeastern shore of Lake Mattamuskeet, arrived at Roanoke Island in October 1817 and remarked in his diary, "The fig & grape here arrive to perfection. The inhabitants supply themselves with good wine, but manufacture little or none for exportation." In June 1823 Thomas Jefferson ordered a 30-gallon barrel of "the pure juice of the grape" through a Plymouth factor named Cox. In 1840 North Carolina was the premier winemaking state in America, its largest vineyard a six-acre farm at Brinkleyville in Halifax County. Sixty years later another Halifax vintner, Paul Garrett, won a prize in Paris for scuppernong wine; in 1904 a sparkling scuppernong called Paul Garrett's Special Champagne took top honors at St. Louis's Louisiana Purchase Exposition. Within a few years, Garrett's sweet Virginia Dare wine was among the most popular vinous drinks of the United States.

When Frank Hollowell of Bayside Plantation, Pasquotank County, put in scuppernongs there in 1973, he cited as his inspiration other up-and-coming growers of that day such as the Wood family in Chowan County and the Sell family in Brunswick County (who perfected an absolutely dry scuppernong wine). Today in Duplin County, the Fussell family operates Duplin Wine Cellars, vintners of a white scuppernong wine, a scuppernong blush, and a sparkling scuppernong with a recipe "developed from an article written by Sidney Weller in 1853" and boasted "to be the oldest and best champagne produced in America." These contemporary growers and vintners have all followed an old tradition, as North Carolina for the better part of two centuries has been an American leader in utilizing its native grapes.

References: Clarence Gohdes, *Scuppernong: North Carolina's Grape and Its Wines* (1982); Robert C. McLean, "A Yankee Tutor in the Old South," *NCHR* 42 (January 1970); Albert E. Radford, Harry E. Ahles, and C. Ritchie Bell, *Manual of the Vascular Flora of the Carolinas* (1968); Bland Simpson, "Nature's Vineyards," *Wildlife in North Carolina* 56 (September 1992).

Bland Simpson

Scuppernong grape arbor beside a dwelling in northeastern North Carolina as depicted in an 1859 engraving in *Harper's New Monthly Magazine*. NCC.

Seaboard Air Line Railway traced its corporate ancestry to the Seaboard Inland Air Line, which was created through an informal agreement in the decade after the Civil War between the Seaboard & Roanoke Railroad (S&R), operating from Portsmouth, Va., to Weldon, and the Raleigh & Gaston Railroad (R&G), extending from Weldon to Raleigh. The two lines desired to protect their joint interests in the developing network of railroads in the region. In 1874 the Virginia legislature gave the S&R the right to acquire connecting companies, and in September 1875 the Seaboard Air Line Agency was formed to implement the legislature's plan. In the nineteenth century the term "air line" commonly referred to a more or less direct route over high ground between cities—in contrast to one that followed the coast or river valleys.

Acting through the two railroads, the Seaboard Air Line Agency acquired the Raleigh & Augusta Air Line Railroad

(R&AAL) in November 1875 and struck an agreement with the Carolina Central Railway (CC) for trackage rights between Hamlet and Charlotte in 1877. Through freight and passenger service was established between Charlotte and Portsmouth, Va., which had steamer connections to Baltimore and the North. Early in 1879 the agency was replaced by the Seaboard Air Line Association (SAL), which controlled the S&R, R&G, R&AAL, and CC.

On 1 Aug. 1893 the SAL was reorganized as the SAL Railway System, although each company retained its corporate identity. In the 1920s, under the presidency of S. David Warfield, the SAL entered on a large-scale expansion into Florida, which was enjoying an enormous land boom. Construction began on the Florida, Western, and Northern Railroad to West Palm Beach and reached Miami early in 1927. The boom burst with the stock market collapse of October 1929, and on 23 Dec. 1930 the SAL entered a long receivership that did not end until reorganization of the company as the Seaboard Air Line Railway on 1 Aug. 1945. At that time it operated 3,857 miles of track.

The late 1940s and 1950s were good to the SAL, and for the first time in its history revenues exceeded those of the rival Atlantic Coast Line Railroad (ACL). Tracks, signaling, and equipment were improved, and the great freight yard at Hamlet—the operating heart of the system, where its lines to Florida met with those to Atlanta and Birmingham and to Richmond—was thoroughly modernized in 1954.

Despite the progress of the 1950s, the U.S. railroad industry was undergoing a change. New highways made long-distance trucking formidable competition, and airlines rapidly increased their share of the passenger and freight markets. Some railroads were in financial trouble and seeking to economize through parallel mergers with competitors. In 1960 the SAL and ACL agreed to merge. One share of SAL stock was to be exchanged for one share in the new company. But the merger was long delayed by litigation in the courts, where communities, including the city of Tampa, Fla., and shippers sought to preserve competition. The U.S. Supreme Court finally ruled in favor of the companies by a unanimous vote, and on 1 July 1967 the ACL merged with the Seaboard Air Line Railway to form the Seaboard Coast Line Railroad. (The redundant name was chosen to preserve the two lines' shortened names "Seaboard" and "Coast Line," as they were generally known.)

After the merger of the SAL and ACL and subsequent mergers leading to the formation of the CSX Transportation Corporation in July 1987, traffic was rerouted in the most efficient manner and a number of SAL lines were abandoned. Through freight traffic on the former SAL main line across North Carolina was diverted to and from Hamlet by way of Pembroke, over the former Carolina Central route to the former ACL main line. The tracks have been pulled up from a point north of Henderson to Petersburg. The Silver Star passenger train from New York to Florida continues to be operated by AMTRAK but uses a Norfolk Southern Corporation connection from Selma on the ACL line to Raleigh. It then operates over the SAL line through Southern Pines, Hamlet, and Columbia, S.C., to and from Florida.

References: Robert Wayne Johnson, *Through the Heart of the South: The Seaboard Air Line Railroad Story* (1995); A. M. Langley, *Seaboard Air Line Album* (1988); R. E. Prince, *Seaboard Air Line Railway: Steam Boats, Locomotives, and History* (1969).

George A. Kennedy

Sea-Gift, an 1873 novel by Edwin Wiley Fuller (1848–76) of Louisburg, presented a lively and romantic picture of student life in Chapel Hill. Autobiographical in some respects, it describes the youth of one John Smith, his career at the University of North Carolina, and his participation in the Civil War. The book contains detailed descriptions of the hazing of freshmen and other aspects of student life and was the first novel set in part in Chapel Hill. It contains a tall tale–telling contest, including a definition of the tall tale presented over 30 years before Mark Twain's essay on the same subject. The plot incorporates the university's "Dromgoole myth," concerning a famous duel fought near Piney Prospect in Chapel Hill. The book came to be known as the "Freshman's Bible" in the late nineteenth century and probably had a bearing on the formation of the Order of the Gimghoul at the university and the construction there of Gimghoul Castle. Elements of the plot of *Sea-Gift* involving a long train ride to enter college also may have influenced Thomas Wolfe in the writing of his novel, *Look Homeward, Angel* (1929), and a scene involving the burning of a plantation house is thought to have been a model for Margaret Mitchell in the writing of *Gone with the Wind* (1936).

Reference: E. T. Malone Jr., "The University of North Carolina in Edwin Fuller's 1873 novel, *Sea-Gift*" (M.A. thesis, UNC-Chapel Hill, 1975).

E. T. Malone Jr.

Seal, State. The design of North Carolina's state seal, officially called the Great Seal of the State of North Carolina, was standardized by the General Assembly in 1971 and modified in 1983 after many variations. The official seal is a circle 2¼ inches in diameter that features the robe-covered figures of "Liberty" and "Plenty" in its center. Liberty is standing and holding a capped pole in her left hand, and in her right hand is a scroll on which is written the word "Constitution." Plenty is seated with her right arm extended, holding three heads of grain in her right hand and the end of an overflowing cornucopia in her left hand. In the background are depictions of mountains and a three-masted ship floating on the ocean. The dates "May 20, 1775" (the date of the so-called Mecklenburg Declaration of Independence) and "April 12, 1776" (the date of the Halifax Resolves) appear at the top and bottom, respectively, of the center part of the seal. Around the outside border of the seal are the phrases "The Great Seal of the State of North Carolina" and *Esse Quam Videri*, the state motto, meaning "to be rather than to seem."

Reference: J. Bryan Grimes, *The History of the Great Seal of the State of North Carolina* (rev. ed., 1974).

Wiley J. Williams

Seaman's Friend Society was organized by a number of prominent businessmen, women, and other citizens in the city of Wilmington to "improve the social, moral, and religious condition of the seamen." In 1853 the society purchased a home and chapel in downtown Wilmington along the Cape Fear River, intended to serve as an "economical, moral boarding house" and hospital. The society cared for nearly 500 sailors a year, providing a temporary home for the mariner who was weary from ocean travel and an environment in which he might successfully be "christianized." The Seaman's Friend Society ended in 1918.

Craig M. Stinson

Seasoning Period is a term describing a time endured by many newcomers to North Carolina and other colonies in the South during which they became acclimated to the weather and living conditions. Humidity and temperature seem to have been especially troublesome to those who arrived from Great Britain.

In a letter to his uncle, Sewallis Shirley, late in July 1765, recently arrived royal governor William Tryon blamed sudden changes in temperature for the sickness his household servants were suffering. He mentioned fevers particularly and noted that a farm girl he brought over "has been so ill that she has done an hours work these two months." In November he wrote the secretary of state, Henry Seymour Conway, of "an illness that has visited me ever since the 3d of August last. It is a compound of every sort of fever; called by the inhabitants the seasoning of this climate."

Seasoning was not restricted to the coastal region. The Moravians in Wachovia noted in their diary for 25 Sept. 1766 that Anglican minister George Micklejohn, who arrived with strong recommendations from England, had been sent to Rowan County by the governor. He was settled in St. Luke's Parish in Salisbury but had been able to preach only once, as he had suffered from fever every day. The following year both Mrs. Tryon, wife of the governor, and their daughter had become ill and moved into the country for their health.

William S. Powell

Secession Movement in North Carolina was the coalition of forces supporting state separation from the American Union as promulgated by John C. Calhoun of South Carolina. After Calhoun's death in 1850, each new setback for the South within the Union led to an increase of secession sentiment. Certain state leaders, including U.S. senator Thomas L. Clingman, had expressed pro-secession views during the 1856 presidential election, when the Republican Party nominated its first candidate for president. Secession was given its greatest impetus, however, by the election of Abraham Lincoln as U.S. president in 1860.

In the 1860 election, Lincoln, the Republican candidate, was not on the North Carolina ballot. The vote was 48,533 for John C. Breckinridge of Kentucky, the southern Democratic choice; 44,039 for John Bell of Tennessee, the Constitutional Union candidate; and 2,690 for Stephen A. Douglas, the regular Democratic nominee. Because Breckinridge supporters backed the Union, the overall vote must be considered evidence of Union sentiment.

Nonslaveholding yeoman farmers made up a majority of the North Carolina population and constituted the core of the Unionist strength. They were disinclined to secede or fight for the preservation of slavery. Also, the Whig Party, which had disintegrated as a national party by 1860, still had a strong following. Whig leaders such as Congressman Zebulon B. Vance and former governor and U.S. senator William A. Graham comprised the bulk of the unconditional Unionist leadership, though other Whigs and conservative Democrats such as William W. Holden, editor of the Raleigh-based *North Carolina Standard*, advocated a "watch and wait" policy while maintaining that secession was a fundamental right of each state. The counties in the west, northeast, and Piedmont were areas of Unionist sentiment.

Democrats like Governor John W. Ellis, Senator Clingman, Congressman Thomas Ruffin, and former congressman William S. Ashe led the secessionists. The major secessionist newspaper was the *Wilmington Journal*, located in slave-heavy New Hanover County. The main areas of secessionist strength were the coastal counties with large slave populations and the counties that bordered South Carolina, especially Mecklenburg. Lincoln's election prompted this group to launch local secession meetings. The first meeting was held in Cleveland County on 12 Nov. 1860, the second in New Hanover on 19 November. A series of similar gatherings were held across the state. The movement was given a boost by the secession of South Carolina on 20 Dec. 1860.

To counter the secessionist trend, the Unionists held meetings of their own. Holden's *Standard* effectively espoused the Union cause, expressing hope of compromise despite the departure of the Deep South states. On 29 Jan. 1861 the General Assembly agreed to put the convention question to the people on 28 February. The legislature also voted to send delegates to the Washington Peace Conference on 4 February.

The convention campaign was vigorously waged. The Unionists were able to set the terms of the debate early, focusing on the question of "Union or Disunion." Secessionist attempts to redefine the campaign based on southern self-defense failed. To the charge that disunion meant war, A. W. Venable of Granville County declared that he would "wipe up every drop of blood shed in the war with this handkerchief of mine."

The Unionists carried the northeastern counties and most of the Piedmont and Mountains. They defeated the secessionists by a vote of 47,323 to 46,672. Because a few Unionists, including Vance, supported the convention call, the delegate elections are more indicative of actual sentiment. Only about a third of the 120 delegates elected were secessionists. The Unionists were helped by positive news from the Peace Conference the day before the election. The debate in the campaign had been injurious to the secessionist cause. On 4 March, a few days after the vote, Lincoln gave his inaugural address, which struck some as conciliatory.

The secessionists did not give up, however. On 22–23 Mar. 1861 delegates from 25 counties assembled in Goldsboro and organized the Southern Rights Party. They urged the legislature to call a convention and demanded that the state join the Confederacy. They posed the new debate in terms of South against North. Despite numerous meetings, by early April North Carolina seemed no nearer to secession than it had been in February. Then came the news that Confederate forces had bombarded Fort Sumter in Charleston Harbor on 12 April, followed on 15 April by Lincoln's call for 75,000 troops. Governor Ellis responded, "You can get no troops from North Carolina." Zebulon Vance was pleading for the Union with his arm upraised when word arrived of Lincoln's summons. "When my hand came down from that impassioned gesticulation," he recalled, "it fell slowly and sadly by the side of a secessionist."

Ellis called a special session of the legislature for 1 May and immediately ordered the seizure of Federal property. When the General Assembly met, it voted for a delegate election on 13 May to an unrestricted convention to meet in Raleigh on 20 May, the anniversary of the so-called Mecklenburg Declaration of Independence. The campaign for the convention was characterized by resignation rather than enthusiasm. Both Unionists and secessionists spoke of the need to act in the face of northern aggression. The major debate—whether North Carolina should separate based on "the right of revolution," as some Unionists advocated, or on the Calhounian doctrine of secession—was over. The radical secessionists favored the latter position.

A total of 122 Democratic and Whig delegates, 108 of whom were native North Carolinians, gathered on 20 May 1861. The delegates held an average of 30.5 slaves each, with the median being 21, which meant that over one-half of the delegates belonged to the small planter class. Sixty-eight delegates had attended college, making them far better educated than those who had elected them. The average personal and real property per delegate was valued at $61,817, placing them among the wealthy citizens of the state.

The convention elected Weldon N. Edwards, a Democratic planter from Warren County, as president. (Edwards defeated William A. Graham of Orange County.) Edwards gave a speech denouncing continued connection with the "Black Republican Union." Onetime Unionist George E. Badger introduced a resolution for separation from the Union based on the right of revolution. An alternate ordinance, simply dissolving the Union and representing the radical position, was proposed by Burton Craige of Rowan County. The Badger proposal was defeated by a vote of 72 to 40. An attempt to modify the Craige ordinance failed. The convention then unanimously passed the ordinance of secession and voted to accept the provisional Constitution of the Confederate States of America. As requested by Governor Ellis, the convention agreed not to put the secession ordinance to a popular vote. On 21 May 1861 the ordinance was signed and President Jefferson Davis proclaimed North Carolina a Confederate state.

The convention represented the high point for the Democratic secessionists, who suffered a major setback one year later when Conservative candidate Zebulon B. Vance was elected governor despite his strong opposition to secession.

References: Kemp P. Battle, "The Secession Convention of 1861," *North Carolina Booklet* (April 1916); Daniel W. Crofts, *Reluctant Confederates: Upper South Unionists in the Secession Crisis* (1989); William C. Harris, *North Carolina and the Coming of the Civil War* (1988); Marc W. Kruman, *Parties and Politics in North Carolina, 1836–1865* (1983); Joseph C. Sitterson, *The Secession Movement in North Carolina* (1939).

Ronnie W. Faulkner

Secotan was a large village of Algonquian-speaking Indians that was encountered in July 1585 along both banks of the Pamlico River by Sir Richard Grenville, an explorer sent by Sir Walter Raleigh. The village was documented in a detailed watercolor drawing by John White in 1585–86. Titled "Indian Village of Secotan," the drawing depicts a well-ordered village with family units, storehouses, fields with growing crops, and individuals performing different tasks. In 1690, Bath, the first town of English settlers in North Carolina, was established in the vicinity of Secotan, which had been abandoned by the Indians.

References: Paul Hulton and David B. Quinn, *The American Drawings of John White, 1577–1590*, vol. 1 (1964); Quinn, *The*

A watercolor drawing of the village of Secotan prepared by John White from observations he made in 1585–86 while a member of the Ralph Lane expedition. Trustees of the British Museum.

Roanoke Voyages, 1584–1590 (2 vols., 1955); Douglas L. Rights, *The American Indian in North Carolina* (2nd ed., 1957).

William S. Powell

Secretary of State is an elective office under the North Carolina Constitution. The office developed from that of secretary of the province, which was first filled in 1675 with the appointment of Robert Holden. The secretary of the province —named by the king of England and serving at His Majesty's pleasure—held largely clerical duties, with most of his attention given to the land office. The state Constitution of 1776, adopted after the colonies declared their independence from Great Britain, provided that the General Assembly "triennially appoint a secretary for this State." The Constitution of 1868 made the secretary of state an elective member of the Executive Department with a four-year term.

The responsibilities of the secretary of state are prescribed by law. Over the years many of these responsibilities have evolved into separate state agencies. By a resolution of the General Assembly of 1831 the secretary was required to collect books for the State Library, and for his services as librarian he received $50 a year. As the first insurance commissioner, he was required to appoint annually investigators of insurance companies doing business in the state and to publish an annual report showing the financial condition of insurance companies. When automobile registration was required in 1909, the secretary of state became responsible for registration and fee collection. In 1921 he began collecting gasoline taxes for the state's road-building program. The issuing of land grants, a function that dated from the first secretary of the province, ceased with the creation of the Property Control Division of the Department of Administration in 1957.

Prior to the construction of the State Legislative Building in 1961 and the employment of an administrative staff, the secretary of state performed a number of services for the General Assembly, including assigning seats in the legislative chambers, enrolling acts and resolutions prior to ratification, and indexing and printing the Session Laws. Most of these duties have been assumed by staff or committees of the General Assembly, but others, such as the publication of the *North Carolina Manual* and the *Directory of State and County Officials*, have remained the responsibility of the secretary of state. The person who holds the office also continues to be the custodian of the ratified acts of the General Assembly, handling the free distribution and sale of the printed Session Laws and journals of the House and Senate. Duties have also shifted to the secretary of state from other departments. Administration of the North Carolina Securities Act was transferred from the Utilities Commission in 1937, and responsibility for commissioning Notaries Public was transferred from the governor in 1971.

Other major functions of the office of secretary of state include chartering business and nonprofit corporations, acting as central filing officer for financing statements under the Uniform Commercial Code, registering trademarks and service marks, administering a land records management program, maintaining an office to inform the business community about all state licensing and regulatory requirements, and registering legislative lobbyists.

Under the Executive Organization Act of 1971, all powers, duties, and functions vested by law in the office of secretary of state were transferred to the Department of the Secretary of State, which was created by the same act, with the secretary of state designated as its head. From 1936 to 1988 the office of secretary of state was held by Thad Eure, who established a record for statewide elective office.

Reference: John L. Cheney Jr., ed., *North Carolina Government, 1585–1979: A Narrative and Statistical History* (1981).

Clyde Smith

Secret Ballot is often called the Australian ballot because the practice of confidential voting started in Australia in the 1850s and rapidly spread to other countries. Numerous American states adopted the secret ballot in the 1890s, but North Carolina maintained partisan ballot voting until the General Assembly passed a new ballot law in 1929.

Under the old system of voting, political parties printed their own ballots with only their own candidates listed. Voting was very public. Party officials and poll workers could tell how a person voted by observing the ballots he took and inserted into the ballot box. This method led to political pressure and vote buying. It did, however, have the advantage of making it easy for the illiterate to vote.

After the turn of the century, pressure gradually increased in North Carolina to eliminate party-produced ballots and replace them with official government ballots listing all candidates for a given office on a single ballot. In 1928 Democrat O. Max Gardner, of Shelby, an early proponent of the secret ballot, was elected governor on a pledge to introduce it in the state. In his inaugural address on 11 Jan. 1929, Gardner stated that North Carolina elections were "fair, honest, and just" but "conditions may still be further improved by the passage of a fair and just secret ballot law."

The first piece of legislation addressed by the 1929 session of the General Assembly was a secret ballot bill presented by J. Melville Broughton of Wake County and T. L. Johnson of Robeson County. There was some opposition in the Senate, primarily from partisans who feared a diminution of the Democratic vote, but the bill finally passed on a vote of 41 to 9. The House approved it by a wider margin—92 to 14—with some amendments that the Senate readily accepted. This ended the use of party ballots in North Carolina.

References: J. Morgan Kousser, *The Shaping of Southern Politics: Suffrage Restriction and the Establishment of the One-Party South, 1880–1910* (1974); Joseph L. Morrison, *Governor O. Max Gardner: A Power in North Carolina and New Deal Washington* (1971); Elmer L. Puryear, *Democratic Party Dissension in North Carolina, 1928–1936* (1962).

Ronnie W. Faulkner

Sectionalism. SEE East-West Rivalry.

Segregation. SEE African Americans; Civil Rights Movement; Education, Public; Greensboro Sit-Ins; *Plessy v. Ferguson*; *Swann v. Charlotte-Mecklenburg Board of Education*.

Semiconductors. SEE Information Technology.

Settlement Patterns. Although there had been earlier attempts at settlement by the Spanish and English, the first permanent colonies in North Carolina took hold during the mid-

seventeenth century and were scattered along the sounds, rivers, and creeks north of Albemarle Sound, a region then claimed by Virginia. The early settlers were primarily English merchants, traders, and farmers from the Jamestown area seeking better opportunities and freedom from taxation. Among them were small numbers of Irish, Scotch-Irish, and Welsh immigrants. Their southern advance was slow and the date of onset obscure. Some colonists arrived with slaves, and records indicate that lands were sometimes granted or sold by local Indians.

Throughout this period, access to unclaimed land was most easily and therefore most frequently accomplished by way of water—the sounds and navigable rivers. Thus, the greatest concentration of early settlements occurred along Albemarle Sound and the Pamlico, Neuse, and Trent Rivers and their tributaries (the Tidewater), giving rise to the state's first established cities: Bath (1705), New Bern (1710), and Edenton (1722). Settlers moving up the Cape Fear River founded Brunswick (ca. 1725), soon to be eclipsed by its upriver rival, Wilmington (ca. 1733). As land near the coast became less available, colonists moved west into the interior along rivers and creeks, reaching the Eno River by about 1735.

By 1663 about 500 people lived between Virginia and Albemarle Sound; by 1675, around 4,000 were situated there. The coastal population in 1730 has been estimated at about 36,000 (including about 6,000 blacks); nonetheless, North Carolina remained the most sparsely settled English colony on the continent. Aside from a few Lowland Scots and Welsh, the majority of settlers throughout the Proprietary period (1663–1729) continued to be English. French Huguenots also located along the upper Neuse River beginning in the 1690s, and German Palatines and Swiss inhabited New Bern from its founding.

With the suppression of piracy and the ending of local Indian wars by 1720, the rate of settlement west of the Coastal Plain accelerated dramatically, continuing throughout the royal period (1729–75) but temporarily slowing down during the French and Indian War (1754–63). Beginning around 1730, migration into the region proceeded largely along two popular routes: northward into the Piedmont and southeast Coastal Plain by way of the Cape Fear River Valley (which had been unsettled until 1667), and southward into the western backcountry via the Great Wagon Road. Some settlers entered the Cape Fear region by way of the "100-mile road" from the vicinity of New Bern.

Among the largest groups traveling north along the Cape Fear River were the Highland Scots, many of whom moved into the region now centered around Fayetteville after 1732. This became the greatest concentration of Highland Scots in America. In a short time, their settlements lay throughout the Upper Cape Fear region today comprising Anson, Bladen, Cumberland, Harnett, Hoke, Moore, Richmond, Robeson, Sampson, and Scotland Counties. At this time a smaller group

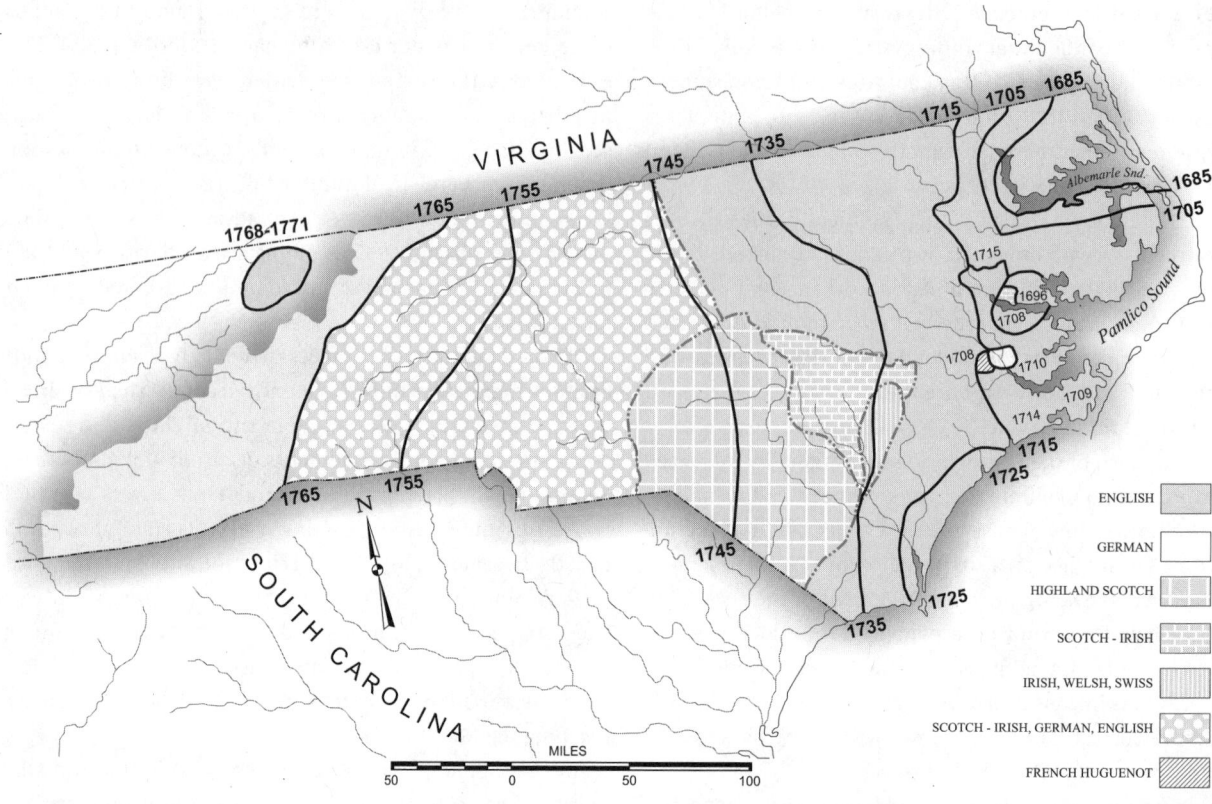

Progress of European settlement, 1685–1771. Map by Mark Anderson Moore, courtesy NCOA&H.

of Welsh immigrants settled primarily west of the Northeast Cape Fear River in parts of modern-day Pender, Duplin, and Sampson Counties.

Coincident with the Highland migration were those of Scotch-Irish and Germans. Utilizing the Great Wagon Road through the Shenandoah Valley of Virginia, they came predominantly from Pennsylvania, but also from New Jersey, Maryland, and Virginia. Most were second- and third-generation farmers and merchants seeking land, tax relief, and, in some cases, greater religious freedom.

The Scotch-Irish (sometimes called Ulster Scots) moved into the North Carolina backcountry, the Piedmont, and onward to South Carolina beginning around 1735. They were highly literate, self-reliant, and industrious, exerting a tremendous influence on the history of the state. By the 1740s Scotch-Irish had settled along the Haw and Eno Rivers, and about 24 years later they were reported west of the Yadkin.

German immigrants, taking much the same route, belonged mainly to Lutheran, Reformed, and Moravian sects, the last comprising the largest and most significant group during the first stages of settlement. Renowned as superior farmers, they located first in present-day Rowan County, then in Cabarrus, Stanly, Union, Mecklenburg, Lincoln, Davie, Davidson, Catawba, and Burke Counties. The Moravians began to arrive in 1753, one year after a party of Moravian brethren from

Pennsylvania purchased a tract of land in modern-day Forsyth County.

The peak period of the settlement of North Carolina lasted from about 1730 until the American Revolution. By 1830 settlement of the entire state was essentially complete.

References: Hugh T. Lefler and Albert Ray Newsome, *North Carolina: The History of a Southern State* (3rd ed., 1973); William S. Powell, *North Carolina through Four Centuries* (1989); Robert W. Ramsey, *Carolina Cradle: Settlement of the Northwest Carolina Frontier, 1747–1762* (1964).

William G. DiNome

SEE ALSO German Settlers; Great Wagon Road; Moravians; Scottish Settlers; Swiss and Palatine Settlers; Welsh Settlers.

Seymour Johnson Air Force Base. Seymour Johnson Field, Goldsboro, was activated on 12 June 1942 as Headquarters, Technical School, Army Air Force Technical Training Command. The following year it also assumed responsibility for preparing Air Corps personnel for deployment overseas as replacements and became the home of the Seventy-fifth Training Wing, which conducted a pretraining school for aviation cadets.

The 326th Fighter Group was assigned to Seymour Johnson

in October 1943 and trained pilots for P-47 Thunderbolt aircraft from January 1944 until the end of World War II. The base also housed a number of German prisoners of war. It became an Air Corps separation center in September 1945 and was deactivated in May 1946.

In the early 1950s Goldsboro mayor Scott B. Berkeley, a World War I aviator, and John Dortch Lewis, a World War II aviator and prisoner of war, led a campaign to reactivate the base, working largely through longtime U.S. congressman Graham A. Barden of Sampson County. On 1 Apr. 1956 Seymour Johnson Air Force Base reopened as part of the Tactical Air Command, and in July it became home to the Eighty-third Fighter-Day Wing. The Eighty-third subsequently was designated the Fourth Tactical Fighter Wing (known as the Fourth Wing). The Fourth is famous for shooting down the greatest number of enemy aircraft in both World War II and the Korean War.

Since its reactivation, the base has been the quarters of the 482nd Fighter-Interceptor Squadron of the Air Defense Command, the 68th Bombardment Wing of the Strategic Air Command, the 19th "Suitcase" Air Force, and other units. The 482nd flew F-102 Delta Darts, and the 68th carried B-52 bombers. KC-10 tanker aircraft were also assigned to the base. The Fourth Wing and its predecessor, the Eighty-third, have flown F-86s, F-100s, F-105s, F-4s, and the F-15E. In the early 2000s the 4th consisted of two operational squadrons and two training squadrons, all equipped with F-15E Strike Eagles. The base was also home to the 916th Air Refueling Wing (USAF Reserve), which flew KC-135R tankers. A minimum security federal prison with 500 inmates was assigned to the base in 1991.

As of the early 2000s Seymour Johnson was the only air force base in the world named for a U.S. Navy pilot. Lt. Seymour Johnson, a test pilot, was killed in a crash near Norbeck, Md., on 5 Mar. 1941. After his death, his mother lived in Goldsboro and for many years served as head of the American Red Cross. The base was also unique in that it enjoyed one of the best reputations in the air force for community relations—a legacy of Berkeley, who was mayor of Goldsboro when the base was reactivated. The base housing development and a major thoroughfare leading to the base are named in Berkeley's honor; the Order of Daedalians chapter at the base bears his name as well. A huge set of air force pilot's wings adorned columns overlooking downtown Goldsboro near city hall, symbolizing the relationship between the civilian and military communities.

Eugene Price

Shad Boats are the official state boats of North Carolina. They were first developed around Roanoke Island after the Civil War, when a shortage of suitable trees for periaugers and an increase in fishing required strong, shallow-draft workboats. This boat type has several names, all linking a locality

Fishermen at Manteo pose with their catch behind a Roanoke Island shad boat, ca. 1900. NCC.

with the vessel's use, including "Dare County shad boat," "spritsail shad boat," "Albemarle Sound boat," "Croatan fishing boat," and "Pamlico Sound boat." The design was limited geographically to the area from Elizabeth City to Ocracoke Island and neighboring sounds. (North Carolina's shad boats should not be confused with late-nineteenth-century V-bottom shad boats made in Florida, Georgia, and South Carolina.)

Shad boats were first built in the 1870s by George Washington Creef, who combined traditional split-log techniques with conventional plank-on-frame construction. The original Creef design was extremely successful and in high demand by coastal fishermen. Creef taught many others to build this vessel, which soon became one of the better and more handsome North Carolina workboats. His boat works produced shad boats from the 1870s through the early 1930s, while other builders turned out similar designs.

The keel was a hewn white cedar trunk, and the curved frames were cut from buttress roots. The hand-shaped keel log reflects descent from the split-log dugouts (periaugers) that utilized a similar centerpiece. Early shad boats had round bottoms with curved frames and a high, square stern to hold nets. Combining cypress frames with cedar or juniper planking made the craft extremely durable. The round bottom, wide beam, and full body, coupled with an upright, raked stem and a raking heart-shaped stern, made the boat extremely stable even in rough water. Most shad boats had no deck except for narrow washboards, or "side-decks." They were powered by a large sprit mainsail and a jib, but many also carried a topsail and occasionally used a flying jib. The combination of the round bottom, sturdy hull, and multiple sails helped fishermen maneuver in the unpredictable sounds.

Gas engines gave later boats greater versatility, but cheaper wood, overuse, and engine vibration made these newer boats much less durable than their sailing predecessors. Engine-powered boats did not require sophisticated hull designs that worked most efficiently in variable winds, so few of the complex, round-hull shad boats were built after the 1920s. There are five shad boats in the North Carolina Maritime Museum in Beaufort, including an original Creef boat.

References: Michael B. Alford, *Traditional Work Boats of North Carolina* (1990); Rodney Barfield, *Seasoned by Salt: A Historical Album of the Outer Banks* (1995); William C. Fleetwood Jr., *Tidecraft* (1995).

Lawrence E. Babits

Shad Festival at Grifton was started in 1971 as a way to promote community spirit and attract visitors to eastern North Carolina. The weekend festival, held each April, celebrates the annual migration of shad up the Neuse River and into creeks such as the Contentnea, which bisects Grifton and once brought steamboats to the town. The Shad Festival boasts more than 30 events, which include a beauty pageant, a "Fishy Tales" lying contest, an art show, "Shad-O" bingo, canoe and kayak races, the "Shad Shoot" archery tournament, a street dance, and plenty of music. The kick-off event for the festival is a shad fishing contest, the winners of which have set four state records for hickory shad taken on hook and line. A parade proceeds down Queen Street, where visitors can also find crafts, a flea market, entertainment, and food. Those who ride the "Shad Shuttle" to the Historical Museum may be surprised to learn that just north of Grifton was the fortified Tuscarora town, Catechna, site of an important battle in 1712. Chief Arnold Hewitt of the Tuscarora Indian Nation in New York came to the 1977 Shad Festival as a special guest.

Because shad is so bony, not much of the fish is actually eaten at the Shad Festival, and other kinds of fish are used for the festival's fish fry and famous fish stew. Eastern North Carolina barbecue is another popular item on the menu.

References: Jerry Bledsoe, *North Carolina Curiosities* (1990); Janet Haseley and Ed Haseley, eds., *The Twenty-seventh Annual Grifton Shad Festival Handbook* (1997).

Rosemary Clifford Neill

Shag Dancing. The shag is a popular dance most commonly associated with the beach towns of North Carolina and South Carolina. It is a two-person, male-led dance with a basic step that allows much room for improvisation and imagination. The dance looks deceptively easy but is actually quite complicated. The origins of the shag are slightly cloudy, but some historians trace its evolution back to early settlers of the Carolina colony who, in an effort to preserve their European musical lineage, formed the St. Cecilia Society in Charles Towne (Charleston), S.C., in the 1760s. Others trace it back even further to African roots. In either case, in the late nineteenth and early twentieth centuries, the slow grind jazz

dances popular in some North Carolina and South Carolina clubs made their way to clubs in the Northeast, and dances such as the Charleston and jitterbug were born, leading eventually to the modern shag.

Although the evolving shag was done to jazz and swing music in the 1920s and 1930s, the modern shag began gaining more popularity on the coast of North Carolina and South Carolina in the 1940s and early 1950s. Billy Jeffers—who deemed himself a "fast dancer," not a shagger—became one of the first "stars" associated with the dance during the 1940s and early 1950s. Next came names such as "Chicken" Hicks and "Big" George Linberry, who helped infiltrate the Carolina coast with the smooth sound of "beach music" and practiced the smooth steps that would become the modern shag. There were many beach club pavilions sporting dilapidated outsides and wooden dance floors where teenagers would sneak off and dance the night away. Probably the most famous of all of these dance clubs was the Pad in Myrtle Beach, S.C. In its prime, the shag became more than just a dance; it was a social phenomenon, with teenagers from all over the Carolinas drawn to its image of daring and excitement.

The first use of the term "shag" most likely appeared in the early 1960s, just when enthusiasm for the dance was waning. In 1954 Hurricane Hazel had demolished most of the old dance pavilions and rock 'n' roll had surpassed shag music in popularity. The shag was revived in the early 1970s, however, when a competitive dance circuit formed in Atlantic Beach inspired a renewed interest in the dance. In the early 2000s, the Society of Stranders (S.O.S.) and the Association of Carolina Shag Clubs listed thousands of members, and there were estimated to be 800,000 people nationwide familiar with the dance.

Reference: Bo Bryan, *Shag: The Legendary Dance of the South* (1995).

Laura Young Baxley

Shakori Indians were one of several small tribes that occupied the Piedmont region of what is now North Carolina during early English colonization. The prehistoric origins of the Shakori are unclear. During his 1711 expedition against warring Tuscarora Indians and their allies, South Carolina Indian fighter John Barnwell claimed that the Shakori and Sissipahaw were identical. During his 1650 exploration of the Virginia-Carolina Piedmont, Edward Bland identified the land between the Meherrin River and the head of the Nottoway River as the "rich old fields" of the Nottoway and "Schockoores." Although Bland did not indicate the location of the Shakori or their relationship with neighboring Indians, the tribe appears to have migrated farther south by 1670.

German explorer John Lederer noted in 1670 that the Shakori were among various tribes located along the Eno River in North Carolina. The tribe may have relocated to this area for both cultural and security reasons. According to Lederer, the Shakori shared similar customs and manners with the neighboring Eno tribe. They also may have sought stronger diplomatic and trade ties with the Eno Indians in order to resist being dominated by the powerful Tuscarora, with whom they periodically fought.

By the early eighteenth century, at least one group of Shakoris was living with the Eno Indians at the town of Adshusheer on the Eno River. The Sissipahaw were located close by on the Haw River. The Shakori-Eno merger occurred on a political as well as cultural level. According to English surveyor and trader John Lawson, the "Shoccories" and the Eno shared a common chief known as Eno-Will. By the time Lawson came into contact with these tribes in 1701, the Indians of the Carolina Piedmont were well within the orbit of the Virginia-Carolina skin and fur trade. Lawson described trade between the Shakori and Tuscarora Indians who probably came from the latter's northern villages. Increased contact with English colonists and traders apparently caused divisions within the Shakori. Eno-Will informed Lawson that his affection for the English had alienated the Anglophobes in his tribe, causing him to fear for his life.

The Shakori's involvement in the skin and fur trade and their close association with the Tuscarora Upper Towns may explain why they played little if any role in the Tuscarora War of 1711–13. On the other hand, South Carolinians accused Eno-Shakori villages of aiding warring Yamassees in 1715. The absence of references to the Shakori after 1715 suggests that they, like other small tribes in the Carolina Piedmont, were assimilated within more powerful neighboring tribes. The Eno and their "confederates," who probably included the Shakori, petitioned the Virginia government in 1715 to settle with the Saponi Indians at Fort Christanna. Between 1736 and 1743, the ethnically diverse Eno migrated to the Catawba River, where they joined forces with the Sissipahaw and other displaced Indians to form the powerful Catawba Nation.

References: James H. Merrell, *The Indians' New World: Catawbas and Their Neighbors from European Contact through the Era of Removal* (1989); H. Trawick Ward and R. P. Stephen Davis Jr., *Indian Communities on the North Carolina Piedmont, A.D. 1000 to 1700* (1993).

Christine S. Devine

Shallow Ford, a rock-bottomed crossing point on the Yadkin River, was the site of several important events in North Carolina history. The ford was used by settlers and traders in the region from about 1750 until about 1920, when highways and bridges rerouted traffic. The course of the Yadkin River at this point forms the boundary between present-day Forsyth County and, to its west, Yadkin County. The Shallow Ford crossing is approximately 600 yards south of the modern bridge on the Huntsville-Lewisville road.

Shallow Ford was an essential link on Great Wagon Road, the frontier road used by immigrants to backcountry North Carolina in the mid-eighteenth century. On 14 Oct. 1780 about 300 Whigs, led by Joseph Cloyd, engaged a similar number of Tories, commanded by Gideon Wright, in a battle near Shallow Ford. The Whigs included about 160 Virginia troops and 140 militiamen from Surry and Rowan Counties. The battle, lasting several hours, ranged over an area that included present-day Huntsville. Fifteen Tories and a single Whig, a captain in the Virginia militia named Henry Francis, were killed in the Whig victory. A tributary of the Yadkin River took the name Battle Branch from this encounter.

On 17 Feb. 1781 Lord Charles Cornwallis's army of 2,500 to 3,000 men crossed the Yadkin at Shallow Ford in pursuit of the American force commanded by Gen. Nathanael Greene. The two armies would meet five weeks later, on 15 Mar. 1781, at the Battle of Guilford Courthouse. A minor engagement resulted from the February 1781 crossing. Joseph Graham's company of Whigs met with the column of Cornwallis's troops en route from Shallow Ford to Salem and, in the conflict, lost one man and had five taken prisoner.

On 11 Apr. 1865 Union cavalry under Gen. George H. Stoneman skirmished with Confederates at Shallow Ford. Moving east from Tennessee across western North Carolina, Stoneman's immediate objective was to destroy factories in Salem engaged in making clothing for southern troops. The detachment that crossed the Yadkin River numbered about 5,000 men. Militia posted at the site stood little chance of slowing their progress. Union accounts state that the Confederates offered "feeble resistance" and fled, leaving behind 100 new muskets.

In 1913 the North Carolina Chapter of the Daughters of the American Revolution placed a series of markers designating a "Daniel Boone Trail" from North Carolina to Kentucky. Two markers were erected at Shallow Ford and another at Huntsville near the John Kelly Tavern building. The state government placed markers dedicated to Shallow Ford and Stoneman's Raid in 1938 and 1941, respectively. These signs were later relocated to sites near the Huntsville-Lewisville bridge.

References: Adelaide L. Fries, J. Edwin Hendricks, and Stuart T. Wright, *Forsyth: The History of a County on the March* (rev. ed., 1976); Robert W. Ramsey, *Carolina Cradle: Settlement of the Northwest Carolina Frontier, 1747–1762* (1964); Frank V. Tursi, *Winston-Salem: A History* (1994).

Michael Hill

Shape-Note Singing is a form of American choral music developed in the early nineteenth century and still sung in sections of the southeastern United States. Shape-note singing is also known as "fasola" singing, after the musical syllables, fa, sol, and la, or "sacred harp" singing, a reference

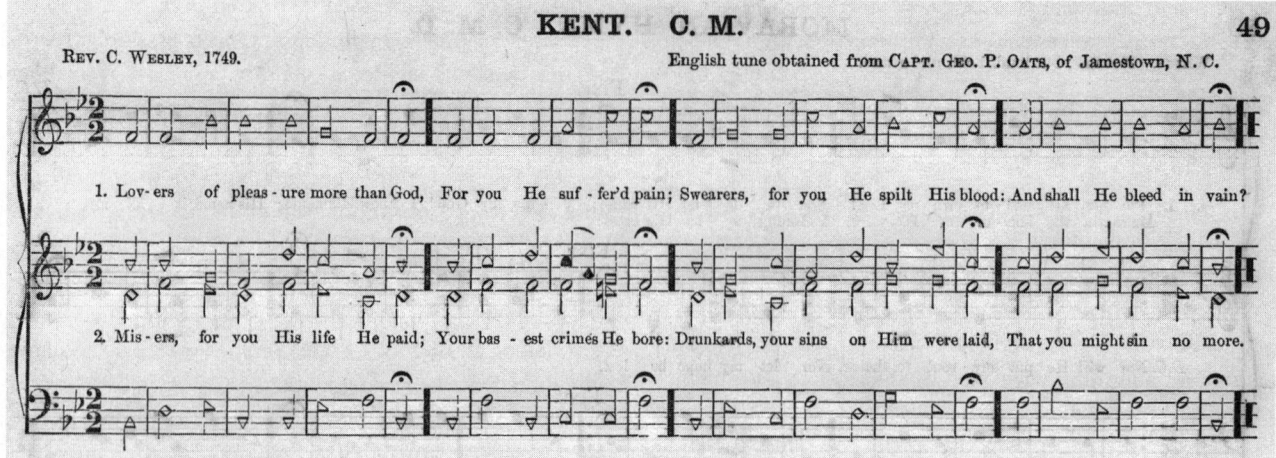

KENT. C. M. 49

Rev. C. Wesley, 1749.   English tune obtained from Capt. Geo. P. Oats, of Jamestown, N. C.

The song "Kent" by Charles Wesley was included in William Hauser's 1878 shape-note songbook *The Olive Leaf*. Hauser credited George Oats of Jamestown as his source for the tune. Music Library, Duke University.

to *The Sacred Harp*, one of many compilations of shape-note music. The term "shape-note" comes from the system of notation used in this music. Instead of using standard notation, in which musical notes have an oval shape, shape-note music assigns a unique shape to a note to indicate its pitch on the staff. Thus, a triangle represents the pitch fa; a circle, sol; a square, la; and a diamond, mi.

Shape-note singing spread rapidly throughout the South. Such was its popularity that between 1801 and 1855 at least 38 shape-note tune books were published. These tune books usually included rudiments of music theory and some instructions on the art of singing. The majority of compositions in each book were hymns and other religious songs, but secular selections included love songs and patriotic tunes. Among the most popular shape-note tune book of the antebellum period was *The Southern Harmony*, compiled by William Walker (1809–75) of South Carolina, one of the most prominent of the southern shape-note singing teachers. Sources for songs in the book included hymn tunes composed by Walker, folk hymns already familiar to many singers, and white spirituals, or sacred texts set to secular folk melodies.

As in other southern states, shape-note music took hold in North Carolina, and North Carolinians contributed to the shape-note tradition. William Hauser (1812–80), born and raised near Bethania in Forsyth County, compiled *The Hesperian Harp* (1848), one of the largest of the shape-note tune books. The tradition of annual shape-note singings also developed in North Carolina with the dedication of the Etowah Baptist Church in 1909 in Henderson County. Participants initially used *The Southern Harmony* but eventually switched to *The Christian Harmony*. The annual singing became so popular that in 1952 it moved from the church to the Etowah Elementary School. The event is traditionally held twice a year, on the first Sunday in May and the first Sunday in September. Singing begins in the morning and, after a break for lunch, resumes in the afternoon.

References: Gilbert Chase, *America's Music: From the Pilgrims to the Present* (3rd ed., 1987); George Pullen Jackson, *White Spirituals in the Southern Uplands: The Story of the Fasola Folk, Their Songs, Singings, and "Buckwheat Notes"* (1933); Mabel Y. Moser, "Christian Harmony Singing at Etowah," *Appalachian Journal* (Spring 1974).

Margaret Foote

Shape-Shifting was one of many superstitions widely accepted by early North Carolinians with little or no understanding of natural phenomena. It was believed that certain people or animals could change form, size, or shape in order to pass through small openings or to appear in a disguise. In the adopted new shape they often worked evil.

William S. Powell

Sharecropping was the mode of labor that supported much of North Carolina's postslavery plantation economy. During Reconstruction, this system of tenant farming offered both planters and laborers, African Americans as well as some poor whites, incentives over the gang labor that predominated during slavery. Planters, strapped for cash in a postbellum economy where money was scarce, offered laborers housing, a mule, tools, and seed to farm a small plot of the planter's land. In return, the sharecropper bought provisions on credit from the planter and reserved the sale and one-half to three-quarters of the crop for the planter. For laborers, sharecropping eliminated the pain and humiliation of gang labor and allowed freedmen to move their families out from direct supervision of white supervisors.

Despite the benefits some sharecroppers accrued from the system, planters profited more. Employers throughout the

South constructed a form of sharecropping that contributed to the horrific poverty of African Americans in the region. Planters, faced with a severe labor shortage at the close of the Civil War, used sharecropping to develop a labor-repressive economy that enabled landowners to maintain economic and political dominance. Sharecropping contracts, designed for a year-long obligation, favored the rights of employers; and Freedmen's Bureau agents, ostensibly the freedmen's advocate, often encouraged freedmen to sign contracts in order to restore stability and order to otherwise chaotic economic conditions. North Carolina laws reinforced planter dominance over croppers. The law defined sharecropping as wage labor. Therefore, croppers were subjected to more managerial supervision than tenants who merely rented land from planters and provided their own supplies. Furthermore, crop lien legislation gave landlords control over the crops, which prevented croppers from selling their goods to merchants elsewhere for better prices.

Economic conditions worsened in the 1880s and 1890s as cotton prices plummeted from 18 cents a pound in 1868 to 5 cents a pound in 1894. North Carolina's poor economic infrastructure offered few forms of credit. The crop lien system intensified laborers' misery as sharecroppers, bound to planters and merchants, pledged their growing crops for food and supplies at interest rates that ranged from 25 percent to 100 percent. By the 1890s, many yeomen, tenants, and sharecroppers revolted against landholders by forming Farmers' Alliances, which established the Populist Party in the mid-1890s. Black and white yeomen, tenants, and croppers drew together to promote reform policies that included the Subtreasury Plan, a system of warehouses intended to store crops until market prices improved. Eventually, the Populist Party dissipated due to friction between leaders, who usually owned land, and rank-and-file tenants and sharecroppers.

Over time, sharecropping declined. New Deal policies and surges in the African American population reversed labor shortages, which enabled planters to turn back to a wage labor system. Programs such as the Agricultural Adjustment Act discouraged farming and released many sharecroppers into the already growing pool of unemployed laborers. Mechanical harvesters further reduced planters' needs for labor. Temporary wage labor proved cheaper than sharecropping contracts, which required year-round management. During World War II, African Americans began to migrate to northern cities for industrial jobs. As the United States embarked upon the postwar years, North Carolina, no longer in need of labor-repressive laws, developed wage labor policies in favor of industrial development.

References: Dwight B. Billings Jr., *Planters and the Making of a "New South": Class, Politics, and Development in North Carolina, 1865–1900* (1979); Margaret Jarman Hagood, *Mothers of the South: Portraiture of White Tenant Farm Women* (1939); Gerald David Jaynes, *Branches without Roots: Genesis of the Black Working Class in the American South, 1862–1882* (1986); Roy G. Taylor, *Sharecroppers: The Way We Really Were* (1984).

Karin Lorene Zipf

SEE ALSO Crop Lien System.

Sharpies were late-nineteenth-century workboats that, according to tradition, were introduced into North Carolina from Long Island Sound by George Ives around 1876. Used in dredging oysters and hauling freight, the sharpie had an upright stem, a flat bottom, a low freeboard, and a round stern; local modifications added closed decking and a cabin. Its rig was initially two-masted with leg-of-mutton sails, but local North Carolina sharpies carried a variety of rigs. The cheap and easily built planked sharpie supplanted the log periauger as a workboat, in part because trees large enough for dugout construction were no longer available and sawn planks were in relative abundance. After 1920 some sharpies were converted to gasoline power, although this modification did not prove entirely satisfactory. Eventually, motorized skiffs and deadrise workboats replaced the sharpie.

References: Michael B. Alford, *Traditional Work Boats of North Carolina* (1990); William C. Fleetwood Jr., *Tidecraft* (1995); Reuel B. Parker, *The Sharpie Book* (1994).

Lawrence E. Babits

Shaw University, founded in Raleigh in 1865, was the first African American institution of higher learning in the South and one of the first in the nation. The university had its beginnings in December 1865, when Henry Martin Tupper, a white educator from Monson, Mass., started a class in theology for the purpose of teaching former slaves how to read and interpret the Bible. From this class evolved the Raleigh Institute (1866), later changed to Shaw Collegiate Institute (1870) and finally incorporated as Shaw University (1875). The school was named for its foremost benefactor, Elijah Shaw of Wales, Mass. The private, Baptist-affiliated liberal arts institute has always been open to both men and women. This coeducational status was assured with the construction, in 1873 of Estey Hall, the first dormitory in the nation devoted exclusively to housing African American women.

Shaw University graduated its first college class in 1878, its first medical school class in 1882, its first law class in 1890, and its first pharmacy class in 1893. The school also had a normal (high school) department, which was changed to the Education Department in 1909. With the discontinuation of the normal department and professional schools (between 1909 and 1926), Shaw became the first African American institution in the South to be devoted exclusively to college and theological work.

Ceramics class at Shaw University, 1954.
Courtesy of NCOA&H. The *Raleigh News and Observer* files.

Shaw has provided North Carolina with many educational leaders. North Carolina Central University, Elizabeth City State University, and Fayetteville State University were all founded by Shaw graduates, and North Carolina Agricultural and Technical State University was housed at Shaw during its first year of operation. Shaw also developed one of the first black studies programs in the country.

In the early 2000s Shaw University enrolled more than 2,400 students in liberal arts and specialized degree programs. It has a strong international studies program, and its Center for Alternative Programs of Education allows students an opportunity to pursue academic degrees through independent study, flexible course scheduling, and credit for prior learning experiences.

References: Wilmoth A. Carter, *Shaw's Universe* (1973); Clara Barnes Jenkins, "A Historical Study of Shaw University" (Ph.D. diss., University of Pittsburgh, 1965); Joseph L. Peacock, "Our Colleges—Shaw University," *Opportunity* 1 (March 1923).

Charles W. Wadelington

Shelby Dynasty, a political machine named for its locus in the town of Shelby, controlled state government for 20 years (1929–49) after gaining power with the 1928 election of Governor O. Max Gardner. At that time leaders of the Democratic Party, which maintained a firm grip on state politics, informally agreed that the eastern and western sections of North Carolina would alternate the one-term governorship. Four years later the Shelby dynasty (or Shelby ring, as it was also called) supported J. C. B. Ehringhaus of Elizabeth City. In 1936 Gardner's brother-in-law Clyde R. Hoey, also of Shelby, won the election. He was succeeded by J. Melvin Broughton of Raleigh and then R. Gregg Cherry of Gastonia.

The conservative-to-moderate faction determined who would run not only for governor but also for other state and congressional offices. After having led the state through both the Great Depression and World War II, the Shelby dynasty engendered discontent by the election of 1948; blacks were dissatisfied, public schools needed more buildings and many repairs, and the road system had not received sufficient attention since the 1920s. The dynasty's candidate in 1948, Charles M. Johnson, lost to W. Kerr Scott, a member of the more liberal "Branchhead Boys," who won on the promise of good roads.

Lee B. Weathers, longtime editor and publisher of the *Shelby Daily Star*, argued that the earliest incarnation of the Shelby dynasty was actually a move to restore democratic government to Cleveland County after the Populist and Republican Fusion had controlled the county government in the 1890s. Among its early leaders were two brothers who both became judges, James L. and E. Y. Webb. James Webb's daughter Faye married O. Max Gardner, and Gardner's sister Bess wed Clyde R. Hoey. Hoey, the Webb brothers, and Odus M. Mull, who served six terms in the North Carolina House of Representatives and six years as chair of the State Democratic Executive Committee, made up the core of the Shelby dynasty under Gardner. Some historians have included Weathers himself as a member of that group, which had such strong influence on local and state politics.

References: Joseph L. Morrison, *Governor O. Max Gardner: A Power in North Carolina and New Deal Washington* (1971); Thomas C. Parramore and Douglas C. Wilms, *North Carolina: The History of an American State* (1988); William S. Powell, *North Carolina through Four Centuries* (1989); Lee B. Weathers, *The Living Past of Cleveland County* (1956).

Paul L. McCraw

SEE ALSO Branchhead Boys.

Shell Castle. For about two decades in the late eighteenth and early nineteenth centuries, the oceangoing trade of most of North Carolina was funneled through one tiny port called Shell Castle. Built on a natural island in the Pamlico Sound close to Ocracoke Inlet, the little port once hummed with activity and was packed with buildings that included one of North Carolina's earliest lighthouses.

Shell Castle was owned by merchants John Gray Blount and John Wallace. North Carolina's shallow sounds and rivers had always restricted oceangoing vessels from trading with the state. Blount and Wallace got around this problem by establishing a new port facility where large ships could transfer their cargoes to barges, which in turn loaded them onto smaller vessels that could ply the shallow waters to New Bern, Edenton, and other ports on the state's sounds and rivers.

In 1789 Blount and Wallace began building their port on a group of oyster beds called Old Rock, which was about a half-mile long and 60 feet wide. They changed the name of the island to Shell Castle after they began building on it. The island was in a good spot to catch trade. It was a solid mass of oyster shells, more resistant to waves and wind than the surrounding sandy islands, and situated next to a deep passage through the shoals of Ocracoke Inlet, called Wallace's Channel. As partners, Blount and Wallace owned lighters and controlled much of the piloting business at the inlet.

To the wharves and warehouses at Shell Castle were added a windmill, a gristmill, a store, a lumber yard, a notary public's office, a tavern, and a main building reported to be 300 feet long, all packed onto its tiny area. The complex was badly damaged in a hurricane in 1806, but the fatal blow was the gradual shoaling of the channels leading to the port around the time of the War of 1812. When ships could no longer get near the port, they took their business to nearby Portsmouth and Ocracoke. Shell Castle was eventually abandoned and its buildings disappeared, although it is still marked on maps and charts of the area.

References: Kenneth E. Burke Jr., *The History of Portsmouth, North Carolina, from Its Founding in 1753 to Its Evacuation in the Face of Federal Forces in 1861* (1976); David Stick, *North Carolina Lighthouses* (1980); Stick, *The Outer Banks of North Carolina, 1584–1958* (1958).

David A. Norris

Shellfish is the popular name for edible mollusks and crustaceans, but fewer than a dozen varieties are caught in sufficient quantities in North Carolina's sounds and offshore waters to be considered part of the state's commercial fishing industry. Though the 2004 catch reported by the North Carolina Division of Marine Fisheries included small numbers of whelks, conchs, scallops, and even stone crab, respectable quantities of oysters, clams, and blue crabs—especially blue crabs—dominate shellfishing in North Carolina. In 2004 more than 76 percent of the state's shellfish poundage was in hard-shell blue crabs.

Blue Crabs. The Atlantic blue crab (*Callinectes sapidus*) is the only crab in North Carolina waters with significant commercial value, although other species, such as the spider crab and calico crab, abound. Blue crabs are generally harvested in the state's sounds, although periodically they are seen in the wash of incoming tides on beaches. The largest populations live in the Albemarle and Pamlico Sounds. Most desirable are the males, or "jimmies," since they yield more meat. Immature females, however, form the basis for "she-crab soup," a popular dish on coastal restaurant menus. Commercially, blue crabs are harvested through the use of pots marked with buoys. Crabs that have just shed their shells in the process of growth are called "soft-shell crabs." Considered delicacies, they are especially commercially valuable in the spring and early summer months.

Historically, crabs were caught and eaten by native peoples and have been noted as a food resource from the earliest European records. Englishmen involved in the Roanoke voyages of the 1580s, including Ralph Lane and Thomas Harriot, commented on the presence of "sea crabbes" that the Native Americans sought for food. In 1709 John Lawson's *A New Voyage to Carolina* described what were almost certainly Atlantic blue crabs: "The smaller flat Crabs I look upon to be the sweetest of all the Species. They are the Breadth of a lusty Man's Hand, or rather larger. These are innumerable, lying in most prodigious quantities, all over the Salts of *Carolina*."

From the colonial period to the early twentieth century, blue crabs were abundant but their use was confined to local gathering for food or fishing bait. Extracting their steamed flesh for packing and canning was a labor-intensive process, and it was difficult to preserve the live crabs and their highly perishable "picked" flesh for transportation to far markets. By the mid-twentieth century, however, demand for the blue crab, combined with faster transportation and better refrigeration techniques, had commercialized crabbing in North Carolina. Although catches in the early 2000s have been smaller than in years past—in 2004 more than 34 million pounds were harvested, with a value of $23 million—the blue crab remains an important seafood resource for the state.

Clams. The clam has been an important food source from coastal waters since prehistoric times. Chroniclers of the Roanoke voyages of the 1580s noted the bounty of shellfish, including clams and other bivalved mollusks, in North Carolina's waters. The state has many edible clam species. Those of greatest commercial value historically have been the northern quahog (*Mercenaria mercenaria*) and the soft-shell clam (*Mya arenaria*). Both are important commercially, the former as "littleneck" or "cherrystone" clams, usually sold live in the shell; and the latter for canning. Techniques for harvesting clams have changed little since the nineteenth century. Clams are taken with rakes or by hand in shallow water. They are also caught with tongs and larger "bull" rakes in deeper water and are dredged in Onslow and Carteret Counties.

The market for North Carolina clams is a relatively recent development due primarily to the fact that the state's waters were far removed from major markets. In the twentieth century, coastal clams were harvested to supply restaurants, wholesale seafood dealers, and the general public. The clam harvest peaked during the 1980s. In 1989, for example, a total of 1.2 million pounds of clams were harvested, with a dollar value of $8.3 million. By 2004 both the size and value of the catch had declined to 548,628 pounds valued at $3.4 million. According to the N.C. Division of Marine Fisheries, the clam fishery has felt the effects of increased fishing pressure, poor water quality, and habitat loss. Experiments with clam "farming," or cultivation in shallow sound waters, have proven successful. In the 1990s at least one Hatteras Island venture tied

Oysters piled high on the deck of a sailing vessel at Washington, N.C., 1884. Courtesy of N C O A & H.

clamming to the tourist economy in a "rake your own clams" business for summer visitors. North Carolina clams continue as primarily a locally used resource, and fresh clam chowder and fritters remain welcome staples on the menus of coastal restaurants.

Oysters. In North Carolina's estuarine waters, oysters (*Crassostrea virginica*) have aroused, but not satisfied, public and private economic hopes and expectations for well over a century. When overfishing resulted in the depletion of the New England oyster beds by the beginning of the nineteenth century, oystermen began moving south. In 1822 North Carolina closed its waters to out-of-state oystermen and forbade dredging by use of drags, scoops, or rakes. Only hand tongs were legal, and North Carolina oystermen were permitted to continue shipping pickled oysters to the West Indies in quantities not to exceed 60 gallons in any one vessel.

In 1858 the state established a procedure by which citizens who were willing to enclose up to 10 acres of suitable estuarine ground and seed it as an artificial oyster bed could secure perpetual fishing rights to it by special license from their local courts. Over the next 30 years, oystermen in Carteret, Dare, Hyde, Onslow, and Pamlico Counties created 52,000 acres of licensed private oyster gardens. After the Civil War, when North Carolina was trying to diversify the foundations of its struggling economy by exploiting its natural resources, it sought to develop its oyster industry. Oyster canneries and shucking houses were established in Elizabeth City, Washington, New Bern, Morehead City, and Beaufort in the late 1880s. North Carolina waters attracted northern oyster pirates. The struggle to expel the pirates in 1890 and 1891 was North Carolina's very pale reflection of the notorious, ongoing, and bloody "oyster war" in Chesapeake Bay. The oyster law of 1891, by which the pirates were forced out, provided a patrol vessel, still maintained today, to police oyster fishing in the state's waters. Also established in 1891 was a supervisory and regulatory board of shellfish commissioners that has evolved into the present-day Marine Fisheries Commission.

Though they were unrecognized by most in the state, seri-

ous problems arose regarding the oyster industry. The state's oystermen had been harvesting virgin stocks that had taken centuries to develop; the rate of oyster population replacement and increase was far lower than supposed, and the species was declining throughout its range. In addition, a series of typhoid outbreaks in 1883 and 1924, traced to contaminated Chesapeake oysters, resulted in a public scare that nearly halted the market in raw oysters. By 1953 shrimp had replaced oysters as the consumer's shellfish of choice, and oysters have never regained their lost ground. After a record oyster take of 1.8 million bushels in 1902, the annual North Carolina take spiraled downward, with 66,000 bushels in 1976 and 48,707 bushels in 2001.

Various steps have been taken to remedy the situation. Millions of bushels of seed were planted in the late 1930s by workers in various New Deal agencies in addition to the state's ongoing seeding program. An experimental oyster farm was established five miles out of Beaufort on North River in 1940. Numerous biological, ecological, and maricultural studies have been conducted over the past 50 years in the hope of finding solutions to the problems affecting the state's oyster industry. The recommendations of the Blue Ribbon Advisory Council on Oysters' 1995 final report form the basis for a new management program.

References: N.C. Division of Marine Fisheries, "North Carolina Commercial Landings 1999" (June 2000); William W. Warner, *Beautiful Swimmers: Watermen, Crabs, and the Chesapeake Bay* (1976).

Kathy Carter
Additional research provided by George Stevenson and David Stick.

SEE ALSO Oyster War.

Shell Mounds. Large amounts of discarded shells, left in mounds along the coast by early Indian communities, often provide clear evidence of the people who once inhabited the region that became North Carolina. Shellfish were an abundant food source for Native Americans. Shell mounds have been found composed almost entirely of oyster shells (the Cape Creek site on Hatteras Island) or clam and mussel shells (archaeological sites along the Pamlico River). Archaeologists have determined that the creation of these shell mounds began more than 1,000 years ago; it is suggested that the mounds are evidence of seasonal subsistence camps. Sites such as those found on Colington and Roanoke Islands are thought to be primarily shellfish collecting camps. From these shell mounds, archaeologists have concluded that these native peoples were hunter-fisher-gatherers living off what the land afforded. Although the sites appear to have been largely based on the accumulated shells, they were probably occupied for only one season by a few extended families. Inland ravine shell mound sites have the same subsistence pattern but reflect adaptations to shellfish species of the river environment.

References: William G. Haag, *The Archaeology of Coastal North Carolina* (1956); Mark A. Mathis and Jeffrey Crow, eds., *The Prehistory of North Carolina: An Archaeological Symposium* (1983); H. Trawick Ward and R. P. Stephen Davis Jr., *Time before History: The Archaeology of North Carolina* (1999).

John F. Ansley

Shelton Laurel Massacre, which occurred in January 1863, serves as a graphic illustration of the divided loyalties of North Carolinians during the Civil War as well as the tenuous relationship between state and Confederate military authorities. Throughout the war North Carolina's western counties suffered considerable violence and disorder. Strong Unionist sentiment ran through the Mountains, and there was intermittent fighting between residents loyal to the United States and their pro-Confederate neighbors. This situation was reminiscent of the bitter social divisions during the American Revolution. In fact, at times Unionists were referred to as "Tories" by their enemies. Further adding to the chaotic atmosphere were marauding gangs of both Confederate and Union deserters, who took advantage of undermanned local enforcement and a weak Confederate presence to practice rampant banditry and lawlessness.

In early January 1863 Confederate sympathizers near the town of Marshall, the seat of Madison County, suffered a series of raids by Unionist outlaws from nearby Shelton Laurel. Later that month Brig. Gen. Henry Heth dispatched Confederate infantry to the county to quell the disturbances. The operation's harsh objectives made it clear that Confederates held the Unionist renegades in low regard. Heth instructed his subordinates to take no prisoners should there be an engagement. Accordingly, a detachment led by Lt. Col. James A. Keith, a Confederate and native of Marshall eager to avenge the wrong done his townsmen, entered the Shelton Laurel area and embarked on a rampage against the Unionists. Locals were tortured to reveal the names of the bandits, and, once identified, these "Tories" (old men and boys) were apprehended; 13 were eventually shot in cold blood. This brutality brought down upon Keith and his men the wrath of the countryside, and constant sniper fire and attempted ambushes soon compelled them to leave the area.

After the war, Keith was arrested but was spared prosecution by presidential amnesty. No one ever stood trial for the Shelton Laurel killings, North Carolina's worst Civil War atrocity.

References: John G. Barrett, *The Civil War in North Carolina* (1963); James O. Hall, "The Shelton Laurel Massacre: Murder in the North Carolina Mountains," *Blue & Gray* (February 1991); John C. Inscoe and Gordon B. McKinney, *The Heart of Confederate Appalachia: Western North Carolina in the Civil War* (2000); Joe A. Mobley, ed., *The Papers of Zebulon Baird Vance*, vol. 2 (1995); Phillip Shaw Paludan, *Victims: A True Story of the Civil War* (repr., 2004).

David L. Cockrell

Shenandoah, CSS. The CSS *Shenandoah*, commanded by James Iredell Waddell of North Carolina, was one of the most famous "commerce raiders" or "cruisers" commissioned by the Confederate navy to destroy northern merchant shipping during the Civil War. When European nations refused to allow Confederate privateers to sell their prizes in European ports, the Confederate navy looked for other ways to destroy Union ocean commerce and compel northern shipping interests to lobby the U.S. Congress for peace with the South. The commerce raiders supplied the means. They were Confederate naval warships less motivated by profit than privateers.

The *Shenandoah*'s main mission was to destroy the Union whaling fleet and move the war to New England, which, according to Waddell and the South, bore much of the responsibility for the war. Between 27 May and 28 June 1865, the ship captured or destroyed about 25 northern whaling vessels, a blow from which the fleet never recovered. During this time, Waddell learned that Gen. Robert E. Lee had surrendered and Richmond had fallen, but also that President Jefferson Davis was calling for continued resistance. Waddell moved to attack Union shipping in San Francisco, but as he approached the city, a British ship confirmed that Davis had been captured and the South defeated. Rather than surrender to the Union in California or intern the *Shenandoah* in a neutral port remote from European civilization, Waddell decided to sail to England and end its voyage there.

The *Shenandoah* rounded Cape Horn and hauled down the Confederate flag for the last time in Liverpool, England. Waddell surrendered the ship to British authorities on 6 Nov. 1865, nearly seven months after Lee had surrendered at Appomattox Court House. The British released the officers and crew, but the ship itself was turned over to the Union. After an unsuccessful attempt to sail to the United States, the *Shenandoah* was sold to the Sultanate of Zanzibar. In 1879 the *Shenandoah* sank in a storm.

References: Murray Cromwell Morgan, *Dixie Raider: The Saga of the C.S.S.* Shenandoah (1948); Warren F. Spencer, *The Confederate Navy in Europe* (1983).

John R. deTreville

Sheriff is the oldest public office in North Carolina. Established in 1662, the office is rooted in English history before the time of the Norman conquest of England. A sheriff appeared in America in Virginia as early as 1634 and in Massachusetts in 1691. On 9 Oct. 1662 the General Court of Virginia issued a commission to Capt. Samuel Stephens to be "Commander of the Southern Plantation" and authorized him to appoint a sheriff of that region, then part of Virginia. It later became North Carolina.

The sheriff often had to do whatever was necessary for the county's judicial and administrative government, a responsibility that made him a powerful person. Even when his office was conducted in strictest honesty, the sheriff was one of the highest-paid officials in the colonial government. His income came from several sources: fees for executing orders of the court, including warrants, civil papers, and attachments; commissions on collected taxes; a salary paid by the colony; a salary paid by the county for "extraordinary expenses" in performing services for which the legislature permitted no fees; commissions on the sale of estates for which he acted as executor; and other miscellaneous fees.

The sheriff became the chief law enforcement officer in the county. Under other provisions of an 1829 law, each county was subdivided into captain's districts for military purposes. The county court appointed a patrol committee of three for each district, which functioned under the sheriff. Sheriffs, elected to two-year terms, continued through the Civil War. A sheriff's duties, which remained much the same over the decades, included enforcing the criminal law, overseeing the civil process, and executing all court processes. A sheriff also served as bailiff to the court, maintained the county jail, and oversaw the collection of taxes and fees owed the county and state. The North Carolina Constitution of 1868 continued the office of sheriff but did remove the old county court of justices of the peace and establish commissioners to set policy for the administration of county government.

With Great Britain's Metropolitan Police Act of the 1850s, law enforcement began to professionalize and sheriffs were quick to take the lead in North Carolina. By the turn of the century, the state's sheriffs had begun to work for better training and equipment for themselves and their deputies. The early 1900s saw the introduction of such innovations as the use of the automobile and the radio in law enforcement, but many counties, with tight fiscal control, were slow to adequately fund their sheriffs. In the 1920s state official and academician Albert Coates began extensive teaching of law enforcement officers. Working in conjunction with the North Carolina Sheriffs' Association, other law enforcement groups, and municipal and county governments, Coates eventually established the Institute of Government at the University of North Carolina in Chapel Hill. His vision resulted in the modern exhaustive training and certification criteria for deputies and other law enforcement personnel.

The office of sheriff has remained virtually unchanged throughout the decades. The sheriff retains the duties of bailiff, jailer, executive officer of the court, and "keeper of the county." The second paragraph of the sheriff's oath of office remains almost intact from that which was prescribed in 1738. One change has occurred: starting in the 1940s, county commissioners began appointing separate tax collectors—although at least one North Carolina sheriff remained the county tax collector in the early 2000s.

References: Julian P. Boyd, "The Sheriff in Colonial North Carolina," *NCHR* 5 (April 1928); Joan G. Brannon, ed., *Selected North Carolina Statutes Relating to Civil Duties of Sheriffs* (1997).

Frank McGuirt

Sherman's March. During the Civil War, Maj. Gen. William T. Sherman's March to the Sea culminated in the Union's capture of Savannah, Ga., in December 1864. Instead of transferring his veteran army by water to Virginia, where Lt. Gen. Ulysses S. Grant had Gen. Robert E. Lee bottled up around Richmond, Sherman received permission to invade the Carolinas. He particularly wanted to apply the fullest measure of "total war" to South Carolina as punishment for bringing on the war. He planned to move directly on Columbia, S.C., and from there to Fayetteville on the Cape Fear River in North Carolina. Then the Union army would push eastward to Goldsboro, which was connected to the coast by two railroads. Along this route Sherman could cut communication lines, destroy public and industrial property, and dampen morale. By applying total war to the home front, Sherman expected to instill a defeatist psychology in southern civilians and soldiers alike. His ultimate objective was to combine with Grant's forces at Richmond and crush Lee's army, thus ending the war.

During the Carolinas campaign, Sherman's army of 60,000 troops and 2,500 wagons was divided into two wings, sometimes forming a front over 40 miles wide. While Sherman's forces were marching through South Carolina, Gen. Joseph E. Johnston became the new commander of Confederate forces in the Carolinas. Sherman correctly surmised that Johnston would attempt to unite his widely scattered army and fight at a place and time of his own choosing. As early as mid-January 1865, at least one North Carolina newspaper began preparing its readers for invasion. A month later, when Fort Fisher and Wilmington on the coast fell to the Union, a wave of despondency hit the state. Many people, fearing that they might be in Sherman's direct path, hid their valuables in an effort to save them.

Because Sherman had cut himself off from his supply base at Savannah, his men were reduced to foraging extensively from the countryside as they moved through the Carolinas in early 1865. Strict regulations limited foraging parties, but there was a wide discrepancy between these orders and the actions of some of the troops, who operated more as mounted robbers than as disciplined foragers. Much of the wanton destruction of property in the two Carolinas was the work of this self-constituted group, known primarily as "bummers." Unsupervised by officers, these men operated on their own.

The origin of the term "bummer" is obscure; however, by the time of Sherman's March to the Sea in the fall of 1864, it had come into general usage. A member of the general's staff defined a bummer as a "raider on his own account, a man who temporarily deserts a place in the ranks and starts up an independent foraging mission." But most soldiers in Sherman's army designated all foragers "bummers" whether authorized or unauthorized.

By 8 Mar. 1865 Sherman's entire army was on North Carolina soil in the vicinity of Laurel Hill Presbyterian Church (now Scotland County), facing a formidable march. Early on the morning of 10 March at Monroe's Crossroads west of Fayetteville, a part of the cavalry under Brevet Maj. Gen. Judson Kilpatrick was surprised and temporarily driven from the field by Confederate horsemen led by Lt. Gen. Wade Hampton. But the Union force regained control of its camp and thus opened the way for the Federal occupation of Fayetteville the next day.

The town and surrounding countryside suffered much at the hands of Sherman's men, who pillaged and destroyed property, including the arsenal. While at Fayetteville, Sherman took the opportunity to rid his columns of the 30,000 black and white refugees who had been following his army. He considered them "useless mouths."

Leaving Fayetteville, Sherman crossed the Cape Fear and turned east toward Goldsboro. On 16 March a small Confederate force fought a delaying action against Sherman's left wing at Averasboro, and three days later Johnston's entire army of 21,000 troops attacked the left wing at Bentonville about 20 miles west of Goldsboro. The first day's fight was by far the bloodiest, ending in a draw. But the Union went on to win the three-day battle—the largest ever fought on North Carolina soil.

After his victory at Bentonville, Sherman allowed Johnston to withdraw to Smithfield. The Union general moved on to Goldsboro, where, on 23 March, he linked up with additional troops under Maj. Gen. John M. Schofield. After receiving news of the fall of Richmond, Sherman turned toward Raleigh, with Johnston retreating before him. On the evening of 12 April, peace commissions from Raleigh arrived at Sherman's headquarters at Clayton. By this time Gen. Robert E. Lee had surrendered at Appomattox, Confederate troops were evacuating the capital of North Carolina, and Johnston was seeking permission from President Jefferson Davis to contact Sherman about ending hostilities. The generals met on three occasions at the James Bennett home west of Durham. The surrender terms drafted at the first two meetings, on 17 and 18 Apr. 1865, were too generous for authorities in Washington, D.C.; at the third meeting, on 26 April, Sherman and Johnston drafted a more satisfactory agreement. The terms were similar to those Lee received from Grant at Appomattox. Except for the stacking of arms at Greensboro and a few minor skirmishes between Union and Confederate troops, the war in North Carolina was over.

References: John G. Barrett, *Sherman's March through the Carolinas* (1956); Mark L. Bradley, *Last Stand in the Carolinas: The Battle of Bentonville* (1996); Bradley, *This Astounding Close: The Road to Bennett Place* (2000); Jacqueline Glass Campbell, *When Sherman Marched North from the Sea: Resistance on the Confederate Home Front* (2003); Lloyd Lewis, *Sherman: Fighting Prophet* (1932); William Tecumseh Sherman, *Memoirs*, vol. 2 (1875).

John G. Barrett

SEE ALSO Averasboro, Battle of; Bentonville, Battle of; Monroe's Crossroads, Battle of.

Shipbuilding in North Carolina, although never a major industry, has contributed appreciably to the economy of the state's coastal region. Shipyards have been located at a variety of sites throughout coastal North Carolina since the early days of settlement, but with few exceptions they have been engaged in the construction of relatively small vessels. One of the first shipbuilders in the colony was Thomas Harding of Bath, who contracted in 1706 to build a 46-foot sloop for Governor Thomas Cary. Despite the ready availability of building materials in North Carolina's vast forests, however, it appears that most colonial era planters and merchants bought their vessels elsewhere, especially in the New England colonies.

As early as the 1760s, the construction of single-mast sloops gave way to turning out small multimast schooners, most often two-masters. By 1783, a visitor to Washington, N.C., on the Pamlico River said the town had approximately 40 houses, and the chief occupation was "the building of small ships and vessels." The revenue cutter *Diligence* was launched in Washington in 1791, and from then until the outbreak of the Civil War the town continued to be a leader in North Carolina shipbuilding activities, its yards turning out at least two or three vessels each year. A free black named Hull Anderson owned one of the shipyards there between 1830 and 1841 and owned four slaves who were engaged in his shipbuilding activity. By 1850 Beaufort County was probably the most important shipbuilding center in the state.

With the increase of maritime activity on the Cape Fear River, shipbuilding assumed growing importance in the Wilmington area. Nineteenth-century shipyards were located in Elizabeth City, New Bern, Beaufort, and Southport, where the 126-foot long steamer *Rowan* was launched in 1847. It was not unusual for small shipyards to be located at isolated sites in places such as Hyde County, the upper reaches of the Chowan River, and Smith Island or Bald Head near Cape Fear, where pilot boats were the specialty.

The Civil War saw an even greater degree of specialization, as shipyard construction was limited almost entirely to vessels for the use of the Confederacy. The most famous of these were the CSS *Albemarle*, a ram built at Plymouth, and her sister ship, the CSS *Neuse*, which was built at the shipyard at White-

Sailing ship under construction at the Wilmington Iron Works in the late 1800s. Courtesy of NCOA&H.

hall (modern-day Seven Springs), on the Neuse River. Following the war, there was a decline in North Carolina shipbuilding activities that continued into the twentieth century, when most shipyards were engaged primarily in ship repair work. Yards such as Meadows in New Bern built trawlers, tugs, and small steamers and, when war production began in 1917, constructed quantities of standardized cargo vessels and submarine chasers.

The Great Depression of the 1930s virtually terminated North Carolina shipbuilding until the start of World War II. The Maritime Commission developed a new large yard at Wilmington that was operated by Newport News Shipbuilding as the North Carolina Shipbuilding Company. It constructed 125 Liberty ships between February 1942 and August 1943, followed by 64 C2-type standard fast freighters. Other firms, notably Barbour Boat Works in New Bern, built wooden minesweepers and escort vessels.

After World War II, the North Carolina Shipbuilding Company closed but other firms continued to operate. Barbour switched to steel construction, building trawlers, fish factory ships, ferries, tugs, and small warships. Other small yards, mainly in the Beaufort and Wanchese areas, built wooden or steel vessels for fisheries. By the 1990s several specialized shipyards were turning out ferry boats at New Bern, sleek sportfishing boats at Harkers Island and Wanchese, and everything from utility outboards to small recreational sailboats elsewhere.

References: Joseph A. Goldenberg, *Shipbuilding in Colonial America* (1976); William N. Still Jr., *Confederate Shipbuilding* (1969).

David Stick
Paul E. Fontenoy

SEE ALSO Harkers Island Boats; Ironclads; Liberty Ships.

Shipwrecks in past centuries were so prevalent along the North Carolina coast—the shallow waters offshore strewn with the ruins of wrecked vessels—that the area became known as the "Graveyard of the Atlantic." At one spot, part

of the pilothouse of a recently sunken trawler almost touches the skeletonlike timbers of a wooden schooner. At another, the eerie hulk of a German submarine rises from the ocean floor. In the vicinity of the North Carolina capes, where the sand shoals are in constant flux, the outline of an entire vessel can be visible to a diver one day but indiscernible beneath the sand the next.

Conditions at Cape Hatteras, long dreaded by mariners, are a major reason for the large number of shipwrecks. There, the cold waters flowing down the coast from the north collide with the warm Gulf Stream current coursing up from the tropics. During the heyday of the coasting trade in the nineteenth century, southbound sailing vessels often were unable to round Cape Hatteras for weeks because of the combined forces of the steady northbound Gulf Stream flow and the prevailing winds from the southwest. Old-timers at Kinnakeet, north of the cape, have recounted seeing as many as 150 sailing ships, tacking back and forth, waiting for the wind to change. Often, when the shift finally came and the wind blew suddenly from the north, one or more of the tacking vessels would end up on the shore.

The absence of a dependable harbor of refuge between Chesapeake Bay and Beaufort Inlet, a distance of more than 200 miles, also contributed to the enormous toll of shipping, especially along the Outer Banks. Inlets had a tendency to close without warning, and the channels in even the more established ones shifted nonstop. Also, it was difficult for a mariner unfamiliar with the low-lying coastline to figure out the difference between an inlet and a low section of beach, and more than one shipwreck resulted when the master finally realized that the inlet toward which he had been heading was a mirage.

The loss of more than 1,000 vessels has been verified in the shipwreck inventory conducted at the Outer Banks History Center on Roanoke Island. Undoubtedly hundreds more were lost before accurate records were kept, or they simply disappeared without a trace. The carnage started early, with the loss of Spanish ships returning home via the Gulf Stream route

Local residents and perhaps crew members pose on the wreck of the *Priscilla*, which ran aground at Gull Shoal in Dare County in August 1899. NCC.

after looting the treasure troves of the Caribbean and Central America.

Early explorers and colonists, including those sent by England's Sir Walter Raleigh, suffered their share of misfortunes. As the Carolina settlement grew, seaborne traffic increased between the ports of the colony and its trading partners in such divergent places as New York, Barbados, and London. The sailing vessels proved no match for the elements, especially when hurricanes struck; newspapers throughout the colonies frequently printed reports of shipwrecks during storms.

Even the largest sailing craft—brigs, barks, and schooners—seldom carried a crew of more than a dozen or so and only a handful of passengers, if any. The introduction of the steamboat resulted in a dramatic change, for the sleek new steam packets were designed specifically to carry passengers. These long, narrow craft—better suited for service on interior waters than for the run from northern ports to Charleston, S.C., or Savannah, Ga.—maintained steady speeds of up to ten miles an hour. Fitted out with what were often advertised as commodious accommodations, they appealed to ever-increasing numbers of travelers, who had to choose between an overland trip that could take weeks or the uncertainty of passage by sail.

The first reported wreck of a steamboat on the North Carolina coast occurred in October 1836, when the navigator of the packet *William Gibbons*, miscalculating that he had cleared Cape Hatteras on the run from New York, turned to the southwest heading and ran his vessel ashore. Residents of Chicama-

comico, where the *William Gibbons* ended up at night on the inner bar, assisted with the rescue of its 140 passengers, including 32 women and 14 children, and no lives were lost. Less than a year later, when the *Home* ran aground at Ocracoke, those on board were less fortunate. Only about 40 of the 130 passengers and crew survived, despite a chronicle of heroism seldom equaled in the annals of North Carolina shipwrecks. The next year approximately 100 people died when the steam packet *Pulaski* foundered off the New River.

The carnage along the coast has been especially heavy during times of war. More than 60 vessels were lost, by shipwreck or gunfire, during the Civil War; at least 15, most sunk by German submarines, in World War I; and approximately 90 more in less than a three-year period during World War II, including three German submarines and many of their victims.

Two shipwrecks within a span of less than three months in the winter of 1877–78—the USS *Huron* at Nags Head with approximately 100 crewmen lost and the *Metropolis* at Currituck Beach with 85 dead—resulted in quick action by Congress to increase the number of lifesaving stations along the North Carolina coast. Surfmen from these stations, originally members of the U.S. Lifesaving Service and later the U.S. Coast Guard, saved hundreds of vessels and rescued untold numbers of shipwreck victims. There was little they could do, however, when the five-masted schooner *Carroll A. Deering* was discovered hard aground on Diamond Shoals one stormy night in January 1921, its sails fluttering in the wind, food set out in the galley, but no sign of human life on board. The mystery of this "Ghost Ship of Diamond Shoals" was never solved.

The advent of radar, loran, sonar, and other breakthroughs in technology ended the time when shipwrecks were the norm along the North Carolina coast.

References: Bland Simpson, *Ghost Ship of Diamond Shoals: The Mystery of the* Carroll A. Deering (2002); James Sprunt, *Derelict: An Account of Ships Lost at Sea in General Commercial Traffic and a Brief History of Blockade Runners Stranded along the North Carolina Coast, 1861–1865* (1920); David Stick, *Graveyard of the Atlantic: Shipwrecks of the North Carolina Coast* (1952).

David Stick

SEE ALSO Graveyard of the Atlantic; *Huron*, USS; Lifesaving Service, U.S.

Shivaree, or chivaree, was a traditional Mountain folk custom staged during the first night that a bride and groom, following the honeymoon, moved into their new residence (even if it happened to be with relatives in their old residence). The attendant loud noises and merrymaking ensured that no one in the neighborhood could sleep through the excitement. The house was surrounded by friends and neighbors, some carrying lighted pine knots. As the parade of well-wishers encircled the house, the men fired guns into the air, the women and children banged on pots or clanged cowbells, and a few creative participants beat the cadence with their own version of a string band. This chaos continued until the couple appeared at the door and invited everyone inside. Simple shivarees required the bride to offer treats of candy or apples, while the groom produced cigars for the men. The women participating in the event brought gifts to help the new housewife set up her household.

An old-fashioned shivaree was not a native North Carolina custom but likely made its way into the Mountain region with the early German or Scotch-Irish settlers. The custom of shivaree was common in New England and the Midwest. Each region imprinted a special twist on the tradition, but there are features to a shivaree shared by all groups.

The merits of a shivaree were numerous. Everyone in the community participated—young and old, male and female. The newlyweds certainly met their neighbors in a friendly if raucous manner and were, in turn, properly initiated into the community. Another important feature of the custom was the collective good cheer and feeling of community everyone shared. Finally, and perhaps most importantly, shivarees were an old-fashioned diversion that was just plain fun.

References: J. B. Hicklin, "Mountain Chivaree," *The State* (14 Apr. 1941); Hellen K. Moore and Ferne Shelton, eds., *Pioneer Superstitions: Old-Timey Signs and Sayings* (1968); Vernon Sechriest, "The Bellin' of Old Man Carter," *The State* (January 1983).

Marilyn Wright

Shoffner Act, introduced by state senator T. M. Shoffner of Alamance County and passed in 1870, empowered the governor to suspend habeas corpus and use militia to restore order in counties where Ku Klux Klan terrorism raged out of control. Governor William W. Holden invoked the act that year to suppress the Klan in Alamance and Caswell Counties, igniting the so-called Kirk-Holden War and leading to Holden's impeachment and removal from office.

References: J. G. de Roulhac Hamilton, *Reconstruction in North Carolina* (1914); Allen W. Trelease, *White Terror: The Ku Klux Klan Conspiracy and Southern Reconstruction* (1971).

Allen W. Trelease

Shooting in the New Year, although thought to have been more widespread in North Carolina during the colonial and antebellum eras (the Moravians complained about the observance), is a ritual that by 2006 had died out completely except in portions of Lincoln and Gaston Counties. In this ritual, descendants of German settlers welcome the New Year by traveling from house to house, chanting and firing black powder muskets. The "shooters" begin their annual tradition at the stroke of midnight on New Year's Day. One man, designated the crier, calls "Halloo" three times to alert those in the house, and then gives a rhyming chant. Of uncertain origin, the chant is part sermon and part good wishes for the coming year. It has been said to resemble speeches in English mummer plays. Following the chant, the shooters step forward one at a time to fire their muskets. Loaded to make the most smoke and noise possible, the guns are fired from the hip at knee level. Once all have fired, the shooters are ushered into the home for coffee and food. The practice became somewhat institutionalized in 1963 when the "Cherryville New Year's Shooters" were federally chartered.

As it is practiced in modern times, the New Year's shoot is thought to be a combination of English and German folk customs, but it primarily grew out of the German tradition of shooting guns to ward off evil spirits. In one incarnation of the tradition, the "Shooting of Witches," boys in certain parts of Germany would stand in a circle on New Year's Eve and fire three times into the air. The Pennsylvania Dutch, at one time, shot among their fruit trees on New Year's Eve to ensure a good harvest.

References: Bill Sharpe, "The New Year Shooters: The Oddest Holiday Custom in North Carolina Was Brought to the Hills of Gaston County by German Immigrants 200 Years Ago," *The State* 22 (January 1955); Kay Valentine, "Shooting in the New Year: The Roar of Old Muskets Echoing over the Gaston Hills Marks a Tradition Unchanged by the Centuries," *The State* 41 (January 1974).

Kevin Cherry

Short Ballot movement set forth the principles that only those offices important enough to attract and deserve public examination should be elective, and that only a few offices should be filled by election at any one time. The movement began in the United States in 1909, led by Woodrow Wilson, then president of Princeton University. The short ballot issue was closely linked with a general drive to centralize government responsibility by decreasing the number and/or lengthening the terms of a few elective offices and simplifying governmental organization.

At least since 1915, North Carolina governors had pointed out the need for a short ballot and fewer elected officials to achieve satisfactory administrative management within the state government. In that year Governor Locke Craig told state lawmakers: "If the General Assembly should clothe the governor with the power to *appoint all* of the administrative officials of the state, except those named in the Constitution, it would accomplish a reform of immense benefit." In his 1917 inaugural address, Governor Thomas W. Bickett urged the legislature to enact a law that all state administrative officers "whose election by the people is not required in the Constitution shall be hereafter appointed by the Governor."

In 1930 Governor O. Max Gardner received the results of a survey that he had commissioned from the Brookings Institution. Based on the findings, Gardner recommended that the legislature adopt a short ballot, cut the number of state officials to be elected, and expand the governor's appointive power on the premise that if the chief executive was responsible for a broad program, he should have commensurate authority to appoint the officials who would carry it out. The General Assembly of 1931 enacted some of Gardner's proposals into law but not the short ballot.

As North Carolina state government continued to grow, the need to simplify and streamline the executive branch concerned governors and legislators from time to time. Reorganization has become a constant feature. For example, in 1969 Governor Robert W. Scott established the State Government Reorganization Study Commission, and in May 1970 he appointed a 50-member citizen Committee on State Government Reorganization. In November 1970 voters approved a constitutional proposal requiring the executive branch to be reduced to 25 departments by the end of 1975. Scott's committee recommended implementation of the constitutional amendment in two phases. With strong support from Scott, the General Assembly ratified the Executive Organization Act of 1971. This measure divided the executive branch into two groups: agencies headed by elected officials and those headed by appointed administrators. The General Assembly passed the Executive Organization Act of 1973. The initial reorganization was in fact mostly completed by the mandated time—the end of 1975, followed in the 1980s and 1990s by additional legislation to further reorganize executive departments.

In the early 2000s several key offices, in addition to the governor and lieutenant governor, remained elective, including the attorney general, the secretary of state, the state treasurer, the superintendent of public instruction, and the commissioners of agriculture, insurance, and labor.

References: Paul V. Betters, *State Centralization in North Carolina* (1932); Roma Sawyer Cheek, *A Preliminary Study of Government Management in North Carolina* (1950); Hugh T. Lefler and Albert R. Newsome, *North Carolina: The History of a Southern State* (3rd ed., 1973); *North Carolina Manual, 1999–2000* (2000).

Wiley J. Williams

SEE ALSO Brookings Institution.

Shorthand was used as a means of rapid writing in ancient Greece, but a scheme akin to the modern form was developed in England beginning in the sixteenth century based on the way words were spelled. Joseph Gales, an English-born journalist who used shorthand in his work, moved to Raleigh in September 1799 and established the *Raleigh Register* in October. He soon was employed by the state not only to record the debates of the General Assembly and other official meetings but also to print them. These documents, together with Gales's newspaper, gave North Carolinians very accurate records of much public business. By 1830 another newspaper editor, native Richard Creecy, had mastered "stenography."

In 1837 in England, Isaac Pitman's phonetic system introduced the use of both sounds and abbreviations, speeding the process of getting the spoken word on paper. It was published in the United States twenty years later, and in 1858–59 Goldsboro lawyer Needham B. Cobb diligently taught himself the system. He was the first-known stenographer in North Carolina and, after about a year, prepared a shorthand primer for the instruction of his eldest son, Collier.

After becoming a Baptist minister, Cobb employed his skill in preparing sermons and taking church minutes. During Reconstruction, at the trial of a former Confederate officer for alleged cruelty to Union prisoners at Salisbury, efforts were made to get Cobb to record the proceedings. Convinced of the officer's innocence, he refused, and a reporter had to be brought in from the North. After the trial ended, Cobb taught stenography to a private class in Raleigh and to ten students at Wake Forest College.

Reference: N. B. Cobb, "The History of Shorthand Writing in North Carolina," *Biennial Report of the Superintendent of Public Instruction of North Carolina* (1900).

William S. Powell

Signories, or "seignories," were territories over which an official, a group of officials, or an individual had dominion.

The Fundamental Constitutions of Carolina on 1 Mar. 1669 directed that the province be divided into counties, with each county further divided into eight signories held by the eight Lords Proprietors. A signory was to consist of 12,000 acres, and manorial courts were to be held by feudal lords in the signories as well as in other places.

References: J. Bryan Grimes, comp., *North Carolina Wills and Inventories* (1912); Mattie Erma Edwards Parker, ed., *North Carolina Charters and Constitutions, 1578–1897* (1963).

William S. Powell

Silk. Early travel writers and government officials speculated that the climate and soil of the land that would become North Carolina would readily support the growing of silkworms. The Carolina charter of 1663 mentioned silk, and several royal governors tried to encourage silk production. Silk had for centuries been a Chinese monopoly, until silkworm eggs were smuggled from China to the West. Silk is made by the caterpillar of the silkworm moth (*Bombyx mori*). Mulberry leaves are the best food for silkworm larvae, and since mulberry trees grew readily in much of North Carolina, eager entrepreneurs were tempted to try to make fortunes from silk. Antebellum sources reported that 3,000 silkworm cocoons, weighing about nine pounds, would yield a pound of silk, and that an acre of mulberry trees would support 500,000 silkworms. Many families set up silk production on a small scale, planting mulberry trees in their yards and using attics as space for caring for the silkworms. In 1840, with cotton bringing seven or eight cents per pound, the lure of raising silk, which when reeled from the cocoons sold for four dollars per pound, was considerable.

Enthusiasm for silk cultivation reached its peak in North Carolina in the antebellum period and died down rapidly soon after. The activity of planting mulberry trees and raising silkworms was jokingly called "*Morus multicaulis* mania." Many merchants sold mulberry trees and silkworm eggs; a Raleigh bookstore with such a sideline sold the eggs at ten dollars an ounce in 1840. Several factors were blamed for the end of the silk "mania" in North Carolina, among them the shortage of skilled, economical labor and the lack of knowledge and preparation on the part of many of the investors.

Numerous silk mills, which processed imported silk into thread, opened in North Carolina in the late nineteenth and early twentieth centuries. The last silk mill in the state, in Greensboro, operated until the 1930s. In the end, the attempts at producing silk in North Carolina left only a few lasting results: a great number of mulberry trees, including some very large, gnarled ones at the Charles B. Aycock Birthplace State Historic Site near Fremont, and Silk Hope, the name of a community in Chatham County.

References: Billy Arthur, "Silk Purse or Sow's Ear," *Our State* 63 (February 1996); Elizabeth Reid Murray, *Wake: Capital County of North Carolina* (1983).

David A. Norris

Silver, Frankie, Murder Case. On 12 July 1833 an estimated 10,000 people crammed into a space behind the Burke County Courthouse in Morganton to see Frances "Frankie" Silver—described as a "bright-eyed, very pretty little woman"—hanged for murdering her husband Charles. She is considered to have been the first white woman ever executed in North Carolina. Reportedly jealousy prompted Silver to decapitate her sleeping husband with an ax one night in their cabin on the Toe River in modern Mitchell County. Alfred Silver, half brother of the slain man, said years later that it had been hoped that Frankie would make a public confession before the execution, but that her father, Isaiah Stewart, shouted from the crowd, "Die with it in you, Frankie."

According to some authorities, Frankie Silver was a victim of poor legal advice and should have been acquitted. B. S. Gaither, the clerk of court at the trial, was quoted as saying there was evidence that Charles Silver was often physically abusive, and that if his wife had admitted the killing and pleaded self-defense she probably would have been found not guilty.

The story of Frankie Silver has become an enduring part of North Carolina folklore and the subject of numerous books, articles, and films.

References: Sharyn McCrumb, *The Ballad of Frankie Silver* (1998); Daniel W. Patterson, *A Tree Accurst: Bobby McMillon and Stories of Frankie Silver* (2000).

Noel Yancey

Silver Fusion was a national political movement of the 1890s in which North Carolina played a leading role. The movement originated with the desire for the free coinage of silver at a ratio of 16 ounces of silver to 1 ounce of gold, as provided for in the Coinage Act of 1837. The coinage of silver had been discontinued in 1873. This act of "demonetization" and the subsequent depression, by virtue of proximity, seemed related and led to widespread belief that ending silver coinage was a "Crime of '73."

The silver cause was given a significant boost in 1892–93 because of three developments: the election of Democrat Grover Cleveland, an advocate of the gold standard, as president; the adverse economic impact of the panic of 1893; and Cleveland's repeal of the Sherman Silver Purchase Act as a solution to the economic crisis. A split in the Democratic Party occurred along sectional lines, with western and southern politicians on one side and easterners on the other. At the same time, the Populist, or People's, Party was drawn into the struggle on the side of silver. The greater part of the Republican Party continued to uphold the gold standard as the conservative course.

In 1894 the North Carolina Populist Party allied itself with the Republican Party in what is called the "Fusion" campaign. The two parties united over electoral issues, ignoring numerous differences in order to dislodge the Democrats and take control of the legislature. Two years later U.S. senator Marion Butler, leader of the North Carolina Populists, was chairman of the national People's Party. A fellow North Carolina Fusionist, Republican James J. Mott, was chairman of the National Silver Party.

Silver Democrats, led by former governor Thomas J. Jarvis and *Raleigh News and Observer* editor Josephus Daniels, were in the forefront of the state party by 1896. Daniels, as national committeeman, persuaded the North Carolina delegation to the Democratic National Convention to endorse William Jennings Bryan of Nebraska for president on 8 July 1896. After his nomination two days later, Bryan said of the North Carolina delegates: "Next to Nebraska, I owe them more than any other people."

The impetus for a fusion of reform forces around the silver issue was overwhelming. Mott had stated that North Carolina Fusion demonstrated "the practicability and safety of men of different parties cooperating to carry out a great measure." At his urging, the National Silver Party had nominated Bryan and Arthur Sewall, a Maine shipbuilding magnate. Butler, despite misgivings about Bryan's devotion to reform, went before the Populist Party convention to urge the Nebraskan's candidacy. The party concurred, but not before nominating Thomas Watson of Georgia in place of Sewall. After some haggling, the North Carolina parties agreed to a joint ticket of presidential electors consisting of six Democrats and five Populists.

Bryan carried North Carolina by a vote of 175,216 to 154,446 for Republican William McKinley, but the Republicans triumphed nationally. The Populist Party was especially weakened by the campaign, which had the effect of damaging its state-level alliance with the Republicans. Two years later, a successful "white supremacy campaign" swept the Democrats back into power. Fusion was at an end.

Free coinage as an emotional issue transcended its consequences. Silver fusion represented a pragmatic effort to build a political coalitions around currency reform, one of the great issues of the Gilded Age. North Carolina, both by action and example, played a historically significant role in the national fusion of silver forces.

References: Robert F. Durden, *The Climax of Populism: The Election of 1896* (1965); Ronnie W. Faulkner, "North Carolina Democrats and Silver Fusion Politics, 1892–1896," *NCHR* 59 (July 1982); Lawrence Goodwyn, *Democratic Promise: The Populist Moment in America* (1976); Stanley D. Jones, *The Presidential Election of 1896* (1964).

Ronnie W. Faulkner

Silversmithing is usually considered one of the luxury trades, involving the manufacture of silver utensils of a wide variety. These include flatware (forks and spoons); knife handles (holloware); bowls; tea, coffee, and chocolate pots; serving trays; tankards and cups; and many other accessories, including jewelry. Silversmithing in North Carolina developed more rapidly than in other southern colonies because importation to the colony was limited by the poor coastal harbors. The demand, although somewhat limited in the eighteenth century, increased steadily as the population of the colony grew. The large oceangoing ships from England could not easily trade with citizens of the colony, but smaller coastal schooners from New England and the middle colonies as well as the West Indies established a lucrative silver trade with the early settlers to eastern North Carolina. Silversmiths also were among the numerous settlers who followed the Great Wagon Road from southeastern Pennsylvania during the last half of the eighteenth century. As the century came to an end, silversmiths were working throughout the state in the more populated areas.

References: John Bivins and Forsyth Alexander, *The Regional Arts of the Early South* (1994); George Barton Cutten, *Silversmiths of North Carolina, 1696–1860* (1984); North Carolina Museum of Art, *Two Hundred Years of Visual Arts in North Carolina* (1976).

Michael H. Lewis

Simkins v. Cone. In 1962 dentist George Simkins, physician Alvin Blount, and other African American physicians and their patients sued Moses H. Cone Memorial Hospital and Wesley Long Community Hospital in Greensboro, charging that they had denied "the admission of physicians and dentists to hospital staff privileges, and the admission of patients to hospital facilities, on the basis of race." The plaintiffs argued that the two hospitals, which had received a combined total of $3.2 million in state and federal construction funds under the 1946 Hill-Burton Hospital Survey and Construction Act, had violated their rights under the Equal Protection clause of the Fourteenth Amendment. The plaintiffs also sought declaratory judgment that the sections of the Hill-Burton Act and Public Health Service Regulations providing for separate-but-equal facilities and services were unconstitutional in violation of the Fifth and Fourteenth Amendments. U.S. attorney general Robert F. Kennedy filed an amicus brief on behalf of the plaintiffs.

On 5 Dec. 1962 the U.S. District Court, Fourth Circuit, upheld the defendants' claim that participation in the Hill-Burton program had not rendered the private, nonprofit hospitals "instrumentalities of the state" and therefore they were outside the provenance of the Fifth and Fourteenth Amendments. In November 1963 the U.S. Court of Appeals, Fourth Circuit, overturned the federal district court ruling, finding that private hospitals that participated in the Hill-Burton program were indeed connected to the government—both state and federal—and were thus obligated by the prohibitions against racial discrimination outlined in the Fifth and Fourteenth Amendments. The court also found unconstitutional the sections in the original Hill-Burton Act that provided for separate-but-equal hospital accommodations and services.

The *Simkins* decision marked the first time that federal courts applied the Equal Protection clause of the Fourteenth Amendment to prohibit racial discrimination by a private entity. This revised the precedent set by the 1883 civil rights cases, in which the Supreme Court narrowly interpreted the Equal Protection clause to prohibit discrimination only by government agencies that were clearly public in character. The broadened definition of "state action" that resulted from *Simkins* made it possible for Congress to pass the 1964 Civil Rights Act the next year, outlawing segregation in public accommodations and prohibiting racial discrimination in employment.

Until the *Simkins* ruling, most hospitals in North Carolina and throughout the South did not accept black patients on an equal basis and did not allow black physicians to admit patients or train as interns. Only at North Carolina's nine all-black hospitals could African American patients and physicians be guaranteed equal access, but such facilities were often overcrowded and unable to afford medical equipment considered standard in most white hospitals. By 1963 a few public hospitals had desegregated, although most still assigned black patients to separate, inferior wards. Almost no hospitals in North Carolina—public or private—permitted black physicians to obtain staff privileges until after *Simkins*.

Reference: U.S. Commission on Civil Rights, North Carolina Advisory Committee, *Equal Protection of the Laws in North Carolina* (1962).

Karen Kruse Thomas

Simmons Sea-Skiff. From 1950 through the 1960s, T. N. Simmons and his son built hundreds of small boats on the North Carolina coast that many regarded as the best sport-fishing and recreational power boats available. Never manufactured on a large scale, the vessels were simply purchased shortly after Simmons finished them. He initially used juniper in their construction, though he later switched to mahogany for the frames and ⅜-inch marine plywood for planking. Most models had an outboard motor as well. Although large motors became available and were used on the boat, Simmons insisted that an 18-horsepower engine was the correct size for his unusual skiff.

Simmons sea-skiffs, both beautiful and seaworthy, are regarded as classics by their owners. In the early 2000s the U.S. Army Corps of Engineers maintained three of these boats for use in putting down survey stakes and similar duties; other owners and builders included residents of several foreign countries in addition to those of southeastern North Carolina.

References: David Carnell, "Mister Simmons' Wonderful Boat," *Wildlife in North Carolina* (June 1987); Bob Simpson and Mary Simpson, "In Search of the Simmons Sea Skiff," *Small Boat Journal* (November 1986).

Gene Purcell

Singing. SEE Hymnody; Moravian Music; Shape-Note Singing.

Sir Walter Hotel, built in 1922 on Raleigh's Fayetteville Street, was part of a large boom in Raleigh's development during the 1920s. Gen. Albert Cox and Josephus Daniels's Capitol Construction Company built the hotel for $750,000. B. H. Griffin, owner of the famed Yarborough House across the street, became a partner and ran the hotel. For many years the Sir Walter Hotel was the preferred location for political gatherings, weddings, debutante balls, and parties of all types. The Sphinx Club, a "gentlemen's retreat," thrived in the hotel as well. Political campaigns and associated events, such as the Jefferson-Jackson Dinner, always took place in the hotel. In the 1960s, the hotel's role as "third chamber of the legislature" and "in" place for social gatherings declined with the expansion of the legislative building in Raleigh and the emergence of the Velvet Cloak Inn and other hotels.

The Sir Walter Hotel can boast its share of intriguing stories and memorable events, perhaps the most publicized of which was the Kluckhorn murder case of 1955. From his hotel room in the Sir Walter, Richard Kluckhorn, a textbook salesman, shot and killed Bernice Seawell of Arlington, Va, on 13 May of that year. It was later discovered that he had been "dry firing" with his gun, which went off accidentally, hitting Seawell in

Lobby of the Sir Walter Hotel. Courtesy of NCOA&H.

the parking lot across the street. Kluckhorn was convicted of involuntary manslaughter.

In 1964 the Sir Walter Hotel was sold to a corporation headed in part by John A. Williams. Williams bought out his partners and in 1967 donated the hotel to the state. The state sold the hotel in 1969 to Plaza Associates, which traded the hotel, along with other properties, to Kidd Brewer for the land on which Crabtree Valley Mall was developed. By 1979 the Sir Walter Hotel had been converted into subsidized housing apartments, and it continues to serve this function. It is currently owned by the Raleigh-based partnership Sir Walter Associates.

References: Bess Ballentine and Nell Joslin Styron, "Tales of the Sir Walter," *The State* 48 (September 1980); Ballentine and Styron, "Tales of the Sir Walter: Part II," *The State* 48 (October 1980); James Vickers, *Raleigh, City of Oaks: An Illustrated History* (1997).

Laura Young Baxley

Sir Walter Raleigh Award for Fiction

was established in 1952 by the Historical Book Club of North Carolina to recognize the year's best book of fiction, drama, short stories, or poetry written by a North Carolinian. A replica of the statuette of Sir Walter Raleigh that crowns the master cup is usually given each year to the author or authors of the original book judged as being most worthy of recognition, though it is sometimes given for meritorious achievement over a period of years. Paul Green won the first award for his outstanding literary career. Other winners have included Daphne Athas, Doris Betts, Fred Chappell, John Ehle, Charles Frazier, Kay Gibbons, Reynolds Price, and Lee Smith. The competition, open to residents of North Carolina, is handled through the secretary of the North Carolina Literary and Historical Association.

References: H. G. Jones, "Sir Walter Raleigh Award," *Carolina Comments* (March 1972); Richard Walser, "North Carolina Awards in Literature and History," *NCHR* 31 (April 1954).

H. G. Jones

Sissipahaw Indians.

In 1701 Englishman John Lawson visited the Sissipahaw town on the Haw River in present-day Alamance County. Believed to have been a Siouan-speaking people, the Sissipahaw were also known as the Saxapahaw, the name by which they are remembered in historical documents. They were so closely associated with the Shakori that some scholars think they may have been one and the same. In 1711, when the Saxapahaw refused to join Tuscarora Chief Hancock's plans to make war on white Carolina settlements, a Tuscarora party attacked them, destroying their town and scattering the people. Some Saxapahaw warriors joined the invading South Carolina army of Col. John Barnwell to fight the Tuscarora, while others may have fled to the Waccamaw.

After the Tuscarora War ended in 1713, the Saxapahaw joined with other Indian groups in the Yamassee War. The survivors of that conflict probably then joined the diverse and powerful Catawba Nation.

References: Douglas L. Rights, *The American Indian in North America* (2nd ed., 1957); H. Trawick Ward and R. P. Stephen Davis Jr., *Indian Communities on the North Carolina Piedmont, A.D. 1000 to 1700* (1993).

Michael D. Green

Skiing.

From its modest beginnings, snow skiing has grown into an important part of the economy and culture of western North Carolina. Skiing on snow has been practiced in northern Europe for over 4,000 years but did not become a recreational pursuit until the late nineteenth century. The two main types of competitive skiing include Alpine, or downhill, skiing and Nordic, or cross-country, skiing. Exactly when snow skiing was first practiced in North Carolina is unknown. A photograph appearing in *North Carolina: A Guide to the Old North State*, published by the Works Progress Administration in 1939, shows a group of skiers on an unnamed snow-covered hill in Banner Elk. An article in *The State* magazine claims that the first organized ski club in the South was organized in 1940 at Lees-McRae College. Certainly by the 1950s, snow skiing was becoming a popular pastime in western North Carolina. Skiers were engaging in Nordic skiing on Clingman's Dome in the Great Smoky Mountains National Park, while downhill skiers at Roan Mountain were discussing erecting a tow rope as early as 1951. In addition, there were people skiing along the slopes of Mount Mitchell, and several individuals there supported an effort to get the state to develop a lodge and snow skiing facilities.

Organized commercial ski operations began in North Carolina in December 1961, when Tom Alexander opened the Cata-

Skiing on Sugar Mountain near Banner Elk. Photograph courtesy of North Carolina Division of Tourism, Film, and Sports Development.

loochee Ski Slopes in a pasture on a hillside behind his ranch in Haywood County. The name was soon changed to Cataloochee Ranch and Ski Area. Alexander utilized snow-making equipment, at the time in its early stages of development, to produce snow on his pasture. For his efforts, Alexander is often referred to as the "Father of Southern Skiing."

At Blowing Rock, Bill Thalheimer led an effort to create the state's first commercial ski operations, but bad weather hampered construction, and it was not until the spring of 1962 that his slopes opened to the public. The Blowing Rock Ski Lodge (modern-day Appalachian Ski Mountain) between Boone and Blowing Rock featured three slopes serviced with tow ropes and the first T-bar type lift used in North Carolina. This also was the first facility in the state equipped with lights for night skiing.

In 1964 Grover, Harry, and Spencer Robbins, brothers active in development efforts in western North Carolina, opened two small ski slopes at Hound Ears Club near Boone. Though small in scale, their operation drew rave reviews. Other small-scale resorts opened in the mid-1960s, including Sapphire Valley near Cashiers and High Meadows near Roaring Gap.

Efforts to create the ski complex that became Seven Devils began in 1964. Six investors from Winston-Salem acquired 1,288 acres in Avery and Watauga Counties. Seven Devils finally began snow skiing operations in the spring of 1967. One of the most influential individuals in the snow skiing enterprises in western North Carolina was Tom Brigham, a dentist from Birmingham, Ala., whose goal was to create a ski resort in the South along the lines of the famous New England resorts. Brigham began searching for a location for his southern ski resort in the late 1950s. After studying numerous sites, he settled on the Banner Elk area and began purchasing land at Beech Mountain in 1961. By 1962 trails had been cut, but an economic downturn dried up financing.

The project advanced little until 1966, when Brigham joined forces with the Robbins brothers of Hound Ears fame. They set out to build what was dubbed the "Disneyland of Southern Skiing." By December of 1967, Beech Mountain was open, deemed to have the highest skiing in the East and featuring the region's first cabin-type gondola lifts. Brigham moved on in 1968 to begin development of another ski area, Sugar Mountain. Located between Linville and Banner Elk, this 3,000-acre resort opened in the fall of 1969. Major features for the site included the distinction of having the "greatest vertical drop south of New England" (1,200 feet).

References: "The Ski Slopes are Swinging," *The State* (15 Jan. 1970); Bill Wright, "Amazing Rise of the Tar Heel Snowbird," *The State* (15 Jan. 1968).

John Hairr

SEE ALSO Beech Mountain/Land of Oz; Cataloochee Ranch and Ski Area.

Slate Belt. The Carolina Slate Belt refers to a region of low-grade metamorphosed volcanic rock characterized by slaty cleavages. This region is one of several belts crossing North Carolina in a general southwest to northeast direction. The Charlotte Belt exhibits a medium to high grade of metamorphosed rock to the west of the Carolina Slate Belt, while to the east lies the Triassic Basin. Some of the rock has been quarried near Hillsborough for local use, most notably on the Duke University campus in Durham.

The term "Carolina Slate Belt" was first used by Henry B. C. Nitze and George B. Hanna in 1896 for Professor Denison Olmsted's *Report on the Geology of North Carolina* (3 vols., 1824–27). They confirmed the age of the belt as pre-Cambrian period. The region was an arc of volcanic islands similar to Japan today, and much explosive material settled in the surrounding seas. Lava flows were numerous. The later tectonic movements led to consolidation, metamorphism, and erosion.

References: Fred Beyer, *North Carolina, the Years before Man: A Geologic History* (1991); P. A. Carpenter III, *Metallic Mineral Deposits of the Carolina Slate Belt*, North Carolina Department of Natural Resources and Community Development Bulletin no. 84 (1976).

Jean H. Seaman

Slater Fund. In 1882 John Fox Slater, a textile manufacturer and philanthropist from Norwich, Conn., established a $1 million fund exclusively for the education of blacks in southern states. The goal of the fund—which benefited several educational projects in North Carolina—was to uplift recently emancipated African Americans and their future children through a "Christian education." Slater designated former U.S. president Rutherford B. Hayes to head the fund. Other trustees included Chief Justice of the Supreme Court Morrison R. Waite; William E. Dodge, cofounder of Phelps-Dodge Corporation; Daniel C. Gilman, president of Johns Hopkins University; and Alfred A. Colquit, governor of Georgia.

Slater requested that teacher training receive priority. Schools that did the best work in preparing black men and women to teach black children—thus helping as many schools at all levels possible—were targeted for funding, along with those schools that recognized and introduced industrial training. The fund supported improvements in salaries and facilities.

The fund's first connection to North Carolina was made through Simon Green Atkins, founder and principal of Slater Industrial Academy, which was established in honor of Slater in September 1892. The school grew and eventually became Winston-Salem State University (1969). A second connection between the Slater Fund and the education of North Carolina blacks was the work of Nathan Carter Newbold. In 1913 Newbold became the state's first director of black education, a position created by funds from the General Education Board. Following a state educational survey, in 1920 Newbold outlined to the State Board of Education a plan to create an entire Division of Negro Education. The plan was approved, $15,000 was appropriated by the General Assembly, and Newbold was named division director, serving for 37 years until his retirement in 1950. Under his leadership, black education experienced remarkable growth in the 1920s, and the idea of publicly supported black schools gained wider acceptance. As a result of his close work with philanthropies, moneys from the Slater and Jeanes Funds, as well as the General Education Board, were utilized efficiently and effectively.

The Slater Fund also was used to establish the state's County Training School System in 1911. The fund agreed to appropriate $500 if counties would match it with $750 and aim to stretch the school session to ten months out of the year. In all, the Slater Fund contributed more than $15,000 to this system, primarily funded through the public schools. One school in each of several counties was selected and called a county training school. Besides offering some of the usual secondary school courses, these schools offered useful industrial courses and some simple teacher training courses. At one time there were nearly 50 such schools; these in time became standard or accredited high schools.

Between 1882 and 1937—when the Southern Education Fund was formed by the merger of the Slater, Jeanes, Peabody Education, and Virginia Randolph Funds—African American institutions in North Carolina received a total of more than $600,000 from the Slater Fund.

References: Will W. Alexander, *The Slater and Jeanes Funds* (1934); Wade H. Boggs, *State-supported Higher Education for Blacks in North Carolina, 1877–1945* (1972); Hugh V. Brown, *A History of the Education of Negroes in North Carolina* (1961).

Wiley J. Williams

SEE ALSO Jeanes Fund.

Slave Clandestine Economy

Slave Clandestine Economy refers to a variety of private agricultural and business endeavors undertaken by some North Carolina slaves. In 1771 a Scottish visitor to North Carolina was somewhat surprised to find that the daily routine of plantation slaves included time for them to work "in their own private fields, consisting of 5 or 6 acres of ground, allowed them by their master, for planting rice, corn, potatoes, tobacco, &c." The visitor was describing the task system of slave labor that endured from long before the American Revolution until the Civil War, for slaveholders often permitted their bondsmen and women time to cultivate their own garden plots. The system benefited both masters, who used it as an incentive, and slaves, who could supplement their meager diets with vegetables and fruits. It also led to participation by the slave population in secret economic activities such as bartering crops for whiskey or wine, unloading their surplus to other blacks who acted as factors, and selling cash crops to local merchants.

That these practices flourished in the early national period was demonstrated on three occasions between 1779 and 1788, when state legislators rewrote a law of 1742 prohibiting slaves from "dealing and Trafficking." It was their intention to prevent slaves from buying, selling, trading, bartering, or borrowing "any Commodities whatsoever." Judging by later petitions to the General Assembly from concerned citizens and subsequent laws, slave "dealing and Trafficking" were not curtailed; indeed, as time went on they seem to have increased.

Although many slaves probably had access to a garden plot and traded or bartered at one time or another, sometimes even with their master's permission, a small number of them participated in the more sophisticated aspects of the clandestine economy. Unlike its neighbors to the north, North Carolina did not develop iron and coal industries that could employ significant numbers of slaves, although it did participate fully in slave hiring. Hired blacks sometimes received limited extra compensation for their work beyond the contract payment to the master; at other times they actually worked for wages. Commenting on the effect of paying wages to slaves, famed landscape architect Frederick Law Olmsted wrote that "negroes in the swamp [making shingles] were more sprightly and straightforward in their manner and conversation than any field hand plantation negroes that I saw." From the owners there were no complaints of "'rascality' or laziness." Working for wages permitted slaves to purchase various commodities and even to own property.

Wages also made it possible for a few ambitious slaves to move into a "gray area" between slavery and freedom, either by hiring themselves out or accumulating enough money to gain some independence. The Society of Friends (Quakers) and other antislavery groups helped to perpetuate these practices by purchasing slaves and allowing them "virtual freedom." Those who opposed them often petitioned the General Assembly for new laws to stop the uncontrolled movement of slaves, or they filed suit against a particular African American; however, such charges were difficult to prove, and judges sometimes sided with blacks who had acquired a "reputation for freedom." Self-hired and virtually free, they often were among the most skilled and talented blacks and engaged in a variety economic activities, including trade with plantation slaves. They worked as carpenters, coopers, cabinetmakers, masons, fishermen, market women, and even contractors.

In 1802 white mechanics in New Hanover County asked the North Carolina legislature to prohibit slaves from working as free mechanics and undertaking contracts "on their own account, at sometimes less than one half the rate that a regular bred white mechanic could afford to do it." According to their petition, slaves occasionally hired gangs of 8 to 12 other bondsmen and bondswomen who worked entirely "for their own benefit." Half a century later, quasi-free slave contractors in the county still conducted a brisk construction business.

Such activities, of course, were unusual, as most slaves labored for their masters in the tobacco, rice, or cotton fields. Although the extent of the clandestine slave economy has not been thoroughly studied, there is little doubt that a significant number of slaves in North Carolina participated in various business undertakings that were neither condoned by their masters nor permitted under the law.

Reference: John Hope Franklin, "Slaves Virtually Free in Ante-Bellum North Carolina," *Journal of Negro History* 28 (July 1943).

Loren Schweninger

Slave Codes. The increasing number of black slaves in colonial America created suspicion and fear among the general population and led to a backlash of white reaction known as slave codes. Virginia was the first of the 13 colonies to adopt such regulations, using earlier Caribbean slave codes as models. Other colonies quickly followed suit, patterning their codes after the Virginia laws.

Slave codes varied slightly from colony to colony, but most made bondage a lifelong condition and ensured that all descendants of slaves would be slaves as well. Other codes prohibited them from voting, owning property, testifying in court against whites, gathering in large numbers, traveling without permission, or marrying whites. Slave codes also gave white masters nearly total control over the lives of slaves, permitting owners to use such corporal punishments as whipping, branding, maiming, and torture. Although white masters could not legally murder their slaves, some did and were never prosecuted. Colonial North Carolina, still tied to South Carolina until 1729, had few slaves in the late seventeenth century, but by 1710 there were around 900. The colony's growing number of blacks led to the creation of a slave code by 1715.

After the Revolutionary War, most states, especially those in the South, developed new slave codes. After the 1830s these laws became increasingly stringent, due to the tensions produced by the Nat Turner Rebellion in Southampton County, Va., and the rise of the abolitionist movement in the North. The new regulations clearly defined slaves as property, rather than as people, and outlawed teaching them to read and write. Slaves could not leave the plantation without their master's permission, strike a white person even in self-defense, buy or sell goods or hire themselves out, or visit the homes of whites or free blacks.

Enforcement of slave codes varied. In times of peace, masters gave slaves more freedom; but in times of unrest, they rigorously enforced the slave codes both through the courts and by establishing slave patrols. Composed of white men who took turns covering a particular area of their county, slave patrols watched for runaways or assisted owners in enforcing the slave codes on their plantations.

Slave codes ended with the Civil War but were replaced by other discriminatory laws known as "black codes" during Reconstruction (1865–77). The black codes were attempts to control the newly freed African Americans by barring them from engaging in certain occupations, performing jury duty, owning firearms, voting, and other pursuits. At first, the U.S. Congress opposed black codes by enacting legislation such as the Civil Rights Acts of 1866 and 1875 and the Thirteenth, Fourteenth, and Fifteenth Amendments to the U.S. Constitution. But by the time of the so-called Compromise of 1877, civil rights for blacks had eroded, as Congress, the U.S. Supreme Court, and northerners lost interest in the issue. The slave codes essentially lived on in Jim Crow laws and other forms of discrimination until successfully challenged in the civil rights era of the 1950s and 1960s.

References: Lerone Bennett Jr., *Before the Mayflower: A History of Black America* (1993); Jeffrey J. Crow, Paul D. Escott, and Flora J. Hatley, *A History of African Americans in North Carolina* (2002); John Hope Franklin and Alfred A. Moss Jr., *From Slavery to Freedom: A History of Negro Americans* (6th ed., 1988); Eugene D. Genovese, *Roll, Jordan, Roll: The World the Slaves Made* (1974).

Alan K. Lamm

SEE ALSO Black Codes; Slave Patrols.

Slave Names. Some scholars of slavery have come to view the names and naming of slaves as a meaningful gauge of many aspects of slave life and culture and of how their customs changed over time. Anthropologist Meyer Fortes's observation that the naming practices of any society "epitomize personal experiences, historical happenings, attitudes to life, and cultural ideas and values" holds particularly true for African American slaves. Extensive records of slaveholding over several generations exist for a number of North Carolina plantations, most notably the Skinner and Hayes plantations in Chowan County; Pettigrew plantations in Tyrrell, Washington, and Wake Counties; Bennehan-Cameron plantation in Orange County; Hargrove plantation in Granville County; Arrington plantations in Nash and Edgecombe Counties; Avery plantation in Burke County; and Lenoir plantation in Caldwell County. Along with records from churches, manumission societies, slave traders, and estate settlements, these documents provide a vast pool of data from which to trace patterns and trends from the colonial period through emancipation.

Evidence indicates that many slave parents named their children after the first generation or so of family members brought to America. Recognizable patterns of change in names and naming practices are evident from the mid-eighteenth century to the early nineteenth century and on through the 1860s. They reflect an acculturation process by which generations of slaves, increasingly removed from the direct influence of the first enslaved African transplants, adopted the conventions of their owners, eventually creating a culture and value system all their own. The names they gave their children provide a valuable, if limited, index of that process over time.

Slaves remained nameless from the time of their capture until their purchase by American masters. Quite a few slaves were allowed to keep their original African names or names assigned them elsewhere (as reflected by the frequency of Spanish and Portuguese names among the first generation of Carolina slaves). Throughout the colonial period, as many as one-fifth of the slaves in North Carolina retained African names; Quash, Cuffee, Mingo, Sambo, Mustapha, and Sukey were among the most common recorded. Slaves often transferred such names to later generations in modified form or relied on African naming traditions, such as "day names" or names reflecting the order of birth among siblings.

Although masters often assigned names to newly purchased slaves that were whimsical, satirical, or condescending in intent, the frequent appearance of classical names—Venus, Cato, Hercules, Bacchus, Pompey—reflect planters' own educations and libraries. Slaves themselves sometimes chose names denoting weather conditions at the time of their child's birth or some distinctive feature of his or her appearance. Geographic names were common, as were the names of ships or distant ports for slaves born in places such as Wilmington or New Bern. Beginning in the early nineteenth century, more biblical names were given to slave children, a reflection of the widespread attempts to Christianize slave communities and their greater exposure to Bible stories.

With the Civil War and emancipation of approximately 360,000 slaves in North Carolina, changes in African American names became indicative of a new value system and sense of self-identity among freedpeople. Whereas slaves had perpetuated African, classical, or other unusual names from one generation to the next—creating a distinctive nomenclature unlike that of southern whites—free blacks began to use more traditionally Anglicized versions of their first names.

References: Cheryll Cody, "'There Was No Absalom on the Ball Plantation': Slave-Naming Practices in the South Carolina Low Country, 1720–1865," *American Historical Review* 92 (June 1987); Eugene D. Genovese, *Roll, Jordan, Roll: The World the Slaves Made* (1974); Herbert G. Gutman, *The Black Family in Slavery and Freedom, 1750–1925* (1976); John C. Inscoe, "Carolina Slave Names: An Index to Acculturation," *Journal of Southern History* 59 (November 1983).

John C. Inscoe

Slave Narratives, firsthand accounts of African Americans who experienced slavery, are essential tools in the study of American history and literature and have played a central role in national debates about slavery, freedom, and American identity. The recorded experiences of African American slaves are also arguably one of North Carolina's greatest contributions to American literature as a whole. Following emancipation, the autobiography was the most popular literary tool of black writers; slave narratives outnumbered novels written by African Americans until the Great Depression. Along with their fictional descendants, the state's slave narratives continue to challenge readers to explore questions of race, social justice, and the meaning of freedom.

Narratives of the antebellum period, usually written by fugitive slaves, focused primarily on the experiences of African Americans held in bondage in the South. Many antebellum narrators depicted slavery as a condition of extreme physical, intellectual, emotional, and spiritual deprivation. Their accounts stirred dialogue between blacks and whites about slavery and freedom, as former slaves wrote both to enlighten white readers about the realities of institutional slavery and to convince them that the black people were deserving of full human rights.

Published slave narratives began to appear throughout the English-speaking world in the late eighteenth and early nineteenth centuries through the efforts of abolitionists, and a significant number sold in the tens of thousands. The autobiographies of Frederick Douglass, William Wells Brown, and Harriet Jacobs (a native of Edenton) were some of the most influential slave narratives of the antebellum period. Jacobs's autobiographical *Incidents in the Life of a Slave Girl: Written by Herself* (1861) contributed extensively to the study of African American women's slave experience. The book is considered one of the two most important American slave narratives—*Narrative of the Life of Frederick Douglass: An American Slave* (1845) is the other—as well as one of the most significant canonical works of African American literature.

Dismissed by many whites as antislavery propaganda, such narratives provide eyewitness accounts of personal struggles, sorrows, aspirations, and triumphs during slavery. They reveal the complex relationship between white master and black slave, in addition to the tremendous efforts of blacks to build and shape their personal lives and communities. Many ex-slaves escaped to the North only to find that their concept of freedom clashed with the reality of racism in the so-called free states. The struggles of former slaves as free citizens of color in the North increasingly appeared in narratives of the 1840s and 1850s.

Former slaves continued to record their experiences after the Civil War. In part, they wanted to ensure that the reunited nation did not forget the evils of the institution that had threatened its existence. When white southern writers and regional boosters of the 1880s and 1890s nostalgically recounted the myths of slavery and "the moonlight-and-magnolias" plantation to northern white audiences, the narratives of ex-slaves were among the few accounts providing a reliable, firsthand portrayal of what slavery had actually been like.

Slave narratives written after emancipation often depicted slavery as a trial wherein the resiliency, industry, and ingenuity of the slave was tested and ultimately validated. Thus, some newly freed African Americans used the genre to argue their capability and readiness to participate in the post–Civil War social and economic order. Booker T. Washington's *Up from Slavery* (1901) is probably the most famous example of the late nineteenth- and early twentieth-century slave narrative.

In the 1930s the Federal Writers' Project, a New Deal program commissioned by the Works Progress Administration (WPA), conducted interviews with formerly enslaved African Americans. The accounts of 176 former slaves provided rare, firsthand reminiscences of slave life in nineteenth-century North Carolina. Although most of the subjects were young during the Civil War, many were able to recall their living conditions under slavery. One woman said that she and her family faced constant hunger, forcing them to steal from their master. Her clothing was also inadequate: she and other slaves received only one pair of shoes a year; when the shoes wore out, they went barefoot. Education on her plantation was strongly discouraged, and any slave found with a book would be sold as punishment.

North Carolina's slave narratives portray the sexual exploitation of black women by white owners as one of the most horrific aspects of slavery. Several WPA interviewees corroborated this testimony. One woman, recalling her master's penchant for carnal interludes with his female slaves, told an interviewer that slaves on her plantation called such men "Carpet Gitters."

Treatment by slaveholders varied. One former slave recounted that one night his mother was taken from her bed and sold without his knowledge. On another occasion he was tied to a tree and brutally beaten until blood flowed down his back. A woman recalled being publicly flogged after she broke some of the master's dishes. Other plantations owners vehemently opposed physical abuse and refused to divide families through sale. Some owners allowed social outlets for their slaves, such as religious meetings, corn shuckings, and dances; others taught their slaves to read and write. Varied accounts of slave quarters also exist: some were comfortable, others Spartan. A few freedpeople looked back on slavery with a sense of loss. One woman lamented the absence of slavery's cradle-to-grave care, while a man recalled his mother claiming that "her master was better than other folks."

Slave narratives have contributed extensively to African American literary and cultural traditions. They also have directly influenced certain classic American works, from Harriet Beecher Stowe's *Uncle Tom's Cabin* (1852) and Mark Twain's *Huckleberry Finn* (1884) to contemporary novels such as William Styron's *The Confessions of Nat Turner* (1967) and Toni Morrison's *Beloved* (1987).

References: William L. Andrews, ed., *The North Carolina Roots of African American Literature: An Anthology* (2006); Andrews and Henry Louis Gates Jr., *Slave Narratives* (2000); Paul D. Escott, *Slavery Remembered: A Record of Twentieth-Century Slave Narratives* (1979); George P. Rawick, ed., *The American Slave: A Composite Autobiography* (19 vols., 1972–76).

Allyson C. Criner
Steven E. Nash

Slave Patrols, constabulary bands of white citizens, enforced North Carolina's slave codes from the mid-eighteenth century until the end of the Civil War. A duty of all white men until the 1830s, patrolling connected nonslaveholders with the slave system, reinforcing poor whites' legal supremacy and control over blacks.

North Carolina, unlike other southern states and perhaps due to the lack of major slave rebellions, was slow to establish formal slave patrols. South Carolina first addressed the issue in 1704, ordering its militia to punish any African American caught away from home without a pass. Virginia introduced a patrol system in 1726 that restricted the guards to the apprehension of slaves. The North Carolina General Assembly did not organize patrols until 1753, although earlier laws had recognized the right of any white citizen to apprehend slaves who ran away or otherwise violated the laws of the colony. The 1753 statute required the county courts to appoint, when necessary, "three freeholders in each district as searchers" to comb slave quarters for weapons at least four times a year. Throughout the century of its existence, the slave patrol in North Carolina remained a civil organization controlled by the county courts; the state militia was called out only in periods of serious unrest.

As an aspect of daily life, the slave patrol fluctuated in importance. Its primary duties were to check the passes of slaves and free blacks and break up gatherings of African Americans. In the absence of slave disturbances, patrollers sometimes neglected their duties or viewed them more as social occasions. Patrols often were ridiculed by slaves and scorned by slaveholders, who feared abuse of their chattel. Patrolling was rarely lucrative; authorities used fines, small salaries, or dismissal from other civic obligations to induce conscientious performance.

The rise of the abolitionist movement in the late 1820s stirred fears of slave insurrections across the state. In 1830 the legislature increased the maximum punishment to 39 lashes and authorized patrols to arrest anyone, white or black, caught trading with a slave. The new law also required the county courts to establish an oversight committee to appoint the patrol and hear any complaints against it.

Despite the lack of major slave uprisings in the state, Virginia's Nat Turner Rebellion in August 1831 produced criticism of the patrol system in North Carolina. In response, new laws permitted officials to call out the militia in times of hysteria caused by runaway slaves but did not allow its complete takeover of patrol duties. Nevertheless, after 1831 the patrol system lost much of its prestige. In the cases of *State v. Isham Hailey* (1845), *State v. Caesar (a Slave)* (1849), and *State v. Jacob Boyce* (1849), the North Carolina Supreme Court curtailed the powers of the slave patrol.

The efficacy of the state's slave patrols is unclear. Unremarkable in their daily operations and varying over place and time, the patrols provided white owners assurance, however superficial, that their chattel would not rise up against them. For blacks, the patrol served as a constant reminder of their absolute lack of freedom. After the Civil War, whites attempted to regain control of African Americans through black codes. The Ku Klux Klan's campaigns of violence and intimidation served many of the same purposes as the antebellum slave patrols.

References: B. F. Callahan, "The North Carolina Slave Patrol" (M.A. thesis, UNC-Chapel Hill, 1973); George P. Rawick, ed., *The American Slave: A Composite Autobiography* (19 vols., 1972–76).

Daniel J. Salemson

Slave Rebellions were a recurring fear in North Carolina throughout much of its early history, although the state never experienced a large-scale revolt. Instead, it responded to internal rumors and rebellions that occurred in other states. The first major shock to white North Carolinians came in 1739, when slaves in South Carolina orchestrated the Stono Rebellion. Because it took place near the North Carolina border, the insurrection induced North Carolina slaveholders in 1741 to restrict their slaves' ability to carry guns.

The period between 1775 and 1800 was a turbulent time for North Carolina slave owners, as the American Revolution destabilized race relations in the state. As the people won independence from Great Britain and then struggled to define the new American nation, they kept a constant watch over their slaves. Many slaves were themselves involved in social and political pursuits. Black men fought for both sides in the Revolutionary War, and many supported the principles of liberty and democracy. During the war, white North Carolinians investigated numerous rumors of slave revolts. In 1775 whites in Wilmington gained peace of mind by disarming all blacks, imposing a 9:00 P.M. curfew, and requiring an oath of allegiance from their slaves. A posse of Beaufort County whites rounded up more than 40 African Americans believed to be plotting an insurrection, including the 2 alleged leaders. These men reportedly planned to kill white families and burn their houses on 8 July 1775 as they traveled to "black country" for weapons and a new black-led government.

Reacting to disturbances in the West Indies, especially the bloody Saint Domingue (Haiti) revolt in 1791, North Carolina restricted the influx of Caribbean slaves in 1794. A year later the law was revised, and in 1798 Governor Samuel Ashe banned the importation of all West Indian slaves to permit the state to settle its own domestic difficulties. A Granville County slave named Quillo had organized a massive revolt to take place in April 1794. His failed plan included holding elections for an African American government and uniting with insurrectionists in neighboring Person County to kill all in their path. In 1798 three slaves, arrested in Bertie County for planning a revolt of 150 slaves, received 39 lashes after being found guilty of a high misdemeanor.

The alarm of a "slave conspiracy" in 1802 actually involved a series of actions taken by whites in response to threats of a slave revolt. Arrests, trials, and the execution of two slaves in Nottoway County, Va., in January 1802 proved to be the beginning of two successive waves of conspiracy scares. The first wave was confined to southeastern Virginia, except for brief excitements in Halifax and Northampton Counties, N.C., during February. The second wave began with new suspicions in Halifax County, Va., in April and spread rapidly to nearly all of eastern Virginia and North Carolina. Discovery of an alleged plot to burn Norfolk prompted slave arrests, trials, and executions from Currituck County eastward and southward in late May and June. Annapolis, Md., was also affected.

White panic was especially evident in Bertie County, where 11 slaves were executed. Others were put to death in Hertford, Halifax, Edgecombe, Currituck, Camden, and Perquimans Counties. Altogether, about 19 slaves were executed in North Carolina and 10 in Virginia, in addition to numerous others reportedly killed by vigilantes and militia. Many more suffered whippings, the cropping of ears, and deportation. Neither trials nor investigations in both states produced credible evidence of actual plotting, but public tranquility did not return until midsummer. Some tightening of slave codes resulted, but there were no further widespread alarms in this area for nearly three decades.

Two rumors of slave rebellions, both originating in Virginia, swept through North Carolina prior to the Civil War. The first followed the brutal murder of 59 white men, women, and children in Southampton County, Va., under the direction of a self-anointed slave preacher named Nat Turner on 21 Aug. 1831. Turner's revolt elicited waves of North Carolina militia seeking to protect the state from similar unrest. One group, the Governor's Guards, reportedly killed 40 slaves while helping to suppress a rebellion in Cross Keys, Va. In this climate of heightened fear, white North Carolinians discovered a suspected uprising in Duplin County, where after hours of torture on 5 Sept. 1831 a slave confessed to devising the plot. On 4 October the insurrectionists were to begin marching south to Wilmington, killing white families along the way; on the coast they would be joined by a force of about 2,000 blacks and blaze a path of destruction on their return north to Fayetteville. The alleged leaders—slaves named Dave and Jim—were killed by a mob on 9 Sept. 1831. Their deaths did not stop the spread of terror to Wilmington, where on 17 September, several slaves confessed to planning an additional revolt.

Several years later John Brown, a white abolitionist of questionable mental stability, led an ill-fated raid on the arsenal at Harpers Ferry, Va. (now West Virginia) to procure weapons for a slave revolt to end slavery. In the attempt, Brown and his men were captured on 16 Oct. 1859 by U.S. Marines under the command of Col. Robert E. Lee. While initial reports in North Carolina exaggerated Brown's numerical strength, the seeming disinterest of black North Carolinians prevented the panic that followed the Nat Turner Rebellion. Nevertheless, in the wake of the raid numerous state newspapers clamored for a better slave patrol system. Black social outlets, including churches, were restricted as white North Carolinians perceived Brown's plan as part of a larger northern conspiracy to undermine southern society. Although his mission failed, Brown inspired a backlash among whites against all things "non-southern," which intensified the sectionalism in North Carolina leading to secession and the Civil War.

References: Kent Blaser, "North Carolina and John Brown's Raid," *Civil War History* 24 (1978); Jeffrey J. Crow, "Slave Rebelliousness and Social Conflict in North Carolina, 1775 to 1802," *William and Mary Quarterly* 37 (1980); Crow, Paul D. Escott, and Flora J. Hatley, *A History of African Americans in North Carolina* (2002); Charles Edward Morris, "Panic and Reprisal: Reaction in North Carolina to the Nat Turner Insurrection, 1831," *NCHR* 62 (January 1985).

Steven E. Nash
Thomas C. Parramore

SEE ALSO Negro Head Road.

A broadside circulated in the Stokes County area in 1836 advertising the sale of land and slaves. NCC.

Slavery. Although slaves had come straight from Guinea to the Carolina colony in the late 1600s, direct importation was not as extensive as in other southern colonies. With the increased demand for cash crops in European markets and the need for fertile land, the British Lords Proprietors in 1663 offered additional acreage for every male and female slave brought into Carolina during the first five years of white settlement. The labor-intensive cash crops of tobacco, rice, and indigo made the use of slaves a "necessary" solution to the inadequate labor supply in the early eighteenth century. Most of this need was met through the natural increase of slave populations, which outpaced slave imports by 1720. After the Carolinas officially split in 1729, North Carolina had 6,000 slaves compared to South Carolina's 32,000.

While geographic barriers made slave trading difficult in North Carolina, they did not totally prevent it. The port at Wilmington was used extensively in the delivery of slaves to the Lower Cape Fear region. However, the barrier islands along the northern coast did not permit access to the natural harbors from the Atlantic Ocean, making the direct importation of slaves into the northern part of the Carolina colony virtually impossible. Many owners in North Carolina purchased their slaves via overland routes from South Carolina, Georgia, and the Chesapeake region.

Agricultural patterns determined the distribution of slaves in North Carolina. Settled in the 1720s by South Carolina planters, the Lower Cape Fear produced rice and naval stores with slave labor. Slavery also prospered along a tier of counties bordering Virginia that concentrated on the cultivation of tobacco. By 1860, 19 counties in the Coastal Plain and Piedmont counted black majorities, and 12 of the 19 produced at least 1,000 400-pound bales of cotton. Commercial crops thus depended heavily on slave labor. Even in the North Carolina Mountains, where it was impossible to grow staple crops, slaves engaged in a variety of economic activities, including manufacturing, mining, construction, and livestock management.

At the time of the French and Indian War (1754–63), a slave cost approximately £60 to £80. During the 1780s the price escalated to as much as £180. An African slave in Charles Towne (Charleston, S.C.), bound for North Carolina, brought $300 in 1804. By 1840 a prime field hand cost about $800. Twenty years later field hands sold for $1,500 to $1,700, women $1,300 to $1,500, and artisans as much as $2,000.

As the American Revolution produced a temporary lull in slave importation, the natural increase of the slave population allowed southern states to sell their human property at a profit. North Carolina attempted to reduce slave imports as early as August 1774, when the Provincial Congress meeting in New Bern resolved "that we will not import any slave or slaves, or purchase any slave or slaves, imported or brought into this Province by others, from any part of the world, after the first day of November next." This prohibition of the slave trade is repeated several times in North Carolina records.

By the end of the Revolutionary War, the nation sought to regain economic stability by reopening the African and West Indian trade, especially in the Carolinas and Georgia. This action met with increased resistance in the Upper South states of the Chesapeake area and in North Carolina, partly because it would cut into profits of interregional trade and partly because of the mainly imagined fear that slave rebellions would spread from the West Indies.

In 1786 North Carolina again banned slave importation; it increased the prohibitive duty on imported Africans, which was later repealed in 1790. Prohibitive laws became more specific in 1794, barring the importation not only of slaves but also of indentured servants by "land or water routes." One year later, legislators passed the "Act against West Indian Slaves," which expressly prevented the importation of slaves by individuals emigrating from the West Indies. White slaveholders in North Carolina made up 31 percent of the population in 1790 and 27.7 percent in 1860. Only 2 percent of these slaveholders owned more than 50 slaves, and only 3 percent attained the rank of planter (owning 20 or more slaves). In 1860 the vast majority of slaveholders (70.8 percent) owned fewer than 10 slaves.

In 1800 and 1807 Congress barred U.S. citizens from exporting slaves, and as of 1 Jan. 1808 it prohibited any engagement in the international slave trade. The disposition of confiscated slaves was left up to individual states. In 1816 North Carolina and several other states passed the Act to Dispose of Illegally Imported Slaves, opting to sell all slaves who had been imported after 1808 with the proceeds benefiting the state treasury.

Although federal and state laws banned the importation of slaves nationwide, these same laws kept the prices high for slaves in the Lower South. The "need" for slaves in the Cotton Belt, the natural increase of slave populations, and the stagnant economy of the Upper South in the late eighteenth and early nineteenth centuries all bolstered the interregional sale of slaves. Between 1810 and 1820, 137,000 slaves were sent from the Chesapeake states and North Carolina to Alabama, Louisiana, Mississippi, and Texas. The sluggish economy of the 1820s–30s led to the sale of thousands more North Carolina slaves to the Cotton Belt.

By any measure, most slaves were ill-fed, ill-housed, and ill-clothed. In the 1780s a traveler observed: "The keep of a negro here does not come to a great figure, since the daily ration is but a quart of maize, and rarely a little meat or salted fish." Each year male slaves received "a suit of coarse woolen cloth, two rough shirts, and a pair of shoes." Conditions had scarcely improved during the antebellum period. Slaves supplemented their owner-supplied diet of cornmeal and fat pork by hunting, fishing, and raising vegetable gardens. Dark, smoky, and crowded, slave cabins were insubstantial structures with dirt floors, unglazed windows, and wattle-and-daub chimneys.

Despite their abhorrent conditions, slaves tried to preserve families and develop cultural defenses against white oppression. Conversion to Christianity before the Revolution came slowly; slaves continued to worship African spirits and to practice African rituals such as the "ring shout." A nineteenth-century observer, who witnessed a Jonkonnu celebration at Somerset Place plantation in Washington County, compared the celebration to a Muslim festival that he had attended in Egypt. Nevertheless, by the nineteenth century Christianity had swept through the state's slave quarters. Baptists and Methodists proved especially effective in converting slaves, who then adapted Christian practices and teachings to their own purposes. Blacks founded separate churches in Fayetteville, Wilmington, New Bern, and Edenton. Some slaves conducted prayer meetings in secret. One former slave recalled a practice that probably derived from West African ceremonies: "We turned down pots on the inside of the house at the door to keep master and missus from hearing the singing and praying."

In the eighteenth century slaves continued to use an extensive pool of African names for their children, but by the nineteenth century their naming patterns showed strong family ties. Slaves were named for fathers, grandfathers, aunts, and uncles. African crafts, medicine, conjury, dance, music, song, and folklore endured. Such cultural persistence allowed slaves to construct their own value system, which their owners never could entirely suppress.

After the Civil War ended in 1865, North Carolina's more than 360,000 newly emancipated African Americans continued these traditions in various forms. In the immediate aftermath of war, African Americans sought precisely those rights and freedoms that had been denied them under slavery: normalization of marriage, equal political and civil rights, education, and the right to own property. With freedom came new opportunities but also numerous new hardships, rooted in whites' deep and brutal acrimony toward blacks' social, economic, and political pursuits. While African Americans moved forward through this markedly hostile environment, remnants of both their African and slave experiences continued to inform their lives and serve as the core of a unique and lasting African American culture.

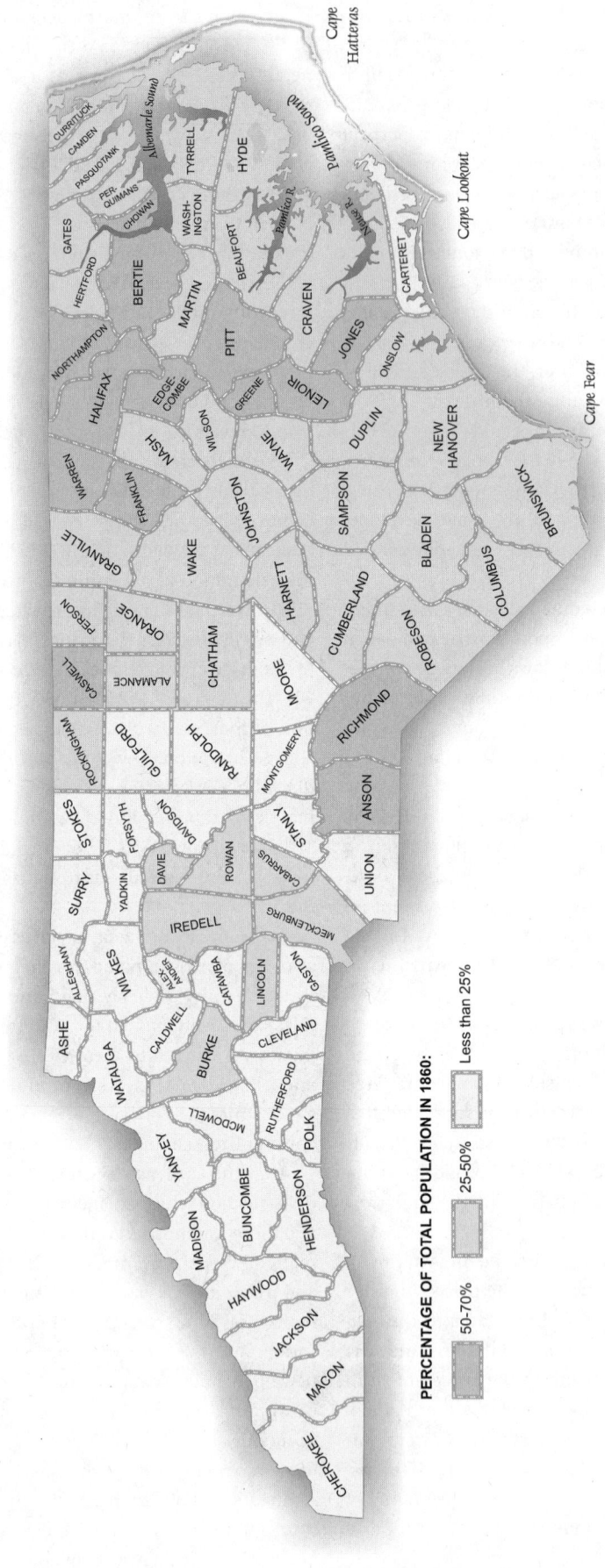

PERCENTAGE OF TOTAL POPULATION IN 1860:

50-70%   25-50%   Less than 25%

Slave population, 1860, showing percentage by county. Map by Mark Anderson Moore, courtesy NCOA&H.

References: Jeffrey J. Crow, Paul D. Escott, and Flora J. Hatley, *A History of African Americans in North Carolina* (2002); John Hope Franklin and Alfred A. Moss Jr., *From Slavery to Freedom: A History of Negro Americans* (6th ed., 1988); Herbert G. Gutman, *The Black Family in Slavery and Freedom, 1750–1925* (1976); Everett Jenkins Jr., *Pan-African Chronology: A Comprehensive Reference to the Black Quest for Freedom in Africa, the Americas, Europe, and Asia, 1400–1865* (1953); Marvin L. Michael Kay and Lorin Lee Cary, *Slavery in North Carolina, 1748–1775* (1995); Michael Tadman, *Speculators and Slaves: Masters, Traders, and Slaves in the Old South* (1989); Hugh Thomas, *The Slave Trade: The Story of the Atlantic Slave Trade, 1440–1870* (1997).

> *Jeffrey J. Crow*
> Additional research provided by Amelia Dees-Killette and Diane Huff.

SEE ALSO Ad Valorem Taxation of Slaves; Colonization Societies; Manumission Societies; Slave Clandestine Economy; Slave Codes; Slave Names; Slave Narratives; Slave Patrols; Slave Rebellions; *State v. John Mann*; *State v. Negro Will*; Underground Railroad.

Slaves' Midsummer Holiday, when slave laborers were permitted a few days off, occurred after crops were laid by and before harvesting began. On 28 Aug. 1862 Catherine Ann Devereux Edmondston of Halifax County wrote in her diary that it was "the Negroes Midsummer holiday, and as all of them but Fanny & Dolly have gone down to the Plantation dinner, the premises are deserted." She referred to "the annual three days holiday" as if it occurred regularly. In sections of the South with large slave populations, summer was a likely time for a slave insurrection and one that whites often dreaded for that reason. The Nat Turner Rebellion at Southampton County, Va., occurred on 21 Aug. 1831.

Reference: Beth G. Crabtree and James E. Patton, eds., *Journal of a Secesh Lady: The Diary of Catherine Ann Devereux Edmondston, 1860–1866* (1979).

> *William S. Powell*

Sloop Point Plantation, located in eastern Pender County, was constructed around 1726, making it the oldest surviving house in North Carolina. John Baptista Ashe acquired a land grant including an estimated 1,000 acres, extending across what is today U.S. 17 to the Intracoastal Waterway. The name derived from an early shipyard and port that served as a center for sloops arriving in the region from other colonies, the Caribbean, and England. The sloops made landfall at the plantation.

A single broad roof of long rafters integrates the piazza into the main room structure of the house, a feature typical of the Caribbean trading areas. Between two interior fireplaces serviced by one large chimney, twin doors lead to an outside porch. The doors swing in and out from the corners of the fireplaces in such a way that one room at a time opens to the porch. When fastened at an angle, the doors provide a passageway from room to room. Another unusual feature of the house is its ingenious cooling system. Near the rear of the house is a hole in the floor that allows cool air from underneath to ventilate a bedroom. At the front of the house, an opening in the porch ceiling allows air to rise to a closet on the second floor and into the front bedrooms.

The plantation operated an early saltworks. The process involved taking salt water from nearby waterways and allowing the water to evaporate in large cast iron pans left out in the sun. The salt residue, or brine, was then collected for distribution. Salt sold for as much as $64.00 per bushel during the Civil War. It was an essential staple much in demand, especially for preserving meats. Rusted relics of early salt pans can still be found at the plantation. Local legend maintains that pirates buried their treasure at Sloop Point, although such treasure has never been found.

A careful restoration of the old plantation house was completed in 1989. The interior of the house still retains much of the colonial wood flooring, paneling, doors, and windows.

References: John V. Allcott, *Colonial Homes in North Carolina* (1963); Catherine W. Bishir, *North Carolina Architecture* (1990); Mills Lane, *Architecture of the Old South: North Carolina* (1990).

> *Beverly Tetterton*

Smithfield Herald, established in 1882 by F. T. Booker, E. G. Smith, and John W. Lassiter (who was not a close relative of the family that later controlled the *Herald* through much of the twentieth century), was the oldest newspaper still operating in Johnston County in the early 2000s. The newspaper was started the same year that Smithfield acquired its first railroad, signaling the beginning of commercial growth for the Johnston County seat, which had not advanced beyond courthouse-village status since its incorporation in 1777.

Thomas J. Lassiter Sr., a schoolteacher, became editor of the *Herald* in 1896. His untimely death in 1920 prompted his widow, Rena Bingham Lassiter, to follow him as editor. Her son, Thomas J. Lassiter Jr., joined her in 1933, after his graduation from college. His career as editor and publisher extended until 1980, when the Lassiter family sold the *Herald* to the News and Observer Publishing Company of Raleigh. Wingate Lassiter served the *Herald* as a third-generation editor until 1994.

The *Smithfield Herald* received journalistic acclaim throughout the twentieth century. In 1922, under editor Rena Lassiter, it won an award as the best semiweekly or weekly newspaper in the state—the first time the North Carolina Press Association had bestowed such an honor. In 1982

Thomas J. Lassiter Jr. was inducted into the North Carolina Journalism Hall of Fame in recognition of his long career of editorial and community leadership. In 1995 the *Herald* became a property of California-based McClatchy Newspapers when McClatchy purchased the *Raleigh News and Observer* and its subsidiaries.

Wingate Lassiter

Smith-Graham Senate Race. The sudden death of U.S. senator J. Melville Broughton on 6 Mar. 1949 caught North Carolinians by surprise and set the stage for a momentous political brawl. The task of appointing Broughton's successor fell to Governor W. Kerr Scott, a maverick in state politics. Seeking to strengthen his hand, Scott launched a campaign to find a successor to Broughton favorable to his own liberal political agenda and sympathetic to the national Democratic policies of President Harry S Truman.

After an inordinate delay in naming a successor, Scott's decision produced the most explosive surprise in North Carolina's modern political history: Scott named Frank Porter Graham, the 62-year-old president of the University of North Carolina and considered "the most renowned southern liberal of his time." Scott chose Graham because he was not a lawyer, had never sought political office, and was recognized as a great humanitarian who cared about the dispossessed. Graham's friends and admirers believed him to be the noblest of North Carolinians—an educator who had spent his life in selfless service to others, whose voice on such difficult matters as race relations and social policy was enlightened and progressive. Graham's adversaries judged him to be a liberal dreamer, a person of unsound judgment who was hostile to the beliefs and mores of the state and whose career had been marred by association with disloyal organizations, most notably in matters of race and politics.

When Graham agreed to run for a full term in 1950, the attacks on him began. Radio commentator Fulton Lewis Jr. disclosed that the Security Board of the Atomic Energy Commission had recently denied Graham a top-secret security clearance because it questioned the soundness of his judgment and some of his political associations. The board's decision was overturned by the full commission, but the revelation was an ominous harbinger of things to come.

Graham, despite his controversial past, had substantial political strengths, including the strong support of the Scott organization, the Truman administration, organized labor, and Jonathan Daniels, editor of the *Raleigh News and Observer*. His Democratic primary challengers included Pinetown pig farmer Olla Ray Boyd and former U.S. senator Robert R. "Our Bob" Reynolds, although neither emerged as a serious threat. Graham's most formidable opponent, Raleigh attorney Willis Smith, entered the fray in February 1950. A former Speaker of the North Carolina House of Representatives and president of

Flyer produced by the Know the Truth Committee portraying the choice between Willis Smith and Frank Porter Graham in the 1950 U.S. Senate election in racial terms. NCC.

the American Bar Association, Smith was part of the conservative "plutocracy" that had governed North Carolina since the 1930s.

From the outset, Smith went on the attack. He denounced socialism and communism, implying that Graham was unaware of the threat posed by either. He opposed the Federal Employment Practices Commission (FEPC) as an invasion of state rights. Smith accused Graham of supporting the FEPC and, as a member of Truman's Civil Rights Commission, of desiring to end statutory racial segregation. Graham, the nonpolitician, responded meekly to the attacks and solicited neither votes nor campaign contributions. He did correctly note that he opposed the FEPC and the use of federal force to compel integration. Smith continued to paint Graham as a "pink" and a muddle-headed academic who had long associations with groups named by the U.S. attorney general as subversive. Graham refrained from personal attacks, but his office slammed Smith as a rich corporate lawyer who was unconcerned about the needs of working-class North Carolinians.

Just prior to the first primary vote, a new emphasis on racial issues emerged with incendiary handbills disseminated across the state. Especially inflammatory was the charge that Graham had appointed a young African American, Leroy Jones, to West Point. The charge was false, but the racial issue had now been broached.

When the votes were counted in the first primary, Graham received 303,605 (48.9 percent) to Smith's 250,222 (40.5 percent). Reynolds and Boyd garnered 10.6 percent. Graham had come agonizingly close (5,634) to a clear majority but had failed to win the election outright, and Smith was entitled to call for a runoff. While Smith considered his course, the U.S. Supreme Court handed down three major decisions affecting southern race relations. The most important for North Carolina was *Sweatt v. Painter*, in which the Court ordered the University of Texas to integrate its law school. These decisions marked the beginning of the end of all-white public education in the South and set off racial alarms throughout the region. A young Jesse Helms and other Smith supporters broadcast advertisements calling on people to rally at Smith's residence, imploring him to aggressively attack Graham's liberalism. Smith quickly obtained the necessary funds and the enthusiastic support required for a second primary.

Having called for a runoff, the Smith forces went on the offensive, declaring Senator Graham a communist sympathizer and charging that blacks were guilty of "bloc-voting" for Graham in the first primary. One flyer, titled "White People Wake Up," claimed that Graham favored "race-mingling" in the work place, hotels, restaurants, and schools. The result was a racial pandemic. Opponents verbally attacked Graham on the stump, and his backers received threatening telephone calls.

In an astounding turnaround, Smith won the second primary 281,114 to 261,789, mainly because white voters in the east abandoned Graham. Graham had been rejected in a campaign of savage intensity by those he seemed to care about the most—poor members of the working class and farmers. Smith proponents succeeded in using communist and race issues to defeat a candidacy sympathetic to both racial and economic equality. The campaign was a triumph of tradition over liberalism and undermined North Carolina's image as progressive on race issues. In the general election in November, Smith defeated Republican E. R. Gavin 364,912 to 177,753.

References: Warren Ashby, *Frank Porter Graham: A Southern Liberal* (1980); Samuel Lubell, *The Future of American Politics* (3rd ed., 1965); Paul Luebke, *Tar Heel Politics: Myth and Realities* (1990); Julian M. Pleasants and Augustus M. Burns, *Frank Porter Graham and the 1950 Senate Race in North Carolina* (1990).

Augustus M. Burns
Julian M. Pleasants

Smith Richardson Foundation is an independent organization started in 1935 by North Carolinia businessman H. Smith Richardson and his wife, Grace Jones Richardson. The foundation, today based in Connecticut, is ranked in the top 100 foundations in the United States by total assets. The trustees make grants to further the foundation's mission to "contribute to important public debates and to help address serious public policy challenges facing the United States." Through domestic and international grant programs, the foundation supports projects that address social, economic, and governmental institutions and help to develop policies that advance the country's interests and values in the world. In its early years, the Smith Richardson Foundation supported projects to encourage judicial reform in North Carolina and to strengthen anticommunist organizations. In later years, the foundation funded a Richardson Fellows (later North Carolina Fellows) program at colleges and universities to help young people develop leadership skills and established the Center for Creative Leadership to study and teach creativity and leadership.

As a young man, Richardson entered the business started by his father, which was to become the Vick Chemical Company. Richardson became president of the company after his father's death in 1919 and led it until his retirement in 1957. After retirement, Richardson devoted more time to philanthropy, using his foundation to support local charitable interests and expand on his belief in the power of individuals to capitalize on the opportunity afforded them in a democratic society. Richardson believed that citizens have a responsibility to support society's institutions and that "the time and thought of able men [should be] applied to the increasingly weighty problems of government and the serious social questions which now confront us." The Smith Richardson Foundation trustees continue to support programs that are consistent with this vision.

Cecelia Moore

SEE ALSO Vick Chemical Company.

Smokehouses, sometimes called meat houses, have been used in North Carolina since the early 1700s as a means of preserving meats through exposure to a constant, concentrated smoke. Typically situated near the kitchen, the smokehouse was one of the most important domestic outbuildings in North Carolina homesteads in the days before freeze-drying, deep-freezing, and vacuum packaging. In November, when the weather turned cold, hogs were slaughtered and the meat saturated with a heavy coating of salt. After hanging the hams from hooks within the smokehouse, a fire was started to provide the smoke necessary to cure the meat. This fire was often started in the middle of the dirt floor, but sometimes a large wash pot was stuffed with wood, ignited, smothered, and left to smolder in the middle of the smokehouse. The smoking of hams or other meats could go on for days or even weeks, depending on the desired product.

Log smokehouses predominated in the western part of North Carolina, while frame construction was more prevalent in the east. Log smokehouses were chinked in order to prevent freezing inside and to keep vermin and insects out. Additionally, a stone or concrete barrier was placed about six inches deep around the smokehouse to keep rats from tunneling into the smokehouse. Double-stud construction of smokehouses was used for two reasons. The weight of a number of curing hams was quite considerable, and the close studs helped support the structure against collapse. Double-studded smokehouses were also constructed in hopes of repelling thieves of the two-legged variety. Somerset Plantation, in Washington County, has a good example of a large smokehouse with studs to discourage theft. If a thief was tempted by the smell of smoked meat and pried off the weatherboarding to help himself, he would not be able to fit between the studs.

Emphasizing the importance placed on the smokehouse and its contents is the fact that many main houses remained open and unlocked while smokehouses were securely padlocked and bolted. Some smokehouses doubled as potato houses and canned good storage; the loss of these necessities was to be guarded against at virtually any cost.

References: Catherine W. Bishir, *North Carolina Architecture* (1990); Carl R. Lounsbury, ed., *An Illustrated Glossary of Early Southern Architecture and Landscape* (1994).

Brian Bullard

Snake Handling is the practice of certain Christian sects most often found in the southern Appalachian Mountains. Their other rituals sometimes involve the drinking of strych-

Snake handling at a nondenominational church in Canton, 1985. Photograph by Bob Scott. Courtesy of the *Asheville Citizen-Times*.

nine, the handling of fire, speaking in unknown tongues (glossolalia), and the laying on of hands for healing of the sick. Members are usually from small, poor communities, feeling little connection to the world away from their mountains. It is believed that George Went Hensley began the twentieth-century practice of snake handling during the summer of 1909 in a remote section of southeast Tennessee, later establishing the "Church of God with Signs Following." His beliefs and practices spread to North Carolina and throughout the southern Appalachians, as well as to parts of the Midwest, where many unemployed mountain people had relocated to find jobs.

Several Bible verses are used by snake handlers to validate their beliefs and practices, in particular Mark 16:17–18, which describes believers "taking up serpents" as signs of faith. Snake handlers consider these words to be commands, not merely suggestions. They believe these words are binding to all who profess belief in the Gospels: God takes over their faculties, allowing them to carry out God's instructions without harm to themselves.

In October 1948, a three-day snake handling "convention" was held in Durham for "people who believed in and practiced the gifts and signs of the Spirit of God." The convention was hosted by Col. Hartman Bunn of Zion Tabernacle in Durham, and ministers and followers came from Virginia, Tennessee, and Kentucky, as well as other towns in North Carolina. At the time, North Carolina Supreme Court cases were pending against Bunn and Benjamin Ralph Massey (who was known as the snake tender of Zion Tabernacle) for having earlier violated a city ordinance against the public handling of snakes. The convention went on as planned, but several arrests were made and numerous poisonous snakes were seized.

Later, in December 1948, Bunn went before the North Carolina Supreme Court, where he stated that the practice of handling snakes was an important part of his religion and that forbidding these actions violated the constitutional freedom of religion. The state attorney general, T. Wade Bruton, argued in return that even though the laws could not regulate what people believed, if their religious practices endangered them, the state could regulate those practices. The next year, the North Carolina General Assembly passed a law declaring that the handling of poisonous reptiles was a "public nuisance and criminal offense." Although in North Carolina, as in most states, the handling of poisonous snakes is illegal, the practice still continues in anonymity in some rural areas.

References: Steven Michael Kane, "Snake Handlers of Southern Appalachia" (Ph.D. diss., Princeton University, 1979); Weston La Barre, *They Shall Take up Serpents: Psychology of the Southern Snake-Handling Cult* (1962).

Antoinette Satterfield

Snap Dragon was the most successful North Carolina privateer in combat with the British fleet in the War of 1812. The schooner was built on the West River in Maryland in 1808 and originally named the *Zephyr*. The *Snap Dragon*'s length was 85.5 feet, its beam 12.5 feet, its draft 8.67 feet, and its weight 147.42 tons. It carried six guns and a crew of 80. Capt. Otway Burns, a skipper of legendary skill and intrepidity, commanded the *Snap Dragon* on three profitable cruises between 1812 and 1814: two in West Indian waters and one near Nova Scotia and Newfoundland. The schooner harried the invading fleet, preventing the arrival of British troops and supplies on American shores, while securing prizes of goods and capturing enemy vessels to enlarge and outfit the small U.S. fleet. During these three cruises, several British ships engaged in battle with the small American craft. Burns captured 42 English vessels and their cargo, valued at more than $4 million, and took more than 300 English officers and sailors prisoner.

Able and swift as it was, the *Snap Dragon* could not have made its remarkable voyages without the genius of Burns. On its fourth cruise, under another skipper (Burns remained ashore, crippled with rheumatism), the schooner was captured by a British sloop of war off Nova Scotia.

Jaquelin Drane Nash

Snipe Hunting in North Carolina denotes one of two forms of recreation. The first, probably the more common, involves a practical joke wherein pranksters take an unsuspecting initiate into the woods at night to hunt for an imaginary bird, only to leave him or her confused and alone in the darkness. A second type of snipe hunting involves a bird that exists in reality rather than legend. The common snipe (*Capella delicata*), known variously as Wilson's snipe, bog snipe, and jacksnipe, inhabits both brackish and freshwater marshes in the coastal plain and affords rigorous winter sport to hunters who flush the birds while slogging through marshland and muddy fields in chest waders or hip boots. The common snipe's larger and more widely disseminated cousin, the woodcock (also known as the timberdoodle or swamp partridge), is more often than not called "snipe" by North Carolina hunters. In the northeastern states the woodcock is a major game bird, but in North Carolina it more often serves as a target of opportunity for quail hunters than as a specific object of pursuit.

Reference: Raiford Trask, "Hit or Miss Snipe," *Wildlife in North Carolina* 55 (February 1991).

Jerry Leath Mills

Soccer, known as football outside of the United States, is the most popular team sport in the world, although it was slow to gain popularity in North Carolina. The modern form of the sport was introduced in England in the 1830s and was played in parts of the United States shortly thereafter, especially in urban areas with large numbers of European immigrants. A handful of North Carolina high schools fielded soccer teams as early as the 1920s, and Duke University had a men's team in 1935. College soccer began to pick up momentum after World War II. The member schools of the Atlantic Coast Conference, which was formed in 1953, competed in soccer from its inception. Duke University, the University of North Carolina, and North Carolina State fielded men's teams in the 1950s. Wake Forest University did not field its first men's team until 1980.

The National Collegiate Athletic Association (NCAA) held its first soccer tournament in 1959, giving the sport a boost. Duke won the men's NCAA title in 1986, while the University of North Carolina at Chapel Hill captured the 2001 title. The University of North Carolina at Greensboro won the NCAA Division III national championship in 1982, 1983, 1985, 1986, and 1987.

In 1972 Congress passed the Education Amendments Act. Title IX of this bill mandated that universities receiving federal money fund women's sports equally with men's sports. This spawned a revolution in women's competitive sports and led to the establishment of what is arguably the most dominant collegiate sports program in history. The University of North Carolina at Chapel Hill started its women's soccer program in 1979 and captured the Association of Intercollegiate Women's Athletics title in 1981.

The following year, the NCAA began overseeing women's collegiate athletics. UNC won the inaugural NCAA title in 1982. From that period through the 2003 season, UNC captured 17 of 22 national titles, all won under the tutelage of coach Anson Dorrance. The UNC women's program has also produced the core of the U.S. national team. Mia Hamm, who played for UNC from 1989 through 1993, became the most accomplished female soccer player in history. UNC's success has overshadowed other women's soccer programs in the state, although several schools have competed well for decades. North Carolina State University in 1988 and Duke in 1992 were NCAA runners-up, both falling to UNC in the title game.

North Carolina has hosted several minor league professional soccer teams. The Women's United Soccer Association was a major league that lasted only three seasons before suspending operations in 2003. The Cary-based Carolina Courage won the 2002 league title.

The North Carolina High School Athletic Association (NCHSAA) held state soccer championships for boys on a sporadic basis beginning in 1927 and annually beginning in 1966. Girls' state championships were inaugurated in 1986. All but the smallest high schools field soccer teams for both boys and girls. In the 2002–3 academic year, 8,539 boys and 7,317 girls played for NCHSAA soccer programs. Soccer is also an extremely popular youth sport in North Carolina. In 2006 thousands of children participated in the North Carolina Youth Soccer Association, while many others played for other organizations.

References: Mia Hamm, *Go for the Goal: A Champion's Guide to Winning in Soccer and Life* (1999); David Smale, *Nothin' Finer, Carolina: The History of UNC Women's Soccer* (1993).

Jim L. Sumner

Socialist Party of North Carolina

Socialist Party of North Carolina (SPNC), formed in 1996, is the modern affiliate of the national Socialist Party, which was organized in July 1901 by the merger of the Social Democratic Party, under Eugene V. Debs, with the reformer wing of the Socialist Labor Party, under Morris Hillquit. The SPNC has small, organized groups in Raleigh and Jacksonville. In the 2000 presidential election, for the first time since 1936, a Socialist Party member was an official write-in candidate in North Carolina. In the early 2000s the SPNC was involved in a variety of causes, including a boycott of Mt. Olive Pickles and People of Faith against the Death Penalty. Again as a write-in, the national Socialist Party presidential candidate in 2004, Walter Brown, received about 300 votes in North Carolina.

Wiley J. Williams

Society for the Propagation of the Gospel in Foreign Parts.

Society for the Propagation of the Gospel in Foreign Parts. King William III's grant of a charter to the Society for the Propagation of the Gospel in Foreign Parts (SPG) on 16 June 1701 brought to fruition the designs of Thomas Bray, Bishop Henry Compton, and other leading English churchmen to foster and support Anglican missions in colonial British America. A pioneering voluntary association of interested clergy and laity, the SPG sought initially to recruit missionaries for work among Native Americans and African Americans. When these ventures proved unsuccessful, the society focused its attention upon white settlements. With funds derived from members' annual subscriptions and special collections, the SPG during the eighteenth century employed well over 300 Anglican clergy and schoolmasters willing to undertake overseas assignments. It thereby greatly aided the bishop of London in discharging his extradiocesan responsibility for the spiritual welfare of Britain's colonial possessions and provided the impetus and organization for overseeing the expansion of the Church of England both in newly settled areas such as the Carolinas and Georgia and in the dissenter strongholds of New England and the Middle Colonies.

Daunting obstacles—climate, hazardous travel, an ethnically and religiously heterogeneous population, dispersed settlement, cultural impoverishment, and social and political instability—meant that the hopes of a flourishing and encompassing Anglican Church in North Carolina were often dashed. John Urmston, an early missionary, graphically described the colony as "this hell of a hole." But what success there was in forming and sustaining Anglican congregations came largely through the efforts of the SPG and its clergymen.

References: Hugh Talmage Lefler, "The Anglican Church in North Carolina," in Lawrence Foushee London and Sarah McCulloh Lemmon, eds., *The Episcopal Church in North Carolina, 1701–1959* (1987); Henry Paget Thompson, *Into All Lands: The History of the Society for the Propagation of the Gospel in Foreign Parts, 1701–1950* (1951).

John K. Nelson

Society of the Cincinnati

Society of the Cincinnati was formed at the close of the American Revolution by commissioned officers of the Continental Army who wanted to keep alive the ideals for which they had fought and to bond themselves and their descendants in fraternal fellowship. Under the leadership of Maj. Gen. Henry Knox, the General Society was organized on 13 May 1783 at Verplanck House, Baron von Steuben's headquarters near Fishkill, N.Y. Branches in each of the 13 original states and in France were established later the same year. George Washington served as the first president general of the society and remained in office until his death in 1799. The North Carolina Chapter of the Society of the Cincinnati was founded in Hillsborough in October 1783 and, under the presidency of Brig. Gen. Jethro Sumner of Warren County, included 66 charter members. The North Carolina Society has grown to almost 500 members and is now one of the largest and most active of the American state branches.

The society's name commemorates Lucius Quintius Cincinnatus, a fifth-century B.C. Roman farmer and soldier who, having laid down his plow and led the republic to victory over invaders, resigned his office and returned to farming. Most of General Washington's officers were civilians who, like Cincinnatus, wanted to resume their peacetime vocations after the Revolution. America's oldest hereditary and patriotic organization, the Society of the Cincinnati today consists of approximately 3,200 descendants of American Continental Army or French army and navy officers. Membership passes by descent and is usually limited to one living member for each Revolutionary War officer.

The society's modern interests are largely historical. Many state branches preserve important historical records, publish historical books, and provide scholarship grants for historical research. The General Society of the Cincinnati has a notable Revolutionary War library-museum in its headquarters at Anderson House in Washington, D.C. The library-museum is open to the public.

Armistead Jones Maupin
Additional research provided by W. Keats Sparrow.

Soil Conservation.

Soil Conservation. Climate and landscape make much of North Carolina susceptible to soil erosion. Intensity and duration of rainfall, the measures of the rain's erosive power, are greater in the Southeast than elsewhere in the continental

United States. During the nineteenth century, inefficient farming practices contributed significantly to the erosion of North Carolina's complex and varied soils; when North Carolina cotton, tobacco, and corn farmers hitched animal power to plows and cultivators to clean-till widely spaced rows, gullies opened on the landscape and the rivers ran red with clay sediments.

Southerners struggled to invent indigenous methods of soil conservation. Nicholas T. Sorsby, a North Carolina native, developed a system of farming around horizontal (contour) plowing and hillside ditching. Written first for the North Carolina Agricultural Society, his *Horizontal Plowing and Hillside Ditching* (1860) was the only book available on these conservation methods prior to the Civil War. Priestly H. Mangum developed the Mangum terrace around 1885 on his farm near Wake Forest. The broad-based terrace became widely adopted in the South and was advocated by various state agricultural agencies. The North Carolina Agricultural Experiment Station in West Raleigh experimented with terracing and by 1896 advocated Mangum terraces to the state's farmers. By 1915 Cleveland County had terraces on 6,000 acres, earning the moniker, the "county of terraces." Terracing was hardly a panacea and in fact sometimes concentrated runoff, causing gullies. Crop rotations of grasses, hay, legumes, or close-growing small grain crops protected the soil from raindrop impact through part of the year and added organic matter to the topsoil, thus increasing the rate of rainfall infiltration. However, the system of agriculture based on clean cultivated row crops made soil conservation a difficult proposition.

Hugh Hammond Bennett, a native of Anson County, earned the title "father of soil conservation" through his efforts to awaken the country to the impact of soil erosion on food production and the economic health of rural communities. Bennett graduated from the University of North Carolina in 1903 and joined the Bureau of Soils in the U.S. Department of Agriculture (USDA). His concern over soil was born of tramping southern fields while making soil surveys. In September 1933, after waging a campaign to start some watershed-based demonstrations of soil conservation with New Deal emergency employment funds, he became head of the Soil Erosion Service, later the Soil Conservation Service (SCS), an agency of the USDA whose main purpose was to help farmers use their land and water resources wisely, thus preventing or reducing loss of soil by flood or erosion. One of several demonstration projects in North Carolina included the Bennett home place in the Brown Creek watershed. When the Soil Conservation Service began extending help to landowners through locally organized and directed soil conservation districts, the Brown Creek Soil Conservation District became, on 4 Aug. 1937, the first recognized by the USDA. The SCS, today the Natural Resources Conservation Service, continues to work with districts, farmers, and local governments and groups throughout the state on soil conservation and other resource matters.

Beginning in the fall of 1934, the Soil Erosion Service and the National Resources Board undertook a national reconnaissance erosion survey; all 100 North Carolina counties have at least one published soil survey for comparison and land management purposes, and certain soil types are named after North Carolina locations: Alamance, Ashe, Conetoe, Fuquay, Georgeville, Goldsboro, Hyde, Mayodan, Pungo, Secrest, Wadesboro, Wake, and White Store. In this survey, erosion was found not to be severe in the Coastal Plain due to the region's gentle slopes combined with sandy soils, which allow rapid infiltration of rainfall and produce some of the richest farmland.

The story in the Piedmont and Mountain regions was very different. The loamy soil of the Piedmont is mostly sandy, red clay, producing some of the best farmland in the state with the greatest variety of crops, including cotton, tobacco, timber, small grains, hay, and corn. In the Mountains, the soils are usually a grayish brown loam, stony, shallow, and on steep slopes, allowing extensive pastureland and some crops of corn, hay, cabbage, and burley tobacco on properly terraced land. However, a soil type designated as Cecil, which covered large areas of the Piedmont, originally had a surface layer of sandy loam 12 to 14 inches thick underlain by 2 to 6 feet of heavy clay. The surface layer had been removed on much of the area. Statewide, the survey teams calculated that 9 percent of the land exclusive of water and large cities had lost three-fourths of its topsoil, 30 percent of the land had lost one-fourth to three-fourths of its topsoil, and 13 percent of the area had been gullied to some extent.

Two trends in land use have reduced soil erosion from cropland in North Carolina. First, there was a decrease in statewide cropland from about 7.7 million acres in 1949 to less than 5 million acres by the late 1990s. Second, land used for crops has been shifting from the Mountains and the Piedmont to the gentler slopes of the Coastal Plain. Comparing 1949 with 2004, Piedmont cropland shrank from 3.4 million acres to 929,000 acres, and Mountain cropland acreage decreased from 819,222 acres to 308,000 acres. Cropland in the Sandhills dropped from 128,648 acres to 61,469 by the early 1990s, and in the same period Coastal Plain cropland declined less severely from about 2.1 to 1.8 million acres. The flatwoods of the Coastal Plain remained fairly constant, with 932,254 acres in 1949 and 897,634 acres by 1992. The Tidewater section actually increased in total acreage, from 334,063 acres in 1949 to 565,448 acres in 1992.

References: Arthur R. Hall, "Soil Erosion and Agriculture in the Southern Piedmont: A History" (Ph.D. diss., Duke University, 1948); William D. Lee, *The Early History of Soil Survey in North Carolina* (1984); Angus McDonald, *Early American Soil Conservationists* (1941); Roy W. Simonson, *Historical Aspects of Soil Survey and Soil Classification* (1987).

Douglas Helms
Additional research provided by Joan E. Freeman.

A contemporary interpretive demonstration of slave labor outside the plantation house at Somerset Place. Photograph by Charles E. Jones. North Carolina Department of Transportation.

Somerset Place is located in Washington County seven miles south of Creswell on Lake Phelps. Originally consisting of more than 100,000 acres, Somerset between 1785 and 1865 was one of the state's most prosperous plantations as well as one of the largest in the Upper South, producing rice, corn, wheat, lumber, and other products. The plantation had a workforce of almost 200 by 1790, including black and white, slave and free. During Somerset's 80-year existence, it was home to more than 850 enslaved men, women, and children, 80 of whom were brought directly to the plantation from their West African homeland in 1786. The plantation was operated solely as a business investment for more than 40 years, but in 1829 it became home to Josiah Collins III, his wife Mary, and their six sons. Josiah Collins III inherited the property from his grandfather, Josiah Collins I, who along with two partners had acquired the land and planned its early development.

By the mid-nineteenth century, the Somerset complex included some 50 structures, ranging from barns and stables to a saw, gristmills, a hospital, and homes. The abolition of slavery in 1865 ended the plantation labor system, and the Somerset property for a number of years was occupied by a variety of tenants. In the late 1930s it became a part of Pettigrew State Park administered by the Department of Conservation and Development. In the 1950s historical research and archaeological investigation led to modest restoration, and in 1954 a report to the newly formed Historic Sites Division of the Department (now Office) of Archives and History inspired action leading to the restoration and preservation of Somerset Place as a North Carolina State Historic Site. Interpretive activity at the site came to be directed toward the role of slave labor on plantations and the role of the planter class in slaves' lives. Reunions of descendants of slaves who had lived at Somerset are held there periodically.

References: Wayne K. Durrill, "Origins of a Kinship Structure in a Slave Community: The Blacks of Somerset Place, 1786–1862" (M.A. thesis, UNC-Chapel Hill, 1981); Richard F. Knapp, ed., *North Carolina's State Historic Sites: A Brief History and Status Report* (1995).

William S. Powell

Sons of Confederate Veterans. With its international headquarters located at Elm Springs Plantation in Columbia, Tenn., and a significant contingent in North Carolina, the Sons of Confederate Veterans is the oldest organization of male descendants of men who served the Confederacy. Its purposes are historical, benevolent, patriotic, and educational. To become a member of the Sons of Confederate Veterans, one must show lineal or collateral ties to a member of the Confederate army or navy who honorably served, was a prisoner of war, was honorably discharged, or served the Confederacy as a member of Congress. Membership is open to male descendants with a minimum age of 12 years.

At the reunion of the United Confederate Veterans in Richmond, Va., on 1 July 1896, Gen. Stephen D. Lee rose to address the assembly and to give his charge and commission to the sons of the men who had worn the Gray. With his charge the United Sons of Confederate Veterans was born. The organization's name was shortened to its present form, Sons of Confederate Veterans, in 1912.

As in the beginning, North Carolina's modern Sons of Confederate Veterans are involved in a multitude of civic projects. The erection of monuments and preservation of battlefields throughout the state remain favored projects. The restoration and maintenance of cemeteries and graveyards is also of high priority. The group gives scholarships, research grants, and gifts of books to libraries and raises funds for the publication of archival records and the support of state and regional archives. Gen. Robert E. Lee's birthday, Confederate Flag Day, and Confederate Memorial Day are some of the annual events publicly celebrated by the Sons of Confederate Veterans at county courthouses and the North Carolina State Capitol. In 2005 the organization had approximately 3,500 active members in North Carolina.

Charles C. Davis

Sons of Liberty. SEE Stamp Act.

Sons of the Revolution in the State of North Carolina, a social, literary, and patriotic society, was organized by ten men who met at the state library in Raleigh on 25 Oct. 1893. Membership was limited to men 21 years of age and older who were lineal descendants of active participants in the movement for independence during the Revolutionary War. Participation was defined as being such that might have subjected one to trial for treason by the British government if the war had been lost. At the first meeting Governor Elias Carr was elected president of the society; among the other officers were Kemp Plummer Battle, Marshall DeLancey Haywood, Daniel Harvey Hill, and Samuel A. Ashe. Carrying out the objectives of the society, members undertook to install portraits of revolutionary leaders in public buildings, to present programs on anniversaries of significant events, to mark notable historic sites, to encourage the study of history in the state, and otherwise to keep alive knowledge of the role of the state in attaining independence.

Reference: James Vann Comer, *Sons of the Revolution in the State of North Carolina, Inc., and Its Predecessor: North Carolina Society of the Sons of the Revolution* (1990).

William S. Powell

Sororities. SEE Fraternities and Sororities.

Soul City, a small town located one mile off U.S. 1 between Warrenton and Manson in Warren County, is a symbol of black economic aspiration fueled by the civil rights gains of the 1960s and 1970s. McKissick Enterprises, headed by civil rights activist Floyd B. McKissick (1922–91), financed the development of an African American community mainly with federal loan guarantees, grants, and contracts totaling $31 million from 1971 to 1978. With completion of the infrastructure, including a water treatment plant, hope abounded for the community's success. However, job-creating industries did not come, and housing construction dragged. The developer also faced damaging federal audits and political opposition, eventually defaulting in 1980.

Although the federal government foreclosed on the Soul City project, the community continued to grow. In the mid-1980s the Z. Smith Reynolds Foundation gave a grant of $20,000 to renovate the historic Green Duke House and turn it into a Jobs Link Center. By the early 2000s Soul City was a 5,000-acre development with a few hundred occupants and assets that included a fire station, a janitorial supplies manufacturer, a poultry-processing plant, the Healthco Clinic, the Floyd McKissick Assisted Living Center, a Head Start preschool center, and recreational facilities.

References: Jason Alston, "Soul City's Dream Is Unfulfilled, but Not Dead," *Durham Herald-Sun*, 30 Aug. 2003; Osha Gray Davidson, *The Best of Enemies: Race and Redemption in the New South* (1996); Floyd B. McKissick, *Three-Fifths of a Man* (1969).

Raymond Gavins

South Atlantic Quarterly. SEE Literary Journals.

South Dakota v. North Carolina, a U.S. Supreme Court case decided in 1904, raised the question of whether the origi-

Model home in the Green Duke subdivision at Soul City, 1977. Courtesy of NCOA&H. The *Raleigh News and Observer* files.

nal jurisdiction of the Supreme Court extended to a dispute in which one state (South Dakota) attempted to sue another state (North Carolina) for the value of bonds issued by the latter state. Although the legal issues were substantial, the decision's origin in and long-term effect on North Carolina politics were equally pronounced.

The author of the lawsuit was Daniel L. Russell Jr., Republican governor of the state from 1897 to 1901. Russell conceived the plan in 1900, while his party was collapsing from the onslaught of white supremacy Democrats. Russell knew that during Reconstruction southern legislatures had issued large numbers of bonds—some the product of corruption, some not—to finance various public improvements, especially railroad construction. By the 1890s the legal problem confronting bondholders was an inability to enforce the written terms of the bonds. After regaining power in southern state governments during the 1870s, Democrats passed laws that readjusted or repudiated bond debt, which was largely held by persons outside the South. Often a bond's owner was offered pennies on the face value dollars of the bond. Equally significant, rulings by lower federal courts that the Eleventh Amendment prevented federal claims against readjustment left the bondholders with no judicial remedy.

Russell's plan to avoid the legal barrier was simple: he would arrange the donation of a small number of adjusted bonds to a state for charitable purposes and then represent the state in an original proceeding against the issuing state in the U.S. Supreme Court. Victory in the high court would significantly raise the value of the remaining bonds, forcing settlement on southern repudiators from Virginia to Texas. Russell's services to the bondholders would also make him a rich man.

Russell searched for a state that would accept a small number of bonds as a donation to its charitable institutions. For this purpose, in December 1900 he contacted his political ally, North Carolina Populist Marion Butler, who was nearing the end of a six-year term in the U.S. Senate. Although Butler did not know that North Carolina bonds would be used, he contacted several Senate colleagues about the possibility of a donation. Eventually he enlisted Senator Charles Pettigrew of South Dakota to endorse a donation act. While the South Dakota donation proceeded, Butler and Russell began to organize the collection of bonds from other southern states so that the bonds could be called in after the anticipated Supreme Court triumph.

The North Carolina bonds were given to South Dakota in the summer of 1901, and South Dakota filed documents asking the Supreme Court to hear the case the following November. At that time, Russell and Butler's role in the suit was unknown to the Democrats now in charge of North Carolina government, but evidence gathered by lawyers for the state in 1902 and 1903 revealed some of their activities in the South Dakota transaction. Thereafter the Democratic press portrayed the scheme as a traitorous act of defeated Populist and Republican leaders. Conveniently for Democrats, Fusion was linked to Republican Reconstruction through the bonds.

The Supreme Court heard oral arguments regarding the case on 13 Apr. 1903 and 8 Jan. 1904. Although the Eleventh Amendment to the U.S. Constitution expressly prohibited a federal court to hear suits brought against one state by citizens of another state, the Supreme Court, by a five-to-four vote, required North Carolina to pay South Dakota $27,400, the full value of ten bonds issued to the Western North Carolina Railroad by the General Assembly of 1866–67. The bonds had been secured by a second mortgage on stock in the state-owned North Carolina Railroad.

South Dakota v. North Carolina was a significant decision of constitutional law that had lasting political effects in North Carolina, particularly for Butler. He left the Populist Party in 1904 and, like many other former Populists in the state, became a Republican. Butler sought to make North Carolina Republicanism resemble the progressive Republican Parties of the Midwest, but his efforts were hampered by the bond issue. Democrats were able to use the case and Butler's larger bond collection plans to discredit the Republican Party of the early twentieth century by linking it to the Republicanism of Reconstruction, Fusion, and African American voting.

References: Robert F. Durden, *Reconstruction Bonds and Twentieth-Century Politics: South Dakota v. North Carolina* (1962); James L. Hunt, "Marion Butler and the Populist Ideal, 1863–1938" (Ph.D. diss., University of Wisconsin, 1990); John V. Orth, *The Judicial Power of the United States: The Eleventh Amendment and American Constitutional Law* (1986).

James L. Hunt

Southeastern Baptist Theological Seminary in Wake Forest is owned and operated by the Southern Baptist Convention for the purpose of providing religious education and professional training for ministers. At its annual meeting in Chicago in May 1950, the Southern Baptist Convention adopted a recommendation that a new seminary be organized and located in North Carolina. The new school was at first housed in the Music-Religion Building of Wake Forest College (now Wake Forest University) in Wake Forest. Southeastern Baptist Theological Seminary officially opened in September 1951, becoming the fourth seminary operated by the Southern Baptist Convention.

The impetus for the establishment of a new seminary was the tremendous growth of the Southern Baptist Convention during the middle of the twentieth century. Many ministers from the southeastern region of the United States found it difficult to relocate to the cities where the three existing seminaries were located. Furthermore, those three schools were experiencing record growth in enrollment.

Wake Forest College moved to Winston-Salem in 1956. Previously, in 1950, the Southern Baptist Convention had voted to purchase the campus for the sum of $1.6 million. Following the move of Wake Forest College, the seminary undertook an extensive renovation of the campus to improve facilities for growing enrollment, which by 1986 had reached 1,200. The seminary experienced a major change in 1987 as a result of the so-called inerrancy controversy in the Southern Baptist Convention. The board of trustees, dominated by fundamentalists, came into conflict with the school's administration and faculty over what they perceived as a liberalization of theology, leading to the resignation of the school's president, Randall Lolley. Under the presidency of Lewis Drummond, continuing conflict between the faculty and trustees caused sharp divisions and led to a decline in student enrollment. Through Drummond's leadership, the seminary affirmed its commitment to fundamentalist principles and established new faculty guidelines. Paige Patterson succeeded Drummond in 1992 as president of the seminary.

In 1994 the trustees established Southeastern Baptist Theological College, later Southeastern College at Wake Forest, for classes leading to a bachelor's degree. The Seminary Program and College Program operate as integral parts of the institution. Southeastern Baptist Theological Seminary maintains its focus on missions and evangelism. In the early 2000s the school had an enrollment of more than 2,200.

Glenn Jonas

Southeastern Center for Contemporary Art (SECCA),

located in Winston-Salem, serves as a nonprofit community resource and revolving exhibit space for American contemporary art. SECCA is dedicated to encouraging scholarship and research in contemporary art as well as supporting the creation of new artworks. It began in 1956 as an exhibition space devoted to work by local artists. The center received a new home when industrialist James G. Hanes willed his 32-acre estate to SECCA in 1972. Renovation of Hanes's mansion, plus construction of a gallery addition and receiving area, was completed in 1976. During this period SECCA initiated an artist support program, the National Endowment for the Arts/SECCA Southeastern Artists Fellowships (later known as SECCA/R. J. Reynolds Artists Fellowships). SECCA expanded that program nationally in 1981, initiating the Awards in the Visual Arts (AVA). For ten years, AVA awarded artists fellowships along with funding museum exhibitions and a purchase program.

In 1990, with a new 24,500-square-foot addition, SECCA shifted its focus to exhibiting the work of major contemporary artists around the country while maintaining a commitment to southeastern artists. Completion of the McChesney Scott Dunn Auditorium enabled the center to offer programs in contemporary music, drama, dance, and film as well as lectures and conferences on contemporary art issues. In 1994 SECCA initiated the Artist and the Community Project. Structured as a series of residencies resulting in the creation of new work, participating artists focus on issues critical to the local community. Working with other community-based institutions from schools to social service agencies, the program forges a link between artists and community members.

SECCA continues to present the diversity of American contemporary art and encourage creative excellence in the visual arts. A distinctive feature of SECCA's galleries is their illumination by natural light showing through wall-sized glass windows, designed so that no artwork falls prey to the sun's potentially injurious rays. The center offers 21,000 square feet of exhibit space and a 300-seat auditorium.

SECCA at times has come under fire from religious groups and members of Congress, such as retired U.S. senator from North Carolina Jesse Helms. Helms and others, angered by work that they considered blasphemous or pornographic, demanded greater accountability by the National Endowment for the Arts (NEA) and threatened to slash NEA budgets. For instance, great outcry arose in 1989 over a 40 × 40-inch photograph by New York's Andres Serrano, who received $15,000 for his work from the NEA through SECCA. The photograph, titled *Piss Christ*, shows a wood and plastic crucifix submerged in the artist's urine. The artist said that his work was "not meant to be an attack on Christ [but was] questioning organized religion and the commercialization of Christ."

Kelly Kress

Southern Christian Leadership Conference (SCLC),

established in 1957 in Atlanta and headed by Martin Luther King Jr. (1929–68), influenced North Carolina civil rights activism through 1975. The SCLC built a mass membership with local affiliates, mainly black churches and civic groups committed to ending segregation by nonviolent direct action. Activist ministers and laymen directed its statewide crusade. Black United Methodist pastor Douglas E. Moore, King's former Boston University classmate, led Durham's 1957 and 1960 lunch counter sit-ins and helped to mentor the student freedom movement. In addition, the SCLC's state field secretary, Golden A. Frinks, organized nationally reported interracial demonstrations in Williamston (1963–64), Hyde County (1968–69), and Wilmington (1971).

References: Taylor Branch, *Parting the Waters: America in the King Years, 1954–63* (1988); David C. Carter, "The Williamston Freedom Movement: Civil Rights at the Grass Roots in Eastern North Carolina, 1957–1964," *NCHR* 76 (1999).

Raymond Gavins

Southern Folklife Collection (SFC) at the University of

North Carolina at Chapel Hill is among the leading folklife archives in the country, containing extensive documentary material for southern traditional and vernacular culture, including musical and oral traditions as well as mainstream media production. Centered around the John Edwards Memorial Collection and the UNC Folklore Archives, the SFC is especially rich in materials documenting the emergence of old-time, country-western, hillbilly, bluegrass, blues, gospel, Cajun, and zydeco music.

With materials donated by Ralph Steele Boggs, Arthur Palmer Hudson, and Guy B. Johnson, among others, the UNC Folklore Curriculum faculty established the Folklore Archives in 1968. The John Edwards Memorial Foundation formed in California in 1962 as an archive and research center named for the young Australian record collector. Following Edwards's death in 1960, his remarkable collection of American country music records, along with a wealth of correspondence and other research materials, was strengthened by additions from his American friends and colleagues, including Eugene Earle, Archie Green, D. K. Wilgus, Ken Griffis, Ed Kahn, and Norm

Cohen. In 1983 UNC purchased the John Edwards Memorial Collection, and in the fall of 1986, the UNC Folklore Archives and the Edwards collection were combined to form the Southern Folklife Collection. The SFC is a component of the Manuscripts Department of the UNC-Chapel Hill Academic Affairs Library, which also houses the Southern Historical Collection and the UNC University Archives. The Southern Folklife Collection officially opened for research during the Sounds of the South Conference at UNC in April 1989.

The Southern Folklife Collection contains nearly 82,000 sound recordings, including cylinders, acetate discs, wire recordings, 78-rpm and 45-rpm discs, LPs, cassettes, CDs, and open-reel tapes. Moving image materials include over 3,000 video recordings and 18 million feet of motion picture film. Paper-based materials include thousands of photographs, song folios, posters, manuscript materials, ephemeral items and research files.

Bruce E. Baker

Southern Highland Craft Guild (SHCG) was established

in 1930 and has worked steadily since then to document, encourage, support, and exhibit the handicrafts of the people of North Carolina and the Southeast. Olive Dame Campbell was instrumental in the beginnings of the organization. After her husband's death in 1919, Campbell embarked upon a study of the folk schools of Denmark and surrounding countries. This trip inspired the founding of the John C. Campbell Folk School and, after visiting a cooperative crafts shop in Finland, the first steps toward organizing the SHCG.

Other leaders interested in handicrafts revival efforts recognized the need for an organized cooperative effort to preserve, support, and market handicraft skills and products. In December 1928, a group gathered in Penland to discuss the state and place of handicrafts in the region, how an organized cooperative might work, and what it could accomplish. These representatives agreed to work toward establishing the Southern Mountain Handicraft Guild. The group mounted a comprehensive exhibition of the region's handicrafts for the first time at the spring 1930 meeting of the Conference of Southern Mountain Workers. At this gathering, members passed the constitution and by-laws for the guild. For the first time, regional schools, producing centers, and artisans were aware of what each institution produced and understood the possibilities for transforming the handicraft tradition into a visible and meaningful part of the region's economy.

Guild members organized a research library, started a membership directory, and planned new exhibitions. In 1931 Frances Goodrich conveyed the ownership of Allanstand Cottage Industries and its salesroom to the guild, providing a space to showcase and market members' handicrafts. At its spring 1935 meeting, the guild dropped "mountain" from its name and substituted "highland" to reflect the broad goals of

the organization and the refined image its members wanted to convey about their handiwork.

In July 1948 the Southern Highland Handicraft Guild (SHHG) and Southern Highlanders, Inc. sponsored its first craftsman fair in Gatlinburg, Tenn. The fair connected visitors with the best crafts and their makers and clearly showed the importance of handicrafts in the life of southern Appalachia. The SHHG and Southern Highlanders, Inc., merged in 1951, and the annual fair moved to Asheville, where the guild was now located. In the 1960s the guild sponsored two fairs each year in Gatlinburg and Asheville and initiated a new era of management and growth. The National Endowment for the Arts, the Appalachian Regional Commission, national museums and galleries, and individual consumers had fully accepted the uniqueness, beauty, and value of southern handicrafts.

In the late 1970s, the Appalachian Regional Commission allocated funds to build a Southern Highlands Folk Art Center on the Blue Ridge Parkway outside of Asheville. The center, opened in 1980, provided a home for the Southern Highland Craft Guild, preserving the region's handicraft heritage and encouraging new ways of expressing beauty. The Folk Art Center also provided a popular marketplace for the exhibition and sale of southern Appalachian handicrafts.

By the early 2000s, the Southern Highland Craft Guild had more than 700 members in nine states, producing crafts that reflect both the important traditions of the southern Appalachian region and the contemporary forms arising from the growth and diversity of the southern crafts movement. The Folk Art Center welcomes 300,000 visitors each year who come to view the finest in traditional and contemporary craft of the Southern Appalachians or take part in the many educational events that are held throughout the year.

References: Garry Barker, *The Handicraft Revival in Southern Appalachia, 1930–1990* (1991); Allen H. Eaton, *Handicrafts of the Southern Highlands* (rev. ed., 1973).

Dennis W. Cross

Southern Historical Collection. SEE Historical Collections.

Southern National Bank. SEE Branch Banking and Trust Company.

Southern Part of Heaven is a phrase coined by author

William Meade Prince in 1950 for the title of his volume of reminiscences of growing up in Chapel Hill. Prince was drawing on an old, probably apocryphal anecdote about a Dr. Kluttz, a Franklin Street store owner in the early years of the twentieth century. As Prince relates it, Kluttz, on his deathbed, inquires of his Presbyterian minister, Parson Moss, what heaven is like, and Moss replies: "Dr. Kluttz, I believe Heaven must be a lot like Chapel Hill in the spring."

Prince's title has long held the status of a beloved cliché in Chapel Hill and continues to be cited in both promotional and sarcastic contexts. An example of the latter is a suggestion, not infrequently made, that in light of Chapel Hill's and the greater Research Triangle's development, population growth, and demographic change in recent years, the label should be emended to the "Southern Part of New Jersey."

References: William Meade Prince, *The Southern Part of Heaven* (1950); James Vickers, *Chapel Hill: An Illustrated History* (1985).

Jerry Leath Mills

Southern Power Company.

Benjamin N. and James B. Duke (sons of Washington Duke, the tobacco magnate and prominent philanthropist), along with partners Walker Gill Wylie and William States Lee, incorporated the Southern Power Company in New Jersey on 22 June 1905. The move came after several years of cautious preliminary investigations and was influenced by the brilliant technical expertise of Lee, who became chief engineer of the Catawba Power Company in 1902 and who later was elected as the first southerner to be president of the American Institute of Electrical Engineers. The Dukes had invested in Catawba Power since 1902, and as part of the deal forming Southern Power they acquired Catawba.

Concentrating on industrial users and the wholesale selling of power, the Dukes had not originally intended to supply individuals in residential areas. Soon, however, there were pressures to retail power to residential customers and small businesses and to operate a streetcar system in Charlotte and other communities such as Greenville and Spartanburg in South Carolina and Greensboro, Durham, and Winston-Salem in North Carolina. In some cities Southern Power also owned and operated natural gas supplies and waterworks. As a result, the Southern Public Utilities Company was organized in 1913 as the retailing and streetcar arm of Southern Power.

From its inception, the Southern Power Company was a highly successful, pioneering hydroelectric venture that played a key role in the industrialization of the Piedmont Carolinas. On 18 Nov. 1924 its name was changed to Duke Power Company, which on 18 June 1997 merged with PanEnergy Corporation to create Duke Energy Corporation.

References: Robert F. Durden, *The Dukes of Durham, 1865–1929* (1975); Durden, *Electrifying the Piedmont Carolinas: The Duke Power Company, 1904–1997* (2001); Carl F. Horn Jr., *The Duke Power Story, 1904–1973* (1973).

Wiley J. Williams

Southern Railway System,

formed from the remnants of several failing Virginia lines, was incorporated in Virginia in 1894 and began operating the same year (its earliest predecessor line was actually the South Carolina Canal and Rail Road Company, chartered in 1827, which ran the nation's first regularly scheduled passenger train and later the first night operation). By 1894 the Southern Railway was comprised of at least 125 consolidated railroads, with 75,000 freight cars, over 1,400 locomotives, and more than 21,000 employees. Among those rail lines were several based in North Carolina, including the Carolina & Northwestern Railway, the Atlantic, Tennessee, and Ohio Railroad, and the Atlanta & Charlotte Airline Railway. By 1896 construction had begun on a new rail yard and rail shops in Rowan County; the facility and adjacent town were named Spencer in honor of the Southern's first president, Samuel Spencer.

Attempting to stay true to its corporate motto, "Southern Serves the South," the railroad, headquartered in Washington, D.C., extended throughout much of the South, with main facilities in Spencer, Knoxville, Chattanooga, Atlanta, and Birmingham. By the time the line running from Meridian, Miss., to New Orleans was acquired in 1916, the railroad extended 8,000 miles across 13 states—its territorial limits for almost half a century.

Several noted North Carolinians played a role in the development of the Southern Railway. Among them, John Motley Morehead and Alexander B. Andrews served as president of two of the Southern's predecessor lines, the North Carolina Railroad and the Western North Carolina Railroad, respectively.

The Southern was efficient and innovative. By mid-1953, it was the first large railroad to convert its entire operation from steam to diesel engines. Known for excellent passenger service, especially on the Southern Crescent running from Washington, D.C., to New Orleans through Piedmont North Carolina, the Southern also developed novel systems to manage and move freight, such as its oversized grain hopper car known as "Big John." In 1979 the Linwood yard opened in Davidson County, replacing the freight yard a few miles south in Spencer. The former yards and shops at Spencer were donated to the state and reopened as the North Carolina Transportation Museum.

In 1982 the Southern merged with another well-managed railroad, the Roanoke-based Norfolk & Western Railroad. The merger formed the Norfolk Southern Railroad, with headquarters in Norfolk. By the early 2000s most of the old Southern Railway lines and facilities operated under the Norfolk Southern name.

References: Burke Davis, *The Southern Railway: Road of the Innovators* (1985); Albert S. Eggerton Jr., *Out of the Past and into the Future: The Bicentennial Story of Southern Railway* (1976); Duane Galloway and Jim Wrinn, *Southern Railway's Spencer Shops, 1896–1996* (1996).

Warren L. Bingham

Southern Tenant Farmers' Union (STFU) was created in response to both the deepening economic depression and the reduction in cotton acreage mandated by the New Deal's 1933 Agricultural Adjustment Act. Primarily a phenomenon of the upper Mississippi Delta's cotton plantation culture, the union was founded by a racially integrated group of sharecroppers and small businessmen in Arkansas in 1934. Its leaders included H. L. Mitchell and Clay East, both dedicated socialists and natives of the Delta. Violence against STFU organizational efforts in 1935 produced national publicity that, in turn, generated much-needed financial aid.

The STFU's impact on North Carolina was indirect and diffuse. To be sure, legislation in the late 1930s helped tenant farmers in the east, but the STFU never crossed the mountains in its organizational drives. The STFU papers are housed in the Southern Historical Collection at the University of North Carolina at Chapel Hill.

References: Donald H. Grubbs, *Cry from the Cotton: The Southern Tenant Farmers' Union and the New Deal* (1971); Robert F. Martin, *Howard Kester and the Struggle for Social Justice in the South, 1904–1977* (1991).

W. H. Cobb

South Lowell Academy was the inspiration of John Archibald McMannen, a lay preacher of the Methodist Church, and his close friend, Claiborn Parrish. With a board of trustees made up of themselves and three local physicians, McMannen and Parrish established a classical academy at South Lowell in what is today Durham County in 1849. Its first headmaster was the Reverend James A. Dean, a graduate of Wesleyan College in Connecticut, who gave the school a luster it maintained even after his departure for larger arenas.

A brick dormitory for the students who flocked there from all parts of the state, as well as a hotel, were soon added to the school, mills, and general store that made up the community. A preparatory school for Randolph-Macon College, the academy became a cultural center with a library, lecture program, debating and temperance societies, and the electrifying preaching of McMannen, who could also play the fiddle. In 1856 Edward Scott added to the school's attraction with a medical school.

The general poverty caused by the Civil War and its aftermath depleted South Lowell's pool of applicants, though the school continued at least until 1897, when it was still listed in the state business directory.

Reference: Jean B. Anderson, *Durham County* (1990).

Jean B. Anderson

South Mills, Battle of. The Battle of South Mills, a Civil War engagement also known as the Battle of Sawyer's Lane and the Battle of Camden, occurred in Camden County on 19 Apr. 1862 at the south end of the Dismal Swamp Canal. After the Confederacy lost Roanoke Island, New Bern, and Fort Macon, the Union's Maj. Gen. Ambrose E. Burnside sought to blow up the locks of the canal at South Mills. He hoped to prevent the Confederates from passing their small ironclad gunboats through the canal to Albemarle Sound and threatening Union forces in the region. Burnside mounted an expedition in cooperation with Federal gunboats to move up the Pasquotank River. Brig. Gen. Jesse L. Reno commanded the expedition of 3,000 men.

Soon after midnight on the morning of 19 April, Reno's force landed about four miles below Elizabeth City. Local Confederates, led by Col. Ambrose R. Wright, had prepared for the enemy. They dug a ditch across the road with marsh woodland at each end, then filled it with wood from fences and buildings and set it on fire to block the Union's movement. This ditch, known as "the roasted ditch," is still extant.

Wright, commanding 900 men, stationed five companies and three guns in a ditch crossing the road on which Reno was advancing. Reno's troops arrived late in the morning and deployed for attack. Wright's outnumbered men held off the Union force for four hours, until they had exhausted their ammunition. Wright fell back and assumed another defensive position, but Reno's men were too shaken and exhausted to follow.

Reno himself was troubled by inaccurate rumors of massive Confederate reinforcements assembling at Norfolk and abandoned the expedition, returning that night to the Federal ships below Elizabeth City. In the engagement, Reno lost 13 killed, 101 wounded, and 13 missing. Wright lost 6 killed, 19 wounded, and 3 captured.

References: John G. Barrett, *The Civil War in North Carolina* (1963); Daniel H. Hill, *Bethel to Sharpsburg*, vol. 1 (1926); Robert Underwood Johnson and Clarence Klough Buel, eds., *Battles and Leaders of the Civil War*, vol. 1 (1884).

Paul Branch
Thomas L. Norris Jr.

South Pacolet River, Battle of. The Battle of South Pacolet River, a Revolutionary War engagement, occurred along the North Carolina–South Carolina border on the night of 14–15 July 1780 as a result of Loyalist colonel Alexander Innes having sent a Major Dunlap with 70 dragoons from Prince's Fort to pursue Col. John Jones's 35 Georgians. Jones was traveling northward through the upcountry to join the first Whig force he could find. Pretending to be Loyalists, Jones's troops had killed or captured about 40 South Carolina Loyalists at Gowen's Old Fort late on 13 July. Fleeing northward, Jones joined Col. Charles McDowell's force north of Earle's Ford on the South Pacolet River on 14 July. That night Dunlap attacked the combined camps of Jones and McDowell, killing two men and wounding six. Outnumbered, Dunlap retreated to Prince's Fort, and Col. Edward Hampton pursued and killed several of Dunlap's men. These events strengthened the Whig cause in the upcountry.

Reference: John S. Pancake, *This Destructive War: The British Campaign in the Carolinas, 1780–1782* (1985).

John L. Bell

Southwest Creek, Battle of. SEE Wyse Fork, Battle of.

Spanish-American War, fought over Cuban independence and lasting less than six months in 1898, afforded North Carolinians a brief interlude in a period of intense political confrontations. In response to President William McKinley's call for troops following the sinking of the USS *Maine* on 15 Feb. 1898, North Carolina recruited two regiments of white troops and a third of black enlisted men and officers. North Carolina, Illinois, and Kansas were the only states to recruit all-black regiments for service. A number of problems plagued the 1st and 2nd North Carolina Regiments, including large numbers of desertions, medical discharges, low morale, oppressive heat, and a lack of training in loading, aiming, and firing rifles.

Raleigh's Camp Bryan Grimes was the training facility for the 1st North Carolina Regiment, the first state unit raised for the war. As that camp became crowded, the 2nd Regiment transferred to the North Carolina State Fairgrounds. On 18 May 1898 Col. W. H. S. Burgwyn of the 2nd Regiment announced that the new camp would be named Camp Dan Russell after the state's governor, Daniel Lindsay Russell. The regiment pitched tents on the grounds and made use of the existing fair buildings, holding dress parade in the enclosure inside the racetrack. The temporary camp served as a mobilization and training facility for North Carolina volunteers during the war.

By early July half of the troops were sick and excused from duty. An outbreak of typhoid fever killed seven men and sent many to the camp hospital. Boredom, delays in pay, and a lack of sufficient uniforms and weapons contributed to morale and discipline problems at the post. Many men deserted, and wanted criminals appeared in the ranks, damaging the 2nd Regiment's reputation.

Since the 2nd Regiment left for new posts in Georgia and Florida in late July 1898, by 2 August only a surgeon, a chaplain, a few guards, and a handful of attendants remained in the camp hospital caring for 27 patients, some with typhoid fever. When the 2nd Regiment returned to Raleigh in September at the end of the war, they occupied Camp Bryan Grimes. By October 1898 the North Carolina State Fair had taken over the site of Camp Dan Russell.

The Catawba County Boys, Company A, 1st North Carolina Regiment, Seventh Army Corp, pose beside a tent at Camp Cuba Libre in Jacksonville, Fla., 30 July 1898. Courtesy of NCOA&H.

The first three companies of the 3rd North Carolina Regiment—Companies A, B, and C, with approximately 380 men—were designated the Russell Black Battalion and arrived at Fort Macon (near Beaufort and Morehead City) on 30 May 1898. They established Camp Russell, a temporary encampment in close proximity to the fort. Seven additional companies of black volunteers arrived in early July, and on 19 July the ten companies were mustered into service as the 3rd Regiment of North Carolina.

On 14 Sept. 1898 the 3rd Regiment moved to Camp Poland near Knoxville, Tenn., remaining there until 21 November, when it proceeded to Camp Haskell near Macon, Ga., for winter encampment. At Macon, the Third passed in review before President McKinley on 21 December and was disbanded during the first week of February 1899.

At the time of the Spanish-American War, the North Carolina State Guard contained five divisions of naval reserves. The state's first fallen soldier, and the first naval officer to be killed in the conflict, was Ens. Worth Bagley of Raleigh. Bagley was killed in action at Cardenas, Cuba, on 11 May 1898. The most widely acclaimed North Carolina army hero of the war was Lt. William E. Shipp of Lincolnton. On 1 July he was killed in action while leading troops of the 10th Cavalry Regiment in the charge up San Juan Hill near Santiago. Some observers maintained that this charge saved the "Rough Riders" and future president Theodore Roosevelt from destruction. Camp Bryan Grimes was renamed Camp Shipp-Bagley in honor of those two heroes.

Members of the 3rd Regiment experienced the Spanish-American War in a way uniquely related to their racial identity. Although many blacks had disagreed about intervention in Cuba—considering the issues of repression and racism on the home front of paramount concern—the declaration of war against Spain put their role in a different perspective. The war afforded African Americans an opportunity to prove themselves, furthering black status and identity while establishing their patriotism and national loyalty. Black troops were, moreover, determined to take on more than a menial role. Although blacks had previously contributed two infantry battalions to the State Guard, by 1898 their numbers had dwindled to a single company (the Charlotte Light Infantry) enrolled in the militia.

Governor Russell involved Senators Jeter C. Pritchard and Marion Butler, his close friend J. C. L. Harris in Washington, D.C., and in-state black leaders, such as George H. White and Henry P. Cheatham, in the effort to secure a full regiment of black volunteers. The governor appointed Col. James H. Young —the former editor of the influential *Raleigh Gazette*, a previous Wake County representative in the General Assembly, and an active member of the Republican Party—as commander of the 3rd Regiment. Russell's Democratic rivals interpreted this decision as a bid for black political support, and Russell, Young, and the 3rd Regiment all withstood considerable acrimony. The resentment created by their presence in both Knoxville and Macon made black troops realize that they would return home to face civilian life in an atmosphere highly charged with racial hatred from hostile newspapers, police forces, and citizens—a situation exemplified by the Wilmington race riot that followed the heated white supremacy political campaign of October–November 1898.

References: Willard B. Gatewood Jr., "North Carolina's Negro Regiment in the Spanish-American War," *NCHR* 48 (October 1971); George H. Gibson, "Attitudes in North Carolina Regarding the Independence of Cuba, 1868–1898," *NCHR* 43 (January 1966); Edward A. Johnson, *History of Negro Soldiers in the Spanish-American War, and Other Items of Interest* (1899); Joseph F. Steelman, *North Carolina's Role in the Spanish-American War* (1975).

Wiley J. Williams
Additional research provided by David A. Norris and Robert C. Voigt.

Spanish Invasions of the North Carolina coast in the 1740s were an offshoot of a series of disputes between England and Spain, beginning with the War of Jenkins' Ear (1739–42), in which the American colonies were unwitting participants. The hostilities began in late April 1741, when two Spanish privateers, one of them a high stern black sloop with about 100 men on board, appeared off the Outer Banks. By early May they had captured six vessels, including two registered in Edenton and another in Pasquotank.

Emboldened by this success, the Spaniards moved ashore at Ocracoke, building a tent town and establishing a base of operations from which they were able to control the movement of ships through Ocracoke Inlet and harass vessels sailing along the coast. In the process they burned several houses and destroyed great numbers of cattle on the coast in addition to fitting out several smaller vessels for operations in the sounds. Finally, in August, North Carolina merchants and shipowners joined together and fitted out the letter-of-marque ship *William* with a crew of 100 men and a small schooner with

which to engage the Spaniards. When the *William* and its consort reached Ocracoke Inlet, the Spaniards abandoned their tent camp and left the coast.

As the War of Jenkins' Ear wore down, the Spanish privateers continued their periodic raids through the spring of 1742. Hardly had that ended, however, when the English and Spanish were fighting again, this time in King George's War. This conflict, known in Europe as the War of the Austrian Succession, eventually pitted Great Britain, Austria, and the Netherlands against Prussia, France, and Spain. It was fought principally in Europe, but there were several sizable campaigns in the Americas. Four companies of North Carolina volunteers totaling about 400 troops were part of a 3,600-man force of Americans under Governor William Gooch of Virginia.

In the summer of 1747 several small Spanish vessels "came creeping along the shore from St. Augustine full of armed men, mostly mulattos and negros" and made a series of landings on the coast at Ocracoke, Core Sound, Bear Inlet, and Cape Fear, "where they killed several of his Majesty's subjects, burned some ships and several small vessels, carried off some negros, and slaughtered a vast number of black cattle and hogs." Before leaving the Carolina coast they also captured the town and port of Beaufort, despite the defensive efforts of the local militia. In the process, ten Spanish prisoners were taken, and the invaders abandoned the town after only a few days of occupation.

The final Spanish attack, early in the fall of 1748, was launched against Brunswick and resulted in the invaders' brief occupation of the town. Meanwhile, during the fighting taking place on the Cape Fear River opposite Brunswick, one of the Spanish vessels, the *Fortuna*, caught fire and blew up. Though all of its officers were killed, several sailors were taken prisoner. When the other Spanish ships sailed down the river to Smith Island, they sent back a flag of truce. A prisoner exchange was arranged, marking the end of the Spanish invasions of the North Carolina coast.

References: Robert J. Cain, ed., *Records of the Executive Council, 1735–1754* (1988); Hugh T. Lefler and William S. Powell, *Colonial North Carolina: A History* (1973).

David Stick
Robert J. Cain

Spanish Moss (*Tillandsia usneoides*) is not actually a moss but rather a member of the pineapple family. Deriving its nutrients from the air, Spanish moss is not parasitic and usually favors hardwood trees. This fibrous plant bears tiny yellow flowers and is found in the eastern regions of North Carolina, generally in low woods and maritime forests. The gray-green tendrils drape gracefully from branches and can extend up to 20 feet. Spanish moss was made into clothing by Native Americans, and a wad of it served as a diaper for infants.

Streamers of it were twisted into rope during the Civil War. Gathered in quantity, it was buried in sandy soil until the growing part rotted, leaving the tough inner strands, which were used to stuff mattresses, cushions, or upholstered furniture. An enduring symbol of the South and southern culture, Spanish moss is often found lending an air of mystique to novels and poetry.

Lisa D. Smith

Speaker Ban Law was adopted on 25 June 1963, the last day of the legislative session, after just over one hour of debate. It prohibited speeches on North Carolina public college campuses by "known" members of the Communist Party, persons "known" to advocate the overthrow of the constitutions of North Carolina or the United States, or individuals who had pleaded the Fifth Amendment in order to decline answering questions concerning communist subversion.

The statute has been viewed as a conservative response to UNC-Chapel Hill liberalism in general and to the support of civil rights by university personnel in particular. Its sponsors —Secretary of State Thad Eure, drafter of the bill; T. Clarence Stone, president of the State Senate; Clifton Blue, Speaker of the State House; and legislators Ned Delamar and Phil Godwin—used an Ohio house bill as their model. The Ohio bill had been brought to their attention by Jesse Helms in a WRAL-TV editorial on 21 June 1963. After Godwin introduced the bill, the normal rules of consideration were suspended. Four minutes later, Speaker Blue declared that it had passed the House on a voice vote. The measure was immediately sent to the Senate, where Stone pushed it through in three readings and

voice votes. He did not recognize anyone who wished to speak against it.

William C. Friday, president of the University of North Carolina System, and the university community were caught completely unprepared for this challenge to academic freedom, but they reacted quickly. On 28 Oct. 1963 the University Board of Trustees agreed to support the repeal or modification of the law. Since North Carolina chief executives had no veto power at the time, Governor Terry Sanford appointed a special committee to review the law on 21 Oct. 1964. That committee subsequently recommended transferring control and authority over speakers to university trustees.

The Southern Association of Colleges and Schools, the chief accrediting body of southern colleges, reported on 19 May 1965 that the Speaker Ban interfered with the "necessary authority" of the UNC administration and thus might be harmful to the university's academic status. At the request of President Friday, newly elected governor Dan Moore on 1 June 1965 proposed that the General Assembly create a study commission to examine the law and remedies that might be considered in a special legislative session. On 5 November the study commission proposed a compromise that was approved by the legislature in a special session. This revised law changed the ban to restrictions on speakers exercised by university trustees under strict guidelines.

Student leaders at Chapel Hill opposed the compromise; they wanted no regulations or limitations on speakers. The issue heated up when the Students for a Democratic Society invited Frank Wilkinson, a leader of the movement to abolish the House Un-American Activities Committee, and Herbert Aptheker, an avowed communist, to speak at Chapel Hill. Friday tried to persuade the trustees to allow the men to appear under very strict guidelines, but the trustees refused.

Student body president Paul Dickson III, a 24-year-old veteran, was unwilling to accept the trustees' decision and worked with Friday throughout the fall of 1964 and winter of 1965 to resolve the conflict. Once the trustees had opted for a hard line, Friday urged Dickson to begin litigation. Dickson arranged for Frank Wilkinson to speak from the public sidewalk—across the university wall—to Chapel Hill students assembled on the campus side. This confrontation of 2 Mar. 1966, and a similar one when Aptheker spoke on 9 March, laid the basis for Dickson's court challenge of the 1965 revised Speaker Ban Law.

Dickson, with the covert support of Friday and the counsel of attorneys McNeill Smith and William Van Alstyne, had set a legal trap for the legislature. On 19 Feb. 1968 a three-judge federal district court in Greensboro ruled that the Speaker Ban Law was unconstitutional and violated First Amendment protections of free speech. Governor Moore did not appeal the decision. On 17 May 1995 the General Assembly finally repealed the Speaker Ban Law, which had been essentially unenforce-

Banned speaker Frank Wilkinson (left) is introduced by student body president Paul Dickson from a public sidewalk on Franklin Street as students seated on the UNC campus listen, 2 Mar. 1966. Photograph by Jock Lauterer. NCC.

able for 27 years. Frank Wilkinson returned to Chapel Hill to speak at the UNC Law School on 27 Feb. 1997.

References: William J. Billingsley, *Communists on Campus: Race, Politics, and the Public University in Sixties North Carolina* (1999); Billingsley, *Speaker Ban: The Anti-Communist Crusade in North Carolina, 1963–1970* (1994); William A. Link, "William Friday and the North Carolina Speaker Ban Crisis, 1963–1968," *NCHR* 72 (April 1995).

W. Lee Johnston Jr.

Speaker of the Assembly,

called the manager of the House of Burgesses in colonial North Carolina, was the most important person in the legislature and possibly the key individual in the legislative process. A sitting member of the Lower House chosen by a majority of his fellow assemblymen at the beginning of each session, the Speaker moderated the proceedings of the body while preserving and protecting its privileges. It was his responsibility, after meeting with and receiving the governor's approval, to call the Assembly to order, to determine who might be admitted, and to interpret the rules of the Lower House. He recognized all speakers, decided what matters could come before the House, and directed all debate. The Speaker was also responsible for amending bills and assisting in the appointment of committees, both temporary and standing. To minimize conflict on the floor, questions of order were directed to the Speaker, who sought to "explain but not to sway the house with arguments or disputes." No meeting of the Lower House was legal without the Speaker's presence, and in the event that a quorum was as few as 15 members, one of them had to be the Speaker. In addition, no bill could become law without his signature.

Successful speakers of the Assembly required not only leadership qualities but also political and oratorical skills in order to form a working consensus of the membership, to represent the House before the governor and the North Carolina Council, and to act as spokesman of the people. Chief among those who occupied the Speaker's chair and exemplified these traits were Edward Moseley, Samuel Swann, and John Harvey at different times between 1708 and 1774.

Whereas Moseley, Swann, and Harvey enabled the Lower House to function more effectively, productively, and aggressively, post-1776 Speakers were less influential. The speakership, which ceased to be the primary focus of opposition to governmental policies after the adoption of the state Constitution of 1776, became instead only one of several means of political training or service available for state leaders. Even though Thomas Benbury occupied the Speaker's chair for six years (1778–82, 1784) and Stephen Cabarrus held it for ten years between 1789 and 1805, the importance of sitting in the House of Commons, as it was now called, including the speakership, was seen as less desirable than comparable service in the State Senate, the governorship, or the U.S. Congress.

References: Charles S. Cooke, *The Governor, Council, and Assembly in Royal North Carolina* (1912); Charles L. Raper, *North Carolina: A Study in English Colonial Government* (1904); William L. Saunders, ed., *The Colonial Records of North Carolina* (10 vols., 1886–88).

Louis P. Towles

Spirit of the Age was a temperance newspaper established in 1849 in Raleigh by Alexander M. Gorman, who earlier had served as the foreman of the *Raleigh Register*'s office. It began as the organ for the North Carolina chapter of the Sons of Temperance. Initially a small paper, it gradually enlarged and eventually became one of the most popular four-page newspapers in North Carolina. The addition of a power press in the early 1850s permitted Gorman to expand the paper's physical layout. By 1860 the *Spirit of the Age* boasted the largest circulation of any newspaper in the state.

The evils of using alcohol dominated its pages. Stories often focused on how it harmed families, describing in heartbreaking detail the tribulations of abused and shamed wives, children who lacked food and clothing, and husbands who had lost all sense of pride. The *Spirit of the Age* also carried literary features (mostly dealing with family-oriented themes) from some of the better-known North Carolina writers of the time.

Gorman's paper was a financial success until the beginning of the Civil War, when the temperance issue took a backseat to secession and military matters. The result was a rapid loss of patronage. During the conflict Gorman sold the paper's office and presses to John G. Williams and became the associate editor of another Raleigh journal. Williams continued to print the *Spirit of the Age* until almost the end of the war, when he finally closed shop. In 1871 the Raleigh printing company Edwards and Broughton attempted to resurrect the newspaper but gave it up after a couple of years.

References: George Washington Paschal, *A History of Printing in North Carolina* (1946); R. H. Whitaker, *Whitaker's Reminiscences, Incidents and Anecdotes* (1905).

David McGee

Spray Water Power and Land Company,

established in 1889 by James Turner Morehead, was a hydroelectric power, textile, and land development company that created the Spray industrial complex on the Smith River in the present-day town of Eden. Its antecedent had been a textile firm created by James Barnett and John Motley Morehead (James Turner Morehead's father and later a governor of North Carolina). The firm of Barnett and Morehead had operated a variety of mills, a cotton gin, a blacksmith shop, and a general store.

After the formation of the power and land development company, James Turner Morehead turned its operation over to his son-in-law, B. Frank Mebane, and a nephew, W. R.

Walker, so that he could then devote his time to more challenging chemical and metal alloy experimentation. The Morehead family interests were now under the direction of Mebane and Walker, who secured northern capital for embarking on a long-range comprehensive textile development of the power resources. Beginning with Spray Cotton Mills in 1896, several mills were built in rapid succession: Nantucket (1898), American Warehouse (1899), Lily (1900), Spray Woolen and Morehead (1902), Rhode Island (1903), and German-American in Draper (1906). All of these mills remained in the company except Spray Cotton Mills, which was sold in 1897 to Karl von Ruck, whose relatives, the Bishoprics, developed the mill into a successful family-owned business during the twentieth century. The Spray corporation—which included three mills, Spray Cotton and Nova Yarns in Eden and a plant at Mt. Holly—maintained an industry-wide reputation for customer satisfaction and high-quality yarns. The company announced its closing in 2001 after 105 years of operation.

Although later divested of its textile interests and water-power rights, the Spray Water Power and Land Company, still under the ownership and management of Morehead descendants, retained large tracts of land that have continued to be developed.

Reference: James E. Gardner, *Eden: Past and Present, 1880–1980* (1982).

Lindley S. Butler

Square Dancing

Square Dancing in North Carolina is inseparably linked to the history and culture of the state's Mountain region. The earliest square dances featured several couples keeping dance figures square through the entire set, but North Carolina's Appalachian style of square dancing is characterized by couples breaking from a ring to perform the Wagon Wheel, Four Leaf Clover, Cage the Birdie, Shoo-Fly-Shoo, and other dances before returning to the ring formation. Square dancing has been defined by the use of a caller, a tradition that developed about 1812. The caller made it unnecessary to memorize the dance beforehand. Appalachian dance music has traditionally included fiddle and banjo and a repertoire of old-time string band and folk tunes, but square dancers, particularly the precision-step cloggers, often perform to Nashville-style country, with drums, electric bass and guitar, and steel guitar sometimes substituting for the fiddle. Appalachian dance has also absorbed the stylish dress and more choreographed routines of the Western or "cowboy" square dances.

Square dances were originally performed in homes to celebrate holidays and community events such as corn shuckings, barn raisings, and barbecues. The calls and pace of the dances often differed according to region. Communities and valleys often had their own versions of fiddle tunes, and dance steps also varied.

North Carolina has produced its own square dancing stars that helped put the dance into the international arena and define its modern characteristics. Bascom Lamar Lunsford, the "Minstrel of the Appalachians," was born in Mars Hill in 1882 and became one of the foremost promoters of folk festivals. His influential Mountain Dance and Folk Festival in Asheville was first held in 1928 and has attracted thousands of visitors every year. Sam Queen of Haywood County set square dance standards until his death in 1969 at age 80. He developed a rapid double shuffle clogging step that became popular in mountain dance groups. Lunsford and Queen helped organize the National Folk Festival in St. Louis in 1934.

Local square dance groups abound in North Carolina, and clogging has become a popular form of entertainment, particularly in tourist areas of the Mountains. The town of Waynesville, for example, closes its Main Street on Friday nights in the summer to allow dancing in front of the county courthouse, where bleachers are provided for spectators.

References: S. Foster Damon, *The History of Square Dancing* (1957); Frank H. Smith, *The Appalachian Square Dance* (1955); Susan Eike Spalding and Jane Harris Woodside, eds., *Communities in Motion: Dance, Community, and Tradition in America's Southeast and Beyond* (1995).

Karl Rohr

Stagecoaches

Stagecoaches, drawn by teams of two to six horses, were public vehicles that ran scheduled, long-distance routes between designated towns by changing horses at predetermined stops. They took their name from the fact that they undertook journeys in stages, usually 10- to 15-mile laps. By extension, the word "stage" came to refer not only to these laps but also to the places where the coaches stopped and even to the vehicles themselves. In the colonies, stagecoaches began as heavy wagons with backless benches; flat roofs supported by posts left the sides open except in bad weather, when leather curtains could be rolled down. Wagon bodies gradually gave way to more boxlike, closed vehicles. Stagecoaches improved in the 1810s, when egg-shaped vehicles, suspended on leather straps mounted on frames, became the norm.

Stagecoach travel in North Carolina began just after the American Revolution. In 1786 a traveler from Suffolk, Va., to Wilmington, N.C., reported that "the stages" had been established only a short time before and were not yet adequately coordinated. As a result, passengers frequently experienced long delays at transfer points. The establishment of stagecoach lines was left to individual entrepreneurs or to companies of investors; unlike some states, which licensed early stage lines, North Carolina exercised no oversight at either the state or local level. Capt. Nathaniel Twining ran an early line in the eastern part of the state, although service varied in efficiency, comfort, and safety before competing lines forced improvements.

Stagecoach in front of the Hotel Iredell in Statesville, ca. 1900. NCC. Photograph by William Jasper Simpson.

Whatever the quality of service, travel by stagecoach was difficult. Even the most comfortable vehicles were stifling in summer and freezing in winter. If the windows were left open, dust from the road stirred up by the horses and carriage wheels would cover everything inside. Passengers often rode from dawn to late evening and were likely to be roused at 4:00 A.M. to continue a journey. Roads were execrable, and if horses or carriage wheels became mired in mud, passengers had to get out and walk or literally put a shoulder to the wheel. Coaches were also delayed by breakdowns—broken axles were common. Fording streams was also routine, and if the water level was high, patrons could expect to get wet inside their carriage. Moreover, vehicles frequently overturned.

Another uncertainty was the type of accommodations provided at stage stops. Almost uniformly, visitors complained that the inns and taverns in North Carolina were filthy, served unpalatable food, provided rude service, and offered no privacy. According to some travelers, female passengers were forced to crowd into one room, men had to wash in a trough in the yard and to sleep two to a bed, and dinners of chicken swimming in black grease were served with lumps of soggy dough instead of bread.

A travelers' guide from the 1840s listed 18 stage routes in North Carolina with all their stops; 7 originated in Raleigh, radiating out in all directions. In the west, Col. Valentine Ripley of Hendersonville was part owner of a major stage line—Rutledge, Pool, and Ripley—that connected Greenville, Tenn., and Greenville, S.C., via Asheville, Hendersonville, and Flat Rock. Because the terrain was so rough in western North Caro-

lina, travel by stage required changes of teams every eight to ten miles and often six horses instead of the usual four.

Despite their discomfort, stagecoach passengers generally did not complain and often developed a camaraderie with other riders. As stagecoaches were on the verge of extinction, travelers by railroad (which had doomed the stage lines) began to lament their passing and the loss of excitement and intimate contact with villages, countryside, and fellow passengers that stage travel had offered.

References: Thomas D. Clark, *Travels in the Old South: A Bibliography* (1956); Alice Morse Earle, *Stage-Coach and Tavern Days* (1900); Randle B. Truitt, *Trade and Travel around the Southern Appalachians* (1935).

Jean B. Anderson

Stagville, an eastern Orange County (now Durham County) plantation of several thousand acres, initially belonged to Virginia-born merchant Richard Bennehan (1743–1825). Bennehan came to North Carolina in 1768 to manage a store on Little River owned by Scottish merchant William Johnston. He began to purchase plantation lands near the Johnston store in 1776, and in the same year he married Mary Amis, a member of a planter family from Northampton County. In 1787 Bennehan bought the core of what would become Stagville Plantation from the widow Judith Stagg. She and her husband Thomas had operated a tavern at the site, which was probably even then known as "Stagville."

Bennehan built a new store and dwelling on the Stagg tract, where he and Mary raised two children, Rebecca and Thomas. At the end of the eighteenth century, Bennehan ranked among the area's most successful planters, owning 3,914 acres and 42 slaves of working age. His lands produced crops of tobacco and cereal grains, as well as livestock. Located near the intersection of the road between Person County and Wake County and the Great Trading Path (running approximately along the modern Interstate 85 corridor) the store prospered, as well. It served for many years, moreover, as the Stagville post office. In addition, Bennehan, a Federalist in political orientation, was a friend to many highly placed North Carolinians, including James Iredell and William R. Davie. Reflective of his status, he was named to a commission charged with building the State Capitol, and he served as a trustee of the University of North Carolina in Chapel Hill.

Stagville's long-term destiny was affected in 1803 when Rebecca Bennehan married Duncan Cameron, a lawyer and planter who was to play a leading role in the state's judicial, political, and banking affairs. Duncan and Rebecca were to make their home at Fairntosh Plantation, one mile south of the Bennehan house at Stagville. Thomas Bennehan never married, however, and upon his death in 1847 Stagville passed to the Cameron family. Under the ownership of Duncan and

Rebecca's son, Paul, it was part of one of the largest complexes of plantations in the antebellum South, encompassing lands in Granville, Orange, Person, and Wake Counties. The old Bennehan house became an overseer's dwelling, while Paul Cameron resided at Fairntosh and at his Hillsborough home, Burnside. More than 100 slaves lived at Stagville Plantation, most housed at the Horton Grove quarter. Following the Civil War, many former slaves and their descendants continued to reside at Stagville, working the land as sharecroppers.

After Paul Cameron's death in 1891, Stagville was inherited by his son Bennehan, who continued farming operations there. Stagville subsequently passed to Bennehan Cameron's daughter Isabelle, who sold the property in 1950. It was purchased in 1954 by Liggett & Myers Tobacco Company, which used the Stagville acreage to raise both field crops and livestock. In 1976 Liggett & Myers, in cooperation with the Historic Preservation Society of Durham, donated 71 of Stagville's core acres to the state, and Historic Stagville became a North Carolina State Historic Site. The gift included the Bennehan house as well as four Horton Grove slave houses (ca. 1851) and the enormous Stagville barn (1860). The result was the creation of the Stagville Center, a facility used for teaching historic preservation theory and technology and African American history. The remaining lands of Stagville farm were purchased in 1984 by Durham Research Properties. Together with Fairntosh and Snow Hill farms (both former Cameron plantations), it became the 5,200-acre Treyburn complex, one of the largest residential, commercial, and industrial developments in the Southeast.

References: Jean Bradley Anderson, *Piedmont Plantation: The Bennehan-Cameron Family and Lands in North Carolina* (1985); Richard F. Knapp, ed., *North Carolina's State Historic Sites: A Brief History and Status Report* (1995); Charles Richard Sanders, *The Cameron Plantation in Central North Carolina (1776–1973) and Its Founder Richard Bennehan* (1974).

Kenneth McFarland

Stamp Act, passed by the British Parliament on 22 Mar. 1765, incited many public protests in North Carolina and other colonies. The act placed a duty on all legal and business documents, licenses, cards, dice, and published materials in the American colonies. The duty stamp, long used in England as a source of revenue, was intended to raise £60,000 annually to meet the expenses of maintaining troops in the colonies to ensure their safety after the Seven Years War (1756–63). In an attempt to make the imperial system work more efficiently in America, England had established the New Colonial Policy in 1763. Under the policy, old laws were more vigorously enforced and new regulations were put into place. As a result, widespread feelings of revolt began to develop in the colonies.

Resistance began immediately after the passage of the Stamp Act, which the colonists considered a tyrannical violation of the principle of English liberty and taxation without representation. The Sons of Liberty in North Carolina formed one of the most active Patriot intercolonial associations opposing the Stamp Act. The Sons of Liberty contested the 1765 law because it was passed by Parliament instead of by the local assemblies, which was the tradition for tax bills. Members of the Sons of Liberty in North Carolina were influential citizens who gained support among the lower classes. They included such political leading lights as John Ashe, James Moore, Hugh Waddell, Cornelius Harnett, and other members of the Assembly as well as Moses John De Rosset, mayor of Wilmington, and Maurice Moore, an assemblyman and judge in Salisbury. Other members were planters and gentlemen from the rural areas of eastern North Carolina who organized and participated in mob protests alongside poorer farmers and townsmen, artisans, seamen, and the unemployed. Official opposition to the Stamp Act was restricted to the Sons of Liberty because Governor William Tryon prevented the election of delegates to the Stamp Act Congress in October 1765 that had been formed to challenge the act.

In October and November 1765 the Sons of Liberty kindled protests in New Bern, Cross Creek, and Edenton, but they were most successful in Wilmington. There, at a mob rally, the earl of Bute was burned in effigy for supporting the Stamp Act. The mob, 500 strong, drank to "LIBERTY, PROPERTY, and no STAMP DUTY." On Halloween night, citizens held a mock funeral for "liberty." The act was to go into effect the following day, but a crowd of nearly 400 forced the resignation of the newly appointed stamp master, William Houston. The mob also compelled Andrew Steuart, printer of Wilmington's *North-Carolina Gazette*, to resume printing on unstamped paper.

Alarmed by the influence of the Sons of Liberty, Tryon invited many of its leaders to dinner in an attempt to win their support for the tax. But this manipulation only strengthened their opposition. Commerce languished at the closed port of Cape Fear as Tryon insisted on compliance with the Stamp Act and the assemblymen openly opposed it.

Tensions boiled over in January 1766, when two ships, the *Dobbs* from Philadelphia and the *Patience* from St. Christopher, West Indies, sailed into Cape Fear. Neither had the mandatory stamped clearance papers from their previous ports. Under the command of Capt. Jacob Lobb, the British sloop *Viper* seized both ships, as well as the *Ruby* a few days later.

The seizure of the merchant ships by Lobb, and the decision of Attorney General Robert Jones to try the case in Halifax, Nova Scotia, caused a fierce reaction. Led by the Sons of Liberty, angry citizens of New Hanover, Brunswick, Bladen, and Duplin Counties drew up an "association" that pledged them "at any risque whatever" to prevent the Stamp Act's enforcement. Wilmington's merchants resolved to stop selling supplies to the British warships. A boat's crew that put into Wilmington to obtain supplies for the *Viper* and the *Diligence* was arrested and jailed, and the boat itself was dragged through the streets in a noisy demonstration. British authority was further defied by armed colonists who seized the customs house in Brunswick Town and occupied Fort Johnston. Also confronting Governor Tryon at his home, they demanded to see Lobb, whom they thought Tryon was protecting. Most of them departed when they learned that Lobb was on his ship.

On the afternoon of 20 February, rebel leaders met with Lobb, who was the senior British naval officer in the province, aboard the *Diligence*. Lobb agreed at last to release the seized vessels, on the grounds that they had not been able to acquire the necessary stamped paper at their previous ports, and to let the ships leave North Carolina without stamped papers. Lobb and several officials of the North Carolina colony were made to swear that they would make no effort to enforce the Stamp Act. The stock of stamped paper on the *Diligence* was eventually returned to England. The colonists had succeeded in preventing any enforcement of the hated Stamp Act in North Carolina, and their actions were influential in Parliament's decision to repeal the act in March 1766. During the next decade, as relations with Britain continued to deteriorate, colonists would remember the successful protest of the "gentlemen, freeholders, and inhabitants" of North Carolina.

References: Lindley S. Butler, *North Carolina and the Coming of the Revolution, 1763–1776* (1976); Robert L. Ganyard, *The Emergence of North Carolina's Revolutionary State Government* (1978); Edmund S. Morgan and Helen M. Morgan, *The Stamp Act Crisis* (1953).

Edward Smith
John F. Ansley
Additional research provided by Amelia Dees-Killette and David A. Norris.

Stanly County, located in the Piedmont region of North Carolina, was formed in 1841 from Montgomery County and named for John Stanly, a Speaker of the North Carolina House of Commons and, later, a U.S. congressman. Early inhabitants of the area included the Saura (Cheraw), Keyauwee, and Tuscarora Indians, followed by German, Dutch, Scotch-Irish and English settlers. Albemarle, the county seat, was incorporated in 1857 and named for George Monck, the duke of Albemarle and one of the Lords Proprietors. Other communities in the county include Badin, Misenheimer, Richfield, New London, Locust, Stanfield, and Lambert. The Yadkin–Pee Dee River, Badin Lake, the Uwharrie Mountains, Morrow Mountain, and Little and Cucumber Creeks are a few of Stanly County's significant physical features.

Pfeiffer University, which was founded in 1885, is located in Stanly County. The county also has a variety of historic landmarks, such as the "City of Albemarle" Antique Fire Engine (1922), the Hall House (1912), and the Albemarle Town Cemetery (1844). Cultural attractions include the Snuggs House Museum, the Morrow Mountain State Park and Museum, and the Uwharrie Players theater company. The county hosts annual events and festivals such as the Best of Badin Festival, Oktoberfest, the Norwood Arbor Day Festival, Beach Blast, Festival of Trees, and Downtown Albemarle Christmas.

Stanly County produces agricultural goods such as corn, soybeans, wheat, cotton, forage, and cattle and other livestock. Manufactured products include yarn, aircraft tires, ladies knitwear, manufactured homes, draperies, popcorn, and circuit breakers. Gold has also historically been mined in Stanly County. The Barringer Mine (1829) introduced subsurface gold mining to North Carolina. In 2004 the county's population was an estimated 59,000.

Reference: Ivey Lawrence Sharpe and Edgar Pepper Fletcher III, *Stanly County, USA: The Story of an Area and an Era, 1841–1991* (1990).

Jay Mazzocchi

SEE ALSO Pfeiffer University.

Stars and Bars served as the first national flag of the Confederate States of America from 4 Mar. 1861 until 1 May 1863. The name derived from the blue canton with a circle of white stars and the three red, white, and red bars in the flag's field. Early flags contain seven stars for the original seven states of the Confederacy. Later examples include 11 stars and occasionally even 12 or 13 for the border states of Missouri and Kentucky. Because of its close resemblance to the Union's Stars and Stripes, the design was dropped in 1863. Even in modern times, most native-born southerners erroneously refer to the Confederate army's post-1863 battle flag as the Stars and Bars.

Although the flag committee had specifically requested design proposals from the public, no official credit was given at the time for the originator of the Stars and Bars. In the early twentieth century controversy arose between two men, their families, and their home states over the question of who should receive credit for the flag's design. Maj. Orren Randolph Smith of North Carolina and Nicola Marschall of Alabama both claimed to have designed the Stars and Bars. Each man received support from his family, his home state, and local veterans and patriotic groups. Smith maintained he had submitted a model of the flag to the Confederate Provisional Congress in Montgomery in February 1861 and had flown an example of his design in Louisburg and made still another copy for a local militia company. Marschall stated he had presented several patterns, including the one adopted.

Both men produced notarized affidavits to support their claims. Smith's crusade was continued by his daughter after his death in 1913, and Marschall's by his family following his death in 1917. The legislative bodies of North Carolina and Alabama each passed resolutions endorsing the flag's designer as a citizen of their state. The controversy received such attention that the United Confederate Veterans, Sons of Confederate Veterans, and Confederate Southern Memorial Association formed committees to investigate the claims of the two men. All three organizations issued statements that while there was no conclusive evidence for either party, the greater evidence supported Smith's claim. Since then, new information has given additional credence to Marschall's claim. It is quite possible that the two men submitted designs so alike that each believed he was the father of the Stars and Bars.

References: Devereaux D. Cannon Jr., *The Flags of the Confederacy: An Illustrated History* (1988); Sons of Confederate Veterans, *The Stars and Bars: Report of the "Stars and Bars" Committee* (1917).

Tom Belton

State Art Society. The North Carolina State Art Society, precursor to the North Carolina Museum of Art, began with the work of the North Carolina Literary and Historical Association, a private organization founded by citizens committed to the state's cultural heritage. In 1924 a fine arts society was organized as a branch of the Literary and Historical Association. *Progressive Farmer* editor Clarence Poe chaired the society's executive committee, with publisher John F. Blair as founding president. In 1925 the society sponsored an art exhibition, and it held its first annual meeting a year later. In 1927 Blair persuaded Robert F. Phifer, a prominent New York industrialist and North Carolina native, to bequeath a gift of his private art collection and a substantial monetary endowment. The same year, the society was chartered by the state as the North Carolina State Art Society, Inc. In 1929 the legislature passed a law providing for a board of directors, but included no provision for state financial support.

The State Art Society received additional support in 1935, when the Works Progress Administration (WPA) designated Raleigh to receive funding through the Federal Art Project and to establish the first Federal Art Center in the nation. In 1939 the General Assembly provided the society with a state art gallery and office space in the former Supreme Court Building. Both the gallery and the art center continued until 1943 under the joint sponsorship of the society and the WPA. With federal aid about to end, the legislature of 1943 authorized the governor and the council of state to grant the society an annual allotment from the state's contingency and emergency fund. In the same year, Governor J. Melville Broughton assembled a citizen's committee to discuss establishing a permanent state art gallery.

In 1947 committee member Robert Lee Humber persuaded businessman and philanthropist Samuel H. Kress of New York to donate $1 million to North Carolina for the purchase of art, contingent upon the state's commitment of an equal amount.

In April 1951 Governor W. Kerr Scott praised the 1947 appropriation as an investment in visual education. The General Assembly voted to release the appropriation and the Kress Foundation confirmed its agreement. Later Governor Scott established the State Art Commission, provided for under the 1947 law. The commission, working in consultation with W. R. Valentiner, a noted art scholar, identified for purchase nearly 200 works of artists from American, British, French, Spanish, Flemish, and Dutch schools.

The 1953 General Assembly authorized conversion of the former State Highway Building into a museum and appropriated funds for its renovation, operation, and maintenance and for staff salaries. The North Carolina Museum of Art (NCMA) opened in April 1956. In 1960 the Kress Foundation released to the museum 71 works of art, the foundation's largest gift to any regional museum and second only to its gift to the National Gallery of Art.

The General Assembly of 1961 formally established the NCMA as a state institution and agency. Following the transfer of governance to the NCMA, the Art Society continued to promote the public's appreciation of art. Through memberships, private gifts, memorial funds, and bequests, the society also acquired works of art for the NCMA.

By the Executive Organization Act of 1971, the State Art Society and the NCMA were transferred to the Department of Art, Culture, and History, renamed by the Executive Organization Act of 1973 as the Department of Cultural Resources. In 1977 the General Assembly formally amended the statutes relating to the Art Society by deleting "State" from its official title. The revised law recognized the society's long-standing role as a membership arm of the NCMA and as a means for citizens to support the NCMA through individual or corporate memberships and participation in the society's diverse programs. Groundbreaking ceremonies for a new art museum were conducted in September 1977, a dedication was given in May of 1981, and a grand opening for the public was held in April 1983.

Reference: Lucy Cherry Crisp, *History of the North Carolina State Art Society* (1956).

Wiley J. Williams

SEE ALSO North Carolina Museum of Art.

State Bank of North Carolina was chartered in 1810 by the state legislature and opened its doors in early 1811. The bank began operations with a central bank in Raleigh, branches at Edenton, New Bern, Wilmington, Fayetteville, Tarboro, and Salisbury, and $1.6 million in capital. It was authorized to issue loans to the U.S. government for up to $100,000 and to any state for up to $50,000.

The War of 1812 disrupted banking in many states, including North Carolina, although the State Bank of North Carolina appears to have remained stable. However, it soon faced competition from the federal government. In 1817 Congress chartered the Second Bank of the United States (BUS) and opened a branch in Fayetteville. The BUS secured notes from banks and then submitted the notes with a demand for payment in specie. Banks were required to comply with such requests from note holders and often forced to call in their own loans to meet the obligations of the large number of notes held by the BUS.

In 1819 the state legislature extended the State Bank's charter to 1838, when it would then be liquidated. In 1832 the bank declared a stock dividend of 50 percent and announced that it was almost ready to cease operations. That same year Congress rechartered the BUS. The BUS required all state banks to redeem their notes upon demand in specie, which finally caused the liquidation of the State Bank.

The 1832–33 state legislature created a new entity, the Bank of North Carolina. The venture was not completed because private citizens failed to purchase enough stock. In the next legislative session the Bank of North Carolina's charter was remodeled, and the institution was given a new name: Bank of the State of North Carolina. By 1835 this state bank possessed ten branches, including branches in New Bern and Tarboro and a main office in Raleigh. After the liquidation of the Bank of the State of North Carolina in 1860, the 1858–59 session of the General Assembly chartered yet another new entity, the Bank of North Carolina. In 1861 this bank had branches in Wilmington, Fayetteville, Tarboro, Windsor, Milton, Charlotte, and Morganton. It went bankrupt when it was forced to pay off debts after the Civil War, providing at least one-quarter of the money in gold. Ultimately stockholders lost more than $1.5 million.

Although the names of these institutions changed, the people chartering, directing, and holding stock in North Carolina's state banks remained largely the same. On 23 June 1866 the state repealed all charters previously granted to state banks, including the Bank of North Carolina, which was liquidated. The Raleigh headquarters building of the pioneering State Bank of North Carolina still stands at the head of New Bern Avenue, just a block from the capitol building.

References: William A. Blair and W. A. Clark, *A Historical Sketch of Banking in North Carolina [and] The History of the Banking Institutions Organized in South Carolina Prior to 1860* (1899; repr., 1980); T. Harry Gatton, *Banking in North Carolina: A Narrative History* (1987).

W. Carson Dean

State Bureau of Investigation (SBI).

Created in 1925 by the General Assembly, the State Bureau of Identification was attached to the prison department, with the deputy warden designated as director. A fingerprint laboratory and offices of the bureau were located at the prison, and the bureau's budget would come from appropriations made to the prison. The bureau's responsibilities included receiving and collecting police information; locating, identifying, and keeping criminal records in the state and from other states; compiling and publishing such information and making it available to state and local law enforcement officials; conducting surveys and studies to determine the source of criminal conspiracies; and receiving the fingerprints of every felon from chiefs of police and sheriffs throughout the state.

In 1937 the legislature established the State Bureau of Identification and Investigation (SBII) and placed it under the direct supervision and control of the governor. To the responsibilities of the State Bureau of Identification were added the investigation of mob violence and election fraud and fraud involving social security, and, when ordered by the governor, assistance to local law enforcement. In addition, the SBII would maintain accurate statistics on crime and criminals in the state and receive monthly updates from the courts on all felony convictions. Reports on crime statistics, previously sent to the attorney general, would now go directly to the bureau, although the attorney general maintained the right to inspect and utilize them. The General Assembly also provided for the creation of a modern crime laboratory with professional staff.

When the legislature transferred the duties, responsibilities, materials, and funds of the SBII to a newly created Department of Justice in 1939, a new State Bureau of Investigation was organized within the department. Except for those duties pertaining to crime statistics, which were to be performed by the department's Division of Crime and Criminal Statistics, all SBII responsibilities would be assumed by the new bureau. To protect sources, evidence, and other information, the General Assembly of 1947 directed that SBI records on criminals and criminal activity could be made public only by court order or by request of district solicitors involved in criminal investigations.

During the 1950s and 1960s, a number of laws affecting the SBI were enacted. In 1961, for example, the bureau was authorized to license private detectives in the state, and in 1965, to investigate arson and damage to, theft of, or misuse of state-owned property.

Under the Executive Organization Act of 1971, the SBI became a division of the re-created Department of Justice. Legislation passed in 1987, 1989, and 1991 gave the SBI additional responsibilities, including background checks of appointees awaiting confirmation by the General Assembly, administration of the department's Police Information Network, and the immediate investigation of suspected child abuse.

The modern SBI is divided into three major areas of operation: Field Investigation, the Crime Laboratory, and the Division of Criminal Information. The latter brought the state's law enforcement community into the computer age through the great amount of up-to-date information it has collected and stored, such as driver's licenses, motor vehicle registrations, wanted and missing persons, stolen property, warrants, stolen vehicles, firearms registration, drug trafficking, and parole and probation histories.

Wiley J. Williams

State Capitol, located on Union Square in central Raleigh, has been the seat of North Carolina government since its completion in 1840. Raleigh had been chosen as the permanent capital city in 1792. After the statehouse on the site burned in 1831—and after the General Assembly had voted not to move the capital to Fayetteville—the legislature in 1833 appropriated funds to build a new capitol building where the old one had stood, incorporating a similar cross-shaped design with a central domed rotunda.

The neoclassical design of the North Carolina State Capitol reflects the contributions of several different architects, including Ithiel Town, Alexander Jackson Davis, William Nichols Jr., and William Strickland. Scottish-born David Paton ultimately supervised the majority of the construction and was responsible for many of the building's features. The resulting structure is considered one of the best-preserved examples of Greek Revival architecture in America. The capitol's interior reflects the features of ancient Greek temples, while its Doric-style exterior columns were modeled after the columns of the Parthenon. The chambers for the State Senate and House of Representatives are designed in similarly classical fashion.

The final cost of the State Capitol building was more than $532,000, a massive sum for the era. The completion of the building—and the simultaneous completion of the Raleigh & Gaston Railroad—was celebrated in Raleigh in June 1840 with dinners, dances, parades, and train rides enjoyed by crowds from throughout the state and beyond. The entire North Carolina state government was situated within the building's walls until 1888, when the Supreme Court and the State Library

relocated. In 1963 members of the General Assembly moved their offices to the State Legislative Building a block away. The modern-day capitol building houses the offices of the governor and lieutenant governor and their staffs.

A replica of an Antonio Canova statue of George Washington (the original of which was destroyed in the 1831 fire) stands in the center of the State Capitol rotunda, and many plaques and busts line the walls. On the grounds are a variety of monuments and statues, including those honoring North Carolina's three presidents (Andrew Jackson, James K. Polk, and Andrew Johnson), the women of the Confederacy, and veterans of the Civil War and the Vietnam War. The State Capitol building is a North Carolina State Historic Site.

References: Catherine W. Bishir, *North Carolina Architecture* (1990); Cecil D. Eliot, "The North Carolina State Capitol," *Southern Architect* 5 (June 1958); Richard F. Knapp, ed., *North Carolina's State Historic Sites: A Brief History and Status Report* (1995).

Wiley J. Williams

SEE ALSO Confederate Monuments; Union Square.

State Fair. The North Carolina State Fair, created in 1853 by the North Carolina State Agricultural Society, was designed as the society's principal agency for the promotion of both scientific agriculture and industry. The initial fair was held on a 16-acre site approximately one mile east of the capitol in Raleigh that both Wake County and the city of Raleigh helped the society acquire. In 1855 the state legislature began to provide the society with an annual subsidy of $1,500 to help cover the fair's operating costs. The fair was an immediate hit with North Carolinians and, under the leadership of society president Thomas Ruffin from 1855 to 1859, became a fixture on the state's social calendar. The Civil War closed the fair until 1869 when, led by Kemp P. Battle, the Agricultural Society re-

The North Carolina State Capitol. Photograph courtesy of North Carolina Division of Tourism, Film, and Sports Development.

The Halifax County Exhibit at the North Carolina Exposition of 1884, held in conjunction with the state fair that year. NCC.

The State Fairgrounds, 1928. Photograph by Ben Dixon MacNeill. NCC.

furbished the fairgrounds and sponsored a fair. In 1873, again aided by the city of Raleigh, the society obtained a new fairground of 55 acres located west of the capitol on Hillsborough Street and next to the North Carolina Railroad.

A virtually bankrupt Agricultural Society lacked the funds to conduct a fair in either 1926 or 1927, leading to a series of events that placed the fair under state control and at its present location. In 1927 the state legislature designated a 200-acre tract of land on Hillsborough Street near North Carolina State University as the fair's new home, and new buildings were constructed with funds from Wake County and the sale of the Agricultural Society's old fairgrounds and buildings. The fair reopened in 1928, and in 1930 it was placed under the control of the State Board of Agriculture. Seeking to avoid the expense of the fair, the state leased its operation to circus promoter George Hamid in 1930. In his 1936 successful campaign for state commissioner of agriculture, W. Kerr Scott promised to return the fair to state management, a promise he fulfilled in 1937 when he convinced the legislature to make the fair a division of the Department of Agriculture. The fair has continued to operate under the auspices of the Department of Agriculture since then, always enjoying strong gubernatorial support. Completion of the Dorton Arena in 1953, the fair's centennial year, provided a performance venue that was hailed as an architectural marvel and that quickly became the symbol of the modern fair. The 1970s also saw major additions to the fair's physical plant with the completion of the Graham,

Scott, and Holshouser Buildings, each named for a prominent North Carolina political figure.

From its inception, the state fair's emphasis was on instructing farmers in the latest advances in scientific agriculture. During the nineteenth century, the Agricultural Society sponsored lectures on a variety of scientific agriculture topics, including irrigation, crop rotation, chemistry in agriculture, and the need for practical agricultural education. Attendance at these lectures was poor, however, and well before the turn of the century the exhibit had replaced the lecture as the fair's primary method of educating the public. The fair became the state's premier showcase of blooded livestock, the most recent and efficient agricultural implements, and crop yields of superior quality and quantity produced with scientific farming methods. It remained the most important venue for introducing the state's farmers to the latest developments in agriculture even after the founding of other agricultural educational institutions, such as North Carolina State University, in the late nineteenth and early twentieth century. The fair, however, never became the significant showcase for industrial development that its founders had envisioned. While some industries did exhibit at the fair, the majority of exhibits continued to feature livestock, crops, and agricultural products, implements, and processes.

One of the Agricultural Society's original goals for the state fair was social, to provide an event that would attract and encourage interaction among people from all sections of the

Nicole Kirkland reacts to an affectionate lick from her Ayrshire cow Vavavavroom, winner of the summer yearling competition at the 2003 state fair. Photograph by John L. White. *Raleigh News and Observer.*

state. In this, the fair succeeded admirably, and its social appeal quickly vied with, and soon surpassed, its significance as an instructional institution. The antebellum fair attracted crowds with simple, homegrown entertainment. Marching bands and parading military units representing North Carolina cities, horse races, and political orations, frequently by the governor, became staples of the nineteenth-century fair. By the turn of the century, the modern midway had emerged, with its "freak" shows, girlie or "hoo-chee-koo-chee" shows, thrill shows, and featured attractions. Although independent attractions continued to play the fair, in the twentieth century the entertainment became even more organized. George Hamid, owner of a circus and Atlantic City's Million Dollar Pier, supplied circus-type acts for performances at the fair's grandstand from 1929 into the 1960s, and in 1948 the James E. Strates Shows contracted to supply most of the midway's shows and rides for a number of years. The fair also continued to attract politicians, including presidential candidates William Jennings Bryan and Franklin D. Roosevelt and Presidents Theodore Roosevelt, Harry Truman, Gerald Ford, and George H. W. Bush. Especially in election years, both the Republican and Democratic Parties continued to appeal to fairgoers, and many of their candidates for statewide office appeared there.

Fair week has ever been, and remains, an integral part of the social life of North Carolina and the capital city of Raleigh. It is a week of parties and politics, organizational meetings and reunions, college football and cultural events, and crowds of North Carolinians representing communities from every corner of the state. The Agriculture Society's concept of an instructional fair, modified by the public's demand for a festival, has resulted in a genuinely unique institution that belongs to and is esteemed by the citizenry of the state. In 2005 the North Carolina State Fair boasted an attendance of 796,000 visitors. Among the many events, food stands, and attractions available

to them were the "Village of Yesteryear," racing pigs, tractor pulls, demolition derbies, stunt shows, a petting zoo, dozens of rides, artistic and handicraft shops and displays, and a variety of musical performances.

Reference: Melton McLaurin, *The North Carolina State Fair: The First 150 Years* (2003).

Melton McLaurin

State Historic Sites Program began as a small operation in the North Carolina Department of Archives and History in Raleigh in October 1955. When the program was created, the General Assembly transferred to it, from the Department of Conservation and Development, responsibility for several historic sites; it soon administered a dozen sites across the state. In 1969 the State Historic Sites Program was joined by the state history museum and a fledgling historic preservation program to become the Division of Historic Sites and Museums. After five years it was split to form the North Carolina Museum of History and the Historic Sites Section, the latter agency combining traditional historic sites functions with federally funded statewide preservation and survey operations.

In October 1975, when there were 19 field units, the program was divided into three sections: Historic Sites, Historic Preservation (soon also to include archaeology), and State Capitol/Visitor Services. A few years later the Historic Sites Section subdivided into five branches: Administration, Archaeology, Interpretations, Operations, and Property Development. By 1995 the program employed 135 full-time staff members and had an operating budget of more than $5 million.

By 2006 the program included 27 State Historic Sites (see map, p. 1076), a home office, and two regional field offices. The Raleigh staff provides overall management and technical support for the historic sites, which stretch from Manteo to Asheville. Regional management teams, composed of personnel elected periodically from field sites, represent their sites and regions in planning priorities across the state and working with the teams in the home office. Of the sites, the most heavily visited are Fort Fisher, the North Carolina Transportation Museum, and Reed Gold Mine. Collectively, the sites annually offer more than 75 special programs and events, ranging from Civil War reenactments to dramas and festivals.

Reference: Richard F. Knapp, ed., *North Carolina's State Historic Sites: A Brief History and Status Report* (1995).

Richard F. Knapp

State Legislative Building in Raleigh was authorized by the North Carolina General Assembly of 1959 to be built as a permanent home for the legislative branch of the state government. The 1957 General Assembly had created the State Legislative Building Commission of seven members, chaired

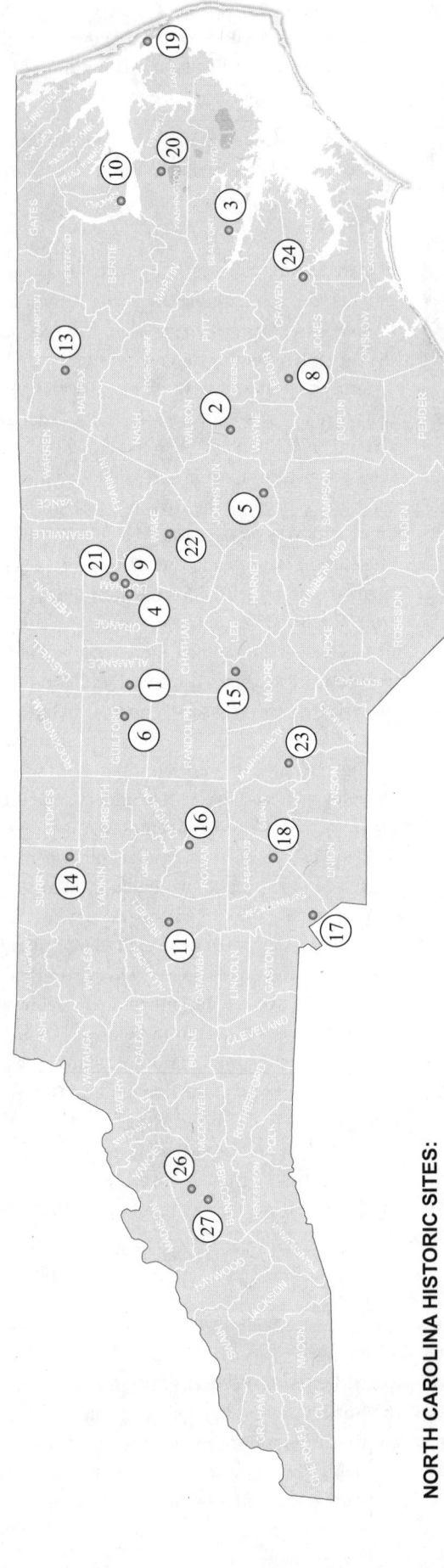

NORTH CAROLINA HISTORIC SITES:

1. Alamance Battleground
2. Charles B. Aycock Birthplace
3. Historic Bath
4. Bennett Place
5. Bentonville Battlefield
6. Charlotte Hawkins Brown Museum
7. Brunswick Town / Fort Anderson
8. CSS *Neuse*
9. Duke Homestead
10. Historic Edenton
11. Fort Dobbs
12. Fort Fisher
13. Historic Halifax
14. Horne Creek Living Historical Farm
15. House in the Horseshoe
16. North Carolina Transportation Museum
17. James K. Polk Memorial
18. Reed Gold Mine
19. Roanoke Island Festival Park
20. Somerset Place
21. Historic Stagville
22. State Capitol
23. Town Creek Indian Mound
24. Tryon Palace Historic Sites & Gardens
25. USS *North Carolina* Battleship Memorial
26. Zebulon B. Vance Birthplace
27. Thomas Wolfe Memorial

State Historic Sites. Map by Mark Anderson Moore, courtesy NCOA&H.

by Thomas J. White. The bill creating this commission emphasized that the purpose of the building was to house only the legislative branch and its auxiliaries. The Legislative Building Commission was given authority to acquire land, hire architects, approve plans and specifications, enter into contracts for the state, and expend funds for the construction, furnishing, and equipping of the building for $4.5 million. The architects for the building were Edward D. Stone, John Holloway, and Ralph Reeves. The commission chose a 5.5-acre site a block north of the State Capitol. It contained two city blocks; Halifax Street between Jones and Lane Streets was closed to join the blocks. The site is bounded by Jones, Salisbury, Lane, and Wilmington Streets. Bids for the building were received in December 1960, and construction was begun by Rea Construction Company in early 1961. In 1961 the General Assembly added another $1 million for the building. Total costs were $5.5 million, or $1.24 for every citizen of North Carolina at the time. The building was first occupied by the General Assembly on 6 Feb. 1963.

The State Legislative Building was described by one reporter at the structure's dedication as North Carolina's "pagoda" because of its copper-covered, pyramidal roofs and indoor and outdoor gardens. It is a modern, functional, and artistic building with elements of historical style and structure. The building is 242 feet square, on a 340-foot base podium of North Carolina granite, with walls and columns of Vermont marble. The columns form a colonnade surrounding the building reaching 24 feet from the podium to the roof of the second floor.

A 28-foot terrazzo mosaic of the Great Seal of North Carolina covers the podium leading to the main entrance. Inside, the red-carpeted, 22-foot-wide stairs extend to the third floor and the public galleries of the House and Senate. Unique garden courtyards are surrounded by committee rooms and members' offices. The House and Senate chambers are on the second floor. Each chamber is 5,180 square feet; they occupy the west and east wings and are divided by a rotunda. When their main brass doors are opened, the presiding officers of each chamber face each other. Massive brass chandeliers accent the natural lighting provided by windows and skylights. American walnut, brass, red carpets, and gold-and-black upholstery add to the building's character. Renovations to the building in the 1980s created more offices and expanded meeting rooms.

In 1982 the Legislative Office Building on Jones Street opened. Approximately one-half of the members of the General Assembly have moved their offices there, as have several of the support divisions of legislative services. The west side of the Legislative Building faces a long plaza surrounded by government office buildings, and to the east are the North Carolina Museum of History and the North Carolina Museum of Natural Sciences.

Reference: Ralph Bernard Reeves Jr., ed., *The Dedication of the State Legislative Building, Raleigh, North Carolina* (1966).

W. Lee Johnston Jr.

State Parks. The North Carolina State Parks System began in 1915, when Mount Mitchell, the highest mountain peak east of the Mississippi River, was bought by the state to save it from destructive lumbering practices. This purchase was followed in 1924 by the acquisition of the Fort Macon Military Reservation. In the late 1920s and 1930s, a number of other areas were acquired as well. As there was no specific agency to administer them, they were placed under the State Division of Forestry until 1935, when a Branch of State Parks was created within the Division of Forestry.

Between the years 1934 to 1941, North Carolina's early parks experienced a period of rapid development through Depression-era New Deal programs such as the Civilian Conservation Corps and the Works Progress Administration. Following the end of World War II, high public demand for recreation facilities spurred continued growth of the state parks system and the expansion of the Branch of State Parks into a separate Division of State Parks in 1948. Since 1969, the state parks system has mushroomed in size thanks to the easing of former legislative restrictions on acquiring land for new state parks.

Canoeing at Umstead State Park near Raleigh. Photograph courtesy of North Carolina Division of Tourism, Film, and Sports Development.

Rock formations tower above the surrounding landscape at Hanging Rock State Park in Stokes County. Photograph courtesy of North Carolina Division of Tourism, Film, and Sports Development.

At the beginning of the twenty-first century, the North Carolina State Parks System, under the administration of the Division of Parks and Recreation, oversaw 50 units contained within three categories: state parks, state recreation areas, and state natural areas. These units contain more than 135,000 acres of land stretching from the mountains to the sea. The system is administered to serve the citizens of North Carolina and their guests by protecting and preserving scenic and natural areas of statewide importance, providing many unique opportunities for recreation as well as scientific and cultural research.

North Carolina's state parks and their years of acquisition are Mount Mitchell (1915); Fort Macon (1924); Morrow Mountain (1935); Hanging Rock (1936); Jones Lake, Singletary Lake, and Pettigrew (1939); William B. Umstead (1943); Cliffs of the Neuse (1945); Hammocks Beach (1961); Lake Norman (1962); Pilot Mountain (1968); Carolina Beach (1969); Stone Mountain (1969); Raven Rock (1970); Crowder's Mountain, Eno River, Medoc Mountain, and Merchant's Millpond (1973); Goose Creek (1974); Jockey's Ridge (1975); South Mountains (1975);

Lake Waccamaw (1976); New River (1977); Lake James (1987); Lumber River (1989); and Gorges (1999). The four State Recreation Areas are Kerr Lake (1951), Jordan Lake (1982), Falls Lake (1983), and Fort Fisher (1986). In 2002 the North Carolina Division of Parks and Recreation began a long-range planning initiative called New Parks for a New Century, which by 2006 had identified 44 sites across the state as potential new recreation areas, natural areas, and parks.

The New River State Park in Ashe County was begun after a protest of a proposed power dam on the New River, which flows north from the northwestern North Carolina Blue Ridge Mountains. It is likely the oldest river in North America and is thought to have been named by Peter Jefferson, Thomas Jefferson's father, when he surveyed the North Carolina–Virginia border in 1749. The General Assembly voted in 1975 to name 26.5 miles of the New River a State Scenic River, the same portion becoming part of the national Wild and Scenic River System in August 1976. North Carolina then created the state park, which includes the 26.5 miles of the New River, declared in 1998 an American Heritage River.

The first state natural area, Weymouth Woods Sandhills Nature Preserve, was donated to the state in 1963. The third, the Theodore Roosevelt State Natural Area, was donated by Roosevelt's heirs in 1971. Unlike those of a state park, the long-term management objectives of a state natural area may include little or no public facilities and very limited public access. A few of the state natural areas are open to the public and staffed; some are managed as satellites of staffed state park units, while others are managed by other conservation agencies under leases or special agreements. The North Carolina state natural areas, with years of acquisition, are Weymouth Woods (1963); Bushy Lake (1970); Theodore Roosevelt (1971); Dismal Swamp and Chowan Swamp (1974); Masonboro Island (1976); Hemlock Bluffs and Mitchells Mill (1976); Bald Head Island (1979); Mount Jefferson (originally a state park, converted to a natural area in 1993); Run Hill (1995); Occoneechee Mountain (1997); Beech Creek Bog (2001); Elk Knob (2001); and Lower Haw River (2003).

In 1976 the Natural Heritage Program was created within the Division of Parks and Recreation. The purpose of this program was to create a statewide inventory of natural diversity and rare species and to make recommendations for the protection of outstanding areas and rare species habitats. To encourage the protection of important natural areas, the program also developed a State Registry of Natural Heritage Areas. Owners of natural areas may register a site by entering into voluntary agreements with the state to protect and manage the natural area for its natural heritage values. The registry provides a vehicle for program staff to inform landowners about the special ecological values on their property and provides recognition for those landowners who agree to protect those

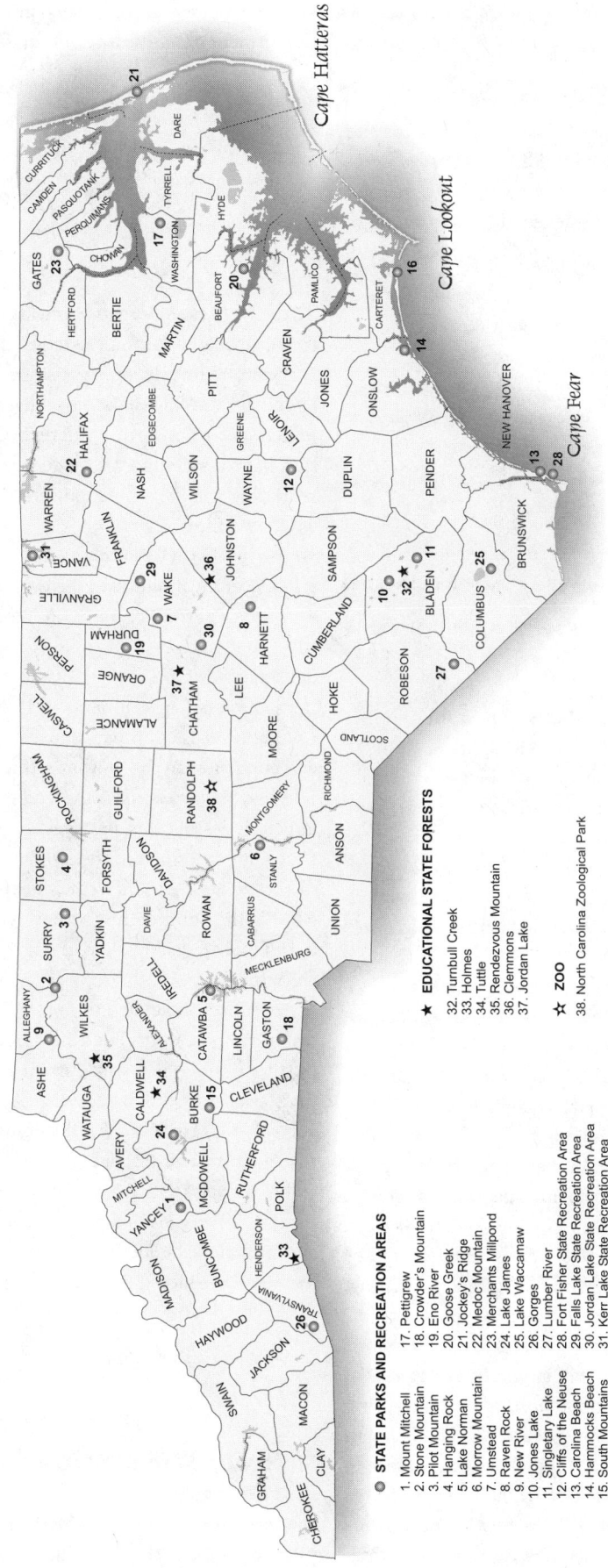

Cape Hatteras

Cape Lookout

Cape Fear

● STATE PARKS AND RECREATION AREAS

1. Mount Mitchell
2. Stone Mountain
3. Pilot Mountain
4. Hanging Rock
5. Lake Norman
6. Morrow Mountain
7. Umstead
8. Raven Rock
9. New River
10. Jones Lake
11. Singletary Lake
12. Cliffs of the Neuse
13. Carolina Beach
14. Hammocks Beach
15. South Mountains
16. Fort Macon
17. Pettigrew
18. Crowder's Mountain
19. Eno River
20. Goose Creek
21. Jockey's Ridge
22. Medoc Mountain
23. Merchants Millpond
24. Lake James
25. Lake Waccamaw
26. Gorges
27. Lumber River
28. Fort Fisher State Recreation Area
29. Falls Lake State Recreation Area
30. Jordan Lake State Recreation Area
31. Kerr Lake State Recreation Area

★ EDUCATIONAL STATE FORESTS

32. Turnbull Creek
33. Holmes
34. Tuttle
35. Rendezvous Mountain
36. Clemmons
37. Jordan Lake

☆ ZOO

38. North Carolina Zoological Park

State parks system. Map by Mark Anderson Moore, courtesy NCOA&H.

values. There are now 357 sites totaling 598,764 acres on the Registry of Natural Heritage Areas, including both public and privately owned lands.

Other state land preservation efforts include the Wildlife Game Lands program, which encompasses 333,000 acres and is managed by the North Carolina Wildlife Resources Commission; Educational State Forests, of which there are six; and the North Carolina Coastal Reserve, which includes a total of eight sites, four of which are within the federal National Estuarine Research Reserve.

References: Association of Southeastern State Parks Directors, *Histories of Southeastern State Parks Systems* (1977); Walter C. Biggs Jr. and James F. Parnell, *State Parks of North Carolina* (1989); North Carolina Division of Parks and Recreation, *System-wide Plan for the North Carolina State Parks System* (2000); Thomas J. Schoenbaum, *The New River Controversy* (1979).

Gordon Neal Diem
Carol A. Tingley
Additional research by Paul Branch and Elizabeth H. Conner.

SEE ALSO Mount Mitchell; New River; Weymouth Woods Sandhills Nature Preserve.

State Planning Board was established in North Carolina during the Great Depression as part of President Franklin D. Roosevelt's New Deal. In 1933 Secretary of the Interior Harold Ickes created the National Planning Board to advise him in the preparation of the public works program of the National Industrial Recovery Act. The National Planning Board sought to stimulate state planning by offering the services of a consultant to those states that formed planning boards. Most states complied.

Governor J. C. B. Ehringhaus, encouraged by the state engineer and the North Carolina League of Municipalities, appointed the first State Planning Board in North Carolina in 1935 to facilitate the flow of federal funds to the state. The state board cooperated with the National Planning Board on its national surveys on public works, drainage, and recreation as well as a program to develop the Southern Highlands Region. It designated as major state projects three national programs: rural electrification, control of soil erosion, and rural rehabilitation. The State Planning Board also conducted studies on transportation, industry, agriculture, commercial fishing, population trends, public welfare, and housing for blacks.

As the fear of postwar economic crises subsided, interest in state planning waned. Across the nation, interest in "economic development," with its connotations of free enterprise, was rising. When the State Planning Board was abolished in 1947, its functions of economic development and assistance to local planning boards were continued by the North Carolina Department of Conservation and Development. In the 1960s the idea of a state planning agency was revived, and subsequently a State Planning Division was established within the Department of Administration in Raleigh.

References: Koleen "Kay" Alice Haire, "The Evolution of City and Regional Planning in North Carolina, 1900–1950" (Ph.D. diss., Duke University, 1967); Albert Lepawsky, *State Planning and Economic Development in the South* (1949); Howard W. Odum, *Folk, Region, and Society: Selected Papers of Howard W. Odum* (1964).

Kay Haire Huggins

State Rights. Before its ratification, much of the opposition to the U.S. Constitution related to the fear of giving too much authority to the federal government. Such fear was based largely on the high-handed policies of the English king and Parliament prior to the American Revolution. The Constitution was thus a compromise document, with the 13 states surrendering many of their powers to the federal government while retaining others.

In 1793 North Carolinian James Iredell delivered an important dissenting opinion in the U.S. Supreme Court on the state rights view of the Constitution. When a majority of the Court ruled that an individual could sue a state in federal court, Iredell insisted that the Constitution did not grant that power to the national government, and he reiterated the view of the Constitution as a compact between sovereign states. This view was confirmed in the Eleventh Amendment.

From the 1790s until the end of the Civil War, there was almost incessant conflict over the issue of state rights, with states and regions on one side and the U.S. government on the other. Southerners were concerned about northern disregard for the rights of the southern states to manage their internal affairs, especially where those affairs concerned the ownership of slaves.

Secession, which led to the Civil War, was the most severe test of the state rights doctrine. After the conflict, the principle of state rights was invoked in an effort to abolish civil rights for blacks and other minority groups, and to prevent the passage of child labor and antilynching laws. After World War II the federal government's ability to control subsidies to the states, as well as its regulation of interstate commerce, effectively nullified most assertions of state rights. The federal subsidy program extended its influence into many areas that were formerly considered the prerogative of the states.

Reference: Hugh T. Lefler and Albert R. Newsome, *North Carolina: The History of a Southern State* (3rd ed., 1973).

Wiley J. Williams

Statesville Record and Landmark, among the oldest daily newspapers in North Carolina, began as the *Landmark*, a weekly, on 19 June 1874. John B. Hussey, a native of Duplin County, was the first editor and publisher. In early 1877 he sold the paper to J. S. Ramsey but remained its editor. Three years later Ramsey sold out, and a new, dynamic editor, Joseph Pearson Caldwell, took over. During the next 12 years Caldwell turned the *Landmark* into what many contemporaries called "the best newspaper in North Carolina, weekly or daily." The *Landmark* became a kind of "news Bible" for Piedmont North Carolinians, maintaining a progressive editorial policy coupled with a fiscally conservative Democratic stance.

Through the *Landmark*, Caldwell, a Statesville native, promoted progress in the area. As a result of his influence, Statesville was one of the first small cities in North Carolina to have an electric light plant. Caldwell also promoted manufacturing as a "way of life for the Piedmont and economic salvation for Statesville." In January 1892, in partnership with D. A. Tompkins, he took over the *Charlotte Chronicle*, changing the name back to the *Observer*. Caldwell sold a half interest in the *Landmark* to Rufus Reid Clark, a Mooresville native who had been on the staff for almost a decade. As editor, Clark continued the progressive editorials and industrial promotion that had marked Caldwell's tenure. In 1895 he changed the weekly *Landmark* to a semiweekly, printing issues every Monday and Thursday. In 1908, after buying Caldwell's remaining half interest in the paper, Clark increased the paper's size to eight pages, putting local news on page one instead of the third page.

In 1907 Pegram A. Bryant joined the *Landmark* staff as a local editor but soon became business manager. In 1918 he bought the paper from Clark and continued as publisher until 1953. Instead of turning the semiweekly into a daily, Bryant began a new publication on 1 Sept. 1920 called the *Statesville Daily* while continuing to publish the Monday and Thursday issues of the *Landmark*.

Beginning in 1931, Bryant experienced competition from a new semiweekly, the *Statesville Record*. This paper had several owners until 1938, when Chester E. Middlesworth, a newspaper publisher from Shamokin, Pa., bought it and rapidly expanded its readership, making it a daily in early 1941 and changing its name to the *Statesville Daily Record*. Middlesworth died unexpectedly in 1946, and his widow brought in J. P. Huskins of Greensboro to serve as editor and general manager with an ownership interest. Huskins, a strong Democrat and brilliant editorial writer who also served in the North Carolina House of Representatives, moved the newspaper forward in both readership and technology. In 1949 the *Statesville Daily Record* became the first newspaper in the state to utilize the new Fairchild scanning engraving system. This permitted a photo engraving to be readied for printing within minutes, whereas the established zinc metal engravings took hours.

Local competition ended in 1953, when the *Landmark* and the *Statesville Daily* were purchased by the *Statesville Daily Record* and merged into one daily afternoon publication, the *Statesville Record and Landmark*. In September 1979 Park Communications, a large media conglomerate, bought the *Record and Landmark*, which became a "flagship publication" among more than 132 newspapers in the Park group. Media General, a major communications company, acquired Park Communications in early 1997.

Reference: Homer Keever, *100th Anniversary—The* Landmark (1974).

Chester Paul Middlesworth

State v. John Mann, an 1829 North Carolina Supreme Court decision, is probably the most notorious judicial opinion on the relationship between master and slave ever rendered by a state court. Written by Justice Thomas Ruffin, *Mann* stands for the proposition that masters were not subject to criminal indictment for a battery committed on their slaves.

John Mann, the defendant, had hired a slave woman, Lydia, from her owner. When Lydia fled minor punishment, Mann shot and wounded her. The grand jury of Chowan County indicted Mann for battery; superior court judge Joseph J. Daniel (later Ruffin's colleague on the North Carolina Supreme Court) charged the petit jurors assembled to hear the evidence that if they believed the punishment inflicted by the defendant was cruel, unwarranted by, and disproportional to Lydia's offense, the defendant was guilty under law because he was not Lydia's true master. The jury returned a verdict of guilty, and Mann appealed to the state supreme court.

That Ruffin took considerable pains over *Mann* is evidenced by the three drafts of the opinion that survive among his personal papers. Reversing Mann's conviction, Ruffin reasoned that a slave is "one doomed in his own person, and his posterity, to live without knowledge, and without the capacity to make anything his own, and to toil that another may reap the fruits." A slave would accept such a fate only if his master wielded "uncontrolled authority over [the slave's] body." If this authority were subjected to judicial scrutiny, it would naturally be diminished and the relationship between master and slave destroyed.

Passages from Ruffin's opinion were used by northern abolitionists as evidence of a slaveholder's admission of the moral perversity of slavery. Indeed, Ruffin, one of the largest planters in Alamance and Orange Counties and the owner of many slaves, began his *Mann* opinion with the observation that "the struggle . . . in the judge's own breast between the feelings of the man and the duties of the magistrate is a severe one, presenting a strong temptation to put aside such questions, if it be possible." One commentator gloated over Ruffin's discomfort: "The moral wrong of slavery is . . . admitted, along with the most resolute determination to support it, by not allowing the rights of the master to come under judicial investigation."

By contrast, Harriet Beecher Stowe, who later wrote the

celebrated antislavery novel *Uncle Tom's Cabin* (1852), sounded a note of respect for Ruffin's candor, reporting that *Mann* had excited "strong interest" among English judges because of its "scorn of dissimulation" and "severe strength and grandeur . . . which approached to the heroic." To later historians *Mann*, with its clearly unsettling implications, expounded a doctrine of absolute dominion of master over slave that served as a reference point for southern appellate judges throughout the antebellum period.

Although some of Ruffin's language in *Mann* may have been excessive, the holding of the case was in fact limited; technically, the decision merely settled the legal consequences of a nonfatal battery of a slave by a master or hirer. After *Mann*, a master could still be indicted for killing a slave; ten years later this possibility was chiseled directly into North Carolina law by Ruffin, who had by then become chief justice of the state supreme court.

A further restraint on a hirer's or overseer's authority left intact by *Mann* was the threat of civil suit for damages. The master as plaintiff could seek to have civil liability imposed on a hirer or overseer for conduct similar to that of John Mann toward Lydia. Civil liability could have been only a marginal deterrent to such behavior, however, because *Mann* left masters —the primary employers of slaves—considerable discretion to punish slaves as their own sense of humanity dictated. By removing nonfatal batteries on slaves from the scrutiny of judicial eyes, *Mann*, with its notable blend of squeamishness and severity, cast a ghastly light over North Carolina slave law and the reputation of its author that has endured for more than a century and a half.

References: Patrick S. Brady, "Slavery, Race, and the Criminal Law in Antebellum North Carolina: A Reconsideration of the Thomas Ruffin Court," *North Carolina Central Law Journal* 10 (1978–79); Eugene D. Genovese, *Roll, Jordan, Roll: The World the Slaves Made* (1974); A. E. Keir Nash, "A More Equitable Past? Southern Supreme Courts and the Protection of the Antebellum Negro," *North Carolina Law Review* 48 (1969).

Martin H. Brinkley

State v. Manuel, argued before the North Carolina Supreme Court in 1838, was the first case to decide that a free black person was a citizen of the state. The case was initiated in Sampson County, where manumitted slave William Manuel was convicted of assaulting a white man and fined $20. Since Manuel did not have the money to pay the fine, the court determined that the sheriff of Sampson County "should hire out the defendant to any person who would pay the said fine for his services for the shortest space of time."

Manuel's attorney appealed to the state supreme court on the grounds that state law permitted a debtor to plead "insolvency from imprisonment for debt" and thus be free to find

employment and pay off the debt on his own. Manuel did not have this option. In the court's opinion, written by William Gaston, the defendant had not been allowed to declare insolvency because of the color of his skin, a justification that violated the guarantees of the state constitution. The 18-page opinion discussed the history and demise of the concept of imprisonment for debt, whether a fine was in fact a debt, the nature of citizenship in the British Empire and the United States, the purposes of constitutional government, and the rights and duties of citizens under a constitution.

Although Manuel still had to pay the fine for his crime, the North Carolina Supreme Court decision permitted him to declare insolvency. More important, as a free black, he was legally a citizen of the state and thus could not be denied any rights guaranteed under the constitution.

Reference: J. H. Schauinger, *William Gaston: Carolinian* (1949).

Alexander R. Stoesen

State v. Negro Will, a celebrated 1834 North Carolina Supreme Court decision standing for the general proposition that if a slave in self-defense, under circumstances strongly calculated to excite passions of terror and resentment, kills his overseer or master, the homicide is not murder but manslaughter. Justice William Gaston wrote the opinion for a unanimous court.

On 22 Jan. 1834 Negro Will, a slave of James S. Battle of Edgecombe County, engaged in an altercation with Battle's slave foreman, Allen, regarding the possession of a hoe. As a result of the dispute, Will broke the hoe and then went to a nearby cotton mill to work. On learning of Will's conduct, Battle's white overseer, Baxter, seized his loaded gun, mounted his horse, and ordered Allen to follow with a cowhide whip. Accosted by Baxter, Will attempted to run away, whereupon Baxter emptied the gun into his back. The wounded fugitive continued to flee but was intercepted by Baxter. In the ensuing struggle, Will delivered a fatal knife wound to Baxter's arm. The Edgecombe County Superior Court found Will guilty of murder in the first degree and sentenced him to die.

After investigating the matter, Battle became convinced that Will had acted in self-defense under extreme provocation. Determined to see that Will received justice, the slave owner engaged two leading members of the bar, Bartholomew F. Moore and George Washington Mordecai, to represent him; to Moore, Battle paid the extraordinary fee of $1,000. Moore and Mordecai took Will's appeal to the state supreme court, where they were opposed by Attorney General J. R. Daniel.

In his brief and oral argument before the supreme court, Moore demanded that the law display a humane attitude toward Will. He maintained that Chief Justice Thomas Ruffin's 1829 decision in *State v. John Mann*, in which Ruffin had written that "the power of the master must be absolute in order to render the submission of the slave perfect," was abhorrent and at variance with prior case law. Although it disagreed with Moore on this point, the court unanimously reversed Will's conviction.

Writing for himself, Ruffin, and Justice Joseph J. Daniel, Justice Gaston reasoned that, had the homicide been committed by free man upon free man, it could have been no more than manslaughter; if between master and apprentice, the deed could have been attributed to "a brief fury" that did not leave the mind capable of the sort of calm, rational thought required for murder. In forceful language, he continued: "If the passions of the slave be excited into unlawful violence by the inhumanity of a master . . . is it a conclusion of law that such passion must spring from diabolical malice?"

Gaston's opinion was lauded by moderate antislavery forces throughout the country; passages were quoted in prominent newspapers and law journals. In silent tribute, abolitionist commentators ignored the decision, presumably because it had scant potential for propaganda. Beginning in the 1890s, historians praised *Will*'s "humanity;" the case supposedly did much to abate the harshness of prior law, such as Ruffin's opinion in *Mann*.

References: John S. Bassett, "The Case of the State v. Will," *Trinity College Historical Papers* 2 (1898); George Gordon Battle, "The State of North Carolina v. Negro Will, a Slave of James S. Battle: A Cause Célèbre of Antebellum Times," *Virginia Law Review* 12 (1924); Patrick S. Brady, "Slavery, Race, and the Criminal Law in Antebellum North Carolina: A Reconsideration of the Thomas Ruffin Court," *North Carolina Central Law Journal* 10 (1978–79); J. Herman Schauinger, "William Gaston and the Supreme Court of North Carolina," *NCHR* 21 (April 1944).

Martin H. Brinkley

SEE ALSO *State v. John Mann*.

State v. Worth. Daniel Worth, a Wesleyan Methodist minister, came to North Carolina in 1857 as an agent of the American Missionary Society. By 1859, 130 new members had joined the churches he served in Guilford and Randolph Counties. His popularity enabled him to denounce the use of liquor, tobacco, and "other fripperies," but his ultimate motive was to attack slavery and to disseminate abolitionist literature. He insisted that religion and antislavery sentiments should be synonymous. In 1859 Worth began to distribute *The Impending Crisis of the South*, a vigorous antislavery book written by Hinton Rowan Helper. Worth's action might have been ignored earlier, but John Brown's raid on Harpers Ferry in the same year had raised fear, anxiety, and passions to a fever pitch throughout the South.

Helper's book was considered an "incendiary publication" under the North Carolina code, which had been amended in 1830 in response to David Walker's *Appeal to the Coloured Citizens of the World* calling for a black rebellion to crush slavery. In late 1859 Worth sold and delivered a copy of *Impending Crisis* to George W. Bowman, a white resident of Guilford County. Subsequently indicted for distributing an incendiary publication that urged slaves to insurrection—a capital offense—he was arrested, refused counsel, and heard 15 witnesses describe his activities. He was bound over for the spring term of Guilford Superior Court on a $5,000 bond, which was then doubled to ensure "good behavior."

Before being tried in Greensboro, Worth was tried in Randolph County and found guilty of the same charge. He was sentenced to a year in jail, but the requirement that he be flogged was dropped. On 27 Apr. 1860 a second trial was held in Greensboro, where this time he was represented by counsel. Attorneys for the defense argued that the 1830 statute did not contain the word "book," but rather used the words "pamphlet or paper" and thus did not refer to *Impending Crisis*. Moreover, the sale to Bowman was a personal matter that did not constitute "distribution." Finally, since Bowman was white and had not given the book to slaves or free blacks, nor read it aloud in their presence, he had not violated the law.

The state contended that Helper's book was an incendiary publication covered by the law given the statute's use of the word "paper." The state also demonstrated that Worth had distributed copies of the book to persons other than Bowman and argued that it was unnecessary to prove that slaves or free blacks had been his target because of the book's "wicked intent" to "excite slaves to insurrection." Worth was convicted, and an appeal to the North Carolina Supreme Court failed.

Authorities set Worth's bond at the purposely low figure of $3,000 in the hope that he would leave the state before sentencing and thus avoid becoming a martyr for the abolitionist cause. This is exactly what happened: Worth jumped bail and was spirited through Virginia to the North. Although he continued to work as an abolitionist, his commitment was always overshadowed by the fact that he had been unwilling to accept a very public imprisonment that might have greatly aided the antislavery movement.

References: Gail Williams O'Brien, *The Legal Fraternity and the Making of a New South Community, 1848–1882* (1986); Nobel J. Tolbert, "Daniel Worth: Tar Heel Abolitionist," *NCHR* 39 (July 1962).

Alexander R. Stoesen

SEE ALSO *Impending Crisis of the South*; Walker's *Appeal*.

Stay Law is a piece of legislation that gives debtors extra time to pay their creditors before their property is seized for payment. Several states passed such a law, beginning in the years of economic upheaval after the American Revolution and continuing through much of the nineteenth century. North Carolina passed a stay law as early as 1794, and it remained in effect for more than 20 years. This statute called for debtors to have extensions of from 20 days to 6 months to pay their debts after a judgment of a justice of the peace. A stay law in 1809 gave similar extensions for debt payment until 1 Apr. 1810.

To protect debtors racked by economic hard times caused by the War of 1812, the General Assembly passed another stay law on 16 Dec. 1812. That statute, also known as the "suspension act," was to remain in effect until 1 Feb. 1814, but it was overturned as unconstitutional by the North Carolina Supreme Court in the case of *Jones v. Crittenden*. A stay law of the early Reconstruction era was also struck down as unconstitutional in 1869.

David A. Norris

Steamboats. In North Carolina, the concept of travel by steamboat was first introduced in 1815, when Archibald D. Murphey chaired a legislative committee on inland navigation. The first steamboat entered the state in 1818, when the New Bern Steamboat Company welcomed the arrival of the *Norfolk* to New Bern. The steamer was built in Norfolk, Va., the city for which it was named.

Three weeks behind the *Norfolk*, the first steamer built in North Carolina was launched at Fayetteville by James Seawell. The *Henrietta* was a hardy 100-foot side-wheeler, with a 15-foot beam and a 4-foot draught. The ship could carry 100 tons of cargo and 30 passengers. Seawell entered the business with a seven-year monopoly on steam trade between Fayetteville and Wilmington, a typical arrangement provided early steamboat companies by the state to encourage their business.

The *Henrietta* was almost a prototype of North Carolina steamers. In size and shape, local steamboats did not change significantly over the next 100 years. They were built with a simple flat-bottom hull and usually two-story decking, the bottom for freight and fuel and the top for passenger cabins. A pilot house was mounted forward on the second deck; the engine and boiler rooms were below, one fore, the other aft.

The river steamer *Cape Fear* docked at Fayetteville, ca. 1875. Rare Book, Manuscript, and Special Collections Library, Duke University.

All were shallow-draught to accommodate the low waters of the state's rivers and sounds. The *Henrietta* was atypical only in its 42-year length of service. Most steamers had a much shorter life due to boiler explosions and other accidents that frequently sank them.

The second steamboat built in North Carolina and the third to begin operations in the state was the *Prometheus*, a small stern-wheeler constructed at Beaufort by Otway Burns, naval hero and noted privateer in the War of 1812. The *Prometheus* plied the waters of the Cape Fear River between Wilmington and Smithville (modern Southport). The steamboat's small engine was no match for the strong coastal currents encountered at the mouth of the river, and the vessel was soon retired from service. Its most notable run may have been in 1819, when it ferried President James Monroe from Wilmington to Smithville as part of his Southern tour.

Other steamboat companies, including the Old Dominion Line, Cape Fear Steamboat Company, and Lutterloh Line, were established in the 1820s and 1830s. Their steamers ranged in size from the 40-ton *Union* to the exceptional 460-ton *Southern Star*, built at Murfreesboro. Speed and tonnage were important factors in the competitive steamboat business. Vessels made slow time down the Cape Fear, Black, Tar, and Neuse Rivers, but they transported freight and passengers faster and more easily than wagons.

Most North Carolina steamboats were 80 to 120 feet long, with a 12- to 15-foot beam. They were constructed without ribs, using instead side planking fastened by bolts. They were powered by 50- to 100-horsepower steam engines, and the majority were stern-wheelers, since they maneuvered better in the crooked and narrow rivers of North Carolina than did side-wheelers. The rivers were so twisting in places that lines were attached to trees along the banks to hand-pull or windlass a steamer around a curve.

Steamboat technology improved as the nineteenth century progressed, but North Carolina generally stayed with what was known and trusted. Some midcentury steamers were more elaborate and could carry more cargo, but they essentially followed the formula initially set by the *Henrietta*.

Wilmington increasingly drew the steamship trade to its docks in the second half of the nineteenth century. Not only local steamers tied daily to its wharves, but also foreign-built hulls from Britain and Europe called at the port city. The New York–Wilmington SS Line offered weekly passage aboard the *Fanita*, *Pioneer*, and *Benefactor*.

In 1896 the North Carolina Board of Agriculture listed 37 steamship companies and owners that were registered in the state with an aggregate value of $289,000. Steamboats carried mail and passengers to the Outer Banks, opened commerce between inland cities and coastal ports, and brought foreign trade to the state. The cumbersome vessels dominated freight and passenger service in eastern North Carolina until the combustible engine brought roads to the coastal plain in the 1920s.

References: Tucker R. Littleton, "North Carolina's First Steamboat," *The State* (November 1977); Thomas H. Sloan, *Inland Steam Navigation in North Carolina, 1818–1900* (1971); Herbert S. Southgate, "Pioneer Skipper," *The State* (October 1985).

Rodney D. Barfield
David A. Norris

SEE ALSO Dan River Steam Navigation Company; French Broad Steamboat Company.

Step Dancing, or "soulstepping," is a form of competitive dance exhibition developed by African American fraternities and sororities in North Carolina and other southern states. The dances feature synchronized movements and percussive beats. Step dancing is a showcase for exhibiting a team's individual style and showing its unity. Its origins can be found in the traditions of competitive drill teams and marching bands and take their movement patterns from African and slave dances such as patting juba and ring shouts.

While the beginning of step dancing dates back to older fraternity rituals, the term "stepping" became popular in the 1980s. Popularized on the campuses of historically black colleges and universities, the informal shows evolved to public exhibitions, often used as fund-raisers for charitable causes. One of the most popular step shows, the East Coast Step Show, originated on the campus of North Carolina's Fayetteville State University in 1998. College step teams come from throughout the East and South to compete, with the prize money designated for the winning team's community projects.

In recent years, step dancing organizations in the United States have established cultural ties to the Gumboot dancers of South Africa through Step Afrika!, an organization that hosts an international festival each year in Soweto, South Africa.

References: Elizabeth C. Fine, *Soulstepping: African American Step Shows* (2003); Susan Eike Spalding and Jane Harris Woodside, eds., *Communities in Motion: Dance, Community and Tradition in America's Southeast and Beyond* (1995).

Cecelia Moore

Stickball, a Native American game similar to lacrosse and called "anetsa" by the Cherokee Indians, was once played throughout the United States. The game was played by two teams with an equal number of men. The object was to get a tiny, walnut-sized, leather-covered ball through a goal using sticks shaped somewhat like small tennis rackets. The size of the field depended on the size of the teams and the availability of suitable terrain. The Cherokees were among the first to play consistently on a field about 100 yards in length, although some fields were much larger. There was no time limit; the first team to score 12 times won. Any strategy to score was acceptable, including biting, choking, and even banging each other on the head with the rackets. There were no time-outs or substitutions, but if a player was knocked out his opponent had to leave the game also.

Although a less violent form of stickball is played primarily as entertainment today, the Cherokees once considered anetsa as the "little brother of war," an important training experience for future conflicts. As a precursor to such training, Cherokees sometimes participated in a pregame ritual in which players were scratched with a bone set in eagle feathers until they bled from 100 different wounds. There is evidence that the Cherokees once settled a land dispute with another tribe on the outcome of a stickball game. These contests, often surrounded by much ceremony, were the state's first large-scale spectator sporting events, attracting huge crowds, including local whites, during the nineteenth century. Many whites, in fact, adopted the game, which came to be played by Confederate soldiers and timber workers in the Mountain region of North Carolina. Stickball remains an important link between modern times and early Cherokee society.

Reference: James Mooney, "Cherokee Ball Play," *Journal of Cherokee Studies* 7 (Spring 1982).

William L. Anderson
Additional research provided by Charles Battle.

Stokes County, located in the Piedmont region of north central North Carolina, was formed in 1789 from Surry County and named for Capt. John Stokes, a Revolutionary War officer and a member of the North Carolina House of Commons. It is partially bordered by the state of Virginia. Early inhabitants of the area included the Saura (Cheraw) and other Siouan Indians; European settlers included the Scotch-Irish and the Moravians and other Germans. The county seat, Danbury, was named after a plantation belonging to Governor Alexander Martin; it was incorporated only in 1957, although it had been considered the county seat since 1849, when it replaced Germantown. Other Stokes County communities include King, Walnut Cove, Pinnacle, Gap, Lawsonville, Prestonville, and Meadows. Hanging Rock State Park is one of Stokes County's most popular natural destinations. Other notable physical features include the Dan and Yadkin Rivers, Beaverdam Creek, Hidden Falls, and Window Falls.

Among the historic sites and landmarks located in Stokes County are Historic Danbury, which preserves several fine examples of early twentieth-century architecture; Moratock Iron Furnace, built in 1843; the Rock House, the ruins of a two-story fieldstone structure built around 1770; and Sheppard's Mill, built in the early twentieth century. County cultural institutions include the Dan River Arts Market and the Stokes Art

Council. The county hosts several festivals and annual events, such as the Stokes County Agricultural Fair, Kingfest, Festival on the Dan, King Christmas Parade, the Stokes County Craft Fair, and the Stokes Stomp.

Stokes County generates forest products and agricultural commodities such as tobacco, livestock, and corn. Manufactured products include copper tubing, elastic, cotton yarn, and medical equipment. The estimated population of Stokes County was just under 46,000 in 2004.

Jay Mazzocchi

Stoneman's Raid, conducted by the Union's Maj. Gen. George Stoneman in late March and April 1865, constituted one of the last military operations in the Civil War. Stoneman's cavalry, about 6,000 strong, entered North Carolina from Tennessee in late March, intending to cut off Gen. Robert E. Lee's escape routes in the event of his expected defeat in Virginia. Moving rapidly through Boone and Wilkesboro, Stoneman veered northward into Virginia, severing rail lines around Lynchburg and Christiansburg. By 9 April (coincidentally the day of Lee's surrender) his men were back in North Carolina. At Germanton, north of Salem, he divided his command.

One brigade under Brig. Gen. William J. Palmer was detailed to capture Salem and then move eastward to cut railroads north and south of Greensboro. This was done swiftly, one column burning a bridge over Reedy Fork north of Greensboro, apparently only minutes after Jefferson Davis and the Confederate cabinet, fleeing Virginia, had passed over it. Other columns destroyed trains, bridges, a gun factory, and commissary stores between Greensboro and High Point. Still others sent to destroy rail bridges toward Lexington encountered stiff resistance and withdrew. All of this occurred on 11 April.

Meanwhile, Stoneman took the larger part of his command southward, rejoining Palmer's Brigade on 12 April at Salisbury. There they repeated the previous day's work on a much larger scale. Salisbury had become a major collection point for Confederate supplies and armaments of every kind. The Federal troops destroyed several miles of railroad track together with depots, warehouses, mills, arms and ammunition, and the recently vacated Salisbury Prison. The destruction consumed two days, and flames could be seen for 15 miles at night. Strong Confederate resistance beat off efforts to destroy a long railroad bridge over the Yadkin River north of town. Having accomplished most of what he set out to do, Stoneman headed back toward Tennessee. On the way his men burned more provisions at Statesville and Newton and another long railroad bridge over the Catawba River just inside South Carolina. They also plundered residents of Morganton and Asheville, although they generally confined themselves to legitimate military targets. The raid ended on 26 April, having lasted almost one month.

References: John G. Barrett, *The Civil War in North Carolina* (1963); Chris J. Hartley, " 'Like an Avalanche': George Stoneman's 1865 Cavalry Raid," *Civil War Regiments* 6 (1998); Ina W. Van Noppen, "The Significance of Stoneman's Last Raid," NCHR 38 (January 1961).

Allen W. Trelease

Stonewall Jackson Manual Training and Industrial School.

In late nineteenth-century North Carolina, young men convicted of criminal offenses were subjected to the same harsh sentences and punishments as hardened adult criminals. In 1890 James P. Cook, a resident of Concord and editor of the local daily newspaper, the *Standard*, witnessed a sentence of "three years and six months at hard labor on the Cabarrus County Chain Gang" imposed on a 13-year-old boy convicted of petty theft. Distressed at the sight of the lad taken from the courtroom chained to a convicted adult criminal, Cook devoted the next 17 years to a campaign for the establishment of a training school for boys.

Supporters of such a school, particularly the benevolent organization King's Daughters of North Carolina, finally convinced the state legislature to embrace their "radical" idea. A special committee of the King's Daughters in 1906 successfully campaigned for the school through public meetings, newspaper articles and editorials, and the dissemination of pamphlets describing the success of reformatories in other states. Success in the legislature was finally assured when sponsors of the bill gained the support of the Confederate veterans in the General Assembly, proposing that the new institution be named in honor of beloved Confederate general Thomas J. "Stonewall" Jackson, who died during the Battle of Chancellorsville. The act establishing the Stonewall Jackson Manual Training and Industrial School in Concord became law on 2 March 1907.

Governor R. B. Glenn named James P. Cook to the school's first board of trustees. The board then elected Cook as its chairman, a position he held for almost two decades. At a public meeting in Concord on 30 Sept. 1907, the citizens of Cabarrus County appointed a committee to raise funds and locate land to be donated to the training school trustees to secure placement of the new school within Cabarrus County. The fund-raising effort was successful, and the school was located on a site that is now within the Concord city limits. In November 1907, the executive committee of the trustees named Professor Walter Thompson, then superintendent of Concord public schools, the first superintendent of instruction at Stonewall Jackson Training School.

From the beginning, school officials insisted that a quality education be offered to the young people committed to their care. The school was proud of its staff of certified teachers, its library, and its visual aids and resource materials. In addition to more traditional academic instruction, young men re-

Boys at the Stonewall Jackson Training School, ca. 1937. NCC. Original photograph owned by H. Lee Pharr.

ceived training in a useful trade. Students worked in the shoe shop, machine shop, sewing room, print shop, barber shop, textile plant, and on the school's farm or in its dairy barn. For many years, students in the print shop published a magazine, called the *UPLIFT*, under the supervision of printing instructor Jesse C. Fisher. Young men learned modern farming techniques raising their food in school fields. Others helped tend the herd of dairy cows that furnished milk and ice cream for the school. "Big Buck," a prize-winning bull, presided over a large herd of Hertford beef cattle that furnished meat for the school kitchen.

Legislative policy eventually shifted away from the incarceration of juvenile offenders found guilty of "status" offenses such as truancy and undisciplined behavior. As a result, the Stonewall Jackson population had dwindled by the early 2000s to an average of 150 young men, from a peak population of 500 juveniles at the school's zenith. The crimes committed by juveniles confined at the school tend to be much more violent than

20 years ago; many are drug- and weapons-related offenses. Consequently, a fence has been installed to prevent students from leaving the grounds.

Reference: Samuel G. Hawfield, *History of Stonewall Jackson Manual Training and Industrial School* (1946).

Clarence E. Horton Jr.

Streetcars, also known as street railways or trolley cars, began operating in Wilmington and Raleigh in 1887. Initially drawn by horses, they were soon powered by electricity, first in Asheville in 1889 and the next year in Winston and Salem; Wilmington made the conversion to electric streetcars in 1892. Charlotte's trolley cars appeared in 1891, and those in Durham and Greensboro began operating in 1902. Concord, Gastonia, Goldsboro, High Point, Salisbury, Spencer, Southern Pines, and Pinehurst also featured streetcars.

To satisfy riders, some streetcar companies had two sets of

A crowded streetcar in Concord, ca. 1910. NCC.

cars—closed ones for winter weather and breezy, open ones for the summer. Many companies developed outlying amusement parks (sometimes called "electric parks"), picnic areas, or similar attractions to draw prospective riders. Wrightsville Beach's interurban line from Wilmington included the well-known Lumina dance pavilion, and the Charlotte street railway's Lakewood Park even provided a small lake for sailboating. With some exceptions, most of North Carolina's streetcars were replaced by motor buses by the 1930s.

References: Michael J. Dunn, "Age of the Trolley Cars," *The State* (1 July 1969); William S. Powell, *North Carolina through Four Centuries* (1989).

Wiley J. Williams

Stretch-Out was a term applied by textile mill workers when additional production quotas were applied by their supervisors after a previous quota had been met. The workers were pressured to increase production with little or no further incentive.

Reference: Jacquelyn Dowd Hall and others, *Like a Family: The Making of a Southern Cotton Mill World* (1987).

William S. Powell

Strolling Players consisting of actors, musicians, jugglers, comedians, and other entertainers who moved about from place to place to perform apparently appeared first in North Carolina in Currituck in 1702. Anthony Aston, a British lawyer, arrived in Charles Towne (Charleston, S.C.) that year "full of Lice, Shame, Poverty, Nakedness, and Hunger," and there "turned Player and Poet, and wrote one Play on the subject of the Country." He then went to the Albemarle region of North Carolina, where he remained a month through the generosity of Allen and Abraham Waights. No copy of his play is known to have survived.

A group called the American Company of Comedians

toured North Carolina in the fall of 1787, presenting productions in Halifax, New Bern, and Wilmington. The latter place boasted an "elegant theatre." A company of comedians from New York toured eastern North Carolina in 1788. At various times singers, dancers, acrobats, rope-dancers, ventriloquists, and exhibitors of natural and artificial curiosities, wax works, and scientific apparatus also appeared throughout the state.

A well-educated but poor young London actor, William Augustus Richards, was a member of a company of actors passing through North Carolina when the group folded after appearing in Warrenton. Richards became a teacher in a local academy and in 1796, while teaching in the preparatory school at the University of North Carolina in Chapel Hill, he and his young charges presented two plays at commencement. These have been described as "the first dramatic performances ever given at any state university in America." The significance of that statement is considerably reduced, however, when it is acknowledged that there were no other state universities at that time.

Reference: Archibald Henderson, "Strolling Players in Eighteenth Century North Carolina," *The Carolina Play-book* 15 (March, June 1942).

William S. Powell

Student Nonviolent Coordinating Committee (SNCC) was one of the most influential organizations to participate in the civil rights movement of the 1960s. Although SNCC is best known for its role in the Freedom Rides of 1961 and is often associated with voter registration and other civil rights activism in Alabama and Mississippi, it had significant roots in North Carolina. After a sit-in by four black students from the North Carolina Agricultural and Technical College in Greensboro on 1 Feb. 1960 sparked a wave of similar demonstrations around the state and region, the Southern Christian Leadership Conference (SCLC) quickly moved to consolidate grassroots student activism and map a strategy for further protests. At the urging of its interim executive director, Ella Baker, the SCLC hosted a conference at Shaw University in Raleigh on 15–17 Apr. 1960 to unite student activists who had been newly energized by the sit-in movement.

Baker, a Norfolk, Va., native who had grown up in Littleton, N.C., before attending Shaw, persuaded the SCLC to bring the conference to her alma mater and to provide gas money to students who attended. Once the meeting convened, Baker successfully advocated that the nascent organization be student-directed rather than under the SCLC umbrella. Representatives of other bodies, such as the National Association for the Advancement of Colored People (NAACP) and the Congress of Racial Equality, also were present, lobbying students to affiliate with their groups. The weekend keynote speaker, the Reverend James Lawson of Nashville, criticized established

SNCC organizer Ella Baker, 1964.
Photograph copyright 1978 George Ballis/Take Stock.

groups such as the NAACP as too slow and conservative. In a rousing sermon, the Reverend Martin Luther King Jr. addressed 1,600 conference delegates and Raleigh citizens in Memorial Auditorium on Saturday night, urging students to adopt the nonviolent philosophy of Mohandas K. Gandhi and, if necessary, face jail time for peaceful protest. The conference concluded with the formal creation of SNCC.

The committee held its first meeting in Atlanta on 13 May 1960, hired one staffer, and set up an office independent of the SCLC. Its first president was Marion Barry, a Fisk University student who later became mayor of Washington, D.C. That fall, SNCC helped coordinate sit-ins and other acts of nonviolent civil disobedience throughout the South. In the spring of 1961, following a U.S. Supreme Court decision ending segregation of the transportation industry, SNCC members confronted violent opposition as Freedom Riders on buses that carried integrated groups of passengers from Washington, D.C., and Nashville through the Carolinas, Georgia, Alabama, and Mississippi. Later, the activists played a key role in the 1963 March on Washington and constituted the "shock troops" and frontline leaders during the Mississippi Freedom Summer of 1964. Historian John Hope Franklin called them "probably the most courageous and the most selfless" civil rights workers.

In 1966 Stokely Carmichael, a former Shaw student and a participant in the 1961 Freedom Rides, was elected chairman of SNCC. Under his leadership, the committee grew increasingly militant, with significant links to the Black Power movement. SNCC was disbanded in 1970.

References: Taylor Branch, *Parting the Waters: America in the King Years, 1954–1963* (1988); Ellen Cantarow, *Moving the Mountain: Women Working for Social Change* (1980); Clayborne Carson, *In Struggle: SNCC and the Black Awakening of the 1960s* (1981); David J. Garrow, *Bearing the Cross: Martin Luther King, Jr., and the Southern Christian Leadership Conference* (1986); Mary King, *Freedom Song:*

A Personal Story of the Civil Rights Movement (1987); Barbara Ransby, *Ella Baker and the Black Freedom Movement: A Radical Democratic Vision* (2003); Howard Zinn, *SNCC: The New Abolitionists* (1964).

Michael Hill

Submarine Attacks. The North Carolina coast saw considerable activity by German submarines, or U-boats, in both World War I and World War II. Because the state was located midway along the eastern seaboard, enemy U-boats could easily attack merchant ships moving north or south along the coastal sea lanes. With ships sometimes sunk within sight of the coast and wreckage and bodies washed ashore, North Carolinians living along the barrier islands from Currituck to Cape Fear experienced the wars with an immediacy denied their inland compatriots. U-boats targeted predominantly merchant ships and trade vessels, rather than naval warships, waging economic warfare against the Allies and hoping to strangle Allied war production.

In World War I, Germany's belated development of long-range submarines delayed their deployment, but beginning in May 1918, three of six large cruiser/minelayer class U-boats operating off the U.S. coast made attacks off North Carolina. The first U-boat to arrive, *U-151*, sank four Allied ships during 5–9 June in the first raids off North Carolina by an enemy warship since the War of 1812. During 4–6 Aug. 1918, the *U-140* sank four other ships, including the Diamond Shoals lightship. In mid-August, the minelayer *U-117* planted mines across the shipping lanes at Wimble Shoals, north of Cape Hatteras, sinking the British tanker *Mirlo*. The *U-117* also sank another ship off North Carolina before returning home. The U-boat attacks ended only when the armistice took effect in November 1918.

The destruction caused by this handful of submarines in 1918 was minor compared to the carnage wrought by German U-boats during World War II. Within weeks of the nation's entry into the conflict in December 1941, the Battle of the Atlantic reached U.S. waters, the German navy recognizing the exposure and vulnerability of American merchant ships along the Atlantic Coast. Once again the North Carolina coast became a major operational area; in 1942 the region off Cape Hatteras earned the nickname "Torpedo Junction."

A fully loaded oil tanker, the *Allen Jackson*, is believed to have been the first victim of the U-boat attacks along the North Carolina coast, sinking about 60 miles off Cape Hatteras on 18 Jan. 1942. The first German submarine operation against the U.S. coast began in January 1942, when five large Type IX U-boats cruised between Nova Scotia and Cape Hatteras. Of these, the *U-66* sank five ships off North Carolina, including the Canadian passenger liner *Lady Hawkins*, with its 250 crew and passengers lost at sea; the *U-123* sank or damaged four

A U.S. Navy blimp protects an Atlantic convoy in 1943. During World War II, Weeksville was a base for blimps that patrolled the Atlantic Ocean off the coasts of North Carolina and Virginia for German submarines. National Archives (neg. 65729, U.S. Navy).

ships; and the *U-125* sank one ship. As fast as they could be refitted and readied for sea, other U-boats, including those of the medium Type VII classes that carried enough fuel to reach the U.S. coast, kept up the pressure. In February 1942 U-boats sank eight more Allied ships within a zone up to 200 miles off the North Carolina coast.

In March 1942 larger numbers of U-boats operated off North Carolina, sinking or damaging 25 ships (the *U-124* alone wrecked 5 of them). U-boat attacks previously concentrated north and east of Cape Hatteras were now occurring off Cape Lookout and Cape Fear as the German submarines cruised south along the coast. The strikes were close to shore because the shipping lanes had been tightened as a defensive measure. Cape Hatteras was judged to be so dangerous that merchant ships were ordered to pass it only in daylight to lessen the likelihood of attack.

During the last 20 days of March 1942, U-boats claimed 23 ships off the North Carolina coast. In the single worst night for shipping of the war, U-boats destroyed 5 ships on 18 March. In April, attacks from as many as 17 different U-boats reached a peak, with 27 Allied ships sunk or damaged within the 200-mile zone off North Carolina. The first four months of 1942 saw nearly 70 ships torpedoed and sent to the ocean bottom. In fact, more than 90 percent of the ships lost at Torpedo Junction during the four years of submarine attacks went down between January and July 1942.

Antisubmarine defenses along the coast tightened, however, and the tide began to turn. Local fishing and pleasure boats, converted into patrol boats, joined additional aircraft, U.S. Navy and Coast Guard antisubmarine vessels, and even a number of British armed trawlers to provide greater protection to merchant ships and local convoys. Sheltered moorings where ships could anchor overnight and form convoys were created at Cape Lookout in April 1942 and at Cape Hatteras the following month. Thereafter, the German toll on shipping diminished significantly.

On 14 Apr. 1942 the destroyer *Roper* sank the *U-85*, the first U-boat to be sunk by the U.S. Navy, off Nag's Head. In May the navy began the formal convoying of merchant ships, causing U-boat sinkings to fall off dramatically. Two warships were sunk during the month, but so was a second U-boat, the *U-352*, off Cape Lookout. In June ten Allied ships were torpedoed, but in July the number dropped to three. Two U-boats, *U-701* and *U-576*, were sunk, and a third was severely damaged by air attack. At this point the Germans withdrew most of their U-boats from the East Coast because of their lack of success in penetrating the tightened defenses. For the rest of the war, German operations along the East Coast were limited to occasional nuisance raids by individual submarines.

In 1943 only one navy warship and two merchant ships were sunk off North Carolina; one ship was damaged in 1944. In April 1945 a number of U-boats mounted a final operation against the U.S. coast, sinking one ship and damaging another off North Carolina. The *U-548* was sunk in this action.

References: James T. Cheatham, *The Atlantic Turkey Shoot: U-boats off the Outer Banks in World War II* (1990); Michael Gannon, *Operation Drumbeat: The Dramatic True Story of Germany's First U-Boat Attacks along the American Coast in World War II* (1990); David Stick, *Graveyard of the Atlantic: Shipwrecks of the North Carolina Coast* (1952).

Paul Branch
Daniel W. Barefoot

SEE ALSO Coast Guard, U.S.; *Mirlo* Rescue.

Substitutes (Civil War).

As the Civil War dragged on and enthusiasm for volunteer enlistments lagged, both sides resorted to conscription to fill their ranks. This practice became even less popular and seemed even more unfair because the draft laws allowed men of means to hire substitutes to take their places. Under the Confederate conscription law, a draftee could evade service by hiring someone who was exempt from the draft to replace him—someone under or over the mandatory conscription age, one whose trade or profession exempted him, or a foreign national. Generally, the "principal," as those supplying substitutes were called, paid a fee to the government as well as a large sum to his substitute. Prices for hiring substitutes in the South reportedly ranged as high as $3,000 in specie and even higher in Confederate currency. At such prices, only the wealthy could afford substitutes. The substitute laws reinforced the perception that the war was "a rich man's war and a poor man's fight." Many soldiers earning scanty military pay simmered with anger over serving with the richly rewarded substitutes, whom they considered little better than mercenaries. Other men served halfheartedly, hoping somehow to hire substitutes of their own.

Although many soldiers and civilians thought that it was wrong to hire substitutes, the practice was widespread. The number of substitutes in the Confederate army is difficult to determine, though some wartime estimates ranged from 50,000 to 150,000. Newspapers carried many ads from men seeking, or offering service as, substitutes. There were even "brokers" who took fees for finding substitutes. Many substitutes quickly deserted or were unfit for military service due to their age, poor health, or alcoholism. Because of such abuses, the Confederate Congress tightened the rules regarding substitution and finally abolished the practice. Men who had hired substitutes found themselves again subject to conscription when the laws changed. They were given a specified length of time to report for duty, and their substitutes still in the service were retained as well.

North Carolina became embroiled in controversy with the Confederate War Department over these changes in the draft laws. In February 1864 Chief Justice Richmond M. Pearson of the North Carolina Supreme Court ruled that it was unconstitutional to force men into the army if they had furnished substitutes. Eventually, however, the full state supreme court reversed Pearson's judgment, confirming the Confederate government's right to annul substitute contracts.

References: Gordon B. McKinney, *Zeb Vance: North Carolina's Civil War Governor and Gilded Age Political Leader* (2004); Memory F. Mitchell, *Legal Aspects of Conscription and Exemption in North Carolina, 1861–1865* (1965); Albert Burton Moore, *Conscription and Conflict in the Confederacy* (1924); Richard E. Yates, *The Confederacy and Zeb Vance* (1958).

David A. Norris

Subtreasury Plan

was among the leading political issues of the 1890s in North Carolina and other states. The plan sought to revolutionize credit and marketing arrangements for staple crops, particularly cotton. A prominent version of the Subtreasury Plan required the federal government to construct warehouses, or subtreasuries, in counties that marketed crops with an annual value of $500,000. At harvest, farmers could deposit crops in the warehouses and receive negotiable federal notes for up to 80 percent of the value of the crops. The farmer had one year to sell the crop and then satisfy the notes and a 1 percent per year interest charge. A fee for storage would also be charged. Unsold crops could be liquidated at auction.

The Subtreasury Plan was radical because agricultural credit in North Carolina in the 1890s was generally provided by merchants and landlords. Credit from these sources, which was necessary to see a farmer through the growing season, was always expensive and often extortionate. Consequently, the Subtreasury Plan sought to revolutionize rural credit by transferring its burdens and profits from local private lenders to the national government.

The political force behind the Subtreasury Plan was the Farmers' Alliance. The national Alliance, influenced by the failure of its marketing and purchasing cooperatives, endorsed the scheme at its 1889 meeting in St. Louis. Historians have disagreed about the origins of the Subtreasury Plan. Some have credited it to Charles W. Macune, a leading member of the Farmers' Alliance in Texas, who presented the plan to delegates in St. Louis. Others have stressed the contribution of Harry Skinner, a Greenville lawyer. Skinner, who would later become a Populist congressman from North Carolina, wrote articles in 1888 and 1889 supporting a government warehouse and note scheme. One of his writings, published in *Frank Leslie's Magazine* in November 1889, was read to the Farmers' Alliance delegates in St. Louis. North Carolinian Leonidas L. Polk, a member of the committee led by Macune that presented the Subtreasury Plan in St. Louis, was aware of Skinner's proposal.

The Subtreasury Plan became the leading political issue among North Carolina Alliance members in 1890. The principal figures in the ensuing contest were Polk, president of the national Farmers' Alliance, and North Carolina's Democratic U.S. senator, Zebulon B. Vance. In early 1890 Vance agreed to introduce the Subtreasury Plan in the Senate, but he expressed his personal opposition to the proposal. Vance's opinion, based on his conviction that Congress lacked constitutional authority to loan money directly to citizens, prompted a storm of criticism from the official organ of the North Carolina Alliance, Polk's Raleigh-based *Progressive Farmer*. The attack on the Democratic leader, in turn, engendered hostility toward Polk by opponents of the Alliance and even many Alliance members. Polk's antagonists portrayed the Subtreasury Plan as a wild and paternalistic interference by government in private finance. Although the Subtreasury Plan was endorsed by several local North Carolina Democratic platforms in 1890, and Alliance members extracted pledges of support for it from many Democratic candidates, the controversy divided the party in the elections held that year.

The Polk-Vance conflict was the high point of Subtreasury Plan politics. To be sure, thousands of North Carolina farmers continued to promote the plan after 1890. It was reaffirmed directly or indirectly at each of the Alliance's national and state meetings until 1896. Moreover, with the appearance of North Carolina Populism in 1892, the idea won formal support from a statewide political organization. North Carolina Populists defended the Subtreasury Plan through the 1890s. Yet widespread discussion of the plan by the Alliance and the Populist Party declined sharply after 1892, and the measure was never seriously considered by Congress.

The Alliance's Subtreasury Plan pitted private lenders and laissez faire ideologues against the credit and marketing interests of a new class of commercial farmers. North Carolina growers were caught between the crippling forces of expensive credit and declining prices and the presumed benefits of commercial production, and many concluded that the Subtreasury Plan was a panacea. However, the plan had significant weaknesses. First, it would serve to encourage, not control, production. There was therefore no guarantee that the federal government would not be left with enormous bad debts if prices driven by increasing surpluses declined below the value of the notes. The Subtreasury Plan also did not address other market constraints, including purchasing monopolies and foreign competition that could push prices below the cost of production despite the availability of inexpensive loans. On the other hand, conservatives' unequivocal rejection of the plan was unwarranted. The crop financing system of the late nineteenth century was patently unjust, and the government's currency contraction policy was equally antidebtor. By creating general access to cheap capital, and by seeking to create more equitable markets, the Subtreasury Plan attempted to resolve two genuine hindrances to southern rural capitalism. The plan's proponents hoped to create both more competition and greater financial independence for farmers by arguing that the government was the appropriate dispenser of rural credit.

References: John D. Hicks, *The Populist Revolt: A History of the Farmers' Alliance and the People's Party* (1931); Robert C. McMath Jr., *Populist Vanguard: A History of the Southern Farmers' Alliance* (1975); Lala C. Steelman, *The North Carolina Farmers' Alliance: A Political History, 1887–1893* (1985).

James L. Hunt

Suedliche Post (Southern Post) was a short-lived German-language newspaper founded in Goldsboro in 1869 by August Heinrich Christian Julius Bonitz (who usually signed his name Julius A. Bonitz). The newspaper sought to benefit the substantial number of German-speaking residents in the area. Bonitz, a native of Clausthal-Zellerfeld, Germany, had settled in Goldsboro, where he published the successful English-language papers *Daily Rough Notes* and the *Messenger*, both stoutly "advocating the supremacy of the white race." In addition, he was agent for the Carolina Immigration Association, which encouraged foreigners to buy land in North Carolina; the *Die Suedliche Post* was its "adopted organ." Only three issues of the paper are known to be preserved; the last (number 9) was dated 27 Nov. 1869.

H. G. Jones

Sugar Act, officially titled the American Revenue Act, was passed by British Parliament in April 1764 in cooperation with Prime Minister George Grenville. The act was intended to reduce the large national debt incurred during the Seven Years War (1756–63), to raise money to garrison troops in the colonies to ensure their safety, and to strengthen imperial control over the colonies. The Sugar Act revised the ineffective Molasses Act of 1733 by reducing the duty on foreign molasses by half; increasing the duties on various types of sugar; levying new taxes on coffee, indigo, wine, silk, and other textiles; and establishing procedures for the more effective collection of taxes. American colonists preferred to deal with foreign planters because foreign molasses was cheaper. Moreover, foreign planters bought colonial goods such as slaves, lumber, flour, fish, and meat, and they paid in hard currency, which was greatly needed in the colonies.

North Carolina colonists viewed the Sugar Act as taxation without representation as well as an economic threat. They consequently lodged a protest in the North Carolina Assembly.

References: John R. Alden, *The South in the Revolution* (1962); Oscar T. Barck Jr. and Hugh T. Lefler, *Colonial America* (1968); Lindley S. Butler, *North Carolina and the Coming of the Revolution, 1763–1776* (1976).

Carmen Miner Smith

Sugar Creek, War of. In the spring of 1765, men from the Sugar Creek and Reedy Creek neighborhoods in newly created Mecklenburg County attacked a crew surveying plantations on approximately 1.2 million acres granted to English merchant Henry McCulloh two decades earlier. This so-called War of Sugar Creek was one of a series of mob actions in the 1750s and 1760s in which settlers on the southwestern North Carolina frontier attempted to thwart the designs of McCulloh and other speculators, notably Governor Arthur Dobbs and Englishman John Selwyn. The terms of these huge grants varied somewhat, but in general they called for the settlement of white Protestants at a ratio of one person per 200 acres. The speculators enjoyed cancellation of quitrents for a decade. At the end of the ten years, unoccupied land in excess of the 1:200 ratio would revert to the Crown.

Although McCulloh had some success in settling people on similar large grants in the Cape Fear River Valley, these western tracts were almost completely vacant prior to the French and Indian War. Dobbs discovered only 75 families during a 1755 tour of his western holdings, then in Anson County. By 1762, when he revisited the area, there were many more settlers who, according to Dobbs, had banded together to resist his plans to be their landlord. At one point, a group of them chased Dobbs and his survey party on horseback and nearly got into a gun battle with Dobbs, who soon left for the coast, never to return to the backcountry.

Citing the disturbance of the late "war" with the French, McCulloh had convinced the Crown to alter the terms of the grants, giving the speculators until 1765 to determine just how many people had settled on the tracts by 1760, to conduct surveys of plantations, and to come to terms with the occupants. In 1761 McCulloh dispatched his able son, Henry Eustace,

to see to this phase of the operations. Henry also acted as agent for Dobbs and for George Augustus Selwyn, who had inherited his father's western claims. Henry McCulloh encountered dogged resistance among the settlers, now led by militia captain Thomas Polk, who had recently arrived from Pennsylvania and who would later become a hero of the Revolution in North Carolina. Polk and his men relied more on intimidation than actual violence to frustrate the speculators, although violence may have been used. In 1767 the McCullohs and their associates finally returned to the Crown most of their land along the border with South Carolina.

References: William S. Powell, James K. Huhta, and Thomas J. Farnham, eds., *The Regulators in North Carolina: A Documentary History, 1759–1776* (1971); Charles G. Sellers Jr., "Private Profits and British Colonial Policy: The Speculations of Henry McCulloh," *William & Mary Quarterly* 8 (October 1951).

James P. Whittenburg

Suicide in North Carolina, as in every state, affects a small but significant percentage of the population. The frequency of the tragedy has in the last few decades reflected nationwide trends, with large increases in several age and gender groups. In the early 2000s North Carolina ranked twenty-first among states in the overall suicide rate, with an occurrence of 12.7 suicides per 100,000 people. An average of 960 North Carolinians commit suicide each year. These relatively high numbers are alarming since in the not-so-distant past, the state's suicide rate was well below the national average.

Historically, suicide has occurred less frequently in the South than in any other region of the nation. This has been viewed as a consequence of southern culture, with its traditional emphasis on religious values, individualistic spirit, and respect for personal honor. In particular, Christianity's condemnation of suicide as an unforgivable sin—an act of defiance toward God that leaves no opportunity for repentance or contrition—made it a wholly unacceptable escape from life's troubles for early North Carolinians and other colonists. Suicide was considered a grave felony, and although colonial authorities in the seventeenth and eighteenth centuries were obviously unable to punish the felons themselves, they found retribution in other ways. For example, a suicide victim's body may have been pierced with a stake and shamefully buried, with all of the victim's belongings forfeited to the king (even when the person had dependents). Those related to the victim were often treated as pariahs within the community.

The harsh nature of such legal and social reactions to suicide reflected early North Carolinians' views on the crime and generally worked as an effective deterrent to would-be suicides. Only the most desperate, depressed, or mentally ill individuals took their own lives. For example, in the mid-1800s some slaves in North Carolina reportedly committed suicide to avoid what they believed to be imminent, severe punishment. Others did so simply to end a life of pure misery.

A relatively low suicide rate continued in North Carolina and throughout the South well into the twentieth century. However, as North Carolina and other southern states became more urbanized, their suicide rates increased. In general, the latter half of the twentieth century saw a dramatic rise in North Carolina's suicide rate as its population—and its prosperity—increased. In 1972 white males in North Carolina, many of them farmers, killed themselves 48 percent more frequently than they had ten years earlier. This "suicide boom" did not reverse in succeeding decades. Between 1980 and 1995 the state's overall suicide rate increased 13 percent, from 11.2 to 12.6 suicides per 100,000 people. While the suicide rate among blacks across most age groups remained low, there were major increases in suicide among younger blacks. For instance, during this period suicide among blacks aged 10–14 rose a frightening 233 percent. Overall, teen suicides increased as well at a smaller but still alarming rate.

Since suicide is a personal and often secretive act, it is nearly impossible to find a blanket cause for its increase in frequency in North Carolina. Nevertheless, various economic and cultural changes in the state have greatly affected many North Carolinians. Primarily, the steady move from an agrarian to an industrial culture—with all its inherent stress—disrupted the traditional lifestyles of many citizens. The great increase in rural suicides in the eastern part of the state, for example, came as many farmers struggled economically, watching their sons and daughters leave their farms for the cities and taking with them the dream of continuing the family business. Additionally, as the modern world becomes more technologically advanced, traditional Christianity has ceased to inform the lives of many people. Significant moral obstacles to suicide have therefore largely been removed. The disintegration of familial relationships, the stress resulting from economic pressures, the wide availability of alcohol and drugs, and other societal changes are also considered important factors in the state's suicide rate.

References: Kathryn B. Surles, *Suicide in North Carolina*, State Center for Health Studies Report, no. 110 (1998); Leslie Wayne, "A Rising Tide of Suicide," *Raleigh News and Observer*, 29 Aug. 1971.

Jay Mazzocchi

Summer School, the first in the United States, was established by University of North Carolina president Kemp P. Battle in 1877, primarily to train teachers. It convened on 3 July for a six-week session attended by both men and women. It was suspended in 1884, having enrolled 2,480 teachers and other students. Resumed in 1894, the summer school continued for 11 more years, with a total enrollment of 1,541. After a two-year

hiatus, the summer school at the university resumed in 1907 and has continued ever since.

William S. Powell

Sunday Schools. The Sunday school as an instrument for teaching children originated in Gloucester, England, about 1780. Philanthropist Robert Raikes originated the idea out of his concern for the ignorance and rowdy behavior of the children of the poor. By the 1790s several schools existed in America, particularly in Philadelphia, where before 1800 more than 2,000 children received instruction in reading and copying from the Bible. The schools were operated by various religious or humanitarian groups, with the former especially emphasizing religious and moral instruction. Presbyterians and Methodists enthusiastically supported these opportunities to teach the children of the unchurched poor.

The first Sunday school in North Carolina was organized by Gottlieb Schober, pastor of the Hopewell Lutheran Church (now Hopewell Moravian Church) near Salem in 1813, with instruction in reading and singing. Under Schober's leadership, the Moravian Single Sisters taught English and German to some 25 children of non-Moravian farmers. The results were gratifying, and the Sunday school concept spread to surrounding counties under Moravian leadership.

Because North Carolina's backcountry had but a few field schools for those who could afford to pay, Sunday schools offered a vital opportunity for the children of yeoman farmers. While religious education was important from the beginning, training in reading, spelling, arithmetic, and writing often proved more enduring. In Stokes County alone, some 1,200 children marched through the streets of Salem in 1830 in the parade of students initiating a new school season. Schober, president of the county Sunday School Union, led the procession at age 74 and acknowledged his pride in seeing "so many young people from our neighborhood, who through the Sunday Schools not only have an opportunity to learn to read, but also to become acquainted with the word of God."

The Sunday school movement waned in the late antebellum period in North Carolina, particularly as the number of public schools began to grow within the state. But in more isolated areas, Sunday schools continued to be the only opportunity for children to gain a degree of literacy. By the late nineteenth century, the American Sunday School Union gained new momentum through the development of a systematic curriculum of biblical study, the International Uniform Lessons, with various denominations providing their own literature for teachers and students to emphasize particular perspectives. The Christian nurture of children remained important throughout the twentieth century, and the need for religious education of all age groups was acknowledged. In the early 2000s, Sunday schools continue to serve an important role in religious and biblical education in many communities.

References: Anne M. Boylan, *Sunday School: The Formation of an American Institution, 1790–1880* (1988); Thomas W. Laqueur, *Religion and Respectability: Sunday Schools and Working Class Culture, 1780–1850* (1976); Jerry L. Surratt, *Gottlieb Schober of Salem: Discipleship and Ecumenical Vision in an Early Moravian Town* (1983).

Jerry L. Surratt

Sundials. Evidence of the use of sundials in North Carolina has been found as early as the colonial period. In May 1772 it was noted that Christian Gottlieb Reuter intended to build two "sun clocks" for the Moravian community of Salem. In 1811 John Stirewalt of Rowan County had a sundial constructed on the south wall of his brick house. In 1833 Henry Barnard of St. John's College, Md., was in Chapel Hill and commented on the sundial in Professor Elisha Mitchell's garden there. The carved sandstone pedestal of another one stands in the Presbyterian churchyard in Fayetteville. A large sundial, adjacent to the Morehead Planetarium in Chapel Hill and very near the site of Mitchell's garden, was constructed in 1956 with a gnomon approximately 24 feet long and 20 feet high. The sundial has become an oft-visited landmark on the University of North Carolina at Chapel Hill campus.

References: Adelaide L. Fries, ed., *Records of the Moravians in North Carolina*, vols. 2 (1925) and 5 (1941); Rener J. Roher, *Sundials: History, Theory, and Practice* (1965).

William S. Powell

Sunset Law, an act of the 1977 General Assembly sponsored by state senator Willis P. Whichard, provided for the periodic review of specific licensing and regulatory agencies of state government to determine which should be terminated, continued, or reestablished. Major state departments were not affected. The purpose of this act was to eliminate many statutes whose goals had been accomplished or that were deemed no longer necessary.

William S. Powell

Superstitions. SEE Folklore.

Supreme Court of North Carolina is a seven-member tribunal occupying the apex of the state's General Court of Justice and possessing appellate jurisdiction to review the decisions of lower courts and administrative boards within the executive branch of state government. Acting on a bill introduced by William Gaston of New Bern, the General Assembly in November 1818 created the separate supreme court contemplated by the Constitution of 1776, which empowered the legislature to appoint "Judges of the Supreme Courts of Law and Equity" and "Judges of Admiralty." Composed of a chief justice and two "judges," the new tribunal was commissioned to exercise exclusive appellate jurisdiction over questions of law and equity arising in the superior courts. The first meeting of the court took place on 1 Jan. 1819, and soon the court began holding two sittings, or "terms," a year. The governor, with the assistance and advice of the Council of State, temporarily filled vacancies on the supreme court until the end of the next session of the General Assembly.

The legislature's creation of an independent appellate judiciary ran counter to the reforming democratic spirit of Jacksonian North Carolina. From the beginning, opponents objected to the judges' salaries, which at $2,500 per year were considered extravagant (at the time the governor annually received only $2,000). The judges' right to "hold office during good behavior," a virtual guarantee of life tenure, angered reformers who regarded the court as an elitist institution too far removed from the people. The growing population of the western counties, naturally given to criticizing an unresponsive, distant state government dominated by eastern planters, protested the long journeys their lawyers had to undertake to argue cases from the overburdened western circuits before the supreme court. To their voices were added those of superior court judges, who resented being reversed on appeal. Throughout the 1820s regular attacks were leveled at the North Carolina Supreme Court by legislators who believed that the chief justice and the two judges should be elected by popular vote.

The 1829 election to the bench of former superior court judge and State Bank of North Carolina president Thomas Ruffin effectively ensured the supreme court's survival, as he single-handedly transformed the common law of the state into an instrument of economic change. Ruffin's writings on the issue of eminent domain—the right of the state to seize private property for the public good—paved the way for the expansion of railroads into North Carolina, enabling the state to embrace the Industrial Revolution. Ruffin's opinions on various subjects were cited as persuasive authority by appellate tribunals nationwide.

The supreme court survived the Civil War, during which its docket was greatly diminished under the leadership of Chief Justice Richmond Pearson. Four major reforms befell the court as a result of North Carolina's adoption of a new constitution in 1868. First, in an extensive revision of the judicial article, the court became a "constitutional" tribunal that owed its existence to the fundamental law of the state rather than to legislative enactment. Second, the number of judges was increased from three to five, with the chief justice retaining his title and his brethren receiving the appellation "associate justices." Third, the justices, including the chief justice, were to be elected by the people for eight-year terms. In the event of a vacancy, the governor was to appoint a substitute to sit until after the next general election of members of the General Assembly.

The twentieth century called upon the supreme court justices to decide a variety of cases related to the responsibilities and limitations of a growing state bureaucracy. Many of these governmental controversies had at their root questions regarding separation of powers: the principle that the executive, legislative, and judicial branches of government should be, in the words of the North Carolina Declaration of Rights, "forever separate and distinct." At the same time the court continued to handle modifications to common law, fashioning new doctrines to meet the demands of a rapidly changing state. The 1980s and 1990s occasionally saw the justices interpret the state constitution as a more capacious vessel of individual rights than its federal counterpart.

The primary function of the modern Supreme Court of North Carolina is to decide questions of law arising in the lower courts and before state administrative agencies. The justices spend most of their time outside the courtroom reading written case records, studying briefs prepared by lawyers, researching applicable law, and writing opinions detailing the reasoning on which the court's determinations are based. The General Assembly in 1937 passed legislation raising the number of justices to seven. The concurrence of four justices generally is required for a decision; each of the seven justices participates in every case except in unusual situations where a justice may feel compelled to recuse, or withdraw, from sitting.

In addition to cases awaiting decision, the justices consider numerous petitions in which a party seeks to bring a case before the court for adjudication. Although most of these requests are denied, the justices read hundreds of records and briefs and spend many hours in conference deliberating their merits. Each justice writes approximately 250 printed pages of opinions every year. These opinions are published in the *North Carolina Reports* and in several unofficial publications; they may be found in major law libraries throughout the world.

References: David M. Britt, "Update of the History of the Supreme Court of North Carolina," *North Carolina Reports* 326 (1990); Walter Clark, "History of the Supreme Court of North Carolina," *North Carolina Reports* 177 (1919); John V. Orth, *The North Carolina State Constitution: A Reference Guide* (1993).

Martin H. Brinkley

Surfing. One of the first instances of a Hawaiian-type surfboard being constructed and used on the North Carolina coast was in the late 1930s, when Tom Fearing of Manteo built one so long and heavy that it took two people to carry it to the water. The riders of Fearing's board were never able to catch a wave and stand up on it Hawaiian style, but it was used extensively for years as a paddle board on which two or even three people could go out to the wrecks a quarter of a mile or so offshore for fishing. In the early 1950s, the Kitty Hawk Craft Shop was selling handmade juniper boards averaging almost 3 feet in length and 15 to 18 inches in width, which were the forerunners of the modern boogie board. By the early 1960s, similar small boards were being manufactured of Styrofoam, but neither the wooden nor Styrofoam types were large enough for stand-up surfing. At about that same time, however, modified versions of Hawaiian surfboards were appearing on North Carolina's beaches, most of them eight or ten feet in length.

The beaches north of Cape Hatteras are especially well suited for surfing because they extend in a north-south direction and receive the full effect of large waves emerging from far out in the Atlantic. Not long after the first surfers appeared on the North Carolina coast, there were signs of conflict as pier operators claimed the surfers were ruining the fishing and resort owners expressed concern over the possibility of surfers injuring bathers in the ocean surf. In most areas, the local authorities now restrict surfing to specified areas.

Riding a surfboard today is quite a different experience from riding one in the early days of North Carolina surfing. Major improvements were the addition of a fin or "skeg" at the rear of the board to serve as a fixed rudder and a leash connecting board and rider, allowing some measure of control after a fall. The greatest change, however, has been in the length of the boards, which has gradually decreased until some of the most popular boards in use for stand-up surfing are not much longer than the original handmade boogie boards.

Another form of surfing, known as windsurfing or sailboarding, has evolved for use when large waves are not available. In this form, the surfer stands on a board while using a sail instead of a wave for propulsion.

References: Lane DeGregory, "A Retro Wave," *The Coast* (31 Mar. 1996); Ron Stoner, "South to Kitty Hawk," *Surfer* (July 1967).

David Stick

SEE ALSO Windsurfing.

Surplus, Federal (1836). Distribution of the U.S. government's surplus revenue in 1836 helped inaugurate an era of unprecedented development in North Carolina, particularly in the realm of public education. Although the $1.5 million distributed in the state may seem small by modern standards, it was an unexpectedly generous sum in 1836. Its proceeds transformed the moribund Literary Fund, established a decade earlier, into a nearly inexhaustible source of revenue for local schools, lasting until the end of the Civil War. On a political level, the surplus ushered in more than a decade of Whig political supremacy in North Carolina, coming after a lengthy battle on the national level between Democratic president Andrew Jackson and his congressional opponents, the Whigs, led by Henry Clay.

In 1833 Jackson had vetoed an earlier distribution bill that sought to return federal funds from the sale of western lands to the states after the national debt had been repaid. But the issue refused to die, and Jackson was forced to accept the compromise bill of 1836. By then even Democrats, while distrustful of federal encroachment on state rights, were clamoring for the revenue to reduce state taxes and pay off the state debt. In some states, however, the more progressive Whigs successfully advocated use of the money for internal improvements (primarily railroads and swamp drainage) and state aid to public education. In North Carolina, Whigs engineered a legislative compromise that kept $100,000 for state operating expenses but devoted the remainder to purchasing bank stock ($600,000) and railroad securities ($533,000) and financing internal projects, such as swamp drainage ($200,000). The stock and securities were assigned to the Literary Fund, where the accrued dividends allowed annual financing for the state's first "common," or public, schools.

The distribution proved an immediate bonanza for two unfinished railroads—the Wilmington & Raleigh (later renamed the Wilmington & Weldon) and the Raleigh & Gaston—that had run out of private construction funds before the state took up their cause. Despite strong opposition from Democrats, the Whigs soon committed $500,000 of the Literary Fund's new money to the 161-mile Wilmington-Weldon system, which in 1840 was the world's longest. Also in 1840 the Raleigh & Gaston Railroad was completed after the legislature agreed to endorse its bonds. The state would eventually commit more than $1 million to the Wilmington-Weldon line, which began paying dividends after 1850. The failing Raleigh-Gaston line, which the state was forced to buy in 1845, proved less lucrative. Meanwhile, the swamp-drainage project was ineffective and the investment considered almost a total loss; the Literary Fund paid out $200,000 to drain Mattamuskeet, Pungo, and Alligator Lakes and open savanna lands in Carteret County, but it saw no return on its investments.

It was the public schools that benefited most from the Literary Fund's expenditures after 1836. The public school law of 1839 permitted an annual expenditure by the fund of $40 for every school district in the state; this raised an additional $20 in taxes and supplied a school building for at least 50 white pupils. By 1840 Rockingham County voters had authorized the first free common school in the state; within six more years, every county had at least one public school. More than 100,000 children were enrolled in 1850, when 2,657 individual schools were in operation. The Literary Fund, which boasted more than $2 million in 1850, remained solvent until 1865, when poor investments and the postwar financial collapse virtually wiped out its capital.

For all its limitations, the experiment in federal revenue sharing was more successful in North Carolina than in other states, where speculators and unwise investments quickly used up the distributions. Although the surplus distributions were theoretically issued as loans to the states, they were never required to be repaid; many states expected the federal largess to continue indefinitely, but for political and economic reasons, this did not occur. The next attempt at federal revenue sharing did not occur until the 1970s, more than a century later.

References: Hugh T. Lefler and Albert R. Newsome, *North Carolina: The History of a Southern State* (3rd ed., 1973); Marcus C. S. Noble, *A History of the Public Schools of North Carolina* (1930).

Benjamin R. Justesen

SEE ALSO Literary Fund.

Surry County,

Surry County, located at the juncture of the Piedmont and Mountain regions of North Carolina and partially bordering the state of Virginia, was formed in 1771 from Rowan County and was named after either the English County of Surrey (birthplace of royal governor William Tryon) or the Saura (Cheraw) Indians who populated the area. Early inhabitants apart from the Saura were other Siouan Indians and the Cherokee, followed by English and German settlers. Dobson, the county seat, was incorporated in 1891 and was named for either William Dobson, a local justice of the peace in 1776, or William P. Dobson, a member of the General Assembly in 1814. Other communities in the county include Mount Airy, Level Cross, Ararat, Bottom, Elkin, and Toast. Pilot Mountain State Park is a much-visited natural site in Surry County, featuring a huge ancient quartzite stone monadnock visible for many miles. Flowing within Surry County are the Yadkin, Mitchell, and Ararat Rivers and numerous creeks, including Red Hill, Beaver, Toms, and Johnson. Mount Airy, "the Granite City," is home to the largest open-faced granite quarry in the world.

The original Siamese twins, Eng and Chang Bunker, are buried at White Plains Baptist Church. Notable among Surry County landmarks and historic sites is the downtown area of Mount Airy, Andy Griffith's hometown. The town boasts several structures connected to the fictional town of Mayberry in the *Andy Griffith Show* television series, including the Snappy Lunch, Old City Hall, Floyd's City Barber Shop, and the Andy Griffith Playhouse. Other cultural institutions include the Charles H. Stone Memorial Library, the Horne Creek Living Historical Farm, and the Foothills Theatre. The county hosts many festivals and annual events, such as the Surry County Agricultural Fair, the Autumn Leaves Festival, Mayberry Days, the Yadkin Valley Pumpkin Festival, and the Elkin Mid-Summer Invitational Tennis Tournament.

Surry County agricultural commodities include tobacco, corn, soybeans, strawberries, apples, swine, beef cattle, dairy products, sheep, and poultry. Manufactured products include hosiery, apparel, textiles, concrete blocks, polished granite, precision tools, blankets, and yarns. Mined in Surry County are minerals such as feldspar, quartz, and mica, in addition to granite. The population of the county was estimated at 72,200 in 2004.

Jay Mazzocchi

SEE ALSO *Andy Griffith Show*; Horne Creek Living Historical Farm; Pilot Mountain.

Surveyors. From colonial times through the twentieth century, land surveying in North Carolina was an imperfect art at best, using old measurements such as furlongs, chains, and rods (or perches or poles) and imprecise boundaries such as trees or gulleys to map out often vague property lines. In the first half of the eighteenth century, the colony was blessed with the services of two first-class geographers, the surveyors-general John Lawson and Edward Moseley. Lawson made a reconnaissance deep into the Carolinas and in 1709 published *A New Voyage to Carolina*, his account of that journey, with an excellent map and drawings of the fauna. Some 20 years later, Moseley produced his well-known 1733 map of the colony. He also had the distinction of participating in three of the four major surveys of that day, which permanently shaped North Carolina's geography and influenced its ethnic distribution. These included the running of the line dividing Virginia and North Carolina (made famous by the narrative written by Virginian William Byrd), the line dividing North Carolina and South Carolina, the southern parallel of the Granville District, and the tracts of the 1.2 million acres granted to Henry McCulloh.

In the revolutionary era and the early years of statehood, North Carolina was served by a new generation of surveyors such as John Daniel, one of the original donors of land to the new state university. He worked mainly in the New Hope Creek watershed of Orange and Chatham Counties, and many of his original plats are in the envelopes of the state land grants. His map of the prominence between Morgan and Bolin Creeks is the earliest of what is now Chapel Hill.

A century later, in the days of Reconstruction and the new state constitution, the management of local taxes was taken from the courts and given to county commissioners, resulting in an immediate need for new and accurate county maps. Between the late 1870s and the mid-1890s many counties ordered maps from surveyor-engineer-cartographers such as Fendol Bevers (Wake), Will Spoon (Alamance), George Tate (Orange), and Lemuel Johnson, a mathematician at Trinity College (Davidson, Randolph, and Durham).

Not until the twentieth century and the advent of aerial surveys did county maps achieve a reliable accuracy. In the years just before World War I, the U.S. Department of Agriculture released an excellent series of soil maps, and the first of the U.S. Geological Survey maps appeared. By the twenty-first century, surveying had been enhanced by remarkable developments in field equipment—utilizing radio beams, lasers, and even global positioning via satellites—that rendered a previously unimagined accuracy.

References: Harry Roy Merrens, *Colonial North Carolina in the Eighteenth Century: A Study in Historical Geography* (1964); William S. Powell, *The First State University* (3rd ed., 1992).

David Southern

Swain County, located in the Mountain region of North Carolina, was formed in 1871 from Jackson and Macon Counties and named for David Lowry Swain, governor of North Carolina and president of the University of North Carolina in Chapel Hill. It is situated along the Tennessee–North Carolina border. Early inhabitants of the area included the Cherokee Indians; early European settlers were Scotch-Irish and German. Bryson City, the county seat, was incorporated in 1887 as Charleston; the name was changed in 1889 in honor of Capt. Thaddeus Dillard Bryson, the founder of the town. Other Swain County communities include Cherokee, Birdtown, Ela, Lauada, Wesser, Almond, and Nantahala.

Two of Swain County's principal features are large sections of the Great Smoky Mountains National Park and the Qualla Boundary, the reservation of the Eastern Band of Cherokee Indians, with Cherokee as its primary town. These dominate the economy of the county, bringing thousands of tourists to the area year round and giving Swain County its distinctive cultural identity. Fontana Lake, a reservoir created by Fontana Dam, built during the New Deal, is a popular recreational area for swimming, boating, fishing, and hiking. Whitewater rafting on the Tuckasegee, Oconaluftee, and Little Tennessee Rivers is another popular activity in the county.

Although tourism is the main source of revenue in Swain County, the county also gains income from forestry and from agricultural commodities such as burley tobacco, tomatoes, boxwoods, ornamentals and other nursery crops, Christmas trees, beef cattle, and dairy products. Minerals in the county include kyanite, pegmatite, clay, feldspar, quartz, garnet, pyrite, magnetite, and thulite.

Swain County is the site of several historic landmarks, among them Nantahala No. 2 Truss Bridge, built in 1899; the Kituwah Indian Mound, once the center of an early Cherokee settlement along the Tuckasegee River; and Oconaluftee Indian Village, established in 1952 and part of the Great Smoky Mountains National Park. Prominent among the county's cultural institutions are the Museum of the Cherokee Indian and the long-running outdoor drama *Unto These Hills*, presented in Cherokee and telling the story of the Eastern Cherokees' removal to Oklahoma on the Trail of Tears. Other cultural attractions include the Smoky Mountain Community Theatre, the Cherokee Cyclorama Wax Museum, the Qualla Arts and Crafts Mutual, and the Cherokee Heritage Museum and Gallery. The county hosts festivals and annual events such as

Bryson City Riverfest, the Fourth of July Freedom Fest, the Fireman's Day Festival, the Bryson City Chili Cookoff, and the Cherokee Blue Grass Festival. In 2004 the estimated population of Swain County was 13,400.

Jay Mazzocchi

SEE ALSO Cherokee Indians; Great Smoky Mountains National Park; Museum of the Cherokee Indian; Oconaluftee Indian Village.

Swamps. Most of the largest remaining swamps (or "dismals," as early settlers called them) in the eastern United States are located in North Carolina's coastal plain. Much of North Carolina's swamplands are bottomland hardwood river swamps, while other swampy areas, including the mysterious Carolina Bays, are in fact pocosins—naturally occurring, freshwater evergreen shrub-bogs that are elevated above nearby lands. The definition of this Indian word, variously spelled "percoarson," "poquosin," and "pequessen," is "swamp on a hill."

The best-known North Carolina swamps include the Great Dismal Swamp National Wildlife Refuge, the Roanoke River National Wildlife Refuge, the Alligator River National Wildlife Refuge, the Pocosin Lakes National Wildlife Refuge, the East Dismal, the Great Alligator Dismal, the Little Dismal, the Angola Swamp, the Holly Shelter Swamp, the Raft Swamp, the Gum Swamp, and the Green Swamp. The alternating nature of North Carolina's eastern territories (rivers, sounds, swamps, and forests) gave early travelers considerable difficulty moving from north to south, giving rise to a correspondingly considerable negative reputation for the coastal plain and sound country as being wet, wild, impenetrable, interminable, and monotonous if not downright terrifying. Along with the timbering operations that have gone on since European colonization, the North Carolina swamps have seen military activity during the American Revolution and the Civil War; been havens for escaped slaves (some of whom gathered and formed colonies and redoubts, while others traveled in secrecy from swamp to swamp); served as sites for illegal distilleries, such as the famously huge moonshine operation in East Lake during Prohibition; and been enormously altered by large-scale draining, land-clearing, and farming operations, particularly in the third quarter of the twentieth century (for example, First Colony Farms on the Albemarle peninsula and Open Ground Farms in the Open Ground Pocosin of eastern Carteret County).

Because of the more recent allied efforts of many conservation groups and state and federal agencies, significant eastern swamp and wetland territories have become state forests, game lands, and national wildlife refuges. However forbidding the swamps may still seem to much of the population, there has nonetheless been a tremendous change in the general attitude about the necessity of preserving and protecting these swamps and lowlands as filters, habitats, flood absorbers, and incomparable sources of renewal in every possible regard.

References: Bob Benner and Tom McCloud, *A Paddler's Guide to Eastern North Carolina* (1987); Jack Temple Kirby, *Poquosin: A Study of Rural Landscape and Society* (1995); Brook Meanley, *Swamps, River Bottoms, and Canebrakes* (1972); Douglas Neil Rader, *Carolina Wetlands: Our Vanishing Resource* (1989); Bland Simpson, *The Great Dismal: A Carolinian's Swamp Memoir* (1990).

Bland Simpson

SEE ALSO Great Dismal Swamp; Pocosins.

Swannanoa Gap Tunnel, a 1,832-foot-long railway tunnel through Swannanoa Mountain near Asheville, was completed on 11 Mar. 1879. After chipping away the final barrier, workers tunneling from opposite sides of the mountain were elated to discover that the two tunnels lined up perfectly. James H. Wilson, chief engineer of the Western North Carolina Railroad, immediately sent a telegram to Governor Zebulon B. Vance stating that "daylight entered Buncombe County this morning through the Swannanoa Tunnel." The first train finally steamed through the tunnel into Asheville on 3 Oct. 1880.

Plans for the Swannanoa Gap Tunnel were drawn up after the Civil War in an effort to make Asheville a railway hub for North Carolina's western counties. Of the large number of workers employed, many were convicts serving misdemeanor sentences, and approximately 120 perished during construction. The tunnel, which cost about $120,000 to build, was cut with the help of nitroglycerine, marking an early use of the explosive in engineering.

References: Lou Harshaw, *Trains, Trestles, and Tunnels: Railroads of the Southern Appalachians* (1977); Mitzi Schaden Tessier, *Asheville: A Pictorial History* (1982).

Rich Weidman

Swann's Revisal is the familiar name of the first book published in the colony of North Carolina. The book—whose partial official title was *A Collection of All the Public Acts of Assembly, of the Province of North-Carolina: Now in Force and Use. Together with the Titles of all such Laws as are Obsolete, Expir'd, or Repeal'd.*—was a compilation of all of the laws of North Carolina ever passed, whether still in force or not. It appeared in 1751 as a 338-page volume from the press of James Davis, who had only recently moved to New Bern from Williamsburg, Va., as the colony's first printer. Prior to that time, the session laws of the colony were copied by hand and available for those who needed them. Errors were sometimes made by an amanuensis during the copying procedure, and variant copies caused problems in court.

Under Governor Gabriel Johnston in 1746, a three-man

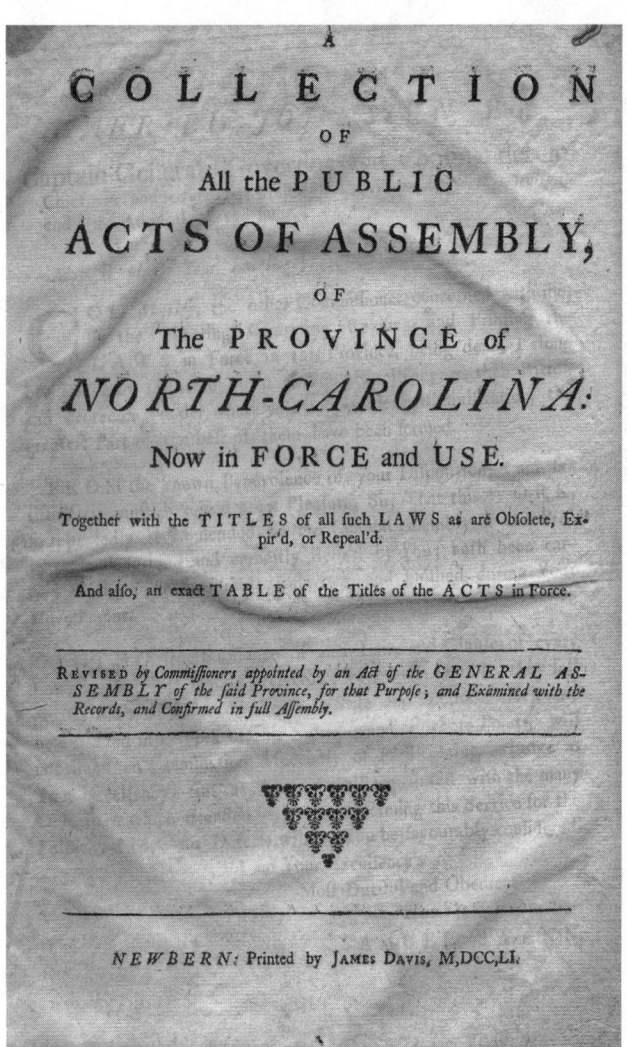

Title page of the first book published in the colony of North Carolina, a 1751 collection of all the laws that had been passed by the Assembly. NCC.

commission was named to compile the laws. One of them declined to serve while another, Edward Moseley, did some work on the collection but died before it was finished. Only Samuel Swann saw the task to its completion, and his name has been forever attached to the document. The book was bound in leather that in time yellowed, thereby providing its other nickname: "Yellow Jacket." This name might also have been suggested by someone who had been "stung" by newly revealed laws.

Reference: Douglas C. McMurtrie, *Eighteenth-Century North Carolina Imprints* (1938).

William S. Powell

Swann v. Charlotte-Mecklenburg Board of Education,

argued before the U.S. Supreme Court in 1971, established court-ordered busing of students as a constitutional means of desegregating public schools. The case originated in the combined Charlotte–Mecklenburg County school system in 1965, when attorney Julius L. Chambers filed suit on behalf of ten pairs of African American parents. The lawsuit, named for six-year-old James E. Swann, contended that the school board's pupil assignment plan—still largely racially based—was insufficient to eliminate the inequalities of the formerly segregated system.

Under pressure from the plaintiffs and the U.S. Office of Education, the school board formulated a new plan for the coming year based on geographic attendance zones for all but 10 schools and pledged to make assignments entirely on a geographic basis by 1967–68. Both the U.S. District Court and the Fourth Circuit Court of Appeals upheld the proposal.

By many measures, the school board's plan was a success, for in 1968 only two urban school districts in the entire country (San Francisco and Toledo) were more desegregated than Charlotte-Mecklenburg. Despite this apparent achievement, the plaintiffs sought to reopen the case, charging that the community, because of various forms of governmentally sanctioned discrimination, was one of the most residentially segregated in the nation and that only through extensive busing could the schools reach the level of desegregation required by law. Federal district court judge James B. McMillan accepted this argument and in April 1969 concluded that there still existed an illegal system of schools identifiable by race.

McMillan directed the school board to develop a new plan that met his criteria for racially neutral schools. In February 1970 he accepted, with minor changes, the board's plan for desegregating the secondary schools of Charlotte and Mecklenburg County through busing. The board had refused to consider a similar degree of busing for the lower grades, however, and McMillan approved a plan for the elementary schools, prepared by a Rhode Island consultant, that required substantial busing as the only means to eliminate all predominately African American schools.

In May the Fourth Circuit Court of Appeals affirmed McMillan's order relating to junior and senior high schools but instructed him to review his requirements for elementary schools according to a test of "reasonableness." The school board and McMillan were unable to agree on an alternative plan, and in September the consultant's plan was implemented with the busing of approximately 43,000 students, more than double the number bused the previous year. In the meantime, the school board and the plaintiffs appealed to the U.S. Supreme Court.

Although Chief Justice Warren Burger initially attempted to persuade his colleagues to reverse McMillan, the high court delivered its unanimous opinion upholding the judge on 20 Apr. 1971. Even this decision did not immediately end the case, as McMillan and the school board continued to disagree over annual adjustments to the pupil assignment plan. Not until July 1975 was McMillan satisfied that the burden of busing was sufficiently distributed between the races and within the white community to end his supervision of the school system and close the case.

At first the effort to desegregate the Charlotte-Mecklenburg schools divided the races and provoked significant unrest, but in time many residents began to take pride in their relatively peaceful and successful adjustment to new social relationships. In 1974 students from West Charlotte High School invited their peers from the embattled Boston public schools to observe how Charlotte had dealt with the challenge of integration; some observers have linked the city's growth and prosperity in the 1980s to the school board's continued commitment to fully integrated schools. The case also showed African Americans and middle-income whites that they too could influence the political process, and in 1977 a biracial coalition won a referendum to replace the long-standing practice of at-large city council elections with a system based on representation by districts. The debate over the extent and value of busing continues, however, and in the early 1990s specialized magnet schools in inner-city neighborhoods were introduced as a partial alternative to busing.

References: Davison M. Douglas, *Reading, Writing, and Race: The Desegregation of the Charlotte Schools* (1995); Frye Gaillard, *The Dream Long Deferred* (1988); Bernard Schwartz, *Swann's Way: The School Busing Case and the Supreme Court* (1986).

Robin Brabham

SEE ALSO Pupil Assignment Act.

Swan's Quarter, Battle of. The Civil War battle at Swan's Quarter occurred on 3 Mar. 1863 during a Union expedition led by Capt. Colin Richardson. His command included Company G from the 1st North Carolina Infantry (U.S.). Accompanied by the gunboat *North State*, Richardson set out from New Bern aboard the steamer *Escort* on a foraging expedition. On 3 March, on a country road near Swan's Quarter, Richardson and his force of 250 artillery, cavalry, and infantry ran into an ambush consisting of about 80 unidentified Confederate troops. Despite their distinct advantage, the Federals were thrown into confusion and had to be rallied before they could contend with the smaller opposing force. Once the howitzers were brought to bear, the ambushers slowly began a fighting withdrawal from the outskirts of Lake Landing back to and through the hamlet of Swan's Quarter. Basing his decision on a rumor that 200 or more Confederates were on the road leading out of Swan's Quarter, Richardson abandoned his expedition and retreated to New Bern, passing through Swan's Quarter, Fairfield, Skeet, and Lake Landing on the way to his ships. Richardson reported 4 men dead and 15 wounded.

Reference: E. B. Long and Barbara Long, *The Civil War Day by Day: An Almanac, 1861–1865* (1971).

Charles C. Davis

Sweet Milk is a southern term referring to fresh, unprocessed whole milk. The term has been used less and less as the regional differences between the South and other areas of the United States have diminished. North Carolina folklore suggests some interesting applications of sweet milk. Some claim it should be drunk as a remedy for snake bite. It is also said to be essential in extinguishing house fires caused by lightning, keeping witches away, and, when used in a poultice of sweet potato leaves, relieving inflammation in the fingers or other parts of the body.

Wiley J. Williams

Swiss and Palatine Settlers. Emigrants from Bern, Switzerland, and the German Palatinate, led by a minor Swiss nobleman, Baron Christoph von Graffenried, are credited with establishing New Bern (North Carolina's second-oldest town) as well as being among the earliest settlers of Craven and Jones Counties. The Swiss were paupers whom the city government of Bern looked upon as undesirables and wished to remove from the area. The German Palatines, who were larger in number, were primarily residents from the Palatinate area located along the Rhine River. They had suffered from repeated wars, particularly the then-ongoing War of the Spanish Succession (1701–14), and an exceptionally harsh winter in 1708 that induced thousands to flee their homeland for better lives elsewhere. Many Palatines were lured by advertisements distributed by agents from Carolina and Pennsylvania who hoped to attract settlers to their still sparsely settled colonies. Others were influenced by the writings of a German pastor extolling the glories of the New World, which hinted that Queen Anne of England might grant passage to America to Palatines.

Queen Anne did in fact see her country as the protector of European Protestantism and looked favorably upon the idea of providing aid to the impoverished German emigrants, many, though not all, of whom were Protestants. Her intent coincided with the need of the Proprietors of Carolina and Pennsylvania for settlers. By 1709, as suffering increased in Germany, 1,000 refugees a week began making their way up the Rhine River and over to England. Within a short time, London was crowded with homeless refugees who lived in tents along the banks of the Thames River. Colonization was seen as one solution to the problem.

The idea of a settlement in Carolina was conceived by Georg Ritter and Company of Bern, which saw an American colony as as an opportunity to profit from mining ventures in the New World and financial grants from the Bernese and English governments for transporting the settlers to Carolina. The company purchased 10,000 acres between the Neuse and Cape Fear Rivers from the Carolina Proprietors, who offered the land at a low price. Graffenried himself purchased 5,000 acres and was given a title of nobility in the colony under the feudal system designated by the Fundamental Constitutions of Carolina. He also assumed direction of the entire project.

In January 1710 the Palatines sailed from Gravesend under John Lawson, surveyor general of Carolina, while Graffenried himself remained in England to await the Swiss. They endured an overly long voyage of 13 weeks, during which more than half of them died from close confinement, meager provisions, spoiled meat, and other hardships. Off the coast of Virginia, one of the ships, filled with supplies, was plundered by a French privateer. These misfortunes were followed by a fever epidemic when the Palatines reached land.

The survivors proceeded to the Chowan River, where they purchased supplies from planter Thomas Pollock, and then traveled through the sounds to the Neuse River. Lawson settled them at the fork of the Neuse and the Trent River. During the summer, almost all fell ill, and many sold their clothes to English settlers in the area in return for food.

When Graffenried arrived with the Swiss, he acted swiftly to relieve the situation. Adequate supplies were unavailable locally as a result of instability created by the Cary Rebellion, so he sent to Virginia and Pennsylvania for provisions. In order to avoid friction with the Indians, Graffenried paid them for the same lands that he had already purchased from the Carolina Proprietors. He then began to develop the settlement which he called Neuse Bern, or Bern on the Neuse. This was later corrupted by the English into the present name, New Bern. Lots of 250 acres, located primarily along the Trent River, were assigned to families, while artisans, including carpenters, blacksmiths, and shoemakers, were to reside in town. Graffenried designed the town in the shape of a cross, with the intention of placing a church in the center. After a shaky beginning, the settlement began to prosper; the combined total of Swiss and German settlers was approximately 400.

On 22 Sept. 1711, the Tuscarora Indians, angered by the enslavement of tribe members and "sharp" trading practices by settlers, surprised and killed approximately 130 persons along the Neuse, Trent, and Pamlico Rivers. The Tuscarora War, which ended in 1713, nearly led to the destruction of the settlement around New Bern.

Graffenried fell deeply into debt and was unable to obtain provisions for his settlement. He returned to England in 1713, hoping to borrow funds. Unsuccessful, he gave up his colony as a failure. The Palatines lost their lands to Pollock, who assumed ownership as Graffenried's chief creditor. In 1749 they were granted equivalent lands, which were spread out over an extensive area, thereby effectively dispersing Graffenried's original settlers.

The small number of settlers remaining, after losses due to disease, war, and the hardships of the ocean voyage, intermarried with residents of other nationalities, and the Swiss-German community blended into the population at large. Their family names, however—including Metz (Metts), Kernegee (Kornegay), Eibach (Ipock), Mueller (Miller), and Kuntz (Koonce)—are still prominent in eastern Carolina.

References: Alonso Thomas Dill Jr., "Eighteenth Century New Bern: A History of the Town and Craven County, 1700–1800, Part 2," NCHR 22 (January 1945); Barbara Thorns, ed., *The Heritage of Craven County, North Carolina* (1984); Alan D. Watson, *A History of New Bern and Craven County* (1987).

Donald E. Collins

Tarboro Daily Southerner, one of the oldest daily newspapers in North Carolina, was first published in 1826 as the *Tarborough Free Press.* According to tradition, the word "free" was dropped from the title because the first publisher and editor, George Howard, declined to print a controversial article submitted by a political opponent. The disappointed contributor wanted to know what was "free" about a paper that would not publish opinions contrary to its own. Howard saw the logic in this, and the paper forthwith became the *Tarborough Press.* In 1852 it was renamed the *Tarboro Daily Southerner.*

Howard, a native of Baltimore, had published a paper in Halifax before moving to Tarboro. In 1844 his 14-year-old son George Howard Jr. joined his father at the *Daily Southerner.* Six years later young Howard became editor, and there is no evidence of his father's further connection with the paper. Since his duties from the first had been editorial, George Jr. presumably was one of the youngest, if not the youngest, newspaper editor in North Carolina history. Meanwhile, he was graduated from the University of North Carolina in 1852.

In 1863 the Howard family sold the *Daily Southerner* to L. D. Pender, who was the editor during the Civil War. A severe paper shortage reduced its size to two pages, and it missed its publication date on more than one occasion. Around the time of the Union raid on Tarboro on 19 July 1863, the newspaper did not appear. On resuming publication, the *Daily Southerner* contained no mention of the raid; the editor simply noted that "for reasons which we deem unnecessary here to state, the Southerner has suspended for several weeks past."

From the Civil War until 2006, the *Tarboro Daily Southerner* had many owners (among them, Governor Henry Toole Clark), many editors, and several names. Four family names have been associated with the paper for many years at a time: first the Howards for over 40 years; Frank Powell for 35 years; and the Bourne and Creech families, who owned or edited the paper for well over half a century. By 2006 the *Daily Southerner* was owned by Community Newspaper Holdings, Inc., a media group headquartered in Birmingham, Ala.

Jaquelin Drane Nash

Tar Heel is the nickname for a native or resident of North Carolina as well as for the state itself, which is known as the Tar Heel State. The term appears to have come into popular use after the Civil War, despite its clear connection to North Carolina's prominent role in the naval stores (tar, turpentine, and pitch) industry going back to prerevolutionary times. Its earliest known use is in a diary entry written by 2nd Lt. William B. A. Lowrance of the 46th Regiment North Carolina Troops. In an entry dated 6 Feb. 1863, Lowrance, encamped in Pender

or Onslow County, wrote: "I know now what is meant by the piney woods region of North Carolina and the idea occurs to me that it is no wonder we are called 'tar heels.'"

Almost every North Carolina company formed for Confederate service adopted a nickname, but not a single one used the term Tar Heel. Stories abound regarding the derogatory origin of the term. Circumstantial evidence indicates that the term was originally coined in 1862 as an insulting name for North Carolina soldiers in the Army of Northern Virginia by soldiers of other states, particularly Virginia. Capt. William McWillie of Richard Anderson's staff recalled that at Fredericksburg, Va., troops called out to a passing North Carolina brigade, "Now tar heels when you get out yonder clap your foot down and stick."

North Carolina soldiers quickly learned to return the fire. Mississippians hurled the intended insult at a limping North Carolina mountaineer immediately after Second Fredericksburg in May 1863. After the Confederate lines on Marye's Heights had been broken and later restored, the North Carolina soldier replied, "Yes, damn you. If yer hadder had some tar on yer own heels yestiddy, yer would er stuck to them thar works better, and we wouldn't er had to put yer back thar."

Despite its initial derogatory intent, the term soon was adopted by North Carolina soldiers themselves. The official seal of approval of Tar Heel as a nickname for North Carolinians came when Governor Zebulon B. Vance visited the Army of Northern Virginia on 28 Mar. 1864. As it was described in a letter home the next day by Pvt. Walter Battle of the 4th Regiment North Carolina Troops, Vance made a point of using the term: "He [Governor Vance] said it did not sound right to him to address us as 'Fellow Soldiers,' because he was not one of us—he used to be until he shirked out of the service for a little office down in North Carolina, so now he would address us as 'Fellow Tar Heels,' as we always stick."

Evidence indicates that the term "Tar Heel" permanently moved from insult to honored nickname at the Battle of Reams Station in Virginia on 25 Aug. 1864. Upon learning of the leading role of the North Carolina brigades in that signal Confederate victory, Gen. Robert E. Lee reportedly cried out, "Thank God for the Tar Heel boys." Tradition has long attested to this incident. While no source directly proves such an utterance, Lee did write a letter to Vance praising the conduct of the North Carolina troops at Reams Station.

Following the Civil War, the use of "Tar Heel" rapidly became widespread in North Carolina. The first known postwar printed use of the term was in sheet music published in Baltimore in 1866 by William C. Miller, entitled "Wearin' of the Grey," written by "Tar Heel." The town of Tar Heel in Bladen

County was settled in 1874, although not incorporated until 1963.

The University of North Carolina football team changed its name from the White Phantoms to the Tar Heels in the 1920s, and all of the university's sports teams came to bear the moniker. The term—often erroneously rendered as one word, "tarheel"—is the standard nickname for North Carolina and North Carolinians alike. It is also commonly used throughout the state in the names of many businesses, services, and organizations.

References: B. A. Botkin, ed., *A Treasury of Southern Folklore* (1947); William S. Powell, "What's in a Name?," *Tar Heel* (March 1982); Michael W. Taylor, *To Drive the Enemy from Southern Soil: The Letters of Colonel Francis Marion Parker and the History of the Thirtieth Regiment N.C.T.* (1998).

Michael W. Taylor

Tar River Navigation Company. The Tar River—rising in Person County and flowing southeast to Beaufort, where it becomes the Pamlico River—first drew legislative attention in 1784, when the General Assembly directed the Pitt, Edgecombe, and Halifax County courts to clear the river of obstructions in their respective jurisdictions. The Tar River Navigation Company was subsequently incorporated in 1816 and given control of the Tar from its source to Greenville and of its tributaries (except Fishing Creek, for which the Fishing Creek Navigation Company was incorporated by the same act). Capitalized at $75,000, the Tar River company was permitted to charge a toll on traffic using the river to compensate for its efforts to improve the navigability of the Tar. The incorporating statute (amended in 1818) also promised a state stock subscription of $8,000. From the outset the company faced almost insurmountable obstacles, not only from the river itself but also from opponents of internal improvements in the region. Although investors subscribed to $56,000 worth of stock, many subsequently refused to meet this obligation and the company had to bring lawsuits (settled by 1825) to force payment.

The Tar River Navigation Company contracted for the construction of a lock and dam at Pippin's Falls for $3,110, but the contractor abandoned the work before completion. Concerned about protecting the public's investment, the legislature in 1823 instructed the state treasurer to withdraw the state's subscription to stock until he could determine that the company had been legally organized, that individual subscribers were buying their shares, and that the company agreed to have its operations managed by the Board of Internal Improvements. Apparently the company failed to meet these criteria, for the state only purchased $1,200 of its $8,000 stock subscription. According to an 1834 report by the Board of Internal Improvements, the stockholders had not met for many years; the company presumably was defunct.

References: Guion G. Johnson, *Ante-Bellum North Carolina: A Social History* (1937); Charles C. Weaver, *Internal Improvements in North Carolina Previous to 1860* (1903).

Alan D. Watson

Task System, in which workers were paid not by the hours they worked but by the number and quality of specific tasks they performed, was common in the industrial economy of late nineteenth-century North Carolina. This system was used primarily in traditional industries such as textiles, tobacco, and furniture manufacture. Since management was able to control what it considered an average or above-average output, thereby manipulating the wage scale, the task system kept workers at a tremendous disadvantage. Many employees' reluctance to join unions, which promised to seek better pay and better working conditions, further weakened their position.

The task system was part of an industrial management trend that relied on so-called scientific theories to scrutinize and enhance worker task performance. On the national scene, Frederick W. Taylor, the "father of scientific management," with followers like Henry L. Gantt and Lillian E. Gilbreth, developed a system of manufacturing management that provided coordination and efficiency control of machines, materials, and workers. Gantt, for instance, devised a task-and-bonus system of compensation, a forerunner of later incentive plans. Under this system, workers received a guaranteed wage, but if they accomplished a measurable amount of extra work, they were paid a bonus (a percentage of the base rate). Taylor's doctrine included theories such as time and motion study, production planning, and inventory control. He also claimed that it was possible to determine "scientifically" how a particular human task might be done most efficiently. Labor unions and other pro-labor forces condemned the Taylor system because it diminished or in some cases removed the human qualities involved in job performance.

Wiley J. Williams

Taxes, State. North Carolina first imposed income taxes in 1849, when it levied a 3 percent tax on interest, dividends, profits, wages, and salaries and a fixed fee of $3.00 on citizens with incomes in excess of $500. Aimed at the growing class of merchants and craftsmen viewed by the agricultural society as undertaxed by the existing state tax system (an ad valorem tax on real property and the poll tax), the new assessment was intended to tax those who did not earn their income primarily from land. From its inception the income tax was an important, though variable, part of the state's tax structure. By 1854 it produced 56 percent of total tax revenues, compared to 44 percent from real property and poll taxes. After the Civil War, however, the income tax was not a major revenue source, as it was collected by local officials who had no way of verifying an honest listing of income.

The 1868 state constitution authorized the General Assembly to tax "trades, professions, franchises, and incomes" but added the provision that "no income shall be taxed when the property from which the income is derived, is taxed." Widespread complaints persisted that the rate of taxation on nonproperty income was too low compared to the rate on property income. In 1903 the State Tax Commission recommended a remedy to this alleged inequity: the state would relinquish use of the property tax, leaving it solely as a local tax source and thus eliminating the incentive for counties to underassess property. The state would then rely solely on income, license, franchise, and inheritance taxes. The 1913 General Assembly proposed a constitutional amendment to implement the recommendation, which was rejected by voters in 1914. But in 1919 the legislature enacted a proposed constitutional amendment to permit the taxation of all income, including income from property, which passed by a large margin in 1920. The legislature also passed a Revaluation Act, which called for a statewide revaluation of all property under the supervision of the State Tax Commission.

In 1921 the General Assembly reformulated the state tax system under the principle that the sources of state and local taxes should be separate. To replace property tax revenues, it enacted a state-administered personal income tax and a corporation income tax, then created the North Carolina Department of Revenue to administer, enforce, and collect the new taxes. The new personal income tax, including exemptions, deductions, and a system of progressive rates, was based on a model developed by the National Tax Association. With the reforms of 1921, North Carolina became one of the first states to relinquish the property tax and to adopt a state-administered income tax. In doing so, the state government lost a source of revenue that had accounted for over 30 percent of its total revenue in 1919. However, the state more than offset the revenue loss by passing a gasoline tax.

In the early 1930s the responsibility for financing schools, roads, and prisons was shifted from counties to the state and a retail sales tax of 3 percent was enacted. The system of taxation and government finance that emerged during the 1931–33 period has remained essentially unchanged. North Carolina relies primarily on personal and corporate income and retail sales taxes, which vary widely from month to month, for raising general state revenue.

A number of studies and investigations of North Carolina's tax structure have been undertaken through the years, and citizens' groups, such as the North Carolina Tax Relief Association and the Taxpayers' League, have worked for changes in the system. At the governmental level, the Tax Study Commission was the designation for various commissions created or authorized by the General Assembly in 1955, 1957, 1965, 1967, and 1971. The purpose of the commissions was to examine a variety of tax situations and inequities in the state and suggest ways to eliminate them. All of these commissions held public hearings and received assistance from state agencies (such as the Department of Revenue, the Department of Tax Research, the Office of the State Treasurer, and the Institute of Government at the University of North Carolina at Chapel Hill) and from professional and other organizations. Governors Luther H. Hodges and Dan K. Moore—chief executives during the time of the 1955–68 Tax Study Commissions—enthusiastically supported them. Hodges, in a June 1955 address on a statewide radio and television network, said that the creation of that year's commission was one of the most significant measures passed by the legislature.

The tax commissions uncovered several serious flaws in the state's tax system. For example, in 1958 the Tax Study Commission reported that ratios of assessed value to actual market value of real estate varied considerably from county to county and within the same county, and that different types of property were often assessed at different percentages of market value in a given county (such as real estate at 40 percent, automobiles at 6 percent, and retail inventories at 50 percent).

In 1977 the Revenue Laws Study Committee, previously a subcommittee of the Legislative Research Commission, was established as a permanent legislative commission dedicated to tax issues. The committee effectively replaced the earlier Tax Study Commissions, examining revenue laws and making recommendations to the legislature.

Although tax laws often change, by the early 2000s North Carolinians paid income taxes in four different tax brackets with rates ranging from 6 percent to 8.25 percent. The state sales tax was 4.5 percent, but various additional local rates in certain areas lifted the total sales tax to 7 percent or more.

References: Leslie E. Carbert, *The Impact of State and Local Taxes in North Carolina and the Southeastern States* (1976); Lucille Howard, *A Study of North Carolina Taxes and the Impact on Taxpayers* (1989); Charles D. Liner, *Business Taxation and Economic Development in North Carolina* (1983); Liner, "Changes in North Carolina's Tax System: The Last Decade," *Popular Government* 57 (Summer 1991).

Wiley J. Williams

SEE ALSO North Carolina Tax Relief Association; Taxpayers' League.

Taxpayers' League was formed in Buncombe County in early 1928 to promote fiscal responsibility and electoral reform in local government. The Buncombe County league was organized because a political ring had incurred excessive debt, leading to the highest local property tax rate in the state. Asheville had built roads, buildings, parks, and reservoirs far beyond its needs. In fact, city government was in danger of insolvency. A real estate boom had collapsed by 1928, leaving the Central Bank and Trust Company holding much worthless real estate paper. In danger of failure, the bank persuaded the political ring to deposit $4.6 million of Asheville's funds. The city had borrowed the money, enough to continue operations for two years. The Taxpayers' League discovered this scam but did not publicize it for fear it would produce a run on the bank, causing a bank failure and the loss of the city's money. When in late 1930 the bank failed anyway, the league turned its efforts to reforming city government and persuading the state to provide local government services in order to reduce property taxes.

By early 1930, 14 counties had similar taxpayer organizations, all striving for lower property taxes. Soon opponents of high property taxes saw the need for a statewide organization; subsequently, representatives from 46 counties formed the North Carolina Tax Relief Association. Its main objective was to secure lower property taxes, but it also urged the state to assume control of local roads and schools and to pay for them with a sales tax. Taxpayer leagues like the one in Buncombe County thus led the property tax revolt that culminated with the state taking over roads, prisons, and schools and shifting part of the property tax burden to gas and sales taxes.

Reference: John L. Bell Jr., *Hard Times: Beginnings of the Great Depression in North Carolina, 1929–1933* (1982).

John L. Bell

SEE ALSO North Carolina Tax Relief Association.

Teacherage was a building, often in a rural setting but on school grounds and resembling a private home, that provided living accommodations for schoolteachers. The term came into general use largely in the first quarter of the twentieth century when public schools began to be opened in rural areas of North Carolina. The teacherage was sometimes managed by a matron or local residents or was operated cooperatively by the residents themselves. The building provided private or shared bedrooms, dining facilities, parlors or reception rooms, and bathrooms. The availability of a comfortable teacherage attracted teachers to schools that otherwise would have had difficulty filling staff vacancies.

William S. Powell

Telegraph was an electronic means for the rapid and reliable transmission of coded information over extended distances. In time it was also perfected to interpret and print the electronic symbols into readable text. By 1848 a telegraph line, which had begun at Washington, D.C., passed through Richmond and reached Raleigh en route to Wilmington. People who lived along the projected route kept North Carolinians informed by mail almost daily of its progress. Use of this new means of communication made possible the creation of new time zones, the use of railroad timetables, the transmission of news to newspapers, personal communication, and other conveniences of a modern lifestyle.

The *Raleigh Register* was the first newspaper in North Carolina to employ the telegraph to receive news, and it boasted of publishing its news 24 hours ahead of other papers in the state. Professor Collier Cobb of the University of North Carolina knew and taught telegraphy and also was a pioneer user of shorthand. As the use of these two cutting-edge skills spread among the state's youth, it heralded the decline of an epithet that had previously been used to describe North Carolina: the "Rip Van Winkle State."

Reference: Guion G. Johnson, *Ante-Bellum North Carolina: A Social History* (1937).

William S. Powell

Telephones began to appear in North Carolina beginning in 1879, three years after Alexander Graham Bell's new invention had first been introduced at the Centennial Exposition in Philadelphia. On 10 March of that year, a telephone was installed in the office of B. W. Starnes, manager of Western Union's Raleigh office, and local businessmen soon came to realize the instrument's utility. On 20 Sept. 1879 the first North Carolina exchange opened in Raleigh, in the rear of the Western Union office at "Battle's Corner," the intersection of Fayetteville and Martin Streets. The enterprise expanded to 30 stations and remained in business only one year. During 1879, however, the first long-distance lines in North Carolina were erected between Raleigh and Goldsboro, and the first long-distance call in the state was made on 14 Apr. 1879 between Raleigh and Wilmington.

On 1 Apr. 1882, Southern Bell began a new operation in Raleigh with 29 subscribers. The new exchange offered 24-hour service, with a day operator and a night operator. In September 1898 the Interstate Telephone Company opened an exchange in Raleigh, followed by the Raleigh Telephone Company, with 600 subscribers, in 1900. Thus Raleigh enjoyed the distinction of having three telephone systems in operation at once. Interstate Telephone merged with Southern Bell in 1907 and became Capital City Telephone Company, resuming the Southern Bell name in 1912. In 1922 Southern Bell purchased Raleigh Telephone Company and became the sole provider in the market.

Efforts to offer telephone service in the Charlotte area also began in 1879. Western Union manager E. R. Dodge began operations on 17 Apr. 1880 with 34 stations, but the business closed in 1882. Southern Bell initiated its maiden effort in Charlotte in 1879, installing its first telephone in T. C. Smith's drugstore on 18 Jan. 1880. The exchange opened in April 1880 but operated for less than three years. A successful effort finally came in July 1884, when Queen City Telephone Company began operations with 64 telephones.

As the nineteenth century drew to a close, telephone exchanges began cropping up in most North Carolina cities. In July 1889 an exchange opened in Greensboro with nine stations; Southern Bell bought the company in 1903. Southern Bell began operations in Wilmington in 1890 with 200 stations and in Winston-Salem the following year with 52 stations. The Procter Telephone Company brought service to Asheville in 1898, and Southern Bell opened a competing exchange in that region the following year.

The telephone dramatically changed the lives of North Carolinians and all Americans. Many subscribers almost instantly felt less isolated and more connected to their communities. Doctors, law enforcement officers, and firefighters were suddenly a mere phone call away. Business deals could be consummated in minutes over long distances, rather than by the slower, more cumbersome exchange of telegrams. Families could inquire about the health of loved ones and share news. Telephone-related terms such as "operator," "central," "information," and "party line" came into common usage. Telephone operators (almost exclusively females) became popular, as they could locate almost anyone at any time, knew the weather forecast, and had a wealth of other useful information. The telephone began to be glamorized in popular music and later in motion pictures.

Despite its popularity, however, the telephone industry was a for-profit business, and Bell and other large companies tended to concentrate in urban areas, where the capital investment needed for lines and equipment was lower and profits high. North Carolina was predominantly rural, and consequently much of the state was left without telephone service. Businessmen in smaller towns began to organize their own telephone companies, and farmers bought equipment and switchboards to set up their own "farmer's lines." Later, the rural lines were connected to the nearest telephone company and were finally replaced by rural multiparty lines.

In 1941 the Office of the Utility Commissioner became the North Carolina Utilities Commission, with a chairman and two full-time commissioners. This commission supervised the post–World War II boom in demand for telephone services. Companies could barely meet the requests for installations. The popular new dial service rapidly replaced the old systems, and innovations in cable technology improved the quality of message transmission and reduced system failures. The coming of the Information Age, coupled with telephone industry deregulation and consumer demand for a full range of services, have combined to produce breathtakingly rapid changes in telecommunications. Through satellite transmissions, cellular phones, and access to the Internet, the telephone industry has seemingly decreased the size of the world, just as the first crank telephones installed little more than a century ago gave many North Carolinians a newfound sense of community.

Reference: Edwin A. Clement, *The North Carolina Telephone Story: The First Ninety-Eight Years, 1879–1977* (1978).

Clarence E. Horton Jr.

Television Stations came to North Carolina beginning in the late 1940s, changing the lives of North Carolinians by providing them instant access to events, images, and ideas that had previously been unimagined. The state's first commercial TV stations were established in July 1949, when WBTV in Charlotte and WFMY-TV in Greensboro went on the air; both stations were properties of Jefferson Standard Life Insurance Company (Jefferson-Pilot Corporation). Live network television came to North Carolina on 30 Sept. 1950, when WBTV and WFMY-TV carried the University of North Carolina–Notre Dame football game from South Bend, Ind. In 1956 WRAL-TV of the Capital Broadcasting Company in Raleigh went on the air as an NBC affiliate.

North Carolina's first educational, or public, TV station (and the tenth in the United States) was WUNC-TV in Chapel Hill, which first broadcast in 1955 after years of Federal Communications Commission hearings on public TV allocations. UNC-Chapel Hill president Gordon Gray and other university officials played key roles in bringing public TV to the state, arguing for the importance of a statewide educational TV network. WUNC-TV's first regular program was a UNC-Wake Forest basketball game. Since then, WUNC, as part of the national Public Broadcasting System, has focused chiefly on educational, historical, and cultural programming, including local shows such as *North Carolina People* and *North Carolina Now*.

Local news programming has been arguably the commercial stations' most important contribution to North Carolina culture. Individual commercial stations have considered it an

Jim Tucker, star of the *Old Rebel–Pecos Pete Show*, and his boxer, Troubles, 1958. The popular children's program on WFMY-TV in Greensboro was locally produced. Photograph by WFMY-TV. NCC.

essential public service to alert viewers to dangerous weather conditions such as hurricanes and, in their aftermath, to fundraising efforts for food, clothing, and money. At election time, North Carolina's local stations devote considerable attention to candidates and issues.

With the rise of cable television in the 1980s, a growing number of local communities developed their own "public access" and government access networks to feature proceedings of local government bodies, community interest programs, and other programming developed by individual citizens. Cable companies were required to provide such public access to network space and equipment as part of their licensing agreements with the federal government and local municipalities, but changes in cable regulations through the 1990s reduced public access and the diversity of local programs produced. North Carolina's public access programs rarely rivaled the creativity or notoriety of programs developed in the nation's major urban areas, but by the early 2000s cities including Charlotte, Greensboro, Chapel Hill, and Raleigh had public access channels with robust local support.

In 1996 James Fletcher Goodmon, the chief executive officer of Capitol Broadcasting Company, made WRAL-TV the nation's first station to transmit TV signals digitally. Some experts believe this may be one of the biggest changes in television since the introduction of color in the 1950s. By the early 2000s there were about 50 TV stations, both public and commercial, in the state. Only a handful of these were independent, with the others affiliates of the major national ABC, NBC, CBS, Fox, UPN, and WB networks.

References: Harry Kenneth Smith, "Development of Educational Broadcasting in North Carolina, 1922 to 1972" (M.A. thesis, UNC-Chapel Hill, 1972); James Vickers, *Raleigh, City of Oaks: An Illustrated History* (1982).

Wiley J. Williams

Temperance Movement in North Carolina, which had as its goal the elimination or severe restriction of alcoholic beverage consumption in the state, is often equated with the formation of temperance societies, beginning in Guilford County in 1822. Yet a governmental regulatory measure that addressed public drunkenness appeared as early as 1715. This law also required any person who wished to retail liquor that was not produced on a farm to obtain a license from the governor. Other laws restricted "tippling houses" (later called "saloons") by compelling all liquor retailers to furnish food and lodging for their guests and gave county courts the power to grant liquor licenses. In the late eighteenth century, Protestant ministers, church organizations, and a variety of churchgoers (especially Baptists, Methodists, and Presbyterians) launched their own crusades against public drunkenness and disorderly conduct.

Two years after the organization of the American Temperance Society in Boston in 1826, two societies in North Carolina affiliated with the national organization appeared. Four years later there were 31 affiliates, including the Orange County Temperance Society, founded in Hillsborough in 1829. The Asheville Temperance Society, organized in April 1831, was the first in the western region of the state. The Pleasant Hill Temperance Society of Alamance County, formed about 1833, existed for more than 75 years. The North Carolina Temperance Society, created in 1839, sought to bring the scattered local units into an effective state organization but did not succeed.

The Washingtonian movement, which originated in Baltimore, came to North Carolina in 1841, followed by the Sons of Temperance in 1843. The Sons was a beneficial as well as a temperance association, retaining the total abstinence pledge of the Washingtonians. Other societies included the Daughters of Temperance, introduced at Raleigh in 1848, and the Cadets of Temperance, an outgrowth of the Sons of Temperance, which began in Wadesboro in 1849.

The Woman's Christian Temperance Union (WCTU), the most prominent temperance society in North Carolina after the Civil War, was organized at Greensboro in 1883 by Frances E. Willard, president of the national WCTU. Its wide range of reform programs included women suffrage, equal rights, child welfare, prison life, international arbitration, world peace, narcotics and tobacco control, child labor, juvenile delinquency, prostitution, and gambling. Two WCTU publications appeared in the state: the *Anchor* and the *North Carolina White Ribbon*.

The Civil War only temporarily stopped the activism for legal measures to eradicate the evils attributed to the liquor traffic. In 1881 the General Assembly reacted to this pressure by authorizing a referendum on prohibition statewide. The result was the crushing defeat of temperance proponents by a vote of 166,325 to 48,370. Yet the issue was not dead. Prohibitionists went to work in their own communities, and by 1900 they had eliminated legal liquor sales in many rural areas and small towns by means of local referendums. They were further strengthened in 1902, when the North Carolina Anti-Saloon League was established. Other events favored the prohibitionists—the Democratic Party became decidedly dry, the Watts Act of 1903 outlawed rural distilleries, and the Ward Law of 1905 dried up all but the state's 80 towns with populations of 1,000 or more.

A second referendum on statewide prohibition was set for May 1908, with Governor Robert B. Glenn leading the antiliquor campaign. The temperance forces carried the day (by a vote of 113,612 to 69,416), and North Carolina went dry in 1909, a decade before the Eighteenth Amendment established national Prohibition. North Carolina thus became the first state to adopt Prohibition by a direct vote of the people. The state retained its antiliquor law for four years after the nation passed the Twenty-first Amendment ending Prohibition.

Legal liquor returned to the state in 1935, when in its closing hours the General Assembly passed the Pasquotank Act, which permitted counties to sell liquor in state-owned stores regulated by an alcoholic control board. In 1937 a statewide local-option law was enacted. In that year the State Board of Alcoholic Control was created by the General Assembly "to establish a system of control over beverages whose alcoholic content exceeded 21 percent." The act included regulation of the manufacture, sale, and possession of these beverages, and no county could sell liquor without approval of its voter majority. By legislative acts of 1935, 1945, and 1949 the board, which changed its name to the North Carolina Alcoholic Beverage Control (ABC) Commission, also obtained authority to regulate the consumption of wine, beer, and other malt beverages and sold liquor through ABC stores, which were given control of all aspects of whiskey production, possession, and sale in the state. In the 1970s the legislature approved "liquor-by-the-drink" at bars and restaurants, subject to local laws and limitations.

References: Guion G. Johnson, *Ante-Bellum North Carolina: A Social History* (1937); Daniel Jay Whitener, "History of the Temperance Movement in North Carolina, 1715 to 1908" (Ph.D. diss, UNC-Chapel Hill, 1932); Whitener, *Prohibition in North Carolina, 1715–1945* (1945).

Wiley J. Williams

SEE ALSO Anti-Saloon League; Turlington Act.

Temple of Israel, begun in 1875, is the oldest Jewish house of worship in North Carolina. Jews, mainly of German descent, had been a prominent part of the Wilmington population since the eighteenth century but had not had a permanent place to worship. The Jewish population of Wilmington increased during the Civil War. In 1867 an Orthodox congregation, the Wilmington Hebrew Congregation, was organized by Rabbi E. M. Myers of Charleston. This group was short-lived, but a Reform congregation was organized in 1872 and three years later began building the Temple of Israel.

Recently discovered information ascribes the design of the temple to Philadelphia architect Samuel Sloan. Previously it had been attributed to Alex Strausz, a local builder and congregation member. If Sloan was the designer, the Temple of Israel is the third Wilmington house of worship he designed. The others are the current First Baptist Church and the previous First Presbyterian Church, both begun in 1859. The temple's Moorish-style building, which was restored in 1982 and 2000, features twin towers with onion domes painted gold. The main body of the building is covered by a gable roof and spans the two towers.

Reference: Tony P. Wrenn, *Wilmington, North Carolina: An Architectural and Historical Portrait* (1984).

Janet K. Seapker

Tennessee, Formation of. Prior to the American Revolution, white settlers were building cabins along the Watauga and Nolichucky Rivers in the western part of the North Carolina colony. In 1772 they drew up a compact called the "Watauga Association." Four years later they petitioned North Carolina to extend its jurisdiction over their area, and the following year North Carolina created Washington County with boundaries that included all of modern Tennessee. Between 1779 and 1788 the state legislature established six additional counties in the Tennessee country: Sullivan (1779), Greene (1783), Davidson (1783), Sumner (1787), Hawkins (1787), and Tennessee (1788).

In 1784 the General Assembly ceded the state's western lands to the United States, then revoked the cession later that year. Nevertheless, the frustrated settlers, led by John Sevier, organized the State of Franklin with a constitution, a separate legislative body, and Sevier as governor. The Continental Congress, as well as Virginia and North Carolina, refused to recognize the new state, and it soon collapsed. In 1789 North Carolina ceded its western lands to the newly established federal government, and on 1 June 1796 Tennessee was admitted to the Union as the sixteenth state. Sevier was elected governor.

References: Noel B. Gerson, *Franklin: America's "Lost State"* (1968); Hugh T. Lefler and Albert R. Newsome, *North Carolina: The History of a Southern State* (3rd ed., 1973); William S. Powell, *North Carolina through Four Centuries* (1989).

Wiley J. Williams

SEE ALSO Franklin, State of.

Tennis in its modern form developed in England in the late nineteenth century. In the United States, it was one of the first sports in which women participated in competitive situations. The sport was played as early as the 1880s at the University of North Carolina, when the University Tennis Club was formed. Reports from Pinehurst and Asheville mentioned tennis in the following decade. Pinehurst first hosted its Midwinter Championship in 1911. The North Carolina Open championships were first held in 1912, while the state high school championships were first held in 1916. Many top players, such as Bill Tilden, played in Pinehurst's North and South Tournament in the 1920s.

Competitive college tennis in the state dates back to the early part of the twentieth century. The University of North Carolina had a team in 1907, while North Carolina State University's first team dates from 1922. The UNC men became a dominant team in the 1930s and held their rank under coaches

John Kenfield (1928–55), Don Skakle (1959–80), and Allen Morris (1981–93). UNC won 15 Southern Conference titles from 1930 through 1953, claimed 22 Atlantic Coast Conference (ACC) titles in a 25-year period from 1954 through 1978, and produced All-American players such as Bitsy Grant (1931), Vic Seixas (1948), and Freddie McNair (1970–73). Other schools, including Duke University and North Carolina State University, began challenging UNC's supremacy during the 1970s.

Women's tennis was a later arrival on the state's college campuses. UNC's Laura Dupont won the 1970 U.S. Lawn Tennis Association's collegiate national championship at a time when the National Collegiate Athletic Association (NCAA) did not have national championships for women. The following year women's tennis became a varsity sport at UNC. By the early 1980s, most colleges in the state fielded women's teams and offered full scholarships to the top players, as had already been done for male players. Duke University, which began its program in 1973, became the dominant women's team, capturing the ACC title every year from 1988 through 1995 and finishing in the NCAA championship top eight five times during that period. Duke's top players included Julie Exum (1990–93) and Susan Sabo (1988–91).

Other top players from North Carolina were Bo Roddey, Whit Cobb, John Sadri, Buck Archer, and Tim Wilkinson. Durham's John Lucas, who gained fame as a basketball player at the University of Maryland and in the professional ranks, won three state tennis championships in high school and played professionally. Althea Gibson, the first black woman to become a world-class tennis player, honed her game under the tutelage of Hubert Eaton of Wilmington in the late 1940s.

Tennis continued to gain popularity as a recreational sport, especially following World War II. Although still associated with exclusive country clubs, tennis soon appeared on many public courts and in municipal programs. It was not a major spectator sport in the state, however, nor has North Carolina been the site of any major professional tennis tournaments, although the Raleigh Heat played in the World Team Tennis League from 1990 to 1993. This was a professional league that operated for a brief period in the summer, mostly with second-rank professional players.

Reference: Carlyle Lewis, *North Carolina Tennis History* (1978).

Jim L. Sumner

Terrapins, members of the tortoise order, are similar in appearance to many of the most common types of turtles. Best known of the North Carolina terrapins are the diamondbacks (*Malaclemys terrapin*), which breed in marshy areas near the seacoast and were once a minor, though lucrative, part of the state's commercial fishing industry. Diamondback terrapin soup, made with sherry and a thick cream sauce, was considered a delicacy in northern cities before the Civil War.

The first recorded commercial terrapin catch in North Carolina occurred in February 1849, when the keeper of the Bodie Island lighthouse, using a specially designed dredge, caught 2,150 diamondbacks that he sold in Norfolk, Va., for $400. By 1880 the total marketed yield in the state was 123,000 pounds, but thereafter the terrapin fishery declined, with only occasional catches reported after World War II.

By the early 2000s, diamondbacks were threatened sufficiently by net fishermen and coastal development to be categorized as a "species of special concern." At the same time, the unique coloring and design on their shells has resulted in their being sought mainly by herpetologists and hobbyists.

References: R. E. Coker, *The Natural History and Cultivation of the Diamond-back Terrapin* (1906); "Hardluck Terrapin," *Wildlife in North Carolina* 64 (February 2000).

David Stick

Terrorism. SEE Homeland Security.

Test Oath was an attempt by colonial leaders to ensure the loyalty of those holding public office in prerevolutionary North Carolina. The First Provincial Congress, initially called simply a convention, met on 25 Aug. 1774 and drew up a "test" or oath to be taken by its delegates. Members of the Provincial Council, the Committees of Safety, and other agencies also were required to subscribe to the oath, which read in part: "We, the subscribers, professing our allegiance to the King . . . do solemnly profess, testify and declare, that we do absolutely believe that neither the Parliament of Great Britain, nor any constituent member thereof, have a right to impose taxes on these Colonies to regulate the internal policy thereof; and that all attempts, by fraud or force, to establish and exercise such claims and powers, are violations of the peace and security of the people, and ought to be resisted to the utmost." The oath concluded with a pledge to uphold all of the "acts, resolutions, and regulations" established by the Provincial Congress.

Reference: William L. Saunders, ed., *Colonial Records of North Carolina*, vol. 10 (1890).

William S. Powell

Textbook Commission originated in the early twentieth-century efforts of Governor Charles B. Aycock and other leaders to raise educational levels in North Carolina. In the beginning, only rural elementary schools came under legislative provisions for uniform selection of textbooks and only one basal textbook per course was authorized for use throughout the state. When high school textbooks were standardized, adoptions were initially at the county level. In 1945 the elementary and secondary textbook committees were combined to create a unified State Textbook Commission composed of professional educators. The size, composition, and duties of the commission changed over time, but the ultimate responsibility for issuing book contracts has rested consistently with the State Board of Education. Major changes have included the shift to an established adoption cycle, the inclusion of lay members, multiple adoptions per course, and more freedom of choice at the local level.

In 1977 the size of the State Textbook Commission was increased to 14 members; in addition to 12 educators, 2 parents were appointed. By 1990 criteria for suitable textbooks were being issued by the state superintendent of public instruction with the aid of the Curriculum Review Committee, and regional textbook evaluation advisory committees were assisting the State Textbook Commission in its work. In 1999 legislation expanded the membership of the commission to a total of 23, including 15 educators and 8 parents. Modifications in law and policy have resulted in the present-day system, which permits local flexibility in textbook choice while maintaining a statewide course of study for all public schools.

References: Allison W. Honeycutt, "Textbook Development," *North Carolina Education* (February 1936); Claude C. Warren and E. Michael Latta, *The Origin and the Development of the North Carolina Textbook Commission* (1990).

George-Anne Willard

Textiles, various forms of fibers, yarn, cloth, and other materials, along with the clothing and apparel made from textiles, have been among North Carolina's most important products since the early nineteenth century. As the textile industry expanded and North Carolina became a worldwide leader in textile production, the poor working conditions of the state's mills, often populated by women and children, became the focal point of aggressive but generally fruitless union activity. After decades of high production, the industry began to face massive economic challenges during the 1970s as foreign imports of clothing and apparel increased dramatically. Further elimination of trade restrictions resulting from treaties such as the North Atlantic Free Trade Agreement (NAFTA) between the United States, Canada, and Mexico, which went into effect in 1994, severely affected North Carolina's textile industry. Despite many factory closings and job losses, however, North Carolina in 2004 continued to be a national leader in textile production, employing more than one-quarter of the textile workers and 6 percent of the apparel workers in the United States.

The Rise of the North Carolina Textile Industry

North Carolina possessed many resources, both natural and economic, that made the state an ideal environment for a booming textile industry. These resources included a mild climate, plenty of accessible waterpower, a wealth of raw ma-

A senior textiles class at North Carolina State College, 1938. Courtesy of NCOA&H.

terials in the form of cotton and lumber, and an abundance of cheap labor. During the first century of textile manufacturing, from the 1820s to the 1920s, North Carolina's textile mills produced a lower-grade yarn and cloth consumed by a local market. Before the Civil War, mills sold their yarns to nearby farm families who operated carding machines, spinning wheels, and hand looms to make their own clothes. A superintendent of the Rocky Mount Mills recalled that in the 1850s he sold most of the coarse yarn produced at the mill "in five pound bundles for the country trade—this was woven by country women on hand looms." He sold surplus yarn for "coarse filling for the Philadelphia market."

A handful of products from North Carolina achieved recognition beyond the communities in which they were manufactured. In Randolph County, Henry Elliott stamped the label "Cedar Falls" on bundles of yarn produced at his mill along the Deep River, and the Salem jeans produced by Francis and Henry Fries in Forsyth County became well known as a durable product for "negro clothing" on southern plantations. The best-known textile product in the early decades of the industry were the Alamance Plaids produced by Edwin M. Holt, who in 1853 had learned of a dyeing process that enabled him to produce the South's first colored cloth on a power loom.

The Civil War stimulated a major conversion of the textile industry from yarn spinning to the manufacture of material for the war effort. The Confederate government entered into contracts with every mill in North Carolina for coats, pants, and other articles of clothing as well as sacks and bags. The two regiments from Salem wore woolen Salem jeans into battle. John Motley Morehead's mill in Leaksville (Rockingham County) furnished blankets, while the Cedar Falls mill became the leading supplier of shirts and underwear by war's end. During the last months of the conflict, the Confederacy drew its entire supply of textile goods from North Carolina.

To assist the former Confederacy's crippled economy, the U.S. Congress passed a law exempting federal taxes on cotton textiles manufactured in the same district where the cotton was grown. New England textile manufacturers closed their mills and moved south to exploit this competitive edge as well as the cheaper labor. In the late nineteenth and early twentieth centuries, North Carolina mills resumed their practice of producing yarn for local consumption and selling the surplus to mills in northern cities, especially New York and Philadelphia. Although a few mills in North Carolina wove their own cloth in addition to making yarn, the national reputation of the state's textile industry remained tied to the production of coarse yarns. North Carolina's textile manufacturers produced lower-grade yarns at a relatively low cost with inexpensive equipment and a largely unskilled labor force. Those mills with weaving departments produced heavy woven goods such as unbleached cloth, plaids, ginghams, denims, toweling, socks, flannel for industrial fabrics, and clothing for working people. Many of the state's most prominent manufacturers of woven goods, such as Cannon Mills and Cone Mills, began during these later decades of the nineteenth century.

An increased demand for American-made textile goods during the World War I era, particularly for military uniforms, blankets, and other apparel, stimulated the North Carolina textile industry and resulted in a large increase in the number of textile mills in the state. By 1921 North Carolina mills were producing $191 million worth of textiles annually, more than twice the production of 1914. This growth continued after the war, and by 1923 North Carolina had overtaken Massachusetts as the leading textile-producing state in the nation (by value of product).

Mill Villages, Labor Disputes, and Twentieth-Century Technologies

In the late nineteenth century, numerous company-owned mill villages developed around the textile mills of North Carolina and other southern states. Typically, one- and two-story timber houses were constructed in rows with small yards, brick pier foundations, tin roofs, porches, and a simple functional design. The size of the houses varied from three to six rooms. Workers rented their houses from the company for ten cents a week per room, with deductions made from the renter's paycheck. The company provided water, coal, and electricity without charge.

Mill owners also built churches, parks, swimming pools, stores, offices, and libraries for employees and families living in mill villages. They sent social workers to organize clubs for all age groups, to visit homes, and to provide transportation to out-of-town hospitals. Companies staged outdoor movies in the summer and held special events and band concerts. Companies also provided a Christmas tree to each household with a gift for every child, often arranged travel and educational tours, and even supported the town baseball team and gave the players (who were also mill workers) paid time off for the season's demands.

By 1900 the vast majority of North Carolina's mill workers lived in mill villages. Although offering some advantages to the workers, these villages were generally more beneficial to mill owners. By keeping their workers content, dependent, and loyal, owners were able to maintain total control of their workforce and ensure the economic success of the mill. The lives of workers in mill towns, in fact, were almost completely dictated by the schedule and requirements of the company factory. Because of the textile industry's reliance on unskilled labor, many North Carolina mills employed entire families, including women and children who were age 12 and above. The workday was long, usually 10 to 12 hours, mill hands worked six days a week, and the work conditions were harsh and unhealthy. Often very young children assisted older family members with simple, easy work in the factories until they were old enough to take on heavier jobs.

While many mill villages were abandoned and demolished as the mills closed, some eventually grew into larger towns. Kannapolis, near the Cannon Mills site in Cabarrus County, and Cramerton, which developed around May Mills in Gaston County, are two such towns. Glencoe Village, a 105-acre site in Alamance County, and Edenton Mill Village in Chowan County were rehabilitated by Preservation North Carolina and the houses sold for restoration as single-family homes. (Both sites are listed in the National Register of Historic Places.)

Despite the many hardships experienced by North Carolina's mill workers, the textile industry proved to be resistant to most labor union activities in the state. The first major labor union to focus on North Carolina's textile industry was the American Federation of Labor in 1898, followed by the United Textile Workers Union in 1919. Several strikes, such as the violent Gastonia strike of 1929, organized primarily by the National Textile Workers Union, did little to improve textile working conditions but succeeded in turning the plight of the state's mill workers into an international cause. Federal labor laws passed as part of the Roosevelt Administration's New Deal, particularly the Fair Labor Standards Act of 1938, addressed some of the most egregious workplace practices of textile mills, especially those involving child labor. Further unionization attempts throughout the first half of the twentieth century included the Harriet-Henderson Mills strike of the late 1950s, which again resulted in violence but little progress for North Carolina textile workers.

The adoption of man-made fibers introduced profound changes in North Carolina's textile industry. Rayon, created in 1855 by a Swiss chemist, was the first of these new products. A regenerated wood cellulose product, rayon was produced commercially in France and later in the United States in 1910. Other important synthetic fibers developed during the first half of the century included acetate, first produced by the Celanese Corporation in 1924; nylon, first produced commercially by DuPont in 1939; vinyon (1939); saran (1941); metallic fibers (1946); modacrylic, developed by Union Carbide in 1949; olefin (1949); and acrylic (1950). Nylon, the most popular and widely utilized of these new fibers, was used to make sewing thread and women's hosiery. During World War II, nylon replaced silk in tires, tents, ropes, and various military supplies. North Carolina provided more textile products to the military than any other state, in the form of blankets, sheets, clothing, tents, bandages, and parachutes. At the end of the war, nylon also became popular in carpeting and automotive upholstery. Another popular fiber has been acrylic, introduced by DuPont in 1950 as a substitute for wool. The first wash-and-wear products consisted of 60 percent acrylic and 40 percent cotton.

Burlington Industries, Inc., led by J. Spencer Love, became the driving force behind the growth of synthetic textiles. Love founded the company in 1923, and it grew through a strategy of acquisitions and mergers and through the adoption of synthetic fibers, especially rayon in the years before World War II. The extraordinary demand of the war years enabled Burlington to expand as a supplier of more than 50 products for the government. Burlington's corporate growth continued in the 1950s and the early 1960s, as revealed in the company's statistical profile for 1967: 130 plants in 15 states and 11 countries, with 83,000 employees. In North Carolina that year, 40,000 people (almost 20 percent of all textile employees in the state) worked at Burlington's 78 plants in 47 communities. No other industrial enterprise was as pervasive in the state.

In the 1970s, new environmental regulations, focused on polluted wastewater and air produced by textile manufacturing, and labor union activity, centered on low wages and poor working conditions, impacted the state's textile industry. Brown lung disease (byssinosis)—an asthma-like narrowing of the air passages caused by chronic inhaling of particles of cotton and other substances prevalent in mills producing yarn, thread, or fabric—was identified as a deadly occupational hazard for thousands of North Carolina's mill workers. During this period, the J. P. Stevens Company lost several court cases related to its labor policies and became known in labor and legal circles as the nation's "number one labor law violator." Meanwhile, the lure of low capital and wage costs began to drive textile manufacturing into Asia, South America, and Central America. Between 1974 and 1984, textile imports nearly tripled, while at the same time, efforts to strengthen the U.S. dollar meant that American goods increased in price. By the mid-1980s, imports accounted for 43 percent of the clothing bought in the United States. By 1990 the trade imbalance in apparel had grown to nearly $25 billion.

The textile industry tried to rebound through legislation and automation, spending, for example, a total of $1.9 billion on new equipment ranging from robots to high-speed weaving machines that use jets of water or air instead of shuttles. In the late 1970s and early 1980s Burlington reinvested 85 percent of its cash flow into new equipment, $1.5 billion over one seven-year period. Some companies remained viable by emphasizing specialty products that competed less with imports. Collins & Aikman turned to automotive carpeting, furniture upholstery and commercial carpeting. Smaller family- and worker-owned companies often managed to stay afloat through such specialization. The industry in 1983 launched a promotional campaign called "Crafted with Pride in the U.S.A." with help from several major retailers, urging Americans to buy clothing bearing those labels.

Decline, Consolidation, and the Future of Textiles in the State

Decline, mergers, and takeovers marked the North Carolina textile industry beginning in the 1980s, with Fieldcrest buying Cannon Mills, West Point–Pepperell buying J. P. Stevens, and Burlington spending millions to block takeover efforts. Often, the changes proved painful for employees, who lost jobs and sometimes benefits such as company pensions, and for communities built around textile operations. Between 1975 and 1985, more than 800 mills closed nationwide, and employment in North Carolina's textile mills fell from an all-time high of 293,600 in 1973 to 211,300 in 1986. Many former textile mills have been transformed into housing or retail shops or have met the wrecking ball.

The effects of numerous free trade agreements, notably NAFTA in 1994 and treaties with African and Caribbean nations in 2000, led to a vast increase in textile and apparel imports and, consequently, numerous plant closings in North Carolina. Approximately 100,000 jobs were lost in textiles in the state from 1997 to 2002, with an additional 70,000 lost in the apparel industry during that same period. In 2003 one of the biggest job losses in North Carolina history occurred when Kannapolis-based Pillowtex closed five plants, eliminating 4,000 jobs. Burlington Industries, mired in debt and struggling to emerge from Chapter 11 bankruptcy protection after years of being pounded by cheaper Asian imports, spent $3.5 million in 1998 for a stake in a small company using nanotechnology—the ability to manipulate individual atoms to create new materials—to produce fabrics that repel water, wine, and other liquids. In 2004 New York financier Wilbur Ross purchased Burlington Industries, which became, along with Cone Mills, part of the giant International Textile Group.

By 2006 the North Carolina textile industry had begun to focus on new technologies and specialized products outside the realm of apparel. Students at N.C. State's College of Textiles, for example, were working with high-tech fabrics that can withstand heat and force and textile products ranging from artificial hearts and optical fibers to under-coverings for roadways. Many large textile companies, facing continued high labor costs and trade deficits, began to establish a future built on marketing technology to other companies rather than on actual production.

References: Mildred Gwin Andrews, *The Men and the Mills: A History of the Southern Textile Industry* (1987); Brent D. Glass, *The Textile Industry in North Carolina: A History* (1992); Jacquelyn Dowd Hall and others, *Like a Family: The Making of a Southern Cotton Mill World* (1987); Harriet L. Herring, *Passing of the Mill Village: Revolution in a Southern Institution* (1949).

Brent D. Glass
Kelly Kress
Additional research provided by Gene Purcell and Douglas A. Wait.

SEE ALSO Burlington Industries; Cannon Mills; Chatham Manufacturing Company; Coleman Manufacturing Company; Cone Mills Corporation; Cotton Mills; Gastonia Strike; Glencoe; Hanes Brands; Harriet-Henderson Cotton Mills Strike.

Thalian Association is the name of a succession of amateur theatrical companies active in Wilmington for more than 200 years. Wilmington gentlemen organized the first "theatrical corps" sometime around 1788, reportedly inspired by a local appearance by a traveling professional company. The name was derived from that of Thalia, the Greek muse of comedy. The troupe used the theater in the Innes Academy, at the northeast corner of Third and Princess Streets, as a stage for its performances.

Innes Academy was named for James Innes, who came to the Cape Fear area about 1735. In his will he bequeathed "all my books and 100 pound Sterling or the equivalent there unto in currency of the country for the use of a free school for the benefit of the youth of North Carolina." For this purpose he also willed a plantation. On 28 Apr. 1803, the trustees of the Wilmington Academy began advertising for bids for "a house in the town of Wilmington suitable for an Academy and Theatre." By December 1806 the academy building was sufficiently finished for the gentlemen of the Thalian Association to present the first of several performances in the new theater. The bill was the *Lovers Vows*, a comedy in five acts, and David Garrick's farce, *Neck or Nothing*. The performances were presented as a benefit for the completion of the academy.

Throughout the first half of the nineteenth century, Innes Academy was the predominant site for performances of drama in Wilmington. In addition to the Thalians, professional touring companies also played there. In 1850 the theater was leased for extended engagements of the Jefferson & Ellsler Company. Joseph Jefferson, at this time in his early twenties, would become one of the most beloved actors of the American theater. Of his arrival in Wilmington, Jefferson wrote, "the days were spent in preparing the dusty old rat-trap of a theatre for the opening."

Wilmington's Thalian Hall. Photograph by Tim Buchman. Courtesy of Preservation North Carolina.

On 12 Aug. 1856, the Thalian Association signed over its interest in the Innes Academy to the city of Wilmington, which was planning a new city hall on the site. In return, the Thalians were granted a lease on a municipal theater planned for the building's east wing, on condition that the group pay half the cost of equipping and furnishing the theater and agree to an annual rent. On 12 Oct. 1858, the new Thalian Hall had its gala opening.

The modern Thalian Association has presented at least one production each year since World War II. Members of the group have also been active in the preservation of Thalian Hall. Thalians successfully lobbied for funds for major restorations of the theater in 1938–41, 1947–52, and 1974–75. After several renovations and additions, the most recent completed in 1990, the building still serves Wilmington in its intended capacity.

References: Mary B. Broadfoot, "Thalian Hall," *Lower Cape Fear Historical Society Bulletin*, no. 13 (February 1970); Donald J. Rulfs, "The Professional Theater in Wilmington," NCHR 28 (April–October 1951); Tony P. Wrenn, *Wilmington, North Carolina: An Architectural and Historical Portrait* (1984).

Bennett L. Steelman
Beverly Tetterton

Theaters. SEE Dramatic Arts; Opera Houses.

Thirteenth Amendment to the U.S. Constitution, sent to the states for ratification in February 1865 with the unanimous support of congressional Republicans and the firm endorsement of President Abraham Lincoln, contained two short sections. The first prohibited slavery and involuntary servitude except as punishment for convicted criminals. The second pronounced in arguably vague terms that Congress had the power to enforce this prohibition "by appropriate legislation." The amendment reflected the North's determination, after four years of Civil War, to make legal, permanent, and more encompassing Lincoln's 1863 Emancipation Proclamation. However, what rights would be granted the former slaves and what powers Congress had under the enforcement clause were left ambiguous.

After Lincoln's assassination, President Andrew Johnson made clear to the South that ratification of the Thirteenth Amendment was one of his minimum requirements for readmission to the Union. The proceedings and results in North Carolina were typical of the actions southern states offered in response. On 29 Nov. 1865, two days after the new North Carolina legislature convened, Rufus Y. McAden introduced a resolution for approval of the Thirteenth Amendment. Debate centered on the second section. Many North Carolinians feared that this provision would allow Congress to regulate civil rights, thus depriving the states of their traditional control over race relations and legal privileges. Supporters tried to assure doubters that Secretary of State William H. Seward was correct in his interpretation that the "clause is really restraining in its effect, instead of enlarging the power of Congress." Faced with the knowledge that rejection of the amendment meant the continuation of federal control over the state, the North Carolina House approved the amendment 100 to 4.

In the Senate, the same debate ensued, but on 4 December that body also ratified the amendment. But opposition forces quickly regrouped, and on the same day Senator A. D. McLean of Cumberland County introduced a resolution "touching" the Thirteenth Amendment; the resolution explicitly stated that North Carolina ratified the amendment only "in the sense given to it" by Seward, "to wit: That it does not enlarge powers of Congress to legislate on the subject of freed men within the States." Although the General Assembly clearly understood that McLean's resolution had no legal effect, both houses endorsed it.

By 15 Dec. 1865, the necessary three-fourths of the states had ratified the Thirteenth Amendment and Seward proclaimed it in effect. With that action slavery, already recognized as ended in North Carolina after the state's 1865 constitutional convention, was now legally and permanently terminated by the U.S. Constitution.

References: Roberta Sue Alexander, *North Carolina Faces the Freedmen: Race Relations during Presidential Reconstruction, 1865–67* (1985); Herman Belz, *A New Birth of Freedom: The Republican Party and Freedmen's Rights, 1861–1866* (1976); Michael L. Benedict, *A Compromise of Principle: Congressional Republicans and Reconstruction, 1863–1869* (1974); Harold M. Hyman and William M. Wiecek, *Equal Justice under Law: Constitutional Development, 1835–1875* (1982).

Roberta Sue Alexander

Thomas Built Buses, Inc., headquartered in High Point, is one of the largest manufacturers of school and commercial transit buses in North America. Perley A. Thomas, known in the industry as "Mr. P.A.," learned his trade as a yacht and streetcar designer in Detroit and Cleveland after leaving his Canadian farm in 1900. He subsequently obtained the job of chief engineer for a small streetcar manufacturer known as the Southern Car Company in the tiny North Carolina town of High Point. The company was growing, selling every streetcar it could produce, but stiff competition put it out of business in 1916.

Thomas then worked independently as a skilled wood craftsman until a call came from the Southern Public Utilities Company—later renamed the Duke Power Company—which needed to renovate some of its streetcars. He called upon a few others who had worked for Southern Car and sent a repair crew to Charlotte, staying home to see if he could develop a new business. When he won a contract to refurbish streetcars for the U.S. Navy shipyard in Mobile, Ala., Thomas and sons Willard and Norman launched a firm bearing their name. The Depression of the 1930s nearly sank the Thomas company, coming at a time when power companies and municipal governments were looking for new ways to administer public transportation at minimal cost.

In 1936 the state of North Carolina advertised for bids for the construction of 500 buses for its school system. With a carefully prepared bid of $195 for a 17-foot bus, $205 for a 19-footer, and $225 for a 21-footer, Thomas's successful proposal reinvigorated his company. By 1972 the number of executives and family heirs in the Thomas Built organization was well over 100, and the idea of taking the company public was explored but dropped when management worked out arrangements for a leveraged buyout of most of the stockholders. The family maintained a majority on the board while being joined for the first time by new outside directors. By 1997 there were only two Thomases and two other men who had married Thomases active in day-to-day operations.

Modern school buses are built with all-steel bodies that reflect a continued emphasis on safety for their young riders. The Thomas Built company competes with builders of school bus bodies in nearly every state in the Union and a few that seek a national niche. The firm had sales of about $400 million in 1996. In 1998 it became part of the Freightliner LLC group, a Daimler-Chrysler company. Still headquartered in High Point and privately held, with several manufacturing facilities, Thomas Built Buses had about 1,600 employees worldwide in the early 2000s and was producing approximately 14,000 vehicles annually.

Reference: Clint Johnson, *From Rails to Roads: The History of Perley A. Thomas Car Works and Thomas Built Buses* (1996).

Joe Exum Brown

Thomas's Legion was formed during the Civil War by William Holland Thomas, the only white man ever to become chief of the Eastern Band of Cherokee Indians. Believing that North Carolinians would not tolerate Cherokee neutrality in the war and seeing an opportunity to procure state recognition of these Indians as citizens, Thomas enlisted more than 400 Cherokees in service to the South. He eventually commanded two companies of Cherokees and six companies of whites. Their first skirmish occurred in September 1862 at Baptist Gap, Tenn., near the Virginia state line. During the battle the grandson of the famous Junaluska was killed—infuriating the Cherokees, who scalped several Union soldiers. By the end of September, Thomas was promoted to colonel of his legion. This command comprised 11 infantry companies (the first 2 of which were Cherokee), 8 cavalry companies, and 1 light artillery battalion. It included the most prominent whites and Cherokees from western North Carolina and became known as Thomas's Legion of Indians and Highlanders or simply Thomas's Legion, although it was often mistakenly called the 69th North Carolina Regiment.

In February 1864 Thomas's men were surprised ten miles west of Quallatown in the Battle of Deep Creek, which resulted in a Union victory. For the most part, the Cherokees saw little combat during the Civil War. They served primarily as guards and rounded up deserters. However, Thomas and his "legion" are credited with firing the last Confederate shots of the Civil War at Waynesville in May 1865.

References: Vernon H. Crow, *Storm in the Mountains: Thomas' Confederate Legion of Cherokee Indians and Mountaineers* (1982); E. Stanly Godbold Jr. and Mattie U. Russell, *Confederate Colonel and Cherokee Chief: The Life of William Holland Thomas* (1990).

William L. Anderson

SEE ALSO Deep Creek, Battle of.

Thomasville Female College was a nineteenth-century academy for girls that grew out of a series of previously established Christian schools in the Davidson County town of Thomasville. The school's history actually began in 1856, when John W. Thomas, considered the founder of Thomasville,

bought the Glen Anna Female Seminary and housed it in a new building north of the railroad on the eastern edge of his land. Thomas took over as president of the school. The 1857 graduating class consisted of five women, whose diplomas were given to them at the graduation ceremony not by Thomas but by Braxton Craven, the president of nearby Trinity College. (The two schools were closely linked.)

Thomas soon renamed his institution Thomasville Female College, but the exact date of this change is not known. An 1861 letter from Thomas to a prospective student's father listed the contemporary expenses of the school: "Board and washing, $25 for session; Tuition in English, $7.50 for session; Music, $8 for session; French, $4 for session; [and] Latin, $4 for session." A catalog from that era emphasized the strictness of the school's social environment: "The discipline of the institution combines mildness with firmness, inculcating strict order, prompt obedience, correct deportment and industry.... Students persisting in violations of morality or good order, or incurably indolent, will be promptly dismissed as unworthy a place in this or any other well regulated literary institution." None of Thomasville's students was allowed to "receive calls from gentlemen during study hours, at unreasonable hours and by no means on the Sabbath." The dipping of snuff was also "strictly forbidden."

Thomasville Female College continued to operate during the Civil War, although many of its northern teachers left at the start of the conflict. In 1885 Baptist minister J. N. Stallings arrived to help run the school. Soon after Stallings took over the entire administration, the student body began to dwindle and several quality teachers left. In 1888 Stallings abandoned the Thomasville campus and moved the college to High Point in hopes of regaining the school's previous success. After four years of struggle, however, the college closed.

References: J. W. Cannon, "Old School for Girls Has Place in History Despite Hectic Career," *Greensboro Daily News*, 3 Jan. 1932; Mary Green Matthews, *Wheels of Faith and Courage: A History of Thomasville, North Carolina* (1951).

Jay Mazzocchi

Thomas Wolfe Memorial, located in Asheville, is centered around the rambling Victorian home where the novelist spent his childhood and adolescence. The house was built in 1883, in the Queen Anne style, and enlarged many times, as Wolfe's mother operated it as a boardinghouse called "Old Kentucky Home" for several decades starting in 1906. Wolfe was born on 3 Oct. 1900 in a smaller house that stood two blocks away, but Old Kentucky Home served as the model for the boardinghouse named "Dixieland" in his epic autobiographical novel, *Look Homeward, Angel* (1929).

The rooms of Old Kentucky Home have been preserved almost intact, with the original Wolfe family pieces arranged

Old Kentucky Home in Asheville, late 1980s. Photograph by Tim Buchman. Courtesy of Preservation North Carolina.

much as they were during Wolfe's youth. At first frowned upon in his hometown for the unflattering portrait he painted of it in his novels (*Look Homeward, Angel* was banned from the Asheville public library for seven years), Wolfe was later celebrated as one of the city's most famous citizens. His youthful home came to be seen as worth preserving as part of the nation's literary history. A classic of twentieth-century Americana, the house has been preserved as an attraction for people from around the world since 1971 as a National Historic Landmark and since 1976 as a North Carolina State Historic Site.

In 1998 a fire severely damaged many of the house's rooms. A number of artifacts and furnishings were subsequently restored, and architects rebuilt the damaged home. The house was closed to visitors for several years, although the visitors center, exhibit hall, and audiovisual program remained open, and the site continued to host special events. All sections of the Thomas Wolf Memorial were reopened in 2004.

References: Wilson Angley, "Historical Research Report: Thomas Wolfe and the Old Kentucky Home" (30 Oct. 1974); David H. Donald, *Look Homeward: A Life of Thomas Wolfe* (1987); Richard F. Knapp, ed., *North Carolina's State Historic Sites: A Brief History and Status Report* (1995); George W. McCoy, "Asheville and Thomas Wolfe," *NCHR* 30 (April 1953).

Ted Mitchell

Thompson Children's Home had its beginning in the work of two men—Benjamin Bronson of St. Peter's Episcopal Church in Charlotte and Edwin A. Osborne, a recent convert to the Episcopal faith. Bronson initiated the effort by facilitating the purchase of more than 250 acres on what was then the outskirts of Charlotte in order to establish a much-needed school for local youths. On part of the property, he opened a denominational academy in 1870. It was named for the Lewis Thompson family, which furnished much of the initial fund-

ing. Although the effort failed for lack of management, the idea was not lost, and in the 1870s Osborne, long interested in educating and caring for "destitute orphans" of every faith, approached Bronson about using the abandoned school for that purpose. In 1866, at Osborne's instigation, the Episcopal Diocese of North Carolina accepted 61 acres and two buildings and paid part of the debt associated with the Bronson school.

Osborne, the orphanage's first superintendent (1886–98), worked energetically to make his dream a reality. Beginning without money and with the existing facilities in poor condition, he solicited food, used clothing and furniture, and money. With the latter he refurbished the old structures, built new ones, and hired a staff to assist him. By 1888 the school had 30 children, a number that would double within 12 years.

In 1898 Osborne resigned and was replaced by Walter J. Smith (1898–1922). William H. Wheeler (1922–40) and M. D. Whisnant (1940–65) also served as superintendents. Smith and Wheeler tapped new sources of revenue and virtually rebuilt the school. By the 1950s, however, needs were changing. There were fewer orphans, meaning declining numbers at Thompson each year, and children lacking one or both parents were increasingly being served by federal or state agencies. It became clear that Osborne's vision was no longer valid and that the church could not indefinitely fund a traditional but archaic institution.

Two independently based reports supported this conclusion, and under superintendent Robert Noble (1965–78) and director John Powell the mission of the institution was dramatically changed. Instead of concentrating upon orphans, the school would now focus upon the treatment of emotionally disturbed children between the ages of 6 and 12. These children would be drawn from across the state and were to be housed in specially designed treatment cottages. The centers were to be served 24 hours a day with rotating staffs.

Now named Thompson Children's Home, the institution was moved from inner Charlotte, which had gradually surrounded the orphanage, to a 40-acre location on the outskirts of the city. With branches at Fletcher and Goldsboro, a child development center in Charlotte, and a strong foster care system, Thompson Children's Home provides a variety of services to more than 300 children and families annually.

References: Lawrence Foushee London and Sarah McCulloh Lemmon, eds., *The Episcopal Church in North Carolina, 1701–1959* (1987); Barbara Lockman, *A Century's Child: The Story of Thompson Children's Home, 1886–1986* (1986).

Louis P. Towles
Additional research provided by Sheila Bumgarner.

Threshing. Mechanized threshing machines probably did not reach North Carolina until the first quarter of the nineteenth century. Before that time few farmers and planters in

Wheat-threshing gang with their livestock and machinery, probably in Chatham County, July 1912. NCC. Original photograph owned by H. T. Eddins of Durham.

the state grew enough wheat, rye, barley, or oats to justify the purchase of a stationary threshing machine. In the 1850s, however, wheat became a viable cash crop in a number of central and southern Piedmont counties, making threshing machines fairly common. North Carolina newspapers frequently carried ads for threshing machines in the decades that followed.

Early stationary threshing machines were often called "groundhog" threshers because when in operation, they appeared to be digging into the ground and kicking refuse out from behind them. Groundhog threshers were comprised of a rotating toothed or studded cylinder, housed within a box, that beat the grain from the heads as sheaves were fed into it. A variation on this design called for a solid ribbed wheel set upright. As the wheel rotated, sheaves of grain were forced against the wheel and the ribs knocked the grain from the heads.

Until the advent of steam engines (and later gas engine tractors), threshing machines were powered by draft animals hitched to "horse powers" that transferred their motion to the machine. Two types of horse powers were used well into the

twentieth century: an inclined treadmill and a circular sweep. By the Civil War, stationary combined threshers and separators could thresh, clean, and bag as many as 200 bushels a day. After the Civil War, threshing technology improved rapidly. By the late 1920s the combined thresher-separator had reached its technological zenith. In 1927, a combined harvester, thresher, and separator was invented that allowed the farmer to cut, thresh, and clean in one operation. Until the late 1930s, this "combine," as it was known, was pulled by teams of horses or mules or a by tractor. In the late 1930s, a self-propelled combine was invented that eliminated the need for an external pulling source.

Although North Carolina was never a major national grain producer, much of the culture that became associated with threshing in the West also flourished in the state. Traveling threshers who followed the south-to-north wheat harvest on the Great Plains had their counterparts in North Carolina. And just as in the West, threshing parties emerged from this communal activity, replete with feasts and dances after the work was completed. With the invention of the combine in 1927, however, this once-common rural activity soon passed into memory.

References: Cornelius O. Cathey, *Agriculture in North Carolina before the Civil War* (1966); Thomas D. Isern, *Bull Threshers and Bindlestiffs: Harvesting and Threshing on the North American Plains* (1990).

Charles LeCount

Thyatira Church and Community. Thyatira Presbyterian Church, located ten miles west of Salisbury, is believed to have been in existence since 1753 under various names, including Lower Meeting House and Cathey's Meeting House. The surrounding community in its early days was composed mainly of Scotch-Irish immigrants who settled first in Pennsylvania and then moved down to North Carolina. The community also had a small population of Pennsylvania Germans. Thyatira sided with the "old school" Presbyterians during the Great Awakening, disapproving of the exuberant actions exhibited by many during the worship services of the movement. This could be attributed to the community's staunch Scotch-Irish and German roots.

One of the church's most influential ministers, Samuel McCorkle, assumed his duties on 2 Aug. 1777. McCorkle, a native of the Thyatira community, believed that religion and education should be joined. To this end, he established Zion-Parnassus Academy, a classical school believed to have been the first normal school in America. This school became one of the finest in the state and produced many students who went on to be early graduates of the University of North Carolina in Chapel Hill—the establishment of which was championed by McCorkle, who became one of the school's original trustees.

This commitment to education can also be seen in how McCorkle ran Thyatira Church. McCorkle broke the church, both white and black communicants, into small groups, a rough equivalent to modern Sunday school programs, where the scriptures and catechism were taught. Thyatira served as a leader in education throughout the early days of North Carolina. Its effects can been seen not only in its support of the University of North Carolina, but in its role in the 1837 founding of Davidson College, a Presbyterian liberal arts school, as well.

Reference: Walter L. Lingle, *Thyatira Presbyterian Church, Rowan County, North Carolina, 1753–1948* [ca. 1948].

Marc Sanders

Tick War was a term that newspaperman Ben Dixon MacNeill applied to a controversy on Hatteras and Ocracoke Islands following passage by the General Assembly in 1919 of an act requiring that cattle and horses be disinfected as a precaution against tuberculosis and glanders, respectively. The law was not especially burdensome on mainland farms with fenced-in livestock, but on the Outer Banks, where cows and horses ranged freely, it was more troublesome. The independent-minded inhabitants of the Outer Banks looked on incredulously when state and federal employees—called "tick doctors" by the local residents—arrived on Hatteras and Ocracoke and began building concrete vats in which horses and cattle were to be dipped. Government officials were puzzled over the relatively small number of animals brought to be disinfected, and the matter got out of hand when some of the vats were mysteriously blown up at night. When news of the problem reached inland, MacNeill was sent by the *Raleigh News and Observer* to Ocracoke, from where he wired tongue-in-cheek stories about the Tick War. Only after the officials gave up and left the islands were "upwards of 200 cattle and as many horses" led from the marshes, where they had been hidden from the "tick doctors."

Reference: H. G. Jones, "Outer Bankers of North Carolina Won 'Tick War,'" *Washington Daily News*, 1 Feb. 1978.

H. G. Jones

Time Zones were determined locally until the coming of railroads. Schedules then became essential, particularly for trains traveling in an east-west direction. In the decade before 1880, the need for standardization became critical and the subject was widely discussed. The United States observed almost 100 conflicting local sun times until the fall of 1883, when a General Time Convention met in Chicago on 11 October and a Southern Time Convention convened in New York on 17 October. As a result, at noon on Sunday, 18 Nov. 1883, four times zones across the nation were established. Most of North Carolina fell into the Eastern Standard Time zone, but the western limit for that zone ran through Asheville at 82 W 33′, thereby leaving a portion of western North Carolina in the Central Standard Time zone. This remained the case until 1946, when most of the municipalities in the western counties passed local ordinances changing to Eastern Standard Time. On 28 Sept. 1947 North Carolina adopted Eastern Standard Time statewide.

During World War I, North Carolina adopted Daylight Time for the periods 31 Mar.–27 Oct. 1918 and 30 Mar.–26 Oct. 1919. Between 1 Aug. 1941 and 9 Feb. 1942, state offices operated on Daylight Time; from 9 Feb. 1942 to 30 Sept. 1945, North Carolina implemented what President Franklin D. Roosevelt called "War Time." From 1946 to 1965 North Carolina did not observe Daylight Time, but since 1966 the state has followed the national schedule.

References: Doris Chase Doane, *Time Changes in the U.S.A.* (1981); U.S. Department of Transportation, *Standard Time in the United State: A History of Standard and Daylight Saving Time in the United States and an Analysis of the Related Laws* (1970).

William S. Powell

Tobacco, although not the primary component of North Carolina's economy that it once was, continues to be a major influence on the economic and cultural identity of the state. From the earliest years of European settlement, during which tobacco quickly rose to become the colony's leading export, through the era of the state's "Big Tobacco" companies and the late twentieth-century decline of the industry, the story of North Carolina agriculture has been told largely through tobacco farming and its related products. Despite shifting economic and societal trends and several far-reaching legal and governmental actions, in the early 2000s North Carolina remained a national leader in the production of several types of tobacco. Roughly 50 percent of the nation's flue-cured tobacco, which supplies flavor and aroma in cigarettes, is produced in the state. Burley, or dark leaf tobacco, which acts as a filler for cigarettes, is also grown in large volume. More than half of North Carolina's 100 counties continue to depend on the production of some type of tobacco as an economic base.

Abandoned dwelling being used as a curing barn for burley tobacco in Watauga County, 1960. NCC.

Development and Growth of the North Carolina Tobacco Industry

Tobacco usage for ritualistic and medicinal purposes has been traced backed by archaeologists to about 800 B.C., and in many modern cultures, including that of some Native Americans, tobacco still has a ceremonial function. In 1492 Christopher Columbus noted the use of tobacco by American Indians. In Jamestown, Va., John Rolfe, more widely recognized as the husband of Pocahontas, first industrialized tobacco in 1612. After four failed efforts by others to establish a permanent colony on North American soil, Rolfe introduced a milder and sweeter tobacco variety. His "scientific" expertise in cultivation and curing, along with commercial ingenuity and foresight, parlayed tobacco into a staple trade item with England. It became the basic economic force that brought permanence and success to the country's social beginnings, while also directly creating a plantation economy based on slave labor.

In the late sixteenth century, Sir Walter Raleigh's Roanoke colonists in the region that became North Carolina found that the Native Americans raised tobacco—the Indian's "holy herb"—and that it was smoked by all ages and both genders in clay pipes and also used as snuff. The settlers began to grow Indian crops, and in time tobacco became Carolina's leading "money crop" or export to the British Isles and Europe. It was grown in the Albemarle Sound area, in the Roanoke River Valley, and later in Granville County and other counties bordering Virginia.

Tobacco production was encouraged by agricultural legislation passed by nearly every Assembly, the vast majority of whose members were engaged in agriculture or related industries—as were perhaps 95 percent of the colonists. This was a natural development resulting from the abundance, fertility, and inexpensiveness of land, as well as the imperative need of the people for self-sufficiency. However, in North Carolina, as elsewhere in colonial America, agricultural practices were generally backward and unscientific. Land was tilled year after year until the soil was exhausted, then new ground was cleared and cultivated. There was little or no crop rotation, barnyard manures were not used, commercial fertilizers were unknown, and there was a scarcity of tools and implements. In addition, tobacco growing, primarily in the Coastal Plain but also in the Piedmont, required a great deal of labor, leading to the growth of the slave population in the colony.

Tobacco production in North Carolina continued to increase throughout the eighteenth and nineteenth centuries. By 1850 the state was producing approximately 12 million pounds a year, and by 1860 that figure had skyrocketed to 33 million pounds. Part of this increase came as a result of the discovery of a new type of tobacco leaf and a new curing process. In about 1852 Abisha and Elisha Slade of Caswell County perfected the production of bright yellow tobacco using charcoal instead of wood as the fuel for curing tobacco grown on a bright, sandy, and relatively infertile soil. The new flue-curing process had been accidentally discovered in 1839 by a young slave named Stephen (who later became known as Stephen Slade). Stephen fell asleep while watching a barn of curing leaf tobacco. When he awoke, he rushed to his nearby charcoal pit, seized several charred butts of logs, and placed them on the dying embers. The result was 600 pounds "of the brightest yellow tobacco ever seen." At first it was thought that this curing process was the secret of producing bright leaf tobacco, but later it was found that the soil was the principal factor.

The Rise of "Big Tobacco"

Tobacco manufacturing was developed largely by men who had experience in growing and selling tobacco or who had lived on farms where tobacco was raised. There were many small tobacco factories in counties along the Virginia border—especially Granville, Person, Caswell, Rockingham, and Stokes—as well as Burke, Iredell, Orange, Rowan, and other counties before 1840. But it took the visits of Confederate and Union armies to the Piedmont, particularly to Durham, to popularize these products. During the Civil War, especially in 1865 when Union general William T. Sherman's troops invaded the state, soldiers discovered the quality of bright leaf smoking tobacco. The idle troops—pending arrangement of terms between Sherman and Confederate general Joseph E. Johnston at Bennett Place—looted John R. Green's tobacco factory at Durham. They found Bull Durham Smoking Tobacco to be the mildest and best they had ever tried.

After the war, the soldiers began writing back to Durham for more bright leaf products. The tobacco industry shed its local character and began its rise to national importance. The Dukes—Washington and sons Benjamin N., James B. "Buck", and Brodie L.—were among the first to take advantage of this new demand. Washington Duke, mustered out of the Confederate army, returned to his farm near Durham, where he found that some tobacco had been overlooked by the marauding soldiers. He began grinding tobacco, which he packed and sold under the brand name Pro Bono Publico to soldiers and the public. By 1874 Duke and his sons were manufacturing smoking tobacco. That year R. J. Reynolds also built his first factory in Winston. James B. Duke decided to start making cigarettes, which by 1880 (following their first commercial production, being rolled by hand, in New York about 1864) had become economically important. Although crude cigarette-making machines had been invented in the United States in the 1870s, a more practical device with which to roll cigarettes was invented by James A. Bonsack, a Virginian. That machine —capable of turning out 120,000 cigarettes a day, the equivalent of 40 steady hand rollers working 10 hours—was set up in the W. Duke, Sons and Company factory in 1884. The Duke firm thus gained a great commercial advantage over competitors.

By the turn of the twentieth century, North Carolina was internationally recognized as America's leading source of tobacco. Even though it was widely known as "Virginia bright leaf," European customers still understood the North Carolina origins and looked to the state as the world's major supplier. Cigarettes were fast replacing cigars and chewing tobacco as the most popular means of tobacco consumption in the United States. Interested in forming a combination of the larger cigarette manufacturers, James B. Duke played a key role in organizing the American Tobacco Company, of which he became president, in 1890. In the following years, American Tobacco and its various offshoots gained control of the market not only for cigarettes but also for smoking tobacco, snuff, and practically all tobacco products except cigars. The federal government's antitrust action against this corporate giant was launched in 1907 and ended in 1911, when the Su-

preme Court ordered its dissolution. The old American Tobacco and its closely related subsidiaries were divided into a new American Tobacco Company, Liggett-Myers, P. Lorillard, Philip Morris, Brown and Williamson, and R. J. Reynolds. James B. Duke soon disassociated himself from the tobacco industry and joined brother Benjamin and George W. Watts in the development of hydroelectric power.

While North Carolina–based tobacco companies came to dominate the industry, the arduous work associated with tobacco cultivation continued to control the lives of thousands of North Carolinians and influence much of the state's rural culture. Tobacco farms and barns were common and easily recognizable features of the North Carolina landscape. Tobacco farming demanded constant attention during all its phases, from planting, tending, and harvesting the crops by hand to curing and transporting the product to market. Successful farming was a year-round process requiring experienced laborers, often working long hours under grueling conditions. From the demise of the plantations following the Civil War through much of the twentieth century, entire families and, in many cases, whole communities lived, worked, and participated in celebrations and diversions fitted to the seasonal requirements of tobacco farming.

During the Great Depression, when crop prices fell drastically, farmers in North Carolina and other agricultural states suffered tremendous hardships. In an effort to improve their situation, Congress passed various bills affecting crop production and prices, the most significant and far-reaching of which was the Agricultural Adjustment Act of 1938. This act established a system of production quotas for several key crops, including tobacco. These quotas—differing in size and calculated from a formula using past production figures of individual tobacco farms—put limits on the amount of tobacco that each producer could sell in the market, thus guaranteeing higher leaf prices. Over the decades, individual producers sold their quotas to larger landowners, who consequently gained increased production rights and a greater share in the market. Quotas were often rented, as well, further strengthening the economic position of the larger farms. The quota system, with its consistently strong price supports, continued to control tobacco production throughout the remainder of the twentieth century. Under this system, North Carolina's tobacco growers became the most productive in the nation. The mid-twentieth century represented a high-water mark for the industry. Growers produced nearly 1 billion pounds of leaf in 1955, the largest amount ever produced in the state.

Meanwhile, Durham (home of American Tobacco and Liggett-Myers), Winston-Salem (R. J. Reynolds and Brown and Williamson), Reidsville (American Tobacco), and Greensboro (Brown and Williamson) were considered to be among the nation's leading tobacco-manufacturing centers. (Philip Morris, the fifth of what became the "Big Five" tobacco companies, located in Concord in 1983.)

Legal Challenges and the Decline of the Industry

Even as production levels reached an all-time high, the tobacco industry in the United States and North Carolina began its decline in the early 1950s, beginning with health-related magazine articles, congressional hearings on smoking and health in 1957, and the U.S. Surgeon General's *Report on Smoking and Health* (1964). A wave of civil lawsuits against the tobacco industry between the mid-1970s and 1995 reflected smokers' concerns, with the filing of more than 400 unsuccessful suits. In 1994, however, the first class-action suits were brought against tobacco companies, including a suit by 60 law firms in five states. These suits represented about 40 million smokers and 50 million ex-smokers claiming to be addicts or suffering physical ailments as a result of using tobacco products. The solidarity of the tobacco companies was broken in 1996, when the Liggett Group (the fifth-largest firm) agreed to settle its part of the suit. Liggett agreed to finance an anti-smoking campaign, not to oppose new government regulations, and to make the first damage payments ever by a tobacco company. Shortly afterward, two former Philip Morris employees confirmed charges that tobacco companies manipulated nicotine levels to keep smokers addicted. Another class-action suit followed, this time involving 60,000 flight attendants who said they were forced to inhale secondary smoke in airplanes.

In the mid-1990s the states of Florida, West Virginia, Minnesota, and Mississippi filed suits for the medical costs they incurred in treating smokers. Other states, including North Carolina, subsequently challenged tobacco companies on similar public health grounds. In November 1998 a legal arrangement between four major U.S. cigarette manufacturers and 46 states, called the Master Settlement Agreement (MSA), was instituted. Under the MSA, cigarette companies agreed to pay the states $206 billion over the following 25 years in compensation for Medicaid costs. These funds, called Phase I funds, represented the largest amount of MSA money to be paid to the states. A second fund in the amount of $5.15 billion, called Phase II, was to be paid by tobacco companies directly to tobacco farmers and allotment holders in the tobacco-growing states.

North Carolina's share of Phase I payments equals $4.6 billion over 25 years, and the state's Phase II payments amount to just under $2 billion. In order to distribute Phase I funds equitably, the North Carolina General Assembly created three programs, each with a specific focus. The Golden LEAF Foundation, created in 1999, is a nonprofit corporation that controls the distribution of 50 percent of the Phase I funds. Operating under a board of directors appointed by the governor, the foundation's stated purpose is to improve the economic conditions of distressed North Carolina communities, in particular those that were previously dependent upon tobacco. The Golden LEAF Foundation gives grants to nonprofit and governmental groups and invests in various economic programs designed to improve and diversify the state's economy, especially in areas such as biotechnology, alternative agricultural products, and alternative fuels. Career training and job creation is one of its primary goals.

The Health and Wellness Trust Fund, recipient of 25 percent of North Carolina's Phase I funds, is a state agency that gives grants to programs related to health and medical issues. The other 25 percent of the funds are controlled by the Tobacco Trust Fund Commission, an 18-member board operating under the state treasurer. The commission is organized to give direct assistance to those unemployed as a result of tobacco-related issues. These include tobacco farmers, quota holders, and others working in the tobacco industry whose lives have been adversely affected by the decline of tobacco.

As part of the MSA, "Big Tobacco" companies also agreed to abide by certain marketing limits, such as being barred from marketing to minors. In 2001, however, there were charges that tobacco companies were still targeting teenagers. In March of that year the attorney generals of California and other states sued Reynolds (maker of Winston and Camel cigarettes) for breaching the terms of the agreement. The Federal Trade Commission reported that the Big Five companies had spent a record $8.24 billion on advertising in 2000. While the companies stopped using outdoor billboards, as required, they put their funds into other publicity venues such as retail store displays and print advertising.

As the tobacco industry faltered, demand fell, and tobacco imports grew, the production quota and price support system, in place since 1938, became increasingly ineffective. In 2004 the quota system, so long the underpinning of North Carolina tobacco farming and a key reason for the continued existence of many small tobacco farms, was eliminated through the passing of the federal Fair and Equitable Tobacco Reform Act. The act initiated a massive buyout program funded at $10 billion over ten years to compensate quota holders and tobacco growers in relation to the size of the quotas they owned. Cigarette manufacturers and importers with shares in the U.S. market were to fund the buyout. While the ultimate effects of the buyout are unfolding, industry analysts believe that the end of the quota system and all federal regulation of tobacco production will undoubtedly result in a significant decrease in the number of small tobacco farms in the state.

In 2006 North Carolina remained one of the top tobacco-producing regions in the world, however, with the state's more than 10,000 tobacco farmers selling approximately $620 million worth of the product annually. Economic and societal trends, however, have led to immense growth in the state's output of other agricultural products, notably hogs ($2 billion), broiler chickens ($2 billion), and soybeans ($290 million). In total, these new areas of production have come to redefine North Carolina agriculture and fill the void left by the tobacco industry's decline.

Tobacco warehouse in Wilson, 1926. NCC.

References: Jerome E. Brooks, *Green Leaf and Gold: Tobacco in North Carolina* (2nd ed., 1997); Philip J. Hilts, *Smoke Screen: The Truth behind the Tobacco Industry Cover-Up* (1996); Roy Norr, "Cancer by the Carton," *Reader's Digest* 61 (December 1952); North Carolina Rural Economic Development Center, *The Economic Impact of the 1998 Tobacco Settlement on the North Carolina Economy* (2000).

 W. W. Yeargin
 Additional research provided by Wiley J. Williams.

SEE ALSO American Tobacco Company; Brown and Williamson Tobacco Company; Bull Durham Tobacco; R. J. Reynolds Tobacco Company; W. Duke Sons and Company.

Tobacco Auctions, highlighted by the unique chant of the tobacco auctioneer, were one of North Carolina's most interesting cultural phenomena. They took place in the state's many tobacco market towns, found as far west as the Asheville burley tobacco auction, east in the flue-cured auction in Greenville, and south in Tabor City and other towns near the South Carolina border. Complete with the chanting auctioneer, the animated warehouse sales leader, and an array of buyers nodding and winking as they bid on each "lot" or "pile," tobacco auctions drew farmers, merchants, tobacco buyers, and curious onlookers. Their importance to local economies was immense: when the auction was over, locals knew by the prices paid to the farmers whether or not they would enjoy a good economic year.

The contemporary "loose-leaf" tobacco auction, during which the tobacco was made available for buyers to inspect at length, premiered in 1858 in Danville, Va., and became the primary method of selling bright leaf tobacco in North Carolina. This method was necessitated, in part, by a chronic distrust between tobacco buyers and those who produced, planted, or sold tobacco.

By 2006, following the economic and cultural upheavals affecting the tobacco industry, tobacco auctions had become largely a thing of the past.

W. W. Yeargin

Tobacco Belts are areas that traditionally have a large number of tobacco warehouses or markets. The largest tobacco belt in North Carolina is the Eastern Belt. It consists of approximately 65 tobacco warehouses, situated in 18 market towns beginning on the north side of the South River and extending northward to Ahoskie. By the late nineteenth century, tobacco production had begun spreading out of the Piedmont region of the state and into many eastern counties. Among the primary reasons for this movement were the diseases and soil depletion experienced in the Piedmont, the adventurous nature of some farmers, and the need for economic expansion. Farmers found it expedient to create markets for their tobacco near to the site of production, and soon the tobacco marketing industry had organized itself in the form of the Eastern Belt, though that term itself was not yet in use.

North Carolina's Border Belt lies along both sides of the North Carolina and South Carolina line, spreading north to the South River in North Carolina. There are approximately 49 warehouses situated in 15 market towns in the Border Belt. North Carolina Border Belt market towns include Chadbourn, Fair Bluff, Fairmont, Lumberton, Whiteville, Clarkton, and Tabor City; South Carolina market towns include Loris, Darlington-Timmonsville, Conway, Florence, and Mullins.

The Old and Middle Belt denotes a tobacco belt that has some of the oldest tobacco market towns in North Carolina. The term "middle" refers to its geographical location in the state. Historically, tobacco production moved westward across Virginia, from Jamestown into Lynchburg, down to Danville, then east and westward along the Virginia–North Carolina border. The modern-day Old and Middle Belt in North Carolina has dozens of tobacco warehouses situated in nine market towns. These towns range from Louisburg in the east to Mount Airy in the west.

The growing, harvesting, and marketing season of North Carolina's Border Belt is usually about one week behind that of the Eastern Belt and two weeks behind the Old and Middle Belt.

W. W. Yeargin

Tomato Clubs, promoting the involvement of young girls in finding ways to increase the production of agricultural crops, were started by the North Carolina Department of Agriculture in 1911 at the prompting of the U.S. Department of Agriculture. Each tomato club member was challenged to grow and can as many tomatoes as she could on one-tenth of an acre of land. Girls in Guilford County started tomato clubs through the efforts of educator Jane S. McKimmon, who held canning club "short courses" at Elon College and Peace Institute, teaching the proper methods of sterilizing and sealing cans. By 1916 thousands of cans of tomatoes and other foods had been produced. McKimmon's efforts eventually led to a vigorous network of 4-H Clubs across the state.

Marilyn Wright

Tombstones. Because of a lack of native stone in the coastal region where European settlement began, the earliest North Carolina grave site memorials were stakes or crosses made of wood, especially cypress, and have almost entirely disappeared. Fieldstones were used where available, but only wealthy settlers could afford hewn stone brought in from elsewhere. Many early graves were marked by small pyramids of brick. By the mid-eighteenth century and for a hundred years thereafter, barrel vaults of brick became common among landowners. However, no extant engraved markers that date to before the 1750s are known. Soapstone, relatively easy to carve, was commonly used in the western counties between about 1750 and 1825. Marble became popular after 1840 and granite soon thereafter.

Throughout North Carolina, the vertical headstone has always been the most common grave marker. Added footstones became common during the mid-1700s and into the 1800s, giving the visual impression of a bed. During the mid-1800s a French-style grave marker appeared, typified by headstone, footstone, and side rails with bedded or potted plants inside. Affluent families as long ago as the late 1700s sometimes chose horizontal "ledger" stones, rectangular, body-length slabs laid flat on the ground atop the grave, possibly to discourage grave robbers. These ledger stones frequently have notable epitaphs. Variations include the table stone, raised upon low brick pilings (usually four or six); chest or "box" graves; and altar tombs.

Commercially carved stones begin to appear in North Carolina after about 1830. Prior to that, stones were often carved by artisans for whom stonework was an avocation or secondary occupation. Their carvings typically consist of simple, often baleful, motifs such as the spirit skull (or "death's-head"), the hourglass, the scythe, the finger pointed heavenward, and the secular urn. With the gradual shift in attitudes toward death associated with the Great Awakening of the 1730s and 1740s, such carvings became softened and more hopeful; the death's-head, for instance, took on wings, and was later replaced by winged cherubs and beatific angels. Other common symbols include anchors (especially at seaside cemeteries), the dove, broken pillars or felled trees, and the Christian cross and crown.

By the late 1800s tombstone design had achieved a high level of sophistication in the cemeteries of North Carolina's major municipalities, often realized in monumental mausoleums designed as temple replicas. Simple epitaphs common until the mid-nineteenth century—usually consisting of no more than the deceased's name and age—gradually took on more detail, often recording age by the year, month and day, as well as the places of birth and death. By the mid-1800s, a lengthy epitaph was often suggestive of affluence. By the close of the nineteenth century, epitaphs became enormously varied and elaborate, sometimes recording the cause of death or quotations from devotional verse. Some are humorous, while others contain references understandable only to the deceased's acquaintances.

The early twentieth century saw a return to brevity and a reawakened interest in symbolic epitaphs. In modern-day North Carolina, as elsewhere, tombstones are most frequently mass-produced, with the stonecutter adding only inscriptions. Stone plaques, set horizontally at ground level, are common since they permit easier, more cost-effective grounds maintenance.

References: Henry King, *Tar Heel Tombstones and the Tales They Tell* (1990); M. Ruth Little, *Sticks and Stones: Three Centuries of North Carolina Gravemarkers* (1998).

William G. DiNome

SEE ALSO Fraktur.

Tornadoes are the fiercest storms that occur on earth. They are cyclonic, with winds that can easily exceed 200 miles per hour for short periods blowing counterclockwise around a low-pressure center. Tornadoes usually develop at the base of a thundercloud and also develop readily during hurricanes. Their wind is sufficient to pick up and incorporate small debris and may move much larger objects, often causing virtually total destruction in their path. North Carolina tornadoes tend to move to the northeast along with their parent thunderstorm, but deviations and jumps are common. The typical tornado track in the state is a few hundred yards wide and a few miles long, although there is often a series of four or five tornadoes associated with a single thunderstorm, widening the path of destruction.

During the period between 1950 and 1995, North Carolina experienced more than 600 tornadoes, ranking it twenty-second among the states in terms of tornado frequency, with a relatively higher number of deaths (82) and injuries (1,952) and amount of property damage ($377 million worth) associated with these storms. There have been marked changes in tornado activity in North Carolina from decade to decade. Whereas during both the 1950s and 1960s the state had fewer than 100 tornadoes, the 1970s had closer to 200 and the 1980s, 150. The 1990s experienced a huge jump in the number of storms, having well over 300—1996 alone had 51 tornadoes, and 1998 broke that record with 66 tornadoes through the end of November—and the early 2000s have thus far had more

storms than either the 1950s or the 1960s. Thankfully, a general decrease in tornado-related deaths, a decline attributed to better forecasts and warnings, has accompanied the increase in storms.

The tornado outbreak of 28 Mar. 1984 was arguably the worst in recent North Carolina history. A series of twisters stretched from Newberry, S.C., northeast to Ahoskie, N.C., leaving 44 dead and 800 injured in the state. Other major events, such as the coastal storm of 28 Nov. 1988 and the 5 May 1989 outbreak in the Triangle area, each of which killed four people, further contributed to a decade seemingly full of tornadoes and destruction. Another of North Carolina's worst tornadoes occurred on 27 Mar. 1994, affecting 40 counties and killing two people while causing $20 million in damages. On 20 Mar. 1998 several tornadoes resulted in over $7 million in damages and killed two people in Rockingham County. With Tropical Storm Bonnie passing through the area, a 13 Aug. 2004 tornado injured about 32 people and killed 3.

Most tornadoes occur in the southern portions of the Coastal Plain and Piedmont. The highly populated counties, notably Mecklenburg and Cumberland, commonly record a large number of storms. There are relatively few tornadoes in the Mountains, although one of the severest outbreaks within the last 40 years, on 3–4 Apr. 1974, affected the extreme western counties from Transylvania westward. Six tornadoes were responsible for six deaths and almost $15 million in damage to buildings, crops, and forests.

Reference: David M. Ludlum, *Early American Tornadoes, 1586–1870* (1970).

Peter J. Robinson

Torpedo Junction. SEE Submarine Attacks.

Torrence's Tavern, located ten miles east of Beattie's Ford across the Catawba River on the road to Salisbury in present-day Iredell County, was the site of a stinging Revolutionary War defeat that the Whig militia suffered at the hands of the British cavalry under Lt. Col. Banastre Tarleton. After successfully crossing the Catawba River on the morning of 1 Feb. 1781, British commander Lord Charles Cornwallis dispatched Tarleton with his green-clad cavalry and the 23rd Regiment Bose Infantry to pursue the fleeing militiamen. Prisoners taken by the cavalrymen revealed that the Whigs had fled Beattie's Ford upstream as well and were falling back toward Salisbury.

Heavy rains made progress difficult, especially for the British infantry, so Tarleton decided to divide his forces in an effort to overtake the enemy. The 23rd Regiment was posted along the Salisbury road five miles from Beattie's Ford, while the horsemen continued their pursuit. Three miles farther along, Tarleton learned that the Whig militiamen he was pursuing were planning to rendezvous with militia from Rowan and Mecklenburg Counties a few miles farther on at Torrence's Tavern.

A motley assemblage of people had gathered at Torrence's on that day—among them militiamen, fugitives from the morning's battle, and "South Carolina refugees." Col. Joseph Graham noted, "Being wet, cold and hungry, they began to drink spirits, carrying it out in pailsful." Amid the mass of wagons, horses and humanity clogging the road, someone sounded the alarm that Tarleton was near. This created a great deal of confusion among the Whigs. Capt. Nathaniel M. Martin attempted to organize a hasty defense and ordered the militiamen to take cover behind a fence and fight the enemy from there.

Detached so far in advance of his support, with his confidence still hurting from the recent defeat at the Battle of Cowpens, Tarleton hesitated to attack. But considering his superior numbers and his ability to retreat to safety if necessary, he decided to make one charge at the enemy. Another key point in his decision was the inclement weather, the heavy rain giving a decided advantage to his saber-wielding troopers.

The fight that followed was brief but intense. One of the first victims of the British attack was Martin, who was pinned under his dead horse and captured. The Whig militia fired one volley, then broke into a retreat. Whig chroniclers have often downplayed the results of the British victory at Torrence's Tavern, maintaining that the few casualties suffered were unarmed old men. In addition, Tarleton is often accused of exaggerating these events, mainly to make up for his earlier defeat at Cowpens. But in his report of 17 Mar. 1781 to Lord George Germain, Cornwallis remarked on the importance of the engagement at Torrence's Tavern: "This stroke, with our passage of the ford, so effectually dispirited the militia, that we met with no further opposition on our march to the Yadkin."

References: John S. Pancake, *This Destructive War: The British Campaign in the Carolinas, 1780–1782* (1985); Banastre Tarleton, *A History of the Campaigns of 1780 and 1781 in the Southern Provinces of North America* (1787).

John Hairr

Tory was a political term originally applied to members of the political party in England that favored the policies of the monarchy and the established church over the king's opponents in Parliament. During the American Revolution, adherents of the royal government who opposed the Revolution were called "Tories" or "Loyalists." The province of North Carolina was believed to have had one of the highest percentages of Loyalists of all the rebellious colonies. It is not surprising that many wealthy merchants and planters with financial ties to England were Tories, as were many Crown officials and Anglican clergymen. However, Tories were members of every level of society and lived in every part of the colony. Some Tories were German immigrants to the piedmont. In addition, many former Regulators, Piedmont frontiersmen who had rebelled against the colonial government, were Tories during the war. The former Regulators had no serious grievances against the Crown itself, but they believed that the provincial government was dominated by corrupt and powerful eastern planters.

Another strong Tory element was the Scottish immigrant population concentrated along the Cape Fear River Valley. Despite their participation in a failed rebellion against the British monarchy in 1746, many Scots in North Carolina remained loyal to the British. Some held to an oath they had taken to support the king; many others thought that a monarchy was the only practical kind of government and feared repression or anarchy without it; and some prominent Scottish leaders still had estates in Scotland. Loyalist forces included black soldiers; some were legally freemen, but many were former slaves. In exchange for military service, the British offered to emancipate the slaves of Patriot owners.

Early in the Revolutionary War, Governor Josiah Martin was optimistic about the prospects of raising Tory military units in North Carolina to join British regulars in putting down the rebellion. The Tories, mostly Highland Scots with some former Regulators who were to join Martin, were defeated and dispersed at the Battle of Moore's Creek Bridge on 27 Feb. 1776. From then until the arrival in North Carolina in September 1780 of British forces under Lord Charles Cornwallis, Tory resistance in the colony was limited, such as the avoidance of loyalty oaths or military service for the Whigs, clandestine plots, and sporadic armed conflict.

When the army of Cornwallis marched into North Carolina in 1780, a number of Tories joined the British. A substantial Tory force, under Maj. Patrick Ferguson, was raised to protect Cornwallis's left flank and end Patriot resistance in the west. Instead, on 7 Oct. 1780 Ferguson was decisively defeated at the Battle of King's Mountain, just south of the North Carolina boundary.

Although Cornwallis was ultimately disappointed that more Tories did not join him, Loyalist North Carolinians were important participants in most of his battles. Lt. Col. John Hamilton's regiment of North Carolina Volunteers was one of the units that surrendered with Cornwallis at Yorktown. North Carolina Tories served in other British provincial regiments and in Loyalist militia units, as well. When the last British regulars left North Carolina on 18 Nov. 1781, armed resistance by Tories continued. Col. David Fanning led a force of North Carolina Tories who captured Governor Thomas Burke during a raid on Hillsborough on 12 Sept. 1781. Fanning's troops continued fighting as late as May 1782. A combined force of British regulars and Tories from Charleston, S.C., captured Beaufort on 5 Apr. 1782 and held it for a short time.

Tories in North Carolina were punished by Confiscation Acts, passed from 1776 to 1782, that allowed their lands to be seized. They also faced violent persecution from the Whigs, especially in areas remote from British troops. However, many Tories who survived the war and remained in North Carolina were relieved by the Act of Pardon and Oblivion in 1783.

During and after the Revolution, thousands of Tories, including many from North Carolina, moved either forcibly or voluntarily to British possessions elsewhere, including Nova Scotia, New Brunswick, Bermuda, the Bahamas, and Florida, or to England or Scotland. A few black Loyalists eventually immigrated to the British colony of Sierra Leone in West Africa.

References: Jeffrey J. Crow, "What Price Loyalism? The Case of John Cruden, Commissioner of Sequestered Estates," *NCHR* 58 (July 1981); Robert O. Demond, *The Loyalists in North Carolina during the Revolution* (1940); Carole Watterson Troxler, *The Loyalist Experience in North Carolina* (1976).

David A. Norris

SEE ALSO Loyalists; Moore's Creek Bridge, Battle of.

Tory Hole. SEE Elizabethtown, Battle of.

Tory Oak, sometimes referred to as the Cleveland Oak, grew for possibly three centuries in what is now the town of Wilkesboro. The exact age of this famous tree will never be known, and all that remains is an 11-foot-tall, mortar-filled, deteriorating dark stump. The tree is famous for the role it played in the American Revolution, when Col. Ben Cleveland, a leading Patriot in western North Carolina, used its spreading limbs to hang at least five Tories during the fall of 1779. Two of the five had plundered the Lincoln County home of George Wilfong, been apprehended by Cleveland's scouts, and brought to the Wilkes County courthouse. There, Cleveland summarily administered his justice, using Wilfong's clothesline (which the thieves had used to steal his horses) to hang the two Loyalists.

The enraged British forces sent a captain and two soldiers to capture Cleveland. They nearly accomplished this aim, but instead found themselves taken prisoner; shortly thereafter, they too were dangling from the huge branches of the Tory Oak.

For many years afterward, the Tory Oak stood nobly as a familiar landmark of the struggle for independence. In 1980 the tree had the distinction of being North Carolina's "champion" black oak, with a circumference of 14 feet, a crown height of 50 feet, and an overall limb spread of 40 feet. It withstood the strain of three operations to remove rotten portions, which were replaced with concrete mortar. The rotting continued, however, and two-thirds of the tree was felled by heavy winds in June 1989. In 1992 the National Park Service designated the Tory Oak site as a Certified Protected Site of the Overmountain Victory National Historic Trail.

Joan S. Baity

The reconstructed mound and temple at Town Creek Indian Mound State Historic Site. Photograph courtesy of North Carolina Division of Tourism, Film, and Sports Development.

Tory War. SEE American Revolution; Lindley's Mill, Battle of; Loyalists.

Town Creek Indian Mound is located five miles southeast of Mount Gilead in Montgomery County. More than 600 years ago, migrating Indians selected this spot overlooking the Little River for a ceremonial center. The Town Creek center served as a fortified refuge and a place to discuss matters important to the people of the Pee Dee culture, as well as a site for religious ceremonies and feasts, which often lasted several days. When white settlers arrived in the eighteenth century, the Pee Dee Indians had long been living elsewhere, probably with the Catawba. When whites occupied the site where the Pee Dee had lived, they left the mound alone but farmed the land around it.

Beginning in the late nineteenth century, people untrained in archaeological techniques from time to time excavated the site in hopes of finding a treasure or other valuable objects. In 1936, however, under Joffre L. Coe, a student at the University of North Carolina in Chapel Hill, careful archaeological excavations began. Coe's thorough work, continuing into the late twentieth century, produced a unique record of professional excavations.

In 1937 the landowner, L. D. Frutchey, donated the site to the state for scientific excavation and the creation of a state park, and Town Creek Indian Mound became the first North Carolina State Historic Site. Transferred to the Department of Archives and History in 1955, the modern-day site includes a visitors center, two temples, a burial house, and a stockade, in addition to the mound. Restorations are based on extensive archaeological and documentary research.

References: Joffre L. Coe, *Town Creek Indian Mound: A Native American Legacy* (1995); Richard F. Knapp, ed., *North Carolina's State Historic Sites: A Brief History and Status Report* (1995);

Douglas L. Rights, *The American Indian in North Carolina* (2nd ed., 1957).

Alexis W. Locklear

Town Documentaries were films made for the entertainment or promotion of small North Carolina towns from about 1913 to the early 1950s. Hundreds of these films recorded events such as athletic contests and celebrations, were edited, and then were shown to the town's population at public screenings. The number of itinerant filmmakers who traveled the state is probably much greater than is presently known. (No official figures on filmmaking in North Carolina exist before the establishment of the state film office in 1980.)

Lexington native H. Lee Waters was perhaps the most prolific and talented of these filmmakers, shooting about 117 documentaries. His series, entitled *Movies of Local People*, was enormously popular and allowed him to make a good living during the Depression after his studio portrait business had slackened. Waters's films were artfully produced compared to the more static and predictable town documentaries produced by other filmmakers. Typically, they were very democratic, portraying people in all walks of life going about their daily business: leaving work, walking the streets, or simply relaxing on a Saturday afternoon. His visits to various towns sometimes coincided with important events like a fire or a festival, which he recorded as well. In many places, Waters's arrival was such an occasion that schools let out so that he could film the student body exiting the building, row after row, class after class. Waters's films were silent, but his screenings usually elicited running commentaries from the locals in attendance.

Less well known and much less documented are the films of Holly Smith, who made more than 100 town documentaries in the Carolinas while working out of Charlotte. (Smith ran a film and camera shop, and the films were intended to promote his business.) Don Parrisher, who made a similarly large number of films about the state (although only a handful are known to exist), worked in the same style as Smith. Both men usually created a 30-minute promotional film that featured a near-standard script with voice-over narration and starred the town's leading white business and civic leaders. These films, where they exist, remain particularly interesting for their depiction of tobacco auctions, manufacturing processes, new car lots, men's and women's fashions, food preparation, school yards, an occasional ball game, and dances and other recreational events.

Town documentaries never enjoyed a market beyond their specific audiences. Newsreels and features, on the other hand, displayed North Carolina scenes and stories to the world. Of the many newsreels made in the state, the best source for extant footage remains the Movietone collection at the University of South Carolina, which has more than 120 reels shot in North Carolina. These include an Asheville visit in 1925 by presidential hopeful Alfred E. Smith, Jack Dempsey's training sessions in Hendersonville in 1926, and the textile strikes of Gastonia, Belmont, and Kannapolis in 1934.

Most of the town documentaries and other early films made in North Carolina have been lost, although small samples are recovered almost every year. Duke University maintains a collection of Waters's town documentaries. The National Archives junked a large collection in the 1980s, including footage of tobacco festivals held in Wilson in the late 1930s and early 1940s. But the archives retained a large number of North Carolina–related documentaries, and several museums, local archives, and stock footage companies around the country have collected films that are of importance to North Carolina history. Fewer than ten of Smith's and Parrisher's films are known to exist in private collections.

References: Alex Albright, "North Carolina's Early Movies," *The State* (July 1986); Tom Whiteside, "The Cameraman Is Coming to Town," *The State* (July 1986); J. W. Williamson, *Southern Mountaineers in Silent Films* (1994).

Alex Albright

Town Milk. The Tarboro Municipal Milk Plant was established in 1918 in response to a severe outbreak of typhoid fever, dysentery, and colitis that claimed the lives of several Tarboro children and left many of all ages weak and ill. That year the town (population 6,400) had obtained its entire milk supply raw and untreated from surrounding farms. There were no large commercial dairies with refrigerated delivery anywhere nearby. Epidemics had been traced to untreated "farm milk" before, but the outbreak in 1918 was severe enough to stir the citizens to drastic action. An ordinance was passed by the town council prohibiting any raw milk to be sold within the town limits. A small pasteurizing plant was set up in a section of the town water plant, and bottles and sterilizing equipment were purchased. A horse-drawn milk wagon and driver were soon delivering safe, pasteurized milk to the townspeople.

As a nonprofit venture, the new "town milk" plant was able to sell its product for a price lower than that charged for raw milk in neighboring communities. There was little or no bootlegging of unprocessed milk, and infant health in the community improved significantly. Soon a new building was erected and motorized distribution replaced the horse-drawn wagon.

At the time it was established, the venture was unique in the nation, and, as far as was known, in the world. Officials from other states and abroad came to Tarboro to investigate the methods and results of the town milk experiment. By 1938 there were similar plants in cities throughout the United States as well as in Wellington, New Zealand, and Rome, Italy.

Tarboro's townspeople were satisfied with their town milk for almost half a century, until wholesale pasteurization and distribution by large companies proved too competitive. In 1965 the plant closed its doors; according to government reports, it was again the only municipal milk plant in operation in the United States at that time.

Reference: U.S. Dept. of Agriculture, *The Municipal Milk Distribution in Tarboro, N.C.* (1938).

Jaquelin Drane Nash

Towns and Cities. Formally established by the colonial government, towns began appearing in eastern North Carolina in the early eighteenth century. By definition, the word "town" was initially applied to population centers "larger than a village but smaller than a city," but as time passed, the words "town" and "city" came to have identical meanings in North Carolina and are now legally interchangeable. Consequently, a municipal government in North Carolina is covered by exactly the same laws regardless of whether it is called a town or a city.

Among the first towns to be established in the state were Bath in 1705, New Bern in 1710, and Edenton in 1722, all of which were located near rivers with sufficient channel depth to accommodate the largest vessels able to navigate the sounds and adjacent waters. As settlement spread, larger concentrations of people were usually found in the vicinity of seaports, trading centers, and county seats, thus calling for the provision of services and facilities not needed in sparsely populated areas. Municipal governments were subsequently formed to maintain the roads, public wells, health and safety ordinances, and volunteer fire departments and town watches. Acts authorizing the establishment of new towns often set aside land for public wharves, courthouses and jails, and occasionally common areas (the forerunners of public squares and parks). Unlike their northern counterparts, however, North Carolina cities and towns were slow to industrialize, and features such as water systems and police departments were late additions.

Townships were first established in North Carolina with the adoption of the Constitution of 1868, which called for a new plan of local government known as the Township and County Commissioner Plan. Borrowed from Pennsylvania, the plan divided each county into townships, with the voters in each electing two justices of the peace and a clerk to serve as the governing body. These township boards were given control of roads and bridges within their jurisdiction, as well as taxes and finances, and had the responsibility of assessing taxable property for final action by the county commissioners. The clerk of the board served as treasurer of the township and was elected for a two-year term, as were the justices of the peace. Other township officials included a three-member school committee and one or more constables.

Townships were convenient administrative subdivisions, particularly for the purpose of building and maintaining roads, although by the early twentieth century they were viewed as little more than "geographical expressions," stripped of all corporate powers. By that time most justices of the peace were appointed, either by the legislature or the governor, and their judicial powers were limited to misdemeanor criminal cases and civil cases involving no more than $50. It seemed that the bold township experiment of 1868 had run its course.

Towns and cities themselves continued to grow in North Carolina in terms of both area and population, and developments such as water and sewer systems, telephones lines, street lighting, and public transportation were introduced—first as private franchises and later as publicly owned utilities. Municipal governments organized school districts, built libraries, and oversaw the paving of streets for automobile usage. Although the Great Depression momentarily halted the expansion of cities and towns, the state provided assistance for roads, libraries, and education, and public works programs designed to combat unemployment resulted in many municipal improvement projects. Legislation enacted in 1959 allowed municipal governments to annex adjacent urban territories and empowered them to zone and regulate land development. In the 1970s environmental protection measures were also adopted.

As the twentieth century drew to a close and a new century dawned, most cities adopted the council-manager form of government—by which a council, presided over by the mayor, creates municipal policy and appoints a manager as chief administrator. By the early 2000s, half of North Carolina's population resided in towns and cities, with the state's municipal population growing at an unprecedented rate.

References: David M. Lawrence and Warren Jake Wicker, eds., *Municipal Government in North Carolina* (1996); Paul W. Wager, *County Government in North Carolina* (1928).

David Stick
Additional research provided by Robert Blair Vocci.

Track and Field in North Carolina is associated largely with colleges and high schools, most of which have track-and-field and cross-country teams for both genders. Track-and-field activities in North Carolina colleges date back to the 1880s. High school state championships in the sport were first held in 1913. Track and field has rarely been a revenue-producing sport, and cutbacks in scholarships have hindered it at the college level.

North Carolina has produced a handful of world-class track athletes. Charlotte's Jim Beatty ran the first indoor sub-four-minute mile in 1962. Twelve years later, Tony Waldrop of Polk County set the world indoor mile record. Both Beatty and Waldrop attended the University of North Carolina at Chapel Hill, as did Floyd "Chunk" Simmons, a Charlotte native who won bronze medals in the grueling ten-event decathlon in the 1948 and 1952 Olympics. Top women track athletes included Raeford's Kathy McMillan, a 1976 Olympic silver medalist in the high jump, and Raleigh's Julie Shea, who won numerous state high school championships before going on to a successful career at North Carolina State University.

A number of nonnatives have gained acclaim during and after their college careers at North Carolina universities. North Carolina Central University runner Lee Calhoun captured gold medals in the 110-meter high hurdles in the 1956 and 1960 Olympics, while Vince Matthews of Johnson C. Smith University won a gold medal in the 1968 Olympics in the 4 × 400 meter relay and a gold medal in the 1972 Olympics 400-meter run. Duke University's Dave Sime was a record-setting sprinter in the mid-1950s and won a silver medal in the 1960 Olympics. Joan Benoit, who attended N.C. State in the early 1980s, won the first Olympic marathon for women in 1984. North Carolina Central was the home of a number of prominent African runners in the 1970s, including Kenyans Robert Ouko and Julius Sand, who ran on the Kenyan gold medal 4 × 400 meter relay team in the 1972 Olympics. California native Marion Jones, a track and basketball standout at UNC-Chapel Hill, became the first woman to win five medals at one Olympics. In Sydney in 2000, Jones won gold medals in the 100-meter dash, the 200-meter dash, and the 1,600-meter relay and bronze medals in the long jump and 400-meter relay.

The best-known track-and-field coach from the state was Dr. LeRoy Walker, head coach of the North Carolina Central team from 1945 through 1974. He coached the Ethiopian and Israeli track teams in the 1960 Olympics and was head coach of the 1976 U.S. Olympic track-and-field team. In 1992 Walker was named president of the U.S. Olympic Committee. Duke University's Al Buehler was coach or manager of three U.S. Olympic teams, while George Williams of Saint Augustine's College was assistant coach of the 1996 U.S. track team. Williams presided over the state's most successful track program. Saint Augustine's captured seven National Collegiate Athletic Association (NCAA) Division II national outdoor men's team titles from 1989 through 1995.

Durham, bolstered by the long presence of Walker and Buehler, has been the track-and-field capital of the state. Duke University has hosted a number of international track meets involving the world's top athletes. These meets include the 1971 and 1994 United States–Pan Africa meets, the 1974 United States–Soviet Union meet, the 1975 United States–Pan Africa–West Germany meet, and the 1980 NCAA championships. Several world-class athletes also train at local campus facilities in the Research Triangle area.

The recreational running boom that began in the 1970s has added to the state's running population but had little impact on the sport's popularity as a spectator sport. Road races, such as the *Charlotte Observer* Marathon, which began in 1977, are held across the state.

Reference: Jim Sumner, *A History of Sports in North Carolina* (1990).

Jim L. Sumner

Trading Ford was a shallow area of the Yadkin River located about seven miles northeast of Salisbury. As one of the few places where the Yadkin could be crossed on foot or horseback, Trading Ford was a focal point for the movement of people through Piedmont North Carolina for hundreds of years. Early European explorers followed old, well-established Indian trading routes that crossed the Yadkin at Trading Ford and connected the Indians of eastern North Carolina and Virginia with those of western North Carolina and beyond. As he followed this path in 1701, English explorer John Lawson paused at Trading Ford to stay with a tribe of Saponi Indians encamped there. Today, parts of highways I-85 and U.S. 64 follow the general direction of these trading paths.

In the mid-eighteenth century, Trading Ford saw the migration of German and Scotch-Irish settlers traveling down the Great Wagon Road from Pennsylvania, New Jersey, and Maryland in search of unclaimed lands. One fork of this road merged with the Indian trading path north of the Yadkin River before crossing Trading Ford. Like a highway interchange, the area attracted early settlements along the banks of the Yadkin and its tributaries in present-day Rowan and Davidson Counties. Among the early inhabitants of the "Jersey Settlement" on the Davidson County side of Trading Ford was the Ellis family, whose plantation would become the birthplace of antebellum governor John W. Ellis.

In February 1781 Trading Ford played a minor role in the Revolutionary War in North Carolina. After the Battle of Cowpens, Patriots under Gen. Nathanael Greene marched north from Charlotte to avoid the British army led by Lord Charles Cornwallis. The Americans arrived at Trading Ford in the evening and safely crossed to the other side, taking all boats with them. The British troops arrived shortly afterward, but rains had caused the Yadkin to rise, and without boats they had no means of catching the Americans.

Although a bridge had been built across the Yadkin by the mid-nineteenth century, Trading Ford remained in use and was sketched in 1849 by Benson Lossing for his *Pictorial Field-Book of the Revolution*. As a result of a dam built at High Rock in the 1920s, much of the lowlands near Trading Ford were flooded, and the ford no longer is passable. However, the islands located near it are still visible to the east of the I-85 bridge.

References: James S. Brawley, *The Rowan Story, 1753–1953: A Narrative History of Rowan County, North Carolina* (1953); Robert W. Ramsey, *Carolina Cradle: Settlement of the Northwest*

Carolina Frontier, 1747–1762 (1964); Douglas L. Rights, *The American Indian in North Carolina* (2nd ed., 1957).

William H. Bingham Jr.

Trail of Tears. SEE Cherokee Indians.

Transportation, North Carolina Department of.

SEE Highway Commission.

Transylvania Company was organized as Louisa Company in 1774 to invest in vacant, nonpatented wild lands within the chartered limits of North Carolina and Virginia. In the fall of that year, Captain Nathaniel Hart visited the Overhill Cherokees at their Otari towns to negotiate for the lease or purchase of an immense tract of land between the Kentucky and Cumberland Rivers. Early in 1775 new articles of copartnership, renamed the Transylvania Company, were entered into to define the terms of the joint venture more clearly. The Transylvania partners took what was purported to be an absolute conveyance of the millions of acres in question from the Cherokee chiefs. Headquartered in Williamsboro, this unincorporated association was, at its largest, composed of nine influential North Carolinians: Richard Henderson, John Williams, Thomas Hart, Nathaniel Hart, David Hart, John Luttrell, Leonard H. Bullock, James Hogg, and William Johnson.

In March 1775 Daniel Boone, working for the Transylvania Company, and a party of about 30 woodsmen blazed a primitive trail from the Holston River in East Tennessee across the mountains at Cumberland Gap to open this area to settlement. Boone's trail, the Wilderness Road, became the main route to the new settlements.

Transylvania Company's so-called purchase from the Indians was publicly denounced by the governors of Virginia and North Carolina, however, and the scheme was invalidated. The Virginia legislature nullified the arrangement by creating Kentucky County in December 1776, and in 1778 that body granted 200,000 acres on the Green River to the Transylvania associates as compensation. The copartners turned to the Cumberland River and formulated plans to colonize French Lick in 1779–80 with another proprietary arrangement, the Cumberland Compact. In 1783 the General Assembly of North Carolina terminated Transylvania's control but granted the copartners 200,000 acres in Powell's Valley in East Tennessee.

References: Archibald Henderson, *The Significance of the Transylvania Company in American History* (1935); William S. Lester, *The Transylvania Colony* (1935).

Wiley J. Williams

Transylvania County is located in the Mountain region of southwestern North Carolina along the South Carolina border. It was formed in 1861 from portions of Jackson and Henderson Counties. Its county seat, Brevard, was established in 1861 but not incorporated until 1889. Its other communities include Cedar Mountain, Cherryfield, Lake Toxaway, Little River, Penrose, Pisgah Forest, and Sapphire.

The forests and mountains of Transylvania County were home to the Cherokee Indians until federal legislation in 1830 forced the relocation of most North Carolina Cherokee to Oklahoma. English, Scotch-Irish, and Welsh settlers came to the region by way of Cherokee trading paths and river routes along the Davidson River and other tributaries in the French Broad River and Savannah River basins, but the county remained lightly populated through the early nineteenth century, home primarily to yeoman farmers. In the late nineteenth century, industrialist George Vanderbilt acquired large tracts of forest land in the county, and in 1895 he hired Carl A. Schenck to manage the lands for timber harvest and conservation. The lands today comprise portions of Pisgah National Forest, nearly 83,000 acres of which is located in Transylvania County. The Cradle of Forestry in America historic site in northern Transylvania County, on the site of the Biltmore Forest School founded by Schenck in 1898, commemorates the role of the school and the county in the development of modern forestry. The county remains an important producer of timber and timber products.

The growth of Brevard and the county generally increased beginning in 1895, when the Henderson & Brevard Railroad (later the Transylvania Railroad Company) came to town. The railroad brought increased commerce and tourism, which in turn sparked development of luxurious resort towns such as Lake Toxaway. A major human and ecological disaster struck, however, when the Lake Toxaway dam broke during a major flood that struck western North Carolina in 1916. The flood destroyed many small farming communities downstream, left Lake Toxaway dry, and led to the failure of the resort. Piles of timber debris from the 1916 flood can still be seen in the area today.

In 1934 Brevard College was founded on the campus of Epworth School, an important early institute for girls and young women in western North Carolina. The college in time earned a strong reputation for education in the arts and in the environmental sciences. Brevard's reputation as an artistic community was also enhanced by the Brevard Music Center, established in 1945 and home to one of the finest summer music festivals and master class programs in the country. By the early twenty-first century, Transylvania County was firmly established as a popular mountain destination for tourists drawn to the county's natural environment and recreational opportunities. The county is popularly billed as the "Land of Waterfalls" on account of its more than 250 falls, including Looking Glass Falls, Sliding Rock Falls, and Whitewater Falls, which, at some 411 feet, is considered the highest cascade east of the Rocky Mountains. Gorges State Park, near Sapphire, was established in 1999 on land purchased from Duke Energy Corporation. The estimated population of Transylvania County was 29,700 in 2004.

Peter Bangma

SEE ALSO Biltmore Forest School; Brevard College; Brevard Music Center

Travel and Tourism. North Carolina's mountains, beaches, scenic attractions, and historic sites annually draw millions of visitors, and even greater numbers of people visit the state's largest cities. Professional sports franchises and events, convention centers catering to businesses and organizations, and unique shopping opportunities have made metropolitan areas such as Charlotte, Raleigh and Durham, Greensboro, and Winston-Salem the state's most popular and profitable tourist destinations.

Before the Civil War, various Coastal, Piedmont, and Mountain communities were noted for their healthful climate, mineral springs, hotels and resorts, and grand scenery. Leisure travelers from inside and outside the state made extensive use of these areas, but such economic activity remained a seasonal, local concern. A true statewide travel and tourism industry did not emerge until the 1880s as developments in transportation created new possibilities for tourism on a larger scale. Tourists from southern and northeastern states began to enjoy rail access to a variety of North Carolina resorts from the mountains to the Atlantic beaches. This opened the state to new groups of potential visitors, and developers soon set about constructing large resorts to accommodate and entertain them. Travel during this period was still limited to the wealthy elite, and new facilities such as Asheville's Battery Park Hotel, Raleigh's Yarborough House, and New Bern's Hotel Albert reflected the refined tastes of visitors. By the First World War, cities offering unique natural or recreational attractions, such as Asheville, Pinehurst, and Wilmington, attracted thousands of tourists each year.

By the 1920s, the Department of Conservation and Development began to promote North Carolina as a tourist destination in official state publications. In 1933 Governor O. Max Gardner, recognizing the emerging importance of tourism to the state's economy, ordered the creation of a Bureau of State Advertising, a new agency devoted to tourism promotion. Gardner's successors all appointed some type of citizens' committee to advise state officials on tourism-related matters and backed a variety of promotional and construction projects to better attract potential visitors. By the 1950s, tourism was a leading component of the state's economy, accounting for more than $100 million annually.

These developments occurred at a time of important growth in the state's tourism infrastructure. Much of this growth came as a result of federal New Deal programs aimed at combating the Great Depression. During the 1930s, the state saw the establishment of important attractions such as the Great Smoky Mountains National Park, the Blue Ridge Parkway, and the Cape Hatteras National Seashore, as well as several national forests. These large public attractions emerged as cornerstones of tourism development within their respective regions.

After World War II, the wealthy elite no longer dominated North Carolina tourism. Motor lodges replaced luxury resorts as the lodging of choice among vacationers. This democratization of travel led to the development of a ski industry, amusement parks such as Carowinds (near Charlotte) and Ghost Town in the Sky (in Maggie Valley), and numerous other local attractions. The state's many Atlantic beaches continued to attract North Carolinians as well as travelers from other eastern states. In the 1990s the Cherokee Indian Reservation added bingo and video gambling to its list of attractions in an effort to draw larger numbers of visitors. During the 1950s, cultural tourism emerged, catering to a traveling public interested in history, architecture, and traditional crafts. Public and private historical attractions such as the Bentonville Battlefield, the Thomas Wolfe House, the Biltmore House, and Tryon Palace continued to draw thousands of visitors each year. Natural attractions remained popular despite increased commercialization of the travel and tourism industry. By the 1980s, the Great Smoky Mountains National Park emerged as the most visited national park in America. National and state preserves across the state continue to draw large numbers of visitors who enjoy fishing, hiking, boating, or simply taking in the natural landscape.

Expansion of the travel and tourism industry initially benefited owners of small motels, restaurants, gasoline stations, and similar businesses. Communities had a vested interest in promoting tourism and extending hospitality to visitors because income generated by tourism stayed in the local community. By the 1960s and 1970s, large national motel chains, franchised eateries, and other businesses slowly eroded the market of many smaller, locally owned businesses. Organizations that own many of North Carolina's large commercial attractions are often headquartered outside the state. While generating revenue and providing profit for many, tourism workers do not share in the industry's prosperity. Tourism workers, often women and minorities, are among the lowest-paid laborers in the state.

By 2006 the Division of Tourism, Film, and Sports Development had become North Carolina's central tourism agency, overseeing a $12.6 billion–a-year industry created by approximately 49 million annual visitors to the state.

Reference: Howard L. Preston, *Dirt Roads to Dixie: Accessibility and Modernization in the Modern South* (1991).

Richard D. Starnes

SEE ALSO Resorts.

Travelers' Rooms were small, porch-like rooms attached to the outside of houses usually situated along stage coach routes and were intended for the use of any passing traveler who needed accommodations. The rooms, often at the back of the houses, contained one or more beds and a minimum of other furniture. As a rule there was no charge for such accommodations, and, since most travelers' rooms had no doors leading inside the house, the owner of the house might have little or no contact with his overnight "guest." The practice of attaching travelers' rooms evolved in rural areas where there were few or no inns, residences were scattered, and travel was difficult. The reputation for "southern hospitality" may have originated because of this practice. Travelers' rooms may be seen at the King-Bazemore House (1763) near Windsor in Bertie County, at Mill Prong House (1790s) near Wagram in Scotland County, and elsewhere.

Reference: Guion G. Johnson, *Ante-Bellum North Carolina: A Social History* (1937).

William S. Powell

Travels of William Bartram is the familiar title by which the 522-page volume by naturalist William Bartram (1739–1823) is generally referred. The work documents his four-year journey through large portions of the Southeast, much of which he and his naturalist father John Bartram had visited during William's youth, sometimes making their headquarters with relatives in Bladen County.

Published by subscription in Philadelphia in 1791, Bartram's account was officially titled *Travels through North & South Carolina, Georgia, East & West Florida, the Cherokee Country, the Extensive Territories of the Muscogulges, or Creek Confederacy, and the Country of the Chactaws; Containing an Account of the Soil and Natural Productions of Those Regions, together with Observations on the Manners of the Indians.* Bartram made a very careful study of plants and animals, discovering new species in some cases and treating all with a reverence and awe stemming from his Quaker upbringing, which taught him that God's creations were perfect and right. He also recorded the customs and history of the Seminole, Cherokee, and Creek Indian Nations, becoming one of the earliest white authorities on these peoples. Though Bartram's interests as a naturalist were broad, his descriptions of alligators are particularly memorable. His accounts of a female alligator's care of her eggs and young and of the struggle to the death of two very large alligators illustrate both his observational skills and his exceptional literary talent.

Having received a classical education at the Philadelphia Academy, Bartram became a careful author and artist; his skill enabled him to record his observations with both words and brush. His *Travels* is an early example of the style of nature writing that combined scientific observation and documentation with anecdotes and personal impressions of the natural world and its inhabitants. Bartram received both criticism and praise for his brilliant combination of scientific and religious ideas and for employing not only a scientific vocabulary but also lyrical description and everyday language to communicate his observations. His work had an immense impact in the scientific community as well as among philosophers, writers, and the general public in America and abroad. In fact, Romantic poets William Wordsworth and Samuel Taylor Coleridge drew from his descriptions, while naturalist writer Henry David Thoreau was influenced by his merging of science and poetry in unabashed admiration of the natural world. Bartram himself became an adviser to younger naturalists of his own day as well as an advocate of a distinctively American scientific identity. Contemporary ecologists and historians still refer to his *Travels* for its meticulous descriptions of nature and Indian society.

Reference: Brad Sanders, *Guide to William Bartram's* Travels: *Following the Trail of America's First Great Naturalist* (2002).

William S. Powell

Treasurer was one of seven "chief officers" whom the Lords Proprietors intended to manage the province of North Carolina. The treasurer, as envisioned in the Fundamental Constitutions of 1669, was to deal with "all matters that concern the public revenue and treasury" and was to be aided by 6 counselors (undertreasurers) and 12 assistants (auditors). This office, like others in the colony, was slow to mature. Early governors acted as their own treasurers due to insufficient revenues until the staggering debts accrued from the Cary Rebellion and the Tuscarora War necessitated a more efficient system for raising taxes. Accordingly, in 1711 the governor and his council appointed treasurers for each of the seven precincts of the province. Three years later, the Lower House of the Assembly joined the Upper House and Governor Edward Hyde named Edward Moseley as treasurer of North Carolina and overseer of all precinct treasurers. Moseley, possibly the most able politician of his era, held the posts from 1714 to 1735. He returned in 1735 as treasurer for the southern district of North Carolina and remained in that position until his death in 1749, sharing what had once been a unified office with William Downing (1735–39), treasurer of the northern district. Eleazer Allen (1749–50), John Starkey (1750–65), and John Ashe (1765–75) succeeded Moseley in the south, while Thomas Barker (1748–52), John Haywood (1752–64), and Joseph Montford (1764–75) followed Downing in the north.

In 1776 the new state of North Carolina required all treasurers to be appointed with the approval of both the House of Commons (formerly the House of Burgesses) and the recently appointed Senate and banned all receivers of public moneys from sitting in the General Assembly or participating in the government. In 1784 the office of treasurer, then consisting of seven district treasurers, was reduced to one officeholder with a two-year term; he was placed on salary, without commission, and his office was moved from Edenton to Hillsborough, a more central location. Memucan Hunt was the first person to serve as singular treasurer of the state. In 1795 the treasury was relocated to the new capital city of Raleigh. At the same time, many of the treasurer's record-keeping functions were transferred to the comptroller-general, who was empowered to keep "distinct records" for all receivers of public moneys and to have these available at all times for inspection by the legislature.

The office of treasurer, in the process, had lost its political significance and had become what it was originally intended to be: a fiscal office. The state constitution of 1868 changed the term of the treasurer to four years and made it a publicly elected post. North Carolina's state treasurers have generally been diligent overseers of the public money, avoiding political or fiscal scandal. The modern office, with the state's previously modest budget growing to more than $17 billion annually and its trust funds reaching about $30 billion, is a far cry from the simple accounting office of earlier times. The treasurer is a member of the Council of State and works closely with the governor on all fiscal and budgetary matters. The officeholder is also the state's banker, investment officer, administrator of governmental employee retirement and benefit systems, and official in charge of helping local governments maintain success in fiscal matters.

References: John L. Cheney Jr., ed., *North Carolina Government, 1585–1974: A Narrative and Statistical History* (1981); Charles L. Raper, *North Carolina: A Study in English Colonial Government* (1904).

Louis P. Towles

Trees. SEE Forests.

Trenton, Battle of. The Civil War action known as the Battle of Trenton, generally considered a skirmish, occurred on 6 Dec. 1863 in Jones County on the banks of Chinquapin Creek, about six miles west of Trenton. The Union's Capt. C. H. Roche left New Bern to retrieve the families of three Confederate deserters who subsequently joined the 2nd North Carolina Infantry, a regiment fighting for the Union. Roche sent a force of 23 men to Trenton to get two of the families. The men crossed the Trent River and rescued the two families without encountering Confederate troops.

Roche took his remaining 50 men farther up the Trent road to remove the third family. On their way to the area known as Chinquapin Chapel, where the family lived, the Union troops confronted a dozen cavalry from the 66th North Carolina State Troops. The Confederates removed the planks from the bridge spanning Beaver Dam Creek, hoping to pre-

vent Roche's advance. The numerically superior Union force drove the enemy back, repaired the bridge, and continued its march. But at Chinquapin Creek, Roche found that the North Carolina troops had destroyed the bridge there and were waiting for him on the opposite side. He dispersed the Confederates with his howitzer but did not cross the creek for fear he would encounter a substantial Confederate force. Roche and his men abandoned their efforts to retrieve the third family, rejoined the other troops, and returned to New Bern that same evening. Roche reported one man killed and one wounded. According to the Confederacy's Brig. Gen. Seth M. Barton, three North Carolinians were wounded in the battle.

Reference: Surena B. Henderson, comp., *Jones County: 200 Years, 1779–1979* (1979).

Thomas J. Farnham

Trinity College began in 1839 when Methodist and Quaker farm families in Randolph County joined together to start a subscription school named Union Institute. When the school's first principal, Brantley York, moved on to other church-related tasks in 1842, his young assistant, Braxton Craven, assumed the responsibility for the school. For the following four decades, Craven waged an unceasing effort to keep the school alive.

Craven's chief challenge was to find financial support, and in 1849 he turned to the state for a recharter of the school as Normal College, with teacher training as its prime mission. Financial support continued to be scarce, however, and in 1859 Craven sought support from the North Carolina Methodists. Under Methodist sponsorship, the college changed its name to Trinity College and adopted a liberal arts curriculum. Though financial difficulties remained, enrollment grew and the college managed to survive the Civil War and Reconstruction without closing.

Craven's death in 1882 after 40 years of leadership brought more uncertainty to Trinity College, but the intervention and leadership of three well-to-do Methodist businessmen—J. W. Alspaugh, Julian S. Carr, and James A. Gray—saved the school. A new president, the Yale-educated John F. Crowell, improved the curriculum and, more important, conceived the idea of moving the college from its isolated, rural setting to a more vibrant, urban location. With key support from Washington Duke and fellow Methodist and townsman Julian S. Carr, Trinity College moved to Durham, opening there in 1892. The Duke family continued its commitment to the institution, and in 1896, when Washington Duke offered to give the college $100,000 for endowment if it would admit women on an "equal footing" with men, the college promptly accepted the offer, making Trinity a pioneer in the South in women's education.

With steady financial support from the Duke family and a growing reputation for quality, Trinity had become by the time

Troublesome Creek Ironworks as sketched in the late 1800s or early 1900s. NCC.

of World War I one of the stronger liberal arts colleges in the South. Soon after the war, President William P. Few revived earlier dreams of making Trinity a university. With the help of Benjamin N. Duke and others, Few approached the wealthiest member of the family, James B. Duke, with the idea. J. B. Duke's establishment of the Duke Endowment in 1924 gave Few the funds to achieve his goal. Trinity thus became and remained what Few conceived of as the liberal arts "heart" of Duke University.

References: Nora C. Chaffin, *Trinity College, 1839–1892: The Beginnings of Duke University* (1950); Earl W. Porter, *Trinity and Duke, 1892–1924: Foundations of Duke University* (1964).

Robert F. Durden

Troublesome Creek Ironworks was originally established as Speedwell Furnace in 1770 in what is now southern Rockingham County by Joseph Buffington, a Quaker ironmaster from Chester County, Pa. Using a lottery to raise capital, Buffington purchased the nearby "mine hill" of Henry Work and the site on the creek where he constructed a rock dam for waterpower, a bloomery to produce pig iron, and a forge for making finished iron items. Buffington sold the ironworks in 1772, probably discovering through practice what is now known through scientific analysis: that the titaniferous

magnetite ore in the area contains too high a concentration of titanium dioxide to produce high-quality iron. This factor established a pattern of failure in all of the attempts to produce iron there.

By the time of the American Revolution, the furnace was in disrepair, but in the course of the maneuvering of the Southern Campaign of 1781, the site became a bivouac and rendezvous for both the British and the American armies. After the war, the ironworks property, which also included a sawmill, was acquired by veterans Col. Archibald Lytle of Hillsborough and Cols. Peter and Constantine Perkins of Pittsylvania County, Va. The earliest effort to establish a grist and flour mill on the property was in 1782, and by the end of the decade the mill was operating. The repaired iron furnace was sold to George Hairston and John Marr of Henry County, Va., who hired Benjamin Jones as the manager. Between 1790 and 1792 Jones ran the furnace with 35 slaves. During his southern tour in 1791, President George Washington, with whom Jones had served in the war, stopped at the ironworks for a visit.

After 1806 James Patrick, a miller, purchased the property from the John Marr estate. In 1810 Patrick had two of the three mills in the county and his flour, described as "first quality," was sold as far away as Petersburg, Va., and Fayetteville. The Patricks retained ownership of the property until after the Civil War. In 1869–71 the old iron mine, now owned by Levi Shaw, was leased by Thomas Graham of Philadelphia, who owned the North Carolina Center Iron Company, with furnaces in Guilford County near Friendship. Opened as the Dannemora Mine, the site produced ore as late as 1880. The old mill, burned and rebuilt in 1915, was operated by the Tilman W. Griffin family until after World War II. At an auction in 1968 the ironworks tract was sold to James G. W. McClamrock of Greensboro, who had long dreamed of preserving the property, and he eventually gave the mill site to the Rockingham County Historical Society.

Lindley S. Butler

Trucks and Trucking. North Carolina truck manufacturing began in Wilson and Henderson in the 1910s. In about 1914 Hackney Brothers Wagon Company, a Wilson firm founded in 1854 by Willis Napolean Hackney that made buggies (horse-drawn vehicles) and wagons, turned to the manufacture of automobile bodies. The bodies could be fitted to the chassis of trucks and buses. In the 1920s—a period when tiny rural schools were being consolidated into larger school districts—Hackney Brothers became one of the nation's leading manufacturers of school bus bodies. Later the company switched to building refrigerated truck bodies made to customer specifications. The firm was sold in 1996 to Transportation Technologies, which manufactures delivery and emergency vehicle truck bodies, trailers, and fire equipment.

In 1907 Richard J. Corbitt, a successful buggy maker in Henderson, entered the automotive manufacturing business by producing a chain-driven vehicle that he called the "motor buggy." Although fewer than 100 cars were ever produced at the Corbitt Motor Company's Henderson plant, Corbitt as early as 1913 began to manufacture trucks, an enterprise that marked the firm's major focus in succeeding years. Custom-made trucks were manufactured for the U.S. Army in World War I, and their use spread to 23 foreign countries. During World War II, more than 4,000 standard trucks were manufactured at the Corbitt plant for the war effort. The company also designed and manufactured specialty vehicles for military use both before and after the war. Corbitt's T-33 military truck was at the time of its production the second-largest truck in the world and the most versatile in range of power and speed. The truck weighed 25 tons and was powered by a radial air-cooled aircraft engine. Because of material shortages, postwar production levels were held to a maximum of 150 diesel truck tractors per month. The company, the largest truck manufacturer in the South at the time, was sold in 1952 and later disbanded.

While the importance of Wilson and Henderson as truck manufacturing centers declined, other cities became hubs for the building of trucks, truck bodies, truck parts, or accessories. Freightliner Corporation, a subsidiary of Daimler-Chrysler and the nation's largest truck builder, had several plants in North Carolina in the early 2000s. Its large truck assembling plant at Mount Holly was Gaston County's larg-

est employer (with about 3,000 workers). Other Freightliner plants were in Cleveland, Gastonia, and High Point, where the company produces Thomas Built Buses for public school systems and other uses.

North Carolina's truck transportation industry has grown from a small operation in the 1920s to a vast system transporting a substantial portion of the state's freight and other materials—often at the expense of the railroads and air freight carriers. The trucking industry in the early twenty-first century represented about 80 percent of the state's commercial freight transportation market. Private carriers, comprising by far the largest component of the industry, were owned or leased and operated by industrial concerns, farmers, and others. So-called exempt carriers (those exempt from certain government regulations) transported only special kinds of goods or used their trucks only for specific purposes, such as hauling certain agricultural products or carrying newspapers.

The trucking industry is particularly sensitive to economic climates and changes in government regulations, particularly at the federal level. For example, three major companies—Hennis, McLean, and Pilot—moved their headquarters to Winston-Salem before 1950 only to declare bankruptcy by 1989. Other problems have plagued the industry. Low pay, particularly for drivers, has at times left thousands of driver slots unfilled. Many truckers have retired because of long absences from their families or monotony on long hauls. Others have left because of dissatisfaction with regulations at all levels of government, such as restrictions prohibiting trucks in certain lanes of interstate highways and in certain streets in localities, as well as maximum weight, width, and height limits. To cope with higher fuel costs, carriers have often absorbed these costs through surcharges or increases in basic rates.

Charlotte in 2006 was home to the most trucking companies in the state, continuing the city's reputation as a large manufacturing and distribution center. Asheville, Fayetteville, Wilmington, Durham, Greensboro, Hickory, High Point, Raleigh, and Winston-Salem/Kernersville were also large centers of trucking operations. Interstate highways have made the entire state accessible to major markets across the country, particularly in the Northeast and Southeast.

References: Clyde C. Carter, *State Regulation of Commercial Motor Carriers in North Carolina* (1958); Charles Lavoy Hilton, "A Study of the Regulated For-Hire Motor Carrier Industry in North Carolina, 1946–1956" (M.A. thesis, UNC-Chapel Hill, 1957); Robert E. Ireland, *Entering the Auto Age: The Early Automobile in North Carolina, 1900–1930* (1990).

Wiley J. Williams
Additional research provided by Janet M. Hackney and Robert E. Ireland.

Tryon Palace is the restored and reconstructed mansion and government house originally built for North Carolina's

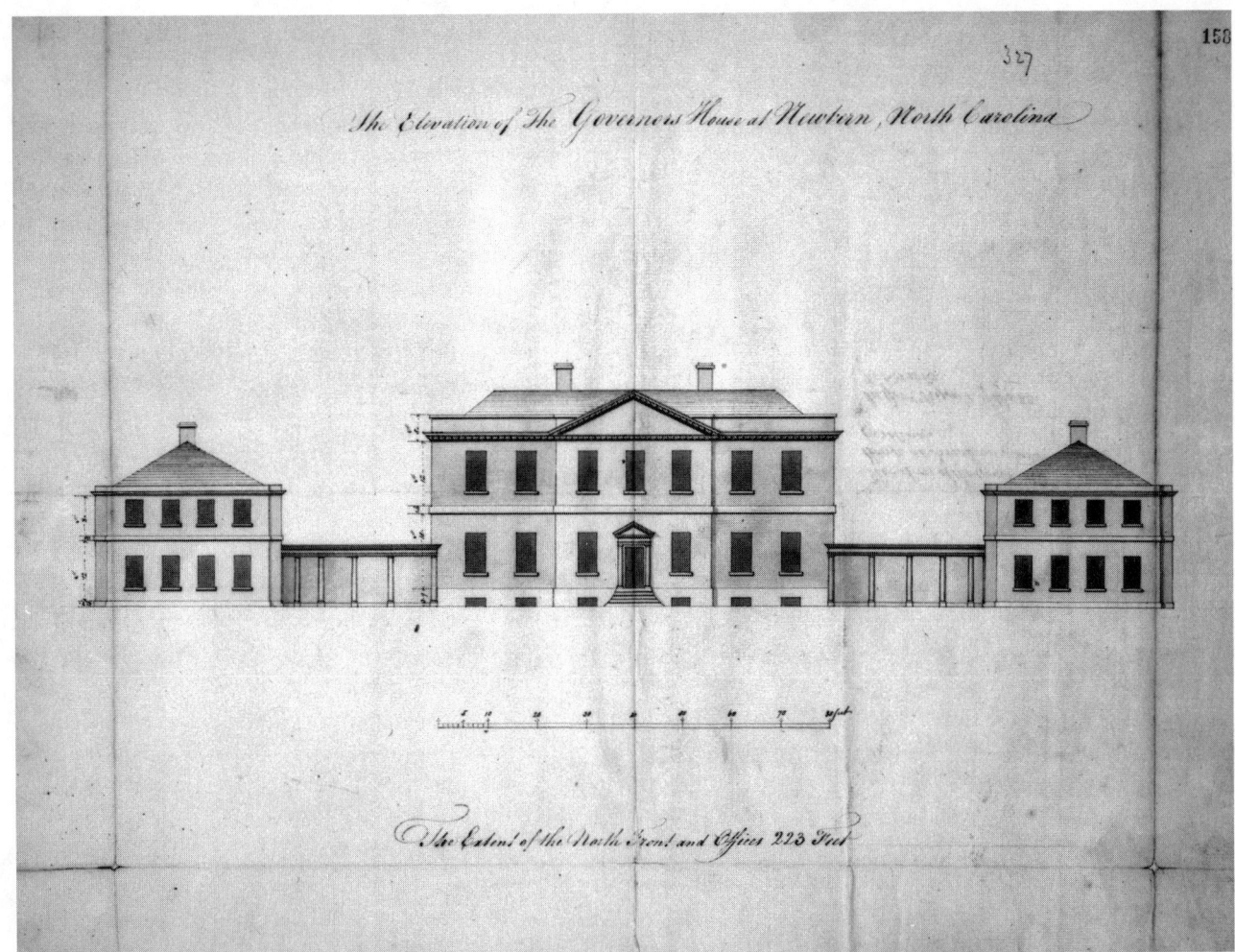

3ʒ

The Elevation of the Governors House at Newbern, North Carolina

The Extent of the North Front and Offices 223 Feet

Plans showing the front elevation of Tryon Palace designed by John Hawks in 1767. The original plans are in the British Public Records Office. Courtesy of NCOA&H.

royal governor William Tryon in 1770. Rising from the banks of the Trent River at the foot of George Street in New Bern, the building is an exact replica of the palace known in colonial America as "the finest government house in the colonies." Following the death of Governor Arthur Dobbs on 29 Mar. 1765, Tryon assumed the office of royal governor and promptly selected New Bern as the site of the capital of the colony. When the colonial Assembly convened in that city on 8 Nov. 1766, Tryon presented a request for an appropriation with which to construct a grand building in New Bern that would serve as the house of colonial government as well as the governor's residence. Less than a month later, the Assembly acceded to the governor's wishes by earmarking £5,000 for the purchase of land and the commencement of construction. The appropriated sum was borrowed from a fund that had been established for the construction of public schools. To replenish the depleted school fund, a poll tax and a levy on alcoholic beverages were imposed.

Tryon had laid the groundwork for the building, which would be known in his time as "Tryon's Palace," before he sailed from England for North Carolina to assume his duties as lieutenant governor in 1764. To assure that his future government house would be of the highest quality, he had persuaded John Hawks, a talented architect, to accompany him to the colony.

On 9 Jan. 1767 Hawks and Tryon executed a contract, which outlined the particulars for the construction of a massive brick structure with wings on either side. A year later, an additional £10,000 was appropriated to ensure completion of the project. When a strong hurricane struck New Bern in September 1769, two-thirds of the buildings in the city were lost, but the palace, then well under roof, survived the storm.

Tryon staged a grand gala to celebrate the official opening of the palace on 5 Dec. 1770. After years of moving from site to site, the colony's seat of government had been established permanently in an imposing structure. However, the extravagance of the palace and the taxes levied to pay for its construction further inflamed many backcountry residents,

Portrait of Lady Margaret Wake Tryon, wife of royal governor William Tryon, painted by an unknown artist in the mid-eighteenth century. Lady Tryon played a prominent role in the cultural development of the North Carolina colony. Courtesy of Norwich Castle Museum and Art Gallery.

whose grievances were given voice by dissidents known as the Regulators. Consequently, Tryon spent the remainder of his tenure in North Carolina mired in controversy and conflict with the western dissidents. He left North Carolina to assume the governorship of New York in June 1771.

Josiah Martin, Tryon's successor as governor of North Carolina, took up residence in the palace on 11 Aug. 1771. He proceeded to fill the building with lavish furnishings at a time when the seeds of revolution were being sown in North Carolina and Britain's other American colonies. As the revolutionary fervor reached a fever pitch in North Carolina, Martin grew concerned for his safety in New Bern and fled the palace on 29 May 1776 in a coach bound for Cape Fear.

Abandoned by the royal governor, Tryon Palace fell into temporary disrepair. On 16 Jan. 1777, in the Council Chambers, Richard Caswell took the oath of office as the first governor of the state of North Carolina. Caswell promptly obtained legislative authority to restore the buildings and grounds of the first capitol of the state. Most of Martin's furniture was confiscated by the new government and purchased at auction for use in the palace.

Abner Nash succeeded Caswell as governor on 17 Apr. 1780, but he was forced to abandon the palace soon thereafter as Lord Charles Cornwallis's army threatened to enter North

Carolina. To aid in the war effort, much of the eight tons of lead that had been used in the construction of the palace was removed and melted into musket balls. After the departure of Nash, the legislature met in the palace two more times, considering on each occasion bills that addressed the repair of the palace and the appointment of caretakers for it. These caretakers were encouraged to rent out rooms in the structure to help defray the expenses of its operation and maintenance. Some consideration was given to selling the palace in an attempt to balance the state budget.

In the wake of the successful conclusion of the Revolutionary War, Tryon Palace continued to deteriorate. Vandals and thieves stripped the building of its valuables, and vagrants took shelter and brawled in the very rooms where the affairs of state had been conducted. Richard Dobbs Spaight, the previous owner of several lots on which the palace had been erected, took the oath of office as governor in the building on 14 Dec. 1792. Two years later, as the new State Capitol in Raleigh neared completion, the state legislature met for the final time at the palace, thus ending the reign of the building as the state's seat of government.

On the evening of 27 Feb. 1798, when a torch accidentally ignited some dry hay, the central portion of the palace burst into flames. By morning, Tryon Palace was mostly a smoldering ruin. Only the west wing survived the conflagration, and over the next 150 years, it was used alternately as a warehouse, a dwelling, a stable and carriage house, a school, and a chapel. In 1925 some interest in rebuilding Tryon Palace on its original site was generated by the Daughters of the American Revolution, historians, and local citizens, but the Great Depression intervened. By 1931 the west wing had been converted into an apartment building.

Renewed interest in a possible restoration inspired Governor Gregg Cherry to create the 25-member Tryon Palace Commission in 1945. The original palace site, which by that time was covered with 54 deteriorating houses fit for demolition, was acquired by the commission with a legislative appropriation of $227,000. Maude Moore Latham, a New Bern native who had played in the palace ruins as a child, served as commission chairperson and also provided substantial financial resources for the project. She established a living trust of $250,000, acquired $125,000 worth of antique furnishings, and bequeathed an additional $1.12 million for the restoration that she did not live to see completed.

In 1951 William G. Perry, of the Boston firm that had restored Colonial Williamsburg in Virginia, was appointed restoration architect. He benefited from two original copies of the palace drawings by Hawks. One set was found in the New-York Historical Society Library, and the other was located at the British Public Record Office in London.

In addition to the extensive historical research that went into the project, archaeological evidence proved beneficial once excavation began. Five feet under George Street, workmen located the original foundations. As the excavations progressed, interior designers were aided by the discovery of pieces of marble, brass, molding, and glass. Completed at a cost of $3.5 million, the restored Tryon Palace was opened to the public on 8 Apr. 1959. It quickly became one of the most heavily visited historic sites in the state.

References: Alonzo T. Dill, *Governor Tryon and His Palace* (1955); William S. Powell, ed., *The Correspondence of William Tryon and Other Selected Papers, 1758–1818* (2 vols., 1980–81); Peter B. Sandbeck, *The Historical Architecture of New Bern and Craven County, North Carolina* (1988); Alan D. Watson, *A History of New Bern and Craven County* (1987).

Daniel W. Barefoot

Tryon's Line, running roughly north to south across western North Carolina, came about as a result of the Royal Proclamation of 1763 at the end of the French and Indian War. It was intended to stop conflict between encroaching white settlers and the American Indians, whose land was being occupied. Officials delayed the running of the line for a time to allow the Cherokee a full hunting season. With much pomp and an impressive show of authority, Governor William Tryon initiated the survey on 4 June 1767 following a formal observance of the birthday of King George III. After two days in the field, Tryon returned to New Bern, leaving the actual running of the line to an appointed three-man commission. The work was completed on 13 June, but the Indians agreed to delay the enforcement of the provisions until the end of the growing season so that settlers whose farms now fell within the Indians' domain could harvest their crops.

Initially the establishment of Tryon's Line was beneficial, but as the white population grew the purpose and authority of the line were ignored. Before the beginning of the American Revolution, North Carolina's frontier families and Indians had reverted to their former conflicts.

References: Louis DeVorsey Jr., *Indian Boundaries in the Southern Colonies, 1763–1775* (1966); William S. Powell, ed., *The Correspondence of William Tryon and Other Selected Papers*, vol. 1 (1980).

William S. Powell

Turlington Act. In 1923 Zebulon Vance Turlington (1877–1969) of Iredell County introduced a measure in the General Assembly to make the state's law conform to the Eighteenth (Prohibition) Amendment to the U.S. Constitution and the Federal Volstead Act. Authorship of the Turlington Act is attributed to Heriot Clarkson, of Charlotte, a vehement prohibitionist who subsequently served on the North Carolina Supreme Court. The act defined the alcoholic content of beverages and made it illegal "to manufacture, sell, barter, transport, import, export, deliver, furnish, purchase, or possess intoxicating liquor." Sacramental and medical uses were permitted. Personal consumption of alcohol was legal only in the home, but the law remained silent on the illegality of obtaining and transporting the contraband to the home.

"Wet" forces tried unsuccessfully to repeal the act, particularly after the end of national Prohibition in 1933. In 1935 the General Assembly passed the New Hanover Act and the Pasquotank Act. These counties and 16 others were authorized to decide by local option vote whether or not to permit liquor sales. Based on the findings of a commission headed by Victor S. Bryant, the legislature passed "An Act to Provide for the Manufacture, Sale, and Control of Alcoholic Beverages in North Carolina." This ABC law established state control over the sale of alcohol in those areas that permitted liquor sales. As late as 1966, state supreme court justice Susie Sharp ruled that "the Turlington Act is still the primary law in every area which has not elected to come under the ABC Act."

Reference: Michael Crowell, "A History of Liquor-by-the-Drink Legislation," *Campbell Law Review* 1 (1979).

Jerry C. Cashion

Turnpikes. The era of turnpikes or toll roads in nineteenth-century North Carolina spanned more than 40 years but contributed only modestly to the development of transportation in the state. With the notable exception of the Buncombe Turnpike, inadequate financing, local and political rivalries, ineffective administration, and the eventual effects of railroads combined to limit the economic and commercial impact of most turnpikes.

Interest in turnpikes began after the War of 1812, when visionary state leader and jurist Archibald D. Murphey championed them as a way to link the western counties with river ports. He called for a turnpike to be constructed from the north fork of the Catawba River in Burke County to the Yellow Mountain on the Tennessee border and for another to run from Raleigh to a convenient terminus on the Neuse River. The state's experiment with turnpikes began in 1818, when the General Assembly authorized the Plymouth Turnpike Company. Four years later it amended this act when it gave the company permission to dig a canal in conjunction with the turnpike, which was to link Pungo Creek in Hyde County with Plymouth in Washington County; however, the company never finished the project. Meanwhile, Horton's Turnpike opened, running from Wilkesboro on the Yadkin to Deep Gap, then through southwestern Ashe County and on to Jonesborough. Built without state aid, this road was badly designed, poorly built, and inadequately maintained.

In the 1820s the legislature endorsed Murphey's internal improvements program and appropriated money for the construction of roads from Rutherfordton to Asheville, Jefferson to the Tennessee line, Old Fort to Asheville and Huntsville, and Surry County to the Virginia line, as well as for the Tennessee River Turnpike, Plymouth Toll Road, and Buncombe Turnpike. The Buncombe Turnpike, which connected Greenville, S.C., with Greeneville, Tenn., via the Saluda Gap, Asheville, and Warm Springs, N.C., was completed in 1827; it became one of the few state-financed internal improvement projects to pay dividends. In the late 1820s it was the longest (about 75 miles), finest, and most traveled highway in the state, becoming the major route from Kentucky and Tennessee to South Carolina and Georgia for enormous herds of cattle, horses, mules, and hogs.

Sectional and partisan jealousies severely undermined efforts to duplicate the success of the Buncombe Turnpike. Throughout the 1840s, eastern Whigs repeatedly defeated attempts to appropriate state funds for a turnpike from Raleigh west to the Tennessee line. Finally, in 1854 the General Assembly approved the construction of the Western Turnpike, which ran through Buncombe County from Asheville across the French Broad River to Waynesville, Webster, Franklin, and Murphy, then west to Ducktown, Tenn., across the Stansbury Mountain chain. Among other turnpikes, the most prominent linked Salisbury, Lincolnton, and Rutherfordton. In the 1850s the state incorporated a number of lesser turnpike companies, including the Jonathan's Creek and Tennessee Mountain, Pigeon River, Tuckasege and Keowee, Qualla Town and Oconaluftee, Tuckasege and Nantahala, Macon County, and Cheoih Turnpikes.

References: Ora Blackmun, *Western North Carolina: Its Mountains and Its People to 1880* (1977); Thomas E. Jeffrey, *State Parties and National Politics: North Carolina, 1815–1861* (1989); F. A. Sondley, *A History of Buncombe County, North Carolina* (2 vols., 1930).

Charles H. McArver

SEE ALSO Buncombe Turnpike.

Tuscarora Indians occupied much of the North Carolina inner Coastal Plain at the time of the Roanoke Island colonies in the 1580s. They were considered the most powerful and highly developed tribe in what is now eastern North Carolina and were thought to possess mines of precious metal. White settlers on Albemarle Sound fought sporadically with the Tuscarora from 1664 to 1667, the conflict apparently begun by the encroachment of a group of refugee Virginia Quakers on lands claimed by the tribe. Whites thereafter avoided further encroachment, recognizing the west side of Chowan River as Tuscarora country until after 1700. (A fur-trading post at the mouth of Salmon Creek, however, operated by mutual consent throughout the period as a monopoly and source of income for Carolina governors.)

A considerable fur trade with the Tuscarora began to develop in Virginia perhaps as early as the 1650s, and the Tuscarora became for a time a formidable presence in Virginia affairs. About 1701 Virginia began tolerating white encroachment on Indian lands west of Blackwater River, and the Chowan frontier immediately dissolved. Whites began pushing into lands of the Meherrin tribe, probably also Iroquoian and understood to be clients of the Tuscarora. The Tuscarora Upper Towns, those under the sway of Chief Tom Blount and occupying sites along the upper Neuse, Tar, and Roanoke Rivers, had sufficiently profitable relations with the whites to accept the new situation as long as they were not directly threatened. The Lower Towns, on the lower Neuse River and the Catechna (now Contentnea) Creek, led by Chief Hancock, were less disposed to do so. Importuned by small coastal tribes who were harassed by white settlements from Bath to New Bern between 1701 and 1711, Hancock and the Lower Towns in September 1711 staged what was evidently intended as a warning attack on white settlements.

The wanderings of Christoph von Graffenried and John Lawson in Tuscarora territory proved to be the flash point. The two men were taken hostage by the Tuscarora in September 1711, and Lawson was subsequently put to death. The brutal and swift English response soon developed into the full-scale Tuscarora War, during which successive expeditions of whites and non-Tuscarora Indians from South Carolina in 1712 and 1713 took on Hancock's forces. Hancock and his people built and employed forts as part of their defensive strategy. The Tuscarora forts were built after 22 Sept. 1711, when a surprise attack upon the colonists on the Cape Fear River killed many settlers. Between October and December 1711, the Tuscarora, expecting a counterattack, turned their living areas into forts and withdrew their families, their crops, and their animals into these structures. Although not unlike European forts, the Tuscarora structures were variations of their circular and square palisade defense perimeters that predated the arrival of the whites. Probably due to the influence of the Europeans, the Tuscarora added thistle bushes outside fort walls and trenches inside the palisades, and at least one fort, Fort Neoheroka, possessed a strong redoubt to cover its entrance.

In late December 1711, Col. John "Jack" Barnwell, with 366 Indians and 30 white militia, marched over 300 miles from South Carolina to the aid of the North Carolinians fighting the Tuscarora. In January 1712 his command besieged and captured Fort Narhantes, 20 miles from New Bern, killing or taking prisoner nearly 400 Indians. Barnwell, with the aid of approximately 150 North Carolina militia, then moved against the larger and better-prepared Fort Hancock on Catechna Creek. An uncoordinated assault in early March failed, and Barnwell withdrew until 7 April, when he again moved against Fort Hancock. This time he approached the fort cautiously, over the course of ten days, by siege trenches. When his men were within 11 yards of the palisades, he ordered the space between the trenches and the walls to be filled by a "great quantity" of lightwood that he intended to set on fire in order to burn the palisades. Others of his command began bombarding Catechna with cannon. At this point, the Indians threatened to kill their white captives, and Barnwell agreed to a peace that required the Tuscarora to cede all territory between the Neuse and the Cape Fear Rivers. He and his Indians then returned to South Carolina.

In early 1713 South Carolina sent James Moore at the head of another expedition of whites and Indian allies aimed at destroying the Tuscarora. The last great stand of the Tuscarora took place at Fort Neoheroka on 20–23 Mar. 1713. Fort Hancock had been built according to state-of-the-art European ideas under the direction of an escaped South Carolina slave named Harry, and Fort Neoheroka may have been a product of the same direction. A marsh to the south offered access to the fort only along a narrow ridge. The fort's earthen walls (with loopholes for firing), topped by tall palisades of logs angled against still taller blockhouses, were surrounded by a moat and trenches; within were second walls and underground bunkers for noncombatants.

Moore's men overran the trenches and raised a blockhouse and battery near the walls high enough to permit firing into Fort Neoheroka. On 20 March the attackers dug a tunnel to a portion of the outer wall and tried to blow it apart, but the effort failed because of defective powder. A subsequent charge carried part of the outer works and made it possible to set fire to a blockhouse and other parts of the fort. Still, three days of desperate hand-to-hand fighting were required for the South Carolinians to gain control, the defenders showing themselves, according to Baron von Graffenried, "unspeakably brave. . . . Wounded savages . . . on the ground still continued to fight. There were about 200 who were burned up in a redoubt and . . . in all about 900, including women and children were dead and captured." Moore had 151 casualties, including 47 killed. This action ended the war-making capacity of the Tuscarora.

Tom Blount's Upper Town Tuscarora, who had aided the European settlers in the war and even handed over Chief Hancock to the whites toward its close, were rewarded with a reservation. Lands on the north side of the Roanoke River between Quitsna Swamp and Deep Creek in southwestern Bertie County were secured in 1717 for this purpose. (An earlier reserved tract between the Neuse and Pamlico Rivers had proved unsatisfactory to Blount and his people.) The location of the reservation is shown on Moseley's map of 1733, Collett's map of 1770, and Price and Strother's 1808 map, where it is assigned its popular name, Indian Woods Reservation.

The Tuscaroras who had opposed the settlers removed to Niagara County, N.Y., to join the Five Nations, thereafter the Six Nations. After several legal exchanges, the Tuscarora executed a deed to the state in 1831 extinguishing their title, right, and interest in the North Carolina land. Some 645 families or clans of Tuscaroras remained in the South, however, migrating to other parts of North Carolina, South Carolina, and Virginia. Their descendants eventually came together and reformed into four communities in and around Robeson County—the Tuscarora Nation East of the Mountain, the Tuscarora Tribe of North Carolina, the Southern Band Tuscarora Indian Tribe, and the Tuscarora Nation of North Carolina—none of which, as of the early 2000s, was officially recognized by the state of North Carolina.

References: Thomas C. Parramore, "The Tuscarora Ascendancy," *NCHR* 59 (October 1982); Parramore, "With Tuscarora Jack on the Back Path to Bath," *NCHR* 64 (April 1987); Herbert J. Paschal Jr., "The Tuscarora Indians in North Carolina" (M.A. thesis, UNC-Chapel Hill, 1953).

Thomas C. Parramore
Additional research provide by George Stevenson, Harry L. Thompson, and Louis P. Towles.

Tweetsie Railroad, the central attraction of a "Wild West" theme park of the same name in Watauga County, dates back to 1866, when the Tennessee legislature granted the East Tennessee & Western North Carolina Railroad Company (ET&WNC) permission to construct a 34-mile line through the rugged Blue Ridge chain from Johnson City, Tenn., to the iron mines in Cranberry, N.C. Philadelphia engineer Col. Thomas Matson supervised construction, and the railroad began operating in 1882. Several small logging lines were built as feeder lines to it as business boomed, especially with the purchase of the Carnegie iron furnace in Johnson City. In 1916 the line was extended to Boone, and passenger service provided access to the formerly isolated area as the railroad also brought lumber out of the mountains. Another extension expanded the line 12 more miles to Hampton, Tenn., which made Tweetsie Railroad one of the largest narrow-gauge lines in the nation. Narrow gauge means the track is only three feet wide, which is significantly narrower than most train tracks.

Destructive floods in August 1940 and competition with modern roads brought about unprofitable conditions for the railroad. On 13 July 1950, the ET&WNC officially shut down. Tweetsie Locomotive #12, the only remaining locomotive of the railroad's original 13, was bought by a group of railroad enthusiasts and moved to Virginia. Soon after, Hurricane Hazel destroyed the railroad tracks, forcing the group to sell the locomotive. It found a new owner in movie cowboy Gene Autry, who intended to use it in his films. This ownership was short-lived. Autry, unable to transport the locomotive to California, sold it for one dollar to Gene Robbins Jr., a native of the North Carolina mountains. Robbins intended to ship the locomotive back to Blowing Rock. North Carolina governor Luther Hodges declared 20 May 1956 as "Tweetsie Homecoming Day." Instead, however, the locomotive underwent extensive restoration in Hickory and was not moved to Blowing Rock until 23 May 1957, when it was accompanied by some of the original ET&WNC rail cars. Later that summer, Tweetsie Locomotive #12 and the cars made a widely welcomed maiden run on new tracks just miles from the old station in Boone. In awe of the many hairpin turns that the railroad navigated, people briefly used the nickname "Stemwinder" for the train. But "Tweetsie" —in recognition of the shrill "tweet-tweet" of the locomotive's whistle—soon became the official name.

Riding the three-mile loop on the Tweetsie Railroad is an amusing adventure that includes helping a U.S. marshal thwart the hijacking attempts of wild Indians or train robbers. Other attractions at the Tweetsie Railroad theme park include live entertainment such as the Palace Saloon Show, Bluegrass Bands, the Rainmaker, and the Tweetsie Clogging Jamboree, and a chair lift to Miner's Mountain that offers a panoramic view of the surrounding area. The Tweetsie Railroad is part of the National Registry of Historic Places.

Brad Minsley

Tyrrell County is located on the southern shore of Albemarle Sound, in the Coastal Plain of northeastern North Carolina. Named for Sir John Tyrrell, one of the Lords Proprietors, the county was formed in 1729 from Chowan, Bertie, Currituck and Pasquotank Counties. It is bordered to the east by the intracoastal waters of the Alligator River. Its county seat, Columbia, was incorporated in 1793 as Elizabeth Town and renamed in 1801. Other communities in the county include Gum Neck, Kilkenny, Fort Landing, Frying Pan Landing, Newfoundland, and Woodley.

Tyrrell County is dominated by its coastlands and its swamps, and the terrain has limited development and population growth since the county was founded. In 2004 Tyrrell County was the state's least populous, with an estimated 4,100 residents. But it is a popular location for fishing and other water sports, hunting, and bird watching. The 110,000-acre Pocosin Lakes National Wildlife Refuge was established in 1990 and is headquartered in Columbia. The refuge and surrounding county lands are home to one of the last large habitats for black bears on the eastern seaboard. Pocosin Arts in Columbia is among the premier arts organizations in the state.

Peter Bangma

U

Ugly Club had been organized by a small body of students at the University of North Carolina in Chapel Hill by 1831 for the avowed purpose of helping homesick students overcome their malady. As altruistic as that motivation may have appeared, it was soon forgotten, and in time the Ugly Club came to be regarded as the beginning of hazing. The acknowledged ugliest man on campus was accorded the leading role in the club, and others nearly as unsightly were granted membership. New students who showed signs of homesickness were called upon to attend a meeting, where they were greeted with, among other things, "horns and tin pans and lusty lungs." Escaping from the presence of these unattractive men and their noise theoretically made the once-homesick students glad to retreat to the quiet of their rooms for a good night's sleep.

Richard B. Creecy, a freshman at the university in 1831, wrote that he was homesick when an acquaintance invited him to a meeting on the top floor of South Building. Creecy wrote that the door was opened by the ugliest man he had ever seen, "dressed in the most uncouth style." He wore a dunce cap with horns on it. The president of the club "marched around the room, mumbling some cabalistic words, while we stood alone in the middle of the hall, feeling very much like a fool." Creecy was obliged against his will to dance around the room, to sing a song, and to "wrestle" with the leader. In the latter engagement the freshman was about to throw the president of the club when he was taken by a surprise grasp. The president was winded but succeeded in blackening Creecy's face with grease and making a pun on his name ("greasy").

Those who survived such antics became acclimated to campus life and lost the inclination toward homesickness. Club activity, however, eventually degenerated into such excessive rowdiness that it resulted in damage to property, the use of firearms on campus, attacks on the faculty, and other behavior requiring strong action by the faculty and trustees, including dismissal of some students.

Reference: Kemp P. Battle, *History of the University of North Carolina, 1789–1868*, vol. 1 (1907).

William S. Powell

Umstead Act, named for U.S. congressman and North Carolina governor William B. Umstead and passed originally in 1939, was enacted by the North Carolina legislature to prevent state-owned agencies from selling merchandise in direct competition with private merchants. The act was passed in an attempt to prevent the government from competing with its taxpaying citizens. The original act excluded several state-run institutions from the law, including counties and municipalities, the North Carolina School for the Blind, state correctional institutions or agencies, and others. Since its ratification in 1939, the act has been amended several times. In 1973 a large amendment to the Umstead Act was ratified, creating further exceptions and updating its provisions. Some colleges are mentioned in the original act, and in 1973 the exemption was expanded to all the campuses in the University of North Carolina System. In 1997 exemptions were extended to the Centennial Campus of North Carolina State University and the North Carolina Zoological Park in Asheboro.

Laura Young Baxley

Underground Railroad was a secret system of individuals who assisted fugitive slaves in their quest for freedom prior to the Civil War. The term, used between about 1830 and 1860, refers to the swift, "invisible" way in which the slaves escaped. Usually they hid during the day and moved at night. The fugitives and the people who helped them used railroad terms as code words: hiding places were "stations," people who aided the runaways were "conductors," and the runaways themselves were "passengers" or "freight." In addition to white members of the Underground Railroad, fugitive slaves relied heavily on fellow slaves and free blacks, who rarely betrayed them. The most famous black leader in the movement was Harriet Tubman, a nonliterate runaway slave who became known as the "Moses" of her people. She returned to the South, including the Blue Ridge Mountains, 19 times to help about 300 African Americans escape to freedom.

The Underground Railroad and the abolitionist movement in North Carolina, as elsewhere, was spearheaded by the Society of Friends (Quakers). In 1809 Quaker slaveholders in Guilford County deeded all of their slaves to the North Carolina Yearly Meeting, which over the next few years spent about $13,000 relocating blacks in northern states, Haiti, and Liberia. The *Greensborough Patriot* (Greensboro) was the state's only abolitionist newspaper. The state's first abolitionist organization was formed in Guilford County in 1816; called the Manumission Society and later the North Carolina Manumission Society, it soon had several chapters and 1,600 members. After legal and other pressures forced the society to disband in 1834, many of its members became active in the Underground Railroad.

As early as 1819, Vestal Coffin had established an Underground Railroad station in Guilford County. His sons Alfred and Addison carried on his work, as did his cousin Levi Coffin. These four, but especially Levi, were unquestionably the best-known of Guilford County's abolitionists. In 1826 Levi moved to Newport (now Fountain City), Ind., where he received the unofficial title of president of the Underground Railroad. His home became known as "Union Station" because of the many runaway slaves who sought temporary refuge there.

The U.S. Congress's Compromise of 1850, which admitted California to the Union as a free state, included the Fugitive Slave Act. Southern states expected that this measure—providing that private citizens as well as officers of the law would assist in apprehending and returning runaway slaves and imposing heavy penalties for failing to comply with the statute—would be effective in returning slaves to their masters. But the act was widely disregarded by northerners. Many officials and individuals in the North not only refused to return the fugitives but also began to play active roles in the Underground Railroad.

The number of slaves aided by the railroad has long been in dispute and subject to widely varying estimates. It most certainly was not the flood of fugitive slaves claimed by antebellum propagandists and later fiction writers (up to 100,000 people). Indeed, the actual number likely represented only a small fraction of the slaves held in bondage.

References: John Spencer Bassett, *Anti-Slavery Leaders of North Carolina* (1898); Charles L. Blackson, "The Underground Railroad: Escape from Slavery," *National Geographic* 166 (July 1984); William S. Powell, *North Carolina: A Bicentennial History* (1977); Powell, *North Carolina through Four Centuries* (1989); Wilbur H. Siebert, *The Underground Railroad from Slavery to Freedom* (1898).

Alex Coffin
Additional research provided by Wiley J. Williams.

Underwater Archaeology. SEE Archaeology.

Underwriter, USS. The USS *Underwriter*, a navy gunboat, fought in the sounds and rivers of North Carolina during the Civil War. Early in 1864 the *Underwriter* was in the Neuse River at New Bern when Confederate forces under Maj. Gen. George E. Pickett mounted an attack to recapture the city. As part of the assault, about 250 Confederate sailors and marines in 14 boats and launches led by Cdr. John Taylor Wood secretly descended the Neuse River from Kinston and found the *Underwriter* anchored north of New Bern, close to the west bank of the river.

In one of the most daring encounters of the war, Wood's command boarded the *Underwriter* shortly after 2:30 A.M. on 2 Feb. 1864, and after vicious hand-to-hand fighting on deck, captured the ship and part of its crew. Five Confederates were killed along with nine Union sailors, including Acting Master Jacob Westervelt, the *Underwriter*'s commander. Many others were wounded. Unfortunately for the Confederates, however, the *Underwriter*'s fires were banked and it lacked sufficient steam to get under way. Once it was clear that the vessel had been captured, Union shore batteries opened fire on the ship.

Wood had no choice but to burn it and retire back up the river, carrying with him the wounded of both sides and the Union prisoners. The *Underwriter* finally blew up and sank as the fire reached its magazine just before sunrise.

References: John S. Carbone, *The Civil War in Coastal North Carolina* (2001); T. J. Scharf, *The History of the Confederate States Navy from Its Organization to the Surrender of Its Last Vessel* (1887); Royce Gordon Shingleton, *John Taylor Wood: Sea Ghost of the Confederacy* (1979).

Paul Branch

Union Churches, found in the backcountry or rural areas of early North Carolina, were buildings that housed two or more families or other groups having similar religious beliefs, a common language, and a desire to further the interests of all parties living in an area of scarce economic resources. The single structure helped preserve the limited assets of the groups involved. Union churches with Evangelical Reformed and Lutheran adherents are known to have existed at Pilgrim, Beck, and Bethany Churches in what is today Davidson County in the eighteenth century. St. Luke's Church on the west side of the Yadkin River, also in present-day Davidson County, housed members of both the Anglican and Lutheran faiths. One of the common bonds within these congregations was the fact that their members spoke German. Traveling ministers of both denominations spoke to the groups in German and English. During the mid-nineteenth century, the North Carolina Railroad built a structure in Company Shops (modern-day Burlington) that was used as a union church. The building had as tenants Baptists, Episcopalians, Lutherans, Methodists, and Presbyterians, and it housed a public school on the second floor, as well as a Masonic lodge. This building was called the "Preaching House."

David R. Koontz

Union County, located in the Piedmont region of North Carolina, was formed in 1842 from Mecklenburg and Anson Counties. Democrats wanted to name it for one of their leaders (Andrew Jackson) and Whigs for one of theirs (Henry Clay), so "Union" was chosen as a compromise. It is situated along the South Carolina border. Early inhabitants of the area included the Waxhaw and Catawba Indians; German, Scotch-Irish, English, and Welsh settlers followed. Monroe, the county seat, was incorporated in 1844 and named for President James Monroe. Other communities in the county include Weddington, Indian Trail, Stallings, Wingate, Marvin, Lake Park, New Salem, and Fairview. Union County's notable physical features include the Rocky River, Lake Twiddy, Lee Branch, and Richardson and Beaverdam Creeks.

President Andrew Jackson was born in the Waxhaws area on the border of North Carolina and South Carolina, and both states claim to be his authentic birthplace. Union County maintains the Museum of the Waxhaws and Andrew Jackson Memorial to honor Jackson. Wingate University was established in Wingate (near Monroe) in 1896. Union County landmarks and historic sites include the Old Union Courthouse, built in 1886; the Confederate Memorial, erected in 1910; and the North Corner Boundary Stone, dated to 1818. Cultural institutions include the Union County Heritage Room; the Jesse Helms Center, an educational institution promoting free enterprise and other values championed by the Monroe native and longtime U.S. senator; the Rainbow Theatre; and the Waxhaw Historical Festival and Drama Association. The county hosts popular festivals and annual events such as the Waxhaw Scottish Fair and Games, the Blooming Arts Festival in Monroe, the Marshville Boll Weevil Festival, and the Weddington Fall Festival.

Part of the fast-growing Charlotte metropolitan area, Union County experienced rapid growth in the late twentieth century. By 2004 it had an estimated population of 151,800. Despite increased urbanization, agriculture remains vital to parts of Union County. Its agricultural goods include soybeans, grains, cotton, eggs, dairy products, poultry, and hogs. Manufactured products include industrial pumps, furniture, textile machinery, and plastic containers.

Reference: Virginia Kendrick, ed., *The Heritage of Union County* (1993).

William S. Powell

SEE ALSO Andrew Jackson Birthplace.

Unionists in North Carolina were citizens who opposed the state's secession from the Union prior to and during the Civil War. After Abraham Lincoln won the presidency in November 1860, the dominant issue in North Carolina was whether the state should leave the Union and join other southern states in a new confederacy. The election of Lincoln, who had pledged to prevent the further extension of slavery, created alarm and despair for the future of North Carolina and the other southern states. The 1860 ballot, however, showed that most North Carolinians opposed secession. William W. Holden, editor of the Raleigh-based *North Carolina Standard*, rejected secession and urged North Carolinians to "watch and wait" until Lincoln and the Republican Party gave tangible proof of their intentions. Federal Whigs, such as William A. Graham, John M. Morehead, and George E. Badger, denied the right as well as the expediency and wisdom of secession.

A minority group of radical Democrats, led by Governor John W. Ellis, favored secession because of Lincoln's election. The events of the winter of 1860–61 steadily weakened Unionist support in the state. In January 1861 the legislature—yielding to increasing pressure—passed the Convention Act, authorizing a vote on 28 February to determine whether to call

a convention and to elect 120 delegates to serve if the referendum passed. Of the 120 delegates chosen at the election, 28 were conditional Unionists, 50 were unconditional Unionists, and 42 were secessionists. Fearing that a convention might lead to secession, however, the voting public turned it down 47,323 to 46,672.

Although most North Carolinians still had no desire to secede, the firing on Fort Sumter and Lincoln's call for troops placed them firmly in the secessionist camp. Governor Ellis informed U.S. secretary of war Simon Cameron that North Carolina would send no troops to aid the government in Washington. In short, the firing on Fort Sumter, Lincoln's call for troops, and his subsequent proclamation blockading southern ports unified the state far more effectively than all the previous arguments of the secessionists. Unionists as well as secessionists applauded the governor's firm stand. All Unionist newspapers, including Holden's *North Carolina Standard*, went over to the secessionist side.

Ellis acted promptly to prepare the state for secession and war. On 1 May 1861 he called for 30,000 volunteers and convened a special session of the General Assembly. That body adjourned 13 days later, the date it had fixed for electing delegates to a convention on the secession question. The convention assembled at Raleigh on 20 May with 120 delegates present. Within an hour after the adoption of an ordinance of secession, the convention ratified the provisional Constitution of the Confederate States of America.

The Unionist cause in North Carolina was not completely extinguished by the state's entry into the Confederacy. Through the leaders of the peace movement, the radical Heroes of America, the guerrilla Buffaloes, and many other formal or informal political groups, fervent Unionism continued to fuel conflicts among the citizenry throughout the war.

References: Daniel W. Crofts, "Union Party of 1861 and the Secession Crisis," *Perspective in American History* 11 (1977–78); Richard Nelson Current, *Lincoln's Loyalists: Union Soldiers from the Confederacy* (1992); John C. Inscoe and Robert C. Kenzer, eds., *Enemies of the Country: New Perspectives on Unionists in the Civil War South* (2001).

Wiley J. Williams

SEE ALSO Buffaloes; Peace Movement; Secession Movement.

Union League of North Carolina was an affiliate of the Loyal League of America, which is believed to have been created in early 1862 by Judge James M. Edmunds of Philadelphia as a patriotic club directed by the Republican Party. Branches quickly formed in New York, Boston, and other cities, and by late 1862 these bodies had created a National Council of Leagues to assist the Republican Party in retaining voter support. The National Council took part in President Abraham Lincoln's reelection drive in 1864 and encouraged the growth of Unionist sentiment among middle and lower class southern whites who wished to return to the Union and among slaves and freedmen who could be weaned from assisting the Confederacy. In 1864 Loyal League organizers appeared in West Virginia, eastern Tennessee, and parts of coastal South Carolina and North Carolina, areas already controlled by Federal troops, to form local Union Leagues.

On 4 July 1865, 2,000 Union Leaguers marched in Raleigh's Independence Day celebration and cheered North Carolina provisional governor William W. Holden, who was known to look favorably on poor white and black concerns. Later that evening, Holden "enthusiastically" received league members and local freedmen at his home. The winter of 1866–67 heightened the political tempo as the national Republican Party swept the fall elections and gained control of Congress. By announcing its intention to grant blacks the vote as well as political and social equality, Congress effectively took over Reconstruction from President Andrew Johnson. In North Carolina, Holden, who had already begun to organize an independent political movement, committed to black equality in January 1867; two months later, after the announcement of Congressional Reconstruction, he launched a state Republican Party.

North Carolina Union Leaguers resisted party control and sought to rule the state organization through the leagues. Since the leagues were at least 80 percent black and represented nearly 40 percent of the state's population that was of African descent, its support was essential for victory. Yet Holden realized that success was equally contingent on a sizable turnout of whites who had difficulty accepting black equality. Accordingly, the governor moved carefully, but by the fall of 1867 he had merged blacks and whites into the state Republican Party, had himself elected as its chair, and reduced the leagues to a component of the party.

Holden worked tirelessly for the Republican Party during 1867 and 1868. New leagues were recruited and old ones strengthened until almost every midland and eastern county supported 2,000 or more leaguers. The Ku Klux Klan soon challenged Holden's efforts. It struck at the basis of his power —the Union Leagues and their leaders—vowing to remove the "dark savages and white ignoramuses wearing the oath of office." Their intimidation was so thorough that many leagues ceased to function and thousands of blacks failed to vote in November 1870. After impeachment charges were brought against him, Holden was tried and removed from office on 22 Mar. 1871. With his fall and the steady pressure of the Ku Klux Klan, the Union Leagues collapsed.

References: Roberta Sue Alexander, *North Carolina Faces the Freedman: Race Relations during Presidential Reconstruction, 1865–1867* (1985); J. G. de Roulhac Hamilton, *Reconstruction in North Carolina* (1914); William C. Harris, *William Woods Holden: Firebrand of North Carolina* (1987).

Louis P. Towles

Union Square, located near the center of Raleigh as laid out in 1792, was designated as the site for the state legislature and served as its location for almost 175 years. The original statehouse, or capitol building, was a rather simple structure built in the square in 1794. After it was destroyed by fire in 1831, an elegant new Greek Revival capitol was erected on the same site and opened in 1840. Outgrown and abandoned by the General Assembly in 1961, the State Capitol now stands restored as the office of the governor and lieutenant governor and as a North Carolina State Historic Site.

Activity on Union Square's surrounding grounds started early and lends itself to division into two distinct phases— functional and commemorative. The functional phase of Union Square's history began in 1792 with the construction of a plank-and-rail fence around the square, replaced with a decorative wrought iron railing in 1848 (then removed in 1899). In 1795 Thomas Atkins constructed outhouses in the northeast and northwest corners of the square, which remained until an indoor plumbing system was installed in the capitol in the 1880s. A growing bureaucracy demanded more space than the statehouse could provide, and in 1814 a one-story, brick office was erected for the governor; it was located where the statue of George Washington now stands and served the state's governors until 1840. Nine years later it was sold and removed from the grounds. The 1816 General Assembly ordered a new office for the secretary of state to be built off the southeast corner of the capitol building. Occupied only by William Hill and his staff, the structure was sold and removed in 1849. A new building was erected for the secretary of the treasury in 1824, also in the southeast quadrant of the square. When the building ceased to be used is not known, but it may have been around 1849, when the square was being cleared of unneeded structures after government officials had moved into the new and larger capitol (1840). One structure not removed was the arsenal, constructed in 1828 to house the military supplies of the state. It stood in the southwest corner until its demolition in 1907, having served as a storage house for nearly 40 years.

Union Square's commemorative phase covers virtually all of the twentieth century. The honoring of individuals important to state's history began in 1900 with a statue of Zebulon B. Vance, followed by tributes to Worth Bagley (1907), Henry Lawson Wyatt (1912), Charles D. McIver (1912), Charles Brantley Aycock (1924), and Samuel A'Court Ashe (1940). Groups receiving commemoration include North Carolina's Confederate soldiers (1892), women of the Confederacy (1914), three U.S. presidents (Andrew Jackson, James K. Polk, and Andrew Johnson; 1948), Vietnam veterans (1987), and veterans of World Wars I and II and the Korean War (1990). Landscaping in 1928 changed the physical appearance of Union Square and led to the present-day walkways and the plantings that represent the variety of trees, flowers, and shrubs native to North Carolina.

References: John L. Cheney Jr., ed., *North Carolina Government, 1585–1979: A Narrative and Statistical History* (1981); Jerry L. Cross, *Construction on Union Square, 1792–1831: A Report on Structures Auxiliary to the Statehouse* (1978); Cross, *Heroes and Heroines on Union Square: The Statues and Monuments on Union (Capitol) Square at Raleigh, North Carolina* (n.d.); John L. Sanders, *The North Carolina State House and Capitol, 1792–1972* (1972).

Jerry L. Cross

Union Volunteer Regiments. Four regiments of white North Carolinians served the Union during the Civil War: the 1st and 2nd North Carolina Union Volunteer Infantry in the Coastal Plain and the 2nd and 3rd North Carolina Union Mounted Infantry in the Mountains. The Union also recruited a black brigade in North Carolina, the African Brigade, which consisted of ex-slaves.

The 1st North Carolina Union Volunteer Infantry was authorized in May 1862 by Maj. Gen. Ambrose E. Burnside, whose army had just completed the conquest of the state's Coastal Plain from the Virginia border south to New Bern. The unit's history, however, dates to the original invasion of the Outer Banks in August 1861 by Maj. Gen. Benjamin F. Butler. Small groups of North Carolina Unionists requested protection from Federal army and navy commanders and proclaimed a willingness to serve in the U.S. Army. The primary function of the 1st North Carolina was defensive duty in and around the occupied towns. Its troops acted as pickets, guards, and gun crews in block houses and were especially useful to Union forces as scouts. Their offensive operations were confined to small-scale expeditions into the countryside, generally in the company of northern units. One exception was Company L, designated as cavalry under Capt. George W. Graham, who had transferred from a New York regiment. This unit gained the respect of Federal commanders as well as widespread publicity in the northern press.

The 2nd North Carolina was formed in the last months of 1863 under Capt. Charles H. Foster, a Maine native who had edited a newspaper in Murfreesboro before the war. This unit suffered from poor organization and bad luck, and its misfortunes resulted in a general lack of respect for North Carolina regiments by Federal commanders. The recruits in the second regiment differed markedly from those in the first. Rather than enlisting only patriotic Unionists, this unit also attracted war-weary Confederate deserters and poor men who were tempted by the $300 bonus and care for their families. Within two months, in February 1864, Confederates commanded by Maj. Gen. George E. Pickett captured an entire company during an attack on New Bern.

The western units, the 2nd and 3rd North Carolina Union Mounted Infantry, were organized in October 1863 and June 1864, respectively, and headquartered in Knoxville, Tenn. Enlisting soldiers for these regiments was not difficult. Unionism was strong in the Mountains, where many residents resented the slaveholding aristocracy of the eastern planters. This was especially evident in Henderson, Transylvania, Yancey, Madison, Mitchell, and Wilkes Counties. Pro-Union sentiment was so strong in Wilkes that Confederates referred to the county as the "Old United States." A Union company organized in Henderson County in 1863 later became Company F, 2nd North Carolina Mounted Union Volunteer Regiment. Early in the war "underground railroads" secretly guided southern Unionists to northern recruiting stations in Tennessee and elsewhere. These men were joined by numerous North Carolinians who had deserted the southern armies following the devastating Confederate defeats at Vicksburg and Gettysburg.

North Carolina's Mountain regiments originated in February 1864 with an order authorizing Maj. George W. Kirk to raise a regiment in eastern Tennessee and western Carolina. Recruits were enlisted for three years and designated as mounted infantry, using privately owned or captured horses. The first regiment was organized in October 1863 with headquarters at Knoxville, Tenn., and Kirk as regimental commander. The 3rd North Carolina Mounted Infantry Regiment was formed in Knoxville in June 1864.

The Confederate population of western North Carolina, which feared incursions into the state, considered Kirk's Volunteers, as the regiments were sometimes called, to be outlaws. Two Federal reports lend credence to this view. In March 1864, five months after the first regiment's formation, the Union division commander, Brig. Gen. T. T. Garrard, viewed it as undisciplined and of little value to his organization. Civilized warfare was certainly violated in a January 1865 order issued to the regiment to take no prisoners and shoot guerrillas, Confederate Home Guards, and partisan rangers whenever and wherever found. There were no actual military campaigns in the Mountains until 1865. But the mountain passes were of strategic importance. The 2nd and 3rd North Carolina Union Mounted Infantry thus did not engage in major battles but fought many small skirmishes.

The African Brigade was formed at a time when few Union army or Federal government officials favored black soldiers, although the groundwork had been laid in Massachusetts by the black 54th and 55th Massachusetts Volunteers. Despite official reticence, the Union army employed blacks as spies, scouts, and guides. Many others worked in civilian support roles in army camps in eastern North Carolina. A March 1863 census of the freed black population in New Bern enumerated 8,500 adult males.

Union authorities planned to raise four black infantry regiments from North Carolina, aided by Governor John A. Andrew of Massachusetts and Col. Edward A. Wild of the 35th Massachusetts Volunteers. They looked for white officers committed to abolition and temperance to mix with black officers. Wild chose James Chaplain Beecher, half brother of abolitionist author Harriet Beecher Stowe, to lead the 1st North Carolina Colored Volunteers (NCCV). On 18 May 1863 Wild began recruiting from among the freedmen gathered in New Bern. The first recruits came from more than 30 North Carolina counties. Equipment was often substandard, but by 25 June Wild pronounced the first regiment complete. On 3 July the unit embarked on its first mission, conducting a raid on the Wilmington & Weldon Railroad that considerably alarmed Confederate North Carolina—raising the specter of massed, armed black men. On 30 July Wild and more than 2,000 soldiers of the African Brigade embarked for Charleston, S.C.

After Wild left North Carolina, recruitment for the 2nd NCCV slowed and formation of the 3rd NCCV was delayed. Although the 3rd was eventually formed, a fourth regiment never materialized. An additional heavy artillery regiment was gradually mustered in from freedmen in occupied North Carolina throughout 1864, but early that year the African Brigade had ceased to exist and its soldiers entered the ranks of the U.S. Colored Troops.

Concerns about ex-slaves serving voluntarily and whites accepting these men proved to be unfounded. Beyond their legacy of a demonstrated commitment to the Union, members of the African Brigade were, through their handpicked officers, exposed to a core set of abolitionist values that aided their transition to emancipation.

References: Richard Nelson Current, *Lincoln's Loyalists: Union Soldiers from the Confederacy* (1992); Wayne K. Durrill, *War of Another Kind: A Southern Community in the Great Rebellion* (1990); Joseph T. Glatthar, *Forged in Battle: The Civil War Alliance of Black Soldiers and White Officers* (1990); Richard Reid, "Raising the African Brigade: Early Black Recruitment in Civil War North Carolina," *NCHR* 70 (July 1993); Reid, "USCT Veterans in Post–Civil War North Carolina," in John David Smith, ed., *Black Soldiers in Blue: African American Troops in the Civil War Era* (2002).

Donald E. Collins

Unitarian Universalist Church. The Universalists were the first religious group in North Carolina to espouse a theology based on a belief in universal salvation—stressing that, since "God is love," there can be no endless punishment or hell for sinners in the afterlife. The first Universalist minister in North Carolina was Abner Kneeland, who preached in Wilmington in 1825. Two years later Jacob Freeze settled in Wilmington, where he began to publish the *Liberalist*. Also in 1827, the Southern Convention of Universalists was organized in the hope of bringing "Universalists into acquaintance with each other, to unite their energies, and make arrange-

ment for preaching." At that time one of the few Universalist churches in the South was the First Universalist Church of Sampson County. Hopes for a Universalist organization in the South faded, although the denomination continued to survive in small numbers well into the twentieth century.

Unitarianism is a faith based on individual freedom of belief, the free use of reason in religion, a united world community, and liberal social action. While Unitarian churches existed in Georgia and South Carolina before the Civil War, no efforts were made to organize permanent congregations in North Carolina until after World War II. The first Unitarian congregation to be organized in the state was in Charlotte in 1947. It is the largest in the state and has over 350 members. A second church was founded in Asheville in 1950, a third in Greensboro in 1951, and a fourth in Winston-Salem in 1953. The next decade saw the creation of congregations in Greenville in 1961 and Durham in 1966. A fellowship was organized in Franklin in 1976. The 1980s saw the organization of similar congregations in Fayetteville (1987), Hendersonville (1981), Hickory (1983) and Harrisburg, near Concord in Cabarrus County (1988). A lesbian, gay, bisexual, transgender, and heterosexual, "intentionally welcoming congregation" was organized in Kernersville in Forsyth County in 1994.

In 1961 the American Unitarian Association and the Universalist Church of America merged to form the Unitarian Universalist Association (UUA). All modern-day Unitarian and Universalist churches in North Carolina are members of the UUA, although the titles used by some churches may vary. Two churches in North Carolina use only the name Universalist in their titles. These are the First Universalist Church of Sampson County, organized at Red Hill near Clinton in 1834, and the Outlaw's Bridge Universalist Church near Seven Springs in Wayne County, which dates from 1905. The congregations at Charlotte, Hickory, and Morehead City use only the name Unitarian. Fourteen other North Carolina congregations are listed as Unitarian Universalist. The Community Church of Chapel Hill retains its original name although it joined the UUA in 1993.

In the early 2000s there were approximately 4,000 members of these churches along with just over a hundred "friends." Some congregations use the term "fellowship" even though that term is technically used for smaller congregations without a minister. Larger congregations with ministers use the term "church." All of the congregations in North Carolina are also members of the Thomas Jefferson District of the UUA, which includes the Carolinas, most of Virginia, eastern Tennessee, and three congregations in Georgia.

Reference: Blanche Raper Zimmerman, *New Dimensions of the Spirit: The Story of Unitarian-Universalists of Winston Salem* (1982).

Alexander R. Stoesen

United Church of Christ (UCC) is one of the largest Christian denominations in the United States, with just under 1.4 million members in approximately 6,000 congregations. The church was created through the 1957 merger of the Evangelical and Reformed Church and the Congregational Christian Church, which were adherents to German Calvinist, or Reformed, and Puritan, or congregationalist, traditions that date back to the fifteenth century. The 1957 merger was based upon the founding of a parent church that espoused social reform, peace, human rights, ecumenism, and church autonomy.

The UCC traces its roots in North Carolina to the work of James O'Kelly, a former Methodist minister who left that church in the early 1800s over a dispute with the hierarchy. Until his death in 1827, O'Kelly recruited churches of all denominations under the banner of congregationalism and organized the Christian Church of North Carolina. In the late 1860s, black Christian and Congregational Churches followed his example by creating their own denominations. These churches and the Christian Church of North Carolina merged in 1931 to form the National Council of Congregational Churches. Twenty-six years later this organization, too, became part of the UCC.

The UCC in the early 2000s had approximately 55,000 members in more than 200 congregations in North Carolina.

References: L. H. Gunnemann, *The Shaping of the United Church of Christ* (1977); Douglas Horton, *The United Church of Christ: Its Origins, Organization and Role in the World Today* (1962); Anne Russell, Marjorie Megivern, and Kevin Coughlin, *North Carolina Portraits of Faith: A Pictorial History of Religions* (1986).

Louis P. Towles

SEE ALSO Evangelical and Reformed Church.

United Confederate Veterans. SEE Veterans' Groups.

United Daughters of the Confederacy. SEE Veterans' Groups.

United Holy Church of America, a primarily African American Christian body founded in Durham in 1894, was an outgrowth of the Holiness movement. The church, initially under the leadership of married couple Charles Christopher Craig and Emma Elizabeth Craig, was first known as the Holy Church of North Carolina and then as the Holy Church of North Carolina and Virginia. In 1918 its name was changed to the United Holy Church of America. The church is Methodist in background but Holiness and Pentecostal in doctrine. It espouses "entire sanctification" and the baptism of the Holy Spirit (or "second blessing"), encouraging, but not requiring, speaking in tongues as a sign of true conversion or as a prerequisite for full membership in the church. The church also believes in divine healing and includes baptism by water, the Lord's Supper, and foot washing among its religious acts.

In the twentieth century the United Holy Church grew through mission activities across the United States. By the beginning of the twenty-first century, it was estimated that there were 50,000 members in 470 congregations in the nation, with 25 churches and 1,500 members in North Carolina. Educational, missionary, youth, and social service programs were available through the United Holy Church general headquarters in Greensboro.

References: Chester W. Gregory, *History of the United Holy Church of America, Inc., 1886–1986* (1986); William Clair Turner, *United Holy Church of America: A Study in Black Holiness-Pentecostalism* (1984).

Louis P. Towles

United States v. American Tobacco Company was a 1911 U.S. Supreme Court case in which the Court found that a large number of persons and corporations—including North Carolinians James Buchanan Duke, George W. Watts, and Benjamin N. Duke, as well as the American Tobacco Company, the R. J. Reynolds Tobacco Company, and Blackwell's Durham Tobacco Company—had violated the federal Sherman Antitrust Act of 1890 by seeking to monopolize practically all sectors of the tobacco industry. The ruling was among the earliest Supreme Court decisions applying the Sherman Act.

The American Tobacco Company was organized in 1890 by James B. Duke, a member of W. Duke, Sons and Company of Durham. At the time, the Dukes' Durham operation was already a leader in the emerging business of manufactured cigarettes. The new American Tobacco Company, capitalized at $25 million, allied five large existing tobacco companies, one of which was W. Duke, Sons and Company. From the moment it was formed, the American Tobacco Company possessed a near monopoly on sales of manufactured cigarettes. By 1908, when the government began the federal lawsuit that led to the Supreme Court decision, the company had extended its monopoly in the United States to most other branches of the tobacco industry, including plug tobacco, smoking tobacco, snuff, and little cigars.

The antitrust case was commenced in a New York federal court. After that court held that the American Tobacco Company was guilty of violating the Sherman Act, but found other defendants not guilty of any violation, both the United States and the American Tobacco Company appealed. The Supreme Court effectively extended the finding of guilt to all parties and remanded the matter to a federal circuit court in New York, with instructions to dissolve the combination. In November 1911 the circuit court, seeking to destroy unified control over the affected branches of the tobacco industry, divided the monopoly's assets among several corporations, including a new

American Tobacco Company, the Liggett and Myers Tobacco Company, the P. Lorillard Company, and the R. J. Reynolds Tobacco Company.

The Supreme Court's ruling had two particularly significant results for North Carolina. First, James B. Duke's association with the American Tobacco Company ended in 1911. Duke's business attention was partly redirected to the development of hydroelectric power in North Carolina and South Carolina through the Southern Power Company, which had been incorporated in 1905. Second, the R. J. Reynolds Tobacco Company, in 1913, introduced its Camel brand, which eventually captured a substantial share of the cigarette market.

The 1911 Supreme Court decision did not end monopolistic practices among cigarette manufacturers. By 1946 the R. J. Reynolds Tobacco Company, the American Tobacco Company, and the Liggett and Myers Tobacco Company were once again before the Supreme Court. The Court affirmed a conviction against them for violating the Sherman Act by unlawful price fixing and monopolizing both the purchase of raw tobacco and the marketing of cigarettes.

References: Reavis Cox, *Competition in the American Tobacco Industry, 1911–1932* (1933); Robert F. Durden, *The Dukes of Durham, 1865–1929* (1975); Nannie M. Tilley, *The R. J. Reynolds Tobacco Company* (1985).

James L. Hunt

University Magazine. SEE Literary Journals.

University of North Carolina at Asheville.
In 1927 William Henry Jones, the principal of Biltmore School near Asheville, and Alonzo Carlton Reynolds, the Buncombe County Schools superintendent, established Buncombe County Junior College, the first public junior college in the United States to offer free tuition. The following year the College of the City of Asheville was similarly established by the city school board.

The two colleges operated as free public institutions until 1930, when a financial crisis forced the city college to close and the county college to charge tuition. The name of the surviving institution was changed to Biltmore Junior College in 1930, and it became in effect the successor to both colleges. The name was changed again to Biltmore College in 1934 and to Asheville-Biltmore College in 1936. The school remained under the control of the city school board and enjoyed some city support. In 1955 the General Assembly voted a modest appropriation, increasing the amount in 1957. Under the provisions of the Community College Act of 1957, Asheville-Biltmore was the first institution to qualify as a state-supported community college, with a board of trustees appointed by the governor, the Asheville City Council, the Buncombe County Board of Commissioners, and the city and county boards of education.

In 1958 the voters of Asheville and Buncombe County approved a $500,000 bond issue for capital funds for the college. This sum, plus funds allocated by the state, enabled the college to launch the first phase of its expansion program in 1959. It was also in this year that the college acquired land in north Asheville. The first two buildings on this campus were completed and occupied for the fall term of 1961. Earlier in 1961, voters had again approved, by a very decisive majority, a $750,000 bond issue (as well as a tax levy) for the further development of the college. Local capital funds and matching funds from the state provided for the construction of five additional buildings. Also in 1961 Governor Terry Sanford appointed the Governor's Commission on Education beyond the High School. This commission examined the future needs for higher education in North Carolina and submitted its report in August 1962. The commission's recommendations were then submitted to the General Assembly, which passed the Omnibus Higher Education Act in 1963. The action converted Asheville-Biltmore to a state senior college, effective 1 July 1963.

As a state senior college, the aims and purposes of Asheville-Biltmore were significantly changed. The school graduated its first four-year class in 1966—the same year its board of trustees passed a resolution stating its intention to see the school become the University of North Carolina at Asheville. After two years of discussion, in April 1968 a committee of the board of trustees of the consolidated University of North Carolina System visited the school to determine whether the college should be incorporated into the University of North Carolina. Their findings were favorable and were adopted by the full board of trustees on 2 Dec. 1968. The legislature gave its approval, and on 1 July 1969, Asheville-Biltmore College became the University of North Carolina at Asheville.

The University of North Carolina at Asheville is distinctive within the University of North Carolina System as the only designated liberal arts university (designated as such by the UNC Board of Governors in 1992) and one of only six public universities nationwide to be so designated. It offers 30 majors in the arts, humanities, and natural and social sciences and is noted for its required four-course humanities sequence and its undergraduate research program. In the early 2000s the university had a total enrollment of more than 3,200 students served by 290 faculty members.

Wiley J. Williams

University of North Carolina at Chapel Hill.
North Carolina's first state constitution, drafted in 1776, contained a provision for public support of education. However, it was not until 1789 that the state succeeded in chartering an institution, a "university supported by permanent funds and well endowed." When the University of North Carolina opened its doors in 1795, it became the first state institution of higher

Faculty of the University of North Carolina at Chapel Hill process to a convocation on University Day, late 1990s. The Old Well appears in the background. Photograph by Justin Smith. UNC-Chapel Hill News Services.

learning in the nation. Patriot leader and Revolutionary War hero William Richardson Davie led the fight to establish the university, an effort that sprang out of the mutual strivings for enlightenment and freedom of the backcountry settlers of Piedmont North Carolina and the plantation federalists of the Coastal Plain.

The first trustees selected the site for the new institution —New Hope Chapel Hill in Orange County—for several reasons. It was centrally located in the state, near the intersection of the roads from Petersburg to Pittsboro and from New Bern to Salisbury; perhaps most important, local landowners were willing to be generous in their donations, offering 1,386 acres and £798 in funds. In return, they were awarded the right to have "one student educated at the said university free from any expense of tuition."

Without the assistance of regularly state-appropriated funds during its first half century, the small institution served as a collegiate training academy for the state's leaders during the entire antebellum period. Constantly assailed by sectarian controversies and financial emergencies, the university closed its doors during the turmoil of Reconstruction following the Civil War. Under the leadership of President Kemp Plummer Battle, it reopened in 1875 and steadily moved toward renewed vitality and regional eminence. In 1885 a teacher training program became an established part of the curriculum. In 1894 the law school was incorporated, and in 1897 the university began to admit women to postgraduate courses. Three years later Sallie Walker Stockard became the first woman to earn a degree from the university, receiving a master's degree with a thesis on the history of Alamance County. At the end of the century there were 512 students enrolled, with a faculty of 35. By the commencement of 1900, 31 master's degrees and seven doctoral degrees had been awarded, the first of each in 1883.

In the first two decades of the twentieth century, the University of North Carolina moved into its own in areas of liberal arts and scientific renown. The first Phi Beta Kappa chapter in North Carolina was established at the university in 1904, and in 1913 the Bureau of Extension was created to make the school's resources more widely available across the state. By 1907 a University Woman's Club had been organized. The university continued to grow, reaching an enrollment of 2,600 students and a faculty of 222 full- and 85 part-time members in 1930. In 1931 the university joined the Women's College at Greensboro (later the University of North Carolina at Greensboro) and North Carolina State College at Raleigh (later North Carolina State University) to form the consolidated University of North Carolina System, controlled by a board of trustees and having a single president with offices on the Chapel Hill campus.

Through its second century, the university, now officially the University of North Carolina at Chapel Hill, thrived. The state added additional campuses to the consolidated system, bringing its total number of schools to 16. The Chapel Hill campus continued to remain in a leadership position. It established the Institute of Government (now the School of Government), the first of its kind in the nation, in 1942. The School of Public Health was established in 1936 and the Division of Health Affairs in 1949, making the university one of the few in the nation with schools in the five health professions—dentistry, nursing, medicine, pharmacy, and public health. Culturally, the Chapel Hill campus led as well. The university dedicated the Playmakers Theatre as the first building devoted to the study of theater on a public campus in 1925. The Morehead Planetarium opened in 1949, and the Ackland Art Museum in 1958. UNC's first radio station, now WUNC-FM, had its beginnings in 1953 when students began broadcasting part-time from Swain Hall; and a public television station (now WUNC-TV) was started in 1955. The university admitted African American students for the first time in 1955, following the 1951 order

Seminar in the UNC-Chapel Hill School of Education. Photograph by Dan Sears. UNC-Chapel Hill News Services.

by federal courts to integrate its law, medical, and graduate schools.

By the early 2000s UNC-Chapel Hill's academic offerings spanned more than 100 fields, including 84 bachelor's, 165 master's, and 108 doctoral degrees as well as professional degrees in dentistry, medicine, pharmacy, and law. Five health schools and UNC Hospitals constitute one of the nation's most complete academic medical centers and are integrated with liberal arts, basic sciences, and high-tech academic programs. The University of North Carolina at Chapel Hill has approximately 2,690 faculty members serving more than 25,000 undergraduate and graduate students from every North Carolina county, the other 49 states, and nearly 100 foreign countries. About 81 percent of the school's undergraduates are from North Carolina.

References: William S. Powell, *The First State University: A Pictorial History of the University of North Carolina* (3rd ed., 1992); William D. Snider, *Light on the Hill: A History of the University of North Carolina at Chapel Hill* (1992); Louis R. Wilson, *The University of North Carolina under Consolidation, 1931–1963: History and Appraisal* (1964).

William D. Snider

University of North Carolina at Charlotte

began as a temporary junior college established to ease an enrollment crisis created by World War II veterans seeking an education under the GI Bill of Rights. Its development into North Carolina's fourth-largest university parallels the rise of many other urban universities across the United States, all established in response to a dramatic increase in public demand for higher education during the postwar era. In 1946 state officials, anticipating overcrowding at traditional colleges and universities, moved to create temporary college centers across the state, operating under the auspices of the Extension Division of the University of North Carolina at Chapel Hill. With an enrollment of 278 men and women, the Charlotte Center opened on 23 Sept. 1946 as the largest of 14 such institutions. It operated as a night school in the facilities of Charlotte's Central High School and offered credits transferable to any senior institution in the state. When the enrollment crisis eased in 1949, state officials closed the temporary centers, but Charlotte residents, who had long sought a public institution of higher learning for their community, arranged to have the city school board take over the center and operate it as Charlotte College, funded by local revenues.

In 1958 Charlotte College became part of the North Carolina Community College System. In 1961 it was moved to what would become a 1,000-acre campus about ten miles northeast of Charlotte. In 1964 it became a four-year college, and in 1965, with an enrollment of 1,815, it became the fourth campus of the consolidated University of North Carolina System.

Initially a school for commuters, the University of North Carolina at Charlotte in 1968 opened its first residence halls and began to grow rapidly. In 1969 it began offering programs leading to master's degrees and in 1993 programs leading to Ph.D. degrees. In August 2000 the Board of Governors of the University of North Carolina System reclassified it a doctoral/research university.

The modern University of North Carolina at Charlotte is comprised of seven colleges: Architecture, Arts and Sciences, Business Administration, Education, Engineering, Information Technology, and Nursing and Health Professions. It draws students from across North Carolina and the nation and around the world. In the early 2000s it had an enrollment of more than 18,000 students. The university serves both students and the Charlotte community through its research centers, including the C. C. Cameron Applied Research Center and the Ben Craig Center. Its affiliation with the 3,200-acre University Research Park, established in 1966 to encourage industry-university relationships, has been successful, resulting in more than 40 companies employing approximately 25,000 workers.

References: Mike Hermann, *Vision, Engineering and Science: The Founding of the C. C. Cameron Applied Research Center* (1999); Arnold K. King, *The Multicampus University of North Carolina Comes of Age, 1956–1986* (1987); Ken Sanford, *Charlotte and UNC-Charlotte, Growing up Together* (1996).

Jack Claiborne

University of North Carolina at Greensboro

was chartered on 18 Feb. 1891 as the North Carolina State Normal and Industrial School with an initial appropriation of $10,000. It was the work largely of Charles Duncan McIver and Edwin A. Alderman, who had been advocating for years for a state normal school for teachers, particularly women, who comprised most of the public school teachers. Several localities desired the school, but Greensboro won the bidding war, pledging $30,000 in additional funds.

The school became a college in 1897, and baccalaureate degrees followed in 1903. The teacher training curriculum was accompanied from the beginning by training in domestic science and commercial subjects. In time, the liberal arts assumed prominence alongside expanded offerings in education, home economics, and music. In 1919 the institution was renamed the North Carolina College for Women, and in 1931, when it joined the University of North Carolina at Chapel Hill and North Carolina State College in Raleigh in the new consolidated University of North Carolina System, it became the Woman's College of the University of North Carolina. So it remained until 1963, when it emerged as the University of North Carolina at Greensboro (UNCG) with coeducation and a broader educational mission.

The initial site in 1891 was a ten-acre tract on what was then the western edge of Greensboro. The campus grew to nearly 200 acres surrounded by urban, residential neighborhoods. The student body numbered 223 by the end of the first year—as many as the campus and neighboring private homes could accommodate. By the early 2000s, the university had more than 13,000 students. The nature of the student body changed vastly over the years. The most obvious changes were racial desegregation, which began with the admission of the first two black students in 1956, and coeducation, which began officially in 1963. Fully as important, UNCG has become a commuter as well as a residential campus, with more than half of the students living in the greater Greensboro area.

Although postgraduate training began early in the institution's history, UNCG granted its first doctorate in 1963. The earliest doctoral programs were in professional areas such as education, home economics, and physical education, areas in which the Woman's College had already established strong graduate programs. Doctoral programs in English and psychology soon followed. The modern university offers master's degrees in 68 fields and doctorates in 14. Its arts programs are nationally known. Weatherspoon Art Museum houses what is considered to be the most outstanding permanent collection of contemporary art in the Southeast. UNCG is also one of only six higher educational institutions in North Carolina approved to have a Phi Beta Kappa chapter.

References: Elisabeth Ann Bowles, *A Good Beginning: The First Four Decades of the University of North Carolina at Greensboro* (1967); Allen W. Trelease, *Changing Assignments: A Pictorial History of the University of North Carolina at Greensboro* (1991).

Allen W. Trelease

University of North Carolina at Pembroke was established on 7 Mar. 1887 as Croatan Normal School by the General Assembly at the request of the Lumbee Indians and other Native Americans in the state. Its purpose was to train Native American public school teachers. The school enrolled 15 students in the first year. In 1911 the legislature renamed the school the Indian Normal School of Robeson County, then changed it in 1913 to the Cherokee Indian Normal School of Robeson County. This name remained until 1941, when it was changed to Pembroke State College. Until 1953 the school was the only state-supported, four-year college for Native Americans in the nation.

In 1969 the General Assembly granted the institution regional university status as Pembroke State University. Three years later it became part of the 16-campus University of North Carolina System. Effective 1 July 1996 the school officially became the University of North Carolina at Pembroke.

The University of North Carolina at Pembroke is a regional public university that offers more than 50 undergraduate degree programs and 14 graduate degree programs. The student body of more than 4,300 students is considered one of the most diverse in the country. The university's collection of American Indian art and artifacts in its Native American Resource Center draws visitors each year from across the nation and abroad. Its Givens Performing Arts Center—the cultural center of the region—is home to performing arts series and local events. A Regional Center for Economic, Community and Professional Development provides a variety of services, including research planning, assessment, consulting, conference design, and customized training. The center also offers a variety of programs in community health, rural education, small business consulting, public safety, and management development.

References: David K. Eliades and Linda Ellen Oxendine, *Pembroke State University: A Centennial History* (1986); Clifton Oxendine, "Pembroke State College for Indians," NCHR 22 (January 1945).

Wiley J. Williams

University of North Carolina at Wilmington first opened its doors in the fall of 1947 as Wilmington College, a county-supported junior college. Classes had begun a year earlier as part of the General Assembly's plan to accommodate rising enrollment caused by returning veterans. One of 14 such temporary regional institutions that operated under the Extension Division of the University of North Carolina, Wilmington College continued to operate as a junior college under the auspices of the New Hanover County Board of Education.

In 1957 the General Assembly passed the Community College Act, and Wilmington College became one of the first three community colleges in the state. By 1961 it had become a four-year institution. In 1969 Wilmington College joined the consolidated University of North Carolina System and became the University of North Carolina at Wilmington. It began offering graduate degree programs in 1977 and was designated a Comprehensive Level 1 university in 1985.

The modern University of North Carolina at Wilmington occupies a 661-acre tract of land with 70 buildings. It has a combined enrollment of more than 10,000 undergraduate and graduate students and ranks fourth highest in the UNC system for average freshman SAT scores. The university has moved away from its early emphasis on vocational training and now offers degrees from the College of Arts and Sciences; the Schools of Business, Education, and Nursing; and its renowned program in marine biology at the Center for Marine Science Research. It also offers a Ph.D. in marine biology, one of only two such programs on the East Coast.

Craig M. Stinson

University of North Carolina Press is a separately incorporated, not-for-profit publishing company affiliated with the University of North Carolina and located in Chapel Hill. It was founded on 13 Mar. 1922, making it the oldest university press in the South and one of the oldest in the nation. The press was organized by ten UNC faculty members and three members of the UNC-Chapel Hill Board of Trustees in order to publish books and periodicals prepared by the faculty as well as university catalogs and bulletins, and "to promote generally, by publishing deserving books, the advancement of the arts and sciences, and the development of literature." Louis Round Wilson, the university librarian, was chosen as the press's first director. In 1923 the press produced its first book, *The Saprolegniaceae*, a study of water molds, by W. C. Coker. In 1932 Wilson was succeeded by William T. Couch, who headed the press from then until 1945.

Most UNC Press titles are scholarly material devoted chiefly to the humanities and social sciences, but the press also publishes some trade books (ranging from nature guides to cookbooks) each season. Original fiction formed part of the press's publishing program for some years, beginning with Bernice Kelly Harris's *Purslane* in 1939, but is no longer issued under the press imprint.

Since its founding, the press has maintained a focus on regional research, publishing many distinguished works about North Carolina and the American South. This focus was a hallmark of Couch's tenure as director, when the press issued numerous books by faculty members associated with UNC's Institute for Research in Social Science. The UNC Press was among the first publishing organizations to establish a continuing program of books by and about African Americans, a strength of its list throughout the twentieth century and into the twenty-first. Women's studies became an important focus beginning in the 1970s. The press has also published a number of important documentary collections—including *The Papers of General Nathanael Greene*, *The Papers of John Marshall*, and *The Black Abolitionist Papers*—and reference works, among them the *Dictionary of North Carolina Biography*, the *North Carolina Atlas*, and the *Encyclopedia of Southern Culture*. UNC Press titles have won hundreds of prestigious awards, including the National Book Award, the Pulitzer Prize in History, and major prizes given by scholarly societies, such as the American Historical Association and the Organization of American Historians, and professional organizations, such as the American Bar Association and the American Institute of Architects. In the early 2000s the UNC Press had more than 1,300 titles in print.

Lillian E. Craton

University of North Carolina System is comprised of 16 constituent institutions throughout the state that form a multicampus public university. Consolidation of the state's public educational institutions began in 1931, when Governor O. Max Gardner proposed consolidating the University

of North Carolina (now the University of North Carolina at Chapel Hill), North Carolina State College of Agriculture and Engineering (now North Carolina State University), and the North Carolina College for Women (now the University of North Carolina at Greensboro). His primary objectives were to eliminate unnecessary duplication of functions of the three institutions and to create a nationally distinctive university. But it was a report on governmental efficiency and economy commissioned by the state from the Brookings Institution in 1930 that gave the final impetus to consolidation. Frank Porter Graham, then president of the University of North Carolina in Chapel Hill, served as the system's first president, and a single board of trustees, consisting of 100 members, was appointed with full authority to manage the three campuses.

Additions to the consolidated UNC System followed. In 1965 the General Assembly added a fourth campus, the University of North Carolina at Charlotte, and in 1969 it added the University of North Carolina at Asheville and the University of North Carolina at Wilmington. In 1971 the General Assembly passed legislation bringing into the University of North Carolina System the state's ten remaining senior institutions: Appalachian State University, East Carolina University, Elizabeth City State University, Fayetteville State University, North Carolina Agricultural and Technical State University, North Carolina Central University, North Carolina School of the Arts, Pembroke State University (renamed the University of North Carolina at Pembroke in 1996), Western Carolina University, and Winston-Salem State University.

Each of the 16 constituent institutions is headed by a chancellor, who is chosen by the UNC Board of Governors on the president's recommendation and is responsible to the president. Each institution has a board of trustees, consisting of eight members elected by the UNC Board of Governors, four appointed by the governor, and the president of the student body, who serves ex officio. Each board has extensive powers over the operations of its institution on delegation from the Board of Governors.

In the early 2000s the 16 campuses had a combined enrollment of nearly 170,000 students and offered more than 200 degree programs. In addition to an array of liberal arts programs, the system has 2 medical schools and a teaching hospital, 2 law schools, a veterinary school, a school of pharmacy, 10 nursing programs, 15 schools of education, 3 schools of engineering, and a specialized school for performing artists. The UNC System presidents under consolidation have been Frank Porter Graham (1932–49); Gordon Gray (1949–55); William C. Friday (1956–86); C. D. Spangler Jr. (1986–97); Molly Corbett Broad (1997–2005); and Erskine Bowles (2005–).

References: Hugh T. Lefler and Albert R. Newsome, *North Carolina: The History of a Southern State* (3rd ed., 1973); Donald A. Lockmiller, *The Consolidation of the University of North Carolina* (1942); William S. Powell, *The First State University: A Pictorial*

History of the University of North Carolina (3rd ed., 1992); Louis R. Wilson, *The University of North Carolina under Consolidation, 1931–1963: History and Appraisal* (1964).

Wiley J. Williams

University v. Foy, a case decided by the North Carolina Supreme Court in 1805, was brought by the University of North Carolina to protect property it had acquired pursuant to its statutory right to escheats—property owned by a person who dies without a will or known heirs and which passes to the state. The political background of the case was a struggle between the Anti-Federalists, who controlled the General Assembly, and the university, described as a "hotbed of Federalists." In an early exercise of judicial review, the state supreme court upheld the university's right to the property.

John V. Orth

Unto These Hills. SEE Outdoor Dramas.

Utilities, Regulation of. The regulation of utilities in North Carolina has always reflected the tension between the goals of private business and the needs of the public. It has been shaped by massive technological change, changes in the respective roles of the federal government and the states, and changes in ideas about economic fairness, government's regulatory function, monopoly, and business competition.

Since the late nineteenth century, North Carolina law has defined public utilities to include companies transporting freight or passengers by railroad, motor trucks, and buses; certain forms of communication service, especially by telephone and telegraph; and certain kinds of industrial and residential services, including electricity, natural gas, and water and sewer distribution, collection, and treatment. The most important aspect of state control has been the power to determine the rates utilities can charge for services. Political justification for extensive regulation stems from the belief that citizens are entitled to the benefits of public utility services at reasonable rates.

The development of modern public utilities regulation can be traced to the construction of a comprehensive railroad network after the Civil War. The increasing size and monopoly status of railroads drove rural shippers dependent on railroads and anxious for low rates to support more regulation. The shippers' efforts culminated in the creation of the Board of Railroad Commissioners, or the Railroad Commission (1891–99), by the Farmers' Alliance–dominated 1891 General Assembly. This measure placed the rates of telegraph, telephone, steamboat, and canal companies under the control of the Railroad Commission. Between 1920 and 1941 there was substantial public debate about the commission's future structure and role. Eventually, this produced a reconfiguration of utility regulation that recognized the special character of utility business.

After World War II, growing demands for utility services resulted in a more bureaucratic regulatory structure. In 1949 legislation increased the size of the Utilities Commission (created in 1941) and allowed it to reorganize its internal operations. At that point the commission's full-time staff was placed into separate divisions for accounting, electricity, telephone, motor passenger, and motor freight. Between the early 1960s and the late 1970s the regulation of utilities in North Carolina was characterized by utilities' numerous demands for rate increases.

By the late 1980s, the number of large electric and telephone rate increase cases, which had been a primary focus of utility regulation in North Carolina between 1974 and 1988, had dramatically declined. In addition, although rate regulation had initially been directed to the transportation sector, especially railroads, by the mid-1990s private passenger train service had been obsolete in the state for more than two decades. Even intrastate railroad freight rates and service issues had been deregulated or preempted by federal law. Federal deregulation and preemption also affected the intrastate motor freight and motor passenger industries, which had been an important object of regulation in North Carolina from the 1930s to the 1980s. Most dramatically, traditional rate regulation in the telephone and electric industries was challenged in the 1980s and 1990s by technological transformations and related antiregulatory policies at the federal level.

Despite the broad trend toward deregulation, utility regulation in North Carolina by the early 2000s remained a complex administrative task. In the 1990s, for example, the Utilities Commission had resolved a large number of utility matters. It conducted almost 1,000 proceedings in 1994 and regulated more than 2,000 companies, including those providing electric service, telecommunications service, water and sewer service, natural gas service, and various forms of transportation services, such as intrastate buses, railroads, and motor freight.

References: J. C. D. Blaine, *Rate-Making and the North Carolina Utilities Commission: A Study in Public Policy* (1962); Frank Hanft, "Control of Utility Rates in North Carolina," *North Carolina Law Review* 13 (June 1934); Annie Sarah Ramsey, "Utility Regulation in North Carolina, 1891–1941: Fifty Years of History and Progress," NCHR 22 (April 1945).

James L. Hunt

Uwharrie National Forest, headquartered at Troy, is one of America's smallest national forests, occupying a little over 50,000 acres in Montgomery, Randolph, and Davidson Counties in the central North Carolina Piedmont. The youngest of the four North Carolina national forests, Uwharrie was established in 1961 from land purchased by the federal government in 1934 to resettle farmers. It is not one continuous unit but discrete parcels of land separated by privately owned tracts. The Uwharrie Mountains, which form the forest's backbone, give it its name, which, according to legend, comes from the name of an Indian tribe indigenous to the area. These thickly wooded, low-lying ridges are some of the oldest in North America, theorized to have begun as volcanoes on the ocean floor. Some, such as Morrow Mountain, have peaks; but these ancient mountains, worn down from a possible height of 20,000 feet by rivers and time, rise only about 1,000 feet from the Piedmont Plateau. Uwharrie National Forest, unlike the national forests of the mountains and the shore, is a sanctuary of hardwoods, pines, and rocks. Nifty Rocks features huge boulders, some as tall as 15 feet.

True to its slogan, "Land of Many Uses," Uwharrie National Forest attracts visitors to hunt game birds and deer, hike on trails such as the Uwharrie National Recreation Trail, and camp and picnic at the Badin Lake Recreation Area on the forest's western border. The Uwharrie Wildlife Management Area covers 13,000 acres and, as a result of stocking in 1945, boasts a large deer population. Rivers and lakes for fishing and water sports abound. Badin Lake, Lake Tillery, and the Yadkin and Pee Dee Rivers run the length of the western boundary; the Uwharrie River flows through the center of the forest. The rich ecosystem sustains numerous species of wildflowers and shrubs. The nation's first gold rush took place near Uwharrie National Forest in 1799; abandoned mines pepper the area. The Russell Mine, active in the late 1800s, is among the largest.

References: G. Nicholas Hancock, *Guide to the Uwharrie Trail in the Uwharrie National Forest* (1983); Alan Hodge, "Pint-Sized Paradise," *The State* 61 (1993); Sharyn Kane and Richard Keaton, *Southern National Forests* (1993).

Angelyn H. Patteson

V

Vacation Bible School (VBS) is a vital part of children's ministries for thousands of Christian churches throughout North Carolina. While VBS has its roots in Southern Baptist churches, the ministry has spread to nearly all Protestant denominations as well as to the Roman Catholic Church. Local congregations use VBS as a means of continuing children's ministry when school is not in session. It serves students primarily in the elementary grades, although some churches offer programs for youth and adults as well. Additionally, many churches view VBS as an essential part of their outreach ministry for the "unchurched," attracting families who do not attend church regularly but wish to provide their children with this experience.

VBS was originally called "Every Day Bible School" when it began in 1901. In its earliest incarnations, programs and curricula were limited. Teaching activities were confined to Bible study and storytelling, and programs tended to be regimented and routine. VBS programs began to improve when Christian educators began to recognize the importance of teaching the Bible with a heavy emphasis on child participation. The "glue, scissors, juice, and cookies" activities of yesteryear can no longer compete with video games, virtual reality, and computers. Therefore, churches have become more creative with their programs, using tools such as multimedia, dramatic presentations, and live music.

The earliest VBS programs ran as long as six weeks, but over the course of the twentieth century, churches generally shortened the length of the program to two weeks. In deference to families taking vacations during the summer, most modern-day congregations in North Carolina limit their VBS programs to one week. Moreover, with some school systems in North Carolina implementing year-round schooling and with both parents in many families working full time, many churches now offer their VBS programs in the evening. In some larger congregations, churches may offer both morning and evening programs to accommodate the needs of participants.

Rusty Rains

"Vale of Humility between Two Mountains of Conceit" is a phrase describing North Carolina that originated from a speech given by Mary Oates Spratt Van Landingham on 6 Mar. 1900. That day, she spoke on the "native literature" of North Carolina before the Mecklenburg Historical Society in Charlotte. Referencing North Carolina's location between South Carolina and Virginia, Van Landingham said, "Where there are mountains of conceit, there are apt to be valleys of humility." The term has remained a source of tongue-in-cheek pride for North Carolinians.

William S. Powell

Vance County, located in the Piedmont region of North Carolina, was formed in 1881 from Granville, Warren, and Franklin Counties and named for Zebulon Baird Vance, governor of North Carolina and U.S. congressman and senator. It is situated along the Virginia border. Early inhabitants of the area included the Occaneechi Indians, followed by German, Scotch-Irish, and English settlers. Henderson, the county seat, was incorporated in 1841 and named for Leonard Henderson, chief justice of the North Carolina Supreme Court from 1829 to 1833. Other communities in the county include Middleburg, Gillburg, Gill, Williamsboro, Greystone, and Epsom. Kerr Lake State Recreation Area brings thousands of visitors to Vance County for boating, waterskiing, and fishing. Other notable physical features of the county include the Tar River, Roland Pond, and Island, Anderson, and Tabbs Creeks.

Rose's department stores were started in Henderson by brothers Paul H. Rose and T. B. Rose in 1915. Vance County landmarks and historic sites include the county courthouse (1884) and St. John's Episcopal Church (1773). Cultural institutions include the Kerr Lake Art Society and the Vance County Historical Museum. The county hosts festivals and annual events such as the Vance County Regional Fair, the Memorial Day Weekend Concert in the Park, and the Kerr Lake Art Show.

Vance County agricultural commodities include tobacco, soybeans, horticultural crops, dairy products, and livestock. Manufactures include textiles, glass containers, manufactured homes, apparel, metal fabrications, lumber and wood products, pet food, plastics, and home furnishings. The min-

Vacation Bible School at the Chapel of the Cross in Chapel Hill, June 2002. Photograph by Susana Vera. *Raleigh News and Observer.*

A cluster of Venus flytraps (with spiked "traps") and pitcher plants growing in southeastern North Carolina. Photograph by Johnny Randall.

erals tungsten, heubnerite, rutile, and sillimanite are mined in the county. The estimated population of Vance County was 43,800 in 2004.

Jay Mazzocchi

Venus Flytrap (*Dionaea muscipula*), one of the few carnivorous plants on earth, grows naturally along a small section of the North Carolina and South Carolina coastline within a 75-mile radius of Wilmington. It prospers only in humid, boggy areas such as the Carolina Bays. The traps, which grow in a rosette, are formed by pairs of modified leaves that resemble clam shells and have spikes along their edges; the inner surfaces of the leaves are equipped with reddish glands that attract insects and arachnids. When an insect touches this surface twice in rapid succession, tiny hairs act as a trigger to close the trap rapidly. Digestion requires seven to ten days depending upon the size of the insect. In 1750 North Carolina's royal governor, Arthur Dobbs, called attention to this unusual plant, described as a "carnivorous vegetable" by botanist William Bartram in 1794. Charles Darwin described it in *Insectivorous Plants* (1875) as "the most wonderful plant in the world."

In 1934 the Venus flytrap was made the official flower of the Garden Clubs of North Carolina, and after a number of years it grew in popularity. Poachers began to dig the plant for sale; the Venus flytrap was officially protected by legislation in 1956.

References: William C. Coker, "Distribution of Venus's Fly Trap," *Elisha Mitchell Scientific Society Journal* 43 (July 1928); W. Charles Nelson, *Aphrodite's Mousetrap* (1990); Patricia R. Roberts, "Response of Venus Fly Trap," *Ecological Monographs* 28 (April 1958).

Craig M. Stinson

Verrazano Expedition. Florentine Giovanni da Verrazano in 1523–24 explored the southern and central coast of what

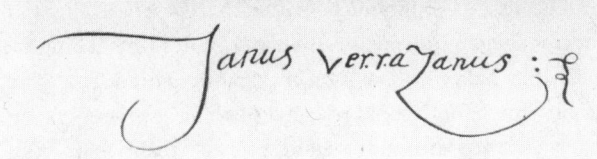

Giovanni da Verrazano. NCC.

became North Carolina while carrying out a reconnaissance of North America for the king of France. He made landfall around 21 Mar. 1524 at a spot he named "Selva di Lauri" (Forest of Laurels), probably in the vicinity of Cape Fear, and sailed south. In this direction he discovered "Campo di Cedri" (Field of Cedars), but no harbor. Eager "not to meet with the Spaniards," he turned back to the north. On the Feast of the Annunciation (5 Apr. 1524), he reached the area between present-day Cape Lookout and Cape Hatteras. Verrazano's opinion that the land of "Annunciata," as he called this part of the Outer Banks, was an isthmus separating the Atlantic Ocean from an arm of the Pacific influenced the mapping and exploration of North America for nearly a century.

Reference: Lawrence C. Wroth, *The Voyages of Giovanni da Verrazzano, 1524–1528* (1970).

Wynne Dough

Vestry in early modern England was the gathering of parishioners to transact parish business. The term derives from the place in parish churches where vestments, utensils, and vessels used in worship were held, where clergy robed, and where official records ordinarily would have been stored. Given the

A reunion of Confederate veterans near Brevard, 1911. NCC.

size of parishes in American colonies where the Church of England was established by law, a "select" vestry, composed of an elected or designated small number of lay persons serving together with the parish minister, replaced this historic practice of a general gathering of parishioners.

In North Carolina, as in Virginia, 12 laymen (vestrymen) managed the affairs of the parish, including the hiring of a minister, the building and maintenance of churches, care for the disadvantaged and handicapped, and the levying of funds to carry out these functions. North Carolina's first vestry met in Chowan Parish on 15 Dec. 1701, members having been named in the Vestry Act of 1701. Following initial election, vestries typically became self-perpetuating ruling bodies unless election or new legislative appointment resulted from the division or consolidation of the parish or the legislative dissolution of the existing body. Where the parish system was effectively instituted, as in Virginia, the vestry became the form of local governance most closely related to the everyday activities of the people.

References: Hugh T. Lefler, "The Anglican Church in North Carolina," in Lawrence Foushee London and Sarah McCulloh Lemmon, eds., *The Episcopal Church in North Carolina, 1701–1959* (1987); Robert E. Rodes Jr., *Law and Modernization in the Church of England: Charles II to the Welfare State* (1991).

John K. Nelson

Veterans' Groups. The first national organization established for the purpose of bringing veterans together in the new American republic was the Society of the Cincinnati, established at the end of the Revolutionary War in 1783. The society was organized by Maj. Gen. Henry Knox, made up of former officers of the Continental Army, and led by George Washington. In addition to more serious pursuits, the group served as a social club established so that veterans could visit and reminisce. Membership rights were passed on to the eldest son, and chapters were established in every state, including North Carolina.

After the end of the American Civil War in 1865, war veterans from both the Union and Confederacy formed veterans' societies. Those who fought for the Union formed the Grand Army of the Republic (GAR), started in Illinois in 1866 by Richard J. Oglesby, John Logan, and Benjamin F. Stephenson. The GAR included elaborate anti-Confederate rites and rituals and promoted fraternal relations among Union veterans, aid for disabled and needy veterans, support for the widows and orphans of veterans, and allegiance to the United States. The GAR grew rapidly and by 1867 virtually every northern state as well as several former Confederate states, including North Carolina, had chapters. Many of North Carolina's Union veterans, as well as northerners who had moved to the state after the war, joined the GAR. In all, North Carolina had 13 GAR chapters, including those located in Wilmington, Elizabeth City, New Bern, Raleigh, Charlotte, Asheville, Edenton, and Bryson City.

Confederate veterans organized a host of local soldiers' reunion groups, which finally came together in 1889 in New Orleans to form the United Confederate Veterans (UCV). John B. Gordon was chosen the first commander of the organization. Like its counterpart the GAR, the UCV included elaborate rituals and a military-style organizational chart that extended up from local units or "camps" all the way to the national level, called the "general headquarters." At the height of its popularity, the UCV had 1,855 camps with 160,000 members, with all but six camps located in former Confederate states. The UCV focused on issues such as petitioning state governments for veterans' pensions, establishing veterans' homes, raising money for Confederate monuments, and education.

The UCV held its first reunion in 1890 in Chattanooga. The 1890s also saw the soldiers' reunion movement aided by a new force, the "Lost Cause" cult, which romanticized the Old South at a time when the pain and misery of the war years had slowly faded from memory and when many Confederate veterans were dying at a growing rate. Ironically, the Lost Cause even became popular in the North in the 1890s, with northern theaters regularly featuring romantic plays about the antebellum South.

In 1895 the United Daughters of the Confederacy (UDC) was established in the capital of the "New South," Atlanta. This organization was largely responsible for creating the hundreds of Confederate monuments and statues that still stand in courthouse squares and other prominent places across the South. The Sons of Confederate Veterans was formed in 1896 to honor and remember those who fought for the Confederacy. Both groups were inspired by the 1896 gathering in Richmond, Va., of 10,000 old Confederate soldiers, many of them poor, who marched in a parade, honored the widow of Jefferson Davis, and reminisced about the war.

The UCV and GAR, after clashing during the early years of their existences, began a period of reconciliation in 1898, brought on by the national patriotism inspired during the Spanish-American War. By the early twentieth century, as time mellowed many bitter feelings, the two groups even began holding joint soldiers' reunions. The last UCV meeting took place in 1951 and was attended by its three surviving members. Like the GAR, however, the UCV lives on through its auxiliary units, which continue to actively promote Civil War history and heritage.

The United States fought other wars that eventually led to the formation of additional veterans' groups in North Carolina and the rest of the country. Beginning in 1899, veterans from the Spanish-American War (1898) and Philippine Insurrection (1899–1901) founded local organizations in order to push for veterans' benefits. These groups included the American Veterans of Foreign Service, which was established in Columbus, Ohio, and the Colorado Society, Army of the Philippines, organized in Denver. In Pennsylvania, the Philippine War Veterans and the American Veterans of the Philippine and China Wars were established, and in 1905 merged to form the American Veterans of Foreign Service. Finally in 1913, the Colorado and Pennsylvania groups joined to form the Army of the Philippines-Cuba and Puerto Rico, later changing the name to the Veterans of Foreign Wars (VFW). The modern VFW, headquartered in Kansas City, Mo., has 1.8 million members in 9,000 local posts worldwide, including several as part of the VFW Department of North Carolina. Membership is open to all veterans who are U.S. citizens and have earned an overseas campaign ribbon.

After World War I, veterans of that conflict formed the American Legion, which was chartered by Congress in 1919.

Like other soldier groups, the American Legion sought to gain benefits for veterans. In 1921 the organization was largely responsible for lobbying Congress to create the U.S. Veterans Bureau, known today as the Veterans Administration. By 1931 membership in the American Legion had reached 1 million. With the outbreak of World War II, the American Legion amended its charter to allow veterans of that conflict to join. The American Legion also played a large role in convincing President Franklin D. Roosevelt to issue the GI Bill of Rights in 1944, which has since helped millions of veterans attend college and purchase homes.

The American Legion subsequently opened membership to veterans of or those serving during the wars in Korea and Vietnam, the invasions of Grenada and Panama, and the Persian Gulf War. It continues to promote veterans' issues as well as many other social concerns. In 2006 the North Carolina American Legion had approximately 40,000 members in more than 200 posts throughout the state.

References: Richard Nelson Current, *Lincoln's Loyalists: Union Soldiers from the Confederacy* (1992); James West Davidson and others, *Nation of Nations: A Narrative History of the American Republic* (3rd ed., 1998); C. Vann Woodward, *Origins of the New South, 1877–1913* (1974).

Alan K. Lamm

SEE ALSO American Legion; Society of the Cincinnati; Sons of Confederate Veterans.

Veto. SEE Governor.

Vice Presidents, U.S. Two North Carolina natives have held the office of vice president of the United States. The first, William Rufus King, was born in Sampson County and was elected to the post as Franklin Pierce's Democratic running mate in 1852. He died just after his inauguration. The second, Andrew Johnson, was born in Raleigh and joined Abraham Lincoln's 1864 ticket as the only southern senator supporting the Union. After Lincoln's assassination in 1865, Johnson assumed the presidency.

David Smith

Vick Chemical Company began as a small cold remedy company in Greensboro and grew into a diversified Fortune 500 corporation with sales in more than 160 countries around the world. In 1905 Lunsford Richardson, a pharmacist and former teacher, started the company (until 1911 called the Vick Family Remedies Company) to manufacture and market the many different medications he had been developing since the 1890s. His eldest daughter served as secretary and his eldest son became the sales manager. Growth came through concentrating on Richardson's most popular product, Vicks VapoRub, a vaporizing salve for colds. Utilizing free samples and billboard and newspaper advertising, VapoRub expanded from the Southeast into the Northeast, and by 1917 it had reached the diffused population west of the Mississippi.

After Richardson's death in 1919 his two sons, H. Smith and Lunsford Richardson, and his son-in-law William Y. Preyer oversaw the business's accelerating growth. The company expanded sales to foreign markets, automated production in Greensboro and Philadelphia, listed Vicks stock on the New York Stock Exchange (1925), and moved company headquarters to New York City. Vicks began marketing other cold products such as nose drops and cough drops, and it diversified into prescription drugs, toiletries, and other fields. The company name was changed to Richardson-Merrell in 1960 and to Richardson-Vicks in 1981, when the Merrell pharmaceutical division was sold to Dow Chemical. Sales passed the $1 billion mark in 1979, and by 1983 health care and consumer brands such as Oil of Olay, Clearasil, Pantene, Vidal Sassoon, Fixodent, and Thompson's Water Seal represented more than 75 percent of company sales.

In September 1985 Unilever, one of the world's largest manufacturers of personal care products, sought to acquire Vicks. Seeing no way to head off the takeover after a three-week battle, Vicks turned to a "white knight" and on 7 October sold the company to Procter & Gamble. Vicks VapoRub, past the century mark, continued as one of Procter & Gamble's major products.

References: Locke Craig Raper, *Vick Chemical Company: A Case Study in Innovation* (1991); H. Smith Richardson, *Early History and Management Philosophy of Richardson-Merrell* (1975).

Norris W. Preyer

Vietnam War, fought in Southeast Asia from 1957 to 1975, was a protracted, ultimately unsuccessful attempt by the United States to prevent North Vietnamese communists from overrunning South Vietnam. U.S. participation in the conflict caused sufficient national turmoil to divide the nation and alter its future course. The financial cost of the war was $150 billion, and more than 58,000 Americans were killed.

As they did in World War II and the Korean War, North Carolina's numerous military installations provided training, supply, and support for many soldiers and airmen who served during the Vietnam era. Fort Bragg was at the forefront of U.S. involvement in the war when the Fifth Special Forces Group (Airborne) was activated in 1961. This unit, known as the Green Berets, trained personnel in counterinsurgency for deployment in the Republic of South Vietnam. On 11 July 1963 Maj. Gen. William C. Westmoreland arrived to take command of Fort Bragg. Westmoreland became deputy chief on 2 Mar. 1964 and later commander of U.S. forces in Vietnam. More than 200,000 young men underwent basic combat training at Fort Bragg between 1966 and 1970. At the peak of the war in 1968, the base's military population reached 57,840.

From December 1961 until the spring of 1963, the 464th Troop Carrier Wing rotated aircraft and crews from Pope Air Force Base to Tan Son Nhut and Da Nang for airlift duties in South Vietnam. Popularly referred to as "Mule Train," after the military codeword for the first squadron to be deployed, the Pope mission was the first conventional U.S. Air Force unit to see action in Vietnam. As the United States became more involved in the war, the need to train large numbers of aircrews for the unique capabilities of the C-130 led to the organization of an aircrew replacement training unit at Pope Air Force Base. The drop zones, low-level routes, and dirt landing zones at Fort Bragg became familiar to many men bound for Southeast Asia.

Throughout the Vietnam War, Marine Corps Air Station Cherry Point deployed three A-6 Intruder squadrons to the Far East and was a constant source of replacements for aircrews and enlisted aviation personnel. Camp Lejeune was an essential base for training and deploying Marine Corps personnel to Vietnam.

Of the 216,348 servicemen from North Carolina who served in the Vietnam War, 1,302 were killed in action and approximately 300 died from other causes. Two North Carolinians received the Medal of Honor. One of them, Lawrence Joel of Winston-Salem, was the first living black man to receive the award. Fourteen other Medal of Honor recipients were born in North Carolina but had enlisted in other states. A statue titled *After the Firefight*, located on the State Capitol grounds in Raleigh, commemorates the contributions of North Carolina's Vietnam veterans. The North Carolina Vietnam Veterans Memorial, a brick wall listing the names of the North Carolinians killed or missing, is located in the Vietnam Veterans Memorial Park on Interstate 85 north of Lexington. North Carolina Vietnam Veterans, Inc., works to resolve remaining prisoner of war and missing soldier issues.

Reference: Phillip B. Davidson, *Vietnam at War: The History, 1946–1975* (1988).

Jo Ann Williford

SEE ALSO Camp Lejeune; Cherry Point Marine Corps Air Station; Fort Bragg; Pope Air Force Base.

Viewpoint was a series of more than 3,000 TV and radio editorials broadcast to much of North Carolina from 21 Nov. 1960 to 11 Nov. 1976. The series was originated by Jesse Helms, then an executive vice president of Capitol Broadcasting Corporation and news director for its WRAL TV and radio stations. Carried on WRAL-TV as well as the state's Tobacco Radio Network (later the North Carolina News Network), *Viewpoint* reached much of Piedmont and eastern North Carolina and, during its heyday, offered Helms a powerful platform for espousing his views on political and social issues. But the influence of the program and its host proved far more significant and long lasting. Helms skillfully used the power of the media to elevate himself and his views to statewide prominence, and, when he declared in 1970 that he would change his party affiliation from Democrat to Republican, it helped catalyze a shift that already had begun in eastern North Carolina. Many in Helms's audience followed suit, dramatically altering the state's political geography. Two years later, Helms would leave *Viewpoint* and use his fame to help launch his successful campaign for a seat in the U.S. Senate.

Helms, the son of a Monroe police and fire chief, attended Wingate and Wake Forest Colleges before beginning a lengthy career in the print and broadcast media. After holding editorial positions at the *Raleigh News and Observer* and *Raleigh Times*, he served in the navy during World War II. Soon after the war, Helms was hired as a news anchor at WRAL-AM radio. It was there that he first honed his use of mass media for political purposes. While covering the 1950 U.S. Senate race between Willis Smith and Frank Porter Graham, Helms produced and paid for radio ads that promoted Smith's candidacy. A year after Smith defeated Graham in a heated campaign marked by race-baiting and accusations that Graham was a communist sympathizer, Helms joined Smith in Washington, D.C., as a staff assistant. After Smith's death in 1953, Helms returned to Raleigh and became executive director of the North Carolina Bankers Association. There, he used the association's trade magazine, the *Tarheel Banker*, as an outlet for sharply written editorials on such issues as free enterprise, school desegregation, and community mores. He went on to serve two terms as a Raleigh city councilman before returning to WRAL-TV in 1960 to run its news operation.

Helms's five-minute weeknight *Viewpoint* editorials were the natural culmination of these experiences, and he harnessed the growing power of broadcast media with remarkable savvy. He covered a wide range of topics, frequently linking national and international issues with more local issues. Among his frequent targets were what he saw as overtly liberal or immoral aspects of American culture, including the excesses of big government, a "left-wing" bias in national TV network programming, the abuse of academic freedom, the evils of communism, a lax criminal justice system, the inadequate compensation of police and fire personnel, and a wasteful and unnecessary welfare system. He touted an agenda that supported the free enterprise system, the death penalty, prayer in public schools, and a strong national defense. He strongly opposed abortion, "subversive" civil rights activities, the Equal Rights Amendment, and the "sex, drugs, and rock 'n' roll" of the radical counterculture.

Another of Helms's favorite targets was the perceived liberalism of the University of North Carolina at Chapel Hill, which represented for him much of what ailed 1960s America. Although he was not shy in voicing his disdain for the university,

Helms is wrongly credited with the famous remark that there was no need to build a zoo in North Carolina when the state could just "put a fence around Chapel Hill." In fact, that statement was made by editorialist Chub Seawell, who also argued that the university had no right to use academic freedom to help "god-denying liars" espouse their version of the truth.

Helms's final *Viewpoint* editorial gave no indication of his permanent departure, but, several days later, A. J. Fletcher, chairman of the board and chief executive officer of the Capitol Broadcasting Corporation, announced on the air that Helms intended to run for a seat in the U.S. Senate. That last *Viewpoint* editorial, number 2,762, which detailed his plan to take a leave of absence in order to seek the Republican nomination in North Carolina, ended Helms's work at WRAL. Although his 1972 election as the state's first Republican U.S. senator in the twentieth century was hardly the opening chapter in his influential and controversial political career, it did mark the beginning of its most significant phase.

WRAL suspended broadcasts of *Viewpoint* in February 1972 but resumed them on 8 Feb. 1973 with a new editorialist, William P. Cheshire, who continued to write and present the segments through 11 Nov. 1976. Without Helms as the driving force behind the series and with the increased popularity of FM radio, *Viewpoint* lost its prominence. WRAL eventually replaced it with fewer regular editorial segments by a wider range of commentators.

References: Howard E. Covington Jr. and Marion A. Ellis, eds., *The North Carolina Century: Tar Heels Who Made a Difference, 1900–2000* (2002); Ernest B. Furgurson, *Hard Right: The Rise of Jesse Helms* (1986); Paul Luebke, *Tar Heel Politics 2000* (1998).

Philip McFee
Additional research provided by Wiley J. Williams.

SEE ALSO Helms-Hunt Senate Race; Smith-Graham Senate Race.

Vine Hill Academy in Scotland Neck was chartered in 1809 by the North Carolina legislature and became one of the most successful schools in the eastern part of the state. Its first trustees were William Ruffin Smith, James Smith Jr., Peyton Randolph Tunstall, Marmaduke Norfleet, Josiah Nelms, Willis Powell, John Anthony, and Simmons J. Baker. The school apparently took its name from Vine Hill, Baker's home in Scotland Neck.

In 1810 the legislature passed an act enabling Vine Hill's trustees to raise $500 by lottery for the school. By 1837 there was a separate building for the female department, which was under the direction of a "Miss Rowan" and a "Miss Hanks" from New York. The available courses for men at the time were listed as Greek, Latin, rhetoric, logic, algebra, geometry, navigation, and surveying. Courses available to women included ancient and modern history, universal geography, chemistry, astronomy, moral and intellectual philosophy, natural theology, elements of elocution, French, botany, and drawing. The female department of Vine Hill operated only intermittently and was suspended in 1847 for want of patronage, according to school records. In succeeding years it operated on an irregular schedule.

During the Civil War, many Vine Hill graduates served with the Confederate army, although the school managed to stay open during and after the war. After a substantial system of public education began in North Carolina in the early twentieth century, Vine Hill was closed and a new public graded school opened on the site. When Scotland Neck High School closed as a result of school consolidation in the 1980s, there was some question as to who would own the property, since the original deed had specified the land was to accommodate a school or other public use. Town offices were moved into the renovated school rooms, and other rooms were used for public purposes, thus maintaining the civic purpose of the deed.

During its long history, Vine Hill educated many prominent North Carolinians. Among these were Judge William Horn Battle of the state supreme court, Attorney General Bartholemew Figures Moore, Meredith College president Charles Brewer, Governor William Walton Kitchin, Senator Claude Kitchin, and Louis Round Wilson, later head of the University Library at Chapel Hill.

David Bryant Gammon

Violence, Group. Group violence has occurred in many forms in North Carolina from the colonial era until the present day, perpetrated both by private citizens and public authorities and motivated by political differences, poverty, racism, labor unrest, and other forces. One of the earliest and best-known groups of North Carolinians who resorted to violence was the Regulators, who formally organized in the Piedmont in 1768. Frustrated by their failure to get redress from corrupt government officials, the Regulators turned to violence until they were eventually crushed by the forces of royal governor William Tryon at the Battle of Alamance in May 1768.

The American Revolution caused massive rifts in North Carolina society, leading to group violence apart from the formal military battlegrounds of the war. As the conflict dragged on, sporadic violence and resistance to government demands became more persistent and widespread. Small bands of private citizens, both Patriot and Loyalist, violently harassed their fellow citizens and occasionally experienced persecution at the hands of government agents. Chaos and violence reigned in the North Carolina Piedmont after the British army swept through the Carolinas in 1780–81. In the war's aftermath, with little government authority in place, marauding bands burned houses, robbed and sometimes murdered innocent victims, and waged pitched battles in towns and neighborhoods throughout the new state.

Although such conflicts, often rooted in economic hardship and ineffective local government, continued to occur during the early and mid-eighteenth century, the most prevalent and troubling form of group violence in North Carolina became that occurring between white citizens and African Americans. The inherent violence of the slave system, which depended in large part on physical force and intimidation for its survival, often led to widespread fear of slave insurrections and consequential violent incidents. Following the Nat Turner Rebellion in Virginia in 1831, for example, various North Carolina militia and mobs suppressed supposed "copycat" insurrections in the state—at one location killing as many as 40 slaves who reputedly were organizing a rebellion.

The Civil War brought numerous instances of nonmilitary violence to the state as citizens again became motivated by vastly divergent political and social loyalties. Lawlessness reigned, particularly in the Mountain region, and violent conflicts often occurred. Confederate authorities were forced to send troops repeatedly into the same area in the 1860s "to quell, neutralize, and capture hundreds of deserters, draft dodgers, and militant Unionists." The Home Guard, organized to keep order, protect key military sites, and round up deserters, often used unnecessary and brutal violence to achieve these ends. Perhaps the most infamous conflict involving the Home Guard was in relation to the Lowry Band, a group of men led by Lumbee Indian Henry Berry Lowry that waged guerrilla war against authorities during the final year of the Civil War and for several years afterward. After members of the Home Guard had killed Lowry's father and brother, reputedly for theft and avoiding conscription, Lowry and his followers—Lumbee, black, and white—murdered about 18 men before Lowry disappeared mysteriously in 1872.

The political and economic turmoil of the Reconstruction years, combined with the uneasy coexistence of whites and newly freed blacks in North Carolina society, led to years of sporadic violence and civil injustice incited by racial prejudice. Although the Ku Klux Klan (KKK) and similar organizations appeared during Reconstruction in the eastern counties of Jones and Lenoir, white violent activity also saw more reprisals in the east, where the size of the African American population and its participation in the local militia discouraged organized attacks by whites. Most of the night riding, physical assaults, and murders perpetrated by the KKK occurred in the Piedmont counties of Alamance, Caswell, Chatham, Orange, Cleveland, and Rutherford.

By the final decades of the nineteenth century, strained race relations had turned into full-blown, politically motivated violence in many places throughout the state. At Reconstruction's end, North Carolina's Democrats—temporarily removed from power by the biracial Republican Party following the enfranchisement of black men in 1868—began to employ violence as part of their efforts to regain control of the state and overturn black political advances. Using a strategy fueled by "white supremacy," the Democrats regained prominence by the end of the century. Although lynching or mob actions perpetrated by whites against black citizens were epidemic in the South in the 1890s and thereafter, these violent events never reached the level of intensity in North Carolina as they did in Deep South states such as Mississippi and Georgia. However, the Wilmington race riot of 1898 stands as an egregious exception. Remarks published by Alexander Manly, editor of the *Daily Record*, an African American newspaper in Wilmington, set off a wave of mob violence that ended with an estimated 250 African American deaths and immeasurable bad will between the state's white and black communities. Ultimately, the Wilmington race riot contributed to the disfranchisement of most blacks and many whites in North Carolina, helped install a one-party, Democratic-led system in the state, and ushered in a legally segregated social order.

Violence involving labor disputes occurred in 1929 as textile workers, plagued by a decade of cost-cutting measures and technological change, confronted another round of wage cuts. Conflict between striking workers and the police in Gastonia received much national attention—partly because the strike was led by the communist-sponsored National Textile Workers Union and also because of the deaths of Gastonia police chief O. F. Aderholt and the strikers' balladeer, Ella Mae Wiggins. The carnage was worse at a subsequent strike in Marion, however, even though the walkout was initiated locally and led by the adamantly anticommunist United Textile Workers Union. The McDowell County sheriff and his deputies fired on picketers when they arrived at a mill for a second walkout, wounding 25 workers. Six of them eventually died. Sporadic violence between workers and local police and National Guardsmen also occurred in North Carolina during the General Textile Strike of 1934, although South Carolina suffered the worst casualties.

In the 1920s KKK activity increased in North Carolina and in many parts of the United States, as it did again during the civil rights movement of the 1950s and 1960s. Although the Federal Bureau of Investigation and other law enforcement agencies did not consider the North Carolina KKK as violent as its Deep South counterparts, North Carolina Klansmen did engage in occasional bombings, dynamiting, and, at one point, a two-county spree of burnings and shootings into black homes. One of the state's most famous KKK incidents took place on 18 Jan. 1958 near Maxton, where about 1,500 Lumbee Indian activists disrupted a KKK rally days after Klansmen had placed burning crosses in the yards of an Indian family in a Lumberton neighborhood and a white woman romantically involved with a Lumbee man. Shots were fired before KKK members fled the scene. Although there were no deaths and only one injury, the "Battle of Maxton" received widespread media attention.

The civil rights movement spawned several other instances of violence in North Carolina involving white and black participants. In some communities, blacks took up arms to defend themselves and their rights while whites organized in violent opposition to their cause. In Monroe in the mid-1950s, members of the National Association for the Advancement of Colored People (NAACP), led by Robert Franklin Williams, armed themselves against persistent attacks on black neighborhoods by local members of the KKK. When the home of NAACP member Albert E. Perry was attacked by a Klan motorcade, a Williams-led, armed squad drove it off. After taking part in further hostilities between Monroe's white and black citizens as well as conflicts with leaders of the NAACP and the civil rights movement, Williams eventually fled to Cuba, where he began to broadcast a cultural and political program known as *Radio Free Dixie*.

In 1970 the state endured another infamous racial murder when Henry D. Marrow Jr., an African American, was attacked and killed by three white men who believed that Marrow had "flirted" with a local white woman. The acquittal of the three whites led to violent uprisings in Oxford and other places, as many blacks rioted, some burning tobacco warehouses in the town. Another notorious act by the North Carolina KKK occurred in 1979, when Klansmen drove a nine-car caravan into a black district in Greensboro and opened fire during an anti-Klan rally organized by members of the Communist Workers Party. Five people were killed and a number of others wounded. In federal court, none of the perpetrators was convicted of murder, and only a small number were found guilty of violating the marchers' civil rights. The event is still a painful memory to Greensboro citizens, who as late as the early 2000s formed a Truth and Reconciliation Commission to explore the history of the incident and ways of bringing the community together in light of past racial conflict.

References: W. Fitzhugh Brundage, ed., *Under Sentence of Death: Lynching in the South* (1997); David S. Cecelski and Timothy B. Tyson, *Democracy Betrayed: The Wilmington Race Riot of 1898 and Its Legacy* (1998); David M. Chalmers, *Hooded Americanism: The History of the Ku Klux Klan* (1987); Paul D. Escott and Jeffrey J. Crow, "The Social Order and Violent Disorder: An Analysis of North Carolina in the Revolution and the Civil War," *Journal of Southern History* 52 (August 1986); Jacquelyn Dowd Hall and others, *Like a Family: The Making of a Southern Cotton Mill World* (1987); Timothy B. Tyson, *Blood Done Sign My Name: A True Story* (2004); Tyson, *Radio Free Dixie: Robert F. Williams and the Roots of Black Power* (1999).

Gail Williams O'Brien
Jay Mazzocchi

SEE ALSO "Death to the Klan" March; Gastonia Strike; Ku Klux Klan; Lowry Band; Lynching; Red Shirts; Regulator Movement; Slave Rebellions; Wilmington Race Riot.

Virginia was the name applied to that part of the New World granted to Sir Walter Raleigh by England's Queen Elizabeth I, the "virgin queen." It appears for the first time on the seal issued to Raleigh as "Lord and Governor of Virginia" at some unspecified date prior to 25 Mar. 1585. He was entitled to discover, hold, and occupy "such remote heathen and barbarous landes . . . not actually possessed of any Christian Prynce and inhabited by Christian people." Raleigh based exploratory expeditions in and attempted to colonize the area of coastal North America that is now North Carolina. His men also ranged northward into the Chesapeake Bay. Even though Raleigh's attempts were unsuccessful, the name "Virginia" became attached to newer colonization efforts that resulted in the establishment of Jamestown in 1607. The site of the 1584–90 activity came to be called "Ould Virginia."

References: Philip L. Barbour, ed., *The Complete Works of Captain John Smith (1580–1631)*, vol. 2 (1986); David B. Quinn, ed., *The Roanoke Voyages*, vol. 1 (1955).

William S. Powell

Virginia Electric & Power Company

Virginia Electric & Power Company was organized in 1909 and initially owned and operated electric street railways and streetlights in Richmond, Va. In the 1920s the company expanded its business into northeastern North Carolina. By 1928 Virginia Power operated approximately 30 miles of electric distribution lines in the state, all near the Virginia border in eastern North Carolina. By 1950 the company served about 30,000 North Carolina customers through more than 2,000 miles of distribution lines.

In the 1950s and 1960s Virginia Power greatly expanded its North Carolina operations. Most significantly, after a protracted legal contest that was resolved in 1953 in the U.S. Supreme Court, Virginia Power built a dam and power plant on the Roanoke River at Roanoke Rapids. A second large hydroelectric dam, Gaston, was also constructed by the company on the Roanoke River.

Despite long-term growth in revenue and customers, the North Carolina operations of Virginia Power suffered several significant setbacks after 1970. Nonetheless, the company remained one of the state's leading utilities. In 1991 North Carolina Power (after 1985 the name of an unincorporated division of Virginia Power that oversaw North Carolina operations) had more than $140 million in annual sales in 20 northeastern counties, including the northern Outer Banks. North Carolina Power provided electricity to more than 94,000 customers. By the early 2000s the company was the third-largest privately owned supplier of electric service in North Carolina.

Reference: Erwin H. Will, *The Past, Interesting; the Present, Intriguing; the Future, Bright: A Story of Virginia Electric and Power Company* (1965).

James L. Hunt

Visual Arts. Although North Carolina's major contributions to American fine arts have been primarily in the fields of literature and music, the state's visual artists have also produced many works that have gained both regional and national attention. Without a large, ethnically diverse, and artistically fertile cultural center such as those in the Northeast and on the West Coast, the state has struggled to develop its own consistently strong and unique visual arts reputation. North Carolina's artistic heritage is far from negligible, however, and has been manifested in numerous media that slowly have grown in popularity over the centuries. Besides painting, portraiture, photography, and other visual forms, the North Carolina arts tradition is steeped in the folk ethos, diverse in its output, and, while not nationally prolific, marked by a strong sense of communal history and purpose.

The history of the state's visual arts is rooted in both its natural environment and educational heritage. Many North Carolina artists have received formal instruction but seek their inspiration in natural settings, while others develop their work based on traditional means and modes. Though the state's artists work in a number of genres, utilizing a bevy of different methods and processes, their cultural and artistic vision is intrinsically linked to their natural geography. As long as the state provides inspiring settings, artists will come, learn, and be moved to create.

Early North Carolina Painting and Portraiture

European artistic tradition graced North Carolina for the first time when John White created his documentary sketches of Native Americans at Roanoke Island in 1585. But the historical record of arts in North Carolina runs dry for the bulk of the seventeenth and eighteenth centuries. By the late eighteenth century, itinerant artists were visiting the new state, often advertising not only their willingness to do portraits but their desire to do decorative painting as well. F. J. Belanger, an immigrant from Martinique, decorated the walls of St. John's Masonic Temple in Wilmington in addition to doing portraits and profiles. William Bartram, who resided in North Carolina for a few years, wrote his famous *Travels of William Bartram* (1791) about his trips throughout the South, including documentary illustrations—watercolors of flora and fauna—in the tradition of White.

Itinerant painters initially found portrait subjects in early towns such as Edenton, New Bern, and Wilmington—centers of shipping, fishing, or general commerce. Some North Carolinians seeking to be immortalized in portraits turned to prominent artists such as John Singleton Copley and Thomas Sully, while others sought out local artists Jacob Marling of Raleigh, William Ranney of Fayetteville, and others. Another popular choice was William Garl Browne, a painter of numerous portraits of President Zachary Taylor, who moved to Raleigh in 1837 and continued his prolific career well into the 1880s.

In 1817, at the direction of the legislature, Governor William Miller searched for an artist to paint two portraits of President George Washington for the statehouse. English-born Thomas Sully, a Gilbert Stuart protégé, first painted the portrait of Washington hanging in the house chamber of the State Capitol in Raleigh, a copy of his teacher's *Landsdowne* portrait of Washington, before crafting another copy; it was saved when the building burned in 1831. The second portrait commissioned from Sully was too large for its designated place in the statehouse, so the artist released the state from the deal. That portrait, titled *The Passage of the Delaware*, became the property of the Museum of Fine Arts in Boston.

With Sully working on commission and Browne becoming increasingly prolific, the mid-nineteenth century was arguably the zenith of portraiture in North Carolina. Early twentieth-century portrait painters were more scarce, but they included Mary Arnold Nash and Mary Graves Rees, both of Chapel Hill. Cuthbert Lee of Asheville also painted portraits of a number of North Carolinians. Although portraiture saw regular practice in the twentieth century, it was not as prevalent as in previous centuries.

A Growing Artistic Community in the State

The beauty and diversity of North Carolina's natural environment inspired a generation of painters in the mid-nineteenth century. Attention to the geographic richness of the region, long admired by indigenous artists, was perfectly suited to European movements such as French naturalism. The pull of the mountains both influenced and attracted numerous painters. In 1854 William C. A. Frerichs, a native of Ghent, Belgium, brought his expertise in European art to the Greensboro Female Academy. Frerichs developed a thematic fascination with western North Carolina that continued even after his departure for New York in the mid-1860s. Conversely, Elliott Daingerfield was raised in North Carolina but became an established New York artist. However, as early as 1886 he began to spend his summers in Blowing Rock, and his influence attracted many artists to that location. Daingerfield's own work was largely landscapes—a "vision of order" in which the artist became one with his subject.

Although North Carolina's budding artistic community was not celebrated nationally, it had influence, and as lesser artists followed established painters to the area, a cooperative spirit came to steer much of the artistic development. Education became a focus of many artists, such as Elizabeth Augusta Chant, who established an art school in Wilmington in the mid-1920s and mentored many others. Her school developed a number of fine pupils, including Claude Howell, whose vibrant scenes of coastal life made him one of the area's best-known painters. In 1931 a group of artists—among them, Daingerfield, Charles Baskerville, Isabelle Bower Henderson, James McLean, Mabel Pugh, Frances Speight, and Mary Tannahill—banded together as the North Carolina Association of Professional Artists and

sponsored juried shows. In fact, Howell had won the juried show prize in 1937 and used the notoriety to launch his career as a professional artist. Robert Gwathmey, Virginia-born and partially educated in North Carolina, became a leader of the Social Realist movement of the 1930s and 1940s. Gwathmey often depicted the degradation and struggles of poor blacks in North Carolina and other southern states in modern, strikingly colorful paintings.

Producing and Teaching Art in North Carolina Colleges and Universities

North Carolina institutes of higher learning, through their ability to both feature and foster artists, became centers for art in the twentieth century. Good painters have abounded in academic settings, such as the schools that became part of the University of North Carolina System: Howell at Wilmington, Kenneth Ness and George Kachergis at Chapel Hill, and Howard Thomas at Greensboro. In 1963 the General Assembly founded the residential public institution for training in the performing arts that would become the North Carolina School of the Arts (NCSA), which also offers a diverse curriculum of multimedia instruction. In 1973, a year after the NCSA was merged with the state university system, the Art Institute of Charlotte became the latest in the nationwide system of similar institutes. Currently, the state continues a strong art education presence in such organizations as the North Carolina Art Education Association (affiliated with the National Art Education Association), which offers annual scholarships and awards, in addition to networking for its members.

Through the efforts of educators to promote and develop a spirited artistic conscience within the state, more progressive, modern artists appeared in the mid- to late twentieth century. Artists such as Mary Leath Thomas and Jim Moon, both abstract in nature, had moderate exposure in the 1940s, but the most prominent wave of modernism was, once more, born from an educational vein. At Black Mountain College, Josef Albers introduced avant-garde ideas that would influence art on a national level. From 1933 to 1956, Black Mountain was the center of revolutionary artistic thought, attracting luminaries such as Willem de Kooning, Jacob Lawrence, Robert Motherwell, Irene Cullis, Susan Moore, Howard Thomas, Clare Leighton, Ken Noland, Angelica Reckendorf, and others.

The public frescoes of Ben Long, both religious and secular, have brought worldwide artistic attention to North Carolina since 1974, the year Long painted his first fresco in Beaver Creek. Long attended the University of North Carolina at Chapel Hill and, after serving in Vietnam, studied at the Art Students' League in New York City and with fresco artist Pietro Annigoni in Florence, Italy. His works are as emotionally compelling as they are large, particularly his portrayal of the human figure. His 15 North Carolina frescoes include *The Agony in the Garden*, *The Resurrection of Christ*, and *The Pentecost* at St. Peter's Catholic Church in Charlotte (1989), a massive, labor-oriented piece in the lobby of the Bank of America Corporate Center in Charlotte (1992), and a work at the Charlotte-Mecklenburg Police Department (1997) depicting various elements of poverty and criminal activity. His paintings and frescoes are also on display in Italy, France, and New York City. Long lives in Asheville, where he teaches his techniques to students at the Fine Arts League of Asheville, which he founded.

The Evolution of Photography

In 1839 French artist Louis J. M. Daguerre announced the discovery of the daguerreotype, one of the earliest and most successful forms of photography. The art spread quickly from the northeastern United States into the Midwest and South. The first daguerreotype operator to find his way into North Carolina may have been an itinerant named Dr. Davis at Halifax in May 1842. Between then and the end of the century, more than 600 photographers practiced their trade in the state, most traveling in wagons or by stage along its main north-south roads. Consequently, the early centers for photographic activity were in the more populated areas, including Raleigh, Fayetteville, Wilmington, New Bern, Hillsborough, Greensboro, Salisbury, and Charlotte. The early itinerants in North Carolina set up makeshift studios in numerous locales, but, as the trade grew, so did the demand, spawning permanent, thriving studios. Roughly a decade after the daguerreotype's introduction to the region, Jesse H. Whitehurst, one of the foremost pioneer daguerreotypists and promoters of the art, is believed to have opened the first permanent gallery in North Carolina at Wilmington in January 1853.

The impending Civil War, along with the development of the ambrotype, a thin negative on glass, boosted interest in the medium, but the war interrupted or ended the careers of most photographers in North Carolina. Commercial photography underwent a resurgence in the postwar period, and the number of professional photographers increased steadily as the population recovered. New photographic methods made it possible to produce more pictures for less money, piquing interest not only in documentary photography but also in formal portraiture.

While generally reserving daguerreotypes, ambrotypes, and tintypes for portraits, photographers produced most outdoor views in the form of cartes-de-visite, stereoscopic views, and large format prints. In the 1870s operators increasingly took the camera outside to capture scenic and interesting views of the North Carolina landscape. Thus, similar to the state's painters, many North Carolina photographers found their focus in the state's natural corridors.

Two important innovations—the gelatin dry-plate developing process and flexible film—occurred during the latter part of the nineteenth century, enabling practitioners to achieve increased productivity and efficiency and leading to the growth of amateur photography. As the century grew to a close, the once male-dominated, upper-class hobby became more egalitarian in nature. Although women had been assisting in galleries, they were slow to take up the trade in North Carolina. The first commercial female photographer in the state likely was Mrs. H. H. Davison, who began work in Oxford in 1882. By the late 1890s several women had stepped behind the camera. African American photographers were an equally rare entity following the proliferation of simple photo technology. Horace Davis, possibly the first, operated a gallery in New Bern by 1870 and 10 years later worked in Raleigh.

The turn of the nineteenth century introduced a new breed of photographer, whose North Carolina epitome was the legendary Bayard Wootten of New Bern. Born in 1875, Wootten took up the trade because of its increasing affordability, as did many others of her day. Becoming immersed in the growing and more accessible world of photography, she formed a close relationship with members of the Women's Federation of the Photographers Association of America, a group that, by its very existence, spoke for the changing face of the medium. Recording rural southern life both for herself and for the government, Wootten's work, especially during her Depression-era heyday, aesthetically and professionally rivaled that of similar documentarian Walker Evans. It continued to inspire female photographers such as North Carolinian Elizabeth Matheson throughout the twentieth century.

Another photographer with a keen eye for documenting the changing face of North Carolina history was Grandfather Mountain owner and preservationist Hugh Morton, who snapped photos of noteworthy North Carolinians for decades before his death in 2006. Many other photographers work in the state; most make a living in portraiture, in the various forms of media, or in the recording for hire of important personal or corporate events, while also scanning the state for artistic impressions. Beginning in the 1990s, the use of digital cameras in conjunction with computers once again revolutionized this industry nationwide.

North Carolina Art Museums, Exhibits, and Centers

North Carolina works of art and portraiture near the end of the twentieth century took on a new dimension in museums across the country, where a number of images by both North Carolinian and regional painters widened the scope of what had been primarily local art. An exhibit, *Painting in the South*, planned at the Virginia Museum in 1983, was a landmark effort to bring together major southern painters. Included were twentieth-century North Carolina artists Howell, Speight, Noland, and Thomas, as well as Hobson Pittman, Victor Huggins, Vernon Pratt, Victor Faccinto, and Romare Bearden. Although the bulk of noteworthy artists in North Carolina are painters, often naturalists, the increasingly healthy artistic temperament in the state has helped foster many kinds of art, from portraiture to pottery.

North Carolina portraits are indexed at both the Frick Art

Reference Library in New York City and the National Portrait Gallery in Washington, D.C. In 1963 Laura MacMillan compiled *The North Carolina Portrait Index, 1700–1860* on behalf of the National Society of the Colonial Dames in the State of North Carolina. A nod to the one-time proliferation of portraiture in the state, the index documents over 500 portraits, while Cuthbert Lee's *Portrait Register* also touts many North Carolinians.

Within the state, both the North Carolina Museum of History and the Ackland Art Museum at UNC-Chapel Hill have outstanding collections of North Carolina portraits. UNC's Philanthropic Society pioneered portrait collecting in the state by establishing a policy of collecting alumni portraits in 1821. Among the society's first acquisitions was a portrait of Joseph Caldwell, then president of the university. The Dialectic Society soon followed in 1926 with a portrait of university founder William R. Davie. The two debating societies merged in 1974, creating the Dialectic and Philanthropic Societies Foundation, Inc., and the more than 100 portraits in the joint collection were entrusted to the foundation.

In addition to university arts programs, several organizations and institutions serve as galleries for local artists as well as resource, teaching, and outreach facilities. The North Carolina Arts Council, created in 1964, aids and supports the state's artistic community through its Visual Arts Program and in many other ways. The council also administered the Artworks for State Buildings Program, which between 1982 and 2000 brought publicly commissioned sculptures and other pieces of art to various parks, municipal buildings, and corporate offices throughout the state. Founded in the mid-twentieth century, the Sawtooth Center for Visual Art and the Southeastern Center for Contemporary Art, both in Winston-Salem, have become important centers for both established and emerging artists in the state. Other museums include the North Carolina Museum of Art in Raleigh, Louise Wells Cameron Art Museum in Wilmington, Mint Museums in Charlotte, Nasher Museum of Art at Duke University, and museums on other college campuses.

References: David S. Bundy, Ella-Prince Knox, and Donald B. Kuspit, *Painting in the South, 1564–1980* (1983); Ola Maie Foushee, *Art in North Carolina: Episodes and Developments, 1585–1970* (1973); Stephen E. Massengill, comp., *Photographers in North Carolina: The First Century, 1842–1941* (2004); North Carolina Museum of Art, *Two Hundred Years of Visual Arts in North Carolina* (1976).

Bruce E. Baker
Martha Belle Caldwell
Additional research provided by Philip McFee, Stephen E. Massengill, and Jo Ann Williford.

SEE ALSO Black Mountain College; Folk Art; Folk Festivals; Louis Orr Etchings; Louise Wells Cameron Art Museum; Mint Museum of Art; North Carolina Museum

of Art; Penland School of Crafts; Sawtooth Center for Visual Art; Southeastern Center for Contemporary Art; State Art Society.

Vital Statistics. North Carolina recognized the need for birth and death records during the colonial period. A colonial act of 1715 required county officials to register births and deaths in their jurisdiction "till there be a clerk of the Parish Church." But the law was never taken seriously and few births were actually registered. In 1767 Governor William Tryon noted that only two counties in the North Carolina colony, Perquimans and Pasquotank, showed evidence that they had attempted to register births.

By 1879 county superintendents of health were required to make monthly reports of vital statistics to the State Board of Health. A subsequent measure enacted in 1881 directed all persons listing property for taxation to present the township assessor with the number of births and deaths in his family from the previous year. However, since this measure did not apply to citizens who did not own property, it excluded a large segment of the population. After the turn of the century, there was an increasing need for legal proof of birth and residence for a variety of reasons, such as social security programs and passport applications. Consequently, the General Assembly responded with the statewide Model Vital Statistics Law, requiring county officials to register all births starting in October 1913.

Under this statute, a newborn had to be registered within five days of birth by the physician or midwife who assisted in the child's delivery. If an attendant was not present, it became the duty of the father or mother to report the birth. The 1913 law required that additional information be included with the birth record, including the date of birth, full name of the child, length of pregnancy, and birth weight and sex of the child. The certificate also had to list information about the parents, such as their full name, residence, race, education, age, birthplace, and occupation, as well as the number of living and dead children previously born to the mother, whether the parents were married, and if the mother had had a blood test for syphilis. The certificate was to contain the attending physician's signature and the name of the registrar. Citizens born before 1913 who needed legal proof of birth could apply for a delayed birth certificate at their local Register of Deeds Office in the county of their birth.

The 1715 act was also not enforced with regard to death statistics, and once again only Perquimans and Pasquotank Counties made any effort to register deaths. Nearly 200 years passed before substantial legislation was adopted to record deaths. In 1909 a statute required the registration of deaths occurring in cities with populations of 1,000 people or more, although Raleigh and Wilmington had already begun keeping vital records in 1885 and 1903, respectively. Registrars, appointed by local officials, were directed to issue a death certificate within three days of death or removal. Every month copies of the certificates were forwarded to the State Register of Vital Statistics. As part of the Model Vital Statistics Law passed by the General Assembly in March 1913, all deaths were to be recorded by the county registrar beginning in October of that year. In most counties the local Register of Deeds records deaths, although in some counties the local Health Department performs that duty.

Kyle S. Kendrick

Volcanoes. The geologic record suggests volcanic activity in what is now North Carolina primarily occurred in two phases of the middle Proterozoic era, between 850 and 500 million years ago, first while the ancient North American and Euro-African plates were moving apart, then while these same plates were colliding. During the first phase, 840 to 800 million years ago, eruptions occurred under the ancient Iapetus Sea and on land. Volcanic ash and lava flows deposited underwater and interbedded with layers of mud and sand are now part of the Ashe Formation stretching from Ashe and Watauga Counties in North Carolina into Franklin County, Va. The first eruptions on land occurred about 820 million years ago on the Piedmont Terrane, along the present North Carolina–Virginia border in the environs of Mount Rogers. These eruptions continued for at least 220 million years and deposited some 3,000 meters of volcanic and sedimentary rock.

The second phase of volcanic activity, beginning around 750 million years ago and lasting more than 300 million years, occurred along an arc of island volcanoes on the Avalon Terrane, a collision zone between the Iapetus Sea and the Theic-Rheic Ocean. Intense folding and metamorphism have destroyed most evidence of these eruptions, but the rocks created are present in the Carolina State Belt stretching southward through the midsection of the state. The eastern boundary of the belt is undetermined as it lies beneath the Coastal Plain, while the western boundary roughly passes near Greensboro, Thomasville, Lexington, Salisbury, Charlotte, and into South Carolina. Remnant volcanic necks and masses of igneous rock are evident in Orange and Chatham Counties, suggesting an early center of volcanic activity near Chapel Hill, dated at around 700 million years old, and near Hillsborough, dated at about 650 million years old.

Volcanic eruptions may have occurred during the middle Eocene epoch, about 47 million years ago, in the northern and western regions of the state, but erosion has removed all cones or other evidence of such activity. Also, volcanic ash deposits (bentonite) in the Castle Hayne Formation in the Coastal Plain are not believed to be native to the region, but possibly deposited by winds from a volcanic center in Virginia or from eruptions forming the island of Bermuda. There are no known active volcanoes in North Carolina today despite some geologic instability on the coast.

References: Fred Beyer, *North Carolina, the Years before Man: A Geologic History* (1991); Mary-Russell Roberson and Kevin G. Stewart, *The Geologic Story of the Carolinas: A Field Guide* (2006).

William G. DiNome

Voluntary Associations. SEE Civic Clubs.

W

Waccamaw Indians were a Siouan-speaking tribe, probably related to the so-called Cape Fear Indians, who populated parts of modern-day southeastern North Carolina. At the time of the first English settlement attempts in the late sixteenth century, the Waccamaw were among several small, autonomous tribal groups ("eastern Siouans") whose territory and hunting grounds extended from just south of the Neuse River down the coast to the lower Cape Fear and inland to Green Swamp and the junction of the Pee Dee and Waccamaw Rivers. They are thought to have been seminomadic river-dwellers who subsisted on hunting and some farming, often on high-ground "islands" within swamps. They lived in dome-shaped bark houses, practiced shamanism, and exhibited distinctive mortuary customs.

The Waccamaw's relationship with European settlers was based on trade (including guns and slaves), alliances, aid, and friendship, yet was all the while marred by European-borne disease, displacement due to European settlement, hostility, and outright warfare. The Tuscarora War (1711–13) and the Yamassee War (1715), in which the Waccamaw fought against the settlers, critically reduced the the tribe's numbers and strength and evidently resulted in their retreat to the isolated swamps near Lake Waccamaw for protection. Some settled with the Catawba, a Siouan tribe to the west. History records practically nothing of the Waccamaw through the remaining eighteenth century until 1790, when the U.S. Census recorded common Waccamaw surnames among inhabitants living in small, isolated communities.

In 1910 the Waccamaw's earliest known governmental body was created, the Council of the Wide Awake Indians, whose primary objective was twofold: to obtain public funding for Indian schools and, later, to attain federal recognition. The council's educational efforts resulted in the opening of the first publicly funded Waccamaw school in 1933, with more to follow; however, these Indian schools were notoriously ill-funded, fueling the council's campaign for federal recognition beginning around 1940. Ultimately the Indian-only schools were dissolved, along with segregation, in 1967. The first official use of the name "Waccamaw Siouan" (the third name officially adopted by the tribe since 1913) appeared in print in 1949, when a bill to grant the Waccamaw federal recognition was introduced in Congress. The bill was defeated the following year. Since then the tribe has focused its efforts on economic development and self-sufficiency. During the 1960s and 1970s, changes in federal policies regarding public funding and economic assistance allowed the Waccamaw and other tribal groups to benefit from several government programs without federal recognition.

Members of the modern-day Waccamaw Siouan tribe are concentrated near Lake Waccamaw in southeastern North Carolina. Most of the approximately 1,500 Waccamaws live in three major communities: Ricefield (Bladen County), Saint James (Columbus County), and Buckhead (straddling the Bladen-Columbus county line). Though not officially recognized by the federal government, they are one of the tribes recognized since 1971 by the North Carolina Commission of Indian Affairs (which Waccamaws and other tribal leaders helped to form the year before). They are closely related by religious denomination, politics, and, to a small degree, intermarriage (they are largely endogamous) to two other Indian groups, the Lumbee and Coharie. The Waccamaw are predominantly Christian and, among the Christians, overwhelmingly Baptist.

Tribal leadership is provided by the Waccamaw Siouan Development Association (WSDA), a nonprofit group founded in 1972. It consists of a nine-member board of directors, elected by secret ballot open to all tribal members over age 18, plus a chief, whose political role, beyond advising the board, is largely symbolic. In designing the WSDA as an agency for economic development, the Waccamaw pioneered a strategy for both self-determination and the articulation of their Indian identity that has achieved some substantial successes since 1978 and has been imitated by other unrecognized tribes in the state. Today most working Waccamaws are employed in the construction, forest and paper, and apparel industries. About 6 percent are full-time farmers. While the Waccamaw do not occupy a reservation, the WSDA owns a small tract as tribal land and a community building for governmental and ceremonial activities.

With community Indian schools eliminated and federal recognition dubious, the introduction of the powwow festival in the 1960s has become a central focus of Waccamaw activity. Held annually in October, the Waccamaw powwow resembles that of many other Indian groups around the nation and plays a central role in articulating Waccamaw identity.

References: Patricia Barker Lerch, "State-Recognized Indians of North Carolina, Including a History of the Waccamaw Sioux," in J. Anthony Paredes, ed., *Indians of the Southeastern United States in the Twentieth Century* (1992); Ruth Y. Wetmore, *First on the Land: The North Carolina Indians* (1975).

William G. DiNome

Wachovia was the name used to designate a large tract of land in the northern Piedmont of North Carolina purchased by the Moravians, or the Unity of Brethren, from John Lord Carteret, Earl Granville, in 1752. Moravians from Pennsylvania and from Europe settled the tract in the decades following, building the villages of Bethabara and Bethania, the town of Salem, and the rural congregations of Friedberg and Friedland.

The Unity of Brethren (*Unitas Fratrum*) arose in the areas of Eastern Europe known as Bohemia and Moravia (presently the Czech Republic) after the martyrdom of Jan Hus in 1415. These Christians believed in a strong biblical foundation for faith, experiential religion, and evangelical preaching of the Christian message. After enduring persecution in the ensuing centuries, in 1727 some remnants of the faithful were given asylum on the estate of Nicholas Ludwig, Count von Zinzendorf, in Saxony, north of Dresden. From their communal village named Herrnhut, Moravian missionaries traveled throughout Western Europe and to the New World to establish Bethlehem, Nazareth, and Lititz in Pennsylvania.

Organized on economic communalism, these towns quickly stabilized and spawned yet other communities. Count Zinzendorf, now an ardent Moravian, learned of available land in the royal colony of North Carolina. Earl Granville, a descendant of one of the original Lords Proprietors, had declined to sell his share to the Crown in 1729. Therefore, while North Carolina was a royal colony, Granville controlled a large territory on which he hoped to settle prosperous colonists. Moravians saw an opportunity to acquire a large piece of land where they might work and worship in peace, with the Crown and the church providing security from oppression. In 1752 agreement was reached in principle for the Moravians to purchase a significant tract in the northern sector of the colony.

Granville's eastern North Carolina lands were mostly settled, but surveyors accompanying Moravian August Gottlieb Spangenberg located a tract of 98,985 acres on the three forks of Muddy Creek, east of the Yadkin River in what is today Forsyth County. Upon viewing such bountiful territory of hills and valleys, Spangenberg was reminded of a beautiful ancestral estate of Count Zinzendorf in south Austria near the Danube, which was named *Der Wachau*. He suggested that the North Carolina tract be named to honor the Zinzendorf family for its assistance to the Moravian survival and resurgence. Both *Wachau* and the Latin form, Wachovia, were used by Moravians to refer to their North Carolina land and the developments therein for a hundred years. Only in the 1850s, when Wachovia land was sold to non-Moravians and the new county seat of Winston was established adjacent to the northern boundary of Salem, did the distinctive Moravian term diminish in usage.

Wachovia remains associated with its Moravian heritage and is familiar to citizens of Winston-Salem. But for most North Carolinians, it is recognized as the name of a prominent banking interest, Wachovia Corporation, which traces its roots to 1879, the year the First National Bank of Salem moved to nearby thriving Winston and became the Wachovia National Bank.

References: Adelaide L. Fries, ed., *Records of the Moravians in North Carolina*, vol. 1 (1922); Fries, Stuart T. Wright, and J. Edwin Hendricks, *Forsyth: The History of a County on the March* (1976).

Jerry L. Surratt

Wachovia Corporation traces its origins to 1866, when the First National Bank of Salem opened, with Israel Lash as president. Following Lash's death in the late 1870s, his nephew William Lemly closed the Salem office and moved to Winston, reopening the bank in 1879 as Wachovia National Bank. Wachovia is the Latin form of the name "Wachau," which was given to the tract of land in the Piedmont settled by Moravians in 1753. The name honored the settlers' connection to the Wachau Valley along the Danube River.

With the advent of trust companies in 1891, a new enterprise, the Wachovia Loan and Trust Company, opened as a second Wachovia in 1893. The two enterprises merged in 1910, three years before the towns of Winston and Salem merged. The new Wachovia Bank and Trust Company had deposits of $4 million, with capital stock of $1.25 million and total resources of $7 million. It was the largest bank in the South and the largest trust operation between Baltimore and New Orleans.

In 1985, after deregulation and the beginning of interstate banking, Wachovia merged with First Atlanta Corporation to create First Wachovia Corporation, an $18 billion interstate bank holding company with dual headquarters in Winston-Salem and Atlanta. Six years later the institution was joined by South Carolina National. L. M. ("Bud") Baker Jr. became chief executive officer of the corporation in 1993.

By 1997 Wachovia was involved in major expansion throughout the Southeast. The acquisition of 1st United Bankcorp in Florida, combined with mergers with Central Fidelity Banks, Inc., and Jefferson Bankshares, Inc., in Virginia, gave Wachovia a retail network of more than 800 banking offices and 1,100 automated teller machines throughout Virginia, North Carolina, South Carolina, Georgia, and Florida. In 2001 Wachovia Corporation merged with First Union Bank; the new company, continuing under the Wachovia name, was headquartered in Charlotte. By 2006, after a merger with Southtrust Corporation, Wachovia was the fourth-largest bank holding company in the nation, with $542 billion in assets, 3,200 financial centers, and 97,000 employees.

References: Pamela L. Moore, "From Absent to No. 1 in Va.," *Charlotte Observer* (25 June 1997); Wachovia Corporation, *A History of Banking and Wachovia* (1994).

Alex Coffin

Wahab's Plantation, Battle of. The Revolutionary War battle of Wahab's Plantation took place on 21 Sept. 1780 between present-day Monroe, N.C., and Lancaster, S.C. Earlier in the month the British army, commanded by Lord Charles Cornwallis, had moved north from Camden, S.C., into the Waxhaw area of North Carolina and South Carolina to secure provisions from civilian farms. During an outbreak of malaria, the British had encamped to gather food and allow their sick to heal. The infamous commander of the British Legion, Lt. Col. Banastre Tarleton, was himself incapacitated by yellow fever and confined to bed. He transferred command of his troops to his deputy, Maj. George Hanger, who led the men during the Battle of Wahab's Plantation.

Young Patriot leader William Richardson Davie, who had grown up in the Waxhaw area, decided to ambush the British and Tory troops as they ravaged the countryside. In the early morning of 21 September, Davie skirted the right flank of Cornwallis's larger armed force encamped on Waxhaw Creek. He learned that the British Legion, recruited from Loyalist colonists, had quartered at the plantation house of Patriot militia captain James Alexander Wahab (or "Wauchope"). About daybreak, as the British sentries were changing, Davie attacked the plantation house through the heavy cover of a cornfield. With only 150 men, Davie used a hit-and-run tactic against the 300 to 400 British soldiers. This move was made even more risky by the encampment of the 71st Highland Regiment (Fraser's Highlanders) overlooking the plantation. Knowledge of the topography and a stealthy advance enabled Davie's force to attack and retreat by the time the reinforcements of the 71st Regiment could arrive. Davie's only loss was 1 man wounded, reportedly by friendly fire, compared to Hanger's 15 or 20 dead and about 40 wounded. By his own account, Davie also managed to capture 96 horses and 120 stands of arms, although other sources list fewer. The plantation was burned by the British in the aftermath of the battle, as was customary, and Cornwallis subsequently moved his troops to Charlotte, where they clashed again with Davie.

Though a small confrontation in the Revolutionary War, the Battle of Wahab's Plantation is particularly representative of the war in the South. Patriot colonists fought Loyalist colonists at the very home of one of the combatants. Whereas Hanger was English, Davie had grown up in a frontier Presbyterian community of Scotch-Irish who formed the basis of his troops, and he led them more by charisma and trust than according to any strict military training. The sudden attack and retreat tactic, akin to Francis Marion's in South Carolina, is also indicative of the different manner of fighting in the southern theater.

Reference: John Buchanan, *The Road to Guilford Courthouse: The American Revolution in the Carolinas* (1997).

David L. Pope

Wake County, located in the Piedmont region of North Carolina, was formed in 1771 from Johnston, Cumberland, and Orange Counties and named for Margaret Wake Tryon, the wife of royal governor William Tryon. Early inhabitants of the area included the Sissipahaw and Occaneechi Indians; English and Scotch-Irish settlers later populated the region. Raleigh was established as the county seat in 1771 under the name Wake County Courthouse; the name was changed to Raleigh, in honor of Sir Walter Raleigh, when the city became the capital of North Carolina in 1792. Other Wake County cities and towns, all within what is fast becoming a solid ring of urban and suburban development surrounding Raleigh, include Cary, Garner, Fuquay-Varina, Holly Springs, Apex, Morrisville, Wake Forest, Zebulon, Wendell, and Knightdale. Notable bodies of water within the county include the Neuse River, Wake Forest Reservoir, Falls, Wheeler, Crabtree, and Bass Lakes, and Swift, Sycamore, and Hominy Creeks.

Wake County is one of North Carolina's most urbanized counties, with an estimated population of nearly 724,000 in 2004. It is dominated by the state government and its ancillary institutions, multiple large businesses and corporations located in Research Triangle Park (which straddles the line between Wake and Durham Counties) and other locales around Raleigh, and its outstanding colleges and universities—North Carolina State University (1887), Peace College (1857), Shaw University (1865), Saint Augustine's College (1867), and Meredith College (1891). Important cultural and historical landmarks and institutions abound in Raleigh and vicinity and include the State Capitol (1833–40); the Governor's Mansion (1891); the State Legislative Building (1961); the Joel Lane House (1760s), the oldest house in Raleigh; Mordecai Historic Park (1785); and the North Carolina State Fairgrounds. Important institutions and attractions include the North Carolina Museum of History, the North Carolina Museum of Art, the North Carolina Museum of Natural Sciences, Raleigh Ensemble Players, Exploris, Raleigh Little Theatre and Rose Garden, the North Carolina Symphony Orchestra, North Carolina State University Crafts Center Gallery, the North Carolina Literary and Historical Association, the North Carolina State Archives, and the Wendell Post Office Museum. William B. Umstead State Park is one of Wake County's many recreational areas. The county hosts popular festivals and annual events such as the North Carolina State Fair, Saint Patrick's Day Parade, the state Special Olympics Summer Games, the International Festival, Executive Mansion Christmas, the Today and Yesteryear Festival, and Rolesville Fireman's Day.

Wake County farmers continue to produce agricultural goods such as nursery and landscape plants, vegetables, and tobacco. Manufactured products include high-tech items such as digital electronics, telecommunications equipment, measuring devices, and pharmaceuticals. Also produced are electric switch gears, flooring, and refrigeration equipment. Minerals such as soapstone, corundum, beryl, graphite, kyanite, pyrite, and magnesite are mined in the county.

Reference: Elizabeth Reid Murray, *Wake: Capital County of North Carolina* (1983).

William S. Powell

SEE ALSO Joel Lane House; Meredith College; North Carolina Museum of Art; North Carolina Museum of History; North Carolina State University; Raleigh; Research Triangle Park; Saint Augustine's College; Shaw University; State Capitol.

Wake Forest University was founded in Wake Forest in 1834 by the North Carolina Baptist State Convention as a "literary and manual labor" school for young men. By 1838, however, the manual labor component was dropped, and Wake Forest College became a liberal arts college whose mission was to provide education for prospective Baptist ministers. The college quickly established itself as a respectable liberal arts institution, growing slowly but steadily throughout the nineteenth and early twentieth centuries.

With the aid of a wealthy Winston-Salem family, Wake Forest's Bowman Gray School of Medicine was founded in 1941. That same year the undergraduate school was awarded a chapter of Phi Beta Kappa. By 1949 student enrollment had grown to more than 2,000, and the schools of business administration and religion were established. But the decade of the 1950s brought the most significant change to the institution since its founding. With the promise of major financial support from the Z. Smith Reynolds Foundation of Winston-Salem, the trustees of Wake Forest College and the Baptist State Convention agreed to move the campus from the town of Wake Forest to Winston-Salem.

Under the leadership of Harold Tribble (1950–67), the move was completed in 1956, and the old campus was sold to the newly formed Southeastern Baptist Theological Seminary. In 1967 Wake Forest College became Wake Forest University. In 1979 a new relationship was initiated between the Baptist State Convention and the university by which the century-old ties with the Baptists were loosened. By the terms of this new relationship, the institution relinquished funding that came through the Baptist Convention and received more flexibility in the selection of future trustees.

Wake Forest University by the early 2000s had a total enrollment of nearly 6,500 students and offered 34 academic majors. In addition to the Bowman Gray School of Medicine and the Wayne Calloway School of Business and Accountancy, the university has a law school, a graduate school in arts and sciences, and a divinity school.

Reference: George Washington Paschal, *History of Wake Forest College* (2 vols., 1948).

Anne Moore

Waldensians. In 1893 the Waldensians, or Waldenses, a Protestant sect that had emerged before the Reformation, settled a colony, named Valdese, in Burke County, eight miles east of Morganton. (The word "Valdese" is Italian for Waldensian.) The Waldensians had lived in the Cottian Alps in northwestern Italy on the French border. Their written history dates to the twelfth century; the leader for whom they are named, Peter Waldo, was a wealthy merchant from Lyons, France, who sold his worldly goods after a friend's death and became a preacher. The Waldensians were persecuted for more than 400 years before being granted full legal and political rights in 1848 by King Charles Albert of Piedmont and Sardinia. Waldensian groups migrated to other parts of the world, but the largest number came to Burke County in North Carolina.

The American who promoted the emigration was Marvin F. Scaife, a capitalist from Pittsburgh who also owned land in the Morganton area. Scaife went to Rome and talked with Matteo Prochet, chairman of the Committee of Evangelization of the Waldensian Church. Colonization plans took shape, and the Waldenses sent two delegates, Jean Bounous and Louis Richard, to inspect land in Burke County. In late May 1893, 29 colonists under the leadership of Charles Albert Tron reached Burke County. Tron could speak English, but the others spoke only Italian and French. The settlement was named Valdese.

In June 1893, the Valdese Corporation, which included Waldenses and American capitalists including Scaife, was established and purchased about 10,000 acres of land for $25,000 on credit from the Morganton Land Company. Tron, who negotiated the contract for the settlers, returned to Italy in July. Enrico Vinay, a Waldensian pastor, succeeded him and directed the affairs of the colony. During the week of 20 Aug. 1893, 25 more emigrants arrived, and another 178 were added to the community in November.

The Waldensian settlers encountered many hardships. The infertility of the soil made farming difficult, and the layout of the land forced people to live at some distance from their nearest neighbors. The language barrier posed problems in communicating with Burke County residents who offered assistance. Fortunately, the Reverend Barthelemy Soulier arrived with his bride in June 1894, and his wise and strong leadership brought stability to the colony. The Valdese Corporation was dissolved, and families purchased individual farms. Soulier remained in the colony for seven years.

Religion was the controlling influence in the lives of the early Waldensian settlers. The church in Valdese, which was part of the Waldensian Church of Italy, united in 1895 with the Presbyterian Church, similar in government and theology, and was admitted to the Concord Presbytery on 9 July 1895. A church building was completed in 1899. Baptists, Methodists, and other denominations established churches in the area as early as 1914. Education was also given much emphasis in Waldensian culture. The first children to arrive attended a local

Waldensian schoolchildren and teacher (standing beside steps) at Valdese, ca. 1905. NCC.

school, but since they spoke no English, the Waldenses established a separate facility in January 1894 and succeeded in employing a series of competent, missionary-minded teachers. In 1905 the Waldensian school came under the auspices of the Burke County school system.

While some progress was made in the area of farming, the success and prosperity of the Waldensian settlement was assured by industrial achievement. The Waldensian Hosiery Mill, established in 1901, paved the way for the growth of industry, and Valdese became one of the nation's leading hosiery manufacturing centers. The Valdese Manufacturing Company was created in 1913 to make cotton yarns. The Waldensian Bakery, built in 1915, at first delivered bread by horse and buggy. The establishment of other factories, banks, general stores, and restaurants promoted growth of the community and its prosperity. On 17 Feb. 1920, the town of Valdese was incorporated. The Waldenses continued to occupy outlying areas around Valdese such as Reynaud and Gardiole, and in time the population became more cosmopolitan.

In 1938 the *Morganton News Herald* began to print "News of the Week in Valdese," and in 1943 a newspaper, the *Valdese News*, appeared. The Old Colony Players of Valdese has presented *From This Day Forward*, an outdoor drama in two acts, each summer since 1968. The play, which features authentic costumes and folk dances, portrays the Waldensian heritage. Tron Hall was established as a museum of artifacts and litera-

ture of early Valdese in 1958; the rapid growth of depositories led to the opening of a new facility, the Waldensian Museum, in 1975. The Valdese Chamber of Commerce was founded in 1930 and has cooperated with many civic, fraternal, patriotic, and service organizations in promoting town improvements.

References: Maxine McCall and Kays Gary, *What Mean These Stones?: A Centennial Celebration of Valdese, North Carolina* (1993); George B. Watts, *The Waldenses of Valdese* (1965).

Lala Carr Steelman

Walker's *Appeal*, actually titled *Appeal to the Coloured Citizens of the World*, was an emotionally charged, powerful antislavery pamphlet published by black Wilmington native David Walker in September 1829 and widely distributed across the South. It appeared in three editions, probably printed in Boston. Although Walker himself was born free, taking the legal rank of his mother, he was deeply troubled by the slave status of his father, who died before Walker was born. After traveling widely, young Walker settled in Boston, where he dealt in second-hand clothing and was active in antislavery causes.

No record has been found of Walker's education, but in his writing there is evidence of literary ability and historical knowledge. His *Appeal* advocates the overthrow of the slave system, through violence if necessary. Even such abolitionist leaders as William Lloyd Garrison objected to Walker's overly

The opening of Article I of David Walker's 1829 antislavery pamphlet.
NCC.

radical ideas and tone. Nevertheless, the *Appeal* was intended to strengthen blacks' resolve and give them hope of freedom. Reaction among slave owners in North Carolina, Georgia, and Virginia, where copies were smuggled in from Boston and New York, was, predictably, prompt and harsh.

References: Clement Eaton, "A Dangerous Pamphlet in the Old South," *Journal of Southern History* 2 (August 1936); Peter P. Hinks, ed., *David Walker's* Appeal to the Coloured Citizens of the World (2000).

William S. Powell

Wallpaper, first known as "wall hanging," appeared in the New England colonies by 1700 and was available in the South by the 1740s. In 1758 plans were made to establish a new capital for North Carolina, to be named George City; the interior of the two-story "Dwelling-House" for the governor was to be plastered and "ornamented with Paper." This may be the earliest reference to wallpaper in North Carolina.

Wallpaper was advertised in the *Virginia Gazette* in 1766. The Joseph Hewes House in Edenton (ca. 1765) had a soft, gray-blue paper with foliage in deep, natural shades of green with flowers, a temple, and musical instruments in shades of rose, salmon, lavender, and blue. There are other instances of surviving wallpaper in North Carolina. One is found at Rosedale Plantation, built by Archibald Frew near Charlotte in

1815. The plantation has three rooms with paper of two block-printed designs about 21 by 18 inches. One design is of children at play, while the other depicts what appears to be a gravestone inscribed "A la Fidelite." Oak Lawn, also near Charlotte, dates from 1818, but its wallpaper depicting the voyage of Captain Cook was printed in France between 1804 and 1806.

Reference: Catherine Lynn, *Wallpaper in America from the Seventeenth Century to World War I* (1980).

William S. Powell

Walton War was the name of a boundary dispute between North Carolina and Georgia that flared into a brief but deadly armed conflict in 1804 in modern Transylvania County. When the area was first being settled, there was uncertainty as to whether it was in South Carolina or North Carolina, with settlers having migrated to the area from both states. In 1797 surveyor John Clark Kirkpatrick made an attempt (as part of the surveying of the Indian line by Andrew Pickens for South Carolina and Benjamin Hawkins for North Carolina) to ascertain the boundary between North Carolina and South Carolina. Kirkpatrick's line divided the settlement but left most of it in South Carolina.

In 1802 the portion of the settlement south of the line was ceded to Georgia as part of the federal agreement whereby Georgia ceded Alabama and Mississippi to the federal government. This settlement was then organized by the Georgia legislature as Walton County. Those holding North Carolina land grants in the vicinity, however, did not recognize Georgia's authority over the area. This resulted in a number of incidents in December 1804 in which Walton County officials sought to impose Georgia law on the North Carolina settlers and collect taxes. In one of these confrontations, North Carolina constable John Hafner was killed when he was struck in the head with the butt of the musket of Georgia official Samuel McAdams. The North Carolina militia was ordered into the area to arrest the offending Georgia officials. All of the Walton officers ultimately escaped from jail before trial and fled to Georgia and South Carolina because they were under capital indictment for Hafner's murder. This exertion of authority by North Carolina, however, demonstrated that the settlement was too remote from the seat of power in Georgia for that state to enforce any legitimate claim.

By 1807 Georgia and North Carolina had agreed that the dividing line between the two states should be the thirty-fifth parallel. A joint survey by the presidents of the University of Georgia and the University of North Carolina revealed that the entire settlement was in North Carolina. Georgia did not recognize the validity of this survey until 1811, when it was confirmed by an independent survey performed by Andrew Ellicott (who located the boundary at Ellicott's Rock).

Although the Georgians who had been arrested in Hafner's

death had fled, North Carolina granted amnesty to the other Walton County officials and reintegrated them into the settlement.

References: Cal Carpenter, *The Walton War and Tales of the Great Smoky Mountains* (1979); Martin Reidinger, *The Walton War and the Georgia–North Carolina Boundary Dispute* (1981).

Martin Reidinger

Wampus is the name of a semimythical creature believed to inhabit Iredell County and adjacent counties. It was a source of particular concern in the early 1930s. Sightings and hearings of the creature followed much the same patterns as present-day sightings of flying saucers, Bigfoot, and Elvis Presley. The physical attributes of the wampus varied greatly. It was said to be silver or black, the size of a dog or a colt, with or without a horn, and with or without "big red eyes." Tracks were occasionally described as "web-footed," although others maintained that the creature had "front paws like a lion and hind feet like a bear." Most observers agreed that it had a "keen holler," although descriptions of the sound it made ranged from that of "a hurt woman" to that of "an elephant with his head in a rain barrel."

The wampus apparently made its first appearance in Iredell County in the fall of 1890 and was duly reported in the *Statesville Landmark*, edited by Joseph P. Caldwell. It is suspected that Caldwell invented the varmint to sell newspapers during an otherwise slow news period, but stories of some kind of bear-dog-cat animal continued to circulate long after Caldwell left for the *Charlotte Observer*. Real or not, the threat of the wampus was used effectively as a bugbear by parents: "Child, you'd better be home before dark, or the wampus is liable to get you."

References: O. C. Stonestreet III, "Summer of the Wampus," *The State* (July 1994); "The Wampus Is Dead—Long Live the Wampus," *Statesville Landmark*, 8 Sept. 1931; "Wampus Wandering thru South Iredell," *Mooresville Enterprise*, 30 Apr. 1931.

O. C. Stonestreet III

War of 1812. Disputes between the United States and Great Britain over neutrality laws, the impressment of American sailors by British warships, and the suspicion that the British were inciting Indian wars on the American frontier caused Congress to declare war on Britain on 18 June 1812. North Carolina governor William Hawkins quickly notified President James Monroe that the state would cooperate fully in executing the war.

North Carolinians served in both the regular army and the militia during the war. When the conflict began, the regular army had fewer than 7,000 troops; when it ended, there were more than 38,000 regulars. The 10th Regiment contained the most North Carolinians, although men from the state served in the 12th, 13th, 15th, and 43rd Regiments as well as the 2nd U.S. Artillery and other units.

The U.S. military planned to invade British Canada, defend the coast against British incursions, and protect the frontier from Indian attacks. America suffered a great setback when Gen. William Hull surrendered Detroit, with 2,000 U.S. troops, to the British on 16 Aug. 1812. His defeat inspired stronger support for the war effort in North Carolina. In Mecklenburg County, 100 men who were past militia age, including many Revolutionary War veterans, drilled at a militia muster and pledged, if it became necessary, to fight the British a second time.

After Hull's disaster, Americans were heartened by news of the brilliant exploits of the U.S. Rifle Regiment and one of its officers, Capt. Benjamin Forsyth of North Carolina. Forsyth led his men on scouting missions, skirmishes, swift raids, and assaults in larger army operations, such as the capture of York, Ontario (modern Toronto), on 26 Apr. 1813, and rose to the rank of lieutenant colonel. He was killed in battle at Odell Town, Canada, on 28 June 1814. Forsyth County is named in his honor.

Although U.S. forces suffered numerous defeats and disappointments on land, a string of victories at sea made many Americans into long-remembered heroes. Capt. Johnston Blakeley was an Irish immigrant who had for a time made North Carolina his home. His ship, the *Wasp*, won single-ship duels with the British warships *Reindeer* and *Avon* and captured several valuable merchant vessels. On a cruise in 1814, the *Wasp* disappeared without a trace. In consideration of Blakeley's service, his widow and daughter received generous pensions from the General Assembly.

American privateers captured or destroyed many British vessels during the war. The most famous was the *Snap Dragon*, whose captain was Otway Burns of Swansboro. On his first voyage in 1812–13, Burns seized eight vessels; on his second voyage in 1813, the *Snap Dragon* returned so full of loot that the crew was forced to sleep on deck.

British naval vessels and privateers harassed coastal shipping throughout the war. As the federal government was unable to spare enough troops or ships to protect the North Carolina coast, the state militia assumed most of the burden for its defense. The British sent landing parties ashore at several places. In November 1813 three barges of armed men from the British privateer *Mars* captured several American vessels anchored at New Inlet. The British were foiled by the local militia, which managed to capture one barge and drive off the others. In another large raid in October 1814, this time against Currituck Inlet, the British captured three ships and burned three more but left as the local militia arrived.

In the most serious attack against North Carolina during the war, Ocracoke and Portsmouth were captured for a few days in July 1813. A British fleet, consisting of a large warship and assorted smaller craft (19 barges, according to one observer, each carrying 40 men) under Adm. Sir George Cockburn, reached Ocracoke about 9:00 P.M. on 11 July. In short order, the British seized the town of Portsmouth on the south side of the inlet, Ocracoke on the north side, and the maritime base known as Shell Castle in the middle. Although the British captured two privateers, the *Anaconda* and the *Atlas*, the revenue cutter *Mercury* outran the enemy ships, reaching New Bern in time to thwart any surprise strike on the mainland. News of the British invasion spread, and militia companies from as far away as Raleigh quickly marched to guard New Bern and other coastal towns.

The British remained at Ocracoke and Portsmouth, looting and vandalizing homes and rounding up provisions and livestock, until 16 July, sailing before the militia could reach Ocracoke. The commander warned that the entire North Carolina coast was under blockade, but there is no indication that the fleet ever returned to enforce it. Governor Hawkins later requested, but failed to receive, federal help in building and manning forts to protect the state from another British invasion.

As the war dragged on, more North Carolina militiamen were called into service. In early 1814 about 1,000 men from the western counties, under the command of Col. Jesse A. Pearson, marched from Salisbury to take part in fighting against the Creek Indians in Georgia and Alabama, but they arrived too late for more than garrison duty and some punitive raids. After the British burned Washington, D.C., on the night of 23–24 August, the federal government called up another 7,000 North Carolina militiamen. Two North Carolina regiments were sent to Norfolk, which was feared to be the target of an enemy attack. The North Carolinians witnessed a British naval bombardment but did not take part in any fighting; kept in readiness until the end of the war, they lost many men from disease. Other militia companies were sent to protect New Bern and Wilmington.

The War of 1812 came to an abrupt end when the Treaty of Ghent was signed on 24 Dec. 1814. Orders had been issued for another regiment of North Carolina detached militia to rendezvous at Wadesboro, travel to the Mississippi Territory, and join forces under Gen. Andrew Jackson. The general smashed a British army at the Battle of New Orleans on 8 Jan. 1815 before news of the treaty reached America, and the Wadesboro rendezvous was canceled.

Despite the humiliating disasters, bad luck, and poor leadership that beset some of the American forces, most North Carolinians supported the War of 1812. Approximately 1,200 residents volunteered for the regular army. Federal records indicate that 18 North Carolina soldiers were killed in action, and many more died from disease. The war had few direct lasting effects on the state, which was far from most of the fighting, as militia units were rarely sent outside of their own boundaries. Indirectly, however, ending the threat of Indian wars and foreign intervention in the trans-Appalachian South paved the way for increased out-migration from North Carolina as dissatisfied citizens sought better opportunities in the west.

References: William S. Dudley, ed., *The Naval War of 1812: A Documentary History*, vol. 1 (1985); Sarah McCulloh Lemmon, "Dissent in North Carolina during the War of 1812," *NCHR* 49 (April 1972); Lemmon, *North Carolina and the War of 1812* (2000).

David A. Norris
Additional research provided by David Stick.

SEE ALSO *Snap Dragon*; *Wasp*.

Warren County, formed in 1779 from no-longer-extant Bute County, is located along the Virginia–North Carolina line in the northeastern Piedmont. It was an early center of the state's tobacco- and cotton-growing plantation economy and the birthplace of many of its early political leaders. The county seat, Warrenton, was established in the same year as the county, and both are named for Joseph Warren, revolutionary Patriot and physician killed in the Battle of Bunker Hill. The town of Macon, incorporated in 1889, was named for Nathaniel Macon (1757–1837), who called the county home and served as Speaker of the U.S. House of Representatives and as a U.S. senator. Other Warren County communities include Arcola, Elberon, Inez, Liberia, Manson, Norlina, Ridgeway, Vaughn, and Wise; the town of Littleton is partly in the county and partly in Halifax County to the east.

The lands that became Warren County were home to significant populations of Tuscarora, Haliwa, and Saponi Indians. Inland migration by English settlers placed these Indian groups under increasing pressure in the first decades of the eighteenth century. The modern-day Haliwa-Saponi tribe, linked to the Indian people who remained in the area, was formally recognized by the state in 1979, with Warren County as part of its home territory. Warren County's plantations were among the most prosperous in North Carolina. The county was also home to one of the largest free black populations in antebellum North Carolina.

After the Civil War, the county's agricultural economy failed to recover, but its black landholders and a new population of freedmen made the county an important if short-lived cradle of black political clout during Reconstruction. John Hyman, the first African American to represent North Carolina in the U.S. Congress, hailed from the county. Whites and blacks in Warren County and other surrounding "Black Belt" counties endured economic misfortunes as the state's northeastern counties failed to enjoy the industrial growth seen elsewhere in the state. After World War II, the region's blacks began to find their voices, and many of them played important roles in the local and statewide movements for civil rights. One of the most prominent was Littleton native Ella Baker, a key figure in the founding of the Student Nonviolent Coordinating Committee. In the 1970s civil rights leader Floyd B. McKissick worked to build a new town in Warren County called Soul City, a community meant to foster and celebrate the aspirations of African Americans but one that failed to meet expectations.

In the early 2000s Warren County remained largely rural, with an economy primarily based in agriculture and light industry. In warm-weather months, people from North Carolina and Virginia travel in significant numbers to Kerr Lake and Lake Gaston, two man-made lakes that are partially located in the county and offer opportunities for boating, swimming, fishing, and other outdoor activities. The area has also maintained a strong commitment to preserving its historic architecture from the early nineteenth century; Warrenton's historic district is listed on the National Register of Historic Places. The estimated population of Warren County was 20,000 in 2004.

Peter Bangma

SEE ALSO Haliwa Indians; Saponi Indians; Soul City.

Warren Junto was the nickname of a group of politicians, led by Nathaniel Macon and all having some connection to Warren County, who were instrumental in the growth of the Jeffersonian Republican Party in North Carolina during early statehood. As President Thomas Jefferson's chief lieutenant in North Carolina, Macon, with his group, contributed greatly to Jefferson's success in the state in the 1800 presidential election. The *Raleigh Register*, the party's official organ, also played a significant role.

References: Weldon N. Edwards, *Memoir of Nathaniel Macon of North Carolina* (1862); Delbert H. Gilpatrick, *Jeffersonian Democracy in North Carolina, 1789–1816* (1967).

Wiley J. Williams

Warrenton Female Academy was founded by Jacob Mordecai (1762–1838) in 1809 as a means of livelihood after his commodities brokerage was bankrupted by the Embargo of 1807. Over the years, he was assisted with the teaching by his son Solomon and his daughters Rachel, Julia, Caroline, Judith, and Ellen. The school gained immediate repute for its excellence and attracted the daughters of planters from all over North Carolina and southern Virginia. Students were to be taught the full range of subjects of any classical male academy as well as needlework, music, and dancing.

Having accumulated a modest fortune by 1818, Mordecai decided to retire from teaching and move to Virginia. He sold the building to his son-in-law Achilles Plunkett and two Philadelphians, Joseph Andrews and Thomas P. Jones, who con-

tinued the school. Plunkett shortly afterward withdrew to start his own school, but Warrenton Female Academy survived and maintained its strong reputation under various principals until the Civil War shut it down. The restored school building remained standing in the early 2000s.

References: Charles L. Coon, *North Carolina Schools and Academies, 1790–1840* (1915); Stanley L. Falk, "The Warrenton Female Academy," NCHR 35 (July 1958); Lizzie W. Montgomery, *Sketches of Old Warrenton* (1924).

Jean B. Anderson

Warren Wilson College, a Presbyterian institution located ten miles east of Asheville, traces its origins to the Asheville Farm School, a missionary endeavor that opened in 1894 with 25 students. From its inception, the school had "academics, work, and Christian service" as its major priorities. In 1924 the Asheville Farm School graduated its first high school class; in addition to pursuing their studies, students were mandated to work in order to pay their bills. (This tradition continues at Warren Wilson to the present day; matriculants engage in useful labor for at least 15 hours per week.)

In 1942 the Asheville Farm School combined with the Dorland-Bell School (Hot Springs) and Mossop School (Harriman, Tenn.) to become Warren Wilson Vocational Junior College and Associated Schools. This new name honored Warren H. Wilson (1867–1937), a prominent churchman who had served as secretary of the Town and Country Life Division of the National Board of the Presbyterian Church (U.S.A.). In 1946 the school added a "university preparatory" department, but each student was still committed to 20 hours of practical labor per week.

After World War II, Warren Wilson became more cosmopolitan in scope; during the 1950s, nearly one-quarter of the student body was international. Racial integration took place in 1952; 1961 graduate Nicholas Mugo, Warren Wilson's first African student, would later serve as Kenya's ambassador to Great Britain, Ethiopia, and the United Nations. The high school curriculum was discontinued in 1957, and in 1969 the college graduated its first four-year class. In 1971 Reuben Holden, a Yale alumnus, became Warren Wilson's president. During his tenure (1971–73) the college officially severed its ties with the Presbyterian Board of National Missions, although not with the Presbyterian Church. Under Holden's leadership, Warren Wilson implemented programs in Appalachian studies, environmental studies, and intercultural studies, as well as a master of fine arts in creative writing.

By the early 2000s Warren Wilson College had approximately 775 students served by 57 full-time faculty members. The school's Outdoor Leadership Program has marked a significant addition to its modern curriculum. In 1991 the Swannanoa Gathering, a series of summer workshops and other events exploring various folk arts, was founded. The gathering is held on the Warren Wilson campus each July and August.

References: Gary Govert, "Switched on Calvin," *Carolina Lifestyle* 6 (September 1982); Reuben A. Holden, *Warren Wilson College: A Centennial Portrait* (1994); Henry W. Jensen, *A History of Warren Wilson College* (1974).

James I. Martin Sr.

Washington, N.C., Attack on.

The September 1862 attack on Washington, N.C., marked the first major Confederate attempt to recapture eastern North Carolina towns taken by Union forces earlier in the Civil War. Before sunrise on 6 September, Maj. Stephen D. Pool and his roughly 700 men from the 1st North Carolina Artillery and the 8th, 17th, and 55th North Carolina Infantry launched a surprise attack on Washington. Pool's first column overwhelmed Union pickets on the west side of Washington and stormed through the town. During the fighting, the Union gunboat *Picket* exploded and sank. Pool's second column encountered stiffer resistance but was soon able to push through the Unionist defenders into town as well.

Col. Edward E. Potter commanded Washington's defending forces, which included the 1st North Carolina Union Volunteers. Union cavalry fanned out through the streets, but resistance proved too heavy. Potter withdrew his artillery and infantry to permit the Union gunboat *Louisiana* to open fire on the town. Its heavy guns turned the tide and the Confederates withdrew.

The Union lost 8 killed, 36 wounded, and 12 missing or captured as well as the *Picket* and 20 of its crew killed (including the captain) and 6 wounded. Confederate losses were at least 13 killed, 57 wounded, and about 20 captured.

References: John G. Barrett, *The Civil War in North Carolina* (1963); Walter Clark, ed., *Histories of the Several Regiments and Battalions from North Carolina in the Great War, 1861–1865*, vols. 1–3 (1901); Louis H. Manarin and Weymouth T. Jordan, eds., *North Carolina Troops, 1861–1865: A Roster*, vols. 6, 13 (1968, 2003).

Paul Branch

Washington, N.C., Siege of.

The Confederate siege of Union-occupied Washington, N.C., extended from 30 March to 16 April 1863. The primary goal was to capture the town, but if that was not possible, the secondary goal was to tie up the garrison and keep Union forces on the defensive. Earlier, Maj. Gen. John G. Foster, leading the Union Department of North Carolina, arrived at Washington to assume command of about 1,200 men, including the 1st North Carolina Union Volunteers. Three gunboats supported this force. Foster ordered reinforcements, but before they could arrive, the Confederacy's Maj. Gen. Daniel H. Hill approached the town on 30 March with about 5,000 troops. Since the element of surprise was lost and a direct assault had little chance of success, Hill besieged the town while his supply wagons gathered provisions from the region. The Confederates erected an earthwork battery, Fort Hill, six miles below Washington at Hill's Point, and its guns prevented Union transports from reaching Washington with reinforcements. Foster and his small garrison were surrounded.

The siege involved several engagements—mostly exchanges between Confederate batteries and Union gunboats and town defenses. On the night of 13 April, however, the Union steamer *Escort* succeeded in running the blockade to Washington carrying supplies, ammunition, and reinforcements. As a result, during 15–16 April Hill abandoned the siege and withdrew his forces. Although he failed to capture Washington, Hill did manage to throw the Union forces on the defensive and to gather large quantities of food from Union-held areas.

References: John G. Barrett, *The Civil War in North Carolina* (1963); Hal Bridges, *Lee's Maverick General: Daniel Harvey Hill* (1991); Douglas S. Freeman, *Lee's Lieutenants: A Study in Command*, vol. 2 (1946).

Paul Branch

Washington, Statues of.

The only statues of first U.S. president George Washington in North Carolina are two located at the State Capitol in Raleigh. The movement to place a statue of Washington in the state began in 1815. With the state in a patriotic fervor following the War of 1812, the General Assembly unanimously adopted a resolution instructing Governor William Miller "to purchase on behalf of this State a full length statue of General Washington."

Nathaniel Macon, a North Carolina congressman from Warren County, sent letters of inquiry searching for a sculptor. Thomas Jefferson recommended well-known Italian sculptor Antonio Canova to do the work. The amount of $10,000 was appropriated during the following session of the General Assembly, and Canova was then commissioned to sculpt the statue. Canova depicted Washington as a Roman soldier, complete with tunic, sandals, and sword. Despite what was certainly by North Carolina standards of the day an unorthodox depiction of the "father of the country," the statue, carved of carrara marble, was well received and considered a great work of art. It arrived in 1821 and was installed in the statehouse, which was remodeled to provide a fitting showcase for the work. It occupied that place of honor until June 1831, when the statehouse burned, severely damaging the statue.

This event led to the state's purchase of a copy of Jean Antoine Houdon's 1788 life-size marble statue of Washington cast by Richmond founder William J. Hubard. This second statue of Washington depicted him in his traditional revolu-

Schoolchildren view Canova's statue of George Washington, 1972. Courtesy of NCOA&H.

tionary uniform as he appeared in 1785 at the age of 54, prior to his election as president. Many North Carolinians were not pleased with this statue, as they expected it to portray Washington as he appeared in his final days. Dedication ceremonies for the statue were scheduled for 4 July 1857 at the capitol, although the statue barely arrived on time. The dedication ceremonies began at 5:00 P.M. that day, with a procession led by the Oak City Guard that began at the south end of Fayetteville Street.

In 1910 the Italian government presented the state with a plaster replica of the Canova statue, and interest was renewed in acquiring a marble one. The General Assembly established a commission in 1923 to arrange for reproduction of the work, but the advent of the Great Depression once again dashed hopes for its replacement. Finally, in 1963, a new commission was appointed that succeeded in contracting with Italian artist Romano Vio to recarve the work using Canova's original model. The "duplicate original" arrived in Raleigh in 1970 and was installed on the same spot in the capitol rotunda designated for it 130 years earlier.

Howard Draper

Washington County, located in the Coastal Plain region of North Carolina, was formed in 1799 from Tyrrell County and named for President George Washington. It is partially bordered by the Albemarle Sound. Early inhabitants of the area included Algonquian Indians, followed by English settlers. Plymouth, the county seat, was incorporated in 1807 and named for Plymouth, Mass. Other Washington County communities include Roper, Creswell, Cherry, Scuppernong, Pleasant Grove, Westover, Hinson, and Wenona. Besides Albemarle Sound, notable bodies of water in the county include the Roanoke and Scuppernong Rivers, Phelps and Pungo Lakes, Beaver Dam and Kendrick Creeks, and East Dismal Swamp. The Pocosin

Lakes National Wildlife Refuge is located in the southeastern corner of the county.

Washington County historic sites include Garrett's Island Home, built in the mid-eighteenth century; Westover Plantation and Homestead Farm, both built in the mid-nineteenth century; and Somerset Place, built in the late eighteenth century and today a North Carolina State Historic Site. As a consequence of the Battle of Plymouth (1864), Confederate forces recaptured the town and reopened the Roanoke River. Cultural attractions include the Port O' Plymouth Roanoke River Museum and the Washington County Arts Council. The county hosts festivals and annual events such as Riverfest, Civil War Living History Weekend, Somerset Homecoming, Indian Heritage Week, and Plymouth Farm-City Festival.

Washington County agricultural products include corn, soybeans, peanuts, tobacco, cotton, cabbage, sage, beans, potatoes, hogs, and poultry. Manufactured products include wood pulp, paper, plywood, lumber, pallets, clothing, rope, and processed peanuts. Washington County's estimated population was 13,500 in 2004.

Jay Mazzocchi

SEE ALSO Plymouth, Battle of; Somerset Place.

Washington Monument in Washington, D.C., contains a block of North Carolina white marble five feet long and three feet high bearing a sculptured bas-relief of the state seal and the inscription "North Carolina Declaration of Independence, May 1775." It was presented to the Washington National Monument Society on 22 Feb. 1853 with a suitable address by Congressman David S. Reid "in the presence of a numerous and distinguished company" gathered at the site. All 50 states, as well as many cities and patriotic organizations, have donated such memorial stones, which are located in the monument's interior.

William S. Powell

Washington's Southern Tour, which began on 9 Apr. 1791, was a journey that George Washington had been contemplating since before his inauguration as president of the United States. In May 1789 he decided to visit every state in the country "in order to become better acquainted with their principal characters and internal circumstances." He began traveling shortly after taking office. He had been to all the northeastern states by the end of August 1790 but had delayed a trip to the southern states largely because one of them—North Carolina—had yet to ratify the U.S. Constitution. Once that was accomplished, on 13 Nov. 1790, he started making plans to journey to the South.

With a carefully devised "line of march" and accompanied only by his senior secretary, Maj. William Jackson, and a handful of servants, Washington left Mount Vernon to investigate conditions in three states he had never seen: North Carolina, South Carolina, and Georgia. He traveled in a lightweight carriage; a wagon, the only other vehicle in his simple entourage, followed with his luggage.

By 16 Apr. 1791 Washington had passed through Virginia and reached Halifax, N.C. He found the town less than impressive: "It seems to be in a decline & does not it is said contain a thousand souls." From Halifax he made his way to Tarboro, where he encountered a humble but sincere welcome. On 19 April he "dined at a trifling place called Greenville" and then headed off in the direction of New Bern accompanied, much to his regret, by the Pitt Light Horse. (Of all the endless annoyances Washington encountered while traveling, he found none to be a greater nuisance than breathing the dust of other men's horses.)

Everything about Washington's stay in New Bern seemed to delight him, including his "exceedingly good lodgings" in the home of John G. Stanly, the entertainments at the Tryon Palace, and the beautiful women with whom the town apparently was amply endowed. His only complaint, certainly a minor one, involved the failure of his hosts to offer him griddle cakes during his stay.

Washington had nothing positive to say about the accommodations or the countryside between New Bern and Wilmington, but he found his reception in Wilmington, where he spent two days, nearly equal to what he had experienced in New Bern. He left Wilmington on 26 April, destined for South Carolina and Georgia.

After stops in Charleston, Savannah, Augusta, Columbia, and Camden, Washington returned to North Carolina on 27 May. Thirteen members of the Salisbury Military Company rode with him to Charlotte, which, like Greenville, he found to be a "trifling place," although he did enjoy dinner at the home of Gen. Thomas Polk. Congressman John Steele, who would later become a part of his administration, joined Washington in Charlotte and accompanied him to Salisbury. His impressions of Salisbury and Salem were favorable.

Governor Alexander Martin met Washington in Salem. The president was eager to learn what North Carolinians thought about their new ties to the federal government. Martin assured him that opposition to ratification was fast dissipating, that North Carolina officials would soon be taking oaths to uphold the Constitution, and that the state had no sympathy with land companies that attempted to usurp lands the federal government recognized as belonging to Native Americans. That was all good news. The next day, 1 June, Washington and Martin surveyed the location at Guilford Courthouse where Americans under Nathanael Greene and Englishmen commanded by Lord Charles Cornwallis had fought just a short decade before.

The battlefield visit really marked the end of Washington's southern tour. The rest of his trip was largely a matter of returning home, and by 12 June he was back at Mount Vernon.

References: John C. Fitzpatrick, ed., *The Diaries of George Washington* (4 vols., 1925); Douglas Southall Freeman, *George Washington: A Biography* (6 vols., 1948–1954); Archibald Henderson, *Washington's Southern Tour, 1791* (1923).

Thomas J. Farnham

Wasp was a privateer commanded by Capt. Johnston Blakeley during the War of 1812. The sloop was still under construction at Newburyport, Mass., when Blakeley received his appointment on 13 Aug. 1813. He hired a crew of 173 and supervised the completion of the ship, which carried 20 carronades and 2 long 12-pounder guns. The *Wasp* sailed on 1 May 1814 with orders to inflict damage on British shipping on the coast of western Europe and then to conduct a naval campaign against English allies along the Spanish coast, afterward returning to New Orleans. Blakeley's orders were to destroy any captured prizes rather than reduce his crew by returning them to American ports and under no circumstances to engage a British naval fighting ship.

From 1 May to 6 July the *Wasp* destroyed six commercial vessels. One, the *Reindeer*, put up a spirited fight and severely damaged the foremast, rigging, and sail of the *Wasp*. Blakeley limped his wounded ship to the port at L'Orient, France, to rest his men and repair his vessel. On 27 August the *Wasp* departed for the Spanish coast on the second leg of its mission. Soon Blakeley spotted a convoy of ten merchant ships under the protection of a British 74-gun frigate. With expert seamanship he cut one, the *Mary*, from the line, took his prize, and burned the vessel before the frigate could maneuver into attack position. Blakeley withdrew the *Wasp* to safer waters, but later that afternoon, another brig in the convoy fell well behind the main line. Blakeley engaged the *Avon* in a 47-minute battle and secured its surrender. But several members of the convoy returned before his crew could board, and the *Wasp* retreated under cover of advancing darkness.

Three weeks later Blakeley and the *Wasp* captured three more prizes: the *Three Brothers*, the *Bacchus*, and the *Atalanta*. As neither a flag nor official papers clearly established the *Atalanta*'s nationality and the captain had no wish to destroy a non-British allied vessel, he sent the brig, commanded by a prize crew of his own men, to Savannah, Ga., where it arrived on 14 Nov. 1814. Last seen by the Swedish vessel *Adonis* on 9 Oct. 1914, the *Wasp*, with captain and crew, mysteriously disappeared.

References: K. P. Battle, "A North Carolina Naval Hero and His Daughter," *North Carolina Booklet* 4 (1901); Sarah McCulloh Lemmon, *North Carolina and the War of 1812* (2000).

Jerry L. Cross

SEE ALSO Blakeley Silver Service.

Watauga Club. Organized on 26 May 1884 in Raleigh, the Watauga Club sprang out of the desire of a group of young, professional North Carolinians to look toward the future rather than remain transfixed by the losses of the past. The club, while avoiding partisan politics, attracted a youthful membership intensely interested in the economic and social betterment of North Carolina. Under the guidance of a young attorney, William Joseph Peele, and aided by several young men destined to rise to positions of leadership—among them Walter Hines Page and Josephus Daniels—the club pushed for the establishment of an industrial school in North Carolina. Col. Leonidas L. Polk, editor of the *Progressive Farmer*, took up the club's campaign, and in 1887 the North Carolina College of Agriculture and Mechanic Arts (now North Carolina State University) was chartered.

Because of member criticism of what Page called "the mummies," the established leadership of the state, many looked with skepticism on the progressive ideas of the Watauga Club. At its largely unpublicized dinner meetings, the club's membership called for improved roads and schools, modern agricultural methods, and farmers' institutes. In the words of one early member, the Watauga Club was always on the look out for any chance to extend "the opportunities of the common man."

After an energetic start, the club drifted into inactivity in the 1890s, but it became active again toward the end of the century in promoting a textile department for the new college. As its membership gradually aged, the Watauga Club lost some of its youthful energies and was quiescent until it was re-energized during the 1920s under the leadership of Clarence Poe, who had succeeded Polk as editor and publisher of the *Progressive Farmer*. Poe remained the club's president from 1925 through 1955, during which time the group regularly invited incoming governors and other important state leaders into its membership.

During modern times, the Watauga Club has maintained a regular membership of some two dozen professional, academic, and business leaders from Raleigh and surrounding cities. North Carolina State University has memorialized the club by establishing the Watauga Medal for leadership and also by naming several campus buildings for the club and several of its members, including Page, Daniels, Peele, and Poe.

References: Jeri Gray, *A Century of the Watauga Club and Its Role in State History* (1984); Richard Walser, *The Watauga Club* (1980).

William D. Snider

SEE ALSO "Mummy Letters."

Watauga County, located in the Mountain region of North Carolina, was formed in 1849 from Ashe, Wilkes, Caldwell, and Yancey Counties and named after the Watauga River ("Watauga" is an Indian word meaning "beautiful river"). It is situated along the Tennessee–North Carolina border. Early inhabitants of the area included the Cherokee Indians, followed by Scotch-Irish, German, Dutch, Swedish, and French settlers. Boone, the county seat, was incorporated in 1871 and named for Daniel Boone, who camped in the area during hunting season. Appalachian State University was established in 1899 in Boone; it is now one of the 16 member schools of the consolidated University of North Carolina. Other Watauga County communities include Seven Devils, Beech Mountain, Valle Crucis, Sugar Grove, Deep Gap, and Sherwood. Notable physical features of the county include the Watauga River, the South Fork of the New River, State Line Ridge, Dugger Mountain, Hanging Rock Ridge, and Egg Knob. Blowing Rock, a massive cliff adjacent to the John's River Gorge, attracts thousands of visitors annually.

Watauga County's location in the Blue Ridge Mountains has led to tourism's becoming its principal industry; visitors can enjoy skiing, horseback riding, golf, whitewater rafting, hiking, caving, snowboarding, mountain biking, and rock climbing at numerous locations throughout the county. The county's cultural attractions, many celebrating its mountain heritage, include the outdoor drama *Horn in the West*, telling the story of Daniel Boone and the Revolutionary War in western North Carolina; the Appalachian Cultural Museum; the Appalachian Heritage Museum; the Grandfather Mountain Nature Museum; the Hickory Ridge Homestead Museum; and the Blowing Rock Stage Company. Tweetsie Railroad, the oldest theme park in North Carolina, features a historic narrow-gauge steam locomotive and numerous western-themed rides. The county hosts annual events and festivals such as the Firefly Festival, the Scottish Highland Games, Valle Country Fair, International Festival, Wilderness Bike Ride, and Gospel Singing Jubilee.

Watauga County produces agricultural goods such as tobacco, horticultural crops, beef cattle, and poultry. Manufactured products include saw blades and other tools, electronic components, woven goods, wood products, crushed stone, furniture, and textiles. Copper and calcite are mined in the county. In 2004 Watauga County had an estimated population of 42,800.

Jay Mazzocchi

SEE ALSO Appalachian State University; Tweetsie Railroad.

Watauga Settlement was the first community established in North Carolina's western frontier and holds the distinction of being perhaps the first American settlement west of the Appalachian Mountains. In the mid-1700s a mixture of English, Highland Scot, and Scotch-Irish pioneers came to the Watauga River Valley, bringing with them a strong sense of self-reliance and a fierce desire for self-government. In fact, these hardy settlers temporarily established one of the first self-governing political bodies to emerge in the American colonies. The settlers' energetic ability to defend their territory helped maintain the integrity of North Carolina's western border during the revolutionary period and advanced the cause of European settlement in the mountainous regions.

An enterprising Virginian named William Bean was the first recorded traveler to the Watauga area. Others followed his lead, among them Daniel Boone, who reputedly killed a bear in the vicinity. Political unrest in the Piedmont, including the Regulator Movement, brought an infusion of immigrants to the mountains. The nature of this migration led British colonial authorities to issue royal edicts forbidding settlement of the western lands by "absconded debtors, indentured servants, and outlaws," or "overmountain people," as they were generally called. Bean and James Robertson, who had come from Orange County in 1770, were not to be undone, however, and shrewdly began negotiations with the local Cherokee tribes to lease the land they had settled. Thus, in 1772 was born the Watauga Association, an independent political entity that constructed its own laws and enforced them by its own court system. Many historians have hailed this as a milestone event in American history, representing a pioneering effort at establishing self-government.

Western settlement increased as the Cherokee's influence waned after their defeat in Lord Dunmore's War and as eastern political turmoil, soon to crystallize into a revolutionary movement, drove more colonists to seek isolation in the mountain region. In 1775, Richard Henderson, with the assistance of Daniel Boone, negotiated a large land purchase from the Cherokee. Simultaneously, the Watauga settlers acquired from the Cherokee legal ownership of their area for the sum of two thousand pounds.

The outbreak of war between the colonists and England thrust new responsibilities on the mountain men. No longer able to avoid the conflict, they became the protectors of the new state of North Carolina and its western borders. To formalize their political status, the Wataugans created the Washington District (probably the first political entity to bear the name of the future president) and sought annexation by the state government. In 1776 British influence led the Cherokee into a futile effort to regain the vast mountainous lands. The tribe began to attack western settlements but achieved nothing beyond provoking a furious response by the westerners, aided by troops sent by four nearby states. This crushing defeat of the Cherokee set the stage for their ultimate removal several decades later.

Eminent Wataugans, such as John Sevier, who had played a key role in the Cherokee Campaign, soon turned their energies to the defeat of the British. In 1780 England again invaded the southern colonies in a last-ditch effort to win the war. Continental defeats earlier that year left only the Carolinas' irregu-

lar military forces to contest the British advance. As the westward wing of Lord Charles Cornwallis's army penetrated the mountainous areas, the Wataugans gathered together to meet the threat. The result was the Battle of King's Mountain (7 Oct. 1780), in which the British force was annihilated. Thus the Wataugans played a significant role in the failure of the British master plan of 1780 and the subsequent collapse of efforts to subdue the rebellious colonies.

After the Revolution, the independent nature of the Wataugans again became apparent as a group of them sought to create their own state of Franklin. In August 1784, at a convention held in Jonesborough, a state government was hastily constructed, with Sevier assuming the governor's seat. North Carolina, seeing most of its western lands usurped by the unruly mountain men, contested the existence of the fledgling state. Franklin's lack of recognition by the Confederation government sealed its fate, and by 1788 the state ceased to exist (its territory later became part of the state of Tennessee).

The legacy of the Watauga Settlement remains strong in western North Carolina, where many people adamantly retain their clannish nature but tourism now largely fuels the economy. Western counties that once composed the settlement area now carry the names of early pioneers, such as Henderson and McDowell. The county of Watauga stands as a reminder of the region's heritage of being part of the first community west of the Appalachians.

References: John Preston Arthur, *A History of Watauga County, North Carolina* (1915); Arthur, *Western North Carolina: A History, 1730–1913* (1914); Max Dixon, *The Wataugans* (1976).

David L. Cockrell

SEE ALSO Franklin, State of; King's Mountain, Battle of; Overmountain Victory National Historic Trail.

Water Conservation. SEE Conservation Movement.

Waterfalls. The 75-mile-wide chain of the Blue Ridge Mountains of North Carolina contain some of the most spectacular waterfalls and cascades to be found anywhere in the continental United States. The Blue Ridge Mountains are a very old range, and geologists believe that about 250 million years ago this chain reached heights of over 15,000 feet. Across the vast march of time the jagged cliffs eroded to reveal the beautiful rolling peaks of about 6,000 feet that exist today. In the process, some of the state's most spectacular scenery can be found along its western rivers and streams.

Perhaps North Carolina's most famous waterfall is Linville Falls, located on the Linville River in Burke County. Linville Falls is a dramatic triple fall that consists of an initial drop of 15 feet, after which the flow disappears into a quartzite cliff. There, out of view, it cascades 60 feet before reappearing for a final 45-foot descent into a deep pool. The gorge formed by the

Whitewater Falls near Sapphire. Photograph copyright Keith Longiotti.

Brevard, another magnificent waterfall can be found on Looking Glass Creek, a tributary of the Davidson River. Looking Glass Falls is a sheer drop of about 60 feet. Because of its easy access (it can be viewed from the parking area), it is one of the most well-known waterfalls in North Carolina. At 411 feet, Whitewater Falls on the Whitewater River near Sapphire is by far the largest waterfall in the state, as well as the highest waterfall east of the Rocky Mountains. The Horsepasture River, also in the Sapphire-Cashiers area, boasts a gradient of over 2,000 feet in six miles, making it home to numerous waterfalls, including Drift Falls (30 feet), Turtleback Falls (20 feet), Rainbow Falls (200 feet), and Stairway Falls (a series of 10- to 12-foot falls).

References: Kevin Adams, *North Carolina Waterfalls: Where to Find Them, How to Photograph Them* (1994); Nicole Blouin, Steve Bordonaro, and Marilou Wier Bordonaro, *Waterfalls of the Blue Ridge* (1994); Brian Boyd, *Waterfalls of the Southern Appalachians* (1993).

Joseph Paul Hoffman

Waterfowl. Ducks, geese, swans, and other waterfowl have played a prominent role in the lives of many North Carolinians, especially those living in the vicinity of the coastal sounds. These birds all breed in the far northwestern part of the North American continent, some as far north as 1,000 miles above Hudson Bay. In the fall they head south for the winter, following four established migratory routes: the Pacific, Central, Mississippi, and Atlantic Flyways. Those terminating their flight in North Carolina use the Atlantic Flyway, which crosses the Great Lakes and continues the southern trek from Pennsylvania to Delaware, Maryland, and Virginia before reaching North Carolina. Beginning in 1934, the federal government acquired Lake Mattamuskeet in Hyde County and transformed it into a 50,000-acre National Wildfowl Refuge, then added the 43,000-acre Swanquarter Refuge and the 398,000-acre Pea Island Refuge. All three are managed by the Fish and Wildlife Service, which carries on programs for growing appropriate feeds for the different types of birds and controlling hunting activity.

Ducks and other waterfowl are of the family Anatidae, characterized by having a broad, flat bill, short legs, and webbed feet. Geese also belong to the Anatidae family and are often included in the general duck category, though they are easily distinguished by having a shorter and more pointed bill than the much smaller ducks and a shorter neck than the larger swan. Herons, long-legged wading birds; bitterns; and egrets are members of the Ardeidae family. They generally inhabit marshlands, mudflats, and lake edges, and 12 of the 60 species known worldwide are present in North Carolina.

Early visitors to North Carolina commented on the tremendous number of wildfowl they saw. Currituck Sound was

river is nearly 1,500 feet high, and the river drops away from the falls another 2,000 feet over the next 12 miles.

Another dramatic waterfall in the Linville area is Elk Falls on the Elk River in Avery County. Although the Elk boasts numerous waterfalls, Elk Falls is the most spectacular. Dropping abruptly 85 feet, the Elk River plunges into a pool of unknown depth. Divers have never reached the bottom, and several legends mention Confederate silver being hidden somewhere in the pool.

Numerous waterfalls may be found in the Nantahala National Forest in Jackson, Macon, and Transylvania Counties. One of the most spectacular is Lower Cullasaja Falls on the Cullasaja River in Macon. With a thundering descent of about 250 feet, this waterfall is one of the highest in the state. Several other dramatic falls can be viewed along the way to Lower Cullasaja Falls. Just beyond the Sequoyah Lake Dam are the Kalakaleskies Falls, a series of cascades ranging from 3 to 45 feet. These falls are fairly accessible, and all may be seen within a quarter of a mile from the parking area below the dam. Another waterfall along the way is Bridal Veil Falls, a series of several drops ranging from 30 to 80 feet. These falls derive their name from a Cherokee legend claiming that if a maiden walked behind the cascading water, she would be married by winter.

In the Pisgah National Forest of Transylvania County near

noted especially for the quantity and variety of ducks wintering there, while Pamlico Sound was noted for its Canada geese and brant, though ducks were in abundance there as well. Before recreational hunters discovered Currituck and Pamlico, local market gunners supplied large quantities of waterfowl for table fare in the north. The canvasback duck, which tended to raft far out on the open sounds, was considered one of the premier delicacies. Redheads also remained far out on the reefs, while mallards and black ducks were the easiest to kill because they tended to feed near shore.

Three kinds of geese populate North Carolina sounds and lakes in winter, the most common being the Canada goose, which is often seen year-round in the state. The others are brant, a smaller variety of goose having a black neck and head, and the snow goose, which is recognizable by its white plumage and black-tipped wings. While disease and a shortage of feeding areas have combined to cause a decrease in the brant population so severe that these birds are seldom encountered now, the numbers of snow geese wintering at Pea Island in the Cape Hatteras National Seashore and elsewhere seem to have been maintained.

Records of herons in North Carolina date back to the state's early history, with mentions in works such as Thomas Harriot's *A Briefe and True Report of the New Found Land of Virginia* (1588). John Lawson, in *A New Voyage to Carolina* (1709), mentions the gray heron, the abundant, slow-flying white heron, and three types of bittern. Common permanent residents of the state include the great blue heron, the largest heron in America; the little blue heron, listed as a species of special concern in the state; the tricolored heron, also a species of special concern; the yellow-crowned night heron; the black-crowned night heron; the great egret; and the snowy egret, another species of special concern. The cattle egret, an African native, reached North Carolina by 1956 and along with the green heron is now a common summer resident.

The state's egret population did not escape the whims of late nineteenth-century fashion. A vogue for the plumes of the great egret and the snowy egret, used to adorn women's hats, led to such a massive killing of these birds that they were nearly exterminated. In the early twentieth century, laws were passed to protect the egret, and the North Carolina population has risen through the decades. Although some species have had dips in numbers at various times, the general egret, heron, and bittern populations remain stable in North Carolina.

As duck and goose hunting gained in popularity on the North Carolina sounds, the most experienced of those engaging in the sport learned to make use of different hunting methods in different locations. Among the most productive were the coffin-like batteries used by hunters who seemed to thrive on discomfort, though the batteries were subsequently banned, as was the use of live decoys. Elevated stake blinds, built in the summers to accustom the fowl to their presence by the beginning of hunting season, covered mile after mile of sand reefs in Pamlico Sound. The use of brush blinds or boxes along the shore was especially prevalent in Currituck Sound.

Visiting hunters had to find someplace to stay, and by the latter part of the nineteenth century, affluent sportsmen began buying up large tracts of land, often extending from sound to ocean, and forming hunting clubs—complete with clubhouses and quarters for the caretakers and their families as well as boats, decoys, and private ponds. As their numbers increased, the clubs began to fit into size-related categories, ranging from corporation and partnership clubs, each with 10 to 20 members, to single-ownership clubs. Relatively few of these clubs have survived, however, a result of the decrease in the population of fowl, increasing restrictions on the number and type of birds that can be killed, and the intrusion of developers who have bought up many of the club properties and turned them into resort facilities.

References: William Neal Conoley Jr., *Waterfowl Heritage: North Carolina Decoys and Gunning Lore* (1982); James Hancock and James Kushlan, *The Herons Handbook* (1984); Eloise F. Potter, James E. Parnell, and Robert P. Teulings, *Birds of the Carolinas* (1980).

David Stick
Margaret Foote

SEE ALSO Decoys.

Waterwheels harnessed the volume, force, and gravity of various bodies of water in North Carolina to provide the leading source of natural, inanimate power before the advent of the steam engine and industrialization. The effectiveness of waterwheels in supplying power to grain, flour, and oil mills lay in their engineering simplicity and adaptability to the task at hand. Three different types of vertical wheels—overshot, undershot, and breastshot—utilized various properties of flowing water, which meant that virtually any moving body of water could power a wheel and, consequently, machinery. Although a single waterwheel actually only powered one turning shaft, gears and cams magnified those revolutions into power for numerous purposes. While waterwheels are usually associated with flour and grain milling, North Carolina had water-powered mills that produced woolen cloth, bore rifle barrels, and pounded rags into paper.

When Oliver Evans developed and patented the first wholly automated water-powered flour mill, Moravians purchased one of the first (and only) licenses for the system. The engineering concepts involved in such an operation were basically general knowledge and no one wanted to pay for them. This helps explain why waterwheels continued to be a popular source of power in North Carolina (especially in undeveloped, rural areas) well into the twentieth century and why few records other than licenses to operate them exist to document their history.

References: Johanna Miller Lewis, "The Salem Congregational Mill," in Frances Griffin, ed., *Three Forks of Muddy Creek*, vol. 13 (1988); Johanna Carlson Miller, "Mills on the Wachovia Tract, 1756–1849" (M.A. thesis, Wake Forest University, 1985).

Johanna Miller Lewis

Wayne County, located in the Coastal Plain region of North Carolina, was formed in 1779 from Dobbs County and named for Revolutionary War general "Mad Anthony" Wayne. Early inhabitants of the area included the Saponi and Tuscarora Indians; English and Scotch-Irish settlers later populated the region. Goldsboro—named for Maj. Mathew Tilghman Goldsborough, assistant engineer on the Wilmington & Weldon Railroad, which passed through Wayne County—was incorporated in 1847 and replaced Waynesboro as the county seat in 1850. Other Wayne County communities include Mount Olive, Walnut Creek, Seven Springs, Eureka, Pikeville, Dobbersville, and Dudley. Notable physical features of the county are the Neuse River, Quaker Neck Lake, Burden and Kelley Creeks, Sasser Millpond, Juniper and Thoroughfare Swamps, and Exum Mill Run.

Seymour Johnson Air Force Base was established on the outskirts of Goldsboro in 1942 and has exerted a great influence on the city and its environs. Wayne County historic sites include the Weil House (1875), Paramount Theatre (1868), Goldsboro City Hall (1910), and the Governor Charles B. Aycock Birthplace, a mid-nineteenth-century homestead and 1893 schoolhouse. Cultural institutions include the Paramount Center for the Performing Arts, the Community Arts Council, the Stagestruck Theatre Company, the Goldsboro Civic Ballet, and the Wayne County Museum. Mount Olive College was founded in the county in 1951. The county hosts annual events and festivals such as the Wayne Regional Agricultural Fair, North Carolina Pickle Festival at Mount Olive (home of a leading pickle-producing company, which shares the town's name), and Fremont Daffodil Festival.

Wayne County agricultural products include cucumbers, soybeans, tobacco, corn, wheat, vegetables, cotton, poultry, and swine. Manufactured products include pickles and relishes, furniture, apparel, commercial baking equipment, and electric transformers. The estimated population of Wayne County was 115,000 in 2004.

Jay Mazzocchi

SEE ALSO Charles B. Aycock Birthplace; Seymour Johnson Air Force Base.

W. Duke, Sons and Company. Washington Duke returned to his small farm in what was then Orange County as a penniless Confederate veteran in the early summer of 1865. Aided by his three children still at home—Mary E., Benjamin N., and James B. Duke—the hard-working farmer soon hit on the idea of the home manufacture of smoking tobacco, which he peddled from a wagon in the populous eastern portion of the state.

In 1874 Washington Duke decided to abandon farming altogether and to follow his oldest son, Brodie L. Duke, to the fast-growing new town of Durham. There the Dukes joined a number of other small tobacco manufacturers who hoped to grow rich in the business. An important development came in 1878 when, for $14,000, young George W. Watts of Baltimore purchased a one-fifth interest in the newly formed W. Duke, Sons and Company.

All of the small tobacco businesses were overshadowed by the W. T. Blackwell Company with its famous Bull Durham brand of smoking tobacco. Despairing of ever catching up to, much less overtaking, the Blackwell company, the youngest of the Dukes, James, persuaded his father and other partners to gamble on machine-made cigarettes, even though the established cigarette producers in Richmond, Va., and elsewhere believed that smokers much preferred the custom-made, hand-rolled product. The Duke firm, nevertheless, negotiated a secret contract with the company that controlled the cigarette-producing machine invented by and named after Virginian James A. Bonsack.

Beginning in 1885, the Duke firm's gamble on the machine paid off handsomely, and within five years W. Duke, Sons and Company, had become the largest cigarette manufacturer in the nation. Partly through limiting access to the Bonsack machine, James B. Duke joined with four other leading cigarette manufacturers to form the American Tobacco Company in 1890, and the 33-year-old became president of the "trust." After that date, W. Duke, Sons and Company, gradually lost its separate identity. In the twentieth century a large Liggett and Myers plant would stand approximately where the first Duke factory in Durham had been, and some of the old brick warehouses would find new lives as condominiums and a fashionable shopping mall.

Reference: Robert F. Durden, *The Dukes of Durham, 1865–1929* (1975).

Robert F. Durden

Weapemeoc Indians, also known as the Yeopim Indians, were a branch of Algonquian-speaking peoples living in sprawling villages along the northern rim of the Albemarle Sound when the Roanoke Island colonists arrived in the 1580s. The subtribes of the Weapemeoc included the Pasquotank, Perquimans, and Poteskeet. They were partly agricultural and raised several varieties of beans (pulse), melons, and gourds, as well as corn, squash, and other vegetables. They were also food-gatherers, hunting turkeys and deer. During the summer months, fish, shellfish, raspberries, strawberries, walnuts, hickory nuts, and acorns supplemented their diet. Severe outbreaks of epidemic diseases during the seventeenth century seem to have devastated the Weapemeocs, who are believed to have had 700 to 800 warriors in 1586, roughly the same in 1600, and only 200 by 1700. One of the Weapemeoc settlements to survive was within modern-day Perquimans County, the name of which was reportedly derived from the name of the Indians who lived there.

References: Maurice A. Mook, "Algonkian Ethnohistory of the Carolina Sound," *Journal of the Washington Academy of Sciences* 34 (15 June, 15 July 1944); Theda Perdue, *Native Carolinians: The Indians of North Carolina* (1985); Douglas L. Rights, *The American Indian in North Carolina* (2nd ed., 1957); Eugene Waddell, *Indians of the South Carolina Lowcountry, 1562–1751* (1980).

Michael D. Green

Weaver College, a coeducational Methodist institution, operated in the Buncombe County town of Weaverville from 1873 until 1934. Prior to the establishment of what was originally known as Weaverville College, an academy founded in 1851 by the local Sons of Temperance stood on the site chosen for the campus. Montraville Weaver contributed the land on which the first buildings were situated. Through gifts and purchases, the campus grew to 55 acres. Initially the college was governed by a local board of trustees independent of any denomination. The school's first president was James A. Regan. Only in 1883 was the property deeded to the Methodist Episcopal Church and the school placed under the supervision of the Western North Carolina Conference.

In 1912 the school was renamed Weaver College and changed from four-year to junior college status. Preparatory classes continued to be offered. Student activities revolved around literary societies and the sports programs. Graduates of Weaver include North Carolina chief justice Walter H. Stacy, Congressman Zeb Weaver, and University of North Carolina professor Hugh T. Lefler.

The Western North Carolina Conference decided in 1933 to merge Weaver and Rutherford Colleges to create a single coeducational Methodist junior college on the grounds of the old Brevard Institute. In the fall of 1934, 30 Weaver students and 5 faculty members moved to the new Brevard College. Brevard continues to preserve the earlier institution through the Weaver Room of the library and the Weaver College Bell Tower. In Weaverville two structures remain from the original campus: the 1874 administration building, now used as a Masonic temple, and a dormitory.

References: William S. Powell, *Higher Education in North Carolina* (1970); F. A. Sondley, *A History of Buncombe County, North Carolina* (1930); Douglas Swaim, ed., *Cabins and Castles: The History and Architecture of Buncombe County, North Carolina* (1981).

Michael Hill

A weaver works at a loom at Penland School of Crafts, 1930. Photograph by Bayard Wootten. NCC.

Weaving, the process of producing textiles on a loom, in North Carolina dates back to the colonial period of the state's history. From that time into the early nineteenth century, weaving functioned as a domestic or home industry in North Carolina, meaning that weavers owned their own looms on which to produce fabric necessary to make clothing, linens, and other accessories. But domestic weaving did not produce the majority of fabric used in North Carolina during this time; most was instead imported from Great Britain and Europe. Domestic production augmented the offering of imported fabrics and sometimes filled special orders.

With the advent of waterpower and steam power, weaving and other aspects of textile production were mechanized with spinning jennys and power looms. One of the first such mechanized mills in North Carolina, complete with mill "operatives" as the labor force, was owned and operated by the Fries brothers in Salem. In the twentieth century, companies such as Hanes, Cone, and Chatham dominated the national textile industry and provided employment for thousands of North Carolinians. Small-scale weavers continued to spin their wares in smaller communities and also as part of the folk arts movement that has continued to gain followers into the early 2000s.

Reference: Johanna Miller Lewis, *Artisans in the North Carolina Backcountry* (1995).

Johanna Miller Lewis

Weights and Measures. Among the responsibilities of the Church of England parishes in early North Carolina was the purchase and maintenance of a set of sealed weights and measures as the standards for each county. This requirement was different from the law in England, where weights and measures were the responsibility of the justices of the peace and their constables. In compliance with a law passed by the

A collection of weights and measures held at the Orange County Museum in Hillsborough. Photograph by Jerry Cotten.

colonial Assembly in 1702, the vestry of St. Paul's Parish in Chowan County by 1703 had ordered a set of weights and measures from Boston to be kept by Edward Smithwick, a church warden.

A statute of 1715 required the set of weights and measures to include "Five half hundreds, One Quarter of an Hundred, Four pounds Weight, Two pounds, One pound & two Half pound weights—A pair of Brass scales together with a Brass or Copper Yard and of measures an Half Bushel, Peck, Gallon, Pot, Pottle [half-gallon], Quart & pint." The "Eldest of the Church wardens . . . or other such person as shall be appointed by the vestry" was to keep the standards in his house. Anyone having weights, measures, or steelyards (a type of balance in which a weight was moved along an iron rod) not officially sealed in England was to take them to the warden to have them checked. Approved weights, measures, and steelyards were designated with the letters "N.C.," with the warden using a metal stamp, or a branding iron in the case of wooden measures (evidently the half bushel and peck containers).

Official weights and measures were considered an important protection for consumers. The colonial Assembly at various times passed laws to punish merchants and others who cheated buyers. The 1715 law fined offenders 20 shillings for each count of using weights, measures, or steelyards that were not officially stamped or sealed. In 1741 the law was changed so that the weights and measures would be provided by the justices of each county. The justices were to levy a tax to pay for them and appoint a Standard Keeper to take charge of them.

Laws protecting citizens from unscrupulous merchants continued to be energetically enforced throughout the nineteenth and twentieth centuries. A comprehensive clarification of these laws, the North Carolina Weights and Measures Act (Chapter 81-A of the North Carolina General Statutes),

was passed by the General Assembly in 1975. The act is primarily enforced by the Standards Division of the North Carolina Department of Agriculture and Consumer Services, which tests the accuracy of all weighing and measuring devices and price-scanning systems used in the state. Violators receive stiff monetary penalties, which are then used to the benefit of the North Carolina public school system.

David A. Norris

Welfare. SEE Poverty.

Well Sweep was an ingenuous device utilized to draw water from a well without ropes or pulleys. It appeared throughout North Carolina on nineteenth-century farms and plantations; both subsistence farmers and their wealthier neighbors used them. The only materials needed to construct a well sweep were wooden poles, which could be obtained locally. A vertical post was mounted by the well hole. The post held a horizontal pole, or sweep, which was heavier at one end and rested on the ground. A long, thin pole with an attached bucket or pail was placed at the other end. A person would pull the thin pole and bucket down into the well and fill it with water, and the sweep's weight would then lift the bucket up.

The well sweep came to be replaced by pulleys and cranks and eventually by mechanical pumps. Although photographic evidence exists of a few still in use during the early years of the twentieth century, well sweeps were uncommon by mid-century.

An 1881 drawing (titled *Carolina Home*) depicting a woman pouring water from a bucket suspended from a well sweep. NCC.

Reference: John Michael Vlach, *Back of the Big House: The Architecture of Plantation Slavery* (1993).

Patricia Phillips Marshall

Welsh Settlers. The Welsh settlement of the Cape Fear region in the early eighteenth century extended 80 to 90 miles inland along the creeks flowing into the Cape Fear and the Northeast Cape Fear Rivers. These bodies of water included Rockfish, James's, Swift's, and Smith's Creeks, Black Mingo and Goshen Swamps, and the Black River near Elizabethtown. This region today covers parts of the counties of Bladen, Columbus, Duplin, Onslow, Jones, Brunswick, and Sampson. The Welsh settlement was spread out because of the naval stores industry; when the British Parliament granted a bounty on naval stores in North Carolina, this encouraged Welsh settlers to migrate from Pennsylvania (later New Castle County, Del.) to the colony in the 1720s. The Welsh settlement in North Carolina preceded the Welsh settlement that began in South Carolina in 1736 on the upper Pee Dee River near the present town of Society Hill.

Welsh settlers in North Carolina were primarily Presbyterians of a strongly Calvinist bent who had attended the Pencader Hundred Presbyterian Church in Pennsylvania. They, along with immigrants from Scotland and Ireland, organized the colony's first Presbyterian congregations in the 1730s and 1740s, and the churches they established had a strong cultural influence in the region. Rock Fish and Hopewell Presbyterian Churches in Duplin County are examples of churches begun by Welsh settlers in the eighteenth century, and their graveyards have tombstones bearing Welsh surnames such as Morgan, Edwards, Thomas, Evans, James, Jones, Williams, and Wells. These surnames are very prominent in the modern Cape Fear.

References: Edward George Hartman, *Americans from Wales* (1983); George Lloyd Johnson Jr., *The Frontier in the Colonial South: South Carolina Backcountry, 1736–1800* (1997); Hugh Meredith, *An Account of the Cape Fear Country, 1731* (1922).

Lloyd Johnson

A map created by Edward Moseley in 1733 documenting two Welsh settlements along the Cape Fear and Northeast Cape Fear Rivers in southeastern North Carolina. Map Collection (MC no. 17), Special Collections Department, Joyner Library, East Carolina University, Greenville.

Wesleyan Church, headquartered in Indianapolis and with theological connections to the Methodist Church, resulted from the merger (1966–68) of two small but similar denominations, the Wesleyan Methodist Church and the Pilgrim Holiness Church. Some articles of faith were reworded or updated; overlapping conferences, districts, and educational institutions were combined or eliminated; and boundaries among select churches were realigned by mutual consent. But, by common agreement, basic doctrines remained unchanged, and despite the schism of some communities from each of the merging denominations, the union was a marked success.

The Wesleyan Methodist Church in America was created in early 1843 as a result of a schism from the Methodist Episcopal Church over slavery, holiness, and the arbitrary use of episcopal power by the parent church. For more than 20 years the church focused its energies upon the antislavery movement, but by 1867 attention shifted dramatically to revivalism, holiness, and evangelizing, and a church that had heretofore been eastern in locale now directed itself west, north, and south.

North Carolina was one of the primary objectives of this new focus because of earlier commitments. In 1848 first one and then three missionaries had been sent into Alamance County, where they established a number of small churches before being driven out three years later by violence and the local courts. In 1871 two native-born ministers with church support returned to the state and successfully established the Wesleyan Methodist Church. By 1879 North Carolina was a separate conference that was to become and to remain the largest in the South. While the state denomination, headquartered at Colfax after 1927, grew slowly, it was by 1968, on the eve of the merger with the Pilgrim Holiness Church, the largest conference in the national Wesleyan Methodist Church, with 6,340 members.

In North Carolina, the Pilgrim Holiness Church and Wesleyan Methodist Church united 153 congregations and 9,829 members in the merger. By the early 2000s, North Carolina's 158 Wesleyan churches had nearly doubled their membership since 1968 to more than 17,500 members.

References: Lee M. Haines and Paul W. Thomas, *An Outline History of the Wesleyan Church* (1985); Ira F. McLeister and Roy S. Nicholson, *Conscience and Commitment: History of the Wesleyan Methodist Church of America* (1976).

Louis P. Towles

Wesleyan Female College

Wesleyan Female College in Murfreesboro was founded and constructed between 1852 and 1855 by the Virginia Conference of the Methodist Episcopal Church to give the "fair daughters [of Virginia and North Carolina] advantages equal to any in the land." The site was chosen because Murfreesboro had an established reputation as a "cultured town." Equally as important to the region's Methodist population was its rivalry with the state's Baptists, who had founded Chowan Female College in Murfreesboro in 1848. As Wesleyan was completed, competition quickly developed between the two schools, with enrollment figures, administrative prosperity, and even the quality of landscaping as points of intense comparison and pride.

Despite able leadership under presidents Joseph Davis, Cornelius Riddick, Paul Whitehead, William Starr, and E. E. Parham, Wesleyan failed to survive. Quarrels between the school's trustees and its presidents limited the effectiveness of the latter's office, and the transfer of the institution in 1881 to the North Carolina Conference of the Methodist Church did not improve Wesleyan's already weak financial base. Perhaps even more devastating was the Civil War, when classes were suspended and school facilities were used as stables and barracks by Confederate cavalry. Wesleyan also suffered a number of fires. One in 1877 forced the closure of the school for four years while it was rebuilt; another in 1893 completely devastated the main building. These and other problems led to the institution's abandonment before 1900.

Reference: William E. Stephenson, "The Davises, the Southalls, and the Founding of Wesleyan Female College, 1854–1859," *NCHR* 57 (July 1980).

Louis P. Towles

Western Carolina University

Western Carolina University began as Cullowhee Academy, a primary-level subscription school for boys and girls established in 1888 in Jackson County. When the academy's first teacher left after one year, community leaders hired a young Virginian, Robert Lee Madison, as principal. It was Madison who proposed what he called the "Cullowhee Idea": that the state appropriate $3,000 annually to an existing high school in each congressional district to support a normal department to train rural teachers. The legislature instead gave Madison $1,500 for a normal department at Cullowhee alone. In 1901 the school received its first capital improvement money from the state, and four years later the legislature changed the name to Cullowhee Normal and Industrial School. It became the model for the creation of Appalachian Training School for Teachers in Boone in 1903 and East Carolina Teachers Training School in Greenville in 1907.

Cullowhee, like Appalachian Training School, was essentially a high school with a teacher training program, though by 1913 both schools had begun the transition to junior college status. In 1925 Cullowhee changed its name to Cullowhee State Normal School (CSNS) and began a four-year evolution that transferred the high school to the county and implemented a four-year college program granting the bachelor of science degree in education. In 1929 CSNS was granted a new charter by the state and renamed Western Carolina Teachers College (WCTC). The new degree program and a popular summer school changed the composition of the student body by attracting students from across the state. In 1942 WCTC began to offer graduate courses in education in its summer program in cooperation with the University of North Carolina and introduced a pioneering program in guidance and counseling.

In 1953 the school's name was changed yet again, this time to Western Carolina College. It became the first of North Carolina's white state-supported colleges to admit an African American student when Levern Hamlin attended summer school in 1957. In 1967 Western Carolina College became Western Carolina University and was designated a regional university. It became part of the University of North Carolina System in 1972.

Western Carolina University has continued to emphasize quality teaching, high academic standards, faculty-student research, and the assessment of student learning. The founding of the Faculty Center for Excellence in Teaching and Learning and the North Carolina Center for the Advancement of Teaching symbolize these efforts. In 1997 Western Carolina University became the first institution in the UNC System to require students to own computers. In the early 2000s the university had a total enrollment of just over 7,000 students. The 265-acre campus includes Hunter Library, the largest collection in western North Carolina, and 5,700 computer data ports on campus in residence hall rooms, electronic classrooms, and laboratories.

References: William Earnest Bird, *The History of Western Carolina College: The Progress of an Idea* (1963); Curtis W. Wood and H. Tyler Blethen, *A Mountain Heritage: The Illustrated History of Western Carolina University* (1989).

Curtis W. Wood

Western Carolinian was founded in Salisbury on 13 June 1820, with Jacob Krider and Lemuel Bingham as editors. The western counties of North Carolina, more sparsely populated than those in the east, had long needed a newspaper to voice its desire for equal representation in the state legislature and otherwise serve its interests. Salisbury, as the region's largest city, was an ideal location for such a paper. In most antebellum political newspapers, national politics received the majority of the editorial attention, but the *Western Carolinian* was a leader in the movement to increase coverage of state issues. The obvious determination of western North Carolina —so forcefully confirmed on the pages of the *Carolinian*—led other editors to take sides on these issues, which included the establishment of a public school system and a public college in the west, internal improvements, the convening of a constitutional convention, the need for a state penitentiary, the care of the handicapped, and free suffrage for all white males. Although it changed hands and political affiliations several times, the *Western Carolinian* remained a strong advocate of the economic growth and political rights of western counties until it ceased publication in 1844.

Reference: Thad Stem Jr., *The Tar Heel Press* (1973).

Wiley J. Williams

Western College of North Carolina, chartered by the General Assembly in 1820, was anticipated to be a degree-granting, nonsectarian institution similar to the state's first university, which had opened in Chapel Hill in 1795. The college was intended for the education of young men living west of the Yadkin River. A board of 25 trustees was named, and certain positions were intended to be filled at the board's initial meeting the following May at the courthouse in Lincolnton. Provisions made for the college's governance included the naming of a president, secretary, and treasurer, while not more than 20 additional trustees might also be named later. Among other specified functions, the trustees were to select a convenient site for the school and appoint professors and tutors.

In Salisbury the recently established *Western Carolinian* published full reports on the trustees' activities and printed an exchange of letters on the proposed college from readers. The majority opinion ultimately did not favor the college; one opponent wrote that those who supported it "must have for their object the baptism of some petty grammar school, or some mushroom academy, with the dignified name of College."

Initial reaction to the idea of Western College had been encouraging enough that three trustees were promptly appointed to examine sites in Burke, Lincoln, and Mecklenburg Counties. Presbyterian minister James McRee was named college president and began working to secure financial support for the institution. Impressive sums of money were pledged in the early stages of the campaign, and there were signs of interest in the college from South Carolina and Georgia. After a four-year struggle, however, Western College became a victim of the east-west political and cultural conflict that had plagued North Carolina for several generations. Sectional leaders in the state were unable to pull together for the common good, and the projected plans collapsed. The idea of establishing a college in the western part of North Carolina was taken up by Presbyterians, however, and Davidson College was founded in 1837.

References: Charles L. Coon, ed., *North Carolina Schools and Academies: A Documentary History* (1915); Cornelia R. Shaw, *Davidson College* (1923).

William S. Powell

Western North Carolina Railroad. Before the North Carolina Railroad was completed in 1856, a crop failure in the west prompted citizens to push for a railroad to connect the eastern and central counties with Asheville. In response, the legislature agreed to build two important extensions of the North Carolina Railroad—the Atlantic & North Carolina Railroad from Goldsboro to Beaufort and the Western North Carolina Railroad from Salisbury to Morganton. The route from Goldsboro to Beaufort was finished in 1858, but work on the Salisbury-to-Morganton track was very slow and costly.

After the Civil War, which virtually halted construction, the state in 1866 subscribed $4 million to the Western North Carolina Railroad to continue the project. John A. Hunt finished the rest of Charles F. Fisher's work east of Morganton, and plans were made for completion of the next section from Morganton to Old Fort. With no ready cash on hand, the railroad's president and stockholders were eager for governmental aid. The state constitutional convention of 1868 and the Republican State Convention authorized the issuance of bonds totaling $6.4 million to extend the road from Morganton to Asheville. In the same year George W. Swepson and Gen. Milton S. Littlefield secured absolute control of the Western North Carolina Railroad by purchasing 2,000 of the 3,080 bonds issued.

The railroad then became a victim of Swepson and Littlefield's corruption. During the administration of Governor William W. Holden, the two men issued worthless securities, participated in fraudulent stock subscriptions, and built a huge debt. The road was pillaged, Littlefield and his cronies fled the state, and Holden was impeached.

After the so-called Littlefield scandal, the state bought the Western North Carolina Railroad for $665,000 in 1870. The same year the Democratic-controlled legislature cut off financial support to the railroads and leased the Western North Carolina to other companies such as the Richmond & Danville Railroad. Construction of the Western North Carolina Railroad stopped in Murphy in 1891 before an extension to Ducktown, Tenn., could be completed. In 1894 the railroad was reorganized as the Southern Railway Company.

References: William Hutson Abrams Jr., "The Western North Carolina Railroad" (M.A. thesis, Western Carolina University, 1976); Cecil Kenneth Brown, *A State Movement in Railroad Development: The Story of North Carolina's First Effort to Establish an East and West Trunk Line Railroad* (1928); Hugh T. Lefler and Albert R. Newsome, *North Carolina: The History of a Southern State* (1963).

Vincent Castano
Donald W. Kern

Wetlands is the descriptive and legal term for many thousands of acres in North Carolina. Most broadly, wetlands encompass all lands that are generally, frequently, occasionally, or intermittently submerged, coursed across, soaked, touched, or in some way affected by water, whether by lunar or wind tide, rainfall, or seasonal flood. These include every sort of terrain, such as coastal marsh (the vast Cedar Island marshes in Carteret County), river swamp (the Roanoke River bottomlands of Northampton, Halifax, Bertie, Martin, and Washington Counties), pocosin thickets, Carolina Bays, and even the small fen nearly a mile high atop Bluff Mountain in Ashe County.

The U.S. Environmental Protection Agency in 1985 cited the factors endangering North Carolina's pocosins. Federal and state environmental restrictions on what use, if any, may be made of particular wetland parcels now affect virtually every sort of agricultural, municipal, and resort development, particularly in the river, swamp, and sound country of North Carolina's coastal plain. While the ecological and environmental values of these areas—as wildlife habitats, seafood nurseries, and pollutant filters—are today far more acknowledged and appreciated than they were only a generation ago, there has been and continues to be much controversy over the designation and subsequent governmental regulation of wetlands. In some cases under current law and practice, a property owner may be allowed to fill or otherwise alter one wetland tract if another tract, similar in size and nature, is set aside in perpetuity as a "mitigation" property. With population in the state's coastal counties rapidly rising, the nature and care of wetlands will continue to be a central matter of public land-use policy in North Carolina.

References: Lawrence S. Earley, "Wetlands in the Highlands," *Wildlife in North Carolina* 53, no. 10 (October 1989); Jack Temple Kirby, *Poquosin: A Study of Rural Landscape and Society* (1995); Brook Meanley, *Swamps, River Bottoms, and Canebrakes* (1972); Douglas Neil Rader, *Carolina Wetlands: Our Vanishing Resource* (1989); Bland Simpson, *Into the Sound Country: A Carolinian's Coastal Plain* (1997).

Bland Simpson

SEE ALSO Great Dismal Swamp; Pocosins; Swamps.

Wet Year. The year 1842 saw North Carolina's coast pounded by two severe hurricanes. The remoteness of many of the state's coastal settlements at the time, particularly those on the Outer Banks, and the lack of good transportation and communications made warning citizens of approaching storms difficult. As a result, people most often did not have time to leave their homes before the advancing storms struck and sometimes could not even return to shore or secure their boats. Although hurricanes generally were not given names before the mid-twentieth century, these two anonymous storms caused such massive devastation and loss of life that their place in North Carolina history is secure.

The season's first storm struck on 12 July 1842, following two months of nearly constant rain. This hurricane caused immense damage, destroying bridges, mills, homes, fences, ships, stores, livestock, crops, and supplies. The 27 July *Washington Whig* reported that this storm was "more violent than had ever before been experienced by the oldest citizens of Portsmouth and Ocracoke." The worst effects were felt on the Outer Banks, particularly Portsmouth, and many people were killed and injured. Floodwaters continued to rise and cause damage for days afterward. Little over a month later, on 23 August, another hurricane hit the slowly recovering and rebuilding coast, bringing more misery and ruin. At least three ships, along with their crews, were lost during this storm. Although coastal residents were by no means unaccustomed to severe weather during the state's fall hurricane season, the immense havoc wreaked by these storms far exceeded their expectations, making the "wet year" of 1842 one of the state's worst pre-twentieth-century natural disasters.

Reference: Jay Barnes, *North Carolina's Hurricane History* (3rd ed., 2001).

Michael Thomas Smith

Wetzell's Mill, Battle of. The Battle of Wetzell's (or Whitsall's) Mill was a Revolutionary War engagement that took place in northeastern Guilford County on 6 Mar. 1781. Lord Charles Cornwallis made an attempt to cut off advance elements of Gen. Nathanael Greene's army that were commanded by Col. Otho Williams. Williams's forces were well south of the rest of Greene's army and separated from it by the waters of Reedy Fork Creek. The British army, consisting of 1,000 infantry under Lt. Col. James Webster and Lt. Col. Banastre Tarleton's cavalry, moved out in the early morning, taking advantage of a thick fog to cover their movements. Before the British could cut off Williams's line of escape, the movement was discovered and the Continentals commenced a hasty retreat north up the road to reunite with the rest of the army. Riflemen and cavalry forces under Col. Henry "Light Horse Harry" Lee provided cover and delayed the British long enough for Williams to get his troops ten miles up the road across the ford over Reedy Fork Creek at Wetzell's Mill.

Believing that the crossing would be a good place to make a stand and check the progress of the British, Williams posted some Continental troops in line of battle covering the ford. The men under Lee and Cols. William Washington and William Campbell were to retire before being overwhelmed and follow the rest of Williams's force north to join Greene's army near the Haw River.

The Continentals put up a stiff resistance at the creek, initially turning back an effort by the British to cross. But Webster personally led a second attack in which his men made it across the creek and up the bank beyond. In the face of the fierce, aggressive move, the Continental lines broke and continued their retreat north.

Both sides are believed to have lost about 50 men in the encounter; Tarleton recorded British losses as "about thirty." More important from his perspective, however, was the opportunity the British lost in not exploiting the victory at Wetzell's Mill by vigorously moving north and either attacking Greene's main army or disrupting their resupply and reinforcement efforts. Instead, Cornwallis directed the British army to fall back to more friendly territory at Bell's Mill on Deep River.

References: John S. Pancake, *This Destructive War: The British Campaign in the Carolinas, 1780–1782* (1985); Anthony J. Scotti Jr., *Brutal Virtue: The Myth and Reality of Banastre Tarleton* (2002).

John Hairr

Weymouth Woods Sandhills Nature Preserve, part

of the North Carolina State Parks System, is a 676-acre natural area located one mile southeast of Southern Pines in Moore County. Established in 1963 as the first nature preserve in the state parks system, the original 400 acres of Weymouth Woods were a gift to the state of North Carolina from Katharine Lamont Boyd, widow of the novelist James Boyd.

The natural area deeded by the Boyds to the people of North Carolina preserves a part of the ecosystem of the Sandhills, a region marked by sandy ridges of longleaf pine and scrub oak between hardwood-filled bottomlands. Early settlers in south-central North Carolina called this area the "pine barrens" because of its extensive forests of longleaf pine. In addition to sizable stands of old-growth longleaf pines, Weymouth Woods is home to rare and endangered species such as the red-cockaded woodpecker, the pine barrens tree frog, and the bog spicebush.

Reference: North Carolina Division of Parks and Recreation, *Weymouth Woods Sandhills Nature Preserve* (1996).

Lynn Roundtree

Whaling began as a shore-based activity on the North Carolina coast as early as 1666. With the eventual depletion of whale populations off their immediate coast, New Englanders soon made the transition to pelagic (open-sea) whaling, a change that foreshadowed their rise to international domination of the industry during the so-called golden age of whaling in the mid-nineteenth century. North Carolinians, however, continued shore-based forms of whaling with little interruption until 1916, when the last reported capture occurred near Cape Lookout. Pelagic whale ships from New England continued to visit the North Carolina coast, pursuing sperm and right whales in the "Hatteras ground" near the edge of the Gulf Stream.

Documentation from the colonial period reveals that North Carolina whale products were lucrative enough to provoke lawsuits among the citizens, to tempt government officials into fraud and embezzlement of tax revenues, to be used as a political issue, and to be recognized as an official medium of currency. During the Proprietary period, annual captures off the North Carolina coast may have exceeded 25 whales in good years.

From at least the Civil War until the demise of the industry, North Carolina's shore-based whaling was centered

An 1856 engraving from *Harper's Monthly* showing small whaling boats similar to those launched by crews off the Outer Banks in the nineteenth century. UNC-Chapel Hill Library.

on Shackleford Banks just west of Cape Lookout. The year-round fishing and seasonal whaling industries were sufficient to induce the establishment of several permanent settlements on Shackleford, including Diamond City, whose population may have numbered as many as 500 during its prime. One particularly curious feature of North Carolina shore whaling was the fishermen's habit of naming individual right whales at the time of their capture. Recorded examples include the "Little Children" whale that was killed by young boys; the "George Washington" whale that was captured on the president's birthday; and the "Cold Sunday" whale that was taken on a day "so cold that flying ducks froze solid while in flight." Other named whales included the "Lee," the "Big Sunday," the "John Rose," the "Mullet Pond," the "Lady Hayes," and the "Haint Bin Named Yit." Best known, however, was the "Mayflower" whale, whose skeleton is on permanent display at the North Carolina State Museum of Natural Sciences in Raleigh, where harpoons and other whaling instruments used on the Outer Banks are also exhibited.

Reference: Marcus B. Simpson Jr. and Sallie W. Simpson, "The Pursuit of Leviathan: A History of Whaling on the North Carolina Coast," NCHR 65 (January 1988).

Marcus B. Simpson Jr.

Whammy, the bane of lead-footed North Carolina drivers during the 1950s and 1960s, was officially a "Speed Watch," the first mechanical device used by North Carolina authorities to detect vehicle speeds. Made by the same company that later developed the "Breathalyzer," the Whammy easily obviated the old subjective estimation methods used by law enforcement personnel. Drivers charged with violations upon evidence from this high-precision device had little chance of escaping conviction and the legal costs and higher insurance rates that ensued.

A law officer would set up a Whammy operation by secluding his or her vehicle near the road and rigging the equipment, which involved placing two air-filled rubber hoses perpendicularly across the roadway, exactly 132 feet apart, then connecting both hoses to a clocking mechanism mounted inside the car. It calculated speed by factoring the known distance traveled and the time needed to cover that distance. Pressure from a vehicle tire on the first hose started a timer, and pressure on the other stopped it; a toggle switch allowed the officer to clock vehicles from both directions. If the timer indicated a speeding vehicle had passed over the apparatus, the officer had to disconnect both hoses, toss them aside, and pursue the offender. Whammy victims may find a little solace in knowing that law officers disliked the contraption, which was almost impossible to assemble and disassemble without soiling their uniforms. As an old patrol hand put it, "the Whammy was the filthiest, aggravatin'est thing to put down and to take up!"

Whammys were used consistently by North Carolina Highway Patrol officers until about 1970, when they were replaced by more technologically advanced devices. The nickname "Whammy," which seems to have been unique to North Carolina, almost certainly came from Al Capp's *Li'l Abner* comic strip character Evil Eye Fleegle, who could inflict harm or destruction with the "whammy," a baleful stare from his distended eyeball.

Whitmel M. Joyner

Chapel Hill police officers calibrating a speed-detection device in 1961. Photograph by Roland Giduz. NCC.

Whig Party was formed during the 1830s by the union of diverse factions that opposed the policies of President Andrew Jackson and the Democratic Party. Many supported Henry Clay, a proponent of internal improvements, protective tariffs, and a national bank. Advocates of state rights challenged Jackson's threat to use force to make South Carolina accept an unpopular import tariff in 1832. Jackson, a strong, assertive president, heavily wielded his power, frequently not only vetoing bills but also pushing his own agenda in Congress. His opponents called him "King Andrew" and began to call themselves "Whigs," taking the name of the opposition party in Britain. Whigs favored an active role for government, particularly in promoting internal improvement projects to aid transportation and public institutions such as schools, mental hospitals, and penitentiaries. The Whigs also endorsed a strong national bank to boost investment and tariffs to protect American industries.

The new Whig Party found many supporters in North Carolina, especially in the west and the Albemarle Sound region.

Most of the east, which was dominated by wealthy planters, remained firmly Democratic. In the election of 1836, Whig candidate Edward B. Dudley won the governor's race, and Whigs received a large minority in the General Assembly and a slight majority of the state's congressional seats. The elections of 1840 further increased the power of the Whig Party: voters elected its candidate, John Motley Morehead, to the governorship, and the legislature chose Whigs Willie P. Mangum and William A. Graham to represent North Carolina in the U.S. Senate. The Whigs thus controlled state politics from 1836 to about 1850. In 1854 future governor Zebulon B. Vance won his first election, as the Whig candidate for a seat in the North Carolina House of Commons.

Among its major accomplishments in North Carolina, the Whig Party counted the expansion of railroads, creation of the state public school system (1839), and establishment of the first state school for the deaf and the blind and of the first state mental asylum, then called Dix Hill (later Dorothea Dix Hospital). The Whig years also saw an increase in the number of newspapers and publishers and of private academies and colleges, as well as a decline in illiteracy.

The Whigs actually began losing their hold on North Carolina in the late 1840s. Many of their national policies—fostering strong banks and protective tariffs, promoting industrial development—were of little interest to the citizens of an agrarian state such as North Carolina. Although southern Whigs did not oppose slavery, the Democrats were much more emphatic in actively supporting slavery and resisting abolition.

The Whig Party disintegrated during the 1850s. In the North, its remnants formed much of the foundation of the new Republican Party. The decade and a half of Whig control had permanently changed North Carolina, turning the so-called Rip Van Winkle State into a leading power in the South. As the Whig Party disappeared, its progressive policies were adapted and put into practice by many leaders of the revitalized Democratic Party of the 1850s. For the election campaign of 1860, the Whig Party was briefly revived in North Carolina as a Unionist alternative to secessionist Democrats and northern Republicans. During the Civil War, North Carolina Whigs evolved into the Conservative Party, which often opposed Jefferson Davis's administration and endorsed stronger individual and state rights.

References: Michael F. Holt, *The Rise and Fall of the American Whig Party* (1999); Marc W. Kruman, *Parties and Politics in North Carolina, 1836–1865* (1983); Herbert Dale Pegg, *The Whig Party in North Carolina* (1968).

David A. Norris

SEE ALSO Conservative Party.

Whimmy-Diddle, also known as the Gee-Haw Whimmy-Diddle ("gee" and "haw" are the commands shouted to oxen on a farm), is a toy made out of a stick of mountain laurel that was traditionally made by mountain parents for their children. Notches are cut down the stick and a propeller is put at the end. When another stick is rubbed against the notches exactly right, the propeller spins. With a lot of practice, the user is able to make the propeller go right or left as desired.

References: Florence H. Pettit, *How to Make Whirligigs and Whimmy Diddles and Other American Folkcraft Objects* (1972); Roy Underhill, *The Woodwright's Companion: Exploring Traditional Woodcraft* (1983).

Elia Bizzarri

Whiskey making and distribution has been part of North Carolina's commerce and culture from the beginning of European settlement. Whiskies in North America are made from a mash of rye, corn, barley, wheat, or other grains, which is fermented and aged in wooden barrels of various styles and conditions. Distilled spirits and the art of making them were important in European heritage, and, after the American Indians introduced the settlers to corn, the crop became an instant staple of local whiskey makers. In western North Carolina counties, settlers raised fine apple crops in addition to corn, and with apple cider came apple brandy. Whiskey-making stills, mostly single-family operations, could be found throughout the region.

In the 1600s and 1700s, taverns were places of social gathering in the Carolinas, and some towns grew up around crossroads establishments. There were laws against drunkenness but not against selling or making whiskey; some attempts at prohibition of alcoholic beverages came as early as 1852, but the movement garnered little attention by the state's General Assembly. By the middle of the 1800s, whiskey was a major commodity for producers in western North Carolina. Farmers in the mountains and foothills realized that, without adequate roads or train service, bringing a load of corn to market was not worth the wagon space. Distilling the corn into whiskey (usually bourbon) was much more economical and brought greater returns.

In the second half of the nineteenth century, producers in the western counties took their distilled spirits to Statesville for further distribution. Statesville was "the end of the line" for train service to the west for some time, so it became the logical shipping point for whiskey distribution across the Carolinas. It is estimated that during the 1880s, as many as 450 distilleries were shipping their products through Statesville. A freight agent of the Atlantic, Tennessee, and Ohio Railroad reported that between September 1879 and March 1880, nearly 57,000 gallons of whiskey had been shipped from Statesville on his railroad. A large amount of whiskey was also shipped on the Western Railroad in that period.

Major wholesale liquor houses were established in Statesville and prospered from the 1880s until the early 1900s, when statewide Prohibition came in 1909. In 1883 P. B. Key & Co. established a distributorship for whiskey. (Key was the grand nephew of Francis Scott Key, author of the "Star Spangled Banner.") The Julius Lowenstein family was a leader in whiskey distribution throughout the Carolinas. Some of the better whiskey of the period was bottled under the Lowenstein name. When whiskey making was declared illegal, the Lowensteins moved to Atlanta and founded the Norris Candy Company.

In 1905 the Watts law, named for Iredell County's state representative Alston D. Watts, was passed in Raleigh, prohibiting the manufacture and sale of liquor outside incorporated towns. It also established local-option elections, which generally went against the liquor interests, "drying up" many towns. After Prohibition was established by the Eighteenth Amendment in 1919, whiskey production continued through the illegal efforts of bootleggers, whose "moonshine" became a way of life in various parts of the state, particularly the western counties. Legal whiskey returned after Prohibition was ended by the Twenty-first Amendment in 1933, although most areas were dry until 1935. No significant commercial distilleries were established in the state.

In 1937 the General Assembly approved local-option elections to sell whiskey and other spirits solely through Alcoholic Beverage Control Commission (ABC) stores, which were given control of all aspects of whiskey production, possession, and sale in the state. Later, "liquor-by-the-drink" at bars and restaurants was approved, subject to a local-option election and certain limitations.

Reference: Joseph Earl Dabney, *Mountain Spirits: A Chronicle of Corn Whiskey from King James' Ulster Plantation to America's Appalachians and the Moonshine Life* (1974).

Chester Paul Middlesworth

SEE ALSO Moonshine.

Whistler's Mother. Wilmington-born Anna Mathilda McNeill Whistler was the mother of artist James Abbott McNeill Whistler and the subject of his most famous painting. Although officially titled *Arrangement in Black and Grey No. 1: The Artist's Mother*, the painting is popularly known as *Whistler's Mother*.

Anna Whistler was born in 1804 in a two-story brick house on the corner of Fourth and Orange Streets in Wilmington. Her father had settled in North Carolina in 1785. Anna married George Washington Whistler, and their first child, James, was born in 1834 in Lowell, Mass. When James was nine years old, the Whistler family moved to Russia, where Maj. Whistler worked as construction engineer for the St. Petersburg-to-

U.S. postage stamp issued on Mother's Day 1934, based on James Whistler's 1871 painting of his North Carolina–born mother, Anna McNeill Whistler. Courtesy of William S. Powell.

Moscow railroad. A cholera epidemic in St. Petersburg forced Anna to take her children to England in 1848, where James studied art. When Maj. Whistler died from cholera that year, Anna returned the family to the United States. After attending West Point, James returned to Europe in 1855 to resume his study of art. Anna joined her son in London in 1863. James Whistler painted the famous portrait of his mother in his London home in 1871.

After completion, the painting was exhibited in a number of art galleries throughout London but did not receive immediate acclaim. Anna died in 1881, and a few months later, the portrait went to America, where it was shown in Pennsylvania and New York. Although denied a permanent place in the Royal Academy in London, the painting gradually drew praise and admiration. Shipped to Paris for sale in 1891, it was purchased by the French government for 4,000 francs.

As a prelude to its acceptance into the collection of the Louvre, French authorities exhibited *Whistler's Mother* in the Luxembourg, where the painting was favorably compared to the works of Rembrandt, Titian, and Velázquez. In 1927, 24 years after the death of the artist, the portrait of his North Carolina–born mother earned James Whistler his place among the masters at the Louvre, a first for an American-born artist.

In 1932 the painting returned to the United States for a coast-to-coast exhibition. During the American tour, the U.S. Postal Service issued a 1934 Mother's Day stamp of Anna Whistler. State highway historical markers designate the site of her birthplace in Wilmington as well as the site of Oak Forest, her family's plantation in Bladen County.

References: Daniel W. Barefoot, *Touring the Backroads of North Carolina's Lower Coast* (1995); Kate R. McDiarmid, *Whistler's Mother: Her Life, Letters and Journal* (1936); Elizabeth Mumford, *Whistler's Mother* (1936).

Daniel W. Barefoot

White Citizens' Councils were established during the 1950s in reaction to federal initiatives to end racial segregation in the South. Historically, they were similar to the various white supremacy groups that grew out of the extreme racial tensions defining southern culture after the Civil War. The nation's first White Citizens' Council was founded in July 1954 in Indianola, Miss., in the aftermath of the U.S. Supreme Court's school desegregation ruling in *Brown v. Board of Education of Topeka, Kansas*. As part of the massive resistance that swept across the South in the mid-1950s, the White Citizens' Council embarked on a mission to interpose the *Brown* decision, attack the National Association for the Advancement of Colored People, and build support through a nationwide propaganda campaign. Citizens' councils appeared in other states, including North Carolina, where the most influential group, the White Patriots, was formed on 22 Aug. 1955 to circumvent the *Brown* ruling.

These citizens' councils were careful to distinguish themselves rhetorically from the more explicit forms of Jim Crow oppression—particularly the Ku Klux Klan—by declaring their disdain for violence. Despite this public stance, individual members did become linked to acts of violence, and the councils greatly contributed to the racial unrest in the mid- to late-1950s South.

References: Numan V. Bartley, *The Rise of Massive Resistance: Race and Politics in the South during the 1950s* (1969); Neil McMillen, *The Citizens' Council: Organized Resistance to the Second Reconstruction, 1954–1964* (1994).

J. Christopher Schutz
Elizabeth Gillespie McRae

SEE ALSO White Patriots of North Carolina.

White Doe, Legend of. The mysterious disappearance between 1587 and 1590 of the English colonists on Roanoke Island, known as the "Lost Colony," spawned numerous legends and ghost stories among the people who later settled in coastal North Carolina. The most popular of these tales concerns Virginia Dare, born on Roanoke Island on 18 Aug. 1587 and the first child of English parentage born in the New World.

Nine days after the birth of the child, Virginia's grandfather John White, the governor of the Roanoke Island colony, set sail for England in an attempt to obtain assistance for the colonists. According to legend, not long after White's departure, Wanchese, one of the local Indians who visited England with White, launched an attack against the colonists. Among the few survivors of the massacre were Ananias and Eleanor Dare and their daughter, Virginia.

Manteo, another Indian who visited England with White, rescued the Dare family. Virginia's parents died, and Manteo's people cared for the little girl, whom they called Winona. Under the tutelage of Manteo, she learned the ways of the forest as she grew into womanhood.

Many of the local Indians competed for Winona, but she chose the handsome Okisko. When she rejected Chico, a sly old witch doctor, he resolved that if he could not have her love, no one would. Using his powerful magic, Chico cast a spell on the young woman, transforming her into a snow-white doe. During the years that followed, the magnificent animal was seen moving gracefully about the island landscape. Sometimes the doe gazed toward the sea as if longing for the return of John White. In the meantime, the heartbroken Okisko sought to reclaim his lost love. He traveled to the shores of Lake Mattamuskeet to consult with Wenaudon, a mighty medicine man known to be Chico's rival. Wenaudon obliged the young brave by providing him with a magic oyster shell–tipped arrow. Wenaudon assured Okisko that if the special arrow pierced the heart of the white doe, she would change back to the lovely young maiden known to the brave as Winona.

For many months the unusual deer eluded hunters, causing great consternation among the Indians on the island. Sensing the anxiety of his braves, the evil Wanchese ordered a hunt for the white deer. A determined Okisko, armed with his special arrow, began the hunt hoping to be the first to find the beautiful deer. He spotted her bounding from the forest at the water's edge. However, at the same moment, Wanchese also caught a glimpse of the animal. Okisko let his magical arrow fly, and it found its way into the heart of the target. Unfortunately, at the same time Wanchese sent a silver arrow, a gift from Queen Elizabeth, into the deer's heart.

A thick gray mist covered the white doe as the wounded animal collapsed. When the mist dissipated, Okisko was thrilled to find Virginia Dare, or Winona, lying on the ground. But as he took her into his arms, his elation turned to despair when he saw that the silver arrow had killed the love that he had lost and found once again. He wrapped her body in his mantle and buried her in the middle of the fort abandoned years earlier by Virginia Dare's kinsmen.

Well into the twentieth century, hunters emerged from the forests of Roanoke Island with tales of a strange deer that eluded them in the wilderness. It appeared suddenly in the darkness of midnight and vanished in the mist of dawn. Longtime residents of the island who heard the story time after time had no doubt that the identity of the mysterious phantom deer was the ghost of Virginia Dare.

References: Nancy Roberts, *North Carolina Ghosts and Legends* (1991); Richard Walser, *North Carolina Legends* (1980); Charles Harry Whedbee, *Legends of the Outer Banks and Tar Heel Tidewater* (1966).

Daniel W. Barefoot

White Furniture Company was organized in Mebane in 1881 by brothers William E. and David A. White, sons of Mebane cofounder Stephen A. White. The factory was incorporated as the White-Rickel Furniture Company on 9 May 1896. There were three principal incorporators, including A. J. Rickel from Manchester, Ohio, who moved to the area looking to invest in the furniture industry. By 1899 he had sold his interest in the Mebane plant, and thereafter the firm was known as the White Furniture Company.

In addition to manufacturing window materials, the White brothers contracted for building jobs. The mass production of building materials eventually led to the standardization of architectural forms throughout the state. The White Furniture Company's success in this lucrative industry led to the production of fine furniture in 1896. Specializing in furnishings for bedrooms and dining rooms, the company continued to prosper. Always on the cutting edge of technology, White Furniture became one of the first plants in the South to utilize electrically powered machinery. In 1905 the company became the first southern furniture manufacturer to be awarded a contract with the U.S. government, supplying furniture to military personnel working on the Panama Canal. Eventually the company supplied solid mahogany furniture for the quarters of army officers throughout the United States and the Far East. In 1912 White Furniture provided the furnishings for Asheville's famed Grove Park Inn, many of which are still in use.

During the Jamestown Exposition of 1907, White Furniture received an award as the top manufacturer of furniture in the country and a blue ribbon for best furniture display. Eventually the company became known for its elegant mahogany dining room furnishings. The pieces produced by White Furniture featured classical designs with attention given to details, such as the selection of fine, kiln-dried woods. Carefully crafted inlays became the company's trademark.

In 1940 White Furniture expanded its business and opened a factory in Hillsborough. During World War II, the company again received government contracts. In 1982, the factory building itself was placed on the National Register of Historic Places. In 1985 the Hickory White Furniture Company, which had no connection to the Mebane firm, purchased White Furniture, ending family ownership after 104 years. Subsequently, in 1993, Hickory White downsized its operation, closing the Mebane plant and consolidating all of its activities in Hickory.

Reference: Bill Bamberger and Cathy N. Davidson, *Closing: The Life and Death of an American Factory* (1998).

Sheila Bumgarner

Whitehall, Battle of. The Civil War battle of Whitehall occurred on 15–16 Dec. 1862 at present Seven Springs in Wayne County when the Confederacy's Brig. Gen. B. H. Robertson and the Union's Maj. Gen. John G. Foster clashed during Foster's attempt to capture the railroad junction at Goldsboro. Late on 15 Dec. 1862 Union cavalry scouts reached Whitehall shortly after Confederate troops crossed north over the bridge spanning the Neuse River, set it on fire, and took up defensive positions. Foster's cavalry rolled hundreds of barrels of pitch to the riverbank and set them on fire to light the Confederate positions. Union artillery attempted to destroy the frame of the Confederate ironclad *Neuse* that was under construction while the cavalrymen exchanged fire with Robertson's pickets. After several hours of futile conflict, the infuriated cavalrymen burned the village and returned to camp.

The next day Foster arrived at Whitehall and engaged the enemy, attempting to make the Confederates believe that his men intended to cross the river. Foster thought that he could then slip the rest of his army past Whitehall to attack a railroad trestle four miles south of Goldsboro. But the Confederates were not fooled and the battle lasted until sunset. By nightfall on 16 December, most of Foster's army had marched west, leaving a small force at Whitehall to remove the wounded and bury the dead.

On 18 December Foster withdrew back through Whitehall and retired to New Bern. After his withdrawal, a Confederate patrol made an alarming discovery. One hundred Union troops had been left unburied on the field, and a 100-yard-long pit was filled with dead soldiers. Despite promotions for Foster and his men, many northern newspapers rated the expedition a disaster because of the extensive Union losses and the fact that Foster failed to capture the crucial railroad junction at Goldsboro.

References: John G. Barrett, *The Civil War in North Carolina* (1963); Walter Clark, ed., *Histories of the Several Regiments and Battalions from North Carolina in the Great War, 1861–1865*, vol. 5 (1901); Frank Moore, ed., *Rebellion Record: A Diary of American Events* (1862).

L. George Williams

White Patriots of North Carolina. On 22 Aug. 1955, following the U.S. Supreme Court's 1954 decision in *Brown v. Board of Education of Topeka, Kansas*, 356 men and women formed the White Patriots of North Carolina to circumvent the Court's ruling. Made up of mostly lawyers, ministers, professors, teachers, and a few textile magnates and state politicians, the Patriots pledged to maintain "the purity and culture of the white race and of Anglo-Saxon institutions." In addition to white supremacy, they vowed to preserve state rights and promote "friendly racial relations." Led by Wesley Critz George, a University of North Carolina biology professor, John W. Clark, a UNC trustee, and C. L. Shuping, a Greensboro attorney, the Patriots mobilized to frustrate plans to desegregate the North Carolina public schools.

With the help of members from 59 of the state's 100 counties, the White Patriots sent recruitment letters, advertised on the radio and television, and held public meetings to spread their white supremacist message. Members urged white North Carolinians not to let "the negro destroy the white race"; racial mixing, they claimed, would destroy the white race and produce a "mongrel population." Capitalizing on Cold War fears, the Patriots also charged that proponents of desegregation were communists.

In 1956 the White Patriots focused on the Democratic primaries, battling to defeat the three North Carolina congressmen—Thurmond Chatham, Charles Deane, and Harold Cooley—who had refused to sign the Southern Manifesto, a House document opposing the *Brown* decision. From January to May, the Patriots held mass public meetings in Greensboro, Burlington, Hillsborough, Graham, Asheboro, and Charlotte. Speakers such as state representative Byrd Satterfield and former assistant attorney general I. Beverly Lake asked audiences if they wanted a "white or mulatto posterity," denounced Governor Luther Hodges's passive plan of voluntary segregation, and pilloried Chatham, Deane, and Cooley. Accusing North Carolina of faltering "behind every other state in the South," Satterfield urged North Carolinians to step up their resistance efforts.

As a result of these efforts, two of the three congressmen lost their bid for reelection. Retiring White Patriot president W. C. George later claimed that his organization had inspired North Carolinians to actively oppose integration. Although the Patriots continued to lobby school boards and harass the families of black children admitted to white schools, their influence waned under the leadership of Troy attorney Horace McCall. Eventually the White Patriots gave way to other white supremacist groups in North Carolina, such as the Defenders of States' Rights.

Reference: Numan Bartley, *The Rise of Massive Resistance: Race and Politics in the South during the 1950s* (1969).

Elizabeth Gillespie McRae

White Trash, or "poor white trash," was a term designating the lowest social class among whites in antebellum North Carolina. Other derogatory names for this group included "rednecks," "crackers," "pecker-woods," and "clay-eaters." These landless tenants and laborers often lived in shacks on the outskirts of towns or in mountain hovels. Although most North Carolina whites were poor, they did not belong to the white trash category, held in contempt even by some black slaves. The term "white trash" connoted many negative characteristics, most notably poverty, ignorance, laziness, and perhaps even criminality. Beginning especially in the 1920s, sociologists, anthropologists, social workers, and economists drew a clear distinction between whites who are poor (a nondisparaging designation) and white trash (a disparaging or offensive term). By the end of the twentieth century "white trash" had become, especially when used for comic purposes, a designation that described a people, mostly in the South, whose tastes, values, and culture were remarkably lowbrow.

References: Charles C. Bolton, *Poor Whites of the Antebellum South: Tenants and Laborers in Central North Carolina and Northeast Mississippi* (1994); John Shelton Reed, *Southern Folk, Plain and Fancy: Native White Social Types* (1986).

Wiley J. Williams

White-Water Rafting is a large and economically significant tourist industry in the North Carolina mountains, with hundreds of thousands of visitors flocking to experience the challenge of running the state's rivers such as the Nantahala, the French Broad, the Nolichucky, and the Pigeon. As early as the 1920s, white-water enthusiasts began exploring the rivers of the Southeast for recreation. Generally, these early adventurers were severely hampered by the inadequacy of their equipment, which often consisted of cedar or canvas canoes. In the 1960s and early 1970s, private boaters, often in homemade fiberglass kayaks or aluminum canoes, began logging "first descents" on many rivers throughout the Southeast. Often with the aid of little more than a topographical map, intrepid souls such as Ramone Eaton, Fritz Orr, Bob Benner, Hugh Caldwell, and Frank Bell, among many others, began to explore the more remote rivers and streams of the region.

In 1972 Payson Kennedy, a member of the faculty of the Georgia Institute of Technology, and Horace Holden, a Presbyterian minister and canoeing partner of Kennedy's, along with their wives and children, located an interesting piece of property along the banks of the Nantahala River near Bryson City. The two families knew the area well as they had spent many summers in North Carolina running rivers, hiking, and camping. Holden found that the local 14-room motel, restaurant, and gas station known as the Tote'n'Tarry was for sale by the local sheriff. That summer, the Holdens and Kennedys secured the property for $150,000 and founded the Nantahala Outdoor Center (NOC). After purchasing military surplus rafts, the limited partnership began leading trips down the Nantahala and Chattooga Rivers (in Georgia and South Carolina). That summer, more than 1,200 people took advantage of this new industry. With all of the summer's profits reinvested, the NOC enhanced their fleet with rafts purchased from a manufacturer in West Virginia. The following year, Payson Kennedy resigned from Georgia Tech, cashed in his retirement, and went into the business of outdoor adventure permanently. Although the company is still based in Bryson City and the original river trips are the mainstay of the business, the NOC offers boating trips throughout the United States as well as destinations such as Costa Rica, Chile, Honduras, Mexico, Corsica, Nepal, France, Morocco, and New Zealand.

Although the NOC represents the first commercial rafting company in North Carolina, many other organizations have emerged in the state as well. In 1979 Glenn Goodrich, of Stamford, Conn., and the owners of the West Virginia–based Mountain River Tours founded Carolina Wilderness Adventures in Hot Springs. Goodrich had worked for Mountain River Tours during summers as a raft guide while completing a computer science degree at Ohio State University. In 1981 Carolina Wilderness acquired Black Canyon River Tours, located along the Nolichucky River in Tennessee. The company offers guided trips on the French Broad, Nolichucky, and Pigeon Rivers. Other white-water rafting companies include the French Broad River Company in Marshall, Blue Ridge Rafting in Hot Springs, and Cherokee Adventures in Erwin, Tenn.

The white-water trips offered in North Carolina typically fall within the Class I–IV range, meaning that they are suitable for beginners as well as those with more experience. Some North Carolina river locales have been used as training facilities for U.S. Olympic kayaking teams. The best river trips typically occur during March, April, May, and June, as water levels are generally highest during those months.

Joseph Paul Hoffman

Wildcat Division, a World War I unit officially known as the Eighty-first National Army Division, was organized in August 1917 with drafted soldiers, mostly from North Carolina, South Carolina, and Florida. Approximately one-third of the soldiers were North Carolinians from almost every part of the state. Two regiments—the 321st Infantry and the 316th Field Artillery—and the 321st Ambulance Company were made up almost exclusively of North Carolinians. The division was called the "Wildcat" Division in recognition of the irascible wildcats that inhabited southern states and after Wildcat Creek, which ran near Camp Jackson, S.C., where the unit was mobilized. The men adopted a wildcat silhouette as a shoulder patch, the first insignia worn by troops in the American Expeditionary Force.

In 1918 the Wildcat Division sailed for Europe where, after additional combat instruction, it was sent on 19 September to the St. Dié sector of France's Vosges Mountain region. There, as part of the French Seventh Army, the division held what was considered a quiet front, although it fought off German trench raids and endured artillery bombardments. On 19 October the Eighty-first was relieved and ordered to the rear to await transfer to the American 1st Army, which was fighting in the Meuse-Argonne offensive. While serving in the St. Dié sector, the division suffered 116 casualties.

In early November 1918 the Eighty-first moved to the front lines near Verdun, where its infantry regiments attacked German lines on the morning of 9 November. From the outset the division encountered heavy machine gun and artillery fire; heavy fog and smoke hindered visibility but also likely saved American lives in the attack. By late afternoon, the 322nd Infantry Regiment had captured the ruined village of Moranville. On the south side of the forest, the 324th Infantry Regiment slowly pushed the enemy back but then abandoned much of the ground by withdrawing to a safer position. The day's fighting produced mixed results, with success north of Bois de Manheulles and frustration south of the forest.

When on the night of 10 November Wildcat Division commanders received no official confirmation of rumors that an armistice might be signed the next day, the 321st and 323rd Infantry Regiments planned a dawn attack on the main German trench line. At daybreak the 321st went "over the top" for the first time and attacked enemy trench positions north of Bois de Manheulles, slowly advancing through heavy fog and shell and machine gun fire. At 10:30 A.M. the 323rd began to fight its way through the barbed wire entanglements along the German main trench line into and south of Bois de Manheulles; some Americans entered German trenches and many were either killed or pinned down under enemy fire. At 11:00 A.M. the firing abruptly stopped when the armistice of 11 Nov. 1918 ended hostilities.

Following the armistice, the Wildcat Division marched 175 miles to a rest area and in early June returned to the United States. During the short time the Eighty-first was in combat, it suffered 248 killed and 856 wounded.

References: Felix E. Brockman, *Here, There, and Back* (1925); C. Walton Johnson, *Wildcats: History of the 321st Infantry, 81st Division* (1919).

R. Jackson Marshall III

Wildflowers. North Carolina's wildflowers have long been recognized as one of the state's most treasured resources. Native Americans and early settlers valued wildflowers as sources of food and medicine, while today botanists study the role of wildflowers within the state's ecology. An amazing diversity of wildflowers grows within North Carolina. The fire pink, violet, wood sorrel, jack-in-the-pulpit, swamp rose, birdfoot violet, and duckweed are but a few of the state's nearly 3,000 species of wildflowers, some of which have interesting associations in the area or are unique in some way.

The blooms of Confederate violets, for instance, are a variegated cream with splotches of violet-gray, often at a glance appearing gray, the color of Confederate army uniforms. The pitcher plant is carnivorous, using the downward-facing hairs of its tubular leaf to trap insects and secreting fluid to digest them. Many wildflowers are found in nearly all counties of the state, including the flowering dogwood (the state flower), rabbit tobacco, the cardinal flower, and the Carolina lily. Other wildflowers are unique to a region. Pinkshell azalea is native to just a few Mountain counties; seaside goldenrod and beach evening primrose grace only the coast. Several nonnative wildflowers have spread throughout the state. The dandelion, ox-eye daisy, Queen Anne's lace, chicory, common plantain, and woolly mullein are among the wildflowers introduced to North Carolina from the Old World.

Wildflowers play a vital role in North Carolina's various ecosystems. Sea oats prevent dune erosion, while saltmeadow cordgrass seeds are food for migrating birds. The cattail offers a refuge for the red-winged blackbird to nest; its seeds and stems are eaten by painted turtles; and its rhizomes are food to the muskrat. Bumblebees, butterflies, wasps, and beetles collect pollen from button bush, lyre-leaved sage, and butterfly weed. The early spring bloom of the skunk cabbage is one of the first sources of pollen available to various insects; the rolled-up leaves of the same plant are food to black bears.

Wildflowers have also been a source of food and medicine for many North Carolinians. Native Americans found the root of duck potato edible and shared this knowledge with the early colonists. Cherokee women brewed a tea from the partridge berry because they believed it would ease the pangs of childbirth. An extract is drawn from the bark and leaves of witch hazel to make an astringent. One of the most well-known medicinal flowers is ginseng; Native Americans used this wildflower to treat cough and headache.

Writings and illustrations dating from the time of the earliest explorations of North Carolina through the present day illustrate a strong interest in the state's wildflowers. In *A Briefe and True Report of the New Found Land of Virginia* (1588), for example, Thomas Harriot notes the value of sassafras in curing many diseases. Over a century later, John Lawson remarks upon the rich wealth of wildflowers within the state in *A New Voyage to Carolina* (1709), and John Brickell notes the medicinal properties of some wildflowers in *The Natural History of North-Carolina* (1737).

The watercolors of Mark Catesby in *The Natural History of Carolina, Florida, and the Bahama Islands* (1731–47) include wildflowers native to the Carolina colony, such as the bay-leaved smilax, the pinxter flower, and the yellow lady slipper. In *The Travels of William Bartram* (1791), the naturalist describes a visit to western North Carolina in which he saw Cherokee maidens reclining "under the shade of floriferous and fragrant native bowers of Magnolia, Azalea, Philadelphus, [and] perfumed Calycanthus." Reporting on his 1841 visit to Ashe County, Asa Gray, perhaps the most important American botanist of the nineteenth century, writes of observing leather flower, spiderwort, dwarf iris, bluets, galax, and ginseng. In *North with the Spring* (1951) Edwin Way Teale lists specific wildflowers he saw near Tryon, later writing in detail about four carnivorous wildflowers of the coastal plain near Wilmington: sundew, butterwort, pitcher plant, and Venus flytrap.

Several botanical gardens, such as the Botanical Gardens of Asheville, the North Carolina Botanical Garden in Chapel Hill, and the Elizabethan Gardens of Roanoke Island, include wildflowers. Since 1985 large beds of wildflowers have been sown along state highways as part of the North Carolina Department of Transportation's Wildflower Program.

References: J. Anthony Alderman, *Wildflowers of the Blue Ridge Parkway* (1997); Dunes of Dare Garden Club, *Wildflowers of the Outer Banks: Kitty Hawk to Hatteras* (1980); William S. Justice, C. Ritchie Bell, and Anne H. Lindsey, *Wild Flowers of North Carolina* (2nd ed., 2005); Albert E. Radford, Harry E. Ahles, and Bell, *Manual of the Vascular Flora of the Carolinas* (1968).

Margaret Foote
Additional research provided by William S. Powell.

SEE ALSO Ginseng; Venus Flytrap.

Wild Horses. Celebrated "wild ponies," actually stunted feral horses, ran loose over much of the Outer Banks until the late 1930s, when the General Assembly abolished free range north of Hatteras Inlet. Five herds of these "Banker" ponies survived by the early 2000s. Many have five lumbar vertebrae and 17 pairs of ribs, traits that frequently characterize Arabians, Barbaries, Andalusians, and descendants such as the Lipizzaner and the Spanish mustang but can occur in all breeds.

Outer Banks horses are genetically closest to one another, the herd of Cumberland Island, Ga., and fairly recent American saddle and harness breeds. The Currituck Banks herd has a unique genetic marker, a fact that some enthusiasts, not taking into account the 300 years of local, systematic exploitation that would have affected the line, have taken as proof that the herd's ancestors came from a sixteenth-century Spanish ship. There have also been efforts, highly selective at best, to trace Banker horses to Ponce de León or the Lost Colony. However, because horses have been in North America for five centuries, discovering the specific roots of any of the Outer Banks' herds is very unlikely. Early settlers of the eastern seaboard tended to put their livestock on uninhabited islands, which required no fencing and usually had few large predators. Horses could have reached the Outer Banks anytime be-

Wild horses grazing in a marsh on Shackleford Banks. Photograph courtesy of North Carolina Division of Tourism, Film, and Sports Development.

tween the 1650s, when stockmen first came down from Virginia, and the early twentieth century, when summer visitors stopped bringing their own mounts.

Cape Lookout National Seashore supports 100-odd horses on Shackleford Banks, where annual "pony pennings" were once a popular attraction. Around 1947 a local doctor released several Shackleford horses and others on Carrot Island, near Beaufort; harsh conditions and mercy killing have reduced this herd from 70 members in 1986 to fewer than 20. The Ocracoke herd had shrunk to about 100 by 1952, when the National Park Service acquired most of the island. Though Boy Scout Troop 290 became a mounted unit while it cared for several privately donated local horses, eventually the Cape Lookout Seashore bought most of these horses, having dispersed the rest of the herd. By 1974 only 10 remained, but veterinary care, supplemental feeding, and the ministrations of an Andalusian stud have brought the population back up to 27.

Since the opening of N.C. 12 in 1984, the Currituck Banks herd, perhaps 60–100 individuals in several bands, has attracted its own tax-exempt support group and inspired a great deal of journalism, merchandising, and controversy. Because the Currituck National Wildlife Refuge excludes horses as nonwildlife, the herd wanders an increasingly crowded county "sanctuary" comprising developed and undeveloped private property. The tiny, probably related band that occupied Back Bay National Wildlife Refuge has been confined to private property in Virginia.

Because of the small size of the horse populations, maintaining genetic diversity and protecting and preserving the herds are significant concerns. Exchanging fertile adults among the Outer Banks herds may reduce inbreeding, and state and federal aid as well as several foundations such as the Foundation for Shackleford Horses and the Corolla Wild Horse Fund seek to solve other problems plaguing the Banker horses.

References: E. Gus Cothran, *Genetic Analysis of the Feral Horse Populations of the Outer Banks* (1993); Gary S. Dunbar, *Historical Geography of the North Carolina Outer Banks* (1958); Hope Ryden, *America's Last Wild Horses* (rev. ed., 1978); Ben B. Salter, *Portsmouth Island Short Stories and History: Wild Horse Report* (1992).

Wynne Dough

Wildlife in North Carolina is abundant despite the state's large human population and increasing urbanization. Approximately 1,270 species of mammals, birds, reptiles, fish, amphibians, and mollusks can be found, of which nearly 200 species are protected by state or federal endangered species laws. North Carolina's three main regions—Mountain, Piedmont, and Coastal Plain—are themselves divided into dozens of habitats for animals. These habitats range from the spruce fir forests of high mountains, which are remnants of the last

Ice Age and harbor several species of hardy animals, to the longleaf pine savanna and pocosins, which have their own distinct residents.

Along the coast, salt marshes are the most important environments for both humans and animals. Like every other wetland, marshes swarm with life. For many fish and shellfish species, the salt marsh is their nursery. Crabs, oysters, shrimp, flounder, mussels, bluefish, croakers, egrets, herons, and multitudes of other creatures live, or certainly feed, in the salt marshes of the coast. Along the "ocean hardbottom," sea turtles, clams, corals, and hundreds of fish species frequent the fertile, rocky outcrops of old river channels that were covered up as the sea level rose at the end of the last Ice Age. The diversity of the dozens of habitats in the state has provided havens for the many animal species that have populated North Carolina throughout its history.

Reptiles and Amphibians. At least 71 species of reptiles are known to inhabit the state or its coastal waters. Representatives of four orders or suborders of reptiles, including alligators, lizards, snakes, and turtles, have been identified. The diversity of reptilian species is greatest in the Coastal Plain, which offers a wide range of habitats and a relatively mild climate. The rolling terrain and moderate climate of the Piedmont also support a diverse assemblage of reptiles. The geologically ancient Mountain terrain provides a more diverse range of habitats than the Piedmont, but the colder climate limits the number of reptilian species that inhabit this region.

Many species of reptiles and amphibians in North Carolina are threatened by human activity. Some of the larger reptiles, including all of the marine turtles and alligators, have been decimated by hunting; now considered endangered species, they are protected by American and international law. Populations of numerous species of smaller reptiles are declining due to habitat destruction by humans.

Twelve species of lizards have been identified in the state. A single colony of the spiny Texas horned lizard is known to exist in Onslow County. Other species include the northern fence lizard, the green anole, five species of skinks, and the six-lined racerunner.

Thirty-seven species of snakes are known to live within the state boundaries, with 31 local species of nonvenomous snakes representing the diverse worldwide Colubridae family inhabiting a wide variety of habitats. Well-known members of this family include the garter, black racer, corn, black rat, ringneck, hognose, milk, coachwhip, and king snakes. The semiaquatic cottonmouth inhabits marshes, swamps, rivers, and streams of the Coastal Plain and the eastern Piedmont. Five species of Viperidae, the poisonous family of snakes with the characteristic heat-sensitive pit between the eye and nostril on either side of a wide head, are found in North Carolina. Three species—the eastern diamondback, pygmy, and timber—are rattlesnakes. The poisonous copperhead can be found in or near forests in all parts of North Carolina. Copperheads inflict the most snake bites to humans in the state, but only one human fatality has been documented in the last century.

Twenty-one species of turtles have been reported in North Carolina or its adjacent coastal waters. The largest of these ancient reptiles are marine turtles. The leatherback sea turtle, the world's largest living turtle, has been observed along the coast but probably does not go ashore to lay eggs. Four other species of marine turtles—the loggerhead, green, Atlantic hawksbill, and Atlantic ridley—range along local coastal waters and estuaries, but only the loggerhead turtle commonly builds nests on beaches, primarily south of Cape Lookout. Numerous other species of aquatic and terrestrial turtles live in North Carolina. The largest of these is the common snapping turtle, which should be treated with caution because of its powerful jaws.

Numerous indigenous salamander, frog, and toad species live in practically every habitat in the state. Important frog species include the bullfrog, Carolina gopher frog, river frog, and southern leopard frog. There are also a number of tree frog species, such as the southern cricket frog, green tree frog, and southern peeper frog. Toad species include the American toad, oak toad, and southern toad. Salamanders abound in North Carolina and the Southeast, living in or near rivers, creeks, and swamps. The state's giant salamander population includes the Neuse River waterdog and the dwarf waterdog. Lungless salamanders include the southern two-lined salamander, dwarf salamander, Junaluska salamander, and eastern mud salamander. The red-spotted newt is also a species of salamander in the state.

Fish. North Carolina has a rich diversity of fish species. English observers during the Roanoke voyages of the 1580s noted many species, confirmed in 1709 by naturalist-surveyor John Lawson, including sharks, Spanish mackerel, mullet, shad, fat-backs (menhaden), skates, eels, bluefish, red drum, rockfish, flounder, herring, sea trout, and many others. Among the freshwater species are trout, several varieties of perch, carp, catfish, sturgeon, and pike. *Fish and Fisheries of the United States*, an 1887 study commissioned by the U.S. Census Bureau, revealed the continuing diversity of North Carolina's waters.

The abundance of fish species in the coastal waters continued into the twentieth century, although sometimes (as in the case of rockfish) in tandem with strict federal regulation to preserve and regenerate some species. For certain other species, like sturgeon and shad, their commercial profitability led to a severe decline: sturgeon are all but absent from North Carolina waters, and shad are only beginning to recover. Although overfishing has often been cited as the main cause of species decline, disappearance of wetlands spawning habitat and poor water quality also have seriously harmed many species.

Bass are found throughout North Carolina's fresh and salt waters. Largemouth bass and white perch like warm, muddy waters, while the Roanoke, rock, spotted, redeye, and smallmouth bass all prefer cooler streams with rocky bottoms. Roanoke, rock, and redeye bass and white perch are native to the state. White perch and white bass may migrate from coastal waters upriver to spawn. North Carolina also has an estimated 4,000 trout streams, many of them in the Great Smoky Mountains National Park, along the Blue Ridge Parkway, and in the Cherokee Indian Reservation.

At the beginning of the twenty-first century, the North Carolina Division of Marine Fisheries listed the following fish species as viable, or able to sustain numbers without intervention: Atlantic menhaden, black sea bass south of Hatteras, king mackerel, Spanish mackerel, spot, spotted ("speckled") sea trout, and striped bass in deep ocean waters. Species in decline included the southern flounder, American shad, and all sharks. Those in "stressed but recovering" status were Atlantic croaker, bluefish, summer flounder, hickory shad, striped bass in sounds, and weakfish (winter sea trout).

Birds. With a great diversity of land forms, climate, and vegetation, North Carolina has habitats suitable for a remarkable variety of birds—by some estimations, approximately 80 percent of all species occurring in eastern North America. Slightly more than 10 percent of species on the official list are hunted as game birds. Bird watching is one of the most popular hobbies in the United States, with millions of dollars spent on the activity each year. From waves of spring migrants flowing through the Blue Ridge Mountains to the spectacular winter accumulations of waterfowl on the coast, North Carolina offers a breathtaking display of bird life that provides great enjoyment to its bird-watching citizens and many visitors from other states and nations.

The composition of the bird population in North Carolina is constantly changing. It is usually broken down into residents, summer visitors, winter visitors, transients, and stragglers. Residents, meaning species rather than individual birds, are present year-round. For example, the American robins that are present in the state during the summer usually move south in the winter and are replaced by northern birds. Summer visitors are found only in the summer months and usually breed in North Carolina. Winter visitors spend the winter months in the state and include many of the ducks, geese, and swans that are hunted as game birds. Transients pass through the state during spring and fall migration as they travel to breeding grounds in the North or wintering territory in the South. Although most migratory birds follow the same routes in spring and fall, a few vary their routes and will pass through the state in only one season. Despite extensive study, bird migration is still not fully understood. Stragglers or accidentals are birds that have wandered outside their usual range.

Although most changes in the range occupied by birds occur naturally, humans sometimes become the change agent, as with the introduction of the house sparrow (1850) and European starling (1870) from Europe. One of the more interesting cases is that of the house finch, a western species that was illegally trapped and shipped by California cage-bird dealers to New York for sale as "Hollywood finches." When the traffic was stopped by the U.S. Fish and Wildlife Service under the Migratory Bird Treaty Act, some dealers on Long Island released their birds in 1940. These house finches flourished and gradually spread south. First seen in North Carolina in the winter of 1962–63, the house finch now breeds throughout the state.

The nineteenth-century slaughter to near extinction of gulls, terns, egrets, and other species for their feathers, used in the millinery trade, raised concerns that resulted in legal protection for nongame birds. In North Carolina, T. Gilbert Pearson assembled an interested group on 11 Mar. 1902 to form the Audubon Society of North Carolina. At its request, the state legislature in 1903 passed a law providing for full protection of nongame birds, nonresident hunting licenses, and a system of wardens to enforce the law. This statute was the forerunner of today's management program administered by the North Carolina Wildlife Commission. Migratory birds are protected under the U.S. Migratory Bird Treaty Act (1918), and the role of the federal government has been broadened more recently by such laws as the Endangered Species Act (1973). In addition to government agencies, many private organizations, including local chapters of the National Audubon Society, Carolina Bird Club, Inc., North Carolina Wildlife Federation, Ducks Unlimited, and Nature Conservancy, play an important role in bird conservation and habitat protection.

Numerous songbirds and garden birds populate North Carolina. Some common species are the American goldfinch, blue jay, Carolina chickadee, Carolina wren, northern cardinal (the North Carolina state bird), gray catbird, barn swallow, pine warbler, red-bellied woodpecker, yellow-bellied sapsucker, ruby-throated hummingbird, tufted titmouse, white-breasted nuthatch, and white-throated sparrow. Shorebirds and game birds include various ducks species, geese, gulls and terns, pelicans, egrets, herons, and osprey.

The subfamily Accipitridae includes hawks, eagles, ospreys, and kites, diurnal raptors that have hooked beaks and hooked claws. In North Carolina, the species most common are the sharp-shinned hawk, cooper's hawk, and northern goshawk. A second subfamily of hawk, Buteoninae, encompasses a group generally referred to as "buteos" or "buzzard hawks." These large, thick-bodied hawks have long, wide wings and short tails; they are often seen soaring high in the sky, scanning the area for prey. Species in the state include the red-tailed hawk, rough-legged hawk, and red-shouldered hawk.

The bald eagle (*Haliaeetus leucocephalus*) is by far the largest of the hawks that inhabit North Carolina. Mature birds are easily recognized because of their great size, their white heads and white tails, and their massive yellow beaks. Eagles feed mainly on birds, small mammals, and fish. Their great flying speed allows them to capture waterfowl in flight and even rabbits that are running for cover. In North Carolina, eagles are most easily seen in the Lake Mattamuskeet area, although they reside—never in large numbers—in many places in the state.

The osprey (*Pandion haliaetus*), frequently called "fish hawk" or "sea eagle"—the only member of the family Pandionidae—is one of the most widely distributed raptors in the world, being present on all continents except Antarctica. In North Carolina, the osprey is found only on the Atlantic coastline, as it rarely lives far from the ocean, though many nest and hunt in the bays and rivers just inland.

Wild turkeys (*Meleagris gallopavo*), the largest game birds in the United States, are native to America and the ancestors of all domestic turkeys. Due to unrestricted hunting and habitat destruction from the clearing of forests, the wild turkey all but disappeared from many sections of North Carolina from the 1880s to the 1920s. In 1937 the Pittman-Robertson Act established funding for wildlife restoration and research. Despite earlier efforts to restore wild turkey populations in North Carolina, they only began to flourish in the 1970s and 1980s, largely due to the National Wild Turkey Federation, which acquired wild turkeys from other states to supplement states in need of birds, and moratoriums placed on turkey hunting. By the twenty-first century, North Carolina's turkey population was well on the way to being fully restored.

Mammals. Native to North Carolina, white-tailed deer are an integral part of the state's history and modern culture, being "every man's big game animal." The male deer (buck) has long been a symbol of power and speed, and the female (doe) figures prominently in ancient legends as the embodiment of grace and beauty. Native Americans depended on the white-tail for meat and a number of important artifacts. European settlers continued this tradition of harvesting deer for survival articles; from famous residents such as Daniel Boone to the most obscure, frontier men and women wore "buckskins." White settlers also opened a commercial trade in deer hides for internal and overseas ventures.

Partially due to strict regulation of hunting, elimination of wild predators, and increased cultivation of food, the white-tailed population has recovered from earlier declines to reach an all-time high. North Carolina's herd is estimated at between 1.5–2 million, approximately 10 percent of the national total. In many areas deer numbers have risen along with human development to the point that many residents are calling for increased hunting seasons and higher bag limits.

Two species of wildcats live in North Carolina. The cougar or mountain lion—a large, unspotted cat with tawny-colored fur and a long tail—though not widespread, is occasionally seen in the southern Appalachian Mountains and the coastal swamps, possibly due more to the releasing of pet cougars than to any significant wild population. The bobcat is the only short-tailed cat indigenous to the mid-Atlantic region. Smaller and having a spotted coat, this solitary and secretive hunter of rodents and rabbits appears in most parts of the state.

The black bear (*Ursus americanus*) is the only species of bear found in North Carolina. It originated in North America and is the most adaptable member of the bear family with a very wide range. In North Carolina, black bears are found from the Coastal Plain into the Appalachian Mountains, with the greatest concentration in the Great Smoky Mountains National Park region along the North Carolina–Tennessee border. While some North Carolina counties still allow the hunting of bears, it is estimated that during the 1990s about one-third of the bears killed in southern Appalachia were taken illegally and often sold to Asian markets.

Between 1900 and 1920 red wolves were extirpated from most of the eastern portion of their range, including North Carolina, and by 1980 they were determined to be extinct in the wild. The red wolf was first reintroduced in the United States in 1987, when four pairs were released into Dare County's 120,000-acre Alligator River National Wildlife Refuge. Additional releases were made, and the first reproduction in the wild occurred in 1988. By the late 1990s there were approximately 50 red wolves living in the Alligator River refuge and nearby Pocosin Lakes National Wildlife Refuge. These wolves help control North Carolina's exploding white-tailed deer populations, also keeping them healthy by preying on the weak and ensuring that only the stronger animals survive to reproduce.

All 16 species of bats found in North Carolina eat insects, from mosquitoes and moths to beetles, crickets, and flies. Even the smallest species eat a lot of insects; some experts believe that a healthy bat colony, rather than anything manmade, is the best way to keep the mosquito population down. Some bats also eat crop-destroying pests. As the public has become more aware of the helpful nature of bats, measures have been started to preserve their numbers. At Chimney Rock Park, several caves in which bats roost have been permanently closed to the public. Bat boxes (artificial roosts) are becoming a common sight in some neighborhoods around the state.

Twenty-nine species of whales are known to inhabit the coastal waters of North Carolina. They are divided into two groups: the order Mysticeti, or baleen whales, and the order Odontoceti, or toothed whales. Baleen whales are distinguished by the large strips of whalebone, or baleen, that hang down from their upper jaws, which they use to eat. Six species of baleen whales frequent the state's coastal waters: the minke whale, Bryde's whale, sei whale, fin whale, black right whale, and humpback whale.

Toothed whales have teeth instead of baleen in their mouths and one blow hole as opposed to the baleen's two. Because of their teeth, members of the order Odontoceti are able to prey upon much larger marine animals than the baleen whales can. Toothed whales found in North Carolina waters include the false killer whale, killer whale, long-finned pilot whale, short-finned pilot whale, melon-headed whale, goose-beaked whale, True's beaked whale, dense-beaked whale, Gervais' beaked whale, dwarf sperm whale, pygmy sperm whale, and sperm whale. Dolphins and porpoises are also considered to be toothed whales. Species found off North Carolina include the harbor porpoise, bridled spotted dolphin, Atlantic spotted dolphin, striped dolphin, Atlantic white-sided dolphin, saddle-backed dolphin, and bottle-nosed dolphin.

North Carolina has many other thriving mammals, including rabbits, raccoons, opossums, beavers, and chipmunks. Foxes, both red and gray, live throughout the state. Wild boars (*Sus scrofa*), not present in the United States before 1890, were introduced into North Carolina at Hooper's Bald in Graham County in 1912, when George Moore of the Whiting Manufacturing Company imported 14 boars from Germany and Russia to join other exotic animals on a large, fenced tract he intended to develop as a game preserve. By the early 1920s, the population had multiplied and many boars had escaped from the preserve; over the next quarter-century wild boars became well established in modern-day Nantahala National Forest and its environs.

Perhaps the most unusual mammal in North Carolina is the flying squirrel. A web of thin, furry skin on both sides of the body extending from the foreleg to the hindleg permits it to perform acrobatic feats. Although the flying squirrel is still fairly common in the state, it is rarely seen because it is nocturnal, resting by day and foraging for food, principally nuts and seed, by night.

References: Jim Dean and Lawrence S. Earley, eds., *Wildlife in North Carolina* (1987); Doug Elliott, "Bats Aren't So Bad," *Wildlife in North Carolina* 54 (November 1990); John A. Fussell III, *A Birder's Guide to Coastal North Carolina* (1994); David S. Lee and James F. Parnell, *Endangered, Threatened, and Rare Fauna of North Carolina* (1990); Margaret Martin, *A Long Look at Nature* (2001); William M. Palmer and Alvin L. Braswell, *Reptiles of North Carolina* (1995); Eloise F. Potter, James F. Parnell, and Robert P. Teulings, *Birds of the Carolinas* (1980); Fred C. Rohde and others, *Freshwater Fishes of the Carolinas, Virginia, Maryland, and Delaware* (1994); William D. Webster, James F. Parnell, and Walter C. Biggs Jr., *Mammals of the Carolinas, Virginia, and Maryland* (1985).

Lee Plummer Templeton
Douglas A. Wait
Additional research provided by Larkin Bell, Kathy Carter, Evan L. Erickson, Joan E. Freeman, John Hairr, William C. Harris, Jerry Leath Mills, Clyde Smith, and Jean Snow.

SEE ALSO Alligators; Audubon Society of North Carolina; Beavers; Cardinal; Carolina Panther; Carolina Parakeet;

Eagles; Endangered Species; Fishing, Recreational; Hunting; Opossums; Terrapins; Waterfowl.

Wilkes County, located in the Mountain region of North Carolina, was formed in 1777 from Surry County and named for the English statesman John Wilkes, a member of the Parliament who fought for American independence. Early inhabitants of the area included the Tutelo and Cherokee Indians; the region was later inhabited by German and Scotch-Irish settlers. Wilkesboro, the county seat, was incorporated in 1847 and named for the county. Other Wilkes County communities include Ronda, Roaring River, North Wilkesboro, Moravian Falls, Boomer, Ferguson, Millers Creek, Mulberry, Wilbar, and Austin. Physical features significant to the county are the Yadkin River and the W. Kerr Scott Reservoir.

"Tom Dooley" of legend and song was hanged in 1868 for the murder of Laura Foster in Ferguson. Wilkes County landmarks and historic sites include the Old Wilkes County Jail, built in 1858; the Robert Cleveland House, built in the late eighteenth century; Claymount Hill, built in 1870; and the Wade Hampton Harris Memorial Bridge, built in 1931. Cultural attractions include the Wilkes Symphony Orchestra, Wilkes Art Gallery, Wilkes Playmakers, and the Whippoorwill Academy and Village, including the Tom Dooley Art Museum. Natural attractions within the county include Stone Mountain State Park and the Rendezvous Mountain Educational State Forest. The county hosts festivals and annual events such as MerleFest, Brushy Mountain Apple Festival, Wilkes Agricultural Fair, Lowe's Balloons over the Blue Ridge, Mountain Bike Ride, and North Wilkesboro Fireworks Celebration.

Wilkes County farms produce such commodities as flue-cured tobacco, apples, poultry, and beef cattle; forestry is an important source of revenue in the county as well. Manufactured goods include hardboard siding, tools, milling equipment, glass products, lingerie, furniture, shoes, and hosiery. Wilkes County had an estimated population of 67,000 in 2004.

Jay Mazzocchi

SEE ALSO "Ballad of Tom Dooley"; MerleFest.

William R. Kenan Jr. Charitable Trust was established by bequest from the estate of chemist and industrialist William R. Kenan Jr., a native North Carolinian and a member of the University of North Carolina class of 1894. Though he lived much of his adult life as a civic and business leader in Lockport, N.Y., he remained very interested in North Carolina and was an especially generous benefactor to his alma mater.

Upon Kenan's death in 1965, approximately $95 million in assets—the bulk of Kenan's estate—went to the establishment of the trust. The bequest directed the trust to fund grants for religious, charitable, scientific, literary, or educational purposes. Education was Kenan's foremost interest. The trust's first major gift was in 1966—a $5 million endowment to establish the William R. Kenan Jr. Professorships. The professorships continue as one of the trust's main programs, and many of America's leading colleges and universities have received grants. The University of North Carolina at Chapel Hill has been the primary beneficiary of these professorships.

The Kenan Trust has established a number of other programs to fulfill its mission, in areas including family literacy, the arts, science and technology, and secondary school grants. Operated from offices in Chapel Hill, the trust is one of the largest of its kind in the South. It is governed by a small number of trustees and managed by an executive director. By the early 2000s the Kenan Trust's assets had grown to more than $300 million, and more than $260 million had been distributed or committed.

Warren L. Bingham

Wilmington is situated between the Cape Fear River and the Atlantic Ocean in New Hanover County. It was known as New Liverpool, New Town, and Newton before being incorporated as Wilmington in 1739–40, named in honor of Spencer Compton, earl of Wilmington, who was a patron of Gabriel Johnston, North Carolina's royal governor at the time.

In 1765 Wilmington was the scene of the American colonies' first successful armed resistance to the Stamp Act. During the Revolution, local Patriots, called Sons of Liberty, butted heads with local Loyalists, many of whom were Highland Scots. In January 1781 Wilmington was occupied by British forces commanded by Maj. James Henry Craig, who used the city as his headquarters while orchestrating skirmishes in the region. In April 1781 he was joined by Lord Charles Cornwallis, who later that month left Wilmington on his fateful march to Yorktown.

From the Revolutionary War through the first few decades of the nineteenth century, Wilmington was a backwater town. Antebellum growth was hampered by a paucity of good roads via which to bring produce to the little port. Thanks to a series of navigational improvements to the Cape Fear River and the city's ports during the mid-nineteenth century, and the invention of steam-powered vessels and railroads, Wilmington began to enjoy steady growth, with exports moving through the port far exceeding imports. Rice, peanuts, flax, cotton, and, most important, naval stores left the banks of the Cape Fear River for destinations all over the world. During this time, Wilmington also became the terminus of the Wilmington & Weldon, Wilmington & Manchester, and Wilmington, Charlotte, and Rutherford Railroads.

At the outbreak of the Civil War, the port suffered from losing its export trade, but within a short time it more than made up for it by becoming a home port to the lucrative blockade-running business. Functioning as "the lifeline of the Confederacy," the blockade-runners brought into Wilmington the military armaments and supplies needed to fuel the Confederate army. The town's official status changed from town to city in 1866. Wilmington's river- and railroad-related businesses continued to grow throughout the nineteenth century. Prosperity was apparent in street and wharf improvements and the construction of fine homes, churches, and public buildings.

The 1940s and the Second World War brought an influx of newcomers and a renewed energy to Wilmington. The North Carolina Shipbuilding Company employed thousands of workers who delivered 243 new ships for the war effort. In 1945 the North Carolina legislature approved the State Ports Authority, which provided support for transforming the World War II shipyard into a first-class port facility. In 1947 access to higher education became a reality when Wilmington College, now the University of North Carolina at Wilmington, opened its doors. In 1948 several community leaders organized the first North Carolina Azalea Festival, which continues to be a much-heralded and well-attended spring event.

In 1961 the USS *North Carolina*, the only American battleship to take part in all 12 major naval offensives in the Pacific during World War II, was berthed on the west side of the Cape Fear River across from the central city. A strong historic preservation movement, initiated in the 1970s, brought much of the old town back to its former elegance, and tourism began to flourish. In 1984 a major movie company constructed a 32-acre film studio within the city limits, boosting the local economy and prompting some to tout Wilmington as "the Hollywood of the East." In 1990 Interstate 40 was completed, linking Wilmington and its port to the rest of the state and nation. During the 1990s Wilmington became one of the fastest-growing cities in the nation. In 2005 Wilmington had a population of around 100,000, making it North Carolina's ninth-largest city.

References: Diane Cobb Cashman, *Cape Fear Adventure: An Illustrated History of Wilmington* (1982); Alan D. Watson, *Wilmington, Port of North Carolina* (1992).

Beverly Tetterton

SEE ALSO Azalea Festival; Filmmaking; Fort Fisher; *North Carolina*, USS; Ports and Harbors; Shipbuilding; Wilmington & Weldon Railroad; Wilmington Campaign of 1781.

Wilmington, css. The CSS *Wilmington* was the last of three ironclad warships built by the Confederate navy in Wilmington during the Civil War. Work began on the CSS *Raleigh* and CSS *North Carolina* in the spring of 1862, but neither vessel proved satisfactory. The *Raleigh* ran aground in Cape Fear in May 1864 and was written off. The *North Carolina* leaked badly and in September 1864 sank at its moorings. In late May 1864 the Confederate secretary of the navy, Stephen R. Mallory, dis-

patched naval shipbuilder John L. Porter to Wilmington to build a new ironclad.

Construction on the *Wilmington* began immediately. Most of the timber came from South Carolina, and iron plating, salvaged from the *Raleigh* and *North Carolina*, was readily available in Wilmington. Although the work progressed quickly, the ship was unfinished when Fort Fisher fell on 15 Jan. 1865. When Union forces occupied Wilmington on 22 February, the *Wilmington*—nearly completed—went up in flames as retreating Confederates destroyed the navy yard to prevent its capture.

References: William N. Still Jr., *Confederate Shipbuilding* (1987); Still, *Iron Afloat: The Story of the Confederate Armorclads* (1985).

Edwin L. Combs

Wilmington & Weldon Railroad (W&W) was the new name adopted in February 1855 by the Wilmington & Raleigh Railroad (completed in 1840), which ran from Wilmington to Weldon by way of Goldsboro and Rocky Mount, bypassing Raleigh. As a central rail link along the Atlantic Coast, it carried heavy traffic during the Civil War and made a considerable profit (in Confederate currency) for its owners. Because the W&W had its own facilities for rerolling iron rails and did not lie in the path of military action until the very end of the war, it suffered somewhat less than many other roads of the region and entered the Reconstruction period dilapidated but intact.

For 20 years after the war, Robert R. Bridgers of Edgecombe County served as president of the W&W. With backers including the Walters family of Baltimore, he developed interlocking directorates, leases, and traffic agreements (using the W&W as a base) that led to the formation of the Atlantic Coast Line Company and the eventual merger with the Atlantic Coast Line Railroad (ACL). In November 1872 the W&W had been leased to its southern connection, the Wilmington, Columbia, and Augusta, but the lease lapsed when the latter road failed to pay the W&W dividend in 1877. Bridgers and his associates acquired control of the Wilmington, Columbia, and Augusta in October 1879, and in June 1885 they leased it to the W&W for 99 years.

In 1898, under Henry Walters's plan to develop an Atlantic Coast Line system, the W&W acquired the southern half of the Cape Fear & Yadkin Valley Railway, with lines from Wilmington to Fayetteville and Sanford as well as from Fayetteville to Bennettsville, S.C. Two years later, the W&W and the Norfolk & Carolina (which connected the W&W at Tarboro with Norfolk), along with connecting roads in Virginia and South Carolina, as well as the Plant System lines in Georgia and Florida shortly afterward, all merged with the ACL, ending the corporate existence of the W&W.

The ACL, however, established its executive and administrative offices in Wilmington, and the northern half of the former W&W (from Weldon to Wilson) became part of the ACL main line. In 1988 a 26-mile stretch of the original W&W from Castle Hayne, north of Wilmington, to Wallace was abandoned, breaking the physical integrity of the historic road. The old freight station on the Cape Fear River survives as a museum of the history of the W&W, the ACL, and North Carolina railroading, but the old passenger station in Wilmington was destroyed.

References: H. D. Dozier, *A History of the Atlantic Coast Line Railroad* (1920); R. E. Prince, *Atlantic Coast Line Railroad: Steam Locomotives, Ships, and History* (1966).

George A. Kennedy

Wilmington, Brunswick, and Southern Railroad

(WB&S), originally known as the Town Creek Railroad and Lumber Company, was chartered in 1907 by local interests to provide freight and passenger service between a connection with the Atlantic Coast Line Railroad and the Seaboard Air Line Railway at Navassa, west of the Cape Fear River bridge, the heart of Brunswick County, and Southport. A 30-mile line was completed in November 1911 by a rather indirect route through Town Creek and Bolivia. According to local legend, the abbreviation WB&S inspired the nickname "Willing, But Slow" when a small locomotive, despite valiant puffing, was unable to start a trainload of World War I soldiers on holiday until many of them got off and gave the train a push. Unlike other Wilmington railroads, the WB&S remained an independent operation throughout its history. Service was discontinued in 1941 and the road abandoned in 1943.

Reference: Charles Kernan, *Rails to Weeds: Searching Out the Ghost Railroads around Wilmington* (1988).

George A. Kennedy

Wilmington Campaign of 1781,

the last important Revolutionary War campaign in North Carolina, was directed toward removing the British enclave in Wilmington that had supported Loyalist depredations throughout the Cape Fear Valley and jeopardized the state government. In January 1781 a small British force commanded by the energetic Maj. James H. Craig of the 82nd Regiment occupied Wilmington, primarily to establish a supply base for the invasion of North Carolina by Lord Charles Cornwallis. The port became a haven for Cornwallis's battered army after the Battle of Guilford Courthouse, but the support that Craig made available to Loyalist commanders in the interior, most notably Col. David Fanning, threatened Whig control of the state in the internecine conflict sometimes called the "Tory War."

In August 1781 the return of capable militia under Gen. Griffith Rutherford, who had been exchanged after nearly a year as a British prisoner, gave the state a commander who could mount a campaign against Wilmington. Ordering a muster in the Salisbury District on 15 September, Rutherford had an army of 1,100 men within two weeks. He moved toward Campbellton on 1 October and combined forces with Gen. John Butler, which gave the little army a total of 1,050 infantry and 350 cavalry. As the force moved toward Wilmington, a cavalry skirmish on 15 October at Rockfish Creek scattered a Loyalist unit. The Whig cavalry scouts backtracked to the Loyalist camp near McFall's Mill, where, in a running fight, the Loyalists were dispersed. Two days later Rutherford sent his entire force into Raft Swamp to flush out Loyalists and deny them a refuge.

Resting at Brown Marsh prior to their final drive on Wilmington, the army was addressed by Governor Alexander Martin. On 23 October Rutherford sent a mounted unit of 300 men under Col. Robert Smith to the southwest side of Cape Fear to cut the port off from overland contact while the main army descended on Wilmington from the north. Smith's blocking force encountered outposts and cleared them with skirmishing at Moore's Plantation and later fought at Seven Creeks with South Carolina Loyalists.

Whig casualties from these engagements were light, prompting the company surgeon to go home. Major Craig's correspondence with his superior officers at Charleston shows that he viewed Rutherford's force as more nuisance than threat. Supply problems prevented Craig from attacking his besiegers before receiving orders to evacuate his position. In the wake of the surrender of Cornwallis at Yorktown, Va., on 19 Oct. 1781, the British high command had decided to abandon Wilmington. On 18 November Rutherford and his men entered Wilmington, the British transport ships still in full view heading down Cape Fear to the Atlantic.

References: John Hairr, *Colonel David Fanning: The Adventures of a Carolina Loyalist* (1998); Gregory De Van Massey, "The British Expedition to Wilmington, January–November, 1781," NCHR 64 (October 1989).

Lindley S. Butler
John Hairr

Wilmington Race Riot

of 10 Nov. 1898 constituted the most serious incident of racial violence in the history of North Carolina. It has been variously called a revolution, a race war, and more accurately a coup d'état. The outbreak stemmed from an editorial published on 18 Aug. 1898 by the *Wilmington Daily Record*, an African American newspaper edited by Alexander Manly. In response to an appeal for the lynching of black rapists made by crusader Rebecca Felton in Georgia on 11 Aug. 1897, Manly wrote that white women "are not any more particular in the matter of clandestine meetings with colored men than are the white men with colored women." Moreover, Manly argued, many accusations of rape were simply cases

Remains of the printing press of Alexander Manly's *Wilmington Daily Record* after his newspaper building was burned by a white mob in 1898. NCC.

where a black man was having an affair with a white woman. Because it involved the sensitive issue of interracial sexual relations, the editorial struck a raw nerve with many whites and led to bitter denunciations of Manly in the Democratic press.

The entire thrust of the white supremacy campaign, in which the Democrats were attempting to regain control of state government, had been racially inflammatory. It was no surprise that after the Democrats, bolstered by bands of armed Red Shirts, overturned Republican-Populist Fusionist control of the state in the 8 November election, the Wilmington Democratic Party leadership decided to discipline Manly and take over the city administration. An order was issued under the name of Alfred M. Waddell, a former congressman and the Democratic candidate for mayor, that editor Manly leave the city with his press and inform Waddell of the action by 7:30 A.M. on 10 November. Unfortunately, Manly had already left Wilmington and the response by local black leaders to Waddell's ultimatum did not reach him in time to forestall the subsequent violence. A white mob of 400–500 people marched on the *Daily Record* office, smashed the press, and burned down the building. The rioters delayed a black fire company long enough to ensure destruction of the property. Thereafter white bands roamed the city, hunting down Fusionists and indiscriminately shooting into neighborhoods believed to be black political strongholds. Many African Americans fled to the forest outside of town. Waddell, backed by armed men, demanded and received the resignation of the entire city board of aldermen, including Republican mayor Silas P. Wright. Waddell immediately took over as mayor and appointed Democratic aldermen.

Republican governor Daniel L. Russell belatedly directed the state militia to stop the violence, but Walker Taylor, the Democratic commander of the guard at Wilmington, arrested only blacks. The new all-white city government forced selected white Fusionists, deemed "decidedly persona non grata," to leave town. In his *Memoirs*, Waddell boasted that the rioting Democrats had "choked the Cape Fear with [black] corpses." In fact, the most-often-cited estimates of black casualties place the number at 11 killed and 25 wounded. Only 3 whites were wounded. Nevertheless, one report noted that at least 2 whites were killed, and another placed the total death toll as high as 250.

Most modern accounts of the violence discount contemporary partisan news stories that a black mob, near the corner of Fourth and Harnett or Nixon Streets, fired the first shots in the riot. From the casualties it is clear that white Democrats did most of the shooting, while blacks were largely defending themselves.

The Wilmington race riot marked a bloody end to increased black participation in North Carolina politics, which had been made possible by Fusionist control of state government from 1894 to 1898. The emergence of an essentially all-white electorate and one-party Democratic rule was solidified two years later with the adoption of the disfranchisement amendment to the state constitution.

The painful legacy of the Wilmington race riot continues to be the subject of study. In 2005, after nearly a decade of research, a special commission formed by the General Assembly under the auspices of the Office of Archives and History released a report chronicling the riot and identifying its long-term effects on African American life in the area. The document concludes that the violence actually resulted from the actions by local whites to gain permanent and unchallenged control of the city. Because of the perceived success of the insurrection, Wilmington blacks were politically dispossessed and had no effective representation until the national civil rights initiatives of the 1960s.

References: David S. Cecelski and Timothy B. Tyson, *Democracy Betrayed: The Wilmington Race Riot of 1898 and Its Legacy* (1998); John DeSantis, "North Carolina City Confronts Its Past in Report on White Vigilantes," *New York Times*, 19 Dec. 2005; Helen G. Edmonds, *The Negro and Fusion Politics in North Carolina, 1894–1901* (1951); Bennett L. Steelman, "Black, White, and Gray: The Wilmington Race Riot in Fact and Legend," *North Carolina Literary Review* 2 (Spring 1994).

Ronnie W. Faulkner

Wilmington Sea Coast Railroad, also known as the Wilmington & Sea Coast Railroad, was chartered in 1887 to provide transportation between Wilmington and Wrightsville Beach. On 12 June 1888 a standard-gauge line for operation with steam engines was completed at a cost of about $30,000; it covered 10.3 miles from a junction with the Wilmington & Weldon Railroad at Wilmington to Hammocks, just across Banks Channel from Wrightsville Beach. At Hammocks, passengers transferred to the 1.5-mile Sea View (later Ocean View) Railway, built in 1889, to cross the channel on a trestle to

Atlantic Station at Wrightsville Beach. Among the promoters of the road were William A. Berry and William Lattimer of Wilmington; Lattimer was its first president (the *Bessie*, the first locomotive, was named for Lattimer's daughter). In 1889 the Wilmington Sea Coast purchased the Ocean View to provide through service, and in April 1902 the entire line was electrified and merged with the Wilmington street car system to become the Consolidated Railways, Light, and Power Company.

References: Charles Kernan, *Rails to Weeds: Searching Out the Ghost Railroads around Wilmington* (1988); Henry B. McKoy, *Wilmington, N.C.—Do You Remember When?* (1957).

George A. Kennedy

Wilmington Star, North Carolina's oldest continuously published daily newspaper, was founded by Maj. William Henry Bernard, a Confederate veteran, on 23 Sept. 1867 as the *Wilmington Evening Star* (soon renamed the *Wilmington Morning Star*). Under Bernard, the paper was unabashedly Democratic, voicing support for Democrats at all levels of government and bitter criticism of Republicans. Moreover, it was an ardent advocacy of white supremacy—a view never more strongly demonstrated than in its coverage of the Wilmington race riots of 1898. The newspaper remained Democratic until World War II, when it became politically independent.

In 1909 failing health forced Bernard's retirement, and he sold the paper to the Wilmington Star Company. In 1927 the R. W. Page Corporation of Columbus, Ga., bought the *Star* and in the latter part of 1929 acquired the *Wilmington News-Dispatch*, an afternoon daily. A combined Sunday edition of the *Star* and the *News-Dispatch* began to appear on 29 Sept. 1929 as the *Sunday Star-News*. In 1940 R. W. Page purchased the *Star*, the *News*, and the *Sunday Star-News* from his own parent company, naming the new corporation Star-News Newspapers. In addition to his journalistic expertise, Page was widely recognized as a leader in the quest for better ports, serving as the first chairman of the State Ports Authority. He continued as president and publisher of the *Star* until his death in February 1955, when his son, Rye B. Page, succeeded him. Family ownership of Star-News Newspapers ended when the New York Times Company bought the business in 1975.

As a morning paper in what was for many years North Carolina's largest city and only ocean port, the *Star* attracted ambitious and talented journalists to Wilmington from across the state. James A. Parham of Robeson County left the *Star* in 1917 to become managing editor of the *Charlotte Observer*, helping to build that paper into the state's largest daily. In 1929 Alfred G. Dickson went to Wilmington as a reporter, beginning a 45-year career spent almost entirely with the *Star-News* papers. He was named managing editor in 1936, editor in 1947, executive editor in 1955, and assistant to the publisher in 1970, two years before his retirement. In 1966 he won a 1965 Sigma Delta Chi (national journalism fraternity) Distinguished Service Award for editorials condemning links between the Ku Klux Klan and law enforcement officers.

Jay Jenkins of Shelby came home from World War II and joined the staff of the *Star*, where he built credentials that led him to positions at the *Raleigh News and Observer* and later the *Charlotte Observer*. For many years he was considered the "dean" of the state's capital news corps. David Brinkley, a native Wilmingtonian and winner of many awards for excellence in TV reporting and commentary, got his first job (1938–40) in journalism as a *Star-News* reporter. He went on to gain national recognition for his work on the *Huntley-Brinkley Report* on NBC television, for coverage of political conventions beginning in 1956, and for ABC's *This Week with David Brinkley* after 1981.

Wiley J. Williams

Wilmington Ten. On 6 Feb. 1971, after weeks of racial tension over integration of the public school system in Wilmington, a white-owned grocery store in a black neighborhood was firebombed. A year later Ben Chavis, a representative of the Commission for Racial Justice, eight black students, and one white woman were arrested, brought to trial, and convicted of the crime. Much national media coverage was given to the "Wilmington Ten," as they were subsequently called, whose sentences ranged from 23 to 24 years. CBS's *60 Minutes*, the *New York Times Magazine*, the Soviet newspaper *Izvestia*, and Amnesty International all focused on the human rights issues involved in the convictions. Protests from around the country were loud, but the North Carolina Court of Appeals found nothing wrong in the way the trials had been conducted. Governor James B. Hunt Jr. refused to pardon the convicted bombers but did reduce their sentences. Nine of the ten were released in the fall of 1978, and Chavis was given his freedom in December 1979. In December 1980 the U.S. Circuit Court of Appeals overturned the convictions, concluding that the initial trial had been unfair and therefore had denied the accused their constitutional rights.

Reference: Jeffrey J. Crow, Paul D. Escott, and Flora J. Hatley, *A History of African Americans in North Carolina* (2002).

Craig M. Stinson

Wilson Collegiate Institute, a private, nonsectarian school located in the eastern North Carolina town of Wilson, opened on 2 Jan. 1872 with 17 students and was chartered by the General Assembly on 24 January of that same year. Founded by Primitive Baptist–affiliated town leaders, the school was granted the right to confer degrees and diplomas in literature, science, and art. The building that housed the institute—constructed in 1859 as the Wilson Female Academy—had been converted to use for a short period as a Confederate military hospital during the Civil War. It was purchased by the founders of Wilson Collegiate Institute in November 1871.

The success of the institute, which grew to an enrollment of 303 during the 1883 term, is attributed to the leadership of the schoolmaster, Sylvester Hassell, an 1862 graduate of the University of North Carolina in Chapel Hill. By 1871 Hassell, an elder in the Primitive Baptist church, had established a reputation as a scholar and educator. He had taught mathematics and languages at the State Normal University in Wilmington, Del., and for a short time served as principal of the New Castle Institute in the same state. An early proponent of coeducation, Hassell equipped the school with a library of 1,200 volumes and more than 60 periodicals, recruited a distinguished faculty, and developed a comprehensive, classical curriculum that offered classes in business, science, mathematics, English, philology, and music. He established what is reported to have been the first practical agricultural department in the eastern part of the state and was a pioneer in strawberry cultivation in North Carolina.

Several students of the Wilson Collegiate Institute ascended to positions of leadership at the national, state, and local level. Perhaps most noteworthy was Josephus Daniels, who grew up in Wilson and started his newspaper career there. Daniels went on to become the editor of the *Raleigh News and Observer*, served as secretary of the navy under President Woodrow Wilson, and eventually was appointed ambassador to Mexico. Charles B. Aycock, governor of North Carolina from 1901 to 1905, also attended the institute.

Wilson Collegiate Institute made a significant contribution to the education of people in Wilson and eastern North Carolina between the Civil War and the advent of public graded schools in the state. In the fall of 1886 Hassell gave up his responsibilities at the school and returned to his home town of Williamston. One of his pupils, Silas E. Warren, took over the school's administration and remained as schoolmaster until his untimely death in 1894. The school's enrollment had dropped to 63 students, most of them female. According to published accounts, the institute property changed ownership during the ensuing years, but efforts to maintain the facility as an educational institution failed.

References: Josephus Daniels, *Tar Heel Editor* (1941); Clark Gerow Shreve, "The Development of Education to 1900 in Wilson" (M.A. thesis, UNC-Chapel Hill, 1941).

Phillip Arthur Mooring

Wilson County, located in the Coastal Plain region of North Carolina, was formed in 1855 from Edgecombe, Nash, Johnston, and Wayne Counties; it was named for Louis Dicken Wilson, a delegate to the constitutional convention of 1835, member of the General Assembly, and hero of the Mexican War. Early inhabitants of the area included the Tuscarora Indians,

followed by English settlers. Wilson, the county seat, was incorporated in 1849 and has the same namesake as the county. Other Wilson County communities include Elm City, Saratoga, Sims, Black Creek, Buckhorn Crossroads, and Stantonsburg. Notable physical features of the county include the Buckhorn Reservoir, Mill Run, and Marsh, Hominy, Cattail, Aycock, and Goss Swamps.

Wilson County is known for its pork barbecue and produces agricultural goods such as tobacco, soybeans, wheat, sweet potatoes, cucumbers, cotton, swine, and poultry. Manufactured products include tires, apparel, glass bottles, fire protection equipment, and fiberglass tubs and showers.

Wilson County landmarks and historic sites include the Lucas-Barnes House, built in 1853, and the James Scarborough House, built ca. 1821, as well as several buildings within the Historic Wilson district—notable among them the Atlantic Coast Line Railroad Passenger and Freight Station, constructed in 1924. BB&T (Branch Banking and Trust Company) was established in 1872 in Wilson. Barton College, also in Wilson, was established, as Atlantic Christian College, in 1902. Wilson County cultural institutions include the Arts Council of Wilson, the Children's Theatre, the British Brass Band, the Play House, and Imagination Station. The county hosts festivals and annual events such as the Spring Festival, Whirligig Festival, Halloween Party and Parade, and Downtown Lights Up and Christmas Parade. In 2004 Wilson County's population was estimated to be 76,400.

Elizabeth Bayley

Windmills were so common along the North Carolina coast at the time of the Civil War that Charles F. Johnson, a Union soldier stationed on Hatteras Island, later wrote that there were "a greater number than I supposed were in existence in the whole country." Johnson may have exaggerated, but the sites of more than 100 eighteenth- and nineteenth-century windmills have been located in Carteret, Hyde, and Dare Counties alone. These were parts of gristmills, which were used almost exclusively for grinding corn. Many were located on isolated barrier islands populated primarily by fishermen and often separated from the nearest cornfield by expanses of broad, narrow sounds. Gristmills existed in this unlikely location because of a barter system in which Outer Banks fishermen traded surplus fish products—including shrimp, considered inedible but used for fertilizer—to mainland farmers for their surplus corn.

Windmills used along North Carolina's coast were almost all of the post mill design, so named because a massive center pole, up to two feet in diameter, supported the entire structure, including the elevated mill and mill house and the four large sails. This type of windmill was unique because it could be rotated to pick up wind from any direction. Early post mills in the Cape Fear region were used primarily to pump water to

Pelletier's windmill on the shore of the White Oak River, about two miles upstream from Swansboro, ca. 1900. NCC. Original photograph owned by Lionel Walter Pelletier, Stella.

flood rice fields, although at one time they were used for flooding salt ponds with seawater in an effort to produce salt. In interior areas, more traditional tower mills were used extensively by North Carolinians to pump water.

North Carolina holds the modern record for the world's largest windmill, a 325-ton experimental structure erected atop Howard's Knob near Boone in the late 1970s. The twin-bladed rotor, mounted on a 140-foot tower, had a wingspan of 200 feet, greater than that of the largest passenger airplane. The project, designed to provide electrical power for 300 to 500 families in the Boone area, was fraught with problems. After four years the operation was discontinued, and the windmill described more accurately as "the world's largest wind-driven generator" was removed. Further development of wind power in the North Carolina mountains and along the coast was being pursued by various groups in the early 2000s.

Reference: Tucker R. Littleton, "When Windmills Whirled on the Tar Heel Coast," *The State* 48 (October 1980).

David Stick

Windsurfing, or boardsailing, is a water sport enjoyed by many North Carolinians and others traveling to the state's Atlantic Coast. In windsurfing, which is closely related to tra-

ditional sailing, the sailor stands on a board powered by a sail attached to it by a universal joint. Although believed to have been invented in the United States in the 1960s, the sport first gained popularity in Europe before being reimported to the United States in the 1970s. It achieved Olympic status in 1984. From the beginning, the Outer Banks of North Carolina have provided some of the best windsurfing on the East Coast. The wind is frequently ample and usually consistent, and the shallow waters of the sound make it an easy place to sail. In addition, the relative mildness of the climate makes it possible to sail throughout the year, especially if using cold-weather gear.

Ted James, who opened Fox Watersports in Buxton in 1976, was one of the first people to windsurf in waves on the Atlantic side of the Outer Banks. Rental equipment for windsurfing could be hired as early as 1978. Ralph Buxton began teaching windsurfing in Nags Head in 1980. Windsurfing did not become an economic force in North Carolina until the early 1980s. Sales of windsurfing gear and cottage rentals have become a significant industry on the Outer Banks. While the sport saw declining demographics in the United States in the 1990s, the Outer Banks still boasts several full-service windsurfing shops.

The southern Outer Banks sees the most windsurfing activity. Cottages have been built directly on the water to rent to windsurfers. The "Canadian Hole," a launch site located about two miles north of Buxton, was named for the many visitors from Canada. Although the Outer Banks remains the epicenter of windsurfing in North Carolina, other coastal locations such as Wilmington, Bogue Sound, and sites near Morehead City (Harkers Island) also provide good sailing venues and a range of conditions.

Inland lake windsurfing may actually be the norm for most sailors in North Carolina. A necessary precondition for inland windsurfing in North Carolina was the creation of large, man-made facilities such as the B. Everett Jordan Lake and Lake Norman. Local windsurfing clubs such as the Triangle Boardsailing Club, the Triad Windsurfing Club, and the International Board Sailing Club of Charlotte have actively promoted the sport since the late 1970s by sponsoring races, regattas, and instruction, and by promoting clean water and free access. *MindJibe*, the newsletter of the Triangle Boardsailing Club, has been published since the early 1980s.

Reference: Mary Ellen Riddle and Thomas Yocum, *The Insiders' Guide to North Carolina's Outer Banks* (1995).

John B. Rutledge

Wine and Wine Making. North Carolina is home to the nation's first cultivated wine grape, the scuppernong, which is a variety of the muscadine grape (*Vitis rotundifolia*) and grows in abundance from the coast to the foothills. The "Mother Vineyard" of scuppernong grapes was discovered on Roanoke

An 1870s drawing of grapes being crushed at the C. G. Garrett and Company Vineyards and Wine Cellars in Halifax County. NCC. Courtesy of Christopher Terrell.

Island by members of the Raleigh expeditions in 1584. For nearly four centuries, North Carolinians have harvested the scuppernong and other grapes to produce wine for private and commercial use. One of the earliest accounts of wines produced in the colony came from the journal of Irish physician John Brickell, who resided in Edenton in 1737. Brickell noted that "there are but few vineyards planted in the colony at present, for I have seen but one small one at Bath-Town and another the Neus (New Bern) of the White Grape. . . . I have drank the wine it produced and it was exceedingly good." Several southern botanists and farmers, including Thomas Jefferson, tried to encourage production of grapes for wine throughout the late 1700s and early 1800s.

Farmers who chose to cultivate scuppernongs found it a lucrative business. The agricultural journal the *Star* reported in 1811 that, during the previous season, 1,369 gallons of wine had been manufactured in an unnamed North Carolina county. A single scuppernong vine can cover an entire acre and produce, even without cultivation, a ton of fruit yielding five barrels of wine. The *American Farmer* reported on 1 Oct. 1819 that "wine is made along the Cape Fear River from Fayetteville to the sea. . . . and the farmers use it as freely as cider is used in

New England. It is common for a farmer to make 8–10 barrels of wine annually for his own use, and many sell considerable quantities."

For the average North Carolinian during this time, however, the drink of choice was "hard" liquor, whiskey or brandy that was readily available everywhere in the region. For most people, wine was a tonic concocted of blackberries or dandelion petals that was used primarily for soothing the bowels. Wine from the scuppernong and other muscadine grape varieties was largely a coastal specialty, enjoyed by gentry and small farmers who produced homemade wine from their backyard vine.

In the early 1800s, there appears to have been no standard method of producing wine. Some vintners pressed the grapes with a cider press, then mixed four parts unfermented juice with one part applejack brandy. Others let the must (the crushed grape mixture) ferment, then drew it off into clean casks, where they mixed three parts juice to one part brandy. Some added honey, while others found the wine's distinctive, musky taste to be sweet enough on its own.

By 1840 grape and wine advocates had encouraged grape plantings, as vineyards and wineries were flourishing across

Sampling wine at Westbend Vineyards near Winston-Salem. Photograph courtesy of North Carolina Division of Tourism, Film, and Sports Development.

the eastern half of the state. Prior to the Prohibition era, in fact, North Carolina ranked as the leading wine producer in the United States. Before the Civil War brought wine making to a halt, there were 25 wineries in the state, with such names as Tokay, Medoc, Cognac, Niagara, Vina Vista, and Catawba. Medoc, located in Halifax County, was the state's largest winery, producing 60 barrels annually.

After the war, vineyards and wineries again sprang up at Castle Hayne, Conover, Eagle Springs, Edenton, Gibson, Holly Ridge, Icard, Littleton, Louisburg, Manteo, Murphy, Peachland, Pettigrew State Park, Samarcand, Tryon, Warrenton, and Willard. In 1900 Paul Garrett, a former Medoc salesman, established his own winery at Littleton. During the next 16 years, he built a wine empire created largely on the distinctive taste of the North Carolina scuppernong. His Virginia Dare red and white wines were the best-selling wines in the nation and won the grand prize at the Louisiana Purchase Exposition in 1904. Garrett's empire, whose production headquarters moved to Virginia and then New York as the southern states became dry, managed to outlast Prohibition. His North Carolina wines gradually lost their distinctive flavor, however, as dry congressmen continued to discourage planting grapes as a cash crop. Upon Garrett's death in 1940, the winery went out of existence.

Wine and grape production in the state remained at an all-time low until 1950, when farmers in Onslow County planted 25 acres of scuppernongs and then established a winery as a market for their grapes. Encouraged by their success, farmers across North Carolina began planting grapes for wine production. In 1972 Jack Kroustalis's Westbend Vineyards in Lewisville became North Carolina's first winery to produce wine made from the same varieties of grapes used to make California and French wines (*Vitis vinifera*).

North Carolina's most famous home became the site of what would become one of the country's most visited wineries when, in the early 1970s, horticulturists at the Biltmore Estate near Asheville began experimenting with French hybrid vines in the estate's gardens. In 1979 the first bottles of Biltmore Estate wines sold out as quickly as they were offered for sale. Biltmore heir William Cecil hired noted French wine maker Phillipe Jourdan to direct the wine-making operations and created a multimillion-dollar winery and tasting room on the estate grounds. Biltmore Estate annually produces about 75,000 cases of wine in 15 varieties and welcomes thousands of visitors through its doors.

By the early 2000s several successful wineries were operating in the state, including Bennett Vineyards, the Biltmore Wine Company, Chateau Laurinda, Dennis Vineyards, Duplin Wine Cellars, Germanton Vineyard and Winery, Martin Vineyards, North Carolina Waldensian Winery, Silohouse Vineyard and Winery, the Teensy Winery, Villar Vintners of Valdese, and Westbend Vineyards. Annually these wineries produce approximately 250,000 gallons of wines made from both European and native grape varieties. North Carolina–produced wine sales contribute about $4 million to the economy each year.

References: Clarence Gohdes, *Scuppernong, North Carolina's Grape and Its Wines* (1982); Carol Byrne Hall, "Fine Wine Finds Its Time," *Raleigh News and Observer*, 4 Sept. 2001; Thomas Pinney, *A History of Wine in America from the Beginning to Prohibition* (1989); Dudley Price, "Industry Needs Aging: N.C. Wineries, Still Just Getting Started, Struggle for Recognition and Respect," *Raleigh News and Observer*, 22 Jan. 2005; Pamela Watson, *Carolina Wine Country: The Complete Guide* (1998).

Elizabeth Scheld Glynn

SEE ALSO Mother Vineyard; Scuppernong Grape.

Wingate University was established in 1896 in Union County, 26 miles southeast of Charlotte, by the Baptist Associations of Union County, N.C., and Chesterfield County, S.C. The school was built on a ten-acre tract that boasted fine oak trees, an all-weather spring, close proximity to the Meadow Branch Baptist Church, and access to the Seaboard Air Line Railway. It offered a complete education from first grade through high school. The trustees, led by John W. Bivens, named the new school for Washington Manley Wingate, a successful president of Wake Forest College.

As the state expanded its public schools, Wingate's enrollment gradually moved toward boarding students in the upper years of high school. In 1923 Wingate became a college, offering the first two years of general education leading to a baccalaureate degree. In the same year, the school became one of several colleges supported by the Baptist State Convention of North Carolina. The economic crisis of the stock market crash and Depression in the 1930s pushed Wingate to the edge of extinction. The convention withdrew support in 1930, students had no money for tuition, and faculty salaries went for the most part unpaid. The administration building burned to the ground in 1932. But school president Coy Muckle and a few determined teachers opened the spring session in the rooms of Wingate Baptist Church, adjacent to the campus. Within a few years a new central building arose on the ashes of the old, attesting the determination of the trustees and local Baptists to keep the school alive. That central building, memorializing President C. C. Burris, who guided the institution from 1936 to 1953, remains as the home to the liberal arts instruction of the college.

The North Carolina Baptists resumed financial support of the college in 1949, and the Southern Association of Colleges and Schools granted membership and accreditation for Wingate in 1952. In 1955 Charles A. Cannon of Kannapolis became interested in the school. Cannon saw Wingate as a place where the children of textile workers and others in the middle class might receive an opportunity to attain higher education. He began to invest in the renewal of the physical plant and the expansion of the curriculum, providing first-class facilities for the growing student body, which reached 1,500 in the late 1960s.

In 1977, under the leadership of Thomas E. Corts, Wingate added upper level college courses and majors, granting its first baccalaureate degrees in 1979. Also in 1979, the college launched Winternational, a program of international study and travel for sophomores; the school built into its tuition the cost of an international experience during the Christmas holidays so that all students could spend ten days in London, Paris, or Amsterdam. Other majors and graduate work in education and business were added during the 1980s, eventually gaining Wingate university status. Modern-day Wingate University has approximately 1,300 students and offers 36 undergraduate majors and 2 graduate programs.

References: Carolyn C. Gaddy, *"Saturday before the Second Sabith": The History of Meadow Branch–Wingate Baptist Church, 1810–1984* (1984); Hubert I. Hester, *The Wingate College Story* (1972).

Jerry L. Surratt

Winston-Salem is heir to a rich heritage produced by the mingling of two distinct historical streams. Known for many years as the Twin City, it was officially formed in 1913 when Salem, founded in 1766 by Moravian settlers, and Winston, established in 1849 as the seat of newly created Forsyth County, merged into a single municipality. From consolidation until the Great Depression, Winston-Salem was the largest and most industrialized city in the state, with an economy dominated by locally developed manufacturing concerns in tobacco and textiles.

A wide array of Winston-Salem's financial, industrial, commercial, and civic enterprises grew out of or benefited from the wealth created by tobacco. Wachovia National Bank opened in 1879, and in the 1880s new railroad connections were built to the north and west. In 1901 and 1902, two brothers who had made fortunes from the sale of their tobacco interests to the American Tobacco trust reinvested their proceeds in textiles; John Wesley Hanes organized the antecedent of Hanes Hosiery Mills, and Pleasant Henderson Hanes founded P. H. Hanes Knitting Company to produce men's underwear. R. J. Reynolds Tobacco Company introduced Camel cigarettes in 1913, and Reynolds soon commanded more than half of the burgeoning national market for cigarettes. The philanthropies of the leading industrial families—the Reynoldses, the Grays, and the Haneses—ornamented the community with new schools, hospitals, churches, and parks.

Of the many businesses that came to Winston-Salem beginning in the mid-twentieth century, by far the most important was the Western Electric Company, which arrived in 1946 and was soon producing a wide range of military and civilian electronics and communications equipment. By the early 1970s it had prompted a host of related businesses to locate in and around Winston-Salem, and its nearly 7,000 employees made it the city's second largest employer after R. J. Reynolds.

The 1980s saw many corporations that had formerly dominated the economy of Winston-Salem disappear or slip out of local control. As early as 1979, the Hanes Corporation, formed in 1965 by the merger of Hanes Hosiery and Hanes Knitting, was bought out by the Sara Lee Corporation. In the trucking industry, federal deregulation created a far more competitive environment that eventually brought the demise of all the major trucking lines based in Winston-Salem. The Western Electric plants, already subsumed into AT&T, closed down as the telephone giant lost its long-distance monopoly in 1984 and was broken up by the U.S. Justice Department. Locally based Piedmont Airlines was bought by USAir in 1987 and lost its separate identity in 1989. By far the greatest blow, however, was the metamorphosis of R. J. Reynolds. Since 1970 the tobacco company had been part of a diversified conglomerate, R. J. Reynolds Industries, which merged in 1987 with the Nabisco Corporation to form RJR Nabisco. In 1990 the last of the huge complex of Reynolds factories in downtown Winston-Salem closed. By the mid-1990s and early 2000s, health care, centering on the mammoth Baptist Hospital/Bowman Gray School of Medicine complex, employed more of the city's workers than any other field.

Winston-Salem boasts several important cultural and historical institutions. The Winston-Salem Arts Council, established in 1949 to promote and coordinate activities in the visual and performing arts, became the first permanent organization of its kind in the United States. The heart of Salem, threatened by urban growth and modernization, became the focus of "an adventure in historical preservation" that began in 1950 with the establishment of Old Salem, Inc.; within 15 years much of the early nineteenth-century appearance of the area was restored, and Salem had become one of the leading town museums in the country.

The Moravian-established Salem College and Academy (1772) and Winston-Salem State University (founded in 1892 as Slater Industrial Academy, a school for black students) are two of the city's important educational institutions. Winston-Salem's higher education resources were greatly expanded in 1939, when Wake Forest College (modern Wake Forest University) accepted an endowment from the estate of Bowman Gray, late president of Reynolds Tobacco, to underwrite expansion of its medical school from two years to four years, provided the school moved to Winston-Salem and became affiliated with the North Carolina Baptist Hospital, located in the city since 1923. After World War II, the success of the medical school led to the entire university being moved to Winston-Salem (from Wake County); the first classes were held on the new campus in 1956. In 1963 educational opportunities in Winston-Salem were further enhanced when the General Assembly chose the city as the site for the North Carolina School of the Arts.

With a population of approximately 200,000, Winston-Salem was North Carolina's fifth-largest city in 2005.

References: Fambrough L. Brownlee, *Winston-Salem: A Pictorial History* (1977); Adelaide Fries, Stuart Thurman Wright, and J. Edwin Hendricks, *Forsyth: The History of a County on the March* (1976); Frank V. Tursi, *Winston-Salem: A History* (1994).

John A. Hutcheson Jr.

SEE ALSO Moravians; R. J. Reynolds Tobacco Company; Salem; Salem Academy and Salem College; Wachovia Corporation; Wake Forest University; Winston-Salem State University.

Winston-Salem Bible College,

formerly the Christian Institute, began in 1945 in a storefront building on Wheeler Street in Winston-Salem. After a shaky beginning during which the college was forced to close its doors twice due to inadequate financing, it reopened in 1950 as a "special purpose" undergraduate institution whose mission was to educate and train workers for evangelism in areas not currently reached by existing churches, especially in the African American community. In 1976 the college moved to a new location on Northampton Drive. During the 1960s and 1970s it expanded and began to train workers from Central America, South America, Africa, and the Caribbean as well as students from the United States. An emphasis on urban ministry and a desire to foster communication between people of different cultures emerged. The college soon had trained more than 70 ministers in the Triad area of North Carolina and 30 percent of the ministers in the region's Independent Christian Churches. The student body of the modern Winston-Salem Bible College

averages about 70 percent black, 15 percent white, and 10 percent foreign.

References: W. Ray Kelley, *Urban Ministry Training in an Inter-Racial Environment* (1995); Kelley, *Winston-Salem Bible College: How It All Began* (1993).

Helen Losse

Winston-Salem Journal, located in North Carolina's fifth-largest city, is one of the state's most influential newspapers, and several of its owners, editors, and reporters have gone on to play significant roles in the national media. Editorially, the *Journal* has supported many local and statewide causes that reflected the desires of some of the city's elite business and philanthropic households, such as the Hanes, Reynolds, Babcock, and Gray families. This was reflected in the paper's support for the restoration of Old Salem, the relocation of Wake Forest University to Winston-Salem in 1956, and the establishment of the North Carolina School of the Arts in the city.

The *Winston-Salem Journal* was founded by Charles Landon Knight and James Robert Justice on 3 Apr. 1897. Knight was the father of John S. and James L. Knight, who later built Knight Ridder, Inc., the largest newspaper chain in the country in terms of total circulation. By 1925 the *Journal* was engaged in cutthroat competition with its local rival, the *Daily Sentinel*. After five months of feuding, *Sentinel* owner Frank Gannett—founder of the Gannett Company, another of the nation's premier newspaper companies and owner of *USA Today*—sold his paper to the Winston-Salem Journal Company.

In 1971 the *Journal* and *Sentinel* were awarded the Pulitzer Prize primarily for their year-long campaign in print to save territory in western North Carolina and Virginia from the hazardous effects of strip mining. When reporters discovered that the Gibbsite Corporation was planning to buy mineral rights in order to strip-mine the land, a stream of articles had appeared in both papers throughout 1970 about the dangers it would pose to the environment and its residents. Facing media criticism and regional opposition, Gibbsite announced its intention to allow its options on the land to lapse.

The *Sentinel* continued to circulate until declining readership forced it to cease publication in 1985. The *Journal*, purchased in 1969 by Media General, Inc., a publicly owned communications company, has remained the primary daily newspaper for Winston-Salem. Soaring production costs and declining readership forced the paper to downsize in 1995, resulting in the dismissal of 86 employees. Other moves to economize and respond to changing markets have included the complete computerization of editing and design procedures, as well as establishing a *Journal* website on the Internet in 1996.

Many talented journalists spent time at the *Winston-Salem Journal*, including Tom Wicker and Marjorie Hunter, who later worked for the *New York Times*; Joe Doster, who left the *Charlotte Observer* to become publisher of the *Journal*; and Chester Davis and Roy Thompson, who dominated the feature-writing contests of the North Carolina Press Association from the 1940s to the 1960s.

By the early 2000s the *Winston-Salem Journal* had a daily circulation of about 93,000 and served residents of Forsyth and other counties in northwestern North Carolina and southwestern Virginia. The *Journal* has begun to shift its emphasis from national events to more community coverage in an effort to compete with other media.

Reference: Frank V. Tursi, *The* Winston-Salem Journal—*Magnolia Trees and Pulitzer Prizes* (1996).

Catherine A. Whittenburg

Winston-Salem State University was founded in Winston-Salem as the Slater Industrial Academy, a school for African Americans, on 28 Sept. 1892. Housed in a one-room frame structure, the school had 25 pupils and 1 teacher. In 1895 it was recognized by the state of North Carolina, and two years later it was chartered by the General Assembly as Slater Industrial and State Normal School.

In 1925 the General Assembly recognized the school's leadership in the field of elementary teacher training by granting it a new charter, extending its curriculum above normal school level, and changing its name to Winston-Salem Teachers College. The school thus became the first African American institution in the nation to grant degrees for teaching in the elementary grades. In 1953 a nursing school was established at the college, awarding graduates the degree of bachelor of science. The state legislature once again revised the college's charter in 1957 by authorizing expansion of the curriculum to include secondary education and any other specific types of training as directed and determined by the State Board of Higher Education. The General Assembly also approved changing the school's name from Winston-Salem Teachers College to Winston-Salem State College in 1963, and to Winston-Salem State University (WSSU) in 1969. Two years later, the General Assembly reorganized higher education in North Carolina, and in 1972 WSSU became one of the 16 constituent institutions of the University of North Carolina System.

By the early 2000s WSSU enrolled more than 2,900 students from all over the United States and many foreign countries. Majors are offered in traditional fields such as English and business and in newer fields such as commercial music and sports management. Graduate programs are offered through an interinstitutional arrangement. The school's 94-acre campus is the home of a sculpture garden and the Diggs Art Gallery. The university also owns a 250-acre camp, Camp Robert Vaughn, located about 20 miles from the main campus.

References: "Historical Sketch," *Winston-Salem State University Catalog* (1985); William S. Powell, *Higher Education in North Carolina* (1970).

Charles W. Wadelington

Winton, Burning of. Winton, the seat of Hertford County, was burned by Federal troops on 20 Feb. 1862. It was the first North Carolina town burned by Union forces during the Civil War and the only one burned completely. On 19 February a flotilla of eight Union gunboats steamed up the Chowan River. As the vessels approached Winton's wharf, Confederate artillery and infantry opened up from the river bluff, but the boats sustained no serious damage.

When the flotilla returned the next morning, Winton was deserted, but several buildings had clearly been used for Confederate billeting and storage. These were torched, resulting in a blaze that left only one small house standing. The Hertford County Courthouse had been destroyed in 1830, and virtually all records from 1830 to 1862 were consumed in this fire, along with several dozen houses, stores, and other buildings. The cooperation of Union army and navy forces in the action constituted one of the first amphibious operations in the history of the American military.

Reference: Thomas C. Parramore, "The Burning of Winton in 1862," *NCHR* 39 (Winter 1962).

Thomas C. Parramore

Wireless Experiments that Reginald Aubrey Fessenden (1866–1932) conducted in North Carolina for the U.S. Weather Bureau from January 1901 to August 1902 led to important advances in radiotelegraphy and radiotelephony. After making voice transmissions between towers a mile apart on Cobb Island, Md., in 1900, Fessenden built a more advanced network stretching from Cape Hatteras, N.C., to Cape Henry, Va. In April 1902 he heard musical notes at his headquarters on Roanoke Island sent from Cape Hatteras, about 50 miles away, and before long he was "talking with Hatteras."

Disagreements with the Weather Bureau ended this project but not Fessenden's interest in radio. In 1906 he established the first transatlantic wireless circuit between Scotland and his new base in Massachusetts. On 24 and 31 December of that year he astonished telegraph operators along the eastern seaboard and at sea, many of whom used unlicensed copies of his equipment, with broadcasts of music and speech. The Radio Corporation of America eventually bought Fessenden's bankrupt National Electric Signaling Company and partly on that account became a communications giant. The combative inventor Fessenden patented more than 500 devices, including the fathometer (used to measure ocean depths), but earned little public recognition. State highway historical markers stand near the former sites of his towers on Hatteras and Roa-

One of Reginald Fessenden's "apparatus shelters" and wire antennas erected at Manteo and Cape Hatteras. Courtesy of NCOA&H.

noke Islands, but other attempts to memorialize him in North Carolina have failed.

Reference: Helen M. Fessenden, *Fessenden: Builder of Tomorrows* (repr., 1974).

Wynne Dough

Witchcraft. Belief in witchcraft influenced people for hundreds of years, and many unexplained occurrences were considered supernatural in origin. In America, the New England colonies were the scene of notorious witchcraft trials, but the southern colonies generally escaped such serious consequences. In 1679 North Carolina law directed local officers to investigate felonies, witchcraft, enchantments, sorceries, and magic arts, among other crimes. The next year, a woman in Perquimans Precinct was jailed on a charge of witchcraft. Court records describe such women as "concerned with familiar Spirits under ye Notion of a Wich."

By the early years of the eighteenth century, witchcraft trials in Massachusetts were ending, and North Carolina courts stopped convicting those accused of such activity. Some cases apparently were either dropped, not prosecuted, or lack complete records. More interesting are cases in which the court rejected charges of witchcraft. In 1706 Walter Tanner accused Mary Rookes of being a witch, which she denied. The court believed her and fined Tanner five shillings. Rookes also faced a similar charge brought by Thomas Collins, who claimed she had bewitched his wife. The court again found her innocent and fined Collins one shilling and costs.

Belief in witches and the supernatural has prevailed throughout the ages. Early settlers in North Carolina believed the Indians could "raise great Storms of Wind and that there were many frightful Apparitions that appear above the Fires during the time of their Conjuration." In April 1768 royal governor William Tryon issued commissions to a number of men to keep the peace, empowering them to hear cases involving charges of "Enchangments, Sorceries, Art Magick," and related causes.

In 1805 the Reverend Brantley York wrote that the belief in witchcraft was widespread in Piedmont North Carolina. He noted much talk of witches and ghosts and observed that people thought witches could change into animals. Witches were also said to be able to enter a house or room through a keyhole and to cast spells on people, animals, and crops.

Men were not immune from charges of witchcraft. In the eighteenth century, Henry Norman was charged with witchcraft, and Duncan McFarland of Laurel Hill in Richmond County was in court at almost every session in the early nineteenth century charged with a variety of transgressions, often including witchcraft.

Although belief in witchcraft, and groups of those professing their belief, has continued in North Carolina, the stereotypical image of witches as evil or dangerous does not persist in any significant way. Many towns are home to organized pagan or wiccan organizations and witch covens, including Shelby's North Carolina Piedmont Church of Wicca, Charlotte's Sacred Oak Grove Coven, Greensboro's Royal Order of the Knights of Herne, Havelock's Shadowwind Coven, Lexington's Gathering of the Silver Rose, and Raleigh's Coven Greyshadow. In addition to practicing traditional witchcraft, these groups express an underlying spirituality in a variety of ways and often have an environmentalist focus.

William S. Powell

Womanless Weddings, often staged by men's civic and fraternal groups, were popular entertainment in North Carolina and other southern states prior to the advent of television. They consisted of a mock wedding in which males dressed the roles of the entire wedding party, including the bride, mother of the bride, bridesmaids, and flower girl. These events were often fund-raisers, since many in the community were more than willing to pay admission to see their male neighbors in ridiculous female attire. Some organizations continue to stage womanless wedding fund-raisers.

"Tom Thumb" weddings, a "cousin" of womanless weddings, were also popular in the early primary grades of the state's public schools. These were usually yearly events in which the youngest students played the bride and groom and their classmates the wedding guests—many of them dressed as nursery rhyme characters.

Lisa Brantley Kobrin

Women. From Virginia Dare's birth on Roanoke Island in 1587 to Elizabeth Dole's election as a U.S. senator in 2002, many North Carolina women have been leaders or participants in important historical events and trends. Countless others—of all races—have lived, worked, and shaped their homes and communities in relative obscurity. Written histories of North Carolina have often focused on topics relating to the work and accomplishments of men, and even in the early 2000s North Carolina women remained marginalized in many ways. Large numbers worked in low-skill jobs in a time of increasing demand for a technologically advanced workforce. Equity of pay for women and men remained an issue. The number of female-headed households continued to increase, while many of the women heading households had low-paying jobs and children to support. At the same time, North Carolina women of ability and energy, regardless of race or class, have enhanced women's opportunities in politics, the arts, and the professions.

Women's Roles in Precolonial and Colonial North Carolina

Agriculture long dominated North Carolina's economy and society, and women constituted an invaluable source of agricultural labor. Native Americans after about 1000 B.C. developed villages with fields of squash, corn, sunflowers, pumpkins, beans, and other vegetables tended by women. Women provided most of the agricultural and domestic labor, and all residences, fields, and agricultural tools belonged to them. The matrilineal kinship system followed by Native Americans—in which children traced their lineage through their mothers rather than their fathers—also reinforced the influence of women. Native American women enjoyed considerable freedom over their choice of husbands or in deciding to divorce. If a couple parted, the man returned to his mother's house. Indian women's authority and autonomy surprised and shocked Europeans in colonial North Carolina.

Most of the first Euro-Americans who moved into North Carolina from Virginia in the 1650s were either servants or women married to poor farmers seeking land in the fledgling colony. Many women expected to marry and become mothers, and single women were sometimes scorned. Women headed no more than 5 percent of the colony's households. The Lords Proprietors, who received their charter to Carolina in 1663, actively encouraged the immigration of women by offering them land grants to settle in the colony. Female indentured servants also received a grant of land after their period of servitude ended, and colonists received headrights for each slave, male or female, they imported into the colony.

Southern women well into the twentieth century lived under a patriarchal system that placed white men at the top of a hierarchy that enforced women's economic and social subordination. Married women under English common law were *femes covert* who held no property rights. Their legal status was subsumed under that of their husbands. Only widows or single white women could own property under common law. White men were legally the masters of their wives and children and, until the end of the Civil War, of the enslaved African Americans who worked their land. Enslaved black women stood at the bottom of the hierarchal structure. Native American women, who were nonwhite but free, were also marginalized in North Carolina.

Farm life on the frontier was a harsh existence on isolated subsistence acreages occupied by men and women struggling to survive by raising a few crops and perhaps some hogs and chickens. Women needed to be self-reliant, industrious, and able to withstand harsh and sometimes dangerous living conditions. Education remained rare, except among the Moravians, who built schools for both boys and girls in the eighteenth century.

The colony matured slowly before rapid settlement in the 1750s. Families who lived in small towns or on larger plantations accumulated wealth from land speculation; the cultivation of rice, cotton, and tobacco; and the production of naval stores. The wealthiest educated their sons and daughters by hiring tutors, although most women received only a rudimentary education in reading, writing, and math. Town women shaped their communities through domestic and public work and the support of churches. Some women became midwives and nurses or ran taverns, inns, boardinghouses, ferries, and shops. A few worked as attorneys during the early colonial period. Many were regular communicants in denominational churches that emerged in North Carolina, especially after the First Great Awakening in the 1730s, raising money for their churches. A few Quaker women became traveling ministers for their faith, as well.

African slaves appeared in the colony by the 1680s, with more men than women being imported at first. They lived under slave codes that controlled their lives. Enslaved men and women endured hard work, poor food, and inadequate shelter during much of the colonial period, yet they formed families and larger slave networks despite these hardships. Slave marriages were not legal, but owners found it beneficial to accept slaves' marriage arrangements. Children born to slave women became the property of the slaveholder. By 1767 nearly 41,000 slaves lived in North Carolina. That number had increased to 100,000 by 1790.

Women in the Revolutionary Era and Early Statehood

During the American Revolution, North Carolina women experienced the disruptions of war while assessing their roles in the new republic. Patriot women supported economic boycotts of English goods, made bandages, nursed the wounded, made and wore homespun, faced personal danger, and maintained farm operations in a time of inflation and shortages. Loyalist women often faced the scorn of their Patriot neighbors; some, like Scottish-born Flora MacDonald, were forced from their homes. New Bern women solved commodity shortages by sharing the single remaining needle in town and pinning their dresses with thorns. Fifty-one women in Edenton signed a petition in support of the political "resolves" of 1774 and asserted it was their duty to do so. The "Edenton Tea Party" indicated that astute urban women understood politics and considered their support of the new republic as an important responsibility.

Improved educational opportunities represented one of the major advancements for women in the new state of North Carolina, although most politicians generally avoided educational reform in the early 1800s. Wealthy planters who educated their daughters hired tutors or sent their daughters to schools outside the state. As private academies developed in the state, more daughters of the elite attended these institutions for instruction in math, history, reading, literature, and the ornamental arts, as well as in the "female attributes" of piety and modesty. About 300 female academies opened their doors in the state between 1820 and 1860. Salem Academy opened to non-Moravians in 1804; Quakers started the New Garden Boarding School (later Guilford College) in 1837; Methodists chartered the Greensboro Female College in 1838; and Episcopalians established Saint Mary's School in 1842. These and other denominational and family-run schools varied in quality, but they generally improved educational opportunities for girls in the state.

Church denominations sent missionaries to Native American communities in North Carolina to teach Christianity and train Indian children in what were deemed proper gender roles. They were instructed in English instead of their native languages, although some tribes escaped the influence of missionaries and retained their native customs.

The children of free blacks in the state, both male and female, had access to some education. Many became apprentices, while others worked for their parents. The 1850 census listed 42 percent of free blacks as being literate, many having been taught by Quakers, Presbyterians, or Methodists. Free black parents, in turn, taught their children to read and write.

In 1839 North Carolina established a public school system for white boys and girls. By 1853 there were 40,000 students enrolled in public schools. Many families questioned the need to educate farm girls, however, and fewer yeoman girls than boys attended public schools.

Life in Antebellum North Carolina

The seasonal routines of agrarian life defined North Carolina culture throughout most of the antebellum era. Women of the state's planter elite generally met the expectations of southern society rather than seeking independent careers. Southern patriarchy gave planter women stronger ties with their male relations than with women of other classes and races. Planter women supervised complex households of slaves and children. The work was never-ending, even for women who escaped much of the drudgery by using servants and slaves. Planter women also faced repeated pregnancies. Many found the unceasing demands and lack of privacy exhausting.

Elite women who lived in towns escaped the agrarian responsibilities of plantation women, and some used their time to work in volunteer groups. They began attending political gatherings after about 1840, and a few wrote and published under pseudonyms in newspapers and literary journals. Educated, intelligent women used their talents to create opportunities for themselves while remaining southern "ladies."

Meanwhile, slave women worked from dawn until dusk and then had to care for their own families at night. House slaves might develop skills as midwives, weavers, and cooks and obtain special status within the white and slave communities. Enslaved women left few records of their experiences, but interviews conducted in the 1930s with former North Carolina slaves indicate the importance of religion and family in the slave community and the anguish caused by the separation of families. These accounts also reveal how slave mistresses enforced their authority through whippings, poor food, and threats to put slaves "in their pocket," meaning to sell them if they caused trouble. The difficulty slave women faced in caring for their own children and babies when forced always to put the needs of the white family first are well documented. Additionally, they faced the threat of sexual assault by their owners, as strikingly described by Harriet Jacobs in her book *Incidents in the Life of a Slave Girl, Written by Herself* (1861).

Religious revivals swept the state in repeated waves during the nineteenth century. Yeoman women participated in emotionally charged services to seek salvation and to express themselves in meetings. They fed and housed traveling ministers. Women from all classes joined churches to obtain a degree of independence. More women than men became church members during the nineteenth century. Baptist women as early as 1810 raised money for church missionary work, and women of other denominations followed. Groups of women started charitable organizations in New Bern, Fayetteville, Wilmington, Raleigh, and Elizabeth City for the worthy poor. Antebellum society accepted this work outside the home as an extension of women's roles as wives and mothers.

Marriage was a civil contract in North Carolina, but women remained unequal partners. Women hoped for affectionate marriages, but the gap between these expectations and reality troubled many wives. The sexual double standard applied to white men displeased many women. Some husbands were poor businessmen, as well. If women chose unwisely in their partners, the legal system offered little help. Divorce proved difficult to obtain in a state controlled by men determined to maintain white male authority over wives and slaves. The courts often protected a husband's right to chastise his wife.

Secession and Civil War

The coming of the Civil War placed all white women in the forefront of supporting the Confederate cause. Women ran the farms, plantations, and businesses while men left to fight in increasingly bloody battles. A diary kept by Halifax County plantation mistress Kate Edmondston, and published more than a century after the war as *Journal of a Secesh Lady*, recorded the impact of the war on women in the state. Women had to rely on themselves and make important decisions. Some welcomed the challenge and independence, but others found it stressful and resented the demands placed on them.

North Carolina's secession elicited immediate and enthusiastic support from many of its women, who worked together to make uniforms, tents, cartridges, bandages, and other military supplies. Some worked in hospitals, organized food drives, and raised funds for war equipment. They wrote patriotic poetry and fiercely criticized southern men who failed to enlist. One woman, Sarah Pritchard Blalock, disguised herself as a man and joined the Twenty-sixth North Carolina Regiment to remain near her husband. As Union troops advanced into eastern North Carolina, many women and children became refugees dependent upon friends and strangers for shelter during times of inflation and food shortages. Public schools for the first time employed more women as teachers than men, at a time when many women needed the income.

Huge numbers of North Carolinians lost family members during the war. The state sent more soldiers to fight for the Confederacy than any other state, and it sustained the greatest number of casualties. Yeoman families in particular suffered as the war dragged on. Facing starvation (flour that had cost $18.00 a barrel in 1862 jumped to a price of $500 a barrel in 1865), they resisted Confederate authority. Some women staged food riots to seize flour and other commodities. They wrote heartfelt letters to Governor Zebulon B. Vance demanding an end to the war and assistance in feeding their families. Yeoman women also wrote letters to their men in the army urging them to come home. By 1864 many North Carolina soldiers had deserted to help their families. The state's Home Guard shot deserters and did not hesitate to torture yeoman women to try to force them to reveal where their male relations were hiding. The protection accorded southern ladies did not apply to women of the yeoman class in many instances.

Slave women's work also fed and clothed the Confederacy, but those who lived near towns occupied by northern troops fled to Union lines. In New Bern and other areas under Federal control, they worked for northern troops as cooks and laundresses and ran boardinghouses. They set up schools to educate black children and helped create new communities such as James City. When the war ended, many slave owners were shocked when former slaves quickly left plantations in search of better lives and opportunities.

Women Help Shape the New South

Women's reactions to the Confederacy's defeat reflected racial, gender, and class differences. There were 25,000 more women than men in North Carolina at the end of the war. Widowed, married, or single, women struggled with poverty. Many accepted paid work to support themselves or their families for the first time. North Carolina's 1868 constitutional convention wrote a new constitution that improved married women's property rights (which also had the effect of helping husbands by protecting property from creditors). More women in the state entered college to improve their knowledge and skills. Educated women, both black and white, turned a critical eye on society and organized women's voluntary associations to promote social change.

Black women sought to reunite families, educate their children, and work with their husbands to build better lives for themselves and their race. Many found that their only chance to work—for poor wages and under harsh conditions—was in domestic service, agricultural labor, or the state's emerging tobacco factories. They were not allowed into the textile mills of the New South, which hired only whites. By 1890 more than 42 percent of black women worked outside their homes, as compared to about 15 percent of white women.

Self-sufficient farms declined with the emergence of a cash crop economy in the 1880s. These crops fed the tobacco and cotton factories, but as a result farm families grew less food for themselves and incurred more debt to merchants who charged high prices and interest. Women, black or white, who had viewed themselves as partners in the farming enterprise felt undervalued as their unpaid contributions lost value in the family economy. Many farmers became so indebted that they lost their farms. By 1890 one-third of white farmers and nearly three-quarters of black farmers in North Carolina were tenants or sharecroppers.

At the same time, industry expanded in the state. By 1904 North Carolina cotton mills contained half the looms and spindles in the South. Mill owners needed cheap local labor to run the machinery. They welcomed white women and children as workers because they could pay them less and because women and children rarely challenged male authority. By 1880 women and children composed 75 percent of the state's mill workers. Durham's tobacco factories employed women in larger numbers, too, offering work to black women as well as white. By 1910 North Carolina's 272,990 female workers represented the highest percentage of working women (34.2 percent) in the nation. Among those working in the lower classes, about half worked in agriculture, and the other half worked as domestic servants or in cotton mills and tobacco factories.

Discontented black and white farm families joined Republicans and agrarian reformers in the Farmers' Alliance and Populist Party in the 1880s and 1890s to challenge entrenched political and business interests in North Carolina that controlled industry and farm prices. About 25,000 women joined the Farmers' Alliance in the state. They pressed for reforms such as the establishment and funding of public schools and colleges for black and white women with some success. White supremacy campaigns launched by the Democrats in 1898 and 1900 limited interracial cooperation, however, until the end of Jim Crow laws, disfranchisement, and segregation in the 1950s and 1960s.

Following the Civil War, elite white women faced diminished income and an independent black labor class. The eldest generation, who had lived longest with slave labor, largely rejected the aspirations of black families. The younger generations of elite white women proved more assertive in building new lives. Some preferred being single and working to support themselves. North Carolina women such as Mary Bayard Clarke and Frances Christine Fisher Tiernan became writers who achieved literary success in the 1870s and 1880s. Women used organizational skills developed during the Civil War to provide service to the state. Raleigh women in May 1866 formed the Wake County Ladies' Memorial Association to establish a cemetery for Confederate dead. In May 1867 they opened one of the first Confederate cemeteries in the South. Women in many other towns did the same. Elite young women who married did their own housework, often with labor-saving devices such as stoves and washing machines or with the help of black women servants. They enjoyed their success in creating modern households.

The overwhelming number of elite working women accepted jobs as teachers in public and private schools and eventually changed the face of instruction in North Carolina. By the 1930s, women made up 80 percent of the state's teaching population. New institutions of higher learning were established, such as the State Normal and Industrial College for white women in Greensboro (now UNC-Greensboro) and Saint Augustine's College for black men and women in Raleigh. Careers as nurses or doctors, librarians, or other professionals became possible, although less than 3 percent of the state's working women were engaged in professional work in 1900. This percentage increased to 10 percent by 1940.

Many women were led by their changing self-image to volunteer in organizations that would benefit the public welfare. White and black women joined the Woman's Christian Temperance Union (WCTU) in the 1880s and worked together to combat alcohol abuse. Black women organized the WCTU Number 2 in 1889, in which they set priorities not only for temperance but also for improving the legal status of their race. In 1908 temperance women achieved victory when North Carolina voters approved statewide Prohibition.

White women's patriotic and memorial groups, such as the United Daughters of the Confederacy, were organized in the 1890s during a period of increased racial strife. These groups controlled the content of textbooks, fostered the literature of the Lost Cause, and preserved class and racial authority. They also participated in white supremacist campaigns that led to the disfranchisement of black men in 1900.

By the twentieth century, North Carolina's organized women confidently advocated public reform. They were not radical feminists. They believed educated women had a duty to study their society, identify problems, and implement solutions. They joined the North Carolina Federation of Women's Clubs (NCFWC), the YWCA, church societies, and temperance groups and set goals for the state's future. The NCFWC, from 1902 on, proved pivotal in persuading the General Assembly to pass welfare legislation for improved sanitation, public libraries, better schools, and much more. The group successfully campaigned in 1913 to have women placed on public school boards, even though women were not yet allowed to vote. Despite the achievements accomplished jointly with black women in groups such as the North Carolina Federation of Colored Women's Clubs, most white organized women remained silent about the treatment of blacks. Not surprisingly, urban black women supported civic reform to help their race as well as their neighborhoods. Leaders such as Charlotte Hawkins Brown challenged white women's unquestioning acceptance of the inferiority of the black race.

Women Earn the Right to Vote

Democratic politicians and businessmen resisted women reformers on some issues as the century progressed, often because women wanted changes that threatened men's political and economic power. Women's pursuit of protective legislation for women and children workers in factories and mills angered them. The women suffrage movement raised alarm bells, because the subordination of women remained a cornerstone of white supremacy, and women suffrage opened the door to black women voters. This stopped many white women from supporting the suffrage movement.

Many North Carolina women and men believed, however, that women, as citizens and taxpayers, should have the vote. In 1913 women organized the Equal Suffrage Association of North Carolina (ESA), welcomed men and women as members, and campaigned vigorously for the vote. Its leaders hoped women's work during World War I would increase support for suffrage in the state. Women volunteered in the Red Cross, grew victory gardens, rolled bandages, conserved grain, and did two-thirds of the work in Liberty Loan campaigns. Nonetheless, women suffrage remained an unpopular idea in the state, and North Carolina's legislature declined to ratify the Nineteenth Amendment in 1920. The state belatedly ratified the amendment in 1971.

The Nineteenth Amendment ensured women's entry into state politics, although many women remained apathetic about voting. Women entered local and state government as librarians, clerks, managers, and agency heads. Some were elected to the North Carolina General Assembly, although between 1921 and 1961 only 13 women served in that capacity. In 1920 Lillian Exum Clement of Buncombe County became the first woman to serve in a state legislature in the South.

Led by Gertrude Weil of the ESA and the NCFWC, women organized the North Carolina League of Women Voters to prepare women for their roles as voters and citizens. The league, together with the Legislative Council of North Carolina Women, pressed an active reform agenda aimed at improving the lives of women and children, including support for the federal Sheppard-Towner Act that funded a health program for mothers and children. Their battle with businessmen to conduct a survey of working conditions in the state's mills failed, however, when men blocked outside studies of work conditions. Support for the league wavered in the 1930s after it supported the Loray textile strike in Gastonia that led to the murder of North Carolina labor activist Ella Mae Wiggins. Weil and other white women condemned the murder and subsequent acquittal of the perpetrators, but their voices failed to sway many in the state.

Activism and the Expansion of Women's Opportunities and Public Influence

Labor conditions turned women workers into activists. New restrictions on child labor increased the number of married women who worked in industry to augment family incomes. The Great Depression also forced married women to seek employment. By 1940 women represented nearly 72 percent of the textile workforce. Working conditions were brutal. Manufacturers, interested in profits and controlling labor, brought in more machinery, fired slow or elderly workers, and increased the workload of the remaining employees.

World War II marked another milestone, as North Carolina women were encouraged to work in factories, munitions plants, and the military to help the war effort. In 1940 one out of every four women in the state worked outside the home. Women kept agricultural production moving, participated in bond drives, conserved food, organized scrap metal drives, joined the Red Cross and the USO, and opened their homes to soldiers' wives who came to the state to visit their husbands. More than 7,000 North Carolina women joined one of the military services.

The war ended with men returning to their former jobs and women being urged to return to their homes. In North Carolina, which historically had a large workforce of women, nearly two-thirds stayed at work. Black women still found work mostly in domestic service, but their experiences during the war later encouraged black women and black men as well to challenge segregation in the state. After the 1954 U.S. Supreme Court decision in *Brown v. Board of Education*, black women in Greensboro organized interracial meetings at churches and the YWCA to discuss integration. When the Greensboro sit-ins occurred in 1960, women joined the movement, although activists such as Ella Baker decried the limited leadership roles allowed black women.

North Carolina women gained visibility in the twentieth century as artists, writers, and musicians. Etta Baker, for example, was nationally recognized for her blues guitar music, and Shirley Caesar enjoyed an illustrious career as one of America's premier gospel singers. Visual artists Clare Leighton, Angelica Reckendorf, and Susan Moore were key members of the influential artistic community centerd at Black Mountain College in the mid-twentieth century. Betty Adcock, Lee Smith, Doris Betts, Wilma Dykeman, Elizabeth Spencer, Kathryn Byer, and Maya Angelou are among many women writers in the state who have helped create a distinctive southern literature respected and enjoyed by readers around the world.

The feminist movement of the 1960s and 1970s challenged and transformed many assumptions about women's roles in the home and workplace. Full equality with men remained elusive, however, in job opportunities, education, and politics. Governor Terry Sanford appointed the Governor's Commission on the Status of Women in 1963, with Duke University professor Anne Firor Scott as chair, to study and report on North Carolina women. The commission clearly delineated that the number of working women had increased by 80 percent between 1940 and 1960, with most women in low-paying jobs without benefits. The report urged pay equity for women and improved child-care options. In 1973, when women activists lobbied the state legislature to ratify the Equal Rights Amendment (ERA), they assumed women suffering from job discrimination, lower wages, fewer health benefits, and limited access to quality day care would support its passage. Instead, many women, as well as men, fearing what they saw as a threat to the South's traditional family values, regarded the ERA as a feminist attack rather than a women's issue and successfully lobbied against it. The legislature voted the amendment down three times, the last time in 1982.

In the late twentieth century, women assumed greater leadership roles in the state legislature, although men continued to hold most of the important legislative posts or appointments on boards and commissions. Women have served as chairs of the Senate Appropriations Committee, as House and Senate minority leaders, and as Speaker pro tempore of the

House. Beverly Perdue, a state senator from Craven County, became North Carolina's first female lieutenant governor in 2000 and won reelection in 2004. Nonetheless, in 2004 women made up only 20.6 percent of the state legislature, although they constituted the majority of the state's population.

In 1992 Eva Clayton became the first woman and, along with Mel Watt, the first African American since Reconstruction to be elected to the U.S. Congress from North Carolina. In 2005 Elaine Marshall started her third term as secretary of state in North Carolina, and Cherie Berry began her second term as head of the Department of Labor. Women headed five of the state's major governmental departments as well. More women found advancement in the field of law. In 2002, 57 percent of the entering class at UNC-Chapel Hill's School of Law was female. Only one female justice sat on the North Carolina Supreme Court in 2005, but 7 out of 15 justices on the state's Court of Appeals were women.

References: Albert Coates, *By Her Own Bootstraps: A Saga of Women in North Carolina* (1975); Donald G. Mathews and Jane S. De Hart, *Sex, Gender, and the Politics of ERA: A State and the Nation* (1990); Kathryn L. Nasstrom, "'More Was Expected of Us': The North Carolina League of Women Voters and the Feminist Movement in the 1920's," *NCHR* 68 (July 1991); North Carolina Council for Women, *Status of Women in North Carolina* (1994); Margaret Supplee Smith and Emily Herring Wilson, *North Carolina Women: Making History* (1999).

Terrell A. Crow
Additional research provided by Ansley Herring Wegner.

SEE ALSO American Association of University Women; Equal Rights Amendment; League of Women Voters; North Carolina Equal Suffrage Association; Women Suffrage.

Women's Association for the Betterment of Public Schoolhouses.

Interest in education and child welfare were major themes for women reformers in late nineteenth- and early twentieth-century North Carolina. In a speech to students in 1902 at the North Carolina Normal and Industrial College for Women at Greensboro (now the University of North Carolina at Greensboro), Charles D. McIver exhorted students to labor as mothers and teachers to improve public education for white children in North Carolina. His speech planted the seeds for the formation of the Women's Association for the Betterment of Public Schoolhouses in North Carolina (WABPS). Although originally founded as a student organization, the group saw its membership skyrocket with the enrollment of middle class white women.

The WABPS served as a major vehicle for women reformers in North Carolina who hoped the organization could combat both illiteracy and poverty within the state. Between 1902 and 1910, the association constructed hundreds of schoolhouses. The widespread popularity of the program was at least partially due to the building of schools at the local level. Because of its success, other states launched similar programs with North Carolina as a model. Like other social programs in this period, the WABPS focused only on whites. In a somewhat parallel program, African American women supported the growth of black schoolhouses in rural communities through the Rosenwald Fund. Through contributions raised at picnics, ice cream socials, and rallies they matched school building funds provided through the Rosenwald program. By the early 1930s, North Carolina had constructed more Rosenwald schools than any other southern state. While both the WABPS and the Rosenwald Fund increased the number and conditions of school buildings, they were largely unsuccessful in their efforts to eradicate poverty.

References: Thomas E. Hatchett, "The Rosenwald Schools and Black Education in North Carolina," *NCHR* 65 (October 1988); James L. Leloudis II, "School Reform in the New South: The Women's Association for the Betterment of Public School Houses in North Carolina, 1902–1919," *Journal of American History* 69 (March 1983).

Tom Belton

SEE ALSO Rosenwald Fund.

Women Suffrage movement in North Carolina began in 1894 with the formation of the North Carolina Equal Suffrage Association in Asheville. Association president Helen Morris sought a state amendment extending the vote to women, and Senator J. L. Hyatt of Yancey County introduced a bill to this effect in the 1897 legislative session. The Senate leader, however, reflecting the sentiment of his colleagues, referred it to the Committee on Insane Asylums, where it died. Little was attempted or accomplished during the next 15 years. The state's women suffrage movement lay dormant, as it did in much of the rest of the nation.

The movement revived in late 1913 with Gertrude Weil's formation of the North Carolina Equal Suffrage League in Charlotte. Weil, a Smith College (Massachusetts) graduate, was the daughter of a German Jewish immigrant who had settled in Goldsboro just before the Civil War. She was one of the South's "new women" who had acquired some postsecondary education, participated in a range of club activities, and enjoyed paid working experiences as the region began to modernize. The Equal Suffrage League helped develop local groups while lobbying legislators and publicizing its cause through pamphlets and speeches. In 1915 Lilian Exum Clement of Asheville started a branch of the Congressional Union, later renamed the National Woman's Party, a more militant group determined to obtain suffrage through a federal amendment. Still, the 1915 legislature voted down all attempts to grant

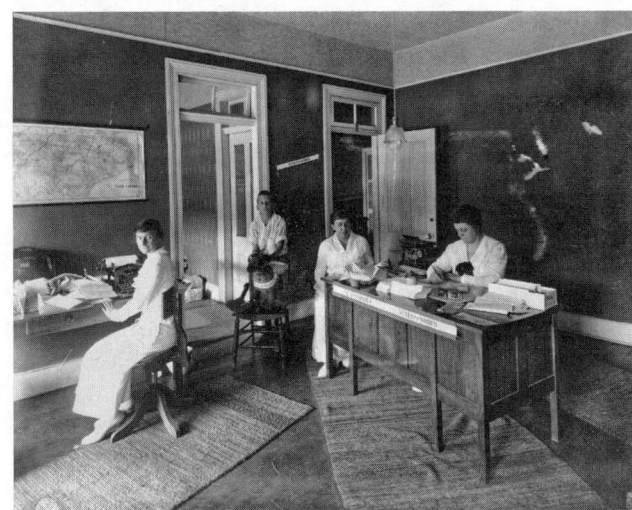

Office of the North Carolina Equal Suffrage League, 1920. Gertrude Weil is at the far left. Courtesy of NCOA&H.

women the vote; representatives from the agricultural counties with the largest African American populations led the opposition. Much of the controversy over women suffrage concerned race: antisuffragists feared that allowing women to vote would increase pressure to reverse laws that prevented African Americans from voting.

As they did elsewhere, suffragists stepped up their efforts in North Carolina after the outbreak of World War I, convinced that women's contribution to the war effort would compel President Woodrow Wilson and Congress to relent. But their activism gained little support in the General Assembly. Legislative initiatives aimed at allowing women to vote in the primaries, the municipal elections, or all elections were defeated as late as 1919. Suffrage activism, however, was more effective on the national stage. On 10 Jan. 1918 the U.S. House of Representatives approved the Nineteenth (or Susan B. Anthony) Amendment—with the affirmative vote of only one North Carolina representative, Edwin Y. Webb. In the Senate, North Carolinians Furnifold M. Simmons and Lee S. Overman joined the minority opposition in the final tally on 4 June 1919.

Congressional adoption of the Nineteenth Amendment prompted antisuffrage organization in North Carolina in the summer of 1920, when Mary Hilliard Hinton of Wake County formed a state branch of the Southern Rejection League in Raleigh, assisted by the National Association Opposed to Women's Suffrage. The state's antisuffrage movement derived its strongest support from politicians eager to retain the control they had obtained after Reconstruction; the textile mill industry, which feared the impact of women's votes on child labor issues; and railroad officials, who worried that women would target them in the progressive attack on corruption in big business. Yet the Southern Rejection League in Raleigh was a small group of perhaps only 20 active members, although Raleigh men also organized the States' Rights Defense

League at the same time. Moreover, North Carolina can claim the only southern antisuffrage journal, the *State's Defense*, but this too was a last-minute affair, published only four times before the ratification battle ended.

In August 1920 Governor Thomas W. Bickett called a special session of the General Assembly to vote the Nineteenth Amendment up or down. President Wilson sent Bickett a telegram urging ratification, but the governor responded with the hope that Tennessee, then also meeting in a special convention, would relieve the pressure on North Carolina by being the thirty-sixth and final state to vote for ratification. Bickett nevertheless encouraged the legislature to ratify the amendment, arguing for a graceful accession to the inevitable. On 17 August the State Senate, by a vote of 25 to 23, postponed consideration of women suffrage until the 1921 session. After the Tennessee legislature had voted for ratification on 18 August, the North Carolina General Assembly met to consider the amendment the next day. Despite Tennessee's approval, the General Assembly still rejected the measure by a vote of 71 to 41, arguing that women suffrage would threaten the sanctity of the family, state rights, and white supremacy. With ratification a fait accompli and thus with nothing to gain nationally, legislators sought not to alienate the prevailing antisuffrage sentiment at home. Not until 1971 did the General Assembly of North Carolina endorse the Nineteenth Amendment.

References: Albert Coates, *By Her Own Bootstraps: A Saga of Women in North Carolina* (1975); Elna C. Green, *Southern Strategies: Southern Women and the Woman Suffrage Question* (1997); Jane DeHart Mathews, "The Status of Women in North Carolina," in Lindley S. Butler and Alan D. Watson, eds., *The North Carolina Experience: An Interpretive and Documentary History* (1984); Kathryn L. Nasstrom, "'More Was Expected of Us': The North Carolina League of Women Voters and the Feminist Movement in the 1920s," *NCHR* 68 (July 1991); Anastatia Sims, *The Power of Femininity in the New South: Women's Organizations and Politics in North Carolina, 1880–1930* (1997).

Caroline Pruden

SEE ALSO League of Women Voters; North Carolina Equal Suffrage Association.

Woodcarving evolved into a true art form among North Carolinians, with works ranging from intricate caricatures and animals popular with the Cherokee and Mountain people to decoys carved by duck hunters along the Outer Banks. The Cherokees held woodcarving in high regard. Traditionally, they took up woodcarving for practical purposes such as making wooden bowls for cooking and masks for use in dances and ceremonial occasions. For leisure, the Cherokees enjoyed carving animals such as bears, deer, and snakes. They used native woods such as walnut, cherry, buckeye, holly, and apple. Cherokee carvings are distinguished by their smooth finish as well as the clear lacquer used to bring out colors and wood textures. Wildfowl decoy carving has been a folk tradition since the middle of the nineteenth century, corresponding to the rise of hunting clubs along the Outer Banks.

Efforts to conserve and support woodcarving and other traditional crafts began in earnest around the turn of the century. In 1902 George Washington Vanderbilt's wife Edith founded Biltmore Industries, a school of mountain crafts in Asheville. In 1925 Olive Dame Campbell and Marguerite Butler founded the John C. Campbell Folk School in honor of Campbell's late husband, who had always dreamed of opening such a school. The Campbell School is the oldest school of traditional crafts in the country, and woodcarving has always been one of its staple courses. Another internationally known craft school, the Penland School of Crafts, is nestled in the mountains of Mitchell County. Lucy Morgan, director of the nearby Appalachian School, opened the school in the 1920s to preserve a way of life she felt was rapidly disappearing with the onslaught of the Industrial Revolution. Penland, which incorporated in 1929 as a nonprofit educational institution, continues to shape the American crafts movement and consistently produces some of the best craftspeople in the United States. In 1961, woodworkers throughout western North Carolina and eastern Tennessee organized a guild called the Appalachian Woodworkers for the preservation of their craft.

The tradition of woodcarving continues into the early 2000s. The Qualla Arts and Crafts Mutual in Cherokee features the work of contemporary Native American carvers. One of the country's most popular caricature carvers, Tom Wolfe, maintains a studio in downtown West Jefferson. Wolfe has authored nearly 40 books on carving, and his original pieces fetch prices from $125 to over $10,000. Woodcarvings from other contemporary artists are also found along the Blue Ridge Parkway at the Northwest Trading Post, the Parkway Craft Center in Moses Cone Mansion, and the Folk Art Center.

References: Brad Campbell and Jay Fields, *The Craft Heritage Trails of Western North Carolina* (1998); Irv Green and Andrea Gross, *Handcrafted in the Blue Ridge* (1997); Rodney L. Leftwich, *Arts and Crafts of the Cherokee* (1970); Daniel W. Patterson and Charles G. Zug III, eds., *Arts in Earnest: North Carolina Folklife* (1990).

Rich Weidman

SEE ALSO Decoys; John C. Campbell Folk School; Penland School of Crafts; Southern Highland Craft Guild.

Woodmen of the World is a national fraternal benefit society founded on 6 June 1890 during a meeting at the Paxton Hotel in Omaha, Neb. Its founder, Joseph Cullen Root, was also the founder of the Modern Woodmen of America, a fraternal benefit society that began in 1882 and had operations in nine central western states. The organization has worked through the decades on a number of service projects that have had a large impact on North Carolina. In the early 2000s the state had about 150 adult lodges and 90 youth lodges serving approximately 110,000 members. Only 12 of North Carolina's 100 counties do not have lodges, though the organization's long-range goals include construction of lodges in those locations, and its philanthropy continues throughout the state.

An important project of the Woodmen has been the North Carolina Orphan's Christmas Party, which raises money for gifts for the state's orphans. Another project adopted by the organization was inspired by a 1997 promise that Woodmen would visit the more than 700 nursing homes in the state and provide an activity annually for the residents. By the early 2000s, more than 450 of the state's nursing homes had been visited.

Among the organization's other civic activities and achievements have been the donation of a drinking fountain to the Tryon Palace Commission in New Bern in 1957; the building of a children's camp, Fresh Air Camp, in 1958–59 by Woodmen of Asheboro on land donated by two Woodmen members; the hosting of camping trips for youngsters at Sportsman Club units at Lake Waccamaw, Camp Lookout, White Lake, and Fort Barnwell; the honoring of safe drivers; the presentation of wheelchairs to those in need; the sponsorship of the American History Awards, a history essay competition and scholarship program; and the presentation to North Carolina schools of *The American Patriot's Handbook*, containing the Constitution.

North Carolina's Woodmen are also active in disaster relief, a project that began after the western North Carolina lodges were called on to provide assistance to the town and residents of Macon, Ga., following a 1994 flood. Working with the American Red Cross, Woodmen today coordinate donations that are sent wherever they are needed. After Hurricane Floyd hit eastern North Carolina in September 1999, Woodmen filled more than 238 tractor trailers with donated items ranging from clothing and furniture to food and school supplies and distributed the goods to those in need.

Suzy Barile

Woolly Worm. The fuzzy brown and black creature commonly called the woolly worm or woolly bear is the larval form of the tiger moth (*Isia isabella*). Woolly worms appear in early fall, when they feast on common plants, and emerge in spring from the pupa stage as moths.

North Carolina's Mountain peoples have long relied on the woolly worm's markings to predict the severity of the upcoming winter. The belief that the coloration of the woolly worm's coat matches the harsh and mild periods of the winter has several variations. For instance, the 13 bands on the caterpillar's body, colored brown and black, are said to correspond to the 13 weeks of winter, and the darker a band, the harsher that week will be. Another version holds more generally that a predomination of dark bands means a hard winter, and a majority of brown bands predicts a mild season.

"Reading the worms" is a popular fall pastime in the North Carolina Mountains. Banner Elk hosts an annual Woolly Worm Festival at which the main events are the woolly worm races. Caterpillars race on three-foot strings in heats until a champion is found, and the winning woolly worm is used for the upcoming winter's prediction. The Center for Woolly Worm Studies at Appalachian State University in Boone conducts annual studies on about 500 woolly bear caterpillars in a more scientific attempt to predict the winter weather.

References: Jerry Bledsoe, *Carolina Curiosities* (1990); Horton Cooper, *North Carolina Folklore and Miscellany* (1972).

Angelyn H. Patteson

Work Songs are sung as an accompaniment to work, primarily manual labor. They are usually traditional in nature, circulating among workers in a given occupation. Tasks such as shucking oysters, hoeing crops, and cutting wood involve repetitious action, and workers often sing to pace the work and pass the time. Other tasks, including hauling in fishing nets, involve the coordination of effort among several workers. For these tasks, song provides a cue for physical action as well as a way to pass the time. In the 1920s, Guy B. Johnson and Howard W. Odum studied work songs in North Carolina, collecting many of their texts from laborers on the University of North Carolina campus in Chapel Hill. As the nature of work changed with increasing industrialization the need for these songs decreased, but some work songs specific to particular activities and conditions persisted. Many songs emerged from the textile industry that commented on the conditions of work in the mills.

Reference: Howard W. Odum and Guy B. Johnson, *Negro Workaday Songs* (1926).

Bruce E. Baker

SEE ALSO Menhaden Chanteymen.

World's Columbian Exposition. In 1892 the United States celebrated the 400th anniversary of Christopher Columbus's first voyage and the following year staged the World's Columbian Exposition, held in Chicago from May to November 1893. The exposition attracted 27 million visitors to its more than 600 acres of grounds and exhibit halls. Most states and many foreign countries contributed exhibits, some large enough to fill entire buildings.

In 1891, in preparation for the World's Columbian Exposition, the North Carolina General Assembly authorized a Board of World's Fair Managers of North Carolina, which selected exhibits showing the "natural and industrial products" as well as the history and culture of the state. Alexander B. Andrews and

Thomas B. Keough represented North Carolina as state commissioners on the World's Columbian Commission, with Elias Carr and G. A. Bingham serving as alternates. The commission also appointed "lady managers" from each state; Florence Hill Kidder and Mary Roberts Price served as North Carolina's lady managers, with Sallie Southall Cotten and Virginia Stella Devine serving as alternates.

The North Carolina board decided not to construct a separate North Carolina building at the Chicago exposition, instead concentrating on exhibits in the halls dedicated to agriculture, forestry, mines and mining, fisheries, and horticulture. The agriculture exhibit displayed North Carolina products and a selection of soil samples showing "the strata from the surface to a depth of several feet." The forestry exhibit held samples of over 100 types of wood native to North Carolina, each four feet long and four inches wide and collected by Gifford Pinchot, forester of the Vanderbilt estate outside of Asheville. There was also a display of 500 different medicinal herbs and plants from the state.

The North Carolina mines and mining exhibit held a vast mineral collection from the state, including over 180 varieties of gems; gold ore and nuggets; iron, silver, and copper ore; building stone; and a 300-pound mica crystal. The fisheries exhibit held mounted specimens of fish and waterfowl native to the state, fishing traps, nets, and other equipment. The horticulture exhibit, the smallest set up by North Carolina, held a selection of wines and some fresh and preserved fruits from the state. There were also North Carolina exhibits in the Woman's Building and in a space in the rotunda of the Government Building dedicated to the history of the 13 original states.

The North Carolina exhibits won a total of 157 medals and awards—more than all the other southeastern states put together. After the exposition, the North Carolina display cases and exhibits were taken to Raleigh and placed in the State Museum (the forerunner of the North Carolina Museum of Natural Sciences).

Reference: William Stephenson, "Sally Southall Cotten and the Chicago World's Fair of 1893," NCHR 58 (October 1981).

David A. Norris

World War I ranks as one of the deadliest wars in American military history, and North Carolina shared in the devastating loss of human life. In only five months of fighting on the western front, 50,554 Americans were either killed in action or died from wounds and 198,059 men were injured. Another 69,540 men died from disease or other causes in France or the United States. North Carolina sent a total of 86,457 men to fight in France. Of that number, 629 were killed in combat, 204 later died of wounds, 3,655 were injured but recovered, and 1,542 died of disease. Some North Carolinians were singled out by the U.S. government for special achievements during the war.

Tents and barracks at Camp Greene near Charlotte. Wade Harris Papers, no. P-317, Southern Historical Collection, Wilson Library, UNC-Chapel Hill.

Robert L. Blackwell, of Person County, who served in the Thirtieth "Old Hickory" Division, was the only North Carolinian to received the Medal of Honor, which was awarded posthumously. Another 200 soldiers from North Carolina received the Distinguished Service Cross, and 12 men were awarded the Distinguished Service Medal. All of North Carolina's World War I veterans were offered a service medal by the state.

North Carolina's Response to War and North Carolinians in Combat

On 5 Apr. 1917 the U.S. House of Representatives passed a resolution declaring war against Germany. North Carolinians' initial reaction was supportive but not enthusiastic. On 5 June President Woodrow Wilson instituted draft registration, and in North Carolina more than 100 percent of eligible men registered—implying that many young men lied about their age in order to be included. The state registered 480,491 men, 142,505 of whom were African American. From the 65 percent found to be physically fit for military service, 40,740 whites and 20,082 African Americans were initially called up.

More North Carolinians were drafted than volunteered, although it is evident that most were willing to serve if called. Some residents joined the war effort even before the United States declared war. Kiffin Yates Rockwell of Asheville, for example, went to France with his brother Paul in August 1914 and joined the French Foreign Legion. Both men were wounded on the western front, Paul in December 1914 and

The results of a tin can drive in front of the Crescent Theater in Statesville during World War I. NCC.

Kiffin in May 1915. Approximately 1,612 North Carolinians evaded the draft.

Many men from North Carolina joined the regular army and served with the First and Second Divisions, becoming the first to reach France in the winter of 1918. Others joined local National Guard units that became part of the Thirtieth, or Old Hickory, Division, and approximately one-third of the draftees in the Eighty-first "Wildcat" Division were North Carolinians. Most North Carolina African Americans served in the Ninety-third Division. The engineer regiment in the Forty-

An Armistice Day parade in Statesville, 1920. NCC.

second Division also contained many men from the state. The Thirtieth and Forty-second and units of the Ninety-third arrived in France in the spring of 1918 and the Eighty-first, in August.

In the spring of 1918, Germany initiated five offensives against Allied lines. At Chateau-Thierry and Belleau Wood, U.S. divisions stopped the German advance and took the offensive. North Carolinians served in all of the major battles on the western front in 1918. As part of the American army, they fought in the Battles of 2nd Marne and St. Mihiel and in the Meuse-Argonne, the last major campaign of the war. As part of the British army, the Old Hickory Division fought at Ypres and the Somme and was credited with breaking the Hindenburg Line in September 1918. North Carolina African Americans in the Ninety-third Division fought in the French army with distinction. The Eighty-first Division arrived to fight in the Meuse-Argonne only days before the war ended. On 11 Nov. 1918 the Eighty-first's North Carolinians went over the top. After five hours of savage fighting that morning, the battle was stopped by the armistice ending the war.

Contributions to Victory on the Home Front

At home, North Carolinians contributed to the war effort in numerous ways and at times struggled with the economic and cultural impact of the war. Soldiers poured into training camps in the state, civilians volunteered for war work, factories new and old hummed with war production, and shortages of labor, food, and fuel touched everyone. The state's Council of Defense, under chairman D. H. Hill, encouraged morale and patriotism, stimulated food production and conservation, kept a register of vacant rooms for soldiers and war plant workers, provided legal aid for soldiers, reported the citizens and property of enemy nations, and helped control vice near army camps, among other responsibilities. The council received no state funds but was paid for by donations from wealthy North Carolinians.

The American Red Cross in North Carolina expanded in size and increased the number of local chapters. It ran canteens at railroad stations to feed traveling soldiers, aided needy families of soldiers, and donated clothing and other items for military hospitals and war refugees. The War Camp

Community Service (WCCS), which operated in towns near military camps or hospitals, including Charlotte, Raleigh, Fayetteville, Southport, Asheville, Waynesville, and Hot Springs, organized entertainment troupes, lounges, reading and writing rooms, clubhouses, and excursions for soldiers. The Charlotte chapter set up a theater and converted the old Presbyterian Hospital into a hotel for soldiers' families. In Charlotte and other towns, separate facilities for black soldiers were established under the auspices of the WCCS. After the armistice in 1919, the WCCS opened more centers to welcome and assist returning veterans.

North Carolina schoolchildren collected scrap metal, planted gardens, bought thousands of 25-cent war savings stamps, and gathered walnut shells to be burned, crushed, and used in filters for gas masks. College students volunteered to help harvest crops or work with the Red Cross. Many male students joined the Students' Army Training Corps, similar to today's ROTC. Governor Thomas Walter Bickett asked churches to ring its bells for two minutes every night at 7:00 until the war was won.

When a scarcity of farmworkers and the heavy strain on railroads from military and industrial requirements threatened to cause food shortages, a "Feed Yourself" campaign promoted by Bickett was so successful that the state produced four times as much food in 1918 as it had the year before. More than 56,000 new gardens were planted by North Carolinians, who were urged to grow, can, dry, or preserve as much of their own food as possible. Even garbage was saved to feed hogs or to be processed into soap, fertilizer, or explosives. To conserve food, "meatless" and "wheatless" days were instituted. Restaurants were encouraged to save food as much as possible. But only sugar was officially rationed.

There were shortages in other commodities as well. New construction, except for farm buildings, required a permit from the Council of Defense. Shoes, gasoline, and coal were scarce. In the fall of 1917 railroads in North Carolina had so little coal that they impressed shipments bound for industries and home use to keep their trains moving. To conserve coal, citizens were asked to cut as much firewood as possible, and in 1918 most nonessential businesses were closed from 18 January to 25 March. From 6 Nov. 1917 until the end of the war, a "Lightless Night Order" permitted electric signs to be lit only from 7:45 to 11:00 and never on Thursday and Sunday nights.

War industries brought jobs, but they also contributed to labor shortages and overcrowding in some cities. Several ships were built in Wilmington, Morehead City, and Elizabeth City; artillery shells were manufactured at the Raleigh Iron Works; a plant in Sanford produced munitions; and a plant in High Point made airplane propellers.

The war touched North Carolina directly when the Diamond Shoals lightship (U.S. Light Vessel No. 71) was sunk by cannon fire from the German U-boat *U-140* on 6 Aug. 1918.

Throughout the war coastal communities dealt with fallout from submarine activities in the Atlantic. The largest military camp in the state was Camp Greene, near Charlotte, which at one time housed 65,000 men. Camp Polk, a training center for tank crews, was assembled near Raleigh. While the camp was under construction, the men trained at the State Fairgrounds. Work on Camp Polk stopped when the war ended. Camp Bragg, an artillery training camp near Fayetteville, was established in September 1918. It remained open after the war and grew into the modern installation of Fort Bragg.

During the conflict, North Carolina housed a significant number of German prisoners of war (POWs). The internment of POWs fell under the jurisdiction of the War Department, which operated camps in Fort Douglas, Utah; Fort Oglethorpe, Ga.; and, later, Fort McPherson, Ga. A fourth internment camp, run by civilians under the Department of Labor, was nestled in the sleepy hamlet of Hot Springs, N.C., in the heart of the Blue Ridge Mountains. The POWs interred at Hot Springs were merchant marines arrested when their ships, mostly luxury liners and cargo vessels bottled up in U.S. ports, were seized in April 1917. Because these men were noncombatants and therefore not officially POWs, they fell under the custody of the Labor Department and the technical charge of noncompliance with immigration laws. The initial group of 1,800 merchant crewmen was later joined by an additional 500 seamen from ships captured in Panama and the Philippines. While in Hot Springs, these POWs constructed barracks and mess halls surrounded by barbed wire on the lawn of the Mountain Park Hotel.

References: Sarah McCulloh Lemmon, *North Carolina's Role in the First World War* (1975); George C. Lewis and John Mewha, *History of Prisoner of War Utilization by the United States Army, 1776–1945* (1955); Jacqueline Burgin Painter, *The German Invasion of Western North Carolina: A Pictorial History* (1992).

R. Jackson Marshall III
Additional research provided by David A. Norris and Rodney J. Steward.

SEE ALSO Old Hickory Division; Submarine Attacks; Wildcat Division.

World War II was fought on three continents, with North Carolinians serving in every major theater. Hostilities began in earnest on 1 Sept. 1939, when Nazi Germany invaded Poland, prompting Great Britain and France to declare war in defense of Poland. America joined the Allies (Great Britain, France, and the Soviet Union) against the Axis Powers (Germany, Italy, and Japan) in December 1941, after the Japanese bombing of the Pearl Harbor naval base in Hawaii.

More than 362,500 North Carolinians (including 69,000 African Americans and 7,000 women) served in the armed forces during the war. Casualties included 6,458 battle deaths and more than 3,000 deaths from other causes. World War II in Europe ended when Germany surrendered on 8 May 1945. The war in the Pacific lasted several months longer, officially concluding on 2 September, when the Japanese signed a treaty of surrender aboard the USS *Missouri*.

North Carolina Contributions in Battle and on the Home Front

The largest group of North Carolinians involved in one operation served in the Thirtieth Division, nicknamed "Old Hickory" after President Andrew "Old Hickory" Jackson and composed of troops primarily from North Carolina, South Carolina, and Tennessee—states with which Jackson had been connected. The division had fought in World War I, then functioned as a National Guard unit; it was recalled into service in 1940. Under the command of Maj. Gen. Leland S. Hobbs, the Thirtieth took part in the invasion of Normandy and engagements throughout France and Belgium before meeting Russian forces at the Elbe River on 8 May 1945. The men of Old Hickory earned numerous medals and citations. Many North Carolinians also served with the Fourth and Eightieth Infantry Divisions. Soldiers in the Fourth were the first American troops to enter Paris, and the Eightieth liberated several German concentration camps. The Sixty-fifth General Hospital in England was sponsored by Duke University in Durham.

Many North Carolinians distinguished themselves in service. Harnett County's Gen. William C. Lee, known as the "Father of the Airborne," was primarily responsible for the establishment of the U.S. Airborne Command. Fighter pilot George C. Preddy, of Greensboro, killed in action in 1944, was the state's leading ace. Maj. Margaret Craighill, of Southport, a physician, was the first woman to be directly commissioned in the medical corps. Six North Carolinians were awarded the Medal of Honor.

The naval war came close to home, when German submarines sank many Allied ships off the North Carolina coast. The area around Hatteras acquired the moniker "Torpedo Junction" because so many ships were sunk there. Forty-one American ships participating in the war were named for North Carolina–related people and places, including the famed battleship USS *North Carolina*, which engaged in much of the fighting in the Pacific.

North Carolina industries also made significant contributions to the war effort. Between 1941 and 1945 the North Carolina Shipbuilding Company of Wilmington built dozens of Liberty ships and other vessels. The state provided many important materials to the armed forces, including more textile goods than any other state. North Carolina was fourth in the production of lumber supplied to the military.

At home, citizens prepared for defense under the auspices of the Office of Civilian Defense. Each county established a defense council to help the population plan for defense and to encourage their participation in wartime programs. As taxes covered only 46 percent of the cost of the war, the government depended on loans from banks and citizens to finance the remainder. These loans came in the form of war bonds and stamps that were sold by banks, theaters, civic clubs, and other volunteers. Eight national campaigns to boost the sale of bonds were launched during and immediately after the war. Millions of dollars were raised in North Carolina, which exceeded its goal in every campaign.

The need for war matériel and supplies and the interruption in shipping certain items created shortages around the state. Local rationing boards, directed by the Office of Price Administration, were organized to oversee the allotment of items such as gasoline, rubber, sugar, coffee, and building materials that were in short supply. The Office of Civilian Defense and the North Carolina Salvage Committee directed the recycling of materials such as metal, rubber, nylon hosiery, and paper under the motto, "Get into the Scrap." Because so many men departed for the military, women entered the workforce in record numbers. "Rosie the Riveter" became the symbol for women taking over jobs vital to the war effort. Work release programs were instituted to enable prisoners to fill some of the shortages.

World War II Military Installations in the State

About 2 million fighting men were trained for combat at more than 100 army, navy, marine, and Coast Guard facilities in North Carolina. Several of these bases remained active after the war ended. Fort Bragg, established in 1918, expanded in the early months of the war to become the largest artillery post in the world. Camp Lejeune, a marine base in Jacksonville, housed training facilities for the "devil dogs" canine corps. Cherry Point Marine Air Station provided training grounds for simulated landings and fighter pilots. An Army Air Force Technical Training School at Seymour Johnson Air Force Base opened in Goldsboro in 1941.

Camp Battle, named after Confederate major general Cullen A. Battle, began operating in December 1941 northwest of New Bern as a base for army units protecting bridges over the Neuse and Trent Rivers as well as for the 111th Infantry, a Pennsylvania National Guard unit stationed there in 1942. The Asheville Naval Convalescent Hospital, where 6,663 sailors and patients from Holland, Great Britain, France, and China were treated, opened on 23 May 1943 in the 225-room Appalachian Hall in Kenilworth Park. Capt. William A. Angwin was its commanding officer until the convalescent home closed on 10 Apr. 1946. Camp Butner, a U.S. Army infantry camp named for Maj. Gen. Henry Wolfe Butner, a native of Surry County and commander of the First Artillery Brigade in World War I, began operations on 4 Aug. 1942. Located on approximately 40,000 acres in Granville, Person, and Durham Counties, this base conducted training exercises for an estimated 30,000 soldiers.

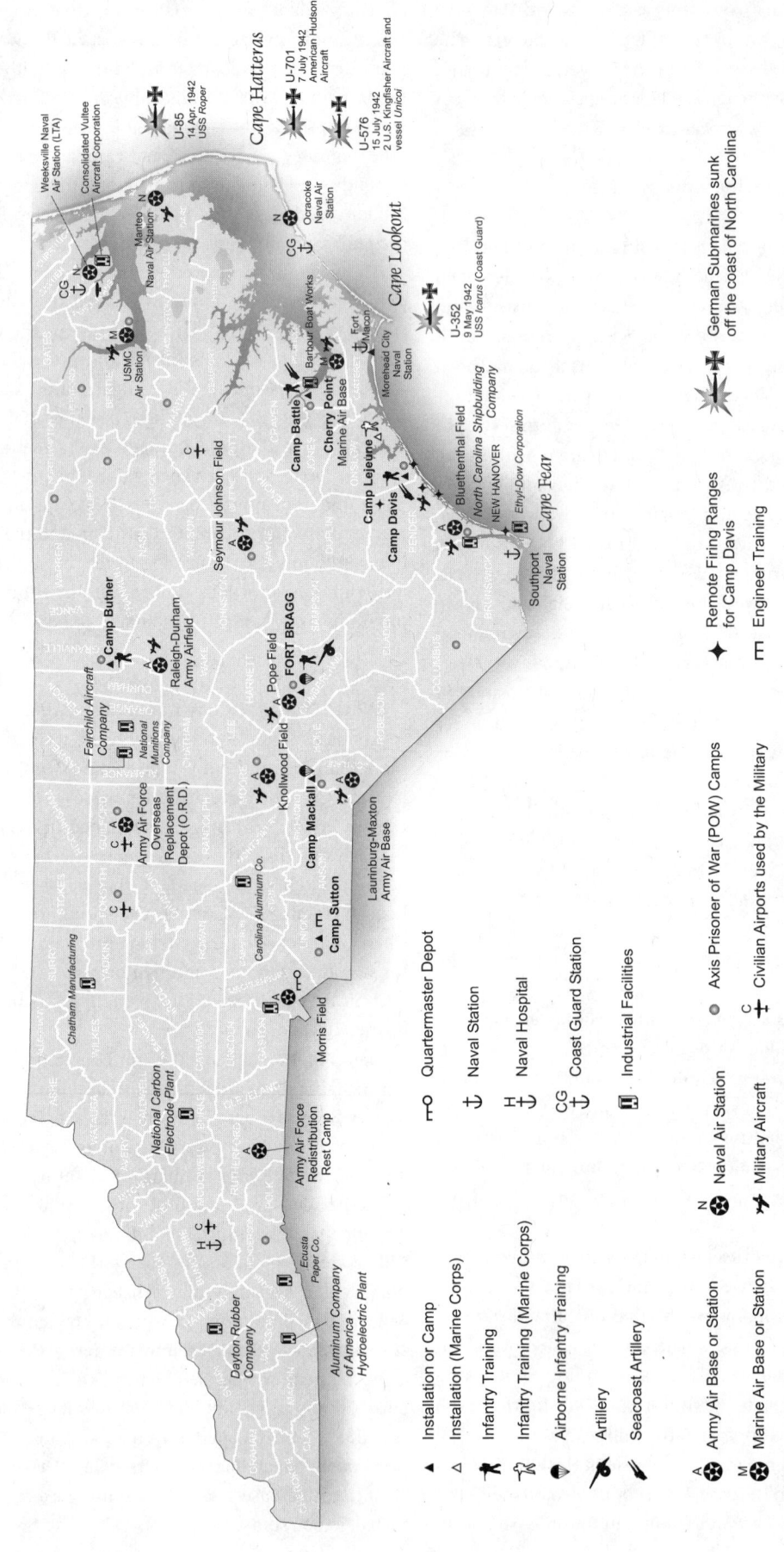

Map Legend

Weeksville Naval
Air Station (LTA)

Consolidated Vultee
Aircraft Corporation

Cape Hatteras

U-701
7 July 1942
American Hudson
Aircraft

U-85
14 Apr. 1942
USS *Roper*

U-576
15 July 1942
2 U.S. Kingfisher Aircraft and
vessel *Unicoi*

Manteo
Naval Air Station

Ocracoke
Naval Air
Station

Cape Lookout

U-352
9 May 1942
USS *Icarus* (Coast Guard)

USMC
Air Station

Barbour Boat Works

Fort Macon

Morehead City
Naval Station

North Carolina Shipbuilding
Company

Bluethenthal Field

Ethyl-Dow Corporation

NEW HANOVER

Cape Fear

Camp Battle

Cherry Point
Marine Air Base

Camp Lejeune

Camp Davis

Southport
Naval
Station

Seymour Johnson Field

Camp Butner

Fairchild Aircraft
Company

National
Munitions
Company

Raleigh-Durham
Army Airfield

Pope Field

FORT BRAGG

Knollwood Field

Army Air Force
Overseas
Replacement
Depot (O.R.D.)

Camp Mackall

Laurinburg-Maxton
Army Air Base

Carolina Aluminum Co.

Chatham Manufacturing

Camp Sutton

Morris Field

National Carbon
Electrode Plant

Army Air Force
Redistribution
Rest Camp

Aluminum Company
of America -
Hydroelectric Plant

Dayton Rubber
Company

Erusta
Paper Co.

German Submarines sunk
off the coast of North Carolina

Remote Firing Ranges
for Camp Davis

Engineer Training

Legend

- Quartermaster Depot
- Naval Station
- Naval Hospital
- Coast Guard Station
- Industrial Facilities
- Axis Prisoner of War (POW) Camps
- Civilian Airports used by the Military

- Installation or Camp
- Installation (Marine Corps)
- Infantry Training
- Infantry Training (Marine Corps)
- Airborne Infantry Training
- Artillery
- Seacoast Artillery

- Army Air Base or Station
- Marine Air Base or Station
- Naval Air Station
- Military Aircraft

Principal military installations, camps, industries, and facilities during
World War II. Map by Mark Anderson Moore, courtesy NCOA&H.

Camp Davis, the first antiaircraft base in the country and an army coastal artillery training center located on 46,683 acres in Onslow and Pender Counties, was built between December 1940 and April 1941. At its peak in 1943, more than 100,000 soldiers and civil service workers were stationed there. The camp was named in honor of Maj. Gen. Richmond Pearson Davis, a native of Statesville, commander of the 151st Field Artillery Brigade in France during World War I and later chief of artillery for the Ninth Corps. Camp Mackall, dedicated on 1 May 1943 in memory of 22-year-old Pvt. John T. Mackall, the first World War II paratrooper to lose his life in action, was a military training installation adjacent to Fort Bragg in Richmond and Scotland Counties. A portion of the camp survived after the war and was used as a wilderness training area by soldiers of the Special Forces (Green Berets). Camp Mackall was the center of training for glider pilots and soldiers and the site of early experiments in glider techniques; thousands of fledgling army paratroopers and glidermen prepared for battle there. Late in the war it was also the home of the 555th Parachute Infantry Battalion, the only combat unit of paratroopers composed of black soldiers.

Camp Sutton, on the outskirts of Monroe, was named for the city's first war casualty, Frank Howie Sutton, a Royal Canadian Air Force volunteer who died on 7 Dec. 1941 during fighting near Tobruk, North Africa. In March 1942 Camp Sutton was established as an expanded temporary military facility for about 18,000 overflow troops from Fort Bragg. When its training center was shut down in October 1944, it became a prisoner of war (POW) camp. After it closed in March 1946, the camp's 2,000 acres were annexed to the city of Monroe, doubling its size and providing a site for later industrial development.

Bluethenthal Field, New Hanover County's second airfield, was dedicated on 30 May 1928 in memory of Arthur Bluethenthal, the first Wilmingtonian killed in World War I. The field had served as a civilian airport until the day after Pearl Harbor, when the Army Air Corps moved in—two squadrons of army P-40 pursuit planes had already been stationed at the airfield to defend the area from enemy bombers—and banned civilian flying. The "Wilmington Army Airport" then swallowed up neighboring farms and houses, increasing its size to over 1,200 acres. First employed as a base for bombers on coastal patrol, it later was used for pilot training on P-47 fighter aircraft. During World War II the federal government invested $11 million in the airfield. After the war, the airport was returned to the county and came to be called the New Hanover County Airport in the 1950s.

The Elizabeth City Coast Guard Air Station opened on 15 Aug. 1940 with 10 aircraft but ended the war with 55. Placed under navy command in November 1941, the station patrolled the Atlantic from the Virginia capes to Cape Lookout. Its aircraft escorted convoys and flew antisubmarine patrols, although they were not sufficiently armed to sink U-boats until late 1943, when the worst of the submarine devastation was already over. The pilots' most important function, therefore, was rescuing survivors of sunken ships. From December 1941 to July 1944 the air station recovered or assisted 186 persons. In late 1944 the station adjusted its mission to air-to-sea rescue. During the war the station shared the airfield with a coast artillery air squadron and a naval blimp unit, and the Coast Guard operated various schools there.

Laurinburg-Maxton Army Air Base, activated on 28 Aug. 1942, covered more than 5,000 acres in Scotland County. Its initial purpose was to offer both aircraft transport and training for infantry and airborne troops. The federal government deactivated the base shortly after the war and eventually deeded the property to the towns of Laurinburg and Maxton; by the mid-1950s the former military base had become an industrial park.

What became the Weeksville Naval Air Station was constructed in 1942 on 640 acres in Pasquotank County approximately four miles south of Elizabeth City. It served as a base for blimps to patrol the coast and escort coastal shipping. In 1947 the station began its second era with lighter-than-air ships designed with new technology. Two blimp squadrons and an antisubmarine helicopter squadron were based at Weeksville until 31 May 1957, when the blimp squadrons were decommissioned. The 1,000-foot-long hanger, known as Airdock 2, the largest wooden building in the world, was destroyed by fire on 3 Aug. 1995.

The Charlotte Quartermaster Depot, part of the Quartermaster Corps of the U.S. Army, opened on 15 May 1941 to supply bases in the Carolinas with items ranging from toothbrushes and bar soap to M1 Garand rifles and gun oil. Eventually the 72-acre site featured 1.2 million square feet of warehouse space and 400,000 square feet of open ground. In early 1942 the depot employed 80 army personnel and more than 2,500 civilians. By the mid-1940s it was one of the most significant depots in the southeastern United States. After the war, it was taken over by an American Graves Registration unit, which worked to deliver the identified remains of 5,170 deceased soldiers to their families in North Carolina, South Carolina, Virginia, Tennessee, and Georgia. The depot was deactivated in January 1949.

North Carolina's other important wartime bases were the Lake Lure Army Air Force Rest and Redistribution Center, Knollwood Field at Winston-Salem, the Elizabeth City Marine Air Corps Station, Morris Field at Charlotte, the Pineville Naval Station, Pope Field in Fayetteville, the Overseas Replacement Depot in Greensboro, and the Raleigh-Durham Army Air Field.

Prisoners of War Held in North Carolina

About 10,000 German POWs were detained at 18 military installations in the state. In North Carolina, as throughout

America, German prisoners participated in compulsory work programs until their forced repatriation to Germany in the spring of 1946. The first German POWs to enter the country came from the *U-352*, sunk by the Coast Guard cutter *Icarus* off the Outer Banks on 9 May 1942. After their initial debarkation at Charleston, S.C., the survivors from the original 44-man crew were taken to Fort Bragg and later transferred to locations outside North Carolina.

In the spring of 1944 the federal government created a nationwide POW program to bolster a waning cadre of civilian and military maintenance workers on military bases and to assist the civilian war-related industries of farming, lumbering, and pulpwood cutting. North Carolina's first German POW work contingents, mostly prisoners from Field Marshal Rommel's Afrika Korps, captured in Tunisia in May 1943, arrived at Camp Davis, Camp Mackall, Camp Sutton, and Wilmington Naval Hospital (New Hanover County) in the spring of 1944. By the fall, after the Allied invasion of Normandy, the POW program in North Carolina, and across the United States, had expanded further. Administered through two major base camps at Fort Bragg and Camp Butner, the state added five more branch camps. There were 300 to 500 prisoners each at Ahoskie, Goldsboro (Seymour Johnson Air Force Base), New Bern, Williamston, and Winston-Salem. A year later still more camps were established as branches of Camp Butner at Moore General Hospital in Carthage, Edenton, Greensboro, Hendersonville, Roanoke Rapids, Scotland Neck, and Whiteville.

Approximately 3,000 Italian POWs—later given relative freedom and new opportunities when Italy received Allied status in the fall of 1943—arrived at Camp Butner in September 1943. By October these prisoners were engaged in work projects such as road building, social conservation, and farming. Branch camps for 500 men each were also set up for picking peanuts in Tarboro, Windsor, and Scotland Neck. New volunteer Italian Service Units were activated by mid-February 1944, and volunteers were transferred to various training centers, including Camp Sutton, which operated as a POW camp starting in March 1944; the camp held 3,500 Italian collaborators until July 1944 and 1,000 German POWs until March 1946. The Italian POW base camp at Butner and its branch camps were phased out and replaced by German POW encampments by May 1944; the Italian POWs, found to be difficult to handle, were relocated outside the state by the end of July.

Camp Butner was the most unusual POW facility in North Carolina. This 5,000-man camp housed a compound of between 700 and 900 non-German, anti-Nazi prisoners who had been captured as members of the German armed forces. Most were Poles, Czechs, French, and Dutch, but there were also Belgian, Russian, and even Mongolian prisoners. About 500 POWs, chiefly Czechoslovakians and Poles, were repatriated to their own national armies after appropriate screening.

A covert national program for the reeducation and democratization of Germans had its most obvious successes at Camp Butner, Fort Bragg, and Camp Mackall. Selected American films and courses in American geography, history, and politics, provided under the rubric of "intellectual diversion," were intended to attract POW interest and change attitudes. After the war ended in Europe, POWs were shown films of the liberated German concentration camps. After viewing such a film at Camp Butner, 1,000 Germans burned their Wehrmacht uniforms voluntarily. At Fort Bragg, beginning in July 1945, army education officers taught 36 courses weekly; of special interest to the POWs were classes on agricultural science, industrialism around the world, and South American and African geography. By late 1945 officers at Fort Bragg claimed, with both pride and exaggeration, that 95 percent of their POW students were familiar with American life and democracy. In September 1945 the POWs at Camp Mackall formed four political parties and elected a camp spokesman and company leader.

North Carolina's POW experience was further distinguished by a successful escape. Kurt Rossmeisl, a former member of Field Marshal Rommel's elite 10th Panzer Division, fled from Camp Butner on 4 Aug. 1945. He lived in Chicago under the name of Frank Ellis until 1959, when he turned himself in to the Cincinnati, Ohio, field office of the Federal Bureau of Investigation.

References: Mary Best, ed., *North Carolina's Shining Hour: Images and Voices from World War II* (2005); Robert D. Billinger Jr., "Behind the Wire: German Prisoners of War at Camp Sutton, 1944–46," *NCHR* 61 (October 1984); Spencer Bidwell King Jr., *Selective Service in North Carolina in World War II* (1949); Arnold Krammer, *Nazi Prisoners of War in America* (1979); Sarah McCulloh Lemmon, *North Carolina's Role in World War II* (1964); David A. Stallman, *A History of Camp Davis* (1990); J. Gordon Vaeth, *Blimps and U-Boats: U.S. Navy Airships in the Battle of the Atlantic* (1992).

Robert D. Billinger Jr.
Jo Ann Williford
Additional research provided by John L. Bell, Tom Belton, Michael Hill, Joshua Howard, Roy Parker Jr., William S. Powell, and Beverly Tetterton.

SEE ALSO Camp Lejeune; Cherry Point Marine Corps Air Station; Fort Bragg; Liberty Ships; Moore General Hospital; Naval Section Bases; *North Carolina*, USS; Old Hickory Division; Overseas Replacement Depot; Refugees (World War II); Seymour Johnson Air Force Base; Submarine Attacks.

Wreath from the Woods of Carolina. Painter, musician, sculptor, and writer Mary Ann Bryan Mason (1802–81) was the first woman in North Carolina known to have written and illustrated a children's book, titled *A Wreath from the Woods of Carolina* (1859). Nine colored lithographs of native wildflowers distinguish the volume from the children's literature of the late antebellum period, and the first ten chapters begin with a Bible verse. The book's ten stories attempt to teach piety and morals to children through relatively heavy-handed didacticism. The book was published in New York by the General Protestant Episcopal School Union and Church Book Society.

Wiley J. Williams

Wright Brothers National Memorial. On 2 Mar. 1927 Congress authorized the establishment of the Kill Devil Hills Monument National Memorial to commemorate Orville and Wilbur Wright's achievement of the first successful flights of a power-driven, heavier-than-air machine. The area, 428 acres located in Dare County off U.S. 158, was transferred from the War Department to the National Park Service on 10 Aug. 1933. In December 1953 its name was changed to the Wright Brothers National Memorial.

The facility includes a visitors center with exhibits telling the story of the Wright brothers' historic flights, an information desk, and administrative offices. The exhibition area offers a sweeping panoramic view of the Wrights' reconstructed 1903 camp and markers on the ground that designate the take-off and landing points of the first flights. Nearby is West Hill, the 91-foot-high sand dune that was the setting of the Wrights' gliding experiments in 1901–3. (The National Park Service has stabilized the dune by seeding it with special grasses adapted to sandy soil.)

The actual Wright Brothers Memorial sits atop Kill Devil Hill. Dedicated in 1932, the memorial is a triangular pylon 60 feet high made of gray granite from Mount Airy. Its sides are ornamented with outspread wings in bas-relief, giving the impression of a gigantic bird about to take flight. Stairs lead to the top of the shaft, and an observation platform offers a splendid view of the surrounding area, including dunes and Albemarle Sound. The monument's inscription reads: "In commemoration of the conquest of the air by the brothers Wilbur and Orville Wright conceived by Genius, achieved by Dauntless Resolution and Unconquerable Faith."

Although the memorial is a unit of the National Park Service, the North Carolina Department of Cultural Resources manages the First Flight Centennial Commission. Both the National Park Service and the commission actively prepared for the activities that culminated in the one-hundredth anniversary of the Wright brothers' flight in December 2003.

Wiley J. Williams

Wyse Fork, Battle of. The Civil War battle of Wyse Fork, also known as the Battle of Southwest Creek, was a fierce engagement between Union and Confederate forces near Kinston on 8–10 Mar. 1865. The Union army of Maj. Gen. Wil-

liam T. Sherman had entered North Carolina in early March 1865 headed for Goldsboro. Three divisions under Maj. Gen. Jacob D. Cox had left New Bern to join forces with Sherman. Meanwhile, Gen. Joseph E. Johnston, who had recently assumed command of all Confederate forces in North Carolina, began to assemble an army with which to strike Sherman. Anxious to prevent a junction of the forces of Sherman and Cox, Johnston instructed Gen. Braxton Bragg to slow the progress of Cox's 13,000-man corps as it marched west from New Bern.

Bragg, a native North Carolinian, chose to make a stand several miles east of Kinston at Southwest Creek. Two seasoned major generals from North Carolina commanded his force: Robert F. Hoke and Daniel Harvey Hill. By the time Bragg, Hoke, and Hill met on the night of 7 March to plan an attack the next day, the Confederates were strongly entrenched on the west bank of the creek. Cox had positioned his troops across the waterway.

In the early morning hours of 8 March, Hoke made an undetected crossing of the creek, flanked the Federals, and slammed into their rear. Hill crossed over about noon, and by day's end the Confederates had secured one of the last southern field victories of the war. Not only had Cox sustained significant losses in killed and wounded, but also Hoke had captured 1,500 of his soldiers. Nonetheless, the Confederate success at Southwest Creek that day was merely temporary.

On 8 March, in the wake of the Federal debacle, much-needed Union reinforcements arrived on the scene, and Maj. Gen. John M. Schofield, Union leader of the Department of North Carolina, took command. During the next two days, Hoke and Hill attempted to exploit their success, but they encountered stubborn resistance, with neither army gaining further advantage. Bragg ordered the Confederates to fall back toward Kinston on the night of 10 March. Just over one week later, the same Confederate soldiers would take the field at Bentonville, the last and largest battle of the war in North Carolina.

Although the Battle of Wyse Fork did not play a significant role in the outcome of the war, it did provide General Johnston with the time he desperately needed to put together an army to confront Sherman. It also served as a lethal reminder to Union forces that the Confederate soldiers in North Carolina were still willing to fight.

References: Daniel W. Barefoot, *General Robert F. Hoke: Lee's Modest Warrior* (1996); John G. Barrett, *The Civil War in North Carolina* (1963); Mark L. Bradley, *Last Stand in the Carolinas: The Battle of Bentonville* (1996); William R. Trotter, *Ironclads and Columbiads: The Civil War in North Carolina* (1989).

Daniel W. Barefoot

X

X-Ray Experiments. On 8 Nov. 1895 Professor Wilhelm Roentgen of the University of Würzburg, Germany, accidentally discovered that electricity, when passed through a glass vacuum tube known as a Crookes' tube, emanates invisible rays that pass completely through the human body, producing photographs of bones and localizing foreign bodies. As soon as an Associated Press account of the new invisible "X" rays was published in the United States on 6 Jan. 1896, American scientists attempted to duplicate Roentgen's experiments.

Henry Louis Smith, professor of natural philosophy at Davidson College, immediately realized that the college laboratory contained the same equipment Roentgen had used to produce the new mystery rays. On 22 Feb. 1896 Smith fired a bullet into the hand of a cadaver (obtained from nearby North Carolina Medical College) and used X-rays to make a

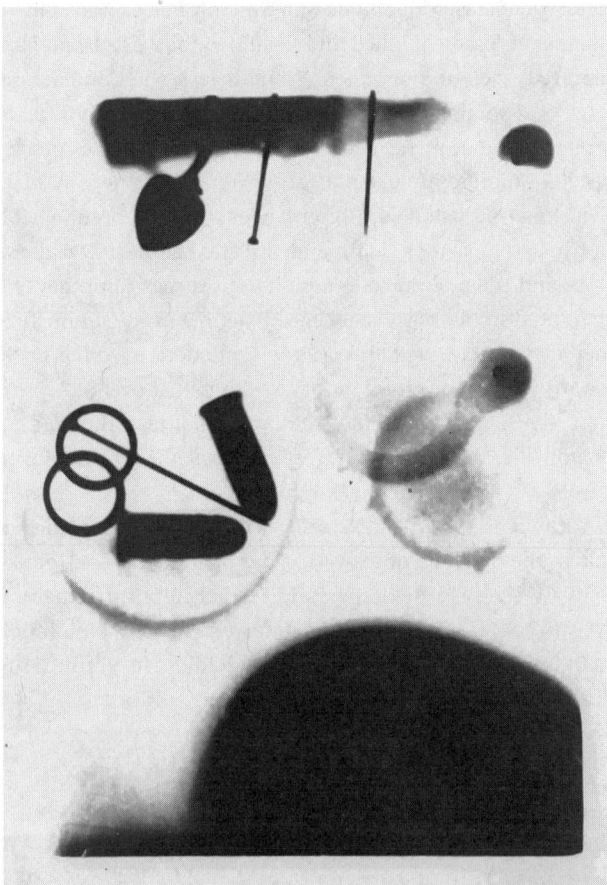

Three students at Davidson College surreptitiously made this X-ray of several objects, including the finger of a cadaver (top), on 12 Jan. 1896. Their X-ray is thought to be the first made in the South. Courtesy of the Davidson College Archives.

photograph clearly showing the bullet's location in the hand. On 27 February an account of his work and an artist's rendition of the photograph appeared in the *Charlotte Observer*. The article caused a sensation in southern medical circles. Although similar experiments were being conducted at Yale and Columbia Universities, it is believed that Smith's "radiograph" locating a foreign object in the human body was the first to be made in the South and one of the first in the United States.

Smith, later president of Davidson College, could also claim credit for the earliest use of X-rays to locate a foreign body in a patient's trachea, enabling surgeons to perform a lifesaving procedure. In the latter part of 1897, a young Cabarrus County girl named Ellen Harris swallowed a small brass sewing thimble. As her condition worsened, examining physicians were unable to determine if the thimble remained in her throat or if some other illness threatened her. At the request of her parents, Smith traveled 25 miles to the Rocky River section of Cabarrus, transporting his batteries and equipment in a wagon. He determined the location of the thimble and marked its location with ink. Ellen was then taken to the Charlotte Surgical Institute for surgery. In order to convince the skeptical surgical team to operate on the child's throat, however, Smith had to haul his equipment to Charlotte and demonstrate the object's location for them. With the aid of the images, the surgeon, C. A. Misenheimer, was able to remove the thimble. News of the lifesaving procedure was widely publicized in area newspapers; afterward Smith was called on several times to locate foreign bodies for removal through surgery.

An interesting and controversial side note to Smith's successful use of X-rays concerns three undergraduate students at Davidson during that period. Having read accounts of Roentgen's experiments in the popular press, juniors Osmond Barringer, Eben Hardie, and Pender Porter decided to make a photograph using the Roentgen procedure. On Sunday evening, 12 Jan. 1896, they secretly used equipment in the Davidson laboratory to expose a plateful of small objects, including the finger of a cadaver, to rays from a Crookes' tube for three hours. The resulting photograph clearly showed how the new rays passed through items of various densities. The three students remained silent about the photograph, fearing expulsion for breaking into the laboratory and dissecting rooms. Years later they broke their silence to claim credit for their early accomplishment, which is preserved in the Davidson library and is now recognized as one of the first X-ray photographs made in the United States. Smith always indignantly denied the students' claim, however, contending that their effort followed his earlier successes and was based on his classroom demonstrations.

References: "Cathode Rays at Davidson," *Charlotte Observer*, 27 Feb. 1896; R. H. Lafferty, "Some Southern Pioneers in X-Ray: An Historical Note," *Radiology* (September 1926); "Radiology in North Carolina, 1896–1916," *North Carolina Medical Journal* 18 (July 1957).

Clarence E. Horton Jr.

Y

Yadkin College, located near the Yadkin River in Davidson County, was opened in 1856 by the Methodist Protestant Church on land donated by Henry W. Walser. One of three institutions of higher education founded by Methodists in North Carolina—the others were Jamestown Female Academy and High Point College (now High Point University)—Yadkin initially offered only preparatory programs. It was rechartered as a college by the legislature in February 1861, but the Civil War forced it to close within a few months. A preparatory program operated briefly in 1865, and in 1867 Yadkin reopened as a secondary school. In 1873 Shadrach Simpson became the school's president, developed a college curriculum, admitted women for the first time, and built a new three-story building. His departure in 1883 marked the beginning of a decline in Yadkin's program to that of a junior college and, finally, a high school. The final director of Yadkin Collegiate Institute, as it became known under a new legislative charter, was William T. Totten, who in 1883 had been the last of the 19 students who received college degrees from Yadkin. Totten enrolled more than 100 students at the beginning of the twentieth century, but the establishment of public schools in North Carolina brought a decline in enrollment, and he closed the school's doors for the last time in 1924.

References: Virginia C. Fick, *Country College on the Yadkin: A Historical Narrative* (1984); Olin B. Michael, *Yadkin College, 1856–1924: A Historic Sketch* (1939).

Richard B. McCaslin

Yadkin County, located in the Piedmont region of northwestern North Carolina in the foothills of the Blue Ridge Mountains, was formed in 1850 from Surry County and named for the Yadkin River. Early inhabitants of the area included the Tutelo and Saponi Indians, followed by German, Scotch-Irish, Welsh, and English settlers. Quakers also migrated to the area in the eighteenth century. Yadkinville, the county seat, was chartered in 1857 and named after the county. Other Yadkin County communities include Arlington, Jonesville, Boonville, East Bend, Courtney, Lone Hickory, Center Brooks, Marler, Smithtown, and Forbush. Notable physical features of the county include the Yadkin River, Brushy Mountains, Fox Knob, and Cobb, Beaverdam, Fall, Lineberry, Froeman, Cranberry, and Deep Creeks.

Yadkin County produces agricultural goods such as grains, tobacco, corn, soybeans, apples, livestock, and poultry. Manufactured products include textiles, hosiery, plastics and styrofoam, furniture, apparel, and stainless steel. Minerals such as feldspar, agate, jasper, limestone, mica, and iron ore are found in the county.

Yadkin County landmarks include the Tulbert House, built around 1852; Bourman Mill Dam, built in the late nineteenth century; and Deep Creek Friends Meeting Cemetery, established around 1801. Richmond Hill, once a law school and home of North Carolina Supreme Court chief justice Richmond Pearson, is now a historic park. Cultural institutions in Yadkin County include the Charles Bruce Davis Museum of Art, History, and Science and the Yadkin Arts Council. The county hosts popular events and festivals such as the Yadkinville Harvest Festival, Yadkinville Annual Magic Show, Boonville Heritage Days Festival, and Yadkinville Bluegrass Contest and Fiddlers' Convention. Yadkin County's estimated population was 37,000 in 2004.

References: Frances H. Casstevens, *Heritage of Yadkin County* (1981); William E. Rutledge, *Illustrated History of Yadkin County, 1850–1908* (1981).

Elizabeth Bayley

Yadkin–Pee Dee River rises as the Yadkin River in Watauga County near the town of Blowing Rock and flows southeast through Caldwell County; it turns northeast and flows through Wilkes County and along the Surry-Yadkin, Davidson-Rowan, Davie-Forsyth, Yadkin-Forsyth, Davie-Davidson County lines, and part of the Montgomery-Stanly County line. It joins the Uwharrie River in Montgomery County to form the Pee Dee River. The Pee Dee River then travels along the Stanly-Montgomery and Anson-Richmond County lines into South Carolina, where it drains into Winyah Bay.

The Yadkin River has been the site of human civilization for at least 12,000 years, earning it the nickname of the "Tigris and Euphrates of the Carolinas." It was formerly called the Sapona River, after the peoples who originally inhabited its banks, until the name was changed between 1709 and 1733. The origin of the word "Yadkin" is unknown; different spellings appeared throughout the eighteenth century, including "Yatkin," "Atkin," and "Reaktin." The name "Pee Dee" probably came from either the Catawba Indian word *pi'ri* (something good) or *pfhere* (smart, expert, or capable).

The size of the Yadkin–Pee Dee's North Carolina watershed is 7,213 square miles, and the river is 435 miles long. There are 81 North Carolina municipalities within its river basin, including Wilkesboro, Salisbury, and Lexington. In the early 2000s the area had a population of more than 1.2 million. The river has experienced various environmental problems, most notably a huge amount of sediment generated by the farmland erosion along its banks. Various soil-conservation plans have begun to solve some of the river's sediment problems, as scientists continue to study both that issue and others affecting the Yadkin's water quality and overall health.

Reference: T. Edward Nickens, "Father Yadkin," *Wildlife in North Carolina* 63 (November 1999).

Elizabeth Bayley

Yadkin River Navigation Company was chartered in 1818 as part of the internal improvements program of progressive state senator Archibald D. Murphey, who, between 1816 and 1819, proposed far-reaching educational, economic, and governmental reforms to improve the quality of life in North Carolina. His plan for internal improvements—water-based transportation facilities and roads to promote trade—called for making the major river systems navigable and connecting them with canals and all-weather roads. Interest by legislators led to the naming of a Board of Internal Improvements in 1819, the hiring of a British engineer later that year, and the appropriation of funds to help finance the projects.

The Yadkin River, flowing north to south across the piedmont (then becoming the Pee Dee River through upper South Carolina), was a vital segment of Murphey's program. Plans called for the Yadkin, Catawba, and Deep Rivers to be connected with the Cape Fear to the Atlantic Ocean at Wilmington, and through the Pee Dee to the Atlantic at Georgetown, S.C. At places where the Yadkin could not be made navigable by straightening or deepening the channel (such as the Narrows and the Uwharrie Mountains area), canals, roads, or portage railroads would be built. A rock canal wall at Bean Shoals on the Yadkin between Yadkin and Forsyth Counties, about 16 feet high and ¼ mile long, indicates the way the numerous rocky shoals of the river were to be bypassed.

The Yadkin River Navigation Company project failed due to insurmountable construction difficulties, lack of funds (in part the result of the economic panic of 1819), and the hostility of eastern legislators toward promoting development and growth in the Piedmont and Mountains. Work ceased by the mid-1820s. Two towns, Clinton and Fulton, were planned on the Yadkin in southern Davie County; town lots were sold but no construction was begun. From 1847 to the 1850s and later in the 1880s, efforts to make the Yadkin navigable were again undertaken without success.

References: Hugh T. Lefler and Albert R. Newsome, *North Carolina: The History of a Southern State* (1954); James W. Wall, *History of Davie County* (1969).

James W. Wall

Yamassee War, although fought in what is now South Carolina, involved many North Carolina Indian tribes. The war began on 15 Apr. 1715 as a reaction to the abusive trade practices that white traders imposed on the Indians. Yamassee warriors and those from other tribes fell upon a party of white traders and their families, killing about 90 of them. In response, an expedition from Charles Towne (modern-day Charleston, S.C.) killed several Yamassee leaders in a series of battles.

At the time the war broke out, South Carolina could produce fewer than 1,500 men capable of bearing arms, so South Carolina governor Charles Craven appealed to North Carolina and Virginia for assistance. Virginia sent guns, and North Carolina sent a force of 100 white men and a company of Tuscarora Indians under the command of Cols. Maurice Moore and Theophilus Hastings. Hastings took about half of the men south by boat, while Moore marched overland with the rest to join forces with Governor Craven. On his march south, Moore learned that the Waccamaw and Cape Fear Indians were planning an ambush. With a force of 60 whites and 60 Indians, Moore marched directly into the Indian towns, seizing a large quantity of ammunition and arms and capturing 80 Indian slaves. Craven's plan to join Moore in a campaign against the Saura (Cheraw) was thwarted because he was forced to turn back and protect Charles Towne against an Indian attack from the south.

Initially, the Cherokee remained neutral during the Yamassee War despite efforts by both sides to gain their support. But when Moore led an army of 300 men into Cherokee country to conduct negotiations on behalf of South Carolina, his mission was successful and marked the turning point in the war. By the spring of 1716, most of the Yamassee had settled in Florida. Other Indian tribes, including the Catawba and the Santee, made peace by fall. Subsequently, the Catawba turned on their former allies, killing many of the Waxhaw and Waccamaw Indians and scattering or enslaving the rest.

Reference: Ruth Y. Wetmore, *First on the Land: The North Carolina Indians* (1975).

Wiley J. Williams

Yancey County, located in the Mountain region of North Carolina and partially bordering the state of Tennessee, was formed in 1833 from Burke and Buncombe Counties and named for Bartlett Yancey, U.S. congressman from 1813 to 1817. Its county seat, Burnsville, was also established in 1833 and named for Otway Burns, a privateer in the War of 1812 and later a member of the General Assembly, who, though a native of Onslow County, supported equal political representation for the western part of the state. Other Yancey County communities include Bald Creek, Busick, Celo, Day Brook, Green Mountain, Hamrick, Micaville, Murchison, Pensacola, Ramseytown, Sioux, and Swiss.

Like other mountain counties, Yancey County was inhabited before European settlement by Cherokee Indians; in 1989 remains of a prehistoric Indian village and burial ground were uncovered in Burnsville on the campus of Cane River Middle School. English, Scotch-Irish, and Irish immigrants were the first Europeans to settle in the county's valleys, creating small farms and agricultural communities that persisted through the nineteenth and twentieth centuries. Since the early twentieth century, the county's primary crop has been burley tobacco, air-cured in barns that are one of the region's architectural hallmarks. Development of the Black Mountain Railroad (later the Yancey Railroad) fostered the mining industry in the county after 1911; Micaville, near the county's eastern border, was an important twentieth-century center for the mica industry. The completion of the Blue Ridge Parkway, which runs along the county's southern border, and the improvement of other highways, brought increased tourism in the twentieth century as well, and today the county is a popular destination for hiking, camping, and other outdoor recreation.

Yancey County is perhaps best known as the home of Mount Mitchell, which at 6,684 feet is the highest peak east of the Mississippi River. The mountain is named for University of North Carolina professor Elisha Mitchell, who died in his attempt to establish its elevation and is buried at its peak. In 1915 Mount Mitchell State Park became North Carolina's first state park. Overall, the county boasts five of the ten highest peaks in the eastern United States in the Black Mountains, regarded as some of the oldest on earth. Yancey County has the highest average elevation of any county in the state. Significant portions of the Pisgah National Forest are located in the county. Yancey County's estimated population was 18,000 in 2004.

Peter Bangma

Yaupon (from the Catawba Indian word *yop*, meaning "tree"), an evergreen shrub or small tree found on the coastal plain from Virginia to Texas and up the Mississippi Valley to Arkansas, made a popular tea in the North Carolina area during the colonial period. Its caffeine-rich leaves and twigs, toasted in earthen pots, were the most common botanical ingredient of black drink, a religious, medicinal, and social beverage used in many Indian societies, evidently as far north as the Great Lakes. As the scientific name of yaupon, *Ilex vomitoria*, implies, Indians sometimes used black drink as an emetic, usually after adding seawater or other nausea-producing substances. A pure infusion of yaupon leaves is harmless, however, and many find its flavor pleasant.

Settlers quickly learned of the stimulant and diuretic properties of yaupon and introduced it to Europe. By the early eighteenth century it had followed chocolate, coffee, and Asian tea from apothecary shops, which dispensed it as a treatment for smallpox and kidney stones, into aristocratic salons. Cured leaves sold for a half-guinea a pound in England, and for a

time yaupon was an important export of the Carolina colony. English, French, Spanish, Portuguese, Italian, Dutch, and German had names for yaupon, more than two dozen in all. Yaupon was inexpensive and popular in the Carolinas and Georgia through the colonial period, but its association with the rural southern poor eroded its acceptability as demand increased for coffee, Asian tea, and (after the Civil War) carbonated soft drinks. The drinking of yaupon tea persisted on the Outer Banks until the early 1900s. Since then, government officials, home economists, and innkeepers have unsuccessfully tried to revive the practice for the sake of patriotism, frugality, or nostalgia.

North Carolina's Yaupon Beach (Brunswick County), Yaupon Creek (Pamlico County), Yaupon Hammock Gut (Carteret County), and Yaupon Hill (Dare County) are named for the plant.

References: Nancy Davis and Kathy Hart, *Coastal Carolina Cooking* (1986); Gary S. Dunbar, *Historical Geography of the North Carolina Outer Banks* (1958).

Wynne Dough

Year without a Summer. The Indonesian volcano Tambora catastrophically erupted in the late spring of 1815, casting well over a million tons of dust into the upper atmosphere. These particles caused not only spectacular sunsets around the world for the next several months, but also a drop in the temperature during the following year worldwide, especially in North America and Europe. The year 1816 opened in the eastern United States with unseasonably mild, spring-like weather that continued almost uninterrupted by wintry days into the month of April. As the days grew longer, however, the air became colder, and New England experienced summer frosts and ice, which froze young buds on the trees and destroyed planting after planting of spring grains until it was too late to put in a crop. North Carolina, too, had major difficulties; providential rains in August saved the corn crop in its coastal counties, but losses were severe in the Piedmont and western counties. Heavy frosts fell in New England and south through North Carolina on 22 August. Because of the abnormal weather worldwide, British newspapers declared that the year 1816 would be remembered as "the year in which there was no summer."

George Stevenson

Yellow-Dog Democrat, a popular term sometimes applied to ultra-loyal supporters of Democratic candidates for public office, came into use in the third decade of the twentieth century. In 1928 Democratic senator Tom Heflin of Alabama supported Republican Herbert Hoover in his campaign for the presidency. Heflin's detractors, in response to his defection, declared that they would vote for a "yellow dog" before they would cast a ballot for a Republican. The term, used as both a compliment and an insult, has continued to appear in North Carolina political speech.

Dennis Isenbarger

Yeomen constituted a class of people in colonial society that generally owned and worked their own land, ranking below the gentry in the social order. The term was applied in North Carolina to the largest body of settlers. As a group, yeomen have been described in general terms as strong, fearless, simple in tastes, crude in manners, provincial in outlook, democratic in social relations, tenacious of their rights, sensitive to encroachments on their personal liberties, and, when interested at all in religion, earnest, narrow, and dogmatic. It was these people, in the minds of outsiders, who characterized the colony.

References: R. D. W. Connor, *Race Elements in the White Population of North Carolina* (1920); Guion G. Johnson, *Ante-Bellum North Carolina: A Social History* (1937).

William S. Powell

YMCA and YWCA. Both the Young Men's Christian Association and the Young Women's Christian Association were founded in London—in 1844 and 1855, respectively. The YMCA arrived in the United States in Boston in 1851; the YWCA was first established in New York City in 1858. The first YMCA in North Carolina was formed in Wilmington in 1857, followed by pre–Civil War associations in Charlotte, Raleigh, Salisbury, and Washington and on the campus of the University of North Carolina in Chapel Hill. North Carolina's YMCA movement was completely halted by the Civil War, but associations were reorganized in such places as Raleigh and Charlotte in the late 1860s. By 1876 nine associations, either new or reorganized, were in existence. By 1922 there were 22 YMCAs in the state, including some at colleges and universities.

While the early YMCAs in North Carolina had ladies' auxiliaries, it was not until the early decades of the twentieth century that the YWCA movement reached the state. It is known that there were YWCAs in Asheville, Charlotte, Greensboro, and Winston-Salem before the end of the first decade of the twentieth century, as well as student associations at a number of colleges and at the School for the Blind in Raleigh. (The YWCA at UNC was not organized until 1935.)

Particularly after World War I, young girls and women moved in large numbers from farms and small towns to jobs in the textile mills and offices of cities. In such a new environment, women needed a safe, inexpensive, and comfortable place to live, wholesome recreation, and a chance to learn new skills—in short, opportunities to develop their full potential as women. The YWCA was one of the organizations to which they turned to help them realize that goal.

Organizationally, YMCAS and YWCAS are independent agencies, and each local Y exercises a high degree of autonomy in developing its programs. Through the years Ys have shared many common concerns and offered many similar services (housing, educational/vocational programs, camping, counseling, child care, citizenship activities, etc.)—services that local boards of directors and volunteer and professionally trained staff consider appropriate for their communities. For instance, not all Ys offer lodging, and in some communities a YMCA serves both girls and boys, as in Chapel Hill–Carrboro, Burlington, Durham, Fayetteville, and Sanford. The greater Asheville, Charlotte, Greensboro, Raleigh, Rocky Mount, Wilmington, and Winston-Salem areas all have one or more YMCAS and YWCAS.

YMCA summer camps in North Carolina began in 1912 when Camp Greenville, a coeducational camp, was established by the Greenville, S.C., YMCA at Cedar Mountain in Transylvania County. Various organizations followed suit, until by the 2000s there were dozens of summer camps in the state. The YMCA ran the largest number of these camps, while private owners, churches, the 4-H Club, the Boy Scouts, and other groups ran several each.

Camp Sea Gull and Camp Seafarer are two of North Carolina's most successful YMCA summer camps. Camp Edgerton near Raleigh was the first camp of the Raleigh YMCA. Small and inadequate, Edgerton may have been the spur for visionary Wyatt Taylor, then general secretary of the YMCA, to turn his attention toward the coast, where he dreamed of establishing a camp that would change the lives of hundreds, perhaps thousands, of young people.

Camp Sea Gull was opened in 1948 on the banks of the Neuse River at Minnesott Beach. The camp grew rapidly, offering two camping sessions for boys and one precamp for girls. In response to popular demand, Camp Seafarer for girls was opened in 1961, with each camp located on 350 wooded acres with excellent access to the river and the ocean. Each year children ages 6 to 16 from all over the United States and several foreign countries enroll. In 1997, 37 states and 12 foreign countries were represented, with a total of 2,700 campers. The Capital Area YMCA's metro business office reports that an estimated $1.2 million is spent annually in Pamlico, Craven, and Carteret Counties as a result of these camps. The annual payroll for year-round camp employees, exclusive of summer staff, is approximately $1 million. These employees include electricians, plumbers, landscapers, and caretakers.

References: Heriot Clarkson, *A Story of the Progress of the Kingdom through the Young Men's Christian Association of the Carolinas* [1936?]; Stephen Beauregard Weeks, *A History of the Young Men's Christian Association Movement in North Carolina, 1857–1888* (1888);

Randy Young, "YMCA Brings All Parts of Community Together," *Chapel Hill News*, 11 Apr. 2001.

Max P. Rogers
Additional research provided by Wiley J. Williams.

Young Men's Institute in Asheville, backed by businessman and philanthropist George W. Vanderbilt, opened in 1893 as a community center for black construction workers at his Biltmore House and Asheville's increasingly segregated African American citizens. By 1906 a black-led supervisory committee had assumed ownership of the center's building. The large brick structure provided blacks with space for a wide variety of business, civic, educational, religious, and social activities until 1977, when it closed. The Young Men's Institute building is listed on the National Register of Historic Places.

References: Catherine W. Bishir, Michael T. Southern, and Jennifer F. Martin, *A Guide to the Historic Architecture of Western North Carolina* (1999); H. G. Jones, *North Carolina Illustrated, 1524–1984* (1983); Sydney Nathans, *The Quest for Progress: The Way We Lived in North Carolina, 1870–1920* (1983).

Raymond Gavins

Z

Zebulon B. Vance, USS. The USS *Zebulon B. Vance* was launched in Wilmington on 6 Dec. 1941, one day before the Japanese attack on Pearl Harbor. At the ceremony, North Carolina governor J. Melville Broughton proclaimed, "As we salute this ship and launch it today, we shall have a proud part in the overthrow of the aggressor who seeks to dominate the entire world." A few minutes later he and 13,000 other North Carolinians watched the ship splash into the Cape Fear River.

Named for the state's legendary Civil War and Reconstruction governor, the *Vance* represented the first of 125 Liberty ships built in Wilmington during World War II. The North Carolina Shipbuilding Company, a subsidiary of Newport News Shipbuilding and Dry Dock Company, began constructing a shipyard on the Cape Fear River's east side in February 1941. In 1944 the Truman Committee (created to study defense-related contracts) reported that the North Carolina yard produced vessels at "the lowest average cost per ship . . . of any of the 16 yards building Liberty ships in 1943."

The *Vance* measured 441.5 feet long and was 56 feet wide at the beam. Its gross tonnage of 7,177 drew 27 feet of water; powered by a 2,500-HP engine, the *Vance* could reach a running speed of 11 to 14 knots. The ship had quarters for 44 officers and enlisted men but "none for passengers." Construction costs were estimated at $1.5 million.

For most of the war the *Vance* served as a freighter. It survived floating mines and a near miss by a torpedo and took part in the invasion of North Africa. Near the war's end the *Vance* was converted into a hospital ship and renamed the USS *John J. Meany.* After the war it was transferred to the Army Transportation Corps and once again named the *Zebulon B. Vance.* The vessel was used to convey British and other war brides to the United States.

References: North Carolina Shipbuilding Company, *Five Years of North Carolina Shipbuilding* (1946); Alan D. Watson, *Wilmington: Port of North Carolina* (1992).

Harry S. Warren

Zebulon B. Vance Birthplace, a North Carolina State Historic Site established in 1955 and located 12 miles northeast of Asheville on Reems Creek Road near Weaverville, serves as a memorial to North Carolina's Civil War governor and U.S. senator Zebulon B. Vance (1830–94). The site, where Vance spent his early childhood, is representative of an 1830s mountain farmstead. The modern State Historic Site consists of a two-story, five-room log house reconstructed around the original chimneys, six log outbuildings, and a visitors center. Throughout the year, visitors can learn about the Vance family through exhibits, a media presentation, and guided tours of the house and grounds. Seasonal demonstrations of the skills and trades needed to survive in the mountains during the early years of the nineteenth century are also offered.

References: Frontis W. Johnston, "Zebulon B. Vance: A Personality Sketch," *NCHR* 30 (April 1953); Richard F. Knapp, ed., *North Carolina's State Historic Sites: A Brief History and Status Report* (1995); Richard E. Yates, *The Confederacy and Zeb Vance* (1958).

David Tate

Zion-Parnassus Academy was an eighteenth-century classical school located in Rowan County about a mile east of Thyatira Church (believed to be the oldest Presbyterian church in western North Carolina). The school's founder (and Thyatira's minister), Samuel Eusebuis McCorkle, hoped to establish a school that would stress religious as well as classical learning. Its name recalled the Hill of Zion, the residence of King David and his successors, and Parnassus, the Greek mountain sacred to Apollo (god of youth, music, and prophecy) and the Muses (goddesses of poetry, art, and science).

Patterned after David Caldwell's school in Guilford County, Zion-Parnassus added a department for teacher training. For this reason, McCorkle's academy has been referred to as the first normal school in America. Forty-five ministers emerged from Zion-Parnassus before it closed around the beginning of the eighteenth century, as did many lawyers, judges, and state officials. In 1798, when the fledgling University of North Carolina held its first commencement, six of the seven graduates were from Zion-Parnassus.

References: William Henry Foote, *Sketches of North Carolina* (1846); James Hurley and Julia Goode Engam, *The Prophet of Zion-Parnassus* (1934).

Steve Suther

Zoning as a procedure to control land use in North Carolina developed along three lines: building regulation, planning-related land-use regulation, and environmental regulation. Building regulation originated during the colonial period when the Assembly directly regulated some types of construction in municipal charters, such as the provision in a 1740 Edenton charter prohibiting wooden chimneys. In the nineteenth century the legislature gradually shifted from a mandatory approach for local governments to an "enabling" approach, in which localities were authorized but no longer directed to regulate construction matters, such as fire hazards, structural safety, and unsanitary and unhealthful conditions.

In 1905 the General Assembly went beyond merely authorizing local codes by enacting a state building law that governed construction in all towns with a population over 1,000. The law required such towns to select a building inspector (often the fire chief if no other inspector was appointed) and designated the state commissioner of insurance responsible for overseeing these inspectors.

In 1933 the legislature took a second pioneering step with the creation of the State Building Code Council. This measure recognized that construction technology and materials were changing so rapidly that a government untrained in construction matters and often meeting only every other year could not write, amend, and administer building regulations without an understanding of the process. The council, composed largely of professionals from the construction industry, was charged with writing a code, amending it to reflect changes, and hearing appeals from local inspectors concerning its correct interpretation. The council's first State Building Code was published in 1936 and ratified by the General Assembly in 1941. In 1957, based on recommendations by the Commission on Reorganization of State Government, the 1933 law that created the Building Code Council was largely rewritten.

North Carolina has gone further than most states in centralizing the legislature's role in adopting building regulations. The State Building Code, however, does not contain all state building regulations. Others are located elsewhere in the General Statutes, including electrical materials required to ensure the safety of hot water heaters, as well as safety standards for trailers, fire escapes, and hotels. Some departments and agencies are empowered to adopt and enforce regulations that fall within their areas of competence, such as the Commissioner of Labor's duty to oversee boiler and pressure vessels.

Planning-related land-use regulations, which deal with building use and location, also date from colonial times. Most of today's land-use regulations result from what is now known as city or county planning. Beginning in 1950, the General Assembly granted counties the power to create planning boards, zone and enact subdivision regulations, and establish other regulatory control measures already enjoyed by cities. It authorized the creation of regional planning commissions, regional economic development commissions, and economic development commissions in 1961 and regional councils of government in 1971. On 4 May 1982 the North Carolina Supreme Court reversed a long-standing legal doctrine by giving local governments the flexibility to base planning and zoning decisions solely on aesthetics. This followed a 1979 ruling involving the Oakwood Historic District of Raleigh in which the court held that historic preservation was a valid reason for letting the city enforce ordinances establishing architectural standards in a designated area.

The third line of land-use regulation, environmental laws and regulations, is concerned with protecting and managing the quality of the human environment, specifically air, water, and land. Environmentalism, involving federal, state, and local governments and private organizations, took hold in the 1960s and continues to evolve. North Carolina has enacted laws to control air and water pollution, drinking water quality, pesticide use, mining practices, radiation protection, hazardous waste and toxic substances disposal, and other concerns. In many cases the federal government sets environmental standards and the states develop the administrative machinery for achieving these standards. Thus, in many cases the state is essentially the conduit for a federal program. Local involvement in environmental control varies with the specific program involved.

References: Philip P. Green, *Zoning in North Carolina* (1952); Charles D. Liner, ed., *State-Local Relations in North Carolina: Their Evolution and Current Status* (1985).

Wiley J. Williams

Z. Smith Reynolds Foundation. Zachary Smith Reynolds was the youngest child of tobacco magnate Richard Joshua Reynolds and Katharine Smith Reynolds and one of the earliest licensed airplane pilots in the nation. When his estate was settled after his tragic death, his two sisters, Mary R. Babcock and Nancy Susan Reynolds, and his brother, R. J. Reynolds Jr., donated their shares, totaling more than $7 million, from his estate to form a charitable trust in memory of their brother. The Z. Smith Reynolds Foundation was incorporated on 21 Aug. 1936 as a general purpose family foundation. Its grants are restricted to nonprofit, tax-exempt organizations in North Carolina. Its first grant was for $100,000 in December 1937 to the North Carolina State Board of Health to help in the fight against venereal disease.

Reynolds's uncle Will Reynolds died in 1951, and his will established the William N. Reynolds Trust with $14 million, the income from which is designated for the Z. Smith Reynolds Foundation. Income from the Z. Smith Reynolds Trust and the William N. Reynolds Trust, along with interest from some short-term investments made by the foundation, are the source of funding for the Z. Smith Reynolds Foundation. It is the fourth-largest philanthropic organization in the state and among the 100 largest in the nation, with assets in excess of $330 million.

References: Emily Herring Wilson, *For the People of North Carolina: The Z. Smith Reynolds Foundation at Half-Century, 1936–1986* (1988); Z. Smith Reynolds Foundation, *Annual Report* (1995).

Anna Withers Bair

Contributors

Douglas Carl Abrams
Alex Albright
Roberta Sue Alexander
John Allen
Michael J. Allingham
Jean B. Anderson
Norman D. Anderson
William L. Anderson
Rod Andrew Jr.
Edwin R. Andrews
Wilson Angley
John F. Ansley
Robert G. Anthony Jr.
William G. Apple
Walter Ashe
William T. Auman

Lawrence E. Babits
Pat Bailey
Anna Withers Bair
Joan S. Baity
Bruce E. Baker
Susan Bales
Peter Bangma
Daniel W. Barefoot
Rodney D. Barfield
Suzy Barile
John G. Barrett
Jim Bartley
Clare R. Arthur Bass
Jerry S. Bates
Charles Battle
Laura Young Baxley
Elizabeth Bayley
Jeffery Beam
John J. Beck
H. M. Bell
John L. Bell
Larkin Bell
Tom Belton
Kent Benfield
Anne M. Berkley
William Irwin Berryhill Jr.
Martha Bethea
Robert D. Billinger Jr.
Warren L. Bingham
William H. Bingham Jr.
Catherine W. Bishir

Elia Bizzarri
Dan Blair
Faye Terres Blalock
Susan L. Blalock
H. Tyler Blethen
Michael Bonner
Sanford L. Boswell
Joan S. Boudreaux
Charles H. Bowman Jr.
Miriam Boyer
Robin Brabham
Tess Bradstreet
Paul Branch
Grace R. Brashear
Leslie S. Bright
Martin H. Brinkley
G. Eugene Brown
Joe Exum Brown
Louis A. Brown
A. J. Bullard
Brian Bullard
Lee Bumgarner
Sheila Bumgarner
Augustus M. Burns
Lindley S. Butler

Robert J. Cain
Martha Belle Caldwell
Robert M. Calhoon
Brooke Calton
Karl E. Campbell
Jeremy T. Canipe
Linda F. Carnes-
    McNaughton
Joanne G. Carpenter
Dawson V. Carr
Grady L. E. Carroll Sr.
Kathy Carter
Robert W. Carter Jr.
Jerry C. Cashion
Vincent Castano
William S. Caudill
Sue Cause
Ellen Fitzgibbons Causey
John C. Cavanagh
David S. Cecelski
Kevin Cherry
Jack Claiborne

James M. Clifton
Andrew Cline
Amy Elizabeth Cloud
W. H. Cobb
David L. Cockrell
Peter A. Coclanis
Joffre L. Coe
Alex Coffin
J. Timothy Cole
Donald E. Collins
Nayda Swonger Colomb
Edwin L. Combs
Stephen C. Compton
Robin Conley
Elizabeth H. Conner
Lura Lincoln Cook
Bryna R. Coonin
Owen Cordle
Lillian E. Craton
James Credle
C. Daniel Crews
Allyson C. Criner
Dennis W. Cross
Jerry L. Cross
Jeffrey J. Crow
Terrell A. Crow
Tony L. Crumbley

Bryan Dalton
Dennis F. Daniels
Charles C. Davis
David K. Davis
R. P. Stephen Davis Jr.
Sion Dayson
W. Carson Dean
Virginia Renna Deaton
Amelia Dees-Killette
John R. deTreville
Christine S. Devine
Gordon Neal Diem
William G. DiNome
Hoyt Doak
Marian Dodd
Robert J. Dodge
Rebecca Dotterer
Wynne Dough
Sarah Spink Downing
Howard Draper

Robert F. Durden
John B. Dysart

David M. Egner
Sonya Elam
Robert Elliot
Charles B. Ellis
Clyde Ellis
Maie El-Sourady
Barry Engber
Evan L. Erickson
Phillip W. Evans

Thomas J. Farnham
Ronnie W. Faulkner
Joseph Ferrell
Virginia Gunn Fick
William G. Fick Jr.
William C. Fields
W. W. Finlator
Peter Graham Fish
Gregory B. Fishel
Paul E. Fontenoy
Margaret Foote
Benjamin Eagles
    Fountain Jr.
Jim Fowlkes
Diane Frazier
Joan E. Freeman
R. Neil Fulghum
Martha Walker Fullington
Clegg M. Furr
J. Elizabeth Furr

David Bryant Gammon
T. Harry Gatton
Raymond Gavins
Robert C. Gibbs
Brent D. Glass
Elizabeth Scheld Glynn
Maggie Goloboy
Ron Gooding
Michael D. Green
Dorothy S. Gregory

Janet M. Hackney
Nancy E. Hagan
John Hairr

Rachel Hake
Lisa Coston Hall
Stephanie Hall
Speed Hallman
Ed L. Hand
Elizabeth Hardin
Terry M. Harper
Opal Watts Harrington
Henry Harris
Laura Harris
William C. Harris
Millie Hart
Anna Harvin
Susan Tucker Hatcher
Marianne B. Hayworth
Laura Hegyi
Will M. Heiser
Douglas Helms
Christopher E. Hendricks
Kimberly Hewitt
William Hicks
Don Higginbotham
Michael Hill
Joseph Paul Hoffman
Charles J. Holden
Ron Holland
Andy Hollins
Ruth E. Homrighaus
Davyd Foard Hood
Clarence E. Horton Jr.
Andrew Hosfeld
Jeffrey Allen Howard
Joshua Howard
John Huang
Diane Huff
Hart Huffines
Kay Haire Huggins
Nathaniel C. Hughes Jr.
John L. Humber
Charles R. Humphreys
James L. Hunt
Melanie Hurdis
John A. Hutcheson Jr.

John C. Inscoe
Robert E. Ireland
Dennis Isenbarger

Claude V. Jackson
Mateusz Jakubowski
Richard A. Jenkins
Leonard T. Jernigan

Andy Johnson
Bob Johnson
K. Todd Johnson
Lloyd Johnson
W. Lee Johnston Jr.
Harley E. Jolley
Glenn Jonas
Garett Jones
H. G. Jones
James R. Jones
Lu Ann Jones
Sheridan R. Jones
Victor T. Jones Jr.
Weymouth T. Jordan Jr.
Deborah Joy
Gail B. Joyner
Whitmel M. Joyner
William S. Joyner
Cheryl F. Junk
Benjamin R. Justesen

M. Keith Kapp
Geoffrey Katz
Jim Keighton
Roy W. Kelley
Donna E. Kelly
Thomas S. Kenan
Kyle S. Kendrick
George A. Kennedy
John R. Kennedy
Sean Kenniff
Robert C. Kenzer
Donald W. Kern
Fred W. Kiger
Deena Deese Kilmon
L. J. Kimball
Roger N. Kirkman
Richard F. Knapp
Nola Reed Knouse
Lisa Brantley Kobrin
David R. Koontz
Emily Koos
William G. Kornegay
Anne A. Kratzer
Kelly Kress
Paul E. Kuhl
Wallace Kuralt

Alan K. Lamm
Wingate Lassiter
David W. Latham
E. Michael Latta

Richard W. Lawrence
Dennis R. Lawson
Elmer Lawson
Charles LeCount
Donald R. Lennon
Lynne S. Lepley
William E. Leuchtenburg
Edward A. Lewis
Johanna Miller Lewis
Michael H. Lewis
Catherine Liao
Stewart Lillard
Jo White Linn
Beverly Littlejohn
Alexis W. Locklear
Helen Losse
James Lutzweiler

Andrew L. Mackie
Tom Magnuson
E. T. Malone Jr.
Edwin H. Mammen
Matthew J. Mancini
Patricia Phillips Marshall
R. Jackson Marshall III
Brenden Martin
James I. Martin Sr.
Athena Masci
Julian Mason
Stephen E. Massengill
Donald G. Mathews
Sister Evelyn Mattern
Scott Matthews
Timothy P. Mattimoe
Armistead Jones Maupin
Jay Mazzocchi
Charles H. McArver
Richard B. McCaslin
W. J. McCoy
Paul L. McCraw
William J. McCrea
Kenneth McFarland
Michael McFee
Philip McFee
Barry McGee
David McGee
Eileen McGrath
Frank McGuirt
Joshua McKaughan
Gordon B. McKinney
Henry A. McKinnon Jr.
Melton McLaurin

Douglas J. McMillan
Jim McPherson
Patty McQuillan
Barbara McRae
Elizabeth Gillespie McRae
Michael R. McVaugh
Susan Jelinek Mellage
Carol K. W. Melton
David Menconi
Arthur Menius
Eli F. Merritt
Deborah Raenette Meyer
Chester Paul Middlesworth
Nancy Smith Midgette
Jerry Leath Mills
Brad Minsley
Memory F. Mitchell
Ted Mitchell
Thornton W. Mitchell
Sarah Mobley
J. Field Montgomery Jr.
Monica Moody
Anne Moore
Cecelia Moore
David G. Moore
Fred Moore
Mark Anderson Moore
Phillip Arthur Mooring
Bill Moose
Laura Morgan
J. B. Morris
Patrick Morton
Stephen Moyer
Sally Mullikin
Elizabeth Reid Murray
Raymond L. Murray
Chris Myers

Jaquelin Drane Nash
Steven E. Nash
Larry K. Neal Jr.
Rosemary Clifford Neill
John K. Nelson
John D. Neville
Jonathan Noffke
David A. Norris
Thomas L. Norris Jr.

Gail Williams O'Brien
Oliver H. Orr Jr.
John V. Orth
Ginny Orvedahl

Ken Otterbourg
Willis H. Overby
Linda Oxendine

John Paden
Jacqueline Burgin Painter
Karl M. Park
Randall E. Parker
Roy Parker Jr.
Thomas C. Parramore
Angelyn H. Patteson
Susan Pearson
Michael R. Pelt
Patricia L. Pertalion
Aili K. Petersen
Amy Curtin Pini
Julian M. Pleasants
Jan-Michael Poff
David L. Pope
Natalie Popovic
Joseph C. Porter
Matthew C. Porter
Joey Powell
Ted Powell
William S. Powell
Norris W. Preyer
Eugene Price
J. L. Price
William S. Price Jr.
Caroline Pruden
William H. Pruden III
Gene Purcell
Tom Purcell
Rosamond Putzel
Timothy D. Pyatt

Rusty Rains
Richard Rankin
Shannon L. Reavis
John Shelton Reed
Tony Reevy
Martin Reidinger
Kirstin Reimer
Mary Keene Remsburg
Robert L. Remsburg III
Zoe Rhine
Bernadette Rider

Surry Roberts
Peter J. Robinson
Charles E. Roe
Dawn Marie Rogers
Max P. Rogers
Leonard Rogoff
Karl Rohr
Randall B. Rosenburg
Lynn Roundtree
Barbara Rowe
John B. Rutledge

Darby Sadler
Daniel J. Salemson
Marc Sanders
Antoinette Satterfield
J. Christopher Schutz
Christoph E. Schweitzer
Loren Schweninger
Jean H. Seaman
Janet K. Seapker
Linda Sellars
Melissa Semcer
Lisa C. Shaffer
Taylor Shaw
Mary Bates Sherwood
Nancy P. Shires
Richard A. Shrader
Bland Simpson
Marcus B. Simpson Jr.
Mark Simpson-Vos
Annie Marie Smith
Carmen Miner Smith
Clyde Smith
David C. Smith
Edward Smith
Lisa D. Smith
Michael Thomas Smith
William S. Smith
William W. Smith
William D. Snider
Jean Snow
Courtney Sorrell
David Southern
W. Keats Sparrow
R. S. Spencer Jr.
Donna J. Spindel

Richard W. Starbuck
Richard D. Starnes
R. M. Steele
Bennett L. Steelman
Lala Carr Steelman
Richard A. Stephenson
Shelby Stephenson
Robert J. Stets
Alesia K. Stevenson
George Stevenson
Rodney J. Steward
David Stick
Glenn Ellen Starr Stilling
Craig M. Stinson
Alexander R. Stoesen
O. C. Stonestreet III
Martha Stoops
William B. Strong
Jim L. Sumner
Jerry L. Surratt
T. David Sustar
Steve Suther

David Tate
Charles E. Taylor
Margaret Taylor
Michael W. Taylor
Lee Plummer Templeton
Beverly Tetterton
Karen Kruse Thomas
Harry L. Thompson
Michael D. Thompson
William H. Thompson Jr.
Sarah C. Thuesen
Thomas K. Tiemann
Carol A. Tingley
Nahal Toosi
Christopher P. Toumey
Louis P. Towles
Allen W. Trelease
Carole Watterson Troxler
George W. Troxler
Lisa R. Turney

Renné Vance
Robert Blair Vocci
Robert C. Voigt

Charles W. Wadelington
Douglas A. Wait
James W. Wall
Richard Walser
Harry S. Warren
Alan D. Watson
Robert D. Weaver
Ansley Herring Wegner
Rich Weidman
Michael L. Wells
Joseph W. Wescott II
Ruth Y. Wetmore
Willis P. Whichard
Scott Whisnant
Ila M. White
Joyce White
Peter S. White
Clarence E. Whitefield
Carolyn Sparks Whittenburg
Catherine A. Whittenburg
James P. Whittenburg
George-Anne Willard
Jeaneane Williams
L. George Williams
Wiley J. Williams
David L. Williamson
Jo Ann Williford
Paul F. Wilson
Curtis W. Wood
Thomas Woodbury
Ann S. Wright
Marilyn Wright
James Wrinn
Kathleen B. Wyche

Noel Yancey
W. W. Yeargin
Maurice C. York

Joseph E. Zaytoun
Katherine Zeisel
Carmena B. Zimmerman
Karin Lorene Zipf
Richard L. Zuber

Index

Indians and, 607, 700; Mississippian Indian tradition, 33–34, 60, 156, 208; mountain sites, 59–60; Newbold-White House and, 791; in northeastern North Carolina, 47; Paleo-Indian period, 32, 33, 58–59, 99; pottery and, 60, 902; pre–European settlement periods and sites, 33–34, 58–60, 700; privies and, 912; *Queen Anne's Revenge*, 888; Saura Indians and, 1007; shell mounds, **1028–29**; tobacco and, 1120; Town Creek Indian Mound, 33, 156, 758, **1127–28**; Tryon Palace, 1138–39; underwater, 60–61, 460, 888; Woodland period, 33–34, 58, 59, 60, 208. *See also* American Indians; Cherokee Indians; Tuscarora Indians

Archaic period. *See* Archaeology: Archaic period

Archdale, John, 172, 927

Archer Aluminum, 977

Archie K. Davis Fellowships, 837

Architecture, **61–64**; Art Deco, 68; barns, **92–94**; brick making and, 147; College of Design, 63, **254**, 779; Gothic Revival, 62, 218–19; Greek Revival, 1073, 1146; Louis Orr etchings, **695–96**; university programs in, 351, 695. *See also specific structures*

Archives and History, Department of. *See* Archives and History, Office of

Archives and History, Division of. *See* Archives and History, Office of

Archives and History, Office of, **64**, 318; archaeology/underwater archaeology, 64, 460, 888; *Carolina Comments*, **183–84**, 817–18; Civil War rosters, **238–40**; colonial and state records and, 255; Crittenden Award and, 313; establishment of, 64, 318; historical markers, 571–72, 609; historic preservation, 459, 460, 574, 863, 954, 1056; plantation names and, 890; reorganization (1973), 406; Wilmington race riot and, 1209. *See also* Historical Commission; North Carolina State Archives; State Historic Sites Program

A.R.C. record label, 951

Arctic, CSS, 625

Arden, 220

Area Health Education Centers, 923

Areas of Environmental Concern, 250

Arends, Johann Gottfried, 704

Arey, E. C., 1002

Arey, John A., 324

Argillite, 748

Argyll Colony, **64–65**, 602, 1012

Arista Cotton Mill, 386

Armorial bearings, **65**

Armories, **65–66**, 1146; Asheville Armory, **69–70**; Fayetteville Arsenal and Armory, 65–66, 419; Salisbury Arsenal, **1002**; Wilmington Armory, 66

Armstrong, Roy, 765

Army Air Corps (AAC), 767, 778, 943, 1020–21, 1233

Army Air Force (AAF), 659, 860, 1020, 1231

Army Worm, **66**

Arrears, **66**

Arrington, Nick, 251–52

Arrogance (rock band), 985

Arrowhead Monument, 723

Artesian wells, **66**

Arthur, Billy, 856

Arthur, Gabriel, 841, 1007

Artificial reefs, **66–67**, 671

Art Institute of Charlotte, 1166

Artist and the Community Project, 1059

Arts and Libraries, Office of, 318

Arts festivals. *See* Folk festivals

Artworks for State Buildings Program, 1168

Asbestos, 748–49

Asbury, Daniel, 79

Asbury, Francis, 224, 253, 590

Ascaridol, 634

Ashcakes, 145

Ashe, John, 40, 1133

Ashe, John Baptista, 1049

Ashe, Samuel, 67, 155, 296, 946, 1045

Ashe, Samuel A., 495, 506, 577, 725, 944, 1146

Ashe, William Willard, 279, 801

Asheboro, 946

Asheboro & Montgomery Railroad, 1

Ashe County, 28, **67**. *See also* Franklin, State of; Ore Knob Copper Mine

Asheville, **67–68**; architecture in, 62, 63, 68; Christian Science and, 220; city planning and,

226, 227, 1105; Civil War and, 68, 69–70, 739; filmmaking and, 430; fires at, 432; Good Roads campaign and, 513; Greek Orthodox Church in, 854; Grove Park Inn, **542–43**, 967, 1198; historical societies and, 573–74; Missionary District of Asheville, **752–53**; Mountain Dance and Folk Festival, 155, 249, 442, 448, **768**; music/opera/theater in, 243, 353, 851; as nineteenth-century resort, 966–67; racket store in, 932; railroads and, 1003, 1099; Rhododendron Festival, 768; Riverside Cemetery, 976; schools of, 70–71, 120, 379, 947; Southern Highland Craft Guild and, 1060; Taxpayers' League, **1105–6**; Thomas Wolfe Memorial, **1116–17**; tuberculosis treatment at, 611; University of North Carolina at Asheville, 68, 155, **1150**, 1154; visual arts and, 1167; Warren Wilson College, **1178–79**; Western North Carolina Railroad and, 1191; writers and, 427–28, 429; Young Men's Institute, **1242**. *See also* Biltmore Estate; Buncombe Turnpike; Wolfe, Thomas

Asheville, Battle of, 68

Asheville, USS, 68–69

Asheville Armory, 69–70

Asheville-Buncombe Technical Community College, 262

Asheville Citizen-Times, **70**, 347, 795

Asheville Community Theater, 353

Asheville Country Club, 300, 543

Asheville Female College, 70

Asheville Normal and Collegiate Institute, **70–71**

Asheville Poetry Review, 684

Asheville School, 71

Asheville Symphony Orchestra, 243

Asian immigrants, 604, 626, 758

Assemblies of God, **71**, 879

Associated Press (AP), 796

Association of Carolina Shag Clubs, 1022

Association of Southern Agricultural Workers, 687

Aston, Anthony, 1088

Athas, Daphne, 428

Atkins, James, 70

Atkins, Simon Green, 834, 1040

Atkins, Thomas, 1146

Atkinson, Thomas, 398, 947

Atlantic & North Carolina Railroad, 787, 788, 789, 827, 828, 937, 939, 968

Atlantic & Western Railway Company, **71–72**

Atlantic Beach, 968

Atlantic Beer and Ale, 109

Atlantic Christian College, 94, 183, 343, 1211

Atlantic Coast Conference (ACC), 97, 98, 452, 536, 537, 1053

Atlantic Coast Line Railroad (ACL), **72**, 166, 172, 247, 317, 637, 939, 941, 1015, 1207–8

Atlantic Collegiate Institute, 73

Atlantic Research Corporation, 984

Atlantic, Tennessee, and Ohio Railroad, 623

Attachment Clause, 73

Atticus, **73–74**

Attmore, John Alonzo, 789

Attorney General, 74, 1069, 1082. *See also* State Bureau of Investigation

Atwood, Harry, 79

Auditor, State, 74

Audubon Society of North Carolina (ASNC), **74–75**, 279, 594, 1204

Augusta Conference, 75

Aurora borealis. *See* Northern lights

Austin, Louis E., 797

Australian ballot. *See* Secret ballot

Austrian Succession, War of (1740–48), 1064

Automobiles, **75–76**, 305; courtship customs and, 307; driver's licenses, **355**; Highway Commission, **564**; moonshine and, 76, 760; vs. railroads, 941; registration of, 1018; whammy and, 1194. *See also* Highway Patrol; Highways; Roads; Trucks and trucking

Auto racing, **76–78**, 161, 761, 831

Autry, Gene, 1141

Autumn Leaves Festival, 443

Averasboro, Battle of, 78, 319, 552, 1031

Averitt, Richard, 661

Avery, Isaac E., 503

Avery, Waightstill, 78, 671, 929

Avery County, **78–79**, 108, 309, 315; Crossnore School, 316; iron ore deposits, 624, 625. *See also* Beech Mountain/Land of Oz; Grandfather Mountain;

Battle, William Horn, 667, 973, 985

Battle, William S., 986

Battle of the Atlantic. *See* Submarine attacks

Battle of the Bees. *See* McIntyre's Farm, Battle of

Battleships bombed by Billy Mitchell, **102–3**, 526

Batts, Nathaniell, 103, 114, 716, 869, 1002

Batts House, **103–4**, 716, 1002

Bauer, Adolphus Gustavus, 519, 732

Baum, L. Frank, 108

Baum, Paul F., 445

Bavier, Frances, 51

Bayard, Elizabeth Cornell, 104

Bayard v. Singleton, **104**, 274

Bayboro, 864

Bayes, Ronald H., 894

Bay River, 864

Bay River Indians, 722. *See also* Bear River Indians

Bay trees, 864, 1014

Bazemore, Levi, 223

B.C. Powders, 556

Beaches. *See* Resorts

Beachey, Lincoln, 79

Beach music, 952, 1022

Beacon Island Lighthouse, 676

Beal, Fred E., 657

Bean, William, 1183

Beard, David, 554

Beards, **104**

Bear Grass, 990

Bear River Indians, **104–5**

Beat poetry, 894

Beat the bounds, **105**

Beatty, Jim, 831, 1129

Beaufort, 189, 820, 1032

Beaufort, Battle of, **105**

Beaufort, css, 389, 767

Beaufort County, 101, 102, **105–6**, 1031. *See also* Bath

Beaufort County Community College, 262

Beaufort County Historical Society, 863

Beaufort Inlet, 177, 615, 676

Beauregard, P. G. T., 738

Beauty shops, **106–7**

Beavers, **107**, 394

Bechtler, Augustus, 107–8, 322

Bechtler, Christopher, 107–8, 322

Bechtler Mint, **107–8**, 322, 993

Beck, Samuel E., 774

Bedford, Jonas, 697–98

Bedfordshire, HMS, 147–48

Beech Creek Bog State Natural Area, 1078

Beecher, James Chaplain, 1148

Beech Mountain/Land of Oz, 79, **108**, 1040

Beech trees, 455

Beer and breweries, **108–9**

Beers, Clifford, 919

Beery, Benjamin W., 190

Beery's Shipyard, 190

Bees, Battle of the. *See* McIntyre's Farm, Battle of

Beeswax, 583

Behrends, Richard D., 6

Belanger, F. J., 1165

Belk, **109–10**, 384, 627, 932

Belk, John, 109–10

Belk, William Henry, 109–10, 908, 932

Bell, Alexander Graham, 1106

Bell, C. Ritchie, 807

Bell, John, 1016

Belmont, 21, 110

Belmont Abbey College, 110, 491

Belmont Abbey Players, 353

Benbury, Thomas, 1066

Benefit of clergy, **110**

Benevolent and Protective Order of Elks, 228

Ben Folds Five, 985

Ben Hur (Wallace), 967

Bennehan, Rebecca, 1068

Bennehan, Richard, 1068

Bennehan, Thomas, 1068–69

Bennett, Harold C., 6

Bennett, Hugh Hammond, 1055

Bennett, James, 1031

Bennett, Lyman, 111

Bennett, Richard, 410

Bennett Advertising, 6

Bennett College, **110–11**, 203, 536, 537

Bennett Place, **111–12**, 238, 363, 757

Bennett Women's Choir, 536

Benoit, Joan, 1130

Benson, 771–72

Benson, John, 537

Bentonville, Battle of, 78, **112–13**, 238, 512, 965, 1031, 1235

Bentonville Battlefield, **113**, 637

Berkeley, John, Lord, 691

Berkeley, Scott B., 1021

Berkeley, William, 318, 667, 691, 910

Bernard, Germain, 556

Bernard, William Henry, 1210

Bernice Bienenstock Furniture Library, **113–14**

Berry, Cherie, 1224

Berry, Harriet "Hattie" Morehead, 501, 514

Bertie, Henry, 114

Bertie, James, 114

Bertie County, **114**, 307, 1045. *See also* Batts House

Bertie; or, Life in the Old Field (Throop), 1002

Beryl, 749

Best, Johnny, 631

Bethabara, **114–15**, 478, 573, 602, 764, 998, 1171. *See also* Salem

Bethania, 52, 55, 853, 1171

Bethel Regiment, **115**, 420

Better Baby Contests, **115**

Better Homes and Gardens, 911

Bettis's Bridge, Battle of, **115–16**, 678

Betts, Doris, 428, 429, 836

B. Everett Jordan Lake, 660

Beveridge, James, 814

Beverley, Robert, 841

Bevington, Helen Smith, 893

Biblical Recorder, 89

Bicentennial Commission, 45

Bicentennial Mall (Raleigh), 45

Bickett, Thomas W., 657, 778, 1035, 1225, 1230

Bickley, George W. L., 651

Biddle, Henry J., 636

Biddle, Mary Duke, 357, 636, 1006

Bienenstock, Bernice, 114

Bienenstock, Nathan (Sandy), 113–14

Big Bethel Church, Va., Battle of, 115, 236–37, 432

Biggs, Asa, 641

Biggs, J. Crawford, 806

Biggs, Timothy, 318

Big Ore Bank, **116**, 624

Big Star stores, 540, 541

Bikle, Louis A., 809

Billboards, 6

Billings, Rhoda, 806

Bill Monroe and the Blue Grass Boys, 131

Bill of Rights, 53, 287, 288

Biltmore Estate, 889; Biltmore Forest School, **116–17**, 118, 279, 454, 690, 889, 1131; Biltmore homespun, 119; Biltmore House, 62, 68, **117–19**, 1242; Biltmore House gardens, 116, 184, 574; Biltmore Industries, **119**, 1226; Biltmore Village, 118, 119, 226; wines of, 1214

Bingham, Daniel H., 981

Bingham, G. A., 1227

Bingham, John Archibald, 120, 569

Bingham, Lemuel, 1191

Bingham, Robert, 120

Bingham, William (father of William James Bingham), 119–20, 569

Bingham, William (son of William James Bingham), 120

Bingham, William James, 120, 569

Bingham School, **119–21**, 569

Biographical History of North Carolina (Ashe), 577

Biosphere Reserves, 522, 533, 770

Biotechnology, 121, 714; Burroughs Wellcome Fund, **159**; Laboratory Corporation of America Holdings (LabCorp), **656**

Birch, John, 634

Bird, William E., 574

Birds. *See* Audubon Society of North Carolina; Waterfowl; Wildlife

Birth and death records. *See* Vital statistics

Birth control, 922–23

Birth of a Nation, The (film), 240, 244, 352, 427, 655

Biscuits, 146, 160

Bishop, Francis Gladden, 766

Bishop of Durham clause, **121**, 180, 182–83

Bishop of London, **121–22**

Bittle, D. H., Mrs., 705, 758

Black and Tan Constitution, **122**, 290. *See also* Constitution of 1868

Black Arts Movement, 894

Blackbeard (Edward Teach) 101, 106, 505, 599, 858, 887–88

Blackbeard (outdoor drama), 101

Blackbeard: A Comedy, in Four Acts; Founded on Fact (Sawyer), 351

Black bears, 531, 595, 1205

Blackburn, Charles, Jr., 836

Black codes, **122**, 229, 283, 401, 467, 949, 1042, 1045

Black-eyed pea, **122–23**, 599

Black freemasonry, **123**

Black Mountain, 424

Black Mountain College, **123–24**, 155, 442, 630, 894, 956, 1166, 1223

Black Mountain Developmental Center, 731

Black Mountain Railroad, 1240

Black Mountains, 500, 769, 1240

Black Panther Party, **124–25**, 234, 777. *See also* Wilmington Ten

Black Pioneers, 360, 698, 991

Black Power Movement, 234, 261, 1089

Blacks. *See* African Americans

Black Second. *See* Congressional districts

Capps, Jimmy, 952
Card, Orson Scott, 429
Cardinal, **179**
Carl Sandburg Home National
    Historic Site, 276
Carlton, Rosa Lee, 449
Carlyle, Irving E., 518
Carlyle Commission. *See*
    Governor's Commission on
    Education beyond High
    School
Carmichael, Cartwright, 96
Carmichael, Stokely, 1089
Carnation Company, 324, 325
Carnegie, Andrew, 179, 925
Carnegie Corporation, 179, 925
Carnegie libraries, **179–80**, 925
Carnivore Preservation Trust, 205
Carolana, 180, 557, 855
Carolina, **180**, 524, 557, 855
Carolina Ballet, 325
Carolina Bays, **180–81**, 1099
Carolina Beach, 597, 615, 969
Carolina Beach State Park, 1078
Carolina Beach Inlet, 615
Carolina canary grass, 525
Carolina Caribbean Corporation,
    108
Carolina Central Railway, **181–82**,
    1015
Carolina charters (1663, 1665),
    182–83, 188, 200; Bishop of
    Durham clause, 121, 180, 182–
    83; Chancery Court, **199–200**;
    conscription and, 277;
    instructions to royal governors
    and, 618; land grants and, 524,
    557, 661; Lords Proprietors
    and, 691; manors and, 710;
    religion and, 222; and rights as
    Englishmen, 284, **973**; silk
    and, 1036; slavery and, 7; state
    boundaries and, 141
Carolina Charter Tercentenary
    Commission, **183**
Carolina Christian College, 94,
    183
Carolina, Clinchfield, and Ohio
    Railroad, 939
Carolina College for Women, **183**
Carolina Comments, **183–84**, 817
Carolina Cougars, 98
Carolina Elephant Tokens. *See*
    Elephant tokens
"Carolina Emerald," 749
Carolina Female College, **184**
Carolina Hotel, **184**, 968
Carolina Hurricanes, 602, 942
Carolina Immigration
    Association, 1092
Carolina Indian Voice, **184–85**

Carolina Inn, 570
Carolina Israelite, **185**, 797
Carolina Jazz Festival, 443
Carolina Journal, 636
Carolina League (baseball), 95
Carolina panther, **185–86**
Carolina Panthers, 452, 588, 725
Carolina parakeet, **186–87**, 394
Carolina Peacemaker, **187**, 797
Carolina Playmakers, 352, 529,
    856, 857
Carolina Political Union (CPU),
    187
Carolina Power & Light Company
    (CP&L), **187–88**, 386–87, 838,
    883
Carolina Quarterly, 683–84
Carolinas, separation of, 141–42,
    188–89, 691, 1046, 1175
Carolinas Cotton Growers
    Cooperative. *See* North
    Carolina Cotton Growers
    Association
Carolina Slate Belt. *See* Slate Belt
Carolinas-Virginia Nuclear Power
    Associates, Inc., 387, 838
Carolina Tar Heels, 951
Carolina Theatre, 362, 363
Carolina Thunderbirds, 601
Carolina Times, 797
Carolina Tungsten Company, 751
Carolina Union Farmer, 416
Carolina Wilderness Adventures,
    1200
Carolina Yacht Club, 969
Carolinian, 797
Carowinds, 48
Carpetbaggers. *See*
    Reconstruction
Carr, Elias, 415, 416, 621, 813, 1057,
    1227
Carr, Julian Shakespeare, 481, 578,
    925, 944, 1134
Carr, Lalla Ruth, 925
Carrie Heath Schwenning
    Scholarship Fund, 31
Carrier, Willis H., 21
Carrigan, William A., 25
Carroll, John, 986
Carroll A. Deering (schooner), 505,
    1033–34
Carrow, Samuel T., 719
Carruth, F. E., 295
Carson, Fiddlin' John, 951
Carson, John, 189
Carson, Jonathan Logan, 189
Carson, Samuel Price, 189
Carson House, **189**, 723
Cartagena Expedition. *See*
    Jenkins' Ear, War of
Carter, Edward, 720

Carter, Isobel Gordon, 445
Carter, Jimmy, 963
Carteret, George, first baron
    Carteret of Hawnes, 524, 691
Carteret, John, second Earl
    Granville, 189, 319, 478, 641,
    691; land grants and, 395, 502,
    524, 661–62, 1171; Moravians
    and, 524, 662, 764, 1170–71
Carteret, Peter, 318
Carteret Community College, 262
Carteret County, 189, 1027. *See
    also* Cape Lookout National
    Seashore; Fort Macon; Harkers
    Island boats; Hoi Toiders
Carteret County Telephone, 594
Carthage, 761
Cary, Thomas, 101, 190, 1031
Cary Rebellion, 101, **190**, 222, 638,
    927, 1002, 1102
Case, Everett, 96–97
Case Farms, 658, 665
Cashwell, Gaston B., 581
Casinos, 38, 212, 490, 1132
Cassatt, Mary, 695
Cassidey, James, 190
Cassidey's Shipyard, **190**
Cassiterite. *See* Tin
Casso, Peter, 48, 617
Casso's Inn, 617
Castle Hayne, 876, 1169
Castle McCulloch Gold Mill, **190**
Castro, Fidel, 935
Caswell, Richard, 41, 65, 84, 191,
    458, 669, 731, 742; burial site
    (and memorial), 787; Camden,
    Battle of, and, 43, 164;
    Constitution of 1776 and, 284;
    as first governor, 286, 469, 548,
    688; Moore's Creek Bridge,
    Battle of, and, 563, 762–63;
    Provincial Congresses and,
    918; Tryon Palace and, 1138
Caswell (wooden gunboat), 546
Caswell County, **191**
Caswell Developmental Center,
    731
Caswell Training School, 383
Cataloochee Ranch and Ski Area,
    191, 555, 1039–40
Cataloochee Trail, **191–92**
Catalpa tree, 192
Catalpa worm, 192
Catawba College, 192, 241, 375,
    404, 955, 990
Catawba County, 167, **192–93**. *See
    also* Lenoir-Rhyne College
Catawba Indians/Nation, 52, 75,
    141, 192, **193–94**, 1006, 1007,
    1023, 1039; American

Revolution and, 194, 241;
    trading and, 608
Catawba Power Company, 358,
    1061
Catawba River, 48, **194**, 725, 867,
    1006, 1007; Cowan's Ford,
    Battle of, and, 308;
    hydroelectric generation on,
    358, 386, 678; North Carolina
    Catawba Company, 807–8;
    Torrence's Tavern and, 1125
Catawba Trail, 608
Catawba Valley Community
    College, 262
Catawba wine, 467
Catesby, Mark, 1201
Cathcart, William, 664
Cathey, William, 194
Cathey's Fort, **194**
Catholic News and Herald
    (Charlotte), 987
Cato Institute, 636
Cat-throwing incident, **194–95**
Cattle drives, **195**, 687. *See also*
    Drovers
Caucasian, **195**
Caudle, Lloyd, 831
Cavanagh, Jack, 404–5
Caves and caverns, **195–96**
Cayuga Indians, 1006
Cecil, John Francis Amherst, 119
Celanese Corporation, 1113
Cement, **196**
Cemeteries, national and state,
    196–97, 441, 483
Census, U.S., 64, 730, 1013, 1170.
    See also Demography
Centennial Exposition
    (Philadelphia, 1876), 1106
Center for Creative Leadership,
    1051
Center for Environmental
    Farming Systems, 15
Center for Marine Science
    Research, 1153
Center for Medicare and Medicaid
    Services, 923
Center for Plant Conservation, 807
Center for Advanced Study in the
    Behavioral Sciences (Palo Alto,
    Calif.), 778
Center for Woolly Worm Studies,
    1227
Central Campaign Committee for
    the Promotion of Public
    Education, 379
Central Carolina Bank & Trust
    Company (CCB), **197–98**,
    1105–6
Central Carolina Community
    College, 262

Deer, 595, 1204; white-tailed, 186, 1204
Deertongue, 334
Defence of the Revolutionary History of the State of Carolina, A, 847
Dega. *See* Montagnards
Deitrick, William Henley, 351
De Kalb, Johann, 164
De Kooning, Willem, 123
DeLacy, John D., 787
Delamar, Ned, 1065
Delaware, USS, 27
Delco Lights, **334**
De León, Ponce, 1201
De Leon, Thomas Cooper, 663
Delgado Mill, 831
Demesne land, **334**
Democratic Party, 256–57, **334–37**, 1144; Aycock, Charles B., and, 200, 330, 335, 954; bloc voting and, 129, 1051; Bourbons, 142–43; *Caucasian*, 195; conservatism and, 282, 283, 896; Convention of 1875 and, 290; "Dawn of a New Day," **330**; Dixiecrats, 347, 896; election law and, 385; Farmers' Alliance and, 415–16; Fusion of Republicans and Populists and, 487–88; Gideon's Band and, 505–6; and Helms-Hunt Senate race, 129, **558–59**; Mexican War and, 734–35; Populist Party and, 897–98; *Progressive Farmer* and, 914–15; Reconstruction and, 340, 949–50; Redeemer Democrats, **953**; Red Shirts, **953–54**; Republican Party and, 962–63; rise of, 895–96; secession and, 1017; Shelby dynasty and, 1026; silver fusion and, 1036–37; and Smith-Graham Senate race, 129, **1050–51**, 1162; *South Dakota v. North Carolina* and, 1057–58; Subtreasury Plan and, 1092; violence, group, and, 1163–64; Whig Party and, 1194, 1195; white supremacy campaigns and, 1209; *Wilmington Star* and, 1210; yellow-dog Democrat, **1240–41**. *See also* Disfranchisement; Progressivism
Demography, 7, 13, 38, **337–38**; Latino population, 664; Metropolitan Statistical Areas, 885; Piedmont Urban Crescent, 885; poverty and, 905; slavery and, 1048

Denmark, James W., 914
Denmark, Juanita Polk, 914
Dentistry, **338–39**; dental clinics, 922
Dentzel, Gustave A., 47
DePeyster, Abraham, 650
Depression. *See* Great Depression
De Quejo, Pedro, 407
De Richebourg, Philippe, 593
Desertion, Civil War, 154, **339–40**, 582, 1029, 1147, 1163; Heroes of America and, 560–61; Linville Caverns and, 196; peace movement and, 871–72; substitutes and, 1091
De Soto, Hernando, 208, 215, 340, 408, 500
De Soto expedition, 60, 99, **340**, 408, 500, 707, 1007
Dessen, Sarah, 429
D'Estaing, Charles Hector, 991
Destructives, **340**
Dett, R. Nathaniel, 536
Devil's Horse's Hoof Prints, **341**
Devil's Tramping Ground, 205, **341**, 446
Devine, Virginia Stella, 1227
Dew, Thomas, 410
Dewey, John, 123
Dewey, Thomas, 347
Deyo, Ruth, 820
Dial, Adolph, 700
Diamondbacks. *See* Terrapins
Diamond City, 177, 597, 676, 1194
Diamondhead Corporation, 184
Diamonds, 749
Diamond Shoals, 176, 505, 526, 675–76, 1033–34
Diamond Shoals lightship, 677, 1089
Dickens, Charles, 663
Dickinson, John, 878
Dickinson, Matthew, 695
Dickinson, Samuel, 319
Dickson, Alfred G., 1210
Dickson, James H., 612
Dickson, Paul, III, 1065
Dickson, Samuel, 70
Dictionary of North Carolina Biography (Powell), 577
Diggs, Edward O., 12
Diggs Art Gallery, 1217
Diligence, HMS, 1070
Dillard, James H., 632
Dimock, Susan, 727
DIMON, Inc., 2
Dinner on the grounds, **341**
Dinosaurs. *See* Fossils
Diphtheria, 610
Directory of State and County Officials, 1018

Dirigibles, 79
Dirt eaters, **341–42**
Disciples of Christ, 94, 183, 221, **342–43**
Disfranchisement, **343–44**, 898, 954, 963; of African Americans, from 1899, 8–9, 11, 230, 274, 291, 330, 335, 343–44, 385, 678, 706; Bassett affair and, 100; of Cherokee Indians, 210–11; of free blacks, 1835, 288; grandfather clause and, 11, 343, 521; lily-white politics and, 678; newspapers and, 796; poll tax, 11, 285, 343, 521, 897; of poor whites, 343
Dismal Swamp Canal, 26, 167, 168, **344–46**, 389, 532, 799
Dismal Swamp State Natural Area, 1078
Dissenters, **346**, 526, 959, 1054
Divorce, **346–47**, 1221
Dix, Dorothea Lynde, 905, 919
Dix, Elijah, 919
Dixiecrats, **347**, 896
Dixon, Amzi Clarence, 481
Dixon, Henry, 164
Dixon, Thomas, Jr., 240, 244, 351, 427, 655
Dixon Brothers, 303
Doak, Samuel, 720
Doar, Harriet, 797
Dobbs, Arthur, 149, 426, 459, 1158; borough towns and, 139; boundaries, state, and, 141; burial site, 998; Church of England and, 222; currency and, 321; death of, 1137; Enfield riots and, 395–96; and French and Indian War, 478; integral society and, 619; King's Bounty and, 648–49; militias, colonial, and, 747; Regulator Movement and, 958; as royal governor, 153, 545, 554, 707; Sugar Creek, War of, and, 1093
Dobbs, Edward Brice, 478
Dobson, 1097
Dobson, William, 1097
Dobson, William P., 1097
Dodge, E. R., 1106
Dog breeds, **348**. *See also* Plott hound
Dog racing, **348**
Dogwood, **348–49**
Dogwood festivals, **349**
Dole, Bob, 777
Dole, Elizabeth, 703, 953
Doodlebugs, **349–50**

Dope wagons, **350**
Doratt, Charles, 809
Doris Duke Center Garden, 1006
Dorland, Luke, 350
Dorland-Bell School, **350**
Dorothea Dix Hospital. *See* Psychiatric hospitals
Dorothea Dix School of Nursing, 919
Dortch Act of 1883 (N.C.), 378
Dorton, J. S. "Doc," 350
Dorton Arena, 63, **350–51**, 1074
Doub, J. B., 1002
Doug Clark and the Hot Nuts, 952
Dougherty, Blanford Barnard, 54
Dougherty, Dauphin Disco, 54
Doughton, Robert Lee, 28
Douglas, Stephen A., 132, 1016
Douglas International Airport (Charlotte), 767
Douglass, Frederick, 1043
Douglass, Robert M., 719
Dowell, Saxie, 631
Downing, Fanny M., 664
Downing, William, 1133
Doyle, John, 723
Drake, Daniel, 747
Drake, Sir Francis, 46, 410, 872–73
Dramatic arts, **351–54**; community theater, 353; professional theater, 353–54; strolling players, **1088**; Thalian Association, 351, **1114**. *See also* Carolina Playmakers; Opera houses; Outdoor dramas
Draper, Earle S., 226–27
Drawbridges, **354**
Dred (Stowe), **354**, 532
Dreier, Theodore, 123
Drexel Furniture Company, **354–55**
Dreyer, Ernst, 292
Drinking water, 225
Driver's licenses, **355**
Dromgoole, Peter, 506
Droughts, 246, 358
Drovers, **355**, 687
Drowning Creek, Battle of. *See* Bettis's Bridge, Battle of
Drugstores, **355–56**
Drummond, Lewis, 1058
Drummond, William, 520, 854, 1012
Duche, Andrew, 207
Duck hunting. *See* Waterfowl
Dudley, Edward B., 385, 626, 775, 1195
Dudley, Guilford Lafayette, 172
Dueling, **356–57**, 616
Duke, Benjamin N., 646, 1006, 1121, 1186; American Tobacco

Farmworkers Legal Services of North Carolina, 736

Farquhar, Robroy, 353

Farris, William, 901

Fashion. *See* Clothing and fashion

Fassifern School, **418–19**

Fatback, **419**

Faulkner, William, 772

Fayetteville, 139, 319, **419–20**, 1011; Cape Fear Valley Scottish Festival, **176**; Confederate Women's Home, **274**; establishment of, 174, 419; fire at, 431–32; freemasonry in, 123; Methodist College, 733–34; Museum of the Cape Fear, **774**; Sherman's March and, 1031; as state capital, 179, 419. *See also* Fort Bragg

Fayetteville Academy, **420**, 432

Fayetteville and Western Plank Road Company, 55, 978

Fayetteville Arsenal and Armory, 65–66, 419

Fayetteville Dogwood Festival, 349

Fayetteville Independent Light Infantry Company (FILI), **420**

Fayetteville Light Infantry Company, 420

Fayetteville Observer, 137, 172, 419, **420–22**, 795

Fayetteville State University, 420, **422**

Fayetteville Technical Community College, 263, 420

Fayetteville Times, 421

Fearing, Tom, 1096

Federal Art and Music Projects, 529, 1071

Federal Bureau of Investigation (FBI), 331

Federal Communications Commission (FCC), 914, 935, 1107

Federal Deposit Insurance Corporation (FDIC) creation, 85

Federal Emergency Relief Administration (FERA), 528–29, 828

Federal Employment Practices Commission (FEPC), 1050

Federal Highway System, 565, 567

Federal Home Loan Bank Board, 1008

Federal Housing Administration, 1008

Federalists, 52–53, 895, 929–30, 962, 1155; banking and, 86, 87; Federalist Party, **422–23**

Federal Reserve System, 85, 323, 865

Federal Writers' Project (FWP), **423**, 1044

Federation of North Carolina Historical Societies, 574

Feeder Ditch, 532

Fee system, **423–24**

Feldspar, 749

Fellowship of Reconciliation, 258

Fellowship of Southern Churchmen (FSC), 259, **424**

Felton, Rebecca, 1208

Feminism. *See* Women

Fences, **424–25**, 686, 1201

Fenn, Elizabeth A., 635

Ferber, Edna, 102

Fergus, John, 727

Ferguson, Patrick, 43, 649–50, 860, 1126

Fernándes, Simon, 30–31, 692

Fernandez, Domingo, 408

Ferrell, Wes, 831

Ferries, **425–26**, 615, 858, 975; Blossom's Ferry, **130**; Hill's Ferry, **569–70**; Smith's Ferry, 637; Sneads Ferry, 794

Fessenden, Reginald A., 463, 858, 1217

Festival for the Eno, 426, 443

Festival Rodin, 822

Fetzer, Robert A., 765

Fetzer, Tom, 777

Few, William P., 358–59, 632, 956, 1135

Fiction, **426–29**; *Fool's Errand, A* (Tourgée), **451**; *Matilda Berkely; or, Family Anecdotes* (Gales), 427, 721–22; North Carolina Writers Conference, **836**; North Carolina Writers' Network, **836**; O. Henry Festival, **843**; pseudonyms and, 918; Roanoke-Chowan Group, 682, **980–81**; *Sea-Gift*, **1015**; slave narratives and, 1043; *Wreath from the Woods of Carolina, A* (Mason), **1234–35**. *See also* Literary awards; Literary journals; Poetry

Fiddle, 848–50, 1067

Fiddler's Grove: A Celebration of Old-Time Music (film), 850

Fieldcrest Cannon, Inc., 1113

Field names, **429–30**

Fiesta del Pueblo, 443, 665

Fifteenth Amendment (U.S. Constitution), 142, 343, 949, 950, 963. *See also* Disfranchisement

Figg and Mueller Engineers, 679

Figure Eight Island, 969

Fillmore, Millard, 40

Filmmaking, **430–31**; at Lake Lure, 967, 993; North Carolina Film Board and, **814**; silent movies, 568, 967; town documentaries, **1128**; Wilmington and, 792, 1207

Finch, Harriet, 705

Finch, Jerry, 705

Finley, Ned, 430

Finney, Charles G., 771

Fire departments, **431–32**

Firehouse (rock band), 985

Firemen's Relief Fund, 432

"First at Bethel, farthest to the front at Gettysburg and Chickamauga, and last at Appomattox," 432

First Citizens Bank & Trust Company, **432–33**

First Colony Farms, 168

First Colony Inn, 968

First Flight Centennial Commission, 318, 1235

First for Freedom (outdoor drama), 548

First Great Awakening. *See* Great Awakening

"First in Freedom," **433**

First National Bank of Charlotte, 86

First National Bank of Salem, 1171

First Union Bank Corporation, 87, **433**, 512

First Universalist Church of Sampson County, 1148

First Wachovia Corporation, 1171

Fish. *See* Wildlife

Fish and Fisheries of the United States, 1203

Fisher, Charles F., 739, 743, 879, 1191

Fisher, Frances Christine. *See* Reid, Christian

Fisher, Jesse C., 1087

Fisheries Commission Board, 279

Fishing, commercial, **433–34**, 615, 783, 858, 987–88; at Salmon Creek, 1002–3; shellfish and, 1027–28; terrapins, 1110; World's Columbian Exposition and, 1227

Fishing, recreational, 162, **434–36**, 864, 1038; artificial reefs, 66–67, 671

Fishing camps, **436–37**

Fishing Tackle Loaner Program, 435

Fish stews, **437**, 1022

Fiske, F. A., 473

Fitzgerald, F. Scott, 432

Fitzgerald, Zelda, 432

Fitzgerald Act. *See* National Apprenticeship Act of 1937 (U.S.)

Flag, state, **437–38**, 548, 549, 725

Flatfooting, 154, 248

Flat Rock, 276, 967

Flat Rock Playhouse, 353, 559

Flatt, Lester, 131, 933

Flax, 559, 679

Fleming, W. W., 457

Flentrop organs, 854

Fletcher, 854

Fletcher, Alfred Johnson, 243, 1162

Fletcher, Elizabeth Utley, 243

Fletcher, Floyd, 187

Fletcher, Fred, 934

Fletcher, Inglis, 388, 389, 428, 836

Fletcher, John, 580

Fletcher, Maria Beale, 754

Flinn, Andrew, 568

Flogging, **438–39**, 950

Floods, 246–47, 358, 373

Flora MacDonald College, **439**, 440, 562, 995

Flora MacDonald Highland Games and Gathering of Scottish Clans, 562

Flora MacDonald homesite, **439–40**

Florida, Western, and Northern Railroad, 1015

Floyd, John B., 739

Floyd, Raymond, 513

Flumes, 690

Flying Squadron. *See* Four-Minute Men

Flying squadrons, 440, 657

Flying squirrel, 1205

Folger, Timothy, 545

Folk art, **440–42**; decoys, 332–33, 1225, 1226; dyes and dyeing, 365; fraktur, **467–68**; John C. Campbell Folk School, **635**; Mountain Heritage Center, **768–69**; Penland School of Crafts, **877**; pine needle art, **886–87**; quilts, **930**; rag rugs, 440; Southern Folklife Collection, 570, **1059–60**; tombstones, 441, **1124–25**; weaving, 119, **1187**; woodcarving and, 1225–26. *See also* Black Mountain College; Pottery; Southern Highland Craft Guild

Folk Art Center. *See* Southern Highland Craft Guild

Folk festivals, 67, 79, 192, 325, **442–44**, 555; Azalea Festival,

Penderlea Homesteads, 875–77
Pender Stores, 540
Penick, Edwin A., 997
Penland, 53, 877, 1060
Penland School of Crafts, 53, 755, 877, 1226
Penmanship, 877–78
Penn, Betsy, 466
Penn, Charles A., 46
Penn, John, 41, 327, 572
Penn, William, 927
Pennant, Elias, 410
Pennington, William, 153
Pennsylvania Dutch. *See* German settlers
Pennsylvania Farmer, 878
Pennsylvania Railroad, 937
Pentecostal Free Will Baptist Church, 560
Pentecostal Holiness Church, 581, 600, **878–79**
Pentecostalism, 71, 223, 1149
Pentes, Jack, 108
People's Bible School. *See* John Wesley College
People's Ticket, **879–80**
Pepsi-Cola, 310, 356, 437, **880–81**
Perdue, Beverly, 1224
Periauger, **881**, 1021, 1025
Periodicals. *See* Magazines, periodicals, and newsletters
Perkins, Benjamin, 568
Perkins, Constantine, 1135
Perkins, Frances, 522
Perkins, Peter, 1135
Perkins, Samuel Huntington, 1014
Perley, Fred A., 770
Permatech, 30
Perquimans County, 693, **881**, 927, 1187. *See also* Newbold-White House
Perquimans County Restoration Association, Inc., 791
Perquimans Indians, 881
Perry, Albert E., 1164
Perry, Sam L., 406
Perry, William G., 1138
Pershing, John J., 778
Persian Gulf War (1991), 737, **881–82**
Person, Joe, Mrs., 869
Person, Thomas, 616, 839, 883
Personal names, **882–83**
Person County, **883**, 1045
Person Place, 470, 694
Person's Ordinary, 616
Pesticides, 366
Peter, Johann Friedrich, 763
Peters, Thomas, 698, 991
Petersburg, Va., 980
Peterson, C. A., 178

Petrillo, J. C., 951
Petroglyphs, 638
Pettigrew, Charles, 398, 1058
Pettigrew, James J., 503, 504, 788
Pettigrew, William Shepard, 996
Pettigrew State Park, 1078
Petty, Lee, 77
Petty, Richard, 77
Pfeiffer, Annie Merner, 883
Pfeiffer, Henry, 883
Pfeiffer University, **883**, 1070
Pfohl, James Christian, 147
Phelps, David, 314
Phelps, Jonathon, 881
P. H. Hanes Tobacco Company, 549
Phifer, John, 929
Phifer, Robert F., 1071
Philip Morris tobacco company, 1121, 1122
Philippine Insurrection (1899–1901), 1160
Phillips, Samuel Field, 890–91
Phillips Brothers County Ham, Inc., 301–2
Phipps, Meg Scott, 17
Phosphate, 750
Photographs, collections of, 570
Photography. *See* Visual arts
Pianos, **883–84**
Pickens, S. V., 479
Picket, USS, **884**, 1179
Pickett, George E., 154, 504, 789, 1144, 1147
Pickin' for Merle (TV series), 732
Pictorial Field-Book of the Revolution (Lossing), 1130
Piedmont. *See* Geography
Piedmont Airlines, 80, 1215
Piedmont & Northern Railway, 294–95, 358
Piedmont blues, 135, 362
Piedmont Community College, 263
Piedmont Heights, 158
Piedmont League (baseball), 95
Piedmont Railroad, 827
Piedmont Urban Crescent, 370, 371, 499, 827, **884–85**, 937
Piedmont Village Tradition, 59
Piedmont Wagon Company, **885**
Pierce, Anna, 747
Pierce, Franklin, 132, 1160
Pierce, Julian T., 235, 702
Pietists, 696
Pigeon River, 1200
Pig pickin'. *See* Barbecue
Pilgrim Holiness Church, 1189, 1190
Pillowtex, 161, 170, 1113
Pilmore, Joseph, 733

Pilot Club International, 229
Pilot Life Insurance, 97
Pilot Mountain, 50, **885–86**, 1078
Pilot Mountain State Park, 1097
Pinchot, Gifford, 116–17, 118, 279, 454, 1227
Pinckney's Treaty (1795), 754
Pinckney, Homer, 890
Pine bark beetles, **886**
Pinehurst, 184, 226, 300, 512, 761, 968, 1109
Pine Knoll Shores, 57, 968
Pine needle art, **886–87**
Pine trees, **887**; loblolly, 455; longleaf, 1, 454, 455, 498, 783, 887, 1193; naval stores and, 783; pine bark beetles, **886**
Pineville, 76, 629
Pinkus, L., 560
Pinto, Solomon, 568
Pirates, 101, 505, 691, 858, **887–88**; oyster war and, 861–62, 1028
Pisgah Forest Pottery, 903
Pisgah Mountains, 500
Pisgah National Forest, 55, 147, 163, 555, 755, **888–89**, 1131, 1240; Biltmore Forest School and, 117, 119; Blue Ridge Parkway and, 133, 158, 559; Civilian Conservation Corps and, 529; Lover's Leap, 591–92; Outward Bound School and, 859; waterfalls in, 1184
Pitcairn Aviation, Inc., 21
Pitman, Isaac, 1035
Pitt, William, earl of Chatham, 205, 889
Pitt Academy, **889**
Pitt Community College, 264
Pitt County, 183, **889**, 966. *See also* East Carolina University
Pittman-Robertson Act of 1937 (N.C.), 1204
Pittsboro, 205, 687
Pittsborough Academy, 943
Plank roads. *See* Roads
Plantation Duty Act of 1673 (Britain), 318, 784, **889–90**
Plantations, 549, 638, 737; Cooleemee Plantation, **292**, 329; Fairntosh Plantation, 1068–69; field names and, 430; gentry, **497–98**; Grove, **541–42**; Hayes Plantation, **554–55**; Oak Forest, 304, 1196; overseers, **861**; names of, **890**; Rosedale, **988**, 1175; Rural Hill Plantation, 562; sharecropping and, 1024–25; slave clandestine economy and, 1041; slave names and, 1042; slaves' midsummer holiday,

1049; Sloop Point Plantation, **1049**; smokehouses, 1052; Somerset Place, **1056**, 1180; Stagville, **1068–69**; Wingfield plantation, 154; women and, 1220
Plant Conservation Program, 394, 507
Playmakers. *See* Carolina Playmakers
PlayMakers Repertory Company, 353
Playmakers Theatre, 1151
Playwrights. *See* Dramatic arts
Pleasant Gardens, 189
Plessy, Homer, 890
Plessy v. Ferguson, 11, 230, **890–91**
P. Lorillard tobacco company, 1121, 1150
Plott, Johannes, 348, 891
Plott hound, 348, **891**
Plowing, 18, 1055
Plowman. See *Arator*
Plunkett, Achilles, 1178
Plymouth, 218, 745, 746, 1180
Plymouth, Battle of, 26, 238, 742, **891–92**, 1180
Plymouth Toll Road, 1140
Plymouth Turnpike Company, 1139
Pocosin Lakes National Wildlife Refuge, 168, 892, 1142, 1180
Pocosins, **892**, 1099, 1192
Poe, Clarence H., 213, 810, 914–15, 1071, 1182
Poet laureate, **892**, 893
Poetry, **892–95**; *Carolina Quarterly* and, 684; Great Dismal Swamp and, 532; Kilmer, Joyce, 775; *Land We Love, The*, and, 663–64; pseudonyms and, 918; Roanoke-Chowan Award, 682, 980, 981; Roanoke-Chowan Group, **980–81**; *Travels of William Bartram* and, 1133
Poliomyelitis, 610, 611, 752, 922
Political parties, **895–96**. *See also* specific parties
Polk, James K., 629, 725, 734, 775, 845, 909
Polk, Leonidas LaFayette, 162; Farmers' Alliance and, 52, 487, 897, 914; immigrants and, 602; North Carolina Farmers' Association and, 621, 813; Populist Party and, 897; *Progressive Farmer* and, 20–21, 487, 914; Subtreasury Plan and, 1092; Watauga Club and, 831, 1182
Polk, Thomas, 671, 929, 1093, 1181

Polk, William, 422, 725, 879, 896
Polk County, **896**. *See also*
　　Isothermal belt
Polkton, 52
Pollock, George, 661
Pollock, Thomas, 1002, 1102
Poll tax, 11, 285, 343, 521, **897**
Pollution. *See* Conservation
　　movement; Environment
Polychlorinated biphenyl (PCB),
　　281
Polygamy, 766
Pond Battery, 746
Pontiac's Conspiracy. *See*
　　Proclamation of 1763
Pool, James H., 855
Pool, John, 4, 852, 950
Pool, Stephen D., 855, 1179
Poole, Charlie, 761, 849, 933, 951
Poole, David Scott, 404, 897
Poole Bills (1920s, N.C.), 404, **897**
Poorhouses, 905
Pop Castle, 616
Pope, Art, 989
Pope, Harley Halbert, 457, 897
Pope, John, 989
Pope, Liston, 810
Pope Air Force Base, 457–58, **897**,
　　1161
Popular Government, 617
Population. *See* Demography
Populist Party, 143, 195, 896, **897–
　　98**; black-white cooperation
　　and, 256; *Caucasian*, **195**;
　　Democratic opposition to, 343,
　　954; farmers and, 335, 415–16,
　　522, 914–15, 1025; Gideon's
　　Band and, 505–6; *Progressive
　　Farmer* and, 914; silver fusion
　　and, 1036–37; *South Dakota v.
　　North Carolina* and, 1058;
　　Subtreasury Plan and, 1092.
　　See also Fusion of Republicans
　　and Populists
Porcelain, 646
Porter, David, 460
Porter, John L., 25–26, 786, 800,
　　942, 1207
Porter, Pender, 1236
Porter, William Sydney. *See*
　　O. Henry
Portis Gold Mine, **898–99**
Ports and harbors, **899–900**
Portsmouth, 177, 614, 1176–77,
　　1192
Pory, John, 410
Postal service, **900–901**. *See also*
　　Airmail service
Post roads, **901**
Poteat, E. McNeill, Jr., 258
Poteat, William, 664

Poteat, William Louis, 404
Potecasi Creek, Battle of, **901**
Potter, Edward E., 986, 1179
Potter, Henry, 524, 641, 664, 787,
　　842–43
Potter, Stanley, 391
Pottery, 668, 761, **902–3**, 946;
　　Jugtown, **643–44**, 761, 903
Potts, Eugene "Genial Gene," 934
Poultry, 20, 623, 658, 687, 714,
　　904–5
Poverty, 19, 54, 527–28, 619, **905–6**;
　　abortion services and, 923;
　　American Indians and, 36–37;
　　Board of Public Charities and,
　　905–6; Fellowship of Southern
　　Churchmen and, 424; Frank
　　Porter Graham Child
　　Development Center and, 470;
　　Great Depression and, 906;
　　highways and, 565; housing
　　and, 906; Kate B. Reynolds
　　Charitable Trust and, 646;
　　North Carolina Conference for
　　Social Service and, 809; North
　　Carolina Fund and, **815**, 859;
　　poorhouses, 905; sharecropping and, 1025;
　　Swiss and Palatine settlers
　　and, 1101–2; white trash and,
　　1199; "Work First" program
　　and, 906
Powell, John, 1117
Powell, Joseph J. W., 292
Powell, Junius K., 906
Powell, William S., 570, 577, 837
Powell Bill (1951, N.C.), **906–7**
Pratt, Charles, earl of Camden,
　　165
Pratt, Joseph Hyde, 133, 501, 514,
　　564
Precincts, **907**
Preddy, George C., 1231
Preliminary Articles (1782), 2
Presbyterian Church, 8, 163, 167,
　　183, 216, 342, 375, 526, **907–8**,
　　960; African Americans and,
　　636; church homecomings,
　　221; educational institutions
　　associated with, 92, 159, 248,
　　316–17, 350, 375, 387–88, 439,
　　569, 636, 668, 759, 870–71,
　　908, 929, 1001–2, 1119, 1178–
　　79, 1191; first settlers, 959;
　　fundamentalism and, 481–82;
　　Gaelic language and, 489–90;
　　Long Street Presbyterian
　　Church, **690–91**; Montreat
　　and, 759; revivals and, 970;
　　Scottish settlers and, 1013;
　　Second Great Awakening and,

　　527; Waldensians and, 1173;
　　Welsh settlers and, 1189. *See
　　also* St. Andrews Presbyterian
　　College; Thyatira Church and
　　community
Presbyterian Junior College for
　　Men, **908**
Preservation. *See* Historic
　　preservation
Preservation North Carolina
　　(PNC), 169, 508, 574–75, 988,
　　1112
Presidents, U.S., **908–9**
Press Office (governor's), 516
Preston, Simon, 809
Preyer, L. Richardson, 129, 859
Preyer, William Y., 1161
Price, Charles Joseph, 688
Price, Daniel O., 617
Price, Jonathan, 968
Price, Joseph, 786
Price, Julian W., 632
Price, Mary Roberts, 1227
Price, Reynolds, 428, 895
Primary Elections Act of 1915
　　(N.C.), 385
Primitive Baptists, 89, 600, 647,
　　1210–11
Primogeniture, **909–10**
Primrose, William S., 812–13
Prince, Henry A., 947
Prince, Turner, 910
Prince, William Meade, 836,
　　1060–61
Princeville, 373, **910**
Printing, **910–11**
Prisoner of War Camps. *See* World
　　War II
Prison Population Stabilization
　　Act of 1987 (N.C.), 868
Prisons: Central Prison, **198**; chain
　　gang, **198–99**, 259, 292, 1086;
　　Committee of One Hundred,
　　259; Confederate Prison
　　(Salisbury), 197, **272–73**, 582,
　　1086; convict labor, **291–92**;
　　debt, imprisonment for, **331**;
　　Governor's Mansion and, 519;
　　overcrowding, 868; parole,
　　868; state penitentiary, 292,
　　950. *See also* Crime rates
Pritchard, Jeter C., 487, 641, 678,
　　898, 976, 1064
Pritchett, Mebane M., 765
Privateers, 850, **911–12**; Jenkins'
　　Ear, War of, and, 1064; *Snap
　　Dragon* (Burns), 911, **1053**,
　　1176; *Wasp* (Blakeley), 125–26,
　　1176, **1181**
Private schools. *See* Education,
　　private

Privies, **912–13**
Pro Bono Publico (tobacco), 1121
Proclamation money, 322
Proclamation of 1763, 209, **913**,
　　1139. *See also* Tryon's Line
Proclamation of Amnesty and
　　Pardon, 289
Procter & Gamble, 1161
Procter Telephone Company,
　　1107
Profanity, **913–14**
Professional Golfers Association
　　(PGA), 512–13
Proffitt, Frank, 449
Progress Energy Carolinas, 188
Progress Energy Center for the
　　Performing Arts, 942
Progressive Farmer, 20–21, 416,
　　487, 621, 813, 897, **914–15**,
　　1071, 1092, 1182
Progressive Party, 195, 896, 898,
　　916
Progressivism, 282, **915–16**
Prohibition, 27, 109, 282, 313, **916**,
　　1195; Anti-Saloon League and,
　　53, 870, 916, 1108; blind tiger
　　and, 127–28; Eighteenth
　　Amendment and, 109, 760,
　　916, 1139, 1196; moonshine
　　and, 760; patent medicines
　　and, 870; Turlington Act and,
　　1139; Twenty-First
　　Amendment and, 1109, 1196;
　　Watts Act of 1903 and, 53, 916,
　　1108, 1196. *See also*
　　Temperance movement
Project Listen, 369
Prometheus (steamboat), 1084
Prophetic Religion, 424
Prostitution, **916–17**; hooker, **584**
Protestant Episcopal Church
　　Publishing Association, **917**
Provincial Congresses, 139, 179,
　　917–18, 965–66, 993; First
　　(New Bern), 41, 372, 917, 965,
　　1110; Second (New Bern), 259,
　　917; Third (Hillsborough), 40,
　　260, 917–18; Fourth (Halifax),
　　41, 296, 548, 918, 966; Fifth
　　(Halifax), 284, 311, 332, 423,
　　548, 549, 671, 763; Gaelic
　　language and, 489; iron and
　　steel industry and, 624; slavery
　　and, 1047; test oath and, 1110
Provincial Council, 179, 260, 878,
　　918
Prudden, Emily, 883
Pseudonyms, **918–19**
Psychiatric hospitals, 588, **919–20**,
　　1195

Line, 1014; Southeastern Railroad, 72; Supreme Court of North Carolina and, 1095; Swannanoa Gap Tunnel, **1099**; Thermal Belt Railway, 181; time zones and, 1119; Transylvania Railroad Company, 1131; vs. trucking, 939, 941, 1015; Tweetsie Railroad, 941, **1141–42**, 1182; utilities, regulation of, and, 1155; Wilmington & Manchester Railroad, 1206; Wilmington & Raleigh Railroad, 620, 937, 1207; Wilmington, Brunswick, and Southern Railroad, **1208**; Wilmington, Charlotte, and Rutherford Railroad, 1206; Wilmington, Columbia, and Augusta Railroad, 1207; Wilmington Sea Coast Railroad, **1209–10**. *See also* Atlantic Coast Line Railroad; North Carolina Railroad; Seaboard Air Line Railway; Southern Railway Company; Western North Carolina Railroad; Wilmington & Weldon Railroad

Rainbow and Ramps Festival, 945

Raleigh, 38–39, 45, 47, 230, 617, 914, 916, **941–42**, 1003, 1172; Andrew Johnson birthplace, **48**; architecture in, 62, 63, 218; Cameron Village, **165**; Central Prison, **198**; Christ Episcopal Church, 62, **218–19**, 427, 947; Civil War and, 1031; Confederate Soldiers' Home, **273–74**; Convention of 1865, 473–74; Dorothea Dix Hospital, 588, 919–20, 1195; East Raleigh–South Park Historic District, 670; Episcopal School for Boys, 398, **399**; fires at, 431, 432, 942; Freedmen's Conventions, 473–74; Governor Morehead School, **517–18**; Governor's Mansion, **519**, 942, 943; Henry Clay Oak, **559–60**; hospitals in, 589; Joel Lane House, **634**, 779; Lafayette's visit, **659**; Meredith College, **732**; Methodist Home for Children, **734**; North Carolina Classical, English, and Mathematical School, 376, **808–9**; North Carolina Debutante Ball, **811–12**; North Carolina Exposition

of 1884, **812–13**; North-Carolina Museum, **821**; North Carolina Museum of Art, 821–23; North Carolina Museum of History, 823–24; North Carolina Symphony and, 833; Oakwood Cemetery, 269, **840**; Oakwood Historic District, 1244; Peace College, **870–71**; Ravenscroft School, **947**; Regional Rail Transit System, 941; Saint Augustine's College, 670, **996**, 1130; Saint Mary's School, 218, 398, 399, 809, 960, **997**; Shaw University, 232, 376, 667, 802, 868, 935, **1025–26**, 1088; Sir Walter Hotel, **1038–39**; as state capital, 150, 178, 179, 285, 370, 496, 1073; state fair, **1073–75**; State Legislative Building, 496, 942, 1018, 1073, **1075**, **1077**; streetcars, 1087–88; telephones and, 1106; television broadcasting, 1108, 1161, 1162; Union Square, **1146–47**; Watauga Club, **1182**. *See also* North Carolina State University; State Capitol

Raleigh, CSS, 190, 625, 767, **942**, 1207

Raleigh, Sir Walter, 179, 941, 1172; Amadas and Barlowe expedition, **30–31**, 34, 408, 858, 982–83; colonization and, 46, 463, 502, 516, 854, 1165; exploration, European, and, 170, 186, 314, 408, 410, 513, 624, 716, 864, 1017, 1165; Lost Colony and, 410, 692, 699, 856; Roanoke voyages and, 326, 391, 408–10, 513, 614, 716, **982–83**, 1017; tobacco and, 1120

Raleigh Academy, **942–43**

Raleigh & Augusta Air Line Railroad, 1014–15

Raleigh & Gaston Railroad, 620, 827, 939, 1014, 1097

Raleigh and Roanoke exhibition, 47

Raleigh Central Labor Union (CLU), 657

Raleigh Concert Band, 243

Raleigh-Durham Army Air Field, **943–44**

Raleigh-Durham International Airport, 81, 943–44

Raleigh Gas Light Company, 780

Raleigh Ice Caps, 602

Raleigh Institute. *See* North

Carolina Classical, English, and Mathematical School

"Raleigh letter," 560

Raleigh National Bank of North Carolina, 86

Raleigh National Cemetery, 197

Raleigh News and Observer, 506, 795, 796, 823, 828, 894, **944–45**, 1210; Bassett affair and, 100; Culture Week and, 319; Dixiecrats and, 347; *Durham Herald-Sun* and, 364; Journalism Hall of Fame and, 638; silver fusion and, 1037; Smith-Graham Senate race and, 1050; Tick War and, 1119

Raleigh Paper Mill, 866

Raleigh Post Office Employees Credit Union, 311

Raleigh Register, 721, 722, 725, 728, 795, 839, 846, 865, 1035, 1106, 1178

Raleigh School of Ballet, 325

Raleigh Standard, 339, 795, 949, 1009

Raleigh Telephone Company, 1106

Raleigh Times, 795

Raleigh Typographical Union, 656

Ramps, **945**

Ramseur, A. L. (Andy), 885

Ramseur, Stephen D., 503, 738

Ramsey, James L., 914

Ramsey, J. S., 1081

Ramsgate Road, **945**

Ramsour's Mill, Battle of, 43, 44, **945–46**

Randolph, John, 930

Randolph, Peyton, 946

Randolph Community College, 264

Randolph County, **946**. *See also* North Carolina Zoological Park; Pottery

Rangers, **946**

Rangers, the (gospel singers), 515

Rankin, Watson S., 130, 915, 921

Ranney, William, 1165

Ransom, Edward D., 290

Ransom, Matt W., 138–39, 740, 901

Ransom, Robert, 546

Rape, 312, 313

Raper, Arthur F., 617

Raper, W. Burkette, 770

Rape Victim Assistance Program, 312

Rasch, Anthony, 126

Raven Rock State Park, 552, 1078

Ravenscroft, John Stark, 398, 947, 996

Ravenscroft School (Raleigh), **947**

Ravenscroft School for Boys (Asheville), **947**

Rawlins, James, 688

Rawls, Leonard, 550–51

Rawls's Mill, Battle of, **947–48**

Ray, Asher H., 694

Ray, Duncan, 151

Ray, Jane Curtis, 694

Ray, John, 781

Ray, John E., 518

Rayner, Kenneth, 40, 780

Rayon, 158, 1112–13

RCA Victor, 303, 951

R. D. W. Connor Award, 682, 818

Rea Construction Company, 1077

Reagan, John Henninger, 271–72

Reagan, Ronald, 81, 777

Real estate, **948**

Reams Station, Battle of, 1103

Receiver General, **948–49**

Reconstruction, 8, 204, 909, **949–51**, 1084; African Americans during, 8, 9, 11, 122, 229–30, 496, 628, 949; American Indians and, 37; black codes, **122**, 229, 283, 401, 467, 949, 1042, 1045; bonds and stocks on railroad companies and, 937, 950, 963, 1057–58; Bragg Committee, **144**; carpetbaggers, 122, 451, 896, 937, 944, 949; Confederate Memorial Day and, 269; Confederate pensions, **271**; Conservative Party and, 283; crime rates and, 312; Democratic Party (Bourbons, Redeemers) and, 142–43, 340, 949–50, 953; economic suffering and, 950; Exodusters, **406–7**; fiction and, 451; Freedmen's Bureau and, 472–73; Heroes of America and, 561; Kirk-Holden War, 705, 950, 1009, 1034; Ku Klux Klan and, 654–55, 705, 953, 1034, 1146, 1163; primary elections and, 385; Republican Party and, 283, 335, 896, 949–50, 962–63, 1009; scalawags, 122, 561, 896, 949–50, **1009**; sharecropping and, 1024–25; Union League, **1145–46**. *See also* Black and Tan Constitution; Fourteenth Amendment

Reconstruction Act of 1867 (U.S.), 401, 467

Reconstruction in North Carolina (Hamilton), 577

Recording industry, **951–53**. *See*

University and, 1215; Winston-Salem and, 1215; women in, 1221, 1223; YWCA and, 1241. *See also* Cotton growing; Cotton mills

Textile Workers Union of America (TWUA), 658; Harriet-Henderson cotton mills strike, **552–53**

Thalheimer, Bill, 1040

Thalian Association, 351, **1114**

Thalian Hall, 851, 1114

Theaters. *See* Dramatic arts; Opera houses

Theatrical Syndicate, 851

Thelonius Monk Quartet, 631

Theodore Park, USS, 671–72

Theodore Roosevelt State Natural Area, 57, 1078

Thermal Belt Railway, 181

Theus, Christian, 955

Thirteenth Amendment (U.S. Constitution), 401, **1115**

This Week with David Brinkley (TV program), 1210

Thomas, Howard, 1166

Thomas, John P., 821

Thomas, John W., 1116

Thomas, Joseph, 342

Thomas, Perley A., 1115

Thomas, Robert K., 700

Thomas, William Holland, 37, 210, 333, 1116

Thomas Built Buses, Inc., **1115–16**, 1136

Thomas S. Kenan Institute for the Arts, 382

Thomas's Legion, **1116**. *See also* Deep Creek, Battle of

Thomasville, 88, 621

Thomasville Female College, **1116**

Thomasville Furniture Industries, 329

Thomas Wolfe Collection, 570

Thomas Wolfe House, 68, 225, 1116–17

Thomas Wolfe Literary Award, 574, 894

Thomas Wolfe Memorial, **1116–17**

Thompson, Bobbie, 849

Thompson, David, 98

Thompson, Ernest, 951

Thompson, Jacob, 330

Thompson, James, 723

Thompson, Joe, 850

Thompson, Lewis, 1117

Thompson, Odell, 850

Thompson, Tommy, 132, 849, 850

Thompson, Viola, 825

Thompson, Walter, 1086

Thompson, W. W., 363

Thompson Children's Home, **1117**

Thomson, Peter, 199

Thomson-Houston Electric Light Company, 386

Thoreau, Henry David, 1133

Thorium, 750

Thornton, Jim, 952

Thornton, Mary Lindsay, 570

Thorp, Benjamin F., 709

Three Mile Island Nuclear Power Plant, 838

Threshing, **1117–19**

Thrift, Julianne Still, 1000

Throop, George Higby, 1002

Thunderstorms, 245

Thurmond, J. Strom, 347

Thyatira Church and community, **1119**, 1243

Tick fever, 686

Tick War, **1119**

Tiernan, Frances Christine Fisher. *See* Reid, Christian

Tilden, Samuel J., 283

Tillet, Toby, 425, 426

Time capsule, 45, 560

Time zones, **1119**

Tin, 750–51

Toast String Stretchers, 850

Tobacco, 45, 371, 390, **1120–23**, 1149; A. C. Monk and Company, 2; American Tobacco Company, **45–46**, 135, 357, 361, 713, 1121, 1149–50, 1186; blue mold, **132–33**; bright leaf tobacco, 1121, 1123; Brown & Williamson Tobacco Company, **150**, 1121; Bull Durham tobacco, 45, **154–55**, 652, 713, 1121, 1186; burley tobacco, 1120, 1240; Camel cigarettes, 976–77, 1150, 1215; chewing tobacco, 150, 976; cigarette manufacture, 45, 46, 150, 528, 976, 1121, 1186, 1215; in colonial times, 411; cultivation, 18, 19–20; deertongue and, 334; exports of, 412; farming, 1121; flue-cured tobacco barns, 62, 93–94; flue-curing process, 191, 528, 637, 1120; folklore and, 444; fundamentalism and, 481; Granville wilt, **525**; Great Depression and, 528; hogshead, **579**; Johnston County and, 637; legal challenges to manufacturers, 1122; Liggett & Myers Tobacco Company, 1069, 1121, 1122, 1150, 1186; Master Settlement Agreement, 1122; National

Recovery Administration and, 530; Piedmont Urban Crescent and, 884; pipe tobacco, 150, 976; Plantation Duty Act of 1673, 318, 889–90; production, 2, 20, 524, 712, 713, 714, 1120–21, 1124; tobacco canoe, 171; transportation for, 362; union activism and, 230, 260; W. Duke, Sons and Company, 45, 1121, 1149, **1186**; William T. Blackwell Company, 45, 46, 155, 652, 1149, 1186; Winston-Salem and, 1215; women in industry, 1221–22; wrapper quality, 579. *See also* R. J. Reynolds Tobacco Company

Tobacco auctions, **1123–24**

Tobacco belts, **1124**

Tobacco Farm Life Museum, 637

Tobacco Radio Network, 1161

Tobacco Research Commission, 798

Tobacco Trust Fund Commission, 1122

Tocqueville, Alexis de, 227

Todman, Norwood, 98

Toilets. *See* Privies

Toll roads, 355, 1140

Tomato clubs, 466, **1124**

Tombstones, 441, **1124–25**. *See also* Fraktur

Tomlinson Chair Company, 485

Tompkins, Daniel A., 204, 417, 1081

Toms, Francis, 927

Tooley, Adam, 869

Topsail Beach, 875

Topsail Inlet. *See* Beaufort Inlet

Topsail Island, 598, 850, 969, 984

Tornadoes, **1125**

Torpedo Junction. *See* Submarine attacks

Torrence's Tavern, **1125–26**

Torrey, Philip H., 166

Tort Claims Act of 1951 (N.C.), 240

Tory, **1126–27**

Tory Hole, 125, 391

Tory Oak, **1127**

Tory Plot. *See* Llewelyn Conspiracy

Tory War. *See* American Revolution; Lindley's Mill, Battle of; Loyalists

Totten, Henry Roland, 807

Totten, Joseph G., 745

Totten, William T., 1238

Touchstone, Caleb, 439

Tourgée, Albion W., 290, 451, 890

Town, Ithiel, 241, 1073

Town Creek Indian Mound, 33, 156, 758, **1127–28**

Town Creek Railroad and Lumber Company. *See* Wilmington, Brunswick, and Southern Railroad

Town documentaries, **1128**

Town milk, **1128–29**

Towns and cities, **1129**

Townshend Acts (1767), 721, 799

Township and County Commissioner Plan, 297, 300, 1129

Tracheal mites, 583–84

Track and field, **1129–30**

Tractors, 18

Trade unions. *See* Labor unions

Trading Ford, **1130–31**

Trail of Tears. *See* Cherokee Indians: Trail of Tears

Training and Standards, Division of, 74

Train wrecks, 707, 953; Bostian Bridge train wreck, **139–41**; Norfolk Southern Railroad and, 799–800; at Saluda Grade, 1003

Transcontinental Gas Pipeline Company (Transco), 780

Transportation: canoes, 170–71, 995; ferries, **425–26**, 569–70, 615, 637, 794, 975; of fish, for market, 434; fords and, 453–54, 534; freight, 977, 1116, 1136; freight rates, 477, 936; gaps and, 491; Hackney Brothers Wagon Company, 1136; Harkers Island Boats, **551**; hogshead, for tobacco transportation, 579; internal improvements, **619–21**; Intracoastal Waterway, **621–22**; for lumber, 1, 520; North Carolina Catawba Company, **807–8**; North Carolina Transportation Museum, **835**; periauger, 1025; ports and harbors and, 899–900; postal service and, 900–901; Railroad Commission, **936**; sharpies, **1025**; Simmons sea-skiffs, **1038**; stagecoaches, **1067–68**; steamboats, **1084–85**; Thomas Built Buses, Inc., **1115–16**, 1136; trucks and trucking, **1136**; wagons, 885, 979; by water, 27, 414, 549, 614, 619–20, 638, 1011. *See also* Automobiles; Aviation; Canals; Highways; Navigation companies; Railroads; River navigation; Roads